9th Edition

THE Adams Jobs Almanac

adams media

Published by Adams Media, an F+W Publications Company
57 Littlefield Street, Avon, MA 02322 U.S.A.
www.adamsmedia.com

ISBN 10: 1-59869-067-1
ISBN 13: 978-1-59869-0675
Manufactured in the United States of America.

J I H G F E D C B A

Because addresses and telephone numbers of smaller companies change rapidly, we recommend you call each company and verify the information before mailing to the employers listed in this book. Mass mailings are not recommended.

While the publisher has made every reasonable effort to obtain and verify accurate information, occasional errors are possible due to the magnitude of the data. Should you discover an error, or if a company is missing, please write the editors at the above address so that we may update future editions.

"This publication is designed to provide accurate and authoritative information with regard to the subject matter covered. It is sold with the understanding that the publisher is not engaged in rendering legal, accounting, or other professional advice. If legal advice or other expert assistance is required, the services of a competent professional person should be sought."

--From a *Declaration of Principles* jointly adopted by a Committee of the American Bar Association and a Committee of Publishers and Associations

This book is available on standing order and at quantity discounts for bulk purchases. For information, call 800/872-5627 (in Massachusetts, 508/427-7100).

CONTENTS

The Employers by Industry

THE NATION'S JOB MARKET: AN OVERVIEW

Employment projections and other information provided in the *Adams Jobs Almanac, 9th Edition* are based on "Occupational Employment Projections to 2014" from the November 2005 *Monthly Labor Review* and *Career Guide to Industries, 2006-07 Edition* published by the U.S. Department of Labor, Bureau of Labor Statistics.

Total U.S. employment will increase by 18.9 million from 145.6 million to 164.5 million during the ten-year period, 2004 – 2014, an average increase over all occupations of 13%. Adding net replacements – job openings created by workers who leave their jobs to work in another occupation, leave the labor force because of retirement or other reasons – results in more than 54.7 million job openings for the period.

While the percentage increase or decrease in employment figure provides an idea of a sector's health, it's important to look at the numerical change in an occupation to obtain a clear picture of opportunities in that field. For example, employment of biomedical engineers is projected to grow almost twice as fast as employment of industrial engineers over the 2004 – 2014 period, 30.7%, compared with 16%. However, the industrial engineer occupation is projected to add about nine times the number of new jobs (28,000 compared with 3,000), because employment was so much larger than for biomedical engineers in 2004 (177,000 compared with 10,000).

Winners and losers

The *Adams Jobs Almanac, 9th Edition*, includes listings of companies in eighteen different industry categories, representing those industries that offer the greatest job growth and consequently, the most employment opportunities for the job seeker. Other fields, while continuing to employ large numbers of people, were not included due to the expectation that current and future conditions would result in below-average job growth.

Industries With Strong Projected Growth (Above Average)

Accounting and Management Consulting
Advertising, Marketing, and Public Relations
Arts, Entertainment, Sports, and Recreation
Biotechnology, Pharmaceuticals, and Scientific R&D
Business Services and Non-Scientific Research
Charities and Social Services
Computer Software, and Services
Educational Services
Environmental and Waste Management Services
Healthcare Services, Equipment, and Products
Hotels and Restaurants
Real Estate

Industries with Average Projected Growth

Architecture, Construction, and Engineering
Financial Services
Legal Services
Retail
Transportation and Travel
Miscellaneous Wholesaling

Industries with Poor Projected Growth

Aerospace
Apparel, Fashion, and Textiles
Automotive
Banking
Chemicals/Rubber and Plastics
Communications: Telecommunications and Broadcasting
Computer Hardware
Electronic/Industrial Electrical Equipment and Components
Fabricated Metal Products and Primary Metals
Food and Beverages/Agriculture
Government
Insurance
Manufacturing
Mining, Gas, Petroleum, Energy Related
Paper and Wood Products
Printing and Publishing
Stone, Clay, Glass, and Concrete Products
Utilities

Accounting And Management Consulting - Accountants and auditors will add 264,000 new positions by 2014, a 22.4% growth, increasing from 1,176,000 to 1,440,000. An increase in the number of businesses, changing financial laws and regulations, and increased scrutiny of company finances will drive growth. Management analyst positions will increase by 122,000 jobs from 605,000 to 727,000, a 20.1% growth. Industry and government will rely on outside expertise to improve the performance of their organizations. Job growth is projected in very large consulting firms with international expertise and in smaller consulting firms that specialize in specific areas, such as biotechnology, healthcare, information technology, human resources, engineering, and marketing.

Advertising, Marketing, And Public Relations - The number of new openings for advertising, marketing, promotions, public relations, and sales managers will increase by 131,000 from 646,000 to 777,000, a 20.3% increase. Growth is spurred by intense domestic and global competition in products and services offered to consumers. However, projected employment growth varies by industry. For example, employment is projected to grow much faster than average in scientific, professional, and related services such as computer systems design and related services and advertising and related services, as businesses increasingly hire contractors for these services instead of additional full-time staff. On the other hand, little or no change in employment is expected in many manufacturing industries.

Aerospace - After recent declines, employment in the aerospace industry is expected to increase modestly by 8%, or 36,000 jobs, from 444,000 to 480,000 positions. Employment in the aerospace industry is slow due to a drastic reduction in commercial transport aircraft orders, caused by a reduction in air travel, the severe financial problems experienced by many airlines, and strong foreign competition in the commercial transport market.

Apparel, Fashion, and Textiles - Having sustained a significant hit in the previous decade, employment in textile, apparel, and furnishings occupations will decline by an additional 161,000 jobs, from 929,000 to 768,000, a 17.3% decrease. The number of openings for fashion designers will increase by 8.4% from 17,000 to 18,000. Employment in the textile and apparel industries will decline, due to greater imports — as import quotas are lifted — and to improved production technology.

Architecture, Construction and Engineering - Architecture and engineering occupations openings are expected to increase 12.5%, from

2,520,000 to 2,835,000, an increase of 315,000 jobs. Employment in construction will increase by 849,000 jobs or 12.4%, from 6,820,000 to 7,669,000 jobs. Demand for new housing and an increase in road, bridge, and tunnel construction will account for the bulk of job growth.

Arts, Entertainment, Sports, and Recreation - Arts, entertainment, and recreation will grow by 25% and add 460,000 new jobs by 2014, increasing from 1,833,000 to 2,293,000 jobs. Most of these new job openings will come from the amusement, gambling, and recreation sector. Job growth will stem from public participation in arts, entertainment, and recreation activities—reflecting increasing incomes, leisure time, and awareness of the health benefits of physical fitness.

Automotive - Employment in motor vehicle and parts manufacturing will increase by 5.6%, adding just 62,000 new jobs for a total of 1,172,000. New jobs for automotive technicians and repairers will grow 14.6% from 1,026,000 to 1,175,000. Productivity gains, job automation, increasing use of contract employees, and international competition will adversely affect employment in this industry.

Banking, Savings And Loans and Other Depository Institutions - Employment in the banking industry is expected to decrease by 1.8%, from 1,783,000 to 1,751,000, a loss of 32,000 jobs. The combined effects of technology, deregulation, mergers, and population growth will continue to affect total employment growth and the mix of occupations in the banking industry. Overall declines in office and administrative support occupations will be offset by growth in some professional, managerial, and sales occupations. Job opportunities should still be favorable for tellers and other administrative support workers because they make up a large proportion of bank employees and have high turnover.

Biotechnology, Pharmaceuticals, and Scientific Research - The number of openings in pharmaceutical and medicine manufacturing should increase by 26.1% or 76,000, from 291,000 to 367,000. Because so many of the pharmaceutical and medicine manufacturing industry's products are related to preventive or routine healthcare, rather than just illness, demand is expected to increase as the population expands. The growing number of older people who will require more healthcare services will further stimulate demand—along with the growth of both public and private health insurance programs, which increasingly cover the cost of drugs and medicines. Openings for life and physical science occupations should grow from 824,000 to 952,000, an increase of 128,000 or 15.5%.

Business Services and Non-Scientific Research - Employment services will gain 1,580,000 jobs, an impressive 45.5% increase, growing from 3,470,000 jobs to about 5 million. Businesses will continue to seek new ways to make their staffing patterns more responsive to changes in demand by hiring temporary employees with specialized skills to reduce costs and to provide the necessary knowledge or experience in certain types of work. Increasing demand for flexible work arrangements and schedules, coupled with significant turnover in these positions, should create plentiful job opportunities for persons who seek jobs as temporaries or contract workers. Building and grounds services occupations should add 356,000 jobs, a 21% growth. Investigation and security service occupations are projected to add 170,000 jobs, a growth of 23.3%.

Charities and Social Services - New openings in community and social services occupations should increase 20.8%, adding 483,000 new jobs and growing the total employment from 2,317,000 to 2,800, 000. Continued rapid growth should result as the elderly population increases rapidly and as greater efforts are made to provide services for the disabled, the sick, substance abusers, and individuals and families in crisis.

Chemicals/Rubber and Plastics - The number of openings in the chemical industry, including soap, paint, rubber, and plastics is projected to decrease by 11.4%, or 160,000 jobs to 1,243, 000. This decrease is due to more efficient production processes and increased plant automation, the state of the national and world economy, company mergers and consolidation, increased foreign competition, the shifting of production activities to foreign countries, and environmental health and safety concerns and legislation.

Communications: Telecommunications and Broadcasting - Employment in the telecommunications industry is expected to decrease 6.5%, a loss of 68,000 jobs. Industry consolidation and strong price competition among telecommunications firms will decrease employment as companies try to reduce their costs. Additionally, technological improvements, such as high-speed wireless data transmission, fiber optic lines, and advanced switching equipment, have massively increased the data transmission capacity of telecommunications networks, and resulted in much higher productivity that will further reduce employment. Telecommunications equipment also is more reliable and requires less monitoring. Broadcasting's 327,000 jobs will increase by 10.7% or 35,000 positions. Factors contributing to the below average rate of growth include industry consolidation, introduction of new technologies, and competition from other media outlets.

Computer Hardware, Software, and Services - Software occupations will increase from 239,000 by 67.4% or 161,000 new positions. An increasing reliance on information technology, combined with falling prices of computers and related hardware, means that individuals and organizations will continue to invest in applications and systems software to maximize the return on their investments in equipment and to fulfill their growing computing needs. The 3,046,000 jobs held by computer specialists, including scientists, engineers, programmers, systems analysts, and database administrators will increase by 957,000 or 31.4%. Job increases will be driven by very rapid growth in computer system design and related services as organizations continue to adopt and integrate increasingly sophisticated technologies. Employment in the computer and electronic product manufacturing industry is expected to decline by 7% or 94,000 jobs to 1,232,000 positions as a result of continued rapid productivity growth, continued increases in imports of products, and outsourcing of some professional functions.

Educational Services - Educational services employ 8,171,000 workers and are expected to increase by 20.3% or 1,662,000 new jobs. Job opportunities for teachers over the next 10 years will vary from good to excellent, depending on the locality, grade level, and subject taught. The total number of job openings, 3,357,000, is attributable to the expected retirement of a large number of teachers. Through 2014, overall preschool to secondary student enrollments, a key factor in the demand for teachers, are expected to rise more slowly than in the past. Overall, employment of postsecondary teachers is expected to grow much faster than the average due to an expected increase in the population of 18-

to 24-year-olds, as a larger percentage of high school graduates attend college, and as more adults return to college to enhance their career prospects or update their skills. The 67,000 child daycare service jobs are expected to increase by 38.5% or 295,000 new jobs. The number of women in the labor force with children young enough to require child daycare will increase steadily. Also, the number of children under age 5 is expected to increase during this period. An unusually large number of job openings also will result each year from the need to replace experienced workers who leave this industry.

Electronic/Industrial Electrical Equipment and Components - The number of new openings for electrical, electronics, and electromechanical assemblers, technicians, engineers, and repairers will increase by 57,000 to 1,461,000, a gain of 4%. Advances in technology, such as faster machines and more automated processes, and a shift of assembly and other production activities to other countries will dampen employment in this industry.

Environmental and Waste Management Services - Occupations including environmental engineers, technicians, scientists and geoscientists, as well as waste treatment operators should grow by 19% or 58,000 jobs, from 303,000 to 361,000. Employment will be stimulated by a need to meet environmental regulations, develop methods of cleaning up existing hazards, and, more generally, respond to increasing public concern for a safe and clean environment.

Fabricated Metal Products and Primary Metals - Employment in the fabricated and primary metal manufacturing industry is expected to decline 5.8% from 1,964,000 to 1,850,000, primarily due to process automation and increasing consolidation in the industry as companies go out of business or are bought by other companies in the industry and their operations merge.

Financial Services - The number of new securities, commodities, and investment openings will increase by 15.7% or 121,000 to 888,000. As people's incomes continue to climb, they will increasingly seek the advice and services of securities, commodities, and financial services sales agents to realize their financial goals. Growth in the volume of trade in stocks over the Internet will reduce the need for brokers for many transactions. Nevertheless, the overall increase in investment is expected to spur employment growth among these workers, with a majority of transactions still requiring the advice and services of securities, commodities, and financial services sales agents. Within this industry, personal financial advisor jobs are projected to increase by 25.9%, adding 41,000 new jobs. Increased investment by businesses and individuals is expected to result in faster-than-average employment growth of financial analysts and personal financial advisors through 2014. Both occupations will benefit as baby boomers save for retirement and as a generally better educated and wealthier population requires investment advice.

Food and Beverages/Agriculture - Agricultural occupations, including agricultural manager, farmer, ranchers, agricultural and food scientists and technicians, and agricultural workers, will lose 149,000 jobs, a 6.8% decrease, from 2,172,000 to 2,023,000 positions. Continued consolidation of farms and technological advancements in farm equipment will dampen employment growth. Food, beverage, and tobacco manufacturing employs 1,692,000 workers and is expected to grow by just 2.6%, or approximately 44,000 new jobs. Despite the rising demand for manufactured food products by a growing population, automation and increasing productivity are limiting employment growth.

Government - Employment in the Federal government is projected to increase by 1.6% or 43,000 jobs to 2,771,000. Job growth generated by increased homeland security needs may be largely offset by projected slow growth or declines in other Federal sectors due to governmental cost-cutting, the growing use of private contractors, and continuing devolution—the practice of turning over the development, implementation, and management of some programs of the Federal Government to State and local governments. State and local governments employ 18,891,000 and are projected to add 2,128,000 jobs, an 11.3% increase. An increasing population and State and local government assumption of responsibility for some services previously provided by the Federal Government are fueling the growth of these services. Despite the increased demand for the services of State and local governments, employment growth will be dampened by budgetary constraints due to a slower growing economy, reductions in Federal aid, especially at the county level, and resistance from citizens to tax increases.

Health Care Services, Equipment, and Products - The number of openings in healthcare practitioners and technical operations and healthcare support occupations will grow 28.3% or 3,000,000 new jobs, from 10,619,000 to 13,625,000 jobs. Rapid growth among health-related occupations reflects an aging population that requires more healthcare, a wealthier population that can afford better healthcare, and advances in medical technology that permit more health problems to be treated more aggressively.

Hotels and Restaurants - Accommodation occupations numbered 1,796,000 in 2004, and should increase by 16.9% or 304,000 jobs over the next decade. Food preparation and serving related occupations – including chefs, cooks, food preparation workers, food service managers, food and beverage serving workers and related workers – employed 8,850,000 and is expected to grow by 1,451,000 new jobs to 10,301,000, a 16.4% increase. Job growth reflects increases in population, dual-income families, and dining sophistication. While job growth will create new positions, the overwhelming majority of job openings will stem from the need to replace workers who leave this large occupational group.

Insurance - Employment in the insurance industry is expected to increase by 9.6%, or 216,000 new jobs, reflecting a growth from 2,260,000 to 2,476,000 jobs. While demand for insurance is expected to rise, downsizing, productivity increases due to new technology, and a trend toward direct mail, telephone, and Internet sales will limit job growth. However, some job growth will result from the industry's expansion into the broader financial services field, and employment in the medical service and health insurance areas is anticipated to grow.

Legal Services - Legal occupations, including lawyers, judges and related workers as well as support staff, employ 1,220,000 workers, and will add 194,000 new jobs, an increase of 15.9%. Employment of lawyers is expected to grow about as fast as the average through 2014, primarily as a result of growth in the population and in the general level of business activities. Budgetary pressures at all levels of government will hold down the hiring of judges, despite rising caseloads, particularly in Federal courts. Paralegal employment, currently 224,000 jobs, is expected to increase much faster than average as organizations presently employing paralegals assign them a growing range of tasks, some of which were formerly performed by lawyers, and as paralegals are increasingly employed in small and medium-sized establishments. The number of self-employed workers in this group is projected to remain unchanged, reflecting the difficulty in establishing new legal practices.

Manufacturing: Miscellaneous Consumer - Manufacturing, across all industries, employed 13.7 million workers in 2004, and is expected to decline by 713,000 jobs, a 5.2% decrease. Productivity gains, job automation, and international competition will adversely affect employment in many manufacturing industries. Certain industries will feel the effects of these factors more than others: appliance manufacturing will lose 24,000 jobs, a 26.7% decline, while furniture manufacturing will shrink by 10,000 jobs for a 1.7% loss.

Manufacturing: Miscellaneous Industrial - Manufacturing, across all industries, employed 13.7 million workers in 2004, and is expected to decline by 713,000 jobs, a 5.2% decrease. Productivity gains, job automation, and international competition will adversely affect employment in many manufacturing industries. Within the industrial sector specifically, industrial machinery manufacturing will lose 147,000 jobs, 12.9% of its total.

Mining, Gas, Petroleum, Energy Related - The approximately 207,000 jobs in the mining industry are expected to fall by 13%, a loss of 27,000 jobs. This continuing long-term decline is due to increased productivity resulting from technological advances in mining operations, consolidation, stringent environmental regulations, and international competition. Oil and gas extraction employs 123,000, and is expected to shrink by 16,000 jobs, or 13%. While some new oil and gas deposits are being discovered in this country, companies increasingly are moving to more lucrative foreign locations reducing the need for employees in the United States.

Paper and Wood Products - Wood products manufacturing employed 548,000 workers in 2004, a number expected to grow by 40,000 or 7.3%. Paper manufacturing, including pulp, paperboard and converted paper products employs about half a million workers and is expected to decline by 12,000, or 2.4%. Forest, conservation, and logging worker jobs are expected to decline by 14,000 jobs or 11.3%. Despite steady demand for lumber and other wood products, employment of timber cutting and logging occupations is expected to decline, primarily because of increased mechanization and increasing imports. Domestic timber producers face increasing competition from foreign producers, who can harvest the same amount of timber at lower cost. As competition increases, the logging industry is expected to continue to consolidate in order to reduce costs, thereby eliminating some jobs.

Printing and Publishing - Printing occupations are expected to decrease by 65,000 jobs, or 9.8%, falling from 665,00 to 600,000 jobs. This decline reflects the increasing computerization of the printing process, growing imports of some types of printed products, and the expanding use of the Internet, which reduces the need for printed materials. Some small and medium-size firms are also consolidating in order to afford the investment in new technology, which is expected to lead to a drop in employment. Newspaper, periodical, book, and directory publisher occupations will increase from 671,000 to 715,000 jobs, a growth of 44,000 jobs, or 6.6%. The demand for, and the output of, printed materials is expected to grow over the 2004-14 period as school enrollments rise, and as substantial growth in the middle-aged and older population spurs adult education and leisure reading. Employment, however, will not grow in line with output because of the increased use of new computerized printing equipment. Also, new business practices within the publishing industry, such as printing-on-demand and electronic publishing, will cut into the production of printed materials. Contributing to this situation is the trend toward outsourcing of work to firms in foreign countries, where books and other materials with long lead times can be produced more cheaply. There are also expected to be fewer newspaper printing jobs as a result of mergers and consolidation within the industry.

Real Estate - Combined real estate and rental and leasing occupations are expected to grow by 18.2%, adding 258,000 jobs by 2014, for a total of 1,675,000 jobs. The bulk of these jobs, 200,000, will come from rental and leasing occupations, representing a 20.7% growth, while real estate brokers and sales agent jobs will grow by just 13%. Growth will be due, in part, to increased demand for housing as the population grows, although increasing use of information technology by agents and customers will tend to limit this growth.

Retail - Employment in retail trade is expected to increase by 1,649,000 jobs or 10.9%, from just over 15 million to 16.7 million. Increases in population, personal income, and leisure time will contribute to employment growth in this industry, as consumers demand more goods.

Stone, Clay, Glass, and Concrete Products - The number of occupations in stone, clay, glass, and concrete products industries is expected to increase by 20,000 jobs, from 505,000 to 525,000, a 3.9% rise. Demand for these products will remain steady, but technological advancements in operations and foreign competition will moderate job growth.

Transportation and Travel - Transportation occupations are expected to increase by 368,000 jobs, 10% to 4,062,000 jobs. Truck transportation, including couriers and messengers industries will grow by 14%, adding 387,000 new jobs, while more modest growth is projected for rail and water transportation, adding 16,000 new jobs or 9.3%. Demand for truck transportation and warehousing services will expand as many manufacturers concentrate on their core competencies and contract out their product transportation and storage functions. Air transportation occupations will increase by 22,000 jobs, or 16.5%, as passenger and cargo traffic continues to expand in response to increases in population, income, and business activity. The travel arrangement and reservation services industry should add 7,000 jobs, just 3%, increasing to 226,000 jobs, due to use of the Internet and industry consolidation.

Utilities: Electric, Gas, and Water - Employment in utilities is projected to decrease by 1.2%, or 7,000 jobs, through 2014. Despite increased output, employment in electric power generation, transmission, and distribution and natural gas distribution is expected to decline through 2014 due to improved technology that increases worker productivity. However, employment in water, sewage, and other systems is expected to increase by 10,000 jobs or 21.7%. Jobs are not easily eliminated by technological gains in this industry because water treatment and waste disposal are very labor-intensive activities.

Miscellaneous Wholesaling - Jobs in wholesale trade are projected to grow by 8.4%, adding 476,000 jobs, compared with the 13% rate of growth projected for all industries combined. Growth will vary, however, depending on the sector of the economy with which individual wholesale trade firms are involved. Consolidation of the industry into larger firms and the spread of new technology (such as electronic commerce) should have their greatest effect on the two largest occupational groups in wholesale trade—office and administrative support, and sales and related occupations. However, as firms provide a growing array of support services, many new jobs will be created and the roles of many workers will change.

HOW TO USE THIS BOOK

Right now, you hold in your hands one of the most effective job-hunting tools available anywhere. In *The Adams Jobs Almanac, 9th Edition*, you will find valuable information to help you launch or continue a rewarding career. But before you open to the book's employer listings and start calling about current job openings, take a few minutes to learn how best to use the resources presented in *The Adams Jobs Almanac, 9th Edition*.

The Adams Jobs Almanac, 9th Edition will help you to stand out from other jobseekers. While many people looking for a new job rely solely on newspaper help-wanted ads, this book offers you a much more effective job-search method -- direct contact. The direct contact method has been proven twice as effective as scanning the help-wanted ads. Instead of waiting for employers to come looking for you, you'll be far more effective going to them. While many of your competitors will use trial and error methods in trying to set up interviews, you'll learn not only how to get interviews, but what to expect once you've got them.

In the next few pages, we'll take you through each section of the book so you'll be prepared to get a jump-start on your competition.

Basics of Job Winning

Preparation. Strategy. Time management. These are three of the most important elements of a successful job search. *Basics of Job Winning* helps you address these and all the other elements needed to find the right job.

One of your first priorities should be to define your personal career objectives. What qualities make a job desirable to you? Creativity? High pay? Prestige? Use *Basics of Job Winning* to weigh these questions. Then use the rest of the chapter to design a strategy to find a job that matches your criteria.

In *Basics of Job Winning,* you'll learn which job-hunting techniques work, and which don't. We've reviewed the pros and cons of mass mailings, help-wanted ads, and direct contact. We'll show you how to develop and approach contacts in your field; how to research a prospective employer; and how to use that information to get an interview and the job.

Also included in *Basics of Job Winning*: interview dress code and etiquette, the "do's and don'ts" of interviewing, sample interview questions, and more. We also deal with some of the unique problems faced by those jobseekers who are currently employed, those who have lost a job, and college students conducting their first job search.

Resumes and Cover Letters

The approach you take to writing your resume and cover letter can often mean the difference between getting an interview and never being noticed. In this section, we discuss different formats, as well as what to put on (and what to leave off) your resume. We review the benefits and drawbacks of professional resume writers, and the importance of a follow-up letter. Also included in this section are sample resumes and cover letters that you can use as models.

The Employer Listings

The *Adams Jobs Almanac, 9th Edition*, includes listings of companies in eighteen different industry categories, representing those industries that offer the greatest job growth and consequently, the most employment opportunities for the job seeker. Each company profile is assigned to one of the industry chapters listed below.

Accounting and Management Consulting
Advertising, Marketing, and Public Relations
Architecture, Construction, and Engineering
Arts, Entertainment, Sports, and Recreation
Biotechnology, Pharmaceuticals, and Scientific R&D
Business Services and Non-Scientific Research
Charities and Social Services
Computer Hardware, Software, and Services
Educational Services
Environmental and Waste Management Services
Financial Services
Health Care: Services, Equipment, and Products
Hotels and Restaurants
Legal Services
Real Estate
Retail
Transportation and Travel
Miscellaneous Wholesaling

Employers are listed alphabetically by state within the industry category. When a company does business under a person's name, like "John Smith & Co.," the company is usually listed by the surname's spelling (in this case "S"). Exceptions occur when a company's name is widely recognized, like "JCPenney" or "Howard Johnson Motor Lodge." In those cases, the company's first name is the key ("J" and "H" respectively).

Many of the company listings offer detailed company profiles. In addition to company names, addresses, and phone numbers, these listings also include contact names or hiring departments, and descriptions of each company's products and/or services. Many of these listings also feature a variety of additional information including:

Positions advertised - A list of open positions the company was advertising at the time our research was conducted. Note: Keep in mind that *The Adams Jobs Almanac, 9th Edition* is a directory of major employers in the area, not a directory of openings currently available. Positions listed in this book that were advertised at the time research was conducted may no longer be open. Many of the companies listed will be hiring, others will not. However, since most professional job openings are filled without the placement of help-wanted ads, contacting the employers in this book directly is still a more effective method than browsing the Sunday papers.

Special programs - Does the company offer training programs, internships, or apprenticeships? These programs can be important to first time jobseekers and college students looking for practical work experience. Many employer profiles will include information on these programs.

Parent company - If an employer is a subsidiary of a larger company, the name of that parent company will often be listed here. Use this information to supplement your company research before contacting the employer.

Number of employees - The number of workers a company employs.

Company listings may also include information on other U.S. locations and any stock exchanges the firm may be listed on.

When using this book, please keep in mind that to save space and avoid repetition, not all business listings were included. Many companies, particularly larger organizations, may have offices in many urban areas and states. By scanning an industry category, you will notice multiple listings for these companies, and while they are not listed for all states, further research, such as visiting the company's website, may reveal an office in your area.

It's also worthwhile to point out that companies in this book are organized by industry, but jobs can cross over many industries. While the healthcare industry employs individuals trained in healthcare, for example, it also employs many whose jobs are not directly health related, including workers in information technology, finance and business, marketing and public relations, and legal areas, to name a few. So, if you're seeking a position in accounting, don't confine your search to the firms listed in the "Accounting and Management Consulting" section.

A note on all employer listings that appear in *The Adams Jobs Almanac, 9th Edition*: This book is intended as a starting point. It is not intended to replace any effort that you, the jobseeker, should devote to your job hunt. Keep in mind that while a great deal of effort has been put into collecting and verifying the company profiles provided in this book, addresses and contact names change regularly. Inevitably, some contact names listed herein have changed even before you read this. We recommend you contact a company before mailing your resume to ensure nothing has changed.

THE BASICS OF JOB WINNING: A CONDENSED REVIEW

This chapter is divided into four sections. The first section explains the fundamentals that every jobseeker should know, especially first-time jobseekers. The next three sections deal with special situations faced by specific types of jobseekers: those who are currently employed, those who have lost a job, and college students.

THE BASICS: Things Everyone Needs to Know

Career Planning

The first step to finding your ideal job is to clearly define your objectives. This is better known as career planning (or life planning if you wish to emphasize the importance of combining the two). Career planning has become a field of study in and of itself.

If you are thinking of choosing or switching careers, we particularly emphasize two things. First, choose a career where you will enjoy most of the day-to-day tasks. This sounds obvious, but most of us have at some point found the idea of a glamour industry or prestigious job title attractive without thinking of the key consideration: Would we enjoy performing the *everyday* tasks the position entails?

The second key consideration is that you are not merely choosing a career, but also a lifestyle. Career counselors indicate that one of the most common problems people encounter in jobseeking is that they fail to consider how well-suited they are for a particular position or career. For example, some people, attracted to management consulting by good salaries, early responsibility, and high-level corporate exposure, do not adapt well to the long hours, heavy travel demands, and constant pressure to produce. Be sure to ask yourself how you might adapt to the day-to-day duties and working environment that a specific position entails. Then ask yourself how you might adapt to the demands of that career or industry as a whole.

Choosing Your Strategy

Assuming that you've established your career objectives, the next step of the job search is to develop a strategy. If you don't take the time to develop a plan, you may find yourself going in circles after several weeks of randomly searching for opportunities that always seem just beyond your reach.

The most common jobseeking techniques are:

- following up on help-wanted advertisements (in the newspaper or online)
- using employment services

- relying on personal contacts
- contacting employers directly (the Direct Contact method)

Each of these approaches can lead to better jobs. However, the Direct Contact method boasts twice the success rate of the others. So unless you have specific reasons to employ other strategies, Direct Contact should form the foundation of your job search.

If you choose to use other methods as well, try to expend at least half your energy on Direct Contact. Millions of other jobseekers have already proven that Direct Contact has been twice as effective in obtaining employment, so why not follow in their footsteps?

Setting Your Schedule

Okay, so now that you've targeted a strategy it's time to work out the details of your job search. The most important detail is setting up a schedule. Of course, since job searches aren't something most people do regularly, it may be hard to estimate how long each step will take. Nonetheless, it is important to have a plan so that you can monitor your progress.

When outlining your job search schedule, have a realistic time frame in mind. If you will be job-searching full-time, your search could take at least two months or more. If you can only devote part-time effort, it will probably take at least four months.

You probably know a few people who seem to spend their whole lives searching for a better job in their spare time. Don't be one of them. If you are presently working and don't feel like devoting a lot of energy to jobseeking right now, then wait. Focus on enjoying your present position, performing your best on the job, and storing up energy for when you are really ready to begin your job search.

The first step in beginning your job search is to clearly define your objectives.

Those of you who are currently unemployed should remember that *job-hunting is tough work, both physically and emotionally.* It is also intellectually demanding work that requires you to be at your best. So don't tire yourself out by working on your job campaign around the clock. At the same time, be sure to discipline yourself. The most logical way to manage your time while looking for a job is to keep your regular working hours.

If you are searching full-time and have decided to choose several different strategies, we recommend that you divide up each week, designating some time for each method. By trying several approaches at once, you can evaluate how promising each seems and alter your schedule accordingly. Keep in mind that the *majority of openings are filled without being advertised.* Remember also that positions advertised on the Internet are just as likely to already be filled as those found in the newspaper!

If you are searching part-time and decide to try several different contact methods, we recommend that you try them sequentially. You simply won't have enough time to put a meaningful amount of effort into more than one method at once. Estimate the length of your job search, and then allocate so many weeks or months for each contact method, beginning with Direct Contact. The purpose of setting this schedule is not to rush you to your goal but to help you periodically evaluate your progress.

The Direct Contact Method

Once you have scheduled your time, you are ready to begin your search in earnest. Beginning with the Direct Contact method, the first step is to develop a checklist for categorizing the types of firms for which you'd like to work. You might categorize firms by product line, size, customer type (such as industrial or consumer), growth prospects, or geographical location. Keep in mind, the shorter the list the easier it will be to locate a company that is right for you.

Next you will want to use this *JobBank* book to assemble your list of potential employers. Choose firms where *you* are most likely to be able to find a job. Try matching your skills with those that a specific job demands. Consider where your skills might be in demand, the degree of competition for employment, and the employment outlook at each company.

Separate your prospect list into three groups. The first 25 percent will be your primary target group, the next 25 percent will be your secondary group, and the remaining names will be your reserve group.

After you form your prospect list, begin working on your resume. Refer to the Resumes and Cover Letters section following this chapter for more information.

Once your resume is complete, begin researching your first batch of prospective employers. You will want to determine whether you would be happy working at the firms you are researching and to get a better idea of what their employment needs might be. You also need to obtain enough information to sound highly informed about the company during phone conversations and in mail correspondence. But don't go all out on your research yet! You probably won't be able to arrange interviews with some of these firms, so save your big research effort until you start to arrange interviews. Nevertheless, you should plan to spend several hours researching each firm. Do your research in batches to save time and energy. Start with this book, and find out what you can about each of the firms in your primary target group. For answers to specific questions, contact any pertinent professional associations that may be able to help you learn more about an employer. Read industry publications looking for articles on the firm. (Addresses of associations and names of important publications are listed after each section of employer listings in this book.) Then look up the company on the Internet or try additional resources at your local library. Keep organized, and maintain a folder on each firm.

The more you know about a company, the more likely you are to catch an interviewer's eye. (You'll also face fewer surprises once you get the job!)

Information to look for includes: company size; president, CEO, or owner's name; when the company was established; what each division does; and benefits that are important to you. An abundance of company information can now be found electronically, through the World Wide Web or commercial online services. Researching companies online is a convenient means of obtaining information quickly and easily. If you have access to the Internet, you can search from your home at any time of day.

You may search a particular company's Website for current information that may be otherwise unavailable in print. In fact, many companies that maintain a site update their information daily. In addition, you may also search articles written about the company online. Today, most of the nation's largest newspapers, magazines, trade publications, and regional business periodicals have online versions of their publications. To find additional resources, use a search engine like Yahoo! or Alta Vista and type in the keyword "companies" or "employers."

If you discover something that really disturbs you about the firm (they are about to close their only local office), or if you discover that your chances of getting a job there are practically nil (they have just instituted a hiring freeze), then cross them off your prospect list. If possible, supplement your research efforts by contacting individuals who know the firm well. Ideally you should make an informal contact with someone at that particular firm, but often a direct competitor or a major customer will be able to supply you with just as much information. At the very least, try to obtain whatever printed information the company has available -- not just annual reports, but product brochures, company profiles, or catalogs. This information is often available on the Internet.

Getting the Interview

Now it is time to make Direct Contact with the goal of arranging interviews. If you have read any books on job-searching, you may have noticed that most of these books tell you to avoid the human resources office like the plague. It is said that the human resources office never hires people; they screen candidates. Unfortunately, this is often the case. If you can identify the appropriate manager with the authority to hire you, you should try to contact that person directly.

The obvious means of initiating Direct Contact are:

- Mail (postal or electronic)
- Phone calls

Mail contact is a good choice if you have not been in the job market for a while. You can take your time to prepare a letter, say exactly what you want, and of course include your resume. Remember that employers receive many resumes every day. Don't be surprised if you do not get a response to your inquiry, *and don't spend weeks waiting for responses that may never come.* If you do send a letter, follow it up (or precede it) with a phone call. This will increase your impact, and because of the initial research you did, will underscore both your familiarity with and your interest in the firm. Bear in mind that your goal is to make your name a familiar one with prospective employers, so that when a position becomes available, your resume will be one of the first the hiring manager seeks out.

If you send a fax, always follow with a hard copy of your resume and cover letter in the mail. Often, through no fault of your own, a fax will come through illegibly and employers do not often have time to let candidates know.

DEVELOPING YOUR CONTACTS: NETWORKING

Some career counselors feel that the best route to a better job is through somebody you already know or through somebody to whom you can be introduced. These counselors recommend that you build your contact base beyond your current acquaintances by asking each one to introduce you, or refer you, to additional people in your field of interest.

The theory goes like this: You might start with 15 personal contacts, each of whom introduces you to three additional people, for a total of 45 additional contacts. Then each of these people introduces you to three additional people, which adds 135 additional contacts. Theoretically, you will soon know every person in the industry.

Of course, developing your personal contacts does not work quite as smoothly as the theory suggests because some people will not be able to introduce you to anyone. The further you stray from your initial contact base, the weaker your references may be. So, if you do try developing your own contacts, try to begin with as many people that you know personally as you can. Dig into your personal phone book and your holiday greeting card list and locate old classmates from school. Be particularly sure to approach people who perform your personal business such as your lawyer, accountant, banker, doctor, stockbroker, and insurance agent. These people develop a very broad contact base due to the nature of their professions.

Another alternative is to make a "cover call." Your cover call should be just like your cover letter: concise. Your first statement should interest the employer in you. Then try to subtly mention your familiarity with the firm. Don't be overbearing; keep your introduction to three sentences or less. Be pleasant, self-confident, and relaxed. This will greatly increase the chances of the person at the other end of the line developing the conversation. But don't press. If you are asked to follow up with "something in the mail," this signals the conversation's natural end. Don't try to prolong the conversation once it has ended, and don't ask what they want to receive in the mail. Always send your resume and a highly personalized follow-up letter, reminding the addressee of the phone conversation. *Always* include a cover letter if you are asked to send a resume, and treat your resume and cover letter as a total package. Gear your letter toward the specific position you are applying for and prove why you would be a “good match” for the position.

Unless you are in telephone sales, making smooth and relaxed cover calls will probably not come easily. Practice them on your own, and then with your friends or relatives.

DON'T BOTHER WITH MASS MAILINGS OR BARRAGES OF PHONE CALLS

Direct Contact does not mean burying every firm within a hundred miles with mail and phone calls. Mass mailings rarely work in the job hunt. This also applies to those letters that are personalized -- but dehumanized -- on an automatic typewriter or computer. Don't waste your time or money on such a project; you will fool no one but yourself.

The worst part of sending out mass mailings, or making unplanned phone calls to companies you have not researched, is that you are likely to be remembered as someone with little genuine interest in the firm, who lacks sincerity -- somebody that nobody wants to hire.

If you obtain an interview as a result of a telephone conversation, be sure to send a thank-you note reiterating the points you made during the conversation. You will appear more professional and increase your impact. However, unless specifically requested, don't mail your resume once an interview has been arranged. Take it with you to the interview instead.

You should never show up to seek a professional position without an appointment. Even if you are somehow lucky enough to obtain an interview, you will appear so unprofessional that you will not be seriously considered.

Preparing for the Interview

As each interview is arranged, begin your in-depth research. You should arrive at an interview knowing the company upside-down and inside-out. You need to know the company's products, types of customers, subsidiaries, parent company, principal locations, rank in the industry, sales and profit trends, type of ownership, size, current plans, and much more. By this time you have

probably narrowed your job search to one industry. Even if you haven't, you should still be familiar with common industry terms, the trends in the firm's industry, the firm's principal competitors and their relative performance, and the direction in which the industry leaders are headed.

You should arrive at an interview knowing the company upside-down and inside-out.

Dig into every resource you can! Surf the Internet. Read the company literature, the trade press, the business press, and if the company is public, call your stockbroker (if you have one) and ask for additional information. If possible, speak to someone at the firm before the interview, or if not, speak to someone at a competing firm. The more time you spend, the better.

Even if you feel extremely pressed for time, you should set aside several hours for pre-interview research.

If you have been out of the job market for some time, don't be surprised if you find yourself tense during your first few interviews. It will probably happen every time you re-enter the market, not just when you seek your first job after

HELP WANTED ADVERTISEMENTS

Only a small fraction of professional job openings are advertised. Yet the majority of jobseekers -- and quite a few people not in the job market -- spend a lot of time studying the help wanted ads. As a result, the competition for advertised openings is often very severe.

A moderate-sized employer told us about their experience advertising in the help wanted section of a major Sunday newspaper:

It was a disaster. We had over 500 responses from this relatively small ad in just one week. We have only two phone lines in this office and one was totally knocked out. We'll never advertise for professional help again.

If you insist on following up on help wanted ads, then research a firm before you reply to an ad. Preliminary research might help to separate you from all of the other professionals responding to that ad, many of whom will have only a passing interest in the opportunity. It will also give you insight about a particular firm, to help you determine if it is potentially a good match. That said, your chances of obtaining a job through the want ads are still much smaller than they are with the Direct Contact method.

getting out of school.

Tension is natural during an interview, but knowing you have done a thorough research job should put you more at ease. Make a list of questions that you think might be asked in each interview. Think out your answers carefully and practice them with a friend. Tape record your responses to the problem questions. (*See also in this chapter: Informational Interviews.)* If you feel particularly unsure of your interviewing skills, arrange your first interviews at firms you are not as interested in. (But remember it is common courtesy to seem enthusiastic about the possibility of working for any firm at which you interview.) Practice again on your own after these first few interviews. Go over the difficult questions that you were asked.

Take some time to really think about how you will convey your work history. Present “bad experiences” as “learning experiences.” Instead of saying “I hated my position as a salesperson because I had to bother people on the phone,” say “I realized that cold-calling was not my strong suit. Though I love working with people, I decided my talents would be best used in a more face-to-face atmosphere.” Always find some sort of lesson from previous jobs, as they all have one.

Interview Attire

How important is the proper dress for a job interview? Buying a complete wardrobe, donning new shoes, and having your hair styled every morning are not enough to guarantee you a career position as an investment banker. But on the other hand, if you can't find a clean, conservative suit or won't take the time to wash your hair, then you are just wasting your time by interviewing at all.

Personal grooming is as important as finding appropriate clothes for a job interview. Careful grooming indicates both a sense of thoroughness and self-confidence. This is not the time to make a statement -- take out the extra earrings and avoid any garish hair colors not found in nature. Women should not wear excessive makeup, and both men and women should refrain from wearing any perfume or cologne (it only takes a small spritz to leave an allergic interviewer with a fit of sneezing and a bad impression of your meeting). Men should be freshly shaven, even if the interview is late in the day, and men with long hair should have it pulled back and neat.

Men applying for any professional position should wear a suit, preferably in a conservative color such as navy or charcoal gray. It is easy to get away with wearing the same dark suit to consecutive interviews at the same company; just be sure to wear a different shirt and tie for each interview.

Women should also wear a business suit. Professionalism still dictates a suit with a skirt, rather than slacks, as proper interview garb for women. This is usually true even at companies where pants are acceptable attire for female employees. As much as you may disagree with this guideline, the more prudent time to fight this standard is after you land the job.

The final selection of candidates for a job opening won't be determined by dress, of course. However, inappropriate dress can quickly eliminate a first-round candidate. So while you shouldn't spend a fortune on a new wardrobe, you should be sure that your clothes are appropriate. The key is to dress at least as or slightly more formally and conservatively than the position would suggest.

What to Bring

Be complete. Everyone needs a watch, a pen, and a notepad. Finally, a briefcase or a leather-bound folder (containing extra, *unfolded*, copies of your resume) will help complete the look of professionalism.

Sometimes the interviewer will be running behind schedule. Don't be upset, be sympathetic. There is often pressure to interview a lot of candidates and to quickly fill a demanding position. So be sure to come to your interview with good reading material to keep yourself occupied and relaxed.

The Interview

The very beginning of the interview is the most important part because it determines the tone for the rest of it. Those first few moments are especially crucial. Do you smile when you meet? Do you establish enough eye contact, but not too much? Do you walk into the office with a self-assured and confident stride? Do you shake hands firmly? Do you make small talk easily without being garrulous? It is human nature to judge people by that first impression, so make sure it is a good one. But most of all, try to be yourself.

Often the interviewer will begin, after the small talk, by telling you about the company, the division, the department, or perhaps, the position. Because of your detailed research, the information about the company should be repetitive for you, and the interviewer would probably like nothing better than to avoid this regurgitation of the company biography. So if you can do so tactfully, indicate to the interviewer that you are very familiar with the firm. If he or she seems intent on providing you with background information, despite your hints, then acquiesce.

But be sure to remain attentive. If you can manage to generate a brief discussion of the company or the industry at this point, without being forceful, great. It will help to further build rapport, underscore your interest, and increase your impact.

> **The interviewer's job is to find a reason to turn you down; your job is to not provide that reason.**
>
> -John L. LaFevre, author, *How You Really Get Hired*
>
> Reprinted from the 1989/90 *CPC Annual,* with permission of the National Association of Colleges and Employers (formerly College Placement Council, Inc.), copyright holder.

Soon (if it didn't begin that way) the interviewer will begin the questions, many of which you will have already practiced. This period of the interview usually falls into one of two categories (or somewhere in between): either a structured interview, where the interviewer has a prescribed set of questions to ask; or an unstructured interview, where the interviewer will ask only leading questions to get you to talk about yourself, your experiences, and your goals. Try to sense as quickly as possible in which direction the interviewer wishes to proceed. This will make the interviewer feel more relaxed and in control of the situation.

Remember to keep attuned to the interviewer and make the length of your answers appropriate to the situation. If you are really unsure as to how detailed a response the interviewer is seeking, then ask.

As the interview progresses, the interviewer will probably mention some of the most important responsibilities of the position. If applicable, draw parallels between your experience and the demands of the position as detailed by the interviewer. Describe your past experience in the same manner that you do on your resume: emphasizing results and achievements and not merely describing activities. But don't exaggerate. Be on the level about your abilities.

The first interview is often the toughest, where many candidates are screened out. If you are interviewing for a very competitive position, you will have to make an impression that will last. Focus on a few of your greatest strengths that are relevant to the position. Develop these points carefully, state them again in different words, and then try to summarize them briefly at the end of the interview.

Often the interviewer will pause toward the end and ask if you have any questions. Particularly in a structured interview, this might be the one chance to really show your knowledge of and interest in the firm. Have a list prepared of specific questions that are of real interest to you. Let your questions subtly show your research and your knowledge of the firm's activities. It is wise to have an extensive list of questions, as several of them may be answered during the interview.

Do not turn your opportunity to ask questions into an interrogation. Avoid reading directly from your list of questions, and ask questions that you are fairly certain the interviewer can answer (remember how you feel when you cannot answer a question during an interview).

Even if you are unable to determine the salary range beforehand, do not ask about it during the first interview. You can always ask later. Above all, don't ask about fringe benefits until you have been offered a position. (Then be sure to get all the details.)

Try not to be negative about anything during the interview, particularly any past employer or any previous job. Be cheerful. Everyone likes to work with someone who seems to be happy. Even if you detest your current/former job or manager, do not make disparaging comments. The interviewer may construe this as a sign of a potential attitude problem and not consider you a strong candidate.

Don't let a tough question throw you off base. If you don't know the answer to a question, simply say so -- do not apologize. Just smile. Nobody can answer every question -- particularly some of the questions that are asked in job interviews.

Before your first interview, you may be able to determine how many rounds of interviews there usually are for positions at your level. (Of course it may differ quite a bit even within the different levels of one firm.) Usually you can count on attending at least two or three interviews, although some firms are known to give a minimum of six interviews for all professional positions. While you should be more relaxed as you return for subsequent interviews, the pressure will be on. The more prepared you are, the better.

Depending on what information you are able to obtain, you might want to vary your strategy quite a bit from interview to interview. For instance, if the first interview is a screening interview, then be sure a few of your strengths really stand out. On the other hand, if later interviews are primarily with people who are in a position to veto your hiring, but not to push it forward, then you should primarily focus on building rapport as opposed to reiterating and developing your key strengths.

If it looks as though your skills and background do not match the position the interviewer was hoping to fill, ask him or her if there is another division or subsidiary that perhaps could profit from your talents.

After the Interview

Write a follow-up letter immediately after the interview, while it is still fresh in the interviewer's mind (see the sample follow-up letter format found in the Resumes and Cover Letters chapter). Not only is this a thank-you, but it also gives you the chance to provide the interviewer with any details you may have forgotten (as long as they can be tactfully added in). If you haven't heard back from the interviewer within a week of sending your thank-you letter, call to stress your continued interest in the firm and the position. If you lost any points during the interview for any reason, this letter can help you regain footing. Be polite and make sure to stress your continued interest and competency to fill the position. Just don't forget to proofread it thoroughly. If you are unsure of the spelling of the interviewer's name, call the receptionist and ask.

THE BALANCING ACT: Looking for a New Job While Currently Employed

For those of you who are still employed, job-searching will be particularly tiring because it must be done in addition to your normal work responsibilities. So don't overwork yourself to the point where you show up to interviews looking exhausted or start to slip behind at your current job. On the other hand, don't be tempted to quit your present job! The long hours are worth it. Searching for a job while you have one puts you in a position of strength.

Making Contact

If you must be at your office during the business day, then you have additional problems to deal with. How can you work interviews into the business day? And if you work in an open office, how can you even call to set up interviews? Obviously, you should keep up the effort and the appearances on your present job. So maximize your use of the lunch hour, early mornings, and late afternoons for calling. If you keep trying, you'll be surprised how often you will be able to reach the executive you are trying to contact during your out-of-office hours. You can catch people as early as 8 a.m. and as late as 6 p.m. on frequent occasions.

Scheduling Interviews

Your inability to interview at any time other than lunch just might work to your advantage. If you can, try to set up as many interviews as possible for your lunch hour. This will go a long way to creating a relaxed atmosphere. But be sure the interviews don't stray too far from the agenda on hand.

Try calling as early as 8 a.m. and as late as 6 p.m. You'll be surprised how often you will be able to reach the executive you want during these times of the day.

Lunchtime interviews are much easier to obtain if you have substantial career experience. People with less experience will often find no alternative to taking time off for interviews. If you have to take time off, you have to take time off. But try to do this as little as possible. Try to take the whole day off in order to avoid being blatantly obvious about your job search, and try to schedule two to three interviews for the same day. (It is very difficult to maintain an optimum level of energy at more than three interviews in one day.) Explain to the interviewer why you might have to juggle your interview schedule; he/she should honor the respect you're showing your current employer by minimizing your days off and will probably appreciate the fact that another prospective employer is interested in you.

References

What do you tell an interviewer who asks for references from your current employer? Just say that while you are happy to have your former employers contacted, you are trying to keep your job search confidential and would rather that your current employer not be contacted until you have been given a firm offer.

IF YOU'RE FIRED OR LAID OFF: Picking Yourself Up and Dusting Yourself Off

If you've been fired or laid off, you are not the first and will not be the last to go through this traumatic experience. In today's changing economy, thousands of professionals lose their jobs every year. Even if you were terminated with just cause, do not lose heart. Remember, being fired is not a reflection on you as a person. It is usually a reflection of your company's staffing needs and its perception of your recent job performance and attitude. And if you were not performing up to par or enjoying your work, then you will probably be better off at another company anyway.

Be prepared for the question "Why were you fired?" during job interviews.

A thorough job search could take months, so be sure to negotiate a reasonable severance package, if possible, and determine to what benefits, such as health insurance, you are still legally entitled. Also, register for unemployment compensation immediately. Don't be surprised to find other professionals collecting unemployment compensation -- it is for everyone who has lost their job.

Don't start your job search with a flurry of unplanned activity. Start by choosing a strategy and working out a plan. Now is not the time for major changes in your life. If possible, remain in the same career and in the same geographical location, at least until you have been working again for a while. On the other hand, if the only industry for which you are trained is leaving, or is severely depressed in your area, then you should give prompt consideration to moving or switching careers.

Avoid mentioning you were fired when arranging interviews, but be prepared for the question "Why were you fired?" during an interview. If you were laid off as a result of downsizing, briefly explain, being sure to reinforce that your job loss was not due to performance. If you were in fact fired, be honest, but try to detail the reason as favorably as possible and portray what you have learned from your mistakes. If you are confident one of your past managers will give you a good reference, tell the interviewer to contact that person. Do not to speak negatively of your past employer and try not to sound particularly worried about your status of being temporarily unemployed.

Finally, don't spend too much time reflecting on why you were let go or how you might have avoided it. Think positively, look to the future, and be sure to follow a careful plan during your job search.

THE COLLEGE STUDENT: Conducting Your First Job Search

While you will be able to apply many of the basics covered earlier in this chapter to your job search, there are some situations unique to the college student's job search.

THE GPA QUESTION

You are interviewing for the job of your dreams. Everything is going well: You've established a good rapport, the interviewer seems impressed with your qualifications, and you're almost positive the job is yours. Then you're asked about your GPA, which is pitifully low. Do you tell the truth and watch your dream job fly out the window?

Never lie about your GPA (they may request your transcript, and no company will hire a liar). You can, however, explain if there is a reason you don't feel your grades reflect your abilities, and mention any other impressive statistics. For example, if you have a high GPA in your major, or in the last few semesters (as opposed to your cumulative college career), you can use that fact to your advantage.

Perhaps the biggest problem college students face is lack of experience. Many schools have internship programs designed to give students exposure to the field of their choice, as well as the opportunity to make valuable contacts. Check out your school's career services department to see what internships are available. If your school does not have a formal internship program, or if there are no available internships that appeal to you, try contacting local businesses and offering your services. Often, businesses will be more than willing to have an extra pair of hands (especially if those hands are unpaid!) for a day or two each week. Or try contacting school alumni to see if you can "shadow" them for a few days, and see what their daily duties are like.

Informational Interviews

Although many jobseekers do not do this, it can be extremely helpful to arrange an informational interview with a college alumnus or someone else who works in your desired industry. You interview them about their job, their company, and their industry with questions you have prepared in advance. This can be done over the phone but is usually done in person. This will provide you with a contact in the industry who may give you more valuable information -- or perhaps even a job opportunity -- in the future. Always follow up with a thank you letter that includes your contact information.

The goal is to try to begin building experience and establishing contacts as early as possible in your college career.

What do you do if, for whatever reason, you weren't able to get experience directly related to your desired career? First, look at your previous jobs and see if there's anything you can highlight. Did you supervise or train other employees? Did you reorganize the accounting system, or boost productivity in some way? Accomplishments like these demonstrate leadership, responsibility, and innovation -- qualities that most companies look for in employees. And don't forget volunteer activities and school clubs, which can also showcase these traits.

On-Campus Recruiting

Companies will often send recruiters to interview on-site at various colleges. This gives students a chance to interview with companies that may not have interviewed them otherwise. This is particularly true if a company schedules "open" interviews, in which the only screening process is who is first in line at the sign-ups. Of course, since many more applicants gain interviews in this format, this also means that many more people are rejected. The on-campus interview is generally a screening interview, to see if it is worth the company's time to invite you in for a second interview. So do everything possible to make yourself stand out from the crowd.

The first step, of course, is to check out any and all information your school's career center has on the company. If the information seems out of date, check out the company on the Internet or call the company's headquarters and ask for any printed information.

Many companies will host an informational meeting for interviewees, often the evening before interviews are scheduled to take place. DO NOT MISS THIS MEETING. The recruiter will almost certainly ask if you attended. Make an effort to stay after the meeting and talk with the company's representatives. Not only does this give you an opportunity to find out more information about both the company and the position, it also makes you stand out in the recruiter's mind. If there's a particular company that you had your heart set on, but you weren't able to get an interview with them, attend the information session anyway. You may be able to persuade the recruiter to squeeze you into the schedule. (Or you may discover that the company really isn't the right fit for you after all.)

Try to check out the interview site beforehand. Some colleges may conduct "mock" interviews that take place in one of the standard interview rooms. Or you may be able to convince a career counselor (or even a custodian) to let you sneak a peek during off-hours. Either way, having an idea of the room's setup will help you to mentally prepare.

Arrive at least 15 minutes early to the interview. The recruiter may be ahead of schedule, and might meet you early. But don't be surprised if previous interviews have run over, resulting in your 30-minute slot being reduced to 20 minutes (or less). Don't complain or appear anxious; just use the time you do have as efficiently as possible to showcase the reasons *you* are the ideal candidate. Staying calm and composed in these situations will work to your advantage.

LAST WORDS

A parting word of advice. Again and again during your job search you will face rejection. You will be rejected when you apply for interviews. You will be rejected after interviews. For every job offer you finally receive, you probably will have been rejected many times. Don't let rejections slow you down. Keep reminding yourself that the sooner you go out, start your job search, and get those rejections flowing in, the closer you will be to obtaining the job you want.

RESUMES AND COVER LETTERS

When filling a position, an employer will often have 100-plus applicants, but time to interview only a handful of the most promising ones. As a result, he or she will reject most applicants after only briefly skimming their resumes.

Unless you have phoned and talked to the employer -- which you should do whenever you can -- you will be chosen or rejected for an interview entirely on the basis of your resume and cover letter. *Your cover letter must catch the employer's attention, and your resume must hold it.* (But remember -- a resume is no substitute for a job search campaign. *You* must seek a job. Your resume is only one tool, albeit a critical one.)

RESUME FORMAT:
Mechanics of a First Impression

The Basics

Employers dislike long resumes, so unless you have an unusually strong background with many years of experience and a diversity of outstanding achievements, keep your resume length to one page. If you must squeeze in more information than would otherwise fit, try using a smaller typeface or changing the margins. Watch also for "widows" at the end of paragraphs. You can often free up some space if you can shorten the information enough to get rid of those single words taking up an entire line. Another tactic that works with some word processing programs is to decrease the font size of your paragraph returns and changing the spacing between lines.

Print your resume on standard 8 1/2" x 11" paper. Since recruiters often get resumes in batches of hundreds, a smaller-sized resume may be lost in the pile. Oversized resumes are likely to get crumpled at the edges, and won't fit easily in their files.

First impressions matter, so make sure the recruiter's first impression of your resume is a good one. Never hand-write your resume (or cover letter)! Print your resume on quality paper that has weight and texture, in a conservative color such as white, ivory, or pale gray. Good resume paper is easy to find at many stores that sell stationery or office products. It is even available at some drug stores. Use *matching* paper and envelopes for both your resume and cover letter. One hiring manager at a major magazine throws out all resumes that arrive on paper that differs in color from the envelope!

Do not buy paper with images of clouds and rainbows in the background or anything that looks like casual stationery that you would send to your favorite aunt. Do not spray perfume or cologne on your resume. Do not include your picture with your resume unless you have a specific and appropriate reason to do so.

Another tip: Do a test print of your resume (and cover letter), to make sure the watermark is on the same side as the text so that you can read it. Also make sure it is right-side up. As trivial as this may sound, some recruiters check for this! One recruiter at a law firm in New Hampshire sheepishly admitted this is the first thing he checks. *"I open each envelope and check the watermarks on the resume and cover letter. Those candidates that have it wrong go into a different pile."*

Getting it on Paper

Modern photocomposition typesetting gives you the clearest, sharpest image, a wide variety of type styles, and effects such as italics, bold-facing, and book-like justified margins. It is also too expensive for many jobseekers. The quality of today's laser printers means that a computer-generated resume can look just as impressive as one that has been professionally typeset.

A computer with a word processing or desktop publishing program is the most common way to generate your resume. This allows you the flexibility to make changes almost instantly and to store different drafts on disk. Word processing and desktop publishing programs also offer many different fonts to choose from, each taking up different amounts of space. (It is generally best to stay between 9-point and 12-point font size.) Many other options are also available, such as bold-facing or italicizing for emphasis and the ability to change and manipulate spacing. It is generally recommended to leave the right-hand margin unjustified as this keeps the spacing between the text even and therefore easier to read. It is not wrong to justify both margins of text, but if possible try it both ways before you decide.

For a resume on paper, the end result will be largely determined by the quality of the printer you use. Laser printers will generally provide the best quality. Do not use a dot matrix printer.

Many companies now use scanning equipment to screen the resumes they receive, and certain paper, fonts, and other features are more compatible with this technology. White paper is preferable, as well as a standard font such as Courier or Helvetica. You should use at least a 10-point font, and avoid bolding, italics, underlining, borders, boxes, or graphics.

Household typewriters and office typewriters with nylon or other cloth ribbons are *not* good enough for typing your resume. If you don't have access to a quality word processing program, hire a professional with the resources to prepare your resume for you. Keep in mind that businesses such as Kinko's (open 24 hours) provide access to computers with quality printers.

Don't make your copies on an office photocopier. Only the human resources office may see the resume you mail. Everyone else may see only a copy of it, and copies of copies quickly become unreadable. Furthermore, sending photocopies of your resume or cover letter is completely unprofessional. Either print out each copy individually, or take your resume to a professional copy shop, which will generally offer professionally maintained, extra-high-quality photocopiers and charge fairly reasonable prices. You want your resume to represent you with the look of polished quality.

Proof with Care

Whether you typed it or paid to have it produced professionally, mistakes on resumes are not only embarrassing, but will usually remove you from consideration (particularly if something obvious such as your name is misspelled). No matter how much you paid someone else to type, write, or typeset your resume, *you* lose if there is a mistake. So proofread it as carefully as possible. Get a friend to help you. Read your draft aloud as your friend checks the proof copy. Then have your friend read aloud while you check. Next, read it letter by letter to check spelling and punctuation.

If you are having it typed or typeset by a resume service or a printer, and you don't have time to proof it, pay for it and take it home. Proof it there and bring it back later to get it corrected and printed.

If you wrote your resume with a word processing program, use the built-in spell checker to double-check for spelling errors. Keep in mind that a spell checker will not find errors such as "to" for "two" or "wok" for "work." Many spell check programs do not recognize missing or misused punctuation, nor are they set to check the spelling of capitalized words. It's important that you still proofread your resume to check for grammatical mistakes and other problems, even after it has been spellchecked. If you find mistakes, do not make edits in pen or pencil or use white-out to fix them on the final copy!

Electronic Resumes

As companies rely increasingly on emerging technologies to find qualified candidates for job openings, you may opt to create an electronic resume in order to remain competitive in today's job market. Why is this important? Companies today sometimes request that resumes be submitted by e-mail, and many hiring managers regularly check online resume databases for candidates to fill unadvertised job openings. Other companies enlist the services of electronic employment database services, which charge jobseekers a nominal fee to have their resumes posted to the database to be viewed by potential employers. Still other companies use their own automated applicant tracking systems, in which case your resume is fed through a scanner that sends the image to a computer that "reads" your resume, looking for keywords, and files it accordingly in its database.

Whether you're posting your resume online, e-mailing it directly to an employer, sending it to an electronic employment database, or sending it to a company you suspect uses an automated applicant tracking system, you must create some form of electronic resume to take advantage of the technology. Don't panic! An electronic resume is simply a modified version of your conventional resume. An electronic resume is one that is sparsely formatted, but filled with keywords and important facts.

In order to post your resume to the Internet -- either to an online resume database or through direct e-mail to an employer -- you will need to change the way your resume is formatted. Instead of a Word, WordPerfect, or other word processing document, save your resume as a plain text, DOS, or ASCII file. These three terms are basically interchangeable, and describe text at its simplest, most basic level, without the formatting such as boldface or italics that most jobseekers use to make their resumes look more interesting. If you use e-mail, you'll notice that all of your messages are written and received in this format. First, you should remove all formatting from your resume including boldface, italics, underlining, bullets, differing font sizes, and graphics. Then, convert and save your resume as a plain text file. Most word processing programs have a "save as" feature that allows you to save files in different formats. Here, you should choose "text only" or "plain text."

Another option is to create a resume in HTML (hypertext markup language), the text formatting language used to publish information on the World Wide Web. However, the real usefulness of HTML resumes is still being explored. Most of the major online databases do not accept HTML resumes, and the vast majority of companies only accept plain text resumes through their e-mail.

Finally, if you simply wish to send your resume to an electronic employment database or a company that uses an automated applicant tracking system, there is no need to convert your resume to a plain text file. The only change you need to make is to organize the information in your resume by keywords. Employers are likely to do keyword searches for information, such as degree held or knowledge of particular types of software. Therefore, using the right keywords or key phrases in your resume is critical to its ultimate success. Keywords are usually nouns or short phrases that the computer searches for which refer to experience, training, skills, and abilities. For example, let's say an employer searches an employment database for a sales representative with the following criteria:

BS/BA
exceeded quota
cold calls
high energy
willing to travel

Even if you have the right qualifications, neglecting to use these keywords would result in the computer passing over your resume. Although there is no way to know for sure which keywords employers are most likely to search for, you can make educated guesses by checking the help-wanted ads or online job postings for your type of job. You should also arrange keywords in a keyword summary, a paragraph listing your qualifications that immediately follows your name and address (see sample letter in this chapter). In addition, choose a nondecorative font with clear, distinct characters, such as Helvetica or Times. It is more difficult for a scanner to accurately pick up the more unusual fonts. Boldface and all capital letters are best used only for major section headings, such as "Experience" and "Education." It is also best to avoid using italics or underlining, since this can cause the letters to bleed into one another.

Types of Resumes

The most common resume formats are the functional resume, the chronological resume, and the combination resume. (Examples can be found at the end of this chapter.) A functional resume focuses on skills and de-emphasizes job titles, employers, etc. A functional resume is best if you have been out of the work force for a long time or are changing careers. It is also good if you want to highlight specific skills and strengths, especially if all of your work experience has been at one company. This format can also be a good choice if you are just out of school or have no experience in your desired field.

Choose a chronological format if you are currently working or were working recently, and if your most recent experiences relate to your desired field. Use reverse chronological order and include dates. To a recruiter your last job and your latest schooling are the most important, so put the last first and list the rest going back in time.

A combination resume is perhaps the most common. This resume simply combines elements of the functional and chronological resume formats. This is used by many jobseekers with a solid track record who find elements of both types useful.

Organization

Your name, phone number, e-mail address (if you have one), and a complete mailing address should be at the top of your resume. Try to make your name stand out by using a slightly larger font size or all capital letters. Be sure to spell out everything. Never abbreviate St. for Street or Rd. for Road. If you are a college student, you should also put your home address and phone number at the top. Change your message on your answering machine if necessary – RUSH blaring in the background or your sorority sisters screaming may not come across well to all recruiters. If you think you may be moving within six months then include a second address and phone number of a trusted friend or relative who can reach you no matter where you are.

Remember that employers will keep your resume on file and may contact you months later if a position opens that fits your qualifications. All too often, candidates are unreachable because they have moved and had not previously provided enough contact options on their resume.

Next, list your experience, then your education. If you are a recent graduate, list your education first, unless your experience is more important than your education. (For example, if you have just graduated from a teaching school, have some business experience, and are applying for a job in business, you would list your business experience first.)

Keep everything easy to find. Put the dates of your employment and education on the left of the page. Put the names of the companies you worked for and the schools you attended a few spaces to the right of the dates. Put the city and state, or the city and country, where you studied or worked to the right of the page.

The important thing is simply to break up the text in some logical way that makes your resume visually attractive and easy to scan, so experiment to see which layout works best for your resume. However you set it up, *stay consistent*. Inconsistencies in fonts, spacing, or tenses will make your resume look sloppy. Also, be sure to use tabs to keep your information vertically lined up, rather than the less precise space bar.

RESUME CONTENT:
Say it with Style

Sell Yourself

You are selling your skills and accomplishments in your resume, so it is important to inventory yourself and know yourself. If you have achieved something, say so. Put it in the best possible light, but avoid subjective statements, such as "I am a hard worker" or "I get along well with my coworkers." Just stick to the facts.

While you shouldn't hold back or be modest, don't exaggerate your achievements to the point of misrepresentation. Be honest. Many companies will immediately drop an applicant from consideration (or fire a current employee) upon discovering inaccurate or untrue information on a resume or other application material.

Write down the important (and pertinent) things you have done, but do it in as few words as possible. Your resume will be scanned, not read, and short, concise phrases are much more effective than long-winded sentences. Avoid the use of "I" when emphasizing your accomplishments. Instead, use brief phrases beginning with action verbs.

While some technical terms will be unavoidable, you should try to avoid excessive "technicalese." Keep in mind that the first person to see your resume may be a human resources person who won't necessarily know all the jargon -- and how can they be impressed by something they don't understand?

Keep it Brief

Also, try to hold your paragraphs to six lines or less. If you have more than six lines of information about one job or school, put it in two or more paragraphs. A short resume will be examined more carefully. Remember: Your resume usually has between eight and 45 seconds to catch an employer's eye. So make every second count.

Job Objective

A functional resume may require a job objective to give it focus. One or two sentences describing the job you are seeking can clarify in what capacity your skills will be best put to use. Be sure that your stated objective is in line with the position you're applying for.

Examples:

An entry-level editorial assistant position in the publishing industry.
A senior management position with a telecommunications firm.

USE ACTION VERBS

How you write your resume is just as important as *what* you write. In describing previous work experiences, the strongest resumes use short phrases beginning with action verbs. Below are a few you may want to use. (This list is not all-inclusive.)

achieved	developed	integrated	purchased
administered	devised	interpreted	reduced
advised	directed	interviewed	regulated
arranged	distributed	launched	represented
assisted	established	managed	resolved
attained	evaluated	marketed	restored
budgeted	examined	mediated	restructured
built	executed	monitored	revised
calculated	expanded	negotiated	scheduled
collaborated	expedited	obtained	selected
collected	facilitated	operated	served
compiled	formulated	ordered	sold
completed	founded	organized	solved
computed	generated	participated	streamlined
conducted	headed	performed	studied
consolidated	identified	planned	supervised
constructed	implemented	prepared	supplied
consulted	improved	presented	supported
controlled	increased	processed	tested
coordinated	initiated	produced	trained
created	installed	proposed	updated
determined	instructed	published	wrote

Don't include a job objective on a chronological resume unless your previous work experiences are <u>completely</u> unrelated to the position for which you're applying. The presence of an overly specific job objective might eliminate you from consideration for other positions that a recruiter feels are a better match for your qualifications. But even if you don't put an objective on paper, having a career goal in mind as you write can help give your resume a solid sense of direction.

Some jobseekers may choose to include both "Relevant Experience" and "Additional Experience" sections. This can be useful, as it allows the jobseeker to place more emphasis on certain experiences and to de-emphasize others.

Emphasize continued experience in a particular job area or continued interest in a particular industry. De-emphasize irrelevant positions. It is okay to include one opening line providing a general description of each company you've worked at. Delete positions that you held for less than four months (unless you are a very recent college grad or still in school). Stress your results and your achievements, elaborating on how you contributed in your previous jobs. Did you increase sales, reduce costs, improve a product, implement a new program? Were you promoted? Use specific numbers (i.e., quantities, percentages, dollar amounts) whenever possible.

Education

Keep it brief if you have more than two years of career experience. Elaborate more if you have less experience. If you are a recent college graduate, you may choose to include any high school activities that are directly relevant to your career. If you've been out of school for a while you don't need to list your education prior to college.

Mention degrees received and any honors or special awards. Note individual courses or projects you participated in that might be relevant for employers. For example, if you are an English major applying for a position as a business writer, be sure to mention any business or economics courses. Previous experience such as Editor-in-Chief of the school newspaper would be relevant as well.

If you are uploading your resume to an online job hunting site such as CareerCity.com, action verbs are still important, but the key words or key nouns that a computer would search for become more important. For example, if you're seeking an accounting position, key nouns that a computer would search for such as "Lotus 1-2-3" or "CPA" or "payroll" become very important.

Highlight Impressive Skills

Be sure to mention any computer skills you may have. You may wish to include a section entitled "Additional Skills" or "Computer Skills," in which you list any software programs you know. An additional skills section is also an ideal place to mention fluency in a foreign language.

Personal Data

This section is optional, but if you choose to include it, keep it brief. A one-word mention of hobbies such as fishing, chess, baseball, cooking, etc., can give the person who will interview you a good way to open up the conversation.

Team sports experience is looked at favorably. It doesn't hurt to include activities that are somewhat unusual (fencing, Akido, '70s music) or that somehow relate to the position or the company to which you're applying. For instance, it would be worth noting if you are a member of a professional organization in your industry of interest. Never include information about your age, alias, date of birth, health, physical characteristics, marital status, religious affiliation, or political/moral beliefs.

References

The most that is needed is the sentence "References available upon request" at the bottom of your resume. If you choose to leave it out, that's fine. This line is not really necessary. It is understood that references will most likely be asked for and provided by you later on in the interviewing process. Do not actually send references with your resume and cover letter unless specifically requested.

HIRING A RESUME WRITER: Is it the Right Choice for You?

If you write reasonably well, it is to your advantage to write your own resume. Writing your resume forces you to review your experiences and figure out how to explain your accomplishments in clear, brief phrases. This will help you when you explain your work to interviewers. It is also easier to tailor your resume to each position you're applying for when you have put it together yourself.

If you write your resume, everything will be in your own words; it will sound like you. It will say what you want it to say. If you are a good writer, know yourself well, and have a good idea of which parts of your background employers are looking for, you should be able to write your own resume better than someone else. If you decide to write your resume yourself, have as many people as possible review and proofread it. Welcome objective opinions and other perspectives.

When to Get Help

If you have difficulty writing in "resume style" (which is quite unlike normal written language), if you are unsure which parts of your background to emphasize, or if you think your resume would make your case better if it did not follow one of the standard forms outlined either here or in a book on resumes, then you should consider having it professionally written.

Even some professional resume writers we know have had their resumes written with the help of fellow professionals. They sought the help of someone who could be objective about their background, as well as provide an experienced sounding board to help focus their thoughts.

If You Hire a Pro

The best way to choose a writer is by reputation: the recommendation of a friend, a personnel director, your school placement officer, or someone else knowledgeable in the field.

Important questions:

- "How long have you been writing resumes?"
- "If I'm not satisfied with what you write, will you go over it with me and change it?"
- "Do you charge by the hour or a flat rate?"

There is no sure relation between price and quality, except that you are unlikely to get a good writer for less than $50 for an uncomplicated resume and you shouldn't have to pay more than $300 unless your experience is very extensive or complicated. There will be additional charges for printing. Assume nothing no matter how much you pay. It is your career at stake if there are mistakes on your resume!

Few resume services will give you a firm price over the phone, simply because some resumes are too complicated and take too long to do for a predetermined price. Some services will quote you a price that applies to almost all of their customers. Once you decide to use a specific writer, you should insist on a firm price quote *before* engaging their services. Also, find out how expensive minor changes will be.

COVER LETTERS: Quick, Clear, and Concise

Always mail a cover letter with your resume. In a cover letter you can show an interest in the company that you can't show in a resume. You can also point out one or two of your skills or accomplishments the company can put to good use.

Make it Personal

The more personal you can get, the better, so long as you keep it professional. If someone known to the person you are writing has recommended that you contact the company, get permission to include his/her name in the letter. If you can get the name of a person to send the letter to, address it directly to that person (after first calling the company to verify the spelling of the person's name, correct title, and mailing address). Be sure to put the person's name and title on both the letter and the envelope. This will ensure that your letter will get through to the proper person, even if a new person now occupies this position. It will not always be possible to get the name of a person. Always strive to get at least a title.

Be sure to mention something about why you have an interest in the company -- *so many candidates apply for jobs with no apparent knowledge of what the company does!* This conveys the message that they just want any job.

Type cover letters in full. Don't try the cheap and easy ways, like using a computer mail merge program or photocopying the body of your letter and typing in the inside address and salutation. You will give the impression that you are mailing to a host of companies and have no particular interest in any one.

Print your cover letter on the same color and same high-quality paper as your resume.

Cover letter basic format

Paragraph 1: State what the position is that you are seeking. It is not always necessary to state how you found out about the position -- often you will apply without knowing that a position is open.

Paragraph 2: Include what you know about the company and why you are interested in working there. Mention any prior contact with the company or someone known to the hiring person if relevant. Briefly state your qualifications and what you can offer. (Do not talk about what you cannot do).
Paragraph 3: Close with your phone number and where/when you can be reached. Make a request for an interview. State when you will follow up by phone (or mail or e-mail if the ad requests no phone calls). Do not wait long -- generally five working days. If you say you're going to follow up, then actually do it! This phone call can get your resume noticed when it might otherwise sit in a stack of 225 other resumes.

Cover letter do's and don'ts

- *Do* keep your cover letter brief and to the point.
- *Do* be sure it is error-free.
- *Do* accentuate what you can offer the company, not what you hope to gain.
- *Do* be sure your phone number and address is on your cover letter just in case it gets separated from your resume (this happens!).
- *Do* check the watermark by holding the paper up to a light -- be sure it is facing forward so it is readable -- on the same side as the text, and right-side up.
- *Do* sign your cover letter (or type your name if you are sending it electronically). Blue or black ink are both fine. Do not use red ink.
- *Don't* just repeat information verbatim from your resume.
- *Don't* overuse the personal pronoun "I."
- *Don't* send a generic cover letter -- show your personal knowledge of and interest in that particular company.

THANK YOU LETTERS: Another Way to Stand Out

As mentioned earlier, *always* send a thank you letter after an interview (see the sample later in this section). So few candidates do this and it is yet another way for you to stand out. Be sure to mention something specific from the interview and restate your interest in the company and the position.

It is generally acceptable to handwrite your thank you letter on a generic thank you card (but *never* a postcard). Make sure handwritten notes are neat and legible. However, if you are in doubt, typing your letter is always the safe bet. If you met with several people it is fine to send them each an individual thank you letter. Call the company if you need to check on the correct spelling of their names.

Remember to:
- Keep it short.
- Proofread it carefully.
- Send it *promptly*.

FUNCTIONAL RESUME

C.J. RAVENCLAW

129 Pennsylvania Avenue
Washington DC 20500
202/555-6652
e-mail: ravenclaw@dcpress.net

Objective

A position as a graphic designer commensurate with my acquired skills and expertise.

Summary

Extensive experience in plate making, separations, color matching, background definition, printing, mechanicals, color corrections, and personnel supervision. A highly motivated manager and effective communicator. Proven ability to:

- **Create Commercial Graphics**
- **Produce Embossed Drawings**
- **Color Separate**
- **Control Quality**
- **Resolve Printing Problems**
- **Analyze Customer Satisfaction**

Qualifications

Printing:
Knowledgeable in black and white as well as color printing. Excellent judgment in determining acceptability of color reproduction through comparison with original. Proficient at producing four- or five-color corrections on all media, as well as restyling previously reproduced four-color artwork.

Customer Relations:
Routinely work closely with customers to ensure specifications are met. Capable of striking a balance between technical printing capabilities and need for customer satisfaction through entire production process.

Specialties:
Practiced at creating silk screen overlays for a multitude of processes including velo bind, GBC bind, and perfect bind. Creative design and timely preparation of posters, flyers, and personalized stationery.

Personnel Supervision:
Skillful at fostering atmosphere that encourages highly talented artists to balance high-level creativity with maximum production. Consistently beat production deadlines. Instruct new employees, apprentices, and students in both artistry and technical operations.

Experience

Graphic Arts Professor, Ohio State University, Columbus OH (1998-2002).
Manager, Design Graphics, Washington DC (2003-present).

Education

Massachusetts Conservatory of Art, Ph.D. 1996
University of Massachusetts, B.A. 1994

CHRONOLOGICAL RESUME

HARRY SEABORN
557 Shoreline Drive
Seattle, WA 98404
(206) 555-6584
e-mail: hseaborn@centco.com

EXPERIENCE

THE CENTER COMPANY — Seattle, WA
Systems Programmer — 2002-present

- Develop and maintain customer accounting and order tracking database using a Visual Basic front end and SQL server.
- Plan and implement migration of company wide transition from mainframe-based dumb terminals to a true client server environment using Windows NT Workstation and Server.
- Oversee general local and wide area network administration including the development of a variety of intranet modules to improve internal company communication and planning across divisions.

INFO TECH, INC. — Seattle, WA
Technical Manager — 1996-2002

- Designed and managed the implementation of a network providing the legal community with a direct line to Supreme Court cases across the Internet using SQL Server and a variety of Internet tools.
- Developed a system to make the entire library catalog available on line using PERL scripts and SQL.
- Used Visual Basic and Microsoft Access to create a registration system for university registrar.

EDUCATION

SALEM STATE UNIVERSITY — Salem, OR
M.S. in Computer Science. — 1999
B.S. in Computer Science. — 1997

COMPUTER SKILLS

- Programming Languages: Visual Basic, Java, C++, SQL, PERL
- Software: SQL Server, Internet Information Server, Oracle
- Operating Systems: Windows NT, UNIX, Linux

ACCOUNTING & MANAGEMENT CONSULTING

You can expect to find the following types of companies in this section:
Consulting and Research Firms • Industrial Accounting Firms • Management Services • Public Accounting Firms • Tax Preparation Companies

Accountants and auditors will add 264,000 new positions by 2014, a 22.4% growth, increasing from 1,176,000 to 1,440,000. An increase in the number of businesses, changing financial laws and regulations, and increased scrutiny of company finances will drive growth. Management analyst positions will increase by 122,000 jobs from 605,000 to 727,000, a 20.1% growth. Industry and government will rely on outside expertise to improve the performance of their organizations. Job growth is projected in very large consulting firms with international expertise and in smaller consulting firms that specialize in specific areas, such as biotechnology, healthcare, information technology, human resources, engineering, and marketing.

Alabama

FRAZIER & DEETER LLC
2000 Morris Avenue, Suite 1710, Birmingham AL 35203. 205/226-2104. **Fax:** 205/226-2103. **Contact:** Corporate Human Resources. **E-mail address:** hr@frazierdeeter.com. **World Wide Web address:** http://www.frazier-deeter.com. **Description:** Provides a wide-range of tax, auditing, accounting, and advisory services. **Note:** Send resumes to the Atlanta corporate office via email: sarah.werner@frazierdeeter.com or via fax: 404/253-7501. **Positions advertised include:** Experienced Audit Professionals, Entry-level Audit Professionals, Entry-level Tax Professionals.

Arizona

COMPREHENSIVE BUSINESS SERVICES
4431 East Broadway Boulevard, Tucson AZ 85711. 520/881-7514. **Contact:** Human Resources. **Description:** Provides a wide range of accounting services to small business owners nationwide. Services include accounting and record keeping, payroll administration, budget and business planning, and consulting.

DELOITTE & TOUCHE
2901 North Central Avenue, Suite 1200, Phoenix AZ 85012-2799. 602/234-5100. **Fax:** 602/234-5186. **Contact:** Human Resources Department. **World Wide Web address:** http://www.us.deloitte.com. **Description:** An international firm of certified public accountants providing professional accounting, auditing, tax, and management consulting services to widely diversified clients. The company has a specialized program consisting of national industry groups and functional groups that cross industry lines. Groups are involved in various disciplines including accounting, auditing, taxation management advisory services, small and growing businesses, mergers and acquisitions, and computer applications. **Positions advertised include:** Federal Corporate Tax Manager; International Tax Senior; Multistate Tax Senior. **Parent company:** Deloitte Touche Tohmatsu. **Number of employees at this location:** 200. **Number of employees worldwide:** 120,000.

ERNST & YOUNG LLP
One Renaissance Square, Two North Central Avenue, Suite 2300, Phoenix AZ 85004. 602/322-3000. **Fax:** 602/322-3023. **Contact:** Human Resources. **World Wide Web address:** http://www.ey.com. **Description:** A certified public accounting firm that also provides management consulting services. Services include data processing, financial modeling, financial feasibility studies, production planning and inventory management, management sciences, health care planning, human resources, cost accounting, and budgeting systems. **Positions advertised include:** Audit Manager; IT Audit Senior; Real Estate Advisory Associate. **Corporate headquarters location:** New York NY. **Other area locations:** Tucson AZ.

KPMG
400 East Van Buren Street, Suite 1100, Phoenix AZ 85004. 602/253-2000. **Contact:** Human Resources. **World Wide Web address:** http://www.kpmg.com. **Description:** KPMG delivers a wide range of value-added assurance, tax, and consulting services. **Positions advertised include:** Audit Sr. Associate; director, KPMG Forensic. **Corporate headquarters location:** Montvale NJ. **Parent company:** KPMG International has more than 85,000 employees worldwide, including 6,500 partners and 60,000 professional staff, serving clients in 155 countries. KPMG International is a leader among professional services firms engaged in capturing, managing, assessing, and delivering information to create knowledge that will help its clients maximize shareholder value.

PRICEWATERHOUSECOOPERS
1850 North Central Avenue, Suite 700, Phoenix AZ 85004-4563. 602/364-8000. **Contact:** Human Resources. **World Wide Web address:** http://www.pwcglobal.com. **Description:** One of the largest certified public accounting firms in the world. PricewaterhouseCoopers provides public accounting, business advisory, management consulting, and taxation services. **Positions advertised include:** Assurance Senior Associate; Systems Assurance Senior/Assoc.; Manager; Assurance Manager. **Corporate headquarters location:** New York NY. **Other U.S. locations:** Nationwide.

California

BAIN & COMPANY
3 Embarcadero Center, San Francisco CA 94111. 415/627-1000. **Fax:** 415/627-1033. **Contact:** Stephanie Davis, Recruiting Manager. **E-mail address:** stephanie.davis@bain.com. **World Wide Web address:** http://www.bain.com. **Description:** An international management consulting firm that helps major companies achieve higher levels of competitiveness and profitability. Founded in 1973. **Special programs:** Internships. **Corporate headquarters location:** Boston MA. **Other area locations:** Palo Alto CA; Los Angeles CA. **Other U.S. locations:** New York NY; Atlanta GA; Houston TX; Chicago IL. **International locations:** Worldwide.

BEARINGPOINT, INC.
355 South Grand Avenue, Suite 1700, Los Angeles CA 90071. 213/443-4100. **Fax:** 213/626-0620. **Contact:** Human Resources. **World Wide Web address:** http://www.bearingpoint.com. **Description:** Delivers a wide range of value-added assurance, tax, and consulting services. **Positions advertised include:** Management Analyst; PeopleSoft General Ledger consultant; SFA Requirements Analyst; Senior Manager, Insurance. **Corporate headquarters location:** McLean VA. **Other are locations:** Costa Mesa CA; Los Angeles CA; Mountain View CA; Sacramento CA; San Diego CA; San Francisco CA; San Jose CA. **Other U.S. locations:** Nationwide. **Listed on:** New York Stock Exchange. **Stock exchange symbol:** BE.

BENSON & NEFF
One Post Street, Suite 2150, San Francisco CA 94104-5225. 415/705-5615. **Fax:** 415/705-5633. **Contact:** Director of Personnel. **E-mail address:** bn@bensonneff.com. **World Wide Web address:**

http://www.bensonneff.com. **Description:** A certified public accounting firm offering accounting, auditing, tax, computer, and other consulting services. **Corporate headquarters location:** This location. **Operations at this facility include:** Service.

CRAWFORD PIMENTEL & COMPANY, INC.
2150 Trade Zone Boulevard, Suite 200, San Jose CA 95131. 408/942-6888. **Fax:** 408/942-0194. **Contact:** Gene Gauthier, Human Resources. **E-mail address:** recruiting@cpconet.com. **World Wide Web address:** http://www.1040tax.com. **Description:** A public accounting firm that also offers management advisory, technology consulting, and business consulting services. **Special programs:** Training. **Corporate headquarters location:** This location. **Operations at this facility include:** Service. **Listed on:** Privately held. **Number of employees at this location:** 25.

DELOITTE & TOUCHE
50 Fremont Street, Suite 3100, San Francisco CA 94105-2230. 415/783-4000. **Toll-free phone:** 888/APPLYDT. **Fax:** 415/783-4329. **Contact:** Human Resources. **E-mail address:** dtcareers@deloitte.com. **World Wide Web address:** http://www.us.deloitte.com. **Description:** An international firm of certified public accountants providing professional accounting, auditing, tax, and management consulting services to widely diversified clients. **Positions advertised include:** Audit Manager; BDC Director; Business Analyst; CDDT Framework Product Manager; Consultant, Technology Integration; Consultant, Network Security Specialist. **Corporate headquarters location:** Switzerland. **Other area locations:** Statewide. **Other U.S. locations:** Nationwide.

ERNST & YOUNG LLP
303 Almaden Boulevard, San Jose CA 95110. 408/947-5500. **Contact:** Director of Human Resources. **World Wide Web address:** http://www.ey.com. **Description:** A certified public accounting firm that also provides management consulting services. Services include data processing, financial modeling, financial feasibility studies, production planning and inventory management, management sciences, health care planning, human resources, cost accounting, and budgeting systems. **Positions advertised include:** Assurance Manager; Senior Recruiter; Tax Manager; Technology Support Specialist; IT Audit Senior Manager. **Corporate headquarters location:** New York NY. **Other area locations:** Statewide. **Other U.S. locations:** Nationwide.

H&R BLOCK
1745 Van Ness Avenue, San Francisco CA 94109. 415/441-2666. **Recorded jobline:** 888/244-6860. **Contact:** Personnel. **E-mail address:** taxprepcareers@hrblock.com. **World Wide Web address:** http://www.hrblock.com. **Description:** Engaged in consumer tax preparation. H&R Block operates more than 9,500 offices nationwide and prepares more than 10 million tax returns each year. The company is also engaged in a number of other tax-related activities including group tax programs, executive tax service, tax training schools, and real estate awareness seminars. **Other U.S. locations:** Nationwide. **Listed on:** New York Stock Exchange. **Stock exchange symbol:** HRB.

MERCER HUMAN RESOURCE CONSULTING
777 South Figueroa Street, Suite 1900, Los Angeles CA 90017. 213/346-2200. **Fax:** 213/346-2680. **Contact:** Human Resources. **E-mail address:** careers.west@us.wmmercer.com. **World Wide Web address:** http://www.mercerhr.com. **Description:** One of the world's largest actuarial and human resources management consulting firms, providing advice to organizations on all aspects of employee/management relationships. Services include retirement, health and welfare; performance and rewards; communication; investment; human resources administration; risk finance and insurance; and health care provider consulting. **NOTE:** Search and apply for positions online. **Positions advertised include:** Actuarial Analyst; Consultant. **Special programs:** Internships. **Corporate headquarters location:** New York NY. **Listed on:** NASDAQ. **Stock exchange symbol:** MERCS.

PRICEWATERHOUSECOOPERS
400 Capital Mall, Suite 600, Sacramento CA 95814. 916/930-8100. **Contact:** Personnel. **E-mail address:** westpwcjobs@us.pwcglobal.com. **World Wide Web address:** http://www.pwcglobal.com. **Description:** One of the largest certified public accounting firms in the world. PricewaterhouseCoopers provides public accounting, business advisory, management consulting, and taxation services. **Positions advertised include:** Senior Tax Associate; M&A Tax Manager; systems Assurance Manager. **Corporate headquarters location:** New York NY. **Other U.S. locations:** Nationwide.

Colorado

BBC RESEARCH & CONSULTING
3773 Cherry Creek North Drive, Suite 850, Denver CO 80209-3827. 303/321-2547. **Fax:** 303/399-0448. **Contact:** Human Resources. **E-mail address:** bbc@bbcresearch.com. **World Wide Web address:** http://www.bbcresearch.com. **Description:** An economic research and management consulting firm. **Corporate headquarters location:** This location. **Listed on:** Privately held. **Number of employees at this location:** 30.

BOOZ ALLEN HAMILTON
121 South Tejon Street, Suite 900, Colorado Springs CO 80903. 719/387-2000. **Fax:** 719/387-2020. **Contact:** Human Resources. **World Wide Web address:** http://www.boozallen.com. **Description:** A global strategy and technology consulting firm with major areas of expertise in strategy, organization, operations, systems, and technology. **Positions advertised include:** AF Science and Technology Business Development Lead; GIS Engineer; Proposal Analyst and Writer; Proposal Manager. **Corporate headquarters location:** McLean VA. **Number of employees worldwide:** 17,000.

CLIFTON GUNDERSON LLP
370 Interlocken Boulevard, Suite 500, Broomfield CO 80021. 303/466-8822. **Fax:** 303/466-9797. **Contact:** Personnel Director. **World Wide Web address:** http://www.cliftoncpa.com. **Description:** A certified public accounting and consulting firm. **Positions advertised include:** Sr. Audit Associate; Marketing Assistant; Sr. Tax Associate.

GRANT THORNTON LLP
707 17th Street, Suite 3200, Denver CO 80202. 303/813-4000. **Contact:** Managing Partner. **World Wide Web address:** http://www.grantthornton.com. **Description:** An international certified public accounting organization offering consulting and accounting services, as well as strategic and tactical planning assistance to a diverse clientele. **Positions advertised include:** Audit Manager; Tax Manager. **Corporate headquarters location:** Chicago IL. **Other U.S. locations:** Nationwide.

PRICEWATERHOUSECOOPERS
1670 Broadway Avenue, Suite 1000, Denver CO 80202. 720/931-7000. **Contact:** Recruiting. **World Wide Web address:** http://www.pwcglobal.com. **Description:** One of the largest certified public accounting firms in the world. PricewaterhouseCoopers provides public accounting, business advisory, management consulting, and taxation services. **Positions advertised include:** Sr. Tax Associate; Manager, ICAS Implementation; Audit Manager. **Corporate headquarters location:** New York NY. **Other U.S. locations:** Nationwide. **International locations:** Worldwide.

Connecticut

DELOITTE & TOUCHE
10 Westport Road, P.O. Box 820, Wilton CT 06897-0820. 203/761-3000. **Fax:** 203/761-3062. **Contact:** Human Resources. **World Wide Web address:**

http://www.us.deloitte.com. **Description:** An international firm of certified public accountants providing professional accounting, auditing, tax, and management consulting services to widely diversified clients. The company has a specialized program consisting of national industry groups and functional groups that cross industry lines. Groups are involved in various disciplines including accounting, auditing, taxation management advisory services, small and growing businesses, mergers and acquisitions, and computer applications. **Positions advertised include:** Administrator; Administrative Compliance Auditor; Administrative Project Specialist; Administrative U.S. National. **Special programs:** Internships. **Corporate headquarters location:** This location. **Other U.S. locations:** Nationwide. **Parent company:** Deloitte Touche Tohmatsu International. **Number of employees worldwide:** 95,000.

ERNST & YOUNG LLP
Goodwin Square, 225 Asylum Street, Hartford CT 06103. 860/247-3100. **Contact:** Human Resources. **World Wide Web address:** http://www.ey.com. **Description:** A certified public accounting firm that also provides management consulting services. Services include data processing, financial modeling, financial feasibility studies, production planning and inventory management, management sciences, health care planning, human resources, cost accounting, and budgeting systems. **NOTE:** Mail resumes to 200 Clarendon Street, Boston MA 02116. **Positions advertised include:** Tax Compliance Manager; Tax Compliance Senior. **Special programs:** Internships. **Other U.S. locations:** Nationwide. **International locations:** Worldwide.

THE FUTURES GROUP INTERNATIONAL
80 Glastonbury Boulevard, Glastonbury CT 06033. 860/633-3501. **Contact:** Human Resources. **World Wide Web address:** http://www.tfgi.com. **Description:** A business and competitive intelligence consulting firm. **NOTE:** Send resumes to 1 Thomas Circle NW, Suite 200, Washington DC 20005. **Other area locations:** Durham CT **Other U.S. locations:** Washington DC. **International locations:** Worldwide.

KPMG
755 Main Street, One Financial Plaza, Hartford CT 06103-4103. 860/522-3200. **Contact:** Human Resources. **World Wide Web address:** http://www.kpmg.com. **Description:** KPMG delivers a wide range of value-added assurance, tax, and consulting services. **Positions advertised include:** Senior Associates, Audit; Tax Professional. **Corporate headquarters location:** Woodcliff Lake NJ. **Other U.S. locations:** Nationwide. **International locations:** Worldwide. **Parent company:** KPMG International has more than 85,000 employees worldwide including 6,500 partners and 60,000 professional staff, serving clients in 844 cities in 155 countries. KPMG International is a leader among professional services firms engaged in capturing, managing, assessing, and delivering information to create knowledge that will help its clients maximize shareholder value.

McGLADREY & PULLEN, LLP
One Church Street, 8th Floor, New Haven CT 06510. 203/773-1909. **Contact:** Human Resources. **World Wide Web address:** http://www.mcgladrey.com. **Description:** A certified public accounting firm providing audit, tax, management, data processing, and cost systems services. Founded in 1926. **Other U.S. locations:** Nationwide.

MERCER HUMAN RESOURCE CONSULTING
1 State Street, Hartford CT 06103. 860/723-5770. **Contact:** Human Resources. **World Wide Web address:** http://www.mercer.com. **Description:** One of the world's largest actuarial and human resources management consulting firms, providing advice to organizations on all aspects of employee relations. Services include retirement, health and welfare, performance and rewards, communication, investment, human resources administration, risk, finance and insurance, and health care provider consulting. **Corporate headquarters location:** New York NY. **Other U.S. locations:** Nationwide. **International locations:** Worldwide.

<u>Delaware</u>
BELFINT, LYONS & SCHUMAN
1011 Centre Road, Suite 310, Wilmington DE 19805. 302/225-0600. **Fax:** 302/225-0625. **Contact:** Frances Pyle, Human Resources. **E-mail address:** fpyle@belfint.com. **World Wide Web address:** http://www.belfint.com. **Description:** A certified public accounting and business consulting firm. **Positions advertised include:** Senior Audit Associate.

GUNNIP & COMPANY LLP
Little Falls Centre Two, 2751 Centerville Road, Suite 300, Wilmington DE 19808-1627. 302/225-5000. **Fax:** 302/225-5100. **Contact:** Human Resources. **E-mail address:** jobs@gunnip.com. **World Wide Web address:** http://www.gunnip.com. **Description:** Provides accounting, auditing, tax and management services to local, national and international clients. Founded in 1947. **NOTE:** See website for current job openings and to apply online. **Positions advertised include:** Accounting Systems Consultant; Accounts Payable Coordinator; Audit Manager; Audit Senior; Tax Accountant; Tax Manager; Tax Senior.

PHILLIPS & COHEN ASSOCIATES, LTD.
258 Chapman Road, Suite 205, Newark DE 19702. 302/355-3500. **Fax:** 302/368-0970. **Contact:** Human Resources. **E-mail address:** info@phillips-cohen.com. **World Wide Web address:** http://www.phillips-cohen.com. **Description:** A collection agency. Founded in 1997. **Positions advertised include:** Collection Specialist.

TRANSUNION
5300 Brandywine Parkway, Suite 100 Wilmington DE 19803. 302/433-8000. **Contact:** Human Resources. **World Wide Web address:** http://www.transunion.com. **Description:** A business intelligence service provider. Founded in 1968. **NOTE:** See website for current job openings and to apply online. **Corporate headquarters location:** Chicago IL. **Other U.S. locations:** Nationwide. **International locations:** Worldwide. **Operations at this facility include:** TransUnion Settlement Solutions. **Number of employees worldwide:** More than 4000.

<u>District Of Columbia</u>
AMERICAN INSTITUTE OF CERTIFIED PUBLIC ACCOUNTANTS (AICPA)
1455 Pennsylvania Avenue NW, Suite 400, Washington DC 20004-1081. 202/737-6600. **Fax:** 202/638-4512. **Contact:** Human Resources. **E-mail address:** careers@aicpa.org. **World Wide Web address:** http://www.aicpa.org. **Description:** A leading professional organization dedicated to serving the needs of the certified public accounting industry. **Corporate headquarters location:** New York NY. **Other U.S. locations:** Durham NC; Ewing NJ.

CHARLES P. MYRICK CPA
805 15th Street NW, Suite 805, Washington DC 20005. 202/789-8898. **Fax:** 202/789-8680. **Contact:** Human Resources. **E-mail address:** charles@myrickcpa.com. **World Wide Web address:** http://www.myrickcpa.com. **Description:** A certified public accounting firm.

DELOITTE & TOUCHE
555 12th Street NW, Suite 500, Washington DC 20004-1207. 202/879-5600. **Fax:** 202/879-5607. **Contact:** Human Resources. **E-mail address:** dtcareers@deloitte.com. **World Wide Web address:** http://www.us.deloitte.com. **Description:** An international firm of certified public accountants providing professional accounting, auditing, tax, and management consulting services to widely diversified clients. The company has a specialized program consisting of national industry groups and functional groups that cross industry lines. Groups are involved in

various disciplines including accounting, auditing, taxation management advisory services, small and growing businesses, mergers and acquisitions, and computer applications. **Positions advertised include:** Accounting Project Team Manager; Business Process Consultant, Capital Markets Consultant; Federal Control Assurance Manager; Forensic & dispute Services Manager. **Number of employees at this location:** 299.

ERNST & YOUNG LLP
THE E&Y KENNETH LEVENTHAL REAL ESTATE GROUP DIVISION
1225 Connecticut Avenue NW, Washington DC 20036. 202/327-6000. **Fax:** 202/327-6200. **Contact:** Human Resources. **World Wide Web address:** http://www.ey.com. **Description:** A special practice unit of Ernst & Young LLP providing accounting and consulting services to the real estate and financial services industries. Overall, Ernst & Young is a certified public accounting firm that also provides management consulting services. Services include data processing, financial modeling, financial feasibility studies, production planning and inventory management, management sciences, health care planning, human resources, cost accounting, and budgeting systems. **NOTE:** Entry-level positions are offered. **Positions advertised include:** Assurance Manager; Internal Communications Manager; Campus Recruiter. **Corporate headquarters location:** New York NY. **Other U.S. locations:** Nationwide. **Number of employees at this location:** 70.

GARDINER, KAMYA & ASSOCIATES PC
1717 K Street NW, Suite 601, Washington DC 20036. 202/857-1777. **Fax:** 202/857-1778. **Contact:** Human Resources Manager. **E-mail address:** gardkamy@erols.com. **World Wide Web address:** http://www.gkacpa.com. **Description:** Provides auditing and accounting, management consulting, information systems services, and taxation services. **Positions advertised include:** CPA. **Parent company:** Midsnell Group International.

KPMG
2001 M Street NW, Washington DC 20036. 202/533-3000. **Contact:** Director of Human Resources. **World Wide Web address:** http://www.kpmg.com. **Description:** KPMG delivers a wide range of value-added assurance, tax, and consulting services. **NOTE:** For immediate consideration, the company encourages candidates to apply online. Resumes can also be mailed to the following address: KPMG Center, Attn: Resume Processing, 717 North Harwood Street, Suite 3100, Dallas TX 75201. Include job code in all correspondence. **Corporate headquarters location:** Montvale NJ. **Parent company:** KPMG International.

NATIVE AMERICAN CONSULTANTS, INC.
725 Second Street NE, Washington DC 20002. 202/547-0576. **Contact:** Human Resources. **E-mail address:** nac@nativeconsultants.com. **World Wide Web address:** http://www.nativeconsultants.com. **Description:** Provides consulting services to government agencies engaged in research for Native Americans. **NOTE:** Interested applicants should send a resume to the above e-mail address. **Corporate headquarters location:** This location.

PRICEWATERHOUSECOOPERS
1301 K Street NW, Suite 800 West, Washington DC 20005. 202/414-1000. **Fax:** 202/414-1301. **Contact:** Human Resources. **World Wide Web address:** http://www.pwcglobal.com. **Description:** One of the largest certified public accounting firms in the world. PricewaterhouseCoopers provides public accounting, business advisory, management consulting, and taxation services. **Positions advertised include:** Privacy Manager; Contracts Manager; Partnership Tax Director; Sr. Marketing Associate; Federal Security Audit Manager; IT Audit Manager; Transfer Pricing Manager. **Corporate headquarters location:** New York NY. **Other U.S. locations:** Nationwide.

Florida

DELOITTE & TOUCHE
One Independent Drive, Suite 2801, Jacksonville FL 32202-5034. 904/665-1400. **Contact:** Human Resources. **E-mail address:** dtcareers@deloitte.com. **World Wide Web address:** http://www.us.deloitte.com. **Description:** An international firm of certified public accountants providing professional accounting, auditing, tax, and management consulting services to widely diversified clients. The company has a specialized program consisting of national industry groups and functional groups that cross industry lines. Groups are involved in various disciplines including accounting, auditing, taxation management advisory services, small and growing businesses, mergers and acquisitions, and computer applications. **International locations:** Worldwide.

KPMG
One Biscayne Tower, 2 South Biscayne Boulevard, Suite 2800, Miami FL 33131-1802. 305/358-2300. **Contact:** Human Resources Department. **World Wide Web address:** http://www.kpmg.com. **Description:** KPMG delivers a wide range of value-added assurance, tax, and consulting services. **Positions advertised include:** Investigative & Integrity Advisor; International Tax Manager; Investigative Advisor; Corporate Recovery Associate. **Corporate headquarters location:** Montvale NJ. **International locations:** Worldwide. **Parent company:** KPMG International has more than 85,000 employees worldwide including 6,500 partners and 60,000 professional staff, serving clients in 844 cities in 155 countries. KPMG International is a leader among professional services firms engaged in capturing, managing, assessing, and delivering information to create knowledge that will help its clients maximize shareholder value.

O'SULLIVAN CREEL, LLP
P. O. Box 12646, Pensacola FL 32574. 850/435-7400. **Physical address**: 316 South Baylen Street, Pensacola FL 32502. **Fax:** 850/435-2888. **Contact:** Kathy Anthony, Firm Administrator. **World Wide Web address:** http://www.osullivancreel.com. **Description:** A full-service accounting and business consulting firm. Founded in 1981. **Positions advertised include:** Tax Manager; Book Keeper; 401K Pension Administrator. **Special programs:** Co-ops. **Corporate headquarters location:** This location. **Listed on:** Privately held. **Annual sales/revenues:** $5 - $10 million.

PRICEWATERHOUSECOOPERS
222 Lakeview Avenue, Suite 360, West Palm Beach FL 33401. 561/805-8100. **Fax:** 813/348-8502. **Contact:** Human Resources Department. **World Wide Web address:** http://www.pwc.com. **Description:** One of the largest certified public accounting firms in the world. PricewaterhouseCoopers provides public accounting, business advisory, management consulting, and taxation services. **Corporate headquarters location:** New York NY. **Other U.S. locations:** Nationwide.

Georgia

AON CONSULTING
3565 Piedmont Road NE, Suite 600, Atlanta GA 30305. 404/264-3141. **Fax:** 404/240-6160. **Contact:** Human Resources. **World Wide Web address:** http://www.aon.com. **Description:** An international human resources consulting and benefits brokerage firm providing advisory and support services in retirement planning, health care management, organizational effectiveness, compensation, human resources-related communications, and information technologies. **NOTE:** Search for jobs online. For most positions, mail resumes to Aon Consulting Worldwide, P.O. Box 66, Winston-Salem NC 27102, or fax to 336/896-8359 – please see job descriptions for exact contact details. No phone calls regarding employment. **Positions advertised include:** Business Producer; Relationship Specialist; Regional Director of Commercial Market Syndication; Senior Syndicator;

Benefit Specialist; Manager Trainee; Worker's Compensation Claims Adjuster; WC Medical Only Claims Adjuster; Manager of Sales Support. **Corporate headquarters location:** Chicago IL. **Other U.S. locations:** Nationwide. **International locations:** Worldwide. **Listed on:** New York Stock Exchange. **Stock exchange symbol:** AOC. **CEO:** Patrick Ryan. **Number of employees worldwide:** 51,000.

BOOZ ALLEN HAMILTON, INC.
230 Peachtree Street, Suite 2100, Atlanta GA 30303. 404/658-8000. **Fax:** 404/577-5709. **Contact:** Human Resources. **World Wide Web address:** http://www.bah.com. **Description:** A diversified, international management consulting organization offering services in both the commercial and public sectors. Areas of expertise include technology, strategy, and planning, as well as social research and other technical fields. **NOTE:** Please visit website to register, search for jobs, and apply online. Online application is the preferred method of applying. **Corporate headquarters location:** McLean VA. **Other area locations:** Augusta GA. **Other U.S. locations:** Nationwide. **International locations:** Worldwide. **Number of employees worldwide:** 14,000.

DRAFFIN & TUCKER
P,O, Box 6, Albany GA. 31702. 229/883-7878. **Physical address:** 2617 Gillionville Road, Albany GA. 31707. **Contact:** Jeff Wright, Human Resources. **E-mail:** jwright@draffin-tucker.com. **World Wide Web address:** http://www.draffin-tucker.com. **Description:** An accounting firm that serves clients in several southern states, including Georgia, Florida, Alabama, South Carolina, and Texas. Founded 1948.

ERNST & YOUNG LLP
600 Peachtree Street NE, Suite 2800, Atlanta GA 30308-2215. 404/874-8300. **Contact:** Human Resources. **World Wide Web address:** http://www.ey.com. **Description:** A certified public accounting firm that also provides management consulting services. Services include data processing, financial modeling, financial feasibility studies, production planning and inventory management, management sciences, health care planning, human resources, cost accounting, and budgeting systems. **NOTE:** Entry-level positions are also available. Please visit website to search for jobs and apply online. **Positions advertised include:** Risk Management Services Manager; Transaction Tax M&A Senior; Real Estate Advisory Services Manager; Technology Support Specialist; Corporate Finance Analyst; Assurance Manager; Health Sciences Advisory Services Staff; Assistant Director of Software Development. **Corporate headquarters location:** New York NY. **Other U.S. locations:** Nationwide. **International locations:** Worldwide. **Operations at this facility include:** Regional Headquarters. **Number of employees nationwide:** 23,000. **Number of employees worldwide:** 103,000.

GEORGIA MANAGEMENT SERVICES
202 North Westover Boulevard, Albany GA 31707. 229/436-7204. **Contact:** Human Resources. **Description:** Provides bookkeeping, payroll, accounts receivable, accounts payable, and other financial management services to nursing homes.

H&R BLOCK
2800 Old Dawson Road, Albany GA 31707. 229/883-5353. **Contact:** Human Resources Department. **World Wide Web address:** http://www.hrblock.com. **Description:** H&R Block is primarily engaged in consumer tax preparation, operating more than 10,000 U.S. offices and preparing more than 10 million tax returns each year. The company also operates more than 800 offices in Canada. H&R Block has offices in over 750 Sears stores in both the United States and Canada. Many offices operate as franchises, and some operate on a seasonal basis. H&R Block is also engaged in a number of other tax-related activities including Group Tax Programs, Premium Tax Service, Tax Training Schools, and Real Estate Tax Awareness seminars. **NOTE:** Please visit website to search for jobs and apply online. **Corporate headquarters location:** Kansas City MO. **Other area locations:** Statewide. **Other U.S. locations:** Nationwide. **International locations:** Australia; Canada; United Kingdom. **Listed on:** New York Stock Exchange. **Stock exchange symbol:** HRB. **President/CEO:** Mark A. Ernst. **Number of employees worldwide:** 24,000.

HAY GROUP
303 Peachtree Street NE, Atlanta GA 30308. 404/575-8700. **Fax:** 404/575-8711. **Contact:** Personnel. **World Wide Web address:** http://www.haygroup.com. **Description:** An international human resources and management consulting firm that provides services such as total compensation planning, strategic management, business culture, employee surveys, and outplacement. Founded 1943. **NOTE:** Please visit website to register, search for jobs, and apply online. **Positions advertised include:** Consultant. **Corporate headquarters location:** Philadelphia PA. **Other U.S. locations:** Nationwide. **International locations:** Worldwide. **Number of employees worldwide:** 2,200.

HEWITT ASSOCIATES
3350 Riverwood Parkway, Suite 80, Atlanta GA 30339-3370. 770/956-7777. **Fax:** 770/956-8780. **Contact:** Human Resources. **World Wide Web address:** http://www.hewitt.com. **Description:** Hewitt Associates is an international firm of consultants and actuaries specializing in the design, finance, communication, and administration of employee benefit and compensation programs. **NOTE:** There are two Atlanta office locations. Please visit website to search for jobs and apply online. **Positions advertised include:** Client Financial Analyst; Experienced Consultant; Market Learning Consultant; Health Management Design Consultant; Technical Programmer Analyst; Local Market Recruiter; HW Quality Assurance Analyst; Pension Administration Analyst; Business Systems Analyst; HM Project Manager; Communication Consultant; Sales Analyst; Talent Design Consultant. **Corporate headquarters location:** Lincolnshire IL. **Other U.S. locations:** Nationwide. **International locations:** Worldwide. **Operations at this facility include:** Benefits consulting. **Listed on:** New York Stock Exchange. **Stock exchange symbol:** HEW. **CEO:** Dale L. Gifford. **Number of employees worldwide:** 13,000.

KPMG
303 Peachtree Street NE, Suite 2000, Atlanta GA 30308. 404/222-3000. **Contact:** Mr. Chris Beall, Director of Human Resources. **World Wide Web address:** http://www.us.kpmg.com. **Description:** Delivers a wide range of value-added assurance, tax, and consulting services, and is the U.S. member firm of KPMG International, the worldwide professional services firm. KPMG International is a leader among professional services firms engaged in capturing, managing, assessing, and delivering information to create knowledge that will help clients maximize shareholder value. Founded in 1897. **Positions advertised include:** Administrative Assistant; Desktop Support Senior Associate; Audit Manager; Senior Manager; Senior Associate; Manager – CFO Advisory Services; Career Assistance Program Manager; Audit Senior Associate; Senior Designer; Senior Financial Analyst; Senior Associate IRBS; Manager Sales and Transaction Tax. **Corporate headquarters location:** New York NY. **Other U.S. locations:** Nationwide. **International locations:** Worldwide. **CEO:** Eugene D. O'Kelly. **Number of employees nationwide:** 18,000. **Number of employees worldwide:** 100,000.

PRICEWATERHOUSECOOPERS
10 Tenth Street, Suite 1400, Atlanta GA 30309. 678/419-1000. **Fax:** 678/419-1239. **Contact:** Jim Klee, Director of Human Resources. **World Wide Web address:** http://www.pricewaterhousecoopers.com. **Description:** One of the largest certified public accounting firms in the world. PricewaterhouseCoopers provides public accounting, business advisory, management consulting, and taxation services. **NOTE:**

Please visit website to search for jobs and apply online. **Positions advertised include:** BCS Senior Associate; Healthcare Associate; Internal Audit Associate; CIPS Experienced Associate; Service Center Consultant; Recruiting Manager; Health and Welfare SE Practice Leader; Assurance Manager; Real Estate Senior Associate; Campus Recruiting Manager; BCS Data Specialist; Trainer; Transaction Services Manager; Manager. **Corporate headquarters location:** New York NY. **Other U.S. locations:** Nationwide. **International locations:** Worldwide. **Number of employees worldwide:** 120,000.

Hawaii

DELOITTE & TOUCHE LLP
1132 Bishop Street, Suite 1200, Honolulu HI 96813-2870. 808/543-0700. **Fax:** 808/526-0225. **E-mail address:** dtcareers@deloitte.com. **Contact:** Human Resources. **World Wide Web address:** http://www.deloitte.com. **Description:** A professional service firm providing financial consulting. **Positions advertised include:** Corporate Tax Senior; E-Audit Senior; Senior Consultant: Business Process and IT Risk and Control/IT Audit.

Illinois

BDO SEIDMAN, LLP
130 East Randolph Drive, Suite 2800, Chicago IL 60601. 312/240-1236. **Fax:** 312/240-3311. **Contact:** Human Resources. **E-mail address:** r7@bdo.com. **World Wide Web address:** http://www.bdo.com. **Description:** A public accounting and consulting firm. **NOTE:** This company has other Illinois locations. See website for addresses. Apply online. **Positions advertised include:** Business Development Manager; International Tax Manager; Valuation Manager; Administrative Assistant. **Corporate headquarters location:** This location. **Other U.S. locations:** Nationwide.

BANSLEY & KIENER
8745 West Higgins Road, Suite 200, Chicago IL 60631. 312/263-2700. **Fax:** 312/263-6935. **Contact:** Human Resources. **E-mail address:** humanresources@bk-cpa.com. **World Wide Web address:** http://www.bk-cpa.com. **Description:** A certified public accounting firm. **NOTE:** Fax or e-mail resumes. **Positions advertised include:** Senior In-Charge Auditors; Staff Assistants; Payroll Compliance Auditor; Paraprofessionals. **Special programs:** Internships. **Corporate headquarters location:** This location. **Operations at this facility include:** Service.

CLIFTON GUNDERSON LLP
301 Southwest Adams Street, Suite 900, P.O. Box 1835, Peoria IL 61656-1835. 309/671-4500. **Fax:** 309/671-1812. **Contact:** Hannah Tropsha, Human Resources. **E-mail address:** cghr@cliftoncpa.com. **World Wide Web address:** http://www.cliftoncpa.com. **Description:** A certified public accounting and consulting firm. **NOTE:** See website for current job openings. Submit resume by e-mail or fax. **Positions advertised include:** Senior Associate (Various); Tax Manager; Receiving Auditor; Timekeeper; Executive Search Consultant. **Corporate headquarters location:** This location.

HEWITT ASSOCIATES
100 Half Day Road, Lincolnshire IL 60069. 847/295-5000. **Contact:** Human Resources. **World Wide Web address:** http://www.hewitt.com. **Description:** Hewitt Associates is an international firm of consultants and actuaries specializing in the design, financing, communication, and administration of employee benefit and compensation programs. **Positions advertised include:** Programmer Analyst; WM Analyst; Compliance Specialist; Financial Consultant; Client Coordinator. **Corporate headquarters location:** This location. **Other area locations:** Chicago IL. **Other U.S. locations:** Nationwide. **International locations:** Worldwide.

A.T. KEARNEY PROCUREMENT SOLUTIONS
222 West Adams Street, Suite 2500, Chicago IL 60606. 312/648-0111. **Toll-free phone:** 888/327-3842. **Fax:** 312/223-7070. **Contact:** Human Resources. **E-mail services:** atkps_careers@atkearney.com. **World Wide Web address:** http://www.atkearney.com. **Description:** A general management consulting firm. **NOTE:** E-mail resumes. **Positions advertised include:** eSourcing Manager.

GEORGE S. MAY INTERNATIONAL COMPANY
303 South Northwest Highway, Park Ridge IL 60068. 847/825-8806. **Toll-free phone:** 800/999-3020. Fax: 847/825-2951. **Contact:** Human Resources. **World Wide Web address:** http://www.georgesmay.com. **Description:** One of the world's largest and oldest management consulting firms. George S. May International focuses on consulting for small businesses. **NOTE:** Visit the website to submit a resume or download the online application and fax it. **Positions advertised include:** Field Service Representative; Executive Analyst; Staff Executive; Marketing Assistant. **Listed on:** Privately held.

McGLADREY & PULLEN, LLP
20 North Martingale Road, Schaumburg IL 60173. 847/517-7070. **Contact:** Human Resources. **E-mail address:** careers@rsmi.com. **World Wide Web address:** http://www.mcgladrey.com. **Description:** A certified public accounting firm providing audit, tax, management, data processing, and cost systems services. **NOTE:** Entry-level positions are offered. **Positions advertised include:** Audit Manager **Special programs:** Internships. **Corporate headquarters location:** Bloomington MN. **Other U.S. locations:** Nationwide. **Operations at this facility include:** Administration; Service.

PRG-SCHULTZ INTERNATIONAL INC
1901B East Voorhees Street, Danville IL 61834-6250. 217/477-1454. **Contact:** Human Resources. **E-mail address:** personnel@prgx.com. **World Wide Web address:** http://www.prgx.com. **Description:** An auditing firm specializing in recovery of lost profits. **Positions advertised include:** Audit Support Programmer; Sr. Auditor; Staff Auditor. **Corporate headquarters location:** Atlanta GA. **Other U.S. locations:** West Valley City UT; Fort Collins CO. **Listed on:** NASDAQ. **Stock exchange symbol:** PRGX. **Number of employees worldwide:** 2,000.

PRICEWATERHOUSECOOPERS
One North Wacker Drive, Chicago IL 60606. 312/298-2000. **Contact:** Human Resources. **World Wide Web address:** http://www.pwcglobal.com. **Description:** A location of one of the largest certified public accounting firms in the world. PricewaterhouseCoopers provides public accounting, business advisory, management consulting, and taxation services. **NOTE:** Apply online. **Corporate headquarters location:** New York NY. **Other U.S. locations:** Nationwide.

RSM MCGLADREY, INC.
191 North Wacker Drive, Suite 1400, Chicago IL 60606. 312/782-2124. **Contact:** Human Resources. **World Wide Web address:** http://www.rsmmcgladrey.com. **Description:** An accounting firm. **NOTE:** Apply online. **Positions advertised include:** Consulting Actuary; Programmer Analyst; Actuarial Analyst; Audit Senior Associate; Audit Manager.

Indiana

BKD LLP
P.O. Box 44998, Indianapolis IN 46244. 317/383-4000. **Physical address:** 201 North Illinois Street, Suite 700, Indianapolis IN 46204. **Fax:** 317/383-4200. **Contact:** David L. Leising, Recruiter. **E-mail address:** dleising@bkd.com. **World Wide Web address:** http://www.bkd.com. **NOTE:** To reach David Leising directly dial ext. 4215. **Description:** A full-service certified public accounting and consulting firm. **Special programs:** Internships. **Corporate headquarters location:** This location.

BLUE & CO., LLC
12800 North Meridian Street, Suite 400, Carmel IN 46032. 317/848-8920. **Fax:** 317/573-2458. **Contact:**

Human Resources. **E-mail address:** jobs@blueandco.com. **World Wide Web address:** http://www.blueandco.com. **Description:** A public accounting and consulting firm with specialties in health care, manufacturing, construction, litigation support, and retirement planning. **Positions advertised include:** Audit Manager; Tax Accountant; Staff Accountant. **Special programs:** Internships. **Internship information:** Internships are offered January through April. **Corporate headquarters location:** This location. **Other U.S. locations:** KY. **Listed on:** Privately held.

DELOITTE & TOUCHE
111 Monument Circle, Suite 2000, Indianapolis IN 46204. 317/464-8600. **Contact:** Human Resources. **World Wide Web address:** http://www.us.deloitte.com. **Description:** An international firm of certified public accountants providing professional accounting, auditing, tax, and management consulting services to widely diversified clients. The company has a specialized program consisting of national industry groups and functional groups that cross industry lines. Groups are involved in various disciplines including accounting, auditing, taxation management advisory services, small and growing businesses, mergers and acquisitions, and computer applications.

ERNST & YOUNG LLP
111 Monument Circle, Suite 2600, Indianapolis IN 46204. 317/681-7000. **Contact:** Personnel. **World Wide Web address:** http://www.ey.com. **Description:** A certified public accounting firm that also provides management consulting services. Services include data processing, financial modeling, financial feasibility studies, production planning and inventory management, management sciences, health care planning, human resources, cost accounting, and budgeting systems. **International locations:** Worldwide.

GEMINUS CORPORATION
8400 Louisiana Street, Merrillville IN 46410. 219/757-1800. **Fax:** 219/757-1831. **Contact:** Diane Johnson, Human Resources. **E-mail address:** diane.johnson@geminus.org. **World Wide Web address:** http://www. geminus.org. **Description:** Operates Head Start programs and performs accounting, marketing, and human resource functions for Southlake Center for Mental Health, an inpatient and outpatient mental health center, and Tri-City Mental Health, an outpatient mental health center. **Positions advertised include:** Staff Accountant; Collection Specialist; Psychologist; Social Worker; Residential Assistant; Staff Nurse; Clinician; Addictions Therapist; Van Driver. **Special programs:** Internships. **Corporate headquarters location:** This location. **Operations at this facility include:** Service. **Listed on:** Privately held.

Iowa

RSM McGLADREY, INC.
212 North Brady Street, 2nd Floor, Davenport IA 52801. 563/324-0447. **Fax:** 563/324-0211. **Contact:** Human Resources. **E-mail address:** careers@rsmi.com. **World Wide Web address:** http://www.rsmmcgladrey.com. **Description:** One of the largest accounting and consulting firms in the United States with 70 offices from coast to coast. Clients range from large, publicly held corporations to small organizations and individuals. Services rendered include auditing services, tax consulting services, and managerial and operational consulting. **NOTE:** Search posted openings and apply on-line only. No paper resumes are accepted and telephone contact is discouraged. Local branch offices post local ads and applicants may respond as requested. **Positions advertised include:** Accountant; Financial Institution Consultant; Global Systems Administrator; Network Consultant; Network Senior Consultant; Payroll Administrator; Public Accountant; Quality Assurance Analyst; SALT Consulting Analyst; Senior Tax Accountant; Supervisor; Tax Manager. **Parent company:** H&R Block. **Corporate headquarters location:** Bloomington MN. **Other area locations:** Burlington IA; Cedar Rapids IA; Des Moines IA; Dubuque IA; Iowa City IA; Waterloo IA. **Other U.S. locations:** Nationwide. **International locations:** Worldwide. **President/CEO:** Tom Rotherham. **Number of employees:** 4,400

Louisiana

BOOZ ALLEN HAMILTON, INC.
111 Veterans Boulevard, Metairie LA 70005. 504/830-2000. **Fax:** 504/837-8437. **Contact:** Human Resources. **World Wide Web address:** http://www.boozallen.com. **Description:** A diversified, international management consulting organization offering services in both the commercial and public sectors. Areas of expertise include technology, strategy, and planning, as well as social research and many other technical fields. Specific services include corporate strategy and long-range planning, organization design, human resources management, financial management and control, acquisitions and divestiture, information systems and automation, manufacturing, inventory and distribution control, qualitative and quantitative market research, attitudinal and demographic trend research, marketing strategy and positioning, venture management, transportation and environmental systems, technology research, new products and process development, government programs, and regulatory compliance. **Positions advertised include:** ESRI Functional Support Specialist; GIS Data Management Analyst; Information Security Engineer; Oracle DBA; System Architect. **Corporate headquarters location:** McLean VA. **Other U.S. locations:** Nationwide. **International locations:** Worldwide. **Number of employees worldwide:** 17,000.

Maine

BAKER NEWMAN & NOYES
280 Fore Street, Portland ME 04112. 207/879-2100. **Fax:** 207/791-1793. **Contact:** Connie Taggart, Human Resources. E-mail address: ctaggart@bnncpa.com. **World Wide Web address:** http://bnncpa.com. **Description:** A certified public accounting firm that provides a variety of services including audits and tax planning. **NOTE**: Search posted openings and apply on-line, by e-mail or fax. **Positions advertised include:** Staff Accountant; Audit Manager; Audit Senior; Audit Senior Manager; Tax Intern; Tax Accountant; Tax Senior; Tax Manager; Tax Senior Manager; Staff Consultant; Senior Staff Consultant; Manager; Senior Manager; Marketing Staff Consultant. **Other U.S. locations:** Manchester NH; Portsmouth NH.

MACDONALD PAGE SCHATZ FLETCHER & CO., LLC
30 Long Creek Drive, South Portland ME 04106. 207/774-5701. **Fax:** 207/774-7835. **Contact:** Ralph R. Hendrix, Human Resources Manager. **E-mail address:** rrh@macpage.com; cpa@macpage.com. **World Wide Web address:** http://www.macpage.com. **Description:** Engaged in all types of accounting for both individual clients and corporations. **Special programs:** Internships. **Other area locations:** South Portland ME; Camden ME. **Number of employees nationwide:** 80.

Maryland

ARONSON & COMPANY
700 King Farm Boulevard, Suite 300, Rockville MD 20850. 301/231-6200. **Fax:** 301/231-7630. **Contact:** Angel Rutch, Human Resources. **E-mail address:** info@aronsoncompany.com. **World Wide Web address:** http://www.aronsoncompany.com. **Description:** A certified public accounting and consulting firm whose services include audit and assurance, technology/accounting systems, tax, investment banking, litigation support, and valuation. **NOTE:** Resumes may be submitted online. **Positions advertised include:** Accountant; Administrative Assistant; Audit & Accounting Controller; Financial Accounting Consultant; Human Resource Director; Public Accountant; Technical Consultant; Timberline Consultant. **Number of employees at this location:** 100. **Number of employees nationwide:** Over 200.

BEATTY SATCHELL BUSINESS SERVICES, INC.
P.O. Box 1187, Easton MD 21601. 410/822-6950. **Physical address:** 125 Bay Street, Easton MD 21601. **Fax:** 410/820-9042. **Contact:** Human Resources. **Description:** An accounting and business services firm that specializes in taxes, pension administration, and estate planning. **Corporate headquarters location:** This location. **Other area locations:** Denton MD. **Number of employees at this location:** 10. **Number of employees nationwide:** 60.

CLIFTON GUNDERSON LLP
9515 Deereco Road, Suite 500, Timonium MD 21093. 410/453-0900. **Fax:** 410/453-0914. **Contact:** Human Resources. **World Wide Web address:** http://www.cliftoncpa.com. **Description:** A certified public accounting and consulting firm that provides services to customers in the agribusiness, contracting, financial, government, health care, and manufacturing industries. **Positions advertised include:** Assurance Manager; Assurance Associate. **Special programs:** Internships; Tuition Assistance Program; Relocation Program. **Corporate headquarters location:** Peoria IL. **Other area locations:** Calverton MD; Forest Hill MD. **Other U.S. locations:** Nationwide. **Subsidiaries include:** R.S. Wells L.L.C.; CG Financial Services. **CEO:** Carl R. George. **Number of employees nationwide:** Over 1,400.

ERNST & YOUNG LLP
621 East Pratt Street, Baltimore MD 21202. 410/539-7940. **Contact:** Director of Administration. **World Wide Web address:** http://www.ey.com. **Description:** A certified public accounting firm that also provides management consulting services. The company offers assurance and advisory business services, comprehensive support for emerging growth companies, corporate finance solutions, and a wide range of tax services. **NOTE:** Applications are available online. **Positions advertised include:** Technology and Security Risk Services Assurance Associate; Production Assistant; Business Risk Group Manager; Business Risk Auditor. **Special programs:** Internships. **Corporate headquarters location:** New York NY. **Other U.S. locations:** Nationwide. **International locations:** Worldwide. **CEO/Chairman:** James S. Turley. **Sales/revenue:** $10.1 billion. **Number of employees worldwide:** 110,000.

GXS
100 Edison Park Drive, Gaithersburg MD 20878. 301/340-4000. **Fax:** 301/340-5299. **Contact:** Human Resources. **E-mail address:** opportunities@gxs.ge.com. **World Wide Web address:** http://www.gxs.com. **Description:** Provides business productivity solutions through management consulting. **Positions advertised include:** Channel Manager; Business Operations Director. **Special programs:** Internships; Co-ops. **Corporate headquarters location:** This location. **Other U.S. locations:** Nationwide. **International locations:** Worldwide. **Parent company:** General Electric Company (Fairfield CT). **Listed on:** New York Stock Exchange. **Stock exchange symbol:** GE. **CEO:** Harvey Seegers. **Number of employees worldwide:** 230,000.

GRANT THORNTON LLP
2 Hopkins Plaza, Suite 700, Baltimore MD 21201-2998. 410/685-4000. **Contact:** Recruiting Coordinator. **World Wide Web address:** http://www.grantthornton.com. **Description:** An international, certified public accounting organization offering a comprehensive scope of consulting and accounting services as well as strategic and tactical planning assistance to a diverse clientele. **Corporate headquarters location:** Chicago IL. **Other U.S. locations:** Nationwide. **International locations:** Worldwide. **Sales/revenue:** $1.7 billion. **Number of employees nationwide:** Over 3,000. **Number of employees worldwide:** 21,500.

HARITON, MANCUSO & JONES, P.C.
11140 Rockville Pike, Suite 340, North Bethesda MD 20852. 301/984-6400. **Fax:** 301/984-0028. **Contact:** Personnel Director. **Description:** An accounting firm. **Listed on:** Privately held. **Number of employees at this location:** 30.

KPMG
111 South Calvert Street, Baltimore MD 21202-6174. 410/949-8500. **Contact:** Tara C. Huber, Human Resources. **E-mail address:** tchuber@kpmg.com. **World Wide Web address:** http://www.kpmgcampus.com. **Description:** KPMG delivers a wide range of value-added assurance, tax, and consulting services. **Special programs:** Internships; Training. **Corporate headquarters location:** McLean VA. **Other U.S. locations:** Nationwide. **International locations:** Worldwide. **Listed on:** NASDAQ. **Stock exchange symbol:** KCIN. **Sales/revenue:** $13.5 billion. **Number of employees at this location:** Over 200. **Number of employees worldwide:** Over 100,000.

NATIONAL ASSOCIATION OF BLACK ACCOUNTANTS
7249-A Hanover Parkway, Greenbelt MD 20770. 301/474-6222. **Fax:** 301/474-3114. **Contact:** Challenge Okiwe, Program Coordinator. **World Wide Web address:** http://www.nabainc.org. **Description:** A nonprofit membership organization for accounting and business professionals and students. The association has nationwide chapters. Founded in 1969. **Special programs:** Internships. **Corporate headquarters location:** This location. **Operations at this facility include:** Administration. **Listed on:** Privately held. **President:** Kim Griffin-Hunter. **Number of employees at this location:** 10.

PRICEWATERHOUSECOOPERS
250 West Pratt Street, Suite 2100, Baltimore MD 21201-2304. 410/783-7600. **Contact:** Human Resources. **World Wide Web address:** http://www.pwcglobal.com. **Description:** A certified public accounting firms with worldwide operations. PricewaterhouseCoopers provides public accounting, business advisory, management consulting, and taxation services. **NOTE:** Online applications area available. **Positions advertised include:** Senior Associate Auditor; GRMS Internal Audit Associate; HCP Experienced Associate; Middle Market Tax Senior Associate; Middle Market Tax Manager; Business Solutions Development Manager. **Corporate headquarters location:** New York NY. **Other U.S. locations:** Nationwide. **International locations:** Worldwide. **Global Chairman:** Andrew Ratcliffe. **Sales/revenue:** Approximately $14 billion. **Number of employees worldwide:** 125,000.

Massachusetts

ABT ASSOCIATES INC.
55 Wheeler Street, Cambridge MA 02138. 617/492-7100. **Fax:** 617/492-5219. **Contact:** Human Resources. **E-mail address:** abtassoc@rpc.webhire.com. **World Wide Web address:** http://www.abtassoc.com. **Description:** One of the largest government and business consulting and research firms in the country. The company offers policy analysis, technical assistance, program evaluation, and program operation services to governmental clients and provides organizational development, service quality measurement and management, strategic planning, management consulting, and new product development services to business clients. ABT Associates conducts its business through four main practice areas: international economic policy research; business research and consulting; and ABT Associates Clinical Trials. Founded in 1965. **Positions advertised include:** Research Assistant; Analyst, Environmental Policy; Associate Division Manager; Associate Programmer Analyst; Information Analyst; Division Vice President. **NOTE:** Online application preferred. **Corporate headquarters location:** This location. **Other area locations:** Lexington MA; Hadley MA. **Other U.S. locations:** Washington DC; Chicago IL; Bethesda MD. **International locations:** Egypt; South Africa. **Operations at this facility include:** Administration; Research and Development. **Annual sales/revenues:**

More than $100 million. **Number of employees worldwide:** 1,000.

BDO SEIDMAN, LLP
150 Federal Street, Suite 900, Boston MA 02110. 617/422-0700. **Fax:** 617/422-0909. **Contact:** Human Resources. **World Wide Web address:** http://www.bdo.com. **Description:** A public accounting and consulting firm. **Positions advertised include:** Assurance Manager; Information Systems Auditor; Senior Tax Consultant.

BAIN & COMPANY, INC.
131 Dartmouth Street, Boston MA 02116. 617/572-2000. **Contact:** Human Resources. **World Wide Web address:** http://www.bain.com. **Description:** An international management consulting firm that helps major companies achieve higher levels of competitiveness and profitability. Founded in 1973. **Corporate headquarters location:** This location. **Other U.S. locations:** Nationwide. **International locations:** Worldwide. **Number of employees nationwide:** 1,000. **Number of employees worldwide:** 2800.

CERIDIAN EMPLOYER SERVICES
401 Edgewater Place, Suite 220, Wakefield MA 01880. 781/213-8000. **Fax:** 781/213-8499. **Contact:** Human Resources. **World Wide Web address:** http://www.ceridian.com. **Description:** An accounting and auditing services company. **Positions advertised include:** Client Service Analyst. **Parent company:** Ceridian Corporation (Minneapolis MN.)

ERNST & YOUNG LLP
200 Clarendon Street, Boston MA 02116. 617/266-2000. **Contact:** Personnel Manager. **World Wide Web address:** http://www.ey.com. **Description:** A certified public accounting firm that also provides management consulting services. Services include data processing, financial modeling, financial feasibility studies, production planning and inventory management, management sciences, health care planning, human resources, cost accounting, and budgeting systems. **Other U.S. locations:** Nationwide. **International locations:** Worldwide. **Number of employees worldwide:** 77,000.

THE FORUM CORPORATION
265 Franklin Street, Boston MA 02110. 617/523-7300. **Toll-free phone:** 800/367-8611. **Fax:** 617/371-3300. **Contact:** Human Resources. **E-mail address:** careers@forum.com. **World Wide Web address:** http://www.forum.com. **Description:** An international training and consulting firm. Founded in 1971. **Special programs:** Internships. **Office hours:** Monday - Friday, 9:00 a.m. - 5:30 p.m. **Corporate headquarters location:** This location. **Other U.S. locations:** Chicago IL; New York NY. **International locations:** Australia; Canada; England; Hong Kong; Korea; New Zealand; Singapore. **CEO:** Pippa Wicks. **Number of employees at this location:** 115. **Number of employees nationwide:** 260.

GRANT THORNTON LLP
226 Causeway Street, 6th Floor, Boston MA 02114. 617/723-7900. **Contact:** Human Resources. **World Wide Web address:** http://www.grantthornton.com. **Description:** An international certified public accounting organization offering consulting and accounting services as well as strategic and tactical planning assistance to a diversified client base. Founded in 1924. **Positions advertised include:** Auditor; Experienced Tax Manager; Tax Associate; State & Local Tax Manager. **Corporate headquarters location:** Chicago IL. **Other U.S. locations:** Nationwide. **International locations:** Worldwide.

H&R BLOCK
77 Main Street, Andover MA 01810. 978/686-1371. **Contact:** Human Resources. **World Wide Web address:** http://www.hrblock.com. **Description:** Engaged in consumer tax preparation. H&R Block operates more than 9,500 offices nationwide, and prepares more than 10 million tax returns each year. The company has offices in over 750 Sears stores in both the United States and Canada. Many offices operate as franchises, and some operate on a seasonal basis. H&R Block is also engaged in a number of other tax-related activities, including group tax programs, premium tax service, tax training schools, and real estate tax awareness seminars. **Corporate headquarters location:** Kansas City MO. **Other U.S. locations:** Nationwide. **Listed on:** New York Stock Exchange. **Stock exchange symbol:** HRB. **President/CEO:** Mark Ernst.

KPMG
99 High Street, Boston MA 02110-2371. 617/988-1000. **Contact:** Human Resources. **World Wide Web address:** http://www.kpmg.com. **Description:** Delivers a wide range of value-added assurance, tax, and consulting services. **Positions advertised include:** Tax Associate; Transactions Services Manager; Internal Auditor; IT Audit Associate; Corporate Tax Associate; Corporate Tax Associate; Office Services Supervisor; Auditor; Corporate Recovery Associate. **Corporate headquarters location:** Montvale NJ. **Other U.S. locations:** Nationwide. **International locations:** Worldwide. **Parent company:** KPMG International is a leader among professional services firms engaged in capturing, managing, assessing, and delivering information to create knowledge that will help its clients maximize shareholder value. **Number of employees worldwide:** 100,000.

A.T. KEARNEY, INC.
One Memorial Drive, 14th Floor, Cambridge MA 02142-1301. 617/374-2600. **Contact:** Human Resources. **World Wide Web address:** http://www.atkearney.com. **Description:** A general management consulting firm. **NOTE:** Visit website for more information concerning recruiting process. **Parent company:** EDS.

ARTHUR D. LITTLE, INC.
68 Fargo Street, Boston MA 02210. 617/443-0309. **Fax:** 617/443-0166. **Contact:** Human Resources. **E-mail address:** careers.mc@adlittle.com. **World Wide Web address:** http://www.adl.com. **Description:** A management consulting firm. The company offers consulting services including, strategy and organization, technology and innovation, safety and risk management, as well as environmental consulting. **Corporate headquarters location:** This location. **Other U.S. locations:** Houston TX. **International locations:** Asia; Europe; Middle East; South America. **Parent company:** Altran Technologies.

MICROCAL LLC.
22 Industrial Drive East, Northampton MA 01060-2327. 413/586-7720. **Toll-free phone:** 800/633-3115. **Fax:** 413/586-0149. **Contact:** Bill Plumley. **E-mail address:** billplumley@microcalorimetry.com. **World Wide Web address:** http://www.microcalorimetry.com. **Description:** A high-tech manufacturer. **Positions advertised include:** Accountant; Human Resources Specialist.

PALLADIUM GROUP, INC.
55 Old Bedford Road, Lincoln MA 01773. Toll-free phone: 800/773-2399. **Contact:** Human Resources. **E-mail address:** careers@palladiumes.com. **World Wide Web address:** http://www.palladiumes.com. **Description:** A management consulting firm. **Positions advertised include:** Research Manager; Research Analyst; Finance Program Director; Systems Administrator; Business Development Associate.

PRICEWATERHOUSECOOPERS LLP
125 High Street, Boston MA 02110. 617/530-5000. **Contact:** Director of Recruiting. **World Wide Web address:** http://www.pwcglobal.com. **Description:** One of the largest certified public accounting firms in the world. PricewaterhouseCoopers provides public accounting, business advisory, management consulting, and taxation services. **Positions advertised include:** Data Quality Manager; Manager; Executive Assistant;

Actuarial Life Manager; Service Center Clerk; Instructor Trainee; Information Technology Manager. **Special programs:** Internships. **Corporate headquarters location:** New York NY. **Other U.S. locations:** Nationwide. **Number of employees at this location:** 540.

GT REILLY & COMPANY
424 Adams Street, Milton MA 02186-4358. 617/696-8900. **Fax:** 617/698-1803. **Contact:** Director of Personnel. **E-mail address:** pjf@gtreilly.com. **World Wide Web address:** http://www.gtreilly.com. **Description:** A regional accounting firm. **Positions advertised include:** Public Accounting Professional.

Michigan
DPM CONSULTING SERVICES
507 East Maple Road, Troy MI 48083-2806. 248/740-8735. **Fax:** 248/740-8846. **Contact:** Recruiting Department. **E-mail address:** jobs@dpmcs.com. **World Wide Web address:** http://www.dpmcs.com. **Description:** Provides information technology staffing and management consulting. **Corporate headquarters location:** This location.

PLANTE & MORAN, LLP
P.O. Box 307, Southfield MI 48037-0307. 248/352-2500. **Physical address:** 27400 Northwestern Highway, Southfield MI 48034. **Fax:** 248/352-0018. **Contact:** Human Resources Department. **E-mail address:** pmcareers@plante-moran.com. **World Wide Web address:** http://www.plantemoran.com. **Description:** Provides accounting, tax, financial planning, and corporate finance services. **Positions advertised include:** Advanced General Accountant; Tax Professional; Technical Standard Manager; Lotus Notes/PDA Support Specialist. **Special programs:** Internships. **Corporate headquarters location:** This location. **Other area locations:** Statewide. **Other U.S. locations:** OH; IL; TN. **Number of employees nationwide:** Over 1,300.

UNITED AMERICAN HEALTHCARE CORPORATION
300 River Place, Suite 4950, Detroit MI 48207-4291. 313/393-4570. **Contact:** Human Resources. **World Wide Web address:** http://www.uahc.com. **Description:** Provides management consulting services to health care companies. **Corporate headquarters location:** This location. **Listed on:** NASDAQ. **Stock exchange symbol:** UAHC.

Minnesota
EMA, INC.
1970 Oakcrest Avenue, Suite 100, St. Paul MN 55113-2624. 651/639-5600. **Toll-free phone:** 800/800-2110. **Fax:** 651/639-5730. **Contact:** Human Resources. **E-mail address:** hrinfo@ema-inc.com. **World Wide Web address:** http://www.ema-inc.com. **Description:** A specialized consulting firm that works with utilities and manufacturers to help clients develop and implement operational strategies for improving work practices, addressing organizational development, and leveraging technology. Founded in 1975. **NOTE:** Entry-level positions are offered. **Positions advertised include:** Network Support Analyst. **Corporate headquarters location:** This location. **Other U.S. locations:** Phoenix AZ; Tucson AZ; Los Angeles CA; Sacramento CA; San Francisco CA; Orlando FL; Boston MA; Philadelphia PA. **International locations:** Canada. **Listed on:** Privately held. **CEO:** Alan Manning. **Annual sales/revenues:** $21 - $50 million. **Number of employees at this location:** 80. **Number of employees nationwide:** 180. **Number of employees worldwide:** 185.

GRANT THORNTON LLP
200 South Sixth Street, Suite 500, Minneapolis MN 55402. 612/332-0001. **Fax:** 612/332-8361. **Contact:** Human Resources. **World Wide Web address:** http://www.grantthornton.com. **Description:** Grant Thornton LLP is the U.S. member firm of Grant Thornton International, one of the six global accounting, tax, and business advisory organizations. The firm specializes in serving mid-cap, small-cap, and privately held clients, and is a provider of selected non-audit services to selected markets. **Other U.S. locations:** Nationwide.

HEWITT ASSOCIATES
45 South Seventh Street, Suite 2100, Minneapolis MN 55402. 612/339-7501. **Fax:** 612/339-3517. **Contact:** Personnel. **World Wide Web address:** http://www.hewitt.com. **Description:** Hewitt Associates is an international human resources outsourcing and consulting firm delivering a range of human capital management services. **NOTE:** Search and apply for positions online. **Corporate headquarters location:** Lincolnshire IL.

KPMG LLP
4200 Wells Fargo Center, 90 South Seventh Street, Minneapolis MN 55402. 612/305-5000. **Fax:** 612/305-5100. **Contact:** Jodi Sengstock, Human Resources. **E-mail address:** jsengstock@kpmg.com. **World Wide Web address:** http://www.us.kpmg.com. **Description:** KPMG LLP, the U.S. member firm of KPMG International, is an audit, tax, and advisory firm. KPMG International's member firms have 76,000 professionals, 6,700 partners, and operate in 144 countries. **NOTE:** See website for current job openings and application instructions. Applying online at is strongly recommended. Entry-level positions available. **Positions advertised include:** Senior Associate – Federal Tax; Audit Manager. **Corporate headquarters location:** Montvale NJ. **Other U.S. locations:** Nationwide. **International location:** Worldwide. **Parent company:** KPMG International. **CEO:** Tim Flynn.

McGLADREY & PULLEN, LLP
3600 American Boulevard West, Third Floor, Bloomington MN 55431-4502. 952/835-9930. **Contact:** Human Resources. **E-mail address:** mcgladrey@rsmi.com. **World Wide Web address:** http://www.mcgladrey.com. **Description:** A certified public accounting firm providing audit, tax, management, data processing, and cost systems services. **Positions include:** Audit, Sr. Associate; Audit Associate; Tax Manager; Internal Audit Associate. **Corporate headquarters location:** This location. **Other area locations:** Minneapolis MN; Duluth MN; Rochester MN; St. Paul MN.

PERSONNEL DECISIONS INTERNATIONAL (PDI)
2000 Plaza VII Tower, 45 South Seventh Street, Minneapolis MN 55402-1608. 920/997-6995. **Toll-free phone:** 800/633-4410. **Fax:** 612/ 337-3698. **Contact:** Human Resources. **E-mail address:** career@personneldecisions.com. **World Wide web address:** http://www.personneldecisions.com. **Description:** A worldwide consulting firm specializing in talent management. PDI applies behavioral sciences to help organizations define successful performance; measure capabilities and potential; and develop the skills and abilities of individuals, teams and organizations. **Positions advertised include:** Consultant – Sales Effectiveness; Regional Financial Specialist; Senior Consultant; Senior Consultant - Sales Effectiveness; Support Specialist; System Specialist. **Corporate headquarters location:** This location. **Other U.S. locations:** Atlanta GA; Boston MA; Chicago IL; Dallas TX; Denver CO; Detroit MI; Houston TX; Los Angeles CA; New York NY; San Francisco CA; Washington DC.

RSM McGLADREY, INC.
227 West First Street, Suite 700, Duluth MN 55802. 218/727-8253. **Fax:** 218/727-1438. **Contact:** Human Resources. **E-mail address:** jobs@rsmi.com. **World Wide Web address:** http://www.rsmmcgladrey.com. **Description:** Provides accounting and auditing services, business planning, taxation, and consulting services. **NOTE:** Search and apply for positions online. **Corporate headquarters location:** Minneapolis MN. **Other U.S. locations:** Nationwide. **Number of employees nationwide:** 4,000.

SCHECHTER DOKKEN KANTER
100 Washington Avenue South, Suite 1600, Minneapolis MN 55401. 612/332-5500. **Fax:** 612/332-1529. **Contact:** Heather Walsh, Human Resources. **E-mail address:** hwalsh@sdkcpa.com. **World Wide Web address:** http://www.sdkcpa.com. **Description:** A regional accounting and management consulting firm performing audits, accounting, tax, employee benefits plan consulting, litigation support, and management consulting services. **NOTE:** Submit resume by mail or e-mail. **Corporate headquarters location:** This location. **Number of employees at this location:** 50.

TOWERS PERRIN
8000 Norman Center Drive, Suite 1200, Minneapolis MN 55437-1097. 952/842-5600. **Contact:** Kathy Halverson, Office Administrator. **World Wide Web address:** http://www.towers.com. **Description:** A management consulting firm engaged in human resources, risk, and financial management, as well as reinsurance. **Positions advertised include:** Senior Retirement Consultant. **Corporate headquarters location:** Stamford CT. **Other U.S. locations:** Nationwide.

Mississippi

HORNE LLP
P.O. Box 22964, Jackson MS 39225-2964. 601/948-0940. **Physical address:** 200 East Capitol Street, Suite 1400, Jackson MS 39201. **Contact:** Human Resources. **E-mail address:** humanresources@horne-llp.com. **World Wide Web address:** http://www.horne-llp.com. **Description:** An accounting and consulting firm that offers services such as business valuation, litigation support and information technology. **Positions advertised include:** Healthcare Assurance Manager; Data Analyst; General Office Assistant; Help Desk Support Specialist; Senior Client Representative. **Other area locations:** Grenada MS; Gulfport MS; Hattiesburg MS; Laurel MS; Lucedale MS; Oxford MS. **Other U.S. locations:** Mobile AL; New Orleans LA; Nashville TN. **Number of employees nationwide:** 300.

HUFFMAN & COMPANY, CPA
497 Keywood Circle, Suite A, Flowood MS 39232. 601/355-6104. **Fax:** 601/944-0548. **Contact:** Ginger Carter, Office Manager. **E-mail address:** cpahuff@aol.com. **Description:** Provides individual and small business accounting and tax services.

Missouri

DELOITTE & TOUCHE
515 North 6th Street, Saint Louis MO 63101. 314/641-4300. **Fax:** 314/342-1100. **Contact:** Human Resources. **World Wide Web address:** http://www.us.deloitte.com. **Description:** An international firm of certified public accountants providing professional accounting, auditing, tax, and management consulting services to widely diversified clients. The company has a specialized program consisting of national industry groups and functional groups that cross industry lines. Groups are involved in various disciplines including accounting, auditing, taxation management advisory services, small and growing businesses, mergers and acquisitions, and computer applications.

ERNST & YOUNG LLP
1200 Main Street, Suite 1800, Kansas City MO 64105. 816/480-5546. **Contact:** Susan Chapman, Human Resources. **World Wide Web address:** http://www.ey.com. **Description:** A certified public accounting firm that also provides management consulting services. Services include data processing, financial modeling, financial feasibility studies, production planning and inventory management, management sciences, health care planning, human resources, cost accounting, and budgeting systems. **Special programs:** Internships. **Corporate headquarters location:** New York NY. **International locations:** Worldwide.

H&R BLOCK
4400 Main Street, Kansas City MO 64111. 816/753-6900. **Contact:** Human Resources. **World Wide Web address:** http://www.hrblock.com. **Description:** Primarily engaged in consumer tax preparation. H&R Block has offices in over 750 Sears stores in both the United States and Canada. Many offices operate as franchises, and some operate on a seasonal basis. H&R Block is also engaged in a number of other tax-related activities including Group Tax Programs, Premium Tax Service, Tax Training Schools, and Real Estate Tax Awareness seminars. **Corporate headquarters location:** This location. **Listed on:** New York Stock Exchange. **Stock exchange symbol:** HRB. **Number of employees at this location:** 300. **Number of employees nationwide:** 80,000.

KPMG
10 South Broadway, Suite 900, St. Louis MO 63102-1761. 314/444-1400. **Fax:** 314/444-1470. **Contact:** Human Resources Director. **World Wide Web address:** http://www.us.kpmg.com. **Description:** KPMG delivers a wide range of value-added assurance, tax, and consulting services. Founded in 1897. **NOTE:** Search and apply for positions online. **Positions advertised include:** Sr. Manager, Audit; Sr. Manager, Information Risk Management; Sr. Associate, Internal Audit; Manager, Industry Risk-Based Solutions. **Corporate headquarters location:** Montvale NJ. **Parent company:** KPMG International is a leader among professional services firms engaged in capturing, managing, assessing, and delivering information to create knowledge that will help its clients maximize shareholder value.

RUBIN, BROWN, GORNSTEIN & CO. LLP
One North Court, Saint Louis MO 63108. 314/290-3300. **Fax:** 314/290-3400. **Contact:** Human Resources. **E-mail address:** recruiting@rbg.com. **World Wide Web address:** http://www.rbg.com. **Description:** A public accounting firm operating primarily in the St. Louis metropolitan area. Services and specialties include accounting, audit, and tax services; and computer, employee benefit plan, legal support management, personal financial, and acquisition consulting services. The company provides services to accounting firms, automotive dealerships, financial services firms including financial institutions and mortgage banks, government agencies, health care companies, hospitality firms, law firms, manufacturing companies, international business consultants, nonprofit organizations, real estate and construction firms, and retailers. **Positions advertised include:** Health Care Audit Management Professional; Small Business Group Accountant; Internal Auditor. **Special programs:** Internships. **Corporate headquarters location:** This location. **Operations at this facility include:** Administration; Sales; Service. **Number of employees at this location:** 200.

Nevada

DELOITTE & TOUCHE
3773 Howard Hughes Parkway, Suite 490 North, Las Vegas NV 89109. 702/893-3176. **Contact:** Human Resources. **World Wide Web address:** http://www.us.deloitte.com. **Description:** An international firm of certified public accountants providing professional accounting, auditing, tax, and management consulting services to widely diversified clients. The company has a specialized program consisting of national industry groups and functional groups that cross industry lines. Groups are involved in various disciplines including accounting, auditing, taxation management advisory services, small and growing businesses, mergers and acquisitions, and computer applications. **Other U.S. locations:** Nationwide. **Number of employees at this location:** 124. **Number of employees nationwide:** 120,000.

KAFOURY ARMSTRONG & CO.
6140 Plumas Street, Reno NV 89509-6060. 775/689-9100. **Fax:** 775/689-9299. **Contact:** Dessie Felder, Human Resources Director. **E-mail address:** dfelder@kafoury.com. **World Wide Web address:** http://www.kafoury.com. **Description:** An accounting, auditing, and taxation specialist. Founded in 1941. **NOTE:** Entry-level positions are offered. **Positions**

advertised include: Accountant; Auditor. **Corporate headquarters location:** This location. **Other U.S. locations:** Elko NV; Fallon NV; Las Vegas NV; Winnemucca NV; Yerington NV. **Listed on:** Privately held. **Annual sales/revenues:** $5 - $10 million. **Number of employees nationwide:** 140.

PRICEWATERHOUSECOOPERS
3800 Howard Hughes Parkway, Suite 550, Las Vegas NV 89109. 702/691-5400. **Fax:** 702/691-5444. **Contact:** Human Resources Department. **World Wide Web address:** http://www.pwc.com. **Description:** One of the largest certified public accounting firms in the world. PricewaterhouseCoopers provides public accounting, business advisory, management consulting, and taxation services. **Positions advertised include:** Assurance Associate. **Corporate headquarters location:** New York NY. **Other U.S. locations:** Nationwide. **International locations:** Worldwide. **Number of employees worldwide:** Over 124,000.

New Jersey
AON CONSULTING
125 Chubb Avenue, 2nd Floor, Lyndhurst NJ 07071. 201/460-6700. **Contact:** Human Resources. **World Wide Web address:** http://www.aonconsulting.com. **Description:** An international human resources consulting and benefits brokerage firm providing integrated advisory and support services in retirement planning, health care management, organizational effectiveness, compensation, human resources-related communications, and information technologies. **Positions advertised include:** Sr. Retirement Consultant; Health and Welfare Consultant. **Corporate headquarters location:** Chicago IL.

BOWMAN & COMPANY LLP
601 White Horse Road, Voorhees NJ 08043. 856/435-6200. **Fax:** 856/435-0440. **Contact:** John Daniels, Human Resources. **World Wide Web address:** http://www.bowmanllp.com. **Description:** A certified public accounting firm. Founded in 1939. **NOTE:** Fill out application online. Entry-level positions are offered. **Special programs:** Internships; Co-ops. **Corporate headquarters location:** This location. **Other area locations:** Woodbury NJ. **Listed on:** Privately held. **Annual sales/revenues:** $5 - $10 million. **Number of employees at this location:** 90.

DELOITTE & TOUCHE
2 Hilton Court, P.O. Box 319, Parsippany NJ 07054-0319. 973/683-7000. **Fax:** 973/683-7459. **Contact:** Human Resources Department. **World Wide Web address:** http://www.us.deloitte.com. **Description:** An international firm of certified public accountants providing professional accounting, auditing, tax, and management consulting services to widely diversified clients. The company has a specialized program consisting of national industry groups and functional groups that cross industry lines. Groups are involved in various disciplines including accounting, auditing, taxation management advisory services, small and growing businesses, mergers and acquisitions, and computer applications. **Positions advertised include:** Audit Manager; Multistate Tax Manager; Employee Benefits Tax Manager; Healthcare Regulatory Consultant Internal Audit Manager. **Corporate headquarters location:** Wilton CT. **Other U.S. locations:** Nationwide. **Parent company:** Deloitte Touche Tohmatsu International.

ERNST & YOUNG LLP
125 Chubb Avenue, Lyndhurst NJ 07071. 201/872-2200. **Contact:** Human Resources. **World Wide Web address:** http://www.ey.com. **Description:** A certified public accounting firm that also provides management consulting services. Services include data processing, financial modeling, financial feasibility studies, production planning and inventory management, management sciences, health care planning, human resources, cost accounting, and budgeting systems. **Positions advertised include:** Strategic Sourcing Analyst; Balance Sheet Analyst Manager; Infrastructure Engineer; Assistant Coordinator; Software Development Specialist; Production Analyst; Help Desk Analyst; Client Services Assistant; Project Account Manager; Executive Coordinator; Financial Analyst; Information Technology Technologist; Financial Application Support. **Corporate headquarters location:** New York NY.

GRANT THORNTON LLP
399 Thornall Street, 4th Floor, Edison NJ 08837. 732/516-5500. **Fax:** 732/516-5502. **Contact:** Human Resources. **World Wide Web address:** http://www.grantthornton.com. **Description:** An accounting, tax, and business advisory organizations with member firms in 111 countries. **Positions advertised include:** Sr. Tax Associate; Sr. Manager, Accounting Principles; Manager, Accounting Principles.

JACKSON HEWITT INC.
7 Sylvan Way, Parsippany NJ 07054. 973/496-1040. **Contact:** Human Resources. **E-mail address:** careers@tax.com. **World Wide Web address:** http://www.jacksonhewitt.com. **Description:** A full-service company specializing in computerized tax preparation and electronic filing. The foundation of Jackson Hewitt's tax service is Hewtax, a proprietary software program. The company offers a number of filing options including SuperFast Refund, through which customers receive a refund anticipation loan within one to two days of filing; Accelerated Check Refund, which allows Jackson Hewitt to set up a bank account for the IRS to deposit the taxpayer's refund; and a standard electronically filed return. The company also operates a travel agency, Campbell Travel. **Positions advertised include:** Human Resources Generalist; Marketing Coordinator; Online Designer; Director, Sales Promotion Marketing; Staff Accountant; Advertising Copywriter. **NOTE:** Search for current positions by location online.

KPMG
3 Chestnut Ridge Road, Montvale NJ 07645. 201/307-7000. **Contact:** Human Resources. **World Wide Web address:** http://www.kpmg.com. **Description:** KPMG delivers a wide range of value-added assurance, tax, and consulting services. **Corporate headquarters location:** This location. **Other U.S. locations:** Nationwide. **Operations at this facility include:** This location houses the company's administrative offices. **Parent company:** KPMG International is a leader among professional services firms engaged in capturing, managing, assessing, and delivering information to create knowledge that will help its clients maximize shareholder value.

KEPNER-TREGOE, INC.
Research Road, P.O. Box 704, Princeton NJ 08542. 609/921-2806. **Toll-free phone:** 800/537-6378. **E-mail address:** kt-us@kepner-tregoe.com. **Physical address:** 17 Research Road, Princeton NJ 08558. **Contact:** Human Resources. **World Wide Web address:** http://www.kepner-tregoe.com. **Description:** A worldwide management consulting firm. Product categories include strategy formulation, systems improvement, skill development, and specific issue resolution. Industry markets served include automotive, information technology, chemicals, financial services, and natural resources. Founded in 1958. **Positions advertised include:** Consultant; Inside Sales Representative. **Corporate headquarters location:** This location. **International locations:** Worldwide. **Number of employees worldwide:** 225.

MERCER HUMAN RESOURCES CONSULTING
212 Carnegie Center, 4th Floor, Princeton NJ 08543. 609/520-2500. **Fax:** 609/520-2478. **Contact:** Human Resources. **World Wide Web address:** http://www.mercerhr.com. **Description:** One of the world's largest actuarial and human resources management consulting firms, providing advice to organizations on all aspects of employee/management relationships. Services include retirement, health and welfare, performance and rewards, communication, investment, human resources administration, risk,

finance and insurance, and health care provider consulting. **Positions advertised include:** Actuarial Analyst; Actuarial Consultant. **Corporate headquarters location:** New York NY. **Other U.S. locations:** Nationwide. **International locations:** Worldwide. **Parent company:** Marsh & McClennan Companies. **Listed on:** New York Stock Exchange. **Stock exchange symbol:** MMC.

KURT SALMON ASSOCIATES, INC.
103 Carnegie Center, Suite 205, Princeton NJ 08540. 609/452-8700. **Fax:** 609/452-8090. **Contact:** Director of Recruiting. **World Wide Web address:** http://www.kurtsalmon.com. **Description:** Provides management consulting to logistics and consumer products companies.

SIBSON CONSULTING
600 Alexander Park, Suite 208, Princeton NJ 08540. 609/520-2700. **Contact:** Human Resources. **World Wide Web address:** http://www.segalco.com/sibson. **Description:** A management consulting firm. **Positions advertised include:** Associate Consultant; Consultant; Senior Consultant; Principal. **Corporate headquarters location:** This location. **Parent company:** Segal.

New Mexico

GILMORE, GANNAWAY, ANDREWS, SMITH & COMPANY
2724 Wilshire Boulevard, Roswell NM 88201. 505/622-5200. **Toll-free phone:** 800/748-3662. **Toll-free phone:** 800/748-3662. **Fax:** 505/622-5206. **Contact:** Office Manager. **World Wide Web address:** http://www.ggas.com. **Description:** A certified public accounting firm.

KPMG LLP
Two Park Square, Suite 700, 6565 Americas Parkway NE, Albuquerque NM 87110. 505/884-3939. **Contact:** Human Resources. **World Wide Web address:** http://www.us.kpmg.com. **Description:** KPMG LLP, the U.S. member firm of KPMG International, is an audit, tax and advisory firm. KPMG International's member firms have 76,000 professionals, 6,700 partners, and operate in 144 countries. The Albuquerque office of represents one of the largest CPA firms in the state of New Mexico. **NOTE:** See website for current job openings and application instructions. Applying online is strongly recommended. Entry-level positions available. **Positions advertised include:** Seasonal Senior Tax Associate. **Special programs:** Internships. **Corporate headquarters location:** Montvale NJ. **Other U.S. locations:** Nationwide. **International locations:** Worldwide. **Parent company:** KPMG International.

New York

BEARINGPOINT, INC.
757 Third Avenue, New York NY 10017. 212/896-1800. **Corporate headquarters location:** McLean VA. **Other U.S. locations:** Nationwide. **Contact:** Human Resources. **World Wide Web address:** http://www.bearingpoint.com. **Description:** Provides strategic consulting, application services, technology solutions, and managed services to large and medium-sized companies and government organizations. BearingPoint focuses on consumer goods, financial services, high technology, and media industries. **Positions advertised include:** Consultant; Management Analyst.

CT CORPORATION SYSTEM
3 Winners Circle, 3rd Floor, Albany NY 12205. 518/451-8000. **Toll-free phone:** 800/624-0909. **Contact:** Human Resources. **E-mail address:** info@ctadvantage.com. **World Wide Web address:** http://www.ctcorporation.com. **Description:** CT Corporation provides research and accounting services for attorneys. **Positions advertised include:** Staff Accountant; Service Team Leader; Internal Support Analyst; Accounts Receivable Maintenance Clerk; Associate Customer Specialist; Quality Assurance Professional; Receptionist; Project Manager; Desktop Support Analyst; Information Technology Manager; Senior Product Manager; Associate Customer Specialist; Operations Process Management Director; Licensing Support Specialist. **Parent company:** Wolters Kluwer U.S. **Number of employees:** 1,100.

DELOITTE TOUCHE TOHMATSU
dba DELOITTE & TOUCHE LLP
1633 Broadway, New York NY 10019-6754. 212/489-1600. **Fax:** 212/489-1687. **Contact:** Human Resources. **World Wide Web address:** http://www.deloitte.com. **Description:** An international auditing partnership of certified public accountants providing professional accounting, auditing, tax, and management consulting services to widely diversified clients from offices in 140 countries. The company has a specialized program consisting of national industry groups and functional groups that cross industy lines. Groups are involved in various disciplines including accounting, auditing, taxation management advisory services, small and growing businesses, mergers and acquisitions, and computer applications. **NOTE:** Apply online. **Positions advertised include:** Senior Industry Knowledge Manager; Administrative Assistant; Administrative Floater; Executive Assistant; Scheduling Manager; Information Technology Recruiting Manager; Tax Recruiting Manager; Client Advisory Associate; Business Development Manager; Relationship Development Manager; Assurance & Compliance Consultant. **Corporate headquarters location:** This location. **Other locations:** Worldwide. **Subsidiaries include:** Deloitte Consulting. **Chairman:** Piet Hoogendoorn. **Annual sales/revenues:** $12.5 billion. **Number of employees:** 98,000.

ERNST & YOUNG INTERNATIONAL
dba ERNST & YOUNG LLP
5 Times Square, New York NY 10036-6530. 212/773-3000. **Fax:** 212/773-6350. **Contact:** Human Resources. **World Wide Web address:** http://www.ey.com. **Description:** A certified public accounting partnership that also provides accounting and management consulting services. Services include data processing, financial modeling, financial feasibility studies, production planning and inventory management, management sciences, health care planning, human resources, cost accounting, and budgeting systems. **Positions advertised include:** Financial Assistant; Financial Researcher; Bilingual Japanese Administrative Assistant; risk Management Senior Manager; Technology & Security Risk Services Senior; Structured Finance Advisory Services Manager; Risk Management Services Senior; Knowledge Resources Manager; On-Call Advisory Services Senior; Credit Risk Management Advisor. **Corporate headquarters location:** This location. **Other locations:** Worldwide. **Chairman:** James S. Turley. **Annual sales/revenues:** $16.9 billion. **Number of employees:** 107,000.

GUIDELINE
625 Avenue of the Americas, New York NY 10011-2020. 212/645-4500. **Fax:** 212/463-6232. **Contact:** Human Resources. **E-mail address:** careers@guideline.com. **World Wide Web address:** http://www.guideline.com. **Description:** Provides business and management consulting, research, and advisory services. The company also offers seminars, conferences, and publications. Founded in 1969. **Positions advertised include:** Industrial Products and Services Director; Corporate Sales Representative; Business Development Manager; Healthcare Team Consultant; Business Consultant; Associate Consultant. **Corporate headquarters location:** This location. **Other locations:** Nationwide. **Listed on:** Over The Counter. **Stock exchange symbol:** FSVP. **Chairman:** Martin E. Franklin. **Annual sales/revenues:** $22 million. **Number of employees:** 169.

KPMG
757 Third Avenue, New York NY 10017. 212/909-5600. **Contact:** Human Resources. **World Wide Web address:** http://www.kpmg.com. **Description:** KPMG delivers a wide range of value-added assurance, tax, and consulting services including legal and management services. **Positions advertised include:**

Senior Associate; Recruiter; Pharmaceutical Regulatory Manager; Associate Pharmaceutical Regulator; Senior Associate Manager; Project Manager; Senior Internal Auditor; Insurance Practice Auditor; Duplicating Operator; Tax Manager; Quantitative Analyst. **Corporate headquarters location:** Montvale NJ. **Other U.S. locations:** Nationwide. **Parent company:** KPMG International is a professional services firm with more than 85,000 employees worldwide including 6,500 partners and 60,000 professionals, serving clients in 844 cities throughout 155 countries. KPMG International is a leader among professional services firms engaged in capturing, managing, assessing, and delivering information to create knowledge that will help its clients maximize shareholder value. **Number of employees at this location:** 1300.

PRICEWATERHOUSECOOPERS
1301 Avenue of the Americas, New York NY 10019. 646/471-4000. **Contact:** Human Resources. **World Wide Web address:** http://www.pwcglobal.com. **Description:** One of the largest certified public accounting firms in the world. PricewaterhouseCoopers provides public accounting, business advisory, management consulting, and taxation services. **NOTE:** Interested job seekers may apply online. **Positions advertised include:** BCS Senior Associate; Asset Advisory Associate; ISG Manager; Special Situations Associate; Insurance Manager; Senior Operational Effectiveness Associate; Executive Assistant to the Chairman; Corporate Treasury Technology Associate; Treasury and Finance Associate; OGC Secretariat Associate; Change and Learning Solutions Manager. **Corporate headquarters location:** This location. **Other U.S. locations:** Nationwide. **International locations:** Worldwide. **Chairman:** Andrew Ratcliffe. **Sales/revenue:** Over $13 billion. **Number of employees worldwide:** 125,000.

TOWERS PERRIN
335 Madison Avenue, New York NY 10017-4605. 212/309-3400. **Contact:** Recruiting Coordinator. **World Wide Web address:** http://www.towersperrin.com. **Description:** A management consulting firm. **Corporate headquarters location:** This location.

North Carolina
ACENTRON TECHNOLOGIES, INC.
201 South College Street, Suite 2050, Charlotte NC 28244. 704/335-0030. **Toll-free phone:** 888/255-6788. **Fax:** 704-376-7369. **Contact:** Human Resources. **E-mail address:** resume@acentron.com. **World Wide Web address:** http://www.acentron.com. **Description:** A consulting and professional services firm. Founded in 1993. **Positions advertised include:** PeopleSoft Developer; Senior Recruiter; Senior Sales Executive. **Other area locations:** Winston-Salem NC; Greenville SC.

DELOITTE & TOUCHE
150 Fayetteville Street Mall, Suite 1800, Raleigh NC 27601. 919/546-8000. **Fax:** 919/833-3276. **Contact:** Office Administrator. **E-mail address:** dtcareers@deloitte.com. **World Wide Web address:** http://www.us.deloitte.com. **Description:** An international firm of certified public accountants providing professional accounting, auditing, tax, and management consulting services to widely diversified clients. **Corporate headquarters location:** New York NY. **Other area locations:** Charlotte NC; Hickory NC; Research Triangle Park NC. **Other U.S. locations:** Nationwide. **International locations:** Worldwide.

ERNST & YOUNG LLP
100 North Tryon Street, Suite 3800, Charlotte NC 28202. 704/372-6300. **Contact:** Human Resources. **World Wide Web address:** http://www.ey.com. **Description:** A certified public accounting firm that also provides management consulting services. Services include data processing, financial modeling, financial feasibility studies, production planning and inventory management, management sciences, health care planning, human resources, cost accounting, and budgeting systems. **Positions advertised include:** Technology and Security Risk Services; Assurance Senior; Risk Management Services Manager; Business Risk Services Senior Auditor, Internal Audit Services. **Corporate headquarters location:** New York NY. **Other area locations:** Raleigh NC; Greensboro NC. **Other U.S. locations:** Nationwide.

KPMG LLP
301 North Elm Street, Suite 700, Greensboro NC 27401. 336/275-3394. **Contact:** Pam Brown, Personnel Manager. **World Wide Web address:** http://www.kpmgcareers.com. **Description:** KPMG delivers a wide range of value-added assurance, tax, and consulting services. **Corporate headquarters location:** Washington DC. **Parent company:** KPMG International. **Other U.S. locations:** Nationwide. **International locations:** Worldwide. **Number of employees at this location:** 50.

McGLADREY & PULLEN, LLP
P.O. Box 2470, Greensboro NC 27402-2470. 336/273-4461. **Physical address:** 230 North Elm Street, Suite 1100, Greensboro NC 27401. **Fax:** 336/274-2519. **Contact:** Jennifer Parish, Personnel. **World Wide Web address:** http://www.mcgladrey.com. **Description:** A certified public accounting firm providing audit, tax, management, data processing, and cost systems services. **Corporate headquarters location:** Bloomington MN. **Other area locations:** Statewide. **Other U.S. locations:** Nationwide.

PRICEWATERHOUSECOOPERS
214 North Tryon Street, Suite 3600, Charlotte NC 28202. 704/344-7500. **Fax:** 704/344-4100. **Contact:** Personnel. **World Wide Web address:** http://www.pwc.com. **Description:** One of the largest certified public accounting firms in the world. PricewaterhouseCoopers provides public accounting, business advisory, management consulting, and taxation services. **Positions advertised include:** HCP Manager; ITS Senior Associate; ISG Manager; SALT Senior Associate; Income Franchise Manager; Assurance Senior Associate; Financial Services IAS Senior Associate; Executive Assistant of Tax Services; SPA Senior Associate; Credit Risk Management Senior Associate. **Corporate headquarters location:** New York NY. **Other U.S. locations:** Nationwide. **International locations:** Worldwide. **Number of employees worldwide:** 120,000.

Ohio
DELOITTE & TOUCHE
127 Public Square, Suite 2500, Cleveland OH 44114. 216/589-1300. **Fax:** 216/589-1369. **Contact:** Human Resources. **E-mail address:** dtcareers@deloitte.com. **World Wide Web address:** http://www.us.deloitte.com. **Description:** An international firm of certified public accountants providing professional accounting, auditing, tax, and management consulting services to widely diversified clients. The company has a specialized program consisting of national industry groups and functional groups that cross industry lines. Groups are involved in various disciplines including accounting, auditing, taxation management advisory services, small and growing businesses, mergers and acquisitions, and computer applications. **Positions advertised include:** Assurance and Advisory Manager. **Special programs:** Internships. **Corporate headquarters location:** Wilton CT. **Other area locations:** Akron OH; Cincinnati OH; Columbus OH; Dayton OH.

ERNST & YOUNG LLP
312 Walnut Street, 1900 Scripps Center, Cincinnati OH 45202. 513/612-1400. **Fax:** 513/621-5512. **Contact:** Personnel Department. **World Wide Web address:** http://www.ey.com. **Description:** A certified public accounting firm that also provides management consulting services. Services include data processing, financial modeling, financial feasibility studies, production planning and inventory management, management sciences, health care planning, human resources, cost accounting, and budgeting systems. **Positions advertised include:** Senior Assurance

Manager; Assurance Staff Member; Business Risk Services Auditor; Tax Compliance Staff Member; IT Audit Manager. **Corporate headquarters location:** New York NY. **Other area locations:** Akron OH; Canton OH; Cleveland OH; Columbus OH; Dayton OH; Toledo OH. **Other U.S. locations:** Nationwide. **International locations:** Worldwide.

HUDSON ACCOUNTING & FINANCE
Heritage Corporate Center, 6001 East Royalton Road, Suite 150, Broadview Heights OH 44147. 440/457-4700. **Fax:** 440/457-4701. **Contact:** Kristen Babbin. **E-mail address:** Kristen.babbin@hhgroup.com. **World Wide Web address:** http://www.hudson.com. **Description:** Provides executive staffing solutions. **Positions advertised include:** Senior Auditor; Senior Accountant; Financial Analyst; Senior Property Accountant; Staff Accountant; Senior Tax Manager; Internal Auditor.

MEADEN & MOORE, INC.
1100 Superior Avenue East, Suite 1100, Cleveland OH 44114. 216/241-3272. **Fax:** 216/771-4511. **Contact:** Human Resources. **E-mail address:** cleveland@meadenmoore.com. **World Wide Web address:** http://www.meadenmoore.com. **Description:** Engaged in certified public accounting and business consulting. **Positions advertised include:** Audit Manager; Audit Specialist; Tax Manager; Senior Manager Accountant; Staff Accountant.

MERCER HUMAN RESOURCE CONSULTING
10 West Broad Street, Suite 1100, Columbus OH 43215-3475. 614/227-5500. **Fax:** 614/224-7676. **Contact:** Personnel Manager. **World Wide Web address:** http://www.mercerhr.com. **Description:** One of the world's largest actuarial and human resources management consulting firms. The company offers advice to organizations on all aspects of employee/management relationships. Services include retirement, health and welfare, performance and rewards, communication, investment, human resources administration, risk, finance and insurance, and health care provider consulting. **Special programs:** Internships; Co-ops. **Other area locations:** Cincinnati OH; Cleveland OH. **Other U.S. locations:** Nationwide.

PRICEWATERHOUSECOOPERS
B.P. Tower, 27th Floor, 200 Public Square, Cleveland OH 44114-2301. 216/875-3000. **Contact:** Human Resources. **World Wide Web address:** http://www.pricewaterhousecoopers.com. **Description:** One of the largest certified public accounting firms in the world. PricewaterhouseCoopers provides public accounting, business advisory, management consulting, and taxation services. **Positions advertised include:** Senior Associate; Internal Audit Senior Associate; IT Audit Associate; Business Analyst; Tax Manager; Junior Analyst. **Corporate headquarters location:** New York NY. **Other U.S. locations:** Nationwide. **International locations:** Worldwide.

Oregon

DELOITTE & TOUCHE
111 SW Fifth Avenue, Suite 3900, Portland OR 97204. 503/222-1341. **Contact:** Human Resources. **World Wide Web address:** http://www.us.deloitte.com. **Description:** An international firm of certified public accountants providing professional accounting, auditing, tax, and management consulting services to widely diversified clients. The company has a specialized program consisting of national industry groups and functional groups that cross industry lines. Groups are involved in various disciplines including accounting, auditing, taxation management advisory services, small and growing businesses, mergers and acquisitions, and computer applications. **Positions advertised include:** Senior Consultant; Internal Audit Supervisor; Accountant; Consultant. **Other U.S. locations:** Nationwide.

GEFFEN MESHER & COMPANY
888 SW Fifth Avenue, Suite 800, Portland OR 97204. 503/221-0141. **Contact:** Human Resources Department. **E-mail address:** hr@gmco.com. **World Wide Web address:** http://www.gmco.com. **Description:** A diversified accounting and business consulting firm. **Positions advertised include:** Audit Manager.

MOSS ADAMS LLP
Fox Tower, 805 SW Broadway, Suite 1200, Portland OR 97205. 503/242-1447. **Fax:** 503/274-2789. **Contact:** Human Resources. **E-mail address:** portlandor@mossadams.com. **World Wide Web address:** http://www.mossadams.com. **Description:** One of the nation's largest accounting firms offering assurance, consulting, and tax and audit services.

PRICEWATERHOUSECOOPERS
1300 SW Fifth Avenue, Suite 3100, Portland OR 97201. 971/544-4000. **Fax:** 971/544-4100. **Contact:** Personnel. **World Wide Web address:** http://www.pricewaterhousecoopers.com. **Description:** One of the largest certified public accounting firms in the world. PricewaterhouseCoopers provides public accounting, business advisory, management consulting, and taxation services. **Positions advertised include:** Senior Manager; State Tax Income Franchise Generalist; Middle Market Senior Associate; Consumer Products Tax Senior Associate; Middle Market Associate; Senior Associate; Systems Assurance Senior. **Corporate headquarters location:** New York NY. **Other U.S. locations:** Nationwide. **International locations:** Worldwide.

Pennsylvania

DELOITTE & TOUCHE
2500 One PPG Place, Pittsburgh PA 15222. 412/338-7200. **Fax:** 412/338-7380. **Contact:** Kristin Lazzari, Recruiting Director. **World Wide Web address:** http://www.us.deloitte.com. **Description:** An international firm of certified public accountants providing professional accounting, auditing, tax, and management consulting services to widely diversified clients. The company has a specialized program consisting of national industry groups and functional groups that cross industry lines. **Positions advertised include:** International Tax Manager; Consultant; Health Care Manager.

ERNST & YOUNG LLP
2 Commerce Square, 2001 Market Street, Suite 4000, Philadelphia PA 19103-7096. 215/448-5000. **Fax:** 215/448-4069. **Contact:** Thomas G. Elicker, Director of Human Resources. **World Wide Web address:** http://www.ey.com. **Description:** A certified public accounting firm that also provides management consulting services. Services include data processing, financial modeling, financial feasibility studies, production planning and inventory management, management sciences, health care planning, human resources, cost accounting, and budgeting systems. **Positions advertised include:** Assurance Manager; Business Risk Services Manager; Sr. Construction Advisor. **Corporate headquarters location:** New York NY.

HAY GROUP INC.
The Wanamaker Building, 100 Penn Square East, Philadelphia PA 19107-3388. 215/861-2000. **Fax:** 215/861-2111. **Contact:** Personnel. **World Wide Web address:** http://www.haygroup.com. **Description:** An international human resources and management consulting firm that provides a variety of services including total compensation planning, strategic management, business culture, employee surveys, and outplacement. **Positions advertised include:** Development Manager; System Administrator; US Marketing Director; Webmaster; Programmer Analyst. **Corporate headquarters location:** This location. **Number of employees worldwide:** 2200.

KPMG
1600 Market Street, 12th Floor, Philadelphia PA 19103. 267/256-7000. **Fax:** 267/256-7200. **Contact:** Human Resources. **World Wide Web address:** http://www.kpmg.com. **Description:** KPMG delivers a

wide range of value-added assurance, tax, and consulting services. **Corporate headquarters location:** Montvale NJ. **Other U.S. locations:** Nationwide. **International locations:** Worldwide. **Parent company:** KPMG International is a leader among professional services firms engaged in capturing, managing, assessing, and delivering information to create knowledge that will help its clients maximize shareholder value. **Listed on:** NASDAQ. **Stock exchange symbol:** KCIN. **Number of employees worldwide:** 85,000.

PRICEWATERHOUSECOOPERS
2 Commerce Square, Suite 1700, 2001 Market Street, Philadelphia PA 19103. 267/330-3000. **Fax:** 267/330-3300. **Contact:** Human Resources Department. **World Wide Web address:** http://www.pwcglobal.com. **Description:** One of the largest certified public accounting firms in the world. PricewaterhouseCoopers provides public accounting, business advisory, management consulting, and taxation services. **Corporate headquarters location:** New York NY. **Other U.S. locations:** Nationwide.

RIGHT MANAGEMENT CONSULTANTS
1818 Market Street, 33rd Floor, Philadelphia PA 19103. 215/988-1588. **Toll-free phone:** 800/237-4448. **Contact:** Human Resources. **E-mail address:** careers@right.com. **World Wide Web address:** http://www.right.com. **Description:** Provides management and human resources consulting services. Founded in 1980. **Corporate headquarters location:** This location. **Listed on:** NASDAQ. **Stock exchange symbol:** RMCI.

SCHNEIDER, DOWNS & COMPANY
1133 Penn Avenue, Pittsburgh PA 15222-4205. 412/261-3644. **Fax:** 412/261-4876. **Contact:** Amy Parkinson, Human Resources. **E-mail address:** aparknson@sdcpa.com. **World Wide Web address:** http://www.schneiderdowns.com. **Description:** A professional accounting, tax, and business consulting firm. **Positions advertised include:** Audit Manager; Application Support Consultant; Tax Senior; Tax Manager.

SYNYGY, INC.
2501 Seaport Drive, Chester PA 19013. 610/494-3300. **Fax:** 610/664-7343. **Contact:** Stephanie Salamon, Technical Recruiter. **E-mail address:** salamon@synygy.com. **World Wide Web address:** http://www.synygy.com. **Description:** Provides software and services that enable organizations to measure, report, and analyze employee performance. Founded in 1991. **NOTE:** Search and apply for positions online. **Company slogan:** Turning information into action. **Positions advertised include:** System Architect; Associate Business Analyst; Software Documentation Specialist; Software Training Specialist; Assistant General Counsel. **Special programs:** Summer Jobs. **Corporate headquarters location:** This location. **Other U.S. locations:** Phoenix AZ. **Number of employees nationwide:** 500.

Rhode Island
KPMG LLP
600 Fleet Center, 50 Kennedy Plaza, Providence RI 02903. 401/421-6600. **Fax:** 401/421-3570. **Contact:** Ana Hurd. **E-mail address:** ahurd@kpmg.com. **World Wide Web address:** http://www.us.kpmg.com. **Description:** KPMG LLP, the U.S. member firm of KPMG International, is an audit, tax and advisory firm. KPMG International's member firms have 76,000 professionals, 6,700 partners, and operate in 144 countries. In Rhode Island, KPMG is the largest audit and risk advisory services and tax services firm. **NOTE:** See website for current job openings and application instructions. Applying online is strongly recommended. Entry-level positions available. **Positions advertised include:** Seasonal Senior Tax Associate. **Special programs:** Internships. **Corporate headquarters location:** Montvale NJ. **Other U.S. locations:** Nationwide. **International locations:** Worldwide. **Parent company:** KPMG International.

South Carolina
DELOITTE & TOUCHE USA LLP
1426 Main Street, Suite 820, Columbia SC 29201-0001. 803/256-7000. **Fax:** 803/256-4288. **Contact:** Human Resources. **World Wide Web address:** http://www.us.deloitte.com. **Description:** An international firm of certified public accountants providing professional accounting, auditing, tax, and management consulting services to widely diversified clients. The company has a specialized program consisting of national industry groups and functional groups that cross industry lines. Groups are involved in various disciplines including accounting, auditing, taxation management advisory services, small and growing businesses, mergers and acquisitions, and computer applications. Deloitte's Information Dynamics (ID) Service Area designs, develops, and implements services that support data warehousing and data archiving strategies, as well as systems and techniques to capture and distribute information in an enterprise. **Positions advertised include:** Senior Manager, Data Warehousing and Business Intelligence; Manager, Enterprise Information Strategy and Architectures; Manager, Portals and Enterprise Content Management; SAP HR Configuration Consultant; SAP HR Senior Manager. **Other U.S. locations:** Nationwide. **Parent company:** Deloitte Touche Tohmatsu. **Number of employees worldwide:** 30,000.

ELLIOT DAVIS & COMPANY LLP
P.O. Box 6286, Greenville SC 29606. 864/242-3370. **Physical address:** 200 East Broad Street, Greenville SC 29601. **Fax:** 864/242-2896. **Contact:** Human Resources Director. **E-mail address:** hr@elliottdavis.com. **World Wide Web address:** http://www.elliottdavis.com. **Description:** The company ranks in the top 40 corporate accounting firms in the U.S. offering comprehensive tax, audit, and consulting services and is affiliated with the international firm Moore Stephens Elliot Davis, LLC. Founded in 1925. **Positions advertised include:** Senior Tax Accountant; Senior Auditor. **Corporate headquarters location:** This location. **Other area locations:** Statewide.

ERNST & YOUNG LLP
75 Beattie Place, Suite 800, Greenville SC 29601. 864/242-5740. **Contact:** Human Resources. **World Wide Web address:** http://www.ey.com. **Description:** A certified public accounting firm that also provides management consulting services. Services include data processing, financial modeling, financial feasibility studies, production planning and inventory management, management sciences, health care planning, human resources, cost accounting, and budgeting systems. **NOTE:** The company requests resumes to be submitted online. **Positions advertised include:** Technology Support Specialist. **Corporate headquarters location:** New York NY. **Other locations:** Worldwide. **Annual sales/revenues:** $10.1 billion. **Number of employees:** 110,000.

GRANT THORNTON LLP
1320 Main Street, Suite 500, Columbia SC 29201. 803/231-3100. **Fax:** 803/231-3057. **Contact:** Human Resources. **World Wide Web address:** http://www.grantthornton.com. **Description:** Grant Thornton LLP is the U.S. member firm of Grant Thornton International, one of the six global accounting, tax and business advisory organizations. Grant Thornton LLP specializes in serving mid-cap, small-cap, and privately held clients, and provides selected non-audit services to selected markets. Grant Thornton has member firms in 112 countries, including 50 offices in the United States. **Positions advertised include:** Senior Assurance Associate; Audit Associate; Audit Manager; Senior Audit Associate. **Corporate headquarters location:** Chicago IL. **Other U.S. locations:** Nationwide. **International locations:** Worldwide.

KPMG
55 Beattie Place, Suite 900, Greenville SC 29601. 864/250-2600. **Contact:** Jonathan Ridgway, Primary Recruiter. **E-**

mail address: jridgway@kpmg.com. **World Wide Web address:** http://www.kpmgcampus.com. **Description:** Delivers a wide range of value-added auditing, accounting, taxation, and consulting services. **Other area locations:** Greensboro SC. **Other locations:** Worldwide. **Parent company:** KPMG International (Amstelveen, Netherlands). **Number of employees at this location:** 75.

PRESIDION SOLUTIONS, INC.
One Harbison Way, Suite 114, Columbia SC 29212. 803/781-7810. **Toll-free phone:** 800/948-8524. **Contact:** Human Resources Manager. **World Wide Web address:** http://www.presidionsolutions.com. **Description:** Performs general accounting functions, as well as human resources, payroll, and workers' compensation for other companies. **Corporate headquarters location:** Troy MI. **Other locations:** Ten sales offices throughout the state of Florida. **Parent company:** Presidion Corporation (Troy MI).

Tennessee

BDO SEIDMAN, LLP
5100 Poplar Avenue, Suite 2600, Memphis TN 38137. 901/680-7600. **Fax:** 901/680-7601. **Contact:** Human Resources. **World Wide Web address:** http://www.bdo.com. **Description:** A national professional services firm providing assurance, tax, financial advisory and consulting services to private and publicly traded businesses. **NOTE:** Search and apply for positions online. **Positions advertised include:** Assurance Associate; Assurance Manager.

CROWE CHIZEK AND COMPANY LLC
105 Continental Place, Suite 200, Brentwood TN 37024. 615/370-9852. **Fax:** 615/399-3663. **Contact:** Recruiting. **World Wide Web address:** http://www.crowechizek.com. **Description:** A provider of assurance, consulting, risk management, tax and technology services to large and middle market public companies and large privately-held businesses. **NOTE:** For entry-level positions, e-mail resumes to: campus_recruiting@crowechizek.com. Search and apply online for experienced positions. **Positions advertised include:** Litigation Practice Executive; Information Security Audit Manager; Internal audit Manager; Senior Manager. **Other area locations:** Knoxville TN. **Other U.S. locations:** IN; IL; KY; OH; MI; FL. **Parent company:** Horwath International. **Number of employees worldwide:** 1,600.

DELOITTE & TOUCHE LLP
424 Church Street, Suite 2400, Nashville TN 37219. 615/259-1800. **Fax:** 615/259-1862. **Contact:** Human Resources Department. **World Wide Web address:** http://www.us.deloitte.com. **Description:** An international firm of certified public accountants providing professional accounting, auditing, tax, and management consulting services to widely diversified clients. The company has a specialized program consisting of national industry groups and functional groups that cross industry lines. Groups are involved in various disciplines including accounting, auditing, taxation management advisory services, small and growing businesses, mergers and acquisitions, and computer applications. **Corporate headquarters location:** Wilton CT. **Other U.S. locations:** Nationwide. **International locations:** Worldwide. **Number of employees nationwide:** 30,000. **Number of employees worldwide:** 120,000.

ERNST & YOUNG LLP
424 Church Street, Suite 1100, Nashville TN 37219-1779. 615/252-2000. **Fax:** 615/242-9128. **Contact:** Human Resources. **World Wide Web address:** http://www.ey.com. **Description:** A certified public accounting firm that also provides management consulting services. Services include data processing, financial modeling, financial feasibility studies, production planning and inventory management, management sciences, health care planning, human resources, cost accounting, and budgeting systems. **NOTE:** Search and apply for positions online. **Corporate headquarters location:** New York NY. **Other U.S. locations:** Nationwide. **Number of employees worldwide:** 103,000.

KPMG
Suite 900, Morgan Keegan Tower, 50 North Front Street, Memphis TN 38103-1194. 901/523-3131. **Fax:** 901/523-8877. **Contact:** Human Resources. **World Wide Web address:** http://www.us.kpmg.com. **Description:** A provider of assurance, tax and legal, and financial advisory services. **NOTE:** Search and apply for positions online. **Positions advertised include:** Manager, Internal Audit Services; Sr. Manager, Internal Audit Services; Sr. Associate.

Texas

CHESHIER AND FULLER, L.L.P.
14175 Proton Road, Dallas TX 75244-3604. 972/387-4300. **Toll-free phone:** 800/834-8586. **Fax:** 972/960-2810. **Contact:** John Gallagher, Human Resources. **World Wide Web address:** http://www.cheshier-fuller.com. **Description:** Offers accounting, tax, audit, management advisory, business valuation, and litigation support services. Founded in 1956. **Special programs:** Training; Summer Jobs. **Office hours:** Monday - Friday, 8:30 a.m. - 5:30 p.m. **Corporate headquarters location:** This location. **Listed on:** Privately held.

ECKERT, INGRUM, TINKLER, OLIPHANT, & FEATHERSTON, L.L.P.
302 Texas Bank Tower, San Angelo TX 76901. 325/942-1093. **Fax:** 325/942-1093. **Contact:** Hiring Partner. **Description:** An accounting firm involved in bookkeeping, taxes, and auditing of various institutions including schools, governments, and banks. **NOTE:** Entry-level positions are offered. **Corporate headquarters location:** This location.

GRANT THORNTON LLP
Bank One Center, 1717 Main Street, Suite 500, Dallas TX 75201. 214/561-2300. **Fax:** 214/561-2370. **Contact:** Personnel. **World Wide Web address:** http://www.grantthornton.com. **Description:** An international certified public accounting organization offering consulting and accounting services as well as strategic and tactical planning assistance to a diverse clientele. **NOTE:** Entry-level positions are offered. **Special programs:** Internships; Training. **Corporate headquarters location:** Chicago IL. **Other U.S. locations:** Nationwide. **Operations at this facility include:** Administration; Regional Headquarters; Sales; Service. **Listed on:** Privately held. **Annual sales/revenues:** More than $485 million. **Number of employees nationwide:** 2,900. **Number of employees worldwide:** 21,500.

H&R BLOCK
Village At Bachman Lake, 3701 West Northwest Highway, Suite 210, Dallas TX 75220. 214/358-4560. **Contact:** Human Resources. **World Wide Web address:** http://www.hrblock.com. **Description:** Primarily engaged in consumer tax preparation, operating more than 9,500 U.S. offices and preparing more than 10 million tax returns each year. H&R Block has established offices in over 750 Sears stores in both the United States and Canada. The company is also engaged in a number of other tax-related activities including group tax programs, executive tax service, tax training schools, and real estate tax awareness seminars. **Corporate headquarters location:** Kansas City MO. **Other U.S. locations:** Nationwide. **Listed on:** New York Stock Exchange. **Stock exchange symbol:** HRB. **Number of employees nationwide:** 80,000.

HEALTHLINK, INC.
3800 Buffalo Speedway, Suite 550, Houston TX 77098. 713/790-0800. **Fax:** 713/852-2151. **Contact:** Human Resources. **World Wide Web address:** http://www.healthlink.com. **Description:** Offers management consulting services for the health care industry. Healthlink services are organized into three main program areas: re-engineering; strategic information systems and project planning; and implementation. IMG also designs computer-based patient records systems for hospitals and medical

centers. **Corporate headquarters location:** St. Louis MO. **Other U.S. locations:** AR; IL; IN; IA; KY.

ARTHUR D. LITTLE, INC.
2525 South Shore Boulevard, Suite 202, League City TX 77573. 281/334-6970. **Contact:** Human Resources. **World Wide Web address:** http://www.adlittle-us.com. **Description:** Offers services in three areas: management consulting; technology and product development; and environmental, health, and safety consulting. The company's clients include a wide range of firms in manufacturing industries including aerospace, automotive, consumer products, industrial electronics, information and telecommunications, medical products, and pharmaceuticals; process industries including chemicals, energy, food, and metals; and service industries, including financial services, health care, information and communications services, transportation, travel and tourism, and utilities. **Positions advertised include:** Business Analyst; Consultant; Intern.

MERCER MANAGEMENT CONSULTING
1717 Main Street, Suite 4300, Dallas TX 75201. 214/758-1880. **Contact:** Human Resources. **E-mail address:** careers@mercermc.com. **World Wide Web address:** http://www.mercermc.com. **Description:** Provides strategy and management consulting services. **NOTE:** Interested jobseekers may apply online at the company's website or by mailing their resumes to the company's Boston office at John Hancock Tower, 200 Clarendon Street, 12th Floor, Boston MA 02116. **Positions advertised include:** Principal; Senior Associate; Associate; Consultant; Analyst.

PAYCHEX, INC.
4242 Woodcock Drive, Suite 100, San Antonio TX 78228. 512/469-0550. **Contact:** Human Resources. **World Wide Web address:** http://www.paychex.com. **Description:** A payroll accounting firm. It also offers services to help employers track attendance. **NOTE:** Jobseekers should apply at the corporate website which lists openings and contact e-mail addresses. **Other area locations:** Houston TX; Dallas TX; Fort Worth TX; Austin TX. **Corporate headquarters location:** Rochester NY. **Listed on:** NASDAQ. **Stock exchange symbol:** PAYX.

Utah

DELOITTE & TOUCHE
50 South Main Street, Suite 1800, Salt Lake City UT 84144-0458. 801/328-4706. **Fax:** 801/355-7515. **Contact:** Personnel. **E-mail address:** dtcareers@deloitte.com. **World Wide Web address:** http://www.deloitte.com/us. **Description:** An international firm of certified public accountants providing professional accounting, auditing, tax, and management consulting services to widely diversified clients. **Positions advertised include:** Administrative Assistant; Consultant; International Tax Senior. **Special programs:** Internships. **Corporate headquarters location:** New York NY. **Other U.S. locations:** Nationwide. **International locations:** Worldwide. **Number of employees worldwide:** 120,000.

ERNST & YOUNG LLP
60 East South Temple, Suite 800, Salt Lake City UT 84111-1036. 801/350-3300. **Fax:** 801/350-3456. **Contact:** Human Resources. **World Wide Web address:** http://www.ey.com. **Description:** A certified public accounting firm that also provides management consulting services. Services include data processing, financial modeling, financial feasibility studies, production planning and inventory management, management sciences, health care planning, human resources, cost accounting, and budgeting systems. **NOTE:** See website for current job openings and to apply online. **Positions advertised include:** Tax Compliance Manager; Tax Consulting Specialist; Tax Consulting Senior. **Special programs:** Internships. **Corporate headquarters location:** New York NY. **Other U.S. locations:** Nationwide. **International locations:** Worldwide.

KPMG LLP
15 West South Temple, Suite 1500, Salt Lake City UT 84101. 801/333-8000. **Contact:** Human Resources. **World Wide Web address:** http://www.us.kpmg.com. **Description:** KPMG LLP, the U.S. member firm of KPMG International, is an audit, tax and advisory firm. KPMG International's member firms have 76,000 professionals, 6,700 partners, and operate in 144 countries. KPMG's Salt Lake City office is made up of 9 partners, 27 Managers, and over 129 personnel. **NOTE:** See website for current job openings and application instructions. Applying online is strongly recommended. Entry-level positions available. **Positions advertised include:** Senior Associate – Federal Tax; Audit Manager. **Corporate headquarters location:** Montvale NJ. **Other U.S. locations:** Nationwide. **International location:** Worldwide. **Parent company:** KPMG International. **CEO:** Tim Flynn.

PRICEWATERHOUSECOOPERS
One Utah Center, 201 South Main, Suite 900, Salt Lake City UT 84111. 801/531-9666. **Fax:** 801/933-8106. **Contact:** Personnel. **World Wide Web address:** http://www.pricewaterhousecoopers.com. **Description:** One of the largest certified public accounting firms in the world. PricewaterhouseCoopers provides public accounting, business advisory, management consulting, and taxation services. **NOTE:** Please visit website to search for jobs and apply online. **Corporate headquarters location:** New York NY. **Other area locations:** Ogden UT. **Other U.S. locations:** Nationwide. **International locations:** Worldwide.

SAGE FORENSIC ACCOUNTING
136 East South Temple, Suite 2220, Salt Lake City UT 84111. 801/531-0400. **Fax:** 801/328-0400. **Contact:** Personnel. **World Wide Web address:** http://www.sagefa.com. **Description:** Provides services in the areas forensic accounting, business valuation, and economic damage calculation. **Corporate headquarters location:** This location. **Other U.S. locations:** NV.

Vermont

McCORMACK, GUYETTE & ASSOCIATES, PC
66 Grove Street, Rutland VT 05701. 802/775-3221, extension 110. **Fax:** 802/775-1850. **Contact:** Chris Ponton, Administrative Assistant. **E-mail address:** mgachris@sover.net. **World Wide Web address:** http://www.cpa-vermont.com. **Description:** A certified public accounting agency providing a variety of accounting services including payroll, tax preparation, and audits. **Number of employees:** 10.

Virginia

KEARNEY AND COMPANY
4501 Ford Avenue, Suite 1400, Alexandria VA 22302. 703/931-5600. **Fax:** 703-931-3655. **Contact:** Human Resources. **World Wide Web address:** http://www.kearneyco.com. **Description:** Kearney & Company is a CPA firm founded in 1985 that specializes in providing accounting, audit, and information technology services to the federal government. **Positions advertised Include:** Staff Accountant/Auditor; Audit Manager; Systems Programmer; Information Security Analyst.

MERCER HUMAN RESOURCE CONSULTING
1051 East Cary Street, Suite 900, Richmond VA 23219. 804/344-2600. **Fax:** 804/344-2601. **Contact:** Human Resources. **World Wide Web address:** http://www.mercerhr.com. **Description:** One of the world's largest actuarial and human resources management consulting firms, providing advice to organizations on all aspects of employee/management relationships. Services include retirement, health and welfare, performance and rewards, communication, investment, human resources administration, risk, finance and insurance, and health care provider consulting. **NOTE:** Search and apply for positions online. **Positions advertised include:** Actuarial Analyst; Actuarial Intern. **Corporate headquarters location:** New York NY. **Parent company:** Marsh &

McLennan Companies, Inc. **Number of employees worldwide:** 15,000.

ROBBINS-GIOIA, INC.
11 Canal Center Plaza, Suite 200, Alexandria VA 22314. 703/548-7006. **Fax:** 703/548-3724. **Contact:** Human Resources. E-mail address: resume@robbinsgioia.com. **World Wide Web address:** http://www.rgalex.com. **Description:** A management consulting firm. The company's services include cost management, risk management, communication management, configuration management, document management, portfolio management, material management, quality management, issues tracking, requirements/scope management, vendor selection, and planning and scheduling. Founded in 1980. **NOTE:** Entry-level positions are offered. Search and apply for positions online. **Positions advertised include:** Quality Control Consultant; Quality Assurance Consulting Manager. **Corporate headquarters location:** This location. **Other U.S. locations:** Nationwide. **Operations at this facility include:** Administration; Sales; Service. **Listed on:** Privately held. **Number of employees nationwide:** 450.

Washington

LEMASTER & DANIELS
601 West Riverside Avenue, Suite 700, Spokane WA 99201. 509/624-4315. **Contact:** Human Resources. **World Wide Web address:** http://www.lemasterdaniels.com. **Description:** An accounting firm providing accounting, auditing, and tax services to clients. Founded in 1908. **Positions advertised include:** Accountant; Director of Reimbursement. **Corporate headquarters location:** This location.

MERRILL LYNCH HOWARD JOHNSON
187 Parfitt Way SW, Bainbridge Island WA 98110. 206/855-9781. **Contact:** Human Resources. **World Wide Web address:** http://www.ml.com. **Description:** An international benefits consulting company. The company works mainly with 401(k) plans and group benefits for corporations.

MILLIMAN USA
1301 Fifth Avenue, Suite 3800, Seattle WA 98101-2605. 206/624-7940. **Fax:** 206/340-1380. **Contact:** Personnel Department. **E-mail address:** seattle.office@milliman.com. **World Wide Web address:** http://www.milliman.com. **Description:** A nationwide actuarial and consulting firm. **Positions advertised include:** Actuary; Pension Analyst. **Corporate headquarters location:** This location. **Operations at this facility include:** Administration; Service.

MOSS ADAMS LLP
1001 Fourth Avenue, Suite 2830, Seattle WA 98154. 206/223-1820. **Contact:** Human Resources. **World Wide Web address:** http://www.mossadams.com. **Description:** One of the nation's largest accounting and consulting firms. Founded in 1913. **Positions advertised include:** Assurance Services Manager; Tax Analyst; Research and Development Manager; Senior IT Consultant. **Corporate headquarters location:** This location. **Other U.S. locations:** CA; OR.

Wisconsin

BDO SEIDMAN, LLP
330 East Kilbourn Avenue, Suite 950, Milwaukee WI 53202-3143. 414/272-5900. **Fax:** 414/272-1090. **Contact:** Human Resources Department. **World Wide Web address:** http://www.bdo.com. **Description:** A public accounting and consulting firm. **Positions advertised include:** Business Development Manager; Assurance Senior. **Other U.S. locations:** Nationwide.

CLIFTON GUNDERSON L.L.C.
123 North Court Street, Suite One, P.O. Box 329, Sparta WI 54656. 608/269-2424. **Fax:** 608/269-2549. **Contact:** Human Resources. **World Wide Web address:** http://www.cliftoncpa.com. **Description:** A certified public accounting and consulting firm with offices in 14 states and the District of Columbia. **Other area locations:** Statewide. **Other U.S. locations:** Nationwide. **Number of employees nationwide:** 1,500.

GRANT THORNTON LLP
10 College Avenue, Suite 300 Appleton WI 54911. 920/968-6700. **Fax:** 920/968-6719. **Contact:** Personnel. **World Wide Web address:** http://www.grantthornton.com. **Description:** An international, certified, public accounting firm offering a comprehensive scope of consulting and accounting services, as well as strategic and tactical planning assistance to a diverse clientele. **Corporate headquarters:** Pompano Beach FL. **Other area locations:** Fond du Lac WI; Madison WI; Milwaukee WI. **Other U.S. locations:** Nationwide. **Parent company:** Grant Thornton International.

THERMO USCS
120 Bishop's Way, Suite 100, Brookfield WI 53008-0951. 800/558-6377. **Fax:** 262/784-5779. **Contact:** Kristen Aziz, Human Resources. **E-mail address:** kaziz@thermo.com. **World Wide Web address:** http://www.thermo.com. **Description:** Provides equipment asset management services, such as instrument and equipment maintenance management, physical inventory tracking, and cost-of-ownership analysis, to the pharmaceutical and healthcare industries. Founded in 1969. **Corporate headquarters location:** This location. **Parent company:** Thermo Electron Corporation (Waltham MA). **Number of employees nationwide:** 175.

WIPFLI ULLRICH BERTELSON
11 Scott Street, Wausau WI 54403. 715/845-3111. **Fax:** 715/842-7272. **Contact:** Human Resources. **E-mail address:** wipfliinformation@wipfli.com. **World Wide Web address:** http://www.wipfli.com. **Description:** Offers management consulting services in: accounting, auditing, and tax; strategic business planning; human resource consulting; business valuation services; family business services; and marketing consulting. **Positions advertised include:** Proofreader; Staff Accountant, Benefit Plan Services. **Corporate headquarters location:** This location. **Other area locations:** Statewide. **Other U.S. locations:** St Paul MN.

ADVERTISING, MARKETING AND PUBLIC RELATIONS

You can expect to find the following types of companies in this section:
Advertising Agencies • Direct Mail Marketers • Market Research Firms • Public Relations Firms

---

The number of new openings for advertising, marketing, promotions, public relations, and sales managers will increase by 131,000 from 646,000 to 777,000, a 20.3% increase. Growth is spurred by intense domestic and global competition in products and services offered to consumers. However, projected employment growth varies by industry. For example, employment is projected to grow much faster than average in scientific, professional, and related services such as computer systems design and related services and advertising and related services, as businesses increasingly hire contractors for these services instead of additional full-time staff. On the other hand, little or no change in employment is expected in many manufacturing industries.

Alabama

ADVANTAGE MARKETING COMMUNICATIONS
109 20th Street North, Birmingham AL 35203. 205/328-3595. **Fax:** 205/328-9573. **Contact:** Human Resources. **World Wide Web address:** http://www.creativeguys.com. **Description:** A full-service marketing consultancy whose services include corporate recognition programs, trade show programs, product introductions, and company outings.

O2 IDEAS INC.
2160 Highland Avenue South, Birmingham AL 35205. 205/949-9494. **Fax:** 205/949-9449. **World Wide Web address:** http://www.O2ideas.com. **Contact:** Human Resources. **Description:** A multi-cultural marketing communications firm specializing in advertising, brand planning, public relations, event planning.

MEDIA NETWORKS, INC.
2100 Lakeshore Parkway, Birmingham AL 35209. **World Wide Web address:** http://www.mni.com. **Contact:** Human Resources. **Description:** A local market advertising company. Provides advertising and promotional placement into a network of 30 area magazines. **Corporate headquarters location:** Stamford CT. **Parent Company:** Time Warner, Inc.

Arizona

ADVO, INC.
2235 South Central Avenue, Phoenix AZ 85004. 602/252-2518. **Contact:** Human Resources. **World Wide Web address:** http://www.advo.com. **Description:** A direct mail advertising company. **Positions advertised include:** Client Services Account Specialist. **Corporate headquarters location:** Windsor CT. **Other U.S. locations:** Nationwide.

CBS OUTDOOR
3150 South 48th Street, Suite 200, Phoenix AZ 85040. 602/246-9569. **Fax:** 480/829-9389. **Contact:** Human Resources. **World Wide Web address:** http://www.cbsoutdoor.com. **Description:** An outdoor-advertising agency specializing in the design of billboards and posters.

CLEAR CHANNEL OUTDOOR
2850 East Camelback Road, Suite 300, Phoenix AZ 85016. 602/957-8116. **Fax:** 602/381-5753. **Contact:** Human Resources Department. **World Wide Web address:** http://www.clearchanneloutdoor.com. **Description:** Provides outdoor billboard advertising services. **Corporate headquarters location:** This location. **U.S. locations:** Nationwide. **Parent company:** Clear Channel Communications, Inc.

CONTINENTAL PROMOTION GROUP, INC.
1120 West Warner Road, Tempe AZ 85284. 480/606-9300. **Toll-free phone:** 800/554-9838. **Fax:** 480/606-4329. **Contact:** Human Resources. **E-mail address:** hrmcpg@cpginc.com. **World Wide Web address:** http://www.cpginc.com. **Description:** Provides promotional services including rebate offers, sweepstakes, and premium fulfillment. Founded in 1989. **Positions advertised include:** Promotion Coordinator; Promotion Customer Service Rep; Data Entry Clerk. **Corporate headquarters location:** This location. **International locations:** Canada; Ireland; United Kingdom.

BERNARD HODES GROUP
2231 East Camelback Road, Suite 370, Phoenix AZ 85016. 602/956-8989. **Fax:** 602/956-9142. **Contact:** Branch Manager. **World Wide Web address:** http://www.hodes.com. **Description:** An advertising agency specializing in recruitment and employee communications. **Positions advertised include:** Account Coordinator. **Corporate headquarters location:** New York NY. **Other U.S. locations:** Chicago IL; Cambridge MA; Dallas TX. **Parent company:** Omnicom.

E.B. LANE & ASSOCIATES, INC.
733 West McDowell Road, Phoenix AZ 85007. 602/258-5263. **Contact:** Sharon Thompson, Director of Administration. **E-mail address:** sthompson@eblane.com. **World Wide Web address:** http://www.eblane.com. **Description:** A full-service advertising agency specializing in media buying, print media, public relations, radio producing, and television producing. **Corporate headquarters location:** This location.

NEWS AMERICA MARKETING
5020 South Ash Avenue, Suite 107, Tempe AZ 85282. 480/756-2226. **Contact:** Human Resources. **World Wide Web address:** http://www.newsamerica.com. **Description:** An in-store marketing company offering demonstrations, coupon advertising, instant coupon systems, and placard advertising on shopping carts. **Positions advertised include:** Market Manager; Unit Manager; Supervisor; In-Store Representative. **Parent company:** News Corporation.

VOICETRAK INC.
6420 East Tanque Verde Road, Tucson AZ 85715. 520/886-4545. **Contact:** Human Resources. **World Wide Web address:** http://www.voicetrak.com. **Description:** A national media research firm. **Corporate headquarters location:** New York NY. **Parent company:** VMS.

Arkansas

CJRW
303 West Capitol Avenue, Little Rock AR 72201. 501/975-6251. **Toll-free phone:** 888/383-2579. **Fax:** 501/975-4241. **Contact:** Mac Stroud, Human Resources. **E-mail address:** HR@cjrw.com. **World Wide Web address:** http://www.cjrw.com. **Description:** A full-service advertising agency. Services include strategic planning, brand development, market research, advertising development, promotions, creative development, direct marketing, media relations, public relations, public policy, public affairs, executive development, and publication services. **Number of employees at this location:** 90. **Number of employees nationwide:** 140.

CJRW NW
P.O. Box 1968, Fayetteville AR 72702-1968. 479/442-9803. **Physical address:** 3 East Colt Square, Fayetteville AR 72702. **Toll-free phone:** 800/599-9803. **Fax:** 479/442-9803. **Contact:** Human Resources. **Description:** A full-service advertising and promotions

agency. The company's primary focus is on print production including package design, FSIs, and coupons for the retail food business. Founded in 1977. **Special programs:** Internships. **Office hours:** Monday - Friday, 8:00 a.m. - 5:00 p.m. **Corporate headquarters location:** Little Rock AR. **President:** Mark Blackwood. **Number of employees at this location:** 29.

MANGAN HOLCOMB PARTNERS
2300 Cottondale Lane, Suite 300, Little Rock AR 72201. 501/376-0321. **Fax:** 501/376-6127. **Contact:** Human Resources. **World Wide Web address:** http://www.manganholcolm.com. **Description:** An advertising agency.

California
A&R PARTNERS
201 Baldwin Avenue, San Mateo CA 94401. 650/762-2800. **Fax:** 650/762-2801. **Contact:** Human Resources. **E-mail address:** jobs@arpartners.com. **World Wide Web address:** http://www.arpartners.com. **Description:** A public relations firm. **NOTE:** Entry-level positions are offered. **Positions advertised include:** Director; Senior Account Executive; Account Executive; Account Associate. **Special programs:** Internships; Apprenticeships; Training. **Corporate headquarters location:** This location. **Other U.S. locations:** New York NY; Denver CO; Portland OR; Louisville KY; Research Triangle Park NC. **Annual sales/revenues:** $5 - $10 million. **Number of employees nationwide:** Over 80.

ACCESS COMMUNICATIONS
101 Howard Street, 2nd Floor, San Francisco CA 94105. 415/904-7070. **Fax:** 415/904-7055. **Contact:** Human Resources. **E-mail address:** jobs@accesspr.com. **World Wide Web address:** http://www.accesspr.com. **Description:** A public relations firm whose clients include software and other high-tech corporations. **Positions advertised include:** Assistant Account Executive; Senior Account Executive; Account Supervisor. **Corporate headquarters location:** This location. **Other U.S. locations:** New York NY.

BBDO WEST
10960 Wilshire Boulevard, Suite 1600, Los Angeles CA 90024. 310/444-4500. **Fax:** 310/444-4600. **Contact:** Human Resources Director. **World Wide Web address:** http://www.bbdo.com. **Description:** One location of the worldwide network of advertising agencies with related businesses in public relations, direct marketing, sales promotion, graphic arts, and printing. **Corporate headquarters location:** New York NY. **Other area locations:** San Francisco CA. **Other U.S. locations:** Miami FL; Atlanta GA; Chicago IL; Wellesley MA; Southfield MI. **Parent company:** BBDO Worldwide operates 345 offices in 76 countries and 96 cities. The company operates 83 subsidiaries, affiliates, and associates engaged solely in advertising and related operations.

BDS MARKETING
10 Holland, Irvine CA 92618. 949/472-6700. **Fax:** 949/597-2220. **Contact:** Human Resources. **E-mail address:** recruiters@bdsmarketing.com. **World Wide Web address:** http://www.bdsmarketing.com. **Description:** Offers a wide variety of marketing services. BDS Marketing provides ideas for sales promotions, product training, and field marketing. **Positions advertised include:** Account Coordinator; Account Director; Account Executive. **Corporate headquarters location:** This location. **Other U.S. locations:** Nationwide. **Number of employees at this location:** 140. **Number of employees nationwide:** 4,000.

BLANC & OTUS
303 Second Street, Suite 900 South, San Francisco CA 94107. 415/856-5100. **Fax:** 415/856-5193. **Contact:** Barbara Melchin, Human Resources. **E-mail address:** bmelchin@blancandotus.com. **World Wide Web address:** http://www.bando.com. **Description:** A public relations firm that primarily serves the high-tech industry. **Positions advertised include:** Account Executive; Senior Account Executive. **Corporate headquarters location:** This location. **Other U.S. locations:** Atlanta GA; Austin TX; Boston MA. **Parent company:** Hill and Knowlton.

BURSON-MARSTELLER
303 Second Street, 8th Floor, San Francisco CA 94107. 415/591-4000. **Fax:** 415/591-4030. **Contact:** Michele Chase, Managing Director of Human Resources. **E-mail address:** michele_chase@nyc.bm.com. **World Wide Web address:** http://www.bm.com. **Description:** A public relations and public affairs firm. **Positions advertised include:** PR Manager, Technology Practice. **Special programs:** Internships. **Corporate headquarters location:** New York NY. **Other area locations:** Los Angeles CA; Sacramento CA; San Diego CA; San Francisco CA. **Other U.S. locations:** Miami FL; Chicago IL; Pittsburgh PA; Austin TX; Dallas TX. **International locations:** Worldwide. **Parent company:** Young and Rubicam, Inc.

CBS OUTDOOR
1731 Workman Street, Los Angeles CA 90031. 323/222-7171. **Contact:** Human Resources Department. **World Wide Web address:** http://www.cbsoutdoor.com. **Description:** An advertising agency specializing in the design of billboards and posters. **Other U.S. locations:** Nationwide. **Parent company:** CBS Corporation.

CERRELL ASSOCIATES, INC.
320 North Larchmont Boulevard, Los Angeles CA 90004. 323/466-3445. **Fax:** 323/466-8653. **Contact:** Acareli Kotero, Account Coordinator. **E-mail address:** araceli@cerrell.com. **World Wide Web address:** http://www.cerrell.com. **Description:** A public relations company specializing in local public affairs, issues management, and political campaigning. **Special programs:** Internships. **Corporate headquarters location:** This location. **Number of employees at this location:** 30.

CITIGATE CUNNINGHAM
1530 Page Mill Road, Palo Alto CA 94304. 650/858-3700. **Fax:** 650/858-3702. **Contact:** Human Resources. **E-mail address:** careers@cunningham.com. **World Wide Web address:** http://www.cunningham.com. **Description:** A public relations agency specializing in the high-tech industry. **Position advertised include:** Manager; Senior Associate. **Corporate headquarters location:** This location. **Other area locations:** San Francisco CA. **Other U.S. locations:** Cambridge MA. **Parent company:** Incepta Group plc. **Operations at this facility include:** Administration; Service. **Listed on:** Privately held. **Number of employees at this location:** 55.

DDB WORLDWIDE COMMUNICATIONS GROUP INC.
340 Main Street, Venice CA 90291-2524. 310/907-1500. **Fax:** 310/907-1992. **Contact:** James Best, Chief People Officer. **World Wide Web address:** http://www.ddbjobs.com. **Description:** A full-service, international advertising agency. **Corporate headquarters location:** New York NY. **Other area locations:** San Francisco CA. **Other U.S. locations:** Washington DC; Miami FL; Honolulu HI; Chicago IL; Dallas TX; Seattle WA. **Parent company:** Omnicom Group Inc. **Operations at this facility include:** Regional Headquarters. **Listed on:** New York Stock Exchange. **Stock exchange symbol:** DDB.

DAILEY & ASSOCIATES ADVERTISING
8687 Melrose Avenue, Suite G300, West Hollywood CA 90069. 310/360-3100. **Fax:** 310/360-0470. **Contact:** Ms. Jean Anne Hutchinson, Director of Human Resources Administration. **E-mail address:** humanresources@daileyads.com. **World Wide Web address:** http://www.daileyads.com. **Description:** A full-service advertising agency. **Positions advertised include:** Account Executive; Broadcast Buyer; Media Planner; Media Biller; Broadcast Traffic Manager.

DAVIS ELEN ADVERTISING
865 South Figueroa Street, 12th Floor, Los Angeles CA 90017. 213/688-7071. **Fax:** 213/688-7106. **Contact:** Pamela McCarthy, VP/Director of Human Resources **E-mail address:** pammccarthy@daviselen.com. **World Wide Web address:** http://www.daviselen.com. **Description:** A full-service advertising agency. **NOTE:** Entry-level positions are offered. **Special programs:** Internships. **Corporate headquarters location:** This location. **Other area locations:** Solana Beach CA; San Francisco CA; Marina Del Ray CA. **Other U.S. locations:** Portland OR. **International locations:** Mexico; Japan. **Listed on:** Privately held.

DEUTSCH, INC.
5454 Beethoven Street, Los Angeles CA. 310/862-3000. **Fax:** 310/862-3104. **Recorded jobline:** 310/862-3555. **Contact:** Human Resources. **E-mail address:** job_opportunities@deutschinc.com. **World Wide Web address:** http://www.deutschinc.com. **Description:** An advertising agency. **Positions advertised include:** Print Production Manager; Print Traffic Manager; Mailroom Clerk. **Corporate headquarters location:** New York NY.

E-AGENCY, INC.
291 Third Street, Oakland CA 94607. 510/496-2300. **Toll-free phone:** 800/834-4175. **Fax:** 510/496-2322. **Contact:** Human Resources. **E-mail address:** careers@e-agency.com. **World Wide Web address:** http://www.e-agency.com. **Description:** A full-service, interactive marketing communications company that offers online and offline services for corporations, non-profits and governmental agencies. **Corporate headquarters location:** This location.

EDELMAN PUBLIC RELATIONS WORLDWIDE
221 Main Street, Suite 1300, San Francisco CA 94105. 415/222-9944. **Fax:** 415/222-9924. **Contact:** Recruiting. **E-mail address:** san.francisco@edelman.com. **World Wide Web address:** http://www.edelman.com. **Description:** A public relations firm. **Positions advertised include:** Vice President; Senior Account Executive. **Corporate headquarters location:** Chicago IL. **Other area locations:** Mountain View CA; Los Angeles CA. **Special programs:** Internships.

THE FINANCIAL RELATIONS BOARD INC.
8687 Melrose Avenue, 7th Floor, Los Angeles CA 90069. 310/854-8311. **Contact:** Human Resources. **World Wide Web address:** http://www.financialrelationsboard.com. **Description:** A public relations firm that primarily serves the financial industry. **Corporate headquarters location:** Chicago IL. **Other U.S. locations:** New York NY. **Parent company:** Weber Shandwick Financial Communications.

FLEISHMAN-HILLARD INC.
201 California Street, 7th Floor, San Francisco CA 94111. 415/318-4000. **Fax:** 415/318-4010. **Contact:** Human Resources. **World Wide Web address:** http://www.fleishman.com. **Description:** A public relations firm. **Positions advertised include:** Account Supervisor; Vice President Tech PR; Vice President Life Sciences. **Corporate headquarters location:** St. Louis MO. **Other area locations:** Los Angeles CA; Sacramento CA; San Diego CA. **Other U.S. locations:** Nationwide. **International locations:** Worldwide. **Parent company:** Omnicom Group Inc.

FOOTE, CONE & BELDING
600 Battery Street, San Francisco CA 94111. 415/820-8000. **Fax:** 415/820-8087. **Contact:** Human Resources Manager. **E-mail address:** sf-resume@fcb.com. **World Wide Web address:** http://www.fcb.com. **Description:** One of the five largest advertising agencies in the world. Foote, Cone & Belding develops integrated marketing campaigns for a broad range of clients. The firm offers additional services such as merchandising, product research, package design, e-business marketing, direct marketing, sports marketing, and events marketing. **NOTE:** Entry-level positions are offered. **Special programs:** Internships; Training. **Corporate headquarters location:** Chicago IL. **Other U.S. locations:** Nationwide. **Parent company:** True North Communications. **Number of employees at this location:** 400.

GCI GROUP
6100 Wilshire Boulevard, Suite 840, Los Angeles CA 90048. 323/930-0811. **Fax:** 323/930-1241. **Contact:** Stephanie Lapham-Howley, Human Resources. **E-mail address:** working@gcigroup.com **World Wide Web address:** http://www.gcigroup.com. **Description:** A high-tech public relations firm. **Corporate headquarters location:** New York NY. **Other area locations:** San Francisco CA. **Other U.S. locations:** Atlanta GA; Austin TX; Chicago IL.

GALLEN.NEILLY & ASSOCIATES
1981 North Broadway, Suite 400, Walnut Creek CA 94596. 925/930-9848. **Fax:** 925/930-9903. **Contact:** Human Resources. **World Wide Web address:** http://www.gallen.com. **Description:** A public relations firm that primarily serves the commercial real estate industry. **Corporate headquarters location:** This location.

GARTNER GROUP
281 River Oaks Parkway, San Jose CA 95134. 408/468-8000. **Contact:** Human Resources. **World Wide Web address:** http://www.gartner.com. **Description:** A market research company. **Positions advertised include:** Director. **Corporate headquarters location:** Stamford CT. **Listed on:** New York Stock Exchange. **Stock exchange symbol:** IT.

GOLIN HARRIS INTERNATIONAL
430 Pacific Avenue, San Francisco CA 94133. 415/274-7900. **Fax:** 415/274-7933. **Contact:** Human Resources. **E-mail address:** careers@golinharris.com. **World Wide Web address:** http://www.golinharris.com. **Description:** A public relations firm that primarily serves high-tech industries. **Corporate headquarters location:** Chicago IL. **Other area locations:** Irvine CA; Los Angeles CA. **Other U.S. locations:** Nationwide.

GOODGUYS ROD & CUSTOM ASSOCIATION
P.O. Box 9132, Pleasanton, CA 94566. 925/838-9876. **Fax:** 925/820-8241. **Contact:** Edgar Silay, Vice President of Internal Operations. **E-mail address:** edgars@good-guys.com (no attachments, please). **World Wide Web address:** http://www.good-guys.com. **Description:** An automotive event promoter specializing in hot rods. **Corporate headquarters location:** This location.

HILL AND KNOWLTON INC.
303 2nd Street, Suite 900 South, San Francisco 94107. 415/281-7120. **Contact:** Denise Gordon, Human Resources. **E-mail address:** denise.gordon@hillandknowlton.com. **World Wide Web address:** http://www.hillandknowlton.com. **Description:** One of the world's largest public relations/public affairs counseling firms, serving more than 1,000 clients worldwide, Hill and Knowlton Inc. serves clients through more than 60 company offices and through associate arrangements with 50 leading regional firms worldwide. **Special programs:** Internships. **Corporate headquarters location:** New York NY. **Other U.S. locations:** Nationwide.

THE HORN GROUP INC.
612 Howard Street, Suite 100, San Francisco CA 94105. 415/905-4000. **Fax:** 415/977-0333. **Contact:** Director of Training. **World Wide Web address:** http://www.horngroup.com. **Description:** A public relations firm that primarily serves high-tech industries. Founded in 1991. **NOTE:** Entry-level positions are offered. **Special programs:** Internships; Summer Jobs. **Corporate headquarters location:** This location. **Other U.S. locations:** Braintree MA; New York NY. **Listed on:** Privately held. **Annual sales/revenues:** $5 - $10 million. **Number of employees at this location:** 40.

INITIATIVE LOS ANGELES
5700 Wilshire Boulevard, Suite 400, Los Angeles CA 90036. 323/370-8017. **Fax:** 323/370-8974. **Contact:** Cynthia Carranza, Human Resources. **E-mail address:** cynthia.carranza@us.initiative.com. **World Wide Web address:** http://www.initiative.com. **Description:** An advertising agency. **Corporate headquarters location:** This location. **Parent company:** Initiative (New York NY).

MACKENZIE COMMUNICATIONS, INC.
423 Washington Street, 6th Floor, San Francisco CA 94111. 415/403-0800. **Fax:** 415/403-0801. **Contact:** Human Resources. **E-mail address:** info@mackenziesf.com. **World Wide Web address:** http://www.mackenziesf.com. **Description:** A public relations firm that serves a wide range of industries including banking, law, and public service. **Corporate headquarters location:** This location.

OGILVY & MATHER
3530 Hayden Avenue, Culver City CA 90232. 310/280-2200. **Recorded jobline:** 212/237-5627. **Contact:** Mary Jensen, Director of Personnel. **World Wide Web address:** http://www.ogilvy.com. **Description:** An advertising agency. **Corporate headquarters location:** New York NY. **Other U.S. locations:** Nationwide. **Parent company:** WWP Group PLC.

PORTER NOVELLI
550 Third Street, San Francisco CA 94107. 415/975-2200. **Fax:** 415/975-2201. **Contact:** Kim Mesfin, Human Resources. **E-mail address:** bayareacareers@porternovelli.com. **World Wide Web address:** http://www.porternovelli.com. **Description:** A public relations firm primarily serving the high-tech and consumer electronics industries. **Positions advertised include:** Assistant Account Executive; Senior Account Executive. **Corporate headquarters location:** New York NY. **Other U.S. locations:** Atlanta GA; Boston MA; New York NY; Chicago IL; Seattle WA; Washington DC.

PUBLICIS & HAL RINEY
2001 The Embarcadero, San Francisco CA 94133. 415/293-2001. **Fax:** 415/293-2619. **Contact:** Human Resources. **World Wide Web address:** http://www.hrp.com. **Description:** An advertising agency. **Corporate headquarters location:** This location. **Parent company:** Publicis Worldwide.

SAATCHI & SAATCHI ADVERTISING
3501 Sepulveda Boulevard, Torrance CA 90505. 310/214-6000. **Fax:** 310/214-6160. **Contact:** Human Resources. **E-mail address:** rcalhoun@saatchila.com. **World Wide Web address:** http://www.saatchi.com. **Description:** A full-service advertising agency. **Corporate headquarters location:** New York NY. **Other U.S. locations:** Nationwide. **Number of employees worldwide:** 7,000.

SOLEM & ASSOCIATES
550 Kearny Street, Suite 1010, San Francisco CA 94108. 415/788-7788. **Fax:** 415/788-7858. **Contact:** Personnel. **World Wide Web address:** http://www.solem.com. **Description:** A public relations firm that primarily serves the health care, transportation, and government advocacy industries. **Corporate headquarters location:** This location.

STERLING COMMUNICATIONS, INC.
750 University Avenue, Suite 250, Los Gatos CA 95032. 408/395-5500. **Fax:** 408/395-5533. **Contact:** Tiffany Bryant, Human Resources. **E-mail address:** tbryant@sterlingpr.com. **World Wide Web address:** http://www.sterlingpr.com. **Description:** A public relations firm that provides services to technology-based companies. **Positions advertised include:** Account Associate; Account Executive. **Corporate headquarters location:** This location.

TBWA/CHIAT/DAY
55 Union Street, San Francisco CA 94111. 415/315-4100. **Recorded jobline:** 310/305-5385. **Contact:** Human Resources. **E-mail address:** hr-sf@tbwachiat.com. **World Wide Web address:** http://www.tbwachiat.com. **Description:** An advertising agency. **NOTE:** Resumes may be submitted via e-mail or regular mail. Mail resumes to: 5353 Grosvenor Boulevard, Los Angeles CA 90066-6913; hr-sf@tbwachiat.com. **Special programs:** Internships. **Corporate headquarters location:** Los Angeles. **Other U.S. locations:** New York NY. **International locations:** Toronto Canada.

TMP WORLDWIDE
799 Market Street, 8th Floor, San Francisco CA 94103. 415/820-7800. **Fax:** 415/820-0540. **Contact:** Human Resources. **World Wide Web address:** http://www.monsterworldwide.com. **Description:** A B-to-B advertising agency in the recruitment and yellow pages advertising business. **NOTE:** Apply online. **Positions advertised include:** Online Marketing Manager; Associate Creative Director; Producer; Company Public Speaker; Marketing Coordinator. **Corporate headquarters location:** New York NY. **Other area locations:** Glendale CA; Laguna Hills CA; San Diego CA. **Other U.S. locations:** Boston MA; Atlanta GA; Chicago IL. **Parent company:** Monster Worldwide Inc. **Listed on:** NASDAQ. **Stock exchange symbol:** MNST.

J. WALTER THOMPSON COMPANY
111 Sutter Street, San Francisco CA 94104. 415/733-0700. **Fax:** 415/733-0701. **Contact:** Roman Lesnau, Human Resources. **E-mail address:** roman.lesnau@jwt.com. **World Wide Web address:** http://www.jwtworld.com. **Description:** The largest full-service U.S. advertising agency. **NOTE:** Entry-level positions are offered. **Positions advertised include:** Art Director. **Corporate headquarters location:** New York NY. **International locations:** Worldwide. **Parent company:** WPP Group. **Listed on:** NASDAQ. **Stock exchange symbol:** WPPGY. **Number of employees at this location:** 175. **Number of employees worldwide:** 8,500.

YOUNG & RUBICAM WEST
303 2nd Street, 8th Floor South Tower, San Francisco CA 94107. 415/882-0600. **Fax:** 415/882-0601. **Contact:** Ms. Whitney Ball, Human Resources Manager. **World Wide Web address:** http://www.yr.com. **Description:** An international advertising agency. The company operates through three divisions: Young & Rubicam International; Marsteller Inc., a worldwide leader in business-to-business and consumer advertising; and Young & Rubicam USA, with 14 consumer advertising agencies operating through four regional groups (except Young & Rubicam Detroit), and five specialized advertising and marketing agencies. **Positions advertised include:** PT Finance Assistant; Account Executive. **Corporate headquarters location:** New York NY.

Colorado

AMERICOMM DIRECT MARKETING
4760 Oakland Street, Suite 175, Denver CO 80239. 303/371-4400. **Toll-free phone:** 877/737-5478. **Contact:** Human Resources Department. **World Wide Web address:** http://www.americomm.net. **Description:** A direct mail processing company.

BERNARD HODES GROUP
2399 Blake Street, Suite 160, Denver CO 80205. 720/904-0461. **Fax:** 720/904-0490. **Contact:** Human Resources. **World Wide Web address:** http://www.hodes.com. **Description:** An advertising agency specializing in recruitment and employee communications. **Corporate headquarters location:** New York NY. **International locations:** Worldwide. **Parent company:** Omnicom.

MILES ADVERTISING, INC.
1936 Market Street, Denver CO 80202. 303/293-9191. **Toll-free phone:** 800/342-8978. **Contact:** Human Resources. **Description:** A full-service advertising agency specializing in residential real estate. Founded in 1986. **NOTE:** Entry-level positions are offered.

Special programs: Internships. **Corporate headquarters location:** This location. **Listed on:** Privately held. **CEO:** David R. Miles. **Annual sales/revenues:** $11 - $20 million. **Number of employees at this location:** 20.

Connecticut

ADVO INC.
One Targeting Center, Windsor CT 06095. 860/285-6100. **Fax:** 860/285-6236. **Contact:** Human Resources. **World Wide Web address:** http://www.advo.com. **Description:** A direct mail advertising company. **Positions advertised include:** Client Services Account Representative; Client Marketing Manager; System and Process Support Manager; Vice President, Network and Planning Development; Human Resources Assistant. **Corporate headquarters location:** This location. **Other U.S. locations:** Nationwide. **Listed on:** New York Stock Exchange. **Stock exchange symbol:** AD. **Number of employees at this location:** 450. **Number of employees nationwide:** 5,500.

CRONIN & COMPANY
50 Nye Road, Glastonbury CT 06033. 860/659-0514. **Contact:** Human Resources. **E-mail address:** hr@cronin-co.com. **World Wide Web address:** http://www.cronin-co.com. **Description:** An advertising, direct marketing, and public relations firm. **Positions advertised include:** Rainmaker; Computer Production Artist. **Special programs:** Internships.

DIRECT MEDIA, INC.
200 Pemberwick Road, Greenwich CT 06830. 203/532-1000. **Contact:** Human Resources. **World Wide Web address:** http://www.directmedia.com . **Description:** Provides direct marketing services such as list management and brokerage. **Positions advertised include:** Copywriter; Package Insert Coordinator; Insert Media Sales Specialist; List Management Account Executive. **Corporate headquarters location:** This location. **Other U.S. locations:** Conway AR; Walnut Creek CA; Schaumburg IL; Merriam KS; Port Chester NY. **International locations:** Toronto, Ontario. **Number of employees worldwide:** 300.

GARTNER, INC.
56 Top Gallant Road, Stamford CT 06904. 203/964-0096. **Fax:** 203/316-6436. **Contact:** Human Resources. **World Wide Web address:** http:// www.gartner.com. **Description:** Gartner, Inc. is a market research and consulting firm providing strategic decision support. **Special programs:** Internships. **Corporate headquarters location:** This location. **Other U.S. locations:** San Jose CA. **International locations:** Australia; Japan; United Kingdom. **Operations at this facility include:** Research and Development; Sales. **Listed on:** NASDAQ. **Stock exchange symbol:** IT.

IMS HEALTH INC.
1499 Post Road, Fairfield CT 06824. 203/319-4700. **Contact:** Human Resources. **World Wide Web address:** http://www.imshealth.com. **Description:** A leading provider of information solutions to the pharmaceutical and healthcare industries. **Positions advertised include:** Manager, Corporate Finance. **Corporate headquarters location:** This location. **Listed on:** New York Stock Exchange. **Stock exchange symbol:** RX. **Number of employees worldwide:** 6,400.

MBI, INC.
47 Richards Avenue, Norwalk CT 06857. 203/853-2000. **Contact:** Human Resources. **World Wide Web address:** http://www.mbi-inc.com. **Description:** MBI is a direct marketing firm for collectibles including coin and stamp sets, porcelain dolls, porcelain plates, and die-cast vehicles. **Positions advertised include:** General Manager. **Special programs:** Internships. **Corporate headquarters location:** This location. **Number of employees at this location:** 700.

MARKET DATA RETRIEVAL
One Forest Parkway, Shelton CT 06484. 203/926-4800. **Contact:** Human Resources. **World Wide Web address:** http://www.schooldata.com. **Description:** Compiles lists of people to market to schools and other educational facilities. **Parent company:** Dun & Bradstreet Corporation.

MARKETING CORPORATION OF AMERICA
372 Danbury Road, Suite 200, Wilton CT 06897. 203/210-2600. **Contact:** Human Resources. **E-mail address:** careers@mcofa.com. **World Wide Web address:** http://www.mcofa.com. **Description:** A consulting firm. **Other U.S. locations:** San Francisco CA; Minneapolis MN; New York NY.

MASON & MADISON
23 Amity Road, Bethany CT 06524. 203/393-1101. **Contact:** Personnel. **World Wide Web address:** http://www.mason-madison.com. **Description:** An advertising and public relations agency. **Other U.S. locations:** Boston MA; New York NY.

MILLWARD BROWN
501 Kingshighway East, Fairfield CT 06825. 203/335-5222. **Fax:** 203/256-5470. **Contact** Human Resources. **World Wide Web address:** http://www.millwardbrown.com. **Description:** Provides research-based marketing consultancy to assist clients in building profitable brands and e-brands and in providing service. **President:** Eileen Campbell.

MINTZ & HOKE INC.
40 Tower Lane, Avon CT 06001. 860/678-0473. **Fax:** 860/679-9702. **Contact:** Dawn Hassan, Manager of Human Resources. **E-mail address:** jobs@mintz-hoke.com. **World Wide Web address:** http://www.mintz-hoke.com. **Description:** An advertising and public relations firm providing advertising creative development and execution; collateral materials development including brochures, packaging, and signage; direct mail/direct marketing; Internet services; market research; marketing communications planning; media planning, negotiating, and trafficking; positioning strategy development; and public relations services. Founded in 1971. **Company slogan:** The Street Smart Agency. **Special programs:** Internships. **Internship information:** Internships are offered for school credit only in the areas of public relations, graphic design, new business development, and media. **Corporate headquarters location:** This location. **President:** Chris Knopf. **Information Systems Manager:** Ron Perine. **Number of employees at this location:** 65.

NFO WORLDGROUP, INC.
2 Pickwick Plaza, 3rd Floor, Greenwich CT 06830. 203/629-8888. **Contact:** Human Resources. **World Wide Web address:** http://www.nfow.com. **Description:** Provides custom and syndicated market research services, primarily using a proprietary panel of prerecruited consumer households throughout the country. NFO also offers Internet-based custom marketing research. **NOTE:** Send resumes to 2700 Oregon Road, Northwood OH 43619. **Corporate headquarters location:** Canton OH. **International locations:** Worldwide. **Subsidiaries include:** Advanced Marketing Solutions, Inc. (CT) provides custom computer software systems used by clients to quickly access and analyze complex business and consumer information; Payment Systems, Inc. (FL) is a leading supplier of information to the financial services industry in the United States. **Parent company:** The Interpublic Group of Companies, Inc. **Listed on:** New York Stock Exchange. **Stock exchange symbol:** IPG. **Number of employees worldwide:** 15,000.

Delaware

ADVO INC.
300 McIntire Drive, Newark DE 19711. 302/798-3567. **Fax:** 302/861-3552. **Contact:** Human Resources. **World Wide Web address:** http://www.advo.com. **Description:** Provides direct-mail marketing services. Founded in 1929. **NOTE:** See website for current job openings and to apply online. **Positions advertised include:** Regional Account Executive; Shipping Supervisor; District Sales Manager; Client Services

Senior Account Representative; Client Services Account Manager; Quality Manager. **Corporate headquarters location:** Windsor CT. **Number of employees nationwide:** 4,700.

AVALON EXHIBITS
65 Lukens Drive, Newark DE 19720. 302/654-1633. **Fax:** 302/654-5846. **Contact:** Human Resources. **E-mail address:** careers@avalonexhibits.com. **World Wide Web address:** www.avalonexhibits.com. **Description:** Creates branding solutions at industry events within North America and worldwide through the design, fabrication and management of custom exhibits, events and display environments. **NOTE:** Submit employment inquiries and resumes via e-mail. **Corporate headquarters location:** This location. **Other U.S. locations:** Las Vegas NV.

District Of Columbia

HILL AND KNOWLTON INC.
600 New Hampshire Avenue NW, Suite 601, Washington DC 20037. 202/333-7400. **Fax:** 202/944-1968. **Contact:** Human Resources. **World Wide Web address:** http://www.hillandknowlton.com. **Description:** One of the largest public relations/public affairs counseling firms in the world. **Corporate headquarters location:** New York NY. **Other U.S. locations:** San Francisco CA. **International locations:** Worldwide.

KETCHUM
2000 L Street, Suite 300, Washington DC 202/835-8800. **Fax:** 202/835-8879. **Contact:** Carol Cincotta, Director of Human Resources. **E-mail address:** dc.resume@ketchum.com. **World Wide Web address:** http://www.ketchum.com. **Description:** A public relations firm. Founded in 1923. **Positions advertised include:** Account Coordinator; Director Healthcare Media Relations; Government Finance/Contracts Manager; Sr. Financial Analyst; Sr. Research Associate. **Special programs:** Internships. **Other U.S. locations:** Nationwide. **International locations:** Worldwide. **Number of employees worldwide:** 1,200.

MAYA ADVERTISING AND COMMUNICATIONS
1028 33rd Street NW, Suite 200, Washington DC 20007. 202/337-0566. **Fax:** 202/337-0548. **Contact:** Human Resources. **E-mail address:** maya@mayadc.com. **World Wide Web address:** http://www.mayadc.com. **NOTE:** See website listings for contact information regarding specific positions. **Description:** A full service marketing and communications firm with a Latino market specialization. **Positions advertised include:** Part Time Graphic Designer; Part Time Writer.

PORTER NOVELLI INTERNATIONAL
1909 K Street NW, 4th Floor, Washington DC 20006. 202/973-5800. **Fax:** 202/973-5858. **Contact:** Juanita Myrick, Human Resources. **World Wide Web address:** http://www.porternovelli.com. **Description:** An agency specializing in public relations, crisis management, issue advertising, and research. **Positions advertised include:** Budget Analyst; Sr. Account Executive. **Special programs:** Internships. **Corporate headquarters location:** New York NY. **Other U.S. locations:** Atlanta GA; Irvine CA; San Francisco CA; Seattle WA; Los Angeles CA; Chicago IL; Boston MA. **Number of employees at this location:** 65. **Number of employees nationwide:** 700.

THE SMITH COMPANY
4455 Connecticut Avenue NW, Suite 600, Washington DC 20008. 202/895-0900. **Fax:** 202/895-0910. **Contact:** Human Resources. **Description:** Provides telemarketing services. **Positions advertised include:** Accountant.

Florida

BBDO
2 Alhambra Plaza, Suite 600, Coral Gables FL 33134. 305/446-6006. **Contact:** Human Resources. **E-mail address:** ximena.nunez@bbdo.com. **World Wide Web address:** http://www.bbdo.com. **Description:** Part of a worldwide network of advertising agencies with related businesses in public relations, direct marketing, sales promotion, graphic arts, and printing. **Corporate headquarters location:** New York NY. **Other U.S. locations:** Los Angeles CA; San Francisco CA; Atlanta GA; Chicago IL; Wellesley MA; Southfield MI. **Parent company:** BBDO Worldwide operates 83 subsidiaries, affiliates, and associates engaged solely in advertising and related operations.

CATALINA MARKETING CORPORATION
200 Carillon Parkway, St. Petersburg FL 33716. 727/579-5000. **Toll-free phone:** 888/322-3814. **Contact:** Human Resources. **E-mail address:** resume@catalinamarketing.com. **World Wide Web address:** http://www.catmktg.com. **Description:** Provides marketing services for consumer product manufacturers and supermarket retailers. The company's point-of-scan electronic marketing network delivers checkout coupons to consumers at supermarket checkouts based on their purchases. The company also provides Internet information on retail grocery promoters. **NOTE:** Entry-level positions are offered. **Positions advertised include:** Executive Assistant; Human Resources Administrator; Customer Services Technician. **Corporate headquarters location:** This location. **Other U.S. locations:** Nationwide. **International locations:** Europe; Japan. **Subsidiaries include:** Catalina Electronic Clearing Services; Health Resource Publishing Company. **Operations at this facility include:** Administration; Divisional Headquarters. **Listed on:** New York Stock Exchange. **Stock exchange symbol:** POS. **Annual sales/revenues:** $51 - $100 million. **Number of employees at this location:** 170. **Number of employees nationwide:** 500. **Number of employees worldwide:** 1,650.

HUSK JENNINGS GALLOWAY & ROBINSON
6 East Bay Street, Suite 600, Jacksonville FL 32202. 904/354-2600. **Fax:** 904/354-7226. **Contact:** Personnel. **World Wide Web address:** http://www.huskjennings.com. **Description:** An advertising, marketing, and public relations agency. **Positions advertised include:** Administrative Manager; Public Relations Specialist. **Corporate headquarters location:** This location. **Number of employees at this location:** 15.

LANDERS AND PARTNERS, INC.
2857 Executive Drive, Suite 210, Clearwater FL 33762. 727/572-5228. **Fax:** 727/572-5910. **Contact:** Cliff Jones, President. **World Wide Web address:** http://www.landersandpartners.com. **Description:** An advertising agency. **Office hours:** Monday – Friday, 9:00 a.m. – 5:30 p.m.

NATIONWIDE ADVERTISING SERVICE INC.
3510 Bay to Bay Boulevard, Tampa FL 33629. 813/831-1085. **Fax:** 813/831-5086. **Contact:** Office Manager. **World Wide Web address:** http://www.hrads.com. **Description:** With offices in 36 major U.S. and Canadian cities, Nationwide Advertising Service is one of the largest and oldest independent, full-service advertising agencies exclusively specializing in human resources communications, promotions, and advertising. The company offers consultation, campaign planning, ad placement, research, and creative production. **Positions advertised include:** Regional Manager; Account Executive. **Corporate headquarters location:** Cleveland OH. **Other U.S. locations:** Detroit MI; St. Louis MO; Houston TX.

SHAKER ADVERTISING AGENCY
4920 West Cypress Street, Suite 104, Tampa FL 33607. 813/289-1100. **Contact:** Lee Ann Foster, Office Manager. **E-mail address:** hr@shaker.com. **World Wide Web address:** http://www.shaker.com. **Description:** An advertising agency. **Positions advertised include:** Human Resources Generalist. **Corporate headquarters location:** Oak Park IL. **Other area locations:** Miami/Ft. Lauderdale FL.

Other U.S. locations: Oak Park IL; Bloomington IN; Boston MA; East Brunswick NJ; Pittsburgh PA; Milwaukee WI. **Number of employees nationwide:** 243.

TULLY-MENARD, INC.
611 Druid Road East, Suite 407, Clearwater FL 33756. 727/298-8301. **Fax:** 727/298-8408. **Contact:** Mr. Joe Tully, President. **World Wide Web address:** http://www.tullymenard.com. **Description:** An advertising agency. **NOTE:** Part-time jobs are offered. **Office hours:** Monday - Friday, 8:30 a.m. - 5:00 p.m. **Corporate headquarters location:** This location. **Listed on:** Privately held. **Annual sales/revenues:** Less than $5 million.

VAL-PAK DIRECT MARKETING
8605 Largo Lakes Drive, Largo FL 33773. 727/399-3189. **Toll-free phone:** 800/237-2871. **Fax:** 727/399-3085. **Recorded jobline:** 727/399-3012. **Contact:** LaToy Black, Recruiting Specialist. **E-mail address:** latoy_black@valpak.com. **World Wide Web address:** http://www.valpak.com. **Description:** An international direct mail advertising company that designs, prints, and mails more than 15 billion coupons annually. **NOTE:** Entry-level positions and second and third shifts are offered. **Special programs:** Internships. **Office hours:** Monday - Friday, 8:00 a.m. - 5:00 p.m. **Corporate headquarters location:** This location. **Parent company:** Cox Enterprises, Inc. is one of the nation's largest privately held media companies with major holdings in the newspaper, television, radio, and cable industries. **Listed on:** Privately held. **President:** Joseph Bourdow. **Annual sales/revenues:** More than $100 million. **Number of employees at this location:** 1,100. **Number of employees nationwide:** 1,500.

WESTWAYNE, INC.
401 East Jackson Street, Suite 3600, Tampa FL 33602. 813/202-1200. **Fax:** 813/202-1261. **Contact:** Human Resources. **World Wide Web address:** http://www.westwayne.com. **Description:** An advertising and marketing agency. **Positions advertised include:** Account Executive; Media Buyer.

YESAWICH, PEPPERDINE AND BROWN & RUSSELL
423 South Keller Road, Suite 100, Orlando FL 32810. 407/875-1111. **Contact:** Julie Gochnour, Director of Human Resources. **World Wide Web address:** http://www.ypb.com. **Description:** An advertising agency. **Positions advertised include:** Vice President; Account Supervisor. **Corporate headquarters location:** This location.

Georgia

ADVO INC.
7924 Troon Circle, Austell GA 30168. 678/945-4303. **Contact:** Human Resources. **World Wide Web address:** http://www.advo.com. **Description:** Provides direct mail advertising services. **Corporate headquarters location:** Windsor CT. **Other U.S. locations:** Nationwide. **Listed on:** New York Stock Exchange. **Stock exchange symbol:** AD. **CEO:** Gary Mulloy. **Number of employees nationwide:** 3,600.

AMBROSI & ASSOCIATES
213 Thornton Road, Suite 100, Lithia Springs GA 30122-1551. 770/941-4333. **Fax:** 770/739-2316. **Contact:** Human Resources. **E-mail address:** info@ambrosi.com. **World Wide Web address:** http://www.ambrosi.com. **Description:** A full-service advertising and marketing services agency specializing in brand building for multi-channel companies. **Positions advertised include:** Production Artist; Production Manager. **Other U.S. locations:** Chicago IL; New York NY; San Francisco CA. **Parent company:** Schawk.

BBDO
3500 Lenox Road, Suite 1900, Atlanta GA 30326. 404/231-1700. **Contact:** Debbie Lindner, Director of Personnel. **World Wide Web address:** http://www.bbdo.com. **Description:** Part of a worldwide network of advertising agencies with related businesses in public relations, direct marketing, sales promotion, graphic arts, and printing. **NOTE:** Please visit website to take the Career Questionnaire. **Corporate headquarters location:** New York NY. **Other U.S. locations:** Los Angeles CA; San Francisco CA; Chicago IL; Miami FL; Detroit MI; Minneapolis MN. **International locations:** Worldwide. **Parent company:** BBDO Worldwide operates 156 offices in 42 countries. The company has 83 subsidiaries, affiliates, and associates engaged solely in advertising and related operations. **Number of employees nationwide:** 3,400.

BRIGHT HOUSE
8 Puritan Mill, 916 Lowery Boulevard, Atlanta GA 30318. 404/240/2500. **Fax:** 404/240-2501. **Contact:** Human Resources. **E-mail address:** careers@brighthouse.com. **World Wide Web address:** http://www.brighthouse.com. **Description:** An ideation firm specializing in strategic thinking, trend analysis, repositioning, forecasting, new product development, and experiential marketing for business.

CBS OUTDOOR
3745 Atlanta Industrial Drive, Atlanta GA 30331. 404/699-1499. **Fax:** 404/505-7013. **Contact:** Human Resources. **World Wide Web address:** http://www.infoutdoor.com. **Description:** An advertising agency specializing in the design of billboards and posters. **Other U.S. locations:** Nationwide. **Parent company:** VIACOM. **CEO:** Wally Kelly.

COMMUNICATIONS 21
834 Inman Village Parkway, Suite 150, Atlanta GA 30307. 404/814-1330. **Fax:** 404/814-1332. **E-mail address:** jobs@c21pr.com. **Contact:** Human Resources. **World Wide Web address:** http://www.c21pr.com. **Description:** A full service marketing and public relations firm, specializing in media relations, marketing campaigns and brand development. **Positions advertised include:** Full-time and part-time PR professionals. **Special programs:** Internships. **Corporate headquarters location:** This location.

CORPORATE RESOURCE DEVELOPMENT
400 Galleria Parkway, Suite 1500, Atlanta GA 30339. 770/772-4273. **Fax:** 770/754-7828. **Contact:** Human Resources. **E-mail address:** outcomes@crdatlanta.com. **World Wide Web address:** http://www.crdatlanta.com. **Description:** Provides marketing consulting services for management, sales, and marketing industries. The company also develops differentiation strategies for companies selling and marketing products identical to those of their competition.

DEFINITION 6
2115 Monroe Drive, Suite 100, Atlanta GA 30324. 404/870-0323. **Fax:** 404/870-0325. **Contact:** Human Resources. **E-mail address:** recruiting@definition6.com. **World Wide Web address:** http://www.definition6.com. **Description:** A digital marketing and technology firm providing solutions in information architecture, customer relationship management, Internet-based business systems, strategy, interactive marketing, and advanced infrastructure hosting. **Positions advertised include:** Project Coordinator; Senior Infrastructure Engineer; Junior Web Designer; Web Production Specialist; Senior Programmer/Project Manager; Information Architect; Network Deployment Engineer; Project Manager. **Other U.S. locations:** Greensboro NC.

DEMANDG, LLC
1961 North Druid Hills Road, Building B, Suite 101, Atlanta GA 30329. 404/929-0091. **Fax:** 404/321-3397. **Contact:** Human Resources. **E-mail address:** info@demandg.com. **Description:** A marketing firm.

FITZGERALD & COMPANY
3060 Peachtree Road, NW, Suite 500, One Buckhead Plaza, Atlanta GA 30305. 404/504-6900. **Fax:** 770/396-

0301. **Contact:** Maria Beasley, Human Resources. **E-mail Address:** hr@fitzco.com. **World Wide Web address:** http://www.fitzco.com. **Description:** A marketing and communications company comprised of three firms: The Bostford Group, which provides promotion marketing services; Weber Public Relations, which provided public relations services; and MRM providing relationship management services. This is a full-service advertising firm. **Office hours:** Monday – Friday, 9:00 a.m. – 5:00 p.m. **Corporate headquarters location:** This location. **President/CEO:** Jay Shields.

HAYSLETT GROUP
50 Glenlake Parkway, NE, Suite 430, Atlanta 30328. 770/522-8855. **Fax:** 770/522-8898. **Contact:** Human Resources. **World Wide Web address:** http://www.hayslettsorrel.com. **Description:** One of the largest and most successful public relations firms in the Atlanta area. **CEO:** Charlie Hayslett.

INITIATIVE MEDIA NORTH AMERICA
5909 Peachwood Dunwoody NE, Atlanta GA 30328. 678/441-7110. **Fax:** 404/949-3562. **Contact:** Human Resources. **World Wide Web address:** http://www.im-na.com. **Description:** Offers media management and planning services including strategic planning, research, and television optimization. **Corporate headquarters location:** New York NY. **Other U.S. locations:** Nationwide. **International locations:** Worldwide. **Parent company:** The Interpublic Group of Companies.

JONES WORLEY DESIGNS, INC.
723 Piedmont Road, NE, Atlanta GA 30308-0701. 404/876-9272. **Fax:** 404/876-9174. **Contact:** Human Resources. **E-mail address:** info@jonesworley.com. **World Wide Web address:** http://www.jonesworley.com. **Description:** A marketing and communications firm. **Corporate headquarters location:** This location.

MACQUARIUM INTELLIGENT COMMUNICATIONS
1800 Peachtree, NW, Suite 250, Atlanta GA 30309. 404/554-4000. **Fax:** 404/554-4001. **Contact:** Human Resources Manager. **E-mail address:** hr@macquarium.com. **World Wide Web address:** http://www.macquarium.com. **Description:** A marketing communications firm focusing on eBusiness technologies. **Positions advertised include:** Director of Human Resources; Project Manager; Quality Assurance Manager; Executive Assistant; Interactive Flask Designer; Software Engineer – Technical Lead; Software Engineer – Tibco; Solution Architect. **President:** Kevin Foster.

MANNING SELVAGE & LEE
1170 Peachtree Street NE, Suite 400, Atlanta GA 30309. 404/875-1444. **Fax:** 404/892-1274. **Contact:** Human Resources. **E-mail Address:** careers@mlsrp.com. **World Wide Web address:** http://www.mslpr.com. **Description:** Provides public relations services for the health care, real estate, business-to-business, and consumer relations industries. **NOTE:** Please visit website to search for jobs, and to download an employment application or a Self-ID form. **Positions advertised include:** Account Executive. **Special programs:** Internships. **Corporate headquarters location:** New York NY. **Other U.S. locations:** Boston MA; Chicago IL; Detroit MI; Los Angeles CA; San Francisco CA; San Antonio TX; Washington D.C. **International locations:** Worldwide. **CEO:** Lou Capozzi.

J. WALTER THOMPSON COMPANY
10B Glenlake Parkway NE, North Tower, Atlanta GA 30328. 404/365-7300. **Contact:** Director of Human Resources. **World Wide Web address:** http://www.jwtworld.com. **Description:** A full-service advertising agency. Founded 1864. **Corporate headquarters location:** New York NY. **Other U.S. locations:** Nationwide. **International locations:** Worldwide. **CEO:** Bob Jeffrey. **Number of employees worldwide:** 8,500.

WEST WAYNE
1170 Peachtree Street, Suite 1500, Atlanta GA 30309. 404/347-8700. **Fax:** 404/347-8800. **Contact:** Cristi Axon, Director of Human Resources. **E-mail address:** wwijobs@westwayne.com. **World Wide Web address:** http://www.westwayne.com. **Description:** An advertising agency. **NOTE:** Human Resources phone is 404/347-8754; fax is 404/347-8919. Please visit website to search for jobs and apply online. **Positions advertised include:** Administrative Assistant; Senior Broadcast Traffic Manager; Part-time Technology Assistant. **Corporate headquarters location:** This location. **Other U.S. locations:** Tampa FL. **President/CEO:** Jeff Johnson.

Illinois

ACNIELSEN
150 North Martingale Road, Schaumburg IL 60173-2076. 847/605-5000. **Fax:** 847/605-2000. **Contact:** Human Resources. **World Wide Web address:** http://www.acnielsen.com. **Description:** Provides demographic and related information such as television audience rating services and consumer polling for the consumer goods industry. **NOTE:** AC Nielsen has additional locations in Illinois. Search and apply for positions online. **Positions advertised include:** Associate Database Specialist; Analyst; Homescan Client Manager; Marketing Manager; VP Group Client Director. **Corporate headquarters location:** New York NY. **Parent company:** VNU. **Operations at this facility include:** Administration; Regional Headquarters; Research and Development; Sales; Service. **Number of employees worldwide:** 21,000.

AMD INDUSTRIES, INC.
4620 West 19th Street, Cicero IL 60804. 708/863-8900. **Toll-free phone:** 800/367-9999. **Fax:** 708/863-2065. **Contact:** Human Resources Director. **World Wide Web address:** http://www.amdpop.com. **Description:** Manufactures and sells point-of-purchase (P.O.P.) displays. **Corporate headquarters location:** This location. **Listed on:** Privately held.

ABACUS
1100 Woodfield Road, Schaumburg IL 60173. 847/330-1313. **Toll-free phone:** 800/455-6245. **Contact:** Human Resources. **World Wide Web address:** http://www.abacus-us.com. **Description:** Provides cooperative data, data management, list processing, and analytical services for marketers. **Positions advertised include:** Database Analyst; Production Technician; Sr. Implementation Engineer. **Corporate headquarters location:** Lafayette CO. **Parent company:** DoubleClick Inc.

THE BRADFORD GROUP
9333 North Milwaukee Avenue, Niles IL 60714. 847/966-2770. **Fax:** 847/581-8630. **Contact:** Recruiter. **E-mail address:** jobs@collectiblestoday.com. **World Wide Web address:** http://www.thebradfordgroup.com. **Description:** A direct marketer of collectibles. The company also sells products of affiliated companies. **NOTE:** Entry-level positions are offered. Search and apply for positions online. **Positions advertised include:** Marketing Professional; Product Manager; Product Designer; Product Development Associate. **Special programs:** Internships. **Corporate headquarters location:** This location. **Other area locations:** Bensenville IL (Distribution). **Listed on:** Privately held.

LEO BURNETT USA
35 West Wacker Drive, Chicago IL 60601. 312/220-5959. **Contact:** Human Resources. **World Wide Web address:** http://www.leoburnett.com. **Description:** One of the world's largest advertising agencies, with 200 operating units worldwide. Leo Burnett USA also provides direct marketing, promotional, interactive, and public relations services. Founded in 1935. **NOTE:** Apply online at the company's website. **Positions advertised include:** Category Manager/Interactive; Copy Editor; Account Executive; Client Billing Manager; Finance Ops Coordinator; AP Administrator; Systems Architect; Biller; Production Designer. **Special**

programs: Internships. **Number of employees worldwide:** 8,000.

CHICAGO DISPLAY MARKETING CORPORATION
1999 North Ruby Street, Melrose Park IL 60160-1109. 708/681-4340. **Fax:** 708/681-5852. **Contact:** Human Resources. **World Wide Web address:** http://www.chicagodisplay.com. **Description:** Designs and markets advertising display materials for merchandisers and manufacturers.

CORMARK, INC.
1701 South Winthrop Drive, Des Plaines IL 60018. 847/364-5900. **Toll-free phone:** 800/211-9646. **Contact:** Human Resources. **E-mail address:** recruit@cormarkinc.com. **World Wide Web address:** http://www.cormarkinc.com. **Description:** A merchandising company. **Positions advertised include:** Engineer; Graphic Designer; Industrial Design Engineer; Project Engineer. **Corporate headquarters location:** This location.

CUSHMAN/AMBERG COMMUNICATIONS INC.
180 North Michigan Avenue, Suite 1600, Chicago IL 60601. 312/263-2500. **Contact:** Human Resources. **World Wide Web address:** http://www.cushmanamberg.com. **Description:** A public relations agency. Founded in 1952. **Corporate headquarters location:** This location.

DDB CHICAGO, INC.
200 East Randolph Drive, Chicago IL 60601. 312/552-6000. **Contact:** Human Resources. **World Wide Web address:** http://www.ddbchi.com. **Description:** A full-service, international advertising agency. **NOTE:** Apply online at http://www.ddbjobs.com. **Corporate headquarters location:** New York NY. **Other U.S. locations:** Nationwide. **Parent company:** Omnicom Group. **Operations at this facility include:** Administration; Marketing; Research and Development; Service.

EDELMAN
200 East Randolph Drive, Suite 6300, Chicago IL 60601. 312/240-3000. **Fax:** 312/240-2900. **Contact:** Human Resources. **World Wide Web address:** http://www.edelman.com. **Description:** A public relations firm. Founded in 1952. **NOTE:** Apply online at the company's website. **Positions advertised include:** Editorial Supervisor; Senior Account Executive; Administrative Assistant; Print Production Coordinator.

ENERGY BBDO
410 North Michigan Avenue, Chicago IL 60611. 312/337-7860. **Contact:** Julieann Vukovich, Human Resources. **E-mail address:** julieann.vukovich@energybbdo.com. **World Wide Web address:** http://www.energybbdo.com. **Description:** A worldwide advertising agency with related businesses in public relations, direct marketing, sales promotion, graphic arts, and printing. **NOTE:** Contact Human Resources. **Special programs:** Internships. **Corporate headquarters location:** New York NY. **Other U.S. locations:** Los Angeles CA; San Francisco CA; Miami FL; Atlanta GA; Wellesley MA; Southfield MI. **Parent company:** BBDO Worldwide (Omnicom Group) operates 156 offices in 42 countries and 96 cities. The company also operates 83 subsidiaries, affiliates, and associates engaged solely in advertising and related operations. **Operations at this facility include:** Administration; Service.

EURO RSCG WORLDWIDE
36 East Grand Avenue, Chicago IL 60611. 312/337-4400. Fax: 312/337-2316. **Contact:** Teresa Mogush, Director of Talent Development. **E-mail address:** teresa.mogush@eurorscg.com. **World Wide Web address:** http://www.eurorscgchicago.com. **Description:** Euro RSCG Chicago is part of the sixth largest marketing communications agency in the world. **Corporate headquarters location:** New York NY. **Operations at this facility include:** Administration; Research and Development; Sales. **Listed on:** Privately held.

FOOTE CONE & BELDING
101 East Erie Street, Chicago IL 60611. 312/425-5000. **Fax:** 312/425-5010. **Contact:** Human Resources. **E-mail address:** CareersChi@fcb.com. **World Wide Web address:** http://www.fcb.com. **Description:** One of the largest advertising agencies in the world. Foote Cone & Belding analyzes the advertising needs of clients, plans and creates advertising for their products and services, and places advertising in various mass-market media. The firm offers additional services such as the design and production of merchandising and promotional programs, product research, and package design. **Corporate headquarters location:** New York NY. **Other U.S. locations:** Nationwide.

GREENHOUSE COMMUNICATIONS
303 West Erie, Suite 400, Chicago IL 60610. 312/278-6000. Fax: 312/278-6200. **Contact:** Human Resources. **E-mail address:** ledwards@greenhousecom.net. **World Wide Web address:** http://www.greenhousecom.net. **Description:** A full-service advertising agency. Greenhouse Communications also offers public relations services, design, research and strategy, sales promotion, marketing support, and interactive services.

BERNARD HODES ADVERTISING
430 North Michigan Avenue, Suite 1101, Chicago IL 60611. 312/288-2550. **Contact:** Human Resources. **World Wide Web address:** http://www.hodes.com. **Description:** An advertising agency specializing in recruitment and employee communications. **Positions advertised include:** Client Services Account Executive. **Special programs:** Internships. **Corporate headquarters location:** New York NY. **Other U.S. locations:** Phoenix AZ; Cambridge MA; Dallas TX. **Parent company:** Omnicom.

KETCHUM
200 East Randolph Street, Chicago IL 60601. 312/228-6800. **Contact:** Human Resources. **World Wide Web address:** http://www.ketchum.com. **Description:** A communications agency specializing in advertising, public relations, and directory advertising. **NOTE:** Apply online for open positions. **Positions advertised include:** Office Manager/Human Resources Coordinator; Financial Analyst; Corporate Vice President. **Special programs:** Internships. **Corporate headquarters location:** New York NY. **Other U.S. locations:** Nationwide. **International locations:** United Kingdom. **Parent company:** Omnicom.

SCOTT LAUDER ASSOCIATES
1117 South Milwaukee Avenue, Libertyville IL 60048. 847/549-6262. **Contact:** Sandra White, Office Manager. **E-mail address:** swhite@v2gfk.com. **World Wide Web address:** http://www.scottlauderassociates.com. **Description:** Engaged in a variety of business services including custom market research. **NOTE:** Send resumes via e-mail, fax or mail to Ms. White at V2 GfK, 587 Skippack Pike, Blue Bell PA 19422. Fax: 215/283-3201. **Parent company:** V2 GfK (Blue Bell PA).

MARSHALL ASSOCIATES, INC.
680 North Lake Shore Drive, Suite 1214, Chicago IL 60611. 312/266-8500. **Fax:** 312/266-7925. **Contact:** Human Resources. **E-mail address:** jobs@marshassoc.com. **World Wide Web address:** http://www.marshassoc.com. **Description:** Marshall Associates is a sales and merchandising company that sells consumer products to retailers across the country. They act on behalf of specific manufacturers to serve as their direct sales force. Marshall Associates' primary product categories include lawn & garden, toys, sporting goods and furniture. **Positions advertised include:** Inside Sales Representative; In-Store Sales Merchandiser; Receptionist. **Corporate headquarters location:** This location. **Other U.S. locations:** Nationwide.

OGILVY & MATHER
111 East Wacker Drive, Chicago IL 60601. 312/856-8200.**Fax:** 312/856-8420. **Recorded jobline:** 212/237-5627. **Contact:** Human Resources. **World Wide Web address:** http://www.ogilvy.com. **Description:** An advertising agency. **Other U.S. locations:** New York NY. **Parent company:** WWP.

RAPID DISPLAYS
4300 West 47th Street, Chicago IL 60632. 800/356-5775. **Fax:** 773/927-1091. **Contact:** Human Resources. **World Wide Web address:** http://www.rapiddisplays.com. **Description:** Manufactures signs and advertising displays. Founded in 1938. **NOTE:** See website for job listings. Mail or fax resumes. **Positions advertised include:** Estimator; Design Technician; Illustrator; Account Executive; Customer Service. **Operations at this facility include:** This is a sales and production office.

SYNOVATE
222 South Riverside Plaza, Chicago IL 60606. 312/526-4000. **Contact:** Human Resources. **E-mail address:** HR.Resumes@synovate.com. **World Wide Web address:** http://www.synovate.com. **Description:** A market research firm that provides services to the government as well as to national and international companies. **NOTE:** Apply online. **Positions advertised include:** Account Director; Account Group Manager; Associate Data Director; Business Systems Analyst; Executive Assistant. **Other U.S. locations:** Nationwide. **International locations:** Worldwide. **Parent company:** Aegis.

J. WALTER THOMPSON COMPANY
900 North Michigan Avenue, Chicago IL 60611. 312/951-4000. **Contact:** Human Resources. **World Wide Web address:** http://www.jwtworld.com. **Description:** An advertising agency. **NOTE:** Apply online. **Other U.S. locations:** Nationwide.

YOUNG & RUBICAM, INC./CHICAGO
233 North Michigan Avenue, Suite 1600, Chicago IL 60601. 312/596-3000. **Contact:** Human Resources. **World Wide Web address:** http://www.yandr.com. **Description:** An international advertising agency. The company operates through three divisions: Young & Rubicam International; Marsteller Inc., a worldwide leader in business-to-business and consumer advertising; and Young & Rubicam USA, with 14 consumer advertising agencies operating through four regional groups, and five specialized advertising and marketing agencies. **Corporate headquarters location:** New York NY. **Other U.S. locations:** Nationwide. **International locations:** Worldwide. **Subsidiaries include:** Burson-Marsteller provides public relations services throughout the world.

WUNDERMAN
233 North Michigan Avenue, Suite 1500, Chicago IL 60601-5519. 312/596-2500. **Contact:** Human Resources. **World Wide Web address:** http://www.wunderman.com. **Description:** An advertising agency. **Corporate headquarters location:** New York NY.

Indiana
AP IMAGE TEAM INC.
1620-B North Ironwood Drive, South Bend IN 46635. 574/259-7112. **Fax:** 574/259-0574. **Toll-free phone:** 866/259-7112. **Contact:** Human Resources. **E-mail address:** info@APImageTM.com. **World Wide Web address:** www.apimagetm.com. **Description:** A promotional marketing company founded in 1991 that provides web/graphic design services. **Positions advertised include:** Java Programmer; Customer Service Representative.

ADVO INC.
8910 Purdue Road, Suite 650, Indianapolis IN 46268. 317/879-4710. **Contact:** Human Resources. **World Wide Web address:** http://www.advo.com. **Description:** A direct mail advertising company. Founded in 1929. **NOTE:** Send resumes to 10176 Dixie Highway, Florence KY 41042. **Corporate headquarters location:** Windsor CT. **Other U.S. locations:** Nationwide.

ASHER AGENCY, INC.
P.O. Box 2535, Fort Wayne IN 46801-2535. 260/424-3373. **Physical address:** 535 West Wayne Street. Fort Wayne, IN 46802. **Toll-free phone:** 800/900-7031. **Contact:** Tom Borne, President. **E-mail address:** tomb@ asheragency.com. **World Wide Web address:** http://www.asheragency.com. **Description:** An advertising agency.

BOYDEN & YOUNGBLUTT CORP.
120 West Superior Street, Fort Wayne IN 46802. 260/422-4499. Fax: 260/422-4044. **Contact:** Human Resources. **World Wide Web address:** http://www.b-y.net. **Description:** An advertising agency specializing in branding. **Positions advertised include:** Account Executive; Web Designer/Network Administrator.

BURKHART ADVERTISING INC.
1335 Mishawaka Avenue, South Bend IN 46615. **Toll-free phone:** 800/777-8122. **Fax:** 219/236-1953. **Contact:** Human Resources. **E-mail address:** info@burkhartadv.com. **World Wide Web address:** http://www.burkhartadv.com. **Description:** An advertising agency that specializes in outdoor billboards and advertising panels for buses and commuter transit in southern Indiana.

DIALAMERICA MARKETING INC.
2952 East Covenanter Drive, Bloomington IN 47401. 812/332-2628. **Fax:** 812/333-7238. **Contact:** Manager of Human Resources. **World Wide Web address:** http://www.dialamerica.com/bloomington. **Description:** A telemarketing agency. Founded in 1957. **Positions advertised include:** Branch Manager; Branch Office Assistant; Teleservice Representative; Sales Supervisor. **Office hours:** Monday - Friday, 8:00 a.m. - 10:00 p.m. **Corporate headquarters location:** Mahwah NJ. **Other U.S. locations:** Nationwide. **Listed on:** Privately held.

KELLER CRESCENT COMPANY, INC.
110 East Louisiana Street, P.O. Box 3, Evansville IN 47701. 812/464-2461. **Fax:** 812/426-7578. **Contact:** Mr. Chris Feagans, Vice President of Human Resources. **E-mail address:** cooljobs@kellercrescent.com. **World Wide Web address:** http://www.kellercrescent.com. **Description:** A marketing communications company offering advertising, media, public relations, sales promotion, audio/visual production, and marketing services, as well as printing and packaging facilities. **Other area locations:** Indianapolis IN. **Other U.S. locations:** St. Louis MO. **Operations at this facility include:** Administration; Manufacturing; Sales.

LAMAR ADVERTISING COMPANY
1770 West 41st Avenue, Gary IN 46408. 219/980-7046. **Fax:** 219/980-1208. **Contact:** Human Resources. **World Wide Web address:** http://www.lamar.com. **Description:** An advertising agency that specializes in outdoor and transit advertising such as billboards, postings, and bulletins. **Corporate headquarters location:** Baton Rouge LA. **Other U.S. locations:** Nationwide.

MARC USA/INDIANAPOLIS
1314 North Meridian Street, Indianapolis IN 46202. 317/632-6501. **Fax:** 317/632-4438. **Contact:** Julie Muncy, Human Resources Director. **E-mail address:** jmuncy@marcusa.com. **World Wide Web address:** http://www.marc-usa.com/indianapolis. **Description:** An advertising agency that offers integrated marketing, creative development, public relations, and market research. Caldwell VanRiper/MARC also offers new media development for client companies.

MZD (MONTGOMERY ZUKERMAN DAVIS, INC.)
1800 North Meridian Street, Suite 200, Indianapolis IN 46202. 317/924-6271. **Fax:** 317/925-3854. **Contact:**

Human Resources. **World Wide Web address:** http://www.mzd.com. **Description:** An advertising, strategic marketing, and public relations agency. MZD offers creative planning, Website development, market research, promotional assistance, and other marketing services. MZD also owns Telematrix, and offers both video and audio production services, as well as computer graphics development. Founded in 1950. **Corporate headquarters location:** This location. **Other U.S. locations:** Chicago IL; Detroit MI.

ROMAN BRANDGROUP
111 Monument Circle, Suite 2400, Indianapolis IN 46200. 317/686-7800. **Contact:** Shawna Lake, Personnel Manager. **World Wide Web address:** http://www.batesusa.com. **Description:** An advertising agency. **Corporate headquarters location:** New York NY.

RUTTER COMMUNICATIONS NETWORK
420 West Washington Street, Muncie IN 47305. 765/289-2113. **Fax:** 765/284-6970. **Contact:** Human Resources. **E-mail address:** hr@rutter.net. **World Wide Web address:** http://www. rutter.net. **Description:** An advertising firm that specializes in network cable advertising.

WHITECO INDUSTRIES
1000 East 80th Place, Suite 700 North, Merrillville IN 46410. 219/769-6601. **Fax:** 219/757-3510. **Contact:** Personnel. **World Wide Web address:** http://www. whiteco.com. **Description:** An advertising agency specializing in the hotel and real estate industries.

Kentucky
BANDY, CARROLL & HELLIGE ADVERTISING
307 West Muhammad Ali Boulevard, Louisville KY 40202. 502/589-7711. **Fax:** 502/589-0390. **Contact:** Human Resources. **E-mail address:** employment@bch.com. **World Wide Web address:** http://www.bch.com. **Description:** An advertising and public relations agency that specializes in Internet marketing, media, branding, marketing to women, and new product introduction. **Corporate headquarters location:** This location. **Other U.S. locations:** Indianapolis IN. **Annual sales/revenues:** $38 million. **Number of employees at this location:** 38.

BASES
50 West RiverCenter Boulevard, Suite 600, Covington KY 41011. 859/905-4320. **Fax:** 859/905-5000. **Contact:** Jamie Kennedy, Human Resources. **E-mail address:** hr@bases.com. **World Wide Web address:** http://www.bases.com. **Description:** A marketing research firm that specializes in forecasting sales of new consumer packaged goods and products through the use of simulated test markets and market models. **Positions advertised include:** Programmer/Analyst; Associate Tabulation Analyst; Programmer, Data Collection; Research Analyst. **Special programs:** Training. **Corporate headquarters location:** This location. **Other U.S. locations:** Westport CT; Chicago IL; Parsippany NJ. **International locations:** Argentina; Mexico; Brazil; Belgium; Canada; China; France; United Kingdom; Australia. **Parent company:** VNU.

CROWE CHIZEK AND COMPANY LLC
9600 Brownsboro Road, Suite 400, Louisville, KY 40241-1122. 502/326-3996. **Contact:** Human Resources. **World Wide Web address:** http://www.crowechizek.com. **Description:** Provides business solutions in the areas of assurance, benefit plan services, financial advisory, forensic services, performance services, risk consulting, and tax consulting to large and middle market public companies and large privately held businesses. **Positions advertised include:** Associate Sales Representative; CRM Manager; Great Plains Manager; Sr. .Net Development Consultant; Sr. Tax Manager. **Parent company:** Horwath International.

DELOITTE & TOUCHE USA LLP
220 West Main Street, Suite 2100, Louisville KY 40202-2284. 502/562-2000. **Fax:** 502/562-2073. **Contact:** Human Resources. **World Wide Web address:** http://www.deloitte.com. **Description:** Provides services in four areas: audit, tax, consulting, and financial advisory services. **Positions advertised include:** Audit Manager; Data Warehousing and Business Intelligence Manager; Enterprise Information Strategy and Architectures Manager; Portals and Enterprise Content Management Manager. **Corporate headquarters location:** New York NY. **Other U.S. locations:** Nationwide. **Parent company:** Deloitte Touche Tohmatsu.

DOE-ANDERSON ADVERTISING
620 West Main Street, Louisville KY 40202. 502/589-1700. **Fax:** 502/587-8349. **Contact:** Crystal Peterson, Personnel. **E-mail address:** cpeterson@doeanderson.com. **World Wide Web address:** http://www.doeanderson.com. **Description:** A full-service advertising and public relations agency. Founded in 1915. **NOTE:** Entry-level positions are offered. Job seekers may apply online for advertised openings. **Positions advertised include:** Management Supervisor. **Special programs:** Internships. **Corporate headquarters location:** This location. **Listed on:** Privately held. **Sales/revenues:** $125 million. **Number of employees at this location:** 85.

PRICEWEBER MARKETING COMMUNICATIONS, INC.
2101 Production Drive, Louisville KY 40299. 502/499-9220. **Fax:** 502/491-5593. **Contact:** Human Resources Director. **E-mail address:** hr@priceweber.com. **World Wide Web address:** http://www.priceweber.com. **Description:** An advertising agency. **Positions advertised include:** Senior-level Writer; Art Director; Account Manager; Advertising Specialist; Web Developer/Software Designer; Writer; Buyer; Photographer. **Corporate headquarters location:** This location.

RED7E
637 West Main Street, Louisville KY 40202. 502/585-3403. **Fax:** 502/582-2043. **Contact:** Human Resources. **E-mail address:** info@red7e.com. **World Wide Web address:** http://www.red7e.com. **Description:** Red7e provides a broad range of planning, creative, direct marketing, public relations, sales promotion, production, and media services to customers in the construction, health care, restaurant, business, financial, and manufacturing industries. Founded in 1974. **Special programs:** Internships. **Corporate headquarters location:** This location. **Number of employees at this location:** 40.

Louisiana
CITY PRINTING, INCORPORATED
2204 Line Avenue, Shreveport LA 71104. 318/688-6692. **Fax:** 318/226-0971. **Toll-free phone:** 800/256-7445. **Contact:** Human Resources. **E-mail address:** adconcepts@cityprinting.net. **World Wide Web address:** http://www.bumpersickers.com. **Description:** Provides advertising and promotional products to businesses in the form of logo-imprinted pens, mugs, key chains, T-shirts, fundraising ideas, business gifts, and awards.

GREMILLION & POU
2800 Centenary Boulevard, Shreveport LA 71104. 318/424-2676. **Fax:** 318/221-3442. **Contact:** Human Resources. **World Wide Web address:** http://www.gp-ad.com. **Description:** Provides brand assessment and development, strategic planning and development, communications strategies, and market research for businesses. **Presidents:** Anne Gremillion and Robert Pou. **Number of employees at this location:** 20.

Maine
BURGESS ADVERTISING & ASSOCIATES, INC.
1290 Congress Street, Portland ME 04102-2150. 207/775-5227. **Fax:** 207/775-3157. **Contact:** Human Resources. **E-mail address:** adburg@burgessadv.com. **World Wide Web address:** http://www. burgessadv.com. **Description:** A full-service marketing, public relations, and advertising firm.

Burgess Advertising & Associates also offers market research, new media, and collateral services. Founded in 1986. **Company slogan:** Advertising that works. **Corporate headquarters location:** This location.

Maryland

EISNER COMMUNICATIONS
509 South Exeter Street, Baltimore MD 21202. 410/685-3390. **Fax:** 410/685-0387. **Contact:** Sue Friedman, Hiring Manager. **E-mail address:** info@eisnerpetrou.com. **World Wide Web address:** http://www.eisnerpetrou.com. **Description:** An advertising and public relations agency. **Special programs:** Internships. **Corporate headquarters location:** This location. **Other U.S. locations:** Washington DC. **Operations at this facility include:** Administration. **Listed on:** Privately held. **President/CEO:** David M. Petrou. **Number of employees at this location:** 65.

4THOUGHT, INC.
2002 Clipper Park Road, Suite 301, Baltimore MD 21211. 410/554-0100. **Fax:** 410/554-0045. **Contact:** Human Resources. **World Wide Web address:** http://www.4thoughtinc.com. **Description:** A marketing communications firm that focuses on brand development, print collateral, environmental graphics, and interactive web solutions. **Positions advertised include:** Marketing and Design Project Manager.

HARTE-HANKS, INC.
4545 Annapolis Road, Baltimore MD 21227. 410/636-6660. **Fax:** 410/789-0159. **Contact:** Jeff Romans. **E-mail address:** jeff_romans@harte-hanks.com. **World Wide Web address:** http://www.harte-hanks.com. **Description:** Worldwide, direct and targeted marketing company that provides direct marketing services and shopper advertising opportunities to a wide range of local, regional, national and international consumer and business-to-business marketers. **Positions advertised include:** Account Manager; Programmer. **Corporate headquarters location:** San Antonio, Texas. **Other U.S. locations:** Nationwide. **International locations:** Worldwide.

Massachusetts

ALLIED ADVERTISING
545 Boylston Street, 11th Floor, Boston MA 02116. 617/859-4800. **Contact:** Human Resources. **World Wide Web address:** http://www.alliedadvpub.com. **Description:** An advertising agency. **Other U.S. locations:** Nationwide. **International locations:** Toronto.

ARNOLD WORLDWIDE
101 Huntington Avenue, Boston MA 02199. 617/587-8000. **Fax:** 617/587-8070. **Contact:** Human Resources. **E-mail address:** jobs@arn.com. **World Wide Web address:** http://www.arn.com. **Description:** An advertising, marketing, and public relations firm. **Positions advertised include:** Sr. Brand Planner; Graphic Designer; Information Architecture Manager.

BBK HEALTHCARE
320 Needham Street, Suite 150, Newton MA 02464. 617/630-4477. **Contact:** Human Resources. **World Wide Web address:** http://www.bbkhealthcare.com. **Description:** BBK is an integrated advertising and public relations firm serving the health policies, technologies, managed care, and pharmaceutical fields. **NOTE:** Please indicate the department to which you are applying. **Corporate headquarters location:** This location. **Listed on:** Privately held. **Number of employees at this location:** 30.

BRODEUR
855 Boylston Street, 8th Floor, Boston MA 02116. 617/587-2800. **Fax:** 617/587-2828. **Contact:** Human Resources. **E-mail address:** hresources@brodeur.com. **World Wide Web address:** http://www.brodeur.com. **Description:** A public relations firm that provides marketing and corporate communications. **Office hours:** Monday - Friday, 8:30 a.m. - 5:30 p.m.

CITIGATE CUNNINGHAM INC.
One Memorial Drive, 17th Floor, Cambridge MA 02142. 617/494-8202. **Fax:** 617/494-8422. **Contact:** Human Resources. **E-mail address:** careers@citigatecunningham.com. **World Wide Web address:** http://www.citigatecunningham.com. **Description:** A public relations firm that also offers organization strategies, research, and brand positioning. **Parent company:** Incepta Group plc.

COMMONWEALTH CREATIVE ASSOCIATES
345 Union Avenue, Framingham MA 01702. 508/620-6664. **Contact:** Human Resources. **World Wide Web address:** http://www.commcreative.com. **Description:** A full-service advertising agency. **Corporate headquarters location:** This location. **Operations at this facility include:** Administration; Sales. **Listed on:** Privately held. **Number of employees at this location:** 10.

CONE INC.
855 Boylston Street, Boston MA 02116. 617/227-2111. **Contact:** Human Resources. **E-mail address:** hr@coneinc.com. **World Wide Web address:** http://www.conenet.com. **Description:** A strategic marketing communications firm. **Positions advertised include:** Business Development Manager; Account Director.

CYRK, INC.
100 Cummings Center, Suite 250-C, Beverly MA 01915. 978/998-7100. **Fax:** 978/998-6840. **Contact:** Human Resources. **E-mail address:** hr@cyrk.com. **World Wide Web address:** http://www.cyrk.com. **Description:** Designs, develops, manufactures, and distributes products for promotional programs. The company also provides integrated marketing services to national and international clients. Founded in 1976. **Positions advertised include:** Account Manager; Field Sales Representative. **Corporate headquarters location:** Monroe WA. **Other U.S. locations:** Nationwide. **Annual sales/revenues:** More than $100 million.

DEVINE & PEARSON COMMUNICATIONS
300 Congress Street, Quincy MA 02169. 617/472-2700. **Fax:** 617/472-8880. **Contact:** Charlotte Delaney, Office Manager. **World Wide Web address:** http://www.devine-pearson.com. **Description:** An advertising and public relations agency that also offers design and consulting services.

THE FIELD COMPANIES
P.O. Box 78, Watertown MA 02471-0078. 617/926-5550. **Toll-free phone:** 800/369-1593. **Physical address:** 385 Pleasant Street, Watertown MA 02472. **Fax:** 617/924-9011. **E-mail address:** info@fieldcompanies.com. **World Wide Web address:** http://www.fieldcompanies.com. **Contact:** Mr. J. McDonald, Human Resources Representative. **Description:** Provides direct mail services such as list procurement and post office delivery. **NOTE:** Entry-level positions are offered. **Corporate headquarters location:** This location. **Listed on:** Privately held. **Number of employees at this location:** 70.

GRAY RAMBUSCH, INC.
One Washington Mall, 10th Floor, Boston MA 02108-2603. 617/367-0100. **Contact:** Human Resources. **Description:** An advertising firm.

HILL, HOLLIDAY
200 Clarendon Street, Boston MA 02116. 617/437-1600. **Contact:** Director of Human Resources. **E-mail address:** careers@hhcc.com. **World Wide Web address:** http://www.hhcc.com. **Description:** An advertising agency. **Other U.S. locations:** New York NY; San Francisco CA; Miami FL.

BERNARD HODES ADVERTISING
2 Seaport Lane, Suite 900, Boston MA 02210. 617/263-2350. **Fax:** 617/248-3929. **Contact:** Human Resources. **World Wide Web address:** http://www.hodes.com. **Description:** An advertising agency specializing in

recruitment and employee communications. **Corporate headquarters location:** New York NY. **Other U.S. locations:** Nationwide. **International locations:** Worldwide. **Parent company:** Omnicom.

KHJ INTEGRATED MARKETING
One Constitution Center, Boston MA 02129-2025. 617/241-8000. **Contact:** Diana Richards, Human Resources. **E-mail address:** drichards@khj.com. **World Wide Web address:** http://www.khj.com. **Description:** An advertising and public relations firm.

MULLEN AGENCY
36 Essex Street, Wenham MA 01984. 978/468-1155. **Contact:** Human Resources. **E-mail address:** jobs@mullen.com. **World Wide Web address:** http://www.mullen.com. **Description:** A leading advertising and public relations firm. **Positions advertised include:** Interactive Account Director; Account Supervisor; Copywriter. **Other U.S. locations:** Detroit MI; Winston-Salem NC; Pittsburgh PA.

PAN COMMUNICATIONS INC.
300 Brickstone Square, Andover MA 01810. 978/474-1900. **Fax:** 978/474-1903. **Contact:** Personnel. **E-mail address:** info@pancomm.com. **World Wide Web address:** http://www.pancommunications.com. **Description:** A full-service public relations agency specializing in four portfolios: business-to-business, high-technology, fashion and consumer products, and trade shows. Founded in 1995. **NOTE:** Entry-level positions offered. **Company slogan:** Partners in public relations. **Positions advertised include:** Associate; Junior Associate; Account Manager; Senior Account Manager; Director. **Special programs:** Internships. **Corporate headquarters location:** This location. **Annual sales/revenues:** Less than $5 million. **Number of employees at this location:** 45.

TMP WORLDWIDE
63 Kendrick Street, Suite 201, Needham MA 02494. 781/444-1010. **Contact:** Human Resources. **World Wide Web address:** http://www.tmpw.com. **Description:** An advertising agency specializing in human resources and employee communications. **Other U.S. locations:** Santa Monica CA; Sausalito CA. **Listed on:** NASDAQ. **Stock exchange symbol:** TMPW.

Michigan

CAMPBELL-EWALD COMPANY
30400 Van Dyke Avenue, Warren MI 48093. 586/574-3400. **Contact:** Human Resources. **World Wide Web address:** http://www.campbell-ewald.com. **Description:** An advertising agency. **Positions advertised include:** Senior Media Planner; Senior Account Executive; Junior Database Analyst; New Business Administrator; Copywriter; Attorney; Production Artist; Account Supervisor; Recruiter. **Special programs:** Internships. **Corporate headquarters location:** This location. **Other area locations:** Southfield MI. **Other U.S. locations:** Los Angeles CA; New York NY. **International locations:** Frankfurt, Germany; Dubai, United Arab Emirates. **Parent company:** The Interpublic Group of Companies, Incorporated. **Listed on:** New York Stock Exchange. **Stock exchange symbol:** IPG. **Number of employees at this location:** 800.

ENTERTAINMENT PUBLICATIONS, INC.
Maple Corporate Center, 1414 East Maple Road, Troy MI 48083. 248/637-8400. **Fax:** 248/404-1915. **Contact:** Corporate Recruiter. **World Wide Web address:** http://www.entertainment.com. **Description:** Develops and markets discount programs, directories, and promotions. Founded in 1962. **Positions advertised include:** Recruiting Specialist; PeopleSoft Administrator; Division Support Coordinator; Logistics Analyst; Vice President, Merchant Marketing. **Corporate headquarters location:** This location. **Parent company:** Cendant Corporation. **Operations at this facility include:** Administration; Sales; Service. **Listed on:** New York Stock Exchange. **Stock exchange symbol:** CD. **Number of employees at this location:** 300. **Number of employees nationwide:** 1,300.

FELDER COMMUNICATIONS GROUP
50 Louis Street NW, 600 Trade Center, Grand Rapids Michigan 49503. 616/459-1200. **Fax:** 616/459-2080. **Contact:** Mike Schurr, Creative Director. **E-mail address:** mike@felder.com. **World Wide Web address:** http://www.felder.com. **Description:** Felder Communications provides brand elevation campaigns to clients such as engineering firms, hospitals, airports, and websites.

FRANCO PUBLIC RELATIONS GROUP
400 Renaissance Center, Suite 1000, Detroit MI 48243. 313/567-2300. **Fax:** 313/567-4486. **Contact:** Human Resources. **E-mail address:** info@franco.com. **World Wide Web address:** http://www.franco.com. **Description:** A public relations firm. Founded in 1964. **Special programs:** Internships. **Corporate headquarters location:** This location. **Subsidiaries include:** Brightlines Creative; The Comark Group Incorporated. **Number of employees at this location:** 25.

NAS RECRUITMENT COMMUNICATIONS
34405 West Twelve Mile Road, Suite 224, Farmington Hills MI 48331. 248/489-8875. **Fax:** 248/489-9118. **Contact:** Regional Manager. **E-mail address:** nas.de@nasrecruitment.com. **World Wide Web address:** http://www.nasrecruitment.com. **Description:** An independent, full-service advertising agency specializing in human resource communications, promotions, and advertising. The company offers consultation, campaign planning, ad placement, research, and creative production. **Corporate headquarters location:** Cleveland OH. **Other U.S. locations:** Nationwide. **International locations:** Canada. **Parent company:** McCann Worldgroup.

SMZ ADVERTISING
900 Wilshire Drive, Suite 102, Troy MI 48084. 248/362-4242. **Fax:** 248/362-2014. **Contact:** Personnel. **E-mail address:** info@smz.com. **World Wide Web address:** http://www.smz.com. **Description:** Develops and produces advertising and marketing communications materials. **Special programs:** Internships. **Corporate headquarters location:** This location. **Listed on:** Privately held. **Number of employees at this location:** 60.

STONE AND SIMONS ADVERTISING INC.
24245 Northwestern Highway, Southfield MI 48075-2573. 248/358-4800. **Fax:** 248/358-0128. **Contact:** Human Resources. **E-mail address:** humanresources@stonesimons.com. **World Wide Web address:** http://www.stonesimons.com. **Description:** An advertising agency. Founded in 1958. **Corporate headquarters location:** This location. **Number of employees at this location:** 40.

TRANS-INDUSTRIES INC.
1780 Opdyke Court, Auburn Hills MI 48326. 248/364-0400. **Fax:** 248/364-0404. **Contact:** Human Resources. **E-mail address:** inquiries@transindustries.com. **World Wide Web address:** http://www.transindustries.com. **Description:** Produces signs, advertising displays, and lighting and environmental systems for highways, as well as for automotive and commercial applications. **Corporate headquarters location:** This location. **Other area locations:** Waterford MI. **Other U.S. locations:** Wilmington NC. **Subsidiaries include:** Transign, Inc.; Vultron, Inc.; Transmatic, Inc. **Listed on:** NASDAQ. **Stock exchange symbol:** TRNI. **Annual sales/revenues:** $34.5 million. **Number of employees at this location:** Approximately 250.

W.B. DONER & COMPANY
25900 Northwestern Highway, Southfield MI 48075. 248/354-9700. **Fax:** 248/827-0880. **Contact:** Director of Human Resources. **Description:** An advertising agency specializing in print and television campaigns.

Special programs: Internships. **Other U.S. locations:** Tampa FL; Baltimore MD; Boston MA; Cleveland OH; Dallas TX. **International locations:** Brussels; London; Melbourne; Montreal; Sydney; Toronto. **Number of employees worldwide:** 930.

YOUNG & RUBICAM, INC.
550 Town Center Drive, Suite 300, Dearborn MI 48126. 313/583-8000. **Fax:** 313/583-8001. **Contact:** Cathy Coraci, Director of Human Resources. **World Wide Web address:** http://www.yr.com. **Description:** An international advertising agency. Founded in 1923. **NOTE:** Entry-level positions are offered. **Special programs:** Internships. **Corporate headquarters location:** New York NY. **Other U.S. locations:** Nationwide. **International locations:** Worldwide. **Parent company:** WPP Group. **Operations at this facility include:** This location houses Young & Rubicam Advertising, Wunderman Cato Johnson, Burson-Marsteller, and Capital Consulting & Research. **Listed on:** New York Stock Exchange. **Stock exchange symbol:** YNR. **Annual sales/revenues:** Approximately $1 billion. **Number of employees at this location:** 260. **Number of employees nationwide:** Over 11,000.

Minnesota

ADVO INC.
4216 Park Glen Road, Minneapolis MN 55416. 952/929-1441. **Contact:** Human Resources. **World Wide Web address:** http://www.advo.com. **Description:** A direct mail media company. Advo distributes ShopWise branded programs and missing children alert cards through the mail. **Positions advertised include:** Regional Account Executive. **Corporate headquarters location:** Windsor CT.

CAMPBELL MITHUN
222 South Ninth Street, Minneapolis MN 55402. 612/347-1327. **Contact:** K.C. Foley, Human Resources Director. **E-mail address:** careers@campbellmithun.com. **World Wide Web address:** http://www.campbellmithun.com. **Description:** A full-service advertising and marketing communications company. Clients include Betty Crocker, H&R Block, Burger King, Andersen Windows, and Toro. **Other U.S. locations:** Irvine CA; New York NY. **Parent company:** Interpublic Group of Companies Inc.

CARLSON COMPANIES, INC.
CARLSON MARKETING GROUP
P.O. Box 59159, Minneapolis MN 55459. 763/212-5000. **Physical address:** 701 Carlson Parkway, Minnetonka MN 55305. **Contact:** Human Resources. **World Wide Web address:** http://www.carlson.com. **Description:** A highly diversified corporation doing business through a variety of subsidiaries. Business areas include hotels, restaurant operations, and retail and wholesale travel. Carlson Marketing Group (also at this location) provides a variety of marketing services for sporting events and airlines; incentive programs for employees of other companies; and strategic consulting services to help client companies create customer/brand loyalty. **Corporate headquarters location:** This location. **Number of employees nationwide:** 50,000.

CARMICHAEL LYNCH
800 Hennepin Avenue, Minneapolis MN 55403. 612/334-6000. **Fax:** 612/334-6171. **Contact:** Human Resources. **E-mail address:** humanresources@clynch.com. **World Wide Web address:** http://www.carmichaellynch.com. **Description:** An advertising agency offering creative development and campaign management services for both national and regional marketing efforts. The firm also provides public relations and corporate communications services through its Carmichael Lynch Spong consultancy. In addition, Carmichael Lynch's creative design unit, Carmichael Lynch Thorburn, offers services for brand identity and interactive marketing efforts. Founded in 1962. **NOTE:** See website for current job openings and application instructions. Entry-level positions are offered. **Special programs:** Internships; Training. **Corporate headquarters location:** This location. **Parent company:** Interpublic Group of Companies Inc.

COLLE+McVOY
8500 Normandale Lake Boulevard, Suite 2400, Bloomington MN 55437-3800. 952/852-7500. **Fax:** 952/852-8100. **Contact:** Phil Johnson, Recruiting Manager. **World Wide Web address:** http://www.collemcvoy.com. **Description:** A full-service advertising and marketing communications agency. Founded in 1935. **Listed on:** Privately held. **CEO:** John Jarvis. **Number of employees at this location:** 280.

DUFFY & PARTNERS
710 Second Street South, Suite 602, Minneapolis MN 55401. 612/548-2333. **Fax:** 612/548-2334. **Contact:** Sarah Brinkman, Employment Contact. **E-mail address:** sbrinkman@duffy.com. **World Wide Web address:** http://www.duffy.com. **Description:** An advertising agency.

FALLON WORLDWIDE
50 South Sixth Street, Suite 2800, Minneapolis MN 55402. 612/758-2345. **Fax:** 612/758-2346. **Contact:** Human Resources. **World Wide Web address:** http://www.fallon.com. **Description:** A full-service advertising firm. In addition to creative development, the firm offers marketing and branding services, brand and corporate identity consulting, and campaign planning services. Fallon also provides interactive marketing services and website development. **Parent company:** Publicis.

FINGERHUT DIRECT MARKETING INC.
4400 Baker Road, Minnetonka MN 55343. 952/932-3100. **Contact:** Human Resources. **E-mail address:** hrjobs@fingerhut.com. **World Wide Web address:** http://www.fingerhut.com. **Description:** Markets general merchandise including electronics, home furnishings, household goods, women's and men's apparel, and jewelry through catalogs and other direct mail solicitations. Fingerhut Company also operates a specialty food gifts mail order business; rents customer lists; markets various insurance products; and offers and services credit cards. **Other area locations:** St. Cloud MN. **Parent company:** Petters Group Worldwide.

GAGE MARKETING GROUP
10000 Highway 55, Minneapolis MN 55441-6365. 763/595-3800. **Fax:** 763/595-3863. **Contact:** Human Resources. **E-mail address:** hr@gage.com. **World Wide Web address:** http://www.gage.com. **Description:** Provides a wide range of integrated marketing services through the following five divisions: Gage Marketing Communications, Gage In-Store Marketing, Gage Print Services, Gage Trade Support Services, and Gage Automotive. **NOTE:** Search http://www.monster.com for current job openings with Gage. **Corporate headquarters location:** This location. **Other area locations:** Howard Lake MN; Long Lake MN; Maple Plain MN; New Brighton MN; Roseville MN; Wayzata MN. **Other U.S. locations:** Newport Beach CA; Kankakee IL; Plymouth MI; El Paso TX. **International locations:** Mexico.

MARTIN WILLIAMS ADVERTISING INC.
60 South Sixth Street, Suite 2800, Minneapolis MN 55402. 612/340-0800. **Contact:** Human Resources. **E-mail address:** human@martinwilliams.com. **World Wide Web address:** http://www.martinwilliams.com. **Description:** An advertising agency. **Positions advertised include:** Interactive Project Manager; Interactive Account Supervisor; Interactive Traffic Coordinator. **Special programs:** Internships. **Corporate headquarters location:** This location.

OLSON & COMPANY
1625 Hennepin Avenue, Minneapolis MN 55403. 612/215-9800. **Fax:** 612/215-9801. **Contact:** Human Resources. **E-mail address:** jobs@oco.com. **World Wide Web address:** http://www.oco.com.

Description: An advertising agency focusing on corporate advertising and branding.

RISDALL ADVERTISING AGENCY
550 Main Street, New Brighton MN 55112. 651/286-6700. **Fax:** 651/631-2561. **Contact:** John Risdall, Chairman. **E-mail address:** info@risdall.com. **World Wide Web address:** http://www.risdall.com. **Description:** An advertising firm specializing in e-commerce, environmental, high-tech, industrial, and business-to-business advertising. Founded in 1972.

SAXTON-FERRIS
11900 Wayzata Boulevard, Suite 114, Minnetonka MN 55305-2010. 952/544-9300. **Fax:** 952/544-7911. **Contact:** June Ferris, General Manager. **World Wide Web address:** http://www.saxton-ferris.com. **Description:** A national Yellow Pages advertising agency. **NOTE:** Entry-level positions are offered. **Corporate headquarters location:** This location. **Parent company:** Ferris Marketing, Inc. **Operations at this facility include:** Service. **Annual sales/revenues:** $5 - $10 million.

YAMAMOTO MOSS
252 First Avenue North, Minneapolis MN 55401. 612/375-0180. **Toll-free phone:** 888/375-9910. **Fax:** 612/342-2424. **Contact:** Human Resources. **E-mail address:** hr@yamamoto-moss.com. **World Wide Web address:** http://www.yamamoto-moss.com. **Description:** A brand and communication systems design firm. **NOTE:** See website for current job openings. Designers and writers should include non-returnable work samples. **Positions advertised include:** Director of Information Strategy.

Missouri
ARNOLD WORLDWIDE
788 Market Street, Suite 200, St. Louis MO 63101. 314/421-6610. **Fax:** 314/491-5627. **Contact:** Human Resources. **E-mail address:** jobs@arn.com. **World Wide Web address:** www.arnoldworldwide.com. **Description:** An international advertising agency whose client roster includes several nationally advertised brands. **Corporate headquarters:** Boston, MA. **Other U.S. locations:** Boston MA, Los Angeles CA, New York NY, Washington D.C.

BERNSTEIN-REIN ADVERTISING, INC.
4600 Madison Avenue, Suite 1500, Kansas City MO 64112. 816/756-0640. **Toll-free phone:** 800/571-6246. **Fax:** 816/531-5708. **Contact:** Human Resources. **E-mail address:** human_res@bradv.com. **World Wide Web address:** http://www.bradv.com. **Description:** A national advertising agency. **NOTE:** Search and apply for positions online. **Positions advertised include:** Account Executive; Group Account Director; Print Production Manager; Media Buyer. **Corporate headquarters location:** This location. **Number of employees at this location:** 300.

BOASBERG WHEELER COMMUNICATIONS
4700 Belleview, Suite 100, Kansas City MO 64112. 816/531-2100. **Contact:** Sharen Hasted, Office Manager. **World Wide Web address:** http://www.bwcom.com. **Description:** A public relations firm. **Parent company:** Valentine-Radford, Inc.

CBS OUTDOOR
6767 North Hanley Road, St. Louis MO 63134. 314/524-0800. **Fax:** 314/524-5047. **Contact:** Personnel Department. **World Wide Web address:** http://www.cbsoutdoor.com. **Description:** An advertising agency specializing in the design of billboards and billposters. **Other U.S. locations:** Nationwide. **Parent company:** CBS Corporation.

KUPPER PARKER COMMUNICATIONS
8301 Maryland Avenue, Suite 200, St. Louis MO 63105-3644. 314/290-2000. **Fax:** 314/290-2101. **Contact:** Director of Human Resources. **E-mail address:** resumes@kupperparker. com. **World Wide Web address:** http://www.kupperparker.com. **Description:** A full-service advertising agency. **NOTE:** Search for positions online.

NATIONWIDE ADVERTISING SERVICE INC.
1023 Executive Parkway, Suite 16, St. Louis MO 63141. 314/579-0050. **Fax:** 314/579-0575. **Contact:** Regional Manager. **World Wide Web address:** http://www.hrads.com. **Description:** With offices in 37 major U.S. and Canadian cities, Nationwide Advertising Service is one of the largest and oldest independent, full-service advertising agencies specializing in human resource communications, promotions, and advertising. Nationwide Advertising Service offers consultation, campaign planning, ad placement, research, and creative production. **NOTE:** Search and apply for positions online. **Corporate headquarters location:** Cleveland OH. **Other U.S. locations:** Nationwide. **Parent company:** McCann-Erickson WorldGroup.

VML
250 Northwest Richards Road, Suite 255, Kansas City MO 64116. 816/283-0700. **Fax:** 816/283-0954. **Contact:** Human Resources. **World Wide Web address:** http://www.vml.com. **Description:** An advertising firm that blends marketing and technology through strategic campaigns, web interaction, and software design. **Positions advertised include:** Lead Project Manager; Sr. Account Manager; Experience Architect; Research Analyst. **Other U.S. locations:** Dallas TX; White Salmon WA; Jacksonville FL; New York NY.

VALENTINE-RADFORD, INC.
P.O. Box 13407, Kansas City MO 64199. 816/842-5021. **Physical address:** 911 Main Street, Suite 1000, Kansas City MO 64105. **Contact:** Human Resources. **World Wide Web address:** http://www.valrad.com. **Description:** An advertising agency.

WINNTECH
7023 East 12th Terrace, Kansas City MO 64126. 816/241-4002. **Fax:** 816/241-1288. **Contact:** Theresa Lusk, Director of Human Resources. **E-mail address:** theresal@winntech.com. **World Wide Web address:** http://www.winntech.com. **Description:** A full-service design and marketing firm with in-house production capabilities.

Nebraska
BOZELL & JACOBS
13801 FNB Parkway, Omaha NE 68154-5229. 402/965-4300. **Fax:** 402/965-4399. **Contact:** Meg Graves, Human Resources. **World Wide Web address:** http://www.bozelljacobs.com. **Description:** Bozell & Jacobs is one of the largest advertising agencies in its primary operating area of Nebraska, Iowa, Colorado, Kansas, South Dakota, and Missouri. Bozell & Jacobs also offers public relations services such as corporate relations, marketing support, employee relations, financial relations, government affairs, and community relations. The staff includes specialists in marketing, media, account service, creative work, research, public relations, finance, agriculture, and broadcast affairs. **NOTE:** Unsolicited portfolios are welcome. **Special programs:** Internships. **Corporate headquarters location:** New York NY. **Other U.S. locations:** Nationwide. **Parent company:** True North Communications.

EXPERIAN INFORMATION SOLUTIONS, INC.
949 West Bond Street, Lincoln NE 68521-3694. 402/475-4591. **Contact:** Human Resources. **E-mail address:** lincoln.resume@experian.com. **World Wide Web address:** http://www.experian.com. **Description:** Experian is a global information solutions company that supplies consumer and business credit, direct marketing, and real estate information services. Founded in 1946. **NOTE:** Part-time jobs and second and third shifts are offered. **Positions advertised include:** Client Services Analyst; Sales Supervisor. **Special programs:** Internships. **Office hours:** Monday - Friday, 8:00 a.m. - 5:00 p.m. **Corporate headquarters location:** Costa Mesa CA. **Other U.S.**

locations: Nationwide. **International locations:** Worldwide. **Parent company:** GUS plc. **Operations at this facility include:** Sales. **Number of employees at this location:** 700. **Number of employees nationwide:** 4,500. **Number of employees worldwide:** 13,000.

THE GALLUP ORGANIZATION
1001 Gallup Drive, Omaha NE 68102. 402/951-2003. **Fax:** 888/500-8282. **Contact:** Human Resources. **World Wide Web address:** http://www.gallup.com. **Description:** A market research company founded in 1935 that uses scientific polling data to consult clients. **NOTE:** Apply online. **Corporate Headquarters location:** Washington DC.

Nevada
R.H. DONNELLEY
2030 East Flamingo Road, Suite 220, Las Vegas NV 89119. 702/369-3700. **Contact:** Human Resources. **World Wide Web address:** http://www.rhdonnelley.com. **Description:** The company is engaged in selling advertising space in 500 Yellow Pages directories of more than 58 independent telephone companies. R.H. Donnelley also provides telemarketing services. Founded in 1886. **Positions advertised include:** Credit Support Analyst; National Acct Manager; National Sales Representative. **Corporate headquarters location:** Purchase NY. **Operations at this facility include:** This location is an area sales office. **Listed on:** New York Stock Exchange. **Stock exchange symbol:** RHD. **Number of employees nationwide:** 1600.

EDURUS INC.
769 Basque Way, Carson City NV 89706. 775/885-8333. **Fax:** 775/885-8334. **Contact:** Human Resources. **E-mail address:** info@edurus.com. **World Wide Web address:** http://www.edurus.com. **Description:** A full service interactive agency specializing in web-integration. Creates brochures, catalogs, and direct-mail campaigns.

VAL-PAK
3232 West Desert Inn Road, Las Vegas NV 89102. 702/248-9600. **Contact:** Human Resources. **World Wide Web address:** http://www.valpak.com. **Description:** Provides direct marketing services through its monthly mailing of coupons to consumer households. This location is one of 220 franchise offices in the U.S. **Corporate headquarters location:** Largo FL. **Other U.S. locations:** Nationwide. **International locations:** Puerto Rico; Canada. **Parent company:** Cox Enterprises, Inc. **Number of employees worldwide:** Over 1,200.

VANGUARD MEDIA GROUP
300 South 4th Street, Suite 1015, Las Vegas NV 89101. 702/383-4002 **Fax:** 702/382-4692. **Contact:** Human Resources. **E-mail address:** employment@vanmedia.com. **World Wide Web address:** http://www.vanmedia.com. **Description:** An integrated marketing communications agency that delivers brand strategy, marketing, public relations, advertising, and interactive services.

New Hampshire
MARKETING INITIATIVES
15 Constitution Drive, Suite 2G, Bedford NH 03110. 603/645-6239. **Fax**: 603/ 645-6249. **Contact:** Corporate office human resources at 610/ 834-5000. **E-mail address:** gommi@marketinginitiatives.com. **World Wide Web address:** http://www.marketinginitiatives.com. **Description:** A marketing communications consulting group handling a broad range of clients. **Positions advertised include:** Data Warehouse Developer. **Parent company:** IMS Health, Plymouth Meeting, Pennsylvania. **CEO:** Thomas M. DiGiacinto.

New Jersey
CLIENTLOGIC
230 Brighton Road, Clifton NJ 07012. 973/778-5588. **Fax:** 973/778-6001. **Contact:** Human Resources. **E-mail address:** cliftonjobs@clientlogic.com. **World Wide Web address:** http://www.clientlogic.com. **Description:** A direct marketing firm. **Corporate headquarters location:** Nashville TN. **Other area locations:** Weehawken NJ. **Parent company:** Onex Corporation.

HARRIS INTERACTIVE
5 Independence Way, P.O. Box 5305, Princeton NJ 08543. 609/520-9100. **Fax:** 609/987-8839. **Contact:** Jane Giles, Human Resources Manager. **E-mail address:** info@harrisinteractive.com. **World Wide Web address:** http://www.harrisinteractive.com. **Description:** A full-service marketing research firm that provides information for use in strategic and tactical marketing decisions. **NOTE:** Mail employment correspondence to: Human Resources, Job Code # 76, Carlson Road, Rochester NY 14610. **Positions advertised include:** Director, Client Development, Healthcare; VP, Sr. Consultant, Customer Loyalty Management. **Special programs:** Internships. **Corporate headquarters location:** Rochester NY. **Other U.S. locations:** Tampa FL; Chicago IL; Detroit MI; Minneapolis MN. **International locations:** Argentina; England. **Parent company:** Harris Interactive. **Listed on:** NASDAQ. **Stock exchange symbol:** HPOL.

THE HIBBERT GROUP
400 Pennington Avenue, Trenton NJ 08650. 609/394-7500. **Fax:** 609/392-5946. **Contact:** Human Resources. **E-mail address:** hr@hibbertco.com. **World Wide Web address:** http://www.hibbertco.com. **Description:** Offers international direct marketing services including literature fulfillment, data services, telemarketing, and direct mail. **Positions advertised include:** Program Administration; Customer Service Representative. **Corporate headquarters location:** This location. **Other U.S. locations:** Denver CO. **Operations at this facility include:** Administration; Sales; Service. **Number of employees nationwide:** 800.

IMS HEALTH
100 Campus Road, Totowa NJ 07512. 973/790-0700. **Contact:** Human Resources. **World Wide Web address:** http://www.ims-health.com. **Description:** Conducts market research on the health care industry for pharmaceutical companies. **NOTE:** Apply online. **Positions advertised include:** Sr. Consultant; Account Service Representative; Business Process Analyst. **Special programs:** Internships. **Corporate headquarters location:** Plymouth Meeting PA. **Parent company:** Dun & Bradstreet. **Number of employees at this location:** 400.

IMEDIA, INC.
745 US Highway 202/206, Bridgewater NJ, 08807. 908/725-7500. **Fax:** 908-725-7501. **Contact:** Personnel. **World Wide Web address:** http://www.imediaconnection.com. **Description:** Provides public relations and technological consulting services for large companies.

KINESIS MARKETING
26 Washington Street, Morristown NJ 07960. 973/206-1021. **Contact:** Human Resources. **World Wide Web address:** http://www.kinesismarketing.com. **Description:** A marketing communications company producing strategic products along with tactical implementation skills to create marketing programs.

KROLL DIRECT MARKETING
101 Morgan Lane, Suite 120, Plainsboro NJ 08536. 609/275-2900. **Fax:** 609/275-6606. **Contact:** Personnel Manager. **World Wide Web address:** http://www.krolldirect.com. **Description:** A telemarketing company.

MOKRYNSKI & ASSOCIATES
401 Hackensack Avenue, 2nd Floor, Hackensack NJ 07601. 201/488-5656. **Contact:** Human Resources. **World Wide Web address:** http://www.mokrynski.com. **Description:** A direct mailing company that manages, acquires, and sells mailing lists for client companies.

New Mexico

TRAFFICDEVELOPER
1809 Arroyo Chamiso, Santa Fe NM 87505. 505/988-5055. **Contact:** Chris Kramer, President. **E-mail address:** ckramer@trafficdeveloper.com. **World Wide Web address:** http://www.trafficdeveloper.com. **Description:** Full-service search engine optimization and web marketing company. **NOTE:** Trafficdeveloper employs ten contracted individuals depending on project needs, and one full-time specialist who provides link-building and copywriting services.

VERDE STUDIOS
2400 Louisiana Boulevard NE, Building 4 – Suite 250, Albuquerque NM 87502. 505/348-9777. **Fax:** 505/348-9787. **Contact:** Maverick Granger, Managing Director. **E-mail address:** mgranger@verdestudios.com. **World Wide Web Address:** http://www.verdestudios.com. **Description:** Provides high-end creative design, back end web development, and online marketing to a growing customer base in both the commercial and government sectors.

New York

ARNOLD WORLDWIDE
110 Fifth Avenue, New York NY 10011. 212/463-1000. **Fax:** 212/463-1080. **Contact:** Luisa Liriano, Staffing Manager. **E-mail address:** lliriano@am.com. **World Wide Web address:** http://www.arnoldworldwide.com. **Description:** A full-service advertising agency. **Positions advertised include:** Interactive Copywriter; Channel Planner; Senior Interactive Art Director; Senior Information Architect; Senior Interactive Producer; Technical Support Analyst. **Other U.S. locations:** Boston MA; Los Angeles CA; Washington DC.

ASSOCIATED MERCHANDISING CORPORATION (AMC)
500 Seventh Avenue, New York NY 10018. 212/819-6600. **Fax:** 212/819-6701. **Contact:** Personnel. **World Wide Web address:** http://www.theamc.com. **Description:** Performs retail product development and international apparel sourcing services for retail clients operating 53 offices worldwide. Founded in 1916. **Positions advertised include:** Commercial Artist; Customer Service Representative; Product Manager. **Corporate headquarters location:** This location. **Other locations:** Worldwide. **Parent company:** Target Corporation (Minneapolis MN). **President/CEO:** Richard J. Kuzmich. **Number of employees:** 1,200.

BBDO WORLDWIDE INC.
1285 Avenue of the Americas, New York NY 10019. 212/459-5000. **Fax:** 212/459-6645. **Recorded jobline:** 212/459-5627. **Contact:** Human Resources Department. **E-mail address:** nyhrmanagerrecruiting@bbdo.com. **World Wide Web address:** http://www.bbdo.com. **Description:** Operates a worldwide network of advertising agencies in 300 offices in 45 countries with related businesses in public relations, direct marketing, sales promotion, graphic design, graphic arts, and printing. BBDO Worldwide operates 83 subsidiaries, affiliates, and associates in advertising and related operations. Since 1891. **Positions advertised include:** Assistant Media Planner; Assistant National TV Buyer; Corporate Computer Systems Manager; Media Supervisor; National TV Buyer; Media Planner; Assistant Account Executive; Budget Coordinator; Systems Engineer; Administrative Assistant; Accounting Clerk; Finance Manager; Control Coordinator; Print Estimator; Art Director. **Special programs:** Internships. **Corporate headquarters location:** This location. **Other U.S. locations:** Nationwide. **International locations:** Worldwide. **Subsidiaries include:** BBDO Detroit. **Parent company:** Omnicom Group Inc. (New York NY). **Chairman/CEO:** Allen Rosenshine. **Annual sales/revenues:** $1.6 billion. **Number of employees worldwide:** 16,600.

BURSON-MARSTELLER
230 Park Avenue South, New York NY 10003. 212/614-4141. **Fax:** 212/598-6999. **Contact:** Michele Chase, Human Resources Director. **E-mail address:** michele_chase@nyc.bm.com. **World Wide Web address:** http://www.bm.com. **Description:** A full-service public relations agency with 75 offices in 34 countries. Founded in 1953. **Positions advertised include:** Public Relations Specialist. **Special programs:** Internships. **Corporate headquarters location:** This location. **Other U.S. locations:** Los Angeles CA; Sacramento CA; San Diego CA; San Francisco CA; Washington DC; Miami FL; Chicago IL; Pittsburgh PA; Dallas TX. **Subsidiaries include:** Cohn & Wolfe, Public Relations. **Parent company:** WPP Group PLC (London, United Kingdom). **Founding Chairman:** Harold Burson. **Annual sales/revenues:** $175 million. **Number of employees at this location:** 340. **Number of employees worldwide:** 1,600.

CBS OUTDOOR
405 Lexington Avenue, 14th Floor, New York NY 10174. 212/297-6400. **Contact:** Human Resources. **World Wide Web address:** http://www.cbsoutdoor.com. **Description:** An advertising agency specializing in the design of billboards and posters. **Special programs:** Internships. **Other U.S. locations:** Nationwide. **Operations at this facility include:** Administration; Divisional Headquarters; Financial Offices; Marketing; Research and Development; Sales; Service.

CLARITAS INC.
53 Brown Road, Ithaca NY 14850. 607/257-5757. **Fax:** 607/266-0425. **Contact:** Human Resources. **World Wide Web address:** http://www.claritas.com. **Description:** Provides demographic data and target marketing information about the population, consumer behavior, consumer spending, households and businesses within any specific geographic market area in the United States. Claritas' target marketing research and market analysis services are aimed at reducing the cost of customer acquisition and growing customer value. Founded in 1971. **Positions advertised include:** Network Analyst. **Corporate headquarters location:** San Diego CA. **Other U.S. locations:** Arlington VA; Atlanta GA; Chicago IL; Los Angeles CA; New York NY; Wilton CT. **Parent company:** VNU is a demographic, market segmentation research information and media company that includes ACNielsen, Nielsen Media Research, Spectra Marketing Systems, and Scarborough Research.

DDB WORLDWIDE COMMUNICATIONS GROUP, INC.
437 Madison Avenue, New York NY 10022. 212/415-2000. **Fax:** 212/415-3414. **Contact:** James Best, Chief People Officer. **World Wide Web address:** http://www.ddb.com. **Description:** A full-service, international advertising agency operating 200 offices in 100 countries. **Positions advertised include:** Advertising Executive; Media Specialist. **Special programs:** Internships. **Corporate headquarters location:** This location. **Other U.S. locations:** Los Angeles CA; Chicago IL. **Parent company:** Omnicom Group, Inc. (also at this location). **Chairman:** Keith L. Reinhard. **Annual sales/revenues:** $1.2 billion. **Number of employees:** 11,900.

DOREMUS & COMPANY, INC.
200 Varick Street, 11th Floor, New York NY 10014. 212/366-3000. **Fax:** 212/366-3060. **Contact:** Kristin Mooney, Human Resources Director. **E-mail address:** careers@doremus.com. **World Wide Web address:** http://www.doremus.com. **Description:** An agency specializing in corporate and financial advertising. Founded in 1903. **NOTE:** Entry-level positions are offered. **Special programs:** Internships. **Corporate headquarters location:** This location. **Other U.S. locations:** San Francisco CA. **International locations:** London, England; Tokyo, Japan; Frankfurt, Germany; Hong Kong, China. **Parent company:** Omnicom Group Inc. (New York NY). **Annual sales/revenues:** $43.5 million. **Number of employees:** 190

FCB WORLDWIDE
100 West 33rd Street,, New York NY 10001. 212/885-3000. **Fax:** 212/885-2803. **Contact:** Director of

Personnel. **E-mail address:** careersny@fcb.com. **World Wide Web address:** http://www.fcb.com. **Description:** An international advertising agency. FCB/LKP offers additional services including direct marketing, design and production of sales promotion programs; market and product research; package design; and trademark and trade name development. The company operates offices throughout Europe, Asia, and Latin America. **Corporate headquarters location:** This location. **International locations:** Worldwide. **Parent company:** Foote, Cone & Belding Communications.

GOTHAM INC.
100 Fifth Avenue, New York NY 10011. 212/414-7000. **Contact:** Patti Ransom, Director Human Resources. **E-mail address:** jobs@gothaminc.com. **World Wide Web address:** http://www.gothaminc.com. **Description:** Specializes in creating start-up brands with an emphasis on fashion and beauty advertising. Founded in 1994. **CEO:** Stone Roberts.

GREY GLOBAL GROUP
777 Third Avenue, New York NY 10017. 212/546-2000. **Contact:** Human Resources: **E-mail address:** careers@grey.com. **World Wide Web address:** http://www.greyglobalgroup.com. **Description:** An international advertising agency operating in 83 countries.

HILL AND KNOWLTON INC.
909 Third Avenue, New York NY 10022. 212/885-0300. **Fax:** 212/885-0570. **Contact:** Human Resources Department. **World Wide Web address:** http://www.hillandknowlton.com. **Description:** One of the largest public relations/public affairs counseling firms in the world. **NOTE:** Human Resources phone: 212/885-0547. **Positions advertised include:** Senior Account Executive; Healthcare Pharmaceutical Account Representative; Bilingual Spanish/English Accountant; Controller. **Corporate headquarters location:** This location. **Other U.S. locations:** San Francisco CA; Washington DC. **International locations:** Worldwide. **Subsidiaries include:** The Wexler Group. **Parent company:** WPP Group plc (London, United Kingdom). **Chairman/CEO:** Paul Taaffe. **Annual sales/revenues:** $325 million. **Number of employees:** 1,117.

THE INTERPUBLIC GROUP OF COMPANIES, INC.
1114 Avenue of the Americas, New York NY 10036. 212/704-1200. **Fax:** 212/704-1201. **Contact:** Doris Weil, Director of Corporate Human Resources. **E-mail address:** hr@interpublic.com. **World Wide Web address:** http://www.interpublic.com. **Description:** An advertising agency doing business in 130 countries worldwide. The company plans, creates, and implements advertising campaigns in various media through either its own subsidiaries or contracts with local agencies. Other activities include publishing, market research, public relations, product development, and sales promotion. Interpublic's international business groups include McCann-Erickson WorldGroup and The Lowe Group. **Corporate headquarters location:** This location. **Subsidiaries/affiliates include:** Advanced Marketing Services; Deutsch, Inc.; DeVries Public Relations; Draft Worldwide; FutureBrand Worldwide; Hill Holliday; Jack Morton Worldwide Inc.; McCann Relationship Marketing Partners Worldwide; McCann-Erickson WorldGroup; Modem Media, Inc.; Mullen Advertising Inc.; NFO WorldGroup, Inc.; Octagon; Temerlin McClain; Weber Shandwick Worldwide. **Listed on:** New York Stock Exchange. **Stock exchange symbol:** IPG. **Chairman/President/CEO:** David A. Bell. **Annual sales/revenues:** $6.2 billion. **Number of employees:** 52,000.

THE KAPLAN THALER GROUP, LTD.
World Wide Plaza, 825 Eighth Avenue, 34th Floor, New York NY 10019-7498. 212/474-5000. **Fax:** 212/474-5702. **Contact:** Human Resources. **E-mail address:** kaplanthalergroup@kaplanthaler.com. **World Wide Web address:** http://www.kaplanthaler.com. **Description:** A national advertising agency. **Corporate headquarters location:** This location. **Other U.S. locations:** Nationwide. **International locations:** Worldwide. **Parent company:** Publicis (Paris, France). **President/CEO:** Linda Kaplan Thaler. **Annual sales/revenues:** $15 million. **Number of employees:** 48.

KATZ MEDIA GROUP, INC.
125 West 55th Street, 21st Floor, New York NY 10019-5366. 212/424-6000. **Fax:** 212/424-6110. **Contact:** Human Resources. **World Wide Web address:** http://www.katz-media.com. **Description:** An advertising agency with 21 regional offices nationwide. **Positions advertised include:** Sales Assistant; Supervisor/Sales Manager's Assistant; Research Analyst. **Corporate headquarters location:** This location. **Parent company:** Clear Channel Communications (San Antonio TX). **Subsidiaries include:** National Cable Communications; Christal Suburban Radio. **Listed on:** New York Stock Exchange. **Stock exchange symbol:** CCU. **CEO:** Stuart (Stu) O. Olds.

L&P MEDIA
255 River Street, Troy NY 12180. 518/880-0300. **Toll-free phone:** 800/201-5949. **Fax:** 518/880-0390. **Contact:** Human Resources. **E-mail address:** jobs@lpmedia.com. **World Wide Web address:** http://www.lpmedia.com. **Description:** A full-service marketing communications firm that offers marketing communications programs, brand building, advertising/promotion, public/media relations, multi-media environments, and fundraising campaigns. Founded in 1977. **Positions advertised include:** Web and Applications Programmer. **Corporate headquarters location:** This location. **Other U.S. locations:** Guilford CT.

LOWE
150 East 42nd Street, New York NY 10017. 212/605-8000. **Contact:** Human Resources. **E-mail address:** info@loweworldwide.com. **World Wide Web address:** http://www.loweworldwide.com. **Description:** An advertising agency.

LYONS LAVEY NICKEL SWIFT INC.
220 East 42nd Street, 3rd Floor, New York NY 10017. 212/771-3000. **Fax:** 212/771-3010. **Contact:** Human Resources Manager. **E-mail address:** jobs@hmcny.com. **World Wide Web address:** http://www.llns.com. **Description:** An advertising agency for pharmaceutical firms. Founded in 1972. **NOTE:** Entry-level positions are offered. **Positions advertised include:** Vice President Supervisor Aricept; Traffic Coordinator; Account Supervisor; Account Assistant; Media Coordinator; Medical Information Specialist; Medical Editor.

McCANN WORLDGROUP
622 Third Avenue, New York NY 10017. 646/865-6000. **Fax:** 646/487-9610. **Contact:** Human Resources. **World Wide Web address:** http://www.mccann.com. **Description:** An advertising agency with operations in 130 countries. **Corporate headquarters location:** This location. **Other U.S. locations:** Atlanta GA; Chicago IL; Louisville KY; Houston TX; Seattle WA. **International locations:** Worldwide. **Parent company:** The Interpublic Group of Companies, Inc.

MEDICUS NY
1675 Broadway, New York NY 10019-5809. 212/468-3100. **Fax:** 212/468-3187. **Contact:** Emilie Schaum, Director of Human Resources. **World Wide Web address:** http://www.medicusny.com. **Description:** Markets a wide range of pharmaceutical and consumer health products and services to health care professionals, patients, and consumers. Services include advertising and promotions, direct-to-consumer marketing, interactive media, medical education, public relations, publication planning, and sales training. Founded in 1972. **Special programs:** Internships. **Office hours:** Monday - Friday, 9:00 a.m. - 5:00 p.m. **Corporate headquarters location:** This location.

International locations: Worldwide. **Parent company:** Publicis. **Chairman/CEO:** Glenn DeSimone.

MICKELBERRY COMMUNICATIONS
405 Park Avenue, Suite 1003, New York NY 10022. 212/832-0303. **Contact:** Human Resources. **World Wide Web address:** http://www.mickelberry.com. **Description:** A holding company for three marketing companies and a commercial printing group. **Parent company:** Union Capital Corporation.

MINDSHARE
498 Seventh Avenue, New York NY 10018. 212/297-7000. **Fax:** 212/297-7001. **Contact:** Human Resources. **E-mail address:** global.hr@mindshareworld.com. **World Wide Web address:** http://www.mindshareworld.com. **Description:** An advertising and public relations agency. **Positions advertised include:** Account Manager; Account Planner; Creative Designer; Media Specialist. **Corporate headquarters location:** This location and London. **Other locations:** Worldwide. **Number of employees worldwide:** 5,300.

ERIC MOWER AND ASSOCIATES
500 Plum Street, Syracuse NY 13204. 315/466-1000. **Contact:** Human Resources. **E-mail address:** hrrecruiter@eric.mower.com. **World Wide Web address:** http://www.mower.com. **Description:** An advertising agency. **Other area locations:** Buffalo NY; Rochester NY. **Annual sales/revenues:** More than $100 million. **Number of employees at this location:** 150.

THE NPD GROUP, INC.
900 West Shore Road, Port Washington NY 11050. 516/625-0700. **Fax:** 516/625-4866. **Contact:** Human Resources Department. **E-mail address:** recruit99@npd.com. **World Wide Web address:** http://www.npd.com. **Description:** A market research firm offering a full line of custom and syndicated consumer research services including point-of-sale computerized audits, purchase panels, mail panels, telephone research, mathematical modeling, and consulting. Industries covered include consumer packaged goods, apparel, toys, electronics, automotive, sports, books, and food consumption. **Positions advertised include:** Account Manager; Analytic Director; Director of Retail Business Development; Director of Client Development; Manager of Financial Reporting/Analysis; Marketing Coordinator; Research Manager; Senior Account Manager; Technical Specialist; Vice President of Client Development. **Special programs:** Internships. **Corporate headquarters location:** This location. **Other area locations:** New York NY. **Other U.S. locations:** Chicago IL; Hyattsville MD; Greensboro NC; Cincinnati OH; Houston TX. **International locations:** Worldwide. **Number of employees nationwide:** 800.

NIELSEN MEDIA RESEARCH COMPANY
770 Broadway, New York NY 10003-9595. 646/654-8300. **Contact:** Josh Lax, Human Resources. **World Wide Web address:** http://www.nielsenmedia.com. **Description:** Nielsen Media Research measures television show audience sizes and provides this information to broadcast networks and advertising agencies. **NOTE:** Interested job seekers may apply online for specific positions or for general consideration. **Positions advertised include:** Staff Assistant; National Accounts Manager; Meeting and Event Manager; Media Field Interviewer; Executive Staff Assistant; Director of Marketing and Communications; Associate Analyst; Bilingual Technical Field Representative. **Corporate headquarters location:** This location. **Other U.S. locations:** Los Angeles CA; San Francisco CA; Dallas TX; Atlanta GA; Chicago IL; Dunedin FL. **Number of employees at this location:** 195. **Number of employees nationwide:** 3,500.

OGILVY & MATHER
309 West 49th Street, New York NY 10019. 212/237-4000. **Recorded jobline:** 212/237-5627. **Contact:** Human Resources. **World Wide Web address:** http://www.ogilvy.com. **Description:** An advertising agency. **Other U.S. locations:** Nationwide. **International locations:** Worldwide. **Parent company:** WPP Group plc.

PETRY MEDIA CORPORATION
dba BLAIR TELEVISION, INC.
3 East 54th Street, New York NY 10022. 212/230-5900. **Fax:** 212/230-5843. **Contact:** Human Resources Staffing. **World Wide Web address:** http://www.petrymedia.com. **Description:** Provides the media industry with national sales, marketing, and research services. The company's subsidiaries represent 250 TV stations and provides services to advertising agencies and spot TV advertisers. **Positions advertised include:** Sales Assistant; Research Analyst; Sales Associate; Account Executive. **Special programs:** Internships. **Corporate headquarters location:** This location. **Other U.S. locations:** Nationwide. **Subsidiaries include:** Blair Television, Incorporated; Petry Television Incorporated. **Operations at this facility include:** Administration; Research and Development; Sales. **Number of employees at this location:** 250. **Number of employees nationwide:** 500.

POSTERLOID CORPORATION
4862 36th Street, Long Island City NY 11101. 718/729-1050. **Contact:** Human Resources. **World Wide Web address:** http://www.polyvision.com. **Description:** Manufactures and markets indoor menu board display systems for the fast-food and convenience store industries and changeable magnetic display signage used primarily by banks to display interest rates and other information. These displays are custom manufactured for ceiling hanging or for window or counter displays. **Corporate headquarters location:** New York NY. **Parent company:** Alpine Group, Incorporated is active in the defense and commercial electronics and telecommunications wire and cable industries through subsidiaries, Alpine Polyvision, Incorporated and DNE Technologies, Incorporated, both of which operate out of CT, and Superior TeleTec Incorporated in Atlanta GA. **Listed on:** New York Stock Exchange. **Stock exchange symbol:** AGI. **President:** Robert Sudack. **Number of employees at this location:** 55.

PUBLISHERS CLEARING HOUSE
382 Channel Drive, Port Washington NY 11050. 516/883-5432. **Contact:** Human Resources. **World Wide Web address:** http://www.pch.com. **Description:** A direct mail marketing company. Publishers Clearing House is one of the largest sources of new magazine subscribers. The company also conducts continuing research to develop effective promotions for other products and services. **Corporate headquarters location:** This location. **Subsidiaries include:** Campus Subscriptions. **CEO:** Robin B. Smith. **Sales/revenue:** Approximately $400 million. **Number of employees nationwide:** 465.

RUDER-FINN, INC.
301 East 57th Street, New York NY 10022. 212/593-6400. **Fax:** 212/593-6397. **Contact:** Human Resources. **E-mail address:** careers@ruderfinn.com. **World Wide Web address:** http://www.ruderfinn.com. **Description:** Offers a wide range of services in the public relations field. **Special programs:** Executive Training Program. **Corporate headquarters location:** This location. **Other U.S. locations:** Los Angeles CA; San Francisco CA; Chicago IL; Washington DC. **International locations:** China; France; Israel; Singapore; United Kingdom.

SAATCHI & SAATCHI ADVERTISING
375 Hudson Street, New York NY 10014. 212/463-2000. **Contact:** Human Resources. **World Wide Web address:** http://www.saatchi-saatchi.com. **Description:** An advertising agency. **Company slogan:** Nothing is impossible. **Office hours:** Monday - Friday, 9:00 a.m. - 5:00 p.m. **Corporate headquarters location:** This

location. **Other U.S. locations:** Nationwide. **International locations:** Worldwide. **Number of employees at this location:** 500.

SAATCHI & SAATCHI ROWLAND
255 Woodcliff Drive, Suite 200, Fairport NY 14450-4219. 585/249-6100. **Contact:** Human Resources. **World Wide Web address:** http://www.saatchibiz.com. **Description:** A full-service, integrated advertising agency. **Corporate headquarters location:** New York NY. **Other area locations:** Rochester NY. **Other U.S. locations:** Wilmington DE. **International locations:** Switzerland; United Kingdom; China; France; Australia. **Parent company:** Saatchi & Saatchi plc. **President:** Christine Withers.

SUDLER & HENNESSEY INC.
230 Park Avenue South, New York NY 10003-1566. 212/614-4100. **Contact:** Roger Gilmore, Human Resources. **E-mail address:** roger_Gilmore@nyc.sudler.com. **World Wide Web address:** http://www.sudler.com. **Description:** An advertising agency. **NOTE:** Available positions can also be viewed at http://www.hotjobs.com. **Corporate headquarters location:** This location.

THE SUTHERLAND GROUP, LTD.
1160 Pittsford-Victor Road, Pittsford NY 14534. 585/586-5757. **Fax:** 585/784-2254. **Contact:** Manager of Employment Development. **World Wide Web address:** http://www.suth.com. **Description:** A marketing and technology services company that develops customer management programs for *Fortune* 500 companies in information technology, telecommunications, education, and legal industries. **Positions advertised include:** Consultant; Sales and Marketing Associate; Inside Sales Representative; Customer Service Representative; Help Desk Representative. **Corporate headquarters location:** Rochester NY. **Number of employees at this location:** 500.

TBWA/CHIAT/DAY
488 Madison Avenue, 7th Floor, New York NY 10022. 212/804-1000. **Fax:** 212/804-1200. **Contact:** Human Resources. **E-mail address:** resumes@tbwachiat.com. **World Wide Web address:** http://www.tbwachiat.com. **Description:** An advertising agency.

J. WALTER THOMPSON COMPANY
466 Lexington Avenue, New York NY 10017. 212/210-7000. **Contact:** Human Resources. **E-mail address:** nygetajob@jwt.com. **World Wide Web address:** http://www.jwt.com. **Description:** A full-service advertising agency. **Positions advertised include:** Administrative Assistant; Financial Analyst. **Corporate headquarters location:** This location. **Other U.S. locations:** Nationwide. **International locations:** Worldwide. **Parent company:** WPP Group. **Listed on:** NASDAQ. **Stock exchange symbol:** WPPGY.

JANE WESMAN PUBLIC RELATIONS, INC.
322 Eighth Avenue, Suite 1702, New York NY 10001. 212/620-4080. **Fax:** 212/620-0370. **Contact:** Human Resources. **E-mail address:** jane@wesmanpr.com. **World Wide Web address:** http://www.wesmanpr.com. **Description:** Provides book publicity services including press kits, author tours, radio and print publicity, and media training. **Corporate headquarters location:** This location.

YOUNG & RUBICAM, INC.
285 Madison Avenue, 9th Floor, New York NY 10017. 212/210-3000. **Fax:** 212/210-5007. **Contact:** Human Resources. **World Wide Web address:** http://www.yandr.com. **Description:** An international advertising agency. The company operates through three divisions: Young & Rubicam International; Marsteller Inc., a worldwide leader in business-to-business and consumer advertising; and Young & Rubicam USA, with 14 consumer advertising agencies operating through four regional groups, and five specialized advertising and marketing agencies. **Special programs:** Internships. **Corporate headquarters location:** This location. **Other U.S. locations:** Nationwide.

North Carolina

COX TARGET MEDIA (CTM)
6030 US Highway 301 North, Elm City NC 27822-9144. 252/236-4301. **Contact:** Human Resources Manager. **E-mail address:** elmcity_humanresources3@coxtarget.com. **World Wide Web address:** http://www.coxtarget.com. **Description:** A direct marketing company that uses the Valpak advertising envelope filled with coupons to reach more than 45 million households and businesses. **Positions advertised include:** Inserting Supervisor. **Corporate headquarters location:** Largo FL. **Other U.S. locations:** Los Angeles CA; Tampa FL; St. Petersburg FL; Boston MA; Minneapolis MN; Houston TX. **Parent company:** CTM is a subsidiary of Cox Newspapers, which is owned by Cox Enterprises.

HAWKEYE/FFWD
325 Arlington Avenue, Suite 700, Charlotte NC 28203. 704/344-7900. **Contact:** Human Resources. **E-mail address:** mtodd@hawkeyeffwd.com. **World Wide Web address:** http://www.ffwdgroup.com. **Description:** A marketing agency providing direct marketing, advertising, branding, online marketing, customer loyalty, and database marketing services. **Other U.S. locations:** New York NY; Denver CO; Chicago IL; Minneapolis MN; Dallas TX.

THE KING PARTNERSHIP
Trinity Way, 1210 Trinity Road, Raleigh NC 27607. 919/828-2990. **Fax:** 919/828-9889. **Contact:** Rich Styles, President. **World Wide Web address:** http://www.thekingpartnership.com. **Description:** A full-service advertising and public relations agency. The company offers creative advertising work, sports marketing, and media buying services. **Corporate headquarters location:** This location.

McKINNEY & SILVER
318 Blackwell Street, Durham NC 27701. 919/313-4239. **Fax:** 919/313-0805. **Contact:** Lea Daughtridge, Human Resources. **E-mail address:** ldautridge@mckinney-silver.com. **World Wide Web address:** http://www.mckinney-silver.com. **Description:** An advertising agency offering broadcast, media, and print production services. **Special programs:** Internships.

NAS RECRUITMENT COMMUNICATIONS
2920 Highwoods Boulevard, Suite 110, Raleigh NC 27604-1053. 919/872-6800. **Fax:** 919/872-3926. **Contact:** Regional Manager. **E-mail address:** nas.ra@nasrecruitment.com. **World Wide Web address:** http://www.hrads.com. **Description:** With offices in 36 major U.S. and Canadian cities, NAS Recruitment Communications is one of the largest and oldest, independent, full-service advertising agencies exclusively specializing in human resource communications, promotions, and advertising. The company offers consultations, campaign planning, ad placement, research, and creative production. **Corporate headquarters location:** Cleveland OH. **Other U.S. locations:** Nationwide. **International locations:** Toronto, Ontario, Canada. **Parent company:** McCann-Erickson WorldGroup.

SADDLE CREEK CORPORATION
3555 Shamrock Road, Harrisburg NC 28075. 704/454-6300. **Fax:** 704/454-6301. **Contact:** Maria Russell, Human Resources. **E-mail address:** mariar@saddlecrk.com. **World Wide Web address:** http://www.saddlecrk.com. **Description:** A direct mail advertising agency with a broad range of clients. Founded 1966. **Positions advertised include:** Mid-Senior Manager; Warehouse Manager; Forklift Driver; Tractor/Trailer Driver; Customer Service Coordinator. **Corporate headquarters location:** Lakeland FL. **Other U.S. locations:** Southern and Southeastern U.S.

Ohio

THE BERRY COMPANY
3170 Kettering Boulevard, Dayton OH 45439. 937/296-2121. **Fax:** 937/297-4542. **Contact:** Human Resources. **World Wide Web address:** http://www.lmberry.com. **Description:** This location is engaged in the sale and marketing of Yellow Pages advertising. The Berry Company also operates BerryDirect, a chain of centers providing teleservicing; Berry Network Inc., a Yellow Pages placement agency; and Berry Sales & Marketing Solutions, a worldwide chain of marketing consultants. **Corporate headquarters location:** This location. **Parent company:** BellSouth Corporation. **Operations at this facility include:** Administration; Divisional Headquarters; Regional Headquarters; Research and Development; Sales. **President/CEO:** Daniel J. Graham. **Number of employees at this location:** 750. **Number of employees nationwide:** 2,400.

CTRAC COMPUTER SERVICES
16855 Foltz Parkway, Strongsville OH 44149. 440/572-1000. **Fax:** 440/572-3330. **Contact:** Human Resources. **E-mail address:** ctrac@ctrac.com. **World Wide Web address:** http://www.ctrac.com. **Description:** A direct mail service bureau.

FAHLGREN
414 Walnut Street, Suite 515, Cincinnati OH 45202. 513/241-9200. **Contact:** Human Resources. **E-mail address:** jobs@fahlgren.com. **World Wide Web address:** http://www.fahlgren.com. **Description:** An advertising and marketing firm. Founded in 1962. **Other area locations:** Columbus OH.

KINETIC SOLUTIONS
18051 Jefferson Parkway Road, Suite 105, Middleberg Heights OH 44130. 440/243-8322. **Contact:** Human Resources. **E-mail address:** hr@usakinetic.com. **World Wide Web address:** http://www.usakinetic.com. **Description:** Provides targeted marketing/sales management and campaign support in the Columbus area. **Positions advertised include:** Account Executive. **Corporate Headquarters:** This location.

LIGGETT-STASHOWER, INC.
1228 Euclid Avenue, Suite 200, Cleveland OH 44115. 216/373-8231. **Toll-free phone:** 800/877-4573. **Fax:** 877/405-0549. **Contact:** William Niemi, Human Resources Department. **E-mail address:** bniemi@liggett.com. **World Wide Web address:** http://www.liggett.com. **Description:** An advertising agency. **Special programs:** Internships: **Internship information:** Candidates interested in the Internship Program should contact Ian Hopkins, Internship Coordinator. E-mail: ihopkins@liggett.com.

NATIONWIDE ADVERTISING SERVICE INC.
441 Vine Street, Suite 4510, Cincinnati OH 45202. 513/241-3121. **Fax:** 513/241-6643. **Contact:** Personnel. **World Wide Web address:** http://www.hrads.com. **Description:** A full-service advertising agency that specializes exclusively in human resource communications, promotions, and advertising. The company offers consultation, campaign planning, ad placement, research, and creative production. **Corporate headquarters location:** Cleveland OH. **Other area locations:** Columbus OH. **Other U.S. locations:** Nationwide.

WYSE ADVERTISING, INC.
25 Prospect Avenue West, Suite 1700, Cleveland OH 44115. 216/696-2424. **Contact:** Human Resources. **E-mail address:** info@wyseadv.com. **World Wide Web address:** http://www.wyseadv.com. **Description:** An advertising agency. Wyse Advertising, Inc. specializes in account service, broadcast production, information systems, media, print production, and strategic planning. **CEO:** Marc Wyse.

Oregon

ROCKEY HILL & KNOWLTON
One SW Columbia, Suite 650, Portland OR 97258. 503/248-9468. **Fax:** 503/274-7689. **Contact:** Human Resources. **World Wide Web address:** http://www.rockey-seattle.com **Description:** A full-service public relations agency. **Special programs:** Internships. **Corporate headquarters location:** Seattle WA.

WIEDEN AND KENNEDY
224 NW 13th Avenue, Portland OR 97209. 503/937-7530. **Fax:** 503/937-7209. **Contact:** Human Resources Manager. **E-mail address:** jobs@wk.com. **World Wide Web address:** http://www.wk.com. **Description:** An advertising firm involved in television, radio, magazines, billboards, and other media.

Pennsylvania

BURSON-MARSTELLER
One Gateway Center, 20th Floor, Pittsburgh PA 15222. 412/471-9600. **Contact:** Human Resources. **World Wide Web address:** http://www.bm.com. **Description:** A global public relations and public affairs firm. **Subsidiaries include:** Cohn & Wolfe, Public Relations.

DAVIS ADVERTISING INC.
One Bala Plaza, Suite 640, Bala Cynwyd PA 19004. 610/227-0400. **Toll-free phone:** 800/777-3284. **Fax:** 610/227-0397. **Contact:** Human Resources Manager. **E-mail address:** ejohnston@davisadv.com. **World Wide Web address:** http://www.davisadv.com. **Description:** An advertising company specializing in recruitment advertising. **Positions advertised include:** Copywriter.

R. H. DONNELLEY
19 Bert Collins Drive, 11 Keystone Industrial Park, Dunmore PA 18512. 570/348-6900. **Contact:** Personnel. **World Wide Web address:** http://www.rhdonnelley.com. **Description:** Engaged in selling advertising space in the Yellow Pages. Founded in 1886. **Corporate headquarters location:** Purchase NY. **Other U.S. locations:** Los Angeles CA; Miami FL; Chicago IL; New York NY. **Parent company:** Dun & Bradstreet Corporation. **Listed on:** New York Stock Exchange. **Stock exchange symbol:** RHD.

HARTE-HANKS, INC.
2050 Cabot Boulevard West, Langhorne PA 19047. 215/750-6600. **Contact:** Human Resources. **World Wide Web address:** http://www7.harte-hanks.com. **Description:** Provides direct marketing services for various companies and publishes a weekly shopping guide. **Positions advertised include:** Account Coordinator; Account Executive; Account Manager; Administrative Assistant; Business Systems Manager; Database Programmer; Healthcare Copywriter; Print Media Coordinator. **Corporate headquarters location:** San Antonio TX.

ICT GROUP, INC.
100 Brandywine Boulevard, Newtown PA 18940. 215/478-2011. **Toll-free phone:** 800/799-6880. **Contact:** Human Resources Department. **World Wide Web address:** http://www.ictgroup.com. **Description:** A direct marketing agency engaged in telemarketing, customer service, and market research. The company serves the energy, financial services, health care, insurance, media, and telecommunications industries. Founded in 1983. **Positions advertised include:** Sr. Finance Manager; Financial Analyst; Call Center Manager; Paralegal; Director, Client Services. **Corporate headquarters location:** This location. **Listed on:** NASDAQ. **Stock exchange symbol:** ICTG. **Number of employees at this location:** 270. **Number of employees nationwide:** 2,100.

INTER-MEDIA MARKETING SOLUTIONS
204 Carter Drive, West Chester PA 19382. 610/429-1822. **Toll-free phone:** 800/835-3466. **Fax:** 610/429-5137. **Contact:** R. Dougherty, Human Resources. **E-mail address:** jobs@imminc.com. **World Wide Web address:** http://www.intermediamarketing.com. **Description:** A direct marketing and research firm focusing on e-commerce, sales, and customer service management solutions. Founded in 1983. **Positions**

advertised include: Management Trainee; Inbound Customer Service Representative; Outbound Sales Representative.

KETCHUM
6 PPG Place, Pittsburgh PA 15222. 412/456-3500. **Contact:** Human Resources Relationship Manager. **E-mail address:** pit.resume@ketchum.com. **World Wide Web address:** http://www.ketchum.com. **Description:** A public relations and advertising agency that specializes in directory advertising. **Positions advertised include:** Intern, Brand Marketing; Account Coordinator; Account Executive. **Other U.S. locations:** Nationwide. **International locations:** Worldwide.

AL PAUL LEFTON COMPANY, INC.
100 Independence Mall West, Philadelphia PA 19106. 215/923-9600. **Fax:** 215/351-4298. **Contact:** Human Resources. **World Wide Web address:** http://www.lefton.com. **Description:** A full-service advertising and public relations firm. Founded in 1928. **Corporate headquarters location:** This location.

LEVLANE ADVERTISING/PR/INTERACTIVE
The Wanamaker Building, 100 Penn Square East, Philadelphia PA 19107. 215/825-9600. **Fax:** 215/825-9601. **Contact:** Human Resources. **World Wide Web address:** http://www.levlane.com. **Description:** An advertising agency and public relations firm. Founded in 1984. **NOTE:** Entry-level positions are offered. **Special programs:** Internships; Apprenticeships. **Office hours:** Monday - Friday, 9:00 a.m. - 5:30 p.m. **Corporate headquarters location:** This location. **Other U.S. locations:** Boynton Beach FL. **Annual sales/revenues:** $21 - $50 million. **Number of employees at this location:** 40.

NATIONAL FULFILLMENT SERVICES
100 Pine Avenue, Building 4, Holmes PA 19043. 610/532-4700. **Toll-free phone:** 800/637-1306. **Fax:** 610/586-3232. **Contact:** Human Resources. **World Wide Web address:** http://www.nfsrv.com. **Description:** Provides direct marketing services. **Positions advertised include:** Bilingual Spanish/English Customer Service Rep. **Corporate headquarters location:** This location. **Operations at this facility include:** Administration; Sales; Service. Listed on: Privately held. **Number of employees at this location:** 110.

NORTH AMERICAN COMMUNICATIONS
338 3rd Avenue, P.O. Box 39, Duncansville PA 16635. 814/696-3553. **Fax:** 814/696-2535. **Contact:** Ms. Tera Herman, Human Resources. **E-mail address:** HR@nacmail.com. **World Wide Web address:** http://www.nacmail.com. **Description:** A vertically integrated direct mail company. North American Communications performs all phases of production, from printing to mailing. Clients include *Fortune* 500 companies, primarily financial institutions. **Special programs:** Internships. **Internship information:** Internships are offered year-round. Positions are available in engineering, customer service, and accounting, and some positions are paid. Contact Human Resources for more information. **Other U.S. locations:** San Diego CA. **Operations at this facility include:** Administration; Manufacturing; Research and Development. **Annual sales/revenues:** $51 - $100 million. **Number of employees at this location:** 555. **Number of employees nationwide:** 800.

PARAGRAPH
417 North Eighth Street, Suite 300, Philadelphia PA 19123. 215/629-3550. Fax: 215/629-2897. **Contact:** Human Resources. **E-mail address:** info@paragraphinc.com. **Description:** An agency that helps organizations develop their brands. **Positions advertised include:** Sr. Copywriter; Web Developer; Jr. Graphic Designer.

TEN UNITED
420 Fort Duquesne Boulevard, One Gateway Center, Suite 1900, Pittsburgh PA 15222. 412/471-5300. **Fax:** 412/471-3308. **Contact:** Human Resources. **E-mail address:** pghjobs@tenunited.com. **World Wide Web address:** http://www.tenunited.com. **Description:** An advertising and public relations agency.

TIERNEY COMMUNICATIONS
200 South Broad Street, Philadelphia PA 19102. 215/732-4100. **Contact:** Personnel. **World Wide Web address:** http://www.tierneyagency.com. **Description:** A full-service advertising and public relations firm. **Special programs:** Internships. **Other U.S. locations:** Harrisburg PA; Cherry Hill NJ.

TRANSCONTINENTAL DIRECT U.S.A. INC.
75 Hawk Road, Warminster PA 18974. 215/672-6900. **Fax:** 215/957-4366. **Contact:** Human Resources. **E-mail address:** info@transcontinentaldirect.com. **World Wide Web address:** http://www.transcontinentaldirect.com. **Description:** A direct mail marketing company. Founded in 1972. **NOTE:** Search and apply for positions online. **Positions advertised include:** Human Resources Benefit Specialist; Machine Operator. **Other U.S. locations:** Downey CA; Fort Worth TX; Bohemia NY. **Number of employees nationwide:** 1,500.

VERTIS
181 Rittenhouse Circle, Bristol PA 19007. 215/785-0101. **Contact:** Human Resources. **World Wide Web address:** http://www.vertisinc.com. **Description:** Develops a variety of direct marketing services including inline printing and finishing, promotional printing, and personalization technologies.

Rhode Island

BLUESTREAK
155 South Main Street, Suite 100, Providence RI 02903. 401/341-3300. **Fax:** 401/849-3411. **Contact:** Neil Johnson, Human Resources. **E-mail address:** careeers@bluestreak.com. **World Wide Web address:** http://www.bluestreak.com. **Description:** An online direct marketing firm. **NOTE:** See website for current job openings and application instructions. **Positions advertised include:** Account Executive; Web Applications Developer. **Other U.S. locations:** Dallas TX. **International locations:** United Kingdom.

MERCURY PRINT & MAIL
P.O. Box 6447, Providence RI 02940. 401/724-7600. **Fax:** 401/724-9920. **Physical address:** 1110 Central Avenue, Pawtucket RI 02861. **Contact:** Sandra Gauthier, Human Resources. **E-mail address:** hr@mpmri.com. **World Wide Web address:** http://www.mpmri.com. **Description:** Provides printing and direct mail advertising services. Founded in 1953. **NOTE:** Send resumes by mail, fax or e-mail.

South Carolina

ANCHOR SIGN
P.O. Box 6009, Charleston SC 29405. 843/576-3214. **Toll-free phone:** 800/213-3331. **Fax:** 843/747-5807. **Contact:** Darrell Edwards, Human Resources. **E-mail address:** careers@anchorsign.com. **World Wide Web address:** http://www.anchorsign.com. **Description:** Designs, manufactures, and installs electrical signs for regional and national accounts. **Positions advertised include:** Accounts Payable Clerk. **Number of employees nationwide:** 140.

MAGNUM PUBLICATIONS LLC
P.O. Box 3518, West Columbia SC 29171. 803/739-6900. **Toll-free number:** 800/951-3977. **Fax:** 803/739-6901. **Contact:** Office Manager. **E-mail address:** hrdept@magnumnational.com. **World Wide Web address:** http://www.magnumnational.com. **Description:** A publishing and public relations firm serving over 400 cities offering several publications for the real estate industry and providing advertising through three publications for realtors which welcome new residents to the area. **Corporate headquarters location:** This location. **Other area locations:** Camden SC; Cayce SC.

South Dakota

MEDIA ONE ADVERTISING/MARKETING
3918 South Western Avenue, Sioux Falls SD 57105. 605/339-0000. **Contact:** Human Resources. **E-mail**

address: info@m-1.com. **World Wide Web address:** http://www.m-1.com. **Description:** A full-service advertising and marketing agency hat provides integrated marketing resources and in-house production services to national, regional and local clients. The firm helps clients draft long-range marketing plans by offering full in-house production services, including airbrushing, photography, graphic design, and film/video production. Areas of expertise include financial services, manufacturing, tourism/gaming, institutional and retail food, professional services and public relations.

Tennessee

THE ADVERTISING CHECKING BUREAU INC.
1610 Century Center Parkway, Suite 104, Memphis TN 38134. 901/346-9941. **Fax:** 901/345-8812. **Contact:** Human Resources. **World Wide Web address:** http://www.acbcoop.com. **Description:** An advertising agency that provides co-op and trade promotion program management, advertising tracking services and other marketing services.

ADVO INC.
4481 Distriplex Cove, Memphis TN 38118. 901/794-0804. **Fax:** 901/794-0889. **Contact:** Human Resources. **E-mail address:** resumeme@advo.com. **World Wide Web address:** http://www.advo.com. **Description:** A direct mail advertising firm. **NOTE:** Search and apply for positions online. **Corporate headquarters location:** Windsor CT. **Number of employees nationwide:** 3,600.

BUNTIN GROUP
1001 Hawkins Street, Nashville TN 37203. 615/244-5720. **Contact:** Debbie Goodwyn, Human Resources. **E-mail address:** dgoodwyn@buntingroup.com. **World Wide Web address:** http://www.buntingroup.com. **Description:** An advertising agency. Founded in 1972. **Number of employees at this location:** 80.

DYE, VAN MOL, & LAWRENCE
209 Seventh Avenue North, Nashville TN 37219. 615/244-1818. **Fax:** 615/780-3302. **Contact:** Ronald Roberts, Personnel. **E-mail address:** ronald.roberts@dvl.com. **World Wide Web address:** http://www.dvl.com. **Description:** An advertising and public relations firm. Founded in 1980. **Number of employees at this location:** 40.

J. WALTER THOMPSON COMPANY
5050 Poplar Avenue, Suite 1000, Memphis TN 38157. 901/682-9656. **Contact:** Human Resources. **World Wide Web address:** http://www.jwt.com. **Description:** An advertising and public relations firm. **NOTE:** Search and apply for positions or submit resume online. **Other U.S. locations:** Nationwide. **International locations:** Worldwide. **Parent company:** WPP.

Texas

ACKERMAN McQUEEN, INC.
600 Commerce Tower, 545 East John Carpenter Freeway, Suite 600, Dallas TX 75062. 972/444-9000. **Fax:** 972/869-4363. **Contact:** Human Resources. **World Wide Web address:** http://www.am.com. **Description:** A full-service advertising agency. Founded in 1939. **NOTE:** Entry-level positions are offered. **Special programs:** Internships. **Internship information:** Unpaid internships are offered each fall, spring, and summer semester for college credit. **Corporate headquarters location:** Oklahoma City OK. **Other U.S. locations:** Colorado Springs CO; Tulsa OK; San Francisco CA. **International locations:** London England. **Subsidiaries include:** Mercury Group; OK Events. **CEO:** Angus McQueen.

ADVO INC.
8950 Railwood Drive, Houston TX 77078. 713/636-7200. **Fax:** 713/633-0839. **Contact:** Human Resources. **World Wide Web address:** http://www.advo.com. **Description:** A direct mail advertising agency. Specialties include Missing Child cards and the ShopWise program. **NOTE:** Please visit website to search for jobs and apply online. **Corporate headquarters location:** Windsor CT. **Other area locations:** El Paso TX; Dallas TX; San Antonio TX. **Other U.S. locations:** Nationwide. **Listed on:** New York Stock Exchange. **Stock exchange symbol:** AD. **Number of employees nationwide:** 3,600.

AEGIS COMMUNICATIONS GROUP
8001 Bent Branch Drive, Suite 150, Irving TX 75063. 972/830-1800. **Toll-free phone:** 800/332-0266. **Fax:** 972/836-1804. **Contact:** Human Resources Department. **E-mail address:** info@aegiscomgroup.com. **World Wide Web address:** http://www.aegiscomgroup.com. **Description:** A teleservices provider that offers integrated marketing services to large corporations. Services include customer acquisition, customer care, and marketing research. **NOTE:** Please visit website to view job listings. **Positions advertised include:** Vice President – Business Development; Executive Assistant to CEO; Payroll Administrator; Senior IT Support Technician. **Corporate headquarters location:** This location. **Other U.S. locations:** GA; FL; IN; NC; WV; AZ; CA; MO. **Listed on:** NASDAQ. **Stock exchange symbol:** AGIS.

BRSG (BLACK ROGERS SULLIVAN GOODNIGHT)
701 Brazos, Suite, 1010 Austin TX 78701. 512/320-8511. **Fax:** 512/320-8990. **Fax:** 713/783-1592. **World Wide Web address:** http://www.brsg.com. **Contact:** Employment. **Description:** A marketing communications firm. **Special programs:** Internships. **Office hours:** Monday - Friday, 8:00 a.m. - 5:00 p.m. **Corporate headquarters location:** This location. **Operations at this facility include:** Administration; Research and Development.

BROUILLARD COMMUNICATIONS INC
1845 Woodhall Rogers Freeway, Suite 1100, Dallas TX 75201. 214/855-5155. **Fax:** 214/871-7028. **Contact:** Human Resources. **World Wide Web address:** http://www.brouillard.com. **Description:** An advertising agency. **Corporate headquarters location:** New York NY.. **Other area locations:** Dallas TX. **Other U.S. locations:** Chicago IL; San Francisco CA. **International locations:** London England. **Operations at this facility include:** Administration; Divisional Headquarters. **President/CEO:** Bill Lyddan.

BURK ADVERTISING & MARKETING, INC.
2906 McKinney Avenue, Suite 100, Dallas TX 75204. 214/953-0494. **Fax:** 214/953-6236. **Contact:** Human Resources. **World Wide Web address:** http://www.wambam.com. **Description:** An advertising and marketing agency offering a variety of print and multimedia services.

COX MEDIA
401 West Cantu Road, Suite D, Del Rio TX 78840. 830/774-5538. **Fax:** 830/774-5438. **Contact:** Human Resources. **World Wide Web address:** http://www.coxmedia.com. **Description:** Provides advertising services for businesses through major cable networks such as CNN. **NOTE:** Please visit website to search for jobs and apply online. **Corporate headquarters location:** Macon GA. **Other area locations:** Statewide. **Other U.S. locations:** Nationwide. **Parent company:** Cox Communications. **Number of employees nationwide:** 1,400.

DDB NEEDHAM
1999 Bryan Street, Suite 2300, Dallas TX 75201. 214/259-4200. **Contact:** Human Resources Department. **World Wide Web address:** http://www.ddbdallas.com. **Description:** A full-service, international advertising agency. **NOTE:** Job listings can be found on ddbjobs.com. **Internship information:** E-mail resume to Staci Williams at hr@omsdal.com. **Corporate headquarters location:** New York NY.

DECISION ANALYST, INC.
604 Avenue H East, Arlington TX 76011. 817/640-6166. **Toll-free number:** 800/262-5974. **Fax:** 817/640-

6567. **Contact:** Human Resources. **E-mail address:** jobs@decisionanalyst.com. **World Wide Web address:** http://www.decisionanalyst.com. **Description:** A market research and consulting firm offering product testing, tracking research, and Internet surveys. **Corporate headquarters location:** This location.

THE DOZIER COMPANY
2547 Farrington, Dallas TX 75207. 214/744-2800. **Fax:** 214/744-1240. **Contact:** Human Resources. **World Wide Web address:** http://www.thedoziercompany.com. **Description:** A full-service advertising and public relations agency. Founded in 1987. **Special programs:** Internships. **Corporate headquarters location:** This location.

FOGARTYKLEINMONROE
7155 Old Katy Road, Suite 100, Houston TX 77024. 713/862-5100. **Contact:** Debbie Ray-Walder, Human Resources Director. **E-mail address:** drwalder@fkmagency.com. **World Wide Web address:** http://www.fkmagency.com. **Description:** A full-service advertising and public relations agency.

GSD&M ADVERTISING
828 West Sixth Street, Austin TX 78703. 512/242-4736. **Contact:** Marci Rogers, Recruiting Coordinator; at 512/242-5932. **E-mail address:** marci_rogers@gsdm.com. **World Wide Web address:** http://www.gsdm.com. **Description:** An advertising agency. **Positions advertised include:** Media Supervisor; Broadcast Supervisor; Media Research Analyst; Administrative Assistant. **Corporate headquarters location:** This location.

HARTE-HANKS, INC.
P.O. Box 269, San Antonio TX 78216. 210/829-9000. **Physical address:** 200 Concord Plaza Drive, Suite 800, San Antonio TX 78216. **Contact:** Human Resources. **World Wide Web address:** http://www.harte-hanks.com. **Description:** Provides direct marketing services for various companies and publishes a weekly shopping guide. **NOTE:** Interested jobseekers should apply online at the corporate website. **Corporate headquarters location:** This location. **Other U.S. locations:** Nationwide.

BERNARD HODES ADVERTISING
7502 Greenville Avenue, Suite 630, Dallas TX 75231. 214/361-9986. **Contact:** Jill Hawkins, Branch Manager. **World Wide Web address:** http://www.hodes.com. **Description:** An advertising agency specializing in recruitment and employee communications. **Corporate headquarters location:** New York NY. **Other U.S. locations:** Nationwide.

LEAD DOGS
2433 Rutland Drive, Suite 210, Austin TX 78758. 512/990-2000. **Toll-free phone:** 800/336-2616. **Fax:** 512/990-8999. **Contact:** Tina Tripoli, Human Resources Director, ext. 106. **E-mail address:** Ttripoli@leaddogs.com. **World Wide Web address:** http://www.leaddogs.com. **Description:** Provides direct marketing services for high-tech companies including event management and database development. **Positions advertised include:** Marketing Pre-Sales Representative; Account Manager; Call Center Manager.

THE M/A/R/C GROUP
160 Northwestridge Circle, Irving TX 75038. 972/506-3901. **Fax:** 972/506-3612. **Contact:** Human Resources. **World Wide Web address:** http://www.marcgroup.com. **Description:** The M/A/R/C Group is a holding company for M/A/R/C Research and Targetbase. M/A/R/C Research (also at this location) specializes in providing strategic customer research for marketing purposes. Targetbase (also at this location) is a customer relationship management firm. **Positions advertised include:** Telephone Interviewer; Senior Strategic Business Analyst. **Other U.S. locations:** Los Angeles CA; Greensboro NC.

NATIONWIDE ADVERTISING SERVICE INC.
7500 San Felipe, Suite 340, Houston TX 77063. 713/780-0770. **Contact:** Regional Manager. **World Wide Web address:** http://www.hrads.com. **Description:** One of the largest independent, full-service advertising agencies specializing exclusively in human resource communications and promotions. The company offers consultations, campaign planning, ad placement, research, and creative production. **Corporate headquarters location:** Cleveland OH. **Other area locations:** Dallas TX: San Antonio TX. **Other U.S. locations:** Nationwide. **International locations:** Canada. **Parent company:** McCann-Erickson World Group.

PRINT MAILERS
707 West Road, Houston TX 77038. 832/201-2000. **Fax:** 832/201-2001. **Contact:** Human Resources. **World Wide Web address:** http://www.pminet.com. **Description:** Provides turnkey direct marketing, printing, and mailing services.

PUBLICIS USA
14185 North Dallas Parkway, Dallas TX 75254. 972/628-7500. **Contact:** Carey Myers, Human Resources. **E-mail address:** resume@publicis-usa.com. **World Wide Web address:** http://www.publicis-usa.com. **Description:** An advertising agency with four locations nationwide. Founded in 1952. **Parent company:** Publicis Group (Paris.)

THE RICHARDS GROUP
8750 North Central Expressway, Suite 1200, Dallas TX 75231-6437. 214/891-5700. **Contact:** Human Resources. **World Wide Web address:** http://www.richards.com. **Description:** A full-service advertising agency offering public relations, media, direct marketing, promotional marketing, naming, graphic design, and interactive communications services. **Listed on:** Privately held.

TL MARKETING INC.
13808 Research Boulevard, Suite 135, Austin TX 78750. 512/371-7272. **Fax:** 512/371-0727. **Contact:** Human Resources. **Description:** A marketing firm representing manufacturers within the electrical industry. **Corporate headquarters location:** Dallas TX.

TMP WORLDWIDE ADVERTISING AND COMMUNICATIONS
1021 Main Street, Suite 1050, Houston TX 77002. 713/843-8600. **Fax:** 832/366-1185. **Contact:** Carolyn Gaither, Human Resources. **World Wide Web address:** http://www.tmp.com. **Description:** A human resources outsourcing firm. Operations include Monster.com, one of the largest and most successful recruiting Websites; recruitment advertising; executive search and selection; and yellow page advertising. **NOTE:** Apply online at this company's website. **Positions advertised include:** Outside Sales Account Executive. **Corporate headquarters location:** New York NY.

J. WALTER THOMPSON
350 North Saint Paul Street, Suite 2410, Dallas TX 75201. 214/468-4360. **Contact:** Human Resources. **World Wide Web address:** http://www.jwtworld.com. **Description:** One of the largest advertising agencies in the nation. **NOTE:** Apply online at this company's website. **Special programs:** Marketing Fellowship. **Positions advertised include:** Director of Analytics. **Corporate headquarters location:** New York NY. **Other U.S. locations**: Nationwide. **Other area locations:** Worldwide. **Parent company:** WWP. **Number of employees worldwide:** 8,500.

USFI
12100 Ford Road, Suite 100, Dallas TX 75234. 972/444-8381. **Fax:** 972/402-8139. **World Wide Web address:** http://www.usfi.com. **Description:** Provides marketing communications solutions. **NOTE:** Please apply for positions online. **Positions advertised**

include: Account Manager; Graphic Designer; Staff Accountant; Software Engineer.

WITHERSPOON ADVERTISING & PUBLIC RELATIONS
1000 West Weatherford Street, Fort Worth TX 76102. 817/335-1373. **Contact:** Human Resources. **E-mail address:** hr@witherspoon.com. **World Wide Web address:** http://www.witherspoon.com. **Description:** A national advertising and public relations agency. **Corporate headquarters location:** This location. **Operations at this facility include:** Service.

Utah
BONNEVILLE COMMUNICATIONS
5 Triad Center, Suite 700, Salt Lake City UT 84180. 801/237-2600. **Toll-free phone:** 888/8-BONCOM. **Fax:** 801/237-2614. **Contact:** Human Resources. **E-mail address:** bonneville@bonneville.com. **World Wide Web address:** http://www.bonneville.com. **Description:** An advertising agency specializing in public service announcements and direct response. **Corporate headquarters location:** This location.

CONNECT PUBLIC RELATIONS
80 East 100 North, Provo UT 84606. 801/373-7888. **Fax:** 801/373-8680. **Contact:** Janeen Bullock, Human Resources. **E-mail address:** janeenb@connectpr.com. **World Wide Web address:** http://www.connectpr.com. **Description:** A public relations and marketing firm with clients in the computer networking field. Founded in 1990. **Special programs:** Internships. **NOTE:** See website for current job openings. **Corporate headquarters location:** This location. **Other U.S. locations:** San Francisco CA; Washington DC. **Listed on:** Privately held.

CONVERGYS
1400 West 4400 South, Ogden UT 84405. 801/629-6423. **Toll-free phone:** 800/543-6423. **Contact:** Human Resources. **World Wide Web address:** http://www.convergys.com. **Description:** Provides outsourced customer care, human resource, and billing services worldwide. The company operates in three segments: Customer Care; Employee Care; and the Information Management Group. Founded in 1976. **NOTE:** See website for current job openings and to apply online. **Other area locations:** Statewide. **Other U.S. locations:** Nationwide. **International locations:** Worldwide.

MYFAMILY.COM, INC.
360 West 4800 North, Provo UT 84604. 801/705-7000. **Fax:** 801/705-7001. **Contact:** Human Resources. **E-mail address:** jobs@myriad.com. **World Wide Web address:** http://www.myriad.com. **Description:** Operates a network of websites designed for subscribers to hold family discussions, create online family photo albums, maintain a calendar of family events, share family history information, and buy gifts for family members. Its sites include MyFamily.com, Ancestry.com, RootsWeb.com, Genealogy.com, Ancestry.co.uk, and Ancestry.ca. The company also publishes *Ancestry Magazine*, *Genealogical Computing Magazine*, Ancestry Family Tree software, a variety of book titles, and databases on CD-ROM. **Positions advertised include:** Accounting Manager; International Marketing Manager – Canada; International Director of Product Marketing. **Corporate headquarters location:** This location. **CEO:** Dave Moon.

UTAH WOOL MARKETING ASSOCIATION
55 South Iron Street, Suite 2 – Building 657, Tooele UT 84074. 435/843-4284. **Fax:** 435/843-4286. **Contact:** Will Griggs, Manager. **Description:** Provides a variety of marketing and related business and financial services to ranchers, processors, and retailers involved in the production and sale of wool and related products. **Corporate headquarters location:** This location.

YOUNG ELECTRIC SIGN COMPANY
2401 Foothill Drive, Salt Lake City UT 84109. 801/464-4600. **Fax:** 801/483-0998. **Contact:** Human Resources Director. **E-mail address:** jobs@yesco.com. **World Wide Web address:** http://www.yesco.com. **Description:** Manufactures and sells outdoor signs and displays. **NOTE:** See website for current job openings. Submit resume by e-mail; clearly indicate the job reference number or job title in the subject line of your e-mail. **Positions advertised include:** Sign Service Technician; Account Executive; Electronics Design Engineer; Sign Service Apprentice; Junior Software Developer; Service Manager; Branch Manager; **Corporate headquarters location:** This location. **Other area locations:** Ogden UT; Orem UT; St. George UT. **Other U.S. locations:** MI; CA; AZ; NV; CO; ID; OR.

Vermont
THE COMMUNICATORS GROUP
1220 Oak Street, Brattleboro VT 05301. 802/257-4321. **Contact:** Human Resources. **World Wide Web address:** http://www.communicatorsgroup.com. **Description:** An advertising, public relations and communications agency operating in print, radio, and television. **Number of employees:** 14.

Virginia
THE MARTIN AGENCY
One Shockoe Plaza, Richmond VA 23219-4132. 804/698-8000. **Fax:** 804/698-8001. **Contact:** Kay Lawson, Human Resources. **E-mail address:** info_hr@martinagency.com. **World Wide Web address:** http://www.martinagency.com. **Description:** An advertising agency. **Other U.S. locations:** New York NY.

MARTIN FOCUS GROUP
1199 North Fairfax Street, Suite 150, Alexandria VA 22314. 703/519-5800. **Fax:** 703/519-0704. **Contact:** Human Resources. **World Wide Web address:** http://www.martinfocus.com. **Description:** Designs and conduct focus groups throughout the state. **Other area locations:** Richmond VA; Roanoke VA.

TMP WORLDWIDE INC.
8280 Greensboro Drive, Suite 900, McLean VA 22102. 703/269-0100. **Fax:** 703/269-0115. **Contact:** Human Resources. **World Wide Web address:** http://www.tmp.com. **Description:** An advertising and public relations firm specializing in corporate and marketing communications. **Positions advertised include:** Marketing and Communications Account Executive; Contract Administrator; Senior Account Executive. **Parent company:** Monster Worldwide. **Listed on:** NASDAQ. **Stock exchange symbol:** TMPW.

WILLIAMS WHITTLE ASSOCIATES, INC.
711 Princess Street, Alexandria VA 22314. 703/836-9222. **Contact:** Human Resources. **World Wide Web address:** http://www.williamswhittle.com. **Description:** An advertising and public relations firm in categories such as restaurants, health care, telecommunications, real estate, automotive, and women's personal products.

Washington
ACKERLEY PARTNERS
1301 Fifth Avenue, Suite 3525, Seattle WA 98101. 206/624-2888. **Contact:** Personnel Department. **World Wide Web address:** http://www.ackerleypartners.com. **Description:** Operates a group of media and entertainment companies. The Ackerley Group's national operations include an outdoor advertising agency, 14 television stations, three radio stations, and a sports/entertainment division that operates the NBA's Seattle SuperSonics and the WNBA's Seattle Storm. **Corporate headquarters location:** This location. **Listed on:** New York Stock Exchange. **Stock exchange symbol:** AK.

ADVO, INC.
4103 C Street NE, Auburn WA 98002. 253/850-3092. **Contact:** Human Resources. **World Wide Web address:** http://www.advo.com. **Description:** One of the nation's largest full-service direct mail marketing companies. **Company slogan:** The targeter of choice.

Corporate headquarters location: Windsor CT. **Listed on:** New York Stock Exchange. **Stock exchange symbol:** AD.

BURKE GIBSON INC.
702 Third Street SW, Auburn WA 98001-5278. 253/735-4444. **Fax:** 253/833-2916. **Contact:** Human Resources. **World Wide Web address:** http://www.burkegibsoninc.com. **Description:** Designs and manufactures point-of-purchase advertising displays for retail and warehouse sales. **Corporate headquarters location:** This location.

DDB SEATTLE
1000 2nd Avenue, Suite 1000, Seattle WA 98104. 206/442-9900. **Contact:** Human Resources. **World Wide Web address:** http://www.ddbseattle.com. **Description:** An advertising agency. **Positions advertised include:** Online Coordinator. **Parent company:** DDB Needham Worldwide, Inc.

JWT SPECIALIZED COMMUNICATIONS
1191 2nd Avenue, Seattle WA 98101. 206/623-2620. **Contact:** Human Resources. **World Wide Web address:** http://www.jwtworks.com. **Description:** A national advertising agency specializing in personnel recruitment advertising, human resources management systems, and employee communications. **Corporate headquarters location:** Los Angeles CA. **Parent company:** WPP Group.

PUBLICIS
424 Second Avenue West, Seattle WA 98119. 206/285-2222. **Contact:** Personnel Department. **E-mail address:** resume@publicis-usa.com. **World Wide Web address:** http://www.publicisinthewest.com. **Description:** An advertising and public relations agency specializing in the areas of technology, health care, retail, and consumer goods. **Corporate headquarters location:** New York NY.

WHITE RUNKLE ASSOCIATES
518 West Riverside, Spokane WA 99201. 509/747-6767. **Fax:** 509/747-9211. **Contact:** Human Resources. **World Wide Web address:** http://www.whiterunkle.com. **Description:** A full-service advertising, marketing, and public relations firm serving clients throughout the Northwest. Founded in 1980. **Special programs:** Internships. **Corporate headquarters location:** This location. **Number of employees at this location:** 20.

WILLIAMS & HELDE
711 Sixth Avenue North, Suite 200, Seattle WA 98109. 206/285-1940. **Fax:** 206/283-8897. **Contact:** Human Resources Department. **World Wide Web address:** http://www.williams-helde.com. **Description:** An advertising agency. Founded in 1970. **Number of employees at this location:** 10.

West Virginia

CHARLES RYAN ASSOCIATES
300 Summers Street, Suite 1100, Charleston WV 25301. 304/342-0161. **Toll-free phone:** 877/342-0161. **Fax:** 304/342-1941. **Contact:** Human Resources. **E-mail address:** resume@charlesryan.com. **World Wide Web address:** http://www.cryanassoc.com. **Description:** An integrated marketing communications firm with specialties in advertising, public relations, interactive technology and government relations. **NOTE:** Resume forms may be completed online. **Positions advertised include:** Graphic Designer; Senior Graphic Designer. **Other U.S. locations:** Richmond, VA; Lexington, KY.

HESS, STEWART & CAMPBELL, PLCC
252 George Street, Beckley WV 25801. 304/255-1978. **Fax:** 304/255-1971. **Contact:** Human Resources. **E-mail address:** hsccpa@hsc-cpa.com. **World Wide Web address:** http://www.hsc-spa.com. **Description:** A certified public accounting firm. **Other area locations:** Huntington; Oak Hill.

Wisconsin

AB DATA, LTD.
8050 North Port Washington Road, Milwaukee WI 53217. 414/540-5000. **Fax:** 414/540-5050. **Contact:** Human Resources. **World Wide Web address:** http://www.abdata.com. **Description:** A full-service, direct mail marketing company that primarily serves nonprofit and democratic political clients. **NOTE:** Entry-level positions are offered. **Corporate headquarters location:** This location. **Other U.S. locations:** Washington DC. **Listed on:** Privately held. **Annual sales/revenues:** $5 - $10 million. **Number of employees at this location:** 85. **Number of employees nationwide:** 100.

BUSINESS MARKETING ASSOCIATES, INC.
3520 County Road, Wausau WI 54401. 715/675-3900. **Contact:** Human Resources Department. **Description:** Engaged in advertising, marketing, and public relations for individual consumers, as well as business-to-business. Business Marketing Associates specializes in the health care and manufacturing industries. **Positions advertised include:** Account Executive.

THE GESSERT GROUP
5369 North 118th Court, Milwaukee WI 53225. 414/466-3400. **Fax:** 414/466-9369. **Contact:** Human Resources Department. **World Wide Web address:** http://www.gessert.com. **Description:** A marketing and multimedia communications company specializing in the health care industry. The Gessert Group creates marketing and advertising programs for medical device companies and ethical drug manufacturers. **Corporate headquarters location:** This location.

ARCHITECTURE, CONSTRUCTION, AND ENGINEERING

You can expect to find the following types of companies in this section:

Architectural and Engineering Services • Civil and Mechanical Engineering Firms • Construction Products, Manufacturers, and Wholesalers • General Contractors/Specialized Trade Contractors

---

Architecture and engineering occupations openings are expected to increase 12.5%, from 2,520,000 to 2,835,000, an increase of 315,000 jobs. Employment in construction will increase by 849,000 jobs or 12.4%, from 6,820,000 to 7,669,000 jobs. Demand for new housing and an increase in road, bridge, and tunnel construction will account for the bulk of job growth.

Alabama

BE&K ENGINEERING COMPANY
P.O. Box 2332, Birmingham AL 35201. 205/972-6000. **Physical address:** 2000 International Park Drive, Birmingham AL 35243. **Fax:** 205/972-6135. **Contact:** Bruce May, Human Resources Manager. **E-mail address:** bekresumes@bek.com. **World Wide Web address:** http://www.bek.com. **Description:** Provides construction, construction management, engineering, and maintenance services. **Positions advertised include:** Construction Recruiter; Billing Clerk; Cost Specialist; Sr. Instruments/Controls Engineer; Sr. Electrical Designer; Structural/Concrete Designer. **Other U.S. locations:** Mobile AL; Newark DE; Atlanta GA; New York NY; Morrisville NC; Trevose PA; Chester VA. **Parent company:** BE&K, Inc.

CAVALIER HOMES, INC.
CAVALIER HOMES OF ALABAMA, INC.
P.O. Box 300, Addison AL 35540. 256/747-1575. **Fax:** 256/747-8019. **Contact:** Sherry Jones, Personnel Director. **World Wide Web address:** http://www.cavhomesinc.com. **Description:** Cavalier Homes designs, produces, and sells manufactured homes. The company markets homes through approximately 500 independent dealers located in 32 states. Founded in 1984. **Corporate headquarters location:** This location. **Other area locations:** Hamilton AL; Winfield AL. **Other U.S. locations:** Cordele GA; Nashville NC; Robbins NC; Shippenville PA; Fort Worth TX. **Operations at this facility include:** This location houses executive offices and operates two manufacturing facilities, which function under the name Cavalier Homes of Alabama, Inc. **Listed on:** American Stock Exchange. **Stock exchange symbol:** CAV. **Number of employees nationwide:** 1,490.

TEC-MASTERS, INC.
1500 Perimeter Parkway, Suite 215, Huntsville AL 35806. 256/721-6616. **Fax:** 256/830-4093. **Contact:** Linda Case, Human Resources. **E-mail address:** lcase@tecmasters.com. **World Wide Web address:** http://www.tecmasters.com. **Description:** An engineering firm engaged in government defense projects such as weapons and logistics systems and material acquisition support. **Corporate headquarters location:** This location. **Other area locations:** Montgomery AL. **Other U.S. locations:** MD: NJ; GA; FL; ID; OK; MO. **Listed on:** Privately held. **Annual sales/revenues:** $21 - $50 million.

WYLE LABORATORIES
7800 Highway 20 West, Huntsville AL 35806. 256/837-4411. **Fax:** 256/830-2109. **Contact:** Human Resources. **E-mail address:** career@wylelabs.com. **World Wide Web address:** http://www.wylelabs.com. **Description:** Provides engineering and testing services to the aerospace, defense, transportation, energy, and electric utility industries. **Positions advertised include:** Senior Calibration Technician; Project Engineer; Senior Staff Electrical Engineer; Project Manager. **Corporate headquarters location:** El Segundo CA. **Other U.S. locations:** Nationwide.

Alaska

ARCTIC SLOPE REGIONAL CORPORATION
P.O. Box 129, Barrow AK 99723. 907/852-8633. **Fax:** 907/852-5733. **Contact:** Charlotte Brower, Personnel Manager. **World Wide Web address:** http://www.asrc.com. **Description:** Arctic Slope Regional Corporation and its subsidiaries are involved in automotive merchandise sales, busing, commercial construction, communications and television operations, consulting, engineering, environmental remediation, hotel operations, manufacturing, oil field support, petroleum refining and products sales, resource exploration and development, and tourism. The company also participates in various partnerships, joint ventures, and other business activities. **Other area locations:** Anchorage AK.

CHUGACH ALASKA CORPORATION (CAC)
560 E. 34th Avenue, Anchorage AK 99503. 907/563-8866. **Fax:** 907/563-8402. **Contact:** Human Resources. **E-mail address:** resumes@chugach-ak.com. **World Wide Web address:** http://www.chugach-ak.com. **Description:** The Chugach family consists of seven subsidiaries and several joint ventures with over 5,000 employees worldwide. CAC currently targets the following areas of business interests - base operating services, educational services, construction services, environmental services, information technology, telecommunications, and full-service employment services. **Positions advertised include:** AP Technician; Accounts Payable Reviewer; Financial Project Analyst.

LOUNSBURY & ASSOCIATES, INC.
5300 A Street; Anchorage AK 99518. 907/272-5451. **Fax:** 907/272-9065. **Contact:** Human Resources. **Description:** Provides professional services in surveying, engineering, planning and project management. **Positions advertised include:** Civil Engineer.

Arizona

ARIZONA ENGINEERING COMPANY
419 North San Francisco Street, Flagstaff AZ 86001. 928/774-7179. **Fax:** 928/779-1041. **Contact:** Human Resources. **E-mail address:** aec@arizonaengineering.com. **World Wide Web address:** http://www.arizonaengineering.com. **Description:** A consulting firm specializing in engineering and land surveying. Caters to public agencies, institutional and industrial clients, and regulated utilities. **Positions advertised include:** Design Engineer; Project Engineer. **Other area locations:** Phoenix AZ.

R.W. BECK & ASSOCIATES
14635 North Kierland Boulevard, Suite 130, Scottsdale AZ 85254. 480/998-8050. **Fax:** 480/998-1618. **Contact:** Human Resources. **E-mail address:** phoenix@rwbeck.com. **World Wide Web address:** http://www.rwbeck.com. **Description:** R.W. Beck is a diversified professional, technical, and management consulting firm. The company provides construction, environmental, technical, energy, solid waste, and water/wastewater services nationwide. **Positions advertised include:** Sr. Consultant. **Corporate headquarters location:** Seattle WA. **Other U.S. locations:** Nationwide. **Operations at this facility include:** This location is primarily engaged in utility engineering.

BURGESS & NIPLE, INC.
5025 East Washington Street, Suite 212, Phoenix AZ 85034. 602/244-8100. **Contact:** Human Resources. **E-mail address:** hr@burnip.com. **World Wide Web**

address: http://www.burgessniple.com. **Description:** An engineering and architecture firm engaged in study, analysis, and design services. The company specializes in waterworks, wastewater, industrial services, hydropower, energy conservation, transportation, systems analysis, HVAC, and geotechnical. Founded in 1912. **Positions advertised include:** Travel Demand Forecaster; Civil Engineer; Engineer. **Corporate headquarters location:** Columbus OH.

CH2M HILL, INC.
2625 South Plaza Drive, Suite 300, Tempe AZ 85282-3397. 480/966-8188. **Fax:** 480/966-9450. **Contact:** Human Resources. **World Wide Web address:** http://www.ch2m.com. **Description:** CH2M Hill is a group of employee-owned companies operating under the names CH2M Hill, Inc., Industrial Design Corporation, Operations Management International, CH2M Hill International, and CH2M Hill Engineering. The company provides planning, engineering design, and operation and construction management services to help clients apply technology, safeguard the environment, and develop infrastructures. The professional staff includes specialists in environmental engineering and waste management, water management, transportation, industrial facilities, and a broad spectrum of infrastructure systems. Founded in 1946. **Positions advertised include:** Environmental Data Management/Database Analyst; Hydrogeologist; Project Manager; Geotechnical Engineer; Civil Engineer. **Corporate headquarters location:** Greenwood Village CO.

EXPONENT, INC.
23445 North 19th Avenue, Phoenix AZ 85027. 623/582-6949. **Fax:** 623/581-8814. **Contact:** Human Resources. **E-mail address:** hr@exponent.com. **World Wide Web address:** http://www.exponent.com. **Description:** Performs scientific analysis of various cases in areas such as accident reconstruction, biomechanics, construction/structural engineering, aviation and marine investigations, environmental assessment, materials and product testing, warnings and labeling issues, accident statistic data analysis, and risk prevention/mitigation. Founded in 1967. **Positions advertised include:** Managing Engineer; Test Engineer; Systems Engineer; Senior Engineer, Vehicle Engineering. **Corporate headquarters location:** Menlo Park CA. **Listed on:** NASDAQ. **Stock exchange symbol:** EXPO.

GOETTL AIR CONDITIONING INC.
1845 West 1st Street, Tempe AZ 85281. 602/275-1515. **Fax:** 602/470-4275. **Contact:** Human Resources. **World Wide Web address:** http://www.goettl.com. **Description:** Manufactures a broad range of air conditioning, heating, and air distribution products including air conditioning systems and components, heat pumps, and evaporative coolers. **Positions advertised include:** HVAC Installers; A/C Installers. **Corporate headquarters location:** This location.

JMC MECHANICAL
6616 West State Avenue, Glendale AZ 85301. 623/934-3206. **Contact:** Mack Crawley, President. **Description:** A utilities contractor specializing in the installation of air conditioning and plumbing systems.

JACOBS SVERDRUP
875 West Elliot Road, Suite 201, Tempe AZ 85284. 480/763-8600. **Fax:** 425/452-1212. **Contact:** Human Resources. **World Wide Web address:** http://www.jacobs.com. **Description:** An environmental engineering, architectural, and construction firm that offers consulting services, design services, and operations management to a diverse clientele. **NOTE:** Entry-level positions are offered. **Positions advertised include:** Drainage Engineer; Project Specialist; Sr. Project Engineer; Urban Planner. **Special programs:** Internships. **Corporate headquarters location:** Pasadena CA. **Parent company:** Jacobs Engineering Group, Inc. **Operations at this facility include:** Administration; Service. **Listed on:** New York Stock Exchange. **Stock exchange symbol:** JEC. **Annual sales/revenues:** More than $100 million. **Number of employees at this location:** 100. **Number of employees worldwide:** 5,000.

JOHNSON CONTROLS, INC.
2032 West Fourth Street, Tempe AZ 85281. 480/894-9193. **Contact:** Human Resources. **World Wide Web address:** http://www.johnsoncontrols.com. **Description:** Johnson Controls, Inc. provides air conditioning services, air filters, automatic temperature control, chiller services, coil cleaning, lighting services, energy management, facilities management systems, fire alarm systems, heating service, maintenance contracts, refrigeration service, and security systems. **Corporate headquarters location:** Milwaukee WI. **Operations at this facility include:** This location sells, services, and installs fire alarm controls and air conditioning systems. **Listed on:** New York Stock Exchange. **Stock exchange symbol:** JCI. **Number of employees at this location:** 65. **Number of employees worldwide:** 123,000.

KINETICS SYSTEMS
2825 West Thomas Road, Phoenix AZ 85017. 602/685-2000. **Fax:** 602/685-2299. **Contact:** Human Resources. **World Wide Web address:** http://www.kineticsgroup.com. **Description:** One of the largest mechanical contracting firms in Arizona, and one of the top 100 in the country. Kinetics Systems provides a wide array of commercial and industrial services including process piping, heating, ventilating, air conditioning, control systems, ultra-high-purity process piping, plumbing, special projects services, energy audits and retrofits, performance contracting, air and water balance, and backflow prevention. **Positions advertised include:** Estimator. **Special programs:** Training. **Corporate headquarters location:** Santa Clara CA. **Parent company:** Kinetics Group, Inc. **Operations at this facility include:** Administration; Service. **Annual sales/revenues:** $51 - $100 million. **Number of employees at this location:** 135. **Number of employees nationwide:** 600.

KITCHELL CORPORATION
1707 East Highland Avenue, Suite 100, Phoenix AZ 85016. 602/264-4411. **Contact:** Kay Ellis, Director of Human Resources. **World Wide Web address:** http://www.kitchell.com. **Description:** A residential and commercial construction and construction management firm. **Positions advertised include:** Assistant Director/Director of Communications; Assistant Equipment Planner; Communications Manger; Construction Project Manager; Project Director; Project Manager; Project Superintendent; Staff Accountant.

LARSEN SUPPLY COMPANY
7045 West Galveston Street, Chandler AZ 85226. 602/961-0971. **Contact:** Human Resources. **World Wide Web address:** http://www.lasco.net. **Description:** Manufactures and distributes a wide range of plumbing fixtures and supplies.

ANDREW LAUREN INTERIORS
1311 West 21st Street, Tempe AZ 85282. 480/829-0054. **Contact:** Human Resources. **Description:** Engaged in commercial and residential interior decorating and design. **Corporate headquarters location:** This location.

McCARTHY BUILDING COMPANIES, INC.
80 East Rio Salado Parkway, Suite 310, Tempe AZ 85281. 480/449-4700. **Fax:** 480/449-4747. **Contact:** Human Resources. **E-mail address:** phx@mccarthy.com. **World Wide Web address:** http://www.mccarthy.com. **Description:** A privately owned construction firm that also operates a separate division for work on bridges. The company currently provides a wide range of construction-related services under construction management, general contract, and design/build contractual arrangements. **NOTE:** Search and apply for positions online. **Positions advertised include:** Project Engineer; Scheduler; VP of Business Development. **Corporate headquarters location:** St.

Louis MO. **Other U.S. locations:** Irvine CA; Sacramento CA; Seattle WA.

PALM HARBOR HOMES INC.
309 South Perry Lane, Tempe AZ 85281. 480/967-7877. **Toll-free phone:** 800/467-7877. **Contact:** Human Resources. **World Wide Web address:** http://www.palmharbor.com. **Description:** Manufactures, sells, and finances prefabricated homes. **Corporate headquarters location:** Addison TX. **Listed on:** NASDAQ. **Stock exchange symbol:** PHHM.

PERINI BUILDING COMPANY
360 East Coronado Road, Phoenix AZ 85004. 602/256-6777. **Contact:** Human Resources. **World Wide Web address:** http://www.periniwest.com. **Description:** Provides general contracting and construction management services. **Corporate headquarters location:** Framingham MA. **Parent company:** Perini Corporation. **Operations at this facility include:** Administration. **Listed on:** American Stock Exchange. **Stock exchange symbol:** PCR.

PULTE HOMES, INC.
15333 North Pima Road, Suite 300, Scottsdale AZ 85260. 480/598-2100. **Contact:** Human Resources. **World Wide Web address:** http://www.pulte.com. **Description:** One of the largest independent, publicly-owned home-building companies in the United States. Pulte Home Corporation's principal business is the construction and sale of moderately priced, single-family homes. **Positions advertised include:** Cost Accountant; Escrow Officer; CAD Technician; Public Relations Rep. **Corporate headquarters location:** Bloomfield Hills MI. **Listed on:** New York Stock Exchange. **Stock exchange symbol:** PHM. **Number of employees at this location:** 130. **Number of employees nationwide:** 5,000.

CHAS ROBERTS AIR CONDITIONING
9828 North 19th Avenue, Phoenix AZ 85021. 602/331-2678. **Contact:** Dave Patenaude, Human Resources Director. **E-mail address:** hr@chasroberts.com. **World Wide Web address:** http://www.chasroberts.com. **Description:** Sells, installs, and services heating and air conditioning systems. **Positions advertised include:** Service Technician; Installer; Commercial/Custom Home Installer.

STANTEC CONSULTING
201 North Bonita Avenue, Suite 101, Tucson AZ 85745-2999. 520/750-7474. **Fax:** 520/750-7470. **Contact:** Human Resources. **E-mail address:** hr@stantec.com. **World Wide Web address:** http://www.stantec.com. **Description:** An engineering services firm. **Positions advertised include:** CAD Technician; Civil Designer; Electrical Designer/Engineer; Mechanical Designer/Engineer; Sr. Structural Engineer. **Other area locations include:** Phoenix AZ; Scottsdale AZ. **Other U.S. locations include:** Nationwide. **International locations:** Barbados.

THE SUNDT COMPANIES, INC.
1501 West Fountainhead Parkway, Suite 600, Tempe AZ 85282. 480/293-3000. **Fax:** 480/293-3079. **Contact:** Human Resources. **World Wide Web address:** http://www.sundt.com. **Description:** A general contractor providing construction management services. **Positions advertised include:** Project Engineer; Sr. Estimator; Project Administrator. **Other area locations:** Phoenix AZ; Tucson AZ. **Other U.S. locations:** Novato CA; Sacramento CA; San Diego CA; Dallas TX.

SUNDT CONSTRUCTION, INC.
2630 South 20th Place, Phoenix AZ 85034. 602/252-5881. **Contact:** Human Resources. **World Wide Web address:** http://www.sundt.com. **Description:** A general contractor providing construction management services. **Parent company:** The Sundt Companies, Inc.

SUNVEK
7681 East Gray, Scottsdale AZ 85260. 480/951-3223. **Fax:** 480/951-8046. **Contact:** Human Resources. **World Wide Web address:** http://www.sunvek.com. **Description:** Provides a variety of home improvement services including roofing, siding, heating/air conditioning, and plumbing.

SWENGEL-ROBBINS, INC.
837 East Southern Avenue, Phoenix AZ 85040-3144. 602/268-1724. **Contact:** Human Resources. **Description:** A construction management firm specializing in engineering and heavy construction including highways and pipelines.

WESTERN TECHNOLOGIES, INC.
3737 East Broadway Road, Phoenix AZ 85040. 602/437-3737. **Fax:** 602/470-1341. **Contact:** Human Resources. **World Wide Web address:** http://www.wt-us.com. **Description:** Provides engineering, consulting, and testing of environmental, geotechnical, and construction materials. Environmental services include site assessments, investigations, feasibility studies, problem solving, and remedial services. Geotechnical services are provided with use of a wide variety of exploration equipment including highly mobile drilling rigs. Materials Engineering and Testing provides analysis and quality assurance of materials and methods for clients. Materials Research develops methods of improving the strength and durability of conventional construction materials through research into the feasibility of using waste and less expensive or more available materials. Construction Quality Control provides interpretation of geotechnical reports, observation and testing of reinforced steel and concrete, visual and nondestructive evaluation of bolted and welded structural steel components, preparing concrete and asphalt mix designs, as well as sampling and testing many other architectural and structural components. Founded in 1955. **Positions advertised include:** Senior Geotechnical Engineer; Geotechnical Engineer; Environmental Scientist; Geologist; Industrial Hygienist; Senior Engineering Technician. **Corporate headquarters location:** This location. **Listed on:** Privately held. **Annual sales/revenues:** $21 - $50 million. **Number of employees at this location:** 285.

California

ABS CONSULTING
300 Commerce Drive, Suite 200, Irvine CA 92602. 714/734-4242. **Fax:** 714/734-4262. **Contact:** Human Resources. **E-mail address:** employ@abs-group.org. **World Wide Web address:** http://www.absconsulting.com. **Description:** Offers engineering consulting for system safety and reliability and provides probable risk assessment to the energy, defense, petrochemical, and manufacturing industries. **NOTE:** Unsolicited resumes or applications not accepted. **Positions advertised include:** Program Manager; Construction Manager; Resident Engineer; Structural Engineer. **Corporate headquarters location:** Houston TX. **Other U.S. locations:** Nationwide. **International locations:** Worldwide. **Parent company:** ABS Group of Companies, Inc.

ACCO ENGINEERED SYSTEMS
6265 San Fernando Road, Glendale CA 91201. 818/244-6571. **Toll-free phone:** 800/998-2226. **Fax:** 818/247-6533. **Contact:** Human Resources. **E-mail address:** hr_dept01@fastmail.fm. **World Wide Web address:** http://www.accoair.com. **Description:** A mechanical contracting firm that specializes in the design and construction of HVAC systems. Founded in 1934. **Corporate headquarters location:** This location. **Other area locations:** San Leandro CA; Sacramento CA; San Diego CA; Tustin CA. **Other U.S. locations:** Orlando FL; Tampa FL; Kent WA. **Operations at this facility include:** Administration; Engineering and Design; Sales; Service. **Listed on:** Privately held. **Annual sales/revenues:** More than $100 million. **Number of employees at this location:** 300. **Number of employees nationwide:** 1,200.

AECOM TECHNOLOGY CORPORATION
555 South Flower Street, Suite 3700, Los Angeles CA 90071-2300. 213/593-8000. **Contact:** Human Resources. **E-mail address:** aecomcareers@aecom.com. **World Wide Web address:** http://www.aecom.com. **Description:** A leading global engineering and design firm. **Positions advertised include:** Accountant; Audit Supervisor; Benefits Specialist. **Corporate headquarters location:** This location. **Other U.S. locations:** Nationwide. **International locations:** Worldwide. **Number of employees worldwide:** 18,000.

ADVANCED FOAM
1745 West 134th Street, Gardena CA 90249. 310/515-0617. **Fax:** 323/515-3548. **Contact:** Human Resources. **World Wide Web address:** http://www.redicoat.com. **Description:** Manufactures specialty sheets of foam for the construction of buildings. The most popular line of products is called Redicoat. **Corporate headquarters location:** This location.

AMELCO CORPORATION
19208 South Vermont Avenue, Gardena CA 90248-4414. 310/327-3070. **Fax:** 310/327-3599. **Contact:** Human Resources. **World Wide Web address:** http://www.amelco.net. **Description:** Provides specialty construction services primarily electrical and mechanical subcontracting. **Corporate headquarters location:** This location. **Other U.S. locations:** Hawaii. **Stock exchange symbol:** AMLC. **Number of employees nationwide:** 500.

ANTHONY AND SYLVAN SWIMMING POOLS AND SPAS
1228 West Shelly Court, Orange CA 92868. 714/628-9600. **Toll-free phone:** 800/877-6657. **Contact:** Personnel. **World Wide Web address:** http://www.anthony-sylvan.com. **Description:** One of the largest builders of residential swimming pools in the United States. **Positions advertised include:** General Manager, Pool Divisions; Retail Store Manager; Operations Manager; Design Consultant; Sales Coordinator. **Parent company:** Anthony Industries, Inc. **Operations at this facility include:** Administration; Divisional Headquarters. **Listed on:** NASDAQ. **Stock exchange symbol:** SWIM.

BARKER MECHANICAL SERVICES INC.
6800 Sierra Court, Suite L, Dublin CA 94568. 925/560-0280. **Contact:** Human Resources. **E-mail address:** info@barkerms.com. **World Wide Web address:** http://www.barkerms.com. **Description:** Sells and services heating and air-conditioning equipment to commercial and industrial clients.

BECHTEL CORPORATION
P.O. Box 193965, San Francisco CA 94119-3965. 415/768-1234. **Physical address:** 50 Beale Street, San Francisco CA 94105-1895. **Fax:** 415/768-9038. **Contact:** Human Resources. **E-mail address:** staffpx@bechtel.com. **World Wide Web address:** http://www.bechtel.com. **Description:** Operations focus on engineering, construction, financing operations and maintenance, electricity, nuclear fuel, metals, minerals, procurement management, transportation, and pollution control. **Positions advertised include:** Contract Manager; Subcontract Manager. **Special programs:** Co-ops; Summer Jobs. **Corporate headquarters location:** This location. **Other area locations:** Martinez CA; Los Angeles CA; San Diego CA. **Other U.S. locations:** AZ; CO; KY; MD; NY; TN; TX; WA.

BECHTEL NEVADA
P.O. Box 2710, Livermore CA 94551. 925/960-2500. **Fax:** 925/960-2595. **Contact:** Danette Hatfield, Human Resources. **E-mail address:** bnresumes@nv.doe.gov. **World Wide Web address:** http://www.bechtelnevada.com. **Description:** Bechtel Nevada operates in the following areas: engineering, construction, financing operations and maintenance, electricity, nuclear fuel, metals, minerals, procurement management, transportation, and pollution control. **NOTE:** Resumes can be faxed to the corporate headquarters at 702/295-2448 or 702/295-0351. **Positions advertised include:** Senior Scientists; Engineer; Technical Staff. **Other U.S. locations:** DC; NM; NV. **Parent company:** Bechtel Corporation (San Francisco CA). **Operations at this facility include:** This location performs engineering research and development for the Department of Energy. **Number of employees at this location:** 85.

BOYLE ENGINEERING CORPORATION
1501 Quail Street, Newport Beach CA 92660. 949/476-3300. **Fax:** 949/721-7142. **Contact:** Recruiting Manager. **E-mail address:** recruitingmgr@boyleengineering.com. **World Wide Web address:** http://www.boyleengineering.com. **Description:** Provides comprehensive services ranging from project planning and feasibility studies to design and construction phases. The company specializes in the fields of water resources; water treatment and distribution; wastewater collection, treatment, and reuse; streets, highways, and bridges; light and heavy rail; drainage and flood control; and land planning. **Positions advertised include:** Associate Engineer; Assistant Pipeline Engineer. **Corporate headquarters location:** This location. **Other area locations:** Bakersfield CA; Fresno CA; Palmdale CA; Encino CA; Ontario CA; Sacramento CA; San Diego CA; San Luis Obispo CA; Ventura CA. **Other U.S. locations:** CO; FL; NV; NM; TX; UT.

BURKE MERCER
2250 South 10th Street, San Jose CA 95112. 408/297-3500. **Fax:** 408/291-8401. **Contact:** Personnel Director. **World Wide Web address:** http://www.burkemercer.com. **Description:** Manufactures a wide variety of flooring products including carpet base, tile, transition strip accessories, stair tread, and floor adhesives. **Corporate headquarters location:** This location. **Parent company:** Burke Industries, Inc.

CH2M HILL CALIFORNIA INC.
P.O. Box 12681, Oakland CA 94604. 510/251-2888. **Physical address:** 155 Grand Avenue, Suite 1000, Oakland CA 94612. **Fax:** 510/893-8205. **Contact:** Human Resources Department. **World Wide Web address:** http://www.ch2m.com. **Description:** The company provides planning, engineering design, and operation and construction management services to help clients apply technology, safeguard the environment, and develop infrastructure. The professional staff includes specialists in environmental engineering and waste management, water management, transportation, industrial facilities, and a broad spectrum of infrastructure systems. Founded in 1946. **Positions advertised include:** Associate Designer; Transportation Planner Specialist; Senior Human Resources Assistant; Hydrogeologist; Structural Engineer; Project Biologist. **Corporate headquarters location:** Englewood CO. **International locations:** Worldwide. **Parent company:** CH2M HILL. **Operations at this facility include:** Regional Headquarters.

CAL-AIR, INC.
12393 Slauson Avenue, Whittier CA 90606. 562/698-8301. **Fax:** 562/464-3294. **Contact:** Human Resources. **E-mail address:** sozuna@calair.com. **World Wide Web address:** http://www.calair.com. **Description:** A mechanical contractor. Cal-Air Conditioning installs and services air conditioning and heating systems, and is also engaged in energy management and sheet metal fabrication. **NOTE:** Resumes may be submitted by e-mail or fax. Applicants may also mail resumes to: Cal-Air, Inc., **Positions advertised include:** Energy Service Sales Representative; Service Technician. **Corporate headquarters location:** This location. **Other area locations:** Statewide. **Parent company:** Johnson Controls. **Operations at this facility include:** Administration; Divisional Headquarters; Sales; Service. **Number of employees at this location:** 150. **Number of employees nationwide:** 400.

CALPROP CORPORATION
13160 Mindanao Way, Suite 180, Marina Del Rey CA 90292-7903. 310/306-4314. **Fax:** 310/301-0435. **Contact:** Dori Baron, Personnel Manager. **Description:** Builds and sells single-family homes and condominiums in California. Founded in 1961. **Corporate headquarters location:** This location.

CAPITAL PACIFIC HOMES
4100 MacArthur Boulevard, Suite 150, Newport Beach CA 92660. 949/622-8400. **Contact:** Kathy Smith, Human Resources. **E-mail address:** kathy.smith@cph-inc.com. **World Wide Web address:** http://www.capitalpacifichomes.com. **Description:** Builds single-family homes throughout Orange County CA, Las Vegas NV, and Austin TX. **Corporate headquarters location:** This location. **Other U.S. locations:** Mesa AZ; Westminster CO; Austin TX. **Parent company:** Capital Pacific Holdings. **Listed on:** American Stock Exchange. **Stock exchange symbol:** CPH.

THE CLARK CONSTRUCTION GROUP, INC.
7677 Oakport Street, Suite 1040, Oakland CA 94621. 510/430-1700. **Contact:** Human Resources. **E-mail address:** hr@clarkconstruction.com. **World Wide Web address:** http://www.clarkconstruction.com. **Description:** One of the nation's leading general contractors. Construction and renovation projects include sports facilities, civic centers, hotels, educational facilities, laboratories, and office buildings. **NOTE:** Address resumes to: Human Resources, The Clark Construction Group, Inc., P.O. Box 5937, Bethesda MD 20814. Fax: 301/272-8414. **Positions advertised include:** Project Manager; Superintendent; Field Engineer; Office Engineer. **Corporate headquarters location:** Bethesda MD. **Other area locations:** Costa Mesa CA. **Other U.S. locations:** Nationwide.

COAST FOUNDRY AND MANUFACTURING COMPANY
2707 North Garey Avenue, Pomona CA 91767. 909/596-1883. **Toll-free phone:** 800/521-4021. **Fax:** 909/596-2650. **Contact:** Human Resources. **World Wide Web address:** http://www.coastfoundrymfg.com. **Description:** A manufacturer of plumbing supplies. **Corporate headquarters location:** This location. **Number of employees at this location:** 300.

DMJM H&N
515 South Flower Street, Los Angeles CA 90071. 213/593-8100. **Fax:** 213/593-8175. **Contact:** Yvette Mitchell, Director, Recruitment. **E-mail address:** careers@dmjm.com. **World Wide Web address:** http://www.dmjm.com. **Description:** Provides a wide range of architectural/engineering services to the public and private sectors. Operations include transportation, public works, and commercial architecture. **Positions advertised include:** Architect. **Special programs:** Internships. **Corporate headquarters location:** This location. **Other U.S. locations:** San Bernardino CA; San Francisco CA; Santa Monica CA. **Parent company:** AECOM Technology Corporation.

ELIXIR INDUSTRIES
24800 Chrisanta Drive, Suite 210, Mission Viejo CA 92691. 949/860-5000. **Toll-free phone:** 800/421-1942. **Fax:** 949/860-5011. **Contact:** Human Resources. **E-mail address:** elixircorp@elixirind.com. **World Wide Web address:** http://www.elixirind.com. **Description:** Manufactures metal siding, roofing, doors, frame parts, roof vents, roof domes, and related mobile home products. **Corporate headquarters location:** This location. **Number of employees nationwide:** 1,300.

EXPONENT, INC.
149 Commonwealth Drive, Menlo Park CA 94025. 650/326-9400. **Fax:** 650/326-8072. **Contact:** Human Resources Department. **E-mail address:** hr@exponent.com. **World Wide Web address:** http://www.exponent.com. **Description:** A technical consulting firm dedicated to the investigation, analysis, and prevention of accidents and failures of an engineering or scientific nature. The company specializes in accident reconstruction, biomechanics, construction/structural engineering, aviation and marine investigations, environmental assessment, materials and product testing, warning and labeling issues, accident statistical data analysis, and risk prevention/mitigation. Founded in 1967. **Positions advertised include:** Thermal Engineer; Senior Systems Engineer; Administrative Assistant; Civil Engineer; Senior Managing Engineer; Principal/Practice Director; Environmental Engineer; Research Assistant; Senior Software Engineer. **Special programs:** Internships. **Corporate headquarters location:** This location. **Other area locations:** Irvine CA; San Diego CA; Los Angeles CA. **Other U.S. locations:** Nationwide. **Subsidiaries include:** Exponent Environmental Group; Exponent Failure Analysis; Exponent Health Group. **Listed on:** NASDAQ. **Stock exchange symbol:** EXPO. **Annual sales/revenues:** $140 million. **Number of employees nationwide:** 675.

FM GLOBAL
21860 Burbank Boulevard, Suite 300, Woodland Hills CA 91367. 818/704-1133. **Fax:** 818/883-0759. **Contact:** Human Resources. **E-mail address:** jobs@fmglobal.com. **World Wide Web address:** http://www.fmglobal.com. **Description:** A loss-control services organization. The company helps owner/company policyholders protect their properties and occupancies against damage from fire, wind, flood, and explosion; from boiler, pressure vessel, and machinery accidents; and from many other insured hazards. **Corporate headquarters location:** Johnston RI. **Other U.S. locations:** Walnut Creek CA; Norwalk CT; Alpharetta GA; Park Ridge IL; Norwood MA; Novi MI; Plymouth MN; St. Louis MO; Charlotte NC; Parsippany NJ; New York NY; North Olmstead OH; Malvern PA; Plano TX; Houston TX; Reston VA; Bellevue WA. **International locations:** Worldwide. **Number of employees worldwide:** 4,000.

FERGUSON ENTERPRISES, INC.
11552 Monarch Street, Garden Grove CA 92841-1815. 714/893-1936. **Toll-free phone:** 866/312-2672. **Fax:** 714/934-8601. **Contact:** Human Resources. **E-mail address:** resumes@ferguson.com. **World Wide Web address:** http://www.ferguson.com. **Description:** Distributes an extensive variety of building materials throughout the western United States. Major product lines include plumbing supplies, valves and fittings, sprinkler and irrigation products, and solar energy components. Ferguson Enterprises operates over 500 locations in North America. **Corporate headquarters location:** Newport News VA. **Other U.S. locations:** Nationwide. **International locations:** Columbia; Mexico; Puerto Rico. **Parent company:** Wolseley.

FLUOR CORPORATION
One Enterprise Drive, Aliso Viejo CA 92656. 949/349-2000. **Fax:** 949/349-2585. **Contact:** Human Resources Department. **E-mail address:** careers@fluor.com. **World Wide Web address:** http://www.fluor.com. **Description:** Operates within the fields of engineering, global services, coal production, and procurement and construction through four operating groups. Fluor Daniel provides engineering, procurement, and construction services. Fluor Global Services provides a wide range of products and related services including consulting services; equipment rental sales and service; operations; and maintenance services. Fluor Signature Services provides business support services to Fluor Corporation. A.T. Massey Coal Group produces coal for the steel industry. **Corporate headquarters location:** This location. **Listed on:** New York Stock Exchange. **Stock exchange symbol:** FLR. **Number of employees worldwide:** 30,000.

GARDCO LIGHTING
2661 Alvarado Street, P.O. Box 2013, San Leandro CA 94577. 510/357-6900. **Fax:** 510/357-3088. **Contact:** Human Resources. **World Wide Web address:** http://www.sitelighting.com. **Description:** Produces and installs outdoor area lighting and flood lighting for parking lots, pathways, gardens, and garages. **Special**

programs: Internships. **Corporate headquarters location:** San Marcos TX. **Other U.S. locations:** Nationwide. **Parent company:** Genlyte Group. **Number of employees at this location:** 200. **Number of employees nationwide:** 3,000.

GENSLER
Two Harrison Street, Suite 400, San Francisco CA 94105. 415/433-3700. **Fax:** 415/836-4599. **Contact:** Human Resources. **E-mail address:** sf_careers@gensler.com. **World Wide Web address:** http://www.gensler.com. **Description:** Provides architectural space planning, graphics, and interior design services nationwide. **Positions advertised include:** AutoCAD Manager. **Special programs:** Internships. **Corporate headquarters location:** This location. **Other area locations:** Irvine CA; Los Angeles CA; Newport Beach CA; San Diego CA; San Jose CA; San Ramon CA. **Other U.S. locations:** Denver CO; Washington DC; Atlanta GA; Boston MA; Detroit MI; New York NY; Houston TX. **Listed on:** Privately held. **Number of employees at this location:** 175. **Number of employees nationwide:** 800.

GRANITE CONSTRUCTION INC.
P.O. Box 50085, Watsonville CA 95077. 831/724-1011. **Physical address:** 585 West Beach Street, Watsonville CA 95076. **Fax:** 831/761-7871. **Contact:** Brian Fox, Director of Recruiting and Retention. **E-mail address:** brian.fox@gcinc.com. **World Wide Web address:** http://www.graniteconstruction.com. **Description:** A construction company. Founded in 1922. **Positions advertised include:** Legal Secretary/Executive Assistant; Senior Estimator; Senior Financial Analyst. **Special programs:** Internships. **Corporate headquarters location:** This location. **Other U.S. locations:** Nationwide. **Operations at this facility include:** Administration. **Listed on:** New York Stock Exchange. **Stock exchange symbol:** GVA. **Number of employees at this location:** 300. **Number of employees nationwide:** 3,000.

HATHAWAY DINWIDDIE CONSTRUCTION COMPANY
275 Battery Street, Suite 300, San Francisco CA 94111. 415/986-2718. **Fax:** 415/956-5669. **Contact:** Human Resources. **E-mail address:** hr@hdcco.com. **World Wide Web address:** http://www.hdcco.com. **Description:** A full-service general contractor. **Positions advertised include:** Project Engineer; Estimator; Project Manager; Superintendent. **Corporate headquarters location:** This location. **Other area locations:** Los Angeles CA; Santa Clara CA.

HOLMES & NARVER TECHNICAL SERVICES
999 Town & Country Road, Orange CA 92868. 714/567-2400. **Fax:** 714/543-0955. **Contact:** Human Resources. **E-mail address:** careers@dmjm.com. **World Wide Web address:** http://www.dmjmhn.aecom.com/marketsandservices/45/54/index.jsp. **Description:** Provides technical staffing and training, procurement, logistic and IT support, and staff augmentation to Federal and state agencies, commercial concerns and private industries. **Corporate headquarters location:** This location. **Parent company:** DMJM H&N.

HUNTER DOUGLAS
1818 South Oak Street, Los Angeles CA 90015. 213/749-6333x3205. **Fax:** 213/742-0981. **Contact:** Human Resources Department. **World Wide World Address:** http://www.hunterdouglas.com. **Description:** A manufacturer of custom-made windows. **Other U.S. locations:** Augusta GA; Chicago IL. **Parent company:** Hunter Douglas Group (The Netherlands). **Operations at this facility include:** Administration; Regional Headquarters; Sales; Service. **Number of employees at this location:** 350. **Number of employees nationwide:** 500.

JACOBS ENGINEERING GROUP INC.
1111 South Arroyo Parkway, P.O. Box 7084, Pasadena CA 91109-7084. 626/578-3500. **Fax:** 626/578-6916. **Contact:** Human Resources. **World Wide Web address:** http://www.jacobs.com. **Description:** An engineering firm offering a full range of services including environmental studies, feasibility studies, architectural services, engineering/design, procurement, construction, construction management, and construction maintenance. Jacobs Engineering Group is one of the largest engineering and construction companies in the United States. The company specializes in the chemicals and polymers, federal programs, pulp and paper, semiconductor, petroleum refining, facilities and transportation, food and consumer products, and pharmaceuticals and biotechnologies industries. **Positions advertised include:** IT Manager; Project Manager; Security Engineer; Tax Accountant. **Corporate headquarters location:** This location. **Listed on:** New York Stock Exchange. **Stock exchange symbol:** JEC.

JENSEN INDUSTRIES, INC.
1946 East 46th Street, Los Angeles CA 90058. 323/235-6800. **Toll-free phone:** 800/325-8351. **Fax:** 323/235-6816. **Contact:** Human Resources. **E-mail address:** hr@jensen-ind.com. **World Wide Web address:** http://www.jensen-ind.com. **Description:** Primarily engaged in manufacturing building products for residential and commercial industries. The company's products include bath cabinets, vanities, lav-tops, toplights, mailboxes, medicine cabinets, roof vents, range hoods, and monitor panels. **Corporate headquarters location:** This location. **Number of employees at this location:** 200.

KAWNEER COMPANY INC.
P.O. Box 3148, Visalia CA 93278. 559/651-4000. **Physical address:** 7200 Doe Avenue, Visalia CA 93291. **Toll-free phone:** 877/505-3785. **Contact:** Personnel Manager. **World Wide Web address:** http://www.kawneer.com. **Description:** Manufactures and markets fabricated products, including nonresidential architectural building products such as storefronts, building entrances, facings, window framing, and curtainwall systems. **Corporate headquarters location:** Norcross GA. **Other U.S. locations:** AL; IN; KY; PA. **Parent company:** ALCOA Inc. **Operations at this facility include:** Administration; Manufacturing; Sales; Service. **Listed on:** New York Stock Exchange. **Stock exchange symbol:** AA. **Number of employees at this location:** 300. **Number of employees worldwide:** 14,000.

LATHROP CONSTRUCTION ASSOCIATES, INC.
4001 Park Road, P.O. Box 2005, Benicia CA 94510. 707/746-8000. **Contact:** Human Resources. **E-mail address:** info@lathropconstruction.com. **World Wide Web address:** http://www.lathropconstruction.com. **NOTE:** Resumes may be submitted via mail, fax, or e-mail. **Description:** A general contractor that offers a variety of services including construction management, budget development, document review, and cost estimation. **Positions advertised include:** Project Manager; Superintendent; Project Engineer. **Corporate headquarters location:** This location.

LOCUS TECHNOLOGIES
1333 North California Boulevard, Suite 350, Walnut Creek CA 94596. 925/906-8100. **Fax:** 925/906-8101. **Contact:** Human Resources Department. **E-mail address:** humanresources@locustec.com. **World Wide Web address:** http://www.locustec.com. **Description:** A leading environmental consulting, engineering, and remediation services provider. **NOTE:** Candidates should send a resume with salary requirements and references. **Positions advertised include:** Project Scientist; Project Engineer. **Corporate headquarters location:** This location. **Other area locations:** Mountain View CA; Middletown CA; Sacramento CA; Los Angeles CA. **Listed on:** Privately held.

MATICH CORPORATION
P.O. Box 50000, San Bernardino CA 92412. 909/382-7400. **Physical address:** 1596 Harry Sheppard Boulevard, San Bernardino CA 92408. **Fax:** 909/382-

0169. **Contact:** Human Resources. **World Wide Web address:** http://www.matichicm.com. **Description:** An asphalt paving and manufacturing company. Matich Corporation is also a highway contractor and construction management firm. Founded in 1918. **Corporate headquarters location:** This location. **Listed on:** Privately held. **Annual sales/revenues:** $21 - $50 million.

McELROY METAL INC.
P.O. Box 127, Adelanto CA 92301. 760/246-5545. **Physical address:** 17031 Koala Road, Adelanto CA 92301. **Contact:** Human Resources. **World Wide Web address:** http://www.mcelroymetal.com. **Description:** Manufactures metal siding and roofing. **Corporate headquarters location:** Shreveport LA. **Other U.S. locations:** Nationwide. **Annual sales/revenues:** Less than $5 million. **Number of employees at this location:** 35. **Number of employees nationwide:** 300.

PAREX INC.
11290 South Vallejo Court, French Camp CA 95231. 209/983-8002. **Toll-free phone:** 800/780-6953. **Fax:** 209/983-1431. **Contact:** Human Resources Department. **World Wide Web address:** http://www.parex.com. **Description:** A manufacturer of stucco and exterior finishing materials. **Corporate headquarters location:** Redan GA. **Parent company:** Lafarge Mortars.

PARSONS BRINCKERHOFF INC.
303 Second Street, Suite 700 North, San Francisco CA 94107. 415/243-4600. **Fax:** 415/243-9501. **Contact:** Betsy Hume, Human Resources Department. **World Wide Web address:** http://www.pbworld.com. **Description:** Provides total engineering and construction management services from project conception through completion. Services include the development of major bridges, tunnels, highways, marine facilities, buildings, industrial complexes, and railroads. **Positions advertised include:** Environmental Planner. **Special programs:** Internships. **Corporate headquarters location:** New York NY. **Other U.S. locations:** Nationwide. **Subsidiaries include:** Parsons Brinckerhoff Construction Services; Parsons Brinckerhoff International. **Number of employees worldwide:** 9,000.

RIMKUS CONSULTING GROUP, INC.
The City Tower, 333 City Boulevard West, Suite 1805, Orange CA 92868. 714/978-2044. **Fax:** 714/978-2088. **Contact:** Human Resources. **E-mail address:** careers@rimkus.com. **World Wide Web address:** http://ywtf.rimkus.com. **Description:** A diversified engineering consulting firm. Areas of expertise include automotive, chemical, environmental, cargo and roadway assessments. **NOTE:** See website for job listings. Send resumes and cover letters by e-mail or fax. **Positions advertised include:** General Contractor. **Corporate headquarters location:** Houston TX. **Other U.S. locations:** Nationwide. **International locations:** Zurich Switzerland; Kuwait City Kuwait; Madrid Spain.

ROEL CONSTRUCTION COMPANY
P.O. Box 80216, San Diego CA 92138-0216. 619/297-4156. **Physical address:** 3366 Kurtz Street, San Diego CA 92110. **Toll-free phone:** 800/662-7635. **Fax:** 619/297-1522. **Contact:** Personnel Director. **E-mail address:** careers@roel.com. **World Wide Web address:** http://www.roel.com. **Description:** A commercial and residential construction company. Roel Construction also provides tenant improvements, structural concrete construction, construction forensic services, and surety claim services. **Positions advertised include:** Assistant Project Manager; Project Engineer; Architect/Inspector. **Corporate headquarters location:** This location. **Other area locations:** Palm Desert CA; Irvine CA. **Other U.S. locations:** Las Vegas NV.

THE RYLAND GROUP, INC.
24025 Park Sorrento, Suite 400, Calabasas CA 91302. 818/223-7500. **Toll-free phone:** 800/638-1768. **Fax:** 818/223-7655. **Contact:** Human Resources. **E-mail address:** corpcareers@ryland.com. **World Wide Web address:** http://www.ryland.com. **Description:** One of the nation's largest homebuilders and a leading mortgage finance company. The company builds homes in six regions and more than 25 cities. **NOTE:** Search and apply for positions online. **Positions advertised include:** Executive Compensation Analyst; Senior Tax Accountant; Assistant Risk Manager; Senior Auditor. **Corporate headquarters location:** This location. **Other U.S. locations:** Nationwide. **Subsidiaries include:** Ryland Homes specializes in on-site construction of single-family attached and detached homes. Operating out of 34 retail and four wholesale branches, Ryland Mortgage Company works directly with Ryland Homes. **Listed on:** New York Stock Exchange. **Stock exchange symbol:** RYL. **Number of employees at this location:** 600. **Number of employees nationwide:** 3,200.

SOUTHDOWN CALIFORNIA CEMENT
5050 83rd Street, Sacramento CA 95826-4745. 916/383-0526. **Contact:** Human Resources. **Description:** Engaged in the production, sale, and delivery of ready-mixed concrete and aggregates.

STANDARD PACIFIC HOMES
15326 Alton Parkway, Irvine CA 92618. 949/789-1600. **Contact:** Human Resources Department. **E-mail address:** careers@stanpac.com. **World Wide Web address:** http://www.standardpacifichomes.com. **Description:** Designs, builds, and sells houses for residential use. **Positions advertised include:** Assistant Construction Manager. **Corporate headquarters location:** This location. **Listed on:** New York Stock Exchange. **Stock exchange symbol:** SPF. **Annual sales/revenues:** More than $100 million.

SWINERTON INCORPORATED
260 Townsend Street, San Francisco CA 94107. 415/421-2980. **Fax:** 415/984-1306. **Contact:** Marina Aviles, Director of Employment and Staffing. **World Wide Web address:** http://www.swinerton.com. **Description:** A general contracting firm that specializes in consulting, value management, and conceptual design. The company's expertise lies with the assisted living, healthcare, public facilities, renovation and restoration, tenant improvement, and transportation markets. **Positions advertised include:** Contracts Manager; Building Manager; Project Assistant; Project Engineer; Project Manager. **Special programs:** Internships. **Corporate headquarters location:** This location. **Other area locations:** Los Angeles CA. **Other U.S. locations:** Tucson AZ; Denver CO; Portland OR. **Operations at this facility include:** Administration. **Listed on:** Privately held. **Number of employees at this location:** 100. **Number of employees nationwide:** 500.

TRANS-PACIFIC CONSULTANTS
27431 Enterprise Circle West, Temecula CA 92590. 909/676-7000. **Fax:** 909/699-7324. **Contact:** Human Resources. **Description:** A full-service consulting company engaged in land planning, civil engineering, and surveying. **Corporate headquarters location:** This location.

URS CORPORATION
600 Montgomery Street, 26th Floor, San Francisco CA 94111-2728. 415/774-2700. **Fax:** 415/398-1905. **Contact:** Personnel Department. **World Wide Web address:** http://www.urscorp.com. **Description:** An international professional services organization with substantial engineering, training, architectural planning, environmental, and construction management capabilities. **Positions advertised include:** Project Manager; Internal Auditor; Vice President. **Corporate headquarters location:** This location. **Listed on:** New York Stock Exchange. **Stock exchange symbol:** URS. **Number of employees worldwide:** 26,000.

URS CORPORATION
915 Wilshire Boulevard, Suite 700, Los Angeles CA 90017. 213/996-2200. **Fax:** 213/996-2290. **Contact:**

Human Resources Department. **World Wide Web address:** http://www.urscorp.com. **Description:** An architectural, engineering, and environmental consulting firm that specializes in air transportation, environmental solutions, surface transportation, and industrial environmental and engineering concerns. **Positions advertised include:** Civil Geo-technical Engineer; Senior Urban Planner; Senior Water Resources Engineer. **Corporate headquarters location:** San Francisco CA. **Other area locations:** Statewide. **Listed on:** New York Stock Exchange. **Stock exchange symbol:** URS.

WENTZ GROUP
555 Twin Dolphin Drive, Suite 160, Redwood Shores CA 94065. 650/592-3950. **Fax:** 650/593-5632. **Contact:** Human Resources. **E-mail address:** elizabethb@wentzgroup.com. **World Wide Web address:** http://www.wentzgroup.com. **Description:** Provides general construction services. **Positions advertised include:** Senior Project Manager; Project Executive; Superintendent; Estimator; Project Manager. **Corporate headquarters location:** This location. **Other area locations:** Sacramento CA; Newport Beach CA. **Listed on:** Privately held. **Number of employees at this location:** 30.

GEORGE H. WILSON, INC.
P.O. Box 1140, Santa Cruz CA 95061-1140. 831/423-9522. **Physical address:** 250 Harvey West Boulevard, Santa Cruz CA 95660. **Contact:** Administrative Manager. **Description:** Provides plumbing, heating, air conditioning, and metal fabrication services. **Corporate headquarters location:** This location. **Operations at this facility include:** Administration; Manufacturing.

Colorado

AIR PURIFICATION COMPANY
1860 West 64th Lane, Denver CO 80221. 303/428-2800. **Contact:** Bruce Wilde, President and Owner. **World Wide Web address:** http://www.airpurificationcompany.com. **Description:** A wholesaler of air conditioning, heating, and ventilation equipment.

ARINC RESEARCH CORPORATION
1925 Aerotech Drive, Suite 212, Colorado Springs CO 80916-4219. 719/574-9001. **Contact:** Human Resources. **World Wide Web address:** http://www.arinc.com. **Description:** An engineering and management consulting firm providing technical studies, analysis, and evaluations of aircraft, ship systems, communications, and information systems. **Positions advertised include:** Staff Principal Engineer; DAS Administrative Engineer; Test & Evaluation Engineer; Sr. Communications Network Engineer. **Corporate headquarters:** Annapolis MD. **Other U.S. locations:** Nationwide. **International locations:** Worldwide. **CEO:** James L. Pierce.

BLACK & VEATCH
30 Pikes Peak, Suite 200, Colorado Springs CO 80903. 719/667-7010. **Fax:** 719/667-7009. **Contact:** Human Resources Department. **World Wide Web address:** http://www.bv.com. **Description:** An environmental/civil engineering and construction firm serving utilities, commerce, industry, and government agencies in more than 40 countries throughout the world. Black & Veatch provides a broad range of study, design, construction management, and turnkey capabilities to clients in the water and wastewater fields. The firm is one of the leading authorities on drinking water treatment through the use of activated carbon, ozone, and other state-of-the-art processes. Black & Veatch is also engaged in wastewater treatment work including reclamation and reuse projects and the beneficial use of wastewater residuals. Other services are provided for solid waste recycling and disposal, transportation, and storm water management. In the energy field, Black & Veatch is a leader in providing engineering procurement and construction for electric power plants. The firm's areas of expertise include coal-fueled plants, simple and combined-cycle combustion turbines, waste-to-energy facilities, hydroelectric plants, and cogeneration facilities. Black & Veatch's capabilities also include nuclear power projects, advanced technology, air quality control, performance monitoring, plant life management, and facilities modification. In addition, Black & Veatch provides transmission and distribution services. Black & Veatch offers a variety of management and financial services including institutional strengthening, privatization, strategic financial planning, and information management. **Positions advertised include:** Engineering Technician; Engineer; Business Development Director; Civil Engineer; Electrical Engineer. **Corporate headquarters location:** Kansas City MO.

BOYLE ENGINEERING CORPORATION
215 Union Boulevard, Suite 500, Lakewood CO 80228. 303/987-3443. **Fax:** 303/987-3908. **Contact:** Human Resources Department. **World Wide Web address:** http://www.boyleengineering.com. **Description:** Provides professional engineering services to create better infrastructure for public and private clients in the United States and abroad. Services range from project planning and feasibility studies to design and construction phases. The company is engaged in water treatment and distribution; wastewater collection, treatment, and reuse; streets, highways, and bridges construction; light and heavy rail; drainage and flood control; and land planning. **Positions advertised include:** Civil Engineer. **Corporate headquarters location:** Newport Beach CA.

CH2M HILL
6161 South Syracuse Way, Suite 200, Greenwood Village CO 80111. 303/706-0990. **Fax:** 303/706-1861. **Contact:** Human Resources. **World Wide Web address:** http://www.ch2mhill.com. **Description:** Provides mechanical, structural, and environmental engineering services through its operating divisions. **NOTE:** Interested jobseekers should fax resumes to 781/663-3733. **Corporate headquarters location:** Englewood CO. **Other area locations:** Colorado Springs CO; Golden CO. **International locations:** Worldwide. **Subsidiaries include:** CH2M Hill Engineering; Industrial Design Corporation; Operating Management International.

CARTER & BURGESS
707 17th Street, Suite 2300, Denver CO 80202-5131. 303/820-5240. **Fax:** 303/820-2402. **Contact:** Human Resources. **E-mail address:** denverinfo@c-b.com. **World Wide Web address:** http://www.c-b.com. **Description:** An architectural, engineering, and construction management firm with 32 offices in 19 states. **Positions advertised include:** CADD Technician; Design Project Manager; Civil Engineer; Civil Project Engineer; Electrical Engineer; GIS Database Solutions Project Manager; Landscape Architect; Proposal Coordinator; Sr. Marketing Coordinator; Water Resource Engineer. **Number of employees nationwide:** 2,700.

CENTEX HOMES
9250 East Costilla Avenue, Suite 200, Greenwood Village CO 80112. 303/792-9810. **Contact:** Personnel. **World Wide Web address:** http://www.centexhomes.com. **Description:** Builds and sells residential homes nationwide. **Corporate headquarters location:** Dallas TX. **Parent company:** Centex Corporation provides home building, mortgage banking, contracting, and construction products and services. **Listed on:** New York Stock Exchange. **Stock exchange symbol:** CTX.

CREATIVE TOUCH INTERIORS
3251 Lewiston Street, Unit #10, Aurora CO 80011. 303/363-3687. **Contact:** Human Resources. **World Wide Web address:** http://www.ctihome.com. **Description:** Engaged in the installation and refinishing of hardwood floors. The company is also engaged in the installation of carpet, vinyl, ceramic tile, and related floor coverings. Founded in 1959. **Positions advertised include:** Scheduler; Production Assistant; Customer Service Representative; Field Supervisor;

Warehouse Driver; Corian Fabricators; Flooring Trainee.

HENSEL PHELPS CONSTRUCTION COMPANY
420 Sixth Avenue, Greeley CO 80632. 970/352-6565. **Fax:** 970/352-9311. **Contact:** Ron Norby, Vice President. **E-mail address:** careers@henselphelps.com. **World Wide Web address:** http://www.henselphelps.com. **Description:** A commercial construction company. **Number of employees nationwide:** 2,600.

ISEC, INC.
P.O. Box 6849, Englewood CO 80155. 303/790-1444. **Physical address:** 33 Inverness Drive East, Englewood CO 80112. **Contact:** Human Resources. **World Wide Web address:** http://www.isecinc.com. **Description:** Provides contract engineering services. **Corporate headquarters location:** this location. **Number of employees nationwide:** 1,000.

JACOBS ENGINEERING GROUP, INC.
JACOBS FACILITIES, INC.
1527 Cole Boulevard, Golden CO 80401. 303/462-7000. **Fax:** 303/462-7001. **Contact:** Human Resources. **E-mail address:** info@jacobs.com. **World Wide Web address:** http://www.jacobs.com. **Description:** An engineering and construction company that provides engineering, procurement, construction, and maintenance services to clients and industries. These industries include chemicals and polymers, federal programs, pulp and paper, semiconductor, petroleum refining, facilities and transportation, food and consumer products, pharmaceuticals and biotechnologies, and basic resources. Through Jacobs College and other site-specific programs, the company trains more than 5,000 employees per year in project and money management, health and safety, and numerous other performance enhancing topics. **Positions advertised include:** Project Controls Specialist. **Corporate headquarters location:** Pasadena CA. **Listed on:** New York Stock Exchange. **Stock exchange symbol:** JEC.

KIEWIT WESTERN COMPANY
7926 South Platte Canyon Road, Littleton CO 80128-5978. 303/979-9330. **Contact:** Mark Campbell, District Business Manager. **World Wide Web address:** http://www.kiewit.com. **Description:** A general contracting company. **Corporate headquarters location:** Omaha NE. **Parent company:** The Kiewit Companies. **Number of employees at this location:** 115.

MERRICK & COMPANY
2450 South Peoria Street, Aurora CO 80014. 303/751-0741. **Fax:** 303/751-2581. **Contact:** Human Resources. **E-mail address:** info@merrick.com. **World Wide Web address:** http://www.merrick.com. **Description:** A full-service engineering and architectural firm. Merrick & Company specializes in advanced technology, civil infrastructure, government, heavy industrial, and land development services. **Positions advertised include:** Piping Designer. **Corporate headquarters location:** This location. **Other U.S. locations:** Atlanta GA; Albuquerque NM; Los Alamos NM. **Listed on:** Privately held. **Number of employees nationwide:** 320.

NEXUS CORPORATION
10983 Leroy Drive, Northglenn CO 80233. 303/457-9199. **Fax:** 303/457-2801. **Contact:** Human Resources. **World Wide Web address:** http://www.nexuscorp.com. **Description:** Manufactures prefabricated, metal greenhouses.

NOLTE
8000 South Chester Street, Suite 200, Centennial CO 80112. 303/220-6400. **Fax:** 303/220-9001. **Contact:** Human Resources. **Email address:** denver_info@nolte.com. **World Wide Web address:** http://www.nolte.com. **Description:** Nolte is a full-service civil engineering firm with offices in the Western United States and Mexico. Areas of specialty include: flood control and drainage; land planning and development; structural engineering; surveying and mapping; traffic and transportation; water supply, distribution and treatment; wastewater engineering and water recycling; construction and program management. **Positions advertised include:** Sr. Office CM Engineer; Sr. Field CM Engineer; Jr. Surveyor; Sr. Office Surveyor; Sr. Engineer; Engineering Manager. **Number of employees nationwide:** 400.

GERALD H. PHIPPS, INC.
1530 West 13th Avenue, Denver CO 80204-2400. 303/571-5377. **Fax:** 303/629-7467. **Contact:** Human Resources. **E-mail address:** HRInquiries@ghpd.com. **World Wide Web address:** http://www.geraldhphipps.com. **Description:** A general contractor/construction manager for commercial buildings. Gerald H. Phipps, Inc. specializes in building medical complexes, high-tech buildings, universities, schools, offices that tenants finish, public facilities, biotechnology labs, and retail projects. Founded in 1952. **Positions advertised include:** Project Engineer; Superintendent, Concrete Division. **Corporate headquarters location:** This location. **Other area locations:** Colorado Springs CO. **Listed on:** Privately held. **Annual sales/revenues:** More than $100 million. **Number of employees at this location:** 250.

GEORGE T. SANDERS COMPANY
10201 West 49th Avenue, Wheat Ridge CO 80033. 303/423-9660. **Fax:** 303/420-8737. **Contact:** Human Resources. **E-mail address:** jobs@gtsanders.com. **World Wide Web address:** http://www.gtsanders.com. **Description:** An independent wholesale distributor of plumbing and heating supplies. George T. Sanders Company operates seven locations in Colorado. **NOTE:** Entry-level positions and part-time jobs are offered. **Office hours:** Monday - Friday, 7:00 a.m. - 5:00 p.m. **Corporate headquarters location:** This location. **Listed on:** Privately held. **President:** Gary T. Sanders. **Purchasing Manager:** Kirk Anderson. **Annual sales/revenues:** $21 - $50 million.

SCIENCE APPLICATIONS INTERNATIONAL CORPORATION (SAIC)
405 Urban Street, Suite 400, Lakewood CO 80228. 303/969-6000. **Contact:** Human Resources. **World Wide Web address:** http://www.saic.com. **Description:** The largest employee-owned research and engineering firm in the U.S. Founded in 1969. **Positions advertised include:** Engineer; Sr. Water Resource Engineer Program Manager; NEPA Specialist; Environmental Analyst; Sr. Unix Systems Administrator; Network Analyst; Oracle Financial Database Administrator; Network Analyst. **Number of employees worldwide:** 43,000.

SPARTA, INC.
985 Space Center Drive, Suite 100, Colorado Springs CO 80915. 719/570-6998. **Fax:** 719/380-6495. **Contact:** Human Resources. **World Wide Web address:** http://www.sparta.com. **Description:** An employee-owned engineering and advanced technology company providing technical products and services to the defense, intelligence, and homeland security sectors of the federal government. **Positions advertised include:** Analyst; Communications/Systems Engineer; DoD Architect; DoD Architect Programmer; Senior Analyst; Space Systems Analyst; Sr. Configuration Management Analyst; Sr. Space Systems Analyst; Web Engineer; Web Portal Engineer. **Corporate headquarters location:** Lake Forest CA.

TERRACON
4172 Center Park Drive, Colorado Springs CO 80916. 719/597-2116. **Fax:** 719/597-2117. **Contact:** Human Resources. **Email address:** careers@terracon.com. **World Wide Web address:** http://www.terracon.com. **Description:** Terracon is an employee-owned provider of geotechnical, environmental, construction materials, and related services, with more than 70 offices in 25 states. Founded in 1965. **NOTE:** When applying, the position title, Req #, and office location must be specified. **Positions advertised include:** Project

Structural Engineer; Construction Materials Technician. **Other area locations:** Denver CO; Fort Collins CO; Greeley CO; Pueblo CO. **Corporate headquarters location:** Lenexa KS.

TETRA TECH EM INC.
4940 Pearl East Circle, Suite 100, Boulder CO 80301. 303/441-7900. **Fax:** 303/447-5585. **World Wide Web address:** http://www.tetratech.com. **Description:** Provides specialized engineering management consulting and technical services in the areas of resource management, infrastructure, and communications. **Positions advertised include:** Civil/Environmental Engineer; Engineering Intern; Human Health Risk Assessor. **Corporate headquarters location:** Pasadena CA. **Listed on:** NASDAQ. **Stock exchange symbol:** TTEK. **Number of employees worldwide:** 8,000.

TRANE COMPANY
101 William White Boulevard, Pueblo CO 81001. 719/585-3800. **Contact:** Human Resources. **World Wide Web address:** http://www.trane.com. **Description:** Develops, manufactures, and sells air-conditioning equipment. **Corporate headquarters location:** Piscataway NJ. **Parent company:** American Standard Companies, Inc. **Listed on:** New York Stock Exchange. **Stock exchange symbol:** ASD.

U.S. ENGINEERING COMPANY
729 Southeast 8th Street, Loveland CO 80537. 970/669-1666. **Fax:** 970/663-0685. **Contact:** Human Resources Department. **E-mail address:** jobs@usengineering.com. **World Wide Web address:** http://www.usengineering.com. **Description:** A contracting company that installs heating, air conditioning, piping, and sprinkler systems for businesses. **Positions advertised include:** Pre-Construction Engineer; Piping Detailer. **Corporate headquarters location:** Kansas City MO. **Listed on:** Privately held. **Annual sales/revenues:** More than $100 million. **Number of employees at this location:** 300. **Number of employees nationwide:** 600.

UNITED PIPELINE SYSTEMS, INC.
135 Turner Drive, Durango CO 81302. 970/259-0354. **Fax:** 970/259-0356. **Contact:** Project Manager. **World Wide Web address:** http://www.insituform.com. **Description:** Engaged in the restoration of pipes. **Parent company:** Insituform Technologies, Inc. uses various trenchless technologies for restoration, new construction, and improvements of pipeline systems including sewers, gas lines, industrial waste lines, water lines and oil field, mining, and industrial process pipelines. **Listed on:** NASDAQ. **Stock exchange symbol:** INSUA.

VANGUARD RESEARCH, INC.
770 Wooten Road, Colorado Springs CO 80915. 719/596-1174. **Contact:** General Manager. **E-mail address:** hr@vriusa.com. **World Wide Web address:** http://www.vriffx.com. **Description:** Provides engineering and technical support services. **Corporate headquarters location:** Arlington VA. **Other U.S. locations:** Bellevue NE. **President/CEO:** Mel Chaskin. **Facilities Manager:** Lee Morgan. **Number of employees at this location:** 30. **Number of employees nationwide:** 150.

WASHINGTON GROUP INTERNATIONAL
7800 East Union Avenue, Suite 100, Denver CO 80237. 303/843-2000. **Contact:** Human Resources. **World Wide Web address:** http://www.wgint.com. **Description:** An engineering and construction firm operating through five major divisions: Government, Industrial/Process, Infrastructure & Mining, Petroleum & Chemicals, and Power. Washington Group International offers construction, engineering, and program-management services to the environmental, industrial, mining, nuclear-services, power, transportation, and water resources industries. **Positions advertised include:** Estimating Manager; Engineer; Equipment Engineer; Mine Engineer. **Operations at this facility include:** Divisional Headquarters; Service.

WRIGHT WATER ENGINEERS INC.
2490 West 26th Avenue, Suite 100A, Denver CO 80211-4208. 303/480-1700. **Fax:** 303/480-1020. **Contact:** Personnel. **E-mail address:** personnel@wrightwater.com. **World Wide Web address:** http://www.wrightwater.com. **Description:** Specializes in the planning and developing of water resources. **Positions advertised include:** Civil Design Engineer. **Other area locations:** Glenwood Springs CO; Durango CO.

Connecticut

ABB INC.
P.O. Box 5308, Norwalk CT 06856-5308. 203/750-2200. **Physical address:** 501 Merritt Seven, Norwalk CT 06851. **Fax:** 203/750-2263. **Contact:** Human Resources. **World Wide Web address:** http://www.abb.com/us. **Description:** Provides engineering, construction, and sales support services as part of a worldwide engineering firm. Internationally, the company operates in five business segments: oil field equipment and services; power systems; engineering and construction; process equipment; and industrial products. **Corporate headquarters location:** This location. **Other U.S. locations:** Nationwide. **International locations:** Worldwide. **Subsidiaries include:** ABB Lumus Global Inc., Bloomfield NJ; ABB Simcon, Broomfield NJ. **Parent company:** ABB Asea Brown Boveri Ltd. (Baden, Switzerland.) **Number of employees worldwide:** 220,000.

BVH INTEGRATED SERVICES, INC.
50 Griffin Road South, Bloomfield CT 06002. 860/286-9171. **Fax:** 860/242-0236. **Contact:** Human Resources. **E-mail address:** start@bvhis.com. **World Wide Web address:** http://www.bvhis.com. **Description:** Provides mechanical, electrical, structural, and civil engineering services.

J. BROWN/LMC GROUP
1010 Washington Boulevard, 8th Floor, Stamford CT 06901. 203/352-0600. **Contact:** Human Resources. **World Wide Web address:** http://www.jbrown.com. **Description:** An international engineering and construction firm serving the plastics, pharmaceutical, food, biotechnology, chemical, oil, and gas industries. **Other U.S. locations:** San Francisco CA; Chicago IL; Cincinnati OH. **Number of employees nationwide:** 185.

CARRIER CORPORATION
One Carrier Place, Farmington CT 06034-4015. 860/674-3000. **Contact:** Human Resources. **E-mail address:** great.jobs@carrier.utc.com. **World Wide Web address:** http://www.carrier.com. **Description:** Manufactures heating, refrigeration, and air conditioning equipment. **Positions advertised include:** Accountant/Auditor; Data Processor; Electrical/Electronics Engineer; Financial Analyst; Mechanical Engineer. **Corporate headquarters location:** This location.

LORENZ FLUIDYNE
One Riverside Drive, Ansonia CT 06401. 203/735-9311. **Toll-free phone:** 800/765-2676. **Fax:** 203/736-3489. **Contact:** Human Resources. **Description:** Produces plumbing supplies and runs a contract screw machine business.

O&G INDUSTRIES INC.
112 Wall Street, Torrington CT 06790. 860/489-9261. **Contact:** Human Resources. **World Wide Web address:** http://www.ogindustries.com. **Description:** A construction firm providing building construction management, design services, heavy civil construction, environmental remediation, and construction materials. **Positions advertised include:** Accountant; Senior Buildings Estimator; Business Development Manager; Project Manager; Project Engineer. **Corporate headquarters location:** This location. **Other area locations:** Bridgeport CT; Southbury CT.

Delaware

BALTIMORE AIRCOIL COMPANY
1162 Holly Hill Road, Milford DE 19963. 302/422-3061. **Fax:** 302/422-9296. **Contact:** Human Resources. **E-mail address:** hr@baltimoreaircoil.com. **World Wide Web address:** http://www.baltimoreaircoil.com. **Description:** A specialist in the design and manufacture of evaporative cooling equipment, cooling towers, evaporative condensers and closed circuit cooling systems. **Other U.S. locations:** Baltimore MD; Madera CA; Paxton IL. **International Locations:** Worldwide.

CB&I (CHICAGO BRIDGE & IRON COMPANY N.V.)
24 Read's Way, New Castle DE 19720. 302/325-8420. **Fax:** 302/325-8425. **Contact:** Human Resources Department. **E-mail address:** employment@cbi.com. **World Wide Web address:** http://www.chicago-bridge.com. **Description:** A global engineering and construction company specializing in steel plate structures. Founded in 1889. **NOTE:** Mail resume to: CB&I, Attn: Human Resources Dept., One CB&I Plaza, 2103 Research Forest Drive, The Woodlands TX 77380. **Listed on:** New York Stock Exchange. **Stock exchange symbol:** CBI.

M. DAVIS & SONS INC.
200 Hadco Road, Wilmington DE 19804-1000. 302/998-3385. **Toll-free phone:** 800/91-DAVIS. **Fax:** 302/655-0245. **Contact:** Human Resources. **E-mail address:** hr@mdavisinc.com. **World Wide Web address:** http://www.mdavisinc.com. **Description:** Offers industrial and pharmaceutical services including computer aided design/build, custom shop fabrication, shutdown capabilities, electrical services and general industrial/mechanical maintenance. Founded in 1870. **NOTE:** To inquire about current job openings contact Human Resources, apply in person or complete the online employment form. **Positions advertised include:** CAD Operator; Crane Operator; Electrician; Steel Fitter; Insulator; Maintenance Mechanic; Millwright; Pipe Fitter; Plumber; Sheet Metal Mechanic; Welder; Iron Worker; Rigger. **Corporate headquarters location:** This location.

DEACON INDUSTRIAL SUPPLY COMPANY INCORPORATED
P.O. Box 765, 7 East Commons Boulevard, New Castle DE 19720. 302/322-5411. **Fax:** 302/322-3493. **Contact:** Human Resources. **E-mail address:** hr@deaconind.com. **World Wide Web address:** http://www.deaconind.com. **Description:** Distributes valves, gaskets, piping, and commercial plumbing supplies. **Note:** Mail Resumes to 165 Boro Line Road, P.O. Box 62485, King of Prussia PA 19406. **Corporate headquarters location:** King of Prussia PA. **Operations at this facility include:** Administration; Sales; Stock.

EDWARD J. DESETA CO., INC.
322 A Street, Suite 200, Wilmington DE 19801-5355. 302/691-2040. **Fax:** 302/691-2041. **Contact:** Human Resources. **World Wide Web address:** http://www.ejdeseta.com. **Description:** Industrial HVAC contractors and engineers.

HOMSEY ARCHITECTURE INC.
2003 North Scott Street, Wilmington DE 19806. 302/656-4491. **Fax:** 302/656-5956. **Contact:** Human Resources. **E-mail address:** employment@homsey.com. **World Wide Web address:** http://www.homsey.com. **Description:** A full-service architecture firm specializing in architecture, landscaping and interior architectural design. Founded in 1935.

SNYDER, CROMPTON & ASSOCIATES, INC.
3411 Silverside Road, Hagley Building, Suite 202, Wilmington DE 19810. 302/478-6030. **Fax:** 302/478-3775. **Contact:** Jeni Albany, Human Resources Manager. **E-mail address:** jalbany@scaconstructs.com. **World Wide Web address:** http://www.scaconstructs.com. **Description:** Provides construction management and general contracting services. **Positions advertised include:** Carpenters; Construction Foreman/Site Superintendents.

J.F. SOBIESKI MECHANICAL CONTRACTORS, INC.
14 Hadco Road, Wilmington DE 19804. 302/993-0103. **Toll-free phone:** 800/665-0002. **Fax:** 302/993.0119. **Contact:** Human Resources. **E-mail address:** hr@sobieskiinc.com. **World Wide Web address:** http://www.sobieskiinc.com. **Description:** A multi-trade industrial, institutional, commercial and residential contractor specializing in process piping, heating, ventilation, air conditioning, plumbing and fire protection. **Positions advertised include:** Plumbing & HVAC Service Technician; HVAC Commercial Technician; HVAC Installer. **Number of employees at this location:** Over 200.

SPEAKMAN COMPANY
P.O. Box 191, Wilmington DE 19899. 302/764-7100. **Toll-free phone:** 800/537-2107. **Fax:** 800/977-2747. **Contact:** Arlene Lunbeck, Personnel Director. **World Wide Web address:** http://www.speakmancompany.com. **Description:** A manufacturer of plumbing, heating and emergency equipment.

TILCON DELAWARE INC.
3700 Bay Road, Dover DE 19901. 302/734-8632. **Contact:** Human Resources. **World Wide Web address:** http://www.tilconde.com. **Description:** A paving contractor that also provides asphalt, gravel, sand and stone to the construction industry.

District of Columbia

AEPA ARCHITECTS ENGINEERS PC
2421 Pennsylvania Avenue NW, Washington DC 20037. 202/822-8320. **Fax:** 202/457-0908. **Contact:** Director of Operations. **World Wide Web address:** http://www.aepa.com. **Description:** An architectural services firm that specializes in biomedical research facilities. **Corporate headquarters location:** This location. **President:** Alfred H. Liu.

HORNING BROTHERS
1350 Connecticut Avenue NW, Suite 800, Washington DC 20036. 202/659-0700. **Contact:** Human Resources. **E-mail address:** resume@horningbrothers.com. **World Wide Web address:** http://www.horningbrothers.com. **Description:** A residential and commercial development, construction, and management company. **Positions advertised include:** Property Manager. **Corporate headquarters location:** This location. **Operations at this facility include:** Administration; Divisional Headquarters. **Number of employees at this location:** 15. **Number of employees nationwide:** 100.

PARSONS BRINCKERHOFF INC.
1401 K Street NW, Suite 701, Washington DC 20005. 202/783-0241. **Fax:** 202/783-0229. **Contact:** Human Resources. **E-mail address:** careers@pbworld.com. **World Wide Web address:** http://www.pbworld.com. **Description:** An architectural engineering firm. **Positions advertised include:** Financial Analyst. **Special programs:** Internships available. **Corporate headquarters location:** New York NY.

THOMAS SOMERVILLE COMPANY
4912 Sixth Street NE, Washington DC 20017. 202/635-4100. **Fax:** 202/635-4154. **Contact:** Human Resources. **World Wide Web address:** http://www.tsomerville.com. **Description:** A distributor of plumbing, heating, and air conditioning supplies. **Corporate headquarters location:** Upper Marlboro MD. **Other U.S. locations:** Annapolis MD; Hyattsville MD; Baltimore MD; Martinsburg WV; Lancaster PA; York PA; Fairfax VA; Chantilly VA.

TOMPKINS BUILDERS, INC.
1333 H Street NW, Suite 200, Washington DC 20005. 202/789-0770. **Contact:** Manager. **World Wide Web address:** http://www.turnerconstruction.com/tompkins. **Description:** A general construction contractor. **Positions advertised include:** Business Development

Manager; Construction Executive; Cost Engineer; Field Engineer; Safety Engineer; Sr. Estimating Engineer. **Parent company:** Turner Construction Company.

Florida

AJT & ASSOCIATES, INC.
8910 Astronaut Boulevard, Cape Canaveral FL 32920-4225. 321/783-7989. **Contact:** Karen Yorio, Human Resources Representative. **E-mail address:** kareny@ajt-assoc.com. **World Wide Web address:** http://www.ajt-assoc.com. **Description:** Provides environmental science and architectural engineering services.

ATC ASSOCIATES
9955 NW 116 Way, Suite 1, Medley FL 33178. 305/882-8200. **Fax:** 305/882-1200. **Contact:** Human Resources. **World Wide Web address:** http://www.atc-enviro.com. **Description:** Performs comprehensive environmental consulting, engineering, and on-site remediation services. Services include assessment of environmental regulations, investigation of contaminated sites, and the design and engineering of methods to correct or prevent the contamination. The company also performs remedial actions, and emergency response actions in cases of spills and accidental releases of hazardous waste. ATC Associates addresses hazardous and nonhazardous contaminants in municipal and industrial water supplies; in wastewater and storm water from municipal, industrial, and military installations; and in groundwater, soils, and air space. Customers include federal, state, and local government agencies. **Positions advertised include:** NDT Technician.

ALUMA SYSTEMS
6402 East Hanna Avenue, Tampa FL 33610. 813/626-1133. **Toll-free phone:** 800/282-9199. **Contact:** Personnel. **E-mail address:** dtweedy@aluma.com. **World Wide Web address:** http://www.aluma.com. **Description:** Supplies forming, shoring, and scaffolding products to the industrial maintenance and concrete construction industries. **Operations at this facility include:** Sales. **President/CEO:** Jim Demitrieus.

APAC INC.
14299 Alico Road, Fort Myers FL 33913. 239/267-7767. **Contact:** Ms Elaine Paserella, Personnel Manager. **World Wide Web address:** http://www.apac.com. **Description:** APAC provides materials, services, and technology to the construction industry. **Positions advertised include:** Project Manager.

APAC INC.
4655 Jerry L. Maygarden Road, Pensacola FL 32504. 850/439-0880. **Contact:** Human Resources. **World Wide Web address:** http://www.apac.com. **Description:** A contractor specializing in road construction. **Positions advertised include:** Staff Accountant; Administrative Assistant.

APAC INC.
1451 Myrtle Street, Sarasota FL 34234. 941/355-7179. **Contact:** Human Resources. **World Wide Web address:** http://www.apac.com. **Description:** A manufacturer of asphalt. **Positions advertised include:** Operations Manager.

ATLANTIC MARINE, INC.
ATLANTIC DRY DOCK CORPORATION
8500 Heckscher Drive, Jacksonville FL 32226. 904/251-3164. **Toll-free phone:** 800/395-6446. **Fax:** 904/251-1579. **Contact:** Human Resources. **World Wide Web address:** http://www.atlanticmarine.com. **E-mail address:** jaxresumes@atlanticmarine.com. **Description:** Builds, repairs, and converts ships for government, commercial, and consumer markets.

BERTRAM YACHT, INC.
P.O. Box 520774 GMF, Miami FL 33152. 305/633-8011. **Physical address**: 3663 Northwest 21st Street, Miami FL 33142. **Fax:** 954/462-0029. **Contact:** John Marler or Manager of Human Resources. **E-mail address:** jmarler@alliedrichardbertram.com. **World Wide Web address:** http://www.alliedrichardbertram.com. **Description:** A manufacturer of yachts. **Positions advertised include:** Marine Technician Electrician; Outboard Technician; Inboard Technician. **Corporate headquarters location:** This location. **Parent company:** Bertram, Inc. **Operations at this facility include:** Manufacturing. **Number of employees at this location:** 240.

CAMERON ASHLEY BUILDING PRODUCTS
5120 west Clifton Street, Tampa FL 33684. 813/884-0444. **Toll-free phone:** 800/749-4067. **Contact:** Human Resources. **World Wide Web address:** http://www.cabp.com. **Description:** A manufacturer and distributor of aluminum and vinyl building products. Founded in 1967. **Corporate headquarters location:** This location. **Other U.S. locations:** AL; GA; KY; LA; TX. **Listed on:** New York Stock Exchange. **Stock exchange symbol:** CAB. **President:** Steve Gaffney. **Annual sales/revenues:** More than $100 million. **Number of employees at this location:** 100. **Number of employees nationwide:** 500.

CATALINA YACHTS
7200 Bryan Dairy Road, Largo FL 33777. 727/544-6681. **Fax:** 727/546-7303. **Contact:** Georgia B. Law, Human Resources Manager. **E-mail address:** georgiacatalinayachts.com. **World Wide Web address:** http://www.catalinayachts.com. **Description:** A yacht manufacturer. Founded in 1970. **Positions advertised include:** Assembler. **Corporate headquarters location:** Woodland Hills CA. **Number of employees at this location:** 170.

CENTEX ROONEY
7901 SW 6th Court, Plantation FL 33324. 954/585-4000. **Contact:** Human Resources. **World Wide Web address:** http://www.centex.com. **Description:** A construction and general contracting company. **Positions advertised include:** Architectural Manager; Strategic Marketing Manager; Operational Marketing Manager; Division Sales Manager; Draftsperson; Field Manager; Customer Service Manager. **Listed on:** New York Stock Exchange. **Stock exchange symbol:** CTX.

J.W. CONNER & SONS, INC.
4100 East 7th Avenue, Tampa FL 33605. 813/247-4441. **Contact:** Michelle Williams, Human Resources. **Description:** A road and highway contractor.

DEVCON INTERNATIONAL CORPORATION
1350 East Newport Center Drive, Suite 201, Deerfield Beach FL 33442. 954/429-1500. **Contact:** Human Resources. **World Wide Web address:** http://www.devc.com. **Description:** Provides heavy construction services focusing on industrial projects in the Caribbean. **Number of employees at this location:** 640.

EXPONENT FAILURE ANALYSIS ASSOCIATES
4101 SW 71st Avenue, Miami FL 33155. 305/661-7726. **Toll-free phone:** 888/656-3976. **Contact:** Human Resources. **E-mail address:** hr@exponent.com. **World Wide Web address:** http://www.exponent.com. **Description:** Engaged in accident reconstruction, biomechanics, construction/structural engineering, aviation and marine investigations, environmental assessment, materials and product testing, warnings and labeling issues, accident statistic data analysis, and risk prevention/mitigation. Founded in 1967. **NOTE:** All hiring is conducted through the main offices of Exponent, Inc. Please send resumes to: Human Resources, 149 Commonwealth Drive, Menlo Park CA 94025. **Positions advertised include:** Civil Engineering. **Corporate headquarters location:** Menlo Park CA. **Listed on:** NASDAQ. **Stock exchange symbol:** EXPO. **Number of employees nationwide:** 675.

FLORIDA CRUSHED STONE COMPANY
P.O. Box 490180, Leesburg FL 34749-0300. 352/787-0608. 1616 South 14th Street, Leesburg FL 34748.

Contact: Human Resources. **World Wide Web address:** http://www.fcsco.com. **Description:** Manufactures construction materials including cement, aggregates, and pavement components.

FLORIDA ENGINEERED CONSTRUCTION PRODUCTS
P.O. Box 24567, Tampa FL 33623. 813/621-4641. **Fax:** 813/630-5476. **Contact:** Larry Toll, Human Resources. **Description:** Manufactures building materials including precast lintels and sills, prestressed concrete beams and joints, roof trusses, and architectural precast slabs. **Corporate headquarters location:** This location. **Other area locations:** Kissimmee FL; Odessa FL; Sarasota FL; West Palm Beach FL; Winter Springs FL. **Operations at this facility include:** Administration; Divisional Headquarters; Manufacturing; Regional Headquarters; Sales; Service. **Listed on:** Privately held. **Number of employees at this location:** 250. **Number of employees nationwide:** 350.

THE HASKELL COMPANY
111 Riverside Avenue, Jacksonville FL 32202. 904/791-4500. **Contact:** Human Resources. **E-mail address:** recruiter@thehaskellco.com. **World Wide Web address:** http://www.thehaskellco.com. **Description:** Provides architectural, construction, engineering, and real estate services. **Positions advertised include:** Assistant Project Manager; Director of Infrastructure; Director of Software & Integration Systems; Director of Career Development; Project Manager; Project Estimator. **Corporate headquarters location:** This location. **Operations at this facility include:** Regional Headquarters.

HUBBARD CONSTRUCTION COMPANY
1936 Lee Road, Suite 120, Winter Park FL 32789. 407/645-5500. **Contact:** Margaret Collins, Director P of Personnel. **World Wide Web address:** http://www.hubbard.com. **Description:** A general construction contractor that specializes in paving, bridge-building, and highway construction. **Positions advertised include:** Asphalt Operator; Asphalt Trade; Back Hoe Operator; Trade Carpenter; Clerical Staff; Concrete Trade; Dozer Operator; Salary Estimator; Foremen; Laborer; Mechanic; Pile Driver; Quality Control; Roller Operator; Supervisor Truck Driver. **Corporate headquarters location:** This location. **Operations at this facility include:** Administration. **Number of employees at this location:** 750. **Number of employees nationwide:** 1,000.

JENKINS AND CHARLAND, INC.
3590 NW 56th Street, Fort Lauderdale FL 33309. 954/484-7777. **Toll-free phone:** 800/486-8986. **Fax:** 954/484-7834. **Contact:** Human Resources. **E-mail address:** ftl@jcengineers.com. **World Wide Web address:** http://www.jcengineers.com. **Description:** Jenkins and Charland is a construction-engineering firm. **Positions advertised include:** Structural Drafter/Designer; Senior Structural Engineer/ Engineering Manager; Structural Engineer. **Other area locations:** Fort Myers FL; Fort Pierce FL; Jacksonville FL; Sarasota FL; Tampa FL.

MISENER MARINE CONSTRUCTION INC.
5600 West Commerce Street, Tampa FL 33616. 813/839-8441. **Contact:** Human Resources. **E-mail address:** lbosworth@orionmarinegroup.com. **World Wide Web address:** http://www.misenermarine.com. **Description:** Engaged in the heavy marine construction of bridges, docks, piers, underwater pipeline and cable, and foundation piling. **Positions advertised include:** Project Manager; Project Engineer. **Corporate headquarters location:** This location.

NOBILITY HOMES, INC.
P. O. Box 1659, Ocala FL 34478. 352/732-5157. **Physical address:** 3741 Southwest 7th Street, Ocala FL 34474. **Contact:** Human Resources. **E-mail address:** info@mobilityhomes.com. **World Wide Web address:** http://www.nobilityhomes.com. **Description:** Designs and manufactures factory-constructed homes. The company also operates real estate sales centers. **Corporate headquarters location:** This location.

ORIOLE HOMES CORPORATION
6400 Congress Avenue, Suite 2000, Boca Raton FL 33487. 561/999-1860. **Fax:** 561/988-9490. **Contact:** Steve Mahon, Director of Human Resources. **World Wide Web address:** http://www.oriolehomes.com. **Description:** Builds and sells houses and condominiums.

PALM HARBOR HOMES
605 South Frontage Road, Suite C, Plant City FL 33563. 813/719-3335. **Fax:** 813/707-1337. **Contact:** Human Resources. **E-mail address:** mvitko@palmharbor.com. **World Wide Web address:** http://www.palmharbor.com. **Description:** A home manufacturer and seller. **Positions advertised include:** Retail Sales Associate.

PALMER ELECTRIC COMPANY SHOWCASE LIGHTING
875 Jackson Avenue, Winter Park FL 32789. 407/646-8700. **Contact:** Human Resources. **World Wide Web address:** http://www.palmer-electric.com. **Description:** Provides electrical services to commercial and residential customers.

POST, BUCKLEY, SCHUH AND JERNIGAN, INC.
2001 NW 107th Avenue, Miami FL 33172-2507. 305/592-7275. **Fax:** 305/594-9478. **Contact:** Human Resources. **World Wide Web address:** http://www.pbsj.com. **Description:** Offers architectural, engineering, and planning/design consulting services. **Positions advertised include:** Senior Project Manager; Senior Field Representative; Senior Information Solutions Developer; Office Engineer; Senior Estimator; Marketing Assistant; Finance Analyst. **Operations at this facility include:** Administration; Regional Headquarters; Sales; Service. **Number of employees nationwide:** 2,700.

RWA, INC.
3050 North Horseshoe Drive, Suite 270, Naples FL 34104. 239/649-1509. **Fax:** 239/649-7056. **Contact:** Human Resources. **E-mail address:** careers@consult-rwa.com. **World Wide Web address:** http://www.consult-rwa.com. **Description:** RWA is a land development and civil engineering design firm offering solutions to both private and public sector clients. **Positions advertised include:** Director of Engineering; Engineering CAD Technician; GIS CAD Technician; Project Manager/Professional Engineer; Survey Instrument Person; Survey Party Chief. **Corporate headquarters location:** This location. **Other area locations:** Fort Myers FL.

REYNOLDS, SMITH AND HILLS, INC.
P.O. Box 4850, Jacksonville FL 32201-4850. 904/256-2500. **Physical address:** 10748 Deerwood Park Boulevard, Jacksonville FL 32256. **Contact:** Jack Higson, Human Resources Director. **World Wide Web address:** http://www.rsandh.com. **Description:** Offers architectural, engineering, and planning/design consulting services. **Positions advertised include:** Senior Civil Site Design Engineer; Landscape Architect; Intern Architect; Structural Engineer. **Other area locations:** Fort Meyers; Merritt Island; Orlando; Plantation; Tampa. **Other U.S. locations:** Chicago IL; Flint MI; Duluth MN; Austin TX; Houston TX. **Number of employees nationwide:** 375.

TREADWAY INDUSTRIES, LLC
111 Weber Avenue, Leesburg FL 34748. 352/326-3313. **Toll-free phone:** 866/TRYTWAY. **Fax:** 352/787-2888. **Contact:** Human Resources. **E-mail address:** info@treadwayindustries.com. **World Wide Web address:** http://www.treadwayindustries.com. **Description:** Treadway Industries assists customers needing architectural and decorative elements within the U.S. and overseas. The markets Treadway services include Commercial Building, Single and Multi-family Residential, Visual Merchandising, Movie and

Television Set, Themeing and Props, Landscape and Hardscape, and Signage and Entryways. **Positions advertised include:** Project Coordinator.

TRI-CITY ELECTRICAL CONTRACTORS
430 West Drive, Altamonte Springs FL 32714. 407/788-3500. **Contact:** Dori Silberman, Director of Human Resources. **Description:** Performs electrical contracting work for both commercial and residential clients.

WALT DISNEY IMAGINEERING
P.O. Box 10321, Lake Buena Vista FL 32830. 407/566-1900. **Physical address:** 200 Celebration Place, Celebration FL 34747. 407/566-1900. **Fax:** 407/566-4220. **Contact:** Human Resources. **World Wide Web address:** http://www.disney.com. **Description:** Responsible for the design, development, and construction of The Walt Disney Company's premiere attractions, resorts, and entertainment venues. **Positions advertised include:** Software Engineer; Staff Assistant; Principal Software Engineer; Assistant Technical Director. **NOTE:** Entry-level positions are offered. **Company slogan:** We make the magic! **Special programs:** Internships. **Corporate headquarters location:** Glendale CA. **Other U.S. locations:** Orlando FL. **Parent company:** The Walt Disney Company. **Operations at this facility include:** Regional Headquarters. **Listed on:** New York Stock Exchange. **Stock exchange symbol:** DIS. **Number of employees at this location:** 400. **Number of employees nationwide:** 50,000. **Number of employees worldwide:** 60,000.

WALTER INDUSTRIES
4211 West Boy Scout Boulevard, P.O. Box 31601, Tampa FL 33631. 813/871-4811. **Recorded jobline:** 813/871-4100. **Contact:** Employment Manager. **World Wide Web address:** http://www.walterind.com. **Description:** One of the nation's largest industrial companies, with leading interests in home building and financing, natural resources, and industrial manufacturing. **Positions advertised include:** Administrative Assistant; Bill of Material Management Coordinator; Executive Assistant. **Listed on:** New York Stock Exchange. **Stock exchange symbol:** WLT.

WILSON MILLER
3200 Bailey Lane, Suite 200, Naples FL 34105. 239/649-4040. **Toll-free phone:** 800/649-4336. **Fax:** 239/643-5716. **Contact:** Human Resources. **E-mail address:** naples@wilsonmiller.com. **World Wide Web address:** http://www.wilsonmiller.com. **Description:** A planning, design and engineering company. **NOTE:** Search for open positions at the company website. **Positions advertised include:** Business Communications Manager; CADD Tech; Civil Designer; Crew Chief; GIS Analyst; Landscape Architect; Senior Engineer, Project Manager; Senior Project Engineer; Transportation Engineer; Water/Wastewater CADD Designer. **Other area locations:** Destin FL; Fort Myers FL; Tallahassee FL; Tampa FL; Panama City Beach FL; Port Charlotte FL; Sarasota FL.

Georgia

ABCO BUILDERS INC.
2680 Abco Court, Lithonia GA 30058. 770/981-0350. **Fax:** 770/981-5776. **Contact:** Mr. Lynn Bledsoe, Vice President. **World Wide Web address:** http://www.abcobuilders.com. **Description:** A commercial construction firm. Founded 1949. **Corporate headquarters location:** This location. **Number of employees at this location:** 350.

ALBANY ELECTRIC COMPANY
P.O. Box 5228, Albany GA 31706. 229/432-7345. **Physical address:** 800 21st Avenue, Albany GA 31701. **Fax:** 229/436-3869. **Contact:** Human Resources. **E-mail address:** info@metropower.com. **World Wide Web address:** http://www.metropower.com. **Description:** Provides a wide range of electrical contract work including construction, maintenance, service, and design for industrial, commercial, institutional, and residential applications. **Other area locations:** Atlanta GA; Columbus GA; Macon GA; Hazelhurst GA; Norcross GA. **Other U.S. locations:** Greer SC; Andalusia AL; Beloit WI. **Parent company:** MetroPower, Inc.

ALCON ASSOCIATES INC.
201 Baldwin Drive, Albany GA 31707. 229/432-7411. **Fax:** 229/434-1492. **Contact:** Human Resources. **E-mail address:** swashburn@alconassociates.com. **World Wide Web address:** http://www.alconassociates.com. **Description:** Engaged in heavy construction and operates as a general contractor. **NOTE:** Resumes are reviewed for matches with job openings, and are kept on file for one year. **Other area locations:** Columbus GA; Kennesaw GA. **President/CEO:** L.D. Bryan III, P.E.

ALLISON-SMITH COMPANY
2284 Marietta Boulevard, Atlanta GA 30318. 404/351-6430. **Fax:** 404/350-1065. **Contact:** Human Resources. **World Wide Web address:** http://www.allison-smith.com. Founded 1943. **Description:** Provides electrical contracting and engineering services. **President:** Lanny Thomas.

AMERICAN WOODMARK CORPORATION
1017 Highway 42 South, Jackson GA 30233. 770/775-6013. **Fax:** 770/775-0383. **Contact:** Human Resources Director. **World Wide Web address:** http://www.americanwoodmark.com. **Description:** Manufactures and distributes kitchen cabinets and vanities for the remodeling and new home construction markets. The company offers almost 100 cabinet lines in a wide variety of designs, materials, and finishes. **Corporate headquarters location:** Winchester VA. **Other U.S. locations:** Nationwide. **Listed on:** NASDAQ. **Stock exchange symbol:** AMWD. **President/CEO:** James Gosa. **Number of employees nationwide:** 3,800.

APAC, INC.
4005 Windward Plaza Drive, Suite 300, Alpharetta GA 30005. 770/664-5550. **Fax:** 770/664-5410. **Contact:** Human Resources. **E-mail address:** apac@ashland.com. **World Wide Web address:** http://www.apac.com. **Description:** Provides a variety of construction services including asphalt and concrete paving and the excavation and construction of bridges and other structures. **NOTE:** Please visit http://www.ashland.com to search for jobs and apply online. **Positions advertised include: Programmer** Analyst; Senior Sourcing Analyst; Secretary; Purchasing Agent; Payroll Processing Supervisor; Regional Plant Support Specialist; Estimator; Cash Applications Processor; Environmental Health and Safety Manager; Project Manager; Foreman; Credit Analyst; Superintendent. **Corporate headquarters location:** This location. **Other U.S. locations:** Southern and Southeastern States. **Parent company:** Ashland Inc. **Listed on:** New York Stock Exchange. **Stock exchange symbol:** ASH.

ARMSTRONG WORLD INDUSTRIES, INC.
P.O. Box 4288, 4520 Broadway, Macon GA 31203. 478/788-4811. **Fax:** 478/781-9930. **Contact:** Human Resources. **World Wide Web address:** http://www.armstrong.com. **Description:** Armstrong World Industries, Inc. manufactures flooring, ceiling systems, furniture, and industrial specialty products. Founded 1860. **Positions advertised include:** Maintenance Systems Team Manager; Process Engineer; Area Maintenance Team Manager; Sales Executive; Builder Channel Sales Manager. **Corporate headquarters location:** Lancaster PA. **Other area locations:** Atlanta. **Other U.S. locations:** Nationwide. **International locations:** Worldwide. **Listed on:** OTC. **Stock exchange symbol:** ACKHQ. **Number of employees worldwide:** 16,500.

B & E JACKSON
229 Peachtree Street, NE, Suite 300, Atlanta GA 30303. 404/577-4914. **Fax:** 404/577-4419. **Contact:** Edith Jackson, Director of Administration. **E-mail address:** ejackson@bejackson.com. **World Wide Web**

address: http://www.bejackson.com. **Description:** A civil engineering firm whose areas of specialty include road design, hydrology studies, civil site design, GIS data manipulation, and urban planning. Founded 1988. **NOTE:** Please send resumes to 34 Peachtree Street NW, Suite 2100, Atlanta GA 30303. **Corporate headquarters location:** This location. **President:** Birdel F. Jackson.

BEAZER HOMES USA, INC.
3740 Devinci Court Suite 200, Norcross GA 30097. 770/613-4550. **Fax:** 770/613-4551. **Contact:** Benefits Manager. **World Wide Web address:** http://www.beazer.com. **Description:** One of the nation's largest homebuilders. **NOTE:** Please visit website to search for jobs, apply online, and for more specific contact information. **Positions advertised include:** Internal Auditor; Office Manager; Senior Design Associate; CAD Associate; Senior CAD Associate; Design Associate. **Corporate headquarters location:** This location. **Other U.S. locations:** Nationwide. **Listed on:** New York Stock Exchange. **Stock exchange symbol:** BZH.

BELCO ELECTRIC
3118 Marjan Drive, Atlanta GA 30340. 770/455-4556. **Fax:** 770/458-9938. **Contact:** Human Resources. **E-mail address:** joy@belcoinc.com. **World Wide Web address:** http://www.belcoinc.com. **Description:** Electrical contractors and engineers for residential, commercial, and industrial customers. **Positions advertised include:** Electrician; Service Technician; Project Manager Trainee; Administrative Staff. **Corporate headquarters location:** This location.

BYERS ENGINEERING COMPANY
6285 Barfield Road, NE, Atlanta GA 30328. 404/843-1000. **Fax:** 404/843-2278. **Contact:** Human Resources. **E-mail address:** careers-engineering@byers.com. **World Wide Web address:** http://www.byers.com. **Description:** A technical services firm serving the telecommunications and utilities industries. Founded in 1971. **NOTE:** Please visit website to download employment application. **Positions advertised include:** ROW/BICS; Software Data Service Provider. **Corporate headquarters location:** This location. **Founder & CEO:** Kenneth G. Byers, Jr. **Number of employees nationwide:** 300.

CENTER BROTHERS INCORPORATED
45 Ross Road, Savannah GA 31405. 912/232-6491. **Contact:** Human Resources. **Description:** Engaged in commercial, interior drywall installation as well as acoustical ceiling construction.

ELIXIR INDUSTRIES
1300 Pope Drive, Douglas GA 31533. 912/384-2078. **Fax:** 912/384-6480. **Contact:** Human Resources. **E-mail address:** elixirdiv24@elixirind.com. **World Wide Web address:** http://www.elixirind.com. **Description:** Manufactures metal siding, roofing, doors, frame parts, roof vents, and roof domes. Founded 1948. **NOTE:** There are two Douglas offices. **Corporate headquarters location:** Gardena CA. **Other area locations:** Fitzgerald GA 31750. **Other U.S. locations:** Nationwide. **Operations at this facility include:** The Extrusion division (this location) provides service to national and international customer with extrusion product needs, including anodizing, cutting, bending, shearing, machining, heat treating, light assembling, testing, and company-owned trucks. **President:** Christopher A. Sahm. **Number of employees nationwide:** 1,300.

FM GLOBAL
3460 Preston Ridge Road, Suite 400, Building #3, Alpharetta GA 30005. 770/777-3600. **Toll-free phone:** 888/216-9323. **Fax:** 770/777-0414. **Toll-free fax:** 888/216-9327. **Contact:** Human Resources. **World Wide Web address:** http://www.fmglobal.com. **Description:** A loss control service organization, which helps policyholders protect their properties and occupancies from damage caused by fire, wind, flood, and explosion; boiler, pressure vessel, and machinery accidents; and many other insured hazards. **NOTE:** Please visit website to search for jobs and apply online. **Corporate headquarters location:** Johnston RI. **Other U.S. locations:** Nationwide. **International locations:** Worldwide. **President/CEO:** Shivan S. Subramaniam. **Number of employees worldwide:** 5,000.

GREENHORNE & O'MARA, INC.
2211 New Market Parkway, Suite 104, Marietta GA 30067. 770/988-9555. **Toll-free phone:** 866/322-8905. **Fax:** 770/952-0653. **Contact:** Personnel. **World Wide Web address:** http://www.g-and-o.com. **Description:** Provides civil/site, environmental, transportation, and geosciences engineering services. Founded in 1950. **NOTE:** Please visit website to search for jobs and apply online. **Corporate headquarters location:** Greenbelt MD. **Other area locations:** Liburn GA. **Other U.S. locations:** FL; NC; PA; VA; WV. **Listed on:** Privately held.

HARTRAMPF, INC.
7000 Central Parkway, Suite 1475, Atlanta GA 30328. 678/320-1888. **Fax:** 770/522-8115. **Contact:** Carol Lathem, Office Manager. **E-mail address:** hr@hartrampf.com. **World Wide Web address:** http://www.hartrampf.com. **Description:** A full-service engineering and architectural firm. Services provided include architectural, structural, mechanical, electrical, civil, environmental, and municipal engineering; surveying and energy conservation; and economic and technical feasibility studies and reports. **NOTE:** Please mail resumes to 180 Allen Road, Suite 217-N, Atlanta GA 30328-4862. Fax to 404/847-0846. **Special programs:** Internships. **Corporate headquarters location:** This location. **Operations at this facility include:** Service. **Number of employees at this location:** 28.

KAWNEER COMPANY, INC.
555 Guthridge Court, Norcross GA 30092. 770/449-5555. **Fax:** 770/734-1560. **Contact:** Human Resources. **World Wide Web address:** http://www.kawneer.com. **Description:** Manufactures and markets fabricated products including nonresidential architectural building products such as storefronts, building entrances, facings, window framing, and curtainwall systems. **Parent company:** Alcoa Company. **Corporate headquarters location:** This location. **Other US. locations:** Bristol IN; Greenwood IN; Bloomsburg PA; Harrisonburg VA; Hernando MS; Springdale AR; Visalia CA. **International locations:** Canada.

LATEX CONSTRUCTION COMPANY
P.O. Box 917, Conyers GA 30012. 770/760-0820. **Physical address:** 1353 Farmer Road NW, Conyers GA 30012. **Fax:** 770/760-0852. **Contact:** Human Resources. **Description:** Engaged in hydrostatic testing and the manufacture of construction pipelines. **NOTE:** Information regarding employment is available through the phone menu.

LOCKWOOD GREENE
303 Perimeter Center North, Suite 800, Atlanta GA 30346. 770/829-6500. **Fax:** 770/829-6601. **Recorded jobline:** 404/818-8301. **Contact:** Kathy Pileggi, Recruiting Manager. **World Wide Web address:** http://www.lg.com. **Description:** An international consulting, design, and construction firm. **Special programs:** Co-ops. **Corporate headquarters location:** Spartanburg SC. **Other area locations:** Augusta GA; Pooler GA. **Other U.S. locations:** Nationwide. **International locations:** Worldwide. **Operations at this facility include:** This location serves clients in the following industries: power and energy; telecommunications; general manufacturing; government; aerospace; chemicals; health care; and food and beverages. **Parent company:** Philipp Holzmann and J.A. Jones, Inc. **Listed on:** Privately held. **President/CEO:** Fred Brune. **Annual sales/revenues:** More than $100 million. **Number of employees worldwide:** 2,500.

MCMICHAEL'S CONSTRUCTION COMPANY, INC.
90 Almon Road, Covington GA 30014. 770/486-3332. **Fax:** 770/786-9805. **Contact:** Human Resources. **World Wide Web address:** http://www.mcmbuilds.com. **Description:** A construction company that serves the Southeast United States. **Positions advertised include:** Project Manager; Trade Professional; Laborer. **Corporate headquarters location:** This location.

MORRISON HOMES
3655 Brookside Parkway, Suite 400, Alpharetta GA 30022. 770/360-8700. **World Wide Web address:** http://www.morrisonhomes.com. **Description:** Builds residential homes. Founded 1984. **NOTE:** Please visit website to search for jobs and apply online. **Positions advertised include:** IS Functional Analyst; AIX Engineer; CADD Operator. **Corporate headquarters location:** This location. **Other area locations:** Marietta GA. **Other U.S. locations:** TX; CA; CO; FL; AZ. **Parent company:** George Wimpley PLC.

TRAVIS PRUITT & ASSOCIATES, P.C.
4317 Park Drive, Suite 400, Norcross GA 30093. 770/416-7511. **Toll-free phone:** 800/909-7511. **Fax:** 770/416-0659. **Contact:** Human Resources. **E-mail address:** pete@travispruitt.com. **World Wide Web address:** http://www.travispruitt.com. **Description:** A consulting firm specializing in civil engineering, land surveys, and landscape architecture. The company also offers environmental engineering services. Founded in 1972. **Positions advertised include:** CAD Technician; Civil Engineer; Survey Party Chief and Personnel; Survey Technician. **Office hours:** Monday - Friday, 8:00 a.m. - 5:00 p.m. **Corporate headquarters location:** This location. **President:** Travis Pruitt, Sr. **Number of employees at this location:** 105.

PYRAMID MASONRY CONTRACTORS INC.
2330 Mellon Court, Decatur GA 30035. 770/987-4750. **Fax:** 770/981-7142. **Contact:** Human Resources. **World Wide Web address:** http://www.pyramidmasonry.net. **Description:** A special trade contractor engaged in masonry stone setting projects. **Other U.S. locations:** FL; NC. **President:** John C. Doherty.

RHEEM RUUD MANUFACTURING
P.O. Box 2098, Milledgeville GA 31061. 478/453-7575. **Physical address:** 138 Roberson Mill Road, Milledgeville GA 31061. **Contact:** Human Resources. **World Wide Web address:** http://www.rheem.com. **Description:** A national manufacturer of central heating and air conditioning equipment. **Office hours:** Monday – Friday, 8:00 a.m. – 5:00 p.m. **Positions advertised include:** Manufacturing Control Manager.

ROSSER INTERNATIONAL, INC.
524 West Peachtree Street NW, Atlanta GA 30308. 404/876-3800. **Fax:** 404/888-6863. **Contact:** Human Resources. **E-mail address:** employment@rosser.com. **World Wide Web address:** http://www.rosser.com. **Description:** An architectural and engineering design firm. Projects include prisons, stadiums, hangars, commercial retail space, and other facilities. **Positions advertised include:** Design Architect; Business Development Coordinator. **Office hours:** Monday - Friday, 8:00 a.m. - 5:00 p.m. **Corporate headquarters location:** This location. **Other area locations:** Cartersville GA; Jackson GA; Savannah GA. **Listed on:** Privately held. **Number of employees nationwide:** 170.

SEASONS 4 INC.
4500 Industrial Access Road, Douglasville GA 30134. 770/489-0716. **Fax:** 770/489-2938. **Contact:** Human Resources. **World Wide Web address:** http://www.seasons4.net. **Description:** Installs heating and air conditioning units in commercial buildings such as supermarkets. Founded 1971. **Corporate headquarters location:** This location.

SERVIDYNE SYSTEMS, INC.
1945 The Exchange, Suite 325, Atlanta GA 30339. 770/933-4200. **Toll-free phone:** 800/241-8996. **Fax:** 770/953-9922. **Contact:** Corporate Recruiter. **World Wide Web address:** http://www.servidyne.com. **Description:** Provides facilities performance management consulting. Servidyne Systems utilizes systematic engineering processes to prevent and solve building operations problems in order to enhance energy efficiency and labor productivity. **NOTE:** Entry-level positions are offered. **Corporate headquarters location:** This location. **Parent company:** Abrams Industries. **Operations at this facility include:** Administration; Manufacturing; Sales; Service. **Listed on:** NASDAQ. **Stock exchange symbol:** ABRI. **President:** Alan Abrams.

SKANSKA
70 Ellis Street NE, Atlanta GA 30303. 404/659-1970. **Fax:** 404/656-1665. **Contact:** Human Resources. **World Wide Web address:** http://www.skanska.com. **Description:** A construction firm primarily engaged in large-scale commercial and industrial construction projects. **Special programs:** Internships. **Corporate headquarters location:** Sweden. **Other U.S. locations:** Nationwide. **International locations:** Worldwide. **Number of employees worldwide:** 69,700.

TUCKER DOOR & TRIM COMPANY
650 Highway 83, Monroe GA 30655. 770/267-4622. **Contact:** Marion Harris, Sales Manager. **Description:** A manufacturer of doors. The company is also engaged in wholesale millwork.

URS CORPORATION
400 Northpark Town Center, 1000 Abernathy Road NE, Suite 900, Atlanta GA 30328. 678/808-8800. **Fax:** 678/808-8400. **Contact:** Human Resources. **World Wide Web address:** http://www.urscorp.com. **Description:** Develops and alters transportation systems, buildings, and industrial facilities. URS Corporation is also involved in environmental reconstruction and preservation services. Founded in 1969. **Positions advertised include:** Civil Engineer; Graduate Civil Engineer; Graduate Water Resources Engineer; MIS Coordinator; Project Accountant/Accounting Manager; Project Civil Engineer; Project Environmental Scientist; Project Transportation Engineer; Senior Accountant; Senior CADD Designer; Senior Civil-Bridge Engineer; Water Resources Engineer. **Special programs:** Internships; Co-ops. **Corporate headquarters location:** San Francisco CA. **Other U.S. locations:** Nationwide. **International locations:** Worldwide. **Listed on:** New York Stock Exchange. **Stock exchange symbol:** URS. **Number of employees worldwide:** 26,000.

WEATHERLY INC.
1100 Spring Street NW, Suite 308, Atlanta GA 30309. 404/873-5030. **Fax:** 404/873-1303. **Contact:** Ms. G.C. Bailey, Executive Assistant. **E-mail address:** info@weatherlyinc.com. **World Wide Web address:** http://www.chematur.se. **Description:** Designs, engineers, and constructs chemical process plants. **Corporate headquarters location:** This location. **Parent company:** Chematur Engineering. **Operations at this facility include:** Administration; Engineering and Design; Sales; Service.

WELDING SERVICES, INC.
2225 Skyland Court, Norcross GA 30071. 678/728-9100. **Fax:** 770/449-4684. **Contact:** Human Resources. **World Wide Web address:** http://www.weldingservices.com. **Description:** Provides repair welding at nationwide nuclear and fossil fuel power plants. **Corporate headquarters location:** This location. **International locations:** Venezuela; The Netherlands. **Operations at this facility include:** Administration; Manufacturing; Research and Development; Sales; Service.

WHITE PROPERTY ACQUISITIONS
4485 Tench Road, Suite 510, Suwanee GA 30024. 770/452-8778. **Fax:** 770/613-0501. **Contact:** Human Resources. **Description:** A general contracting company that specializes in fire damage repairs.

Founded in 1960. **NOTE:** Entry-level positions are offered. **Corporate headquarters location:** This location. **Listed on:** Privately held. **Annual sales/revenues:** Less than $5 million.

RALPH WHITEHEAD ASSOCIATES
3505 Koger Boulevard, Suite 205, Duluth GA 30096. 770/452-0797. **Fax:** 770/936-9171. **Contact:** Human Resources. **E-mail address:** atl@rwhitehead.com. **World Wide Web address:** http://www.rwhitehead.com. Founded 1961. **Description:** A civil engineering consulting firm. **NOTE:** Please visit website to search for jobs. **Positions advertised include:** Project Manager/Senior Engineer; Highway/Roadway Engineer; Stormwater Services Engineer; Geotechnical Engineer; Project Engineer; Designer; Project Design Engineer – Railway; Project Design/Engineer – Transportation; Engineering Technician – Construction Service. **Corporate headquarters location:** Charlotte NC. **Other U.S. locations:** Overland Park KS; Jacksonville FL; Charleston SC; Rock Hill SC; Raleigh NC; Richmond VA. **Number of employees nationwide:** 120.

JOHN WIELAND HOMES, INC.
P.O. Box 87363, Atlanta GA 30337. 770/996-6065, ext.: 1400. Physical address: 1950 Sullivan Road, Atlanta GA 30337. **Fax:** 770/907-3485. **Contact:** Human Resources. **E-mail address:** hr@jwhomes.com. **World Wide Web address:** http://www.jwhomes.com. **Description:** A real estate developer and construction company specializing in single-family homes. **NOTE:** Please visit website to search for jobs and apply online. **Positions advertised include:** Project Sales Consultant; Pricing Project Coordinator; Loan Officer Part-time Human Resources Assistant; Superintendent; Architectural Product Leader; Estimating Coordinator; Design Consultant; Accounting Coordinator; Licensed Sales Assistant; Architect; Crew Member; Director of Risk Management; Receptionist; Manager of Administration; Corporate Office Manager; Structural Engineer; Boxtruck Driver; Assembler – Windows; Piggyback Driver; Flatbed Driver. **Corporate headquarters location:** This location. **Other U.S. locations:** Mount Pleasant SC; Franklin TN; Morrisville NC; Charlotte NC.

WINTER CONSTRUCTION COMPANY
1330 Spring Street NW, Atlanta GA 30309. 404/588-3300. **Fax:** 404/223-5753. **Contact:** Personnel. **World Wide Web address:** http://www.wintercompanies.com. **Description:** A general contracting and construction company that specializes in commercial construction. **NOTE:** Please visit website to search for jobs and apply online. **Positions advertised include:** Assistant Project Manager; Contract Administrator; Environmental Project Engineer; Estimator; Project Manager; Project Superintendent; Senior Estimator; Senior Project Manager; Superintendent – Institutional; Superintendent – Environmental Services. **Special programs:** Internships. **Corporate headquarters location:** This location. **Parent company:** The Winter Companies (also at this location). **Operations at this facility include:** Administration; Research and Development; Sales; Service. **President/CEO:** Brent Reid.

Hawaii

HAWAIIAN DREDGING CONSTRUCTION COMPANY
P.O. Box 4088, Honolulu HI 96812-4088. 808/735-3211. **Physical address:** 614 Kapahulu Avenue, Honolulu HI 96815-3891. **Fax:** 808/735-7416. **Contact:** Human Resources. **E-mail address:** employment@hdcc.com. **World Wide Web address:** http://www.hdcc.com. **Description:** A full-service contractor of housing, hotels and resorts, bridges, power plants, and marine projects.

PARSONS BRINCKERHOFF INC.
American Savings Bank Tower, Suite 3000, 1001 Bishop Street, Honolulu HI 96813. 808/531-7094. **Fax:** 808/528-2368. **Contact:** Human Resources. **E-mail address:** careers@pbworld.com. **World Wide Web address:** http://www.pbworld.com. **Description:** An engineering and design firm engaged in the design of bridges, tunnels, rapid transit systems, hydroelectric facilities, water supply systems, and marine facilities. **NOTE:** Search and apply for jobs online. **Positions advertised include:** Assistant Civil Engineer; Assistant Planner; CADD Operator; Engineer; Environmental Planner. **Corporate headquarters location:** New York NY. **Other U.S. locations:** Nationwide. **International locations:** Worldwide. **Chairman/CEO:** Tom O'Neill. **Number of employees worldwide:** 9,000.

Idaho

CSHQA, ARCHITECTS/ENGINEERS/PLANNERS
C.W. Moore Plaza, 250 South Fifth Street, Boise ID 83702. 208/343-4635. **Fax:** 208/343-1858. **Contact:** Human Resources. **E-mail address:** hr@cshqa.com. **World Wide Web address:** http://www.cshqa.com. **Description:** Full service engineering and architectural firm, with an office in Donnelly. Founded in 1889. **Positions advertised include:** Interior Designer; Mechanical Designer; Junior Mechanical Engineer; AIT; Architectural Project Manager. **Other U.S. locations:** CA. **President:** Jeffrey A. Shneider, AIA.

POSITRON SYSTEMS
6151 North Discovery Way, Boise ID 83713. 208/672-1923. **Fax:** 208/672-8012. **Contact:** Scott Ritchie, Director of Operations. **E-mail address:** scottr@positronsystems.com. **World Wide Web address:** http://www.positronsystems.com. **Corporate office location:** This location. **Description:** Performs nondestructive testing that identifies structural integrity, fatigue, and embrittlement problems at the atomic level on various components, from aircraft landing struts and wing spars to nuclear power plants and oil refineries. **Other area locations:** Pocatello ID (Test and Analysis center).

SCIENTECH, LLC
200 South Woodruff Avenue, Idaho Falls ID 83402. 208/524-9200. **Contact:** Human Resources. **E-mail address**: employment@scientech.com **World Wide Web address:** http://www.scientech.com. **Description:** Scientech, LLC is a provider of electric generation services and products, safety and risk analysis, information technology and strategic consulting. **NOTE:** Unless otherwise stated on website, e-mail resumes or send to Human Resources Department, 910 Clopper Road, Gaithersburg MD 20878; fax: 301/258-2463. **Positions advertised include:** Electronics Assembler; Quality Assurance Representative; Office Assistant; Lead ANSI Level III Test Technician. **Other U.S. locations:** Nationwide. **Subsidiaries include:** Belfort Engineering. **Listed on:** Privately held. **Number of employees nationwide:** 350.

WASHINGTON GROUP INTERNATIONAL
P.O. Box 73, Boise ID 83729. 208/386-5000. **Physical address:** 720 Park Boulevard, Boise ID 83712 **Fax:** 208/386-7186. **Recorded jobline:** 208/386-6966. **Contact:** Corporate Staffing. **E-mail address:** jobs@wgjobs.com. **World Wide Web address:** http://www.wgint.com. **Description:** Provides integrated engineering, construction and management solutions for businesses and governments worldwide in more than two-dozen major markets. **NOTE:** Entry-level positions are offered. **Positions advertised include:** Payroll Specialist; Human Resource Representative; Construction Engineer; Design Engineer; Project Control Manager; Structural Supervisor. **Special programs:** Internships; Co-ops; Summer Jobs. **Corporate headquarters location:** This location. **Other U.S. locations:** Nationwide. **International locations:** Worldwide. **Listed on:** NASDAQ. **Stock exchange symbol:** WGII. **Number of employees worldwide:** 25,000.

Illinois

ADVANCE MECHANICAL SYSTEMS INC.
2080 South Carboy, Mount Prospect IL 60056-5750. 847/593-2510. **Fax:** 847/593-2536. **Contact:** Human

Resources. **World Wide Web address:** http://www.advmech.com. **Description:** An engineering firm specializing in mechanical and HVAC contracting.

AMBITECH ENGINEERING CORPORATION
1333 Butterfield Road, Suite 200, Downers Grove IL 60515. 630/963-5800. **Fax:** 630/963-8099. **Contact:** Carrie Koenig, Human Resources Manager. **E-mail address:** ckoenig@ambitech.com. **World Wide Web address:** http://www.ambitech.com. **Description:** A consulting and engineering firm engaged in the engineering and design of petroleum refineries, chemical plants, and petrochemical plants including. **NOTE:** See website for application. **Positions advertised include:** 3D Administrator; Instrumentation and Controls Programmer; Mechanical Engineer; Senior Piping Engineer; Senior Process Engineer. **Corporate headquarters location:** This location. **Listed on:** Privately held.

ANNING-JOHNSON COMPANY
1959 Anson Drive, Melrose Park IL 60160. 708/681-1300. **Contact:** Human Resources. **World Wide Web address:** http://www.anningjohnson.com. **Description:** Engaged in a variety of areas including acoustical ceiling, drywall, fireproofing, metal floor decks, metal siding, roofing, and geotechnical fill. Founded in 1940. **Corporate headquarters location:** This location. **Parent company:** Anson Industries Inc.

AXIS INC.
2201 West Townline Road, Peoria IL 61615. 309/691-3988. **Fax:** 309/691-4172. **Contact:** Human Resources. **E-mail address:** careers@axis-inc.com. **World Wide Web address:** http://www.axis-inc.com. **Description:** Engaged in civil and mechanical engineering, information technology, and client-site technical services. Founded in 1987. **NOTE:** See list of job openings at the company's website. Submit resume by e-mail. **Other U.S. locations:** Indianapolis IN. **International locations:** India; United Kingdom.

BELCAN CORPORATION
Woodland Courte Office Center, 3130 Finley Road, Suite 520, Downers Grove IL 60515. 630/786-9900. **Contact:** Human Resources. **E-mail address:** rbanchak@belcan.com. **World Wide Web address:** http://www.belcan.com. **Description:** An engineering and consulting firm offering long-term, client-site consulting services. **NOTE:** Entry-level positions are offered. Search and apply for positions online. **Positions advertised include:** ANSYS/Fluent Application Engineer; Business Development Manager. **Corporate headquarters location:** Cincinnati OH. **Other area locations:** Peoria IL. **Other area locations:** Nationwide. **International locations:** China. **Listed on:** Privately held.

BRICKKICKER
849 North Ellsworth, Naperville IL 60563. 630/420-9900. **Toll-free phone:** 800/821-1820. **Fax:** 630/420-2270.**Contact:** Human Resources. **World Wide Web address:** http://www.brickkicker.com. **Description:** Performs home and building inspections.

BURNSIDE CONSTRUCTION COMPANY
2400 Wisconsin Avenue, Downers Grove IL 60515. 630/515-9999. **Contact:** Human Resources. **World Wide Web address:** http://www.traditions55plus.com. **Description:** A residential construction company. Founded in 1911.

THE CHICAGO FAUCET COMPANY
2100 South Clearwater Drive, Des Plaines IL 60018-5999. 847/803-5000. **Fax:** 847/803-5454. **Contact:** Human Resources. **World Wide Web address:** http://www.chicagofaucets.com. **Description:** Manufactures brass products including plumbing fittings. **Parent company:** Geberit AG.

COMMERCIAL LIGHT COMPANY (CLC)
245 Fencl Lane, Hillside IL 60162. 708/449-6900. **Fax:** 708/449-6942. **Contact:** Human Resources. **World Wide Web address:** http://www.clcats.com. **Description:** An electrical contractor. Founded in 1915.

CTE (CONSOER TOWNSEND ENVIRODYNE ENGINEERS, INC.)
303 East Wacker Drive, Suite 600, Chicago IL 60601. 312/938-0300. **Fax:** 312/938-1109. **Contact:** Director of Human Resources. **E-mail address:** jobs@cte.aecom.com. **World Wide Web address:** http://www.cte.aecom.com. **Description:** Provides engineering consulting for highways, airports, and waste management projects. **NOTE:** Apply online at the company's website or e-mail resumes. **Parent company:** AECOM Technology.

CONTRACTING & MATERIAL COMPANY
9550 West 55th Street, Suite B, McCook IL 60525. 708/588-6000. **Contact:** Human Resources. **World Wide Web address:** http://www.candmcompany.com. **Description:** Provides contract construction services for electrical, pipeline, highway, and heavy construction projects. **NOTE:** Garages are located at 5401 West Harrison Street, Chicago IL 60644-5030.

ELKAY MANUFACTURING COMPANY
2222 Camden Court, Oak Brook IL 60523. 630/574-8484. **Fax:** 630/574-5012. **Contact:** Human Resources. **World Wide Web address:** http://www.elkay.com. **Description:** Manufactures stainless steel sinks, faucets, water coolers, and kitchen cabinets. **NOTE:** Entry-level positions are offered. Apply online for all positions. **Corporate headquarters location:** This location. **Listed on:** Privately held.

ENERFAB
1913 South Briggs Street, Joliet IL 60433. 815/727-4624. **Fax:** 815/727-0776. **Contact:** Human Resources. **World Wide Web address:** http://www.enerfab.com. **Description:** A mechanical engineering company that provides a variety of services including HVAC, power piping, fabrication, and plumbing. **Corporate headquarters location:** Cincinnati OH. **Operations at this facility include:** Chicago regional office on Enerfab's Power Maintenance division.

GANNETT FLEMING
225 West Washington Street, Suite 2200, Chicago IL 60606. 312/924-2899. **Fax:** 312/924-0201. **Contact:** Human Resources. **E-mail address:** employment@gfnet.com. **World Wide Web address:** http://www.gannettfleming.com. **Description:** Provides civil and structural engineering consulting services.

GERBER PLUMBING FIXTURES CORPORATION
2500 Internationale Parkway, Woodridge IL 60517. 630/679-1420. **Fax:** 630/679-1430. **Contact:** Human Resources. **World Wide Web address:** http://www.gerberonline.com. **Description:** Manufactures a variety of bathroom and kitchen plumbing products including faucets, valves, lavatories, toilets, and vanities. **Corporate headquarters location:** This location.

GRAYCOR INC.
One Graycor Drive, Homewood IL 60430. 708/206-0500. **Contact:** Human Resources. **E-mail address:** bill_oneill@graycor.com. **World Wide Web address:** http://www.capitolconstruction.com. **Description:** The company builds industrial, commercial, health care, and educational structures throughout North America, focusing on the Upper Midwest. It offers construction management and design/build services on projects ranging from industrial plant additions to office towers and shopping malls. Graycor also offers blasting, refractory relining, and other maintenance services for power utilities and automotive, food, metals, and waste management companies. It has also recently added an interiors unit. **NOTE:** See website for current job openings and to submit a resume online. **Positions advertised include:** Project Manager; Construction Superintendent. **Other area locations:** Carmi IL; Chicago IL; Palatine IL. **Other U.S. locations:** AZ;

CO; KY; MI; OH; WI. **Subsidiaries include:** Graycor Industrial Contructors; Graycor Construction Company; Graycor Blasting Company; Graycor International.

HANSON ENGINEERS
1525 South Sixth Street, Springfield IL 62703. 217/788-2450. **Fax:** 217/788-2503. **Contact:** Human Resources. **World Wide Web address:** http://www.hansonengineers.com. **Description:** A consulting firm that provides a variety of architectural, engineering, and scientific services. Founded in 1954. **Corporate headquarters location:** This location. **Other U.S. locations:** Nationwide.

HONEYWELL
1500 West Dundee Road, Arlington Heights IL 60004. 847/797-4000. **Contact:** Human Resources. **World Wide Web address:** http://www.honeywell.com. **Description:** Honeywell is engaged in the research, development, manufacture, and sale of advanced technology products and services in the fields of chemicals, electronics, automation, and controls. The company's major businesses are home and building automation and control, performance polymers and chemicals, industrial automation and control, space and aviation systems, and defense and marine systems. **NOTE:** See job listings on Honeywell's website and apply online. **Operation at this facility include:** This location manufactures home heating and air-conditioning controls. **Listed on:** New York Stock Exchange. **Stock exchange symbol:** HON.

KENNY CONSTRUCTION COMPANY
250 Northgate Parkway, Wheeling IL 60090. 847/541-8200. **Fax:** 847/541-8358. **Contact:** Human Resources. **World Wide Web address:** http://www.kennyconstruction.com. **Description:** A construction company that handles various large scale projects such as subways, tunnels, airports, stadiums, buildings, hotels, power plants, mass transit, bridges, highways and all manner of Infrastructure projects. Kenny Construction operates primarily in five operating groups: Tunnels, Transportation, Underground, Building, and Power. **Positions advertised include:** Accounts Payable Clerk, Construction Superintendent, Cost Control Engineer, Office Assistant, Project Engineer, Project Manager. **Corporate headquarters location:** This location.

M+W ZANDER
549 West Randolph Street, Chicago IL 60661. 312/577-3200. **Contact:** Human Resources. **World Wide Web address:** http://www.mw-zander.com. **Description:** An architectural and engineering firm. Founded in 1945.

MACKIE CONSULTANTS, INC.
9575 West Higgins Road, Suite 500, Rosemont IL 60018. 847/696-1400. **Contact:** Human Resources. **Description:** An engineering consulting firm providing a variety of engineering services as well as land surveying and grading.

MOHN CUSTOM INTERIORS
2201 West White Oaks Drive, Springfield IL 62704. 217/787-6251. **Contact:** Manager. **World Wide Web address:** http://www.mohninteriors.com. **Description:** Provides professional interior design and furniture upholstering services. Founded in 1968. **Office hours:** Monday – Friday, 9:00 a.m. – 5:00 p.m.; Saturday – 10:00 a.m. – 12:00 p.m.

F.E. MORAN
2265 Carlson Drive, Northbrook IL 60062. 847/498-4800. **Contact:** Human Resources. **World Wide Web address:** http://www.femoran.com. **Description:** An international mechanical contracting company specializing in fire detection, heating, air conditioning, plumbing, and ventilation systems. **NOTE:** See website for job listings and contact information. **Corporate headquarters location:** This location.

W.E. O'NEIL CONSTRUCTION COMPANY
2751 North Clybourn Avenue, Chicago IL 60614. 773/755-1611. **Fax:** 773/327-4806. **Contact:** Pat McGowan, Organizational Development Director. **E-mail address:** chicago.careers@oneilind.com. **World Wide Web address:** http://www.oneilind.com. **Description:** A general construction company specializing in construction management, general contracting, design/build, and preconstruction. **NOTE:** Jobseekers should indicate the department in which they are interested in a cover letter. **Corporate headquarters location:** This location. **Parent company:** O'Neil Industries, Inc. (also at this location).

PACKER ENGINEERING INC.
1950 North Washington Street, Naperville IL 60563. 630/505-5722. **Toll-free phone:** 800/323-0114. **Fax:** 630/505-3010. **Contact:** Human Resources. **E-mail address:** pejobs@packereng.com. **World Wide Web address:** http://www.packereng.com. **Description:** A multidisciplinary engineering, consulting, and technical services company. The practice includes failure analysis; accident investigation and reconstruction; fire/explosion cause and origin studies; product design evaluations; process design assessments; customized and routine testing; applied research; commercial product development; and litigation support. **NOTE:** Apply online for all positions. Entry-level positions are offered. **Special programs:** Internships. **Internship information:** Paid summer internships are available through The Packer Foundation. For additional information, visit the Foundation's website at http://www.packerfoundation.com/internships. **Corporate headquarters location:** This location. **Other U.S. locations:** Nationwide. **Parent company:** The Packer Group.

PARSONS TRANSPORTATION GROUP
10 South Riverside, Suite 400, Chicago IL 60606. 312/930-5100. **Fax:** 312/930-0018. **Contact:** Technical Recruiter. **World Wide Web address:** http://www.parsons.com. **Description:** Designs and builds roads, bridges, highways, and other transportation infrastructure. **NOTE:** Apply online. **Positions advertised include:** Project Manager; Associate Engineer; Principal Designer. **Corporate headquarters location:** Washington DC.

PATRICK ENGINEERING
4970 Varsity Drive, Lisle IL 60532. 630/795-7200. **Fax:** 630/724-1681. **Contact:** Human Resources. **E-mail address:** hr_jobs@patrickengineering.com. **World Wide Web address:** http://www.patrickengineering.com. **Description:** Offers solid waste planning, architecture, surveying, and engineering services in the civil, transportation, environmental, geotechnical, hydraulic, water resources, structural, and electrical sectors. Founded in 1979. **Other area locations:** Chicago IL; Springfield IL. **Other U.S. locations:** MI: WI; PA.

PERKINS & WILL
330 North Wabash Avenue, Suite 3600, Chicago IL 60611. 312/755-0770. **Toll-free phone:** 800/837-9455. **Fax:** 312/755-4788. **Contact:** Human Resources. **E-mail address:** hr@perkinswill.com. **World Wide Web address:** http://www.perkinswill.com. **Description:** An architectural, interior design and planning firm that serves both commercial and industrial companies. The company also provides an IDP/IDEP program for unlicensed designers. This location also hires seasonally. Founded in 1935. **NOTE:** Mail, fax or e-mail resumes. Entry-level positions and part-time jobs are offered. **Positions advertised include:** Environmental Graphics Designer; Marketing Coordinator. **Corporate headquarters location:** This location. **Other U.S. locations:** Los Angeles CA; Miami FL; Atlanta GA; Minneapolis MN; Charlotte NC; New York NY. **International locations:** Paris, France. **Subsidiaries include:** TY Lin, Inc. **Parent company:** Dar Al Handesah. ~~**Listed on:** Privately held.~~

RAGNAR BENSON INC.
250 South Northwest Highway, Park Ridge IL 60068-5875. 847/698-4900. **Fax:** 847/692-9320. **Contact:** Human Resources. **World Wide Web address:** http://www.ragnarbenson.com. **Description:** An

engineering and construction firm that specializes in design-build, construction management, and general contracting. Founded in 1922. **Positions advertised include:** Project Superintendent.

RAYMOND PROFESSIONAL GROUP, INC.
550 West Van Buren Street, Suite 400, Chicago IL 60607. 312/935-3200. **Fax:** 312/935-3201. **Contact:** Human Resources. **World Wide Web address:** http://www.raymondgroup.com. **Description:** A multidisciplinary engineering consulting firm. Services include electrical, mechanical, and structural engineering.

ROBERTS & SCHAEFER COMPANY
222 South Riverside Plaza, Suite 1800, Chicago IL 60606. 312/236-7292. **Contact:** Human Resources. **World Wide Web address:** http://www.r-s.com. **Description:** A multidisciplinary engineering firm. Founded in 1903.

SARGENT & LUNDY
55 East Monroe Street, Chicago IL 60603. 312/269-2000. **Fax:** 312/269-1960. **Contact:** Kathleen A. Lynch, Human Resources. **E-mail address:** kathleen.a.lynch@sargentlundy.com. **World Wide Web address:** http://www.sargentlundy.com. **Description:** Provides a broad range of engineering services. Founded in 1891. **NOTE:** See website for job listings and contact information. Entry-level and temporary positions are offered. **Corporate headquarters location:** This location. **Other U.S. locations:** Nationwide. **International locations:** Worldwide. **Listed on:** Privately held.

SMITHFIELD CONSTRUCTION GROUP, INC.
400 W. Huron, Chicago IL 60610. 312/266-9800. **Fax:** 312/266-9530. **Contact:** Adrienne Pearlman, Human Resources. **E-mail address:** apearlman@smith-field.com. **World Wide Web address:** http://www.smith-field.com. **Description:** Residential, commercial, and industrial construction company. **Positions advertised include:** Safety Director.

GEORGE SOLLITT CONSTRUCTION COMPANY
790 North Central, Wood Dale IL 60191. 630/860-7333. **Fax:** 630/860-7347. **Contact:** Howard Strong, Vice President of Operations. **World Wide Web address:** http://www.sollitt.com. **Description:** A leading general contractor/construction management firm. Clients include hospitals, schools, and major corporations. Founded in 1838. **NOTE:** Entry-level positions are offered. **Special programs:** Training. **Corporate headquarters location:** This location. **Listed on:** Privately held.

STERLING PLUMBING GROUP, INC.
2900 Golf Road, Rolling Meadows IL 60008. 847/734-1777. **Contact:** Human Resources. **World Wide Web address:** http://www.sterlingplumbing.com. **Description:** Manufactures sinks, faucets, tubs, and toilets as well as other plumbing supplies for kitchens and bathrooms. **NOTE:** For job listings, visit Kohler's website at http://www.hr.kohler.com/careers. Parent company: Kohler.

R&D THIEL INC.
2340 Newburg Road, Belvidere IL 61008. 815/544-1699. **Contact:** Human Resources. **E-mail address:** HumanResources@rdthiel.com. **World Wide Web address:** http://www.rdthiel.com. **Description:** Provides a variety of construction services ranging from carpentry labor to completed residential housing. **NOTE:** See website for job listings and contact information. **Positions advertised include:** Wall Panel Designer; Truss Designers; Carpenter Helpers; Carpenters; Lead Carpenters; Jobsite Foreman. **Corporate headquarters location:** This location.

UNDERWRITERS LABORATORIES INC.
333 Pfingsten Road, Northbrook IL 60062. 847/272-8800. **Fax:** 847/509-6300. **Contact:** Human Resources **E-mail address:** northbrook@us.ul.com. **World Wide Web address:** http://www.ul.com. **Description:** An independent, nonprofit corporation established to help reduce or prevent bodily injury, loss of life, and property damage. Engineering functions are divided between six departments: Electrical Department; Burglary Protection and Signaling Department; Casualty and Chemical Hazards Department; Fire Protection Department; Heating, Air Conditioning, and Refrigeration Department; and Marine Department. The company also provides factory inspection services through offices in the United States and 54 other countries. **Corporate headquarters location:** This location. **Other U.S. locations:** CA; NC; NY; WA. **Operations at this facility include:** Administration; Service.

THE WALSH GROUP
929 West Adams, Chicago IL 60607. 312/563-5400. **Fax:** 312/563-5420. **Contact:** Human Resources. **E-mail address:** agonzalez@walshgroup.com. **World Wide Web address:** http://www.walshgroup.com. **Description:** A construction contracting company. **Positions advertised include:** Payroll Data Entry Clerk; Field Secretary; Project Engineer.

WASHINGTON GROUP INTERNATIONAL
1020 West 31st Street, Suite 300, Downers Grove IL 60515. 630/829-3000. **Fax:** 630/829-3011. **Contact:** Human Resources. **World Wide Web address:** http://www.wgint.com. **Description:** Provides integrated engineering, construction, and management services for businesses and governments worldwide. Markets served include: power generation, transmission and distribution, and clean air solutions; environmental remediation; heavy civil construction; mining; nuclear services; defense, homeland security, and global threat reduction; industrial, chemical, and pharmaceutical processing; manufacturing; facilities operations and management; transportation; and water resources. **Positions advertised include:** Electrical Engineer. **Corporate headquarters location:** Boise ID. **Other U.S. locations:** Nationwide. **Listed on:** NASDAQ. **Stock exchange symbol:** WGII. **Number of employees worldwide:** 25,000.

WICKES INC.
706 Deerpath Drive, Vernon Hills IL 60061. 847/367-6542. **Fax:** 847/3673767. **Contact:** Human Resources. **E-mail address:** humanresources@wickes.com. **World Wide Web address:** http://www.wickes.com. **Description:** One of the largest suppliers of building materials in the United States. Wickes's manufacturing facilities produce prehung door units, window assemblies, roof and floor trusses, and framed wall panels. **Corporate headquarters location:** This location. **Other U.S. locations:** Denver CO; Elwood IN; Ocean Springs MS; Lomira WI. **Listed on:** NASDAQ. **Stock exchange symbol:** WIKS.

Indiana

ATSI, INC.
9200 Calumet Avenue, Suite N500, Munster IN 46321. 219/836-8490. **Fax:** 219/836-8493. **Contact:** Human Resources. **E-mail address:** hrdept@atsiinc.com. **World Wide Web address:** http://www.atsiinc.com. **Description:** A full-service, multi-disciplinary engineering firm that provides engineering services to the industrial and commercial sectors. ATSI specializes in heavy industrial facility design and modifications, high-temperature applications such as blast furnace construction, and analytical engineering. **Positions advertised include:** Sales and Marketing Manager. **Other U.S. locations:** Amherst NY; Cranberry Township PA.

BURGESS & NIPLE, LTD.
251 North Illinois Street, Capital Center, Suite 920, Indianapolis IN 46204. 317/237-2760. **Fax:** 614/459-9433. **Contact:** Human Resources. **E-mail address:** hr@burnip.com. **World Wide Web address:** http://www.burgessniple.com. **Description:** An engineering and architecture firm engaged in study, analysis, and design services. The company specializes in waterworks, wastewater, industrial services,

hydropower, energy conservation, transportation, systems analysis, HVAC, and geotechnical. **NOTE:** Applicants can e-mail or fax resumes using the information provided in this listing. Resumes sent via regular mail should be addressed as follows: Human Resources, Burgess & Niple, 5085 Reed Road, Columbus OH 43220. **Positions advertised include:** Transportation Planner; Travel Demand Forecaster. **Corporate headquarters location:** Columbus OH.

CONSOLIDATED FABRICATION AND CONSTRUCTORS, INC.
3851 Ellsworth Street, Gary IN 46408. 219/884-6150. **Fax:** 219/884-6652. **Contact:** Human Resources. **World Wide Web address:** http://www.consfab.com. **Description:** A mechanical contracting company for industrial applications including the repair of oil refineries and chemical plants. Consolidated Fabrication and Constructors also manufactures and repairs tanks and pressure valves.

CONTINENTAL ELECTRIC COMPANY
P.O. Box 2710, Gary IN 46403. 219/938-3460. **Physical address:** 9501 East Fifth Avenue, Gary IN 46403. **Fax:** 219/938-3469. **Contact:** Human Resources. **World Wide Web address:** http://www.continentalelectric.com. **Description:** Provides electrical contracting services to residential and industrial clients.

FAIRMONT HOMES, INC.
P.O. Box 27, Nappanee IN 46550. 574/773-7941. **Physical address:** 502 South Oakland, Nappanee IN 46550. **Fax:** 574/773-2185. **Contact:** Human Resources. **World Wide Web address:** http://www.fairmonthomes.com. **Description:** Manufactures and markets sectional housing, modular homes, and recreational vehicles nationwide. **Corporate headquarters location:** This location. **Other U.S. locations:** Montevideo MN. **Listed on:** Privately held.

HAGERMAN
P.O. Box 502710 Indianapolis IN 46250-7710. 317/713-0636. **Physical address:** 7930 Castleway Drive, Indianapolis IN 46250. **Contact:** Human Resources. **Fax:** 317/577-6841. **World Wide Web address:** http://www.hagermangc.com. **Description:** Engaged in construction management and general contracting services. **Positions advertised include:** Estimator. **Corporate headquarters location:** This location. **Number of employees at this location:** 100.

HUNT CONSTRUCTION GROUP
P.O. Box 128, Indianapolis IN 46206. 317/241-6301. **Physical address:** 2450 South Tibbs Avenue, Indianapolis IN 46241. **Fax:** 317/227-7830. **Contact:** Human Resources. **E-mail address:** incareers@huntconstructiongroup.com. **World Wide Web address:** http://www.huntconstructiongroup.com. **Description:** A general contract and construction management firm. **NOTE:** No phone calls please. Direct application materials to the attention of: Employment Opportunities. No personal names are necessary. **Positions advertised include:** Project Engineer; Assistant Project Engineer; Superintendent. **Corporate headquarters location:** This location.

INTERNATIONAL STEEL REVOLVING DOOR COMPANY
2138 North Sixth Avenue, Evansville IN 47710. 812/425-3311. **Fax:** 812/426-2682. **Contact:** Human Resources. **World Wide Web address:** http://www.internationalrevolvingdoors.com. **Description:** Designs and builds custom revolving doors. The company also performs metal stamping. Founded in 1963. **Special programs:** Internships; Apprenticeships. **Corporate headquarters location:** This location. **Listed on:** Privately held.

KAWNEER COMPANY
1151 Bloomingdale Road, P.O. Box 639, Bristol IN 46507. 574/848-7616. **Contact:** Human Resources. **World Wide Web address:** http://www.kawneer.com. **Description:** Manufactures and markets nonresidential architectural building products including storefronts, building entrances, facings, window framing, and curtain wall systems. **Parent company:** Alcoa is one of the largest aluminum producers in North America.

LIBERTY HOMES, INC.
P.O. Box 35, Goshen IN 46527-0035. 574/533-0431. **Physical address:** 1101 Eisenhower Drive N, Goshen IN 46526. **Fax:** 574/533-0438. **Contact:** Human Resources. **World Wide Web address:** http://www.libertyhomesinc.com. **Description:** Designs, manufactures, and sells single section and multi-sectional manufactured homes.

MIDLAND ENGINEERING COMPANY
P.O. Box 1019, South Bend IN 46624. 574/272-0200. **Physical address:** 52369 Indiana State Route, South Bend IN 46637. **Fax:** 574/272-7400. **Contact:** Human Resources. **World Wide Web address:** http://www.midlandengineering.com. **Description:** A contract construction firm that focuses on residential work such as roofing, sheet metal, waterproofing, and restoration.

MILLER BUILDING SYSTEMS, INC.
58120 County Road 3 South, Elkhart IN 46517. 574/295-1214. **Fax:** 574/295-2232. **Contact:** Human Resources. **World Wide Web address:** http://www.mbsionline.com. **Description:** Designs, manufactures, and markets prefabricated buildings. **Subsidiaries include:** Miller Structures, Inc. serves both the modular and mobile office market, as well as (through its Residential Division) the modular housing market. The company's main clients are firms that sell, lease, and rent modular and mobile office structures, as well as residential housing builders and dealers. Miller Telecom Services, Inc. is responsible for telecommunication shelters and pre-cast concrete assemblies for prisons, hazardous waste, and material confinement structures. The main market for Miller Telecom is end users with specific requirements for specialized applications.

ORBITAL ENGINEERING
3800 179th Street, Hammond IN 46323. 219/989-3300. **Contact:** Human Resources. **E-mail address:** japhilips@orbitalengr.com. **World Wide Web address:** http://www.orbitaleng.com. **Description:** A design consulting firm providing a variety of engineering services. **Corporate headquarters location:** Pittsburgh PA.

PARKER HANNIFIN CORPORATION
10801 Rose Avenue, New Haven IN 46774. 260/748-6000. **Contact:** Human Resources. **World Wide Web address:** http://www.parker.com. Description: Parker Hannifin Corporation is a worldwide manufacturer of hydraulic products, fluid connectors, electrical power distribution equipment, engine components, and truck drivetrain systems. The company serves the automotive, aerospace, industrial, and semiconductor industries. **NOTE:** Hires through a staffing firm. **Operations at this facility include:** This location manufactures air conditioning and heating equipment.

SQUARE D COMPANY
252 North Tippecanoe Street, Peru IN 46970. 765/472-3381. **Contact:** Human Resources. **World Wide Web address:** http://www.squared.com. **Description:** A manufacturer of electrical distribution products for the construction industry. Products are used in commercial and residential construction, industrial facilities, and machinery, as well as original equipment manufacturers' products. Residential building products feature circuit breakers with an exclusive quick-open mechanism that isolates potential dangers quickly. Square D also equips public buildings such as schools, stadiums, museums, hospitals, prisons, military bases, and wastewater treatment plants with electrical distribution systems.

SUPERIOR CONSTRUCTION COMPANY INC.
P.O. Box 64888, Gary IN 46402. 219/886-3728. **Physical address**: 2045 East Dunes Highway, Gary IN 46401. **Fax:** 219/885-4328. **Contact:** Human Resources. **World Wide Web address:** http://www.superior-construction.com. **Description:** A contract construction company that focuses on nonresidential business and highway construction.

SUPERIOR ENGINEERING LLC
2345 167th Street, Hammond IN 46323. 219/844-7030. **Fax:** 219/844-4217. **Contact:** Human Resources. **World Wide Web address:** http://www.superiorengineering.com **Description:** Offers structural, electrical, and mechanical engineering services.

THERMA-TRU CORPORATION
108 Mutzfeld Road, Butler IN 46721. 260/868-5811. **Contact:** Human Resources. **E-mail address:** mgray@thermatru.com. **World Wide Web address:** http://www.thermatru.com. **Description:** Manufactures fiberglass doors and steel doors. **NOTE:** Interested candidates should mail resumes to: Therma-Tru Corporation, Corporate Human Resources, P.O. Box 8780, Maumee OH 43537.

THE TOWNSEND GILBERT COMPANY
101 Main Street, P.O. Box 128, Parker City IN 47368. **Toll-free phone:** 800/428-8128. **Fax:** 765/468-3131. **Contact:** Human Resources. **World Wide Web address:** http://www.townsendtree.com. **Description:** A construction contracting firm specializing in pipeline, sewer, and marine projects.

UNDERWRITERS LABORATORIES, INC.
110 South Hill Street, South Bend IN 46617. **Toll-free phone:** 800/332-4345. **Fax:** 574/233-8207. **Contact:** Human Resources. **E-mail address:** ehl@ehl.ul.com. **World Wide Web address:** http://www.ul.com. **Description:** A not-for-profit product-safety testing and certification organization. Underwriters Laboratories (UL) has been testing products for more than a century. **Positions advertised include:** EHL Operations Manager; Fire Protection Engineer; Inside Sales; Quality Registration Sales Position; Suppression Reviewer. **Other U.S. locations:** CA; CO; FL; GA; IL; MA; MI; MN; MO; NC; NV; NY; TX; WA.

UNITED TECHNOLOGIES CARRIER SECURITY
7310 West Morris, Indianapolis IN 46231. 317/243-0851. **Contact:** Salaried Human Resources. **World Wide Web address:** http://www.utc.com. **Description:** A commercial manufacturer of HVAC equipment. **NOTE:** Apply online at www.carrier.com. **International locations:** Asia; Australia; Canada; Europe; Latin America; Mexico. **Parent company:** United Technologies provides high-technology products and support services to customers in the aerospace, building, military, and automotive industries worldwide. Products include large jet engines, temperature control systems, elevators and escalators, helicopters, and flight systems. The company markets its products under a variety of brand names including Carrier, Hamilton Standard, Otis, Pratt & Whitney, and Sikorsky.

WATERFURNACE INTERNATIONAL
9000 Conservation Way, Fort Wayne IN 46809. 260/478-5667. **Fax:** 260/479-3284. **Contact:** Human Resources. **E-mail address:** hr@waterfurnance.com. **World Wide Web address:** http://www.waterfurnace.com. **Description:** One of North America's leading manufacturers and distributors of geothermal heating and cooling systems for residential and commercial applications. WaterFurnace products are sold and serviced through commercial representatives and residential authorized dealers, and supported by independent distributors and regional direct-sales branches throughout the United States, Canada, and Australia. **Parent company:** WFI Industries, Ltd. **Operations at this facility include:** Administration; Distribution; Manufacturing; Marketing; Research and Development.

WEIL McLAIN
500 Blaine Street, Michigan City IN 46360. 219/879-6561. **Contact:** Human Resources. **World Wide Web address:** http://www.weil-mclain.com. **Description:** Manufactures heating equipment including boilers for the home construction and industrial markets. **Office hours:** Monday - Friday, 7:30 a.m. - 4:30 p.m.

ZIOLKOWSKI CONSTRUCTION INC.
1005 South Lafayette Boulevard, South Bend IN 46601. 574/287-1811. **Fax:** 574/234-0151. **Contact:** Human Resources Department. **World Wide Web address:** http://www.ziolkowskiconst.com. **Description:** A contract construction company with divisions for general construction, masonry, painting, design and architecture, and interiors.

Iowa

CURRIES COMPANY
1502 12th Street NW, Mason City IA 50401-2542. 641/423-1334. **Fax:** 641/422-2650. **Contact:** Mark Evers, Director of Human Resources. **E-mail address:** mark.evers@doorgroup.com. **World Wide Web address:** http://www.curries.com. **Description:** Part of the ESSEX Total Openings Group, Curries Company manufactures doors and frames for the construction market. The company's custom and pre-engineered products are created with the building designer in mind including doors and frames in a variety of construction systems, styles, fire ratings, and steel types. Founded in 1958. **Affiliates include:** ESSEX Total Openings Group. **Parent company:** ASSA ABLOY Inc. **President:** Jerry Currie.

THE WALDINGER CORPORATION
2601 Bell Avenue, Des Moines IA 50321-1189. 515/284-1911. **Fax:** 515/323-5150. **Contact:** Tim Steele, Human Resources. **World Wide Web address:** http://www.waldinger.com. **Description:** Engaged in mechanical and sheet metal construction. The company also designs, manufactures, installs, and maintains heating, air conditioning, ventilation, piping, and plumbing systems. Founded in 1906. **Positions advertised include:** Accountant; Engineer; Industrial Engineer; Project Manager; Service Manager; Service Sales Representative; Service Technician; Computer Programmer; Draftsperson; Mechanical Engineer. **Office hours:** Monday - Friday, 8:00 a.m. - 5:00 p.m. **Corporate headquarters location:** This location. **Annual sales/revenues:** Over $100 million. **Number of employees:** 1,000.

Kansas

BLACK & VEATCH
11401 Lamar Avenue, Overland Park KS 66211. 913/458-2000. **Fax:** 913/458-2934. **Contact:** Human Resources. **World Wide Web address:** http://www.bv.com. **Description:** An employee-owned global engineering, consulting, and construction company specializing in infrastructure development in energy, water, information, and government markets. Services include conceptual and preliminary engineering services, engineering design, procurement, construction, financial management, asset management, information technology, environmental, security design and consulting, and management consulting services. The company has more than 90 offices worldwide. Founded in 1915. **Positions advertised include:** Lead Mechanical Engineer; Project Estimator; HR Compensation Analyst; Human Resources Associate. **Corporate headquarters location:** This location. **Other U.S. locations:** Nationwide. **International locations:** Worldwide.

MARTIN K. EBY CONSTRUCTION CO., INC.
P.O. Box 1679, Wichita KS 67201-1679. 316/268-3500. **Physical address:** 610 North Main Street, Wichita KS 67203. **Fax:** 316/268-3649. **Contact:** Karman Diehl, Human Resources. **E-mail address:** kdiehl@ebycorp.com. **World Wide Web address:** http://www.ebycorp.com. **Description:** A general

contractor for commercial buildings, treatment plants, pipelines, heavy highways, locks, dams, and power plants. Founded in 1937. **NOTE:** Entry-level positions are offered. **Positions advertised include:** Project Engineer; Superintendent; Project Manager; Estimator; Civil Engineer; Foreman; Carpenter; Bricklayer; Ironworker; Cement Finisher; Laborer. **Special programs:** Internships; Co-ops. **Corporate headquarters location:** This location. **Other U.S. locations:** Maitland FL; Austin TX; Bedford TX. **Parent company:** Eby Corporation. **Listed on:** Privately held. **President:** Rich Bean. **Annual sales/revenues:** More than $170 million. **Number of employees nationwide:** 800.

PARSONS BRINCKERHOFF INC.
dba PARSONS BRINCKERHOFF QUADE & DOUGLAS, INC.
225 North Market Street, Suite 350, Wichita KS 67202. 316/263-6121. **Fax:** 316/263-8989. **Contact:** Human Resources. **World Wide Web address:** http://www.pbworld.com. **E-mail address:** ownbey@pbworld.com. **Description:** Provides complete engineering and construction management services, including the development of major bridges, tunnels, highways, marine facilities, buildings, industrial complexes, and railroads for transportation, power buildings, and telecommunications projects with more than 250 worldwide offices. Founded in 1885. **Special programs:** Internships. **Corporate headquarters location:** New York NY. **Other area locations:** Lenexa KS. **Other U.S. locations:** Nationwide. **International locations:** Worldwide. **Operations at this facility include:** The Wichita office is part of the U.S. infrastructure arm of PB. **Chairman:** Robert (Bob) Prieto. **Annual sales/revenues:** $1.4 billion. **Number of employees worldwide:** 9,300.

Kentucky
BURGESS & NIPLE, LTD.
220 Lexington Green Circle, Suite 110, Lexington KY 40503. 859/273-0557. **Fax:** 859/273-3332. **Contact:** Mark Willis, District Director. **E-mail address:** hr@burnip.com. **World Wide Web address:** http://www.burgessniple.com. **Note:** Applicants can search and submit applications for advertised positions online. **Description:** An engineering and architecture firm engaged in study, analysis, and design services. The company specializes in waterworks, wastewater, industrial services, hydropower, energy conservation, transportation, systems analysis, HVAC, and geotechnical services. Founded in 1912. **Positions advertised include:** Travel Demand Forecaster; Project Engineer. **Corporate headquarters location:** Columbus OH. **Other U.S. locations:** AZ; IN; OH; VA; WV; PA. **Number of employees nationwide:** Approximately 700.

COX INTERIOR, INC.
1751 Old Columbia Road, Campbellsville KY 42718. 270/789-3129. **Toll-free phone:** 800/733-1751. **Fax:** 270/465-7977. **Contact:** Cathy Priddy, Human Resources Department. **E-mail address:** contact@coxinterior.com. **World Wide Web address:** http://www.coxinterior.com. **Description:** Manufactures stair parts, doors, mantels, and other hardwood trim products. Primary materials are poplar, oak, and cherry woods as alternatives to pine. **Corporate headquarters location:** This location. **Operations at this facility include:** Administration; Manufacturing plant. **Number of employees at this location:** 840. **Number of employees nationwide:** Over 905.

JAMES N. GRAY COMPANY
dba GRAY CONSTRUCTION
10 Quality Street, Lexington KY 40507-1450. 859/281-5000. **Fax:** 859/281-9313. **Contact:** Susan Brewer, Human Resources. **E-mail address:** sbrewer@gray.com. **World Wide Web address:** http://www.jngray.com. **Description:** A design and construction firm specializing in commercial construction. Founded in 1960. **Special programs:** Educational Assistance Program. **Other area locations:** Glasgow KY. **Other U.S. locations:** Austin TX; Birmingham AL; Richmond VA. **International locations:** Japan. **Subsidiaries include:** Gray-ICE Builders, Inc. (Anaheim CA); Operations Associates (Greenville SC); WC Construction (Versailles KY). **Sales/revenues:** $330 million. **Number of employees at this location:** 350.

Louisiana
BASIC INDUSTRIES
15981 Airline Highway, Baton Rouge LA 70817. 225/752-4333. **Toll-free phone:** 800/766-7677. **Fax:** 225/756-7666. **Contact:** Human Resources. **World Wide Web address:** http://www.basicindustries.com. **Description:** A diversified company with business segments in refining, petrochemicals, power and utilities, paper and pulp, and maintenance or new construction. The company offers services such as industrial insulating, scaffolding, fireproofing, and asbestos abatement. **NOTE:** For current employment opportunities, contact the Baton Rouge Hiring Center at 16055 Airline Highway, Baton Rouge LA 70817, or by fax at 225/756.7678. **Special programs:** Apprenticeships; Training. **Corporate headquarters location:** This location. **Other U.S. locations:** NC; TX; Washington D.C. **Parent Company:** XServ, Incorporated. **Operations at this facility include:** Sales and Marketing; Safety; Maintenance and Construction Services. **Listed on:** Privately held. **President:** Dean Bordelon. **Sales/revenues:** $158 million.

CDM
1515 Poydras Street, Suite 1350, New Orleans LA 70112. 504/799-1100. **Fax:** 504/412-8260. **Contact:** Human Resources. **World Wide Web address:** http://www.cdm.com. **Description:** An employee-owned, full-service consulting, engineering, construction, and operations firm. CDM provides services through four business units: federal services group, industrial services group, international services group, and public services group. Founded in 1947. **Positions advertised include:** Environmental Engineer; GIS Specialist; Project Engineer; Water Resources Engineer. **Corporate headquarters location:** Cambridge MA. **Other area locations:** Baton Rouge LA; Shreveport LA. **Other U.S. locations:** Nationwide. **Number of employees worldwide:** 3,600.

CONESTOGA-ROVERS & ASSOCIATES
4915 South Sherwood Forest Boulevard, Baton Rouge LA 70816. 225/292-9007. **Fax:** 225/292-3614. **Contact:** Frank Edwards. **E-mail address:** hr@craworld.com. **World Wide Web address:** http://www.craworld.com. **Description:** Provides advice in the fields of engineering, environment, construction, and information technology. Founded in 1976. **NOTE:** Current opportunities for CRA and wholly-owned subsidiaries, as well as CRA affiliated companies, are listed at http://www.workoplis.com. On this website, job seekers can search and apply for available positions. **Positions advertised include:** Environmental Scientist; Geologist. **Corporate headquarters location:** Waterloo ON, Canada. **Other area locations:** Shreveport LA. **Other U.S. locations:** Nationwide. **International locations:** Canada; Mexico; United Kingdom. **Parent Company:** CRA Family of Companies. **Operations at this facility include:** Divisional Headquaters. **Listed on:** Privately held. **Number of employees at this location:** 75. **Number of employees nationwide:** 250. **Number of employees worldwide:** 2,000.

FIBREBOND CORPORATION
1300 Davenport Drive, Minden LA 71055. 318/377-1030. **Toll-free phone:** 800/824-2614. **Fax:** 318/377-5756. **Contact:** Vickie Cullen, Director of Human Resources. **E-mail address:** vickie.cullen@fibrebond.com. **World Wide Web address:** http://www.fibrebond.com. **Description:** Manufactures prefabricated buildings and structures. **Corporate headquarters location:** This location. **Other U.S. locations:** Fairfield CA. **CEO/Chairman:** Claud B. Walker.

LUDWIG BUILDING SYSTEMS
P.O. Box 23134, Harahan LA 70183. 504/733-6260. **Physical address:** 521 Timesaver Avenue, Harahan LA 70123. **Fax:** 504/733-7458. **Contact:** Human Resources. **Description:** Engaged in the manufacture and construction of commercial, retail, and industrial steel buildings. **Corporate headquarters location:** This location. **Operations at this facility include:** Administration; Manufacturing; Sales.

URS CORPORATION
600 Carondelet Street, New Orleans LA 70130-3587. 504/586-8111. **Fax:** 504/522-0554. **Contact:** Human Resources. **E-mail address:** recruiter@urscorp.com. **World Wide Web address:** http://www.urscorp.com. **Description:** A fully-integrated engineering and architectural organization that specializes in the project management, design, and construction management of industrial, private, and government facilities. URS Corporation also provides process and environmental engineering, architectural design, and total support services. **NOTE:** Please visit website to apply online; this is the preferred method of application and resume submission. **Positions advertised include:** 3D Design Coordinator; Administrative Assistant; Architectural Senior Designer; Chemical Engineer; Civil/Structural Drafter; Civil Drafter; Civil Engineer; Civil Senior Designer. **Special programs:** Tuition Reimbursement Program; Professional Development Program; Internships. **Corporate headquarters location:** San Francisco CA. **Other area locations:** Baton Rouge; Lake Charles; Metairie; Shreveport. **Operations at this facility include:** Administration; Engineering; Design. **Listed on:** New York Stock Exchange. **Stock exchange symbol:** URS. **President/CEO/Chairman:** Martin M. Koffel. **Annual sales/revenues:** $3.38 billion. **Number of employees at this location:** 400. **Number of employees worldwide:** 28,000.

Maine

BATH IRON WORKS CORPORATION
700 Washington Street, Bath ME 04530. 207/443-1059. **Fax:** 207/442-1919. **Contact:** Nancy Fortin. **E-mail address:** employment@biw.com. **World Wide Web address:** http://www.gdbiw.com. **Description:** Engineers and builds ships including navy frigates and destroyers. The company also sells shipbuilding and repair technology worldwide. **Other U.S. locations:** Nationwide. **Parent company:** General Dynamics (Falls Church VA). **Listed on:** Privately held.

CIANBRO CORPORATION
P.O. Box 1000, One Hunnewell Square, Pittsfield ME 04967. 207/487-3311. **Fax:** 207/667-2466. **Toll-free phone**: 866/242-2628. **Contact:** Amy Chute, Human Resources Manager. **E-mail address:** jobsnne@cianbro.com. **World Wide Web address:** http://www.cianbro.com. **Description:** An employee-owned, civil and industrial construction company. Cianbro Corporation is primarily involved in facilities construction and renovation in the eastern United States. Founded in 1949. **NOTE**: Search posted openings on-line and reply by e-mail. **Positions advertised include:** Pipewelder; Pipefitter; Structural Welder; First Class Linesman. **Corporate headquarters location:** This location. **Other area locations:** Portland ME. **Other U.S. locations:** Bloomfield CT; Baltimore MD. **Listed on:** Privately held. **Number of employees at this location:** 150. **Number of employees nationwide:** 1,200.

DRAGON PRODUCTS CORPORATION
P.O. Box 1521, Portland ME 04104-1521. 207/774-6355. **Physical address:** 38 Preble Street, Portland ME 04101. **Toll-free phone:** Maine – 800/427-6368; National – 800/828-8352. **Fax:** 207/761-5694. **Contact:** John Slaegle, Human Resources. **E-mail address:** info@dragonproducts.com. **World Wide Web address:** http://www.dragonproducts.com. **Description:** Manufactures, markets, and distributes ready-mix cement. Dragon Products Corporation also manufactures and sells crushed aggregate, sand, and concrete blocks. **NOTE:** Visit corporate web site for link to www.JobsInMaine.com web site. **Corporate headquarters location:** This location. **Other area locations:** Statewide. **Other U.S. locations:** Newington NH; Boston MA.

DURATHERM WINDOW CORPORATION
YORK SPIRAL STAIR
720 Main Street, North Vassalboro ME 04962. 207/872-5558. **Toll-free phone:** 800/996-5558. **Fax:** 207/872-6731. **Contact:** Personnel. **E-mail address:** info@durathermwindow.com. **World Wide Web address:** http://www.durathermwindow.com. **Description:** Manufactures standard and custom wooden window systems, doors, and spiral stairs. Customers include architects, contractors, private residences, retail stores, and companies.

LANE CONSTRUCTION CORPORATION
P.O. Box 103, Bangor ME 04402. 207/945-0850. **Fax:** 207/947-8887. **Physical address:** 1067 Odlin Road, Hermon ME 04401. **Contact:** Vicky Ham, Human Resources. **E-mail address:** HR@LaneConstruction,com, **World Wide Web address:** http://www.laneconstruct.com. **Description:** A construction company specializing in paving. **Corporate headquarters location:** Meridan CT. **Other U.S. locations:** Nationwide.

H.E. SARGENT, INC.
P.O. Box 435, 101 Bennoch Road, Stillwater ME 04489. 207/827-4435. **Fax:** 207/827-6150. **Contact:** Personnel. **World Wide Web address:** http://www.hesargent.com. **Description:** A general and heavy construction firm engaging in earth and civil work.

SHERIDAN CORPORATION
P.O. Box 359, Fairfield ME 04937. 207/453-9311. **Physical address:** 33 Sheridan Road, Fairfield ME 04937. **Fax:** 207/453-2820. **Contact:** Personnel. **E-mail address:** jobs@sheridancorp.com. **World Wide Web address:** http://www.sheridancorp.com. **Description:** A general contractor specializing in residential and commercial construction. **Positions advertised include:** Laborer; Steel Erector; Metal Roof Installer; Form Carpenter; Welder; Metal Siding Installer; Project Supervisor; Rough Carpenter; Steel Fabricator; Crane Operator; Sales Consultant; Administrative Worker; Proposal Coordinator; Project Manager; Health and Safety Personnel; Engineer; CAD Operator. **Other area locations:** Portland ME.

WRIGHT-PIERCE ENGINEERS
99 Main Street, Topsham ME 04086. 207/725-8721. **Fax:** 947/729-8414. **Contact:** Human Resources. **E-mail address:** dma@wright-pierce.com. **World Wide Web address:** http://www.wright-pierce.com. **Description:** A full-service civil and environmental engineering firm. The company specializes in civil and transportation engineering; structural engineering; environmental laboratory services; and water, wastewater, and solid waste treatment. **NOTE:** Search posted listings and apply on-line. **Positions advertised include**: Internship; Civil CAD Technician. **Corporate headquarters location:** This location. **Other area locations:** Portland ME. **Other U.S. locations:** Middletown CT; Portsmouth NH. **Number of employees at this location:** 95.

MARYLAND

ARINC INCORPORATED
2551 Riva Road, Annapolis MD 21401-7465. 410/266-4000. **Fax:** 410/266-3201. **Contact:** Staffing. **World Wide Web address:** http://www.arinc.com. **Description:** An engineering and management consulting firm that provides technical studies, analyses, and evaluations of aircraft and ship communication and information systems. Customers of ARINC include the Department of Defense, the Department of Energy, the Department of Transportation, and the Federal Aviation Administration. **Positions advertised include** Market Research Analyst; GPS Engineer; GPS Software

Engineer; Antenna Electromagnetic Engineer; Analyst; Operation Analyst; Interoperability Test Analyst; Network Test Engineer; Systems Analyst; Pricing Intern; Junior Java Developer; Marketing Communications Writer; Mechanical Design Engineer; Principal Engineer. **Special programs:** Internships. **Corporate headquarters location:** This location. **Other area locations:** Rockville MD; Patuxent River MD; Millersville MD; Baltimore MD. **Other U.S. locations:** Nationwide. **International locations:** Canada; United Kingdom; France; Spain; Germany; China; Japan; Taiwan; Thailand. **Operations at this facility include:** Administration; Research and Development; Sales. **Listed on:** Privately held. **Number of employees at this location:** 2,600. **Number of employees worldwide:** Over 3,000.

ATC ASSOCIATES INC.
8989 Herrmann Drive, Suite 300, Columbia MD 21045. 410/381-0232. **Fax:** 410/381-0247. **Contact:** Wilma Smith, Human Resources. **E-mail address:** AFCJobs@atc-enviro.com. **World Wide Web address:** http://www.atc-enviro.com. **Description:** Provides geotechnical engineering and consulting services to customers in the environmental field. Founded in 1982. **Positions advertised include:** Project Manager. **Corporate headquarters location:** Woburn MA. **Other U.S. locations:** Nationwide. **Number of employees nationwide:** 1,800.

ANALEX
10480 Little Patuxent Pkwy, Suite 400, Columbia MD 21044. 410/740-3026. **Fax:** 410/740-5160. **Contact:** Human Resources. **World Wide Web address:** http://www.analex.com. **Description:** Provides intelligence, systems engineering, and security services in support of national security. Analex focuses on developing technical approaches for the intelligence community, analyzing and supporting defense systems, designing, developing and testing aerospace systems and providing a full range of security support services to the U.S. government. **Positions advertised include:** Systems Engineer. **Listed on:** American Stock Exchange. **Stock exchange symbol:** NLX.

CENTURY ENGINEERING, INC.
32 West Road, Towson MD 21204. 410/823-8070. **Contact:** Ken Stratemeyer, Human Resources. **E-mail address:** kstratemeyer@centuryeng.com. **World Wide Web address:** http://www.centuryeng.com. **Description:** Provides electrical, mechanical, civil, structural, and geotechnical engineering services to private firms and government agencies in the U.S. **NOTE:** Entry-level positions are offered. **Positions advertised include:** Instrument Operations; Environmental Structures Engineer; Hydraulics Engineer; Structural Engineer; Traffic Engineer; Transportation Planner; Electrical Engineer. **Corporate headquarters location:** This location. **Other area locations:** Oakland MD. **Other U.S. locations:** Dover DE; Elkins WV. **CEO:** Francis X. Smyth. **Number of employees at this location:** 100. **Number of employees nationwide:** Approximately 170.

CERTAINTEED CORPORATION
P.O. Box 290, Williamsport MD 21795. 301/223-7900. **Physical address:** 10131 Governor Lane Boulevard, Williamsport MD 21795. **Fax:** 301/582-5510. **Contact:** Human Resources. **World Wide Web address:** http://www.certainteed.com. **Description:** Manufactures and distributes building materials, fiberglass products, and piping products. Principal products are used in residential, commercial, and industrial construction; repair and remodeling; fiberglass reinforcement applications; water and sewer systems; and other underground utility systems. Other products include roofing, acoustical insulation, fiberglass thermal insulation, air handling products, glass fiber, vinyl siding, and PVC piping. **Corporate headquarters location:** Valley Forge PA. **Other area locations:** Hagerstown MD. **Other U.S. locations:** Nationwide. **Parent company:** Saint-Gobain Corporation. **Operations at this facility include:** This location is a vinyl siding and windows manufacturing plant. **Sales/revenues:** Over $2.5 billion. **Number of employees nationwide:** Approximately 7,000.

THE CLARK CONSTRUCTION GROUP, INC.
7500 Old Georgetown Road, Bethesda MD 20814. 301/272-8100. **Fax:** 301/272-1928. **Contact:** Personnel. **E-mail address:** hr@clarkconstruction.com. **World Wide Web address:** http://www.clarkconstruction.com. **Description:** Provides general contract construction. Founded in 1906. **NOTE:** Resumes submitted via e-mail must be in Microsoft Word, WordPerfect, or text file format. **Positions advertised include:** Estimator; Field Engineer; Office Engineer; Project Manager; Safety Representative; Superintendent. **Special programs:** Internships; Co-ops. **Corporate headquarters location:** This location. **Other U.S. locations:** Costa Mesa CA; Oakland CA; Tampa FL; Chicago IL; Boston MA. **Sales/revenue:** $2 billion.

DAVENPORT INSULATION INC.
P.O. Box 57, 15445 Depot Lane, Upper Marlboro MD 20772. 301/627-1800. **Fax:** 301/627-6999. **Contact:** Human Resources. **Description:** A contracting and retail operation specializing in the installation and servicing of insulation and related products.

GAF MATERIALS CORPORATION
1500 South Ponca Street, Baltimore MD 21224. 410/633-7200. **Contact:** Matt Sterrett, Human Resources Manager. **E-mail address:** employment@gaf.com. **World Wide Web address:** http://www.gaf.com. **Description:** Produces prepared roofing, roll roofing, built-up roofing systems, single-ply roofing, and insulation products. Founded in 1886. **Corporate headquarters location:** Wayne NJ. **Other U.S. locations:** Nationwide. **International locations:** Worldwide. **Sales/revenue:** $1.2 billion.

GENERAL PHYSICS CORPORATION
6095 Marshalee Drive, Suite 300, Elkridge MD 21075. 410/379-3600. **Toll-free phone:** 800/727-6677. **Fax:** 410/540-5302. **Contact:** Human Resources. **E-mail address:** hr@gpworldwide.com. **World Wide Web address:** http://www.gpworldwide.com. **Description:** A performance improvement firm that provides training, engineering, and technical services to clients in the aerospace, automotive, defense, government, manufacturing, utility, independent power, pharmaceutical, and process industries. Founded in 1966. **NOTE:** Entry-level positions are offered. **Company slogan:** Leading the world to better performance. **Positions advertised include:** Program Manager Technician; Unix Administrator. **Special programs:** Internships; Training. **Office hours:** Monday - Friday, 8:30 a.m. - 5:00 p.m. **Corporate headquarters location:** This location. **Other area locations:** Aberdeen Proving Ground MD; Edgewood MD. **Other U.S. locations:** Nationwide. **International locations:** Brazil; Canada; Malaysia; Mexico; England. **Parent company:** GP Strategies Corporation. **Operations at this facility include:** Administration. **Listed on:** New York Stock Exchange. **Stock exchange symbol:** GPX. **Sales/revenue:** Approximately $180 million. **Number of employees at this location:** 200. **Number of employees nationwide:** 1,400. **Number of employees worldwide:** 2,200.

INITIAL CONTRACT SERVICES
1505 Bloomfield Avenue, Baltimore MD 21227. 410/525-1800. **Fax:** 410/525-3535. **Contact:** General Manager. **Description:** Provides housekeeping and building maintenance services to a wide range of clientele. **Corporate headquarters location:** Norcross GA. **Other U.S. locations:** Danbury CT; Atlanta GA; New York NY. **Parent company:** Rentokil Initial PLC. **Number of employees nationwide:** Over 3,000.

J.C.J. INC.
P.O. Box 1297, Upper Marlboro MD 20773. 301/780-6420. **Physical address:** 15123 Marlboro Pike, Upper Marlboro MD 20772. **Contact:** Owner. **Description:** A sheet metal and roofing contractor. The company is also

engaged in stainless steel fabrication. **Corporate headquarters location:** This location.

KCI TECHNOLOGIES, INC.
10 North Park Drive, Hunt Valley MD 21030-1846. 410/316-7800. **Fax:** 410/316-7817. **Contact:** Bob Bell, Hiring Manager. **E-mail address:** employment@kci.com. **World Wide Web address:** http://www.kci.com/tech. **Description:** Provides planning, engineering, surveying, geotechnical testing, and construction inspection services. **Positions advertised include:** CADD Designer; 3rd Party Inspector; Accounts Payable Specialist; Administrative Assistant; CADD Drafter; Civil Designer; Engineer; Environmental Scientist; Estimator; Geotechnical Engineer; Human Resources Assistant; Marketing Associate; Planner; Structural Design Clerk. **Corporate headquarters location:** This location. **Other area locations:** Laurel MD; Baltimore MD. **Other U.S. locations:** PA; OH; WV; VA; NC; DE; NC; DC; GA; FL. **Listed on:** Privately held.

JOHN J. KIRLIN, INC.
515 Dover Road, Suite 2100, Rockville MD 20850. 301/424-3410. **Fax:** 301/738-8888. **Contact:** Shane L. Williams, Corporate Director of Human Resources. **E-mail address:** swilliams@johnjkirlin-inc.com. **World Wide Web address:** http://www.johnjkirlin-inc.com. **Description:** Installs mechanical systems, such as HVAC, site utilities, plumbing, and process piping. **NOTE:** Online applications are available. **Positions advertised include:** Senior Project Manager; Estimator; CADD Operator; Mechanical Coordinator; Drafter. **Office hours:** Monday - Friday, 7:30 a.m. - 5:00 p.m. **Corporate headquarters location:** This location. **Other U.S. locations:** Fort Lauderdale FL; Atlanta GA; Baltimore MD; Raleigh NC. **President/CEO:** Wayne T. Day.

A.D. MARBLE & COMPANY, INC.
10989 Red Run Boulevard, Suite 209, Owings Mills MD 21117. 410/902-1421. **Fax:** 410/902-8856. **Contact:** Human Resources. **E-mail address:** jobs@admarble.com. **World Wide Web address:** http://www.admarble.com. **Description:** An employee-owned environmental and engineering consulting firm specializing in environmental studies, regulatory clearance, mitigation and monitoring, cultural resources services, and engineering. **Positions advertised include:** Civil Engineer; Environmental Scientist/Planner.

MILLER & LONG COMPANY, INC.
4824 Rugby Avenue, Bethesda MD 20814. 301/657-8000. **Contact:** Miles Gladstone, Personnel Director. **E-mail address:** hr@millerandlong.com. **World Wide Web address:** http://www.millerandlong.com. **Description:** A construction firm specializing in high-rise concrete construction. Founded in 1947. **NOTE:** Resumes may be submitted via e-mail. **Corporate headquarters location:** This location. **Other area locations:** Baltimore MD. **Other U.S. locations:** Garner NC.

NVR, INC.
3156 Sedgewick Drive, Waldorf MD 20603. 301/374-9486. **Contact:** Human Resources. **E-mail address:** elresumes@nvrinc.com. **World Wide Web address:** http://www.nvrinc.com. **Description:** A homebuilding and mortgage banking company. **Positions advertised include:** Loan Processor; Regional Manager; Unified Construction System (UCS) Group Administrator. **Corporate headquarters location:** This location. **Other area locations:** Statewide. **Other U.S. locations:** Nationwide.

QUANTA SYSTEMS CORPORATION
213 Perry Parkway, Gaithersburg MD 20877-2145. 301/590-3300. **Fax:** 301/590-3325. **Contact:** Human Resources. **World Wide Web address:** http://www.quantasystems.com. **Description:** A research and development engineering company that also manufactures high-technology products and commercial communications equipment. **Positions advertised include:** Business Development Director. **Corporate headquarters location:** Hanover MD. **Parent company:** Compudyne Corporation. **Listed on:** NASDAQ. **Stock exchange symbol:** CDCY.

RWD TECHNOLOGIES, INC.
5521 Research Park Drive, Baltimore MD 21228. 410/869-1000. **Toll-free phone:** 888/RWD-TECH. **Fax:** 410/869-3002. **Contact:** Lisa Heslin, Human Resources. **E-mail address:** jobs@rwd.com. **World Wide Web address:** http://www.rwd.com. **Description:** An engineering consulting firm that offers a broad range of integrated business solutions to increase worker effectiveness and productivity. **NOTE:** Resumes sent via e-mail must be formatted in ASCII text. **Office hours:** Monday – Friday, 8:30 a.m. – 5:15 p.m. **Other area locations:** Baltimore MD. **Other U.S. locations:** Nationwide. **International locations:** Germany; United Kingdom; Belgium; Canada. **Subsidiaries include:** Deutschland GmbH; RWD Technologiens; RWD Technologies Canada; RWD Technologies UK, Limited; RWD Technologies Belgium, B.V.B.A.; Sap Learning Solutions Pte, Limited; SAP Learning Solutions Australia Pty, Limited. **Listed on:** NASDAQ. **Stock exchange symbol:** RWDT. **Number of employees worldwide:** Over 900.

STV GROUP
7125 Ambassador Road, Suite 200, Baltimore MD 21244. 410/944-9112. **Contact:** Human Resources. **E-mail address:** careers@stvinc.com. **World Wide Web address:** http://www.stvinc.com. **Description:** STV Group provides engineering and architectural consulting and design services for a variety of projects. The company operates four business segments including civil engineering, which provides services for the construction of highways, bridges, airports, and marine ports; defense systems engineering, which serves the U.S. Department of Defense regarding the development of equipment and special hardware; industrial process engineering, which consists of services for the development of manufacturing equipment and process systems; and transportation engineering, which involves consulting, design, and construction supervision services for transportation facilities. **Corporate headquarters location:** Douglasville PA. **Other U.S. locations:** Nationwide. **Subsidiaries include:** STV Environmental; STV International; STV Architects; STV Incorporated. **Number of employees at this location:** 120. **Number of employees nationwide:** 1,300.

A.J. SACKETT & SONS COMPANY
1701 South Highland Avenue, Baltimore MD 21224. 410/276-4466. **Contact:** Human Resources. **E-mail address:** sales@ajsackett.com. **World Wide Web address:** http://www.ajsackett.com. **Description:** An engineering services company that also manufactures handling and processing equipment. **President:** Larry Taylor.

TATE ACCESS FLOORS, INC.
P.O. Box 278, Jessup MD 20794. 410/799-4207. **Fax:** 717/246-3437. **Physical address:** 7510 Montevideo Road, Jessup MD 20794. **Contact:** Human Resources. **E-mail address:** joybise@tateaccessfloors.com. **World Wide Web address:** http://www.tateaccessfloors.com. **Description:** Manufactures access flooring and accessories. Founded in 1962. **NOTE:** Mail resumes to 52 Springdale Road, Red Lion PA 17356. **Corporate headquarters location:** This location. **Other U.S. locations:** Nationwide. **Subsidiaries include:** Floating Floors; Innocrete; USG Access Floor Division Assets. **Parent company:** Kingspan Group plc. **Operations at this facility include:** Manufacturing. **Sales/revenue:** Over $150 million.

TRANDES CORPORATION
4601 President's Drive, Suite 360, Lanham MD 20706. 301/459-0200. **Fax:** 301/459-1069. **Contact:** Janine Carran, Director of Human Resources. **E-mail address:** jcarran@trandes.com. **World Wide Web address:** http://www.trandes.com. **Description:** An engineering

contractor providing services to the federal government. Founded in 1972. **Special programs:** Tuition Assistance Program. **Corporate headquarters location:** This location. **Other area locations:** Lexington Park MD. **Other U.S. locations:** Nationwide. **Sales/revenue:** Over $16 million. **Number of employees nationwide:** Over 220.

WILLIAMS SCOTSMAN
8211 Town Center Drive, Baltimore MD 21236. 800/782-1500. **Fax:** 410/931-6063. **Contact:** Human Resources. **E-mail address:** hr@willscot.com. **World Wide Web address:** http://www.willscot.com. **Description:** A national provider of mobile and modular building solutions for the construction, education, commercial, healthcare and government markets. **Corporate headquarters locations:** This location. **Other U.S. locations:** Nationwide.

MASSACHUSETTS

ABBOT BUILDING RESTORATION COMPANY, INC.
28 Allerton Street, Boston MA 02119. 617/445-0274. **Contact:** Human Resources Department. **Description:** Specializes in building restoration. Services include brick masonry and concrete repair.

AMERICAN BILTRITE INC.
57 River Street, Wellesley Hills MA 02481. 781/237-6655. **Fax:** 781/237-6880. **Contact:** Human Resources. **E-mail address:** info@ambilt.com. **World Wide Web address:** http://www.ambilt.com. **Description:** Manufactures hard floor coverings including asphalt felt-based linoleum. **Listed on:** American Stock Exchange. **Stock exchange symbol:** ABL.

ARCADD, INC.
1185 Washington Street, West Newton MA 02465. 617/332-1200. **Fax:** 617/969-3362. **Contact:** Employment. **E-mail address:** arcaddinc@aol.com. **World Wide Web address:** http://www.arcadd.com. **Description:** An architectural design firm.

BALCO INC.
306 Northern Avenue, Boston MA 02210. 617/482-0100. **Contact:** Human Resources. **Description:** A heating, ventilation, air conditioning, and refrigeration contractor engaged in construction and residential building maintenance services. **Corporate headquarters location:** This location. **Other U.S. locations:** Birmingham AL; Rockville MD; Harrisburg PA. **Parent company:** Energy Systems, Inc. **Operations at this facility include:** Administration; Sales; Service. **Number of employees at this location:** 500.

BEALS & THOMAS, INC.
144 Turnpike Road, Southborough MA 01772-2104. 508/786-5431. **Fax:** 508/366-4391. **Contact:** Human Resources. **E-mail address:** hr@btiweb.com. **World Wide Web address:** http://www.btiweb.com. **Description:** A civil engineering firm offering a variety of services including surveying, site planning, and landscape architecture. **NOTE:** Applicants can submit resume online. **Positions advertised include:** Marketing Coordinator; PC/Network Support Technician; Staff Level Civil Engineer; Sr. Civil Engineer.

R.W. BECK, INC.
550 Cochituate Road, P.O. Box 9344, Framingham MA 01701-9344. 508/935-1600. **Fax:** 508/935-1888. **Fax:** 508/935-1666. **Contact:** Human Resources. **E-mail address:** boston@rwbeck.com. **World Wide Web address:** http://www.rwbeck.com. **Description:** A diversified professional, technical, and management consulting firm. The company provides construction, environmental, technical, energy, solid waste, and water/wastewater services nationwide. Founded in 1942. **Positions advertised include:** Engineer. **Corporate headquarters location:** Seattle WA. **Operations at this facility include:** Divisional Headquarters; Regional Headquarters. **Listed on:** Privately held. **Number of employees at this location:** 100. **Number of employees nationwide:** 500.

WILLIAM A. BERRY & SON, INC.
99 Conifer Hill Drive, Suite 410, Danvers MA 01923. 978/774-1057. **Toll-free phone:** 877/774-1057. **Fax:** 978/233-9457. **Contact:** Human Resources. **E-mail address:** careers@berry.com. **World Wide Web address:** http://www.waberry.com. **Description:** A construction management firm. Founded in 1857. **Positions advertised include:** Senior Project Engineer; Project Manager; Sr. Engineer; Project Engineer; MEP Coordinator.

BRYANT ASSOCIATES, INC.
160 North Washington Street, Boston MA 02114-2127. 617/248-0300. **Fax:** 617/248-0212. **Contact:** Human Resources. **E-mail address:** jobs@bryant-engrs.com. **World Wide Web address:** http://www.bryant-engrs.com. **Description:** An engineering and surveying firm. Founded in 1976. **Positions advertised include:** Operations Manager. **Other U.S. locations:** New Ipswich NH; Syracuse NY; Lincoln RI.

CANNON DESIGN
100 Cambridge Street, suite 1400, Boston MA 02114. 617/742-5440. **Contact:** Human Resources. **World Wide Web address:** http://www.cannondesign.com. **Description:** An architectural, interior design, and engineering firm. **Positions advertised include:** Engineer; Project Architect; Educational Planner. **Corporate headquarters location:** Grand Island NY. **Other U.S. locations:** Los Angeles CA; Washington DC; Jacksonville FL; Chicago IL; Baltimore MD; St. Louis MO.

CARLSON ASSOCIATES, INC.
959 Concord Street, 2nd Floor, Framingham MA 01701. 508/370-0100. **Fax:** 508/626-2390. **Contact:** Ms. Saroj Patel, Personnel Manager. **Description:** Provides a variety of architectural services. **Corporate headquarters location:** This location. **Other U.S. locations:** CA; FL; NC. **Subsidiaries include:** Carlson Design/Construction Corporation. **Parent company:** Carlson Holdings Company. **Operations at this facility include:** Administration. **Number of employees at this location:** 40. **Number of employees nationwide:** 95.

CLARK CONSTRUCTION
263 Summer Street, Boston MA 02210. 617/353-1550. **Contact:** Human Resources. **World Wide Web address:** http://www.clarkus.com. **Description:** A general construction contractor. Founded in 1906. **Positions advertised include:** Project Manager; Superintendent; Field Engineer; Office Engineer. **Corporate headquarters location:** Bethesda MD. **Other U.S. locations:** Irvine CA; Oakland CA; Tampa FL; Chicago IL.

COLONIAL SAW
122 Pembroke Street, P.O. Box A, Kingston MA 02364. 781/585-4364. **Fax:** 781/585-9375. **Contact:** Human Resources: **E-mail address:** info@csaw.com. **World Wide Web address:** http://www.csaw.com. **Description:** Produces woodworking and tool grinding technology.

CUTTING EDGE TECHNOLOGIES
250 Nicks Rock Road, Plymouth MA 02360. 508/746-6900. **Toll-free phone:** 800/233-9956. **Fax:** 508/747-4339. **Contact:** Human Resources. **E-mail address:** toolsales@cetdirect.com. **World Wide Web address:** http://www.cetdirect.com. **Description:** 1SO 9002 certified company to make cutting tools that meet standard or special tolerances.

DEWBERRY & GOODKIND
31 St. James Avenue, 3rd Floor, Boston MA 02116. 617/695-3400. **Fax:** 617/695-3310. **Contact:** Personnel. **World Wide Web address:** http://www.dewberry.com. **Description:** An engineering firm specializing in architectural design, environmental consulting, and construction

administration. Founded in 1922. **Positions advertised include:** Civil/Structural Engineer.

ECKLAND CONSULTANTS
131 Tremont Street, 3rd Floor, Boston MA 02111. 617/423-1100. **Fax:** 617/423-1188. **Contact:** Human Resources. **World Wide Web address:** http://www.eckland.com. **Description:** An architecture and engineering consulting firm that specializes in property and environmental assessments for real estate agencies and banks. **Other U.S. locations:** Nationwide.

EDWARDS & KELCEY
343 Congress Street, 2nd Floor, Boston MA 02110. 617/242-9222. **Fax:** 617/242-9824. **Contact:** Human Resources. **E-mail address:** corphr@ekmail.com. **World Wide Web address:** http://www.ekcorp.com. **Description:** An engineering firm specializing in road/highway, traffic, and structural projects. **Positions advertised include:** Architectural Job Captain, Control Systems Engineer; Mechanical Designer; Systems Engineer. **Corporate headquarters location:** Morristown NJ. **Other U.S. locations:** Nationwide. **International locations:** The Netherlands; Puerto Rico.

EXPONENT, INC.
21 Strathmore Road, Natick MA 01760. 508/652-8500. **Contact:** Human Resources Department. **E-mail address:** hr@exponent.com. **World Wide Web address:** http://www.exponent.com. **Description:** A technical consulting firm dedicated to the investigation, analysis, and prevention of accidents and failures of an engineering or scientific nature. The company provides a multidisciplinary approach to analyze how failures occur. The company specializes in accident reconstruction, biomechanics, construction/structural engineering, aviation and marine investigations, environmental assessment, materials and product testing, warning and labeling issues, accident statistical data analysis, and risk prevention/mitigation. Founded in 1967. **Positions advertised include:** Engineer; Sr. Managing Engineer; Chemical Engineer. **NOTE:** Search and apply for positions online. **Other U.S. locations:** Nationwide. **Parent company:** Exponent, Inc. **Listed on:** NASDAQ. **Stock exchange symbol:** EXPO.

FAY, SPOFFORD & THORNDIKE, INC.
5 Burlington Woods, Burlington MA 01803. 781/221-1000. **Fax:** 781/221-1015. **Contact:** Human Resources. **E-mail address:** hr@fstinc.com. **World Wide Web address:** http://www.fstinc.com. **Description:** Engaged in civil, electrical, environmental, and mechanical engineering. **Corporate headquarters location:** This location. **Other U.S. locations:** Cromwell CT; Boston MA; Bedford NH; West Caldwell NJ; Melville NY; New York NY. **Number of employees at this location:** 175.

GALE ASSOCIATES, INC.
163 Libbey Parkway, P.O. Box 890189, Weymouth, MA 02189. 781/335-6465. **Toll-free phone:** 800/659-4753. **Fax:** 781/335-6467. **Contact:** Kathleen A. Forrand, Human Resources Manager. **E-mail address:** kaf@gainc.com. **World Wide Web address:** http://www.gainc.com. **Description:** A national architecture and engineering firm that specializes in the improvement of existing buildings, sites, and infrastructures for both public and private clients. This location also hires seasonally. Founded in 1964. **NOTE:** Entry-level positions and part-time jobs are offered. **Positions advertised include:** Structural Engineer; Building Enveloper Specialist. **Special programs:** Training; Co-ops; Summer Jobs. **Office hours:** Monday - Friday, 8:00 a.m. - 5:00 p.m. **Corporate headquarters location:** This location. **Other U.S. locations:** Mountain View CA; Oakland CA; Winter Park FL; Baltimore MD; Bedford NH. **Operations at this facility include:** Divisional Headquarters. **Listed on:** Privately held. **President:** Harold E. Flight. **Accounting Manager:** Bruce P. White. **Annual sales/revenues:** $5 - $10 million. **Number of employees at this location:** 60. **Number of employees nationwide:** 100.

GANNETT FLEMING
150 Wood Road, Braintree MA 02184. 781/380-7750. **Fax:** 781/380-7754. **Contact:** Human Resources. **E-mail address:** employment@gfnet.com. **World Wide Web address:** http://www.gannettfleming.com. **Description:** An engineering firm offering a wide variety of services including structural, geo-technical, environmental, hazardous waste, bridge design, and tunnel design. **Positions advertised include:** Civil Engineer; Structural Engineer; Architect; Marketing Coordinator; Sr. Project Engineer. **Other U.S. locations:** Nationwide.

GRACE CONSTRUCTION PRODUCTS
62 Whittemore Avenue, Cambridge MA 02140. 617/876-1400. **Contact:** Human Resources. **E-mail address:** careers@grace.com. **World Wide Web address:** http://www.graceconstruction.com. **Description:** As part of W.R. Grace & Company, Grace Construction Products manufactures concrete additives, waterproofing products and systems, and fire protection products. The company has more than 125 plants and sales offices worldwide. **NOTE:** Entry-level positions are offered. **Special programs:** Internships. **Corporate headquarters location:** Columbia MD. **Subsidiaries include:** Darex Container Products (Belgium; Lexington MA); Davison Chemicals (Canada; Columbia MD); Performance Chemicals (Cambridge MA). **Listed on:** New York Stock Exchange. **Stock exchange symbol:** GRA. **CEO:** Paul Norris.

HDR ENGINEERING, INC.
7 Winthrop Square, Boston MA 02110. 617/357-7700. **Contact:** Human Resources. **E-mail address:** careers@hdrinc.com. **World Wide Web address:** http://www.hdrinc.com. **Description:** HDR Engineering, Inc. provides water, transportation, waste, and energy services including studies, design, and implementation for complex projects. **Corporate headquarters location:** Omaha NE. **Operations at this facility include:** This location specializes in a variety of transportation-related engineering projects including bridges, roads, and tunnels. **Parent company:** HDR, Inc.

HNTB CORPORATION
75 State Street, 10th Floor, Boston MA 02109. 617/542-6900. **Contact:** Human Resources. **World Wide Web address:** http://www.hntb.com. **Description:** An architectural engineering firm specializing in the design of highways and bridges. **Positions advertised include:** Traffic Engineer; Aviation Planner; Project Architect; Graphic Designer; division Business Manager; Structural Engineer. **Corporate headquarters location:** Kansas City MO. **Other U.S. locations:** Nationwide.

HARVEY INDUSTRIES, INC.
1400 Main Street, Waltham MA 02451-9180. 781/899-3500. **Toll-free phone:** 800/882-8945. **Contact:** Human Resources. **E-mail address:** jobs@harveyind.com. **World Wide Web address:** http://www.harveyind.com. **Description:** Manufactures windows and doors. The company is also a wholesale distributor of building materials. **Positions advertised include:** Human Resources Supervisor; Imaging Clerk.

HAYES ENGINEERING
603 Salem Street, Wakefield MA 01880. 781/246-2800. **Fax:** 781/246-7596. **Contact:** Business Manager. **E-mail address:** rgraf@hayeseng.com. **World Wide Web address:** http://www.hayeseng.com. **Description:** A civil and environmental engineering firm that also provides land surveying services.

JACOBS SVERDRUP
2 Center Plaza, 7th Floor, Boston MA 02108. 617/742-8060. **Fax:** 617/742-8830. **Contact:** Human Resources. **World Wide Web address:** http://www.sverdrup.com. **Description:** A civil engineering firm engaged in the operation of environmental, transportation, and facilities projects. **Positions advertised include:** Cost Analyst; Electrical Engineer; Geotechnical Engineer;

Mechanical Engineer; Transit Operations Specialist. Transportation Engineer.

LEMESSURIER CONSULTANTS
675 Massachusetts Avenue, Cambridge MA 02139. 617/868-1200. **Fax:** 617/661-7520. **Contact:** Peter Cheevers, Personnel Director. **World Wide Web address:** http://www.lemessurier.com. **Description:** Provides structural engineering consulting services. Founded in 1961. **Positions advertised include:** Experienced CAD Operators.

MAGUIRE GROUP, INC.
33 Commercial Street, Suite 1, Foxborough MA 02035. 508/543-1700. **Contact:** Jan Washburn, Human Resources Manager. **E-mail address:** jwashburn@maguiregroup.com. **World Wide Web address:** http://www.maguiregroup.com. **Description:** An architectural, engineering, and planning firm, serving domestic and international clients. Maguire Group, Inc. is engaged in the design and construction management of industrial commercial buildings; environmental facilities including sewers and treatment plants; hydroelectric power plants; highways, bridges, airports, and mass transit projects; and port and marine facilities. **Positions advertised include:** Architectural Project Manager; Construction Manager; Plumbing Engineer. **Corporate headquarters location:** This location. **Other U.S. locations:** New Britain CT; Portland ME; Portsmouth NH; Atlantic City NJ; Lawrenceville NJ; Harrisburg PA; Philadelphia PA; Pittsburgh PA; State College PA; Providence RI. **International locations:** St. Croix, U.S. Virgin Islands.

MASSACHUSETTS ELECTRIC CONSTRUCTION COMPANY
180 Guest Street, Boston MA 02135-2028. 617/254-1015. **Fax:** 617/254-0706. **Contact:** Human Resources. **World Wide Web address:** http://www.masselec.com. **Description:** An electrical contractor. Services include construction management, value engineering, design, and consultation. **Positions advertised include:** Transit Estimator; Maintenance Engineer. **Other U.S. locations:** Nationwide.

NATIONAL ENGINEERING SERVICE CORPORATION
10 Cedar Street, Suite 27, Woburn MA 01801. 781/938-4747. **Contact:** Human Resources. **Description:** A contract engineering firm engaged primarily in civil engineering projects.

PARSONS
150 Federal Street, Boston MA 02110. 617/946-9400. **Fax:** 617/946-9777. **Contact:** Human Resources. **World Wide Web address:** http://www.parsons.com. **Description:** An employee-owned engineering and construction company specializing in power generation and utilities, general industrial engineering, and environmental engineering. Founded in 1944. **Positions advertised include:** Piping Designer; Project Manager; Engineer; Business Development Manager; Bridge Engineer; Technical Consultant. **Other U.S. locations:** Nationwide. **International locations:** Worldwide.

PARSONS BRINCKERHOFF INC.
75 Arlington Street, 9th Floor, Boston MA 02116. 617/426-7330. **Contact:** Human Resources. **World Wide Web address:** http://www.pbworld.com. **Description:** An engineering and design firm engaged in the design of bridges, tunnels, rapid transit systems, hydroelectric facilities, water supply systems, and marine facilities. **Positions advertised include:** Civil Engineer. **Other U.S. locations:** Nationwide.

PERINI CORPORATION
73 Mt. Wayte Avenue, Framingham MA 01701. 508/628-2000. **Fax:** 508/628-2960. **Contact:** Human Resources. **E-mail address:** dtanner@perini.com. **World Wide Web address:** http://www.perini.com. **Description:** One of the largest heavy and building construction firms in the United States. Worldwide projects include bridges and roads, mass transportation and airport construction, and commercial building construction. Perini also provides engineering and consulting services. Founded in 1894. **Positions advertised include:** Scheduler; Estimator; Project Engineer. **Corporate headquarters location:** This location. **Operations at this facility include:** Administration. **Listed on:** American Stock Exchange. **Stock exchange symbol:** PCR.

SASAKI ASSOCIATES, INC.
64 Pleasant Street, Watertown MA 02472. 617/926-3300. **Fax:** 617/924-2748. **Contact:** Human Resources. **World Wide Web address:** http://www.sasaki.com. **Description:** An architectural and design firm that specializes in architecture, civil engineering, graphic design, interior design, landscape architecture, and urban design. Founded in 1953. **Positions advertised include:** Urban Designer; Architecture Operations Coordinator; Architect; Landscape Designer. **Corporate headquarters location:** This location. **Other U.S. locations:** San Francisco CA; Dallas TX. **Number of employees at this location:** 155. **Number of employees nationwide:** 200.

SEI COMPANIES
88 Black Falcon Avenue, Suite 210, Boston MA 02210-2414. 617/210-1600. **Fax:** 617/210-1800. **Contact:** Human Resources. **E-mail address:** jobsboston@seicompanies.com. **World Wide Web address:** http://www.seicompanies.com. **Description:** A mechanical and electrical engineering firm. **Positions advertised include:** Electrical Engineer; Mechanical Engineer/Designer; Sr. Plumbing/Fire Protection Engineer; Energy Engineer; Project Services Coordinator.

STONE & WEBSTER ENGINEERING CORPORATION
100 Technology Center Drive, Stoughton MA 02072. 617/589-5111. **Fax:** 617/589-1587. **Contact:** Human Resources Department. **World Wide Web address:** http://www.shawgrp.com. **Description:** Provides construction, consulting, engineering, environmental, and procurement services to a variety of industries worldwide. **Positions advertised include:** Principal Mechanical Engineer; Lead Mechanical Engineer. **NOTE:** Apply online. **Office hours:** Monday - Friday, 8:00 a.m. - 4:45 p.m. **Corporate headquarters location:** This location. **Other U.S. locations:** Denver CO; Cherry Hill NJ; New York NY; Chattanooga TN; Houston TX. **Parent company:** The Shaw Group, Inc. **Listed on:** New York Stock Exchange. **Stock exchange symbol:** SGR. **Number of employees at this location:** 1,200. **Number of employees nationwide:** 6,000.

TIGHE & BOND
53 Southampton Road, Westfield MA 01085. 413/562-1600. **Fax:** 413/562-5317. **Contact:** April Lassard, Administrative Assistant. **E-mail address:** alassard@tighebond.com. **World Wide Web address:** http://www.tighebond.com. **Description:** Offers environmental and civil engineering consulting services. **Positions advertised include:** Project Manager; Sr. Hydrogeologist; GIS Analyst; Structural Engineer. **Other area locations:** Worcester MA; Pocasset MA.

VHB/VANASSE HANGEN BRUSTLIN, INC.
101 Walnut Street, P.O. Box 9151, Watertown MA 02471-9151. 617/924-1770. **Fax:** 617/924-2286. **Contact:** Human Resources. **E-mail address:** info@vhb.com. **World Wide Web address:** http://www.vhb.com. **Description:** A civil engineering firm specializing in Transportation, land development, and environmental projects. **Positions advertised include:** Water Quality Specialist; Traffic Engineer; Sr. Traffic Engineer/Project Manager; Land Surveyor; Project Engineer; Sr. Business Systems Programmer/Analyst; Water Resources Engineer; Software Quality Assurance and Implementation Specialist; Sr. Landscape Architect; Transportation Engineer.

VANDERWEIL ENGINEERS
274 Summer Street, Boston MA 02210. 617/423-7423. **Fax:** 617/423-7401. **Contact:** Human Resources. **World Wide Web address:** http://www.vanderweil.com. **Description:** A consulting engineering firm. **Positions advertised include:** Designer; Mechanical Engineer; Project Manager.

WASHINGTON GROUP INTERNATIONAL, INC.
One Broadway, Cambridge MA 02142. 617/494-7000. **Contact:** Human Resources. **World Wide Web address:** http://www.wgint.com. **Description:** Provides design, engineering, and construction services to chemical, petroleum, and other related industrial customers. **Positions advertised include:** Engineer.

Michigan

ADVANCED ENGINEERING SOLUTIONS, INC.
5860 North Canton Center Road, Suite 380, Canton MI 48187. 734/459-9948. **Fax:** 734/459-7590. **Contact:** Human Resources. **World Wide Web address:** http://www.aes-inc.com. **Description:** An engineering and information technology consulting firm. **Positions advertised include:** Embedded Systems Engineer; Industrial Engineer; Manufacturing Process Engineer; Quality Engineer; Test Engineer; Database Administrator; Network Administrator; Java Programmer; C++ Programmer; PeopleSoft Consultant; Cold Fusion Expert. **Corporate headquarters location:** This location.

AMERICAN SHOWER AND BATH CORPORATION
693 South Court Street, Lapeer MI 48446. 810/664-8501. **Contact:** Human Resources. **World Wide Web address:** http://www.asbcorp.com. **Description:** Manufactures products for showers and bathtubs, including wall surrounds, shower enclosure kits, and bathtub and shower doors. **Special programs:** Internships. **Corporate headquarters location:** Moorestown NJ. **Parent company:** Masco Corporation. **Operations at this facility include:** Manufacturing; Sales. **Number of employees at this location:** 100.

ARCADIS GIFFELS
25200 Telegraph Road, Southfield MI 48034. 248/936-8000. **Fax:** 248/936-8111. **Contact:** Human Resources Administrator. **World Wide Web address:** http://www.arcadis-us.com. **Description:** An engineering, architectural, and surveying firm that serves clients in the communications, environmental, infrastructure, and buildings business sectors. **Positions advertised include:** Task Manager. **Corporate headquarters location:** Denver CO. **Other U.S. locations:** Nationwide. **International locations:** Worldwide. **Parent company:** Arcadis NV (the Netherlands). **Listed on:** NASDAQ. **Stock exchange symbol:** ARCAD. **Number of employees at this location:** 500. **Number of employees worldwide:** 8,500.

ATWELL-HICKS, INC.
500 Avis Drive, Suite 100, Ann Arbor MI 48108. 734/994-4000. **Fax:** 734/994-1590. **Contact:** Human Resources. **E-mail address:** careers@atwell-hicks.com. **World Wide Web address:** http://www.atwell-hicks.com. **Description:** A land development consulting firm. AHI provides a wide range of services for commercial and residential land development projects. **Positions advertised include:** Accounting Assistant. **Corporate headquarters location:** This location. **Other area locations:** Brighton MI; Shelby Township MI; Grand Rapids MI. **Other U.S. locations:** Naperville IL; Orlando FL; Tampa FL.

BARTON MALOW COMPANY
26500 American Drive, Southfield MI 48034. 248/436-5024. **Fax:** 248/436-5001. **Contact:** Jose Herrera, Recruiting Manager. **E-mail address:** jose.herrera@bartonmalow.com. **World Wide Web address:** http://www.bmco.com. **Description:** A construction management, program management, and general contracting company engaged in the construction of health facilities and commercial and industrial buildings. **Positions advertised include:** Director of Marketing. **Special programs:** Internships. **Corporate headquarters location:** This location. **Other area locations:** Detroit MI; Oak Park MI. **Other U.S. locations:** Columbus OH; Phoenix AZ; Chantilly VA; Charlottesville VA; Norcross GA; Linthicum MD. **Operations at this facility include:** Administration. **Annual sales/revenues:** Over $1 billion. **Number of employees nationwide:** 1,550.

BRENCAL CONTRACTORS INC.
6686 East McNichols Street, Detroit MI 48212. 313/365-4300. **Fax:** 313/365-4739. **Contact:** Anne Colo, Personnel Director. **Description:** A contracting company specializing in concrete and industrial construction. **Corporate headquarters location:** This location. **Other area locations:** Detroit MI. **Number of employees at this location:** 200.

CUNNINGHAM-LIMP COMPANY
39300 West Twelve Mile Road, Suite 200, Farmington Hills MI 48331. 248/489-2300. **Fax:** 248/489-1247. **Contact:** Personnel. **E-mail address:** info@cunninghamlimp.com. **World Wide Web address:** http://www.cunninghamlimp.com. **Description:** An engineering, architectural, and surveying services company. **Corporate headquarters location:** This location.

DLZ CORPORATION
1425 Keystone Avenue, Lansing MI 48911. 517/393-6800. **Fax:** 517/272-7390. **Contact:** Human Resources. **E-mail address:** hrdept@dlzcorp.com. **World Wide Web address:** http://www.dlzcorp.com. **Description:** A professional consulting firm providing complete architectural, engineering, and environmental services to public and private sector clients. **NOTE:** Send resumes to: DLZ Corporation, Attention: Human Resources, Job Code: #, 6121 Huntley Road, Columbus OH 43229-1003. **Positions advertised include:** Civil Engineer; Entry Level Biologist; Highway Project Manager; Landscape Architect; Registered Surveyor; Survey Crew Chief; Transportation Planner/NEPA Specialist; Wastewater Engineer. **Corporate headquarters location:** Columbus OH. **Other area locations:** Detroit MI; Gaylord MI; Niles MI. **Other U.S. locations:** IN; IL; MA; WV. **Number of employees nationwide:** Over 700.

DENTON ENTERPRISES
22003 Harper Avenue, St. Clair Shores MI 48080. 313/884-5530. **Contact:** Human Resources. **Description:** A contracting company specializing in the construction of streets and highways. **Corporate headquarters location:** This location.

E&L CONSTRUCTION GROUP
P.O. Box 418, Flint MI 48501. 810/744-4300. **Physical address:** 2830 Lippincott Boulevard, Flint MI 48506. **Fax:** 810/744-1735. **Contact:** Kristy Krueger, Administration. **E-mail address:** markk@eandlgroup.com. **World Wide Web address:** http://www.eandlgroup.com. **Description:** A contracting company specializing in the construction of industrial buildings and warehouses. **NOTE:** Entry-level positions are offered. **Other area locations:** Sault Ste. Marie MI. **Number of employees at this location:** 120.

ETKIN SKANSKA CONSTRUCTION COMPANY
407 East Fort Street, Suite 401, Detroit MI 48226-2940. 313/964-0953. **Fax:** 313/964-1153. **Contact:** Controller. **E-mail address:** michigancareers@skanskausa.com. **World Wide Web address:** http://www.skanskausa.com. **Description:** Engaged in the construction of commercial, educational, retail, and hospital buildings. **Corporate headquarters location:** Parsippany NJ. **Other area locations:** Grand Rapids MI; Kalamazoo MI; Southfield MI. **Other U.S. locations:** Nationwide. **Sales/revenue:** $5 billion. **Number of employees at this location:** 200. **Number of employees nationwide:** 5,300.

EXPONENT, INC.
39100 Country Club Drive, Farmington Hills MI 48331. 248/324-9100. **Fax:** 248/324-9199. **Contact:** Human Resources. **E-mail address:** hr@exponent.com. **World Wide Web address:** http://www.exponent.com. **Description:** A technical consulting firm dedicated to the investigation, analysis, and prevention of accidents and failures of an engineering or scientific nature. The company specializes in accident reconstruction, biomechanics, construction/structural engineering, aviation and marine investigations, environment assessment, materials and product testing, warning and labeling issues, accident statistic data analysis, and risk prevention/mitigation. Founded in 1967. **Positions advertised include:** Managing Engineer. **Corporate headquarters location:** Menlo Park CA. **Other U.S. locations:** Nationwide. **International locations:** United Kingdom; Germany. **Parent company:** Exponent. **Listed on:** NASDAQ. **Stock exchange symbol:** EXPO.

FISHBECK, THOMPSON, CARR & HUBER, INC.
1515 Arboretum Drive SE, Grand Rapids MI 49546. 616/575-3824. **Fax:** 616/464-3995. **Contact:** Human Resources. **E-mail address:** humanres@ftch.com. **World Wide Web address:** http://www.ftch.com. **Description:** A firm providing a full range of civil engineering, architectural/engineering, and environmental services to public and private sector clients. **Positions advertised include:** Project Architect; Mechanical CAD Technician; Programmer. **Corporate headquarters location:** This location. **Other area locations:** Farmington Hills MI; Kalamazoo MI; Lansing MI. **Number of employees nationwide:** 260.

JOHN E. GREEN COMPANY
220 Victor Avenue, Highland Park MI 48203. 313/868-2400. **Fax:** 313/868-0011. **Contact:** Personnel Director. **World Wide Web address:** http://www.johnegreen.com. **Description:** A plumbing and heating contracting firm specializing in mechanical and fire protection systems. **Corporate headquarters location:** This location. **Other area locations:** Ann Arbor MI; Lansing MI; Saginaw MI; Petoskey MI; Negaunee MI. **Other U.S. locations:** Nashville TN. **Number of employees at this location:** 200.

HARLAN ELECTRIC COMPANY
2695 Crooks Road, Rochester Hills MI 48309. 248/853-4601. **Contact:** Human Resources. **E-mail address:** info@harlanelectric.com. **World Wide Web address:** http://www.harlanelectric.com. **Description:** Provides power line construction services to electric utilities, telecommunication providers, industrial facilities and government agencies. **Corporate headquarters location:** This location. **Other U.S. locations:** Millbury MA; Carlisle PA. **Parent company:** The MYR Group, Inc. **Number of employees at this location:** 1,900.

HARLEY ELLIS DEVEREAUX
26913 Northwestern Highway, Suite 200, Southfield MI 48034. 248/262-1500. **Fax:** 248/262-1552. **Contact:** Michelle Kaye, Human Resources. **E-mail address:** careers@harleyellis.com. **World Wide Web address:** http://www.harleyellis.com. **Description:** A multidivisional architectural and engineering firm providing comprehensive planning, design, and problem-solving services to commercial, governmental, industrial, and institutional clients. Founded in 1962. **Corporate headquarters location:** This location. **Other U.S. locations:** Cincinnati OH; Chicago IL; Los Angeles CA. **Subsidiaries include:** ENG/6A. **Listed on:** Privately held. **Number of employees at this location:** 100. **Number of employees nationwide:** Over 350.

JAY DEE CONTRACTORS INC.
38881 Schoolcraft Road, Livonia MI 48150. 734/591-3400. **Contact:** Human Resources Department. **E-mail address:** careers@jaydeecontr.com. **World Wide Web address:** http://www.jaydeecontractors.com. **Description:** A tunneling contractor for underground construction projects. **Positions advertised include:** Project Manager; Project Superintendent; Project Engineer; Surveyor; Civil Engineer; Estimator; Experienced Tunnel Laborers; Experienced Operating Engineers; Administrative and Accounting Support Staff. **Special programs:** Internships. **Corporate headquarters location:** This location. **Other area locations:** Detroit MI. **Number of employees at this location:** 100.

KOLTANBAR ENGINEERING COMPANY
P.O. Box 3456, Troy MI 48007-3456. 248/362-2400. **Physical Address:** 950 West Maple Road, Troy MI 48084. **Fax:** 248/362-2316. **Contact:** Personnel Department. **E-mail address:** jobs@koltanbar.com. **World Wide Web address:** http://www.koltanbar.com. **Description:** Provides manufacturing engineering, process development, and planning services. **Special programs:** Internships. **Corporate headquarters location:** This location.

LIFETIME DOORS INC.
30700 Northwestern Highway, Farmington Hills MI 48334. 248/851-7700. **Fax:** 248/851-8534. **Contact:** Human Resources Department. **World Wide Web address:** http://www.lifetimedoors.com. **Description:** A privately held manufacturer of a variety of flush doors. Founded in 1947. **Corporate headquarters location:** This location. **Other U.S. locations:** Los Banos CA; Sacramento CA; Hearne TX; Watseka IL; Easton PA; Denmark SC. **Number of employees nationwide:** Approximately 500.

THE MILLGARD CORPORATION
12822 Stark Road, P.O. Box 510027, Livonia MI 48150. 734/425-8550. **Fax:** 734/425-0624. **Contact:** Human Resources. **World Wide Web address:** http://www.adeptmultimedia.com/millgard/. **Description:** A contractor specializing in deep foundation systems including caissons, high capacity piling and slurry walls/trenches. **Corporate headquarters location:** This location. **Other U.S. locations:** North Andover MA. **Operations at this facility include:** Administration; Divisional Headquarters. **Listed on:** Privately held. **Number of employees at this location:** 100.

PERINI BUILDING COMPANY
535 Griswold, Suite 1818, Detroit MI 48226. 313/965-4888. **Contact:** Personnel Department. **World Wide Web address:** http://www.perini.com. **Description:** A contracting company engaged in the construction of industrial buildings and warehouses. **Corporate headquarters locations:** Framingham MA. **Parent company:** Perini Corporation. **Number of employees at this location:** 200.

PROGRESSIVE ARCHITECTURE ENGINEERING
1811 Four Mile Road NE, Grand Rapids MI 49525-2442. 616/361-2664. **Fax:** 616/361-1493. **Contact:** Human Resources. **E-mail address:** foxj@progressiveae.com. **World Wide Web address:** http://www.progressiveae.com. **Description:** A full-service architectural and engineering firm. **Positions advertised include:** Director of Design. **Special programs:** Medical Reimbursement Program; Tuition Reimbursement Program. **Corporate headquarters location:** This location. **Number of employees at this location:** 150.

PULTE HOMES INC.
100 Bloomfield Hills Parkway, Suite 200, Bloomfield Hills MI 48304. 248/644-7300. **Toll-free phone:** 800/777-8683. **Contact:** Renee Belanger, Human Resources Manager. **World Wide Web address:** http://www.pulte.com. **Description:** One of the largest independent, publicly owned, homebuilding companies in the United States. The principal business of Pulte Home Corporation is the construction and sale of moderately priced, single-family homes. **Positions advertised include:** 401(k) Administrator; Assistant Superintendent; Corporate Audit Manager; Risk Finance Manager; Production Assistant. **Corporate**

headquarters location: This location. **Other U.S. locations:** Nationwide. **Subsidiaries include:** Builders Supply and Lumber; ICM Mortgage Corporation. **Listed on:** New York Stock Exchange. **Stock exchange symbol:** PHM. **Number of employees nationwide:** 10,800.

RANDERS ENGINEERS AND CONSTRUCTORS
3597 Henry Road, Suite 200, Muskegon MI 49441. 231/780-1200. **Fax:** 231/780-0211. **Contact:** Human Resources. **E-mail address:** randers@randers.com. **World Wide Web address:** http://www.randers.com. **Description:** A full-service architectural, construction, development, engineering, and environmental firm. The company also provides turnkey modular systems for complex process operations. **Corporate headquarters location:** This location. **Other U.S. locations:** Cincinnati OH. **Subsidiaries include:** Clark-Trombley Consulting Engineers, Incorporated; Randers Engineering, Incorporated; Randers Group Property Corporation; Randers-EPC Incorporated; Redeco Incorporated.

SMITHGROUP INC.
500 Griswold Street, Suite 1700, Detroit MI 48226. 313/983-3600. **Fax:** 313/442-8098. **Contact:** Human Resources. **E-mail address:** dt-hr@smithgroup.com. **World Wide Web address:** http://www.smithgroup.com. **Description:** A multifaceted architectural and engineering firm engaged in construction, facility management, historic preservation, landscaping, telecommunications, and real estate consulting. **Special programs:** Internships. **Corporate headquarters location:** This location. **Other area locations:** Ann Arbor MI. **Other U.S. locations:** Phoenix AZ; San Francisco CA; Santa Monica CA; Washington DC; Madison WI; Chicago IL. **Operations at this facility include:** Service. **Number of employees at this location:** 250.

TETRA TECH MPS
710 Avis Drive, Ann Arbor MI 48108. 734/665-6000. **Fax:** 734/665-2570. **Contact:** Human Resources. **E-mail address:** careers@ttmps.com. **World Wide Web address:** http://www.ttmps.com. **Description:** An engineering, architectural, and surveying firm. **Positions advertised include:** Civil Engineer. **Special programs:** Internships. **Corporate headquarters location:** This location. **Other area locations:** Statewide. **Other U.S. locations:** Toledo OH. **International locations:** Worldwide. **Subsidiaries include:** McNamee Industrial Services, Incorporated. **Parent company:** Tetra Tech, Incorporated. **Listed on:** NASDAQ. **Stock exchange symbol:** TTEK. **Number of employees nationwide:** 400.

UNIVERSAL FOREST PRODUCTS, INC.
2801 East Beltline Avenue NE, Grand Rapids MI 49525. 616/364-6161. **Contact:** Human Resources. **E-mail address:** jobs@ufp.com. **World Wide Web address:** http://www.ufpinc.com. **Description:** Manufactures and distributes trusses, deck panels, and lattice work. **Positions advertised include:** Senior Benefits Analyst. **Corporate headquarters location:** This location. **Other U.S. locations:** Nationwide. **International locations:** Canada; Mexico. **Listed on:** NASDAQ. **Stock exchange symbol:** UFPI.

UNIVERSAL SYSTEMS
1401 East Stewart Avenue, Flint MI 48505-3698. 810/785-7970. **Fax:** 810/785-7990. **Contact:** Human Resources. **World Wide Web address:** http://www.universalsys.com. **Description:** Provides a variety of services including the design, manufacture, and installation of electrical and control systems. **Corporate headquarters location:** This location.

WADE-TRIM
P.O. Box 10, Taylor MI 48180. 313/961-3650. Physical address: 500 Griswold Avenue, Suite 2500, Detroit MI 48226. **Fax:** 313/961-0898. **Contact:** Tammy Forney, Human Resources. **E-mail address:** tforney@wadetrim.com. **World Wide Web address:** http://www.wadetrim.com. **Description:** A firm providing a full range of engineering, planning, surveying and landscape architecture services for government and industry. **Positions advertised include:** Civil Engineer; GIS Analyst; Construction Technician. **Corporate headquarters location:** This location. **Other area locations:** Bay City MI; Cadillac MI; Flint MI; Gaylord MI; Grand Rapids MI; Taylor MI; Troy MI. **Other U.S. locations:** Tampa FL; Cleveland OH; Pittsburgh PA. **Subsidiaries include:** Facilities Management; Municipal Systems Consulting. **Number of employees nationwide:** Over 400.

Minnesota

ADOLFSON AND PETERSON INC.
6701 West 23rd Street, Minneapolis MN 55426. 952/544-1561. **Fax:** 952/525-2333. **Contact:** Personnel. **E-mail address:** jobs@a-p.com. **World Wide Web address:** http://www.adolfsonpeterson.com. **Description:** A construction company. **Positions advertised include:** Facilities Maintenance Manager; Project Manager; Superintendent. **Other U.S. locations:** CO; AZ; TX.

ANDERSEN CORPORATION
100 Fourth Avenue North, Bayport MN 55003-1096. 651/264-5150. **Contact:** Human Resources. **World Wide Web address:** http://www.andersenwindows.com. **Description:** Manufactures windows and doors. **NOTE:** Search and apply for positions online. **Positions advertised include:** Product Development Engineer; Engineer; Project Manager; Quality Engineer; Production Supervisor; Design Engineer; Pilot Plant Engineering Manager. **Special programs:** Internships.

ARCHITECTURE TECHNOLOGY CORPORATION
9971 Valley View Road, Eden Prairie MN 55344. 952/829-5864. **Fax:** 952/829-5871. **Contact:** Human Resources. **World Wide Web address:** http://www.atcorp.com. **Description:** A computer architectural and networking technologies consulting firm. Founded in 1981. **NOTE:** See website for current job openings. Forward resumes for systems engineering and software architecture positions to: es.resume@atcorp.com. Forward resumes for research positions to: r&d.resume@atcorp.com. **Positions advertised include:** Systems Engineer; Research Staff. **Other U.S. locations:** Washington DC; Ithaca NY; Rome NY.

ARCON CONSTRUCTION COMPANY
43249 Frontage Road, P.O. Box 159, Harris MN 55032. 651/674-4474. **Contact:** Controller/Secretary. **Description:** A contracting firm specializing in highway and street construction.

CERTAINTEED CORPORATION
3303 Fourth Avenue East, Shakopee MN 55379. 952/445-6450. **Contact:** Human Resources. **World Wide Web address:** http://www.certainteed.com. **Description:** CertainTeed Corporation manufactures and distributes building materials, fiberglass products, and piping products. Principal products are used in residential, commercial, and industrial construction; repair and remodeling; fiberglass reinforcement applications; water and sewer systems; and other underground utility systems. Other products include roofing, acoustical insulation, fiberglass thermal insulation, air handling products, glass fiber, vinyl siding, and PVC piping. **Positions advertised include:** Senior Process Engineer. **Corporate headquarters location:** Valley Forge PA. **Parent company:** Compagnie de Saint-Gobain. **Operations at this facility include:** This location manufactures shingles.

CRYSTAL CABINET WORKS, INC.
1100 Crystal Drive, Princeton MN 55371. 763/389-4187. **Fax:** 763/389-0583. **Contact:** Human Resources. **World Wide Web address:** http://www.ccworks.com. **Description:** Manufactures custom-made cabinets. **NOTE:** Apply in person. **Other area locations:** Sauk Rapids MN.

DURA SUPREME
300 Dura Drive, Howard Lake MN 55349. 320/543-4535. **Fax:** 320/543-4597. **Contact:** Human Resources. **E-mail address:** hr@durasupreme.com. **World Wide Web address:** http://www.durasupreme.com. **Description:** Manufactures cabinets. **NOTE:** Apply in person. **Positions advertised include:** Woodworker; Builder; Machine Operator; Material Handler. **Special programs:** Internships. **Corporate headquarters location:** This location. **Operations at this facility include:** Administration; Manufacturing. **Listed on:** Privately held. **Number of employees at this location:** 300.

EGAN COMPANIES, INC.
625 Boone Avenue North, Brooklyn Park MN 55428. 763/544-4131. **Fax:** 763/595-4380. **Contact:** Bonnie Ouradnik, Human Resources. **E-mail address:** bcouradnik@eganco.com. **World Wide Web address:** http://www.eganco.com. **Description:** Mechanical and electrical contractors specializing in commercial and industrial projects.

ELLERBE BECKET
800 LaSalle Avenue, Minneapolis MN 55402-2014. 612/376-2000. **Fax:** 612/376-2271. **Contact:** Human Resources. **E-mail address:** jobs@ellerbebecket.com. **World Wide Web address:** http://www.ellerbebecket.com. **Description:** An architectural and engineering firm engaged in the design of industrial, commercial, corporate, public assembly, educational, and medical buildings nationwide. Founded in 1908. **NOTE:** See website for current job openings. Entry-level positions are offered. **Corporate headquarters location:** This location. **Annual sales/revenues:** More than $100 million. **Number of employees at this location:** 425. **Number of employees nationwide:** 700.

HANS HAGEN HOMES
941 NE Hillwind Road, Suite 300, Fridley MN 55432. 763/586-7200. **Contact:** Personnel Director. **E-mail address:** info@hanshagenhomes.com. **World Wide Web address:** http://www.hanshagenhomes.com. **Description:** A construction company and land development company specializing in townhouses and single-family homes.

HAMMEL GREEN & ABRAHAMSON, INC.
701 Washington Avenue North, Minneapolis MN 55401. 612/758-4566. **Fax:** 612/758-4199. **Contact:** Human Resources Director. **E-mail address:** recruiting@hga.com. **World Wide Web address:** http://www.hga.com. **Description:** An architectural, engineering, and planning firm. **Positions advertised include:** Architect; Plumbing Systems Engineer; Specifier; Industrial Engineer. **Other area locations:** Rochester MN. **Other U.S. locations:** Milwaukee WI; San Francisco CA; Los Angeles CA; Sacramento CA.

HEAT & GLO
20802 Kensington Boulevard, Lakeville MN 55044. **Toll-free phone:** 888/427-3973. **Contact:** Human Resources. **E-mail address:** info@heatnglo.com. **World Wide Web address:** http://www.heatnglo.com. **Description:** Manufactures and installs gas, wood, and electric fireplaces, stoves, and related accessories. **NOTE:** Search and apply for positions online at http://hnicareers.com. **Positions advertised include:** Quality Manager; Executive Assistant. **Corporate headquarters location:** This location. **Parent company:** Hearth & Home Technologies Inc.

GUSTAVE A. LARSON COMPANY
13200 10th Avenue North, Plymouth MN 55441. 612/546-7175. **Contact:** Human Resources Department. **World Wide Web address:** http://www.galarson.com. **Description:** A wholesaler of heating and air conditioning systems, parts, and supplies. **NOTE:** See website for current job openings and to download application. Submit completed application by mail to the corporate office. **Positions advertised include:** Residential HVAC Sales Consultant. **Corporate headquarters location:** Pewaukee WI. **Operations at this facility include:** Sales.

LESTER BUILDING SYSTEMS, LLC
1111 Second Avenue South, Lester Prairie MN 55354. 320/395-2531. **Fax:** 320/395-5393. **Contact:** Human Resources. **E-mail address:** hr@lesterbuildings.com. **World Wide Web address:** http://www.lesterbuildings.com. **Description:** A manufacturer and retailer of pre-engineered wood-frame buildings. **NOTE:** Entry-level positions are offered. **Positions advertised include:** Engineering Technician; Carpenter; Customer Service/Pricing Specialist. **Corporate headquarters location:** This location.

McGOUGH COMPANIES
2737 Fairview Avenue North, St. Paul MN 55113-1372. 651/633-5050. **Fax:** 651/633-5673. **Contact:** Human Resources. **E-mail address:** info@mcgough.com. **World Wide Web address:** http://www.mcgough.com. **Description:** offers a range of real estate and building services through its corporate services, development, construction, and facilities management divisions. **Other area locations:** Rochester MN. **Other U.S. locations:** Phoenix AZ.

McQUAY INTERNATIONAL
13600 Industrial Park Boulevard, Plymouth MN 55441. 763/553-5330. **Toll-free phone:** 800/432-1342. **Fax:** 763/553-5302. **Contact:** Human Resources. **E-mail address:** HRplymouth@mcquay.com. **World Wide Web address:** http://www.mcquay.com. **Description:** McQuay is an international company that engineers, manufactures, sells, and services commercial heating, ventilating, and air conditioning equipment. **Corporate headquarters location:** This location. **Other area locations:** Faribault MN; Owatonna MN. **Operations at this facility include:** Administration; Parts.

MILLER ARCHITECTS AND BUILDERS
P.O. Box 1228, St. Cloud MN 56302. 320/251-4109. **Physical address:** 3335 West St. Germain, St. Cloud MN 56301. **Toll-free phone:** 800/772-1758. **Fax:** 320/251-4693. **Contact:** Personnel Department. **E-mail address:** mktg@millerab.com. **World Wide Web address:** http://www.millerab.com. **Description:** A construction contractor and building firm.

M.A. MORTENSON COMPANY
P.O. Box 710, Minneapolis MN 55440-0710. 763/522-2100. **Physical address:** 700 Meadow Lane North, Minneapolis MN 55422. **Fax:** 763/287-5339. **Contact:** Mr. Dan Haag, Human Services Director. **E-mail address:** jobs@mortenson.com. **World Wide Web address:** http://www.mortenson.com. **Description:** A general construction firm that provides construction management, design-build, general contracting, maintenance and operations, turnkey construction, and project development services. **Positions advertised include:** Assistant Safety Trainer; Design-Build Manager; Field Engineer; Learning and Development Facilitator; Project Accountant; Project Director; Project Engineer. **Special programs:** Internships. **Corporate headquarters location:** This location. **Other U.S. locations:** CO; WA; AZ; HI; WI; IL. **Operations at this facility include:** Administration. **Number of employees nationwide:** 1,800.

NEWMECH CONSTRUCTION
1633 Eustis Street, St. Paul MN 55108. 651/645-0451. **Fax:** 651/642-5591. **Contact:** Human Resources Manager. **E-mail address:** info@newmech.com. **World Wide Web address:** http://www.newmech.com. **Description:** A full-service construction and engineering firm. **NOTE:** See website to download application. Submit completed application by mail.

NORCRAFT COMPANIES, INC.
3020 Denmark Avenue, Suite 100, Eagan MN 55121. 651/234-3300. **Fax:** 651/234-3398. **Contact:** Human Resources. **World Wide Web address:** http://www.norcraftcompanies.com. **Description:** Manufactures wooden kitchen and bath cabinets.

Corporate headquarters location: This location. **Other area locations:** Cottonwood MN. **Other U.S. locations:** Nationwide. **Number of employees at this location:** 50. **Number of employees nationwide:** 1,700.

PCI (PROGRESSIVE CONTRACTORS INC.)
14123 42nd Street Northeast, St. Michael MN 55376-9563. 763/497-6100. **Fax:** 763-497-6101. **Contact:** Human Resources. **E-mail address:** brosso@pciroads.com. **World Wide Web address:** http://www.progressivecontractors.com. **Description:** A contractor specializing in highway and street construction. **NOTE:** Contact Human Resources to inquire about current job openings.

PARK CONSTRUCTION COMPANY
500 73rd Avenue, Suite 120, Minneapolis MN 55432. 763/786-9800. **Fax:** 763/786-2952. **Contact:** Personnel. **World Wide Web address:** http://www.parkconstructionco.com. **Description:** A regional contractor specializing in heavy earth moving, heavy civil, structural, and golf course construction projects.

PARSONS BRINCKERHOFF & QUADE INC.
510 First Avenue North, Suite 550, Minneapolis MN 55403. 612/371-0443. **Fax:** 612/371-4410. **Contact:** Human Resources. **E-mail address:** careers@pbworld.com. **World Wide Web address:** http://www.pbworld.com. **Description:** Provides complete engineering and construction management services including the development of major bridges, tunnels, highways, marine facilities, buildings, industrial complexes, and railroads. **Corporate headquarters location:** New York NY.

RYAN COMPANIES U.S., INC.
50 South 10th Street, Suite 300, Minneapolis MN 55403-2012. 612/492-4000. **Fax:** 612/492-3000. **Contact:** Human Resources. **E-mail address:** opportunity@ryancompanies.com. **World Wide Web address:** http://www.ryancompanies.com. **Description:** Engaged in the design and construction of commercial projects including corporate office, manufacturing, industrial, product distribution, high-tech, medical, and retail buildings. The company also provides property management and turnkey development services. **NOTE:** Entry-level positions and part-time jobs are offered. **Positions advertised include:** Receptionist; Project Assistant **Special programs:** Internships; Training; Co-ops. **Corporate headquarters location:** This location. **Other U.S. locations:** CA; FL; IL; AZ; IA. **Listed on:** Privately held. **Annual sales/revenues:** More than $100 million. **Number of employees nationwide:** 300.

ST. PAUL LINOLEUM & CARPET COMPANY
2956 Center Court, Eagan MN 55121. 651/686-7770. **Contact:** Clemment J. Commers, Owner/President. **World Wide Web address:** http://www.stpaullinocpt.com. **Description:** A commercial floor-covering contractor.

TRUTH HARDWARE
700 West Bridge Street, Owatonna MN 55060. 507/451-5620. **Toll-free phone:** 800/866-7884. **Fax:** 507/451-5655. **Contact:** Human Resources Manager. **E-mail address:** mrodrigz@truth.com. **World Wide Web address:** http://www.truth.com. **Description:** Manufactures hardware for windows, doors, and skylights.

Mississippi

ABMB ENGINEERS, INC.
700 North State Street, Suite 300, Jackson MS 39202. 601/354-0696. **Contact:** Human Resources. **E-mail address:** hr@abmb.com. **World Wide Web address:** http://www.abmb.com. **Description:** Provides engineering services nationwide, specializing in highway and traffic engineering, bridges and other structures, site civil and surveying, and civil works. **NOTE:** Send resume to ABMB Engineers, Inc., 500 Main Street, Baton Rouge LA 70801; fax to 225-765-7244; or e-mail to address above. **Positions advertised include:** Civil Engineer; Traffic Engineer. **Corporate headquarters location:** Baton Rouge LA. **Other area locations:** Vicksburg MS. **Number of employees nationwide:** 100.

ALLEN & HOSHALL LTD.
713 Pear Orchard Road, Suite 100, Ridgeland MS 39157. 601/977-8993. **Fax:** 601/977-8924. **Contact:** Human Resources. **E-mail address:** ahinfo@allenhoshall.com. **World Wide Web address:** http://www.allenhoshall.com. **Description:** Allen & Hoshall Ltd. provides architectural, structural, and civil engineering services. **NOTE:** Corporate hiring is done through the Memphis, Tennessee headquarters location: 1661 International Drive, Suite 100, Memphis TN 38120. **Other area locations:** Hernando MS; Jackson MS; Tunica MS. **Other U.S. locations:** Chattanooga TN; Knoxville TN; Nashville TN. **Number of employees nationwide:** 130.

COOKE DOUGLASS FARR LEMONS/LTD.
3780 I-55 North, Suite 101, Jackson MS 39211. 601/366-3110. **Fax:** 601/366-3181. **Contact:** Human Resources. **E-mail address:** asomers@cdfl.com. **World Wide Web Address:** http://www.cdfl.com. **Description:** Provides architectural, engineering, interior design, planning, landscaping, and graphic design services. Founded in 1961.

CROFT, LLC
P.O. Box 826, McComb MS 39649. 601/684-6121. **Physical address:** 107 Oliver Emmerich Drive, McComb MS 39648. **Toll-free phone:** 800/222-3195. **Fax:** 601/684-0537. **Contact:** Victor C. Donati, Jr., Corporate Human Resources Director. **E-mail address:** donativ@croftllc.com. **World Wide Web address:** http://www.croftmetals.com. **Description:** A national manufacturer of aluminum and vinyl building products. Products include windows, doors, patio doors, and bath and shower enclosures. **Positions advertised include:** Plant Manager; Electrostatic Painter. **Corporate headquarters locations:** This location. **Other U.S. locations:** Oviedo FL; Newton MS; Lumber Bridge NC. **Operations at this facility include:** Manufacturing of aluminum and vinyl window and door units. **Number of employees at this location:** 400. **Number of employees nationwide:** 2,500.

GULF STATES MANUFACTURERS
P.O. Box 1128, Starkville MS 39760. 662/323-8021. **Physical address:** 101 Airport Road, Starkville MS 39759. **Fax:** 662/323-4225. **Contact:** Gary Mitchell, Director of Human Resources. **E-mail address:** gmitchell@gulfstatesmanufacturers.com. **World Wide Web address:** http://www.gulfstatesmanufacturers.com. **Description:** Manufactures pre-engineered metal buildings. Founded in 1968. **Parent company:** MAGNATRAX Corporation. **Number of employees at this location:** 400.

IVEY MECHANICAL COMPANY, LLC
514 North Wells Street, P.O. Box 610, Kosciusko MS 39090. 662/289-3646. **Fax:** 662/289-8602. **Contact:** Danny Brunt, Human Resources. **E-mail address:** danny.brunt@iveymechanical.com. **World Wide Web address:** http://www.iveymechanical.com. **Description:** A mechanical contracting company that provides piping, plumbing, and HVAC services primarily to the correctional, healthcare, commercial, entertainment, industrial, and manufacturing industries. **Positions advertised include:** Sheet Metal Worker. **Other U.S. locations:** GA; AL; NC; KY; TN.

JESCO INC.
2020 McCullough Boulevard, Tupelo MS 38801. 662/842-3240. **Toll-free phone:** 800/280-1792. **Fax:** 662/680-6123. **Contact:** Jerry Stubblefield, President. **World Wide Web address:** http://www.jescoinc.net. **Description:** An industrial contracting company engaged in the construction of buildings, mill work, agricultural buildings, and steel fabrication. Jesco also provides mechanical and electrical services, and industrial maintenance. Established in 1941. **Positions**

advertised include: Electrician. **Corporate headquarters locations:** This location. **Other area locations:** Fulton MS. **Other U.S. locations:** AL; TN. **Annual sales/revenues:** $200 million.

THE MCC GROUP, L.L.C.
24101 Spyder Drive, Pass Christian MS 39571. 228/452-0502. **Contact:** Teasha Sepulveda. **E-mail address:** hr@mccgroup.com. **World Wide Web address:** http://www.mccgroup.com. **Description:** A complete M.E.P. contractor that offers customers mechanical, electrical and plumbing pre-construction and construction services. Founded in 1958. **NOTE:** Resumes must be sent to 3001 17th Street, Metairie LA 70002, or faxed to 504/831-4760. **Positions advertised include:** Project Manager; Mechanical Engineer; Electrical Engineer; Estimator; Field Supervisor. **Corporate headquarters location:** Metairie LA. **Other U.S. locations:** Charlotte NC; Raleigh NC. **Operations at this facility include:** This location is a satellite office, as well as a fabrication facility.

NEEL-SCHAFFER, INC.
666 North Street, P.O. Box 22625, Suite 201, Jackson MS 39202. 601/948-3071. **Fax:** 601/948-3178. **Contact:** Human Resources Department. **E-mail address:** humanresources@neel-schaffer.com. **World Wide Web address:** http://www.neel-schaffer.com. **Description:** A multi-disciplined engineering and planning firm. Founded in 1983. **Positions advertised include:** Engineer. **Corporate headquarters location:** This location. **Other area locations:** Statewide. **Other U.S. locations:** AL; FL; GA; LA; TN; TX.

Missouri

ASCHINGER ELECTRIC COMPANY
863 Horan Drive, P.O. Box 26322, Fenton MO 63026. 636/343-1211. **Fax:** 636/343-9658. **Contact:** Donna L. Kebel, Controller/Office Manager. **E-mail address:** info@aschinger.com. **World Wide Web address:** http://www.aschinger.com. **Description:** An electrical contracting firm specializing in industrial and commercial applications. **Office hours:** Monday - Friday, 8:00 a.m. - 5:00 p.m. **Corporate headquarters location:** This location. **Listed on:** Privately held. **President:** Eric D. Aschinger. **Annual sales/revenues:** $21 - $50 million. **Number of employees at this location:** 200.

BSI CONSTRUCTORS INC.
6767 Southwest Avenue, St. Louis MO 63143. 314/781-7820. **Contact:** Joseph M. Kaiser, Executive Vice President. **World Wide Web address:** http://www.bsistl.com. **Description:** A general contracting and construction management firm. **Corporate headquarters location:** This location. **Number of employees at this location:** 100.

BANK BUILDING CORPORATION
13537 Barret Parkway Drive, Ballwin MO 63131 314/821-2265. **Fax:** 314/821-6443. **Contact:** Personnel. **E-mail address:** jobs@newground.com. **World Wide Web address:** http://www.newground.com. **Description:** A national design and building firm that also provides consulting and planning services. **Operations at this facility include:** Administration; Regional Headquarters. **Other U.S. locations:** IL; CA; NH. **International locations:** Canada.

BLACK & VEATCH
Ward Parkway, P.O. Box 8405, Kansas City MO 64114. 913/458-2000. **Contact:** Hiring Manager. **World Wide Web address:** http://www.bv.com. **Description:** Black & Veatch Corporation is a global engineering, consulting and construction company specializing in infrastructure development in the fields of energy, water and information. Black & Veatch offers conceptual and preliminary engineering services, engineering design, procurement, construction, financial management, asset management, information technology, environmental, security design and consulting, and management consulting services. Founded in 1915. **NOTE:** Search and apply for positions online. **Positions advertised include:** Communications Specialist; Electrical Engineer; **Corporate headquarters location:** Overland Park KS. **Other area locations:** St. Louis MO. **Other U.S. locations:** Nationwide. **International locations:** Worldwide.

BLACK & VEATCH
15450 South Outer Forty Drive, Suite 2000, Chesterfield MO 63017-8522. 636/532-7940. **Fax:** 636/532-1465. **Contact:** Recruiting Department. **World Wide Web address:** http://www.bv.com. **Description:** Black & Veatch Corporation is a global engineering, consulting and construction company specializing in infrastructure development in the fields of energy, water and information. Black & Veatch offers conceptual and preliminary engineering services, engineering design, procurement, construction, financial management, asset management, information technology, environmental, security design and consulting, and management consulting services. Founded in 1915. **NOTE:** Search and apply for positions online. **Corporate headquarters location:** Overland Park KS. **Other area locations:** Kansas City MO. **Other U.S. locations:** Nationwide. **International locations:** Worldwide.

BURNS & McDONNELL
9400 Ward Parkway, Kansas City MO 64114. 816/333-9400. **Fax:** 816/333-3690. **Contact:** Human Resources. **E-mail address:** recruiter@burnsmcd.com. **World Wide Web address:** http://www.burnsmcd.com. **Description:** A consulting firm specializing in architectural and environmental engineering. **Positions advertised include:** Senior Architect; Structural Engineer; Project Assistant. **Corporate headquarters location:** This location. **Other U.S. locations:** Denver CO; Chicago IL; St. Louis MO. **Listed on:** Privately held.

BUTLER MANUFACTURING COMPANY
1540 Genessee Street, Kansas City MO 64102. 816/968-3000. **Fax:** 816/968-3720. **Contact:** Human Resources. **E-mail address:** recruiting@butlermfg.com. **World Wide Web address:** http://www.butlermfg.com. **Description:** Supplies steel and wood frame pre-engineered building systems for a wide variety of commercial, community, industrial, and agricultural applications. The company designs, manufactures, and markets component systems for nonresidential construction including aluminum curtain wall, storefront entrances and doors, and roof accessories. Butler also provides comprehensive design and construction planning, execution, and management services for major purchasers of construction. In addition, the company designs, manufactures, and sells commercial and on-farm grain storage units. **Number of employees nationwide:** 3,065.

CLARK RICHARDSON & BISKUP CONSULTING ENGINEERS, INC.
7410 Northwest Tiffany Springs, Suite 100, Kansas City MO 64153. 816/880-9800. **Fax:** 816/880-9898 **Contact:** Human Resources. **E-mail address:** kcjobs@crbusa.com. **World Wide Web address:** http://www.crbusa.com. **Description:** A design firm primarily involved in facility and process design for high technology industries such as pharmaceutical, biotechnology, specialty chemical, and microelectronics. Founded in 1984. **NOTE:** Search and apply for positions online. **Positions advertised include:** HVAC Engineer; Mechanical Engineer; Process Utility Engineer; Sr. Pharmaceutical Process Engineer; Instrumentation & Controls Engineer; Electrical Engineer. **Other U.S. locations:** NC; PA; CA; MN; NE.

CLIMATE ENGINEERING CORPORATION
152 East Kirkham Avenue, St. Louis MO 63119. 314/968-8400. **Contact:** Personnel. **Description:** Engaged in contract engineering services for plumbing, heating, and air conditioning. **Number of employees at this location:** 100.

CONDAIRE INC.
1141 Reco Drive, St. Louis MO 63126. 314/821-8388. **Fax:** 314/821-6530. **Contact:** Malcolm Sweet, Jr., President. **World Wide Web address:** http://www.condaire.com. **Description:** A mechanical contracting firm engaged in a variety of heating, ventilating, air conditioning, plumbing, and industrial piping services. Founded in 1946. **Corporate headquarters location:** This location. **Listed on:** Privately held. **Annual sales/revenues:** $11 - $20 million. **Number of employees at this location:** 100.

CORRIGAN COMPANY MECHANICAL CONTRACTORS
3545 Gratiot Street, St. Louis MO 63103. 314/771-6200. **Fax:** 314/771-8537. **Contact:** Thomas L. Garbin, Director of Human Resources. **World Wide Web address:** http://www.corrigan.com. **Description:** A mechanical contracting company engaged in heating, air conditioning, and plumbing. Founded in 1896. **NOTE:** Entry-level positions are offered. **Special programs:** Co-ops; Summer Jobs. **President:** Thomas J. Corrigan. **Annual sales/revenues:** More than $100 million. **Number of employees at this location:** 500.

FRU-CON CONSTRUCTION CORPORATION
P.O. Box 100, 15933 Clayton Road, Ballwin MO 63011. 636/391-6700. **Contact:** Human Resources. **E-mail address:** jobs@frucon.com. **World Wide Web address:** http://www.fru-con.com. **Description:** An international construction and engineering firm. **Positions advertised include:** Project Manager; Project Engineer; Estimator; Engineer. **Corporate headquarters location:** This location. **Number of employees at this location:** 1,000.

GOEDECKE COMPANY INC.
4101 Clayton Avenue, St. Louis MO 63110. 314/652-1810. **Contact:** Human Resources. **Description:** Goedecke Company provides construction services including insulation, hard board for industrial buildings, wall systems, sealants, insulation, adhesives, waterproofing, and scaffold rental and erection. **Special programs:** Internships. **Corporate headquarters location:** This location. **Other U.S. locations:** Decatur IL; Evansville IN; Indianapolis IN; Louisville KY; Kansas City MO; Springfield MO. **Operations at this facility include:** This location houses administrative offices only. **Listed on:** Privately held. **Number of employees at this location:** 100.

H.B.D. CONTRACTING INC.
5517 Manchester Avenue, St. Louis MO 63110-1975. 314/781-8000. **Fax:** 314/781-5214. **Contact:** Human Resources Department. **World Wide Web address:** http://www.hbdcontracting.com. **Description:** A general contracting firm specializing in commercial engineering. **Positions advertised include:** Civil Engineer. **Corporate headquarters location:** This location. **Operations at this facility include:** Administration. **Number of employees at this location:** 100.

HBE CORPORATION
11330 Olive Boulevard, St. Louis MO 63141. 314/567-9000. **Fax:** 314/567-0602. **Contact:** Personnel Director. **World Wide Web address:** http://www.hbecorp.com. **Description:** Engaged in the design and construction of hospitals, financial institutions, and hotels. HBE Corporation also operates and manages hotels. **World Wide Web address:** http://www.hbecorp.com. **Positions advertised include:** Architect; Engineer; Construction Manager; Sales Representative. **Corporate headquarters location:** This location. **Operations at this facility include:** Divisional Headquarters.

HARTMAN-WALSH PAINTING COMPANY
7144 North Market Street, St. Louis MO 63133-1899. 314/863-1800. **Fax:** 314/863-6964. **Contact:** Personnel. **World Wide Web address:** http://www.hartmanwalsh.com. **Description:** Provides commercial and industrial painting and waterproofing services.

HELLMUTH, OBATA & KASSABAUM, INC.
1 Metropolitan Square, St. Louis MO 63102. 314/421-2000. **Contact:** Personnel Director. **World Wide Web address:** http://www.hok.com. **Description:** An architectural and structural engineering firm. **Positions advertised include:** Bookkeeper; Senior Project Manager; Interiors Technician. **Other U.S. locations:** Nationwide. **International locations:** Worldwide.

JACOBS FACILITIES INC.
One Financial Plaza, 501 North Broadway, St. Louis MO 63102-1826. 314/335-4000. **Fax:** 314/335-5102. **Contact:** Recruiting Manager. **World Wide Web address:** http://www.jacobs.com. **Description:** An engineering, architectural, and construction firm that provides consulting services, design services, construction management, and construction services. **NOTE:** Search and apply for positions online. Entry-level positions are offered. **Positions advertised include:** Project Hydraulic Modeling Engineer; Plumbing/Fire Protection Design Engineer. **Special programs:** Internships; Summer Jobs. **Corporate headquarters location:** Pasadena CA. **Other U.S. locations:** Nationwide. **International locations:** Worldwide. **Operations at this facility include:** Administration; Regional Headquarters; Sales; Service. **Listed on:** New York Stock Exchange. **Stock exchange symbol:** JEC. **Annual sales/revenues:** More than $100 million. **Number of employees at this location:** 580.

JAY HENGES ENTERPRISES, INC.
4133 Shoreline Drive, Earth City MO 63045. 314/291-6600. **Fax:** 314/291-7630. **Contact:** Personnel. **Description:** Engaged in the installation of carpet, wood, and vinyl floors; insulation and acoustical ceiling work; and the manufacture of portable buildings. **Corporate headquarters location:** This location.

HUDSON SERVICES
P.O. Box 221000, St. Louis MO 63122. 314/965-1929. **Contact:** Mr. C.L. Hudson, President. **Description:** Provides building services, consulting, management, and bookkeeping.

INDEECO
425 Hanley Industrial Court, St. Louis MO 63144. 314/644-4300. **Toll-free phone:** 800/243-8162. **Fax:** 314/644-5332. **Contact:** Human Resources Recruiter. **E-mail address:** recruiter@indeeco.com. **World Wide Web address:** http://www.indeeco.com. **Description:** Engaged in the design and manufacture of custom electric heating equipment for industrial and commercial applications.

INSITUFORM MID-AMERICA, INC.
702 Spirit 40 Park Drive, Chesterfield MO 63005. 636/530-8000. **Toll-free phone:** 800/234-2992. **Fax:** 636/519-8010. **Contact:** Human Resources. **E-mail address:** careers@insituform.com. **World Wide Web address:** http://www.insituform.com. **Description:** Insituform Mid-America, Inc. uses various trenchless technologies for rehabilitation, new construction, and improvements of pipeline systems (sewers; gas lines; industrial waste lines; water lines; oil field mining; and industrial process pipelines). The company's trenchless technologies require little or no excavation and eliminate the need to replace deteriorating pipes. Insituform Mid-America provides a wide variety of technologies including Insituform, PALTEM, Tite Liner, and tunneling. **Listed on:** NASDAQ. **Stock exchange symbol:** INSU. **Number of employees nationwide:** 570. **Number of employees worldwide:** 2,100.

McBRIDE & SON
One McBride & Son Center Drive, Chesterfield MO 63005. 636/537-2000. **Fax:** 636/537-2546. **Contact:** Director of Human Resources. **World Wide Web address:** http://www.mcbridehomes.com. **Description:** A construction company engaged in concrete foundation work, carpentry work, home building, general contracting, real estate sales, property management, and remodeling. **NOTE:** See company

website for application instructions for specific openings. **Positions advertised include:** Administrative Assistant; Craftsman; Project Manager; Sales Representative; Superintendent. **Corporate headquarters location:** This location. **Operations at this facility include:** Administration; Regional Headquarters. **Number of employees at this location:** 400.

McCARTHY CONSTRUCTION COMPANY
1341 North Rock Hill Road, St. Louis MO 63124-1498. 314/968-3300. **Fax:** 314/968-4642. **Contact:** Jan Kraemer, Human Resources. **E-mail address:** jkraemer@mccarthy.com. **World Wide Web address:** http://www.mccarthy.com. **Description:** One of the nation's oldest privately held construction firms. The company provides a wide range of construction-related services under construction management, general contract, and design and building contractual arrangements, and operates a separate division for work on bridges. **Company slogan:** Our goal is to be the best builder in America. **Positions advertised include:** MEP Controls Superintendent; Project Engineer; Insurance and Risk Analyst; Superintendent. **Special programs:** Internships. **Corporate headquarters location:** This location. **Other U.S. locations:** Phoenix AZ; Newport Beach CA; Sacramento CA; San Francisco CA; Las Vegas NV; Dallas TX. **Annual sales/revenues:** More than $100 million. **Number of employees at this location:** 150. **Number of employees nationwide:** 2,000.

MILLSTONE BANGERT INC.
601 fountain Lakes Boulevard, St. Charles MO 63301. 636/949-0038. **Contact:** Human Resources. **Description:** Engaged in road and heavy construction general contracting. **Number of employees at this location:** 100.

MORGAN-WIGHTMAN SUPPLY COMPANY
10199 Woodfield Lane, Saint Louis MO 63132. 314/995-9990. **Fax:** 314/995-9781. **Contact:** Mr. Ken Gudeman, Personnel Department. **World Wide Web address:** http://www.morgan-wightman.com. **Description:** A distributor of wholesale building materials including windows, doors, moldings, and cabinets. **Corporate headquarters location:** This location. **Operations at this facility include:** Administration.

NIEHAUS CONSTRUCTION SERVICES INC.
4151 Sarpy Avenue, St. Louis MO 63110. 314/533-8434. **Fax:** 314/533-1448. **Contact:** Director of Personnel. **World Wide Web address:** http://www.ncs-stl.com. **Description:** Engaged in terrazzo, tile, marble, and mosaic construction.

PARSONS BRINCKERHOFF INC.
1831 Chestnut Street, 7th Floor, St. Louis MO 63103-2225. 314/421-1476. **Fax:** 314/421-1741. **Contact:** Director of Personnel. **World Wide Web address:** http://www.pbworld.com. **Description:** Provides total engineering and construction management services, from project conception through completion, through a worldwide staff of 9,000 professionals and support personnel. Services include the development of major bridges, tunnels, highways, marine facilities, buildings, industrial complexes, and railroads. **NOTE:** Search and apply for positions online. **Positions advertised include:** Sr. CADD Designer; Sr. Supervising Engineer. **Corporate headquarters location:** New York NY. **Other U.S. locations:** Nationwide. **International locations:** Worldwide.

STRUCTURAL SYSTEMS INC.
816 South Kirkwood Road, Kirkwood MO 63122. 314/966-5920. **Fax:** 314/966-6267. **Contact:** Human Resources. **Description:** An architectural and construction firm specializing in fabricated buildings, general contracting, and design/build contracting.

SUBSURFACE CONSTRUCTORS
110 Angelica Street, St. Louis MO 63147. 314/421-2460. **Fax:** 314/421-2479. **Contact:** Personnel Director. **World Wide Web address:** http://www.subsurfaceconstructors.com. **Description:** A foundation contracting firm that provides pile driving and core drilling services.

TARLTON CORPORATION
5500 West Park Avenue, St. Louis MO 63110. 314/633-3300. **Fax:** 314/647-1940. **Contact:** Human Resources. **Wide Web address:** http://www.tarltoncorp.com. **Description:** A general contractor and construction company. **Special programs:** Internships. **Corporate headquarters location:** This location. **Operations at this facility include:** Administration. **Listed on:** Privately held. **Number of employees at this location:** 45.

CHARLES F. VATTEROTT & COMPANY
10449 St. Charles Rock Road, St. Louis MO 63114. 314/427-4000. **Contact:** Personnel Department. **Description:** A residential construction firm.

FRED WEBER INC.
2320 Creve Coeur Mill Road, P.O. Box 2501, Maryland Heights MO 63043-8501. 314/344-0070. **Fax:** 314/344-0970. **Contact:** Jackie O'Leary, VP Human Resources. **E-mail address:** jsoleary@fredweberinc.com. **World Wide Web address:** http://www.fredweberinc.com. **Description:** A contractor specializing in highway construction, stone quarries, asphalt plants, sand plants, and commercial construction.

ZURHEIDE-HERRMANN INC.
4333 Clayton Avenue, St. Louis MO 63110. 314/652-6805. **Contact:** Ronald Dahman, President. **Description:** Provides engineering and architectural services. **Special programs:** Internships. **Corporate headquarters location:** This location. **Other U.S. locations:** Champaign IL. **Operations at this facility include:** Service. **Number of employees at this location:** 35.

Montana
SLETTEN CONSTRUCTION COMPANY
P.O. Box 2467, Great Falls MT 59403. 406/761-7920. **Physical address:** 1000 25th Street North, Great Falls MT 59401. **Fax:** 406/761-0923. **Contact:** Leanna Babcock, Personnel Director. **World Wide Web address:** http://www.slettencompanies.com. **Description:** A general construction contractor with operations in bridge, dam, medical center, light and heavy industrial, and multi-unit housing construction. Sletten Construction is licensed to perform construction in Montana, Wyoming, Washington, Idaho, Nevada, Oregon, California, Arizona, Utah, North and South Dakota, and Colorado. **Special programs:** Internships. **Other U.S. locations:** Phoenix AZ; Las Vegas NV; Boise ID; Cody WY. **Operations at this facility include:** Administration; Regional Headquarters. **Listed on:** Privately held. **Number of employees at this location:** 30. **Number of employees nationwide:** 350.

Nebraska
BONNAVILLA HOMES
111 Grant Street, P.O. Box 127, Aurora NE 68818-0127. 402/694-5250. **Fax:** 402/694-5873. **Contact:** Human Resources. **World Wide Web address:** http://www.bonnavilla.chiefind.com. **Description:** A housing manufacturer. Established in 1970. **NOTE:** Entry-level positions are offered. **Special programs:** Summer Jobs. **Office hours:** Monday - Friday, 8:00 a.m. - 5:00 p.m. **Other U.S. locations:** CO, ND, SD, MT, WY, KS, MN, IA, MO. **Parent company:** Chief Industries, Inc. (Grand Island NE). **NOTE:** Contact Chief Industries at hr@chiefind.com; 3492 W. Old Highway 30 P.O. Box 2078 Grand Island, NE 68802-2078. 308/389-7200. **Operations at this facility include:** Divisional Headquarters; Manufacturing. **Number of employees at this location:** 350.

HDR, INC.
8404 Indian Hills Drive, Omaha NE 68114-4049. 402/399-1000. **Toll-free phone:** 800/366-4411. **Fax:**

402/399-1238. **Contact:** Human Resources. **E-mail address:** careers@hdrinc.com. **World Wide Web address:** http://www.hdrinc.com. **Description:** An architecture and engineering firm that operates worldwide and is employee owned. Founded in 1917. **NOTE:** Entry-level positions and part-time jobs are offered. **Company slogan:** Shaping the future through creative solutions and visionary leadership. **Special programs:** Internships; Co-ops; Summer Jobs. **Corporate headquarters location:** This location. **Other U.S. locations:** Nationwide. **Subsidiaries include:** HDR Architecture, Inc. specializes in the architectural design of health care facilities (hospitals and integrated health care networks, ambulatory care centers, oncology and cardiology centers, diagnostic and treatment centers, and strategic facilities assessment); justice facilities (courthouse and administrative facilities, adult and juvenile detention facilities, and state correctional facilities); and science and technology facilities (research facilities, advanced technology facilities, telecommunications, university science facilities, and manufacturing facilities). HDR Engineering, Inc. provides water, transportation, waste, and energy services including studies, design, and implementation for complex projects. **Listed on:** Privately held. **Chairman/CEO:** Dick Bell. **Information Annual sales/revenues:** $51 - $100 million. **Number of employees at this location:** 450. **Number of employees worldwide:** 3,300.

THE KIEWIT COMPANIES
1000 Kiewit Plaza, Omaha NE 68131. 402/342-2052. **Fax:** 402/271-2939. **Contact:** Human Resources. **E-mail address:** human.resources@kiewit.com. **World Wide Web address:** http://www.kiewit.com. **Description:** One of the largest construction companies in the country. Kiewit's primary markets are the building, power, transportation, water resources, and mining industries. Projects include highways, bridges, high-rise buildings, office complexes, railroads, tunnels, subways, dams, airports, power plants, canals, water treatment facilities, offshore petroleum platforms, and other heavy civil projects. The company has district offices throughout North America. **Positions advertised include:** Structural Design Engineer; Engineer; Superintendent; Business Manager; Internal Auditor. **Special Programs:** Internships, Co-ops. **Corporate headquarters location:** This location. **Other U.S. locations:** Nationwide. **Operations at this facility include:** Administration. **Listed on:** Privately held. **Annual sales/revenues:** More than $100 million. **Number of employees at this location:** 300. **Number of employees nationwide:** 15,000.

Nevada

AMERICAN BUILDINGS COMPANY
2401 Conestoga Drive, Carson City NV 89706. 775/887-2900. **Contact:** Human Resources. **E-mail address:** employment@americanbuildings.com. **World Wide Web address:** http://www.americanbuildings.com. **Description:** Manufactures prefabricated metal buildings. **Positions advertised include:** CAD/Drafting; Engineering; Sales. **Corporate headquarters location:** Eufaula AL. **Parent company:** MAGNATRAX. **Operations at this facility include:** Manufacturing plant. **Number of employees nationwide:** 500. **Other U.S. locations:** Nationwide.

THE LOUIS BERGER GROUP, INC.
500 Amigo Court, Suite 100, Las Vegas NV 89119. 702/736-6632. **Fax:** 702/736-0704. **Contact:** Robert Santonastaso. **E-mail address:** rsantonastaso@louisberger.com. **World Wide Web address:** http://www.louisberger.com. **Description:** A roadway design and engineering company. Founded in 1953. **Corporate headquarters location:** East Orange NJ. **Other U.S. locations:** Nationwide. **Parent company:** The Berger Group.

BLACK & VEATCH
4040 South Eastern Avenue, Suite 330, Las Vegas NV 89119. 702/732-0448. **Fax:** 702/732-7578. **Contact:** Human Resources. **World Wide Web address:** http://www.bv.com. **Description:** An environmental/civil engineering and construction firm serving utilities, commerce, industry, and government agencies in more than 40 countries throughout the world. Black & Veatch provides a broad range of study, design, construction management, and turnkey capabilities to clients in the water and wastewater fields. Other services are provided for solid waste recycling and disposal, transportation, and storm water management. In the energy field, Black & Veatch is a leader in providing engineering procurement and construction for electric power plants. The firm's areas of expertise include coal-fueled plants; simple and combined-cycle combustion turbines; fluidized bed combustion; waste-to-energy facilities; hydroelectric plants; and cogeneration facilities. In the industrial sector, Black & Veatch's experience is focused primarily on projects involving cleanrooms, industrial processes and planning, utility systems, and cogeneration. In addition to engineering, procurement, and construction, Black & Veatch offers a variety of management and financial services, including institutional strengthening, privatization, strategic financial planning, and information management. **Corporate headquarters location:** Overland Park KS. **Other U.S. locations:** Nationwide. **International locations:** Worldwide.

CH2M HILL
2285 Corporate Circle, Suite 200, Henderson NV 89014. 702/369-6175. **Contact:** Human Resources Manager. **World Wide Web address:** http://www.ch2m.com. **Description:** An engineering consulting firm. The company provides planning, engineering design, and operation and construction management services to help clients apply technology, safeguard the environment, and develop infrastructure. The staff includes specialists in environmental engineering and waste management, water management, transportation, industrial facilities, and a broad spectrum of infrastructure systems. Founded in 1946. **Corporate headquarters location:** Englewood CO. **Other U.S. locations:** Nationwide. **International locations:** Worldwide.

CH2M HILL
5370 Kietzke Lane, Reno NV 89511. 775/329-7300. **Contact:** Human Resources. **World Wide Web address:** http://www.ch2m.com. **Description:** An engineering consulting firm. The company provides planning, engineering design, and operation and construction management services to help clients apply technology, safeguard the environment, and develop infrastructure. The staff includes specialists in environmental engineering and waste management, water management, transportation, industrial facilities, and a broad spectrum of infrastructure systems. Founded in 1946. **Corporate headquarters location:** Englewood CO. **Other U.S. locations:** Nationwide. **International locations:** Worldwide.

CALIFORNIA POOLS & SPAS
9037 West Sahara Avenue, Las Vegas NV 89117. 702/254-2654. **Contact:** Personnel Director. **E-mail address:** careers@californiapools.com. **World Wide Web address:** http://www.californiapools.com. **Description:** Constructs spas and swimming pools. **Corporate headquarters location:** West Covina CA. **Other U.S. locations:** AZ; CA; TX.

CAPITAL CABINET CORPORATION
3645 Losee Road, North Las Vegas NV 89030-3324. 702/649-8733, extension 68. **Fax:** 702/649-6512. **Contact:** Clint Pies, Human Resources. **E-mail address:** employment@capitalcabinet.com. **World Wide Web address:** http://www.capitalcabinet.com. **Description:** Manufactures wooden kitchen cabinetry. Founded in 1946. **Positions advertised include:** Finish Room Technician; Cabinet Designer; Sales Representative; Installer. **Other U.S. locations:** Ontario CA.

CARSON TAYLOR HARVEY CONSTRUCTION
255 East Warm Springs Road, Las Vegas NV 89119. 702/876-6013. **Fax:** 702/876-5580. **Contact:** Human

Resources. **E-mail address:** carson-taylor-harvery@taylorconstrgrp.com. **World Wide Web address:** http://www.taylorconstrgrp.com. **Description:** A construction company specializing in commercial and industrial projects. **Corporate headquarters location:** Des Moines IA. **Parent company:** Taylor Construction Group (Des Moines IA).

DESIGN ENGINEERING CORPORATION
2900 South Rancho Drive, Las Vegas NV 89102. 702/871-9069. **Fax:** 702/456-9463. **Contact:** Personnel. **Description:** A design engineering company involved in civil surveying and electrical, structural, and mechanical engineering. **Number of employees at this location:** 50.

GOTHIC LANDSCAPING INC.
4565 West Nevso Drive, Las Vegas NV 89103. 702/252-7017. **Contact:** Human Resources. **Description:** A landscaping company for major builders and construction companies. **Corporate headquarters location:** Los Angeles CA. **Other U.S. locations:** Phoenix AZ. **Number of employees at this location:** 100.

HDR ENGINEERING
770 East Warm Springs Road, Suite 360, Las Vegas NV 89119. 702/938-6000. **Fax:** 702/938-6060. **Contact:** Human Resources. **E-mail address:** careers@hdrinc.com. **World Wide Web address:** http://www.hdrinc.com. **Description:** An architecture and engineering firm. HDR has projects in all 50 states and in 30 foreign countries. The company has 90 locations worldwide. Founded in 1917. **Number of employees nationwide:** 1,600. **Corporate headquarters location:** Omaha NE. **Other U.S. locations:** Nationwide. **International locations:** Worldwide. **Number of employees worldwide:** 3,300.

HUGHES SUPPLY INC
P.O. Box 270668, Las Vegas NV 89127. 702/382-6930. **Physical address:** 855 West Bonanza Road, Las Vegas NV 89106. **Fax:** 702/366-6749. **Contact:** Human Resources. **World Wide Web address:** http://www.hughessupply.com. **Description:** A wholesaler of electrical, waterworks, and plumbing supplies.

JACOBS CIVIL, INC.
2500 North Buffalo Drive, Suite 110, Las Vegas NV 89128. 702/870-2130. **Contact:** Human Resources. **World Wide Web address:** http://www.jacobs.com. **Description:** An environmental, architectural, and construction firm that offers consulting services, design services, and operations management to diverse clientele. **Positions advertised include:** Construction Inspector. **Corporate headquarters location:** Pasadena CA. **Other U.S. locations:** Nationwide. **Parent company:** Jacobs Engineering. **Listed on:** New York Stock Exchange. **Stock exchange symbol:** JEC. **Number of employees worldwide:** 5,000.

KLEINFELDER
6380 South Polaris Avenue, Las Vegas NV 89118. 702/736-2936. **Contact:** Human Resources. **World Wide Web address:** http://www.kleinfelder.com. **Description:** An engineering consulting firm. **Positions advertised include:** Project Professional, Geotechnical; Project Manager; Soils and Materials Technician. **Corporate headquarters location:** San Diego CA. **Other area locations:** Reno, Carson City. **Subsidiaries include:** The Kleinfelder Group, Inc.; Kleinfelder, Inc.; Kleinfelder Mexico, S.A. de C.V.; Spectrum Exploration, Inc., Trinity Engineering/Kleinfelder; GeoSystems.

KRUMP CONSTRUCTION, INC.
825 Steneri Way, Sparks NV 89431. 775/358-5679, extension 151. **Contact:** Karen Albrecht, Director of Corporate Administration. **E-mail address:** karena@krump.com. **World Wide Web address:** http://www.krump.com. **Description:** A contracting company specializing in industrial and warehouse building construction. Founded 1967. **Positions advertised include:** Project Engineer; IT Support Analyst; Superintendent; Project Manager.

LLOYD'S REFRIGERATION, INC.
3550 West Tompkins Avenue, Las Vegas NV 89103. 702/798-1010. **Fax:** 702/798-6531. **Contact:** Human Resources Manager. **E-mail address:** employment@lloydshomepage.com. **World Wide Web address:** http://www.lloydshomepage.com. **Description:** Designs and installs refrigeration systems, air conditioning and ventilation systems, and stainless steel and sheet metal work in both residential and commercial buildings.

MEADOW VALLEY CONTRACTORS, INC.
4635 Andrew Street, Suite F, North Las Vegas NV 89081. 702/643-9472. **Fax:** 702/643-6953. **Contact:** Robert Terril, Area Manager. **E-mail address:** info@meadowvalley.com. **World Wide Web address:** http://www.meadowvalley.com. **Description:** Performs heavy construction services including highway and bridge construction and the paving of airport runways and highways. **Positions advertised include:** Entry Level Construction; Structural Engineer; Project Construction, Civil Engineer. **Corporate headquarters location:** Phoenix AZ. **Subsidiaries include:** Meadow Valley Corporation; Ready Mix Inc. **Listed on:** NASDAQ. **Stock exchange symbol:** MVCO.

NEVADA STATE PLASTERING
3308 Meade Avenue, Las Vegas NV 89102-7893. 702/362-2215. **Contact:** Office Manager. **Description:** A plastering contractor.

QUALITY WOOD PRODUCTS
3001 North Nellis Boulevard, Las Vegas NV 89115. 702/369-3008. **Contact:** Human Resources. **Description:** Manufactures and installs doors in both residential and commercial buildings.

SOUTHERN NEVADA PAVING, INC.
3920 West Hacienda Avenue, Las Vegas NV 89118. 702/876-5226. **Fax:** 702/649-8864. **Contact:** Human Resources. **E-mail address:** hr.southwest@aggregate.com. **World Wide Web address:** http://www.aggregate.com. **Description:** An aggregate, asphalt, and contracting company. **Parent company:** Aggregate Industries. **Number of employees at this location:** 500.

SUPERIOR TILE & MARBLE INC.
4305 South Polaris Avenue, Las Vegas NV 89103-4152. 702/798-7882. **Contact:** Human Resources. **Description:** A tile and marble contracting company. **Corporate headquarters location:** Oakland CA.

WESTERN TECHNOLOGIES, INC.
3611 West Tompkins Avenue, Las Vegas NV 89103-5618. 702/798-8050. **Fax:** 702/798-7664. **Contact:** Human Resources. **E-mail address:** s.allanson@wt-us.com. **World Wide Web address:** http://www.wt-us.com. **Description:** Provides engineering, consulting, and testing of environmental, geotechnical, and construction materials. Environmental services include site assessments, investigations, feasibility studies, problem solving, and remedial services with use of state-of-the-art technology. Materials Engineering and Testing provides analysis and quality assurance of materials and methods for clients. Materials Research develops methods of improving the strength and durability of conventional construction materials through research into feasibility of substituting less expensive or more available materials. Construction Quality Control provides interpretation of geotechnical reports, observation and testing of reinforced steel and concrete, visual and nondestructive evaluation of bolted and welded structural steel components, concrete and asphalt mix designs, as well as sampling and testing many other architectural and structural components. **NOTE:** Entry-level positions are available. **Positions advertised include:** Senior Geotechnical Engineer; Geotechnical Project Engineer; Environmental Scientist; Geologist; Senior Engineering Technician;

Welding Inspector; Structural Steel Technician; Nuclear Gauge Technician; NAQTC or WAQTC Certified Technician; ICC/ICBO Certified Inspector. **Special programs:** Training. **Corporate headquarters location:** Phoenix AZ. **Other U.S. locations:** AZ; CO; NM; TX; UT. **International locations:** Mexico. **Number of employees worldwide:** Over 425.

New Hampshire

AAVID THERMALLOY, LLC

P.O. Box 400, Laconia NH 03247. 603/528-3400. **Physical address:** 67 Primrose Drive, Laconia NH 03246. **Fax:** 603/528-1478. **Contact:** Janis Powell, Human Resources Recruiter. **E-mail address:** powellj@aavid.com. **World Wide Web address:** http://www.aavid.com. **Description:** A thermal engineering and management company that develops and markets solutions to heat-related problems. **Office hours:** Monday – Friday 8:00 a.m. – 5:00 p.m. **Corporate headquarters location:** Concord NH. **Other U.S. locations:** Santa Clara CA; Plano TX. **International locations:** Worldwide. **Parent company:** Aavid Thermal Technologies, Inc. **CEO:** Bharatan R. Patel. **Number of employees at this location:** 700. **Number of employees nationwide:** 1,800.

AMERICAN EXPLOSIVES CORP.

668 First New Hampshire Turnpike, Northwood NH 03261. 603/942-8899. **Fax:** 603/942-8558. **E-mail address:** jobapp@americanexplosives.com. **World Wide Web address:** http://www.americanexplosives.com. **Description:** American Explosives is a drilling and blasting company; its workers are contracted for jobs of all types, everything from highway work to residential neighborhoods. It is the fastest growing company in its field in Southern New Hampshire, Maine, and Vermont. **NOTE:** Apply on-line or e-mail resume. This company has been acquired by Maine Drilling and Blasting, Gardiner, ME and is in ownership transition. **Positions advertised include:** Blaster; Driller; Laborer; Driver; CDL Hazmat. **Number of employees at this location:** 41.

BRONZE CRAFT CORPORATION

P.O. Box 788, Nashua NH 03061-0788. 603/883-7747. **Physical address:** 37 Will Street, Nashua NH 03061. **Toll-free phone:** 800/488-7747. **Fax:** 603/883-0222. **Contact:** Personnel Director. **World Wide Web address:** http://www.bronzecraft.com. **Description:** A sand-cast foundry, Bronze Craft Corporation manufactures architectural products including window and door hardware. The company also supplies finished products to companies like Steinway, GE, and Westinghouse. Operations at this location include machining, polishing, finishing, and assembly. Bronze Craft Corporation also provides customer support including engineering, pattern making, tooling, and repairing. **Office hours:** Monday – Friday, 8:00 a.m. – 5:00 p.m. **Corporate headquarters location:** This location. **Operations at this facility include:** Administration; Manufacturing; Research and Development; Sales; Service. **Number of employees at this location:** 150.

CREARE INC.

P.O. Box 71, Hanover NH 03755. 603/643-3800. **Fax:** 603/643-4657. **Contact:** Human Resources. **E-mail address:** recruit@creare.com. **World Wide Web address:** http://www.creare.com. **NOTE:** Please see website and job listings for information on how to submit electronic applications. **Description:** Provides engineering services to customers worldwide. Services range from basic research to the development of prototype products. Founded in 1961. **Positions advertised include:** Design Engineer; R&D Engineer; Mechanical Detail Drafter; Mechanical Technician; Office Assistant/Receptionist. **Office hours:** Monday - Friday, 8:00 a.m. - 5:00 p.m. **Corporate headquarters location:** This location. **Operations at this facility include:** Administration; Research and Development; Sales; Service. **Number of employees at this location:** 100.

CUSTOMIZED STRUCTURES INC.

P.O. Box 884, Plains Road, Claremont NH 03743. 603/543-1236. **Toll-free phone:** 800/523-2033. **Fax:** 603/542-5650. **Contact:** Human Resources. **World Wide Web address:** http://www.custruct.com. **Description:** Manufactures modular homes and wholesales to residential builders and dealers of modular systems. Customized Structures specializes in homes of wood platform frame construction, designed for single-family housing, two-family housing, and multifamily housing. Each unit includes suggested plans for foundations. **NOTE:** Search posted openings and apply on-line. **Positions advertised include:** CAD Designer; Experienced Tradesmen; Controller Estimator; Cost Accountant. **Number of employees at this location:** 100.

HARVEY INDUSTRIES INC.

725 Huse Street, Manchester NH 03103. 603/669-2121. **Toll-free phone:** 800/562-6237. **Fax:** 603/669-9098. **Contact:** Shelley Holmes, Human Resources. **E-mail address:** jobs@harveyind.com. **World Wide Web address:** http://www.harveyind.com. **NOTE:** Search posted openings and apply online. **Description:** Manufactures windows and doors. The company is also a wholesale distributor of building materials. **Positions advertised include:** First Shift Production Supervisor; Second Shift Production Supervisor; Administrative Clerk; Customer Service Representative; Inside Sales Representative; Second Shift Leadperson; Design Engineer – Windows and Doors. **Corporate headquarters location:** Waltham MA.

NEW ENGLAND HOMES INC.

270 Ocean Road, Greenland NH 03840. 603/436-8830. **Toll-free phone:** 800/800-8831. **Fax:** 603/431-8540. **Contact:** Mile Younus, Human Resources. **E-mail address**: myounus@newenglandhomes.net. **World Wide Web address:** http://www.newenglandhomes.net. **Description:** A manufacturer of modular homes. **NOTE:** Search posted openings and apply online. Must fill out online application form. **Positions advertised include:** Roofer; Framer; CDL-A Driver; Field Set Crew; Entry Level Sales; Estimator. **Number of employees at this location:** 120.

New Jersey

ABB INC.

P.O. Box 6005, North Brunswick NJ 08902. **Physical Address:** 1460 Livingstone Avenue, North Brunswick NJ 08902-6005. 732/932-6000. **Contact:** Human Resources Manager. **World Wide Web address:** http://www.abb.com/us. **Description:** Provides engineering, construction, and sales support services as part of a worldwide engineering firm. Internationally, the company operates through the following business segments: oil field equipment and services; power systems; engineering and construction; process equipment; and industrial products. **Corporate headquarters location:** Norwalk CT. **Other U.S. locations:** New York NY. **Subsidiaries include:** ABB Lumus Global Inc. (Bloomfield NJ); ABB Simcom (Bloomfield NJ); ABB Susa (also at this location). **Parent company:** ABB AG (Baden, Switzerland). **Number of employees worldwide:** 220,000.

ABB LUMMUS GLOBAL INC.

1515 Broad Street, Bloomfield NJ 07003. 973/893-1515. **Fax:** 973/893-2000. **Contact:** Human Resources. **World Wide Web address:** http://www.abb.com/us. **Description:** An engineering firm serving power plants, chemical plants, and petrochemical and oil refineries, as well as other industries such as aviation and storage. **Parent company:** ABB Inc. (Norwalk CT) provides engineering, construction, and sales support services as part of the worldwide engineering firm. Another subsidiary, ABB Simcon (Bloomfield NJ), specializes in chemical engineering. Internationally, the company operates in five business segments: oil field equipment and services, power systems, engineering and construction, process equipment, and industrial products.

AMERICAN STANDARD COMPANIES INC.
One Centennial Avenue, P.O. Box 6820, Piscataway NJ 08854. 732/980-6000. **Contact:** Human Resources. **World Wide Web address:** http://www.americanstandard.com. **Description:** A global, diversified manufacturer. The company's operations consist of four segments: air conditioning products, plumbing products, automotive products, and medical systems. The air conditioning products segment (through subsidiary The Trane Company) develops and manufactures Trane and American Standard air conditioning equipment for use in central air conditioning systems for commercial, institutional, and residential buildings. The plumbing products segment develops and manufactures American Standard, Ideal Standard, Porcher, Armitage Shanks, Dolomite, and Standard bathroom and kitchen fixtures and fittings. The automotive products segment develops and manufactures truck, bus, and utility vehicle braking and control systems under the WABCO and Perrot brands. The medical systems segment manufactures Copalis, DiaSorin, and Pylori-Chek medical diagnostic products and systems for a variety of diseases including HIV, osteoporosis, and renal disease. **Positions advertised include:** Strategic Business Development Analyst; Forecast Analyst; International Tax Assistant; Manager, Retirement Benefits. **Corporate headquarters location:** This location. **International locations:** Worldwide. **Listed on:** New York Stock Exchange. **Stock exchange symbol:** ASD. **Chairman/CEO:** Frederic M. Poses. **Number of employees worldwide:** 57,000.

ARROW GROUP INDUSTRIES, INC.
1680 Route 23 North, P.O. Box 928, Wayne NJ 07474-0928. 973/696-6900. **Fax:** 973/696-8539. **Contact:** Joanne Trezza, Human Resources Director. **E-mail address:** assist@arrowsheds.com. **World Wide Web address:** http://www.sheds.com. **Description:** Manufactures steel storage buildings. **Corporate headquarters location:** This location. **Other U.S. locations:** Breese IL. **Listed on:** Privately held. **Number of employees at this location:** 115. **Number of employees nationwide:** 330.

THE LOUIS BERGER GROUP, INC.
100 Halsted Street, East Orange NJ 07018. 973/678-1960. **Fax:** 973/676-0532. **Contact:** Ms. Terry Williams, Human Resources Manager. **E-mail address:** recruiter@louisberger.com. **World Wide Web address:** http://www.louisberger.com. **Description:** A diversified consulting firm. The company provides cultural, environmental, and transportation-related engineering and planning services in the United States. Louis Berger also aids in urban and rural development projects in Africa, Asia, Latin America, and the Middle East. This location also hires seasonally. Founded in 1940. **NOTE:** Entry-level positions and part-time jobs are offered. **Positions advertised include:** Network Engineer; Human Resources Generalist; Auditor; Sr. Financial Analyst; Accountant. **Special programs:** Summer Jobs. **Corporate headquarters location:** This location. **Other U.S. locations:** Nationwide. **International locations:** Worldwide. **Listed on:** Privately held. **Annual sales/revenues:** More than $100 million. **Number of employees at this location:** 270. **Number of employees nationwide:** 900. **Number of employees worldwide:** 2,000.

BURNS AND ROE ENTERPRISES, INC.
800 Kinderkamack Road, Oradell NJ 07649. 201/265-2000. **Fax:** 201/986-4459. **Contact:** Staffing. **E-mail address:** staffing@roe.com. **World Wide Web address:** http://www.roe.com. **Description:** Engaged in construction, engineering, maintenance, and operation services. The company specializes in the design and engineering of complex facilities. **Special programs:** Internships. **Positions advertised include:** Corporate Security Manager; Civil/Structural Designer; Civil/Structural Engineer; Principal Nuclear Engineer; Sr. Electrical Engineer; Information Technology Manager. **Corporate headquarters location:** This location. **Listed on:** Privately held. **Number of employees at this location:** 600. **Number of employees nationwide:** 1,200. **Number of employees worldwide:** 1,250.

C/S GROUP
3 Werner Way, Lebanon NJ 08833. 908/236-0800. **Fax:** 908/236-0604. **Contact:** Susan Kizies, Director of Human Resources. **E-mail address:** careerops@c-sgroup.com. **World Wide Web address:** http://www.c-sgroup.com. **Description:** Manufactures building materials including wall protection products, sun controls, and fire vents. Founded in 1948. **NOTE:** Entry-level positions and part-time jobs are offered. **Positions advertised include:** Regional Sales Manager. **Corporate headquarters location:** This location. **Other U.S. locations:** Garden Grove CA; Muncy PA. **International locations:** France; Spain; United Kingdom. **Listed on:** Privately held. **Annual sales/revenues:** More than $100 million.

CUH2A
1000 Lenox Drive, Lawrenceville NJ 08648. 609/844-1212. **Fax:** 609/791-7718. **Contact:** Ms. Pat Little, Human Resources. **E-mail address:** plittle@CUH2A.com. **World Wide Web address:** http://www.cuh2a.com. **Description:** The world's largest professional services firm dedicated to facilities solutions for research organizations. Founded in 1962. **Positions advertised include:** Director, Construction Administration. **Corporate headquarters location:** This location. **Other U.S. locations:** Atlanta GA; Chicago IL; San Francisco CA; Washington DC. **International locations:** London; Paris.

CENTEX HOMES
500 Craig Road, Manalapan NJ 07726. 732/780-1800. **Contact:** Human Resources. **World Wide Web address:** http://www.centexhomes.com. **Description:** Centex Homes designs, constructs, and sells homes nationwide. **Positions advertised include:** Purchasing Manager; Entitlements Manager; Estimator. **Other U.S. locations:** Nationwide. **Parent company:** Centex Corporation. **Listed on:** New York Stock Exchange. **Stock exchange symbol:** CTX.

CLAYTON BRICK
2 Porete Avenue, North Arlington NJ 07031. 201/998-7600. **Contact:** Human Resources. **World Wide Web address:** http://www.claytonco.com. **Description:** Engaged in precast concrete panel construction and installation. **NOTE:** For employment information contact the central Clayton Companies office: P.O. Box 3015, 515 Lakewood-New Egypt Road, Lakewood NJ 08701, 732/363-1995, or contact Wayne Tart at 732/905-3156 or by e-mail at waynetart@netscape.com.

EDWARDS AND KELCEY INC.
299 Madison Avenue, P.O. Box 1936, Morristown NJ 07962-1936. 973/267-0555. **Fax:** 973/267-3555. **Contact:** Human Resources. **World Wide Web address:** http://www.ekcorp.com. **Description:** A consulting, engineering, planning, and communications organization whose range of services includes location and economic feasibility studies; valuations and appraisals; cost analyses; computer technology; marketing studies; traffic and transportation studies; soils and foundation analyses; environmental impact studies; master planning; structural surveys; and preliminary and final designs. Services also include preparation of contract documents and observation of construction operations for public transit systems, terminals, railroads, bus depots, parking garages, airports, ports, highways, streets, bridges, tunnels, traffic control systems, military facilities, communications systems, storm and sanitary sewers, water supply and distribution, flood control, and land development. Founded in 1946. **NOTE:** Entry-level positions are offered. **Positions advertised include:** Geotechnical Engineer; Sr. Accountant; Project Manager; Electrical Engineer; Civil Engineer. **Special programs:** Internships. **Corporate headquarters location:** This location. **Other U.S. locations:** Atlanta GA; Chicago IL; Baltimore MD; Boston MA;

Minneapolis MN; Manchester NH; New York NY; Saratoga Springs NY; Cincinnati OH; Chadds Ford PA; West Chester PA; Providence RI; Dallas TX; Houston TX; Leesburg VA; Milwaukee WI. **International locations:** Puerto Rico. **Operations at this facility include:** Administration; Divisional Headquarters. **Listed on:** Privately held. **Annual sales/revenues:** More than $100 million. **Number of employees at this location:** 200. **Number of employees nationwide:** 730.

FM GLOBAL
400 Interpace Parkway, Building C, 3rd Floor, Parsippany NJ 07054-1196. 973/402-2200. **Contact:** District Office. **World Wide Web address:** http://www.fmglobal.com. **Description:** A loss control services organization. The company helps owner company policyholders to protect their properties and occupancies from damage caused by fire, wind, flood, and explosion; boiler, pressure vessel, and machinery accidents; and many other insured hazards. **Corporate headquarters location:** Johnston RI. **Other U.S. locations:** Nationwide. **International locations:** Worldwide.

GAF MATERIALS CORPORATION
1361 Alps Road, Wayne NJ 07470. 973/628-3000. **Toll-free phone:** 800/766-3411. **Contact:** Human Resources. **E-mail address:** employment@gaf.com. **World Wide Web address:** http://www.gaf.com. **Description:** Manufactures roofing materials. **Positions advertised include:** Customer Care Quality Assurance Manager; Sr. Buyer. **Operations at this facility include:** Administration; Manufacturing.

HILL INTERNATIONAL
303 Lippincott Center, Marlton NJ 08053. 856/810-6200. **Fax:** 856/810-1309. **Contact:** Human Resources. **E-mail address:** greggmetzinger@hillintl.com. **World Wide Web address:** http://www.hillintl.com. **Description:** Provides construction management and consulting services. **Positions advertised include:** Cost Estimator; Assistant Controller; Testifying Expert; Vice President of Business Development. **Corporate headquarters location:** This location.

LIPINSKI LANDSCAPING
251 Princeton Hightstown Road, East Windsor NJ 08520-1401. 609/443-1552. **Contact:** Human Resources. **Description:** Provides landscaping services to commercial and residential clients. This location also hires seasonally. **NOTE:** Entry-level positions are offered. **Special programs:** Internships; Apprenticeships; Summer Jobs. **Corporate headquarters location:** This location. **Other U.S. locations:** Princeton NJ. **Annual sales/revenues:** $21 - $50 million. **Number of employees at this location:** 320.

MELARD MANUFACTURING CORPORATION
2 Paulson Avenue, P.O. Box 58, Passaic NJ 07055-5703. 973/472-8888. **Contact:** Personnel. **World Wide Web address:** http://www.masco.com. **Description:** Manufactures a broad range of hardware products including bath accessories and plumbing equipment. **Positions advertised include:** Assistant Controller. **Corporate headquarters location:** This location. **Parent company:** Masco Corporation.

JOS. L. MUSCARELLE, INC.
99 West Essex Street, Route 17, Maywood NJ 07607. 201/845-8100. **Contact:** Joseph Muscarelle, Jr., President. **Description:** Engaged in construction and real estate development.

PATENT CONSTRUCTION SYSTEMS
One Mack Centre Drive, Paramus NJ 07652. 201/261-5600. **Fax:** 201/261-5544. **Contact:** Human Resources and Labor Relations. **E-mail address:** jobs@pcshd.com. **World Wide Web address:** http://www.pcshd.com. **Description:** Manufactures and markets scaffolding as well as concrete forming and shoring products. Founded in 1909. **Positions advertised include:** Director of Engineering. **Parent company:** Harsco Corporation.

PIONEER INDUSTRIES
171 South Newman Street, Hackensack NJ 07601. 201/933-1900. **Contact:** Personnel Director. **World Wide Web address:** http://www.pioneerindustries.com. **Description:** Produces industrial doors, fireproof and theft-proof doors, and other sheet metal specialties. **Corporate headquarters location:** Bloomfield Hills MI. **Parent company:** Core Industries. **Operations at this facility include:** Manufacturing.

SCHIAVONE CONSTRUCTION CO.
150 Meadowlands Parkway, 3rd Floor, Secaucus NJ 07094. 201/867-5070. **Contact:** Recruiting. **Description:** A heavy construction firm engaged in large-scale projects such as highways, tunnels, and bridges. Clients include city, state, and federal governments.

New Mexico

ASCG INCORPORATED
6501 Americas Parkway NE, Suite 400, Albuquerque NM 87110. 505/247-0294. **Fax:** 505/242-4845. **Contact:** Human Resources Manager. **E-mail address:** jobs@ascg.com. **World Wide Web address:** http://www.ascg.com. **Description:** An engineering firm specializing in hydrology, structural, airport design, civil, mechanical, and environmental disciplines. **NOTE:** See website for current job openings and to apply online. **Other U.S. locations:** AK; CO; ID; NM; WA. **Corporate headquarters location:** Anchorage AK. **Parent company:** NANA Regional Corporation.

AMREP SOUTHWEST INC.
333 Rio Rancho Drive NE, Rio Rancho NM 87124. 505/892-9200. **Fax:** 505/896-9180. **Contact:** Human Resources. **World Wide Web address:** http://www.amrepsw.com. **Description:** Founder and principal developer of the city of Rio Rancho, adjoining Albuquerque, New Mexico. Develops commercial, residential and industrial property.

ARMSTRONG CONSTRUCTION COMPANY
P.O. Box 1873, Roswell NM 88202. 505/622-1080. **Physical address:** 3300 South Sunset Avenue, Roswell NM 88201. **Contact:** Charles Yslas, Human Resources. **E-mail address:** charles@armstrongconstruction.com. **World Wide Web address:** http://www.armstrongconstruction.com. **Description:** A contracting company specializing in highway, heavy, and utility construction. Founded in 1922. **Other area locations:** Hobbs NM.

BURN CONSTRUCTION COMPANY, INC.
P.O. Drawer 1869, Las Cruces NM 88004. 505/526-4421. **Contact:** Personnel Director. **Description:** A construction company that provides a variety of services including dirt work, paving, and concrete services. The company also works with utilities and water and wastewater treatment plants. **NOTE:** Apply in person. **Corporate headquarters location:** This location.

D.L.R. GROUP
5285 Daybreak Drive, Farmington NM 87401. 505/327-6068. **Fax:** 505/327-6060. **Contact:** George Trosky, Office Leader. **E-mail address:** gtrosky@dlrgroup.com. **World Wide Web address:** http://www.dlrgroup.com. **Description:** An architectural design firm that specializes in educational, judicial, medical, and recreational projects with 15 offices nationwide. Founded in 1977. **Office hours:** Monday - Friday, 8:00 a.m. - 5:00 p.m. **Corporate headquarters location:** Omaha NE. **Number of employees nationwide:** 545.

THE GARDNER ZEMKE COMPANY
6100 Indian School Road NE, Albuquerque NM 87110. 505/881-0555. **Fax:** 505/888-2191. **Contact:** Human Resources. **Wide Web address:** http://www.gardnerzemke.com. **Description:** An

electrical and mechanical contractor for commercial buildings. **Special programs:** Apprenticeships. **Corporate headquarters location:** This location.

J.B. HENDERSON CONSTRUCTION
10100 Trumbull SE, Albuquerque NM 87123. 505/292-8955. **Contact:** Human Resources. **E-mail address:** bstewart@jbhenderson.com. **World Wide Web address:** http://www.jbhenderson.com. **Description:** Provides architectural, mechanical, pipe, and sheet metal fabrication, as well as design build services, to clients in the private and public sector. The fourth largest general contractor and the second largest mechanical contractor in New Mexico. **NOTE:** For administrative and project management positions, contact the office directly. For construction positions, inquiries must be directed to the local the union offices. **Other area locations:** Los Alamos NM; Rio Rancho NM.

JAYNES COMPANIES
P.O. Box 26841, Albuquerque NM 87125. 505/345-8591. **Physical address:** 2906 Broadway North East, Albuquerque NM 807107. **Contact:** Human Resources. **E-mail address:** info@jaynescorp.com. **World Wide Web address:** http://www.jaynescorp.com. **Description:** Operates five commercial construction companies located in seven offices throughout the Southwest. Nearly 50 years of experience offering design and building, construction management, and expertise in concrete. Privately owned since 1946. **NOTE:** See website for current job openings and application instructions.

KELLY CABLE CORPORATION
3740 Hawkins Street NE, Albuquerque NM 87109. 505/343-1144. **Contact:** Human Resources. **E-mail address:** carmstrong@kellycorporation.com. **World Wide Web address:** http://www.kellycorporation.com. **Description:** A cable television contractor. Kelly Cable Corporation specializes in burying phone cable, as well as installing aerial phone cable. The company also provides construction contracting for utilities. Founded in 1988. **NOTE:** Submit resume by e-mail or mail to 7000 North Broadway, Bldg. 4, Suite 400, Denver CO 80221. Information at 303/430-1414 x508. **Positions advertised include:** Laborers; Operators; SNI Technicians. **Corporate headquarters location:** Denver CO. **Listed on:** Privately held.

KLINGER CONSTRUCTORS LLC
P.O. Box 90850, Albuquerque NM 87199. 505/822-9990. **Physical address:** 8701 Washington Street NE, Albuquerque NM 87113. **Fax:** 505/821-0439. **Contact:** Office Manager. **World Wide Web address:** http://www.klingerconstructors.com. **Description:** A construction company in commercial, industrial, and institutional markets. **NOTE:** Apply in person, or search for positions online. **Parent company:** Klinger Companies, Inc.

SMITH ENGINEERING
210 North Main Street, Roswell NM 88202. 505/884-0700. **Contact:** Sherry Rains. **E-mail address:** sherryr@secnm.com. **World Wide Web address:** http://www.secnm.com. **Description:** An engineering consulting firm providing civil, structural, and environmental engineering, as well as materials testing services. **NOTE:** See website for current job openings and application instructions. **Other area locations:** Albuquerque NM.

WESTERN TECHNOLOGIES, INC.
8305 Washington Place NE, Albuquerque NM 87113-1670. 505/823-4488. **Fax:** 505/821-2963. **Contact:** Human Resources. **E-mail address:** s.allanson@wt-us.com. **World Wide Web address:** http://www.wt-us.com. **Description:** Provides engineering, consulting, and testing of environmental, geotechnical, and construction materials. Twenty offices in six states and Mexico. Founded in 1955. **Positions advertised include:** Senior Geotechnical Engineer; Geotechnical Project Engineer; Senior Environmental Project Manager; Geologist; Industrial Hygienist; Welding Inspector. **Corporate headquarters location:** Phoenix AZ. **Number of employees nationwide:** 425.

New York

AMEC
667 Bay Road, Suite 3B, Queensbury NY 12804. 518/761-243**Fax:** 518/798-5774. **Contact:** Human Resources. **World Wide Web address:** http://www.amec.com. **Description:** One of the largest construction management companies in the world offering a wide range of services including construction management, contracting program management, consulting, and design and construction. Founded in 1936. **Special programs:** Internships. **Corporate headquarters location:** London, United Kingdom. **Subsidiaries include:** AMEC Construction Management, Inc.; Spie S.A. **Listed on:** London Stock Exchange. **Stock exchange symbol:** AMEC. **Annual sales/revenues:** $5 billion. **Number of employees at this location:** 140. **Number of employees nationwide:** 500. **Number of employees worldwide:** 45,000.

ACME ARCHITECTURAL PRODUCTS, INC.
dba ACME STEEL PARTITION COMPANY, INC.
251 Lombardy Street, Brooklyn NY 11222. 718/384-7800. **Contact:** Human Resources. **World Wide Web address:** http://www.acmesteel.com. **Description:** Manufactures commercial interior products including hollow metal doors and frames, partitions, and office panels and furniture, as well as distributing builder's hardware and architectural wood doors.

AMMANN AND WHITNEY
96 Morton Street, New York NY 10014-3326. 212/462-8500. **Fax:** 212/929-5356. **Contact:** Human Resources. **E-mail address:** rdarvie@ammann-whitney.com. **World Wide Web address:** http://www.ammann-whitney.com. **Description:** An engineering firm specializing in structural, civil, architectural, mechanical and electrical engineering, as well as construction inspection services. **Positions advertised include:** Resident Engineer; Construction Inspector; Office Engineer; Senior Architect; Architect; Site Civil Engineer; Structural Drafter; Computer-aided Design Operator; Senior Structural Engineer; Construction Engineer; Design Engineer. **Other U.S. locations:** Wethersfield CT; Washington DC; Boston MA; Hoboken NJ; Philadelphia PA; Richmond VA.

CARRIER CORPORATION
Building ARC, P.O. Box 4808, Carrier Parkway, Syracuse NY 13221-4808. 315/432-6000. **Contact:** Diversity and Staffing. **E-mail address:** great.jobs@carrier.utc.com. **World Wide Web address:** http://www.global.carrier.com. **Description:** Manufactures heating, ventilating, and air conditioning units. Carrier Corporation produces and sells these units for both commercial and residential use. **Positions advertised include:** Mechanical Engineer. **Corporate headquarters location:** Farmington CT. **Parent company:** United Technologies (Hartford CT). **Annual sales/revenues:** $8.8 billion. **Number of employees:** 45,000.

CLOUGH HARBOUR & ASSOCIATES LLP
III Winners Circle, P.O. Box 5269, Albany NY 12205-0269. 518/453-4500. **Fax:** 518/458-1735. **Contact:** Human Resources Department. **E-mail address:** infosys@cha-llp.com. **World Wide Web address:** http://www.cha-llp.com. **Description:** An engineering firm with 20 offices nationwide. Specialties include civil engineering, environmental engineering, highway planning, landscape architecture, communications infrastructure design, urban planning, and geotechnical engineering. **Positions advertised include:** Engineer; Geographic Information System Analyst; Human Resources Manager; Senior Civil Engineer; Senior Planner; Water/Wastewater Engineer. **Corporate headquarters location:** This location. **Other locations:** Nationwide. **Number of employees:** 550.

DREW INDUSTRIES INCORPORATED
200 Mamaroneck Avenue, Suite 301, White Plains NY 10601. 914/428-9098. **Fax:** 914/428-4581. **Contact:**

Human Resources. **World Wide Web address:** http://www.drewindustries.com. **Description:** Drew Industries is the holding company of Kinro, Inc. Kinro is one of the leading producers of aluminum and vinyl windows for manufactured homes, and windows and doors for recreational vehicles. Kinro has nine domestic manufacturing plants. **Corporate headquarters location:** This location. **Subsidiaries include:** Lippert Components, Inc.; Kinro, Inc. **Listed on:** American Stock Exchange. **Stock exchange symbol:** DW. **Annual sales/revenues:** $325 million. **Number of employees:** 2,800.

FOSTER WHEELER LTD.
9431 Foster Wheeler Road, Dansville NY 14437. 716/335-3131. **Fax:** 585/335-3018. **Contact:** Human Resources. **E-mail address:** us_staffing@fwc.com. **World Wide Web address:** http://www.fwc.com. **Description:** Engaged in three business segments: process plants segment, consisting primarily of the design, engineering, and construction of process plants and fired heaters for oil refiners and chemical producers; a utility and engine segment, consisting primarily of the design and fabrication of steam generators, condensers, feedwater heaters, electrostatic precipitators, and other pollution abatement equipment; and an industrial segment that supplies pressure vessels and internals, electrical copper products, industrial insulation, welding wire, and electrodes. **Corporate headquarters location:** Clinton NJ. **Other U.S. locations:** Nationwide. **International locations:** Worldwide. **Listed on:** New York Stock Exchange. **Stock exchange symbol:** FWC. **Annual sales/revenues:** $3.5 billion. **Number of employees:** 9,000.

INDUSTRIAL ACOUSTICS COMPANY, INC.
1160 Commerce Avenue, Bronx NY 10462. 718/430-4541. **Fax:** 718/430-4766. **Contact:** Michele Pisani, Human Resources Department. **E-mail address:** hr@industrialacoustics.com. **World Wide Web address:** http://www.industrialacoustics.com. **Description:** IAC is an international company with engineering and manufacturing capabilities serving the architectural, air conditioning, industrial, medical and life sciences, power plant, and military/commercial aviation markets. The company develops and markets noise control products, turnkey systems for air conditioning and air handling units, jet engine aircraft hush-house test facilities, detention cells, acoustical ceilings for correctional institutions, and other special purpose ceilings. Founded in 1949. **Positions advertised include:** Project Engineer; Auto Cad Drafter/Designer. **Corporate headquarters location:** This location. **International locations:** Germany; United Kingdom. **President/CEO:** Robert E. Schmitt. **Annual sales/revenues:** $100 million. **Number of employees:** 300.

KSW MECHANICAL SERVICES
3716 23rd Street, Long Island City NY 11101. 718/361-6500. **Fax:** 718/784-1943. **Contact:** Human Resources. **Description:** A mechanical contracting firm engaged in the installation of heating, ventilation, and air conditioning systems in commercial buildings. **Corporate headquarters location:** This location. **Listed on:** Over The Counter. **Stock exchange symbol:** KSWW. **Chairman/CEO:** Floyd Warkol. **Annual sales/revenues:** $50 million. **Number of employees:** 45.

PARAMOUNT ELECTRONICS COMPANY
3300 Veterans Memorial Highway, Bohemia NY 11716. 631/737-3030. **Contact:** Human Resources. **Description:** Provides contract drafting services. **Corporate headquarters location:** This location.

PARSONS BRINCKERHOFF INC.
One Penn Plaza, New York NY 10119. 212/465-5000. **Fax:** 212/465-5096. **Contact:** Joe Alberti, Personnel. **E-mail address:** careeres@pbworld.com. **World Wide Web address:** http://www.pbworld.com. **Description:** Provides total engineering and construction management services, including the development of major bridges, tunnels, highways, marine facilities, buildings, industrial complexes, and railroads. Founded in 1885. **Corporate headquarters location:** This location. **International locations:** Worldwide. **Subsidiaries include:** Parsons Brinckerhoff Construction Services; Parsons Brinckerhoff Development Corporation; Parsons Brinckerhoff International; Parsons Brinckerhoff Quade & Douglas. **President/CEO:** Thomas J. O'Neill. **Sales/revenue:** Approximately $1.4 billion. **Number of employees worldwide:** Over 9,000.

ALBERT PEARLMAN, INC.
60 East 42nd Street, Suite 1041, New York NY 10165. 212/687-5055. **Fax:** 212/687-6228. **Contact:** Human Resources. **E-mail address:** randyp@albertpearlman.com. **World Wide Web address:** http://www.albertpearlman.com. **Description:** The largest painting contractor in New York City. **Corporate headquarters location:** This location. **Other locations:** Hackensack, NJ; Long Island, NY.

SLANT/FIN CORPORATION
100 Forest Drive, Greenvale NY 11548. 516/484-2600. **Contact:** Human Resources. **E-mail address:** info@slantfin.com. **World Wide Web address:** http://www.slantfin.com. **Description:** Engaged in the manufacture and sale of heating and cooling equipment for both domestic and foreign markets. **Corporate headquarters location:** This location. **International locations:** Canada. **Number of employees worldwide:** 600.

SLATTERY SKANSKA INC.
16-16 Whitestone Expressway, Whitestone NY 11357. 718/767-2600. **Fax:** 718/767-2411. **Contact:** Larry Bolyard, Director of Human Resources Department. **E-mail address:** larry.bolyard@slattery.skanska.com. **World Wide Web address:** http://www.slatteryskanska.com. **Description:** A heavy construction firm engaged in large-scale projects such as mass transit, sewage treatment plants, highways, bridges, and tunnels. **Positions advertised include:** Estimator; Superintendent; Project Engineer. **Office hours:** Monday - Friday, 8:00 a.m. - 4:30 p.m. **Corporate headquarters location:** This location. **Parent company:** Skanska USA. **Operations at this facility include:** Administration. **Number of employees at this location:** 1,000.

STROBER BROTHERS, INC.
Pier 3, Furman Street, Brooklyn NY 11201. 718/875-9700. **Fax:** 718/246-3060. **Contact:** Human Resources. **World Wide Web address:** http://www.strober.com. **Description:** Strober Organization, Inc. is a supplier of building materials to professional building contractors in the residential, commercial, and renovation construction markets. The company operates 10 building centers across four states, offering a broad selection of gypsum wallboard and other drywall products, lumber, roofing, insulation and acoustical materials, plywood, siding products, metal specialties, hardware and tools, waterproofing, masonry, and steel decking products. The building centers also offer a full spectrum of millwork. Founded in 1912. **Corporate headquarters location:** This location.

TESTWELL LABORATORIES, INC.
47 Hudson Street, Ossining NY 10562. 914/762-9000. **Fax:** 914/762-9638. **Contact:** Personnel Director. **World Wide Web address:** http://www.testwelllabs.com. **Description:** Provides construction materials and environmental testing, inspection, and consulting services for the construction, environmental, and real estate industries. **Corporate headquarters location:** This location. **Other area locations:** Albany NY. **Other U.S. locations:** Miami FL; Mays Landing NJ. **Operations at this facility include:** Administration; Regional Headquarters; Sales; Service. **Number of employees at this location:** 90. **Number of employees nationwide:** 400.

TURNER CORPORATION

375 Hudson Street, New York NY 10014. 212/229-6000. **Contact:** Human Resources. **World Wide Web address:** http://www.turnerconstruction.com. **Description:** A holding company involved in construction, general building, contract management, and real estate development. **Corporate headquarters location:** This location. **Subsidiaries include:** Turner Construction Company; Turner Medical Building Services.

WELSBACH ELECTRIC CORPORATION
P.O. Box 560252, 111-01 14th Avenue, College Point NY 11356-0252. 718/670-7900. **Contact:** Personnel. **World Wide Web address:** http://www.welsbachelectric.com. **Description:** An electrical contractor engaged in the installation and maintenance of streetlights and traffic signals. **Corporate headquarters location:** This location. **Parent company:** EMCOR Group, Inc. **Listed on:** New York Stock Exchange. **Stock exchange symbol:** EME. **President:** Fred Goodman.

North Carolina

APAC – ATLANTIC, INC.
P.O. Box 6939, Asheville NC 28816. 828/665-1180. **Physical address:** 1188 Smokey Park Highway, Candler NC 28715. **Fax:** 828/665-9345. **Contact:** Human Resources. **E-mail address:** aparecruiter@ashland.com. **World Wide Web address:** http://www.apac.com. **Description:** A division of APAC that produces asphalt for federal and state highways, and private and commercial projects. **Positions advertised include:** Marketing Representative. **Corporate headquarters location:** Atlanta GA. **Other area locations:** Statewide. **Other U.S. locations:** Nationwide. **Parent company:** APAC, a subsidiary of Ashland Inc.

FM GLOBAL
14120 Ballantyne Corporate Place, Suite 460, Charlotte NC 28277. 704/752-3080. **Contact:** Human Resources. **E-mail address:** jobs@fmglobal.com. **World Wide Web address:** http://www.fmglobal.com. **Description:** A loss control service organization. FM Global's primary objective is to help owner company policyholders protect their properties and occupancies from damage from fire, wind, flood, and explosion; from boiler, pressure vessel, and machinery accidents; and from many other insured hazards. To accomplish this objective, a wide range of engineering, research, and consulting services are provided, primarily in the field of loss control. **Special programs:** Internships; Co-ops. **Corporate headquarters location:** Johnston RI. **Other U.S. locations:** Nationwide. **International locations:** Worldwide. **Operations at this facility include:** Claims Office.

GREGORY POOLE EQUIPMENT COMPANY
4807 Beryl Road, Raleigh NC 27606. 919/828-0641. **Contact:** Human Resources. **E-mail address:** info@gregorypoole.com. **World Wide Web address:** http://www.gregorypoole.com. **Description:** Manufactures a range of material handling products, power system solutions, and provides construction contracting services. **Positions advertised include:** Rental Store Technician; Hydraulic Shop Tech; Construction Welder; Construction Technician; Construction Master; Technician/Field Service Technician; Construction Component Specialist. **Corporate headquarters location:** This location.

JOYCE ENGINEERING
2301 West Meadowview Road, Henderson Building, Suite 203, Greensboro NC 27407. 336/323-0092. **Fax:** 336/323-0093. **Contact:** Personnel. **E-mail address:** hrreg@joyceengineering.com. **World Wide Web Address:** http://www.joyceengineering.com. **Description:** Provides waste management consulting services. Specializes in providing engineering and environmental solutions. **Positions advertised include:** Geologist/Environmental Scientist. **Corporate headquarters location:** Richmond VA.

T. A. LOVING COMPANY CONSTRUCTION SERVICES
P.O. Drawer 919, Goldsboro NC 27533-0919. 919/734-8400. **Fax:** 919/580-9444. **Contact:** Paula V. Herring, Human Resources Director. **E-mail address:** pherring@taloving.com. **World Wide Web address:** http://www.taloving.com. **Description:** T.A. Loving Company provides complete construction and pre-construction services for the general building, utility and bridge/heavy trades. **Positions advertised include:** Project Manager; Superintendent; Estimator. **Number of employees nationwide:** 300.

OAKWOOD MOBILE HOMES
2518 West Preddy Boulevard, Greensboro NC 27407. 336/299-5611. **Toll-free phone:** 866/551-8175. **Contact:** Human Resources. **World Wide Web address:** http://www.oakwoodhomes.com. **Description:** Manufactures and sells prefabricated housing. **NOTE:** Send resumes to Clayton Homes, Inc., Human Resources, Box 9790, Maryville TN 37802. Fax: 865/380-3789. **Positions advertised include:** Collections Representative. **Special programs:** Internships. **Corporate headquarters location:** This location. **Other U.S. locations:** Nationwide. **Parent company:** Oakwood Homes Corporation. **Operations at this facility include:** Sales; Service. **Listed on:** New York Stock Exchange. **Stock exchange symbol:** OKWHQ.

PARSONS
4701 Hedgemore Drive, Charlotte NC 28209. 704/529-6246. **Fax:** 704/529-0374. **Contact:** Human Resources. **E-mail address:** employment.parsons@parsons.com. **World Wide Web address:** http://www.parsons.com. **Description:** Founded in 1944, Parsons is one of the largest 100% employee-owned engineering and construction companies in the United States. **Positions advertised include:** Project Manager, Senior Designer/Drafter, Engineering Manager, Engineer 6/ Modeler, Executive Administrative Assistant, Environmental Manager, Senior Transportation Planner, Traffic Engineer, Civil Design Engineer, Highway Engineer. **Other area locations:** Cary NC. **Other U.S. locations:** Nationwide. **International locations:** Worldwide. **Number of employees worldwide:** 9,000.

SPX CORPORATION
13515 Ballantyne Corporate Place, Charlotte NC 28277. 704/752-4400. **Fax:** 704/752-7511. **Contact:** Lee Covelli, Human Resources. **E-mail address:** lee.covelli@spx.com. **World Wide Web address:** http://www.spx.com. **Description:** The company operates in three segments: industrial products, building products, and engineering. The industrial products segment produces sanitary pumps for the food and industrial processing industries; submersible water and petroleum pumps; petroleum leak detection equipment; compacting equipment for soil, asphalt, and refuse applications; cooling towers for power generation, industrial, and heating and cooling applications; cast-iron boilers and electrical resistance heaters for industrial and residential customers; industrial machinery and process equipment; and aerospace components. The building products segment manufactures complementary products that encompass architectural metal roofing; side-hinged and rolling steel doors; residential garage doors; pre-engineered metal buildings; loading dock systems and related equipment; and wall, roof, floor, and window systems. It also provides general and specialized contractor services. The engineering segment is comprised of the Litwin companies, which provide worldwide engineering and construction services for the refining and petrochemical, polymers, specialty chemicals, and environmental control markets. Litwin also provides advanced process control and instrumentation capabilities. **NOTE:** Visit http://www.monster.com to search for jobs and apply online. **Corporate headquarters location:** This location. **International locations:** Worldwide. **Operations at this facility include:** Executive Offices. **Listed on:** New York

Stock Exchange. **Stock exchange symbol:** SPW. **Number of employees worldwide:** 22,000.

SOUTHERN INDUSTRIAL CONSTRUCTORS, INC.
6101 Triangle Drive, Raleigh NC 27617-4717. 919/782-4600. **Recorded jobline:** 888/874-2778, extension 4202. **Fax:** 919/782-2935. **Contact:** Human Resources. **World Wide Web address:** http://www.southernindustrial.com. **Description:** An industrial construction firm specializing in the installation of manufacturing processes and equipment. The company operates in 33 states. **Corporate headquarters location:** This location. **Other area locations:** Wilmington NC; Raleigh NC. **Other U.S. locations:** Columbia SC. **Listed on:** Privately held.

TURNER CONSTRUCTION COMPANY
5955 Carnegie Boulevard, Suite 125, Charlotte NC 28209. 704/554-1001. **Fax:** 704/554-5081. **Contact:** Human Resources. **World Wide Web address:** http://www.turnerconstruction.com. **Description:** Turner is a nationwide construction company founded in 1902. **Positions advertised include:** Assistant Engineer, Assistant Estimating Engineer. **Corporate headquarters location:** New York NY. **Other U.S. locations:** Nationwide.

UNDERWRITERS LABORATORIES
12 Laboratory Drive, P.O. Box 13995, Research Triangle Park NC 27709. 919/549-1400. **Fax:** 919/547-6000. **Contact:** Human Resources Director. **E-mail address:** rtpjobs@us.ul.com. **World Wide Web address:** http://www.ul.com. **Description:** An independent, nonprofit corporation established to help reduce or prevent bodily injury, loss of life, and property damage. The organization is engaged in the scientific investigation of various materials, devices, equipment, and construction methods and systems, and in the publication of standards, classifications, specifications, and other information. Underwriters Laboratories also provides a factory inspection service through offices located throughout the United States and in 54 other countries. **Other U.S. locations:** Nationwide. **International locations:** Worldwide. **Operations at this facility include:** Customer Service; Laboratory and Testing Facility. **Number of employees at this location:** 450. **Number of employees worldwide:** 4,000.

<u>North Dakota</u>
ABC SEAMLESS
3001 Fiechtner Drive, Fargo ND 58103. 701/293-5952. **Toll-free phone:** 800/732-6577. **Fax:** 701-293-3107. **Contact:** Don Jennings, General Manager. **E-mail address:** info@abcseamless.com. **World Wide Web address:** http://www.abcseamless.com. **Description:** Manufactures and installs siding, gutters, and replacement windows. **NOTE**: Apply on-line or call 800/732-6577. **Positions advertised include:** Siding and Gutter Installer; Sales Person; Appointment Coordinator. **Corporate headquarters location:** This location. **Other U.S. locations:** Nationwide.

CONCRETE, INC.
5000 DeMers Avenue, Grand Forks ND 58201. 701/772-6687. **Toll-free phone:** 800/732-4261. **Fax:** 701/772-4315. **Contact:** Gerlinde Olson, Human Resources Director. **E-mail address:** gerlinde@coninc.net. **World Wide Web address:** http://www.ciprecast.com. **Description:** Provides a wide range of concrete building services including submitting bids, designing diagrams, manufacturing concrete beams and building materials, and erecting beams. **Positions advertised include**: Receptionist; Secretary; Welder; Carpenter. **Corporate headquarters location:** This location. **Other U.S. locations:** SD; MN. **Parent company:** Wells Concrete Products Company. **Number of employees nationwide:** 150.

FARGO GLASS & PAINT COMPANY, INC.
P.O. Box 3107, Fargo ND 58108-3107. 701/235-4441. **Physical address:** 1801 7th Avenue North, Fargo ND 58102. **Contact:** Human Resources Department. **World Wide Web address**: www.fargoglass.com. **Description:** A wholesale paint, glass, millwork, and floor covering contracting firm.

INDUSTRIAL BUILDERS, INC.
P.O. Box 406, Fargo ND 58107. 701/282-4977. **Physical Address:** 1307 Country Road, 17 North, West Fargo, ND 58078. **Fax:** 701/281-1409. **Contact:** Human Resources Department. **E-mail address:** info@industrialbuilders.com. **World Wide Web address:** http://www.industrialbuilders.com. **Description:** A full-service general construction firm. **NOTE**: Apply online. **Corporate headquarters location:** This location. **President:** Paul W. Diederich.

<u>Ohio</u>
ALSIDE INC.
P.O. Box 2010, Akron OH 44309. 330/929-1811. **Physical address:** 3773 State Road, Cuyahoga Falls OH 44223. **Toll-free phone:** 800/922-6009. **Fax:** 330/922-2142. **Contact:** Human Resources. **World Wide Web address:** http://www.alside.com. **Description:** Manufactures vinyl building products including windows, siding, soffit, trim, and related accessories for the construction and consumer markets. Founded in 1947. **Other U.S. locations:** Nationwide.

ARMSTRONG AIR CONDITIONING, INC.
421 Monroe Street, Bellevue OH 44811-1789. 419/483-4840. **Contact:** Human Resources Director. **World Wide Web address:** http://www.aac-inc.com. **Description:** Manufactures and markets a variety of heating and cooling products including residential gas, oil and electric furnaces; split system cooling units; and heat pumps and package units. The company markets its products under the brand names Air-Ease, Armstrong Air, Concord, and Magic-Pak. **Parent company:** Lennox International Inc.

THE AUSTIN COMPANY
6095 Parkland Boulevard, Cleveland OH 44124. 440/544-2600. **Fax:** 440/544-2684. **Contact:** Human Resources. **E-mail address:** humanres@theaustin.com. **World Wide Web address:** http://www.theaustin.com. **Description:** An engineering, architectural design, and construction firm specializing in industrial, commercial, and government projects. The company markets its services to the air transportation, aerospace, banking, broadcasting, chemical processing, entertainment, food and beverage, general manufacturing, laboratory research and testing, metal processing, newspaper publishing, pharmaceuticals, and telecommunications industries. Founded in 1878. **Corporate headquarters location:** This location. **Other U.S. locations:** Nationwide. **International locations:** Australia; The Netherlands; United Kingdom. **Subsidiaries include:** The Austin Company of U.K. Ltd.; Ragnor Benson Inc. **Listed on:** Privately held. **President/CEO:** J. William Melsop. **Number of employees nationwide:** 610.

BURGESS & NIPLE, LTD.
5085 Reed Road, Columbus OH 43220. 614/459-2050. **Fax:** 614/459-9433. **Contact:** Brenda White, Human Resources. **E-mail address:** hr@burnip.com. **World Wide Web address:** http://www.burgessniple.com. **Description:** An engineering and architecture firm engaged in study, analysis, and design services. The company specializes in waterworks, wastewater, industrial services, hydropower, energy conservation, transportation, systems analysis, HVAC, and geotechnical. **Positions advertised include:** Architect; Civil Engineer; Transportation Engineer; Print Clerk; CADD Technician. **Corporate headquarters location:** This location. **Other area locations:** Akron OH; Cincinnati OH; Painesville OH. **Other U.S. locations:** Payson AZ; Phoenix AZ; Indianapolis IN; Lexington KY; Charleston WV; Parkersburg WV. **Operations at this facility include:** Administration; Divisional Headquarters. **Listed on:** Privately held. **Number of employees at this location:** 275. **Number of employees nationwide:** 480.

CONTECH CONSTRUCTION PRODUCTS INC.
1001 Grove Street, Middletown OH 45044. 513/425-5896. **Contact:** Human Resources. **E-mail address:** jobopportunities@contech-cpi.com. **World Wide Web address:** http://www.contech-cpi.com. **Description:** Contech Construction Products manufactures and markets steel, aluminum, geosynthetic, and plastic construction products for the civil construction market. The company's products are used in a variety of applications including general construction and infrastructure upgrading; airports, culverts, overpasses, railways, roads, stream enclosures, and earth retaining walls; bridge replacement and rehabilitation; and site development, storm water management, soil stabilization, and erosion control. **Corporate headquarters location:** This location. **Other area locations:** Akron OH; Cincinnati OH; Cleveland OH; Columbus OH; Port Clinton OH. **Other U.S. locations:** Nationwide. **Listed on:** Privately held.

CRANE PERFORMACE SIDING
1441 Universal Road, P.O. Box 1058, Columbus OH 43216. 614/443-4841. **Toll-free phone:** 800/366-8472. **Fax:** 800/733-8469. **Contact:** Human Resources. **World Wide Web address:** http://www.vinyl-siding.com. **Description:** Develops, manufactures, and distributes, exterior vinyl siding. Founded in 1947. **Parent company:** Crane Plastics.

DANIS INDUSTRIES CORPORATION
2 River Place, Suite 100, Dayton OH 45405. 937/228-1225. **Fax:** 937/228-0535. **Contact:** Marvin Goldschmidt, Human Resources. **E-mail address:** mgoldschmidt@danis.com. **World Wide Web address:** http://www.danis.com. **Description:** A building construction corporation. Danis Industries Corporation specializes solely in the development and construction of water and wastewater treatment facilities nationwide. Founded in 1916. **Corporate headquarters location:** This location. **Other U.S. locations:** Denver CO; Orlando FL; Columbia MD.

DAVEY TREE EXPERT COMPANY
P.O. Box 5193, 1500 North Mantua Street, Kent OH 44240. 330/673-9511. **Toll-free phone:** 800/445-8733. **Fax:** 330/673-1037. **Contact:** Joseph Gregory (Field openings) jgregory@davey.com and Greg Mazur (Office) gmazur@davey.com. **World Wide Web address:** http://www.davey.com. **Description:** Provides grounds maintenance; tree, shrub, and lawn care; vegetation management; and consulting services nationwide. The Davey Tree Expert Company serves the commercial, residential, and utilities markets. Founded in 1880. **NOTE:** Applications and inquiries can be made on-line using the URL listed above. **Positions advertised include:** Landscape Entomologist; Maintenance Mechanic. **Special programs:** Internships. **Corporate headquarters location:** This location. **Other area locations:** Cleveland OH; Eastlake OH; Mansfield OH; North Royalton OH; Richfield OH; Solon OH.

DOMINION HOMES
5501 Frantz Road, P.O. Box 7166, Dublin OH 43017-0766. 614/761-6000. **Fax:** 614/356-6010. **Contact:** Human Resources. **E-mail address:** careers@dominionhomes.com. **World Wide Web address:** http://www.dominionhomes.com. **Description:** A builder of single-family homes in central Ohio. The company offers two distinct product lines of homes and condominiums.

FM GLOBAL
25050 Country Club Boulevard, Suite 400, North Olmsted OH 44070. 216/362-4820. **Fax:** 216/898-4651. **Contact:** Human Resources. **E-mail address:** jobs@fmglobal.com. **World Wide Web address:** http://www.fmglobal.com. **Description:** A commercial and industrial property management and risk services organization. The company helps policyholders to protect their properties and occupancies from fire, wind, flood, and explosion; boiler, pressure vessel, and machinery accidents; and many other insured hazards. **Corporate headquarters location:** Johnston RI. **Other U.S. locations:** Nationwide. **International locations:** Worldwide.

GREAT LAKES WINDOW CORPORATION
30499 Tracy Road, P.O. Box 1896, Toledo OH 43603. 419/666-5555. **Toll-free phone:** 800/666-0000. **Fax:** 419/661-2926. **Contact:** Human Resources Department. **World Wide Web address:** http://www.greatlakeswindow.com. **Description:** Designs, develops, manufactures, and markets vinyl windows and doors. The company's products include bay and bow windows; casement, awning, and French casement windows; double-hung windows; two- and three-section sliding windows; traditional and specialty garden windows; and sliding and hinged patio doors. **President and CEO:** Mark Watson.

INNOVATIVE TECHNOLOGIES CORPORATION (ITC)
1020 Woodman Drive, Dayton OH 45432-1410. 937/252-2145. **Toll-free phone:** 800/745-8050. **Fax:** 937/254-6853. **Contact:** Judy Conn, Human Resources. **E-mail address:** connj@itc-1.com. **World Wide Web address:** http://www.itc-1.com. **Description:** A general contractor and engineering services firm. The company specializes in defense contracting. Founded in 1987. **Corporate headquarters location:** This location. **Other U.S. locations:** FL; GA; UT.

JACOBS ENGINEERING
1880 Waycross Road, P.O. Box 465600, Cincinnati OH 45240. 513/595-7500. **Fax:** 513/595-7860. **Contact:** Human Resources. **World Wide Web address:** http://www.jacobs.com. **Description:** One of the largest engineering and construction companies in the United States. Jacobs provides engineering, procurement, construction, and maintenance services to selected clients and industries. These industries include chemicals and polymers, federal programs, pulp and paper, semiconductor, petroleum refining, facilities and transportation, food and consumer products, pharmaceuticals and biotechnologies, and basic resources. **Corporate headquarters location:** Pasadena CA. **Other U.S. locations:** Nationwide. **International locations:** Worldwide. **Listed on:** New York Stock Exchange. **Stock exchange symbol:** JEC.

THE KASSOUF COMPANY
9715 Clinton Road, Cleveland OH 44144. 216/651-3333. **Fax:** 216/651-3839. **Contact:** Edward J. Kassouf, President. **World Wide Web address:** http://www.kassouftunnel.com. **Description:** A contractor specializing in sewers, waterlines, and other underground infrastructures.

KIRK & BLUM MANUFACTURING COMPANY
3120 Forrer Street, Cincinnati OH 45209. 513/458-2600. **Toll-free phone:** 800/333-5475. **Fax:** 513/351-5475. **Contact:** Personnel Director. **World Wide Web address:** http://www.kirkblum.com. **Description:** Manufactures ventilation equipment. **Corporate headquarters location:** This location. **Other area locations:** Defiance OH. **Other U.S. locations:** IN; KY; NC; TN.

KOKOSING CONSTRUCTION COMPANY INC.
P.O. Box 226, Fredericktown OH 43019-9159. 740/694-6315. **Physical address:** 16402 Village Parkway, Fredericktown OH 43019-9159. **Fax:** 740/694-1481. **Contact:** Human Resources. **World Wide Web address:** http://www.kokosing-inc.com. **Description:** A general contracting firm engaged in engineering, manufacturing, and construction. **Special programs:** Internships; Co-ops. **Corporate headquarters location:** This location.

KRAFTMAID CABINETRY, INC.
P.O. Box 1055, Middlefield OH 44062. 440/632-1833. **Physical address:** 15535 South State Street, Middlefield OH 44062. **Fax:** 440/632-0032. **Contact:** Chris Allen, Human Resources. **World Wide Web address:** http://www.kraftmaid.com. **Description:** A cabinet manufacturer. Founded in 1969. **Parent**

company: MASCO. **Number of employees nationwide:** 3,000.

MANUFACTURED HOUSING ENTERPRISES, INC.
09302 U.S. Route 6, Bryan OH 43506. 419/636-4511. **Toll-free phone:** 800/821-0220. **Fax:** 419/636-6521. **Contact:** Hal Kinder, Human Resources Manager. **E-mail address:** mhe@bright.net. **World Wide Web address:** http://www.mheinc.com. **Description:** Manufactures mobile and modular homes. The company also provides the chassis and components for its homes including cabinets, countertops, carpeting, and a variety of custom options. **Corporate headquarters location:** This location. **Operations at this facility include:** Administration; Manufacturing; Research and Development; Sales; Service.

MODERN TECHNOLOGIES CORPORATION
4032 Linden Avenue, Dayton OH 45432. 937/252-9199. **Contact:** Human Resources Department. **E-mail address:** hr@modtechcorp.com. **World Wide Web address:** http://www.modtechcorp.com. **Description:** Provides engineering, system support, and management solutions and services to engineering, manufacturing, technical, and government industries. **Positions advertised include:** Lead Analyst; Associate Analyst; Financial Analyst; Accountant; Program Manager. **Corporate headquarters location:** This location. **Other area locations:** Cincinnati OH; Cleveland OH; Columbus OH. **Other U.S. locations:** Nationwide. **International locations:** Worldwide. **Subsidiaries include:** Composite Technologies Corporation. **Parent company:** MTC Technologies, Inc. **Operations at this facility include:** Administration; Divisional Headquarters; Manufacturing; Regional Headquarters; Research and Development. **Listed on:** Privately held.

THE MOSSER GROUP
122 South Wilson Avenue, Fremont OH 43420. 419/334-3801. **Contact:** Human Resources. **E-mail address:** humanresources@mossergrp.com. **World Wide Web address:** http://www.mossergrp.com. **Description:** A general construction and design firm. The Mosser Group specializes in masonry, pre-engineered steel buildings, pre-cast concrete construction, renovations, and tilt-up concrete construction. Founded in 1948. **Special programs:** Internships. **Corporate headquarters location:** This location. **Other U.S. locations:** Toledo OH.

NELSON STUD WELDING
P.O. Box 4019, Elyria OH 44036-2019. 440/329-0400. **Physical address:** 7900 West Ridge Road, Elyria OH 44036-2019. **Contact:** Human Resources. **World Wide Web address:** http://www.nelsonstud.com. **Description:** Produces standard and automatic stud welding systems and related stud fasteners for the construction, metal-working, and transportation industries; and cold-formed parts and specialized handling equipment.

NESCO INC.
6140 Parkland Boulevard, Suite 110, Mayfield Heights OH 44124. 440/461-6000. **Fax:** 440/449-3111. **Contact:** Human Resources. **E-mail address:** hq@nescoinc.com. **World Wide Web address:** http://www.nescoinc.com. **Description:** A holding company that operates through three primary groups. The Industrial Group builds process automation and material handling systems. The Service Group specializes in engineering, design, in-house drafting, and documentation. The Real Estate Group owns and manages a variety of commercial and residential buildings. Founded in 1956. **Corporate headquarters location:** This location. **Other area locations:** Akron OH; Dayton OH; Lorain OH; Middleburg Heights; Parma OH. **Operations at this facility include:** Administration. **Number of employees at this location:** 4,000.

ROPPE CORPORATION
1602 North Union Street, P.O. Box 1158, Fostoria OH 44830. 419/435-8546. **Toll-free phone:** 800/537-9527. **Fax:** 419/435-1056. **Contact:** Personnel. **E-mail address:** hr@roppe.com. **World Wide Web address:** http://www.roppe.com. **Description:** A leading manufacturer of rubber and vinyl flooring products.

RUDOLPH/LIBBE, INC.
6494 Latcha Road, Walbridge OH 43465-9738. 419/241-5000. **Fax:** 419/837-9373. **Contact:** Human Resources. **World Wide Web address:** http://www.rlcos.com. **Description:** A general contractor and construction management firm. **Corporate headquarters location:** This location.

STARK TRUSS COMPANY, INC.
109 Miles Avenue SW, Canton OH 44710. 330/478-2100. **Toll-free phone:** 800/933-2258. **Contact:** Human Resources. **World Wide Web address:** http://www.starktruss.com. **Description:** Manufactures wood, floor, and roof trusses that are used in the construction of buildings and houses. **Other area locations:** Washington Courthouse OH; Marysville OH; Edgerton OH; Beach City OH; Champion OH; New Philadelphia OH. **Other U.S. locations:** IN; KS; MO; KY; SC; TX.

TURNER CONSTRUCTION
1422 Euclid Avenue, Cleveland OH 44115. 216/522-1180. **Contact:** Human Resources. **World Wide Web address:** http://www.turnerconstruction.com. **Description:** An international general contracting and construction management firm. Founded in 1902. **Corporate headquarters location:** New York NY.

URS GREINER
277 West Nationwide Boulevard, Columbus OH 43215-2566. 614/464-4500. **Contact:** Human Resources. **World Wide Web address:** http://www.urscorp.com. **Description:** An architectural, engineering, and planning consulting firm specializing in health care, corrections facilities, colleges/universities, commercial businesses, water/wastewater facilities, and surface transportation. **Positions advertised include:** Principal Architect. **Special programs:** Internships. **Corporate headquarters location:** San Francisco CA. **Other area locations:** Akron OH; Cincinnati OH; Cleveland OH. **Other U.S. locations:** Nationwide. **International locations:** Worldwide. **Parent company:** URS Corporation. **Listed on:** New York Stock Exchange. **Stock exchange symbol:** URS.

USG INTERIORS, INC.
1000 Crocker Road, Westlake OH 44145-1031. 440/871-1000. **Contact:** Human Resources. **World Wide Web address:** http://www.usg.com. **Description:** Manufactures interior construction products including flooring, ceiling grids, room dividers, and wall paneling. **Corporate headquarters location:** Chicago IL.

UNITED McGILL CORPORATION
One Mission Park, Groveport OH 43125. 614/836-9981. **Fax:** 614/836-9843. **Contact:** Celeste Palanondon, Personnel Services Director. **E-mail address:** personnel@unitedmcgill.com. **World Wide Web address:** http://www.unitedmcgill.com. **Description:** An engineering, manufacturing, and construction firm. Products include spiral and rectangular ducts and fittings for HVAC, acoustical equipment, vacuum drying systems, pressure vessels, and air pollution control systems. Founded in 1951. **NOTE:** Entry-level positions are offered. **Subsidiaries include:** McGill AirClean Corporation; McGill AirFlow Corporation; McGill AirPressure Corporation; McGill AirSeal Corporation. **Special programs:** Training. **Corporate headquarters location:** This location. **Other area locations:** Columbus OH; Broadview Heights OH; West Chester OH; Westerville OH. **Other U.S. locations:** Nationwide. **Listed on:** Privately held. **Annual sales/revenues:** $51 - $100 million. **Number of employees nationwide:** 600.

WASHINGTON GROUP INTERNATIONAL
1500 West Third Street, Cleveland OH 44113. 216/523-5600. **Fax:** 216/523-5922. **Contact:** Human Resources.

World Wide Web address: http://www.wgint.com. **Description:** An engineering and construction firm operating through five major divisions: Government, Industrial/Process, Infrastructure & Mining, Petroleum & Chemicals, and Power. Washington Group International offers construction, engineering, and program-management services to the environmental, industrial, mining, nuclear-services, power, transportation, and water resources industries. **Corporate headquarters location:** Boise ID. **Other U.S. locations:** Nationwide. **International locations:** Worldwide. **Number of employees worldwide:** 26,000.

WAXMAN INDUSTRIES, INC.
24460 Aurora Road, Bedford Heights OH 44146. 440/439-1830. **Fax:** 440/439-8678. **Contact:** Personnel. **World Wide Web address:** http://www.waxmanind.com. **Description:** A holding company that supplies plumbing hardware, and floor and surface protection products to the repair and remodeling markets. Waxman Industries, Inc. operates through six divisions: Medal of Pennsylvania, Inc. distributes construction hardware products to independent retailers; WAMI Sales distributes pipe nipples, fittings, valves and related plumbing products to industrial distributors; Waxman Consumer Products Group, Inc. distributes floor, plumbing, and surface protection products to retailers; and CWI, The Orient Group, and TWI are the company's foreign operating divisions that manufacture and package products for distribution. Founded in 1934. **Corporate headquarters location:** This location.

WELDED CONSTRUCTION COMPANY
P.O. Box 470, Perrysburg OH 43552-0470. 419/874-3548. **Physical address:** 26933 Eckel Road, Perrysburg OH 43551. **Fax:** 419/874-4883. **Contact:** Alexandra Shroyer. **E-mail address:** ashroyer@welded.com. **World Wide Web address:** http://www.welded-construction.com. **Description:** A construction company that specializes in the manufacture and installation of pipeline for the natural gas, oil and product pipeline markets. In addition to mainline construction, Welded Construction Company also provides compressor station installation, emergency repair, meter station installation, testing and rehabilitation, and valve replacement.

Oklahoma

AAON, INC.
2425 South Yukon Avenue, Tulsa OK 74107. 918/583-2266. **Fax:** 918/583-6094. **Contact:** Human Resources. **E-mail address:** aaonhr1@aaon.com. **World Wide Web address:** http://www.aaonnet.com. **Description:** Engineers, manufactures, and markets rooftop heating, air-conditioning, and heat recovery equipment. **Corporate headquarters location:** This location. **Other U.S. locations:** Longview TX. **International location:** Burlington Ontario, Canada. **Listed on:** NASDAQ. **Stock exchange symbol:** AAON. **Sales/Revenues:** Approximately $41.7 million.

ARINC
6400 SE 59th Street, Oklahoma City OK 73135. 405/601-6000. **Fax:** 405/601-6041. **Contact:** Sophia Jones, Recruiter. **World Wide Web address:** http://www.arinc.com. **Description:** An engineering and management consulting firm that provides technical studies, analyses, and evaluations of aircraft and ship systems, as well as communication and information systems. Customers of ARINC include the Department of Defense, the Department of Energy, the Department of Transportation, and the Federal Aviation Administration. **NOTE:** ARINC prefers that applications be submitted online. **Positions advertised include:** Avionics Technician; Senior Electrical Engineer; Surveillance Systems Engineer; Project/Radiographic Testing Engineer; Senior Mechanical Engineer; Senior Staff Analyst. **Special programs:** Educational Assistance Program; Training; Internships; Co-ops. **Corporate headquarters location:** Annapolis MD. **Other U.S. locations:** Nationwide. **International locations:** Worldwide. **Sales/Revenue:** $734 million. **Number of employees at this location:** 85. **Number of employees worldwide:** 3,000.

MATRIX SERVICE COMPANY
10701 East Ute Street, Tulsa OK 74116. 918/838-8822, extension 239. **Contact:** Melissa Harvey, Recruiter. **World Wide Web address:** http://www.matrixservice.com. **Description:** Provides specialized on-site maintenance and construction services for petroleum refineries, pipelines, chemical plants, and storage facilities. **Positions advertised include:** Receptionist; Drafter; Drafting Squad Leader. **Special programs:** Training; Tuition Reimbursement; Professional Development Program. **Corporate headquarters location:** This location. **Other area locations:** Catoosa OK. **Other U.S. locations:** Nationwide. **International locations:** Sarnia Ontario, Canada. **Listed on:** NASDAQ. **Stock exchange symbol:** MTRX. **Sales/revenue:** $126.8 million. **Number of employees at this location:** 830. **Number of employees worldwide:** 3,313.

Oregon

ASCENTRON
994 Antelope Road, White City OR 97503. 541/826-2405. **Fax:** 541/826-1205. **Contact:** Human Resources. **E-mail address:** employment@ascentron.com. **World Wide Web address:** http://www.ascentron.com. **Description:** Assembles electro-mechanical products on a contract basis. Founded in 1982. **Positions advertised include:** Controller. **Office hours:** Monday - Friday, 8:00 a.m. - 5:00 p.m. **Corporate headquarters location:** This location.

BLACK & VEATCH
4800 Meadows Road, Suite 200, Lake Oswego OR 97035. 503/699-7556. **Fax:** 503/697-3699. **Contact:** Human Resources. **World Wide Web address:** http://www.bv.com. **Description:** Black & Veatch is an environmental/civil engineering and construction firm serving utilities, commerce, and government agencies in more than 40 countries worldwide. Black & Veatch provides a broad range of study, design, construction management, and turnkey capabilities to clients in the water and wastewater fields. The firm is one of the leading authorities on drinking water treatment through the use of activated carbon, ozone, and other state-of-the-art processes. Black & Veatch is also engaged in wastewater treatment work including reclamation and reuse projects and the beneficial use of wastewater residuals. Other services are provided for solid waste recycling and disposal, transportation, and storm water management. In the energy field, Black & Veatch is a leader in providing engineering procurement and construction for electric power plants. The firm's areas of expertise include coal-fueled plants, simple and combined-cycle combustion turbines, fluidized bed combustion, waste-to-energy facilities, hydroelectric plants, and cogeneration facilities. Black & Veatch's capabilities also include nuclear power projects, advanced technology, air quality control, performance monitoring, plant life management, and facilities modification. In addition, Black & Veatch operates in the transmission and distribution field. In the industrial sector, Black & Veatch focuses on projects involving cleanrooms, industrial processes and planning, utility systems, and cogeneration. In addition to engineering, procurement, and construction, Black & Veatch offers a variety of management and financial services including institutional strengthening, privatization, strategic financial planning, and information management. **Corporate headquarters location:** Overland Park KS. **Operations at this facility include:** This location operates a division engaged in electrical engineering and a division engaged in environmental engineering and wastewater treatment.

CH2M HILL, INC.
P.O. Box 428, Corvallis OR 97339. 541/752-4271. **Physical address:** 2300 NW Walnut Boulevard, Corvallis OR 97330. **Contact:** Human Resources. **World Wide Web address:** http://www.ch2m.com. **Description:** Provides planning, engineering design,

and operation and construction management services to help clients apply technology, safeguard the environment, and develop infrastructure. The professional staff includes specialists in environmental engineering and waste management, water management, transportation, industrial facilities, and a broad spectrum of infrastructure systems. The company operates through three business groups: Energy, Environment, and Systems; Transportation; and Water. Founded in 1946. **Positions advertised include:** Facilities Operations Manager; Project Delivery Leader; Risk Assessor. **Corporate headquarters location:** Greenwood Village CO.

CHAMPION HOMES, INC.
1204 Mill Street, Silverton OR 97381. 503/873-6381. **Contact:** Human Resources Department. **World Wide Web address:** http://www.championoregon.com. **Description:** The Northwest division of one of the largest advanced-design homebuilders in the world. Founded in 1937. **Listed on:** New York Stock Exchange. **Stock exchange symbol:** CHB.

CLARK'S QUALITY ROOFING
4709 NE 148th Avenue, #2, Portland OR 97230. 503/257-7800. **Fax:** 503/257-7806. **Contact:** Troy Fallon, Human Resources. **E-mail address:** info@cqrinc.com. **World Wide Web address:** http://www.cqrinc.com. **Description:** Clark's Quality Roofing specializes in commercial membrane roofing installations. Their professional services include waterproofing, maintenance and repairs, metal roofing installations and sheet metal specialty fabrication. They are certified by leading roof manufacturers to install a wide variety of systems. **Positions advertised include:** Roofer; Foreman; Repair Technician. **Corporate headquarters location:** Salt Lake City UT.

FEI COMPANY
5350 NE Dawson Creek Road, Hillsboro OR 97124-5830. 503/640-7500. **Contact:** Human Resources. **World Wide Web address:** http://www.feic.com. **Description:** FEI Company is a leader in the design, manufacture, and sale of focused ion beam workstations and components based on field emission technology. Founded in 1971. **Listed on:** NASDAQ. **Stock exchange symbol:** FEIC.

FLEETWOOD HOMES OF OREGON
2655 Progress Way, P.O. Box 628, Woodburn OR 97071-0628. 503/981-3136. **Contact:** Personnel. **World Wide Web address:** http://www.fleetwoodhomes.com. **Description:** Manufactures factory-crafted residential homes.

HOFFMAN CORPORATION
805 SW Broadway, Suite 2100, Portland OR 97205. 503/221-8811. **Contact:** Personnel. **E-mail address:** sheri-sundstrom@hoffmancorp.com. **World Wide Web address:** http://www.hoffmancorp.com. **Description:** A full-service commercial and industrial construction company. Founded in 1922. **Positions advertised include:** Electrical Cost Engineer/Estimator, Mechanical Cost Control/Estimator, Project Accountant, Project Scheduler. **Corporate headquarters location:** This location.

MALARKEY ROOFING COMPANY
3131 N Columbia Boulevard, P.O. Box 17217, Portland OR 97217. 503/283-1191. **Contact:** Human Resources. **World Wide Web address:** http://www.malarkey-rfg.com. **Description:** Manufactures roofing products for both residential and commercial use.

MARLETTE HOMES, INC.
400 W Elm Avenue, P.O. Box 910, Hermiston OR 97838. 541/567-5546. **Toll-free phone:** 800/547-2444. **Fax:** 541/567-7851. **Contact:** General Manager. **World Wide Web address:** http://www.marlettehomes.com. **Description:** A manufacturer of homes. Founded in 1953. **NOTE:** This office only accepts resumes for office workers and sales representatives. All production and factory workers are hired through the Oregon State Employment Office. **Other U.S. locations:** Middlebury IN. **Parent company:** Schult Homes Corporation.

PSC, INC.
959 Terry Street, Eugene OR 97402-9150. 541/683-5700. **Toll-free phone**: 800/695-5700. **Fax:** 541/345-7140. **Contact:** Human Resources. **World Wide Web address:** http://www.pscnet.com. **Description:** Develops, manufactures, and markets bar code reading products including fixed-station decoders and portable data terminals, for the automatic identification and data collection market. The company also markets bar code input devices manufactured by others for use with the company's fixed-station decoders and portable data terminals. The company's products are used principally in point-of-sale and point-of-service applications in a wide variety of industries including retail, education, manufacturing, health care, and package delivery. **Positions advertised include:** Customer Account Specialist; Electric Engineer; Mechanical Engineer.

SKYLINE HOMES
550 Booth Bend Road, McMinnville OR 97128. 503/472-3181. **Fax:** 503/472-6463. **Contact:** Human Resources. **E-mail address:** hresources@skylinecorp.com. **World Wide Web address:** http://www.skylinecorp.com. **Description:** Manufactures prefabricated homes. **NOTE:** Human Resources address: P.O. Box 743, Elkhart IN 46515-0743. **Positions advertised include:** Production Worker. **Corporate headquarters location:** Elkhart IN. **Parent company:** Skyline. **Number of employees at this location:** 200.

SWANSON GROUP
2635 Old Highway 99 South, Roseburg OR 97470. 541/492-1103. **Contact:** Human Resources. **E-mail address:** john@sunstuds.com. **World Wide Web address:** http://www.swansongroupinc.com. **Description:** A sawmill specializing in studs and related products for the construction industry.

TURNER CONSTRUCTION COMPANY
1650 NW Naito Parkway, Suite 160, Portland OR 97209. 503/226-9825. **Fax:** 503/226-9836. **Contact:** Human Resources. **World Wide Web address:** http://www.turnerconstruction.com. **Description:** Turner is a nationwide construction company founded in 1902. **Positions advertised include:** Assistant Engineer; Assistant Estimating Engineer. **Corporate Headquarters location:** 375 Hudson Street, New York NY 10014. **Chairman and CEO:** Thomas C. Leppert.

Pennsylvania

ACME MANUFACTURING COMPANY
7601 State Road, Philadelphia PA 19136. 215/338-2850. **Contact:** General Manager. **E-mail address:** merrimanc@acmemfg.com. **World Wide Web address:** http://www.acmemfg.com. **Description:** Manufactures sheet metal products including heating and air conditioning equipment. **Corporate headquarters location:** Auburn Hills MI.

ALLEN-SHERMAN-HOFF
P.O. Box 3006, 185 Great Valley Parkway, Malvern PA 19355-1321. 610/647-9900. **Fax:** 610/648-8724. **Contact:** Human Resources. **World Wide Web address:** http://www.diamondpower.com. **Description:** Engaged in the design engineering of material handling systems for power plants and industrial applications.

AMERICAN INFRASTRUCTURE
1805 Berks Road, P.O. Box 1340, Worcester PA 19490. 610/222-8800. **Fax:** 610/222-4800. **Contact:** Human Resources. **E-mail address:** careers@airecruiting.com. **World Wide Web address:** http://www.americaninfrastructure.com. **Description:** A heavy civil construction company and materials supplier. **Positions advertised include:** Estimator; Field Manager; Project Engineer; Project Manager; Superintendent.

MICHAEL BAKER CORPORATION
P.O. 12259, Pittsburgh PA 15231. 412/269-6300. **Toll-free phone:** 800/642-2537. **Fax:** 412/375-3980. **Physical address:** Airside Business Park, 100 Airside Drive, Moon Township PA 15108. **Contact:** Human Resources. **World Wide Web address:** http://www.mbakercorp.com. **Description:** An architectural and engineering firm that provides engineering, management, and operations services to the construction, energy, environmental, and transportation markets. **Positions advertised include:** Architect; Civil Associate; Civil Engineer; Construction Specialist; Geotechnical Engineer; Design Associate. **Corporate headquarters location:** This location. **Other area locations:** Coraopolis; Philadelphia; Beaver; Harrisburg; Horsham; Gibsonia. **Other U.S. locations:** Nationwide.

BERGER BROTHERS
805 Pennsylvania Boulevard, Feasterville PA 19053. 215/355-1200. **Toll-free phone:** 800/523-8852. **Fax:** 215/355-0913. **Contact:** Nicole Gartzke, Human Resources. **E-mail address:** nicoleg@bergerbros.com. **World Wide Web address:** http://www.bergerbros.com. **Description:** Manufactures roofing and drainage systems. Founded in 1874. **Number of employees at this location:** 250.

BUCHART-HORN, INC. & BASCO ASSOCIATES
The Industrial Plaza of York, 445 West Philadelphia Street, York PA 17401-3383. 717/852-1400. **Toll-free phone:** 800/274-2224. **Fax:** 717/852-1401. **Contact:** Human Resources. **World Wide Web address:** http://www.bh-ba.com. **Description:** Provides consulting, engineering, environmental, project management, administrative, training and architectural services to Federal, municipal, institutional and industrial clients throughout the United States and Europe. **Positions advertised include:** Airport Design Engineer; Director of Aviation Services; Environmental Manager; Sr. Environmental Engineer; Vice President, Federal Program Operations.

BUCKLEY & COMPANY, INC.
3401 Moore Street, Philadelphia PA 19145. 215/334-7500. **Contact:** Joseph Martosella, Vice President. **Description:** A heavy construction firm specializing in highways, bridges, tunnels, and other large-scale construction projects.

CANNON SLINE
Airport Industrial Complex, 10 Industrial Highway, MS 38, Lester PA 19113. 610/521-2100. **Fax:** 610/521-2101. **Contact:** Human Resources. **World Wide Web address:** http://www.cannonsline.com. **Description:** Provides painting, coating, and related services to industrial and commercial clients.

CARLISLE SYNTEC INCORPORATED
1285 Ritner Highway, P.O. Box 7000, Carlisle PA 17013. 717/245-7000. **Toll-free phone:** 800/4-SYNTEC. **Fax:** 717/245-7285. **Contact:** Human Resources Manager. **World Wide Web address:** http://www.carlislesyntec.com. **Description:** Manufactures elastomeric roofing membrane and related building products for the commercial roofing market. **Positions advertised include:** Insulation Product Manager; Software Development Specialist; Industrial Engineer; Mechanical Engineer. **Corporate headquarters location:** Syracuse NY. **Parent company:** Carlisle Companies Inc. **Operations at this facility include:** Divisional Headquarters; Manufacturing; Research and Development; Sales. **Listed on:** New York Stock Exchange. **Stock exchange symbol:** CSL. **Number of employees at this location:** 400. **Number of employees nationwide:** 1,040.

CERTAINTEED CORPORATION
750 East Swedesford Road, P.O. Box 860, Valley Forge PA 19482. 610/341-7000. **Toll-free phone:** 800/233-8990. **Fax:** 610/341-7784. **Contact:** Ms. Kathyrn Ferrante, Human Resources Director. **E-mail address:** ctrecruitment@saint-gobain.com. **World Wide Web address:** http://www.certainteed.com. **Description:** Certainteed Corporation manufactures and distributes building materials, fiberglass products, and piping products. Principal products are used in residential, commercial, and industrial construction; repair and remodeling; fiberglass reinforcement applications; water and sewer systems; and other underground utility systems. Other products include roofing, acoustical insulation, fiberglass thermal insulation, air handling products, glass fiber, vinyl siding, and PVC piping. **Positions advertised include:** Credit Services Analyst; Director of Engineering and Maintenance; Marketing Communications Manager; Materials Manager; Pricing and Data Control Specialist; **Corporate headquarters location:** This location. **Other U.S. locations:** Nationwide. **Parent company:** Saint-Gobain. **Operations at this facility include:** Administration. **Number of employees at this location:** 450. **Number of employees nationwide:** 8,000.

CONESTOGA WOOD SPECIALTIES, INC.
P.O. Box 158, East Earl PA 17519. 717/445-6701. **Physical address:** 245 Reading Road, East Earl PA 17519. **Fax:** 717/445-3428. **Contact:** Recruiter. **World Wide Web address:** http://www.conestogawood.com. **Description:** Manufactures and supplies wood products including panel doors, components, and moldings to the construction industry. **NOTE:** Current openings are listed on http://www.careerbuilder.com. **Special programs:** Internships. **Corporate headquarters location:** This location. **Other U.S. locations:** Jacksonville AR; Darlington MD; Kenly NC; Kramer PA. **Operations at this facility include:** Administration; Divisional Headquarters; Manufacturing; Sales; Service. **Listed on:** Privately held. **Number of employees at this location:** 675. **Number of employees nationwide:** 1,500.

DICK CORPORATION
P.O. Box 10896, Pittsburgh PA 15236. 412/384-1000. **Fax:** 412/384-1424. **Contact:** Vicki Senko, Human Resources Administrator. **E-mail address:** jobs@dickcorp.com. **World Wide Web address:** http://www.dickcorp.com. **Description:** A general construction and construction management corporation. **Positions advertised include:** Project Engineer; System Engineer; Regional Safety Manager.

EXPONENT, INC.
3401 Market Street, Suite 300, Philadelphia PA 19104. 215/594-8800. **Fax:** 215/594-8899. **Contact:** Human Resources. **E-mail address:** hr@exponent.com. **World Wide Web address:** http://www.exponent.com. **Description:** A technical consulting firm dedicated to the investigation, analysis, and prevention of accidents and failures of an engineering or scientific nature. The company provides a multidisciplinary approach to analyze how failures occur. The company specializes in accident reconstruction, biomechanics, construction/structural engineering, aviation and marine investigations, environmental assessment, materials and product testing, warning and labeling issues, accident statistical data analysis, and risk prevention/mitigation. Founded in 1967. **NOTE:** Search and apply for positions online. **Positions advertised include:** Managing Engineer, Biomechanics; RN, Biomechanics; Sr. Engineer. **Corporate headquarters location:** Menlo Park CA. **Listed on:** NASDAQ. **Stock exchange symbol:** EXPO.

FM GLOBAL
101 Lindenwood Drive, Suite 200, Malvern PA 19355. 610/296-3100. **Fax:** 610/993-0892. **Contact:** Human Resources. **World Wide Web address:** http://www.fmglobal.com. **Description:** A loss control services organization. The primary objective of FM Global is to help owner company policyholders to protect their properties and occupancies from damage due to fire, wind, flood, and explosion; boiler, pressure vessel, and machinery accidents; and many other insured hazards. **NOTE:** Resumes for unsolicited positions are not considered. **Corporate headquarters**

location: Johnston RI. **Other U.S. locations:** Nationwide. **International locations:** Worldwide.

FRANCIS, CAUFFMAN, FOLEY, AND HOFFMAN
2120 Arch Street, Philadelphia PA 19103. 215/568-8250. **Fax:** 215/568-2639. **Contact:** Tom Gavin, Director of Human Resources. **E-mail address:** tgavin@fcfh-did.com. **World Wide Web address:** http://www.fcfh-did.com. **Description:** A full-service architectural firm serving the communications, health care, pharmaceutical, and corporate markets. Founded in 1954. **Positions advertised include:** Communications Director; Business development; Healthcare Planner; Project Manager; Project Architect; R&D Architect; Staff Architect. **Other U.S. locations:** Syracuse NY; Baltimore MD.

FUELLGRAF ELECTRIC COMPANY
600 South Washington Street, Butler PA 16001. 724/282-4800. **Fax:** 724/282-1926. **Contact:** Human Resources. **E-mail address:** feco@fuellgraf.com. **World Wide Web address:** http://www.fuellgraf.com. **Description:** An electrical construction and engineering firm. Founded in 1946. **NOTE:** Entry-level positions are offered. **Office hours:** Monday - Friday, 7:00 a.m. - 5:00 p.m. **Corporate headquarters location:** This location. **Other U.S. locations:** Williamsport PA. **Operations at this facility include:** Regional Headquarters. **Annual sales/revenues:** $11 - $20 million. **Number of employees at this location:** 100.

GLASGOW, INC.
Willow Grove Avenue and Limekiln Pike, P.O. Box 1089, Glenside PA 19038-1089. 215/884-8800. **Fax:** 215/884-1465. **Contact:** Human Resources. **World Wide Web address:** http://www.glasgowinc.com. **Description:** A heavy construction and highway contracting firm. **Corporate headquarters location:** This location. **Operations at this facility include:** Administration. **President:** Bruce Rambo.

HERMAN GOLDNER COMPANY
7777 Brewster Avenue, Philadelphia PA 19153. 215/365-5400. **Contact:** Human Resources. **World Wide Web address:** http://www.goldner.com. **Description:** A mechanical construction company. The company also supplies pipes, valves, fittings, and building control systems to the construction industry. **NOTE:** Applications must be mailed or hand delivered to the above address.

HDR ENGINEERING, INC.
3 Gateway Center, 3rd Floor, Pittsburgh PA 15222-1074. 412/497-6000. **Fax:** 412/497-6080. **Contact:** Susan Philipp, Human Resources Manager. **E-mail address:** careers@hdrinc.com. **World Wide Web address:** http://www.hdrinc.com. **Description:** Provides water, transportation, and waste and energy services including studies, design, and implementation for complex projects. **Parent company:** HDR, Inc. is a holding company for both HDR Engineering, Inc. and Henningson, Durham & Richardson, Inc., which specializes in the design of health care facilities including hospitals and integrated health care networks, ambulatory care centers, oncology and cardiology centers, diagnostic and treatment centers, and strategic facilities assessment; justice facilities including courthouse and administrative facilities, adult and juvenile detention facilities, and state correctional facilities; and science and industry facilities including research facilities, advanced technology facilities, telecommunications, university science facilities, and manufacturing facilities. **Corporate headquarters location:** Omaha NE.

HNTB
8 Penn Center, 7th Floor, 1628 John F Kennedy Boulevard, Philadelphia PA 19103. 212/568-6500. **Contact:** Human Resources. **World Wide Web address:** http://www.hntb.com. **Description:** HNTB is engineering, architectural, and planning company involved in public infrastructure projects. **NOTE:** Search and apply for positions or complete profile online. **Positions advertised include:** Highway Engineer; Bridge Engineer; Receptionist.

HRI INC.
1750 West College Avenue, State College PA 16801. 814/238-5071. **Contact:** Human Resources. **Description:** A road construction company.

HARSCO CORPORATION
P.O. Box 8888, Camp Hill PA 17001-8888. 717/763-7064. **Physical address:** 350 Poplar Church Road, Camp Hill PA 17001. **Fax:** 717/612-5619. **Contact:** Human Resources. **E-mail address:** employment@harsco.com. **World Wide Web address:** http://www.harsco.com. **Description:** Harsco Corporation is a diversified industrial manufacturing and service company that conducts business through 10 divisions and has 16 classes of products and services. Operations fall into three groups: Metal Reclamation and Mill Services includes scrap management, slab management systems, iron making, materials handling, equipment rental, recycling technology, aggregate marketing, and nonferrous metallurgical industry services; Infrastructure and Construction includes railway maintenance equipment, industrial grating products, and scaffolding, shoring, and concrete forming equipment; and Process Industry Products includes industrial pipe fittings, process equipment, and gas control and containment equipment. **Positions advertised include:** Network Engineer; Sr. Payroll Specialist; Sr. Director, Internal Audit; Manager, International Tax. **Special programs:** Internships. **Corporate headquarters location:** This location. **Other U.S. locations:** Nationwide. **Listed on:** New York Stock Exchange. **Stock exchange symbol:** HSC. **Number of employees at this location:** 90. **Number of employees worldwide:** 13,000.

GLENN O. HAWBAKER, INC.
1952 Waddle Road, P.O. Box 135, State College PA 16804-0135. 814/237-1444. **Toll-free phone:** 800/350-5078. **Fax:** 814/235-3654. **Contact:** Mr. Page L. Gaddis, Personnel Manager. **E-mail address:** plg@goh-inc.com. **World Wide Web address:** http://www.goh-inc.com. **Description:** Engaged in heavy construction services including paving, road construction, bridge construction, and other related services. Founded in 1952. **Positions advertised include:** Director of Training and Development; Project Administrator; Heavy Equipment Operator. **Special programs:** Internships; Summer Jobs. **Office hours:** Monday - Friday, 8:00 a.m. - 5:00 p.m. **Corporate headquarters location:** This location. **Other area locations:** DuBois PA; Montoursville PA; Turtlepoint PA. **Operations at this facility include:** Administration; Sales. **Listed on:** Privately held. **Annual sales/revenues:** $21 - $50 million. **Number of employees at this location:** 600.

HENKELS & McCOY, INC.
985 Jolly Road, Blue Bell PA 19422-0900. 215/283-7600. **Fax:** 215/283-7659. **Contact:** Vincent Benedict, Director of Personnel. **World Wide Web address:** http://www.henkelsandmccoy.com. **Description:** An engineering and construction firm that specializes in designing, building, and maintaining infrastructure. Founded in 1923. **Positions advertised include:** Mechanical Engineer; Project Scheduler. **Corporate headquarters location:** This location. **Other U.S. locations:** Nationwide. **Listed on:** Privately held. **Number of employees nationwide:** 5,000.

HONEYWELL INC.
1005 South Bee Street, Pittsburgh PA 15220. 412/928-4200. **Contact:** Human Resources. **World Wide Web address:** http://www.honeywell.com. **Description:** Honeywell is engaged in the research, development, manufacture, and sale of advanced technology products and services in the fields of chemicals, electronics, automation, and controls. The company's major businesses are home and building automation and control, performance polymers and chemicals, industrial automation and control, space and aviation

systems, and defense and marine systems. **Corporate headquarters location:** Morristown NJ. **Operations at this facility include:** This location manufactures, sells, and services HVAC equipment. **Listed on:** New York Stock Exchange. **Stock exchange symbol:** HON.

INFRASOURCE SERVICES, INC.
100 West Sixth Street, Suite 300, Media PA 19063. 610/480-8073. **Contact:** Human Resources. **World Wide Web address:** http://www.infrasourceinc.com. **Description:** A provider of infrastructure construction services for electric power, gas, telecommunications, and energy intensive industries in the United States. **Corporate headquarters location:** This location. **Listed on:** New York Stock Exchange. **Stock exchange symbol:** IFS. **Number of employees nationwide:** 4,000.

IRWIN & LEIGHTON, INC.
1030 Continental Avenue, King of Prussia PA 19406. 610/989-0100. **Fax:** 610/989-0200. **Contact:** Personnel. **E-mail address:** info@irwinleighton.com. **World Wide Web address:** http://www.irwinleighton.com. **Description:** A full-service construction services firm. Founded in 1909. **Corporate headquarters location:** This location.

KAWNEER COMPANY, INC.
500 East 12th Street, P.O. Box 629, Bloomsburg PA 17815. 570/784-8000. **Toll-free phone:** 877/505-3756. **Fax:** 570/389-6238. **Contact:** Human Resources. **World Wide Web address:** http://www.kawneer.com. **Description:** Kawneer Company manufactures and markets fabricated products including nonresidential architectural building products such as storefronts, building entrances, facings, window framing, and curtain wall systems. **Other U.S. locations:** Springdale AR; Visalia CA; Jonesboro GA; Franklin IN. **Operations at this facility include:** This location manufactures aluminum doors and windows. **Parent company:** ALCOA. **Operations at this facility include:** Manufacturing. **Listed on:** New York Stock Exchange. **Stock exchange symbol:** AA. **Number of employees at this location:** 485. **Number of employees worldwide:** 14,000.

KEATING BUILDING CORPORATION
The Phoenix, Suite 300, 1600 Arch Street, Philadelphia PA 19103-2028. 610/668-4100. **Fax:** 610/660-4950. **Contact:** Career Coordinator. **E-mail address:** careers@keatingnet.com. **World Wide Web address:** http://www.keatingweb.com. **Description:** A general construction firm that specializes in development, emissions, construction, and housing programs. **NOTE:** Entry-level positions are offered. **Special programs:** Internships. **Corporate headquarters location:** This location. **Other U.S. locations:** CT; FL; NJ; OH. **Operations at this facility include:** Administration. **Annual sales/revenues:** More than $100 million. **Number of employees at this location:** 100. **Number of employees nationwide:** 175.

L. ROBERT KIMBALL & ASSOCIATES, INC.
615 West Highland Avenue, P.O. Box 1000, Ebensburg PA 15931. 814/472-7700 ext. 409. **Fax:** 814/472-7712. **Contact:** Karen Maul, Human Resources. **E-mail address:** hmnres@lrkimball.com. **World Wide Web address:** http://www.lrkimball.com. **Description:** A national, full-service consulting firm specializing in engineering, architecture, mapping sciences, and environmental services. **NOTE:** Entry-level positions are offered. **Positions advertised include:** Structural Engineer; Mechanical Engineer; Business Development Specialist; Secretary; Assistant Manager of Construction Services; Transportation Project Manager. **Special programs:** Training. **Corporate headquarters location:** This location. **Other area locations:** Harrisburg PA; Philadelphia PA; Pittsburgh PA; State College PA. **Other U.S. locations:** Raleigh NC; Cranford NJ; Syracuse NY; Richmond VA. **Operations at this facility include:** Administration; Sales. **Annual sales/revenues:** $21 - $50 million. **Number of employees at this location:** 350. **Number of employees nationwide:** 500.

KLING
2301 Chestnut Street, Philadelphia PA 19103. 215/569-2900. **Fax:** 215/569-5963. **Contact:** Human Resources Department. **E-mail address:** employment@tklp.com. **World Wide Web address:** http://www.tklp.com. **Description:** Provides architectural, engineering, and interior design services. Founded in 1946. **NOTE:** Entry-level positions are offered. **Positions advertised include:** Senior Projects Control Engineer; Junior Projects Control Engineer. **Special programs:** Internships; Training; Co-ops; Summer Jobs. **Office hours:** Monday - Friday, 8:30 a.m. - 5:30 p.m. **Corporate headquarters location:** This location. **Other U.S. locations:** Washington DC; Raleigh NC. **Annual sales/revenues:** $21 - $50 million. **Number of employees nationwide:** 400.

LIMBACH COMPANY
4 Northshore Center, Pittsburgh PA 15212. 412/359-2100. **Fax:** 412/359-2389. **Contact:** Human Resources. **World Wide Web address:** http://www.smcco.org/limbach.htm. **Description:** Construction contractors specializing in plumbing, heating, and air conditioning. **Corporate headquarters location:** Columbus OH. **Parent company:** SMCCO.

M&T COMPANY
3368 West ridge Pike, Pottstown PA 19464. 610/495-9320. **Fax:** 610/495-9317. **Contact:** Personnel Department. **World Wide Web address:** http://www.cdi-gs.com. **Description:** Provides a range of engineering and technical services to the military aviation market. **Parent company:** CDI Corporation.

MI HOME PRODUCTS INC.
650 West Market Street, Gratz PA 17030. 717/365-3300. **Contact:** Debbie Loughren, Human Resources. **World Wide Web address:** http://www.mihomeproducts.com. **Description:** Manufactures metal doors and frames.

JAMES D. MORRISSEY, INC.
9119 Frankford Avenue, Philadelphia PA 19114. 215/333-8000. **Fax:** 215/624-3308. **Contact:** Bruce Angst, Human Resources. **E-mail address:** jobs@jdm-inc.com. **World Wide Web address:** http://www.jdm-inc.com. **Description:** A heavy construction firm that specializes in large-scale projects such as highways and commercial buildings. **Positions advertised include:** Superintendent; Foreman; Estimator's Assistant; Highway Estimator; Bituminous Paving Foreman; Field Office Manager. **Corporate headquarters location:** This location.

OVERHEAD DOOR CORPORATION
23 Industrial Park Road, Lewistown PA 17044-0110. 717/248-0131. **Contact:** Human Resources. **E-mail address:** jobs@overheaddoor.com. **World Wide Web address:** http://www.overheaddoor.com. **Description:** Designs, manufactures, and installs upward-lifting doors including commercial and industrial systems and residential garage doors and openers. Founded in 1923. **Positions advertised include:** Customer Service Representative; Occupational Safety and Health Administrator. **Corporate headquarters location:** Dallas TX.

PACE RESOURCES INC.
P.O. Box 15040, York PA 17405-7040. **Physical address:** 40 South Richland, York PA 17404. 717/852-1300. **Contact:** Frank Weaver, Human Resources Director. **Description:** A holding company for architectural and engineering firms, as well as a testing laboratory, a computer service center, and a printing company. Founded in 1970.

PARSONS CORPORATION
1880 JFK Boulevard, 18th Floor, Philadelphia PA 19103. 215/567-1580. **Fax:** 215/567-1581. **Contact:** Human Resources. **World Wide Web address:** http://www.parsons.com. **Description:** An employee-owned engineering and construction company. The company's major services are the design, engineering, and supervision of the construction of electrical power

generating stations, and electrical transmission and distribution systems, as well as the upgrading and retrofitting of existing power plants. Parsons Power Group also renders services to industrial clients and various government agencies. **Positions advertised include:** Technical Consultant; Designer/Drafter; Principal Engineer; Sr. Engineer; Technical Specialist.

PENN LINE SERVICES
300 Scottdale Avenue, Scottdale PA 15683. 724/887-9110. **Fax:** 724/887-6705. **Contact:** Cynthia Bush, Human Resource Generalist. **E-mail address:** cindy@pennline.com. **World Wide Web address:** http://www.pennline.com. **Description:** A contracting firm that offers a range of specialties including electrical, guardrail, landscaping, and tree trimming services.

STV INCORPORATED
205 West Welsh Drive, Douglassville PA 19518. 610/385-8213. **Fax:** 610/385-8515. **Contact:** Patrick Austin, Human Resources Director. **World Wide Web address:** http://www.stvinc.com. **Description:** Provides engineering and architectural consulting and design services for a variety of projects, as well as construction inspection services for numerous industries, institutions, and sectors. The company operates four business segments including civil engineering, which provides services for the construction of highways, bridges, airports, and marine ports; defense systems engineering, which serves the U.S. Department of Defense in the development of equipment and special hardware; industrial process engineering, which consists of services for the development of manufacturing equipment and process systems; and transportation engineering, which involves consulting, design, and construction supervision services for transportation facilities. Founded in 1945. **Positions advertised include:** Civil and Structural Engineer; Sr. Highway Project Manager; Architect. **Special programs:** Co-ops; Summer Jobs. **Corporate headquarters location:** This location. **Other U.S. locations:** Nationwide. **Parent company:** STV Group Inc. **Operations at this facility include:** Regional Headquarters. **Listed on:** NASDAQ. **Stock exchange symbol:** STVI. **Annual sales/revenues:** $51 - $100 million. **Number of employees at this location:** 275. **Number of employees nationwide:** 1,000.

SARGENT ELECTRIC COMPANY
2801 Liberty Avenue, P.O. Box 30, Pittsburgh PA 15230. 412/391-0588. **Fax:** 412/394-7535. **Contact:** Human Resources. **World Wide Web address:** http://www.sargent.com. **Description:** An electrical contractor.

SHARON TUBE COMPANY
134 Mill Street, P.O. Box 492, Sharon PA 16146. **Toll-free phone:** 800/242-1221. **Fax:** 724/953-1031. **Contact:** Personnel. **World Wide Web address:** http://www.sharontube.com. **Description:** A wholesaler of plumbing and heating supplies. Founded in 1929.

R.M. SHOEMAKER COMPANY
One Tower Bridge, 100 Front Street, Suite 1300, P.O. Box 888, West Conshohocken PA 19428. 610/941-5500. **Fax:** 610/941-4203. **Contact:** Human Resources. **E-mail address:** hr@rmsco.com. **World Wide Web address:** http://www.rmshoemaker.com. **Description:** An industrial and commercial construction company. **Positions advertised include:** Project Manager; Project Superintendent; Project Engineer; Project Accountant; Estimator.

TOLL BROTHERS, INC.
250 Gibraltar Road, Horsham PA 19044. 215/938-8000. **Fax:** 215/938-8291. **Contact:** Personnel. **World Wide Web address:** http://www.tollbrothers.com. **Description:** Designs and builds luxury homes. Founded in 1967. **Positions advertised include:** Accountant; Assistant Bookkeeper; Architectural Designer; Java Programmer; Mortgage Loan Officer; Purchasing Manager. **Corporate headquarters location:** This location. **Other U.S. locations:** Nationwide. **Subsidiaries include:** Coleman Homes; Geoffrey Edmonds & Associates. **Listed on:** New York Stock Exchange. **Stock exchange symbol:** TOL. **Annual sales/revenues:** More than $100 million. **Number of employees at this location:** 200. **Number of employees nationwide:** 2,000.

TRACO INC.
71 Progress Avenue, Cranberry Township PA 16066. 724/776-7000. **Fax:** 724/776-7014. **Contact:** Human Resources. **World Wide Web address:** http://www.traco.com. **Description:** Manufactures, installs, and sells commercial and residential windows. **Positions advertised include:** Estimator; Design Engineer; Human Resource Manager; Project Manager. **Number of employees worldwide:** 2,000.

TRANE COMPANY
400 Business Center Drive, Pittsburgh PA 15205. 412/747-3000. **Fax:** 412/747-4550. **Contact:** Human Resources. **World Wide Web address:** http://www.trane.com/Pittsburgh. **Description:** Trane Company develops, manufactures, and sells air conditioning equipment designed for use in central air conditioning systems for commercial, institutional, industrial, and residential buildings. The company's products are designed to cool water, and to cool, heat, humidify, dehumidify, move, and filter air. Other products include similar systems for buses and rapid transit vehicles, refrigeration equipment for trucks, and pollution control equipment. **Positions advertised include:** Project Manager; Engineering Support; Financial Manager; Account Manager. **Corporate headquarters location:** Tyler TX. **Operations at this facility include:** This location is a sales office.

WASHINGTON GROUP INTERNATIONAL, INC.
301 Chelsea Parkway, Boothwyn PA 19061. 610/497-8000. **Fax:** 610/497-8005. **Contact:** Human Resources. **World Wide Web address:** http://www.wgint.com. **Description:** A diversified corporation engaged in the design, engineering, and construction of industrial plants; architectural and community services; heavy machinery design and construction; industrial facilities; and mining and metallurgy. **Corporate headquarters location:** Boise ID.

WILLIARD LIMBACH
175 Titus Avenue, Suite 100, Warrington PA 18976. 215/488-9700. **Fax:** 215/488-9699. **Contact:** Human Resources Manager. **World Wide Web address:** http://www.williard.com. **Description:** A mechanical/electrical contracting firm specializing in HVAC, electrical, plumbing, and water treatment construction and services. **Corporate headquarters location:** This location.

YORKTOWNE, INC.
P.O. Box 231, Red Lion PA 17356. 717/244-4011. **Toll-free phone:** 800/777-0065. **Physical address:** 100 Redcoe Avenue, Red Lion PA 17356. **Contact:** James Burtnett, Vice President/Human Resources. **E-mail address:** cabinets@yorktwn.com. **World Wide Web address:** http://www.yorktowneinc.com. **Description:** Manufactures and markets kitchen cabinets and bathroom vanities for the residential construction industry. **Parent company:** Elkay Manufacturing Company.

Rhode Island
DIPRETE ENGINEERING ASSOCIATES
2 Stafford Court, Cranston RI 02920. 401/943-1000. **Fax:** 401/464-6006. **Contact:** Karen King. **E-mail address:** Karen@diprete-eng.com. **World Wide Web address:** http://www.diprete-eng.com. **Description:** The firm works on land development projects and other civil and environmental projects throughout New England. It is divided into six project teams assembled by area of expertise: three civil and environmental engineering teams, a land planning and site design team, a surveying services team and an individual sewage disposal system design, testing and inspection team. **NOTE:** See website for current job openings.

Send resumes by mail, fax or e-mail. **Positions advertised include:** Civil/Survey Engineer; Land Planner/Site Designer. **Corporate headquarters location:** This location.

FM GLOBAL
1301 Atwood Avenue, Johnston RI 02919. 401/275-3000. **Toll-free phone:** 800/343-7722. **Fax:** 401/275-3029. **Contact:** Elena Gargana. **E-mail address:** jobs@fmglobal.com. **World Wide Web address:** http://www.fmglobal.com. **Description:** A commercial and industrial property insurance and risk management organization specializing in property protection. Founded in 1835. **NOTE:** You must submit your resume through FM Global's website to be considered for employment opportunities. **Positions advertised include:** Associate Underwriter; Methods Analyst; Lead Business Analyst; Manager; Principal Data Analyst; Software Engineer; Executive Administrative Assistant. **Special programs:** Internships; Co-ops. **Corporate headquarters location:** This location. **Other area locations:** West Glocester RI. **Other U.S. locations:** Nationwide. **International locations:** Worldwide. **Number of employees at this location:** 700. **Number of employees worldwide:** 4,000.

GILBANE BUILDING COMPANY
7 Jackson Walkway, Providence RI 02903. 401/456-5800. **Fax:** 401/456-5936. **Toll-free phone:** 800/GILBANE. **Contact:** Human Resources. **World Wide Web address:** http://www.gilbaneco.com. **Description:** A full-service construction and real estate development company offering services in site selection, financing, programming and construction. The company is involved in all major construction markets including industrial, corporate, health care, education, airports, convention centers and correctional facilities. Founded in 1873. **Office hours:** Monday - Friday, 8:00 a.m. - 5:00 p.m. **NOTE:** See website for current job openings and to apply online. **Positions advertised include:** Graphics Designer/Specialist; Business Development Manager; Internal Auditor; Knowledge Manager; Marketing Manager; Project Engineer; Project Manager; Technical Assistant; Tunnel Safety Manager. **Corporate headquarters location:** This location. **Other U.S. locations:** Nationwide. **Listed on:** Privately held. **Annual sales/revenues:** More than $100 million. **CEO:** Paul Choquette, Jr. **Number of employees at this location:** 200. **Number of employees nationwide:** 1,000.

NORTEK, INC.
50 Kennedy Plaza, Providence RI 02903. 401/751-1600. **Fax:** 401/751-4724. **Contact:** Jane White, Director of Human Resources. **E-mail address:** white@nortek-inc.com. **World Wide Web address:** http://www.nortek-inc.com. **Description:** A diversified manufacturer and distributor of building, remodeling and indoor environmental control products for the residential and commercial construction, do-it-yourself, remodeling and renovation markets. Products include range hoods and other spot ventilation products, heating and air-conditioning systems, indoor air quality systems and specialty electronic products. Established in 1967. **NOTE:** Contact Human Resources to inquire about open positions. **Corporate headquarters location:** This location. **Parent company:** Thomas H. Lee Partners. **CEO:** Richard Bready.

South Carolina

ADC ENGINEERING
1226 Yeamans Hall Road, Hanahan SC 29406. 843/566-0161. **Fax:** 843/566-0162. **Contact:** Donna Yaw, Human Resources. **E-mail address:** email@adcengineering.com. **World Wide Web address:** http://www.adcengineering.com. **Description:** Full service structural engineering roofing, water proofing, consulting and landscaping company. **Positions advertised include:** Auto Cad Technician.

BE & K BUILDING GROUP
201 East McBee Avenue, Suite 300, Greenville SC 29601. 864/250-5000. **Fax:** 864/250-5230. **Contact:** Human Resources. **E-mail address:** bgcareers@bek.com. **World Wide Web address:** http://www.bekbuildinggroup.com. **Description:** An employee-owned, privately held commercial design and construction company. **Positions advertised include:** Project Engineer; Project Manager. **Corporate headquarters location:** This location. **Other U.S. locations:** Atlanta GA; Orlando FL; Providence RI; Raleigh NC; Richmond VA. **International locations:** Mexico. **Parent company:** BE & K Inc. (Birmingham AL). **Number of employees nationwide:** 700.

DAVIS ELECTRICAL CONSTRUCTORS, INC.
429 North Main Street, P.O. Box 1907, Greenville SC 29602. 864/250-2471. **Toll-free phone:** 800/849-3284. **Fax:** 864/250-2567. **Contact:** Bill Dyar, Human Resources Director. **World Wide Web address:** http://www.daviselectrical.com. **Description:** An electrical and instrumentation contractor for power plants, textile manufacturers, and chemical producers. Founded in 1965. **Positions advertised include:** Electrical Engineer; Project Coordinator. **Corporate headquarters location:** This location. **Other U.S. locations:** Baton Rouge LA; Debary FL; Shelby NC; Gulfport MS.

FLUOR ENTERPRISES, INC.
100 Fluor Daniel Drive, Greenville SC 29607-2762. 864/281-8600. **Fax:** 864/281-6913. **Contact:** Human Resources. **E-mail address:** careers@fluor.com. **World Wide Web address:** http://www.fluor.com. **Description:** Operates within the fields of engineering, global services, coal production, and procurement and construction. **Positions advertised include:** Safety Technician; Senior Maintenance Engineering Manager; Senior Estimator; Senior Auditor; Audit Manager; Business Project Analyst; Sales Director; Principal Estimator; Project Manager; Senior Mechanical Estimator; Operations Director. **Corporate headquarters location:** Aliso Viejo CA. **Other U.S. locations:** Nationwide. **International locations:** Worldwide. **Parent company:** Fluro Corporation. **Operations at this facility include:** Fluor Enterprises, Inc.; Fluor Constructors International, Inc. (250 Executive Center Drive, Greenville SC 29615). **Listed on:** New York Stock Exchange. **Stock exchange symbol:** FLR. **Annual sales/revenues:** $10 billion. **Number of employees worldwide:** 51,300.

JACOBS APPLIED TECHNOLOGY
2040 Bushy Park Road, P.O. Box 63125, Goose Creek SC 29445. 843/824-1100. **Fax:** 843/824-1103. **Contact:** Human Resources Manager. **World Wide Web address:** http://www.jacobs.com. **Description:** Designs, fabricates, and constructs propane-air gas plants and process plants for the chemical, petrochemical, fine chemical, specialty chemical, food and beverage, pharmaceutical, and consumer industries. Founded in 1947. **Positions advertised include:** Project Manager. **Parent company:** Jacobs Engineering Group, Inc. (Pasadena CA) provides engineering, procurement, construction, and maintenance services to the chemicals and polymers, federal programs, pulp and paper, semiconductor, petroleum refining, facilities and transportation, food and consumer products, pharmaceutical and biotechnology, and basic resources industries. **Parent company:** Jacobs Engineering Group, Inc. **Operations at this facility include:** Administration; Manufacturing; Sales.

JACOBS SIRRINE ENGINEERS, INC.
1041 East Butler Road, P.O. Box 5456, Greenville SC 29607. 864/676-6000. **Fax:** 864/676-5096. **Contact:** Mary Johnson, Human Resources Representative. **World Wide Web address:** http://www.jacobs.com. **Description:** Provides architectural, engineering, and construction management consulting services. **Positions advertised include:** Civil Inspector; Customer Service Representative; Sales Manager; Civil Engineer; Electrical Engineer; Mechanical Engineer. **Parent company:** Jacobs Engineering Group, Inc.

LOCKWOOD GREENE ENGINEERS, INC.
P.O. Box 491, Spartanburg SC 29304. 864/578-2000. **Physical address:** 1500 International Drive, Spartanburg SC 29303. **Toll-free phone:** 888/LOCKWOOD. **Fax:** 864/599-6400. **E-mail address:** careers@lg.com. **Contact:** Trudy Wofford, Personnel Manager. **World Wide Web address:** http://www.lg.com. **Description:** A consulting firm that provides engineering and architectural design for industrial and commercial clients. Specifically, the company is involved in the planning and project management of industrial plants and production facilities. **Positions advertised include:** Electrical Design Engineer; Marketing Coordinator; Project Manager; Architectural Engineer; Chemical Engineer; Civil Engineer; Computer Programmer; Draftsperson; Electrical Engineer; Industrial Engineer; Mechanical Engineer; Systems Analyst. **Corporate headquarters location:** This location. **Parent company:** J.A. Jones, Inc. (Charlotte NC). **Operations at this facility include:** Computer-aided design, process, and environmental engineering, control systems engineering, computer systems integration and testing, and construction. **Annual sales/revenues:** $1 billion. **Number of employees:** 3,000.

TRICO ENGINEERING CONSULTANTS, INC.
4425 Belle Oaks Drive, North Charleston SC 29405. 843/740-7700. **Contact:** Ian M. Saunders. **E-mail address:** isaunders@tricoengineering.com. **World Wide Web address:** http://www.tricoengineering.com. **Description:** An engineering company that does surveying projects. **Positions advertised include:** Survey Instrument Person. **Corporate headquarters location:** This location.

South Dakota

HILLS MATERIALS COMPANY
P.O. Box 2320, Rapid City SD 57709-2320. 605/394-3300. **Physical location:** 3975 Sturgis Road, Rapid City SD 57702. **Fax:** 605/341-3446. **Contact:** Human Resources. **E-mail address:** jobs@hillsmaterials.com. **World Wide Web address:** http://www.hillsmaterials.com. **Description:** An integrated construction materials business with aggregates, asphalt lay-down and concrete ready-mix operations. Operates four limestone quarries, four sand and gravel pits, three asphalt plants, four ready mix plants, an emulsion plant and a machine shop/equipment repair facility. Founded in 1925. **NOTE:** Please visit website to view current openings and download application form. **Special programs:** Seasonal positions.

LARSON MANUFACTURING COMPANY
2333 Eastbrook Drive, Brookings SD 57006. 605/692-6115. **Contact:** Human Resources. **World Wide Web address**: http://www.larsondoors.com. **Description:** Manufactures storm doors and storm windows. **Corporate headquarters location:** This location.

Tennessee

APAC
1210 Harbor Avenue, P.O. Box 13427, Memphis TN 38113. 901/947-5600. **Fax:** 901/947-5699. **World Wide Web address:** http://www.ashland.com. **Description:** APAC is the largest transportation construction contractor in the U.S. **Positions advertised include:** Quality Control Specialist. **Corporate headquarters location:** Atlanta GA. **Parent company:** Ashland Inc.

ADAMS, CRAFT, HERZ, WALKER
800 Oak Ridge Turnpike, Suite A400, Oak Ridge TN 37830-6988. 865/482-4451. **Fax:** 865/482-4454. **Contact:** Human Resources Department. **World Wide Web address:** http://www.achw.com. **Description:** Provides architectural, engineering, planning, and surveying services.

BARGE, WAGGONER, SUMNER & CANNON
211 Commerce Street, Suite 600, Nashville TN 37201. 615/254-1500. **Contact:** Human Resources. **World Wide Web address:** http://www.bargewaggoner.com. **Description:** An employee-owned design firm offering services in engineering, architecture, planning, landscape architecture, and surveying. **NOTE:** Please apply online. **Positions advertised include:** Civil/Environmental Designer. **Corporate headquarters location:** This location. **Other U.S. locations:** Jasper AL; Dothan AL; Huntsville AL; Montgomery AL; Birmingham AL; Lexington KY; Dayton OH; Morristown TN; Blountville TN; Knoxville TN; Memphis TN; Oak Ridge TN.

BLAINE CONSTRUCTION CORPORATION
6510 Deane Hill Drive, Knoxville TN 37919. 865/693-8900. **Fax:** 865/691-7606. **Contact:** Personnel. **E-mail address:** jobs@blaineconstrcution.com. **World Wide Web address:** http://www.blaineconstruction.com. **Description:** A full-service general contractor serving commercial, industrial, institutional, and specialty construction markets. Founded in 1969. **Other U.S. locations:** Nationwide.

BRUCE HARDWOOD FLOOR COMPANY
160 Rosedale Street, Jackson TN 38302-1334. 731/422-7727. **Contact:** Personnel. **World Wide Web address:** http://www.brucehardwoodfloors.com. **Description:** This facility is a plant that manufactures hardwood flooring. Founded in 1884. **NOTE:** Search and apply for positions online. Unsolicited resumes not accepted. Only electronically submitted applications will be considered. **Positions advertised include:** Continuous Improvement Engineer; Production Supervisor; Quality Manager. **Parent company:** Armstrong World Industries. **Listed on:** New York Stock Exchange. **Stock exchange symbol:** ACK.

CENTEX RODGERS, INC.
2636 Elm Hill Pike, Suite 120, Nashville TN 37214. 615/889-4400. **Fax:** 615/872-1107. **World Wide Web address:** http://www.centex-construction.com. **Description:** Provides healthcare construction management services. Part of the Centex Construction Group. **Parent company:** Centex Corporation.

CLAYTON HOMES AND VANDERBILT MORTGAGE, INC.
P.O. Box 9790, Maryville TN 37802. 865/380-3000. Physical address: 500 Alcoa Trial, Maryville TN 37804. **Fax:** 865/380-3789. **Contact:** Human Resources. **World Wide Web address:** http://www.clayton.net. **Description:** A vertically-integrated builder and seller of low- to medium-priced manufactured homes operating in 49 states. The company provides financing and insurance services to its retail customers and owns and operates 88 manufactured housing communities in 12 states. Founded in 1966. **Corporate headquarters location:** This location. **Parent company:** Berkshire Hathaway. **Operations at this facility include:** Administration. **Number of employees nationwide:** 5,000.

DENARK CONSTRUCTION
1635 Western Avenue, Knoxville, TN 37921. 865/637-1925. **Fax:** 865/637-2837. **Contact:** Human Resources. **E-mail address:** hr@denark.com. **World Wide Web address:** http://www.denark.com. **Description:** Denark Construction is a full-service general contractor/design-builder/construction manager. Denark Construction's services include: design-build teams, construction management, general contracting, light commercial work, and high-end residential. **Positions advertised include:** Project Managers; Project Estimators, Project Engineers, Project Accountants, Entry Level/College Graduates. **Corporate Headquarters:** This location.

FLINTCO, INC.
2179 Hillshire Circle, Memphis TN 38133-6074. 901/372-9600. **Contact:** Human Resources. **World Wide Web address:** http://www.flintco.com. **Description:** A general construction contractor. **Corporate headquarters location:** Tulsa OK.

GOODMAN COMPANY
1810 Wilson Parkway, Fayetteville TN 37334-3559. 931/433-6101. **Fax:** 931/433-1312. **Contact:** Manager

of Human Resources. **World Wide Web address:** http://www.amana-hac.com. **Description:** Designs, develops, manufactures, and sells heating, ventilation, and air conditioning products. **Corporate headquarters location:** Amana IA. **Other U.S. locations:** Nationwide. **Parent company:** Raytheon Corporation. **Operations at this facility include:** Administration; Divisional Headquarters; Manufacturing; Research and Development; Sales; Service. **Number of employees at this location:** 1,000.

W.L. HAILEY AND COMPANY
2971 Kraft Drive, P.O. Box 40646, Nashville TN 37204-0646. 615/255-3161. **Fax:** 615/256-1316. **Contact:** Human Resources. **E-mail address:** humanresources@wlhailey.com. **World Wide Web address:** http://www.wlhailey.com. **Description:** Engaged in heavy construction including pipelines, bridges, tunnels, marine structures, and treatment plants. **Other U.S. locations:** Atlanta GA; Birmingham AL.

HARDAWAY GROUP, INC.
615 Main Street, Nashville TN 37206. 615/254-5461. **Fax:** 615/254-4518. **Contact:** Randy Swinehart, Personnel Director. **E-mail address:** rswinehart@hardaway.net. **World Wide Web address:** http://www.hardaway.net. **Description:** A full-service construction firm. Founded in 1924. **NOTE:** Entry-level positions are offered. **Corporate headquarters location:** This location. **Operations at this facility include:** Administration. **Listed on:** Privately held. **Annual sales/revenues:** More than $100 million. **Number of employees at this location:** 400. **Number of employees nationwide:** 500.

HSB PROFESSIONAL LOSS CONTROL, INC.
P.O. Box 585, Kingston TN 37763-0585. 865/376-1131. Physical address: 164 Locomotive Drive, Lenoir TN 37771. **Fax:** 865/376-5078. **Contact:** Human Resources. **World Wide Web address:** http://www.hsbplc.com. **Description:** Provides engineering services in the areas of fire protection, safety, and environmental protection. **Parent company:** HSB Global Standards

INTERNATIONAL COMFORT PRODUCTS
650 Heil Quaker Avenue, P.O. Box 128, Lewisburg TN 37091. 931/359-3511. **Fax:** 931/270-3312. **Contact:** Employment Manager. **E-mail address:** recruiting@icpusa.com. **World Wide Web address:** http://www.icpusa.com. **Description:** Manufactures and markets central heating and air conditioning units. **NOTE:** Current openings posted online. **Parent company:** United Technologies Corporation.

JACOBS ENGINEERING GROUP INC.
600 William Northern Boulevard, Tullahoma TN 37388. 931/455-6400. **Fax:** 931/393-6210. **Contact:** Employment. **World Wide Web address:** http://www.jacobs.com. **Description:** A professional and engineering services firm supporting NASA, U.S. Department of Defense entities, and private companies. **NOTE:** Search and apply for positions or submit resume online. **Positions advertised include:** IT Help Desk Coordinator. **Corporate headquarters location:** Pasadena CA. **Listed on:** New York Stock Exchange. **Stock exchange symbol:** JEC. **Number of employees at this location:** 200. **Number of employees worldwide:** 4,000.

KIRBY BUILDING SYSTEMS INC.
dba ASSOCIATED BUILDING SYSTEMS
124 Kirby Drive, Portland TN 37148. 615/325-4165. **Fax:** 800/348-7799. **Contact:** Charles Wilcox, Personnel Director. **World Wide Web address:** http://www. kirbybuildingsystems.com. **Description:** Manufactures prefabricated metal buildings and components. **Parent company:** Magnatrax Corporation.

KOHLER COMPANY
2000 North Fifth Street, Union City TN 38261-0769. 731/885-1200. **Fax:** 731/885-0286. **Contact:** Personnel. **World Wide Web address:** http://www.sterlingplumbing.com. **Description:** Manufactures kitchen and bathroom appliance including faucets, sinks, tubs, showers, tub and shower enclosures, and toilets.

LAUREN ENGINEERS AND CONSTRUCTORS
139 Fox Road, Suite 204, Knoxville TN 37922. 865/690-8610. **Fax:** 865/691-0321. **Contact:** Human Resources. **E-mail address:** hr@laurenec.com. **World Wide Web address:** http://www.laurenec.com. **Description:** Provides engineering and design services for the chemical process, steel and metals, and nuclear and fossil power generation industries. **Corporate headquarters location:** Abilene TX. **Number of employees nationwide:** 200.

MARVIN WINDOWS & DOORS
101 Marvin Road, Ripley TN 38063. 731/635-5190. **Contact:** Director of Human Resources. **World Wide Web address:** http://www.marvin.com. **Description:** Manufactures wood windows and doors. **NOTE:** Search and apply for positions online. **Positions advertised include:** Manufacturing/Process Engineer. **Corporate headquarters location:** Warroad MN. Other U.S. locations: OR; ND. **Listed on:** Privately held. **Number of employees at this location:** 800. **Number of employees nationwide:** 4,500.

MEMPHIS HARDWOOD FLOORING
1551 North Thomas Street, Memphis TN 38107. 901/526-7306. **Fax:** 901/525-0059. **Contact:** Human Resources, Plant. **World Wide Web address:** http://www.chickasawflooring.com. **Description:** Manufactures hardwood flooring.

PHILLIPS & JORDAN INC.
6621 Wilbanks Road, Knoxville TN 37912. 865/688-8342. **Fax:** 865/688-8369. **Contact:** Susan Williams, Human Resources. **E-mail address:** swilliams@pandj.com. **World Wide Web address:** http://www.pandj.com. **Description:** A general contractor specializing in land clearing, earthwork, site development, project management, and disaster recovery services. Founded in 1953.

TPI CORPORATION
P.O. Box 4973, Johnson City TN 37602-4973. 423/477-0086. **Fax:** 423/477-8289. **Contact:** Human Resources. **World Wide Web address:** http://www.tpicorp.com. **Description:** Manufactures electric heating, air ventilation, lighting, and control products. **Corporate headquarters location:** This location. **Other U.S. locations:** Nationwide. **Subsidiaries include:** Columbus Electric; Fostoria Industries. **Operations at this facility include:** Administration; Manufacturing; Research and Development; Sales; Service. **Listed on:** Privately held. **Number of employees at this location:** 425.

THETA ENGINEERING
101 East Tennessee Avenue, Oak Ridge TN 37830. 865/482-0056. **Fax:** 865/482-7583. **Contact:** Human Resources. **E-mail address:** humanresources@theta-hq.com. **World Wide Web address:** http://www.theta-hq.com. **Description:** Offers engineering subcontracting and project management support.

VP BUILDINGS
P.O. Box 17967, Memphis TN 38187. 901/748-8000. **Physical address:** 3200 Players Club Circle, Memphis TN 38125. **Toll-free phone:** 800/238-3246. **Fax:** 901/748-9321. **Contact:** Human Resources Department. **E-mail address:** humanresources@vp.com. **World Wide Web address:** http://www.vp.com. **Description:** Designs and manufactures pre-engineered metal building systems for the low-rise, nonresidential market. **Positions advertised include:** Entry Level Engineer; Experienced Structural Engineer; Project Technician. **Corporate headquarters location:** This location. **Other U.S. locations:** Pine Bluff AR; Rainsville AL; Turlock CA; Van Wert OH; St. Joseph MO;

Kernersville NC; Evansville WI. **Parent company:** Grupo IMSA (Mexico).

Texas

ABB LUMMUS GLOBAL
3010 Briar Park Drive, Houston TX 77042. 713/821-5000. **Fax:** 713/821-3589. **Contact:** Personnel Director. **World Wide Web address:** http://www.abb.com/us. **Description:** An engineering firm serving power plants, chemical plants, and petrochemical and oil refineries, as well as other industries such as aviation and storage. **NOTE:** Please visit website to search for jobs and apply online. **Corporate headquarters location:** Zurich Switzerland. **Other U.S. locations:** Nationwide. **International locations:** Worldwide. **Parent company:** ABB Group. **Listed on:** New York Stock Exchange. **Stock exchange symbol:** ABB. **CEO:** Samir Brikho. **Number of employees nationwide:** 9,500. **Number of employees worldwide:** 115,000.

J.D. ABRAMS LP
111 Congress Avenue, Suite 2400, Austin TX 78701-4083. 512/322-4000. **Fax:** 512/322-4018. **Contact:** Mr. Dean Bernal, Vice President of Human Resources. **E-mail address:** dbernal@jdabrams.com. **World Wide Web address:** http://www.jdabrams.com. **Description:** A heavy, civil construction company specializing in public works infrastructure projects. Founded 1966. **Positions advertised include:** Estimator; Project Manager; Project Engineer; Field Engineer; Scheduler; Accountant; Human Resources Representative; Clerk. **Corporate headquarters location:** This location. **Other area locations:** Dallas TX; El Paso TX; Houston TX. **President:** Jon Abrams.

AMERICAN HOMESTAR CORPORATION
2450 South Shore Boulevard, Suite 300, League City TX 77573. 281/334-9700. **Fax:** 281/334-9737. **Contact:** Personnel. **E-mail address:** marketing@hstr.com. **World Wide Web address:** http://www.americanhomestar.com. **Description:** Designs, manufactures, and sells houses throughout the southwestern United States. Founded 1971. **Corporate headquarters location:** This location. **Other U.S. locations:** OK; LA; NM; CO.

APAC TEXAS, INC.
TEXAS BITULITHIC DIVISION
P.O. Box 224048, Dallas TX 75222-4048. 214/741-3531. **Physical address:** 2121 Irving Boulevard, Dallas TX 75207. **Fax:** 214/742-3540. **Contact:** Human Resources. **World Wide Web address:** http://www.apac.com. **Description:** A general contracting company specializing in concrete and asphalt paving work. **NOTE:** The president at this location is Stephen B. Robertson. Please visit website to search for jobs and apply online. **Positions advertised include:** Office Assistant. **Corporate headquarters location:** Alpharetta GA. **Other area locations:** Beaumont TX. **Other U.S. locations:** Southern and Southeastern U.S. **Parent company:** Ashland. **Listed on:** New York Stock Exchange. **Stock exchange symbol:** ASH.

AUSTIN COMMERCIAL INC.
P.O. Box 2879, Dallas TX 75221. 214/443-5700. **Physical address:** 3535 Travis Street, Suite 300, Dallas TX 75204. **Contact:** Human Resources Department. **E-mail address:** aclpjobs@austin-ind.com. **World Wide Web address:** http://www.austin-ind.com. **Description:** A commercial construction company providing general contracting, construction management, and preconstruction services including cost estimating and scheduling. **Positions advertised include:** Safety Manager; Senior MEP Superintendent; Assistant FOM; Superintendent. **Other area location:** Austin TX. **Other U.S. locations:** Phoenix AZ. **Parent company:** Austin Industries. **President:** David Walls.

BAY LTD.
P.O. Box 9908 Corpus Christi TX 78469. 361/693-2100. **Physical address:** 401 Corn Products Road, Corpus Christi TX 78409. **Fax:** 361/289-5005. **Contact:** Porfilio Silva, Personnel. **E-mail address:** silvap@bayltd.com. **World Wide Web address:** http://www.bayltd.com. **Description:** Provides construction and fabrication services to the petroleum industry. **NOTE:** Contact Personnel directly at 361/289-2400. **Corporate headquarters location:** This location. **Other area locations:** Friendswood TX. **Other U.S. locations:** Amerlia LA. **International location:** Mexico. **Parent company:** Berry Contracting Inc.

BECHTEL CORPORATION
P.O. Box 2166, Houston TX 77056. 713/235-2000. **Physical address:** 3000 Post Oak Boulevard, Houston TX 77056. **Fax:** 713/960-9031. **Contact:** Human Resources. **E-mail address:** staffpx@bechtel.com. **World Wide Web address:** http://www.bechtel.com. **Description:** Operates in the following areas: engineering, construction, financing operations, electricity, nuclear fuels, metals, minerals, procurement management, transportation, and pollution control. Founded 1898. **NOTE:** Please visit http://www.bechtel.com/careers to search for jobs. **Positions advertised include:** Senior Engineer' Engineering Supervisor; IS&T Manager; Senior Technical Support Specialist; Senior Designer. **Corporate headquarters location:** San Francisco CA. **Other U.S. locations:** Washington D.C.; San Diego CA; Richland WA; Oak Ridge TN; New York NY; McLean VA; Louisville KY; North Las Vegas NV; Glendale AZ; Frederick MD. **International locations:** Worldwide. **Number of employees worldwide:** 42,000.

BELDON ROOFING COMPANY
P.O. Box 13380, San Antonio TX 78213. 210/341-3100. **Physical address:** 5039 West Avenue, San Antonio TX 78213. **Toll-free phone:** 800/688-7663. **Fax:** 210/341-2959. **Contact:** Human Resources. **E-mail address:** greatjob@beldon.com. **World Wide Web address:** http://www.beldon.com. **Description:** A construction company that specializes in roofing and sheet metal work for all types of buildings. Founded in 1946. **NOTE:** Please visit website to view job listings and access online application. Please note whether your desired position requires an online application. Resumes are not kept on file. **Positions advertised include:** Roofer; Sheet Metal Installer. **Office hours:** Monday - Friday, 8:00 a.m. - 5:00 p.m.

THE BERGAILA COMPANIES
1880 S. Dairy Ashford, Suite 606, Houston TX 77077. 281/496-0803. **Fax:** 281/496-4705. **Contact:** Human Resources. **World Wide Web address:** http://www.bergaila.com. **Description:** An engineering and drafting service contractor. **NOTE:** Please visit individual subsidiaries websites (available through corporate website) for more information about employment. **Subsidiaries include:** Bergaila & Associates, Inc.; BES Engineering.

BERNARD JOHNSON YOUNG, INC.
1100 Louisiana Street, 3rd Floor 380, Houston TX 77002. 713/571-1600. **Fax:** 713/977-4781. **Contact:** Human Resources. **World Wide Web address:** http://www.bjy.com/phoenix. **Description:** An architectural engineering firm. The company also provides technical services, using the Internet to provide a full-time video link to customers. **Special programs:** Internships. **Corporate headquarters location:** This location. **Other area locations:** Dallas TX; Houston TX. **Other U.S. locations:** Rockville MD; Washington D.C.; Peoria IL; Phoenix AZ; American Fork UT; Pleasanton CA. **Operations at this facility include:** Administration; Regional Headquarters; Research and Development; Sales. **Listed on:** Privately held.

BUELL DOOR COMPANY
5200 East Grand Avenue, Dallas TX 75223. 214/827-9260. **Toll-free phone:** 800/556-0155. **Fax:** 214/826-9163. **Contact:** Human Resources. **World Wide Web address:** http://www.buelldoor.com. **Description:** A manufacturer of architectural doors and hardware.

CARTER BURGESS INC.
777 Main Street, Fort Worth TX 76102-5304. 817/735-7161. **Fax:** 817/735-6148. **Contact:** Human Resources. **World Wide Web address:** http://www.c-b.com. **Description:** An architectural, engineering and construction firm specializing in large buildings, such as skyscrapers and public facilities, such as museums. Founded in 1939. **NOTE:** Apply online. **Positions advertised include:** Civil Designer; Mechanical CADD Technician; Mechanical Engineer; Rod Operator; Senior Marketing Coordinator; Instrument Operator; Business Development; Regional Finance Manager. **Special programs:** Internships. **Corporate headquarters location:** This location. **Other area locations:** Austin TX; Dallas TX; Houston TX; Arlington TX; San Antonio TX. **Other U.S. locations:** Nationwide. **Number of employees nationwide:** 2,300.

CAVALIER HOMES, INC.
P.O. Box 5003, Wichita Falls TX 76307. 940/723-5523. **Physical address:** 719 Scott Avenue, Suite 600, Wichita Falls TX 76301. **Contact:** Human Resources. **World Wide Web address:** http://www.cavhomebuilders.com. **Description:** Overall, Cavalier Homes, Inc. designs and manufactures a wide range of homes and markets them through approximately 500 independent dealers nationwide. **Corporate headquarters location:** Addison AL. **Operations at this facility include:** This location houses administrative offices. **Subsidiaries include:** Cavalier Acceptance Corporation provides installment sale financing to qualifying retail customers of these exclusive dealers. **Listed on:** New York Stock Exchange. **Stock Exchange symbol:** CAV.

CENTEX CONSTRUCTION COMPANY, INC.
3100 McKinnon, 7th Floor, Dallas TX 75201. 214/468-4700. **Fax:** 214/468-4505. **Contact:** Human Resources. **E-mail address:** human.resources@checmail.com. **World Wide Web address:** http://www.centex-construction.com. **Description:** A commercial general contractor that provides preconstruction, construction, management, and general contracting services. **NOTE:** Please visit http://www.centex-careers.com to search for jobs and apply online. **Positions advertised include:** Marketing Coordinator. **Corporate headquarters location:** This location. **Other area locations:** San Antonio TX. **Other U.S. locations:** Pasadena CA; Rochester MN; Indianapolis IN; Livonia MI; Fairfax VA; Charlotte NC; Nashville TN; Marietta GA; FL (Multiple locations). **Subsidiaries include:** Centex Rogers; Centex Rooney; Centex Southeast; Centex Southwest; Centex Mid Atlantic. **Parent company:** Centex Corporation. **Listed on:** New York Stock Exchange. **Stock exchange symbol:** CTX. **CEO:** Robert C. Van Cleave.

ELK CORPORATION
14911 Quorum Drive, Suite 600, Dallas TX 75254-1491. 972/851-0500. **Contact:** Human Resources. **World Wide Web address:** http://www.elcor.com. **Description:** Manufactures roofing products including fiberglass asphalt shingles. **Corporate headquarters location:** This location. **Subsidiaries include:** Elk Corporation of Texas. **Listed on:** New York Stock Exchange. **Stock exchange symbol:** ELK.

J.C. EVANS CONSTRUCTION COMPANY
P.O. Box 9647, Leander TX 78641. 512/244-1400. **Physical address:** 301 County Road 271, Leander TX 78646. **Fax:** 512/244-1900. **Contact:** Human Resources. **World Wide Web address:** http://www.jcevans.com. **Description:** A general contracting company. **Positions advertised include:** Concrete Finisher. **Corporate headquarters location:** This location.

EXPONENT, INC.
10899 Kinghurst Drive, Suite 245, Houston TX 77099. 281/879-6161. **Fax:** 281/879-0687. **Contact:** Personnel. **World Wide Web address:** http://www.exponent.com. **Description:** A technical consulting firm dedicated to the investigation, analysis, and prevention of accidents and failures of an engineering or scientific nature. The company provides a multidisciplinary approach to analyze how failures occur. The company specializes in accident reconstruction, biomechanics, construction/structural engineering, aviation and marine investigations, environmental assessment, materials and product testing, warning and labeling issues, accident statistical data analysis, and risk prevention/mitigation. Founded in 1967. **NOTE:** Applications and resumes accepted online or via e-mail. See website. **Corporate headquarters location:** Menlo Park CA. **Parent company:** Exponent. **Listed on:** NASDAQ. **Stock exchange symbol:** EXPO.

FM GLOBAL
5700 Granite Parkway, Suite 700, Plano TX 75024. 972/377-4808. **Fax:** 972/731-1800. **Contact:** Human Resources. **World Wide Web address:** http://www.fmglobal.com. **Description:** A loss control services organization. FM Global helps owner company policyholders to protect their properties and occupancies from damage caused by fire, wind, flood, and explosion; boiler, pressure vessel, and machinery accidents; and many other insured hazards. **Corporate headquarters location:** Johnston RI. **Other U.S. locations:** Nationwide. **International locations:** Worldwide.

FINSA DEVELOPMENT CORPORATION
302 Hanmore Industrial Park, Harlingen TX 78550. 956/425-9017. **Contact:** Human Resources. **World Wide Web address:** http://www.finsa.net. **Description:** A company that constructs, owns, sells, and leases industrial park property.

FUGRO GEOSCIENCES
6100 Hillcroft Street, Houston TX 77081. 713/778-5580. **Contact:** Human Resources. **World Wide Web address:** http://www. fugro.com. **Description:** A conglomerate of international engineering and geoscience consulting firms serving the offshore, industrial, public works, and commercial industries. The firms offer geosciences, earth sciences, and waste management services. **NOTE:** There are 12 different divisions located at this Houston location with separate Human Resource offices. See website for divisions and contact information. **Corporate headquarters location:** The Netherlands.

GAF MATERIALS CORPORATION
4545 Leston Street, Dallas TX 75247. 214/637-1186. **Contact:** Human Resources. **World Wide Web address:** http://www.gaf.com. **Description:** A multiproduct manufacturer with sales in both consumer and industrial construction markets. The company's product line includes building, roofing, and insulation materials for the construction trades; specialty chemicals and plastics; and reprographic products. **Corporate headquarters location:** Wayne NJ. **Other U.S. locations:** Nationwide. **Operations at this facility include:** Manufacturing; Sales. **Listed on:** Privately held.

GENERAL ALUMINUM CORPORATION
1250 Champion Circle Rear, Carrollton TX 75006. 972/484-4964. **Contact:** Human Resources. **Description:** Manufactures aluminum doors and windows, partition screens, sliding glass doors, and related products.

HDR, INC.
17111 Preston Road, Suite 300, Dallas TX 75248. 972/960-4000. **Fax:** 972/960-4185. **Contact:** Human Resources. **World Wide Web address:** http://www.hdrinc.com. **Description:** Offers architectural and engineering design services, in addition to construction consulting and interior design services. The company's three main business sectors are health care, justice, and science and industry. Founded in 1917. **Corporate headquarters location:** Omaha NE. **Other U.S. locations:** Alexandria VA. **Operations at this facility include:** Administration; Marketing;

Regional Headquarters; Service. **Listed on:** Privately held.

HNTB CORPORATION
5910 West Plano Parkway, Suite 200, Plano TX 75093. 972/661-5626. **Fax:** 972/661-5614. **Contact:** Human Resources. **World Wide Web address:** http://www.hntb.com. **Description:** Offers architectural, engineering, and planning services to public agencies and private industry. **NOTE:** Applicants should apply online at the company's website. **Positions advertised include:** Municipal Department Manager; Aviation Project Manager; Municipal Project Manager; Aviation Engineer; Public Involvement Manager. **Corporate headquarters location:** Kansas City MO. **Other area locations:** Austin TX; San Antonio TX. **Other U.S. locations:** Nationwide. **Subsidiaries include:** HNTB Design/Build, Inc.; HNTB International Corporation; HNTB Architecture, Inc. **Operations at this facility include:** Sales. **Listed on:** Privately held.

HALFF ASSOCIATES
8616 Northwest Plaza Drive, Dallas TX 75225. 214/346-6251. **Fax:** 214/217-6451. **Contact:** Susie Nevitt. **E-mail address:** careers@halff.com. **World Wide Web address:** http://www.halff.com. **Description:** Provides architecture and engineering consulting services. **Positions advertised include:** Utility Locators; Structural CADD Technician; Environmental Scientist; Landscape Architect; Land Surveyors; Mechanical/Electrical Engineers. **Other area locations:** Forth Worth TX; Houston TX; McAllen TX; Austin TX; Frisco TX; San Antonio TX.

D.R. HORTON, INC.
1901 Ascension Boulevard, Suite 210, Arlington TX 76006. 817/856-8200. **Fax:** 817/856-8238. **Contact:** Human Resources. **World Wide Web address:** http://www.drhorton.com. **Description:** D.R. Horton, Inc. and its operating subsidiaries are engaged primarily in the construction and sale of single-family homes designed principally for the entry-level and move-up market segments. **NOTE:** Interested jobseekers should see the company's website for contact information. **Operations at this facility include:** Regional office. **Listed on:** New York Stock Exchange. **Stock exchange symbol:** DHI. **Number of employees nationwide:** 4,300.

HOWE-BAKER ENGINEERS, INC.
P.O. Box 956, Tyler TX 75710. 903/597-0311. **Physical address:** 3102 East Fifth Street, Tyler TX 75701. **Contact:** Michael Osborn, Human Resources. **E-mail address:** mosborn@Cblepc.com. **World Wide Web address:** http://www.howebaker.com. **Description:** Provides mechanical, civil, and electrical engineering services. **Positions advertised include:** Process Engineer; Project Engineer; Mechanical Engineer; Civil Engineer; Electrical Engineer.

HUITT-ZOLLARS
3131 Mckinney Avenue, Suite 600, Dallas TX 75204. 214/871-3311. **Fax:** 214/871-0757. **Contact:** Human Resources. **World Wide Web address:** http://www.huitt-zollars.com. **Description:** Provides consulting services in engineering, architecture, planning, landscape architecture, surveying, and construction management. **Positions advertised include:** Land Development Technician; Land Development EIT; Land Development PE.

INSITUFORM TECHNOLOGIES, INC.
16619 Aldine Westfield Road, Houston TX 77032. 281/828-0308. **Contact:** Human Resources. **E-mail address:** careers@insituform.com. **World Wide Web address:** http://www.insituform.com. **Description:** Insituform Technologies, Inc. uses various trenchless technologies for rehabilitation, new construction, and improvements of pipeline systems including sewers; gas lines; industrial waste lines; water lines; and oil field, mining, and industrial process pipelines. **NOTE:** Resumes can also be mailed to 702 Spirit 40 Park Drive, Chesterfield MO 63005, Attention: Human Resources. **Parent company:** Insituform Technologies, Inc. provides a wide variety of technologies including Insituform, PALTEM, Tite Liner, and tunneling. **Operations at this facility include:** This location conducts pipeline rehabilitation. **Listed on:** NASDAQ. **Stock exchange symbol:** INSU.

INTEGRATED ELECTRICAL SERVICES INC.
1800 West Loop South, Suite 500, Houston TX 77027-9408. 713/860-1500. **Toll-free phone:** 800/696-1044. **Fax:** 713/860-1599. **Contact:** Bob Callahan, Human Resources Representative. **World Wide Web address:** http://www.ielectric.com. **Description:** An electrical contractor providing construction and maintenance services to a variety of business segments. The company's services include design and installation work for new and renovation projects, preventative maintenance, and emergency repair work. **Corporate headquarters location:** This location. **Other U.S. locations:** Nationwide. **Listed on:** New York Stock Exchange. **Stock exchange symbol:** IES. **Number of employees nationwide:** 13,000.

JALCO, INC.
P.O. Box 27368, Houston TX 77227. 713/728-8480. **Physical address**: 5148 Lotus Street, Houston TX 77045. **Fax:** 713/729-6553. **Contact:** Nilo S. Cruz, Administrative Officer. **E-mail address:** jalcohou@aol.com. **Description:** A heavy-construction company.

KAUFMAN AND BROAD
9990 Richmond Avenue, Suite 400, Houston TX 77042. 713/977-6633. **Contact:** Human Resources. **World Wide Web address:** http://www.kaufmanandbroad.com. **Description:** A single-family residential homebuilder. **NOTE:** Interested jobseekers must apply online for all positions. This company has locations throughout Texas. **Positions advertised include:** Director of Land Acquisition; Senior Land Development Manager; Land Development Superintendent; Closing Coordinator; Sales Representative; Field Loan Counselor; Studio Assistant; Receptionist; File Clerk; Office Assistant. **Corporate headquarters location:** Los Angeles CA.

KELLOGG, BROWN & ROOT
601 Jefferson Street, Houston TX 77002. 713/753-3022. **Contact:** Human Resources. **World Wide Web address:** http://www.halliburton.com. **Description:** A full-service design, engineering, procurement, construction, and contract management firm. The company serves the process and energy industries worldwide and is primarily involved in hydrocarbon-processing plants including oil-refining units, petrochemical manufacturing plants, ammonia and fertilizer plants, and gas-processing units. **NOTE:** Job listings and applications are available at the company's website. **Special programs:** Internships; Apprenticeships; Graduate. **Corporate headquarters location:** Dallas TX. **Other U.S. locations:** Nationwide. **Operations at this facility include:** Engineering. **Listed on:** New York Stock Exchange. **Stock exchange symbol:** HAL.

LAUREN ENGINEERS & CONSTRUCTORS
901 South First Street, Abilene TX 79602. 325/670-9660. **Fax:** 325/670-9663. **Contact:** Human Resources. **E-mail address:** hr@laurenec.com. **World Wide Web address:** http://www.laurenec.com. **Description:** Designs and builds power plants, refineries, and related large-scale projects. **Positions advertised include:** Process Engineering Manager; Senior Mechanical Engineer. **Corporate headquarters location:** This location. **Other U.S. locations**: Knoxville TN; Duluth GA.

LENNOX INTERNATIONAL, INC.
P.O. Box 799900, Dallas TX 75379-9900. 972/497-5000. **Physical address:** 2140 Lake Park Boulevard, Richardson TX 75080. **Fax:** 972/497-5476. **Contact:** Human Resources. **World Wide Web address:** http://www.lennoxinternational.com. **Description:** Manufactures and services refrigeration, heating and

air-conditioning equipment. **Positions advertised include:** Customer Financial Services Coordinator; Product Manager; Accounting Analyst; Customer Financial Services Administrator; Accounting Support; Pricing Services Analyst. **Special programs:** Internships. **Corporate headquarters location:** This location. **Subsidiaries include:** Armstrong Air Conditioning Inc.; Heatcraft Inc.; Lennox Global Ltd.; Lennox Industries, Inc. **Operations at this facility include:** Administration. **Listed on:** New York Stock Exchange. **Stock exchange symbol:** LII. **Number of employees worldwide:** 21,000.

LOCKWOOD, ANDREWS & NEWNAM, INC.
2925 Briarpark Drive, Suite 400, Houston TX 77042. 713/266-6900. **Toll-free phone:** 800/688-7590. **Contact:** Human Resources. **E-mail address:** hr@lan-inc.com. **World Wide Web address:** http://www.lan-inc.com. **Description:** Provides complete architectural, construction management, engineering, planning, and project management. The company also operates within the fields of infrastructure, thermal energy, and transportation. **NOTE:** A completed application must accompany a resume. The application can be downloaded on the company's website. Part-time jobs are offered. **Positions advertised include:** Bridge Design Engineer; Drafter; Electrical Engineer; Facilities Group Manager; Project Manager; Land Development Project Manager; Transportation Planner. **Special programs:** Internships; Summer Jobs. **Corporate headquarters location:** This location. **Other area locations:** Austin TX; Dallas TX; Fort Worth TX; San Antonio TX; Waco TX: San Marcos TX. **Other U.S. locations:** Phoenix AZ, **Parent company:** Leo A. Daly Company. **Listed on:** Privately held.

LYDA SWINERTON BUILDERS, INC
P.O. Box 680907, San Antonio TX 78268. 210/684-1770. **Physical address**: 12400 San Pedro Avenue, San Antonio TX 78216. **Contact:** Human Resources. **Description:** One of the largest general commercial contractors in Texas. Past projects included the Alamo Dome.

MAREK BROTHERS
3539 Oak Forest Drive, Houston TX 77018. 713/681-2626. **Fax:** 713/681-6540. **Contact:** Human Resources. **E-mail address:** info@marekbros.com. **World Wide Web address:** http://www.marekbros.com. **Description:** A construction contractor. Marek Brothers specializes in drywall and insulation installation for residential and office buildings. **Subsidiaries include:** Oak Forest Lumber & Supply; Markek Interior Systems, Inc.; MEMCO.

MORGAN BUILDING SYSTEM
P.O. Box 660280, Dallas TX 75266-0280. 972/864-7300. **Physical address:** 2780 McCree Road, Garland TX 75041. **Fax:** 972/864-7316. **Contact:** Human Resources. **World Wide Web address:** http://www.morganusa.com. **Description:** Manufactures, transports, and retails re-locatable buildings, spas, recreational vehicles, swimming pools, and decks to consumers, businesses, government buyers, and institutional buyers. **NOTE:** This company has retail locations throughout Texas. Interested jobseekers should consult its website for listings. For sales and office positions, contact Leslie McLeod, at lmcleod@morganusa.com. For all other positions, e-mail resumes to S. Morgan at smorgan@morganusa.com. **Positions advertised include:** Traveling Operational Inventory Auditor; Administrative Assistant (Customer Service); Inside Sales; Spa Technicians; Dispatchers; Yard Foremen; Clerical; Receptionists. **Corporate headquarters location:** This location. **Other U.S. locations:** AL; AR; CO; GA; LA; MO; MS; NM; OK; TN. **Operations at this facility include:** Administration. **Listed on:** Privately held.

MORRISON SUPPLY COMPANY
311 East Vickery Boulevard, Fort Worth TX 76104. 817/336-0451. **Contact:** Charles Allen, Human Resources Manager. **World Wide Web address:** http://www.morsco.com. **Description:** A wholesaler of plumbing and heating equipment, tools, and supplies. **Corporate headquarters location:** This location.

O'HAIR SHUTTERS
P.O. Box 2764, Lubbock TX 79408. 806/765-5791. **Toll-free phone:** 800/582-2625. **Fax:** 888/765-7140. **Contact:** Human Resources. **World Wide Web address:** http://www.ohair.com. **Description:** Manufactures outdoor shutters for homes. **Corporate headquarters location:** This location.

OPTIMIZED PROCESS DESIGNS (OPD)
P.O. Box 810, Katy TX 77493. 281/371-7500. **Physical address:** 25610 Clay Road, Katy TX 77493. **Fax:** 281/371-0132. **Contact:** Human Resources. **World Wide Web address:** http://www.opd-inc.com. **Description:** Designs, engineers, and constructs natural gas treatment facilities. **Parent company:** Koch Industries, Inc. **Listed on:** Privately held.

OVERHEAD DOOR CORPORATION
1900 Crown Drive, Farmer's Branch TX 75234. 972/233-6611. **Contact:** Human Resources. **E-mail address:** jobs@overheaddoor.com. **World Wide Web address:** http://www.overheaddoor.com. **Description:** Manufactures aluminum, steel, fiberglass, and wooden overhead doors, rolling steel fire doors, grilles, and metal insulated entrance doors. Products are distributed through a network of more than 400 authorized distributors in the United States and Canada. The company also manufactures truck and trailer doors. **Corporate headquarters location:** This location. **Other area locations:** Carrollton TX; Corpus Christi TX; Fort Worth TX; Houston TX; Mount Pleasant TX; Richardson TX. **Parent company:** Sanwa Shutter Corporation.

PALM HARBOR HOMES INC.
15303 Dallas Parkway, Suite 800, Addison TX, 75001. 972/991-2422. **Fax:** 512/385-2910. **Contact:** Human Resources. **World Wide Web address:** http://www.palmharbor.com. **Description:** Produces manufactured houses. Founded in 1978. **NOTE:** This company has retail and sales positions located throughout Texas. In addition, it has job openings in Manufacturing and Service. Interested jobseekers should apply online at the company's website. **Special programs:** Sale Training; Quality Training. **Corporate headquarters location:** Addison TX. **Other U.S. locations:** AL; AZ; FL; GA; NC; OH; OR. **Listed on:** NASDAQ. **Stock exchange symbol:** PHHM. **Number of employees nationwide:** 4,100.

QUALITY CABINETS
515 Big Stone Gap Road, Duncanville TX 75137. 972/298-6101. **Contact:** Human Resources. **World Wide Web address:** http://www.qualitycabinets.com. **Description:** Manufactures cabinets. **Corporate headquarters location:** This location. **Parent company:** Texwood Industries.

RAILWORKS
P.O. Box 15217, Houston TX 77220. 713/673-6208. **Contact:** Human Resources. **E-mail address:** careers@railworks.com. **Description:** A railroad construction contractor. **Corporate headquarters location:** White Plains NY. **Operations at this facility include:** This location is the administrative office for the South-Central Division of Railworks. **Listed on:** Privately held. **Number of employees worldwide:** 3,000.

S&B ENGINEERS AND CONSTRUCTORS
7825 Park Place Boulevard, Houston TX 77087. 713/645-4141. **Recorded jobline:** 713/845-7950. **Contact:** Human Resources. **World Wide Web address:** http://www.sbec.com. **Description:** A construction company. **NOTE:** For engineering positions, contact Ken Miller via e-mail at employment@sbec.com or fax to 713/645-4347. For all other positions, mail resumes to Human Resources. **Positions advertised include:** Project Engineer;

Electrical Engineer; Metallurgist/Welding Engineer; Pressure Vessel Engineer; Heat Transfer Engineer; Field Heater Engineer; Civil/Structural Engineer; Project Manager; Senior Estimator; Project Controls Manager. **Office hours:** Monday – Friday, 7:30 a.m. – 4:30 p.m. **Other area locations:** McAllen TX; Austin TX. **Other U.S. locations:** LA; SC; Washington D.C. **International locations:** United Kingdom; India; Saudi Arabia; Singapore. **Listed on:** Privately held.

SOUTHERN INVESTORS SERVICE COMPANY
9 Greenway Plaza, Suite 2900, Houston TX 77046. 713/869-7800. **Contact:** Human Resources. **Description:** Offers commercial construction, real estate development, distribution and installation of construction products, and savings and loan services. **Corporate headquarters location:** This location.

SPAWGLASS CONSTRUCTION INC.
13800 West Road, Houston TX 77041. 281/970-5300. **Fax:** 281/970-5305. **Contact:** Human Resources. **E-mail address:** humanresources@spawglass.com. **World Wide Web address:** http://www.spawglass.com. **Description:** A general construction contractor. **NOTE:** Send resume via e-mail or visit the nearest location. See the company's website for locations' addresses. **Corporate headquarters location:** This location. **Other area locations:** San Antonio TX; Austin TX; Harlingen TX.

TD INDUSTRIES, INC.
P.O. Box 819060, Dallas TX 75381-9060. 972/888-9500. **Physical address:** 13850 Diplomat Drive, Dallas TX 75234. **Fax:** 972/888-9507. **Contact:** Human Resources. **E-mail address:** tddallasjobs@tdindustries.com. **World Wide Web address:** http://www.tdindustries.com. **Description:** A national construction and service company that designs, installs, and repairs HVAC, plumbing, high-purity process piping, and energy management systems in commercial and industrial markets. Founded in 1946. **NOTE:** Entry-level positions are offered. See this company's website for job listings and contact information for all locations. **Positions advertised include:** Quickpen Software Operator; Mechanical Estimator; Building Technician; Administrative Assistant; Lead Change-out Technician; Scheduler; Project Manager; Job Cost Analyst. **Corporate headquarters location:** This location. **Other area locations:** Houston TX; Austin TX; San Antonio TX. **Other U.S. locations:** GA; AZ; Washington D.C. **Listed on:** Privately held.

THORPE CORPORATION
6833 Kirbyville, P.O. Box 330403, Houston TX 77033. 713/644-1247. **Fax:** 713/649-6503. **Contact:** Human Resources. **World Wide Web address:** http://www.thorpeproducts.com. **Description:** An engineering, construction, and refractory company. **NOTE:** Entry-level positions are offered. **Corporate headquarters location:** This location. **Other area locations:** Beaumont TX; Dallas TX. **Other U.S. locations:** Gonzales LA. **Subsidiaries include:** J.T. Thorpe (also at this location); Leacon-Sunbelt, Inc.; Thorpe Products. **Operations at this facility include:** Administration; Manufacturing; Sales; Service. **Listed on:** Privately held.

3D/INTERNATIONAL
1900 West Loop South, Suite 400, Houston TX 77027. 713/871-7000. **Fax:** 713/871-7171. **Contact:** Personnel. **World Wide Web address:** http://www.3di.com. **Description:** An architectural and interior design firm. The company also provides construction management, engineering, environmental consulting, and program management systems. **NOTE:** This company provides its job listings for all its Texas and U.S. locations online at its website. Apply online. **Positions advertised include:** Receptionist; Project Manager; General Superintendent. **Corporate headquarters location:** This location. **Other area locations:** Austin TX; San Antonio TX. **Other U.S. locations:** NM, CA; MI; MN; FL; AZ; UT; Washington D.C. **Operations at this facility include:** Administration; Sales; Service.

TURNER, COLLIE & BRADEN, INC.
P.O. Box 130089, Houston TX 77219. 713/780-4100. **Physical address:** 5757 Woodway, Suite 101 West, Houston TX 77057-1599. **Fax:** 713/780-0838. **Contact:** Human Resources. **World Wide Web address:** http://www.tcb.aecom.com. **Description:** A consulting firm providing technical services including engineering and design for the transportation, public works, environmental, and land development industries and does engineering economics and feasibility studies. Founded in 1946. **NOTE:** Entry-level positions and part-time jobs are offered. **Positions advertised include:** Administrative Clerk. **Special programs:** Internships; Co-ops; Summer Jobs. **Office hours:** Monday - Friday, 7:30 a.m. - 4:30 p.m. **Corporate headquarters location:** This location. **Other area locations:** Austin TX; Dallas TX; San Antonio TX; Fort Worth TX; Pharr TX. **Other U.S. locations:** CO; CA; NV; IL. **Parent company:** AECOM. **Operations at this facility include:** Administration; Divisional Headquarters; Sales. **Listed on:** Privately held.

U.S. HOME CORPORATION
P.O. Box 2863, Houston TX 77252-2863. 713/877-2311. **Physical address:** 10707 Clay Road, Houston TX 77041. **Contact:** Human Resources. **World Wide Web address:** http://www.ushome.com. **Description:** Builds and sells single-family houses. **NOTE:** This company has several locations throughout Texas. For job listings at a specific location, apply online at the corporate website. **Positions advertised include:** Internal Auditor. **Other area locations:** Austin TX; Dallas TX; San Antonio TX; Fort Worth TX; Fredericksburg TX. **Other U.S. locations:** AZ; CA; CO; FL; MD; MI; NV; NJ: NC; OH; VA; Washington D.C. **Parent company:** Lennar. **Listed on:** New York Stock Exchange. **Stock exchange symbol:** LEN. **Number of employees nationwide:** 7,700

THE VISTAWALL GROUP
803 Airport Road, P.O. Box 629, Terrell TX 75160. 972/551-6100. **Toll-free phone:** 800/869-4567. **Fax:** 972/551-6210. **Contact:** Human Resources. **E-mail address:** careers@vistawall.com. **World Wide Web address:** http://www.vistawall.com. **Description:** The Vistawall Group, through its subsidiaries, designs, manufactures, and distributes entrances, storefront and low-rise framing systems, skylight systems, and engineered curtain wall systems. **Positions advertised include:** Contracts Manager/Project Management. **Corporate headquarters location:** This location. **Other area locations:** Dallas TX; Houston TX. **Subsidiaries include:** Moduline Window Systems; Naturalite Skylight Systems; Skywall Translucent Systems; Vistawall Architectural Products. **Parent company:** Butler Manufacturing Company.

WASHINGTON GROUP INTERNATIONAL
10550 Richmond Avenue, Suite 300, Houston TX 77042. 281/529-3100. **Fax:** 281/529-3119. **Contact:** Human Resources. **World Wide Web address:** http://www.wgint.com. **Description:** Provides a variety of technical construction services including design, engineering, and consulting with a customer base consisting mainly of petroleum refining, petrochemical, and chemical plants.

DAVID WEEKLEY HOMES
1111 North Post Oak Road, Houston TX 77055. 713/963-0500. **Fax:** 713/963-0322. **Contact:** Human Resources. **World Wide Web address:** http://www.davidweekleyhomes.com. **Description:** Builds energy-efficient homes and offers multilevel warranties. **NOTE:** Apply online. **Positions advertised include:** Help Desk Associate; Residential Sales Consultant; Residential Construction Superintendent; Marketing Coordinator. **Other area locations:** Austin TX; Dallas TX; San Antonio TX. **Other U.S. locations:** GA; NC; FL; GA; SC; CO; TN.

WHITING-TURNER COMPANY
2301 West Plano Parkway, Suite 104, Plano TX 75075. 469/429-0800. **Fax:** 469/429-0801. **Contact:** Human Resources. **World Wide Web address:**

http://www.whiting-turner.com. **Description:** A construction company that builds state-of-the-art retail and office buildings. Founded in 1909. **NOTE:** Send resume directly to the office. **Positions advertised include:** Architectural Engineers; Civil Engineers; Electrical Engineers; Mechanical Engineers; Structural Engineers; Building Technicians; Construction Managers. **Corporate headquarters location:** Baltimore MD. **Other U.S. locations:** Nationwide.

H.B. ZACHRY COMPANY
537 Logwood, San Antonio TX 78221. 210/475-8000. **Fax:** 210/475-8060. **Recorded jobline:** 800/JOB-SUSA. **Contact:** Larry Cantwell, Professional Employment Manager. **World Wide Web address:** http://www.zachry.com. **Description:** A construction management company operating through the following seven divisions: Process, Power, Heavy, Maintenance & Service, Commercial, International, and Pipeline. The company primarily builds power plants, highways, and pipelines in the southern United States, as well as in foreign countries. H.B. Zachry Company does not handle residential construction contracts. Founded in 1923. **NOTE:** Entry-level positions are offered. This company's website has a complete job listings on its website. Apply online. **Positions advertised include:** Documents Controls; Legal Secretary; Construction Electrical Facilitator; Design Technician; Mechanical Equipment Reliability Improvement Coordinator; Maintenance Supervisor; Civil Field Superintendents; Secretary **Special programs:** Summer Jobs. **Corporate headquarters location:** This location. **Listed on:** Privately held.

Utah

AMSCO WINDOWS
P.O. Box 25368, Salt Lake City UT 84125-0368. 801/972-6441. **Physical address:** 1880 South 1045 West, Salt Lake City UT 84104. **Contact:** Human Resources. **E-mail address:** personnel@amscowindows.com. **World Wide Web address:** http://www.amscowindows.com. **Description:** A window manufacturer. **NOTE:** See website for current job openings and application instructions. **Corporate headquarters location:** This location.

BIG-D CONSTRUCTION CORPORATION
404 West 400 South, Salt Lake City UT 84101. 801/415-6096. **Fax:** 801/415-6996. **Contact:** Randy Price, Human Resources. **E-mail address:** rprice@big-d.com. **World Wide Web address:** http://www.big-d.com. **Description:** A commercial construction firm. Founded in 1967. **Positions advertised include:** Senior Project Manager; Senior Estimator; Craftsmen. **Corporate headquarters location:** This location. **Other U.S. locations:** Lindon UT; Ogden UT. **Listed on:** Privately held. **CEO:** Jack Livingood.

CH2M HILL
215 South State Street, Suite, 1000 Salt Lake City UT 84111. 801/350-5200. **Fax:** 801/355-2301. **Contact:** Human Resources. **E-mail address:** hr@ch2m.com. **World Wide Web address:** http://www.ch2m.com. **Description:** A group of employee-owned companies operating under the names CH2M Hill, Inc., Industrial Design Corporation, Operations Management International, CH2M Hill International, and CH2M Hill Engineering. The company provides planning, engineering design, and operation and construction management services to help clients apply technology, safeguard the environment, and develop infrastructure. The professional staff includes specialists in environmental engineering and waste management, water management, transportation, industrial facilities, and a broad spectrum of infrastructure systems. Founded in 1946. **NOTE:** Search and apply for current job openings online. **Corporate headquarters location:** Englewood CO.

DMJM H&N
1135 South West Temple, Suite A, Salt Lake City UT 84101. 801/363-5085. **Fax:** 801/ 961-7373. **Contact:** Human Resources. **World Wide Web address:** http://www.dmjmhn.com. **Description:** Provides a full range of architectural and engineering services. **NOTE:** Resumes for engineering positions should be addressed to Ed Patience. Resumes regarding architectural positions should be sent to Ralph Stanislaw. **Special programs:** Internships. **Corporate headquarters location:** New York NY. **Other U.S. locations:** Nationwide. **Operations at this facility include:** Divisional Headquarters; Service. **Parent company:** AECOM Technology.

FORSGREN ASSOCIATES
370 East 500 South, Suite 200, Salt Lake City UT 84111. 801/364-4785. **Toll-free phone:** 800/826-9304. **Fax:** 801/364-4802. **Contact:** Human Resources. **E-mail address:** ckemp@forsgren.com. **World Wide Web address:** http://www.forsgren.com. **Description:** A civil engineering firm. **Other area locations:** Farmington UT. **Other U.S. locations:** Wenatchee WA; Boise ID; Rexburg ID; Evanston WY; Ouray CO; Sacramento CA.

JACOBSEN CONSTRUCTION COMPANY, INC.
P.O. Box 27608, Salt Lake City UT 84127-0608. 801/973-0500. **Physical address:** 3131 West 2210 South, Salt Lake City UT 84119. **Fax:** 801/973-7496. **Contact:** Human Resources Department. **E-mail address:** hr-dept@jacobsenconstruction.com. **World Wide Web address:** http://www.jacobsenconstruction.com. **Description:** A general contractor involved in large commercial, industrial, manufacturing, public works, and institutional projects. Founded in 1922. **NOTE:** Entry-level and experienced positions are offered. Please visit website to download application form. **Special programs:** Apprenticeships; Training; Summer Jobs. **Corporate headquarters location:** This location. **Subsidiaries include:** Jacobsen Construction Services. **Listed on:** Privately held. **President/CEO:** Lonnie M. Bullard. **Number of employees nationwide:** 450.

LAYTON CONSTRUCTION
9090 South Sandy Parkway, Sandy UT 84070. 801/568-9090. **Fax:** 801/563-3695. **Contact:** Human Resources. **E-mail address:** hr@laytoncompanies.com. **World Wide Web address:** http://www.layton-const.com. **Description:** Engaged in industrial and commercial construction. **NOTE:** Please visit website to download application form. Resumes are only accepted when accompanies by the application form. **Positions advertised include:** Project Engineer; Designer; Senior Construction Manager; Project Administrator/Project Assistant; Superintendent. **Other U.S. locations:** AR; ID; OR.

THE SHAW GROUP
7090 South Union Park Avenue, Suite 500, Midvale UT 84047-6059. 801/565-1122. **Fax:** 801/565-1761. **Contact:** Human Resources. **World Wide Web address:** http://www.shawgrp.com. **Description:** A construction management company. **Corporate headquarters location:** Baton Rouge LA. **Other area locations:** Clearfield UT. **Other U.S. locations:** Nationwide.

TRANSCORE
488 East 6400 South, Suite 375, Murray UT 84107. 801/293-1920. **Fax:** 801/293-1921. **Contact:** Human Resources. **World Wide Web address:** http://www.transcore.com. **Description:** TransCore is a traffic engineering and transportation-planning firm. **NOTE:** See website for current job openings and to apply online. Or, mail resumes to 8158 Adams Drive, Hummelstown PA 17036; fax to 717/564-8439. **Positions advertised include:** TOC Operator. **Other U.S. locations:** Nationwide. **Parent company:** Roper Industries. **President/CEO:** John Worthington.

WON-DOOR CORPORATION
1865 South 3480 West, Salt Lake City UT 84104. 801/973-7500. **Toll-free phone:** 800/453-8494. **Fax:** 801/977-9749. **Contact:** Personnel. **E-mail address:** personnel@wondoor.com. **World Wide Web address:** http://www.wondoor.com. **Description:** Manufactures sliding partition doors and swinging fire doors. **Corporate headquarters location:** This location.

Other U.S. locations: Nationwide. **International locations:** Canada; Taiwan; United Kingdom; New Zealand; Singapore; Germany.

Vermont

ENGELBERTH CONSTRUCTION, INC.
463 Mountain View Drive, Colchester VT 05446. 802/655-2307. **Fax:** 802/655-2391. **Contact:** Gina Catanzarita, Director of Human Resources. **E-mail address:** ginac@engelberth.com. **World Wide Web address:** http://www.engelberth.com. **Description:** An industrial construction company and general contractor with ongoing contracts at area churches and schools while maintaining a core business in hospital construction. At regional ski resorts, including Killington, Stratton Mountain, and Stowe, the company has construction contracts for building housing and expanding base lodges. **Other U.S. locations:** Keene NH. **Corporate headquarters location:** This location. **Annual sales/revenues:** $80 million. **Number of employees:** 280.

NORTHEASTERN LOG HOMES
492 Scott Highway, P.O. Box 126, Groton VT 05046-0126. 802/584-3336. **Fax:** 802/584-3200. **Contact:** Human Resources. **World Wide Web address:** http://www.northeasternlog.com. **Description:** Manufactures precut log, post, and beam homes. Founded in 1972. **Corporate headquarters location:** This location. **Other U.S. locations:** Kenduskeag ME; Louisville KY; Westfield MA. **Listed on:** Privately held. **Number of employees at this location:** 90.

PIZZAGALLI CONSTRUCTION COMPANY
50 Joy Drive, P.O. Box 2009, South Burlington VT 05403. 802/651-1271. **Fax:** 802/651-1208. **Contact:** Jim Carabell, Employee Development and Personnel Manager. **E-mail address:** resumes@pizzagalli.com. **World Wide Web address:** http://www.pizzagalli.com. **Description:** A general contractor that handles projects including water and wastewater treatment plants; government work including army barracks and prisons; and high school renovations and additions. **Positions advertised include:** Records Retention Coordinator; Project Manager; Superintendent. **Special programs:** Training; Internships; Co-ops. **Corporate headquarters location:** This location. **Other U.S. locations:** Garner NC; South Portland ME. **Subsidiaries/Affiliates include:** Pizzagalli Properties, LLC. **Number of employees at this location:** 95. **Number of employees nationwide:** 1,200.

RUSSELL CONSTRUCTION SERVICES
170 South Main Street, Suite 6, Rutland VT 05701-4599. 802/775-3325, extension 212. **Fax:** 802/775-8287. **Contact:** Jo Muscatello, Human Resources Supervisor. **E-mail address:** jmuscatello@jarc.com. **World Wide Web address:** http://www.jarc.com. **Description:** A construction company and general contractor that builds schools, warehouses, and grocery stores. Founded in 1934. **Positions advertised include:** Welder; Superintendent; Field Engineer.

Virginia

ALCOA HOME EXTERIORS, INC.
185 Johnson Drive, Stuarts Draft VA 24477-0538. 540/337-3663. **Contact:** Human Resources. **World Wide Web address:** http://www.alcoa.com. **Description:** Manufactures vinyl siding for sale to distributors. **NOTE:** Search and apply for positions online. **Corporate headquarters location:** Pittsburgh PA. **Other U.S. locations:** Denison TX; Gaffney SC; Sidney OH; Atlanta GA. **Parent company:** Alcoa, Inc. **Listed on:** New York Stock Exchange. **Stock exchange symbol:** AA. **Number of employees nationwide:** 1,600.

AMSEC LLC
2829 Guardian Lane, Virginia Beach VA 23452. 757/463-6666. **Fax:** 757/463-9110. **Contact:** Human Resources. **World Wide Web address:** http://www.amsec.com. **Description:** An employee-owned company that provides engineering, technical, and program management solutions and services to customers throughout the U.S. with clients primarily in the business of navy and commercial marine engineering, naval architecture, and information technology. **Positions advertised include:** HR Assistant; Associate Contracts Rep; Sr. Vice President of Finance and Accounting; Finance Manager.

AMERICAN WOODMARK CORPORATION
3102 Shawnee Drive, Winchester VA 22601-4208. 540/665-9100. **Contact:** Human Resources Director. **World Wide Web address:** http://www.americanwoodmark.com. **Description:** Manufactures and distributes kitchen cabinets and vanities. The company's products are sold nationally through a network of independent distributors, home centers, major builders, and home manufacturers. Founded in 1980. **NOTE:** Entry-level positions and part-time jobs are offered. **Positions advertised include:** Manager; Auditor; Systems Developer **Corporate headquarters location:** This location. **Other U.S. locations:** AZ; GA; IN; KY; MN; OK; TN; WV. **Listed on:** NASDAQ. **Stock exchange symbol:** AMWD. **Annual sales/revenues:** $564 million. **Number of employees at this location:** 220. **Number of employees nationwide:** 2,600.

MICHAEL BAKER CORPORATION
3601 Eisenhower Avenue, Suite 600, Alexandria VA 22304. 703/960-8800. **Fax:** 703/960-9125. **Contact:** Human Resources Department. **World Wide Web address:** http://www.mbakercorp.com. **Description:** Provides engineering consulting and design services, construction services, and operations and maintenance services. As the company's core business, the engineering group encompasses a broad range of disciplines required to plan, design, and inspect the construction of architectural and engineering projects. Michael Baker's construction group consists of construction management and design, heavy and highway construction, and general construction. Maintains offices in 21 states and six other countries. **NOTE:** Search and apply for positions online. **Positions advertised include:** Technical Manager; Business Systems Analyst; Civil Associate; Civil Engineer; GIS Specialist; Software Systems Developer; Public Relations Specialist; Marketing Coordinator; Planning Associate; Project Manager; Operations Manager; Technical Specialist. **Corporate headquarters location:** Moon Township PA. **Other U.S. locations:** Nationwide. **International locations:** Worldwide. **Listed on:** AMEX. **Stock exchange symbol:** BKR. Number of employees nationwide: 4,400.

BARBER & ROSS COMPANY
255 Fort Collier Road, Winchester VA 22603. 540/722-9199. **Fax:** 540/545-4886. **Contact:** Human Resources. **Description:** Manufactures window units, interior and exterior door units, door entrance products, and other door products and accessories. Founded in 1876. **Corporate headquarters location:** This location. **Other area locations:** Richmond VA. **Other U.S. locations:** Mebane NC; Knox IN. **Number of employees nationwide:** 1,200.

THE CHRISTOPHER COMPANIES
10306 Eaton Place, Suite 450, Fairfax VA 22030. 703/352-5950. **Fax:** 703/352-0960. **Contact:** Human Resources Department. **World Wide Web address:** http://www.christophercompanies.com. **Description:** Engaged in the building of customized homes, condominiums, and townhouse developments in the northern Virginia area. Founded in 1974.

DEWBERRY
8401 Arlington Boulevard, Fairfax VA 22031-4666. 703/849-0525. **Fax:** 703/849-0185. **Contact:** Richard A. Penner, Director of Personnel. **E-mail address:** hr@dewberry.com. **World Wide Web address:** http://www.dewberry.com. **Description:** A full-service architectural and engineering firm. Operations include planning, engineering, architecture, program management, surveying and mapping. Founded in

1956. **NOTE:** Entry-level positions are offered. Search and apply for positions online. **Positions advertised include:** Civil Engineer, Transportation; Project Manager; System Network Engineer. **Special programs:** Internships. **Office hours:** Monday - Friday, 8:00 a.m. - 5:00 p.m. **Corporate headquarters location:** This location. **Other U.S. locations:** 30 offices in 14 states. **Listed on:** Privately held. **Annual sales/revenues:** More than $100 million. **Number of employees at this location:** 800. **Number of employees nationwide:** 1,500.

DAVIS H. ELLIOT COMPANY INC.
P.O. Box 12707, Roanoke VA 24027-2707. 540/344-1294. **Fax:** 540/344-9888. **Contact:** Human Resources. **World Wide Web address:** http://www.davishelliot.com. **Description:** A construction service provider that specializes in commercial and industrial electrical construction, the design and manufacturing of electric control panels, and transmission and distribution line construction and repair. Founded in 1946. **NOTE:** Entry-level positions are offered. **Special programs:** Apprenticeships. **Office hours:** Monday - Friday, 8:00 a.m. - 5:00 p.m. **Corporate headquarters location:** This location. **Other U.S. locations:** Lexington KY; Broken Arrow OK.

EMCOR CONSTRUCTION SERVICES
1420 Spring Hill Road, Suite 500, McLean VA 22102. 703/556-8000. **Fax:** 703/556-0890. **Contact:** Lynn Mauer, Human Resources. **World Wide Web address:** http://www.emcorgroup.com. **Description:** A national electrical construction contractor. **NOTE:** Search and apply for positions online. **Parent company:** EMCOR Group Inc. **Listed on:** New York Stock Exchange. **Stock exchange symbol:** EME.

EXPONENT, INC.
1800 Diagonal Road, Suite 300, Alexandria VA 22314. 571/227-7200. **Fax:** 571/227-7299. **Contact:** Human Resources. **E-mail address:** hr@exponent.com. **World Wide Web address:** http://www.exponent.com. **Description:** An engineering and scientific consulting firm that performs in-depth scientific research and analysis and rapid-response evaluations for clients' technical problems. Founded in 1967. **NOTE:** Search and apply for positions online. **Positions advertised include:** Managing Civil Engineer; Technology Development Engineer; Construction Manager; Construction Engineer. **Corporate headquarters location:** Menlo Park CA. **Other area locations:** Washington DC; Bowie MD. **International locations:** Germany; United Kingdom. **Listed on:** NASDAQ. **Stock exchange symbol:** EXPO.

FERGUSON ENTERPRISES, INC.
12500 Jefferson Avenue, Newport News VA 23602. 757/874-7795. **Fax:** 757/989-2501. **Contact:** Recruiting Department. **E-mail address:** expresumes@ferguson.com. **World Wide Web address:** http://www.ferguson.com. **Description:** A coast-to-coast wholesale distributor, supplying plumbing and builder products, industrial pipe, valves and fittings, heating and cooling equipment, waterworks products, and tool and safety products. Ferguson Enterprises operates over 500 locations in 49 states, D.C. Puerto Rico, and Mexico. Founded in 1953. **NOTE:** Offers entry-level positions. **Other U.S. locations:** Nationwide. **International locations:** Mexico; Puerto Rico. **Parent company:** Wolseley.

HDR INC.
1101 King Street, Suite 400, Alexandria VA 22314-2944. 703/518-8500. **Fax:** 703/518-8649. **Contact:** Human Resources. **World Wide Web address:** http://www.hdrinc.com. **Description:** HDR is an architectural, engineering and consulting firm. **Positions advertised include:** Structural CAD Technician; Interior Designer; Water/Wastewater Project Manager; Sr. Marketing Coordinator; Project Architect; Laboratory Planner; Clean Room Designer; Marketing Coordinator. **Corporate headquarters location:** Omaha NB. **Other area locations:** Norfolk VA; Richmond VA. **Number of employees worldwide:** 4,100.

NATIONWIDE HOMES, INC.
1100 Rives Road, P.O. Box 5511, Martinsville VA 24115. 276/632-7100. **Toll-free phone:** 800/216-7001. **Fax:** 276/666-2537. **Contact:** John Adams, Human Resources Director. **World Wide Web address:** http://www.nationwide-homes.com. **Description:** Builder of modular single-family homes, commercial structures, multi-family residences, and remodeling additions. **NOTE:** Entry-level positions are offered. **Special programs:** Apprenticeships; Summer Jobs. **Office hours:** Monday - Friday, 8:00 a.m. - 5:00 p.m. **Listed on:** Privately held. **President/CEO:** Ronald Evans. **Annual sales/revenues:** $21 - $50 million. **Number of employees at this location:** 450.

PBS&J CORPORATION
11818 Rock Landing Drive, Suite 102, Newport News VA 23606-4395. 757/596-8267. **Fax:** 757/596-8660. **Contact:** Human Resources. **World Wide Web address:** http://www.pbsj.com. **Description:** Provides planning, architectural, engineering, and construction management services. The group targets the transportation and environmental markets, and nearly 80% of its sales are derived from public-sector projects. **Positions advertised include:** CADD Technician; Project Manager; Engineer; Sr. Engineer; Program Assistant. **Corporate headquarters location:** Miami FL.

PIERCE ASSOCIATES
4216 Wheeler Avenue, P.O. Box 9050, Alexandria VA 22304-9050. 703/751-2400. **Fax:** 703/751-2479. **Contact:** Human Resource Manager. **E-mail address:** hr@pai.us. **World Wide Web address:** http://www.pierceassociates.com. **Description:** A contractor specializing in mechanical construction (HVAC, plumbing, and fire protection.) **Corporate headquarters location:** This location. **Listed on:** Privately held. **Number of employees at this location:** 40.

RADIAN INC.
5845 Richmond Highway, Suite 725, Alexandria VA 22303. 703/329-9300. **Toll-free phone:** 800/595-5593. **Fax:** 703/317-2020. **Contact:** Human Resources. **E-mail address:** hr@radianinc.com. **World Wide Web address:** http://www.radianinc.com. **Description:** Radian Inc. is a full-service provider of engineering, logistics, system integration, and life-cycle management services for government and commercial customers. Founded in 1977. **Positions advertised include:** VP of Finance; Supply Technician; Mechanic; Security System Project Engineer; Facilities Security Officer; Accountant; Logistician; Jr. Engineer; Electrician; Installation Technician. **Parent company:** Engineered Support Systems, Inc. (ESSI).

RAYTHEON UTD
8350 Alban Road, Suite 700, Springfield VA 22150. 703/440-8834. **Fax:** 703/455-4676. **Contact:** Human Resources. **E-mail address:** careers@utdinc.com. **World Wide Web address:** http://www.raytheon.com. **Description:** Raytheon UTD provides engineering and scientific analysis, assessment and technology development to federal, state and local government agencies. **NOTE:** Search for positions online. **Positions advertised include:** Civil/Geotechnical Engineer; Sr. Systems Engineer; Instrumentation Engineer.

TIDEWATER SKANSKA, INC.
P.O. Box 57, Norfolk VA 23501. 757/578-4100. **Physical address:** 809 South Military Highway, Virginia Beach VA 23464. **Fax:** 757/420-3551. **Contact:** Human Resources. **E-mail address:** mail@tidewaterskanska.com. **World Wide Web address:** http://www.usacivil.skanska.com. **Description:** A heavy industrial, highway, and bridge contractor with primary operations in the Southeast. **Positions advertised include:** Marine/Bridge Superintendent; Project Engineer; Sr. Purchasing/Sub-Contract Specialist; Sr. Project Manager. **Corporate**

headquarters location: This location. **Parent company:** Skanska USA Civil, Inc. **Listed on:** Privately held. **Annual sales/revenues:** More than $100 million. **Number of employees at this location:** 90. **Number of employees nationwide:** 600.

WILLIAMS INDUSTRIES INC.
P.O. Box 1770, Manassas VA 20109. 703/335-7800. **Physical address:** 8624 J.D. Reading Drive, Manassas VA 20109. **Fax:** 703/335-7802. **Contact:** Human Resources. **World Wide Web address:** http://www.wmsi.com. **Description:** A general construction company for the industrial, commercial, and institutional construction markets. Founded in 1970. **NOTE:** Entry-level positions and second and third shifts are offered. **Special programs:** Apprenticeships. **Office hours:** Monday - Friday, 8:30 a.m. - 4:30 p.m. **Corporate headquarters location:** This location. **Listed on:** NASDAQ. **Stock exchange symbol:** WMSI. **Number of employees nationwide:** 400.

Washington
ANVIL CORPORATION
1675 West Bakerview Road, Bellingham WA 98226. 360/671-1450. **Contact:** Johanna Snyder, Human Resources. **E-mail address:** jsnyder@anvilcorp.com. **World Wide Web address:** http://www.anvilcorp.com. **Description:** An engineering and technical services company that provides a variety of services to the mining, environmental, utilities, transportation, and chemical industries. **Positions advertised include:** NDE Technician. **Corporate headquarters location:** This location.

ROBERT E. BAYLEY CONSTRUCTION
8005 SE 28th Street, Suite 100, Mercer Island WA 98040-9004. 206/621-8884. **Fax:** 206/343-7728. **Contact:** Personnel Department. **World Wide Web address:** http://www.bayley.net. **Description:** A general building contractor specializing in commercial construction. **Corporate headquarters location:** This location.

R.W. BECK, INC.
1001 Fourth Avenue, Suite 2500, Seattle WA 98154. 206/695-4700. **Contact:** Mr. Van Finger, Director of Personnel. **World Wide Web address:** http://www.rwbeck.com. **Description:** A diversified professional, technical, and management consulting firm. The company provides construction, environmental, technical, energy, solid waste, and water/wastewater services nationwide. **NOTE:** Apply online. **Positions advertised include:** Senior Project Manager. **Corporate headquarters location:** This location. **Number of employees at this location:** 175. **Number of employees nationwide:** 500.

BERGER/ABAM ENGINEERS INC.
33301 Ninth Avenue South, Suite 300, Federal Way WA 98003-2600. 206/431-2300. **Fax:** 206/431-2250. **Contact:** Personnel. **E-mail address:** employment@abam.com. **World Wide Web address:** http://www.abam.com. **Description:** A civil engineering and consulting firm specializing in the design of piers and waterfront structures, tanks and reservoirs, bridges, transit guideways, buildings, floating structures, and offshore drilling platforms. Berger/Abam Engineers Inc. also performs concrete material research, advanced computer design analysis, and construction management services. **Positions advertised include:** Document Production Specialist; Civil Engineer. **Corporate headquarters location:** This location.

CH2M HILL
P.O. Box 91500, Bellevue WA 98009-2050. 425/453-5000. **Physical address:** 1100 112th Avenue Northeast, Bellevue WA 98004. **Contact:** Human Resources. **World Wide Web address:** http://www.ch2m.com. **Description:** CH2M Hill is group of employee-owned companies operating under the names CH2M Hill, Inc., Industrial Design Corporation, Operations Management International, CH2M Hill International, and CH2M Hill Engineering. The company provides planning, engineering design, and operation and construction management services to help clients apply technology, safeguard the environment, and develop infrastructure. The professional staff includes specialists in environmental engineering and waste management, water management, transportation, industrial facilities, and a broad spectrum of infrastructure systems. Founded in 1946. **Corporate headquarters location:** Denver CO. **Other U.S. locations:** Nationwide. **Number of employees at this location:** 350. **Number of employees nationwide:** 4,000.

CALLISON ARCHITECTURE
1420 Fifth Avenue, Suite 2400, Seattle WA 98101. 206/623-4646. **Fax:** 206/623-4625. **Contact:** Human Resources. **E-mail address:** employment@callison.com. **World Wide Web address:** http://www.callison.com. **Description:** Provides architectural and design services to the healthcare, hospitality, residential, and retail markets. **Positions advertised include:** Administrative Assistant; Designer; Specification Writer. **Corporate headquarters location:** This location.

CAPITAL DEVELOPMENT COMPANY
711 Sleater Kinney Road Southeast, Lacey WA 98503. 360/491-6850. **Contact:** Human Resources. **Description:** Engaged in a variety of construction activities including contracting, leasing, and property development and management.

COCHRAN ELECTRIC COMPANY INC.
P.O. Box 33524, Seattle WA 98133-0524. 206/367-1900. **Physical address:** 12500 Aurora Avenue North, Seattle WA 98206. **Fax:** 206/368-3218. **Contact:** Personnel Department. **E-mail address:** jobs@cochraninc.com. **World Wide Web address:** http://www.cochran-inc.com. **Description:** Engaged in commercial and industrial electrical work and powerline engineering. **Corporate headquarters location:** This location.

CONTROL SOLUTIONS NORTHWEST
7222 East Nora Avenue, Spokane WA 99212. 509/892-1121. **Contact:** Human Resources. **World Wide Web address:** http://www.invensysibs.com. **Description:** Provides heating, ventilation, and air conditioning services.

DLR GROUP
900 Fourth Avenue, Suite 700, Seattle WA 98164. 206/461-6000. **Contact:** Jill Star, Recruiter. **E-mail address:** jstar@dlrgroup.com. **World Wide Web address:** http://www.dlrgroup.com. **Description:** An architectural design firm that specializes in educational, judicial, medical, and recreational projects.

WAYNE DALTON CORPORATION
2001 Industrial Drive, Centralia WA 98531. 360/736-7651. **Toll-free phone:** 877/827-3667. **Contact:** John Peterson, Human Resources. **World Wide Web address:** http://www.wayne-dalton.com. **Description:** Manufactures garage doors and related items. **Corporate headquarters location:** Mt. Hope OH. **Parent company:** Hardsco Corporation.

EDAW INC.
815 Western Avenue, Suite 300, Seattle WA 98104. 206/622-1176. **Fax:** 206/343-9809. **Contact:** Human Resources. **E-mail address:** humanresources@edaw.com. **World Wide Web address:** http://www.edaw.com. **Description:** Engaged in landscape architecture, environmental planning, and urban design services worldwide. **Corporate headquarters location:** San Francisco CA. **Other U.S. locations:** Irvine CA; Denver CO; Atlanta GA; Alexandria VA. **Operations at this facility include:** Administration; Service. **Number of employees at this location:** 15. **Number of employees nationwide:** 200. **Number of employees worldwide:** 250.

FLUOR FEDERAL SERVICES

1200 Jadwin Avenue, P.O. Box 1050, Richland WA 99352. 509/372-2000. **Contact:** Human Resources. **World Wide Web address:** http://www.fluor.com. **E-mail address:** ffshr@flour.com. **Description:** A full-service engineering and construction company serving the power, industrial, hydrocarbon, and process industries, as well as the federal government. **Parent company:** Fluor Corporation (Irvine CA) is engaged in engineering and construction, as well as the production of various natural resources. Fluor Corporation provides its services to energy, natural resource, industrial, commercial, utility, and government clients. Natural resources mined include gold, silver, lead, zinc, iron ore, coal, oil, and gas. The corporation also provides contract drilling services. **Listed on:** New York Stock Exchange. **Stock exchange symbol:** FLR. **Number of employees worldwide:** 20,000.

HUTTIG BUILDING PRODUCTS
525 South C Street NW, Auburn WA 98001. 253/941-2600. **Fax:** 253/735-9370. **Contact:** Director of Employee Relations. **World Wide Web address:** http://www.huttig.com. **Description:** A wholesale distributor of building materials. **Positions advertised include:** Branch Manager; Outside Sales Representative. **Corporate headquarters location:** Chesterfield MO.

JCV CONSTRUCTORS
325 South Kenyon Street, P.O. Box 80346, Seattle WA 98108-0346. 206/762-4219. **Contact:** Personnel Department. **Description:** Engaged in general contract construction. Founded in 1991. **Annual sales/revenues:** $11 - $20 million. **Number of employees at this location:** 10.

KIEWIT COMPANIES
2200 Columbia House Boulevard, Vancouver WA 98661. 360/693-1478. **Fax:** 360/693-5582. **Contact:** Human Resources Manager. **E-mail address:** human.resources@kiewit.com. **World Wide Web address:** http://www.kiewit.com. **Description:** One of the largest construction companies in the country. Kiewit's primary markets are building, power, transportation, water resources, and mining. Types of projects include highways, bridges, high-rise buildings, office complexes, railroads, tunnels, subways, dams, airports, power plants, canals, water treatment facilities, offshore petroleum platforms, and other heavy civil projects. The company has district offices throughout North America. **Positions advertised include:** Engineer; Project Manager. **Corporate headquarters location:** Omaha NE.

LINDAL CEDAR HOMES INC.
4300 South 104th Place, Seattle WA 98178. 206/725-0900. **Fax:** 206/725-1615. **Contact:** Personnel Department. **E-mail address:** employment@lindal.com. **World Wide Web address:** http://www.lindal.com. **Description:** Manufactures cedar homes and sunrooms. Lindal also provides wholesale lumber, building materials, and related services. **Positions advertised include:** Area Manager. **Corporate headquarters location:** This location.

LANCE MUELLER & ASSOCIATES
130 Lakeside Avenue, Suite 250, Seattle WA 98122. 206/325-2553. **Fax:** 206/328-0554. **Contact:** Lance Mueller, Principal. **E-mail address:** lmueller@lmueller.com. **World Wide Web address:** http://www.lma-architects.com. **Description:** An architectural firm that specializes in commercial projects.

NBBJ ARCHITECTURE DESIGN PLANNING
111 South Jackson Street, Seattle WA 98104. 206/223-5555. **Fax:** 206/621-2300. **Contact:** Personnel. **World Wide Web address:** http://www.nbbj.com. **Description:** An architectural design firm. NBBJ specializes in commercial buildings, health facilities, sports and entertainment complexes, airports, retail centers, government buildings, and senior living facilities. The company is also heavily engaged in urban planning and design, campus planning, and graphic design services. **Positions advertised include:** Architect; Planner; Interior Designer; Graphic Designer. **Other U.S. locations:** Los Angeles CA; San Francisco CA; Research Triangle Park NC; New York NY; Columbus OH. **International locations:** Japan; Norway; Taiwan. **Operations at this facility include:** Service.

NORD COMPANY
300 West Marine View Drive, P.O. Box 1187, Everett WA 98201. 425/259-9292. **Contact:** Personnel Department. **Description:** Produces wood-style and rail-panel doors, louver products, columns and posts, and arch spindles. **Corporate headquarters location:** Clamout Falls OR.

PARSONS BRINCKERHOFF INC.
999 Third Avenue, Suite 2200, Seattle WA 98104-4020. 206/382-5200. **Fax:** 206/382-5222. **Contact:** Personnel. **World Wide Web address:** http://www.pbworld.com. **Description:** An engineering and design firm engaged in the design of bridges, tunnels, rapid transit systems, hydroelectric facilities, water supply systems, and marine facilities worldwide. **Corporate headquarters location:** New York NY.

THE SIMPSON DOOR COMPANY
400 West Simpson Avenue, McCleary WA 98557. 360/495-3291. **Fax:** 360/495-3295. **Contact:** Human Resources. **World Wide Web address:** http://www.simpsondoor.com. **Description:** Manufactures doors. Founded in 1912. **NOTE:** Unsolicited resumes/applications are not accepted. Employment opportunities are usually listed in the corresponding community's newspaper. **Corporate headquarters location:** This location.

URS CORPORATION
Century Square, 1501 Fourth Avenue, Suite 1440, Seattle WA 98101-1616. 206/438-2700. **Contact:** Human Resources. **World Wide Web address:** http://www.urscorp.com. **Description:** An architectural, engineering, and environmental consulting firm that specializes in air transportation, environmental solutions, surface transportation, and industrial environmental and engineering concerns. **Positions advertised include:** Civil Geotechnical Engineer; Electrical Senior Designer; Environmental Technician; Graduate Civil Engineer; Graduate Geologist; Marketing Services Manager; Mechanical Engineer; Principal Environmental Scientist; Project Toxicologist; CADD Designer; Senior Estimator.

UTILX CORPORATION
P.O. Box 97009, Kent WA 98064-9709. 253/395-0200. **Physical address**: 22820 Russell Road, Kent WA 98032. **Fax:** 253/395-1040. **Contact:** Personnel. **E-mail address:** jobs@utilx.com. **World Wide Web address:** http://www.utilx.com. **Description:** Provides installation and maintenance services for underground utilities including electricity, water, gas, and telephone. UTILX's technologies include the FlowMole guided drilling system and the CableCure service for injecting silicon fluids into utility cables to repair damage from water. The company's services are marketed domestically while their products are sold primarily in international markets. **Corporate headquarters location:** This location. **Subsidiaries include:** Flow Mole Limited (UK). **Number of employees at this location:** 100. **Number of employees nationwide:** 500.

WEATHERVANE WINDOW COMPANY
7911 S. 188th Street, Kent WA 98032. 425/827-9669. **Toll-free phone:** 800/634-3433. **Fax:** 425/822-9797. **Contact:** Human Resources. **World Wide Web address:** http://www.weathervanewindows.com. **Description:** Manufactures wood, aluminum-clad wood, and vinyl windows.

HOWARD S. WRIGHT CONSTRUCTION COMPANY
425 Pontius Avenue North, Suite 100, Seattle WA 98109. 206/447-7654. **Fax:** 206/447-7727. **Contact:**

Personnel. **World Wide Web address:** http://www.hswright.com. **Description:** A general contracting company for nonresidential buildings.

West Virginia

BURGESS & NIPLE
1124 Smith Street, Suite 105, Charleston WV 25301. 304/343-9370. **Contact:** Human Resources. **E-mail address:** hr@burnip.com. **World Wide Web address:** http://www.burgessniple.com. **Description:** An engineering and architecture firm engaged in study, analysis, and design services. The company specializes in waterworks, wastewater, industrial services, hydropower, energy conservation, transportation, systems analysis, HVAC, and geotechnical services. **Positions advertised include:** Bridge Engineer, Travel Demand Forecaster. **Corporate headquarters location:** Columbus OH. **Other area locations:** Parkersburg. **Other U.S. locations:** AZ; KY; IN; OH; PA; VA.

PARSONS BRINCKERHOFF INC.
1000 Green River Drive, Suite 101, Fairmont WV 26554. 304/534-4405. **Fax:** 304/534-4406. **Contact:** Human Resources. **E-mail address:** careers@pbworld.com. **World Wide Web address:** http://www.pbworld.com. **Description:** Provides engineering and construction management services, including the development of major bridges, tunnels, highways, marine facilities, buildings, industrial complexes, and railroads. **Special Programs:** Internships; College Campus Visits. **Corporate headquarters location:** New York NY.

VECELLIO & GROGAN, INC.
P.O. Box 2438, Beckley WV 25802-2438. 304/252-6575. **Physical address:** 2251 Robert C. Byrd Drive, Beckley WV 25801. **Toll-free phone:** 800/255-6575. **Fax:** 304/252-4131. **Contact:** Penny Jones, Personnel Manager. **E-mail address:** HR@VecellioGrogan.com. **World Wide Web address:** http://www.vecelliogrogan.com. **Description:** A construction company specializing in highways and bridges. **Positions advertised include:** Foreman; Equipment Operator; Truck Driver; Field Mechanic; Survey Crew; Laborer.

Wisconsin

AZCO, INC.
P.O. Box 567, Appleton WI 54912-0567. 920/734-5791. **Physical address:** 806 Valley Road, Menasha WI 54952. **Fax:** 920/734-7432. **Contact:** Recruiter. **E-mail address:** smitchell@azco-inc.com. **World Wide Web address:** http://www.azco-inc.com. **Description:** An employee-owned full-service integrated construction firm specializing in machinery installation, structural steel construction, construction management, pipe and sheet metal installations, and boiler repair and installation. **Positions advertised include:** Project Manager; Superintendent; Quality Control Inspector; Safety Representative; Project Coordinator. **Other area locations:** Appleton WI.

THE BOLDT COMPANY
2525 North Roemer Road, Appleton WI 54911. 920/739-6321. **Fax:** 920/739-4409. **Contact:** Human Resources. **E-mail address:** resume@boldt.com. **World Wide Web address:** http://www.theboldtcompany.com. **Description:** A construction services firm specializing in the pulp and paper, engineering, and construction industries. **Corporate headquarters location:** This location. **Other area locations:** Madison WI, Milwaukee WI. **Other U.S. locations:** GA, IL, MN, OK. **Subsidiaries include:** Oscar J. Boldt Construction; Boldt Technical Services; Boldt Consulting Services.

BUILDING SERVICE INC. (BSI)
11925 West Carmen Avenue, Milwaukee WI 53225-2134. 414/353-3600. **Fax:** 414/358-5092. **Contact:** Paula Brierton, Human Resources Manager. **E-mail address:** pbrierton@buildingservice.com. **World Wide Web address:** http://www.buildingservice.com. **Description:** Offers interior design and space planning to construction management services for renovations and new construction. **Other area locations:** Appleton WI.

CRESTLINE
888 Southview Drive, Mosinee WI 54455. 715/693-7000. **Fax:** 715/693-8505. **Contact:** Personnel. **World Wide Web address:** http://www.crestlinewindows.com. **Description:** A manufacturer of windows, patio doors, and skylights under the Vetter and Crestline labels. Founded in 1892. **NOTE:** Entry-level positions are offered. **Corporate headquarters location:** This location. **Parent company:** SNE Enterprises, Inc. (also at this location).

CRISPELL-SNYDER, INC.
700 Geneva Parkway, P.O. Box 550, Lake Geneva WI 53147. 262/348-5600. **Toll-free phone:** 800/203-7700. **Fax:** 262/348-9979. **Contact:** Maggie Mentel, Human Resources Director. **E-mail address:** mentelm@crispell-snyder.com. **World Wide Web address:** http://www.crispell-snyder.com. **Description:** Consulting engineers specializing in civil engineering for small municipalities in southeastern and eastern Wisconsin. Crispell-Snyder provides services in the areas of transportation, water resources, wastewater treatment, general public works engineering, studies, grant writing, and structural engineering. **NOTE:** Entry-level positions and part-time jobs are offered. **Positions advertised include:** Senior Public Works Engineer. **Special programs:** Internships; Co-ops; Summer Jobs. **Corporate headquarters location:** This location. **Other area locations:** Germantown WI; Racine WI. **Listed on:** Privately held. **Annual sales/revenues:** Less than $5 million. **Number of employees at this location:** 45. **Number of employees nationwide:** 75.

MARSHALL ERDMAN AND ASSOCIATES
5117 University Avenue, P.O. Box 5249, Madison WI 53705. 608/238-0211. **Toll-free phone:** 800/322-5117, extension 6216. **Fax:** 608/218-4465. **Contact:** Julia Houck. **E-mail address:** jhouck@erdman.com. **World Wide Web address:** http://www.erdman.com. **Description:** Designs and constructs healthcare facilities nationwide. **NOTE:** Entry-level positions and second and third shifts are offered. **Positions advertised include:** Development Analyst; Project Engineer, Electrical; Project Engineer, Plumbing. **Special programs:** Internships. **Corporate headquarters location:** This location. **Other U.S. locations:** Denver CO; Hartford CT; Washington DC; Atlanta GA; Dallas TX. **Listed on:** Privately held. **Annual sales/revenues:** More than $100 million. **Number of employees at this location:** 270. **Number of employees nationwide:** 410.

FLAD & ASSOCIATES, INC.
P.O. Box 44977, Madison WI 53744-4977. 608/238-2661. **Physical address:** 644 Science Drive, Madison WI 53711. **Fax:** 608/238-6727. **Contact:** Human Resources. **E-mail address:** humanresources@flad.com. **World Wide Web address:** http://www.flad.com. **Description:** An architectural and engineering firm specializing in the planning and design of facilities for academic, healthcare, and research, development and production clients. Founded in 1927. **Positions advertised include:** Human Resources/Training; Lab Planner; Project Manager; Project Manager, Healthcare; Senior Interior Designer, Healthcare. **Corporate headquarters location:** This location. **Other U.S. locations:** FL; CT; NC; CA. **Number of employees nationwide:** 300.

GREENHECK FAN CORPORATION
P.O. Box 410, Schofield WI 54476-0410. 715/355-2236. **Fax:** 715/355-2444. **Contact:** Human Resources. **E-mail address:** hr@greenheck.com. **World Wide Web address:** http://www.greenheck.com. **Description:** Manufactures rooftop ventilators, sidewall fans, centrifugal fans, and kitchen ventilation systems. **Positions advertised include:** Application Engineer; International Application Engineer; Product

Development Engineer; Materials Specialist. **Special programs:** Internships. **Corporate headquarters location:** This location. **Other U.S. locations:** Sacramento CA; Frankfort KY. **Operations at this facility include:** Administration; Manufacturing; Research and Development; Sales. **Annual sales/revenues:** More than $100 million. **Number of employees nationwide:** 1,400.

HOMESHIELD
311 East Coleman Street, Rice Lake WI 54868. 715/234-9061. **Fax:** 715/234-1816. **Contact:** Human Resources. **World Wide Web address:** http://www.home-shield.com. **Description:** A leading fenestration supply companies. Homeshield produces window screens, door screens, wood grilles, architectural moldings, window and patio door assemblies, and roll-form metal assemblies. **Positions advertised include:** Product Development Engineer. **Corporate headquarters location:** This location. **Operations at this facility include:** Manufacturing; Research and Development. **Parent company:** Quanex Building Products. **Listed on:** New York Stock Exchange. **Number of employees at this location:** 260. **Number of employees nationwide:** 2,500.

HUFCOR INC.
2101 Kennedy Road, P.O. Box 591, Janesville WI 53547. 608/756-1241. **Toll-free phone:** 800/356-6968. **Fax:** 608/758-8398. **Contact:** Vice President of Human Resources. **E-mail address:** hiring@hufcor.com. **World Wide Web address:** http://www.hufcor.com. **Description:** Manufactures operable partitions, accordion folding doors, glasswall partitions and portable walls. **Positions advertised include:** Production Facilitator; Electronic Tool Maker; Cost Accountant. **Corporate headquarters location:** This location.

KOLBE & KOLBE MILLWORK
1323 South 11th Avenue, Wausau WI 54401-5998. 715/842-5666. **Fax:** 715/845-8270. **Contact:** Ann Micholic, Human Resources. **E-mail address:** amicholic@kolbe-kolbe.com. **World Wide Web address:** http://www.kolbe-kolbe.com. **Description:** Manufactures wooden doors and wood-framed windows. **Positions advertised include:** Pro-E Technician. **Corporate headquarters location:** This location. **Other area locations:** Manawa WI. **Subsidiaries include:** K-K Sales distributes products throughout the Midwest; K-K Way transports products throughout the Midwest; KVW manufactures vinyl windows and doors. **Number of employees at this location:** 1,300.

MEAD & HUNT, INC.
6501 Watts Road, Madison WI 53719. 608/273-6380. **Fax:** 608/273-6391. **Contact:** Human Resources. **E-mail address:** hr@meadhunt.com. **World Wide Web address:** http://www.meadhunt.com. **Description:** Provides planning, design, and construction management services. **Positions advertised include:** Electrical Engineer; Senior Electrical Engineer; Water Resources Senior Project Manager. **Other area locations:** Green Bay WI; La Crosse WI; Milwaukee WI. **Other U.S. locations:** CA: OR; DC; MI; MN. **Number of employees nationwide:** 270.

C.R. MEYER AND SONS COMPANY
895 West 20th Street, P.O. Box 2157, Oshkosh WI 54903-2157. 920/235-3350. **Fax:** 920/235-3419. **Contact:** Human Resources Manager. **E-mail address:** info@crmeyer.com. **World Wide Web address:** http://www.crmeyer.com. **Description:** A privately owned, full-service construction company. Founded in 1888. **Corporate headquarters location:** This location. **Other area locations:** Green Bay WI; Rhinelander WI. **Other U.S. locations:** Augusta GA; Chester PA; Kalamazoo MI; Escanaba MI; Muskegon MI; Coleraine MN; Tulsa OK.

NORTH AMERICAN MECHANICAL, INC.
6135 North American Lane, DeForest WI 53532. 608/241-4328. **Fax:** 608/241-2710. **Contact:** Personnel Department. **E-mail address:** rpeters@naminc.com. **World Wide Web address:** http://www.naminc.com. **Description:** A commercial HVAC contractor. **NOTE:** Entry-level positions and part-time jobs are offered. **Special programs:** Internships; Apprenticeships; Summer Jobs. **Corporate headquarters location:** This location. **Parent company:** Comfort Systems USA, Inc. **Listed on:** New York Stock Exchange. **Stock exchange symbol:** FIX. **Number of employees at this location:** 165.

TOWN & COUNTRY ELECTRIC
2662 American Drive, Appleton WI 54915. 920/738-1500. **Toll-free phone:** 800/677-1506. **Fax:** 920/738-1515. **Contact:** Human Resources. **World Wide Web address:** http://www.faith-technologies.com. **Description:** A commercial and industrial electrical contractor. **Corporate headquarters location:** This location. **Other area locations:** Crivitz WI; Fond du Lac WI; Green Bay WI; La Crosse WI; Madison WI; Milwaukee WI; Sheboygan WI; Stevens Point; Wautoma WI. **Parent Company:** Faith Technologies. **Listed on:** New York Stock Exchange. **Stock exchange symbol:** ESENIOR

TRI-PHASE AUTOMATION, INC.
604 North Shore Drive, Hartland WI 53029. 262/367-6900. **Fax:** 262/367-6910. **Contact:** Human Resources. **E-mail address:** triphase@tri-phase.com. **World Wide Web address:** http://www.tri-phase.com. **Description:** A distributor of mechanical engineering products. **Corporate headquarters location:** This location.

WAUSAU HOMES, INC.
Highway 51 South, P.O. Box 8005, Wausau WI 54402-8005. 715/359-7272. **Contact:** Human Resources. **World Wide Web address:** http://www.wausauhomes.com. **Description:** A company consisting of independently owned and operated builders. **Positions advertised include:** Cost Accountant; Associate Buyer. **Corporate headquarters location:** This location. **Other U.S. locations:** Nationwide. **Number of employees at this location:** 500.

Wyoming

ELKHORN CONSTRUCTION
71 Allegiance Circle, P.O. Box 809, Evanston WY 82930-0809. 307/789-1595. **Fax:** 307/789-7145. **Contact:** Jon Bailey, Estimating/Project Controls Manger. **World Wide Web address:** http://www.elkhornconstruction.com. **Description:** Provides industrial and plant construction and maintenance catering to the oil, gas, power and mining industries. Founded in 1984. **NOTE:** Call to inquire about open positions. Submit resumes by mail or fax. **Corporate headquarters location:** This location. **Other area locations include:** Rock Springs WY. **Other U.S. locations include:** CO; NM; UT; TX. **Subsidiaries include:** Dynamic Services; Eagle Pipeline Construction, Inc.; HOAD, Inc; ProSafe.

STROUT ARCHITECTS
85 West Snow King Avenue, P.O. Box 1250, Jackson Hole WY 83001. 307/733-5778. **Contact:** Roger P. Strout, AIA Principal Architect. **E-mail address:** Rstrout@stroutarchitects.com. **World Wide Web address:** http://www.stroutarchitects.com. **Description:** A commercial and residential architecture firm.

TETON HOMES
P.O. Box 2349, Mills WY 82644. 307/235-1525. **Physical address:** 3283 North Nine Mile Road, Casper WY 82604. **Contact:** Human Resources. **E-mail address:** tetonhomes@alluretech.com. **World Wide Web address:** http://www.tetonhomes.com. **Description:** Teton Homes is a manufacturer of RVs. The company's RV line includes the Grand, the Prestige, and the Tradition. Founded in 1967. **NOTE:** Plant closed during the weeks of Independence Day and Christmas. **Positions advertised include:** Engineering Manager; Construction.

ARTS, ENTERTAINMENT, SPORTS, AND RECREATION

You can expect to find the following types of companies in this section:
Botanical and Zoological Gardens • Entertainment Groups • Motion Picture and Video Tape Production and Distribution • Museums and Art Galleries • Physical Fitness Facilities • Professional Sports Clubs; Sporting and Recreational Camps • Public Golf Courses and Racing and Track Operations • Theatrical Producers and Services

---

Arts, entertainment, and recreation will grow by 25% and add 460,000 new jobs by 2014, increasing from 1,833,000 to 2,293,000 jobs. Most of these new job openings will come from the amusement, gambling, and recreation sector. Job growth will stem from public participation in arts, entertainment, and recreation activities—reflecting increasing incomes, leisure time, and awareness of the health benefits of physical fitness.

Alabama

ALABAMA SHAKESPEARE FESTIVAL
One Festival Drive, Montgomery AL 36117. 334/271-5353. **Toll-free phone:** 800/841-4273. **Contact:** Human Resources. **World Wide Web address:** http://www.asf.net. **Description:** A theater dedicated to the classics and contemporary work in rotating repertory. Founded in 1972. **NOTE:** Applicants should send resumes to department of interest. **Positions advertised include:** General Manager.

Alaska

DENALI NATIONAL PARK AND PRESERVE
P.O. Box 9, Denali Park AK 99755. 907/683-2294. **Fax:** 907/683-9617. **Contact:** Susanne Brown, Human Resources. **World Wide Web address:** http://www.nps.gov/dena. **Description:** A 6-million-acre park. **Positions advertised include:** Park Ranger; Budget Technician; Safety and Occupational Health Specialist. **Special programs:** Internships. **Number of employees at this location:** 100.

KENAI FJORDS NATIONAL PARK
P.O. Box 1727, Seward AK 99664. 907/224-3175. **Physical address:** 1212 Fourth Avenue, Seward AK 99664. **Fax:** 907/224-2144. **Contact:** Human Resources. **World Wide Web address:** http://www.kenai.fjords.national-park.com. **Description:** A 580,000-acre national park established to protect the area's habitat and landscape. The national park supports unaltered natural environments and ecosystems, an ice field wilderness, unnamed waterfalls in unnamed canyons, and glaciers. Authorized commercial guides provide hiking, fishing, and kayaking services. Air charters, boat tours, and charters are also available. **Positions advertised include:** Park Ranger; Park Guide; Visitor Use Assistant; Biological Technician. **Special programs:** Internships.

Arizona

ARIZONA CARDINALS
P.O. Box 888, Phoenix AZ 85001. 602/379-0101. **Contact:** Human Resources. **World Wide Web address:** http://www.azcardinals.com. **Description:** Administrative offices for the NFL team.

ARIZONA DIAMONDBACKS
P.O. Box 2095, Phoenix AZ 85001. 602/462-6500. **Recorded jobline:** 602/379-2088. **Contact:** Personnel. **World Wide Web address:** http://www.azdiamondbacks.com. **Description:** Administrative offices for the professional baseball team.

ARIZONA VETERANS MEMORIAL COLISEUM & EXPOSITION CENTER
P.O. Box 6728, Phoenix AZ 85005. 602/252-6771. **Physical address:** 1826 West McDowell Road, Phoenix AZ 85007. **Contact:** Pamela Stocksdale, Director of Personnel. **Description:** A convention center and arena that hosts a variety of events including the Arizona Exposition & State Fair.

CRAZY HORSE CAMPGROUNDS
1534 Beachcomber Boulevard, Lake Havasu City AZ 86403. 928/855-4033. **Contact:** Manager. **World Wide Web address:** http://www.crazyhorsecampgrounds.com. **Description:** A year-round recreational vehicle park and campground that also houses a market and clubhouse.

GOLD'S GYM
2156 East Baseline Road, Mesa AZ 85204. 480/497-8686. **Contact:** Manager. **World Wide Web address:** http://www.goldsgym.com. **Description:** A full-service health and fitness club complete with weights and cardiovascular equipment, fitness and aerobic instruction, tanning, personal training, and child-care facilities. Overall, Gold's Gym is one of the world's largest health club chains, with over 550 locations. Founded in 1965. **NOTE:** Part-time jobs are offered.

HEARD MUSEUM
2301 North Central Avenue, Phoenix AZ 85004. 602/252-8840. **Contact:** Human Resources. **World Wide Web address:** http://www.heard.org. **Description:** A museum that showcases Native American art and cultural artifacts.

McDUFFY'S SPORTS BAR & OFF-TRACK BETTING
P.O. Box 1570, Tempe AZ 85281. 480/966-5600. **Physical address:** 230 West Fifth Street, Tempe AZ 85281. **Fax:** 480/966-6582. **Contact:** Hiring Manager. **World Wide Web address:** http://www.mcduffys.com. **Description:** Operates a full-service restaurant and bar and offers pool tables, games, and live entertainment. McDuffy's also houses off-track betting facilities. **Other area locations:** Peoria AZ.

MUSEUM OF NORTHERN ARIZONA
3101 North Fort Valley Road, Flagstaff AZ 86001. 928/774-5213. **Fax:** 928/779-1527. **Contact:** Human Resources. **World Wide Web address:** http://www.musnaz.org. **Description:** Offers exhibits and programs on the art, culture, and natural science of the Grand Canyon Region and the Colorado Plateau. Founded in 1928. **Positions advertised include:** Retail Operations Manager; Collections Assistant. **Special programs:** Internships. **Internship information:** Candidates for internships must complete an application. The museum also requires copies of college or university transcripts, and a typewritten statement. For more information, please visit the museum's Website. **Office hours:** Monday - Friday, 9:00 a.m. - 5:00 p.m.

PHOENIX ART MUSEUM
1625 North Central Avenue, Phoenix AZ 85004-1685. 602/257-1880. **Fax:** 602/253-8662. **Contact:** Human Resources Manager. **E-mail address:** hr@phxart.org. **World Wide Web address:** http://www.phxart.org. **Description:** A nonprofit visual arts museum with collections including Asian art, European art, Latin American art, decorative arts, and fashion design. This location also hires seasonally. Founded in 1949. **NOTE:** Entry-level positions, part-time jobs, and second and third shifts are offered. Also, when sending resume, please list the position that you are applying for and send it to the attention of the Human Resources Manager. **Positions advertised include:** Security Shift Captain; Curatorial Assistant. **Special programs:** Internships. **Office hours:** Tuesday - Sunday, 10:00 a.m. - 5:00 p.m. **Corporate headquarters location:** This location. **Listed on:** Privately held. **Number of employees at this location:** 110.

PHOENIX GREYHOUND PARK

P.O. Box 20300, Phoenix AZ 85036-0300. 602/273-7181. **Contact:** Human Resources. **World Wide Web address:** http://www.phoenixgreyhoundpark.com. **Description:** Operates a greyhound racing track. **Parent company:** Delaware North Companies. **Number of employees at this location:** 500.

PHOENIX SUNS
201 East Jefferson Street, Phoenix AZ 85004. 602/379-7900. **Fax:** 602/379-7990. **Recorded jobline:** 602/379-2088. **Contact:** Human Resources. **World Wide Web address:** http://www.nba.com/suns. **Description:** Houses administrative offices for the NBA team. **Corporate headquarters location:** This location.

TURF PARADISE INC.
1501 West Bell Road, Phoenix AZ 85023. 602/942-1101. **Contact:** Human Resources. **World Wide Web address:** http://www.turfparadise.com. **Description:** A 220-acre thoroughbred race track. Turf Paradise also operates a 14-acre mobile home park. **Corporate headquarters location:** This location.

California

AIMS MULTIMEDIA
20765 Superior Street, Chatsworth CA 91311-4409. 818/773-4300. **Toll-free phone:** 800/367-2467. **Fax:** 818/341-6700. **Contact:** Adele Brant, Human Resources. **E-mail address:** info@aimsmultimedia.com. **World Wide Web address:** http://www.aimsmultimedia.com. **Description:** Engaged in educational video production and distribution. **Corporate headquarters location:** This location. **Parent company:** Discovery Education.

ALLIED VAUGHN
5 Thomas Mellon Circle, Suite 128, Brisbane CA 94134. 415/656-2200. **Toll-free phone:** 888/691-3381. **Fax:** 415/656-2299. **Contact:** Human Resources. E-mail address: human.resources@alliedvaughn.com. **World Wide Web address:** http://www.alliedvaughn.com. **Description:** One of the nation's leading independent multimedia manufacturing companies, offering CD-audio and CD-ROM mastering and replication; videocassette and audiocassette duplication; laser video disc recording; off-line and online video editing; motion picture film processing; film-to-tape and tape-to-film transfers; and complete finishing, packaging, warehousing, and fulfillment services. **Other U.S. locations:** Nationwide.

ASCENT MEDIA
2813 West Alameda Avenue, Burbank CA 91505. 818/840-7000. **Fax:** 818/260-2131. **Contact:** Human Resources Department. **E-mail address:** recruiting@ascentmedia.com. **World Wide Web address:** http://www.4mc.com. **Description:** Offers creative and production services to the media and entertainment industries. **Positions advertised include:** Project Manager; Senior Financial Analyst. **Parent company:** Liberty Media Corporation. **Listed on:** New York Stock Exchange. **Stock exchange symbol:** L.

BALLY TOTAL FITNESS
12440 East Imperial Highway, Suite 300, Norwalk CA 90650. 562/484-2875. **Fax:** 562/484-2446. **Contact:** Donielle Williams. **E-mail address:** dwilliams@ballyfitness.com. **World Wide Web address:** http://www.ballyfitness.com. **Description:** One of the world's largest owners and operators of fitness centers. Bally Total Fitness is operated by Bally Health & Tennis Corporation, which, through the subsidiaries it controls, is a nationwide commercial operator of fitness centers in the United States. Bally Health & Tennis operates over 360 fitness centers located in 27 states with approximately 4 million members. **Positions advertised include:** Financial Services Representative; Member Services Representative; Payment Processing. **Special programs:** Internships. **Corporate headquarters location:** Chicago IL. **Other U.S. locations:** Nationwide. **International locations:** Canada. **Parent company:** Bally's Entertainment. **Listed on:** New York Stock Exchange. **Stock exchange symbol:** BFT. **Operations at this facility include:** Regional Service Center.

BAY MEADOWS COMPANY
P.O. Box 5050, San Mateo CA 94402. 650/573-4540. **Physical address:** 2600 South Delaware Street, San Mateo CA 94403. **Fax:** 650/573-4671. **Contact:** Human Resources. **World Wide Web address:** http://www.baymeadows.com. **Description:** Operates Bay Meadows Race Track on the San Francisco Peninsula, and California Jockey Club, an equity real estate investment trust whose principal asset is Bay Meadows Race Track. **Corporate headquarters location:** This location.

BOOMERS PARK
1155 Graves Avenue, El Cajon CA 92021. 619/593-1155. **Fax:** 619/593-6897. **Contact:** Human Resources. **E-mail address:** employment@palaceentertainment.com. **World Wide Web address:** http://www.boomersparks.com. **Description:** An amusement park that features paddle boats, go carts, bumper boats, and a maze that is changed monthly. The park also includes a roller skating rink, arcade, and snack bar. **Corporate headquarters location:** Irvine CA. **Parent company:** Palace Entertainment Company.

CIS HOLLYWOOD
1144 North Las Palmas Avenue, Hollywood CA 90038. 323/463-8811. **Fax:** 323/962-1859. **Contact:** Recruiting. **E-mail address:** srichards@cishollywood.com. **World Wide Web address:** http://www.cishollywood.com. **Description:** Provides video post-production services. **NOTE:** Website includes guidelines for demo reels submission. **Corporate headquarters location:** This location.

CASTLE ROCK ENTERTAINMENT
345 North Maple Drive, Suite 135, Beverly Hills CA 90210. 818/954-6000. **Fax:** 310/285-2345. **Contact:** Human Resources Department. **World Wide Web address:** http://www.castle-rock.com. **Description:** A motion picture and video production company. **Parent Company:** Time Warner Inc. **Listed on:** New York Stock Exchange. **Stock exchange symbol:** AOL.

CREATIVE ARTISTS AGENCY, INC. (CAA)
9830 Wilshire Boulevard, Beverly Hills CA 90212-1825. 310/288-4545. **Fax:** 310/288-4800. **Contact:** Human Resources. **World Wide Web address:** http://www.caa.com. **Description:** Manages and represents actors, directors, and writers in the film and television industries. Founded in 1975. **Number of employees worldwide:** 400.

DEL MAR THOROUGHBRED CLUB
2260 Jimmy Durante Boulevard, P.O. Box 700, Del Mar CA 92014. 858/755-1141. **Contact:** Ann Hall, Director of Human Resources. **E-mail address:** ann@dmtc.com. **World Wide Web address:** http://www.dmtc.com. **Description:** A horse racing facility. Del Mar Thoroughbred Club is a member of the Thoroughbred Racing Association of North America.

DELUXE LABORATORIES, INC.
1377 Serrano Avenue, Hollywood CA 90027. 323/462-6171. **Fax:** 323/461-0608. **Contact:** Human Resources. **World Wide Web address:** http://www.bydeluxe.com. **Description:** A motion picture film developer. **Parent company:** The Rank Group plc.

DIAMOND ENTERTAINMENT CORPORATION dba E-DMEC
800 Tucker Lane, Walnut CA 91789. 909/839-1989. **Fax:** 909/869-1990. **Contact:** Human Resources. **World Wide Web address:** http://www.e-dmec.com. **Description:** Engaged in the distribution and sale of videocassette and DVD titles, including public domain programs and certain licensed programs. The company markets its video and DVD programs to national and regional mass merchandisers, department stores, drug sores, supermarkets, and other similar retail outlets. **Corporate headquarters location:** This location.

Subsidiaries include: Jewel Products International, Inc.

DICK CLARK PRODUCTIONS, INC.
9200 Sunset Boulevard, 10th Floor, Los Angeles CA 90069. 310/786-8900. **Contact:** Human Resources Department. **World Wide Web address:** http://www.dickclarkproductions.com. **Description:** One of the nation's top entertainment companies. The company primarily produces talk shows, made-for-TV movies, and awards shows such as the Golden Globe Awards. **Special programs:** Internships. **Corporate headquarters location:** This location.

THE WALT DISNEY COMPANY
500 South Buena Vista Street, Burbank CA 91521-7235. 818/560-1811. **Contact:** Staffing Services. **World Wide Web address:** http://disney.go.com. **Description:** One of the nation's top film studios. **Positions advertised include:** VP Human Resources; Director, Business Planning; Accountant; Director Organizational Change and Development; Manager, Human Resources Communications; Digital Media Specialist; IT Coordinator. **Corporate headquarters location:** This location. **Listed on:** New York Stock Exchange. **Stock exchange symbol:** DIS.

DISNEYLAND
1313 South Harbor Boulevard, P.O. Box 3232, Anaheim CA 92803. 714/781-1600. **Fax:** 714/781-0065. **Recorded jobline:** 800/766-0888. **Contact:** Professional Staffing Department. **E-mail address:** dl.resort.resumes@Disney.com. **World Wide Web address:** http://www.disney.com. **Description:** One of the largest amusement/theme parks in the world. **Positions advertised include: include:** Capital Planning Manager; Forecasting and Analysis Manager; Senior Catering and Conventions Services Manager; Sous Chef; Senior Accountant; Accounting Assistant; Market Research Manager; Vacation Planner; Candy Maker. **Corporate headquarters location:** Burbank CA. **Parent company:** The Walt Disney Company. **Operations at this facility include:** Resort/Support Functions.

E! ENTERTAINMENT TELEVISION NETWORKS
5750 Wilshire Boulevard, Los Angeles CA 90036. 323/954-2400. **Recorded jobline:** 323/954-2666. **Contact:** Human Resources. **E-mail address:** hr@eentertainment.com. **World Wide Web address:** http://www.eentertainment.com. **Description:** Operates a cable network dedicated to the entertainment and fashion industries. **Positions advertised include:** Rights and Clearance Coordinator; Accounts Payable Clerk; Production Accountant, Coordinator, International Marketing; Director, Research. **Special programs:** Internships. **Internship information:** For more information regarding internships call: 323/954-2710. **Corporate headquarters location:** This location. **Other U.S. locations:** New York NY; Chicago IL; Windsor CT.

FREMANTLEMEDIA NORTH AMERICA, INC.
2700 Colorado Avenue, Suite 450, Santa Monica CA 90404. 310/255-4700. **Contact:** Human Resources. **E-mail address:** hr@fremantlemedia.com. **World Wide Web address:** http://www.fremantlemedia.com. **Description:** Produces, distributes, markets, and promotes television programs and recorded music both domestically and internationally. The company is a leading distributor of television programming in the first-run syndication and distributes, represents, or owns participations in more than 160 television series, over 250 motion pictures, a variety of children's programming, and live-event specials. **Corporate headquarters location:** This location. **Parent company:** RTL Group (London England). **Number of employees at this location:** 125.

GOLD'S GYM
360 Hampton Drive, Venice CA 90291. 310/392-6004. **Fax:** 310/396-1065. **Contact:** Human Resources. **World Wide Web address:** http://www.goldsgym.com. **Description:** A full-service health and fitness club. Each club is complete with weights and cardiovascular equipment, fitness and aerobic classes, tanning, personal training, and childcare facilities. Gold's Gym is one of the world's largest health club chains, with over 550 locations. **NOTE:** Part-time jobs are offered. **Corporate headquarters location:** This location. **Other area locations:** Statewide. **Other U.S. locations:** Nationwide. **Parent company:** Neste Development. **Number of employees at this location:** 40.

SAMUEL GOLDWYN COMPANY
9570 West Pico Boulevard, Suite 400, Los Angeles CA 90035. 310/860-3100. **Contact:** Human Resources. **Description:** Engaged primarily in the financing, production, and distribution of feature-length motion pictures. Samuel Goldwyn Company also finances and distributes television programs intended for licensing to cable and first-run syndication markets, and to U.S. and foreign television networks. **NOTE:** Resumes may be submitted by mail or fax. Address resumes to: Samuel Goldwyn Company, Attention: Human Resources, 10203 Santa Monica Boulevard, Los Angeles CA 90067. Fax: 310/284-9213. **Special programs:** Internships. **Corporate headquarters location:** This location. **Other U.S. locations:** New York NY. **Operations at this facility include:** Administration; Regional Headquarters; Research and Development; Sales. **Number of employees at this location:** 260.

HBO PICTURES
2049 Century Park East, Suite 4100, Los Angeles CA 90067. 310/201-9200. **Contact:** Personnel Department. **World Wide Web address:** http://www.hbo.com/films. **Description:** Produces original, cable network films. **Positions advertised include:** Assistant, HBO Films Development; Executive Assistant, HBO Films Post Production. **Corporate headquarters location:** New York NY. **Parent company:** Time Warner.

HOLLYWOOD PARK INC.
P.O. Box 369, Inglewood CA 90306-0369. 310/419-1500. **Physical address:** 1050 South Prairie Avenue, Inglewood CA 90301. **Contact:** Human Resources Department. **World Wide Web address:** http://www.hollywoodpark.com. **Description:** Owns and operates a horseracing track and gaming casino. **Positions advertised include:** Security Officer. **Corporate headquarters location:** This location. **Parent company:** Churchill Downs Inc. **Listed on:** NASDAQ. **Stock exchange symbol:** CHDN.

IMAGE ENTERTAINMENT, INC.
20525 Nordhoff Street, Suite 200, Chatsworth CA 91311. 818/407-9100. **Contact:** Human Resources. **World Wide Web address:** http://www.image-entertainment.com. **Description:** One of the largest laser disc licensees and distributors in North America. The company distributes thousands of titles ranging from feature films and music videos to family, documentary, and special interest programming to over 2,500 retail outlets. The company releases exclusive titles from licensers such as Disney's Buena Vista Home Video, New Line Home Video, Orion Home Video, Playboy Home Video, and Turner Home Entertainment. **Corporate headquarters location:** This location. **Listed on:** NASDAQ. **Stock exchange symbol:** DISK.

INDUSTRIAL LIGHT + MAGIC
P.O. Box 2459, San Rafael CA 94912. 415/258-2200. **Physical address:** 3155 Kerner Boulevard, San Raffael CA 94901. **Recorded jobline:** 415/448-2100. **Fax:** 415/448-2850. **Contact:** Recruiting. **E-mail address:** hrdept@lucasdigital.com. **World Wide Web address:** http://www.ilm.com. **Description:** A digital effects company engaged in motion picture film production. The company is comprised of Industrial Light & Magic (ILM), a visual effects company; and Skywalker Sound, a state-of-the-art audio facility. **Positions advertised include:** CG Technical Assistant; Digital Matte Artist; Digital Resource Assistant; Database Administrator.

Corporate headquarters location: This location. **Parent company:** Lucas Films Ltd.

INTERNATIONAL CREATIVE MANAGEMENT, INC. (ICM)
8942 Wilshire Boulevard, Beverly Hills CA 90211-1934. 310/550-4198. **Fax:** 310/550-4100. **Contact:** Human Resources. **E-mail address:** careers@icmtalent.com. **World Wide Web address:** http://www.icmtalent.com. **Description:** A talent agency managing film, music, publishing, television, theater, and public affairs clients. The agency also protects intellectual property rights. **Other U.S. locations:** New York NY. **International locations:** London; Paris; Rome. **Number of employees worldwide:** 500.

IWERKS ENTERTAINMENT, INC.
4520 West Valerio Street, Burbank CA 91505-1046. 818/841-7766. **Toll-free phone:** 800/388-8628. **Fax:** 818/840-188. **Contact:** Human Resources. **World Wide Web address:** http://www.iwerks.com. **Description:** Designs, manufactures, installs, and services high-resolution, proprietary motion picture theater attractions in museums, visitor centers, casinos, and newly emerging entertainment venues. The company's attractions are built around a variety of theater systems including fixed and portable simulators, giant screen, 360-degree, and virtual reality theater systems. Business segments include Iwerks Attractions and Technologies, Iwerks Studios, Iwerks Cinetropolis, Iwerks Touring Technologies, and Omni Films International. **NOTE:** Entry-level positions are offered. **Special programs:** Internships. **Corporate headquarters location:** This location.

JOSHUA TREE RECREATION
6171 Sunburst Street, Joshua Tree CA 92252-0838. 760/366-8415. **Contact:** Human Resources. **Description:** Operates the Joshua Tree Park as well as a community center, and offers a variety of classes and outdoor activity programs.

KNOTT'S BERRY FARM
8039 Beach Boulevard, Buena Park CA 90620. 714/220-5200. **Fax:** 714/220-5150. **Recorded jobline:** 714/995-6688. **Contact:** Staffing Department. **World Wide Web address:** http://www.knotts.com. **Description:** This location is an amusement park. Overall, Knott's Berry Farm is engaged in the development and management of family restaurants, retail operations, and specialty food products manufacturing. **Positions advertised include:** Purchasing Assistant; Buyer; Catering Sales Manager; Entertainment Technician. **Special programs:** Internships. **Corporate headquarters location:** This location. **Other area locations:** Irvine CA; Moreno Valley CA; Placentia CA. **Other U.S. locations:** Bloomington MN. **Operations at this facility include:** Administration; Sales.

LASERPACIFIC MEDIA CORPORATION
809 North Cahuenga Boulevard, Hollywood CA 90038. 323/462-6266. **Fax:** 323/464-6005. **Contact:** Personnel. **World Wide Web address:** http://www.laserpacific.com. **Description:** A major supplier of film, videotape, digital sound postproduction, and multimedia services to prime time television shows. **Corporate headquarters location:** This location. **Listed on:** NASDAQ. **Stock exchange symbol:** LPAC. **Chairman and CEO:** James R. Parks. **Annual sales/revenues:** $21 - $50 million. **Number of employees nationwide:** 225.

LIONSGATE ENTERTAINMENT
2700 Colorado Avenue, Suite 200, Santa Monica CA 90404. 310/449-9200. **Fax:** 310/255-3870. **Contact:** Human Resources. **E-mail address:** resumes@lgf.com. **World Wide Web address:** http://www.lionsgatefilms.com. **Description:** Produces, markets, and distributes motion pictures. **Positions advertised include:** Senior Accountant; Finance Coordinator; Budget Analyst. **Corporate headquarters location:** This location. **Other U.S. locations:** New York NY. **Listed on:** New York Stock Exchange. **Stock exchange symbol:** LGF. **Annual sales/revenues:** $426.6 million.

LOS ANGELES ATHLETIC CLUB
431 West Seventh Street, Los Angeles CA 90014. 213/625-2211. **Fax:** 213/625-0128. **Contact:** Human Resources Department. **E-mail address:** laaco.jobs@laac.net. **World Wide Web address:** http://www.laac.com. **Description:** Operates an athletic facility with programs in virtually every sport, as well as concession, banquet, and guest hotel facilities. **Corporate headquarters location:** This location. **Other area locations:** Marina del Rey CA; Orange CA. **Operations at this facility include:** Administration; Sales; Service. **Listed on:** Privately held. **Number of employees at this location:** 240. **Number of employees nationwide:** 370.

LOS ANGELES COUNTY MUSEUM OF ART
5905 Wilshire Boulevard, Los Angeles CA 90036. 323/857-6000. **Fax:** 323/857-4720. **Recorded jobline:** 323/857-6069. **Contact:** Adam Kaplan, Employment Administrator. **E-mail address:** jobs@lacma.org. **World Wide Web address:** http://www.lacma.org. **Description:** A premier visual arts museum. The museum's collection expresses the creativity of cultures from all over the world. Founded in 1938. **NOTE:** Entry-level positions and part-time jobs are offered. No phone calls please. **Positions advertised include:** Director of Conservation; Director of Development Head Librarian; Membership Systems Specialist; Senior Conservation Scientist; Membership Services Assistant. **Special programs:** Internships. **Office hours:** Monday - Friday, 8:00 a.m. - 5:00 p.m.

LOS ANGELES DODGERS
1000 Elysian Park Avenue, Los Angeles CA 90012. 323/224-1500. **Fax:** 323/224-2606. **Contact:** Human Resources. **World Wide Web address:** http://losangeles.dodgers.mlb.com. **Description:** The offices for the National League baseball team. **Positions advertised include:** Stadium Operations Assistant; Security Manager. **Special programs:** Internships.

LOS ANGELES ZOO
5333 Zoo Drive, Los Angeles CA 90027. 323/666-4650. **Contact:** Personnel. **World Wide Web address:** http://www.lazoo.org. **Description:** A zoo that houses a fully equipped animal hospital and animal health center, an animal food commissary, and a horticultural section. **NOTE:** For employment information, contact: Los Angeles City Personnel Department, Room 100, City Hall South, Los Angeles CA 90012. 213/847-9240, http://www.cityofla.org/PER/index.htm. **Number of employees at this location:** 180.

LUCASFILM LTD.
P.O. Box 29901, San Francisco CA 94129. 415/662-1700. **Fax:** 415/662-7460. **Contact:** Human Resources. **World Wide Web address:** http://www.lucasfilm.com. **Description:** A leading film production company specializing in visual and sound effects. **Positions advertised include:** Production Finance Director; Trademark and Legal Assistant; Internal Audit Manager; Senior Human Resources Manager; Director of Publishing; Marketing Manager. **Special programs:** Internships. **Corporate headquarters location:** This location.

MGM INC.
10250 Constellation Boulevard, Los Angeles CA 90067. 310/449-3000. **Recorded jobline:** 310/449-3569. **Contact:** Human Resources Department. **World Wide Web address:** http://www.mgm.com. **Description:** A fully integrated media company providing entertainment through the production and distribution of feature films, television programs, animation, music, and interactive games. **NOTE:** Search and apply for positions online. **Positions advertised include:** Data Warehouse Analyst; Unix Systems Administrator; Category Management Analyst. **Special programs:** Internships. **Corporate**

headquarters location: This location. **Listed on:** New York Stock Exchange. **Stock exchange symbol:** MGM.

THE OAKLAND ATHLETICS (A'S)
7000 Coliseum Way, Oakland CA 94621. 510/638-4900. **Recorded jobline:** 510/638-4900x2817. **Contact:** Human Resources. **E-mail address:** hr@oaklandathletics.com. **World Wide Web address:** http://oakland.athletics.mlb.com. **Description:** Business offices for the Major League Baseball team. **NOTE:** Entry-level positions and part-time jobs are offered. **Positions advertised include:** Stadium Events Staff; Guest Relations Staff. **Special programs:** Internships. **Office hours:** Monday - Friday, 8:00 a.m. - 5:00 p.m. **Corporate headquarters location:** This location. **Listed on:** Privately held.

OAKLAND RAIDERS
1220 Harbor Bay Parkway, Alameda CA 94502. 510/864-5000. **Contact:** Human Resources. **World Wide Web address:** http://www.raiders.com. **Description:** Offices for the National Football League team.

THE OUTDOOR CHANNEL
43445 Business Park Drive, Suite 103, Temecula CA 92590. **Toll-free phone:** 800/770-5750. **Fax:** 951/699-6313. **Contact:** Vicki Windham, Manager of Human Resources. **E-mail address:** vwindham@outdoorchannel.com. **World Wide Web address:** http://www.outdoorchannel.com. **Description:** A national television network. **NOTE:** No telephone call accepted. **Positions advertised include:** Media Research Analyst; Production Assistant; Freelance Camera Operator. **Corporate headquarters location:** This location. **Listed on:** NASDAQ. **Stock exchange symbol:** GLRS.

PARAMOUNT PICTURES CORPORATION
5555 Melrose Avenue, Hollywood CA 90038-3197. 323/956-5000. **Fax:** 323/862-1134. **Recorded jobline:** 323/956-5216. **Contact:** Human Resources – Dept. WEB. **World Wide Web address:** http://www.paramount.com. **Description:** Paramount Pictures Corporation is involved in many aspects of the entertainment industry including motion pictures, television, and video production and distribution. Founded in 1905. **Positions advertised include:** Assistant Product Manager; Financial Analyst; International Product Manager; Business Systems Analyst; Senior Programmer Analyst; Senior Operations Auditor; Senior Financial Analyst; Director of Accounting. **Special programs:** Internships. **Corporate headquarters location:** New York NY. **Parent company:** Viacom, Inc. Other subsidiaries of Viacom include MTV, Blockbuster, Showtime, Nickelodeon, and Simon & Schuster. **Listed on:** New York Stock Exchange. **Stock exchange symbol:** VIA. **Number of employees at this location:** 3,000.

PIXAR ANIMATION STUDIOS
1200 Park Avenue, Emeryville CA 94608. 510/752-3000. **Fax:** 510/752-3151. **Contact:** Recruiting. **E-mail address:** hr@pixar.com. **World Wide Web address:** http://www.pixar.com. **Description:** A computer animation studio. Pixar Animation Studios produces various computer animated entertainment products in the form of feature films and computer software. **Positions advertised include:** Effects Technical Director; Layout Artist; Lighting Technical Director; Animator; Digital Painter; Set Dresser; Facilities Technician; Assistant Controller; Accounting Assistant; Software Engineer; Media Systems Engineer. **Corporate headquarters location:** This location. **Listed on:** NASDAQ. **Stock exchange symbol:** PIXR. **Number of employees at this location:** 430.

SAN DIEGO ZOO
P.O. Box 120551, San Diego CA 92112-0551. 619/231-1515. **Fax:** 619/744-3326. **Recorded jobline:** 619/557-3968. **Contact:** Human Resources. **World Wide Web address:** http://www.sandiegozoo.org. **Description:** One of the nation's largest zoos. **NOTE:** Applications or resumes not accepted online or via e-mail, and are accepted only for current job openings. **Positions advertised include:** Animal Keeper; Human Resources Representative; Administrative Assistant.

SAN JOSE MUSEUM OF ART
110 South Market Street, San Jose CA 95113. 408/271-6840. **Contact:** Human Relations Department. **E-mail address:** hrdept@sjmusart.org. **World Wide Web address:** http://www.sjmusart.org. **Description:** A contemporary art museum. **Positions advertised include:** Development Manager for Individual Giving; Bilingual Studio Arts Educator; Visitor Service Reps. **Special programs:** Internships; Residencies; Volunteer Opportunities.

SAN JOSE SHARKS
525 West Santa Clara Street, San Jose CA 95113. 408/287-7070. **Fax:** 408/999-5797. **Contact:** Human Resources. **E-mail address:** hr@svse.net. **World Wide Web address:** http://www.sj-sharks.com. **Description:** A professional hockey team. **Corporate headquarters location:** This location.

SANTA BARBARA LOCATION SERVICES
REAL TALENT/KIDS
1214 Coast Village, Suite 12, Montecito CA 93108. 805/565-1562. **Fax:** 805/969-9595. **Contact:** Ms. Ronnie Mellen, Owner. **World Wide Web address:** http://www.santabarbara-locations.com. **Description:** Assists the film industry by providing location/production coordination services. Real Talent/Kids (also at this location, 805/969-2222) is a casting company. Founded in 1983. **Number of employees at this location:** 5.

SIX FLAGS MAGIC MOUNTAIN
SIX FLAGS HURRICANE HARBOR
P.O. Box 5500, Valencia CA 91355. 661/255-4801. **Physical address:** 26101 Magic Mountain Parkway, Valencia CA 91355. **Recorded jobline:** 661/255-4800. **Contact:** Alex Hottya, Human Resources. **E-mail address:** ahottya@sftp.com. **World Wide Web address:** http://www.sixflags.com. **Description:** An amusement and water theme park. **Other U.S. locations:** Nationwide. **Corporate headquarters location:** New York NY. **Parent company:** Premier Parks (OK) owns and operates 35 theme parks nationwide. **Listed on:** New York Stock Exchange. **Stock exchange symbol:** PKS.

SONY PICTURES ENTERTAINMENT
10202 West Washington Boulevard, Suite 3900, Culver City CA 90232-3195. 310/244-4000. **Contact:** Human Resources. **E-mail address:** resumes@spe.sony.com. **World Wide Web address:** http://www.sonypictures.com. **Description:** Sony Pictures is involved in motion pictures, television, theatrical exhibitions, and studio facilities and technology. The motion picture business distributes movies produced by Columbia TriStar Pictures. The television business, which encompasses Columbia TriStar Television, Columbia TriStar Television Distribution, and Columbia TriStar International Television, is involved with numerous cable channels and distributes and syndicates television programs such as *Days of Our Lives*. **NOTE:** Search and apply for positions online. **Positions advertised include:** Financial Analyst; Visual Development Artist; Manager, Business Development; Audio Coordinator; Designer. **Special programs:** Internships. **Corporate headquarters location:** This location. **Parent company:** Sony Corporation of America. **Operations at this facility include:** Administration; Sales. **Listed on:** New York Stock Exchange. **Stock exchange symbol:** SNE.

SPELLING ENTERTAINMENT INC.
5700 Wilshire Boulevard, Suite 500, Los Angeles CA 90036. 323/965-5700. **Contact:** Human Resources. **Description:** A leading producer and distributor of television, film, and interactive entertainment. The company comprises Spelling Television, which produces made-for-television movies, miniseries, and one-hour series including *Seventh Heaven* and *Sunset*

Beach; Big Ticket Television, which produces sitcoms for the broadcast and first-run markets; Spelling Films, which produces and distributes feature films; Worldwide Vision, which syndicates the Spelling Entertainment library of more than 20,000 hours of television programming and thousands of feature films; Republic Entertainment, a distributor of home videos for the rental and sell-through markets; Virgin Interactive Entertainment, a developer and publisher of interactive games; and Hamilton products, a licensing and merchandising company that handles Spelling Properties. **Office hours:** Monday - Friday, 9:00 a.m. - 6:00 p.m. **Corporate headquarters location:** This location. **Parent company:** Viacom, Inc. **Listed on:** New York Stock Exchange. **Stock exchange symbol:** VIA. **Number of employees worldwide:** 1,000.

THE SPORTS CLUB COMPANY
1835 Sepulveda Boulevard, Los Angeles CA 90025. 310/479-5200. **Fax:** 310/445-9819. **Recorded jobline:** 310/477-6824. **Contact:** Human Resources. **E-mail address:** hr@thesportsclub.com. **World Wide Web address:** http://www.thesportsclubla.com. **Description:** Owns and operates several health clubs throughout California under the names Sports Club and Spectrum Club. **Corporate headquarters location:** This location. **Listed on:** American Stock Exchange. **Stock exchange symbol:** SCY.

TECHNICOLOR, INC.
4050 Lankershim Boulevard, North Hollywood CA 91604. 818/769-8500. **Contact:** Human Resources. **E-mail address:** hrjobs@technicolor.com. **World Wide Web address:** http://www.technicolor.com. **Description:** Engaged in film processing services for the movie industry. **Corporate headquarters location:** Camarillo CA. **Other area locations:** Burbank CA; Glendale CA; Ontario CA.

UNIVERSAL STUDIOS, INC.
100 Universal City Plaza, Building 1220/1, Universal City CA 91608. 818/777-1000. **Physical address:** 3900 Lankershim Boulevard, Universal City CA 91604. **Recorded jobline:** 818/777-JOBS. **Contact:** Corporate Workforce Planning & Strategic Staffing. **E-mail address:** jobs@unistudios.com. **World Wide Web address:** http://www.universalstudios.com. **Description:** A diversified entertainment company and a worldwide leader in motion pictures, television, music, and home and location-based themed entertainment. The company's main operating divisions include Universal Studios, Universal Studios Recreation Group, Universal Studios Information Technology, Universal Studios Operations Group, Universal Music Group, Universal Pictures, Universal Networks & Worldwide Television Distribution, Universal Studios Consumer Products Group, Universal Studios Online, and Spencer Gifts. **NOTE:** Entry-level positions are offered. Online application recommended. **Positions advertised include:** Senior Financial Analyst; Legal Assistant; Accounting Analyst. **Special programs:** Internships; Training; Co-ops; Summer Jobs. **Corporate headquarters location:** This location. **Other U.S. locations:** Orlando FL; New York NY; Memphis TN; Nashville TN; Dallas TX. **International locations:** Worldwide. **Parent company:** NBC Universal. **Annual sales/revenues:** $6.6 billion. **Number of employees worldwide:** 22,000.

WARNER BROS. STUDIOS (WB TELEVISION NETWORK)
4000 Warner Boulevard, Burbank CA 91522. 818/954-6000. **Recorded jobline:** 818/954-5400. **Contact:** Human Resources. **World Wide Web address:** http://www.warnerbros.com. **Description:** An entertainment/film production company. The company also operates a television network with nationwide affiliates. **NOTE:** Search and apply for positions online. **Positions advertised include:** Traffic Adiminstrator; Finance Coordinator; Manager, Graphics Production; Freelance Online Producer; Freelance Avid Editor; Freelance Writer/Producer. **Corporate headquarters location:** This location. **Parent company:** Time Warner. **Listed on:** New York Stock Exchange. **Stock exchange symbol:** TWX. **Annual sales/revenues:** $6.9 billion.

WILLIAM MORRIS AGENCY, INC.
One William Morris Place, Beverly Hills CA 90212. 310/859-4000. **Fax:** 310/859-4205. **Contact:** Human Resources. **World Wide Web address:** http://www.wma.com. **Description:** One of the largest talent and literary agencies in the world. **NOTE:** Entry-level positions are offered. **Corporate headquarters location:** This location.

Colorado

ANASAZI HERITAGE CENTER BUREAU OF LAND MANAGEMENT
27501 Highway 184, Dolores CO 81323-9217. 970/882-4811. **Fax:** 970/882-7035. **Contact:** Human Resources. **World Wide Web address:** http://www.co.blm.gov/ahc. **Description:** An archeological museum that focuses on the interpretation of the Anasazi culture. **Special programs:** Internships. **Corporate headquarters location:** Washington DC. **Parent company:** U.S. Department of the Interior.

ANDERSON RANCH ARTS CENTER
5263 Owl Creek Road, P.O. Box 5598, Snowmass Village CO 81615. 970/923-3181. **Fax:** 970/923-3871. **Contact:** Employment. **World Wide Web address:** http://www.andersonranch.org. **Description:** Offers 100 summer workshops (one or two weeks long) in painting and drawing, ceramics, sculpture, woodworking, furniture design, photography, creative studies, and children's studies. In the winter, the center runs a studio residency program. The center also offers a visiting artists program for professional and emerging artists. **Positions advertised include:** Director of Marketing and Communications. **Special programs:** Internships.

BRECKENRIDGE OUTDOOR EDUCATION CENTER
P.O. Box 697, Breckenridge CO 80424. 970/453-6422. **Fax:** 970/453-4676. **Contact:** Human Resources. **E-mail address:** boec@boec.org. **World Wide Web address:** http://www.boec.org. **Description:** A nonprofit organization offering year-round wilderness and adventure programs and adaptive skiing opportunities for people with disabilities and other special needs. Activities include downhill and cross-country skiing, ropes courses, rafting, rock climbing, camping, and fishing. Founded in 1976. **Special programs:** Internships. **Corporate headquarters location:** This location.

COLORADO HISTORICAL SOCIETY
1300 Broadway, Denver CO 80203. 303/866-3682. **Fax:** 303/866-4464. **Contact:** Alice Rodriguez, Personnel. **World Wide Web address:** http://www.coloradohistory.org. **Description:** A nonprofit organization that collects, preserves, and interprets the history and prehistory of Colorado and the West through educational programs and museum exhibits. Founded in 1879. **Special programs:** Internships; Summer Jobs. **Corporate headquarters location:** This location. **Number of employees at this location:** 95. **Number of employees nationwide:** 115.

COLORADO ROCKIES
2001 Blake Street, Denver CO 80205. 303/832-8326. **Fax:** 303/312-2028. **Recorded jobline:** 303/312-2490. **Contact:** Human Resources. **World Wide Web address:** http://www.coloradorockies.com. **Description:** The Major League Baseball franchise of the Denver area.

CREEDE REPERTORY THEATRE
124 North Main Street, P.O. Box 269, Creede CO 81130. 719/658-2541. **Fax:** 719/658-2343. **Contact:** Human Resources. **E-mail address:** crt@creederep.com. **World Wide Web address:** http://www.creederep.com. **Description:** A nonprofit theater producing eight plays annually. Founded in 1969. **NOTE:** This location also hires seasonally.

Special programs: Internships. **Number of employees at this location:** 40.

DENVER BRONCOS
13655 Broncos Parkway, Englewood CO 80112. 203/649-9000. **Contact:** Human Resources. **World Wide Web address:** www.denverbroncos.com. **Description:** The executive office of the NFL franchise and former Super Bowl champions.

DENVER CENTER THEATRE COMPANY
1101 13th Street, Denver CO 80204. 303/893-4000. **Recorded jobline:** 303/446-4873. **Contact:** Human Resources. **World Wide Web address:** http://www.denvercenter.org. **Description:** A professional acting troupe that performs a broad range of theatrical productions year-round. Founded in 1978. **Parent company:** Denver Center for the Performing Arts. **Number of employees at this location:** 300.

THE DENVER ZOO
2300 Steele Street, Denver CO 80205-4899. 303/376-4800. **Fax:** 303/376-4801. **Contact:** Human Resources. **E-mail address:** zoohr@denverzoo.org. **World Wide Web address:** http://www.denverzoo.org. **Description:** A zoo featuring year-round exhibits including Bird World and Tropical Discovery. **Positions advertised include:** Zookeeper; School Programs Specialist.

NATIONAL SPORTS CENTER FOR THE DISABLED
P.O. Box 1290, Winter Park CO 80482. 970/726-1540. **Contact:** Human Resources. **World Wide Web address:** http://www.nscd.org. **Description:** Provides outdoor mountain recreational services to children and adults with disabilities. This is a nonprofit company. Founded in 1970. **Positions advertised include:** Recreation Programs Supervisor; National Programs Coordinator. **Special programs:** Internships. **Corporate headquarters location:** This location. **Parent company:** Winter Park Recreation Association. **Annual sales/revenues:** Less than $5 million. **Number of employees at this location:** 55.

NAUTILUS HEALTH AND FITNESS GROUP
1886 Prairie Way, Louisville CO 80027. 303/939-0100. **Fax:** 303/545-1425. **Contact:** Human Resources Department. **World Wide Web address:** http://www.nautilusgroup.com. **Description:** Manufactures and distributes health and fitness products. **Positions advertised include:** Mechanical Engineer. **Special programs:** Internships. **Corporate headquarters location:** Vancouver WA. **Parent company:** The Nautilus Group Inc. **Operations at this facility include:** Administration. **Listed on:** New York Stock Exchange. **Stock exchange symbol:** NLS.

WINTER PARK RESORT
P.O. Box 36, Winter Park CO 80482. 970/726-1536. **Fax:** 303/892-5823. **Recorded jobline:** 888/562-4525. **Contact:** Human Resources. **E-mail address:** wjob@skiwinterpark.com. **World Wide Web address:** http://www.winterparkresort.com. **Description:** A mountain resort offering lodging, skiing, ice-skating, sleigh rides, and hot air balloon rides. **Note:** Applications are accepted online or in-person at the recruiting office in the Administration building. The office is open 7 days a week from 8:00 a.m. to 4:30 p.m. **Positions advertised include:** Lift Electrician; Security Officer; Travel Specialist.

Connecticut
ESPN INC.
935 Middle Street, Bristol CT 06010. 860/585-2000. **Contact:** Human Resources. **World Wide Web address:** http://www.espn.go.com. **Description:** Operates the ESPN, ESPN2, and ESPN Classic all-sports networks. **Corporate headquarters location:** This location.

GOODSPEED OPERA HOUSE
6 Main Street, P.O. Box A, East Haddam CT 06423. 860/873-8664. **Contact:** Human Resources. **E-mail address:** employment@goodspeed.org. **World Wide Web address:** http://www.goodspeed.org. **Description:** A regional theater specializing in the revival and development of musical theater. Founded in 1963. **Positions advertised include:** Scenic Carpenter; Props Assistant; Costume Shop Staff; Wardrobe Staff; Production Assistant. **Special programs:** Internships; Apprenticeships.

HARTFORD CIVIC CENTER
One Civic Center Plaza, Hartford CT 06103. 860/249-6333. **Contact:** Jane Dion, Personnel Director. **World Wide Web address:** http://www.hartfordciviccenter.com. **Description:** Business offices for the civic center, which is host to numerous concerts, sporting events, and entertainers year-round. The Hartford Civic Center is managed by Madison Square Garden. **Special programs:** Internships. **Corporate headquarters location:** This location.

THE HARTFORD STAGE COMPANY
50 Church Street, Hartford CT 06103. 860/525-5601. **Contact:** Human Resources Department. **World Wide Web address:** http://www.hartfordstage.org. **Description:** A professional, not-for-profit theater producing classic, contemporary, and new plays. Founded in 1964. **Number of employees at this location:** 80.

HARTFORD SYMPHONY ORCHESTRA
228 Farmington Avenue, Hartford CT 06105. 860/246-8742. **Contact:** Personnel. **World Wide Web address:** http://www.hartfordsymphony.org. **Description:** Offices for the symphony orchestra. **Corporate headquarters location:** This location.

LIME ROCK PARK
497 Lime Lock Road, Lakeville CT 06039. 860/435-5000. **Contact:** Human Resources. **World Wide Web address:** http://www.limerock.com. **Description:** Operates an automobile road course.

MYSTIC AQUARIUM INSTITUTE FOR EXPLORATION
55 Coogan Boulevard, Mystic CT 06355. 860/572-5955. **Fax:** 860/572-5969. **Contact:** Human Resources. **E-mail address:** humanresources@mysticaquarium.org. **World Wide Web address:** http://www.mysticaquarium.org. **Description:** A nonprofit organization that promotes awareness of the aquatic world through an integration of educational programs, marine-life exhibits, research and development, and ocean exploration. Mystic Aquarium's exhibits include a variety of fish and invertebrates, African black-footed penguins, beluga whales, Stellar's sea lions, northern fur seals, harbor seals, and Atlantic bottlenose dolphins. The organization also offers the Education Center in Hartford, which provides live animal exhibits, classrooms, and a resource center. Founded in 1973. **NOTE:** Entry-level positions, part-time jobs, and second and third shifts are offered. **Positions advertised include:** Exhibit Educator; Instructor; Shipping and Receiving Clerk. **Special programs:** Internships. **Office hours:** Monday - Friday, 9:00 a.m. - 5:00 p.m. **Corporate headquarters location:** This location. **Parent company:** Sea Research Foundation, Inc. **Annual sales/revenues:** Less than $5 million. **Number of employees at this location:** 225.

MYSTIC SEAPORT
P.O. Box 6000, Mystic CT 06355-0990. 860/572-0711. **Physical address:** 75 Greenmanville Avenue, Mystic CT 06355-0990. **Contact:** Human Resources. **World Wide Web address:** http://www.mysticseaport.com. **Description:** A 19th-century maritime museum. **NOTE:** Seasonal positions offered.

THE SCIENCE CENTER OF CONNECTICUT
950 Trout Brook Drive, West Hartford CT 06119. 860/231-2824. **Contact:** Human Resources. **World Wide Web address:** http://www.sciencecenterct.org. **Description:** A science museum, open seven days per week in July and August, and six days per week during the rest of the year (closed on Mondays.) The Science Center of Connecticut has a wide variety of science

exhibits, some of which feature interactive touch screens. Exhibits include a planetarium, an aquarium, special science exhibits for children, math exhibits featuring pool tables, and a walk-in kaleidoscope.

TRANS-LUX CORPORATION
110 Richards Avenue, Norwalk CT 06854. 203/853-4321. **Contact:** Human Resources. **World Wide Web address:** http://www.trans-lux.com. **Description:** Designs, produces, leases, sells, and services large-scale, multicolor, real-time electronic information displays for both indoor and outdoor use. These displays are used primarily in applications for the financial, banking, gaming, corporate, retail, health care, transportation, and sports markets. The company also owns an expanding chain of movie theaters in the western region of the United States and owns real estate in the United States and Canada. **Positions advertised include:** Controller. **Corporate headquarters location:** This location. **International locations:** Australia; Canada. **Subsidiaries include:** Trans-Lux Fair-Play; Trans-Lux Sports; Trans-Lux West. **Listed on:** American Stock Exchange. **Stock exchange symbol:** TLX.

WADSWORTH ATHENEUM MUSEUM OF ART
600 Main Street, Hartford CT 06103. 860/278-2670. **Contact:** Human Resources. **World Wide Web address:** http://www.wadsworthatheneum.org. **Description:** A fine arts museum housing a collection of 19th-century American painting, Renaissance and Baroque European painting, European and American decorative arts, the Amistad Foundation collection of African-American art and artifacts, and the Nutting collection of Colonial American furniture. Founded in 1842.

WORLD WRESTLING FEDERATION ENTERTAINMENT, INC.
1241 East Main Street, P.O. Box 3857, Stamford CT 06902. 203/352-8600. **Contact:** Human Resources. **World Wide Web address:** http://www.wwe.com. **Description:** Develops and markets television programming and pay-per-view broadcasting for the World Wrestling Federation. The company also produces and manages live wrestling events. **Positions advertised include:** Director of Internal Audit; Director of Job Notification. **Special Programs:** Internships. **Corporate headquarters location:** This location.

Delaware

DELAWARE PARK
777 Delaware Park Boulevard, Wilmington DE 19804. 302/994-2521. **Recorded jobline:** 302/994-2521, ext. 7318. **Fax:** 302/892-3071. **Contact:** Human Resources. **E-mail address:** hr@delawarepark.com. **World Wide Web address:** http://www.delawarepark.com. **Description:** Operates a thoroughbred racing facility, slot machines and an 18-hole golf course. **NOTE:** See website for current job openings and application instructions. **Positions advertised include:** Security Officer; Booth Cashier; Slot Technician; Food and Beverage Server; Cook; Plumber; Floor Care; Carpenter; CAD Operator; Director of Strategic Planning; Staff Accountant; Accounting Supervisor; Slot Analyst.

DOVER DOWNS GAMING & ENTERTAINMENT INC.
P.O. Box 1412, Dover DE 19903-0843. 302/674-4600. **Physical address:** 1131 North DuPont Highway, Dover DE 19901. **Fax:** 302/857-3253. **Contact:** Human Resources. **E-mail address:** recruiter@doverdowns.com. **World Wide Web address:** http://www.doverdowns.com. **Description:** A diversified gaming and entertainment company whose operations consist of Dover Downs Slots, a 91,000-square foot video lottery (slots) casino complex; the Dover Downs Hotel and Conference Center; and Dover Downs Raceway, a harness racing track with pari-mutuel wagering on live and simulcast horse races. **NOTE:** See website to download employment application, which can be mailed or faxed to Human Resources. **Listed on:** New York Stock Exchange. **Stock exchange symbol:** DDE.

HAGLEY MUSEUM AND LIBRARY
P.O. Box 3630, Wilmington DE 19807-0630. 302/658-2400. **Fax:** 302/658-5147. **Contact:** Robert Hill, Human Resources. **E-mail address:** rhill@hagley.org. **World Wide Web address:** http://www.hagley.org. **Description:** A nonprofit educational institution dedicated to American business and technological history. The museum examines the development of the DuPont Company's first product, black powder. **NOTE:** See website for current job openings. **Positions advertised include:** Groundskeeper; Museum Education Guide.

WINTERTHUR MUSEUM & COUNTRY ESTATE
Route 52, Winterthur DE 19735. 302/888-4600. **Toll-free phone:** 800/448-3883. **Contact:** Human Resources. **World Wide Web address:** http://www.winterthur.org. **Description:** Henry Francis du Pont's former country estate now houses his collection of American art that dates from 1640 through 1860. The estate also includes a 60-acre garden and a research library for American art studies.

District Of Columbia

AMERICAN SYMPHONY ORCHESTRA LEAGUE
910 17th Street NW, Suite 800, Washington DC 20006. 202/776-0215. **Fax:** 202/776-0224. **Contact:** Rachel Feinberg, Human Resources Assistant. **E-mail address:** hr@symphony.org. **World Wide Web address:** http://www.symphony.org. **Description:** A national service organization for America's professional symphony orchestras. Founded in 1942. **NOTE:** Resumes should be sent to: Rachel Feinberg, Human Resources Assistant, American Symphony Orchestra League, 33 West 60th Street, 5th Floor, New York NY 10023. Fax: 212/262-5198. Phone: 212/262-5161 ext. 245. **Special programs:** Internships. **Internship information:** Internships are available year-round. **Annual sales/revenues:** Less than $5 million. **Number of employees at this location:** 45.

ARENA STAGE
1101 Sixth Street SW, Washington DC 20024-2691. 202/554-9066. **Fax:** 202/488-4056. **Contact:** Administrative Director. **E-mail address:** jobs@arenastage.org. **World Wide Web address:** http://www.arenastage.org. **Description:** A nonprofit theater company. **NOTE:** See website for individual contacts. Internships candidates should consult the website for information regarding deadlines, requirements, and types of internships offered. **Positions advertised include:** Accounting Associate; Publicist; Inbound Sales Representative; Outbound Sales Associate. **Special programs:** Internships; Apprenticeships; Fellowships. **Operations at this facility include:** Production. **Number of employees at this location:** 200.

ATLANTIC VIDEO
650 Massachusetts Avenue NW, Washington DC 20001. 202/408-0900. **Fax:** 202/408-3419. **Contact:** Human Resources. **E-mail address:** hr@atlanticvideo.com. **World Wide Web address:** http://www.atlanticvideo.com. **NOTE:** See website for important instructions regarding applications. No phone calls please. **Description:** Provides production and postproduction services featuring studios, editing facilities, uplinking and downlinking, ancillary graphics, and audio editing facilities. **Positions advertised include:** Sr. Audio Designer/Mixer; Promo Editor; Manager of Information Systems; Cheyron Operator; Video Engineer.

FRIENDS OF THE NATIONAL ZOO
3001 Connecticut Avenue NW, Washington DC 20008. 202/633-3085. **Fax:** 202/673-0289. **Contact:** Human Resources Director. **E-mail address:** jobs@fonz.org. **World Wide Web address:** http://www.fonz.org. **Description:** In support of the mission of the Smithsonian National Zoological Park, Friends of the

National Zoo is a nonprofit company that provides biological education and environmental protection. Founded in 1958. **Positions advertised include:** Deputy Executive Director; Education Specialist; Assistant Manager, Revenue. **Special programs:** Internships; Co-ops; Summer Jobs. **Office hours:** Monday - Friday, 9:00 a.m. - 4:00 p.m. **Corporate headquarters location:** This location. **Listed on:** Privately held. **Number of employees at this location:** 500.

THE JOHN F. KENNEDY CENTER FOR THE PERFORMING ARTS
2700 F Street NW, Washington DC 20566. 202/467-4600. **Fax:** 202/416-8630. **Contact:** Human Resources. **World Wide Web address:** http://www.kennedy-center.org. **Description:** An arts facility presenting more than 3,000 performances each year and home to the National Symphony Orchestra. **Positions advertised include:** NSO Assistant; Manager, International Programming; Assistant Manager, Corporate & Foundation Relations.

NATIONAL CHILDREN'S MUSEUM
955 L'Enfant Plaza North SW, Suite 5100, Washington DC 20024. 202/675-4120. **Fax:** 202/675-4140. **Contact:** Human Resources. **E-mail address:** info@ncm.museum. **World Wide Web address:** http://www.ncm.museum. **Description:** A child-centered museum scheduled to open in 2009. **Positions advertised include:** Vic President of Exhibitions and Programs; Director of Partnerships; Development Officer; Communications Associate.

NATIONAL GALLERY OF ART
Sixth Street & Constitution Avenue NW, Washington DC 20565. 202/737-4215. **Recorded jobline:** 202/842-6298. **Fax:** 202/789-3011. **Contact:** Human Resources. **E-mail address:** staffing@nga.gov. **World Wide Web address:** http://www.nga.gov. **Description:** An art gallery hosting a variety of exhibitions and lectures in art and film. **NOTE:** If applying by mail, send resume to: National Gallery of Art, Personnel Office, 2000B South Club Drive, Landover MD 20785. **Positions advertised include:** Development Specialist; Mechanical Engineering Technician; Program Specialist; Museum Specialist.

NATIONAL MUSEUM OF AFRICAN ART
950 Independence Avenue SW, Washington DC 20560-0708. 202/633-4600. **Fax:** 202/357-4879. **Contact:** Human Resources. **World Wide Web address:** http://www.nmafa.si.edu. **Description:** A museum devoted exclusively to the collection, study, and exhibition of African art. An important research and reference center, the museum houses a collection of over 6,000 objects, a library, photographic archives, and a conservation laboratory. **Parent company:** Smithsonian Institution.

NATIONAL MUSEUM OF AMERICAN HISTORY
750 9th Street NW, Victor Building, Washington DC 20560-0912. 202/633-3553. **Fax:** 202/357-3346. **Contact:** Personnel Office. **World Wide Web address:** http://americanhistory.si.edu. **Description:** A museum that investigates, interprets, collects, preserves, exhibits, and honors the heritage of America. Founded in 1846. **NOTE:** For information regarding other opportunities at the Smithsonian Institution and its various museums, call the Smithsonian's recorded jobline: 202/287-3102. **Company slogan:** The increase and diffusion of knowledge. **Special programs:** Internships. **Internship information:** The museum's internship program is open to persons enrolled in their final two years of high school and through retirement. Please contact the Office of Internships and Fellowships to receive an application packet. **Parent company:** Smithsonian Institution. **Director:** Brent D. Glass.

NATIONAL MUSEUM OF NATURAL HISTORY
10th Street and Constitution Avenue NW, Washington DC 20560-0912. 202/275-1102. **Recorded jobline:** 202/287-3102. **Contact:** Human Resources. **World Wide Web address:** http://www.mnh.si.edu. **NOTE:** Interested applicants may also call the Smithonian's recorded jobline for additional information regarding openings and application procedures. **Description:** A part of the Smithsonian Institution, this museum displays natural history exhibits.

U.S. HOLOCAUST MEMORIAL MUSEUM
100 Raoul Wallenberg Place SW, Washington DC 20024-2126. 202/488-2674. **Fax:** 202/314-0311. **Contact:** Gerard Cataldo, Human Resources. **E-mail address:** gcataldo@ushmm.org. **World Wide Web address:** http://www.ushmm.org. **Description:** A museum dedicated to the education and remembrance of the Holocaust and genocide studies. The museum includes more than 30,000 items in 18 languages. **Positions advertised include:** Security Specialist; Manager, Program Evaluation; Director of Special Events; Exhibits Specialist; Director of Communications.

Florida

ALLIANCE ENTERTAINMENT CORPORATION
4250 Coral Ridge Drive, Coral Springs FL 33065. 954/255-4000. **Fax:** 954/340-7641. **Contact:** Human Resources. **World Wide Web address:** http://www.aent.com. **Description:** Alliance Entertainment operates in two segments of the entertainment industry: the sale and distribution of prerecorded music and related products, and the acquisition and exploration of proprietary rights to recorded music, video, television, CD-ROMs, and books. **Positions advertised include:** Movie Editor; Programmer; Staff Writer. **Corporate headquarters location:** This location.

ALLIED VAUGHN
3438 Maggie Boulevard, Orlando FL 32811-6502. 407/649-0008. **Toll-free phone:** 877/238-8035. **Fax:** 407/649-9005. **Contact:** Personnel. **World Wide Web address:** http://www.alliedvaughn.com. **Description:** One of the nation's leading independent multimedia manufacturing companies, offering CD-audio and CD-ROM mastering and replication; videocassette and audiocassette duplication; off-line and online video editing; motion picture film processing; film-to-tape and tape-to-film transfers; and complete finishing, packaging, warehousing, and fulfillment services. **NOTE:** When sending resumes, please specify the department to which you are applying.

BIG CAT RESCUE
12802 Easy Street, Tampa FL 33625. 813/920-4130. **Contact:** Human Resources Department. **E-mail address:** savethecats@aol.com. **World Wide Web address:** http://www.bigcatrescue.com. **Description:** A nonprofit organization that serves as both a wildlife sanctuary for large exotic cats and a home for over 200 unwanted animals.

BREVARD ZOO
8225 North Wickham Road, Melbourne FL 32940. 321/254-9453. **Fax:** 321/259-5966. **Contact:** Human Resources. **E-mail address:** info@brevardzoo.org. **World Wide Web address:** http://www.brevardzoo.org. **Description:** Features over 400 animals of Latin America, native Florida, and Australia in their natural habitat.

BUSCH GARDENS TAMPA BAY ADVENTURE ISLAND
P.O. Box 9158, Tampa FL 33674. 813/987-5400. **Physical address:** 3605 Bougainvillea Avenue, Tampa FL 33612 **Toll-free phone:** 888/800-5447. **Contact:** Human Resources. **World Wide Web address:** http://www.buschgardens.com. **Description:** A 300-acre theme park featuring shows, rides, attractions, and exotic animals. **NOTE:** All applications must be made in person at the Human Resources Office. A personal interview is required and all applicants must be a minimum of 18 years old. Please be aware that many technical and professional positions are filled by

internal promotions. **Positions advertised include:** Camp Counselor.

CPAMERICA, INC.
2255 Glades Road, Suite 324 A, Boca Raton FL 33431. 561/988-2607. **Contact:** Human Resources. **E-mail address:** cpamerica@worldnet.att.net. **World Wide Web address:** http://www.cpamerica.com. **Description:** A consulting firm organized to market celebrities, entertainers, and concert performers to international corporations. **Corporate headquarters location:** This location. **Other U.S. locations:** Las Vegas NV. **Listed on:** Privately held. **President/CEO:** Jack Wishna. **Number of employees at this location:** 10. **Number of employees nationwide:** 20.

CARIBBEAN GARDENS
1590 Goodlette-Frank Road, Naples FL 34102-5260. 239/262-5409. **Contact:** Human Resources. **E-mail address:** info@caribbeangardens.com. **World Wide Web address:** http://www.caribbeangardens.com. **Description:** A 52-acre botanical and zoological preserve featuring exhibits of endangered plant and animal species. Founded in 1919.

GATORLAND
14501 South Orange Blossom Trail, Orlando FL 32837. 407/855-5496. **Toll-free phone:** 800/393-JAWS. **Contact:** Personnel. **E-mail address:** info@gatorland.com. **World Wide Web address:** http://www.gatorland.com. **Description:** An attraction featuring a cypress swamp walk, a children's water park, a children's petting zoo, and the 10-acre Alligator Breeding Marsh.

GOLDEN BEAR GOLF INC.
11780 U.S. Highway 1, Suite 400, North Palm Beach FL 33408. 561/626-3900. **Contact:** Linda Clark, Personnel Administrator. **World Wide Web address:** http://www.nicklaus.com. **Description:** Franchises golf practice and instruction facilities, operates golf schools, constructs golf courses through Weitz Golf International (also at this location), and sells consumer golf products and apparel. **Corporate headquarters location:** This location. **Operations at this facility include:** Service. **Listed on:** NASDAQ. **Stock exchange symbol:** JACK.

GULF BREEZE ZOO AND BOTANICAL GARDENS
5701 Gulf Breeze Parkway, Gulf Breeze FL 32563. 850/932-2229. **Fax:** 850/932-8575. **Contact:** Personnel. **E-mail address:** information@the-zoo.com. **World Wide Web address:** http://www.the-zoo.com. **Description:** An attraction that offers botanical Japanese gardens, a Safari Line train that drives through 30 acres of cageless animals, and a zoo that features more than 700 animals.

INFINIUM LABS INC
2033 Main Street #309, Sarasota FL 34237. 941/917-0788. **Contact:** Human Resources. **E-mail address:** jobs@infiniumlabs.com. **World Wide Web address:** http://www.infiniumlabs.com. **Description:** A global entertainment and interactive game company. **Positions advertised include:** Legal Assistant.

INTERNATIONAL SPEEDWAY CORPORATION
P.O. Box 2801, Daytona Beach FL 32120-2801. 386/254-2700. **Physical address:** 1801 West International Speedway Boulevard, Daytona Beach FL 32114. **Contact:** Director of Personnel. **World Wide Web address:** http://www.daytonausa.com. **Description:** Organizes stock car, sports car, motorcycle, and go-cart racing events for spectators at six locations, including two in Daytona Beach. Among the major events conducted by the company are late-model stock car races sanctioned by the National Association for Stock Car Auto Racing, Inc. (NASCAR). The company also produces and syndicates race and race-related radio broadcasts through MRN Radio. **Other U.S. locations:** AL; AZ; NY; SC. **Subsidiaries include:** Amercrown Service Corporation conducts food, beverage, and souvenir operations. **Number of employees nationwide:** 4,620.

KERZNER INTERNATIONAL
1000 South Pine Island Road, Suite 800, Plantation FL 33324. 954/809-2000. **Fax:** 954/809-2711. **Contact:** Human Resources. **E-mail address:** kerznerjobs@kerzner.com. **World Wide Web address:** http://www.kerzner.com. **Description:** Owns and operates casinos, resorts, and hotel facilities. **Listed on:** New York Stock Exchange. **Exchange symbol:** KZL.

LION COUNTRY SAFARI
2003 Lion Country Safari Road, Loxahatchee FL 33470-3976. 561/793-1084. **Fax:** 561/793-9603. **Contact:** Ron Cameron, Human Resources. **E-mail address:** rcameron@lioncountrysafari.com. **World Wide Web address:** http://www.lioncountrysafari.com. **NOTE:** Positions available in all departments for those who wish to work with animals. **Description:** Features two parks including the Lion Country park, a 500-acre drive-through, cageless zoo; and Safari World, an amusement park with boat cruises, rides, and animals. Founded in 1967.

LOWRY PARK ZOO
1101 West Sligh Avenue, Tampa FL 33604. 813/935-8552. **Fax:** 813/935-9486. **Contact:** Human Resources. **E-mail address:** information@lowryparkzoo.com. **World Wide Web address:** http://www.lowryparkzoo.com. **Description:** A zoo hosting approximately 600,000 visitors per year. The zoo features 1,500 animals and offers a wide variety of shows and exhibits. **Positions advertised include:** Visitor Services Representative; Custodial Services Representative; Food Services Representative; Camel & Horse Ride Operator; Security Guard; Wild Australia Carriage Driver; Eco Tour Train Driver; Occasional Spanish Interpreter; Instructor / Keeper Outreach; Nite Site Instructor.

M.E. PRODUCTIONS
2000 SW 30th Avenue, Pembroke Park FL 33009. 954/458-4000. **Toll-free phone:** 800/544-0033. **Fax:** 954/458-4003. **Contact:** Hal Etkin, President. **World Wide Web address:** http://www.meproductions.com. **Description:** A production corporation providing sets, lighting, staging, floral arrangements, decor, audio/visual, entertainment, and music services. **Special programs:** Internships. **Corporate headquarters location:** This location. **Operations at this facility include:** Administration; Manufacturing; Sales. **Number of employees at this location:** 60.

MANHATTAN TRANSFER MIAMI
13121 Northwest 42nd Avenue, Opa Locka FL 33054. 305/688-2222. **Contact:** Human Resources. **World Wide Web address:** http://www.mtmiami.com. **Description:** Provides access to the Latin American and Spanish television markets. The company provides numerous production, post-production, and broadcast services to MTV Latino and The Discovery Channel Latin America/Iberia. Services include creative editing, film-to-tape transfer, electronic video editing, computer generated graphics, duplication, and audio services, as well as production and network facilities operations.

MIAMI METROZOO
12400 SW 152nd Street, Miami FL 33177. 305/251-0400. **Contact:** Human Resources. **World Wide Web address:** http://www.miamimetrozoo.com. **Description:** Features Asian River Life, the African Plains Exhibit, and more than 700 cageless, wild animals. **Positions advertised include:** Welder; Zookeeper; Elephant Zookeeper. **NOTE:** Visit http://www.miamidade.gov/jobs for current job postings in the Miami park and recreation area.

PARROT JUNGLE AND GARDENS
1111 Parrot Jungle Trail, Miami FL 33132. 305/2-JUNGLE. **Fax:** 305/400-7293. **Contact:** Human Resources. **E-mail address:** parrots@parrotjungle.com.

World Wide Web address: http://www.parrotjungle.com. **Description:** An attraction dedicated to parrots and the Caribbean. It features a garden with more than 1200 varieties of exotic plants, a primate exhibit, and both free-flying and trained parrot exhibits.

SEA WORLD OF FLORIDA
7007 SeaWorld Drive, Orlando FL 32821. 407/351-3600. **Contact:** Professional Staffing Department. **World Wide Web address:** http://www.seaworld.com. **Description:** A marine-life park offering a variety of shows and exhibits. **Positions advertised include:** Admissions Attendants; Assistant Lead; Beer School Instructor; Cook; Education Admissions Assistant; Filtration Technician; Food Service; Game Host; Maintenance Help; Registered Nurse; Licensed Practical Nurse; Sales Clerk; Sign Maker; Walk Around Character; Warehouse Worker. **U.S. locations:** CA; TX.

TALLAHASSEE MUSEUM OF HISTORY & NATURAL SCIENCE
3945 Museum Drive, Tallahassee FL 32310-6325. 850/576-1636. **Fax:** 850/574-8243. **Contact:** Personnel. **World Wide Web address:** http://www.tallahasseemuseum.org. **Description:** A museum and zoo featuring historical buildings, an environmental science center, and wild animals.

UNIVERSAL STUDIOS FLORIDA
1000 Universal Studios Plaza, Orlando FL 32819. 407/363-8000. **Fax:** 407/363-8006. **Recorded jobline:** 407/363-8080. **Contact:** Human Resources. **World Wide Web address:** http://www.universalstudios.com. **Description:** A diversified entertainment company and a worldwide leader in motion pictures, television, music, and home and location-based themed entertainment. The company's main operating divisions include Universal Studios, Universal Studios Recreation Group, Universal Studios Information Technology, Universal Studios Operations Group, Universal Music Group, Universal Pictures, Universal Networks & Worldwide Television Distribution, Universal Studios Consumer Products Group, Universal Studios Online, and Spencer Gifts. **Positions advertised include:** Oracle Program Analyst; Assistant Manager of Wardrobe; Attractions Supervisor; Executive Assistant; Park Services Supervisor; Front Teller; VIP Tours Supervisor; Brand Marketing Internet Representative; HVAC Technician; Groundskeeper; Gardener; Attractions Spiel Attendant; Certified Dive Technician; Maintenance Technician; Corporate Attorney; Sous Chef; Accounts Payable Manager; Engineer; E-commerce & Wholesale Sales Manager; Assistant Store Manager; Merchandiser; Second Cook; Legal Secretary; Ride Supervisor; Marketing Research Director; Landscape Architect; Cultural Trainer; Contracts Administrator; Animation Control Technician. **NOTE:** Entry-level positions are offered. **Company slogan:** It's a big universe. Where do you fit in? **Special programs:** Co-ops; Summer Jobs. **Corporate headquarters location:** Universal City CA. **Other U.S. locations:** Nationwide. **International locations:** Worldwide. **Parent company:** The Seagram Co. Ltd. **Listed on:** New York Stock Exchange. **Stock exchange symbol:** VOX. **Number of employees at this location:** 12,000.

WET 'N WILD
6200 International Drive, Orlando FL 32819. 407/351-1800. **Toll-free phone:** 800/992-WILD. **Contact:** Human Resources. **E-mail address:** info@wetnwild.com. **World Wide Web address:** http://www.wetnwild.com. **Description:** A water park offering a variety of activities for all ages. **Positions advertised include:** Lifeguard; Front Gate; Surf Sky; Park Services; Food Service; Security Guard; Receptionist; Ride Operator.

Georgia
ALLIANCE THEATRE COMPANY
1280 Peachtree Street NE, Atlanta GA 30309. 404/733-4650. **Contact:** Human Resources. **World Wide Web address:** http://www.alliancetheatre.org. **Description:** A theater company offering a diverse 10-performance season of contemporary plays, musical theater, world and regional premieres, and classics. **Office hours:** Monday - Friday, 9:00 a.m. - 5:00 p.m. **NOTE:** For acting positions, please contact the Casting Director. For open call information, call the Alliance Audition Information Phone Line at 404/733-4622, or the ACPA Hotline at 770/521-8338. For volunteer positions, call the Volunteer Hotline at 404/733-4619. For Usher positions, call the Usher Hotline at 404/733-4761. **Parent company:** The Robert W. Woodruff Arts Center.

ATLANTA BOTANICAL GARDEN
1345 Piedmont Avenue NE, Atlanta GA 30309-3366. 404/876-5859. **Fax:** 404/876-7472. **Contact:** Human Resources Department. **E-mail address:** jobs@atlantabotanicalgarden.org. **World Wide Web address:** http://www.atlantabotanicalgarden.org. **Description:** Offers family entertainment featuring the Fuqua Conservatory, which contains exotic and endangered plants from around the world. The organization also maintains a lake, baseball fields, a tennis center, and bicycle trails. **NOTE:** Volunteer positions are also available. **Positions advertised include:** Security Officer; Administrative Assistant – Part-time; Summer Cam Teacher. **Special programs:** Internships. **Office hours:** Monday - Friday, 8:30 a.m. - 5:00 p.m.

ATLANTA CYCLORAMA
800-C Cherokee Avenue SE, Atlanta GA 30315. 404/658-7625. **Contact:** Director. **World Wide Web address:** http://www.bcaatlanta.com. **Description:** Offers dramatic taped narrations of a day during the Civil War Battle of Atlanta. This domed, 1920s structure features a large, circular painting, viewed from a revolving stage.

ATLANTA MOTOR SPEEDWAY
P.O. Box 500, Hampton GA 30228. 770/946-4211. **Physical address:** 1500 North Highway 41, Atlanta GA 30260. **Contact:** Human Resources. **World Wide Web address:** http://www.atlantamotorspeedway.com. **Description:** One of the NASCAR circuit's fastest tracks. The track hosts two annual Winston Cup championship events and is home to the Wings and Wheels Motor Fair, as well as the Busch Grand National Race. **Listed on:** New York Stock Exchange. **Stock exchange symbol:** TRK. **CEO:** O. Burton Smith.

CARMIKE CINEMAS
P.O. Box 391, Columbus GA 31902-0391. 706/576-3400. **Physical address:** 1301 1st Avenue, Columbus GA 31901. **Fax:** 706/576-3441. **Contact:** Human Resources. **World Wide Web address:** http://www.carmike.com. **Description:** An operator of motion picture theaters in the United States. **Corporate headquarters location:** This location. **Listed on:** NASDAQ. **Stock exchange symbol:** CKEC. **Other U.S. locations:** Nationwide.

CRUNCH FITNESS
3101 Cobb Parkway, Atlanta GA 30339. 770/955-3845. **Toll-free phone:** 800/FITNESS. **Contact:** Human Resources. **World Wide Web address:** http://www.ballyfitness.com. **Description:** One of the world's largest owners and operators of recreational health clubs. **Positions advertised include:** Membership Consultant; Personal Trainer; Child Care Attendant; Group Exercise Instructor; Receptionist; Maintenance Mechanic; Locker Room Attendant; Retail Sales Associate. **Corporate headquarters location:** Chicago IL. **Other area locations:** Roswell GA; Morrow GA; Norcross GA; Tucker GA. **Other U.S. locations:** Nationwide. **Listed on:** New York Stock Exchange. **Stock exchange symbol:** BFT.

DENON DIGITAL INDUSTRIES INC.
1380 Monticello Road, Madison GA 30650. 706/342-3425. **Contact:** Foss Hodges, Personnel Manager. **World Wide Web address:** http://www.denon.com. **Description:** Manufactures prerecorded compact discs.

Founded in 1910. **Corporate headquarters location:** Pinebrook NJ. **Other U.S. locations:** CA. **International locations:** Worldwide.

FERNBANK MUSEUM OF NATURAL HISTORY
767 Clifton Road NE, Atlanta GA 30307. 404/929-6300. **Fax:** 404/378-8140. **Contact:** Human Resources. **E-mail address:** human.resources@fernbank.edu. **World Wide Web address:** http://www.fernbank.edu/museum. **Description:** This facility is one of the city's largest and newest museums and one of the first major U.S. natural history museums built since the early 1900s. The Fernbank Museum offers "A Walk in Time Through Georgia" as its permanent exhibit, as well as a four-story IMAX screen. **NOTE:** Volunteer positions are also available. **Positions advertised include:** Onsite Sales Representative; Member Services Volunteer Representative – Part-time; Exhibit Designer; Busser – Part-time; Dishwasher – Part-time. **Special programs:** Internships.

HIGH MUSEUM OF ART
1280 Peachtree Street NE, Atlanta GA 30309. 404/733-4400. **Fax:** 404/733-4502. **Contact:** Personnel. **World Wide Web address:** http://www.high.org. **Description:** A contemporary art museum. Holdings include 19th- and 20th-century American furniture, 19th-century American landscape paintings, European paintings and sculptures from the 14th through the 19th centuries, African masks and ceremonial figures, folk art, and photography. The museum also offers an education gallery where performances, workshops, and classes are held, and children of all ages can participate in hands-on art activities. Founded in 1905. **Special programs:** Internships; Volunteer Opportunities. **Parent company:** The Robert W. Woodruff Arts Center. **Number of employees at this location:** 150.

SIX FLAGS OVER GEORGIA
P.O. Box 43187, Atlanta GA 30336. 770/948-9290. **Physical address:** 275 Riverside Parkway, SW, Austell GA 30168. **Contact:** Debbie McGraw, Human Resources Manager. **E-mail address:** sgrecrut@sftp.com. **World Wide Web address:** http://www.sixflags.com/parks/overgeorgia. **Description:** A state-of-the-art theme park with more than 100 rides, shows, and attractions. Main attractions include the Looping Starship, Mindbender, and the Great American Scream Machine. **NOTE:** Please visit website to search for jobs, apply online, and to find details about applying for specific jobs. Seasonal, Part-time, and Full-time jobs are offered. **Positions advertised include:** Admission Attendant; Food Services Attendant; Host/Hostess – Games, Housekeeping, Merchandise, Park Services, Rides, Security. **Parent company:** Premier Parks (OK) owns and operates 40 theme parks nationwide. **Listed on:** New York Stock Exchange. **Stock exchange symbol:** PKS.

SONY MUSIC ENTERTAINMENT, INC.
5152 Columbia Drive, Carrollton GA 30117. 770/836-2000. **Contact:** Employment Manager. **World Wide Web address:** http://www.sonymusic.com. **Description:** Produces prerecorded discs and tapes. **Special programs:** Internships. **Corporate headquarters location:** New York NY. **CEO:** Andrew Lack. **Number of employees nationwide:** 15,000.

Idaho
AMERISTAR CASINOS, INC.
550 Blue Lakes Boulevard North, Twin Falls ID 83301. 208/733-2282. **Contact:** Human Resources. **World Wide Web address:** http://www.ameristarcasinos.com. **Description:** Ameristar owns and operates casinos and hotels in four states. Cactus Pete's Resort Casino and The Horseshu Hotel and Casino are located in Jackpot, Nevada, on the Idaho/Nevada border. **NOTE:** Apply for positions online at www.jobflash.com/ameristar. **Positions advertised include:** Beverage Manager; Groundskeeper; Restaurant Chef; Food Server; Casino Shift Manager; Security Officer; Surveillance Agent; Financial Operations Controller; Assistant Housekeeping Manager; Sales Coordinator. **Corporate headquarters location:** Henderson, NV. **Other U.S. locations:** CO; IA; MI; MO. **Listed on:** NASDAQ. **Stock exchange symbol:** ASCA. **President/CEO:** Craig H. Neilsen.

Illinois
ADLER PLANETARIUM & ASTRONOMY MUSEUM
1300 South Lake Shore Drive, Chicago IL 60605. 312/322-0591. **Fax:** 312/322-9909. **Contact:** Marguerite E. Dawson, Human Resources Manager. **E-mail address:** mdawson@adlerplanetarium.org. **World Wide Web address:** http://www.adlerplanetarium.org. **Description:** A planetarium and science museum focusing on astronomy. Founded in 1930. **NOTE:** Entry-level and part-time positions are offered. **Positions advertised include:** Director of Individual Giving; Museum Service Staff. **Special programs:** Internships; Training; Volunteer. **Corporate headquarters location:** This location. **Operations at this facility include:** Administration.

ALLIED VAUGHN
1200 Thorndale Avenue, Elk Grove Village IL 60007. 847/595-2900. **Toll-free phone:** 800/759-4087. **Fax:** 847/595-8677. **Contact:** Human Resources. **E-mail address:** staffing@alliedvaughn.com. **World Wide Web address:** http://www.alliedvaughn.com. **Description:** One of the nation's leading independent multimedia manufacturing companies offering CD-audio and CD-ROM mastering and replication, videocassette and audiocassette duplication, off-line and online video editing, motion picture film processing, film-to-tape and tape-to-film transfers, and complete finishing, packaging, warehousing, and fulfillment services. **Positions advertised include:** Sales Executive. **Corporate headquarters location:** Minneapolis MN.

ART INSTITUTE OF CHICAGO
111 South Michigan Avenue, Chicago IL 60603-6404. 312/443-3600. **Fax:** 312/857-0141. **Contact:** Human Resources. **E-mail address:** aic.jobs@artic.edu. **World Wide Web address:** http://www.artic.edu. **Description:** An art museum that provides educational programs, family workshops, artist demonstrations, and lectures. Exhibits include African and Ancient American Art, Architecture, Arms and Armor, Impressionism and Post-Impressionism, Modern Art, and Textiles. **NOTE:** Part-time and temporary positions available. E-mail or fax resumes and cover letters. An application is available also online. It can be downloaded and e-mailed or faxed. **Positions advertised include:** Helpdesk Supervisor; Auxiliary Board Assistant Director; Evening Associates Assistant Director; Membership Associate Director; Coordinator; Day Security Officer; Housekeeper; Information Systems Assistant. **Special programs:** Volunteer; Internship.

BALLY TOTAL FITNESS HOLDING CORPORATION
8700 West Bryn Mawr Avenue, Chicago IL 60631. 773/399-1300. **Contact:** Personnel Director. **E-mail address:** resumes@ballyfitness.com. **World Wide Web address:** http://www.ballyfitness.com. **Description:** Bally Total Fitness operates 440 facilities in the United States, Mexico, Canada, Korea, the People's Republic of China, and the Caribbean under the brand names Bally Total Fitness, Crunch Fitness, Gorilla Sports, Pinnacle Fitness, Bally Sports Clubs, and Sports Clubs of Canada. **NOTE:** Bally has offices throughout the United States. Their website provides job listings and contact information for each location. See website. **Positions advertised include:** Director of Operational Accounting; Junior Auditor; Senior Auditor. **Special programs:** Internships. **Corporate headquarters location:** This location. **Other U.S. locations:** Nationwide. **Listed on:** New York Stock Exchange. **Stock exchange symbol:** BFT.

BROADVIEW MEDIA
142 East Ontario, 3rd Floor, Chicago IL 60611. 312/337-6000. **Contact:** Human Resources. **World**

Wide Web address: http://www.broadviewmedia.com. **Description:** A full-service film and video production company involved in production, editing, audio, consumer graphics, and distribution, servicing broadcast and cable networks, corporate advertising agencies, and business to business markets. **NOTE:** Entry-level positions are offered.

CHICAGO ACADEMY OF SCIENCES
PEGGY NOTEBAERT NATURE MUSEUM
2340 North Cannon Drive, Chicago IL 60614. 773/755-5100. **Fax:** 773/549-5199. **Contact:** Human Resources. **World Wide Web address:** http://www.chias.org. **Description:** A natural history museum. The Nature Museum, located on the North Pier, offers hands-on exhibits and also runs week-long summer nature camps June through August each year. Founded in 1857. **NOTE:** See website for job listings and specific contact information.

CHICAGO BOTANIC GARDEN
1000 Lake Cook Road, Glencoe IL 60022. 847/835-5440. **Fax:** 847/835-4484. **Contact:** Human Resources. **E-mail address:** employment@chicagobotanic.org. **World Wide Web address:** http://www.chicagobotanic.org. **Description:** Contains horticultural displays used to promote the understanding of plants, gardening, and natural resource conservation. Founded in 1965. **NOTE:** See website for job listings. Submit resumes and cover letters by e-mail. **Positions advertised include:** Controller; Major Gifts Officer; Post-doctoral Research Fellow; Assistant Registrar (Part-Time); Conservation Scientist; Manager, Network Operations; Plant Health Care Technician; Lab Manager; Plant Collections; Conservation Scientist; Environmental Scientist; Soil and Microbial Ecology; Director of Visitor Operations; Project Manager, Special Events. **Special programs:** Internships.

CHICAGO CUBS
Wrigley Field, 1060 West Addison Street, Chicago IL 60613. 773/404-2827. **Contact:** Director of Human Resources. **World Wide Web address:** http://www.cubs.com. **Description:** The administrative offices for the professional baseball team. **NOTE:** See website for current job openings.

CHICAGO SYMPHONY ORCHESTRA
220 South Michigan Avenue, Chicago IL 60604-2508. 312/294-3333. **Fax:** 312/294-3838. **Contact:** Human Resources. **E-mail address:** hr@cso.org. **World Wide Web address:** http://www.cso.org. **Description:** One of the nation's most prestigious orchestras. **Positions advertised include:** Senior Budget Analyst; Vice President for Development; Sales Associate (Part Time); Payroll Assistant (Part Time). **Special programs:** Internships. **Corporate headquarters location:** This location.

CHICAGO TOUR GUIDES INSTITUTE, INC.
27 North Wacker Drive, Suite 400, Chicago IL 60606. 773/276-6683. **Fax:** 773/252-3729. **Contact:** Human Resources Department. **World Wide Web address:** http://www.chicagoguide.net. **Description:** Offers tours of Chicago. The European Language Center (also at this location) hires part-time and full-time foreign language interpreters for U.S. and foreign companies. **Corporate headquarters location:** This location. **Operations at this facility include:** Administration; Service.

CIRCA '21 DINNER PLAYHOUSE
1828 Third Avenue, Rock Island IL 61201. 309/786-2667. **Fax:** 309/786-4119. **Contact:** Dennis Hitchcock, Producer. **E-mail address:** dlaake@circa21.com. **World Wide Web address:** http://www.circa21.com. **Description:** Produces musicals and modern comedies, as well as a series of children's plays and concerts year-round. Circa '21 Dinner Playhouse has produced numerous national tours. Founded in 1977. **NOTE:** Part-time jobs are offered. Interested jobseekers may fill out an application in person at the office or e-mail their resumes. See website for current job openings and application instructions. **Positions advertised include:** Operations Manager; Housekeeper; Cook; Dishwasher; Maintenance Worker. **Special programs:** Internships. **Listed on:** Privately held.

FAIRMOUNT PARK
OGDEN FAIRMOUNT INC.
9301 Collinsville Road, Collinsville IL 62234-1799. 618/345-4300. **Contact:** Human Resources. **World Wide Web address:** http://www.fairmountpark.com. **Description:** A horse racing track.

THE FIELD MUSEUM OF NATURAL HISTORY
1400 South Lake Shore Drive, Chicago IL 60605. 312/922-9410. **Fax:** 312/665-7272. **Contact:** Human Resource. **E-mail address:** hr@fieldmuseum.org. **World Wide Web address:** http://www.fmnh.org. **Description:** A natural history museum. The museum provides both formal and informal educational opportunities for the public and conducts its own research in the fields of anthropology, geology, zoology, and biology. Founded in 1893. **NOTE:** The museum only accepts online applications via its website. Entry-level positions are offered. **Positions advertised include:** Annual Giving Manager; Campaign Manager; Enterprise Application and Project Manager; Major Gifts Office, Prospect Research Coordinator. **Special programs:** Internships; Volunteer. **Corporate headquarters location:** This location. **Operations at this facility include:** Administration; Research and Development; Service. **Listed on:** Privately held.

GOODMAN THEATRE
170 North Dearborn Street, Chicago IL 60601. 312/443-3811. **Contact:** Human Resources. **World Wide Web address:** http://www.goodman-theatre.org. **Description:** A nonprofit theater producing both classic and contemporary works. Founded in 1925. **NOTE:** See the theatre's website for job listings and contact information.

HARPO INC.
110 North Carpenter Street, Chicago IL 60607. 312/633-1000. **Contact:** Human Resources. **World Wide Web address:** http://www.oprah.com. **Description:** Engaged in film and television production. **Corporate headquarters location:** This location. **President:** Oprah Winfrey.

JOHN DEERE HISTORIC SITE
8393 South Main, Grand Detour, Dixon IL 61021. 815/652-4551. **Contact:** Human Resources. **World Wide Web address:** http://www.deere.com. **Description:** The historic site of John Deere, who founded one of the country's largest agricultural manufacturing companies. This location houses a museum and a blacksmith shop.

KNIGHT'S ACTION PARK & CARIBBEAN WATER ADVENTURE
1700 Recreation Drive, Springfield IL 62707. 217/546-8881. **Contact:** Human Resources. **E-mail address:** knightsap@aol.com. **World Wide Web address:** http://www.knightsactionpark.com. **Description:** An action and water park offering bumper boats, batting cages, miniature golf, a driving range, laser tag, and other activities. **NOTE:** E-mail resumes or drop by the park to fill out an application. **Positions advertised include:** Office; Cashier; Maintenance; Ride Operator; Lifeguard; Food Service; Housekeeping; Parking Attendant; Guest Greeter; Landscaping.

KOHL CHILDREN'S MUSEUM
2100 Patriot Boulevard, Glenview IL 60026-8018. 847/832-6888. **Fax:** 847/724-6398. **Contact:** Human Resources. **World Wide Web address:** http://www.kohlchildrensmuseum.org. **Description:** A children's museum with multisensory exhibits and programs intended to enhance children's understanding of themselves and the world around them. **Positions advertised include:** Exhibit Guide. **Special programs:** Internships; Volunteers. **Corporate headquarters location:** This location.

LINCOLN PARK ZOO
2001 North Clark Street, P.O. Box 14903, Chicago IL 60614. 312/742-2000. **Fax:** 312/742-2299. **Contact:** Human Resources. **World Wide Web address:** http://www.lpzoo.com. **Description:** The Greater Chicago area's zoological exhibit, including amusement rides, a train and restaurants. **NOTE:** A completed application must be submitted for any position. See website for job listings, application and submission procedures. Part-time and seasonal positions are offered. **Positions advertised include:** Education Interpreter; Retail Greeter; Production Manager; Curator; Guest Services Attendant. **Special programs:** Volunteer.

LYRIC OPERA OF CHICAGO
20 North Wacker Drive, Chicago IL 60606. 312/332-2244. **Fax:** 312/419-1082. **Contact:** Human Resources. **E-mail address:** jobs@lyricopera.org. **World Wide Web address:** http://www.lyricopera.org. **Description:** Engaged in the study of opera, music, and the fine arts. Lyric Opera is a nonprofit organization that sponsors, produces, and encourages opera and musical performances in Chicago and the surrounding areas. Founded in 1954. **NOTE:** Part-time, seasonal and entry-level positions are offered. See website for job listings. Fax, mail or e-mail resumes. **Special programs:** Internships. **Corporate headquarters location:** This location.

McCORMICK PLACE
2301 South Lake Shore Drive, Chicago IL 60616. 312/791-7000. **Fax:** 312/791-6543. **Recorded jobline:** 312/791-6090. **Contact:** Human Resources Director. **World Wide Web address:** http://www.mccormickplace.com. **Description:** A convention center that features three theaters, 114 meeting rooms, a ballroom, and over 2 million square feet of exhibition space. **NOTE:** An application is required for any position. See website for application. **Positions advertised include:** Production Coordinator.

MUSEUM OF CONTEMPORARY ART
220 East Chicago Avenue, Chicago IL 60611. 312/280-2660. **Toll-free phone:** 800/MCA-7858. **Fax:** 312/397-4095. **Recorded jobline:** 312/397-4050. **Contact:** Susan Kieffer, Human Resources Manager. **E-mail address:** skieffer@mcachicago.org. **World Wide Web address:** http://www.mcachicago.org. **Description:** A nonprofit, contemporary art museum offering exhibitions of international works from 1945 to the present, with a permanent collection of over 1,500 works. **NOTE:** See website for job listings. Submit resumes and cover letters by mail or fax. An application may also be completed in person at the Human Resources Office. Entry-level positions, part-time jobs, and second and third shifts are offered. **Positions advertised include:** Accounts Payable/Payroll Accountant; Coordinator of Interpretive Training; Accounting Assistant; Marketing Coordinator; Media Relations Coordinator; Box Office Associate; Free-Lance Preparators; Gallery Officers; Visitor Services Associate; Coatroom Attendants. **Special programs:** Internships; Summer Jobs. **Office hours:** Monday - Friday, 10:00 a.m. - 5:00 p.m.

MUSEUM OF SCIENCE & INDUSTRY
57th Street & Lake Shore Drive, Chicago IL 60637. 773/684-1414. **Fax:** 773/684-0019. **Contact:** Human Resources. **E-mail address:** Human.Resources@msichicago.org. **World Wide Web address:** http://www.msichicago.org. **Description:** One of the largest science museums in the world. Museum of Science & Industry offers over 800 exhibits. Founded in 1933. **NOTE:** Interested jobseekers may fax, mail or e-mail resumes. Walk-in applicants are also accepted in the Human Resources Office. Part-time and temporary positions are offered. **Positions advertised include:** Demonstrator; Public Programs; Internal Auditor; Program Interpreters; Administration Assistant; Retail Businesses and Technology Services; Director of Marketing; Maintenance Technician; Manager of Program Development. **Special programs:** Internships; Volunteers. **Office hours:** Monday, Tuesday and Wednesday – 10:00 a.m. – 3:00 p.m. **Corporate headquarters location:** This location.

SHEDD AQUARIUM
1200 South Lake Shore Drive, Chicago IL 60605. 312/939-2426. **Contact:** Tina Henry, Human Resources Recruiter. **E-mail address:** jobs@sheddaquarium.org. **World Wide Web address:** http://www.shedd.org. **Description:** An aquarium and oceanarium offering a wide range of exhibits, outreach programs, and educational workshops. **NOTE:** See website for job listings. Part-time positions offered. Mail or e-mail resumes for all positions. **Positions advertised include:** Admissions Associate; Aquarist; Interpretive Naturalist; Membership Associate; Audio-Visual Operator; Multimedia Manager. **Corporate headquarters location:** This location.

SIX FLAGS GREAT AMERICA
542 North Route 21, P.O. Box 1776, Gurnee IL 60031. 847/249-4636. **Contact:** Human Resources. **World Wide Web address:** http://www.sixflags.com. **Description:** A theme park. **NOTE:** Apply in person at the company's Human Resources Office. **Special programs:** Internships. **Office hours:** Monday – Friday, 1:00 p.m. – 5:00 p.m.; Saturday, 11:00 a.m. – 3:00 p.m. **Other U.S. locations:** CA; GA; NJ; TX. **International locations:** Toronto, Canada. **Parent company:** Premier Parks (OK) owns and operates 35 theme parks nationwide. **Operations at this facility include:** Administration; Sales.

STEPPENWOLF THEATRE COMPANY
1650 North Halsted Street, Chicago IL 60614. 312/335-1650. **Fax:** 312/335-0808. **Contact:** Human Resources. **World Wide Web address:** http://www.steppenwolf.org. **Description:** A Tony Award-winning theater company. **NOTE:** See website for job listings and contact information. **Positions advertised include:** Technical Director; Fundraising; Theatre Sales. **Special programs:** Internships; Volunteers.

THE UNITED CENTER
1901 West Madison Street, Chicago IL 60612. 312/455-4500. **Fax:** 312/455-4750. **Contact:** Human Resources. **World Wide Web address:** http://www.united-center.com. **Description:** A state-of-the-art stadium and entertainment facility. The United Center is home to the Chicago Bulls basketball team and the Chicago Blackhawks ice hockey team. **Operations at this facility include:** Administration; Sales; Service.

WMS INDUSTRIES, INC.
3401 North California Avenue, Chicago IL 60618. 773/961-1620. **Fax:** 773/961-1234. **Contact:** Human Resources. **E-mail address:** hr@wmsgaming.com. **World Wide Web address:** http://www.wmsgaming.com. **Description:** WMS Industries operates in three divisions: the gaming division designs and manufactures slot machines; the pinball and cabinets division; and the contract manufacturing division produces coin-operated video games for Midway Games. **Positions advertised include:** BOM Analyst; Electrical Lab Assistant; Lead Artist; Manufacturing Engineer; Planner; Principal Engineer; Software Engineer. **Subsidiaries include:** WMS Gaming Inc. **Listed on:** New York Stock Exchange. **Stock exchange symbol:** WMS.

Indiana
BMG COLUMBIA HOUSE
6550 East 30th Street, Indianapolis IN 46219. 317/542-6000. **Contact:** Human Resources. **World Wide Web address:** http://www.bmg.com. **Description:** Engaged in the production of music and entertainment through 200 music labels, music publishing, direct marketing, and CD and cassette manufacturing. **Special programs:** Internships. **Corporate headquarters location:** New York NY. **Parent company:** Bertelsmann AG.

BRADFORD WOODS OUTDOOR CENTER
5040 State Road 67 North, Martinsville IN 46151. 765/342-2915. **Fax:** 765/349-1086. **Contact:** Human Resources. **E-mail address:** bradwood@indiana.edu. **World Wide Web address:** http://www.bradwoods.org. **Description:** Offers environmental education and recreation programs. Bradford Woods is affiliated with Indiana University. **NOTE:** Seasonal and Part-time positions are available. **Positions advertised include:** Field Instructor; Summer Camp Counselor; Administrative Assistant; Office Services Assistant; Accounting Assistant; Account Representative. **Special programs:** Internships.

THE CHILDREN'S MUSEUM OF INDIANAPOLIS
3000 North Meridian, P.O. Box 3000, Indianapolis IN 46206. 317/334-3322. **Toll-free phone:** 800/820-6214. **Fax:** 317/920-2047. **Contact:** Manager of Recruiting Services. **E-mail address:** hrweb@childrensmuseum.org. **World Wide Web address:** http://www.childrensmuseum.org. **Description:** A nonprofit, interactive museum for children. The Children's Museum of Indianapolis is one of the largest and fourth oldest children's museum in the world. Founded in 1925. **NOTE:** Entry-level positions, part-time jobs, and second and third shifts are offered. **Positions advertised include:** Vertebrate Paleontologist; Dinosphere Interpretation Manager; Chief Development Officer; Planetarium Show Specialist; Educational Gallery Assistant; Box Office Sales Assistant; Visitor Services Assistant. **Special programs:** Internships; Training; Summer Jobs; Scholarships. **Office hours:** Monday - Friday, 9:00 a.m. - 5:00 p.m. **Corporate headquarters location:** This location. **Operations at this facility include:** Research and Development; Sales; Service. **Listed on:** Privately held.

EITELJORG MUSEUM
500 West Washington Street, Indianapolis IN 46204. 317/636-9378. **Fax:** 317/264-1724. **Contact:** Lezlie Laxton, Personnel Coordinator. **E-mail address:** personnel@eiteljorg.com. **Description:** A museum of Native American and Western art. **Positions advertised include:** Exhibit Specialist.

FORT WAYNE CHILDREN'S ZOO
3411 Sherman Boulevard, Fort Wayne IN 46808. 260/427-6800. **Contact:** Human Resources. **World Wide Web address:** http://www.kidszoo.com. **Description:** A children's zoo featuring African, Indonesian Rain Forest, and Australian exhibits. The zoo also offers a miniature train ride and a dugout canoe ride as well as the Wild Wings Bird Show. **Positions advertised include:** Seasonal Zoo Attendant. **Special programs:** Internships; Apprenticeships.

THE INDIANA REPERTORY THEATRE
140 West Washington Street, Indianapolis IN 46202. 317/635-5277. **Contact:** Employment. **E-mail address:** indianarep@indianarep.com. **World Wide Web address:** http://www.indianarep.com. **Description:** A nonprofit theatre operating from October to May of each year. Founded in 1971. **NOTE:** Jobseekers interested in administrative positions should contact Jane Robison, General Manager. Those interested in production positions should contact Josh Friedman, Production Manager.

INDIANAPOLIS COLTS
7001 West 56th Street, Indianapolis IN 46254. 317/297-7000. **Fax:** 317/297-7000. **Contact:** Executive Vice President of Operations. **E-mail address:** info@colts.com. **World Wide Web address:** http://www.colts.com. **Description:** Administrative offices for the National Football League team. **Special programs:** Internships. **Internship information:** Please check the Website for specific internship information. **Corporate headquarters location:** This location.

INDIANAPOLIS MUSEUM OF ART
4000 Michigan Road, Indianapolis IN 46208. 317/923-1331. **Fax:** 317/931-1978. **Recorded jobline:** 317/920-2670. **Contact:** Human Resources. **World Wide Web address:** http://www.ima-art.org. **Description:** One of the largest general art museums in the U.S. **NOTE:** Unsolicited resumes are not accepted. **Special programs:** Internships.

THE INDIANAPOLIS ZOO
1200 West Washington Street, Indianapolis IN 46222. 317/630-2041. **Fax:** 317/630-2194. **Contact:** Human Resources. **E-mail address:** jobs@indyzoo.com. **World Wide Web address:** http://www.indyzoo.com. **Description:** The Indianapolis Zoo's collection includes a hoofed animal complex, a display garden, an education center, and a library. Founded in 1944. **Positions advertised include:** Encounter Keeper; Zoo Educator; Gardener; Seasonal Butterfly Gardener. **Special programs:** Internships.

SPLASH DOWN DUNES
150 East U.S. Highway 20, Porter IN 46304. 219/929-1181. **Contact:** Human Resources. **World Wide Web address:** http://www.splashdowndunes.com. **Description:** A water amusement park. Splash Down Dunes is the largest water park in Indiana and is open during the summer only (May through September).

WOLF PARK
Wolf Park, Battle Ground IN 47920. 765/567-2265. **Fax:** 765/567-4299. **Contact:** Manager. **World Wide Web address:** http://www.wolfpark.org. **Description:** A nonprofit research organization focusing on wolf behavior and preservation. The park offers walking tours, lectures, and seminars to the public. Founded in 1972. **Special programs:** Internships; Co-ops. **Corporate headquarters location:** This location. **Parent company:** North American Wildlife Park Foundation, Inc.

Iowa

AMEDIA NETWORKS. INC.
421 121st Street, Urbandale IA 50323. 515/224-0919. **Toll-free phone:** 888/776-8268. **Fax:** 515/224-0256. **Contact:** Human Resources. **World Wide Web address:** http://www.amedia.com. **Description:** A leading producer of corporate training products and services. The company offers audio, interactive multimedia, and video products. **Positions advertised include:** Account Manager; Multimedia Designer. **Listed on:** NASDAQ.

BINGO KING COMPANY
3211 Nebraska Avenue, Council Bluffs IA 51501. 712/323-1488. **Fax:** 712/323-3215. **Toll-free phone**: 800/465-1700. **Contact:** Human Resources. **E-mail address:** jobs@bkentertainment. **World Wide Web address:** http://www.bingoking.com. **Description:** Manufactures and distributes a line of bingo cards, break-open tickets, ink markers, electronic equipment, supplies, and accessories. Bingo King products are sold primarily to distributors, who resell them to fraternal, charitable, religious, and social organizations; lodges; hospitals; nursing homes; PTA groups; military clubs; and other similar organizations that use products to raise money and provide entertainment. The company's products are also sold to charitable and commercial bingo halls and to government lottery agencies through company-owned retail stores in Canada, mail-order catalogs, and promotional flyers. Through its Colorado-based subsidiary, the company also makes and distributes electronic gaming equipment. **NOTE**: Contact corporate HR office at 905/687-1700, fax: 905/687-4129. **Corporate headquarters location:** St. Catharines, Ontario, Canada. **International locations:** Canada; Mexico. **Subsidiaries include:** Bazaar & Novelty, Canada; Video King, Littleton CO. **Listed on:** NASDAQ. **Stock exchange symbol:** STUA.

Kentucky

CHURCHILL DOWNS, INC.
700 Central Avenue, Louisville KY 40208. 502/636-4400. **Toll-free phone:** 800/28DERBY. **Fax:** 502/635-

0742. **Contact:** Human Resources Manager. **E-mail address:** cdijobs@kyderby.com. **World Wide Web address:** http://www.churchilldowns.com. **Description:** A horse racetrack and home to the Kentucky Derby. The grounds also include the Eclipse Dining Room and Terrace; Silks Restaurant; the Jockey Club and Balcony; the Skye Terrace; the Clubhouse Gardens; the paddock, where the horses are saddled for the races; the Kentucky Derby Museum, one of the world's largest museums dedicated to thoroughbred racing; and the Churchill Downs Sports Spectrum, where wagering is available on live, televised racing from Keeneland, Turfway Park, Ellis Park, and top racetracks around the country. Founded in 1874. **Positions advertised include:** Payroll Manager; Internal Auditor; Marketing Intern; IT Project Manager. **Corporate headquarters location:** This location. **Subsidiaries include:** Arlington Park; Calder Race Course; Churchill Downs; Churchill Downs Simulcast Network; Churchill Downs Simulcast Productions; Ellis Park; Finish Line Off-Track Betting; Hoosier Park at Anderson; Kentucky Downs; Kentucky Off-Track Betting, Inc.; Nasrin Services LLC; Trackside Off-Track Betting. **Listed on:** NASDAQ. **Stock exchange symbol:** CHDN. **Sales/revenues:** $463 million. **Number of employees at this location:** 1,500.

KENTUCKY REPERTORY THEATRE AT HORSE CAVE
101 East Main Street, P.O. Box 215, Horse Cave KY 42749. 270/786-1200. **Fax:** 270/786-5298. **Contact:** Robert Brock, Artistic Director. **E-mail address:** rbrock@kentuckyrep.org. **World Wide Web address:** http://www.kentuckyrep.org. **Description:** A nonprofit repertory theater promoting professional and educational theater programs. **Special programs:** Internships. **Corporate headquarters location:** This location. **Number of employees at this location:** 10.

STAGE ONE
501 West Main Street, Louisville KY 40202-2957. 502/589-5946. **Fax:** 502/588-5910. **Contact:** Human Resources. **E-mail address:** stageone@stageone.org. **World Wide Web address:** http://www.stageone.org. **Description:** A professional theater company that targets youth audiences, their families and the education community.

U.S. FOREST SERVICE
LAND BETWEEN THE LAKES NATIONAL RECREATION AREA
100 Van Morgan Drive, Golden Pond KY 42211. 270/924-2089. **Fax:** 270/924-2060. **Contact:** Greg Barnes. **E-mail address:** rweakly@fs.fed.us. **World Wide Web address:** http://www.lbl.org. **Description:** A designated national recreation area under the management of the USDA Forest Service that additionally features environmental education opportunities. The park's facilities include a living history farm, a nature center, a planetarium and observatory, a horseback riding campground and public horse stable, and an elk and bison prairie interpretive site. **Special programs:** Internships; Apprenticeships.

Louisiana

ELMWOOD FITNESS CENTER
Elmwood Plaza Shopping Center, 1200 South Clearview Parkway, Suite 1200, Harahan LA 70123. 504/733-1600. **Fax:** 504/799-1684. **Contact:** Lorilea Craft, Human Resources. **E-mail address:** lcraft@ochsner.com. **World Wide Web address:** http://www.elmwoodfitness.com. **Description:** A full-service fitness center offering programs for the entire family. Recreational activities include indoor and outdoor pools; racquetball, volleyball, and basketball courts; weight training; and aquatics. The center includes two aerobic studios; the Cardiovascular Health Center; and Kidsports, a facility for children's activities. **NOTE:** Visit the website to search available positions and apply online. **Positions advertised include:** Club Instructor; Fitness Staff; Environmental Services Lead; Pool Operator; Club Staff; Painter/Maintenance; Fitness Equipment Technician; EFC Watch Engineer; Human Resources Advisor. **Other area locations:** Metairie; New Orleans. **Operations at this facility include:** This location is the main health club. **Parent company:** Ochsner Clinic Foundation, a health-care facility.

Maine

MAINE STATE MUSIC THEATRE INC.
22 Elm Street, Brunswick ME 04011. 207/725-8760, ext.: 11. **Fax:** 207/725-1199. **Contact:** Kathy Kacinski, Company Manager. **E-mail address:** jobs@msmt.org. **World Wide Web address:** http://www.msmt.org. **Description:** A nonprofit music theater company that produces five shows per summer. Maine State Music Theatre also trains theater professionals. **Special programs:** Internships. **Corporate headquarters location:** This location.

PORTLAND PIRATES
94 Free Street, Portland ME 04101. 207/828-4665. **Fax:** 207/773-3278. **Contact:** Brian Williams. **E-mail address:** bwilliams@portlandpirates.com. **World Wide Web address:** http://www.portlandpirates.com. **Description:** A minor league professional hockey franchise. The Portland Pirates play in the AHL (American Hockey League) and are an affiliate of the Washington Capitals. The team plays in the Cumberland County Civic Center. The team's offices include the following departments: a ticket office, souvenir sales, media relations, team services, and community relations.

PORTLAND SEA DOGS
P.O. Box 636, Portland ME 04102. 207/874-9300. **Physical address:** 271 Park Avenue, Portland ME 04102. **Toll-free phone:** 800/936-3647. **Contact:** Charlie Eshbach, General Manager. **E-mail address:** ceshbach@seadogs.com. **World Wide Web address:** http://www.portlandseadogs.com. **Description:** A minor league baseball franchise. The Portland Sea Dogs are the AA affiliate of the Florida Marlins Major League Baseball franchise. **Corporate headquarters location:** This location.

PORTLAND STAGE COMPANY
P.O. Box 1458, Portland ME 04104. 207/774-1043. **Physical address:** 25 Forest Avenue, Portland ME 04104. **Fax:** 207/774-0576. Contact: Dan Burston. **E-mail address:** dburston@portlandstage.com. **World Wide Web address:** http://www.portlandstage.com. **Description:** A nonprofit professional theater. Founded 1974. **Special programs:** Internships. **Corporate headquarters location:** This location. **Number of employees at this location:** 30.

SUGARLOAF/USA
5092 Access Road, Carrabasset Valley ME 04947. 207/237-6932. **Toll-free phone**: 800/843-5623. **Fax:** 207/237-6778. **Contact:** Marilyn Curry, Human Resources Director. **World Wide Web address:** http://www.sugarloaf.com. **Description:** An operator of a ski mountain and resort. Features at Sugarloaf include a number of cross-country trails, an Olympic-size ice-skating rink, and an 18-hole golf course. **NOTE:** Search posted openings and apply on-line. **Positions advertised include:** Certified Massage Therapist; Costume Character; Hotel Housekeeper; Lift Dispatcher; Lift Operator; Marketing Services and Interactive Manager; Nordic Pro/Shop Sales; Owner Services Secretary; Race and Event Crew; Security Dispatcher; Security Officer; Snow Shoveler; Sugarloaf Food Service Provider; Water Utilities Technician. **Special programs:** Internships. **Corporate headquarters location:** This location. **Parent company:** American Skiing Company. **Operations at this facility include:** Administration; Sales; Service. **Number of employees at this location:** 750.

SUNDAY RIVER SKI AREA
P.O. Box 450, Bethel ME 04217. 207/824-5160. **Toll-free phone:** 877/476-6956. **Fax:** 207/824-5110. **Contact:** Human Resources Department. **E-mail address:** jobs@sundayriver.com. **World Wide Web address:** http://www.sundayriver.com. **Description:** Operates more than 120 ski trails on eight mountains. **NOTE:** Search posted openings and apply on-line.

Positions advertised include: Lift Operator; Electrician; Hotel Administrative Assistant; Hotel Line Cook; Housekeeper; Rental Technician; Event Staff Member; Snowboard Professional.

THE THEATER AT MONMOUTH
P.O. Box 385, Monmouth ME 04259-0385. 207/933-2952. **Contact:** David Greenham, Producing Director. **E-mail address:** tamoffice@theateratmonmouth.org. **World Wide Web address:** http://www.theateratmonmouth.org. **Description:** A small, professional, summer theater in central Maine, performing in a national historic landmark Victorian opera house. **NOTE:** The theater offers seasonal employment for professionals in the technical, costume, administrative, and performance departments. **Special programs:** Internships. **Corporate headquarters location:** This location. **Operations at this facility include:** Administration; Sales. **Number of employees at this location:** 40.

Maryland

ALLIED VAUGHN
344 Cottswold Place, Riva MD 21140. 410/956-1070. **Fax:** 410/995-1287. **Contact:** Human Resources. **World Wide Web address:** http://www.alliedvaughn. **Description:** An independent multimedia manufacturing company that offers CD-audio and CD-ROM mastering and replication, videocassette and audiocassette duplication, off-line and online video editing, motion picture film processing, film-to-tape and tape-to-film transfers, and complete finishing, packaging, warehousing, and fulfillment services. **Corporate headquarters location:** Minneapolis MN. **Other U.S. locations:** Nationwide. **Subsidiaries include:** TangibleData, Incorporated. **CEO:** Dave Willette.

BALLY TOTAL FITNESS
1 East Joppa Road, Towson MD 21204. 410/337-0088. **Contact:** Human Resources. **World Wide Web address:** http://www.ballyfitness.com. **Description:** Through its subsidiaries, Bally's Total Fitness, operates over 330 fitness centers located in 27 states with approximately 4.2 million members. The fitness centers operate under the Bally's name in conjunction with various others including Holiday Health, Jack LaLanne, Holiday Spa, Chicago Health Clubs, Scandinavian, President's First Lady, Vic Tanny and Aerobics Plus, and the Vertical Clubs. **Positions advertised include:** Management Trainee; Service Manager; Program Instructor; Group Fitness Instructor; Personal Trainer; Lifeguard; Receptionist; Childcare Attendant; Housekeeper. **Special programs:** Internships. **Corporate headquarters location:** Chicago IL. **Other U.S. locations:** Phoenix AZ; Los Angeles CA; Denver CO; Washington DC; Miami FL; Atlanta GA; Chicago IL; Detroit MI; Minneapolis MN; New York NY; Cleveland OH; Philadelphia PA; Dallas TX; Houston TX; Seattle WA. **Listed on:** New York Stock Exchange. **Stock exchange symbol:** BFT.

BALTIMORE BAYHAWKS
600 Washington Avenue, Suite 10, Towson MD 21204. 866/994-2957. **Contact:** Mandy Eysie, Personnel. **E-mail address:** meysie@baltimorebayhawks.com, or kwilliams@baltimorebayhawks.com. **World Wide Web address:** http://www.baltimorebayhawks.com. **Description:** Baltimore's Major League Lacrosse franchise, and the 2002 MLL champions. **Positions advertised include:** Internships.

BALTIMORE ORIOLES
333 West Camden Street, Baltimore MD 21201-2435. 410/685-9800. **Fax:** 410/547-6273. **Contact:** Personnel. **World Wide Web address:** http://www.orioles.mlb.com. **Description:** Administrative offices for the major league baseball team. **Corporate headquarters location:** This location.

BALTIMORE RAVENS
1 Winning Drive, Training Facility, Owings Mills MD 21117. 410/407-4000. **Contact:** HR Department. **E-mail address:** employment@ravens.nfl.com. **World Wide Web address:** http://www.baltimoreravens.com. **Description:** Baltimore's NFL franchise and Super Bowl XXXV champions. **NOTE:** Offers internships.

CHESAPEAKE AND OHIO CANAL NATIONAL HISTORICAL PARK
1850 Dual Highway, Suite 100, Hagerstown MD 21740-6620. 301/739-4200. **Fax:** 301/739-5275. **Contact:** Human Resources. **E-mail address:** choh_superintendent@nps.gov. **World Wide Web address:** http://www.nps.gov/choh. **Description:** Preserves the cultural and national history of the Chesapeake and Ohio Canal, which operated as a transportation route from 1828 to 1924. The canal runs for 184.5 miles along the Potomac River from Washington DC to Cumberland MD. **Special programs:** Internships.

THE NATIONAL AQUARIUM
501 East Pratt Street, Baltimore MD 21202. 410/576-3800. **Contact:** Human Resources. **E-mail address:** jobs@aqua.com. **World Wide Web address:** http://www.aqua.org. **Description:** An aquarium institute focused on environmental conservation. **Positions advertised include:** Publications Manager; Sales Associate; Security Officer; Veterinary Associate; Visitor Advocate. **Special programs:** Internships. **Executive Director:** David M. Pittenger.

OCEAN CITY MD RECREATION & PARKS
P.O. Box 15. Ocean City MD 21842. 410/250-0125. **Physical address:** 200 125th Street, Ocean City MD 21842. **Contact:** Human Resources Manager. **E-mail address:** dcockrell@ococean.com. **World Wide Web address:** http://www.ococean.com. **Description:** Recreation and parks information for Ocean City. **Positions advertised include:** Special Events Operations Manager.

THE PRINCE GEORGE'S PUBLICK PLAYHOUSE FOR THE PERFORMING ARTS
5445 Landover Road, Cheverly MD 20784-1225. 301/277-1710. **Contact:** Hiring Manager. **World Wide Web address:** http://www.pgparks.com. **Description:** A theater offering dramatic, dance, and musical performances year-round. Founded in 1947. **Corporate headquarters location:** This location.

THE WALTERS ART MUSEUM
600 North Charles Street, Baltimore MD 21201-5188. 410/547-9000. **Contact:** Human Resources. **E-mail address:** jobs@thewalters.org. **World Wide Web address:** http://www.thewalters.org. **Description:** Holds the private collections of William and Henry Walters. The Walters Art Gallery sponsors traveling and special exhibitions to supplement the Walters' original collections. **Positions advertised include:** Rentals Events Assistant; Special Events Security Officer. **Special programs:** Internships.

Massachusetts

AMERICAN REPERTORY THEATRE
Loeb Drama Center, 64 Brattle Street, Cambridge MA 02138. 617/495-2668. **Contact:** Robert Orchard, Managing Director. **E-mail address:** information@amrep.org. **World Wide Web address:** http://www.amrep.org. **Description:** A nonprofit theater. **Special programs:** Internships. **Office hours:** Monday - Friday, 9:00 a.m. - 5:00 p.m.

BOSTON BALLET
19 Clarendon Street, Boston MA 02116. 617/456-6204. **Fax:** 617/695-6995. **Contact:** Human Resources. **World Wide Web address:** http://www.bostonballet.org. **Description:** One of the largest dance companies in the United States. Boston Ballet performs a mix of classic story ballets, contemporary ballets, and avant-garde works. Founded in 1965. **Positions advertised include:** Director of Marketing.

BOSTON BRUINS
One Fleet Center Place, Suite 250, Boston MA 02114. 617/624-1050. **Contact:** Human Resources. **World Wide Web address:** http://www.bostonbruins.com.

Description: Administrative and publicity offices for the National Hockey League team. **Corporate headquarters location:** This location.

BOSTON RED SOX BASEBALL CLUB
Fenway Park, 4 Yawkey Way, Boston MA 02215. 617/267-9440. **Contact:** Human Resources. **World Wide Web address:** http://boston.redsox.mlb.com. **Description:** Operates the Boston Red Sox, an American League professional baseball franchise. **Positions advertised include:** Information Technology Technician.

BOSTON SPORTS CLUB
201 Brookline Avenue, Boston MA 02215. 617/266-7400. **Contact:** Human Resources. **Description:** A fully equipped fitness center with free weights, nautilus equipment, a pool, massage therapy, and exercise classes including sports conditioning, aerobics, and yoga.

BOSTON SYMPHONY ORCHESTRA, INC.
301 Massachusetts Avenue, Boston MA 02115. 617/266-1492. **Recorded jobline:** 617/638-9399. **Contact:** Human Resources. **World Wide Web address:** http://www.bso.org. **Description:** Administrative offices for the Boston Symphony Orchestra.

THE CAPITOL THEATRE
204 Massachusetts Avenue, Arlington MA 02474. 781/648-6022. **Contact:** Manager. **Description:** An independently owned, six-screen movie theater. Founded in 1925. **Corporate headquarters location:** This location.

CRANBERRY VALLEY GOLF COURSE
183 Oak Street, Harwich MA 02645. 508/430-5234. **Contact:** Human Resources. **World Wide Web address:** http://www.cranberrygolfcourse.com. **Description:** A town owned and operated golf course.

JACOB'S PILLOW DANCE FESTIVAL, INC.
358 George Carter Road, Becket MA 01223. 413/243-9919. **Fax:** 413/243-4744. **Contact:** Connie Chin, General Manager. **E-mail address:** info@jacobspillow.org. **World Wide Web address:** http://www.jacobspillow.org. **Description:** One of America's oldest dance festivals, presenting 10 weeks of dance performances and conducting a professional dance school each summer. Founded in 1942. **Positions advertised include:** Director of Marketing & PR; Director of Marketing and Public Relations; Operations Coordinator; Marketing and Graphics Associate. **Special programs:** Internships. **Internship information:** Full- and part-time internships are offered.

MEDIEVAL MANOR
246 East Berkeley Street, Boston MA 02118. 617/423-4900. **Contact:** Manager. **World Wide Web address:** http://www.medievalmanor.com. **Description:** A dinner/theater restaurant with a medieval theme.

MUSEUM OF FINE ARTS - BOSTON
465 Huntington Avenue, Boston MA 02115. 617/267-9300. **Fax:** 617/247-2312. **Contact:** Human Resources Department. **World Wide Web address:** http://www.mfa.org. **Description:** One of the largest museums in New England, with a wide spectrum of permanent and featured exhibits. **Positions advertised include:** Curatorial Planning and Project Manager; Assistant Curator; Research Fellow; Corporate Sponsorship Officer; Development Associate; Director, Planned Giving. **Positions advertised include:** Curatorial Specialist. **Corporate headquarters location:** This location.

NATIONAL AMUSEMENTS INC.
200 Elm Street, P.O. Box 9126, Dedham MA 02027-9126. 781/461-1600. **Contact:** Maureen Dixon, AVP, Human Resources. **E-mail address:** mdixon@national-amusements.com. **World Wide Web address:** http://www.nationalamusements.com. **Description:** National Amusements operates the Showcase, Multiplex, Cinema de Lux, and KinoStar movie theater chains, operating 1,425 screens in the U.S. UK, Latin America, and Russia. **Positions advertised include:** Enterprise Project Manager. **Operations at this facility include:** This location houses administrative offices.

NEW ENGLAND AQUARIUM
Central Wharf, Boston MA 02110. 617/973-5200. **Contact:** Human Resources. **World Wide Web address:** http://www.neaq.org. **Description:** An aquarium offering a variety of educational programs, outdoor shows, whale watching trips, and the Aquarium Medical Center. Founded in 1969. **Positions advertised include:** Visitor Assistant; Sales Associate; Lead Sales Associate; Alternate Lead Visitor Attendant; IMAX Theatre Host; Reservation Assistant; Administrative Assistant.

NEW ENGLAND PATRIOTS FOOTBALL CLUB
60 Washington Street, Foxboro MA 02035. 508/543-8200. **Contact:** Human Resources. **World Wide Web address:** http://www.patriots.com. **Description:** Houses the executive offices of the New England Patriots, a member of the National Football League.

OLD STURBRIDGE VILLAGE
One Old Sturbridge Village Road, Sturbridge MA 01566. 508/347-0216. **Fax:** 508/347-0254. **Contact:** Personnel Department. **World Wide Web address:** http://www.osv.org. **Description:** An outdoor history museum representing rural New England during the 1830s. Old Sturbridge Village operates a working farm, a mill, blacksmith and pottery shops, and a variety of other exhibits on 200 acres of land. Old Sturbridge Village also offers a wide range of events including apple cider tasting, archaeology programs, and concerts. **President:** Alberta Sebolt George.

PLIMOTH PLANTATION
P.O. Box 1620, Plymouth MA 02362. 508/746-1622. **Fax:** 508/746-3407. **Contact:** Susan Haverstock, Human Resources. **E-mail address:** shaverstock@plimoth.org. **World Wide Web address:** http://www.plimoth.org. **Description:** An outdoor authentic re-creation of the seventeenth-century Plymouth Colony. The staff plays the parts of the villagers and tour guides. Plimoth Plantation is open seven days a week, 9:00 a.m. - 5:00 p.m. from April through November. Founded in 1947. **Positions advertised include:** Retail Administrative Assistant; Stockroom Supervisor; Apprentice Interpreter.

SANKATY HEAD GOLF CLUB
100 Sankaty Road, Siasconsett MA 02564. 508/257-6655. **Fax:** 508/257-4265. **Contact:** Human Resources. **World Wide Web address:** http://www.sankatygolfclub.org. **Description:** A private golf club on Nantucket Island known for its signature hole next to Sankaty Head Light House. **Golf Professional:** Mark Heartfield.

SIX FLAGS NEW ENGLAND
1623 Main Street, P.O. Box 307, Agawam MA 01001. 413/786-9300. **Fax:** 413/821-0038. **Contact:** Human Resources. **E-mail address:** SFNEHR@sftp.com. **World Wide Web address:** http://www.sixflags.com. **Description:** A 160-acre amusement park with over 100 rides and attractions. Founded in 1940. **NOTE:** Apply online. Applicants must be available to work weekends April and May, daily June though Labor Day, and weekends in September and October. Must be at least 16 years old. Applicants may apply in person or mail in an application. **Parent company:** Premier Parks (OK) owns and operates 35 theme parks nationwide. **CEO:** Kieran Burke.

SUFFOLK DOWNS
111 Waldemar Avenue, East Boston MA 02128. 617/567-3900. **Contact:** Human Resources. **World Wide Web address:** http://www.suffolkdowns.com. **Description:** A thoroughbred racetrack and entertainment facility offering live racing June through

September. In the off-season, the track offers simulcasted broadcasts of races throughout the country.

Michigan

ALLIED VAUGHN
11923 Brookfield Street, Livonia MI 48150. 734/462-5543. **Toll-free phone:** 800/462-5543. **Fax:** 734/462-4004. **Contact:** Human Resources. **E-mail address:** staffing@alliedvaughn.com. **World Wide Web address:** http://www.alliedvaughn.com. **Description:** An independent multimedia manufacturing company that offers CD-audio and CD-ROM mastering and replication, videocassette and audiocassette duplication, laser video disc recording, off-line and online video editing, motion picture film processing, film-to-tape and tape-to-film transfers and complete finishing, packaging, warehousing, and fulfillment services. Founded in 1942. **Corporate headquarters location:** Minneapolis MN. **Other U.S. locations:** Nationwide. **Subsidiaries include:** TangibleData, Incorporated.

THE DETROIT INSTITUTE OF ARTS
5200 Woodward Avenue, Detroit MI 48202. 313/833-7900. **Contact:** Human Resources. **E-mail address:** hrjobs@dia.org. **World Wide Web address:** http://www.dia.org. **Description:** Preserves, collects, and displays works of art and generally furthers the understanding and appreciation of the visual arts. Founded in 1885. **Positions advertised include:** Donor Relations Manager. **Corporate headquarters location:** This location.

G.T.N. INDUSTRIES, INC.
13320 Northend, Oak Park MI 48237. 248/548-2500. **Toll-free phone:** 888/225-5486. **Fax:** 248/548-8614. **Contact:** Kathleen Dargel, Director of Human Resources. **E-mail address:** kdargel@gtninc.com. **World Wide Web address:** http://www.gtninc.com. **Description:** A global production, post production, and new media company. **Special programs:** Internships. **Internship information:** Internships are offered in various departments including: Audio Post; Post Production; Film Transfer; Information Technology; Visual Effects; and Operations. **Corporate headquarters location:** This location. **Other area locations:** Troy MI.

GRACE & WILD STUDIOS, INC.
23689 Industrial Park Drive, Farmington Hills MI 48335. 248/471-6010. **Fax:** 248/471-2312. **Contact:** Human Resources. **E-mail address:** humanresources@gracewild.com. **World Wide Web address:** http://www.gracewild.com. **Description:** Engaged in film and videotape production, film transfer, and related services. **Special programs:** Internships. **Corporate headquarters location:** This location. **Subsidiaries include:** Postique; Griot Editorial; Detroit Power & Light; Projections; IN-GEAR Equipment Rental; Film Craft Lab; Grace & Wild Interactive Development; Grace & Wild Digital Studios.

HANDLEMAN COMPANY
500 Kirts Boulevard, Troy MI 48084. 248/362-4400. **Contact:** Vice President of Personnel. **E-mail address:** careers@handleman.com. **World Wide Web address:** http://www.handleman.com. **Description:** Engaged in the wholesale distribution of prerecorded music, books on tape, and videos. The company is comprised of two segments: Handleman Entertainment Resources and Northcoast Entertainment. **Special programs:** Executive Candidate Training Program; Mentor Program; Educational Assistance Program. **Corporate headquarters location:** This location. **Other area locations:** Romulus MI. **Other U.S. locations:** Nationwide. **International locations:** Canada; Mexico; Brazil; Argentina; United Kingdom. **Subsidiaries include:** Anchor Bay Entertainment; Madacy Entertainment; Entertainment Company. **Listed on:** New York Stock Exchange. **Stock exchange symbol:** HDL. **Annual sales/revenues:** Over $1 billion. **Number of employees worldwide:** 2,300.

THE MIDLAND CENTER FOR THE ARTS
1801 West Saint Andrews Road, Midland MI 48640-2695. 989/631-5930. **Fax:** 989/631-7890. **Contact:** Tine Siegmund, Human Resources. **E-mail address:** siegmund@mcfta.org. **World Wide Web address:** http://www.mcfta.org. **Description:** Provides various types of entertainment including musical comedy, jazz bands, dance groups, and pop artists. Founded in 1943. **Special programs:** Internships. **Internship information:** The company offers summer internships. Applications are accepted year-round.

Minnesota

BROADVIEW MEDIA
4455 West 77th Street, Minneapolis MN 55435. 952/835-4455. **Fax:** 952/835-0971. **Contact:** Red White, Operations Director. **World Wide Web address:** http://www.broadviewmedia.com. **Description:** A full-service production company in film, video, audio, and interactive media. **Other U.S. locations:** Chicago IL.

THE CHILDREN'S THEATRE COMPANY
2400 Third Avenue South, Minneapolis MN 55404-3597. 612/874-0500. **Fax:** 612/874-8119. **Contact:** Human Resources Representative. **World Wide Web address:** http://www.childrenstheatre.org. **Description:** A flagship theatre for young people and families. The full-time staff includes a resident acting company, performing apprentices, and 90 professionals who work with more than 300 technicians and adult and student actors each year. **Positions advertised include:** Janitor; Assistant Technical Director.

DULUTH ENTERTAINMENT CONVENTION CENTER
350 Harbor Drive, Duluth MN 55802. 218/722-5573. **Contact:** Bryan French, Human Resources. **E-mail address:** bfrench@decc.org. **World Wide Web address:** http://www.decc.org. **Description:** A convention center that hosts a variety of sports and entertainment events. **NOTE:** See website to download application, or apply in person. **Positions advertised include:** Cook; Tour Guide; Temporary Laborer.

GUTHRIE THEATER
725 Vineland Place, Minneapolis MN 55403. 612/347-1100. **Fax:** 612/347-0451. **Contact:** Human Resources Department. **E-mail address:** search@guthrietheater.org. **World Wide Web address:** http://www.guthrietheater.org. **Description:** A theater featuring a resident professional repertory company that presents ensemble productions of classical and modern drama. **NOTE:** The Guthrie Theater will be moving to a new facility in 2006.

HAZELTINE NATIONAL GOLF CLUB
1900 Hazeltine Boulevard, Chaska MN 55318. 952/448-4500. **Fax:** 952/448-1726. **Contact:** Human Resources. **World Wide Web address:** http://www.hngc.com. **Description:** A private championship golf club. **NOTE:** See website for types of job openings and application instructions.

HOMETIME
4275 Norex Drive, Chaska MN 55318. 952/448-9912. **Contact:** Jim Hentges. **E-mail address:** jhentges@duplicationfactory.com. **World Wide Web address:** http://www.hometime.com. **Description:** Produces a public television show on home repair. Duplication Factory, a provider of video duplication services, is also at this location.

K-TEL INTERNATIONAL (USA), INC.
2655 Cheshire Lane North, Plymouth MN 55447. 763/268-0226. **Fax:** 763/559-5505. **Contact:** Manager of Human Resources. **World Wide Web address:** http://www.k-tel.com. **Description:** Distributes recorded music products. **Corporate headquarters location:** This location. **Parent company:** K-Tel International, Inc. **Listed on:** NASDAQ. **Stock exchange symbol:** KTEL.

LIEBERMAN COMPANIES, INC.
9549 Penn Avenue South, Bloomington MN 55431. 952/887-5299. **Toll-free phone:** 800/879-0321. **Fax:** 952/887-5656. **Contact:** Personnel. **E-mail address:** info@liebermancompanies.com. **World Wide Web address:** http://www.liebermancompanies.com. **Description:** Distributes equipment, parts, and supplies to the coin-operated amusement, vending, billiard, and gaming industries. **Special programs:** Internships. **Corporate headquarters location:** This location. **Parent company:** LIVE. **Operations at this facility include:** Administration; Sales; Service. **Listed on:** Privately held. **Number of employees at this location:** 60.

MANN THEATRES
711 Hennepin Avenue, Minneapolis MN 55403. 612/332-3303. **Contact:** Human Resources. **World Wide Web address:** http://www.manntheatresmn.com. **Description:** Operates a chain of movie theaters throughout Minnesota. **NOTE:** Apply in person at any Mann Theatre location. **Corporate headquarters location:** This location.

THE MINNEAPOLIS INSTITUTE OF ARTS
2400 Third Avenue South, Minneapolis MN 55404. 612/870-3014. **Fax:** 612/870-3263. **Recorded jobline:** 612/870-3239. **Contact:** Human Resources. **E-mail address:** miajobs@artsmia.org. **World Wide Web address:** http://www.artsmia.org. **Description:** An art museum that stresses the collection of master works of art in the areas of painting; sculpture; decorative arts; prints; drawings; photography; textiles; and Asian, African, Oceanic, and Native American arts. Founded in 1883.

MINNESOTA TIMBERWOLVES
Target Center, 600 First Avenue North, Minneapolis MN 55403. 612/673-1600. **Fax:** 612/673-1387. **Contact:** Human Resources. **E-mail address:** hr@targetcenter.com. **World Wide Web address:** http://www.timberwolves.com. **Description:** Operates an NBA basketball team. **Positions advertised include:** Corporate Sales Manager; Ticketing Specialist; Receptionist; Ticket Sales Representative.

MINNESOTA TWINS
34 Kirby Puckett Place, Minneapolis MN 55415. 612/375-1366. **Contact:** Ms. Raenell Dorn, Vice-President of Human Resources. **E-mail address:** raenelldorn@twinsbaseball.com. **World Wide Web address:** http://www.mntwins.com. **Description:** Operates a Major League Baseball franchise.

MINNESOTA VIKINGS
9520 Viking Drive, Eden Prairie MN 55344. 952/828-6500. **Contact:** Bonnie Lillemoen, Human Resources Manager. **World Wide Web address:** http://www.vikings.com. **Description:** Operates the National Football League team. **Corporate headquarters location:** This location.

SCIENCE MUSEUM OF MINNESOTA
120 West Kellogg Boulevard, St. Paul MN 55102. 651/221-2532. **Fax:** 651/221-4777. **Recorded jobline:** 651/221-4548. **Contact:** Human Resources. **E-mail address:** humanresources@smm.org. **World Wide Web address:** http://www.smm.org. **Description:** Science Museum of Minnesota is a private, nonprofit, educational and research institution organized to collect, study, and preserve objects of scientific significance and to interpret the objects, discoveries, and insights of science for the general public through its exhibits and education programs. The museum has exhibits in anthropology, biology, geography, paleontology, technology, cultural history, and natural history. Additionally, the museum houses a collection of over 1.5 million scientific objects and an Omnitheater that produces and distributes OMNIMAX films shown around the world. **NOTE:** All applications must be faxed, mailed, or brought to the museum. Full- and part-time positions available. Advanced degrees in the natural sciences are required for curatorial positions. **Positions advertised include:** Director of Anthropology; Marketing Specialist/Media Planning; Graphic Production Technician. **Number of employees at this location:** 600.

WALKER ART CENTER
1750 Hennepin Avenue, Minneapolis MN 55403. 612/375-7600. **Fax:** 612/375-7590. **Recorded jobline:** 612/375-7588. **Contact:** Gary White, Human Resources Director. **E-mail address:** gary.white@walkerart.org. **World Wide Web address:** http://www.walkerart.org. **Description:** An international contemporary art museum with exhibition, film/video, and performing arts programming. Also contains a restaurant and gift shop. **NOTE:** Part- and full-time positions available. Use one method only when applying for jobs (mail, fax, or e-mail). **Special programs:** Internships. **Corporate headquarters location:** This location.

THE FREDERICK R. WEISMAN ART MUSEUM
University of Minnesota, 333 East River Road, Minneapolis MN 55455. 612/625-9494. **Contact:** Carol Stafford, Human Resources. **World Wide Web address:** http://www.weisman.umn.edu. **Description:** An art museum affiliated with the University of Minnesota. The museum's collection features early 20th century American artists and a selection of contemporary art. It is also a teaching museum for the University of Minnesota and the community.

Missouri

AMC ENTERTAINMENT INC.
920 Main Street, Kansas City MO 64105. 816/221-4000. **Fax:** 816/480-4625. **Contact:** Human Resources. **E-mail address:** human_resources@amctheatres.com. **World Wide Web address:** http://www.amctheatres.com. **Description:** AMC Entertainment Inc. is one of the largest motion picture exhibitors in the United States. AMC's theater technology ranges from computerized box offices to High Impact Theatre Systems. The company operates 214 theaters with 2,906 screens in 23 states and the District of Columbia. **Corporate headquarters location:** This location. **Subsidiaries include:** American Multi-Cinema Inc. (AMC).

MISSOURI ATHLETIC CLUB
405 Washington Avenue, St. Louis MO 63102-2183. 314/231-7220. **Fax:** 314/213-2327. **Recorded jobline:** 314/539-4437. **Contact:** Human Resources. **World Wide Web address:** http://www.mac-stl.com. **Description:** A private club offering a full gymnasium, heated swimming pool and solarium, multiple private dining rooms and a la carte outlets, a pro shop, and overnight guest accommodations. This location also hires seasonally. Founded in 1903. **NOTE:** Entry-level positions and second and third shifts are offered. **Special programs:** Apprenticeships; Summer Jobs. **Office hours:** Monday - Friday, 8:00 a.m. - 4:30 p.m. **Corporate headquarters location:** This location. **Other area locations:** Town and Country MO. **Number of employees at this location:** 235. **Number of employees nationwide:** 310.

MISSOURI BOTANICAL GARDEN
4344 Shaw Boulevard, St. Louis MO 63110. 314/577-9400. **Fax:** 314/577-9597. **Recorded jobline:** 314/577-9401. **Contact:** Human Resource Management. **E-mail address:** jobs@mobot.org. **World Wide Web address:** http://www.mobot.org. **Description:** A nonprofit cultural organization that promotes the preservation and enrichment of plant life and the environment. Missouri Botanical Garden has been internationally recognized for its botanical research, education programs, and horticulture display. Founded in 1859. **NOTE:** Part-time jobs are offered. Applications may be downloaded and mailed or e-mailed to Human Resource Management. Resumes accepted only for current job openings. Search for openings online. **Special programs:** Internships; Summer Jobs; Volunteer Positions. **Office hours:** Monday - Friday, 9:00 a.m. - 5:00 p.m. **Corporate headquarters location:** This location. **Director:** Dr.

Peter H. Raven. **Number of employees at this location:** 370.

MUNICIPAL THEATRE ASSOCIATION OF ST. LOUIS
The Muny, Forest Park, St. Louis MO 63101. 314/361-1900. **Fax:** 314/361-0009. **Contact:** Employment. **World Wide Web address:** http://www.muny.com. **Description:** A nonprofit theatrical production company that operates a large outdoor theater. Founded in 1919. **Special programs:** Internships; Summer Jobs. **Corporate headquarters location:** This location. **Operations at this facility include:** Sales. **Number of employees at this location:** 20.

THE ST. LOUIS ART MUSEUM
One Fine Arts Drive, Forest Park, St. Louis MO 63110-1380. 314/721-0072. **Fax:** 314/721-6172. **Contact:** Human Resources. **E-mail address:** jhawkins@slam.org. **World Wide Web address:** http://www.slam.org. **Description:** A comprehensive, free, public art museum with diverse collections from cultures worldwide, along with strong educational programs and a regular schedule of special exhibitions. Founded in 1879.

ST. LOUIS SYMPHONY ORCHESTRA
718 North Grand Boulevard, St. Louis MO 63103. 314/533-2500. **Contact:** Personnel Department. **E-mail address:** resume@slso.org. **World Wide Web address:** http://www.slso.org. **Description:** Houses the administrative offices for one of the oldest orchestras in the United States. Founded in 1880. **Positions advertised include:** Network Administrator.

SIX FLAGS ST. LOUIS
I-44 & Six Flags Road, Eureka MO 63025. 636/938-4800. **Contact:** Human Resources Manager. **E-mail address:** jljohnson@sftp.com. **World Wide Web address:** http://www.sixflags.com/stlouis. **Description:** An amusement park. **Positions advertised include:** Cash Control Agent; Food Service Attendant; Host; Hostess; Laborer; Loss Prevention Officer. **Special programs:** Internships. **Other U.S. locations:** Nationwide. **Parent company:** Premier Parks (OK) owns and operates 35 theme parks nationwide. **Operations at this facility include:** Divisional Headquarters; Sales.

SWANK MOTION PICTURES
201 South Jefferson Avenue, St. Louis MO 63103-2579. 314/534-6300. **Toll-free phone:** 800/876-3322. **Contact:** Human Resources. **E-mail address:** humanres@swank.com. **World Wide Web address:** http://www.swankav.com. **Description:** A nontheatrical film distribution and audiovisual equipment rental company. **Special programs:** Internships. **Corporate headquarters location:** This location. **Other U.S. locations:** Nationwide. **Operations at this facility include:** Administration; Regional Headquarters; Sales. **Listed on:** Privately held. **Number of employees at this location:** 100. **Number of employees nationwide:** 900.

Nevada

FERN ADAIR CONSERVATORY OF THE ARTS
3265 East Patrick Lane, Las Vegas NV 89120. 702/458-7575. **Contact:** Staffing. **E-mail address:** info@fernadair.com. **World Wide Web address:** http://www.fernadair.com. **Description:** A dance school offering ballet, tap, hip-hop, tumbling, and jazz lessons, as well as classes in piano, voice, karate, and children's theatre.

GOLD'S GYM
3750 East Flamingo Road, Las Vegas NV 89121. 702/451-4222. **Contact:** Manager. **World Wide Web address:** http://www.goldsgym.com. **Description:** A full-service health and fitness club that offers weights and cardiovascular equipment, fitness and aerobic instruction, tanning, personal training, and child care facilities. Gold's Gym is one of the world's largest health club chains with over 650 locations. **NOTE:** Part-time jobs are offered. **Special programs:** Training; Summer Jobs. **Corporate headquarters location:** Palm Springs CA. **Other U.S. locations:** Nationwide. **Parent company:** Neste Development. **Number of employees at this location:** 40.

SHUFFLE MASTER INC.
1106 Palms Airport Drive, Las Vegas NV 89119-3730. 702/897-7150. **Fax:** 702/897-2284. **Contact:** Human Resources. **E-mail address:** career@sufflemaster.com. **World Wide Web address:** http://www.shufflemaster.com. **Description:** Designs and manufactures automatic card shufflers for the gaming industry. Also designs technology to identify gaming cheats.

WILD ISLAND FAMILY ADVENTURE PARK
250 Wild Island Court. Sparks NV 89434. 775/359-2927, extension 115. **Fax:** 775/359-5942. **Contact:** Darren Young, Operations. **E-mail address:** operations@wildisland.com. **World Wide Web address:** http://www.wildisland.com. **Description:** A family adventure park featuring a waterpark, bowling and billiards, an arcade, mini golf, go-karts, and dining. **Positions advertised include:** Lifeguard; Cashier; Group Sales; Bartender.

New Hampshire

ATTITASH BEAR PEAKS
Route 302, Bartlett NH 03812. 603/374-2368. **Fax:** 603/374-1960. **Contact:** Linda Gauthier, Human Resources. **E-mail address:** lgauthier@attitash.com. **World Wide Web address:** http://www.attitash.com. **Description:** A four season, big mountain resort. **NOTE:** Search posted listings and apply on-line. Paper resumes are also accepted. **Positions advertised include:** Maintenance Technician; Lift Mechanic; Relief Night Auditor; Ski and Snowboard Pro; Daycare/Nursery Staff Member; Lift Operator; Lift Attendant; Rental and Repair Technician; Market Researcher; Retail Associate.

BLACK MOUNTAIN SKI RESORT
P.O. Box B, Jackson NH 03846. 603/383-4490. **Physical address:** Black Mountain Road, Jackson NH 03846. **Contact:** John Fichera, General Manager. **E-mail address:** ski@blackmt.com. **World Wide Web address:** http://www.blackmt.com. **Description:** New Hampshire's oldest ski resort.

CANOBIE LAKE PARK
P.O. Box 190, Salem NH 03079-0190. 603/893-3506. **Physical address:** 85 North Policy Street, Salem NH 03079. **Fax:** 603/890-2404. **Contact:** Personnel Department. **World Wide Web address:** http://www.canobie.com. **NOTE:** Please visit website to download application, or to have an application sent to you. **Description:** A family amusement park. The park offers attractions and rides including steel corkscrew and wooden rollercoasters as well as one of 12 remaining historical carousels in the nation. Founded in 1902. **Positions advertised include:** Ride Operator; Ride Attendant; Games Attendant; Cashier; Gate Attendant; Security Officer; Mechanic; Office Staff; Costume Character; Lifeguard; Midway Sweeper; Matron/Custodian; First Aid Attendant; Landscaping Grounds Crew; Food Service Worker. **Office hours:** Monday – Friday, 10:00 a.m. – 4:30 p.m.

CHANNEL MARINE
96 Channel Lane, P.O. Box 5397, Weirs Beach NH 03247. 603/366-4801. **Toll-free phone:** 800/524-BOAT. **Fax:** 603/366-4101. **Contact:** Brad Davidson, Operations Manager. **E-mail address:** brad@channelmarine.com. **World Wide Web address:** http://www.channelmarine.com. **Description:** Sells and services powerboats. Founded 1946. **NOTE:** Openings posted as needed on-line. **Positions advertised include:** Parts Manager; Marine Service Technician; Assistant Service Manager; Fork Truck Operator.

CLARK'S TRADING POST
U.S. Route 3, North Woodstock NH 03251. 603/745-8913. **Contact:** Human Resources. **E-mail address:**

info@clarkstradingpost.com. **World Wide Web address:** http://www.clarkstradingpost.com. **Description:** A family entertainment spot. Features animal shows, train rides, and a specialty gift shop. **NOTE:** Clark's Trading Post runs on a summer season schedule – from May through October. Call for more detailed dates.

CRANMORE MOUNTAIN RESORT
1 Skimobile Road, P.O. Box 1640, North Conway NH 03860. 603/356-5543. **Toll-free phone:** 800-SUN-N-SKI. **Contact:** Human Resources. **World Wide Web address:** http://www.cranmore.com. **Description:** A ski, snowboard, and tubing resort. **NOTE**: Search posted openings on-line.

LOON MOUNTAIN RECREATION CORPORATION
Rural Route 1, Box 41, Kancamagus Highway, Lincoln NH 03251. 603/745-6281, ext.: 5577. **Toll-free phone:** 800/229-LOON. **Contact:** Barbara Rome, Human Resources. **E-mail address:** jobs.lm@boothcreek.com. **World Wide Web address:** http://www.loonmtn.com. **Description:** A ski resort. Off-season activities include biking, horseback riding, gondola rides, Mountain Man Tours, and numerous arts and crafts fairs. **NOTE:** Please visit website for online application form. **Positions advertised include:** Customer Service Representative; Ski Patrol Ambassador Coordinator; Lift Maintenance Mechanic; Business Plan Developer; F&B Line Worker; Cashier; Grounds and Parking Manager; Sales Manager; Equipment Rental Technician; Shuttle Bus Driver; Children Center Daycare Attendant; Children Center Ski and Snowboard Instructors; Ski and Snowboard Instructors; Custodian.

NORTHERN FOREST HERITAGE PARK
961 Main Street, Berlin NH 03570. 603/752-7202. **Fax:** 603/752-7222. **Contact:** Human Resources Department. **E-mail address:** heritage@ncia.net. **World Wide Web address:** http://www.northernforestheritage.org. **Description:** An on-site logging museum with plans to open an authentic logging camp and hands-on exhibits for tourists. Founded in 1996. **NOTE:** The Park is open May through October.

RAGGED MOUNTAIN RESORT
620 Ragged Mountain Road, Danbury NH 03230. 603/768-3600. **Fax:** 603/768-3929. **Contact:** Human Resources. **E-mail address:** ragged@ragged-mt.com. **World Wide Web address:** http://www.ragged-mt.com. **Description:** A four season ski and golf resort. **NOTE**: Applicants may fax resume only.

STONEWALL FARM
242 Chesterfield Road, Keene NH 03431. 603/357-7278. **Fax:** 603/357-6018. **Contact:** Kathy Harrington, Human Resources. **E-mail address:** kharrington@stonewallfarm.com. **World Wide Web address:** http://www.stonewallfarm.org . **Description:** Stonewell Farm began as a family farm. Over time, it change families – the few families who owned the farm passed it down to their children. In 1989, with no children to pass it on to, Norm Chase sold the farm to Michael Kidder, who transformed it into a place that would benefit the community. Today, Stonewall Farm offers horse drawn hay and sleigh rides, a hiking trail, while maintaining a dairy, sugarhouse, and garden. It is a non-profit organization. **Positions advertised include:** Grant Writer; Teamster. **Office hours:** Monday – Friday, 8:30 a.m. – 4:30 p.m. **President:** Mary Ann Kristiansen.

STORYLAND/MORRELL CORPORATION
Route 16, Glen NH 03838. 603/383-4293. **Contact:** Human Resources. **Fax**: 603/383-6172. **E-mail address:** hr@storylandnh.com. **World Wide Web address:** http://www.storylandnh.com. **Description:** A children's theme park in the White Mountains. Founded in 1954. **NOTE:** Search posted openings online and download application. There are numerous positions available for kids age fourteen and up and for both seasonal and year-round cast members. The season generally lasts from May through October. Story Land encourages people with skills in welding, plumbing, electricity, automotive mechanics, and painting to apply. They also encourage those with interest in management, marketing, and professional staff positions to apply. **Positions advertised include:** Parking Assistant; Pet Kennel Assistant; Live Character; Stage Entertainment/Theatrics; Ride Operator; Grounds Maintenance Worker; Cashier; Sales Assistant; Cook; Food Server; Dishwasher; Greeter.

New Jersey

ASCENT MEDIA EAST
240 Pegasus Avenue, Northvale NJ 07647. 203/912-9970. **Contact:** Human Resources. **World Wide Web address:** http://www.ascentmedia.com. **Description:** Operates an array of satellite antennas capable of transmitting and receiving domestic and international television transmissions. **Corporate headquarters location:** New York NY. **Parent company:** International Post Ltd. provides a wide range of post-production services, primarily to the television advertising industry, and distributes television programming to the international market through its operating subsidiaries. Other subsidiaries of the parent company include Big Picture/Even Time Limited; Cabana; Manhattan Transfer, Inc.; and The Post Edge, Inc. The company's services include creative editorial services, film-to-tape transfer, electronic video editing, computer-generated graphics, duplication, and audio services, all in multiple standards and formats, as well as network playback operations. The company's services are provided in the New York metropolitan area and South Florida.

CMEINFO.COM
1008 Astoria Boulevard, Suite A, Cherry Hill NJ 08033. 856/874-0010. **Contact:** Human Resources. **World Wide Web address:** http://www.cmeinfo.com. **Description:** Produces educational videotapes, audiotapes, and CD-ROMs for professionals in the medical field.

McCARTER THEATRE CENTER FOR THE PERFORMING ARTS
91 University Place, Princeton NJ 08540. 609/258-6500. **Fax:** 609/497-0369. **Contact:** General Manager. **E-mail address:** admin@mccarter.org. **World Wide Web address:** http://www.mccarter.org. **Description:** A performing arts center that produces and presents artists in dramatic, musical, dance, and special events. Established in 1963. **Special programs:** Internships. **Corporate headquarters location:** This location. **Number of employees at this location:** 200.

MOUNTAIN CREEK
200 Route 94, Vernon NJ 07462. 973/827-2000. **Contact:** Human Resources. **World Wide Web address:** http://www.mountaincreek.com. **Description:** Operates as a water amusement park in the summer and a ski resort in the winter.

NEW JERSEY SPORTS & EXPOSITION AUTHORITY
50 State Route 120, East Rutherford NJ 07073. 201/935-8500. **Recorded jobline:** 201/460-4265. **Contact:** Gina Klein, Director of Human Resources. **E-mail address:** hr@njsea.com. **World Wide Web address:** http://www.njsea.com. **Description:** A state-appointed agency responsible for coordinating and running sports and entertainment activities at the Meadowlands Sports Complex, which includes Meadowlands Racetrack (harness and thoroughbred racing, as well as other events), Giants Stadium (New York Giants, New York Jets, concerts, and other events), and Continental Airlines Arena (New Jersey Nets, New Jersey Devils, tennis, track, concerts, and other events). **Corporate headquarters location:** This location.

THE SHAKESPEARE THEATRE OF NEW JERSEY
36 Madison Avenue, Madison NJ 07940. 973/408-3278. **Fax:** 973/408-3361. **Contact:** Joseph Discher,

Artistic Associate. **E-mail address:** njsf@njshakespeare.org. **World Wide Web address:** http://www.njshakespeare.org. **Description:** A nonprofit professional theater devoted to producing the works of Shakespeare and other classic masterworks. Founded in 1962. **NOTE:** Entry-level positions are offered. **Positions advertised include:** Box Office Associate; Casting Internship; Sales Manager; Assistant Production Manager; Scenic Charge Artist. **Special programs:** Internships; Apprenticeships; Training.

SONY MUSIC ENTERTAINMENT
400 North Woodbury Road, Pitman NJ 08071. 856/589-8000. **Contact:** Human Resources. **World Wide Web address:** http://www.sony.com. **Description:** Sony Music is a major recording company. **Operations at this facility include:** This location manufactures CDs and DVDs.

New Mexico

ALBUQUERQUE INTERNATIONAL BALLOON FIESTA
4401 Alameda, Albuquerque NM 87113. 505/821-1000. **Fax:** 505/828-2887. **Contact:** Melissa Fetch, Event Assistant. **E-mail address:** Melissa@balloonfiesta.com. **World Wide Web address:** http://www.balloonfiesta.com. **Description:** The Albuquerque International Balloon Fiesta is held annually during the first week of October. The Fiesta is one of the largest hot air ballooning events in the world with attendance reaching totals of over 1 million. **Positions advertised include:** Balloon Pilot; Balloon Pilot Crew.

BANDELIER EFX
68 Santa Maria, P.O. Box 2555, Corrales NM 87048. 505/345-8021. **Fax:** 505/345-8023. **Contact:** Tim Stevens. **E-mail address:** tstevens@bandelier.com. **World Wide Web address:** http://www.bandelier.com. **Description:** A television production company that specializes in live-action and 30-second animated commercials. **NOTE:** See website for current job openings and application instructions.

CLIFFS AMUSEMENT PARK
4800 Osuna Road NE, Albuquerque NM 87109. 505/881-9373. **Contact:** Human Resources. **World Wide Web address:** http://www.cliffsamusementpark.com. **Description:** An amusement park. **NOTE:** See website to download application.

EXPLORA! SCIENCE CENTER & CHILDREN'S MUSEUM
1701 Mountain Road NW, Albuquerque NM 87104. 505/224-8300. **Contact:** Human Resources. **World Wide Web address:** http://www.explora.mus.nm.us. **Description:** An interactive science exhibit center that features 250 science, technology, and art exhibits.

ISLETA CASINO & RESORT
11000 Broadway SE, Albuquerque NM 87105. 505/724-3907. **Contact:** Human Resources. **World Wide Web address:** http://www.isletacasinoresort.com. **Description:** A gambling casino featuring video gaming, poker, keno, and other games. **NOTE:** Application form may be downloaded. **NOTE:** See website for current job openings and to download application. **Positions advertised include:** Count Manager; Beverage Server; Buffet Attendant; Buffet Cook; Hostess: Transportation Lead; Valet Attendant; Chip Runner; Dealer; Delivery Clerk; Floor Technician; Change Clerk; Agent; Floor Supervisor; Pit Clerk.

NEW MEXICO MUSEUM OF NATURAL HISTORY AND SCIENCE
1801 Mountain Road NW, Albuquerque NM 87104. 505/841-2800. **Contact:** Becky Pate. **E-mail address:** becky.pate@nmmnh.state.nm.us. **World Wide Web address:** http://www.nmmnh-abq.mus.nm.us. **Description:** A museum focusing on nature, artifacts, and prehistoric fossils. **NOTE:** The Museum is a division of the State of New Mexico Department of Cultural Affairs. Employment opportunities can be found at the State Personnel Office web site: http://www.state.nm.us/spo. **Positions advertised include:** Ecology Intern. **Number of employees at this location:** 100.

ROSWELL MUSEUM AND ART CENTER
100 West 11th Street, Roswell NM 88201. 505/624-6744. **Contact:** Human Resources. **World Wide Web address:** http://www.roswellmuseum.org. **Description:** A leading museum of Southwestern art featuring works by such artists as Georgia O'Keefe.

RUIDOSO DOWNS RACING, INC.
P.O. Box 449, Ruidoso Downs NM 88346. 505/378-4431. **Physical address:** 1461 Highway 70 West, Ruidoso Downs NM 88246. **Contact:** Vicki McCabe, Human Resources. **World Wide Web address:** http://ruidownsracing.com. **Description:** A horse racing facility featuring simulcast racing, a casino, and dining areas. The season begins in late May and runs through early September.

SANDIA CASINO
30 Rainbow Road, Albuquerque NM 87113-2156. 800/526-9366. **Fax:** 505/796-7551. **Contact:** Human Resources. **E-mail address:** staffing@sandiacasino.com. **World Wide Web address:** http://www.sandiacasino.com. **Description:** A casino featuring a wide variety of games including poker, black jack, roulette, and craps. Sandia Casino is open 24 hours per day, seven days per week. **NOTE:** See website for current job openings. Apply in person, or submit resume by mail, fax or e-mail. **Positions advertised include:** Player Development Manager; Bus Manager; Marketing Manager; Cage/Vault Manager; Driver; Table Games Floor Supervisor; Table Games Box Person; Baker; Cook; Administrative Support Clerk; Maintenance; Chief Financial Officer; Business Development Specialist; Waste Water Treatment Operator; Staff Accountant; Lifeguard. **Number of employees at this location:** 1,200.

SANTA FE OPERA
P.O. Box 2408, Santa Fe NM 87504-2408. 505/986-5955. **Contact:** Director of Human Resources. **E-mail address:** humanresources@santafeopera.org. **World Wide Web address:** http://www.santafeopera.org. **Description:** An opera company that offers summer performances in its outdoor theater. **NOTE:** Hiring is seasonal, with staff reaching approximately 600 during July and August. Some year-round positions available. Search and apply for positions online. **Positions advertised include:** Production Staff; Summer Maintenance and Grounds Positions; Usher; Opera Shop Cashier; Customer Service Rep; Database Application Specialist.

SANTA FE SKI AREA
2209 Brothers Road, Suite 220, Santa Fe NM 87505. 505/982-4429. **Contact:** Human Resources. **World Wide Web address:** http://www.skisantafe.com. **Description:** This ski area is located in the Sangre de Christo mountain range. The Santa Fe Ski Area has 44 trails. **NOTE:** The majority of the positions here are seasonal temporary positions, running from Thanksgiving to Easter. A job fair for the winter skiing season is held every November when approximately 200 positions are filled. There is usually another hiring session during the Christmas season.

SUNLAND PARK RACETRACK & CASINO
1200 Futurity Drive, Sunland Park NM 88063. 505/874-5200. **Fax:** 505/874-5369. **Contact:** Human Resources. **E-mail address:** sunlandinfo@sunland-park.com. **World Wide Web address:** http://www.sunland-park.com. **Description:** Offers live and simulcast horse racing, slot machines, five restaurants, and meeting rooms. **NOTE:** Search for positions online.

TAOS SKI VALLEY, INC.
P.O. Box 90, Taos Ski Valley NM 87525. 505/776-2291. **Toll-free phone:** 866/968.7386. **Fax:** 505/776-8596. **Contact:** Kirstin Lett, Human Resources

Department. **E-mail address:** kl@skitaos.org. **World Wide Web address:** http://www.skitaos.org. **Description:** One of the top resort skiing areas in North America. The ski area has more than 72 trails and features one of the top-ranked ski schools in the country. **NOTE:** Most positions are entry level and seasonal. Summer and full-time/year-round positions are filled from within the company. Download employment application. **Positions advertised include:** Adult Ski School Instructor; Bussers; Cashiers; Dishwashers; Lift Operations; Line Servers; Parking Lot Shuttle Drivers; Retail Sales.

New York

A&E TELEVISION NETWORKS
235 East 45th Street, New York NY 10017. 212/210-1400. **Fax:** 212/907-9402. **Contact:** Human Resources. **World Wide Web address:** http://www.aetn.com. **Description:** A joint venture of The Hearst Corporation, ABC, Inc., and NBC, the company is a media corporation that provides magazine and book publishing services, distributes home videos, and operates Websites and the A&E and History Channel cable stations. **NOTE:** The company prefers resumes to be faxed to the above number along with the position to which applying and salary requirements. **Positions advertised include:** Affiliate Sales Administration Manager; Inventory Analyst; Legal & Business Affairs Assistant; Traffic Services Assistant; Account Executive. **Corporate headquarters location:** This location. **Subsidiaries include:** The History Channel; Biography Channel; History Channel International; Genealogy.com; Military.com; Mysteries.com.

AMERIC DISC
17 Gaigal Drive, Nesconset NY 11767. 631/360-2300. **Contact:** Human Resources. **World Wide Web address:** http://www.americdisc.com. **Description:** Americ Disc is one of the nation's leading independent multimedia manufacturing companies offering CD-audio and CD-ROM mastering and replication; videocassette and audiocassette duplication; laser video disc recording; off-line and online video editing; motion picture film processing; film-to-tape and tape-to-film transfers; and finishing, packaging, warehousing, and fulfillment services. **Corporate headquarters location:** Quebec, Canada. **Other U.S. locations:** NC; MN.

THE AMERICAN KENNEL CLUB
260 Madison Avenue, 4th Floor, New York NY 10016. 212/696-8200. **Recorded jobline:** 919/816-3896. **Contact:** Vicki Lane Rees, Human Resources Director. **World Wide Web address:** http://www.akc.org. **Description:** An independent, nonprofit organization devoted to the advancement of purebred dogs. The American Kennel Club adopts and enforces rules and regulations governing dog shows, obedience trials, and field trials, and fosters and encourages interest in the health and welfare of purebred dogs. The club also offers a wide range of books and magazines for national distribution. Founded in 1884. **NOTE:** Entry-level positions are offered. Resumes should be sent to: AKC Human Resources Department, P.O. Box 37905, Raleigh NC 27627-7905; or fax: 919/816-4282. **Positions advertised include:** Computer Support Specialist; Administrative Assistant; Desktop Publishing Specialist; Editorial Assistant. **Office hours:** Monday - Friday, 8:30 a.m. - 4:15 p.m. **Corporate headquarters location:** This location. **Other U.S. locations:** Raleigh NC. **Listed on:** Privately held, Not-for-Profit company. **Number of employees at this location:** 75. **Number of employees nationwide:** 450.

AMERICAN MUSEUM OF NATURAL HISTORY
Central Park West at 79th Street, New York NY 10024-5192. 212/769-5000. **Contact:** Human Resources. **World Wide Web address:** http://www.amnh.org. **Description:** A museum of anthropology, astronomy, mineralogy, and zoology. The museum has a research library and 38 exhibition halls and offers educational and research programs. The museum also publishes several in-house and nationally distributed magazines based on research conducted there. Founded in 1869. **Corporate headquarters location:** This location.

AMERICAN SYMPHONY ORCHESTRA LEAGUE
33 West 60th Street, 5th Floor, New York NY 10023. 212/262-5161. **Fax:** 212/262-5198. **Contact:** Human Resources. **E-mail address:** hfield@symphony.org or hr@symphony.org. **World Wide Web address:** http://www.symphony.org. **Description:** A national service organization for America's professional, symphony, chamber, youth, and college orchestras. Founded in 1942. **Positions advertised include:** Executive Assistant to the President; Secretary to the Board of Directors. **Office hours:** Monday - Friday, 9:00 a.m. - 5:30 p.m. **Other U.S. locations:** Washington DC.

APOLLO THEATRE
253 West 125th Street, New York NY 10027. 212/531-5300. **Fax:** 212/749-2743. **Contact:** Human Resources. **World Wide Web address:** http://www.apollotheater.com. **Description:** A nonprofit performing arts theater with performances year-round. **Parent company:** The Apollo Theater Foundation, Inc.

ARISTA RECORDS
888 7th Avenue, New York NY 10019. 212/489-7400. **Fax:** 212/830-2107. **Contact:** Human Resources. **World Wide Web address:** http://www.arista.com. **Description:** Provides sales, promotional, and artist and repertoire activities for Arista Records and its contracted artists. Founded in 1974. **Corporate headquarters location:** This location. **Parent company:** BMG Entertainment. **Operations at this facility include:** Corporate Administration; Sales.

BROADWAY VIDEO INC.
1619 Broadway, 10th Floor, New York NY 10019. 212/265-7600. **Contact:** Vice President of Operations. **E-mail address:** info@broawayvideo.com. **World Wide Web address:** http://www.broadwayvideo.com. **Description:** An entertainment production company offering editing, design, sound, and related services for all types of media. **Corporate headquarters location:** This location. **Founder:** Lorne Michaels.

BROOKLYN ACADEMY OF MUSIC
30 Lafayette Avenue, Brooklyn NY 11217. 718/636-4100. **Fax:** 718/636-4179. **Contact:** Sarah Weinstein, Director of Human Resources. **E-mail address:** hrresumes@bam.org. **World Wide Web address:** http://www.bam.org. **Description:** A nonprofit arts showcase offering dance, opera, and theatrical performances, as well as performances by the Brooklyn Philharmonic Orchestra. Founded in 1859. **NOTE:** Job openings can be found at the stage door located at 116 St. Felix Street. **Positions advertised include:** Marketing Intern; Summer Concerts Intern; BA Mart Internship; Membership Coordinator; Director Human Resources; Marketing Manager E-media.

BROOKLYN BOTANIC GARDEN
1000 Washington Avenue, Brooklyn NY 11225-1099. 718/623-7200. **Fax:** 718/622-7826. **Contact:** Director of Human Resources Department. **E-mail address:** personnel@bbg.org. **World Wide Web address:** http://www.bbg.org. **Description:** Exhibits over 10,000 plants in the Steinhardt Conservatory. Brooklyn Botanic Garden also offers programs teaching hands-on gardening to children ages three to 17. Brooklyn Botanic Garden offers special events such as the Cherry Blossom Festival, student art exhibitions, tours of the Japanese Hill-and-Pond Garden, and the Annual Spring Plant Sale. Founded in 1910. **Positions advertised include:** Grants Writer; Education Coordinator; Gardening Instructor; Vice President of Horticulture; Arborist; Maintainer; Security Guard.

CINE MAGNETICS VIDEO & DIGITAL LABORATORIES
100 Business Park Drive, Armonk NY 10504-1750. 914/273-7500. **Fax:** 914/273-7575. **Contact:** Human

Resources. **E-mail address:** cminfo@cinemagnetics.com. **World Wide Web address:** http://www.cinemagnetics.com. **Description:** Cine Magnetics is involved in video and film duplication and photo finishing. **Corporate headquarters location:** This location. **Other U.S. locations:** Studio City CA.

THE CLOISTERS
Fort Tryon Park, New York NY 10040. 212/923-3700. **Contact:** Assistant Museum Educator. **World Wide Web address:** http://www.metmuseum.org. **Description:** A museum devoted to the art of medieval Europe. The collection includes architectural fragments, sculptures, frescoes, illuminated manuscripts, tapestries, stained glass, and paintings. Established in 1938. **Special programs:** Internships. **Parent company:** The Metropolitan Museum of Art.

COMEDY CENTRAL
1775 Broadway, 9th Floor, New York NY 10019. 212/767-8600. **Contact:** Human Resources. **World Wide Web address:** http://www.comedycentral.com. **Description:** Operator of the Comedy Central cable television network, which produces such shows as The Daily Show and South Park. **NOTE:** The company's stated policy is to not accept postal mail for any reason – apply online through the company Website. However, resumes for production positions will not be considered without reels/tapes. **Positions advertised include:** Writer; Producer; Sales Operations Analyst. **Special programs:** Internships. **Parent company:** Comedy Central is a joint venture between Viacom, Inc., and Time Warner Entertainment Company.

COURTROOM TELEVISION NETWORK LLC
600 Third Avenue, 2nd Floor, New York NY 10016. 212/973-2800. **Fax:** 240/337-8569. **Contact:** Human Resources. **World Wide Web address:** http://www.courttv.com. **Description:** Court TV is a cable television network providing coverage of publicized legal battles and couret proceedings. **Positions advertised include:** Copy Editor; Administrative Assistant; Junior Web Designer; Senior Staff Writer; Production Assistant; Executive Director. **Corporate headquarters location:** This location. **Parent company:** Turner Broadcasting System, Inc. (Atlanta GA).

DUART FILM AND VIDEO
245 West 55th Street, New York NY 10019. 212/757-4580. **Contact:** Supervisor. **World Wide Web address:** http://www.duart.com. **Description:** Involved in motion picture services and television broadcasting.

4KIDS ENTERTAINMENT, INC.
1414 Avenue of the Americas, New York NY 10019. 212/758-7666. **Fax:** 212/980-0933. **Contact:** John Gansley, Human Resources. **World Wide Web address:** http://www.4kidsentertainmentinc.com. **Description:** A vertically integrated merchandising and entertainment company. 4Kids Entertainment is involved in merchandise licensing, toy design, and TV, movie, and music production. **Positions advertised include:** Sales Clerk; Marketing Specialist; Legal Assistant; Accountant; Graphic Designer. **Corporate headquarters location:** This location. **International locations:** London, United Kingdom. **Subsidiaries include:** 4Kids Entertainment International Limited; 4Kids Entertainment Licensing, Inc.; 4Kids Entertainment Home Video, Inc.; 4Kids Productions Inc.; 4Kids Ad Sales, Inc.; Leisure Concepts UK; Leisure Concepts, Inc.; 4Kids Technology, Inc.; The Summit Media Group, Inc.; Websites 4 Kids, Inc.; 4Kids Entertainment Music, Inc. **Listed on:** New York Stock Exchange. **Stock exchange symbol:** KDE. **Chairman/CEO:** Alfred (Al) R. Kahn. **Annual sales/revenues:** $53 million. **Number of employees:** 188.

HBO (HOME BOX OFFICE)
1100 Avenue of the Americas, New York NY 10036. 212/512-1000. **Contact:** Shelley Fischel, Human Resources Director. **World Wide Web address:** http://www.hbo.com. **Description:** Operates HBO, HBO HDTV, and Cinemax, television networks dedicated to movies. Divisions of HBO include: MoreMAX, ThrillerMAX, and ActionMAX. **Positions advertised include:** Financial Operations and Reporting Assistant; Production Coordinator; Attorney; Product Development and Production Supervisor; Financial Analyst; Legal Contract Administrator; Executive Assistant; Compressionist; Writer; Producer. **Other U.S. locations:** Los Angeles CA. **Parent company:** AOL Time Warner Inc. **Chairman/CEO:** Chris Albrecht. **Annual sales/revenues:** $2.5 billion. **Number of employees:** 2,000.

THE HUDSON RIVER MUSEUM OF WESTCHESTER
ANDRUS PLANETARIUM
511 Warburton Avenue, Yonkers NY 10701. 914/963-4550. **Contact:** Human Resources. **World Wide Web address:** http://www.hrm.org. **Description:** A museum of art, history, and science. Collections include 19th-century fine and decorative arts, and 19th- and 20th-century paintings. Andrus Planetarium is the only public planetarium in Westchester County.

IAC/INTERACTIVE CORP
152 West 57th Street, New York NY 10019. 212/314-7300. **Contact:** Human Resources. **World Wide Web address:** http://www.iac.com. **Description:** Operated diversified businesses including retailing, membership and subscriptions, services, media and advertising, and emerging businesses. **Corporate headquarters location:** This location. **Listed on:** NASDAQ. **Stock exchange symbol:** IACI.

LINCOLN CENTER FOR THE ARTS, INC.
NEW YORK CITY BALLET
70 Lincoln Center Plaza, New York NY 10023. 212/875-5255. **Fax:** 212/875-5185. **Contact:** Stacy Tonkas, Human Resources Director. **E-mail address:** humanresources@lincolncenter.org. **World Wide Web address:** http://www.lincolncenter.org. **Description:** An international center for the performing arts presenting live performances of opera, ballet, music, theater, dance, circus, and puppetry. **Positions advertised include:** Institutional Giving Director; Publicist; Human Resources Assistant; Customer Service Representative. **Executive Director:** Scott Noppe-Brandon. **Annual sales/revenues:** $25 million.

MGM/UNITED ARTISTS
ORION PICTURES CORPORATION
1350 Avenue of the Americas, 24th Floor, New York NY 10019. 212/708-0300. **Fax:** 212/708-0377. **Contact:** Human Resources. **World Wide Web address:** http://www.mgm.com. **Description:** Metro-Goldwyn-Mayer Inc. is one of the nation's largest film distribution companies. **Special programs:** Internships. **Corporate headquarters location:** Santa Monica CA. **Subsidiaries include:** MGM Pictures; Movielink, LLC; United Artists Corporation. **Operations at this facility include:** Administration; Sales; Service. **Listed on:** New York Stock Exchange. **Stock exchange symbol:** MGM. **Chairman/CEO:** Alex Yemenidjian. **Annual sales/revenues:** $1.65 billion. **Number of employees at this location:** 250. **Number of employees nationwide:** 1,150.

MADISON SQUARE GARDEN, L.P.
2 Penn Plaza, 16th Floor, New York NY 10121. 212/465-6000. **Fax:** 212/465-6026. **Recorded jobline:** 212/465-6335. **Contact:** Human Resources. **E-mail address:** msghr@thegarden.com. **World Wide Web address:** http://www.thegarden.com. **Description:** Operates sports and entertainment events in the Arena, Rotunda, and Paramount Theatre. Professional sports teams include the NBA's New York Knicks, the WNBA's New York Liberty, and the NHL's New York Rangers. Madison Square Garden also operates the MSG Network (one of the nation's oldest regional cable television sports networks). In addition, Madison Square Garden operates its own restaurants, catering, fast food, and merchandise divisions. **NOTE:** Seasonal and part-time jobs are offered. **Positions advertised include:** Accountant; Marketing Representative;

Financial Analyst; Advertising Clerk; Graphic Designer. **Special programs:** Internships. **Internship information:** Madison Square Garden has a college internship program that runs during the fall, spring, and summer semesters. For application information, call 212/465-6258. **Corporate headquarters location:** This location. **Parent company:** Regional Programming Partners. **Listed on:** Privately held. **Chairman:** James L. Dolan. **Annual sales/revenues:** $790 million.

THE METROPOLITAN MUSEUM OF ART
1000 Fifth Avenue, New York NY 10028-0198. 212/535-7710. **Fax:** 212/472-2764. **Contact:** Employment Office. **E-mail address:** employoppty@metmuseum.org. **World Wide Web address:** http://www.metmuseum.org. **Description:** A museum containing one of the most extensive art collections in the world. Permanent exhibits range from ancient art to modern art. Operations include conservation and curatorial departments, education services, libraries, concerts and lectures, internships, fellowships, publications and reproductions, and exhibitions. The museum also operates The Cloisters in Fort Tryon Park.

THE METROPOLITAN OPERA ASSOCIATION, INC.
Lincoln Center, New York NY 10023. 212/362-6000. **Fax:** 212/870-7405. **Contact:** Lisa Fuld, Human Resources Associate. **E-mail address:** resumes@mail.metopera.org. **World Wide Web address:** http://www.metopera.org. **Description:** The Opera produces approximately 25 operas per year, tours internationally, and performs free outdoor concerts in New York area parks. Founded in 1883. **NOTE:** Entry-level positions, part-time jobs, and second and third shifts are offered.

MULTIMEDIA TUTORIAL SERVICES, INC.
205 Kings Highway, Brooklyn NY 11223. 718/234-0404. **Contact:** Human Resources. **Description:** Produces and markets tutorial education programs, primarily in videotape and also CD-ROM formats, for use by adults and children in homes, work, schools, libraries, and other locales. Principal products consist of a series of 92 videotapes and supplemental materials on mathematics and an interactive, audio-visual, CD-ROM based system for language instruction. The company's videotapes include colorful computer graphics and real life vignettes. **Corporate headquarters location:** This location.

MUSEUM OF MODERN ART
11 West 53rd Street, New York NY 10019. 212/708-9400. **Fax:** 212/333-1107. **Contact:** Human Resources Manager. **E-mail address:** jobs@moma.org. **World Wide Web address:** http://www.moma.org. **Description:** Houses one of the world's foremost collections of modern art. **Special programs:** Internships. **Corporate headquarters location:** This location. **Number of employees at this location:** 550.

NYS THEATRE INSTITUTE
37 First Street, Troy NY 12180. 518/274-3200. **Fax:** 518/274-3815. **Contact:** Arlene Leff, Intern Program Director. **World Wide Web address:** http://www.nysti.org. **Description:** A professional resident theater company that specializes in theater for family audiences with a strong arts and education approach. **Special programs:** Internships.

NEW LINE CINEMA
888 Seventh Avenue, 19th Floor, New York NY 10106. 212/541-8800. **Contact:** Human Resources. **World Wide Web address:** http://www.newline.com. **Description:** Produces and distributes low-budget theatrical motion pictures (generally action/adventure and comedy films targeted at the younger market). The company also acquires distribution rights to films produced by others, and has agreements with distributors in ancillary markets such as home video, pay television, and free television. **Positions advertised include:** Music & Development Assistant; Contract Accounting Assistant. **Special programs:** Internships. **Parent company:** Time Warner, Incorporated.

THE NEW YORK BOTANICAL GARDEN
200th Street & Southern Boulevard, Bronx NY 10458-5126. 718/817-8700. **Contact:** Human Resources. **E-mail address:** hr@nybg.org. **World Wide Web address:** http://www.nybg.org. **Description:** An internationally recognized center for botanical research offering 47 gardens and plant collections. The New York Botanical Garden is dedicated to environmental education and the conservation of plant diversity. Founded in 1891. **Positions advertised include:** Associate Vice President for Development; Director of the Plant Research Laboratory; Institutional Database Administrator; Project Manager; Manager of Public and School Programs; Director of Horticulture for Public Programs; Associate Rose Garden Curator; Gardener for Public Programs; Administrative Assistant; Assistant Gardener; Research Assistant; Herbarium Assistant; Office Assistant; Gate Attendant. **Special programs:** Internships. **Corporate headquarters location:** This location. **Operations at this facility include:** Education; Research and Development.

NEW YORK CITY CENTER
130 West 56th Street, New York NY 10019. 212/247-0430. **Fax:** 212/246-9778. **Contact:** Human Resources. **World Wide Web address:** http://www.nycitycenter.org. **Description:** A theater for dance and musical performances. **Positions advertised include:** Web site/Network Support Administrator. **Corporate headquarters location:** This location. **Operations at this facility include:** Administration.

THE NEW YORK RACING ASSOCIATION
P.O. Box 90, Jamaica NY 11417. 718/641-4700. **Contact:** Human Resources. **World Wide Web address:** http://www.nyracing.com. **Description:** A state-franchised, nonprofit racing association that owns, operates, and manages three horseracing tracks: Aqueduct, Belmont Park, and Saratoga, where pari-mutuel wagering is conducted. These facilities are the site of some of America's most prestigious stakes races: The Wood Memorial, and The Belmont and Travers Stakes.

NEW YORK SHAKESPEARE FESTIVAL
425 Lafayette Street, New York NY 10003. 212/539-8500. **Contact:** General Manager. **Description:** A nonprofit organization involved in many productions: year-round on-Broadway, off-Broadway, on tour around the country, television specials of theatrical works, free Shakespearean productions in Central Park each summer, and the development of new works.

OXYGEN MEDIA, INC.
75 9th Avenue, 7th Floor, New York City NY 10011. 212/651-2000. **Contact:** Human Resources. **E-mail address:** jobs@oxygen.com. **World Wide Web address:** http://www.oxygen.com. **Description:** Produces and broadcasts television programs and Websites geared toward women viewers. **Positions advertised include:** Junior Accountant. **CEO/Chairman:** Geraldine Laybourne. **Number of employees at this location:** 450.

PARAMOUNT CENTER FOR THE ARTS
1008 Brown Street, Peekskill NY 10566. 914/739-2333. **Contact:** Human Resources. **E-mail address:** info@paramountcenter.org. **World Wide Web address:** http://www.paramountcenter.org. **Description:** A former vaudeville house revived as a performing arts facility offering programs in music, theater, film, and dance. **Office hours:** Monday – Friday, 10:00 a.m. – 6:00 p.m., Saturday, 12:00 p.m. – 4:00 p.m.

RADIO CITY ENTERTAINMENT
1260 Avenue of the Americas, New York NY 10020. 212/247-4777. **Contact:** Human Resources. **World Wide Web address:** http://www.radiocity.com. **Description:** A diversified entertainment production

company. **NOTE:** Resumes may be mailed to the Human Resources Department, 2 Penn Plaza, New York NY 10121. **Special programs:** Internships. **Corporate headquarters location:** This location. **Parent company:** Madison Square Garden, L.P.

ROUNDABOUT THEATRE COMPANY, INC.
231 West 39th Street, Suite 1200, New York NY 10018. 212/719-9393. **Fax:** 212/869-8817. **Contact:** Human Resources Department. **E-mail address:** jobs@roundabouttheatre.org. **World Wide Web address:** http://www.roundabouttheatre.org. **Description:** A theater presenting revivals of classic plays. Founded in 1965. **Positions advertised include:** Ticket Services Representative; Tele-Sales Representative. **Special programs:** Internships. **Number of employees at this location:** 50.

SHOWTIME NETWORKS INC.
1633 Broadway, New York NY 10019. 212/708-1600. **Contact:** Human Resources. **World Wide Web address:** http://www.mtv.com. **Description:** Operates a number of premium cable networks including SHOWTIME, SHO2, SHO3, Showtime Extreme, Showtime Beyond, The Movie Channel, The Movie Channel 2, Sundance, and FLIX. **Corporate headquarters location:** This location. **Parent company:** Viacom International Incorporated. **Listed on:** New York Stock Exchange. **Stock exchange symbol:** VIA.

SHUBERT ORGANIZATION, INC.
234 West 44th Street, 7th Floor, New York NY 10036. 212/944-3700. **Contact:** Human Resources. **World Wide Web address:** http://www.shubertorg.com. **Description:** Owns 16 Broadway theatres, the National Theatre in Washington DC, and the Shubert Theatre in Los Angeles CA. The Shubert Organization also produces plays. **Corporate headquarters location:** This location. **Operations at this facility include:** Administration; Sales. **President:** Phillip Smith. **Sales/revenue:** $325 million. **Number of employees nationwide:** 1,450.

SONY PICTURES ENTERTAINMENT
550 Madison Avenue, 7th Floor, New York NY 10022. 212/833-8500. **Fax:** 212/833-6249. **Contact:** Kathleen Alvarez, Human Resources Supervisor. **World Wide Web address:** http://www.sonypictures.com. **Description:** Sony Pictures is involved in motion pictures, television, theatrical exhibitions, and studio facilities and technology. The motion picture business distributes movies produced by Columbia TriStar Pictures. The television business, which encompasses Columbia TriStar Television, Columbia TriStar Television Distribution, and Columbia TriStar International Television, is involved with numerous cable channels and distributes and syndicates television programs such as *Days of Our Lives* and *Dawson's Creek*. Loews Cineplex Entertainment operates state-of-the-art theaters in 385 locations with 2,926 screens in 15 states. Sony Pictures Imageworks specializes in motion picture special effects and production planning through revisualization sequences. **Positions advertised include:** Administrative Assistant; Publicity Breaks Coordinator. **Special programs:** Internships. **Internship information:** Sony Pictures Entertainment offers various fall, spring, and summer internships in its Manhattan and Inwood, Long Island offices. Students must be available to work 15 to 21 hours per week. Majors in film, communications, management, and marketing are a plus, but all majors are welcome. Applicants must have basic office experience, excellent writing skills, and good interpersonal skills. Most internships are for academic credit, but some offer pay or a weekly stipend. **Office hours:** Monday – Friday, 9:00 a.m. – 5:00 p.m. **Corporate headquarters location:** Culver City CA. **Parent company:** Sony Corporation of America. **Operations at this facility include:** Administration; Sales. **Listed on:** New York Stock Exchange. **CEO/Chairman:** John Calley. **Sales/revenue:** $4.8 billion. **Stock exchange symbol:** SNE. **Number of employees at this location:** 100.

SOUTH STREET SEAPORT MUSEUM
12 Fulton Street, New York NY 10038. 212/748-8600. **Fax:** 212/748-8610. **Contact:** Director of Human Resources Department. **World Wide Web address:** http://www.southstseaport.org. **Description:** A maritime history museum. Through educational programs, exhibitions, and the preservation of buildings and ships, the museum interprets the role of the seaport in the development of the city, state, and nation. Founded in 1967. **Special programs:** Internships.

STATEN ISLAND INSTITUTE OF ARTS AND SCIENCES
75 Stuyvesant Place, Staten Island NY 10301. 718/727-1135. **Fax:** 718/273-5683. **Contact:** Human Resources. **Description:** An organization that focuses on Staten Island and its people with strong collections in arts and sciences. Founded in 1881.

STRONG MUSEUM
One Manhattan Square, Rochester NY 14607. 716/263-2700. **Fax:** 716/263-2493. **Contact:** Personnel. **World Wide Web address:** http://www.strongmuseum.com. **Description:** A public educational institution that collects, preserves, and interprets historic artifacts, manuscripts, and other materials that tell the story of everyday life in America after 1820 with a special concentration on the Northeast during the era of industrialization.

UNIVERSAL MUSIC AND VIDEO DISTRIBUTION
137 East State Street, Gloversville NY 12078. 518/725-0604. **Contact:** Personnel Manager. **Description:** A record and cassette manufacturing and distribution facility.

UNIVERSAL MUSIC GROUP
825 Eighth Avenue, 28th Floor, New York NY 10019. 212/333-8000. **Contact:** Human Resources. **World Wide Web address:** http://www.universalstudios.com/music. **Description:** Produces and markets popular and classical records and is active in the areas of film development, production, and distribution, as well as event television, video theater, merchandising, touring, and music publishing. **Subsidiaries include:** MCA; Universal Concerts. **Parent company:** The Seagram Company Ltd.

WARNER BROS. INC.
1325 Avenue of the Americas, 31st Floor, New York NY 10019. 212/636-5600. **Contact:** Department of Human Resources. **World Wide Web address:** http://www.warnerbros.com. **Description:** Offices of the diversified entertainment company. **Parent company:** AOL Time Warner. **Listed on:** New York Stock Exchange. **Stock exchange symbol:** AOL.

WILDLIFE CONSERVATION SOCIETY (WCS) BRONX ZOO
2300 Southern Boulevard, Bronx NY 10460. 718/220-5100. **Fax:** 718/220-2464. **Contact:** Mariam Benitez, Human Resources Director. **E-mail address:** hr@wcs.org. **World Wide Web address:** http://www.wcs.org/home/zoos/bronxzoo. **Description:** Operates the Aquarium for Wildlife Conservation, the Bronx Zoo, the Central Park Wildlife Center, the Prospect Park Wildlife Center, and the Queens Wildlife Center. Wildlife Conservation Society (WCS) also manages the St. Catherine Wildlife Survival Center off the coast of Georgia and nearly 300 international field projects in over 50 nations. Additionally, WCS conducts environmental education programs at local, national, and international levels. **Office hours:** Monday - Friday, 9:00 a.m. - 5:00 p.m.

WILLIAM MORRIS AGENCY, INC.
1325 Avenue of the Americas, New York NY 10019. 212/586-5100. **Fax:** 212/246-3583. **Contact:** Human Resources. **World Wide Web address:** http://www.wma.com. **Description:** One of the largest talent and literary agencies in the world. Founded in 1898. **Positions advertised include:** Agent Trainee. **Special programs:** Training. **Corporate headquarters**

location: Beverly Hills CA. **Other U.S. locations:** Nashville TN; Beverly Hills CA; Miami Beach FL. **Operations at this facility include:** Regional Headquarters. **Number of employees at this location:** 200. **Number of employees nationwide:** 700. **Number of employees worldwide:** 750.

YONKERS RACEWAY
810 Yonkers Avenue, Yonkers NY 10704. 914/968-4200. **Fax:** 914/968-1121. **Contact:** Anita Tripo, Director of Personnel. **World Wide Web address:** http://www.yonkersraceway.com. **Description:** Operates a major harness racing facility, as well as a convention and meeting facility. **Corporate headquarters location:** This location.

North Carolina
THE BILTMORE COMPANY/BILTMORE HOUSE
One North Pack Square, Asheville NC 28801. 828/255-6122. **Toll-free phone:** 800/624-1575. **Fax:** 828/225-6744. **Contact:** Human Resources Manager. **E-mail address:** humanresouces@biltmore.com. **World Wide Web address:** http://www.biltmore.com. **Description:** The Biltmore Company is an organization dedicated to the preservation of the largest privately-owned historic house in America (Biltmore House) and its 50,000-object collection. Founded in 1986. **Positions advertised include:** Systems Support Trainee; Parking Host; Retail Stockroom Supervisor; Sales Manager; Administrative Assistant; Education Program Coordinator; Floral Display Staff; Engineering Services Staff; Housekeeping Staff; Winery Production Staff; Call Direction Host; Food and Beverage Director; Front Desk Supervisor; Operations Specialist; Engineer; Facility Services Crew Leader; Reservation Sales Agent; Concierge; Reception and Ticket Center Host; E-commerce Customer Service and Sales Representative. **Special programs:** Internships. **Number of employees at this location:** 1,500.

CHARLOTTE SYMPHONY ORCHESTRA
201 South College Street, Suite 110, College Street Level, Charlotte NC 28244. 704/972-2003, extension 232. **Fax:** 704/972-2011. **Contact:** A.T. 'Bud' Simmons, Director of Operations. **E-mail address:** buds@charlottesymphony.org. **World Wide Web address:** http://www.charlottesymphony.org. **Description:** Offices of the local symphony orchestra. The symphony plays 115 performances every season, to an accumulated audience of over 250,000. Founded in 1932. **Operations at this facility include:** Administration; Sales; Service.

SPEEDWAY MOTORSPORTS, INC.
P.O. Box 600, Concord NC 28026. 704/455-3239. **Physical address:** 5555 Concord Parkway South, Concord NC 28027. **Fax:** 704/532-3312. **Contact:** Personnel. **World Wide Web address:** http://www.speedwaymotorsports.com. **Description:** Promotes, markets, and sponsors motor sports activities including eight racing events annually sanctioned by NASCAR, five of which are associated with the Winston Cup professional stock car racing circuit and three of which are associated with the Busch Grand National circuit. The company also operates, sanctions, and promotes its Legends Cars, 5/8-scale modified cars, modeled after those driven by legendary early NASCAR racers. Other Speedway Motorsports operations include two ARCA annual stock car races. **NOTE:** Send resumes to P.O. Box 18747, Charlotte NC 28218. **Special programs:** Internships. **Corporate headquarters location:** This location. **Subsidiaries include:** Atlanta Motor Speedway; Bristol Motor Speedway; Infineon Raceway; Las Vegas Motor Speedway; Lowe's Motor Speedway; PRN Radio; Texas Motor Speedway. **Listed on:** New York Stock Exchange. **Stock exchange symbol:** TRK. **Number of employees at this location:** 255.

North Dakota
FARGO PARK DISTRICT
701 Main Avenue, Fargo ND 58103. 701/241-8160. **Fax:** 781/241-8266 **Contact:** Jim Larson, Director of Finance and Human Resources. **E-mail address:** jlarson@fargoparks.com. **World Wide Web address:** http://www.fargoparks.com. **Description:** Handles staffing for maintenance and recreational programs for public parks in the Fargo area. **NOTE:** This location hires seasonally. **Positions advertised include:** Outdoor Recreation Instructor; Little People Sports Sampler Instructor/Supervisor; Adult Volleyball Referee.

Ohio
AKRON ZOOLOGICAL PARK
500 Edgewood Avenue, Akron OH 44307. 330/375-2550. **Contact:** Human Resources. **World Wide Web address:** http://www.akronzoo.org. **Description:** A zoo featuring a variety of special exhibits. **Special programs:** Internships.

BALLETMET COLUMBUS
BALLETMET DANCE ACADEMY
322 Mt. Vernon Avenue, Columbus OH 43215. 614/229-4860. **Fax:** 614/229-4858. **Contact:** Human Resources Department. **E-mail address:** dance@balletmet.org. **World Wide Web address:** http://www.balletmet.org. **Description:** A nonprofit professional dance company. The BalletMet Dance Academy (also at this location) currently ranks as one of the top five professional dance schools in the country. Founded in 1978. **Corporate headquarters location:** This location. **Annual sales/revenues:** Less than $5 million. **Number of employees at this location:** 100.

CEDAR FAIR L.P.
One Cedar Point Drive, Sandusky OH 44870-5259. 419/627-2233. **Fax:** 419/627-2163. **Contact:** Human Resources. **E-mail address:** work@cedarpoint.com. **World Wide Web address:** http://www.cedarfair.com. **Description:** Owns and operates three seasonal amusement parks. Cedar Point, located on Lake Erie between Cleveland and Toledo, is the third-oldest amusement park still in operation in the United States. Knott's Berry Farm is located near Los Angeles, California. Valleyfair, located near Minneapolis-St. Paul, is one of the largest amusement parks in Minnesota and serves a total population of 8 million people. Worlds of Fun and Oceans of Fun are jointly located in Kansas City, Missouri. Dorney Park & Wildwater Kingdom is located near Allentown PA.

CINCINNATI OPERA
Music Hall, 1241 Elm Street, Cincinnati OH 452010. 513/621-1919. **Fax:** 513/744-3520. **Contact:** Human Resources. **E-mail address:** info@cincinnatiopera.com. **World Wide Web address:** http://www.cincyopera.com. **Description:** The second oldest opera company in the United States. The Cincinnati Opera also offers educational and outreach programs to children, aspiring artists, and educators. Founded in 1920.

CINCINNATI PLAYHOUSE
P.O. Box 6537, Cincinnati OH 45206. 513/345-2242. **Physical address:** 962 Mount Adams Circle, Cincinnati OH 45202. **Fax:** 513/345-2254. **Contact:** Personnel. **E-mail address:** admin@cincyplay.com. **World Wide Web address:** http://www.cincyplay.com. **Description:** A professional regional theatre producing classic and contemporary comedies, dramas, musicals, and recent hits during a 10-month season. The Cincinnati Playhouse operates two theatres including The Robert S. Marx Theatre, which houses 628 seats, and the Thompson Shelterhouse, which seats 225. Founded in 1960. **Positions advertised include:** Summer Theatre Day Camp Director; Seasonal Subscription Assistant. **Special programs:** Acting Internships.

CINCINNATI ZOO
3400 Vine Street, Cincinnati OH 45220. 513/559-7706. **Recorded jobline:** 513/559-7706. **Contact:** Personnel. **World Wide Web address:** http://www.cincyzoo.org. **Description:** A zoo and botanical garden housing approximately 700 different animal species and over 3,000 types of plants. The Cincinnati Zoo also operates several research and conservation programs including

the Center for Research and Endangered Wildlife (CREW), Cheetah Conservation, Guam Rail Release, Mountain Gorilla Conservation, and the Zoo Conservation Fund. **NOTE:** Seasonal opportunities are available. **Number of employees at this location:** 170.

CLEVELAND METROPARKS ZOO
4101 Fulton Parkway, Cleveland OH 44144. 216/635-3280. **Recorded jobline:** 216/635-3211. **Fax:** 216/635-3286. **Contact:** Human Resources Department. **E-mail address:** resumes@clevelandmetroparks.com. **World Wide Web address:** http://www.clemetparks.com. **Description:** Features thousands of animals from 7 continents housed on 165 wooded acres and 2 indoor acres of tropics. The Cleveland Metroparks Zoo also offers several education programs including programs for schools and groups at the zoo, programs for schools and groups away from the zoo, distance learning programs, safaris and night tracks, and college-level courses. **NOTE:** Seasonal positions are available. **Special programs:** Internships, Part-Time and Seasonal Employment. **Internship information:** Please visit the zoo's Website for current internship information.

THE CLEVELAND PLAYHOUSE
8500 Euclid Avenue, Cleveland OH 44106. 216/795-7000. **Fax:** 216/795-7005. **Contact:** Personnel. **World Wide Web address:** http://www.clevelandplayhouse.com. **Description:** A theater dedicated to the presentation of new and classical American plays. Founded in 1915. **Positions advertised include:** Telephone Sales Representative. **Internship information:** Visit the Playhouse website or call for current information.

COLUMBUS ZOO AND AQUARIUM
P.O. Box 400, Powell OH 43065-0400. 614/645-3550. **Physical address:** 9990 Riverside Drive, Powell OH 43065. **Contact:** Human Resources Director. **World Wide Web address:** http://www.columbuszoo.org. **Description:** A zoo featuring a wide range of exhibits including "African Forest," "Kangaroo Walk-About," a live coral reef, prairie dogs, and a migratory song bird aviary. **Special programs:** Seasonal Positions; Internships/Mentorships; Volunteer Opportunities. **Internship information:** The zoo offers annual paid Mentorships for college juniors and seniors in the following departments: Human Resources, Visitor Services, and Marketing. Interested candidates should contact Jennifer Koslow for more information. E-mail: jennifer.koslow@columbuszoo.org.

THE ROCK AND ROLL HALL OF FAME AND MUSEUM
One Key Plaza, Cleveland OH 44114. 216/781-7625. **Recorded jobline:** 216/515-1912. **Contact:** Human Resources Department. **World Wide Web address:** http://www.rockhall.com. **Description:** A non-profit institution that houses the permanent Rock and Roll Hall of Fame exhibit as well as other temporary exhibits related to Rock and Roll history. The Museum also produces programs for the public that include concerts, lectures, panel discussions, and teacher education. **NOTE:** Please reference the job number for which you are applying in your cover letter. Candidates may also complete an online application. **Positions advertised include:** Visitor Service Representative; Security Representative; Education Programs Manager. **Special programs:** Internships; Volunteer Opportunities.

Oregon

CHINOOK WINDS CASINO
1777 NW 44th Street, Lincoln City OR 97367-5094. 541/996-5800. **Recorded Jobline:** 888/CHINOOK ext. 8097. **Contact:** Human Resources. **World Wide Web address:** http://www.chinookwindscasino.com. **Description:** A full-service casino. In addition to gaming tables and slot machines, Chinook Winds Casino offers a supervised child care facility, a video arcade, a gift shop, dining facilities, and complementary valet and shuttle services. **Positions advertised include:** Utility Worker; Food and Beverage Worker; Dining Room Busser; Beverage Server; Buffet Server; Banquet Server; Valet Attendant; Blackjack Dealer.

GOLD'S GYM
3589 Fairview Industrial Drive SE, Salem OR 97302. 503/581-4766. **Fax:** 503/391-1267. **Contact:** Hiring Manager. **World Wide Web address:** http://www.goldsgym.com. **Description:** A full-service health and fitness club. Each club is complete with weights and cardiovascular equipment, fitness and aerobic classes, tanning, personal training, and childcare facilities. **NOTE:** Part-time jobs and entry-level positions are offered. **Corporate headquarters location:** Palm Springs CA.

HOLLYWOOD ENTERTAINMENT CORPORATION
9275 SW Peyton Lane, Wilsonville OR 97070. 503/570-1600. **Contact:** Human Resources. **World Wide Web address:** http://www.hollywoodvideo.com. **Description:** Owns and operates more than 1,600 video retail superstores. Each of the company's stores rents videocassettes, DVDs, video games, and video game systems and sells videocassettes, accessories, and confectionery items. **Positions advertised include:** Materials Specialist; Category Manager; Allocation Manager; Lease Compliance Specialist; Security Specialist; Payroll Manager; Operations Supervisor. **Office hours:** Monday - Friday, 8:00 a.m. - 5:00 p.m. **Corporate headquarters location:** This location. **Other U.S. locations:** Nationwide.

LUHR JENSEN & SONS INC.
400 Portway Avenue, P.O. Box 297, Hood River OR 97031. 541/386-3811. **Contact:** Human Resources. **World Wide Web address:** http://www.luhr-jensen.com. **Description:** A manufacturer of sporting goods including fishing lures and the Little Chief Electric Smokehouse, an appliance that smoke-cures meat.

JONES SPORTS COMPANY
17230 NE Sacramento Street, Portland OR 97230. 503/255-1410. **Contact:** Human Resources. **E-mail address:** info@jones-golf.com. **World Wide Web address:** http://www.jonessports.com. **Description:** Manufactures golf bags and related accessories.

LEUPOLD & STEVENS INC.
P.O. Box 688, Beaverton OR 97075-0688. 503/526-5186. **Physical address:** 14400 NW Greenbrier Street, Beaverton OR 97006-4791. **Contact:** Human Resources. **E-Mail Address:** hrdept@leupold.com. **World Wide Web address:** http://www.leupold.com. **Description:** A manufacturer of sports optical equipment such as riflescopes and binoculars. **Positions advertised include:** Sales Forecast Analyst; Sales Service Representative; Tactical Market Specialist. **Corporate headquarters location:** This location.

OREGON COAST AQUARIUM
2820 SE Ferry Slip Road, Newport OR 97365. 541/867-3474. **Fax:** 541/867-6846. **Contact:** Human Resources. **World Wide Web address:** http://www.aquarium.org. **Description:** A nonprofit aquarium offering a variety of special events including an annual music festival, whale watching cruises, artist workshops, bay cruises, and "Breakfast with the Animals." The aquarium focuses on education and features fish and animal species found off the Oregon coast. **NOTE:** Entry-level positions are offered. **Positions advertised include:** Security Officer. **Special programs:** Internships; Summer Jobs. **Office hours:** Monday - Friday, 9:00 a.m. - 6:00 p.m. **Corporate headquarters location:** This location.

OREGON MUSEUM OF SCIENCE AND INDUSTRY (OMSI)
1945 SE Water Avenue, Portland OR 97214. 503/797-4000. **Recorded jobline:** 503/797-4665. **Contact:** Personnel. **E-mail address:** employment@omsi.edu. **World Wide Web address:** http://www.omsi.edu. **Description:** A science museum featuring an Omnimax

theater, the Murdoch Sky Theatre Planetarium, and submarine tours on the U.S.S. Blueback. **NOTE:** OMSI accepts resumes for current open positions only. **Positions advertised include:** Special Projects Educator; Administrative Assistant; Museum Educator; Sales Associate; Summer Camp Counselor.

PORTLAND TRAILBLAZERS BASKETBALL CLUB
One Center Court, Suite 200, Portland OR 97227. 503/235-8771. **Contact:** Human Resources. **E-mail address:** jobs@rosequarter.com. **World Wide Web address:** http://www.rosequarter.com. **Description:** The administrative offices of the Portland Trailblazers, a professional basketball team playing in the National Basketball Association (NBA). **Positions advertised include:** Finance; Internships.

RENTRAK CORPORATION
P.O. Box 18888, Portland OR 97218. 503/284-7581. **Physical address:** One Airport Center, 7700 NE Ambassador Place, 3rd Floor, Portland OR 97220. **Fax:** 503/282-9017. **Contact:** Human Resources Department. **E-mail address:** gti@rentrak.com. **World Wide Web address:** http://www.rentrak.com. **Description:** A video distributor. **NOTE:** Online applications preferred in Adobe Acrobat format, phone calls are discouraged. **Positions advertised include:** Programmer Analyst. **Corporate headquarters location:** This location.

RODGERS INSTRUMENTS LLC
1300 NE 25th Avenue, Hillsboro OR 97124. 503/648-4181. **Fax:** 503/681-6508. **Contact:** Personnel. **E-mail address:** recruiting@rodgers.rain.com. **World Wide Web address:** http://www.rodgersinstruments.com. **Description:** Manufactures pipe and digital organs. **Positions advertised include:** Finishing Technician; Sales Agent; Dealer Salesperson.

SPIRIT MOUNTAIN CASINO
P.O. Box 39, Grand Ronde OR 97347. 503/879-2350. **Toll-free phone:** 800/760-7977. **Fax:** 503/879-2486. **Physical address:** 27100 SW Salmon River Highway, Grand Ronde OR 97396. **Contact:** Human Resources. **World Wide Web address:** http://www.spirit-mountain.com. **Description:** A gaming facility that offers a 100-room lodge, casino gambling, live entertainment, and four restaurants. **Positions advertised include:** Cage Cashier; Lead Main Kitchen Cook; Executive Chef; Administrative Assistant; Bus Person; Wait Staff Member; Hostess; Cashier; Shift Lead; Inventory Systems Administrator; Prep Cook; Valet Attendant; Dealer. **Parent company:** Spirit Mountain Gaming Inc.

24 HOUR FITNESS
1210 NW Johnson Street, Portland OR 97209. 503/222-1210. **Contact:** Human Resources. **World Wide Web address:** http://www.24hourfitness.com. **Description:** A 24-hour fitness club that offers rock climbing, group cycling, personal training, tanning, and child care in addition to cardio and weight training equipment. **Positions advertised include:** Front Desk; Fuel Station Attendant; Kid's Club; Personal Trainer; Sales Counselor. **Corporate headquarters location:** San Ramon CA.

WILD HORSE GAMING RESORT
72777 Highway 331, Pendleton OR 97801-3379. 541/278-2274. **Fax:** 541/966-1990. **Contact:** Human Resources. **E-mail address:** jobs@wildhorseresort.com. **World Wide Web address:** http://www.wildhorseresort.com. **Description:** A casino/hotel that also has an RV park and a championship golf course. **Positions advertised include:** Director of Slot Operations; Director of Information Systems; Administrative Assistant; Tablegames Supervisor.

Pennsylvania

CAMELBACK SKI AREA
Exit 299 I-80, P.O. Box 168, Tannersville PA 18372. 570/629-1661. **Fax:** 570/620-0942. **E-mail address:** cooljobs@skicamelback.com. **World Wide Web address:** http://www.skicamelback.com. **Description:** A ski resort in the Pocono Mountains. **Positions advertised include:** Life Guards; Ambassadors; Customer Service; Janitorial; Water Park/ Lift Attendants; Ticket Sales. **NOTE:** See website for dates on seasonal hiring sessions.

CARNEGIE MUSEUMS OF PITTSBURGH
4400 Forbes Avenue, Pittsburgh PA 15213. 412/622-3310. **Fax:** 412/622-5582. **Contact:** Human Resources Department. **E-mail address:** employment@carnegiemuseums.org. **World Wide Web address:** http://www.carnegiemuseums.org. **Description:** Association of the Andy Warhol Museum, Carnegie Museum of Art, Carnegie Museum of Natural History, and the Carnegie Science Center. **Jobs advertised include:** Campaign Manager.

CINRAM MANUFACTURING
1400 East Lackawanna Avenue, Olyphant PA 18448. 570/383-3291. **Contact:** Human Resources. **World Wide Web address:** http://www.cinram.com. **Description:** Produces compact discs, records, cassettes, and CD-ROMs.

COMCAST-SPECTACOR, LP
3601 South Broad Street, Philadelphia PA 19148. 215/336-3600. **Recorded jobline:** 215/952-4180. **Contact:** Human Resources Manager. **World Wide Web address:** http://www.comcast-spectacor.com. **Description:** A sports/entertainment firm managing the Philadelphia Flyers, 76ers, Wings, Kixx, and Phantoms; Comcast SportsNet; the First Union Spectrum; and the First Union Center. The First Union Spectrum and Center are host to Flyers and Phantoms hockey, 76ers basketball, Kixx soccer and over 500 other sporting, musical, and entertainment events each year. Comcast SportsNet is a 24-hour sports network dedicated to the Philadelphia-area sports world. **NOTE:** Online application is encouraged. **Special programs:** Internships. **Internship information:** A variety of internship opportunities are available to college students during the fall, spring, and summer terms. **Corporate headquarters location:** This location. **Parent company:** Comcast Corporation. **Operations at this facility include:** Administration; Sales; Service. **Listed on:** New York Stock Exchange. **Stock exchange symbol:** CCZ. **Number of employees at this location:** 800.

ELMWOOD PARK ZOO
1661 Harding Boulevard, Norristown PA 19401. 610/277-3825. **Fax:** 610/292-0332. **Contact:** Personnel. **World Wide Web address:** http://www.elmwoodparkzoo.org. **Description:** A zoo featuring over 150 wild animals of North America. **Positions advertised include:** Zookeeper; Food Service; Face Painter; Guest Services; Summer Camp Counselor.

THE FRANKLIN INSTITUTE SCIENCE MUSEUM
222 North 20th Street, Philadelphia PA 19103. 215/448-1200. **Fax:** 215/448-1121. **Contact:** Human Resources. **E-mail address:** employment@fi.edu. **World Wide Web address:** http://sln.fi.edu. **Description:** A nonprofit scientific and educational corporation. The Franklin Institute Science Museum consists of The Science Center, The Mandel Futures Center, The Fels Planetarium, and The Tuttleman Omniverse Theater, with a wide range of interactive and educational exhibits in many different scientific areas. Founded in 1824. **Positions advertised include:** Systems Analyst; Public Relations Assistant; Project Technician.

KENNYWOOD PARK
4800 Kennywood Boulevard, West Mifflin PA 15122. 412/461-0500. **Fax:** 412/464-0719. **Contact:** Personnel. **World Wide Web address:** http://www.kennywood.com. **Description:** A family amusement park, consisting of rides, games, food, and other entertainment and concessions. **NOTE:** See website for seasonal employment schedule.

LONGWOOD GARDENS INC.
Route 1, P.O. Box 501, Kennett Square PA 19348-0501. 610/388-1000. **Fax:** 610/388-2079. **Contact:** Administrative Services. **E-mail address:** jobs@longwoodgardens.org. **World Wide Web address:** http://www.longwoodgardens.org. **Description:** A horticultural display garden. Longwood Gardens also offers a restaurant and meeting facilities. **Positions advertised include:** Director; Research Assistant; Crop Inventory Specialist; Merchandising Coordinator; Groundskeeper; Gardener.

PENN NATIONAL GAMING, INC.
825 Berkshire Boulevard, Suite 203, Wyomissing PA 19610. 610/373-2400. **Fax:** 610/373-7564. **Contact:** Human Resources. **E-mail address:** careers@pngaming.com. **World Wide Web address:** http://www.pngaming.com. **Description:** Operates the Penn National Race Course, off-track wagering facilities, and casinos. **Listed on:** NASDAQ. **Stock exchange symbol:** PENN.

PENN NATIONAL RACE COURSE
P.O. Box 32, Grantville PA 17028. 717/469-2211. **Contact:** Human Resources. **World Wide Web address:** http://www.pnrc.com. **Description:** A thoroughbred racetrack. **Positions advertised include:** VP of Facilities; Training Manager; Assistant Controller. **Parent company:** Penn National Gaming, Inc.

PHILADELPHIA MUSEUM OF ART
P.O. Box 7646, Philadelphia PA 19101-7646. 215/763-8100. **Physical Address:** Benjamin Franklin Parkway & 26th Street, Philadelphia PA 19130. **Fax:** 215/684-7977. **Contact:** Human Resources. **E-mail address:** jobs@philamuseum.org. **World Wide Web address:** http://www.philamuseum.org. **Description:** An art museum housing a collection of European and American paintings and decorative arts, as well as Indian and East Asian art. Founded in 1876. **NOTE:** The museum also has many volunteer opportunities. **Positions advertised include:** Associate Director of Membership; Membership Analyst; Accounts Payable Coordinator; Graphic Designer; Assistant Manager of Visitor Services. **Special programs:** Internships. **Number of employees at this location:** 350.

PHILADELPHIA PARK RACETRACK
3001 Street Road, Bensalem PA 19020. 215/639-9000. **Contact:** Human Services. **E-mail address:** jobs@philadelphiapark.com. **World Wide Web address:** http://www.philadelphiapark.com. **Description:** A thoroughbred racetrack. The company also operates several off-track betting facilities located throughout the greater Philadelphia area.

PHILADELPHIA ZOO
3400 West Girard Avenue, Philadelphia PA 19104. 215/243-1100. **Fax:** 215/243-5219. **Recorded jobline:** 215/243-5276. **Contact:** Human Resources. **E-mail address:** hr@phillyzoo.org. **World Wide Web address:** http://www.phillyzoo.org. **Description:** One of America's first zoos featuring over 2,000 animals and the Peco Primate Reserve exhibit. Founded in 1874. **Positions advertised include:** Vice President, Development; Facilities Engineering Superintendent.

PITTSBURGH PIRATES
PNC Park at North Shore, 115 Federal Street, Pittsburgh PA 15212. 412/323-5000. **Contact:** Human Resources. **World Wide Web address:** http://www.pirateball.com. **Description:** Offices of the Pittsburgh Pirates Major League Baseball team. **NOTE:** Search and apply for positions online.

PITTSBURGH STEELERS
3400 South Water Street, Pittsburgh PA 15203-2349. 412/432-7800. **Fax:** 412/432-7878. **Contact:** Human Resources Department. **World Wide Web address:** http://www.steelers.com. **Description:** Administrative offices of the National Football League's Pittsburgh Steelers.

PITTSBURGH ZOO & AQUARIUM
One Wild Place, Pittsburgh PA 15206-1178. 412/665-3640. **Toll-free phone:** 800/474-4966. **Contact:** Human Resources. **E-mail address:** hr@pittsburghzoo.org. **World Wide Web address:** http://pittsburghzoo.com. **Description:** A zoo featuring the Kids Kingdom, an interactive attraction in which children are encouraged to act like animals.

Rhode Island

HASBRO, INC.
1027 Newport Avenue, P.O. Box 1059, Pawtucket RI 02862-1059. 401/431-8697. **Contact:** Human Resources. **World Wide Web address:** http://www.hasbro.com. **Description:** A major producer and marketer of toys including brand names GI Joe, My Little Pony, Tonka Trucks, Cabbage Patch Kids, Play-Doh and Nerf. The company also has a large stake in the board game market. The Hasbro Playskool affiliate manufactures preschool toys, child-care products, play sets and children's apparel. **NOTE:** See website to search and apply for jobs online. **Positions advertised include:** Associate Graphic Designer; Project Administrator; Project Coordinator; Associate Internet Marketing Manager; Reliability Engineer; Tax Specialist; Instructional Designer; Copywriter; Packaging Graphic Designer; Cost Engineer; Project Engineer; Senior Project Engineer; Associate Brand Manager, Girls Marketing. **Special programs:** Internships. **Corporate headquarters location:** This location. **Other U.S. locations:** Chicago IL; East Longmeadow MA; Seattle WA. **International locations:** Worldwide. Listed **on:** New York Stock Exchange. **Stock exchange symbol:** HAS. **Annual sales/revenues:** More than $100 million.

METRO EAST
One Metro Park Drive, Cranston RI 02910. 401/464-4800. **Fax:** 401/464-4884. **Contact:** Beth Pescarino, Human Resources. **World Wide Web address:** http://www.metroglobal.com. **Description:** Metro East is the distribution division of Metro Global Media, an international adult entertainment and multimedia enterprise. Metro East distributes adult products to over 500 retail outlets throughout the northeast and mid-Atlantic regions. The 64,000 square foot warehouse holds an inventory of over 100,000 items. The warehouse has been re-engineered to accommodate order fulfillment from all of Metro Global Media's divisions, e-commerce traffic from its online superstore AmazingDirect.Com and its direct-to-consumer mail order business. **NOTE:** Call to inquire about current job openings. **Positions advertised include:** Receptionist; Construction Project Coordinator; Carpenter; Construction Assistant; Store Manager; Visual Merchandiser; Interim Store Manager. **Corporate headquarters location:** Chatsworth CA. **Subsidiaries include:** Metro International Distributors, Inc. **Parent company:** Metro Global Media, Inc. **President:** Gregory N. Alves.

ROGER WILLIAMS PARK ZOO
1000 Elmwood Avenue, Providence RI 02907. 401/785-3510. **Fax:** 401/941-3988. **Contact:** Rob Upham, Human Resources. **World Wide Web address:** http://www.rogerwilliamsparkzoo.org. **Description:** Features exhibits and educational programs designed to promote a better understanding of how different types of animals function in their individual habitats. The park also has a working carousel and hosts a number of musical and recreational events throughout the year. Roger Williams Park Zoo is owned and operated by the City of Providence. **NOTE:** See website for current job openings. Submit resumes by mail.

South Carolina

ALABAMA THEATRE
4750 Highway 17 South, North Myrtle Beach SC 29582. 843/272-5758. **Fax:** 843/272-1111. **Contact:** Talent Department. **E-mail address:** bradshaw@alabama-theatre.com. **World Wide Web address:**

http://www.alabama-theatre.com. **Description:** A performing arts showcase featuring dance, comedy and country music performances. **Positions advertised include:** Singer; Dancer; Musician.

CHARLESTON MUSEUM
360 Meeting Street, Charleston SC 29403. 843/722-2996. **Contact:** Human Resources. **E-mail address:** info@charlestonmuseum.org. **World Wide Web address:** http://www.charlestonmuseum.org. **Description:** As the oldest municipal museum in the country, the Charleston Museum features collections of arts, crafts, textiles, and furniture with an emphasis on the history of South Carolina and the Civil War.

RIVERBANKS ZOO & GARDEN
P.O. Box 1060, Columbia SC 29202-1060. 803/779-8717. **Physical address:** 500 Wildlife Parkway, Columbia SC 29210. **Fax:** 803/253-6381. **Contact:** Human Resources Director. **E-mail address:** jobs@riverbanks.org. **World Wide Web address:** http://www.riverbanks.org. **Description:** A zoo featuring over 2,000 animals and a 70-acre botanical garden. **NOTE:** For positions with the zoo's food service, catering and merchandiser, Aramark Sports and Entertainment Services, call 803/779-8717, extension 1303. **Positions advertised include:** Horticulturist; Mammal Keeper; Herpetological Keeper; Night Watch Person; Pony Ride Attendant; Development Director; Hospital Keeper; Guest Services Representative; Curator; Lorikeet Aviary Attendant.

SOUTH CAROLINA STATE MUSEUM
301 Gervais Street, Columbia SC 29201. 803/898-4929. **Fax:** 803/898-4969. **Contact:** Charles Lee, Director of Human Resources. **World Wide Web address:** http://www.museum.state.sc.us. **Description:** A museum featuring art, history, natural history, and science and technology. **Corporate headquarters location:** This location.

WOODLANDS RESORT & INN
125 Parsons Road, Summerville SC 29483. 843/875-2600. **Toll-free phone:** 800/774-9999. **Fax:** 843/875-2603. **Contact:** Human Resources. **E-mail address:** accounting@woodlandsinn.com. **World Wide Web address:** http://www.woodlandsinn.com. **Description:** One of Charleston's most luxurious hotels. AAA Five Diamond. **Positions advertised include:** Pastry Chef; Maintenance Help; Dishwasher; Server.

Tennessee
CAPITOL NASHVILLE
3322 West End Avenue, 11th Floor, Nashville TN 37203. 615/269-2000. **Contact:** Director of Office Services. **World Wide Web address:** http://www.capitol-nashville.com. **Description:** Offices of the record company.

GAYLORD ENTERTAINMENT COMPANY
One Gaylord Drive, Nashville TN 37214. 615/316-6000. **Contact:** Human Resources. **World Wide Web address:** http://www.gaylordentertainment.com. **Description:** Operates convention resorts as well as a number of specialty entertainment and media companies including the Grand Ole Opry, Gaylord Opryland Resort & Convention Center in Nashville, Tennessee, Gaylord Palms Resort & Convention Center, near Orlando, Florida and Gaylord Texan Resort & Convention Center, on Lake Grapevine, near Dallas. **NOTE:** Search and apply for positions online. **Positions advertised include:** Manager, Construction Accounting; Director of Staffing; Director of Compensation and HRIS; Database Administrator. **Listed on:** New York Stock Exchange. **Stock exchange symbol:** GET.

MEMPHIS ZOO
2000 Prentiss Place, Memphis TN 38112. 901/276-9453. **Recorded jobline:** 901/333-6736. **Contact:** Human Resources. **World Wide Web address:** http://www.memphiszoo.org. **Description:** A zoo. **NOTE:** Search for positions and download application online. Phone calls and e-mails are not accepted. Seasonal positions available. **Positions advertised include:** Accounting Manager;

REGAL ENTERTAINMENT GROUP
7132 Regal Lane, Knoxville TN 37918. 865/922-1123. **Fax:** 865/925-0561. **Contact:** Human Resources. **E-mail address:** jobs@regalcinemas.com. **World Wide Web address:** http://www.regalcinemas.com. **Description:** A leading motion picture exhibitor in the eastern United States. The company primarily shows first-run movies at its 562 multiscreen theaters in 39 states. Founded in 1989. **Corporate headquarters location:** This location. **Number of employees nationwide:** 18,300.

SONY BMG - RCA RECORDS
1400 18th Avenue South, Nashville TN 37212. 615/858-1200. **Contact:** Human Resources. **World Wide Web address:** http://www.bmg.com. **Description:** Offices of the national record company. **Corporate headquarters location:** New York NY. **Parent company:** Bertelsmann AG and Sony Corporation.

TENNESSEE RIVERBOAT COMPANY
300 Neyland Drive, Knoxville TN 37902. 865/525-7827. **Toll-free phone:** 800/509-2628. **Contact:** Human Resources. **World Wide Web address:** http://tnriverboat.com. **Description:** The Tennessee Riverboat Company operates the Star of Knoxville riverboat. The Star of Knoxville is an authentic paddle-wheeler with a capacity of 325 passengers. It's main deck seats 144 passengers and is fully enclosed, air conditioned, and heated for year-round operation. The vessel is equipped with two bars, a dance floor, and band stage.

WARNER REPRISE NASHVILLE
20 Music Square East, Nashville TN 37203-4326. 615/748-8000. **Contact:** Human Resources. **World Wide Web address:** http://www.wbrnashville.com. **Description:** A record production company.

Texas
ALLIED VAUGHN
3694 Westchase Drive, Houston TX 77042. 713/266-4269. **Toll-free phone:** 800/394-4546. **Fax:** 713/266-9538. **Contact:** Human Resources. **E-mail address:** human.resources@alliedvaughn.com. **World Wide Web address:** http://www.alliedvaughn.com. **Description:** One of the nation's leading independent, multimedia manufacturing companies, offering CD-audio and CD-ROM mastering and replication; videocassette and audiocassette duplication; laser video disc recording; off-line and online video editing; motion picture film processing; film-to-tape and tape-to-film transfers; and complete finishing, packaging, warehousing, and fulfillment services. **NOTE:** Please visit website to view job listings. **Other area locations:** Irving TX. **Listed on:** Privately held.

AUSTIN MUSEUM OF ART
823 Congress Avenue, Suite 100, Austin TX 78701. 512/495-9224. **Fax:** 512/496-9159. **Contact:** Human Resources. **E-mail address:** jobs@aoma.org. **World Wide Web address:** http://www.amoa.org. **Description:** This museum's collection includes outdoor sculptures. Paintings, photos, and drawings are also on display. The property for this location was donated in 1970s. It also houses an art school.

AUSTIN NATURE CENTER
301 Nature Center Drive, Austin TX 78746. 512/327-8181. **Fax:** 512/306-8470. **Contact:** Personnel. **World Wide Web address:** http://www.ci.austin.tx.us/ansc/ http://www.ci.austin.tx.us/ansc. **Description:** An indoor/outdoor nature center housing exhibits, live animals, interactive games, and discovery labs. Austin Nature Center is situated on an 80-acre preserve, with more than two miles of hiking trails. **NOTE:** Volunteer positions are also available.

CERUTTI PRODUCTIONS
3410 Saddle Point Street, San Antonio TX 78259-3625.

210/403-0800. **Contact:** Mark Cerutti, President. **E-mail address:** Marc@Cerutti.org. **World Wide Web address:** http://www.filcro.com/cerutti.html. **Description:** A video production studio offering talent, engineering, and technical services. **NOTE:** See website for instructions about how to submit resumes and portfolio items. **Positions advertised include:** Production Assistants; Writers; Post Production Assistants; Marketing Assistants; Sales Representatives; Voice-over talent. **Listed on:** Privately held.

CINEMARK USA, INC.
3900 Dallas Parkway, Suite 500, Plano TX 75093-7865. 972/665-1000. **Fax:** 972/665-1004. **Contact:** Human Resources. **World Wide Web address:** http://www.cinemark.com. **Description:** Operates approximately 300 theatres with 3,000 screens nationwide and internationally. Also manages the IMAX theatres. **NOTE:** To apply for corporate, sales, mechanical or management positions, mail resume with specific salary requirements to the Dallas office. For theatre attendant positions, visit the nearest location. See website for locations.

CONTEMPORARY ARTS MUSEUM OF HOUSTON
5216 Montrose Boulevard, Houston TX 77006-6598. 713/284-8250. **Fax:** 713/284-8275. **Contact:** Human Resources. **World Wide Web address:** http://www.camh.org. **Description:** A non-profit museum that showcases modern art from Texas, the United States and abroad. The museum is free to the public. **Special programs:** Internships. **Internship information:** Send resume, cover letter and references to this location's Department of Education and Public Programs.

DALLAS COWBOYS
One Cowboys Parkway, Irving TX 75063. 972/556-9900. **Contact:** Human Resources. **World Wide Web address:** www.dallascowboys.com. **Description:** Administrative offices for the National Football League team. **Corporate headquarters location:** This location.

DALLAS MUSEUM OF ART
1717 North Harwood Street, Dallas TX 75201. 214/922-1215. **Contact:** Scott Gensemer, Director of Human Resources **E-mail address:** sgensemer@dm-art.org. **World Wide Web address:** http://www.dm-art.org. **Description:** Offers a wide range of exhibits in all art media. **Positions advertised include:** Curator of American Art; Carpenter; Exhibitions Assistant; Associate/Assistant Registrar.

DALLAS MUSEUM OF NATURAL HISTORY
P.O. Box 150349, Dallas TX 75315-0349. 214/421-3466. **Fax:** 214-428-4356. **E-mail address:** employment@dmnhnet.org. **Contact:** Employment Manager. **E-mail address:** employment@dmnhnet.org. **World Wide Web address:** http://www.dallasdino.org. **Description:** Operates a natural history museum offering a full range of exhibits and presentations. **Positions advertised include:** Chief Operating Officer; Vice President-Advancement; Director of Education.

DIVERSE WORKS
1117 East Freeway, Houston TX 77002. 713/223-8346. **Fax:** 713-223-4608. **Contact:** Hiring Manager. **World Wide Web address:** http://www.diverseworks.org. **Internship program:** E-mail resume to info@diverseworks.org. **Description:** A nonprofit art gallery and theater for the performing and visual arts. Diverse Works is affiliated with the Cultural Arts Council. **Office hours:** Monday – Friday, 10:00 a.m. – 6 p.m.

EL PASO ART ASSOCIATION
500 West Paisano Drive, El Paso TX 79901. 915/534-7377. **Contact:** Human Resources. **World Wide Web address:** http://www.elpasoartassociation.com. **Description:** Hosts various Shakespeare productions in conjunction with the McKelligon Canyon Amphitheater (also at this location).

THE GRAND 1894 OPERA HOUSE
2020 Post Office Street, Galveston TX 77550. 409/763-7173. **Toll-free phone:** 800/821-1894. **Fax:** 409/763-1068. **Contact:** Maureen Patton, Executive Director. **World Wide Web address:** http://www.thegrand.com. **Description:** A 1040-seat opera house offering ballet, symphony, opera, and other musical and theatrical performances.

GREATER TUNA CORPORATION
3660 Stoneridge Road, Suite C101, Austin TX 78746. 512/328-8862. **Fax:** 512/347-8975. **Contact:** Human Resources. **World Wide Web address:** http://www.greatertuna.com. **Description:** Produces a variety of comedic theater performances including *Greater Tuna,* a political satire shown in theaters nationwide. Other shows have included *A Tuna Christmas* and *Red, White and Tuna.*

HOUSTON MUSEUM OF NATURAL SCIENCE
One Hermann Circle Drive, Houston TX 77030. 713/639-4600. **Contact:** Human Resources. **World Wide Web address:** http://www.hmns.org. **Description:** Offers numerous educational exhibits in many different areas of natural sciences.

HOUSTON SYMPHONY
615 Louisiana Street, Suite 102, Houston TX 77002. 713/224-4240. **Contact:** Human Resources. **E-mail address:** office@houstonsymphony.org. **World Wide Web address:** http://www.houstonsymphony.org. **Description:** A symphony orchestra.

KIMBELL ART MUSEUM
3333 Camp Bowie Boulevard, Fort Worth TX 76107-2792. 817/332-8451. **Fax:** 817/877-1264. **Contact:** Robert Newcombe, Photography Department. **E-mail address:** rnewcombe@kimbellmuseum.org. **World Wide Web address:** http://www.kimbellart.org. **Description:** An art gallery known for its large collection of Asian arts, international art and period pieces. **NOTE:** Mail or e-mail cover letter, resume and references. **Special programs:** Internships.

LADY BIRD JOHNSON WILDFLOWER CENTER
4801 La Crosse Avenue, Austin TX 78739. 512/292-4100. **Contact:** Human Resources. **World Wide Web address:** http://www.wildflower.org. **Description:** A nonprofit organization that serves to educate people on the value and beauty of native plants. Lady Bird Johnson Wildflower Center also houses Wild Ideas: The Store, a retail store offering books, art, and clothing dedicated to generating an interest in plant life; and The Wildflower Cafe, a coffee shop and eatery. **Special programs:** Internships. **Corporate headquarters location:** This location.

LUTCHER THEATER FOR THE PERFORMING ARTS
P.O. Box 2310, Orange TX 77631. 409/745-5535. Physical address: 707 Main Avenue, Orange TX 77630. **Toll-free phone:** 800/828-5535. **Contact:** Human Resources. **World Wide Web address:** http://www.lutcher.org. **Description:** A performing arts theater.

THE MUSEUM OF FINE ARTS - HOUSTON
1001 Bissonnet Street, Houston TX 77005. 713/639-7560. **Fax:** 713/639-7597. **Recorded jobline:** 713/639-7888. **Contact:** Human Resources. **World Wide Web address:** http://www.mfah.org. **Description:** An art museum with exhibits including The Glassell Collection of African Gold, Art of Asia, and Modern and Contemporary Art. **NOTE:** Interested jobseekers must complete an employment profile online at the museum's website. **Positions advertised include:** Administrative Assistant; Assistant Archivist; Cataloger; Library Director; Program Coordinator; Education Manager; Assistant Register; Security Officer. **Special programs:** Internships. **Corporate**

headquarters location: This location. **Number of employees at this location:** 600.

MULTIMEDIA GAMES, INC.
206 Wild Basin Road, Building B, Suite 400, Austin TX 78746. 512/334-7500. **Fax:** 512/334-7695. **Contact:** Human Resources. **E-mail address:** employment@mm-games.com. **World Wide Web address:** http://www.multimediagames.com. **Description:** The company designs, develops, and manufactures video lottery and interactive Class II and Class III gaming systems and games for the Native American, charitable and video lottery gaming markets. **Positions advertised include:** Assembly Manager; Buyer/Planner; Game Designer; Game Programmer; Lead Mechanical Engineer; NOC Analyst; OLAP Database Developer; Production Artist; Sr. International Accountant; Software Developer; Software Test Technician; Systems Architect. **Other U.S. locations:** Tulsa OK.

NESTFAMILY.COM, INC.
1461 South Beltline Road, Suite 500, Coppell TX 75019. 972/402-7100. **Contact:** Human Resources. **World Wide Web address:** http://www.nestfamily.com. **Description:** Develops educational games, CD-ROMs, music, and videotapes for children. Founded in 1988. **Positions advertised include:** Business-to-Business Telesales Representative; Marketing Manager.

PRIMEDIA WORKPLACE LEARNING
4101 International Parkway, Carrollton TX 75007. 972/309-4000. **Fax:** 972/309-4986. **Contact:** Human Resources. **E-mail address:** jobs@pwpl.com. **World Wide Web address:** http://www.pwpl.com. **Description:** Produces and distributes educational videos to academic, corporate, and industrial clients.

SEA WORLD OF TEXAS
10500 Sea World Drive, San Antonio TX 78251-3002. **Physical address**: 2595 North Ellison Drive, San Antonio TX 78251. 210/523-3198. **Contact:** Human Resources. **World Wide Web address:** http://www.seaworld.com. **Description:** Sea World is home to all types of marine life, and includes such entertainment as shows, exhibits, and a water park. **NOTE:** Seasonal, professional and hourly positions offered. Apply at the nearest Sea World location. **Special programs:** Student and Senior Employment.

SIX FLAGS FIESTA TEXAS
197931 Interstate Highway 10 West, San Antonio TX 78257. 210/698-3991. **Contact:** Human Resources. **World Wide Web address:** http://www.sixflags.com. **Description:** A theme park offering attractions, shows, and a water park. **NOTE:** Full-time, part-time and seasonal positions offered. Apply in person or online at the company's website. **Positions advertised include:** Admissions Attendant; Food Services Assistant; Merchandise Host Assistant; Technician. **Office hours:** Monday – Sunday, 9:00 a.m. – 5:00 p.m. **Parent company:** Premier Parks (OK) owns and operates 35 theme parks nationwide.

SIX FLAGS HOUSTON
SIX FLAGS ASTROWORLD, WATERWORLD, & SPLASHTOWN
9001 Kirby Drive, Houston TX 77054. 713/799-1234. **Fax:** 713/799-1030. **Contact:** Human Resources. **World Wide Web address:** http://www.sixflagsjobs.com. **Description:** An amusement and theme park. Six Flags AstroWorld offers seven theme lands based on the nations of the world, past and present. Six Flags AstroWorld has 11 roller coasters and also offers Wonderland, filled with rides and activities for younger children. The park also offers entertainment including shows and concerts. Six Flags WaterWorld offers water slides, waterfalls, a fantasy water playground for kids, a game room, specialty shops, a restaurant, and food stands. Six Flags SplashTown is a family-oriented water park. **NOTE:** Jobseekers can apply online at the company's website or in person, if possible. Six Flags Houston hires over 3,000 employees each season. Entry-level positions, part-time jobs, and second and third shifts are offered. **Positions advertised include:** Ride Worker; Warehouse Worker; Games Host; Food Services Attendant; Admission Attendant. **Special programs:** Internships; Training; Summer Jobs; Senior Jobs. **Internship information:** Some paid summer internships are offered and housing is available. For more information, e-mail or write to the Human Resources Department. **Office hours:** Monday - Friday, 9:00 a.m. - 12:00 p.m., 1:00 p.m. - 6:00 p.m. **Parent company:** Premier Parks (OK) owns and operates 35 theme parks nationwide.

SIX FLAGS OVER TEXAS
HURRICANE HARBOR
13 Alamo Drive, Tuscola TX 76001. 817/640-8900x4216. **Contact:** Human Resources. **World Wide Web address:** http://www.sixflags.com. **Description:** Dallas-area location of the popular amusement park. Rollercoasters, rides, and events are the attraction, including a new SpongeBob SquarePants ride. Hurricane Harbor is a nearby waterpark. **NOTE:** Seasonal, full-time, part-time positions available. Apply online or in person at the park. Hurricane Harbor has its own Human Resources. For job information, call: 817/265-3356 or e-mail sfhhhr@sftp.com. **Positions advertised include:** Host/Hostess; Plumber; Cash Control. **Office hours:** Monday – Friday, 12:00 p.m. – 6:30 p.m.; Saturday, 12:00 p.m. – 5:00 p.m.

THE STRAND THEATRE
2317 Ships Mechanics Row, Galveston TX 77550. 409/763-4591. **Toll-free phone:** 877/STR-AND9. **Contact:** Human Resources. **World Wide Web address:** http://www.galveston-thestrand.org. **Description:** A 200-seat theatre that hosts films, comedy shows, concerts, and children's theatre productions. Founded in 1978. **NOTE:** The Strand Theatre welcomes applications for volunteer positions.

TEXAS STADIUM
2401 East Airport Freeway, Irving TX 75062. 972/438-7676. **Contact:** Human Resources. **Description:** A sporting arena. Texas Stadium is the home field of the Dallas Cowboys professional football team.

24HOUR FITNESS
4600 West Park Boulevard, Plano TX 75093. 972/612-6960. **Fax:** 972/867-6497. **Contact:** Human Resources. **World Wide Web address:** http://www.24hourfitness.com. **Description:** The world's largest sports and fitness center chain. **NOTE:** Please visit website to search for job and apply online. **Positions advertised include:** Front Desk Personnel; Kid's Club Worker; Personal Trainer; Sales Counselor. **Corporate headquarters location:** Carlsbad CA. **Other area locations:** Statewide. **Other U.S. locations:** Western, Southern, and Midwestern U.S. **Operations at this facility include:** This location is a Super Sport Club. **CEO:** Mark S. Mastrov.

WESTERN PLAYLAND INC.
6900 Delta Drive, El Paso TX 79905. 915/772-3914. **Contact:** Human Resources. **World Wide Web address:** http://www.westernplayland.com. **Description:** An amusement park. **NOTE:** A completed application is required for any position. Download application online and mail it.

ZILKER BOTANICAL GARDEN
2220 Barton Springs Road, Austin TX 78746. 512/477-8672. **Contact:** Human Resources. **World Wide Web address:** http://www.zilkergarden.org. **Description:** Covering 22 acres of land, Zilker Botanical Garden is comprised of a multitude of individual gardens including Xeriscape Garden, Herb and Fragrance Garden, and Rose Garden. **Special programs:** Volunteer.

Utah

ALTA SKI AREA
P.O. Box 8007, Little Cottonwood Canyon, Alta UT 84092-8007. 801/359-1078. **Fax:** 801/799-2340. **Contact:** Human Resources. **E-mail address:** info@altaskiarea.com. **World Wide Web address:**

http://www.altaskiarea.com. **Description:** Operates a variety of ski trails. Founded in 1938. **NOTE:** Employment is seasonal. Positions are available from November to April. Please visit website for online application form and to see specific contact information for available positions. **Positions advertised include:** Lift Operator; Snow Cat Operator; Kitchen Help; Snowmaker; Building Maintenance Worker; Ticket Seller; Watson's Shelter Worker; PSIA Certified Instructor; Ski School Sales Personnel; Snow Remover; Ski Patroller; Alf's Restaurant Worker; Ski Shop Employee; Ski Area Mechanic; Parking Attendant.

BRYCE CANYON NATIONAL PARK
P.O. Box 640201, Bryce Canyon UT 84717-0001. 435/834-5322. **Contact:** Human Resources. **World Wide Web address:** http://www.nps.gov/brca. **Description:** A National Park. **NOTE:** Please visit http://www.usajobs.opm.gov to see job listings.

FEATURE FILMS FOR FAMILIES
5286 South 320 West, Suite A-116, Salt Lake City UT 84107. 801/263-8555. **Contact:** Recruiting. **World Wide Web address:** http://www.familytv.com. **Description:** A G-rated video production and distribution company. The company has produced more than 10 family movies. **NOTE:** Second- and third-shifts are available. **Special programs:** Training. **Other area locations:** Roy UT; Price UT; Logan UT; Orem UT; Murray UT. **Other U.S. locations:** Marshalltown IA; Evanston WY.

THANKSGIVING POINT
3003 North Thanksgiving Way, Lehi UT 84043. 801/768-4946. **Toll-free phone:** 888/672-6040. **Fax:** 801/766-5050. **Recorded jobline:** 801/768-4955. **Contact:** Wendy Herzog, Human Resources. **E-mail address:** wendyh@thanksgivingpoint.com. **World Wide Web address:** http://www.thanksgivingpoint.com. **Description:** A family-oriented destination. Offers scenic gardens, educational facilities, restaurants, a golf course, and other activities. **NOTE:** Part- and full-time positions available. See website for current job openings, application instructions, and to download a job application. Submit resume by mail, fax, or e-mail. **Positions advertised include:** General Maintenance Technician/ Journeyman Electrician; Director of Development;

UTAH SYMPHONY
Abravanel Hall, 123 West South Temple, Salt Lake City UT 84101-1496. 801/533-5626. **Fax;** 801/869-9026. **Contact:** Kate Crawford, Office Manager. **E-mail address:** kcrawford@utahsymphonyopera.org. **World Wide Web address:** http://www.utahsymphony.org. **Description:** A symphony that performs year round. **NOTE:** No phone calls regarding employment.

UTAH ZOOLOGICAL SOCIETY
2600 East Sunnyside Avenue, Salt Lake City UT 84108. 801/584-1728. **Fax:** 801/584-1770. **Contact:** Human Resources. **World Wide Web address:** http://www.hoglezoo.org. **Description:** A nonprofit organization that operates the Hogle Zoo. This location also hires seasonally. **NOTE:** See website for current job openings, application instructions, and to download an application. Entry-level positions and part-time jobs are offered. **Positions advertised include:** Food Service Staff; Gate/Guest Services Staff; Gift Sales Staff; Train Engineer. **Special programs:** Internships; Summer Jobs. **Corporate headquarters location:** This location.

Vermont

JAY PEAK SKI & SUMMER RESORT
4850 Vermont Route 242, Jay VT 05859. 802/327-2183. **Fax:** 802/988-4049. **Contact:** Sharyn Kane. **E-mail address:** skane@jaypeakresort.com. **World Wide Web address:** http://www.jaypeakresort.com. **Description:** A four season resort featuring lodging, dining, and other recreational activities located close to the Canadian border. **NOTE:** In-person interviews are required for all positions. **Positions advertised include:** Administrative Golf Superintendent; Administrative Assistant; Snowmaker; Snow Shoveler; Parking Attendant Cashier.

KILLINGTON LTD.
4763 Killington Road, Killington VT 05751. 802/422-6100. **Toll-free phone:** 800/300-9095. **Fax:** 802/422-6294. **Contact:** Tammy L. McKenzie, Recruiting Specialist. **E-mail address:** humres@killington.com. **World Wide Web address:** http://www.killington.com. **Description:** Operates Killington Resort located in central Vermont. Amenities include an 18-hole golf course, a tennis school (USPTA), and winter skiing featuring 7 mountains with 200 trails, 31 lifts and 75 miles of riding terrain. **NOTE:** Applications for winter employment are accepted beginning in August. **Positions advertised include:** Reservations Supervisor; Health Club Attendant; Restaurant Supervisor; Network Administrator; Director of Lodging Operations; Condominium Site Coordinator; Perfect Turn Instructor; Housekeeping Attendant. **Special programs:** Internships.

Virginia

ASH LAWN OPERA SUMMER FESTIVAL
2000 Holiday Drive, Suite 100, Charlottesville VA 22901. 434/293-4500. **Fax:** 434/293-0736 **Contact:** Ms. Judith Walker, General Director. **World Wide Web address:** http://www.ashlawnopera.org. **Description:** A summer festival that produces two operas and one musical theatrical production each season. Ash Lawn-Highland Summer Festival offers preperformance lectures; presents Music at Twilight (including classical and contemporary programs); and offers Summer Saturdays, a theater and music production for children. **Special programs:** Internships; Apprenticeships. **Number of employees at this location:** 60.

BOWL AMERICA INC.
6446 Edsall Road, Alexandria VA 22312. 703/941-6300. **Contact:** Human Resources. **Description:** Engaged in the operation of 18 bowling centers. **Corporate headquarters location:** This location. **Other area locations:** Richmond VA. **Other U.S. locations:** Washington DC; Jacksonville FL; Orlando FL; Baltimore MD. **Listed on:** American Stock Exchange. **Stock exchange symbol:** BWL. **Number of employees nationwide:** 700.

BUSCH GARDENS/WATER COUNTRY USA
One Busch Gardens Boulevard, Williamsburg VA 23187-8785. **Fax:** 757/253-3013. **Recorded jobline:** 757/253-3020. **Contact:** Human Resources. **World Wide Web address:** http://www.buschgardens.com. **Description:** A theme park. **NOTE:** Offers seasonal employment; search and apply online. **Office hours:** Monday - Saturday, 9:00 a.m. - 4:00 p.m. **Parent company:** Anheuser-Busch. **Listed on:** New York Stock Exchange. **Stock exchange symbol:** BUD.

COLONIAL NATIONAL HISTORICAL PARK
P.O. Box 210, Yorktown VA 23690. 757/898-3400. **Contact:** Annette Spragan, Personnel Management Specialist. **World Wide Web address:** http://www.nps.gov/colo. **Description:** A national historical park that preserves, protects, and interprets the site of the first permanent English settlement in the New World (Jamestown) and the site of the last major battle of the American Revolutionary War.

THE COLONIAL WILLIAMSBURG FOUNDATION
P.O. Box 1776, Williamsburg VA 23187. 757/229-1000. **Toll-free phone:** 800/HIS-TORY. **Fax:** 757/220-7259. **Recorded jobline:** 757/220-7129. **Contact:** Sherri Ashby, Human Resources Representative. **E-mail address:** sashby@cwf.org. **World Wide Web address:** http://www.history.org. **Description:** A nonprofit educational organization that acts to preserve and restore 18th-century Williamsburg through historical interpretation. Founded in 1926. **NOTE:** Entry-level positions, part-time jobs, and second and third shifts are offered. Search and apply for positions

online. **Positions advertised include:** Associate Producer; Compensation Analyst; Fabricator. **Special programs:** Internships; Apprenticeships; Summer Jobs. **Corporate headquarters location:** This location. **Number of employees at this location:** 3,500.

FELD ENTERTAINMENT, INC.
8607 Westwood Center Drive, Vienna VA 22182. 703/749-5538. **Fax:** 888/832-4421. **Contact:** Human Resources. **E-mail address:** jobs@feldinc.com. **World Wide Web address:** http://www.feldentertainment.com. **Description:** Operates circuses including Ringling Bros. and Barnum & Bailey Circus, television productions, and ice shows including Walt Disney's World on Ice. Founded in 1967. **Positions advertised include:** Accountant; Administrative Assistant; Broadcast Specialist; International Contracts Manager; Online Marketing Coordinator; Sales Reporting Specialist; Sr. Payroll Specialist; Systems Architect; Treasury Analyst. **Corporate headquarters location:** This location. **Other U.S. locations:** MD; FL.

GOLD'S GYM
2955 South Glebe Road, Arlington VA 22206. 703/683-4653. **Contact:** Human Resources. **World Wide Web address:** http://www.goldsgym.com. **Description:** A full-service health and fitness club. Each club is complete with weights and cardiovascular equipment, fitness and aerobic instruction, tanning, personal training, and childcare facilities. Overall, Gold's Gym is one of the world's largest health club chains, with over 600 locations. **Corporate headquarters location:** Palm Springs CA.

GUNSTON HALL PLANTATION
10709 Gunston Rd, Mason Neck VA 22079. 703/550-9220. **Fax:** 703/550-9480. **Contact:** Human Resources. **World Wide Web address:** http://www.gunstonhall.org. **Description:** A 550-acre plantation house operating as a museum. In the 1700s the plantation was home to George Mason, the author of the Virginia declaration of rights. **NOTE:** Volunteer positions available.

JAMESTOWN-YORKTOWN FOUNDATION
P.O. Box 1607, Williamsburg VA 23187-1607. 757/253-4838. **Toll-free phone:** 888/593-4682. **Fax:** 757/253-5299. **Contact:** Debbie Jarvis, Human Resources. **World Wide Web address:** http://www.historyisfun.org. **Description:** An institution of the commonwealth of Virginia that operates Jamestown Settlement and Yorktown Victory Center, museums that preserve and interpret the first English settlement in the New World and the story of the American Revolution. **Number of employees at this location:** 466 full- and part-time staff and 1,100 volunteers.

Washington

ACKERLEY PARTNERS
1301 Fifth Avenue, Suite 3525, Seattle WA 98101. 206/624-2888. **Contact:** Personnel Department. **World Wide Web address:** http://www.ackerleypartners.com. **Description:** Operates a group of media and entertainment companies. The Ackerley Group's national operations include an outdoor advertising agency, 14 television stations, three radio stations, and a sports/entertainment division that operates the NBA's Seattle SuperSonics and the WNBA's Seattle Storm. **Corporate headquarters location:** This location. **Listed on:** New York Stock Exchange. **Stock exchange symbol:** AK.

THE BURKE MUSEUM OF NATURAL HISTORY & CULTURE
University of Washington, P.O. Box 353010, Seattle WA 98195-3010. 206/543-5590. **Contact:** Department of Human Resources. **World Wide Web address:** http://www.washington.edu/burkemuseum. **Description:** A museum that explores the natural and cultural history of the Pacific Northwest region. The museum houses more than 3 million geological, anthropological, and zoological specimens.

CRYSTAL MOUNTAIN RESORT
33914 Crystal Mountain Boulevard, Crystal Mountain WA 98022. 360/663-2265. **Contact:** Human Resources. **World Wide Web address:** http://www.crystalmt.com. **Description:** A ski resort and lodge.

FUNTASIA FAMILY FUN PARK
7212 220th Street SW, Edmonds WA 98026. 425/775-4263. **Contact:** Human Resources. **World Wide Web address:** http://www.familyfunpark.com. **Description:** An amusement park offering a variety of recreational facilities including a go-cart track, a mini-golf course, bumper cars and boats, a video arcade, and batting cages.

SEATTLE ATHLETIC CLUB/DOWNTOWN
2020 Western Avenue, Seattle WA 98121. 206/443-1111. **Fax:** 206/443-2632. **Contact:** Human Resources. **World Wide Web address:** http://www.sacdt.com. **Description:** A full-service athletic club offering a variety of classes, personal training services, and extensive free weights and cardiovascular equipment. Other club amenities include a swimming pool, a whirlpool, saunas and steam rooms, and basketball and squash courts.

SEATTLE CENTER
305 Harrison Street, Room 104, Seattle WA 98109-4645. 206/684-7221. **Fax:** 206/233-3932. **Recorded jobline:** 206/684-7218. **Contact:** Personnel. **World Wide Web address:** http://www.seattlecenter.com. **Description:** An entertainment complex. The Seattle Center is home to many cultural and athletic organizations including the Seattle Symphony, Seattle Opera, the NBA's Seattle SuperSonics, and the WNBA's Seattle Storm.

SEATTLE CHORAL COMPANY
1518 NE 143rd Street, Seattle WA 98125. 206/365-8765. **Fax:** 206/365-8714. **Contact:** Mr. Fred Coleman, Artistic Director. **World Wide Web address:** http://www.seattlechoralcompany.org. **Description:** An oratorio society performing symphonic and a cappella masterworks. Founded in 1980. **Corporate headquarters location:** This location.

THE SEATTLE MARINERS
P.O. Box 4100, Seattle WA 98104. 206/346-4000. **Fax:** 206/346-4050. **Contact:** Personnel Department. **World Wide Web address:** http://www.mariners.org. **Description:** A professional baseball team playing in Major League Baseball's American League West division. Founded in 1977.

THE SUMMIT AT SNOQUALMIE
P.O. Box 1068, 101 State Route 906, Snoqualmie Pass WA 98068. 425/434-7669. **Contact:** Manager of Human Resources Department. **World Wide Web address:** http://www.summitatsnoqualmie.com. **Description:** Operates four ski areas in the metropolitan Seattle area. This location also hires seasonally. **Corporate headquarters location:** This location. **Number of employees at this location:** 1,200.

THE VICTORY STUDIOS
2247 15th Avenue West, Seattle WA 98119. 206/282-1776. **Toll-free phone:** 888/282-1776. **Fax:** 206/282-3535. **Contact:** Human Resources. **World Wide Web address:** http://www.victorystudios.com. **Description:** Provides video duplication, audio and editing services, and computer graphics services. **Corporate headquarters location:** This location. **Other U.S. locations:** North Hollywood CA. **Operations at this facility include:** Administration. **Annual sales/revenues:** $5 - $10 million. **Number of employees at this location:** 50. **Number of employees nationwide:** 75.

WOODLAND PARK ZOO
5500 Phinney Avenue North, Seattle WA 98103-5858. 206/684-4800. **Contact:** Personnel. **World Wide Web address:** http://www.zoo.org. **Description:** A zoo

located on 92 acres of botanical gardens. Exhibits include over 300 different animal species, as well as the African Savannah, Elephant Forest, Northern Trail, and the Tropical Rain Forest. **Positions advertised include:** Classes/Camp Assistant; Cashier; Drafting and Design Specialist; Outreach and Education Coordinator; Security Officer.

West Virginia

CHARLES TOWN RACES AND SLOTS
U.S. Route 340, Charles Town WV 25414. 304/724-4237. **Toll-free phone:** 800/795-7001. **Fax:** 304/724-4368. **Recorded jobline:** 304/724-4308. **Contact:** Human Resources. **E-mail address:** ctrhr@pngaming.com. **World Wide Web address:** http://www.ctownraces.com. **Description:** Live horse racing, as well as gaming facilities and various dining and drinking selections. **NOTE:** Paper resumes and applications are no longer accepted. Apply online. **Positions advertised include:** Accounts Payable Manager; Bartender; Bus Greeter; Electrician; EMT/Paramedic; Equipment Operator; Group Sales Manager; Maitre'D; Porter; Security Officer.

THE MOUNTAINEER RACE TRACK & GAMING RESORT
P.O. Box 358, Route 2 South, Chester WV 26034. 304/387-2400. **Fax:** 304/387-8417. **Recorded jobline:** 304/387-8175. **Contact:** Eric Miser, Recruiter. **E-mail address:** emiser@mtrgaming.com. **World Wide Web address:** http://www.mtrgaming.com. **Description:** A gaming resort offering slot machines, racetracks, and table gambling. Owned and operated by MTR Gaming Group. **NOTE:** Applications must be completed in person at the Human Resources Office, 300 Jefferson Street, Newell WV 26050; however, applicants can mail or e-mail a resume and cover letter to the Chester WV address, Attn: Human Resources Recruiting. **Listed on:** NASDAQ. **Stock exchange symbol:** MNTG.

Wisconsin

GREEN BAY PACKERS
P.O. Box 10628, Green Bay WI 54307-0628. 920/569-7301. **Physical address:** 1265 Lombardi Avenue, Green Bay WI 54304. **Contact:** Human Resources Department. **World Wide Web address:** http://www.packers.com. **Description:** The administrative offices for the National Football League team. **Corporate headquarters location:** This location.

MADISON CHILDREN'S MUSEUM
100 State Street, Madison WI 53703. 608/256-6445. **Contact:** Executive Director. **World Wide Web address:** http://www.madisonchildrensmuseum.com. **Description:** A children's museum offering a wide variety of activities and programs weekly and monthly.

MADISON OPERA & GUILD
3414 Monroe Street, Madison WI 53711. 608/238-8085. **Fax:** 608/233-3431. **Contact:** Human Resources. **E-mail address:** info@madisonopera.org. **World Wide Web address:** http://www.madisonopera.org. **Description:** A regional opera company that produces two major operas annually and a free operatic event in the summer. **Corporate headquarters location:** This location.

MADISON SYMPHONY ORCHESTRA
222 West Washington Avenue, Suite 460, Madison WI 53703. 608/257-3734. **Fax:** 608/280-6192. **Contact:** Alexis Carreon, Personnel Manager. **E-mail address:** acarreon@madisonsymphony.org. **World Wide Web address:** http://www.madisonsymphony.org. **Description:** This location houses the administrative offices, as well as the box office for the Madison Symphony Orchestra.

MILWAUKEE BALLET COMPANY, INC.
504 West National Avenue, Milwaukee WI 53204. 414/643-7677. **Fax:** 414/649-4066. **Contact:** Controller. **World Wide Web address:** http://www.milwaukeeballet.org. **Description:** A nonprofit professional dance company. Milwaukee Ballet Company also operates a ballet school with over 800 students. The ballet has five series of performances each year and over 25 performances of *The Nutcracker* each December. **Special programs:** Apprenticeships. **Corporate headquarters location:** This location. **Subsidiaries include:** Milwaukee Ballet Orchestra. **Annual sales/revenues:** Less than $5 million. **Number of employees at this location:** 250.

MILWAUKEE PUBLIC MUSEUM
800 West Wells Street, Milwaukee WI 53233. 414/278-6186. **Fax:** 414/278-6100. **Recorded jobline:** 414/278-6151. **Contact:** Human Resources. **E-mail address:** humanresources@mpm.edu. **World Wide Web address:** http://www.mpm.edu. **Description:** A museum open to the public year-round. Exhibits include The Streets of Old Milwaukee, Third Planet Dinosaur Hall, and Costa Rican Rainforest. The museum also operates the Humphrey IMAX Dome Theater and a turn-of-the-century exhibit called A Sense of Wonder. The museum also offers weekend family programs called Afternoon Adventures. **Positions advertised include:** Graphic Designer; Gift Officer; Director of Corporate Relations.

MILWAUKEE REPERTORY THEATRE
108 East Wells Street, Milwaukee WI 53202. 414/224-1761. **Fax:** 414/224-9097. **Contact:** Personnel. **E-mail address:** mailrep@milwaukeerep.com. **World Wide Web address:** http://www.milwaukeerep.com. **Description:** A theater producing a broad range of classical and contemporary theater pieces.

OVERTURE CENTER FOR THE ARTS
201 State Street, Madison WI 53703. 608/258-4177. **Fax:** 608/258-4971. **Contact:** Human Resources Department. **E-mail address:** info@overturecenter.com. **World Wide Web address:** http://www.overturecenter.com. **Description:** Offers performances by the Madison Symphony Orchestra, the Madison Opera, the Madison Repertory Theatre, and the Children's Theatre of Madison.

Wyoming

JACKSON HOLE MOUNTAIN RESORT
3395 West Village Drive, P.O. Box 290, Teton Village WY 83025. 307/739-2728. **Toll-free phone:** 888/DEEP-SNO. **Fax:** 307/739-6255. **Recorded jobline:** 307/739-2604. **Contact:** Human Resources. **E-mail address:** hr@jacksonhole.com. **World Wide Web address:** http://www.jacksonhole.com. **Description:** A ski resort offering a full range of activities throughout the year. Facilities include numerous ski slopes, snow mobile trails, a golf course, hiking trails, and bike trails. Jackson Hole Mountain Resort also offers ski instruction. **NOTE:** See website for job openings and application instructions.

BIOTECHNOLOGY, PHARMACEUTICALS, AND SCIENTIFIC R&D

You can expect to find the following types of companies in this section:
Clinical Labs • Lab Equipment Manufacturers • Pharmaceutical Manufacturers and Distributors

---

The number of openings in pharmaceutical and medicine manufacturing should increase by 26.1% or 76,000, from 291,000 to 367,000. Because so many of the pharmaceutical and medicine manufacturing industry's products are related to preventive or routine healthcare, rather than just illness, demand is expected to increase as the population expands. The growing number of older people who will require more healthcare services will further stimulate demand—along with the growth of both public and private health insurance programs, which increasingly cover the cost of drugs and medicines. Openings for life and physical science occupations should grow from 824,000 to 952,000, an increase of 128,000 or 15.5%.

Alabama

SCIENCE APPLICATIONS INTERNATIONAL CORPORATION (SAIC)
6725 Odyssey Drive Northwest, Huntsville AL 35806-2803. 256/971-6400. **Contact:** Human Resources. **World Wide Web address:** http://www.saic.com. **Description:** The largest employee-owned research and engineering firm in the United States. **NOTE:** Search and apply for positions online. **Positions advertised include:** Ballistic Missile Adversary Requirements; BMDS Integration and Test Lead; Business Manager, Unmanned Ground Vehicle IPT, FCS – HSV; Data Process Engineer; Facilities Maintenance Tech I; GMD Senior Systems Engineer – GSS and GFC; Computer Scientist; IT Security Engineer; Model Analyst; Software Developer; Software Programmer/Developer; Logistics Transportation Consultant; Principle Systems Engineer; Project Control Analyst III; Requirements Analyst; SCRS Software Engineer; SCRS Software Engineer; Software Application Engineer; Systems Analyst/Engineer. **Number of employees worldwide:** 43,000.

SOUTHERN RESEARCH INSTITUTE
2000 Ninth Avenue South P.O. Box 55305, Birmingham AL 35255-5305. 205/581-2000. **Toll-free phone:** 800/967-6774. **Recorded jobline:** 205/581-2609. **Contact:** Human Resources. **E-mail address:** jobs@sri.org. **World Wide Web address:** http://www.sri.org. **Description**: A network of collaborative centers for scientific discovery and technology development for public and private sector clients in the pharmaceutical sciences, homeland security, automotive and engineering industries. **NOTE:** Job applicants must apply online. **Positions advertised include:** Associate Biologist; Biologist; Cancer Biologist; Cell Biologist; Mechanical Engineer; Neuroscientist; Research Assistant; Security Officer. **Corporate headquarters location:** This location. **Other area locations:** Anniston AL; Wilsonville AL. **Other U.S. locations:** Frederick MD; Fort Leonard Wood MO; Research Triangle Park NC. **Operations at this facility include:** Research and Development.

Arizona

BLOOD SYSTEMS LABORATORIES
2424 West Erie Drive, Tempe AZ 85282. 480/675-7010. **Fax:** 480/675-7025. **Recorded jobline:** 888/892-7598. **Contact:** Human Resources. **E-mail address:** jobs@bloodsystems.org. **World Wide Web address:** http://www.bloodsystems.org. **Description:** Blood Systems is one of the nation's largest nonprofit blood service providers. The company collects 800,000 blood donations annually. Founded in 1943. **NOTE:** Entry-level positions and second and third shifts are offered. **Parent company:** Blood Systems. **Other U.S. locations:** Bedford TX. **Operations at this facility include:** Administration; Research. **Annual sales/revenues:** $11 - $20 million. **Number of employees at this location:** 175.

HEALTH FACTORS INTERNATIONAL
429 South Siesta Lane, Tempe AZ 85281. 480/921-1991. **Fax:** 480/921-2084. **Contact:** Human Resources. **World Wide Web address:** http://www.hfi-phx.com. **Description:** Manufactures a wide variety of vitamins and related products.

HOPE PHARMACEUTICALS
8260 East Gelding Drive, Scottsdale AZ 85260. 480/607-1970. **Fax:** 480/607-1971. **Contact:** Human Resources. **World Wide Web address:** http://www.hopepharm.com. **Description:** Develops a variety of pharmaceuticals including medicines for motion sickness and acne treatments.

LABORATORY CORPORATION OF AMERICA (LABCORP)
3930 East Watkins Street, Suite 301, Phoenix AZ 85034. 602/454-8000. **Contact:** Human Resources. **World Wide Web address:** http://www.labcorp.com. **Description:** One of the nation's leading clinical laboratory companies, providing services primarily to physicians, hospitals, clinics, nursing homes, and other clinical labs nationwide. LabCorp performs tests on blood, urine, and other bodily fluids and tissue, aiding the diagnosis of disease. **Positions advertised include:** Microbiology Technologist; Phlebotomist; Lab Supervisor; Cytotechnologist. **Corporate headquarters location:** Burlington NC. **Listed on:** New York Stock Exchange. **Stock exchange symbol:** LH.

MEDICIS PHARMACEUTICAL CORPORATION
8125 North Hayden Road, Scottsdale AZ 85258. 602/808-8800. **Fax:** 602/808-0822. **Contact:** Human Resources. **E-mail address:** employment@medicis.com. **World Wide Web address:** http://www.medicis.com. **Description:** Engaged in the sale and marketing of dermatological pharmaceuticals. **Positions advertised include:** Investor Relations Analyst; Purchasing Director; Contract Coordinator; Developer/Architect. **Corporate headquarters location:** This location. **Listed on:** New York Stock Exchange. **Stock exchange symbol:** MRX. **Annual sales/revenues:** $11 - $20 million.

NATIONAL OPTICAL ASTRONOMY OBSERVATORIES
950 North Cherry Avenue, P.O. Box 26732, Tucson AZ 85726. 520/318-8386. **Fax:** 520/318-8456. **Contact:** Sandra Abbey, Human Resources Manager. **E-mail address:** hrnoao@noao.edu. **World Wide Web address:** http://www.noao.edu. **Description:** Responsible for the development and continuing operation of the Kitt Peak National Observatory, which provides observational frontier research in optical astronomy. **Positions advertised include:** Software Engineer; Data Aide; Mechanical Engineer; Electrical Engineer. **Corporate headquarters location:** Washington DC. **Other U.S. locations:** Hilo HI; Baltimore MD; Sunspot NM. **International locations:** Chile. **Parent company:** AURA. **Number of employees at this location:** 330. **Number of employees worldwide:** 500.

PROCTER & GAMBLE
2050 South 35th Avenue, Phoenix AZ 85009. 602/269-2171. **Contact:** Human Resources Manager. **World**

Wide Web address: http://www.pg.com. **Description:** Procter & Gamble manufactures over 300 laundry, cleaning, paper, beauty, health care, food, and beverage products in more than 140 countries. Brand name products include Cover Girl, Max Factor, Vidal Sassoon, Clearasil, and Noxzema health and beauty products; Pepto-Bismol, Vicks, and NyQuil health care products; Bounce, Downy, Tide, Comet, and Mr. Clean cleaning products; Luvs, Pampers, Always, Tampax, Bounty, Charmin, and Puffs paper products; and Crisco, Folgers, Millstone, Sunny Delight, and Pringles food and beverage products. **Positions advertised include:** Manufacturing Engineer; Plant Technician. **Corporate headquarters location:** Cincinnati OH. **Operations at this facility include:** This location manufactures Metamucil. **Listed on:** New York Stock Exchange. **Stock exchange symbol:** PG.

SONORA QUEST LABORATORIES
1255 West Washington Street, Tempe AZ 85281-1210. 602/685-5000. **Recorded jobline:** 602/685-5555. **Contact:** Human Resources. **World Wide Web address:** http://www.sonoraquest.com. **Description:** Provides diagnostic testing services. **Positions advertised include:** Medical Lab Technician; Medical Technologist; Phlebotomist; Spec Prep Technician.

STERIS LABORATORIES
620 North 51st Avenue, Phoenix AZ 85043. 602/278-1400. **Fax:** 602/447-3385. **Contact:** Personnel. **World Wide Web address:** http://www.watsonpharm.com. **Description:** Manufactures sterile, injectable, generic pharmaceuticals. **Positions advertised include:** Chemist; Manufacturing Manager; Validation Engineer; Scientist. **Corporate headquarters location:** Corona CA. **Parent company:** Watson Pharmaceuticals, Inc. **Listed on:** New York Stock Exchange. **Stock exchange symbol:** WPI.

ZILA PHARMACEUTICALS
5227 North Seventh Street, Phoenix AZ 85014-2800. 602/266-6700. **Contact:** Marlin Steele, Human Resources. **World Wide Web address:** http://www.zila.com. **Description:** Manufactures treatments for cold sores and fever blisters. **Positions advertised include:** Supply Chain Manager. **Corporate headquarters location:** This location. **Parent company:** Zila Inc. **Operations at this facility include:** Administration; Research and Development; Sales; Service. **Listed on:** NASDAQ. **Stock exchange symbol:** ZILA. **Number of employees at this location:** 20.

California

A.P. PHARMA
123 Saginaw Drive, Redwood City CA 94063. 650/366-2626, extension 319. **Fax:** 650/365-6490. **Contact:** Sandra Squires, Human Resources. **E-mail address:** jobs@appharma.com. **World Wide Web address:** http://www.appharma.com. **Description:** A developer and marketer of polymer-based delivery systems and related technologies for use in pharmaceuticals, over-the-counter drugs, toiletries, and specialty applications. **Corporate headquarters location:** This location. **Listed on:** NASDAQ. **Stock exchange symbol:** APPA.

ABAXIS, INC.
3240 Whipple Road, Union City CA 94587. 510/675-6500. **Fax:** 510/441-6151. **Contact:** Personnel. **E-mail address:** jobs@abaxis.com. **World Wide Web address:** http://www.abaxis.com. **Description:** A research and development firm. Abaxis, Inc. is focused on the commercialization of the Piccolo System, which consists of a small, whole-blood analyzer and blood chemistry reagent rotors. The company developed Primary Health Profile, a nine-test reagent rotor marketed to veterinarians. Founded in 1989. **Positions advertised include:** Embedded Software Engineer. **Corporate headquarters location:** This location.

ABBOTT LABORATORIES
820 Mission Street, South Pasadena CA 91030. 818/440-0700. **Contact:** Human Resources. **World Wide Web address:** http://www.abbott.com. **Description:** A health care company that develops pharmaceuticals and medical devices for such conditions as AIDS, diabetes, and cancer. **Corporate headquarters location:** Abbott Park IL. **Other area locations:** Santa Clara CA; Redwood City CA; San Diego CA.

ACCUTECH, LLC
2641 La Mirada Drive, Vista CA 92083. 760/599-6555. **Toll-free phone:** 800/749-9910. **Contact:** Human Resources. **E-mail address:** info@accutech-llc.com. **World Wide Web address:** http://www.accutech-llc.com. **Description:** Develops, manufactures, and markets disposable diagnostic tests for cholesterol measurement. **Corporate headquarters location:** This location.

ALLERGAN, INC.
P.O. Box 19534, Irvine CA 92623. 714/246-4500. **Physical address:** 2525 DuPont Drive, Irvine CA 92612. **Toll-free phone:** 800/347-4500. **Fax:** 714/246-4971. **Contact:** Personnel. **E-mail address:** resume@allergan.com. **World Wide Web address:** http://www.allergan.com. **Description:** Develops, manufactures, and distributes prescription and nonprescription pharmaceutical products in the specialty fields of ophthalmology and dermatology. Allergan, Inc.'s products are designed to treat eye and skin disorders, and to aid contact lens wearers. **Positions advertised include:** Director, Clinical Research; Senior Clinical Data Analyst; Director, Biostatistics; Manager, Medical Writer; Principal Programmer; Biology Professional; Product Manager; Manager, Purification; Director QA. **Special programs:** Internships. **Corporate headquarters location:** This location. **International locations:** Worldwide. **Listed on:** New York Stock Exchange. **Stock exchange symbol:** AGN. **Operations at this facility include:** Administration; Divisional Headquarters; Manufacturing; Research and Development; Sales.

ALLIANCE PHARMACEUTICAL CORPORATION
4660 La Jolla Village Drive, Suite 825, San Diego CA 92122. 858/410-5200. **Fax:** 858/410-5201. **Contact:** Human Resources. **E-mail address:** corpcom@allp.com. **World Wide Web address:** http://www.allp.com. **Description:** Develops, manufactures, and markets pharmaceutical products including Oxygent, a drug used to eliminate the need for blood transfusions during surgery; Liquivent, a drug used to treat acute respiratory illnesses; and Imagent, a diagnostic contrast agent used to enhance ultrasound images. **Listed on:** NASDAQ. **Stock exchange symbol:** ALLP.

ALZA CORPORATION
1900 Charlestown Road, P.O. Box 7210, Mountain View CA 94039-7210. 650/564-5000. **Fax:** 650/564-5656. **Recorded jobline:** 650/494-5319. **Contact:** Darlene Markovich, Human Resources Director. **E-mail address:** jobs@alza.com. **World Wide Web address:** http://www.alza.com. **Description:** Develops, manufactures, and markets therapeutic systems for both humans and animals. Products include drug delivery technologies that focus on the areas of urology and oncology and are used in the treatment of angina, hypertension, respiratory allergies, motion sickness, and nicotine withdrawal. Founded in 1968. **Positions advertised include:** Regulatory Affairs Associate; Research Scientist; Senior Biostatistician; Program Manager; Senior HR Business Partner; Senior Financial Analyst. **Special programs:** Internships. **Corporate headquarters location:** This location. **Other area locations:** Vacaville CA. **Other U.S. locations:** Minneapolis MN. **International locations:** Canada. **Parent company:** Johnson & Johnson. **Operations at this facility include:** Administration; Manufacturing; Research and Development. **Listed on:** New York Stock Exchange. **Stock exchange symbol:** JNJ. **Number of employees at this location:** 1,000.

AMERISOURCEBERGEN
4000 Metropolitan Drive, Orange CA 92868-3502. 714/385-4000. **Toll-free phone:** 800/442-3040. **Fax:** 714/385-1442. **Contact:** Human Resources Recruiting. **E-mail address:** techcareers@amerisourcebergen.com. **World Wide Web address:** http://www.amerisourcebergen.com. **Description:** Distributes pharmaceuticals and medical-surgical supplies. **Positions advertised include:** Project Manager, Systems Assurance; Technical Support Rep; Computer Operator. **Corporate headquarters location:** Valley Forge PA. **Other U.S. locations:** Nationwide (Distribution Centers). **Listed on:** New York Stock Exchange. **Stock exchange symbol:** ABC. **Number of employees nationwide:** 13,000.

AMGEN INC.
One Amgen Center Drive, Thousand Oaks CA 91320-1799. 805/447-1000. **Toll-free phone:** 800/77-AMGEN. **Fax:** 805/447-1985. **Recorded jobline:** 800/446-4007. **Contact:** Human Resources. **E-mail address:** jobs@amgen.com. **World Wide Web address:** http://www.amgen.com. **Description:** Researches, develops, manufactures, and markets human therapeutics based on advanced cellular and molecular biology. Products include EPOGEN, which counteracts the symptoms of renal failure experienced by kidney dialysis patients, and NEUPOGEN, which reduces the incidence of infection in cancer patients who receive chemotherapy. **Positions advertised include:** Associate Director, Marketing; Associate Director, Tax; Associate Director, Early Development; Associate Product Manager; Associate Director, Corporate Communications; Associate Director, Medical Affairs; Associate Scientist; Clinical Trial Specialist; Director, Clinical Research; Engineer; Global Safety Specialist. **Special programs:** Internships. **Corporate headquarters location:** This location. **Other U.S. locations:** Boulder CO; Longmont CO; Washington D.C.; Louisville KY; Cambridge MA; West Greenwich RI; Bothell WA; Seattle WA;. **International locations:** Worldwide. **Listed on:** NASDAQ. **Stock exchange symbol:** AMGN. **Annual sales/revenues:** $8.4 billion. **Number of employees at this location:** 2,280. **Number of employees worldwide:** 12,900.

AMYLIN PHARMACEUTICALS, INC.
9360 Towne Centre Drive, Suite 110, San Diego CA 92121. 858/552-2200. **Fax:** 858/552-2212. **Contact:** Human Resources. **E-mail address:** jobs@amylin.com. **World Wide Web address:** http://www.amylin.com. **Description:** Researches the hormone amylin, which provides drug strategies for treating juvenile- and maturity-onset diabetes, and other metabolic diseases. **Positions advertised include:** Director, Analytical Development; Senior Statistician; Development Scientist; Global Safety Manager; Senior Regulatory Affairs Manager; Director, Clinical Supplies; Senior Director, Corporate Training and Development; Senior Manager, Process Engineering. **Corporate headquarters location:** This location. **International locations:** Oxford England; Munster Germany. **Number of employees at this location:** 100. **Listed on:** NASDAQ. **Stock exchange symbol:** AMLN.

APPLIED BIOSYSTEMS
850 Lincoln Centre Drive, Foster City CA 94404. 650/638-5800. **Toll-free phone:** 800/327-3002. **Fax:** 650/638-5884. **Contact:** Human Resources. **World Wide Web address:** http://www.appliedbiosystems.com. **Description:** Manufactures life science systems and analytical tools for use in such markets as biotechnology, pharmaceuticals, environmental testing, and chemical manufacturing. **Corporate headquarters location:** This location. **Parent company:** Applera Corporation. **Listed on:** New York Stock Exchange. **Stock exchange symbol:** ABI. **Number of employees nationwide:** 900.

ARETE ASSOCIATES
P.O. Box 6024, Sherman Oaks CA 91413. 818/501-2880, extension 432. **Physical address:** 5000 Van Nuys Boulevard, Suite 400, Sherman Oaks CA 91403. **Fax:** 818/501-2905. **Contact:** Human Resources. **E-mail address:** cajobs@arete.com. **World Wide Web address:** http://www.arete.com. **Description:** Provides research and development in the area of signal processing as it applies to atmospheric, oceanographic, and related areas. The company is involved in the mathematical modeling of physical processes, signal and image processing, remote sensing and phenomenology, electro-optics, radar, and acoustics. Founded in 1976. **Positions advertised include:** Research Analyst. **Corporate headquarters location:** This location. **Other U.S. locations:** AZ; FL; VA. **Operations at this facility include:** This location is the Signal & Information Processing Division, as well as Corporate Administration and Research & Development. **Listed on:** Privately held. **Number of employees at this location:** 90. **Number of employees nationwide:** 170.

AVIGEN INC.
1301 Harbor Bay Parkway, Alameda CA 94502. 510/748-7150. **Fax:** 510/748-7371. **Contact:** Human Resources. **E-mail address:** hr@avigen.com. **World Wide Web address:** http://www.avigen.com. **Description:** Dedicated to the development of gene therapy products and delivery technology for the treatment of series and chronic diseases. **Positions advertised:** Scientist, Neurobiology; Assistant Controller. **Corporate headquarters location:** This location.

BD BIOSCIENCES
2350 Qume Drive, San Jose CA 95131-1807. 408/432-9475. **Toll-free phone:** 877/222-8995. **Fax:** 408/954-2347. **Contact:** Personnel. **World Wide Web address:** http://www.bdbiosciences.com. **Description:** BD Biosciences serves laboratories worldwide with research and clinical applications in immunology, hematology, and cell biology. The company also provides products and instruments for infectious disease diagnosis, which screen for microbial presence; grow and identify organisms; and test for antibiotic susceptibility. Products for the industrial microbiology market are used for food testing, environmental monitoring, and biopharmaceutical fermentation media. Tissue culture products help advance the understanding of diseases and potential therapies. **Positions advertised include:** Systems Engineer; Scientist; Reagent Development Associate; System Specialist; Director, Program Management. **Corporate headquarters location:** Franklin Lakes NJ. **Other U.S. locations:** Nationwide. **International locations:** Worldwide. **Listed on:** New York Stock Exchange. **Stock exchange symbol:** BOX. **Number of employees at this location:** 500. **Number of employees worldwide:** 3,000.

BAXTER BIOSCIENCE
One Verizon Way, Westlake Village CA 91362-3811. 805/372-3000. **Fax:** 805/372-3002. **Contact:** Human Resources. **World Wide Wed address:** http://www.baxter.com. **Description:** Manufactures biological and biopharmaceutical products used to threat clotting disorders, immune deficiency and blood volume. **Corporate headquarters location:** This location. **Parent company:** Baxter Healthcare Corporation. **Operations at this facility include:** Divisional Headquarters.

BAYER CORPORATION
808 Parker Street, P.O. Box 1986, Berkeley CA 94701. 510/705-5000. **Contact:** Personnel. **World Wide Web address:** http://www.bayerus.com. **Description:** Bayer is engaged in the development, manufacture, and distribution of health care products including pharmaceuticals and a wide range of hospital equipment. **Corporate headquarters location:** Pittsburgh PA. **Other U.S. locations:** Nationwide. **International locations:** Worldwide. **Parent company:** Bayer Group (Germany). **Operations at this facility include:** This location is Bayer's biotechnology headquarters. **Listed on:** New York Stock Exchange. **Stock exchange symbol:** BAY. **Number of employees**

nationwide: 21,000. **Number of employees worldwide:** 120,000.

BECKMAN COULTER, INC.
4300 North Harbor Boulevard, P.O. Box 3100, Fullerton CA 92834-3100. 714/871-4848. **Fax:** 714/773-8283. **Contact:** Employment. **E-mail address:** breahr@beckman.com. **World Wide Web address:** http://www.beckman.com. **Description:** Sells and services a diverse range of scientific instruments, reagents, and related equipment. Products include DNA synthesizers, robotic workstations, centrifuges, electrophoresis systems, detection and measurement equipment, data processing software, and specialty chemical and automated general chemical systems. Many of the company's products are used in research and development and diagnostic analysis. **NOTE:** Second and third shifts are offered. **Positions advertised include:** Senior Documentation Control Specialist; Senior Graphic Designer; Technical Operations Engineer; Finance Compliance Manager; Senior Technical Writer; Manufacturing Associate. **Corporate headquarters location:** This location. **Other area locations:** Brea CA; Carlsbad CA; Palo Alto CA; Porterville CA; San Diego CA. **Other U.S. locations:** Nationwide. **International locations:** Worldwide. **Parent company:** Beckman Instruments, Inc. **Operations at this facility include:** Administration; Manufacturing; Research and Development. **Listed on:** New York Stock Exchange. **Stock exchange symbol:** BEC. **Annual sales/revenues:** $1.8 billion. **Number of employees worldwide:** 11,000.

BIOCATALYTICS INC.
129 North Hill Avenue, Suite 103, Pasadena CA 91106-1955. 626/585-9797. **Fax:** 626/356-3999. **Contact:** Personnel Department. **E-mail address:** info@biocatalytics.com. **World Wide Web address:** http://www.biocatalytics.com. **Description:** A leading provider of technology and services for the application of enzymes. **NOTE:** Accepts resumes from applicants with a B.S., M.S., or P.H.D in microbiology, molecular biology, or biochemistry. **Corporate headquarters location:** This location.

BIOGEN IDEC
5200 Research Place, San Diego CA 92122. 858/401-8000. **Fax:** 858/431-8750. **Contact:** Manager of Human Resources Department. **E-mail address:** resumes@biogenidec.com. **World Wide Web address:** http://www.biogen.com. **Description:** Manufactures chemotherapeutic pharmaceuticals for the treatment of lymphoma. The company is also in the clinical trial phase of drug development for diseases such as arthritis. **Positions advertised include:** Director, Medical Research; Manager, EHS; Senior Scientist; Associate Director, Clinical Development; Manager, Human Resources; Senior Director, Marketing. **Corporate headquarters location:** Cambridge MA. **International locations:** Worldwide. **Listed on:** NASDAQ. **Stock exchange symbol:** IDPH.

BIO-RAD LABORATORIES
1000 Alfred Nobel Drive, Hercules CA 94547. 510/724-7000. **Fax:** 510/741-5817. **Contact:** Human Resources. **World Wide Web address:** http://www.bio-rad.com. **Description:** Develops, manufactures, and markets diagnostic test kits, specialty chemicals, and related equipment used for separating complex mixtures. The company also produces analytical instruments used to detect and measure chemical components in minute quantities, as well as products for electron microscopy. **Positions advertised include:** Administrative Associate; Business Systems Consultant; Chemist; Engineer; Environment Manager; HR Consultant; Manufacturing Engineering Manager; Oracle DBA; Product Manager. **Special programs:** Summer Internships. **Internship information:** Bio-Rad Laboratories offers summer internships for undergraduates. **Corporate headquarters location:** This location. **Other U.S. locations:** Randolph MA; Philadelphia PA. **International locations:** Worldwide. **Operations at this facility include:** Administration; Manufacturing; Research and Development; Service. **Listed on:** American Stock Exchange. **Stock exchange symbol:** BIO.

BIOTIME, INC.
6121 Hollis Street, Emeryville CA 94608. 510/350-2940. **Fax:** 510/350-2948. **Contact:** contacts@biotimemail.com. **World Wide Web address:** http://www.biotimeinc.com. **Description:** Engaged in the research and development of aqueous-based synthetic solutions. Products are used as plasma expanders, organ preservation solutions, or solutions to replace blood volume. Founded in 1990. **Corporate headquarters location:** This location. **Listed on:** American Stock Exchange. **Stock exchange symbol:** BTX.

B. BRAUN MEDICAL, INC.
2525 McGaw Avenue, Irvine CA 92614. 949/660-2000. **Fax:** 949/660-2821. **Recorded jobline:** 949/660-2272. **Contact:** Personnel. **E-mail address:** hr.irvine@bbraun.com. **World Wide Web address:** http://www.bbraunusa.com. **Description:** Manufactures intravenous systems and solutions. The company also offers IV accessories, critical care products, and epidural anesthesia and pharmaceutical devices. **Positions advertised include:** Microbiology Specialist; Metrology Technician; Instructional Designer; Director of Regional Pharmacy Operations; Lead, QC Process Control; Industrial Engineer; Regulatory Affairs Manager. **Corporate headquarters location:** Bethlehem PA. **Other U.S. locations:** Cherry Hill NJ; Allentown PA; Carrollton TX.

CALGENE, INC.
1920 Fifth Street, Davis CA 95616. 530/753-6313. **Fax:** 530/792-2453. **Contact:** Human Resources. **World Wide Web address:** http://www.monsanto.com. **Description:** Develops genetically engineered plants and plant products for the food and seed industries. The company's research and business efforts are focused in three main crop areas: fresh market tomato, edible and industrial plant oils, and cotton. **Corporate headquarters location:** St. Louis MO. **Parent company:** Monsanto Company.

CANCERVAX CORPORATION
2110 Rutherford Road, Carlsbad CA 92008. 760/494-4200. **Fax:** 760/494-4271. **Contact:** Human Resources. **E-mail address:** carlsbadcareers@cancervax.com. **World Wide Web address:** http://www.cancervax.com. **Description:** A biotechnology company focused on the creation of products for the treatment of cancer. **Advertised positions:** Regulatory Science Manager; Senior Scientist; Research Associate. **Corporate headquarters location:** This location. **Other locations:** Marina Del Rey CA.

CATALYST PHARMACEUTICAL RESEARCH LLC.
1111 S. Arroyo Parkway, Suite 200, Pasadena CA 91105. 626/568-8645. **Fax:** 626/568-8667. **Contact:** Human Resources. **E-mail address:** info@catalyspharm.com. **World Wide Web address:** http://www.catalystpharm.com. **Description:** An integrated clinical research organization providing clinical research, biostatistics, and data processing, regulatory, and licensing services support for pharmaceutical development. **Positions advertised include:** Clinical Project Manager; Biostatistician; Regulatory Affairs Manager; Clinical Data Manager; Manager, Clinical Data Management.

CELERA GENOMICS
180 Kimball Way, South San Francisco CA 94080. 650/829-1000. **Toll-free phone:** 877/CELERA1. **Contact:** Human Resources. **World Wide Web address:** http://www.celera.com. **Description:** Engaged in the discovery and development of innovative drugs, with a focus in oncology. **Positions advertised include:** Senior Financial Analyst; Senior Scientist, Biology; Director, Cell Biology; Principal

Scientist; Facilities Planner; Attorney. **Special programs:** Internships. **Corporate headquarters location:** This location. **Other U.S. locations:** Rockville MD. **Parent company:** Applera Corporation. **Listed on:** New York Stock Exchange. **Stock exchange symbol:** CRA. **Number of employees nationwide:** 538.

CELL GENESYS, INC.
500 Forbes Boulevard, South San Francisco CA 94080. 650/266-3000. **Fax:** 650/266-2960. **Contact:** Human Resources. **E-mail address:** hr@cellgenesys.com. **World Wide Web address:** http://www.cellgenesys.com. **Description:** Develops and commercializes gene therapies to treat major life-threatening diseases including cancer, cardiovascular disorders, hemophilia, and Parkinson's disease. **Positions advertised include:** Biostatistician; Process Development Scientist; Research Associate; Senior Clinical Research Associate; Senior Scientist. **Corporate headquarters location:** This location. **Other area locations:** Hayward CA. **Listed on:** NASDAQ. **Stock exchange symbol:** CEGE.

CHIRON CORPORATION
4560 Horton Street, Emeryville CA 94608-2916. 510/655-8730. **Fax:** 510/655-9910. **Contact:** Human Resources. **E-mail address:** jobs@chiron.com. **World Wide Web address:** http://www.chiron.com. **Description:** A biotechnology company that operates within three global health care sectors including biopharmaceuticals, blood testing, and vaccines. The company specializes in products designed to prevent and treat cancer, cardiovascular disease, and infectious diseases. **Positions advertised include:** Corp Business Development Director; Clinical QA Auditor; Clinical Director; Manager, Clinical Research; Associate Director, Investor Relations; Associate Director, Engineering. **Corporate headquarters location:** This location. **Other area locations:** Vacaville CA. **Other U.S. locations:** Annandale NJ; Seattle WA. **International locations:** Canada; France; Germany; Italy; Netherlands; United Kingdom. **Subsidiaries include:** IOLAB. **Listed on:** NASDAQ. **Stock exchange symbol:** CHIR. **Number of employees nationwide:** 1,900.

CHOLESTECH CORPORATION
3347 Investment Boulevard, Hayward CA 94545-3808. 510/732-7200. **Fax:** 510/732-7229. **Contact:** Human Resources. **E-mail address:** ctec_hr@cholestech.com. **World Wide Web address:** http://www.cholestech.com. **Description:** Develops and markets diagnostics systems that measure cholesterol. **Positions advertised include:** Assistant Controller; New Products Marketing Manager; Senior Scientist; Quality Control Analyst. **Corporate headquarters location:** This location. **Listed on:** NASDAQ. **Stock exchange symbol:** CTEC.

CORTEX PHARMACEUTICALS INC.
15231 Barranca Parkway, Irvine CA 92618. 949/727-3157. **Fax:** 949/727-3657. **Contact:** Human Resources. **E-mail address:** hr@cortexpharm.com. **World Wide Web address:** http://www.cortexpharm.com. **Description:** Researches and develops neuro-pharmaceuticals including the brand name AMPALEX which interacts with AMPA receptors and may increase certain types of memory. **Corporate headquarters location:** This location. **Listed on:** American Stock Exchange. **Stock exchange symbol:** COR.

COSMODYNE LLC
3010 Old Ranch Parkway, Suite 300, Seal Beach CA 90740. 562/795-5990. **Fax:** 562/795-5998. **Contact:** Personnel. **World Wide Web address:** http://www.cosmodyne.com. **Description:** Involved in cryogenics research and applications. **Corporate headquarters location:** This location. **Parent company:** Cryogenic Group. **Operations at this facility include:** Administration; Manufacturing; Research and Development. **Listed on:** Privately held. **Number of employees at this location:** 85.

DADE BEHRING, INC.
1584 Enterprise Boulevard, West Sacramento CA 95691. 916/372-1920. **Fax:** 916/374-3213. **Contact:** Professional Employment. **E-mail address:** microscan_recruiter@dadebehring.com. **World Wide Web address:** http://www.dadebehring.com. **Description:** Manufactures and distributes diagnostic instrument systems and other labware that serve clinical and research laboratories worldwide. Dade Behring also offers its customers support services. **Corporate headquarters location:** Deerfield IL. **Other area locations:** Sacamento CA; Los Angeles CA. **International locations:** Worldwide. **Number of employees worldwide:** 7,500.

DIAGNOSTIC PRODUCTS CORPORATION
5210 Pacific Concourse Drive, Los Angeles CA 90045-6900. 310/645-8200. **Toll-free phone:** 800/372-1782. **Fax:** 310/645-9999. **Contact:** Personnel Department. **E-mail address:** resumes@dpconline.com. **World Wide Web address:** http://www.dpcweb.com. **Description:** Manufactures medical immunodiagnostic test kits that are used to diagnose and treat a variety of medical conditions such as allergies, anemia, cancer, diabetes, infectious diseases, reproductive disorders, thyroid disorders, and veterinary applications. **Positions advertised include:** R&D Document Specialist; Manufacturing Supervisor; Clinical Research Associate; Regulatory Affairs Associate; Data Analysis Supervisor; Scientist; Optics Research Scientist. **Corporate headquarters location:** This location. **Operations at this facility include:** Administration; Manufacturing; Research and Development; Sales; Service. **Listed on:** New York Stock Exchange. **Stock exchange symbol:** DP. **Number of employees at this location:** 430.

ELAN PHARMACEUTICALS, INC.
800 Gateway Boulevard, South San Francisco CA 94080. 650/877-0900. **Fax:** 650/553-7138. **Contact:** Recruiter. **E-mail address:** careers@elanpharma.com. **World Wide Web address:** http://www.elan.com. **Description:** A research-based pharmaceutical company with a focus on drug delivery systems and specializing in neurology, cancer, pain management, and infectious diseases. **Positions advertised include:** Accountant; Patent Attorney; Reimbursement Analyst; Scientist. **Corporate headquarters location:** Dublin, Ireland. **Parent company:** Elan Corporation. **Listed on:** New York Stock Exchange. **Stock exchange symbol:** ELN. **Number of employees worldwide:** 2,000.

EXELIXIS, INC.
170 Harbor Way, P.O. Box 511, South San Francisco CA 94083-0511. 650/837-7000. **Fax:** 650/837-8300. **Contact:** Human Resources. **E-mail address:** careers@exelixis.com. **World Wide Web address:** http://www.exelixis.com. **Description:** A genomics-based drug research and development company. **Positions advertised include:** Clinical Scientist; Director, Clinical Oncology Research; Senior Scientist; Vice President, Translational Medicine; Assistant Research Scientist; Safety Technician; Senior Financial Analyst; Director, Operations. **Corporate headquarters location:** This location. **Other U.S. locations:** Portland OR. **Listed on:** NASDAQ. **Stock exchange symbol:** EXEL.

FISHER SCIENTIFIC COMPANY
44560 Osgood Road, Fremont CA 94539. 510/771-1536. **Fax:** 408/565-9852. **Contact:** Joan Rhymes, Human Resources. **E-mail address:** joan.rhymes@fishersci.com. **World Wide Web address:** http://www.fisherscientific.com. **Description:** Manufactures, distributes, and sells a wide range of products used in industrial and medical laboratories. Products include analytical and measuring instruments, apparatuses, and appliances; reagent chemicals and diagnostics; glassware and plasticware; and laboratory furniture. Manufacturing operations are carried out by six operating divisions in 11 U.S. locations. **Corporate headquarters:** Hampton NH. **Other U.S. locations:**

Nationwide. **International locations:** Worldwide. **Listed on:** New York Stock Exchange. **Stock exchange symbol:** FSH. **Number of employees worldwide:** 10,000.

GENELABS TECHNOLOGIES, INC.
505 Penobscot Drive, Redwood City CA 94063-4738. 650/369-9500. **Fax:** 650/368-6080. **Contact:** Employment Department. **E-mail address:** hr@genelabs.com. **World Wide Web address:** http://www.genelabs.com. **Description:** Develops, manufactures, and provides products for the treatment, prevention, and diagnosis of viral and severely debilitating or life-threatening diseases. The company operates through its biopharmaceutical and diagnostic divisions to clinical laboratories and physicians' offices worldwide. **Corporate headquarters location:** This location. **Listed on:** NASDAQ. **Stock exchange symbol:** GNLB.

GENENTECH, INC.
One DNA Way, South San Francisco CA 94080-4990. 650/225-1000. **Fax:** 650/225-6000. **Contact:** Human Resources. **World Wide Web address:** http://www.gene.com. **Description:** A biotechnology company that develops, manufactures, and markets pharmaceuticals using human genetic information. Genentech specializes in products designed to treat growth deficiencies, breast cancer, and AMI. **Positions advertised include:** Automation Engineer; Scientist, Immunology; Head, Adult Endocrinology; Business Process Analyst; Quality Manager; Operations Team Leader. **Corporate headquarters location:** This location. **Other area locations:** Oceanside CA; Redwood City CA; Vacaville CA. **Listed on:** New York Stock Exchange. **Stock exchange symbol:** DNA.

GILEAD SCIENCES
333 Lakeside Drive, Foster City CA 94404. 650/574-3000. **Toll-free phone:** 800/445-3235. **Fax:** 650/578-9264. **Contact:** Human Resources. **E-mail address:** gilead@rpc.webhire.com. **World Wide Web address:** http://www.gilead.com. **Description:** A biopharmaceutical company dedicated to the discovery, development, and commercialization of treatments for human diseases. The company's business is focused on making new therapies available to patients, physicians, and health care systems. The company has also developed treatments for diseases caused by HIV, the Hepatitis B virus, the Herpes simplex virus, human papilloma virus, and the influenza virus. **NOTE:** Entry-level positions are offered. **Positions advertised include:** Head, Commercial Operations; Desktop Support Specialist; Accounting Manager; Senior Research Associate; Senior Maintenance Technician. **Special programs:** Internships. **Corporate headquarters location:** This location. **Other area locations:** San Dimas CA. **Other U.S. locations:** Durham NC. **Listed on:** NASDAQ. **Stock exchange symbol:** GILD. **Annual sales/revenues:** $836 million. **Number of employees at this location:** 270. **Number of employees worldwide:** 1,600.

HEMACARE CORPORATION
21101 Oxnard Street, Woodland Hills CA 91367. 877/310-0717. **Fax:** 818/251-5351. **Contact:** Human Resources Department. **E-mail address:** jobs@hemacare.com. **World Wide Web address:** http://www.hemacare.com. **Description:** Provides blood management systems such as plasma exchange and bone marrow transplantation. The company also operates a donor center. **Positions advertised include:** Registered Nurse; Medical Assistant. **Corporate headquarters location:** This location. **Other area locations:** Los Angeles CA; Sherman Oaks CA. **Other U.S. locations:** Bangor ME; Scarborough ME; Cambridge MA; Yonkers NY. **Subsidiaries include:** Coral Blood Services.

HYCOR BIOMEDICAL INC.
7272 Chapman Avenue, Garden Grove CA 92841. 714/895-9558. **Toll-free phone:** 800/382-2527. **Fax:** 714/933-3222. **Contact:** Human Resources Department. **World Wide Web address:** http://www.hycorbiomedical.com. **Description:** Develops, produces, and markets a broad range of diagnostic and medical products. The company's focus is on allergy diagnostics and therapy, microscopic urinalysis, specialized immunodiagnostics, and laboratory controls. **Corporate headquarters location:** This location. **Listed on:** NASDAQ. **Stock exchange symbol:** HYBD.

IDM PHARMAS, INC.
5820 Nancy Ridge Drive, San Diego CA 92121-2829. 858/860-2500. **Fax:** 858/860-2600. **Contact:** Human Resources. **E-mail address:** usjobs@idm-biotech.com. **World Wide Web address:** http://www.idm-biotech.com. **Description:** A biopharmaceutical company focused on the development of products that activate the immune system to treat cancer. **Positions advertised include:** Senior Quality Assurance Associate. **Corporate headquarters location:** This location. **Other area locations:** Irvine CA. **International locations:** France.

I-FLOW CORPORATION
20202 Windrow Drive, Lake Forest CA 92630. 949/206-2700. **Toll-free phone:** 800/448-3569. **Fax:** 949/206-2664. **Contact:** Human Resources. **E-mail address:** hr@iflo.com. **World Wide Web address:** http://www.iflo.com. **Description:** Manufactures drug delivery systems. The company is also engaged in epidural, chronic, and wound site pain management. **Corporate headquarters location:** This location. **Subsidiaries include:** InfuSystem, Inc. **Listed on:** NASDAQ. **Stock exchange symbol:** IFLO.

THE IMMUNE RESPONSE CORPORATION
5931 Darwin Court, Carlsbad CA 92008. 760/431-7080. **Fax:** 760/431-8636. **Contact:** Human Resources. **World Wide Web address:** http://www.imnr.com. **Description:** Develops treatments in three distinct proprietary areas: HIV-infected patients, autoimmune disease treatment; and gene therapy treatment. **Subsidiaries include:** TargeTech, Inc. **Corporate headquarters location:** This location. **Other U.S. locations:** King of Prussia, PA. **Listed on:** NASDAQ. **Stock exchange symbol:** IMNR.

INSITE VISION INCORPORATED
965 Atlantic Avenue, Alameda CA 94501. 510/865-8800. **Fax:** 510/747-1374. **Contact:** Human Resources. **E-mail address:** careers@insite.com. **World Wide Web address:** http://www.insitevision.com. **Description:** Manufactures ophthalmic pharmaceuticals. InSite Vision is responsible for the development of the DuraSite eyedrop-based drug delivery system, which provides a steady drug flow to the eye over an elapsed period of time. **NOTE:** Submit resume online or to fax number above; do not submit resumes via email. **Corporate headquarters location:** This location. **Listed on:** American Stock Exchange. **Stock exchange symbol:** ISV.

IRIS INTERNATIONAL, INC.
9172 Eton Avenue, Chatsworth CA 91311. 818/709-1244. **Toll-free phone:** 800/PRO-IRIS. **Fax:** 818/700-9661. **Contact:** Human Resources. **E-mail address:** hr@proiris.com. **World Wide Web address:** http://www.proiris.com. **Description:** Manufactures and markets diagnostic urinalysis systems, digital imaging software development, sample collection, sample processing and small benchtop centrifuges and supplies for chemistry, coagulation, cytology, hematology, and urinalysis for the clinical and veterinary markets. **Corporate headquarters location:** This location. **Listed on:** American Stock Exchange. **Stock exchange symbol:** IRI. **Number of employees nationwide:** 65.

INVITROGEN CORPORATION
1600 Faraday Avenue, P.O. Box 6482, Carlsbad CA 92008. 760/603-7200. **Fax:** 760/602-6500. **Contact:** Personnel. **E-mail address:** hr.dept@biosource.com. **World Wide Web address:** http://www.invitrogen.com. **Description:** Licenses, develops, manufactures, markets, and distributes immunological reagents and

enzyme-linked immunosorbent assay (ELISA) test kits used in biomedical research. The ELISA test kits are used by researchers and scientists to detect various immunological molecules in biological fluids found in humans, mice, rats, and primates. Founded in 1989. **NOTE:** Entry-level positions and part-time jobs are offered. **Positions advertised include:** Assay Production Associate; Research Associate; Technical Production Planner; Antibody Production Associate. **Corporate headquarters location:** This location. **Other U.S. locations:** IL; MI; MO; OH; WI; OR; TX; WA. **International locations:** Worldwide.

IRWIN NATURALS FOR HEALTH
NATURE'S SECRET
5310 Beethoven Street, Los Angeles CA 90066. 310/306-3636, extension 3804. **Toll-free phone:** 866/544-7946. **Fax:** 310/306-9280. **Contact:** Human Resources. **World Wide Web address:** http://www.irwinnaturals.com. **Description:** Develops herbal remedies and nutritional products. Nature's Secret is the brand name of the company's line of vitamins. **Parent company:** OMNI Neutraceuticals. **Annual sales/revenues:** $21 - $50 million.

ISIS PHARMACEUTICALS, INC.
1896 Rutherford Road, Carlsbad CA 92008-7208. 760/931-9200. **Fax:** 760/603-4650. **Recorded jobline:** 760/603-3858. **Contact:** Human Resources. **E-mail address:** resume@isisph.com. **World Wide Web address:** http://www.isispharm.com. **Description:** Develops antisense technology drugs and combinatorial drugs to combat cancer and infectious or inflammatory diseases. **Corporate headquarters location:** This location. **Listed on:** NASDAQ. **Stock exchange symbol:** ISIP.

LA JOLLA PHARMACEUTICAL COMPANY (LJP)
6455 Nancy Ridge Drive, San Diego CA 92121-2249. 858/452-6600. **Fax:** 858/626-2851. **Contact:** Human Resources. **E-mail address:** jobs@ljpc.com. **World Wide Web address:** http://www.ljpc.com. **Description:** La Jolla Pharmaceutical Company (LJP) develops highly specific therapeutics to treat antibody-mediated and inflammatory diseases. The company is a leader in B-cell tolerance for treatment of antibody-mediated diseases and conducts Phase II clinical trials for the treatment of lupus. LJP also develops therapeutics for recurrent fetal loss, autoimmune stroke, Rh hemolytic disease of the newborn, myasthenia gravis, and Graves' disease. The company also develops compounds that control inflammation. **NOTE:** Resumes accepted only for posted positions. **Positions advertised include:** Associate Clinical Project Manager; Director, Medical Operations; Senior Clinical Manager. **Corporate headquarters location:** This location. **Listed on:** NASDAQ. **Stock exchange symbol:** LJPC.

LABORATORY CORPORATION OF AMERICA (LABCORP)
5601 Oberlin Drive, Suite 100, San Diego CA 92121. 858/455-1221. **Contact:** Personnel. **World Wide Web address:** http://www.labcorp.com. **Description:** One of the nation's leading clinical laboratory companies, providing services primarily to physicians, hospitals, clinics, nursing homes, and other clinical labs nationwide. LabCorp performs tests on blood, urine, and other body fluids and tissue, aiding the diagnosis of disease. **NOTE:** Search and apply for positions online. **Positions advertised include:** Client Inquiry Representative; Data Entry Operator; Senior Technologist; Cytology Clerk; Histotechnician. **Corporate headquarters location:** Burlington NC. **Other area locations:** San Leandro CA; Los Angeles CA. **Listed on:** New York Stock Exchange. **Stock exchange symbol:** LH.

LAWRENCE BERKELEY NATIONAL LABORATORY
One Cyclotron Road, Mail Stop 937-600, Berkeley CA 94720. 510/486-7950. **Fax:** 510/486-5870. **Contact:** Recruitment. **E-mail address:** employment@lbl.gov. **World Wide Web address:** http://www.lbl.gov. **Description:** A multiprogram national research facility operated by the University of California for the Department of Energy. The oldest of the nine national laboratories, the company's major activities include the Advanced Light Source, Human Genome Center, California Institute for Energy Efficiency, and the Center for Advanced Materials. **NOTE:** Search and apply for positions online. **Positions advertised include:** Administrative Assistant; Executive Assistant; Human Resources Assistant; Software Developer; Systems Administrator; Physicist; Geological Scientist; Biologist; Radiation Safety Technician; Research Associate. **Special programs:** Internships. **Corporate headquarters location:** This location. **Operations at this facility include:** Administration; Research and Development. **Number of employees at this location:** 3,000.

LAWRENCE LIVERMORE NATIONAL LABORATORY
P.O. Box 5510, L-725, Livermore CA 94551-5510. 925/422-9367. **Physical address:** 7000 East Avenue, Livermore CA 94550-9234. **Contact:** Christine Kachiu, Recruiting Specialist. **World Wide Web address:** http://www.llnl.gov. **Description:** Engaged in basic and applied research. The laboratory's research centers around six major programs including weapon studies, magnetic fusion energy, laser isotope separation, laser fusion energy, energy and resources, and biomedical, environmental, and atmospheric sciences. NOTE: Apply online only to open positions. **Positions advertised include:** Chief Financial Officer; Division Office Manager; Program Coordinator; Administrative Specialist; Maintenance Mechanic; Chemist; Biomedical Scientist; Physicist; Software Developer; Computer Scientist. **Corporate headquarters location:** This location. **Operations at this facility include:** Research and Development. **Number of employees nationwide:** 8,000.

LIGAND PHARMACEUTICALS INC.
10275 Science Center Drive, San Diego CA 92121. 858/550-7500. **Fax:** 858/550-7506. **Contact:** Human Resources. **E-mail address:** jobs@ligand.com. **World Wide Web address:** http://www.ligand.com. **Description:** A biopharmaceutical company that researches, develops, and markets small molecule pharmaceutical products that address the medical needs of patients with cancer, cardiovascular and inflammatory diseases, osteoporosis, and metabolic disorders. **NOTE:** Search and apply for positions online. **Positions advertised include:** Director, Clinical Operations; Clinical Research Associate. **Corporate headquarters location:** This location. **Listed on:** NASDAQ. **Stock exchange symbol:** LGND.

MERCK RESEARCH LABORATORIES
3535 General Atomics Court, San Diego CA 92121. 858/202-5000. **Contact:** Human Resources. **World Wide Web address:** http://www.merck.com. **Description:** A biochemistry laboratory involved in neuroscience research. **Positions advertised include:** Business Manager, Acute Care; Animal Care Specialist; Pharmaceutical Sales Representative; Senior Research Biologist; Executive Assistant. **Corporate headquarters location:** Whitehouse Station NJ.

METALLURGICAL LABS INC.
1717 Solano Way, Suite 39, Concord CA 94520. 925/603-1080. **Contact:** Human Resources. **Description:** Engaged in analyzing metal and metal products, as well as performing chemical analyses. **Corporate headquarters location:** This location.

NEKTAR THERAPEUTICS
150 Industrial Road, San Carlos CA 94070. 650/631-3100. **Fax:** 650/631-3150. **Contact:** Human Resources. **World Wide Web address:** http://www.nektar.com. **Description:** Researches, develops, and manufactures aerosol drug delivery systems for the treatment of lung diseases. The system allows macromolecules of drug powder particles to be absorbed by alveoli in the lungs. **NOTE:** Search and apply for positions online.

Positions advertised include: Senior Quality Engineer; Process Engineer; Patent Counsel; Director, Internal Audit; Director, IS Quality Management. **Special programs:** Internships. **Corporate headquarters location:** This location. **Other U.S. locations:** Huntsville AL. **Listed on:** NASDAQ. **Stock exchange symbol:** NKTR.

NEURION PHARMACEUTICALS
180 N. Vinedo Avenue, Pasadena CA 91107. 626/583-5020. **Fax:** 626/395-0683. **Contact:** Human Resources. **E-mail address:** resumes@neurionpharma.com. **World Wide Web address:** http://www.neurionpharma.com. **Description**: A privately held, early-stage pharmaceutical company that discovers and develops safer and more effective pharmaceuticals that target ion channels. **Positions advertised include:** Neurobiology Research Associate.

NUCLEAR PHARMACY SERVICES
501 40th Street, Building B, Bakersfield CA 93301. 661/633-2118. **Fax:** 661/633-0123. **Contact:** Human Resources. **World Wide Web address:** http://www.nps.cardinal.com. **Description:** Compounds, dispenses, and distributes patient-specific intravenous drugs and solutions for use in diagnostic imaging and offers a complete range of pharmacy services. **Corporate headquarters location:** Dublin OH. **Parent company:** Cardinal Health. **Operations at this facility include:** Administration. **Listed on:** New York Stock Exchange. **Stock exchange symbol:** CAH. **Number of employees at this location:** 175.

ONCOLOGY THERAPEUTICS NETWORK
395 Oyster Point Boulevard, Suite 500, South San Francisco CA 94080. 650/952-8400. **Toll-free phone:** 800/482-6700. **Contact:** Human Resources. **World Wide Web address:** http://www.otnnet.com. **Description:** Distributes pharmaceuticals and related products for the treatment of cancer to oncology physicians. **Corporate headquarters location:** New York NY. **Parent company:** Bristol-Myers Squibb. **Listed on:** New York Stock Exchange. **Stock exchange symbol:** BMY.

ONYX PHARMACEUTICALS, INC.
2100 Powell Street, Emeryville CA 94608. 510/597-6500. **Fax:** 510/597-6604. **Contact:** Human Resources. **E-mail address:** resumes@onyx-pharm.com. **World Wide Web address:** http://www.onyx-pharm.com. **Description:** Engaged in the discovery and development of therapeutics based on the genetics of human disease. The company's main focus is on the discovery of cancer treatments. **NOTE:** Search and apply for positions online. **Positions advertised include:** Director, Regulatory Affairs; Medical Science Liaison; Product Manager. **Corporate headquarters location:** This location. **Listed on:** NASDAQ. **Stock exchange symbol:** ONXX.

PDL BIOPHARMA, INC.
34801 Campus Drive, Fremont CA 94555. 510/574-1400. **Fax:** 510/574-1500. **Contact:** Human Resources. **E-mail address:** careers@pdl.com. **World Wide Web address:** http://www.pdl.com. **Description:** A research and development company focused on the development of humanized and human monoclonal antibodies for the treatment and prevention of various diseases. **Positions advertised include:** Administrative Assistant; Clinical Research Associate; Medical Director; Stock/401K Administrator; Business Analyst; Network Analyst; Metrology Technician; Protein Chemistry Director. **Corporate headquarters location:** This location. **Other U.S. locations:** Plymouth MN; Brooklyn Park MN; Edison NJ. **Listed on:** NASDAQ. **Stock exchange symbol:** PDLI.

PHARMAVITE LLC
P.O. Box 9606, Mission Hills CA 91346-9606. 818/221-6200. **Fax:** 818/221-6644. **Contact:** Human Resources. **E-mail address:** cremmers@pharmavite.net. **World Wide Web address:** http://www.pharmavite.com. **Description:** An international manufacturer, marketer, and retailer of vitamins, mineral and herbal supplements with a portfolio of brands that include Nature Made, Nature's resource, SAM-e, and Olay. **Positions advertised include:** Senior Systems Analyst. **Corporate headquarters location:** This location. **Operations at this facility include:** Administration; Research and Development.

PSYCHEMEDICS CORPORATION
5832 Uplander Way, Culver City CA 90230. 310/216-7776. **Toll-free phone:** 800/522-7424. **Contact:** Personnel. **World Wide Web address:** http://www.psychemedics.com. **Description:** A biotechnology company concentrating on diagnostics through the detection and measurement of substances in the body by using hair samples. The first commercial product, a testing service for the detection of abused substances, is provided principally to private sector companies. This drug test detects cocaine, marijuana, opiates, methamphetamine, and PCP. A test for methadone is used in the treatment industry. Psychemedics Corporation's testing methods use a patented technology for performing immunoassays on enzymatically dissolved hair samples with confirmation testing by gas chromatography/mass spectrometry. **Corporate headquarters location:** Acton MA. **Listed on:** American Stock Exchange. **Stock exchange symbol:** PMD. **Number of employees nationwide:** 95.

QUEST DIAGNOSTICS
18433 roscoe Boulevard, Suite 105, Northridge CA 91325. **Toll-free phone:** 800/209-9816. **Contact:** Human Resources. **World Wide Web address:** http://www.questdiagnostics.com. **Description:** One of the largest clinical laboratories in North America, providing a broad range of clinical laboratory services to health care clients such as physicians, hospitals, clinics, dialysis centers, pharmaceutical companies, and corporations. The company offers and performs tests on blood, urine, and other bodily fluids and tissues to provide information for health and well-being. **Positions advertised include:** Account Executive; Account Sales Representative. **Corporate headquarters location:** Teterboro NJ. **Listed on:** New York Stock Exchange. **Stock exchange symbol:** DGX.

QUEST DIAGNOSTICS AT NICHOLS INSTITUTE
33608 Ortega Highway, San Juan Capistrano CA 92675. 949/728-4000. **Fax:** 949/728-4781. **Recorded jobline:** 949/728-4526. **Contact:** Human Resources. **World Wide Web address:** http://www.questdiagnostics.com. **Description:** One of the largest clinical laboratories in North America, providing a broad range of clinical laboratory services to health care clients such as physicians, hospitals, clinics, dialysis centers, pharmaceutical companies, and corporations. The company offers and performs tests on blood, urine, and other bodily fluids and tissues to provide information for health and well-being. **Positions advertised include:** Associate Scientific Director; Laboratory Supervisor; Laboratory Associate; Clinical Laboratory Scientist; Senior Implementation Analyst; Customer Service Assistant. **Corporate headquarters location:** Teterboro NJ. **Other U.S. locations:** Nationwide. **Listed on:** New York Stock Exchange. **Stock exchange symbol:** DGX.

QUESTCOR PHARMACEUTICALS CORPORATION
3260 Whipple Road, Union City CA 94587. 510/400-0700. **Fax:** 510/400-0799. **Contact:** Human Resources. **E-mail address:** hr@questcor.com. **World Wide Web address:** http://www.questcor.com. **Description:** An integrated specialty pharmaceutical company that researches, develops, and markets a variety of pharmaceuticals to the health care industry. The company's products include Emitasol, Ethamolin, Inulin, Glofil-125, and NeoFlo. **NOTE:** Resumes may be submitted via fax at 928/244-3718. **Corporate headquarters location:** This location. **Listed on:** American Stock Exchange. **Stock exchange symbol:** QSC.

QUIDEL CORPORATION
10165 McKellar Court, San Diego CA 92121. 858/552-1100. **Toll-free phone:** 800/874-1517. **Fax:** 858/453-2050. **Contact:** Human Resources. **E-mail address:** hr@quidel.com. **World Wide Web address:** http://www.quidel.com. **Description:** Engaged in the research, development, and manufacture of immunodiagnostic products designed to provide accurate testing for acute and chronic human illnesses. Customers include physicians, clinical laboratories, and consumers. **Positions advertised include:** Manufacturing Engineer; Regulatory compliance Specialist. **Office hours:** Monday - Friday, 8:00 a.m. - 5:00 p.m. **Corporate headquarters location:** This location. **Other area locations:** Santa Clara CA. **Subsidiaries include:** VHA Inc. **Listed on:** NASDAQ. **Stock exchange symbol:** QDEL. **President/CEO:** S. Wayne Kay.

ROCKWELL SCIENTIFIC COMPANY LLC
1049 Camino Dos Rios, Thousand Oaks CA 91360. 805/373-4545. **Fax:** 805/373-4775. **Contact:** Human Resources. **World Wide Web address:** http://www.rockwellscientific.com. **Description:** Rockwell Scientific Company conducts research on projects ranging from disruptive technologies intended to catalyze new business opportunities to technology application and transition. **NOTE:** Search and apply for positions online. **Positions advertised include:** Applied Computational Physicist; Compound Semiconductor Process Engineer; FPA Test Technician; Sensor Test Engineer; Camera Engineer; Senior Cost Accounting Advisor. **Other area locations:** Camarillo CA.

SRI INTERNATIONAL
333 Ravenswood Avenue, Menlo Park CA 94025-3493. 650/859-2000. **Contact:** Personnel. **E-mail address:** careers@sri.com. **World Wide Web address:** http://www.sri.com. **Description:** A multidisciplinary research, development, and consulting organization engaged in government and private industry research. SRI International provides solutions in a variety of areas including pharmaceutical discovery; biopharmaceutical development; education, health, and state policy; engineering sciences; and systems development. **Positions advertised include:** Information Systems Security Officer; Senior Researcher; Senior Secuirty Professional; Web and Graphic Designer. **Corporate headquarters location:** This location. **Listed on:** NASDAQ. **Stock exchange symbol:** STRC.

SCIOS INC.
6500 Paseo Padre Parkway, Fremont CA 94555. 510/248-2405. **Contact:** Human Resources. **E-mail address:** jobs@sciosinc.com. **World Wide Web address:** http://www.sciosinc.com. **Description:** Researches, develops, and manufactures pharmaceuticals for the treatment of cardiovascular and neurological disorders. Founded in 1981. **Positions advertised include:** Accountant; Application Developer; Clinical Research Associate; Senior Medical Writer; Drug Safety Associate; Scientist. **Special programs:** Internships. **Office hours:** Monday - Friday, 8:00 a.m. - 5:00 p.m. **Corporate headquarters location:** This location. **Parent company:** Johnson & Johnson. **Listed on:** NASDAQ. **Stock exchange symbol:** SCIO. **Number of employees nationwide:** Over 700.

SHAKLEE CORPORATION
4747 Willow Road, Pleasanton CA 94588. 925/924-2000. **Fax:** 925/924-2862. **Contact:** Roseanne Jennings, Personnel Manager. **World Wide Web address:** http://www.shaklee.com. **Description:** Manufactures and markets vitamins, minerals, protein powders, and other nutritional products. **Corporate headquarters location:** This location.

SKYEPHARMA INC.
10450 Science Center Drive, San Diego CA 92121. 858/625-2424. **Fax:** 858/678-3999. **Contact:** Human Resources. **E-mail address:** jobs@skyepharma.com. **World Wide Web address:** http://www.skyepharma.com. **Description:** Develops proprietary, injectable material that can encapsulate a wide variety of drugs to provide sustained and controlled delivery. **Positions advertised include:** Process Engineer; Senior Scientist; Systems Control Engineer. **Corporate headquarters location:** This location. **Parent company:** SkyePharma Plc (London). **Listed on:** NASDAQ. **Stock exchange symbol:** SKYE. **Number of employees at this location:** 60.

STANFORD LINEAR ACCELERATOR CENTER
2575 Sand Hill Road, Menlo Park CA 94025. 650/926-3300. **Contact:** Human Resources. **E-mail address:** employment@slac.stanford.edu. **World Wide Web address:** http://www.slac.stanford.edu. **Description:** One of the world's leading research laboratories. SLAC's mission is to design, construct and operate state-of-the-art electron accelerators and related experimental facilities for use in high-energy physics and synchrotron radiation research. Established in 1962. **Positions advertised include:** Financial Management Analyst; Associate Project Director of Civil Construction; Electrical Engineer; Environmental Engineer; Facilities Coordinator; Mechanical Engineer; Pulse Power Electronics Engineer; Computing Information Systems Analyst; Beam Line Engineer; Engineering Physicist; Health Physicist; Physicist; Research Software Developer.

TANABE RESEARCH LABORATORIES USA, INC.
4540 Towne Center Court, San Diego CA 92121. 858/622-7000. **Fax:** 858/558-0650. **Contact:** Human Resources. **E-mail address:** jobs@trlusa.com. **World Wide Web address:** http://www.trlusa.com. **Description:** Researches allergies, rheumatism, asthma, and arthritis. **Corporate headquarters location:** Osaka, Japan. **Parent company:** Tanabe Seiyaku Corporation, Ltd.

THERMO ELECTRON
355 River Oaks Parkway, San Jose CA 95134. 408/965-6000. **Fax:** 408/965-6010. **Contact:** Human Resources. **World Wide Web address:** http://www.thermo.com. **Description:** Manufactures laboratory instruments and supplies for the health care industry. **NOTE:** Contact information may vary. See job postings for more specific instructions. **Positions advertised include:** Software Engineer; Export Customer Service Engineer; Instrument Specialist. **Corporate headquarters location:** Waltham MA. **Parent company:** Thermo Electron Corporation. **Listed on:** New York Stock Exchange. **Stock exchange symbol:** TMO. **Number of employees at this location:** 300.

VICAL INC.
10390 Pacific Center Court, San Diego CA 92121. 858/646-1100. **Fax:** 858/646-1150. **Contact:** Karen Blade, Senior Human Resources Specialist. **E-mail address:** hr@vical.com. **World Wide Web address:** http://www.vical.com. **Description:** Provides research and development services for DNA, gene therapy, cancer, AIDS, and malaria. **Positions advertised include:** Contract Administrator; Manufacturing Engineer; Research Scientist; Environmental Health and Safety Manager. **Corporate headquarters location:** This location. **Listed on:** NASDAQ. **Stock exchange symbol:** VICL.

WATSON PHARMACEUTICALS, INC.
311 Bonnie Circle, Corona CA 92880. 951/493-5300. **Fax:** 951/493-5836. **Contact:** Human Resources. **World Wide Web address:** http://www.watsonpharm.com. **Description:** Produces and distributes off-patent and proprietary pharmaceuticals such as analgesics, dermatological, primary care, antihypertensive, hormonal, generic, and central nervous system treatments. **NOTE:** Search and apply for positions online. **Positions advertised include:** Project Manager; Chemist; Senior Clinical Research Associate; Warehouse Operator; Finance Manager; Laboratory Technician; General Maintenance

Mechanic. **Corporate headquarters location:** This location. **Subsidiaries include:** Circa Pharmaceuticals, Inc.; Oclassen Pharmaceuticals, Inc.; Watson Laboratories, Inc. **Listed on:** New York Stock Exchange. **Stock exchange symbol:** WPI. **CEO:** Dr. Allen Chao.

XENCOR
111 West Lemon Avenue, Monrovia CA 91016. 626/305-5900. **Fax:** 626/305-0350. **Contact:** Recruiting. **E-mail address:** recruiting@xencor.com. **World Wide Web address:** http://www.xencor.com. **Description:** A biotechnology company that develops protein drugs. **Positions advertised:** Associate Director, Marketing; Senior Scientist.

XENOGEN CORPORATION
860 Atlantic Avenue, Alameda CA 94501. 510/291-6100. **Fax:** 510/291-6146. **Contact:** Human Resources. **E-mail address:** employment@xenogen.com. **World Wide Web address:** http://www.xenogen.com. **Description:** Offers real-time in vivo imaging services. Xenogen's in vivo biophotonic imaging system assists pharmaceutical companies in drug discovery and development. **Positions advertised include:** Research Associate. **Corporate headquarters location:** This location. **Other U.S. locations:** Cranbury NJ.

Colorado

AMGEN INC.
4000 Nelson Road, Longmont CO 80503. 303/401-1000. **Contact:** Human Resources. **World Wide Web address:** http://www.amgen.com. **Description:** Researches, develops, manufactures, and markets human therapeutics based on advanced cellular and molecular biology. **Positions advertised include:** Quality Engineer; Sr. Engineer; Validation Engineer; Technical Writer; Sr. IS Project Manager; QA Specialist; Materials Coordinator. **Corporate headquarters location:** Thousand Oaks CA. **Other area locations:** Boulder CO. **Listed on:** NASDAQ. **Stock exchange symbol:** AMGN.

ASPENBIO, INC.
1585 South Perry Street, Castle Rock CO 80104. 303/794-2000. **Contact:** Human Resources. **E-mail address:** info@aspenbioinc.com. **World Wide Web address:** http://www.aspenbioinc.com. **Description:** The company is dedicated to the discovery, development, manufacture and marketing of novel patented products that enhance the reproductive efficiency of animals. The company was founded to produce purified proteins for diagnostic applications and is now a leading supplier of human hormones to many of the nation's largest medical diagnostic companies and research institutions. **Positions advertised include:** Manager of Diagnostic Protein Sales.

BAXTER BIOLIFE PLASMA SERVICES
519 Sable Boulevard, Aurora CO 80011. 303/367-9660. **Contact:** Human Resources. **Description:** BioLife Plasma Services collects high quality plasma that is processed into life-saving plasma-based therapies. **Positions advertised include:** Phlebotomist; Medical Historian. **Corporate headquarters location:** Deerfield IL. **Parent company:** Baxter International, Inc. **Listed on:** New York Stock Exchange. **Stock exchange symbol:** BAX. **Number of employees at this location:** 200. **Number of employees worldwide:** 48,000.

BOLDER BIOTECHNOLOGY, INC.
4056 Youngfield Street, Wheat Ridge CO 80033. 303/420-4420. **Fax:** 303/420-4426. **Contact:** Human Resources. **World Wide Web address:** http://www.bolderbio.com. **Description:** Bolder BioTechnology, Inc. uses advanced protein engineering technologies to create proprietary human protein pharmaceuticals with enhanced therapeutic properties. Products are intended for the treatment of hematological and endocrine disorders, cancer, and infectious disease. **Positions advertised include:** Scientist; Research Associate.

COLORADO SERUM COMPANY
4950 York Street, P.O. Box 16428, Denver CO 80216. 303/295-7527. **Fax:** 303/295-1923. **Contact:** Joe Huff, President. **E-mail address:** colorado-serum@colorado-serum.com. **World Wide Web address:** http://www.colorado-serum.com. **Description:** Develops and manufactures veterinary serums and biologics.

THE HACH COMPANY
P.O. Box 389, Loveland CO 80539-0389. 970/669-3050. **Fax:** 970/669-2932. **Contact:** Human Resources. **World Wide Web address:** http://www.hach.com. **Description:** Manufactures and sells laboratory instruments, process analyzers, and test kits that analyze the chemical content and other properties of water and other aqueous solutions. The company also produces chemicals for use with its manufactured instruments and test kits. **Positions advertised include:** Key Accounts Manager; Catalog Marketing Manager; Web Manager; Business Development Manager; Export Credit Administrator; Telesales Supervisor; Production Engineer; Project Manager. **Corporate headquarters location:** This location. **Other U.S. locations:** Ames IA. **International locations:** Germany. **Parent company:** Danaher Corporation. **Number of employees at this location:** 500. **Number of employees nationwide:** 800.

HEMOGENIX, INC.
4405 North Chestnut Street, Suite D, Colorado Springs CO 80907. 719/264-6250. **Fax:** 719/264-6253. **Contact:** Human Resources. **World Wide Web address:** http://www.hemogenix.com. **E-mail address:** positions@hemogenix.com. **Description:** Develops stem-cell hemotoxicity testing methods. Founded in 2000.

NATURESMART/NBTY
1500 East 128 Avenue, Thornton CO 80241. 303/474-2300. **Contact:** Personnel. **World Wide Web address:** http://www.nbty.com. **Description:** Develops, manufactures, and markets vitamins, nutrients, and herbal supplements.

OSI PHARMACEUTICALS, INC.
2860 Wilderness Place, Boulder CO 80301. 303/546-7600. **Fax:** 303/444-0672. **Contact:** Human Resources. **E-mail address:** employment@osip.com. **World Wide Web address:** http://www.osip.com. **Description:** A biopharmaceutical company dedicated to the discovery, development, and commercialization of treatments for human diseases. The company's business is focused on making new therapies available to patients, physicians, and health care systems. The company has also developed treatments for diseases caused by HIV, the Hepatitis B virus, the Herpes simplex virus, human papillomavirus, and the influenza virus. **Positions advertised include:** Director, clinical Research; Director, Regulatory Affairs; Director, Clinical Operations; Clinical Research Associate. **Corporate headquarters location:** Melville NY. **International locations:** UK. **Listed on:** NASDAQ. **Stock exchange symbol:** OSIP

QLT USA, INC.
2579 Midpoint Drive, Fort Collins CO 80525. 970/482-5868. **Contact:** Human Resources. **E-mail address:** recruitingUSA@qltinc.com. **World Wide Web address:** http://www.qltinc.com. **Description:** A global biopharmaceutical company specializing in developing treatments for cancer, eye diseases and dermatological and urological conditions. **Positions advertised include:** Senior Research Associate; Scientist; Engineering Technician; Quality Control Analyst; Material Handler; Quality Assurance Associate. **Corporate headquarters location:** Vancouver British Columbia Canada.

QUEST DIAGNOSTICS INCORPORATED
695 South Broadway, Denver CO 80209. 303/899-6000. **Fax:** 303/899-6123. **Contact:** Human Resources. **World Wide Web address:** http://www.questdiagnostics.com. **Description:** One of the largest clinical laboratories in

North America, providing a broad range of clinical laboratory services to health care clients, which include physicians, hospitals, clinics, dialysis centers, pharmaceutical companies, and corporations. The company offers and performs tests on blood, urine, and other bodily fluids and tissues to provide information for health and well-being. **Positions advertised include:** Cytology Supervisor; Billing Coordinator; Medical Technolgist. **Corporate headquarters location:** Teterboro NJ. **Other U.S. locations:** Nationwide. **Listed on:** New York Stock Exchange. **Stock exchange symbol:** DGX.

REPLIDYNE, INC.
1450 Infinite Drive, Louisville CO 80027. 303/996-5500. **Fax:** 303/996-5599. **Contact:** Personnel Department. **E-mail address:** employment@replidyne.com. **World Wide Web address:** http://www.replidyne.com. **Description:** A specialty pharmaceutical company focused on developing and commercializing innovative anti-infective products.

ROCHE COLORADO
2075 North 55th Street, Boulder CO 80301. 303/442-1926. **Fax:** 303/938-6413. **Contact:** Human Resources. **E-mail address:** boulder.hr@roche.com. **World Wide Web address:** http://www.rochecolorado.com. **Description:** An international drug development company focusing on oncology. **Positions advertised include:** Disbursement Accountant; Executive Legal Assistant. **Parent company:** Hoffman-LaRoche Inc.

SANDOZ INC MANUFACTURING
2555 West Midway Boulevard, Broomfield CO 80038-0446. 303/466-2400. **Contact:** Human Resources. **World Wide Web address:** http://www.us.sandoz.com. **Description:** Manufactures and distributes generic pharmaceutical products. **Positions advertised include:** Senior Distribution Technician; Lead QC Chemist; Tech Services Scientist; Quality Engineer; Packaging Supervisor; QA Support Specialist. **Parent company:** Novartis Group.

SCIONA, INC.
1401 Walnut Street, Suite 203, Boulder CO 80302. 303/442-4300. **Fax:** 303/442-4301. **Contact:** Director of Operations. **E-mail address:** info@sciona.com. **World Wide Web address:** http://www.sciona.com. **Description:** Sciona researches and develops DNA screens for common gene variants that affect an individual's response to food, medications and the environment. Sciona's field of genetic personalization is a discipline aimed at creating products and services tailored to an individual's genetic makeup.

SIRNA THERAPEUTICS, INC.
2950 Wilderness Place, Boulder CO 80301. 303/449-6500. **Fax:** 303/449-6995. **Contact:** Human Resources. **E-mail address:** jobs@sirna.com. **Description:** Sirna Therapeutics is a biotechnology company focused on developing therapeutics based on RNA interference (RNAi) technology, a field of biology and medicine. The Company is using its proprietary nucleic acid technology and expertise to develop a new class of RNAi-based therapeutics that target human diseases and conditions. **Positions advertised include:** Scientist. **Corporate headquarters location:** San Francisco CA.

**UNIVERSITY CORPORATION FOR ATMOSPHERIC RESEARCH
NATIONAL CENTER FOR ATMOSPHERIC RESEARCH**
P.O. Box 3000, Boulder CO 80307-3000. 303/497-1000. **Physical address:** 1850 Table Mesa Drive, Boulder CO 80305. **Contact:** Human Resources. **World Wide Web address:** http://www.ucar.edu. **Description:** A nonprofit consortium of North American institutions that grants Ph.D. degrees in atmospheric and related sciences. The organization manages the National Center for Atmospheric Research, a research and facilities center sponsored by the National Science Foundation. UCAR also manages over a dozen other programs that enhance the conduct and applications of atmospheric research. **Positions advertised include:** software Engineer/Programmer.

Connecticut
APPLERA CORPORATION
301 Merritt Seven, P.O. Box 5435, Norwalk CT 06856. 203/840-2000. **Toll-free phone:** 800/761-5381. **Fax:** 203/840-2410. **Contact:** Human Resources. **World Wide Web address:** http://www.applera.com. **Description:** A worldwide leader in the development, manufacture, and distribution of analytical and life science systems used in environmental technology, pharmaceuticals, biotechnology, chemicals, plastics, food, agriculture, and scientific research. Founded in 1937. **Positions advertised include:** Financial Analyst; Associate Benefits Administrator; Design Specialist; Travel Specialist. **Corporate headquarters location:** This location. **Subsidiaries include:** Applied Biosystems; Celera Genomics; Celera Diagnostics. **Listed on:** New York Stock Exchange. **Stock exchange symbol:** ABI.

BAYER HEALTHCARE
400 Morgan Lane, West Haven CT 06516. 203/813-2000. **Recorded jobline:** 203/812-5507. **Contact:** Personnel. **World Wide Web address:** http://www.bayerus.com. **Description:** This division conducts business through three major areas of the health care industry: prescription medicine, biological products, and biotechnology. **Corporate headquarters location:** Pittsburgh PA. **Parent company:** Bayer A.G. Worldwide. **Operations at this facility include:** This location is engaged in basic research and drug discovery as part of the Pharmaceutical Division.

BOEHRINGER INGELHEIM PHARMACEUTICALS, INC.
900 Old Ridgebury Road, Ridgefield CT 06877. 203/798-9988. **Contact:** Director of Human Resources. **World Wide Web address:** http://www.boehringer-ingelheim.com. **Description:** Involved in the research, development, manufacture, and marketing of pharmaceutical products used to treat cardiovascular, pulmonary, viral, and immunological diseases. **Corporate headquarters location:** Ingelheim, Germany. **Number of employees nationwide:** 5,100.

BRISTOL-MYERS SQUIBB COMPANY
5 Research Parkway, Wallingford CT 06492. 203/677-6000. **Contact:** Human Resources. **World Wide Web address:** http://www.bms.com. **Description:** Bristol-Myers Squibb is a manufacturer of pharmaceuticals, medical devices, nonprescription drugs, toiletries, and beauty aids. The company's pharmaceutical products include cardiovascular, anti-infective, and anticancer agents; AIDS therapy treatments; central nervous system drugs; and diagnostic agents. Its line of nonprescription products includes formulas, vitamins, analgesics, remedies, and skin care products sold under Bufferin, Excedrin, Nuprin, and Comtrex brand names. Beauty aids include Clairol and Ultress hair care and Nice n' Easy and Clairesse hair colorings, hair sprays, gels, and deodorants. **Corporate headquarters location:** New York NY. **Operations at this facility include:** This location is a pharmaceutical research facility. **Listed on:** New York Stock Exchange. **Stock exchange symbol:** BMY.

CLINICAL LABORATORY PARTNERS
129 Patricia M. Genova Drive, Newington CT 06111. 860/696-8020. **Toll-free phone:** 800/286-9800. **Contact:** Human Resources. **World Wide Web address:** http:// www.clinicallabpartners.com. **Description:** A laboratory that performs several different physician-ordered tests on blood.

DIANON SYSTEMS, INC.
200 Watson Boulevard, Stratford CT 06615. 203/381-4000. **Toll-free phone:** 800/328-2666. **Contact:** Cynthia Yuhlan, Human Resources. **World Wide Web address:** http://www.dianon.com **Description:** A provider of testing services and diagnostic information to focused physician audiences in the United States and Europe. A wide range of laboratory tests are offered,

with applications in the screening, diagnosis, prognosis, and monitoring of cancer and genetic disorders. Screening tests include those for congenital abnormalities; prostate, bladder, and ovarian cancer; and kidney disease. Prognostic testing is available for patients for whom a diagnosis has already been made regarding prostate cancer, bladder cancer, breast cancer, colon cancer, leukemia, and lymphoma. Monitoring tests are used to detect recurrent tumors and to estimate the response to therapy. **NOTE:** Does not accept resumes. Fill out online application. **Corporate headquarters location:** This location. **Other U.S. locations:** AZ; GA; MD; OH; TX. **International locations:** Amsterdam; France; Germany. **Listed on:** NASDAQ. **Stock exchange symbol:** DIAN. **Number of employees nationwide:** 300.

FOLEY LABORATORY SERVICES, INC.
655 Winding Brook Drive, Glastonbury CT 06033. 860/633-2660. **Toll-free phone:** 800/253-5506. **Fax:** 860/652-3259. **Contact:** Human Resources. **World Wide Web address:** http://www.dotdrugtest.com. **Description:** Provides alcohol and drug testing services. **Corporate headquarters location:** This location.

MOORE MEDICAL CORPORATION
389 John Downey Drive, P.O. Box 1500, New Britain CT 06050. 860/826-3600. **Contact:** Human Resources Manager. **World Wide Web address:** http://www.mooremedical.com. **Description:** A national distributor of pharmaceuticals and medical supplies. Primary customers include pharmacies, physicians, dentists, veterinarians, emergency medical services, municipalities, school systems, and correctional facilities. **Positions advertised include:** Customer Service Representative; Inside Sales Representative; Buyer; Field Sales Representative, Occupational Health; Senior Manager, Distribution Center; Returns Processor; Programmer Analyst. **Corporate headquarters location:** This location. **Other U.S. locations:** Hayward CA; Visalia CA; Lemont IL. **Operations at this facility include:** Administration; Sales; Service. **Listed on:** American Stock Exchange. **Stock exchange symbol:** MMD. **Number of employees nationwide:** 425.

NEUROGEN CORPORATION
35 NE Industrial Road, Branford CT 06405. 203/488-8201. **Fax:** 203/481-8683. **Contact:** Human Resources. **World Wide Web address:** http://www.neurogen.com. **Description:** Manufactures and markets neuropharmaceuticals for the treatment of psychiatric and neurological disorders through research involving molecular biology, medicinal chemistry, genetic engineering, and neurobiology. Development has also begun on new psychotherapeutic drugs to aid in treating a wide range of neuropsychiatric disorders including anxiety, psychosis, epilepsy, dementia, sleep- and stress-related disorders, and depression. **Positions advertised include:** Part-time Lab Assistant; Pain Pharmacologist; Research Associate; Senior Scientist. **Corporate headquarters location:** This location. **Listed on:** NASDAQ. **Stock exchange symbol:** NRGN. **Number of employees at this location:** 80.

PFIZER INC.
Eastern Point Road, Groton CT 06340-5146. 860/441-4100. **Contact:** Human Resources. **World Wide Web address:** http://www.pfizer.com. **Description:** Pfizer is a leading pharmaceutical company that distributes products concerning cardiovascular health, central nervous system disorders, infectious diseases, and women's health worldwide. The company's brand-name products include Benadryl, Ben Gay, Cortizone, Desitin, Halls, Listerine, Sudafed, and Zantac 75. **Corporate headquarters location:** New York NY. **Operations at this facility include:** This location develops pharmaceutical products. **Listed on:** New York Stock Exchange. **Stock exchange symbol:** PFE.

PURDUE PHARMA L.P.
201 Tresser Boulevard, Stamford CT 06901-3431. 203/588-8000. **Fax:** 203/588-8850. **Contact:** Human Resources. **World Wide Web address:** http://www.purduepharma.com. **Description:** Purdue is engaged in the research, development, production, sales, and licensing of both prescription and over-the-counter medicines and hospital products. **NOTE:** Candidates must apply online. No hard copy resumes will be considered. **Positions advertised include:** Sr. Statistical Programmer; Program Manager; Staff Accountant; Sr. Auditor; Clinical Research Scientist; Drug Safety Analyst; Library Coordinator; Asst. General Counsel.

QUEST DIAGNOSTICS
3 Sterling Drive, Wallingford CT 06492. 203/949-1260. **Contact:** Human Resources. **World Wide Web address:** http://www.questdiagnostics.com. **Description:** One of the largest clinical laboratories in North America, providing a broad range of clinical laboratory services to health care clients that include physicians, hospitals, clinics, dialysis centers, pharmaceutical companies, and corporations. The company offers and performs tests on blood, urine, and other bodily fluids and tissues to provide information for health and well-being. **Other U.S. locations:** Nationwide. **Listed on:** New York Stock Exchange. **Stock exchange symbol:** DGX.

VION PHARMACEUTICALS
4 Science Park, New Haven CT 06511. 203/498-4210. **Fax:** 203/498-4211. **Contact:** Dan Chapman, Human Resources. **World Wide Web address:** http://www.vionpharm.com. **Description:** Engaged in research to find treatments and therapies for cancer. **Listed on:** NASDAQ. **Stock exchange symbol:** VION.

WATSON PHARMACEUTICALS, INC.
131 West Street, Danbury CT 06810. 203/744-7200. **Contact:** Human Resources. **World Wide Web address:** http://www.watsonpharm.com. **Description:** Manufactures generic prescription drugs. **Corporate headquarters location:** Corona CA. **Other U.S. locations:** Nationwide. **Parent company:** Watson Pharmaceuticals. **Listed on:** New York Stock Exchange. **Stock exchange symbol:** WPI. **Number of employees at this location:** 85.

Delaware

AGILENT TECHNOLOGIES, INC.
2850 Centerville Road, Wilmington DE 19808-1610. 877/424-4536. **Fax:** 302/792-9294. **Contact:** Human Resources. **World Wide Web address:** http://www.agilent.com. **Description:** Agilent Technologies, Inc. provides bio-analytical and electronic measurement solutions to the communications, electronics, life sciences and chemical analysis industries. **NOTE:** See website for current job openings and to apply online. **Corporate headquarters location:** Palo Alto CA. **Operations at this facility include:** R&D.

ASTRAZENECA PHARMACEUTICALS
1800 Concord Pike, P.O. Box 15437, Wilmington DE 19850-5437. 302/886-2200. **Fax:** 302/886-2972. **Contact:** Penny Stoker, Vice President of Human Resources. **World Wide Web address:** http://www.astrazeneca-us.com. **Description** A pharmaceutical company engaged in the research, development, manufacture and marketing of prescription pharmaceuticals, as well as the supply of healthcare services worldwide. It provides medicines designed to fight diseases in such areas as cancer, cardiovascular, gastrointestinal, infection, neuroscience and respiratory. **NOTE:** Must apply for current job openings online. **Special programs:** Entry-Level Positions; Internships. **Corporate headquarters location:** London, United Kingdom. **Other area locations:** Newark DE (Manufacturing; Distribution). **Operations at this facility include:** U.S. Corporate Headquarters.

DADE BEHRING INC.
500 GBC Drive, Newark DE 19702. 302/631-6000. **Contact:** Human Resources. **World Wide Web address:** http://www.dadebehring.com. **Description:**

Dade Behring is a leader in the diagnostics industry, serving more than 24,000 laboratories worldwide with products to assist clinicians in diagnosing medical conditions and in identifying treatment options. **NOTE:** See http://www.monster.com for current job openings and application instructions. **Number of employees worldwide:** 6,500.

LABORATORY CORPORATION OF AMERICA (LABCORP)
212 Cherry Lane, New Castle DE 19720. 302/655-5050. **Contact:** Human Resources. **World Wide Web address:** http://www.labcorp.com. **Description:** A clinical laboratory company providing services primarily to physicians, hospitals, clinics, nursing homes and other clinical labs nationwide. **NOTE:** See website for current job openings and to apply online. **Positions advertised include:** Phlebotomist. **Corporate headquarters location:** Burlington NC. **Other area locations:** Claymont DE; Dover DE; Middletown DE; Newark DE; Wilmington DE. **Listed on:** New York Stock Exchange. **Stock exchange symbol:** LH.

QUEST PHARMACEUTICAL SERVICES
Delaware Technology Park, 3 Innovation Way, Suite 240, Newark DE 19711. 302/369-5601. **Fax:** 302/369-5602. **Contact:** Human Resources. **E-mail address:** careers@questpharm.com. **World Wide Web address:** http://www.questpharm.com. **Description:** A contract research organization for the pharmaceutical industry that runs a GLP-compliant DMPK laboratory, supporting drug discovery and development. **NOTE:** Submit resume by e-mail or fax. **Positions advertised include:** Scientist/Senior Research Scientist; Staff/Associate Scientist.

District Of Columbia
GLAXOSMITHKLINE
1500 K Street NW, Suite 650, Washington DC 20005. 202/715-1000. **Contact:** Human Resources. **World Wide Web address:** http://www.gsk.com. **Description:** A pharmaceutical preparations company whose products include AZT, an AIDS treatment drug; Zantac; and Malarone, medication for malaria. **Positions advertised include:** Oncology Account Manager; Pharmaceutical Sales Rep. **Corporate headquarters location:** United Kingdom. **Other U.S. locations:** Nationwide. **International locations:** Worldwide. **Listed on:** New York Stock Exchange. **Stock exchange symbol:** GSK. **Number of employees nationwide:** 24,000. **Number of employees worldwide:** 110,000.

HOFFMANN-LA ROCHE INC.
1425 K Street NW, Suite 650, Washington DC 20005. 202/408-0090. **Contact:** Human Resources. **World Wide Web address:** http://www.rocheusa.com. **Description:** An international health care organization that develops and manufactures pharmaceuticals, diagnostics, and vitamins. **Positions advertised include:** Division Sales Manager, Oncology; Executive Assistant. **Corporate headquarters location:** Nutley NJ. **Other U.S. locations:** Nationwide. **International locations:** Worldwide. **Subsidiaries include:** Roche Biomedical Laboratories; Roche Diagnostics (ethical pharmaceuticals); Roche Vitamins Inc. **Parent company:** The Roche Group. **Listed on:** Privately held. **Annual sales/revenues:** More than $100 million. **Number of employees nationwide:** 20,000. **Number of employees worldwide:** 66,000.

NATIONAL ACADEMY OF SCIENCES
NATIONAL RESEARCH COUNCIL (NRC)
500 5th Street NW, Washington DC 20001. 202/334-2000. **Fax:** 202/334-1746. **Contact:** Human Resources. **World Wide Web address:** http://www.nasonline.org. **Description:** A federally chartered private corporation whose primary aim is to provide an independent source of counsel to the government on matters of science and technology. Academy members are elected. The academy's research is conducted by the National Research Council (NRC.)

RESEARCH TRIANGLE INSTITUTE (RTI)
701 13th Street NW, Suite 750, Washington DC 20005-3962. 202/728-2080. **Fax:** 202/728-2095. **Contact:** Human Resources. **E-mail address:** jobs@rti.org. **World Wide Web address:** http://www.rti.org. **Description:** A nonprofit, independent research organization involved in many scientific fields, under contract to business; industry; federal, state, and local governments; industrial associations; and public service agencies. The institute was created as a separately operated entity by the joint action of North Carolina State University, Duke University, and the University of North Carolina at Chapel Hill. Close ties are maintained with the universities' scientists, both through the active research community of the Research Triangle region in North Carolina and through collaborative research conducted for government and industry clients. Research Triangle Institute responds to national priorities in health, the environment, advanced technology, and social policy with contract research for the U.S. government including applications in statistics, social sciences, chemistry, life sciences, environmental sciences, engineering, and electronics. **Positions advertised include:** Analyst; Editor/Writer; Financial Administration Specialist; Research Statistician; Sr. Contract Negotiator. **Corporate headquarters location:** Research Triangle Park NC. **Other U.S. locations:** Rockville MD; Cocoa Beach FL; Hampton VA; Atlanta GA; Chicago IL; Waltham MA; Anniston AL. **Number of employees nationwide:** 1,750.

SCIENCE APPLICATIONS INTERNATIONAL CORPORATION (SAIC)
2020 K Street NW, Suite 400, Washington DC 20006. 202/530-8900. **Contact:** Human Resources. **World Wide Web address:** http://www.saic.com. **Description:** The largest employee-owned research and engineering firm in the U.S. with offices in 150 cities worldwide. **Positions advertised include:** Help Desk Specialist; Technical Project Manager. **Number of employees worldwide:** 43,000.

Florida
ABC RESEARCH CORPORATION
3437 SW 24th Avenue, Gainesville FL 32607. 352/372-0436. **Fax:** 352/378-6483. **Contact:** Human Resources. **World Wide Web address:** http://www.abcr.com. **Description:** A laboratory specializing in food and water analysis. **Positions advertised include:** PhD Food Safety Microbiologist; Food Safety Auditor; Quality Assessment Product Manager.

BECKMAN COULTER, INC.
P.O. Box 169015, Miami FL 33116-9015. 305/380-3800. **Physical address:** 11800 147th Avenue SW, Miami FL 33196. **Fax:** 305/380-3689. **Contact:** Human Resources. **World Wide Web address:** http://www.beckmancoulter.com. **Description:** Sells and services a diverse range of scientific instruments, reagents, and related equipment. Products include DNA synthesizers, robotic workstations, centrifuges, electrophoresis systems, detection and measurement equipment, data processing software, and specialty chemical and automated general chemical systems. Many of the company's products are used in research and development and diagnostic analysis. **Positions advertised include:** Sales Consultant. **Corporate headquarters location:** Fullerton CA.

IVAX CORPORATION
4400 Biscayne Boulevard, Miami FL 33137. 305/575-6000. **Contact:** Human Resources. **World Wide Web address:** http://www.ivax.com. **Description:** IVAX Corporation is a holding company with subsidiaries involved in specialty chemicals, pharmaceuticals, personal care products, and medical diagnostics. The company's principal business is the research, development, manufacture, marketing, and distribution of health care products. Brand name products, marketed under the Baker Norton trade name, include the urological medications Bicitra, Polycitra, Polycitra-K, Polycitra-LC, Neutra-Phos, Neutra-Phos-K, Prohim, Urotrol, Lubraseptic Jelly, and Pro-Banthine; and cardiovascular medicines Cordilox, Triam-Co, Amil-

Co, Spiro-Co, and Fru-Co. Other drugs include Proglycem, used to treat hyperinsulinism; Serenance, a neuroleptic used for psychiatric disorders; the respiratory medications Cromogen, Salamol, and Beclazone metered dose inhalers; the Steri-Nebs line of nebulization products; and Eye-Crom and Glaucol. IVAX also markets generic drugs. Through DVM Pharmaceuticals, Inc., IVAX formulates, packages, and distributes veterinary products including DermCaps, a daily dietary supplement; a line of topical therapeutics including ChlorhexiDerm Flush and shampoo, OxyDex shampoo and gel, HyLyt shampoo and rinse, and Relief shampoo, rinse, and spray; two groups of optic products known as Clear and OtiCalm; the DuraKyl and SynerKyl line of ectoparasiticidals; and the wound dressing BioDres. **Positions advertised include:** Administrative Assistant; Inside Sales Call Center Manager; Ivax Legal Secretary; People Soft Application Developer; Research Scientist; Buyer; Cost Accountant: Validation Specialist; Formulation Scientist; System Administrator; Web Producer. **Corporate headquarters location:** This location. **Listed on:** American Stock Exchange. **Stock exchange symbol:** IVX. **Number of employees nationwide:** 2,910.

IVAX PHARMACEUTICALS
4400 Biscayne Boulevard, Miami FL 33137. 305/575-6000. **Toll-free phone:** 800/327-4114. **Contact:** Human Resources Department. **World Wide Web address:** http://www.ivaxpharmaceuticals.com. **Description:** IVAX Pharmaceuticals manufactures generic pharmaceuticals. **Positions advertised include:** Senior Accountant; Regulatory Affairs Manager; Plant Engineer; Director of Systems Development; Validation Manager; Business Analyst; Windows Administrator; Health Information Technician; Senior Production Coordinator. **Parent company:** IVAX Corporation. **Listed on:** American Stock Exchange. **Stock exchange symbol:** IVX.

THE MONTICELLO COMPANY
1604 Stockton Street, Jacksonville FL 32204. 904/384-3666. **Contact:** Human Resources. **World Wide Web address:** http://www.monticellocompanies.com. **Description:** The Monticello Company manufactures and sells over-the-counter pharmaceuticals produced at the company's plant in Mexico. **Corporate headquarters location:** This location. **Operations at this facility include:** This location provides administrative services. **Parent company:** Monticello Companies.

NABI BIOPHARMACEUTICALS
5800 Park of Commerce Boulevard NW, Boca Raton FL 33487. 561/989-5800x5511. **Fax:** 561/989-5874. **Contact:** Human Resources. **World Wide Web address:** http://www.nabi.com. **Description:** Provides plasma and plasma-based products that aid in the prevention and treatment of diseases and disorders. **Corporate headquarters location:** This location. **Other U.S. locations:** Rockville MD. **Listed on:** NASDAQ. **Stock exchange symbol:** NBIO.

NOVEN PHARMACEUTICALS, INC.
11960 SW 144th Street, Miami FL 33186. 305/253-5099. **Fax:** 305/251-1887. **Contact:** Sandra Miller, Human Resources Administrator. **E-mail address:** hrjobs@noven.com. **World Wide Web address:** http://www.noven.com. **Description:** Develops and manufactures transdermal and transmucosal drug delivery systems. **Positions advertised include:** Analytical Chemist; Product Release Supervisor; Controlled Substance Manager. **Listed on:** NASDAQ. **Stock exchange symbol:** NOVN.

PHARMERICA
PHARMACY MANAGEMENT SERVICES, INC. (PMSI)
175 Kelsey Lane, Tampa FL 33619. 813/626-7788. **Toll-free phone:** 800/237-7676. **Contact:** Human Resources. **World Wide Web address:** http://www.pharmerica.com. **Description:** A supplier of pharmaceuticals and related products to long-term care facilities, hospitals, and assisted living communities. PharMerica also provides nurse consultant services, infusion therapy and training, medical records consulting, and educational programs. PMSI (also at this location) offers medical equipment and supplies through mail-order delivery. **Positions advertised include:** Account Executive; Account Manager; Billing Analyst; Business Process Analyst; Cash Application Associate; Cash Associate; Clerical Assistant; Collection Associate; Computer Operator; Web Developer; Shipping, Receiving Clerk; Tax Accountant. **Corporate headquarters location:** This location. **Listed on:** New York Stock Exchange. **Stock exchange symbol:** ABC.

QUEST DIAGNOSTICS INCORPORATED
4225 East Fowler Avenue, Tampa FL 33617. 813/972-7100. **Toll-free phone:** 800/282-6613. **Fax:** 813/972-3986. **Contact:** Human Resources. **World Wide Web address:** http://www.questdiagnostics.com. **Description:** One of the largest clinical laboratories in North America, providing a broad range of clinical laboratory services to health care clients that include physicians, hospitals, clinics, dialysis centers, pharmaceutical companies, and corporations. The company offers and performs tests on blood, urine, and other bodily fluids and tissues to provide information for health and well-being. Founded in 1969. **Positions advertised include:** Histology; Phlebotomy; Technical Laboratory Services; Lab Management; Accounts Receivable Billing Clerk. **Other U.S. locations:** Nationwide. **Listed on:** New York Stock Exchange. **Stock exchange symbol:** DGX. **Annual revenues:** More than $100 million.

RESEARCH TRIANGLE INSTITUTE (RTI)
3000 North Atlantic Avenue, Suite 208, Cocoa Beach FL 32931. 321/799-1607. **Contact:** Human Resources. **E-mail address:** jobs@rti.org. **World Wide Web address:** http://www.rti.org. **Description:** A nonprofit, independent research organization involved in many scientific fields. Clients include federal, state, and local governments, industrial associations, and public service agencies. The institute was created as a separately operated entity by the joint action of North Carolina State University, Duke University, and the University of North Carolina at Chapel Hill. RTI responds to national priorities in health, the environment, advanced technology, and social policy with contract research for the U.S. government including applications in statistics, social sciences, chemistry, life sciences, environmental sciences, engineering, and electronics. The institute operates a 180-acre campus in the center of Research Triangle Park NC, which includes laboratory and office facilities for all technical programs. **Corporate headquarters location:** Research Triangle Park NC. **Other U.S. locations:** Nationwide. **International locations:** England; Indonesia; South Africa. **Number of employees nationwide:** 1,950.

SCHERING-PLOUGH
13900 NW 57th Court, Miami FL 33014. 305/698-4600. **Contact:** Human Resources. **World Wide Web address:** http://www.schering-plough.com. **Description:** Schering-Plough Corporation is engaged in the discovery, development, manufacture, marketing, and testing of pharmaceutical and consumer products. Pharmaceutical products include prescription drugs, over-the-counter medicines, eye care products, and animal health products promoted to the medical and allied health professions. The consumer products group consists of proprietary medicines, toiletries, cosmetics, foot care, and sun care products marketed directly to the public. Products include Coricidin cough and cold medicines and Maybelline beauty products. **Positions advertised include:** Maintenance Supervisor; Production Support Manager; Project Manager; Senior Technical Systems Analyst; Senior Validation Specialist; Production Supervisor. **Listed on:** New York Stock Exchange. **Stock exchange symbol:** SGP.

SCIENTIFIC INSTRUMENTS, INC.
4400 West Tiffany Drive, West Palm Beach FL 33407. 561/881-8500. **Contact:** Leigh Ann Capers, Human

Resources Department. **E-mail address:** info@scientificinstruments.com **World Wide Web address:** http://www.scientificinstruments.com. **Description:** Manufactures temperature-sensing and controlling instruments as well as other laboratory instruments.

Georgia

ALLIANT PHARMACEUTICALS, INC.
333 North Point Center East, Suite 250, Alpharetta GA 30022. 770/817-4500. **Contact:** Human Resources. **E-mail address:** careers@alliantpharma.com. **World Wide Web address:** http://www.alliantpharma.com. **Description:** A specialty pharmaceutical company focused on acquiring, developing, and commercializing proprietary products for the pediatric and pediatric specialty markets. The company's products address the sub-specialties of allergy and immunology, psychiatry, neurology, dermatology, urology, and infectious diseases. Founded in 2004. **Positions advertised include:** Associate Product Manager; Regional Account Manager. **Corporate headquarters location:** This location.

BARD MEDICAL DIVISION
8195 Industrial Boulevard, Covington GA 30014. 770/784-6100. **Toll-free phone:** 800/526-4455. **Fax:** 800/852-1339. **Contact:** Human Resources. **World Wide Web address:** http://www.bardmedical.com. **Description:** A leader in urology medical products, and committed to diagnosing and treating urinary tract infections. **Corporate headquarters location:** Murray Hill NJ. **Parent company:** C.R. Bard. **Listed on:** New York Stock Exchange. **Stock exchange symbol:** BCR.

CRYOLIFE
1655 Roberts Boulevard NW, Kennesaw GA 30144. 770/419-3355. **Toll-free phone:** 800/438-8285. **Fax:** 770/426-0031. **Contact:** Human Resources Manager. **World Wide Web address:** http://www.cryolife.com. **Description:** A biomedical laboratory specializing in cryopreserved transplantable human tissues as well as the development and production of bio-adhesives. Founded in 1984. **Corporate headquarters location:** This location. **Subsidiaries include:** CryoLife International; CryoLife Europa Ltd. **Listed on:** New York Stock Exchange. **Stock exchange symbol:** CRY. **President/CEO:** Stephen G. Anderson. **Annual sales/revenues:** $51 - $100 million. **Number of employees worldwide:** 400.

HUBER ENGINEERED MATERIALS
1000 Parkwood Circle, Suite 1000, Atlanta GA 30339. 678/247-7300. **Toll-free phone:** 800/313-6888. **Fax:** 678/247-2797. **Contact:** Human Resources. **E-mail address:** staffing@huber.com. **World Wide Web address:** http://www.huber.com. **Description:** Engineers a variety of products through science and chemistry. The company's products range from cosmetics to coatings for bridges and ships. **Corporate headquarters location:** This location. **Other area locations:** Fairmont GA; Kennesaw GA; Macon GA; Marble Hill GA; Sandersville GA; Wrens GA. **Other U.S. locations:** Etowah TN; Havre de Grace MD; Hawesville KY; Johnsonburg PA; Kingsport TN; Longview WA; Seattle WA; Marble Falls TX; Quincy IL. **International locations:** Worldwide. **Parent company:** J.M. Huber Corporation.

IMMUCOR
P.O. Box 5625, Norcross GA 30091-5625. 770/441-2051. **Physical address:** 3130 Gateway Drive, Norcross GA 30071. **Toll-free phone:** 800/829-2553. **Fax:** 770/441-3807. **Contact:** Human Resources. **E-mail address:** hr@immucor.com. **World Wide Web address:** http://www.immucor.com. **Description:** An international in vitro diagnostic company that develops, manufactures, and markets products used by blood banks, hospitals, and clinical laboratories to test, detect, and identify properties of the human blood. Founded in 1982. **NOTE:** Entry-level positions are offered. Please visit website to search for jobs and apply online. **Positions advertised include:** Field Service Engineer; Customer Service Representative. **Office hours:** Monday – Friday, 8:30 a.m. – 5:30 p.m. **Corporate headquarters location:** This location. **Other U.S. locations:** Houston TX; Thomas VA. **International locations:** Worldwide. **Listed on:** NASDAQ. **Stock exchange symbol:** BLUD. **Number of employees nationwide:** 500. **President/CEO:** Edward Gallup.

LABORATORY CORPORATION OF AMERICA (LABCORP)
1957 Lakeside Parkway, Suite 542, Tucker GA 30084. 770/939-4811. **Contact:** Human Resources. **World Wide Web address:** http://www.labcorp.com. **Description:** One of the nation's leading clinical laboratory companies, providing services primarily to physicians, hospitals, clinics, nursing homes, and other clinical laboratories nationwide. Labs perform tests on blood, urine, and other bodily fluids and tissue, aiding the prompt and accurate diagnosis of disease. **NOTE:** Please visit website to register, search for jobs, and apply online. **Positions advertised include:** Service Representative/Courier; Patient Services Technician Specialist; Service Representative. **Corporate headquarters location:** Burlington NC. **Other U.S. locations:** Nationwide. **Listed on**: New York Stock Exchange. **Stock exchange symbol:** LH. **Number of employees nationwide:** 23,000.

MERCK & COMPANY, INC.
3517 Radium Springs Road, Albany GA 31705. 229/420-3000. **Contact:** Human Resources. **World Wide Web address:** http://www.merck.com. **Description:** Merck discovers, develops, manufactures, and markets a broad range of pharmaceutical products to improve human and animal health. The Merck-Medco Managed Care Division manages pharmacy benefits for more than 40 million Americans, encourages the appropriate uses of medicines, and provides disease management programs. **NOTE:** Please visit website to search for jobs and apply online. **Positions advertised include:** Hospital Sales Representative; Specialty Sales Representative. **Corporate headquarters location:** Whitehouse Station NJ. **Other U.S. locations:** Rahway NJ; Wilson NC; Danville PA; Elkton VA. **International locations:** Worldwide. **Operations at this facility include:** Manufacturing of prescription drugs. **Listed on:** New York Stock Exchange. **Stock exchange symbol:** MRK. **President/CEO:** Raymond V. Gilmartin.

MERIAL LTD.
3239 Satellite Boulevard NW, Duluth GA 30096. 678/638-3000. **Contact:** Human Resources. **World Wide Web address:** http://www.merial.com. **Description:** Develops veterinary vaccines and pharmaceuticals. **NOTE:** Please visit website to search for jobs and apply online. **Positions advertised include:** Financial Analyst; Associate Manager; Biostatistician; Accountant; Administrative Associate; Director – Financial Analyst; Senior Database Administrator; Senior Manager; Senior Business Analyst; Project Leader. **Corporate headquarters location:** This location. **Other area locations:** Athens GA; Gainesville GA. **Other U.S. locations:** Nationwide. **International locations:** Worldwide. **Subsidiaries include:** Hubbard ISA. **Operations at this facility include:** This location serves as the North American headquarters. **Number of employees worldwide:** 6,500.

MICROMERITICS INSTRUMENT CORPORATION
One Micromeritics Drive, Norcross GA 30093-1877. 770/662-3620. 3678. **Fax:** 770/662-3696. **Contact:** Human Resources. **E-mail address:** hr@micromeritics.com. **World Wide Web address:** http://www.micromeritics.com. **Description:** Produces and distributes laboratory analysis equipment used in various health care and scientific applications including liquid chromatographs. **NOTE:** Please visit website to search for jobs and apply online. **Corporate headquarters location:** This location. **International locations:** China; Italy; Belgium; France; Germany. **Operations at this facility include:** Manufacturing; Research and Development. **Subsidiaries include:**

Alcott Chromatography. **Number of employees worldwide:** 240.

MIKART
1750 Chattahoochee Avenue NW, Atlanta GA 30318. 404/351-4510. **Toll-free phone:** 888/4MIKART. **Fax:** 404/350-0432. **Contact:** Human Resources. **E-mail address:** resumes1@mikart.com. **World Wide Web address:** http://www.mikart.com. **Description:** Engaged in the formulation, manufacturing, and packaging of generic and prescription drugs. **NOTE:** No phone calls regarding employment. **Positions advertised include:** Formulation Scientist; Analytical Methods Development Chemist. **Corporate headquarters location:** This location. **Number of employees at this location:** 170.

PFIZER
P.O Box 2347, Augusta GA 30903. 706/303-6000. **Physical address:** 1736 Lover's Lane, Augusta GA 30901. **Contact:** Human Resources Department. **World Wide Web address:** http://www.pfizer.com. **Description:** Develops and manufactures prescription medicines and other products for both humans and animals. Medicines include Celebrex, Diflucan, Viagra, Zoloft, and Zyrtec. Over the counter products include Benadryl, e.p.t., Listerine, Lubriderm, Rolaids, Sudafed, and Visine. **NOTE:** Please visit the Georgia Department of Labor in person or online – http://www.dol.state.ga.us – for a listing of Pfizer job opportunities. **Office hours:** Monday – Friday, 8:00 a.m. – 4:30 p.m. **Corporate headquarters location:** New York NY. **Other U.S. locations:** Nationwide. **International locations:** Worldwide. **Listed on:** New York Stock Exchange. **Stock exchange symbol:** PFE. CEO: Hank McKinnell. **Number of employees worldwide:** 122,000.

QUEST DIAGNOSTICS INCORPORATED
3175 Presidential Drive, Atlanta GA 30340. 770/452-1590. **Contact:** Human Resources. **E-mail address:** careers@questdiagnostics.com. **World Wide Web address:** http://www.questdiagnostics.com. **Description:** Quest Diagnostics is one of the largest clinical laboratories in North America, providing a broad range of clinical laboratory services to health care clients that include physicians, hospitals, clinics, dialysis centers, pharmaceutical companies, and corporations. The company offers and performs tests on blood, urine, and other bodily fluids and tissues to provide information for health and well-being. **NOTE:** Please visit website to search for jobs. **Positions advertised include:** Phlebotomy Service Floater; Floater; Representative of Phlebotomy Services. **Corporate headquarters location:** Teterboro NJ. **Other area locations:** Statewide. **Other U.S. locations:** Nationwide. **Operations at this facility include:** This location is engaged in specimen collection. **Listed on:** New York Stock Exchange. **Stock exchange symbol:** DGX. **CEO:** Kenneth Freeman. **Number of employees worldwide:** 37,000.

SOLVAY PHARMACEUTICALS
901 Sawyer Road, Marietta GA 30062. 770/578-9000. **Fax:** 770/578-5597. **Contact:** Human Resources. **World Wide Web address:** http://www.solvay.com. **Description:** A manufacturer of prescription drugs. **Corporate headquarters location:** Brussels Belgium. **Other U.S. locations:** Nationwide. **International locations:** Worldwide. **Parent company:** Solvay S.A. **Listed on:** Over-the-Counter. **Stock exchange symbol:** SVYSY. **Number of employees worldwide:** 30,302.

STERICYCLE PHARMACEUTICAL SERVICES
2084-M Lake Industrial Court, Conyers GA 30013. 770/785-9710. **Contact:** Human Resources. **E-mail address:** recruiter@usiinc.net. **World Wide Web address:** http://www.stericycle.com. **Description:** A pharmaceutical company engaged in the disposal of outdated pills and medical products. **Positions advertised include:** Technical Specialist; Account Manager; Account Development Manager. **Corporate headquarters location:** Winston-Salem NC.

Hawaii
CYANOTECH CORPORATION
73-4460 Queen Kaahumanu Highway, Suite 102, Kailua-Kona HI 96740. 808/326-1353. **Fax:** 808/329-4533. **Toll-free phone:** 800/393-1353. **Contact:** Human Resources. **Email address:** info@cyanotech.com. **World Wide Web address:** http://www.cyanotech.com. **Description:** Develops and produces natural products from microalgae. The company manufactures products for use in nutritional supplements, immunological diagnostics, and aquaculture/pigments. **Corporate headquarters location:** This location. **Other U.S. locations:** NV. **Subsidiaries include:** Cyanotech International FSC, Inc.; Nutrex, Inc. **Listed on:** NASDAQ. **Stock exchange symbol:** CYAN. **Number of employees at this location:** 80.

Illinois
ABBOTT LABORATORIES
100 Abbott Park Road, Abbott Park IL 60064-3500. 847/937-6100. **Fax:** 847/937-1511. **Contact:** Human Resources Department. **World Wide Web address:** http://www.abbott.com. **Description:** A *Fortune* 500 company engaged in the design and manufacture of disposable medical devices for hemodynamic monitoring and fluid collection. **NOTE:** Please visit website to search for jobs and apply online. **Positions advertised include:** Secretary; Senior Financial Analyst; Manager of Strategy and Development; Contract Coordinator; Project Engineer; Secretary; Technical Project Leader/Architect; Project Engineer. **Corporate headquarters location:** This location. **Other U.S. locations:** Nationwide. **International locations:** Worldwide. **Listed on:** New York Stock Exchange. **Stock exchange symbol:** ABT. **Number of employees worldwide:** 70,000.

AKORN, INC.
2500 Millbrook Drive, Buffalo Grove IL 60089. 847/279-6100. **Toll-free phone:** 800/535-7155. **Contact:** Human Resources. **World Wide Web address:** http://www.akorn.com. **Description:** A specialty pharmaceutical company engaged in the development, manufacturing, and marketing of branded and multi-source pharmaceutical products focused in the areas of ophthalmology, anesthesia, antidotes, and rheumatology. **Positions advertised include:** Quality Control Chemist; Analytical Scientist; Regulatory Affairs Associate; Microbiologist; Supervisor, Pharmaceutical Production. **Other area locations:** Decatur IL.

ARGONNE NATIONAL LABORATORY
9700 South Cass Avenue, Argonne IL 60439. 630/252-2000. **Contact:** Human Resources. **World Wide Web address:** http://www.anl.gov. **Description:** One of the Department of Energy's largest research centers. Argonne National Laboratory's research falls into three broad categories: engineering research including research on meltdown-proof nuclear reactors, advanced batteries, and fuel cells; physical research including materials science, physics, chemistry, mathematics, and computer science; and energy, environmental, and biological research including research into the causes and cures of cancer, alternate energy systems, and environmental and economic impact assessments. The laboratory is operated by the University of Chicago for the U.S. Department of Energy. **NOTE:** Search and apply for positions online. **Positions advertised include:** Network Administrator; Operational Health Physics Group Leader; Quality Assurance Representative; Senior Financial Analyst; Senior Trainer- Radiological/Nuclear; Senior Technician.

ASTELLAS PHARMA US, INC.
3 Parkway North, Deerfield IL 60015. 847/317-8800. **Fax:** 847/317-1245. **Contact:** Human Resources. **E-mail address:** employment@fujisawa.com. **World Wide Web address:** http://www.astellas.us. **Description:** A pharmaceutical company that markets products in the area of anti-infectives, cardiovasculars, transplantation, and dermatology. **NOTE:** Apply online at the company's website for specific job openings.

Resumes may also be e-mailed for specific job openings. **Positions advertised include:** Assistant/Associate Director Regulatory Affairs; Senior Corporate Records Assistant; Senior Medical Writer; Project Assistant. **Corporate headquarters location:** This location.

COLE-PARMER INSTRUMENT COMPANY
625 East Bunker Court, Vernon Hills IL 60061-1884. 847/549-7600. **Toll-free phone:** 800/323-4340. **Fax:** 847/549-1515. **Contact:** Human Resources. **E-mail address:** hr@coleparmer.com. **World Wide Web address:** http://www.coleparmer.com. **Description:** An international exporter and distributor of scientific instruments for laboratories. **NOTE:** See website for job listings. Apply online or e-mail resumes. **Positions advertised include:** Product Application Specialist; Product Manager; Distribution Specialist; Staff Accountant; Human Resources Coordinator.

DSM DESOTECH INC.
1122 St. Charles Street, Elgin IL 60120. 847/697-0400. **Toll-free phone:** 800/223-7191. **Fax:** 847/468-7795. **Contact:** Human Resources Department. **World Wide Web address:** http://www.dsmdesotech.com. **Description:** A researcher, formulator, and manufacturer of ultraviolet and electron beam curable materials and technology. **NOTE:** Search and apply for open positions online. **Corporate headquarters location:** This location.

DADE BEHRING, INC.
1717 Deerfield Road, Deerfield IL 60015-0778. 847/267-5300. **Fax:** 847/267-5408. **Contact:** Human Resources. **World Wide Web address:** http://www.dadebehring.com. **Description:** Manufactures and distributes diagnostic instrument systems and other labware that serve clinical and research laboratories worldwide. Dade Behring also offers its customers support services. **Positions advertised include:** Bilingual Customer Satisfaction Representative; Office Services Clerk; Systems Analyst. **Corporate headquarters location:** This location. **International locations:** Worldwide.

THE FEMALE HEALTH COMPANY
515 North State Street, Suite 2225, Chicago IL 60610. 312/595-9123. **Fax:** 312/595-9122. **Contact:** Human Resources. **World Wide Web address:** http://www.femalehealth.com. **Description:** Markets and distributes a proprietary female barrier contraceptive product known as the Reality female condom. **Corporate headquarters location:** This location. **Parent company:** Wisconsin Pharmacal Company, Inc. (Jackson WI).

FERMI NATIONAL ACCELERATOR LABORATORY
P.O. Box 500, MS 116, Batavia IL 60510. 630/840-3324. **Fax:** 630/840-2306. **Contact:** Employment Manager. **E-mail address:** employ@fnal.org. **World Wide Web address:** http://www.fnal.gov. **Description:** A federally funded, nonprofit organization dedicated to basic research in the field of high-energy physics. **NOTE:** See website for job listings and contact information. **Special programs:** Internships. **Corporate headquarters location:** Washington DC. **Parent company:** Universities Research Association. **Operations at this facility include:** Research and Development.

FERRO PFANSTIEHL LABORATORIES, INC.
1219 Glen Rock Avenue, Waukegan IL 60085. 847/623-0370. **Fax:** 847/623-9173. **Contact:** Human Resources. **E-mail address:** resume@ferro.com. **World Wide Web address:** http://www.ferro.com. **Description:** A chemical laboratory specializing in the production of carbohydrates and biological chemicals. Clients are primarily pharmaceutical companies. **NOTE:** See website for job requirements and e-mail resumes. **Corporate headquarters location:** Cleveland, OH. **Listed on:** New York Stock Exchange. **Stock exchange symbol:** FOE.

GE HEALTHCARE
3350 North Ridge Avenue, Arlington Heights IL 60004. 847/398-8400. **Fax:** 847/818-6629. **Contact:** Human Resources. **World Wide Web address:** http://www.gehealthcare.com. **Description:** Researches, develops, and manufactures nuclear medicine and radiopharmaceuticals. **NOTE:** For a list of job openings, visit the website. To apply, either fax or e-mail resumes and cover letters, stating desired position. **Operations at this facility include:** Manufacturing; Research and Development.

LEICA MICROSYSTEMS USA
2345 Waukegan Road, Bannockburn IL 60015. 847/405-0123. **Contact:** Human Resources. **World Wide Web address:** http://www.leica-microsystems.us. **Description:** Manufactures and sells microscopes and other scientific instruments.

NEIGHBORCARE
1250 East Diehl Road, Suite 208, Naperville IL 60563. 630/245-4800. **Fax:** 630/505-1319. **Contact:** Human Resources. **World Wide Web address:** http://www.neighborcare.com. **Description:** An institutional pharmacy provider that offers services such as infusion therapy, drug distribution, patient management, educational services, and consulting services for managing health care costs. **Parent company:** Omnicare.

NORTHFIELD LABORATORIES, INC.
1560 Sherman Avenue, Suite 1000, Evanston IL 60201-4800. 847/864-3500. **Fax:** 847/864-0353. **Contact:** Human Resources. **World Wide Web address:** http://www.northfieldlabs.com. **Description:** Develops chemically altered human hemoglobin as an alternative for blood transfusion where acute blood loss has occurred. The company markets PolyHeme, a blood substitute product that carries as much oxygen and loads and unloads oxygen in the same manner as transfused blood. **Listed on:** NASDAQ. **Stock exchange symbol:** NFLD.

OMNICARE
1717 Park Street, Suite 200, Naperville IL 60563. 630/305-8000. **Contact:** Human Resources. **World Wide Web address:** http://www.omnicare.com. **Description:** Provides professional pharmacy, related consulting, and data management services for skilled nursing, assisted living, and other institutional healthcare providers. Omnicare also provides clinical research services for the pharmaceutical and biotechnology industries. **NOTE:** Call to inquire about current job openings.

PFIZER
5500 Forest Hills Road, Rockford IL 61105. 815/877-8081. **Contact:** Human Resources. **World Wide Web address:** http://www.pfizer.com. **Description:** Pfizer is a leading pharmaceutical company that distributes products concerning cardiovascular health, central nervous system disorders, infectious diseases, and women's health worldwide. The company's brand-name products include Benadryl, Ben Gay, Cortizone, Desitin, Halls, Listerine, Sudafed, and Zantac 75. **NOTE:** This company has other locations in Illinois. See website for job listings and locations. Apply online. **Positions advertised include:** Buyer/Planner; Oncology Sales Consultant. **Corporate headquarters location:** New York NY. **Operations at this facility include:** This location manufactures gum. **Listed on:** New York Stock Exchange. **Stock exchange symbol:** PFE.

QUEST DIAGNOSTICS INCORPORATED
1614 W. Central Road, Arlington Heights IL 60005. 847/342-0344. **Contact:** Human Resources. **World Wide Web address:** http://www.questdiagnostics.com. **Description:** Quest Diagnostics is one of the largest clinical laboratories in North America, providing a broad range of clinical laboratory services to health care clients that include physicians, hospitals, clinics, dialysis centers, pharmaceutical companies, and corporations. The company offers and performs tests on

blood, urine, and other bodily fluids and tissues to provide information for health and well-being. **NOTE:** This company has locations throughout Illinois and the United States. See website for locations and job listings. **Operations at this facility include:** This location is a testing laboratory. **Listed on:** New York Stock Exchange. **Stock exchange symbol:** DGX.

SARGENT-WELCH SCIENTIFIC COMPANY
911 Commerce Court, Buffalo Grove IL 60089. 847/465-7527. **Toll-free phone:** 800/727-4368. **Contact:** Human Resources. **E-mail address:** sarwel@sargentwelch.com. **World Wide Web address:** http://www.sargentwelch.com. **Description:** Sargent-Welch Scientific Company is a distributor and manufacturer of a wide range of analytical instruments, scientific apparatus, lab equipment, supplies, chemicals, and furniture. **Corporate headquarters location:** West Chester PA. **Parent company:** VWR Corporation. **Operations at this facility include:** This location houses customer service offices.

SILLIKER LABORATORIES GROUP, INC.
900 Maple Road, Homewood IL 60430. 708/957-7878. **Fax:** 708/957-3798. **Contact:** Margo Neetz, Human Resources Generalist. **E-mail address:** human.resources@silliker.com. **World Wide Web address:** http://www.silliker.com. **Description:** Operates a network of food testing laboratories. The labs test for pathogens and microbes and serve to verify the accuracy of nutritional labeling. Founded in 1967. **NOTE:** See website for job listings. Apply online or e-mail or mail resumes. Entry-level positions and part-time jobs are offered. **Special programs:** Summer Jobs. **Corporate headquarters location:** This location. **International locations:** Worldwide. **Listed on:** Privately held.

Indiana

BAYER HEALTHCARE
P.O. Box 40, Elkhart IN 46515. 574/264-8111. **Physical address:** 1025 North Michigan Street, Elkhart IN 46514. **Fax:** 574/262-7450. **Contact:** William Gross, Human Resources Director. **World Wide Web address:** http://www.bayerus.com. **Description:** Produces citric acid monitoring systems for blood and urine, over-the-counter cold remedy products, and vitamins. **NOTE:** To increase chances of consideration, applicants should submit a resume online in reference to a specific job posting. **Special programs:** Internships; Co-ops.

BINDLEY WESTERN INDUSTRIES, INC.
8909 Purdue Road, Suite 500, Indianapolis IN 46290. 317/704-4602. **Fax:** 317/704-4602. **Contact:** Human Resources. **World Wide Web address:** http://www.bindley.com. **Description:** Distributes prescription pharmaceuticals to drug stores, hospitals, clinics, and other health care providers. The company also distributes non-pharmaceutical products including health and beauty aids. **Corporate headquarters location:** This location. **Parent company:** Cardinal Health. **Listed on:** New York Stock Exchange. **Stock exchange symbol:** BDY.

BRISTOL-MYERS SQUIBB
2400 West Lloyd Expressway, Evansville IN 47721. 812/429-7800. **Contact:** Human Resources. **World Wide Web address:** http://www.bms.com. **Description:** A pharmaceutical and related health care products company. **Positions advertised include:** Manager, Enterprise Application Integration; Category Leader; Occupational Health Nurse; Manager, Training and Development; Project Manager; Manager, External Manufacturing; Sr. Product Development Scientist; Sr. Nutrition Scientist; Sr. Principal Research Scientist; Sr. Process Engineer; External Planning Manager; Production Assurance Specialist; QA Analyst; Manager, Consumer Marketing. **Corporate headquarters location:** New York NY. **Listed on:** New York Stock Exchange. **Stock exchange symbol:** BMY. **Number of employees worldwide:** 43,000.

CENTRAL INDIANA REGIONAL BLOOD CENTER
3450 North Meridian Street, Indianapolis IN 46208. 317/916-5150. **Fax:** 317/916-5085. **Contact:** Human Resources. **E-mail address:** employment @cirbc.org. **World Wide Web address:** http://www.cirbc.org. **Description:** A nonprofit blood center and one of the nation's largest blood banking institutions. The Central Indiana Regional Blood Center provides blood services as well as bone and tissue products. Founded in 1952. **Positions advertised include:** Blood Collection Technician; Components Technician; Director of Testing; Field Recruiter; Laboratory Assistant; Materials Handler; Telephone Recruiter.

COVANCE LABORATORIES INC.
8211 Scicore Drive, Indianapolis IN 46214. 317/271-1200. **Contact:** Human Resources. **World Wide Web address:** http://www.covance.com. **Description:** A life sciences firm providing biological and chemical research services. Covance Laboratories is also a supplier of laboratory animals and biological products. Clients include research institutes, industrial companies, government agencies, and manufacturers of pharmaceuticals, chemicals, food, and cosmetics. **Positions advertised include:** Assistant Buyer; Technical Associate; Extraction Analyst; Pathologist Associate; Special Chemistry Technologist. **Corporate headquarters location:** Princeton NJ.

ELI LILLY AND COMPANY
Lilly Corporate Center, Indianapolis IN 46285. 317/276-2000. **Contact:** Human Resources. **World Wide Web address:** http://www.lilly.com. **Description:** Discovers, develops, manufactures, and sells a broad line of human health products and pharmaceuticals including diagnostic products; monoclonal antibody-based diagnostic tests for colon, prostate, and testicular cancer; medical devices; patient vital-signs measurement and electrocardiograph systems; implantable cardiac pacemakers and related medical systems; and anti-infectives and diabetic care products. The company also produces animal health products such as animal antibiotics and special animal feed additives. **NOTE:** Jobseekers are encouraged to apply via the Website: https://jobs.lilly.com. **Positions advertised include:** Analytical Chemist; Associate Biologist; Associate Environmental Consultant; Associate Project Manager; Behavioral Pharmacologist; Biologist, Cancer Research; Clinical Data Management Coordinator. **Corporate headquarters location:** This location. **Listed on:** New York Stock Exchange. **Stock exchange symbol:** LLY.

MEAD JOHNSON NUTRITIONALS
2400 West Lloyd Expressway, Evansville IN 47721. 812/429-5000. **Contact:** Employment. **World Wide Web address:** http://www.meadjohnson.com. **Description:** Engaged in the research, manufacture, and marketing of pharmaceutical and nutritional products for the consumer and pharmaceutical markets. **Corporate headquarters location:** This location. **Parent company:** Bristol-Myers Squibb Company. **Number of employees at this location:** 2,500. **Number of employees worldwide:** 5,000.

MID-AMERICA CLINICAL LABORATORIES
2560 North Shadeland Avenue, Indianapolis IN 46219. 317/803-1010. **Fax:** 317/803-0097. **Contact:** Jane Lloyd, Human Resources. **E-mail address:** hr@macl1.com. **World Wide Web address:** http://www.maclonline.com. **Description:** This location houses administrative offices. Overall, Mid-America Clinical Laboratories provide lab services for Community East Hospital.

PATHOLOGISTS ASSOCIATED
1200 West White River Boulevard, Muncie IN 47303. 765/284-7795. **Fax:** 765/741-5604. **Contact:** Human Resources. **World Wide Web address:** http://www.palab.com. **Description:** A clinical laboratory that provides services for Ball Memorial Hospital. **NOTE:** Interested applicants should complete the employment application available on the website.

Submit applications to: Pathologists Association, Attention: Human Resources Department, 1200 West White River Boulevard, Muncie IN 47303. **Positions advertised include:** Phlebotomist; Medical Technologist; Lab Supply Coordinator; Specimen Processing Assistant.

SCHWARZ PHARMA MANUFACTURING
1101 C Avenue West, Seymour IN 47274. 812/523-5400. **Contact:** Rhonda Wells, Human Resources Manager. **World Wide Web address:** http://www.schwarzusa.com. **Description:** Specializes in the manufacture of prescription cardiovascular pharmaceuticals, such as treatments for high blood pressure. Schwarz Pharma Manufacturing also produces tablet and liquid cough suppressants, analgesics, cold medications, and other nonprescription drugs under the Schwarz label.

SERADYN INC.
7998 Georgetown Road, Suite 1000, Indianapolis IN 46268. 317/610-3800. **Contact:** Human Resources Department. **World Wide Web address:** http://www.seradyn.com. **Description:** Seradyn consists of three distinct divisions: Diagnostics, Particle Technology, and Photovolt. Products include industrial and diagnostic instruments, as well as a full line of medical diagnostic reagents. **Corporate headquarters location:** This location. **Operations at this facility include:** This location manufactures medical test kits. **Parent company:** Mitsubishi Chemical Corporation.

Iowa

AIN COMPANY, LLC
1223 Oakes Drive, Iowa City IA 52245. 319/621-7995. **Contact:** Human Resources. **E-mail address:** info@aincompany.com. **World Wide Web address:** http://www.aincompany.com. **Description:** Develops software for simulating neurobiology.

AMES LABORATORY
105 Technical and Administrative Services Facility (TASF), Iowa State University, Ames IA 50011-3020. 515/294-2680. **Fax:** 525/294-5741. **Contact:** Human Resources. **World Wide Web address:** http://www.ameslab.gov. **Description:** A U.S. Department of Energy laboratory operated by Iowa State University. The lab performs basic and applied energy research. **NOTE:** Applicants must apply online at http://www.iastatejobs.com. **Positions advertised include:** Administrator; Scientist; Engineer; Chemist; Physicist. **Operations at this facility include:** Research and Development.

BIOFORCE NANOSCIENCES
1615 Golden Aspen Drive, Suite 101, Ames IA 50010. 515/233-8333. **Fax:** 515/233-8337. **Contact:** Human Relations. **E-mail address:** hr@bioforcenano.com. **World Wide Web address:** http://www.bioforcenano.com. **Description:** A rapidly expanding developer of ultra-miniaturized array technologies for biomolecular analysis. **NOTE**: Search posted openings and apply on-line. **Positions advertised include:** Molecular/Cell Biology Research Associate.

FORT DODGE ANIMAL HEALTH
800 Fifth Street NW, Fort Dodge IA 50501. 913/664-7000. **Contact:** Kevin Scarich, Human Resources, ext.: 2361. **E-mail address:** fprtdodge@trackcarriers.com. **World Wide Web address:** http://www.wyeth.com. **Description:** Formerly part of the American Home Products Corporation, this division manufactures and distributes prescription and over-the-counter animal health care products distributing to over 100 countries and specializing in veterinary biological vaccines. Founded in 1912. **NOTE:** Inquiries and resumes may be sent to the company headquarters: Staffing Manager, 9225 Indian Creek Parkway, Suite 400, Overland Park KS 66210, or fax: 913/664-7195. **Corporate headquarters location:** Overland Park KS. **Affiliates include:** Wyeth Pharmaceuticals; Wyeth Research; Wyeth Consumer Healthcare. **Parent company:** Wyeth (Collegeville PA). **Operations at this facility include:** Manufacturing of pharmaceuticals and biological vaccines. **Number of employees at this location:** 450. **Number of employees nationwide:** 1,700. **Number of employees worldwide:** 4,000.

INTEGRATED DNA TECHNOLOGIES, INC.
1710 Commercial Park, Coralville IA 52241. 319/626-8400. **Toll-free phone:** 800/328-2661. **Fax:** 319/626-9611. **Contact:** Heidi Skow, Human Resources Assistant. **E-mail address:** hskow@idtdna.com. **World Wide Web address:** http://www.idtdna.com. **Description:** Integrated DNA Technologies, Inc. researches and supplies oligonucleotide synthesis to biotechnology firms. Since 1987. **NOTE:** For sales positions contact executive offices: IDT, 8930 Gross Point Road, Suite 700, Skokie IL 60077. May search posted openings and apply on-line or submit resume by e-mail. **Positions advertised include:** Customer Service Representative; Senior Enterprise Applications Specialist; Senior Database Administrator; Senior Technical Writer; Order Administrator; Entry-Level Enterprise Applications Specialist; Patent Technical Assistant; Programmer/Business Analyst. **Corporate headquarters location:** This location. **Operations at this facility include:** Administration; Research and Development.

NEWLINK GENETICS CORPORATION
2901 South Loop Drive, Suite 3900, Ames IA 50010. 515/296-5555. **Fax:** 515/296-5557. **Contact:** Shelley Kinnear. **E-mail address:** skinnear@linkp.com. **World Wide Web address:** http://www.newlinkgenetics.com. **Description:** A biopharmaceutical company that works to produce diagnostic and therapeutic agents to improve the lives of cancer patients. **NOTE**: Search openings and apply on-line. **Positions advertised include:** Computational Biologist; Transgenic Mouse Breeding Colony Technician; Senior and Postdoctoral Scientists.

NOVARTIS ANIMAL HEALTH US INC.
1447 140th Street, Larchwood IA 51241. 712/477-2811. **Contact:** Human Resources. **World Wide Web address:** http://www.novartis.com. **Description:** Novartis engaged in research and development of vaccines for farm animals and domestic animals. This branch focuses on farm animal pharmaceutical research and development. **NOTE**: Search posted openings and apply on-line via corporate web site only. No paper resumes will be accepted. **Corporate headquarters location:** Greensboro, North Carolina.

PHARMACOM CORPORATION
100 Oakdale Campus, Iowa City IA 52242. 319/335-4771. **Fax:** 319/335-4482. **Contact:** Human Resources. **E-mail address:** corporate@pharmacom.us. **World Wide Web address:** http://www.pharmacom.us. **Description:** Develops lab-on-a-chip technology. **NOTE:** Search posted openings and apply online only. No paper resumes accepted and no telephone contact. **Positions advertised include:** Research Scientist; Nanotechnologists; Software Developers; Bioinformatics Scientists; Lab Technicians; Microelectronic Engineers.

PIONEER HI-BRED INTERNATIONAL, INC.
400 Locust Street, Suite 700, P.O. Box 14454, Des Moines IA 50306. 515/248-4800. **Toll-free phone:** 800/247-6803 ext.4000. **Fax:** 515/248-4999. **Contact:** Frank Forest, Human Resources. **E-mail address:** apply@pioneer.com. **World Wide Web address:** http://www.pioneer.com. **Description:** A biotechnology company and the largest soybean seed and corn producer, the company genetically engineers high-yield hybrid seeds for farmers growing animal feeds. The company manufactures seeds for alfalfa, canola, sorghum, sunflowers, wheat, silage and hay inoculants. Founded in 1926. **NOTE:** Entry-level positions and part-time jobs are offered. Search posted openings and apply on-line only. No paper resumes are accepted. Telephone contact is discouraged. **Positions advertised include:** Administrative Assistant; Postdoctoral Researcher; Human Resource Director; Human Resource Manager; Laboratory Technician; Market Research Analyst; Production Technician;

Public Relations Coordinator; Purchasing Operations Manager; Research Associate; Research Coordinator; Research Scientist; Security Officer; Senior Application Developer. **Special programs:** Internships. **Corporate headquarters location:** This location. **International locations:** Worldwide. **Parent company:** Dupont. **President:** Richard L. (Rick) McConnell. **Annual sales/revenues:** $2 billion. **Number of employees:** 5,000.

Kansas

QUEST DIAGNOSTICS

10101 Renner Boulevard, Lenexa KS 66219. 913/888-1770. **Contact:** Human Resources. **World Wide Web address:** http://www.questdiagnostics.com. **Description:** Provides medical and drug testing for the insurance industry as well as for employees to detect the existence of infection, cardiovascular disease, HIV, and tobacco use. The company's tests are specifically designed to provide a standardized format to assist insurance companies in objectively evaluating the mortality or morbidity risk posed by policy applicants. Formerly Home Office Reference Laboratory, the company is a centralized laboratory in the Kansas City area that provides testing and information services including risk assessment information, healthcare services, and drug testing to determine eligibility and premium payment levels. Testing uses individual specimens as well as telephone inspections and motor vehicle reports. The company also performs substance abuse testing, urinalysis, and Pap smears. **NOTE:** Apply online only. **Positions advertised include:** Marketing Representative; Buyer Position; Currier Supervisor Positions; Associate C Engineer Position; Medical Lab Tech; Setup Associate; Technical Account Manager; Account Marketing Associate. **Other U.S. locations:** Nationwide. **International locations:** Canada.

SNYDER MEMORIAL RESEARCH FOUNDATION

1407 Wheat Road, Winfield KS 67156. 620/221-4080. **Fax:** 620/221-2684. **Contact:** Human Resources. **E-mail address**: tsmith@snydermri.org. **World Wide Web address:** http://www.snydermri.org. **Description:** A foundation focusing on biomedical and cancer research. **Positions advertised include:** Biological Scientist. **Operations at this facility include:** Research and Development. **President:** Jim Barnthouse. **Number of employees at this location:** 10.

Kentucky

OMNICARE, INC.

100 East RiverCenter Boulevard, Suite 1600, Covington KY 41011-1558. 859/392-3300. **Fax:** 859/392-3330. **Contact:** Human Resources. **E-mail address:** human.resources@omnicare.com. **World Wide Web address:** http://www.omnicare.com. **Description:** Provides pharmaceutical services to long-term care facilities including nursing homes and rehabilitation centers. **NOTE:** Resumes may be submitted via e-mail. **Corporate headquarters location:** This location. **Other U.S. locations:** Nationwide. **Subsidiaries include:** Omnicare Senior Pharmacy Services; Omnicare Geriatric Pharmaceutical Care; Omnicare Health management Programs; Omnicare Senior Health outcomes; Omnicare Information Solutions; Omnicare Clinical Research; Omnicare PBM Plus; excelleRx; RxCrossroads. **Listed on:** New York Stock Exchange. **Stock exchange symbol:** OCR.

QUEST DIAGNOSTICS

2277 Charleston Drive, Lexington KY 40505. 859/299-3866. **Toll-free phone:** 800/366-7522. **Fax:** 859/293-7406. **Contact:** Barbara Senters, Human Resources. **World Wide Web Address:** http://www.questdiagnostics.com. **Description:** Provides a broad range of clinical laboratory services to health care clients that include physicians, hospitals, clinics, dialysis centers, pharmaceutical companies, and corporations. The company performs tests on blood, urine, and other bodily fluids and tissues to provide information for health and well-being. **NOTE:** Online applications are available. **Positions advertised include:** Route Service Representative; Phlebotomy Services Representative; Genomics & Esoteric Test Specialist; Specimen I Technician. **Corporate headquarters location:** Teterboro NJ. **Other area locations:** Bowling Green KY; Frankfort KY; Louisville KY. **Other U.S. locations:** Nationwide. **International locations:** Mexico; United Kingdom; Germany; France; Belgium; Brazil. **Listed on:** New York Stock Exchange. **Stock exchange symbol:** DGX.

Louisiana

BASF CORPORATION

8800 Line Avenue, Shreveport LA 71106. 318/861-8200. **Fax:** 318/861-8297. **Contact:** Human Resources. **E-mail address:** recruiting@basf.com. **World Wide Web address:** http://www.basf.com. **Description:** A chemical company whose diverse product line includes plastics, colorants and pigments, dispersions, fine chemicals, automotive and industrial coatings, crop-protection agents, and oil and gas. **NOTE:** Entry-level positions are offered. Job seekers may submit applications online, as paper resumes are no longer accepted. **Special programs:** Internships; Professional Development Program; Tuition Reimbursement Program; Employee Stock Purchase Program. **Corporate headquarters location:** Mount Olive NJ. **Other area locations:** Geismar LA. **Other U.S. locations:** Nationwide. **International locations:** Worldwide. **Subsidiaries include:** BASF Aktiengesllschaft; BASF Canada; BASF Mexicana. **Parent company:** BASF AG. **Operations at this facility include:** Production; Laboratory; Administration; Maintenance. **Listed on:** New York Stock Exchange; major European stock exchanges in Frankfurt, London, Paris, and Zurich. **Stock exchange symbol:** New York (BF); Frankfurt (BAS); London (BFA); Paris (BA); Zurich (BAS). **CEO/Chairman:** Klaus Peter Lobbe. **Sales/revenues:** $29 billion. **Number of employees at this location:** 205. **Number of employees nationwide:** 12,000. **Number of employees worldwide:** Over 93,000.

JACOBS ENGINEERING GROUP, INC.

4949 Essen Lane, Baton Rouge LA 70809. 225/769-7700. **Fax:** 225/768-5087. **World Wide Web address:** http://www.jacobs.com. **Description:** Provides professional technical services, including scientific consulting, construction, and engineering, to companies worldwide. Specialties include aerospace, oil and gas, biotechnology, pulp and paper, buildings, and pharmaceuticals. **NOTE:** Search current job openings and apply online. Submit a resume if available positions do not meet interests. **Positions advertised include:** Control Systems Engineer; Document Controller; Electrical Engineer; Engineering Project Manager; Field Draftsperson; JMMS Support Analyst; Material Controller; PC Support Technician; Piping Designer; Project Engineer; Senior Buyer; Scheduler/Planner; Structural Designer. **Corporate headquarters location:** Pasadena CA. **Other area locations:** Lake Charles. **Other U.S locations:** Nationwide. **International locations:** Worldwide. **Listed on:** New York Stock Exchange. **Stock exchange symbol:** JEC. **Director/President:** Craig L. Martin. **Annual Revenues:** $5 billion.

QUEST DIAGNOSTICS

4648 South Interstate 10 Service Road West, Metairie LA 70001. 504/889-2307. **Fax:** 504/889-2678. **Contact:** Dee Vu. **World Wide Web address:** http://www.questdiagnostics.com. **Description:** Provides a broad range of clinical laboratory services to health care clients such as physicians, hospitals, clinics, dialysis centers, pharmaceutical companies, and corporations. The company offers and performs tests on blood, urine, and other bodily fluids and tissues to provide information for health and well-being. **NOTE:** Search current job listings and apply online. **Positions advertised include:** Phlebotomy Services Representative. **Corporate headquarters location:** Teterboro NJ. **Other area locations:** Baton Rouge; Kenner; New Orleans. **Other U.S. locations:** Nationwide. **Listed on:** New York Stock Exchange.

Stock exchange symbol: DGX. **CEO/Chairman:** Surya N. Mohapatra. **Annual sales/revenues:** $5.1 billion. **Number of employees nationwide:** 27,000.

Maine

THE BAKER COMPANY
P.O. Drawer E, 161 Gatehouse Road, Sanford ME 04073. 207/324-8773. **Toll-free phone:** 800/992-2537. **Fax:** 207/324-3869. **Contact**: Joel Plourde, Human Resources. **E-mail address:** jplourde@bakerco.com. **World Wide Web address:** http://www.bakerco.com. **Description:** Designs and manufactures air containment and clean air products for life science, pharmaceutical, industrial, and medical applications. **Corporate headquarters location:** This location. **Other U.S. locations:** Nationwide. **Number of employees at this location:** 180.

BINAX INC.
10 Southgate Road, Scarborough ME 04074. 207/730-5700. **Fax:** 207/730-5710. **Toll-free phone:** 800/323-3199. **Contact:** Human Resources. **E-mail address:** ddende@binax.com. **World Wide Web address:** http://www.binax.com. **Description:** A biotechnology company focused on developing technology for rapid diagnostic testing. **NOTE**: No telephone contact allowed. Cover letter is required. Search posted openings and apply on-line, by e-mail, or fax. **Positions advertised include:** Senior Manager Critical Reagents; Director Quality Systems Regulatory Compliance; Manufacturing Engineer; Machine Operator. **Corporate headquarters location:** This location.

BIODESIGN INTERNATIONAL
60 Industrial Park Road, Saco ME 04072. 207/283-6500. **Toll-free phone:** 888/530-0140. **Fax:** 207/283-4800. **Contact:** S. Enman, Human Resources. **E-mail address:** senmam@biodesign.com. **World Wide Web address:** http://www.biodesign.com. **Description:** Manufactures and markets polyclonal and monoclonal antibodies, purified antigens, and assay development reagents. BIODESIGN International also offers custom services for research and industrial clients. Custom services include antibody production, analysis, conjugation, and other laboratory processes. Founded in 1987. **Positions advertised include:** Marketing/Product Manager; Technical Sales Representative. **Corporate headquarters location:** This location.

ENVIROLOGIX
500 Riverside Industrial Parkway, Portland ME 04103-1486. 207/797-0300. **Fax:** 207/797-7533. **Toll-free phone:** 866/408-4597. **Contact:** Peter Johnson, Human Resources. **E-mail address:** hr-web@envirologix.com. **World Wide Web address:** http://www.envirologix.com. **Description:** Develops and produces rapid test kits for identifying molds, fungi, and natural toxins. **NOTE:** Employment application is available online.

IDEXX LABORATORIES, INC.
One IDEXX Drive, Westbrook ME 04092. 207/856-0300. **Toll-free phone:** 800/548-6733. **Fax:** 207/856-0625. **Contact:** Donalee Santoro, Human Resources. **World Wide Web address:** http://www.idexx.com. **Description:** Develops and commercializes advanced biotechnology-based and chemistry-based detection systems for veterinary, food, and environmental testing applications. The veterinary products are used to detect and monitor diseases, physiologic disorders, immune status, hormone and enzyme levels, blood chemistry and electrolyte levels, blood counts, and other substances or conditions in animals. The food and environmental products are used to detect various microbiological and chemical contaminants in food products and water, and the biomedical products are used in clinical research, pharmaceutical development, and other life applications. **NOTE:** Search posted openings and apply on-line. No paper resumes are accepted and telephone contact is discouraged. **Other area locations:** Portland ME. **Other U.S. locations:** Nationwide. **International locations:** Worldwide. **Number of employees worldwide:** 500.

IMMUCELL CORPORATION
56 Evergreen Drive, Portland ME 04103. 207/878-2770. **Toll-free phone:** 800/466-8235. **Fax:** 207/878-2117. **Contact:** Human Resources. **E-mail address:** info@immucell.com. **World Wide Web address:** http://www.immucell.com. **Description:** Develops, manufactures, and markets milk-derived, passive, antibody products to prevent gastrointestinal diseases in both humans and animals. The company's business is to utilize its core technology (the production of commercial quantities of pathogen-specific antibodies from cow's milk) in two business areas that share research, development, and manufacturing technologies and resources: human disease treatment and prevention products, and dairy and beef animal health products. **NOTE**: Search openings and apply on-line as available at www.jobsinme.com. **Listed on:** NASDAQ. **Stock exchange symbol:** ICCC.

THE JACKSON LABORATORY
600 Main Street, Bar Harbor ME 04609. 207/288-6000. **Fax:** 207/288-6106. **Contact:** Sandy McFarland, Human Resources. **E-mail address:** jobs@jax.com. **World Wide Web address:** http://www.jax.org. **Description:** The Jackson Laboratory is an independent, nonprofit institution. A staff of more than 30 scientists conducts research directed toward two general goals: the development of new knowledge of mammalian genetics, and the investigation of basic biological processes and their relationships to human diseases. In addition to research, the laboratory distributes nearly 2 million mice annually and offers research-training programs for high school, undergraduate, graduate, and postdoctoral level students. **NOTE:** Only online applications accepted. **Positions advertised include:** Grants Coordinator; Senior Product Coordinator; Human Resourcse Information Systems Assistant; Production Technician Trainee; Technical Information Services Specialist; Data Architect; Security Guard; Environmental Monitoring Technician; Research Assistant; Laboratory Technician; Director of Directed Research; Biomedical Technologist; Database User Support Specialist; Manager – Biostatistician; Scientific Curator – Various Departments; Senior Veterinarian. **Corporate headquarters location:** This location. **Number of employees at this location:** 650.

MAINE BIOTECHNOLOGY SERVICES, INC.
1037-R Forest Avenue, Portland ME 04103. 207/797-5454. **Toll-free phone:** 800/925-9476. **Fax:** 207/797-5595. **Contact:** Human Resources. **E-mail address:** msullivan@mainebiotechnology.com. **World Wide Web address:** http://www.mainebiotechnology.com. **Description:** A contracting firm that produces monoclonal and polyclonal antibodies for biotechnology companies.

Maryland

ALBA THERAPEUTICS CORPORATION
800 West Baltimore Street, Suite 400, Baltimore MD 21201. 410/319-0780. **Fax:** 410/319-0799. **Contact:** Human Resources. **E-mail address:** careers@albatherapeutics.com. **World Wide Web address:** http://www.albatherapeutics.com. **Description:** A biopharmaceutical company focused on the development, production, and marketing of pharmaceuticals for the treatment of inflammatory and immune mediated diseases. **Positions advertised include:** Clinical Research Assistant; Senior Accountant.

ALION SCIENCE AND TECHNOLOGY
185 Admiral Cochrane Drive, Annapolis MD 21401. 410/573-7000. **Fax:** 410/573-7033. **Contact:** Human Resources. **World Wide Web address:** http://www.alionscience.com. **Description:** A research and development company whose primary customer is the U.S. government. **Positions advertised include:** Assistant Programming Analyst; Assistant Engineer; Research Communications Analyst. **Note:** Applicants can search and submit for specific jobs listed currently online. **Corporate headquarters location:** McLean VA. **Other area locations:** Lanham MD. **Other U.S.**

locations: IL; NY; FL; PA; AL; IN; MI; VA; WA. **Operations at this facility include:** Administration; Research and Development. **CEO/Chairman:** Bahman Atefi. **Number of employees at this location:** 500. **Number of employees nationwide:** 1,700.

ALPHARMA USPD
7205 Windsor Boulevard, Baltimore MD 21244. 410/298-1000. **Toll-free phone:** 800/638-9096. **Fax:** 410/298-8187. **Contact:** Human Resources. **World Wide Web address:** http://www.alpharma.com. **Description:** Alpha, Incorporated is an international pharmaceutical company that develops, manufactures, and markets specialty generic and proprietary human pharmaceuticals and animal health products. Business segments include The Animal Health Division, which manufactures and markets antibiotics and other feed additives to the poultry and swine industries; The Aquatic Animal Health Division, which serves the aquaculture industry and is a manufacturer and marketer of vaccines for farmed fish; and The Fine Chemicals Division, which is a basic producer of specialty bulk antibiotics. **NOTE:** Online applications are available. **Positions advertised include:** Validation Engineer; Training Specialist; Microbiologist; Quality Control Analytical Lab Supervision; Technical Service Metrology Supervisor. **Corporate headquarters location:** Fort Lee NJ. **Other area locations:** Columbia MD; Owing Mills MD. **Other U.S. locations:** Elizabeth NJ; Lincolnton NC. **International locations:** Oslo, Norway. **Operations at this facility include:** This location is part of Alpha, Incorporated's U.S. Pharmaceuticals Division and manufactures liquid pharmaceuticals, creams, and ointments. **Listed on:** New York Stock Exchange. **Stock exchange symbol:** ALO. **Annual sales/revenues:** More than $100 million. **Number of employees at this location:** 600. **Number of employees nationwide:** 1,200.

BIORELIANCE
14920 Broschart Road, Rockville MD 20850-3349. 301/738-1000. **Fax:** 301/738-1033. **Contact:** Human Resources. **E-mail address:** info@bioreliance.com. **World Wide Web address:** http://www.bioreliance.com. **Description:** A contract service organization that provides development and nonclinical services to biotechnology and pharmaceutical companies. BioReliance provides development, testing, and manufacturing services that cover the product from preclinical development through licensed production. **Positions advertised include:** Account Management; Business Analyst; Chemical Repository Coordinator; Desktop Supply Specialist; Laboratory Assistant; Laboratory Directory; Maintenance Technician; QA Auditor; Receptionist; Financial Analyst; Study Director; Test Article Reception. **Corporate headquarters location:** This location. **Other U.S. locations:** Bethesda MD. **International locations:** Heidelberg, Germany; Tokyo, Japan; Stirling, Scotland. **Listed on:** NASDAQ. **Stock exchange symbol:** BREL. **CEO:** Capers McDonald. **Number of employees worldwide:** Approximately 600.

CAMBREX BIOSCIENCE WALKERSVILLE, INC.
8330 Biggs Ford Road, Walkersville MD 21793. 301/898-7025. **Fax:** 301/845-2435. **Contact:** Human Resources. **E-mail address:** human.resources@cambrex.com. **World Wide Web address:** http://www.cambrex.com. **Description:** Manufactures cell culture products used to develop drugs and vaccines. Cell culture products include living cell cultures; chemically defined nutrient medics necessary for growing the cell cultures; and sera used to supplement the media. BioWhittaker, Incorporated also manufactures endotoxin detection products, which aid pharmaceutical and medical device manufacturers in determining whether their products are safe for humans. **NOTE:** Entry-level positions are offered. **Positions advertised include:** Controllership Financial Representative; Staff Accountant; Accounting Manager; Tax Research & Plan Manager; Treasurer; Facilities Technician; Maintenance Technician; Human Resources Director; Manufacturing Manager; Fermentation Support; Quality Assurance Technician; Material Handler; Operations Technician; Quality Assurance Analyst. **Special programs:** Internships; Training; Summer Jobs; Tuition Reimbursement Program; Scholarship Program. **Office hours:** Monday - Friday, 8:00 a.m. - 5:00 p.m. **Corporate headquarters location:** East Rutherford NJ. **Parent company:** Cambrex Corporation. **Listed on:** New York Stock Exchange. **Stock exchange symbol:** CBM. **CEO:** James A. Mack. **Sales/revenues:** Approximately $530 million. **Number of employees worldwide:** Over 2,000.

CELERA GENOMICS GROUP
45 West Gude Drive, Rockville MD 20850. 240/453-3000. **Toll-free phone:** 877/235-3721. **Fax:** 240/453-4000. **Contact:** Human Resources. **World Wide Web address:** http://www.celera.com. **Description:** Engaged in the discovery and development of therapies for cancer, autoimmune and inflammatory diseases such as asthma and rheumatoid arthritis. Founded in 1998. **Positions advertised include:** Senior Associate Scientist, Cell Biology. **Other U.S. locations:** Alameda CA; San Francisco CA. **Parent company:** Applera Corporation. **Listed on:** New York Stock Exchange. **Stock exchange symbol:** CRA.

CHESAPEAKE BIOLOGICAL LABORATORIES, INC.
1111 South Paca Street, Baltimore MD 21230-2591. 410/843-5000. **Toll-free phone:** 800/441-4225. **Fax:** 410/843-4414. **Contact:** Human Resources. **E-mail address:** info@cblinc.com. **World Wide Web address:** http://www.cblinc.com. **Description:** A pharmaceuticals manufacturing company that provides sterile finish processing and specializes in single-dose vials and syringes. **Special programs:** Training and Development Program.

EMERGENT BIOSOLUTIONS
300 Professional Drive, Suite 100, Gaithersburg MD 20879. 301/590-0129. **Fax:** 301/590-1251. **Contact:** Human Resources. **World Wide Web address:** http://www.antexbio.com. **Description:** Develops pharmaceuticals to treat, detect, and prevent infectious diseases. **Positions advertised include:** Director of Formulation Development; Director of Process and Analytical Development; Manager of Analytical Methods; Quality Assurance/Regulatory Manager. **Corporate headquarters location:** This location.

HUMAN GENOME SCIENCES, INC.
14200 Shady Grove Road, Rockville MD 20850-3338. 301/309-8504. **Fax:** 301/309-1845. **Contact:** Human Resources. **E-mail address:** resume@hgsi.com. **World Wide Web address:** http://www.hgsi.com. **Description:** A biotechnology research firm employing cell biology, molecular biology, genomic research, and other sciences in order to discover ways to prevent and cure diseases by using the body's own proteins to make pharmaceuticals. The company is also involved in the isolation and characterization of human genes. **Positions advertised include:** Associate Director; Bio Processing Associate; Engineering Scientist; Cleaning & Analytical Validation Manager; Clinical Applications Systems Administration; Clinical Systems Administration Custodian. **Special programs:** Educational Assistance Program. **Corporate headquarters location:** This location. **Listed on:** NASDAQ. **Stock exchange symbol:** HGSI. **CEO/Chairman:** William A. Haseltine.

JOHNS HOPKINS UNIVERSITY APPLIED PHYSICS LABORATORY
11100 Johns Hopkins Road, Laurel MD 20723-6099. 240/228-3172, or 443/778-3172. **Fax:** 240/228-5274. **Contact:** Employment Office. **E-mail address:** recruiter0@jhuapl.edu. **World Wide Web address:** http://www.jhuapl.edu. **Description:** A nonprofit research and development laboratory, the Applied Physics Laboratory (APL) of Johns Hopkins University makes contributions in defense, space, and biomedicine. **NOTE:** Entry-level positions are offered. To contact the employment office directly, call

240/228-3172. **Positions advertised include:** Network Technician; Telecommunications Engineer; Network Workstation Support Engineer; Network Support Section Supervisor; Senior Administrative Specialist; Maintenance Electrician; Project Manager; Biomechanical Engineer; Aerosol Facility Test Operator; Electrical Engineer; Mechanical Engineer; Post-Doctoral Epidemiologist; Spacecraft Systems Engineer; Space/Atmospheric Physicist; Computer Science Researcher; Strike Warfare Project Manager. **Special programs:** Continuing Education Program; Scholarship Program. **Number of employees at this location:** 3,350.

MARTEK BIOSCIENCES CORPORATION
6480 Dobbin Road, Columbia MD 21045. 410/740-0081. **Fax:** 410/740-2985. **Contact:** Human Resources. **E-mail address:** jobs@martekbio.com. **World Wide Web address:** http://www.martekbio.com. **Description:** Engaged in the research, development, and production of nutritional supplements, food ingredients, reagents, and pharmaceuticals drawn from the ocean's microalgae supply. Founded in 1985. **Positions advertised include:** Clinical Research Associate; Clinical Research Manager; Competitive Intelligence Analyst; Molecular Bio Research Associate. **Corporate headquarters location:** This location. **Other U.S. locations:** Boulder CO; Winchester KY. **Listed on:** NASDAQ. **Stock exchange symbol:** MATK. **President:** Richard J. Radmer. **Number of employees nationwide:** 172.

MEDIMMUNE, INC.
One Medimmune Way, Gaithersburg MD 20878. 301/398-0000. **Fax:** 301/527-4215. **Contact:** Human Resources. **E-mail address:** JobOpenings@medimmune.com. **World Wide Web address:** http://www.medimmune.com. **Description:** Researches and develops biopharmaceuticals for the infectious disease and organ transplant markets. **Positions advertised include:** Clinical Data Analyst; Director of Project Planning and Alliance Management; Associate Scientist; Administrative Assistant; Clinical Liaison; Senior Project Engineer; Accounting Assistant. **Note:** Do not e-mail resumes. Only include your contact information and information request. **Special programs:** Educational Assistance Program. **Corporate headquarters location:** This location. **Other area locations:** Frederick MD. **Other U.S. locations:** CA; PA. **International locations:** United Kingdom; the Netherlands. **Subsidiaries include:** Medimmune Oncology; U.S. Bioscience; Medimmune Vaccines. **Listed on:** NASDAQ. **Stock exchange symbol:** MEDI. **Founder/Chairman:** Wayne D. Hockmeyer. **Sales/revenue:** $619 million. **Number of employees nationwide:** Over 1,500.

OSIRIS THERAPEUTICS, INC.
2001 Aliceanna Street, Baltimore MD 21231-3043. 410/522-5005. **Fax:** 410/522-5519. **Contact:** Human Resources. **E-mail address:** hr@osiristx.com. **World Wide Web address:** http://www.osiristx.com. **Description:** Osiris Therapeutics is a clinical stage biotechnology company founded for the purpose of commercializing stem cell products harvested from a readily available but non-controversial source (adult bone marrow). **Positions advertised include:** Manufacturing Associate/Cell Technician. **Corporate headquarters location:** This location.

QUEST DIAGNOSTICS INCORPORATED
5411 Old Frederick Road, Suite 9, Baltimore MD 21229-2126. 410/744-0606. **Fax:** 410/869-0972. **Contact:** Personnel. **World Wide Web address:** http://www.questdiagnostics.com. **Description:** Provides a broad range of clinical laboratory services to health care clients that include physicians, hospitals, clinics, dialysis centers, pharmaceutical companies, and corporations. The company performs tests on blood, urine, and other bodily fluids and tissues to provide information for health and well-being. **NOTE:** Apply online. **Positions advertised include:** Quality Assurance; Sales Associate; Marking Associate; Specimen Processor; Medical Operator; Administrative Assistant; Laboratory Management; Accounts Receivable; Human Resources Manager. **Corporate headquarters location:** Teterboro NJ. **Other U.S. locations:** Nationwide. **Operations at this facility include:** This location is a laboratory facility. **Listed on:** New York Stock Exchange. **Stock exchange symbol:** DGX.

SCIENCE APPLICATIONS INTERNATIONAL CORPORATION (SAIC)
1129 Business Parkway South, Suite 10, Westminster MD 21157. 410/876-0280. **Contact:** Human Resources. **World Wide Web address:** http://www.saic.com. **Description:** A research and engineering firm offering technology development, computer systems integration, technical support, and computer hardware and software products. Services are aimed at the energy, environment, health care, information technology, Internet, maritime, national security, space, telecommunications, transportation, and logistics fields. **NOTE:** Must apply online. Part-time and temporary positions are offered. **Positions advertised include:** Subcontracts Supervisor; Public Legislative Affairs Analyst; Biology Tech Writer; Systems Engineer; Regulatory Affairs; Scientist; Biomedical R&D Support Specialist; Document Specialist; Finance Analyst; Budget Analyst; Conference Administration Assistant; Word Processing Assistant; Clinical Quality Assurance Associate; Research Associate; Webmaster; Logistic Specialist; Clinical Project Manager; Post Doctoral Fellow; Visiting Scientist; Quality Assurance Manager. **Corporate headquarters location:** San Diego CA. **Listed on:** Privately held. **President/CEO:** J.R. Beyster. **Sales/revenue:** $6.1 billion. **Number of employees nationwide:** 1,100. **Number of employees worldwide:** Over 41,000.

SPHERIX INC.
12051 Indian Creek Court, Beltsville MD 20705. 301/419-3900. **Fax:** 301/623-2330. **Contact:** Human Resources. **E-mail address:** hrdept@spherix.com. **World Wide Web address:** http://www.spherix.com. **Description:** Develops and maintains hotlines for public and professional inquiries about the health care and government industries. Spherix also provides information technology services and develops biotech products. **Positions advertised include:** National Pharmaceutical Account Manager; National Government Account Manager; Customer Service Call Center Representative. **Office hours:** Monday - Friday, 8:00 a.m. - 5:30 p.m. **Corporate headquarters location:** This location. **Other area locations:** Cumberland MD. **Listed on:** NASDAQ. **Stock exchange symbol:** SPEX. **President:** David Affeldt. **Number of employees at this location:** 300. **Number of employees nationwide:** 500.

Massachusetts

ABBOTT BIORESEARCH CENTER
100 Research Drive, Worcester MA 01605. 508/849-2500. **Fax:** 508/755-8511 **Contact:** Human Resources. **E-mail address:** abcjobs@abbott.com. **World Wide Web address:** http://www.abbott.com/AbbottBioresearch. **Description:** Engaged in immunology and oncology research for the development of pharmaceuticals. **Positions advertised include:** Sr. Research Associate; Associate Director, Toxicology; QC Manager; Purchasing Manager; Sr. Scientist; Sr. Business Systems Analyst. **Corporate headquarters location:** Abbott Park IL. **Parent company:** Abbott Laboratories. **Other U.S. locations:** Nationwide. **International locations:** Worldwide.

ACAMBIS INC.
38 Sidney Street, 4th Floor, Cambridge MA 02139. 617/761-4200. **Fax:** 617/494-1741. **Contact:** Human Resources. **E-mail address:** careers@acambis.com. **World Wide Web address:** http://www.acambis.com. **Description:** Discovers and develops oral vaccines and noninjected antibody products to prevent and treat diseases that infect the human body at its mucous membranes. These tissues include the linings of the gastrointestinal, respiratory, and genitourinary tracts

and the surfaces of the eyes. Acambis is pursuing three principal product development programs that target diseases that have high rates of incidence including viral pneumonia in children, peptic ulcer disease, and antibiotic-associated diarrhea and colitis. **Positions advertised include:** Clinical Trial Manager; Regulatory Affairs Manager; Process Development Associate; QA Documentation Associate; Project Manager. **Corporate headquarters location:** Cambridge, England. **Listed on:** NASDAQ. **Stock exchange symbol:** ACAM.

ADVANCED MAGNETICS, INC.
61 Mooney Street, Cambridge MA 02138. 617/497-2070. **Fax:** 617/547-2445. **Contact:** Human Resources. **E-mail address:** contactus@advancedmagnets.com. **World Wide Web address:** http://www.advancedmagnetics.com. **Description:** Engaged in the development and manufacture of MRI contrast agents for the detection of cancer and other diseases. **Listed on:** American Stock Exchange. **Stock exchange symbol:** AVM.

ALKERMES, INC.
88 Sidney Street, Cambridge MA 02139. 617/494-0171. **Contact:** Human Resources. **World Wide Web address:** http://www.alkermes.com. **Description:** A pharmaceutical company that produces drug delivery systems for pharmaceutical agents. Alkermes produces four proprietary delivery systems including Cereport blood-brain permeabilizer, ProLease and Medisorb injectable sustained-release systems, RingCap and Dose Sipping oral delivery systems, and AIR pulmonary delivery systems. **Positions advertised include:** Clinical Manager; Drug Safety Associate; Medical Director; Statistical Programmer; Development Engineer; Scientist; Quality Control Microbiologist Supervisor; Regulatory Affairs Director; Regulatory Affairs Manager; Strategic Procurement Manager. **NOTE:** Apply and submit resumes online. **Corporate headquarters location:** This location. **Other area locations:** Chelsea MA. **Other U.S. locations:** Cincinnati OH. **Listed on:** NASDAQ. **Stock exchange symbol:** ALKS.

AMERICAN SCIENCE & ENGINEERING, INC.
829 Middlesex Turnpike, Billerica MA 01821. 978/262-8700. **Fax:** 978/262-8804. **Contact:** Human Resources. **E-mail address:** service@as-e.com. **World Wide Web address:** http://www.as-e.com. **Description:** Researches, develops, produces, and sells instrumentation for X-ray research for use in government space science programs and other scientific applications. The company also manufactures and sells a load management and automatic remote meter-reading system for public utilities; and develops, manufactures, and markets X-ray equipment. **Positions advertised include:** Principal Mechanical Engineer; Engineering Manager; Business Systems Analyst; Program Manager. **Corporate headquarters location:** This location. **Operations at this facility include:** Administration; Manufacturing; Research and Development; Sales; Service. **Listed on:** American Stock Exchange. **Stock exchange symbol:** ASE.

ANIKA THERAPEUTICS
160 New Boston Street, Woburn MA 01801. 781/932-6616. **Fax:** 781/935-7803. **Contact:** Personnel. **E-mail address:** contact@anikatherapeutics.org. **World Wide Web address:** http://www.anikatherapeutics.com. **Description:** Develops and commercializes products using hyaluronic acid (HA) for medical and therapeutic applications. Products include AMVISC, a high molecular weight HA product that is used as a viscoelastic agent in ophthalmic surgical procedures including cataract extraction and intraocular lens implantation; HYVISC, a high molecular weight HA product used for the treatment of joint dysfunction in horses due to noninfectious synovitis associated with equine osteoarthritis; ORTHOVISC, a high molecular weight, injectable HA product for the symptomatic treatment of osteoarthritis of the knee; and INCERT, a chemically modified, cross-linked form of HA designed to prevent the formation of post-surgical wound adhesions. Founded in 1993. **Positions advertised include:** Sr. Financial Analyst; Sr. Manufacturing Operator; Quality Assurance Manager. **Special programs:** Internships. **Corporate headquarters location:** This location. **Listed on:** NASDAQ. **Stock exchange symbol:** ANIK.

ANTIGENICS INC.
3 Forbes Road, Lexington MA 02421-7305. 781/674-4400. **Fax:** 781/674-4200. **Contact:** Human Resources. **E-mail address:** recruiter@antigenics.com. **World Wide Web address:** http://www.antigenics.com. **Description:** Develops diagnostic and vaccine products to fight AIDS, cancer, and other diseases. **Positions advertised include:** VP Clinical Development; Regulatory Affairs Associate; Clinical Research Associate; Director, Business Development; Medical Director. **Corporate headquarters location:** New York NY. **Other area locations:** Woburn, MA. **International locations:** The Netherlands. **Listed on:** NASDAQ. **Stock exchange symbol:** AGEN.

APPLIED SCIENCE LABORATORIES
175 Middlesex Turnpike, Bedford MA 01730. 781/275-4000. **Fax:** 781/275-3388. **Contact:** Human Resources. **E-mail address:** asl@a-s-l.com. **World Wide Web address:** http://www.a-s-l.com. **Description:** Develops and manufactures eye tracking systems and technology. The company also provides contract research. **Corporate headquarters location:** This location. **Parent company:** Applied Science Group, Inc.

ARIAD PHARMACEUTICALS, INC.
26 Landsdowne Street, Cambridge MA 02139. 617/494-0400. **Contact:** Kathy Lawton, Manager, Human Resources. **E-mail address:** human.resources@ariad.com. **World Wide Web address:** http://www.ariad.com. **Description:** A biopharmaceutical company that uses gene regulation and signal transduction to develop therapeutic products. Founded in 1991. **Positions advertised include:** Director, Clinical Safety and Pharmacovigilence; Manager, clinical Operations; Staff Scientist; Sr. Biostatistician; Sr. QA Specialist; Research Associate. **NOTE:** When mailing resumes, address to Job Code:___ before the above address. Job codes can be found on the website. **Corporate headquarters location:** This location. **Listed on:** NASDAQ. **Stock exchange symbol:** ARIA.

ASTRAZENECA
50 Otis Street, P.O. Box 4500, Westborough MA 01581. 508/366-1100. **Contact:** Human Resources. **World Wide Web address:** http://www.astrazeneca.com. **Description:** Develops pharmaceuticals to fight infections, cardiovascular and gastrointestinal diseases, cancer, and asthma and other respiratory problems. Other products developed by AstraZeneca are used as anesthetics and to control pain. **Positions advertised include:** Research Associate; Pharmaceutical Sales; Sr. Scientist; Purchasing Manager; Administrative Coordinator; Facilities Technician; Product Operation; Machine Adjuster; CAD Leader; Patent Attorney; Chemist; Training Specialist; Scientist.

ATHENA DIAGNOSTICS, INC.
377 Plantation Street, 4 Biotech Park, Worcester MA 01605. 508/756-2886. **Toll-free phone:** 800/394-4493. **Fax:** 508/753-5601. **Contact:** Human Resources. **E-mail address:** employment@athenadiagnostics.com. **World Wide Web address:** http://www.athenadiagnostics.com. **Description:** A reference laboratory that develops and commercializes diagnostics and therapeutics for neurological and neurogenic disorders. **Corporate headquarters location:** South San Francisco CA. **Parent company:** Elan Pharmaceuticals, Inc. **Operations at this facility include:** Administration; Manufacturing; Research and Development; Sales; Service. **Listed on:** NASDAQ. **Number of employees at this location:** 65.

AVANT IMMUNOTHERAPEUTICS, INC.
119 Fourth Avenue, Needham MA 02494-2725. 781/433-0771. **Fax:** 781/433-3113. **Contact:** Human

Resources. **E-mail address:** info@avantimmune.com. **World Wide Web address:** http://www.avantimmune.com. **Description:** A biopharmaceutical company specializing in the understanding and treatment of diseases caused by misregulation of the body's natural defense systems. **Positions advertised include:** Project Management Associate. **Corporate headquarters location:** This location. **Other area locations:** Fall River MA. **Listed on:** NASDAQ. **Stock exchange symbol:** AVAN.

BBI DIAGNOSTICS
375 West Street, West Bridgewater MA 02379. 508/580-1900. **Contact:** Human Resources. **World Wide Web address:** http://www.bbii.com. **Description:** A clinical laboratory that provides diagnostic testing specifically for HIV-1 (AIDS), HTLV-1, HIV-2, and Viral Hepatitis. **Parent company:** SeraCare Life Sciences, Inc.

BAYER DIAGNOSTICS
63 North Street, Medfield MA 02052. 508/359-7711. **Contact:** Human Resources. **World Wide Web address:** http://www.bayerdiag.com. **Description:** Develops, manufactures, and sells clinical diagnostic systems. Bayer Diagnostics specializes in critical care, laboratory, and point-of-care testing. **NOTE:** Search for positions on monster.com. **Other area locations:** Norwood MA. **International locations:** Worldwide. **Parent company:** Bayer Group. **Number of employees nationwide:** 4,500.

BIOGEN IDEC
14 Cambridge Center, Cambridge MA 02142. 617/679-2000. **Fax:** 617/679-2617. **Contact:** Human Resources. **E-mail address:** resumes@biogen.com. **World Wide Web address:** http://www.biogen.com. **Description:** Develops and commercializes drugs produced by genetic engineering. Products include alpha interferon, sold by Schering-Plough, and Hepatitis B vaccines, sold by Merck and SmithKline Beecham. **Positions advertised include:** Associate Customer Service Director; Manufacturing Associate; Commodity Analyst; Medical Coder; Sales Analyst; Data Support Administrator; Web Architect; Associate Scientist; Business Analyst; Business Project Manager; Development Engineer; Documentation Specialist. **Special programs:** Internships. **Corporate headquarters location:** This location. **Other U.S. locations:** Research Triangle Park NC. **International locations:** France. **Operations at this facility include:** Administration; Manufacturing; Research and Development. **Listed on:** NASDAQ. **Stock exchange symbol:** BGEN. **Number of employees nationwide:** 430.

BIOPURE CORPORATION
11 Hurley Street, Cambridge MA 02141. 617/234-6500. **Fax:** 617/234-6505. **Contact:** Personnel. **E-mail address:** hr@biopure.com. **World Wide Web address:** http://www.biopure.com. **Description:** A pharmaceutical company that develops oxygen-based therapeutic products. **Positions advertised include:** Biostatistics Data Manager; Clinical Project Manager; Clinical Operations Director; Regulatory Affairs Drug Safety Specialist. **Listed on:** NASDAQ. **Stock exchange symbol:** BPUR.

BIOSPHERE MEDICAL INC.
1050 Hingham Street, Rockland MA 02370. 781/681-7900. **Fax:** 781/792-2745. **Contact:** Human Resources. **World Wide Web address:** http://www.biospheremed.com. **Description:** Biomedical company focused on embolotherapy. **International locations:** France.

BRISTOL-MYERS SQUIBB COMPANY
331 Treble Cove Road, Building 300-2, Billerica, MA 01862. 978/667-9531. **Contact:** Human Resources. **World Wide Web address:** http://www.bms.com. **Description:** Manufactures pharmaceuticals including Coumadin, Sinemet, Cardiolite, Thallium, and I.V. Persantine. **Positions advertised include:** International Brand Manager Cardiolite; Research Scientist Assistant; Technical Transfer Representative; Accounts Receivable Representative; Process Engineer; Technician Principal; Principal Quality Scientist; Planner; Buyer; Assistant Vet Services Technician; Occupational Health; Purchase Agent; Customer Service Representative; Lead Person; Project Custodian. **Corporate headquarters location:** New York NY. **Listed on:** New York Stock Exchange. **Stock exchange symbol:** BMY.

THE CBR INSTITUTE FOR BIOMEDICAL RESEARCH
800 Huntington Avenue, Boston MA 02115. 617/731-6470. **Fax:** 617/278-3416. **Contact:** Human Resources. **E-mail address:** jobs@cbrinstitute.com. **World Wide Web address:** http://www.cbr.med.harvard.edu. **Description:** Provides molecular diagnostic and genetic typing services for the purpose of identity testing, matching potential donors for patients, and diagnosis of inherited diseases. The company also provides blood testing services to detect diseases for early treatment, as well as the testing new medical treatments and diagnostic products. **Special programs:** Internships. **Corporate headquarters location:** This location. **Parent company:** The CBR Institute is a nonprofit organization affiliated with Harvard Medical School that conducts research on the functions and uses of components of blood and other tissue and trains medical and scientific personnel in research. **Operations at this facility include:** Research and Development. **Number of employees at this location:** 150.

CHARLES RIVER LABORATORIES
251 Ballardvale Street, Wilmington MA 01887. 978/658-6000. **Fax:** 978/658-4150. **Contact:** Human Resources Manager. **E-mail address:** jobs@criver.com. **World Wide Web address:** http://www.criver.com. **Description:** A commercial supplier of laboratory animals including mice, rats, and guinea pigs for use in medical and scientific research. Users include chemical and pharmaceutical companies, government agencies, universities, commercial testing laboratories, hospitals, and others. **Positions advertised include:** Manager, Computer Operations & Operating Systems; Product Marketing Administrator, Transgenics; Sr. Analyst, Corporate Accounting; Sr. Technologist, Diagnostic Support; Administrator, Corporate Engineering. **Corporate headquarters location:** This location. **Operations at this facility include:** Administration; Manufacturing; Research and Development; Sales; Service. **Listed on:** New York Stock Exchange. **Stock exchange symbol:** CRL. **Number of employees nationwide:** 1,100.

CORNING INC.
45 Nagog Park, Acton MA 01720-3413. 978/635-2200. **Contact:** Human Resources. **World Wide Web address:** http://www.corning.com. **Description:** Corning's Science Products Division is engaged in the design, development, manufacture, and sale of disposable plastic research labware. **Positions advertised include:** Business Development Manager; Midwest Area Sales Manager. **NOTE:** Summer internships are available. **Other U.S. locations:** Nationwide. **International locations:** Worldwide. **Listed on:** New York Stock Exchange. **Stock exchange symbol:** GLW.

CHARLES STARK DRAPER LABORATORY, INC.
555 Technology Square, Mail Stop 44, Cambridge MA 02139-3563. 617/258-1000. **Fax:** 617/258-1113. **Contact:** Personnel. **E-mail address:** hr@draper.com. **World Wide Web address:** http://www.draper.com. **Description:** A private, nonprofit corporation dedicated to scientific research, development, and education. **Positions advertised include:** Test Engineer; Systems Engineer; Communications Engineer; Software Engineer; Avionics Engineer; Robotics Engineer. **Corporate headquarters location:** This location.

CUBIST PHARMACEUTICALS
65 Hayden Avenue, Lexington MA 02421. 781/860-8660. **Fax:** 781/861-0566. **Contact:** Human Resources.

E-mail address: hr@cubist.com. **World Wide Web address:** http://www.cubist.com. **Description:** Pharmaceutical company focused on the production of antiinfective drugs. **Positions advertised include:** Manager, Contract Operations; QC Analyst; Executive Coordinator, Technical Operations; Sr. Recruiter; Sr. Clinical Trials Manager; Sr. Toxicologist; Clinical Data Manager. **Corporate headquarters location:** This location.

DYAX CORPORATION
300 Technology Square, Cambridge MA 02139-3515. 617/225-2500. **Contact:** Human Resources. **World Wide Web address:** http://www.dyax.com. **Description:** Engaged in producing protein and peptide separations as well as screening technology products. Dyax Corporation also develops nuclear medicine to help alleviate clotting problems. **Positions advertised include:** Procurement Manager; Program Management Director; System Administrator. Subsidiaries include: Dyax s.a. (Belgium); Biotage Division (Charlottesville VA); Biotage UK (England). Listed on: New York Stock Exchange. Stock exchange symbol: DYAX.

GPC BIOTECH
610 Lincoln Street, Waltham MA 02451. 781/890-9007. **Fax:** 781/890-9005. **Contact:** Human Resources. **E-mail address:** hr.waltham@gpc-biotech.com. **World Wide Web address:** http://www.gpc-biotech.com. **Description:** A transatlantic genomics drug discovery company that specializes in proprietary genomics, proteomics, and drug discovery technologies designed to improve the process of drug development. Founded in 1992. **Positions advertised include:** Associate Director, Internal Audit and Controls. **Office hours:** Monday - Friday, 8:30 a.m. - 5:00 p.m. **Listed on:** Privately held. **Number of employees at this location:** 75.

GENVEC INC.
Building 96, 13th Street, Charlestown Navy Yard, Charlestown MA 02129. 617/242-9100. **Fax:** 617/242-0070. **Contact:** Human Resources. **E-mail address:** resume@genvec.com. **World Wide Web address:** http://www.genvec.com. **Description:** A biotechnology company that specializes in cell transplantation technology designed to treat diseases characterized by cell dysfunction or cell death. Founded in 1989. **Special programs:** Co-ops. **Office hours:** Monday - Friday, 8:00 a.m. - 5:30 p.m.

GENZYME BIOSURGERY
64 Sidney Street, Cambridge MA 02139-4136. 617/494-8484. **Contact:** Human Resources. **World Wide Web address:** http://www.genzyme.com. **Description:** Develops tissues grown from human cells for medical use. **Corporate headquarters location:** Cambridge MA. **Other U.S. locations:** Nationwide. **International locations:** Worldwide. **Parent company:** Genzyme Corporation (Cambridge MA). **Listed on:** NASDAQ. **Stock exchange symbol:** GENZ. **Annual sales/revenues:** $51 - $100 million. **Number of employees nationwide:** 3,140. **Number of employees worldwide:** 3,700.

GENZYME CORPORATION
One Kendall Square, Building 1400, Cambridge MA 02139-1562. 617/252-7500. **Contact:** Human Resources. **World Wide Web address:** http://www.genzyme.com. **Description:** An international, diversified health care products company focused on developing and delivering practical solutions to specific medical needs. The company's activities and products are organized into six primary business areas: Therapeutics, Surgical Products, Genetics, Pharmaceuticals, Diagnostic Services, and Tissue Repair. Founded in 1981. **Special programs:** Internships; Co-ops; Summer Jobs. **Office hours:** Monday - Friday, 8:30 a.m. - 5:00 p.m. **Corporate headquarters location:** This location. **Other U.S. locations:** Nationwide. **International locations:** Worldwide. **Listed on:** NASDAQ. **Stock exchange symbol:** GENZ. **Annual sales/revenues:** $51 - $100 million. **Number of employees nationwide:** 3,140. **Number of employees worldwide:** 3,700.

IDERA PHARMACEUTICALS
345 Vassar Street, Cambridge MA 02139. 617/679-5500. **Contact:** Human Resources. **E-mail address:** hr@iderapharma.com. **World Wide Web address:** http://www.iderapharma.com. **Description:** A pharmaceutical research and development company focused on the treatment of viral diseases, cancer, and diseases of the eye. **Listed on:** American Stock Exchange. **Stock exchange symbol:** IDP

IMMUNOGEN INC.
128 Sidney Street, Cambridge MA 02139. 617/995-2500. **Fax:** 617/995-2510. **Contact:** Human Resources. **E-mail address:** resume@immunogen.com. **World Wide Web address:** http://www.immunogen.com. **Description:** ImmunoGen Inc. is engaged in the research and development of pharmaceuticals, primarily for the treatment of cancer. The company's product line consists of proprietary toxins or drugs coupled with highly specific targeting agents. **Positions advertised include:** Patent Agent; Validation Engineer; Principal Development Director; Analytical Development Scientist/ Chemistry Scientist; Chemistry Research Associate; Process Development Research Associate. **Corporate headquarters location:** This location. **Operations at this facility include:** This location is a research facility. **Listed on:** NASDAQ. **Stock exchange symbol:** IMGN.

INDEVUS PHARMACEUTICALS, INC.
33 Hayden Avenue, Lexington MA 02421. 781/861-8444. **Fax:** 781/860-5600. **Contact:** Human Resources, Tessa Cooper. **E-mail address:** hr@indevus.com. **World Wide Web address:** http://www.indevus.com. **Description:** Develops medical products for multiple therapeutic areas, primarily urology, gynecology and men's health. **Corporate headquarters location:** This location. **Positions advertised include:** Corporate Controller; Information Technology Systems Administrator. **Listed on:** NASDAQ. **Stock exchange symbol:** IDEV.

KLA-TENCOR
200 Friberg Parkway, Suite 4003, Westborough MA 01581. 508/898-0091. **Fax:** 508/366-9104. **Contact:** Human Resources. **World Wide Web address:** http://www.kla-tencor.com. **Description:** Manufactures electron scanning microscopes.

MIT LINCOLN LABORATORY
244 Wood Street, Lexington MA 02420-9108. 781/981-7066. **Fax:** 781/981-7086. **Contact:** Human Resources Department. **E-mail address:** resume@ll.mit.edu. **World Wide Web address:** http://www.ll.mit.edu. **Description:** A federally funded, nonprofit research center of the Massachusetts Institute of Technology (MIT). Lincoln Laboratory applies science, by means of advanced technology, to critical problems of national security. Problems focus on space surveillance, tactical systems, free space and terrestrial optical communications, and air traffic control systems. Founded in 1951. **Positions advertised include:** Engineer; Analyst; Laboratory Assistant; Biologist. **Office hours:** Monday - Friday, 8:30 a.m. - 5:00 p.m. **Corporate headquarters location:** This location. **Operations at this facility include:** Research and Development. **Number of employees at this location:** 2,200.

MACROCHEM CORPORATION
110 Hartwell Avenue, Lexington MA 02421-3134. 781/862-4003. **Fax:** 781/862-4338. **Contact:** Human Resources. **E-mail address:** hr@macrochem.com. **World Wide Web address:** http://www.macrochem.com. **Description:** Engaged in the development and commercialization of advanced drug delivery systems for the transdermal delivery of enzyme, protein, and drug compounds for therapeutic, over-the-counter, and cosmetic applications. SEPA, MacroChem's worldwide-patented compound, accelerates the passage of drugs through the skin and

other biomembranes. **Corporate headquarters location:** This location. **Listed on:** NASDAQ. **Stock exchange symbol:** MCHM.

MATRITECH, INC.
330 Nevada Street, Newton MA 02460. 617/928-0820. **Toll-free phone:** 800/320-2521. **Fax:** 617/928-0821. **Contact:** Human Resources. **E-mail address:** hr@matritech.com. **World Wide Web address:** http://www.matritech.com. **Description:** A biotechnology company using proprietary nuclear matrix protein technology to develop and commercialize innovative serum-, cell-, and urine-based NMP diagnostics that enable physicians to detect and monitor the presence of bladder, breast, colon, cervical, and prostate cancers. Founded in 1987. **Corporate headquarters location:** This location. **Listed on:** NASDAQ. **Stock exchange symbol:** NMPS. **CEO:** Stephen D. Chubb. **Annual sales/revenues:** Less than $5 million. **Number of employees at this location:** 55.

MILLENNIUM PHARMACEUTICALS, INC.
40 Landsdowne Street, Cambridge MA 02139. 617/679-7000. **Toll-free phone:** 800/390-5663. **Fax:** 617/663-3735. **Contact:** Human Resources. **E-mail address:** info@minm.com. **World Wide Web address:** http://www.mlnm.com. **Description:** Engaged in genomics research and development. **Positions advertised include:** Research Assistant; Project Manager; Clinical Data Manager; Medical Director; Manager, Quality Assurance; Scientist; Engineer. **Other U.S. locations:** San Diego CA. **International locations:** England; Japan. **Listed on:** NASDAQ. **Stock exchange symbol:** MLNM.

MILLIPORE CORPORATION
290 Concord Road, Billerica MA 01821. 978/715-4321. **Contact:** Employment Manager. **World Wide Web address:** http://www.millipore.com. **Description:** Manufactures microporous filters and filtration devices used for the analysis, separation, and purification of fluids. Products are used in the fields of health care, pharmaceuticals, micro-electronics, biological sciences, and genetic engineering. **Positions advertised include:** Technology Manager; Product Manager Consultant; Process Development Scientist Manager; Quality Engineer. **Corporate headquarters location:** This location. **Listed on:** New York Stock Exchange. **Stock exchange symbol:** MIL. **Number of employees worldwide:** 4,200.

NEW ENGLAND BIOLABS, INC.
240 County Road, Ipswich MA 01938-2723. 978/927-5054. **Contact:** Human Resources. **E-mail address:** resumes@neb.com. **World Wide Web address:** http://www.neb.com. **Description:** A medical research laboratory that manufactures products for molecular biology research with a specialization in restriction endonucleases. **Positions advertised include:** Marketing Communications Manager; Research Associate; Postdoctoral Fellow; Development and Production Coordinator.

NOVEON
207 Lowell Street, Wilmington MA 01887. 978/642-5000. **Fax:** 978/657-4371. **Contact:** Human Resources. **E-mail address:** edelehanty@thermadics.com. **World Wide Web address:** http://www.thermedics.com. **Description:** A supplier of custom manufactured thermoplastic polyurethanes.

NUTRAMAX PRODUCTS INC.
51 Blackburn Drive, Gloucester MA 01930. 978/282-1800. **Fax:** 978/282-3794. **Contact:** Human Resources. **E-mail address:** hr@nutramax.com. **World Wide Web address:** http://www.nutramax.com. **Description:** Manufactures pharmaceutical and personal care products. **Positions advertised include:** Domestic Sales Representative; International Sales Representative. **Corporate headquarters location:** This location. **Operations at this facility include:** Administration; Manufacturing; Sales. **Number of employees at this location:** 250. **Number of employees nationwide:** 525.

ORGANOGENESIS INC.
150 Dan Road, Canton MA 02021. 781/575-0775. **Fax:** 781/401-1299. **Contact:** Human Resources. **World Wide Web address:** http://www.organogenesis.com. **Description:** Designs, develops, and manufactures medical therapeutics containing living cells and/or natural connective tissue components. The company's products are designed to promote the establishment and growth of new tissues to restore, maintain, or improve biological function. Organogenesis's product development focus includes living tissue replacements, organ assist treatments, and guided tissue regeneration scaffolds. **Positions advertised include:** Product Associate; Facilities Technician; Quality Control Microbiologist; Human Resources Director. **Corporate headquarters location:** This location. **Listed on:** AMEX. **Stock exchange symbol:** ORG.

OSCIENT PHARMACEUTICALS CORPORATION
1000 Winter Street, Suite 2200, Waltham MA 02451. 781/398-2300. **Fax:** 781/893-9535. **Contact:** Human Resources. **E-mail address:** hrjobs@oscient.com. **World Wide Web address:** http://www.oscient.com. **Description:** Develops and commercializes pharmaceuticals. **Positions advertised include:** Medical Director; Sr. Financial Analyst; Sr. Quality Assurance manager; Territory Manager. **Corporate headquarters location:** This location. **Operations at this facility include:** Administration; Research and Development. **Listed on:** NASDAQ. **Stock exchange symbol:** OSCI

PIERCE BOSTON TECHNOLOGY CENTER
35A Cabot Road, Woburn MA 01801-1059. 781/970-0350. **Fax:** 781/937-3096. **Contact:** Human Resources. **World Wide Web address:** http://www.endogen.com. **Description:** Develops, manufactures, and markets diagnostic test kits that test for HIV and cancer. Products are sold in the United States to private and government institutions, university hospitals, medical centers, and large commercial laboratories via a direct sales force. **Corporate headquarters location:** Rockford IL. **Parent Company:** Pierce Chemical Corporation. **NOTE:** Please send all resumes to: Pierce Chemical Corporation, P.O. Box 117, Rockford IL 61105.

PSYCHEMEDICS CORPORATION
125 Nagog Park, Acton MA 01720. 978/206-8220. **Contact:** Human Resources Department. **World Wide Web address:** http://www.psychemedics.com. **Description:** A biotechnology company concentrating on diagnostics through the detection and measurement of substances in the body using hair samples. The first commercial product, a testing service for the detection of drugs, is provided principally to private sector companies. This test identifies traces of cocaine, marijuana, opiates, methamphetamines, and PCP. Psychemedics's testing methods use patented technology for performing immunoassays on enzymatically dissolved hair samples with confirmation testing by gas chromatography or mass spectrometry. **Corporate headquarters location:** This location. **Other U.S. locations:** Culver City CA. **Listed on:** American Stock Exchange. **Stock exchange symbol:** PMD. **Number of employees nationwide:** 95.

QUEST DIAGNOSTICS INCORPORATED
415 Massachusetts Avenue, Cambridge MA 02139-4102. 617/547-8900. **Fax:** 617/868-7962. **Contact:** Human Resources. **World Wide Web address:** http://www.questdiagnostics.com. **Description:** One of the largest clinical laboratories in North America, providing a broad range of clinical laboratory services to health care clients that include physicians, hospitals, clinics, dialysis centers, pharmaceutical companies, and corporations. The company offers and performs tests on blood, urine, and other bodily fluids and tissues to provide information for health and well-being. **Positions advertised include:** Phlebotomy Services

Representative; Account Manager; Medical Technologist; Billing Supervisor; Processing Associate.

REPLIGEN CORPORATION
41 Seyon Street Building #1, Suite 100, Waltham MA 02453. 781/250-0111. **Toll-free phone:** 800/622-2259. **Fax:** 781/259-0015. **Contact:** Human Resources. **World Wide Web address:** http://www.repligen.com. **Description:** Researches and manufactures pharmaceutical products. **Positions advertised include:** QA Specialist; QC Associate; Sales and Marketing Associate.

SEPRACOR, INC.
84 Waterford Drive, Marlborough MA 01752. 508/481-6700. **Fax:** 508/357-7490. **Contact:** Human Resources. **World Wide Web address:** http://www.sepracor.com. **Description:** Develops new and improved versions of prescription drugs. Sepracor's products are known as Improved Chemical Entities (ICE Pharmaceuticals) and are used in the allergy, asthma, gastroenterology, neurology, psychiatry, and urology markets. **Positions advertised include:** CRM Manager; Supply Manager; Director, Respiratory Marketing; Director, Medical Affairs; Clinical Monitoring Manager; Vice President, Regulatory Affairs; Sr. Corporate Counsel; Principal Scientist; Compensation Analyst; Patent Liaison; Associate Director, Pharmacology. **Corporate headquarters location:** This location. **Listed on:** NASDAQ. **Stock exchange symbol:** SEPR.

SERONO, INC.
One Technology Place, Rockland MA 02370. 781/982-9000. **Toll-free phone:** 800/283-8088. **Contact:** Human Resources. **World Wide Web address:** http://www.seronousa.com. **Description:** Manufactures prescription pharmaceuticals for the treatment of a variety of diseases including multiple sclerosis and cancer. **Positions advertised include:** Sr. Marketing Manager; Manager, Clinical Quality; Sr. Scientist Medicinal Chemistry; Director of Medical Affairs; Project Manager; Clinical Research Scientist; Director, Brand Marketing. **Corporate headquarters location:** This location. **Operations at this facility include:** Administration; Manufacturing; Research and Development; Sales; Service. **Listed on:** Privately held. **Number of employees at this location:** 150. **Number of employees nationwide:** 370.

SHIRE PLC
700 Main Street, Cambridge MA 02139. 617/349-0200. **Contact:** Human Resources. **World Wide Web address:** http://www.shire.com. **Description:** Engaged in the research and development of specialty pharmaceuticals. **Positions advertised include:** Research & Design Specialist; Quality Control Analyst; Bioengineer; Staff Scientist; Warehouse Manager; Inventory Control Coordinator; Material Planner; Operations Analysis Manager; Financial Planning Analyst; Regulatory Documentation Coordinator. **Listed on:** NASDAQ. **Stock exchange symbol:** TKTX.

SHUSTER LABORATORIES, INC.
85 John Road, Canton MA 02021. 781/821-2200. **Toll-free phone:** 800/444-8705. **Fax:** 781/821-9266. **Contact:** Human Resources. **E-mail address:** resumes@shusterlabs.com. **World Wide Web address:** http://www.shusterlabs.com. **Description:** An independent consumer products testing, quality assurance and R&D firm. Services include technical consulting, product development, product evaluation and testing, custom quality assurance programs, laboratory testing, regulatory affairs, auditing, consumer testing and sensory research. **Positions advertised include:** Lab Associate. **Parent company:** STR.

STERIS-ISOMEDIX SERVICES
435 Whitney Street, Northborough MA 01532. 508/393-9323. **Contact:** Human Resources. **World Wide Web address:** http://www.steris.com. **Description:** Provides contract sterilization services to manufacturers of prepackaged products such as health care and certain consumer products. The company uses gamma radiation and ethylene oxide in these operations. **Positions advertised include:** Field Service Representative. **Corporate headquarters location:** Mentor OH.

THERION BIOLOGICS CORPORATION
76 Rogers Street, Cambridge MA 02142-1119. 617/475-7500. **Fax:** 617/475-7249. **Contact:** Human Resources. **E-mail address:** excellence@therionbio.edu. **World Wide Web address:** http://www.therionbio.com. **Description:** Develops therapeutic vaccines to extend and improve the lives of cancer patients. **Positions advertised include:** Team Leader, Materials; Process Development Scientist; QC Compliance Support Analyst; QC Bioanalytical Analyst; Research Associate.

VENTURE TECHNOLOGIES, INC
85 Rangeway Road, North Billerica MA 01862. 978/667-9890. **Fax:** 978/671-0114. **Contact:** Human Resources. **World Wide Web address:** http://www.venturetechnologies.com. **Description:** Designs and develops products that analyze, measure, control, and communicate. Areas of expertise include electronic engineering, software engineering, mechanical engineering, industrial design, and wireless design. **Positions advertised include:** Sr. Software Engineer; BSD/Linux Software Engineer; Sr. Electrical Engineer; Sr. Mechanical Engineer; RF Development Engineer.

VERTEX PHARMACEUTICALS INCORPORATED
130 Waverly Street, Cambridge MA 02139. 617/444-6100. **Fax:** 617/444-6680. **Contact:** Human Resources. **World Wide Web address:** http://www.vpharm.com. **Description:** Develops drugs for viral, autoimmune, inflammatory, and neurodegenerative diseases. Vertex Pharmaceuticals also develops oral active pharmaceuticals for drug-resistant cancer and hemoglobin disorders. **Positions advertised include:** Stock Plan Administrator; Scientist; Solid State Materials Scientist; Sr. Research Associate; Principal Statistical Programmer; Outsourcing Specialist; Business/Systems Analyst; Communications Specialist; Staff Investigator. **Corporate headquarters location:** This location. **Subsidiaries include:** Altus Biologics Inc. (Cambridge MA); Versal Technologies, Inc. (Cambridge MA); Vertex Pharmaceuticals (Europe) Limited (United Kingdom); Vertex Securities Corporation (Cambridge MA). **Listed on:** NASDAQ. **Stock exchange symbol:** VRTX.

VIACELL, INC.
245 First Street, Cambridge MA 02142. 617/914-3400. **Toll-free phone:** 866/842-2355. **Contact:** Human Resources. **E-mail address:** careers@viacellinc.com. **World Wide Web address:** http://www.viacellinc.com. **Description:** A biotechnology company focused on enabling the widespread use of human cells as medicine. ViaCell is developing proprietary stem cell product candidates intended to address cancer, cardiac disease, and diabetes. **Positions advertised include:** Clinical Consultant/Inside Sales; Entry Level Sales/Expedition Group; Professional Product Marketing Manager; Senior Scientist; Vice President, Medical Affairs.

WATERS CORPORATION
34 Maple Street, Milford MA 01757. 508/478-2000. **Fax:** 508/872-1990. **Recorded jobline:** 508/482-3332. **Contact:** Human Resources. **World Wide Web address:** http://www.waters.com. **Description:** Produces a range of instruments, information management systems, and chromatography products for high-performance liquid chromatography and related applications. Waters Corporation's products are also used in fundamental research directed toward a better understanding of the chemical, physical, and biological composition of compounds, as well as in the detection, measurement, and identification of compounds of interest across a wide range of industries. Founded in

1958. **NOTE:** Entry-level positions and second and third shifts are offered. **Positions advertised include:** Research Chemist; Electrical Engineer; Financial Analyst; Software Engineer; Sr. Technical Writer. **Office hours:** Monday - Friday, 8:00 a.m. - 4:30 p.m. **Corporate headquarters location:** This location. **Other U.S. locations:** Nationwide. **International locations:** Worldwide. **Operations at this facility include:** Regional Headquarters. **Listed on:** New York Stock Exchange. **Facilities Manager:** William Stares. **Annual sales/revenues:** More than $100 million. **Number of employees at this location:** 950. **Number of employees worldwide:** 2,000.

WHITEHEAD INSTITUTE FOR BIOMEDICAL RESEARCH
9 Cambridge Center, Cambridge MA 02142-1479. 617/258-5000. **Fax:** 617/258-6294. **Contact:** Human Resources **E-mail address:** resumes@wi.mit.edu. **World Wide Web address:** http://www.wi.mit.edu. **Description:** A nonprofit research and teaching institution that specializes in programs regarding AIDS and cancer research, developmental biology, genetics, infectious diseases, and structural biology. **Positions advertised include:** Research Scientist; Programmer; Technical Assistant. **Corporate headquarters location:** This location.

WOODS HOLE OCEANOGRAPHIC INSTITUTION
Mail Stop 15, 14 Maury Lane, Woods Hole MA 02543-1120. 508/289-2253. **Fax:** 508/457-2173. **Contact:** Human Resources. **E-mail address:** hr@whoi.edu. **World Wide Web address:** http://www.whoi.edu. **Description:** A private, nonprofit oceanography research institute. **Positions advertised include:** Assistant Scientist; Chief Scientist; Engineering Assistant; Part Time Helper; Postdoctoral Investigator; Research Assistant; Security Guard; Electrician.

WYETH GENETICS INSTITUTE
35 Cambridge Park Drive, Cambridge MA 02140. 617/876-1170. **Contact:** Human Resources. **World Wide Web address:** http://www.wyeth.com. **Description:** Performs biotechnology research contributing to the application and creation of recombinant DNA technology. **Positions advertised include:** Scientist; SR. Research Scientist; Sr. Director Biometrics; Associate Technician; Patent Counsel; Sr. Clinical Writer. **Other area locations:** Andover MA. **Other U.S. locations:** St. Louis MO. **International locations:** Germany. **Parent company:** American Home Products Corporation (Madison NJ).

Michigan

DIFCO LABORATORIES
BD BIOSCIENCES
920 Henry Street, Detroit MI 48201. 313/442-8800. **Toll-free phone:** 800/638-8663. **Contact:** Human Resources Manager. **World Wide Web address:** http://www.bdbiosciences.com. **Description:** Engaged in the manufacture of microbiological products such as dehydrated culture media, diagnostic reagents, and capital equipment. **Special programs:** Scholarship Programs. **Corporate headquarters location:** San Jose CA. **Other U.S. locations:** Rockville MD; Bedford MA; San Diego CA. **International locations:** Worldwide. **Parent company:** Becton, Dickinson and Company (Franklin Lakes NJ). **Listed on:** New York Stock Exchange. **Stock exchange symbol:** BDX. **Number of employees at this location:** 300. **Number of employees worldwide:** Approximately 3,000.

PERRIGO COMPANY
515 Eastern Avenue, Allegan MI 49010. 269/673-8451. **Fax:** 269/673-9128. **Contact:** Employment Specialist. **World Wide Web address:** http://www.perrigo.com. **Description:** Manufactures and sells pharmaceuticals, vitamins, and personal care products. These products are sold under individual store brand names such as Tylenol, Advil, and One-A-Day. **Positions advertised include:** Quality Assurance Auditor; Regulatory Affairs Project Manager; Automated Systems Engineer; Research Scientist; Facilities Engineer; Sourcing Manager; Analytical Senior Chemist; Marketing Information Manager. **Corporate headquarters location:** This location. **Other area locations:** Holland MI; Montague MI; **Other U.S. locations:** SC; NJ; CA. **International locations:** England; Mexico. **Operations at this facility include:** Administration; Divisional Headquarters; Manufacturing; Research and Development; Sales. **Listed on:** NASDAQ. **Stock exchange symbol:** PRGO. **Annual sales/revenues:** Over $800 million. **Number of employees worldwide:** Approximately 4,000.

PFIZER GLOBAL RESEARCH AND DEVELOPMENT
2800 Plymouth Road, Ann Arbor MI 48105. 734/622-7000. **Fax:** 734/622-3310. **Contact:** Human Resources. **World Wide Web address:** http://www.pfizer.com. **Description:** The industry's largest pharmaceutical research and development organization. **Positions advertised include:** Administrative Specialist; Scientist; Corporate Counsel; Patent Counsel; Financial Analyst; Marketing Manager; Clinical Pharmacometrician. **Special programs:** Internships; Co-ops. **Corporate headquarters locations:** New York NY. **Other U.S. locations:** Cambridge MA; New London CT; Groton CT; La Jolla CA. **International locations:** Canada; France; Japan; United Kingdom. **Operations at this facility include:** Administration; Divisional Headquarters; Research and Development. **Listed on:** New York Stock Exchange; London Stock Exchange; Swiss Euronext. **Stock exchange symbol:** New York Stock Exchange (PFE); London and Swiss Stock Exchanges (PFZ). **Annual sales/revenues:** $45.2 billion. **Number of employees at this location:** 2,700. **Number of employees worldwide:** 122,000.

PFIZER INC.
188 Howard Avenue, Holland MI 49424-6517. 616/392-2375. **Contact:** Human Resources. **World Wide Web address:** http://www.pfizer.com. **Description:** The world's largest research-based pharmaceutical company. Pfizer researches, develops, manufactures, and markets pharmaceutical products for human and animal healthcare. **Positions advertised include:** Senior Development Scientist; Human Resources Generalist; Associate Chemist; Manufacturing Engineer; Validation Associate; Compliance Engineer; Web Developer. **Special programs:** Internships; Co-ops. **Corporate headquarters locations:** New York NY. **Other U.S. locations:** Nationwide. **International locations:** Worldwide. **Operations at this facility include:** This location is a Pharmaceutical Sciences Pilot Plant. **Listed on:** New York Stock Exchange; London Stock Exchange; Swiss Euronext. **Stock exchange symbol:** New York Stock Exchange (PFE); London and Swiss Stock Exchanges (PFZ). **Annual sales/revenues:** $45.2 billion. **Number of employees worldwide:** 122,000.

Minnesota

BECKMAN COULTER, INC.
1000 Lake Hazeltine Drive, Chaska MN 55318-1084. 612/448-4848. **Fax:** 612/368-1140. **Contact:** Human Resources. **E-mail address:** chaskahr@beckman.com. **World Wide Web address:** http://www.beckman.com. **Description:** Sells and services a diverse range of scientific instruments, reagents, and related equipment. Products include DNA synthesizers, robotics workstations, centrifuges, electrophoresis systems, detection and measurement equipment, data processing software, and specialty chemical and automated general chemical systems. **Positions advertised include:** Sr. Quality Assurance Scientist; Production Scientist; Sr. Software Development Engineer; Technical Support Engineer. **Operations at this facility include:** Administration; Manufacturing; Research and Development; Sales; Service. **Listed on:** New York Stock Exchange. **Stock exchange symbol:** BEC. **Number of employees worldwide:** 10,000.

CIMA LABS INC.
10000 Valley View Road, Eden Prairie MN 55344. 952/947-8728. **Fax:** 952/947-8770. **Contact:** Human Resources. **E-mail address:** hr@cimalabs.com. **World

Wide Web address: http://www.cimalabs.com. **Description:** Develops, formulates, and manufactures a pharmaceutical drug delivery system. CIMA LABS INC.'s main product is a fast-dissolving tablet for individuals who have difficulty swallowing pills. Founded in 1986. **NOTE:** Entry-level positions are offered. **Corporate headquarters location:** This location. **Parent company:** Cephalon, Inc.

DIASORIN INC.
1951 Northwest Avenue, P.O. Box 285, Stillwater MN 55082-0285. 651/439-9710. **Fax:** 651/351-5700. **Contact:** Human Resources. **E-mail address:** hr@diasorin.com. **World Wide Web address:** http://www.diasorin.com. **Description:** A private company that develops and manufactures reagents for use in infectious disease, hepatitis, endocrinology, bone and mineral metabolism, cancer, brain injury, cardiac, therapeutic drug monitoring, and autoimmunity. **Special programs:** Internships; Summer Jobs. **International locations:** Worldwide. **Number of employees at this location:** 325.

IMMUNOCHEMISTRY TECHNOLOGIES, LLC
9401 James Avenue South, Suite 155, Bloomington MN 55431. 952/888-8788. **Contact:** Personnel. **E-mail address:** hr@immunochemistry.com. **World Wide Web address:** http://www.immunochemistry.com. **Description:** Develops, manufactures, and optimizes custom-designed immunoassays in kit form. Immunochemistry Technologies also provides protein purification, modification, and conjugation services, as well as antibody production. Founded in 1994. **NOTE:** Entry-level positions are offered. **Corporate headquarters location:** This location. **Listed on:** Privately held. **Number of employees at this location:** 15.

MEDTOX SCIENTIFIC INC.
402 West County Road D, St. Paul MN 55112-3522. 651/636-7466. **Toll-free phone:** 800/832-3244. **Fax:** 651/628-6160. **Contact:** Personnel. **World Wide Web address:** http://www.medtox.com. **Description:** A drug testing and toxicology laboratory.

PDL BIOPHARMA, INC.
3955 Annapolis Lane, Plymouth MN 55447. 763/551-1778. **Fax:** 763/551-1780. **Contact:** Human Resources. **World Wide Web address:** http://www.pdl.com. **Description:** A research and development company focused on the development of humanized and human monoclonal antibodies for the treatment and prevention of various diseases. **Positions advertised include:** Maintenance Technician; Application Analyst; Business Analyst; Metrology Technician; Scientist, Cell Culture; Scientist, Purification; Manufacturing Supervisor: Manager, Quality Assurance. **Corporate headquarters location:** Fremont CA. **Other area locations:** Brooklyn Park MN.

PADDOCK LABORATORIES, INC.
3940 Quebec Avenue North, New Hope MN 55427. 763/546-4676. **Toll-free phone:** 800/328-5113. **Fax:** 763/546-4842. **Contact:** Human Resources. **E-mail address:** employment@paddocklabs.com. **World Wide Web address:** http://www.paddocklabs.com. **Description:** Manufactures generic pharmaceuticals. Founded in 1977. **NOTE:** See website for current job openings. Submit resume by e-mail. **Positions advertised include:** Laboratory Analyst; Regulatory Affairs Analyst; Regulatory Affairs Director; Formulations Development Director; Account Representative. **Number of employees at this location:** 250.

QUEST DIAGNOSTICS INCORPORATED
600 West County Road D, Suite 11, St. Paul MN 55112-3519. 651/635-1500. **Contact:** Personnel. **World Wide Web address:** http://www.questdiagnostics.com. **Description:** One of the largest clinical laboratories in North America, providing a broad range of clinical laboratory services to health care clients that include physicians, hospitals, clinics, dialysis centers, pharmaceutical companies, and corporations. The company offers and performs tests on blood, urine, and other bodily fluids and tissues to provide information for health and well-being. **Positions advertised include:** Phlebotomy Service Floater; Cyto Tech Assistant;

R&D SYSTEMS
TECHNE CORPORATION
614 McKinley Place Northeast, Minneapolis MN 55413. 612/379-2956. **Toll-free phone:** 800/343-7475. **Fax:** 612/656-4434. **Contact:** Human Resources. **E-mail address:** hr@rndsystems.com. **World Wide Web address:** http://www.rndsystems.com. **Description:** R&D Systems is a specialty manufacturer of biological products with two operating divisions: Biotechnology and Hematology. Founded in 1976. **Positions advertised include:** HR Administrative Assistant; Product Launch Coordinator; Production Specialist; Research Associate; Technical Sales Representative. **Special programs:** Internships. **Corporate headquarters location:** This location. **Parent company:** Techne Corporation (also at this location) is a holding company whose subsidiaries manufacture hematology control products, biotech products, and biological products. **Number of employees at this location:** 190.

SOLVAY PHARMACEUTICALS
210 Main Street West, Baudette MN 56623. 218/634-3500. **Fax:** 218/634-3540. **Contact:** Human Resources. **E-mail address:** careers@solvay.com. **World Wide Web address:** http://www.solvaypharmaceuticals-us.com. **Description:** Develops a variety of prescription pharmaceuticals used to treat psychiatric, hormonal, and gastrointestinal disorders. **NOTE:** Search and apply for positions online. **Other U.S. locations:** Marietta GA. **Number of employees worldwide:** 30,000.

SYNGENTA SEEDS
7500 Olson Memorial Highway, Golden Valley MN 55427. 763/593-7333. **Fax:** 763/593-7828. **Contact:** Human Resources. **World Wide Web address:** http://www.syngenta.com. **Description:** A researcher, producer, and marketer of agricultural seeds and products. **NOTE:** Submit resume by fax, or search and apply online at http://agcareers.com. **Parent company:** Syngenta AG (Switzerland). **Listed on:** New York Stock Exchange. **Stock exchange symbol:** SYT.

UPSHER-SMITH LABORATORIES
6701 Evenstad Drive, Maple Grove MN 55369. 763/315-2000. **Toll-free phone:** 800/654-2299. **Fax:** 763/315-2300. **Contact:** Human Resources Department. **E-mail address:** uslhr@upsher-smith.com. **World Wide Web address:** http://www.upsher-smith.com. **Description:** Manufactures prescription and nonprescription pharmaceuticals. **NOTE:** Submit applications by e-mail or mail. **Positions advertised include:** Quality Assurance Analyst; Machine Operator; Manufacturing Technician; Senior Scientist; Associate Chemist. **Other area locations:** Minneapolis MN.

VIROMED LABORATORIES
6101 Blue Circle Drive, Minnetonka MN 55343. 952/563-3300. **Fax:** 952/563-4152. **Contact:** Jackie Williams, Human Resources. **E-mail address:** hr@viromed.com. **World Wide Web address:** http://www.viromed.com. **Description:** A medical laboratory that provides laboratory testing services to the healthcare, transplant medicine, pharmaceutical, and biotechnology industries. **NOTE:** Search and apply for positions online at http://www.labcorpcareers.com and select "Minnesota—Minneapolis/Minnetonka" as the location. **Positions advertised include:** Lab Supervisor I; Accountant; Technician; Associate Director of Molecular Genetics; QA Analyst.

Missouri

AMERICAN CHEMICAL SOCIETY, KANSAS CITY SECTION
425 Volker Boulevard, Kansas City MO 64110-2299. 816/753-7600. **Fax:** 816/753-8420. **Contact:**

Personnel. **World Wide Web address:** http://www.mriresearch.org. **Description:** Engaged in all types of scientific research in the areas of health, agricultural and food safety, national defense, engineering, and energy. **NOTE:** Applications may be submitted online (preferred method). **Other U.S. locations:** FL; MD; CO.

AVENTIS PHARMACEUTICALS
10236 Marion Park Drive, Kansas City MO 64137-1405. 816/966-5100. **Contact:** Human Resources. **World Wide Web address:** http://www.aventis.com. **Description:** Manufactures prescription pharmaceuticals. **NOTE:** Search and apply for positions online. **Positions advertised include:** Diabetes Scientific Manager/Specialist; External Manufacturing Specialist; Sales Representative. **Corporate headquarters location:** Strasbourg, France.

CENTOCOR
4766 LaGuardia Drive, St. Louis MO 63134. 314/426-5000. **Fax:** 314/426-6229. **Contact:** Human Resources. **E-mail address:** wyeth@trackcareers.com. **World Wide Web address:** http://www.wyeth.com. **Description:** Performs biotechnology research contributing to the application and creation of recombinant DNA technology. **Corporate headquarters location:** Madison NJ. **Other U.S. locations:** Nationwide. **Operations at this facility include:** Administration; Manufacturing. **Number of employees worldwide:** 52,000.

D&K HEALTHCARE RESOURCES
8235 Forsyth Boulevard, Clayton MO 63105. 314/727-3485. **Fax:** 314/727-5759. **Contact:** Human Resources. **World Wide Web address:** http://www.dkwd.com. **Description:** Distributes pharmaceuticals and health and beauty aids to retailers and hospitals. **Corporate headquarters location:** This location. **Listed on:** NASDAQ. **Stock exchange symbol:** DKWD.

FOREST PHARMACEUTICALS, INC.
3721 Laclede Avenue, Earth City, MO 63045. 314/493-7000. **Contact:** Personnel Department. **World Wide Web address:** http://www.forestpharm.com. **Description:** Distributes pharmaceutical products for Forest Laboratories, Inc. **Corporate headquarters location:** New York NY. **Parent company:** Forest Laboratories, Inc. develops, manufactures, and sells both branded and generic forms of ethical drug products, as well as nonprescription pharmaceutical products sold over –the counter, which are used for the treatment of a wide range of illnesses. **Listed on:** American Stock Exchange. **Stock exchange symbol:** FRX.

IVX ANIMAL HEALTH
3915 South 48th Street Terrace, St. Joseph MO 64503. 816/364-3777. **Fax:** 816/364-3778. **Contact:** Human Resources. **E-mail address:** tkarr@psiqv.com. **World Wide Web address:** http://www.psiqv.com. **Description:** A manufacturer of generic animal pharmaceuticals.

JONES PHARMACEUTICALS, INC.
1945 Craig Road, St. Louis MO 63146. 314/576-6100. **Fax:** 314/469-5749. **Contact:** Human Resources. **World Wide Web address:** http://www.kingpharm.com. **Description:** A specialty pharmaceutical manufacturer that targets specific areas. The company produces endocrine products for the treatment of thyroid disease; manufactures and markets a variety of veterinary pharmaceuticals; and markets pharmaceuticals used in hospitals. **NOTE:** Search and apply for positions online. **Positions advertised include:** Quality Systems Analyst. **Parent company:** King Pharmaceuticals. **Corporate headquarters location:** Bristol TN. **Listed on:** New York Stock Exchange. **Stock exchange symbol:** KG.

KV PHARMACEUTICAL COMPANY
2503 South Hanley Road, St. Louis MO 63144. 314/645-6600. **Contact:** Staffing Department. **E-mail address:** staffing@kvpharmaceutical.com. **World Wide Web address:** http://www.kvpharmaceutical.com. **Description:** KV Pharmaceutical Company researches, develops, produces, and sells drug delivery products. **NOTE:** Second and third shifts are offered. Search and apply for positions online. **Positions advertised include:** Packaging Supervisor; Document Control Specialist; Staffing Specialist; Research Scientist; DEA Compliance Inspector; Inspector/Auditor. **Office hours:** Monday - Friday, 8:00 a.m. - 4:30 p.m. **Corporate headquarters location:** This location. **Listed on:** New York Stock Exchange. **Stock exchange symbol:** KVA. **Annual sales/revenues:** More than $100 million. **Number of employees nationwide:** 550.

MALLINCKRODT, INC.
1600 North Z, Saint Louis MO 63102. 314/654-2000. **Contact:** Personnel. **E-mail address:** employment@tycohealthcare.com. **World Wide Web address:** http://www.mallinckrodt.com. **Description:** Manufactures and markets healthcare products through three main specialty groups. The Imaging Group provides magnetic resonance, nuclear medicine, and X-ray products. The Pharmaceuticals Group provides pharmaceutical products for addiction therapy and pain relief. The Respiratory Group manufactures airway management systems and respiratory devices. **NOTE:** Jobseekers should send resumes to Corporate Employment, 675 McDonnell Boulevard, P.O. Box 5840, St. Louis MO 63134. **Corporate headquarters location:** This location. **Parent company:** TYCO International. **Number of employees worldwide:** 13,000.

PM RESOURCES
13001 St. Charles Rock Road, Bridgeton MO 63044. 314/291-6724. **Fax:** 314/291-2657. **Contact:** Plant Manager. **Description:** Formulates and distributes animal health products including feed additives, medicated treatments, anthelmintics, nutritional supplements, cleaners and disinfectants, and pest control products. **Parent company:** Agri-Nutritional Group.

PFIZER
One Pfizer Way, Lees Summit MO 64081. 816/524-5580. **Contact:** Human Resources. **World Wide Web address:** http://www.pfizer.com. **Description:** A leading pharmaceutical company that distributes products concerning cardiovascular health, central nervous system disorders, infectious diseases, and women's health worldwide. The company's brand-name products include Benadryl, Ben Gay, Cortizone, Desitin, Halls, Listerine, Sudafed, and Zantac 75.

QUEST DIAGNOSTICS INCORPORATED
11636 Administration Drive, St. Louis MO 63146. 314/567-3905. **Contact:** Human Resources Department. **World Wide Web address:** http://www.questdiagnostics.com. **Description:** One of the largest clinical laboratories in North America, providing a broad range of clinical laboratory services to health care clients that include physicians, hospitals, clinics, dialysis centers, pharmaceutical companies, and corporations. The company offers and performs tests on blood, urine, and other bodily fluids and tissues to provide information for health and well-being. **NOTE:** Search and apply for positions online. **Other U.S. locations:** Nationwide.

STERIS CORPORATION
7405 Page Avenue, St. Louis MO 63133. 314/290-4600. **Contact:** Human Resources. **World Wide Web address:** http://www.steris.com. **Description:** Develops, manufactures and markets infection prevention, contamination prevention, microbial reduction and surgical support systems, products, technologies and services for healthcare, scientific, food, research and industrial customers. **NOTE:** Search and apply for positions online. **Positions advertised include:** Associate Scientist. **Corporate headquarters location:** Mentor OH. **Listed on:** New York Stock Exchange. **Stock exchange symbol:** STE. **Number of employees worldwide:** 5,100.

VI-JON LABORATORIES, INC.
8515 Page Avenue, St. Louis MO 63114. 314/427-1000. **Fax:** 314/427-1010. **Contact:** Human Resources Manager. **E-mail address:** hr@vijon.com. **World Wide Web address:** http://www.vijon.com. **Description:** Wholesalers of a variety of pharmaceuticals and cosmetics. **NOTE:** Search for positions online. **Positions advertised include:** Buyer; Sr. Buyer; Material Planning Coordinator; Chemical Processing Manager; **Corporate headquarters location:** This location. **Operations at this facility include:** Manufacturing. **Listed on:** Privately held. **Number of employees at this location:** 100.

Montana

GLAXOSMITHKLINE
553 Old Corvallis Road, Hamilton MT 59840. 406/363-6214. **Contact:** Human Resources. **World Wide Web address:** http://www.gsk.com. **Description:** Involved in the research and development of immunotherapeutics to prevent or treat cancer, autoimmune diseases, and infectious diseases. **NOTE:** Must apply online at corporate web site, no paper resumes are accepted. **Positions advertised include:** Development Assistant/Associate. **Operations at this facility include:** Manufacturing and Adjuvant **Number of employees nationwide:** 380.

PHARMERICA
1130 17th Avenue South, Great Falls MT 59405. 406/452-3713. **Toll-free phone:** 877/975-2273. **Contact:** Rich Mosholder, Human Resources. **World Wide Web address:** http://www.pharmerica.com. **Description:** A supplier of pharmaceuticals and related products to long-term care facilities, hospitals, and assisted living communities. PharMerica also provides nurse consultant services, infusion therapy and training, medical records consulting, and educational programs. **Corporate headquarters location:** Tampa FL. **Other U.S. locations:** Nationwide. **Parent company:** AmerisourceBergen Corporation. **Listed on:** New York Stock Exchange. **Stock exchange symbol:** ABC.

SGM BIOTECH, INC.
10 Evergreen Drive, Suite E, Bozeman MT 59715. 406/585-9535. **Fax:** 406/585-9219. **Contact:** Human Resources. **World Wide Web address:** http://www.sgmbiotech.com. **Description:** Manufactures biological indicators and products that visually indicate when sterilization is complete by evaluating the common sterilization processes of ethylene oxide gas, steam, and dry heat.

Nebraska

MDS PHARMA SERVICES
621 Rose Street, Lincoln NE 68502-0837. 402/476-2811. **Fax:** 402/476-7598. **Contact:** Human Resources. **World Wide Web address:** http://www.mdsps.com. **Description:** Offers a complete range of clinical trials, analytical and statistical services, and consumer product research. These services are provided from facilities and offices in the United States, Europe, and Japan, and in more than 1,000 clinical investigation sites. MDS Pharma Services performs all types of Phase I studies including complete bioavailability and bioequivalence studies and pharmacokinetic/ pharmacodynamic clinical studies with healthy and special populations, as well as offering data analysis and customized reporting. MDS Pharma Services also designs and manages complete Phase II, III, and IV multicenter clinical studies. **Positions advertised include:** Clinical Study Design Technician; Proposal Development Coordinator; Principal Investigator; Instrument Specialist; Regulatory Submission Coordinator; Scientific Writer; Senior Pharmacokineticscist; Clinical Conduct Associate; Scientist; Extraction Analyst; Clinical Research Nurse; Custodian. **NOTE:** Please see website for online application form. **Other U.S. locations:** Nationwide. **International locations:** Worldwide. **Parent company:** MDS Inc. **Listed on:** New York Stock Exchange. **Stock exchange symbol:** MDZ.

NATURE TECHNOLOGY CORPORATION
4701 Innovation Drive, Lincoln NE 68521. 402/472-6530. **Fax:** 402/472-6532. **Contact:** Dr. Claude Hodgson. **E-mail address:** hodgson@natx.com. **World Wide Web address:** http://www.natx.com. **Description:** Provides vector design, development, and manufacturing assistance to the biotech and biopharmaceutical industries for the construction of genes in living cells and organisms.

PFIZER ANIMAL HEALTH
601 West Cornhusker Highway, Lincoln NE 68521. 402/475-4541. **Contact:** Human Resources. **World Wide Web address:** http://www.pfizer.com. **NOTE:** Please see website for online application form. **Description:** Manufactures veterinary biologicals and pharmaceuticals. **Corporate headquarters location:** New York, NY. **Other U.S. locations:** Nationwide. **International locations:** Worldwide. **Listed on:** New York Stock Exchange. **Stock exchange symbol:** PFE.

PHARMA CHEMIE
1877 Midland Street, P.O. Box 326, Syracuse NE 68446-0326. 402/269-3195. **Fax:** 402/269-3196. **Contact:** Human Resources. **World Wide Web address:** http://www.pharma-chemie.com. **Description:** Produces a full line of animal nutritional supplements.

VETERINARY DIAGNOSTIC CENTER
Fair Street and East Campus Loop, P.O. Box 82646, Lincoln NE 68501-2646. 402/472-1434. **Fax:** 402/472-3094. **Contact:** Human Resources. **E-mail:** vdc@unl.edu. **World Wide Web address:** http://vbms.unl.edu/nvdls.shtml. **Description:** A veterinary diagnostic laboratory, part of the Nebraska Veterinary Diagnostic System at University of Nebraska at Lincoln, that identifies animal diseases. **NOTE:** Human Resources phone is 402/472-3101. Part of University of Nebraska at Lincoln.

Nevada

BUTLER ANIMAL HEALTH SUPPLY, LLC
4795 Longley Lane, Reno NV 89502. 775/848-1747. **Contact:** Human Resources. **World Wide Web address:** http://www.accessbutler.com. **Description:** A distributor of veterinary pharmaceuticals and biological products to veterinarians. **Corporate headquarters location:** Dublin OH. **Other U.S. locations:** Nationwide. **International locations:** Worldwide. **Listed on:** Privately held. **Number of employees at this location:** 50.

CARDINAL HEALTH LAS VEGAS
61 Spectrum Boulevard, Las Vegas NV 89101. 702/438-4494. **Contact:** Human Resources. **World Wide Web address:** http://www.cardinal.com. **Description:** Manufactures and distributes pharmaceuticals, as well as medical supplies and equipment. **Corporate headquarters location:** Dublin OH. **Other U.S. locations:** Nationwide. **International locations:** Worldwide. **Parent company:** Cardinal Health, Inc. **Operations at this facility include:** This location manufactures radioactive drugs that are distributed to businesses and hospitals in the Las Vegas area. **Listed on:** New York Stock Exchange. **Stock exchange symbol:** CAH. **Sales/revenue:** Over $50 billion. **Number of employees worldwide:** 55,000.

DOLISOS AMERICA INC.
3014 Rigel Avenue, Las Vegas NV 89102. 702/871-7153. **Contact:** Human Resources. **World Wide Web address:** http://www.dolisosamerica.com. **Description:** A manufacturer of homeopathic remedies. **Parent company:** Boiron.

LABORATORY CORPORATION OF AMERICA (LABCORP)
888 Willow Street, Reno NV 89502. 775/334-3400. **Contact:** Human Resources Manager. **World Wide Web address:** http://www.labcorp.com. **Description:** One of the nation's leading clinical laboratory companies, providing services primarily to physicians, hospitals, clinics, nursing homes, and other laboratories nationwide. LabCorp performs tests on blood, urine,

and other bodily fluids and tissue, aiding the prompt and accurate diagnosis of disease. **Corporate headquarters location:** Burlington NC. **Other U.S. locations:** Nationwide. **Operations at this facility include:** Administration. **Listed on:** New York Stock Exchange. **Stock exchange symbol:** LH. **Number of employees nationwide:** 23,000.

QUEST DIAGNOSTICS
4230 Burnham Avenue, Suite 144, Las Vegas NV 89119-5410. 702/733-7866. **Toll-free phone:** 800/433-2750. **Contact:** Human Resources. **World Wide Web address:** http://www.questdiagnostics.com. **Description:** A medical testing laboratory offering over 500 diagnostic determinations. **Positions advertised include:** Transcriptionist; Medical Technologist; Assistant Controller; Billing Coordinator; Route Service Rep; Laboratory Assistant; Specimen Technician; Phlebotomy Services Representative.

STEINBERG DIAGNOSTIC MEDICAL IMAGING
P.O. Box 36900, Las Vegas NV 89133-6900. 702/732-6090. **Physical address:** 2950 South Maryland Parkway, Las Vegas NV 89109-2257. **Fax:** 702/731-5067. **Contact:** Human Resources Manager. **E-mail address:** mlayugan@sdmi-lv.com. **World Wide Web address:** http://www.sdmi-lv.com. **Description:** A radiology lab. **Positions advertised include:** Mammography Technologist; MRI Technologist; RN-Special Procedures; Ultrasound Technologist.

New Hampshire
FISHER SCIENTIFIC INTERNATIONAL INC.
1 Liberty Lane, Hampton NH 03842. 603/926-5911. **Fax:** 603/929-2379. **Contact:** Human Resources. **World Wide Web address:** http://www.fisherscientific.com. **Description:** One of the largest providers of instruments, equipment, and other products to the scientific community. The company offers a selection of products and services to research centers and industrial customers worldwide. Fisher Scientific serves scientists engaged in biomedical, biotechnology, pharmaceutical, chemical, and other fields of research and development in corporations, the educational and research institutions, and government agencies. The company also supplies clinical laboratories, hospitals, environmental testing centers, remediation companies, quality control laboratories, and other industrial facilities. In addition, Fisher Scientific represents its customers as a third-party purchaser of maintenance materials and other basic supplies. **NOTE:** Search posted openings nationwide and apply on-line only. No paper resumes are accepted and telephone contact is discouraged. **Corporate headquarters location:** This location. **Other U.S. locations:** Tustin CA; Suwanee GA; Hanover Park IL; Houston TX. **International locations:** Worldwide. **Listed on:** New York Stock Exchange. **Stock exchange symbol:** FSH. **Annual sales/revenues:** More than $100 million. **Number of employees at this location:** 110. **Number of employees worldwide:** 10,000.

MILLIPORE CORPORATION
11 Prescott Road, Jaffrey NH 03452. 603/532-8711. **Contact:** Scott Loumer, Human Resources Manager. **World Wide Web address:** http://www.millipore.com. **Description:** Millipore Corporation manufactures microporous filters and filtration devices used for the analysis, separation, and purification of fluids. Products are used in the fields of health care, pharmaceuticals, micro-electronics, biological sciences, and genetic engineering. **NOTE:** Search posted openings nationwide and apply online only. No paper resumes are accepted. **Positions advertised include:** Document Control Coordinator; Production Supervisor; Quality Supervisor; Finance Manager; Shipper/Receiver; Process Technician; Validation Engineer; Quality Assurance Inspector; HVAC Technician. **Office hours:** Monday – Thursday, 6:30 a.m. – 4:00p.m.; Friday, 6:30 a.m. – 3:00 p.m. **Corporate headquarters location:** Bellirica MA. **Operations at this facility include:** This location manufactures filtration devices for the pharmaceutical industry. **Listed on:** New York Stock Exchange. **Stock exchange symbol:** MIL. **Number of employees worldwide:** 4,200.

New Jersey
ABBOTT POINT-OF-CARE
104 Windsor Center Drive, East Windsor NJ 08520. 609/443-9300. **Fax:** 609/426-3907. **Contact:** Human Resources. **E-mail address:** hr_usa@i-stat.com. **World Wide Web address:** http://www.abbottpointofcare.com. **Description:** Develops, manufactures, and markets medical diagnostic products for blood analysis. **NOTE:** Entry-level positions and part-time jobs are offered. **Positions advertised include:** Sr. Product Manager; Director Product Development Program Management; Sr. Quality Systems Specialist; Sr. Mechanical Engineer; Process Improvement Engineer. **International locations:** Kanata, Ontario, Canada. **Listed on:** New York Stock Exchange. **Stock exchange symbol:** ABT.

ALFACELL CORPORATION
225 Belleville Avenue, Bloomfield NJ 07003. 973/748-8082. **Fax:** 973/748-1355. **Contact:** Human Resources. **World Wide Web address:** http://www.alfacell.com. **Description:** Developing ribonuclease protein-based therapy for the treatment of cancer and other life-threatening diseases.

ALPHARMA INC.
One Executive Drive, Fort Lee NJ 07024. 201/947-7774. **Toll-free phone:** 800/645-4216. **Fax:** 201/947-6145. **Contact:** Human Resources. **World Wide Web address:** http://www.alpharma.com. **Description:** A multinational pharmaceutical company that develops, manufactures, and markets specialty generic and proprietary human pharmaceuticals and animal health products. The U.S. Pharmaceuticals Division is a market leader in liquid pharmaceuticals and a prescription market leader in creams and ointments. The International Pharmaceuticals Division manufactures generic pharmaceuticals and OTC products. Other divisions include the Animal Health Division, which manufactures and markets antibiotics and other feed additives for the poultry and swine industries; the Aquatic Animal Health Division, which serves the aquaculture industry and is a manufacturer and marketer of vaccines for farmed fish; and the Fine Chemicals Division, which is a basic producer of specialty bulk antibiotics. **Corporate headquarters location:** This location. **Listed on:** New York Stock Exchange. **Stock exchange symbol:** ALO.

ALTEON INC.
6 Campus Drive, Parsippany NJ 07054. 201/934-5000. **Fax:** 201/934-8880. **Contact:** Human Resources Department. **E-mail address:** careers@alteon.com. **World Wide Web address:** http://www.alteonpharma.com. **Description:** A pharmaceutical company engaged in the discovery and development of novel therapeutic and diagnostic products for treating complications associated with diabetes and aging. **Positions advertised include:** Clinical Research Associate; Clinical Team Manager; Regulatory & Quality Assurance Manager. **Listed on:** American Stock Exchange. **Stock exchange symbol:** ALT.

ASTRALIS, LTD.
75 Passaic Avenue, Fairfield NJ 07004. 973/227-7168. **Fax:** 973/227-7169. **Contact:** Human Resources. **E-mail address:** info@astralisltd.com. **World Wide Web address:** http://www.astralisltd.com. **Description:** A biotechnology firm focusing on the research and development of novel treatments for immune system disorders and skin diseases such as psoriasis.

BASF CORPORATION
KNOLL PHARMACEUTICALS
100 Campus Drive, Florham Park NJ 07932. 973/245-6000. **Fax:** 973/245-6002. **Contact:** Liz Roman, Director of Human Resources. **World Wide Web address:** http://www.basf.com. **Description:** BASF Corporation is an international chemical products organization, doing business in five operating groups:

Chemicals; Coatings and Colorants; Consumer Products and Life Sciences; Fiber Products; and Polymers. **Positions advertised include:** Procurement Agent; Product Manager; Sr. Attorney/Counsel; Manager, Editorial Services; Corporate Paralegal; Business Development Rep. **Corporate headquarters location:** This location. **Operations at this facility include:** This location serves as the U.S. headquarters and houses management offices and the pharmaceutical division, Knoll Pharmaceuticals. **Listed on:** New York Stock Exchange. **Stock exchange symbol:** BF. **Number of employees worldwide:** 125,000.

BARRIER THERAPEUTICS
600 College Road East, Suite 3200, Princeton NJ 08540-6697. 609/945-1200. **Fax:** 609/945-1212. **Contact:** Human Resources. **E-mail address:** hr@barriertherapeutics.com. **World Wide Web address:** http://www.barriertherapeutics.com. **Description:** A pharmaceutical company focused on the discovery, development, and commercialization of pharmaceutical products that address major medical needs in the treatment of dermatological diseases and disorders. **Positions advertised include:** Associate Director/Director, Clinical Pharmacokinetics; Associate Director/Director, Quality Assurance & Regulatory Compliance; Director, US Regulatory Affairs.

BERLEX LABORATORIES, INC.
340 Changebridge Road, P.O. Box 1000, Montville NJ 07045-1000. 973/487-2000. **Contact:** Human Resources. **World Wide Web address:** http://www.berlex.com. **Description:** Researches, manufactures, and markets ethical pharmaceutical products in the fields of cardiovascular medicine, endocrinology and fertility control, diagnostic imaging, oncology, and central nervous system disorders. Berlex Laboratories has three strategic units: Berlex Drug Development & Technology (New Jersey), Oncology/Central Nervous System (California), and Berlex Biosciences (California). The company also owns Berlex Drug Development and Technology and operates a national sales force. The sales force, which is divided into three geographic regions, markets the complete line of Berlex products including BETASERON, which is used to treat multiple sclerosis. **Positions advertised include:** Director, Drug Safety Management; IT Project Manager; Director, Medical Affairs; Manager, Clinical Quality Assurance; Regulatory Toxicologist. **Corporate headquarters location:** This location. **Parent company:** Schering AG (Germany).

BIO-REFERENCE LABORATORIES
481 Edward H. Ross Drive, Elmwood Park NJ 07407. 201/791-2600. **Fax:** 201/475-8730. **Contact:** Human Resources. **E-mail address:** jobs@bioreference.com. **World Wide Web address:** http://www.bio-referencelabs.com. **Description:** Operates a clinical laboratory. Bio-Reference offers a list of chemical diagnostic tests including blood and urine analysis, blood chemistry, hematology services, serology, radioimmunological analysis, toxicology (including drug screening), Pap smears, tissue pathology (biopsies), and other tissue analyses. Bio-Reference markets its services directly to physicians, hospitals, clinics, and other health facilities. **Corporate headquarters location:** This location. **Listed on:** NASDAQ. **Stock exchange symbol:** BRLI.

BIOVAIL PHARMACEUTICALS, INC.
700 Route 202/206 North, Bridgewater NJ 08807. 908/927-1400. **Fax:** 908/927-1401. **Contact:** Human Resources. **World Wide Web address:** http://www.biovail.com. **Description:** A specialty pharmaceutical company engaged in the formulation, clinical testing, registration, manufacture, and commercialization of pharmaceutical products utilizing advanced drug-delivery technologies. **Positions advertised include:** Network Administrator; Operations Change Coordinator; Database Administrator; Systems Administrator; Sr. Director, US Regulatory Affairs; Manager, Organization Development; Manager, Clinical Operations and Outsourcing; Manager, Sales Training and Development; Manager, Contract Development.

BRACCO DIAGNOSTICS INC.
107 College Road East, Princeton NJ 08540. 609/514-2200. **Toll-free phone:** 800/631-5245. **Fax:** 609/514-2424. **Contact:** Human Resources. **E-mail address:** jobsearch@bracco.com. **World Wide Web address:** http://www.bracco.com. **Description:** Researches and develops diagnostic pharmaceuticals and nuclear medicine imaging products. **NOTE:** Resumes may be submitted on-line at the above Website. Job listings provide e-mail addresses and contact information. **Positions advertised include:** Programmer. **Parent company:** Bracco S.p.A. **Number of employees worldwide:** 2,300.

BRADLEY PHARMACEUTICALS, INC.
383 Route 46 West, Fairfield NJ 07004-2402. 973/882-1505. **Fax:** 973/575-5366. **Contact:** Human Resources. **E-mail address:** personnel@bradpharm.com. **World Wide Web address:** http://www.bradpharm.com. **Description:** Manufactures and markets over-the-counter and prescription pharmaceuticals, and health-related products including nutritional, personal hygiene, and internal medicine brands. Founded in 1985. **Positions advertised include:** Product Manager; Sales Assistant Training Manager; Quality Assurance Director; Pharmaceutical Sales Representative; Telemarketing. **Corporate headquarters location:** This location. **Subsidiaries include:** Doak Dermatologics Company Inc. (Westbury NY); Kenwood Therapeutics. **Listed on:** NASDAQ. **Stock exchange symbol:** BPRX.

BRISTOL-MYERS SQUIBB COMPANY
P.O. Box 5335, Princeton NJ 08543-5335. 609/252-4000. **Fax:** 609/897-6412. **Contact:** Employment Department. **World Wide Web address:** http://www.bms.com. **Description:** Bristol-Myers Squibb manufactures pharmaceuticals, medical devices, nonprescription drugs, toiletries, and beauty aids. The company's pharmaceutical products include cardiovascular drugs, anti-infectives, anticancer agents, AIDS therapy treatments, central nervous system drugs, diagnostic agents, and other drugs. Nonprescription products include formulas, vitamins, analgesics, remedies, and skin care products. Nonprescription drug brand names include Bufferin, Excedrin, Nuprin, and Comtrex. Beauty aids include Clairol and Ultress hair care, Nice 'n Easy and Clairesse hair colorings, hair sprays, gels, and deodorants. **Positions advertised include:** Medical Marketing Director; Global Marketing Director; Clinical Scientist Associate; Research Scientist Associate; Clinical Protocol Manager; Clinical Scientist; Research Investigator; Research Assistant; Territory Business Sales Associate; Accounting Director; Principal Accountant; Associate Manager; Administrative Assistant; Counsel Patent Associate; Director Marketing Research; Manager. **Corporate headquarters location:** New York NY. **Operations at this facility include:** This location is engaged in the research and manufacture of various pharmaceuticals and personal care products. **Listed on:** New York Stock Exchange. **Stock exchange symbol:** BMY.

CELATOR PHARMACEUTICALS, INC.
303B College Road East, Princeton NJ 08540. 609/243-0123. **Fax:** 609/243-0202. **Contact:** Human Resources. **E-mail address:** hr@celatorpharma.com. **World Wide Web address:** http://www.celatorpharma.com. **Description:** A privately held biopharmaceutical company developing new and more effective therapies to treat cancer. **Positions advertised include:** Director, Drug Metabolism and Pharmacokinetics; Clinical Project Manager; Scientist, Process Development; Associate Technician, Process Development; Quality Control Sr. Analyst; Quality Control Analyst; Scientist.

CELGENE CORPORATION
86 Morris Avenue, Summit NJ 07901. 908/673-9000. **Fax:** 732/271-4184. **Contact:** Human Resources. **E-mail address:** jobs@celgene.com. **World Wide Web**

address: http://www.celgene.com. **Description:** Engaged in the development and commercialization of a broad range of immunotherapeutic drugs designed to control serious disease states. Celgene also manufactures and sells chiral intermediates, key building blocks in the production of advanced therapeutic compounds and certain agrochemical and food-related products. The focus of Celgene's immunotherapeutics program is the development of small molecule compounds that modulate bodily production of tumor necrosis factor alpha, a hormone-like protein. Elevated levels of this cytokine are believed to cause symptoms associated with several debilitating diseases such as HIV and AIDS-related conditions, sepsis, and inflammatory bowel disease. **NOTE:** Search and apply for positions online. Resumes only accepted for current openings. **Positions advertised include:** Associate Director Clinical Operations; Associate Director QC; Attorney; Manager Sales Operations; Clinical Operations Coordinator; Clinical Pharmacologist; Data Manager; Manager Scientific and Medical Writing; Medical Reviewer; Sr. SAS Programmer; QC Analyst; Product Manager Strategic Marketing. **Corporate headquarters location:** This location. **Listed on:** NASDAQ. **Stock exchange symbol:** CELG.

CELSIS LABORATORY GROUP
165 Fieldcrest Avenue, Edison NJ 08837. 732/346-5100. **Contact:** Human Resources. **E-mail address:** info@celsis.com. **World Wide Web address:** http://www.celsislabs.com. **Description:** An independent testing laboratory specializing in toxicology, microbiology, and analytical chemistry. **Number of employees at this location:** 50.

CORIELL INSTITUTE FOR MEDICAL RESEARCH
403 Haddon Avenue, Camden, NJ 08103. 856/966-7377. **Fax:** 856/964-0254. **Contact:** Charlotte Tule, Director of Human Resources. **E-mail address:** ctule@coriell.org. **World Wide Web address:** http://www.coriell.org. **Description**: Coriell is an independent, not-for-profit research organization. In addition to research programs in stem cell biology, genetic diversity, and human genetic diseases, Coriell operates the world's largest repositories of human cells for use in research. Founded in 1953. **Positions advertised include:** Postdoctoral Fellow; Research Associate/Senior Postdoctoral.

COVANCE INC.
210 Carnegie Center, Princeton NJ 08540. 609/452-4953. **Toll-free phone:** 888/COV-ANCE. **Fax:** 609/452-9854. **Contact:** Human Resources. **World Wide Web address:** http://www.covance.com. **Description:** One of the world's largest and most comprehensive drug development services companies. Covance Inc. provides preclinical testing, health economics consulting, biomanufacturing, and clinical support services. Founded in 1993. **NOTE:** Entry-level positions are offered. **Positions advertised include:** Business Analyst. **Positions advertised include:** Sr. Medical Writer; Sr. Project Manager; Sr. Manager, External Communications; Business Process Improvement Leader; IT Portfolio Management Analyst. **Corporate headquarters location:** This location. **Other U.S. locations:** Berkeley CA; Richmond CA; Walnut Creek CA; Washington DC; Tampa FL; Indianapolis IN; Kalamazoo MI; Research Triangle Park NC; Reno NV; Allentown PA; Denver PA; Radnor PA; Nashville TN; Alice TX; Cumberland VA; Vienna VA; Madison WI. **International locations:** Worldwide. **Subsidiaries include:** Berkeley Antibody Company, Inc. provides a variety of preclinical services. GDXI, Inc. provides electrocardiogram analysis for clinical trials. **Listed on:** New York Stock Exchange. **Stock exchange symbol:** CVD.. **Number of employees at this location:** 1,000. **Number of employees worldwide:** 7,700.

CYTOGEN CORPORATION
650 College Road East, Suite 3100, Princeton NJ 08540. 609/750-8200. **Toll-free phone:** 800/833-3533. **Fax:** 609/452-2476. **Contact:** Human Resources. **E-mail address:** hrdirector@cytogen.com. **World Wide Web address:** http://www.cytogen.com. **Description:** Develops products for the targeted delivery of diagnostic and therapeutic substances directly to sites of disease, using monoclonal antibodies. Proprietary antibody linking technology is used primarily to develop specific cancer diagnostic imaging and therapeutic products. Founded in 1981. **Positions advertised include:** Medical Oncologist; Medical Science Liaison; New Business Development. **Corporate headquarters location:** This location. **Listed on:** NASDAQ. **Stock exchange symbol:** CYTO. **Number of employees at this location:** 120.

DSM NUTRITIONAL PRODUCTS, INC.
45 Waterview Boulevard, Parsippany NJ 07054-1298. 973/257-8500. **Fax:** 973/257-8600. **Contact:** Human Resources. **World Wide Web address:** http://www.dsm.com. **Description:** The world's leading supplier of vitamins, carotenoids and other chemicals to the feed, food, pharmaceutical, and cosmetic industries.

DERMA SCIENCES, INC.
214 Carnegie Center, Suite 100, Princeton NJ 08540. 609/514-4744. **Toll-free phone:** 800/825-4325. **Fax:** 609/514-0502. **Contact:** Human Resources. **E-mail address:** info@dermasciencesinc.com. **World Wide Web address:** http://www.dermasciences.com. **Description:** Engaged in the development, marketing, and sale of proprietary sprays, ointments, and dressings for the management of certain chronic, nonhealing skin ulcerations such as pressure and venous ulcers, surgical incisions, and burns.

ENZON, INC.
20 Kingsbridge Road, Piscataway NJ 08854-3998. 732/980-4500. **Fax:** 732/980-5911. **Contact:** Human Resources. **E-mail address:** hr@enzon.com. **World Wide Web address:** http://www.enzon.com. **Description:** A biopharmaceutical company that develops advanced therapeutics for life threatening diseases, primarily in the area of oncology. **Positions advertised include:** Human Resources Specialist; Manufacturing Manager; Accounting Manager; Associate Director; Quality Assurance Clerk; Validation Specialist; Application Engineer; Research Associate; Clinical Project Manager; Computer Support Specialist; Clinical Research Assistant. **Office hours:** Monday - Friday, 8:30 a.m. - 5:00 p.m. **Corporate headquarters location:** Bridgewater NJ. **Listed on:** NASDAQ. **Stock exchange symbol:** ENZN. **President/CEO:** Peter Tombros. **Annual sales/revenues:** $11 - $20 million. **Number of employees at this location:** 55. **Number of employees nationwide:** 90.

FISHER SCIENTIFIC COMPANY
One Reagent Lane, Fair Lawn NJ 07410. 201/796-7100. **Contact:** Michelle Valvano, Personnel Manager. **World Wide Web address:** http://www.fisherscientific.com. **Description:** Fisher Scientific manufactures, distributes, and sells a wide range of products used in industrial and medical laboratories. Products include analytical and measuring instruments, apparatus, and appliances; reagent chemicals and diagnostics; glassware and plasticware; and laboratory furniture. Customers are primarily industrial laboratories, medical and hospital laboratories, and educational and research laboratories. Manufacturing operations are carried out by six operating divisions in 11 U.S. locations. **Positions advertised include:** Chemical Packager; Process Engineer; Production Planner. **Operations at this facility include:** This location produces reagents. **Listed on:** New York Stock Exchange. **Stock exchange symbol:** FSH.

GENMAB INC.
457 North Harrison Street, Princeton NJ 08540. 609/430-2481. **Fax:** 609/430-2482. **Contact:** Human Resources. **World Wide Web address:** http://www.genmab.com. **Description:** A publicly-traded international biotechnology company that creates and develops fully human monoclonal antibody-based

products for the treatment of life-threatening and debilitating diseases such as cancer, infectious disease, rheumatoid arthritis and other inflammatory conditions. **Parent company:** Genmab A/S (Copenhagen Denmark).

GENTA
Two Connell Drive, Berkeley Heights NJ 07922. 908/286-9800. **Contact:** Human Resources. **E-mail address:** jobs@genta.com. **World Wide Web address:** http://www.genta.com. **Description:** A biopharmaceutical company focused on the identification, development and commercialization of drugs for the treatment of patients with cancer. **Positions advertised include:** Customer Services/Distribution/Logistics Manager; Director, Product Communication; Manager, Sales Operation; Product Director; Sr. Packaging Development Engineer/Manager; Medical Writer; National Sales Director; Director, Medical Science Liaison; Associate Director/Director Drug Product Manufacturing.

GLAXOSMITHKLINE CORPORATION
257 Cornelison Avenue, Jersey City NJ 07302. 201/434-3000. **Contact:** Human Resources. **World Wide Web address:** http://www.gsk.com. **Description:** Develops, manufactures, and sells products in four general categories: denture, dental care, oral hygiene, and professional dental products; proprietary products; ethical pharmaceutical products; and household products. Dental-related products include Polident denture cleansers. **Positions advertised include:** Pharmaceutical Sales Representative. **Listed on:** New York Stock Exchange. **Stock exchange symbol:** GSK.

GLAXOSMITHKLINE PHARMACEUTICALS
101 Possumtown Road, Piscataway NJ 08854. 732/469-5200. **Contact:** Human Resources Manager. **World Wide Web address:** http://www.gsk.com. **Description:** Manufactures penicillin. **Positions advertised include:** Analytical Chemist; Clinical Operations Project Manager. **Corporate headquarters location:** Philadelphia PA. **Parent company:** GlaxoSmithKline Corporation is health care company engaged in the research, development, manufacture, and marketing of ethical pharmaceuticals, animal health products, ethical and proprietary medicines, and eye care products. **Listed on:** New York Stock Exchange. **Stock exchange symbol:** GSK.

HOFFMANN-LA ROCHE INC.
340 Kingsland Street, Nutley NJ 07110-0119. 973/235-5000. **Contact:** Director of Staffing. **World Wide Web address:** http://www.rocheusa.com. **Description:** An international health care organization that develops and manufactures pharmaceuticals, diagnostics, and vitamins. **NOTE:** Entry-level positions, part-time jobs, and second and third shifts are offered. **Positions advertised include:** Account Manager; Associate Clinical Director; Clinical Director; Clinical Pharmacology Study Manager; Coordinator, Drug Regulatory Affairs; Director Global Alliance. **Corporate headquarters location:** This location. **Other U.S. locations:** Nationwide. **International locations:** Worldwide. **Subsidiaries include:** Roche Biomedical Laboratories; Roche Diagnostics (ethical pharmaceuticals); Roche Vitamins Inc. **Parent company:** F. Hoffmann-La Roche Ltd. **Operations at this facility include:** Divisional Headquarters. **Listed on:** Privately held. **Annual sales/revenues:** More than $100 million. **Number of employees at this location:** 6,000. **Number of employees nationwide:** 20,000. **Number of employees worldwide:** 80,000.

HUNTINGDON LIFE SCIENCES
Mettlers Road, P.O. Box 2360, East Millstone NJ 08875. 732/873-2550. **Fax:** 732/873-8513. **Contact:** Human Resources. **E-mail address:** careers@princeton.huntingdon.com. **World Wide Web address:** http://www.huntingdon.com. **Description:** Provides contract biological safety (toxicological) testing services on a worldwide basis through two laboratories in the United States and the United Kingdom. The toxicology divisions of Huntington Life Sciences conduct studies designed to test pharmaceutical products, biologicals, chemical compounds, and other substances in order to produce the data required to identify, quantify, and evaluate the risks to humans and the environment resulting from the manufacture or use of these substances. These divisions also perform analytical and metabolic chemistry services. Huntington Life Sciences also performs clinical trials of new and existing pharmaceutical and biotechnology products and medical devices. The company is engaged in the clinical development process including analytical chemistry, evaluation of clinical data, data processing, biostatistical analysis, and the preparation of supporting documentation for compliance with regulatory requirements. Founded in 1952. **NOTE:** Entry-level positions, part-time jobs, and second and third shifts are offered. **Positions advertised include:** Animal Technician; Bioanalytical Analyst; Business Development Professional; Lab Assistant. **Special programs:** Summer Jobs. **Office hours:** Monday - Friday, 8:30 a.m. - 5:00 p.m. **Corporate headquarters location:** Cambridgeshire, England. **Parent company:** Huntingdon Life Sciences, Ltd. **President:** Alan Staple. **Annual sales/revenues:** $51 - $100 million. **Number of employees at this location:** 200. **Number of employees worldwide:** 1,500.

IGI, INC.
105 Lincoln Avenue, P.O. Box 687, Buena NJ 08310. 856/697-1441. **Fax:** 856/697-2259. **Contact:** Human Resources. **World Wide Web address:** http://www.askigi.com. **Description:** A diversified company engaged in three business segments: animal health products, cosmetic and consumer products, and biotechnology. The animal health products business produces and markets poultry vaccines, veterinary products, nutritional supplements, and grooming aids. The cosmetic and consumer products business produces and markets dermatologic, cosmetic, and consumer products. The biotechnology business develops and markets various applications of IGI's lipid encapsulation technology, primarily for human medicines and vaccines. Founded in 1977. **Corporate headquarters location:** This location.

IMCLONE SYSTEMS INCORPORATED
33 ImClone Drive, Branchburg NJ 08876. 908/218-9588. **Fax:** 908/704-8325. **Contact:** Human Resources. **World Wide Web address:** http://www.imclone.com. **Description:** A biopharmaceutical company dedicated to developing breakthrough biologic medicines in the area of oncology. **Positions advertised include:** Analyst, Field and Technical Operations; Associate Instrument Technician; Clinical Research Associate; Clinical QA Auditor; Compliance Support Analyst; Development Analyst; Development Scientist; Director, Biostatistics; Director Regulatory, Investigational Products; Documentation Coordinator; Drug Safety Data Coordinator; Formulation Associate; HR Coordinator; Manager, Process Engineering; Manager, QC; Manager, Enterprise Systems; Manager, Downstream Validation; Manufacturing Operators, Cell Culture, Purification, Bioservices; Manufacturing Engineer; Medical Affairs Operations Assistant; Medical Writer; Principal Engineer. **Corporate headquarters location:** New York NY. **Operations at this facility include:** Manufacturing, product development, finance, clinical, regulatory and quality assurance and commercial operations.

IMMUNOMEDICS, INC.
300 American Road, Morris Plains NJ 07950. 973/605-8200. **Fax:** 973/605-8282. **Contact:** Human Resources. **E-mail address:** hr@immunomedics.com. **World Wide Web address:** http://www.immunomedics.com. **Description:** Manufactures products to treat and detect infectious diseases and cancer. Products include LeukoScan, a diagnostic imaging tool that can scan for cancers such as osteomyelitis. **Positions advertised include:** Clinical Research Associate; Manager, Clinical Operations; Pharmacokinetic Technologist.

Listed on: NASDAQ. **Stock exchange symbol:** IMMU.

IVAX PHARMACEUTICALS INC.
140 LeGrand Avenue, Northvale NJ 07647. 201/767-1700. **Fax:** 201/767-1700. **Contact:** Personnel. **World Wide Web address:** http://www.ivaxpharmaceuticals.com. **Description:** Produces ethical pharmaceuticals for the cardiovascular, nervous, digestive, and respiratory systems. **Positions advertised include:** Chemist; Manager QC; Process Operator; QA Specialist. **Corporate headquarters location:** Miami FL.

JANSSEN PHARMACEUTICA INC.
1125 Trenton-Harbourton Road, Titusville NJ 08560. 609/730-2000. **Contact:** Human Resources. **World Wide Web address:** http://www.janssen.com. **Description:** A pharmaceutical research company that specializes in prescription drugs for use in a range of fields including dermatology and psychiatry. **NOTE:** Check current job postings and apply on-line at the Johnson & Johnson career Website: http://www.jnj.com/careers. **Parent company:** Johnson & Johnson (New Brunswick NJ).

LABORATORY CORPORATION OF AMERICA (LABCORP)
116 Millburn Avenue, Suite 211, Millburn NJ 07041. 973/912-8617. **Contact:** Human Resources. **World Wide Web address:** http://www.labcorp.com. **Description:** The company is one of the nation's leading clinical laboratory companies, providing services primarily to physicians, hospitals, clinics, nursing homes, and other clinical labs nationwide. LabCorp performs tests on blood, urine, and other body fluids and tissue, aiding the diagnosis of disease. **NOTE:** Direct employment correspondence to: LabCorp Human Resources, 309 East Davis Street, Burlington NC 27215. **Corporate headquarters location:** Burlington NC. **Operations at this facility include:** This location is a blood-drawing facility.

LIFECELL CORPORATION
One Millennium Way, Branchburg NJ 08876. 908/947-1100. **Fax:** 908/947-1200. **Contact:** Human Resources. **E-mail address:** hr@lifecell.com. **World Wide Web address:** http://www.lifecell.com. **Description:** Designs, manufactures, and produces products dealing with skin grafts for burn patients and with the preservation of transfusable blood platelets (blood cells that control clotting). LifeCell's main product, AlloDerm, removes the cells in allograft skin (from a cadaveric donor) that the patient's own immune system would normally reject. This technology enables the AlloDerm to become populated with the patient's own skin cells and blood vessels. Founded in 1986. **Listed on:** NASDAQ. **Stock exchange symbol:** LIFC.

LUNDBECK RESEARCH USA, INC.
215 College Road, Paramus NJ 07652. 201/261-1331. **Contact:** Human Resources. **World Wide Web address:** http://www.lundbeckresearch.com. **Description:** Researches and develops pharmaceuticals for the treatment of psychiatric and neurological disorders. **Positions advertised include:** Sr. Scientist; Research Associate; Patent Attorney.

MEDAREX, INC.
707 State Road, Princeton NJ 08540-1437. 908/479-2400. **Fax:** 908/479-2420. **Contact:** Human Resources. **E-mail address:** humanresources@medarex.com. **World Wide Web address:** http://www.medarex.com. **Description:** Researches and develops antibody-based pharmaceutical products to be used for the treatment of AIDS and other infectious diseases; cancers (including breast, ovarian, prostate, colon, and pancreatic); autoimmune diseases; and cardiovascular disease. These products bind to cells in the immune system and to the diseased cells, then stimulate the immune system to destroy the diseased cells. Founded in 1987. **Positions advertised include:** Accountant; Research Analyst. **NOTE:** Submit resume and search for current opportunities online. **Corporate headquarters location:** Princeton NJ.

MEDPOINTE INC.
265 Davidson Avenue, Suite 300, Somerset NJ 08873. 732/564-2200. **Contact:** Human Resources. **World Wide Web address:** http://www.medpointepharma.com. **Description:** A major manufacturer of ethical drugs and consumer products. Health care products include tranquilizers, laxatives, antibacterials, analgesics, decongestants, and cold and cough remedies. The company also manufactures tests for pregnancy, mononucleosis, rubella, and meningitis. Consumer products include Arrid antiperspirants and deodorants, Trojan condoms, hair lotions, and pet care items. **NOTE:** Entry-level positions and second and third shifts are offered. **Corporate headquarters location:** This location. **Other area locations:** North Brunswick NJ. **Other U.S. locations:** Decatur IL. **Number of employees nationwide:** 2,200.

MERCK & COMPANY, INC.
One Merck Drive, P.O. Box 100, Whitehouse Station NJ 08889-0100. 908/423-1000. **Contact:** Human Resources. **World Wide Web address:** http://www.merck.com. **Description:** A worldwide organization engaged in discovering, developing, producing, and marketing products for health care and the maintenance of the environment. Products include human and animal pharmaceuticals and chemicals sold to the health care, oil exploration, food processing, textile, paper, and other industries. Merck also runs an ethical drug mail-order marketing business. **Corporate headquarters location:** This location. **Other U.S. locations:** Albany GA; Montvale NJ; Rahway NJ; Wilson NC; West Point PA; Elkton VA. **Listed on:** New York Stock Exchange. **Stock exchange symbol:** MRK.

NAPP TECHNOLOGIES
401 Hackensack Avenue, Hackensack NJ 07601. 201/843-4664. **Fax:** 201/843-4737. **Contact:** Personnel. **E-mail address:** tom.smith@napptech.com. **World Wide Web address:** http://www.napptech.com. **Description:** Produces bulk pharmaceuticals, cosmetic raw materials, and fine chemicals. **Corporate headquarters location:** This location.

NOVARTIS PHARMACEUTICALS CORPORATION
59 Route 10, East Hanover NJ 07936. 973/503-7500. **Contact:** Human Resources. **World Wide Web address:** http://www.novartis.com. **Description:** Novartis Pharmaceuticals Corporation is one of the largest life science companies in the world. The company has three major divisions: health care, agribusiness, and nutrition. The health care division specializes in pharmaceuticals, both proprietary and generic, and ophthalmic health care. The agribusiness division is involved in seed technology, animal health, and crop protection. The nutrition sector includes medical, health, and infant nutrition. **Corporate headquarters location:** This location. **Other area locations:** Summit NJ. **Operations at this facility include:** This location houses administrative offices and Novartis Pharmaceuticals' primary research facility.

NOVO NORDISK PHARMACEUTICALS INC.
100 College West, Princeton NJ 08540. 609/987-5800. **Fax:** 609/921-8082. **Contact:** Human Resources. **World Wide Web address:** http://www.novo-nordisk.com. **Description:** One of the world's largest producers of industrial enzymes and insulin for the treatment of diabetes. **Positions advertised include:** Customer Care Administrator; Clinical Administrator; Medical Writer; Medical Information Scientist; Clinical Project Manager; Technical Rate Administrator; E-business Manager; Tax Accountant; Brand Manager; Clinical Administrator; Human Resources Generalist; Clinical Project Manager; Project Associate; Strategic Information Manager. **Parent company:** Novo Nordisk A/S (Baysvaerd, Denmark).

ORGANON INC.
56 Livingston Avenue, Roseland NJ 07068. 973/325-4500. **Toll-free phone:** 800/241-8812. **Fax:** 973/669-6144. **Contact:** Human Resources. **E-mail address:**

wohr@organon-usa.com. **World Wide Web address:** http://www.organon-usa.com. **Description:** A worldwide leader in pharmaceutical research and development in the fields of reproductive medicine, anesthesiology, central nervous system disorders, thrombosis, and immunology. **NOTE:** Entry-level positions and part-time jobs are offered. **Positions advertised include:** Pharmaceutical Scientist. **Special programs:** Internships; Summer Jobs. **Office hours:** Monday - Friday, 8:00 a.m. - 4:30 p.m. **Corporate headquarters location:** This location. **Parent company:** Akzo Nobel. **Annual sales/revenues:** More than $100 million. **Number of employees at this location:** 1,200.

ORTHO-McNEIL, INC.
1000 Route 202 North, P.O. Box 300, Raritan NJ 08869-0602. 908/218-6000. **Contact:** Human Resources. **World Wide Web address:** http://www.ortho-mcneil.com. **Description:** Develops and sells pharmaceutical products including women's health, infectious disease, and wound healing products. **Positions advertised include:** National Account Manager; Clinical Research Associate. **NOTE:** All hiring is done out of the corporate offices. Resumes should be sent to Johnson & Johnson Recruiting Services, Employment Management Center, Room JH-215, 501 George Street, New Brunswick NJ 08906-6597. **Parent company:** Johnson & Johnson (New Brunswick NJ).

OSTEOTECH INC.
51 James Way, Eatontown NJ 07724. 732/542-2800. **Fax:** 732/542-9312. **Contact:** Human Resources. **E-mail address:** hr@osteotech.com. **World Wide Web address:** http://www.osteotech.com. **Description:** Processes human bone and connective tissue for transplantation and develops and manufactures biomaterial and device systems for musculoskeletal surgery. Osteotech is a leader in volume and quality of tissue processing for the American Red Cross and the Musculoskeletal Tissue Foundation. Founded in 1986. **NOTE:** Entry-level positions and second and third shifts are offered. **Company slogan:** Innovators in musculoskeletal tissue science. **Positions advertised include:** Clinical Research Technician; Clinical Research Associate; Auditor Associate; Processing Technology. **Special programs:** Training. **Office hours:** Monday - Friday, 8:00 a.m. - 5:00 p.m. **Corporate headquarters location:** This location. **Other U.S. locations:** Nationwide. **International locations:** The Netherlands. **Listed on:** NASDAQ. **Stock exchange symbol:** OSTE. **President:** Richard Bauer. **Annual sales/revenues:** $21 - $50 million. **Number of employees at this location:** 180. **Number of employees nationwide:** 200. **Number of employees worldwide:** 225.

PFIZER
100 Route 206 North, Peapack NJ 07977. 908/901-8000. **Contact:** Human Resources. **World Wide Web address:** http://www.pfizer.com. **Description:** Pfizer manufactures and markets agricultural products, performance chemicals used in consumer products, prescription pharmaceuticals, and food ingredients. **Corporate headquarters location:** This location. **Operations at this facility include:** This location houses administrative offices. **Number of employees worldwide:** 60,000.

QMED, INC.
25 Christopher Way, Eatontown NJ 07724. 732/544-5544. **Fax:** 732/544-5404. **Contact:** Human Resources. **E-mail address:** jobs@qmedinc.com. **World Wide Web address:** http://www.qmedinc.com. **Description:** Designs, manufactures, and markets testing devices that enable medical professionals to perform minimally invasive diagnostic procedures for certain illnesses, such as silent myocardial ischemia, venous blood flow insufficiencies, and diabetic neuropathy. **Positions advertised include:** Licensed Practical Nurse; Patient Education Nurse; Help Desk Manager; Information Technology Developer; Registered Nurse; Operations Program Analyst; Accounting Manager; Medical Assistant; Customer Service Specialist; Account Manager. **Listed on:** NASDAQ. **Stock exchange symbol:** QEKG.

QUEST DIAGNOSTICS INCORPORATED
1290 Wall Street West, Lyndhurst NJ 07071. 201/393-5000. **Toll-free phone:** 800/222-0446. **Fax:** 201/462-4715. **Contact:** Personnel. **World Wide Web address:** http://www.questdiagnostics.com. **Description:** One of the largest clinical laboratories in North America, providing a broad range of clinical laboratory services to health care clients that include physicians, hospitals, clinics, dialysis centers, pharmaceutical companies, and corporations. The company offers and performs tests on blood, urine, and other bodily fluids and tissues to provide information for health and well-being. **Positions advertised include:** Technologist; Histotechnologist; Assistant Administrator; Phlebotomy Service Representative; Pathologist Representative; Group Leader; Field Operations Manager; Customer Service Representative; Dispatcher; Imaging Clerk. **Corporate headquarters location:** This location. **Other U.S. locations:** Nationwide. **Listed on:** New York Stock Exchange. **Stock exchange symbol:** DGX.

SGS U.S. TESTING COMPANY INC.
291 Fairfield Avenue, Fairfield NJ 07004. 973/575-5252. **Toll-free phone:** 800/777-8378. **Fax:** 973/575-7175. **Contact:** Personnel. **E-mail address:** hrustc@yahoo.com. **World Wide Web address:** http://www.ustesting.sgsna.com. **Description:** An independent laboratory specializing in the testing of a variety of industrial and consumer products. Services include biological, chemical, engineering/materials, environmental, electrical, paper/packaging, textiles, certification programs, and inspections. **Positions advertised include:** Account Executive, Outside Sales. **Other U.S. locations:** Nationwide. **Parent company:** SGS North America. **Operations at this facility include:** Administration; Sales; Service.

SANOFI-AVENTIS
200-400 Crossing Boulevard, Bridgewater NJ 08807. 908/304-7000. **Contact:** Human Resources. **World Wide Web address:** http://www.sanofi-aventis.us. **Description:** An international pharmaceutical company working with respiratory, cardiac, and osteopathic medications. **Positions advertised include:** Animal Care Technician; Associate Chemist; Associate Scientist; Epidemiologist; Global Change Coordinator; Global Program Manager; Manager. **Operations at this facility include:** Marketing; Research and Development.

SAVIENT PHARMACEUTICALS, INC.
One Tower Center 14th Floor, East Brunswick NJ 08816. 732/418-9300. **Fax:** 732/418-9235. **Contact:** Human Resources. **E-mail address:** hr@savientpharma.com. **World Wide Web address:** http://www.savientpharma.com. **Description:** Develops, manufactures, and markets novel therapeutic products. The company specializes in preclinical studies, research and development, and biotechnology derived products. **Positions advertised include:** Area Manager; Controller; Sales Manager; Director of Marketing. **Corporate headquarters location:** This location. **International locations:** Rehovot, Israel.

SCHERING-PLOUGH CORPORATION
2000 Galloping Hill Road, Kenilworth NJ 07033. 908/298-4000. **Contact:** Human Resources Department. **World Wide Web address:** http://www.schering-plough.com. **Description:** Engaged in the discovery, development, manufacture, and marketing of pharmaceutical and consumer products. Pharmaceutical products include prescription drugs, over-the-counter medicines, eye care products, and animal health products promoted to the medical and allied health professions. The consumer products group consists of proprietary medicines, toiletries, cosmetics, and foot care products. Brand names include Coricidin, Maybelline, Claritin, Coppertone, and Dr. Scholl's. **Positions advertised include:** Associate

Manager; Compliance Manager; Computer Systems Validation Specialist; Mechanical Supervisor; Porter; Premium Buyer; CAD Operator; Validation Engineer; Computer Systems Administrator; Staff Validation Specialist; Publishing Technician; Medical Writer. **Note:** Current positions are updated on the website. **Corporate headquarters location:** This location. **Other area locations:** Statewide. **International locations:** Worldwide.

TEVA PHARMACEUTICALS USA
8 Gloria Lane, Fairfield NJ 07004. 973/575-8618. **Contact:** Human Resources. **World Wide Web address:** http://www.tevapharmusa.com. **Description:** Manufactures and markets generic pharmaceuticals. The company focuses on therapeutic medicines for the analgesic, cardiovascular, dermatological, and anti-inflammatory markets. **Corporate headquarters location:** This location. **Other area locations:** Elmwood Park NJ; Fairfield NJ; Paterson NJ; Waldwick NJ. **Other U.S. locations:** Mexico MO. **Number of employees nationwide:** 790.

UNIGENE LABORATORIES, INC.
110 Little Falls Road, Fairfield NJ 07004. 973/882-0860. **Fax:** 973/227-6088. **Contact:** Human Resources. **World Wide Web address:** http://www.unigene.com. **Description:** A biopharmaceutical research and manufacturing company that has developed a patented method to produce calcitonin, a leading drug for treating osteoporosis. Founded in 1980. **Corporate headquarters location:** This location. **Other U.S. locations:** Boonton NJ. **Listed on:** NASDAQ. **Stock exchange symbol:** UGNE. **President:** Warren P. Levy, Ph.D. **Annual sales/revenues:** $5 - $10 million. **Number of employees at this location:** 65.

UNILEVER HOME & PERSONAL CARE USA
45 River Road, Edgewater NJ 07020. 201/945-8550. **Contact:** Human Resources. **World Wide Web address:** http://www.unilever.com. **Description:** Researches and develops household and personal care products. **Corporate headquarters location:** Greenwich CT. **Annual sales/revenues:** More than $100 million. **Number of employees at this location:** 500.

WATSON PHARMACEUTICALS
360 Mount Kemble Avenue, P.O. Box 1953, Morristown NJ 07962. 973/355-8300. **Fax:** 973/355-8301. **Contact:** Human Resources. **World Wide Web address:** http://www.watsonpharm.com. **Description:** Manufactures generic drugs. **Positions advertised include:** Meeting & Travel Services Manager; System Analyst Developer; Associate Director Regulatory Affairs; Sales Automation Manager; Accountant; Administrative Assistant; Analytics & Sales Information Director. **Corporate headquarters location:** This location. **Listed on:** New York Stock Exchange. **Stock exchange symbol:** WPI. **Number of employees nationwide:** 1,500.

WYETH CORPORATION
5 Giralda Farms, Madison NJ 07940. 973/660-5000. **Contact:** Human Resources. **World Wide Web address:** http://www.wyeth.com. **Description:** Wyeth is one of the world's largest research-driven pharmaceutical and health care products companies. It is a leader in the discovery, development, manufacturing and marketing of pharmaceuticals, vaccines, biotechnology products, and non-prescription medicines. The Company's major divisions include Wyeth Pharmaceuticals, Wyeth Consumer Healthcare and Fort Dodge Animal Health. **Positions advertised include:** Regional Manager; Clinical Research Associate; Manager of Information Management; Project Manager; Human Resources Assistant; Forecasting Analyst; Trade Promotion Manager; Category Manager. **Corporate headquarters location:** This location. **Number of employees worldwide:** 53,000.

XENOGEN BIOSCIENCES
5 Cedarbrook Drive, Cranbury NJ 08512. 609/860-0806. **Fax:** 609/860-8515. **Contact:** Human Resources. **E-mail address:** employment@xenogen.com. **World Wide Web address:** http://www.xenogen.com. **Description:** Offers real-time in vivo imaging services. Xenogen's in vivo biophotonic imaging system assists pharmaceutical companies in drug discovery and development. **Corporate headquarters location:** Alameda CA.

ZENOTECH, INC
1 Deer Park Drive, Suite H-6, Monmouth Junction NJ 08852. 732/438-1622. **Fax:** 732/438-1623. **Contact:** Human Resources. **E-mail address:** careers@zenotechlabs.com. **World Wide Web address:** http://www.zenotechlabs.com. **Description:** Develops and manufactures generic biopharmaceuticals and markets them worldwide. **Positions advertised include:** Mammalian Cell Culture Biologist; Bacterial Fermentation Scientist; Protein Purification Scientist; Quality Control Biochemist; Formulation Development Biotechnologist; Finance Manager.

New Mexico

EXAGEN DIAGNOSTICS
801 University Boulevard SE, Suite 209, Albuquerque NM 87106. 505/272-7966. **Fax:** 505/272-7965. **Contact:** Human Resources. **E-mail address:** info@exagendiagnostics.com. **World Wide Web address:** http://www.exagendiagnostics.com. **Description:** Exagen Diagnostics discovers, validates, and commercializes small sets of genomic markers, providing prognostic reagents for commercial laboratory testing and for pharmaceutical use in clinical trials. **NOTE:** Search and apply for positions online. **Positions advertised include:** Marketing Director; Scientist; Controller; Information Technology Manager; Molecular Biology Technician.

EXPRESS SCRIPTS
4500 Alexander Boulevard NE, Albuquerque NM 87107. 505/345-8080. **Contact:** Human Resources. **E-mail address:** opportunities@express-scripts.com. **World Wide Web address:** http://www.express-scripts.com. **Description:** A pharmacy benefit management company that serves 50 million members in managed care organizations, insurance carriers, third-party administrators, employers, and union-sponsored benefit plans through facilities in eight states and Canada. **NOTE:** Search and apply for positions online. **Listed on:** NASDAQ. **Stock exchange symbol:** ESRX. **Number of employees worldwide:** 7,500.

GENZYME GENETICS
2000 Vivigen Way, Santa Fe NM 87505. 505/438-1111. **Fax:** 505/438-1120. **Contact:** Human Resources. **World Wide Web address:** http://www.genzymegenetics.com. **Description:** A diagnostic laboratory specializing in prenatal and oncology testing as well as prenatal genetic counseling services. **NOTE:** Search and apply for positions online. **Positions advertised include:** Lab Supervisor. **Special programs:** Internships; Co-ops. **Other U.S. locations:** Nationwide. **Parent company:** Genzyme Corporation. **Number of employees worldwide:** 8,000.

LOS ALAMOS NATIONAL LABORATORY
P.O. Box 1663, Los Alamos NM 87545. 505/667-8622. **Physical address:** Bikini Atoll Road, SM 30, Los Alamos NM 87545. **Fax:** 505/665-5419. **Contact:** Resume Service Center. **E-mail address:** jobs@lanl.gov. **World Wide Web address:** http://www.lanl.gov. **Description:** A national laboratory engaged in research and development in a wide range of areas including quality and planning; energy and environment; materials science; nuclear materials and security; biotechnology and biomedicine; instrumentation; sensors and transducers; physics; and high-performance computing, modeling, and simulation. Operated by the University of California for the National Nuclear Security Administration of the U.S. Department of Energy. **NOTE:** See website for current job openings and application instructions. Entry-level positions are offered. **Positions advertised include:** Administrative Specialist; Associate Director; Auditor; Biochem Lab Tech; Chief of Staff; Staff

Member; Project Leader; Deputy Group Leader; Group Leader; Division Leader; Program Manager; Security Specialist; Team Leader; Computer Technician. **Number of employees at this location:** 10,700.

LOVELACE RESPIRATORY RESEARCH INSTITUTE
2425 Ridgecrest Drive SE, Albuquerque NM 87108. 505/348-9400. **Fax:** 505/348-4976. **Contact:** Human Resources. **E-mail address:** hrmail@llri.org. **World Wide Web address:** http://www.lrri.org. **Description:** A private not-for-profit biomedical research institute that is focused solely on respiratory disease research. **NOTE:** See website for current job openings. Include job number when applying for a position. **Positions advertised include:** Institute Compliance Manager; Sr. Research Technologists; Laboratory Technician; Senior Buyer; Word Processor; Science Camp Counselor. **Internship information:** Postdoctoral positions are available year-round. Please call for more information. **Corporate headquarters location:** This location. **Number of employees at this location:** 320.

PHARMERICA
2720 Broadbent Parkway NE, Suite A, Albuquerque NM 87107. 505/343-1113. **Fax:** 505/343-9769. **Contact:** Human Resources. **World Wide Web address:** http://www.pharmerica.com. **Description:** A supplier of pharmaceuticals and related products to long-term care facilities, hospitals, and assisted living communities through 83 pharmacies in 35 states. PharMerica also provides nurse consultant services, infusion therapy and training, medical records consulting, and educational programs. **NOTE:** Search and apply for positions online or contact local facility. **Corporate headquarters location:** Tampa FL. **Parent company:** AmerisourceBergen Corporation. **Number of employees nationwide:** 5,000.

PHYSICAL SCIENCE LABORATORY
P.O. Box 30002, Las Cruces NM 88003-8002. 505/522-9100. **Contact:** Regina Galvan, Personnel Manager. **E-mail address:** personnel@psl.nmsu.edu. **World Wide Web address:** http://www.psl.nmsu.edu. **Description:** Provides a wide range of research and development services in geothermal and wind energy, as well as providing contract services to the Department of Defense. A part of New Mexico State University. **NOTE:** Search for positions online. **Positions advertised include:** Research Chemist; Atmospheric Scientist; Administrative Assistant; Instructional Coordinator; Jr. Computer Software Engineer; Sr. Computer Software Engineer. **Corporate headquarters location:** This location.

QUEST DIAGNOSTICS INCORPORATED
7510 Montgomery NE, Suite 10, Albuquerque NM 87109. 505/889-7144. **Contact:** Operations Manager. **World Wide Web address:** http://www.questdiagnostics.com. **Description:** Quest Diagnostics is one of the largest clinical laboratories in North America, providing a broad range of clinical laboratory services to health care clients that include physicians, hospitals, clinics, dialysis centers, pharmaceutical companies, and corporations. The company offers and performs tests on blood, urine, and other bodily fluids and tissues to provide information for health and well-being. **Corporate headquarters location:** Teterboro NJ. **Other U.S. locations:** Nationwide. **Operations at this facility include:** This location takes blood samples. **Listed on:** New York Stock Exchange. **Stock exchange symbol:** DGX.

SANDIA NATIONAL LABORATORIES
P.O. Box 5800, MS 1023, Albuquerque NM 87105-1023. 505/844-3441. **Physical address:** 1515 Eubank Boulevard SE, Albuquerque, NM 87123. **Contact:** Human Resources. **E-mail address:** empsite@sandia.gov. **World Wide Web address:** http://www.sandia.gov. **Description:** A research facility. Areas of focus include nuclear energy research and maintaining and securing nuclear weaponry. Funded by the U.S. Department of Energy and managed by Lockheed Martin Corp. **NOTE:** Search and apply for positions online. **Positions advertised include:** Attorney; Bayesian Statistician; Cataloging Librarian; Complex Systems Engineer; Computer Software Research/Development; Economist; Electronic Engineer; Explosives Engineer; Mechanical Engineer; Medical Administrative Support; Operations Research Analyst; Optical Modeling; Project Staff; Pulsed Power Designer; Software Developer; Systems Engineer; Vulnerability Analyst. **Other area locations:** Carlsbad NM. **Other U.S. locations:** CA. **Number of employees nationwide:** 8,600.

New York

ADVANCED BIOPHOTONICS, INC.
125 Wilbur Place, Suite 120, Bohemia NY 11716. 631/244-8244. **Fax:** 631/244-7960. **Contact:** Lisa Mackenzie, Director of Human Resources. **E-mail address:** lmackenzie@advancedbp.com. **World Wide Web address:** http://www.advancedbp.com. **Description:** Develops functional medical imaging applications using advanced infrared technology for the observation and measurement of changes of photonic activity within tissue. Imaging technology is used by clinicians and researchers in disease detection, disease management, and drug discovery applications. **Positions advertised include:** Clinical Research Manager; Senior Software Developer.

ADVION BIOSCIENCES, INC.
15 Catherwood Road, Ithaca NY 14850. 607/266-0665. **Fax:** 607/266-0749. **Contact:** Human Resources. **E-mail address:** careers@advion.com. **Description:** A developer of automated, chip-based technology designed to boost the sensitivity, data quality and sample throughput for electrospray mass spectrometers. Founded in 1993. **Positions advertised include:** Assistant Scientist; Technical Writer; Method Development Scientist; Product Application Scientist; Support Analyst.

AMERICAN STANDARDS TESTING BUREAU INC.
P.O. Box 583, New York NY 10274-0583. 212/943-3160. **Physical address:** 40 Water Street, New York NY 10004. **Toll-free phone:** 800/221-5170. **Fax:** 212/825-2250. **Contact:** John Zimmerman, Director, Professional Staffing. **World Wide Web address:** http://www.astm.org. **Description:** Offers lab consulting and forensic services to the government and various industries. The company specializes in biotechnology, environmental sciences, forensics, engineering, failure analysis, and products liability. **Positions advertised include:** Aerospace Engineer; Biomedical Engineer; Chemical Engineer; Clerical Supervisor; Chemist; Environmental Engineer. **Corporate headquarters location:** This location. **Other U.S. locations:** Nationwide. **Operations at this facility include:** Administration; Divisional Headquarters; Research and Development; Sales. **Annual sales/revenues:** $50 million. **Number of employees at this location:** 430.

BARR LABORATORIES, INC.
223 Quaker Road, P.O. Box 2900, Pomona NY 10970-0519. 845/362-1100. **Fax:** 845/362-2774. **Contact:** Human Resources. **World Wide Web address:** http://www.barrlabs.com. **Description:** Barr Laboratories is a leading independent developer, manufacturer, and marketer of off-patent pharmaceuticals. **Positions advertised include:** R&D Documentation Specialist; Senior Validation Engineer; Quality Control Manager; Quality Control Chemist; Technical Group Leader Quality Control; External Auditor. **Corporate headquarters location:** This location. **Other locations:** NJ; OH; PA; OH. **Operations at this facility include:** Development and production laboratories; Administration; Manufacturing; Research & Development; Pharmacy operations. **Listed on:** New York Stock Exchange. **Stock exchange symbol:** BRL. **Chairman/CEO:** Bruce L. Downey. **Annual sales/revenues:** $1.2 billion. **Number of employees:** 1,075.

BIOSPECIFICS TECHNOLOGIES CORPORATION
35 Wilbur Street, Lynbrook NY 11563. 516/593-7000. **Fax:** 516/593-7039. **Contact:** Human Resources. **World Wide Web address:** http://www.biospecifics.com. **Description:** An industry leader in the production and development of enzyme pharmaceuticals used for wound healing, tissue regeneration, and tissue remodeling. Biospecifics Technologies Corporation produces Collagenase Santyl ointment, an enzyme used for the treatment of chronic wounds and dermal ulcers. **NOTE:** Resumes should be mailed or faxed to the above address. **Positions advertised include:** Clinical Lab Technician. **Office hours:** Monday - Friday, 9:00 a.m. - 5:00 p.m. **Listed on:** NASDAQ. **Stock exchange symbol:** BSTC. **Annual sales/revenues:** $8.2 million. **Number of employees:** 48.

BRISTOL-MYERS SQUIBB COMPANY
345 Park Avenue, New York NY 10154-0037. 212/546-4000. **Fax:** 212/546-4020. **Contact:** Stephen E. Bear, Human Resources Director. **World Wide Web address:** http://www.bms.com. **Description:** Manufacturer of pharmaceuticals, medical devices, nonprescription drugs, toiletries, and beauty aids. The company's pharmaceutical products include cardiovascular drugs, anti-infective agents, anticancer agents, AIDS therapy treatments, central nervous system drugs, diagnostic agents, and other drugs. The company's line of nonprescription products includes formulas, vitamins, analgesics, remedies, and skin care products sold under the brand names Bufferin, Excedrin, Nuprin, and Comtrex. Beauty aids include Clairol and Ultress hair care, Nice 'n Easy hair colorings, hair sprays, gels, and deodorants. **NOTE:** Resumes may be sent to the company's human resources address: Bristol-Myers Squibb Company, P.O. Box 5335, Princeton NY 08543-5335; or by fax to: 609/897-6412. **Positions advertised include:** Chemist. **Corporate headquarters location:** This location. **Subsidiaries include:** ConvaTec; Mead Johnson & Company. **Listed on:** New York Stock Exchange. **Stock exchange symbol:** BMY. **Chairman/CEO:** Peter R. Dolan. **Annual sales/revenues:** $18.1 billion. **Number of employees:** 46,000.

DARBY GROUP COMPANIES, INC.
300 Jericho Quadrangle, Jericho NY 11753. 516/683-1800. **Fax:** 516/688-2820. **Contact:** Debra Leff, Human Resources Department. **World Wide Web address:** http://www.darbygroup.com. **Description:** A manufacturer and distributor of over-the-counter drugs, pharmaceuticals, and vitamins operating 12 distribution facilities nationwide. **Corporate headquarters location:** This location. **Other U.S. locations:** Nationwide. **Subsidiaries include:** Dental Division; Medical Division; Burns Veterinary Supply; Darby Corporate Solutions. **Chairman:** Michael Ashkir. **Annual sales/revenues:** $625 million. **Number of employees:** 1,500.

DAXOR CORPORATION
The Empire State Building, 350 Fifth Avenue, Suite 7120, New York NY 10118. 212/330-8500. **Fax:** 212/244-0806. **Contact:** Human Resources. **World Wide Web address:** http://www.daxor.com. **Description:** Promotes the safety of the American Blood Banking System. The company's Idant Division also researches cryobiology for artificial insemination purposes and operates one of the largest sperm banks in the United States. **Subsidiaries include:** IDANT Laboratories. **Listed on:** American Stock Exchange. **Stock exchange symbol:** DXR. **Chairman/President/CEO:** Joseph Feldschuh. **Annual sales/revenues:** 2.7 million. **Number of employees:** 30.

E-Z-EM INC.
1111 Marcus Avenue, Suite LL26, Lake Success NY 11042. 516/333-8230. **Fax:** 516/302-2915. **Contact:** Human Resources. **E-mail address:** hr@ezem.com. **World Wide Web address:** http://www.ezem.com. **Description:** E-Z-EM is a worldwide producer of barium sulfate contrast systems for use in GI tract X-ray examinations. The company operates in two industry segments: diagnostic products and surgical products. The diagnostic products segment includes both contrast systems, consisting of barium sulfate formulations and related apparatus used in X-ray, CT-scanning, and other imaging examinations; and noncontrast systems, which include interventional radiology products, custom contract pharmaceuticals, gastrointestinal cleansing laxatives, X-ray protection equipment, and immunoassay tests. **Corporate headquarters location:** This location. **Listed on:** American Stock Exchange. **Stock exchange symbol:** EZM. **Annual sales/revenues:** $122 million. **Number of employees:** 932.

EMISPHERE TECHNOLOGIES, INC.
765 Old Saw Mill River Road, Tarrytown NY 10591-6751. 914/347-2220. **Fax:** 914/347-2498. **Contact:** Barbara Mohl, Human Resources Director. **E-mail address:** jobs@emisphere.com. **World Wide Web address:** http://www.emisphere.com. **Description:** Researches and develops oral drug delivery systems. **Positions advertised include:** Analytical Research Associate; Drug Delivery Research Associate; Patent Paralegal; Documentation Control Professional; Laboratory Animal Technician. **Listed on:** NASDAQ. **Stock exchange symbol:** EMIS. **Chairman/CEO:** Michael M. Goldberg. **Annual sales/revenues:** $3.4 million. **Number of employees:** 241.

ENZO BIOCHEM, INC.
dba ENZO CLINICAL LABS
60 Executive Boulevard, Farmingdale NY 11735. 631/755-5500. **Fax:** 631/863-0143. **Contact:** Human Resources. **World Wide Web address:** http://www.enzo.com. **Description:** Through its subsidiaries, the company is engaged in the research, development, marketing, and manufacturing of health care products. Enzo's products and services are sold to scientists and medical personnel worldwide. The company has proprietary technologies and expertise in manipulating and modifying genetic material and other biological molecules. Founded in 1976. **Positions advertised include:** Phlebotomist; Histotechnologist; Grosser. **Subsidiaries include:** Enzo Therapeutics, Inc. is developing antisense genetic medicines to combat cancer, viral, and other diseases. Enzo Diagnostics, Inc. develops and markets proprietary DNA probe-based products to clinicians and researchers. EnzoLabs, Inc. provides diagnostic testing services to the New York medical community. **Corporate headquarters location:** This location. **Parent company:** Enzo Biochem. **Listed on:** New York Stock Exchange. **Stock exchange symbol:** ENZ. **Chairman/CEO:** Elazar Rabbani. **Annual sales/revenues:** $54 million. **Number of employees:** 231.

FOREST LABORATORIES, INC.
909 Third Avenue, 24th Floor, New York NY 10022-4731. 212/421-7850. **Fax:** 212/750-9152. **Contact:** Human Resources. **E-mail address:** staffing@frx.com. **World Wide Web address:** http://www.frx.com. **Description:** Develops, manufactures, and sells branded and generic prescription drugs for the treatment of cardiovascular, central nervous system, pulmonary, and women's health problems. In the United States, Forest Laboratories' ethical specialty products and generics are marketed directly by the company's subsidiaries Forest Pharmaceuticals and Inwood Laboratories. In the United Kingdom, Ireland, and certain export markets, Forest Laboratories products are marketed directly by the company's subsidiaries, Pharmax Ltd. and Tosara Group. **Positions advertised include:** Sales Force Automation Analyst; Forecast Analyst; Licensing Secretary; Product Manager; Senior Product Manager; Customer Planning Long Term Care/Government Manager; Customer Planning Analyst; Customer Planning Pharmacy Benefit Manager; Business Development Assistant Director; Respiratory Product Manager; Senior Respiratory Product Manager. **Special programs:** Internships; Co-ops; Summer Jobs. **Office hours:** Monday - Friday, 9:00 a.m. - 5:00 p.m. **Corporate**

headquarters location: This location. **Other U.S. locations:** St. Louis MO; Jersey City NJ; Commack NY; Farmingdale NY; Inwood NY; Cincinnati OH. **International locations:** Ireland; United Kingdom. **Subsidiaries include:** Forest Pharmaceuticals, Inc.; Inwood Laboratories, Inc.; Pharmax Ltd.; Tosara Group. **Operations at this facility include:** Accounting/Auditing; Administration; Financial Offices; Marketing; Sales. **Listed on:** New York Stock Exchange. **Stock exchange symbol:** FRX. **President:** Howard Solomon. **Annual sales/revenues:** $1.6 billion. **Number of employees at this location:** 350. **Number of employees nationwide:** 3,731.

E. FOUGERA & COMPANY
SAVAGE LABORATORIES
60 Baylis Road, Melville NY 11747. 631/454-6996. **Contact:** Human Resources Manager. **E-mail address:** hr@altanainc.com. **World Wide Web address:** http://www.fougera.com. **Description:** Manufactures various generic pharmaceuticals including multisource topicals and ophthalmics. Products include surgical lubricants, antifungal creams, hydrocortisone ointments, and other generic treatments. **Corporate headquarters location:** This location. **Parent company:** Altana, Inc. (also at this location) also owns Savage Laboratories, which manufactures ethical pharmaceuticals. **Positions advertised include:** Microbiologist; Quality Assurance Monitor; Analytical Services Supervisor.

HI-TECH PHARMACAL CO., INC.
369 Bayview Avenue, Amityville NY 11701. 631/789-8228. **Fax:** 631/789-8429. **Contact:** Carole Wood, Human Resources Manager. **World Wide Web address:** http://www.hitechpharm.com. **Description:** Develops, manufactures, and markets prescription and generic liquid and semi-solid drugs, as well as nutritional products. Hi-Tech Pharmacal manufactures more than 100 generic products marketed under the company's own brand names. **Subsidiaries include:** Health Care Products manufactures branded items marketed under the H-T, Sooth-It, and Diabetic Tussin brands. **Listed on:** NASDAQ. **Stock exchange symbol:** HITK. **Chairman:** Bernard Seltzer. **Annual sales/revenues:** $33 million. **Number of employees:** 164.

IMCLONE SYSTEMS INC.
180 Varick Street, 6th Floor, New York NY 10014-4606. 212/645-1405. **Fax:** 212/645-2054. **Contact:** Human Resources Director. **World Wide Web address:** http://www.imclone.com. **Description:** Engaged primarily in the research and development of therapeutic products for the treatment of cancer and cancer-related diseases. **Positions advertised include:** Chemistry Research Associate; Chemistry Research Scientist; Modeling Chemistry Senior Scientist; Facilities Worker; Immunology Research Associate; Immunology Scientist; Immunology Senior Scientist; Intellectual Property Law Clerk; Molecular & Cell Biology Senior Scientist. **Corporate headquarters location:** This location. **Other locations:** Somerville NJ. **Listed on:** NASDAQ. **Stock exchange symbol:** IMCLE. **Annual sales/revenues:** $33 million. **Number of employees:** 400.

NALGE NUNC INTERNATIONAL
75 Panorama Creek Drive, Rochester NY 14625-2385. 716/586-8800. **Contact:** Human Resources. **World Wide Web address:** http://www.nalgenunc.com. **Description:** Manufactures ultrafiltration and centrifugal devices for use in biological and genetic research. **Positions advertised include:** New Product Manager; Product Development Project Leader. **Office hours:** Monday – Friday, 8:00 a.m. – 5:00 p.m. **Other U.S. locations:** Duluth GA; Naperville IL. **International locations:** Worldwide.

NOVO NORDISK OF NORTH AMERICA
405 Lexington Avenue, Suite 6400, New York NY 10174. 212/983-1730. **Contact:** Human Resources Department. **World Wide Web address:** http://www.novonordisk-us.com. **Description:** A holding company whose divisions produce insulin, industrial enzymes, and other drugs and bioindustrial items. The Health Care Group is the diabetes care division that develops and manufactures insulin and delivery systems related to the treatment of diabetes. The Biopharmaceuticals division develops, produces, and markets products for the treatment of coagulation and other blood disorders as well as growth disorders. The Bioindustrial division consists of detergents, providing enzymes to the detergent industry. **NOTE:** Human Resources is located at 100 Overlook Center, Suite 200, Princeton NJ 08540. 609/987-5800. Jobseekers may apply for positions online. **Positions advertised include:** Managed Care Account Executive; Pharmaceutical Sales Representative. **Other U.S. locations:** Davis CA; Clayton NC; Franklinton NC; Princeton NJ; Seattle WA. **Parent company:** Novo Nordisk A/S (Baysvaerd, Denmark). **Operations at this facility include:** This location is the corporate service office for North America. **Listed on:** New York Stock Exchange. **Stock exchange symbol:** NVO. **President:** Martin Soeters. **Number of employees at this location:** 25. **Number of employees nationwide:** 1,000. **Number of employees worldwide:** 13,000.

OSI PHARMACEUTICALS, INC.
41 Pinelawn Road, Melville NY 11747. 631/962-2000. **Fax:** 631/752-3880. **Contact:** Human Resources. **E-mail address:** employment@osip.com. **World Wide Web address:** http://www.osip.com. **Description:** A biopharmaceutical company utilizing proprietary technologies to discover and develop products for the treatment and diagnosis of human diseases. The company conducts a full range of drug discovery activities from target identification through clinical candidates for its own products and in collaborations and co-ventures with other major pharmaceutical companies. **NOTE:** Jobseekers may apply for positions online. **Positions advertised include:** Purchasing Specialist. **Corporate headquarters location:** This location. **Other area locations:** Farmingdale NY; Uniondale NY. **Other U.S. locations:** Boulder CO. **International locations:** England. **Listed on:** NASDAQ. **Stock exchange symbol:** OSIP. **President:** Dr. Colin Goddard.

PDK LABS INC.
145 Ricefield Lane, Hauppauge NY 11788. 631/273-2630. **Contact:** Human Resources. **E-mail address:** info@pdklabs.com. **World Wide Web address:** http://www.pdklabs.com. **Description:** PDK Labs manufactures and distributes over-the-counter pharmaceutical products and vitamins. The company's line of products primarily consists of nonprescription caffeine products, pain relievers, decongestants, diet aids, and a broad line of vitamins, nutritional supplements, and cosmetics. The company markets its products through direct mail, regional distributors, and private label manufacturing.

PRECISION PHARMA
155 Duryea Road, Melville NY 11747. 631/752-7314. **Fax:** 631/752-7354. **Contact:** Human Resources. **E-mail address:** hr@precisionpharma.com. **World Wide Web address:** http://www.precisionpharma.com. **Description:** Precision Pharma is a leader in the field of pathogen inactivation of blood products. The company's technologies are designed to address the risk of viral contamination of blood products. Founded in 1995. **Positions advertised include:** Fractionation Technician; Mechanic. **Corporate headquarters location:** This location. **President/CEO:** James A. Moose.

PROCTER & GAMBLE PHARMACEUTICAL INC.
P.O. Box 191, Norwich NY 13815. 607/335-2111. **Contact:** Human Resources. **World Wide Web address:** http://www.pg.com. **Description:** This location manufactures pharmaceutical prescription products including Asacol, Vrontex, Dantrium, Dantrium-IV, Didronel, Macrobid, and Macrodantin. Overall, Procter & Gamble manufactures over 300 laundry, cleaning, paper, beauty, health care, food, and

beverage products in more than 140 countries. Brand-name products include Cover Girl, Max Factor, Vidal Sassoon, Clearasil, and Noxzema health and beauty products; Pepto-Bismol, Vicks, and NyQuil health care products; Bounce, Downy, Tide, Comet, and Mr. Clean cleaning products; Luvs, Pampers, Always, Tampax, Bounty, Charmin, and Puffs paper products; and Crisco, Folgers, Millstone, Sunny Delight, and Pringles food and beverage products. **Corporate headquarters location:** Cincinnati OH. **Other U.S. locations:** Nationwide. **International locations:** Worldwide. **Listed on:** New York Stock Exchange. **Stock exchange symbol:** PG. **Number of employees worldwide:** Over 100,000.

QUEST DIAGNOSTICS INCORPORATED
175 Jericho Turnpike, Suite 304, Syosset NY 11791. 516/677-7717. **Contact:** Human Resources. **World Wide Web address:** http://www.questdiagnostics.com. **Description:** Quest Diagnostics is one of the largest clinical laboratories in North America, providing a broad range of clinical laboratory services to health care clients that include physicians, hospitals, clinics, dialysis centers, pharmaceutical companies, and corporations. The company offers and performs tests on blood, urine, and other bodily fluids and tissues to provide information for health and well-being. **NOTE:** Online applications are available. **Positions advertised include:** Laboratory Manager; District Sales Manager; Billing Supervisor; **Corporate headquarters location:** Teterboro NJ. **Other U.S. locations:** Nationwide. **International locations:** Worldwide. **Operations at this facility include:** This location is a clinical laboratory. **Listed on:** New York Stock Exchange. **Stock exchange symbol:** DGX. **Sales/revenue:** Over $4 billion. **Number of employees worldwide:** 33,400.

REGENERON PHARMACEUTICALS, INC.
777 Old Saw Mill River Road, Suite 10, Tarrytown NY 10591. 914/345-7400. **Fax:** 914/345-7790. **Contact:** Human Resources. **E-mail address:** jobs@regeneron.com. **World Wide Web address:** http://www.regeneron.com. **Description:** A research company that develops pharmaceuticals to treat neurological, oncological, inflammatory, allergic, and bone disorders as well as muscle atrophy. **Positions advertised include:** Senior Director; Medical Program Coordinator; Endocrinologist; Biostatistician; Assay Development Associate Director; Quality Auditor; Eye Angiogenesis; Bioreactor Development Associate Director; Cell Line and Process Development Research Associate. **Special programs:** Internships. **Corporate headquarters location:** This location. **Other area locations:** Rensselaer NY. **Listed on:** NASDAQ. **Stock exchange symbol:** REGN.

SANDOZ, INC.
1999 Marcus Avenue, New Hyde Park NY 11042. 516/478-9700. **Contact:** Human Resources. **World Wide Web address:** http://www.sandoz.com. **Description:** A developer and manufacturer of generic pharmaceuticals. **Positions advertised include:** Quality Control Chemist. **Corporate headquarters location:** Princeton NJ. **Parent company:** Novartis AG. **Listed on:** New York Stock Exchange. **Stock exchange symbol:** NVS. **Number of employees nationwide:** 1,500.

SCIENTIFIC INDUSTRIES, INC.
70 Orville Drive, Bohemia NY 11716. 631/567-4700. **Toll-free phone:** 888/850-6208. **Contact:** Personnel. **World Wide Web address:** http://www.scientificindustries.com. **Description:** Manufactures and markets laboratory equipment including vortex mixers and miscellaneous laboratory apparatuses including timers, rotators, and pumps. The company develops and sells computerized control and data logging systems for sterilizers and autoclaves. Scientific Industries' products are used by hospital laboratories, clinics, research laboratories, pharmaceutical manufacturers, and medical device manufacturers. **Corporate headquarters location:** This location. **Listed on:** NASDAQ. **Stock exchange symbol:** SCND. **President/CEO:** Helena Santos.

STERIS-ISOMEDIX SERVICES
23 Elizabeth Drive, Chester NY 10918. 845/469-4087. **Contact:** Human Resources. **World Wide Web address:** http://www.steris.com/isomedix. **Description:** Provides contract sterilization services to manufacturers of prepackaged health care and consumer products. **Corporate headquarters location:** Mentor OH.

STIEFEL LABORATORIES INC.
Route 145, Building 6290, Oak Hill NY 12460. 518/239-6901. **Fax:** 518/239-8402. **Contact:** Human Resources. **World Wide Web address:** http://www.stiefel.com. **Description:** This location is the research and manufacturing headquarters. Overall, Stiefel Laboratories Inc. is engaged in the manufacture, research, sale, and distribution of medicated skin products. **International locations:** Worldwide.

UNDERWRITERS LABORATORIES INC.
1285 Walt Whitman Road, Melville NY 11747-3801. 631/271-6200. **Fax:** 631/271-8259. **Contact:** Employment Coordinator. **E-mail address:** melville@us.ul.com. **World Wide Web address:** http://www.ul.com. **Description:** An independent, nonprofit organization that specializes in product safety testing and certification worldwide. **Special programs:** Summer Jobs. **Corporate headquarters location:** Northbrook IL. **Other U.S. locations:** Santa Clara CA; Research Triangle Park NC; Camas WA. **Number of employees at this location:** 800. **Number of employees worldwide:** 4,000.

WATSON PHARMACEUTICALS
33 Ralph Avenue, P.O. Box 30, Copiague NY 11726-1297. 631/842-8383. **Contact:** Personnel Director. **World Wide Web address:** http://www.watsonpharm.com. **Description:** Manufactures brand-name and generic pharmaceuticals in the areas of dermatology, women's health, neuropsychiatry, and primary care. **Positions advertised include:** Scientist; Chemist; Documentation Coordinator; Validation Engineer; Training Manager; Scheduler; Packaging Manager.

WYETH
401 North Middletown Road, Pearl River NY 10965-1299. 845/732-5000. **Contact:** Personnel Director. **World Wide Web address:** http://www.wyeth.com. **Description:** Manufactures both prescription and nonprescription pharmaceutical and hospital products including pharmaceuticals for the treatment of infectious diseases, mental illness, cancer, arthritis, skin disorders, glaucoma, tuberculosis, and other diseases; adult and pediatric vaccines; vitamin, multivitamin, and mineral products; and Davis & Geck surgical sutures, wound closure devices, and other hospital products. **Corporate headquarters location:** Madison NJ. **Listed on:** New York Stock Exchange. **Stock exchange symbol:** WYE.

WYETH PHARMACEUTICALS
211 Bailey Road, West Henrietta NY 14586-9728. 585/272-7000. **Contact:** Human Resources. **World Wide Web address:** http://www.wyeth.com. **Description:** Engaged in the research and manufacture of ethical and over-the-counter pharmaceuticals. **Operations at this facility include:** Manufacturing; Research and Development.

ZEPTOMETRIX
872 Main Street, Buffalo NY 14202. 716/882-0920. **Toll-free phone:** 800/274-5487. **Contact:** Human Resources. **World Wide Web address:** http://www.zeptometrix.com. **Description:** A vertically integrated biotechnology company concentrating in the field of human retroviruses. The company markets and sells a line of diagnostic and research products that are used by organizations that perform biomedical research including public and private universities, hospitals, and public health labs.

North Carolina

AAIPHARMA
2320 Scientific Park Drive, Wilmington NC 28405. 910/254-7000. **Toll-free phone:** 800/575-4224. **Fax:**

910/815-2300. **Contact:** Human Resources. **World Wide Web address:** http://www.aaipharma.com. **Description:** A provider of product development and support services to the pharmaceutical, biotechnology, and medical device industries. Services range from testing through an integrated series of services. **Positions advertised include:** Business Development Specialist; Associate Project Manager, Clinical Distribution; Senior Analyst, SAP Sales and Distribution; Contracts Attorney; Legal Support Assistant; Senior Oracle Support Analyst, Helpdesk PC Technician; Microbiologist; Quality and Compliance Specialist; Scientist; Senior Packaging Operator; Clinical Trial Materials Coordinator; Pharmacist, Clinical Trials Materials; Document and Data Specialist; Chemist, Biotech; Pharmaceutical Manufacturing Operator. **Corporate headquarters location:** This location. **Other area locations:** Morrisville NC; Chapel Hill NC. **Other U.S. locations:** Kansas City KS; Natick MA; Charleston SC. **International locations:** Canada; Germany; France; The Netherlands; Japan.

AFFINERGY INC.
617 Davis Drive, Suite 100, Durham NC 27713. 919/433-2221. **Fax:** 919-882-9124. **Contact:** Jonathan Gindes. **E-mail address:** jobs@affinergy.com. **World Wide Web address:** http://www.affinergy.com. **Description:** Affinergy develops site-specific biological systems using biofriendly binders that selectively adhere to proteins, drugs, cells, and biomaterial surfaces. Affinergy is focused on developing coatings and medical devices for the orthopedic and cardiovascular markets. **Positions advertised include:** Controller and Operations Manager; Research Scientist, Peptide Chemist; Research Scientist, Phage Display; Research Scientist, Assay Development; Postdoctoral Scientist, Peptide Chemistry.

ALMAC DIAGNOSTICS
4204 Technology Drive, Durham NC 27704. 919/479 8850. **Fax:** 919/471 2633. **Contact:** Human Resources. **E-mail address:** recruit@almac-sciences.com. **World Wide Web address:** http://www.almac-diagnostics.com. **Description:** Almac Diagnostics has two divisions: The Genomic Services business provides gene express and bioinformatics services to academia, biotech, and pharmaceutical companies; the Research and Development Division develops new tests to change future cancer management. **Positions advertised include:** General Manager. **Other U.S. locations:** Audubon PA; Yardley PA; San Francisco CA. **Parent company:** Almac Sciences Group is a global leader in the research, development, and delivery of pharmaceutical services. **Number of employees worldwide:** 2,000.

ALPHAVAX, INC.
P.O. Box 110307, Research Triangle Park NC 27709-0307. 919/595-0400. **Fax:** 919/595-0401. **Contact:** Human Resources. **E-mail address:** humanresources@alphavax.com. **World Wide Web address:** http://www.alphavax.com. **Description:** A biotechnology company developing vaccines with broad applications against infectious disease, cancer, and biodefense threats. Development is currently targeting pandemic influenza and cytomegalovirus as well as HIV, prostate, and breast cancer. Founded in 1998. **Positions advertised include:** Quality Assurance Manager; Quality Control Analyst. **Corporate headquarters location:** This location. **Other area locations:** Lenoir NC.

BAYER CROPSCIENCE
2 T.W. Alexander Drive, P.O. Box 12, Research Triangle Park NC 27709. 919/549-2000. **Toll-free phone:** 800/842-8020. **Fax:** 919/549-2641. **Contact:** Human Resources. **World Wide Web address:** http://www.bayercropscienceus.com. **Description:** Involved in the research and development of pesticides and herbicides. **NOTE:** Please visit http://www.bayerjobs.com to search for jobs. **Other U.S. locations:** Kansas City MO. **International locations:** Monheim, Germany. **Parent company:** Bayer AG. **Operations at this facility include:** This location is the business headquarters of the company's NAFTA Region. **Listed on:** New York Stock Exchange. **Stock exchange symbol:** BAY. **Number of employees at this location:** 500.

CHARLES RIVER LABORATORIES, INC.
11000 Weston Parkway, Suite 100, Cary NC 27513. 919/460-9005. **Fax:** 919/462-2200. **Contact:** Human Resources. **E-mail address:** hr.usa@inveresk.com. **World Wide Web address:** http://www.criver.com. **Description:** Provides research services to pharmaceutical companies for studies that include FDA drug approval. **Positions advertised include:** Manager, Clinical Monitoring; Project Team Assistant; Telecommunications/Facility Specialist; Financial Analyst; Associate Director Systems; Medical Director; Senior Clinical Research Associate; Clinical Research Associate; Executive Assistant; Associate Director; Clinical Project Manager; Senior Biostatistician; Director of Proposal Development. **Corporate headquarters location:** Wilmington MA. **Other area locations:** Durham NC; Raleigh NC. **International locations:** Worldwide.

EMBREX INC.
P.O. Box 13989, Research Triangle Park NC 27709-3989. 919/941-5185. **Physical address:** 1040 Swabia Court, Durham NC 27703. **Fax:** 919/314-2550. **Contact:** Personnel. **E-mail address:** employment@embrex.com. **World Wide Web address:** http://www.embrex.com. **Description:** Develops and manufactures an automated, egg-injection system, eliminating the need for manual vaccination of newly hatched broiler chicks. Its patented INOVOJECT system inoculates up to 50,000 eggs per hour. The company's research also includes viral neutralizing factors, immunomodulators, gene vaccines, and performance enhancement products that alter bird physiology for early delivery. **Positions advertised include:** Facilities Technician; Inventory and Manufacturing Accountant; Research Associate; Supervisor of Shipping and Receiving; Production Manager; Lead Process Operator. **Corporate headquarters location:** This location. **Other area locations:** Statewide. **International locations:** Argentina; Brazil; China; Korea; Malaysia. **Subsidiaries include:** Embrex Europe Ltd. **Listed on:** NASDAQ. **Stock exchange symbol:** EMBX. **Number of employees nationwide:** 240.

GLAXOSMITHKLINE
3030 Cornwallis Road, Research Triangle Park NC 27709. 919/483-2100. **Toll-free phone:** 888/825-5249. **Fax:** 919/315-1053. **Contact:** Director or Human Resources Operations. **World Wide Web address:** http://www.gsk.com. **Description:** A pharmaceutical preparations company whose products include AZT, an AIDS treatment drug; Zantac; and Malarone, a medication for malaria. **Positions advertised include:** Administrative Assistant; Advisor/Manager Respiratory Commercial Analysis; Assistant Scientist; Assistant Clinical Supplies Project Leader; Associate Program Manager; Chemical Engineer; Clinical Pharmacokineticist; Clinical Pharmacology Disease Area Manager; Director of Business Integration; Health Enhancement Manager; Epidemiologist; Pharmaceutical Sales Representative. **Special programs:** Internships. **Corporate headquarters location:** London, England. **Other area locations:** Zebulon NC. **Other U.S. locations:** PA; NJ; DE; MA; MI; SC. **International locations:** Worldwide. **Operations at this facility include:** Administration; Research and Development. **Listed on:** New York Stock Exchange. **Stock exchange symbol:** GSK. **Number of employees worldwide:** 100,000.

KING PHARMACEUTICALS, INC.
4000 Centre Green Road, Suite 300, Cary NC 27513. 919/653-7001. **Contact:** Human Resources. **World Wide Web address:** http://www.kingpharm.com. **Description:** A pharmaceutical development firm specializing in cardiovascular drugs. Founded 1994.

Positions advertised include: Director of Medicinal Chemistry; Senior Scientist of Data Sciences. **Corporate headquarters location:** Bristol TN. **Other area locations:** Statewide. **Other U.S. locations:** Nationwide. **Listed on:** New York Stock Exchange. **Stock exchange symbol:** KG.

LABORATORY CORPORATION OF AMERICA (LABCORP)
309 East Davis Street, P.O. Box 2230, Burlington NC 27216. 336/584-5171. **Toll-free phone:** 800/331-2843. **Contact:** Human Resources. **World Wide Web address:** http://www.labcorp.com. **Description:** One of the nation's leading clinical laboratory companies, providing services primarily to physicians, hospitals, clinics, nursing homes, and other clinical labs nationwide. LabCorp performs tests on blood, urine, and other body fluids and tissue, aiding the diagnosis of disease. **Positions advertised include:** Senior Cytogenetics Technologist; Laboratory Director; National Managed Care Executive Director; Senior Programmer/Analyst; Lead Project Analyst/Engineer. **Special programs:** Internships. **Corporate headquarters location:** This location. **Other U.S. locations:** Nationwide. **Operations at this facility include:** Administration; Regional Headquarters; Research and Development; Sales; Service. **Listed on:** New York Stock Exchange. **Stock exchange symbol:** LH. **Number of employees nationwide:** 23,000.

MERCK MANUFACTURING
4633 Merck Road West, Wilson NC 27893. 252/243-3261. **Toll-free phone:** 800/473-2011. **Contact:** Human Resources. **World Wide Web address:** http://www.merck.com. **Description:** Manufactures pharmaceuticals for Merck & Company, Inc. **Corporate headquarters location:** Whitehouse Station NJ. **Other U.S. locations:** Nationwide. **International locations:** Worldwide. **Parent company:** Merck & Company, Inc. is a worldwide organization engaged primarily in the business of discovering, developing, producing, and marketing products for the maintenance of health and the environment. Products include human and animal pharmaceuticals and chemicals sold to the health care, oil exploration, food processing, textile, paper, and other industries. Merck & Company, Inc. also runs an ethical drug mail-order marketing business. **Operations at this facility include:** This location is a pharmaceutical plant that packages many of Merck's well-known prescription drugs, as well as manufactures Zocor, Singulair, medication for AIDS patients, and other medications for those suffering from high blood pressure or ulcers. **Listed on:** New York Stock Exchange. **Stock exchange symbol:** MRK. **Number of employees at this location:** 425.

NATIONAL INSTITUTE OF ENVIRONMENTAL HEALTH SCIENCES
111 Alexander Drive, P.O. Box 12233, Research Triangle Park NC 27709. 919/541-0218. **Recorded jobline:** 919/541-4331. **Contact:** Lindsay Lloyd. **E-mail address:** lloyd3@niehs.nih.gov. **World Wide Web address:** http://www.niehs.nih.gov. **Description:** A component of the Department of Health and Human Services, the National Institute of Environmental Health Services specializes in biomedical research programs, communication strategies, and prevention and intervention efforts. The focus of the Institute is to reduce human illness and dysfunction caused by the environment. **Positions advertised include:** Health Science Administrator; Administrative Assistant; External Program Specialist; Secretary of Office Automation; Student Assistant; Program Specialist. **Special programs:** Fellowships; Internships. **Corporate headquarters location:** This location. **Other U.S. locations:** Bethesda MD.

QUINTILES TRANSNATIONAL CORPORATION
P.O. Box 13979, Research Triangle Park NC 27709-3979. 919/998-2000. **Physical address:** 4709 Creekstone Drive Durham NC 27703. **Fax:** 919/998-2094. **Contact:** Human Resources. **E-mail address:** hr.info@quintiles.com. **World Wide Web address:** http://www.quintiles.com. **Description:** A contract pharmaceutical research company. Provides professional services for pharmaceutical and biotechnology companies, as well as healthcare providers. Founded 1982. **Positions advertised include:** Administrative Assistant; Alliance Management Director; Analyst; Associate Clinical Scientist; Employee Premium Services; Global Account Executive; IT Security Architect; Pricing Analyst; Project Manager; Project Specialist; Scientific Specialist; Senior Administrative Assistant; Senior Contracts Manager; Vice President of Market Development. **Corporate headquarters location:** This location. **Other area locations:** Morrisville NC. **Other U.S. locations:** Nationwide. **International locations:** Worldwide. **Parent company:** Pharma Services Acquisition Corporation.

RESEARCH TRIANGLE INSTITUTE (RTI)
3040 Cornwallis Road, P.O. Box 12194, Research Triangle Park NC 27709-2194. 919/541-6000. **Fax:** 919/316-3791. **Contact:** Supervisor of Employment Services. **E-mail address:** jobs@rti.org. **World Wide Web address:** http://www.rti.org. **Description:** A nonprofit, independent research organization involved in many scientific fields, under contract to business; industry; federal, state, and local governments; industrial associations; and public service agencies. The institute was created as an independent entity by the joint action of North Carolina State University, Duke University, and the University of North Carolina at Chapel Hill; however, close ties are maintained with the universities' scientists, both through the active research community of the Research Triangle Park region and through collaborative research for government and industry clients. RTI responds to national priorities in health, the environment, advanced technology, and social policy with contract research for the U.S. government including applications in statistics, social sciences, chemistry, life sciences, environmental sciences, engineering, and electronics. Founded in 1958. **NOTE:** Entry-level positions are offered. **Positions advertised include:** Accountant; Accounting Manager; Acquisitions Specialist; Administrative Assistant; Analyst; Biological Lab Assistant; Biologist; Business Development Director; Call Center Services Supervisor; Chemist; Contract Billing Specialist; Economist; Engineer; Environmental Engineer; Maintenance Supervisor; Postdoctoral Chemist; Senior Research Scientist Toxicologist. **Corporate headquarters location:** This location. **Other area locations:** Durham NC; Raleigh NC; Greenville NC. **Other U.S. locations:** Washington DC; Cocoa Beach FL; Hampton VA; Rockville MD; Atlanta GA; Chicago IL; Waltham MA; Anniston AL. **International locations:** United Arab Emirates; Indonesia; England; South Africa; El Salvador. **Subsidiaries include:** RTI Polska LLC. **Listed on:** Privately held. **Annual sales/revenues:** More than $100 million. **Number of employees at this location:** 1,400.

SYNGENTA BIOTECHNOLOGY, INC.
3054 Cornwallis Road, P.O. Box 12257, Research Triangle Park NC 27709-2257. 919/541-8500. **Contact:** Human Resources. **World Wide Web address:** http://www.syngentabiotech.com. **Description:** Researches and develops products to improve crop protection and to increase crop production. **Corporate headquarters location:** This location. **Parent company:** Syngenta (Switzerland). **Listed on:** New York Stock Exchange. **Stock exchange symbol:** SYT. **Number of employees worldwide:** 19,000.

TENGION
3929 Westpoint Boulevard, Winston Salem NC 27103. 336/722-5855. **Contact:** Human Resources. **E-mail address:** careers@tengion.com. **World Wide Web address:** http://www.tengion.com. **Description:** A biotechnology company that develops bioengineered tissues based on proprietary advances in autologous tissue engineering technology and optimal biomaterials. Founded in 2003. **Positions advertised include:** Senior Scientist, Process Development and Engineering; Scientist, Product Engineering; Research Technician;

Technician; Preclinical Study Coordinator; Electrician. **Corporate headquarters location:** King of Prussia PA. **Operations at this facility include:** R&D.

TYCO HEALTHCARE/MALLINCKRODT
8800 Durant Road, Raleigh NC 27616. 919/878-2930. **Contact:** Human Resources. **World Wide Web address:** http://www.mallinckrodt.com. **Description:** Tyco Healthcare/Mallinckrodt, Inc. provides specialty chemicals and human and animal health products worldwide through Tyco Healthcare/Mallinckrodt and two other technology-based businesses: Mallinckrodt Chemical, Inc. and Mallinckrodt Veterinary, Inc. **Corporate headquarters location:** Hazelwood MO. **Other U.S. locations:** Nationwide. **International locations:** Worldwide. **Operations at this facility include:** This location manufactures dyes used in CT scans.

Ohio

BATTELLE
505 King Avenue, Columbus OH 43201. 614/424-5901. **Contact:** Employment Advisor. **E-mail address:** employment@battelle.org. **World Wide Web address:** http://www.battelle.org. **Description:** An international technology organization that serves industry and government by generating, applying, and commercializing technology through research and development. With a wide range of scientific and technical capabilities, Battelle serves clients worldwide. **NOTE:** Resumes are only accepted for advertised positions and a specific job reference number must accompany every resume. Available positions are listed on the company's Website, and interested jobseekers are encouraged to apply using the online form available there. **Positions advertised include:** Research Scientist; Technician; Principal Synthesis Chemist; Pesticide Chemist; Office Assistant; Senior Internal Auditor; Payroll Tax Assistant. **Special programs:** Internships. **Corporate headquarters location:** This location. **Operations at this facility include:** Administration; Research and Development. **Number of employees at this location:** 2,000. **Number of employees nationwide:** 8,000.

CSA INTERNATIONAL
8501 East Pleasant Valley Road, Independence OH 44131-5575. 216/524-4990. **Contact:** Human Resources Manager. **World Wide Web address:** http://www.csa-international.org. **Description:** Performs certification testing and operates research labs for gas-fired equipment. **Operations at this facility include:** Research and Development; Service.

CARDINAL HEALTH, INC.
7000 Cardinal Place, Dublin OH 43017. 614/757-5000. **Toll-free phone:** 800/234-8701. **Fax:** 614/757-8602. **Recorded jobline:** 614/757-5627. **Contact:** Human Resources Department. **World Wide Web address:** http://www.cardhealth.com. **Description:** A wholesale distributor of pharmaceuticals, medical and surgical products, and related health supplies. The company also distributes merchandise typically sold in retail drug stores, hospitals, and health care provider facilities. Cardinal Health provides specialized support services to assist clients such as order-entry and confirmation, inventory control, monitoring pricing strategies, and financial reporting. The company has developed an in-pharmacy computer system that provides prices, patient profiles, financial data, and management services. **Positions advertised include:** Senior Programmer Analyst; Graphic Designer; Compensation Analyst; Administrative Assistant; Buyer Assistant; Project Engineer; Credit Collections Specialist; Quality Assurance Analyst; Business Systems Analyst; Financial Analyst; Senior Tax Analyst; Human Resources Manager; Senior Auditor. **Special programs:** Internships. **Corporate headquarters location:** This location. **Subsidiaries include:** Medicine Shoppe International, Inc.; National PharmPak Services, Inc.; PCI Services, Inc.; ScriptLINE. **Listed on:** New York Stock Exchange. **Stock exchange symbol:** CAH. **Annual sales/revenues:** $21 - $50 million. **Number of employees at this location:** 1,300. **Number of employees nationwide:** 30,000. **Number of employees worldwide:** 36,000.

METCUT RESEARCH ASSOCIATES, INC.
3980 Rosslyn Drive, Cincinnati OH 45209-1196. 513/271-5100. **Toll-free phone:** 800/966-2888. **Fax:** 513/271-9511. **Contact:** Human Resources. **E-mail address:** hr@metcut.com. **World Wide Web address:** http://www.metcut.com. **Description:** A materials engineering research and development firm engaged in specimen testing. **Corporate headquarters location:** This location. **President and CEO:** John P. Kahles.

NEOPROBE CORPORATION
425 Metro Place North, Suite 300, Dublin OH 43017. 614/793-7500. **Toll-free phone:** 800/793-0079. **Fax:** 614/793-7520. **Contact:** Human Resources. **E-mail address:** info@neoprobe.com. **World Wide Web address:** http://www.neoprobe.com. **Description:** Conducts research involving cancer diagnosis and treatment. The company is developing and commercializing products worldwide that are based on its proprietary, core RIGS technology. The RIGS system combines small radiation detectors and disease-targeting agents designed to provide surgeons with immediate information about the location of diseased tissue during surgery. **Listed on:** New York Stock Exchange. **Stock exchange symbol:** NEOP. **CEO:** David Bupp.

OMNICARE PHARMACY OF PERRYSBURG
P.O. Box 1030, Perrysburg OH 43552-1030. 419/661-2200. **Physical address:** 7643 Ponderosa Road, Perrysburg OH 43551. **Contact:** Human Resources Department. **World Wide Web address:** http://www.omnicarewesthaven.com. **Description:** Distributes pharmaceuticals to nursing homes.

PATHEON PHARMACEUTICALS
2110 East Galbraith Road, Cincinnati OH 45237. 513/948-9111. **Contact:** Human Resources Coordinator. **E-mail address:** CRO_Recruiting@patheon.com. **World Wide Web address:** http://www.patheon.com. **Description:** Develops, manufactures, and markets pharmaceutical products. The company specializes in products related to allergies, arthritis, cardiology, diabetes, infectious diseases, oncology, and respiratory disorders. **Positions advertised include:** Commercial Business Manager. **Corporate headquarters location:** Mississauqua Ontario.

RICERCA BIOSCIENCES LLC
7528 Auburn Road, P.O. Box 1000, Concord OH 44077. 440/357-3300. **Toll-free phone:** 888/763-4797. **Fax:** 440/350-7923. **Contact:** Human Resources. **World Wide Web address:** http://www.ricerca.com. **Description:** Provides research and development services on a contract basis to clients primarily in the agricultural, pharmaceutical, and specialty chemicals industries. The company also helps clients develop new products, improve existing products, and support the registration of products for regulatory compliance. **Positions advertised include:** Medical Chemist; Synthetic Chemist; Process Chemist; Chemical Process Development Engineer. **Corporate headquarters location:** This location. **Parent company:** Ishihara Sangyo Kaisha, Ltd. (Japan). **Number of employees at this location:** 300.

ROSS PRODUCTS
625 Cleveland Avenue, Columbus OH 43215-1724. 614/624-7677. **Contact:** Staffing Department. **World Wide Web address:** http://www.abbott.com. **Description:** Develops and markets adult and pediatric nutritionals. The company's products include Isomil and Similac infant formulas as well as Ensure adult nutritionals. Founded in 1888. **Positions advertised include:** Project Engineer; Research Scientist; Help Desk Manager; Quality Assurance Project Leader; Senior Engineer; Senior Financial Analyst; Customer Relations Coordinator; Maintenance Supervisor; Maintenance Mechanic. **Parent company:** Abbot Laboratories is a health care company that develops,

manufactures and markets products and services for the prevention, diagnosis, treatment, and cure of a variety of diseases. The company specializes in developing treatments for diabetes, pain management, respiratory infections, HIV/AIDS, pediatrics and animal health. **Operations at this facility include:** Divisional Headquarters.

WIL RESEARCH LABORATORIES
1407 George Road, Ashland OH 44805. 419/289-8700. **Contact:** Human Resources. **E-mail address:** info@wilresearch.com. **World Wide Web address:** http://www.wilresearch.com. **Description:** A contract pharmaceutical and chemical laboratory. **NOTE:** Entry-level positions are offered. Interested candidates should submit a completed employment application (which may be downloaded from the website), along with a resume for review. **Positions advertised include:** Reproductive Toxicologist; Juvenile Toxicologist; Biologist; Staff Pathologist; Research Assistant; Formulations Specialist; Chemist; Report Writer; Auditor; Histologist. **Number of employees at this location:** 175.

Oklahoma

DIANON SYSTEMS, INC.
840 Research Parkway, Oklahoma City OK 73104. 800/634-9330. **Fax:** 405/290-4413. **Contact:** Human Resources. **World Wide Web address:** http://www.dianon.com. **Description:** Provides physicians and health care companies with pathology services to detect cancers and genetic diseases. **Corporate headquarters location:** Stratford CT. **Parent company:** LabCorp, Inc.

Oregon

ELECTRO SCIENTIFIC INDUSTRIES, INC. (ESI)
13900 NW Science Park Drive, Portland OR 97229. 503/641-4141. **Fax:** 503/671-5571. **Contact:** Human Resources. **World Wide Web address:** http://www.esi.com. **Description:** Electro Scientific Industries, Inc. designs and builds advanced production equipment used throughout the world in electronics manufacturing. The principal end markets for products made using ESI equipment include the computer, telecommunications, and automotive industries. ESI's principal product lines include precision, high-speed test equipment for ceramic capacitor manufacturing; laser manufacturing systems for semiconductor yield improvement; precision laser and mechanical drilling systems for electronic interconnection; machine vision systems; and advanced laser trimming systems for the precise tuning of electronic circuits. Founded in 1949. **Positions advertised include:** Electro Mechanical Integrator; Laser/Optics Manufacturing Supervisor; Operations Specialist; Checkout Technician. **Corporate headquarters location:** This location. **Operations at this facility include:** Administration; Manufacturing; Research and Development; Sales; Service.

HACH ULTRA ANALYTICS
481 California Avenue, Grants Pass OR 97526. **Toll-free phone:** 800/866-7889. **Fax:** 541/472-6566. **Contact:** Roxanne McClure, Human Resources Department. **World Wide Web address:** http://www.hachultra.com. **Description:** Manufactures particle-monitoring instruments used to size and count particles in air, liquids, and gases. Primary markets (both domestic and international) are the pharmaceutical, semiconductor, fluid power, and aerospace industries. **Positions advertised include:** Support Engineer. **Corporate headquarters location:** Newport CA.

HATFIELD MARINE SCIENCE CENTER
2030 SE Marine Science Drive, Newport OR 97365. 541/867-0100. **Fax:** 541/867-0138. **Contact:** Human Resources. **E-mail address:** hmsc@oregonstate.edu. **World Wide Web address:** http://www.hmsc.orst.edu. **Description:** A research and teaching facility operated by Oregon State University. The Hatfield Marine Science center offers estuarine and marine education and research, a base for oceanographic studies, and a variety of laboratory capabilities.

KAISER PERMANENTE CENTER FOR HEALTH RESEARCH
3800 North Interstate Avenue, Portland OR 97227. 503/335-2400. **Contact:** Human Resources. **E-mail address:** information@kpchr.org. **World Wide Web address:** http://www.kpchr.org. **Description:** Conducts health care research including clinical trials, intervention studies, and social economic studies. **Corporate headquarters location:** Oakland CA.

MOLECULAR PROBES, INC.
29851 Willow Creek Road, Eugene OR 97402. 541/335-0338. **Toll-free phone:** 800/438-2209. **Fax:** 541/335-0305. **Contact:** Human Resources. **World Wide Web address:** http://www.probes.com. **Description:** A biotechnology company that develops fluorescent technology for biochemistry, cell biology, diagnostics, immunology, microbiology, molecular biology, and neuroscience research and studies. **Positions advertised include:** Biosciences Associate Scientist; Biosciences Quality Control Manager; Cell Biologist; Paralegal; Patent Attorney; Senior Manager; Staff Scientist; Technical Editor; Technical Writer.

NEUROCOM INTERNATIONAL INC.
9570 SE Lawnfield Road, Clackamas OR 97015-9611. 503/653-2144. **Contact:** Human Resources. **World Wide Web address:** http://www.onbalance.com. **Description:** Specializes in balance and mobility and manufactures medical equipment for the treatment of chronic dizziness and mobility disorders.

OREGON MEDICAL LABORATORIES
123 International Way, Springfield OR 97477. 541/349-8464. **Toll-free phone:** 800/826-3616. **Fax:** 541/984-8255. **Contact:** Human Resources. **E-mail address:** jobs@omlabs.com. **World Wide Web address:** http://www.omlabs.com. **Description:** A clinical laboratory that provides testing and consultation services to area hospitals and physicians. Oregon Medical Laboratory is also a certified drug-testing facility. **Positions advertised include:** IS Help Desk Specialist; Technical Specialist, Blood Bank; Chief Financial Officer; Medical Technologist. **Corporate headquarters location:** This location.

QUEST DIAGNOSTICS INCORPORATED
6600 SW Hampton Street, Portland OR 97223. 503/306-1010. **Toll-free phone:** 800/222-7941. **Fax:** 503/306-1540. **Contact:** Janet Napoleon, Director Human Resources. **World Wide Web address:** http://www.questdiagnostics.com. **Description:** Quest Diagnostics is one of the largest clinical laboratories in North America, providing a broad range of clinical laboratory services to health care clients that include physicians, hospitals, clinics, dialysis centers, pharmaceutical companies, and corporations. The company offers and performs tests on blood, urine, and other bodily fluids and tissues to provide information for health and well-being. **Positions advertised include:** Medical Transcriptionist; Phlebotomy Services Representative. **Corporate headquarters location:** Teterboro NJ. **Other U.S. locations:** Nationwide. **Operations at this facility include:** This location is a diagnostic laboratory performing clinical testing for clients throughout the Pacific Northwest.

WELCH ALLYN PROTOCOL, INC.
8500 SW Creekside Place, Beaverton OR 97008. 503/530-7500. **Fax:** 503/526-4200. **Contact:** Manager of Human Resources Department. **World Wide Web address:** http://www.protocol.com. **Description:** A manufacturer of portable systems for monitoring patients' vital signs. **Positions advertised include:** Assembler; Buyer; Marketing Director; QA Director; Engineering Technician. **Corporate headquarters location:** This location. **Operations at this facility include:** Administration; Manufacturing; Research and Development; Sales; Service.

Pennsylvania

ACCUWEATHER, INC.
385 Science Park Road, State College PA 16803. 814/237-0309. **Fax:** 814/235-8599. **Contact:** John Graham, Human Resources Manager. **E-mail address:** resume@accuwx.com. **World Wide Web address:** http://www.accuweather.com. **Description:** One of the world's leading commercial weather services providing information and products to customers nationwide. Founded in 1962. **NOTE:** Entry-level positions and second and third shifts are offered. **Positions advertised include:** Forecaster; Production Manager; Marketing Manager Multimedia; Purchasing Assistant; Administrative Assistant; Account Executive; Meteorological Programmer. **Special programs:** Internships. **Corporate headquarters location:** This location. **Subsidiaries include:** Perfect Date. **Number of employees at this location:** 320.

AMERICAN COMPETITIVENESS INSTITUTE
One International Plaza, Suite 600, Philadelphia PA 19113. 610/362-1200. **Fax:** 610/362-1341. **Contact:** Human Resources. **E-mail address:** info@aciusa.org. **World Wide Web address:** http://www.aciusa.org. **Description:** A scientific research corporation dedicated to the advancement of electronics manufacturing processes and materials for The Department of Defense and industry. Founded in 1992. **Positions advertised include:** Government Program(s) Manager/Coordinator; Director, Army Sustainment Center; Project Engineer/Program Manager; Senior Digital Design Engineer; Senior Member of Technical Staff; Senior RF Engineer; Technical Writer/Editor-Communications.

AMERISOURCEBERGEN CORPORATION
1300 Morris Drive, Suite 100, Chesterbrook PA 19087-5594. 610/727-7000. **Toll-free phone:** 800/829-3132. **Fax:** 610/727-3611. **Contact:** Lisa Hickman, Human Resources Manager. **World Wide Web address:** http://www.amerisourcebergen.com. **Description:** A large pharmaceutical distribution company serving hospitals, nursing homes, clinics, and pharmacy chains. The company also provides health and beauty aids, general merchandise, inventory control, emergency delivery, and marketing and promotional services. **Positions advertised include:** Coordinator, Proposal Development; Product Manager; Portfolio Analyst. **Corporate headquarters location:** This location. **Other U.S. locations:** Orange CA. **Listed on:** New York Stock Exchange. **Stock exchange symbol:** ABC. **Annual sales/revenues:** More than $100 million.

APPTEC
4751 League Island Boulevard, Philadelphia PA 19112. 215/218-5500. **Toll-free phone:** 800/622-8820. **Fax:** 215/218-5990. **Contact:** Human Resources. **E-mail address:** facjobs.phila@apptec-usa.com. **World Wide Web address:** http://www.apptec-usa.com. **Description:** Provides testing, contract research and development, and cGMP manufacturing services for the biopharmaceutical/biotechnology and medical device/medical product industries. **Positions advertised include:** Manufacturing Director; Metrology Manager; QC/Environmental Manager; Metrology Associate; Process Development Scientist. **Corporate headquarters location:** St. Paul MN.

BIO-IMAGING TECHNOLOGIES, INC.
826 Newtown-Yardley Road, Newtown PA 18940-1721. 267/757-3000. **Fax:** 267/757-3005. **Contact:** Maria Kraus, Controller. **E-mail address:** careers@bioimaging.com. **World Wide Web address:** http://www.bioimaging.com. **Description:** Processes and analyzes data for clinics and labs. The company receives lab data from clinical tests, including MRIs and ultrasounds, and then digitizes the information.

BIOSIS
3501 Market Street, Philadelphia PA 19104. 215/386-0100. **Toll-free phone:** 800/336-4474. **Fax:** 215/243-2208. **Contact:** Dana Felt, Senior Human Resources Generalist. **E-mail address:** info@biosis.org. **World Wide Web address:** http://www.biosis.org. **Description:** A nonprofit educational organization. Its mission is to foster the growth, communication, and use of biological knowledge. BIOSIS offers one of the world's largest collections of abstracts and bibliographical references of biological and medical literature available for public use. Founded in 1926. **NOTE:** Entry-level positions are offered. Search and apply for positions online. **Corporate headquarters location:** This location. **International locations:** Worldwide. **Subsidiaries include:** BIOSIS (UK). **Parent company:** Thomson Scientific. **Operations at this facility include:** Administration; Marketing; Production; Sales. **Annual sales/revenues:** $21-$50 million. **Number of employees at this location:** 250.

CELLOMICS, INC.
100 Technology Drive, Pittsburgh PA 15219. 412/770-2200. **Fax:** 412/770-2440. **Contact:** Human Resources. **E-mail address:** humanresources@cellomics.com. **World Wide Web address:** http://www.cellomics.com. **Description:** Develops research components for pharmaceutical and biotechnology companies to aid in faster, more efficient drug discovery processes. Cellomics, Inc. delivers genomic- and cell-based solutions. Founded in 1996. **Positions advertised include:** Marketing Programs Manager; Technical Writer; BioAssay Scientist; Sr. Software Engineer; Informatics Support Specialist. **Corporate headquarters location:** This location. **Parent company:** Fisher Biosciences.

CENTOCOR, INC.
800/850 Ridgeview Drive, Horsham PA 19044. 610/651-6000. **Fax:** 610/651-6100. **Contact:** Human Resources. **World Wide Web address:** http://www.centocor.com. **Description:** Develops biopharmaceutical therapeutics and diagnostic products for cardiovascular, inflammatory, and infectious diseases, and cancer. Centocor concentrates on research, development, and manufacturing with a technological focus on monoclonal antibodies, peptides, and nucleic acids. **NOTE:** On-line applications can be made via the Johnson and Johnson Careers Website. **Positions advertised include:** Director, Clinical Research; Associate Director, Marketing Compliance; Sr. Tax Analyst; Director, Channel Management; Finance Management. **Corporate headquarters location:** This location. **Subsidiaries include:** Centocor B.V. (the Netherlands); Centocor U.K. Limited (England); and Nippon Centocor K.K. (Japan). **Parent company:** Johnson & Johnson. **Listed on:** New York Stock Exchange. **Stock exchange symbol:** JNJ.

CEPHALON, INC.
41 Moores Road, Frazer PA 19355. 610/344-0200. **Fax:** 610/738-6312. **Contact:** Ms. Pat Vandenberg, Recruiting. **World Wide Web address:** http://www.cephalon.com. **Description:** Develops, manufactures, and markets pharmaceutical products for the treatment of neurological disorders, sleep disorders, and cancer. **Positions advertised include:** Sr. Programmer Analyst; Functional Business Analyst; Market Research Analyst; Clinical Materials Sr. Associate; Maintenance Information Team Leader. **Corporate headquarters location:** This location. **Subsidiaries include:** Cephalon Development Corporation; Cephalon International Holdings, Inc.; Cephalon Investments, Inc.; Cephalon Property Management, Inc.; Cephalon Technology, Inc. **Listed on:** NASDAQ. **Stock exchange symbol:** CEPH.

FISHER SCIENTIFIC
2000 Park Lane, Pittsburgh PA 15275. 412/490-8300. **Fax:** 412/490-8900. **Contact:** Human Resources. **World Wide Web address:** http://www.fishersci.com. **Description:** Offers a selection of more than 150,000 products and services to research centers and industrial customers worldwide. Fisher Scientific serves scientists engaged in biomedical, biotechnology, pharmaceutical, chemical, and other fields of research and development in companies, educational and research institutions, and government agencies. The company also supplies clinical laboratories, hospitals, environmental testing centers, remediation companies, quality-control

laboratories, and other industrial facilities. **Positions advertised include:** Analyst, Cross Referencing; Bio/Pharma Segment Director. **Listed on:** New York Stock Exchange. **Stock exchange symbol:** FSH. **Number of employees worldwide:** 19,500.

GENAERA CORPORATION
5110 Campus Drive, Plymouth Meeting PA 19462. 610/941-4020. **Fax:** 610/941-5399. **Contact:** Human Resources Department. **E-mail address:** resume@genaera.com. **World Wide Web address:** http://www.genaera.com. **Description:** A biopharmaceutical company engaged in the development of medicine for infectious and genetic diseases. The company's clinical development efforts are focused on oncology with ongoing research efforts in respiratory and infectious diseases. **Listed on:** NASDAQ. **Stock exchange symbol:** GENR. **Number of employees at this location:** 40.

GLAXOSMITHKLINE CORPORATION
One Franklin Plaza, P.O. Box 7929, Philadelphia PA 19101-7929. 215/751-4000. **Contact:** Personnel Department. **World Wide Web address:** http://www.us.gsk.com. **Description:** GlaxoSmithKline Corporation is a health care company engaged in the research, development, manufacture, and marketing of ethical pharmaceuticals, animal health products, ethical and proprietary medicines, and eye care products. The company's principal divisions include GlaxoSmithKline Pharmaceuticals, GlaxoSmithKline Animal Health, and GlaxoSmithKline Consumer Healthcare. The company is also engaged in many other aspects of the health care field including the production of medical and electronic instruments. Through its subsidiary, Menley & James Laboratories, the company also manufactures proprietary medicines including Contac Cold Capsules, Sine-Off sinus medicine, Love cosmetics, and Sea & Ski outdoor products. **NOTE:** Online application is encouraged. **Corporate headquarters location:** This location. **Operations at this facility include:** This location is the U.S. headquarters. **Listed on:** New York Stock Exchange. **Stock exchange symbol:** GSK. **Number of employees nationwide:** 24,000.

LIFESENSORS INC.
271 Great Valley Parkway, Malvern PA 19355. 610/644-8845. **Fax:** 610 644 8616. **Contact:** Careers at LifeSensors. **E-mail address:** luthra@lifesensors.com. **World Wide Web address:** http://www.lifesensors.com. **Description:** A biotechnology company that discovers, develops, manufactures, and markets protein expression technologies based on advances in cellular and molecular biology. LifeSensors markets to academic and government research institutions, and pharmaceutical and biotechnology companies. **Positions advertised include:** Sr. Scientist, Molecular Biology; Sr. Scientist, Protein Chemistry.

McNEIL CONSUMER HEALTH CARE
JOHNSON & JOHNSON MERCK CONSUMER PHARMACEUTICALS CO.
7050 Camp Hill Road, Fort Washington PA 19034-2292. 215/273-7000. **Contact:** Human Resources. **World Wide Web address:** http://www.tylenol.com. **Description:** Manufactures and markets a wide range of consumer pharmaceutical products, including Tylenol. Johnson & Johnson Merck Consumer Pharmaceuticals Company (also at this location) develops and markets a variety of over-the-counter items. **NOTE:** Search and apply for positions through the corporate website: http://www.jnj.com. **Positions advertised include:** Manager, Conventions, Exhibits and Medical Meetings; Regulatory Communications Professional. **Parent company:** Johnson & Johnson (New Brunswick NJ).

MERCK & COMPANY, INC.
P.O. Box 4, West Point PA 19486. 215/652-5000. **Physical address:** 770 Sumneytown Pike, West Point PA 19486. **Contact:** Human Resources. **World Wide Web address:** http://www.merck.com. **Description:** Merck & Company is a worldwide organization engaged primarily in the business of discovering, developing, producing, and marketing products for the maintenance of health and the environment. Products include human and animal pharmaceuticals and chemicals sold to the health care, oil exploration, food processing, textile, and paper industries. Merck also runs an ethical drug, mail-order marketing business. **Positions advertised include:** Director, Development Planning and Integration; Manager Financial Systems and Process; Chemist; Sr. Research Biologist; Applications Services, Sr. Analyst; Director, Labor Relations. **Corporate headquarters location:** Whitehouse Station NJ. **Operations at this facility include:** This location researches and manufactures prescription drugs, and performs administrative and human resources functions.

MYLAN LABORATORIES INC.
1500 Corporate Drive, Suite 400, Canonsburg PA 15321. 724/514-1800. **Contact:** Human Resources. **E-mail address:** resume@myanlabs.com. **World Wide Web address:** http://www.mylan.com. **Description:** One of the nation's largest manufacturers of generic pharmaceutical products in finished tablet, capsule, and powder dosage forms for resale by others under their own labels. Mylan Laboratories, through its subsidiaries, also develops and manufactures wound care products. **Positions advertised include:** Quality Control Specialist; Formulation Specialist; Legal Secretary; Senior Regulatory Affairs Associate. **Corporate headquarters location:** This location. **Listed on:** New York Stock Exchange. **Stock exchange symbol:** MYL. **Number of employees nationwide:** 1,240.

OMNICARE CLINICAL RESEARCH
630 Allendale Road, King Of Prussia PA 19406. 484/679-2400. **Toll-free phone:** 800/290-5766. **Fax:** 484/679-2505. **Contact:** Human Resources Department. **World Wide Web address:** http://www.omnicarecr.com. **Description:** Develops pharmaceuticals. **Positions advertised include:** Study Initiation Coordinator; Project Manager; Revenue Coordinator; Programmer/Analyst; Director, Regulatory Affairs. **Corporate headquarters location:** Covington KY.

ORASURE TECHNOLOGIES, INC.
220 East First Street, Bethlehem PA 18015. 610/882-1820. **Fax:** 610/882-1830. **Contact:** Jill Manning. **World Wide Web address:** http://www.orasure.com. **Description:** Produces biomedical diagnostic products. **Positions advertised include:** Director, Clinical Trials; Staffing Manager; Validation Engineer; Regulatory Manager; Quality Engineer. **Corporate headquarters location:** This location.

ORTHO-McNEIL PHARMACEUTICAL
Welsh Road at McKean Road, Spring House PA 19477-0776. 215/628-5000. **Contact:** Employment Manager. **World Wide Web address:** http://www.ortho-mcneil.com. **Description:** Develops and sells pharmaceutical products including women's health, infectious disease, and wound healing products. **NOTE:** Jobs are posted on the Johnson & Johnson corporate Website: http://www.jnj.com. **Corporate headquarters location:** This location. **Parent company:** Johnson & Johnson (New Brunswick NJ). **Operations at this facility include:** Administration; Manufacturing; Research and Development.

ORTHOVITA
45 Great Valley Parkway, Malvern PA 19355. 610/640-1775. **Fax:** 610/640-2603. **Contact:** Human Resources Department. **E-mail address:** jointheteam@orthovita.com. **World Wide Web address:** http://www.orthovita.com. **Description:** A biomaterials company with proprietary technologies applied to the development of BioStructures, synthetic biologically active tissue engineering products for restoration of the human skeleton used in spine surgery and in the repair of osteoporotic fractures. **Positions advertised include:** Manufacturing Associate; Sr. Cost Accountant; Human Resources/Payroll Administrator; Director/Manager, Budget and Forecast.

PFIZER
400 West Lincoln Avenue, Lititz PA 17543. 717/626-2011. **Fax:** 717/627-9548. **Contact:** Human Resources. **World Wide Web address:** http://www.pfizer.com. **Description:** Pfizer is a leading pharmaceutical company that distributes products concerning cardiovascular health, central nervous system disorders, infectious diseases, and women's health worldwide. The company's brand-name products include Benadryl, Ben Gay, Cortizone, Desitin, Halls, Listerine, Sudafed, and Zantac 75. **Corporate headquarters location:** New York NY. **Operations at this facility include:** This location is a manufacturing and distribution facility.

PURESYN
87 Great Valley Parkway, Malvern PA 19355. 610/640-0800. **Fax:** 610/640-0808. **Contact:** Human Resources. **E-mail address:** jointheteam@puresyn.com. **World Wide Web address:** http://www.puresyn.com. **Description:** Develops, manufactures and markets products and services for the separation and purification of nucleic acids and other biological molecules. **Positions advertised include:** Quality Assurance Specialist.

QUEST DIAGNOSTICS INCORPORATED
20826 Route 19, Cranberry Township PA 16066-6019. 724/776-3223. **Contact:** Human Resources Department. **World Wide Web address:** http://www.questdiagnostics.com. **Description:** One of the largest clinical laboratories in North America, providing a broad range of clinical laboratory services to health care clients that include physicians, hospitals, clinics, dialysis centers, pharmaceutical companies, and corporations. The company offers and performs tests on blood, urine, and other bodily fluids and tissues to provide information for health and well-being. **Positions advertised include:** Billing Coordinator; Specimen Technician; Customer Service Representative; Payroll Management Team Leader. **Other U.S. locations:** Nationwide.

REPRODUCTIVE SCIENCE INSTITUTE
950 West Valley Road, Suite 2401, Wayne PA 19087. 610/964-9663. **Fax:** 610/964-0536. **Contact:** Personnel. **World Wide Web address:** http://www.ihr.com/rsi. **Description:** A medical laboratory specializing in hormonal studies and endocrinology research. **Other area locations:** Wyomissing PA; Jenkintown PA.

SANOFI PASTEUR
Discovery Drive, Box 187, Swiftwater PA 18370-0187. 570/839-7187. **Fax:** 570/839-0561. **Contact:** Human Resources Department. **World Wide Web address:** http://www.us.aventispasteur.com. **Description:** A pharmaceutical manufacturing firm with an emphasis on developing vaccines to prevent diseases such as Lyme disease, AIDS, and malaria. **NOTE:** Search and apply for positions online. **Positions advertised include:** Business Information Systems Analyst; Senior Auditor; Laboratory Coordinator; Filing & Packaging Technician.

SARTORIUS BBI SYSTEMS
2800 Baglyos Circle, Bethlehem PA 18020. 610/866-4800. **Toll-free phone:** 800/258-9000. **Fax:** 610/866-4890. **Contact:** Human Resources. **E-mail address:** info@sartorius-bbi-systems.com. **World Wide Web address:** http://www.bbraunbiotech.com. **Description:** Manufactures custom-built fermentation/cell culture bioreactor systems. B. Braun Biotech also produces a line of accessory products for laboratories including shakers, homogenizers, freeze-dryers, and heating/cooling circulator baths.

VWR SCIENTIFIC PRODUCTS
1310 Goshen Parkway, West Chester PA 19380. 610/431-1700. **Fax:** 610/436-1763. **Contact:** Human Resources. **E-mail address:** hrwc@vwr.com. **World Wide Web address:** http://www.vwrsp.com. **Description:** Provides laboratory equipment, chemicals, and supplies to the scientific marketplace worldwide. VWR Scientific is organized into five operating units that are aligned to serve specific market niche opportunities both in North America and overseas. VWR Scientific, the company's main domestic operating unit, is a full-line distributor of scientific supplies, laboratory chemicals and apparatus, and research equipment. VWR Scientific Products serves customers in a wide variety of markets including pharmaceuticals, biotechnology, chemicals, environmental testing, food, electronics, and education. VWR Canada provides the Canadian marketplace with a single coast-to-coast supplier. **Positions advertised include:** Director, Sales Training & Development; HRIS Director; Compensation Analyst; Sr. Programmer Analyst; E-Business Support Coordinator; Project Manager. **Corporate headquarters location:** Pompano Beach FL. **Number of employees nationwide:** 1,635.

WEST PHARMACEUTICAL SERVICES
101 Gordon Drive, P.O. 645, Lionville PA 19341-0645. 610/594-2900. **Fax:** 610/594-3011. **Contact:** Employment Supervisor. **World Wide Web address:** http://www.westpharma.com. **Description:** Researches and develops drug molecule delivery systems; designs and manufactures packaging components, systems, and devices that deliver and differentiate drugs and health care products; provides contract laboratory services; and performs commercialization processes for the manufacturing, filling, and packaging of drug and health care products. **Positions advertised include:** Supervisor, Regulatory Affairs; Principal Chemist. **Corporate headquarters location:** This location. **International locations:** Worldwide. **Listed on:** New York Stock Exchange. **Stock exchange symbol:** WST. **Number of employees at this location:** 300.

WISTAR INSTITUTE OF ANATOMY AND BIOLOGY
3601 Spruce Street, Philadelphia PA 19104. 215/898-3700. **Fax:** 215/898-2204. **Contact:** Jo-Ann Mendel, Human Resources Director. **World Wide Web address:** http://www.wistar.upenn.edu. **Description:** A nonprofit, biomedical research facility. As a federally designated Basic Cancer Research Center, the institute emphasizes cancer studies in addition to searching for ways to prevent and cure other devastating diseases. Wistar Institute develops model systems and tools for biomedical research, such as cell lines, monoclonal antibodies, viral vectors, and other products of genetic engineering. **Positions advertised include:** Associate Professor; Lab Assistant; Postdoctoral Researcher; Research Assistant.

WYETH PHARMACEUTICALS
500 Arcola Road, Collegeville PA 19426. 610/902-1200. **Contact:** Personnel Director. **World Wide Web address:** http://www.wyeth.com. **Description:** Produces a wide range of pharmaceutical products and proprietary medicines. **NOTE:** Entry-level positions are offered. **Positions advertised include:** Director, Project Management; Manager, External Supply; Director Clinical Affairs; Director Quality Management; Sr. Compensation Analyst; Trial Support Manager; Analyst; Sr. Clinical Scientist; Product Director. **Special programs:** Summer Jobs. **Corporate headquarters location:** Radnor PA. **Listed on:** New York Stock Exchange. **Stock exchange symbol:** WYE.

<u>Rhode Island</u>

AMGEN INC.
40 Technology Way, West Greenwich RI 02817. 401/392-1200. **Toll-free phone:** 800/842-6436. **Contact:** Human Resources. **World Wide Web address:** http://www.amgen.com. **Description:** The world's largest biotechnology company. Named by FORTUNE magazine in 2006 as one of the "100 Best Companies to Work For." Founded in 1980. **NOTE:** See website for job openings and to apply online. All resumes are processed centrally. It is not necessary to address a cover letter to a specific individual. **Positions advertised include:** Administration Coordinator; Area Human Resources Manager; Associate Scientist; Business Analyst; Engineer; Engineering Project Manager; Lab Manager; Manufacturing Associate; Project Specialist; Quality Assurance Specialist.

Corporate headquarters location: Thousand Oaks CA. **Other U.S. Locations:** CO; KY; MA; D.C.; WA. **International locations:** Worldwide. **Operations at this facility include:** Manufacturing. **Listed on:** NASDAQ. **Stock exchange symbol:** AMGN. **Chairman/President/CEO:** Kevin W. Sharer. **Number of employees worldwide:** 14,000.

STERALOIDS, INC.
P.O. Box 689, Newport RI 02840-0689. 401/848-5422. **Fax:** 401/848-5638. **Contact:** Human Resources. **World Wide Web address:** http://www.steraloids.com. **Description:** Engaged in the supply of hormones and steroids to scientists and researchers.

South Carolina
GLAXOSMITHKLINE PLC
65 Windham Boulevard, Aiken SC 29805. 803/649-3471. **Contact:** Human Resources Manager. **World Wide Web address:** http://www.gsk.com. **Description:** A health care company engaged in the research, development, manufacture, and marketing of ethical pharmaceuticals, animal health products, ethical and proprietary medicines, and eye care products. **Positions advertised include:** Sales Representative. **Corporate headquarters location:** Middlesex, United Kingdom. **Operations at this facility include:** Production of Aquafresh toothpaste and Vivarin sleep inhibitors. **Listed on:** New York Stock Exchange. **Stock exchange symbol:** GSK. **Annual sales/revenues:** $32 billion. **Number of employees worldwide:** 107,900.

LABORATORY CORPORATION OF AMERICA (LABCORP)
25 Woods Lake Road, Suite 602, Greenville SC 29607. 864/232-0636. **Contact:** Human Resources. **World Wide Web address:** http://www.labcorp.com. **Description:** One of the nation's leading clinical laboratory companies, providing services primarily to physicians, hospitals, clinics, nursing homes, and other clinical labs nationwide. LabCorp performs tests of blood, urine, and other body fluids and tissue, as well as aiding the diagnosis of disease. Founded in 1971. **Positions advertised include:** Technical Specialist; Service Representative. **Corporate headquarters location:** Burlington NC. **Listed on:** New York Stock Exchange. **Stock exchange symbol:** LH. **Annual sales/revenues:** $3.3 billion. **Number of employees:** 20,000.

PERRIGO COMPANY
P.O. Box 1968, Greenville SC 29602. 864/288-5521. **Physical address:** 4615 Dairy Drive, Greenville SC 29607. **Contact:** Sharon Garrison. **E-mail address:** sgarriso@perrigo.com. **World Wide Web address:** http://www.perrigo.com. **Description:** Manufactures and sells generic pharmaceuticals, vitamins, and personal care products for the store brand market, nationally and internationally. **Positions advertised include:** Lean Sigma Black Belt. **Corporate headquarters location:** Allegan MI. **Other locations:** CA; MI; NJ. **International locations:** England; Mexico. **Operations at this facility include:** Vitamin manufacturing; Warehouse and Distribution Center also in Greenville SC. **Listed on:** NASDAQ. **Stock exchange symbol:** PRGO. **Annual sales/revenues:** $826 million. **Number of employees nationwide:** 4,250.

Tennessee
CHASE SCIENTIFIC GLASS, INC.
234 Cardiff Valley Road, Rockwood TN 37854. 865/354-1212. **Toll-free phone:** 800/451-4351. **Fax:** 865/354-3853. **Contact:** Human Resources. **E-mail address:** sroy@chasescientific.com. **World Wide Web address:** http://www.chasescientific.com. **Description:** Manufactures laboratory, hospital, and scientific glassware including test tubes and slides.

COVANCE INC.
150 4th Avenue North, Suite 600, Nashville TN 37219. 615/313-6700. **Contact:** Human Resources. **World Wide Web address:** http://www.covance.com/careers. **Description:** A drug development services company. **NOTE:** Search and apply for positions or submit resume online. **Positions advertised include:** Clinical Research Associate; Trial Logistics Associate. **Corporate headquarters location:** Princeton NJ. **Listed on:** New York Stock Exchange. **Stock exchange symbol:** CVD. **Number of employees worldwide:** 6,500.

GALBRAITH LABORATORIES, INC.
P.O. Box 51610, Knoxville TN 37950-1610. 865/546-1335. **Physical address:** 2323 Sycamore Drive, Knoxville TN 37921-1700. **Toll-free phone:** 877/449-8797. **Fax:** 865/546-7209. **Contact:** Jim Cummings, Manager of Human Resources. **E-mail address:** labinfo@galbraith.com. **World Wide Web address:** http://www.galbraith.com. **Description:** One of the world's largest microanalytical laboratories. Galbraith provides laboratory services to all segments of industry, government, and the academic world. These services include analysis for all elements, trace analyses, physical property testing, environmental testing, compendium methods, and assays. Industry-specific expertise covers pharmaceuticals, pulp and paper, plastics, environmental testing, agriculture, chemicals, petroleum, textiles, and mining. Founded in 1950.

KING PHARMACEUTICALS, INC.
501 Fifth Street, Bristol TN 37620. 423/989-8000. **Toll-free phone:** 800/776-3637. **World Wide Web address:** http://www.kingpharm.com. **Description:** A vertically integrated branded pharmaceutical company. **NOTE:** Search and apply for positions online. **Positions advertised include:** Supervisor, Medicaid; Contract Coordinator; Financial Analyst; Senior Project Manager; Manager, Contract Quality Assurance. **Corporate headquarters location:** This location. **Listed on:** New York Stock Exchange. **Stock exchange symbol:** KG.

PROTHERICS
5214 Maryland Way, Suite 405, Brentwood TN 37027. 615/327-1027. **Fax:** 615/320-1212. **Contact:** Human Resources Department. **World Wide Web address:** http://www.protherics.com. **Description:** An international biopharmaceutical company, engaged in the development, production and commercialization of immunopharmaceuticals and cancer therapies. **Corporate headquarters location:** London.

QUEST DIAGNOSTICS INCORPORATED
525 Mainstream Drive, Nashville TN 37228. 615/687-2000. **Contact:** Human Resources. **World Wide Web address:** http://www.questdiagnostics.com. **Description:** One of the largest clinical laboratories in North America, providing a broad range of clinical laboratory services to health care clients, which include physicians, hospitals, clinics, dialysis centers, pharmaceutical companies, and corporations. The company offers and performs tests on blood, urine, and other bodily fluids and tissues to provide information for health and well-being. **NOTE:** Search and apply for positions online. **Corporate headquarters location:** Teterboro NJ. **Operations at this facility include:** This is a major laboratory facility.

SCHERING-PLOUGH CORPORATION
3030 Jackson Avenue, Memphis TN 38151. 901/320-2011. **Contact:** Human Resources Department. **World Wide Web address:** http://www.schering-plough.com. **Description:** Engaged in the discovery, development, manufacture, and marketing of pharmaceutical and consumer products. Pharmaceutical products include prescription drugs, over-the-counter medicines, eye care products, and animal health products promoted to the medical and allied health professions. The consumer products group consists of proprietary medicines, toiletries, cosmetics, and foot care products marketed directly to the public. Products include Coricidin cough and cold medicines, Dr. Scholl's foot care products, and Coppertone skincare products. **NOTE:** Search and apply for positions online. **Positions advertised include:** Customer Logistics Manager; Sr. Scientist; Financial Operations analyst;

Sr. Systems Analyst; Scientist; Deductions Resolution Specialist; Sr. Customer Support Specialist. **Corporate headquarters location:** Kenilworth NJ. Other **U.S. locations:** Nationwide. **International locations:** Worldwide. **Operations at this facility include:** This location houses administrative offices for HealthCare Products. **Number of employees nationwide:** 2,000. **Number of employees worldwide:** 30,500.

Texas

ABBOTT DIAGNOSTICS
1921 Hurd Street, Irving TX 75038. 972/518-6000. **Contact:** Human Resources. **World Wide Web address:** http://www.abbott.com. **Description:** Designs, develops, and manufactures automated laboratory instruments, primarily used in the fields of clinical chemistry, microbiology, and therapeutic drug monitoring. **NOTE:** Please visit website to search for jobs and apply online. **Positions advertised include:** Technical Support Personnel; Information Technology Specialist. **Special programs:** Internships; Co-ops; Summer programs. **Corporate headquarters location:** Abbott Park IL. **Other U.S. locations:** Nationwide. **International locations:** Worldwide. **Parent company:** Abbott Laboratories is an international manufacturer of a wide range of health care products including pharmaceuticals, hospital products, diagnostic products, chemical products, and nutritional products. **Listed on:** New York Stock Exchange. **Stock exchange symbol:** ABT. **Number of employees worldwide:** 70,000.

ALLERGAN, INC.
P.O. Box 2675, Waco TX 76702-2675. 254/666-3331. **Physical address:** 8301 Mars Drive, Waco TX 76712. **Fax:** 254/666-3011. **Contact:** Human Resources. **World Wide Web address:** http://www.allergan.com. **Description:** Develops, manufactures, and distributes prescription and nonprescription pharmaceutical products in the specialty fields of ophthalmology and dermatology. **NOTE:** Please visit website to search for jobs and apply online. **Positions advertised include:** Controller; Compliance Officer. **Special programs:** Internships. **Corporate headquarters location:** Irvine CA. **Listed on:** New York Stock Exchange. **Stock exchange symbol:** AGN. **President/CEO:** David E.I. Pyott. **Number of employees worldwide:** 5,200.

AMBION, INC.
2130 Woodward, Austin TX 78744-1832. 512/651-0200. **Toll-free phone:** 800/888-8804. **Fax:** 512/651-0201. **Contact:** Human Resources. **World Wide Web address:** http://www.ambion.com. **Description:** Develops and supplies RNA-based life science research and molecular biology products. Ambion specializes in the development of products for stabilizing, synthesizing, handling, isolating, storing, detecting, and measuring RNA. **Positions advertised include:** Scientist; Section Leader; Post Doctoral Associate; Chemist; Process Development Chemist; Engineer; Sr. Specialist, Web Development; Programmer Analyst; Manager, Planning/Scheduling; Manufacturing Supervisor; Material Handler; Production Technician; Sr. Specialist Marketing; Marketing Manager; Product Manager; Business Systems Analyst.

APPLIED BIOSYSTEMS
13215 North Promenade Boulevard, Stafford TX 77477. 281/340-6200. **Fax:** 281/340-6210. **Contact:** Human Resources. **World Wide Web address:** http://www.appliedbiosystems.com. **Description:** Manufactures products for genetic analysis, molecular agriculture, and human and microbial identification. **NOTE:** Please visit website to search for jobs. **Corporate headquarters location:** Foster City CA. **Listed on:** New York Stock Exchange. **Stock exchange symbol:** ABI.

CARRINGTON LABORATORIES
2001 Walnut Hill Lane, Irving TX 75038. 972/518-1300. **Fax:** 972/550-7556. **Contact:** Human Resources. **E-mail address:** info@carringtonlabs.com. **World Wide Web address:** http://www.carringtonlabs.com. **Description:** Develops, manufactures, and markets a number of wound care products, pharmaceutical products, and veterinary products, all of which are based on complex carbohydrates derived from aloe vera. Products include Carrasyn Hydrogel Wound Dressing; CarraSorb H Calcium Alginate Wound Dressing; CarraFilm Transparent Film Dressing; CarraSorb M Freeze-Dried Gel; DiaB, a line of wound care products for diabetics; and RadiaCare, a line of products to treat radiation dermatitis. **Corporate headquarters location:** This location. **Subsidiaries include:** DelSite; Finca Sabila; Sabila Industrial; Caraloe, Inc. manufactures and markets nutritional aloe drinks. **Parent company:** AVACARE, Inc. **Listed on:** NASDAQ. **Stock exchange symbol:** CARN. **President/CEO:** Dr. Carlton E. Turner.

DPT LABORATORIES INC.
307 East Josephine Street, San Antonio TX 78215. 210/223-3281. **Fax:** 210/476-0794. **Contact:** Human Resources. **E-mail address:** hr.sa@dptlabs.com. **World Wide Web address:** http://www.dptlabs.com. **Description:** Provides pharmaceutical manufacturing and development services from prototype development to worldwide distribution. **NOTE:** Entry-level positions and second and third shifts are offered. Corporate headquarters location: 318 McCullough Street, San Antonio TX. **Positions advertised include:** Packaging Engineer; Industrial Engineer; Account Coordinator; Administrative Assistant.

ENCYSIVE PHARMACEUTICALS
7000 Fannin, Floor 20, Houston TX 77030. 713/796-8822. **Fax:** 713/578-6720. **Contact:** Human Resources. **World Wide Web address:** http://www.tbc.com. **Description:** A pharmaceutical research and development firm that specializes in pharmaceuticals for the treatment of acute cardiovascular conditions. **Positions advertised include:** Senior Research Technician. **Corporate headquarters location:** Bellaire TX. **Listed on:** NASDAQ. **Stock exchange symbol:** ENCY.

FISHER SCIENTIFIC COMPANY
9999 Veterans Memorial Drive, Houston TX 77038. 281/668-0005. **Contact:** Human Resources. **World Wide Web address:** http://www.fisherscientific.com. **Description:** One of the oldest and largest providers of instruments, equipment, and other products to the scientific community. The company offers a selection of more than 150,000 products and services to research centers and industrial customers worldwide. Fisher serves scientists engaged in biomedical, biotechnology, pharmaceutical, chemical, and other fields of research and development; and scientists in companies, educational and research institutions, and government agencies. The company also supplies clinical laboratories, hospitals, environmental testing centers, remediation companies, quality control laboratories, and other industrial facilities. In addition, Fisher represents its customers as a third-party purchaser of maintenance materials and other basic supplies. **NOTE:** Submit resume online at the company's website.

LABORATORY CORPORATION OF AMERICA (LABCORP)
4207 James Casey Street, Suite 101, Austin TX 78745. 512/443-0538. **Fax:** 210/735-0512. **Contact:** Human Resources. **World Wide Web address:** http://www.labcorp.com. **Description:** One of the nation's leading clinical laboratory companies, providing services primarily to physicians, hospitals, clinics, nursing homes, and other clinical labs nationwide. LabCorp performs tests on blood, urine, and other body fluids and tissue, aiding the diagnosis of disease. **NOTE:** This company has locations in Houston and Dallas. For a complete list of jobs and locations, see the company's website. **Corporate headquarters location:** Burlington NC. **Other U.S. locations:** Nationwide. **Operations at this facility include:** This location is a blood-drawing facility. **Listed on:** New York Stock Exchange. **Stock exchange symbol:** LH. **Number of employees nationwide:** 19,600.

LYNNTECH INC.
3900 State Highway 6, South, College Station TX 77845. 979/694-5255. **Fax:** 979/694-5271. **Contact:** Human Resources. **E-mail address:** hrlynntech@lynntech.com. **World Wide Web address:** http://www.lynntech.com. **Description:** Offers a broad range of research services including environmental and genetic research. Lynntech receives most of its business from government contracts. **Corporate headquarters location:** This location.

MYLAN BERTEK DOW HICKAM PHARMACEUTICALS INC.
12720 Dairy Ashford, Sugar Land TX 77478. 281/240-1000. **Fax:** 281/240-0002. **Contact:** Human Resources. **World Wide Web address:** http://www.mylan.com. **Description:** Develops drugs for viral, autoimmune, inflammatory, and neurodegenerative diseases as well as developing oral active pharmaceuticals for drug-resistant cancer and hemoglobin disorders.

NATIONAL INSTITUTIONAL PHARMACY SERVICES, INC. (NIPSI)
8977 Interchange Drive, Houston TX 77054. 713/668-7596. **Contact:** Human Resources. **Description:** Provides a full range of prescription drugs, enteral and perenteral nutritional therapy products, and infusion therapy products. The company offers antibiotic therapy, pain management, and chemotherapy services to over 520 facilities. NIPSI operates a network of 22 pharmacies in nine states.

PPD DEVELOPMENT
4009 Banister Lane, Austin TX 78704. 512/447-2663. **Contact:** Human Resources. **World Wide Web address:** http://www.ppdi.com. **Description:** Provides research and development services for companies in the biotechnology and pharmaceutical industries. **Positions advertised include:** Clinical Data Associate; Project Manager; Clinical Research Associate; Project Manager; Medical Writer; Senior Scientist. **Parent company:** PPD, Inc. **Listed on:** NASDAQ. **Stock exchange symbol:** PPDI.

PHARMERICA
3019 Interstate Drive, San Antonio TX 78219. 210/227-5262. **Contact:** Human Resources. **World Wide Web address:** http://www.pharmerica.com. **Description:** A supplier of pharmaceuticals and related products to long-term care facilities, hospitals, and assisted living communities. PharMerica also provides nurse consultant services, infusion therapy and training, medical records consulting, and educational programs. This company has locations throughout Texas and the United States. **NOTE:** PharMerica lists its Texas locations on its website and job listings for each location. Interested jobseekers are encouraged to visit the website and apply online. **Corporate headquarters location:** Tampa FL.

QUEST DIAGNOSTICS INCORPORATED
8933 Interchange Drive, Houston TX 77054. 713/667-5829. **Contact:** Human Resources. **World Wide Web address:** http://www.questdiagnostics.com. **Description:** One of the largest clinical laboratories in North America, providing a broad range of clinical laboratory services to health care clients that include physicians, hospitals, clinics, dialysis centers, pharmaceutical companies, and corporations. The company offers and performs tests on blood, urine, and other bodily fluids and tissues to provide information for health and well-being. **NOTE:** This company has second and third shift positions. **Positions advertised include:** Phlebotomist Services Representative; Medical Technologist; Route Service Representative. **Other area locations:** Irving TX: Fort Worth TX; Beaumont TX; San Antonio TX; Austin, TX; Dallas TX. **Listed on:** New York Stock Exchange. **Stock exchange symbol:** DGX.

SOUTHWEST RESEARCH INSTITUTE
P.O. Drawer 28510, San Antonio TX 78228-0510. 210/684-5111. **Physical address:** 6220 Culebra Road, San Antonio TX 78238. **Fax:** 210/522-3990. **Contact:** Human Resources. **E-mail address:** humanresources@swri.org. **World Wide Web address:** http://www.swri.org. **Description:** An independent, nonprofit, applied engineering and physical science research and development organization. Research is conducted in areas such as automation, intelligent systems, and advanced computer technology; biosciences/bioengineering; nuclear waste regulatory analyses; electronic systems and instrumentation; encapsulation and polymer research; engines, fuels, and lubricants; environmental science; fire technology; fluid and machinery dynamics; engineering and materials sciences; nondestructive evaluation research and development; and space sciences. **Special programs:** Internships. **Corporate headquarters location:** This location. **Listed on:** Privately held. **Number of employees nationwide:** 2,800.

TEXAS VETERINARY MEDICAL DIAGNOSTIC LABORATORY
P.O. Box 3200, Amarillo TX 79116-3200. 806/353-7478. **Physical address:** 6610 Amarillo Boulevard West, Amarillo TX 79106. **Toll-free phone:** 888/646-5624. **Fax:** 806/359-0636. **Contact:** Human Resources. **World Wide Web address:** http:// tvmdl.tamu.edu. **Description:** A diagnostic laboratory that performs medical testing on animals to assist veterinarians with diagnosis and prognosis. Test fields include chemistry, hematology, urology, toxicology, serology, histology, bacteriology, and necropsies. **Office hours:** Monday - Friday, 8:00 a.m. - 5:00 p.m.; Saturday, 8:00 a.m. - 12:00 p.m. **Other U.S. locations:** College Station TX; Gonzales TX; Center TX.

REPROS THERAPEUTICS INC.
2408 Timberloch Place, Suite B-7, The Woodlands TX 77380. 281/719-3400. **Fax:** 281/719-3446. **Contact:** Human Resources. **World Wide Web address:** http://www.reprosrx.com. **Description:** Researches, develops, and markets biopharmaceutical products that deal with a variety of issues including hormonal and reproductive system disorders. **Corporate headquarters location:** This location.

VIAGEN, INC.
12357-A Riata Trace Parkway, Suite 100, Austin TX 78727. 512/401-5900. **Toll-free phone:** 866/878-1301. **Fax:** 512/401-5919. **Contact:** Human Resources. **E-mail address:** employment@viagen.com. **World Wide Web address:** http://www.viagen.com. **Description:** Provides advanced livestock genetic technologies, including cloning. ViaGen's compilation of livestock genomic data and patented breeding and product identification processes are used in the cattle, swine, and equine industries to obtain superior genetics.

Utah

ARUP LABORATORIES
500 Chipeta Way, Salt Lake City UT 84108-1221. 801/583-2787. **Toll-free phone:** 800/242-2787. **Fax:** 801/584-2712. **Contact:** Linda Ivie, Human Resources. **E-mail address:** iviel@aruplab.com. **World Wide Web address:** http://www.arup-lab.com. **Description:** Performs esoteric and general laboratory testing for hospitals, reference laboratories, and independent laboratory clients. ARUP Laboratories provides a broad range of tests including analytical determinations on biological fluids and tissues. **NOTE:** See website to search for jobs and apply online. **Positions advertised include:** Administrative Assistant; Business Research Analyst; Client Service Representative; Medical Technologist; Phlebotomist; Proposal/Contract Assistant. **Corporate headquarters location:** This location. **Number of employees nationwide:** 1,400.

CEPHALON, INC.
4745 Wiley Post Way, Salt Lake City UT 84116. 801/595-1405. **Fax:** 801/595-1406. **Contact:** Recruitment Manager. **World Wide Web address:** http://www.cephalon.com. **Description:** Develops, manufactures, and markets pharmaceutical products for the treatment of neurological disorders, sleep disorders, and cancer. Founded in 1987. **NOTE:** See website for

current job openings and to apply online. **Positions advertised include:** Steam Engineer/Maintenance Specialist; Pharmaceutical Manufacturing Technician. **Corporate headquarters location:** Frazer PA. **International locations:** Germany; France; United Kingdom. **Listed on:** NASDAQ. **Stock exchange symbol:** CEPH.

DESERET LABORATORIES
1414 East 3850 South, St. George UT 84790. 435/628-8786. **Toll-free phone:** 800/632-2993. **Fax:** 435/673-1202. **Contact:** Human Resources. **E-mail address:** hrmgr@deseretlabs.com. **World Wide Web address:** http://www.deseretlabs.com. **Description:** Manufactures vitamins and botanicals and conducts research and development pertaining to its product line.

FRESENIUS MEDICAL CARE
475 West 13th Street, Ogden UT 84404. 801/626-4515. **Fax:** 801/399-1802. **Contact:** Human Resources Manager. **E-mail address:** ogden.hr@fmc-na.com. **World Wide Web address:** http://www.fmcna.com. **Description:** A pharmaceutical drug manufacturer specializing plastic blood-banking disposables, intravenous devices, and specialty solutions. The company markets these products to both home care patients and medical institutions in the United States and abroad. **Corporate headquarters location:** Lexington MA. **Other U.S. locations:** Nationwide.

IDAHO TECHNOLOGY, INC.
390 Wakara Way, Salt Lake City UT 84108. 801/736-6354. **Toll-free phone:** 800/735-6544. **Fax:** 801/588-0507. **Contact:** Human Resources. **E-mail address:** hr@idahotech.com. **World Wide Web address:** http://www.idahotech.com. **Description:** A research and development company for molecular biological equipment. Idaho Technology also manufactures and assembles thermocyclers. **NOTE:** Please visit website for online application form if desired. **Positions advertised include:** Staff Accountant; Technical Training Specialist; Mechanical Engineer; Software Engineers; Research Associates; Laboratory Technician. **Corporate headquarters location:** This location.

IDEASPHERE INC.
1525 West Business Park Drive, Orem UT 84058. 801/225-5525x123. **Toll-free phone:** 800/572-5076. **Fax:** 801/225-5899. **Contact:** Human Resources. **Description:** IdeaSphere produces natural and organic vitamins, nutrients, and other products. Products include tablets, capsules, powder drink mixes, nutritional snacks, and bars. **NOTE:** Part-time jobs and second- and third-shifts are offered. **Special programs:** Summer Jobs. **Corporate headquarters location:** Grand Rapids MI.

LABORATORY CORPORATION OF AMERICA (LABCORP)
5199 South Green Street, Murray UT 84123. 801/288-9000. **Toll-free phone:** 800/444-4522. **Contact:** Human Resources. **World Wide Web address:** http://www.labcorp.com. **Description:** One of the nation's leading clinical laboratory companies, providing services primarily to physicians, hospitals, clinics, nursing homes, and other clinical labs nationwide. LabCorp performs tests on blood, urine, and other body fluids and tissue, aiding the diagnosis of disease. **NOTE:** See website for current job openings and to apply online. **Positions advertised include:** Customer Service Support Representative; Specimen Accesioner; Specimen Processor; Technician; Technologist Trainee. **Corporate headquarters location:** Burlington NC. **Other U.S. locations:** Nationwide. **Listed on:** New York Stock Exchange. **Stock exchange symbol:** LH. **Number of employees nationwide:** 23,000.

MOXTEK, INC.
452 West 1260 North, Orem UT 84057. 801/225-0930. **Fax:** 801/221-1121. **Contact:** Human Resources. **World Wide Web address:** http://www.moxtek.com. **Description:** Manufactures components for analytical instruments and engineers new products for X-ray analysis of materials. **NOTE:** See website for current job openings and to apply online. **Positions advertised include:** Process Technician; Materials Scientist.

MYRIAD GENETICS
320 Wakara Way, Salt Lake City UT 84108. 801/582-3600. **Fax:** 801/584-3640. **Contact:** Human Resources. **E-mail address:** jobs@myriad.com. **World Wide Web address:** http://www.myriad.com. **Description:** A biopharmaceutical company engaged in the development and marketing of therapeutic and molecular diagnostic drugs and products. **NOTE:** No phone calls regarding employment. See website for current job openings and application instructions. **Positions advertised include:** Account Executive; Customer Service Specialist; Laboratory Technician; National Accounts Manager; Regional Medical Specialist; Research Associate; Vice President of Clinical Research; Receiving Clerk. **Corporate headquarters location:** This location. **CEO:** Peter D. Meldrum.

NPS PHARMACEUTICALS
383 Colorow Drive, Salt Lake City, UT 84108. 801/583-4939. **Fax:** 801/583-4961. **Contact:** Human Resources. **World Wide Web address:** http://www.npsp.com. **Description:** Engaged in treatment therapy research for diseases such as osteoporosis. **NOTE:** Please visit website to search for jobs and apply online. **Positions advertised include:** DMPK Lab Assistant/Research Associate; Records Management Specialist. **Corporate headquarters location:** This location. **Other U.S. locations:** Parsippany NJ. **International locations:** Ontario Canada.

NATURE'S SUNSHINE
P.O. Box 19005, Provo UT 84605-9005. 801/342-4300. **Physical address:** 75 East 1700 South, Provo UT 84606. **Fax:** 801/798-4126. **Contact:** Human Resources. **E-mail address:** hr@natr.com. **World Wide Web address:** http://www.naturessunshine.com. **Description:** Produces herbs and vitamins in capsule form. Nature's Sunshine manufactures over 200 vitamin and health products. **Positions advertised include:** Associate Order Sales Representative; Commission Service Analyst; Compliance Analyst; International Accounting Specialist. **Corporate headquarters location:** This location. **Other area locations:** Spanish Fork, UT. **International locations:** Worldwide.

NATURE'S WAY
1375 North Mountain Springs Parkway, Springville UT 84663. 801/489-1500. **Toll-free phone:** 800/962-8873. **Fax:** 801/489-1700. **Contact:** Human Resources. **E-mail address:** andreacl@naturesway.com. **World Wide Web address:** http://www.naturesway.com. **Description:** Manufactures health foods including herbs and vitamins. Founded in 1969. **NOTE:** Call on Tuesday and Friday afternoons to inquire about current job openings. Entry-level positions and second- and third-shifts are offered. This firm does not accept unsolicited resumes. An application must be submitted in order to be considered for employment. **Company slogan:** To advance healthy living through natural choices. **Corporate headquarters location:** This location.

NUTRACEUTICAL CORPORATION
1400 Kearns Boulevard, Park City UT 84060. 435/655-6000. **Toll-free phone:** 800/669-8877. **Fax:** 800/767-8514. **Recorded jobline:** 800/669-3009. **Contact:** Human Resources. **World Wide Web address:** http://www.nutraceutical.com. **Description:** Produces nutritional and herbal supplements. **NOTE:** Entry-level positions, part-time jobs, and second- and third-shifts are offered. **NOTE:** Please visit website to search for jobs and apply online. **Positions advertised include:** Marketing Analyst; Product Brand Manager. **Special programs:** Internships; Summer Jobs. **Corporate headquarters location:** This location. **Other area locations:** Orem UT; Ogden UT. **Subsidiaries include:** Woodland Publishing. **Listed on:** Privately held.

Number of employees worldwide: 600. **CEO:** Frank W. Gay II.

RICHARDS LABORATORIES OF UTAH, INC.
55 East Center Street, Pleasant Grove UT 84062. 801/785-2500. **Contact:** Human Resources. **Description:** A microbiology laboratory, an environmental laboratory, and a bioremediation facility.

SCIENCE APPLICATIONS INTERNATIONAL CORPORATION (SAIC)
2675 Industrial Drive, Suite 303, Ogden UT 84401. 801/399-1487. **Contact:** Laurie Lucas. **World Wide Web address:** http://www.saic.com. **Description:** A leading government services contractor offering a wide range of technical support and project management services. It provides networking, software development, and systems integration, as well as technical analysis and research for many federal and state agencies, and it offers maintenance and technical support to various branches of the military. **NOTE:** See website for current job openings and to apply online. **Positions advertised include:** Junior Business Analyst; Project/Account Manager. **Other area locations:** Layton UT; Ogden UT; Tooele UT. **Other U.S. locations:** Nationwide. **International locations:** Worldwide.

SONIC INNOVATIONS, INC.
2795 East Cottonwood Parkway, Suite 660, Salt Lake City UT 84121. 801/365-2800. **Fax:** 801/365-3003. **Contact:** Susan Marker, Human Resources. **E-mail address:** smarker@sonici.com. **World Wide Web address:** http://www.sonici.com. **Description:** Designs and manufactures advanced hearing aids, using a successful and tiny chip. **Corporate headquarters location:** This location. **Other U.S. locations:** Eagan MN. **International locations:** Canada; Denmark, Australia; New Zealand. **Listed on:** NASDAQ. **Stock exchange symbol:** SNCI. **President/CEO:** Samuel L. Westover.

WATSON PHARMACEUTICALS
577 Chipeta Way, Salt Lake City UT 84108-1222. 801/588-6200. **Fax:** 801/588-6212. **Contact:** Human Resources. **World Wide Web address:** http://www.watsonpharm.com. **Description:** A researcher, developer, and manufacturer of branded and generic pharmaceutical products. **NOTE:** Please visit website to search for jobs and apply online. **Positions advertised include:** Biostatistician; Clinical Data Specialist; Manager – Analytical R&D; Chemist; Process Operator; Scientist; Clinical Programmer Analyst; Direct Quality Assurance; Process Operator; Maintenance Supervisor; Secretary; General Maintenance Mechanic; Process Operator; Validation Engineer; Packaging Operator; Data Entry Clerk; Quality Auditor Associate. **Corporate headquarters location:** Corona CA. **Listed on:** New York Stock Exchange. **Stock exchange symbol:** WPI. **Number of employees at this location:** 320.

Vermont

AUTUMN HARP INC.
61 Pine Street, Bristol VT 05443. 802/453-4807. **Fax:** 802/453-4903. **Contact:** Human Resources. **E-mail address:** jobs@autumnharp.com. **World Wide Web address:** http://www.autumnharp.com. **Description:** A private label, full service, custom manufacturer of cosmetics and personal care products. Founded in 1977. **Positions advertised include:** Compounder/Batcher; Production Worker; Sales Executive; Technical Information Officer; Quality Assurance Administrative Assistant.

BIO-TEK INSTRUMENTS, INC.
Highland Park, P.O. Box 998, Winooski VT 05404. 888/451-5171. **Fax:** 802/655-7941. **Contact:** Human Resources. **E-mail address:** hrresumes@biotek.com. **World Wide Web address:** http://www.biotek.com. **Description:** Designs, develops, and markets microplate instrumentation and software. Founded in 1968. **Positions advertised include:** Senior Mechanical Engineer; Receptionist. **Corporate headquarters location:** This location. **Operations at this facility include:** Global Sales; Service; Distribution Support.

GREEN MOUNTAIN ANTIBODIES, INC.
One Mill Street, Suite 1-7, Burlington VT 05401. 802/865-6230. **Fax:** 802/865-0115. **Contact:** Human Resources. **E-mail address:** info@greenmoab.com. **World Wide Web address:** http://www.greenmoab.com. **Description:** Provides services to medical researchers such as developing custom hybridomas, culturing cells, and immunochemistry. **Corporate headquarters location:** This location.

MYLAN TECHNOLOGIES INC.
110 Lake Street, St. Albans VT 05478. 802/527-0175, extension 331. **Toll-free phone:** 800/532-5226. **Fax:** 802/527-1364. **Contact:** Kimberly Messier, Senior Human Resources Consultant. **E-mail address:** mtihr@mylanlabs.com. **World Wide Web address:** http://www.mylantech.com. **Description:** A pharmaceutical company manufacturing generic antibiotics, antidepressants, anti-inflammatories, beta-blockers, and laxatives. The company also manufactures transdermal drug delivery systems, coating and laminates for the transdermal administration of drugs, patches for wound care therapy, and surgical drapes. Founded in 1961. **Positions advertised include:** Production Supervisor; Assistant Scientist; Senior Quality Assurance Auditor; Stability Scientist; Process Engineer. **Corporate headquarters location:** Pittsburgh PA. **Other locations:** IL; MI; NC; PA; WV. **Subsidiaries/Affiliates include:** Mylan Pharmaceuticals; UDL Laboratories. **Parent company: Listed on:** New York Stock Exchange. **Stock exchange symbol:** MYL. **Annual sales/revenues:** $1.1 billion. **Number of employees nationwide:** 2,200.

Virginia

ABBOTT LABORATORIES
Business Route 29 North, P.O. Box 479, Altavista VA 24517. 434/369-3100. **Contact:** Human Resources. **World Wide Web address:** http://www.abbott.com. **Description:** Manufactures pharmaceuticals and liquid nutrition products including Similac, Pedialyte, and Ensure. The company also manufactures anesthetics, blood pressure monitors, and I.V. systems. **NOTE:** Offers internships. Search and apply for positions online. **Corporate headquarters location:** Abbott Park IL. **Other U.S. locations:** Nationwide. **International locations:** Worldwide. **Listed on:** New York Stock Exchange. **Stock exchange symbol:** ABT. Number of employees worldwide: 70,000.

BATTELLE
1550 Crystal Drive, Arlington VA 22202-4135. 703/413-8866. **Contact:** Human Resources. **World Wide Web address:** http://www.battelle.com. **Description:** Battelle is a global science and technology enterprise that develops and commercializes technology and manages laboratories for customers. With the national labs it manages or co-manages, the company oversees 19,000 staff members and conducts $2.9 billion in annual research and development. **Positions advertised include:** Missile Defense Systems Engineer; Intelligence Analyst; Research Scientist; Counter Intelligence Analyst; Sr. Health Research Scientist; system and Network Administrator; Information Security Analyst. **Corporate headquarters location:** Columbus OH.

CEL-SCI CORPORATION
8229 Boone Boulevard, Suite 802, Vienna VA 22182. 703/506-9460. **Fax:** 703/506-9471. **Contact:** Human Resources. **World Wide Web address:** http://www.cel-sci.com. **Description:** Develops immune system-based treatments for cancer and infectious diseases. CEL-SCI Corporation is involved in the research and development of natural human interleukin-2 and cytokine-related products and processes using proprietary cell culture technologies. Founded in 1983. **Corporate headquarters location:** This location. **Subsidiaries include:** Viral

Technologies, Inc. is a privately held company engaged in the development of a vaccine for AIDS. **Listed on:** American Stock Exchange. **Stock exchange symbol:** CVM. **Number of employees at this location:** 10. **Number of employees nationwide:** 30.

COVANCE LABORATORIES INC.
9200 Leesburg Pike, Vienna VA 22182. 703/893-5400. **Contact:** Human Resources. **World Wide Web address:** http://www.covance.com. **Description:** A life sciences firm providing drug development services. Clients include global pharmaceutical and biotech companies. **NOTE:** Search and apply for positions online. **Positions advertised include:** Study Technician; Health and Safety Specialist; Anatomic Pathologist; Business Continuity Program Manager; Resource Planning Associate; Medical Technologist. **International locations:** 18 countries. **Operations at this facility include:** Administration; Research and Development. **Listed on:** New York Stock Exchange. **Stock exchange symbol:** CVD. Number of employees worldwide: 6,500.

FAIRFAX IDENTITY LABORATORY
601 Biotech Drive, Richmond VA 23235. **Toll-free phone:** 800/735-9224. **Fax:** 804/648-2641. **Contact:** Human Resources. **E-mail address:** jobs@givf.com. **World Wide Web address:** http://www.fairfaxidlab.com. **Description:** Provides diagnostic, treatment, genetic and reproductive testing, and cryobank services. **Parent company:** Commonwealth Biotechnologies, Inc.

FAIRFAX MEDICAL LABORATORIES
4200 Pleasant Valley Road, Chantilly VA 20151. 703/222-2313. **Fax:** 703/263-7961. **Contact:** Human Resources Manager. **World Wide Web address:** http://www.fairfaxmedicallab.com. **Description:** A full-service medical laboratory that provides comprehensive clinical laboratory services. Founded in 1984. **Positions advertised include:** Cytologist; Histologist; Medical Technologist; Phlebotomist.

MERCK & COMPANY, INC.
2778 South East Side Highway, Elkton VA 22827. 540/298-1211. **Contact:** Human Resources. **World Wide Web address:** http://www.merck.com. **Description:** Merck is a worldwide organization engaged in discovering, developing, producing, and marketing products for the maintenance of health and the environment. Products include human and animal pharmaceuticals and chemicals sold to the health care, oil exploration, food processing, textile, paper, and other industries. Merck also runs an ethical drug mail-order marketing business. **NOTE:** Search and apply for positions online. **Corporate headquarters location:** Whitehouse Station NJ. **Operations at this facility include:** This location manufactures pharmaceuticals. **Listed on:** New York Stock Exchange. **Stock exchange symbol:** MRK.

RESEARCH TRIANGLE INSTITUTE (RTI)
One Enterprise Parkway, Suite 310, Hampton VA 23666-5845. 757/827-8450. **Fax:** 757/827-3273. **Contact:** Human Resources Department. **E-mail address:** jobs@rti.org. **World Wide Web address:** http://www.rti.org. **Description:** A nonprofit, independent research organization involved in many scientific fields, under contract to business; industry; federal, state, and local governments; industrial associations; and public service agencies. RTI works in the areas of health, environmental protection, advanced technology, education and training, and economic and social development. **NOTE:** Search and apply for positions online. **Corporate headquarters location:** Research Triangle Park NC. **Other U.S. locations:** Washington DC; Cocoa Beach FL; Atlanta GA; Rockville MD; Chicago IL; Waltham MA; Anniston AL. **Number of employees nationwide:** 2,300.

SCIENCE & TECHNOLOGY CORPORATION
10 Basil Sawyer Drive, Hampton VA 23666-1393. 757/766-5800. **Fax:** 757/865-1294. **Contact:** Human Resources. **E-mail address:** jobs@stcnet.com. **World Wide Web address:** http://www.stcnet.com. **Description:** A research and development government contractor engaged in atmospheric sciences and meteorology, remote sensing, scientific data processing and modeling, chemical/biological defense, test and evaluation, programming support, and biology, astrobiology and microgravity research. Founded in 1979. **NOTE:** Search and apply for positions online. **Corporate headquarters location:** This location. **Other U.S. locations:** AL; CA; CO; FL; MD; NH; TX; UT. **Listed on:** Privately held. **President/CEO:** Dr. Adarsh Deepak. **Annual sales/revenues:** $21 - $50 million. **Number of employees at this location:** 65. **Number of employees nationwide:** 300.

Washington

AMGEN
1201 Amgen Court West, Seattle WA 98119-3105. 206/265-7000. **Fax:** 206/621-1399. **Contact:** Human Resources. **World Wide Web address:** http://www.amgen.com. **Description:** A leading biopharmaceutical company focused on the discovery, manufacture, and marketing of products to treat immune system disorders. **NOTE:** Apply online. **Positions advertised include:** Business Analyst; Engineer; Facilities Maintenance Technician; Global Project Manager. **Corporate headquarters location:** Thousand Oaks CA. **Other area locations:** Bothell WA. **Operations at this facility include:** Administration; Manufacturing; Research and Development.

BIO-RAD LABORATORIES
6565 185th Avenue NE, Redmond WA 98052. 425/881-8300. **Contact:** Human Resources. **World Wide Web address:** http://www.bio-rad.com. **Description:** Engaged in the research and development of diagnostic test equipment used to detect blood viral disease.

CARDINAL HEALTH DISTRIBUTION
P.O. Box 1589, Auburn WA 98001-1589. 253/939-5550. **Physical address:** 801 C Street NW, Auburn WA. **Fax:** 253/833-9402. **Contact:** Human Resources. **World Wide Web address:** http://www.cardinal.com. **Description:** A nationwide wholesale distributor of pharmaceuticals, medical and surgical products, and related health supplies. The company also distributes merchandise typically sold in retail drug stores, hospitals, and health care provider facilities. Cardinal Distribution also provides its clients with such specialized support services as order entry and confirmation, inventory control, monitoring pricing strategies, and financial reporting. The company has developed an in-pharmacy computer system that provides prices, patient profiles, financial data, and management services. **Corporate headquarters location:** Dublin OH. **Other U.S. locations:** Nationwide. **Operations at this facility include:** Regional Headquarters; Warehouse/Distribution; Wholesaling. **Number of employees at this location:** 175. **Number of employees nationwide:** 3,000.

CELL THERAPEUTICS, INC.
201 Elliott Avenue West, Suite 400, Seattle WA 98119. 206/282-7100. **Fax:** 206/272-4010. **Recorded jobline:** 800/656-2355. **Contact:** Human Resources. **E-mail address:** resume@ctiseattle.com. **World Wide Web address:** http://www.cticseattle.com. **Description:** Researches and develops oncology products designed to manage cancer and cancer treatment side effects. Founded in 1992. **Corporate headquarters location:** This location. **Listed on:** NASDAQ. **Annual sales/revenues:** $5 - $10 million. **Number of employees at this location:** 190.

DYNACARE LABORATORY
1229 Madison Street, Suite 650, Seattle WA 98104. 206/386-2672. **Fax:** 206/386-2991. **Contact:** Human Resources. **E-mail address:** jobsdnw@dynacare.com. **World Wide Web address:** http://www.dynacare.com. **Description:** A medical laboratory. **Positions advertised include:** Lab Assistant; Phlebotomist; Medical Technologist; Assistant Supervisor of Specimen Processing; Route Representative. **Listed on:**

NASDAQ. **Stock exchange symbol:** DNCR.

EPOCH PHARMACEUTICALS, INC.
21720 23rd Drive SE 150, Bothell WA 98021. 425/482-5555. **Fax:** 425/482-5550. **Contact:** Human Resources. **World Wide Web address:** http://www.epochpharm.com. **Description:** Developing oligonucleotides as new therapeutic compounds and for use in diagnostic testing. Utilizing proprietary and unique technology in the design, synthesis, and chemical modification of oligonucleotides, the company is developing gene blockers that act by specifically binding to and inactivating the DNA of disease-associated genes; protein blockers that act by selective inhibition of certain proteins that are central to the growth and reproduction of cells and viruses; and DNA probe-based diagnostic systems for the rapid identification of certain disease pathogens. **Listed on:** NASDAQ. **Stock exchange symbol:** EBIO.

HOLLISTER-STIER LABORATORIES, LLC
3525 North Regal Street, Spokane WA 99207. 509/489-5656. **Fax:** 509/482-1792. **Contact:** Human Resources. **E-mail address:** human_resources@Hollister-stier.com. **World Wide Web address:** http://www.hollister-stier.com. **Description:** Engaged in the development and manufacture of allergy medication. **Positions advertised include:** Senior Validation Specialist; Accountant; Environmental Monitoring Technician; Warehouse Clerk; Pollen Collector.

ICOS CORPORATION
22021 20th Avenue SE, Bothell WA 98021. 425/485-1900. **Fax:** 425/489-0356. **Contact:** Human Resources. **E-mail address:** hr@icos.com. **World Wide Web address:** http://www.icos.com. **Description:** Discovers and develops new pharmaceuticals by targeting early stages of the chronic inflammatory process and by seeking points of intervention that may lead to more specific and efficacious drugs. ICOS's signal transduction programs in PDE inhibitors and cell cycle checkpoint modulators have yielded additional approaches to treating inflammatory conditions, as well as male erectile dysfunction, cardiovascular diseases, and cancer. **Positions advertised include:** Building Facilities Coordinator; Clinical Pharmacist; Purchasing Assistant; Payroll Specialist; Senior Staff Scientist. **Corporate headquarters location:** This location. **Number of employees at this location:** 200.

LABORATORY CORPORATION OF AMERICA (LABCORP)
21903 Sixty-eighth Avenue, South, Kent WA 98032. 253/395-4000. **Contact:** Human Resources. **World Wide Web address:** http://www.labcorp.com. **Description:** One of the nation's leading clinical laboratory companies, providing services primarily to physicians, hospitals, clinics, nursing homes, and other clinical labs nationwide. LabCorp performs tests on blood, urine, and other body fluids and tissue, aiding the diagnosis of disease. **Positions advertised include:** Account Representative; Medical Laboratory Sales Representative. **Corporate headquarters location:** Burlington NC. **Listed on:** New York Stock Exchange. **Stock exchange symbol:** LH.

MDS PHARMA SERVICES
22011 30th Drive SE, Bothell WA 98021-4444. 425/487-8200. **Contact:** Human Resources. **World Wide Web address:** http://www.mdsps.com. **Description:** Engaged in pharmaceutical research and development.

MERIDIAN VALLEY CLINICAL LAB, INC.
515 West Harrison Street, Suite 200, Kent WA 98032. 253/859-8700. **Contact:** Human Resources Department. **World Wide Web address:** http://www.meridianvalleylab.com. **Description:** Engaged in testing related to adrenal steroids and allergies. The lab also performs stool analyses. **Corporate headquarters location:** This location.

NEORX CORPORATION
300 Elliot Avenue West, Suite 500, Seattle WA 98119. 206/281-7001. **Fax:** 206/284-7112. **Contact:** Human Resources. **E-mail address:** hr@neorx.com. **World Wide Web address:** http://www.neorx.com. **Description:** Develops treatments for cancer and cardiovascular disease. The company's focus is on targeting therapeutic agents on diseased or injured cells, while sparing normal tissues the full impact of these treatments. The company's cardiovascular program is focused primarily on reducing reclosure of coronary arteries following balloon angioplasty. **Corporate headquarters location:** This location. **Listed on:** NASDAQ. **Number of employees at this location:** 80.

PACIFIC NORTHWEST NATIONAL LABORATORY
902 Battelle Boulevard, P.O. Box 999, Richland WA 99352. 509/375-2121. **Toll-free phone:** 888/375-PNNL. **Contact:** Human Resources. **World Wide Web address:** http://www.pnl.gov. **Description:** A national laboratory engaged in basic and applied research in energy, material and chemical sciences, earth and environmental engineering, waste technology, environmental restoration, and nuclear-related areas. **Positions advertised include:** Duty Forecaster; Senior Atmospheric Scientist; HR Generalist; Program Director. **Special programs:** Internships. **Corporate headquarters location:** Columbus OH. **Operations at this facility include:** Research and Development. **Number of employees at this location:** 4,800.

PATHOLOGY ASSOCIATES MEDICAL LABORATORIES
110 West Cliff Avenue, Spokane WA 99204. 509/755-8600. **Contact:** Human Resources. **E-mail address:** hr@paml.com. **World Wide Web address:** http://www.paml.com. **Description:** A laboratory that performs blood, tissue, and drug tests. **Corporate headquarters location:** This location.

QUEST DIAGNOSTICS INCORPORATED
1737 Airport Way South, Suite 200, Renton WA 98055. 206/623-8100. **Fax:** 206/624-5488. **Contact:** Human Resources Department. **World Wide Web address:** http://www.questdiagnostics.com. **Description:** One of the largest clinical laboratories in North America, providing a broad range of clinical laboratory services to health care clients, which include physicians, hospitals, clinics, dialysis centers, pharmaceutical companies, and corporations. The company offers and performs tests on blood, urine, and other bodily fluids and tissues to provide information for health and well-being. **Positions advertised include:** Specimen Processor; Phlebotomy Services Representative; Pricing Manager.

TARGETED GENETICS CORPORATION
1100 Olive Way, Suite 100, Seattle WA 98101. 206/623-7612. **Fax:** 206/521-4782. **Recorded jobline:** 206/521-7300. **Contact:** Human Resources. **E-mail address:** careers@targen.com. **World Wide Web address:** http://www.targen.com. **Description:** Develops gene therapy products for the treatment of certain acquired and inherited diseases. The principal focus is on three product development programs that address high-risk diseases for which there are no known cures: cytoxic T lymphocyte, (CTL)-based, immunotherapy for infectious diseases and cancer; in vivo adeno-associated virus, (AAV)-based, therapy for cystic fibrosis and other diseases; and stem cell therapy. The company approaches gene therapy through multiple delivery systems including retroviral vector delivery, AAV vector delivery, and nonviral vector delivery. **Positions advertised include:** Quality Assurance Associate. **Special programs:** Internships. **Corporate headquarters location:** This location. **Operations at this facility include:** Research and Development. **Annual sales/revenues:** Less than $5 million. **Listed on:** NASDAQ. **Stock exchange symbol:** TGEN. **Number of employees at this location:** 80.

TRIPATH IMAGING, INC.
8271 154th Avenue NE, Redmond WA 98052. 425/869-7284. **Toll-free phone:** 800/636-7284. **Fax:**

425/869-5325. **Contact:** Human Resources. **World Wide Web address:** http://www.tripathimaging.com. **Description:** Engaged in the research and development of technologies to automate the interpretation of medical images. The company's initial products are automated screening systems that are used to analyze and classify Pap smears. These screening systems use high-speed video microscopes, image interpretation software, and field-of-view computers to recognize, analyze, and classify individual cells within the complex images on a Pap smear. These products include the AutoPap QC and the AutoPap Screener. **Corporate headquarters location:** Burlington NC. **Number of employees at this location:** 100.

West Virginia

MYLAN PHARMACEUTICALS, INC.
781 Chestnut Ridge Road, Morgantown WV 26504. 304/599-2595. **Toll-free phone:** 800/826-9526. **Fax:** 304/598-5406. **Contact:** Human Resources. **E-mail address:** resume@mylanlabs.com. **World Wide Web address:** http://www.mylanpharms.com. **Description:** Manufactures a broad range of pharmaceuticals including analgesics, antibiotics, antidepressants, anti-inflammatory drugs, diuretics, and muscle relaxants. **Positions advertised include:** Product Safety Specialist; Scientist; Research Scientist; Quality Assurance Reviewer; Quality Assurance Chemist; Chemist; Senior Chemist; Recruiter; Senior Manager, CMC. **Special programs:** Internships; Summer Jobs. **Corporate headquarters location:** Pittsburgh PA. **Parent company:** Mylan Laboratories Incorporated. **Listed on:** New York Stock Exchange. **Stock exchange symbol:** MYL. **Number of employees at this location:** 900.

Wisconsin

ABS GLOBAL, INC.
1525 River Road, P.O. Box 459, De Forest WI 53532. 608/846-3721. **Toll-free phone:** 800/356-5331. **Fax:** 608/846-6442. **Contact:** Human Resources. **E-mail address:** hr_abs@absglobal.com. **World Wide Web address:** http://www.absglobal.com. **Description:** Manufactures artificial insemination products for cattle. The company is a world leader in bovine DNA, in vitro fertilization, and cell cloning research. **Positions advertised include:** ABS Representative; Accountant; Customer Service Representative. **Special programs:** Internships.

AMERICAN AG-TEC INTERNATIONAL, LTD.
1711 Woolsey Street, P.O. Box 569, Delavan WI 53115-0569. 262/728-8815. **Fax:** 262/728-8131. **Contact:** Human Resources. **E-mail address:** info@ag-tec.com. **World Wide Web address:** http://www.ag-tec.com. **Description:** A company dedicated to international markets within the agriculture industry, focusing primarily on genetic development and biotechnology, technology transfers and licensing, seeds and seed production, and agricultural production. **Corporate headquarters location:** This location.

CHIMERX
6143 North 60th Street, Milwaukee WI 53218. 414/535-9506. **Toll-free phone:** 800/626-7833. **Fax:** 414/535-9508. **Contact:** Human Resources. **E-mail address:** info@chimerx.com. **World Wide Web address:** http://www.chimerx.com. **Description:** As the retail division of Molecular Biology Resources, Inc., CHIMERx offers DNA ladders, modifying enzymes, restriction endonucleases, nucleic acid labeling products, and other ancillary molecular agents for the research community. **Special programs:** Internships. **Corporate headquarters location:** This location. **Other area locations:** Madison WI. **Parent company:** Molecular Biology Resources, Inc. **Listed on:** Privately held.

COVANCE, INC.
3301 Kinsman Boulevard, Madison WI 53704. 608/241-4471. **Fax:** 608/242-2624. **Contact:** Human Resources Manager. **World Wide Web address:** http://www.covance.com. **Description:** A life sciences firm providing biological and chemical research services. Covance is also a supplier of laboratory animals and biological products. **Positions advertised include:** Research Associate; Study Coordinator; Analyst; Client Service Coordinator; Operations Manager. **Corporate headquarters location:** Princeton NJ. **Other U.S. locations:** Nationwide. **International locations:** Worldwide. **Operations at this facility include:** This nonclinical facility provides additional drug development capacity to pharmaceutical and biotechnology companies. **Listed on:** New York Stock Exchange. **Stock exchange symbol:** CVD.

INVITROGEN CORPORATION
501 Charmany Drive, Madison WI 53719. 608/204-5000. **Toll-free phone:** 800/791-1400. **Fax:** 608/204-5200. **Contact:** Human Resources. **World Wide Web address:** http://www.invitrogen.com. **Description:** Manufactures drug discovery screening products and services. **Positions advertised include:** Drug Discovery Business Area Manager; Research Associate; Scientist; Senior Scientist. **Parent company:** Invitrogen.

PROMEGA CORPORATION
2800 Woods Hollow Road, Madison WI 53711. 608/274-4330. **Toll-free phone:** 800/356-9526. **Fax:** 608/277-2516. **Contact:** Human Resources Department. **E-mail address:** hr@promega.com. **World Wide Web address:** http://www.promega.com. **Description:** Designs and manufactures biological reagents and systems for the life sciences industry. Founded in 1978. **Positions advertised include:** R& D Scientist; Production Scientist; Senior Software Developer; VP Marketing; Marketing Coordinator; Director of Human Resources; Associate General Counsel. **Corporate headquarters location:** This location. **Other U.S. locations:** San Luis Obispo CA.

PROTOPROBE, INC.
10437 Innovation Drive, Suite 303, Milwaukee WI 53226-4815. 414/774-2670. **Toll-free phone:** 800/432-3711. **Fax:** 414/774-0767. **Contact:** Human Resources. **E-mail address:** protoprb@protoprobe.com. **World Wide Web address:** http://www.protoprobe.com. **Description:** Researches protein chemistry, immunology, molecular and cellular biology, and focuses on antibody technology and tools to research and treat cancer in humans. Research is performed for the federal government and research companies. **Corporate headquarters location:** This location.

BUSINESS SERVICES & NON-SCIENTIFIC RESEARCH

You can expect to find the following types of companies in this section:
Adjustment and Collection Services • Cleaning, Maintenance, and Pest Control Services • Credit Reporting Services • Detective, Guard, and Armored Car Services • Security Systems Services • Miscellaneous Equipment Rental and Leasing • Secretarial and Court Reporting Services

---

Employment services will gain 1,580,000 jobs, an impressive 45.5% increase, growing from 3,470,000 jobs to about 5 million. Businesses will continue to seek new ways to make their staffing patterns more responsive to changes in demand by hiring temporary employees with specialized skills to reduce costs and to provide the necessary knowledge or experience in certain types of work. Increasing demand for flexible work arrangements and schedules, coupled with significant turnover in these positions, should create plentiful job opportunities for persons who seek jobs as temporaries or contract workers. Building and grounds services occupations should add 356,000 jobs, a 21% growth. Investigation and security service occupations are projected to add 170,000 jobs, a growth of 23.3%.

Alabama

ASI
350 Voyager Way, Huntsville AL 35806. 256/890-0083. **Fax:** 256/890-0242. **Contact:** Human Resources. **E-mail address:** asi@asi-hsv.com. **World Wide Web address:** http://www.asi-hsv.com. **Description:** A management and technical solutions company working in the areas of information technology, systems engineering and program management, engineering and scientific analysis, and organizational and professional development. Founded in 1992. **Positions advertised include:** Program Control Analyst; NASA Research Analyst; Sr. Configuration Management Specialist; Program Manager – GMD; Sr. Quality/Mission Assurance Engineer; System Engineer/Analyst. **Other area locations:** Montgomery AL. **Other U.S. locations:** Nationwide. **Number of employees nationwide:** 350.

BAIL BONDS EXPRESS AGENCY, INC.
2301 15TH Street, Tuscaloosa AL 35401-4612. 205/759-1048. **Toll-free phone:** 800/536-8075. **Fax:** 205/759-1054. **Contact:** Human Resources. **E-mail address: World Wide Web address:** http://www.bailbondsexpress.com. **Description:** A bail bonds agency.

DIGITAL FUSION SOLUTIONS, INC.
4940-A Corporate Drive, Huntsville AL 35805. 256/837-2620. **Fax:** 256/837-0988. **Contact:** Human Resources. **E-mail address:** resumes@digitalfusion.com. **World Wide Web address:** http://www.digitalfusion.com. **Description:** An information technology and engineering services company providing services to both government and commercial customers. **Positions advertised include:** Sr. Software Engineer; Principal Computer Scientist; Sr. System Analyst; Contracts Administrator; Project Manager; Principal Engineer; Security Assistant; Electrical Engineer.

EBSCO INDUSTRIES INC.
P.O. Box 1943, Birmingham AL 35201-1943. 205/991-6600. **Physical address:** 5724 Highway 280 East, Birmingham AL 35242. **Fax:** 205/995-1518. **Recorded jobline:** 205/991-1477. **Contact:** Human Resources. **E-mail address:** jobs@ebsco.com. **World Wide Web address:** http://www.ebscoind.com. **Description:** A diverse company whose principal operations include a magazine subscription service. EBSCO Industries' primary customers are academic libraries. **NOTE:** This company offers entry-level positions. **Positions advertised include:** Application Developer; Java/JavaScript Programmer; Manufacturing Accountant; Programmer Analyst; SQL Database Administrator; Technology Architect. **Corporate headquarters location:** This location. **Other U.S. locations:** Nationwide. **Operations at this facility include:** Administration; Service. **Listed on:** Privately held. **Annual sales/revenues:** More than $100 million. **Number of employees at this location:** 700. **Number of employees nationwide:** 3,500. **Number of employees worldwide:** 4,500.

ERC, INCORPORATED
555 Sparkman Drive, Executive Plaza, Suite 1622, Huntsville AL, 35816. 256/430-3080. **Fax:** 256/430-3081. **Contact:** Human Resources. **E-mail address:** hr@erc-incorporated.com. **World Wide Web address:** http://www.erc-incorporated.com. **Description:** A privately-held small business providing high technology services and products in the areas of engineering, systems integration and management services; research and development; test and evaluation; and information technology to NASA, the Army and the Air Force. Founded in 1988. **Positions advertised include:** ISS Systems Management Engineer; Electro Optics Engineer; Mechanical Engineer; Instrumentation Technician II; Test Engineer - Sensors/Seekers; Supply Technician; SR Software Engineer; Software Developer; Electronic Technician – Maintenance; Plasma Engineer/Physicist; Energetic Materials Support Chemist; Electrical & Computer Systems Engineer; Programmer IV; Propulsion Test Systems Engineer; Computer Scientist; Engineer II. **Corporate headquarters location:** This location. Other U.S. locations: Pasadena CA; Stennis Space Center, MS; Houston TX; Edwards AFB, CA; Denver CO; Washington DC.

EXPODISPLAYS
3401 Mary Taylor Road, Birmingham AL 35235. 205/439-8213. **Fax:** 205/439-8201. **Contact:** Human Resources. **E-mail address:** hr@expodisplays.com. **World Wide Web address:** http://www.expodisplays.com. **Description:** A manufacturer and designer of custom displays and exhibits. **Positions advertised include:** Graphics Production; Exhibit Project Manager; Cabinet Maker.

SNELLING SEARCH
1813 University Drive, Suite 201, Huntsville AL 35801. 256/382-3000. **Fax:** 256/382-6691. **Contact:** George Barnes, Executive Recruiter. **World Wide Web address:** http://www.snelling.com/huntsville. **Description:** A full-service staffing firm. **Positions advertised include:** Mechanical Engineer; Business Banker; Outside Sales; Gov't Accountant; Financial Analyst; Fire Control Systems Engineer; Product Marketing Manager; Senior Loan Officer; Technical Recruiter; Commercial Loan Officer; Bank Branch Manager; Auditor; Bank City President; Asst. Bank Branch Manager; Cost Accountant; Manufacturing Engineer w/ DOD.

THE WACKENHUT CORPORATION
6610 Old Madison Pike, Suite 105B, Huntsville AL 35806. 256/837-0126. **Fax:** 256/837-9732. **Contact:** Human Resources. **E-mail address:** recruitment@wackenhut.com. **World Wide Web address:** http://www.wackenhut.com. **Description:** Provides contract security services to corporations, government agencies, and industrial and commercial customers. **Positions advertised include:** Custom

Protection Officer. **Corporate headquarters location:** Palm Beach Gardens FL. **Other area locations:** Birmingham AL; Montgomery AL. **Other U.S. locations:** Nationwide. **International locations:** Worldwide. **Parent company:** Group 4 Securicor. **Number of employees worldwide:** 40,000.

WEST CORPORATION
5000 Bradford Drive, Huntsville AL 35805. 256/864-9600. **Toll-free phone:** 800/815-5146. **Fax:** 256/864-9703. **Contact:** Human Resources. **E-mail address:** hsvjobs@west.com. **World Wide Web address:** http://www.west.com. **Description:** A provider of outsourced communication solutions to many of the world's largest companies, specializing in customer acquisition, customer care, and interactive voice response services. **Positions advertised include:** Operations Team Supervisor; Customer Service Agent. **Corporate headquarters location:** Omaha NE.

Alaska
COMPUCOM ALASKA LEARNING CENTER
3000 C Street, Suite 102, Anchorage AK 99503. 907/562-4488. **Fax:** 907/762-9160. **Contact:** D. Renee Rasmussen, District Service Manager. **E-mail address:** rrasmuss@compucom.com. **World Wide Web address:** http://www.compucomalaska.com. **Description:** Provides computer hardware and software training for companies and business professionals. Founded in 1981. **Positions advertised include:** Microsoft Certified Trainer; Microsoft and Adobe Instructor. **Other U.S. locations:** Nationwide. **Parent Company:** Compucom.

CHUGACH ALASKA CORPORATION (CAC)
560 E. 34th Avenue, Anchorage AK 99503. 907/563-8866. **Fax:** 907/563-8402. **Contact:** Human Resources. **E-mail address:** resumes@chugach-ak.com. **World Wide Web address:** http://www.chugach-ak.com. **Description:** The Chugach family consists of seven subsidiaries and several joint ventures with over 5,000 employees worldwide. CAC currently targets the following areas of business interests - base operating services, educational services, construction services, environmental services, information technology, telecommunications, and full-service employment services. **Positions advertised include:** AP Technician; Accounts Payable Reviewer; Financial Project Analyst.

Arizona
AT SYSTEMS SECURITY
3001 West Indian School Road, Suite 218, Phoenix AZ 85017. 602/264-4193. **Recorded jobline:** 800/315-8442. **Contact:** Human Resources. **E-mail address:** newcareers@atsystemsinc.com. **World Wide Web address:** http://www.atsystemsinc.com. **Description:** Provides security guard services to a variety of clients.

ALLIEDBARTON SECURITY SERVICES.
702 East Osborne Street, Suite 160, Phoenix AZ 85014. 602/381-1795. **Fax:** 602/381-0265. **Contact:** Personnel. **World Wide Web address:** http://www.alliedsecurity.com. **Description:** Provides detective, guard, and armored car services. **Positions advertised include:** Security Officer; EMT.

AMERICAN BUILDING MAINTENANCE INDUSTRIES
2632 West Medtronic Way, Tempe AZ 85281. 480/968-8300. **Fax:** 480/921-8734. **Contact:** Branch Manager. **World Wide Web address:** http://www.abm.com. **Description:** Provides janitorial and maintenance services for clients who own or manage commercial buildings of 50,000 square feet or more. **Special programs:** Internships. **Corporate headquarters location:** San Francisco CA. **Parent company:** ABM Industries Inc. **Listed on:** New York Stock Exchange. **Stock exchange symbol:** ABM.

AUTOMATIC DATA PROCESSING (ADP)
7474 West Chandler Boulevard, Chandler AZ 85226. 480/961-4553. **Contact:** Human Resources. **World Wide Web address:** http://www.adp.com. **Description:** A *Fortune* 500 company providing a variety of data processing services. ADP's Employer Services, the largest division, provides payroll processing, tax, and personnel reporting. Other services include brokerage, dealer, financial, and collision estimating services. **Positions advertised include:** Client Account Rep; contract Sales Recruiter; Payroll Implementation Specialist. **Corporate headquarters location:** Roseland NJ. **Operations at this facility include:** Accounting/Auditing; Production; Regional Headquarters; Sales; Service. **Listed on:** New York Stock Exchange. **Stock exchange symbol:** ADP.

CAREMARK
9501 East Shea Boulevard, Scottsdale AZ 85260. 480/391-4683. **Contact:** Human Resources. **World Wide Web address:** http://www.caremark.com. **Description:** Manages prescription drug benefit programs. **Positions advertised include:** PRC Technician; Director of Finance; Manager IT Audit; Sr. Pricing Analyst; Manager of Rebate Reporting; Senior Financial Analyst; Database Administrator; Project Leader. **Corporate headquarters location:** Nashville TN. **Other area locations:** Phoenix AZ. **Operations at this facility include:** Administration; Service. **Listed on:** New York Stock Exchange. **Stock exchange symbol:** CMX. **Number of employees at this location:** 1,100.

DYNAMIC SCIENCE, INC. (DSI)
8433 North Black Canyon Highway, Suite 200, Phoenix AZ 85021. 602/995-3700. **Fax:** 602/995-4091. **Contact:** Human Resources. **E-mail address:** dsi@exodyne.com. **World Wide Web address:** http://www.exodyne.com. **Description:** Services cover the spectrum of developmental and operational test support and evaluation; operation and maintenance of integrated test ranges; communications system operations and maintenance; facility operation and maintenance; transportation systems research and development; aircraft and vehicle operation and maintenance; and data collection, processing, and management. DSI provides services to a broad customer base including U.S. government defense and civilian agencies, state and local governments, academic institutions, and domestic and international private industry. DSI operates through three divisions: The Defense Technical Services Division, The Exodyne Services Division, and The Research, Science, and Technology Division. Founded in 1942. **Positions advertised include:** General Manager; Air Traffic Controller; Division General Manager. **Parent company:** Exodyne, Inc.

EDS (ELECTRONIC DATA SYSTEMS)
2222 West Dunlop Avenue, Suite 300, Phoenix AZ 85021. 602/997-7391. **Contact:** Human Resources. **World Wide Web address:** http://www.eds.com. **Description:** Provides consulting, systems development, systems integration, and systems management services for large-scale and industry-specific applications. Founded in 1962. **Corporate headquarters location:** Plano TX. **Listed on:** New York Stock Exchange. **Stock exchange symbol:** EDS. **Number of employees nationwide:** 54,000. **Number of employees worldwide:** 120,000.

LOOMIS, FARGO & COMPANY
849 West 24th Street, Tempe AZ 85282. 480/829-3552. **Fax:** 480/829-3932. **Contact:** Human Resources. **World Wide Web address:** http://www.loomisfargo.com. **Description:** Provides armored transportation, cash vault services, and ATM services. **Positions advertised include:** Area Controller; Area Fleet Manager. **Corporate headquarters location:** Houston TX. **Other U.S. locations:** Nationwide. **Listed on:** Privately held.

NAVIGANT CONSULTING
Collier Center, 201 East Washington Street, Suite 1700, Phoenix AZ 85004. 602/257-0075. **Fax:** 602/254-6163. **Contact:** Human Resources. **World Wide Web address:** http://www.navigantconsulting.com. **Description:** Provides accounting, financial, economic, engineering, and consulting services related to business

disputes. **Special programs:** Internships. **Corporate headquarters location:** Chicago IL. **Other U.S. locations:** Nationwide. **Operations at this facility include:** Administration. **Listed on:** New York Stock Exchange. **Stock exchange symbol:** NCI.

RENTAL SERVICE CORPORATION
6929 East Greenway Parkway, Suite 200, Scottsdale AZ 85254. 480/905-3300. **Contact:** Personnel. **World Wide Web address:** http://www.rscrental.com. **Description:** Rents a broad line of general equipment to industrial and construction companies, government agencies, municipalities, and homeowners. Some of the company's equipment includes heavy industrial machinery such as backhoes and forklifts, and personal rentals such as lawnmowers. **Positions advertised include:** Fixed Asset Accountant; Fleet Coordinator; Business Process Analyst; Sr. Compensation Analyst. **Other U.S. locations:** AZ; CA; FL; LA; TX. **Subsidiaries include:** RSC Equipment Rental; Prime Energy.

RURAL/METRO CORPORATION
9221 East Via de Ventura, Scottsdale AZ 85258. 480/994-3886. **Fax:** 480/606-3268. **Contact:** Human Resources. **E-mail address:** recruiting@rmetro.com. **Description:** Provides emergency and non-emergency medical transportation services, fire protection, and other safety-related services. **World Wide Web address:** http://www.ruralmetro.com. **Positions advertised include:** Accounts Payable Specialist; Collector; Financial Analyst. **Special programs:** Internships. **Corporate headquarters location:** This location. **Other U.S. locations:** Nationwide. **Operations at this facility include:** Administration; Sales. **Listed on:** NASDAQ. **Stock exchange symbol:** RURL. **Number of employees at this location:** 200. **Number of employees nationwide:** 4,400.

SECURITAS
1607 South Pantano Road, Suite 401, Tucson AZ 85710. 520/296-3833. **Fax:** 520/296-2464. **Contact:** Human Resources. **World Wide Web address:** http://www.pinkertons.com. **Description:** One of the oldest and largest nongovernmental security service organizations in the world. The company's principal business is providing high-quality security, investigative, and consulting services to commercial, industrial, institutional, governmental, and residential clients. Pinkerton Security operates through more than 125 offices in the United States, Canada, and Great Britain. Major services include industrial and nuclear plant security, institutional security, commercial and residential building security, retail security, construction security, patrol and inspection services, community security, sports and special events services, K-9 patrol services, courier services, inventory services, investigation services, security consultation, and equipment evaluation. **Parent company:** Securitas AB (Stockholm, Sweden.)

UNICON, INC.
3140 North Arizona Avenue, Suite 113, Chandler AZ 85225. 480/926-2368. **Fax:** 480/558-2320. **Contact:** Human Resources. **E-mail address:** hr@unicon.net. **World Wide Web address:** http://www.unicon.net. **Description:** Provides services and systems that allow clients to measure training, learning, knowledge and change management initiatives. Founded in 1993. **Positions advertised include:** Business Analyst; Deployment Specialist; Software Developer; System Administrator; uPortal Consultant; Web Developer II. **Corporate headquarters location:** This location. **Other U.S. locations:** El Segundo CA. **Listed on:** Privately held. **President/CEO:** Ray Barker.

THE WACKENHUT CORPORATION
3220 East Harbour Drive, Suite 200, Phoenix AZ 85034. 602/431-0020. **Fax:** 602/454-0870. **Contact:** Human Resources. **World Wide Web address:** http:/www.wackenhut.com. **Description:** A diversified provider of services to government, industrial, commercial, and professional organizations and agencies worldwide. The corporation has offices throughout the United States and in 49 other countries on six continents. The Wackenhut Corporation specializes in security-related services including physical security, investigations, the management of correctional and detention facilities, rehabilitative programs, and information security. The company also provides educational services and training; facility management; food service to jails and prisons; design, financial services, and construction management for correctional facilities; and fire prevention and emergency services. The Wackenhut Corporation is a leader in the privatization of public services to municipal, state, and federal governments worldwide. Founded in 1954. **Special programs:** Summer Jobs. **Corporate headquarters location:** Palm Beach Gardens FL. **Other area locations:** Tucson AZ. **Parent company:** Group 4 Securicor (London). **Listed on:** New York Stock Exchange. **Stock exchange symbol:** WAK.

YOH COMPANY
4000 North Central Avenue, Suite 1450, Phoenix AZ 85012. 602/235-9739. **Toll-free phone:** 888/825-9295. **Fax:** 602/280-1022. **Contact:** Human Resources. **E-mail address:** Phoenix@yoh.com. **World Wide Web address:** http://www.yoh.com. **Description:** Delivers long- and short-term temporary and direct placement of technology and professional personnel for the information technology community in the Phoenix Valley and surrounding areas. **Positions advertised include:** Java Developer; System Administrator; Document Librarian; Project Manager; .Net Application Architect. **Other area locations:** Tucson AZ. **Parent company:** Day & Zimmerman.

Arkansas

ACXIOM CORPORATION
1 Information Way, Little Rock AR 72202. 501/342-1000. **Contact:** Cindy Childers HR Supervisor. **World Wide Web address:** http://www.acxiom.com. **Description:** An information retrieval services company. Founded 1969. **NOTE:** Search and apply for positions online. **Positions advertised include:** Administrative Assistant; Client Delivery Analyst; Client Representative; Consultant; Data Acquisitions Manager; Data Administrator; Database Administrator; Database Developer; Decision Support Analyst; Financial Analyst; Industry Solutions Architect; Product Manager; Sales Account Manager; Software Developer; Solutions Developer. **Corporate headquarters location:** This location. **Listed on:** NASDAQ. **Stock exchange symbol:** ACXM.

IKON NORTH AMERICA
10825 Financial Centre Parkway, Little Rock AR 72211. 501/663-4044. **Toll free phone:** 888/456-6457. **Fax:** 501/663-0842. **Contact:** Human Resources. **E-mail address:** resumes@ikon.com. **World Wide Web address:** http://www.ikon.com. **Description:** Business communication and supply company. **NOTE:** Entry level positions available. **Corporate headquarters location:** Malvern PA. **Other area locations:** Fort Smith AR; Jonesboro AR; Pine Bluff AR; Rogers AR. **Other U.S. locations:** Nationwide. **International locations:** Worldwide. **Listed on:** New York Stock Exchange. **Stock exchange symbol:** IKN.

MILLBROOK DISTRIBUTION SERVICES, INC.
P.O. Box 790, Harrison AR 72602. 870/741-3425. **Fax:** 870/365-3280. **Recorded jobline:** 800/375-6455, ext. 90001. **Contact:** Human Resources. **World Wide Web address:** http://www.millbrookds.com. **Description:** Arranges displays of nonfood items and specialty food items in grocery stores. **Corporate headquarters location:** Leicester MA.

California

ABM INDUSTRIES INCORPORATED
160 Pacific Avenue, Suite 222, San Francisco CA 94111. 415/733-4000. **Fax:** 415/733-7333. **Contact:** Human Resources. **E-mail address:** hrresumes@abm.com. **World Wide Web address:** http://www.abm.com. **Description:** A national contract maintenance firm providing janitorial, maintenance,

and building management products and services in more than 60 metropolitan areas throughout the United States and Canada. **Positions advertised include:** Compensation Manager; Data Center Operator; Data Security Analyst; Documentation Specialist; Project Manager; Senior Internal Auditor. **Corporate headquarters location:** This location. **Listed on:** New York Stock Exchange. **Stock exchange symbol:** ABM. **Number of employees nationwide:** 70,000.

ADT SECURITY SERVICES
3551 Arden Road, Hayward CA 94545-3922. 650/345-6948. **Toll-free phone:** 800/228-0530. **Contact:** Human Resources. **World Wide Web address:** http://www.adt.com. **Description:** Designs, programs, markets, and installs protective systems to safeguard life and property from hazards such as burglary, hold-up, and fire. ADT Security Services has over 180,000 customers in the United States, Canada, and Western Europe. **NOTE:** Job openings are listed at http://www.monster.com. **Corporate headquarters location:** Boca Raton FL. **Parent Company:** Tyco Fire & Security. **Operations at this facility include:** Administration; Sales; Service.

ARAMARK UNIFORM SERVICES
P.O. Box 7891, Burbank CA 91510. 818/973-3700. **Physical address:** 115 North First Street, Burbank CA 91502. **Toll-free phone:** 800/ARAMARK. **Contact:** Human Resources. **World Wide Web address:** http://www.aramark-uniform.com. **Description:** One of America's largest uniform providers with over 400,000 customers. The company offers uniforms to reinforce corporate identities or to meet specialized demands for static control and flame resistance and provides a variety of products including walk-off mats, cleaning cloths, disposable towels, and other environmental control items. **Positions advertised include:** Customer Information Specialist; Assistant Regional Controller; Account Manager. **Corporate headquarters:** This location. **Parent company:** ARAMARK (Philadelphia PA). **Listed on:** New York Stock Exchange. **Stock exchange symbol:** RMK. **Number of employees worldwide:** 200,000.

AUTOMATIC DATA PROCESSING (ADP)
3300 Olcott Street, Santa Clara CA 95054. 408/988-6565. **Toll-free phone:** 800/225-5237. **Contact:** Human Resources. **World Wide Web address:** http://www.adp.com. **Description:** Automatic Data Processing is engaged in payroll processing services including unemployment claims management, and local, state, and federal tax filing. **Positions advertised include:** Implementation Specialist; Implementation Manager; Major Account Sales Rep. **Corporate headquarters location:** Roseland NJ. **Operations at this facility include:** This location is part of the major accounts division. **Listed on:** New York Stock Exchange. **Stock exchange symbol:** ADP. **Number of employees at this location:** 500. **Number of employees nationwide:** 20,000.

CJ LASER BUSINESS SERVICES
654 14th Street, Oakland CA 94612. 510/832-2828. **Fax:** 510/832-1969. **Contact:** Store Manager. **Description:** Provides laser printer repair services and reconditions toner cartridges. **Corporate headquarters location:** This location.

COMPUTER HORIZONS CORPORATION
1411 West 190th Street, Suite 470, Gardena CA 90248-4324. 310/771-0770. **Toll-free phone:** 800/711-2421. **Fax:** 310/771-0777. **Contact:** Human Resources. **World Wide Web address:** http://www.computerhorizons.com. **Description:** A full-service technology solutions company offering contract staffing, outsourcing, re-engineering, data migration, downsizing support, and network management. The company has a worldwide network of 43 offices. Founded in 1969. **Corporate headquarters location:** Mountain Lakes NJ. **Other area locations:** San Francisco CA. **Other U.S. locations:** Nationwide. **International locations:** Canada; England. **Listed on:** NASDAQ. **Stock exchange symbol:** CHRZ.

CONGRUENT SOFTWARE
2977 Ygnacio Valley Road, Suite 414, Walnut Creek CA 94598-3535. 925/934-9750. **Fax:** 925/934-9718. **Contact:** Human Resources. **E-mail address:** info@congruentsoft.com. **World Wide Web address:** http://www.congruentsoft.com. **Description:** A technical services and contingent staffing company. **Corporate headquarters location:** Bellevue WA. **International locations:** India; Mauritius.

COPART, INC.
4665 Business Center Drive, Fairfield CA 94534. 707/639-5000. **Contact:** Personnel. **E-mail address:** jobs@copart.com. **World Wide Web address:** http://www.copart.com. **Description:** Copart auctions salvage vehicles as a service to vehicle suppliers, principally major insurance companies. Copart services numerous vehicle suppliers including many of the largest insurance, financial, and rental car companies in the country. **Positions advertised include:** Assistant General Manager. **Corporate headquarters location:** This location. **Other area locations:** Statewide.

DUN & BRADSTREET, INC.
dba D&B
725 South Figueroa Street, Los Angeles CA 90017. 213/430-9209. **Contact:** District Manager. **E-mail address:** hrsourcing@dnb.com. **World Wide Web address:** http://www.dnb.com. **Description:** Provides business-to-business credit, marketing, and investment management services. **Positions advertised include:** Relationship Manager. **Corporate headquarters location:** Short Hills NJ. **Parent company:** The Dun & Bradstreet Corporation. **Operations at this facility include:** Sales. **Listed on:** New York Stock Exchange. **Stock exchange symbol:** DNB. **Number of employees worldwide:** 6,100.

ELECTRO RENT CORPORATION
6060 Sepulveda Boulevard, Van Nuys CA 91411-2512. 818/787-2100. **Toll-free phone:** 800/688-1111. **Fax:** 818/786-1602. **Contact:** Human Resources. **E-mail address:** maya@electrorent.com. **World Wide Web address:** http://www.electrorent.com. **Description:** Rents and leases electronic equipment including test and measurement instruments, workstations, personal computers, and data communication products. **NOTE:** E-mail is the preferred method of resume submission. **Positions advertised include:** Inside Sales Representative; Account Development Representative; Senior RF Technician. **Corporate headquarters location:** This location. **Other U.S. locations:** Nationwide. **Listed on:** NASDAQ. **Stock exchange symbol:** ELRC. **Annual sales/revenues:** More than $100 million. **Number of employees at this location:** 200. **Number of employees nationwide:** 500.

ELECTRONIC CLEARING HOUSE, INC. (ECHO)
730 Paseo Camarillo, Camarillo CA 93010. 800/262-3246, extension 8530. **Fax:** 805/419-8683. **Contact:** Human Resources. **E-mail address:** hr@echo-inc.com. **World Wide Web address:** http://www.echo-inc.com. **Description:** Provides credit card processing and debit card processing services, as well as services for merchant accounts, check guarantee, check verification, check conversion, check representment, check collection, and Automated Clearing HOUSE (ACH) check processing. **Positions advertised include:** Salesperson. **Corporate headquarters location:** This location. **Subsidiaries include:** National Credit Card Reserve Corporation; XpressCheX, Inc.; ECHO Payment Services, Inc.; Computer Based Controls, Inc. **Listed on:** NASDAQ. **Stock exchange symbol:** ECHO.

FAIR ISAAC CORPORATION
200 Smith Ranch Road, San Rafael CA 94903. 415/472-2211. **Toll-free phone:** 800/999-2955. **Fax:** 415/492-9381. **Contact:** Human Resources. **E-mail address:** info@fairisaac.com. **World Wide Web address:** http://www.fairisaac.com. **Description:** Develops and provides data management software and services for the consumer credit, personal lines

insurance, and direct marketing industries. Founded in 1956. **Positions advertised include:** Analytic Science Lead; Analystic Science Engineer; Business Consulting Manager; Director. **Corporate headquarters location:** Minneapolis MN. **Other area locations:** Emeryville CA; Irvine CA; San Diego CA; San Jose CA. **Subsidiaries include:** Dynamark (Minneapolis MN); European Analytic Products Group (Birmingham, England). **Listed on:** New York Stock Exchange. **Stock exchange symbol:** FIC.

IDEALAB
130 West Union Street, Pasadena CA 91103. 626/585-6900. **Fax:** 626/535-2701. **Contact:** Human Resources. **E-mail address:** info@cph.com. **World Wide Web address:** http://www.idealab.com. **Description:** Idealab generates ideas for new technology-based businesses and creates, capitalizes, and operates a separate company to conduct each new business. **Positions advertised include:** Combustion Engineer; Test Engineer.

INAWORD
1601 Cloverfield Boulevard, 2nd Floor, South Tower, Santa Monica CA 90404. 310/460-3200. **Toll-free phone:** 800/805-9673. **Fax:** 800/805-7994. **Contact:** Human Resources. **E-mail address:** info@inaword.net. **World Wide Web address:** http://www.inaword.net. **Description:** Offers language translation services on documents including patents, legal documents, product labels, manuals and user guides, advertising copy, and Web material. The company also provides interpreters for meetings and training seminars and electronic publishing services. **Corporate headquarters location:** This location.

JETRO SAN FRANCISCO
235 Pine Street, Suite 1700, San Francisco CA 94104. 415/392-1333. **Fax:** 415/788-6927. **Contact:** Human Resources Department. **World Wide Web address:** http://www.jetro.org/sanfrancisco. **Description:** A nonprofit organization that provides assistance to area businesses regarding trade and investment opportunities in Japan. This location also has a Japanese information center that is open to the public. **Corporate headquarters location:** This location.

PITNEY BOWES MANAGEMENT SERVICES
801 South Grand Avenue, Suite 6, Los Angeles CA 90017. 213/746-4855. **Contact:** Human Resources. **E-mail address:** staffing@pb.com. **World Wide Web address:** http://www.pb.com. **Description:** A facility management company specializing in reprographics, facsimiles, mailroom, supply room, file room, and other related office services. **Special programs:** Internships. **Corporate headquarters location:** Stamford CT. **Other U.S. locations:** Chicago IL; New York NY; Dallas TX. **Parent company:** Pitney Bowes Inc. **Operations at this facility include:** Administration; Divisional Headquarters; Regional Headquarters; Sales.

PRUDENTIAL OVERALL SUPPLY
1661 Alton Parkway, Irvine CA 92606. 949/250-4855. **Toll-free phone:** 800/767-5536. **Fax:** 949/261-1947. **Contact:** Human Resources Manager. **E-mail address:** hrjobs@pos-clean.com. **World Wide Web address:** http://www.pos-clean.com. **Description:** An industrial laundry service. Founded in 1932. **NOTE:** Entry-level positions are offered. **Positions advertised include:** General Manager; Service Manager; Plant Superintendent; District Sales Manager; Corporate Sales Representative; Maintenance Mechanic. **Corporate headquarters location:** This location. **Other U.S. locations:** Phoenix AZ; Tucson AZ; Fresno CA; Los Angeles CA; San Diego CA; San Jose CA. **Operations at this facility include:** Administration; Manufacturing; Sales; Service. **Listed on:** Privately held. **Annual sales/revenues:** More than $100 million. **Number of employees at this location:** 100. **Number of employees nationwide:** 2,000.

PYRAMID SCREENING TECHNOLOGY, INC.
5994 West Las Positas Boulevard, Suite 225, Pleasanton CA 94588. 925/460-9228. **Fax:** 925/460-9230. **Contact:** Human Resources. **World Wide Web address:** http://www.pyramidst.com. **Description:** Provides applicant screening services for client companies. **Corporate headquarters location:** This location.

QUEST DISCOVERY SERVICES, INC.
P.O. Box 49051, San Jose CA 95161-9051. 408/441-7000. **Physical address:** 2025 Gateway Plaza, San Jose CA 95110. **Fax:** 408/441-7070. **Contact:** Human Resources. **E-mail address:** jobs@questds.com. **World Wide Web address:** http://www.questds.com. **Description:** Provides litigation support services such as deposition reporting, process serving, and large volume copy work. **NOTE:** Mail resumes to: Quest Discovery Services, Inc., Attention: Human Resources, P.O. Box 49051, San Jose CA 95161-9051. **Corporate headquarters location:** This location.

SECURITAS SECURITY SERVICES
1506 Brookhollow Drive, Suite 114, Santa Ana CA 92707. 714/245-6800. **Fax:** 714/245-6823. **Contact:** Human Resources. **World Wide Web address:** http://www.securitasinc.com. **Description:** One of the world's largest suppliers of global, total security solutions. The company provides a broad array of security-related services to address the protection needs of customers through its 650 offices in the United States. Securitas U.S.A. has grown tremendously through its acquisition of companies such as Pinkerton, Wells Fargo, Burns, American Protective Services, and First Security. **Special programs:** Internships. **Corporate headquarters location:** Parsippany NJ. **Other U.S. locations:** Nationwide. **Parent company:** Securitas (Sweden).

SOURCECORP
20500 Belshaw Avenue, Carson CA 90746. 310/763-7575. **Fax:** 310/763-7211. **Contact:** Human Resources. **E-mail address:** careers@srcp.com. **World Wide Web address:** http://www.srcp.com. **Description:** Provides full-service records management for businesses through data storage and imaging services. Data is stored on both disk and microfilm. **Corporate headquarters location:** Dallas TX. **Other area locations:** Burbank CA; Corona CA; Oakland CA. **Listed on:** NASDAQ. **Stock exchange symbol:** SRCP.

UNDERWRITERS LABORATORIES INC.
455 E. Trimble Road, San Jose CA 95131. 408/754-6500. **Fax:** 408/689-6500. **Contact:** Human Resources Department. **E-mail address:** scjobs@ul.com. **World Wide Web address:** http://www.ul.com. **Description:** An independent, nonprofit corporation established to help reduce or prevent bodily injury, loss of life, and property damage. Underwriters Laboratories accomplishes its objectives by scientific investigation of various materials, devices, equipment, constructions, methods, and systems; and by the publication of standards, classifications, specifications, and other information. Engineering functions are divided between six departments: Electrical; Burglary Protection and Signaling; Casualty and Chemical Hazards; Fire Protection; Heating, Air-Conditioning, and Refrigeration; and Marine. The company also performs factory inspections. **Corporate headquarters location:** Northbrook IL.

WESTERN OILFIELDS SUPPLY COMPANY dba RAIN FOR RENT
P.O. Box 2248, Bakersfield CA 93303. 661/399-9124. **Physical address:** 3404 State Road, Bakersfield CA 93308. **Fax:** 661/393-6897. **Contact:** Human Resources Director. **E-mail address:** careers@rainforrent.com. **World Wide Web address:** http://www.rainforrent.com. **Description:** Engaged in the rental, sale, and installation of liquid handling systems, pumps, tanks, and irrigation systems to industrial and agricultural customers. Founded in 1934. **NOTE:** Search for positions online. **Office hours:** Monday - Friday, 8:00 a.m. - 5:00 p.m. **Corporate headquarters location:** This location. **Other area locations:** Riverside CA. **Other U.S. locations:** Nationwide. **International locations:** Mexico.

Number of employees at this location: 150. **Number of employees nationwide:** 435.

Colorado

ACS STATE & LOCAL SOLUTIONS, INC.
1999 Broadway, Suite 2700, Denver CO 80202. 303/295-2860. **Contact:** Human Resources. **E-mail address:** recruiter@acs-inc.com. **World Wide Web address:** http://www.acs-inc.com. **Description:** An IT and business services consultancy. Founded in 1988. Positions **advertised include:** Sr. Consultant, Investment Analyst; Business Analyst Manager; Sr. Consultant Retirement Actuary. Corporate headquarters **location:** Dallas TX.

ADT SECURITY SERVICES
14200 East Exposition Avenue, Aurora CO 80012. 303/338-8200. **Contact:** Human Resources. **World Wide Web address:** http://www.adt.com. **Description:** Sells and installs security systems and provides electronic monitoring and maintenance services for homes and businesses. ADT has approximately 170,000 subscribers. Founded in 1993. **Positions advertised include:** Sales Representative. **Other area locations:** Denver CO. **Other U.S. locations:** Miami FL; Atlanta GA; Shreveport LA; Dallas TX; Houston TX. **Number of employees nationwide:** 685.

AON INNOVATIVE SOLUTIONS
13922 Denver West Parkway, Building 54, Golden CO 80401. 303/279-2900. **Contact:** Director of Human Resources. **World Wide Web address:** http://www.aon.com. **Description:** A provider of third-party administrative services including claims adjudication, customer service in-bound call handling, telemarketing, and fulfillment/order taking. **Positions advertised include:** Sr. Programmer/Analyst; Sr. Staff Accountant. **Corporate headquarters location:** Chicago IL. **Other U.S. locations:** Nationwide. **International locations:** Worldwide. **Parent company:** Aon Corporation. **Operations at this facility include:** Administration; Sales; Service. **Listed on:** New York Stock Exchange. **Stock exchange symbol:** AOC. **Number of employees at this location:** 200.

AUTOMATIC LAUNDRY COMPANY
P.O. Box 39365, Denver CO 80239. 303/371-9274. **Contact:** Human Resources. **World Wide Web address:** http://www.automaticlaundry.com. **Description:** Leases laundry room space and installs coin-operated laundry equipment in apartment complexes.

BRINK'S INC.
6703 East 47th Avenue Drive, Denver CO 80216. 303/355-2071. **Fax:** 303-355-9954. **Contact:** Human Resources. **World Wide Web address:** www.brinksinc.com. **Description:** An armored security service specializing in transporting currency. **Corporate headquarters location:** Dallas TX.

COMPUTER RESEARCH, INC.
10170 Church Ranch Way, Suite 300, Westminster CO 80021-6061. 303/297-9200. **Contact:** Human Resources. **E-mail address:** crimail@crixnet.com. **World Wide Web address:** http://www.crix.com. **Description:** Provides data processing, accounting, and record-keeping services for approximately 60 investment securities firms and banks throughout the country. Clients use Computer Research, Inc. systems to maintain their customer accounts and firm records in compliance with financial industry and regulatory agency reporting requirements. These systems include a number of proprietary computer programs that the company maintains and operates, linking clients to its data centers in Pittsburgh and Denver (this location.) The programs provide online retrieval, reports, and records on a day-to-day basis using data supplied by the clients. **Positions advertised include:** Mainframe Developer; Applications Developer; CSR.

FIRST DATA CORPORATION
6200 South Quebec Street, Greenwood Village CO 80111. 303/488-8000. **Contact:** Human Resources. **World Wide Web address:** http://www.firstdata.com. **Description:** A holding company. Through its subsidiaries, First Data provides credit card issuing and merchant transaction processing services, e-commerce solutions, money transfers, and other business services. **NOTE:** Apply online. **Positions advertised include:** Sr. Tax Specialist; Manager, Content Management; Project Manager; Sr. Financial Analyst. **Corporate headquarters location:** This location. **Subsidiaries include:** First Data Resources. **Other U.S. locations:** Phoenix AZ; Palo Alto CA; Sunrise FL; Atlanta GA; Omaha NE; Nashville TN. **Listed on:** New York Stock Exchange. **Stock exchange symbol:** FDC.

INFORMATION HANDLING SERVICES (IHS)
15 Inverness Way East, Englewood CO 80112. 303/790-0600. **Contact:** Director of Human Resources. **E-mail address:** info@ihs.com. **World Wide Web address:** http://www.ihs.com. **Description:** Assimilates and indexes technical, engineering, federal, and regulatory information and transfers it to microform and electronic media. **Positions advertised include:** Senior Systems Engineer; Production Clerk. **Corporate headquarters location:** This location. **Parent company:** Information Handling Services Group.

LOOMIS FARGO & COMPANY
600 South Cherry Street, Suite 314, Denver CO 80246. 303/825-0376. **Fax:** 303/355-6383. **Contact:** Personnel. **E-mail address:** employment@loomisfargo.com. **World Wide Web address:** http://www.loomisfargo.com. **Description:** An armored security service specializing in transporting currency. **Corporate headquarters location:** Houston TX. **Other area locations:** Colorado Springs CO; Fort Collins CO; Grand Junction CO; Vail CO. **Other U.S. locations:** Nationwide.

THE PRODUCT LINE, INC.
5000 Lima Street, Denver CO 80239. 720/374-3800. **Fax:** 720/374-3720. **Contact:** Betti Scronce, Director of Human Resources. **E-mail address:** tpljob@tpli.com. **World Wide Web address:** http://www.tpli.com. **Description:** Provides call center services to national and international corporations. Founded in 1982. **Corporate headquarters location:** This location. **Operations at this facility include:** Administration; Sales; Service. **Listed on:** Privately held. **Number of employees at this location:** 300.

RENTAL SERVICE CORP.
481 West 84th Avenue, Thornton CO 80260. 303/428-7466. **Contact:** Human Resources. **World Wide Web address:** http://www.rentalservice.com. **Description:** A general construction equipment rental company. **Parent company:** Atlas Copco Group.

SHAMROCK DELIVERY SERVICES
6484 South Quebec Street, Englewood CO 80111. 303/220-1700. **Fax:** 303/220-0752. **Contact:** Human Resources. **World Wide Web address:** http://www.shamrockdelivery.com. **Description:** A delivery/courier service. Founded in 1989. **Positions advertised include:** Driver.

SOURCE ONE MANAGEMENT, INC.
1225 17th Street, Suite 1500, Denver CO 80202. 303/832-8600. **Fax:** 303/832-1910. **Contact:** Director of Human Resources. **E-mail address:** resumes@sourceone.com. **World Wide Web address:** http://www.sourceone.com. **Description:** Provides staffing for government and private sector management and information technology contracts. **Positions advertised include:** Records Clerk. **Corporate headquarters location:** This location. **Other U.S. locations:** DC; MT; ND; SD; WA. **Operations at this facility include:** Administration; Service. **Listed on:** Privately held. **Number of employees at this location:** 15. **Number of employees nationwide:** 200.

STARTEK, INC.
100 Garfield Street, Suite 300, Denver CO 80206. 303/262-4500. **Contact:** Human Resources Department. **E-mail address:** jobs@startek.com. **World Wide Web address:** http://www.startek.com. **Description:** Provides process management services to *Fortune* 500 customers and other major corporations worldwide. Services include logistics management, e-commerce support, Internet support, technical support, order processing, packaging, distribution, inventory management, product assembly, manufacturing, fulfillment, and customer support. **Positions advertised include:** Client Service Director; Corporate Procurement Director; Sr. Financial Analyst; Director of Corporate Strategy; Director of Compensation and Benefits. **Corporate headquarters location:** This location. **Other U.S. locations:** LA; TX; VA; IL; WY; OK. **International locations:** Canada. **Listed on:** New York Stock Exchange. **Stock exchange symbol:** SRT.

Z-AXIS CORPORATION
5445 DTC Parkway, Suite 450, Greenwood Village CO 80111. 303/713-0200. **Fax:** 303/713-0299. **Contact:** Heidi O'Neil, Controller. **E-mail address:** jobs@zaxis.com. **World Wide Web address:** http://www.zaxis.com. **Description:** Designs visual evidence for legal cases using computer-generated animation and graphics. **Positions advertised include:** Flash/Lightwave Animator. **Corporate headquarters location:** This location. **Other U.S. locations:** San Francisco CA; Chicago IL; New York NY.

Connecticut

CONNECTICUT ON-LINE COMPUTER CENTER, INC.
135 Darling Drive, Avon Park South, Avon CT 06001. 860/678-0444. **Fax:** 860/677-1169. **Contact:** Sue W. Kittredge, Director of Human Resources. **World Wide Web address:** http://www.cocc.com. **Description:** A data processing service bureau for the banking industry. The company serves banks throughout New England and New York State. **NOTE:** Entry-level positions are offered. **Positions advertised include:** IT Internal Audit Specialist; Reconcilement Clerk; Database Administrator. **Corporate headquarters location:** This location. **Listed on:** Privately held. **Annual sales/revenues:** $11 - $20 million. **Number of employees at this location:** 250.

EMCOR GROUP, INC.
301 Merritt Seven, 6th Floor, Norwalk CT 06851. 203/849-7800. **Contact:** Elissa Hall, Human Resources. **World Wide Web address:** http://www.emcorgroup.com. **Description:** Emcor is a diversified business services company engaged primarily in developing, integrating, and maintaining electrical and mechanical systems for the commercial construction industry. In addition to electrical and mechanical construction services, the company also provides complete facilities management services across a number of market sectors, including healthcare, hotels/hospitality, education, government/public, transportation, water/wastewater, pharmaceutical, and others. **Positions advertised include:** Desktop Support Specialist. **Corporate headquarters location:** This location. **Other U.S. locations:** Nationwide. **International locations:** Worldwide. **Listed on:** New York Stock Exchange. **Stock exchange symbol:** EME.

FISERV, INC.
151 National Drive, Glastonbury CT 06033. 860/633-9990. **Contact:** Human Resources. **World Wide Web address:** http://www.fiserv.com. **Description:** FiServ, Inc. provides data processing services to banks and credit institutions. The company also offers PC banking and e-commerce technology. **Positions advertised include:** Product Specialist. **Corporate headquarters location:** Brookfield WI. **Other U.S. locations:** Nationwide. **Listed on:** NASDAQ. **Stock exchange symbol:** FISV. **Number of employees nationwide:** 16,000.

GUARDSMARK, INC.
10 Columbus Boulevard, 2nd Floor, Hartford CT 06106. 860/560-7777. **Contact:** Human Resources. **World Wide Web address:** http://www.guardsmark.com. **Description:** Provides security, life safety, fire and protective, investigative, and consulting services. **Corporate headquarters location:** Memphis TN.

KEANE
39 Old Ridgebury Road, Suite 8, Danbury CT 06810-5108. 203/744-8877. **Fax:** 203/794-1176. **Contact:** Human Resources. **E-mail address:** info.ct@keane.com. **World Wide Web address:** http://www.keane.com. **Description:** Keane collaborates with Global 2000 and government agencies to produce software to help the agencies business strategies. **Positions advertised include:** Managing Director. **Corporate headquarters location:** Boston MA. **Other area locations:** Rocky Hill CT. **Other U.S. locations:** Nationwide. **International locations:** Coventry, England; London, England; New Delhi, India; Hyderabad, India. **Listen on:** American Stock Exchange. **Stock Exchange Symbol:** KEA.

McBEE
45 South Main Street, West Hartford CT 06107. 860/236-3500. **Toll-free phone:** 800/662-2331. **Contact:** Human Resources. **World Wide Web address:** http:// www.mcbeeinc.com. **Description:** Supplies specialized business forms to small businesses in the United States and Canada. Founded in 1906. **Positions advertised include:** Sales Representative.

PINKERTON CONSULTING & INVESIGATIONS
321 Research Parkway, Meriden CT 06450. 203/237-7778. **Contact:** Human Resources. **World Wide Web address:** www.ci-pinkerton.com. **Description:** America's first private investigation firm. Specializes in security solutions to corporate problems. **Corporate headquarters location:** Parsippany NJ. **Other U.S. locations:** Nationwide. **International locations:** Worldwide.

RESEARCH INTERNATIONAL
1010 Washington Boulevard, 6th Floor, Stamford CT 06901. 203/358-0900. **Fax:** 312/787-4156. **Contact:** Human Resources. **E-mail address:** greatjobs@research-int.com. **World Wide Web address:** http://www.research-int.com. **Description:** A company specializing in custom market research. Company teams up with clients and coaches them on making their own companies thrive. **Positions advertised include:** Senior Research Manager. **Other U.S. locations:** Nationwide. **International locations:** Worldwide.

STR SPECIALIZED TECHNOLOGY RESOURCES
10 Water Street, Enfield CT 06082. 860/749-8371. **Fax:** 860/749-8234. **Contact:** Carol Dyjak, Business Administration & Human Resources Manager. **World Wide Web address:** http://www.strlab.com. **Description:** Provides testing and quality assurance services to assist in product development and safety evaluation of consumer products, industrial products, and raw materials. Services include regulatory compliance, product design evaluation and development, in-process quality control audits, factory audits, post-production quality assurance, preshipment verification, and management information reporting. **NOTE:** Entry-level positions and second and third shifts are offered. **Positions advertised include:** Technician Assistant; Per Diem Apparel/Textile Inspector; Extruder Operator. **Listed on:** Privately held. **Annual sales/revenues:** $21 - $50 million.

SECURITAS
1042 Main Street, East Hartford CT 06108. 860/289-6496. **Contact:** Human Resources. **World Wide Web address:** http://www.securitasinc.com. **Description:** Offers a wide range of protective services and contract security guard programs to businesses and government

agencies. Burns International Security Services also provides electronic security systems and security planning consultation. **Parent company:** Burns International Services Corporation.

TOWERS PERRIN
One Financial Plaza, Hartford CT 06103-2613. 860-727-9400. **Contact:** Human Resources. **World Wide Web address:** http://www.towersperrin.com. Towers Perrin is a global professional services firm that helps organizations around the world optimize performance through effective people, risk and financial management. The firm provides innovative solutions to client issues in the areas of human resource strategy, design and management; actuarial and management consulting to the financial services industry; and reinsurance intermediary services. **NOTE:** Search and apply for positions online. **Positions advertised include:** Senior Claims Consultant; Disability Consultant; Actuarial Consultant (Property/Casualty); Analyst (non-actuary). **Subsidiaries include:** Tillinghast.

THE WACKENHUT CORPORATION
1010 Wethersfield Avenue, Suite 201, Hartford CT 06114. 860/296-4775. **Contact:** Human Resources. **World Wide Web address:** http://www.wackenhut.com. **Description:** The Wackenhut Corporation is a diversified provider of services to government, industrial, commercial, and professional organizations and agencies worldwide. The corporation has offices throughout the United States and in 49 other countries on six continents. The company also provides educational services and training, facility management, food service to jails and prisons, design, financial services and construction management for correctional facilities, and fire prevention and emergency services. The Wackenhut Corporation is a leader in the privatization of public services to municipal, state, and federal governments worldwide. Founded in 1954. **Corporate headquarters location:** Palm Beach Gardens FL. **Other U.S. locations:** Nationwide. **Operations at this facility include:** This location specializes in security-related services including physical security, investigations, the management of correctional and detention facilities, rehabilitative programs, and information security. **Listed on:** New York Stock Exchange. **Stock exchange symbol:** WAK. **Chairman/CEO:** George R. Wackenhut.

Delaware

AT SYSTEMS
P.O. Box 1223, Wilmington DE 19899-1223. 302/762-5444. **Physical address:** 4200 Governor Printz Boulevard, Wilmington DE 19802. **Recorded jobline:** 800/248.8526. **Fax:** 302/762-8941 **Contact:** Human Resources. **E-mail address:** careers@atsystemsinc.com. **World Wide Web address:** http://www.atsystemsinc.com. **Description:** Provides cash management services, such as armored transportation, cash vault processing and ATM services, for large and small retail and banking customers across America. **NOTE:** Apply in person, or submit resume by fax or e-mail. **Corporate headquarters location:** Pasadena CA.

FAIR ISAAC CORPORATION
10 Corporate Circle, Suite 200, New Castle DE 19720. 302/324-8015. **Fax:** 302/324-7967. **Contact:** Human Resources. **World Wide Web address:** http://www.fairisaac.com. **Description:** Fair Isaac Corporation, along with its subsidiaries, provides analytic, software and data management products and services to automate and improve decisions. Founded in 1956. **NOTE:** See website for current job openings and to apply online. **Operations at this facility include:** This location is a sales office. **Listed on:** New York Stock Exchange. **Stock exchange symbol:** FIC. **Number of employees nationwide:** 3,000.

J.R. GETTIER & ASSOCIATES INCORPORATED
2 Centerville Road, Wilmington DE 19808. 302/652-2700. **Fax:** 302/652-8699. **Contact:** Heather Shupe, Human Resources. **E-mail address:** hshupe@gettier.com. **World Wide Web address:** http://www.gettier.com. **Description:** Provides protective, investigative and security services in Delaware, Maryland, New Jersey and Pennsylvania. **NOTE:** Send resume by mail, fax or e-mail. **Positions advertised include:** Strike Security Team; Guard Team; Investigations Team; Executive Protection Team.

NIXON UNIFORM SERVICE, INC.
2925 Northeast Boulevard, Wilmington DE 19802. 302/764-7550. **Fax:** 302/351-1621. **Toll-free phone:** 888/649-6687. **Contact:** Human Resources. **E-mail address:** jobs@uniformservice.com. **World Wide Web address:** http://www.uniformservice.com. **Description:** Rents and sells casual wear, linens, medical garments and uniforms. **Positions advertised include:** Sales Representatives; Route Service Representatives; Production Associates; Management (various). **Special programs:** Internships. **Corporate headquarters location:** This location. **Other U.S. locations:** DC; MD; NJ; PA. **Number of employees at this location:** 300.

ONESOURCE
1007 North Orange Street, Wilmington DE 19899. 302/498-5199. **Fax:** 302/498-5202. **Contact:** Human Resources. **World Wide Web address:** http://www.one-source.com. **Description:** OneSource offers both contract and on-demand building services that include cleaning services, engineering and maintenance services, landscape and golf course maintenance, aviation support services, and staffing and specialty services. **NOTE:** For hourly positions, apply in person. For management/administrative positions, see website. **Corporate headquarters location:** Atlanta GA. **Other area locations:** Dover DE.

ORKIN
101 Johnson Way, New Castle DE 19720. 302/325-4410. **Contact:** Human Resources. **World Wide Web address:** http://www.orkin.com. **Description:** Pest control company.

SECURITAS
6 Denny Road, Suite 300, Wilmington DE 19809. 302/764-1070. **Fax:** 302/764-9602. **Contact:** Human Resources. **World Wide Web address:** http://www.pinkertons.com. **Description:** Provides professional detective and security services to both commercial and private customers. Founded in 1909. **NOTE:** Call to inquire about current job openings. **Other U.S. locations:** Nationwide.

District Of Columbia

ACCENTURE
800 Connecticut Avenue NW, Suite 600, Washington DC 20006. 202/533-1100. **Fax:** 202/533-1111. **Contact:** Human Resources. **World Wide Web address:** http://www.accenture.com. **Description:** Accenture is a management consulting, technology services, and outsourcing company. **Positions advertised include:** HR Transformation Consultant; SAP Sr. Manager; Healthcare Program Manager.

THE ADVISORY BOARD COMPANY
2445 M Street, NW, Washington DC 20037. 202/266-5600. **Contact:** Human Resources. **World Wide Web address:** http://www.advisoryboardcompany.com. **Description:** The Advisory Board, a membership of 2,500 of the country's largest health systems and medical centers, provides best practices research and analysis to the health care industry, focusing on business strategy, operations and general management issues. **Positions advertised include:** .NET Software Engineer; Academy Consultant; Academy Research Analyst; Associate Director, Educational Services; Business Analyst; Content Factory Architect; Data Associate.

THE AMERICAN ENTERPRISE INSTITUTE
1150 Seventeenth Street NW, Washington DC 20036. 202/862-5800. **Fax:** 202-862-7177. **Contact:** Director of Human Resources. **E-mail address**: Jobs@aei.org. **World Wide Web address:** http://www.aei.org.

Description: A private, nonpartisan, not-for-profit institution dedicated to research and education on issues of government, politics, economics, and social welfare. Founded in 1943. **Positions advertised include:** Magazine Editor; Research Assistant; Staff Assistant; Development Assistant; Marketing Assistant.

AMERICAN INSTITUTES FOR RESEARCH
1000 Thomas Jefferson Street NW, Suite 200, Washington DC 20007. 202/342-5000. **Fax:** 202/944-5454 **Contact:** Human Resources. **E-mail address:** resumes@air.org. **World Wide Web address:** http://www.air.org. **Description:** A non-profit research and analysis organization with a concentration on education, health, individual and organizational performance, and quality of life issues. Founded in 1946. **Positions advertised include:** Research Assistant; Training and Development Manager; Accounting Assistant; Quality Assurance Associate; Sr. AP Analyst; Director Software Engineering; Sr. Software Specialist; Sr. Contracts Specialist. **Corporate headquarters location:** This location. **Other U.S. locations:** Palo Alto CA; Concord MA.

AQUENT
1333 H Street NW, Suite 630 East, Washington DC 20005. 202/293-5700. **Contact:** Tracy Donovan. **E-mail address:** dcrecruiting@aquent.com. **World Wide Web address:** http://www.aquent.com. **Description:** A professional services firm whose specialties include marketing, information technology, and financial services. **Positions advertised include:** Web Developer; Promotions Manager; User Designer; Production Manager; Product Marketing Manager; Sr. Copywriter. **Corporate headquarters location:** Boston MA. **Other U.S. locations:** Nationwide. **International locations:** Worldwide.

ARMS CONTROL ASSOCIATION
1150 Connecticut Avenue NW, Suite 620, Washington DC 20036. 202/463-8270. **Fax:** 202/463-8273. **Contact:** Assistant to the Director. **World Wide Web address:** http://www.armscontrol.org. **Description:** An organization providing information on arms control issues. **Positions advertised include:** Research Analyst.

BOOZ ALLEN HAMILTON
700 Thirteenth Street NW, Suite 1100, Washington DC 20005. 202/508-6500. **Fax:** 202/508-6565. **Contact:** Human Resources. **World Wide Web address:** http://www.boozallen.com. **Description:** A global strategy and technology consulting firm specializing in strategy, organization, operations, systems, and technology. Founded in 1914. **Positions advertised include:** Budget Analyst; Financial Analyst; Business Systems Analyst; Maritime Analyst; NATO Medical Planner; Integration Specialist; Integrated Logistics Engineer; Information Operations Analyst. **Corporate headquarters location:** McLean VA. **Number of employees worldwide:** 17,000.

THE BROOKINGS INSTITUTION
1775 Massachusetts Avenue NW, Washington DC 20036-2188. 202/797-6210. **Fax:** 202/797-2479. **Contact:** Human Resources. **E-mail address:** hrjobs@brookings.edu. **World Wide Web address:** http://www.brook.edu. **Description:** A private, nonprofit organization devoted to research, education, and publishing in the fields of economics, government, foreign policy, and the social sciences. Its activities are carried out through three research programs (Economic Studies, Governmental Studies, Foreign Policy Studies); the Center for Public Policy Education; Information Technology; and the Brookings Press. **Positions advertised include:** Financial Manager; Development Coordinator; Sr. External Affairs Officer; Budget Coordinator; Outreach Director; Research Assistant. **NOTE:** This institution does not accept unsolicited resumes. Check the website for a listing of open positions. Positions are also posted on the Washington Post's website. **Special programs:** Internships; Fellowships. **President:** Strobe Talbott.

CENTER FOR STRATEGIC & INTERNATIONAL STUDIES (CSIS)
1800 K Street NW, Suite 400, Washington DC 20006. 202/887-0200. **Fax:** 202/775-3199. **Contact:** Human Resources. **E-mail address:** employment@csis.org. **World Wide Web address:** http://www.csis.org. **Description:** A nonprofit, public policy research institute. **NOTE:** Entry-level positions are offered. **Positions advertised include:** Gift and Database Coordinator; Post-Conflict Reconstruction Project Coordinator. **Special programs:** Internships available. **Number of employees at this location:** 240.

CORPORATE EXECUTIVE BOARD
2000 Pennsylvania Avenue NW, Suite 6000, Washington DC 20006. 202/777-5000. **Fax:** 202/777-5100. **Contact:** Human Resources. **E-mail address:** jobs@executiveboard.com. **World Wide Web address:** http://www.executiveboard.com. **Description:** A B2B content provider whose information is geared to helping its clients improve corporate strategies, processes, and their general business framework. **Positions advertised include:** IT Recruiting Specialist; Desktop Publishing Specialist; Manager, Editorial Group; Proofreader; Controller; Business analyst; Java Developer. **Special programs:** Internships available. **Listed on:** NASDAQ. **Stock exchange symbol:** EXBD.

LEVICK STRATEGIC COMMUNICATIONS
1900 M Street NW, Suite 400, Washington DC 20036. 202/973-1318. **Fax:** 202/973-1301. **Contact:** Marie Leiter, Human Resources Department. **E-mail address:** mleiter@levick.com. **World Wide Web address:** http://www.levick.com. **Description:** Communications strategist and counselor to financial institutions and corporations.

LUCIDEA
529 14th Street NW, Suite 545, Washington DC 20045. 202/777-1199. **Fax:** 202/777-1179. **Contact:** Human Resources. **E-mail address:** careers@lucidea.com. **World Wide Web address:** http://www.lucidea.com. **Description:** An Internet and web software developer.

SCIENCE APPLICATIONS INTERNATIONAL CORPORATION (SAIC)
2020 K Street NW, Suite 400, Washington DC 20006. 202/530-8900. **Contact:** Human Resources. **World Wide Web address:** http://www.saic.com. **Description:** The largest employee-owned research and engineering firm in the U.S. with offices in 150 cities worldwide. **Positions advertised include:** Help Desk Specialist; Technical Project Manager. **Number of employees worldwide:** 43,000.

UNITED STATES SERVICE INDUSTRIES (USSI)
1424 K Street NW, 4th Floor, Washington DC 20005. 202/783-2030. **Contact:** Human Resources. **E-mail address:** communications@ussiclean.com. **World Wide Web address:** http://www.ussiclean.com. **Description:** A building maintenance company offering janitorial services. **Other U.S. locations:** VA; FL; MD.

THE WEINBERG GROUP
1220 Nineteenth Street NW, Suite 300, Washington DC 20036. 202/833-8077. **Contact:** Personnel. **E-mail address:** careers@weinberggroup.com. **World Wide Web address:** http://www.weinberggroup.com. **Description:** A scientific and regulatory consulting firm that helps clients improve manufacturing processes, clear regulatory hurdles, and defend products in the courts and the media. **Positions advertised include:** Researcher; Consultant; Sr. Consultant; Sr. Director; Vice President. **Other U.S. locations:** San Francisco CA; New York NY.

Florida

ADP TOTAL SOURCE
701 Northpoint Parkway, Suite 340, West Palm Beach FL 33407. 561/615-7478. **Toll-free phone:** 800/447-3237. **Contact:** Personnel. **World Wide Web address:** http://www.adptotalsource.com. **Description:** Provides benefits, payroll, and related human resources services.

Positions advertised include: Human Resource Manager; Client Account Representative; 401K Conversion Manager; Human Resource Consultant; Time & Attendance Implementation Manager; Administrative Assistant Executive.

ACHIEVEGLOBAL
8875 Hidden River Parkway, Suite 400, Tampa FL 33637. 813/631-5517. **Fax:** 813/631-5796. **Contact:** Human Resources. **World Wide Web address:** http://www.achieveglobal.com. **Description:** Provides training and consulting services in sales performance, customer service, leadership, and teamwork. AchieveGlobal offers programs in 70 countries and more than 40 languages. **Positions advertised include:** Product Logistics Specialist; Lead Coordinator; Training Performance Consultant, Spanish. **Corporate headquarters location:** This location.

ALIG TECHNOLOGY GROUP, INC.
499 Sheridan Street, Suite 317A, Dania Beach FL 33004. 954/924-1009. **Fax:** 954/925-4270. **Contact:** Human Resources. **E-mail address:** hr3@aligtech.com. **World Wide Web address:** http://www.aligtech.com. **Description:** Provides Internet development, design, and consulting services to corporate clients with an emphasis on the real estate industry including commercial and residential markets. **Positions advertised include:** Experienced Web Developer; Experienced Web Designer.

AMERICAN DOCUMENT MANAGEMENT
101 Northeast Third Avenue, Suite 1250, Ft. Lauderdale FL 33301. 954/462-5400. **Fax**: 954/463-7500. **Contact:** Human Resources. **E-mail address:** resume@amdoc.com. **World Wide Web address:** http://www.amdoc.com. **Description:** Provides litigation support, regional and in-house scanning centers, hosted retrieval, and forms processing for businesses in the corporate, private and governmental sectors. **Positions advertised include:** Account Executive; Document Analyst. **Corporate headquarters location:** This location. **Other U.S. locations:** Indianapolis IN.

ARAMARK CORPORATION
1301 Riverplace Boulevard, Suite C-20, Jacksonville FL 32207. 904/396-5037. **Contact:** Human Resources. **World Wide Web address:** http://www.aramark.com. **Description:** ARAMARK is one of the world's leading providers of managed services. The company operates in all 50 states and 10 foreign countries, offering a broad range of services to businesses of all sizes including many *Fortune* 500 companies and thousands of universities, hospitals, and municipal, state, and federal government facilities. ARAMARK's businesses include Food, Leisure, and Support Services including Campus Dining Services, School Nutrition Services, Leisure Services, Business Dining Services, International Services, Healthcare Support Services, Conference Center Management, and Refreshment Services; Facility Services; Correctional Services; Industrial Services; Uniform Services, which includes Wearguard, a direct marketer of work clothing; Health and Education Services including Spectrum Healthcare Services and Children's World Learning Centers; and Book and Magazine Services. **Positions advertised include:** Training Manager; District Management Trainee; Accounts Manager. **Operations at this facility include:** This location is a cafeteria. **Corporate headquarters location:** Philadelphia PA. **Number of employees nationwide:** 150,000. **Listed on:** New York Stock Exchange. **Stock exchange symbol:** RMG.

ARMOR HOLDINGS, INC.
13386 International Parkway, Jacksonville FL 32218. 904/741-5400. **Contact:** Human Resources. **World Wide Web address:** http://www.armorholdings.com. **Description:** Develops, manufactures, and markets security products including body armor to corporate and government clients worldwide. Armor Holdings, Inc. also provides security solutions such as risk analysis and electronic surveillance. **Corporate headquarters location:** This location. **Other U.S. locations:** Nationwide. **International locations:** Worldwide. **Listed on:** New York Stock Exchange. **Stock exchange symbol:** AH. **Annual sales/revenues:** More than $100 million.

FIRST AMERICAN REAL ESTATE SOLUTIONS
1800 NW 66th Avenue, Fort Lauderdale FL 33313. 954/792-2000. **Contact:** Human Resources. **World Wide Web address:** http://www.firstamres.com. **Description:** Maintains credit reports and provides information services for the real estate industry. **Positions advertised include:** Account Executive; Development Territory Manager. **NOTE:** Please send resumes to: Human Resources, 5601 East La Palma Avenue, Anaheim CA 92802. **Operations at this facility include:** Administration; Manufacturing; Regional Headquarters; Research and Development; Sales; Service. **Number of employees at this location:** 320. **Number of employees nationwide:** 1,200.

G&K SERVICES, INC.
7037 Commonwealth Avenue, Suite 28, Jacksonville, FL 32220. 904/786-2220. **Contact:** Human Resources. **World Wide Web address:** http://www.gkservices.com. **Description:** Provides uniform services to more than 85,000 businesses including those in the automotive, high-tech, maintenance/repair, and manufacturing industries. G&K's services include designing uniform programs that fit customers' needs; helping customers select a company logo, garment style, and colors; and introducing the uniform program to customers' employees. Products include executive wear, industrial wear, flame-resistant garments, clean room uniforms, treated dust mops, linens, and wiping towels. G&K also provides delivery of clean garments on a weekly basis. **Positions advertised include:** Territory Sales Representative; Route Manager; District Sales Manager; Route Sales Manager; Account Manager. **Other U.S. locations:** Nationwide. **International locations:** Canada. **Listed on:** NASDAQ. **Stock exchange symbol:** GKSRA. **Number of employees nationwide:** 8,000.

OSI COLLECTION SERVICES
5022 Gate Parkway North, Suite 204, Jacksonville FL 32256. 904/380-2600. **Contact:** Human Resources. **Description:** A collection agency. **Corporate headquarters location:** This location.

PALM COAST DATA LTD.
11 Commerce Boulevard, Palm Coast FL 32164. 386/445-4662. **Contact:** Lynn Lawson, Director of Human Resources. **World Wide Web address:** http://www.palmcoastd.com. **Description:** Manages subscription lists for publishing companies. Founded in 1984. **Positions advertised include:** Proof Print Operator; Data Entry Assistant Supervisor; Imaging Verifier; Agency Customer Service Clerk; Mail Sorter; Building Custodian; Machine Maintenance Worker; PC Programmer; Mailing Services Director; Customer Service Manager; Business Analyst; Customer Service Manager; Customer Service Representative; Data Entry Home Keyer. **Parent company:** DIMAC Direct.

SPHERION
2050 Spectrum Boulevard, Fort Lauderdale FL 33309. 954/938-7600. **Contact:** Human Resources. **World Wide Web address:** http://www.spherion.com. **Description:** Spherion is an executive search firm that offers professional recruiting, testing, and assessment services. **Positions advertised include:** PeopleSoft Production Support Analyst; Staffing Branch Coordinator; Real Estate Financial Analyst; Business Analyst Process Base; Novell Engineer; Internal Auditor; Project Accountant; Controller; Outside Sales Representative; User Interface Design; Staffing Coordinator; Entry Level Staff Accountant; Online Marketing Manager; Sales Representative; Internal Auditor; Build Engineer. **Corporate headquarters location:** This location. **Other U.S. locations:** Nationwide. **International locations:** Worldwide. **Operations at this facility include:** This location houses administrative offices only. **Listed on:** New

York Stock Exchange. **Stock exchange symbol:** SFN. **Number of employees worldwide:** 500,000.

TEAM STAFF RX
1901 Ulmerton Road, Suite 450, Clearwater FL 33762. 727/456-3600. **Toll-free phone:** 800/345-9642. **Fax:** 727/299-9065. **Contact:** Human Resources. **World Wide Web address:** http://www.teamstaffrx.com. **Description:** Team Staff Rx offers a full line of employer services including payroll processing, permanent and temporary placement of personnel, in-house hardware and software systems, outsourcing, facility management, employee leasing, and insurance services. **Positions advertised include:** C T Technologist; Special Procedures Technologist; Clinical Pharmacist; Staff Pharmacist; Radiological Pharmacist; Radiological Technologist; Pharmacy Director; MRI Technologist; Pharmacist. **Listed on:** NASDAQ. **Stock exchange symbol:** TSTF. **Number of employees nationwide:** 20,000.

THE WACKENHUT CORPORATION
3974 Woodcock Drive, Suite 100, Jacksonville FL 32207. 904/398-1640. **Toll-free phone:** 800/254-4411. **Fax:** 904/396-6716. **Contact:** Human Resources. **World Wide Web address:** http://www.wackenhut.com. **Description:** Provides physical security services, correction services, and related products to businesses, governments, and individuals from more than 150 domestic and foreign offices. Specific services include security guard services; corrections staffing; private investigative services; the assembly and sale of electronic security equipment and systems; the training of security guards and fire and crash rescue personnel; providing fire protection and emergency ambulance service to municipalities; security consulting; planning, designing, and implementing integrated security systems; and providing specialized services to the nuclear power industry. Wackenhut has 90 offices located in most major United States cities. **Office hours:** Monday - Friday, 8:30 a.m. - 5:00 p.m. **Corporate headquarters location:** Palm Beach Gardens FL. **International locations:** Worldwide. **Subsidiaries include:** Wackenhut Corrections, Inc.; Wackenhut International. **Listed on:** New York Stock Exchange. **Stock exchange symbol:** WAK. **Number of employees nationwide:** 40,000.

Georgia

ADT SECURITY SERVICES
2821 Harley Court, Columbus GA 31909-2769. 706/653-1388. **Contact:** Human Resources. **World Wide Web address:** http://www.adtsecurityservices.com. **Description:** Designs, programs, markets, and installs protective systems to safeguard life and property from hazards such as burglary, hold-up, and fire. **NOTE:** Please visit website or visit monster.com to search for jobs, and to apply online. **Office hours:** Monday – Friday, 8:00 a.m. – 5:00 p.m. **Corporate headquarters location:** Boca Raton FL. **Other area locations:** Statewide. **Other U.S. locations:** Nationwide. **International locations:** Worldwide. **Parent company:** Tyco International LTD. **Listed on:** New York Stock Exchange. **Stock exchange symbol:** TYC. **Annual revenues:** More than $100 million. **Number of employees worldwide:** 15,000.

AKS INCORPORATED
401 16th Street, Suite 1371, Atlanta GA 30363. 404/892-6620. **Contact:** Human Resources. **E-mail address:** jobs@aksincorporated.com. **World Wide Web address:** http://www.aksincorporated.com. **Description:** A placement firm specializing in civil, mechanical, and electrical engineers, and architects. Founded in 2002. **Positions advertised include:** PLC Controls Engineer; Project Architect/Intern.

APCO (AUTOMOBILE PROTECTION CORPORATION)
P.O. Box 88230, Atlanta GA 30356 **Physical address:** 6010 Atlantic Boulevard, Norcross GA 30071. **Toll-free phone:** 888/EASY-400. **Fax:** 770/246-2453. **Contact:** Human Resources. **E-mail Address:** jobs@easycare.com **World Wide Web address:** http://www.easycare.com. **Description:** Provides products and services to automobile dealers to enhance customer satisfaction. Services include the EasyCare Certified Pre-Owned Vehicle Program, an extended service contract for dealers and their customers. APCO promotes the vehicle service contracts, engages in customer service for the service contracts, and also arranges for insurance carriers that cover the dealer's cost of making repairs during the contract. Founded in 1984. **Positions advertised include:** Claims Adjuster; Customer Service Representative. **Corporate headquarters location:** This location. **Other U.S. locations:** Nationwide. **Subsidiaries include:** The Aegis Group, Inc. **Parent company:** Ford Motor Company. **President/CEO:** Larry I. Dorfman.

AARON RENTS, INC.
309 East Paces Ferry Road NE, Atlanta GA 30305. 404/231-0011. **Contact:** Human Resources. **World Wide Web address:** http://www.aaronrents.com. **Description:** Rents and sells residential and office furniture and business equipment from 574 stores in 42 states. Founded 1955. **Positions advertised include:** Customer Service Representative; Bilingual Manager in Training; Manager in Training; Consumer Electronics Repair Technician; Operational Auditor. **Corporate headquarters location:** This location. **Other U.S. Locations:** Nationwide. **International locations:** Ontario Canada. **Operations at this facility include:** Administration. **Listed on:** New York Stock Exchange. **Stock exchange symbol:** RNT. **Number of employees nationwide:** 3,900. **CEO:** R. Charles Loudermilk, Sr.

ALLIANCE DATA SYSTEMS
3200 Windy Hill Road Southeast, Atlanta GA 30339. 770/933-5600. **Contact:** Human Resources. **World Wide Web address:** http://www.alliancedatasystems.com. **Description:** Alliance Data Systems provides transaction, credit and marketing services to large consumer based businesses within the retail, petroleum, financial services, utility and hospitality markets. **Positions advertised include:** Project Manager; Sr. Systems Programmer Analyst; Sr. Business System Analyst; Manager, Applications Development. **Corporate headquarters location:** Dallas TX. **Listed on:** New York Stock Exchange. **Stock exchange symbol:** ADS.

ALLIED BARTON SECURITY SERVICE
1360 Peachtree Street, Suite 1050, Atlanta GA 30309. 770/492-1997. **Fax:** 770/492-1984. **Contact:** Human Resources. **World Wide Web address:** http://www.alliedsecurity.com. **Description:** One of the largest national contract security officer companies in the nation. Allied Security provides loss prevention services to private businesses and governmental agencies. **NOTE:** Please visit website for online application form. **Corporate headquarters location:** King of Prussia PA. **Other U.S. locations:** Nationwide. **Number of employees nationwide:** 20,000.

ARISTA INFORMATION TECHNOLOGY
2150 Boggs Road, Building 400, Suite 430, Duluth GA 30096. 678/473-1885. **Fax:** 678/473-1051. **Contact:** Human Resources. **World Wide Web address:** http://www.aristainfo.com. **Description:** A full service laser printing and mailing company. **NOTE:** Please visit website for online application form. **Corporate headquarters location:** This location. **Other U.S. locations:** NC.

CDM
2030 Powers Ferry Road, Suite 325, Atlanta GA 30339. 770/952-8643. **Fax:** 770/952-9893. **Contact:** Human Resources. **World Wide Web address:** http://www.cdm.com. **Description:** A consulting, engineering, construction and operations firm aiding its clients in improving the environment in numerous ways. Founded 1947. **NOTE:** Please visit website to search for jobs and apply online. **Positions advertised include:** Environmental Engineer. **Corporate headquarters location:** Cambridge MA. **Other U.S. locations:** Nationwide. **International locations:** Worldwide. **Number of employees worldwide:** 3,600.

DATAMATX, INC.
3146 Northeast Expressway NE, Atlanta GA 30341-5345. 770/936-5600. **Toll-free phone:** 800/943-5240. **Fax:** 770/936-5614. **Contact:** Jennifer Hall, Director of Human Resources. **E-mail address:** hr@datamatx.com. **World Wide Web address:** http://www.datamatx.com. **Description:** Provides data processing services, laser printing, and mail services. Founded in 1976. **NOTE:** Entry-level positions are offered. **Other U.S. locations:** Phoenix AZ; Richmond VA. **Operations at this facility include:** Administration; Research and Development; Sales; Service. **Listed on:** Privately held. **Number of employees nationwide:** 170.

DEKALB OFFICE ENVIRONMENTS
1320 Ridgeland Parkway, Alpharetta GA 30004. 770/360-0200. **Fax:** 770/360-0305. **Contact:** Human Resources Manager. **E-mail address:** humanresources@dekalboffice.com. **World Wide Web address:** http://www.dekalboffice.com. **Description:** Sells office furniture and provides facilities management services including reconfiguration, design, warehousing, project management, installation, and refinishing. **Positions advertised include:** Account Executive. **Corporate headquarters location:** This location. **Operations at this facility include:** Administration; Sales; Service. **President:** John H. Rasper. **Number of employees at this location:** 140.

FAIR, ISAAC AND CO., INC.
3550 Engineering Drive, Suite 200, Norcross GA 30092. 770/810-8000. **Contact:** Dawn Ridz, Human Resources Recruiter. **E-mail address:** dawnridz@fairisaac.com. **World Wide Web address:** http://www.fairisaac.com. **Description:** Develops and provides data management software and services for the consumer credit, personal lines insurance, and direct marketing industries. Founded in 1956. **NOTE:** Contact is located at corporate office. Fax is 858/202-2056. Please visit website to search for jobs and apply online. **Corporate headquarters location:** San Rafael CA. **Other U.S. locations:** Nationwide. **International locations:** Worldwide. **Subsidiaries include:** CRMA Consulting; DynaMark, Inc.; Risk Management Technologies. **Listed on:** New York Stock Exchange. **Stock exchange symbol:** FIC. **President:** Thomas Grudnowski. **Number of employees nationwide:** 2,000.

FIRST DATA CORPORATION
250 Williams Avenue NW, Atlanta GA 30303. 404/521-1943. **Contact:** Human Resources. **World Wide Web address:** http://www.firstdatacorp.com. **Description:** A holding company. **NOTE:** Please visit website to search for jobs and apply online. **Positions advertised include:** In-House Sales Executive; MER/Account Executive; Human Resources Assistant; PB Manager; Administrative Assistant; Data Entry Operator; PB Lead; PB Coordinator; Warehouse Clerk; Mail Insert Machine Operator. **Corporate headquarters location:** Greenwood Village CO. **Subsidiaries include:** First Data Resources; First Data POS. **Listed on:** New York Stock Exchange. **Stock exchange symbol:** FDC. **CEO:** Charlie Fote. **Number of employees worldwide:** 30,000.

IKON OFFICE SOLUTIONS
1738 Bass Road, Building 3, Macon GA 31210. 478/238-7200. **Toll-free phone:** 800/800/1060. **Fax:** 912/471-2369. **E-mail address:** resumes@ikon.com. **World Wide Web address:** http://www.ikon.com. **Description:** One of the world's largest providers of copier and printer technologies. IKON hopes to aid companies in their management of large workloads by providing the best technology and service. **NOTE:** Please visit website to search for jobs and apply online. **Positions advertised include:** Accounts Payable Associate; Cash Operations Associate; Logistics Assistant; Lease Collections Supervisor; Collector; Commercial Credit Analyst; IT Project Manager; Customer Service Representative; Recruiter; Named Account Representative; Bi-lingual Collector. **Corporate headquarters location:** Malvern PA. **Other area locations:** Statewide. **Other U.S. locations:** Nationwide. **International locations:** Canada; Denmark; France; Germany; Mexico; United Kingdom; Ireland. **Operations at this facility include:** This location serves as the main area office. **Listed on:** New York Stock Exchange. **Stock exchange symbol:** IKN. **Number of employees worldwide:** 7,000.

JUDGE INC.
2500 Northwinds Parkway, Suite 300, Alpharetta GA 30004. 678/297-0800. **Fax:** 678/297-9014. **Contact:** Human Resources. **E-mail address:** atlantajobs@judge.com. **World Wide Web address:** http://www.judgeinc.com. **Description:** A technical recruiting firm specializing in the food processing, pharmaceutical, retail, distribution, and information technology industries. Founded 1970. **Positions advertised include:** Production Supervisor; HAACP Coordinator. **Corporate headquarters location:** Conshohocken PA. **Other U.S. locations:** Arlington TX; Jacksonville FL; Laguna Hills CA; Tampa FL; Edison NJ.

LASON, INC.
216 Bullsboro Drive, Newnan Atlanta GA 30263. 770/250-2600. **Fax:** 678/797-3967. **Contact:** Human Resources. **E-mail address:** jobs@lason.com. **World Wide Web address:** http://www.lason.com. **Description:** An information processor handling data entry and processing, systems analysis, and clerical support. **NOTE:** Please visit website to search for jobs. E-mail applications are preferred. **Positions advertised include:** Sales Executive. **Corporate headquarters location:** Troy MI. **Other US. locations:** Nationwide. **International locations:** Canada; Mexico; India. **CEO:** Ronald D. Risher.

MANHATTAN ASSOCIATES
2300 Windy Ridge Parkway, Suite 700, Atlanta GA 30339. 770/955-7070. **Fax:** 770/955-0302. **E-mail address:** careers@manh.com. **World Wide Web address:** http://www.manh.com. **Description:** A leading supply chain execution company, providing companies with the means to ship inventory faster. **NOTE:** Please visit website to search for jobs and apply online. **Positions advertised include:** Call Center Consultant; RFID Consultant; Senior Software Consultant; WMS Labor Management Software Expert; Corporate Catering and Food Coordinator; Demand Generation Representative; Junior Business Analyst; Program Manager; Software Analyst; Senior Software Analyst; Technical Lead; Technical Support Consultant; Senior Internet Software Engineer; Software Engineer. **Corporate headquarters location:** This location. **Other U.S. locations:** Burlington MA; Carmel IN; Mishawaka IN; Vienna VA. **International locations:** Worldwide. **Listed on:** NASDAQ. **Stock exchange symbol:** MANH. **President/CEO:** Richard Haddrill.

MILLER/ZELL INC.
4715 Frederick Drive SW, Atlanta GA 30336. 404/691-7400. **Fax:** 404/699-2189. **Contact:** Brenda B. Redding, Manager of Personnel Administration. **E-mail address:** recruitme@millerzell.com. **World Wide Web address:** http://www.millerzell.com. **Description:** Purchases store fixtures, furniture, displays, prefabricated building products, and interior design products; prints graphics and point-of-purchase signage and fixtures; and provides fixtures, graphics, and service to retail companies. **NOTE:** Please visit website to search or jobs and apply online. **Positions advertised include:** Corporate Training Director; Print Planner; Senior Programmer/Analyst, JD Edwards. **Corporate headquarters location:** This location. **Other U.S. locations:** New York NY; Washington D.C. Bentonville AR. **International locations:** Worldwide. **Operations at this facility include:** Administration; Manufacturing; Sales. **CEO:** Sandy Miller. **Number of employees at this location:** 350.

NDCHEALTH CORPORATION
4 Corporate Square NE, Atlanta GA 30329. 404/728-2000. **Toll-free phone:** 800/225-5632. **Fax:** 404/728-3904. **Contact:** Director of Staffing. **E-mail address:**

careers@ndchealth.com. **World Wide Web address:** http://www.ndchealth.com. **Description:** A provider of information systems and services to the health care market. NDCHealth offers patient eligibility, claims processing, consulting, billing and other services to doctors, hospitals, pharmacies, government agencies, and managed care organizations. The company's clients include more than 55,000 pharmacies, 100,000 physicians, and more than 1,200 hospitals. Founded 1977. **NOTE:** Please visit website to search for jobs and apply online. **Positions advertised include:** Director of Finance; Training Specialist; Senior Payroll Representative; Senior Paralegal; Senior Administrative Assistant; Senior Recruiter; Lead Systems Engineer; Senior Financial Analyst; Manager – Training and Development; Maintenance Electrician; Senior Attorney; Senior Internal Auditor; Director - IHR. **Corporate headquarters location:** This location. **Other U.S. locations:** Nationwide. **International locations:** Canada; Germany; United Kingdom. **Listed on:** New York Stock Exchange. **Stock exchange symbol:** NDC. **President/CEO:** William Hoff. **Number of employees worldwide:** 1,800.

ONESOURCE
1600 Parkwood Circle, Suite 400, Atlanta GA 30339. 770/436-9900. **Contact:** Human Resources. **World Wide Web address:** http://www.2onesource.com. **Description:** Provides facility management including janitorial and landscaping services. **Corporate headquarters location:** This location. **Other area locations:** Statewide.

PRG-SCHULTZ INTERNATIONAL, INC.
600 Galleria Parkway, Suite 100, Atlanta GA 30339. 770/779-3900. **Toll-free phone:** 800/752-5894. **Fax:** 770/779-3250. **Contact:** Personnel. **E-mail address:** personnel@prgx.com. **World Wide Web address:** http://www.prgx.com. **Description:** A profit-recovery firm. Profit recovery group offers services in logistics, tax, communications, and payables. **NOTE:** Please visit website to download application form. Visit http://www.monster.com to search for jobs and apply online. **Positions advertised include:** Reports Analyst; Network Operations Analyst; Regional Human Resources Manager. **Corporate headquarters location:** This location. **Other U.S. locations:** San Juan Capistrano CA; West Valley City UT; Fort Collins CO; New York NY; Parsippany NJ. **International locations:** Worldwide. **Listed on:** NASDAQ. **Stock exchange symbol:** PRGX. **President/CEO:** John Cook. **Annual sales/revenues:** More than $100 million. **Number of employees worldwide:** 3,500.

RDA CORPORATION
980 Hammond Drive, Suite 350, Atlanta GA 30328. 770/668-9200. **Toll-free phone:** 877/678-9200. **Fax:** 770/668-9280. **Contact:** Human Resources Manager. **World Wide Web address:** http://www.rdacorp.com. **Description:** Provides IT integration and security services. Founded in 1988. **NOTE:** Please visit website to search for jobs and apply online. **Corporate headquarters location:** Baltimore MD. **Other U.S. locations include:** IL, PA; VA. **CEO:** Don Awalt. **Number of employees nationwide:** 206.

RAILCAR MANAGEMENT, INC.
1819 Peachtree Road, NE, Suite 303, Atlanta GA 30309. 404/355-6734. **Fax:** 404/352-8814. **Contact:** Rachel M. Emigh, Assistant Vice President of Human Resources. **E-mail address:** hr@railcarmgt.com. **World Wide Web address:** http://www.railcarmgt.com. **Description:** Provides IT services and e-Commerce solutions to the railroad industry. Founded in 1979. **NOTE:** No phone calls regarding employment. **Corporate headquarters location:** This location.

REFLEX SECURITY, INC.
5730 Glenridge Drive, Suite 10, Atlanta GA 30328. 770/408-2034. **Contact:** Recruiting. **E-mail address:** careers@reflexsecurity.com. **World Wide Web address:** http://www.reflexsecurity.com. **Description:** Reflex Security, Inc. is a provider of intrusion detection and prevention network security technology solutions. The company's flagship product is an automated intrusion response system that identifies, analyzes, and responds to internal and external network security threats in real-time, without the need of human intervention. **Positions advertised include:** Account Executive; Customer Engineer; Senior Software Developer; Senior Quality Assurance (QA) Tester; Inside Sales.

ROLLINS INC.
P.O. Box 647, Atlanta GA 30301. 404/888-2000. **Physical address:** 2170 Piedmont Road NE, Atlanta GA 30324. **Fax:** 404/888-2672. **Recorded jobline:** 404/888-2125. **Contact:** Human Resources. **E-mail address:** jobs@rollinscorp.com. **World Wide Web address:** http://www.rollinscorp.com. **Description:** A nationwide chain providing termite and other pest control services. **Positions advertised include:** Vice President of Training; Orkin National Accounts Receivable Representative; Commercial Sales Director; Accounts Payable Telecom Specialist; Customer Service Assistant; Corporate Controller; Collector; Senior Claims Adjuster; New Customer Specialist. **Corporate headquarters location:** This location. **Other U.S. locations:** Nationwide. **Subsidiaries include:** Orkin Pest Control. **Listed on:** New York Stock Exchange. **Stock exchange symbol:** ROL. **President/CEO:** Gary W. Rollins.

SECURITAS SECURITY SERVICES
400 Chastain Center, Suite 410, Kennesaw GA 30144. 770/426-5262. **Fax:** 770/426-5480. **Contact:** Human Resources. **World Wide Web address:** http://www.pinkertons.com. **Description:** America's largest security provider. **Positions advertised include:** Account Executive. **Other U.S. locations:** Nationwide. **International locations:** Worldwide. **Operations at this facility include:** Regional Headquarters for the Southeast. **Number of employees worldwide:** 200,000.

SECURITAS – PINKERTON
2801 Buford Highway, Suite 400, Atlanta GA 30329. 404/633-1140. **Contact:** Personnel Manager. **World Wide Web address:** http://www.securitasinc.com. **Description:** The company offers a full range of specialized protective services including premier property and high-rise services, health care and hospital services, special event services, ATM services, and patrol services. The company serves thousands of companies worldwide with investigation services, threat assessment services, and executive protection. **NOTE:** Please visit website to search for jobs. **Corporate headquarters location:** Chicago IL. **Other area locations:** Statewide. **Other U.S. locations:** Nationwide. **International locations:** Worldwide. **Operations at this facility include:** District offices. **International locations:** Worldwide. **Number of employees worldwide:** 93,000.

WORLD MARKETING ATLANTA.
1961 South Cobb Industrial Boulevard, Smyrna GA 30082. 770/431-2500. **Toll-free phone:** 800/962-4514. **Fax:** 770/431-2517. **Contact:** Human Resources. **E-mail address:** frontdesk@ace-marketing.com. **World Wide Web address:** http://www.acemarketingservices.com. **Description:** Offers a variety of mailing services including total project planning, package design, computer processing, production management, lettershop operation, warehousing and fulfillment, and list brokerage. **Positions advertised include:** Second Shift Lettershop Mechanic; Machine Operator; Procurement Coordinator; In-Process Auditor; Warehouseman. **Parent company:** World Marketing. **Operations at this facility include:** Administration; Manufacturing; Sales. **Listed on:** Privately held.

Hawaii

HAWAII PROTECTIVE ASSOCIATION LIMITED
1290 Maunakea Street, Suite A, Honolulu HI 96817-4119. 808/537-5938. **Contact:** Jeanie Aio, Operations Supervisor. **Description:** A security firm that provides uniformed guards and motorized patrols to various

clients throughout the state of Hawaii. **NOTE:** Entry-level positions are offered. Applicants must come in-person to fill out an application. **Positions advertised include:** Security Officer. **Number of employees at this location:** 400.

Illinois

ACXIOM CORPORATION
1501 Opus Place, Downers Grove IL 60515-5727. 630/964-1501. **Contact:** Human Resources. **World Wide Web address:** http://www.acxiom.com. **Description:** Provides a variety of services including data integration services, data products, and information technology outsourcing. **NOTE:** Entry-level positions offered. Apply online for all positions. **Positions advertised include:** Client Executive; Client Representative; Decision Support Analyst. **Special programs:** Internships. **Corporate headquarters location:** Little Rock AR. **Listed on:** NASDAQ. **Stock exchange symbol:** ACXM.

ADVANCED TECHNOLOGY SERVICES, INC.
8201 North University, Peoria IL 61615. 309/693-4000. **Fax:** 309/693-4164. **Contact:** Human Resources. **E-mail address:** info@advancedtech.com. **World Wide Web address:** http://www.advancedtech.com. **Description:** Provides manufacturers with production equipment maintenance, information technology, and spare parts repair services. Founded in 1985. **Positions advertised include:** Systems Engineer; Application Technician; Business Analyst; Calibration Coordinator.

ASTRO BUILDING SERVICES INC.
2510 North Illinois Street, Belleville IL 62226. 618/235-4006. **Contact:** Human Resources. **Description:** Provides contract floor cleaning and shining services to retail stores.

AUDIT BUREAU OF CIRCULATIONS (ABC)
900 North Meacham Road, Schaumburg IL 60173. 847/605-0909. **Toll-free phone:** 800/285-2220. **Fax:** 847/605-9771. **Contact:** Human Resources. **E-mail address:** recruit@accessabc.com. **World Wide Web address:** http://www.accessabc.com. **Description:** A nonprofit membership organization created by advertisers and publishers to ensure that circulating facts and statistics are compliant with industry bylaws and rules. Founded in 1914. **NOTE:** Entry-level positions are offered. **Positions advertised include:** Audit Manager; Technical Reviewer; Programmer; Shipping Clerk; Field Auditor. **Special programs:** Training. **Office hours:** Monday - Friday, 7:30 a.m. - 5:00 p.m. **Corporate headquarters location:** This location. **Other U.S. locations:** Nationwide. **Operations at this facility include:** Administration; Regional Headquarters.

AUTOMATIC DATA PROCESSING, INC. (ADP)
100 Northwest Point Boulevard, Elk Grove Village IL 60007. 847/718-2000. **Contact:** Senior Employment Specialist. **World Wide Web address:** http://www.adp.com. **Description:** Automatic Data Processing (ADP) helps over 300,000 clients improve their business performance by providing computerized transaction processing, data communications, and information services. The company's services include payroll, payroll tax, and human resource information management; brokerage industry market data; back-office and proxy services; industry-specific services to auto and truck dealers; and computerized auto repair and replacement estimating for auto insurance companies and body repair shops. **NOTE:** Search and apply for positions online. **Positions advertised include:** Help Desk Coordinator; Express Representative; Product Manager; Senior Computer Operator; Staffing Specialist; Program Manager; Billing Specialist; CVR Regional Director; Tax Data Representative. **Corporate headquarters location:** Roseland NJ. **Operations at this facility include:** Administration; Regional Headquarters; Sales; Service. **Listed on:** New York Stock Exchange. **Stock exchange symbol:** ADP.

CANON BUSINESS SOLUTIONS
425 North Martingale Road, Suite 100, Schaumburg IL 60173. 847/706-3480. **Fax:** 847/706-3419. **Contact:** Renette Makanoeich, Recruiter. **E-mail address:** rmakanoeich@solutions.canon.com. **World Wide Web address:** http://www.solutions.canon.com. **Description:** Offers customized solutions for business offices. Canon Business Solutions markets the full line of Canon office equipment including copiers, laser printers, fax machines, and scanners. Founded in 1974. **NOTE:** Entry-level positions are offered. **NOTE:** Apply online at this website for open positions. **Positions advertised include:** Sales Manager; Field Service Technician. **Corporate headquarters location:** Japan. **Other area locations:** Downers Grove IL; Chicago IL. **Parent company:** Canon Inc. **Listed on:** New York Stock Exchange. **Stock exchange symbol:** CAJ.

DIAMONDCLUSTER INTERNATIONAL
875 North Michigan Avenue, Suite 3000, John Hancock Center, Chicago IL 60611. 312/255-5000. **Fax:** 312/255-6000. **Contact:** Aneeta Muradali, Human Resources. **World Wide Web address:** http://www.diamondcluster.com. **Description:** A management consulting company offering expertise in business strategy, technology, and program management to companies in the financial services, insurance, telecommunications, healthcare, and the public sector worldwide. Founded in 1994. **NOTE**: Apply online at this company's website. **Special programs:** Internships. **Corporate headquarters location:** This location. **Other U.S. locations:** NY; Washington DC. **International locations:** United Kingdom; Spain; Germany; France; Brazil; India; United Arab Emirates. **Listed on:** NASDAQ. **Stock exchange symbol:** DTPI.

ELECTRO RENT CORPORATION
200 West Mark Street, Woodale IL 60191. 630/860-3991. **Contact:** Human Resources. **World Wide Web address:** http://www.electrorent.com. **Description:** Rents and leases electronic equipment including test and measurement instruments, workstations, personal computers, and data communication products. **Corporate headquarters location:** Van Nuys CA. **Other U.S. locations:** Nationwide.

EXPERIAN
955 American Lane, Schaumburg IL 60173. 847/517-5600. **Contact:** Human Resources. **World Wide Web address:** http://www.experian.com. **Description:** Maintains credit reports and provides information services for the real estate industry. **NOTE:** Send resumes to: Experian, Human Resources Department, 475 Anton Boulevard, Building D, Costa Mesa CA 92626. Resumes may also be faxed to 714/830-2444. **Positions advertised include:** Information Security Operations Analysts; Technical Support Representative; Client Integration Services Analyst; Senior Business Analyst, Custom/Hosted Database Solutions. **Other U.S. locations:** Nationwide.

FRY, INC.
740 Pasquinelli Drive, Suite 100, Westmont IL 60559. 630/850-9144. **Toll-free phone:** 800/FRY-6858. **Fax:** 630/850-8043. **Contact:** Human Resources. **World Wide Web address:** http://www.fry.com. **Description:** Fry, Inc. designs, develops, and manages high scale ebusiness brands, applications, and systems. Fry was one of the first companies to offer ecommerce, branding sites, and extranets to its clients. **Positions advertised include:** Account Director; Director of Business Development; E-commerce Project Manager; Office Manager; Proposal Writer. **Corporate headquarters location:** Ann Arbor MI. **Other U.S. locations:** New York NY.

GREAT LAKES MAINTENANCE & SECURITY CORPORATION
8734 South Cottage Grove, Suite 200, Chicago IL 60619-6924. 773/994-1899. **Contact:** Human Resources. **Description:** Provides maintenance, cleaning, and security guard services.

LANTER DELIVERY SYSTEMS
One Caine Drive, Madison IL 62060 618/452-5300x257. **Fax:** 618/452-5931. 305B South Lee, Bloomington IL 61701. 309/828-5383. **Contact:** Human Resources. **World Wide Web address:** http://www.lanterdeliverysystems.com. **Description:** A chain of courier companies located in the Midwest providing delivery service throughout the United States and Canada. **Corporate headquarters location:** Madison WI. **Other U.S. locations:** KS; GA; IN; KY.

LEXISNEXIS
70 West Madison, 22nd Floor, Chicago IL 60602. 312/236-7903. **Contact:** Human Resources. **E-mail address:** Employment.HR@lexisnexis.com. **World Wide Web address:** http://www.lexisnexis.com. **Description:** Offers searching, filing, and retrieval services for law firms and financial organizations. This facility provides document service and storage for the Midwest region. **NOTE:** Apply online.

McCOY SECURITY, INC.
20 East Jackson, Suite 1400, Chicago IL 60604. 312/322-4900. **Fax:** 312/322-0078. **Contact:** Personnel Manager. **E-mail address:** jobs@mccoysecurity.com. **World Wide Web address:** http://www.mccoysecurity.com. **Description:** A security firm providing primarily unarmed guards and patrolmen in the greater Chicago area. **NOTE:** Call or an appointment, e-mail resume or complete the online application.

MERRILL LYNCH RETIREMENT GROUP
300 South Wacker Drive, Suite 2600, Chicago IL 60606. 312/697-1040. **Contact:** Human Resources. **World Wide Web address:** http://www.ml.com. **Description:** Specializes in employee benefits consulting on a national basis for over 30 years. **NOTE:** See website for job listings and apply online. **Corporate headquarters location:** New York NY. **Other U.S. locations:** San Francisco CA; Seattle WA. **Operations at this facility include:** Divisional Headquarters.

NORTH CENTRAL REGIONAL EDUCATIONAL LAB INC.
1120 East Diehl Road, Suite 200, Naperville IL 60563. 630/649-6500. **Contact:** Human Resources. **E-mail address:** jobs@learningpt.org. **World Wide Web address:** http://www.ncrel.org. **Description:** A nonprofit organization that promotes education by providing information access through research-based resources to teachers, parents, students, and policymakers. Founded in 1984. **NOTE:** For job listings, visit http://www.learningpt.org/employ/. **Positions advertised include:** Applied Research and Development Director; Program Specialist; Senior Research Associate; Program Associate.

OFFICEMAX INC.
150 East Pierce Road, Itasca IL 60143. 630/438-7800. **Contact:** Human Resources. **World Wide Web address:** http://www.officemax.com. **Description:** A business-to-business distributor of office and computer supplies, furniture, paper products, and promotional products. Founded in 1964. **NOTE:** Apply online. **International locations:** Australia; Canada; United Kingdom; France; Germany; Spain. **Corporate headquarters location:** This location. **Listed on:** New York Stock Exchange. **Stock exchange symbol:** OMX.

SCOTTISH DEVELOPMENT INTERNATIONAL
1020 31st Street, Lower Level 20, Downers Grove IL. 60515. 630/968-6555. **Contact:** Human Resources Department. **World Wide Web address:** http://www.scottishdevelopmentinternational.com. **Description:** A nonprofit, economic development agency for the British government engaged in attracting new business to Scotland.

SERVICEMASTER COMPANY
3250 Lacey Road, Suite 600, Downers Grove IL 60515. 630/663-2000. **Fax:** 901/766-1157. **Contact:** Gina DePompei, People Services Director. **E-mail address:** careers@servicemaster.com. **World Wide Web address:** http://www.servicemaster.com. **Description:** A housekeeping, maintenance, and management company that provides services to residential, commercial, educational, industrial, and health care facilities in 50 states, Washington DC, and 15 foreign countries. Other services include lawn care (through TruGreen and ChemLawn), cleaning and restoration, pest control, radon testing, and child care. **NOTE:** E-mail or fax resumes to the attention of Corporate People Services – Careers. Resumes may also be mailed to the Corporate People Services – Careers' office at ServiceMaster Consumer Services, 860 Ridge Lake Boulevard, Suite AL-1099, Memphis TN 38120. **Corporate headquarters location:** This location. **Listed on:** New York Stock Exchange. **Stock exchange symbol:** SVM.

SIEMENS BUSINESS SERVICES
3041 Woodcreek Drive, Suite 100, Downers Grove IL 60515. 630/724-8000. **Fax:** 630/336-1222. **Contact:** Recruiter. **E-mail address:** careers@sbs.siemens.com. **World Wide Web address:** http://www.sbs-usa.siemens.com. **Description:** Provides systems integration services and resells software. **NOTE:** See website for job listings.

SMITH, BUCKLIN AND ASSOCIATES
401 North Michigan Avenue, Suite 2200, Chicago IL 60611. 312/644-6610. **Fax:** 312/673-6580. **Contact:** Human Resources. **E-mail address:** ChicagoHR@smithbucklin.com. **World Wide Web address:** http://www.smithbucklin.com. **Description:** Provides daily management services for nonprofit organizations worldwide and for full-service and contract clients.

TOPCO ASSOCIATES, INC.
7711 Gross Point Road, Skokie IL 60077. 847/676-3030. **Fax:** 847/329-3621. **Contact:** Dennis Pieper, Human Resources Manager. **E-mail address:** dpieper@topco.com. **World Wide Web address:** http://www.topco.com. **Description:** A leader in private label procurement and brand management for the supermarket and food service industries. The company specializes in procuring, packaging, and distributing corporate brands, perishables, and pharmaceutical products. **NOTE:** Fax or e-mail resumes to Mr. Pieper. **Corporate headquarters location:** This location. **Other U.S. locations:** Visalia CA; Lakeland FL. **Listed on:** Privately held.

Indiana

LOOMIS FARGO
122 North College Avenue, Indianapolis IN 46202. 317/632-3421. **Fax:** 317/955-1278. **Contact:** Human Resources. **World Wide Web address:** www.loomisfargo.com. **Description:** An armored car service specializing in transporting currency. **Other U.S. locations:** Nationwide.

MAGNUM SECURITY SERVICES
601 South Bend Avenue, South Bend IN 46617. 574/232-9653. **Contact:** Human Resources. **Description:** Provides security guards and other security personnel for commercial establishments.

MOODY'S KMV
130 South Main Street, Suite 300, South Bend IN 46601. 574/472-5700. **Toll-free phone:** 800/523-2627. **Fax:** 574/245-7670. **E-mail address:** resumes@mkmv.com. **World Wide Web address:** http://www.moodyskmv.com. **Description:** Provider of quantitative credit analysis tools to lenders, investors, and corporations. **Positions advertised include:** Advisory Services Associate; Application Support Engineer; Global Client Services Associate; Quality Assurance Engineer; Senior Software Engineer. **Other U.S. locations:** CA; NY. **International locations:** Tokyo, Japan; London, UK; Relgate, UK.

NATIONAL ASSOCIATION OF THE SELF-EMPLOYED
8610 East 106th Street, Suite 200, Fishers IN 46038. 317/571-0307. **Contact:** Human Resources. **World**

Wide Web address: http://www.nase.org. **Description:** A professional association that offers members a wide range of services including group hospitalization insurance.

SECURITAS USA
4265 Counselors Road, Indianapolis IN 46240. 317/569-1149. **Contact:** Human Resources. **World Wide Web address:** http://www.securitasinc.com. **Description:** Offers a wide range of protective services and contract security guard programs to businesses and government. **Other U.S. locations:** Nationwide

TELESERVICES DIRECT
6050 Corporate Way, Indianapolis IN 46278. 317/216-2240. **Fax:** 317/216-2248. **Contact:** Human Resources. **E-mail address:** jobs@teleservicesdirect.com. **World Wide Web address:** http://www.teleservicesdirect.com. **Description:** Providers of outsourced telemarketing solutions. **NOTE:** Search and apply for positions online. **Positions advertised include:** Call Center Team Leader; Senior Account Executive. Corporate headquarters location: This location.

WALKER INFORMATION
3939 Priority Way South Drive, Indianapolis IN 46240. 317/843-3939. **Fax:** 317/843-8584. **Contact:** Human Resources. **E-mail address:** walkerhr@walkerinfo.com. **World Wide Web address:** http://www.walkerinfo.com. **Description:** Provides marketing research and data collection for clients. Walker Information collects data from its clients' customers using the Internet, paper questionnaires, and telephone interviewing. Founded in 1939. **NOTE:** Entry-level positions are offered. **Special programs:** Internships. **Corporate headquarters location:** This location. **International locations:** Hamburg, Germany; Toronto, Canada. **Listed on:** Privately held.

Kentucky

ACS
1084 South Laurel Road, London KY 40744. 606/878-7900. **Contact:** Human Resources. **World Wide Web address:** http://www.acs-inc.com. **Description:** Affiliated Computer Services, Incorporated provides business process and information technology outsourcing solutions to a wide range of clients. **Positions advertised include:** Data Entry Operator; Software Developer. **Special programs:** Internships; Training; Career Development Program. **Corporate headquarters location:** Dallas TX. **Other area locations:** Lexington KY; Liberty KY; Louisville KY; Pikeville KY; Richmond KY. **Other U.S. locations:** Nationwide. **International locations:** Worldwide. **Sales/revenues:** $5 billion. **Number of employees worldwide:** Over 55,000.

AUTOMATIC DATA PROCESSING, INC. (ADP)
13425 Eastpoint Center Drive, Suite 124, Louisville KY 40223. 859/971-9696. **Contact:** Sales Manager. **World Wide Web address:** http://www.adp.com. **Description:** Provides computerized transaction processing, data communications, and information services through its four primary businesses. This location is the head office for the Employer Services Division which provides payroll processing, payroll tax filing, job costing, labor distribution, automated bill payment, management reports, unemployment compensation management, human resource information, and benefits administration support to over 300,000 businesses. Other divisions include Claims, Dealer, and Brokerage Services. **Positions advertised include:** Business Analyst; HRIS Implementation Consultant; Major Account Sales Representative. **Special programs:** Tuition Reimbursement Program; Scholarship Program; Internships. **Corporate headquarters location:** Roseland NJ. **Other area locations:** Elk Grove KY; Florence KY. **Other U.S. locations:** Nationwide. **Listed on:** New York Stock Exchange. **Stock exchange symbol:** ADP. **Sales/revenues:** $8.5 billion. **Number of employees nationwide:** 25,000. **Number of employees worldwide:** Over 40,000.

CONCORD CUSTOM CLEANERS
P.O. Box 55910, Lexington KY 40555-5910. 859/422-4800. **Physical address:** 1850 Bryant Road, Suite 400, Lexington KY 40509. **Fax:** 859/422-4801. **Contact:** Human Resources. **E-mail address:** info@concordcustomcleaners.com. **World Wide Web address:** http://www.concordcustomcleaners.com. **Description:** A retail chain of dry cleaning stores that operates 120 locations across the U.S. Founded in 1957. **Corporate headquarters location:** This location. **Other U.S. locations:** Nationwide.

HK SYSTEMS INC.
2100 Litton Lane, Hebron KY 41048. 859/334-3400. **Fax:** 859/334-2329. **Contact:** Human Resources. **E-mail address:** hr.mke@hksystems.com. **World Wide Web address:** http://www.hksystems.com. **Description:** The company develops, implements and supports integrated solutions for the management of enterprise-wide inventory, distribution, logistics management and automated material handling systems. HK Systems also manufactures automated guided vehicles, automated storage and retrieval machines, conveyors, palletizers, and sortation equipment. **Corporate headquarters location:** New Berlin WI. **Other U.S. locations:** Bountiful UT; Salt Lake City UT; Montgomery AL; Charlotte NC; Duluth GA; Gainsville GA; Grapevine TX; Novi MI; St. Louis MO. **International locations:** Mississauga, Ontario, Canada. **Subsidiaries include:** Irista. **Sales/revenues:** $250 million. **Number of employees worldwide:** 1,200.

Maine

CANTEEN SERVICES COMPANY
P.O. Box 895, Bangor ME 04402-0895. 207/945-5688. **Physical address:** 244 Perry Road, Bangor ME 04401. **Toll-free phone:** 800/432-7919. **Fax:** 207/947-3430. **Contact:** Human Resources Department. **E-mail address:** bangor@canteenmaine.com. **World Wide Web address:** http://www.canteenmaine.com. **Description:** Sells, rents, and services vending machines. Canteen Services Company also offers catering and office coffee services. **Other area locations:** Saco ME; Lewiston ME.

CRITICAL INSIGHTS
120 Exchange Street, Portland ME 04101. 207/772-4011. **Fax:** 207/772-7027. **Contact:** Nancy Harman. **E-mail address:** insights@criticalinsights.com. **World Wide Web address:** http://www.criticalinsights.com. **Description:** A strategic market and public opinion research firm. **NOTE:** Reach listed contact at 207/780-8096. **Positions advertised include:** Day/Evening Interviewer.

DRESSER & ASSOCIATES
243 Route 1, Scarborough ME 04074. 207/885-0809. **Toll-free phone:** 866/885-7212. **Fax:** 207/885-0816. **Contact:** Human Resources. **E-mail address:** mfdresser@dresserassociates.com. **World Wide Web address:** http://www.dresserassociates.com. **Description:** An operational management and performance consultancy. **NOTE:** Search posted openings on-line; respond by e-mail. **Positions advertised include:** Inside Sales Representative; Account Executive; Software Implementation Consultant.

MCBEE/DELUX
1321 Washington Avenue, Portland ME 04103. 207/797-5908. **Fax:** 207/797-0312. **Toll-free phone:** 800/662-2331. **Contact:** Rebecca Doman, Human Resources. **E-mail address:** info@mcbeeinc.com. **World Wide Web address:** http://www.mcbeeinc.com. **Description:** Produces specialized business forms including check and payroll forms. Founded 1908. **Positions advertised include:** Sales Representative. **Corporate headquarters location:** Thorofare NJ. **Parent company:** Delux Checks.

Maryland

ABS CONSULTING
4 Research Place, Suite 200A, Rockville MD 20850. 301/907-9100. **Contact:** Human Resources. **E-mail address:** ABSGRPEMP@eagle.org. **World Wide Web address:** http://www.absconsulting.com. **Description:** Provides consulting services to clients in the education, industrial, government, transportation, healthcare, and finance industries. **Special programs:** Tuition Reimbursement Program. **Corporate headquarters location:** Houston TX. **Other U.S. locations:** Nationwide. **International locations:** Worldwide. **Subsidiaries include:** ABS Group, Incorporated; EQE International, Incorporated. **President:** Christopher J. Wiernicki. **Sales/revenues:** Over $130 million. **Number of employees worldwide:** Over 1,100.

ADP
401 North Washington Street, Suite 200, Rockville MD 20850. 301/296-7000. **Toll-free phone:** 800/205-8881. **Fax:** 301/296-7017. **Contact:** Human Resources. **World Wide Web address:** http://www.adpims.com. **Description:** Provides transaction processing and information-based business services. **NOTE:** Apply online. **Positions advertised include:** Controller Regional Business Unit; Director, Product Marketing; Major Accounts Outside Sales Representative; Technical Editor Associate; Administrative Assistant. **Corporate headquarters location:** Roseland NJ. **Other U.S. locations:** Lake Mary FL; Honolulu HI; Westmont IL; Norristown PA. **Listed on:** New York Stock Exchange. **Stock exchange symbol:** ADP. **Sales/revenues:** Over $6 billion.

AON CONSULTING
10451 Mill Run Circle, Owings Mills MD 21117. 410/363-5500. **Fax:** 410/363-5697. **Contact:** Human Resources Director. **World Wide Web address:** http://www.aon.com. **Description:** Aon is an international human resources consulting and benefits brokerage firm providing integrated advisory and support services in retirement planning, health care management, organizational effectiveness, compensation, human resources-related communications, and information technologies. **Positions advertised include:** Plant Manager. **Corporate headquarters location:** Chicago IL. **Other area locations:** Baltimore MD. **Other U.S. locations:** Nationwide. **International locations:** Worldwide. **Listed on:** New York Stock Exchange. **Stock exchange symbol:** AOC. **CEO/Chairman:** Patrick G. Ryan. **Sales/revenues:** Over $8 billion. **Number of employees worldwide:** Over 53,000.

BOOZ ALLEN HAMILTON
201 North Charles Street, Suite 1201, Baltimore MD 21201. 410/752-4400. **Fax:** 410/752-2543. **Contact:** Human Resources. **World Wide Web address:** http://www.boozallen.com. **Description:** A strategy and technology consulting firm serving Fortune 500 companies and government agencies. Founded in 1914. **NOTE:** Search and apply for positions online. If mailing resume, send to: Booz Allen Hamilton, 8283 Greensboro Drive, McLean VA 22102-3838. **Positions advertised include:** Chemical Biological Defense Expert; Sr. Cost Analyst; Electrical Technical Advisor; Information System Security Engineer; Mechanical Engineer; Network Performance Analysis Team Lead; Oracle Database Developer/Administrator; Remote Systems Administrator. **Corporate headquarters location:** McLean VA. **Number of employees worldwide:** 17,000.

CANTEEN VENDING SERVICE
4501 Auth Place, Suitland MD 20746. 301/702-1267. **Toll-free phone:** 800/357-0012. **Fax:** 301/702-1984. **E-mail address:** randy.morris@each.compass-usa.com. **Contact:** Carlson Knight, Human Resources. **World Wide Web address:** http://www.canteen-usa.com. **Description:** Operates a food and vending service, as well as several cafeterias. **Positions advertised include:** Branch Manager; Customer Service Manager; Supervisor; Route Driver. **Parent company:** Compass Group (also at this location) is a national contract food service management firm, serving 10,000 clients across the United States and in Canada. The three principal operating divisions of Service America are Dining Services, which concentrates on Corporate America; Vending Services, one of the largest vending machine operators in the country with over 60,000 units; and Recreation Services, which provides food for convention centers, sports arenas, and performing arts centers.

DALE CARNEGIE TRAINING
11140 Rockville Pike, Suite 650, Rockville MD 20852. 301/770-2444. **Contact:** Personnel. **E-mail address:** Carla_lee@dalecarnegie.com. **World Wide Web address:** http://www.washingtondc.dalecarnegie.com. **Description:** A professional services institute offering training for sales people in the areas of motivation, time management, and leadership. Founded in 1912. **Corporate headquarters location:** New York NY.

FAIR, ISAAC AND CO., INC.
8140 Corporate Drive, Suite 200, Baltimore MD 21236. 410/931-7800. **Fax:** 410/931-7801. **Contact:** Human Resources. **E-mail address:** info@fairisaac.com. **World Wide Web address:** http://www.fairisaac.com. **Description:** Provides consulting services to financial institutions, service organizations, and government support institutions. Services include statistical analysis, database development and reporting, and actuarial management of customer portfolios through software decision support systems. **Positions advertised include:** Business Risk Consulting Director; Business Risk Consulting Manager. **Special programs:** Tuition Reimbursement Program. **Corporate headquarters location:** San Rafael CA. **Other U.S. locations:** Nationwide. **International locations:** Worldwide. **Subsidiaries include:** Nykamp Consulting Group, Incorporated; Prevision; Risk Management Technologies; Credit and Risk Management Associates. **Listed on:** New York Stock Exchange. **Stock exchange symbol:** FIC. **CEO:** Thomas G. Grudnowski.

GREATER BALTIMORE ALLIANCE
111 South Calvert Street, Suite 2220, Baltimore MD 21202-6180. 410/468-0100. **Toll-free phone:** 888/298-4322. **Fax:** 410/468-3383. **Contact:** Director. **E-mail address:** info@greaterbaltimore.org. **World Wide Web address:** http://www.greaterbaltimore.org. **Description:** A nonprofit, regional, economic development corporation. The organization provides services to employers moving to the greater Baltimore area and works to improve existing regional businesses. **Corporate headquarters location:**. This location. **President/CEO:** Ioanna T. Morfeissis.

LANIER WORLDWIDE, INC.
300 Red Brook Boulevard, Suite 110, Owings Mills MD 21117. 443/394-6064. **Fax:** 443/394-6068. **Contact:** Bridgette Black. **E-mail address:** bblack@lanier.com. **World Wide Web address:** http://www.lanier.com. **Description:** A business services company that provides document management solutions. **Positions advertised include:** Collections Supervisor; Commercial Sales Representative; Senior Operations Analyst. **Corporate headquarters location:** Atlanta GA. **Other U.S. locations:** Nationwide. **International locations:** Worldwide. **President and CEO:** Nori Goto.

LOCKHEED MARTIN ASPEN SYSTEMS
2277 Research Boulevard, Rockville MD 20850. 301/519-5000. **Fax:** 301/330-8946. **Contact:** Human Resources. **World Wide Web address:** http://www.aspensys.com. **Description:** Provides a broad range of analytical, technical, and information support services in the energy, environment, health, housing, education, justice, and legal services fields. These support services reach both the private and public sectors at the national, regional, state, and local levels. Founded in 1970. **Special programs:** Training; Tuition Reimbursement Program; Scholarship Opportunities. **Subsidiaries include:** Hunter Medical,

Incorporated; StaffXpress. **President:** Al Lampert. **Number of employees nationwide:** Over 1,600.

MASTER SECURITY INC.
10944-D Beaver Dam Road, Hunt Valley MD 21030. 410/584-8789. **Contact:** Human Resources. **E-mail address:** hr@mastersecurity.us. **World Wide Web address:** http://www.mastersecurity.us. **Description:** Provides security guards for malls and private buildings including apartments and corporate offices.

NEWROADS, INC.
2 North Maple Avenue, Ridgely MD 21660. 410/634-2060. **Contact:** Human Resources. **E-mail address:** info@newroads.com. **World Wide Web address:** http://www.newroads.com. **Description:** Provides outsourced operations solutions to companies engaged in one-to-one direct commerce. **Corporate headquarters location:** Charlotte NC.

PROFESSIONAL MAILING AND DISTRIBUTION SERVICES (PMDS)
9050 Junction Drive, Annapolis Junction MD 20701-1150. 301/604-3305. **Fax:** 301/953-2838. **Contact:** Human Resources. **E-mail address:** info@pmds.com. **World Wide Web address:** http://www.pmds.com. **Description:** PMDS offers complete turnkey services that include publications and subscription processing; membership database maintenance; meeting registration and planning; automated mailing services; and additional support services. The company's client base is composed of membership associations and nonprofit organizations. **NOTE:** Entry-level positions are offered. **Corporate headquarters location:** This location. **Listed on:** Privately held. **President:** Rita Hope Counts. **Number of employees at this location:** Over 200.

Massachusetts

AM-PM CLEANING CORPORATION
1560 Trapelo Road, Waltham MA 02451. 781/622-1444. **Contact:** Human Resources. **Description:** Provides cleaning and maintenance service. **NOTE:** Entry-level positions and part-time jobs are offered. **Company slogan:** Maintaining an atmosphere of excellence. **Corporate headquarters location:** This location. **General Manager:** J. Kenneth Fosealdo. **Sales Manager:** Karen Perkins. **Annual sales/revenues:** $11 - $20 million. **Number of employees at this location:** 650.

ARAMARK UNIFORM SERVICES
P.O. Box 568, Lawrence MA 01842. 978/685-1936. **Physical Address:** 110 Glenn Street, Lawrence MA 01843. **Contact:** Human Resources. **World Wide Web address:** http://www.aramark-uniform.com. **Description:** Offers uniforms to reinforce corporate identities or to meet specialized demands for static control and flame resistance. The company also provides a variety of products including walk-off mats, cleaning cloths, disposable towels, and other environmental control items. **Parent company:** ARAMARK (Philadelphia PA) is one of the world's leading providers of managed services. The company operates in all 50 states and 10 foreign countries, offering a broad range of services to businesses of all sizes including many *Fortune* 500 companies and thousands of universities, hospitals, and municipal, state, and federal government facilities. The company is employee-owned.

AUTOMATIC DATA PROCESSING (ADP)
225 Second Avenue, Waltham MA 02454. 781/890-2500. **Contact:** Human Resources. **World Wide Web address:** http://www.adp.com. **Description:** A data processing and computing services firm that provides commercial services such as payroll, accounts receivable, accounts payable, financial statement preparation, tax services, and unemployment compensation management; financial services including general and specialized management oriented online services to major corporations, large financial institutions, and the government; dealer services in the auto, truck, and industrial equipment trade; collision estimating services; and pension services. **Positions advertised include:** Call Center Analyst; Area Trainer; Division Technologist; TotalSource Sales Associate. **Corporate headquarters location:** Roseland NJ. **Operations at this facility include:** Service. **Listed on:** New York Stock Exchange. **Stock exchange symbol:** ADP.

CASS INFORMATION SYSTEMS, INC.
900 Chelmsford Street, Lowell MA 01851. 978/446-0101. **Fax:** 978/323-6624. **Contact:** Human Resources. **E-mail address:** humanresourcesbos@cassinfo.com. **World Wide Web address:** http://www.cassinfo.com. **Description:** Cass Information Services is a provider of information services. These logistics-related services include the processing and payment of freight charges, preparation of transportation management reports, auditing of freight charges, and rating of freight shipments. Cass Information Systems operations are divided between its Payment Systems Group and its Software Systems Group. **NOTE:** Jobseekers should send resumes to: Human Resources, 900 Chelmsford Street, Lowell MA 01851-8101. **Subsidiaries include:** Cass Bank & Trust is a bank that provides a full range of banking services to individual, corporate, and institutional customers. **Parent company:** Cass Commercial Corporation. **Other U.S. locations:** Bridgeton MO; Columbus OH. **Operations at this facility include:** This location operates as part of the Payment Systems Group. **Listed on:** NASDAQ. **Stock exchange symbol:** CASS.

DUN & BRADSTREET, INC.
1800 West Park Drive, Suite 300, Westborough MA 01581. 508/871-8000. **Contact:** Human Resources. **E-mail address:** hrsourcing@dnb.com. **World Wide Web address:** http://www.dnb.com. **Description:** Provides business-to-business credit, marketing, and investment management services. **Corporate headquarters location:** Short Hills NJ. **Parent company:** The Dun & Bradstreet Corporation. **Listed on:** New York Stock Exchange. **Stock exchange symbol:** DNB. **CEO:** Allan Loren. **Number of employees worldwide:** 9,000.

FORRESTER RESEARCH
400 Technology Square, Cambridge MA 02139. 617/497-7090. **Contact:** Human Resources. **World Wide Web address:** http://www.forrester.com. **Description:** An independent research firm that provides technology consulting services to business. **Positions advertised include:** Corporate Communication Manager; Editing Manager; Web Developer; Client Care Specialist; Financial Services Analyst; Research Advisor; Healthcare Analyst; Sales Associate; Healthcare Associate; Applications Analyst; Business Development Director; Account Executive; Research Associate. **Corporate headquarters location:** This location. **Other U.S. locations:** San Francisco CA. **International locations:** England; Germany; The Netherlands. **Listed on:** NASDAQ. **Stock exchange symbol:** FORR.

IRON MOUNTAIN INC.
745 Atlantic Avenue, Boston MA 02111. 617/357-4455. **Fax:** 617/ **Contact:** Human Resources. **Fax:** 617/368-9117. **E-mail address:** jobs@ironmountain.com. **World Wide Web address:** http://www.ironmountain.com. **Description:** One of the nation's largest record management companies. Iron Mountain provides businesses with storage facilities for their records. **Positions advertised include:** Software Engineer; Security Administrator; Labor Relations Manager; Systems Engineer; Quality Assurance Manager. **Corporate headquarters location:** This location. **Other U.S. locations:** Nationwide. **Listed on:** NASDAQ. **Stock exchange symbol:** IRM.

MAIL COMPUTER SERVICE INC. (MCS)
321 Manly Street, West Bridgewater MA 02379. 508/584-6490. **Fax:** 508/584-2890. **Contact:** Human Resources. **World Wide Web address:** http://www.mailcompserv.com. **Description:** A full-service mail house. Mail Computer Service Inc.'s mass-

mailing services include data processing, mail processing, digitizing, lasering, and printing. **Positions advertised include:** Client Service Account Manager.

MAINTENANCE CHEMICAL SUPPLIERS INC.
135 Oak Hill Way, Brockton MA 02301. 508/436-7624. **Fax:** 508/436-7630. **Contact:** Human Resources. **World Wide Web address:** http://www.mcs1.com. **Description:** Provides maintenance and janitorial services. The company is also involved in the direct sale of industrial chemical products. **Corporate headquarters location:** This location.

MASS BUYING POWER (MBP)
1076 Washington Street, Hanover MA 02339. 781/829-4900. **Contact:** Human Resources. **E-mail address:** massbuy@massbuy.com. **World Wide Web address:** http://www.massbuy.com. **Description:** Provides discount purchasing benefits for employees of member companies. Mass Buying Power offers discounts on a wide variety of products and services including automobiles, major household appliances, furniture, consumer loans, and home improvements. Mass Buying Power also operates a full-service travel agency specializing in discount travel packages. Founded in 1967. **Corporate headquarters location:** This location. **Listed on:** Privately held.

McGRAW-HILL COMPANIES, INC.
24 Hartwell Avenue, Lexington MA 02421. 781/863-5100. **Contact:** Human Resources. **World Wide Web address:** http://www.mcgraw-hill.com. **Description:** McGraw-Hill Companies, Inc. provides computer-accessible economic information, models, forecasts, analyses, software, and consulting services to clients in industry, government, and business. **Positions advertised include:** Business Development Manager. **Corporate headquarters location:** New York NY. **Other area locations:** Boston MA. **Listed on:** New York Stock Exchange. **Stock exchange symbol:** MHP.

MILHENCH SUPPLY COMPANY
121 Duchaine Road, New Bedford MA 02745. 508/995-8331. **Toll-free phone:** 800/642-7570. **Fax:** 508/995-4187. **Contact:** Human Resources. **World Wide Web address:** http://www.milhench.com. **Description:** A supplier of janitorial & maintenance, industrial packaging, safety & material handling & storage supplies.

SECURITAS USA
One Harborside Drive, Boston MA 02128. 617/568-8700. **Contact:** Human Resources. **World Wide Web address:** http://www.securitasusa.com. **Description:** A contract security agency providing uniformed security officers, investigative services, and security system installation.

UNITED RENTALS
133 Southampton Street, Boston MA 02118. 617/445-6750. **Contact:** Human Resources. **E-mail address:** careerinfo@ur.com. **World Wide Web address:** http://www.unitedrentals.com. **Description:** Rents construction equipment and supplies. **Positions advertised include:** District Manager. **Corporate headquarters locations:** Greenwich CT. **Other U.S. locations:** Nationwide. **Listed on:** NYSE. **Stock exchange symbol:** URI.

WSI CORPORATION
400 Minuteman Road, Andover MA 01810. 978/983-6300. **Fax:** 978/983-6406. **Contact:** Human Resources. **E-mail address:** jobs@wsi.com. **World Wide Web address:** http://www.wsi.com. **Description:** Provides weather-driven business solutions for professionals in the aviation, media and energy markets, and multiple federal and state government agencies. **Positions advertised include:** Sr. Software Engineer; Director/Senior Product Manager; Media Design Specialist; On-Air Graphic and Application Specialist; Sr. Automation SQA Engineer; Business Aviation Product Manager; Airline Product Manager. **Parent company:** Landmark Communications.

WORKSCAPE
123 Felton Street, Marlborough MA 01752. 508/573-9000. **Toll-free phone:** 888/605-9620. **Fax:** 508/573-9500. **Contact:** Human Resources. **E-mail address:** hr@workscape.com. **World Wide Web address:** http://www.workscape.com. **Description:** Workscape provides a full range of outsourced HR solutions including benefits administration, compensation management, performance management, employee self-service and manager self-service, as well as an employee portal. **Positions advertised include:** Business Analyst; Development Project Manager; Database Developer; Perl Programmer/Production Control Engineer; Principal Software Engineer; Sales/Marketing Assistant; Senior Software Engineer; Service Manager; Solutions Consultant. **Corporate headquarters location:** This location.

YANKEE GROUP
31 St. James Avenue, Boston MA 02116-4114. 617/956-5000. **Contact:** Human Resources. **World Wide Web address:** http://www.yankeegroup.com. **Description:** A business consulting firm specializing in telecommunications and wireless/mobile communications; IT hardware, software and services; consumer technologies, media and entertainment. Founded in 1970. **Positions advertised include:** Staff Accountant; Human Resources Generalist; Associate Account Executive; Business Development Associate.

Michigan

AUTOMATIC DATA PROCESSING (ADP)
175 Jackson Plaza, Ann Arbor MI 48106. 734/769-6800. **Contact:** Human Resources. **World Wide Web address:** http://www.adp.com. **Description:** A computer software and data processing firm specializing in software development, sales, and support; remote computing services; and telecommunications. There are four divisions of Automatic Data Processing at this location: Automotive Claims Services; Dealer Services; Interactive Personnel and Payroll; and Network Services-Division Headquarters. **Positions advertised include:** Autosource Service Representative; Technical Support Representative; Database Administrator; Internet Administrator. **Corporate headquarters location:** Roseland NJ. **Other U.S. locations:** Nationwide. **International locations:** Worldwide. **Operations at this facility include:** Divisional Headquarters; Service. **Listed on:** New York Stock Exchange. **Stock exchange symbol:** ADP. **Number of employees worldwide:** Over 40,000.

HHA SERVICES
22622 Harper Avenue, St. Clair Shores MI 48080. 586/771-3040. **Toll-free phone:** 800/442-1140. **Fax:** 810/771-3044. **Contact:** Jennifer Feddersen, Recruiting Manager. **E-mail address:** jfeddersen@hhaservices.com. **World Wide Web address:** http://www.hhaservices.com. **Description:** Offers contract services for maintenance, food service, transportation, security, clinical engineering, housekeeping, laundry, and linen supply. Founded in 1974. **Positions advertised include:** Regional Director of Sales; Regional Director of Operations; Director of Facilities Management; Senior Area Manager; Director of Environmental Services/Housekeeping. **Special programs:** Training; Tuition Reimbursement Program; Relocation Assistance Program. **Corporate headquarters location:** This location. **Other U.S. locations:** Austin TX. **Listed on:** Privately held.

JANI-KING OF MICHIGAN, INC.
27777 Franklin Road, Suite 900, Southfield MI 48034. 248/936-0040. **Fax:** 248/936-0049. **Contact:** Tracy Greene, Human Resources. **E-mail address:** detops-5-25-04@janiking.net. **World Wide Web address:** http://www.janiking.com. **Description:** A commercial cleaning franchise company. **Positions advertised include:** Operations Manager. **Corporate headquarters:** Addison TX. **Parent company:** Jani-King International.

METRO PLANT SERVICES
19648 Purlington Street, Livonia MI 48152. 248/426-3000. **Contact:** Human Resources. **E-mail address:** mpfflorist@aol.com. **Description:** Provides houseplants and offers related interior plant arrangement services. Metro Plant Services' facilities include greenhouses.

MINNESOTA

AMERIPRIDE SERVICES
10801 Wayzata Boulevard, Minnetonka MN 55305. 612/738-4200. **Fax:** 952-738-3169. **Contact:** Jeremiah Munson, Human Resources. **E-mail address:** jeremiah.munson@ameripride.org. **World Wide Web address:** http://www.ameripride.com. **Description:** A linen and uniform rental and supply company. **Other area locations:** Statewide. **Other U.S. locations:** Nationwide. **International locations:** Canada.

BOWNE & CO.
333 South 7th Street, Suite 2110, Minneapolis MN 55402. 612/330-0900. **Fax:** 612/330-0930. **Contact:** Human Resources. **World Wide Web address:** http://www.bowne.com. **Description:** The company offers services to create, manage, translate, and distribute transactional and compliance-related documents. **Corporate headquarters location:** New York NY. **Operations at this facility include:** Bowne Financial Print.

DATA RECOGNITION CORPORATION
13490 Bass Lake Road, Maple Grove MN 55311. 763/268-2000. **Contact:** Human Resources. **E-mail address:** resumes@datarecognitioncorp. **World Wide Web address:** http://www.datarecognitioncorp.com. **Description:** Processes educational tests and surveys. **NOTE:** See website for current job openings. Submit resume by e-mail. Entry-level positions and second and third shifts are offered. **Positions advertised include:** Inserter Operator; Bindery Operator; Business Development Consultant; Associate Software Developer; Senior Software Developer; Quality Assurance Analyst; Test Development Specialist. **Special programs:** Internships. **Corporate headquarters location:** This location. **Listed on:** Privately held. **Number of employees at this location:** 150.

FAIR ISAAC CORPORATION
901 Marquette Avenue, Suite 3200, Minneapolis MN 55402-3232. 612/758-5200. **Fax:** 612/758-5201. **Contact:** Human Resources. **World Wide Web address:** http://www.fairisaac.com. **Description:** Fair Isaac Corporation, along with its subsidiaries, provides analytic, software and data management products and services to automate and improve decisions. The company operates in four segments: Strategy Machine Solutions, Scoring Solutions, Professional Services and Analytic Software Tools. The Scoring Solutions segment develops FICO scores that are used by credit card organizations, as well as mortgage and auto loan originators, to prescreen solicitation candidates to evaluate applicants for new credit and review existing accounts. Founded in 1956. **Corporate headquarter locations:** This location. **Listed on:** New York Stock Exchange. **Stock exchange symbol:** FIC. **Number of employees nationwide:** 3,000.

FUJITSU CONSULTING
110 Cheshire Lane, Minnetonka MN 55305. 952/258-6000. **Toll-free phone:** 877/446-2676. **Fax:** 952/258-6001. **Contact:** Human Resources. **World Wide Web address:** http://www.fujitsu.com/us. **Description:** A provider of management and technology consulting to business and government, Fujitsu Consulting is the North American consulting and services arm of Fujitsu. **Parent company:** Fujitsu Limited.

G&K SERVICES INC.
5995 Opus Parkway, Suite 500, Minnetonka MN 55343. 952/912-5500. **Contact:** Human Resources. **World Wide Web address:** http://www.gkcares.com. **Description:** A linen supply service. **Positions advertised include:** Marketing Analyst; Territory Sales Representative; Accounts Receivable Representative. **Corporate headquarters location:** This location. **Listed on:** NASDAQ. **Stock exchange symbol:** GKSRA.

GFK CUSTOM RESEARCH INC.
8401 Golden Valley Road, P.O. Box 27900, Minneapolis MN 55427-0900. 763/542-0800. **Fax:** 763/542-0864. **Contact:** Human Resources. **E-mail address:** hr@gfkcustomresearch.com. **World Wide Web address:** http://www.gfkcustomresearch.com. **Description:** A marketing research firm that consults with major corporations to meet business research information needs. **NOTE:** Submit resume by e-mail or mail. **Positions advertised include:** Senior Director, Account Management; Client Service Team Leader; Project Manager; Research Analyst; Technical Specialist; Research Designer; Qualitative Researcher; Analyst; Database Marketing Specialist. **Parent company:** Gfk.

HSBC FINANCE CORPORATION
10900 Wayzata Boulevard, Minnetonka MN 55305. 952/525-5020. **Contact:** Human Resources. **E-mail address: World Wide Web address:** http://www.hsbcusa.com. **Description:** HSBC Finance Corporation is the consumer finance arm of HSBC – North America, one of the top ten financial services organizations in the United States. The company's businesses serve more than 60 million customers in five key areas: personal financial services, consumer finance, commercial banking, private banking, and corporate investment banking and markets. **Parent company:** HSBC Holdings. **Operations at this facility include:** Credit Card Services.

I.C. SYSTEM
444 Highway 96 East, St. Paul MN 55127-2557. 651/481-6467. **Fax:** 651/481-6422. **Contact:** Human Resources. **E-mail address:** hr@icsystem.com. **World Wide Web address:** http://www.icsystem.com. **Description:** An accounts receivable/collections services management company founded in 1938. **Positions advertised include:** Account Executive; Developer; Operations Manager; SQL Database Administrator; Web Dialer Administrator. **Other U.S. locations:** Nationwide. **Number of employees:** 900.

MARSDEN BUILDING MAINTENANCE COMPANY
1717 University Avenue West, St. Paul MN 55104. 651/641-1717. **Fax:** 641/641-0523. **Contact:** Human Resources. **World Wide Web address:** http://www.marsden.com. **Description:** Provides contract janitorial services. **Corporate headquarters location:** This location. **Other area locations:** Hopkins MN; Rochester MN. **Other U.S. locations:** Des Moines IA; Omaha NE; Phoenix AZ; Stevens Point WI; Milwaukee WI; Madison WI; Green Bay WI; Sheboygan WI; Racine WI; Appleton WI.

QUESTAR DATA SYSTEMS, INC.
2905 West Service Road, Eagan MN 55121. 651/688-0089. **Toll-free phone:** 800/688-0126. **Fax:** 651/688-0546. **Contact:** Human Resources. **E-mail address:** careers@questarweb.com. **World Wide Web address:** http://www.questarweb.com. **Description:** A full-service survey research and consulting firm that works with clients to develop, conduct, and analyze surveys in the areas of public sector research, organizational consulting, and service quality research. **Positions advertised include:** Research Analyst; Senior SQL Developer/DBA; Programmer/Analyst – CEM; Senior Account Executive. **Corporate headquarters location:** This location.

SCICOM DATA SERVICES
10101 Bren Road East, Minnetonka MN 55343. 952/933-4200. **Toll-free phone:** 800/488-9087. **Contact:** Human Resources. **E-mail address:** info@scicom.com. **World Wide Web address:** http://www.scicom.com. **Description:** Provides document and mail processing services, marketing publication services, and information management.

SECURITAS SECURITY SERVICES
4000 Olson Memorial Highway, Suite 200, Golden Valley MN 55422. 763/287-3122. **Fax:** 763/287-3123. **Contact:** Branch Manager. **World Wide Web address:** http://www.securitasinc.com. **Description:** One of the world's largest suppliers of global, total security solutions. The company provides a broad array of security-related services to address the protection needs of more than 20,000 customers through 220 offices in the United States, Canada, Mexico, Europe, and Asia. **NOTE:** For Security Officer positions, contact the office. For all other positions, please visit website to search for jobs and apply online. **Corporate headquarters location:** Stockholm, Sweden. **Other area locations:** Duluth MN. **Other U.S. locations:** Nationwide. **International locations:** Worldwide. **Number of employees worldwide:** 200,000.

TOWERS PERRIN
8000 Norman Center Drive, Suite 1200, Minneapolis MN 55437-1097. 952/842-5600. **Contact:** Kathy Halverson, Office Administrator. **World Wide Web address:** http://www.towers.com. **Description:** A management consulting firm engaged in human resources, risk, and financial management, as well as reinsurance. **Positions advertised include:** Senior Retirement Consultant. **Corporate headquarters location:** Stamford CT. **Other U.S. locations:** Nationwide.

Mississippi
AFFILIATED COMPUTER SERVICES, INC.
2847 Virlilia Road, Flora MS 39071. 601/879-8211. **Contact:** Human Resources. **E-mail Address:** info@acs-inc.com. **World Wide Web address:** http://www.acs-inc.com. **Description:** Provides business process outsourcing (BPO) and information technology outsourcing (ITO). **Positions advertised include:** Business Systems Analyst; CSR Coordinator; Java Programmer; Business Analyst; Financial Analyst; Pharmacy Services Manager; System Engineer. **Corporate headquarters location:** Dallas TX. **Other area locations:** Ridgeland MS. **Listed on:** New York Stock Exchange. **Stock exchange symbol:** ACS.

CENTRAL SERVICE ASSOCIATION
93 South Coley Road, Tupelo MS 38801. 662/842-5962. **Fax:** 662/840-1329. **Contact:** Human Resources. **World Wide Web address:** http://www.csa1.com. **Description:** Provides billing services for electric and water utilities. Founded in 1938. **Positions advertised include:** Information Systems Representative.

PEOPLE LEASE
689-B Towne Center, Ridgeland MS 39157. 601/987-3025. **Toll-free phone:** 800/723-3025. **Fax:** 601/987-3029. **Contact:** Human Resources. **E-mail address:** mail@peoplelease.com. **World Wide Web address:** http://www.peoplelease.com. **Description:** Provides payroll preparation and other human resources management services, as well as offering personal and commercial insurance policies. Founded in 1984.

Missouri
ALLIED SECURITY INC.
1910 Pine Street, Suite 400, St. Louis MO 63103. 314/241-4220. **Toll-free phone:** 800/609-9673. **Fax:** 314/241-6899. **Contact:** Personnel Director. **World Wide Web address:** http://www.alliedsecurity.com. **Description:** Provides contract security guard services. **NOTE:** Apply for positions online. **Positions advertised include:** Manager; Security Officer; Sales Representative. **Office hours:** Monday - Friday, 8:00 a.m. - 4:00 p.m. **Corporate headquarters location:** King of Prussia PA. **Other U.S. locations:** Nationwide. **Operations at this facility include:** Administration; Sales. **Listed on:** Privately held. **Number of employees at this location:** 400.

AON CONSULTING WORLDWIDE
8182 Maryland Avenue, Suite 550, Clayton MO 63105. 314/725-9966. **Fax:** 314/725-2262. **Contact:** Human Resources. **World Wide Web address:** http://www.aon.com. **Description:** Offers human capital consulting services. **NOTE:** Search and apply for positions online. **Positions advertised include:** Health and Welfare Consultant; Communication Consultant. **Other area locations:** Clayton MO. **Other U.S. locations:** Nationwide.

AUTOMATIC DATA PROCESSING (ADP)
12200 Webber Hill Road, St. Louis MO 63127. 314/525-3000. **Contact:** Human Resources Manager. **World Wide Web address:** http://www.adp.com. **Description:** Automatic Data Processing (ADP) helps clients improve their business performance by providing computerized transaction processing, data communications, and information services. The company processes paychecks for over 17 million wage earners and issues 32 million W-2s to employees annually. The company's services include payroll, payroll tax, and human resource information management; brokerage industry market data; back-office and proxy services; industry-specific services to auto and truck dealers; and computerized auto repair and replacement estimating for auto insurance companies and body repair shops. **NOTE:** Search and apply for positions online. **Positions advertised include:** Field Engineer; Associate AE; SBS Outside Sales Associate; Associate Implementation Specialist. **Corporate headquarters location:** Roseland NJ.

CLEAN UNIFORM COMPANY
1316 South Seventh Street, St. Louis MO 63104-3634. 314/421-1220. **Fax:** 314/421-4902. **Contact:** Office Manager. **World Wide Web address:** http://www.cleanuniform.com. **Description:** Engaged in the rental and laundering of uniforms, dust mops, and dust mats. **Number of employees at this location:** 100.

CLEAN-TECH COMPANY
2815 Olive Street, St. Louis MO 63103. 314/652-2388. **Contact:** Vice President of Operations. **Description:** Engaged in a variety of services including janitorial and security guard services.

EXPRESS SCRIPTS, INC.
14000 Riverport Drive, Maryland Heights MO 63043. 314/770-1666. **Contact:** Director of Human Resources. **World Wide Web address:** http://www.express-scripts.com. **Description:** One of the largest, independent, full-service pharmacy benefit management companies in the United States, serving more than 7 million members through its integrated retail pharmacy network and mail service programs. The company's clients are health plan sponsors including HMOs, insurance companies, third-party administrators, unions, and self-insured companies. The company offers services through a nationwide network of more than 40,000 participating pharmacies with point-of-sale claims administration and two mail service pharmacies. The company also provides benefit design consultation and drug utilization review and formulates management services through its pharmacy benefit management programs. In addition, Express Scripts offers other ancillary services designed to control medical costs: IVTx offers infusion therapy through six sites in the East, Midwest, and Southwest, and OPTx offers a national vision program through a full-service vision laboratory and a network of ophthalmologists and optometrists. **Corporate headquarters location:** This location. **Other U.S. locations:** Tempe AZ; St. Louis MO. **Listed on:** NASDAQ. **Stock exchange symbol:** ESRX. **Annual sales/revenues:** More than $100 million. **Number of employees at this location:** 850.

LOOMIS FARGO & COMPANY
2220 Mason Lane, Ballwin MO 63021. 314/835-9070. **Fax:** 314/835-0705. **Contact:** Human Resources. **World Wide Web address:** www.loomisfargo.com. **Description:** An armored car service specializing in transporting currency, serving the St. Louis area. **Other U.S. locations:** Nationwide.

MARITZ, INC.
1375 North Highway Drive, Fenton MO 63099. 636/827-2828. **Contact:** Human Resources. **World**

Wide Web address: http://www.maritz.com. Description: Maritz delivers a wide range of integrated, custom-designed, performance enhancement services. The company's resources include marketing services, all-employee involvement programs, and travel services. Marketing services include sales incentive programs; performance enhancement training; business communications; database marketing; customer satisfaction/surveys; business meetings; data collection/analysis; information services; marketing research; teleservices; fulfillment services; and direct marketing. Employee involvement programs include employee suggestions; cost reduction; quality improvement; safety; team building; and rewards and recognition. Travel services include group travel awards; individual travel awards; business meetings; special events travel; and corporate travel management. **Positions advertised include:** Analyst, IT; Director, IT; Programmer/Developer, IT; Sr. Research Analyst; Sr. Research Manager; Director, Client Operations; Market Development Director; Product Development Manager; Product Manager; Sr. Information Manager. **Number of employees at this location:** 2,500. **Number of employees worldwide:** 5,700.

NATIONAL LINEN SERVICE
P.O. Box 14467, St. Louis MO 63178. 314/865-4500. **Physical address:** 315 Lynch Street, St. Louis MO 63118. **Fax:** 314/773-3828. **Contact:** Human Resources. **World Wide Web address:** http://www.national-linen.com. **Description:** A linen rental service. Primary customers include restaurants, hospitals, hotels, and catering companies. **Corporate headquarters location:** Atlanta GA. **Parent company:** National Services Industries. **Number of employees at this location:** 120. **Number of employees nationwide:** 12,000.

SPANN BUILDING MAINTENANCE COMPANY
3130 Gravois Avenue, St. Louis MO 63118. 314/241-1975. **Contact:** Quintin Clemmons, Personnel. **Description:** A janitorial service. **Corporate headquarters location:** This location. **Operations at this facility include:** Administration; Sales; Service.

WESTERN UNION FINANCIAL SERVICES INC.
13022 Hollenberg Drive, P.O. Box 4430, Bridgeton MO 63044-2409. 314/291-8000. **Toll-free phone:** 800/325-6000. **Contact:** Anne Barrett, Manager of Personnel and Training. **World Wide Web address:** http://www.westernunion.com. **Description:** A customer service center that provides money transfer and message services to the public. Founded in 1851. **NOTE:** Entry-level positions, part-time jobs, and second and third shifts are offered. **Company slogan:** The fastest way to send money worldwide. **Special programs:** Training; Co-ops; Summer Jobs. **Corporate headquarters location:** Greenwood Village CO. **International locations:** Worldwide. **Parent company:** First Data Corporation. **Operations at this facility include:** Service. **Listed on:** New York Stock Exchange. **Stock exchange symbol:** FDC. **Number of employees at this location:** 750. **Number of employees nationwide:** 36,000.

WHELAN SECURITY COMPANY INC.
1750 South Hanley Road, St. Louis MO 63144. 314/644-1974. **Contact:** Human Resources. **World Wide Web address:** http://www.transnationalsecurity.com. **Description:** Provides contract security guard services. **Special programs:** Internships. **Corporate headquarters location:** This location. **Other U.S. locations:** LA; IL; KS; TX. **Operations at this facility include:** Administration; Regional Headquarters; Service. **Listed on:** Privately held. **Number of employees nationwide:** 1,500.

Montana

TOWN PUMP, INC. AND AFFILIATES
P.O. Box 6000, Butte MT 59702. 406/497-6700. **Physical address:** 600 South Main Street, Butte MT 59701. **Fax:** 406/497-6704. **Recorded jobline:** 800/823-3252. **Contact:** Human Resources Director. **E-mail address:** HR@townpump.com. **World Wide Web address:** http://www.townpump.com. **Description:** Owns and operates 62 convenience stores, truck stops, car washes, restaurants, 58 casinos, and eight motels throughout Montana. The company also operates a petroleum transportation and delivery division. Founded in 1954. **NOTE:** Entry-level positions, part-time jobs, and second and third shifts are offered. **Company slogan:** Montana owned and operated. **Positions advertised include:** Car Wash Manager; Convenience Store Manager. **Special programs:** Internships; Training; Summer Jobs. **Office hours:** Monday - Friday, 8:00 a.m. - 5:00 p.m. **Corporate headquarters location:** This location. **Subsidiaries include:** Northwest Petroleum; Town Pump Food Stores; Town Pump Car Wash; Town Pump 5600; Lucky Lil's Casino; Magic Diamond Casino. **Listed on:** Privately held. **Annual sales/revenues:** More than $100 million. **Number of employees at this location:** 100. **Number of employees nationwide:** 1,500.

Nebraska

FIRST DATA CORPORATION
7305 Pacific Street, Omaha NE 68114. 402/777-2000. **Fax:** 402/777-1738. **Contact:** Personnel. **World Wide Web address:** http://www.firstdatacorp.com. **Description:** First Data Corporation offers electronic commerce and payment services to 2 million merchant locations. **Positions advertised include:** Quality Assurance Analyst; TeleCheck Area Representative; Sales Trainer; Associate Customer Engineer; Production Machine Operator. **Corporate headquarters location:** Greenwood Village, CO. **Other U.S. locations:** Atlanta GA. **Operations at this facility include:** Administration; Divisional Headquarters; Sales; Service. **Listed on:** New York Stock Exchange. **Stock exchange symbol:** FDC. **Annual sales/revenues:** More than $100 million. **Number of employees at this location:** 7,000. **Number of employees worldwide:** 29,000.

INFOUSA
5711 South 86th Circle, P.O. Box 27347, Omaha NE 68127. 402/596-8900 **Toll-free phone:** 800/321-0869. **Fax:** 402/592-3109. **Contact:** Jim Stultz, Recruiter. **E-mail address:** jobs@infousa.com. **World Wide Web address:** http://www.infousa.com. **Description:** Provides business and consumer marketing information services including market research services, online information services, and business directories. Information is supplied from the company's proprietary database containing information on about 10 million businesses in the United States and 1 million businesses in Canada. The database of infoUSA is compiled and updated annually from approximately 5,000 yellow page telephone directories, as well as other publicly-available sources including business white pages, directories, annual reports and other SEC filing information, press releases, business magazines, newsletters, and top newspapers. Founded in 1972. **Positions advertised include:** Sales Executive; Accounts Executive; Outbound Telemarketing; General Manager; Software Engineer; Vice resident of Sales. **Office hours:** Monday - Friday, 8:00 a.m. - 5:00 p.m. **Corporate headquarters location:** This location. **Other U.S. locations:** Nationwide. **International locations:** Canada; England. **Listed on:** NASDAQ. **Stock exchange symbol:** IUSA. **Number of employees worldwide:** 2,000.

QUILOGY
13220 Birch Drive, Suite 220, Omaha NE 68164. 402/491-3007. **Contact:** Human Resources. **E-mail address:** resumes@quilogy.com. **World Wide Web address:** http://www.quilogy.com. **Description:** Firm specializing in business solutions. Founded in 1992. **Positions advertised include:** Application Developer; Business Strategist; Database Consultor; Enterprise Architect; Graphic Designer; Multimedia Specialist; Networking Consultant; Technology Trainer; Web Technology Developer; Accountant; Contract Administrator; Marketing/Communications; Recruiter; Technical Sales; Training Sales. **Corporate**

headquarters: St. Charles MO. **Other U.S. locations:** Nationwide.

Nevada

ALARMCO INC.
2007 Las Vegas Boulevard South, Las Vegas NV 89104. 702/382-5000. **Toll-free phone:** 800/390-4180. **Fax:** 702/731-5862. **Contact:** Human Resources. **World Wide Web address:** http://www.alarmco.com. **Description:** Installs and services alarms for businesses and residences. Founded in 1950. **Positions advertised include:** Alarm Installer; Sales Person; Service Technician; Fire Alarm Inspector; Central Station Operator. **Corporate headquarters location:** This location. **Number of employees at this location:** 100.

ALLIEDBARTON SECURITY SERVICES
1515 East Tropicana Avenue, Suite 395, Las Vegas NV 89119. 702/795-3317. **Contact:** Personnel. **World Wide Web address:** http://www.alliedsecurity.com. **Description:** Provides security services to a wide variety of clients including businesses, hospitals, and residential customers. **NOTE:** Apply for positions online. **Corporate headquarters location:** King of Prussia PA. **Other U.S. locations:** 60 offices nationwide. **Parent company:** Allied Security LLC. **Number of employees nationwide:** 20,000.

B'MORE SECURITY & PROTECTION AGENCY
1928 Western Avenue, Suite 5, Las Vegas NV 89102. 702/598-1941. **Contact:** Human Resources. **Description:** An agency providing armed and unarmed security services including bodyguard services, convention security, and NDOT-certified traffic control. Founded in 1989. **Corporate headquarters location:** This location. **Listed on:** Privately held. **Annual sales/revenues:** Less than $5 million. **Number of employees at this location:** 65.

G.E.S. EXPOSITION SERVICES
GEM CAPSTONE DIVISION
950 Grier Drive, Las Vegas NV 89119. 702/263-1500. **Toll-free phone:** 800/443-9767. **Contact:** Human Resources Manager. **E-mail address:** careers@gesexpo.com. **World Wide Web address:** http://www.gesexpo.com. **Description:** Designs, builds, and sets up booths and displays for exhibits and trade shows. **Corporate headquarters location:** This location. **Other U.S. locations:** Nationwide. **International locations:** Canada.

ITS (INTERNATIONAL TOTAL SERVICES)
3305 Spring Mountain Road, Suite 73, Las Vegas NV 89102. 702/251-7944. **Contact:** Human Resources. **Description:** A security firm offering unarmed guard services to a wide range of clients. **Number of employees at this location:** 150.

INTUIT PAYROLL SERVICES
1285 Financial Boulevard, Reno NV 89502. 775/332-8800. **Contact:** Human Resources. **World Wide Web address:** http://www.intuit.com. **Description:** A payroll processor. **Corporate headquarters location:** Mountain View CA. **Other U.S. locations:** Nationwide. **International locations:** Canada; Japan; United Kingdom. **Parent company:** Intuit Inc. **Listed on:** NASDAQ. **Stock exchange symbol:** INTU. **Number of employees worldwide:** 7,500.

JOHNSON CONTROLS, INC.
3579 Red Rock Street, Suite B, Las Vegas NV 89103. 702/798-1979. **Contact:** Branch Manager. **World Wide Web address:** http://www.johnsoncontrols.com. **Description:** Johnson Controls is a global market leader in automotive systems and facility management and control. In the automotive market, it is a major supplier of integrated seating and interior systems, and batteries. For nonresidential facilities, Johnson Controls provides control systems and services including comfort, energy and security management. Founded in 1885. **Corporate headquarters location:** Milwaukee WI. **Operations at this facility include:** As part of the controls segment, this location is involved in the installation and service of facility management and control systems, retrofit and service of mechanical equipment and lighting systems in nonresidential buildings, and on-site management of facility operations and management. **Listed on:** New York Stock Exchange. **Stock exchange symbol:** JCI. **Number of employees worldwide:** 119,000.

LOOMIS FARGO & COMPANY
3370 Palm Parkway, Las Vegas NV 89104. 702/457-0105. **Fax:** 702/207-0148. **Contact:** Personnel. **World Wide Web address:** http://www.loomisfargo.com. **Description:** An armored security service specializing in transporting currency. **NOTE:** Applications will not be mailed to jobseekers. They must be picked up in person. **Corporate headquarters location:** Houston TX. **Other U.S. locations:** Nationwide. **Number of employees at this location:** 45.

SECURITAS USA
5250 Neil Road, Suite 303, Reno NV 89502. 775/828-1590. **Fax:** 775/828-1639. **Contact:** Human Resources. **E-mail address:** human.resources@securitassystems.com. **World Wide Web address:** http://www.pinkertons.com. **Description:** A nongovernmental security service organization. The company's principal business is providing security, investigative, and consulting services to commercial, industrial, institutional, governmental, and residential clients. Major services include industrial and nuclear plant security, institutional security, commercial and residential building security, retail security, construction security, patrol and inspection services, community security, sports and special events services, K-9 patrol services, courier services, inventory services, investigation services, security consultation, and equipment evaluation. **NOTE:** Apply to local office for Security Officer positions; search and apply online for other positions. **Corporate headquarters location:** Chicago IL **Other area locations:** Statewide. **Other U.S. locations:** Nationwide. **Parent company:** Securitas Group. **Sales/revenue:** $5 billion. **Number of employees worldwide:** Over 210,000.

WACKENHUT SERVICES INC.
501 Atlas Drive, North Las Vegas NV 89030. 702/295-1600. **Fax:** 702/227-5131. **Contact:** Human Resources. **E-mail address:** recruitment@wsihq.com. **World Wide Web address:** http://www.wsihq.com. **Description:** Provides armed and unarmed security personnel, paramilitary protective forces, law enforcement officers, fire-rescue services, aviation operations and support, base operation and facility management to government and commercial customers both domestically and internationally. **Corporate headquarters location:** Palm Beach Gardens FL. **Other U.S. locations:** Nationwide. **Parent company:** Wackenhut is a leading provider of contract services to major corporations, government agencies, and a wide range of industrial and commercial customers. The company's security-related services include uniformed security officers, investigations, background checks, emergency protection, and security audits and assessments. Other services include facility operations and management, fire suppression and prevention, and airport crash-fire-rescue. The Corporation's training arm, the Wackenhut Training Institute develops and conducts training programs not only for Company personnel, from security officers to managers, but also for outside proprietary security force personnel. **Corporate headquarters location:** Palm Beach Gardens FL. **Parent company:** Group 4 Securicor. **Operations at this facility include:** Administration; Service. **Number of employees at this location:** 200. **Number of employees nationwide:** 40,000.

New Hampshire

AUTOMATIC DATA PROCESSING (ADP)
105 Gay Street, Manchester NH 03103. 603/629-2337. **Toll-free phone:** 877/237-4711. **Contact:** Human Resources. **World Wide Web Address:** http://www.adp.com. **Description:** ADP offers benefit administration, human resource and retirement services for businesses of any size. **NOTE:** Search posted openings nationwide and apply on-line only. **Position**

advertised include: Administrative Assistant; Benefits Specialist; Bilingual Response Center Associate; Client Account Rep.; Financial Analyst; Implementation Manager-Clackamas; Key Account Executive; Laser District Manager. **Corporate Headquarters**: Roseland, NJ

BRANDPARTNERS
10 Main Street, Rochester NH 03839. 603/335-1400. **Toll-free phone:** 800/732-3999. **Fax:** 603/335-2870. **Contact:** Human Resources. **E-mail address:** job-applications@brandpartners.com. **World Wide Web address:** http://www.brandpartners.com. **Description:** Provides retail services. **NOTE:** Search posted openings online and respond via e-mail, mail or fax. **Positions advertised include:** Architectural Design Manager; Assistant Project Manager; Account Manager; Project Manager- Design/Build; Multimedia Designer; Project Architect/Job Captain; Digital Sales Consultant.

CAMPAGNE ASSOCIATES
195 McGregor Street, Suite 410, Manchester NH 03102. 603/622-4776. **Toll-free phone:** 800/582-3487. **Fax:** 603/622-5192. **Contact:** Diane Stevens, Human Resources. **E-mail address:** info@campagne.com. **World Wide Web address:** http://www.campagne.com. **Description:** Offers fundraising software to non-profit organizations, to aid their fundraising organization and subsequent success. **Positions advertised include:** Controller; Software Sales Professional; Customer Support Representative. **CEO:** Ric Pratte.

ROBERT HALF TECHNOLOGY
1155 Elm Street, 7th floor, Manchester NH 03101. 603/647-6200. **Contact:** Human Resources. **E-mail address:** Manchester@roberthalftechnology.com. **World Wide Web address:** http://www.roberthalftechnology.com. **Description:** Provides staffing solutions to premier organizations worldwide that require technical expertise. Projects range from complex e-business and web development initiatives to enterprise wide application development and technical system support. **NOTE:** Search posted openings and apply online. **Positions advertised include:** Systems Administrator; Data Warehouse Developer; Access Developer; .net Developer, J2ee Developer.

SERVICEMASTER AAA
12 Progress Avenue, Nashua NH 03062. 603/883-4800. **Fax:** 800/883-5646. **Contact:** Human Resources. **E-mail address:** SVMAAA@aol.com. **World Wide Web address:** http://svmaaa.com. **Description:** A residential and commercial cleaning service with two specific divisions: disaster restoration due to flood or fire damage, and carpet/upholstery steam cleaning. **Office hours:** Monday - Friday, 8:00 a.m. - 5:00 p.m.

New Jersey

ADP MAJOR ACCOUNTS MARKETING
15 Waterview Boulevard, Parsippany NJ 07054. 973/404-4000. **Contact:** Human Resources. **World Wide Web address:** http://www.adp.com. **Description:** One of the world's largest providers of computerized transaction processing, data communications, and information services. ADP Major Accounts Division provides outsourcing solutions for companies with 50 to 999 employees. **Positions advertised include:** Client Service Rep; Corporate Payroll Assistant; Group Leader Teledata; Litigation Paralegal; Major Account Sales Rep. **Special programs:** Internships. **Corporate headquarters location:** Roseland NJ. **Listed on:** New York Stock Exchange. **Stock exchange symbol:** ADP. **Annual sales/revenues:** More than $100 million. **Number of employees nationwide:** 25,000.

ADT SECURITY SERVICES
29 Commerce Way, Suite E, Totowa NJ 07512-1154. 973/237-3100. **Contact:** Personnel. **World Wide Web address:** http://www.adt.com. **Description:** Services more than 15,000 burglar, fire, and other alarm systems. ADT Security Services also manufactures a variety of alarms and monitoring equipment for use in alarm service operations and for sale to commercial and industrial users. **Corporate headquarters location:** Boca Raton FL. **Other U.S. locations:** Orlando FL; St. Petersburg FL; Tampa FL; Atlanta GA; Baltimore MD; Rockville MD. **Parent company:** Tyco Fire & Security.

BISYS GROUP, INC.
105 Eisenhower Parkway, Roseland NJ 07068. 973/758-1981. **Contact:** Human Resources. **World Wide Web address:** http://www.bisys.com. **Description:** A national, third-party provider of computing, administrative, and marketing support services to financial organizations. Services are offered through three major business units: Information Services, Loan Services, and Investment Services. The company derives a majority of its revenues from services provided through a single integrated software product, TOTAL PLUS, which includes comprehensive loan and deposit administration; branch automation and electronic banking services; operations and new business systems support; and accounting, financial management, and regulatory reporting services. **Positions advertised include:** Pricing and Market Data Manager; Network Administrator; Corporate Trainer; Investor Services Administrator. **NOTE:** Resumes may be submitted on-line at the above Website. Job postings are listed by location in the "Careers" section. **Listed on:** New York Stock Exchange. **Stock exchange symbol:** BSG.

BOWNE FINANCIAL PRINT
215 County Avenue, Secaucus NJ 07094. 201/271-1000. **Fax:** 201/271-2060. **Contact:** Human Resources. **World Wide Web address:** http://www.bowne.com. **Description:** The world's largest financial printer and leading electronic filer with the SEC. **Positions advertised include:** Computer Operator.

BOWNE MARKETING & BUSINESS COMMUNICATIONS
800 Central Boulevard, Carlstadt NJ 07072. 201/933-5656. **Fax:** 201/635-5295. **Contact:** Human Resources. **World Wide Web address:** http://www.bowne.com. **Description:** Provides web-based and datafed content editing and ordering tools integrated with digital document services and distributed print capabilities.

BRINKS INC
481 New Jersey Railroad Avenue, Newark NJ 07114. 973/824-0778. **Fax:** 973/824-1396. **Contact:** Human Resources. **World Wide Web address:** www.brinksinc.com. **Description:** An armored security service specializing in transporting currency. **Corporate headquarters location:** Dallas TX.

CHM PARTNERS INTERNATIONAL
466 Southern Boulevard, Chatham NJ 07928. 973/966-1600. **Fax:** 973/966-6933. **Contact:** Human Resources. **E-mail address:** solutions@chm-partners.com. **World Wide Web address:** http://www.chm-partners.com. **Description:** Provides retained executive search and management consulting services, specializing in senior-level executive and board searches.

CENDANT CORPORATION
10 Sylvan Way, Parsippany NJ 07054-0642. 973/428-9700. **Fax:** 973/496-5966. **Contact:** Human Resources. **E-mail address:** cendant.jobs@cendant.com. **World Wide Web address**: http://www.cendant.com. **Description:** Provides a wide range of business services including dining services, hotel franchise management, mortgage programs, and timeshare exchanges. Cendant Corporation's Real Estate Division offers employee relocation and mortgage services through Century 21, Coldwell Banker, ERA, Cendant Mortgage, and Cendant Mobility. The Travel Division provides car rentals, vehicle management services, and vacation timeshares through brand names including Avia, Days Inn, Howard Johnson, Ramada, Travelodge, and Super 8. The Membership Division offers travel, shopping, auto, dining, and other financial services through Travelers Advantage, Shoppers Advantage,

Auto Vantage, Welcome Wagon, Netmarket, North American Outdoor Group, and PrivacyGuard. **Positions advertised include:** Commercial Marketing Associate; Mortgage Processor; Staff Accountant; Financial Analyst; International Treasury Manager; Marketing Manager; Executive Assistant; Regional Business Consultant; Staff Accountant; Director; Finance Manager; Administrative Assistant; Marketing Communications Manager. **Corporate headquarters location:** New York NY. **Listed on:** New York Stock Exchange. **Stock exchange symbol:** CD. **President/CEO:** Henry Silverman. **Number of employees at this location:** 1,100. **Number of employees worldwide:** 28,000.

COMPUTER OUTSOURCING SERVICES, INC. (COSI)
2 Christie Heights Street, Leonia NJ 07605. 201/840-4753. **Fax:** 201/363-9675. **Contact:** Human Resources. **World Wide Web address:** http://www.cosi-us.com. **Description:** Provides payroll, data processing, and tax filing services to companies in book publishing, apparel, direct response marketing, and other industries. **Corporate headquarters location:** This location. **Listed on:** NASDAQ. **Stock exchange symbol:** COSI.

DUN & BRADSTREET
103 JFK Parkway, Short Hills NJ 07078. 973/921-5500. **Contact:** Human Resources. **World Wide Web address:** http://www.dnb.com. **Description:** A holding company. **Positions advertised include:** Automotive Solutions Leader; Product Strategy Leader; Channel Management Leader; Communications Consultant; MBA Project Leader & Recruiter; Administrative Assistant Sales; Teleweb Leader; Global Marketing & Promotions Leader; New Customer Acquisitions Manager; Sales Support Coordinator; Marketing Coordinator; Financial Analyst; Director Marketing Strategy; Product Marketing Manager; Program Manager; Communications Executive Assistant; Principal Consultant; Human Resources Director. **Subsidiaries include:** Dun & Bradstreet, Inc. provides information to the business community about other companies including data on credit and marketing. Moody's Investor Services provides ratings and other financial market information to assist individuals and companies in assessing investment opportunities. **Listed on:** New York Stock Exchange. **Stock exchange symbol:** DNB. **Number of employees worldwide:** 12,000.

FAULKNER INFORMATION SERVICES
116 Cooper Center, 7905 Browning Road, Pennsauken NJ 08109-4319. 856/662-2070. **Toll-free phone:** 800/843-0460. **Fax:** 856/662-3380. **Contact:** Human Resources. **E-mail address:** faulkner@faulkner.com. **World Wide Web address:** http://www.faulkner.com. **Description:** An independent publishing and research company specializing in providing technical information to end users and communication and IT professionals. Faulkner Information Services publishes more than a dozen standard information services in both print and electronic formats. The company provides comprehensive intelligence on products, vendors, technological advancements, and management issues associated with a wide range of technologies from open systems and client/server to enterprise networking, workgroup computing, and telecommunications. Faulkner also offers custom research and publication capabilities in such areas as market studies, customer satisfaction surveys, competitive analysis reports, and custom databases. **Positions advertised include:** Freelance Author; Experienced Editor. **Corporate headquarters location:** This location. **Operations at this facility include:** Administration; Research and Development; Sales; Service. **Number of employees at this location:** 45.

HSBC
200 Somerset Corporate Boulevard, Bridgewater NJ 08807. 908/685-0630. **Contact:** Personnel. **World Wide Web address:** http://www.hsbc.com. **Description:** Provides data processing services for the insurance and banking industries. **Positions advertised include:** Sr. Marketing Manager; Sr. Analyst Business Systems; Sr. Analyst Database Administrator; EBusiness Engineering Consultant.

LOOMIS FARGO & COMPANY
701 Kingstand Avenue, Lyndhurst NJ 07071. 201/939-2700. **Fax:** 201/939-1934. **Contact:** Personnel. **E-mail address:** employment@loomisfargo.com. **World Wide Web address:** http://www.loomisfargo.com. **Description:** An armored security service specializing in transporting currency. **NOTE:** Search and apply online. **Positions advertised include:** Cash Management Services Manager. **Other area locations:** Pennsauken NJ. **Other U.S. locations:** Nationwide.

GREG MANNING AUCTIONS, INC.
775 Passaic Avenue, West Caldwell NJ 07006. 973/882-0004. **Fax:** 973/882-3499. **Contact:** Personnel. **E-mail address:** info@gregmanning.com. **World Wide Web address:** http://www.gregmanning.com. **Description:** Conducts public auctions of rare stamps, stamp collections, and stocks. Items included in the auctions are rare stamps; sports trading cards and sports memorabilia; rare glassware and pottery; pre-Colombian art objects; Egyptian, Middle Eastern, and Far Eastern antiquities; and rare coins. **Corporate headquarters location:** New York NY. **Parent company:** Escala Group. **Listed on:** NASDAQ. **Stock exchange symbol:** ESCL.

MATHEMATICA POLICY RESEARCH, INC.
P.O. Box 2393, Princeton NJ 08543-2393. 609/799-3535. **Contact:** Personnel Department. **E-mail address:** researchrecruiting@mathematica-mpr.com. **World Wide Web address:** http://www.mathematica-mpr.com. **Description:** An employee-owned company that conducts social policy research (both data collection and data analysis) for government agencies, foundations, and private sector clients. The company specializes in health, labor, welfare, education, child care, and food and nutrition. **Positions advertised include:** Public Health Researcher; Education Researcher; Research Assistant; Human Services Policy Analyst; Health Policy Analyst; Survey Division Secretary; Survey Researcher; Statistician; Survey Specialist. **Corporate headquarters location:** This location. **Other U.S. locations:** Washington DC. **Operations at this facility include:** Service. **Number of employees at this location:** 200.

MINTAX, INC.
41 Arthur Street, East Brunswick NJ 08816. **Toll-free phone:** 800/873-1000. **Fax:** 732/257-5500. **Contact:** Human Resources. **World Wide Web address:** http://www.mintax.com. **Description:** Offers consulting services to corporations for obtaining tax credits and governmental incentives. **Positions advertised include:** Incentives Compliance Analyst; Sr. Business Development Executive; Trade Analyst; Accounting/Tax Consultant; Telemarketer; Sales and Use Tax Analyst.

SCIENCE MANAGEMENT LLC
SMC CONSULTING
745 Routes 202/206, Bridgewater NJ 08807. 908/722-0300. **Fax:** 908/722-0421. **Contact:** Personnel. **E-mail address:** info@smcmgmt.com. **World Wide Web address:** http://www.smcmgmt.com. **Description:** Works with IBM to provide disaster recovery services to large corporations. SMC Consulting (also at this location) provides management consulting services. **Corporate headquarters location:** This location.

TEAMSTAFF, INC.
300 Atrium Drive, Somerset NJ 08873. 732/748-1700. **Toll-free phone:** 800/565-8303. **Fax:** 732/748-3220. **Contact:** Human Resources. **E-mail address:** peo@teamstaff.com. **World Wide Web address:** http://www.teamstaff.com. **Description:** A full-line provider of human resource management services to employers in a wide variety of industries. Services include professional employer organization (employee leasing) services, placement of temporary and

permanent staffing, and payroll and payroll tax service preparation. **Corporate headquarters location:** This location.

New Mexico
AKAL SECURITY
7 Infinity Loop, Espanola NM 87532. 505/753-7832. **Toll-free phone:** 888/325-2527. **Fax:** 505/753-8689. **Contact:** Human Resources. **World Wide Web address:** http://www.akalsecurity.com. **Description:** Provides security services to businesses, private homes, and government facilities. Founded in 1980. **NOTE:** Search and apply for positions online. **Positions advertised include:** Security Officers; Court Security Officers. **Corporate headquarters:** This location. **Other area locations:** Albuquerque NM; Santa Fe NM. **Other U.S. locations:** Nationwide.

ABM JANITORIAL SERVICES
740 San Mateo Boulevard NE, Suite A1, Albuquerque, NM 87108. 505/262-2809. **Contact:** Human Resources. **World Wide Web address:** http://www.abm.com. **Description:** ABM Janitorial Services provides basic cleaning (such as vacuuming, window washing, and dusting), general maintenance, and sanitation services for corporate, retail, and medical facilities. Other clients include universities, public venues, and transportation. **NOTE:** Call to inquire about current job openings. **Parent company:** ABM Industries.

LOOMIS FARGO & COMPANY
624 Industrial Avenue NE, Albuquerque NM 87107. 505/344-9444. **Fax:** 505/344-5305. **Contact:** Human Resources. **E-mail address:** employment@loomisfargo.com. **World Wide Web address:** www.loomisfargo.com. **Description:** An armored car service specializing in transporting currency. **NOTE:** For Guard/Driver positions, apply in person. See website for all other positions. **Other U.S. locations:** Nationwide.

MEDICARE SERVICES
6301 Indian School Road, Suite 990, Albuquerque NM 87110. 505/872-2576. **Contact:** Human Resources. **World Wide Web address:** http://www.oknmmedicare.com. **Description:** Processes forms for Medicare Part B claims. **NOTE:** Resumes should be sent to Human Resources, 701 NW 63rd Street, Oklahoma City OK 73116.

NORTHROP GRUMMAN
100 Sun Avenue NE, Albuquerque NM 87109. 505/998-8100. **Contact:** Human Resources. **World Wide Web address:** http://www.northropgrumman.com. **Description:** An information technology services firm whose operating subsidiaries provide research and development and contract support to clients in the following industries: national defense, communications, energy, transportation, environmental, and other areas. **NOTE:** Search and apply for positions online. **Positions advertised include:** Software Engineer; Writer/Editor; Word Processing Specialist; Security Coordinator; Airborne Laser Performance Analyst.

ROBERT HALF TECHNOLOGY
6501 Americas Parkway NE, Suite 675, Albuquerque NM 87110. 505/888-6225. **Fax:** 505/884-4559. **Contact:** Human Resources. **E-mail address:** albuquerque@roberthalftechnology.com. **Description:** Provides flexible staffing solutions to premier organizations worldwide that require technical expertise on demand. Projects range from complex e-business and web development initiatives to enterprise wide application development and technical system support. **Positions advertised include:** Database Administrator; Programmer Analyst; Technical Writer; PC Technician.

TECH REPS, INC.
1300 Eubank Boulevard SE, Albuquerque NM 87123-3336. 505/998-5830. **Fax:** 505/998-5848. **Contact:** Human Resources Department. **E-mail address:** resumes@ktech.com. **World Wide Web address:** http://www.ktech.com. **Description:** A full-service communications company that provides technical documentation and visual media services for commercial firms and government agencies. Services include technical writing, production, and illustration and graphic design. Founded in 1974. **Positions advertised include:** Component Characterization Specialist; Mechanical Technician; Administrative Assistant; Environmental Scientist; Graphic Artist; Software Developer; Technical Writer. **Corporate headquarters location:** This location. **Parent company:** Ktech Corporation.

New York
ADT SECURITY SERVICES
335 West 16th Street, New York NY 10011. 212/627-2500. **Contact:** Human Resources. **World Wide Web address:** http://www.adt.com. **Description:** Designs, programs, markets, and installs protective systems to safeguard life and property from hazards such as burglary, hold-up, and fire. ADT Security Services has over 180,000 customers in the United States, Canada, and Western Europe. Founded in 1874. **Positions advertised include:** Commercial Sales Representative. **Corporate headquarters location:** Boca Raton FL. **Parent company:** Tyco International Ltd. **Listed on:** New York Stock Exchange. **Stock exchange symbol:** TYC.

ADECCO SA
175 Broad Hollow Road, Melville NY 11747. 631/844-7650. **Fax:** 631/844-7022. **Contact:** Human Resources. **World Wide Web address:** http://www.adeccousa.com. **Description:** Provides a wide variety of job search and placement services, from temporary placements to executive recruitment. **Corporate headquarters location:** Zurich, Switzerland. **Other locations:** Worldwide. **Subsidiaries include:** Lee Hecht Harrison. **Operations at this facility include:** North American headquarters. **Listed on:** New York Stock Exchange; Swiss Exchange. **Stock exchange symbol:** ADO; ADEN. **Annual sales/revenues:** $18 million. **Number of employees worldwide:** 700,000.

ALLIEDBARTON SECURITY SERVICES
330 West 34th Street, 18th Floor, New York NY 10001. 212/481-5777. **Fax:** 212/689-7521. **Contact:** Human Resources. **World Wide Web address:** http://www.alliedbarton.com. **Description:** A full-service corporate security firm that provides contract guard services, electronic security, and investigative services. **Positions advertised include:** Security Guard. **Corporate headquarters location:** King of Prussia PA. **Other area locations:** Albany NY; Elmsford NY; Syosset NY. **Other U.S. locations:** Nationwide. **Subsidiaries/Affiliates include:** Spectaguard Inc. **Parent company:** MacAndrews & Forbes. **Operations at this facility include:** Divisional Office. **Annual sales/revenues:** $500 million. **Number of employees:** 19,000.

AMERICAN CLAIMS EVALUATION, INC.
One Jericho Plaza, 3rd Floor, Wing B, Jericho NY 11753. 516/938-8000. **Fax:** 516/938-0405. **Contact:** Gary J. Knauer, CFO, Treasurer, Secretary, & Human Resources VP. **Description:** American Claims Evaluation, Inc. provides a full range of vocational rehabilitation and disability management services through its wholly owned subsidiaries. The company is a health care cost containment services company that verifies the accuracy of hospital bills submitted to its clients for payment. Such clients include commercial health insurance companies, third-party administrators, health maintenance organizations, and self-insured corporate clients. **Corporate headquarters location:** This location. **Subsidiaries include:** RPM Rehabilitation & Associates, Inc. **Listed on:** NASDAQ. **Stock exchange symbol:** AMCE. **Chairman/President/CEO:** Gary Gelman. **Annual sales/revenues:** $1.3 million. **Number of employees:** 22.

AMERICAN STUDENT LIST COMPANY, LLC
330 Old Country Road, Mineola NY 11501-4143. 516/248-6100. **Fax:** 516/248-6364. **Contact:** Human

Resources. **World Wide Web address:** http://www.americanstudentlist.com. **Description:** A leading provider of direct marketing information of preschool children and students from elementary schools, high schools, colleges, and post-graduate schools throughout the United States. Lists are rented primarily to various colleges, educational institutions, financial institutions, magazine publishers, and national organizations. Lists are available for all geographic areas of the United States and are provided to customers in the form of mailing labels, magnetic tape, or computer diskettes. **Other U.S. locations:** Boca Raton FL. **Parent company:** Havas Advertising (Levallois-Perret Cedex, France).

ASSOCIATED TEXTILE RENTAL SERVICE INC.
5586 Main Street, Williamsville NY 14221. 716/626-1076. **Contact:** Human Resources. **Description:** This location is the corporate office for the business rental company. Associated Textile Rental Service deals primarily in linens, tablecloths, and uniforms for restaurants. **Corporate headquarters location:** This location. **Other locations:** New Hartford NY; Fort Lauderdale FL; Rochester NY. **Number of employees at this location:** 10.

BRINKS INC
652 Kent Avenue, Brooklyn NY 11211. 718-260-2200. **Contact:** Personnel. **World Wide Web address:** http://www.brinksinc.com. **Description:** An armored security service specializing in transporting currency. **Other U.S. locations:** Nationwide.

CT CORPORATION SYSTEM
3 Winners Circle, 3rd Floor, Albany NY 12205. 518/451-8000. **Toll-free phone:** 800/624-0909. **Contact:** Human Resources. **E-mail address:** info@ctadvantage.com. **World Wide Web address:** http://www.ctcorporation.com. **Description:** CT Corporation provides research and accounting services for attorneys. **Positions advertised include:** Staff Accountant; Service Team Leader; Internal Support Analyst; Accounts Receivable Maintenance Clerk; Associate Customer Specialist; Quality Assurance Professional; Receptionist; Project Manager; Desktop Support Analyst; Information Technology Manager; Senior Product Manager; Associate Customer Specialist; Operations Process Management Director; Licensing Support Specialist. **Parent company:** Wolters Kluwer U.S. **Number of employees:** 1,100.

CARBON CONSULTING GROUP
121 East 24th Street, 2nd Floor, New York NY 10010. 212/228-0360. **Fax:** 212/228-0390. **Contact:** Human Resources. **E-mail address:** hr@carboncg.com. **World Wide Web address:** http://www.carboncg.com. **Description:** Offers a range of services for customers in the financial, media, and pharmaceutical industries including software design, software development, creative services, project management, and support services. **Positions advertised include:** Senior Technical Analyst; Project Manager; Business Analyst.

CASCADE LINEN SERVICES
835 Myrtle Avenue, Brooklyn NY 11206. 718/963-9600. **Contact:** Human Resources. **Description:** Provides commercial linen supply and rental services for hotels, restaurants, and medical institutions. **Corporate headquarters location:** This location.

CENDANT CORPORATION
9 West 57th Street, 37th Floor, New York NY 10019. 973/428-9700. **Fax:** 212/413-1918. **Contact:** Terence P. Conley, Human Resources. **World Wide Web address:** http://www.cendant.com. **Description:** Provides a wide range of business services including dining services, hotel franchise management, mortgage programs, and timeshare exchanges. Cendant Corporation's Real Estate Division offers employee relocation and mortgage services through Century 21, Coldwell Banker, ERA, Cendant Mortgage, and Cendant Mobility. The Travel Division provides car rentals, vehicle management services, and vacation timeshares through brand names including Avia, Days Inn, Howard Johnson, Ramada, Travelodge, and Super 8. The Membership Division offers travel, shopping, auto, dining, and other financial services through Travelers Advantage, Shoppers Advantage, Auto Vantage, Welcome Wagon, Netmarket, North American Outdoor Group, and PrivacyGuard. Founded in 1997. **NOTE:** Paper resumes are no longer accepted. **Positions advertised include:** International Relocation Consultant; Partner Marketing Manager; Hotel Manager; Field Auditor. **Corporate headquarters location:** This location. **Subsidiaries include:** Avis Group Holdings, Inc.; Budget Group, Inc.; Century 21 Real Estate Corporation; Coldwell Banker Real Estate Corporation; Days Inn Worldwide Inc.; Fairfield Resorts, Inc.; Galileo International, Inc.; Howard Johnson International Inc.; Jackson Hewitt Inc.; NRT Incorporated; PHH Arval; Ramada Franchise Systems Inc.; Super 8 Motels, Inc.; Travelodge Hotels, Inc.; Trendwest Resorts, Inc. **Listed on:** New York Stock Exchange. **Stock exchange symbol:** CD. **Chairman/President/CEO:** Henry R. Silverman. **Annual sales/revenues:** $14 billion. **Number of employees worldwide:** 85,000.

COMMAND SECURITY CORPORATION
1133 Route 55, Lexington Park, P.O. Box 340, Lagrangeville NY 12540. 845/454-3703. **Fax:** 845/454-0075. **Contact:** Debra Miller, Office Manager. **E-mail address:** dmiller@commandsecurity.com. **World Wide Web address:** http://www.cscny.com. **Description:** CSC principally provides uniformed and nonuniformed security services from its 16 operating offices to commercial, financial, industrial, aviation, and government clients. Security services include providing guards for access control, theft prevention, surveillance, vehicular and foot patrol, and crowd control. **Positions advertised include:** Security Guard. **Corporate headquarters location:** This location. **Other U.S. locations:** CA; CT; FL; IL; MA; NJ; PA. **Subsidiaries include:** COMGUARD. **Listed on:** Over The Counter. **Stock exchange symbol:** CMMD. **Chairman/President/CEO:** William C. Vassell. **Annual sales/revenues:** $84 million. **Number of employees nationwide:** 3,600.

CYBERDATA, INC.
20 Max Avenue, Hicksville NY 11801. 516/942-8000. **Fax:** 516/942-0800. **Contact:** Job Opportunities Department. **E-mail address:** jobs@cyberdata.com. **World Wide Web address:** http://www.cyberdata.com. **Description:** Provides an array of information-based services for client companies including information management, storage, and dissemination. CyberData, Inc. offers a mass fax service through a large number of modems. **Positions advertised include:** Computer Programmer; Sales Representative.

DICE INC.
3 Park Avenue, 33rd Floor, New York NY 10016. 212/725-6550. **Fax:** 212/725-6559. **Contact:** Jeff Deese, Human Resources Director. **World Wide Web address:** http://www.dice.com. **Description:** Provides online services to IT companies and operates a job board Website for technology professionals. The technical resources offered include hundreds of technical books, a retail store, and information on the newest technologies. Founded in 1994. **NOTE:** Mail Resumes to: Human Resources, 4101 NW Urbandale Drive, Urbandale IA 50322. **Corporate headquarters location:** This location. **Other locations:** Urbandale IA; Alpharetta GA; Augustine FL. **Subsidiaries include:** MeasureUp; dice.com. **Listed on:** Over The Counter. **Stock exchange symbol:** DICEQ. **Chairman/President/CEO/Director:** Scot W. Melland. **Annual sales/revenues:** $56 million. **Number of employees:** 153.

ESQUIRE DEPOSITION SERVICES
216 East 45th Street, 8th Floor, New York NY 10017. 212/687-8010. **Fax:** 212/557-5972. **Contact:** Human Resources. **World Wide Web address:** http://www.esquiredeposition.com. **Description:** A court reporting firm using state-of-the-art technology to

provide printed and computerized transcripts, video recordings of testimony from depositions, and speech recognition systems to the legal profession primarily in metropolitan New York City and Southern California. The company's technologies include real-time transcription, interactive real-time transcription, full-text search and retrieval programs, compressed transcripts, and multimedia technology systems. **Parent company:** The Hobart West Group. **Annual sales/revenues:** $200 million.

GUARDIAN CLEANING INDUSTRIES
161 Avenue of the Americas, New York NY 10013. 212/645-9500. **Contact:** Human Resources. **World Wide Web address:** http://www.guardian.baweb.com. **Description:** An industrial/commercial maintenance firm providing cleaning and exterminating services.

HEALTH MANAGEMENT SYSTEMS, INC.
401 Park Avenue South, New York NY 10016. 212/685-4545. **Fax:** 212/889-8776. **Contact:** Lewis D. Levetown, Director Human Resources. **E-mail address:** recruit@hmsy.com. **World Wide Web address:** http://www.hmsy.com. **Description:** The company works with government health agencies, Medicaid, and Medicare to recover overpaid healthcare expenses from providers by supplying information management services and software. HMS provides financial systems and consulting, retroactive insurance claims reprocessing, data processing, and third-party liability recovery services. **Corporate headquarters location:** This location. **Other U.S. locations:** Nationwide. **Affiliates include:** Accordis. **Parent company:** HMS Holdings Corp. (also at this location). **Chairman/CEO:** William (Bill) F. Miller III. **Annual sales/revenues:** $59 million. **Number of employees:** 433.

INTERPOOL, INC.
633 Third Avenue, 27th Floor, New York NY 10017. 212/986-3388. **Contact:** Human Resources. **World Wide Web address:** http://www.interpool.com. **Description:** Leases containers and chassis, primarily to container shipping lines. The company is one of the world's leading lessors of intermodal dry cargo containers and one of the largest lessors of intermodal container chassis in the United States. Founded in 1968. **Corporate headquarters location:** Princeton NJ. **International locations:** Worldwide. **Subsidiaries include:** Interpool Limited conducts the international container leasing business. **Listed on:** New York Stock Exchange. **Stock exchange symbol:** IPX. **Annual sales/revenues:** $300 million. **Number of employees:** 200.

LEWIS TREE SERVICE
300 Lucius Gordon Drive, West Henrietta NY 14586. 585/436-3208. **Fax:** 585/235-5864. **Contact:** Human Resources. **E-mail address:** hr@lewistree.com. **World Wide Web address:** http://www.lewistree.com. **Description:** Lewis Tree Service is an employee-owned company with operations nationwide that provides complete vegetation management services specializing in working with utility companies at sites where trees obstruct the proper functioning of a particular utility. Founded in 1938. **Positions advertised include:** Climber/Operator; Crew Leader; General Foreman; Bucket Trimmer; Spray Technician; Work Coordinator. **Number of employees:** 1,350.

LOOMIS FARGO & COMPANY
58 Ellicott Road, Cheektowaga NY 14277. 716/684-9600. **Fax:** 716/684-5644. **Contact:** Personnel. **World Wide Web address:** http://www.loomisfargo.com. **Description:** An armored security service specializing in transporting currency. **NOTE:** Applications will not be mailed to jobseekers. They must be picked up in person. **Other U.S. locations:** Nationwide.

JOHN C. MANDEL SECURITY BUREAU INC.
611 Jackson Avenue, Bronx NY 10455. 718/402-5002. **Fax:** 718/402-5004. **Contact:** Personnel Department. **World Wide Web address:** http://www.johncmandel.com. **Description:** Provides security services through armed and unarmed guards on an around-the-clock basis throughout the New York City metropolitan area. Clients range from private housing developments and projects to a wide range of commercial and industrial customers. **Corporate headquarters location:** This location. **Other locations:** Amenia NY; Brooklyn NY.

MERCER HUMAN RESOURCE CONSULTING
1166 Avenue of the Americas, New York NY 10036. 212/345-7000. **Fax:** 212/345-7414. **Contact:** National Recruiting Coordinator. **World Wide Web address:** http://www.mercerhr.com. **Description:** An actuarial and human resources management consulting firm with 140 offices in 40 countries worldwide. The company offers advice to organizations on all aspects of employee/management relationships. Services include retirement, health and welfare, performance and rewards, communication, investment, human resources administration, risk, finance and insurance, and health care provider consulting. **Positions advertised include:** Actuarial Analyst; Actuarial Consultant; Administrative Assistant; Compensation Analyst; Consultant; Administrative Assistant Floater; Senior Consultant. **Corporate headquarters location:** This location. **Other U.S. locations:** Nationwide. **International locations:** Worldwide. **Parent company:** Marsh & McLennan Companies, Inc. **Number of employees:** 13,000.

ONESOURCE FACILITY SERVICES
429 West 53rd Street, New York NY 10019. 212/408-6200. **Contact:** Human Resources. **World Wide Web address:** http://www.2onesource.com. **Description:** Provides a variety of services including janitorial, landscaping, and pest control to public institutions, retail stores, schools, industrial facilities, and commercial buildings. **Corporate headquarters location:** Atlanta GA.

PAYCHEX, INC.
911 Panorama Trail South, Rochester NY 14625-0397. 585/218-5100. **Fax:** 585/264-8555. **Contact:** Human Resources. **E-mail address:** jobopps@paychex.com. **World Wide Web address:** http://www.paychex.com. **Description:** Paychex, Incorporated is a national payroll processing and payroll tax preparation company for small to medium-sized businesses. While payroll is the core business, the company also provides other ancillary products and services including Taxpay, direct deposit, check signing and insertion, Section 125 cafeteria plans, insurance services, 401(k) recordkeeping, employee management services, and employee benefits pooling. Paychex has over 100 locations, serving more than 300,000 clients nationwide. Founded in 1971. **Positions advertised include:** Computer Operator; Data Center Quality Process Supervisor; Taxpayment Service Customer Support Representative; Senior Buyer/Purchasing Representative; Warehouse/Distribution Manager; Accounting Specialist; Collections Supervisor; Recovery Specialist; Risk Analysis Supervisor; National Sales Support Representative; Outside Sales Representative. **Special programs:** Internships; Training; Co-ops. **Corporate headquarters location:** This location. **Other U.S. locations:** Nationwide. **Listed on:** NASDAQ. **Stock exchange symbol:** PAYX. **Number of employees at this location:** 1,500. **Number of employees nationwide:** 5,000.

PAYPRO CORP.
450 Wireless Boulevard, Hauppauge NY 11788. 631/777-1100. **Fax:** 631/777-1103. **Contact:** Human Resources. **E-mail address:** hrit@payprocorp.com. **World Wide Web address:** http://www.payprocorp.com. **Description:** A payroll solutions provider that offers related services such as time and attendance solutions, unemployment cost containment, 401K administration, cafeteria plans, and labor-related tax credits. **Positions advertised include:** Computer Operator/Product Support; Technical Support Specialist.

THE RAYMOND CORPORATION
South Canal Street, P.O. Box 130, Greene NY 13778-

0130. 607/656-2311. **Fax:** 607/656-9005. **Contact:** Mary Alice Porter, Human Resources. **E-mail address:** staffing@raymondcorp.com. **World Wide Web address:** http://www.raymondcorp.com. **Description:** Designs, manufactures, sells, and leases materials handling systems. **Positions advertised include:** Programmer/Analyst; Engineering Technical Specialist; Regional Manager; Warehouse Worker/Assembler; Digital Imaging Specialist; Engineer; Information Analyst. **Corporate headquarters location:** This location. **Subsidiaries include:** R.H.E. Ltd.; Raymond Industrial Equipment, Limited; Raymond Leasing Corporation; Raymond Sales Corporation; Raymond Transportation Corporation; The Raymond Export Corporation.

REED BUSINESS INFORMATION
360 Park Avenue South, New York NY 10014. 646/746-6400. **Fax:** 646/746-7433. **Contact:** Director of Human Resources. **World Wide Web address:** http://www.reedbusiness.com. **Description:** Reed Business Information is a leading business-to-business magazine publisher with more than 80 specialty publications serving 16 major service and industry sectors including media, electronics, research and technology, computers, food service, and manufacturing. **Corporate headquarters location:** This location. **Other U.S. locations:** Nationwide. **International locations:** Worldwide. **Parent company:** Reed Elsevier Group plc. **Operations at this facility include:** This location publishes several magazine titles including *Broadcasting & Cable*, *Childbirth, Daily Variety*, *Graphic Arts Monthly*, *Library Journal*, *Modern Bride*, *Motor Boat*, and *Publishers Weekly*. **Listed on:** New York Stock Exchange. **Stock exchange symbol:** ENL; RUK. **Number of employees at this location:** 500. **Number of employees worldwide:** 12,000.

SANBORN MAP COMPANY
629 Fifth Avenue, Pelham NY 10803. 914/738-1649. **Fax:** 914/738-1680. **Contact:** General Manager. **E-mail address:** pelham@sanborn.com. **World Wide Web address:** http://www.sanbornmap.com. **Description:** A mapping and geographical information service, Sanborn Map Company is a data source for AM/FM, GIS, and environmental investigations. Sanborn's operations are organized through three units: Mapping, Custom Databases, and Environmental Data Services. Mapping involves building footprint maps showing street addresses and building details based on actual field inspections. Sanborn's Environmental Data Services operation uses an archive of maps dating back to 1867 to show building and land use including underground tanks and pipes, types of material stored, and owners and occupants of properties. The company's Custom Databases operation produces databases and designed digital map files based on Sanborn's existing map collection and its current field survey services. Information collected from the field survey services include land and building uses, housing unit counts, building vacancy status, building construction details, and building condition. **Corporate headquarters location:** This location. **Other area locations:** Rochester NY. **Other U.S. locations:** Chesterfield MO; San Antonio TX; Columbus OH; Colorado Springs CO; Charlotte NC. **Operations at this facility include:** Administration; Manufacturing; Research and Development; Sales. **CEO:** Pankaj Desai. **Number of employees at this location:** 35.

SOUTHWORTH-MILTON
294 Ainsley Drive, Syracuse NY 13210. 315/476-9981. **Fax:** 315/476-0660**Contact:** Jill Parcels, Human Resources. **E-mail address:** jill_parcels@smilton.com. **World Wide Web address:** http://www.southworth-milton.cat.com. **Description:** Sale and lease of Caterpillar brand heavy machinery. . **Corporate headquarters location:** This location. **Number of employees at this location:** 30.

TEMCO SERVICE INDUSTRIES INC.
One Park Avenue, 1st Floor, New York NY 10016. 212/889-6353. **Contact:** Human Resources. **World Wide Web address:** http://www.temcoservices.com. **Description:** Offers a wide variety of maintenance, security, and related services through a workforce directed by a network of experienced managers. The company operates in the following areas: Building Maintenance Services; Engineering Maintenance Services; Extermination and Security Services; and Incineration and Heat Recovery Systems. **Corporate headquarters location:** This location. **International locations:** Belgium. **Operations at this facility include:** Administration; Sales; Service.

WINFIELD SECURITY
35 West 35th Street, New York NY 10001. 212/947-3700. **Contact:** Human Resources. **World Wide Web address:** http://www.winfieldsecurity.com. **Description:** Provides security guard services for office buildings, schools, businesses, and manufacturers. **Corporate headquarters location:** This location. **Other area locations:** Bronx NY; Brooklyn NY; Queens NY. **Other U.S. locations:** Bloomfield NJ.

WINSTON RESOURCES, INC.
535 Fifth Avenue, Suite 701, New York NY 10017. 212/557-5000. **Contact:** Human Resources. **Description:** Winston Resources is a network of recruiting companies. Winston Resources has seven owned offices and 21 offices licensed or franchised under various names. Businesses include a wide range of industries. Founded in 1967. **Corporate headquarters location:** This location.

WUNDERMAN
285 Madison Avenue, New York NY 10017. 212/941-3000. **Contact:** Careers. **World Wide Web address:** http://www.wunderman.com. **Description:** Provides communications and database technologies for the marketing industry through the company's international research and development marketing lab. **Positions advertised include:** Chief of Staff; Assistant Account Executive; Account Executive. **International locations:** Worldwide. **President/CEO:** David Sable.

North Carolina

JEFFERSON-PILOT FINANCIAL
100 North Greene Street, Greensboro NC 27401. 336/691-3000. **Physical address: Fax:** 336/691-3797. **Contact:** Human Resources. **E-mail address:** gsojobs@jpfinancial.com. **World Wide Web address:** http://www.jpfinancial.com. **Description:** A holding company whose principal insurance subsidiaries are Jefferson-Pilot Life Insurance Company, Jefferson-Pilot Fire and Casualty Company, and Jefferson-Pilot Title Insurance Company. The company also operates radio and television stations and produces televised sports programs. **Positions advertised include:** Manager of Internal Auditing; Supply Clerk; Quality Assurance Analyst; Audio-Visual Specialist; Customer Service Team Leader; Production Supervisor; Manager of Financial Reporting; Senior Accountant; Quality Assurance Analyst; JPSC Marketing Assistant; Business Analyst; Communications Specialist; Insurance Agent; Annuity Product Management; Actuarial Clerk; Manager of Annuity Product Compliance; Marketing Specialist; File Clerk. **Corporate headquarters location:** This location. **Other U.S. locations:** Concord NH; Omaha NE. **Parent company:** Jefferson-Pilot Corporation. **Listed on:** New York Stock Exchange. **Stock exchange symbol:** JP.

RENTAL SERVICE CORPORATION
dba RSC RENTAL EQUIPMENT
3022 Griffith Street, Charlotte NC 28203. 704/522-8338. **Fax:** 704/522-6449. **Contact:** Ronnie Rockett, General Manager. **E-mail address:** s472mgr@rentalservice.com. **World Wide Web address:** http://www.rscrental.com. **Description:** Engaged in equipment rental and sale to the industrial and construction markets. **Corporate headquarters location:** Scottsdale AZ. **Other area locations:** Statewide. **Other U.S. locations:** Nationwide. **International locations:** Canada; Mexico. **Parent company:** Atlas Copco Group. **Operations at this**

facility include: Sales; Service. **Listed on:** Privately held. **Number of employees nationwide:** 6,000.

SECURITAS
5108 Reagan Drive, Suite 14, Charlotte NC 28206. 704/597-0626. **Toll-free phone:** 800/232-7465. **Recorded jobline:** 888/591-4473. **Contact:** Human Resources. **World Wide Web address:** http://www.securitasinc.com. **Description:** Offers a wide range of protective services and contract security guard programs to businesses and government. Burns International Security Services also provides electronic security systems and security planning consultation. **Corporate headquarters location:** Chicago IL. **Other U.S. locations:** Nationwide. **Number of employees nationwide:** 93,000.

TEKSYSTEMS
200 South College Street, Suite 1900, Charlotte NC 28202. 704/357-4500. **Toll-free phone:** 800/380-5473. **Fax:** 704/357-4490. **Contact:** Leigh Crenshaw. **E-mail address:** lcrenshaw@teksystems.com. **World Wide Web address:** http://www.teksystems.com. **Description:** Provides Information Technology services and staffing. **Positions advertised include:** Unix Systems Administrator; Information Security Manager; Desktop Support; Data Modeler; Financial Business Systems Analyst; Oracle Developer. **Other area locations:** Statewide. **Other U.S. locations:** Nationwide.

UNIFIRST
4700 Dwight Evans Road, Charlotte NC 28217. 704/523-9593. **Toll-free phone:** 800/347-7888. **Fax:** 704/525-9443. **Contact:** Human Resources. **E-mail address:** employment@unifirst.com. **World Wide Web address:** http://www.unifirst.com. **Description:** Provides laundry rental and cleaning services for hotels and restaurants. **NOTE:** Fax resumes to 978/657-5821, Attention: Director of Recruiting. Mail resumes to 68 Jonspin Road, Wilmington MA 01887. **Corporate headquarters:** Wilmington MA. **Other area locations:** Durham NC; Goldsboro NC; Kernersville NC; Rocky Mount NC; Wilmington NC. **Other U.S. locations:** Nationwide. **International locations:** Canada. **Parent company:** UniFirst Corporation. **Listed on:** New York Stock Exchange. **Stock exchange symbol:** UNF.

Ohio

CASS INFORMATION SYSTEMS, INC.
2675 Corporate Exchange Drive, Columbus OH 43231. 614/839-4500. **Fax:** 614/839-4299. **Contact:** Human Resources Manager. **World Wide Web address:** http://www.cassinfo.com. **Description:** A provider of logistics-related information services that include processing and payment of freight charges, preparation of transportation management reports, auditing of freight charges, and rating of freight shipments. Cass Information Systems operations are divided between its Payment Systems Group and its Software Systems Group. Founded in 1956. **NOTE:** Entry-level positions are offered. **Parent company:** Cass Commercial Corporation is also the parent company of Cass Bank & Trust, a wholly-owned bank that provides a full range of banking services to individual, corporate, and institutional customers. Cass Bank & Trust operates through its main bank in Sunset Hills MO, two downtown St. Louis facilities, and through its West Port facility in Maryland Heights MO. **Other U.S. locations:** Lowell MA; Bridgeton MO. **Listed on:** NASDAQ. **Stock exchange symbol:** CASS. **Annual sales/revenues:** $5 - $10 million. **Number of employees at this location:** 130. **Number of employees nationwide:** 650.

CINTAS CORPORATION
P.O. Box 625737, Cincinnati OH 45262-5737. 513/459-1200. **Physical address**: 6800 Cintas Boulevard, Mason OH 45040. **Toll-free phone:** 800/786-4367. **Fax:** 513/573-4159. **Contact:** Human Resources. **World Wide Web address:** http://www.cintas-corp.com. **Description:** Designs, manufactures, and distributes uniforms and ancillary products through rental and direct sale for companies throughout the United States. Cintas Corporation has 300 locations in 39 states. **Positions advertised include:** Accountant; Customer Service Representative; Data Warehouse Analyst; Travel Consultant. **Listed on:** NASDAQ. **Stock exchange symbol:** CTAS. **Number of employees nationwide:** 23,000.

FIESTA SALONS, INC.
6363 Fiesta Drive, Columbus OH 43235-5200. 614/766-6363. **Contact:** Human Resources. **World Wide Web address:** http://www.fiestasalons.com. **Description:** Operates a chain of hair and tanning salons. **Positions advertised include:** Cosmetologist; Stylist; Receptionist/Intern; Associate Manager; Educator; Division Manager. **Corporate headquarters location:** This location.

GBS CORPORATION
P.O. Box 2340, North Canton OH 44720. 330/494-5330. **Physical address:** 7233 Freedom Avenue NW, North Canton OH 44720. **Contact:** Laurie Quinn, Human Resources Director. **E-mail address:** hr@gbscorp.com. **World Wide Web address:** http://www.gbscorp.com. **Description:** Specializes in information management through its various business units, which print business forms, sell telephones, and offer computer services. Divisions include GBS Forms & Systems; GBS Filing Systems; GBS Computer Systems; GBS Labeling Systems; and GBS Communications. Founded in 1971. **Corporate headquarters location:** This location. **Other U.S. locations:** Tampa FL; Livonia MI; Malvern OH; Stow OH; Youngstown OH. **Operations at this facility include:** Administration; Divisional Headquarters. **Number of employees at this location:** 100. **Number of employees nationwide:** 450.

HYDROCHEM INDUSTRIAL SERVICES
11580 Lafayette Drive Northwest, P.O. Box 592, Canal Fulton OH 44614-9445. 330/854-4526. **Contact:** Human Resources. **E-mail address:** jobs@hydrochem.com. **World Wide Web address:** http://www.hydrochem.com. **Description:** An industrial cleaning company that provides heavy-duty cleaning services such as high-pressure water blasting and vacuuming for industrial plants. **NOTE:** Resumes are accepted by e-mail or fax. Fax resumes to: 713/393-5953. Please specify job code. **Corporate headquarters location:** Deer Park TX. **Other area locations:** Canton OH; Lima OH; Stratton OH; Youngstown OH. **Other U.S. locations:** Nationwide.

KABLE FULFILLMENT SERVICE OF OHIO
1290 Mount Vernon Avenue, Marion OH 43302. 740/725-5164. **Contact:** Nancy Headley, Human Resources Director. **E-mail address:** nheadley@kable.com. **World Wide Web address:** http://www.kable.com. **Description:** Engaged in marketing, data gathering, data processing, storing, and lettershop services for publishing and product fulfillment clients. **Positions advertised include:** Data Entry Corrections Clerk; Assistant Account Executive; Accounting Clerk. **Special programs:** Internships. **Corporate headquarters location:** Mount Morris IL. **Parent company:** Kable News Company, Inc. **Operations at this facility include:** Administration; Divisional Headquarters; Service. **Number of employees at this location:** 470. **Number of employees nationwide:** 1,500.

LOOMIS FARGO & COMPANY
36 Bissell Street, Youngstown OH 44505. 330/746-3246. **Fax:** 330/746-8939. **Contact:** Personnel. **World Wide Web address:** http://www.loomisfargo.com. **Description:** An armored security service specializing in transporting currency. **NOTE:** Applications will not be mailed to jobseekers. They must be picked up in person. **Other U.S. locations:** Nationwide.

MANATRON
4105 Executive Drive, Beavercreek OH 45430. 440/284-0580. **Toll-free phone:** 800/776-7227. **Fax:** 269/567-2912. **Contact:** Personnel Manager. **E-mail**

address: recruiter@manatron.com. **World Wide Web address:** http://www.manatron.com. **Description:** Provides real estate appraisal, mapping services, and data processing services for local tax jurisdictions and departments of local government. **NOTE:** Resumes are accepted by e-mail or fax. **Positions advertised include:** Sales Executive. **Corporate headquarters location:** Portage MI. **Other U.S. locations:** Nationwide. **Parent company:** Manatron, Inc. **Operations at this facility include:** Divisional Headquarters. **Listed on:** NASDAQ. **Stock exchange symbol:** MANA. **Number of employees at this location:** 50.

PAYCHEX, INC.
5450 Frantz Road, Suite 100, Dublin OH 43016. 614/210-0400. **Contact:** Human Resources. **World Wide Web address:** http://www.paychex.com. **Description:** A payroll processing and payroll tax preparation company for small- to medium-sized businesses. Started in 1971. **NOTE:** See website for instructions on how to submit a resume via e-mail. Resumes can also be mailed or faxed to specific office locations. **Positions advertised include:** Account Executive; Branch Manager; Client Service Representative; Computer Operator; Distribution Specialist; District Sales Assistant; Payroll Specialist; Receptionist; Sales Representative; Sales Management; Technical Support Specialist. **Corporate headquarters:** Rochester NY. **Other area locations:** Uniontown OH; Cincinnati OH; Miamisburg OH; Holland OH. **Other U.S. locations:** Nationwide. **CEO:** B. Thomas Golisano.

THE REYNOLDS & REYNOLDS COMPANY
115 South Ludlow Street, Dayton OH 45402. 937/485-2000. **Contact:** Human Resources. **World Wide Web address:** http://www.reyrey.com. **Description:** An integrated information systems company providing business services. The company has three major divisions: business forms including continuous-feed forms, lottery and entertainment tickets, and stock forms; computer products with turnkey systems; and financial services. Other products include computerized user systems for vertical marketplaces. Major clients include small businesses, financial institutions, automobile dealers, hospitals, and health care organizations. **NOTE:** Search and apply for positions online. **Positions advertised include:** Automotive Business Consultant; Business Systems Analyst; Senior Database Administrator; Sales Proposal and Process Analyst; Collection Analyst; New Markets Product Manager. **Corporate headquarters location:** This location. **Listed on:** New York Stock Exchange. **Stock exchange symbol:** REY.

ROTO-ROOTER, INC.
2500 Chemed Center, 255 East Fifth Street, Cincinnati OH 45202-4725. 513/762-6184. **Fax:** 513/762-6590. **Contact:** Wendy Gross, Human Resources. **World Wide Web address:** http://www.rotorooter.com. **Description:** A provider of plumbing and drain cleaning services and one of the largest providers of residential appliance and air conditioning repair services through the sale of service contracts. The Roto-Rooter network of franchises and company-owned operations provides drain cleaning services to approximately 90 percent of the U.S. population and plumbing services to 72 percent. Founded in 1935. **Corporate headquarters location:** This location. **Subsidiaries include:** Service America; Vitas Healthcare. **Parent company:** Chemed Corporation. **Operations at this facility include:** Administration; Divisional Headquarters; Regional Headquarters; Sales. **Listed on:** NASDAQ. **Stock exchange symbol:** RRR. **Number of employees nationwide:** 3,357.

SECURITAS
1717 Brittain Road, Suite 314, Akron OH 44310. 330/633-0700. **Fax:** 330/633-1324. **Contact:** Human Resources. **World Wide Web address:** http://www.securitasusa.com. **Description:** Offers a full range of specialized protective services including premier property and high-rise services, health care and hospital services, special event services, ATM services, and patrol services. The company serves thousands of companies worldwide with investigation, threat assessment, and executive protection services. **Corporate headquarters location:** Westlake Village CA. **Other U.S. locations:** Nationwide.

TNS NFO
2700 Oregon Road, Northwood OH 43619. 419/666-8800. **Fax:** 419/661-8595. **Contact:** Human Resources. **World Wide Web address:** http://www.tns-global.com. **Description:** Provides custom and syndicated market research services primarily using a proprietary panel of pre-recruited consumer households throughout the country. Formerly known as NFO WorldGroup, TNS NFO is now part of one of the largest market research organizations in the world. **Company slogan:** The sixth sense of business. **Positions advertised include:** Senior Research Analyst; Statistical Analyst; Panel Support Specialist; Market Product Coordinator. **Corporate headquarters:** Greenwich CT. **Subsidiaries include:** Payment Systems, Inc. (FL), a leading supplier of information to the financial services industry in the United States; Advanced Marketing Solutions, Inc. (CT) provides custom computer software systems used by clients to quickly access and analyze complex business and consumer information.

VAN DYNE CROTTY, INC.
3233 Newmark Drive, Miamisburg OH 45342. 937/236-1500. **Toll-free phone:** 800/826-3963. **Fax:** 937/435-8432. **Contact:** Human Resources. **World Wide Web address:** http://www.vandynecrotty.com. **Description:** Provides uniform leasing and textile services. **Positions advertised include:** Service Representative; Sales Representative. **Corporate headquarters location:** This location. **Other area locations:** Cleveland OH; Toledo OH. **Operations at this facility include:** Administration; Sales; Service. **Listed on:** Privately held. **Number of employees at this location:** 250. **Number of employees nationwide:** 750.

VOLT SERVICES GROUP
4027 Colonel Glenn Highway, Suite 100, Beavercreek OH 45431. 937/431-5239. **Fax:** 937/431-5280. **Contact:** Human Resources. **E-mail address:** dayton056999@volt.com. **World Wide Web address:** http://www.volt.com. **Description:** Provides staffing solutions in telecommunications and Information Technology. **Positions advertised include:** Forklift Operator; Electronic Assembler.

Oklahoma
MPSI SYSTEMS, INC.
4343 South 118th East Avenue, Tulsa OK 74146. 918/877-6774. **Toll-free phone:** 800/727-6774. **Contact:** Bill Webb, Director of Human Resources. **E-mail address:** hr@mpsisys.com. **World Wide Web address:** http:// www.mpsisys.com. **Description:** Provides convenience retailers with data and decision support systems to increase profitability. **Corporate headquarters location:** This location. **International locations:** Brazil; China; England; Japan; Singapore; South Africa; South Korea. **Listed on:** OTC. **Stock exchange symbol:** MPSI. **Number of employees nationwide:** 120. **Number of employees worldwide:** 300.

Oregon
BARRETT BUSINESS SERVICES, INC.
2828 SW Kelley Avenue, Portland OR 97201. 503/220-0988. **Toll-free phone:** 800/494-5669. **Fax:** 503/220-0987. **Contact:** Human Resources. **World Wide Web address:** http://www.barrettbusiness.com. **Description:** Provides employees for a diverse set of customers including forest products and agriculture-based companies, electronics manufacturers, transportation and shipping enterprises, professional firms, and general contractors. In a professional employer arrangement, Barrett becomes a co-employer of the client-company's workforce and assumes responsibility for handling some or all of the personnel-related

matters, including payroll and payroll taxes, employee benefits, health insurance and workers' compensation coverage, risk management, and related administrative responsibilities. **Positions advertised include:** Marketing Manager; Bookkeeper; Truck Driver; Landscaper; Welder. **Corporate headquarters location:** This location. **Subsidiaries include:** D&L Personnel Department Specialists, Inc.; JRL Services, Inc.

J.H. BAXTER AND COMPANY
120 Alva Park, P.O. Box 10797, Eugene OR 97440-2797. 541/689-3020. **Toll-free phone:** 800/776-9321. **Fax:** 541/689-8319. **Contact:** Joe Harbert, District Manager. **World Wide Web address:** http://www.jhbaxter.com. **Description:** J.H. Baxter and Company operates through three areas of business: chemical licensing, timberland management, and wood treatment. **NOTE:** As the sales office and the manufacturing plant share a post office box, jobseekers should indicate to which location they are applying. Jobseekers interested in working in sales should direct resumes to the above contact name. Jobseekers interested in working at the plant should direct resumes to Jim Burkert, Plant Manager. **Corporate headquarters location:** San Mateo CA. **Operations at this facility include:** This location houses sales offices.

HERTZ EQUIPMENT RENTAL CORPORATION
4939 NE Columbia Boulevard, Portland OR 97218. 503/287-5789. **Fax:** 503/287-4326. **Contact:** Human Resources. **E-mail address:** jgodaert@hertz.com. **World Wide Web address:** http://www.hertzequip.com. **Description:** A construction equipment rental company. **Positions advertised include:** Mechanic; Driver; Sales Coordinator.

INITIAL SECURITY
3720 SW 141st Avenue, Suite 100, Beaverton OR 97005. 503/626-6444. **Fax:** 503/626-4044. **Contact:** Human Resources Department. **E-mail address:** initial@initialsecurity.com. **World Wide Web address:** http://www.initialsecurity.com. **Description:** Provides a variety of security services including consulting, guards, investigations, patrols, strike coverage, and special events. Founded in 1928.

POORMAN-DOUGLAS CORPORATION
10300 SW Allen Boulevard, Beaverton OR 97005. 503/350-5800. **Contact:** Human Resources Department. **World Wide Web address:** http://www.poorman-douglas.com. **Description:** Provides data processing services for other businesses.

SECURITAS
103 SW 4th Street, Portland OR 97204. 503/226-1233. **Contact:** Human Resources. **E-mail address:** hr@ci-pinkerton.com. **World Wide Web address:** http://www.pinkertons.com. **Description:** Operating for more than 130 years, Pinkerton's Inc. is one of the oldest and one of the largest nongovernmental security services organizations in the world today. The company's principal business is providing high-quality security, investigative, and consulting services to a multitude of commercial, industrial, institutional, governmental, and residential clients. Pinkerton's operates from 129 offices in the United States, Canada, and Great Britain. Major services include industrial and nuclear plant security, institutional security, commercial and residential building security, retail security, construction security, patrol and inspection services, community security, sports and special events services, K-9 patrol services, courier services, inventory services, investigation services, security consultation, and equipment evaluation.

SIMPLEXGRINNELL
6305 SW Rosewood Street, Lake Oswego OR 97035. 503/683-9000. **Contact:** Human Resources. **World Wide Web address:** http://www.simplexgrinnell.com. **Description:** Manufactures and installs fire alarm, sprinkler, and detection systems. Founded in 1850. **Positions advertised include:** Administrative; Hard Analysis; Manufacturing; Sales; System Programming; Corporate Departments. **Corporate headquarters location:** Exeter NH. **Other U.S. locations:** Nationwide. **International locations:** Worldwide. **Parent company:** Tyco International Ltd.

STARPLEX CROWD MANAGEMENT
5775 SW Jean Road, Lake Oswego OR 97035. 503/222-5957. **Contact:** Human Resources. **E-mail address:** custserv@starplexcms.com. **World Wide Web address:** http://www.starplexcms.com. **Description:** Provides crowd management services for special events.

TRM CORPORATION
5208 NE 122nd Avenue, Portland OR 97230. 503/257-8766. **Toll-free phone:** 800/877-8762. **Fax:** 800/998-3721. **Contact:** Angela Childers, Human Resources. **E-mail address:** angelachilders@trm.com. **World Wide Web address:** http://www.trm.com. **Description:** A leading provider of self-service photocopying centers. The company owns, maintains, and monitors over 34,000 ATMs and photocopiers located in independent retail establishments such as pharmacies, stationery stores, hardware stores, convenience stores, and gift shops. **Corporate headquarters location:** This location. **International locations:** Belgium; Canada; France; United Kingdom.

THE WACKENHUT CORPORATION
5319 SW Westgate Drive, Suite 125, Portland OR 97221-2411. 503/291-1005. **Fax:** 503/291-1073. **Contact:** Human Resources. **World Wide Web address:** http://www.wackenhut.com. **Description:** The Wackenhut Corporation is a diversified provider of services to government, industrial, commercial, and professional organizations and agencies worldwide. The Wackenhut Corporation specializes in security-related services including physical security, investigations, the management of correctional and detention facilities, rehabilitative programs, and information security. The company also provides educational services and training, facility management, food service to jails and prisons, design, financial services and construction management for correctional facilities, and fire prevention and emergency services. The Wackenhut Corporation is a leader in the privatization of public services to municipal, state, and federal governments worldwide. Founded in 1954. **Other U.S. locations:** Nationwide. **International locations:** Worldwide. **CEO:** George R. Wackenhut.

WEBTRENDS CORPORATION
851 SW 6th Avenue, Suite 700, Portland OR 97204. 503/294-7025. **Toll-free phone:** 888/932-8736. **Fax:** 503/294-7130. **Contact:** Personnel. **World Wide Web address:** http://www.webtrends.com. **Description:** Develops and markets e-business solutions designed to help businesses manage their Internet infrastructure, e-commerce strategies, and e-marketing activities. **Corporate headquarters location:** San Jose CA. **Parent company:** NetIQ.

Pennsylvania

ADT SECURITY SERVICES, INC.
2858 Banksville Road, Pittsburgh PA 15216. 412/572-8000. **Contact:** Human Resources. **World Wide Web address:** http://www.adt.com. **Description:** ADT designs, programs, markets, and installs protective systems to safeguard life and property from hazards such as burglary, robbery, and fire. **NOTE:** See http;//www.monster.com for a listing of available jobs at ADT. **Corporate headquarters location:** Boca Raton FL. **Operations at this facility include:** This location is a sales and service office.

ALLIED SECURITY INC.
3606 Horizon Drive, King of Prussia PA 19406. 610/239-1100. **Toll-free phone:** 800/437-8803. **Fax:** 610/239-1107. **Contact:** Human Resources. **World Wide Web address:** http://www.alliedsecurity.com. **Description:** One of the largest national contract security officer companies in the United States. Allied Security provides loss prevention services to private businesses and government agencies. **Positions**

advertised include: Payroll Coordinator; Benefits Coordinator. **Special programs:** Internships. **Office hours:** Monday - Friday, 8:00 a.m. - 5:00 p.m. **Corporate headquarters location:** This location. **Subsidiaries include:** Allsafe Security Inc. **Operations at this facility include:** Administration; Sales; Service. **Listed on:** Privately held. **Annual sales/revenues:** More than $100 million. **Number of employees at this location:** 45. **Number of employees nationwide:** 8,000.

ANSWERTHINK, INC.
225 Washington Street, Conshohocken PA 19428. 610/234-5500. **Fax:** 610/234-5550. **Contact:** Human Resources. **World Wide Web address:** http://www.answerthink.com. **Description:** A business and technology consulting firm. Answerthink's portfolio of offerings includes benchmarking, business transformation, business applications, and business intelligence services. Founded in 1997. **Positions advertised include:** Java/Portal/Application Developer; Kronos Application Consultant; Outlooksoft Application Consultant; SAP Production Planning Lead. **Listed on:** NASDAQ. **Stock exchange symbol:** ANSR.

ARAMARK CORPORATION
ARAMARK LEISURE SERVICES GROUP
ARAMARK Tower, 1101 Market Street, Philadelphia PA 19107. 215/238-3000. **Contact:** Personnel. **World Wide Web address:** http://www.aramark.com. **Description:** One of the world's leading providers of managed services. The company operates in all 50 states and 10 foreign countries, offering a broad range of services to businesses of all sizes including most *Fortune* 500 companies and thousands of universities; hospitals; and municipal, state, and federal government facilities. ARAMARK Corporation is employee-owned. The company is among the market leaders in all of its businesses, which are: Food, Leisure and Support Services, including Campus Dining Services, School Nutrition Services, Leisure Services, Business Dining Services, International Services, Healthcare Support Services, Conference Center Management, and Refreshment Services; Facility Services; Correctional Services; Industrial Services; Uniform Services, which includes Wearguard, a direct marketer of work clothing; Health and Education Services, including Spectrum Healthcare Services and Children's World Learning Centers; and Book and Magazine Services. **Listed on:** New York Stock Exchange. **Stock exchange symbol:** RMK. **Corporate headquarters location:** This location. **Number of employees worldwide:** 240,000.

ARAMARK FACILITY SERVICES
ARAMARK Tower, 1101 Market Street, Philadelphia PA 19107. 215/238-2000. **Contact:** Human Resources. **World Wide Web address:** http://www.aramark.com. **Description:** Provides housekeeping and maintenance services. **Corporate headquarters location:** This location. **Parent company:** ARAMARK Corporation is one of the world's leading providers of managed services. The company operates in all 50 states and 10 foreign countries, offering a broad range of services to businesses of all sizes, including most *Fortune* 500 companies and thousands of universities; hospitals; and municipal, state, and federal government facilities. ARAMARK is employee-owned. The company is among the market leaders in all of its businesses, which are: Food, Leisure and Support Services, including Campus Dining Services, School Nutrition Services, Leisure Services, Business Dining Services, International Services, Healthcare Support Services, Conference Center Management, and Refreshment Services; Facility Services; Correctional Services; Industrial Services; Uniform Services, which includes Wearguard, a direct marketer of work clothing; Health and Education Services including Spectrum Healthcare Services and Children's World Learning Centers; and Book and Magazine Services. **Listed on:** New York Stock Exchange. **Stock exchange symbol:** RMK. **Number of employees worldwide:** 240,000.

ASSOCIATED CREDIT BUREAU SERVICES INC.
5910 Hamilton Boulevard, Allentown PA 18106. 610/398-7300. **Toll-free phone:** 866/530-2227. **Contact:** Joslyn Buss, Manager, Human Resources. **E-mail address:** careers@acbsi.com. **World Wide Web address:** http://www.acbsi.com. **Description:** A full-service business information company providing consumer credit information and employment reports to a variety of businesses, state and local governments, retailers, and schools. Founded in 1916. **Corporate headquarters location:** This location.

AUTOMATIC DATA PROCESSING (ADP)
1125 Virginia Drive, Fort Washington PA 19034. 215/283-6274. **Contact:** Human Resources. **World Wide Web address:** http://www.adp.com. **Description:** Provides computerized transaction processing, record keeping, data communications, and information services. ADP helps more than 300,000 clients improve their business performance by providing services such as payroll, payroll tax, and human resource information management; brokerage industry market data, back office, and proxy services; industry-specific services to auto and truck dealers; and computerized auto repair and replacement estimating for auto insurance companies and body repair shops. Employer Services, Brokerage Services, Dealer Services, and Claims Services are the company's four largest businesses. **NOTE:** Search and apply for positions online. **Corporate headquarters location:** Roseland NJ. **Listed on:** New York Stock Exchange. **Stock exchange symbol:** ADP. **Number of employees at this location:** 250.

CDI BUSINESS SOLUTIONS
1717 Arch Street, 35th Floor, Philadelphia PA 19103. 215/569-2200. **Fax:** 215/569-1300. **Contact:** Human Resources. **World Wide Web address:** http://www.cdicorp.com. **Description:** Provides engineering and information technology outsourcing solutions and professional staffing to customers in the aerospace, process & industrial, IT, life sciences and government services sectors.

DAY & ZIMMERMANN, INC.
1818 Market Street, Philadelphia PA 19103. 215/299-8000. **Contact:** Human Resources. **World Wide Web address:** http://www.dayzim.com. **Description:** Provides a wide range of professional services including engineering design, construction, and procurement; clean room design and validation; construction management; technical services; automation and data processing consulting; mass real estate appraisal; security guard services; munitions manufacturing services; naval ship alterations; and logistical support. **NOTE:** See website for current openings and application details. **Positions advertised include:** ABAP Developer; Assistant Project Director; Billing Specialist; Director, Human Resources and Diversity; Human Resource Coordinator; Payroll Services Specialist. **Corporate headquarters location:** This location. **Operations at this facility include:** Administration; Sales; Service. **Number of employees at this location:** 200. **Number of employees nationwide:** 20,000.

HEALTHCARE SERVICES GROUP
3220 Tillman Drive, Suite 300, Bensalem PA 19020. 215/639-8191. **Toll-free phone:** 800/363-4274. **Fax:** 215/639-2152. **Contact:** Human Resources. **E-mail address:** jobs@hcsgcorp.com. **World Wide Web address:** http://www.hcsgcorp.com. **Description:** Provides cleaning and laundering services for nursing homes and hospitals. **Other area locations:** Doylestown PA. **Corporate headquarters location:** This location.

HOSPITAL CENTRAL SERVICES INC.
2171 28th Street SW, Allentown PA 18103. 610/791-2222. **Fax:** 610/791-2919. **Contact:** Human Resources. **E-mail address:** hr@hcsc.org. **World Wide Web address:** http://www.hcsc.org. **Description:** Provides management services for hospitals including laundry

services, physician billing, and the operation of blood centers. . **Positions advertised include:** Database Analyst.

THE ICS GROUP, LTD.
1 East Uwchlan Avenue, Suite 101, Exton PA 19341. 610/594-0600. **Fax:** 610/594-7720. **Contact:** Human Resources. **World Wide Web address:** http://www.theicsgroup.com. **Description:** Provides temporary, temp-to-hire, and direct hire personnel to the Delaware Valley business community.

MACINTOSH LINEN AND UNIFORM RENTAL
1202 West Allen Street, Allentown PA 18102. 610/437-5435. **Contact:** Human Resources. **Description:** Rents linen and uniforms to a variety of industries including restaurants, hospitals, and nursing homes.

NCO GROUP, INC.
507 Prudential Road, Horsham PA 19044. 215/441-3000. **Toll-free phone:** 800/220-2274. **Contact:** Human Resources. **World Wide Web address:** http://www.ncogroup.com. **Description:** Provides accounts-receivable and delinquency management, collection services, billing, market research, and telemarketing services to a variety of businesses. Founded in 1926. **Corporate headquarters location:** This location. **Listed on:** NASDAQ. **Stock exchange symbol:** NCOG.

NAVIGANT CONSULTING, INC.
Bell Atlantic Tower, 1717 Arch Street, Suite 4800, Philadelphia PA 19103. 215/832-4400. **Fax:** 215/832-4401. **Contact:** Human Resources. **World Wide Web address:** http://www.navigantconsulting.com. **Description:** Navigant is an independent consulting firm providing litigation, financial, healthcare, energy, and operational consulting services to government agencies, legal counsel, and large companies. **NOTE:** Search and apply for positions online. **Other area locations:** Pittsburgh PA.

PAYCHEX, INC.
7450 Tilghman Street, Suite 107, Allentown PA 18106. 610/398-7518. **Fax:** 610/398-8632. **Contact:** Human Resources. **World Wide Web address:** http://www.paychex.com. **Description:** A payroll processing and payroll tax preparation company for small to medium-sized businesses. **Positions advertised include:** Customer Service Payroll Specialist. **Corporate headquarters location:** Rochester NY. **Other U.S. locations:** Nationwide. **Number of employees nationwide:** 3,300.

STIVERS STAFFING
1 Penn Center Plaza, 1617 JFK Boulevard, Suite 825, Philadelphia PA 19103. 215/561-1355. **Fax:** 215/567-2876. **E-mail address:** philly@stivers.com. **World Wide Web address:** http://www.stivers.com. **Description:** Places applicants into a wide range of careers and companies. **Positions advertised include:** Mailroom Staff; Receptionist; Administrative Assistant.

THE WACKENHUT CORPORATION
200 Butler Avenue, Suite 200, Lancaster PA 17601. 717/397-3443. **Fax:** 717/397-3507. **Contact:** Personnel. **World Wide Web address:** http://www.wackenhut.com. **Description:** Provides physical security services, correction services, and products to businesses, governments, and individuals through more than 150 domestic and foreign offices. Specific services include security and corrections staffing; security guard and fire and crash rescue personnel training; fire protection and emergency ambulance service; and security consulting. Wackenhut has 90 offices located in most major United States cities. **Positions advertised include:** Security Officer; Sales Representative; Armed Custom Protection Officer. **Subsidiaries include:** Wackenhut Corrections, Inc.; Wackenhut International.

Rhode Island
GTECH CORPORATION
55 Technology Way, West Greenwich RI 02817. 401/392-1000. **Fax:** 401/392-4950. **Contact:** Janice Gordon, Human Resources. **E-mail address:** janice.gordon@gtech.com. **World Wide Web address:** http://www.gtech.com. **Description:** Supplies computerized systems and services for government-authorized lotteries. Subsidiaries operate online lottery networks; sell, deliver, and install turn-key online lottery systems under contract agreements; and design, manufacture, and provide point-of-sale terminals used in its online lottery networks. **NOTE:** See website for current positions. Resumes must be submitted online. **Positions advertised include:** Internal Auditor; Senior Financial Analyst; Integration Engineer; IT Asset Manager; Director of Innovation; Senior Game Design Analyst. **Special programs:** Internships; Apprenticeships. **Corporate headquarters location:** This location (soon to be relocating to downtown Providence). **Other area locations:** Coventry RI; Cranston RI; Newport RI; Warwick RI. **Other U.S. locations:** Nationwide. **International locations:** Worldwide. **Parent company:** Lottomatica. **Listed on:** New York Stock Exchange. **Stock exchange symbol:** GTK. **Annual sales/revenues:** More than $1.25 billion. **Number of employees at this location:** 1,500. **Number of employees worldwide:** 5,300.

IBIS CONSULTING
291 Promenade Street, Providence RI 02908. 401/453-9000. **Fax:** 401/453-1034. **Contact:** Human Resources. **E-mail address:** hr@ibisconsulting.com. **World Wide Web address:** http://www.ibisconsulting.com. **Description:** A firm specializing in the automated collection and analysis of large-scale e-mail and electronic data for discovery. Ibis regularly acts as advisor to top litigators, legislators and information technology executives on the preservation, collection and processing of electronic evidence. **NOTE:** See website for current job openings. Send resume by e-mail. **Positions advertised include:** Second-Shift Desktop Support Technician; Business Development Consultant; Executive Assistant; Business Development Manager; Receptionist; Client Service Associate; Consultant, Client Services; Engineering Executive; Software Developer. **Corporate headquarters location:** This location. **Other U.S. locations:** Los Angeles CA.

RDW GROUP
125 Holden Street, Providence RI 02908. 401/521-2700. **Contact:** Heather Smith, Human Resources. **E-mail address:** hsmith@rdwgroup.com. **World Wide Web address:** http://www.rdwgroup.com. **Description:** A communications agency providing advertising, marketing, public relations and interactive services for clients throughout New England. **NOTE:** Phone inquiries not accepted. **Other U.S. locations:** Boston MA; Worcester MA.

South Carolina
DEFENDER SERVICES
P.O. Box 1775, Columbia SC 29202-1775. 803/776-4220. **Physical address:** 9031 Garner's Ferry Road, Columbia SC 29209. **Fax:** 803/776-1580. **Contact:** Nicky McCarter, President. **E-mail address:** nickym@defenderservices.com. **World Wide Web address:** http://www.defenderservices.com. **Description:** Offers cleaning, painting, floor sanding, maintenance, yard work, grounds work, housekeeping, trash removal, and security. **Corporate headquarters location:** This location. **Other area locations:** Anderson SC; Charleston SC; Greenwood SC; Lancaster SC. **Other U.S. locations:** Nationwide. **Number of employees nationwide:** 7,000.

DIVERSCO INTEGRATED SERVICES INC.
105 Diversco Drive, P.O. Box 5527, Spartanburg SC 29307. 864/699-2368. **Toll-free phone:** 800/277-3420. **Fax:** 864/579-9578. **Contact:** Raina Tuten, Human Resources Manager. **World Wide Web address:** http://www.diversco.com. **Description:** Provides outsourcing services including janitorial and building maintenance, security, temporary staffing, food processing equipment, sanitation, and contract services to industrial clients. **Corporate headquarters location:** This location. **Other locations:** Nationwide.

Parent company: Diversco Holdings, Inc. (also at this location). **Subsidiaries include:** Personnel Management, Inc.; Spartan Security. **Number of employees nationwide:** 9,000.

GENERAL PHYSICS CORPORATION
958 Millbrook Avenue, Suite 7, Aiken SC 29803. 803/649-0515. **Fax:** 803/649-3017. **Contact:** Human Resources. **E-mail address:** hr@gpworldwide.com. **World Wide Web address:** http://www.genphysics.com. **Description:** Provides training, engineering, and technical services to clients in the aerospace, automotive, defense, government, manufacturing, utility, independent power, pharmaceutical, and process industries. **Corporate headquarters location:** Elkridge MD. **International locations:** Canada; India; UK. **Subsidiaries include:** GP Environmental; GP Technologies. **Parent company:** GP Strategies Corporation.

South Dakota
VERIFICATIONS, INC.
1425 Mickelson Drive, Suite 100, Watertown, SD 57201. 605/884-1200. **Toll-free phone:** 800/247-0717. **Fax:** 605/884-1140. **Contact:** Human Resources. **World Wide Web address:** http://www.verificationsinc.com. **Description:** A privately held corporation that conducts employment screening and application processing services for clients from a broad range of industries, with the majority of checks performed for Fortune 500 companies. **NOTE:** Contact Human Resources about current job openings. **Corporate headquarters location:** Minneapolis MN. **Other area locations:** Aberdeen SD; Mitchell SD. **Other U.S. locations:** ND.

Tennessee
BEARINGPOINT, INC.
3200 West End Avenue, Suite 500, HQ West End Center, Nashville TN 37203. 615/783-1620. **Fax:** 615/783-1619. **Contact:** Human Resources. **World Wide Web address:** http://www.bearingpoint.com. **Description:** A business consulting, systems integration, and managed services firm providing business and technology strategy, systems design, architecture, applications implementation, and network infrastructure services to business, government agencies, and other organizations. **NOTE:** Search and apply for positions online. **Positions advertised include:** Financial Solutions Development Lead; Hyperion Reporting Analysis Consultant. **Corporate headquarters location:** McLean VA. **Listed on:** New York Stock Exchange. **Stock exchange symbol:** BE. **Number of employees worldwide:** 16,000.

CLIENTLOGIC
Two American Center, 3102 West End Avenue, Suite 1000, Nashville TN 37203. 615/301-7100. **Contact:** Human Resources. **E-mail address:** nashvillejobs@clientlogic.com. **World Wide Web address:** http://www.clientlogic.com. **Description:** ClientLogic is an international provider of integrated customer management solutions including integrated customer acquisition, list management and brokerage, database design and development, multi-channel customer and technical support, eCommerce services, and warehousing/fulfillment. The company operates in 52 locations in 12 countries throughout North America, Europe and Asia. **NOTE:** Search for positions at: Monster.com. **Positions advertised include:** Market Research Specialist; Paralegal/Compliance Specialist. **Corporate headquarters location:** This location. **Parent company:** Onex Corporation (Canada). **Number of employees worldwide:** 16,500.

COMDATA HOLDINGS CORPORATION
5301 Maryland Way, Brentwood TN 37027. 615/370-7000. **Fax:** 615/370-7828. **Contact:** Human Resources. **E-mail address:** resumes@comdata.com. **World Wide Web address:** http://www.comdata.com. **Description:** Comdata provides credit and debit processing and reporting for commercial fleets and merchants, electronic cash, gift and smart/chip card programs for retailers and governmental agencies, payroll services for food, retail and other service industries, and point-of-sale equipment, software and auxiliary services for merchants and convenience stores. **Positions advertised include:** Applications Specialist; Credit Implementation Representative; Retention Account Executive; Sr. Manager, Corporate Communications; Technical Representative; Wintel Systems Administrator. **Corporate headquarters location:** This location. **Other U.S. locations:** Los Angeles CA; Denver CO; Atlanta GA; Cincinnati OH; Dallas TX. **International locations:** Toronto, Canada. **Parent company:** Ceridian Corporation. **Operations at this facility include:** Administration; Sales; Service. **Number of employees nationwide:** 1,800.

CORRECTIONS CORPORATION OF AMERICA
10 Burton Hills Boulevard, Nashville TN 37215. 615/263-3000. **Toll-free phone:** 800/624-2931. **Fax:** 615/263-3140. **Contact:** Personnel. **E-mail address:** humanresources@correctionscorp.com. **World Wide Web address:** http://www.correctionscorp.com. **Description:** A leading private-sector provider of detention and correctional services to federal, state, and local governments. The company designs, finances, constructs, renovates, and manages jails and prisons, and provides escort and court services and long-distance transportation of inmates. Its expertise covers adult and juvenile offenders, at all levels of security classification. **Corporate headquarters location:** This location. **Subsidiaries include:** CAA International furnishes similar services abroad in Puerto Rico, Australia, and the United Kingdom. **Listed on:** New York Stock Exchange. **Stock exchange symbol:** CXW. **Number of employees nationwide:** 15,000.

GUARDSMARK, INC.
22 South Second Street, Memphis TN 38103-2695. 901/522-7800. **Contact:** Recruitment Manager. **World Wide Web address:** http://www.guardsmark.com. **Description:** Provides security, life safety, and fire and protective services, as well as background screening, investigative services, and consulting. Founded in 1963. **Corporate headquarters location:** New York NY. **Other U.S. locations:** Nationwide. **Listed on:** Privately held. **Annual sales/revenues:** More than $100 million. **Number of employees at this location:** 125. **Number of employees nationwide:** 14,000.

INNLINK, LLC
130 Maple Drive North, Hendersonville TN 37075. 615/264-8000. **Toll-free phone:** 800/525-4658. Fax: 615/264-1898. **Contact:** Human Resources. **E-mail address:** info@innlink.com. **World Wide Web address:** http://www.innlink.com. **Description:** Provides reservation products and services for hotels and hotel companies. **Parent company:** ShoLodge, Inc.

MURRAY GUARD, INC.
P.O. Box 10248, Jackson TN 38308. 731/668-3400. **Physical address:** 58 Murray Guard Drive, Jackson TN 38305. **Toll-free phone:** 800/238-3830. **Contact:** Danny Underwood, Vice President of Human Resources. **World Wide Web address:** http://www.murrayguard.com. **Description:** A security services firm. Founded in 1967. **NOTE:** Complete application online. **Corporate headquarters location:** This location.

QUALITY COMPANIES, INC.
P.O. Box 18428, Memphis TN 38181-0428. 901/367-8200. **Physical address:** 4690 Hungerford Road, Memphis TN 38118. **Contact:** Human Resources. **Description:** Engaged in the marketing of incentive programs for other companies, as well as individual and group travel programs.

Texas
ACS, INC.
2828 North Haskell, Building 1, Dallas TX 75204. 214/841-6111. **Contact:** Human Resources. **World Wide Web address:** http://www.acs-inc.com. **Description:** A full-service provider of data processing services, computer outsourcing, facilities management, electronic transaction processing, and telecommunications services. The firm owns several

data centers across the United States and a telecommunications network that encompasses leading-edge technologies. The company uses many different computer platforms including IBM, Amdahl, Hewlett-Packard, Tandem, and UNIX-based systems. **Positions advertised include:** Software Support Analyst; Vice President – Network Services; Real Estate Associate; Global Licensing Analyst; Payroll Tax Specialist; HR Specialist; Executive Administrative Assistant; HRIS Analyst; Network Solutions Technical Architect; Network Security Analyst; e-learning Instructional Designer; Export Compliance Officer; Development Specialist; Senior Project Manager; Senior Accountant; Call Center Team Manager; Accounting Manager. **Corporate headquarters location:** This location. **Other U.S. locations:** Nationwide. **Listed on:** New York Stock Exchange. **Stock exchange symbol:** ACS. **Number of employees worldwide:** 40,000.

ADT SECURITY SERVICES
2400 Lacy Lane, Carrollton TX 75006. 512/832-0122. **Fax:** 512/832-2988. **Contact:** Paul Ebersol, Human Resources. **World Wide Web address:** http://www.adtsecurityservices.com. **Description:** Designs, installs, sells, and monitors fire and burglar alarm systems for commercial and industrial retail customers. ADT Security also offers armed and unarmed security guards. **Corporate headquarters location:** Boca Raton FL. **Parent company:** Tyco International, Ltd. **Listed on:** New York Stock Exchange. **Stock exchange symbol:** TYC. **Number of employees nationwide:** 15,000.

ACE AMERICA'S CASH EXPRESS INC.
8530 Cinderbed Road, Irving TX 75038. 972/550-5000. **Fax:** 972/582-1410. **Contact:** Human Resources. **E-mail address:** employment@acecashexpress.com. **World Wide Web address:** http://www.acecashexpress.com. **Description:** One of the largest check cashing companies in the United States, offering check cashing services for government and payroll checks. **NOTE:** Contact Human Resources directly at 972/550-5106. Please visit website for a listing of store positions. **Corporate headquarters location:** This location. **Other U.S. locations:** Nationwide. **Listed on:** NASDAQ. **Stock exchange symbol:** AACE.

ALLIED SECURITY INC.
4501 Attwater Avenue, Texas City TX 77590. 409/941-0388. **Contact:** Human Resources. **World Wide Web address:** http://www.alliedsecurity.com. **Description:** One of the largest contract security officer companies in the nation. Allied Security provides loss prevention services to private businesses and government agencies. **NOTE:** Please visit website to fill out online application form. **Corporate headquarters location:** King of Prussia PA. **Other area locations:** Dallas TX; Houston TX; San Antonio TX. **Other U.S. locations:** Nationwide.

ASSOCIATED BUILDING SERVICES COMPANY
1910 Napoleon Street, Houston TX 77003. 713/844-7800. **Fax:** 713/621-1429. **Contact:** Human Resources. **E-mail address:** resumes@abslink.com. **World Wide Web address:** http://www.abslink.com. **Description:** One of the largest facility maintenance contractors in the nation. Founded 1945. **NOTE:** Contact the hiring office at 713/844-7884. **Positions advertised include:** Janitor; Supervisor; Sales Personnel; Project Manager; Branch Manager; District Manager; Operations Manager. **Corporate headquarters location:** This location. **Other area locations:** Dallas TX; The Woodlands TX; Austin TX; San Antonio TX. **Other U.S. locations:** WA; OR; CO; TN; AZ; VA.

AUTOMATIC DATA PROCESSING (ADP)
2735 North Stemmons Freeway, Dallas TX 75207. 214/630-9311. **Toll-free phone:** 800/829-2237. **Contact:** Human Resources. **World Wide Web address:** http://www.adp.com. **Description:** Provides computerized transaction processing, record keeping, data communications, and information services. ADP helps more than 500,000 clients improve their business performance by providing services such as payroll, payroll tax, and human resource information management; brokerage industry market data, back office, and proxy services; industry-specific services to auto and truck dealers; and computerized auto repair and replacement estimating for auto insurance companies and body repair shops. The company's four largest businesses are Employer Services, Brokerage Services, Dealer Services, and Claims Services. **NOTE:** Please visit website to search for jobs and apply online. Online applications are preferred. **Positions advertised include:** New Account Coordinator; Corporate Sales Manager; Supervisor – Quality Control; Client Service Representative; Implementation Specialist; MADM; SBS Outside Sales Associate; Program Manager; Project Leader Implementation; Banking Representative; Overflow Operator; Client Technical Analyst; Account Executive; Manager – Financial Services; Network Technical Support Specialist; Customer Support Executive; Tax Service Representative; human Resources Director. **Special programs:** Co-ops; Internships. **Corporate headquarters location:** Roseland NJ. **Other U.S. locations:** Nationwide. **International locations:** Worldwide. **Listed on:** New York Stock Exchange. **Stock exchange symbol:** ADP.

BAKER HUGHES INC.
P.O. Box 4740, Houston TX 77210-4740. 713/439-8600. **Physical address:** 3900 Essex Lane, Suite 1200, Houston TX 77027. **Fax:** 713/439-8699. **Contact:** Human Resources. **World Wide Web address:** http://www.bakerhughes.com. **Description:** Provides vital information to many segments of the energy industry through high-technology data acquisition operations. **NOTE:** Please visit website to search for job and apply online. **Positions advertised include:** HS&E Specialist; Formation Evaluation Analyst; Parts Finisher; Legal Secretary; Facilities Specialist; Senior Financial Benefits Specialist; Manufacturing Engineer; Electro-Mechanical Technician; HR Administrator; Ethics Director; Accounting Clerk; International Tax Specialist; Technical Support Engineer; Directional Driller. **Corporate headquarters location:** This location. **Other U.S. locations:** Western and Southern U.S. **International locations:** Worldwide. **Operations at this facility include:** Administration; Divisional Headquarters; Manufacturing; Regional Headquarters; Research and Development; Sales. **Listed on:** New York Stock Exchange. **Stock exchange symbol:** BHI. **President/CEO:** Mike Wiley. **Number of employees worldwide:** 24,500.

THE BENCHMARK COMPANY
907 South Congress Avenue, Suite 7, Austin TX 78704. 512/707-7500. **Fax:** 512/707-7757. **Contact:** Human Resources Department. **E-mail address:** thebenc@earthlink.net. **World Wide Web address:** http://www.thebenchmarkcompany.net. **Description:** Gathers data and research about radio listeners. Benchmark is also involved in researching broadcasting companies. **President/CEO:** Dr. Robert E. Balon.

BLACKMON MOORING STEAMATIC
308 Arthur Street, Fort Worth TX 76107. 817/810-9200. **Toll-free phone:** 877/730-1948. **Fax:** 817/810-5639. **Contact:** Human Resources. **World Wide Web address:** https://www.blackmonmooring.com. **Description:** A high-tech restoration and cleaning firm with affiliate companies involved in providing environmental services. BMS Enterprises Inc. has specific technical expertise with electronics and wet document recovery. The company provides disaster restoration services following fire and water catastrophes. BMS Enterprises Inc. is also involved in providing HVAC services to improve indoor air quality. **Corporate headquarters location:** This location. **Operations at this facility include:** Administration; Research and Development; Sales; Service. **Listed on:** Privately held.

CGI
300 Burnett Street, Fort Worth TX 76113. 817/348-3681. **Contact:** Human Resources. **World Wide Web**

address: http://www.cgi.com. **Description:** CGI provides technical, outsourcing and consulting services to a wide variety of companies worldwide. **NOTE:** This company offers entry-level positions. Jobseekers must create an employment profile at the company's website. **Corporate headquarters location:** Montreal CA. **Listed on:** New York Stock Exchange. **Stock exchange symbol:** GIB. **Number of employees worldwide:** 20,000.

CISCO-EAGLE
2120 Valley View Lane, Dallas TX 75234. 972/406-9330. **Toll-free phone:** 800/877-3861. **Fax:** 972/406-9577. **Contact:** Human Resources. **E-mail address:** personnel@cisco-eagle.com. **World Wide Web address:** http://www.cisco-eagle.com. **Description:** Cisco-Eagle's expertise in is warehouse management, including warehouse space and design, process flow, material handling, labor needs and technology. They also sell warehouse furnishings, such as benches, ladders, pallets; containers; carts and trucks. **Corporate headquarters location:** This location. **Other U.S. locations:** OK; AK. **Operations at this facility include:** This location serves as the company's main engineering office and warehouse.

CONVERGYS
12031 North Freeway, Houston TX 77060. 281/765-3900. **Contact:** Human Resources. **World Wide Web address:** http://www.convergys.com. **Description:** This company provides billing, customer and service support to large businesses, especially utilities. **NOTE:** This company provides a complete list of job openings at each of its Texas locations. See website and apply online. **Corporate headquarters location:** Cincinnati OH. **Other area locations:** Austin TX; Dallas TX: Irving TX; Lubbock TX: Brownsville TX; Killeen TX; Pharr TX. **Other U.S. locations:** Nationwide. **International locations:** Worldwide. **Number of employees worldwide:** 50,000.

THE DWYER GROUP
P.O. Box 3146, 1010 North University Parks Drive, Waco TX 76707. 254/745-2400. **Fax:** 254/745-2590. **Contact:** Human Resources. **World Wide Web address:** http://www.dwyergroup.com. **Description:** An international provider of specialty services through a group of service-based franchisers. **Subsidiaries include:** Rainbow International Carpet Dyeing & Cleaning Company has more than 300 franchises in the United States, 30 franchises in Canada, and more than 140 franchise operations in 16 other foreign countries. Rainbow specializes in indoor restoration and cleaning services including upholstery and drapery cleaning, carpet dyeing and cleaning, ceiling cleaning, deodorization, and comprehensive fire and water damage restoration and cleanup. Mr. Rooter Corporation is a complete residential and commercial plumbing service company, with a total of 300 franchises in the United States. Aire Serv Heating & Air Conditioning, Inc. is a franchiser of heating, ventilation, and air conditioning maintenance and repair services. The primary client base for its franchisees includes residential and light commercial applications. Aire Serv has nearly 40 U.S. franchises. Mr. Electrician electrical contracting service franchise. Glass Doctor is a residential, business and auto glass franchisor. DreamMaker Bath & Kitchen by Worldwide offers kitchen and bath remodeling franchise opportunities.

FIRST AMERICAN FLOOD DATA SERVICES
11902 Burnet Road, Suite 400, Austin TX 78758. 512/834-9595. **Toll-free number:** 800/447-1772. **Fax:** 800/447-2258. **Contact:** Judy Ellison, Human Resources Director. **World Wide Web address:** http://floodcert.com. **Description:** Determines whether properties are in a flood zone for mortgage companies and banks.

FISERV, INC.
595 Orleans Street, Beaumont TX 77701. 409/839-0600. **Contact:** Human Resources. **World Wide Web address:** http://www.fiserv.com. **Description:** An independent provider of data processing outsourcing capabilities and related products and services for financial institutions. FiServ's system applications are designed to increase the operating efficiency, customer service, and marketing capability of banks, credit unions, mortgage banks, savings institutions, and other financial intermediaries. **Corporate headquarters location:** Brookfield WI. **Other area locations:** Statewide. **Other U.S. locations:** Nationwide. **Listed on:** NASDAQ. **Stock exchange symbol:** FISV.

THE FREEMAN COMPANIES
1421 W. Mockingbird Lane, Dallas TX 75247. 214/670-9000. **Toll-free phone:** 888/670-3060. **Contact:** Human Resources. **World Wide Web address:** http://www.totalshowcase.com. **Description:** Offers set-up and display services for theater productions; trade shows and conventions.

GC SERVICES
332 West Highway 190, Copperas Cove, TX 76522. 254/547-4994. **Contact:** Human Resources. **World Wide Web address:** http://www.gcserv.com. **Description:** A collection agency. **Positions advertised include:** Account Reconciliation Clerk; Accounting Manager; Accounts Payable Analyst; Inventory Reconciliation Clerk; Remittance Processing Supervisor. **Corporate headquarters location:** This location: **Other U.S. locations:** Nationwide.

HOOVER'S, INC.
5800 Airport Boulevard, Austin TX 78752. 512/374-4500. **Fax:** 512/374-4501. **World Wide Web address:** http://www.hoovers.com. **Description:** A leading provider of business information for sales, marketing, business development, and other professionals who need intelligence on U.S. and global companies, industries, and people. This information is available through an online service, corporate intranets and distribution agreements with licensees, as well as via print and CD-ROM products. **NOTE:** Search and apply for positions online. **Positions advertised include:** Applications Manager; Direct Marketing Program Coordinator; Director of Retention Marketing; Editorial Operations Analyst; Industry Editor; Product Marketing Specialist - Large Accounts; Sales Operations Analyst; Saleslogix Programmer; VP Acquisition Marketing; VP Managing Editor. **Parent company:** Dun & Bradstreet.

HYDROCHEM INDUSTRIAL SERVICES
P.O. Box 478, Baytown TX 77522-0478. 281/834-7767. **Physical address:** 3600 Bayway Drive, Baytown TX 77520. **Fax:** 713/393-5953. **Contact:** Human Resources. **E-mail address:** jobs@hydrochem.com. **World Wide Web address:** http://www.hydrochem.com. **Description:** An industrial cleaning company that provides heavy-duty cleaning services such as high-pressure water blasting and vacuuming for industrial plants. **Positions advertised include:** Equipment Trainee. **Corporate headquarters location:** Canal Fulton OH.

INITIAL SECURITY
3355 Cherry Ridge Street, Suite 200, San Antonio TX 78230. 210/349-6321. **Toll-free phone:** 800/683-7771. **Fax:** 210/349-0213. **Contact:** Human Resources. **E-mail address:** initial@initialsecurity.com. **World Wide Web address:** http://www.initialsecurity.com. **Description:** Offers security guard services throughout the greater San Antonio area. **NOTE:** This company offers entry-level positions and training.

LOOMIS, FARGO & COMPANY
611 South Presa Street, San Antonio TX 78210. 210/226-0195. **Contact:** Human Resources. **World Wide Web address:** http://www.loomisfargo.com. **Description:** Provides armored transportation, cash vault, and ATM services. **NOTE:** This company has locations throughout Texas and the United States. See the company's website for job listings by location and for mailing addresses. **Corporate headquarters location:** Houston TX. **Other U.S. locations:** Nationwide.

NATIONAL LINEN SERVICE
620 Yorktown Road, Dallas TX 75208. 214/741-1751. **Contact:** Human Resources Manager. **World Wide**

Web address: http://www.national-linen.com. **Description:** A service that launders and delivers various kinds of linens including tablecloths and napkins to hotels and restaurants. **Positions advertised include:** Sales Representative. **Other area locations:** Lubbock TX; Wichita Falls TX. **Other U.S. locations:** Nationwide.

OCEANEERING INTERNATIONAL, INC.
11911 FM 529, Houston TX 77041. 713/329-4500. **Fax:** 713/329-4869. **Contact:** Human Resources. **World Wide Web address:** http://www.oceaneering.com. **Description:** Offers underwater diving, equipment, and related services to marine and space companies. Oceaneering sells also under the trade name of Solus Schall. Founded in 1964. This company has offices throughout Texas. **NOTE:** See the company's website for job listings by location and for specific contact information. **Corporate headquarters location:** This location. **Other U.S. locations:** Nationwide. **International locations:** Worldwide. **Listed on:** New York Stock Exchange. **Stock exchange symbol:** OII. **Number of employees worldwide:** 3,500.

PEROT SYSTEMS CORPORATION
2300 West Plano Parkway, Plano TX 75057-8427. 972/577-0000. **Toll-free phone:** 888/407-3768. **Fax:** 972/340-6100. **Contact:** Human Resources. **World Wide Web address:** http://www.perotsystems.com. **Description:** Operated by the former presidential candidate Ross Perot, this company provides technology consulting and outsourcing for global companies primarily in the engineering, financial, government and healthcare markets. Founded in 1988, it is on the Fortune 1000 list of companies. **NOTE:** Apply online. **Positions advertised include:** Senior Recruiter; Human Resources Analyst; Senior Developer/Team Lead; Technical Writer; Project Manager; Infrastructure Strategist. **Corporate headquarters location:** This location. **Other area locations:** Lubbock TX; Dallas TX. **Other U.S. location:** Nationwide. **Listed on:** New York Stock Exchange. **Stock exchange symbol:** PER.

PHILIP SERVICES CORPORATION
5151 San Felipe, Suite 1600, Houston TX 77056. 713/623-8777. **Contact:** Human Resources. **World Wide Web address:** http://www.contactpsc.com. **Description:** Provides specialized turn-around maintenance and environmental, electrical, and instrumentation contracting services. Principal markets include petroleum refiners, natural gas processors, petrochemical firms, oil producers, and paper and pulp companies throughout the United States and Europe. Services include turnkey heat exchanger maintenance, tower and vessel maintenance, petroleum and petrochemical storage tank cleaning, and sludge control. In addition, Philip Services Corporation offers turnaround management services, supervising all aspects of periodic maintenance projects. The company also installs electrical and instrumentation systems for offshore production platforms and petrochemical facilities.

QUANTUM RESEARCH INTERNATIONAL
7505B Lockheed Drive, El Paso TX 79925. 915/772-2700. **Fax:** 915/772-2250. **Contact:** Human Resources. **World Wide Web address:** http://www.quantum-intl.com. **Description:** Engaged in weapons research and general engineering for the army. **NOTE:** Mail resumes to 991 Discovery Drive, Huntsville, AL 35806; or fax them to 256/971-1802; or e-mail them to personnel@quantum-intl.com. **Corporate headquarters location:** Huntsville AL.

RIA
2395 Midway Road, Carrollton TX 75006. 972/250-7000. **Fax:** 972/250-7763. **Contact:** Human Resources. **World Wide Web address:** http://www.riahome.com. **Description:** One of the world's largest providers of solutions for tax research, compliance, and information. **NOTE:** This company prefers that jobseekers apply online at its corporate website: http://www.thomsoncareers.com. **Parent company:** Thomson Tax and Accounting.

SECURITAS
9441 LBJ Freeway, Suite 25, Dallas TX 75243. 972/238-5994. **Contact:** Human Resources. **World Wide Web address:** http://www.pinkertons.com. **Description:** Offers a full range of specialized protective services including property and high-rise services, health care and hospital services, special event services, ATM services, and patrol services. The company serves thousands of companies worldwide with investigation, threat assessment, and executive protection services. **NOTE:** Securitas has more than 50 locations throughout Texas. The company offers security, management and support positions. Jobseekers interested in security positions must apply at the nearest Securitas office. A list of offices can be found on the website as well as information about job qualifications. Management and support positions are listed on the corporate website along with contact information. **Positions advertised include:** Business Development Manager; Office Assistant; Branch Manager; Area Manager; Account Manager; Human Resources Manager; Recruiter; Scheduling Manager. **Corporate headquarters location:** Westlake Village CA. **Other U.S. locations:** Nationwide. **International locations:** Worldwide. **Operations at this facility include:** This location is engaged in industrial and private security, investigation, and security consulting. **Number of employees:** 200,000.

SERVICE CORPORATION INTERNATIONAL (SCI)
1929 Allen Parkway, Houston TX 77219. 713/522-5141. **Contact:** Human Resources. **World Wide Web address:** http://www.sci-corp.com. **Description:** Engaged in the operation of cemeteries and also provides cremation services and grief counseling. **NOTE:** Apply online at this company's website. **Positions advertised include:** Attorney; Senior Web Developer; Location Manager; Assistant Sales Manager. **Corporate headquarters location:** This location. **Other U.S. locations:** Nationwide. **International locations:** Worldwide. **Listed on:** New York Stock Exchange. **Stock exchange symbol:** SRV.

THE WHITNEY SMITH COMPANY, INC.
301 Commerce Street, Suite 1950, Fort Worth TX 76102. 817/877-0014. **Fax:** 817/877-3846. **Contact:** Human Resources. **World Wide Web address:** http://www.whitneysmithco.com. **Description:** A human resources consulting firm that provides professional assistance in all human resources disciplines, employee relations, compensation, recruitment, benefits, safety and training, and audits and litigation support.

TELECHECK SOUTHWEST
5251 Westheimer, Suite 1000, Houston TX 77056-5404. 713/331-7700. **Contact:** Human Resources. **World Wide Web address:** http://www.telecheck.com. **Description:** A check verification company. **NOTE:** Apply online at this company's website. **Corporate headquarters location:** This location. **Other U.S. locations:** Nationwide.

TURNER INDUSTRIES
P.O. Box 1029, Beaumont TX 77704. 409/722-8031. **Physical address**: 2005 Industrial Park Road, Nederland TX 77627. **Contact:** Human Resources. **Description:** Provides plant maintenance, including shut-downs and turn-arounds; pipe fabrication; tank cleaning; hauling; and rigging services. **Other area locations:** Texas City TX. **Other U.S. locations:** Nationwide. **Parent company:** Turner Industries.

WARRANTECH CORPORATION
2200 Highway 121 Suite 100, Bedford TX 76021. 817/785-6601. **Toll-free phone:** 800/833-8801. **Contact:** Human Resources. **World Wide Web address:** http://www.warrantech.com. **Description:** Provides extended service contracts and limited warranties to retailers, distributors, and manufacturers of automobiles, recreational vehicles, automotive components, home appliances, home entertainment products, computers and peripherals, and office and

communications equipment. **NOTE:** Apply online. **Positions advertised include:** Application Developer. **Corporate headquarters location:** This location. **Other U.S. locations:** Stamford CT.

WEST TELESERVICES
11330 IH-10 West, Building 3000, San Antonio TX 78249. 210/690-6900. **Toll-free phone:** 800/521-6000. **Contact:** Human Resources. **E-mail address:** westjobs@west.com. **World Wide Web address:** http://www.west.com. **Description:** A telemarketing company that deals with both outbound (phone sales) and inbound (phone orders) calls. This location handles inbound and outbound calling for *Fortune* 500 companies. **NOTE:** This company requires that interested jobseekers apply in person. The website provides job listings for each location as well as location addresses and office hours. **Positions advertised include:** Customer Service Representative; Interactive Sales Representative; Marketing Representative; Teleservices Representative. **Special programs:** Internships. **Other area locations:** Beaumont TX; El Paso TX; Harlingen TX; Killeen TX; Lubbock TX; Universal City TX; Waco TX; Sherman TX. **Listed on:** NASDAQ. **Stock exchange symbol:** WSTC.

Utah

ALORICA
8285 West 3500 South, Magna UT 84044. 801/907-3000. **Fax:** 801/907-3611. **Contact:** Human Resources. **E-mail address:** hr@alorica.com. **World Wide Web address:** http://www.alorica.com. **Description:** Provides outsourced customer service operations through its call centers Contact center services include technical support, customer service, help desk, billing, and sales (inbound and outbound). **NOTE:** See website for current job openings and application instructions. **Other area locations:** Chino CA.

BURRELLESLUCE
1687 West 820 North, Provo UT 84601. 801/374-6920. **Contact:** Eleanor Lovland, Human Resources. **E-mail address:** elovland@burrellesluce.com. **World Wide Web address:** http://www.burrellesluce.com. **Description:** A media monitoring company. Public relations and business professionals use Burrelles*Luce* to measure PR activity, track competitors, and retrieve important business news from around the world. **Corporate headquarters location:** Livingston NJ.

RR DONNELLEY
630 West 1000 North, Logan UT 84321. 435/755-4000. **Fax:** 435/755-4330. **Contact:** Human Resources. **World Wide Web address:** http://www.rrdonnelley.com. **Description:** Produces images and words, and provides printing and mailing services to companies in publishing, healthcare, and retail industries, among others. **NOTE:** See website for current job openings and to apply online. **Other U.S. locations:** Nationwide. **International locations:** Worldwide. **Parent company:** RR Donnelley. **Number of employees worldwide:** 47,000.

EVOLUTION GROUP INC.
150 West Civic Center Drive, Sandy UT 84070. 801/858-1400. **Fax:** 801/858-1398. **Contact:** Human Resources. **E-mail address:** inquire@evogroupinc.com. **World Wide Web address:** http://www.evogroupinc.com. **Description:** Specializes in outsourcing companies' group benefit programs, human resources, insurance services, and financial services.

FRANKLINCOVEY
2200 West Parkway Boulevard, Salt Lake City UT 84119. 801/975-1776. **Toll-free phone:** 800/827-1776. **Fax:** 801/817-8747. **Contact:** Human Resources. **World Wide Web address:** http://www.franklincovey.com. **Description:** Provides training seminars and products designed to improve individual productivity through effective time management. The company also offers other training and consulting services. **NOTE:** See website for current job openings and to download application. Submit completed application and resume by fax or mail. **International locations:** Worldwide. **Listed on:** New York Stock Exchange. **Stock exchange symbol:** FC. **Number of employees worldwide:** 2,500.

HARRIS INTERACTIVE INC.
1998 South Columbia Lane, Orem UT 84097. 801/226-1524. **Fax:** 801/226-3483. **Contact:** Jon Hansen, Recruiter. **E-mail address:** jhansen@harrisinteractive.com. **World Wide Web address:** http://www.harrisinteractive.com. **Description:** A market research, polling, and consulting firm. **NOTE:** Please visit website for current job openings and to apply online. **Positions advertised include:** HR Professional; Telephone Center Supervisor; Trainer; Telephone Interviewer. **Corporate headquarters location:** Rochester NY. **Other U.S. locations:** Nationwide. **International locations:** United Kingdom; Belgium; France; China.

LOOMIS, FARGO & CO.
563 West 500 South, Suite 340, Bountiful UT 84010. 801/397-8507. **Fax:** 801/397-8155. **E-mail address:** employment@loomisfargo.com. **World Wide Web address:** http://www.loomisfargo.com. **Description:** Provides security escorts, armored transportation, and protection services. **NOTE:** See website for current job openings and application instructions. **Positions advertised include:** Driver/Guard; Branch Manager; Customer Service Representative; Transportation Supervisor. **Corporate headquarters location:** Houston TX. **Other area locations:** Salt Lake City UT; Saint George UT. **Other U.S. locations:** Nationwide. **Parent company:** Securitas AB.

MANAGEMENT & TRAINING CORPORATION
500 North Marketplace Drive, P.O. Box 10, Centerville UT 84014. 801/693-2600. **Toll-free phone:** 800/574-4682. **Fax:** 801/693-2900. **Contact:** Human Resources. **World Wide Web address:** http://www.mtctrains.com. **Description:** As a government contractor, Management & Training Corporation manages the operation of Job Corps centers nationwide; manages the operations of low- to minimum-security correctional facilities; and provides building maintenance services. **Special programs:** Internships; Training. **Corporate headquarters location:** This location. **Other area locations:** Clearfield UT. **Other U.S. locations:** Nationwide. **International locations:** Ontario Canada; Queensland Australia. **Listed on:** Privately held.

PAYCHEX, INC.
10757 South Riverfront Parkway, Suite 200, South Jordan UT 84095. 801/561-3473. **Fax:** 801/561-3644. **Contact:** Human Resources Manager. **E-mail address:** fieldrecruiting@paychex.com; jobopps@paychex.com. **World Wide Web address:** http://www.paychex.com. **Description:** A national payroll processing and payroll tax preparation company for small- to medium-sized businesses. The company also provides human resource products and services including employee handbook services, Section 125 cafeteria plans, insurance services, and 401(k) record keeping. Paychex has 94 locations and serves nearly 225,000 clients nationwide. **NOTE:** See website for current job openings, or contact Human Resources by telephone. **Positions advertised include:** Customer Service Representative. **Special programs:** Internships; Co-ops. **Corporate headquarters location:** Rochester NY. **Other U.S. locations:** Nationwide.

SECURITAS SECURITY SERVICES
5525 South 900 East, Salt Lake City UT 84117. 801/262-5678. **Toll-free phone:** 800/232-7465. **Fax:** 801/266-7935. **Contact:** Branch Manager. **World Wide Web address:** http://www.securitasinc.com. **Description:** One of the world's largest suppliers of global, total security solutions. The company provides a broad array of security-related services to address the protection needs of more than 20,000 customers through 220 offices in the United States, Canada, Mexico, Europe, and Asia. Pinkerton counts approximately half of the *Fortune* 500 companies as its clients. **NOTE:** For Security Officer positions, contact

the office. For all other positions, please visit website to search for jobs and apply online. **Corporate headquarters location:** Stockholm, Sweden. **Other area locations:** Magna UT. **Other U.S. locations:** Nationwide. **Number of employees worldwide:** 200,000.

Vermont

A.N. DERINGER, INC.
64-66 North Main Street, P.O. Box 1309, St. Albans VT 05478-1012. 802/524-8116. **Toll-free phone:** 800/523-4357. **Fax:** 802/524-8297. **Contact:** Human Resources. **World Wide Web address:** http://www.anderinger.com. **Description:** Offers a wide range of international trade services from customs house brokerage and freight forwarding to warehousing, cargo insurance, global transportation and confidential business consultation, operating 33 offices in the U.S. and agents worldwide. Founded in 1919. **Positions advertised include:** Human Resources Generalist; Maintenance. **Other area locations:** Burlington VT; Derby Line VT; Highgate Springs VT. Norton VT; St. Albans VT. **Other U.S. locations:** Nationwide. **International locations:** Worldwide. **Number of employees nationwide:** 550.

Virginia

ALION SCIENCE AND TECHNOLOGY
1750 Tysons Boulevard, Suite 1300, McLean, VA 22102. 703/918-4480. **Contact:** Human Resources. **World Wide Web address:** http://www.alionscience.com. **Description:** A privately held, employee-owned global research and development company primarily serving the U.S. government. Founded in 1936. **NOTE:** Search and apply for positions online. **Positions advertised include:** Director, Contracts/Procurement. **Corporate headquarters location:** This location. **Other area locations:** Alexandria VA. **Number of employees worldwide:** 1,700.

AMERICAN BUILDING MAINTENANCE (ABM)
113 Clermont Avenue, Alexandria VA 22304. 703/461-7501. **Fax:** 703/236-0288. **Contact:** Human Resources. **World Wide Web address:** http://www.abm.com. **Description:** Provides maintenance services for area offices. ABM operates 76 branch offices in 40 states. **Corporate headquarters location:** San Francisco CA. **Other U.S. locations:** Nationwide. **Operations at this facility include:** Service. **Listed on:** New York Stock Exchange. **Stock exchange symbol:** ABM. Number of employees nationwide: 43,000.

APPLIED ORDNANCE TECHNOLOGY, INC.
100 Greenspring Drive, Stafford VA 22554. 540/657-2680. **Fax:** 540/288-9905. **Contact:** Human Resources. **World Wide Web address:** http://www.aot.com. **Description:** Provides engineering and management services to support weapons engineering, environmental engineering, ordnance design, information technology, system safety, and gun and ammunition systems. **NOTE:** Search and apply for positions online. **Positions advertised include:** Training Analyst; Sr. Systems Analyst; Systems Safety Engineer. **Corporate headquarters location:** Waldorf MD.

THE BRINK'S COMPANY
1801 Bayberry Court, P.O. Box 18100, Richmond VA 23226. 804/289-9600. **Fax:** 804/289-9768. **Contact:** Human Resources. **E-mail address:** info@BrinksCompany.com. **World Wide Web address:** http://www.pittston.com. **Description:** The Brink's Company is a global leader in business and security services with three operating units: Brink's, Incorporated, a provider of secure transportation and cash management services; Brink's Home Security, a residential alarm company; and BAX Global, providing supply chain management and transportation solutions. **NOTE:** Search and apply for positions online. **Positions advertised include:** Tax Counsel, State and Local; Manager of Taxes, International. **Corporate headquarters location:** This location. **Other U.S. locations:** Darien CT. **Listed on:** New York Stock Exchange. **Stock exchange symbol:** PZB. **Annual sales/revenues:** $4 billion. **Number of employees worldwide:** 50,000.

THE CNA CORPORATION
4825 Mark Center Drive, Alexandria VA 22311. 703/824-2004. **Contact:** Human Resources. **World Wide Web address:** http://www.cna.org. **Description:** A non-profit organization that provides independent research and analysis to inform the work of public sector leaders. **Positions advertised include:** Research Specialist; Project Control Analyst; Editor; Pricing Analyst; Business Analyst; Sr. Accountant. **Number of employees nationwide:** 600.

CALIBER ASSOCIATES
10530 Rosehaven Street, Suite 400, Fairfax VA 22030. 703/385-3200. **Fax:** 703/385-3206. **Contact:** Human Resources. **E-mail:** careers@caliber.com. **World Wide Web Address:** http://www.caliber.com. **Description:** Caliber Associates is a consulting firm, providing research and consulting services that help clients develop and manage effective human services programs and policies for the public good. **Positions advertised include:** Research Associate; Juvenile Justice Manager; Project Manager; Executive Director, National Child Care Information Center. **Parent company:** ICF Consulting.

CALIBRE
6354 Walker Lane, Suite 300, Alexandria VA 22310-3252. 703/797-8500. **Toll-free phone:** 888/225-4273. **Fax:** 703/797-8501. **Contact:** Human Resources. **World Wide Web address:** http://www.calibresys.com. **Description:** An employee-owned management and technology services company. The company develops solutions to solve management, technology, and program challenges for defense, federal civil, state and local government, and commercial customers. **Positions advertised include:** Analyst; Contracts Analyst; Environmental Engineer; GIS Technician; Program Analyst; Safety Training Manager; Sr. Analyst; Sr. Programmer/Analyst; Systems Accountant. **Corporate headquarters location:** This location.

CINTAS CORPORATION
P.O. Box 1207, Culpeper VA 22701. 540/825-2300. **Contact:** Human Resources. **World Wide Web address:** http://www.cintas.com. **Description:** Provides uniform rental, industrial laundering, and restroom cleaning services. Operates 351 facilities in the U.S. and Canada, including 15 manufacturing plants and seven distribution centers. **Positions advertised include:** Service Sales Rep. **Corporate headquarters location:** Cincinnati OH. **Other U.S. locations:** Nationwide. **Operations at this facility include:** Administration; Divisional Headquarters; Manufacturing; Regional Headquarters; Sales; Service. **Listed on:** NASDAQ. **Stock exchange symbol:** CTAS. **Number of employees at this location:** 140. **Number of employees worldwide:** 27,000.

CORT BUSINESS SERVICES
11250 Waples Mill Road, Suite 500, Fairfax VA 22030. 703/968-8500. **Toll-free phone:** 888/669-2678. **Fax:** 703/968-8550. **Contact:** Director of Human Resources. **E-mail address:** jobs@cort1.com. **World Wide Web address:** http://www.cort1.com. **Description:** A national provider of rental furniture, accessories, and related services in the rent-to-rent segment of the furniture rental industry. The segment serves both corporate and individual customers. CORT focuses on corporate customers by offering office and residential furniture and related accessories through a direct sales force of approximately 450 salespeople and a network of 94 showrooms in 26 states and the District of Columbia. Corporate customers include *Fortune* 500 companies, small businesses and professionals, and owners and operators of apartment communities. **Corporate headquarters location:** This location.

FC BUSINESS SYSTEMS, INC.
3060 Williams Drive, Suite 600, Fairfax VA 22031-4648. 703/752-8400. **Fax:** 703/560-1396. **Contact:** Manager of Personnel Department. **E-mail address:**

jobs@amerind.com. **World Wide Web address:** http://www.fcbs.com. **Description:** Provides engineering and IT services to government customers. Founded in 1984. **NOTE:** Search and apply for positions online. **Corporate headquarters location:** This location. **Parent company:** General Dynamics. **Number of employees nationwide:** 1,100.

GEOEYE
21700 Atlantic Boulevard, Dulles VA 20166. 703/480-7500. **Fax:** 703/450-9570. **Contact:** Human Resources. **E-Mail address:** recruiter@orbimage.com. **World Wide Web address:** http://www.geoeye.com. **Description:** GeoEye is a leading global provider of geospatial imagery products and services, with a constellation of digital remote sensing satellites complemented by data from other optical, aerial and radar sources. **NOTE:** Search and apply for positions on Website. **Positions advertised include:** Federal; DoD Sales Manager; IT System Engineer; Manager, Network and Ground Operations; Science and Production Engineer Manager.

ICF CONSULTING
9300 Lee Highway, Fairfax VA 22031. 703/934-3000. **Fax:** 703/934-3740. **Contact:** Employment Manager. **E-mail address:** info@icfconsulting.com. **World Wide Web address:** http://www.icfconsulting.com. **Description**: ICF Consulting is a management, technology, and policy consulting firm that develops solutions in five markets: energy, environment, homeland security, community development, and transportation. Since 1969, ICF Consulting has served major corporations, government at all levels, and multinational institutions. **NOTE:** Entry-level positions available. Search and apply for positions online. **Positions advertised include:** Associate; Associate for Emergency Management; Configuration Management Specialist; Contracts Specialist; Data Administrator; Director/VP, Business Development, Homeland Security; Energy Management and Efficiency Expert; Housing and Community Development Associate. **Corporate headquarters location:** This location. **Other U.S. locations:** Nationwide. **International locations:** Lisbon, Portugal; London, England; Moscow, Russia; Rio de Janeiro, Brazil; Toronto, Canada.

ITC LEARNING CORPORATION
1616 Anderson Road, Suite 109, McLean VA 22102. 703/442-0670. **Toll-free phone:** 800/638-3757. **Fax:** 703/852-7174. **Contact:** Personnel. **E-mail address:** learning@itclearning.com. **World Wide Web address:** http://www.itclearning.com. **Description:** A full-service training company specializing in the development, production, marketing, and sale of both off-the-shelf and custom-designed multimedia training courseware for commercial, educational, and government organizations. The company also markets, sells, and distributes linear training products (primarily videotape and text-based) through its Training Department. Founded in 1977. **Corporate headquarters location:** This location. **Other U.S. locations:** Atlanta GA. **International locations:** Australia; United Kingdom. **Subsidiaries include:** CI Acquisition Corporation. **Annual sales/revenues:** $21 - $50 million. **Number of employees at this location:** 45. **Number of employees nationwide:** 100.

INSTITUTE OF DEFENSE ANALYSES
4850 Mark Center Drive, Alexandria VA 22311-1882. 703/845-2000. **Fax:** 240/282-8314. **Contact:** Employment Office. **E-mail address:** resumes@ida.org. **World Wide Web address:** http://www.ida.org. **Description:** Provides defense system evaluation, testing, and simulation for the government. The non-profit, federally funded Institute of Defense Analyses also offers technical support services. **Positions advertised include:** Administrative Officer; Network System Analyst; Micro-Computer Technician; Research Assistant; Analyst, Intelligent Systems; Defense Resource Analyst; Satellite Test and Evaluation Analyst; Undersea Warfare Analyst; Cost Research and Analysis. **Special programs:** Internships. **Internship information:** The institute offers several paid internships every summer. Applications are accepted January through March. Candidates are asked to send a cover letter and resume by fax or e-mail. **Corporate headquarters location:** This location. **Number of employees at this location:** 750.

MARTIN FOCUS GROUP
1199 North Fairfax Street, Suite 150, Alexandria VA 22314. 703/519-5800. **Fax:** 703/519-0704. **Contact:** Human Resources. **World Wide Web address:** http://www.martinfocus.com. **Description:** Designs and conduct focus groups throughout the state. **Other area locations:** Richmond VA; Roanoke VA.

MERCER HUMAN RESOURCE CONSULTING
1051 East Cary Street, Suite 900, Richmond VA 23219. 804/344-2600. **Fax:** 804/344-2601. **Contact:** Human Resources. **World Wide Web address:** http://www.mercerhr.com. **Description:** One of the world's largest actuarial and human resources management consulting firms, providing advice to organizations on all aspects of employee/management relationships. Services include retirement, health and welfare, performance and rewards, communication, investment, human resources administration, risk, finance and insurance, and health care provider consulting. **NOTE:** Search and apply for positions online. **Positions advertised include:** Actuarial Analyst; Actuarial Intern. **Corporate headquarters location:** New York NY. **Parent company:** Marsh & McLennan Companies, Inc. **Number of employees worldwide:** 15,000.

SERCO
2650 Park Tower Drive, Suite 800, Vienna VA 22180. 571/226-5000. **Contact:** Human Resources. **E-mail address:** resumes@serco.com. **World Wide Web address:** http://www.serco-na.com. **Description:** Serco provides a broad range of services to the U.S. Military, the U.S. Postal Service, US Federal Aviation Administration, Canadian Department of National Defence, Ontario Ministry of Transportation, as well as other federal civilian agencies, state and local governments, and commercial customers. **NOTE:** Search and apply for positions online. **Positions advertised include:** Software Engineer and Systems Analyst; Director Of Communications. **Special programs:** Training. **Corporate headquarters location:** This location. **Other U.S. locations:** Nationwide. **International locations:** Worldwide. **Number of employees nationwide:** 6,000. **Number of employees worldwide:** 40,000.

SPARKS PERSONNEL SERVICES
11490 Commerce Park Drive, Suite 100, Reston VA 20191. 703/620-6444. **Fax:** 703/620-2968. **Contact:** Human Resources. **World Wide Web address:** http://www.sparkspers.com. **Description:** Staffing firm that places personnel In a variety of businesses and positions. **NOTE:** Search and apply for positions through website. **Positions advertised include:** Administrative Assistant; Customer Service Rep; Executive Assistant; Marketing Specialist.

SYSTEM PLANNING CORPORATION
1000 Wilson Boulevard, Suite 3000, Arlington VA 22209-2211. 703/351-8200. **Fax:** 703/351-8261. **Contact:** Director of Staff Development. **E-mail address:** recruiting@sysplan.com. **World Wide Web address:** http://www.sysplan.com. **Description:** Provides high-technology systems and support for national security initiatives and policy. Customers include state and local governments, major aerospace companies, and architectural and engineering firms. **NOTE:** Search and apply for positions online. **Positions advertised include:** Emergency Planning Expert; Information Assurance Engineer; Image/Signal Processing Engineer; Avionics Test Engineer. **Corporate headquarters location:** This location.

TALLYGENICOM CORPORATION
4500 Daly Drive, Suite 100, Chantilly VA 20151. 703/633-8700. **Fax:** 703/222-7629. **Contact:** Dick

Gooch, Manager of Human Resources. **World Wide Web address:** http://www.tallygenicom.com. **Description:** TallyGenicom offers a wide selection of ultra-reliable business and industrial printers, printing solutions, printer supplies, printer parts, and service. They provide a full range of impact and laser printers, including line matrix, serial matrix, industrial ink jet, monochrome laser and color laser**Positions advertised include:** HR Representative. **Corporate headquarters location:** This location. **Other area locations:** Waynesboro VA. **Other U.S. locations:** Kent WA. **Operations at this facility include:** This location manufactures printers and relays. **Number of employees nationwide:** 2,150.

VSE CORPORATION
2550 Huntington Avenue, Alexandria VA 22303-1499. 703/329-4277. **Fax:** 703/329-4623. **Recorded jobline:** 703/329-4784. **Contact:** HR/Recruiter. **E-mail address:** hr@vsecorp.com. **World Wide Web address:** http://www.vsecorp.com. **Description:** Offers engineering services, logistical support services, and data processing services. **NOTE:** Search and apply for positions online. **Positions advertised include:** Engineering Technician. **Other U.S. locations:** NJ; MD; FL; CA; MI; GA. **Listed on:** NASDAQ. **Stock exchange symbol:** VSEC. **Number of employees at this location:** 200. **Number of employees nationwide:** 1,200.

Washington

ADT SECURITY SERVICES
11824 North Creek Parkway North, 105 N, Bothell WA 98011. 206/624-3103. **Contact:** Human Resources. **World Wide Web address:** http://www.adtsecurityservices.com. **Description:** Designs, installs, sells, and monitors fire and burglar alarm systems for commercial and industrial retail customers. The company also offers armed and unarmed security guards. **Corporate headquarters location:** Boca Raton FL. **Other U.S. locations:** Nationwide.

AMERICAN BUILDING MAINTENANCE
16 East Columbia Drive, Kennewick WA 99336. 509/582-9776. **Toll-free phone:** 800/678-4270. **Fax:** 509/582.5224. **Contact:** Human Resources. **World Wide Web address:** http://www.cbvcp.com. **Description:** American Building Maintenance (ABM) provides nationwide maintenance services to commercial and residential facilities. ABM was founded over 75 years ago. ABM offers a variety of services including janitorial, lighting maintenance, floor care, janitorial supplies, window cleaning, and carpet cleaning. **Positions advertised include:** Janitorial; Maintenance. **Corporate headquarters location:** This location. **Other U.S. locations:** Nationwide.

LABOR READY, INC.
P.O. Box 2910, Tacoma WA 98402-2910. 253/383-9101. **Physical address**: 1015 A Street, Tocoma WA 98402. **Toll-free phone:** 800/610-8920. **Fax:** 800/850-9559. **Contact:** Human Resources. **World Wide Web address:** http://www.laborready.com. **Description:** Provides temporary employees, primarily to construction, warehousing, landscaping, and manufacturing businesses. Founded in 1989. **Corporate headquarters location:** This location. **Other U.S. locations:** Nationwide. **International locations:** Canada; Puerto Rico; United Kingdom. **Listed on:** New York Stock Exchange. **Stock exchange symbol:** LRW. **Annual sales/revenues:** More than $100 million.

LOOMIS FARGO & COMPANY
3702 South G Street, Tacoma WA 98418. 253/475-4225. **Fax:** 253-475-2356. **Contact:** Personnel. **World Wide Web address:** http://www.loomisfargo.com. **Description:** An armored security service specializing in transporting currency. **NOTE:** Applications will not be mailed to jobseekers. They must be picked up in person. **Other U.S. locations:** Nationwide.

LYNX MEDICAL SYSTEMS
15325 SE 30th Place, Suite 200, Bellevue WA 98007. 425/641-4451. **Contact:** Human Resources. **E-mail address:** humanresources@lynxmed.com. **World Wide Web address:** http://www.lynxmed.com. **Description:** Offers coding, billing, transcription, and consulting services to professional medical groups, health care facilities and systems, and third-party payers. **Positions advertised include:** CDM Coordinator; Inpatient/Outpatient Coding Specialist; Sales Manager; Executive Assistant. **Corporate headquarters location:** This location. **Other U.S. locations:** Waterloo IA.

MUZAK LLC
P.O. Box 80416, Seattle WA 98108. 206/763-2517. **Physical address:** 200 South Orcas Street, Seattle WA 98108. **Contact:** Personnel Department. **E-mail address:** corporate@nbbi.com. **World Wide Web address:** http://www.muzak.com. **Description:** Provides satellite delivered and on-site music services to commercial and retail establishments delivered both directly and through franchised dealers worldwide. Muzak serves approximately 300,000 locations worldwide through over 200 sales and service locations. **Corporate headquarters location:** Fort Mill SC.

NORTHWEST PROTECTIVE SERVICES, INC.
2700 Elliott Avenue, Seattle WA 98121. 206/448-4040. **Fax:** 206/448-2461. **Contact:** Human Resources. **World Wide Web address:** http://www.nwprotective.com. **Description:** Provides contract security services. **Positions advertised include:** Security Officer. **Corporate headquarters location:** This location. **Other area locations:** Spokane WA; Tacoma WA. **Other U.S. locations:** Portland OR. **Operations at this facility include:** Service. **Number of employees nationwide:** 700.

SECURITAS USA
2510 North Pines Road, Suite 1, Spokane WA 99206. 509/927-2552. **Contact:** Human Resources. **World Wide Web address:** http://www.securitas.com. **Description:** One of the world's largest suppliers of global, total security solutions. The company provides a broad array of security-related services including business intelligence, investigations, security systems integration, and consulting.

SIEMENS BUSINESS SERVICES, INC.
4500 150th Avenue NE, Overlake North, Building A, Redmond WA 98052. 425/556-3800. **Contact:** Personnel. **World Wide Web address:** http://www.siemens.com. **Description:** Provides systems integration, help desk, and PC repair services to *Fortune* 1000 companies and federal clients. **Corporate headquarters location:** Norwalk CT. **Other U.S. locations:** Nationwide. **Listed on:** New York Stock Exchange. **Stock exchange symbol:** SI.

SOLUCIENT
411 108th Avenue NE, Suite 800, Bellevue WA 98004. 425/455-2652. **Toll-free phone:** 800/290-8982. **Fax:** 425/451-9736. **Contact:** Human Resources. **E-mail address:** becareers@solucient.com. **World Wide Web address:** http://www.solucient.com. **Description:** Provides data processing services and develops software for the health care industry. **Positions advertised include:** Quality Assurance Manager; Receptionist; Senior Program Manager; Senior Technical Writer. **Corporate headquarters location:** Evanston IL.

VERISIGN
P.O. Box 2909, Olympia WA 98501. 360/493-6000. **Physical address:** 4501 Intelco Loop SE, Lacy WA 98503. **Contact:** Human Resources. **E-mail address:** jobs@verisign.com. **World Wide Web address:** http://www.verisign.com. **Description:** Operates intelligent infrastructure services that enable people and business to find, connect, secure, and transact across global networks. **Corporate headquarters location:**

Mountain View CA. **Listed on:** NASDAQ. **Stock exchange symbol:** VRSN.

THE WACKENHUT CORPORATION
1035 Andover Park West, Suite 210, Tukwila WA 98188. 253/872-1555. **Fax:** 253/395-8099. **Contact:** Human Resources. **World Wide Web address:** http://www.wackenhut.com. **Description:** Provides physical security services, correction services, and related products to businesses, governments, and individuals from more than 150 offices worldwide. Specific services include security guard services; corrections staffing; private investigative services; the assembly and sale of electronic security equipment and systems; the training of security guards and fire and crash rescue personnel; providing fire protection and emergency ambulance service to municipalities; security consulting; planning, designing, and implementing integrated security systems; and providing specialized services to the nuclear power industry. **Corporate headquarters location:** Palm Beach Gardens FL. **Other U.S. locations:** Nationwide. **Number of employees nationwide:** 40,000.

Wisconsin

ADECCO STAFFING
2915 South 108th Street, West Allis WI 53227-3519. 414/771-6005. **Contact:** Human Resources. **World Wide Web address:** http://www.adeccousa.com. **Description:** Offers staffing, career services, executive search and e-recruitment. **Corporate headquarters location:** Melville NY. **Other area locations:** Statewide. **Other U.S. locations:** Nationwide. **Parent company:** Adecco SA. **Listed on:** New York Stock Exchange. **Stock exchange symbol:** ADO.

AUTOMATIC DATA PROCESSING (ADP)
330 East Kilborn Avenue, Suite 875, Milwaukee WI 53202. 414/273-4444. **Contact:** Human Resources Department. **World Wide Web address:** http://www.adp.com. **Description:** Offers technology-based solutions through four business units: employer services offers HR, payroll and benefits administration; brokerage services provides securities processing and investor communication services; dealer services provides computing solutions for auto and truck dealers; and claims services provides auto repair estimating and claims processing. **Positions advertised include:** Major Accounts Sales Representatives; SBS Sales Outside Sales Associate. **Corporate headquarters location:** Roseland NJ. **Operations at this facility include:** This location is a Major Account Services Center. **Listed on:** New York Stock Exchange. **Stock exchange symbol:** ADP.

FISERV, INC.
255 Fiserv Drive, P.O. Box 979, Brookfield WI 53008-0979. 262/879-5000. **Toll-free phone:** 800/872-7882. **Fax:** 262/879-5013. **Contact:** Human Resources Department. **World Wide Web address:** http://www.fiserv.com. **Description:** Provides information management systems and services to the financial industry, including transaction processing, outsourcing, business process outsourcing and software and systems solutions. **Positions advertised include:** Business Analyst; Client Services Supervisor; Conversion Programmer Analyst; Corporate Attorney; Specialist, Project Management; Director of Marketing Services; HRIS Administrator; MicroProducts Systems Analyst; Network Engineer. **Corporate headquarters location:** This location. **Other area locations:** Statewide. **Other U.S. locations:** Nationwide. **International locations:** Worldwide. **Listed on:** NASDAQ. **Stock exchange symbol:** FISV. **Annual sales/revenues:** More than $100 million. **Number of employees at this location:** 8,500.

GREATLAND CORPORATION
3130 South Ridge Road, Green Bay WI 54304. 920/339-4407. **Fax:** 920/337-4187. **Contact:** Melissa Englebert. **E-mail address:** menglebert@greatland.com. **World Wide Web address:** http://www.greatland.com. **Description:** A national provider of products and services for the financial, tax and accounting services markets. Founded in 1974. **Positions advertised include:** Accounts Receivable/Collections Clerk; Assistant Marketing Manager; Business Development Manager; Market Specialist; Project Manager; Senior Systems Analyst; Software Support Associate; Requirements and Technical Writing Analyst. **Corporate headquarters location:** Grand Rapids MI.

HOME ENTRY SERVICES
2605 Kennedy Road, P.O. Box 592, Janesville WI 53545. 608/757-2445. **Fax:** 608/757-0012. **Contact:** Kristin Williams, Human Resources. **Description:** A data entry company that allows homeworkers to log into the Internet to process work digitally from images instead of paper.

LOOMIS FARGO & COMPANY
603 South Oneida Street, Green Bay WI 54303. 920/494-0124. **Fax:** 920/494-0749. **Contact:** Personnel. **E-mail address:** employment@loomisfargo.com. **World Wide Web address:** http://www.loomisfargo.com. **Description:** An armored security service specializing in transporting currency. **Corporate headquarters location:** Houston TX. **Other area locations:** Milwaukee WI; Madison WI. **Other U.S. locations:** Nationwide.

METAVANTE CORPORATION
4900 West Brown Deer Road, Milwaukee WI 53223. 414/357-2290. **Toll-free phone:** 800/236-3282, extension 42200. **Contact:** Human Resources. **World Wide Web address:** http://www.metavante.com. **Description:** Provides technology for financial institutions including customer relationship management, electronic banking, electronic funds transfer, financial account processing, and wealth management. **NOTE:** Entry-level positions and second and third shifts are offered. **Special programs:** Internships; Training; Summer Jobs. **Corporate headquarters location:** This location. **Other U.S. locations:** GA; CA; MI; FL; MA; IL; NJ. **Parent company:** Marshall & Ilsley Corporation. **Operations at this facility include:** Administration; Research & Development; Sales; Service. **Listed on:** New York Stock Exchange. **Stock exchange symbol:** MI.

MOORE WALLACE RESPONSE MARKETING SERVICES
1333 Scheuring Road, De Pere WI 54115. 920/499-0811. **Fax:** 920/339-1676. **Contact:** Human Resources. **World Wide Web address:** http://www.mwrms.com. **Description:** Provides a wide range of direct mailing services. **Corporate headquarters location:** Bannockburn IL. **Other area locations:** Green Bay WI. **Other U.S. locations:** IN; OH; CA; NY; IL; MD. **Parent company:** RR Donnelley. **Operations at this facility include:** Manufacturing.

SECURITAS SECURITY SERVICES USA, INC.
2501 South Oneida Street, Appleton WI 54915. 920/739-9271. **Fax:** 920/739-6252. **Contact:** Human Resources. **World Wide Web address:** http://www.securitas.com. **Description:** Securitas offers a full range of specialized protective services including Premier Property/High-Rise Services, Healthcare/Hospital Services, Special Event Services, ATM Services, and Patrol Services. **Operations at this facility include:** This location is a district office of the international investigation and security company. **Parent company:** Securitas.

Wyoming

AFFINION GROUP
3001 East Pershing Boulevard, Cheyenne WY 82001. 307/771-2700. **Contact:** Karen Walgren, Human Resources. **E-mail address:** jobs@affiniongroup.com. **World Wide Web address:** http://www.affiniongroup.com, or http://www.trilegiant.com. **Description:** Trilegiant, Trilegiant Loyalty Solutions and Progeny Marketing Innovations recently merged to become Affinion Group, which is an affinity direct marketer of value-added membership, insurance and package

enhancement programs and services to consumers. Affinion Group currently offers its programs and services worldwide through more than 4,500 affinity partners in a wide variety of industries, including financial services, retail, travel, telecommunications, utilities and Internet. **Corporate headquarters location:** Norwalk CT. **Operations at this facility include:** Administration; Call Center; Sales; Service. **Number of employees nationwide:** 3,600.

CHARITIES AND SOCIAL SERVICES

You can expect to find the following types of companies in this section:
Social and Human Service Agencies • Job Training and Vocational Rehabilitation Services • Nonprofit Organizations

---

New openings in community and social services occupations should increase 20.8%, adding 483,000 new jobs and growing the total employment from 2,317,000 to 2,800, 000. Continued rapid growth should result as the elderly population increases rapidly and as greater efforts are made to provide services for the disabled, the sick, substance abusers, and individuals and families in crisis.

Arizona

AMERICAN RED CROSS
6135 North Black Canyon Highway, Phoenix AZ 85015-1892. 602/336-6660. **Fax:** 602/336-5770. **Recorded jobline:** 602/336-6666. **Contact:** Human Resources. **E-mail address:** hr@arizonaredcross.org. **World Wide Web address:** http://www.arizonaredcross.org. **Description:** A humanitarian organization that aids disaster victims, gathers blood for crisis distribution, trains individuals to respond to emergencies, educates individuals on various diseases, and raises funds for other charitable establishments. **Positions advertised include:** Instructor. **Corporate headquarters location:** Washington DC. **Other U.S. locations:** Nationwide.

BIG BROTHERS BIG SISTERS OF AMERICA
202 South First Avenue, Suite 101, Yuma AZ 85364. 928/782-7422. **Contact:** Human Resources. **World Wide Web address:** http://www.bbbsa.org. **Description:** Provides volunteer and professional services to assist children and youth in achieving their highest potential as they grow to become responsible men and women, through over 505 Big Brothers Big Sisters agencies nationwide. Across the country, more than 75,000 children are matched with adult volunteers. The agencies also provide an array of counseling, referral, and family support services to parents and children in over 110,000 families each year. Additional programs focus on children with special needs including those with physical disabilities or learning disabilities, as well as those who are abused, neglected, or have dropped out of school. Special prevention and intervention programs at many agencies address the problems of drug abuse, teen pregnancy, foster care, and juvenile delinquency. **Corporate headquarters location:** Philadelphia PA.

EASTER SEALS ARIZONA
2075 South Cottonwood Drive, Tempe AZ 85282. 602/252-6061. **Toll-free phone:** 800/626-6061. **Fax:** 602/252-6065. **Contact:** Human Resources. **E-mail address:** hr@azseals.org. **World Wide Web address:** http://www.eastersealsarizona.org. **Description:** Provides treatment and support services for disabled individuals.

GOODWILL INDUSTRIES OF CENTRAL ARIZONA
417 North 16th Street, Phoenix AZ 85006. 602/254-2222. **Fax:** 602/258-7047. **Contact:** Human Resources. **E-mail address:** hr@goodwillaz.org. **World Wide Web address:** http://www.goodwillcentralaz.org. **Description:** Besides operating over 1,400 thrift stores nationwide, Goodwill is a nonprofit provider of employment training for the disabled and the poor. **Positions advertised include:** Store Manager; Youth Services Program Coordinator; Youth Services Case Manager; Career Center Educator; Case Manager; Event Coordinator; Community Based Instructor. **Special programs:** Internships. **Corporate headquarters location:** Bethesda MD. **Other U.S. locations:** Nationwide. **Parent company:** Goodwill Industries International. **Number of employees at this location:** 225.

LA FRONTERA CENTER, INC.
502 West 29th Street, Tucson AZ 85713. 520/838-3945. **Contact:** Human Resources. **World Wide Web address:** http://www.lafrontera.org. **Description:** A nonprofit, community-based, behavioral health center that provides mental health and chemical dependency services to residents of Pima County. The center operates 30 programs in 23 different facilities throughout Pima County. La Frontera Center provides services for infants born to addicted mothers, children with developmental disabilities, chemically dependent adults, and homeless adults with mental illnesses. The center also provides outreach, rehabilitation, and substance abuse recovery programs. Founded in 1968. **Positions advertised include:** Behavioral Health Technician; Case Manager; Case Manager Aide; Clinical Supervisor; Clinician; LPN. **Office hours:** Monday - Friday, 8:00 a.m. - 5:00 p.m.

PARENTS ANONYMOUS, INC.
202 South First Avenue, Suite 103, Yuma AZ 85364. 928/329-7372. **Contact:** Human Resources. **World Wide Web address:** http://www.parentsanonymous.org. **Description:** Operates the nation's largest and oldest child abuse prevention, education, and treatment programs.

PRESCOTT YMCA OF YAVAPI COUNTY, INC.
750 Whipple Street, Prescott AZ 86301. 928/445-7221. **Fax:** 928/445-5135. **Contact:** Human Resources. **World Wide Web address:** http://www.prescottymca.org. **Description:** A community-based, service organization dedicated to building the spirit, mind, and body of each individual with programs unique to each community. With programs emphasizing education, health, and recreation, the YMCA serves men, women, and children of all ages, religions, races, and abilities, with a focus on youth. **Corporate headquarters location:** Chicago IL.

THE SALVATION ARMY
P.O. Box 52177, Phoenix AZ 85072. 602/267-4100. **Physical address:** 2707 East Van Buren Street, Phoenix AZ 85008. **Contact:** Ms. Robin Harvey, Personnel Director. **World Wide Web address:** http://www.tsasw.org. **Description:** A nonprofit organization providing several service programs including day-care centers, programs for people with disabilities, substance abuse programs and tutoring for at-risk students. The Salvation Army targets its programs to assist alcoholics, battered women, drug addicts, the elderly, the homeless, people with AIDS, prison inmates, teenagers, and the unemployed. **Other U.S. locations:** Nationwide.

VISIONQUEST
600 North Swan Road, P.O. Box 12906, Tucson AZ 85732. 520/881-3950. **Fax:** 520/881-3269. **Contact:** Human Resources. **E-mail address:** jobs@vq.com. **World Wide Web address:** http://www.vq.com. **Description:** A social service organization providing troubled kids and teens with recreational alternatives. VisionQuest allows participants to engage in such outdoor activities as camping and sailing. **NOTE:** Entry-level positions are offered. **Positions advertised include:** Child Care Worker. **Corporate headquarters location:** This location. **Other U.S. locations:** PA; TX. **Subsidiaries include:** Lodgemakers. **Operations at this facility include:** Administration. **Listed on:** Privately held. **Number of employees at this location:** 60. **Number of employees nationwide:** 1,050.

California

AMERICAN CANCER SOCIETY
1700 Webster Street, Oakland CA 94612. 510/832-7012. **Toll-free phone:** 800/ACS-2345. **Fax:** 510/893-0951. **Contact:** Human Resources. **World Wide Web address:** http://www.cancer.org. **Description:** A nationwide, community-based, nonprofit, voluntary health organization dedicated to eliminating cancer as a major health problem by funding cancer research and public education. The society helps patients directly by offering services including transportation to treatment and rehabilitation services. **Positions advertised include:** Vice President of Corporate Relations. **Special programs:** Internships. **Corporate headquarters location:** Atlanta GA. **Other U.S. locations:** Nationwide.

AMERICAN RED CROSS
3650 Fifth Avenue, San Diego CA 92103. 619/542-7400. **Fax:** 619/260-3528. **Contact:** Cindy DiPiero, Director of Personnel. **E-mail address:** redcross.careers@sdarc.org. **World Wide Web address:** http://www.sdarc.org. **Description:** A humanitarian organization that aids disaster victims, gathers blood for crisis distribution, trains individuals to respond to emergencies, educates individuals on various diseases, and raises funds for other charitable establishments. **Positions advertised include:** Response Coordinator; Associate Disaster Liaison. **Corporate headquarters location:** Washington DC. **Other U.S. locations:** Nationwide.

BIENVENIDOS CHILDREN'S CENTER
205 East Palm Street, Altadena CA 91001. 626/798-7222. **Fax:** 626/798-8444. **Contact:** Human Resources. **World Wide Web address:** http://www.bienvenidos.org. **Description:** Runs a foster family agency and a group residential home for children who are placed into state custody by the courts. Bienvenidos Children's Center also provides outpatient mental health services to children aged birth to 21 years.

BOY SCOUTS OF AMERICA
SANTA CLARA COUNTY COUNCIL
970 West Julian Avenue, San Jose CA 95126. 408/280-5088. **Fax:** 408/280-5162. **Contact:** Sharon Bartholomew, Administrative Assistant. **E-mail address:** sharon@sccc-scouting.org. **World Wide Web address:** http://www.sccc-scouting.org. **Description:** Western regional office of the national scouting organization for young adults. The Boy Scouts of America has 340 local councils nationwide. **Corporate headquarters location:** Irving TX.

CATHOLIC CHARITIES
P.O. Box 4900, Santa Rosa CA 95402. 707/528-8712. **Physical address:** 987 Airway Court, Santa Rosa CA 95405. **Fax:** 707/575-4910. **Contact:** Personnel. **E-mail address:** smmcarty@srcharities.org or amullan@srcharities.org. **World Wide Web address:** http://www.srcharities.org. **Description:** Provides social service programs for the needy in several counties of California. **Positions advertised include:** Office Assistant, Homeless Services; Director of Development; Bilingual Program Coordinator.

CENTER FOR GOVERNMENT STUDIES
10951 West Pico Boulevard, Suite 120, Los Angeles CA 90064. 310/470-6590. **Fax:** 310/475-3752. **Contact:** Human Resources. **E-mail address:** slevin@cgs.org. **World Wide Web address:** http://www.cgs.org. **Description:** A non-profit organization dedicated to studying and implementing governmental reforms. **Special programs:** Internships. **Corporate headquarters location:** This location.

COVENANT HOUSE CALIFORNIA
1325 North Western Avenue, Hollywood CA 90027-5615. 323/461-3131. **Fax:** 323/957-7421. **Contact:** Human Resources. **E-mail address:** info@covdove.org. **World Wide Web address:** http://www.covenanthouseca.org. **Description:** An international human service agency for homeless and runaway adolescents. **Corporate headquarters location:** New York NY. **Other area locations:** Oakland.

EXCEPTIONAL CHILDREN'S FOUNDATION
8740 West Washington Boulevard, Culver City CA 90232. 310/204-3300. **Fax:** 310/845-8057. **Contact:** Human Resources. **E-mail address:** hrecf@ecf.net. **World Wide Web address:** http://www.ecf-la.org. **Description:** A nonprofit, educational service that provides schooling for children and adults with developmental disabilities. **Positions advertised include:** Developmental and External relations Coordinator; Educators; Developmental Instructor; Counselor; Registered Nurse Supervisor; Certified Nursing Assistant; Case Manager. **Corporate headquarters location:** This location.

FILIPINOS FOR AFFIRMATIVE ACTION
310 8th Street, Suite 306, Oakland CA 94607. 510/465-9876. **Fax:** 510/465-7548. **Contact:** Ms. Lillian Galedo, Executive Director. **E-mail address:** lgaledo@filipinos4action.org. **World Wide Web address:** http://www.filipinos4action.org. **Description:** A private, nonprofit, advocacy organization that provides employment and immigration assistance, information, and other services to the Filipino community. **Corporate headquarters location:** This location. **Other area locations:** Union City CA.

GOODWILL INDUSTRIES OF SOUTHERN CALIFORNIA
342 North San Fernando Road, Los Angeles CA 90031. 323/223-1211. **Fax:** 323/539-2046. **Contact:** Human Resources. **E-mail address:** resumes@goodwillsocal.org. **World Wide Web address:** http://www.goodwillsocal.org. **Description:** Besides operating 1,400 thrift stores nationwide, Goodwill is a nonprofit provider of employment training for the disabled and the poor. **Positions advertised include:** Retail Store Manager; Employment Specialist; Contracts Director; Job Coach; Education Coordinator. **Corporate headquarters location:** Bethesda MD. **Other U.S. locations:** Nationwide.

INTEGRATED COMMUNITY SERVICES
3020 Kerner Boulevard, Suite A, San Rafael CA 94901. 415/455-8481. **Fax:** 415/455-8483. **Contact:** Donna Lemmon, Executive Director. **E-mail address:** donna@connectics.org. **World Wide Web address:** http://www.connectics.org. **Description:** Provides job placement services and independent living skills training for individuals with disabilities. **Positions advertised include:** Job Coach; Independent Living Skills Trainer.

LUMETRA
One Sansome Street, Suite 600, San Francisco CA 94104-4448. 415/677-2000. **Fax:** 415/677-2195. **Contact:** Human Resources. **E-mail address:** humanresources@lumetra.com. **World Wide Web address:** http://www/lumetra.com. **Description:** A non-profit organization dedicated to improving the quality and safety of healthcare. **Positions advertised include:** Assistant Appeals Manager; Communications Specialist; Quality Improvement Advisor; Senior Appeals Specialist. **Corporate headquarters location:** This location. **Other U.S. locations:** Columbia MD.

NATIONAL MEMORY IMPAIRMENT INSTITUTE
646 Brea Canyon Road, Suite 110, Walnut CA 91789. 888/672-6577. **Fax:** 909/612-8417. **Contact:** Human Resources. **E-mail address:** info@nmi2.org. **World Wide Web address:** http://www.nmi2.org. **Description:** A non-profit organization dedicated to developing formal standards of care and a national certification program for individuals caring for the memory impaired. **Corporate headquarters location:** This location.

PUBLIC POLICY INSTITUTE OF CALIFORNIA
500 Washington Street, Suite 800, San Francisco CA 94111. 415/291-4400. **Fax:** 415/291-4401. **Contact:** Human Resources. **E-mail address:**

resumes@ppic.org. **World Wide Web address:** http://www.ppic.org. **Description:** A non-profit organization dedicated to independent, objective research on policy issues affecting Californians. **Positions advertised include:** Research Associate; Communications Analyst; Production Associate; Program Director. **Special programs:** Internships. **Corporate headquarters location:** This location.

ORANGE COUNTY ASSOCIATION FOR RETARDED CITIZENS
225 West Carlkarcher Way, Anaheim CA 92801-2499. 714/744-5301. **Contact:** Human Resources. **E-mail address:** info@orangecountyarc.org. **World Wide Web address:** http://www.orangecountyarc.org. **Description:** A supported employment program where adults with mental disabilities provide product packaging and assembly. **Corporate headquarters location:** This location.

REGIONAL CENTER OF ORANGE COUNTY
P.O. Box 22010, Santa Ana CA 92702-2010. 714/796-5100. **Contact:** Personnel. **E-mail address:** jabernatha@rcocdd.com. **World Wide Web address:** http://www.rcocdd.com. **Description:** A nonprofit organization dedicated to helping individuals with all types of learning disabilities ranging from mental retardation to cerebral palsy. **Positions advertised include:** Service Coordinator; **Corporate headquarters location:** This location. **Operations at this facility include:** Administration; Service. **Listed on:** Privately held. **Number of employees at this location:** 200.

THE SALVATION ARMY
180 East Ocean Boulevard, Long Beach CA 90802. 562/436-7000. **Fax:** 562/491-8699. **Contact:** Personnel. **World Wide Web address:** http://www.salvationarmy.org. **Description:** A nonprofit organization providing several service programs including day-care centers, programs for people with disabilities, substance abuse programs and tutoring for at-risk students. The Salvation Army targets its programs to assist alcoholics, battered women, drug addicts, the elderly, the homeless, people with AIDS, prison inmates, teenagers, and the unemployed. **Corporate headquarters location:** Alexandria VA.

SAN JOSE JOB CORPS CENTER
3485 East Hills Drive, San Jose CA 95127. 408/937-3207. **Fax:** 408/254-5667. **Contact:** Human Resources. **E-mail address:** coronav@jcdc.jobcorps.org. **Description:** Offers vocational and educational training for youths. **Positions advertised include:** Administration Director; Career Preparation Counselor; Admissions Counselor. **Corporate headquarters location:** Rochester NY. **Number of employees at this location:** 200. **Parent company:** Career Systems Development Corporation.

SIERRA CLUB
85 Second Street, 2nd Floor, San Francisco CA 94105. 415/977-5500. **Recorded jobline:** 415/977-5744. **Contact:** Human Resources Department. **E-mail address:** resumes@sierraclub.org. **World Wide Web address:** http://www.sierraclub.org. **Description:** A national, volunteer-based, nonprofit company chiefly concerned with the maintenance and preservation of national natural resources, wildlife, and wilderness areas. **NOTE:** Please call the jobline for a listing of available positions before sending a resume. **Positions advertised include:** Senior Member Services Representative; Publicity Manager; Senior Editor; Associate Editor. **Corporate headquarters location:** This location.

YMCA OF THE EAST BAY
2330 Broadway, Oakland CA 94612. 510/451-8039. **Fax:** 510/987-7449. **Contact:** Human Resources Director. **World Wide Web address:** http://www.ymca.com. **Description:** The YMCA provides health and fitness; social and personal development; sports and recreation; education and career development; and camps and conferences to children, youths, adults, the elderly, families, the disabled, refugees and foreign nationals, YMCA residents, and community residents, through a broad range of specific programs. Founded in 1879. **NOTE:** Entry-level positions are offered. **Special programs:** Internships; Training. **Corporate headquarters location:** Chicago IL. **Other U.S. locations:** Nationwide. **Number of employees at this location:** 650. **Number of employees nationwide:** 20,000.

Colorado

COMPASSION INTERNATIONAL
12290 Voyager Parkway, Colorado Springs CO 80921. 719/487-7000. **Contact:** Recruitment. **World Wide Web address:** http://www.ci.org. **Description:** A Christian organization that aids poverty-stricken children throughout the world. **Positions advertised include:** Corporate Audit Specialist; Editorial Specialist; Feature Writer Specialist; International Communications Specialist; IT Software Development Specialist.

DEVELOPMENTAL DISABILITY RESOURCE CENTER (DDRC)
11177 West 8th Avenue, Suite 300, Westminster CO 80215. 303/233-3363. **Contact:** Human Resources. **World Wide Web address:** http://www.ddrcco.com. **Description:** A nonprofit organization that provides services to individuals with developmental disabilities. **Positions advertised include:** Home Host Provider; Vocational Instructor Supervisor; Early Intervention Speech/Language Therapist.

DIVISION FOR DEVELOPMENTAL DISABILITIES
3824 West Princeton Circle, Denver CO 80236. 303/866-7450. **Fax:** 303/866-7470. **Contact:** Kerry Stern, Acting Director. **Description:** A nonprofit organization that provides services to individuals with developmental disabilities.

EAST DENVER YMCA
3540 East 31st Avenue, Denver CO 80205. 303/322-7761. **Contact:** Human Resources. **World Wide Web address:** http://www.ymca.com. **Description:** One of the nation's largest and most comprehensive nonprofit service organizations. The YMCA provides health and fitness, social and personal development, sports and recreation, education and career development, and camps and conferences to children, youths, adults, the elderly, families, disabled individuals, refugees and foreign nationals, YMCA residents, and community residents through a broad range of specific programs.

GOODWILL INDUSTRIES OF DENVER
6850 North Federal Boulevard, Denver CO 80221. 303/650-7700. **Contact:** Human Resources. **E-mail address:** info@goodwilldenver.org. **World Wide Web address:** http://www.goodwilldenver.org. **Description:** Operates 1,400 thrift stores nationwide and provides employment training for the disabled and the disadvantaged. **Other U.S. locations:** Nationwide. **Annual sales/revenues:** $5 - $10 million. **Number of employees at this location:** 290.

MARCH OF DIMES BIRTH DEFECTS FOUNDATION
1325 South Colorado Boulevard, Suite B508, Denver CO 80222. 303/692-0011. **Contact:** Director. **E-mail address:** co611@modimes.org. **World Wide Web address:** http://www.modimes.org. **Description:** March of Dimes operates the Campaign for Healthier Babies that includes programs of research, community services, education, and advocacy. March of Dimes chapters across the country work with their communities to determine and meet the needs of women, babies, and families. Through specially designed programs, women are provided access to prenatal care. **Corporate headquarters location:** White Plains NY.

MILE HIGH UNITED WAY
2505 18th Street, Denver CO 80211-3939. 303/433-8383. **Contact:** Human Resources. **World Wide Web**

address: http://www.unitedwaydenver.org. **Description:** A nonprofit organization made up of volunteers and human service professionals. Mile High United Way provides disaster relief, emergency food and shelter, and rehabilitation and development services to needy individuals. Founded in 1887. **NOTE:** Entry-level positions are offered. **Office hours:** Monday - Friday, 8:00 a.m. - 5:00 p.m. **Annual sales/revenues:** $21 - $50 million. **Number of employees at this location:** 65.

PARKPLACE RETIREMENT COMMUNITY
111 Emerson Street, Denver CO 80218. 303/744-0400. **Contact:** Human Resources. **World Wide Web address:** http://www.arclp.com. **Description:** A retirement community. Founded in 1978. **NOTE:** Search and apply for positions online. **Corporate headquarters location:** Brentwood TN. **Parent company:** American Retirement Corporation. **Listed on:** New York Stock Exchange. **Stock exchange symbol:** ACR.

SENIORS INC.
5840 East Evans Avenue, Denver CO 80222. 303/300-6900. **Fax:** 303/300-6950. **Contact:** Human Resources. **World Wide Web address:** http://www.seniorsinc.org. **Description:** Provides programs and services for older persons that promote and enhance independent living. Founded in 1969. **Positions advertised include:** Resource Development Associate Manager. **Special programs:** Internships. **Corporate headquarters location:** This location. **Operations at this facility include:** Administration; Sales; Service. **Number of employees at this location:** 30.

UNITED CEREBRAL PALSY OF COLORADO, INC.
2200 South Jasmine Street, Denver CO 80222. 303/691-9339. **Fax:** 303/691-0846. **Contact:** Human Resources. **World Wide Web address:** http://www.cpco.org. **Description:** A nonprofit organization that provides education, childcare, and employment services, as well as information and referrals. The organization is also engaged in donation pickup. **Corporate headquarters location:** This location. **Number of employees at this location:** 30.

THE URBAN LEAGUE OF METROPOLITAN DENVER
5900 East 39th Avenue, Denver CO 80207. 303/388-5861. **Fax:** 303/388-3523. **Contact:** Personnel. **World Wide Web address:** http://www.denverurbanleague.org. **Description:** A nonprofit organization that sponsors a variety of social programs including employment services and career and outplacement counseling. **Corporate headquarters location:** This location.

Connecticut

BIG BROTHERS BIG SISTERS OF SOUTHWESTERN CONNECTICUT
2470 Fairfield Avenue, Bridgeport CT 06605. 203/366-3766. **Fax:** 203/384-8861. 203/366-3766. **Contact:** Human Resources. **World Wide Web address:** http://www.bbbsa.org. **Description:** Provides volunteer and professional services to assist children in achieving their highest potential through over 505 Big Brothers/Big Sisters agencies nationwide. Across the country, more than 75,000 children are matched with adult volunteers. The agencies also provide counseling and family support services to parents and children in over 110,000 families each year. Additional programs focus on children with special needs including the handicapped, learning-disabled, and school dropouts, as well as those who are abused and neglected. Special prevention and intervention programs at many agencies address the problems of drug abuse, teen pregnancy, foster care, and juvenile delinquency. **Corporate headquarters location:** Philadelphia PA. **Other U.S. locations:** Nationwide.

CARING COMMUNITY
84 Waterhole Road, Colchester CT 06415. 860/267-4463. **Contact:** Human Resources. **Description:** Operates group homes for the mentally retarded.

COMMUNITY ACTION COMMITTEE OF DANBURY
66 North Street, Danbury CT 06810. 203/744-4700. **Contact:** Human Resources. **Description:** A nonprofit organization that provides daycare, heating assistance, Head Start programs, counseling, bill payment assistance, and rental assistance services to low-income families.

COMMUNITY RENEWAL TEAM (CRT)
555 Windsor Street, Hartford CT 06120. 860/560-5600. **Fax:** 860/560-5664. **Contact:** Human Resources. **World Wide Web address:** http://www.crtct.org. **Description:** Provides employment education and energy assistance to community residents. The agency also administers Head Start daycare at other locations throughout the community. **Positions advertised include:** Internal Auditor; Medical Advocate; Recreation Coordinator; Part-Time Counselor; Case Manager; Program Nurse.

CONNECTICUT COALITION AGAINST DOMESTIC VIOLENCE
90 Pitkin Street, East Hartford CT 06108. 860/282-7899. **Fax:** 860/282-7892. **Contact:** Executive Director. **World Wide Web address:** http://www.ctcadv.org. **Description:** Provides support services to battered women and their children. **Positions advertised include:** Family Violence Victim Advocate; Community Educator; Program Advocacy Specialist. **Parent company:** National Coalition Against Domestic Violence is a nonprofit public education and advocacy organization and a coalition of direct service programs. The coalition works toward the prevention of domestic violence by bringing about societal change. Activities of the coalition include public education and advocacy, technical assistance to member groups, information and technical assistance to public agencies and legislative committees, and professional training for law enforcement and human service workers. In addition, the coalition staff prepares policy statements and offers assistance and expertise in the preparation of protocols and practices for a wide variety of public and private entities.

CONNECTICUT DEPARTMENT OF SOCIAL SERVICES
25 Sigourney Street, Hartford CT 06106. 860/424-5060. **Toll free phone:** 800/473-8909. **Contact:** Human Resources. **World Wide Web address:** http://www.dss.state.ct.us. **Description:** Assists the elderly, disabled, families, and individuals through the Rehabilitation Act, the Food Stamps Act, the Older Americans Act, the Social Security Act, and the state welfare program.

EASTER SEALS GOODWILL INDUSTRIES REHABILITATION CENTER
95 Hamilton Street, New Haven CT 06511. 203/777-2000. **Contact:** Director. **World Wide Web address:** http://www.newhavengoodwill.easterseals.com. **Description:** Easter Seals provides treatment and support services for disabled individuals. Goodwill Industries Rehabilitation Center (also at this location) provides employment training and operates 1,400 retail stores nationwide.

NORTHERN MIDDLESEX YMCA
99 Union Street, Middletown CT 06457. 860/347-6907. **Contact:** Human Resources. **World Wide Web address:** http://www.middlesexymca.org. **Description:** One of the nation's largest and most comprehensive nonprofit service organizations. The YMCA provides health and fitness, social and personal development, sports and recreation, education and career development, and camps and conferences to children, youths, adults, the elderly, families, disabled individuals, refugees and foreign nationals, YMCA residents, and community residents through a broad range of specific programs.

THE SALVATION ARMY
1313 Connecticut Avenue, Bridgeport CT 06607. 203/367-1087. **Contact:** Human Resources. **World**

Wide Web address: http://www.salvationarmy.org. **Description:** A nonprofit organization providing several service programs including day-care centers, programs for people with disabilities, substance abuse programs and tutoring for at-risk students. The Salvation Army targets its programs to assist alcoholics, battered women, drug addicts, the elderly, the homeless, people with AIDS, prison inmates, teenagers, and the unemployed. **Corporate headquarters location:** Alexandria VA. **Other U.S. locations:** Nationwide. **International locations:** Worldwide.

SAVE THE CHILDREN
54 Wilton Road, Westport CT 06880. 203/221-4030. **Toll-free phone:** 800/728-3843. **Contact:** Personnel. **World Wide Web address:** http://www.savethechildren.org. **Description:** A nonprofit organization that works to raise funds for disadvantaged children worldwide. **Positions advertised include:** Marketing Manager; Outbound Call Center Representative; Deputy Director of Education; Education Specialist; Program Specialist; Family Planning/Reproductive Health Advisor; AVP Planning, Monitoring and Evaluation. **Corporate headquarters location:** This location.

TECHNOSERVE INC.
49 Day Street, Norwalk CT 06854. 203/852-0377. **Fax:** 203/838-6717. **Contact:** Stacey Daves-Ohlin, Director of Human Resources. **World Wide Web address:** http://www.technoserve.org. **Description:** A private, nonprofit development aid organization that works with low-income people and development institutions in Africa, Latin America, and Eastern Europe to help establish or strengthen self-help enterprises. **NOTE:** See website for details on positions. All applicants should be fluent in French; only senior level applicants should apply. **Positions advertised include:** Trade Specialist; Agribusiness Specialist; Finance Specialist; Business Specialist Service Provider. **Special programs:** Internships. **Corporate headquarters location:** This location. **Other U.S. locations:** Washington DC. **Number of employees at this location:** 25. **Number of employees nationwide:** 220.

UNITED WAY OF CONNECTICUT
30 Laurel Street, Hartford CT 06106. 860/493-6800. **Contact:** Human Resources. **World Wide Web address:** http://www.unitedway.org. **Description:** A nonprofit organization that operates referral and crisis intervention services for pregnant women and parents. **Other U.S. locations:** Nationwide.

UNITED WAY OF STAMFORD
62 Palmers Hill Road, Stamford CT 06902. 203/348-7711. **Contact:** Human Resources. **World Wide Web address:** http://www.unitedway.org. **Description:** A nonprofit organization that offers referral and crisis intervention services for pregnant women and parents. **Other U.S. locations:** Nationwide.

Delaware

AMERICAN RED CROSS OF THE DELMARVA PENINSULA
100 West 10th Street, Wilmington DE 19801. 302/656-6620. **Fax:** 302/656-8797. **Contact:** Human Resources. **E-mail address:** jobs@redcrossdelmarva.org. **World Wide Web address:** http://www.redcrossdelmarva.org. **Description:** Helps local families when disaster strikes; teaches lifesaving skills such as first aid, CPR and water safety; and provides free training in disaster preparedness. The organization covers 9 counties and serves over 1 million people. **NOTE:** See website for current job openings and application instructions. **Positions advertised include:** Development Manager, Finance Director.

DELAWARE GUIDANCE SERVICES
1213 Delaware Avenue, Wilmington DE 19806. 302/652-3948. **Fax:** 302/652-8297. **E-mail address:** lchristina@delawareguidance.org. **World Wide Web address:** http://www.delawareguidance.org. **Contact:** Human Resources. **Description:** Provides mental health services for children, youth and their families. Operates treatment centers in New Castle, Kent and Sussex counties. **NOTE:** See website for current job openings. Send resume by mail, fax or e-mail. **Positions advertised include:** Mental Health Outpatient Therapist; Mental Health Aide; Nurse Practitioner. **Special programs:** Internships. **Corporate headquarters location:** This location. **Number of employees at this location:** 10. **Number of employees statewide:** 60.

YWCA DELAWARE
233 North King Street, Wilmington DE 19801. 302/658-7161. **Contact:** Human Resources. **World Wide Web address:** http://www.ywca.org. **Description:** Provides social services for women, including childcare, housing, mortgage counseling and career counseling.

District Of Columbia

AARP
601 E Street NW, Washington DC 20049. **Toll-free phone:** 888/687-2277. **Contact:** Human Resources. **World Wide Web address:** http://www.aarp.org. **Description:** With 35 million members, AARP is the leading nonprofit, nonpartisan membership organization for people age 50 and over in the United States. **Positions advertised include:** Sr. Developer; Program Specialist, International Affairs; Manager, Business Analysis; Sr. Strategic Analyst; Director, Advocacy Management; Sr. Strategic Planner; Benefits Manager; Sr. Corporate Attorney.

AMERICAN COUNCIL OF THE BLIND (ACB)
1155 15th Street NW, Suite 1004, Washington DC 20005. 202/467-5081. **Toll-free phone:** 800/424-8666. **Fax:** 202/467-5085. **Contact:** Human Resources. **E-mail address:** info@acb.org. **World Wide Web address:** http://www.acb.org. **Description:** ACB is a national membership organization established to promote the independence, dignity, and well-being of blind and visually impaired people. ACB is one of the largest organizations of blind people in the United States with over 70 state and special interest affiliates and a national network of chapters and members. By providing numerous programs and services, ACB enables blind people to live and work independently and to advocate for their rights. Founded in 1961. **Corporate headquarters location:** This location. **Operations at this facility include:** This location houses administrative offices.

AMERICAN RED CROSS
2025 E Street, NW, Washington DC 20006. 202/303-4498. **Contact:** Director of Human Resources. **World Wide Web address:** http://www.redcross.org. **Description:** A humanitarian organization that aids disaster victims, gathers blood for crisis distribution, trains individuals to respond to emergencies, educates individuals on various diseases, and raises funds for other charitable establishments. **Positions advertised include:** Associate, Financial Policy and Procedure; Audit Manager; Sr. Financial Analyst; Debt Manager; Documentation and Training Manager; Caseworker; Systems Analyst; Logistics Analyst; Director, Compliance. **Special programs:** Internships available. **Corporate headquarters location:** This location. **Other U.S. locations:** Nationwide.

B'NAI B'RITH INTERNATIONAL
2020 K Street, 7th Floor, Washington DC 20006. 202/857-6600. **Contact:** Director of Human Resources. **E-mail address:** hr@bnaibrith.org. **World Wide Web address:** http://www.bnaibrith.org. **Description:** A Jewish social services and political action organization. B'Nai B'Rith has seven district offices located across the United States. **NOTE:** Human Resources phone: 202/857-6510. **Special programs:** Internships. **Corporate headquarters location:** This location. **Operations at this facility include:** Administration; Public Affairs.

CENTER FOR INTERNATIONAL POLICY
1717 Massachusetts Avenue NW, Suite 801,

Washington DC 20036. 202/232-3317. **Fax:** 202/232-3440. **E-mail address:** cip@ciponline.org. **World Wide Web Address:** http://www.ciponline.org. **Description:** Promotes a U.S foreign policy based on international demilitarization and respect for basic human rights.

CHILD WELFARE LEAGUE OF AMERICA
440 First Street NW, 3rd Floor, Washington DC 20001-2085. 202/638-2952. **Fax:** 202/638-4004. **Contact:** Human Resources. **E-mail address:** hr@cwla.org. **World Wide Web address:** http://www.cwla.org. **Description:** A national, nonprofit organization with almost 800 affiliated public and private agencies that together serve more than 2 million children and their families every year. Child Welfare League of America and its agencies offer services for the many areas of child welfare including adoption, child daycare, child protection, family foster care, chemical dependency prevention and treatment, and housing and homelessness. **Positions advertised include:** Program Coordinator; Publications Coordinator; Contract Accountant; Sr. Government Affairs Associate.

CORPORATION FOR NATIONAL AND COMMUNITY SERVICE (CNS)
1201 New York Avenue NW, Washington DC 20525. 202/606-5000. **Fax:** 202/565-2782. **Contact:** Human Resources. **E-mail address:** jobs@cns.gov. **World Wide Web address:** http://www.cns.gov. **NOTE:** Candidates should e-mail or fax resumes. **Description:** A governmental organization geared toward matching jobseekers and volunteers with community service jobs. CNS organizes AmeriCorps, National Senior Services Corps, and Learn & Serve America. **NOTE:** Please call or visit the Website to view available positions and application procedures. **Positions advertised include:** Sr. Grants Officer; Human Capital Specialist; Training Specialist. **Special programs:** Internships. **Corporate headquarters location:** This location. **Other U.S. locations:** Nationwide.

FAMILY AND CHILD SERVICES OF WASHINGTON DC
929 L Street NW, Washington DC 20001. 202/289-1510. **Fax:** 202/371-0863. **Contact:** Nolia C. Melton, Director of Human Resources. **E-mail address:** resumes@fcsdc.com. **World Wide Web address:** http://www.familyandchildservices.org. **Description:** A private, nonprofit, social services organization offering a broad range of services including counseling, adoption, family daycare, foster care, and summer and winter camping for children, as well as services for the elderly. **Positions advertised include:** Crisis Line Volunteer Coordinator; Social Worker; Program Assistant; Child Development Specialist. **Special programs:** Internships. **Corporate headquarters location:** This location.

FARMWORKERS JUSTICE FUND
1010 Vermont Avenue NW, Suite 915, Washington DC 20005. 202/783-2628. **Fax:** 202/783-2561. **Contact:** Ms. Baez. **E-mail address:** fjf@nclr.org. **World Wide Web address:** http://www.fwjustice.org. **Description:** Farmworkers Justice Fund helps migrant and seasonal farmworkers improve their wages and working conditions, labor and immigration policy.

NATIONAL DEMOCRATIC INSTITUTE FOR INTERNATIONAL AFFAIRS
2030 M Street NW, Fifth Floor, Washington DC 20036. 202/728-5500. **Fax**: 202/728-5520. **Contact:** Human Resources. **E-Mail address:** contact@ndi.org. **World Wide Web address:** http://www.ndi.org. **Description:** National Democratic Institute For International Affairs is a nonprofit organization working to expand and promote democracy worldwide. **Positions advertised include:** Internal Audit Manager; Program Officer; UNIX Systems Administrator; Deputy Regional Director.

NATIONAL TRUST FOR HISTORIC PRESERVATION
1785 Massachusetts Avenue NW, Washington DC 20036. 202/588-6000. **Fax:** 202/588-6059. **Contact:** Human Resources Director. **E-mail address:** jobs@nthp.org. **World Wide Web address:** http://www.nthp.org. **Description:** A nonprofit organization that encourages public participation in the preservation of buildings, objects, sites, and districts that are significant to the history and culture of the nation. Founded in 1949. **Positions advertised include:** Individual Giving Manager; Assistant Asset Manager; Associate Director, Preservation Conferences; Vice President of Development; Director of Strategic Services; Program Officer.

SO OTHERS MIGHT EAT (SOME)
71 O Street NW, Washington DC 20001-1258. 202/797-8806. **Fax:** 202/265-3849. **Contact:** Human Resources. **E-mail address:** some@some.org. **World Wide Web address:** http://www.some.org. **Description:** Provides food, clothing, and medical and dental assistance to the needy.

Florida

AMERICAN CANCER SOCIETY
3901 NW 79th Avenue, Suite 224, Miami FL 33166. 305/594-4363. **Contact:** Human Resources. **World Wide Web address:** http://www.cancer.org. **Description:** A nationwide, community-based, nonprofit, voluntary health organization dedicated to eliminating cancer as a major health problem by funding cancer research and public education. The society helps patients directly by offering services including transportation to treatment and rehabilitation services. **Positions advertised include:** Community Representative.

AMERICAN RED CROSS
2018 Lewis Turner Boulevard, Fort Walton FL 32547. 850/314-0316. **Contact:** Manager. **World Wide Web address:** http://www.redcross.org. **Description:** A humanitarian organization that aids disaster victims, gathers blood for crisis distribution, trains individuals to respond to emergencies, educates individuals on various diseases, and raises funds for other charitable establishments. **Corporate headquarters location:** Washington DC. **Other U.S. locations:** Nationwide.

BAYFRONT YMCA
750 West Retta Esplanade, Punta Gorda FL 33950. 941/637-0797. **Contact:** Personnel. **Description:** The YMCA is one of the nation's largest and most comprehensive service organizations. The YMCA provides health and fitness programs; promotes social and personal development; offers sports and recreation; implements education and career development programs; and organizes camps and conferences for individuals of all ages and backgrounds. **Corporate headquarters location:** Chicago IL. **Other U.S. locations:** Nationwide. **Operations at this facility include:** Offers a variety of classes in aerobics, yoga, and tai chi and social events.

BRADENTON YMCA
3805 59th Street West, Bradenton FL 34209. 941/792-7484. **Contact:** Human Resources. **E-mail address:** manateeymca@aol.com. **World Wide Web address:** http://www.manateeymca.org. **Description:** Offers a variety of aerobics and workout classes. Bradenton YMCA's facilities include an indoor heated pool and a gym. **Positions advertised include:** Front Desk Receptionist. **Corporate headquarters location:** Chicago IL. **Other U.S. locations:** Nationwide.

CATHEDRAL RESIDENCES
601 North Newnan Street, Jacksonville FL 32202. 904/798-5360. **Contact:** Human Resources. **World Wide Web address:** http://www.cathedralresidences.org. **Description:** A nonprofit organization that focuses on the needs of elderly citizens. Cathedral Foundation operates independent living apartments and a nursing home, and provides various community services.

ST. AUGUSTINE FAMILY YMCA
500 Pope Road, St. Augustine FL 32080. 904/471-9622. **Contact:** Michelle Cooligan, Program Director.

World Wide Web address: http://www.ymcaffc.org. **Description:** One of the nation's largest and most comprehensive service organizations. The YMCA provides health and fitness, social and personal development, sports and recreation, education and career development, and camps and conferences to children, youths, adults, the elderly, families, the disabled, refugees and foreign nationals, YMCA residents, and community residents through a broad range of specific programs. **Positions advertised include:** Wellness Coach; Yoga Instructor; Courtesy Counter Front Desk Clerk; Child Watch Associate. **Corporate headquarters location:** Chicago IL. **Other U.S. locations:** Nationwide.

ST. PETERSBURG YMCA
70 35th Street South Petersburg, FL 33602. 727/895-9622. **Contact:** Human Resources. **Description:** One of the nation's largest and most comprehensive service organizations. The YMCA provides health and fitness, social and personal development, sports and recreation, education and career development, and camps and conferences to children, youths, adults, the elderly, families, the disabled, refugees and foreign nationals, YMCA residents, and community residents through a broad range of specific programs. **Corporate headquarters location:** Chicago IL. **Other U.S. locations:** Nationwide.

Georgia
AMERICAN CANCER SOCIETY
1599 Clifton Road NE, Atlanta GA 30329. 404/320-3333. **Fax:** 404/982-3677. **Contact:** Human Resources. **E-mail address:** acs.jobs1@cancer.org. **World Wide Web address:** http://www.cancer.org. **Description:** A nationwide, community-based, nonprofit, voluntary health organization dedicated to eliminating cancer as a major health problem by funding cancer research and public education. The society helps patients directly by offering services including transportation to treatment and rehabilitation services. Founded in 1913. **Positions advertised include:** Director – Fundraising Communications; Director – National Media Relations; Online Fundraising Project Manager; HRMS Analyst; Manager – Evaluation Services; Administrative Specialist; Coordinator – CRM Projects; Network Security Engineer; Server Administrator; Assistant Controller; Associate Medical Editor; Director – Sampling and Statistics; Manager – Planned Giving Promotions; Director – Estate & Asset Services; Web Services Administrator; HelpDesk Support Analyst. **Special programs:** Internships. **Corporate headquarters location:** This location. **Other U.S. locations:** Nationwide. **Operations at this facility include:** Administration; Service.

AMERICAN RED CROSS
1955 Monroe Drive NE, Atlanta GA 30324-4888. 404/876-3302. **Fax:** 404/575-3086. **Contact:** Human Resources. **E-mail address:** cbattle@arcatl.org. **World Wide Web address:** http://www.redcrossatlanta.org. **Description:** A humanitarian organization that aids disaster victims, gathers blood for crisis distribution, trains individuals to respond to emergencies, educates individuals on various diseases, and raises funds for other charitable establishments. **NOTE:** Volunteer positions are also available. **Positions advertised include:** Youth Program Specialist; Media Relations Specialist; Data Entry Associate; Health Specialist. **Special programs:** Internships. **Corporate headquarters location:** Washington DC. **Other area locations:** Decatur GA; Lawrenceville GA; Marietta GA; Morrow GA. **Other U.S. locations:** Nationwide. **CEO:** Tim English. **Number of employees at this location:** 125.

ARTHRITIS FOUNDATION
P.O. Box 7669, Atlanta GA 30357-0669. 404/872-7100. **Physical address:** 1330 West Peachtree Street, Atlanta GA 30309. **Fax:** 404/872-0457. **Contact:** Human Resources. **E-mail address:** resume@arthritis.org. **World Wide Web address:** http://www.arthritis.org. **Description:** Engaged in research to find a cure for arthritis. Also provides information to educate those who have the disease. **Corporate headquarters location:** This location. **Positions advertised include:** Vice President – Strategic Marketing Alliances; Manager – Year Round Program; Maintenance Technician; Group Vice President – Major Donor Relations; Regional Director – Charitable Estate Planning. **President/CEO:** John H. Klippel.

ATLANTA UNION MISSION
P.O. Box 1807, Atlanta GA 30301. 404/367-2244. **Physical address:** 2353 Bolton Road NW, Suite 300, Atlanta GA 30318. **Contact:** T.J. Elison, Human Resources Manager. **E-mail address:** tj.elion@myaum.org. **World Wide Web address:** http://www.aumcares.org. **Description:** One of the largest homeless shelter service groups in the Southeast. Founded 1938. **NOTE:** Contact Human Resources directly at 404/526-4321. Volunteer positions are also available. **President/CEO:** David Coleman.

ATLANTA URBAN LEAGUE INC.
100 Edgewood Avenue NE, Suite 600, Atlanta GA 30303. 404/659-1150. **Fax:** 404/659-5326. **Contact:** Employment Programs. **World Wide Web address:** http://www.nul.org. **Description:** Provides a variety of services including job search assistance and training, housing counseling, summer youth programs, and mortgage counseling. Founded in 1920. **Corporate headquarters location:** New York NY. **Parent company:** National Urban League.

BOY SCOUTS OF AMERICA
P.O. Box 440728, Kennesaw GA 30160. 770/421-1601. **Physical address**: 50 Chastain Court Boulevard, Kennesaw GA 30144. **Contact:** Personnel. **World Wide Web address:** http://www.scouting.org. **Description:** The national scouting organization for young adults. **Corporate headquarters location:** Irving TX. **Other U.S. locations:** Nationwide. **Operations at this facility include:** Regional Headquarters. **Number of employees nationwide:** 3,950.

BOYS & GIRLS CLUBS OF AMERICA
1275 Peachtree Street NE, Atlanta GA 30309. 404/487-5700. **Toll-free phone:** 800/854-CLUB. **Contact:** Human Resources Department. **E-mail address:** info@bgca.org. **World Wide Web address:** http://www.bgca.org. **Description:** A private, nonprofit organization providing developmental programs for disadvantaged young people. **NOTE:** Please visit website to search for jobs and apply online. Volunteer positions are also available. **Positions advertised include:** Federal Grants Compliance Auditor; Director – Teen Services; Senior Director – Delinquency Prevention; Supply Services Assistant; Warehouse Assistant; Program Assistant – Urban Services; Regional Service Director; Marketing Manager; Health PE Director; Director of Operations. **Corporate headquarters location:** This location. **Other U.S. locations:** Nationwide. **President:** Roxanne Spillet.

CARE USA
151 Ellis Street NE, Atlanta GA 30303. 404/681-2552. **Fax:** 404/589-2651. **Contact:** Human Resources. **World Wide Web address:** http://www.careusa.org. **Description:** An independent, nonprofit, cooperative organization. CARE USA is a member of CARE International, an umbrella organization that coordinates the program activities of the member organizations. CARE's purpose is to help the developing world's poor in their efforts to achieve social and economic well-being. CARE offers disaster relief, technical assistance, training, food, and other material resources and management in combinations appropriate to local needs and priorities. CARE also advocates public policies and programs that support these services. Founded in 1945. **NOTE:** Volunteer programs are also available. Please visit website to register, search for jobs, and apply online. **Positions advertised include:** Sexual and Reproductive Health Team Leader; Senior Advisor – Inter-Agency CG. **Office hours:** Monday - Friday, 8:30

a.m. - 5:00 p.m. **Corporate headquarters location:** This location. **Other U.S. locations:** Nationwide. **International locations:** Worldwide.

CHRISTIAN CITY
7290 Lester Road, Union City GA 30291-2317. 770/964-3301. **Fax:** 770/964-7041. **Recorded jobline:** 770/964-3301, Ext. 773. **Contact:** Human Resources Department. **E-mail address:** milliec@christian-city.org. **World Wide Web address:** http://www.christiancity.org. **Description:** A nonprofit company operating a home for children, retirement homes, a convalescent center, and an Alzheimer's care center. Founded in 1964. **NOTE:** Volunteer positions, entry-level positions and second and third shifts are offered. **Company slogan:** Multiple ministries. One mission. **Positions advertised include:** Activity Aids; Administrative Support; Chaplain; Courtesy Officers; Dietary Staff; Foster Parents; Housekeeping; Laundry Worker; Maintenance Worker; LPN; RN; CNA; Social Worker. **Special programs:** Summer Jobs. **Corporate headquarters location:** This location. **Listed on:** Privately held. **President/CEO:** Robert L. Crutchfield. **Number of employees at this location:** 400.

COOPERATIVE BAPTIST FELLOWSHIP
P.O. Box 4343, Macon GA 31208-4343. 478/742-1191. **Physical address**: 2465 Hillcrest Avenue, Macon GA 31204. **Fax:** 478/742-6150. **Contact:** Human Resources. **E-mail address:** contact@cbfga.org. **World Wide Web address:** http://www.cbfga.org. **Description:** A foundation dedicated to providing support to Baptist churches around the world and to providing missionaries. **Corporate headquarters location:** This location. **Other area locations:** Statewide.

THE DEVEREUX GEORGIA TREATMENT NETWORK
1291 Stanley Road NW, Kennesaw GA 30152. 770/427-0147. **Toll-free phone:** 800/342-3357. **Contact:** Michele Washington, Human Resources. **E-mail address:** mwashin2@devereux.org. **World Wide Web address:** http://www.devereux.org. **Description:** Operates a 125-bed, nonprofit, residential facility. The center provides counseling, vocational training, family counseling, and educational services for adolescents between 11 and 17 years of age who exhibit behavior disorders or delinquent behavior. **NOTE:** Please visit website to search for jobs and apply online. **Positions advertised include:** Clinical Therapist; Cook; Direct Care Professional; Head Nurse; Human Resources Assistant; LPN/LVN; RN; Special Education Teacher; Therapeutic Staff Support. **Corporate headquarters location:** Villanova PA. **Other U.S. locations:** Nationwide. **CEO:** Ronald Burd. **Number of employees nationwide:** 4,500.

EASTER SEALS SOCIETY
P.O. Box 847, Dublin GA 31040. 478/275-8850. **Physical address:** 602 Kellam Road, Dublin GA 31021. **Contact:** Human Resources. **World Wide Web address:** http://www.easter-seals.org. **Description:** Provides treatment and support services for disabled individuals. **NOTE:** Please visit website or contact your local office to lean about employment opportunities. **Corporate headquarters location:** Chicago IL. **Other area locations:** Albany GA; Atlanta GA; Augusta GA; Columbus GA; Roswell GA.

GOODWILL INDUSTRIES OF ATLANTA, INC.
2201 Glenwood Avenue SE, Atlanta GA 30316. 404/486-8400. **Fax:** 404/371-9041. **Contact:** Human Resources. **E-mail address:** humanresources@ging.org. **World Wide Web address:** http://www.ging.org. **Description:** Operates 1,400 thrift stores nationwide. Goodwill is also a nonprofit provider of employment training for the disabled and the disadvantaged. **NOTE:** Entry-level positions are offered. **Positions advertised include:** Assistant Store Manager; Production Associate; Floor Associate; Trailer Attendant; Floor Supervisor; Director of Skills Development. Truck Driver. **Special programs:** Training. **Corporate headquarters location:** Rockville MD. **Other area locations:** Statewide. **Other U.S. locations:** Nationwide. **International locations:** Worldwide. **Parent company:** GII. **Listed on:** Privately held. **President/CEO:** George W. Kessinger. **Number of employees worldwide:** 72,000.

HABITAT FOR HUMANITY INTERNATIONAL
121 Habitat Street, Americus GA 31709-3498. 229/924-6935. **Toll-free phone:** 800/422-4828. **Contact:** Human Resources. **E-mail address:** hrstaffing@habitat.org. **World Wide Web address:** http://www.habitat.org. **Description:** A nonprofit, ecumenical, Christian housing ministry whose mission is to build housing for the poor around the world. **NOTE:** Please visit website to search for jobs. Volunteer positions are also available. **Positions advertised include:** Global Village Registration Coordinator; Video Producer; Media Specialist; Director of Collaborative Development; Web Communications Manager; Traffic Coordinator; User Interface Specialist; Senior Financial Analyst; Mail Processing Center Assistant; Application Support Analyst – Financial Systems; Controller; Cashier; Compensation Manager. **Corporate headquarters location:** This location. **Other U.S. locations:** Nationwide.

HEAD START PROGRAM
4332 Rosemont Drive, Columbus GA 31904. 706/327-2682. **Contact:** Human Resources. **World Wide Web address:** http://www2.acf.dhhs.gov/programs/hsb. **Description:** A state- and federally funded program for low-income families with young children. Founded in 1965. **NOTE:** Please visit website to search for jobs. **Other area locations:** Statewide. **Other U.S. locations:** Nationwide.

MISSION TO THE WORLD
1600 North Brown Road, Lawrenceville GA 30043-8141. 678/823-0004. **Fax:** 678/823-0027. **Contact:** Courtney Rogers, Personnel. **E-mail address:** crogers@mtw.org. **World Wide Web address:** http://www.mtw.org. **Description:** Provides support services including funding and advisory services to missionaries for the Presbyterian Church of America. **NOTE:** Contact Personnel directly at Ext. 278. **Special programs:** Internships. **Corporate headquarters location:** This location.

UNITED WAY OF METROPOLITAN ATLANTA INC.
100 Edgewood Avenue NE, Second Floor, Atlanta GA 30303. 404/527-7200. **Contact:** Human Resources. **E-mail address:** cberube@unitedwayatlanta.org. **World Wide Web address:** http://www.unitedwayatl.org. **Description:** Through a network of volunteers and local charities, United Way organizations throughout America help meet the health and human care needs of millions of people. The United Way system includes approximately 1,900 community-based organizations. United Way volunteers raise funds that are used for human services ranging from disaster relief, emergency food and shelter, and crisis intervention to daycare, physical rehabilitation, and youth development. **NOTE:** Please visit website to search for jobs. **Positions advertised include:** Grant Accountant; Building Accountant. **Corporate headquarters location:** Alexandria VA. **Parent company:** United Way of America is the national service and training center, supporting its members with national services that include advertising, training, corporate relations, research, networks, and government relations.

YMCA OF METRO ATLANTA
100 Edgewood Avenue NE, Suite 1100, Atlanta GA 30303. 404/588-9622. **Contact:** Human Resources. **E-mail address:** comments@ymcaatl.org. **World Wide Web address:** http://www.ymcaatlanta.org. **Description:** One of the nation's largest and most comprehensive service organizations. The YMCA provides health and fitness; social and personal development; sports and recreation; education and career development; and camps and conferences to

children, youths, adults, the elderly, families, the disabled, refugees and foreign nationals, YMCA residents, and community residents, through a broad range of specific programs. **NOTE:** Volunteer positions are also available. **Other U.S. locations:** Nationwide.

YWCA OF BRUNSWICK
144 Scranton Connector, Brunswick GA 31525-0514. 912/265-4100. **Fax:** 912/265-8059. **Contact:** Katie O'Shea, Human Resources Director. **World Wide Web address:** http://www.ywcabrunswickga. **Description:** An organization that represents more than 25 million women worldwide. YWCA is committed to empowering women to overcome racism and injustice. YWCA provides shelter to women and children who are homeless or have been victims of domestic violence. Day care services include training programs for baby sitters and other child care providers. YWCA also offers employment training including GED and ESL courses, Welfare-to-Work programs, and career counseling workshops. The organization is a member of the YWCA/Nike Sports Program and the United States Olympic Committee. **NOTE:** Please visit website to see job listings, and to download application form. **Positions advertised include:** Executive Director; After School Activity Leader; Facilities Assistant; Lifeguard; Child Care Associate Teacher; After School Site Coordinator; Swim Instructor; Membership Services Assistant. **Corporate headquarters location:** New York NY. **Other area locations:** Macon GA; Marietta GA; Atlanta GA.

Hawaii
CHILD AND FAMILY SERVICES
91-1841 Fort Weaver Road, Ewa Beach HI 96706. 808/681-1423. **Fax:** 808/681-1486. **Recorded jobline:** 808/543-8483. **Contact:** Julia Sandoval, Director of Human Resources. **E-mail address:** jsandoval@cfs-hawaii.org. **World Wide Web address:** http://www.childandfamilyservice.org. **Description:** A private, non-profit, human services organization. Works to strengthen families and assist the proper development of children. **Positions advertised include:** Administrator; Autism Consultant; Child Development Specialist; Domestic Violence Specialist; Mental Health Specialist; Program Director; Crisis Outreach Specialist; Exercise Leader. **Other area locations:** Statewide.

Illinois
AMERICAN RED CROSS OF GREATER CHICAGO
Rauner Center, 2200 West Harrison Street, Chicago IL 60612. 312/729-6100. **Fax:** 312/729-6306. **Contact:** Human Resources. **E-mail address:** chicagohr@usa.redcross.org. **World Wide Web address:** http://www.chicagoredcross.org. **Description:** A humanitarian organization that aids disaster victims, gathers blood for crisis distribution, trains individuals to respond to emergencies, educates individuals on various diseases, and raises funds for other charitable establishments. **Positions advertised include:** Technical Curriculum Specialist; Fulfillment Associate; Graphic Designer; Manager of Marketing. **Special programs:** Internships; Volunteering. **Corporate headquarters location:** Washington DC. **Other U.S. locations:** Nationwide.

ANIXTER CENTER
6610 North Clark Street, Chicago IL 60626-4062. 773/973-7900. **Fax:** 773/973-5268. **Contact:** Debbie Thom, Human Resources Director. **E-mail address:** specirno@anixter.org. **World Wide Web address:** http://www.anixter.org. **Description:** A nonprofit job training and rehabilitation organization for people with developmental disabilities. **NOTE:** Part-time positions offered. **Positions advertised include:** Advocate; Certified Nursing Assistant; Certified Occupational Therapist; Certified Special Educators; Child Care Worker; Mental Health Professional; Occupational Therapy Consultant; Substance Abuse Counselor; Teaching Assistant/Substitute Teacher.

ASPIRE OF ILLINOIS
9901 Derby Lane, Westchester IL 60154-3709. 708/547-3550x3577. **Fax:** 708/547-4067. **Contact:** Michael Quirk, Human Resources Administrator. **E-mail address:** mquirk@aspireofillinois.org **World Wide Web address:** http://www.aspireofillinois.org. **Description:** A private, nonprofit agency serving the developmental, residential, and vocational needs of adults and children with developmental and mental disabilities. **NOTE:** Apply in person at the Human Resources Office. **Special programs:** Internships; Volunteers. **Corporate headquarters location:** This location. **Listed on:** Privately held.

CATHOLIC CHARITIES OF THE ARCHDIOCESE OF CHICAGO
721 North LaSalle Street, Chicago IL 60610. 312/655-7000. **Fax:** 312/831-1321. **Recorded jobline:** 312/655-7118. **Contact:** Employment Services. **World Wide Web address:** http://www.catholiccharities.net. **Description:** A network of private social service organizations that provides food, shelter, and clothing to more than 10 million poor and homeless people each year. **NOTE:** This organization provides a complete list of open positions and contact information on its website. See website. **Positions advertised include:** Intake/Marketing Specialist; Supervisor; Bi-Lingual Receptionist/Clerk; Social Work/Coordinator.

CHICAGO YOUTH CENTERS
104 South Michigan Avenue, 14th Floor, Chicago IL 60603-5902. 312/795-3500. **Fax:** 312/795-3520. **Contact:** Human Resources. **E-mail address:** asykes@chicagoyouthcenters.org. **World Wide Web address:** http://www.chicagoyouthcenters.org. **Description:** The largest independent youth services agency based in Chicago. Provides recreational and educational opportunities for kids in depressed areas of Chicago. **NOTE:** See website for current job openings.

RAY GRAHAM ASSOCIATION
2801 Finley Road, Downers Grove IL 60515. 630/620-2222. **Fax:** 630/628-2351. **Contact:** Human Resources. **E-mail address:** rgajobs@yahoo.com. **World Wide Web address:** http://www.ray-graham.org. **Description:** A consumer-driven organization that responds to the needs of people with disabilities and their families. **NOTE:** An application is required for any position and must be completed in person at the Human Resources office. **Positions advertised include:** Dietary Technician; Lab Technician; Community Support Specialist; ADT/AM Aide. **Corporate headquarters location:** This location. **Operations at this facility include:** Administration.

JANE ADDAMS HULL HOUSE ASSOCIATION
1030 West Van Buren, Chicago IL 60607. 312/906-8600. **Fax:** 312/235-5287. **Contact:** Staffing Coordinator. **World Wide Web address:** http://www.hullhouse.org. **Description:** A nonprofit, multiservice social agency dedicated to helping people build better lives for themselves and their families. Jane Addams Hull House Association has 6 community centers and 35 satellite locations throughout metropolitan Chicago. The organization serves approximately 225,000 people from geographically, culturally, and economically diverse backgrounds each year. **NOTE:** See website for job listings and contact information. **Positions advertised include:** Literacy Aide; Case Management Supervisor; Program Supervisor; Caseworker; Administrative Assistant. **Corporate headquarters location:** This location.

KNOX COUNTY COUNCIL FOR DEVELOPMENTAL DISABILITIES
2015 Windish Drive, Galesburg IL 61401. 309/344-2600. **Contact:** Deputy Executive Director. **World Wide Web address:** http://www.kccdd.com. **Description:** A nonprofit agency serving people with developmental disabilities. **Special programs:** Volunteers. **Corporate headquarters location:** This location. **Operations at this facility include:** Administration; Manufacturing; Service.

KREIDER CENTER
P.O. Box 366, Dixon IL 61021. 815/288-6691. **Physical address:** 500 Anchor Road, Dixon IL. **Contact:** Human Resources. **Description:** Provides residential and day services for adults with mental disabilities.

LIONS CLUBS INTERNATIONAL
300 West 22nd Street, Oak Brook IL 60523-8842. 630/571-5466. **Contact:** Human Resources. **World Wide Web address:** http://www.lionsclubs.org. **Description:** An international service organization. This location is the headquarters for the International Activities and Program Planning Division. **NOTE:** See website for job listings.

MARYVILLE CITY OF YOUTH
1150 North River Road, Des Plaines IL 60016. 847/294-1999. **Fax:** 847/824-7190. **Contact:** Human Resources Department. **World Wide Web address:** http://www.maryvilleacademy.org. **Description:** A residential home for orphaned and homeless children. Founded in 1882. **Positions advertised include:** Family Educator. **Special programs:** Volunteers. **Corporate headquarters location:** This location.

METROPOLITAN FAMILY SERVICES
One North Dearborn, Chicago IL 60602. 312/986-4000. **Fax:** 312/986-4347. **Contact:** Human Resources. **E-mail address:** resumes@metrofamily.org. **World Wide Web address:** http://www.metrofamily.org. **Description:** A nonprofit, social services agency that provides counseling and support services to low-income families and individuals. The agency operates 23 other locations in the Chicago area. Positions advertised include: Bi-lingual Social Worker; Program Supervisor; Social Worker or Counselor. **Special programs:** Internships. **Corporate headquarters location:** This location. **Operations at this facility include:** Administration; Service.

ROTARY INTERNATIONAL
One Rotary Center, 1560 Sherman Avenue, Evanston IL 60201. 847/866-3000. **Fax:** 847/866-5766. **Contact:** Human Resources. **World Wide Web address:** http://www.rotary.org. **Description:** Rotary International is one of the largest international, nonprofit, service organizations in the world. Founded in 1905. **Special programs:** Internships. **Corporate headquarters location:** This location. **Operations at this facility include:** This location provides administrative services to Rotary clubs including publicity and the administration of humanitarian and scholarship programs funded by the Rotary Foundation.

THE WOODLAWN ORGANIZATION (TWO)
6040 South Harper Avenue, Chicago IL 60637. 773/288-5840. **Contact:** Human Resources. **World Wide Web address:** http://www.wearewoodlawn.org. **Description:** Provides social services including a detoxification center, a child abuse treatment center, mental health facilities, two early childhood development programs, secretarial and word-processing training programs, a youth try-out employment project, and HUD real estate management services. **Corporate headquarters location:** This location. **Operations at this facility include:** Administration.

YMCA OF METROPOLITAN CHICAGO
801 North Dearborn, Chicago IL 60610. 312/932-1200. **Contact:** Human Resources. **World Wide Web address:** http://www.ymcachgo.org. **Description:** One of the nation's largest and most comprehensive service organizations. The YMCA provides health and fitness; social and personal development; sports and recreation; education and career development; and camps and conferences to children, youths, adults, the elderly, families, the disabled, refugees and foreign nationals, YMCA residents, and community residents, through a range of programs. **Special programs:** Internships.

Indiana
ARC OPPORTUNITIES, INC.
235 West 300 North, Howe IN 46746. 260/463-2653. **Fax:** 260/463-2046. **Contact:** Human Resources. **E-mail address:** info@arcopportunities.com. **World Wide Web address:** http://www.thearclink.org. **Description:** ARC Opportunities offers a skills workshop and some contract factory work opportunities for handicapped adults and helps these individuals attain jobs in the community. ARC also hosts the First Steps program, which aids infants and children with physical and learning disabilities.

AREA FIVE AGENCY ON AGING AND COMMUNITY SERVICES
1801 Smith Street, Logansport IN 46947. 574/722-4451. **Fax:** 574/722-3447. **Contact:** Human Resources. **World Wide Web address:** http://www.areafive.com. **Description:** A social services organization that offers nursing home placement for the elderly, childcare services, and home weatherizing services. Area Five also hosts the local Head Start Program. **Positions advertised include:** Case Manager.

ASSOCIATION OF RETIRED AMERICANS
6505 East 82nd Street, Suite 130, Indianapolis IN 46250. 317/915-2500. **Fax:** 317/915-2510. **Contact:** Human Resources. **World Wide Web address:** http://www.ara-usa.org. **Description:** Provides insurance discounts, hearing and vision care discounts, and car rental discounts for members.

BIG SISTERS OF CENTRAL INDIANA
2960 North Meridian Street, Suite 150, Indianapolis IN 46208. 317/921-2201. **Fax:** 317/921-2202. **Contact:** Human Resources. **World Wide Web address:** http://www.bbbsci.org. **Description:** Provides volunteer and professional services to young girls. The agency also provides an array of counseling, referral, and family support services to parents and children. Additional programs focus on children with special needs including physical or learning disabilities, as well as those who are abused, neglected, or have dropped out of school. Special prevention and intervention programs at many agencies address the problems of drug abuse, teen pregnancy, foster care, and juvenile delinquency. **Other U.S. locations:** Nationwide.

CENTRAL INDIANA COUNCIL ON THE AGING (CICOA)
4755 Kingsway Drive, Suite 200, Indianapolis IN 46205. 317/254-5465. **Fax:** 317/803-6273. **Contact:** Human Resources. **World Wide Web address:** http://www.cicoa.org. **Description:** Coordinates in-home services such as home health care and respite care for elderly individuals.

COMMUNITY ACTION PROGRAM (CAP)
P.O. Box 188, Covington IN 47932. 765/793-4881. **Physical address:** 418 Washington Street, Covington IN 47932. **Fax:** 765/793-4884. **Contact:** Human Resources. **Description:** A community service center that offers energy assistance services, weatherizing and housing services, and other community programs. CAP also hosts the local Head Start program.

COMMUNITY ACTION SOUTHERN INDIANA
1613 East Eighth Street, Jeffersonville IN 47130. 812/288-6451. **Fax:** 812/284-8314. **Contact:** Human Resources. **Description:** A community service center that offers energy assistance services, weatherizing and housing services, and other community programs. CAP also hosts the local Head Start program. Community Action Southern Indiana also sponsors several programs for youth including Four Cs (a developmental program for toddlers), Head Start, and Achieve.

COMMUNITY CENTERS OF INDIANAPOLIS, INC.
2236 East Tenth Street, Indianapolis IN 46201. 317/633-8210. **Fax:** 317/638-3675. **Contact:** Dean Johns, Human Resources. **World Wide Web address:** http://www.enn.org. **Description:** A service organization that operates 14 community service centers in Indianapolis. Services include individual and family counseling, assessment, and referral, as well as emergency assistance food and clothing banks; housing revitalization; senior citizen activities, hot lunches,

residential facility, and homemaker assistance; transportation for low-income seniors and disabled persons to center-related activities; summer day camp; summer youth activities; tutoring and remedial education; outpatient and residential drug and alcohol treatment programs for adolescents; recreation and social development for all ages; training for job readiness and job skills seminars; well baby clinics, health clinics, and a dental clinic; Women, Infants and Children nutrition programs (WIC); food stamp distribution; immigration and naturalization help; ESL classes; library extensions; and offices for the Indiana State Employment Service.

COMMUNITY HARVEST FOOD BANK
999 East Tillman Road, Fort Wayne IN 46816. 260/447-3696. **Fax:** 260/447-4859. **Contact:** Jane Avery, Executive Director. **E-mail address:** info@communityharvest.org. **World Wide Web address:** http://www. communityharvest.org. **Description:** Collects and distributes food donations. The food bank operates as part of a group of over 400 agencies in northeast Indiana and Allen County. Founded in 1983.

GEMINUS CORPORATION
8400 Louisiana Street, Merrillville IN 46410. 219/757-1800. **Fax:** 219/757-1831. **Contact:** Diane Johnson, Human Resources. **E-mail address:** diane.johnson@geminus.org. **World Wide Web address:** http://www. geminus.org. **Description:** Operates Head Start programs and performs accounting, marketing, and human resource functions for Southlake Center for Mental Health, an inpatient and outpatient mental health center, and Tri-City Mental Health, an outpatient mental health center. **Positions advertised include:** Staff Accountant; Collection Specialist; Psychologist; Social Worker; Residential Assistant; Staff Nurse; Clinician; Addictions Therapist; Van Driver. **Special programs:** Internships. **Corporate headquarters location:** This location. **Operations at this facility include:** Service. **Listed on:** Privately held.

GIRL SCOUTS OF LIMBERLOST
2135 Spy Run Avenue, Fort Wayne IN 46805. 260/422-3417. **Contact:** Human Resources. **World Wide Web address:** http://www.girlscouts.org. **Description:** A social service organization aimed at meeting the social and developmental needs of adolescent girls. **Corporate headquarters location:** New York NY. **Parent company:** Girl Scouts USA.

NEW HORIZONS REHABILITATION, INC.
P.O. Box 98, Batesville IN 47006. 812/934-4528. **Physical address:** 237 Six Pine Ranch Road, Batesville IN 47006. **Fax:** 812/934-2522. **Contact:** Marie Dausch, Executive Director. **World Wide Web address:** http://www.nhrehab.org. **Description:** A nonprofit job service that helps people with disabilities find jobs within the community. **Office hours:** Monday – Friday, 7:30 a.m. – 4:00 p.m.

UNITED WAY OF CENTRAL INDIANA
3901 North Meridian Street, Indianapolis IN 46208. 317/923-1466. **Fax:** 317/921-1388. **Contact:** Human Resources. **World Wide Web address:** http://www.uwci.org. **Description:** An organization that raises and distributes funds for community service needs. **Special programs:** Internships; Volunteer Opportunities. **Internship information:** Paid and unpaid internships are offered in a variety of areas throughout the year. **Other U.S. locations:** Nationwide.

UNITED WAY OF HOWARD COUNTY
210 West Walnut, Room 201, Kokomo IN 46901. 765/457-6691. **Contact:** Carl Graber, President. **World Wide Web address:** http://www.unitedwayhoco.org. **Description:** An organization that raises and distributes funds for community service needs. **Special programs:** Internships. **Other U.S. locations:** Nationwide.

WOLF PARK
Wolf Park, Battle Ground IN 47920. 765/567-2265. **Fax:** 765/567-4299. **Contact:** Manager. **World Wide Web address:** http://www.wolfpark.org. **Description:** A nonprofit research organization focusing on wolf behavior and preservation. The park offers walking tours, lectures, and seminars to the public. Founded in 1972. **Special programs:** Internships; Co-ops. **Corporate headquarters location:** This location. **Parent company:** North American Wildlife Park Foundation, Inc.

YMCA CAMP POTAWOTAMI
P.O. Box 38, South Milford IN 46786. 260/351-2525. **Physical address**: 1755 East 700 Street, Wolcottville IN 46795. **Toll-free phone:** 800/966-9622. **Fax:** 260/351-3915. **Contact:** Executive Director. **World Wide Web address:** http://www.camp-potawotami.org. **Description:** The YMCA provides health and fitness, social and personal development, sports and recreation, education and career development, and camps and conferences to children, youths, adults, the elderly, families, and the disabled. **Operations at this facility include:** This location is a resident camp offering programs to children, families, and organizations throughout the Midwest.

Kansas

AMERICAN RED CROSS
1900 East Douglas Street, Wichita KS 67209. 316/219-4070. **Contact:** Personnel. **World Wide Web address:** http://www.midwaykansas.redcross.org. **Description:** A humanitarian organization that aids disaster victims, gathers blood for crisis distribution, trains individuals to respond to emergencies, educates individuals on various diseases, and raises funds for other charitable establishments. **Other area locations:** Throughout Kansas. **Other U.S. locations:** Nationwide.

Kentucky

THE CABBAGE PATCH SETTLEMENT HOUSE, INC.
1413 South Sixth Street, Louisville KY 40208. 502/634-0811. **Fax:** 502/637-9943. **Contact:** Lisa Griffin, Human Resources. **E-mail address:** lgriffin@cabbagepatch.org. **World Wide Web address:** http://www.cabbagepatch.org. **Description:** An independently funded, nonprofit, Christian charity that assists underprivileged, inner-city individuals through daycare, family services, and recreational/educational programs. Services include an Educational Opportunities Program, counseling, financial assistance for struggling families, childcare, and youth recreation and development programs. Founded in 1910. **Corporate headquarters location:** This location. **Annual sales/revenues:** $1.6 million. **Number of employees at this location:** 30.

RESCARE INCORPORATED
10140 Linn Station Road, Louisville KY 40223. 502/394-2168. **Fax:** 502/394-2235. **Contact:** People Department. **E-mail address:** mlstewart@rescare.com. **World Wide Web address:** http://www.rescare.com. **Description:** Provides support and training service for people with mental disabilities or other developmental disabilities. **NOTE:** To contact Human Resources directly, call 502/394-2168. **Positions advertised include:** A/R Analyst; Revenue & Cash A/R Manager; Chief Compliance Officer; Computer Hardware Specialist; Labor Relations Director; Financial Analyst; Human Resource Information Specialist Analyst; Payroll Assistant. **Other U.S. locations:** Nationwide. **International locations:** Canada; Puerto Rico. **Listed on:** NASDAQ. **Stock exchange symbol:** RSCR. **Number of employees worldwide:** Approximately 29,000.

Maine

COASTAL ENTERPRISES, INC.
P.O. Box 268, Wiscasset ME 04578. 207/882-7552. **Physical address:** 36 Water Street, Wiscasset ME 04578. **Fax:** 207/882-7308. **Contact:** Personnel Department. **E-mail address:** cei@ceimaine.org. **World Wide Web address:** http://www.ceimaine.org. **Description:** A non-profit social and economic development organization. **Other area locations:**

Portland; Lewiston; Augusta; Sanford; Fairfield; Farmington; Unity; Bangor.

CUMBERLAND COUNTY YMCA
70 Forest Avenue, P.O. Box 1078, Portland ME 04101. 207/874-1111. **Fax:** 207/874-1114. **Contact:** Charlene Turner, Human Resources. **E-mail address:** cturner@cumberlandymca.org. **World Wide Web address:** http://www.cascobayymca.org. **Description:** Provides a wide range of social and educational services including health and lodging. Founded 1853. **NOTE:** For childcare positions, resumes should be directed to Pam Washington, Director of Childcare. For positions in finance, resumes should be directed to Ludmila Tutunaru, Director of Finance. You may search for and apply to jobs through http://jobsinme.com. Volunteer positions are also available. **Positions advertised include:** Youth Program Assistant; Teen Program Assistant; Substitute Childcare Provider. **Special programs:** Internships, including health and lodging. **Other area locations:** Freeport ME; New Gloucester ME; Standish ME.

H.O.M.E., INC.
P.O. Box 10, 90 School House Road, Orland ME 04472. 207/469-7961. **Fax:** 207/469-1023. **Contact:** Father Randy Eldridge, Internship Coordinator. **E-mail address:** padre@homecoop.net. **World Wide Web address:** http://www.homecoop.net/index.html. **Description:** Provides self-sufficiency instruction to individuals. In addition, this nonprofit company provides education, an outlet for people to sell their crafts, and health care for low-income individuals. H.O.M.E., Inc. also gives job-training workshops and provides housing. Founded in 1970. **Special programs:** Internships. **Internship information:** Interns receive training, room and board, and a small stipend. **Corporate headquarters location:** This location. **Number of employees at this location:** 55.

Maryland
CALL FOR ACTION, INC.
5272 River Road, Suite 300, Bethesda MD 20816-1405. 301/657-8260. **Contact:** Human Resources. **World Wide Web address:** http://www.callforaction.org. **Description:** A nonprofit consumer group engaged in mediation between manufacturers and dissatisfied consumers through a network of consumer hotlines. **Office hours:** Tuesday – Friday, 11:00 a.m. – 1:00 p.m. **Corporate headquarters location:** This location. **Other U.S. locations:** Nationwide. **International locations:** Buenos Aires, Argentina.

THE CHIMES, INC.
4814 Seton Drive, Baltimore MD 21215. 410/358-6677. **Toll-free phone:** 800/CHI-MES1. **Fax:** 410/358-1747. **Recorded jobline:** 410/358-6006. **Contact:** Human Resources. **E-mail address:** hrmail@chimes.org. **World Wide Web address:** http://www.chimes.org. **Description:** A nonsectarian, nonprofit agency that offers a broad range of vocational, rehabilitative, residential, educational, and support services for thousands of individuals in central Maryland, northern Virginia, and Washington DC. The Chimes helps children, adults, and senior citizens with mental and related disabilities to lead more independent lives. Founded in 1947. **Positions advertised include:** Single and Multi Site Job Coach; Food Service Manager; House Manager; Research Proven Technician; Program Coordinator; Instructor; Executive Assistant; Accounts Payable Manager; Environmental Services. **Office hours:** Monday – Thursday, 9:00 a.m. – 3:00 p.m. **Corporate headquarters location:** This location. **Other U.S. locations:** CA; DE; DC; IA; VA. **International locations:** Israel. **President/CEO:** Terry Allen Perl. **Number of employees nationwide:** 600.

COOPERATIVE HOUSING FOUNDATION
8601 Georgia Avenue, Suite 800, Silver Spring MD 20910. 301/587-4700. **Fax:** 301/587-7315. **Contact:** Human Resources. **E-mail address:** hrrec@chfhq.org. **World Wide Web address:** http://www.chfhq.org. **Description:** A foundation providing housing, economic, infrastructure, and health assistance. **NOTE:** When submitting via e-mail, attach resume and cover letter as separate documents. **Positions advertised include:** Communications Assistant; Security Offices; Short Term Consultant; A/R Accountant; Credit Manager; Credit Analyst; Operations Support Officer; Municipal Financial Specialist; Program Officer; Program Manager. **Corporate headquarters location:** This location. **Operations at this facility include:** Regional Headquarters. **President/CEO:** Michael Doyle.

EPISCOPAL MINISTRIES TO THE AGING
576 Johnsville Road, Eldersburg MD 21784. 410/970-2000. **Contact:** Human Resources. **World Wide Web address:** http://www.emaseniorcare.org. **Description:** A nonprofit company that provides a variety of programs and services to the elderly. EMA operates two residential and outpatient facilities, a continuing care retirement community, a research and development institute devoted to the care of the aging, and various other retirement and nursing facilities in the Baltimore area. **NOTE:** Entry-level positions and second and third shifts are offered. See Website for further information on Human Resource contacts for the Copper Ridge, Fairhaven, and Buckingham's Choice facilities. **Positions advertised include:** Director of Budget and Cost; Maintenance Technician; LPN; Registered Nurse; Unit Clerk; Laundry Assistant; Sous Chef; Certified Medicine Aide; Wait Staff; Server/Cashier; Beautician; Housekeeping Assistant; Assistant Director of Activities. **Special programs:** Training; Tuition Reimbursement Program; Scholarship Program. **Office hours:** Monday - Friday, 9:00 a.m. - 5:00 p.m. **Corporate headquarters location:** This location. **Subsidiaries include:** Fairhaven Incorporated is a continuing care retirement community with 420 residents in independent living, assisted living, and comprehensive care units. Copper Ridge, Incorporated is a nursing facility specializing in care for the memory-impaired, with accommodations for 126 residents in its assisted living and comprehensive care units. Buckingham's Choice is a continuing care retirement community. **Number of employees nationwide:** Over 1,000.

MELWOOD TRAINING CENTER
5606 Dower House Road, Upper Marlboro MD 20772. 301/599-8000. **Fax:** 301/599-0180. **Recorded jobline:** 866/447-1340. **Contact:** Corporate Recruiting Manager. **E-mail address:** cdougher@melwood.org. **World Wide Web address:** http://www.melwood.org. **Description:** A private, nonprofit agency providing services for individuals with disabilities. Founded in 1963. **NOTE:** Entry-level and seasonal positions, part-time jobs, and second and third shifts are offered. The Corporate Recruiting Office is located at 9666 Pennsylvania Avenue, Upper Marlboro MD 20772. To contact directly, call 301/599-7913 or fax to 301/599-7915. **Positions advertised include:** Community Support Assistant; Resident Service Counselor; Assistant Cook; Writing Assistant; Summer Life Guard; Van Driver. **Company slogan:** Growing together. **Special programs:** Internships; Training; Summer Jobs. **Office hours:** Monday - Friday, 8:00 a.m. - 5:00 p.m. **Corporate headquarters location:** This location.

NATIONAL FEDERATION OF THE BLIND
NATIONAL CENTER FOR THE BLIND
1800 Johnson Street, Baltimore MD 21230. 410/659-9314. **Contact:** Human Resources. **World Wide Web address:** http://www.nfb.org. **Description:** An organization geared toward helping blind people. The organization provides literature and public education about blindness; equipment to assist the blind; and offers the Job Opportunities for the Blind program that helps blind persons who are seeking employment. Founded in 1940.

ROCK CREEK FOUNDATION
12120 Plum Orchard Drive, Suite B, Silver Spring MD 20904. 301/586-0900. **Fax:** 301/587-8724. **Contact:** Human Resources. **World Wide Web address:** http://www.ddamaryland.org/rockcreek.htm.

Description: A national training site engaged in creating opportunities for disabled adults. Individuals are aided in community integration through avenues such as educational, volunteer, and employment opportunities.

Massachusetts

ACTION FOR BOSTON COMMUNITY DEVELOPMENT (ABCD)
178 Tremont Street, Boston MA 02111. 617/357-6000. **Contact:** Human Resources, Department 161. **E-mail address:** hr@bostonabc.org. **World Wide Web address:** http://www.bostonabcd.org. **Description:** A nonprofit, community action, human services agency helping low-income residents make the transition from poverty to self-sufficiency. ABCD provides programs and services including job training, education, weatherization, housing services, fuel assistance, the Urban College Program, child care including Head Start and daycare, and elder service programs. **NOTE:** Submit applications in Microsoft Word only. **Positions advertised include:** Health Coordinator; Graphic Designer. **Corporate headquarters location:** This location. **Operations at this facility include:** Administration; Research and Development.

ADAMS/CHESHIRE HEADSTART PROJECT
46 Howland Avenue, Suite 3, Adams MA 01220. 413/743-5150. **Contact:** Human Resources. **Description:** A state- and federally funded daycare program for low-income families with children between the ages of three and five.

AIDS ACTION COMMITTEE
294 Washington Street 5th Floor, Boston MA 02108. 617/437-6200. **Fax:** 617/437-6445. **Recorded jobline:** 617/450-1435. **Contact:** Human Resources. **E-mail address:** resumes@aac.org. **World Wide Web address:** http://www.aac.org. **Description:** A nonprofit organization providing services to people living with HIV, and their families; combating the AIDS epidemic through education; and advocating fair and effective AIDS policy and funding. The AIDS Action Committee is the largest AIDS service organization in New England. Founded by a small group of volunteers, the organization now includes a full-time professional staff supported by several thousand volunteers. The group operates through several segments, all of which offer employment and volunteer opportunities. They include clinical services, housing, financial and legal, counseling, education, training, development, fundraising, public policy, government relations, communications, grant writing, administration and finance, AR/AP, human resources, MIS, computer operations, and facilities. Founded in 1983. **Positions advertised include:** Clinical Specialist; Associate Director of Major Gifts; Bilingual Hotline Coordinator; Field Interviewer. **NOTE:** Please call the jobline for current openings. Indicate the position of interest in your cover letter. **Special programs:** Internships. **Corporate headquarters location:** This location. **Operations at this facility include:** Administration. **Number of employees at this location:** 100.

BIG BROTHERS BIG SISTERS
101 State Street, Suite 601, Springfield MA 01103-2071. 413/781-4730. **Contact:** Human Resources. **Description:** Provides a mentor program for underprivileged children by pairing them with an adult volunteer.

CATHOLIC CHARITIES
75 Kneeland Street, 8th Floor, Boston MA 02111. 617/482-5440. **Fax:** 617/482-9737. **Contact:** Human Resources. **E-mail address:** resumes@ccab.org. **World Wide Web address:** http://www.ccab.org. **Description:** A social service agency. Services include career counseling, alternative education, immigration refugee services and relief, family guidance, shelter and ministry programs, substance abuse services, and English-as-a-Second-Language (ESL) programs. **Positions advertised include:** Clinical Programs Director; Agency Counselor; LSCW Social Worker.

CEREBRAL PALSY OF THE SOUTH SHORE CHILDREN'S DEVELOPMENTAL DISABILITIES CENTER
43 Old Colony Avenue, Quincy MA 02170. 617/479-7443. **Contact:** Human Resources. **Description:** An outpatient rehabilitation and treatment center for children from birth to eight years old who have disabilities. The onsite treatment facilities also include a school and a daycare center. **Positions advertised include:** Nurse; Social Worker; Therapist.

CITIZENS ENERGY CORPORATION
88 Black Falcon Avenue, Center Lobby, Suite 342, Boston MA 02210. 617/338-6300. **Contact:** Controller. **E-mail address:** inform@citizensenergy.com. **World Wide Web address:** http://www.citizensenergy.com. **Description:** A nonprofit organization aimed at providing needy families with affordable home heating oil.

EDUCATION DEVELOPMENT CENTER, INC.
55 Chapel Street, Newton MA 02458. 617/969-7100. **Contact:** Human Resources. **World Wide Web address:** http://www.edc.org. **Description:** One of the world's leading educational nonprofit research and development firms specializing in early childhood development, K-12 education, health promotion, learning technologies, and institutional reform. Founded in 1958. **Company slogan:** Promoting human development through education. **Positions advertised include:** Sr. Assistant Director of Grants and Contracts; Technology/Curriculum Specialist; Project Assistant. **Corporate headquarters location:** This location. **Other U.S. locations:** Washington DC; New York NY. **International locations:** The Netherlands. **Listed on:** Privately held. **Annual sales/revenues:** $21 - $50 million. **Number of employees at this location:** 310. **Number of employees nationwide:** 400.

FEDERATED DORCHESTER NEIGHBORHOOD HOUSES
269 East Cottage Street, Dorchester MA 02125. 617/282-5034. **Fax:** 617/265-6020. **Contact:** Human Resources. **E-mail address:** aarroyo@fdnh.org. **World Wide Web address:** http://www.fdnh.org. **Description:** A nonprofit, human service agency with eight locations. **NOTE:** Entry-level positions and part-time jobs are offered. **Positions advertised include:** Case Manager; Operations and Administration Coordinator; Community Outreach Coordinator; Teen Recreation Worker. **Special programs:** Internships; Summer Jobs. **Corporate headquarters location:** This location. **Number of employees at this location:** 450.

HABITAT FOR HUMANITY BOSTON
273 Summer Street, 3rd Floor, Boston MA 02210. 617/423-2223. **Contact:** Human Resources. **World Wide Web address:** http://www.habitatboston.org. **Description:** A nonprofit organization that builds homes for the homeless. **Corporate headquarters location:** Americus GA. **Other U.S. locations:** Nationwide.

HEAD START PROJECT
62 First Street, Pittsfield MA 01201. 413/499-0137. **Contact:** Human Resources. **E-mail address:** lmcallops@nhsa.org. **World Wide Web address:** http://www.nhsa.org. **Description:** A state- and federally-funded program for low-income families with young children.

HISTORIC NEW ENGLAND
141 Cambridge Street, Boston MA 02114. 617/227-3956. **Contact:** Human Resources. **World Wide Web address:** http://www.historicnewengland.org. **Description:** A nonprofit society founded to preserve New England's domestic buildings and artifacts. It is among the country's largest regional preservation organizations, owning 43 historic properties, 34 of which are open as house museums. Founded in 1910. **Special programs:** Internships. **Corporate headquarters location:** This location. **Other U.S. locations:** CT; ME; NH; RI. **Number of employees at**

this location: 45. **Number of employees nationwide:** 100.

THE ITALIAN HOME FOR CHILDREN
1125 Center Street, Jamaica Plain MA 02130. 617/524-3116. **Contact:** Director. **E-mail address:** hr@italianhome.org. **World Wide Web address:** http://www.italianhome.org. **Description:** A residential treatment center for emotionally disturbed children. The Italian Home for Children provides counseling and schooling for approximately 60 youths, aged six to 13. **Positions advertised include:** Childcare Worker; Quality Improvement Associate; Director of Child Care Training Services. **Number of employees at this location:** 100.

**JANE DOE INC.
MA COALITION AGAINST SEXUAL ASSAULT & DOMESTIC VIOLENCE**
14 Beacon Street, Suite 507, Boston MA 02108. 617/248-0922. **Fax:** 617/248-0902. **Contact:** Human Resources. **E-mail address:** jobs@janedoe.org. **World Wide Web address:** http://www.janedoe.org. **Description:** A nonprofit public education and advocacy organization. Jane Doe Inc. operates more than 30 programs across the state.

**MASSACHUSETTS AUDOBON SOCIETY
MOOSE HILL WILDLIFE SANCTUARY**
293 Moose Hill Street, Sharon MA 02067. 781/784-5691. **Contact:** Director. **World Wide Web address:** http://www.massaudubon.org. **Description:** A nonprofit organization involved in educating the community about the environment and promoting conservation efforts. The sanctuary offers a wide range of programs including Owl Prowls, family camp-outs, summer camp for children, and maple sugaring tours. The sanctuary also has its own art gallery featuring bimonthly exhibits of works by local artists. **NOTE:** Moose Hill Wildlife Sanctuary welcomes applicants for volunteer positions. **Positions advertised include:** Adventure Camp Instructor: After Camp Instructor. **Corporate headquarters location:** Lincoln MA.

MELMARK NEW ENGLAND
50 Tower Office Park, Woburn MA 01801. 781/932-9211. **Fax:** 781/932-0189. **Contact:** Recruiting Department. **E-mail address:** recruiter@melmarkne.org. **World Wide Web address:** http://www.melmarkne.org. **Description:** A non-profit organization, serving children with autism, neurological disorders, and acquired brain injuries. **Positions advertised include:** ABA Counselor; Classroom Teacher; Speech Language Pathologist.

MORGAN MEMORIAL GOODWILL INDUSTRIES, INC.
1010 Harrison Avenue, Boston MA 02119-2540. 617/541-1400. **Fax:** 617/541-1495. **Contact:** Toni Preston, Director of Human Resources. **World Wide Web address:** http://www.goodwillmass.org. **Description:** A nonprofit human services agency. Programs include training, employment, and career services for persons with disabilities and others who face barriers to employment; and youth services including a live-in summer camp in central Massachusetts for inner-city youth, ages 7 through 16. The organization also operates nine retail stores. **NOTE:** Volunteer opportunities are offered. **Positions advertised include:** Retail Supervisor; Computer Instructor; Case Manager; Developmental Specialist; Balance Sheet Accountant. **Special programs:** Internships. **President/CEO:** Joanne K. Hilferty.

OLD COLONY ELDERLY SERVICES, INC.
P.O. Box 4469 Brockton MA 02301 508/584-1561. **Physical address:** 144 Main Street, Brockton MA 02301. **Contact:** Human Resources. **Description:** Provides various services to the elderly including transportation and in-home care.

PINE STREET INN, INC.
444 Harrison Avenue, Boston MA 02118. 617/892-9100. **Fax:** 617/521-7667. **Contact:** HR Employment Coordinator. **World Wide Web address:** http://www.pinestreetinn.org. **Description:** Provides shelter, transitional programs, and housing for men, women, and children. **Operations at this facility include:** Administration; Service. **Number of employees at this location:** 650.

**PROJECT BREAD
WALK FOR HUNGER**
145 Border Street, Boston MA 02128. 617/723-5000. **Contact:** Human Resources. **World Wide Web address:** http://www.projectbread.org. **Description:** Supports nearly 500 food pantries, soup kitchens, homeless shelters, food banks, and other emergency feeding programs in 119 Massachusetts communities. Project Bread's Technical Assistance Program trains over 200 volunteers and staff, provides over 100 programs with one-on-one management assistance, and holds training series. Project Bread's transportation program, Food Drive for the Hungry, operated jointly with the American Red Cross, provides transportation to pick up low-cost or donated food. Since it began in 1969, the Walk for Hunger has become one of the nation's largest annual, one-day fundraisers for the hungry.

THE SALVATION ARMY
187 Columbus Avenue, Boston MA 02116-5197. 617/542-5420. **Fax:** 617/338-7990. **Contact:** Divisional Personnel Secretary. **World Wide Web address:** http://www.salvationarmy.org. **Description:** A nonprofit organization providing several service programs including day-care centers, programs for people with disabilities, substance abuse programs and tutoring for at-risk students. The Salvation Army targets its programs to assist alcoholics, battered women, drug addicts, the elderly, the homeless, people with AIDS, prison inmates, teenagers, and the unemployed. **Corporate headquarters location:** Alexandria VA. **Other U.S. locations:** Nationwide. **Operations at this facility include:** Administration; Divisional Headquarters. **Number of employees at this location:** 50.

UNITED WAY OF MASSACHUSETTS BAY
51 Sleeper Street, Boston MA 02210. 617/624-8000. **Fax:** 617/624-9114.**Contact:** Human Resources. **World Wide Web address:** http://www.uwmb.org. **Description:** Through a vast network of volunteers and local charities, the United Way helps to meet the health and human-care needs of millions of people. The United Way is comprised of approximately 1,900 organizations. **Other U.S. locations:** Nationwide.

Michigan

AUSABLE VALLEY COMMUNITY MENTAL HEALTH
511 Griffin Road, West Branch MI 48661. 989/345-5571. **Fax:** 989/345-4111. **Contact:** Human Resources. **Description:** Provides mental health and substance abuse treatment services on an outpatient basis. **Corporate headquarters location:** This location.

COMMUNITY MENTAL HEALTH FOR CENTRAL MICHIGAN
2603 West Wackerly Road, Midland MI 48640. 989/631-2320. **Fax:** 989/631-9903. **Contact:** Human Resources. **World Wide Web address:** http://www.cmhcm.org. **Description:** Provides outpatient therapy, case management services, and children's intensive services. **Corporate headquarters location:** This location. **Other area locations:** Gladwin MI; Harrison MI; Mount Pleasant MI; Big Rapids MI; Reed City MI.

FOCUS HOPE
1355 Oakman Boulevard, Detroit MI 48238. 313/494-4775. **Fax:** 313/494-4287. **Contact:** Human Resources. **E-mail address:** hr@focushope.edu. **World Wide Web address:** http://www.focushope.edu. **Description:** An organization providing civil rights advocacy and operating a food center. **Number of employees statewide:** Over 800.

GOODWILL INDUSTRIES OF GREATER DETROIT
3111 Grand River Avenue, Detroit MI 48208. 313/964-3900, extension 331. **Fax:** 313/964-3972. **Contact:** Human Resources. **E-mail address:** snoland@goodwilldetroit.com. **World Wide Web address:** http://www.goodwilldetroit.org. **Description:** Besides operating 1,400 thrift stores nationwide, Goodwill is a nonprofit provider of employment training for the disabled and the poor. **Positions advertised include:** Support Coordination Specialist. **Corporate headquarters location:** This location. **Other U.S. locations:** Nationwide.

L.A.D.D. INC. (LIVING ALTERNATIVES FOR THE DEVELOPMENTALLY DISABLED)
8054 Ortonville Road, P.O. Box 965, Clarkston MI 48347. 248/625-3870. **Contact:** Human Resources. **E-mail address:** eastofficecoordinator@laddinc.net. **World Wide Web address:** http://www.laddinc.net. **Description:** Establishes group homes for developmentally disabled adults. Founded in 1978. **Positions advertised include:** Professional Care Technician; Assistant Manager; Manager; Area Supervisor; Quality Assurance Supervisor; Office Coordinator; Director of Operations; Administrator. **Corporate headquarters location:** This location. **Other area locations:** Statewide.

STARR COMMONWEALTH
13725 Starr Commonwealth Road, Albion MI 49224. 517/629-5591, extension 2459. **Toll-free phone:** 800/837-5591. **Fax:** 517/629-2317. **Contact:** Dennis Eddy, Recruitment Coordinator. **E-mail address:** eddyd@starr.org. **World Wide Web address:** http://www.starr.org. **Description:** A private, non-profit service organization for troubled youth offering long-term residential care, alternative education, and foster care. **NOTE:** Summer jobs and temporary positions are offered. **Positions advertised include:** Public Relations Specialist; Youth Specialist; Marketing Services Coordinator; Teacher/Counselor. **Corporate headquarters location:** This location. **Other area locations:** Battle Creek MI; Detroit MI. **Other U.S. locations:** Columbus OH; Van Wert OH. **Number of employees nationwide:** Over 500.

UNITED WAY FOR SOUTHEASTERN MICHIGAN
1212 Griswold Street, Detroit MI 48226. 313/226-9200. **Fax:** 313/226-9210. **Contact:** Human Resources. **E-mail address:** resume@uwsem.org. **World Wide Web address:** http://www.uwsem.org. **Description:** Through a vast network of volunteers and local charities, the United Way helps to meet the health and human-care needs of millions of people. The United Way includes approximately 1,900 organizations. **Positions advertised include:** Special Events Director; Grants Manager; Director of Diversity Relationships; Editorial Associate; Editorial Service Manager; Graphic Design Associate.

UPCAP SERVICES
2501 14th Avenue South, P.O. Box 606, Escanaba MI 49829. 906/786-4701. **Fax:** 906/786-5853. **Contact:** Human Resources. **World Wide Web address:** http://www.upcapservices.com. **Description:** An agency on aging. UPCAP contracts and manages services for the elderly including personal care, meal delivery, and homemaker aid. Founded in 1961. **Corporate headquarters location:** This location. **Other area locations:** Marie MI; Munising MI; Marquette MI; Manistique MI; Ironwood MI; Iron Mountain MI; Houghton MI.

YMCA OAK PARK
900 Long Boulevard, Lansing MI 48911. 517/694-3901. **Fax:** 517/694-2945. **Contact:** Tiffeny Forrest, Executive Director. **E-mail address:** tforrest@ymcaoflansing.org. **World Wide Web address:** http://www.ymcaoflansing.org. **Description:** One of the nation's largest and most comprehensive service organizations. The YMCA provides health and fitness; social and personal development; sports and recreation; education and career development; and camps and conferences to children, youths, adults, the elderly, families, the disabled, refugees and foreign nationals, YMCA residents, and community residents, through a range of programs. **Corporate headquarters location:** Chicago IL. **Other U.S. locations:** Nationwide. **International locations:** Worldwide.

Minnesota

AMERICAN REFUGEE COMMITTEE
430 Oak Grove Street, Suite 204, Minneapolis MN 55403. 612/872-7060. **Toll-free phone:** 800/875-7060. **Fax:** 612/607-6499. **Contact:** Colleen Striegel, Human Resources. **E-mail address:** colleens@archq.org. **World Wide Web address:** http://www.archq.org. **Description:** An international nonprofit, nonsectarian organization that provides humanitarian assistance and training to refugees. **Positions advertised include:** Regional Manager; Human Resources Specialist. **International locations:** Guinea; Liberia; Sierra Leone; Rwanda; Sudan; Uganda; Pakistan; Thailand; Kosovo; Macedonia; Serbia and Montenegro; Sri Lanka.

INDUSTRIES INC.
500 South Walnut Street, Mora MN 55051. 320/679-2354. **Contact:** Human Resources. **Description:** Provides job training and placement services for individuals who are mentally challenged.

LIGHTHOUSE FOR THE BLIND
4505 West Superior Street, Duluth MN 55807. 218/624-4828. **Toll-free phone:** 800/422-0833. **Fax:** 218/624-4479. **Contact:** Human Resources. **World Wide Web address:** http://www.lighthousefortheblind-duluth.org. **Description:** Provides rehabilitative services, teaches skills, and sells products to people who are blind and visually impaired.

MRCI WORKSOURCE
P.O. Box 328, Mankato MN 56002. 507/386-5600. **Physical address:** 15 Map Drive, Mankato MN 56001. **Fax:** 507/345-5991. **Recorded jobline:** 800/733-9935; 507/386-4747. **Contact:** Human Resources. **World Wide Web address:** http://www.mrci.info. **Description:** A provider of community-based, supported employment services for people with disabilities or disadvantages, with sites in nine metropolitan and southern Minnesota counties. **Positions advertised include:** Day Training and Habilitation Team Leader/Instructor.

OCCUPATIONAL DEVELOPMENT CENTER
1520 Highway 32 South, P.O. Box 730, Thief River Falls MN 56701. 218/681-4949. **Contact:** Human Resources. **World Wide Web address:** http://www.odcmn.com. **Description:** Provides disabled people with an environment where they can enhance job skills, and aids them in finding employment. **Positions advertised include:** Part-Time Job Coach.

AMHERST H. WILDER FOUNDATION
919 Lafond Avenue, St. Paul MN 55104-2198. 651/642-4033. **Fax:** 651/642-4033. **Contact:** Human Resources. **E-mail address:** jobs@wilder.org. **World Wide Web address:** http://www.wilder.org. **Description:** A nonprofit, health and human services organization operating over 100 programs. **NOTE:** Entry-level positions are offered. **Positions advertised include:** Administrative Specialist; Compliance Specialist; Contracts & Grants Specialist; Division Director of Supportive Housing and Employment Services; Bilingual Counselor I/II; Peer Recovery Specialist – Bilingual; Social Worker. **Special programs:** Internships. **Corporate headquarters location:** This location. **Number of employees at this location:** 1,300.

Mississippi

BOYS & GIRLS CLUBS OF CENTRAL MISSISSIPPI
1450 West Capital Street, Jackson MS 39204. 601/969-7088. **Fax:** 601/969-7089. **Contact:** Bob Ward, Vice

President of Operations. **E-mail address:** bward@bgccm.net. **World Wide Web address:** http://www.bgccm.net. **Description:** A youth development organization that assists young people from disadvantaged economic, social, and family circumstances. **NOTE:** To volunteer, contact volunteer@bgccm.net. **Corporate headquarters location:** Atlanta GA. **Other area locations:** There are three other Boys & Girls Clubs in Jackson MS, as well as others statewide. **Other U.S. locations:** Nationwide. **Parent company:** United Way.

THE UNITED WAY OF THE CAPITAL AREA
P.O. Box 23169, Jackson MS 39225. 601/948-4725. **Physical address:** 843 North President Street, Jackson MS 39202. **Fax:** 601/968-8596. **Contact:** Administrative Assistant. **World Wide Web address:** http://www.myunitedway.com. **Description:** The United Way provides community and emergency services to families and children. Community and living services include daily living needs, aid for the homeless, HIV/AIDS education, housing, 24-hour crisis counseling, disaster relief, emergency assistance, military family services, elderly services, and services for victims of sexual assault. Services to families and children include counseling in areas of teen pregnancy, family violence, illiteracy, child abuse, adoption, speech and hearing, and emergency shelter for children. Health and Rehabilitation Services include drug/alcohol treatment, health research, health screening, mental illness, medication assistance, training and employment for the handicapped, and developmental services for mentally and physically handicapped individuals. Youth Development Services assist in dropout prevention, tutoring, child care, after school care, water safety, safe places, recreational activities, camping opportunities, and character building. **Corporate headquarters location:** Alexandria VA.

YMCA OF METROPOLITAN JACKSON
840 East River Place, Suite 503, Jackson MS 39202-3488. 601/948-0818, extension 202. **Fax:** 601/968-3874. **Contact:** Tina Voltz, Human Resources. **E-mail address:** tina@jacksony.org. **World Wide Web address:** http://www.jacksony.org. **Description:** The YMCA provides health and fitness; social and personal development; sports and recreation; education and career development; and camps and conferences to children, youths, adults, the elderly, families, the disabled, refugees and foreign nationals, YMCA residents, and community residents, through a broad range of specific programs. **NOTE:** For volunteer opportunities, contact Christy Coward at 601/948-0818, extension 120, or by e-mail at ccoward@jacksony.org. **Other U.S. locations:** Nationwide.

Missouri
CARDINAL RITTER INSTITUTE
7601 Watson Road, St. Louis MO 63119. 314/961-8000. **Fax:** 314/962-7140. **Contact:** Human Resources. **E-mail address:** jkohlberg@ccstl.org. **World Wide Web address:** http://www.ccstl.org/cri. **Description:** An organization that specializes in providing home health care, housing, social services, employment programs, and volunteer programs to the elderly. **Corporate headquarters location:** This location. **Number of employees at this location:** 350.

HUMANE SOCIETY OF MISSOURI
1201 Macklind Avenue, St. Louis MO 63110. 314/647-8800. **Fax:** 314/647-4317. **Contact:** Human Resources. **E-mail address:** hr@hsmo.org. **World Wide Web address:** http://www.hsmo.org. **Description:** One of the oldest and largest humane societies in the United States, providing emergency field services in St. Louis County. The organization investigates cruelty and neglect to animals statewide, and operates two animal shelters and two veterinary clinics. The society provides public relations and educational programs and operates a rehabilitation farm for large animals. **Positions advertised include:** Client and Animal Service specialist; Adoption Counselor; Development Data Specialist. **Special programs:** Internships. **Corporate headquarters location:** This location. **Operations at this facility include:** Service.

JEWISH COMMUNITY CENTERS
2 Millstone Campus Drive, Carlyn H. Wohl Building, St. Louis MO 63146. 314/432-5705. **Contact:** Director of Personnel. **Description:** A service organization whose facilities include a swimming pool, fitness center, and racquetball courts.

JUDEVINE CENTER FOR AUTISM
1101 Olivette Executive Parkway, St. Louis MO 63132. 314/432-6200. **Fax:** 314/849-2721. **Contact:** Human Resources. **E-mail address:** hr@judevine.org. **World Wide Web address:** http://www.judevine.org. **Description:** A pioneer agency providing services to children and adults with autism and related conditions in the areas of independent living, employment, training, family support, and professional development. **Positions advertised include:** Program Manager; Supported Living Coordinator; Employment Technician; **Operations at this facility include:** Administration; Divisional Headquarters; Regional Headquarters; Research and Development; Service. **Number of employees at this location:** 400.

MERS/MISSOURI GOODWILL INDUSTRIES INC.
1727 Locust Street, St. Louis MO 63103. 314/241-3464. **Contact:** Human Resources Director. **E-mail address:** employment@mersgoodwill.org. **World Wide Web address:** http://mersgoodwill.org. **Description:** Provides vocational rehabilitation services for clients needing evaluation, work adjustment, business career training, computer training, and placement services. **Special programs:** Internships. **Operations at this facility include:** Administration. **Number of employees at this location:** 200.

YMCA OF GREATER ST. LOUIS
1528 Locust Street, St. Louis MO 63103-1816. 314/436-4100. **Contact:** Jean Hubler, Vice President of Human Resources. **World Wide Web address:** http://www.ymca.com. **Description:** The YMCA provides health and fitness, social and personal development, Provides health and fitness, social and personal development, sports and recreation, education and career development, and camps and conferences to children, youths, adults, the elderly, families, the disabled, refugees and foreign nationals. **NOTE:** Search for positions online.

Nebraska
UNIVERSITY OF NEBRASKA MEDICAL CENTER
P.O. Box 6159, Omaha NE 68198-7420. 402/559-4000. **Physical address:** 44th and Emile, Omaha NE 68198-5470. **Recorded jobline:** 402/559-5443. **Contact:** Human Resources. **NOTE:** Human Resources number is 402/559-4071. Please see website for online application form and for guidelines on how to apply for any open positions. **World Wide Web address:** http://www.unmc.edu. **Description:** Provides family-focused services and supports individuals with disabilities.

Nevada
AMERICAN HEART ASSOCIATION (AHA) CLARK COUNTRY DIVISION
2355 Red Rock Street, Suite 103, Las Vegas NV 89146. 702/367-1366. **Fax:** 702/367-1975. **Contact:** Barbara Wood, Director. **World Wide Web address:** http://www.americanheart.org. **Description:** The American Heart Association is one of the oldest and largest national, nonprofit, voluntary health associations dedicated to reducing disability and death from cardiovascular diseases and stroke. The AHA, also called the Heart Fund, is a community-based organization with about 2,100 state and metropolitan affiliates, divisions, and branches throughout the United States and Puerto Rico. AHA-funded research has yielded such discoveries as CPR, bypass surgery, pacemakers, artificial heart valves, microsurgery, life-

extending drugs, and new surgical techniques to repair heart defects. The American Heart Association develops interactive public education programs and trains about 5 million Americans per year in emergency care procedures; these training systems are used by millions more worldwide. Founded in 1924. **Corporate headquarters location:** Dallas TX. **Other U.S. locations:** Nationwide.

AMERICAN RED CROSS
1771 East Flamingo Road, Suite 206B, Las Vegas NV 89119. 702/791-3311. **Fax:** 702/791-3372. **Contact:** Melissa Cooper, Human Resources Coordinator. **E-mail address:** melissac@redcrosslasvegas.org. **World Wide Web address:** http://www.redcrosslasvegas.org. **Description:** A humanitarian organization that aids disaster victims, gathers blood for crisis distribution, trains individuals to respond to emergencies, educates individuals on various diseases, and raises funds for other charitable establishments. **Corporate headquarters location:** Washington DC. **Other U.S. locations:** Nationwide.

BOY SCOUTS OF AMERICA
7220 South Paradise Road, Las Vegas NV 89119. 702/736-4366. **Contact:** Jim Reed, Director of Field Service. **World Wide Web address:** http://www.scouting.org. **Description:** A national scouting organization for young adults. The Boy Scouts of America has 340 local councils nationwide. **Corporate headquarters location:** Irving TX.

COMMUNITY SERVICES AGENCY & DEVELOPMENT CORPORATION
1090 East 8th Street, Reno NV 89512. 775/786-6023. **Fax:** 775/786-5743. **Contact:** Human Resources. **World Wide Web address:** http://www.csareno.org. **Description:** A human service organization whose operations include the Head Start program, a rental assistance program, and a homeownership assistance program. **Positions advertised include:** Site Supervisor; Head Teacher; Assistant Teacher; Substitute Teacher.

GIRL SCOUTS OF THE SIERRA NEVADA
605 Washington Street, Reno NV 89503. 775/322-0642. **Toll-free phone:** 800/222-5406. **Fax:** 775/322-0701. **Contact:** Janie Galvin, Executive Assistant. **E-mail address:** jagalvin@gssn.org. **World Wide Web address:** http://www.gssn.org. **Description:** Part of the national scouting organization, Girl Scouts of the United States of America. **NOTE:** Apply for positions online. **Positions advertised include:** Group/School Coordinator; Drop-In Center Director. **Corporate headquarters location:** New York NY.

MARCH OF DIMES BIRTH DEFECTS FOUNDATION
3650 North Rancho Drive, Suite 106, Las Vegas NV 89130. 702/732-9255. **Contact:** Director. **E-mail address:** nv411@marchofdimes.com. **World Wide Web address:** http://www.modimes.org. **Description:** The mission of the March of Dimes Birth Defects Foundation is to improve the health of babies by preventing birth defects and infant mortality. The March of Dimes carries out this mission through the Campaign for Healthier Babies, which includes programs of research, community services, education, and advocacy. Birth defects are the primary focus of March of Dimes research efforts. Every year, hundreds of grants are awarded to scientists to help find cures to over 3,000 known birth defects. March of Dimes chapters across the country work with their communities to determine and meet the needs of women, babies, and families. **Other U.S. locations:** Nationwide.

RENO FAMILY YMCA
1300 Foster Drive, Reno NV 89509. 775/329-1311. **Contact:** Director. **World Wide Web address:** http://www.ymca.com. **Description:** One of the nation's largest and most comprehensive service organizations. The YMCA provides the opportunity for health and fitness; social and personal development; sports and recreation; education and career development; and camps and conferences for individuals of all ages and backgrounds. **Corporate headquarters location:** Chicago IL. **Other U.S. locations:** Nationwide.

ST. JUDE'S RANCH FOR CHILDREN
100 St. Jude's Street, Boulder City NV 89005. 702/294-7100. **Toll-free phone:** 800/492-3562. **Contact:** Human Resources Department. **E-mail address:** hr@stjudesranch.org. **World Wide Web address:** http://www.stjudesranch.org. **Description:** A residential facility specializing in the treatment of children with emotional problems, particularly those who have suffered from neglect or abuse. **Special programs:** Internships. **Corporate headquarters location:** This location. **Other U.S. locations:** Bulverde TX; New Braunfels TX.

THE SALVATION ARMY
P.O. Box 28369, Las Vegas NV 89126. 702/642-3811. **Physical address:** 2035 Yale Street, North Las Vegas NV 89030. **Contact:** Human Resources. **World Wide Web address:** http://www.salvationarmy.org. **Description:** The Salvation Army is a Christian organization that offers services such as food, medical attention, and daycare for the homeless nationwide. **Other U.S. locations:** Nationwide. **International locations:** Worldwide. **Operations at this facility include:** This location houses the main administrative offices for the Nevada branches of the charitable organization.

New Hampshire

AMERICAN CANCER SOCIETY
Gail Singer Memorial Building, 360 Route 101, Unit 8, Bedford NH 03110. 603/472-8899. **Fax**: 603/472-7093. **Contact**: Peter Ames. **E-Mail Address**: peter.ames@cancer.org. **World Wide Web Address**: http://www.cancer.org. **Description**: With chartered divisions throughout the country and over 3, 400 local offices, the American Cancer Society is committed to fighting cancer through balanced programs of research, education, patient service, advocacy, and rehabilitation. **NOTE:** Search posted openings on-line. **Positions advertised include:** Grassroots Advocacy Coordinator.

COMMUNITY ALLIANCE OF HUMAN SERVICES
27 John Stark Highway, P.O. Box 188, Newport NH 03773. 603/863-7708. **Contact:** Barbara Brill, Director of Fiscal and IT Services. **E-mail address:** bbrill@communityalliance.net. **World Wide Web address:** http://www.communityalliance.net/employment. **Description:** Provides a range of human services including residential programming, counseling, court liaisons, parental aides, diversions, and mentoring. **Positions advertised include:** Certified Nurse's Aide; Licensed Practical Nurse; Registered Nurse; Childcare Teacher.

NEW HAMPSHIRE VOCATIONAL REHABILITATION OFFICE DEPARTMENT OF EDUCATION
101 Pleasant Street, Concord NH 03301. 603/271-3471. **Fax:** 603/271-7095. **Contact:** Barbara Cochrane, Human Resources. **E-mail address:** bcochrane@ed.state.nh.us. **World Wide Web address:** http://www.ed.state.nh.us/education. **Description:** Assists disabled persons in obtaining or maintaining employment. **NOTE:** The state of New Hampshire requires an application to be filled out for any of these positions; a resume cannot be submitted instead of an application. Please visit website to download the application and see application process details. **Office hours:** Monday 0 Friday, 8:00 a.m. – 4:30 p.m. **Corporate headquarters location:** This location. **Other U.S. locations:** Berlin NH; Keene NH; Lebanon NH; Manchester NH; Nashua NH; Portsmouth NH.

RIVERBEND COMMUNITY MENTAL HEALTH
P.O. Box 2032, Concord NH 03302-2032. 603/228-1551. **Fax:** 603/225-2803. **Contact:** Human Resources. **E-mail address:** hr@riverbendcmhc.org. **World Wide**

Web address: http://www.riverbendcmhc.org. **Description:** An organization providing outpatient, group, and family therapy; case management; psychiatric treatment; 24-hour emergency and assessment services; a crisis intervention program; and supervised residential living. Founded in 1963. **NOTE:** Entry-level positions and second and third shifts are offered. **Positions advertised include:** Residential Rehabilitation Specialist; Children's Respite Care; Psychiatric Rehabilitation Case Manager; Emergency Service Clinician; Internship Director/Child Clinical Psychologist; Child and Family Therapist; Custodian; Admissions Clinical Coordinator; Clinician; Intensive Case Manager; Child and Family Therapist; Admissions Coordinator; Family Support Therapist; Residential Rehabilitation Specialist – Part-time; Substitute Van Driver – Part-time; LPN – Part-time. **NOTE:** Search posted openings and apply online. Volunteer positions are available. **Special programs:** Internships; Training. **Office hours:** Monday - Friday, 8:00 a.m. - 5:00 p.m. **Corporate headquarters location:** This location. **Other area locations:** Franklin NH; Henniker NH; Hillsboro NH. **President:** Dale K. Klatzker. **Annual sales/revenues:** $11 - $20 million. **Number of employees at this location:** 250.

YMCA CAMP BELKNAP
P.O. Box 1546 Wolfeboro NH 03894. 603/569-3475. **Physical address:** Route 109, Tuftonboro NH 03894. **Fax:** 603/569-1471. **Contact:** Gene Clark, Director. **E-mail address:** clarks@campbelknap.org. **World Wide Web address:** http://www.campbelknap.org. **Description:** YMCA-affiliated overnight summer camp, providing valuable camping, recreational, and physical skills to male campers. **Positions advertised include:** Assistant Chef/Cook; Associate Nurse.

New Jersey

AMERICAN RED CROSS
332 West Front Street, Plainfield NJ 07060. 908/756-6414. **Contact:** Human Resources. **World Wide Web address:** http://www.redcross.org. **Description:** A humanitarian organization that aids disaster victims, gathers blood for crisis distribution, trains individuals to respond to emergencies, educates individuals on various diseases, and raises funds for other charities. **Other U.S. locations:** Nationwide.

THE ARC OF BERGEN AND PASSAIC COUNTIES, INC.
223 Moore Street, Hackensack NJ 07601. 201/343-0322. **Fax:** 201/343-0401. **Contact:** Human Resources. **E-mail address:** arcbpc@aol.com. **World Wide Web address:** http://www.arcbergenpassaic.org. **Description:** A nonprofit organization that works with mentally disabled people to improve their quality of life.

COMMUNITY OPTIONS INC.
16 Farber Road, Princeton NJ 08540. 609/951-9900. **Fax:** 609/951-9112. **Contact:** Recruiter. **E-mail address:** resume@comop.org. **World Wide Web address:** http://www.comop.org. **Description:** A private, nonprofit organization that works with adults who have developmental disabilities to find them housing and employment opportunities. **Positions advertised include:** Recruiter; Grant Writer; Training Specialist; Human Resources Assistant. **Corporate headquarters location:** This location. **Other area locations:** Forked River NJ; Morristown NJ; Trenton NJ; Wayne NJ.

HOPE HOUSE
19-21 Belmont Avenue, Dover NJ 07801. 973/361-5555. **Fax:** 973/361-5290. **Contact:** Human Resources. **E-mail address:** information@hopehousenj.org. **World Wide Web address:** http://www.hopehouse.com. **Description:** A nonprofit organization that provides AIDS outpatient, substance abuse, and family counseling; does house cleaning for the elderly; and performs household chores for home-bound individuals. Hope House also operates a 40-bed residential facility for children and adolescents. **Positions advertised include:** Executive Director; Counselor. **NOTE:** Send resume to the following address attention Human Resources. Hope House, P.O. Box 851, Dover NJ, 07801. Fax resume to: 973/361-6586.

HOPES
124 Grand Street, Hoboken NJ 07030. 201/656-3711. **Contact:** Human Resources. **Description:** A nonprofit organization funded by the state of New Jersey that sponsors programs such as Head Start and a medical transportation program for senior citizens.

URBAN LEAGUE OF HUDSON COUNTY
253 Martin Luther King Jr. Drive, Jersey City NJ 07305. 201/451-8888. **Contact:** Human Resources. **World Wide Web address:** http://www.ulohc.org. **Description:** A nonprofit organization that sponsors a variety of social programs including employment services and parenting programs.

New Mexico

AMERICAN RED CROSS
192 Monroe Street NE, Albuquerque NM 87108. 505/265-8514. **Fax:** 505/265-5389. **Contact:** Sonni McCullum, Human Resources. **E-mail address:** mccullums@usa.redcross.org. **World Wide Web address:** http://www.redcrossalbq.org. **Description:** A humanitarian organization that aids disaster victims, gathers blood for crisis distribution, trains individuals to respond to emergencies, educates individuals on various diseases, and raises funds for other charitable establishments. **Other U.S. locations:** Nationwide.

CHILD AND FAMILY SERVICES, INC. OF LEA COUNTY
950 East Snyder Street, Hobbs NM 88240. 505/397-7336. **Fax:** 505/393-0420. **Contact:** Laurie Pellissier, Human Resources Coordinator. **Description:** A nonprofit, full-service, Head Start preschool and daycare program that sponsors the summer food program in Lea County and coordinates with the Foster Grandparent Program. **NOTE:** Entry-level positions are offered. **Special programs:** Internships; Apprenticeships; Training. **Corporate headquarters location:** This location. **Other U.S. locations:** Lovington NM.

GOODWILL INDUSTRIES OF NEW MEXICO
5000 San Mateo NE, Albuquerque NM 87109. 505/881-6401. **Fax:** 505/884-3157. **Contact:** Human Resources Manager. **World Wide Web address:** http://www.goodwillnm.org. **Description:** Besides operating 1,400 thrift stores nationwide, Goodwill is a nonprofit provider of employment training for the disabled and the poor. Goodwill found work for more than 100,000 jobseekers between 1990 and 1995. **NOTE:** Apply in person.

UNITED WAY OF CENTRAL NEW MEXICO
2340 Alamo Avenue SE, Second floor, Albuquerque NM 87106. 505/247-3671. **Fax:** 505/242-3576. **Contact:** Human Resources. **World Wide Web address:** http://www.uwcnm.org. **Description:** Through a network of volunteers and local charities, local United Way organizations throughout America help meet the health and human care needs of millions of people. The United Way system includes approximately 1,900 community-based organizations. United Way of America operates a national service and training center, supporting its members with national services that include advertising, training, corporate relations, research, networks, and government relations.

New York

ALCOHOLICS ANONYMOUS (A.A.)
P.O. Box 459, Grand Central Station, New York NY 10163. 212/870-3400. **Physical address:** 475 Riverside Drive, 11th Floor, New York NY 10115. **Contact:** Human Resources. **World Wide Web address:** http://www.alcoholics-anonymous.org. **Description:** Alcoholics Anonymous (A.A.) is a fellowship of men and women who share their experiences with each other so that they may work on their common problems and help others to recover from alcoholism. A.A. consists of 89,000 local groups in 141 countries. Founded in 1935. **Corporate headquarters location:** This location.

Subsidiaries include: A.A. World Services, Inc. operates at this location with 100 employees coordinating with local groups, with A.A. groups in treatment and correctional facilities, and with members and groups overseas. A.A. literature is prepared, published, and distributed through this office. The A.A. Grapevine, Inc. publishes the *A.A. Grapevine,* the fellowship's monthly international journal. The magazine has a circulation of about 119,000 in the United States, Canada, and other countries. A.A. Grapevine, Inc. also produces a selection of cassette tapes and anthologies of magazine articles.

AMERICAN FOUNDATION FOR THE BLIND
11 Penn Plaza, Suite 300, New York NY 10001. 212/502-7600. **Toll-free phone:** 800/232-5463. **Fax:** 212/502-7777. **Contact:** Kelly Bleach, Director of Personnel. **E-mail address:** afbinfo@afb.net. **World Wide Web address:** http://www.afb.org. **Description:** A nonprofit organization. The American Foundation for the Blind (AFB) is a leading national resource for people who are blind or visually impaired, the organizations that serve them, and the general public. AFB operates through four primary areas of activity: development, collection, and dissemination of information; identification, analysis, and resolution of critical issues; education of the public and policymakers on the needs and capabilities of people who are blind or visually impaired; and production and distribution of talking books and other audio materials. Founded in 1921.

AMERICAN RED CROSS OF NENY
33 Everett Road, Albany NY 12205. 518/458-8111. **Fax:** 518/459-8268. **Contact:** Human Resources. **E-mail address:** nunnally@redcrossneny.org. **World Wide Web address:** http://www.redcrossneny.org. **Description:** The American Red Cross of Northeastern New York is part of the national humanitarian organization that aids disaster victims, gathers blood for crisis distribution, trains individuals to respond to emergencies, educates individuals on various diseases, and raises funds for other charitable establishments. **NOTE:** Human Resources phone extension: x3016. **Positions advertised include:** Volunteer Coordinator. **Special programs:** Internships. **Corporate headquarters location:** Washington DC. **Other U.S. locations:** Nationwide.

AMERICAN SOCIETY FOR THE PREVENTION OF CRUELTY TO ANIMALS
424 East 92nd Street, New York NY 10128. 212/876-7700. **Fax:** 212/876-0014. **Contact:** Human Resources. **E-mail address:** hr@aspca.org. **World Wide Web address:** http://www.aspca.org. **Description:** The society is involved in six primary areas: animals as pets; humane education; animals for sport and entertainment; experimentation on animals; animal industries; and protection of wild animals and endangered species. Founded in 1866. **NOTE:** Human Resources phone: 212/876-0014. **Positions advertised include:** Director of Medicine; Veterinarian; Custodian; Executive Assistant to COO; Assistant Director; Animal Behavior Counselor.

BEDFORD STUYVESANT RESTORATION CORPORATION
1368 Fulton Street, Brooklyn NY 11216-2630. 718/636-6930. **Contact:** Human Resources. **E-mail address:** info@restorationplaza.org. **World Wide Web address:** http://www.restorationplaza.org. **Description:** A nonprofit community development corporations promoting the economic revitalization of the Bedford Stuyvesant section of Brooklyn since 1967.

THE BOYS' CLUB OF NEW YORK (BCNY)
287 East 10th Street, New York NY 10009. 212/533-2550. **Contact:** Hiring. **World Wide Web address:** http://www.bcny.org. **Description:** Provides a variety of services to young men in the New York City area. BCNY's educational program has helped hundreds of young men to attend leading prep schools and colleges, offering support and counseling to help them succeed. BCNY's job training program offers teenage members their first work experience in top-flight New York companies. The club offers a year-round program serving boys between 6 and 17 years old. Founded in 1876. **Corporate headquarters location:** This location.

CAPITAL DISTRICT YMCA
P.O. Box 12640, Albany NY 12212-2640. 518/869-3500. **Physical address:** 151 Vly Road, Albany NY 12212-5005. **Contact:** Human Resources Manager. **World Wide Web address:** http://www.cdymca.org. **Description:** One of the nation's largest and most comprehensive service organizations. The YMCA provides health and fitness, social and personal development, sports and recreation, education and career development, and camps and conferences to children, youths, adults, and the elderly, families, the disabled, refugees and foreign nationals, YMCA residents, and community residents, through a broad range of specific programs. **Positions advertised include:** Member Service Representative; Lifeguard; Childcare Associate; Maintenance Custodian; Swimming Instructor; Head Toddler Teacher; Fitness Coach; Membership Receptionist; Teen Program Assistant; Group Exercise Coordinator.

CATHOLIC CHARITIES OF THE DIOCESE OF BROOKLYN & QUEENS
191 Joralemon Street, Brooklyn NY 11201. 718/722-6001. **Fax:** 718/722-6096. **Contact:** Sister Ellen Patricia Finn. **World Wide Web address:** http://www.ccbq.org. **Description:** A network of private social service organizations that provides food, shelter, and clothing to disadvantaged individuals. **Positions advertised include:** Social Worker; Case Aid; Staff Psychiatrist; Service Clinician; Case Manager; Social Service Assistant; Driver; Administrative Assistant; Program Coordinator. **Other locations:** Brooklyn NY; Queens NY.

CHILDREN'S AID SOCIETY
105 East 22nd Street, New York NY 10010. 212/949-4800. **Contact:** Human Resources Manager. **E-mail address:** jobs@childrensaidsociety.org. **World Wide Web address:** http://www.childrensaidsociety.org. **Description:** Provides early, intensive, and long-term support to thousands of city children and their families through various programs and services including medical and dental care, foster care, group homes, adoption, homemakers, emergency assistance, food distribution, Head Start, tutoring, mentors, community centers, community schools, counseling, court diversion programs, camps, sports, arts, dance, theater, chorus, internships, jobs, teen pregnancy prevention, leadership projects, college and prep/college scholarships, and services to the homeless. Founded in 1853. **NOTE:** Jobseekers may submit an application online. **Positions advertised include:** Accounts Payable Supervisor; Purchasing Manager; Clinical Nurse Administrator; Summer Camp Group Leader; Lifeguard; Social Worker; Medical Receptionist; Senior Social Worker; Gym/Recreation Specialist; Nutritionist; Nurse; Head Teacher; Violence Prevention Coordinator; Center Director; Family Services Director; Foster Care Social Worker; Homefinding Supervisor; Substance Abuse Specialist; Education Coordinator. **Corporate headquarters location:** This location. **Other locations:** Throughout the New York City metropolitan area. **Operations at this facility include:** Administration; Regional Headquarters.

CHILDREN'S VILLAGE
Westmore Hall, 1st Floor, Dobbs Ferry NY 10522. 914/693-0600 ext. 1214. **Fax:** 914/674-4512. **Contact:** Human Resources Department. **E-mail address:** recruiter@childrensvillage.org. **World Wide Web address:** http://www.childrensvillage.org. **Description:** A nonprofit organization that operates a residential treatment center for emotionally disturbed children. **Positions advertised include:** Social Worker; Assistant Director; Registered Nurse; Financial Analyst; Administrative Assistant; Child Care Worker; Sociotherapist; Cyber Café Supervisor. **Corporate**

headquarters location: This location. **Other locations:** Harlem NY.

COMMUNITY COUNSELING SERVICES COMPANY
461 Fifth Avenue, New York NY 10117. 212/695-1175. **Contact:** Human Resources Department. **E-mail address:** careers@ccsfundraising.com. **World Wide Web address:** http://www.ccsfundraising.com. **Description:** A nationwide fundraising company that organizes campaigns for nonprofit clients. **Positions advertised include:** Capital Campaign Director.

COMMUNITY SERVICE SOCIETY OF NEW YORK
105 East 22nd Street, New York NY 10010. 212/254-8900. **Fax:** 212/614-5336. **Contact:** Personnel Manager. **E-mail address:** cssemployment@cssny.org. **World Wide Web address:** http://www.cssny.org. **Description:** A nonprofit, social advocacy organization that conducts policy analysis and research, provides training and technical assistance to strengthen community-based organizations, and develops service programs that respond to the complex problems faced by the poor in New York City. **Positions advertised include:** Volunteer Program Coordinator; Training Manager; Program Manager; Program Specialist; Contract Coordinator; Experience Corps Program Coordinator.

THE FORD FOUNDATION
320 East 43rd Street, New York NY 10017. 212/573-5000. **Fax:** 212/351-3677. **Contact:** Human Resources. **World Wide Web address:** http://www.fordfound.org. **Description:** One of the largest philanthropic organizations in the United States. This private, nonprofit institution donates funds for educational, developmental, research, and experimental efforts designed to produce significant advances in a wide range of social problems. The company also operates several overseas field offices in Asia, Latin America, the Middle East, and Africa. **Corporate headquarters location:** This location. **Other locations:** Worldwide.

FOSTER HOME SERVICES
JEWISH CHILD CARE ASSOCIATION
120 Wall Street, 12th Floor, New York NY 10005. 212/425-3333. **Fax:** 212/652-4731. **Contact:** Human Resources. **World Wide Web address:** http://www.jewishchildcareny.org. **Description:** Provides social services for children including the placement of abused children in foster homes, as well as training programs for future foster parents. Founded in 1822. **NOTE:** See website for a current listing of job openings with detailed application information. **Positions advertised include:** Registered Nurse; Social Worker; Residential Milieu Counselor; Recruiter/Trainer. **Corporate headquarters location:** This location. **Operations at this facility include:** Administration; Service.

GIRL SCOUTS OF THE UNITED STATES OF AMERICA
420 Fifth Avenue, New York NY 10018-2798. 212/852-8000. **Toll-free phone:** 800/478-7248. **Fax:** 212/852-6514. **Contact:** Staffing Department. **World Wide Web address:** http://www.girlscouts.org. **Description:** Girl Scouts is a non-profit national scouting organization for girls. **Positions advertised include:** Inventory Management Director; Adult Development & Instructional Design Consultant. **Corporate headquarters location:** This location. **Chairperson:** Cynthia Bramlett Thompson. **Annual sales/revenues:** 41.6 million. **Number of employees:** 480.

HENRY STREET SETTLEMENT
265 Henry Street, New York NY 10002. 212/766-9200. **Contact:** Human Resources. **World Wide Web address:** http://www.henrystreet.org. **Description:** Provides various social services including daycare, home care, housekeeping, Meals on Wheels, work training for 16- to 21-year-olds, after-school homework help, shelter for battered women, and care for pregnant teenagers. **Positions advertised include:** Shelter Director; Case Manager; Mental Health Care Social Worker; Information Systems Technician; Support Specialist; ESOL Instructor; Residence Assistant; Accounting Manager; Program Director; Training Coordinator; Youth Counselor; Parent Advocate Coordinator; Case Manager; Parent Advocate; Office Assistant; Case Manager; Docent Opportunity; Housekeeper; Job Developer.

JEFFERSON REHABILITATION CENTER
380 Gaffney Drive, P.O. Box 41, Watertown NY 13601. 315/788-2730. **Fax:** 315/788-8557. **Contact:** Human Resources. **E-mail address:** ttgagnon@jeffrehabcenter.org. **World Wide Web address:** http://www.jeffrehabcenter.org. **Description:** A health and rehabilitation center with a manufacturing facility. Jefferson Rehabilitation operates several area sites. The company is a nonprofit organization working with handicapped individuals, treating both physical impairments and mental retardation. **Positions advertised include:** Applied Behavior Specialist Assistant; Registered Nurse; Qualified Mental Retardation Professional Assistant; Maintenance Worker; Secretary; Residence Manager Aide; Cook/ Housekeeper; Direct Care Staff; Occupational Trainer; Food Services Helper/Bus Aide; therapy Aide.

JEWISH COMMUNITY CENTER ASSOCIATION
15 East 26th Street, 10th Floor, New York NY 10010-1579. 212/532-4949. **Fax:** 212/481-4174. **Contact:** C. Carlson, Personnel Manager. **E-mail address:** info@jcca.org. **World Wide Web address:** http://www.jcca.org. **Description:** The nonprofit, national coordinating body for the Jewish Community Center movement in North America. The association has more than 50 area locations and serves as the continental coordinating body for the Jewish Community Center Movement in North America associated with over 275 JCCs, YM-YWHAs and camps operating over 500 sites in the U.S. and Canada. **Corporate headquarters location:** This location. **Other locations:** Nationwide. **International locations:** Israel.

JUST ONE BREAK, INC.
570 7th Avenue, New York NY 10018. 212/785-7300. **Fax:** 212/785-4513. **Contact:** Recruiter. **E-mail address:** jobs@justonebreak.com. **World Wide Web address:** http://www.justonebreak.com. **Description:** A nonprofit organization that helps people with disabilities find employment. Founded in 1947.

LIGHTHOUSE INTERNATIONAL
111 East 59th Street, New York NY 10022-1202. 212/821-9200. **Toll-free phone:** 800/829-0500. **Fax:** 212/821-9707. **Recorded jobline:** 212/821-9419. **Contact:** Nicole Ruderman, Recruiting Coordinator. **E-mail address:** nruderman@lighthouse.org. **World Wide Web address:** http://www.lighthouse.org. **Description:** Enables people who are blind or partially blind to lead independent lives through education, research, information, career and social services, and vision rehabilitation. Lighthouse International serves more than 5,000 persons. **Positions advertised include:** School Nurse; Vision Rehabilitation Assistant; Administrative Coordinator; Job Coach. **Special programs:** Internships. **Other area locations:** Brooklyn NY; Poughkeepsie NY; Queens NY; White Plains NY. **Number of employees at this location:** 305. **Number of employees nationwide:** 375.

LITTLE FLOWER CHILDREN'S SERVICES OF NEW YORK
2450 North Wading River Road, Wading River NY 11792. 631/929-6200 ext. 157. **Fax:** 631/929-6121. **Contact:** Human Resources. **E-mail address:** jobs@lfchild.org. **World Wide Web address:** http://www.littleflowerny.org. **Description:** Provides adoption and foster care services, foster homes for individuals who are mentally handicapped, intermediate care facilities, residential treatment facilities, and therapeutic foster boarding homes. Little Flower Children's Services cares for more than 2,600 children

annually. **Positions advertised include:** Caseworker; Youth Counselor; Direct Care Worker; Registered Nurse; Licensed Practical Nurse; Secretary; Clerk; Maintenance Worker; Grounds Keeper; Kitchen Worker; Driver. **Special programs:** Internships. **Corporate headquarters location:** This location. **Other locations:** Brooklyn NY; Queens NY. **Number of employees:** 650.

LOWER WEST SIDE HOUSEHOLD SERVICES CORPORATION
250 West 57th Street, Suite 1511, New York NY 10107-1511. 212/307-7107. **Fax:** 212/956-2308. **Contact:** Human Resources. **E-mail address:** contact@homecareny.org. **World Wide Web address:** http://www.homecareny.org. **Description:** A nonprofit company that provides home health care services to the elderly, infants, toddlers, and adults living in the five boroughs of New York City and Westchester County. Services include nursing, custodial care, nutrition, social work, and arrangements for medical equipment. The agency also provides free custodial care for individuals and families infected with HIV/AIDS. **NOTE:** Second and thirds shifts are offered. Founded in 1969. **Positions advertised include:** Service Coordinator; Data Entry Clerk; Home Health Aide; Licensed Practical Nurse; Occupational Therapist; Physical Therapist; Social Worker; Speech-Language Pathologist. **Special programs:** Training. **Office hours:** Monday - Friday, 8:00 a.m. - 5:00 p.m. **Corporate headquarters location:** This location. **Other U.S. locations:** Scarsdale NY. **Number of employees at this location:** 250.

MARCH OF DIMES BIRTH DEFECTS FOUNDATION
1275 Mamaroneck Avenue, White Plains NY 10605. 914/428-7100. **Fax:** 914/997-4479. **Contact:** Mary Jane Scott, Human Resources. **E-mail address:** recruiter@marchofdimes.com. **World Wide Web address:** http://www.marchofdimes.com. **Description:** A private foundation operating the Campaign for Healthier Babies, which includes programs of research, community service, education, and advocacy. Birth defects are the primary focus of March of Dimes research efforts. The foundation's 55 chapters across the country work with their communities to determine and meet the needs of women, children, and families. Through specially designed programs, women are provided with access to prenatal care. Founded in 1938 by President Franklin Roosevelt to prevent polio. **Positions advertised include:** Assistant Design Director; Senior Designer; Program Quality Improvement Manager; External Program Grants Manager; Director of Program Services. **Corporate headquarters location:** This location. **Other U.S. locations:** Nationwide. **Chairman:** Gary D. Forsee. **Annual sales/revenues:** $218 million.

MARYKNOLL FATHERS AND BROTHERS
P.O. Box 302, Maryknoll NY 10545. 914/941-7590. **Contact:** Human Resources. **World Wide Web address:** http://www.maryknoll.org. **Description:** Maryknoll Fathers and Brothers is an international order of religious missionaries. Founded in 1911. **Special programs:** Summer Jobs. **Corporate headquarters location:** This location. **Other locations:** Chicago IL; Los Angeles CA; Minneapolis MN; New York NY; Ossining NY; Washington DC.

NEW YORK STATE COALITION AGAINST DOMESTIC VIOLENCE
350 New Scotland Avenue, Albany NY 12208. 518/482-5465. **Contact:** Sherry Frohman, Executive Director of Human Resources. **Description:** An organization providing support and services to battered women and their children. **Parent company:** National Coalition Against Domestic Violence is a nonprofit public education and advocacy organization and a coalition of direct service programs, currently composed of 33 member organizations offering services to battered women and their children. Activities of the coalition include public education and advocacy; technical assistance to member groups; information and technical assistance to public agencies and legislative committees; and professional training for law enforcement and human service workers. In addition, the coalition staff prepares policy statements and offers assistance and expertise in the preparation of protocols and practices for a wide variety of public and private entities.

THE SALVATION ARMY
960 Main Street, Buffalo NY 14202. 716/883-9800. **Contact:** Director of Operations. **World Wide Web address:** http://www.salvationarmy.org. **Description:** A nonprofit organization providing several service programs including day-care centers, programs for people with disabilities, substance abuse programs and tutoring for at-risk students. The Salvation Army targets its programs to assist alcoholics, battered women, drug addicts, the elderly, the homeless, people with AIDS, prison inmates, teenagers, and the unemployed. **Corporate headquarters location:** West Nyack NY. **Other U.S. locations:** Nationwide. **International locations:** Worldwide.

U.S. FUNDS FOR UNICEF
333 East 38th Street, 6th Floor, New York NY 10016. 212/686-5522. **Contact:** Employment Manager. **World Wide Web address:** http://www.unicefusa.org. **Description:** Organized for educational and charitable purposes, U.S. Funds for UNICEF aims to increase awareness of the needs of children around the world. **Special programs:** Internships. **Corporate headquarters location:** This location. **Other U.S. locations:** Los Angeles CA; Washington DC; Atlanta GA; Chicago IL; Boston MA; Houston TX. **Operations at this facility include:** Administration; Divisional Headquarters. **Listed on:** Privately held. **Number of employees at this location:** 100.

UNITED CEREBRAL PALSY ASSOCIATIONS OF NEW YORK STATE
330 West 34th Street, 14th Floor, New York NY 10001. 212/947-5770. **Fax:** 212/594-4538. **Contact:** Human Resources Department. **E-mail address:** info@cerebralpalsynys.org. **World Wide Web address:** http://www.cpofnys.org. **Description:** A nonprofit health care organization that provides services to persons with developmental disabilities. **Special programs:** Internships. **Corporate headquarters location:** Washington DC. **Other area locations:** Bronx NY; Brooklyn NY; Queens NY; Staten Island NY. **Operations at this facility include:** Administration; Divisional Headquarters. **Annual sales/revenues:** $51 - $100 million. **Number of employees at this location:** 1,700.

UNITED WAY OF NEW YORK CITY
2 Park Avenue South, 2nd Floor, New York NY 10016-1601. 212/251-2500. **Contact:** Human Resources. **World Wide Web address:** http://www.unitedwaynyc.org. **Description:** A nonprofit organization that offers referral and crisis intervention services for pregnant women and parents.

WESTCHESTER COMMUNITY OPPORTUNITY PROGRAM
2269 Saw Mill River Road, Building 3, Suite G-16, Elmsford NY 10523-3833. 914/592-5600. **Contact:** Personnel. **Description:** A county-sponsored, nonprofit social services agency operating through numerous community action programs that provides clinical services, employment training programs, energy programs, and a wide range of other community services. **Corporate headquarters location:** This location.

YWCA
610 Lexington Avenue, New York NY 10022. 212/755-4500. **Fax:** 212/838-1279. **Contact:** Human Resources. **E-mail address:** info@ywcanyc.org. **World Wide Web address:** http://www.ywcanyc.org. **Description:** Provides counseling, physical fitness activities, a shelter, and daycare facilities for women and their children. **Corporate headquarters location:** This location. **Other U.S. locations:** Nationwide.

North Carolina

AMERICAN RED CROSS
THE CAROLINAS BLOOD SERVICES REGION
2425 Park Road, P.O. Box 36507, Charlotte NC 28236. 704/376-1661. **Fax:** 704/370-0244. **Recorded jobline:** 704/347-8464. **Contact:** Chapter Manager. **World Wide Web address:** http://www.redcrossblood.org. **Description:** A humanitarian organization that aids disaster victims, gathers blood for crisis distribution, trains individuals to respond to emergencies, educates individuals on various diseases, and raises funds for other charitable establishments. **Special programs:** Internships. **Corporate headquarters location:** Washington DC. **Other U.S. locations:** Nationwide.

AMERICAN RED CROSS
PITT COUNTY CHAPTER
601 F Country Club Drive, Greenville NC 27834. 252/355-3800. **Fax:** 252/355-8831. **Contact:** Ms. Deborah Horn, Executive Director. **E-mail address:** dhorn@pittredcross.org. **Wide Web address:** http://www.pittredcross.org. **Description:** A humanitarian organization that aids disaster victims, gathers blood for crisis distribution, trains individuals to respond to emergencies, educates individuals on various diseases, and raises funds for other charitable establishments. **Corporate headquarters location:** Washington DC. **Other U.S. locations:** Nationwide.

DECI (DURHAM EXCHANGE CLUB INDUSTRY, INC.)
1717 Lawson Street, Durham NC 27703. 919/596-1341. **Fax:** 919/596-6380. **Recorded jobline:** 919/596-1346, extension 501. **Contact:** Human Resources. **E-mail address:** deci@deci.org. **World Wide Web address:** http://www.deci.org. **Description:** A private, nonprofit, community-based, vocational rehabilitation facility. Founded in 1966. **NOTE:** Entry-level positions are offered. **Positions advertised include:** Production Supervisor. **Special programs:** Internships; Summer Jobs. **Number of employees at this location:** 85.

NORTH CAROLINA BIOTECHNOLOGY CENTER
15 T.W. Alexander Drive, Research Triangle Park NC 27709-3547. 919/541-9366. **Contact:** Human Resources. **World Wide Web address:** http://www.ncbiotech.org. **Description:** A nonprofit agency dedicated to supporting biotechnology research, development, and commercialization in North Carolina. **Corporate headquarters location:** This location.

PIEDMONT BEHAVIORAL HEALTH CARE
245 LePhillip Court NE, Concord NC 28025. 704/721-7000. **Fax:** 704/721-7010. **Contact:** Personnel. **World Wide Web address:** http://www.piedmontbhc.org. **Description:** Provides a variety of programs and educational services for individuals with mental health needs, substance abuse issues, and developmental disabilities. **Positions advertised include:** Care Coordinator; Case Manager; Child and Youth Provider Relations Manager; Community Relations Specialist; DD Case Management Services Administrator; Health Care Technician. **Corporate headquarters location:** This location. **Other area locations:** Salisbury NC; Albemarle NC; Monroe NC.

RESIDENTIAL SERVICES INC.
111 Providence Road, Chapel Hill NC 27514. 919/942-7391, extension 121. **Fax:** 919/933-4490. **E-mail address:** mail@rsi-nc.org. **World Wide Web address:** http://www.rsi-nc.org. **Description:** A private, non-profit organization that provides living options, counseling and personal care to children and adults with developmental disabilities. **Positions advertised include:** Direct Support Professional; Supervisor of Support Services; Direct Support Coordinator.

WINSTON-SALEM INDUSTRIES FOR THE BLIND
7730 North Point Drive, Winston-Salem NC 27106-3310. 336/759-0551. **Toll-free phone:** 800/242-7726. **Fax:** 336/759-0990. **Contact:** Annette Clinard, Human Resources Manager. **E-mail address:** aclinard@wsifb.com. **World Wide Web address:** http://www.wsifb.com. **Description:** Provides training and employment workshops for the blind. Founded 1936. **Positions advertised include:** Retail Store Cashier. **Corporate headquarters location:** This location. **Other area locations:** Asheville NC.

North Dakota

FRASER, LTD.
2902 South University Drive, Fargo ND 58103 701/232-3301. **Fax:** 701/237-5775. **Contact:** Junelle Christianson, Director of Program Operations. **World Wide Web address:** http://www.fraserltd.org. **E-mail address:** fraser@fraserltd.org. **Description:** A social service agency. In addition to counseling, residential facilities, and other services to the elderly and developmentally disabled, childcare services are available. **NOTE:** For jobs in the childcare field, ask for the Childcare Coordinator. **Operations at this facility include:** An Adult Retirement Program and Residential Facilities; Fraser Hall Group Homes for the developmentally disabled; the Independent Living Training Program which encompasses Intermediate Care Facility Training, Transitional Community Living, and Minimally Supervised Living Arrangements; Fraser Childcare Services. **Number of employees at this location:** Over 130.

LUTHERAN SOCIAL SERVICES OF NORTH DAKOTA
P.O. Box 389, Fargo ND 58107. 701/235-7341. **Physical address:** 1325 11th Street South, Fargo ND 58103. **Fax:** 701/471-3296. **Contact:** Rob Johnston, Human Resources. **E-mail address:** rjohnston@lssnd.org. **World Wide Web address:** http://www.lssnd.org. **Description:** One of North Dakota's largest private social service agencies. Lutheran Social Services offers a wide range of programs and services including adoption assistance, pregnancy counseling, residential treatment for emotionally disturbed children, youth advocacy services, and addiction outreach. The organization also offers a variety of services to the elderly including rehabilitation, companion services, independent living, and social and educational programs for the handicapped. **NOTE:** See Website for a regularly updated list of job openings, apply on line. **Positions advertised include:** Senior Companion; Attendant Care Worker; Mentor for Native Americans. **Office hours:** Monday, Wednesday, Friday, 8:00 a.m. – 5:00 p.m.; Tuesday, Thursday, 8:00 a.m. – 8:30 p.m. **Other area locations:** Bismarck ND; Grand Forks ND, Minot ND; Williston ND. **Operations at this facility include:** Center for New Americans; Independent Living Program; Youth Court Program; Great Plains Food Banks; Multicultural Children Services.

Ohio

AMERICAN CANCER SOCIETY, OHIO DIVISION
5555 Frantz Road, Dublin OH 43017. 614/718-4416. **Toll-free phone:** 800/686-4357. **Fax:** 614/718-4417. **Contact:** Tina Carper, Director of Employee Relations. **World Wide Web address:** http://www.cancer.org. **Description:** A nationwide, community-based, nonprofit, voluntary health organization dedicated to eliminating cancer as a major health problem by funding cancer research and public education. The society helps patients directly by offering services including transportation to treatment and rehabilitation services. **NOTE:** Entry-level positions and part-time jobs are offered. **Special programs:** Internships; Training; Summer Jobs. **Corporate headquarters location:** This location. **Other area locations:** Cincinnati OH; Cleveland OH; Youngstown OH. **Other U.S. locations:** Nationwide. **Annual sales/revenues:** $21 - $50 million. **Number of employees at this location:** 235. **Number of employees nationwide:** 1,000.

AMERICAN RED CROSS
995 East Broad Street, Columbus OH 43205. 614/253-7981. **Fax:** 614/253-4081. **Recorded jobline:** 614/251-1455. **Contact:** Human Resources. **E-mail address:**

gcjobs@usa.redcross.org. **World Wide Web address:** http://columbus.redcross.org. **Description:** A humanitarian organization that aids disaster victims, gathers blood for crisis distribution, trains individuals to respond to emergencies, educates individuals on various diseases, and raises funds for other charitable establishments. **NOTE:** Resumes must be sent in regards to a specific position. **Positions advertised include:** Procurement Technician; Accounting Coordinator; Manager of Chapter Services; Special Events Coordinator. **Corporate headquarters location:** Washington DC. **Other U.S. locations:** Nationwide.

CINCINNATI ASSOCIATION FOR THE BLIND
2045 Gilbert Avenue, Cincinnati OH 45202. 513/487-4213. **Toll-free phone:** 888/687-3935. **Contact:** Jennifer Glassmeyer, Human Resources Department. **E-mail address:** jennifer.glassmeyer@cincyblind.org. **World Wide Web address:** http://www.cincyblind.org. **Description:** An association that offers a variety of services for the blind including mobility instruction, rehabilitation teaching, computer training, and talking book programs. **Positions advertised include:** Accounting Clerk; Computer Access Specialist. **Special programs:** Volunteering opportunities available.

CINCINNATI HAMILTON COMMUNITY ACTION AGENCY
1740 Langdon Farm Road, Cincinnati OH 45237. 513/569-1840. **Fax:** 513/569-1251. **Contact:** Human Resources. **Description:** An agency that offers food vouchers, home energy assistance, Head Start programs, rent assistance, and utility bills assistance.

CYSTIC FIBROSIS FOUNDATION
2011 Madison Road, Cincinnati OH 45208. 513/533-9300. **Fax:** 513/533-9301. **Contact:** Executive Director. **World Wide Web address:** http://www.cff.org/cincinnati.htm. **Description:** A nonprofit national foundation dedicated to developing a treatment and cure for cystic fibrosis. The Cystic Fibrosis Foundation offers cystic fibrosis care centers nationwide; provides grants to scientists conducting research about cystic fibrosis; operates several cystic fibrosis research centers; supports clinical trials; and offers free brochures, fact sheets, and videos pertaining to the disease. **Corporate headquarters location:** Bethesda MD. **Other area locations:** Dayton OH; Columbus OH; Lyndhurst OH.

LOTT INDUSTRIES
2001 Collingwood Boulevard, Toledo OH 43620. 419/255-0064. **Toll-free phone:** 888/399-5688. **Fax:** 419/255-6432. **Contact:** Human Resources. **World Wide Web address:** http://www.lottindustries.com. **Description:** A nonprofit organization that employs mentally disabled individuals to conduct a variety of services, including packaging, document disposal, and mailing preparation

THE SALVATION ARMY
P.O. Box 596, 114 East Central Parkway, Cincinnati OH 45201. 513/762-5600. **Fax:** 513/762-5679. **Contact:** Personnel. **E-mail address:** swo@salvationarmy-usaeast.org. **World Wide Web address:** http://www.salvationarmy.org. **Description:** A nonprofit organization providing several service programs including day-care centers, programs for people with disabilities, substance abuse programs and tutoring for at-risk students. The Salvation Army targets its programs to assist alcoholics, battered women, drug addicts, the elderly, the homeless, people with AIDS, prison inmates, teenagers, and the unemployed. **Corporate headquarters:** This is the divisional headquarters. **Other U.S. locations:** Nationwide.

SHELTER ADULT WORKSHOP (SAW)
1275 Lakeside Avenue, Cleveland OH 44114. 216/241-8230. **Fax:** 216/861-0253. **Contact:** Roberta Jupin, Personnel. **World Wide Web address:** http://www.ccbmrdd.org. **Description:** A facility that employs mentally retarded and developmentally disabled individuals. Through nine locations nationwide, individuals are involved in light factory work including mailing, assembly, and packaging. SAW is affiliated with the Cuyahoga County Board of Mental Retardation. **Other area locations:** Beachwood OH; Euclid OH; Maple Heights OH; Parma OH; Rocky River OH.

YMCA OF CENTRAL OHIO
40 West Long Street, Columbus OH 43215. 614/224-1142. **Fax:** 614/224-0639. **Contact:** Lori Leist, Human Resources Director. **E-mail address:** lleist@ymca-columbus.com. **World Wide Web address:** http://www.ymca-columbus.com. **Description:** One of the nation's largest and most comprehensive nonprofit service organizations. The YMCA provides health and fitness; social and personal development; sports and recreation; education and career development; and camps and conferences to children, youths, adults, the elderly, families, disabled individuals, refugees and foreign nationals, YMCA residents, and community residents through a broad range of specific programs. This location also hires seasonally. **NOTE:** Entry-level positions and part-time jobs are offered. **Positions advertised include:** Supportive Housing Program Case Manager; Swimming/Water Fitness Lifeguard; Custodian; Childcare Teacher; Camp Counselor. **Special programs:** Summer Jobs. **Other U.S. locations:** Nationwide. **International locations:** Worldwide. **President/CEO:** John Bickley. **Number of employees at this location:** 800.

Oklahoma

BIOS
309 East Dewey Avenue, Sapulpa OK 74066. 918/227-3734. **Toll-free phone:** 888/920-3600. **Fax:** 918/227-8378. **Contact:** Stacy Bonham. **E-mail address:** sbonham@bioscorpok.com. **World Wide Web address:** http://www.bioscorpok.com. **Description:** Provides residential services to people with developmental disabilities by teaching life, community, social, and vocational skills. **NOTE:** Online applications are available. **Special programs:** College Reimbursement Plan. **Positions advertised include:** PRN HTS; Habilitation Training Specialist; Program Coordinator; Employment Training Specialist. **Corporate headquarters location:** This location. **Other area locations:** Bartlesville OK; Muskogee OK; Oklahoma City OK; Enid OK.

Oregon

AMERICAN RED CROSS
3131 North Vancouver Avenue, Portland OR 97227. 503/284-1234. **Recorded jobline:** 503/280-1474. **Contact:** Human Resources Department. **World Wide Web address:** http://www.redcross.org. **Description:** A humanitarian organization that aids disaster victims, gathers blood for crisis distribution, trains individuals to respond to emergencies, educates individuals on various diseases, and raises funds for other charitable establishments.

GOODWILL INDUSTRIES
1943 SE Sixth Avenue, Portland OR 97214-3579. 503/238-6100. **Contact:** Human Resources. **E-mail address:** hr@goodwill.org. **World Wide Web address:** http://www.goodwill.org. **Description:** A nonprofit provider of employment training for the disabled and the poor. Goodwill Industries also operates approximately 1,400 thrift stores nationwide. **Positions advertised include:** Business Partnerships Manager; Government Relations Manager; Technical Trainer; Resource Development Director; Communications Specialist; User Support Specialist.

THE SALVATION ARMY
1785 NE Sandy Boulevard, Portland OR 97232. 503/234-0825. **Contact:** Human Resources. **World Wide Web address:** http://www.salvationarmy.org. **Description:** A nonprofit organization providing several service programs including day-care centers, programs for people with disabilities, substance abuse programs and tutoring for at-risk students. The Salvation Army targets its programs to assist

alcoholics, battered women, drug addicts, the elderly, the homeless, people with AIDS, prison inmates, teenagers, and the unemployed.

UNITED WAY
619 SW 11th Avenue, Suite 300, Portland OR 97205-2646. 503/228-9131. **Fax:** 503/226-9385. **Contact:** Human Resources. **World Wide Web address:** http://www.unitedway-pdx.org. **Description:** Through a network of volunteers and local charities, United Way organizations throughout America help meet the health and human care needs of millions of people. **Positions advertised include:** Development Officer. **Corporate headquarters location:** Alexandria VA. **Other U.S. locations:** Nationwide.

YMCA OF GRANTS PASS
1000 Redwood Avenue, P.O. Box 5439, Grants Pass OR 97527-0439. 541/474-0001. **Contact:** Human Resources. **World Wide Web address:** http://www.ymca.com. **Description:** One of the nation's largest and most comprehensive service organizations. The YMCA provides health and fitness, social and personal development, sports and recreation, education and career development, and camps and conferences to children, youths, adults, the elderly, families, the disabled, refugees and foreign nationals, YMCA residents, and community residents, through a broad range of specific programs.

Pennsylvania

AMERICAN RED CROSS
700 Spring Garden Street, Philadelphia PA 19123. 215/451-4000. **Contact:** Human Resources. **E-mail address:** Phillyjobs@usa.redcross.org. **World Wide Web address:** http://www.redcross.org. **Description:** in addition to domestic disaster relief, the American Red Cross offers services in five other areas: community services that help the needy; support and comfort for military members and their families; the collection, processing and distribution of lifesaving blood and blood products; educational programs that promote health and safety; and international relief and development programs. **Positions advertised include:** Staff Nurse; Sr. Manager, Operations; Reference Technologist; Process Control Associate; Lab Assistant; Account Manager.

ARTHRITIS FOUNDATION
219 North Broad Street, 2nd Floor, Philadelphia PA 19107. 215/564-9800. **Contact:** Branch Director. **World Wide Web address:** http://www.arthritis.org. **Description:** The Arthritis Foundation is a nonprofit organization that is engaged in research to find a cure for arthritis and to educate those who have the disease. Founded in 1948. **NOTE:** The foundation encourages applicants for volunteer positions**Office hours:** Monday - Friday, 8:30 a.m. - 4:30 p.m. **Corporate headquarters location:** Atlanta GA. **Number of employees nationwide:** 650.

BIG BROTHERS/BIG SISTERS OF AMERICA
230 North 13th Street, Philadelphia PA 19107. 215/567-7000. **Contact:** Human Resources. **E-mail address:** nationalcareers@bbbsa.org. **World Wide Web address:** http://www.bbbsa.org. **Description:** The National Office of Big Brothers/Big Sisters of America. Provides volunteer and professional services to assist children and youth in achieving their highest potential as they grow. There are over 505 Big Brothers/Big Sisters agencies nationwide where more than 75,000 children are matched with adult volunteers. The agency also provides counseling, referral, and family support services to parents and children in more 110,000 families each year. Additional programs focus on children with special needs including physical or learning disabilities, as well as those who are abused, neglected, or have dropped out of school. Special prevention and intervention programs at many agencies address the problems of drug abuse, teen pregnancy, foster care, and juvenile delinquency. Founded in 1904. **Positions advertised include:** Associate Director of Information Technology Services; Associate Director of Training; Director of Hispanic Mentoring; Director of Research and Evaluation. **Corporate headquarters location:** This location. **Other U.S. locations:** Nationwide.

ENERGY COORDINATING AGENCY
1924 Arch Street, Philadelphia PA 19103. 215/988-0929. **Fax:** 215/988-0919. **Contact:** Human Resources. **World Wide Web address:** http://www.ecasavesenergy.org. **Description:** A private, non-profit corporation dedicated to ensuring that low and moderate income people have access to safe, affordable and reliable sources of energy and water. **Positions advertised include:** Director of Conservation Services.

HOPE ENTERPRISES INC.
136 Catawissa Avenue, P.O. Box 1837, Williamsport PA 17703-1837. 570/326-3745. **Fax:** 570/326-1258. **Contact:** Human Resources Department. **E-mail address:** info@heionline.org. **World Wide Web address:** http://www.heionline.org. **Description:** Offers workshop training for individuals with mental disabilities. Hope Enterprises also operates over 20 group homes, a preschool, and an adult training facility that teaches domestic skills and personal hygiene. **Positions advertised include:** Accounting Clerk; Active Treatment Aide; ATF Trainer; Behavior Specialist; Custodian; Job Coach; Teacher; Van Driver. **Number of employees worldwide:** 450.

KEYSTONE AREA COUNCIL OF THE BOY SCOUTS OF AMERICA
One Baden-Powell Lane, P.O. Box 389, Mechanicsburg PA 17055. 717/766-1591. **Fax:** 717/795-8721. **Contact:** Human Resources. **World Wide Web address:** http://www.keystonebsa.org. **Description:** The national scouting organization for young adults. The Boy Scouts of America has 340 local councils nationwide. **Corporate headquarters location:** Irving TX.

NEW CASTLE YOUTH DEVELOPMENT CENTER
Rural Route 6, Box 21-A, Frew Mill Road, New Castle PA 16101. 724/656-7300. **Fax:** 724/656-7414. **Contact:** Personnel. **Description:** A residential correction facility for juvenile offenders. **Office hours:** Monday - Friday, 8:00 a.m. - 5:00 p.m. **Parent company:** Philadelphia Department of Public Welfare. **Executive Director:** Robert Liggett. **Number of employees at this location:** 470.

THE SALVATION ARMY
P.O. Box 6176, Erie PA 16512. 814/456-4239. **Physical address:** 1209 Sassafras Street, Philadelphia PA 16501. **Contact:** Human Resources. **World Wide Web address:** http://www.salvationarmy.org. **Description:** A nonprofit organization providing several service programs including day-care centers, programs for people with disabilities, substance abuse programs and tutoring for at-risk students. The Salvation Army targets its programs to assist alcoholics, battered women, drug addicts, the elderly, the homeless, people with AIDS, prison inmates, teenagers, and the unemployed.

SKILLS OF CENTRAL PENNSYLVANIA, INC.
341 Science Park Road, Suite 6, State College PA 16803. 814/238-3245. **Fax:** 814/238-5117. **Contact:** John Fox, Human Resources Director. **E-mail address:** jfox@skillsgroup.org. **World Wide Web address:** http://www.skillsofcentralpa.org. **Description:** A nonprofit company offering services for individuals with mental or physical disabilities. **Positions advertised include:** Residential Services Assistant; Vocational Training Services Assistant; Community Support Specialist; Employment Training Specialist.

SOUTHERN HOME SERVICES
57 East Armat Street, Philadelphia PA 19144. 215/842-4800. **Contact:** Personnel. **World Wide Web address:** http://www.southernhome.org. **Description:** Operates a child and family treatment center. Southern Home Services provides children's services including after-school programs, foster care, and residential care.

NOTE: Entry-level positions and second and third shifts are offered. **Parent company:** Tabor Services, Inc. **Annual sales/revenues:** $5 - $10 million. **Number of employees at this location:** 160.

SUNCOM INDUSTRIES INC.
128 Water Street, P.O. Box 46, Northumberland PA 17857. 570/473-8352. **Fax:** 570/473-0159. **Contact:** Peggy Vitale, Chief Executive Officer. **World Wide Web address:** http://www.suncom.org. **Description:** Operates a workshop for people with physical and mental disabilities. **Facilities Manager:** Roger Dietz.

THRESHOLD REHABILITATION SERVICES
1000 Lancaster Avenue, Reading PA 19607. 610/777-7691. **Fax:** 610/777-1295. **Contact:** Human Resources. **E-mail address:** hr@trsinc.org. **World Wide Web address:** http://www.trsinc.org. **Description:** Provides rehabilitation services to individuals with emotional, physical, or mental disabilities.

Rhode Island
RHODE ISLAND COALITION AGAINST DOMESTIC VIOLENCE
422 Post Road, Suite 202, Warwick RI 02888-1524. 401/467-9940. **Fax:** 401/467-9943. **Contact:** Deborah DeBare, Executive Director. **E-mail address:** ricadv@ricadv.org. **World Wide Web address:** http://www.ricadv.org. **Description:** A nonprofit public education and advocacy organization and a coalition of direct service programs, offering services to battered women and their children. Activities of the coalition include public education and advocacy; technical assistance to member groups, information and technical assistance to public agencies and legislative committees, and professional training for law enforcement and human service workers. In addition, the coalition staff prepares policy statements and offers assistance and expertise in the preparation of protocols and practices for a wide variety of public and private companies. Incorporated in 1979. **NOTE:** See website for current job openings with the Rhode Island Coalition Against Domestic Violence or one of its member agencies. **Positions advertised include:** Community Education Coordinator - Women's Center of Rhode Island; Court Advocate - Women's Center of Rhode Island; Family Advocate - Women's Center of Rhode Island.

South Carolina
THE AMERICAN RED CROSS BLOOD SERVICES
CAROLINAS BLOOD SERVICES REGION
2751 Bull Street, Columbia SC 29201 803/251-6000. **Fax:** 803/251-6191. **Recorded jobline:** 803/251-6035. **Contact:** Human Resources Manager. **E-mail address:** redcrossjobssc@usa.redcross.org. **World Wide Web address:** http://www.redcrossblood.org. **Description:** A nonprofit, blood collection and distribution organization serving over 100 hospitals and medical centers in an 82-county area covering North Carolina, parts of South Carolina, Georgia, and Tennessee distributing 1,500 blood products daily. **NOTE:** Entry-level positions, part-time jobs, and second and third shifts are offered. **Positions advertised include:** Collections Technicians Specialist; Lab Technician: Tele Recruiter. **Special programs:** Training. **Corporate headquarters location:** Charlotte NC. **Other U.S. locations:** Nationwide. **Parent company:** American Red Cross (Washington DC). **Operations at this facility include:** Central South Carolina Chapter. **Number of employees:** 1,050.

BERKELEY CITIZENS, INC.
1301 Old Highway 52 South, P.O. Drawer 429, Moncks Corner SC 29461. 843/761-0300. **Fax:** 843/761-0303. **Contact:** Human Resources. **E-mail address:** bciadmin@bciservices.org. **World Wide Web address:** http://www.berkeleycitizens.org. **Description:** Provides support services for people with mental retardation, head and spinal cord injuries, autism, and related disabilities. **Positions advertised include:** Conifer Associate; House Manager.

HABITAT FOR HUMANITY
CENTRAL SOUTH CAROLINA HABITAT FOR HUMANITY
209 South Sumter Street, Columbia SC 29201. 803/252-3570. **Fax:** 803/252-7525. **Contact:** Director. **E-mail address:** info@habitatcsc.org. **World Wide Web address:** http://www.habitatcsc.org. **Description:** A non-profit, social services organization that builds homes for the homeless. **NOTE:** The majority of this organization's staff consists of volunteers. **Special programs:** Internships. **Corporate headquarters location:** Americus GA. **Other U.S. locations:** Nationwide.

MARCH OF DIMES BIRTH DEFECTS FOUNDATION
240 Stoneridge Drive, One Graystone Building, Suite 206, Columbia SC 29210. 803/252-5200. **Toll-free phone:** 800/277-2773. **Fax:** 803/799-4549. **Contact:** Carryl Krohne, Human Resources. **E-mail address:** sc447@marchofdimes.com. **World Wide Web address:** http://www.marchofdimes.com. **Description:** Operates the Campaign for Healthier Babies, which includes programs of research, community services, education, and advocacy. March of Dimes chapters across the country work with their communities to determine and meet the needs of women, babies, and families. Through specially designed programs, women are provided access to prenatal care and empowered to improve their futures and those of their children. **Positions advertised include:** Senior Community Director.

MUSCULAR DYSTROPHY ASSOCIATION
2700 Middleburgh, Suite 240, Columbia SC 29204. 803/799-7435. **Contact:** Muroslav Cuturic, MD. **World Wide Web address:** http://www.mdausa.org. **Description:** A social services organization that provides funding for research to cure neuromuscular diseases. The group also offers support groups, summer camps, and educational programs. **Positions advertised include:** Health Care Services Coordinator. **Corporate headquarters location:** Tucson AZ. **Other area locations:** Charleston SC; Greenville SC. **Other U.S. locations:** Nationwide.

THE SALVATION ARMY
P.O. Drawer 2786, Columbia SC 29202-1374. 803/765-0260. **Physical address:** 2025 Main Street, Columbia SC 29201. **Fax:** 803/254-6465. **Contact:** Head Secretary. **World Wide Web address:** http://www.salvationarmysouth.org. **Description:** A nonprofit organization providing several service programs including day-care centers, programs for people with disabilities, substance abuse programs and tutoring for at-risk students. The Salvation Army targets its programs to assist alcoholics, battered women, drug addicts, the elderly, the homeless, people with AIDS, prison inmates, teenagers, and the unemployed. **Other U.S. locations:** Nationwide.

South Dakota
BADLANDS NATIONAL PARK
25216 Ben Reifel Road, P.O. Box 6, Interior SD 57750. 605/433-5361. **Fax:** 605-433-5248. **Contact:** Human Resources. **E-mail address:** badl_information@nps.gov. **World Wide Web address:** http://www.nps.gov/badl. **Description:** Badlands National Park consists of 244,000 acres of sharply eroded buttes, pinnacles and spires blended with the largest protected mixed-grass prairie in the United States. The Badlands Wilderness Area covers 64,000 acres. **NOTE:** See http://www.badlands.national-park.com for information about the many different job possibilities in and around Badlands National Park. **Special programs:** Internships, Volunteer positions.

BLACK HILLS NATIONAL FOREST
25041 North Highway 16, Custer SD 57730. 605/673-9200. **Contact:** Personnel Department. **E-mail address:** r2blackhillswebinfo@fs.fed.us. **World Wide Web address:** http://www.fs.fed.us/outernet/bhnf. **Description:** Organization protecting Black Hills National Forest. **NOTE:** Employees are recruited

through various methods, some of which require you to contact another organization. Contact information for each of these groups is available on the Black Hills website under "Jobs." **Special programs:** Summer Jobs; Volunteer positions.

NATIONAL PARK SERVICE WINDCAVE NATIONAL PARK
Rural Route 1, Box 190, Hot Springs SD 57747-9430. 605/745-4600. **Fax:** 605/745-4207. **Contact:** Human Resources. **World Wide Web address:** http://www.nps.gov/wica. **Description:** Protects and preserves caves in the national park and maintains the park's natural resources. **NOTE:** Search for jobs through the USAJOBS website - http://www.usajobs.opm.gov.

Tennessee

AMERICAN RED CROSS
836 Commercial Court, Murfreesboro TN 37129-3667. 615/893-4272. **Contact:** Human Resources. **World Wide Web address:** http://www.redcross.org. **Description:** A humanitarian organization that aids disaster victims, gathers blood for crisis distribution, trains individuals to respond to emergencies, educates individuals on various diseases, and raises funds for other charitable establishments.

NATIONAL MULTIPLE SCLEROSIS SOCIETY
4219 Hillsboro Road, Suite 306, Nashville TN 37215. 615/269-9055. **Toll-free phone:** 800/269-9055. **E-mail address:** tns@nmss.org. **Contact:** Human Resources Department. **World Wide Web address:** http://www.msmidsouth.org. **Description:** A national nonprofit organization providing services such as health care equipment and financial aid. **Other U.S. locations:** Nationwide.

THE SALVATION ARMY
631 Dickerson Road, Nashville TN 37207. 615/242-0411. **Contact:** Human Resources. **World Wide Web address:** http://www.salvationarmy.org. **Description:** A nonprofit organization providing several service programs including day-care centers, programs for people with disabilities, substance abuse programs and tutoring for at-risk students. The Salvation Army targets its programs to assist alcoholics, battered women, drug addicts, the elderly, the homeless, people with AIDS, prison inmates, teenagers, and the unemployed.

Texas

AIDS SERVICES OF AUSTIN
7215 Cameron Road, Austin TX 78752. 512/406-6111. **Fax:** 512/452-3299. **Contact:** Personnel. **E-mail address:** asa.mail@asaustin.org. **World Wide Web address:** http://www.asaustin.org. **Description:** This organization has 600 volunteers that work together to assist the community and individuals who are HIV-positive. AIDS Services of Austin is involved in philanthropy, wellness educational programs, safe sex seminars, counseling, and financial aid for HIV-positive individuals. **NOTE:** Volunteer positions are also available. **Special programs:** Internship. **Office hours:** Monday – Friday, 8:30 a.m. – 5:30 p.m.

AMERICAN HEART ASSOCIATION (AHA)
7272 Greenville Avenue, Dallas TX 75231. 214/373-6300. **Contact:** Human Resources Department. **E-mail address:** aharesume@heart.org. **World Wide Web address:** http://www.americanheart.org. **Description:** A national, nonprofit, voluntary health associations dedicated to reducing disability and death from cardiovascular diseases and stroke. The association trains about 5 million Americans per year in emergency care procedures. Founded in 1924. **NOTE:** Please visit website to view job listings. **Positions advertised include:** National Senior Account Manager, Healthcare; Senior Bilingual Editor/Writer; Manager, Food Certification Communications; Accounts Payable Supervisor; Staff Accountant; Senior Financial Systems Analyst; Director, ECC Healthcare Markets; Project Coordinator, Emergency Cardiovascular Care Programs; Director, Foundation Giving; Developer, Java, Web, VB; E-Business Architect; Marketing Information Consultant; Director of Healthcare Strategy; Virtual Customer Manager. **Special programs:** Internships. **Corporate headquarters location:** This location. **Other U.S. locations:** Nationwide. **CEO:** M. Cass Wheeler.

AMERICAN RED CROSS
3642 East Houston Street, San Antonio TX 78219. 210/224-5151. **Toll-free phone:** 800/775-6803. Fax: 210/226-9973. **Contact:** Human Resources. **E-mail address:** infosatx@usa.redcross.org. **World Wide Web address:** http://www.saredcross.org. **Description:** A humanitarian organization that aids disaster victims, gathers blood for crisis distribution, trains individuals to respond to emergencies, educates individuals on various diseases, and raises funds for other charitable establishments. **NOTE:** Please visit website to view job listings and to fill out online job application. **Positions advertised include:** Instructor; Associate Director of Financial Development. **Corporate headquarters location:** Washington D.C.

BAYTOWN YMCA
201 West YMCA Drive, Baytown TX 77521-4121. 281/427-1797. **Contact:** Employment. **Wide Web address:** http://www.ymcahouston.org. **Description:** One of the nation's largest and most comprehensive service organizations. The YMCA provides health and fitness services, social and personal development, sports and recreation, education and career development, and camps and conferences to children, youths, adults, the elderly, families, the disabled, refugees and foreign nationals, YMCA residents, and community residents, through a broad range of programs. **NOTE:** Please visit website to download and view job listings. **Positions advertised include:** Membership/Marketing Director; Director of Center Operations; Program Director; Membership Coordinator; Group Executive; Director of Communications; Pre-School Care Giver; Day Camp Counselor; Gymnastics Instructor; Swim Instructor; Lifeguard; Aerobics Instructor; Tai Chi Instructor; After School Child Care Giver; Group Fitness Instructor. **Corporate headquarters location:** Chicago IL.

BETTY HARDWICK CENTER
2616 South Clack, Abilene TX 79606. 325/690-5100. **Fax:** 325/690-5136. **Contact:** Human Resources. **World Wide Web address:** http://bhcmhmr.org. **Description:** An outpatient counseling facility for mentally challenged people. **NOTE:** Please visit website to view jobs listings and apply online. **Positions advertised include:** Contract Foster Care Provider; HCS Trainer; Skills Trainer.

BOY SCOUTS OF AMERICA
P.O. Box 152079, Irving TX 75015-2079. 972/580-2000. **Physical address:** 1325 West Walnut Hill Lane, Irving TX 75015-2079. **Contact:** Professional Selection and Placement. **World Wide Web address:** http://www.scouting.org. **Description:** The national scouting organization for young men. Boy Scouts of America has more than 300 local councils nationwide. **Special programs:** Internships. **Corporate headquarters location:** This location. **Other U.S. locations:** Nationwide. **Listed on:** Privately held.

CHILD CARE ASSOCIATES
P.O. Box 7935, Fort Worth TX 76111. 817/838-0055. **Physical address:** 3000 East Belknap, 3rd Floor, Fort Worth TX 76111. **Contact:** Human Resources. **World Wide Web address:** http://www.childcareassociates.org. **Description:** A nonprofit daycare association. The organization's primary function is assisting low-income families in finding affordable daycare. **NOTE:** Please visit website to view job listings. There area several offices located in Fort Worth. **Positions advertised include:** Assistant Center Director; Center Director; Cook; Early Head Start Teacher; Housekeeper; Teacher; Teacher Assistant; Disabilities Services Assistant; Mentor Teacher; Secretary/Clerk. **Corporate headquarters location:** This location. **Other area locations:** Denton TX; Plano TX; Abilene TX.

CHILDREN'S NUTRITION RESOURCE CENTER (CNRC)
1100 Bates Street, Houston TX 77030. 713/798-7000. **Contact:** Human Resources. **E-mail address:** cnrc@bcm.tmc.edu **World Wide Web address:** http://www.bcm.tmc.edu/cnrc. **Description:** Researches the nutrition needs of children, pregnant women, and nursing mothers. **NOTE:** Please visit website to view job listings, apply online, or download application form. **Positions advertised include:** Senior Research Assistant. **Parent company:** Baylor College of Medicine and the U.S. Department of Agriculture.

COMMUNITIES IN SCHOOL
2150 West 18th Street, Suite 100, Houston TX 77008. 713/654-1515. **Fax:** 713/655-1302. **Contact:** Human Resources Department. **World Wide Web address:** http://www.cishouston.org. **Description:** A social service agency offering school programs to prevent dropouts. **NOTE:** Volunteer positions are also available. **Other area locations:** Statewide. **Other U.S. locations:** Nationwide.

E.O.A.C.
500 Franklin Avenue, Waco TX 76701. 254/753-0331. **Contact:** Employment. **Description:** Offers Head Start programs for three- and four-year-olds; charter school for children ages five years through third grade; Youth in Action, an alcohol and drug prevention program for teenagers; assistance with rent and utilities payments; and a variety of services for the homeless. **Operations at this facility include:** This is the central office of E.O.A.C.

THE GLADNEY CENTER
6300 John Ryan Drive, Fort Worth TX 76132-4122. 817/922/6088. **Toll-free number:** 800/452-3639. **Contact:** Human Resources. **World Wide Web address:** http://www.gladney.org. **Description:** A nonprofit adoption agency providing services to young women who seek adoptive parents for their infants; individuals seeking to build their families through adoptions; and adoptees. Founded in 1887.

GOODWILL INDUSTRIES
460 Wall Street, Beaumont TX 77701. 409/838-9911. **Fax:** 409/832-1822. **Contact:** Human Resources. **World Wide Web address:** http://www.goodwillbmt.org. **Description:** A nonprofit provider of employment training for the disabled and the poor, operating 1,800 thrift stores nationwide. **Other U.S. locations:** Nationwide. **Parent company:** Goodwill Industries International, Inc.

HARMONY FAMILY SERVICES
305 Grape Street, Abilene TX 79601. 325/672-7200. **Contact:** Human Resources. **Description:** A social services agency that offers many programs including a residential treatment center for runaway and homeless youths.

HOUSTON AREA URBAN LEAGUE
1301 Texas Avenue, Houston TX 77002. 713/393-8700. **Contact:** James Lacy, Manager of Operations. **World Wide Web address:** http://www.haul.org. **Description:** A social service agency that also provides employment services.

LIGHTHOUSE OF HOUSTON
3602 West Dallas Street, P.O. Box 130345, Houston TX 77219-0435. 713/527-9561. **Contact:** Human Resources. **World Wide Web address:** http://www.thelighthouseofhouston.org. **Description:** A nonprofit organization for the blind offering adult day care, recreational activities, and social services.

MARTIN LUTHER HOMES OF TEXAS INC.
520 East Donegan Street, Suite 2, Seguin TX 78155. 830/372-3075. **Contact:** Human Resources. **World Wide Web address:** http://www.mosiacinfo.org. **Description:** An agency that provides housing and support services for individuals with mental retardation. This company is now part of Mosaic, an organization created by the Lutheran Church.

NEIGHBORHOOD CENTERS INC.
P.O. Box 271389, Houston TX 77277-1389. 713/669-5256. **Fax:** 713/669-5349. **Recorded jobline:** 713/669-5389. **Contact:** Diana Salazar, Human Resources. **E-mail address:** diana.salazar@neighborhood-centers.org. **World Wide Web address:** http://www.neighborhood-centers.org. **Description:** A human services organization offering a variety of programs to assist low-income families. Some of the programs offered include Healthy Start, which provides prenatal services and Early Head Start, which promotes the emotional and physical growth of children. Founded in 1907. **Positions advertised include:** Process Analyst; Family Service Worker; Assistant Children's Activity Leader; Athletic Specialist; Parent Educator; Program Support Coordinator; Driver; Maintenance Engineer; Receptionist; Bus Driver; Building Service Worker. **Parent company:** United Way.

OAKS TREATMENT CENTER
1407 West Stassney Lane, Austin TX 78745. 512/464-0200. **Toll-free phone:** 800/843-6257. **Fax:** 512/464-0439. **Contact:** Human Resources. **World Wide Web address:** http://www.psysolutions.com/facilities/oaks. **Description:** A residential and treatment center for children and young adults with behavioral, emotional, or developmental disabilities. **NOTE:** See website for job listings. **Positions advertised include:** Speech/Language Pathologist; Occupational Therapist; Collector; RN. **Corporate headquarters location:** This location. **Parent company:** Psychiatric Solutions Inc. (PSI).

PANHANDLE COMMUNITY SERVICES
P.O. Box 763, Clarendon TX 79226. 806/874-2573. **Contact:** Human Resources. **Description:** Offers housing, energy, transportation, and food banks for homeless and low-income families.

SALVATION ARMY TEXAS DIVISION
6500 Harry Hines Boulevard, Dallas TX 75235. 214/956-6000. **Contact:** Human Resources. **World Wide Web address:** http:www.salvationarmytexas.org. **Description:** A world-renown Christian volunteer organization that helps distribute money, food, clothing and other items to those in need, whether due to economic or social hardship, natural disaster or war. Also operates thrift stores. **NOTE:** In addition to the Texas division's office, the Salvation Army has several thrift stores throughout the state. See the website for locations.

SPINDLETOP MENTAL HEALTH & MENTAL RETARDATION
2750 South Eighth Street, Beaumont TX 77701. 409/839-1000. **Contact:** Human Resources. **Description:** A crisis resolution and counseling center providing addiction recovery programs throughout six counties in Texas.

THE RONALD McDONALD HOUSE OF GALVESTON
P.O. Box 1045, Galveston TX 77553. 409/762-0609. **Fax:** 409/762-5338. **Contact:** Human Resources. **E-mail address:** ronmcd@galveston.com. **World Wide Web address:** http://www.rmgalveston.org. **Description:** A nonprofit organization providing support services for families of children afflicted with serious illnesses.

TOWN NORTH YMCA
4332 Northaven Road, Dallas TX 75229. 214/357-8431. **Fax:** 214/357-2986. **Contact:** Human Resources. **World Wide Web address:** http://www.ymcadallas.org. **Description:** One of the nation's largest and most comprehensive nonprofit service organizations. The YMCA provides health and fitness, social and personal development, sports and recreation, education and career development, and camps and conferences to children, teens, adults, seniors, families, disabled individuals, refugees and foreign nationals, YMCA residents, and community residents through a broad range of specific programs. **NOTE:** An application is required for any position at any YMCA. Applications

can be found on the website and can be faxed. There are 18 other YMCAs in the Greater Dallas area. See website for additional locations and job listings. **Other U.S. locations:** Nationwide.

UNITED WAY OF METROPOLITAN DALLAS
1800 North Lamar, Dallas TX 75202. 214/978-0000. **Contact:** Human Resources. **World Wide Web address:** http://www.unitedwaydallas.com. **Description:** A nonprofit organization that helps to meet the health and human-care needs of Dallas area residents. Overall, the United Way includes approximately 1,900 organizations. **Special programs:** Internships. **Office hours:** Monday - Friday, 8:15 a.m. - 5:00 p.m. **Corporate headquarters location:** Alexandria VA.

Utah

AMERICAN CANCER SOCIETY
941 East 3300 South, Salt Lake City UT 84106. 801/483-1500. **Fax:** 801/483-1558. **Contact:** Human Resources. **World Wide Web address:** http://www.cancer.org. **Description:** A nationwide, community-based, nonprofit, voluntary health organization dedicated to eliminating cancer as a major health problem by funding cancer research and public education. The society helps patients directly by offering services including transportation to treatment and rehabilitation services. **NOTE:** Volunteer positions are also available. Please see website for details on how to apply for specific positions. **Special programs:** Internships. **Corporate headquarters location:** Atlanta GA. **Other area locations:** Orem UT. **Other U.S. locations:** Nationwide.

AMERICAN RED CROSS
465 South 400 East, Salt Lake City UT 84111. 801/323-7000. **Toll-free phone:** 800/328-9272. **Contact:** Human Resources. **E-mail address:** info@utahredcross.org. **World Wide Web address:** http://www.utahredcross.org. **Description:** A humanitarian organization that aids disaster victims, gathers blood for crisis distribution, trains individuals to respond to emergencies, educates individuals on various diseases, and raises funds for other charitable establishments. **NOTE:** Please visit website to search for jobs, register, and apply online. **Other U.S. locations:** Nationwide. **International locations:** Worldwide.

CENTRAL UTAH ENTERPRISES
1170 South 350 East, Provo UT 84606. 801/375-0414. **Fax:** 801/374-8086. **Contact:** Human Resources. **Description:** Provides job skill training for jobseekers with disabilities.

MARCH OF DIMES
757 East South Temple Street, Suite 120, Salt Lake City UT 84102. 801/746-5540. **Fax:** 801/746-5546. **Contact:** Amy Hansen, State Director. **E-mail address:** ahansen@marchofdimes.com. **World Wide Web address:** http://www.marchofdimes.com. **Description:** An organization dedicated to preventing birth defects and infant mortality through the Campaign for Healthier Babies, which includes programs of research, community services, education, and advocacy. March of Dimes chapters across the country work with their communities to determine and meet the needs of women, children, and families. Through specially designed programs, women are provided access to prenatal care. **Corporate headquarters location:** White Plains NY.

RONALD McDONALD HOUSE
935 East South Temple, Salt Lake City UT 84102-1411. 801/363-4663. **Fax:** 801/363-0092. **Contact:** Human Resources. **World Wide Web address:** http://www.rmhc.com. **Description:** Offers housing for families of children who are hospitalized due to acute or chronic illnesses. The facility allows families to remain close to the medical facilities that are caring for their children. **NOTE:** Call to inquire about current job openings. Volunteer positions also available. **Corporate headquarters location:** Oak Brook IL. **Other U.S. locations:** Nationwide. **International locations:** Worldwide.

YWCA
322 East 300 South, Salt Lake City UT 84111-2699. 801/537-8600. **Contact:** Human Resources. **E-mail address:** saltlakecity@ywconnect.org. **World Wide Web address:** http://www.ywca.com. **Description:** Provides counseling, physical fitness activities, a shelter, and daycare programs for women. **NOTE:** You must complete an employment application in order to be considered for a position. Please visit website to download employment application. Volunteer positions are also available. **Positions advertised include:** Shelter Advocate; Recreation Activities Specialist; Teen Advocate; Child Care Substitute Teacher; Cook; Janitor. **Corporate headquarters location:** Washington D.C. **Other area locations:** Brigham City UT. **Other U.S. locations:** Nationwide.

Vermont

AMERICAN RED CROSS
29 Mansfield Street, Burlington VT 05401. 802/658-6400. **Fax:** 802/658-6120. **Contact:** Angela Russell, Administrative Coordinator. **E-mail address:** arussell@nvtredcross.org. **World Wide Web address:** http://www.nvtredcross.org. **Description:** A humanitarian organization that aids disaster victims, gathers blood for crisis distribution, trains individuals to respond to emergencies, educates individuals on various diseases, and raises funds for other charitable establishments. **NOTE:** Resumes accepted by e-mail or fax. Phone calls are not accepted.

UNITED WAY OF WINDHAM COUNTY
28 Vernon Street, Suite 410, Brattleboro VT 05301. 802/257-4011. **Fax:** 802/257-4715. **Contact:** Andrea Livermore, Executive Director. **E-mail address:** uwaywind@sover.net. **World Wide Web address:** http://www.unitedwaywindham.org. **Description:** Through a network of volunteers and service programs, United Way of Windham County helps to meet the health and human care needs of its community through 40 annual programs as well as conducting needs assessments, reviewing agency programs, raising money for service programs, and offering comprehensive information and referrals through a help line.

VERMONT NETWORK AGAINST DOMESTIC VIOLENCE & SEXUAL ASSAULT
P.O. Box 405, Montpelier VT 05601. 802/223-1302. **Fax:** 802/223-6943. **Contact:** Coordinator. **World Wide Web address:** http://www.vtnetwork.org. **Description:** A nonprofit, public education and advocacy organization composed of 16 member organizations offering services to battered women and their children. Activities of the coalition include public education and advocacy; technical assistance to member groups; information and technical assistance to public agencies and legislative committees; and professional training for law enforcement and human service workers.

Virginia

AMERICAN RED CROSS
8111 Gatehouse Road, Falls Church VA 22042. 703/206-7330. **Contact:** Human Resources. **World Wide Web address:** www.redcross.org. **Description:** A humanitarian organization that aids disaster victims, gathers blood for crisis distribution, trains individuals to respond to emergencies, educates individuals on various diseases, and raises funds for other charitable establishments. **NOTE:** Search and apply for positions online. **Positions advertised include:** UNIX Systems Administrator; Software Engineer; Network Engineer; Systems Administrator; Systems Analyst; IT Project Manager. **Operations at this facility:** The ARC data center.

NATIONAL ALLIANCE FOR THE MENTALLY ILL (NAMI)
2107 Wilson Boulevard, Suite 300, Arlington VA 22201. 703/524-7600. **Fax:** 703/524-9094. **Contact:**

Director of Human Resources. **World Wide Web address:** http://www.nami.org. **Description:** Provides a wide range of services to families living with mental illness including support groups and special interest networks; up-to-date, scientific information through publications; a toll-free helpline; annual Mental Illness Awareness Week campaigns; advocacy for services; and support for research. Founded in 1979.

NATIONAL WILDLIFE FEDERATION
11100 Wildlife Center Drive, Reston VA 20190-5362. **Toll-free phone:** 800/822-9919. **Contact:** Human Resources. **World Wide Web address:** http://www.nwf.org. **Description:** A nonprofit, conservation society dedicated to preserving the nation's wildlife. Founded in 1936. **NOTE:** Search and apply for positions online. **Positions advertised include:** Sr. Director, Regional Development; Internet Application Developer; Sr. Director of Marketing. **Special programs:** Internships. **Internship information:** Cover letters and resumes should be directed to 1400 16th Street NW, Washington DC 20036. **Corporate headquarters location:** This location. **Other U.S. locations:** Washington DC; Atlanta GA; Winchester VA. **Number of employees at this location:** 300. **Number of employees nationwide:** 500.

UNITED WAY OF AMERICA
701 North Fairfax Street, Alexandria VA 22314-2045. 703/836-7112. **Fax:** 703/683-7811. **Contact:** Human Resources. **World Wide Web address:** http://www.unitedway.org. **Description:** This location is the national service and training center, supporting its members with services that include advertising, training, corporate relations, research, networks, and government relations. Overall, through a vast network of volunteers and local charities, local United Way organizations throughout America help meet the health needs of millions. United Way's history is built on local organizations helping people in their communities. The United Way system includes approximately 1,400 community-based organizations. **Positions advertised include:** Database Administrator; Manager, Field Leadership; Vice President, Membership and Financial Accountability. **Corporate headquarters location:** This location.

Washington
AMERICAN RED CROSS
1900 25th Avenue South, Seattle WA 98144-4708. 206/323-2345. **Contact:** Human Resources. **World Wide Web address:** http://www.redcross.org. **Description:** A humanitarian organization that aids disaster victims, gathers blood for crisis distribution, trains individuals to respond to emergencies, educates individuals on various diseases, and raises funds for other charitable establishments. **Corporate headquarters location:** Washington DC.

CHILDCARE INTERNATIONAL
715 West Orchard Drive, Suite 7, Bellingham WA 98225. 360/647-2283. **Contact:** Human Resources. **World Wide Web address:** http://www.childcare-intl.org. **Description:** Dedicated to the global relief of children in need. The organization's programs include feeding and sponsorship of these children. Founded in 1981.

GOODWILL INDUSTRIES
307 West Columbia Street, Pasco WA 99301. 509/547-7717. **Contact:** Employment. **World Wide Web address:** http://www.goodwill.org. **Description:** Goodwill Industries is a nonprofit provider of employment training for the disabled and the poor, and operates 1,400 thrift stores nationwide. **Corporate headquarters location:** Bethesda MD. **Operations at this facility include:** This location houses the area administrative offices and a thrift store.

IAM CARES
4700 42nd Avenue, Southwest Suite 570, Seattle WA 98116. 206/938-1253. **Toll-free phone:** 800/763-1301. **Fax:** 206/764-0452. **Contact:** Area Project Director. **World Wide Web address:** http://www.iamcareswa.org. **Description:** A nonprofit agency sponsored by the Machinist Union (IAM & AW). IAM Cares provides employment and training services to individuals with disabilities. Founded in 1980. **Special programs:** Internships. **Corporate headquarters location:** Upper Marlboro MD. **Other U.S. locations:** Nationwide. **International locations:** Canada. **Number of employees at this location:** 15. **Number of employees nationwide:** 150.

LIFELONG AIDS ALLIANCE
1002 East Seneca, Seattle WA 98122. 206/328-8979. **Contact:** Human Resources. **E-mail address:** jobs@lifelongaidsalliance.org. **World Wide Web address:** http://www.lifelongaidsalliance.org. **Description:** Provides case management, financial advocacy, and housing assistance to individuals infected with the AIDS virus.

LUTHERAN COMMUNITY SERVICES
433 Minor Avenue North, Seattle WA 98109. 206/694-5700. **Contact:** Human Resources. **World Wide Web address:** http://www.lcsnw.org. **Description:** Provides a variety of social services including counseling, family support, grassroots, and foster care services. Annually, the organization serves more than 20,000 individuals.

OVERLAKE SERVICE LEAGUE
P.O. Box 53203, Bellevue WA 98015-3203. 425/451-1175. **Fax:** 425/451-1088. **Contact:** Special Services. **World Wide Web address:** http://www.overlakeserviceleague.com. **Description:** A social services organization that provides emergency financial assistance, develops and offers several youth programs, and operates a thrift store. Founded in 1911.

TACOMA GOODWILL INDUSTRIES REHABILITATION CENTER INC.
714 South 27th Street, Tacoma WA 98409. 253/272-5166. **Fax:** 253/428-4162. **Contact:** Human Resources. **E-mail address:** resumes@tacomagoodwill.org. **World Wide Web address:** http://www.tacomagoodwill.org. **Description:** Provides vocational rehabilitation programs. **Positions advertised include:** Loss Prevention Analyst; Custodian; Maintenance Worker. **Corporate headquarters location:** Bethesda MD. **Number of employees at this location:** 600.

THE WEST SEATTLE HELPLINE
4517 California Avenue SW, Suite A, P.O. Box 16738, Seattle WA 98116. 206/932-4357. **Fax:** 206/933-8174. **Contact:** Human Resources. **World Wide Web address:** http://www.seattlewesthelpline.org. **Description:** Provides financial assistance to families facing homelessness. The West Seattle Helpline also works closely with other community organizations to provide clothing and food for these families.

West Virginia
BRALEY & THOMPSON, INCORPORATED
1600 7th Street, Parkersburg WV 26105. 304/422-9355. **Toll-free phone:** 800/969-5170. **Fax:** 304/295-5176. **Contact:** Patty Clark, State Administrator. **World Wide Web address:** http://www.btkids.com. **Description:** Provides foster care services and family preservation support. **Other area locations:** St. Albans; Huntington.

THE GREATER GREENBRIER VALLEY COMMUNITY FOUNDATION, INCORPORATED
109 South Jefferson Street, Lewisburg WV 24901. 304/645-5620. **Contact:** Barbara Elliot, Managing Director. **E-mail address:** tggvcf@citynet.net. **World Wide Web address:** http://www.greenbriervalleycommunityfoundation.org. **Description:** Accepts contributions, manages funds and makes charitable distributions.

Wisconsin
ALLIANCE FOR CHILDREN & FAMILIES
11700 West Lake Park Drive, Milwaukee WI 53224-3099. 414/359-1040. **Toll-free phone:** 800/221-2681.

Fax: 414/359-1074. **Contact:** Human Resources Department. **World Wide Web address:** http://www.alliance1.org. **Description:** A national membership organization that provides resources and leadership to over 300 private, nonprofit child- and family-serving organizations in the U.S. and Canada. Founded in 1911. **Corporate headquarters location:** This location. **Parent company:** Families International, Inc.

AMERICAN HEART ASSOCIATION (AHA)
660 East Mason Street, Suite 200, Milwaukee WI 53202. 414/271-9999. **Fax:** 414/271-3299. **Contact:** Personnel. **World Wide Web address:** http://www.americanheart.org. **Description:** One of the oldest and largest national, nonprofit, voluntary health associations dedicated to reducing disability and death from cardiovascular diseases and stroke. The AHA, also called the Heart Fund, is a community-based organization with approximately 2,100 state and metropolitan affiliates, divisions, and branches throughout the United States and Puerto Rico. The American Heart Association runs interactive public education programs and trains 5 million Americans per year in emergency care procedures. Founded in 1924. **Corporate headquarters location:** Dallas TX.

AMERICAN RED CROSS BADGER CHAPTER
4860 Sheboygan Avenue, Madison WI 53705-0905. 608/233-9300. **Fax:** 608/227-1439. **Contact:** Larissa Pertzborn, Human Resources Associate. **E-mail address:** pertzbornl@usa.redcross.org. **World Wide Web address:** http://www.redcross.org/wi/badger. **Description:** A humanitarian organization that aids disaster victims, gathers blood for crisis distribution, trains individuals to respond to emergencies, educates individuals on various diseases, and raises funds for other charitable establishments. **Positions advertised include:** Chief Executive Officer; Emergency Services Director. **Other U.S. locations:** Nationwide.

CHILDREN'S SERVICE SOCIETY OF WISCONSIN
611 56th Street, Suite 300, Kenosha WI 53140. 262/652-5522. **Contact:** Human Resources. **World Wide Web address:** http://www.cssw.org. **Description:** A state agency offering counseling, adoption, and foster parent services. **Positions advertised include:** Child and Family Therapist. **Other area locations:** Statewide.

DANE COUNTY PARENT COUNCIL HEAD START
2096 Red Arrow Trail, Madison WI 53711. 608/270-3416. **Fax:** 608/275-6756. **Contact:** Shaun Thomson, Human Resources Coordinator. **Description:** A family service center that offers a wide range of basic support services for parents including a GED program and free clothing. Head Start (also at this location) is an educational program for children.

FAMILY SERVICE
128 East Olin Avenue, Suite 100, Madison WI 53713. 608/252-1325x1127. **Fax:** 608/252-1333. **Contact:** Nancy Caray, Human Resources Coordinator. **Description:** A private, nonprofit mental health agency with programs that include ATA (Alternatives to Aggression), SAH (Safe at Home), FIT (Families in Transition), and CCCS (Consumer Credit Counseling Services). Founded in 1910. **Special programs:** Internships. **Annual sales/revenues:** Less than $5 million. **Number of employees at this location:** 55.

HOMES FOR INDEPENDENT LIVING OF WISCONSIN
P.O. Box 278, Dousman WI 53118. 262/691-4162. **Fax:** 262/569-9962. **Contact:** Marybeth, HIL Employment. **World Wide Web address:** http://www.hil-wi.com. **Description:** A for-profit agency providing residential support services to people with developmental disabilities through over 70 regionally organized programs in 10 Wisconsin counties. Founded in 1977. **NOTE:** Entry-level positions and second and third shifts are offered. **Corporate headquarters location:** Oconomowoc WI. **Parent company:** Oconomowoc Residential Programs, Inc. provides a variety of human services.

INDIANHEAD COMMUNITY ACTION AGENCY
209 East 3rd Street South, P.O. Box 40, Ladysmith WI 54848-0040. 715/532-5594. **Fax:** 715/532-7808. **Contact:** Human Resources Director. **E-mail address:** info@indianheadcaa.org. **World Wide Web address:** http://www.indianheadcaa.org. **Description:** A nonprofit agency providing a variety of social services including home health care, Head Start programs, a home weatherizing program, and a clothing center. Founded in 1964. **NOTE:** Entry-level positions and part-time jobs are offered. **Corporate headquarters location:** This location. **Number of employees at this location:** 35. **Number of employees nationwide:** 950.

KENOSHA YMCA
720 59th Street, Kenosha WI 53140. 262/654-7292. **Fax:** 262/654-2860. **Contact:** Personnel. **World Wide Web address:** http://www.kenoshaymca.org. **Description:** Provides a wide range of athletic, social and educational services for the community.

OPPORTUNITIES INC. DIVERSIFIED PERSONNEL SERVICES
200 East Cramer Street, Fort Atkinson WI 53538-0278. 920/563-2437. **Toll-free phone:** 800/314-4567. **Fax:** 920/563-4651. **Contact:** Crystal Pontnack. **E-mail address:** crystal@oppinc.com. **World Wide Web address:** http://www.oppinc.com. **Description:** A vocational rehabilitation facility serving adults with all ranges of disabilities. Includes vocational skill training, job placement, employment counseling, assessment, and a full range of therapy services. The company is engaged in subcontract work for other companies in the areas of printing, bindery, mailings, assembly, packaging, and metal fabrication. **Corporate headquarters location:** This location. **Other area locations:** Oconomowoc WI; Watertown WI. **Special programs:** Internships. **Number of employees nationwide:** 500.

RANCH COMMUNITY SERVICES
W187 N8661 Maple Road, Menomonee Falls WI 53051-1800. 262/251-8670, extension 306. **Fax:** 262/251-8878. **Contact:** Human Resources Coordinator. **E-mail address:** careers@ranchwi.org. **World Wide Web address:** http://www.ranchwi.org. **Description:** A nonprofit human services organization devoted to assisting adults with developmental disabilities by helping them to find jobs and providing them with community activities. There are additional locations in Waukesha and Milwaukee Counties. Founded in 1960. **NOTE:** Entry-level positions and second and third shifts are offered. **Positions advertised include:** Certified Nursing Assistant; Community Integration Specialist. **Special programs:** Internships; Training. **Corporate headquarters location:** This location. **Other area locations:** Milwaukee WI. **Annual sales/revenues:** Less than $5 million. **Number of employees at this location:** 150.

ST. COLETTA OF WISCONSIN
W4955 Highway 18, Jefferson WI 53549. 920/674-4330. **Fax:** 920/674-4603. **Contact:** Human Resources. **E-mail address:** recruiter@stcolettawi.org. **World Wide Web address:** http://www.stcolettawi.org. **Description:** A facility for individuals with developmental disabilities that houses a school and other programs. **Corporate headquarters location:** This location. **Other area locations:** Waukesha WI; Arlington Heights WI; Palatine WI; Madison WI. **Number of employees at this location:** 400.

UNITED MIGRANT OPPORTUNITY SERVICES, INC. (UMOS, INC.)
2701 South Chase Avenue, Milwaukee WI 53207. 414/389-6000. **Toll-free phone:** 800/279-8667. **Fax:** 414/671-4833. **Contact:** Human Resources. **World Wide Web address:** http://www.umos.org. **Description:** A nonprofit advocacy corporation

offering a wide range of employment, training, and educational programs and services statewide to enable migrant, seasonal farm workers and other disadvantaged clients to obtain full employment **Corporate headquarters location:** This location. **Number of employees at this location:** 30.

VALLEY PACKAGING INDUSTRIES, INC.
1325 South Perkins Street, Appleton WI 54914. 920/749-5840. **Fax:** 920/749-5850. **Contact:** Human Resources. **E-mail address:** hr@vpind.com. **World Wide Web address:** http://www.vpind.com. **Description:** A nonprofit corporation that provides a broad range of vocational rehabilitation services for disabled persons. Founded in 1956. **Positions advertised include:** Truck Driver; Program Assistant. **Special programs:** Internships. **Corporate headquarters location:** This location. **Other area locations:** Madison WI. **Subsidiaries include:** Madison Packaging & Assembly (Madison WI). **Number of employees at this location:** 250. **Number of employees nationwide:** 900.

WISCONSIN HUMANE SOCIETY
4500 West Wisconsin Avenue, Milwaukee WI 53208. 414/264-6257. **Contact:** Human Resources. **E-mail address:** wrandall@wihumane.org. **World Wide Web address:** http://www.wihumane.org. **Description:** A nonprofit, community-based organization that provides shelter and veterinary care for stray, unwanted, feral, and wild animals and prevents the mistreatment of animals through education and law enforcement. Founded in 1879. **NOTE:** Entry-level positions, part-time jobs, and second and third shifts are offered. **Positions advertised include:** Development Director; Veterinary Technician; Animal Care Technician. **Special programs:** Internships; Summer Jobs. **Listed on:** Privately held. **Annual sales/revenues:** Less than $5 million.

COMPUTER HARDWARE, SOFTWARE, AND SERVICES

You can expect to find the following types of companies in this section:
Computer Components and Hardware Manufacturers • Consultants and Computer Training Companies • Internet and Online Service Providers • Networking and Systems Services • Repair Services/Rental and Leasing • Resellers, Wholesalers, and Distributors • Software Developers/Programming Services • Web Technologies

---

Software occupations will increase from 239,000 by 67.4% or 161,000 new positions. An increasing reliance on information technology, combined with falling prices of computers and related hardware, means that individuals and organizations will continue to invest in applications and systems software to maximize the return on their investments in equipment and to fulfill their growing computing needs. The 3,046,000 jobs held by computer specialists, including scientists, engineers, programmers, systems analysts, and database administrators will increase by 957,000 or 31.4%. Job increases will be driven by very rapid growth in computer system design and related services as organizations continue to adopt and integrate increasingly sophisticated technologies. Employment in the computer and electronic product manufacturing industry is expected to decline by 7% or 94,000 jobs to 1,232,000 positions as a result of continued rapid productivity growth, continued increases in imports of products, and outsourcing of some professional functions.

Alabama

ASI
350 Voyager Way, Huntsville AL 35806. 256/890-0083. **Fax:** 256/890-0242. **Contact:** Human Resources. **E-mail address:** asi@asi-hsv.com. **World Wide Web address:** http://www.asi-hsv.com. **Description:** A management and technical solutions company working in the areas of information technology, systems engineering and program management, engineering and scientific analysis, and organizational and professional development. Founded in 1992. **Positions advertised include:** Program Control Analyst; NASA Research Analyst; Sr. Configuration Management Specialist; Program Manager – GMD; Sr. Quality/Mission Assurance Engineer; System Engineer/Analyst. **Other area locations:** Montgomery AL. **Other U.S. locations:** Nationwide. **Number of employees nationwide:** 350.

ALACAD
2687 John Hawkins Parkway, Birmingham AL 35244. 205/444-3100. **Fax:** 205/444-3111. **Contact:** Human Resources. **World Wide Web address:** http://www.alacad.com. **Description:** Resells computer hardware and software. **Corporate headquarters location:** This location. **Other area locations:** Huntsville AL; Jackson AL. **Other U.S. locations:** Jackson MS. **International Locations:** Cyprus; Singapore; Sweden; United Kingdom.

ALATAX, INC.
3001 Second Avenue South, Birmingham AL 35233. 205/324-0088. **Fax:** 205/324-1538. **Contact:** Human Resources. **World Wide Web address:** http://www.alatax.com. **Description:** Develops revenue enhancement software. **Positions advertised include:** Regional Account Manager. **Corporate headquarters location:** This location. **Parent company:** Portfolio Recovery Associates.

AUTO F/X SOFTWARE
151 Narrows Parkway, Suite E, Birmingham, AL 35242. 205/980-0056. **Fax:** 205/980-1121. **Contact:** Human Resources. **World Wide Web address:** http://www.autofx.com. **Description:** Develops automated and precreated effects and designs software for the graphic arts field.

AVOCENT
4991 Corporate Drive NW, Huntsville AL 35805. 256/430-4000. **Fax:** 256/430-4030. **Contact:** Human Resources. **World Wide Web address:** http://www.avocent.com. **Description:** A supplier of connectivity solutions for enterprise data centers, service providers and financial institutions worldwide. Branded products include switching, extension, intelligent platform management interface (IPMI), remote access and video display solutions. **Positions advertised include:** Marketing Programs Manager; Business Development Manager; Firmware Engineer; Hardware Engineer; SAP BASIS Administrator; Director, Materials; Product Marketing Manager; Program Manager. **Corporate headquarters location:** This location. **Other U.S. locations:** San Diego CA; Sunrise FL; Chelmsford MA; Austin TX; Redmond WA. **International locations:** Canada; Germany; Hong Kong. **Listed on:** NASDAQ. **Stock exchange symbol:** AVCT. **Number of employees worldwide:** 900.

BOKLER SOFTWARE CORPORATION
P.O. Box 261, Huntsville AL 35804. 256/539-9901. **Fax:** 256/883-2629. **Contact:** Human Resources. **E-mail address:** info@bokler.com. **World Wide Web address:** http://www.bokler.com. **Description:** Develops cryptographic software that allows businesses to set up information security systems. **Corporate headquarters location:** This location.

CPSI (COMPUTER PROGRAMS AND SYSTEMS, INC.)
6600 Wall Street, Mobile AL 36695. 251/639-8100. **Toll-free phone:** 800/711-2774. **Fax:** 251/639-8214. **Contact:** Human Resources. **E-mail address:** employment@cpsinet.com. **World Wide Web address:** http://www.cpsinet.com. **Description:** Develops and installs business software for hospitals and other health care providers. CPSI's products assist in office management, electronic billing, and a wide range of other tasks. Founded in 1979.

CINRAM
4905 Moores Mill Road, Huntsville AL 35811. 256/859-9042. **Fax:** 256/859-9932. **Contact:** Human Resources. **World Wide Web address:** http://www.cinram.com. **Description:** Manufactures CD-ROM drives and computer CDs on which companies can store information. **Positions advertised include:** Industrial Equipment Maintenance. **Corporate headquarters location:** Ontario, Canada. **Other U.S. locations:** Richmond IN; Commerce CA; Olyphant PA. **International locations:** Worldwide.

COMMAND ALKON, INC.
1800 International Park Drive, Suite 400, Birmingham AL 35243. 205/879-3282. **Fax:** 205/870-1405. **Contact:** Human Resources. **E-mail:** careers@commandalkon.com. **World Wide Web address:** http://www.commandalkon.com. **Description:** Designs business software for the construction materials industry. **Positions advertised include:** Delphi Programmer Analyst; Network Consultant; Network Administrator; Business Analyst/Spec Writer; Programmer Analyst; Corporate Controller; QA Analyst. **Corporate headquarters location:** This location.

COMPUTER SCIENCES CORPORATION (CSC)
4090 South Memorial Parkway, Huntsville AL 35802. 256/883-1140. **Fax:** 256/880-0367. **Contact:** Human Resources. **World Wide Web address:**

http://www.csc.com. **Description:** Provides information technology solutions and technical services for the Department of Defense and intelligence agencies, federal civilian agencies and state government clients, health care organizations, and other commercial customers. Founded in 1976. **NOTE:** Entry-level positions are offered. **Positions advertised include:** Computer Scientist; Project Control Analyst; System Engineer; Client Services Manager; Technician; Functional Coordinator; Security Administrator; Data Analyst. **Corporate headquarters location:** El Segundo CA. **Listed on:** New York Stock Exchange. **Stock exchange symbol:** CSC. **Number of employees at this location:** 1,000. **Number of employees worldwide:** 78,000.

COMSYS IT PARTNERS, INC.
5330 Stadium Trace Parkway, Suite 335, Birmingham AL 35244. 205/987-8878. **Toll-free phone:** 800/987-8878. **Fax:** 205/403-6068. **Contact:** Human Resources. **World Wide Web address:** http://www.comsys.com. **Description:** A full-service computer consulting firm. **NOTE:** Entry-level positions are offered. **Positions advertised include:** Requirements/Implementation Team Lead; System Analyst; Database Administrator; Technical Consultant; Project Manager; Data Warehouse Requirements Analyst. **Corporate headquarters location:** Houston TX. **Other U.S. locations:** Nationwide. **International locations:** Worldwide. **Listed on:** NASDAQ. **Stock exchange symbol:** CITP. **Annual sales/revenues:** More than $600 million. **Number of employees at this location:** 500. **Number of employees nationwide:** 5,000.

DP ASSOCIATES
4900 Century Street NW, Huntsville AL 35816. 256/837-8300. **Fax:** 256/837-8454. **Contact:** Tommie Batts, Executive Vice President. **E-mail address:** info@dpa-hsv.com. **World Wide Web address:** http://www.dpa-hsv.com. **Description:** Provides contract, technical computer support services for the U.S. government and business.

DRS TEST & ENERGY MANAGEMENT, INC.
110 Wynn Drive, Huntsville AL 35805. 256/895-2006. **Fax:** 256/895-2064. **Contact:** Human Resources. **E-mail address:** humanresources@drs-tem.com. **World Wide Web address:** http://www.pei-idt.com. **Description:** Designs, develops, and produces military hardware and software.

DIEBOLD INFORMATION AND SECURITY SYSTEMS
6767 Old Madison Pike NW, Suite 300, Huntsville AL 35806. 256/922-8000. **Contact:** Human Resources. **Description:** Offers ADP/IT equipment maintenance and IT professional services to federal and state government agencies and commercial firms. **Corporate headquarters location:** Bountiful UT. **Other U.S. locations:** Nationwide. **Listed on:** New York Stock Exchange. **Stock exchange symbol:** DBD.

DIGITAL FUSION SOLUTIONS, INC.
4940-A Corporate Drive, Huntsville AL 35805. 256/837-2620. **Fax:** 256/837-0988. **Contact:** Human Resources. **E-mail address:** resumes@digitalfusion.com. **World Wide Web address:** http://www.digitalfusion.com. **Description:** An information technology and engineering services company providing services to both government and commercial customers. **Positions advertised include:** Sr. Software Engineer; Principal Computer Scientist; Sr. System Analyst; Contracts Administrator; Project Manager; Principal Engineer; Security Assistant; Electrical Engineer.

DYNETICS INC.
P.O. Box 5500, Huntsville AL 35814-5500. 256/922-9230. **Physical address:** 990 Explorer Boulevard, Huntsville AL 35806. **Fax:** 256/922-9260. **Contact:** Human Resources. **E-mail address:** Human.Resources@dynetics.com. **World Wide Web address:** http://www.dynetics.com. **Description:** A research and development firm for the defense, aerospace, and automotive industries. Products and services include software, computer imaging, systems analysis, simulation, computer modeling, and test evaluation. **Positions advertised include:** RAMT Engineer; Systems Engineer; Weapons Systems Engineer; Account Manager; Document Control Specialist; Radar Analyst; Aerospace Engineer. **Corporate headquarters location:** This location. **Other U.S. locations:** Colorado Springs CO; Washington DC; Fort Walton Beach FL; Dayton OH; El Paso TX; San Antonio TX. **Subsidiaries include:** Auburn Engineering (Rochester Hills MI); Aviation and Missile Solutions (AMS) (Huntsville AL); iMs (Integrated Management Solutions) (Huntsville AL); Information Engineering (Huntsville AL). **Operations at this facility include:** Research and Development. **Number of employees at this location:** 400. **Number of employees nationwide:** 800.

ERC, INCORPORATED
555 Sparkman Drive, Executive Plaza, Suite 1622, Huntsville AL, 35816. 256/430-3080. **Fax:** 256/430-3081. **Contact:** Human Resources. **E-mail address:** hr@erc-incorporated.com. **World Wide Web address:** http://www.erc-incorporated.com. **Description:** A privately-held small business providing high technology services and products in the areas of engineering, systems integration and management services; research and development; test and evaluation; and information technology to NASA, the Army and the Air Force. Founded in 1988. **Positions advertised include:** ISS Systems Management Engineer; Electro Optics Engineer; Mechanical Engineer; Instrumentation Technician II; Test Engineer - Sensors/Seekers; Supply Technician; SR Software Engineer; Software Developer; Electronic Technician – Maintenance; Plasma Engineer/Physicist; Energetic Materials Support Chemist; Electrical & Computer Systems Engineer; Programmer IV; Propulsion Test Systems Engineer; Computer Scientist; Engineer II. **Corporate headquarters location:** This location. Other U.S. locations: Pasadena CA; Stennis Space Center, MS; Houston TX; Edwards AFB, CA; Denver CO; Washington DC.

GE FANUC EMBEDDED SYSTEMS
12090 South Memorial Parkway, Huntsville AL 35803. 256/880-0444. **Contact:** Human Resources. **E-mail address:** human.resources@vmic.com. **World Wide Web address:** http://www.gefanuc.com. **Description:** Provides embedded computing and communication hardware and software products and services for government and commercial businesses. **NOTE:** Search and apply for positions online. **Positions advertised include:** Hardware Design Engineer; TECH CDI Systems Engineering. **Corporate headquarters location:** This location. **Other U.S. locations:** Ventura CA.

INTERGRAPH CORPORATION
288 Dunlop Boulevard, P.O. Box 240000, Huntsville AL 35824. 256/730-2000. **Fax:** 256/730-7250. **Contact:** Human Resources. **E-mail address:** jay.cobb@intergraph.com. **World Wide Web address:** http://www.intergraph.com. **Description:** Intergraph develops, manufactures, markets, and maintains interactive computer graphics systems that support the creation, analysis, display, output, and maintenance of virtually every type of design, drawing, map, or other graphic representation. The company's hardware products include workstations, servers, and peripherals. Software products include operating systems, database management applications, and over 1,200 graphics software programs for the CAD/CAM, engineering, design, and manufacturing industries. Clients include companies in the utilities, transportation, building, process, vehicle design, electronics, manufacturing, and publishing industries. **Positions advertised include:** VP of Global Information Technology; Director, Corporate Communications; Director, Tax. **Corporate headquarters location:** This location. **Other U.S. locations:** Nationwide. **International locations:** Worldwide. **Listed on:** NASDAQ. **Stock exchange**

symbol: INGR. **Number of employees worldwide:** 3,700.

JVC DISC AMERICA INC.
One JVC Road, Tuscaloosa AL 35405. 205/556-7111. **Contact:** Victor Hamner, HR Manager. **E-mail address:** vhamner@jvcdiscusa.com. **World Wide Web address:** http://www.jvcdiscusa.com. **Description:** Manufactures DVD's and CD-ROM's. **Corporate headquarters location:** Japan. **Other U.S. locations:** Elk Grove CA.

KONICA MINOLTA PRINTING SOLUTIONS USA, INC.
One Magnum Pass, Mobile AL 36618. 251/633-4300. **Toll-free phone:** 800/523-2696. **Contact:** Todd St. Mary, Human Resources Manager. **E-mail address:** human.resources@minolta-qms.com. **World Wide Web address:** http://www.minolta-qms.com. **Description:** Develops, manufactures, and distributes laser printers and associated supplies and accessories for general office, electronic publishing, graphic design, advanced imaging, and home office applications. **NOTE:** Applications accepted only for open positions. **Positions advertised include:** IT Manager. **Corporate headquarters location:** This location. **Other U.S. locations:** Orlando FL. **International locations:** Worldwide.

MAXVISION CORPORATION
495 Production Avenue, Madison AL 35758. 256/772-3058. **Fax:** 256/772-3078. **Contact:** Human Resources. **E-mail address:** personnel@maxvision.com. **World Wide Web address:** http://www.maxvision.com. **Description:** A designer and manufacturer of Pentium Pro and Alpha-based Windows NT workstations for CAD/CAM/CAE uses. MaxVision is a leading 3-D technology developer. **Corporate headquarters location:** This location.

NEW MILLENIUM TECHNOLOGIES
P.O. Box 899, Huntsville AL 35804. 256/704-2324. **Physical address:** 120 Holmes Avenue, Suite 301, Huntsville AL 35801. **Fax:** 256/704-2327. **Contact:** Human Resources. **E-mail address:** resumes@nm-tech.com. **World Wide Web address:** www.nm-tech.com. **Description:** Provides IT implementation and management solutions. **CEO:** Larry K. Stoltz.

PREMIER PROFESSIONAL SYSTEMS
7047 Old Madison Pike, Suite 350, Huntsville AL 35806-2197. 256/971-2001. **Fax:** 256/971-2008. **Contact:** Human Resources. **E-mail address:** hr@premier-inc.com. **World Wide Web address:** http://www.premier-inc.com. **Description:** Provides software development and implementation. Founded in 1990. **Positions advertised include:** Heavy Equipment Mechanics; Diesel Engine Mechanics. **President:** Jannifer J. Henderson.

SIRSIDYNIX
101 Washington Street SE, Huntsville AL 35801. 256/704-7000. **Fax:** 256/704-7007. **Contact:** Human Resources. **World Wide Web address:** http://www.sirsi.com. **Description:** Develops software for turnkey library systems. **Positions advertised include:** Systems Specialist; Sr. Systems Specialist; Associate Market Consultant. **Corporate headquarters location:** This location. **Other U.S. locations:** Provo UT; St. Louis MO. **International locations:** Australia; Canada; France; Singapore.

UNISYS CORPORATION
2741 Gunter Park Drive West, Montgomery AL 36109. 334/244-2800. **Contact:** Human Resources. **World Wide Web address:** http://www.unisys.com. **Description:** Provides technology services and solutions in consulting, systems integration, outsourcing, infrastructure, and server technology. **Positions advertised include:** Systems Analyst; IT Storage Area Network Engineer; Network Systems/Operations Analyst. **Corporate headquarters location:** Blue Bell PA. **Other area locations:** Birmingham AL. **Other U.S. locations:** Nationwide. **International locations:** Worldwide. **Number of employees worldwide:** 37,000.

VT MILTOPE CORPORATION
3800 Richardson Road South, Hope Hull AL 36043. 334/284-8665. **Fax:** 334/613-6591.**Contact:** Vice President, Administration, Human Resource Department. **E-mail address:** hr@miltope.com. **World Wide Web address:** http://www.miltope.com. **Description:** VT Miltope Corporation manufactures microcomputers and computer peripheral equipment for military and other applications that require reliable operation in severe land, sea, and airborne environments. **Positions advertised include:** Electrical Design Engineer; Electrical Test Engineer; Electro-Mechanical Assembler; General Operator. **Corporate headquarters location:** This location. **Other U.S. locations:** Boulder CO. **Parent company:** Vision Technologies Systems. **Subsidiaries include:** Miltope Business Products, Inc. produces commercial computer printer and document products.

XANTE CORPORATION
2800 Dauphin Street, Suite 100, Mobile AL 36606. 251/473-6502. **Fax:** 251/473-6503. **Contact:** Kathleen Parker, Human Resources Manager. **E-mail address:** employment@xante.com. **World Wide Web address:** http://www.xante.com. **Description:** Develops and manufactures laser printers and peripheral equipment. **Positions advertised include:** U.S. Sales Representative; Software Engineer; Technical Support Representative; Mechanical Engineer; Windows Programmer. **Corporate headquarters location:** This location. **International location:** The Netherlands. **Listed on:** Privately held. **Number of employees at this location:** 190.

XEROX CONNECT, INC.
1000 Urban Center Drive, Suite 600, Birmingham AL 35242. 205/970-4600. **Contact:** Human Resources. **World Wide Web address:** http://www.xeroxconnect.com. **Description:** Offers systems integration services. The company operates in three service groups: Consulting and Design Services, Systems Integration, and Operations and Support Services. **Positions advertised include:** Production Color Sales Executive. **Parent company:** Xerox Corporation.

Alaska

CTG (COMPUTER TASK GROUP, INC.)
4701 Business Park Boulevard, Building J, Anchorage AK 99503. 907/261-6500. **Fax:** 907/261-6520. **Contact:** Human Resources. **World Wide Web address:** http://www.ctg.com. **Description:** Provides information technology staffing and solutions and application management outsourcing. **Corporate headquarters location:** Buffalo NY. **Other U.S. locations:** Nationwide. **International locations:** Worldwide. **Listed on:** New York Stock Exchange. **Stock exchange symbol:** CTG.

DATAFLOW/ALASKA, INC.
800 East Dimond Boulevard, Suite 3-450, Anchorage AK 99515. 907/365-2700. **Fax:** 907/365-2790. **Contact:** Human Resources. **E-mail address:** resumes@dataflowalaska.com. **World Wide Web address:** http://www.dataflowalaska.com. **Description:** Provides systems analysis, programming services, technical support, and training to federal and state agencies. Founded in 1994. **Positions advertised include:** Cold Fusion Programmer. **Corporate headquarters location:** This location. **Other area locations:** Juneau AK.

TOUCH N' GO SYSTEMS, INC.
406 G Street, Suite 210, Anchorage AK 99501. 907/274-6333. **Fax:** 907/274-9493. **Contact:** Human Resources. **E-mail address:** touchngo@touchngo.com. **World Wide Web address:** http://www.touchngo.com. **Description:** Develops network software and provides Website design and management services. Touch N' Go also offers computer network consulting services. **Corporate headquarters location:** This location.

Arizona

ACCENTURE
4742 North 24th Street, Suite 400, Phoenix AZ 85016. 602/337-4000. **Fax:** 602/337-4444. **Contact:** Personnel. **World Wide Web address:** http://www.accenture.com. **Description:** A management and technology consulting firm offering a wide range of services including business re-engineering, customer service system consulting, data system design and implementation, Internet sales systems research and design, and strategic planning. **Positions advertised include:** Project Manager; Architecture and Engineering Lead; Mainframe Technical Architect; Application Architect; Java Technical Specialist. **Corporate headquarters location:** Chicago IL. **Other U.S. locations:** Nationwide. **International locations:** Worldwide.

ACTIVE RECOGNITION TECHNOLOGIES
234 South Extension, Suite 103, Mesa AZ 85210. 480/586-3400. **Fax:** 480/586-3401. **Contact:** Human Resources. **World Wide Web address:** http://www.activerecognition.com. **Description:** A developer of vehicle and license plate recognition software. **Positions advertised include:** Junior QA Tester/Field Installer.

AJILON SERVICES INC.
1201 South Alma School Road, Suite 5100, Mesa AZ 85210. 480/668-4866. **Toll-free phone:** 800/938-2342. **Fax:** 480/464-5366. **Contact:** Personnel. **E-mail address:** recruit.phoenix@ajilon.com. **World Wide Web address:** http://www.ajilon.com. **Description:** Offers computer consulting services, project support, and end user services. **Other area locations:** Scottsdale AZ; Chandler AZ. **Other U.S. locations:** Nationwide.

AMERICAN CYBERNETICS, INC.
1830 West University Drive, Suite 112, Tempe AZ 85281. 480/966-9245. **Fax:** 480/966-1654. **Contact:** Human Resources Department. **Description:** A publisher of programmer editing software, including Multi-Edit for Windows and Windows NT, and Evolve, an XBase programming add-on.

ANALYSTS INTERNATIONAL
11024 North 28th Drive, Phoenix AZ 85029. 602/789-7200. **Fax:** 602/789-6077. **Contact:** Human Resources. **World Wide Web address:** http://www.analysts.com. **Description:** AIC is an international computer consulting firm. The company assists clients in developing systems in a variety of industries using different programming languages and software. This involves systems analysis, design, and development. **Positions advertised include:** Computer Technician; configuration Management Analyst; Project Manager; Sr. Oracle DBA. **Corporate headquarters location:** Minneapolis MN. **Listed on:** NASDAQ. **Stock exchange symbol:** ANLY.

APPLE COMPUTER, INC.
2430 East Camelback Road, Phoenix AZ 85016-4210. 602/977-0285. **Contact:** Human Resources. **E-mail address:** applejobs@apple.com. **World Wide Web address:** http://www.apple.com. **Description:** Apple Computer, Inc. manufactures personal computers and computer-related products for home, business, scientific, industrial, professional, and educational uses. **Positions advertised include:** Apple Solutions Consultant. **Corporate headquarters location:** Cupertino CA. **Operations at this location:** Retail store. **Listed on:** NASDAQ. **Stock exchange symbol:** AAPL.

AVNET, INC.
60 South McKemy Avenue, Chandler AZ 85226. 480/643-6400. **Contact:** Human Resources. **E-mail address:** avnet.staffing@avnet.com. **World Wide Web address:** http://www.avnet.com. **Description:** Avnet, Inc. operates throughout North America and Europe as one of the largest distributors of electronic components and computer products for industrial and military customers. The company also produces and distributes other electronic, electrical, and video communications products. **Positions advertised include:** Distribution Center Rep; Sr. Systems Administrator; Computer Technician. **Corporate headquarters location:** Phoenix AZ. **Other area locations:** Tempe AZ. **Operations at this facility include:** This location manufactures and distributes computers and computer-related products. **Listed on:** New York Stock Exchange. **Stock exchange symbol:** AVT.

CRC INFORMATION SYSTEMS, INC.
16100 North Greenway-Hayden Loop, Scottsdale AZ 85260. 480/443-9494. **Fax:** 480/443-3656. **Contact:** Human Resources. **E-mail address:** imcdonald@crcinfosys.com. **World Wide Web address:** http://www.crcinfosys.com. **Description:** Designs and manufactures computer software for printing and labeling companies. Founded in 1978. **Corporate headquarters location:** This location. **President/CEO:** Henry S. Hebing.

COMPUTER ASSOCIATES INTERNATIONAL, INC.
9201 East Mountain View Road, Suite 200, Scottsdale AZ 85258. 480/657-4000. **Contact:** Recruiting. **E-mail address:** joinca@ca.com. **World Wide Web address:** http://www.ca.com. **Description:** Computer Associates International, Inc. is one of the world's leading developers of client/server and distributed computing software. The company develops, markets, and supports enterprise management, database and applications development, business applications, and consumer software products for a broad range of mainframe, midrange, and desktop computers. Computer Associates serves major business, government, research, and educational organizations. Founded in 1976. **NOTE:** Interested jobseekers should apply online or send resumes to: Computer Associates International, Inc., Human Resources Recruitment, One Computer Associates Plaza, Islandia NY 11749. **Positions advertised include:** Contract Specialist; Principal Architect, ETA; Sales Manager; Sr. Consultant; Sr. Solution Strategist. **Special programs:** Internships; Co-ops. **Corporate headquarters location:** Islandia NY. **Other U.S. locations:** Nationwide. **Operations at this facility include:** This location is a sales and support office. **Listed on:** New York Stock Exchange. **Stock exchange symbol:** CA. **Number of employees at this location:** 15. **Number of employees nationwide:** 4,000. **Number of employees worldwide:** 9,000.

COMPUWARE CORPORATION
4127 East Van Buren, Suite 100, Phoenix AZ 85008. 602/567-6300. **Contact:** Human Resources. **World Wide Web address:** http://www.compuware.com. **Description:** Offers enterprise software and IT services. **Positions advertised include:** QA Analyst; Systems Integration Tester; Web Applications Developer; Java Developer; Programmer/Analyst Web. **Corporate headquarters location:** Detroit MI. **Listed on:** NASDAQ. **Stock exchange symbol:** CPWR.

CONVERGING TECHNOLOGIES, INC.
One South Church Avenue, Suite 2200, Tucson AZ 85701. 520/670-7100. **Fax:** 520/670-7420. **Contact:** Yolanda Bay, Human Resources. **E-mail address:** mvergara@spartacom.com. **World Wide Web address:** http://www.spartacom.com. **Description:** A provider of business software for networking, modem pooling and sharing, and remote control solutions. **Positions advertised include:** Inside Sales Account Manager. **Corporate headquarters location:** This location.

CYMA SYSTEMS, INC.
2330 West University Drive, Suite 7, Tempe AZ 85281. 480/303-2962. **Toll-free phone:** 800/292-2962. **Contact:** Human Resources. **E-mail address:** hr@cyma.com. **World Wide Web address:** http://www.cyma.com. **Description:** Develops and distributes microcomputer-based software focusing on accounting, medical practice management, point-of-sale, and related vertical applications. Founded in 1980. **Corporate headquarters location:** This location. **Operations at this facility include:** Administration;

Manufacturing; Research and Development; Sales; Service. **Number of employees at this location:** 60.

ECT (EVERETT CHARLES TECHNOLOGIES)
3020 South Park Drive, Tempe AZ 85282. 602/438-1112. **Fax:** 602/426-9217. **Contact:** Hiring Supervisor. **World Wide Web address:** http://www.ectinfo.com. **Description:** Engaged in the design and manufacture of printed circuit boards. **Positions advertised include:** Drill Operator; Dry Film Operator; Plating Operator. **Corporate headquarters location:** Pomona CA. **Other U.S. locations:** NY; NH; IL; FL; MN; RI.

ECLIPSYS CORPORATION
444 North 44th Street, Suite 100, Phoenix AZ 85008. 602/389-8000. **Fax:** 602/389-8111. **Contact:** Human Resources. **World Wide Web address:** http://www.eclipsnet.com. **Description:** Provides a variety of computer-related solutions to members of the health care industry. The company's businesses include software development, systems implementation, systems administration, and systems engineering. **NOTE:** Search and apply for positions online. **Company slogan:** The Outcomes Company. **Positions advertised include:** Product Support Specialist. **Corporate headquarters location:** Boca Raton FL. **Listed on:** NASDAQ. **Stock exchange symbol:** ECLP.

FUJITSU COMPUTER SYSTEMS
10429 South 51st Street, Suite 201, Phoenix AZ 85044. 480/477-8450. **Fax:** 480/477-8451. **Contact:** Human Resources. **World Wide Web address:** http://www.fujitsu.com. **Description:** Fujitsu designs, manufactures, develops, markets, and services large-scale, high-performance, general purpose computer systems (both hardware and software.) Customers are primarily large corporations, government agencies, and universities with high-volume data processing requirements. The company markets more than 470 different systems. **NOTE:** Search and apply for positions online. **Corporate headquarters location:** Sunnyvale CA. **Other U.S. locations:** Nationwide. **International locations:** Worldwide. **Operations at this facility include:** This location is a customer service and sales office.

GTCO CALCOMP
14555 North 82nd Street, Scottsdale AZ 85260. 480/948-6540. **Fax:** 480/948-5508. **E-mail address:** az.hr@gtcocalcomp.com. **Contact:** Human Resources. **World Wide Web address:** http://www.gtcocalcomp.com. **Description:** Manufactures computer peripheral equipment including desktop graphics tablets, wide-format scanners, and large-format digitizers. Products are used in engineering, construction, and graphics applications. **Corporate headquarters location:** Columbia MD.

GROUPSYSTEMS
1430 East Fort Lowell Road, Suite 301, Tucson AZ 85719. 520/325-8228. **Toll-free phone:** 800/368-6338. **Contact:** Human Resources. **E-mail address:** careers@Groupsystems.com. **World Wide Web address:** http://www.groupsystems.com. **Description:** Develops group decision support software. **Corporate headquarters location:** Broomfield CO.

HEWLETT-PACKARD COMPANY
1711 West Greentree Drive, Suite 111, Tempe AZ 85284. 480/753-4317. **Contact:** Human Resources. **World Wide Web address:** http://www.hp.com. **Description:** Hewlett-Packard is engaged in the design and manufacture of measurement and computation products and systems used in business, engineering, science, health care, and education. Principal products include integrated instrument and computer systems (including hardware and software); computer systems and peripheral products; and medical electronic equipment systems. **Positions advertised include:** Financial Analyst; Marketing Communications Consulting Manager; MS Sales Specialist; Pre-Sales Consultant; HP Educations Sales Specialist; Handheld Sales Specialist. **Corporate headquarters location:** Palo Alto CA. **Operations at this facility include:** This location is a sales office. **Listed on:** New York Stock Exchange. **Stock exchange symbol:** HWP.

HOOLEON CORPORATION
P.O.Box 589, 304 West Denby Avenue, Melrose NM 88124. 928/634-7515. **Contact:** Human Resources. **World Wide Web address:** http://www.hooleon.com. **Description:** Customizes computer keyboards. **President/CEO:** Joan Crozier.

IBM CORPORATION
9000 South Rita Road, Tucson AZ 85744. 520/799-1000. **Contact:** Human Resources. **World Wide Web address:** http://www.ibm.com. **Description:** IBM is a developer, manufacturer, and marketer of advanced information processing products including computers and microelectronic technology, software, and networking systems. The company also offers information technology services. **NOTE:** Search and apply for positions online. **Corporate headquarters location:** Armonk NY. **Operations at this facility include:** This facility is engaged in the development of data access and storage devices. **Subsidiaries include:** IBM Credit Corporation; IBM Instruments, Inc.; IBM World Trade Corporation. **Listed on:** New York Stock Exchange. **Stock exchange symbol:** IBM.

INDOTRONIX INTERNATIONAL CORPORATION
7373 East Doubletree Ranch Road, Suite 200, Scottsdale AZ 85258. 480/998-2112. **Fax:** 480/998-2202. **Contact:** Human Resources. **World Wide Web address:** http://www.iic.com. **Description:** Develops software. **Positions advertised include:** Systems Administrator. **Corporate headquarters location:** Poughkeepsie NY. **Other U.S. locations:** Sunnyvale CA; Tampa FL; Atlanta GA; Naperville IL; Austin TX; Irving TX: Morrisville NC; Plainsboro NJ.

INSIGHT ENTERPRISES, INC.
6820 South Harl Avenue, Tempe AZ 85283. 480/902-1000. **Fax:** 480/902-1157. **Contact:** Human Resources. **E-mail address:** jobs@insight.com. **World Wide Web address:** http://www.insight.com. **Description:** A direct marketer of name brand computers, computer hardware, and software. Customers include educational institutions, businesses, and both local and national governments worldwide. **Positions advertised include:** Sr. Financial Analyst; Sr. Income Tax Manager; Database Administrator; Marketing Strategy Coordinator; Sales Manager; Sr. Network Consultant. **Special programs:** Internships. **Corporate headquarters location:** This location. **Listed on:** NASDAQ. **Stock exchange symbol:** NSIT. **Annual sales/revenues:** More than $100 million. **Number of employees at this location:** 430.

INTELLIGENT INSTRUMENTATION INC.
3000 East Valencia Road, Suite 100, Tucson AZ 85706. 520/573-0887. **Fax:** 520/573-9671. **Contact:** Personnel. **World Wide Web address:** http://www.instrument.com. **Description:** Manufactures networking hardware and Ethernet data collection systems. **Corporate headquarters location:** This location. **Parent company**: Texas Instruments. **Listed on:** New York Stock Exchange. **Stock exchange symbol:** TXN.

INTUIT INC.
2800 East Commerce Center Place, Tucson AZ 85706. 520/901-3000. **Contact:** Human Resources. **World Wide Web address:** http://www.intuit.com. **Description:** A provider of business and financial management solutions for small and mid-sized businesses, consumers and accounting professionals. Its flagship products and services include QuickBooks®, Quicken® and TurboTax® software. Founded in 1983. **Positions advertised include:** HR Administrator; Director, Outsource Management; Sr. Manager Training and Quality; Sr. Business Analyst; Director, Outsource Management; Communications Manager; Sr. Business Analyst; Sr. Instructional Designer. **Number of employees worldwide:** 7,000.

JDA SOFTWARE GROUP, INC.
14400 North 87th Street, Scottsdale AZ 85260-3649. 480/308-3000. **Fax:** 480/308-3001. **Contact:** Human Resources. **World Wide Web address:** http://www.jda.com. **Description:** Develops software for the retail industry. **Positions advertised include:** Sr. Accountant; Telecom Engineer; Project Manager; Software Engineer; System Engineer; Technical Writer. **Listed on:** NASDAQ. **Stock exchange symbol:** JDAS.

KNOZALL SOFTWARE, INC.
9386 North Linnet Road, Casa Grande AZ 85222. 520/876-5357. **Contact:** Human Resources. **World Wide Web address:** http://www.knozall.com. **Description:** Manufactures networking utilities for local and wide area networks. Founded in 1990. **Corporate headquarters location:** This location.

McKESSON CORPORATION
3200 North Central Avenue, Suite 1700, Phoenix AZ 85012. 602/230-7575. **Contact:** Personnel. **E-mail address:** phxhumanresources@mckesson.com. **World Wide Web address:** http://www.mckesson.com. **Description:** Produces and sells software applications catering to the specific needs of medical facilities. Some of the programs include materials management, financial accounting, patient scheduling for operating rooms, and inventory control for health clinics. **Positions advertised include:** Production Control Engineer; Sr. Proposal Writer; Biotech Reimbursement Marketing Director; MiddleWare Administrator; Clinical Pharmacy Manager. **Corporate headquarters location:** San Francisco CA.

MICROAGE
1330 West Southern Avenue, Tempe AZ 85282. 480/366-2200. **Contact:** Human Resources. **E-mail address:** employment@microage.com. **World Wide Web address:** http://www.microage.com. **Description:** Provides information technology products and services to institutions and governmental agencies throughout the country and corporations worldwide. **Positions advertised include:** Account Executive; Independent Sales Consultant; Sales Operational Specialist. **Corporate headquarters location:** This location. **Subsidiaries include:** MicroAge Channel Services provides purchasing and marketing services for resellers and vendors. MicroAge Infosystems Services coordinates and services large-account marketing efforts in conjunction with franchised resellers. MicroAge Product Services provides distribution, logistics, technical, and outsourcing services. MicroAge Technologies markets to value-added resellers. **Number of employees nationwide:** 6,100.

MOTOROLA COMPUTER GROUP
2900 South Diablo Way, Tempe AZ 85282. 602/438-5720. **Contact:** Human Resources. **World Wide Web address:** http://www.motorola.com. **Description:** Motorola Computer Group supplies embedded computer technology. The Embedded Technologies group manufactures embedded board lines. The Technical Systems group manufactures electronic products used in industrial automation, electronic imaging, and communications applications. The New Ventures group researches emerging technologies. **Positions advertised include:** FSO Application Engineer; Sr. Product Engineering Manager; IC Power Amplifier Designer; NPI Quality Engineer; R&D Engineer. **Corporate headquarters location:** This location. **Operations at this facility include:** This location manufactures computer hardware. **Parent company:** Motorola Inc. **Listed on:** New York Stock Exchange. **Stock exchange symbol:** MOT.

NCR CORPORATION
525 West Alameda Drive, Tempe AZ 85282. 714/529-0231. **Contact:** Human Resources. **World Wide Web address:** http://www.ncr.com. **Description:** NCR Corporation is a worldwide provider of computer products and services. The company provides computer solutions to the retail, financial, and communications industries through several business units. NCR Computer Systems Group develops, manufactures, and markets computer systems; NCR Financial Systems Group is an industry leader in three target areas: financial delivery systems, relationship banking data warehousing solutions, and payments systems/item processing; NCR Retail Systems Group is a world leader in end-to-end retail solutions serving the food, general merchandise, and hospitality industries; NCR Worldwide Services provides data warehousing services solutions and end-to-end networking services, and designs, implements, and supports complex open systems environments; NCR Systemedia Group develops, produces, and markets a complete line of information products to satisfy customers' information technology needs including transaction processing media, auto identification media, business form communication products, managing documents and media, and a full line of integrated equipment solutions. **Positions advertised include:** Quality Technician; Distribution Material Handler. **Corporate headquarters location:** Dayton OH. **Other U.S. locations:** Nationwide. **Operations at this facility include:** This location is a manufacturing facility and sales office. **Listed on:** New York Stock Exchange. **Stock exchange symbol:** NCR. **Annual sales/revenues:** More than $100 million. **Number of employees nationwide:** 19,000. **Number of employees worldwide:** 38,000.

NETPRO COMPUTING, INC.
4747 North 22nd Street, Suite 400, Phoenix AZ 85016. 602/346-3615. **Fax:** 602/346-3610. **Contact:** Human Resources. **E-mail address:** hr@netpro.com. **World Wide Web address:** http://www.netpro.com. **Description:** Designs and sells directory services management software. Founded in 1991. **Positions advertised include:** Business Development Specialist; QA Engineer; Systems Consultant. **Special programs:** Internships; Summer Jobs. **Corporate headquarters location:** This location. **Listed on:** Privately held. **Annual sales/revenues:** $11 - $20 million. **Number of employees at this location:** 85. **Number of employees nationwide:** 95.

PEGASUS SOLUTIONS, INC.
14000 North Pima Road, Suite 100, Scottsdale AZ 85260. 480/624-6000. **Fax:** 480/624-6687. **Contact:** Personnel. **E-mail address:** jobs@pegs.com. **World Wide Web address:** http://www.pegs.com. **Description:** A leading provider of software and other technology solutions for the travel/tourism industry. **Positions advertised include:** Support Analyst; Billing Coordinator; CAT Product Specialist; Data Services Agent; QA Automation Analyst; Software Engineer. **Corporate headquarters:** Dallas TX. **Listed on:** NASDAQ. **Stock exchange symbol:** PEGS.

STRATUS TECHNOLOGIES
4455 East Camelback Road, Suite 115A, Phoenix AZ 85018. 602/852-3000. **Contact:** Human Resources. **World Wide Web address:** http://www.stratus.com. **Description:** Stratus offers a broad range of computer systems, application solutions, middleware, and professional services for critical online operations. **NOTE:** Mail resumes to Stratus Technologies, 111 Powdermill Road, Maynard MA 01754. **Corporate headquarters location:** Maynard MA. **Subsidiaries include:** Shared Systems Corporation provides software and professional services to the financial services, retail, and health care industries. SoftCom Systems, Inc. provides data communications middleware and related professional services that bridge the gap between open distributed systems and legacy mainframe and midrange systems used for online applications. Isis Distributed Systems, Inc. develops advanced messaging middleware products that enable businesses to develop reliable, high-performance distributed computing applications involving networked desktop computers and shared systems. **Operations at this facility include:** This location houses engineering, customer service, and sales personnel.

SYNTELLECT INC.
16610 North Black Canyon Highway, Suite 100, Phoenix AZ 85053. 602/789-2800. **Fax:** 602/789-2899.

Contact: Human Resources. **E-mail address:** hr@syntellect.com. **World Wide Web address:** http://www.syntellect.com. **Description:** Syntellect designs software for businesses that allows customers to access automated voice systems. **Positions advertised include:** Project Manager; Systems Test Engineer; Inside Sales Representative; Manager, Product Development; Sr. Software Engineer. **Corporate headquarters location:** This location. **Parent company:** Enghouse Systems Limited (Canada).

SYSTEMS SOLUTIONS INC.
2108 East Thomas Road, Suite 103, Phoenix AZ 85016. 602/955-5566. **Fax:** 602/955-7795. **Contact:** Human Resources. **E-mail address:** jobs@syspac.com. **World Wide Web address:** http://www.syspac.com. **Description:** Provides Internet services and offers technical services and solutions for Website design, Website hosting, database programming, local- and wide-area networks, computer telephony, and software development. Systems Solutions also offers SYSPAC, a comprehensive library of distribution, inventory control, and accounting software modules. **NOTE:** Entry-level positions are offered. **Special programs:** Training; Summer Jobs. **Office hours:** Monday - Friday, 8:00 a.m. - 5:00 p.m. **Corporate headquarters location:** This location. **Listed on:** Privately held. **Annual sales/revenues:** Less than $5 million. **Number of employees at this location:** 30.

TRISTAR, INC.
3740 East La Salle, Phoenix AZ 85040. 602/333-1600. **Fax:** 602/333-1602. **Contact:** Human Resources. **E-mail address:** HR@TriCadCam.com. **World Wide Web address:** http://www.tristar.com. **Description:** Provides CAD/CAM software, workstations, and staffing services. **Positions advertised include:** Solutions Architect; Associate Webmaster; Inside Sale Representative.

UNISYS CORPORATION
2525 East Camelback Road, Suite 350, Phoenix AZ 85016. 602/224-4200. **Fax:** 602/224-4258. **Contact:** Human Resources. **World Wide Web address:** http://www.unisys.com. **Description:** Provides technology services and solutions in consulting, systems integration, outsourcing, infrastructure, and server technology. **Positions advertised include:** Consultant. **Corporate headquarters location:** Blue Bell PA. **Other U.S. locations:** Nationwide. **Operations at this facility include:** This location houses a sales and engineering facility. **Listed on:** New York Stock Exchange. **Stock exchange symbol:** UIS. **Number of employees worldwide:** 37,000.

Arkansas
ARISTOTLE INTERNET ACCESS
401 West Capitol, Suite 700, Little Rock AR 72201. 501/376-1377. **Contact:** Terry Norris, Human Resources. **E-mail address:** info@aristotle.net. **World Wide Web address:** http://www.aristotle.net. **Description:** Provides Internet access to central Arkansas. The company also offers Website design, Internet applications training, and HTML programming. **Corporate headquarters location:** This location.

COGNITIVEDATA CORPORATION
900 South Shackleford Road, Little Rock AR 72211. 501/975-7580. **Toll free number:** 866/243-7883. **Fax:** 866/243-7817. **Contact:** Mark Guenther, Human Resources. **World Wide Web address:** http://www.cognitivedata.com. **E-mail address:** talent@congitivedata.com. **Description:** Develops, markets and supports data quality solutions for the direct marketing industry. **Positions advertised include:** Direct Mail Database Analyst; Client Account Coordinator; Senior Database Developer; Senior Sales Executive.

DATAFIX
1203 Nettleton Circle, Jonesboro AR 72401. 870/972-5330. **Fax**: 870/972-9619. **Contact:** Steve Taylor, Human Resources. **World Wide Web address:** http://www.data-fix.com. **Description:** Provides repair services for most types of computers and printers. **Other area locations:** Springdale AR; Little Rock AR.

EURONET
17300 Chenal Parkway, Suite 200, Little Rock AR 72223. 501/218-7300. **Fax:** 501/218-7302. **Contact:** Human Resources. **E-mail address:** hr@euronetworldwide.com. **World Wide Web address:** http://swww.euronetworldwide.com. **Description:** Develops payment processing software for the banking industry. Founded in 1975. **NOTE:** All resumes to 4601 College Boulevard, Leawood KS 66211, 913/327-4200. Fax: 913/327-1921. **Corporate headquarters:** Leawood KS. **International locations:** Worldwide. **Listed on:** NASDAQ. **Stock exchange symbol:** EEFT. **Annual sales/revenues:** $5 - $10 million. **Number of employees at this location:** 140.

LOISLAW
105 North 28th Street, Van Buren AR 72956. 479/471-5581. **Fax:** 479/471-5745. **Contact:** Human Resources. **E-mail address:** jobs@loislaw.com. **World Wide Web address:** http://www.loislaw.com. **Description:** An online, full-text database service providing access to state and federal law libraries. The service enables lawyers, business professionals, and government agencies to electronically research thousands of resources from their own computers. The company also publishes the information in CD-ROM format. **Parent company:** WoltersKluwer. **Corporate headquarters location:** This location.

RITTERNET
3300 One Place, P.O. Box 19053, Jonesboro AR 72401. 870/974-9100. **Fax:** 870/336-3402. **Toll-free phone:** 888/659-6009. **Contact:** Human Resources. **E-mail address:** employment@callritter.com. **World Wide Web** address: http://www.ritternet.com. Description: An Internet access service for northeast Arkansas. **Positions advertised include:** Sales Engineer; Telecom Technician.

California
AT&T GOVERNMENT SOLUTIONS
5383 Hollister Avenue, Suite 200, Santa Barbara CA 93111. 805/964-7724. **Contact:** Karen Cashman, Recruiting Manager. **World Wide Web address:** http://www.att.com/gov. **Description:** AT&T Government Solutions creates large-scale, decision-support systems and software engineering environments; applies operations research and mathematical modeling to business and management systems; and implements advanced database technology. **Special programs:** Internships. **Corporate headquarters location:** Vienna VA. **Other area locations:** El Segundo CA; Los Angeles CA; Sacramento CA; San Francisco CA; San Diego CA. **Other U.S. locations:** Nationwide. **Parent company:** AT&T Corporation. **Operations at this facility include:** Research & Development. **Listed on:** New York Stock Exchange. **Stock exchange symbol:** T. **Number of employees at this location:** 120. **Number of employees worldwide:** 1,300.

ACCENTURE
2101 Rosecrans Avenue, Suite 3100, El Segundo CA 90245. 310/726-2700. **Fax:** 310/726-2950. **Contact:** Human Resources Manager. **World Wide Web address:** http://www.accenture.com. **Description:** A management and technology consulting firm. Accenture offers a wide range of services including business re-engineering, customer service system consulting, data system design and implementation, Internet sales systems research and design, and strategic planning. **Corporate headquarters location:** Chicago IL. **Other area locations:** Palo Alto CA; Sacramento CA; San Francisco CA; Walnut Creek CA. **Other U.S. locations:** Nationwide. **International locations:** Worldwide. **Listed on:** New York Stock Exchange. **Stock exchange symbol:** ASN.

ACER AMERICA CORPORATION
2641 Orchard Parkway, San Jose CA 95134. 408/432-6200. **Toll-free phone:** 800/733-2237. **Fax:** 408/922-2918. **Contact:** Professional Staffing. **E-mail address:** careers@acer.com. **World Wide Web address:** http://us.acer.com. **Description:** One of the largest microcomputer manufacturers and OEM suppliers. The company also manufactures a variety of computer peripherals and components including monitors, keyboards, expansion cards, and CD-ROM drives. **Positions advertised include:** Business Manager, Inside Sales; Business Manager, Retail Sales. **Parent company:** Acer Inc. (Taiwan) **Number of employees at this location:** 700. **Number of employees nationwide:** 1,200. **Number of employees worldwide:** 25,000.

ACMA COMPUTERS
1505 Reliance Way, Fremont CA 94539. 510/623-1212. **Toll-free phone:** 800/786-6888. **Fax:** 510/623-0818. **Contact:** Human Resources. **E-mail address:** sales@acma.com. **World Wide Web address:** http://www.acma.com. **Description:** Manufactures custom-engineered computers and servers. **Positions advertised include:** Account Manager; Marketing Communications Specialist; In-House Sales Assistant; Technical Support Engineer; Office Assistant. **Corporate headquarters location:** This location.

ACOM SOLUTIONS INC.
2850 East 29th Street, Long Beach CA 90806-2313. 562/424-7899. **Fax:** 562/424-8662. **Contact:** Human Resources. **E-mail address:** nsmith@acom.com. **World Wide Web address:** http://www.acom.com. **Description:** Develops and markets advanced modular software systems for e-document management, e-payment management, B2B e-commerce management and e-purchasing management. **Positions advertised include:** Regional Sales Manager. **Other U.S. locations:** Los Angeles CA; Duluth GA; St. Paul MN.

ACTEL CORPORATION
2061 Stierlin Court, Mountain View CA 94043-4655. 650/318-4200. **Toll-free phone:** 888/992-2835. **Fax:** 650/318-4600. **Contact:** Human Resources. **World Wide Web address:** http://www.actel.com. **Description:** Designs, manufactures, and markets programmable integrated circuits used in computers, peripherals, telecommunications devices, and consumer electronics. **Corporate headquarters location:** This location. **Other area locations:** Irvine CA; Newbury Park CA. **Other U.S. locations:** Nationwide. **International locations:** Canada; France; Germany; Italy; Japan; Korea; United Kingdom. **Operations at this facility include:** Administration; Manufacturing.

ACTIVANT SOLUTIONS INC.
7683 Southfront Road, Livermore CA 94551. 925/449-0606. **Toll-free phone:** 800/678-7423. **Fax:** 925/449-1037. **Contact:** Human Resources. **E-mail address:** industry.marketing@activant.com. **World Wide Web address:** http://www.activant.com. **Description:** Develops business management software and solutions primarily for the automotive aftermarket, retail agribusiness, hardware, paint, and hardlines and lumber industries nationwide. **Positions advertised include:** Desktop Support Analyst; Information Acquisition Specialist; Senior Systems Analyst; Senior Engineer; Staff Development Engineer. **Corporate headquarters location:** Austin TX. **Other U.S. locations:** Florence AL; Denver CO; Raleigh NC; Newton NJ; San Antonio TX. **International locations:** Canada; France; Ireland, United Kingdom.

ACTIVISION, INC.
3100 Ocean Park Boulevard, Santa Monica CA 90405. 310/255-2000. **Contact:** Human Resources. **World Wide Web address:** http://www.activision.com. **Description:** An international publisher of innovative interactive entertainment software. **Corporate headquarters location:** This location.

ADAPTEC, INC.
691 South Milpitas Boulevard, Milpitas CA 95035. 408/945-8600. **Fax:** 408/22-2533. **Contact:** Human Resources. **World Wide Web address:** http://www.adaptec.com. **Description:** Adaptec provides software and hardware solutions for storage connectivity and data protection, storage networking and networked storage subsystems to leading OEM and distribution channel partners. Adaptec solutions are in use by enterprises, ISPs, medium and small businesses and consumers worldwide. **Positions advertised include:** Senior Staff Engineer; SAP Security Administrator; Business Systems Analyst; Senior Product Manager; OEM Sales Manager. **Corporate headquarters location:** This location. **Other area locations:** Foothill Ranch CA; Laguna Hills CA. **Other U.S. locations:** CO; FL; MA; MN; NC; TX; WA. **Listed on:** NASDAQ. **Stock exchange symbol:** ADPT. **Number of employees worldwide:** 1,560.

ADOBE SYSTEMS, INC.
345 Park Avenue, San Jose CA 95110-2704. 408/536-6000. **Fax:** 408/537-6000. **Contact:** Human Resources. **World Wide Web address:** http://www.adobe.com. **Description:** Develops, markets, and supports computer software products and technologies that enable users to create, display, and print electronic documents for Macintosh, Windows, and OS/2 compatibles. The company distributes its products through a network of original equipment manufacturers, distributors and dealers, value-added resellers, and systems integrators. **Positions advertised include:** Business Systems Analyst; Computer Scientist; Database Operations Manager; Direct Marketing Program Manager; Director, Channel & Licensing Operations. **Corporate headquarters location:** This location. **Other U.S. locations:** Nationwide. **International locations:** Australia; Canada; Denmark; France; Germany; Ireland; Japan; the Netherlands; Norway; Spain; Sweden; UK. **Listed on:** NASDAQ. **Stock exchange symbol:** ADBE. **Number of employees worldwide:** 3,700.

ADVENT SOFTWARE, INC.
301 Brannan Street, 6th Floor, San Francisco CA 94107. 415/543-7696. **Toll-free phone:** 800/685-7688. **Fax:** 415/543-5070. **Contact:** Human Resources. **E-mail address:** jobs@advent.com. **World Wide Web address:** http://www.advent.com. **Description:** Develops financial planning and investment applications for investment managers, financial planners, and brokerage houses. **Positions advertised include:** Applications Engineer; Associate System Administrator; Business Analyst; Data Conversion Analyst; Interface Manager; Product Manager; Professional Services Consultant; Senior Software Engineer. **Corporate headquarters location:** This location. **Other U.S. locations:** Cambridge MA; New York NY. **International locations:** Australia; Europe. **Subsidiaries include:** MicroEdge; Second Street Securities; Advent Market Data. **Listed on:** NASDAQ. **Stock exchange symbol:** ADVS. **Annual sales/revenues:** More than $100 million.

AGILENT TECHNOLOGIES
395 Page Mill Road, P.O. Box 10395, Palo Alto CA 94303. 650/752-5000. **Toll-free phone:** 877/424-4536. **Contact:** Human Resources. **World Wide Web address:** http://www.agilent.com. **Description:** Produces test, measurement, and monitoring devices; semi-conductor products; and chemical analysis. Agilent Technologies' primary clients are communications equipment manufacturers, Internet service providers, and biopharmaceutical companies. **Positions advertised include:** Legal Coordinator; R&D Engineer; Mixed-Signal RFIC Engineer; IT Consultant; Project Manager; R&D Scientist. **Corporate headquarters location:** This location. **Listed on:** New York Stock Exchange. **Stock exchange symbol:** A. **Number of employees nationwide:** 11,500. **Number of employees worldwide:** 28,000.

AJILON SERVICES INC.
1960 East Grand Avenue, Suite 1080, El Segundo CA 90245. 310/335-4800. **Toll-free phone:** 800/811-4274.

Fax: 310/335-4820. **Contact:** Human Resources. **E-mail address:** recruit.la@ajilon.com. **World Wide Web address:** http://www.ajilon.com. **Description:** Offers computer consulting services, project support, and end user services. **Positions advertised include:** Senior Account Manager. **Corporate headquarters location:** Towson MD. **Other area locations:** Simi Valley CA; Burbank CA; Glendale CA. **Other U.S. locations:** Nationwide. **Parent company:** Adecco.

ALLDATA CORPORATION
9412 Big Horn Boulevard, Elk Grove CA 95758-1100. 916/684-5200. **Toll-free phone:** 800/697-2533. **Fax:** 916/684-5225. **Contact:** Human Resources. **E-mail address:** hr@alldata.com. **World Wide Web address:** http://www.alldata.com. **Description:** Provides diagnostic, repair, and estimating information to the professional automotive service industry. **Corporate headquarters location:** This location. **Parent company:** AutoZone. **Number of employees at this location:** 300.

AMDOCS LIMITED
2570 Orchard Parkway, Building C, San Jose CA 95131. 408/965-7000. **Fax:** 408/965-4338. **Contact:** Human Resources. **E-mail address:** jobs.web@amdocs.com. **World Wide Web address:** http://www.amdocs.com. **Description:** Develops customer support management software. **Corporate headquarters location:** Chesterfield MO. **Other U.S. locations:** Boston MA; Champaign IL. **International locations:** Worldwide. **Listed on:** New York Stock Exchange. **Stock exchange symbol:** DOX.

AMPRO COMPUTERS INC.
5215 Hellyer Avenue, Suite 110, San Jose CA 95138-1007. 408/360-0200. **Toll-free phone:** 800/966-5200. **Fax:** 408/360-0222. **Contact:** Human Resources. **E-mail address:** careers@ampro.com. **World Wide Web address:** http://www.ampro.com. **Description:** A leading ISO 9001 manufacturer of board-level PC and PC/AT compatible computer modules for embedded applications and the originator of the PC/104 and PC/104-Plus standards. **Corporate headquarters location:** This location. **Other U.S. locations:** Nationwide. **International locations:** Worldwide. **Listed on:** Privately held. **Annual sales/revenues:** $21 - $50 million. **Number of employees at this location:** 60.

ANACOMP, INC.
15378 Avenue of Science, San Diego CA 92128. 858/716-3400. **Fax:** 858/716-3775. **Contact:** Human Resources. **World Wide Web address:** http://www.anacomp.com. **Description:** Provides document storage solutions; manufactures computer hardware and software; and develops customized financial software. **Positions advertised include:** Credit Services Representative. **Corporate headquarters location:** This location. **Other area locations:** Vista CA. **Other U.S. locations:** Nationwide. **International locations:** Austria; France; Germany; Italy; Netherlands; Sweden; Switzerland; United Kingdom. **Operations at this facility include:** Administration; Engineering and Design; Manufacturing; Marketing; Research and Development; Sales. **Number of employees worldwide:** 1,150.

ANALYSTS INTERNATIONAL CORPORATION (AIC)
1390 Willow Pass Road, Suite 200, Concord CA 94520-7900. 925/687-5522. **Toll-free phone:** 800/698-9411. **Fax:** 925/528-6990. **Contact:** Human Resources Manager. **E-mail address:** jobs@analysts.com. **World Wide Web address:** http://www.analysts.com. **Description:** An international computer consulting firm. The company uses different programming languages and software to assist clients in developing systems for a variety of industries. **Positions advertised include:** Application Consultant; Application Developer; Application Specialist; Business Analyst. **Corporate headquarters location:** Minneapolis MN. **Other area locations:** San Jose CA; Los Angeles CA. **Other U.S. locations:** Nationwide. **International locations:** Canada; United Kingdom. **Listed on:** NASDAQ. **Stock exchange symbol:** ANLY.

AONIX
5930 Cornerstone Court West, San Diego CA 92121. 858/457-2700. **Toll-free phone:** 800/972-6649. **Fax:** 858/824-0212 **Contact:** Human Resources. **E-mail address:** resume@aonix.com. **World Wide Web address:** http://www.aonix.com. **Description:** Develops and markets computer-aided software engineering (CASE) products that allow a network of minicomputers to interact. **Positions advertised include:** Controller. **Corporate headquarters location:** This location. **Other U.S. locations:** Ames IA; Tucson AZ. **International locations:** France; Germany; Sweden; United Kingdom.

APPLE COMPUTER, INC.
One Infinite Loop, MS: 84-3CE, Cupertino CA 95014. 408/996-1010. **Fax:** 408/996-0275. **Recorded jobline:** 408/974-0529. **Contact:** Personnel. **E-mail address:** applejobs@apple.com. **World Wide Web address:** http://www.apple.com. **Description:** Develops, manufactures, and markets personal computer systems and peripherals. The company's desktop publishing and communications products are marketed internationally. Founded in 1976. **Special programs:** Internships. **Corporate headquarters location:** This location. **Other area locations:** Statewide. **Other U.S. locations:** Nationwide. **Operations at this facility include:** Sales. **Listed on:** NASDAQ. **Stock exchange symbol:** AAPL. **Number of employees nationwide:** 10,900.

APPLIED IMAGING CORPORATION
120 Baytech Drive, San Jose CA 95134-2302. 408/719-6400. **Fax:** 408/719-6401. **Contact:** Administration Manager. **E-mail address:** info@aicorp.com. **World Wide Web address:** http://www.aicorp.com. **Description:** Develops software used by hospitals and universities for detecting genetic birth defects. **Corporate headquarters location:** This location. **Other U.S. locations:** League City TX. **International locations:** Newcastle England.

APPLIED MATERIALS, INC.
3050 Bowers Avenue, P.O. Box 58039, Santa Clara CA 95054-3299. 408/727-5555. **Contact:** Corporate Employment. **E-mail address:** jobs@appliedmaterials.com. **World Wide Web address:** http://www.appliedmaterials.com. **Description:** A *Fortune* 500 company that is a leading producer of wafer fabrication systems for the semiconductor industry. The company also sells related spare parts and services. Applied Materials' products include dry etch systems for the creation of circuit paths in semiconductors and implementation products for silicon wafers. **NOTE:** For questions about the application process or a specific position, contact ask_employment@appliedmaterials.com. Resumes may be submitted via the e-mail address listed above. **Positions advertised include:** Account Technologist; Administrative Assistant; Business Process Development Manager; CAD Designer; Customer Engineer; Electrical Engineer; Financial Analyst; Human Resources Division Manager; System Design Engineer; Systems Project Manager; Technical Support Engineer. **Corporate headquarters location:** This location. **Other area locations:** Hayward CA; Irvine CA; Milpitas CA; Ontario CA; Roseville CA. **Other U.S. locations:** Nationwide. **International locations:** Worldwide. **Listed on:** NASDAQ. **Stock exchange symbol:** AMAT. **Number of employees nationwide:** 16,200.

ASANTE TECHNOLOGIES
2223 Oakland Road, San Jose CA 95131. 408/435-8388. **Fax:** 408/432-3042. **Contact:** Human Resources. **E-mail address:** hr@asante.com. **World Wide Web address:** http://www.asante.com. **Description:** Designs, develops, and manufactures Gigabit Ethernet and Fast Ethernet networking systems. **Positions advertised include:** Senior Product Manager; Staff

Software Engineer. **Corporate headquarters location:** This location. **International locations:** Germany; Austria; Switzerland. **Operations at this facility include:** Administration; Research and Development; Sales; Service. **Listed on:** NASDAQ. **Stock exchange symbol:** ASNT. **Annual sales/revenues:** $15.2 million.

ASPYRA INC.
26115-A Mureau Road, Calabasas CA 91302. 818/880-6700. **Toll-free phone:** 800/437-9000. **Fax:** 818/880-4398. **Contact:** Human Resources Department. **E-mail address:** jobs@aspyra.com. **World Wide Web address:** http://www.aspyra.com. **Description:** Designs and manufactures computer-based, clinical information systems and products that automate the acquisition and management of clinical data for the health care industry. The company sells its products and systems to hospitals, clinics, reference laboratories, veterinarians, other health care institutions, and original equipment manufacturers. **Corporate headquarters location:** This location.

AUTO-GRAPHICS, INC.
3201 Temple Avenue, Pomona CA 91768-3279. 909/595-7004. **Toll-free phone:** 800/776-6939. **Fax:** 909/595-3506. **Contact:** Human Resources. **E-mail address:** info@auto-graphics.com. **World Wide Web address:** http://www.auto-graphics.com. **Description:** Provides software and processing services to database and information publishers. Services include the computerized preparation and processing of customer-supplied information to be published in various formats including print, microform, CD-ROM, and/or online computer access. In addition, the company markets CD-ROM hardware and software packages for access to computer generated information. **Positions advertised include:** Inside Sales Representative. **Corporate headquarters location:** This location. **Subsidiaries include:** A-G Canada; Datacat; Dataquad; LibraryCard. **Number of employees at this location:** 115.

AUTODESK, INC.
111 McInnis Parkway, San Rafael CA 94903. 415/507-5000. **Fax:** 415/507-5100. **Contact:** Human Resources. **E-mail address:** resumes@autodesk.com. **World Wide Web address:** http://www.autodesk.com. **Description:** Designs, develops, markets, and supports a line of computer-aided design (CAD), engineering, and animation software products for desktop computers and workstations. **Positions advertised include:** Business Analyst; SQA Engineer; QA Engineer; Marketing Manager; Product Designer; Data Analyst; IT Project Manager; Oracle DBA; Data Architect; Senior Solutions Manager. **Special programs:** Internships. **Corporate headquarters location:** This location. **International locations:** Worldwide. **Number of employees nationwide:** 1,800. **Listed on:** NASDAQ. **Stock exchange symbol:** ADSK.

AUTONOMY INC.
892 Ross Drive, Sunnyvale CA 94089. 408/541-1500.: Human Resources Department. **E-mail address:** autononmy@autonomy.com. **World Wide Web address:** http://www.autonomy.com. **Description:** Develops and markets software tools and applications for searching, retrieving, and filtering information on the Internet. **Positions advertised include:** Marketing Programs Specialist; Senior Consultant; Principal Software Engineer. **Corporate headquarters location:** San Francisco.

AVNET MEMEC
10805 Rancho Bernardo Road, Suite 110, San Diego CA 92127. 858/385-7500. **Contact:** Personnel. **World Wide Web address:** http://www.em.avnet.com. **Description:** Distributes computers and semiconductors. NOTE: Search and apply for positions online. **Positions advertised include:** IT Project Manager; Senior Manager, Corporate Development; Business Systems Analyst.

AZUL SYSTEMS
1600 Plymouth Street, Mountain View CA 94043. 650/230-6500. **Fax:** 650/230-6600. **World Wide Web address:** http://www.azulsystems.com. **Description:** Designs and manufactures server hardware used to create networks. **Positions advertised include:** QA Test Engineer. **Corporate headquarters location:** This location. **International locations:** United Kingdom; Japan. **Listed on:** Privately held.

BEA SYSTEMS, INC.
2315 North First Street, San Jose CA 95131. 408/570-8000. **Toll-free phone:** 800/817-4232. **Fax:** 408/570-8901. **Contact:** Human Resources. **World Wide Web address:** http://www.bea.com. **Description**: Provides application server software and middleware used by developers to establish software application platforms. Its products support transaction processing, billing, customer service, provisioning, and securities trading. **Positions advertised include:** Engineering Director; Marketing Director; Product Management Director; Business Operations Director; Mission Critical Support Director; Solutions Marketing Director; Director/Sr. Director, Solutions Marketing; Engineering Product Manager; Export Compliance Manager; Global Services Alliance Manager; Interactive Marketing Program Manager; International Tax Manager; IT Security Project Manager; Product Marketing Manager; Project Manager, Customer Segmentation; Real Estate Specialist; Revenue Recognition Finance Manager; Revenue Recognition Manager; Senior Director, WW Support Entitlement; Senior HR Business Partner; Senior QA Engineer; Senior Software Engineer; Sr. Director, Vertical Sales, Manufacturing and Pharma; Sr. Export Compliance Analyst; Sr. Architect; Sr. Director, Services IT Liaison; Sr. Financial Analyst; Sr. IT Software Developer; Sr. Manager, Credit and Collections; Sr. Manager, Partner Marketing; Sr. Product Marketing Manager, Competitive Research. **Listed on:** NASDAQ. **Stock exchange symbol:** BEAS.

BMC SOFTWARE, INC.
1030 West Maude Avenue, Sunnyvale CA 94085-2810. 408/546-9000. **Fax:** 408/546-9001. **Contact:** Human Resources. **E-mail address:** resumes@bmc.com. **World Wide Web address:** http://www.bmc.com. **Description:** Develops, markets, and supports standard systems software products to enhance and increase the performance of large-scale (mainframe) computer database management systems and data communications software systems. **Positions advertised include:** Senior Product Developer; Technical Business Analyst; Staff Product Developer. **Corporate headquarters location:** Houston TX. **Other area locations:** San Francisco CA; Mountain View CA; Pleasanton CA; Irvine CA. **Other U.S. locations:** Nationwide. **International locations:** Worldwide. **Listed on:** New York Stock Exchange. **Stock exchange symbol:** BMC. **Number of employees worldwide:** 6,200.

BARRA, INC.
2100 Milvia Street, Berkeley CA 94704-1113. 510/548-5442. **Fax:** 510/548-4374. **Contact:** Human Resources. **E-mail address:** careers@barra.com. **World Wide Web address:** http://www.barra.com. **Description:** Develops, markets, and supports application software and information services used to analyze and manage portfolios of equity, fixed income, and other financial instruments. The company serves more than 750 clients in 30 countries including many of the world's largest portfolio managers, fund sponsors, pension and investment consultants, brokers/dealers, and master trustees. **NOTE:** Entry-level positions are offered. **Positions advertised include:** Research Consultant; Technical Project Consultant; Data Engineer; Market Data Analyst; Data Analyst; Office Clerk. **Special programs:** Internships; Training; Summer Jobs. **Corporate headquarters location:** This location. **Other U.S. locations:** Cranbury NJ; New York NY. **International locations:** Australia; Brazil; England; Germany; Hong Kong; Japan; South Africa. **Operations at this facility include:** Administration; Research and Development; Sales; Service. **Listed on:** NASDAQ. **Stock exchange symbol:** BARZ. **Annual**

sales/revenues: More than $100 million. **Number of employees worldwide:** Over 500.

BELL MICROPRODUCTS INC.
1941 Ringwood Avenue, San Jose CA 95131. 408/451-9400. **Toll-free phone:** 800/800-1513. **Fax:** 408/451-1600. **Contact:** Human Resources. **World Wide Web address:** http://www.bellmicro.com. **Description:** Markets and distributes a select group of computer products to original equipment manufacturers and value-added resellers. Products include logic microprocessors; disk, tape, and optical drives and subsystems; drive controllers; and board-level products. The company also provides a variety of manufacturing and value-added services to its customers including the supply of board-level products to customer specifications on a turnkey basis; certain types of components and subsystem testing services; systems integration and disk drive formatting and testing; and the packaging of electronic component kits to customer specifications. Founded in 1987. **Positions advertised include:** Inside Sales Representative; Hardware Engineer; Retail Product Manager; Warehouse Manager. **Corporate headquarters location:** This location. **Other U.S. locations:** Nationwide. **International locations:** Argentina; Brazil; Canada; Chile; Italy; Mexico; the Netherlands; United Kingdom. **Listed on:** NASDAQ. **Stock exchange symbol:** BELM.

BLIZZARD ENTERTAINMENT
P.O. Box 18979, Irvine CA 92623. 949/955-1380. **Fax:** 949/737-2000. **Contact:** Jack Sterling, Human Resources. **E-mail address:** resumes@blizzard.com. **World Wide Web address:** http://www.blizzard.com. **Description:** Develops and publishes entertainment software such as computer games. **Positions advertised include:** Public Relations Manager; Associate Public Relations Manager. **Corporate headquarters location:** This location.

BLUEBEAM SOFTWARE, INC.
396 West Washington Boulevard, Suite 600, Pasadena CA 91103. **Toll-free phone:** 866/496-2140. 626/296-2140. **Fax:** 626/398-9210. **Contact:** Human Resources. **E-mail address:** hres@bluebeam.com. **World Wide Web address:** http://www.bluebeam.com. **Description:** Bluebeam invents, develops, and commercializes desktop software applications specifically designed to meet the needs of engineers and architects.

BORLAND SOFTWARE CORPORATION
20450 Stevens Creek Boulevard, Suite 800, Cupertino CA 95014. 408/863-2800. **Contact:** Human Resources. **E-mail address:** resume@borland.com. **World Wide Web address:** http://www.borland.com. **Description:** Develops, distributes, and manages tools that allow software developers to create enterprise applications that are known as Information Networks. Borland Software also provides consulting and technical support services. **Positions advertised include:** Integration Engineer; R&D Engineer. **Special programs:** Internships. **Corporate headquarters location:** This location. **Listed on:** NASDAQ. **Stock exchange symbol:** BORL.

BRODERBUND LLC
100 Pine Street, Suite 1900, San Francisco CA 94111. 415/659-2000. **Fax:** 415/659-1877. **Contact:** Alan Byrne, Vice President of Personnel. **E-mail address:** resumes@riverdeep.net. **World Wide Web address:** http://www.broderbund.com. **Description:** Develops, publishes, and markets personal computer software for the home, school, and small business markets. Products include personal productivity and educational software. **Positions advertised include:** Affiliate and Search Engineer Marketing Manager; Associate Producer, Personal Publishing; Technology Architect; Senior Direct Marketing Manager; Art Director; Project Design Manager. **Corporate headquarters location:** This location. **Parent company:** Riverdeep Learning Limited (also at this location). **Number of employees at this location:** 340.

CACI INTERNATIONAL, INC.
1011 Camino Del Rio South, San Diego CA 92108. 619/692-4400. **Contact:** Recruiter. **World Wide Web address:** http://www.caci.com. **Description:** Provides computer consulting services including information technology and facility management support. **NOTE:** Send resumes to: CACI, Attn: Recruiters, 4795 Meadow Wood Lane, Chantilly VA 20151. Fax: 703/961-5031. **Corporate headquarters location:** Arlington VA.

CCH INC.
21250 Hawthorne Boulevard, Torrance CA 90503. 310/543-6200. **Toll-free phone:** 800/PFX-9998. **Fax:** 310/543-6544. **Contact:** Human Resources. **World Wide Web address:** http://www.cch.com. **Description:** One of the nation's largest developers of income tax processing software. The company markets its software products to tax attorneys, tax accountants, and CPAs. **Positions advertised include:** Payroll Specialist. **Corporate headquarters location:** Riverwoods IL. **Other U.S. locations:** Chatsworth CA; Washington DC; Chicago IL; St. Cloud MN. **Parent company:** Wolters Kluwer. **Number of employees at this location:** 400.

CI DESIGN
4320 East Miraloma Avenue, Anaheim CA 92807. 714/646-0111. **Toll-free phone:** 800/576-5487. **Fax:** 714/646-0266. **Contact:** Human Resources. **E-mail address:** stella@cidesign.com. **World Wide Web address:** http://www.ci-design.com. **Description:** Designs and manufactures computer hardware and peripherals including storage and disk drive systems. **Positions advertised include:** Sales Representative. **Special programs:** Internships. **Corporate headquarters location:** This location. **Other U.S. locations:** Nationwide. **International locations:** The Netherlands; Taiwan.

CABLE & COMPUTER TECHNOLOGY
1555 South Sinclair Street, Anaheim CA 92806. 714/937-1341. **Fax:** 714/937-1225. **World Wide Web address:** http://www.c2t.com. **Contact:** Human Resources. **Description:** Manufactures computer emulation hardware for the U.S. government. **Corporate headquarters location:** This location.

CADENCE DESIGN SYSTEMS, INC.
2655 Seely Avenue, San Jose CA 95134. 408/943-1234. **Toll-free phone:** 800/746-6223. **Fax:** 408/428-5001. **Contact:** Human Resources. **World Wide Web address:** http://www.cadence.com. **Description:** Manufactures electronic design automation software. **Positions advertised include:** Product Engineer; Senior Systems Engineer; Software Engineer; Senior Marketing Manager; Legal Specialist; Principal Desgin Engineer. **Special programs:** Internships. **Corporate headquarters location:** This location. **Other area locations:** Irvine CA; San Diego CA; Santa Barbara CA. **Other U.S. locations:** MD; MA; MS; NJ; NC; OR; PA; TX. **International locations:** Canada; England; France; India; Ireland; Italy; Japan; Scotland; Taiwan. **Operations at this facility include:** Administration; Research and Development; Sales. **Listed on:** New York Stock Exchange. **Stock exchange symbol:** CDN. **Number of employees worldwide:** 4,800.

CAM COMMERCE SOLUTIONS
17075 Newhope Street, Suite A, Fountain Valley CA 92708. 714/241-9241. **Fax:** 714/241-9893. **Contact:** Human Resources. **World Wide Web address:** http://www.camcommerce.com. **Description:** Designs, manufactures, markets, and services inventory management, point-of-sale, order entry, and accounting software systems for small to medium-sized retailers and wholesalers. Founded in 1983. **Positions advertised include:** Technical Support Specialist. **Corporate headquarters location:** This location. **Other U.S. locations:** Burlingame CA; Aurora CO; Altamonte Springs FL; Hopkinton MA; St. Louis MO; Saddle River NJ; Henderson NV; Dallas TX. **Listed**

on: NASDAQ. **Stock exchange symbol:** CADA. **Number of employees at this location:** 164.

CHARTERHOUSE SOFTWARE CORPORATION
2801 Townsgate Road, Suite 139, Westlake Village CA 91361. 805/494-5191. **Fax:** 805/494-8191. **Contact:** Human Resources. **World Wide Web address:** http://www.chsoft.com. **Description:** Manufactures and markets accounting software, sells business forms, and offers related consulting services. **Corporate headquarters location:** This location.

CHRONTEL, INC.
2210 O'Toole Avenue, Suite 100, San Jose CA 95131-1326. 408/383-9328. **Fax:** 408/383-9338. **Contact:** Human Resources. **E-mail address:** careers@chrontel.com. **World Wide Web address:** http://www.chrontel.com. **Description:** Manufactures computer microchips. **Positions advertised include:** Analog Design Engineer; Applications Engineer; Firmware and System Design Engineer; Algorithm Design Engineer. **Corporate headquarters location:** This location. **Other area locations:** San Diego CA. **Number of employees at this location:** 100.

CIBER ENTERPRISE SOLUTIONS
1010 Battery Street, San Francisco CA 94111. 415/875-1800. **Fax:** 415/875-1801. **Contact:** Employment Administrator. **E-mail address:** recruitingsf@ciber.com. **World Wide Web address:** http://sanfrancisco.ciber.com. **Description:** A leading software-consulting firm serving clients in a variety of industries. The company is engaged in the implementation of HRMS, financial, distribution, manufacturing, and student systems. **Positions advertised include:** Implementation Consultant. **Corporate headquarters location:** Greenwood Village CO. **Other U.S. locations:** Nationwide. **Parent company:** CIBER, Inc. **Listed on:** New York Stock Exchange. **Stock exchange symbol:** CBR. **Number of employees at this location:** 220.

CISCO SYSTEMS, INC.
P.O. Box 640730, San Jose 95164. 408/526-4000. **Physical address:** 170 West Tasman Drive, San Jose CA 95134. **Fax:** 800/818-9201. **Contact:** Human Resources. **E-mail address:** apply@cisco.com. **World Wide Web address:** http://www.cisco.com. **Description:** Develops, manufactures, markets, and supports high-performance internetworking systems that enable customers to build large-scale integrated computer networks. The company's products connect and manage communications among local and wide area networks that employ a variety of protocols, media interfaces, network topologies, and cable systems. **Positions advertised include:** Product Manager; Software Engineer; IT Analyst; Technical Leader; Commodity Manager; Network Consulting Engineer. **Special programs:** Internships; Co-ops. **Corporate headquarters location:** This location. **International locations:** Worldwide. **Listed on:** NASDAQ. **Stock exchange symbol:** CSCO. **Number of employees nationwide:** 15,000. **Number of employees worldwide:** 34,000.

CNET NETWORKS, INC.
235 Second Street, San Francisco CA 94105. 415/344-2000. **Contact:** Human Resources. **E-mail address:** careers@cnet.com. **World Wide Web address:** http://www.cnet.com. **Description:** A new media company that provides services and information related to computers and technology. Products and services include technology-related Internet sites, television shows, radio shows, and comparison shopping. **Positions advertised include:** Account Coordinator; Account Executive; Associate Data Producer; Associate Designer; Associate Editor; Director Sales Programs; Director of Global Marketing Communications; Executive Editor. **Special programs:** Internships. **Corporate headquarters location:** This location. **Other area locations:** Irvine CA. **Other U.S. locations:** Chicago IL; Louisville KY; Bridgewater NJ; New York NY; Cambridge MA. **International locations:** Worldwide. **Listed on:** NASDAQ. **Stock exchange symbol:** CNET.

COMMUNICATION INTELLIGENCE CORPORATION (CIC)
275 Shoreline Drive, Suite 500, Redwood Shores CA 94065-1413. 650/802-7888. **Fax:** 650/802-7777. **Contact:** Human Resources Department. **E-mail address:** jobs@cic.com. **World Wide Web address:** http://www.cic.com. **Description:** Develops, markets, and licenses handwriting recognition and related technologies for the emerging pen-based computer market. The company has created a natural input recognition system that allows a computer to recognize hand-printed character input. **Positions advertised include:** Inside Sales Representative. **Corporate headquarters location:** This location. **International locations:** China. **Listed on:** NASDAQ. **Stock exchange symbol:** CICI.

COMPUTER ASSOCIATES
10180 Telesis Court, San Diego CA 92121. 858/452-0170. **Contact:** Personnel. **World Wide Web address:** http://www.ca.com. **Description:** One of the world's leading developers of client/server and distributed computing software. The company develops, markets, and supports enterprise management, database and applications development, business applications, and consumer software products for a broad range of mainframe, midrange, and desktop computers. Founded in 1976. **NOTE:** CAI prefers that candidates submit a resume via their online resume builder. **Positions advertised include:** Software Engineer; Senior Technology Specialist. **Corporate headquarters location:** Islandia NY. **Other U.S. locations:** Nationwide. **International locations:** Worldwide. **Operations at this facility include:** This location develops software. **Listed on:** New York Stock Exchange. **Stock exchange symbol:** CA. **Annual sales/revenues:** $3.12 billion. **Number of employees nationwide:** 5,000. **Number of employees worldwide:** Over 15,000.

COMPUTER HORIZONS CORPORATION
1411 West 190th Street, Suite 470, Gardena CA 90248-4324. 310/771-0770. **Fax:** 310/771-0777. **Contact:** Human Resources. **World Wide Web address:** http://www.computerhorizons.com. **Description:** A full-service technology solutions company offering contract staffing, outsourcing, re-engineering, data migration, downsizing support, and network management. The company has a worldwide network of 43 offices. Founded in 1969. **Corporate headquarters location:** Mountain Lakes NJ. **Other area locations:** San Francisco CA. **Other U.S. locations:** Nationwide. **International locations:** Canada; England. **Listed on:** NASDAQ. **Stock exchange symbol:** CHRZ.

COMPUTER SCIENCES CORPORATION
2100 East Grand Avenue, El Segundo CA 90245. 310/615-0311. **Fax:** 310/322-9768. **Contact:** Human Resources. **World Wide Web address:** http://www.csc.com. An information technology services company offering systems design and integration; IT and business process outsourcing; applications software development; Web and application hosting; and management consulting. **Positions advertised include:** Finance Manager; Communications Specialist; Network Engineer; Procurement Specialist; Logistics Manager; Compensation Manager. **Corporate headquarters location:** This location. **International locations:** Canada; Germany; Japan; The Netherlands; Saudi Arabia; South Korea; Spain; United Kingdom. **Operations at this facility include:** This location primarily serves the U.S. government. **Listed on:** New York Stock Exchange. **Stock exchange symbol:** CSC. **Number of employees nationwide:** 20,000. **Number of employees worldwide:** 90,000.

COMPUWARE CORPORATION
1300 Clay Street, Suite 700, Oakland CA 94612. 510/251-8900. **Contact:** Corporate Recruiting. **E-mail**

address: compuware.recruiting@compuware.com. **World Wide Web address:** http://www.compuware.com. **Description:** Develops, markets, and supports an integrated line of systems software products that improve the productivity of programmers and analysts in application program testing, test data preparation, error analysis, and maintenance. Compuware also provides a broad range of professional data processing services including business systems analysis, design, and programming, as well as systems planning and consulting. **NOTE:** Resumes may be submitted online, or by mail or fax. Address resumes to: Corporate Recruiting, Compuware Corporation, One Camous Martius, Detroit MI 48226. Fax: 877/873-6784. **Positions advertised include:** Software Sales Manager; Regional Products Director; Pre-Sales Support Engineer. **Corporate headquarters location:** Detroit MI. **Other area locations:** Irvine CA; Los Angeles CA; San Diego CA. **Other U.S. locations:** Denver CO; St. Louis MO; Cincinnati OH; Cleveland OH; Columbus OH; Nashville TN; McLean VA; Milwaukee WI. **International locations:** Canada; South Africa; United Kingdom. **Listed on:** NASDAQ. **Stock exchange symbol:** CPWR.

COMSYS INFORMATION TECHNOLOGY SERVICES, INC.
2020 Main Street, Suite 150, Irvine CA 94614. 949/885-0220. **Toll-free phone:** 800/276-4727. **Fax:** 949/885-0244. **Contact:** Human Resources. **World Wide Web address:** http://www.comsys.com. **Description:** A computer consulting and contracting firm that provides outsourcing, project support, vendor management, and other specialty services. Founded in 1969. **Corporate headquarters location:** Houston TX. **Other area locations:** Folsom CA; San Francisco CA; Campbell CA. **Other U.S. locations:** Nationwide. **Parent company:** COMSYS IT Partners, Inc.

CONVERA
1808 Aston Avenue, Suite 290, Carlsbad CA 92008. 760/438-7900. **Fax:** 703/804-8133. **Contact:** Human Resources. **E-mail address:** recruit@convera.com. **World Wide Web address:** http://www.convera.com. **Description:** Designs, develops, markets, and supports computer software products used for the document imaging and multimedia information retrieval marketplaces. The company also offers consulting, training, maintenance, and systems integration services. In addition, the company performs research and development under contract and licenses proprietary software products for use in office, identification, and multimedia information retrieval systems. The company distributes its products through direct sales, distributors, select resellers, and vertical market suppliers. **Positions advertised include:** IT Security Specialist; Linux System Administrator; Crawler software Engineer; Information Retrieval Software Engineer. **Corporate headquarters location:** Vienna VA. **Operations at this facility:** Training. **Listed on:** NASDAQ. **Stock exchange symbol:** CNVR.

CORNERSTONE PERIPHERALS TECHNOLOGY, INC.
225 Hammond Avenue, Fremont CA 94539. 510/580-8900. **Fax:** 510/580-8998. **Contact:** Human Resources. **E-mail address:** hr@cptmail.com. **Description:** Designs computer displays and graphics controller cards. Founded in 1986. **Special programs:** Internships. **Corporate headquarters location:** This location. **International locations:** Munich, Germany. **Listed on:** Privately held. **Number of employees at this location:** 55.

CREATIVE LABS, INC.
1901 McCarthy Boulevard, Milpitas CA 95035. 408/428-6600. **Fax:** 408/546-6305. **Contact:** Recruiting. **World Wide Web address:** http://www.creative.com. **Description:** Creative Labs provides multimedia products and peripherals for personal computers. Products include graphics and audio cards, multimedia upgrade kits, portable media players, mp3 players, web cameras, and speakers. **Positions advertised include:** Assistant Controller; Brand Manager, Audio; Test Engineer; Financial Support Analyst; Marcom Manager; Marketing Copywriter. **Corporate headquarters location:** This location. **Other area locations:** Fremont CA; Scotts Valley CA. **Other U.S. locations:** Stillwater OK. **International locations:** Canada; Latin America. **Parent company:** Creative Technology, Ltd. **Operations at this facility include:** Administration; Research and Development; Manufacturing. **Listed on:** NASDAQ. **Stock exchange symbol:** CREAF.

DCL
48641 Milmont Drive, Fremont CA 94538. 510/651-5100. **Fax:** 510/651-2261. **Contact:** Human Resources. **E-mail address:** careers@dclcorp.com. **World Wide Web address:** http://www.discopylabs.com. **Description:** A supply chain management company. **Corporate headquarters location:** This location. **Other area locations:** Ontario CA.

D-LINK SYSTEMS, INC.
17595 Mt. Hermann, Fountain Valley CA 92708-4160. 800/326-1688. **Contact:** Human Resources. **E-mail address:** hr@dlink.com. **World Wide Web address:** http://www.dlink.com. **Description:** Manufactures networking, connectivity, and data communications products. The company's product line includes adapters, hubs, switches, routers, and print servers. **Positions advertised include:** Web Programmer; Manager, Channel Programs; Senior Account Executive; Director, MSO Sales; Program Manager. **Corporate headquarters location:** This location.

DTC COMPUTER SUPPLIES
P.O. Box 2834, Rancho Cucamonga CA 91729-2834. 909/466-7680. **Physical address:** 9033 9th Street, Rancho Cucamonga CA 91730. **Toll-free phone:** 800/700-7683. **Fax:** 909/466-7682. **Contact:** Human Resources Department. **World Wide Web address:** http://www.dtc1.com. **Description:** Manufactures magnetic computer tape and distributes computer supplies. **Corporate headquarters location:** This location.

DATA TECHNOLOGY CORPORATION (DTC)
1700 Space Park Drive, Santa Clara CA 95054. 408/745-9320. **Contact:** Human Resources. **Description:** Develops and manufactures computer peripherals including printers, disk drives, terminals, controllers, and supplies. Products are marketed to both original equipment manufacturers and distributors. **Corporate headquarters location:** This location.

DECISIONONE
2323 Industrial Parkway West, Hayward CA 94545. 510/266-3000. **Contact:** Scott, Hagenbuch, Human Resources. **E-mail address:** scott.hagenbuch@decisionone.com. **World Wide Web address:** http://www.decisionone.com. **Description:** DecisionOne is an international supplier of plug-compatible computer equipment and accessories. Products include disk and tape storage devices, terminals, intelligent workstations and systems, controllers, printers, airline reservation systems, and a comprehensive range of computer supplies. The company operates in 27 countries around the world. **Corporate headquarters location:** Frazer PA. **Operations at this facility include:** This location repairs computer monitors.

DISKEEPER CORPORATION
7590 North Glenoaks Boulevard, Burbank CA 91504. 818/771-1600. **Fax:** 818/252-5514. **Contact:** Human Resources. **E-mail address:** ppo@diskeeper.com. **World Wide Web address:** http://www.diskeeper.com. **Description:** Develops and markets systems software and applications for the Windows NT operating system. **Positions advertised include:** Staff Accountant; Vice President of Public Relations; Axapta Programmer; GUI Designer; Senior Software Engineer. **Corporate headquarters location:** This location. **Listed on:** Privately held. **Annual sales/revenues:** $21 - $50 million. **Number of employees at this location:** 160.

EMC
2201 Dupont Drive, Suite 500, Irvine CA 92612. 949/833-1442. **Contact:** Human Resources. **World Wide Web address:** http://software.emc.com. **Description:** Develops client/server software. **Positions advertised include:** Associate Customer Engineer; Partner Solutions Lead; Customer Engineer; Tech Solutions Project Manager; Adivsory Commercial Technology Consultant; Solutions Business Analyst; Regional Coordinator. **Other U.S. locations:** Dallas TX; Englewood CO; Bellevue WA; South Jordan UT; Cambridge MA. **Parent company:** EMC Corporation (Hopkinton MA).

EMC DOCUMENTUM
6801 Koll Center Parkway, Pleasanton CA 94566. 925/600-6800. **Fax:** 925/600-6850. **Contact:** Human Resources. **World Wide Web address:** http://software.emc.com. **Description:** Develops client/server software for document management. **Positions advertised include:** Senior Financial Analyst. **Other U.S. locations:** Dallas TX; Englewood CO; Bellevue WA; South Jordan UT; Cambridge MA. **Parent company:** EMC Corporation (Hopkinton MA).

EDGE DYNAMICS, INC.
1001 Marshall Street, Suite 500, Redwood City CA 94063. 650/780-7800. **Toll-free phone:** 866/737-EDGE. **Fax:** 650/780-7801. **Contact:** Human Resources. **World Wide Web address:** http://www.edgedynamics.com. **Description:** Edge Dynamics provides pharmaceutical manufacturers enterprise software for commerce optimization, solutions that optimize sales, distribution, and supply chain operations while complementing traditional transaction management and analytic systems. **Corporate headquarters location:** This location. **Other U.S. locations:** Philadelphia PA.

ELECTRO RENT CORPORATION
6060 Sepulveda Boulevard, Van Nuys CA 91411-2512. 818/787-2100. **Toll-free phone:** 800/688-1111. **Fax:** 818/786-1602. **Contact:** Human Resources. **E-mail address:** maya@electrorent.com. **World Wide Web address:** http://www.electrorent.com. **Description:** Rents and leases electronic equipment including test and measurement instruments, workstations, personal computers, and data communication products. **NOTE:** E-mail is the preferred method of resume submission. **Positions advertised include:** Inside Sales Representative; Account Development Representative; Senior RF Technician. **Corporate headquarters location:** This location. **Other U.S. locations:** Nationwide. **Listed on:** NASDAQ. **Stock exchange symbol:** ELRC. **Annual sales/revenues:** More than $100 million. **Number of employees at this location:** 200. **Number of employees nationwide:** 500.

ELECTRONIC ARTS, INC.
209 Redwood Shore Parkway, Redwood City CA 94065. 650/628-1500. **Contact:** Human Resources. **World Wide Web address:** http://www.ea.com. **Description:** Creates, markets, and distributes interactive entertainment software for use primarily on independent game systems and IBM-compatible PCs. **Positions advertised include:** SW Engineer; Peoplesoft Developer/Analyst; Compensation Consultant; Product Manager; Art Director; Audio Engineer; Category Manager. **Corporate headquarters location:** This location. **Other area locations:** Chicago IL; Los Angeles CA; Louisville KY. **Other U.S. locations:** Orlando FL. **Listed on:** NASDAQ. **Stock exchange symbol:** ERTS. **Number of employees worldwide:** 4,400.

EMBEE TECHNOLOGIES
16592 Millikan Avenue, Irvine, CA 92606. 949/266-1700. **Fax:** 949/435-1595. **Contact:** Human Resources. **E-mail address:** sales@embeetech.com. **World Wide Web address:** http://www.embeetech.com. **Description:** Provides a portfolio of business and technology solutions to enable our clients to improve their business performance. Embee's core portfolio comprises IT, wireless and structured cabling services. **Positions advertised include:** Account Executive, Network Project Manager/Consultant, Network Engineer, Project Manager Cabling & Wireless. **Parent company:** Embee Inc.

EMULEX CORPORATION
3333 Susan Street, Costa Mesa CA 92626-7112. 714/662-5600. **Toll-free phone:** 800/EMULEX-1. **Fax:** 714/241-0792. **Contact:** Sadie Herrera, Director of Human Resources. **E-mail address:** hr@emulex.com. **World Wide Web address:** http://www.emulex.com. **Description:** Emulex Corporation specializes in intelligent interface technology for the computer industry. Emulex designs, manufactures, and markets data storage and network connectivity products, as well as advanced integrated circuits. **Positions advertised include:** Senior Customer Program Manager; Senior Product Marketing Manager; Marketing Director; Supply Chain Specialist; OEM Support Engineer Senior Engineer; VP, Marketing. **Corporate headquarters location:** This location. **Other U.S. locations:** Bolton MA; Longmont CO; Bothell WA. **Listed on:** NASDAQ. **Stock exchange symbol:** EMLX.

ENCAD, INC.
6059 Cornerstone Court West, San Diego CA 92121. 858/452-0882. **Toll-free phone:** 800/45-ENCAD. **Fax:** 858/457-5831. **Contact:** Human Resources. **E-mail address:** jobs1@encad.com. **World Wide Web address:** http://www.encad.com. **Description:** ENCAD, Inc. designs, develops, manufactures, and markets wide-format, color ink-jet printers and plotters. Typical users are in industries utilizing computer-aided design; architectural, engineering, and construction design; geographic information systems such as surveying and mapping; and graphic arts such as digital photo imaging and editing, sign-making, three-dimensional renderings, and presentation graphics. **Positions advertised include:** Product Manager. **Corporate headquarters location:** This location. **Parent company:** Kodak.

EPLUS, INC.
1900 Point West Way, Suite 120, Sacramento CA 95815. 916/568-1555. **Toll-free phone:** 800/827-5711. **Fax:** 916/568-1590. **Contact:** Human Resources. **E-mail address:** resumes@eplus.com. **World Wide Web address:** http://www.eplus.com. **Description:** Leases and sells computers and other IT equipment. ePlus also develops online software products that provide supply chain management solutions including electronic procurement, e-financing, and e-asset management. **Corporate headquarters location:** Herndon VA. **Other area locations:** Del Mar CA; Sunnyvale CA. **Other U.S. locations:** Nationwide. **Listed on:** NASDAQ. **Stock exchange symbol:** PLUS.

EPICOR SOFTWARE CORPORATION
18200 Von Karman Avenue, Suite 1000, Irvine CA 92612. 949/585-4000. **Fax:** 949/585-4093. **Contact:** Mary Lou Wilkins, Human Resources. **E-mail address:** careers@epicor.com. **World Wide Web address:** http://www.epicor.com. **Description:** Develops financial and manufacturing software for use in a client/server environment. Epicor Software focuses exclusively on mid-market companies. Founded in 1984. **Positions advertised include:** Senior Financial Analyst; Marketing Programs Manager; Senior Applications Specialist; IS Support Administrator. **Corporate headquarters location:** This location. **Other area locations:** Oakland CA; Gold River CA; San Diego CA. **Other U.S. locations:** Nationwide. **International locations:** Worldwide. **Listed on:** NASDAQ. **Stock exchange symbol:** EPIC. **Annual sales/revenues:** $153 million. **Number of employees worldwide:** 950.

EVEREX COMMUNICATIONS INC.
5020-A Brandin Court, Fremont CA 94538. 510/687-0075. **Fax:** 510/683-2021. **Contact:** Human Resources. **E-mail address:** jobs@everexcomm.net. **World Wide Web address:** http://www.everexcomm.net. **Description:** Focuses upon wireless Gateway and

Internet appliance network solutions targeted at the small business and home environments. **Corporate headquarters location:** This location. **Operations at this facility include:** Administration; Manufacturing; Sales; Service. **Listed on:** Privately held.

EXCITE INC.
555 Broadway, Redwood City CA 94063. 650/568-6000. **Fax:** 650/568-6030. **Contact:** Human Resources Department. **E-mail address:** positions@staff.excite.com. **World Wide Web address:** http://www.excite.com. **Description:** An Internet search engine that offers Web navigation services and features site reviews, editorial columns, news, and regional information. **Positions advertised include:** Marketing Manager; Sales Planner; Graphic Designer; System Operator. **Corporate headquarters location:** This location. **Parent company:** IAC Search & Media. **Listed on:** NASDAQ. **Stock exchange symbol:** XCIT.

FAIR ISAAC CORPORATION
200 Smith Ranch Road, San Rafael CA 94903. 415/472-2211. **Toll-free phone:** 800/999-2955. **Fax:** 415/492-9381. **Contact:** Human Resources. **E-mail address:** info@fairisaac.com. **World Wide Web address:** http://www.fairisaac.com. **Description:** Develops and provides data management software and services for the consumer credit, personal lines insurance, and direct marketing industries. Founded in 1956. **Positions advertised include:** Analytic Science Lead; Analystic Science Engineer; Business Consulting Manager; Director. **Corporate headquarters location:** Minneapolis MN. **Other area locations:** Emeryville CA; Irvine CA; San Diego CA; San Jose CA. **Subsidiaries include:** Dynamark (Minneapolis MN); European Analytic Products Group (Birmingham, England). **Listed on:** New York Stock Exchange. **Stock exchange symbol:** FIC.

FILEMAKER INC.
P.O. Box 58168, Santa Clara CA 95052. 408/987-7000. **Physical address:** 5201 Patrick Henry Drive, Santa Clara CA 95054. **Contact:** Human Resources. **E-mail address:** filemaker_hr@filemaker.com. **World Wide Web address:** http://www.filemaker.com. **Description:** Develops software including FileMaker Pro 5 and FileMaker Server 5, database systems that are designed for Windows and Macintosh operating systems. **Positions advertised include:** SQA Engineer; Senior Technical Support Engineer; Software Engineer Intern. **Special programs:** Internships. **Corporate headquarters location:** This location.

FILENET CORPORATION
3565 Harbor Boulevard, Costa Mesa CA 92626-1420. 714/327-3400. **Contact:** Kenneth Ross, Employment Manager. **World Wide Web address:** http://www.filenet.com. **Description:** FileNet develops and markets electronic content management software and e-business solutions. Products and services are used to help corporations and organizations build intranets, create electronic portals to streamline information management, and to create, process, edit, organize, and store all forms of digital content for Internet applications. **Positions advertised include:** Internal Audit Manager; Benefits Analyst; Learning Technologist; Business Systems Manager; Application Systems Lead; Web System Lead; Senior System Administrator; Principal Engineer. **Special programs:** Internships. **Corporate headquarters location:** This location. **Other U.S. locations:** Nationwide. **Listed on:** NASDAQ. **Stock exchange symbol:** FILE. **Number of employees at this location:** 800. **Number of employees worldwide:** 1,700.

FUJITSU COMPUTER PRODUCTS OF AMERICA INC.
1255 East Arques Avenue, Sunnyvale CA 94085-4701. 408/746-7000. **Fax:** 408/894-1700. **Contact:** Human Resources. **E-mail address:** fcpajobs@us.fujitsu.com. **World Wide Web address:** http://www.fujitsu.com/us. **Description:** Fujitsu Computer Products of America manufactures hard drives, magneto-optical drives, printers, scanners, and tape drives. **Positions advertised include:** ASIC Design Engineer; Senior Customer Support Engineer; Business Development Manager; Inside Sales Professional; Product Specialist. **Corporate headquarters location:** This location. **Other area locations:** Irvine CA. **Other U.S. locations:** Austin TX; Burlington MA; Houston TX; Longmont CO. **Parent company:** Fujitsu, Ltd. (Japan). **Operations at this facility include:** Administration.

FUJITSU COMPUTER SYSTEMS
1250 East Arques Avenue, Sunnyvale CA 94085-3470. 408/746-6000. **Toll-free phone:** 800/538-8460. **Fax:** 408/992-2674. **Contact:** Human Resources. **World Wide Web address:** http://www.fpc.fujitsu.com. **Description:** Designs, develops, manufactures, markets, and services large-scale, high-performance, general-purpose computer systems. Customers are primarily large corporations, government agencies, and large universities with high-volume data processing requirements. **Positions advertised include:** Plasma Display Operations Engineer; Alliances Account Executive. **Special programs:** Internships. **Corporate headquarters location:** This location. **Other U.S. locations:** Nationwide. **International locations:** Germany; Ireland; Italy; Portugal; Switzerland; United Kingdom. **Parent company:** Fujitsu, Ltd. **Operations at this facility include:** Administration; Manufacturing; Research and Development; Sales; Service. **Listed on:** NASDAQ. **Stock exchange symbol:** FJTSY. **Number of employees at this location:** 3,500. **Number of employees nationwide:** 6,000. **Number of employees worldwide:** 9,500.

FUJITSU MICROELECTRONICS AMERICA, INC.
1250 East Arques Avenue, Sunnyvale CA 94088-3470. 408/737-5600. **Fax:** 408/737-5999. **Contact:** Human Resources. **E-mail address:** careers@fma.fujitsu.com. **World Wide Web address:** http://www.fujitsu.com/us/micro. **Description:** Fujitsu Microelectronics, Inc. manufactures microprocessors, Ethernet decoders and encoders, discrete chips, and memory products. **Corporate headquarters location:** This location. **Parent company:** Fujitsu, Ltd. (Japan). **Operations at this facility include:** This location houses administrative offices.

FUSIONWARE CORPORATION
3931 MacArthur Boulevard, Suite 212, Newport Beach CA 92660. 949/250-4800. **Fax:** 949/752-6772. **Contact:** Human Resources. **E-mail address:** sales@fusionware.net. **World Wide Web address:** http://www.fusionware.net. **Description:** Engaged in systems and software integration services. **Corporate headquarters location:** Friday Harbor WA. **Operations at this facility include:** Sales; Service.

GATEWAY, INC.
7565 Irvine Center Drive, Irvine CA 92618. 949/471-7000. **Toll-free phone:** 800/846-2000. **Fax:** 949/471-7041. **Contact:** Human Resources. **World Wide Web address:** http://www.gateway.com. **Description:** A leading provider of personal computers, digital cameras, camcorders, and systems and networking products. **Positions advertised include:** Senior Software Engineer; Senior Manager, Commodity Procurement; Consumer Electronics Engineer. **Corporate headquarters location:** This location. **Other U.S. locations:** Kansas City MO; Sioux City SD. **Number of employees worldwide:** 1,900. **Listed on:** New York Stock Exchange. **Stock exchange symbol:** GTW.

GOOGLE INC.
1600 Ampitheatre Parkway, Mountain View CA 94043. 650/623-4000. **Fax:** 650/618-1499. **Contact:** Human Resources. **E-mail address:** jobs@google.com. **World Wide Web address:** http://www.google.com. **Description:** Operates the world's largest Internet search engine. **Positions advertised include:** Software Engineer; Web Specialist; Product Marketing Manager; Financial Analyst; Senior Accountant; Corporate Legal

Assistant; Business Analyst; Executive Assistant. **Corporate headquarters location:** This location.

GLASSHOUSE TECHNOLOGIES, INC.
4305 Hacienda Drive, Suite 350, Pleasanton CA 94588. 925/225-9130. **Fax:** 925/225-9144. **Contact:** People Strategy and Services Team. **E-mail address:** careers@glasshouse.com. **World Wide Web address:** http://www.glasshouse.com. **Description:** A consulting firm providing data storage strategies and solutions for the financial services, health care, biopharmaceutical, and technology sectors. Founded in 2001. **Positions advertised include:** IT Manager; Senior Storage Consultant; Engagement Partner; Project Manager. **Corporate headquarters location:** Framingham MA. **Other area locations:** Carlsbad CA. **Other U.S. locations:** Minneapolis MN; New York NY; Durham NC; Hartford CT; Washington DC. **Listed on:** Privately held.

GLOBAL INFORMATION DISTRIBUTION (GID)
2635 Zanker Road, San Jose CA 95134-2107. 408/232-5500. **Fax:** 408/232-5501. **Contact:** Personnel. **E-mail address:** jscheurer@gid-it.com. **World Wide Web address:** http://www.gid-it.com. **Description:** Manufactures film-based imaging printers and storage/retrieval hardware. **Corporate headquarters location:** This location. **Parent company:** International GID Group (Cologne, Germany).

GOLDEN RAM
8 Whatney, Irvine CA 92618. 949/460-9000. **Toll-free phone:** 800/222-8861. **Fax:** 949/460-7600. **Contact:** Personnel. **E-mail address:** jobs@goldenram.com. **World Wide Web address:** http://www.goldenram.com. **Description:** Manufactures third-party memory modules for computers to increase RAM. **Positions advertised include:** Sales Representative. **Corporate headquarters location:** This location.

GRECO SYSTEMS
7171 Alvarado Road, La Mesa CA 91941. 619/466-4242. **Contact:** Personnel. **E-mail address:** hr@grecosystems.com. **World Wide Web address:** http://www.grecosystems.com. **Description:** Manufactures industrial computer software and hardware systems for communication and storage in factory automation facilities. **Corporate headquarters location:** This location. **Parent company:** e-DNC, Inc. **Listed on:** Privately held. **Annual sales/revenues:** $5 - $10 million. **Number of employees at this location:** 60.

HANSEN INFORMATION TECHNOLOGIES
11092 Sun Center Drive, Rancho Cordova CA 95670. 916/921-0883. **Toll-free phone:** 800/821-9316. **Fax:** 916/921-6620. **Contact:** Human Resources Coordinator. **World Wide Web address:** http://www.hansen.com. **Description:** A supplier of application software that helps manage the operations of government. **Positions advertised include:** Software Engineer, Billing & Tax; Business Analyst Assets; Business Analyst Technical Services; Configuration Specialist CDR; Integration Specialist Assets; Integration Specialist CDR; MIS Analyst Technical Services; Project Manager CDR; Project Manager Migrations; Quality Assurance Technician Technical Services; Sales Engineer; Senior Software Engineer; Software Engineer Financial; Software Engineer - GIS Solutions.

HELLO COMPUTERS INC.
99 West Tasman Drive, Suite 101, San Jose CA 95134. 408/435-0801. **Toll-free phone:** 877/794-3556. **Fax:** 408/273-6891. **Contact:** Human Resources. **E-mail address:** staffing@hellocomputers.com. **Description:** Provides IT training, staffing and other computer-related services. **Corporate headquarters location:** This location.

HEWLETT-PACKARD COMPANY
3000 Hanover Street, Palo Alto CA 94304-1185. 650/857-1501. **Fax:** 650/857-5518. **Contact:** Human Resources. **World Wide Web address:** http://www.hp.com. **Description:** Hewlett-Packard designs and manufactures measurement and computation products and systems used in business, engineering, science, health care, and education. Principal products include integrated instrument and computer systems such as hardware and software, peripheral products, and electronic medical equipment and systems. Products are sold through retail stores, warehouses, resellers, mail-order catalogs, and telemarketers. The company conducts business in more than 90 countries. **Positions advertised include:** Software Territory Sales Representative; Research Associate; Advertising Director; Marketing Science Research Intern; Senior Experience Designer. **Special programs:** Internships. **Corporate headquarters location:** This location. **Other area locations:** Statewide. **Other U.S. locations:** Nationwide. **International locations:** Worldwide. **Listed on:** New York Stock Exchange. **Stock exchange symbol:** HPQ. **Number of employees worldwide:** 142,000.

HITACHI DATA SYSTEMS
750 Central Expressway, Santa Clara CA 95050-2627. 408/970-1000. **Fax:** 408/727-8036. **Contact:** Human Resources. **E-mail address:** hrresumes@hds.com. **World Wide Web address:** http://www.hds.com. **Description:** Hitachi Data Systems manufactures mainframe computers. **Positions advertised include:** Database Administrator; Business Analyst; Attorney; Global Storage Manager. **Corporate headquarters location:** This location. **Parent company:** Hitachi Ltd. **Operations at this facility include:** Sales; Marketing. **Listed on:** New York Stock Exchange. **Stock exchange symbol:** HIT.

HITACHI VIA MECHANICS USA
2325 Paragon Drive, Suite 10, San Jose CA 95131. 408/392-9560. **Contact:** Human Resources. **World Wide Web address:** http://www.hitachi-via-usa.com. **Description:** Manufactures graphics tablets with pressure sensitive pens for computers. **Parent company:** Hitachi Ltd. **Listed on:** New York Stock Exchange. **Stock exchange symbol:** HIT.

HOYA CORPORATION USA
101 Metro Drive, Suite 500, San Jose CA 95110. 408/441-3300. **Contact:** Human Resources. **World Wide Web address:** http://www.hoya.co.jp. **Description:** Develops, produces, and markets glass, thin-film, rigid disks for use in hard drives for mobile computing applications. **NOTE:** Entry-level positions are offered. Resumes should be sent to: Human Resources, Hoya Corporation USA, 3400 Edison Way, Fremont CA 94538. **Corporate headquarters location:** This location. **Subsidiaries include:** Continuum; Probe Tech. **Parent company:** Hoya Corporation (Japan). **Listed on:** Privately held. **Number of employees at this location:** 185. **Number of employees worldwide:** Over 3,000.

HYPERION SOLUTIONS CORPORATION
5450 Great America Parkway, Santa Clara CA 95054. 408/588-8000. **Fax:** 408/588-8500. **Contact:** Human Resources. **World Wide Web address:** http://www.hyperion.com. **Description**: Develops business performance management software. **Positions advertised include:** Curriculum Developer; Instructor; Senior Consultant; Partner Technical Account Manager; Project Manager, Custom Training; Domain Leader; Project Manager, Planning; Senior Product Manager, Analytic Services; Manager Software Engineering; Senior Compensation Analyst; Software Architect; Financial Analyst; Advisory Software Engineer; Principal Performance Engineer; System Architect Engineer; Senior Manager, Quality Engineering. **Listed on:** NASDAQ. **Stock exchange symbol:** HYSL. **Number of employees worldwide:** 2,500.

IBM ALMADEN RECEARCH CENTER
650 Harry Road, San Jose CA 95120. 408/927-1733. **Toll-free phone:** 800/IBM4YOU. **Fax:** 408/927-4307. **Contact:** Human Resources. **World Wide Web address:** http://www.almaden.ibm.com. **Description:**

An industrial research laboratory that focuses on basic and applied research in computer science, magnetic and optical storage technology, physical and materials science and technology, and scientific and technical application software. **Positions at this facility include:** Advisory Software Engineer; Software Engineer; Circuit Design Engineer; Instrumentation Engineer. **Corporate headquarters location:** White Plains NY. **Parent company:** IBM Corporation. **Operations at this facility include:** Research and Development. **Listed on:** New York Stock Exchange. **Stock exchange symbol:** IBM.

IAMBIC SOFTWARE
1270 Oakmead Parkway, Suite 214, Sunnyvale CA 94085. 408/882-0390. **Contact:** Human Resources. **E-mail address:** jobs@iambic.com. **World Wide Web address:** http://www.iambic.com. **Description:** Develops and manufactures software applications for the handheld computing market. **Positions advertised include:** Software Engineer; Technical Support Engineer. **Corporate headquarters location:** This location.

IMAGE MICROSYSTEMS, INC.
6301 Chalet Drive, Commerce CA 90040. 562/776-3333. **Fax:** 562/776-3322. **Contact:** Human Resources. **World Wide Web address:** http://www.imagemicro.com. **Description:** A reseller of computer hardware and software. **Corporate headquarters location:** This location. **Other U.S. locations:** Austin TX.

IMATION CORPORATION
300 South Lewis Road, Camarillo CA 93012-8485. 805/482-1911. **Contact:** Human Resources. **World Wide Web address:** http://www.imation.com. **Description:** Develops data storage products, medical imaging and photo products, printing and publishing systems, and customer support technologies and document imaging, and markets them under the trademark names Dry View laser imagers, Matchprint and Rainbow color proofing systems, Travan data cartridges, and LS-120 diskette technology. **Corporate headquarters location:** Oakdale MN. **Listed on:** New York Stock Exchange. **Stock exchange symbol:** IMN.

INFONET SERVICES CORPORATION
2160 East Grand Avenue, El Segundo CA 90245-5024. 310/335-2600. **Fax:** 310/335-2679. **Contact:** Ken Montgomery, Human Resources Department. **E-mail address:** ken_montgomery@infonet.com. **World Wide Web address:** http://www.infonet.com. **Description:** Provides networking services to international corporations. Founded in 1970. **Positions advertised include:** Marketing Communications Specialist; Financial Analyst; Customer Care Support Analyst; Senior Billing Specialist. **Corporate headquarters location:** This location. **Listed on:** New York Stock Exchange. **Stock exchange symbol:** IN.

INFORMATION BUILDERS INC.
1731 Technology Drive, Suite 750, San Jose CA 95110. 408/453-7600. **Fax:** 408/453-5824. **Contact:** Human Resources. **E-mail address:** employment_opportunities@ibi.com. **World Wide Web address:** http://www.informationbuilders.com. **Description:** A software development firm. Products include WebFOCUS, FOCUS Solutions, EDA Middleware, and SmartMart Data Warehouse. Other services include software support and sales. **Positions advertised include:** Regional Technical Operations Manager. **Corporate headquarters location:** New York NY. **Other U.S. locations:** Nationwide. **Number of employees nationwide:** 1,800.

INFORMIX SOFTWARE, INC.
4100 Bohannon Drive, Menlo Park CA 94025. 650/926-6300. **Contact:** Human Resources. **World Wide Web address:** http://www.informix.com. **Description:** Provides database technology to build, deploy, run, and evolve applications. Informix products include distributed database management systems, application development tools, and graphical- and character-based productivity software. **Corporate headquarters location:** This location. **Other U.S. locations:** Englewood CO; Downers Grove IL; Lenexa KS; Portland OR. **International locations:** England; Singapore. **Parent company:** IBM. **Operations at this facility include:** Administration; Research and Development; Sales. **Listed on:** New York Stock Exchange. **Stock exchange symbol:** IBM. **Number of employees at this location:** 800. **Number of employees nationwide:** 1,300.

INGRAM MICRO
1600 East Saint Andrew Place, P.O. Box 25125, Santa Ana CA 92799-5125. 714/566-1000. **Contact:** Human Resources Department. **World Wide Web address:** http://www.ingrammicro.com. **Description:** Distributes microcomputer products including desktop and notebook PCs, servers, CD-Rom drives, printers, and software. **Positions advertised include:** Supply Chain Coordinator; Marketing Manager; Senior Copywriter; Financial Analyst; Senior Contract Negotiator; Business Process Improvement Manager. **Corporate headquarters location:** This location. **Listed on:** New York Stock Exchange. **Stock exchange symbol:** IM. **Number of employees worldwide:** 11,300.

INTEL CORPORATION
2200 Mission College Boulevard, P.O. Box 58119, Santa Clara CA 95052-8119. 408/765-8080. **Contact:** Staffing Department. **World Wide Web address:** http://www.intel.com. **Description:** One of the largest semiconductor manufacturers in the world. Other products include supercomputers; embedded control chips and flash memories; motherboards; multimedia hardware; personal computer enhancement products; and the design and marketing of microcomputer components, modules, and systems. Intel sells its products to original equipment manufacturers and other companies that incorporate them into their products. **Positions advertised include:** Audit Specialist; CAD Engineer; Senior Press Relations Specialist; Hardware Test Engineer; Manufacturing Engineer; Product Engineer; Patent Attorney; Device Engineer; Principal Research Scientist; Software Engineer. **Corporate headquarters location:** This location. **Listed on:** NASDAQ. **Stock exchange symbol:** INTC.

INTELLICORP
2900 Lakeside Drive, Suite 221, Santa Clara CA 94054. 408/454-3500. **Fax:** 408/454-3529. **Contact:** Human Resources Department. **E-mail address:** jobs@intellicorp.com. **World Wide Web address:** http://www.intellicorp.com. **Description:** Designs, develops, and markets software development tools and provides related training, customer support, and consulting services. IntelliCorp provides its customers with object-oriented software tools for the design, development, and delivery of scalable client/server applications. **NOTE:** Resumes must be e-mailed; resumes submitted by postal mail or fax will not be accepted. **Positions advertised include:** Regional Sales Manager; Senior Marketing Executive; IPC Technical Consultant. **Corporate headquarters location:** This location. **Other U.S. locations:** Nationwide. **International locations:** Europe.

INTERNATIONAL MICROCOMPUTER SOFTWARE, INC. (IMSI)
100 Rowland Way, 3rd Floor, Novato CA 94945. 415/878-4000. **Fax:** 415/897-2544. **Contact:** Jackie Wandrey, Human Resources. **World Wide Web address:** http://www.imsisoft.com. **Description:** A leading developer of productivity software for business and home use. The company's Home Living Media division focuses on CD-ROM multimedia software for learning and education. IMSI's three primary product lines are business, consumer productivity, and multimedia learning software. **Corporate headquarters location:** This location.

INTERVOICE, INC.
EDIFY EDUCATION SERVICES
2840 San Tomas Expressway, Santa Clara CA 95051. 972/454-8769. **Contact:** Human Resources. **E-mail address:** careers@edify.com. **World Wide Web**

address: http://www.intervoice.com. **Description:** Develops voice self-service systems for business customers. **Positions advertised include:** Senior Product Manager; Senior Software Engineer; Senior Accountant; Client Services Sales Manager. **Corporate headquarters location:** Dallas TX. **Operations at this facility include:** This location is a training center.

INTUIT, INC.
2632 Marine Way, Mountain View CA 94043. 650/944-6000. **Contact:** Human Resources. **World Wide Web address:** http://www.intuit.com. **Description:** Develops and markets personal finance and small business accounting software and also offers support services. Products include Quicken, which allows users to organize and manage personal finances. **Positions advertised include:** Senior Administrative Assistant; Engineering Manager; Senior PeopleSoft Application Developer; Marketing Operations Manager. **Corporate headquarters location:** This location. **Other U.S. locations:** AZ; MA; MI; NV; NY; TX; UT; VA. **International locations:** Canada; Japan; United Kingdom. **Listed on:** NASDAQ. **Stock exchange symbol:** INTU. **Number of employees worldwide:** 6,700.

JUNIPER NETWORKS, INC.
1194 North Mathilda Avenue, Sunnyvale CA 94089-1206. 408/745-2000. **Toll-free phone:** 888/586-4737. **Fax:** 408/745-2100. **Contact:** Human Resources. **World Wide Web address:** http://www.juniper.net. **Description:** Manufactures computer networking equipment such as IP platforms and provides the appropriate services. **Positions advertised include:** Director of Mergers & Acquisitions; Technical Instructor. **Corporate headquarters location:** This location. **Other U.S. locations:** Nationwide.

KAY COMPUTERS
722 Genevieve Street, Suite N, Solana Beach CA 92075. 858/481-0225. **Fax:** 858/481-4363. **Contact:** Human Resources. **World Wide Web address:** http://www.kaycomputers.com. **Description:** Manufactures personal computers. **Corporate headquarters location:** This location.

KEANE, INC.
133 Technology Drive, Suite 200, Irvine CA 92618. 949/450-4600. **Toll-free phone:** 800/315-8306. **Fax:** 949/450-4601. **Contact:** Human Resources. **E-mail address:** careers@keane.com. **World Wide Web address:** http://www.keane.com. **Description:** A software development and consulting firm providing systems and software applications to the transportation, finance, health care, and insurance industries. **Positions advertised include:** Engagement Manager; Account Executive. **Corporate headquarters location:** Boston MA. **Listed on:** American Stock Exchange. **Stock exchange symbol:** KEA.

KENSINGTON TECHNOLOGY GROUP
333 Twin Dolphin Drive, Sixth Floor, Redwood Shores CA 94065. 650/572-2700. **Toll-free phone:** 800/243-2972. **Fax:** 650/572-9675. **Contact:** Human Resources. **E-mail address:** jobs@kensington.com. **World Wide Web address:** http://www.kensington.com. **Description:** Designs and markets computer accessories, peripherals, and software for the computer aftermarket. Products include mice and trackballs, joysticks, gamepads, surge suppressor systems, cable and lock security devices, and carrying cases. **NOTE:** Entry-level positions are offered. Search and apply for positions online. **Positions advertised include:** Channel Development Representative; Sales Planning Analyst; ID Product Designer; Sales Support Specialist. **Special programs:** Internships. **Office hours:** Monday - Friday, 8:00 a.m. - 5:00 p.m. **Corporate headquarters location:** This location. **Parent company:** ACCO Brands, Inc. **Listed on:** New York Stock Exchange. **Stock exchange symbol:** ABD.

KINGSTON TECHNOLOGY
17600 Newhope Street, Fountain Valley CA 92708. 714/435-2600. **Toll-free phone:** 877/546-4786. **Fax:** 714/435-35269955. **Contact:** Human Resources. **E-mail address:** jobs@kingston.com. **World Wide Web address:** http://www.kingston.com. **Description:** A leading independent manufacturer of more than 2,000 memory, processor, and other peripheral products. Founded in 1987. **NOTE:** Entry-level positions are offered. **Positions advertised include:** Sales Account Manager. **Corporate headquarters location:** This location. **International locations:** France; Germany; Ireland; Taiwan; United Kingdom. **Listed on:** Privately held. **Annual sales/revenues:** More than $100 million. **Number of employees worldwide:** 1,200.

KONTRON AMERICA
14118 Stowe Drive, Poway CA 92064-7147. 858/294-4558. **Fax:** 858/677-0898. **Contact:** Human Resources. **World Wide Web address:** http://www.kontron.com. **Description:** A manufacturer of ruggedized PC chassis and a reseller of computer hardware. **NOTE:** Search and apply for positions online. **Positions advertised include:** Order Entry Administrator; Senior Program Manager; Material Handler; Executive Assistant. **Corporate headquarters location:** This location. **Other area locations:** Hayward CA. **Other U.S. locations:** Eden Prairie MN; Pittsburgh PA.

LSI LOGIC
1621 Barber Lane, Milpitas CA 95035. 408/954-3108. **Fax:** 408/433-8918. **Contact:** Human Resources. **World Wide Web address:** http://www.lsilogic.com. **Description:** Designs and markets integrated circuits that implement the compression, decompression, and transmission of digital full-motion video and still images for consumer electronics, communications, and computer applications such as video CD players, direct broadcast of television programming by satellites, and multimedia computing. Founded in 1988. **NOTE:** Search and apply for positions online. **Corporate headquarters location:** This location. **Other area locations:** Irvine CA; Los Angeles CA; San Diego CA. **U.S. locations:** Nationwide. **International locations:** China; France; Germany; Italy; the Netherlands; Sweden; United Kingdom. **Number of employees worldwide:** 600. **Listed on:** New York Stock Exchange. **Stock exchange symbol:** LSI.

LANTRONIX
15353 Barranca Parkway, Irvine CA 92618. 949/453-3990. **Fax:** 949/453-7165. **Contact:** Human Resources. **E-mail address:** employment@lantronix.com. **World Wide Web address:** http://www.lantronix.com. **Description:** Provides network-enabling technology that allows for configuring and communicating over the Internet and shared networks. **Positions advertised include:** Cost Accountant; Senior Software Engineer; Test Engineer. **Corporate headquarters location:** This location. **Annual sales/revenues:** $21 - $50 million. **Listed on:** NASDAQ. **Stock exchange symbol:** LTRX.

LOGITECH, INC.
6505 Kaiser Drive, Fremont CA 94555. 510/795-8500. **Fax:** 510/792-8901. **Contact:** Human Resources Manager. **World Wide Web address:** http://www.logitech.com. **Description:** Designs, develops, manufactures, and markets computer hardware and software products. Logitech is a leading worldwide manufacturer of computer pointing devices including mice, trackballs, and joysticks, and imaging devices such as scanners and cameras for PC, MAC, and other platforms. **Special programs:** Internships. **Corporate headquarters location:** This location. **Other U.S. locations:** Framingham MA; Dallas TX. **Parent company:** Logitech International S.A. **Operations at this facility include:** Administration; Research and Development; Sales. **Listed on:** NASDAQ. **Stock exchange symbol:** LOGI. **Number of employees at this location:** 350.

LOTUS DEVELOPMENT CORPORATION
425 Market Street, 25th Floor, San Francisco CA 94105. 415/545-3800. **Contact:** Human Resources. **World Wide Web address:** http://www.lotus.com. **Description:** Develops, manufactures, and markets

applications software and services that meet the evolving technology and business applications requirements of individuals, work groups, and entire organizations. **Corporate headquarters location:** Cambridge MA. **Parent company:** IBM Corporation. **Listed on:** New York Stock Exchange. **Stock exchange symbol:** IBM.

LUCAS ARTS ENTERTAINMENT COMPANY
1110 Gorgas Avenue, P.O. Box 29908, San Francisco CA 94129. 415/472-3400. **Fax:** 415/444-8438. **Contact:** Recruiting. **World Wide Web address:** http://www.lucasarts.com. **Description:** An international developer and publisher of entertainment software, some of which incorporate a Star Wars theme. **Positions advertised include:** Financial Analyst; Producer; Senior Character Technical Director; Marketing Coordinator. **Corporate headquarters location:** This location.

LUCENT TECHNOLOGIES INTERNETWORKING SYSTEMS
1288 San Luis Obispo Street, Hayward CA 94544. 510/475-5000. **Contact:** Human Resources. **World Wide Web address:** http://www.lucent.com. **Description:** Develops, manufactures, markets, and supports a family of high-performance, multiservice wide area network (WAN) switches that enable public carrier providers and private network managers to provide cost-effective, high-speed, enhanced data communications services. These products direct and manage data communications across wide area networks that utilize different network architectures and services, and are designed to support, on a single platform, the major high-speed packet data communications services. These services include frame relay, switched multimegabit data service, and asynchronous transfer mode. The company markets its products to interexchange carriers, local exchange carriers, competitive access providers, other public network providers, and private network managers. **Corporate headquarters location:** Murray Hill NJ. **Listed on:** New York Stock Exchange. **Stock exchange symbol:** LU. **Number of employees worldwide:** 32,500.

MAI SYSTEMS CORPORATION HOTEL INFORMATION SYSTEMS
26110 Enterprise Way, Suite 200, Lake Forest CA 92630. 949/598-6000. **Toll-free phone:** 800/497-0532. **Fax:** 949/598-6324. **Contact:** Human Resources. **World Wide Web address:** http://www.maisystems.com. **Description:** A worldwide provider of information systems solutions software for the hospitality industry and mid-size manufacturers and distributors. **Positions advertised include:** Cognos Developer. **Corporate headquarters location:** This location. **Other U.S. locations:** San Francisco CA; Boston MA; Tampa FL; Washington DC; Whitehouse Station NJ; Dallas TX. **International locations:** China; Indonesia; Malaysia; Singapore; United Kingdom. **Operations at this facility include:** Administration; Manufacturing; Research and Development; Sales; Service. **Listed on:** American Stock Exchange. **Stock exchange symbol:** NOW.

MSC SOFTWARE CORPORATION
2 MacArthur Place, Santa Ana CA 92707. 714/540-8900. **Fax:** 714/784-4491. **Contact:** Human Resources, Professional Staffing. **E-mail address:** msc.jobs@mscsoftware.com. **World Wide Web address:** http://www.mscsoftware.com. **Description:** Develops, markets, and supports software for computer-aided engineering. **Positions advertised include:** Consulting Engineer; Manager of Compensation; Web Developer; Logistics Administrator. **Corporate headquarters location:** This location. **Listed on:** New York Stock Exchange. **Stock exchange symbol:** MNS.

MTI TECHNOLOGIES CORPORATION
17595 Cartwright Road, Irvine CA 92614. 949/251-1101. **Fax:** 949/251-1102. **Contact:** Human Resources. **E-mail address:** jobs@mti.com. **World Wide Web address:** http://www.mti.com. **Description:** Designs, manufactures, markets, and services high-performance storage solutions for the DEC, IBM, and open UNIX systems computing environments. These storage solutions integrate MTI's proprietary application and embedded software with its advanced servers and industry standard storage peripherals. Products include NetBacker client/server application software, Infinity Automated Tape Library Series, and other systems and related application software. **Positions advertised include:** Open Software Implementation Engineer; Storage Solution Architect; Project Manager. **Corporate headquarters location:** This location.

MACROMEDIA, INC.
601 Townsend Street, San Francisco CA 94103. 415/252-2000. **Fax:** 415/832-2020. **Contact:** Personnel. **World Wide Web address:** http://www.macromedia.com. **Description:** Develops multimedia software for the Web. **NOTE:** Search and apply for positions online. **Positions advertised include:** Developer Support and Services Engineer; Director, Communications software Engineering; International Development Engineer; Principal Technical Writer; Media Director; Marketing Analyst. **Special programs:** Internships. **Parent company:** Adobe Systems Incorporated.

MAXTOR CORPORATION
500 McCarthy Boulevard, Milpitas Ca 95035. 408/894-5000. **Fax:** 408/952-3600. **Contact:** Human Resources. **E-mail address:** staffing_ca@maxtor.com. **World Wide Web address:** http://www.maxtor.com. **Description:** Manufactures hard disk drives and related electronic data storage equipment for computers, as well as related components for original equipment manufacturers. **Positions advertised include:** Assistant Treasurer; Senior Staff roduct Manager; Senior Technician; Senior Engineer Reliability. **Special programs:** Internships. **Corporate headquarters location:** This location. **International locations:** Hong Kong; Singapore. **Listed on:** New York Stock Exchange. **Stock exchange symbol:** MXO.

MCAFEE, INC.
3965 Freedom Circle, Santa Clara CA 95054. 408/988-3832. **Contact:** Human Resources. **World Wide Web address:** http://www.mcafee.com. **Description:** Designs, manufactures, markets, and supports antivirus software and other security products. Products include VirusScan, an antivirus software, and SpamKiller. **Positions advertised include:** Senior Product Marketing Manager; Technical Support Engineer; Competitive Researcher; Business Development Manager; Corporate Development Analyst; Hardware Engineer; Senior Software Development Engineer. **Corporate headquarters location:** This location. **Other U.S. locations:** Plano TX.

MENTOR GRAPHICS CORPORATION
1001 Ridder Park Drive, San Jose 95131. 408/436-1500. **Toll-free phone:** 800/547-3000. **Fax:** 408/436-1501. **Contact:** Human Resources. **World Wide Web address:** http://www.mentor.com. **Description:** A provider of electronic design software and hardware used by companies to aid in the design and production of electronics. **NOTE:** Search and apply for positions online. **Positions advertised include:** Marketing Director; Product Marketing Manager; Technical Marketing Engineer; Software Development Engineer; Senior Financial Analyst. **Corporate headquarters location:** Wilsonville OR. **Listed on:** NASDAQ. **Stock exchange symbol:** MENT.

MERCURY INTERACTIVE CORPORATION
379 North Whisman Road, Mountain View CA 94043-3969. 650/603-5200. **Fax:** 650/603-5300. **Contact:** Personnel. **World Wide Web address:** http://www.mercury.com. **Description:** Develops automated software quality tools for enterprise applications testing. The company's products are used to isolate software and system errors prior to application deployment. **Positions advertised include:** Senior Manager of Business Development; Director, Business Transformation; Technical Enablement

Manager; Application Support Engineer; Contracts Negotiator; Treasury Operations Manager. **Corporate headquarters location:** This location. **Listed on:** NASDAQ. **Stock exchange symbol:** MERQ. **Annual sales/revenues:** $506 million.

MERISEL, INC.
200 Continental Boulevard, El Segundo CA 90245. 310/615-3080. **Toll-free phone:** 800/637-4735. **Fax:** 310/535-8134. **Contact:** Personnel. **E-mail address:** hr@merisel.com. **World Wide Web address:** http://www.merisel.com. **Description:** A wholesaler of computer hardware and software products. Merisel distributes the products to computer resellers throughout the United States and Canada. **Positions advertised include:** Inside Sales Representative. **Office hours:** Monday - Friday, 8:30 a.m. - 5:30 p.m. **Corporate headquarters location:** This location. **Other U.S. locations:** Marlborough MA; Cary NC. **International locations:** Canada. **Listed on:** NASDAQ. **Stock exchange symbol:** MSEL. **Annual sales/revenues:** $96 million.

MICRO 2000, INC.
1100 East Broadway, 3rd Floor, Glendale CA 91205. 818/547-0125. **Toll-free phone:** 800/864-8008. **Contact:** Personnel Director. **World Wide Web address:** http://www.micro2000.com. **Description:** Develops and markets computer diagnostic products for troubleshooting. Founded in 1990. **Positions advertised include:** Appointment Setter; Sales Representative; QA Technician. **Corporate headquarters location:** This location. **International locations:** Australia; Germany; Holland; United Kingdom. **Listed on:** Privately held. **Annual sales/revenues:** $5 - $10 million. **Number of employees at this location:** 45.

MICROSOFT CORPORATION
1065 La Avenida Street, Mountain View CA 94043. 650/693-1001. **Contact:** Human Resources Department. **E-mail address:** jobs@microsoft.com. **World Wide Web address:** http://www.microsoft.com. **Description:** Microsoft designs, sells and supports a product line of microcomputer software for business, home, and professional use. Microsoft also manufactures related books and hardware products. Software products include spreadsheets, desktop publishing, project management, graphics, word processing, and database applications, as well as operating systems and programming languages. **NOTE:** Register online to submit resume, create profile, or create job search agent. **Positions advertised include:** Database Analyst; Consultant; Hardware Design Engineer; Operations Analyst; Program Manager; Software Development Engineer; Systems Engineer; Human Resources Generalist; Marketing Manager. **Corporate headquarters location:** Redmond WA. **Other area locations:** Sacramento CA; San Francisco CA. **Operations at this facility include:** This location is a research and design office. **Listed on:** NASDAQ. **Stock exchange symbol:** MSFT.

MIDWAY HOME ENTERTAINMENT INC.
10110 Mesa Rim road, San Diego CA 92191 858/658-9500. **Contact:** Human Resources. **E-mail address:** hr@midwaygames.com. **World Wide Web address:** http://www.midway.com. **Description:** Develops video game software. **Positions advertised include:** Acquisition and Traffic Manager; Cinematic Art Director; Localization Coordinator. **Corporate headquarters location:** Chicago IL. **Operations at this facility include:** This location is a research and development facility. **Listed on:** New York Stock Exchange. **Stock exchange symbol:** MWY.

MIPS TECHNOLOGIES, INC.
1225 Charleston Road, Mountain View CA 94043-1353. 650/567-5000. **Fax:** 650/567-5150. **Contact:** Susan Raskin, Director of Human Resources. **E-mail address:** susan@mips.com. **World Wide Web address:** http://www.mips.com. **Description:** Designs 32- and 64-bit RISC processors for license to semiconductor suppliers. The company's products are then embedded in such items as digital cameras, handheld computing devices, and video game systems. **NOTE:** Search and apply for positions online. **Positions advertised include:** Senior Programmer; Multi Media Market Development Manager; Design Verification Engineer; Senior Core Engineer. **Corporate headquarters location:** This location. **Listed on:** NASDAQ. **Stock exchange symbol:** MIPS. **Annual sales/revenues:** $39 million.

MITCHELL INTERNATIONAL
9889 Willow Creek Road, San Diego CA 92131. 858/578-6550. **Toll-free phone:** 800/854-7030. **Fax:** 858/530-4636. **Contact:** Michael Dean Galvin, Staffing Manager. **E-mail address:** michael.galvin@mitchell.com. **World Wide Web address:** http://www.mitchell.com. **Description:** Provides printed information and electronic software products for the automotive industry. **Positions advertised include:** Automotive Editor; Configuration Mgmt Analyst; Corporate business Decision Analyst; Contract Technical Recruiter. **Special programs:** Internships. **Corporate headquarters location:** This location. **Other U.S. locations:** Chicago IL; Detroit MI; McLean VA; Milwaukee WI. **Subsidiaries include:** EH Boeckh (Milwaukee WI); Mitchell-Medical (VA); NAG's (Detroit MI). **Parent company:** Hellman & Friedman LLC. **Number of employees nationwide:** Over 700.

MUSITEK
410 Bryant Circle, Suite K, Ojai CA 93023. 805/646-8051. **Toll-free phone:** 800/676-8055. **Fax:** 805/646-8099. **Contact:** Personnel. **World Wide Web address:** http://www.musitek.com. **Description:** Develops music software including MIDISCAN, which converts printed sheet music into multitrack MIDI files. **Corporate headquarters location:** This location.

NETIS TECHNOLOGY, INC.
P.O. Box 700357, San Jose CA 95170-0357. 408/263-0368. **Fax:** 408/216-7762. **Contact:** Human Resources. **E-mail address:** hr@netistech.com. **World Wide Web address:** http://www.netistech.com. **Description:** Provides systems integration and networking services. The company also manufactures personal computers and offers a network consulting service. Founded in 1989. **Corporate headquarters location:** This location. **Listed on:** Privately held. **Number of employees at this location:** 20.

NETSCAPE COMMUNICATIONS CORPORATION
P.O. Box 7050, Mountain View CA 94039-7050. 650/254-1900. **Physical address:** 466 Ellis Street, Mountain View CA 94043. **Fax:** 650/528-4124. **Contact:** Human Resources. **World Wide Web address:** http://www.netscape.com. **Description:** An Internet service provider. The company also provides developmental tools, commercial applications, and client/server software. **Positions advertised include:** Technical Support Engineer; Quality Assurance Manager; Senior Technical Project Manager; Software Engineer. **Special programs:** Internships. **Corporate headquarters location:** This location. **Other area locations:** Half Moon Bay CA; Sunnyvale CA; San Francisco CA. **Other U.S. locations:** Nationwide. **Parent company:** Time Warner. **Listed on:** New York Stock Exchange. **Stock exchange symbol:** AOL.

NETWORK APPLIANCE, INC.
495 East Java Drive, Sunnyvale CA 94089. 408/822-6000. **Fax:** 408/822-4501. **Contact:** Human Resources. **E-mail address:** ntapjobs@netapp.com. **World Wide Web address:** http://www.netapp.com. **Description:** Develops data storage equipment for corporate networks. **NOTE:** Search and apply for positions online. **Positions advertised include:** ATA Storage Development Engineer; Business Analyst; Business Systems Analyst; Database Application Engineer; Director of Legal; Disk Drive Sustaining Engineer. **Corporate headquarters location:** This location. **Other U.S. locations:** Morrisville NC; Cranberry

Township PA; Waltham MA. **Listed on:** NASDAQ. **Stock exchange symbol:** NTAP. **Number of employees worldwide:** 2,345. **Annual sales/revenues:** $1.2 billion.

NEW HORIZONS WORLDWIDE
1900 South State College Boulevard, Anaheim CA 92806. 714/940-8000. **Fax:** 714/938-6004. **Contact:** Personnel. **E-mail address:** career.corp@newhorizons.com. **World Wide Web address:** http://www.newhorizons.com. **Description:** Offers computer training classes to individuals and businesses. New Horizons Worldwide operates over 240 centers worldwide. Founded in 1982. **NOTE:** Search and apply for positions online. **Positions advertised include:** Treasury Director; Proposal Writer; E-Learning Specialist; Product Specialist; Regional Vice President. **Corporate headquarters location:** This location. **Other U.S. locations:** Nationwide. **International locations:** Worldwide. **Listed on:** NASDAQ. **Stock exchange symbol:** NEWH. **Annual sales/revenues:** $139 million.

NORTEL NETWORKS
2603 Camino Ramon, San Ramon CA 94583. 925/867-2000. **Contact:** Human Resources. **E-mail address:** work@nortelnetworks.com. **World Wide Web address:** http://www.nortelnetworks.com. **Description:** Designs, produces, and supports multimedia access devices for use in building corporate, public, and Internet networks. The primary focus of the company's services is the consolidation of voice, fax, video, and data and multimedia traffic into a single network link. **Company slogan:** How the world shares ideas. **Office hours:** Monday - Friday, 8:00 a.m. - 5:00 p.m. **Corporate headquarters location:** Ontario Canada. **Other U.S. locations:** Nationwide. **International locations:** Worldwide. **Parent company:** Nortel. **Listed on:** New York Stock Exchange; Toronto Stock Exchange. **Stock exchange symbol:** NT. **President/CEO:** William Owens. **Annual sales/revenues:** $9.8 billion. **Number of employees worldwide:** 37,000.

NORTHROP GRUMMAN INFORMATION TECHNOLOGY
222 North Sepulveda Boulevard, Suite 1310, El Segundo CA 90245. 310/640-1050. **Contact:** Human Resources. **World Wide Web address:** http://www.it.northropgrumman.com. **Description:** Develops state-of-the-art software and information technology systems for the U.S. military and government. **Positions advertised include:** Software Engineer; Senior Embedded Systems Developer. **Corporate headquarters location:** Herndon VA. **Other U.S. locations:** Greenbelt MD; Falls Church VA; Dallas TX; Chantilly VA. **Operations at this facility include:** Research and Development. **Listed on:** New York Stock Exchange. **Stock exchange symbol:** NOC. **Number of employees worldwide:** 19,000.

NOVELL, INC.
1735 Technology Drive, Suite 790, San Jose CA 95110. 408/961-1037. **Contact:** Human Resources. **World Wide Web address:** http://www.novell.com. **Description:** Novell, Inc. develops software tools and systems, works in partnership with other companies, and provides computer network management services. **NOTE:** Search and apply for positions online. **Corporate headquarters location:** Waltham MA. **Other U.S. locations:** Nationwide. **International locations:** Worldwide. **Operations at this facility include:** This location is involved in marketing, software engineering, and administration. **Listed on:** NASDAQ. **Stock exchange symbol:** NOVL. **Number of employees nationwide:** 7,900.

NVIDIA CORPORATION
2701 San Tomas Expressway, Santa Clara CA 95050. 408/486-2000. **Fax:** 408/486-2200. **Contact:** Human Resources. **E-mail address:** hr@nvidia.com. **World Wide Web address:** http://www.nvidia.com. **Description**: Develops programmable graphics processor technologies for computing, consumer electronics, and mobile devices. **Positions advertised include:** Sr. ASIC Design Engineer; Architecture Engineer; Sr. Physical Design Engineer; System Software Engineer; 3D Tools Architect; Timing Methodology Engineer; NForce Sr. Product Manager; Video Systems Architect. **Other U.S. locations:** Nationwide. **Listed on:** NASDAQ. **Stock exchange symbol:** NVDA. **Number of employees worldwide:** 3,000.

OBJECTIVITY, INC.
640 West California Avenue, Suite 210, Sunnyvale CA 94086-2486. 408/992-7100. **Toll-free phone:** 800/767-6259. **Fax:** 408/992-7171. **Contact:** Human Resources. **E-mail address:** hr@objectivity.com. **World Wide Web address:** http://www.objectivity.com. **Description:** Manufactures computer database software. **NOTE:** Resumes may be submitted by mail, fax, or e-mail. **Corporate headquarters location:** This location.

OPTICAL RESEARCH ASSOCIATES
3280 East Foothill Boulevard, Suite 300, Pasadena CA 91107-3103. 626/795-9101. **Fax:** 626/795-9102. **Contact:** Human Resources. **World Wide Web address:** http://www.opticalres.com. **Description:** A supplier of imaging and illumination design/analysis software. Founded in 1963. **Positions advertised include:** Optical Illumination Software Engineer; Technical Business Analyst; Software Project Manager; Contract Software Test Engineer; Director, Illumination Engineering; Product Planner; Optical Sales Engineer. **Other U.S. locations:** Westborough MA; Tucson AZ; Novi MI.

OPTIMAL SYSTEMS SERVICES
2722 South Fairview Street, Santa Ana CA 92704-5947. 714/957-8500. **Toll-free phone:** 800/253-3434. **Fax:** 714/957-8705. **Contact:** Human Resources. **World Wide Web address:** http://www.oss.opmr.com. **Description:** Provides consulting, networking, software support, and maintenance services. **Corporate headquarters location:** This location. **Parent company:** Optimal Robotics Inc.

ORACLE CORPORATION
500 Oracle Parkway, LTN-1, Redwood Shores CA 94065. 650/506-7000. **Contact:** Recruiting. **E-mail address:** resumes_us@oracle.com. **World Wide Web address:** http://www.oracle.com. **Description:** Designs and manufactures database and information management software for business, and provides consulting services. **NOTE:** Search and apply for positions online. **Positions advertised include:** Software Development Manager; Applications Developer; Product Management Director; Support Engineer. **Corporate headquarters location:** This location. **Other U.S. locations:** Nationwide. **Operations at this facility include:** Administration; Sales. **Listed on:** NASDAQ. **Stock exchange symbol:** ORCL. **Number of employees nationwide:** 41,000.

OVERTURE SERVICES, INC.
74 North Pasadena Avenue, Pasadena CA 91103. 626/685-5600. **Fax:** 626/685-5601. **Contact:** Human Resources. **World Wide Web address:** http://www.overture.com. **Description:** Provides marketing services to companies doing business online. **Positions advertised include:** Account Executive; Associate Marketing Manager; Business Planning Analyst; Customer Service Representative; Development Manager; Network Support Engineer; Senior Java Developer; Senior Product Manager. **Special programs:** Internships. **Corporate headquarters location:** This location. **Other area locations:** Carlsbad CA; Sunnyvale CA. **Other U.S. locations:** Chicago IL; New York NY. **Parent company:** Yahoo! Inc. **Number of employees at this location:** Over 800.

PC PROFESSIONAL INC.
1615 Webster Street, Oakland CA 94612. 510/465-5700. **Fax:** 510/465-8327. **Contact:** Human Resources.

E-mail address: resume@pcprofessional.com. **World Wide Web address:** http://www.pcprofessional.com. **Description:** A value-added reseller of various types of computer hardware to corporate and consumer customers. **Positions advertised include:** Sales Account Manager; Field Service Engineer. **Corporate headquarters location:** This location.

PCMALL
2555 West 190th Street, Torrance CA 90504. 310/354-5600. **Toll-free phone:** 800/555-6255. **Contact:** Human Resources. **E-mail address:** salesrecruit@pcmall.com **World Wide Web address:** http://www.pcmall.com. **Description:** A leading reseller of computer products to businesses, governmental and educational institutions, and consumers. Founded in 1987. **Positions advertised include:** Manager of Data Mining and Analytics; Category Marketing Manager; Purchasing Manager; Account Executive. **Corporate headquarters location:** This location. **Listed on:** NASDAQ. **Stock exchange symbol:** MALL. **Annual sales/revenues:** $975 million.

PARASOFT CORPORATION
101 East Huntington Drive, Monrovia CA 91016. 626/256-3680. **Fax:** 626/256-6884. **Contact:** Human Resources. **E-mail address:** jobs@parasoft.com. **World Wide Web address:** http://www.parasoft.com. **Description:** Develops software using C and C++. **NOTE:** Submit resumes via e-mail or fax. **Positions advertised include:** Software Engineer; Sales Engineer; Technical Writer; Inside Sales Representative; Public Relations Specialist. **Corporate headquarters location:** This location.

PEREGRINE SYSTEMS INC.
3611 Valley Centre Drive, San Diego CA 92103. 858/481-5000. **Fax:** 858/481-1751. **Contact:** Human Resources. **World Wide Web address:** http://www.peregrine.com. **Description:** Designs and manufactures help-desk software. **NOTE:** Search and apply for positions online. **Positions advertised include:** Contract Technical Recruiter; Senior Software Engineer; Financial Analyst; Senior Revenue Accountant; Analytical Application Engineer. **Corporate headquarters location:** This location. **Listed on:** NASDAQ. **Stock exchange symbol:** PRGN.

PERFORMANCE TECHNOLOGIES
4669 Murphy Canyon Road, Suite 250, San Diego CA 92123. 858/627-1700. **Fax:** 858/627-1710. **Contact:** Human Resources. **E-mail address:** info@pt.com. **World Wide Web address:** http://www.pt.com. **Description:** Develops systems, platforms, components, and software for the communications infrastructure. Customers include the communications, military, and commercial markets. **NOTE:** Search for positions online. **Corporate headquarters location:** Rochester NY. **Other area locations:** San Luis Obispo CA. **Other U.S. locations:** Norwood MA. **Listed on:** NASDAQ. **Stock exchange symbol:** PTIX.

PHOENIX TECHNOLOGIES LTD.
915 Murphy Ranch Road, Milpitas CA 95035. 408/570-1000. **Toll-free phone:** 800/677-7305. **Fax:** 408/570-1001. **Contact:** Human Resources. **World Wide Web address:** http://www.phoenix.com. **Description:** Phoenix Technologies designs, develops, and markets systems software and end user software products. The Peripherals Division designs, develops, and supplies printer emulation software, page distribution languages, and controller hardware designs for the printing industry. The PhoenixPage imaging software architecture enables printer manufacturers to offer products that are compatible with the PostScript language, the PCL printer language, and other imaging standards. Phoenix Technologies' PC Division works with leading vendors and standards committees to ensure that Phoenix products enable manufacturers to develop and deploy next-generation PCs quickly and cost-effectively. The company's Package Products Division is a single-source publisher of MS-DOS, Windows, and other software packages. **NOTE:** Entry-level positions are offered. **Positions advertised include:** Senior Product Marketing Manager; Oracle Applications Developer; Director, QA and Operations; Principal Engineer. **Special programs:** Internships. **Corporate headquarters location:** This location. **Other U.S. locations:** Norwood MA; Durham NC; Beaverton OR; Austin TX; Houston TX; Brookfield WI. **International locations:** Worldwide. **Listed on:** NASDAQ. **Stock exchange symbol:** PTEC. **Annual sales/revenues:** $85 million. **Number of employees at this location:** 140. **Number of employees worldwide:** 800.

PINNACLE SYSTEMS
280 North Bernardo Avenue, Mountain View CA 94043. 650/526-1600. **Fax:** 650/526-1601. **Contact:** Human Resources. **E-mail address:** resume@pinnaclesys.com. **World Wide Web address:** http://www.pinnaclesys.com. **Description:** Develops digital and video-editing tools for both professional and consumer markets. Products include DVExtreme, a digital special effects system; and Studio 400, a video-editing system for consumers. **Positions advertised include:** Marketing Manager; Manufacturing Engineering Manager; Product Manager; Program Manager; Quality Engineer. **Corporate headquarters location:** This location. **Listed on:** NASDAQ. **Stock exchange symbol:** PCLE.

POLYCOM, INC.
4750 Willow Road, Pleasanton CA 94588-2708. 925/924-6000. **Toll-free phone:** 800/765-9266. **Fax:** 925/924-6100. **Contact:** Human Resources. **World Wide Web address:** http://www.polycom.com. **Description:** Creates, develops, and markets a variety of innovative videoconferencing devices and systems. **NOTE:** Search and apply for positions online. **Positions advertised include:** Assistant Corporate Controller; Financial Manager; Senior Applications Integegration Engineer; Senior Software Engineer. **Corporate headquarters location:** This location. **Listed on:** NASDAQ. **Stock exchange symbol:** PLCM. **Number of employees worldwide:** Over 1,000.

PORTRAIT DISPLAYS, INC.
6663 Owens Drive, Pleasanton CA 94588. 925/227-2700. **Fax:** 925/227-2705. **Contact:** Human Resources Department. **E-mail address:** hr@portrait.com. **World Wide Web address:** http://www.portrait.com. **Description:** A manufacturer of pivoting, portrait-capable computer monitors. The company's software line allows the user to view and edit documents in either landscape, or portrait orientation, and offers an image rotation function as well. **Positions advertised include:** Senior Sales/Application Engineer; Software Engineer; Software Development Manager. **Office hours:** Monday - Friday, 9:00 a.m. - 5:00 p.m. **Corporate headquarters location:** This location. **Listed on:** Privately held.

PRINTRONIX INC.
14600 Myford Road, P.O. Box 19559, Irvine CA 92623. 949/863-1900. **Toll-free phone:** 800/665-6210. **Fax:** 714/368-2940. **Contact:** Human Resources. **E-mail address:** employment@printronix.com. **World Wide Web address:** http://www.printronix.com. **Description:** Designs, manufactures, and markets impact line printers and laser printers for use with minicomputers, microcomputers, and other computer systems. **Positions advertised include:** Industrial Engineer; Worldwide Product Manager; Human Resources Administrative Assistant; Warehouse Supervisor; Accounting Supervisor; Business Development Manager. **Corporate headquarters location:** This location. **Operations at this facility include:** Administration; Manufacturing; Research and Development; Sales; Service. **Listed on:** NASDAQ. **Stock exchange symbol:** PTNX.

PROGRESS SOFTWARE CORPORATION
1720 South Amphlett Boulevard, Suite 300, San Mateo CA 94402. 650/372-3647. **Fax:** 650/341-8432.

Contact: Human Resources. **World Wide Web address:** http://www.progress.com. **Description:** A software company. **Corporate headquarters location:** Bedford MA. **Listed on:** NASDAQ. **Stock exchange symbol:** PRGS.

PROMISE TECHNOLOGY INC.
580 Cottonwood Drive, Milpitas CA 95035. 408/228-6300. **Fax:** 408/228-6407. **Contact:** Human Resources. **E-mail address:** humanresources@promise.com. **World Wide Web address:** http://www.promise.com. **Description:** Manufactures high-performance hard drive controller cards for use in IBM computers. **Positions advertised include:** Technical Support Specialist; Senior Software Engineer; Hardware Engineer, Advanced Storage; Product Test Engineer; Staff Accountant. **Corporate headquarters location:** This location.

QAD INC.
6450 Via Real, Carpinteria CA 93013. 805/684-6614. **Fax:** 805/565-4202. **Contact:** Tom Adam, Corporate Recruiter. **E-mail address:** tma@qad.com. **World Wide Web address:** http://www.qad.com. **Description:** QAD develops software including MFG/PRO, a software package designed to aid in supply and distribution management for large companies. **NOTE:** Search and apply for positions online. **Positions advertised include:** Senior International Tax Analyst; Project Manager; Corporate Financial Systems Administrator; Test Automation Engineer. **Corporate headquarters location:** This location. **Operations at this facility include:** This location houses administrative offices. **Listed on:** NASDAQ. **Stock exchange symbol:** QADI.

QLOGIC CORPORATION
26650 Aliso Viejo Parkway, Aliso Viejo CA 92656. 949/389-6000. **Toll-free phone:** 800/662-4471. **Fax:** 949/389-6009. **Contact:** Human Resources. **E-mail address:** hr@qlogic.com. **World Wide Web address:** http://www.qlogic.com. **Description:** Develops, manufactures, and markets network connectivity components. Founded in 1985. **NOTE:** Search and apply for positions online. **Positions advertised include:** Analog Circuit Design Engineers; Layout Engineer; Principal DVT Engineer; Embedded Software Engineer; Foundry Engineering Manager; Principal Software Engineer. **Corporate headquarters location:** This location. **Listed on:** NASDAQ. **Stock exchange symbol:** QLGC. **Annual sales/revenues:** More than $100 million.

QANTEL TECHNOLOGIES
3506 Breakwater Court, Hayward CA 94545-3611. 510/731-2080. **Toll-free phone:** 800/666-3686. **Fax:** 510/731-2075. **Contact:** Human Resources. **E-mail address:** jobs@qantel.com. **World Wide Web address:** http://www.qantel.com. **Description:** Manufactures coprocessor systems and related peripherals. **Positions advertised include:** Applications Software Developer; Java/Web Developer; Manufacturing Software Product Manager; Software Development Project Manager. **Corporate headquarters location:** This location.

QUADRAMED
1050 Los Vallecitos Boulevard, Suite 105, San Marcos CA 92069. 760/752-5160. **Toll-free phone:** 800/767-6374. **Fax:** 760/752-5172. **Contact:** Human Resources Department. **E-mail address:** resume@quadramed.com. **World Wide Web address:** http://www.quadramed.com. **Description:** Develops and markets specialized decision support software designed to improve the organizational and clinical effectiveness of hospitals, academic medical centers, managed care providers, large physician groups, and other health care providers. **Corporate headquarters location:** Reston VA. **Listed on:** NASDAQ. **Stock exchange symbol:** QMDC.

QUALITY SYSTEMS, INC.
18191 Von Karman Avenue, Suite 450, Irvine CA 92612. 949/255-2600. **Toll-free phone:** 800/888-7955. **Fax:** 949/255-2605. **Contact:** Human Resources. **E-mail address:** hr@qsii.com. **World Wide Web address:** http://www.qsii.com. **Description:** Develops and markets computerized information processing systems primarily to group dental and medical practices. The systems provide advanced computer-based automation in various aspects of group practice management including the retention of patient information, treatment planning, appointment scheduling, billing, insurance claims processing, electronic insurance claims submission, allocation of income among group professionals, managed care reporting, word processing, and accounting. Founded in 1973. **NOTE:** Entry-level positions are offered. **Positions advertised include:** Programmer Analyst; Customer Support Representative. **Special programs:** Internships. **Corporate headquarters location:** This location. **Other U.S. locations:** Horsham PA; Atlanta GA. **Listed on:** NASDAQ. **Stock exchange symbol:** QSII. **Number of employees nationwide:** 230.

QUANTUM CORPORATION
1650 Technology Drive, Suite 700, San Jose CA 95110-1382. 408/944-4000. **Fax:** 408/944-4040. **Contact:** Human Resources. **E-mail address:** jobs@quantum.com. **World Wide Web address:** http://www.quantum.com. **Description:** Designs, manufactures, and markets small hard disk drives used in desktop PCs, workstations, and notebook computers. **NOTE:** Search and apply for positions online. **Positions advertised include:** Software Engineer; Systems Management Architect; Finance Project Manager. **Corporate headquarters location:** This location. **Listed on:** New York Stock Exchange. **Stock exchange symbol:** DSS. **Annual sales/revenues:** $870 million. **Number of employees nationwide:** 2,455.

QUICK EAGLE NETWORKS
830 Maude Avenue, Mountain View CA 94043. 650/962-8282. **Fax:** 650/962-7950. **Contact:** Human Resources. **E-mail address:** jobs@quickeagle.com. **World Wide Web address:** http://www.quickeagle.com. **Description:** Develops, manufactures, and markets high-speed digital access products for the WAN marketplace. **Positions advertised include:** Accounting Manager; Vice President, Engineering; Hardware Product Architect; Hardware Engineer; Technical Writer. **Corporate headquarters location:** This location.

QUICKLOGIC CORPORATION
1277 Orleans Drive, Sunnyvale CA 94089-1138. 408/990-4000. **Fax:** 408/990-4040. **Contact:** Human Resources. **E-mail address:** jobsusa@quicklogic.com. **World Wide Web address:** http://www.quicklogic.com. **Description:** Manufactures and distributes field programmable logic units. **Positions advertised include:** Marketing Communications Specialist; ERP Report Developer. **Corporate headquarters location:** This location. **International locations:** Toronto Canada; Bangalore India. **Listed on:** NASDAQ. **Stock exchange symbol:** QUIK.

RAINING DATA CORPORATION
25A Technology Drive, Irvine CA 92614-5846. 949/442-4400. **Fax:** 949/250-8187. **Contact:** Human Resources. **E-mail address:** hr@rainingdata.com. **World Wide Web address:** http://www.rainingdata.com. **Description:** Develops, markets, and supports software products for the development and deployment of applications for accessing multiuser databases in workgroup and enterprisewide client/server computing environments. The company's products are used by corporations, system integrators, small businesses, and independent consultants to deliver custom information management applications for a wide range of uses including financial management, decision support, executive information, sales and marketing, and multimedia authoring systems. In addition to these products, Raining Data provides consulting, technical support, and training to help plan, analyze, implement, and maintain applications software based on the company's technology. **Corporate headquarters**

location: This location. **Listed on:** NASDAQ. **Stock exchange symbol:** RDTA.

RATIONAL SOFTWARE CORPORATION
18880 Homestead Road, Cupertino CA 95014. 408/863-9900. **Contact:** Human Resources. **World Wide Web address:** http://www.rational.com. **Description:** Develops, markets, and supports embedded software products for Web and e-commerce applications. The company's products operate on both Windows and UNIX systems. **Corporate headquarters location:** This location. **International locations:** Worldwide. **Parent company:** IBM.

RICOH BUSINESS SYSTEMS
1123A Warner Avenue, Tustin CA 92780. 714/481-4020. **Fax:** 714-481-4132. **Contact:** Human Resources. **World Wide Web address:** http://www.ricoh-/usa.com/rbs. **Description:** Develops, manufactures, and markets data handling and output equipment. The company's products include printers and digital communications equipment. **Parent company:** Ricoh Corporation.

RICOH DIGITAL CAMERA DIVISION
242 East Airport Drive, Suite 102, San Bernardino CA 92408. 909/890-9039. **Fax:** 909/890-9045. **Contact:** Human Resources. **World Wide Web address:** http://www.ricohzone.com. **Description:** The Digital Camera Division is a leader in the development, manufacture, distribution and OEM licensing of imaging products. **Corporate headquarters location:** West Caldwell NJ. **Parent company:** Ricoh Corporation.

RICOH ELECTRONIC DEVICES
One Ricoh Square, 1100 Valencia Avenue, Tustin CA 92780. 714/566-2500. **Contact:** Human Resources. **E-mail address:** jobs@rei.ricoh.com. **World Wide Web address:** http://www.rei.ricoh.com. **Description:** A manufacturer of advanced office automation equipment including digital copiers, peripherals, thermal media, and toner. **NOTE:** Search and apply for positions online. **Positions advertised include:** Process Training Coordinator; QA Engineer; Buyer; Manufacturing Engineer; Production Technician. **Other area locations:** Santa Ana CA; Irvine CA. **Other U.S. locations:** Lawrenceville GA.

RIVERDEEP, INC.
100 Pine Street, Suite 1900, San Francisco CA 94111. 415/659-2000. **Fax:** 415/659-1877. **Contact:** Human Resources. **E-mail address:** resumes@riverdeep.net. **World Wide Web address:** http://www.riverdeep.com. **Description:** Produces education software. **Positions advertised include:** Database Marketing Manager; Channel Marketing Manager; Technology Architect; Executive Producer, Schools; Senior Instructional Designer; Director of Technology. **Corporate headquarters location:** This location. **Other U.S. locations:** Cedar Rapids IA; Boston MA.

SAP AMERICA, INC.
18101 Von Karman Avenue, Suite 900, Irvine CA 92612. 949/622-2200. **Fax:** 949/622-2201. **Contact:** Human Resources. **World Wide Web address:** http://www.sap.com. **Description:** Develops a variety of client/server computer software packages including programs for finance, human resources, and materials management applications. **NOTE:** Search and apply for positions online. **Corporate headquarters location:** Newtown Square PA. **Other U.S. locations:** Nationwide. **International locations:** Germany. **Parent company:** SAP AG. **Listed on:** New York Stock Exchange. **Stock exchange symbol:** SAP. **Number of employees nationwide:** 3,000. **Number of employees worldwide:** 30,000.

SMS TECHNOLOGIES, INC.
9877 Waples Street, San Diego CA 92121. 858/587-6900. **Fax:** 858/457-2069. **Contact:** Personnel Manager. **E-mail address:** resumes@smstech.com. **World Wide Web address:** http://www.smstech.com. **Description:** Provides turnkey electronic manufacturing services to the telecommunications, medical electronics, computer, and industrial equipment industries. **NOTE:** Second and third shift positions are offered. **Positions advertised include:** Manufacturing Engineer; RF Technicians; Program Manager. **Special programs:** Training. **Corporate headquarters location:** This location. **Operations at this facility include:** Administration; Divisional Headquarters; Manufacturing; Research and Development. **Listed on:** Privately held. **CEO:** Robert L. Blumberg. **Annual sales/revenues:** $21 - $50 million. **Number of employees at this location:** 200.

SAFENET, INC.
6 Venture, Suite 315, Irvine CA 92618. 949/450-7300. **Contact:** Human Resources. **E-mail address:** humanresources@safenet-inc.com. **World Wide Web address:** http://www.safenet-inc.com. **Description:** Develops security-related technology such as secure Web servers and Virtual Pirate Network acceleration boards, Internet software distribution solutions, data, voice, and satellite security systems, and smart card readers. **NOTE:** Resumes may be submitted via mail, fax, or e-mail. Send resumes to: Safenet, Inc., Attention: Human Resources, 4690 Millenium Drive, Belcamp MD 21017. Fax: 410/931-7524. **Corporate headquarters location:** Belcamp MD. **Listed on:** NASDAQ. **Stock exchange symbol:** SFNT.

SAGE SOFTWARE, INC.
56 Technology Drive, Irvine CA 92618-2301. 949/753-1222. **Toll-free phone:** 800/854-3415. **Fax:** 949/753-0374. **Contact:** Human Resources. **World Wide Web address:** http://www.sagesoftware.com. **Description:** Develops, markets, and supports high-end microcomputer accounting software. **Positions advertised include:** Design Analyst; Senior Customer Support Analyst; Senior Accountant; Financial Analyst; Copy Writer; Director, Installed Base Sales. **Corporate headquarters location:** This location. **Parent company:** Sage Group plc (London England). **Number of employees nationwide:** 2,100.

SANDISK CORPORATION
140 Caspian Court, Sunnyvale CA 94089. 408/542-0500. **Fax:** 408/542-0604. **Contact:** Human Resources. **E-mail address:** careers@sandisk.com. **World Wide Web address:** http://www.sandisk.com. **Description:** Manufactures computer components including memory cards. **Positions advertised include:** Developer; Business Systems Analyst; Design Engineer; Industrial Design Engineer; Software Engineer; Accountant. **Corporate headquarters location:** This location. **Listed on:** NASDAQ. **Stock exchange symbol:** SNDK. **Annual sales/revenues:** Over $1 billion.

SAPIENT CORPORATION
225 Broadway, Suite 1575, San Diego CA 92101. 619/342-4500. **Fax:** 305/359-3235. **Contact:** Director of Hiring. **World Wide Web address:** http://www.sapient.com. **Description:** Provides systems integration, consulting, and software integration services. Founded in 1991. **NOTE:** Search and apply for positions online. **Corporate headquarters location:** Cambridge MA. **Other area locations:** San Diego CA. **Other U.S. locations:** Atlanta GA; Detroit MI; Miami FL; Jersey City NJ; Washington DC; Chicago IL. **International locations:** England; Germany; India. **Listed on:** NASDAQ. **Stock exchange symbol:** SAPE. **Annual sales/revenues:** $184 million.

SAVVIS COMMUNICATIONS
17836 Gillette Avenue, Irvine CA 92614. 949/608-2739. **Contact:** Human Resources. **World Wide Web address:** http://www.savvis.net. **Description:** A global IT utility provider that delivers hosting, network, and application services to 110 cities in 45 countries. **NOTE:** Search and apply for positions online. **Positions advertised include:** Senior Network Systems Engineer; Senior Program Manager. **Corporate headquarters location:** St. Louis MO.

SCIENCE APPLICATIONS INTERNATIONAL CORPORATION
10260 Campus Point Drive, San Diego CA 92121. 858/826-7624. **Contact:** Human Resources. **E-mail address:** jobs@saic.com. **World Wide Web address:** http://www.saic.com. **Description:** Offers technology development, computer system integration, and technology support services. Founded in 1969. **NOTE:** Search and apply for positions online. **Positions advertised include:** Project Control Analyst; Tax Accountant; Executive Assistant; Human Resources Assistant; Programmer; Senior Software Engineer; Network Engineer; Senior Mechanical Engineer; Senior Radio Engineer. **Special programs:** Internships. **Corporate headquarters location:** This location. **Other area locations:** Statewide. **Subsidiaries include:** AMSEC; Carreker-Antinori; Danet; GSC; Global Integrity Corp.; Hicks & Assoc.; INTESA; Leadership 2000; Network Solutions, Inc.; PAI. **Annual sales/revenues:** $6.7 billion. **Number of employees worldwide:** 43,000.

SCITECH SOFTWARE INC.
180 East Fourth Street, Suite 300, Chico CA 95928. 530/894-8400. **Fax:** 530/894-9069. **Contact:** Human Resources. **E-mail address:** career@scitech.com. **World Wide Web address:** http://www.scitechsoft.com. **Description:** A leading developer of operating system drivers for embedded systems.

SEAGATE TECHNOLOGY
920 Disc Drive, Scotts Valley CA 95067-0360. 831/438-6550. **Contact:** Human Resources. **World Wide Web address:** http://www.seagate.com. **Description:** Designs and manufactures data storage devices and related products including hard-disk drives, tape drives, software, and systems for a variety of computer-related applications and operating systems. **Positions advertised include:** Senior Programmer Analyst; Office Assistant; Senior Accountant; Investigator. **Corporate headquarters location:** This location. **Other U.S. locations:** OK. **Annual sales/revenues:** $6.5 billion. **Number of employees nationwide:** 87,000.

SECURE COMPUTING
4810 Harwood Road, San Jose CA 95124-5206. 408/979-6100. **Toll-free phone:** 800/692-5625. **Fax:** 408/979-6501. **Contact:** Human Resources. **World Wide Web address:** http://www.securecomputing.com. **Description:** Provides a variety of network security products, including firewalls, user identification and authorization software, and Web filtering applications. Its firewall and virtual private network (VPN) gateways enable companies to securely manage and maintain network access for employees, customers, and partners. Secure Computing also provides software that enables network administrators to restrict access to specific Web sites to streamline system resources and improve employee productivity. **NOTE:** Search and apply for positions online. **Listed on:** NASDAQ. **Stock exchange symbol:** SCUR.

SEEBEYOND
800 East Royal Oaks Drive, Monrovia CA 91016-6347. 626/471-6000. **Fax:** 626/471-6100. **Contact:** Human Resources. **World Wide Web address:** http://www.seebeyond.com. **Description:** Develops data interface engines and database software for enterprisewide solutions. Products include e*Gate, an enterprise integration program. **Positions advertised include:** Business Process Architect; Engagement Manager; Senior Consultant; Software Engineer. **Corporate headquarters location:** This location. **Parent company:** Sun Microsystems, Inc.

SHARP SYSTEMS OF AMERICA (SSA)
5901 Bolsa Avenue, Huntington Beach CA 92647. 714/903-4600. **Fax:** 714/903-4716. **Contact:** Human Resources. **E-mail address:** hr@sharpsystems.com. **World Wide Web address:** http://www.sharp-business.com. **Description:** a division of Sharp Electronics Corporation. SSA markets, sells and supports computing systems technologies and products for corporate business environments throughout North America.

SIEBEL SYSTEMS, INC.
2207 Bridgepointe Parkway, San Mateo CA 94404. 650/295-5000. **Toll-free phone:** 800/647-4300. **Contact:** Human Resources. **World Wide Web address:** http://www.siebel.com. **Description:** A leading provider of e-commerce application software. **NOTE:** Search and apply for positions online. **Positions advertised include:** Curriculum Developer; Lead Software Engineer; Senior QA Design Engineer; Senior Recruiter; Senior Financial Analyst; Senior Public Relations Manager. **Corporate headquarters location:** This location. **Parent company:** Oracle. **Annual sales/revenues:** $1.35 billion. **Number of employees worldwide:** 5,000.

SIEMENS MEDICAL SOLUTIONS HEALTH SERVICES
3010 Old Ranch Parkway, Suite 450, Seal Beach CA 90740. 562/340-4000. **Contact:** Recruiter. **World Wide Web address:** http://www.siemensmedical.com. **Description:** Siemens Medical Solutions is a leading provider of health care information systems and service solutions to hospitals, multi-entity health care corporations, integrated health networks, physician groups, and other health care providers in North America and Europe. Siemens Medical Solutions also provides a full complement of solutions for the newly emerging community health information networks, which includes payers and employers as well as providers. The company offers a comprehensive line of health care information systems including clinical, financial, administrative, ambulatory, and decision support systems, for both the public and private health care sectors. These systems are offered on computers operating at the customer site, at the Siemens Information Services Center, or as part of a distributed network. The company also provides a portfolio of professional services including systems installation, support, and education. In addition, the company provides specialized consulting services for the design and integration of software and networks, facilities management, information systems planning, and systems-related process reengineering. **NOTE:** Please contact the corporate Human Resources Department for employment information: 601/219-6300. **Corporate headquarters location:** Malvern PA. **Other U.S. locations:** Nationwide. **Operations at this facility include:** This location is a technical support office. **Listed on:** New York Stock Exchange. **Stock exchange symbol:** SI. **Number of employees worldwide:** 31,000.

SILICON GRAPHICS INC. (SGI)
1500 Crittenden Lane, Mountain View CA 94043. 650/960-1980. **Contact:** Human Resources. **World Wide Web address:** http://www.sgi.com. **Description:** Manufactures a family of workstation and server systems that are used by engineers, scientists, and other creative professionals to develop, analyze, and simulate complex, three-dimensional objects. **Positions advertised include:** Public Relations Director; Internal Audit Director; Administrator. **Corporate headquarters location:** This location. **Listed on:** New York Stock Exchange. **Stock exchange symbol:** SGI. **Number of employees worldwide:** 3,100.

SIMPLETECH, INC.
3001 Daimler Street, Santa Ana CA 92705. 949/476-1180. **Toll-free phone:** 800/367-7330. **Fax:** 949/476-0852. **Contact:** Human Resources. **E-mail address:** jobs@simpletech.com. **World Wide Web address:** http://www.simpletech.com. **Description:** Designs and manufactures computer memory products, portable storage devices, and PC cards. Founded in 1990. **NOTE:** Second and third shifts are offered. **Positions advertised include:** Product Marketing Manager; Account Representative; Software Engineer; Director, Product Engineering. **Corporate headquarters location:** This location. **International locations:** Canada; Scotland. **Listed on:** NASDAQ. **Stock**

exchange symbol: STEC. **Annual sales/revenues:** $211 million. **Number of employees at this location:** 300. **Number of employees nationwide:** 430.

SMART MODULAR TECHNOLOGIES
4211 Starboard Drive, Fremont CA 94538. 510/623-1231. **Contact:** Human Resources Department. **E-mail address:** careers@smartm.com. **World Wide Web address:** http://www.smartm.com. **Description:** Manufactures and distributes computer components including PC cards and memory modules. **Positions advertised included:** Senior PCB Designer; SEC Reporting Manager; Inventory Analyst. **Corporate headquarters location:** This location. **Other area locations:** Irvine CA. **Parent company:** Selectron. **Listed on:** New York Stock Exchange. **Stock exchange symbol:** SLR.

SMITH MICRO SOFTWARE, INC.
51 Columbia Street, Suite 200, Aliso Viejo CA 92656. 949/362-5800. **Fax:** 949/362-2300. **Contact:** Human Resources. **E-mail address:** jobs@smithmicro.com. **World Wide Web address:** http://www.smithmicro.com. **Description:** A computer consulting firm. **Positions advertised include:** Sales Representative; Customer Support Technician. **Corporate headquarters location:** This location. **Other U.S. locations:** Boulder CO. **Listed on:** NASDAQ. **Stock exchange symbol:** SMSI.

SOLID OAK SOFTWARE, INC.
P.O. Box 6826, Santa Barbara CA 93160. 805/967-9853. **Fax:** 805/967-1614. **Contact:** Human Resources. **World Wide Web address:** http://www.solidoak.com. **Description:** Develops access-control software. **Corporate headquarters location:** This location.

SPANSION INC.
915 Deguigne Drive, P.O. Box 3453, Sunnyvale CA 94088-3453. 408/962-2500. **Contact:** Human Resources. **World Wide Web address:** http://www.spansion.com. **Description**: Manufactures and markets flash memory devices for use in electronic devices such as wireless telephones, networking equipment, and automotive subsystems. The company was formed in 2003 by a joint venture between Advanced Micro Devices and Fujitsu. **Positions advertised include:** AMHS Equipment Engineer; Associate Engineer; Business Operations/Production Control; Business Development Analyst; Business Development Marketing Manager; CAD Design Engineer; Calibre SVRF Engineer; Corporate Counsel Corporate Marketing Manager. **Listed on:** NASDAQ. **Stock exchange symbol:** SPSN.

SPEAR TECHNOLOGIES
595 Market Street, 4th Floor, San Francisco CA 94105. 415/593-2999. **Fax:** 415/593-3207. **Contact:** Human Resources. **E-mail address:** jobs@speartechnologies.com. **World Wide Web address:** http://www.speartechnologies.com. **Description:** Develops, markets, and supports a line of maintenance management software for the transportation industry. **Positions advertised include:** Human Resources Manager; Senior Software Engineer; Senior Quality Engineer. **Corporate headquarters location:** This location. **Other U.S. locations:** Hartford CT. **International locations:** Netherlands. **Parent company:** Hansen Information Technologies. **Number of employees at this location:** 225.

SPECTRAL DYNAMICS INC.
2730 Orchard Parkway, San Jose CA 95134-2012. 408/678-3500. **Contact:** Personnel. **World Wide Web address:** http://www.spectraldynamics.com. **Description:** Specializes in the design and manufacture of computer-controlled test, measurement, and development systems and software for a wide variety of customers in three high-tech markets: electronic equipment manufacturers, mechanical equipment manufacturers, and semiconductor manufacturers. Products are used for design verification testing and process improvement. **Corporate headquarters location:** This location.

SPESCOM SOFTWARE
10052 Mesa Ridge Court, Suite 100, San Diego CA 92121-2916. 858/625-3000. **Fax:** 858/625-3010. **Contact:** Human Resources. **E-mail address:** resumes@spescom.com. **World Wide Web address:** http://www.spescomsoftware.com. **Description:** Designs, develops, integrates, and markets electronic document management software for industrial, utility, commercial, and government applications. **Positions advertised include:** Configuration Management Consultant. **Corporate headquarters location:** This location. **International locations:** England. **Parent company:** Spescom Limited (South Africa). **Number of employees at this location:** 85.

SUN MICROSYSTEMS, INC.
4150 Network Circle, UMIL 15-106, Santa Clara CA 95054. 650/960-1300. **Toll-free phone:** 800/555-9786. **Contact:** Human Resources. **World Wide Web address:** http://www.sun.com. **Description:** Produces high-performance computer systems, workstations, servers, CPUs, peripherals, and operating systems software. Products are sold to engineering, scientific, technical, and commercial markets worldwide. **NOTE:** Search and apply for positions online. **Corporate headquarters location:** This location. **Subsidiaries include:** Forte Software Inc. manufactures enterprise application integration software. **Listed on:** NASDAQ. **Stock exchange symbol:** SUNW. **Number of employees nationwide:** 26,300.

SUNGARD FINANCIAL SYSTEMS INC.
23975 Park Sorrento, Suite 400, Calabasas CA 91302. 818/223-2200. **Fax:** 818/223-2201. **Contact:** Human Resources. **E-mail address:** jobs@sungard.com. **World Wide Web address:** http://www.sungard.com. **Description:** Develops and sells investment portfolio software for financial institutions. **Corporate headquarters location:** Wayne PA. **Parent company:** SunGard Data Systems provides specialized computer services, mainly proprietary investment support systems for the financial services industry and disaster recovery services. The company's disaster recovery services include alternate-site backup, testing, and recovery services for IBM, DEC, Prime, Stratus, Tandem, and Unisys computer installations. The company's computer service unit provides remote-access IBM computer processing, direct marketing, and automated mailing services. **Listed on:** New York Stock Exchange. **Stock exchange symbol:** SDS.

SUNRISE TELECOM
302 Enzo Drive, San Jose CA 95138. 408/363-8000. **Fax:** 408/363-8313. **Contact:** Human Resources. **World Wide Web address:** http://www.sunrisetelecom.com. **Description:** Manufacturer of telecommunication equipment used for fiber optics, cable, and Internet products and services. **NOTE:** See website for job listings. To apply, mail or fax resumes. Entry-level positions offered. Search and apply for positions online. **Positions advertised include:** Purchasing Agent; Manufacturing Test Engineer; IP Hardware Engineer; Windows Application Software Engineer; Regional Sales Manager; National Sales/Marketing Engineer; Product Manager. **Corporate headquarters location:** This location. **Other U.S. locations:** GA. **International locations:** Canada; Italy; China; Germany, Japan. **Listed on:** NASDAQ. **Stock exchange symbol:** SRTI.

SYBASE, INC.
One Sybase Drive, Dublin CA 94568. 925/236-5000. **Contact:** Human Resources. **World Wide Web address:** http://www.sybase.com. **Description:** Develops, markets, and supports a full line of relational database management software products and services for integrated, enterprisewide information management systems. **NOTE:** Search and apply for positions online. **Positions advertised include:** Finance Director; Senior Product Support Analyst; Senior PR Specialist; Senior Software Engineer; Senior Project and Planning Manager. **Corporate headquarters location:** This location. **Listed on:** New York Stock Exchange. **Stock**

exchange symbol: SY. **Number of employees worldwide:** 4,000.

SYMANTEC CORPORATION
20330 Stevens Creek Boulevard, Cupertino CA 95014. 408/517-8000. **Contact:** Human Resources Staffing. **E-mail address:** jobs@symantec.com. **World Wide Web address:** http://www.symantec.com. **Description:** Symantec Corporation is a global organization that develops, manufactures, and markets software products for individuals and businesses. The company is a vendor of utility software for stand-alone and networked personal computers. In addition, the company offers a wide range of project management products, productivity applications, and development languages and tools. The company is organized into several product groups that are devoted to product marketing, engineering, technical support, quality assurance, and documentation. Founded in 1982. **Positions advertised include:** Senior Senior Accountant; Senior Administrative Specialist; Accounting Manager. **Special programs:** Internships. **Corporate headquarters location:** This location. **Operations at this facility include:** This location houses finance, sales, and marketing operations. **Listed on:** NASDAQ. **Stock exchange symbol:** SYMC. **Number of employees nationwide:** 1,200.

SYMBOL TECHNOLOGIES, INC.
6480 Via Del Oro, San Jose CA 95119. 408/528-2700. **Fax:** 408/528-2780. **Contact:** Professional Staffing. **E-mail address:** jobopps@symbol.com. **World Wide Web address:** http://www.symbol.com. **Description:** Designs, manufactures, and sells various lines of portable and nonportable computers and systems for business information and bill collection applications. Clients include retail food stores, drug stores, and hardware stores. **NOTE:** Resumes should be sent to Human Resources Department, Symbol Technologies, Inc., One Symbol Plaza, Holtsville NY 11742-1300. **Positions advertised include:** Business Development Services Specialist; Network Product Development Engineer; Mobile Solutions Software Architect; Software Development Manager. **Corporate headquarters location:** Holtsville NY. **Operations at this facility include:** Education; Repairs; Sales; Systems/Software Services. **Listed on:** New York Stock Exchange. **Stock exchange symbol:** SBL.

SYNNEX CORPORATION
44201 Nobel Drive, Fremont CA 94538. 510/656-3333. Fax: 510/668-3495. **Contact:** Human Resources. **E-mail address:** staffing@synnex.com. **World Wide Web address:** http://www.synnex.com. **Description**: An information technology supply chain services company that provides IT distribution, contract assembly services, and logistics services to original equipment manufacturers and value-added resellers. **Positions advertised include:** Accounts Payables Analyst; Program Manager; Associate Product Manager; Resident Planner; Supply Chain Analyst; Outside CTI Sales Representative; Business Development Representative-CAT; Vendor Claims Specialist; Benefits Analyst; Field Account Executive-Solutions Architect; Inventory/Procurement Analyst; Product Manager; Business Development Representative-AMD; Business Development Representative-Storage; Compensation Analyst; Internal Auditor.

SYNOPSYS INC.
700 East Middlefield Road, Mountain View CA 94043. 650/584-5000. **Toll-free phone:** 800/541-7737. **Contact:** Human Resources Department. **E-mail address:** employment@synopsys.com. **World Wide Web address:** http://www.synopsys.com. **Description:** Develops, markets, and supports high-level design automation software for designers of integrated circuits and electronic systems. **NOTE:** Search and apply for positions online. **Positions advertised include:** Compliance Analyst; Senior Applications Consultant; Corporate Applications Engineer; Financial Analyst; Marketing Director; Public Relations Specialist; Software Engineer; R&D Engineer. **Corporate headquarters location:** This location. **Listed on:** NASDAQ. **Stock exchange symbol:** SNPS. **Number of employees at this location:** 415. **Number of employees worldwide:** 4,000.

TELE ATLAS
1605 Adams Drive, Menlo Park CA 94025. 650/328-3825. **Contact:** Human Resources. **E-mail address:** jobs@teleatlas.com. **World Wide Web address:** http://www.teleatlas.com. **Description:** Develops digital mapping software for the automotive and transportation industries. **NOTE:** Search and apply for positions online. **Positions advertised include:** Senior Software Engineer. **Corporate headquarters location:** Lebanon NH.

3COM CORPORATION
575 Anton Boulevard, Suite 300, Costa Mesa CA 92626. 310/348-8110. **Contact:** Human Resources. **World Wide Web address:** http://www.3com.com. **Description:** 3Com is a *Fortune* 500 company delivering global data networking solutions to organizations around the world. 3Com designs, manufactures, markets, and supports a broad range of ISO 9000-compliant global data networking solutions including routers, hubs, remote access servers, switches, and adapters for Ethernet, Token Ring, and high-speed networks. These products enable computers to communicate at high speeds and share resources including printers, disk drives, modems, and minicomputers. **Positions advertised include:** Account Executive. **Special programs:** Internships. **Corporate headquarters location:** Marlborough MA. **Other area locations:** Santa Clara CA; Los Angeles CA. **Operations at this facility include:** Administration; Manufacturing; Research and Development; Sales; Service. **Listed on:** NASDAQ. **Stock exchange symbol:** COMS. **Annual sales/revenues:** More than $100 million. **Number of employees nationwide:** 5,000.

TITAN CORPORATION
3033 Science Park Road, San Diego CA 92121. 858/552-9500. **Contact:** Personnel. **World Wide Web address:** http://www.titan.com. **Description:** A leading provider of information technology and communications services and products primarily used by US government agencies such as the Department of Defense and the Department of Homeland Security. Founded in 1981. **NOTE:** Search and apply for positions online. **Positions advertised include:** Applications Programmer; Chief Scientist; Configuration Manager; Field Engineer; Financial Analyst; Junior Software Engineer. **Corporate headquarters location:** This location. **Parent company:** L-3 Communications. **Listed on:** New York Stock Exchange. **Stock exchange symbol:** TTN. **Annual sales/revenues:** Approximately $2 billion. **Number of employees worldwide:** 12,000.

TOSHIBA AMERICA INFORMATION SYSTEMS INC.
9740 Irvine Boulevard, Irvine CA 92718. 949/583-3000. **Fax:** 949/587-6436. **Contact:** Human Resources. **E-mail address:** employment@tais.com. **World Wide Web address:** http://www.toshiba.com. **Description:** Develops, markets, and supports computers, printers, fax machines, security imaging systems, industrial video products, voice processing systems, and medical and PC cameras. **NOTE:** Apply online or e-mail resume as a word attachment. **Positions advertised include:** Finance Manager; Tax Specialist; Senior Engineer; Technical Support Specialist; Sales Support Representative. **Corporate headquarters location:** New York NY. **Parent company:** Toshiba America Inc.

TRIDENT MICROSYSTEMS
1090 East Arques Avenue, Sunnyvale CA 94085-4601. 408/991-8800. **Fax:** 408/733-1087. **Contact:** Human Resources. **E-mail address:** trid-hr@tridentmicro.com. **World Wide Web address:** http://www.tridentmicro.com. **Description:** Designs, develops, and markets integrated graphics ICs and multimedia audio/visual chips for

PCs. Founded in 1988. **Positions advertised include:** Investor Relations Specialist. **Corporate headquarters location:** This location. **Other U.S. locations:** Chandler AZ. **Operations at this facility include:** Sales; Technical Support. **Listed on:** NASDAQ. **Stock exchange symbol:** TRID. **Number of employees at this location:** 300.

TRIMBLE NAVIGATION LIMITED
935 Stewart Drive, Sunnyvale CA 94085. 408/481-8000. **Toll-free phone:** 800/874-6253. **Contact:** Human Resources. **E-mail address:** jobs@trimble.com. **World Wide Web address:** http://www.trimble.com. **Description**: Develops global positioning system (GPS) technology as well as other positioning technologies, and provides advanced GPS components, wireless communications, and software. **Positions advertised include:** Test Engineer; Project Manager; Software Engineer; Project Leader; Financial Analyst; Sr. Financial Analyst; New Product Introduction Specialist; MarCom Manager; SEC Analyst; Member Technical Staff; Product Applications Engineer; Sr. Consolidations Accountant; Senior Tax Analyst; FAS 109 Tax Manager; Associate FAS 109 Tax Controller; Supplier Quality Engineer Manager; Master Scheduler/Planner; Worldwide Technical Services Manager; TMS/System Engineer; Firmware Engineer; MTS-System Engineer. **Other area locations:** Santa Clara CA. **Other U.S. locations:** Chandler AZ; Corvallis OR; Dayton OH; Westminster CO. **Listed on:** NASDAQ. **Stock exchange symbol:** TRMB. **Number of employees worldwide:** 2,400.

UNISYS CORPORATION
10850 Via Frontera, San Diego CA 92127. 858/451-3000. **Fax:** 858/451-4656. **Contact:** Human Resources Manager. **World Wide Web address:** http://www.unisys.com. **Description:** Provides technology services and solutions in consulting, systems integration, outsourcing, infrastructure, and server technology. **Positions advertised include:** Accounting Analyst. **Corporate headquarters location:** Blue Bell PA. **Other U.S. locations:** Nationwide. **Operations at this facility include:** This location is a manufacturing facility. **Listed on:** New York Stock Exchange. **Stock exchange symbol:** UIS. **Number of employees worldwide:** 49,000.

VERANCE
4435 Eastgate Mall, Suite 350, San Diego CA 92121. 858/202-2800. **Fax:** 858/202-2801. **Contact:** Human Resources Staffing. **E-mail address:** jobs@verance.com. **World Wide Web address:** http://www.verance.com. **Description:** Creates software to manage the copyright and legal distribution of computerized audio and visual files. **NOTE:** See website for job listings. E-mail resumes. **Positions advertised include:** Database Development Engineer; Electro Mechanical Assembler; Hardware Configuration Manager; Systems Administrator; Watermark Engine Software Engineer. **Corporate headquarters location:** This location. **Other area locations:** Los Angeles CA. **Other U.S. locations:** NY; IL.

VERIFONE, INC.
2099 Gateway Place, Suite 600, San Jose CA 95110. 408/232-7800. **Fax:** 916/630-2566. **Contact:** Human Resources. **E-mail address:** jobs@verifone.com. **World Wide Web address:** http://www.verifone.com. **Description:** VeriFone develops, manufactures, and services software for electronic payment systems that are used in a variety of industries including consumer, financial, and health care. **Positions advertised include:** Controller of SEC Reporting; Controller Revenue Recognition. **Corporate headquarters location:** This location. **Parent company:** GTCR Golder Rauner.

VERISIGN, INC.
487 East Middlefield Road, Mountain View CA 94043. 650/961-7500. **Fax:** 650/961-7300. **Contact:** Human Resources. **World Wide Web address:** http://www.verisign.com. **Description**: The company provides telecom carriers and other enterprise customers with digital commerce and communication products and services including address billing and payment, clearing and settlement, content delivery, domain name registration, Internet security, network connectivity and interoperability, and network databases interactions. **Positions advertised include:** Sales Development Representative; Sr. Accountant; Software Development Engineer; Project Manager; Quality Assurance Engineer; Sales Engineer; Authentication Supervisor; Quality Assurance Manager; Project Manager; HR Specialist; Security Engineer; Product Management Director; Business Systems Analyst; Network Engineer; Order Fulfillment Analyst; Corporate Communications Specialist; Telecom Engineer; Strategic Performance Analyst. **Corporate headquarters location:** This location. **Listed on:** NASDAQ. **Stock exchange symbol:** VRSN. **Number of employees worldwide:** 4,000.

VIEWSONIC CORPORATION
381 Brea Canyon Road, Walnut CA 91789. 909/444-8888. **Fax:** 909/468-1252. **Contact:** Human Resources. **World Wide Web address:** http://www.viewsonic.com. **Description:** Manufactures computer monitors, flat-panel displays, and projectors for the business, education, entertainment, and professional markets. **Corporate headquarters location:** This location. **Office hours:** Monday - Friday, 7:00 a.m. - 6:00 p.m. **CEO:** James Chu. **Number of employees at this location:** 400. **Number of employees worldwide:** Over 600.

VISIONEER, INC.
5673 Gibraltar Drive, Suite 150, Pleasanton CA 94588. 925/251-6300. **Fax:** 925/416-8604. **Contact:** Human Resources. **E-mail address:** careers@visioneer.com. **World Wide Web address:** http://www.visioneer.com. **Description:** Develops software for flatbed and sheet-fed scanners. **Office hours:** Monday - Friday, 8:00 a.m. - 5:00 p.m. **Corporate headquarters location:** This location. **CEO:** Larry Smart. **Annual sales/revenues:** $51 - $100 million.

VISUAL MATRIX CORPORATION
3320 North San Fernando Boulevard, Burbank CA 91504. 818/843-4831. **Fax:** 818/843-6544. **Contact:** Human Resources. **E-mail address:** jobs@visual-matrix.com. **World Wide Web address:** http://www.visual-matrix.com. **Description:** A developer and manufacture of video signal processing technology. **Positions advertised:** Hardware Engineer; Electronics Engineer; Project Engineer; Firmware Designer; Software Designer.

VITESSE SEMICONDUCTOR CORPORATION
741 Calle Plano, Camarillo CA 93012. 805/388-3700. **Toll-free phone:** 800/848-9773. **Contact:** Human Resources. **World Wide Web address:** http://www.vitesse.com. **Description:** Designs and manufactures software systems used in a variety of electronic industries. Founded in 1984. **NOTE:** See website for job listings. Apply online. Entry-level positions are offered. **Positions advertised include:** Process Engineering Technician; Systems Architecture; Technical Writer; Assembly Engineer; Key Accounts Manager; Systems Engineering Technician; Product Marketing Manager. **Corporate headquarters location:** This location. **Other U.S. locations:** MA; CO; TX; NJ. **Listed on:** NASDAQ. **Stock exchange symbol:** VTSS. **Number of employees worldwide:** 800.

VIVENDI UNIVERSAL GAMES
6080 Center Drive, 10th Floor, Los Angeles CA 90045. 310/431-4000. **Contact:** Corporate Recruiter. **E-mail address:** careers@vugames.com. **World Wide Web address:** http://www.vugames.com. **Description:** A publisher and distributor of multimedia educational and entertainment software for both the home and school markets. **Special programs:** Internships. **Corporate**

headquarters location: This location. **Listed on:** New York Stock Exchange. **Stock exchange symbol:** VE.

WESTERN DIGITAL CORPORATION
20511 Lake Forest Drive, Lake Forest CA 92630. 949/672-7000. **Fax:** 949/672-5466. **Contact:** Director of Compensation. **E-mail address:** resumix@ripley.wdc.com. **World Wide Web address:** http://www.westerndigital.com. **Description:** Engaged in information storage management. Western Digital is a leader in manufacturing hard disk drives for servers, workstations, and individual computers. **NOTE:** Search and apply for positions online. **Positions advertised include:** Administrative Assistant; Engineering Program Director; Principal Engineering Software Developer; Senior Test Engineer; Lead Claims Processor. **Corporate headquarters location:** This location. **Other area locations:** Fremont CA; San Jose CA. **Listed on:** New York Stock Exchange. **Stock exchange symbol:** WDC.

WIND RIVER SYSTEMS
500 Wind River Way, Alameda CA 94501. 510/748-4100. **Fax:** 510/749-2302. **Contact:** Staffing Department. **E-mail address:** resumes@careers-windriver.com. **World Wide Web address:** http://www.wrs.com. **Description:** A software engineering and development firm. **Positions advertised include:** Alliance Marketing Manager; Compiler Engineer; Data Administrator; Editor; Flash Guru. **Corporate headquarters location:** This location. **Other area locations:** Sunnyvale CA. **Listed on:** NASDAQ. **Stock exchange symbol:** WIND.

WONDERWARE CORPORATION
26561 Rancho Parkway South, Lake Forest CA 92630. 949/727-3200. **Fax:** 949/639-1830. **Contact:** Employment. **E-mail address:** employment@wonderware.com. **World Wide Web address:** http://www.wonderware.com. **Description:** A developer of industrial applications software. **Positions advertised include:** Senior Software Development Engineer; Human Resources Consultant; Senior Technical Support Specialist; Principal Marketing Research Analyst. **Corporate headquarters location:** This location.

WYSE TECHNOLOGY
3471 North First Street, San Jose CA 95134. 408/473-1200. **Fax:** 408/473-2080. **Contact:** Human Resources. **E-mail address:** wysejobs@wyse.com. **World Wide Web address:** http://www.wyse.com. **Description:** Manufactures workstations that access information from a server rather than from a hard drive. **NOTE:** Search and apply for positions online. **Positions advertised include:** Business Analyst; Network Engineer; Oracle Database Administrator. **Corporate headquarters location:** This location. **CEO:** Douglas Chance. **Facilities Manager:** Lee Perry.

XILINX, INC.
2100 Logic Drive, San Jose CA 95124-3400. 408/559-7778. **Fax:** 408/559-7114. **Contact:** Ms. Chris Taylor, Vice President of Human Resources. **E-mail address:** jobs@xilinx.com. **World Wide Web address:** http://www.xilinx.com. **Description:** A leading supplier of field programmable gate arrays and related development system software used by electronic systems manufacturers. **NOTE:** Apply online. Hard copy resumes are not accepted. **NOTE:** Search for positions and submit resume online. **Positions advertised include:** Applications Engineer; Process Development Engineer; Product Engineer; Senior Research Engineer; Business Development Analyst; IT Architecture Intern; Corporate Paralegal; Web Publishing Specialist. **Special programs:** Internships. **Corporate headquarters location:** This location. **Operations at this facility include:** Administration; Manufacturing; Research and Development; Sales; Service. **Listed on:** NASDAQ. **Stock exchange symbol:** XLNX. **Number of employees at this location:** 850. **Number of employees worldwide:** 2,770.

YAHOO! INC.
701 First Avenue, Sunnyvale CA 94089. 408/349-3300. **Fax:** 408/349-3301. **Contact:** Nancy Larocca, Staffing Manager. **World Wide Web address:** http://www.yahoo.com. **Description:** A global Internet communications, commerce, and media company that offers a comprehensive branded network of services to millions of users each month. Founded in 1994. **NOTE:** The company does not accept phone calls regarding employment. Search and apply for positions online. **Positions advertised include:** Senior Financial Analyst; Software Engineer; Corporate Development Manager; Business Development Manager; Marketing Director; Web Development Manager; Customer Care Agent; Senior Business Intelligence Engineer. **Special programs:** Internships. **Office hours:** Monday - Friday, 8:00 a.m. - 6:00 p.m. **Corporate headquarters location:** This location. **Other U.S. locations:** Nationwide. **International locations:** Worldwide. **Listed on:** NASDAQ. **Stock exchange symbol:** YHOO. **Number of employees at this location:** 1,300. **Number of employees worldwide:** 2,000.

ZENDEX CORPORATION
6780A Sierra Court, Dublin CA 94568. 925/828-3000. **Fax:** 925/828-1574. **Contact:** Human Resources. **World Wide Web address:** http://www.zendex.com. **Description:** Manufactures a variety of computers, computer boards, and PCs for use in industrial applications. **Corporate headquarters location:** This location.

ZYXEL COMMUNICATIONS INC.
1130 North Miller Street, Anaheim CA 92806-2001. 714/632-0882. **Fax:** 714/632-0858. **Contact:** Human Resources. **E-mail address:** jobs@zyxel.com. **World Wide Web address:** http://www.us.zyxel.com. **Description:** ZyXEL is a manufacturer of computer modems, routers, and ISDN terminal adapters. **Positions advertised include:** Marketing Coordinator. **Corporate headquarters location:** Taiwan.

Colorado

ADP SECURITIES INDUSTRY SOFTWARE (ADP/SIS)
dba ADP/SIS
4725 Independence Street, Wheat Ridge CO 80033. 303/590-6000. **Fax:** 303/590-6420. **Contact:** Human Resources. **World Wide Web address:** http://www.sis.adp.com. **Description:** Develops financial software for brokerage houses and related companies. **Positions advertised include:** Finance Director; Tandem Technical Consultant; Education Specialist.

AGI
7150 Campus Drive, Suite 260, Colorado Springs CO 80920. 719/573-2600. **Fax:** 719/573-9079. **Contact:** Human Resources. **E-mail address:** hr@agi.com. **World Wide Web address:** http://www.agi.com. **Description:** AGI provides analysis and visualization software to national security and space professionals for integrated analyses of land, sea, air, and space assets. **Corporate headquarters location:** Exton PA.

AT&T GOVERNMENT SOLUTIONS
985 Space Center Drive, Suite 310, Colorado Springs CO 80915. 719/596-5395. **Contact:** Human Resources. **World Wide Web address:** http://www.att.com/gov. **Description:** AT&T Government Solutions provides knowledge-based professional services and technology-based product solutions to government and commercial customers. AT&T Government Solutions also provides studies and analysis capabilities for policy development and planning; modeling and simulation of hardware and software used in real-time testing of sensor, weapon, and battlefield management command, control, and communication systems; and testing and evaluation. **NOTE:** Please see company Website for more details on applying for a position. **Positions advertised include:** Analyst; Intel Analyst; Project Manager. **Corporate headquarters location:** Santa Barbara CA. **Other U.S. locations:** Nationwide. **Operations at this facility include:** This location develops software for

the U.S. government. **Parent company:** AT&T Corporation. **Listed on:** New York Stock Exchange. **Stock exchange symbol:** T. **Number of employees worldwide:** 1,300.

ALTIA
5030 Corporate Plaza Drive, Colorado Springs CO 80919. 719/598-4299. **Fax:** 719/598-4392. **Contact:** Human Resources. **E-mail address:** info@altia.com. **World Wide Web address:** http://www.altia.com. **Description:** Manufactures feature prototyping software for engineers and marketing professionals. **Corporate headquarters location:** This location.

ANALYSTS INTERNATIONAL CORPORATION (AIC)
5445 DTC Parkway, Suite 320 A, Englewood CO 80111. 303/721-6200. **Fax:** 303/721-6403. **Contact:** Manager of Human Resources. **World Wide Web address:** http://www.analysts.com. **Description:** AIC is an international, computer consulting firm. The company assists clients in developing systems using various programming languages and software. **Positions advertised include:** Sr. SQL Developer. **Corporate headquarters location:** Minneapolis MN. **Listed on:** NASDAQ. **Stock exchange symbol:** ANLY.

ASPEN SYSTEMS, INC.
3900 Youngfield Street, Wheat Ridge CO 80033-3865. 303/431-4606. **Fax:** 303/431-7196. **Contact:** Personnel. **World Wide Web address:** http://www.aspsys.com. **Description:** A manufacturer of high-performance workstations and servers for the OEM, VAR, and retail industries. **Positions advertised include:** Computer Production Engineer. **Corporate headquarters location:** This location.

AUTO-TROL TECHNOLOGY CORPORATION
12500 North Washington Street, Denver CO 80241-2400. 303/452-4919. **Toll-free phone:** 800/233-2882. **Fax:** 303/252-2249. **Recorded jobline:** 303/252-2007. **Contact:** Human Resources. **E-mail address:** careers@auto-trol.com. **World Wide Web address:** http://www.auto-trol.com. **Description:** Develops and markets software for the CAD/CAM/CAE, technical illustration, network configuration, and technical information management industries. Auto-Trol Technology Corporation integrates computer hardware, operating systems, proprietary graphics software, and applications software into systems for process plant design, civil engineering, discrete manufacturing, facilities layout and design, mechanical design, technical publishing, and network configuration management. **NOTE:** Entry-level positions are offered. **Positions advertised include:** Test Engineer; Consultant/Project Manager; Sales Representative. **Special programs:** Internships. **Corporate headquarters location:** This location. **Other U.S. locations:** Nationwide. **Annual sales/revenues:** $5 - $10 million. **Number of employees at this location:** 200.

BAKER ATLAS
1625 Broadway, Suite 1300, Denver CO 80202. 303/629-9250. **Contact:** Human Resources. **World Wide Web address:** http://www.bakeratlas.com. **Description:** Baker Atlas develops and markets proprietary computer software, provides management services for the petroleum and mining industries, and provides electronic data processing services. **Positions advertised include:** Well Planner. **Corporate headquarters location:** Houston TX. **Operations at this facility include:** This location develops software for the oil and gas industries. **Parent company:** Baker Hughes. **Listed on:** New York Stock Exchange. **Stock exchange symbol:** BHI.

CGI-AMS
14033 Denver West Parkway, Golden CO 80401. 303/215-3500. **Contact:** Director of Human Resources. **World Wide Web address:** http://www.cgi.com. **Description:** Assists large organizations in solving complex management problems by applying information technology and systems engineering solutions. Industries and markets served include financial service institutions, insurance companies, federal agencies, state and local governments, colleges and universities, telecommunications firms, health care providers, and energy companies. **Listed on:** New York Stock Exchange. **Stock exchange symbol:** GIB.

CHESS INC.
410 Raritan Way, Denver CO 80204. 303/573-5133. **Contact:** Human Resources Department. **World Wide Web address:** http://www.chessinc.com. **Description:** Engaged in the repair and sale of computer equipment and printers. **Other area locations:** Colorado Springs CO. **Positions advertised include:** Account Executive; Parts Administrator; Administrative Assistant; Accounts Receivable Clerk; Service Technician.

CIBER, INC.
5251 DTC Parkway, Suite 600, Greenwood Village CO 80111. 303/779-6242. **Toll-free phone:** 800/242-3799. **Fax:** 303/779-6244. **Contact:** National Recruiting. **World Wide Web address:** http://www.ciber.com. **Description:** Provides consulting for client/server development, mainframe and legacy systems, industry-specific analysis, application-specific analysis, and network development. **Positions advertised include:** Systems Administrator; SQL DBA/ETL Architect; Business Intelligence Developer. **Corporate headquarters location:** This location. **International locations:** Canada; United Kingdom. **Listed on:** New York Stock Exchange. **Stock exchange symbol:** CBR.

COMPUTER SCIENCES CORPORATION (CSC)
460 Wooten Road, Suite 144, Colorado Springs CO 80916. 719/799-2880. **Contact:** Human Resources. **World Wide Web address:** http://www.csc.com. **Description:** An information technology services company offering systems design and integration; IT and business process outsourcing; applications software development; Web and application hosting; and management consulting. **Positions advertised include:** Network Administrator; Network Engineer; Computer Scientist. **Corporate headquarters location:** El Segundo CA. **Other area locations:** Denver CO; Broomfield CO; Greenwood Village CO. **Listed on:** New York Stock Exchange. **Stock exchange symbol:** CSC. **Number of employees worldwide:** 80,000.

COMSTOR
295 Interlocken Boulevard, Suite 100, Broomfield CO 80021. 303/222-4747. **Toll-free phone:** 800/543-6098. **Fax:** 303/222-4875. **Contact:** Human Resources. **World Wide Web address:** http://www.comstor.com. **Description:** Distributes computers, internetworking products, and peripherals and provides related services. Founded in 1986. **NOTE:** Entry-level positions are offered. **Office hours:** Monday - Friday, 8:00 a.m. - 5:00 p.m. **Corporate headquarters location:** Chantilly VA. **Other U.S. locations:** Tarrytown NY; Pittsburgh PA; Omaha NE. **Number of employees at this location:** 140. **Number of employees nationwide:** 370.

CONVERGYS
10225 Westmoor Drive, Westminster CO 80021. 720/887-7800. **Contact:** Human Resources. **World Wide Web address:** http://www.convergys.com. **Description:** Provides customer care, human resources, and billing services through outsourced solutions, consulting services, and software support to industries including communications, financial services, technology, and consumer products. **Positions advertised include:** Implementation Technical Analyst. **Listed on:** New York Stock Exchange. **Stock exchange symbol:** CVG.

EDS (ELECTRONIC DATA SYSTEMS CORPORATION)
833 Boulder Road Southwest, Louisville CO 80027-2452. 303/665-1500. **Contact:** Human Resources. **World Wide Web address:** http://www.eds.com. **Description:** Provides consulting, systems development, systems integration, and systems

management services for large-scale and industry-specific applications. Founded in 1962. **Positions advertised include:** Business Services Analyst. **Corporate headquarters location:** Plano TX. **Other U.S. locations:** Nationwide. **Listed on:** New York Stock Exchange. **Stock exchange symbol:** EDS. **Number of employees nationwide:** 50,000.

EMC CORPORATION
1099 18th Street, 17th Floor, Denver CO 80202. 303/293-9331. **Contact:** Human Resources. **World Wide Web address:** http://www.emc.com. **Description:** Provides products, services, and solutions for information storage and its management with solutions that integrate networked storage technologies, storage systems, software, and services. **Positions advertised include:** Commercial Technology Consultant; Federal Account Manager; Partner Manager; Regional Network Specialist; Sr. Systems Engineer. **Corporate headquarters location:** Hopkinton MA. **Other area locations:** Boulder CO; Englewood CO; Colorado Springs CO.

EAST CENTRAL NEIGHBORHOOD LINK
2546 15th Street, Denver CO 80211. 303/830-0123. **Contact:** Ted Pinkowitz, President. **World Wide Web address:** http://www.ecentral.com. **Description:** Provides Internet access, e-mail accounts, and home pages on the Web to companies and individuals.

ENSCICON CORPORATION
555 Zang Street, Suite 100, Lakewood CO 80228. 303/980-8600. **Fax:** 303/832-6700. **Contact:** Staffing. **E-mail address:** info@enscicon.com. **World Wide Web address:** http://www.enscicon.com. **Description:** Provides computer science engineering and high-tech consulting services. Founded in 1994. **Positions advertised include:** Project Scheduler; I&C Lead Engineer; Lead Electrical Engineer; Project Geologist; Project Manager; Process Engineer; Mechanical Engineer. **Corporate headquarters location:** This location. **Other U.S. locations:** Portland OR. **Listed on:** Privately held. **President:** William Smith.

EXABYTE CORPORATION
2108 55th Street, Boulder CO 80301. 303/442-4333. **Contact:** Human Resources. **World Wide Web address:** http://www.exabyte.com. **Description:** Designs, manufactures, and markets cartridge tape subsystems for data storage applications. The company's products are used in a broad spectrum of computer systems based on 8mm helical scan, 4mm helical scan, and quarter-inch technologies. Products are used in various computer systems ranging from personal computers to supercomputers. A large majority of its units are used with workstations, network file servers, and minicomputers. **Positions advertised include:** Business Development Rep; Manufacturing Support Engineer; Software Tools Engineer. **Corporate headquarters location:** This location. **Listed on:** NASDAQ. **Stock exchange symbol:** EXBT.

FRONTRANGE SOLUTIONS
1125 Kelly Johnson Boulevard, Colorado Springs CO 80920. 719/531-5007. **Fax:** 719/536-0620. **Contact:** Human Resources Department. **World Wide Web address:** http://www.frontrange.com. **Description:** Develops software for support center markets such as help desks, customer service, and MIS/IS departments. **Positions advertised include:** Consultant; Customer Account Rep; Customer Support Specialist; Inside Sales Rep; Technical Analyst.

GOLDEN SOFTWARE, INC.
809 14th Street, Golden CO 80401-1866. 303/279-1021. **Toll-free phone:** 800/972-1021. **Fax:** 303/279-0909. **Contact:** Human Resources. **World Wide Web address:** http://www.goldensoftware.com. **Description:** Develops contouring, mapping, and graphing software for Windows and DOS operating systems. **Corporate headquarters location:** This location.

HARRIS CORPORATION
1999 Broadway Street, Suite 4000, Denver CO 80202-3050. 303/237-4000. **Contact:** Human Resources. **World Wide Web address:** http://www.broadcast.harris.com. **Description:** Develops software for television and radio stations.

HEWLETT PACKARD
305 Rockrimmon Boulevard South, Colorado Springs CO 80919. 719/548-2000. **Contact:** Human Resources. **World Wide Web address:** http://www.hp.com. **Description:** Designs, manufactures, sells, and services computers, associated peripheral equipment, and related software and supplies. Applications and programs include scientific research, computation, communications, education, data analysis, industrial control, time sharing, commercial data processing, graphic arts, word processing, health care, instrumentation, engineering, and simulation. **NOTE:** Apply online. **Positions advertised include:** ITSM Problem Manager; Associate Consultant; Microsoft Subject Matter Expert; Enterprise Inside Sales Rep; Customer Service Engineer. **Corporate headquarters location:** Palo Alto CA. **Listed on:** New York Stock Exchange. **Stock exchange symbol:** HPQ.

IBM CORPORATION
6300 Diagonal Highway, Boulder CO 80301. 303/443-9905. **Toll-free phone:** 800/796-9876. **Recorded jobline:** 800/964-4473. **Contact:** Human Resources. **World Wide Web address:** http://www.ibm.com. **Description:** IBM is a developer, manufacturer, and marketer of advanced information processing products including computers and microelectronic technology, software, networking systems, and information technology-related services. The company has operations in the United States, Canada, Europe, Middle East, Africa, Latin America, and Asia. **NOTE:** Search and apply for positions online. **Corporate headquarters location:** Armonk NY. **Operations at this facility include:** This facility is engaged in the manufacture of magnetic discs and tapes. **Subsidiaries include:** IBM Credit Corporation; IBM Instruments, Inc.; IBM World Trade Corporation. **Listed on:** New York Stock Exchange. **Stock exchange symbol:** IBM.

INFOR GLOBAL SOUTIONS
5555 Tech Center Drive, Suite 300, Colorado Springs CO 80919. 719/590-8940. **Fax:** 719/528-1465. **Contact:** Human Resources. **E-mail address:** infor.careers@infor.com. **World Wide Web address:** http://www.infor.com. **Description:** Provider of enterprise business solutions to the manufacturing and distribution industries. **Corporate headquarters location:** Atlanta GA. **Other U.S. locations:** Columbus OH; Grand Rapids MI; East Greenwich RI; Hampton NH; Duluth GA; Malvern PA; Northville MI.

INTRADO, INC.
1600 Dry Creek Road, Longmont CO 80503. 720/494-5800. **Fax:** 720/494-6652. **Contact:** Human Resources. **E-mail address:** HR@intrado.com. **World Wide Web address:** http://www.intrado.com. **Description:** Develops public safety computer software and systems that implement emergency communication networks with telephone service providers. **Positions advertised include:** Incident Administrator; Accounting Manager; Sr. Software Engineer; Product Marketing Manager; Sr. System Administrator; Data Analyst. **Corporate headquarters location:** This location. **Listed on:** NASDAQ. **Stock exchange symbol:** TRDO.

ISYS SEARCH SOFTWARE
8775 East Orchard Road, Suite 811, Englewood CO 80111. 303/689-9998. **Contact:** Human Resources. **E-mail address:** employment@isys-search.com. **World Wide Web address:** http://www.isys-search.com. **Description:** Manufactures text retrieval software. Products include ISYS HindSite Internet utilities; ISYS Web, for online publishing; ISYS Image, for data capture and full-text search; ISYS Electronic Publisher, a retrieval and authoring tool; and ISYS for Adobe Acrobat, a search engine with PDF files.

MANAGED BUSINESS SOLUTIONS (MBS)
1201 Oakridge Drive, Suite 320, Fort Collins CO 80525. 970/224-1016. **Fax:** 970/416-1543. **Contact:** Human Resources. **E-mail address:** careers@mbshome.com. **World Wide Web address:** http://www.mbshome.com. **Description:** MBS specializes in application development, application management and support, and IT resource management. Founded in 1993. **Positions advertised include:** Java Developer; Technical Writer; Tech Solution Specialist; .NET Developer; MPE System Operator.

MAXTOR CORPORATION
2452 Clover Basin Drive, Longmont CO 80503. 303/651-6000. **Fax:** 303/678-2379. **Contact:** Human Resources. **E-mail address:** staffing@maxtor.com. **World Wide Web address:** http://www.maxtor.com. **Description:** Maxtor Corporation produces hard disk drives and related electronic data storage equipment for computers, as well as related components for original equipment manufacturers. **Positions advertised include:** Database Administrator; Product Support Rep. **Corporate headquarters location:** Milpitas CA. **Operations at this facility include:** This location is a research and development facility. **Listed on:** New York Stock Exchange. **Stock exchange symbol:** MXO.

McKESSON CORPORATION
285 Century Circle, Louisville CO 80027. 303/926-2000. **Contact:** Human Resources. **World Wide Web address:** http://www.mckesson.com. **Description:** McKesson Corp. is an information solutions company that provides information systems and technology to health care enterprises including hospitals, integrated delivery networks, and managed care organizations. McKesson's primary products are Pathways 2000, a family of client/server-based applications that allows for the integration and uniting of health care providers; STAR, Series, and HealthQuest transaction systems; TRENDSTAR decision support system; and QUANTUM enterprise information system. The company also offers outsourcing services that include strategic information systems planning, data center operations, receivables management, business office administration, and major system conversions. **Positions advertised include:** Technical Support Manager; Cardiology Sales Product Specialist; Technical Support Engineer; Director, Business Analysis. **Corporate headquarters location:** San Francisco CA. **Operations at this facility include:** This location designs and installs software for the medical industry. **Subsidiaries include:** HBO & Company (UK) Limited; HBO & Company Canada Ltd.

OCTAGON SYSTEMS
6510 West 91st Avenue, Suite 110, Westminster CO 80031. 303/430-1500. **Contact:** Personnel. **E-mail address:** hrstaffing@octagonsystems.com. **World Wide Web address:** http://www.octagonsystems.com. **Description:** Manufactures personal computers for extreme environments. Founded in 1981. **Positions advertised include:** Director of Operations. **Corporate headquarters location:** This location. **Listed on:** Privately held. **Number of employees at this location:** 70.

1MAGE SOFTWARE INC.
6025 South Quebec Street, Suite 300, Englewood CO 80111. 303/773-1424. **Fax:** 303/796-0587. **Contact:** Human Resources. **E-mail address:** jobs@1mage.com. **World Wide Web address:** http://www.1mage.com. **Description:** Develops and markets image recording and storage systems to convert paper records into electronic format. 1mage Software also offers installation and support services. **Corporate headquarters location:** This location.

ORACLE
12320 Oracle Boulevard, Colorado Springs CO 80921. 719/577-8000. **Fax:** 719/757-2037. **Contact:** Human Resources. **World Wide Web address:** http://www.oracle.com. **Description:** the world's largest enterprise software company. **Positions advertised include:** Contract Renewal Rep; Support Engineer; Sr. Consultant. **Corporate headquarters location:** Redwood Shores CA. **Other area locations:** Denver CO. **Listed on:** NASDAQ. **Stock exchange symbol:** ORCL.

QUARK, INC.
1800 Grant Street, Suite 800, Denver CO 80203. 303/894-8888. **Fax:** 303/894-3649. **Contact:** Human Resources Department. **E-mail address:** work@quark.com. **World Wide Web address:** http://www.quark.com. **Description:** Develops software including QuarkXPress, one of the leading products in desktop publishing. **Positions advertised include:** VP, Customer Care; VP, Human Resources; VP, Marketing; Project Coordinator; Quality Assurance Engineer; Sr. Software Engineer; Software Architect; Manager, Web Services. **International locations:** Worldwide.

SI INTERNATIONAL
4040 East Bijou Street, Colorado Springs CO 80909. 719/235-4100. **Fax:** 719/380-8702. **Contact:** Human Resources. **World Wide Web address:** http://www.si-intl.com. **Description:** A provider of information technology and network solutions primarily to the federal government, focusing on federal IT modernization, homeland security, and space systems modernization. Founded in 1998. **Positions advertised include:** Manager New Program Development; Principal Contracts Administrator; Video Network Engineer; Systems Engineer; Senior IT Systems Engineer; Associate Network Engineer. **Corporate headquarters location:** Reston VA. **Other area locations:** Denver CO; Fort Collins CO.

SANMINA-SCI CORPORATION
702 Bandley Drive, Fountain CO 80817. 719/382-2000. **Contact:** Human Resources. **World Wide Web address:** http://www.sanmina-sci.com. **Description:** Sanmina-SCI Corporation is an electronics contract manufacturer serving the fastest-growing segments of the global electronics manufacturing services market. Sanmina-SCI provides end-to-end manufacturing solutions to OEMs primarily in the communications, defense and aerospace, industrial and medical instrumentation, multimedia, and computer and server technology sectors. **Positions advertised include:** Quality Engineer; Program Administrator; Buyer; Supply Chain Manager. **Corporate headquarters location:** San Jose CA. **Other U.S. locations:** Nationwide. **International locations:** Canada; France; Ireland; Mexico; Scotland; Singapore; Thailand. **Operations at this facility include:** This location produces a wide range of assemblies for mass storage products including small tape backup devices, large multiple-disk array systems, and high-capacity optical storage units. **Listed on:** NASDAQ. **Stock exchange symbol:** SANM.

SEAGATE TECHNOLOGY
389 Disc Drive, Longmont CO 80503. 720/684-1000. **Contact:** Human Resources. **World Wide Web address:** http://www.seagate.com. **Description:** Designs and manufactures data storage devices and related products including hard drives, tape drives, software, and systems for many computer-related applications and operating systems. These products include 2.5-inch and 3.5-inch drives with memory storage capacity between 150 megabytes and one gigabyte. **Positions advertised include:** Applications Engineer; Concept Market Development Director; Firmware Engineer; Servo Engineer; Sr. Analyst, Product Marketing; Electrical Design Engineer. **Corporate headquarters location:** Scotts Valley CA.

SPECTRA LOGIC
1700 North 55th Street, Boulder CO 80301-2725. 303/449-6400. **Fax:** 303/939-8844. **Contact:** Human Resources. **E-mail address:** hireme@spectralogic.com. **World Wide Web address:** http://www.spectralogic.com. **Description:** Manufactures backup hardware and automated tape libraries. Founded in 1979. **NOTE:** Entry-level positions are offered. **Positions advertised**

include: Disk/RAID Engineer; Firmware Engineer; Project Coordinator; Operations Engineer; Supply Chain Specialist; Hardware Support Technician. **Special programs:** Internships. **Internship information:** For detailed internship information, visit the company's Website. **Corporate headquarters location:** This location. **International locations:** UK; China. **Listed on:** Privately held. **Number of employees at this location:** 150. **Number of employees worldwide:** 300.

SPECTRUM HUMAN RESOURCE SYSTEMS CORPORATION
707 Seventeenth Street, Suite 3800, Denver CO 80202-3438. 303/592-3200. **Toll-free phone:** 800/334-5660. **Fax:** 303/595-9970. **Contact:** Recruiter. **E-mail address:** info@ spectrumhr.com. **World Wide Web address:** http://www.spectrumhr.com. **Description:** Develops computer software for use in human resources management, benefits administration, and training development administration. Founded in 1984. **NOTE:** Entry-level positions are offered. **Positions advertised include:** HR Systems Implementation Programmer. **Corporate headquarters location:** This location. **Listed on:** Privately held. **Annual sales/revenues:** $5 - $10 million. **Number of employees at this location:** 100. **Number of employees nationwide:** 115.

STORAGETEK
One StorageTek Drive, Louisville CO 80028-0001. 303/673-5151. **Contact:** Human Resources. **World Wide Web address:** http://www.stortek.com. **Description:** StorageTek supplies high-performance computer information storage and retrieval systems for mainframe and mid-frame computers and networks. Products include automated cartridge systems, random access subsystems, and fault-tolerant disk arrays. The company also distributes equipment; sells new peripherals, software, and hardware; and offers support services. **Corporate headquarters location:** This location. **Parent company:** Sun Microsystems. **Operations at this facility include:** Administration; Manufacturing; Research and Development.

SUN MICROSYSTEMS, INC.
500 Eldorado Boulevard, Broomfield CO 80021. 303/464-4000. **Contact:** Human Resources. **World Wide Web address:** http://www.sun.com. **Description:** Sun Microsystems Inc. produces high-performance computer systems, workstations, servers, CPUs, peripherals, and operating system software. The company also developed a microprocessor called SPARC. **Corporate headquarters location:** Santa Clara CA. **Operations at this facility include:** This location is a sales office. **Subsidiaries include:** Forte Software Inc. manufactures enterprise application integration software. **Listed on:** NASDAQ. **Stock exchange symbol:** SUNW.

SUNGARD INSURANCE SYSTEMS
14280 East Jewell Avenue, Suite 200, Aurora CO 80012. 303/283-5300. **Contact:** Human Resources. **World Wide Web address:** http://www.sungardinsurance.com. **Description:** Develops financial software for insurance companies. **Parent company:** SunGard Data Systems, Inc. **Listed on:** New York Stock Exchange. **Stock exchange symbol:** SDS.

SYKES ENTERPRISES INC.
777 North Fourth Street, Sterling CO 80751. 970/522-6638. **Contact:** Human Resources. **E-mail address:** careers@sykes.com. **World Wide Web address:** http://www.sykes.com. **Description:** Provides computer outsourcing services, hardware and software technical support, systems consulting and integration, and documentation development. **Corporate headquarters location:** Tampa FL. **Other U.S. locations:** Nationwide. **International locations:** The Netherlands; Philippines. **Listed on:** NASDAQ. **Stock exchange symbol:** SYKE.

T-NETIX, INC.
7108 South Alton Drive, Centennial CO 80112. 720/488-9481. **Contact:** Human Resources Department. **E-mail address:** humanresources@t-netix.com. **World Wide Web address:** http://www.t-netix.com. **Description:** Manufactures software for fraud prevention and advanced call processing. **Corporate headquarters location:** Carrollton TX. **Subsidiaries include:** Cell-Tel, Tampa FL. **Parent company:** Securus.

XAWARE INC.
5555 Tech Center Drive, Suite 200, Colorado Springs CO 80919. 719/884-5400. **Fax:** 719/884-5492. **Contact:** Human Resources. **E-mail address:** careers@xaware.com. **World Wide Web address:** http://www.xaware.com. **Description:** XAware, Inc. is a provider of information integration, conversion, and exchange solutions that helps companies transform and extend existing information assets into standards-based information services. **Positions advertised include:** Professional Services Staff; Sales Operations Specialist.

XI GRAPHICS
1801 Broadway, Suite 1710, Denver CO 80202-3800. 303/298-7478. **Toll-free phone:** 800/946-7433. **Fax:** 303/298-1406. **Contact:** Employment. **E-mail address:** jobs@xig.com. **World Wide Web address:** http://www.xig.com. **Description:** Develops a line of products that enhance the graphics capabilities of PC hardware. Products include X Windows display servers, OpenGL development, and custom development. **Operations at this facility include:** Customer Service; Financial Offices; Sales; Technical Support. **Listed on:** Privately held.

ZYKRONIX INC.
357 Inverness Drive South, Suite 300C, Englewood CO 80112. 303/799-4944. **Fax:** 303/799-4978. **Contact:** Human Resources. **E-mail address:** hr@zykronix.com. **World Wide Web address:** http://www.zykronix.com. **Description:** Designs and manufactures PCs that are used mainly for industrial applications. Founded in 1990. **President/CEO:** David M. Ghaemi. **Corporate headquarters location:** This location.

Connecticut

ANTEON CORPORATION
Oral School Road, Suite 105, Mystic CT 06355. 860/572-9600. **Fax:** 860/599-6516. **Contact:** Jennifer Dauster-Bevacqua, Human Resources Administrator. **World Wide Web address:** http://www.anteon.com. **Description:** A leading provider of technology-based solutions in the areas of engineering, information technology, and interactive multimedia services. **Positions advertised include:** Telecommunications Analyst. **Corporate headquarters location:** Fairfax VA. **Other U.S. locations:** Nationwide. **International locations:** Germany; Italy; United Kingdom. **Listed on:** New York Stock Exchange. **Stock exchange symbol:** ANT. **Annual sales/revenues:** More than $100 million. **Number of employees nationwide:** 5,400.

CTI ELECTRONICS CORPORATION
110 Old South Avenue, Stratford CT 06615. 203/386-9779. **Contact:** Human Resources. **World Wide Web address:** http://www.ctielectronics.com. **Description:** Manufactures computer peripherals including keyboards, trackballs, and joysticks. **Corporate headquarters location:** This location.

COMPUTER ASSOCIATES
1351 Washington Boulevard, Suite 800, Stamford CT 06902. 203/352-6800. **Toll-free phone:** 800/243-9462. **Fax:** 203/937-3015. **Contact:** Human Resources. **World Wide Web address:** http://www.ca.com. **Description:** Computer Associates International is one of the world's leading developers of client/server and distributed computing software. The company develops, markets, and supports enterprise management, database and applications development, business applications, and consumer software products for a broad range of mainframe, midrange, and desktop computers. Computer Associates International serves

major business, government, research, and educational organizations. **Positions advertised include:** Sales Executive; Customer Relationship Manager. **Corporate headquarters location:** Islandia NY. **Other U.S. locations:** Nationwide. **Listed on:** New York Stock Exchange. **Stock exchange symbol:** CA. **Annual sales/revenues:** More than $100 million.

COMPUTER HORIZONS CORPORATION
500 Winding Brook Drive, Glastonbury CT 06033. 860/633-4646. **Fax:** 860/657-9817. **Contact:** Personnel. **World Wide Web address:** http://www.computerhorizons.com. **Description:** A full-service technology solutions company offering contract staffing, outsourcing, re-engineering, migration, downsizing support, and network management. **Corporate headquarters location:** Mountain Lakes NJ. **Other U.S. locations:** Nationwide. **Listed on:** NASDAQ. **Stock exchange symbol:** CHRZ. **Number of employees nationwide:** 3,600.

CORPORATE INFORMATION TECHNOLOGIES
314 Farmington Avenue, Suite 130, Farmington CT 06032. 860/676-2720. **Fax:** 860/676-8273. **Contact:** Human Resources. **World Wide Web address:** http://www.corpit.com. **Description:** Provides computer consulting services and software solutions to healthcare, insurance, and technology companies. Corporate Information technologies' services include application development and project management; desktop/LAN support; Helpdesk support; Mainframe support; Network administration and architecture; server/application hosting and administration; and Website and e-business development, programming, and hosting.

FISERV, INC.
151 National Drive, Glastonbury CT 06033. 860/633-9990. **Contact:** Human Resources. **World Wide Web address:** http://www.fiserv.com. **Description:** FiServ, Inc. provides data processing services to banks and credit institutions. The company also offers PC banking and e-commerce technology. **Positions advertised include:** Product Specialist. **Corporate headquarters location:** Brookfield WI. **Other U.S. locations:** Nationwide. **Listed on:** NASDAQ. **Stock exchange symbol:** FISV. **Number of employees nationwide:** 16,000.

GENERAL DATACOMM, INC.
6 Rubber Avenue, Naugatuck CT 06770. 203/729-0271. **Fax:** 203/729-5734. **Contact:** Anne Davino, Human Resources. **E-mail address:** jobs@gdc.com. **World Wide Web address:** http://www.gdc.com. **Description:** Provides business solutions for enterprise and telecommunications networks based on Asynchronous Transfer Mode (ATM) products and services. General DataComm operates in three areas: ATM products, internetworking products, and network access products. The company designs, assembles, markets, installs, and maintains products and services that enable telecommunications common carriers, corporations, and governments to build, upgrade, and manage their global telecommunications networks. General DataComm's networks transmit information via telephone lines, microwaves, satellites, fiber-optic cables, and other media between computers and terminals or information processing systems. Founded in 1969. **Corporate headquarters location:** This location. **International locations:** Canada; Columbia. **Annual sales/revenues:** More than $100 million. **Number of employees worldwide:** 150.

HYPERION SOLUTIONS
900 Long Ridge Road, Stamford CT 06902. 203/703-3000. **Fax:** 203/322-3904. **Contact:** Human Resources. **World Wide Web address:** http://www.hyperion.com. **Description:** Hyperion Solutions develops, markets, and supports a family of network-based business information software products for large multidivision or multilocation companies worldwide. The product line provides executives, managers, and analysts with the capability to collect, process, access, and analyze critical business information in a timely manner, using networked personal computers. **Positions advertised include:** Compensation Manager; Financial Applications Instructor; Partner Technical Account Manager; Administrative Assistant; Performance Engineer; Software Engineer. **Special programs:** Internships. **Corporate headquarters location:** Sunnyvale CA. **Other U.S. locations:** Nationwide. **Operations at this facility include:** Administration; Divisional Headquarters; Regional Headquarters; Research and Development; Sales; Service. **Listed on:** NASDAQ. **Stock exchange symbol:** HYSL. **Number of employees worldwide:** 2,300.

IPC INFORMATION SYSTEMS, INC.
42 Pequot Park Road, Westbrook CT 06498. 860/399-5981. **Contact:** Human Resources. **World Wide Web address:** http://www.ipc.com. **Description:** Provides network communications solutions for the financial industry. Through its Information Transport Systems (ITS) business, the company provides its customers with voice, data, and video solutions through the design, integration, implementation, and support of local and wide area networks. ITS solutions incorporate the latest technology and are supported by a team of systems engineers. **Corporate headquarters location:** New York NY. **Other U.S. locations:** Nationwide. **Listed on:** NASDAQ. **Stock exchange symbol:** IPCR. **Annual sales/revenues:** $21 - $50 million. **Number of employees at this location:** 70. **Number of employees nationwide:** 200. **Number of employees worldwide:** 250.

IMAGE GRAPHICS, INC.
917 Bridgeport Avenue, Shelton CT 06484. 203/926-0100. **Toll-free phone:** 888/464-6243. **Contact:** Personnel. **World Wide Web address:** http://www.igraph.com. **Description:** A systems integrator for imaging and cold systems. The company also manufactures high-resolution electronic data recorders. **Corporate headquarters location:** This location.

INSURITY
170 Huyshope Avenue, Hartford CT 06106. 860/616-7721. **Contact:** Human Resources. **E-mail address:** hr@insurity.com. **World Wide Web address:** http://www.insurity.com. **Description:** Develops insurance software to process workers' compensation claims. **Positions advertised include:** Database Programmer; Project Manager; Quality Assurance Analyst; Support Specialist; Programmer Analyst; Client Service Analyst. **Corporate headquarters location:** This location. **Other area locations:** East Hartford CT. **Other U.S. locations:** Cumming GA; Red Wing MN; Richardson TX.

MILLENNIATHREE
290 Pratt Street, Mail Stop 13, Meriden CT 06450. 203/235-1806. **Contact:** Human Resources. **Description:** Provides Web design and hosting services as well as a variety of graphic design services.

NEW TECHNOLOGY SOLUTIONS, INC.
432 Washington Avenue, North Haven CT 06473. 203/234-1404. **Fax:** 203/239-7230. **Contact:** Human Resources. **World Wide Web address:** http://www.newtechusa.com. **Description:** Provides Microsoft Windows and VB developer training. The company offers seminars, on-site training programs, videos, and other related services. Founded in 1993. **Positions advertised include:** Systems Engineer; Senior Systems Engineer; Systems Architect; Practice Manager; Business Development Manager; Technical Services Director. **Corporate headquarters location:** This location. **Other U.S. locations:** Waltham MA; Providence RI.

PORTRAIT INTERNATIONAL, INC.
639 Research Parkway, Suite 100, Meriden CT 06450. 203/782-2300. **Contact:** Human Resources. **World Wide Web address:** http://www.aitgroup.com. **Description:** A software development and applications

company that specializes in telemarketing, marketing, sales, and customer service application software for the IBM midrange, UNIX client/server market. **Other U.S. locations:** Irvine CA; Cleveland OH. **International locations:** Australia; England; Paris.

QUEUE INC.
1 Controls Drive, Shelton CT 06484. 203/446-8100. **Toll-free phone:** 800/232-2224. **Contact:** Personnel. **World Wide Web address:** http:// www.queueinc.com. **Description:** Develops educational software. Queue's products range from early education software to more advanced levels in the areas of history, art, math, literature, language arts, test preparation, and typing.

RCG INFORMATION TECHNOLOGY, INC.
628 Hebron Avenue, Building 2, Suite 200, Glastonbury CT 06033. 860/278-1234. **Contact:** Human Resources. **World Wide Web address:** http://www.rcgit.com. **Description:** Provides computer consulting services. **Corporate headquarters location:** Edison NJ. **Other U.S. locations:** Washington DC; Orlando FL; Chicago IL; New York NY; Westchester NY; Philadelphia PA; Dallas TX; Houston TX. **International locations:** Philippines; South Africa.

SCAN-OPTICS, INC.
169 Progress Drive, Manchester CT 06040. 860/645-7878. **Fax:** 860/645-7995. **Contact:** Human Resources. **E-mail address:** mdarrell@scanoptics.com. **World Wide Web address:** http://www.scanoptics.com. **Description:** Scan-Optics designs and manufactures information processing systems used for imaging, data capture, document processing, and information management. Scan-Optics systems make it possible to process very large volumes of paper using features such as high-speed paper movement, optical character recognition, intelligent character recognition, high-speed image capture, image processing, and image storage and retrieval systems. Scan-Optics systems encompass hardware, software, and integration technologies for complete solutions. Typical applications for Scan-Optics systems include the processing of credit card sales drafts, mail order forms, federal and state tax forms, health care forms, automobile registrations, shareholder proxies, and payroll time cards. **Corporate headquarters location:** This location. **Other U.S. locations:** Dallas TX. **International locations:** England.

SPEAR TECHNOLOGIES
800 Maine Street South, Suite 210, 3rd Floor, Southbury CT 06488. 203/262-1161. **Contact:** Human Resources. **Description:** Develops, markets, and supports maintenance management software for the transportation industry. **Corporate headquarters location:** Oakland CA. **International locations:** England.

Delaware

COMPUTER AID, INC. (CAI)
901 Market Street, Suite 1200, Wilmington DE 19801. 302/888-5500. **Fax:** 302/888-5799. **Contact:** Human Resources Department. **E-mail address:** staffing@compaid.com. **World Wide Web address:** http://www.compaid.com. **Description:** A computer consulting company providing software development, maintenance outsourcing, e-commerce and other web-related services to companies as well as federal, state and local governments. **Positions advertised include:** Senior Technical Recruiter; Programmer Analyst; Solution Consultant; Programmer; Helpdesk Institute Pool. **Other U.S. locations:** Nationwide. **International locations:** Worldwide.

COMPUTER SCIENCES CORPORATION (CSC)
400 Commerce Drive, Newark DE 19713. 302/391-6000. **Contact:** Human Resources. **World Wide Web address:** http://www.csc.com. **Description:** An information technology services company offering systems design and integration; IT and business process outsourcing; applications software development; Web and application hosting; and management consulting. Founded in 1959. **NOTE:** See website for current job openings and application instructions. **Positions advertised include:** Application Developer; Computer Scientist; System Analyst; Financial Analyst. **Corporate headquarters location:** El Segundo CA. **Number of employees worldwide:** 80,000.

EDS (ELECTRONIC DATA SYSTEMS CORPORATION)
Bristol Building · 248 Chapman Road, Suite 100, Newark DE 19702. 302/454-7622. **Contact:** Human Resources. **E-mail address:** careers@eds.com. **World Wide Web address:** http://www.eds.com. **Description:** A global technology services company that provides information technology and business process outsourcing services to clients in the manufacturing, financial services, healthcare, communications, energy, transportation, and consumer and retail industries as well as to governments around the world. **NOTE:** See website for current job openings and to apply online. **Positions advertised include:** Business Services Analyst; Information Analyst; Insurance Analyst. **Corporate headquarters location:** Plano TX.

FAIR ISAAC CORPORATION
10 Corporate Circle, Suite 200, New Castle DE 19720. 302/324-8015. **Fax:** 302/324-7967. **Contact:** Human Resources. **World Wide Web address:** http://www.fairisaac.com. **Description:** Fair Isaac Corporation, along with its subsidiaries, provides analytic, software and data management products and services to automate and improve decisions. Founded in 1956. **NOTE:** See website for current job openings and to apply online. **Operations at this facility include:** This location is a sales office. **Listed on:** New York Stock Exchange. **Stock exchange symbol:** FIC. **Number of employees nationwide:** 3,000.

INFOQUEST SYSTEMS, INC.
15 Innovation Way, Suite 120, Newark DE 19711. 302/456-3392. **Toll-free phone:** 800/414-9899. **Fax:** 302/368-7544. **Contact:** Human Resources. **E-mail address:** jobs@iqsi.com. **World Wide Web address:** http://www.iqsi.com. **Description:** Develops software for the health care industry that assists with billing patients and scheduling appointments; attaches dictation to patients' files; and sends appointment reminders. **Corporate headquarters location:** This location.

District Of Columbia

AKQA, INC.
3255 Grace Street NW, Washington DC 20007. 202/551-9900. **Fax:** 202/551-9930. **Contact:** Human Resources Manager. **E-mail address:** DCjobs@akqa.com. **World Wide Web address:** http://www.akqa.com. **Description:** A digital marketing agency. AKQA's list of clients includes: AT&T, BMW Group, De Beers, Kit Kat, Microsoft, MTV, Nike, Sainsbury's, Smithsonian, Texas Instruments, Visa, and Xbox. **Positions advertised include:** Designer; Copywriter; Producer; Flash Developer. **Corporate headquarters location:** This location. **Other U.S. locations:** San Francisco CA; New York NY. **International locations:** London, England; Singapore.

ALIGNED DEVELOPMENT STRATEGIES, INC. (ADSI)
1925 K Street, NW, Suite 105, Washington DC 20006. 202/659-2807. **Fax:** 202/659-2810. **Contact:** Human Resources. **E-mail address:** info@goadsi.com. **World Wide Web address:** http://www. goadsi.com. **Description:** A consulting firm specializing in IT and e-Business for corporate and government entities. **Positions advertised include:** Oracle Database Administrator; Java/JSP Developer; Director of Government Marketing; Web Development Instructor; ASP.NET Web Developer; Network Security Specialist; Network Systems Administrator.

IBM CORPORATION
1301 K Street NW, Washington DC 20006. 202/515-

5100. **Contact:** IBM Staffing Services. **World Wide Web address:** http://www.ibm.com. **Description:** International Business Machines (IBM) develops, manufactures, and markets advanced information processing products including computers and microelectronic technology products, software, and networking systems and provides information technology-related services. **Positions advertised include:** Business Development Architect; Client Services Leader; Communications Systems Analyst; Creative Director; Database Administrator; Federal Systems Analyst. **Corporate headquarters location:** Armonk NY. **Operations at this facility include:** This location operates as a business support center. **Subsidiaries include:** IBM Credit Corporation; IBM Instruments, Inc.; IBM World Trade Corporation. **Listed on:** New York Stock Exchange. **Stock exchange symbol:** IBM.

INSLAW INC.
1156 15th Street NW, Washington DC 20005-2707. 202/828-8600. **Fax:** 202/659-0755. **Contact:** Tom Nolasco. **World Wide Web address:** http://www.inslawinc.com. **Description:** Designs, manufactures, and markets case tracking management software for the legal industry.

Florida

ACD SYSTEMS OF AMERICA
8550 Northwest 33rd Street, Suite 101, Miami FL 33122. 305/596-5644. **Fax:** 305/406-9802. **Contact:** Human Resources. **World Wide Web address:** http://www.acdcorporate.com. **Description:** Develops and markets digital imaging software. **Corporate headquarters location:** British Columbia Canada. **Positions advertised include:** Macintosh Software Developer.

AMICAS, INC.
325 Bill France Boulevard, Daytona Beach FL 32114. **Contact:** Human Resources. **World Wide Web address:** http://www.amicas.com. **Description:** Develops medical image and information management software for radiology departments. AMICAS offers radiology information systems, picture archiving and communications (PACS) systems, Web-based and wireless image and report distribution tools, and billing systems for the ambulatory and acute care radiology markets. **Positions advertised include:** Technical Support Analyst. **Corporate headquarters location:** Boston MA. **Listed on:** NASDAQ. **Stock exchange symbol:** AMCS.

AT&T GOVERNMENT SOLUTIONS
1980 North Atlantic Avenue, Suite 1030, Cocoa Beach FL 32931. 321/784-4030. **Fax:** 321/784-2009. **Contact:** Human Resources Department. **World Wide Web address:** http://www.att.com. **Description:** This division of AT&T creates large-scale, decision-support systems and software engineering environments; applies operations research and mathematical modeling to business and management systems; and implements advanced database technology. AT&T also provides studies and analysis capabilities for policy development and planning; modeling and simulation of hardware and software used in real-time testing of sensor, weapon, and battlefield management command, control, and communication systems; and testing and evaluation. AT&T's services are offered primarily to government and commercial customers. **Other U.S. locations:** Nationwide. **Operations at this facility include:** This location provides technical services and systems engineering.

ADERANT NORTH AMERICA
2255 Killearn Center Boulevard, Tallahassee FL 32309. 850/224-2200. **Contact:** Human Resources. **World Wide Web address:** http://www.aderant.com. **Description:** Develops financial software. Established in 1981. **NOTE:** Entry-level positions and part-time jobs are offered. **Special programs:** Training; Co-ops; Summer Jobs. **Corporate headquarters location:** Sydney, Australia. **Other U.S. locations:** Nationwide. **International locations:** Worldwide. **CEO:** Neil H. Gamble. **Number of employees worldwide:** 1,600.

ALLEN SYSTEMS GROUP INC.
1333 Third Avenue South, Naples FL 34102. 239/435-2200. **Contact:** Human Resources. **World Wide Web address:** http://www.allensysgroup.com. **Description:** Supplies *Fortune* 1000 companies with system management, file transfer, and help desk software. **Positions advertised include:** Analyst Relations Manager; Accounts Payable Manager; Accounts Receivable Manager; Staff Accountant; Staff Attorney. **Corporate headquarters location:** This location.

AMERICAN RIBBON & TONER COMPANY
2895 West Prospect Road, Fort Lauderdale FL 33309. 954/733-4552. **Fax:** 954/733-0319. **Contact:** Personnel. **E-mail address:** info@ribbontoner.com. **World Wide Web address:** http://www.ribbontoner.com. **Description:** Manufactures ribbons and toner cartridges for printers, fax machines, and copiers.

ANALYSTS INTERNATIONAL CORPORATION (AIC)
3835 NW Boca Raton Boulevard, Suite 300C, Boca Raton FL 33431. 561/750-8588. **Contact:** Human Resources. **E-mail address:** bocajobs@analysts.com. **World Wide Web address:** http://www.analysts.com. **Description:** AIC is an international computer consulting firm. The company uses different programming languages and software to assist clients in developing systems for a variety of industries. **Corporate headquarters location:** Minneapolis MN.

ANSWERTHINK CONSULTING GROUP
1001 Brickell Bay Drive, Suite 3000, Miami FL 33131. 305/375-8005. **Contact:** Human Resources. **E-mail address:** careers@answerthink.com. **World Wide Web address:** http://www.answerthink.com. **Description:** Provides computer consulting and IT services to *Fortune* 1000 companies. **Positions advertised include:** Consultant; Manager. **Corporate headquarters location:** Atlanta GA. **Other U.S. locations:** Fremont CA; Chicago IL; Burlington MA; Iselin NJ; Marlton NJ; New York NY; Hudson OH; Conshohocken PA; Dallas TX. **Listed on:** NASDAQ. **Stock exchange symbol:** ANSR.

AVINEON
15500 Light Wave Drive, Suite 200, Clearwater FL 33760. 727/539-1661. **Fax:** 727/539-0954. **Contact:** Human Resources. **World Wide Web address:** http://www.avineon.com. **Description:** Provides automated mapping, facility management, and geographic information system technologies to government and industries worldwide. **Note:** Formerly Agra Baymont. **Other U.S. locations:** Nationwide. **International locations:** Worldwide.

AVIONYX, INC.
1918 Dairy Road, West Melbourne FL 32904. 321/728-7975. **Toll-free phone:** 800/636-2833. **Fax:** 321/728-4049. **Contact:** Human Resources. **E-mail address:** jobs@avionyx.com. **World Wide Web address:** http://www.avionyx.com. **Description:** Provides full life cycle embedded software engineering services for commercial avionics systems requiring stringent development and testing standards such as DO-178B. **Positions advertised include:** Junior Software Test Engineer; IT Manager/Tech Support; Senior Software Engineer/Manager; Software/Hardware Project/Program Manager; Software Quality Engineer.

BELL MICROPRODUCTS LATIN AMERICA
7630 NW 25th Street, Miami FL 33122. 305/477-6406. **Contact:** Human Resources. **World Wide Web address:** http://www.fti-inc.com. **Description:** Distributes a full-line of computer products to Latin America. The company also provides training, service, and technical support. **Positions advertised include:** Distributor Supervisor; Inside Sales Representative; Marketing Programs Representative; Outside Sales Representative; RMA Clerk; Warehouse Manager.

BENEFIT TECHNOLOGY INC.
2701 South Bayshore Drive, Suite 401, Miami FL 33133. 305/285-6900. **Contact:** Human Resources. **World Wide Web address:** http://www.benefittechnology.com. **Description:** Develops Visual Basic software for life insurance companies.

BOCA RESEARCH
1601 Clint Moore Road, Suite 200, Boca Raton FL 33487. 561/241-8789. **Contact:** Human Resources. **World Wide Web address:** http://www.bocaresearch.com. **Description:** Manufactures computer components including network cards and video cards. **Corporate headquarters location:** This location. **Office hours:** Monday – Friday, 8:00 a.m. – 7:30 p.m.

CPA SOFTWARE
1 Pensacola Plaza, Pensacola FL 32501. 850/434-2685. **Toll-free phone:** 800/272-7123. **Fax:** 850/852-0470. **Contact:** Administrative Manager. **World Wide Web address:** http://www.cpasoftware.com. **Description:** Develops software for certified public accountants. **Positions advertised include:** Programmer/Analyst; Customer Service Representative; Data Conversion Specialist; Sales/Marketing Professional; Classroom Instructor. **Corporate headquarters location:** This location. **Parent company:** Fenimore Software Group, Inc. **Number of employees at this location:** 100.

CTG (COMPUTER TASK GROUP, INC.)
1335 Gateway Drive, Suite 2013, Melbourne FL 32901. 321/725-1300. **Contact:** Human Resources. **World Wide Web address:** http://www.ctg.com. **Description:** A computer consulting firm that performs programming and networking services for corporate clients. **Corporate headquarters location:** Buffalo NY. **Other U.S. locations:** Nationwide. **Listed on:** New York Stock Exchange. **Stock exchange symbol:** CTG.

CARECENTRIC
14788 Indigo Lakes Circle, Naples FL 34104. 239/352-3332. **Toll-free phone:** 800/441-2331. **Fax:** 770/801-0789. **Contact:** Human Resources. **World Wide Web address:** http://www.carecentric.com. **Description:** Develops and publishes software for the home health care industry. **NOTE:** Jobseekers should send a resume to CareCentric, 6600 Powers Ferry Road, Atlanta GA 30339. **Positions advertised include:** Software Demo & Support Specialist. **Corporate headquarters location:** Atlanta GA. **Annual sales/revenues:** $11 - $20 million. **Number of employees at this location:** 100. **Number of employees nationwide:** 300.

CITEL AMERICA, INC.
1515 NW 167th Street, Park Center Boulevard, Suite 6-303, Miami FL 33169. 305/621-0022. **Contact:** Human Resources Department. **E-mail address:** citel4u@ix.Netcom.com. **World Wide Web address:** http://www.citelprotection.com. **Description:** Manufactures surge protectors for computers. **Positions advertised include:** Sales Engineer.

CITRIX SYSTEMS, INC.
6400 Northwest 6th Way, Fort Lauderdale FL 33309. 954/267-3000. **Fax:** 954/267-3018. **Contact:** Human Resources. **E-mail address:** resume@citrix.com. **World Wide Web address:** http://www.citrix.com. **Description:** Develops application server software and services. Founded in 1989. **Positions advertised include:** Customer Care Manager; Supervisor Disbursement; Test Engineer; Build Engineer; Corporate Consultant; Order Entry Representative; Marketing Operations Analyst; Product Marketing Manager; Technical Software Trainer. **Corporate headquarters location:** This location. **Listed on:** NASDAQ. **Stock exchange symbol:** CTXS. **Annual sales/revenues:** More than $100 million.

COLAMCO INC.
975 Florida Central Parkway, Suite 1100, Longwood FL 32750. 407/331-3737. **Toll-free phone:** 800/327-2722. **Contact:** Human Resources. **World Wide Web address:** http://www.colamco.com. **Description:** Sells and distributes IT products to a customer base made up of primarily small businesses.

COMPUTER ASSOCIATES INTERNATIONAL, INC.
4601 Touchton Road East, Jacksonville FL 32246. 904/371-6200. **Contact:** Human Resources. **World Wide Web address:** http://www.cai.com. **Description:** Computer Associates International is one of the world's leading developers of client/server and distributed computing software. The company develops, markets, and supports enterprise management, database and applications development, business applications, and consumer software products for a broad range of mainframe, midrange, and desktop computers. Computer Associates International serves major business, government, research, and educational organizations. **Positions advertised include:** Associate Consultant; Call Center Program Manager; Consultant; Telesales Professional. **Corporate headquarters location:** Islandia NY. **Other U.S. locations:** Nationwide. **Annual sales/revenues:** More than $100 million. **Listed on:** New York Stock Exchange. **Stock exchange symbol:** CA. **CEO:** Sanjay Kumar.

COMSYS INC.
300 Northwest 82nd Avenue, Suite 411, Plantation FL 33324. 954/475-1456. **Contact:** Human Resources Department. **World Wide Web address:** http://www.comsys.com. **Description:** Offers contract computer consulting services. **Positions advertised include:** Biz Talk Consultant; Data Warehouse Developer; Designer; Programmer; HP - Unix Administrator; Information Analyst; Network Engineer; Testers; UAT Lab Technologist. **Corporate headquarters location:** Houston TX. **Other U. S. locations:** Nationwide.

CONCURRENT COMPUTER CORPORATION
2881 Gateway Drive, Pompano Beach FL 33069. 954/974-1700. **Toll-free phone:** 800/666-4544. **Fax:** 954/973-5398. **Contact:** Human Resources. **E-mail address:** resumes@ccur.com. **World Wide Web address:** http://www.ccur.com. **Description:** Provides networking systems, servers, software, technical support, and other services to companies in academic, aerospace/defense, CAD engineering, and scientific industries. **Positions advertised include:** Industry Marketing Manager. **Special programs:** Internships. **Corporate headquarters:** Duluth GA. **Listed on:** NASDAQ. **Stock exchange symbol:** CCUR. **Number of employees at this location:** 300. **Number of employees nationwide:** 425.

CONVERGYS
160 Lorum Road, Sunrise FL 33323. 954/851-9200. **Contact:** Human Resources. **World Wide Web address:** http://www.convergys.com. **Description:** A computer software company specializing in the telecommunications industry. **Positions advertised include:** Analyst; Assistant Coordinator. **Special programs:** Internships. **Corporate headquarters location:** Cincinnati OH. **Operations at this facility include:** Regional Headquarters; Research and Development; Sales; Service. **Listed on:** New York Stock Exchange. **Stock exchange symbol:** CVG.

DRS TACTICAL SYSTEMS
3520 U.S. Highway 1, Palm Bay FL 32905. 321/727-3672. **Fax:** 321/725-0496. **Contact:** Human Resources. **World Wide Web address:** http://www.paravant.com. **Description:** Manufactures rugged hand-held computer systems and software for the military. **Positions advertised include:** Production Manager; Electrical Engineer; Optical Engineer; Optical Worker; Quality Engineer; Electrician Technician; Mechanical Engineer; Test Manager; Controller; Program Manager; Quality Engineer; Analog Design Electrical Engineer. **Listed on:** NASDAQ. **Stock exchange symbol:** PVAT.

ECI TELECOM
1201 West Cypress Creek Road, Fort Lauderdale FL 33309. 954/772-3070. **Fax:** 954/351-4404. **Contact:**

Human Resources. **World Wide Web address:** http://www.ecitele.com. **Description:** Provides wide-area network systems for voice and data systems. **Corporate headquarters location:** This location. **Other U.S. locations:** Calabasas CA; Clearwater FL; Orlando FL; Herndon VA. **International locations:** Worldwide. **Operations at this facility include:** Administration; Manufacturing; Research and Development. **Listed on:** NASDAQ. **Stock exchange symbol:** ECIL. **Number of employees at this location:** 220.

ENCORE REAL TIME COMPUTING, INC.
1700 NW 66th Avenue, Suite 103, Fort Lauderdale FL 33313. 954/377-1100. **Fax:** 954/377-1145. **Contact:** Human Resources Department. **E-mail address:** info@encore.com. **World Wide Web address:** http://www.encore.com. **Description:** Encore specializes in the manufacture of minicomputers for aerospace, defense, simulation, energy, and information systems. **Special programs:** Internships. **Positions advertised include:** Hardware Engineer. **Corporate headquarters location:** This location. **Operations at this facility include:** Administration; Research and Development; Service.

EXECUTRAIN OF FLORIDA
One Urban Center, 4830 West Kennedy Boulevard, Suite 700, Tampa FL 33609. 813/288-2000. **Contact:** Human Resources. **E-mail address:** info@executrain.com. **World Wide Web address:** http://www.executrain.com/tampa. **Description:** Trains businesses and employees in the use of computer software and offers IT certification programs. **Other U.S. locations:** Nationwide. **International locations:** Worldwide.

FDP CORPORATION
2140 South Dixie Highway, Miami FL 33133. 305/858-8200. **Fax:** 305/858-0295. **Contact:** Human Resources. **E-mail address:** jobs@insurance.sunguard.com. **World Wide Web address:** http://www.fdpcorp.com. **Description:** Develops financial software for insurance agencies. **Positions advertised include:** Sales Executive.

FIDELITY
11601 North Roosevelt Boulevard, St. Petersburg FL 33716. 727/556-9000. **Fax:** 727/227-5005. **Contact:** Manager of Employment. **E-mail address:** recruit3@certegy.com. **World Wide Web address:** http://www.certegy.com. **Description:** Offers payment authorization services for financial institutions and retail establishments via national online computer systems that enable authorization of check and credit card transactions. **NOTE:** Equifax lists all job opportunities through Norrell Services. Call any local Norrell office for further information. **Positions advertised include:** Accountant; Business Analyst; AVP Risk Operations; Business Consultant; Client Relations Coordinator; Collections Account Manager; Database Analyst; Data Entry Operator; Programmer Analyst; Quality Control Specialist; Collections Supervisor. **Corporate headquarters location:** Atlanta GA. **Operations at this facility include:** Administration; Divisional Headquarters; Regional Headquarters; Research and Development; Sales Service. **Listed on:** New York Stock Exchange. **Stock exchange symbol:** EFX.

FISCHER INTERNATIONAL SYSTEMS CORPORATION
3584 Mercantile Avenue, Naples FL 34104. 239/643-1500. **Fax:** 239/643-3772. **Contact:** Human Resources. **World Wide Web address:** http://www.fisc.com. **Description:** Develops and sells software for electronic mailings, directories, and security.

GENERAL DYNAMICS INC. (ADVANCED INFORMATION SYSTEMS)
960 John Sims Parkway West, Niceville FL 32578-1823. 850/678-2126. **Fax:** 850/678-3977. **Contact:** Human Resources. **World Wide Web address:** http://www.veridian.com. **Description:** General Dynamics provides engineering systems integration and technical services to government agencies. **Positions advertised include:** Defense Analysis Specialist; Systems Engineer. **Other U.S. locations:** Nationwide. **Operations at this facility include:** This location offers computer support to nearby Air Force bases. **Number of employees nationwide:** Over 5,000.

HTE INC.
1000 Business Center Drive, Lake Mary FL 32746. 407/304-3235. **Contact:** Human Resources. **World Wide Web address:** http://www.hteinc.com. **Description:** Develops software for the government, education, law enforcement, and public safety markets. **Positions advertised include:** Applications Specialist; Customer Account Executive; Installation Specialist; Software Engineer; Support Analyst. **Listed on:** NASDAQ. **Stock exchange symbol:** HTEI. **Annual revenues:** $51 - $100 million. **Number of employees at this location:** 500.

HARRIS CORPORATION
1025 West NASA Boulevard, Mail Stop 19, Melbourne FL 32901. 321/727-9207. **Toll-free phone:** 800/4HA-RRIS. **Contact:** Human Resources. **World Wide Web address:** http://www.harris.com. **Description:** A communications equipment company that provides broadcast, network, government, and wireless support products and systems. **NOTE:** Send resumes to: Harris Corporation, Resume Processing, P.O. Box 549238, Suite 107, Waltham MA 02454. **Positions advertised include:** Engineering Administration; Program Manager Support Assistant; Word Processor Proposal Center; Corporate Legal Administrator; Lead Senior Auditor; Contracts Manager; Engineering Specialist; Information Systems Security Supervisor. **Corporate headquarters location:** This location. **International locations:** Worldwide. **Operations at this facility include:** Administration; Manufacturing; Research and Development; Sales; Service. **Listed on:** New York Stock Exchange. **Stock exchange symbol:** HRS. **President/CEO:** Phillip W. Farmer. **Number of employees worldwide:** 10,000.

HARRIS TECHNICAL SERVICES CORPORATION
1225 Evans Road, Melbourne FL 32904. 321/952-7550. **Toll-free phone:** 888/952-9468. **Fax:** 321/733-7570. **Contact:** Human Resources. **World Wide Web address:** http://www.harris.com. **Description:** Develops software solutions for commercial and government applications. **NOTE:** Entry-level positions are offered. Send resumes to: Harris Corporation, Resume Processing, P.O. Box 549238, Suite 107, Waltham MA 02454. **Positions advertised include:** Software Engineer; Quality Control Manager; Process Systems Engineer; Information Security Engineer; Communications Infrastructure Systems Engineer; Information and Transportation Systems Engineer; Business Development Manager; Quality Engineer. **Office hours:** Monday - Friday, 8:00 a.m. - 5:00 p.m. **International locations:** Worldwide. **Parent company:** Harris Corporation. **Listed on:** New York Stock Exchange. **Stock exchange symbol:** HRS. **President/CEO:** Phillip W. Farmer. **Number of employees worldwide:** 10,000.

HUMMINGBIRD, INC.
124 Marriott Drive, Tallahassee FL 32301. 850/942-3627. **Contact:** Cyndi Utt, Human Resources. **World Wide Web address:** http://www.hummingbird.com. **Description:** Develops document management software. Hummingbird also provides education, consulting, and support services for its products. **Positions advertised include:** Quality Assurance Analyst; Clarity System Analyst. **Listed on:** NASDAQ. **Stock exchange symbol:** HUMC.

HYPERION SOLUTIONS
401 East Las Olas Boulevard, Ft. Lauderdale FL 33301. 954/332-2410. **Fax:** 954/332-2411. **Contact:** Human Resources. **World Wide Web address:** http://www.hyperion.com. **Description:** Provides proprietary software to help businesses manage their

operations. **Positions advertised include:** Staff Accountant. **International locations:** Worldwide. **Average annual revenue:** 490 million. **Listed on:** NASDAQ. **Exchange symbol:** HYSL.

IBM CORPORATION
8051 Congress Avenue, Boca Raton FL 33487. 561/241-1997. **Toll-free phone:** 800/426-4968. **Contact:** Human Resources. **World Wide Web address:** http://www.ibm.com. **Description:** This location operates as a regional sales office. Overall, IBM is the developer, manufacturer, and marketer of advanced information processing products including computers and microelectronic technology, software, networking systems, and information technology-related services. **NOTE:** Jobseekers should send a resume to IBM Staffing Services, 1DPA/051, 3808 Six Forks Road, Raleigh NC 27609. **Corporate headquarters location:** Armonk NY. **Subsidiaries include:** IBM Credit Corporation; IBM Instruments, Inc.; IBM World Trade Corporation.

IBIS LLC
999 West Yamato Road, Suite 100, Boca Raton FL 33431. 561/982-7400. **Fax:** 561/237-2851. **Contact:** Human Resources. **E-mail address:** contact@ibisit.com. **World Wide Web address:** http://www.ibisit.com. **Description:** A technology & service company working to develop internet solutions. **Positions advertised include:** Chief Financial Advisor; Corporate Counsel; Publisher Account Manager; Publisher Account Representative; Client Services Associate; Commercial Legal Assistant; Director of Business Development; Internet Business Development Manager; Internet Marketing Specialist; Technical Support; Help Desk Representative.

IKON OFFICE SOLUTIONS TECHNOLOGY SERVICES
5100 West Lemon Street, Tampa FL 33601. 813/261-2000. **Fax:** 813/267-2500. **Contact:** Kim McDaniels, Human Resources. **World Wide Web address:** http://www.ikon.com. **Description:** Provides client/server and workflow consulting, network integration, product fulfillment, and technical training. Founded in 1988. **Positions advertised include:** 3rd Shift Copy Machine Operator; Account Executive Outside Sales. **Other area locations:** Fort Lauderdale FL; Jacksonville FL; Orlando FL; Tallahassee FL. **Other U.S. locations:** Pittsburgh PA. **Operations at this facility include:** Sales. **Listed on:** New York Stock Exchange. **Stock exchange symbol:** IKN. **Annual sales/revenues:** $51 - $100 million. **Number of employees at this location:** 100. **Number of employees nationwide:** 210.

INTELLECT TECHNICAL SOLUTIONS
Bay Vista Complex, 15950 Bay Vista Drive #130, Clearwater FL 33760. 727/533-9797. **Toll-free phone:** 800/599-8781. **Fax:** 727/533-0685. **Contact:** Chris Chiappetta, Human Resources. **E-mail address:** chrisc@intellectcorp.com **World Wide Web address:** http://www.intellectcorp.com. **Description:** A full service provider of technology consultants. **Positions advertised include:** Marketing Consultant; Sales Consultant.

ISYS/BIOVATION
6925 Lake Ellenor Drive, Suite 135, Orlando FL 32809. 407/859-2881. **Contact:** Human Resources. **World Wide Web address:** http://www.isysbiov.com. **Description:** Designs computer hardware and software to help manage laboratory information for hospitals, universities, and doctors' offices.

KHAMELEON SOFTWARE
400 North Ashley Drive, Suite 2600, Tampa FL 33602. 813/223-4148. **Contact:** Human Resources. **E-mail address:** hr@khameleonsoftware.com. **World Wide Web address:** http://www.khameleonsoftware.com. **Description:** Provides software design, consulting, and related services to e-focused, software, and system-integration businesses. **Special programs:** Internships. **Corporate headquarters location:** This location. **Other U.S. locations:** San Francisco CA; Atlanta GA; New York NY.

LOCKHEED MARTIN TACTICAL DEFENSE SYSTEMS
P.O. Box 6000, Clearwater FL 33758. 813/855-5711. **Physical address:** 3655 Tampa Road, Oldsmar FL 34677. **Fax:** 813/854-7225. **Contact:** Human Resources. **World Wide Web address:** http://www.lockheedmartin.com. **Description:** This location is a computer hardware manufacturing facility. Overall, Lockheed Martin Tactical Defense Systems designs and builds 16-bit and 32-bit technical computing systems used in mil-spec environments. Applications include electronic warfare, signal intelligence, radar, sonar, and imaging where digital signal processing or general purpose computing is required. The company is also involved in systems engineering, software development tools, computer systems, and integrated workstations of commercial architectures for proof-of-concept program phases. **NOTE:** Entry-level positions and second shifts are offered. **Positions advertised include:** Accountant; Software Engineer; Technician. **Special programs:** Training. **Corporate headquarters location:** Bethesda MD. **Other U.S. locations:** Nationwide. **International locations:** Worldwide. **Parent company:** Lockheed Martin Corporation. **Listed on:** New York Stock Exchange. **Stock exchange symbol:** LMT. **Number of employees at this location:** 500.

MPS GROUP
One Independent Drive, Jacksonville FL 32202. 904/360-2900. **Toll-free phone:** 877/MOD-ISIT. **Fax:** 904/360-2110. **Contact:** Human Resources. **World Wide Web address:** http://www.modisit.com. **Description:** Provides a wide range of computer consulting services. **Positions advertised include:** MSI Consultant; Seibel Systems Business Analyst; Net Developer; Quality Assurance Technical Writer. **Corporate headquarters location:** This location. **Other U.S. locations:** Nationwide. **International locations:** Canada; United Kingdom; Western Europe.

MACACADEMY/WINDOWS ACADEMY FLORIDA MARKETING INTERNATIONAL, INC.
102 East Granada Boulevard, Ormond Beach FL 32176-1712. 386/677-1918. **Toll-free phone:** 800/527-1914. **Fax:** 386/677-6717. **Contact:** Human Resources. **World Wide Web address:** http://www.macacademy.com. **Description:** Offers CD-ROM and video training for several PC and MacIntosh computer applications. The company also offers live seminars and on-site training in the United States, the United Kingdom, Australia, and Japan.

MAILSTREET
7890 Peters Road, Suite G102, Plantation FL 33324. 954/880-8965. **Toll-free phone:** 866/433-8787. **Fax:** 954/252-4506. **Contact:** Human Resources. **World Wide Web address:** http://www.mailstreet.com. **Description:** Provides Microsoft Exchange Server based email and collaboration hosting services. Founded in 2001. **Positions advertised include:** Support Engineer; Customer Service Representative. **Parent company:** Apptix, Inc.

McKESSONHBOC
1025 Greenwood Boulevard, Suite 500, Lake Mary FL 32746. 407/804-5000. **Fax:** 407/804-5005. **Contact:** Human Resources. **World Wide Web address:** http://www.hboc.com. **Description:** Provides information systems and technology to health care enterprises including hospitals, integrated delivery networks, and managed care organizations. McKessonHBOC's primary products are Pathways 2000, a family of client/server-based applications that allow the integration and uniting of health care providers; STAR, Series, and HealthQuest transaction systems; TRENDSTAR decision support system; and QUANTUM enterprise information system. The company also offers outsourcing services that include strategic information systems planning, data center

operations, receivables management, business office administration, and major system conversions. **Positions advertised include:** New Business Enterprise Vice President; Network Communications Analyst. **Corporate headquarters location:** San Francisco CA. **Other U.S. locations:** San Diego CA; Chicago IL; Minneapolis MN; Bedminster NJ; Dallas TX. **Subsidiaries include:** HBO & Company (UK) Limited; HBO & Company Canada Ltd. **Number of employees nationwide:** 470.

MODCOMP INC.
1550 South Powerline Road, Deerfield Beach FL 33442. 954/571-4600. **Contact:** Julie Slovin, Human Resources Manager. **World Wide Web address:** http://www.modcomp.com. **Description:** Manufactures computers designed for industrial automation, energy transportation, and communication applications. Founded in 1970.

MODUS OPERANDI
122 4th Avenue, Indialantic FL 32903. 321/984-3370. **Contact:** Human Resources. **E-mail address:** hr_jobs@modusoperandi.com. **World Wide Web address:** http://www.modusoperandi.com. **Description:** Designs high-tech software for the U.S. government.

NETWORK INFOSERVE, INC.
8370 West Hillsborough Avenue, Suite 201, Tampa FL 33615. 813/888-9208. **Fax:** 813/888-9481. **Contact:** Human Resources. **E-mail address:** jobs@niicorp.com. **World Wide Web address:** http://www.niicorp.com. **Description:** Engaged in systems integration.

NEXTIRAONE SYSTEMS
1601 Northwest 136th Avenue, Sunrise FL 33323. 954/846-1601. **Contact:** Human Resources. **World Wide Web address:** http://www.nextiraone.com. **Description:** Manufactures data communications equipment including WANs, LANs, and access products. The company also offers related services including project management, installation, consultation, network integration, maintenance, disaster recovery, and training. **Other U.S. locations:** Irvine CA; Acton MA; Hackensack NJ; Dallas TX.

OCE PRINTING SYSTEMS USA
5600 Broken Sound Boulevard NW, Boca Raton FL 33487. 561/997-3100. **Contact:** Human Resources. **World Wide Web address:** http://www.oceusa.com. **Description:** Services computer printers and copiers. **Positions advertised include:** Trainer; Field Service Engineer; Buyer.

PARADYNE CORPORATION
8545 126th Avenue North, Largo FL 33773. 727/530-2000. **Fax:** 727/530-8216. **Contact:** Human Resources. **World Wide Web address:** http://www.paradyne.com. **Description:** Manufactures and distributes WAN solutions including DSL, T1, and service-level management products. **Positions advertised include:** Mechanical Engineer; R&D Technician; Facilities Technician; Hardware Engineer; Support Engineer; EMS Development Engineer, **Special programs:** Internships. **Listed on:** NASDAQ. **Stock exchange symbol:** PDYN. **Number of employees at this location:** 2,150.

PAYFORMANCE CORPORATION
10550 Deerwood Park Boulevard, Suite 300, Jacksonville FL 32256. 904/997-6777. **Fax:** 904/997-8017. **Contact:** Human Resources. **World Wide Web address:** http://www.payformance.com. **Description:** Develops computer hardware and software designed for payment automation systems. Payformance Corporation provides services to over 3,000 corporate customers worldwide. **Positions advertised include:** Customer Service Representative; Product Manager. **Corporate headquarters location:** This location.

PAYSYS INTERNATIONAL
900 Winderley Place, Suite 140, Maitland FL 32751. 407/660-0343. **Contact:** Human Resources. **World Wide Web address:** http://www.paysys.com. **Description:** Develops credit card processing software.

PREMIO COMPUTER
8784 NW 18th Terrace, Miami FL 33172. 305/471-0199. **Contact:** Human Resources. **World Wide Web address:** http://www.premiopc.com. **Description:** A reseller of computers.

PYGMY COMPUTER SYSTEMS INC.
12651 South Dixie Highway, Suite 405, Miami FL 33156. 305/253-1212. **Toll-free phone:** 800/447-7469. **E-mail address:** support@pygmy.com. **Fax:** 305/255-1876. **Contact:** Personnel. **World Wide Web address:** http://www.pygmy.com. **Description:** Resells pocket computers and associated software.

SUN MICROSYSTEMS, INC.
3501 Quadrangle Boulevard, Suite 150, Orlando FL 32817. 407/380-0058. **Contact:** Human Resources. **World Wide Web address:** http://www.sun.com. **Description:** Sun Microsystems produces high-performance computer systems, workstations, servers, CPUs, peripherals, and operating system software. Products include a microprocessor called SPARC. Products are sold to engineering, scientific, technical, and commercial markets worldwide. **Positions advertised include:** Finance Accounting; Project Operations Support; Mission Critical Technical Support; Sales; Sales Management; Global Account Development; Account Management; Pre Sales Technical Support; Customer Service Program Sales; Technical Consultant; Project Manager; Systems Engineer; General Controller; Sales Representative. **Corporate headquarters location:** Palo Alto CA. **Other U.S. locations:** Nationwide. **International locations:** Worldwide. **Operations at this facility include:** This location manufactures mainframe computers. **Subsidiaries include:** Forte Software Inc. manufactures enterprise application integration software. **Listed on:** NASDAQ. **Stock exchange symbol:** SUNW. **CEO:** Scott McNealy. **Annual sales/revenues:** More than $100 million. **Number of employees worldwide:** 40,000.

TECH DATA CORPORATION
5350 Tech Data Drive, Clearwater FL 33760. 727/539-7429. **Contact:** Human Resources. **E-mail address:** jobs@techdata.com. **World Wide Web address:** http://www.techdata.com. **Description:** Distributes microcomputer-related hardware and software products to value-added resellers and computer retailers throughout the United States, Canada, Europe, Latin America, and the Caribbean. Tech Data Corporation purchases its products in large quantities directly from manufacturers and publishers, maintains an inventory of more than 25,000 products, and sells to an active base of over 50,000 customers. Tech Data Corporation provides its customers with products in networking, mass storage, peripherals, software, and systems from more than 600 manufacturers and publishers. Founded in 1974. **NOTE:** Entry-level positions and second and third shifts are offered. **Positions advertised include:** Compliance Coordinator; Communications Analyst; Applications Developer; Systems Application Manager; Systems Programmer; Accountant; Assistant Accountant; Credit Analyst; Credit Processor; Financial Analyst; Majors Vendor Reconciliation Specialist; Financial Analyst; Associate Counsel; Vendor Associate Manager. **Corporate headquarters location:** This location. **Other U.S. locations:** CA; GA; IN; NJ; TX. **International locations:** Canada; The Caribbean; Europe; Latin America; Middle East. **Subsidiaries include:** Computer 2000 AG (Germany); Tech Data Canada Inc. (Ontario, Canada); Tech Data Education, Inc. (Clearwater FL); Tech Data Finance, Inc. (Walnut Creek CA); Tech Data France, SNC (Bobigny, France); Tech Data Latin America (Miami FL); Tech Data Pacific, Inc. (Clearwater FL); Tech Data Product Management, Inc. (Clearwater FL). **Operations at this facility include:** Administration; Divisional Headquarters; Regional Headquarters; Sales; Service. **Listed on:** NASDAQ. **Stock exchange**

symbol: TECD. **CEO:** Steven A. Raymund. **Annual sales/revenues:** More than $100 million.

TINGLEY SYSTEMS
31722 State Road 52, P.O. Box 700, San Antonio FL 33576. 352/588-2250. **Contact:** Human Resources. **E-mail address:** tsi@tingsley.net. **World Wide Web address:** http://www.tingleysystems.com. **Description:** Develops software for the health care industry.

TYBRIN CORPORATION
1030 Titan Court, Fort Walton Beach FL 32547. 850/337-2500. **Toll-free phone:** 800/989-2746. **Contact:** Human Resources. **E-mail address:** support@b2secure.com. **World Wide Web address:** http://www.tybrin.com. **Description:** Tybrin Corporation provides engineering and computer support services to government and commercial customers. Founded in 1972. **Positions advertised include:** Access Analyst; Access Engineer; Lead Linux Administrative Program; Project Cost Analyst; Project Scheduler; Recruiter; Systems Test Engineer; Travel Accounting Clerk. **Corporate headquarters location:** This location. **Other U.S. locations:** Nationwide. **Listed on:** Privately held. **Number of employees nationwide:** 825.

UNISYS CORPORATION
7000 West Palmetto Park Road, Suite 201, Boca Raton FL 33433. 561/750-5800. **Contact:** Human Resources. **World Wide Web address:** http://www.unisys.com. **Description:** Provides technology services and solutions in consulting, systems integration, outsourcing, infrastructure, and server technology. **Positions advertised include:** Human Resources Business Partner; Microsoft Technology Consultant; Project Manager; Software Developer. **Corporate headquarters location:** Blue Bell PA. **Other U.S. locations:** Nationwide. **International locations:** Worldwide. **Operations at this facility include:** This location is a regional headquarters office. **Listed on:** New York Stock Exchange. **Stock exchange symbol:** UIS. **Number of employees worldwide:** 39,000.

VANN DATA SERVICES, INC.
200 West International Speedway, Daytona Beach FL 32114. 386/238-1200. **Fax:** 386/238-1454. **Contact:** Human Resources. **E-mail address:** jobs@vanndata.com. **World Wide Web address:** http://www.vanndata.com. **Description:** Computer service, sales and solutions company. **CEO:** George Van Arnam.

VERITAS SOFTWARE
401 East Las Olas Boulevard, Fort Lauderdale FL 33301. 954/332-2333. **Contact:** Human Resources. **World Wide Web address:** http://www.veritas.com. **E-mail address:** jobs@veritas.com. **Description:** Develops and markets backup software. **Positions advertised include:** Latin America Sales Director. **Corporate headquarters:** Mountain View CA. **Other U.S. locations:** Nationwide. **International locations:** Worldwide. **Listed on:** NASDAQ. **Stock exchange symbol:** VRTS. **Number of employees worldwide:** Over 5,000.

Georgia

ACCENTURE
100 Peachtree Street NE, Suite 1300, Atlanta GA 30303. 404/880-9100. **Contact:** Personnel. **World Wide Web address:** http://www.accenture.com. **Description:** A management and technology consulting firm. Accenture offers a wide range of services including business re-engineering; customer service system consulting; data system design and implementation; Internet sales systems research and design; and strategic planning. **NOTE:** Search and apply for jobs online. **Other U.S. locations:** Nationwide. **International locations:** Worldwide. **Listed on:** New York Stock Exchange. **Stock exchange symbol:** ACN. **CEO:** Joe W. Forehand. **Number of employees worldwide:** 86,000.

ADVANCED CONTROL SYSTEMS, INC.
P.O. Box 922548, Norcross GA 30010-2548. 770/446-8854. **Physical address:** 2755 Northwoods Parkway, Norcross GA 30071. **Toll-free phone:** 800/831-7223. **Fax:** 770/446-3502. **Contact:** Elaine Meggs, Human Resources. **E-mail address:** humanresources@acsatlanta.com. **World Wide Web address:** http://www.acsatlanta.com. **Description:** Manufactures distribution and energy management software and related hardware components. Founded 1975. **NOTE:** No phone calls regarding employment. **Positions advertised include:** Programmer. **Other U.S. locations:** CA; TX. **CEO:** John Muench.

AGENTEK, INC.
5900 Windward Parkway, Suite 400, Atlanta GA 30005. 678/393-1808. **Fax:** 678/393-9950. **Contact:** Human Resources. **E-mail address:** jobs@agentek.com. **World Wide Web address:** http://www.agentek.com. **Description:** Provides mobile communication solutions to help businesses improve visibility, communication, productivity, and service delivery. **Positions advertised include:** Project Manager; Software Engineer; Quality Assurance Engineer; Technical Support Representative.

AGILYSYS
11545 Wills Road, Suite 100, Alpharetta GA 30004. 770/625-7500 **Toll-free phone:** 800/448-6177. **Fax:** 770/625-7525. **Contact:** Human Resources Department. **World Wide Web address:** http://www.agilysys.com. **Description:** Provides enterprise computer technology solutions consisting of server and storage hardware, software, and services. Agilysys serves customers in a variety of industries and the public sector. **Positions advertised include:** Marketing Specialist; Team Leader; Account Rep; HR Manager; Systems Integration Specialist; QA Analyst. **Corporate headquarters location:** Mayfield Heights OH. **Other U.S. locations:** Boca Raton FL; Solon OH; Cleveland OH; Chicago IL; Burlington MA; New York NY. **International locations:** China; Canada. **Listed on:** NASDAQ. **Stock exchange symbol:** AGYS.

AMDOCS
1145 Sanctuary Parkway, Suite 110, Alpharetta GA 30004. 678/393-2260. **Fax:** 678/393-2276. **Contact:** Human Resources. **World Wide Web address:** http://www.amdocs.com. **Description:** Supplies operations support software used by telecommunications service providers to deliver voice, data, and wireless services to their customers. Amdocs also provides software to automate customer relationship management, sales, and billing operations, as well as publishing software for creating print and online directories. In addition, the company offers outsourced customer service and data center operations. **Positions advertised include:** Clarify Implementation Deployment Support; Consultant; Sr. Consultant; Java Programmer; Solution Sales Director; Software Engineer. **Corporate headquarters location:** St. Louis MO. **Other U.S. locations:** Jersey City NJ; El Dorado Hills CA; Charlotte NC; San Jose CA; Champaign IL. **Listed on:** New York Stock Exchange. **Stock exchange symbol:** DOX. **Number of employees worldwide:** 13,000.

AMERICAN MEGATRENDS, INC.
6145-F Northbelt Parkway, Norcross GA 30071-2976. 770/246-8600. **Fax:** 770/246-8790. **Contact:** Human Resources. **World Wide Web address:** http://www.ami.com. **Description:** Provider of BIOS technology, motherboards, utilities, and storage solutions. **Corporate headquarters location:** This location. **International locations:** China; Germany; India; Japan; Korea; Taiwan.

AMERICAN POWER CONVERSION CORPORATION (APC)
400 Galleria Parkway Southeast, Atlanta GA 30339. 678/385-6620. **Contact:** Human Resources. **World Wide Web address:** http://www.apc.com. **Description:** Manufactures uninterruptible power supply devices, surge protectors, cooling products, and power conditioning equipment to protect computers and

other electronic devices from damage due to electrical power failures and surges. APC also offers power management software and installation and maintenance services. Founded in 1981. **Positions advertised include:** Systems Engineer; Partner Development Manager; Senior Field Service Engineer; Air Team Lead. **Corporate headquarters location:** West Kingston RI. **Listed on:** NASDAQ. **Stock exchange symbol:** APCC. **Number of employees worldwide:** 6,500.

AMERICAN SOFTWARE, INC.
470 East Paces Ferry Road, Atlanta GA 30305. 404/261-4381. **Toll-free phone:** 800/726-2946. **Fax:** 404/261-5206. 238-8499. **Contact:** Human Resources. **Description:** Develops, markets, and supports integrated supply-chain management and financial-control systems software. The company's multiplatform enterprise software applications are primarily used for forecasting and inventory management, purchasing and materials control, and order processing and receivables control. The company also provides consulting and outsourcing services. **Corporate headquarters location:** This location. **Operations at this facility include:** Administration; Research and Development; Sales; Service. **Listed on:** NASDAQ. **Stock exchange symbol:** AMSWA. **CEO:** James Edenfield. **Annual sales/revenues:** $51 - $100 million. **Number of employees nationwide:** 440.

AMERICA'S BEST COMPUTER DISTRIBUTORS INC. (ABCD)
108 Old Montgomeryville Road, Milledgeville GA 31061. 478/454-2299. **Toll-free phone:** 800/733-3988. **Fax:** 478/452-0737. **Contact:** Human Resources. **World Wide Web address:** http://www.abcd4less.com. **Description:** Distributes computer hardware and accessories. The company also provides on-site repairs and technical support services.

ANALYSTS INTERNATIONAL CORPORATION (AIC)
3169 Holcomb Bridge Road, Suite 210, Norcross GA 30071. 770/446-6971. **Toll-free phone:** 800/597-5995. **Fax:** 770/446-3028. **Contact:** Human Resources. **E-mail address:** atlantajobs@analysts.com. **World Wide Web address:** http://www.analysts.com. **Description:** AiC is an information systems consulting firm. AiC provides analytical and programming services including consulting, systems analysis, design, programming, instruction, and technical writing. **NOTE:** Please visit website to register, search for jobs, and apply online. **Corporate headquarters location:** Minneapolis MN. **Other U.S. locations:** Nationwide. **International locations:** Canada; United Kingdom. **Operations at this facility include:** Regional Headquarters. **Listed on:** NASDAQ. **Stock exchange symbol:** ANLY. **Annual sales/revenues:** More than $100 million. **President/CEO:** Mike LaVelle. **Number of employees worldwide:** 4,500.

ANSWERTHINK CONSULTING GROUP
1117 Perimeter Center, Suite 500, Atlanta GA 30338. 770/225-3600. **Fax:** 707/225-3650. **Contact:** Personnel. **World Wide Web address:** http://www.answerthink.com. **Description:** Provides computer consulting and IT services to *Fortune* 1000 companies. Founded 1997. **NOTE:** Please visit website to search for jobs and apply online. **Positions advertised include:** SAP Professional. **Corporate headquarters location:** This location. **Other U.S. locations:** Burlington MA; Chicago IL; Hudson OH; Miami FL; New York NY; Conshohocken PA. **International locations:** Eschborn Germany; London England. **Listed on:** NASDAQ. **Stock exchange symbol:** ANSR. **Number of employees worldwide:** 1,600.

ASPECT SOFTWARE
4450 Rivergreen Parkway, Duluth GA 30096. 770/239-4000. **Fax:** 770/239-4444. **Contact:** Human Resources Manager. **World Wide Web address:** http://www.davox.com. **Description:** Davox Corporation develops, markets, implements, supports, and services outbound and inbound/outbound management systems software for call center operations. Founded 1981. **NOTE:** Please visit website to search for jobs and apply online. **Corporate headquarters location:** Westford MA. **Other U.S. locations:** Irvine CA; Miami FL; Oak Brook IL; Fort Washington PA; Richardson TX. **International locations:** Worldwide. **Operations at this facility include:** This location is a sales office. **President/CEO:** James D. Foy.

AUTOMATED SYSTEMS DESIGN (ASD)
645 Hembree Parkway, Suite D, Roswell GA 30076. 770/740-2300. **Toll-free phone:** 800/CABLING. **Fax:** 603/590-0079. **Contact:** Human Resources. **World Wide Web address:** http://www.asd-usa.com. **Description:** Installs cabling for computer networks. **President:** Bob Eskew. **Number of employees at this location:** 30.

CSC CONSULTING
2 Ravinia Drive, Suite 1150, Atlanta GA 30346. 770/677-3200. **Contact:** Human Resources. **World Wide Web address:** http://www.csc.com. **Description:** An independent provider of information technology consulting, systems integration, and outsourcing to industry and government. The company's services include management consulting as well as education and research programs in the strategic use of information resources and the design, engineering, development, integration, installation, and operation of computer-based systems and communications systems. CSC also provides consumer credit-related services, automated systems for health care organizations, financial insurance services, and data processing services. The company's principal markets are the U.S. federal government, U.S. commercial markets, and various international markets. Founded in 1959. **Positions advertised include:** Application Development Manager; Programmer Analyst; Strategic Management Specialist; Business Developer; System Administrator; Technician; Application Developer; Application Designer. **Corporate headquarters location:** El Segundo CA. **Listed on:** New York Stock Exchange. **Stock exchange symbol:** CSC. **Number of employees worldwide:** 90,000.

CSL TESCOM
8601 Dunwoody Place, Atlanta GA 30350. 678/250-1100. **Contact:** Human Resources. **World Wide Web address:** http://www.tescom-usa.com. **Description:** Provides software quality assurance and testing. **Positions advertised include:** QA Engineer; Performance Engineer; Automated Testing Specialist; Enterprise Software and ERP Project Management/ Implementation; Mercury QuickTest Pro QA Consultant.

CHECKFREE CORPORATION
4411 East Jones Bridge Road, Norcross GA 30092. 678/375-3387. **Contact:** Human Resources. **World Wide Web address:** http://www.checkfreecorp.com. **Description:** Provides a wide range of services and products that enable consumers, businesses, and financial institutions to conduct business over the Internet. CheckFree operates in three divisions: Electronic Commerce, Investment Services, and Software. Founded in 1981. **NOTE:** Please visit website to search for jobs and apply online. No phone calls regarding employment. **Positions advertised include:** Applications Specialist; Senior Business Process Consultant; Director Database Engineer; Revenue Accounting Manager; Insurance Sales Specialist; VP of Marketing, Strategy, and Business Development; Event Manager; Staff Project Manager; Senior Network Engineer; Software Engineer; Senior Database Administrator; Regional Sales Manager; Facilities Engineer; Manager of Operations; Project Manager; Six Sigma Black Belt; Corporate Business Continuity Program Manager. **Corporate headquarters location:** This location. **Other U.S. locations:** Nationwide. **International locations:** Canada, United Kingdom. **Listed on:** NASDAQ. **Stock

exchange symbol: CKFR. **Number of employees worldwide:** 3,300.

COLORGRAPHIC COMMUNICATIONS CORPORATION
P.O. Box 80448, Atlanta GA 30366. 770/455-3921. **Physical address:** 5980 Peachtree Road, Atlanta GA 30341. **Toll-free phone:** 877/943-3843. **Contact:** Human Resources. **World Wide Web address:** http://www.colorgraphic.net. **Description:** Manufactures graphic adapter boards that allow split screens on computers. **Office hours:** Monday – Friday, 9:00 a.m. – 5:30 p.m.

COMPREHENSIVE COMPUTER CONSULTING (CCC)
7000 Central Parkway, Suite 1000, Atlanta GA 30328. 770/512-0100. **Toll-free phone:** 888/451-1136. **Fax:** 770/512-0101. **Contact:** Human Resources Department. **World Wide Web address:** http://www.cccupclose.com. **Description:** Provides businesses with long-term, contract computer consultants. Founded 1978. **NOTE:** CCC uses the following Websites to post job listings: Computerjobs.com; and Dice.com. You may also submit your resume at their website by completing the online form. **Positions advertised include:** NET Developer; AutoLisp/AutoCad Developer; Capacity Planner; Digital System Installation & Operations Expert; Enterprise IT Architect; Functional Peoplesoft Consultant; Help Desk Personnel; Infrastructure/Network/SAN Analyst; Java/WebSphere Developer; Network Architect; Oracle Programmer. **Corporate headquarters location:** This location. **Other U.S. locations:** AL; NC; TX.

COMPUTER & CONTROL SOLUTIONS, INC. (CCSI)
2050 Mount Industrial Boulevard, Tucker GA 30084. 770/491-1131. **Toll-free phone:** 800/959-3525. **Fax:** 770/493-7033. **Contact:** Human Resources. **E-mail address:** hr@rackmountequipment.com. **World Wide Web address:** http://www.ccsisystems.com. **Description:** Provides systems integration services. **Positions advertised include:** Sales Personnel; Assembly Technician; Repair Technician.

COMPUTER ASSOCIATES INTERNATIONAL, INC.
2002 Summit Boulevard, Atlanta GA 30319. 404/946-1000. **Contact:** Human Resources. **World Wide Web address:** http://www.ca.com. **Description:** Computer Associates International is one of the world's leading developers of client/server and distributed computing software. The company develops, markets, and supports enterprise management, database and applications development, business applications, and consumer software products for a broad range of mainframe, midrange, and desktop computers. The company serves major business, government, research, and educational organizations. Founded in 1976. **NOTE:** Please visit website to search for jobs, and to find more specific contact information. **Positions advertised include:** Consultant; Principal Consultant; Senior Consultant; Vice President – Finance and Administration; Account Director. **Corporate headquarters location:** Islandia NY. **Other U.S. locations:** Nationwide. **International locations:** Worldwide. **Operations at this facility include:** This location sells software and provides technical support. **Listed on:** New York Stock Exchange. **Stock exchange symbol:** CA. **President/CEO:** Sanjay Kumar. **Number of employees nationwide:** 17,000.

COMPUTER HORIZONS CORPORATION
3340 Peachtree Road NE, Suite 160, Atlanta GA 30326. 404/814-3777. **Toll-free phone:** 800/662-3971. **Fax:** 404/814-3788. **Contact:** Human Resources. **World Wide Web address:** http://www.computerhorizons.com. **Description:** A full-service technology solutions company offering contract staffing, outsourcing, re-engineering, migration, downsizing support, and network management services. Founded 1969. **Office hours:** Monday - Friday, 9:00 a.m. - 5:00 p.m. **Corporate headquarters location:** Mountain Lakes NJ. **Other U.S. locations:** Nationwide. **International locations:** Canada; India. **Listed on:** NASDAQ. **Stock exchange symbol:** CHRZ. **President/CEO:** William J. Murphy. **Number of employees worldwide:** 3,000.

COMPUTER INTELLIGENCE2, INC.
Governor's Ridge, 1642 Powers Ferry Road, Building 12, Suite 300, Marietta GA 30067. 770/425-2267. **Toll-free phone:** 888-657-3278. **Fax:** 770/425-1338. **Contact:** Human Resources. **World Wide Web address:** http://www.ci2.com. **Description:** Provides computer based technologies and services. **Corporate headquarters location:** This location. **Other U.S. locations:** Washington, D.C.

EMC CORPORATION
2850 Premiere Parkway, Duluth GA 30097. 770/814-3600. **Fax:** 678/457-0003. **Contact:** Human Resources. **World Wide Web address:** http://www.emc.com. **Description:** EMC Corporation designs, manufactures, markets, and supports high-performance data storage products. The company also provides related services for selected mainframe and mid-range computer systems primarily manufactured by IBM and Unisys. **NOTE:** Please visit website to search for jobs and apply online. You may also mail resumes to corporate office at P.O. Box 65, Nutting Lake MA 01865, or fax to 508/435-8829. **Positions advertised include:** Account Manager; Channel Sales Representative; Senior Account Manager; Software Account Manager; Business Continuity Systems Integrator; Client Solutions Lead; Practice Manager; Managed Services Storage Architect. **Corporate headquarters location:** Hopkinton MA. **Other U.S. locations:** Nationwide. **International locations:** Worldwide. **Operations at this facility:** This is a sales office. **Listed on:** New York Stock Exchange. **Stock exchange symbol:** EMC. **Number of employees nationwide:** 13,100. **Number of employees worldwide:** 23,600.

EMAG
3495 Piedmont Road, Building 11, Suite 500, Atlanta GA 30305. 404/995-6060. **Toll-free phone:** 800/364-9838. **Fax:** 404/872-8247. **Toll-free fax:** 800/334-8273. **Contact:** Human Resources. **World Wide Web address:** http://www.emaglink.com. **Description:** EMEG provides document storage solutions, manufactures computer hardware and software, and develops customized financial software. **Corporate headquarters location:** This location. **Other U.S. locations:** NY; CA; TX. **International locations:** United Kingdom. **Operations at this facility include:** This location provides optical disk storage for IBM computers. Optical disks, also called laser disks, store data in the form of text, music, or pictures and are read by a laser that scans the surface. **Office hours:** Monday - Friday, 8:00 a.m. - 6:00 p.m. **Number of employees worldwide:** 200.

EARTHLINK, INC.
1375 Peachtree Street, Level A, Atlanta GA 30309. 404/815-0770. **Contact:** Human Resources. **World Wide Web address:** http://www.earthlink.net. **Description:** Provides Internet access and Web hosting services to individuals and small businesses. Founded in 1994. **NOTE:** Please visit website to search for jobs and apply online. **Positions advertised include:** Software Engineer; Manager – Broadband Provisioning Applications Development; Solutions Center Tier 2 Analyst; Senior Cost Analyst; Account Manager; Senior Manager – Partner Performance; Client Support Analyst; Technical Writer; Data Analyst; Project Analyst; Manager – Special Projects; Web Developer; Director – Procurement; Training Coordinator; Network Abuse Engineer; Security Analyst; Interface Design Director. **Corporate headquarters location:** This location. **Other U.S. locations:** San Francisco CA; Pasadena CA. **Listed on:** NASDAQ. **Stock exchange symbol:** ELNK.

ELESYS NORTH AMERICA, INC.
70 Crestridge Drive, Suite 150, Suwanee GA 30024. 770/904-3400. **Contact:** Human Resources. **E-mail**

address: jobs@elesys-na.com. **World Wide Web address:** http://www.elesys-na.com. **Description:** Develops electronic automotive safety systems for automobile manufacturers. **NOTE:** Please visit website to search for jobs and apply online. **Positions advertised include:** Senior Manager, Human Resources. **Office hours:** Monday – Friday, 8:00 a.m. – 4:30 p.m. **Corporate headquarters location:** This location. **Other U.S. locations:** Plymouth MI. **International locations:** Japan. **Operations at this facility include:** Administration; Market Development. **President:** Akio Kobayashi. **Number of employees at this location:** 42. **Number of employees worldwide:** 325.

EXTENSITY
66 Perimeter Center East, Atlanta GA 30346-1805. 404/239-2000. **Fax:** 404/239-2404. **Contact:** Human Resources. **World Wide Web address:** http://www.extensity.com. **Description:** Develops and markets business applications software in the areas of human resources, materials management, manufacturing, healthcare, and higher education. Products include the SmartStream series of financial software. **NOTE:** Please visit website to search for jobs and apply online. **Positions advertised include:** Accounts Receivable Administrator; Billing Analyst; Hosted Operations Systems Administrator; Senior Accountant; Senior Business Systems Analyst; Senior Financial Analyst. **Corporate headquarters location:** Ontario Canada. **Other U.S. locations:** Nationwide. **International locations:** Worldwide. **President/CEO:** Charles S. Jones. **Number of employees worldwide:** 2,400.

FAIR, ISAAC AND CO., INC.
3550 Engineering Drive, Suite 200, Norcross GA 30092. 770/810-8000. **Contact:** Dawn Ridz, Human Resources Recruiter. **E-mail address:** dawnridz@fairisaac.com. **World Wide Web address:** http://www.fairisaac.com. **Description:** Develops and provides data management software and services for the consumer credit, personal lines insurance, and direct marketing industries. Founded in 1956. **NOTE:** Contact is located at corporate office. Fax is 858/202-2056. Please visit website to search for jobs and apply online. **Corporate headquarters location:** San Rafael CA. **Other U.S. locations:** Nationwide. **International locations:** Worldwide. **Subsidiaries include:** CRMA Consulting; DynaMark, Inc.; Risk Management Technologies. **Listed on:** New York Stock Exchange. **Stock exchange symbol:** FIC. **President:** Thomas Grudnowski. **Number of employees nationwide:** 2,000.

FIRSTWAVE TECHNOLOGIES, INC.
5775 Glen Ridge Drive, Building E, Suite 400, Atlanta GA 30328. 770/250-0360. **Toll-free phone:** 800/540-6061. **Fax:** 770/431-1201. **E-mail address:** careers@firstwave.net. **Contact:** Human Resources. **World Wide Web address:** http://www.firstwave.com. **Description:** Develops, markets, and supports software systems that automate the integrated sales, marketing, and customer service functions of business organizations in a wide range of industries. These sales performance solutions provide end users with closed-loop business solutions. Founded in 1984. **Corporate headquarters location:** This location. **International locations:** United Kingdom. **Operations at this facility include:** Administration; Research and Development; Sales; Service. **Listed on:** NASDAQ. **Stock exchange symbol:** FSTW. **CEO:** Richard Brock. **Annual sales/revenues:** $21 - $50 million.

GLENAYRE
11360 Lakefield Drive, Duluth GA 30097. 770/283-1000. **Fax:** 770/283-3993. **Contact:** Human Resources. **E-mail address:** gtti@glenayre.com. **World Wide Web address:** http://www.glenayre.com. **Description:** Develops communication network administration software. **Corporate headquarters location:** This location. **Other U.S. locations:** TX; IL. **International locations:** Worldwide. **Listed on:** NASDAQ. **Stock exchange symbol:** GEMS. **CEO:** Clarke H. Bailey.

HEBCO INC.
7980 Industrial Highway, Suite B, Macon GA 31216. 478/788-9340. **Fax:** 478/784-9087. **Contact:** Randy Williams. **E-mail address:** hebco@hebco.com. **World Wide Web address:** http://www.hebco.com. **Description:** Provides computer engineering and technical services. **Corporate headquarters location:** Oklahoma City OK. **Other U.S. locations:** AR; PA.

HYPERION SOFTWARE CORPORATION
3200 Town Point Drive, Suite 175, Kennesaw GA 30144. 678/797-6540. **Fax:** 678/797-6541. **Contact:** Human Resources. **World Wide Web address:** http://www.hysoft.com. **Description:** Hyperion Software Corporation develops financial applications for managers and analysts. **NOTE:** Please visit website to search for jobs and apply online. **Corporate headquarters location:** Sunnyvale CA. **Other U.S. locations:** Nationwide. **International locations:** Worldwide. **Operations at this facility include:** Regional sales office. **Listed on:** NASDAQ. **Stock exchange symbol:** HYSL. **Number of employees worldwide:** 2,600.

IBM CORPORATION
4111 Northside Parkway NW, Atlanta GA 30327. 404/238-7000. **Toll-free phone:** 800/426-4968. **Fax:** 800/262-2494. **Contact:** IBM Staffing Services. **World Wide Web address:** http://www.ibm.com. **Description:** IBM is a developer, manufacturer, and marketer of advanced information processing products including computers and microelectronic technology, software, networking systems, and information technology-related services. **NOTE:** Please visit website to search for jobs and apply online. **Positions advertised include:** Application Architect; Associate Service Delivery Representative; Business Operations/Program Manager; Portal/Lotus Specialist; Systems Services Representative; Technical eLearning Consultant. **Corporate headquarters location:** White Plains NY. **Other area locations:** Statewide. **Other U.S. locations:** Nationwide. **International locations:** Worldwide. **Operations at this facility include:** This location is a sales office. **Subsidiaries include:** IBM Credit Corporation; IBM Instruments, Inc.; IBM World Trade Corporation. **Listed on:** New York Stock Exchange. **Stock exchange symbol:** IBM. **CEO:** Samuel J. Palmisano.

INDUS INTERNATIONAL
3301 Windy Ridge Parkway, Atlanta GA 30339. 770/952-8444. **Fax:** 770/955-2977. **Contact:** Human Resources. **E-mail address:** recruiter_east@Indus.com. **World Wide Web address:** http://www.indus.com. **Description:** Develops software for client/server asset care applications used by manufacturing companies. **Corporate headquarter locations:** This location. **Other U.S. locations:** Columbia SC; Englewood Cliffs NJ; Pittsburg PA; Richland WA; San Francisco CA. **International locations:** Canada; United Kingdom; France; Australia; Japan; Dubai. **Listed on:** NASDAQ. **Stock exchange symbol:** IINT. **President/CEO:** Gregory J. Dukat. **Number of employees worldwide:** 600.

INFOR
1000 Windward Concourse Parkway, Suite 100, Alpharetta GA 30005. 770/418-2000. **Contact:** Human Resources. **E-mail address:** hr@infor.com. **World Wide Web address:** http://www.infor.com. **Description:** Develops software for select manufacturing and distribution industries. **Corporate headquarters location:** This location. **Other U.S. locations:** Chicago IL; Shrewsbury NJ. **CEO:** Jess Solomon.

INTELLINET
Two Concourse Parkway, Suite 100, Atlanta GA 30328. 404/442-8000. **Fax:** 404/442-8001. **Contact:** Human Resources. **E-mail address:** careers@intellinet.com. **World Wide Web address:** http://www.intellinet.com. **Description:** An information technology services firm. **Positions advertised include:** BizTalk Consultant; Consultant / Senior Consultant, Development; Consultant/Senior

Consultant, Exchange; Business Intelligence Consultant; Business Development Manager; Sharepoint Specialist. **Other U.S. locations:** Birmingham AL; Charlotte NC; New York NY; Tampa FL; Washington DC.

INTERACTIVE BUSINESS SYSTEMS, INC. (IBS)
515 Crossville Road, Suite 210, Roswell GA 30075. 678/277-9407. **Fax:** 678/277-2577. **Contact:** Human Resources. **E-mail address:** atlanta@ibs.com. **Description:** IBS provides technology solutions across the areas of business, applications and infrastructure, specializing in the insurance and health care industries. **NOTE:** Submit resume and apply for positions online. **Positions advertised include:** Healthcare IT Project Manager; .NET C# Software Developer; QA Tester with Compuware & Insurance; Quality Assurance Analyst (Senior); Actuate Database Report Developer/Analyst; Linux Network Change Management Analyst; LINUX Network Engineer. **Corporate headquarters location:** Oak Brook IL.

INTERWOVEN
14 Piedmont Center, Suite 1500, 3525 Piedmont Road, Atlanta GA 30305-1530. 404/264-8000. **Fax:** 404/264-8300. **Contact:** Human Resources. **E-mail address:** jobs@mediabin.com. **World Wide Web address:** http://www.mediabin.com. **Description:** Develops digital imaging technologies and software. Founded in 1987. **Corporate headquarters location:** Sunnyvale CA. **Other U.S. locations:** Newport Beach CA; Bethesda MD; Chicago IL; Waltham MA; Dallas TX; New York NY; Bellevue WA. **International locations:** Worldwide. **Listed on:** NASDAQ. **Stock exchange symbol:** IWOV. **CEO:** Martin Brauns. **Number of employees worldwide:** 700.

IVIVITY
5555 Oakbrook Parkway, Suite 280, Norcross GA 30093-2286. 678/990-1550. **Fax:** 678/990-1551. **Contact:** Human Resources. **World Wide Web address:** http://www.ivivity.com. **Description:** A technology provider of intelligent storage infrastructure components and building blocks to storage networking and storage infrastructure OEMs. **Positions advertised include:** Operations Analyst; Product Manager; Field Application Engineer. **Corporate headquarters location:** This location. **President and CEO:** David Coombs.

JDA SOFTWARE GROUP
1090 Northchase Office Parkway, Suite 300, Marietta GA 30067-6402. 770/424-0100. **Contact:** Human Resources. **World Wide Web address:** http://www.jda.com. **Description:** Develops inventory control software. **NOTE:** Search and apply for jobs online. **Corporate headquarters location:** Scottsdale AZ. **Other U.S. locations:** Andover MA; Campbell CA; Columbus OH; Ann Arbor MI; St Louis Park MN; Naperville IL; Irving TX; Parsippany NJ. **International locations:** Worldwide. **Listed on:** NASDAQ. **Stock exchange symbol:** JDAS. **Number of employees worldwide:** 1,300.

LECTRA SYSTEMS, INC.
889 Franklin Road SE, Marietta GA 30067-7945. 770/422-8050. **Fax:** 770/422-1503. **Toll-free phone:** 877/453-2872. **Fax:** 800/746-8760. **Contact:** Human Resources. **World Wide Web address:** http://www.lectra.com. **Description:** Manufactures CAD/CAM systems for the textiles and leather processing industries. **NOTE:** Contact Human Resources directly at 800/746-3416. Please visit website to search for jobs and apply online. **Positions advertised include:** Strategic Account Manager; Welcome Center Representative; Communications Manager. **Corporate headquarters location:** Paris France. **Number of employees worldwide:** 1,520.

LEICA GEOSYSTEMS GIS & MAPPING
5051 Peachtree Corners Circle, Suite 100, Norcross GA 30092. 770/776-3400. **Toll-free phone:** 877/463-7327. **Fax:** 404/248-9400. **Contact:** Human Resources. **E-mail address:** human.resources@leicaus.com. **World Wide Web address:** http://gis.leica-geosystems.com. **Description:** Designs geographic imaging software, which provides solutions for spectral analysis, digital photogrammetry, and map composition. One of the largest digital mapping companies in the world. The company provides the hardware and software used for the Geospatial Imaging Chain. **Positions advertised include:** Regional Sales Manager; Software Engineer; Airborne Sensor Support Engineer; Digital Photogrammetry Support Engineer; Marketing Communications Writer; Product Manager; Product Specialist; Remote Sensing Specialist; Software Engineer; Systems Integration Technician; Business Analyst; Controller Operations; Design Electro Mechanical Engineer; Key Account Manager; Strategic Purchaser. **Corporate headquarters location:** This location. **Other U.S. locations:** San Diego CA; Westford MA. **International locations:** Heerbrugg Switzerland.

McKESSON INFORMATION SOLUTIONS
5995 Windward Parkway, Alpharetta GA 30005. 404/338-6000. **Contact:** Human Resources. **World Wide Web address:** http://www.mckhboc.com. **Description:** Provides information systems and technology to health care enterprises including hospitals, integrated delivery networks, and managed care organizations. McKesson's primary products are Pathways 2000, a family of client/server-based applications that allows the integration and uniting of health care providers; STAR, Series, and HealthQuest transaction systems; TRENDSTAR decision support system; and QUANTUM enterprise information system. The company also offers outsourcing services that include strategic information systems planning, data center operations, receivables management, business office administration, and major system conversions. **Positions advertised include:** Senior Business Analyst; Product Support Analyst; Business Analyst R&D and Services; Manager of Financial Planning and Analysis; Senior Financial Analyst; Senior Oracle Database Administrator; Enterprise Vice President – Sales; Sales Support Product Consultant; Staff Accountant; Technology Licensing Attorney; Auditor; Project Manager – Clinical Demo Systems; Sales Associate; Network/Desktop Systems Specialist; Enterprise Sales Executive; HRIS Call Center Analyst; Security Infrastructure Engineer. **Corporate headquarters location:** San Francisco CA. **Other U.S. locations:** Carrollton TX. **Parent company:** McKesson Corporation. **Listed on:** New York Stock Exchange. **Stock exchange symbol:** MCK.

MERCURY INTERACTIVE CORPORATION
5 Concourse Parkway, Suite 2350, Atlanta GA 30328. 770/804-5895. **Fax:** 770/804-5894. **Toll-free phone:** 800/TEST-911. **Contact:** Human Resources Department. **World Wide Web address:** http://www.mercuryinteractive.com. **Description:** Mercury Interactive is a developer of automated software quality (ASQ) tools for enterprise applications testing. The company's products are used to isolate software and system errors prior to application deployment. **Positions advertised include:** Consulting Project Manager; Expert Consultant – Technology Integration; Process Engineer; Solution Consultant; Application Delivery Testing Systems Engineer. **Corporate headquarters location:** Sunnyvale CA. **Other U.S. locations:** Nationwide. **Operations at this facility include:** This location is a sales office. **Listed on:** NASDAQ. **Stock exchange symbol:** MERQ. **CEO:** Amnon Landan. **Annual sales/revenues:** More than $100 million. **Number of employees worldwide:** 2,322.

NCR CORPORATION
2651 Satellite Boulevard, Duluth GA 30096. 770/623-7000. **Contact:** Human Resources. **World Wide Web address:** http://www.ncr.com. **Description:** A provider of computer products and services. The company provides computer solutions to three targeted industries: retail, financial, and communication. NCR Computer Systems Group develops, manufactures, and

markets computer systems. NCR Financial Systems Group is an industry leader in financial delivery systems, relationship banking data warehousing solutions, and payments systems/item processing. NCR Retail Systems Group is a world leader in end-to-end retail solutions serving the food, general merchandise, and hospitality segments. NCR Worldwide Services provides data warehousing services solutions; end-to-end networking services; and designing, implementing, and supporting complex open systems environments. NCR Systemedia Group develops, produces, and markets a complete line of information products to satisfy customers' information technology needs including transaction processing media, auto identification media, business form communication products, managing documents and media, and a full line of integrated equipment solutions. **Positions advertised include:** Pricing Director; Financial Planning Analyst; Compris Controller; GIS IC Food; Sales Representative; Channel Marketing Manager; Industrial Design Engineer; Product Management Business Analyst; Production Planning Manager. **Corporate headquarters location:** Dayton OH. **Other U.S. locations:** El Segundo CA; San Diego CA; Columbia SC. **International locations:** Worldwide. **Listed on:** New York Stock Exchange. **Stock exchange symbol:** NCR. **Number of employees worldwide:** 29,000.

NORTEL NETWORKS
5405 Windward Parkway, Alpharetta GA 30004. 770/708-4000. **Contact:** Human Resources. **World Wide Web address:** http://www.nortel.com. **Description:** Nortel Networks designs, produces, and supports multimedia access devices for use in building corporate, public, and Internet networks. The primary focus of the company's services is the consolidation of voice, fax, video, and data and multimedia traffic into a single network link. **NOTE:** Please visit website to search for jobs and apply online. **Corporate headquarters location:** Ontario, Canada. **Other U.S. locations:** Richardson TX; Santa Clara CA; Simi Valley CA; San Ramon CA; Billerica MA; Triangle Park NC; Schaumburg IL. **Operations at this facility include:** This location develops software. **Listed on:** New York Stock Exchange. **Stock exchange symbol:** NT. **President/CEO:** Frank A. Dunn.

NOVA INFORMATION SYSTEMS, INC.
One Concourse Parkway, Suite 300, Atlanta GA 30328. 770/396-1456. **Toll-free phone:** 800/226-9332. **Contact:** Human Resources. **E-mail address:** novaresume@novainfo.com. **World Wide Web address:** http://www.novainfo.com. **Description:** Develops and markets credit and debit card processing software. **Office hours:** Monday – Friday, 8:30 a.m. – 5:30 p.m. **Corporate headquarters location:** This location. **Other U.S. locations:** Knoxville TN. **Listed on:** New York Stock Exchange. **Stock exchange symbol:** NIS. **Annual sales/revenues:** More than $100 million. **CEO:** Edward Grzedzinski. **Number of employees nationwide:** 1,500.

OPEN SOLUTIONS
3098 Piedmont Road NE, Suite 200, Atlanta GA 30305. 404/262-2298. **Toll-free phone:** 800/275-4374. **Fax:** 404/233-4815. **Contact:** Human Resources. **World Wide Web address:** http://www.libertysite.com/fitech. **Description:** Designs software for credit unions. Founded 1977. **Corporate headquarters location:** This location. **Other area locations:** Louisville GA. **Listed on:** Privately held. **Other U.S. locations:** Greensboro NC. **Parent company:** Liberty Enterprises Inc.

ORACLE - PEOPLESOFT
3353 Peachtree Road NE, Suite 600, Atlanta GA 38326. 404/439-5900. **Contact:** Human Resources. **World Wide Web address:** http://www.peoplesoft.com. **Description:** Creates a variety of software. Founded 1987. **NOTE:** Please visit website to search for jobs and apply online. **Positions advertised include:** PGS Manager; Client Executive Healthcare; Staff Proposal Specialist; Revenue Management Systems Solution Consultant; Senior Consultant. **Corporate headquarters location:** Pleasanton CA. **Other area locations:** Atlanta GA. **Other U.S. locations:** Nationwide. **International locations:** Worldwide. **Listed on:** NASDAQ. **Stock exchange symbol:** PSFT. **Number of employees worldwide:** 12,000.

PER-SE TECHNOLOGIES, INC.
1145 Sanctuary Parkway, Suite 200, Alpharetta GA 30004. 770/237-4300. **Toll-free phone:** 877/737-3773. **Contact:** Human Resources. **World Wide Web address:** http://www.per-se.com. **Description:** A provider of comprehensive business management services, financial and clinical software, and Internet solutions to physicians and other healthcare professionals. **Positions advertised include:** Senior Software Engineer; Product Director; Corporate Communications Associate; Staff Financial Analyst; Help Desk Administrator; Senior Coding Consultant; Healthcare Consulting Sales Director; Practice/Account Manager; Client Enrollment Specialist. **Corporate headquarters location:** This location. **Other U.S.** locations: Nationwide. **Listed on:** NASDAQ. **Stock exchange symbol:** PSTI. **President/CEO:** Phillip M. Pead. **Number of employees nationwide:** 5,000.

SED INTERNATIONAL
4916 North Royal Atlanta Drive, Tucker GA 30085. 770/491-8962. **Toll-free phone:** 800/444-8962. **Fax:** 770/938-1235. **Toll-free fax:** 800/329-2733. **Contact:** Human Resources Department. **E-mail address:** humanresources@sedintl.com. **World Wide Web address:** http://www.sedonline.com. **Description:** A wholesaler of computer systems and cellular phones. Founded 1980. **NOTE:** Please visit website for job listings. **Positions advertised include:** Inside Sales Representative. **Corporate headquarters location:** This location. **Other U.S. locations:** City of Industry CA; Dallas TC; Miami FL. **International locations:** Argentina; Puerto Rico; Columbia. **Listed on:** NASDAQ. **Stock exchange symbol:** SECX. **CEO:** Mark Diamond. **Number of employees worldwide:** 287.

SAGE SOFTWARE
SMALL BUSINESS SOLUTIONS
1505 Pavilion Place, Norcross GA 30093. 770/724-4000. **Contact:** Human Resources. **E-mail address:** humanresources@bestsoftware.com. **World Wide Web address:** http://www.peachtree.com. **Description:** Develops, manufactures, and markets accounting software. **NOTE:** Please visit website to search for jobs and apply online. No phone calls regarding employment. **Positions advertised include:** Web Managing Editor; Inside Software Sales Representative; Design Analyst – Windows GUI; Associate Marketing Manager; ACT Lead Qualifying Sales Representative; Shipping and Receiving Clerk; Customer Support Manager; Vice President of Product Management; Director of Corporate Sales; Network Engineer; Senior Marketing Manager; Vice President of Direct Mail. **Corporate headquarters location:** This location. **Parent company:** Best Software.

SAMPO TECHNOLOGY CORPORATION
5550 Peachtree Industrial Boulevard, Suite 100, Norcross GA 30071. 770/449-6220. **Fax:** 770/447-1109. **Contact:** Personnel Manager. **World Wide Web address:** http://www.sampotech.com. **Description:** Distributes computer monitors. **Corporate headquarters location:** Taiwan. **Other U.S. locations:** Irvine CA. **International locations:** The Netherlands; China; Philippines. **Operations at this facility include:** Administration; Sales; Service. **CEO:** H.C. Ho. **Number of employees worldwide:** 1,500.

SIMTROL
2220 Norcross Parkway, Suite 255, Norcross GA 30071. 678/533-1200. **Fax:** 770/441-1823. **Toll-free phone:** 800/474-6876. **Contact:** Human Resources. **World Wide Web address:** http://www.simtrol.com . **Description:** Designs, produces, and markets tailored

software for interactive group video conferencing systems. Using standard telecommunication transmissions, Simtrol products allow many people at different geographic locations to see and hear one another on live television. **Corporate headquarters location:** This location. **CEO:** Rick Egan.

SOLARCOM, LLC
One Sun Court, Norcross GA 30092. 770/449-6116. **Fax:** 770/582-7233. **Contact:** Recruiting Department. **E-mail address:** recruiting@solarcom.com. **World Wide Web address:** http://www.solarcom.com. **Description:** An IT consulting firm providing services in the areas of enterprise systems, internetworking, storage technologies, business recovery and hosting, and financial solutions. **Positions advertised include:** Carrier Services Sales; Leasing Consultant; Channel Account Manager; Storage Sales Representative; Compaq Account Executive; Parts Sales Rep.

SUNGARD DATA SYSTEMS
11560 Great Oaks Way, Suite 200, Alpharetta GA 30022. 770/587-6800. **Fax:** 770/587-6808. **Contact:** Human Resources. **World Wide Web address:** http://www.sungard.com. **Description:** Develops financial software for insurance companies. **NOTE:** Please visit website to search for jobs. Visit http://www.sungard.apply2jobs.com to apply online. **Positions advertised include:** Manager of Professional Services; Consultant. **Corporate headquarters location:** Wayne PA. **International locations:** Worldwide. **Parent company:** SunGard Financial Systems. **Listed on:** New York Stock Exchange. **Stock exchange symbol:** SDS. **President/CEO:** Cristobal I. Conde. **Number of employees at worldwide:** 10,000.

TASQ TECHNOLOGY
2155 Barrett Park Drive, Suite 215, Kennesaw GA 30144. 770/218-5000. **Contact:** Human Resources. **World Wide Web address:** http://www.tasq.com. **Description:** Provides point-of-sale equipment and resolutions for electronic payment purposes. **Corporate headquarters location:** Rocklin CA. **Parent company:** First Data Corporation.

TRIDIA CORPORATION
1000 Cobb Place Boulevard NW, Building 200, Suite 220, Kennesaw GA 30144-3684. 770/428-5000. **Toll-free phone:** 800/582-9337. **Fax:** 770/428-5009. **Contact:** Human Resources. **World Wide Web address:** http://www.tridia.com. **Description:** A provider of SCO UNIX-based solutions and a software developer and reseller. The company's product line includes DOUBLEVISION remote control software, which allows a user to connect to another user's screen. Founded 1987. **Office hours:** Monday – Friday, 8:30 a.m. – 5:00 p.m. **Corporate headquarters location:** This location. **CEO:** Vincent Frese, II.

UNISYS CORPORATION
5550-A Peachtree Parkway, 3rd Floor, Norcross GA 30092. 770/368-6000. **Fax:** 770/368-6152. **Contact:** Human Resources. **World Wide Web address:** http://www.unisys.com. **Description:** Provides technology services and solutions in consulting, systems integration, outsourcing, infrastructure, and server technology. **NOTE:** Please visit website to register, search for jobs, and apply online. **Positions advertised include:** Portfolio Sales Executive; Mail Clerk; CRM Manager; Client Focus Manager. **Corporate headquarters location:** Blue Bell PA. **Other area locations:** Savannah GA. **Other U.S. locations:** Nationwide. **International locations:** Worldwide. **Operations at this facility include:** This location provides information services and global customer support. **Listed on:** New York Stock Exchange. **Stock exchange symbol:** UIS. **Number of employees worldwide:** 37,000. **President/CEO:** Lawrence A. Wrinbach.

VCG INC.
1805 Old Alabama Road, Roswell GA 30076. 770/246-2300. **Toll-free phone:** 800/318-4983. **Fax:** 770/449-3638. **Contact:** Missy DuToit, Human Resources Manager. **E-mail address:** hr@vcgsoftware.com. **World Wide Web address:** http://www.vcgsoftware.com. **Description:** Distributes computer hardware and staffing software. Founded in 1976. **NOTE:** Please visit website to search for jobs. **Positions advertised include:** Data Migration Engineer; Regional Sales Manager; Application Support Representative; C++ Analyst; Quality Assurance Analyst; Web Design Developer. **Corporate headquarters location:** This location. **Operations at this facility include:** Accounting/Auditing; Customer Service; Marketing; Sales. **Annual sales/revenues:** $11 - $20 million.

VERSO TECHNOLOGIES
400 Galleria Parkway, Suite 300, Atlanta GA 30339. 678/589-3500. **Fax:** 678/589-3750. **Contact:** Julie Prye, Vice President of Human Resources. **E-mail address:** jobs@verso.com. **World Wide Web address:** http://www.verso.com. **Description:** Develops and installs wINNfinity and LANmark management systems. Founded 1984. **NOTE:** Please visit website to search for jobs. No phone calls regarding employment. **Positions advertised include:** Training and Installation Specialist; Bilingual Customer Care Agent; Customer Care Agent; Senior Software Engineer. **Corporate headquarters location:** This location. **Other U.S. locations:** Oakbrook Terrace IL. **Listed on:** NASDAQ. **Stock exchange symbol:** VRSO. **CEO:** Steve Odom. **Number of employees nationwide:** 450.

WEST INFORMATION CENTER
245 Peachtree Center Avenue, Suite 1000, Atlanta GA 30303. 404/881-0454. **Toll-free phone:** 800/336-5768. **Fax:** 404/881-0873. **Contact:** Human Resources. **World Wide Web address:** http://www.westlaw.com. **Description:** An online information company that provides access to public and court records for clients such as lawyers, bankers, investigators, and those involved with commercial transactions and business litigation. **Parent company:** Thompson West.

Hawaii

CTA
550 Paiea Street, Suite 210, Honolulu HI 96819. 808/839-2200. **Fax:** 808/839.4844. **Contact:** Judy Bishop, General Manager. **E-mail address:** info@cta.net. **World Wide Web address:** http://www.cta.net. **Description:** A Business Services company that assists companies with staffing, applications development, and systems engineering. **Positions advertised include:** Payroll Specialist; Customer Claims; Senior Information Processor; Administrative Assistant; Accounting Assistant; Human Resources Assistant; Bilingual Service Representative; Executive Administrative Assistant.

HIPOINT SOFTWARE, LLC
Interstate Building, 1314 South King Street, Suite 864, Honolulu HI 96814. 808/597-8851. **Fax:** 808/597-8861. **Contact:** Human Resources. **E-mail address:** info@hipointsoftware.com. **World Wide Web address:** http://www.hipointsoftware.com. **Description:** A computer consulting firm specializing in data collection and management applications for distribution companies. **Corporate headquarters location:** This location. **Other U.S. locations:** New York NY.

HON-CAD
1000 Bishop Street, Suite 500, Honolulu HI 96813. 808/440-5008. **Fax:** 808/440-5001. **Contact:** Bill Clisham. **E-mail address:** resumes@honcad.com. **World Wide Web address:** http://www.hon-cad.com. **Description:** As the CAD division of HONCAD Corporation, Hon-CAD provides professional CAD training, services, and products to Hawaii's architecture, engineering, and construction markets. **Positions advertised include:** CAD Applications Engineer.

SYNCADD VIVID DATA
1833 Kalakaua Avenue, Suite 1000, Honolulu HI 96815. 808/941-8286. **Fax:** 808/941-7173. **Contact:**

Human Resources. **E-mail address:** contact@syncadd.com. **World Wide Web address:** http://www.syncadd.com. **Description:** A technology company that focuses on managing real estate property assets and resources using the Vivid Data Platform. The platform allows for the integration of a variety of technologies, including GIS, CAD, GPS, and laser devices.

TECHNOLOGY INTEGRATION GROUP
1220 Kapiolani Boulevard, Suite 410, Honolulu HI 96814. 808/524-6652. **Contact:** Maranda Kidwell. **E-mail address:** maranda.kidwell@tig.com. **World Wide Web address:** http://www.tig.com. **Description:** Provides IT software, hardware, and support to clients of all sizes. **NOTE:** Fax all resumes to Corporate Headquarters at 858/566-7293. **Positions advertised include:** Account Executive. **Corporate headquarters location:** San Diego CA. **Other U.S. locations:** Nationwide. **Operations at this facility include:** Sales; Customer Support; Technical Services. **Annual sales/revenue:** $200 million. **Number of employees nationwide:** 320.

VERIFONE, INCORPORATED
Mililani Technology Park, 100 Kahelu Avenue, 1st Floor, Mililani HI 96789-3909. 808/623-2911. **Fax:** 916/630-2566. **Contact:** Human Resources. **World Wide Web address:** http://www.verifone.com. **Description:** Develops and manufactures credit card transaction terminals and secure payment solutions. The company specializes in the automation and delivery of secure payment transactions. **Corporate headquarters location:** San Jose CA. **Parent company:** Hewlett Packard. **Operations at this facility include:** Research and Development. **Listed on:** New York Stock Exchange. **Stock exchange symbol:** PAY. **Number of employees worldwide:** 1,000.

Idaho

AMS SERVICES INC.
7600 North Mineral Drive, Suite 400, Coeur d'Alene ID 83814. 800/444-4813. **Contact:** Human Resources. **World Wide Web address:** http://www.amsworld.com. **Description:** Develops and markets insurance software. **Corporate headquarters location:** Bothell WA. **Other U.S. locations:** CT; FL; TX.

ADAGER CORPORATION
The Adager Way, Sun Valley ID 83353-3000. 208/726-9100. **Toll-free phone:** 800/533-7346. **Fax:** 208/726-8191. **Contact:** Human Resources. **E-mail address:** info@adager.com. **World Wide Web address:** http://www.adager.com. **Description:** A specialized database utility firm. Adager's hardware is oriented to any type of HP3000 hardware, operating system, or IMAGE/SQL version. **Number of employees at this location:** 4. **President:** Rene Wok

AGENCY SOFTWARE, INC.
215 West Commerce Drive, Hayden Lake ID 83835. 208/762-7188. **Toll-free phone:** 800/342-7327. **Fax:** 208/762-1265. **Contact:** Human Resources Department. **World Wide Web address:** http://www.agencysoft.com. **Description:** Develops software for the insurance industry and employs a small staff in sales, technical support, quality assurance and software development. The company advertises its open positions in The Coeur d'Alene Press newspaper. **Number of employees at this location:** 15. **President:** Mitch McInelly

EMERGECORE NETWORKS LLC
8850 West Emerald Street, Boise ID 83704. 208/947-8555. **Fax:** 208/947-8556. **Contact:** Human Resources. **E-mail address:** jobs@emergecore.com. **World Wide Web address:** http://www.emergecore.com. **Description:** Develops integrated IT solutions for small businesses.

HEWLETT PACKARD
11311 Chinden Boulevard, Boise ID 83714. 208/396-6000. **Fax:** 208/396-3457. **Contact:** Human Resources. **World Wide Web address:** http://www.hp.com. **Description:** HP is a technology solutions provider to consumers, businesses and institutions globally. The company's offerings span IT infrastructure, global services, business and home computing, and imaging and printing. At HP Boise, Imaging and Printing Systems is the largest group on site. Also based in Boise is HP Services (HPS), which integrates all product support and repair activities. Another significant business is the Network Storage Solutions Organization (NSS). Idaho Falls has a sales and service office. **NOTE:** Search and apply for positions online. **Corporate headquarters location:** Palo Alto CA. **Other U.S. locations:** Nationwide. **International locations:** Worldwide.

IANYWHERE SOLUTIONS, INC.
5777 North Meeker Avenue, Boise ID 83713. 208/322-7575. **Toll-free phone:** 800/235-7576. **Fax:** 208/327-5004. **Contact:** Charlene Hofstetter, Human Resources. **E-mail address:** charlene.hofstetter@sybase.com. **World Wide Web address:** http://www.ianywhere.com. **Description:** Sybase acquired Extended Systems and integrated it into its iAnywhere subsidiary. iAnywhere's business is mobile and embedded databases, mobile management and security, mobile middleware and synchronization and Bluetooth® and infrared protocol technologies. **NOTE:** Apply online at www.sybase.coom. **Positions advertised include:** Intern/Co-op Tech; Product Support Analyst. **Corporate headquarters location:** Dublin, CA. **International locations:** Worldwide. **Operations at this facility include:** Administration; Sales; Service; Technical Support. **Listed on:** New York Stock Exchange. **Stock exchange symbol:** SY.

MPC COMPUTERS
906 East Karcher Road, Nampa ID 83687. 208/893-3434. **Toll-free phone:** 800/828-0416. **Fax:** 208/893-7044. **Contact:** Human Resources. **E-mail address:** jobs@mpccorp.com. **World Wide Web address:** http://www.mpccorp.com. **Description:** A wholly owned subsidiary of HyperSpace Communications, MPC provides computer products and IT solutions to mid-sized businesses, government agencies and education organizations. Also provides customer and product support. **NOTE:** Unsolicited resumes and applications are not accepted. See website for current openings. Apply for open positions via e-mail, fax or mail, indicating job title and number. **Positions advertised include:** Associate General Counsel; Programmer Analyst; Business Acquisition Specialist; Inside Sales Rep – Federal; Manager of Finance; Engineering Technician – Regression; Forecast Planner; Purchasing Specialist; Account Executive – Idaho. **Corporate headquarters location:** This location. **Parent company:** HyperSpace Communications. **Listed on:** American Stock Exchange. **Stock exchange symbol:** HCO.

MICRON TECHNOLOGY, INC.
8000 South Federal Way, P.O. Box 6, Boise ID 83707-0006. 208/368-4000. **Fax:** 208/363-2322. **Recorded jobline:** 800/932-4991. **Contact:** Human Resources. **E-mail address:** jobs@micron.com. **World Wide Web address:** http://www.micron.com. **Description:** Micron manufactures and markets DRAMs, NAND flash memory, CMOS image sensors, other semiconductor components and memory modules for use in leading-edge computing, consumer, networking, and mobile products. **NOTE:** See website to search and apply for positions. **Positions advertised include:** ESD/Latch-Up Senior R&D Engineer; Gas Support Technician; Cost Accounting Manager. **Special programs:** Internships; College Recruiting. **Corporate headquarters location:** This location. **Other area locations:** Meridian ID; Nampa ID. **Other U.S. locations:** CA; IL; MN; NC; NH; NY; OR; TX; UT; VA. **International Locations:** Worldwide. **Listed on:** New York Stock Exchange. **Stock exchange symbol:** MU. **Number of employees at this location:** 7,825. **Number of employees nationwide:** 11,400. **Number of employees worldwide:** 16,900

PROCLARITY CORPORATION
500 South 10th Street, Boise ID 83702. 208/344-1630. **Fax:** 208/343-6128. **Contact:** Human Resources. **E-mail address:** employment@proclarity.com. **World Wide Web address:** http://www.proclarity.com. **Description:** Expanding on the Microsoft business intelligence platform, ProClarity's solutions allow business professionals to monitor business performance, visualize and explore multi-dimensional data and perform root-cause analysis. **NOTE:** Apply for open positions online. **Positions advertised include:** Accounts Payable Accountant; Marketing Intern; Product Specialist Internship; Senior Business Intelligence Consultant. **Corporate office location:** This location. **Worldwide locations**: France; Germany; Netherlands; United Kingdom. **CEO**: Bob Lokken.

TREETOP TECHNOLOGIES INC.
6148 Discovery Way, Suite 105, Boise ID 83713. 208/342-5668. **Fax:** 208/345-8808. **Contact:** Human Resources. **E-mail address:** resumes@treetoptech.com. **World Wide Web address:** http://www.treetoptech.com. **Description:** A computer consulting company that designs IT portfolios for organizations to improve cost effectiveness and efficiency. **NOTE:** See website for current positions. **Corporate headquarters location:** This location. **Other U.S. locations:** Nationwide. **International locations:** Singapore.

Illinois

ACCENTURE
161 North Clark Street, 44th Floor, Chicago IL 60601. 312/693-0161. **Fax:** 312/693-0507. **Contact:** Human Resources. **World Wide Web address:** http://www.accenture.com. **Description:** A management and technology consulting firm. Accenture offers a wide range of services including business re-engineering; customer service system consulting; data system design and implementation; Internet sales systems research and design; and strategic planning. **NOTE:** Search and apply for positions online. **Positions advertised include:** Administrative Assistant; Senior Accountant; Analytics Manager; HR Transformation Consultant. **Corporate headquarters location:** Bermuda. **Other U.S. locations:** Nationwide. **International locations:** Worldwide. **Listed on:** New York Stock Exchange. **Stock exchange symbol:** ACN. **Number of employees worldwide:** 75,000.

ADVANCED SYSTEM DESIGNS, INC.
100 Yordy Road, Morton IL 61550. 309/263-7944. **Toll-free phone:** 877/273-4968. **Fax:** 309/263-7721. **Contact:** Human Resources. **World Wide Web address:** http://www.asd.net. **Description:** A provider of information technology solutions with five areas of focus: IBM, Microsoft, security, networks, and business intelligence. **Positions advertised include:** Lead Technical Consultant; Microsoft .NET Application Developer; SQL Server Developer; Systems Engineer.

ALERI
Two Prudential Plaza, 41st Floor, Chicago IL 60601. 312/540-0100. **Fax:** 312/540-0717. **Contact:** Human Resources. **E-mail address:** careers@aleri.com. **World Wide Web address:** http://www.aleri.com. **Description:** Designs and develops solutions for financial institutions including the ATLAS software product line, a series of financial transaction processing systems that allow companies to increase productivity and reduce operating costs. Founded in 1999.

AMDOCS
2109 Fox Drive, Champaign IL 61820. **Toll-free phone:** 888/727-8508. **Fax:** 217/351-8256. **Contact:** Human Resources. **World Wide Web address:** http://www.amdocs.com. **Description:** Provides customer service software. **Positions advertised include:** Vendor Manager; Facility Supervisor; Sr. Mainframe Infrastructure & Application Analyst. **Corporate headquarters location:** St. Louis MO. **Other U.S. locations:** Nationwide.

ANALYSTS INTERNATIONAL CORPORATION (AIC)
1101 Perimeter Drive, Suite 830, Schaumburg IL 60173-5060. 847/619-4673. **Fax:** 847/605-9489. **Contact:** Senior Staffing Assistant. **E-mail address:** jobs@analysts.com. **World Wide Web address:** http://www.analysts.com. **Description:** Analysts International is an international computer consulting and staffing firm. The company assists clients in analyzing, designing, and developing systems using different programming languages and software. **NOTE:** Search and apply for jobs online. A minimum of one to two years of programming experience is required. **Corporate headquarters location:** Minneapolis MN. **Other U.S. locations:** Nationwide. **Listed on:** NASDAQ. **Stock exchange symbol:** ANLY. **Annual sales/revenues:** More than $100 million.

APPLIED SYSTEMS, INC.
200 Applied Parkway, University Park IL 60466. 708/534-5575. **Fax:** 708/534-8016. **Contact:** Human Resources. **E-mail address:** careers@appliedsystems.com. **World Wide Web address:** http://www.appliedsystems.com. **Description:** Provides computer systems integration and design services to the insurance industry. **NOTE:** Search for positions online. Submit resume by e-mail or fax. **Positions advertised include:** Account Manager; Agency Consultant; Business Development Representative; Developer; Engagement Manager; Operations Administrator; PC Support Technician; Product Consultant.

CA, INC.
2400 Cabot Drive, Lisle IL 60532. 630/505-6000. **Contact:** Human Resources. **World Wide Web address:** http://www.ca.com. **Description:** A leading international provider of computer services for businesses. **NOTE:** See website for current job openings and to apply online. **Positions advertised include:** Architect; Customer Information Representative; Quality Assurance Engineer; Sales Executive; Security Architect. **Corporate headquarters location:** Islandia NY. **Other area locations:** Bloomington IL; Chicago IL **Other U.S. locations:** Nationwide. **International locations:** Worldwide. **Listed on:** New York Stock Exchange. **Stock exchange symbol:** CA.

CDW CORPORATION
200 North Milwaukee Avenue, Vernon Hills IL 60061. 847/465-6000. **Fax:** 847/465-3444. **Contact:** Human Resources. **E-mail address:** careers@cdw.com. **World Wide Web address:** http://www.cdw.com. **Description:** Operates as a direct marketer of multi-brand information technology products and services, reselling name-brand computers and peripherals to businesses, government agencies, and educational institutions through catalog, phone, and online sales. **NOTE:** Apply online. **Corporate headquarters location:** This location. **Listed on:** NASDAQ. **Stock exchange symbol:** CDWC. **Annual sales/revenues:** More than $100 million.

CHICAGO MICROSYSTEMS, INC.
1825 Elmdale Avenue, Glenview IL 60026-1297. 847/998-9970. **Fax:** 847/998-9975. **Contact:** Human Resources. **World Wide Web address:** http://www.chimicro.com. **Description:** Chicago Microsystems, Inc. (CMI) is a full-service information technology consulting firm serving clients throughout the Chicago Metro area. CMI specializes in serving the education and small business markets.

COMPUTER HORIZONS CORPORATION RECRUITING CENTER, MIDWEST REGION
6400 Shafer Court, Suite 420, Rosemont IL 60018. 847/698-6800. **Toll-free phone:** 800/877-2421. **Fax:** 847/698-6823. **Contact:** Staffing Manager. **World Wide Web address:** http://www.computerhorizons.com. **Description:** Computer Horizons is a full-service technology solutions company offering contract staffing, outsourcing, re-engineering, migration, downsizing support, and network management. Founded in 1969. **NOTE:** Apply online at the

company's website. **Corporate headquarters location:** Mountain Lakes NJ.

COMPUTER SCIENCES CORPORATION (CSC)
2021 Spring Road, Suite 200, Oak Brook IL 60061. 630/574-0100. **Contact:** Human Resources. **World Wide Web address:** http://www.csc.com. **Description:** Provide customers in industry and government with IT services and solutions, including systems design and integration; IT and business process outsourcing; applications software development; Web and application hosting; and management consulting. Founded in 1959. **NOTE:** Search and apply for positions online. **Listed on:** New York Stock Exchange. **Stock exchange symbol:** CSC. **Number of employees worldwide:** 90,000.

COMPUWARE CORPORATION
475 Martingale Road, Suite 800, Schaumburg IL 60173. 630/285-8560. **Fax:** 630/285-8572. **Contact:** Human Resources. **E-mail address:** compuware.recruiting@compuware.com. **World Wide Web address:** http://www.compuware.com. **Description:** Develops, markets, and supports an integrated line of systems software products that improve the productivity of programmers and analysts in application program testing, test data preparation, error analysis, and maintenance. Compuware also provides a broad range of professional data processing services including business systems analysis, design, and programming, as well as systems planning and consulting. **NOTE:** Apply online to open positions. **Corporate headquarters location:** Detroit MI.

CONVERGYS
2 Pierce Place, Itasca IL 60143-3153. 630/775-1700. **Fax:** 630/775-8890. **Contact:** Human Resources. **World Wide Web address:** http://www.convergys.com. **Description:** Provides outsourced customer care, human resource, and billing services worldwide. The company operates in three segments: Customer Care; Employee Care; and the Information Management Group. Founded in 1976. **NOTE:** See website for current job openings and to apply online. **Other area locations:** Chicago IL. **Other U.S. locations:** Nationwide. **International locations:** Worldwide.

CORPORATE DISK COMPANY
4610 Prime Parkway, McHenry IL 60050. 815/331-6000. **Toll-free phone:** 800/634-3475. **Fax:** 815/331-6030. **Contact:** Human Resources. **World Wide Web address:** http://www.disk.com. **Description:** Manufactures and develops software packages and provides related support services.

DATA COMMUNICATION FOR BUSINESS INC. (DCB INC.)
2949 County Road, 1000 East, Dewey IL 61840. 217/897-6600. **Fax:** 217/897-1331. **Contact:** Human Resources. **World Wide Web address:** http://www.dcbnet.com. **Description:** Manufactures and markets data communications equipment. The company also aids in network installation by providing assistance with accessory equipment, communications lines and suppliers, site planning, and installation.

DATALOGICS INC.
101 North Wacker Drive, Suite 1800, Chicago IL 60606. 312/853-8200. **Fax:** 312/853-8282. **Contact:** Human Resources. **E-mail address:** recruiting@datalogics.com. **World Wide Web address:** http://www.datalogics.com. **Description:** Develops and markets software for publishing companies. **Positions advertised include:** Development Engineer; Sales Engineer/Web Developer; Sales Manager. **Corporate headquarters location:** This location.

EBIX INC.
1900 East Golf Street, Suite 1050, Schaumburg IL 60173. 847/789-3047. **Fax:** 847/619-4773. **Contact:** Human Resources. **World Wide Web address:** http://www.ebix.com. **Description:** Develops agency management applications and software for the insurance industry. **NOTE:** See website for current job openings. Send resumes to EBIX, Inc., 5 Concourse Parkway, Suite 3200, Atlanta GA 30328.

EDGE SYSTEMS, INC.
1805 High Point Drive, Suite 103, Naperville IL 60563-9359. 630/810-9669. **Fax:** 630/810-9228. **Contact:** Human Resources Director. **E-mail address:** careers@edge.com. **World Wide Web address:** http://www.edge.com. **Description:** Engaged in document services and content-management consulting. **Corporate headquarters location:** This location. **Other area locations:** Chicago IL (Sales).

ELECTRO RENT CORPORATION
200 West Mark Street, Woodale IL 60191. 630/860-3991. **Contact:** Human Resources. **World Wide Web address:** http://www.electrorent.com. **Description:** Rents and leases electronic equipment including test and measurement instruments, workstations, personal computers, and data communication products. **Corporate headquarters location:** Van Nuys CA. **Other U.S. locations:** Nationwide.

FUJITSU COMPUTER SYSTEMS
9399 West Higgins Road, Suite 250, Rosemont IL 60018. 847/692-6940. **Fax:** 847/692-3331. **Contact:** Human Resources. **World Wide Web address:** http://www.computers.us.fujitsu.com. **Description:** Designs, develops, manufactures, markets, and services more than 470 large-scale, high-performance, general purpose computer systems. Customers are primarily large corporations, government agencies, and large universities with high-volume data processing requirements. **Corporate headquarters location:** Sunnyvale CA. Other area locations: Rosemont IL (Fujitsu Computer Systems). Operations at this facility include: This is a office for Fujitsu Computer Systems. **Parent company:** Fujitsu Limited.

FUTURESOURCE
955 Parkview Boulevard, Lombard IL 60148. 630/620-8444. **Contact:** Human Resources. **World Wide Web address:** http://www.futuresource.com. **Description:** An online, real-time, financial news provider.

GALILEO INTERNATIONAL
9700 West Higgins Road, Suite 400, Rosemont IL 60018. 847/518-4000. **Contact:** Human Resources. **World Wide Web address:** http://www.galileo.com. **Description:** Designs and installs software for the travel industry that provides access to inventory, scheduling, and pricing information. **NOTE:** Apply online at this company's website. **Corporate headquarters location:** Parsippany NJ. **Other U.S. locations:** Centennial CO. **International locations:** UK; Saudi Arabia; India. **Operations at this facility include:** This office is a corporate regional office.

GREENBRIER & RUSSEL, INC.
1450 East American Lane, Suite 1700, Schaumburg IL 60173. 847/706-4000. **Toll-free phone:** 800/453-0347. **Fax:** 847/706-4020. **Contact:** Sherry Greer, Recruiter. **E-mail address:** recruiting@gr.com. **World Wide Web address:** http://www.gr.com. **Description:** Provides strategic business solutions through technical services and software. The company offers technical and management consulting, information systems training, and a range of intranet and client/server software. The consulting division is a national practice that focuses on helping clients meet business goals through the use of technology. The company's training division offers instructor-led intranet, client/server, AS/400, and DB2 classes. **NOTE:** Entry-level positions are offered. **Positions advertised include:** Senior Business Objects Developer; Data Warehouse Architect; MS Analysis Services Consultant; Oracle Application DBA; Student Systems Functional Consultant; CRM Functional Consultant. **Corporate headquarters location:** This location. **Other U.S. locations:** Milwaukee WI; Appleton WI; Minneapolis MN; Atlanta GA; Dallas TX.

HEALTH MANAGEMENT SYSTEMS
820 West Jackson Boulevard, Chicago IL 60607. 312/962-6100. **Contact:** Laura Pontarelli, Human Resources Director. **World Wide Web address:** http://www.hmsy.com. **Description:** Develops software for the health insurance and health care industries. **NOTE:** Entry-level positions are offered. **Corporate headquarters location:** New York NY. **Other U.S. locations:** Nationwide. **Operations at this facility include:** Administration; Research and Development; Sales; Service. **Listed on:** Privately held.

HEWITT ASSOCIATES
100 Half Day Road, Lincolnshire IL 60069. 847/295-5000. **Contact:** Human Resources. **World Wide Web address:** http://www.hewitt.com. **Description:** Hewitt Associates is an international firm of consultants and actuaries specializing in the design, financing, communication, and administration of employee benefit and compensation programs. **Positions advertised include:** Programmer Analyst; WM Analyst; Compliance Specialist; Financial Consultant; Client Coordinator. **Corporate headquarters location:** This location. **Other area locations:** Chicago IL. **Other U.S. locations:** Nationwide. **International locations:** Worldwide.

IBM CORPORATION
One IBM Plaza, Chicago IL 60611. 312/245-6383. **Contact:** IBM Staffing Services. **World Wide Web address:** http://www.ibm.com. **Description:** IBM is a developer, manufacturer, and marketer of advanced information processing products including computers and microelectronic technology, software, networking systems, and information technology-related services. **Corporate headquarters location:** Armonk NY. **International locations:** Africa; Asia; Canada; Europe; Latin America; Middle East. **Operations at this facility include:** This location is a marketing office. **Listed on:** New York Stock Exchange. **Stock exchange symbol:** IBM.

INFORMATION RESOURCES, INC.
150 North Clinton Street, Chicago IL 60661. 312/726-1221. **Fax:** 312/726-5304. **Contact:** Human Resources. **World Wide Web address:** http://www.infores.com. **Description:** Develops and maintains computerized proprietary databases, decision support software, and analytical models to assist clients, primarily in the consumer packaged goods industry, in testing and evaluating their marketing plans for new products, media advertising, price, and sales promotions. **NOTE:** Apply online. **Corporate headquarters location:** This location. **Other U.S. locations:** Atlanta GA; Los Angeles CA; San Francisco CA; Darien CT; Waltham MA; Fairfield NJ; Cincinnati OH; Richmond VA; Fairfield NJ. **Operations at this facility include:** Administration.

INGENIENT TECHNOLOGIES, INC.
1701 West Golf Road, Tower 1, Suite 300, Rolling Meadows IL 60008. 847/357-1980. **Fax:** 847/357-1981. **Contact:** Human Resources. **E-mail address:** hr@ingenient.com. **World Wide Web address:** http://www.ingenient.com. **Description:** A technology company that develops multimedia product solutions based upon embedded Digital Signal Processors (DSPs) and General Purpose Processors (GPPs). **NOTE:** Search for open positions on the company website. **Positions advertised include:** Business Development Manager; Design Verification and Testing Engineer; Firmware Engineers; Hardware Engineers; Senior DSP Engineer; WindowsCE Software Engineer. **Corporate headquarters location:** This location. **Other U.S. locations:** Baltimore MD.

INRULE TECHNOLOGY
224 North Des Plaines, Suite 603, Chicago IL 60661. 312/648-1800. **Fax:** 312/873-3851. **Contact:** Rick Chomko, Chief Product Officer. **E-mail address:** resume@inrule.com. **World Wide Web address:** http://www.inrule.com. **Description:** Manufacturer of software (InRuleSuite) that helps streamline the development of program coding. Primary clients are those in the insurance, finance, manufacturing and professional markets. **NOTE:** E-mail resumes. **Listed on:** Privately held.

INSIGHT ENTERPRISES, INC.
444 Scott Drive, Bloomingdale IL 60108-3111. 630/924-6700. **Toll-free phone:** 800/321-2437. **Contact:** Human Resources. **World Wide Web address:** http://www.corp.insight.com. **Description:** Sells and distributes computer hardware, software and peripherals to *Fortune* 500 companies. Founded in 1988. **Positions advertised include:** Wireless Sales Engineer; Corporate Sales Representative; Inside Sales Representative; Procurement Specialist; Software Sales Engineer. **Office hours:** Monday - Friday, 8:00 a.m. - 5:00 p.m. **Corporate headquarters location:** This location. **Other U.S. locations:** Nationwide. **Listed on:** NASDAQ. **Stock exchange symbol:** NSIT.

KLEINSCHMIDT INC.
450 Lake Cook Road, Deerfield IL 60015. 847/945-1000. **Contact:** Human Resources. **World Wide Web address:** http://www.kleinschmidt.com. **Description:** Offers third-party computer networking services.

LAKEVIEW TECHNOLOGY
1901 South Meyers Road, Suite 600, Oak Brook Terrace IL 60181. 630/282-8100. **Toll-free phone:** 800/573-8371. **Fax:** 630/282-8500. **Contact:** Human Resources. **E-mail address:** hr@lakeviewtech.com. **World Wide Web address:** http://www.lakeviewtech.com. **Description:** Resells IBM products and services. LAS also provides training, education, and software development services.

McKESSON CORPORATION
1400 South Wolf Road, Wheeling IL 60090. 847/537-4800. **Toll-free phone:** 800/323-8154. **Fax:** 847/537-4866. **Contact:** Recruiter. **World Wide Web address:** http://www.mckesson.com. **Description:** Produces and sells software applications catering to the specific needs of medical facilities. Some of the programs include materials management, financial accounting, patient scheduling for operating rooms, and inventory control for health clinics. Founded in 1974. **NOTE:** See website for job listings and apply online. Entry-level positions are offered. **Positions advertised include:** VP Health Systems National Accounts; Sales Support Product Demonstrator; Staff Pharmacist; Director of National Accounts; Product Manager/Development Manager. **Special programs:** Internships. **Corporate headquarters location:** San Francisco CA. **Other U.S. locations:** Boulder CO. **Listed on:** New York Stock Exchange. **Stock exchange symbol:** MCK.

MERCURY INTERACTIVE CORPORATION
10255 West Higgins Road, Suite 620, Rosemont IL 60018. 847/803-3176. **Fax:** 847/803-5686. **Contact:** Human Resources. **World Wide Web address:** http://www.mercuryinteractive.com. **Description:** Mercury Interactive is a developer of automated software quality (ASQ) tools for enterprise applications testing. The company's products are used to isolate software and system errors prior to application deployment. **NOTE:** See website for job listings and apply online. **Corporate headquarters location:** Sunnyvale CA. **Operations at this facility include:** This location is a sales office. **Listed on:** NASDAQ. **Stock exchange symbol:** MERQ.

MIDWAY GAMES INC.
2704 West Roscoe Street, Chicago IL 60618. 773/961-2222. **Contact:** Human Resources. **World Wide Web address:** http://www.midway.com. **Description:** Develops a wide variety of coin-operated arcade and home video game entertainment and software products. Midway produces games for Sony, Nintendo, and Saga platforms. **Positions advertised include:** Executive Producer; Financial Planning Analyst. **Special programs:** Internships. **Corporate headquarters location:** This location. **International locations:** Midway Games Limited, London England. **Listed on:** New York Stock Exchange. **Stock exchange symbol:** MWY.

PC WHOLESALE
444 Scott Drive, Bloomingdale IL 60108. 630/307-1700. **Contact:** Human Resources. **World Wide Web address:** http://www.pcwholesale.com. **Description:** Distributes computer systems, peripherals, and supplies to an international client base. PC Wholesale also offers support services. Founded in 1989. **Corporate headquarters location:** This location. **Other U.S. locations:** MN; NJ: GA.

PEOPLESOFT
233 South Wacker Drive, 45th Floor, Chicago IL 60606. 312/651-8000. **Contact:** Human Resources. **World Wide Web address:** http://www.oracle.com. **Description:** PeopleSoft designs, markets, and supports a wide variety of business software applications. **Corporate headquarters location:** Redwood Shores CA. **Other U.S. locations:** Nationwide. **International locations:** Worldwide. **Parent company:** Oracle. **Operations at this facility include:** This location serves as the Midwestern U.S. Regional Headquarters for the company. **Listed on:** NASDAQ. **Stock exchange symbol:** PSFT.

PITNEY BOWES DOCUMENT MESSAGING TECHNOLOGIES
220 Western Court, Suite 100, Lisle IL 60532. 630/435-7500. **Contact:** Human Resources. **World Wide Web address:** http://www.pbdmt.com. **Description:** Develops information management software for customer service, marketing, and systems integration applications. **Parent company:** Pitney Bowes Inc.

QUADRAMED
440 North Wells, Suite 505, Chicago IL 60610. 312/396-0700. **Toll-free phone:** 800/634-0800. **Fax:** 312/396-0800. **Contact:** Human Resources. **E-mail address:** resume@quadramed.com. **World Wide Web address:** http://www.quadramed.com. **Description:** Develops and markets specialized decision support software designed to improve the organizational and clinical effectiveness of hospitals, academic medical centers, managed care providers, large physician groups, and other health care providers. **NOTE:** See website for job listings. Apply online or e-mail resumes. Resumes may also be faxed to the company's corporate office in Santa Ana CA at 714/371-1700. **Positions advertised include:** Nurse Consultant; Support Analyst.

RIVERGLASS, INC.
60 Hazelwood Drive, Suite 216, Champaign IL 61820. 630/578-4271. **Contact:** Human Resources. **E-mail address:** careers@riverglassinc.com. **World Wide Web address:** http://www.riverglassinc.com. **Description:** Develops business software that helps organizations collect, manage, and analyze information. **Positions advertised include:** Research Engineer; Software Usability Consultant. **Other area locations:** West Chicago IL.

S.I. TECH, INC.
P.O. Box 609, Geneva IL 60134. 630/761-3640. **Fax:** 630/761-3644. **Contact:** Ramesh Sheth, Human Resources Manager. **World Wide Web address:** http://www.sitech-bitdriver.com. **Description:** Manufactures and markets fiber-optic products such as modems, multiplexers, F.O. hubs, LAN/WAN products, short-haul modems, and cable assemblies for data communications use. Founded in 1984. **Office hours:** Monday - Friday, 7:00 a.m. - 7:00 p.m. **Corporate headquarters location:** This location. **Listed on:** Privately held.

SPSS INC.
233 South Wacker Drive, 11th Floor, Chicago IL 60606. 312/651-3000. **Contact:** Human Resources. **World Wide Web address:** http://www.spss.com. **Description:** Develops, markets, and supports statistical software. **NOTE:** See this company's website for job listings. Apply online.

SSA GLOBAL
500 West Madison, Suite 2200, Chicago IL 60661. 312/258-6000. **Fax:** 312/474-7500. **Contact:** Human Resources. **E-mail address:** careersops@ssaglobal.com. **World Wide Web address:** http://www.ssaglobal.com. **Description:** System Software Associates develops, markets, and supports an integrated line of business application, computer-aided software engineering (CASE), and electronic data interchange (EDI) software, primarily for IBM minicomputers and workstations. **NOTE:** See website for job listings and mail or e-mail resumes. **Corporate headquarters:** This location. **Other U.S. locations:** Nationwide. **International locations:** Worldwide.

SSS RESEARCH, INC.
600 S. Washington Street, Suite 100, Naperville IL 60540. 630/548-2332. **Fax:** 630/281-4466. **Contact:** Human Resources. **E-mail address:** info@sss-research.com. **World Wide Web address:** http://www.sss-research.com. **Description:** A software research and development firm that designs systems for national defense, intelligence, and other high priority government missions. Founded in 2003.

SILVON SOFTWARE INC.
900 Oakmont Lane, Suite 400, Westmont IL 60559. 630/655-3313. **Contact:** Human Resources. **World Wide Web address:** http://www.silvon.com. **Description:** Develops sales tracking software. **NOTE:** See website for job listings and contact information.

SOLUCIENT
1007 Church Street, Suite 700, Evanston IL 60201. 800/366-7526. **Contact:** Human Resources. **World Wide Web address:** http://www.solucient.com. **Description:** Solucient provides healthcare business intelligence to the healthcare industry. The company maintains the nation's largest healthcare database, comprised of more than 22.6 million hospital discharges per year. Serving a client base of more than 3,300 customers, Solucient provides information resources to more than 2,000 hospitals, as well as many of the largest pharmaceutical manufacturers in the United States. **Positions advertised include:** Desktop Services Supervisor; Director of Vendor Management; Senior Systems Database Administrator. **Corporate headquarters location:** This location.

STARTSPOT MEDIAWORKS, INC.
1840 Oak Avenue, Evanston IL 60201. 847/866-1830. **Fax:** 847/866-1880. **Contact:** Human Resources. **World Wide Web address:** http://www.startspot.com. **Description:** Develops a group of informational websites that work as search engines. StartSpot's sites include: LibrarySpot is library resource site; BookSpot offers book reviews and reading lists, along with lists of authors, publishers, and the latest news on happenings in the book world; GourmetSpot offers advice and links to some of the best recipes, restaurants, culinary equipment, and wine available; EmploymentSpot provides information and related links for jobseekers.

TECHNIUM, INC.
8745 West Higgins Road, Suite 350, Chicago IL 60631. 773/380-0555. **Fax:** 773/380-0568. **Contact:** Jim Archuleta, Human Resources. **E-mail address:** jarchuleta@technium.com. **World Wide Web address:** http://www.technium.com. **Description:** Technium provides computer consulting services focusing on client/server technologies. The company's client base represents a variety of industries, from consumer products and health care to financial services and software. Technium provides a full range of services to deploy client/server applications including architecture planning, application analysis, visualization, and design; graphical user interface development, using Visual C++, Visual Basic, PowerBuilder, and Delphi; object-oriented development with C, C++, and Smalltalk; relational database development in SQL Server, Microsoft Access, Oracle, and Sybase; and decision support systems development

using OLAP and Data Warehousing technologies. **NOTE:** E-mail resumes. Entry-level positions are offered. **Special programs:** Training. **Corporate headquarters location:** This location. **Other U.S. locations:** Dallas TX; Milwaukee WI. **Listed on:** Privately held.

THOMAS ELECTRONICS
300 South LaLonde Avenue, Addison IL 60101. 315/923-2051. **Fax:** 315/923-4401. **Contact:** Human Resources. **World Wide Web address:** http://www.thomaselectronics.com. **Description:** Manufactures deflective yokes for CRTs. **NOTE:** Resumes should be mailed to Thomas Electronics Human Resources Department, 208 Davis Parkway, Clyde NY 14433.

3COM CORPORATION
3800 Golf Road, Rolling Meadows IL 60008. 847/262-7000. **Contact:** Human Resources. **World Wide Web address:** http://www.3com.com. **Description:** 3Com is a billion-dollar *Fortune* 500 company delivering global data networking solutions to organizations around the world. 3Com designs, manufactures, markets, and supports a broad range of ISO 9000-compliant global data networking solutions including routers, hubs, remote access servers, switches, and adapters for Ethernet, Token Ring, and high-speed networks. These products enable computers to communicate at high speeds and share resources including printers, disk drives, modems, and minicomputers. **NOTE:** Apply online. **Positions advertised include:** Customer Operations Representative; Program Manager; Software Engineer; Technical Voice Education Developer; Product Engineer.

TIGER DIRECT
175 Ambassador Drive, Naperville IL 60540. 630/355-3000. **Contact:** Human Resources. **World Wide Web address:** http://www.tigerdirect.com. **Description:** Manufactures a wide variety of computer supplies including hardware, software, and computer office equipment. **Operations at this facility include:** This location is a distribution center.

TRI-COR INDUSTRIES, INC.
5 Eagle Center, Suite 8, O'Fallon IL 62269. 618/632-9804. **Fax:** 618/632-9805. **Contact:** Bill Welsch, Deputy Manager. **E-mail address:** b.welsch@tricorind.com. **World Wide Web address:** http://www.tricorind.com. **Description:** Develops software for Department of Defense applications and offers technical support. **NOTE:** Submit resumes and cover letters indicating area of interest. E-mail resumes to Mr. Welsch or download the application found on the website and fax it to his attention. **Corporate headquarters location:** Lanham MD.

THE TRIZETTO GROUP
500 Technology Drive, Naperville IL 60563. 630/369-5300. **Contact:** Human Resources. **E-mail address:** recruiting@rims.com. **World Wide Web address:** http://www.trizetto.com. **Description:** Develops technology products and services for healthcare organizations. **Corporate headquarters location:** Newport Beach CA.

UNISYS CORPORATION
2611 Corporate West Drive, Lisle IL 60532. 630/505-7522. **Contact:** Human Resources. **World Wide Web address:** http://www.unisys.com. **Description:** Provides technology services and solutions in consulting, systems integration, outsourcing, infrastructure, and server technology. **Corporate headquarters location:** Blue Bell PA. **Other U.S. locations:** Nationwide. **Operations at this facility include:** This location is a sales office. **Listed on:** New York Stock Exchange. **Stock exchange symbol:** UIS.

WOLFRAM RESEARCH, INC.
100 Trade Center Drive, Champaign IL 61820. 217/398-0700. **Fax:** 217/398-0747. **Contact:** Human Resources. **E-mail address:** resumes@wolfram.com. **World Wide Web address:** http://www.wri.com. **Description:** Develops mathematical software and services including Mathematica. **Positions advertised include:** NKS Development Director; Project Assistant; Numerical Computation Developer; Analysis Developer; Symbolic Computation Developer; Software Quality Engineer; Academic Account Sales Executive; Commercial Sales Representative; Technical Product Manager.

Indiana

ADVANCED MICROELECTRONICS, INC.
6001 East Old Highway 50, Vincennes IN 47591. 812/726-4500. **Fax:** 812/726-4551. **Contact:** Human Resources. **E-mail address:** info@advancedmicro.com. **World Wide Web address:** http://www.advancedmicro.com. **Description:** Provides computer repair services and computer sales. **Positions advertised include:** Software Engineer; Sales Account Representative; Field Service Technician; Network Engineer.

ANALYSTS INTERNATIONAL CORPORATION (AIC)
5750 Castle Creek Parkway North, Suite 100, Indianapolis IN 46250. 317/842-1100, ext.: 125. **Toll-free phone**: 800/783-1101. **Contact:** Human Resources. **World Wide Web address:** http://www.analysts.com. **Description:** An international computer consulting firm. The company assists clients in analyzing, designing, and developing systems using different programming languages and software. Founded in 1966. **Office hours:** Monday - Friday, 7:30 a.m. - 5:00 p.m. **Corporate headquarters location:** Minneapolis MN. **Other U.S. locations:** Nationwide. **Operations at this facility include:** Regional Headquarters. **Listed on:** NASDAQ. **Stock exchange symbol:** ANLY.

APTERA SOFTWARE, INC.
5120 Investment Drive, Fort Wayne IN 46808. 260/969-1410. Fax: 260/484-9842. **Contact:** Human Resources. **E-mail address:** careers@apterasoftware.com. **World Wide Web address:** http://www.apterasoftware.com. **Description:** Creates web-based management software and custom software for businesses in the Midwest. **Positions advertised include:** Business Development Manager; Software Architect. **Corporate headquarters location:** This location.

BELL TECH.LOGIX
5604 Fortune Circle South, Suite G-N, Indianapolis IN 46241. 317/227-6700. **Contact:** General Manager. **World Wide Web address:** http://www.belltechlogix.com. **Description:** Bell Tech.logix is a leading distributor of computer-related electronic components, semiconductors, and microcomputer products. **Operations at this facility include:** This location is engaged in computer product development, training, and systems engineering.

CARLETON INC.
P.O. Box 570, South Bend IN 46624. 574/243-6040. **Physical address:** 3975 William Richardson Drive, South Bend IN 46628. **Toll-free phone:** 800/433-0090. **Fax:** 574/243-6060. **Contact:** Human Resources. **World Wide Web address:** http://www.carletoninc.com. **Description:** Develops software for the consumer credit and credit insurance industries. Carleton also sells preprogrammed, hand-held computers.

COMPUTER HORIZONS CORPORATION
3815 River Crossing Parkway, Suite 100, Indianapolis IN 46240. 317/576-1000. **Contact:** Human Resources. **World Wide Web address:** http://www.computerhorizons.com. **Description:** A full-service technology solutions company offering contract staffing, outsourcing, re-engineering, migration, downsizing support, and network management. **Corporate headquarters location:** Mountain Lakes NJ. **Other U.S. locations:** Nationwide. **President and CEO:** William J. Murphy.

CONTINENTAL DESIGN & ENGINEERING
2710 Enterprise Drive, Anderson IN 46013. 765/778-9999. **Toll-free phone:** 800/875-4557. **Fax:** 765/778-3078. **Contact:** Cathy Mellinger, Director of Technical Recruiting. **E-mail address:** cdcin@continental-design.com. **World Wide Web address:** http://www.continental-design.com. **Description:** Continental Design & Engineering provides computer-aided engineering and design services. **Corporate headquarters location:** This location. **Other U.S. locations:** Troy MI. **Operations at this facility include:** This location houses administrative offices as well as the engineering and design center.

DIGITECH
8455 Castlewood Drive, Suite C, Indianapolis IN 46250. 317/863-0025. **Fax:** 317/863-0029. **Contact:** Human Resources. **E-mail address:** info@itdept4u.com. **World Wide Web address:** http://www.itdept4u.com. **Description:** An **Error! Contact not defined.** services company. **Positions advertised include:** Network Technician. **NOTE:** Search and apply for positions online.

FISERV, INC.
3575 Moreau Court, Suite 2, South Bend IN 46628. 574/282-3300. **Contact:** Human Resources. **World Wide Web address:** http://www.fiserv.com. **Description:** Develops software for the mortgage industry. **Positions advertised include:** Executive Assistant; Project Manager. **Other U.S. locations:** Nationwide. **Listed on:** NASDAQ. **Stock exchange symbol:** FISV.

HURCO COMPANIES, INC.
One Technology Way, Indianapolis IN 46268. 317/293-5309. **Contact:** Human Resources Manager. **E-mail address:** info@hurco.com. **World Wide Web address:** http://www.hurco.com. **Description:** Designs, manufactures, and sells computer numerical control (CNC) systems and software, as well as CNC machine tools for the international machine tool industry.

MAILCODE
1500 Kepner Drive, P.O. Box 5625, Lafayette IN 47903-5625. 765/447-8888. **Fax:** 765/447-1828. **Contact:** Human Resources. **E-mail address:** careers@mailcode.com. **World Wide Web address:** http://www.mailcode.com. **Description:** Develops, manufactures and delivers mail processing software solutions. Their various software applications include local, remote and voice encoding, as well as OCR technologies. **Positions advertised include:** Senior Accounting Clerk; Application Engineer; Development Controls Engineer, Electrical; Director, International Sales; Process Engineering Technician; Senior Software Engineer. **Corporate headquarters location:** This location. **Parent Company:** Pitney Bowes.

MEDAVANT
2533 Centennial Boulevard, Suite B, Jeffersonville IN 47130. 812/944-3865. **Contact:** Human Resources. **World Wide Web address:** http://www.medavanthealth.com. **Description:** Manufactures computer components and installs computer systems for the clinical laboratory industry.

ONTARIO SYSTEMS CORPORATION
1150 West Kilgore Avenue, Muncie IN 47305. 765/751-7000. **Fax:** 765/751-7818. **Contact:** Human Resources Specialist. **E-mail address:** careers@ osntariosystems.com. **World Wide Web address:** http://www.ontariosystems.com. **Description:** Develops software for businesses that offer accounts receivable management, collection, and teleservicing services. **NOTE:** Part-time jobs are offered. **Company slogan:** People are our foundation. **Positions advertised include:** Systems Analyst; Technical Communicator. **Special programs:** Training. **Office hours:** Monday - Friday, 8:00 a.m. - 5:00 p.m. **Corporate headquarters location:** This location. **Other U.S. locations:** Berlin OH; Cle Elum WA. **Subsidiaries include:** CDS Leopold; Sherry Labs. **Parent company:** Ontario Corporation. **Listed on:** Privately held.

POWERWAY, INC.
6919 Hillsdale Court Indianapolis, IN 46250. 317/598-1760. **Toll-free phone:** 800/964-9004. **Fax:** 317/598-1740. **Contact:** Human Resources. **E-mail address:** info@powerwayinc.com. **World Wide Web address:** http://www.powerwayinc.com. **Description:** Powerway is a software company that delivers innovative technology solutions that help manufacturing companies accelerate time to market and improve product quality while reducing risks and costs. **Positions advertised include:** Database Designer. **International locations:** Mexico; UK.

THEORIS INC.
10000 Allisonville Road, Fishers IN 46038-2008. 317/849-4444. **Fax:** 317/576-6934. **Contact:** Recruiting Coordinator. **E-mail address:** info@theoris.com. **World Wide Web address:** http://www.theoris.com. **Description:** A computer consulting firm. **NOTE:** Address all employment inquiries to the corporate office. **Corporate headquarters location:** This location.

TRUEVISION
7340 Shadeland Station, Suite 200, Indianapolis IN 46256. 317/841-0332. **Fax:** 317/577-8779. **Contact:** Human Resources. **World Wide Web address:** http://www.pinnaclesys.com. **Description:** Develops PC digital video cards for desktop video production. **Corporate headquarters location:** Mountainview CA.

Iowa

AVG AUTOMATION
P.O. Box 1327, Bettendorf IA 52722. 630/668-3900. **Physical address:** 4140 Utica Ridge Road, Bettendorf IA 52722. **Fax:** 563/359-9094. **Contact:** Linda Wooten, Human Resources Manager. **World Wide Web address:** http://www.avg.net. **Description:** The AVG Group of companies, which includes former Uticor Technologies, manufactures computer hardware, monitors, message displays, motion controls, operator interface technologies, and other electronic products.

ADVANCED TECHNOLOGIES GROUP, INC.
1601 48th Street, Suite 220, West Des Moines IA 50266. 515/221-9344. **Fax:** 515/221-1266. **Contact:** Tej Dhawan, Human Resources. E-mail address: Jobs2003@a-t-g.com. **World Wide Web address:** http://www.a-t-g.com. **Description:** Web design and technology consulting service for corporations and state agencies and is a certified Microsoft Windows platform consulting service. Founded in 1991. **NOTE:** Search posted openings and apply on-line; paper resumes are not accepted. **Positions advertised include**: Telephony Solutions Developer and Systems Analyst. **Listed on:** Privately held. **Chairman/CEO:** Atul Gupta. **Annual sales/revenues:** $6.1 million. **Number of employees:** 45.

BRODERBUND, RIVERDEEP AND THE LEARNING COMPANY
222 Third Avenue SE, Cedar Rapids IA 52401. 319/378-7392. **Fax:** 319/395-0217. **Contact:** Human Resources. **World Wide Web address:** http://www.broderbund.com. **Description:** Develops more than 80 software programs for a wide range of business applications and provides technical support services. **Corporate headquarters location:** Novato CA. **Other U.S. locations:** CA; MA; WA. **International locations:** Ireland; Israel. **Parent company:** Riverdeep Group, PLC (Dublin, Ireland).

R.K. DIXON COMPANY
5700 Utica Ridge Road, Davenport IA 52807. 563/344-9100. **Contact:** Human Resources. **Toll-free phone:** 800/553-0023. **E-mail address:** employment@rkdixon.com. **World Wide Web address:** http://www.rkdixon.com. **Description:** Sells and services copiers, fax machines, and filing systems, and installs computer networks for offices. Authorized Canon dealer at some locations. Founded in 1983.

Other area locations: Dubuque IA. **Other U.S. locations:** Bloomington IL; Peoria IL; Rockford IL; Springfield IL. **Subsidiaries include:** Copy Products Corporation; Network Integration Services. **President:** Bryan Dixon. **Number of employees:** 150.

EAGLE POINT SOFTWARE CORPORATION
4131 Westmark Drive, Dubuque IA 52002-2627. 563/556-8392. **Toll-free phone:** 800/678-6565. **Fax:** 563/582-3286. **Contact:** Human Resources. **E-mail address:** hr@eaglepoint.com. **World Wide Web address:** http://www.eaglepoint.com. **Description:** Develops integrated software for the architectural, landscaping, civil engineering, and structural marketplaces. Founded in 1983. **Positions advertised include:** Field Business Consultant; Administrative Assistant; Architect; Civil Engineer; Landscape Architect. **Office hours:** Monday - Friday, 8:00 a.m. - 5:00 p.m. **Corporate headquarters location:** This location. **Other U.S. locations:** Church Hill TN. **Subsidiaries include:** Land Development Today Magazine. **Listed on:** Privately held. **President/CEO:** John F. Biver. **Annual sales/revenues:** $17 million. **Number of employees:** 130.

FOUNDATION FOR MEDICAL CARE/ENCOMPASS
6000 Westown Parkway, West Des Moines IA 50266-7771. 515/223-2900. **Fax:** 515/453-8118. **Contact:** Ronna Pochter, Vice President. **E-mail address:** rpochter@ifmc.org. **World Wide Web address:** http://www.ifmc.org. **Description:** IFMC seeks to optimize the quality of medical care and health through collaborative relationships, education, and health information management. IFMC employs more than 500 people in seven offices throughout the United States. **NOTE**: Search posted listings and apply on-line. **Positions advertised include:** Coordinator, Review; Coordinator, Review Medical Support; Coordinator, Review Disease Management; Coordinator, Review Enhanced Primary Care Case Management; Manager, Government; Assistant, Review II.

KEANE, INC.
383 Collins Road NE, Cedar Rapids IA 52402. 319/393-3343. **Fax:** 319/378-1836. **Contact:** Christine Miller, Human Resources. E-mail address: christine_m_miller@keane.com. **World Wide Web address:** http://www.keane.com. **Description:** Keane offers businesses a variety of computer consulting services and also assists in project management. Founded in 1965. **Corporate headquarters location:** Boston MA. **Other U.S. locations:** Nationwide. **Operations at this facility include:** Design, development, and managing of software for corporations and health care facilities. **Listed on:** American Stock Exchange. **Stock exchange symbol:** KEA. **Chairman:** John F. Keane, Sr. **Annual sales/revenues:** $873 million. **Number of employees nationwide:** 7,800.

McKESSON CORPORATION
700 Locust Street, Suite 500, Dubuque IA 52001. 563/556-3131. **Fax:** 563/557-3951. **Contact:** Paul Kirincic, Human Resources. **World Wide Web address:** http://www.mckesson.com. **Description:** A leading provider of management information systems, related support services, and electronic data interchange services for medical group practices, faculty practice plans, and medical enterprises. **NOTE:** Search posted openings and apply on-line. **Parent company:** McKesson Information Solutions. **Operations at this facility include:** Administration; Research and Development; Service.

MICROFRONTIER, INC.
P.O. Box 231, Winterset, IA 50237. 515/462-5930. **Toll-free phone**: 800/388-8109. **Contact:** Human Resources. E-mail address: mfi@microfrontier.com. **World Wide Web address:** http://www.microfrontier.com. **Description:** Develops graphic arts software. Founded in 1987. **NOTE:** Entry-level positions are offered. **Positions advertised include:** Computer Programmer; Marketing Specialist; Sales Representative; Software Engineer. **Number of employees at this location:** 15.

RADISYS CORPORATION
1240 Office Plaza Drive, W. Des Moines IA 50266. 515/223-8000. **Toll-free phone**: 800/475-9000. **Fax:** 515/327-2484. **Contact:** Human Resources. **World Wide Web address:** http://www.radisys.com. **Description:** Develops embedded systems software for a wide range of applications including development of the OS-9 real-time operating system, Intel IXP 1200 Network Processor solutions, the Microcode Solutions Library, and consulting services projects. **NOTE:** Search posted openings and apply on-line at corporate web site only. **Corporate headquarters location:** Hillsboro OR. **Other U.S. locations:** Boca Raton FL; Charlotte NC; Cheshire CT; Cranbury and Mount Laurel NJ; Flower Mound TX; Marlboro MA; San Diego CA. **International locations:** Worldwide. **Operations at this facility include:** This site serves as the headquarters for RadiSys' Microwave Software, part of the Communications Software Division. This branch hires almost exclusively software engineers. **Listed on:** NASDAQ. **Stock exchange symbol:** RSYS. **Chairman:** C. Scott Gibson. **Annual sales/revenues:** $200 million. **Number of employees:**18.

WORKSTREAM
505 North Fourth Street, Fairfield IA 52556. 641/472/7720. **Toll-free phone:** 866/470-9675. **Fax:** 641/472-7105. **Contact:** Human Resources at corporate office on-line only. **World Wide Web address:** http://www.workstreaminc.com. **Description:** Develops and provides human resource-related business software and services. Founded in 1996. **NOTE:** Search and apply for positions online only. No paper resumes will be accepted. Home office work may be available. **Corporate headquarters location:** Ottawa Canada. **Other U.S. locations:** FL; CA. **Listed on:** NASDAQ. **Stock exchange symbol:** WSTM.

Kansas

ACTUATE CORPORATION
12980 Metcalf Avenue, Suite 300, Overland Park KS 66213. 913/851-2200. **Contact:** Corporate Offices. **Toll free phone**: 888/422-8828. **World Wide Web address:** http://www.actuate.com. **Description:** A provider of information delivery software products and services. The company offers a platform for retrieving business information from corporate databases as well as designing spreadsheet technology for Web-based computing. Founded in 1993. **NOTE**: Must contact corporate office for all employment inquiries. **Corporate headquarters location:** South San Francisco CA. **Other U.S. locations:** Nationwide. **International locations:** Worldwide. **Operations at this location:** Actuate's F-1 Division. **Listed on:** NASDAQ. **Stock exchange symbol:** ACTU. **Chairman:** Nicholas Nierenberg. **Annual sales/revenues:** $109 billion. **Number of employees worldwide:** 575.

AEROCOMM
11160 Thompson Avenue, Lenexa KS 66219. 913/492-2320. **Toll-free phone:** 800/492-2320. **Fax:** 913/492-1243. **Contact:** Human Resources Department. **E-mail address:** rf@aerocomm.com. **World Wide Web address:** Opening posted on-line http://www.aerocomm.com. **Description:** Designs, manufactures, and markets Instant Wireless data communications for equipment manufacturers and spread spectrum data radios for OEM integration or commercial plug-and-play. **Positions advertised include:** Inside Sales Representative; OEM Sales Representative; RF Technician. **Corporate headquarters location:** This location. **Other U.S. locations:** Salt Lake City UT. **Listed on:** Privately Held.

BALANCE INNOVATIONS LLC
13400 West 99th Street, Lenexa KS 66215. 913/599-1177. **Fax:** 913/599-1179. **Contact:** Human Resources. **E-mail address:** info@balanceinnovations.com. **World Wide Web address:**

http://www.balanceinnovations.com. **Description:** Develops software for cash management in retail businesses. Products are designed to improve such operations as revenue balancing, check processing, cash forecasting, and tracking of non-cash tender items. Founded in 1991. **Positions advertised include:** Software QA Analyst; Technical Support Analyst; Administrative Assistant.

CONTROL SYSTEMS INTERNATIONAL INC.
8040 Neiman Road, Lenexa KS 66214. 913/599-5010. **Fax:** 913/599-5013. **Contact:** Human Resources. **E-mail address:** mktg@csiks.com. **World Wide Web address:** http://www.ucos,com/employment. **Description:** Manufactures networking systems that aid in fuel distribution management. Founded in 1968. **NOTE:** Entry-level positions are offered. **Positions advertised include:** Electrical/Electronics Engineer; Software Engineer. **Corporate headquarters location:** This location. **Other U.S. locations:** Irvine CA. **International locations:** London, England. **Listed on:** Privately held. **Annual sales/revenues:** $21 - $50 million. **Number of employees worldwide:** 160.

COVANSYS CORPORATION
dba PDA SOFTWARE SERVICES, INC.
7701 College Boulevard, Overland Park KS 66210. 913/469-8700. **Fax:** 913/469-5814. **Contact:** Alison Davy, Human Resources. **E-mail address:** adavy@covansys.com. **World Wide Web address:** http://www.pdainc.com. **Description:** As of June 2002 Covansys Corp. acquired PDA, which had been a wholly owned subsidiary of Selective Insurance Group, Inc. Founded in 1975 PDA develops and maintains information systems for states that are required to meet federal tracking mandates of the WIC Program (Women, Infants & Children) and offers the Web-based product, FloodConnect for private insurers managing flood insurance through the National Flood Insurance Program. The company provides software consulting, application development and processing services, which include Web development, and data exchange for federal and state agencies as well as for insurance, agrochemical, and pharmaceutical industries. **NOTE:** Apply to corporate office via main web site. **Positions advertised include:** IIPAA Privacy Consultant; Director/Senior Director. **Corporate headquarters location:** Farmington Hills MI. **Listed on:** NASDAQ. **Stock exchange symbol:** CVNS. **Co-Chairmen:** Ned Lautenbach and Rajendra Vattikuti. **Annual sales/revenues:** CVNS: $383 million; PDA: $18 million. **Number of employees at this location:** 190. **Number of employees worldwide:** 4,500

DYNAMICS RESEARCH CORPORATION
106 South 5th Street, Leavenworth KS 66048. 913/758-1551. **Contact:** Human Resources. **World Wide Web address:** http://www.drc.com. **Description:** Delivers technical and information technology services to the Department of Defense and state government agencies. **Positions advertised include:** Collective Training Directorate Team Lead; Historical Writer; Military Analyst; Program Manager; Sr. Military analyst; Tactical Operation Center and Staff Training System Developer. **Corporate headquarters location:** Andover MA. **Other U.S. locations:** Nationwide.

ENGENIO TECHNOLOGY
3718 North Rock Road, Wichita KS 67226. 316/636-8000. **Contact:** Ariel Morillo, Human Resources. **World Wide Web address:** http://www.engenio.com. **Description:** Manufactures and designs communications systems and storage semiconductors that access, interconnect, and store data, voice, and video. The company produces standard and custom integrated circuits specializing in broadband and wireless communications, consumer electronics, and data networking. In addition to its system-on-a-chip devices the company supplies servers, storage network solutions, and software for storage area networks. Founded in 1981. **Positions advertised include:** Human Resources Administrative Assistant; Failure Analysis Technician; Director of Manufacturing Engineering; Material Handler; Production Planning and Control; Manufacturing Manager; Storage Assembly Specialist; Buyer; Test Engineering Technician; Design Engineer; Applications Engineer. **Other U.S. locations:** Nationwide. **International locations:** Worldwide. **Number of employees worldwide:** 6,000.

IBM
16011 College Boulevard, Lenexa KS 66219. **Contact:** Human Resources. **World Wide Web address:** http://www.ibm.com. **Description:** Provides database technology to build, deploy, run, and evolve applications. Products include powerful distributed database management systems, application development tools, and graphic- and character-based productivity software for delivering information to every significant desktop platform. **NOTE:** Call HR nationwide, 800/796-9876. Resumes may be submitted via IBM's Global Employment website. **Positions advertised include:** Senior Software Engineer; Services Support Representative; Customer Engineer; Computer Programmer. **Special programs:** Internships. **Corporate headquarters location:** White Plains NY. **Other area locations:** Overland Park KS; Shawnee Mission KS; Topeka KS; Wichita KS. **U.S. locations:** Nationwide. **International locations:** Worldwide. **Subsidiaries include:** Hitachi Global Storage Technologies; IBM Canada Ltd; IBM-Microelectronics; IBM-Hardware; IBM-Services; IBM-Software; Lotus Development Corporation; Tivoli Software. **Listed on:** New York Stock Exchange. **Stock exchange symbol:** IBM. **Annual sales/revenues:** $81 billion. **Number of employees worldwide:** 320,000

MEDIWARE INFORMATION SYSTEMS, INC.
11711 West 79th Street, Lenexa KS 66214. 913/307-1000. **Fax:** 913/307-1111. **Contact:** Human Resources. **E-mail address:** jobs@mediware.com. **World Wide Web address:** http://www.mediware.com. **Description:** Develops software and data management systems for pharmacies, hospitals, surgical centers, and blood banks specializing in clinical information systems to manage health care facilities. Provides pharmacy stock control systems through its British subsidiary, JAC. Founded in 1980. **Positions advertised include:** Clinical Project Manager; Implementation Consultant; Implementation Specialist; National Sales Director. **Other U.S. locations:** Scotts Valley CA; Melville NY; Lake Oswego OR; Dallas TX. **International locations:** United Kingdom. **Listed on:** NASDAQ. **Stock exchange symbol:** MEDW. **Chairman/Secretary:** Lawrence Auriana. **Annual sales/revenues:** $31 million.

MICROTECH COMPUTERS, INC.
4921 Legends Drive, Lawrence KS 66049. 785/841-9513. **Fax:** 785/841-1809. **Contact:** Personnel. **Email address**: hr@microtechcomp.com. **World Wide Web address:** http://www.microtechcomp.com. **Description:** Develops, manufactures, markets, installs, and services personal computers and related equipment. Primary customers are end users, retailers, corporations, and government agencies. Founded in 1986. **NOTE**: Openings posted through local media ads. **Company slogan:** Your key business partner. **Corporate headquarters location:** This location. **Other area locations:** Shawnee Mission KS; Topeka KS. **Subsidiaries include:** A-Plus Open; MicroOpen; Atipa Technologies. **Operations at this facility include:** Accounting; Administration; Distribution; Manufacturing; Research and Development; Sales; Support Service; Warehouse. **Listed on:** Privately held. **President:** Mike Zheng. **Annual sales/revenues:** $5 million. **Number of employees:** 80.

Kentucky
AJILON CONSULTING
One Paragon Centre, Suite 430, 6060 Dutchmans Lane, Louisville KY 40205. 502/454-5840. **Toll-free phone:** 800/364-9078. **Fax:** 502/454-9742. **Contact:** Rebecca Tinley, Human Resources. **E-mail address:** recruit.louisville@ajilon.com. **World Wide Web address:** http://www.ajilonconsulting.com. **Description:** Offers computer consulting services,

project support, and end user services with specializations in the areas of information technology, communications, finance and accounting, and legal and office. **Positions advertised include:** e*Gate Integration Developer; Documentum Developer. **Special programs:** Tuition Reimbursement Program. **Corporate headquarters location:** Baltimore MD. **Other U.S. locations:** Nationwide. **International locations:** Worldwide. **Subsidiaries include:** Software Quality Partners; Computer People, Inc. **Parent company:** Adecco. **Number of employees worldwide:** 10,000.

ANALYSTS INTERNATIONAL CORPORATION (AIC)
2365 Harrodsburg Road, Suite B-450, Lexington KY 40504-3342. 859/223-0001. **Toll-free phone:** 800/279-8433. **Fax:** 859/224-4389. **Contact:** Corporate Recruiter. **E-mail address:** jobs@analysts.com. **World Wide Web address:** http://www.analysts.com. **Description:** An international computer consulting firm. The company assists clients in developing systems in a variety of industries using different programming languages and software. Founded in 1966. **NOTE:** Job seekers may apply online for specific positions or general consideration. **Positions advertised include:** Development Engineer; Engineering Technologist; ERP Application Consultant; Facilities Engineer; Industrial Designer; JAVA Programmer; Senior Siebel EIM Consultant. **Corporate headquarters location:** Minneapolis MN. **Other area locations:** Bowling Green KY; Louisville KY; Paducah KY. **Other U.S. locations:** Nationwide. **International locations:** Canada; United Kingdom. **Subsidiaries include:** Sequoia Services Group; Managed Services Group; IT Supplemental Resources. **Listed on:** NASDAQ. **Stock exchange symbol:** ANLY. **Number of employees worldwide:** Over 3,000.

COMPUTER ANALYTICAL SYSTEMS, INC.
1418 South Third Street, Louisville KY 40208. 502/635-2019. **Toll-free phone:** 800/977-3475. **Fax:** 502/636-9157. **Contact:** Human Resources. **E-mail address:** info@c-a-s-i.com. **World Wide Web address:** http://www.c-a-s-i.com. **Description:** A technical consulting firm offering a variety of services including database development and maintenance, custom programming, hardware/software sales solutions, networking, and systems integration and management. Founded in 1988.

IBM CORPORATION
230 Lexington Green Circle, Suite 500, Lexington KY 40503. **Toll-free phone:** 800/796-9876. **Contact:** Staffing Services. **World Wide Web address:** http://www.ibm.com. **Description:** An advanced information technologies company that manufactures and markets a wide range of products, including computer systems, software, networking systems, microelectronics, and storage devices. **Positions advertised include:** Oracle I/T Migration Specialist; Planning Leader; Business Development Executive; Competitive Sales Specialist; Remedy Consultant; BI Architect; Business Objects Developer; Analog Circuit Design; Service Management Architect. **Special programs:** Training. **Corporate headquarters location:** Armonk NY. **Other U.S. locations:** Nationwide. **International locations:** Worldwide. **Subsidiaries include:** Hitachi Global Storage Technologies; IBM Canada Limited; IBM Global Services; IBM Software; Lotus Development Corporation; Tivoli Software. **Operations at this facility include:** This location develops document conferencing software applications for end users. **Listed on:** New York Stock Exchange. **Stock exchange symbol:** IBM. **Sales/revenues:** $81 billion. **Number of employees worldwide:** 350,000.

KEANE, INC.
9300 Shelbyville Road, Suite 205, Louisville KY 40222. 502/423-9958. **Contact:** Human Resources. **E-mail address:** careers@keane.com. **World Wide Web address:** http://www.keane.com. **Description:** Offers businesses a variety of computer consulting services. Keane also develops, markets, and manages software for its clients and assists in project management. **Positions advertised include:** Programmer/Analyst; Quality Assurance Analyst. **Special programs:** Tuition Assistance Program; Training. **Corporate headquarters location:** Boston MA. **Other area locations:** Lexington KY. **Other U.S. locations:** Nationwide. **International locations:** London, UK; Coventry, UK; Halifax, Nova Scotia, Canada; Noida, India; Hyderabad, India. **Subsidiaries include:** Metro Information Services. **Listed on:** American Stock Exchange. **Stock exchange symbol:** KEA. **Sales/revenues:** $212.5 million. **Number of employees worldwide:** 9,000.

LEXMARK INTERNATIONAL, INC.
740 New Circle Road NW, Lexington KY 40550. 859/232-2379. **Contact:** Recruiting Office. **E-mail address:** recruiting@lexmark.com. **World Wide Web address:** http://www.lexmark.com. **Description:** Develops, manufactures, and markets laser and inkjet printers, typewriters, computer keyboards, and related supplies, services and solutions. **Positions advertised include:** Hardware Engineering–Student; National Promotions Manager; IT Program Manager; Software Engineer–Student; Embedded Control Engineer; Publications Program Manager; Financial Operations Specialist; Channel Solutions Manager; Electrophotographic Engineer. **Special programs:** Internships; Co-ops. **Corporate headquarters location:** This location. **Other U.S. locations:** Boulder CO. **International locations:** Worldwide. **Operations at this facility include:** Administration; Manufacturing; Research and Development; Sales. **Listed on:** New York Stock Exchange. **Stock exchange symbol:** LXK. **Sales/revenues:** $5.2 billion. **Number of employees at this location:** 4,000. **Number of employees worldwide:** 13,000.

LEXNET, INC.
268 Southland Drive, Suite 120, Lexington KY 40503. 859/266-1141. **Fax:** 859/268-6196. **Contact:** Human Resources. **E-mail address:** jobs@lexnetinc.com. **World Wide Web address:** http://www.lexnetinc.com. **Description:** Provides computer network consulting and training. **Positions advertised include:** Sales Consultant; Hardware Technician; System Engineer; AccPac Accounting Support; Application Specialist; Citrix Engineer; Printer Engineer. **Corporate headquarters location:** This location.

MEDIAPLEX SYSTEMS
5111 Commerce Crossing, Suite 200, Louisville KY 40229-2100. 502/810-5000. **Fax:** 502/810-5179. **Contact:** Personnel. **World Wide Web address:** http://www.adwaresystems.com. **Description:** Provide management information systems solutions through content management, workflow/project management, and media management for the marketing communications industry. **Other U.S. locations:** Los Angeles CA; Indianapolis IN; New York NY. **International locations:** Toronto, Canada. **Parent company:** Valueclick. **Operations at this facility include:** Development & Support.

METTLER TOLEDO INC.
2549 Richmond Road, Suite 400, Lexington KY 40509. 859/266-3000. **Contact:** Human Resources. **World Wide Web address:** http://www.mt.com. **Description:** Provides precision instruments and related services for professional use. **Corporate headquarters location:** Columbus OH. **Other U.S. locations:** Nationwide. **International locations:** Worldwide. **Listed on:** New York Stock Exchange. **Stock exchange symbol:** MTD. **Sales/revenues:** Over $1 billion. **Number of employees nationwide:** 3,000. **Number of employees worldwide:** Over 8,000.

NETGAIN TECHNOLOGIES INC.
2031 Georgetown Road, Lexington KY 40511. 859/255-0155. **Fax:** 859/252-2681. **Contact:** Human Resources. **E-mail address:** info@netgainky.com. **World Wide Web address:** http://www.netgainky.com. **Description:** Provides

professional, business, and IT services to clients in the computer, healthcare, digital output, and phone industries. **Positions advertised include:** Desktop Support Technician; Systems Network Manager; IT Security SOX Auditor. **Other area locations:** Louisville KY. **Other U.S. locations:** Little Rock AR.

POMEROY COMPUTER RESOURCES
1020 Petersburg Road, Hebron KY 41048. 859/846-8727. **Fax:** 859/586-4414. **Contact:** Corporate Recruiting Manager. **World Wide Web address:** http://www.pomeroy.com. **Description:** A full-service systems integration company that sells, installs, and services microcomputers and microcomputer equipment primarily for business, professional, educational, and government customers. The company also offers customer support services including network analysis and design, systems configuration, custom installation, training, maintenance, and repair. Founded in 1992. **NOTE:** Online applications are available. **Positions advertised include:** SOL ASP Java Web Developer; Solutions & RFF Proposal Coordinator. **Corporate headquarters location:** This location. **Other area locations:** Lexington KY; Louisville KY. **Other U.S. locations:** Cincinnati OH; Louisville OH; Kingsport TN; Knoxville TN; Nashville TN. **Subsidiaries include:** Xenas Multimedia. **Listed on:** NASDAQ. **Stock exchange symbol:** PMRY. **Sales/revenues:** $702 million. **Number of employees at this location:** 120. **Number of employees nationwide:** 1,765.

Louisiana
ANTARES TECHNOLOGY SOLUTIONS, INC.
8772 Quarters Lake Road, P.O. Box 80539, Baton Rouge LA 70898-0539. 225/922-7748. **Toll-free phone:** 800/366-8807. **Fax:** 225/922-7749. **Contact:** Human Resources. **E-mail Address:** hr@antaresnet.com. **World Wide Web address:** http://www.antaresnet.com. **Description:** A software design, development, and information technology company. Founded in 1988. **Positions advertised include:** Software Quality Assurance Analyst. **Other area locations:** Metairie LA.

ANTEON CORPORATION
4023 Main Street, Belle Chasse LA 70037. 504/469-5584. **Contact:** Human Resources. **World Wide Web address:** http://www.anteon.com. **Description:** A leading provider of technology-based solutions in the areas of engineering, information technology, and interactive multimedia services. Anteon designs, integrates, maintains, and upgrades systems for national defense, intelligence, emergency response, infrastructure and other high-priority government missions. The company also provides customers with the systems engineering and program management skills necessary to manage the development and operations of their mission-critical systems. **Positions advertised include:** Environmental Engineer; Sr. Database Architect; Sr. Programmer/Analyst; Technical Aide. **Corporate headquarters location:** Fairfax VA. **Other U.S. locations:** Nationwide. **International locations:** Germany; Italy; United Kingdom. **Parent company:** General Dynamics. **Listed on:** New York Stock Exchange. **Stock exchange symbol:** ANT. **Annual sales/revenues:** More than $100 million. **Number of employees nationwide:** 5,400.

APOGEN TECHNOLOGIES
13919 River Road, Suite 230, Luling LA 70070. 985/331/1297. **Contact:** Human Resources. **World Wide Web address:** http://www.apogen.com. **Description:** A provider of technology solutions to the federal government. Apogen's key capabilities include: enterprise architecture, software development and systems integration, network engineering and operations, energy and environmental engineering, program management, and spectral imaging technology. **NOTE:** Search current job openings and apply online. **Positions advertised include:** NT Administrator; Project Planner; Security Systems Engineer; Software Test Manager; Solutions Architect/Lead Developer; SQL Windows Developer; Sr. Security Systems Engineer; Sr. Systems Analyst. **Other area locations:** Mandeville VA. **Other U.S. locations:** McLean VA; Albuquerque NM; Las Vegas NV; Los Alamos NM; Tempe AZ; San Diego CA; Springfield VA. **Parent company:** QinetiQ North America. **Number of employees nationwide:** 1,000.

DATEC
Oakwood Corporate Center, 401 Whitney Avenue, Suite 406, Gretna LA 70056. 504/368-2097. **Fax:** 504/368-2989. **Contact:** Human Resources. **World Wide Web address:** http://www.datecinc.com. **Description:** A certified woman-owned corporation that provides systems support for engineering design, drafting, project management, and fabrication of worldwide offshore production facilities; complemented by on-site training, support and services. **Corporate headquarters location:** Midland TX. **Other area locations:** Baton Rouge LA. **Other U.S. locations:** AL; OK; TX. **Parent Company:** ECAD, Incorporated. **Listed on:** Privately held.

LEWIS COMPUTER SERVICES, INC.
8549 United Plaza Boulevard, Suite 310, Baton Rouge LA 70809. 225/709-2000. **Toll-free phone:** 800/955-3947. **Fax:** 225/709-2010. **Contact:** Human Resources. **E-mail address:** jobs@lewis.com. **World Wide Web address:** http://www.lewis.com. **Description:** Develops software for home health agencies. **NOTE:** Search current job openings and apply online. **Positions advertised include:** Business Analyst; Client Software Trainer; Clinical Software Trainer; Lotus Notes Developer; Manager of Customer Education; MIS Assistant; Product Manager; Recruiter; Technical Support Professional. **Corporate headquarters location:** This location. **Other U.S. locations:** Chicago IL. **President:** Jeffrey Lewis. **Number of employees at this location:** Over 100.

PRE-ENGINEERING SOFTWARE CORPORATION
5800 One Perkins Place Drive, Suite 10-D, Baton Rouge LA 70808. 225/769-3728. **Fax:** 225/769-3661. **Contact:** Human Resources. **E-mail address:** mail@pre-engineering.com. **World Wide Web address:** http://www.pre-engineering.com. **Description:** Develops and publishes software programs and other teaching tools used to reinforce students' math and science skills while encouraging an interest in the engineering field.

SYGNVS INTEGRATED SOLUTIONS, INC.
13405 Seymour Myers Boulevard, Building A, Suite 1, Covington LA 70433-6895. 985/892.7207. **Contact:** Human Resources. **World Wide Web address:** http://www.sygnvs.com. **Description:** A software consulting firm that specializes in business management and integrated accounting software applications. The company also sells, implements, supports, trains, and does custom programming for MAS90 and MAS200. **NOTE:** Job openings are posted at http://back2work.nola.com. Applications can be filed through this website. **Positions advertised include:** Accounting Software Consultant.

TENMAST SOFTWARE
1503 Goodwin Road, Suite 100, Ruston LA 71270. 318/251-2392. **Fax:** 318/251-2205. **Contact:** Human Resources. **World Wide Web address:** http://www.tenmast.com. **Description:** Produces software for managing tenant and financial data, tracking maintenance activities, performing unit inspections, and producing standard HUD and agency-specific reports for Public Housing and Section 8. **NOTE:** Open positions are occasionally posted on the website. Interested applicants should send an e-mail to jamesm@tenmast.com with an attached resume. **Available positions include:** Systems Architect. **Corporate headquarters location:** Lexington KY. **Listed on:** Privately held. **President:** James C. Mauch. **Annual sales/revenues:** $5 million.

Maine

BLUE MARBLE GEOGRAPHICS
345 Water Street, Suite 100, Gardiner ME 04345. 207/582-6747. **Toll-free phone:** 800/ 616-2725. **Fax:** 207/582-7001. **Contact:** Human Resources Department. **E-mail address:** hr@bluemarblegeo.com. **World Wide Web address:** http://www.bluemarblegeo.com. **Description:** Develops and markets mapping software. Products include coordinate and data translator programs, tracking and GPS programs, and a wide array of mapping software development and application tools. Founded in 1993. **NOTE:** Search on-line postings. E-mail is preferred when responding to job openings. **Positions advertised include:** Software Developer; Entry Level Software Salesperson. **Corporate headquarters location:** This location.

BURGESS COMPUTER INC.
101 Centre Street, Bath ME 04530. 207/443-9554. **Fax:** 207/443-3856. **Toll-free phone:** 800/498-8642. **Contact:** Human Resources. **E-mail address:** craig@burgessinc.com. **World Wide Web address:** http://www.burgessinc.com. **Description:** Provides technology consulting and implementation services.

CASCO DEVELOPMENT INC.
2 Portland Fish Pier, P.O. Box 1057, Portland ME 04101. 207/773-0944. **Fax:** 207/773-0524. **Contact:** Hiring Manager. **E-mail address:** jobs@cascodev.com. **World Wide Web address:** http://www.cascodev.com. **Description:** A developer and provider of labor related data collection and reporting software. **NOTE**: Search posted openings on-line.

COMMON CENSUS
90 Bridge Street, 1st Floor, Westbrook ME 04092. 207/854-5454. **Fax:** 207/854-3154. **Toll-free phone**: 800/552-7373. **Contact:** Human Resources. **E-mail address:** hr@commoncensus.com. **World Wide Web address:** http://www.commoncensus.com. **Description:** Produces an operating system that allows businesses to manage employee benefits.

FIRST TEK TECHNOLOGIES INC.
482 Congress Street, Suite 203, Portland ME 04101. 207/699-2885. **Fax:** 207/221-1005. **Contact:** Human Resources. **E-mail address:** erma@first-tek.com. **World Wide Web address:** http://www.first-tek.com. **Description:** An IT and e-commerce solution provider that performs services as well as delivers products. **Positions advertised include:** Program Analyst; Software Engineer; Systems Analyst; Business Analyst. **Other U.S. locations:** North Brunswick NJ; Chicago IL; Sioux Falls SD; Omaha NE; Newark DE; Des Moines IA.

GEEKTEAM.COM
197 Sullivan Road, Greene ME 04236. 207/946-2455. **Fax:** 603/372-4538. **Toll-free phone:** 888/517-7816. **Contact:** Bill Clarke. **E-mail address:** employment@geekteam.com. **World Wide Web address:** http://www.geekteam.com. **Description:** Designs and builds custom web applications. Also develops web-based software products. **Positions advertised include:** Application/Information Architect; Application Programmer.

I-MANY, INC.
511 Congress Street, Suite 600, Portland ME 04101. 207/774-3244. **Fax:** 207/828-0491. **Contact:** Human Resources. **E-mail address**: hr@imany.com. **World Wide Web address:** http://www.imanyinc.com. **Description:** Develops and manufactures contract management software, and provides Internet-based solutions for the medical, surgical, and pharmaceutical fields. **NOTE:** Please visit website for online application form. **Listed on:** NASDAQ. **Stock exchange symbol:** IMNY.

SACO RIVER TECHNOLOGIES
70 Shadagee Road, Saco ME 04072. 207/727-5795. **Fax:** 207/727-5793. **Contact:** Hiring Manager. **World Wide Web address:** http://www.sacorivertech.com. **Description:** Provides a variety of computer services including consulting, programming, and Web design to help clients understand their technology options. Founded in 1991. **Corporate headquarters location:** This location.

SOMIX TECHNOLOGIES INC.
1293 Main Street, Sanford ME 04073. 207/324-8805. **Fax:** 207/324-8683. **Contact:** Human Resources. **E-mail address:** jobs@somix.com. **World Wide Web address:** http://www.somix.com. **Description:** Develops web-based IT and system management applications. **Positions advertised include: Positions advertised include:** Perl Programmer; Sales; Information Systems; Internships.

Maryland

ACS GOVERNMENT SOLUTIONS GROUP, INC.
One Curie Court, Rockville MD 20850. 301/921-7000. **Contact:** Human Resources. **World Wide Web address:** http://www.acs-inc.com. **Description:** Provides contract computer services to the government including data processing and systems integration. **NOTE:** Online applications are available. **Positions advertised include:** Business Analyst. **Special programs:** Internships. **Corporate headquarters location:** Dallas TX. **Other U.S. locations:** Nationwide. **Subsidiaries include:** Analytical Systems Engineering Corporation; Betac Corporation. **Parent company:** Computer Services, Incorporated. **Listed on:** New York Stock Exchange. **Stock exchange symbol:** ACS. **President/CEO:** William Woodard. **Number of employees nationwide:** 4,100.

AJILON SERVICES INC.
901 Dulaney Valley Road, Suite 309, Towson MD 21204. 410/828-0788. **Fax:** 410/321-7918. **Contact:** Janet Metzger, Human Resources. **World Wide Web address:** http://www.ajilon.com. **Description:** Offers computer consulting services, project support, and end user services. **Positions advertised include:** Accounts Payable Supervisor; Payroll Accountant. **Special programs:** Tuition Reimbursement Program. **Other U.S. locations:** Nationwide. **International locations:** Canada. **President/COO:** Mark E. Fusco.

ANALYSYS
1834 East Joppa Road, Baltimore MD 21234-2735. 410/661-9800. **Toll-free phone:** 800/661-9803. **Contact:** Human Resources. **E-mail address:** info@analysys.com. **World Wide Web address:** http://www.analysys.com. **Description:** A provider of IT services to small and mid-sized companies in the central Maryland area. Founded in 1995. **Positions advertised include:** Computer and Information Technology Support/Systems Administrator.

ANTEON CORPORATION
3211 Jermantown Road, Fairfax VA 22030. 703/246-0200. **Contact:** Human Resources. **E-mail address:** careers@anteon.com. **World Wide Web address:** http://www.anteon.com. **Description:** Provides information technology solutions and advanced engineering services to government clients. The company designs, integrates, maintains, and upgrades state-of-the-art systems for national defense, intelligence, emergency response, and other high-priority missions. **Positions advertised include:** Accountant; Contracts Administrator; Financial Analyst; International Contracts Manager; Program Manager; Proposal Specialist; Sr. Pricing Analyst. **Corporate headquarters location:** This location. **Listed on:** New York Stock Exchange. **Stock exchange symbol:** ANT. **Number of employees worldwide:** 7,600 in more than 100 offices.

ATLIS SYSTEMS INC.
8455 Colesville Road, Suite 1050, Silver Spring MD 20910. 301/578-4200. **Fax:** 301/650-2043. **Contact:** President. **E-mail address:** info@atlis.com. **World Wide Web address:** http://www.atlis.com. **Description:** Provides various computer-related services including document coding, systems integration, information processing, and electronic publishing. **NOTE:** Part-time, temporary, and entry-

level positions are offered. **Positions advertised include:** TeX Application Programmer. **Corporate headquarters location:** This location. **Other U.S. locations:** Camp Hill PA.

BENELOGIC, LLC.
2118 Greenspring Drive, Timonium MD 21093. 443/322-2494. **Toll-free phone:** 877/716-8778. **Fax:** 443/322-2496. **Contact:** Human Resources. **E-mail address:** info@benelogic.com. **World Wide Web address:** http://www.benelogic.com. **Description:** Develops software applications designed to simplify employee benefits administration and benefits data transfer. Founded in 2000. **Positions advertised include:** Quality Assurance Engineer; Implementation Analyst; Vendor Operations Analyst; Marketing Intern.

CACI SECURITY GROUP
6835 Deerpath Road, Elkridge MD 21075. 410/796-7200. **Contact:** Human Resources. **E-mail address:** jobs@caci.com. **World Wide Web address:** http://www.caci.com. **Description:** Manufactures access control systems and security systems. The company also provides software support for the U.S. Navy. **NOTE:** Resumes should be sent to: 14151 Park Meadow Drive, Attn: Recruiters, Chantilly VA 20151, or faxed to 703/679-4510. Resumes may also be submitted online. **Positions advertised include:** OPELINT Analyst; All Source Analyst; Team Leader; Security Manager; Program Manager; Project Manager; Operation Research Analyst. **Corporate headquarters location:** Arlington VA. **Other U.S. locations:** Nationwide. **International locations:** England; Scotland. **Parent company:** CACI International, Incorporated. **Listed on:** NASDAQ. **Stock exchange symbol:** CACI.

CENTURY TECHNOLOGIES, INC. (CENTECH)
8403 Colesville Road, Suite 920, Silver Spring MD 20910. 301/585-4800. **Fax:** 301/588-1619. **Contact:** Human Resources. **E-mail address:** resumes@centech.com. **World Wide Web address:** http://www.centech.com. **Description:** A systems integrator that provides telecommunications and networking services to clientele in the public and private sectors. Founded in 1977. **Positions advertised include:** Microsoft Certified Consultant. **Corporate headquarters location:** This location. **Other U.S. locations:** Beavercreek OH; Del City OK. **Number of employees nationwide:** 300.

CISCO SYSTEMS
8865 Stanford Boulevard Suite 201, Columbia MD 21045. 410/309-4800. **Fax:** 410/309-4899. **Contact:** Human Resources. **World Wide Web address:** http://www.cisco.com **Description:** Cisco Systems is the leader for networking and the Internet. **Note:** Applications may be submitted online. **Positions advertised include:** Finance Business Specialist; Safety Manager. **Corporate Headquarters location:** San Jose, CA. **Other U.S. locations:** Nation wide. **International locations:** World Wide. **Listed on:** NASDAQ. **Stock exchange symbol:** CSCO.

COMPRO SYSTEMS, INC.
9 Basswood Court, Baltimore MD 21228. 410/788-7968. **Contact:** Human Resources. **World Wide Web address:** http://www.compro.com. **Description:** Fulfills the automation needs of clients through systems integration, LANs, networking, the Internet, customized application software development, database management, document image processing, and business modeling. ComPro's customers include both government and commercial clients. Founded in 1982. **Positions advertised include:** Queue Coordinator; Help Desk Administrator; Cross Functional Queue Manager; Tools Applicant Support; Network Systems Administrator; Network Storage Area Associate; Sonet Engineer; Service Writer; Configuration Manager; Desktop Support Systems Administrator; UNIX Infrastructure Administrator; Web Architect; Windows NT2000 Server Administrator; Fiber Optics Technician. **Corporate headquarters location:** This location. **International locations:** India. **Listed on:** Privately held. **Sales/revenues:** $11 - $20 million. **Number of employees at this location:** 15. **Number of employees nationwide:** 225.

COMPUTER SCIENCES CORPORATION
15245 Shady Grove Road, Suite 200, Rockville MD 20850. 301/921-3000. **Contact:** Human Resources. **World Wide Web address:** http://www.csc.com. **Description:** An information technology services company offering systems design and integration; IT and business process outsourcing; applications software development; Web and application hosting; and management consulting. **Positions advertised include:** Systems Analyst; Applications Developer; Contract Specialist. **Corporate headquarters location:** El Segundo CA. **Other U.S. locations:** Nationwide. **International locations:** Worldwide. **Subsidiaries include:** DynaCorp. **Operations at this facility include:** This location is the Systems Sciences division headquarters, and primarily serves the U.S. government. **Listed on:** New York Stock Exchange. **Stock exchange symbol:** CSC. **President/COO:** Edward P. Boykin. **Sales/revenue:** $11.3 billion. **Number of employees nationwide:** 20,000. **Number of employees worldwide:** 90,000.

COMSO, INC.
6303 Ivy Lane, Suite 300, Greenbelt MD 20770. 301/345-0046. **Fax:** 301/345-0047. **Contact:** Recruiting. **E-mail address:** recruit@comso.com. **World Wide Web address:** http://www.comso.com. **Description:** A computer systems integration firm. Founded in 1988. **Positions advertised include:** Director of Business; Development Sales. **Other area locations:** Silver Spring MD; Landover MD; Fort Meade MD. **Other U.S. locations:** Arlington VA; McClean VA; Reston VA; Washington D.C.

COMSYS
9737 Washingtonian Boulevard, Suite 500, Gaithersburg MD 20878. 301/921-3600. **Toll-free phone:** 800/926-6797. **Fax:** 301/921-3660. **Contact:** Human Resources. **World Wide Web address:** http://www.comsys.com. **Description:** Provides contract programming and computer and software consulting services. **Positions advertised include:** Contract Administrator; Database Technician; Expert Approval Import Processing; HTML Programmer; Logistic Support Engineer; Mechanical Engineer; Performance Test Coordinator; Resident Source Inspector; Service Level Management; Subcontract Administrator; UNIX Administrator. **Corporate headquarters location:** Houston TX. **Other area locations:** Baltimore MD. **Other U.S. locations:** Nationwide. **President/CEO:** Michael T. Willis.

DRS ELECTRONIC SYSTEMS, INC.
200 Professional Drive, Suite 400, Gaithersburg MD 20879. 301/921-8100. **Fax:** 301/869-5008. **Contact:** Human Resources. **E-mail address:** resume@drs-esg.com. **World Wide Web address:** http://www.drs.com. **Description:** Manufactures and sells a diverse range of electronic products for communication, technological, transportation, and defense applications. **Positions advertised include:** Electrical Engineer; Radar Systems Engineer; Software Engineer; Software Configuration Management Support; Technical Display Software Systems Engineer; UNIX Administration. **Corporate headquarters location:** Parsippany NJ. **Other U.S. locations:** Nationwide. **International locations:** Canada; England. **Parent company:** DRS Technologies, Incorporated is a defense electronic systems supplier that serves customers in both government and commercial sectors. **Listed on:** American Stock Exchange. **Stock exchange symbol:** DRS. **President/Chairman/CEO:** Mark S. Newman.

DRS TECHNICAL AND MANAGEMENT SERVICES CORPORATION
4041 Powder Mill Road, Suite 700, Calverton MD 20705. 301/595-0710. **Fax:** 301/937-5236. **Contact:** Director of Human Resources. **E-mail address:** tamscojobs@tamscohq.com. **World Wide Web**

address: http://www.tamsco.com. **Description:** Offers a variety of ADP-oriented and telecommunications system development, manufacturing, and integration services. These products and services include requirements definition; systems engineering; systems and telecommunications network design; software development; electronics and telecommunications equipment; hardware development and manufacturing; and systems integration and implementation. **Positions advertised include:** Billing Specialist; Accountant Representative; Marketing Specialist. **Corporate headquarters location:** This location. **Other area locations:** Abingdon MD; Lexington Park MD. **Other U.S. locations:** Dayton OH; Warner Robins GA; Fort Gordon GA; Elizabeth City NC; San Diego CA; Ogden UT; Polson MO. **Operations at this facility include:** Administration. **Listed on:** Privately held. **President/CEO:** David R. Gust. **Number of employees at this location:** 40. **Number of employees nationwide:** 500.

DALY COMPUTERS
22521 Gateway Center Drive, Clarksburg MD 20871. 301/670-0381. **Toll-free phone:** 800/955-DALY. **Fax:** 301/963-1516. **Contact:** Human Resources. **E-mail address:** hr@daly.com. **World Wide Web address:** http://www.daly.com. **Description:** An information technologies service provider geared primarily toward the public sector. **Positions advertised include:** Inside Sales Person; Outside Sales Person; Computer Engineer. **Corporate headquarters location:** This location. **Other U.S. locations:** Miami FL; Chicago IL; Harrisburg PA; Richmond VA; Roanoke VA.

DIGICON CORPORATION
1355 Piccard Drive, Suite 200, Rockville MD 20850. 301/721-6300. **Contact:** Maryanne Kozorous, Recruiter. **E-mail address:** careers@digicon.com. **World Wide Web address:** http://www.digicon.com. **Description:** A systems integration firm that provides telecommunications, networking, information technology, and enterprise systems management services. **NOTE:** Resumes submitted online must be in Word format. **Positions advertised include:** Service Center Engineer; Contract Manager; HQ Capture Manager; Oracle Developer; Project Manager; N/H-IT Acquisition Specialist; HQ Network Engineer; Software Engineer Manager; Staff Accountant. **Subsidiaries include:** DTx Incorporated; Digicon Technologies. **Sales/revenue:** Approximately $55 million. **Number of employees nationwide:** Over 300.

DOCUCORP INTERNATIONAL
8455 Colesville Road, Suite 820, Silver Spring MD 20910. 301/589-6300. **Contact:** Human Resources. **E-mail address:** recruiter@docucorp.com. **World Wide Web address:** http://www.docucorp.com. **Description:** Develops business solution software for document management and automation purposes. The company's services include insurance policy production, financial fulfillment, electronic bill presentment and payment, and customer statements and billings. **NOTE:** Resumes should be sent to: Docucorp, Attn: Recruiter, 5910 North Central Expressway, Suite 800, Dallas TX 75206. Fax to: 214/987-8187 **Positions advertised include:** Lead Writer. **Corporate headquarters location:** Dallas TX. **Other U.S. locations:** Atlanta GA; Portland ME; Bedford NH; Dallas TX. **International locations:** London, England. **Listed on:** NASDAQ. **Stock exchange symbol:** DOCC. **President/CEO:** Michael D. Andereck. **Sales/revenue:** $72 billion. **Number of employees nationwide:** 400.

DYNAMAC CORPORATION
2275 Research Boulevard, Suite 300, Rockville MD 20850-3268. 301/417-9800. **Fax:** 301/417-6125. **Contact:** Michael Ray, Human Resources. **E-mail address:** hr@dynamac.com. **World Wide Web address:** http://www.dynamac.com. **Description:** Develops environmental software geared toward database applications. **Positions advertised include:** Litigation Support Specialist; Records Specialist; NEPA Specialist; Webmaster; Administration Assistant. **NOTE:** Resumes submitted via e-mail must be in Microsoft Word or ASCII text format. **Corporate headquarters location:** This location. **Other area locations:** Germantown MD; Aberdeen Proving Ground MD. **Other U.S. locations:** OR; ID; OK; KS; TX; SC; NC; FL; PA. **CEO/Chairman:** Diana MacArthur.

FILETEK, INC.
9400 Key West Avenue, Rockville MD 20850. 301/251-0600. **Fax:** 301/251-1990. **Contact:** Debbie Mobley, Manager of Human Resources. **E-mail address:** employment@filetek.com. **World Wide Web address:** http://www.filetek.com. **Description:** Uses hierarchical relational database technology to design, develop, and deliver mass data storage software systems for large corporations. Founded in 1984. **NOTE:** To contact Human Resources directly, call 301/517-1840. **Special programs:** Tuition Reimbursement Program. **Corporate headquarters location:** This location. **Other U.S. locations:** Nationwide. **International locations:** Belgium; Germany; United Kingdom. **Listed on:** Privately held. **President/CEO:** William C. Thompson. **Number of employees at this location:** 100.

GTCO CALCOMP, INC.
7125 Riverwood Drive, Columbia MD 21046. 410/381-6688. **Toll-free phone:** 800/344-4723. **Fax:** 410/290-9065. **Contact:** Human Resources. **E-mail address:** md.hr@gtcocalcomp.com. **World Wide Web address:** http://www.gtcocalcomp.com. **Description:** Manufactures input peripherals. Founded in 1975. **Positions advertised include:** Sales Representative. **Special programs:** Tuition Reimbursement Program. **Corporate headquarters location:** This location. **Other U.S. locations:** Scottsdale AZ. **International locations:** Vienna, Austria; Munich, Germany. **President:** Eric Timmons. **Number of employees at this location:** 60.

GENERAL DYNAMICS ADVANCED INFORMATION SYSTEMS
2721 Technology Drive, Suite 400, Annapolis Junction MD 20701. 240/456-5500. **Fax:** 240/456-5575. **Contact:** Human Resources. **World Wide Web address:** http://www.gd-ais.com. **Description:** Assists various military branches with software engineering, systems integration, and project development. **NOTE:** Online applications are available. **Positions advertised include:** Principal Engineering Systems; Technical Writing Specialist; Principal Engineer; Lead Engineer; Administrative Assistant; Technical Support Engineer; Information Technology Engineer; Finance Specialist; Software Quality Assurance Engineer. **Corporate headquarters location:** Arlington VA. **Other area locations:** California MD; Aberdeen MD. **Other U.S. locations:** Nationwide. **Operations at this facility include:** This location offers computer support to the Naval Air Warfare Center. **President/CEO:** David H. Langstaff. **Number of employees nationwide:** Over 7,000.

GROUP 1 SOFTWARE, INC.
4200 Parliament Place, Suite 600, Lanham MD 20706-1844. 301/731-2300. **Toll-free phone:** 800/368-5806. **Contact:** Human Resources. **E-mail address:** rachel_holstein@g1.com. **World Wide Web address:** http://www.g1.com. **Description:** Develops, acquires, and markets specialized, integrated list management, mail management, and marketing support software systems. Group 1 Software also publishes list and mail management software products. Founded in 1982. **Positions advertised include:** Sales Executive; Sales Manager; Development Manager; Principal Engineer; Software Engineer; Technical Support Representative; Staff Attorney. **Special programs:** Training. **Corporate headquarters location:** This location. **Other U.S. locations:** CA; GA; IL; MN; NV; NJ; TX; VA; FL. **International locations:** Worldwide. **Operations at this facility include:** Administration; Research and Development; Sales. **Listed on:** NASDAQ. **Stock exchange symbol:** GSOF. **CEO:** Robert S. Bowen. **Sales/revenues:** $21 - $50 million. **Number of employees at this location:** 250. **Number**

of employees nationwide: 325. **Number of employees worldwide:** 365.

HEWLETT PACKARD
6406 Ivy Lane, Greenbelt MD 20770. 301/459-7900. **Toll-free phone:** 800/544-9944. **Contact:** Human Resources. **World Wide Web address:** http://www.hp.com. **Description:** Designs, manufactures, sells, and services computers, peripheral equipment, and related software and supplies. Applications and programs include scientific research, computation, communications, education, data analysis, industrial control, time sharing, commercial data processing, graphic arts, word processing, health care, instrumentation, engineering, and simulation. **NOTE:** Previously Compaq Computer Corporation. The two companies merged in May 2002. **Positions advertised include:** Business Process Transition Manager; Director of Consulting; Global Deployment Manager; Global Solutions Manager; 1TO Operations Consultant; HP Service Tax Manager; Financial Analyst; Program Manager; Project Manager. **Corporate headquarters location:** Palo Alto CA. **Other U.S. locations:** Nationwide. **International locations:** Worldwide. **Operations at this facility include:** This location is a sales office. **Listed on:** New York Stock Exchange. **Stock exchange symbol:** HP. **Sales/revenue:** $72 billion. **Number of employees worldwide:** 140,000.

IBM CORPORATION
6710 Rockledge Drive, Bethesda MD 20817. 301/803-2000. **Toll-free phone:** 800/333-6705. **Contact:** IBM Staffing Services. **World Wide Web address:** http://www.ibm.com. **Description:** International Business Machines Corporation (IBM) is a developer, manufacturer, and marketer of advanced information processing products including computers and microelectronic technology products, software, and networking systems. The company also provides information technology-related services. **NOTE:** Online applications are available. **Positions advertised include:** AIX Storage Area Network Associate; BP Engineer; Client Executive; Data Modeler; Information Technology Architect; Research Program Security Consultant; Pricing Analyst; Siebel Coordinator; Subcontract Administrator; User Case Analyst. **Special programs:** Training. **Corporate headquarters location:** Armonk NY. **Other U.S. locations:** Nationwide. **International locations:** Worldwide. **Subsidiaries include:** IBM Credit Corporation; IBM Instruments, Incorporated; IBM World Trade Corporation. **Operations at this facility include:** This location is an administrative service center. **Listed on:** New York Stock Exchange. **Stock exchange symbol:** IBM. **President/CEO/Chairman:** Samuel J. Palmisano. **Sales/revenue:** Approximately $81 billion. **Number of employees worldwide:** 335,421.

INFORMATION SYSTEMS & NETWORK CORPORATION (ISN)
10411 Motor City Drive, Suite 700, Bethesda MD 20817. 301/469-0400. **Contact:** Human Resources. **World Wide Web address:** http://www.isncorp.com. **Description:** Provides systems integration services to the U.S. government. Founded in 1980. **Corporate headquarters location:** This location.

INFORMATION SYSTEMS AND SERVICES, INC. (ISSI)
8601 Georgia Avenue, Suite 708, Silver Spring MD 20910. 301/588-3800. **Fax:** 301/588-3986. **Contact:** Human Resources. **E-mail address:** info@issinet.com. **World Wide Web address:** http://www.issinet.com. **Description:** Develops and integrates enterprise software. Founded in 1987.

INTERVISE CONSULTANTS, INC.
12 South Summit Avenue, Suite 100, Gaithersburg MD 20877. 240/364-9500. **Contact:** Human Resources. **E-mail address:** nc-resumes@intervise.com. **World Wide Web address:** http://www.intervise.com. **Description:** A computer systems engineering consulting firm whose clientele include commercial firms and government contractors. **Positions advertised include:** Government Professional Services Salesperson. **Corporate headquarters location:** This location. **Other U.S. locations:** Minneapolis MN; Raleigh NC; Dallas TX; McLean VA.

L-SOFT INTERNATIONAL, INC.
8100 Corporate Drive, Suite 350, Landover MD 20785-2231. 301/731-0440. **Toll-free phone:** 800/399-5449. **Fax:** 301/731-6302. **Contact:** Human Resources. **E-mail address:** jobs@lsoft.com. **World Wide Web address:** http://www.lsoft.com. **Description:** Develops mailing list management software. The company's product line includes LISTSERV, an electronic mailing list management product; LSMTP, a program for large quantity delivery of Internet mail; and EASE, which allows users to create mail lists on L-Soft's centrally maintained servers. Founded in 1994. **Positions advertised include:** Senior Custom Support Engineer. **Corporate headquarters location:** This location. **Other area locations:** Bethesda MD. **International locations:** Sweden; United Kingdom.

L3 COMMUNICATIONS TITAN CORPORATION
22290 Exploration Drive, Lexington Park MD 20653-1397. 240/895-7400. **Contact:** Human Resources. **World Wide Web address:** http://www.titansystemscorp.com/groups/cgsg. **Description:** L3 Communications Titan Corporation provides information solutions, system support and products for national defense and civilian agencies. **Positions advertised include:** Acoustic Test Engineer; Administrative Assistant; Avionics Components Engineer; Communication Systems Manager; Test Analyst; Engineering Support; Mechanical Engineer; Network Administrator; Public Safety Communications Engineer; Business Analyst; Software Systems Analyst; Software Engineer. **Corporate headquarters:** San Diego CA. **Other U.S. locations:** Nationwide. **International locations:** Worldwide. **Operations at this facility include:** This location is part of the Systems Technology division of The Titan Corporation, specializing in ship and aviation engineering. **Listed on:** New York Stock Exchange. **Stock exchange symbol:** TTN. **CEO/Chairman:** Gene W. Ray. **Sales/revenue:** $2 billion. **Number of employees worldwide:** 12,000.

MANAGEMENT TECHNOLOGY INC. (MTI)
7700 Old Branch Avenue, Suite C200, Clinton MD 20735. 301/856-4840. **Toll-free phone:** 800/821-8133. **Fax:** 301/868-6227. **Contact:** Recruiting Department. **E-mail address:** personnel@mtiinc.com. **World Wide Web address:** http://www.mtiinc.com. **Description:** Develops and markets a variety of banking and financial software. **Positions advertised include:** Web Developer; Administrative Assistant; Contract Administrator; Business Development Associate; Chief Financial Aide Officer; Corporate IT Recruiter; Computer Programmer. **NOTE:** Entry-level positions are offered. Resumes may be submitted online. **Special programs:** Tuition Reimbursement Program. **Corporate headquarters location:** This location. **Other U.S. locations:** Falls Church VA; Hampton VA; New York NY. **President/CEO:** Pauline C. Brooks.

MANUGISTICS, INC.
9715 Key West Avenue, Rockville MD 20850. 301/255-5000. **Toll-free phone:** 800/331-0728. **Contact:** Human Resources. **E-mail address:** jobs@manu.com. **World Wide Web address:** http://www.manugistics.com. **Description:** Develops decision support software and provides support services for Fortune 500 manufacturing, transportation, and distribution companies. **Positions advertised include:** Accounting Manager; Business Development Manager; Database Developer; Director Industry & Alliance Marketing; Help Desk Specialist; Lead Software Developer; Financial Planning Analyst; Project Analyst; Production Manager; Applications Developer; Corporate Receptionist; Human Resources Generalist; Model Analyst; Program Manager; Proposal Writer; Software Developer C++; Software Manager; Test Manager. **Special programs:** Internships; Training.

Corporate headquarters location: This location. **Other U.S. locations:** Nationwide. **International locations:** United Kingdom; Taiwan; Sweden; Spain; Singapore; the Netherlands; Japan; Italy; Australia; Belgium; Brazil; France; Germany; China. **Operations at this facility include:** Administration; Research and Development; Sales; Service. **Listed on:** NASDAQ. **Stock exchange symbol:** MANU. **CEO/Chairman:** Gregory J. Owens. **Sales/revenue:** $310 million. **Number of employees at this location:** 300. **Number of employees worldwide:** Approximately 2,000.

MERCURY INTERACTIVE CORPORATION
8201 Corporate Drive, Suite 600, Landover MD 20785. 301/459-2163. **Fax:** 301/459-5916. **Contact:** Human Resources. **E-mail address:** jobs@merc-int.com. **World Wide Web address:** http://www-svca.mercuryinteractive.com. **Description:** A developer of automated software quality (ASQ) tools for enterprise applications testing. The company's products are used to isolate software and system errors prior to application deployment. Founded in 1989. **NOTE:** Interested jobseekers should direct resumes to Mercury Interactive, 1325 Borregas Avenue, Sunnyvale CA 94089. **Positions advertised include:** Contract Manager. **Corporate headquarters location:** Sunnyvale CA. **Other U.S. locations:** Nationwide. **International locations:** Worldwide. **Operations at this facility include:** This location is a sales office. **Listed on:** NASDAQ. **Stock exchange symbol:** MERQ. **President/CEO:** Amnon Landan. **Sales/revenue:** $400 million. **Number of employees worldwide:** 1,822.

METASTORM
500 East Pratt Street, Suite 1250, Baltimore MD 21202. 443/874-1300. **Toll-free phone:** 877/321-6382. **Fax:** 443/874-1336. **E-mail address:** recruitment@metastorm.com. **World Wide Web address:** http://www.metastorm.com. **Description:** Provider of business process management (BPM) software for modeling, automating, and controlling processes. **Positions advertised include:** Account Executive (AE); Technical Support Analyst/Software Support Analyst. **Corporate headquarters location:** This location. **International locations:** Künten Switzerland; Wimbledon, London.

MICROLOG CORPORATION OF MARYLAND
20270 Goldenrod Lane, Germantown MD 20876. 301/540-5500. **Fax:** 301/540-5557. **Contact:** Human Resources. **E-mail address:** human.resources@mlog.com. **World Wide Web address:** http://www.mlog.com. **Description:** Designs, assembles, and supports a line of interactive communications systems and application solutions software for customers worldwide. **Corporate headquarters location:** This location. **International locations:** The Netherlands. **Listed on:** OTC. **Stock exchange symbol:** MLOG. **Number of employees at this location:** 105. **Number of employees nationwide:** 300.

MICROS SYSTEMS, INC.
7031 Columbia Gateway Drive, Columbia MD 21046-2289. 443/285-6000. **Fax:** 443/285-0650. **Contact:** Personnel. **E-mail address:** employment@micros.com. **World Wide Web address:** http://www.micros.com. **Description:** Engaged in enterprise systems integration for the leisure and entertainment industries. **NOTE:** Entry-level positions are offered. **Positions advertised include:** Customer Care Account Specialist; Implementation Specialist; Network Specialist; Production Support Specialist; Project Specialist; Credit Representative; Payroll Analyst; Implementation Specialist; Product Specialist; Application Solutions Specialist; Restaurant Director POS Sales; Inside Sales Representative; Sales Executive; Account Executive. **Special programs:** Internships. **Office hours:** Monday – Friday, 8:00 a.m. – 5:00 p.m. **Corporate headquarters location:** This location. **Other U.S. locations:** Nationwide. **International locations:** Worldwide. **Subsidiaries include:** Fidelio Software Corporation; Fidelio Software GmbH. **Operations at this facility include:** Administration; Manufacturing; Regional Headquarters; Research and Development; Sales; Service. **Listed on:** NASDAQ. **Stock exchange symbol:** MCRS. **President/CEO:** Tom Giannopoulos. **Number of employees at this location:** 700. **Number of employees nationwide:** 900. **Number of employees worldwide:** 1,100.

MULTIMAX, INC.
1441 McCormick Drive, Largo MD 20774. 301/925-8222. **Toll-free phone:** 800/339-8828. **Fax:** 301/925-2956. **Contact:** Human Resources Department. **E-mail address:** hrmd@multimax.com. **World Wide Web address:** http://www.multimax.com. **Description:** Provides LAN/WAN design and networking services to customers in the government and commercial sectors. **Positions advertised include:** Business Developer; Account Manager; Federal Information Technology Services Associate; Computer Sales Associate. **Corporate headquarters location:** This location. **Other U.S. locations:** Beavercreek OH; Tinton Falls NJ; Atlantic City NJ; Montgomery AL; Indialantic FL; Nashua NH; Virginia Beach VA; Alexandria VA.

NORTHROP GRUMMAN INFORMATION TECHNOLOGY
4800 Hampden Lane, Suite 1100, Bethesda MD 20814. 301/986-0800. **Contact:** Human Resources. **World Wide Web address:** http://www.northropgrummanit.com. **Description:** Provides information technology services and solutions. **Positions advertised include:** Web Software Designer; Multimedia Designer; Help Desk Associate; Contracts Administrator; Media Producer; Photographer; Graphic Artist; Media Script Writer; Viideographer; Network Manager Engineer. **Special programs:** Internships; Training; Summer Jobs. **Corporate headquarters location:** Herndon VA. **Other U.S. locations:** Nationwide. **International locations:** Germany; Korea. **Listed on:** New York Stock Exchange. **Stock exchange symbol:** NOC.

OPTELECOM, INC.
12920 Cloverleaf Center Drive, Germantown MD 20874. 301/444-2200. **Toll-free phone:** 800/293-4237. **Contact:** Diane Mortazavi, Human Resources Manager. **E-mail address:** humanresources@optelecom.com. **World Wide Web address:** http://www.optelecom.com. **Description:** Designs and manufactures various communication products such as modems and interface cards for video, audio, and data transmission. Optelecom also performs coil windings. **NOTE:** To contact Human Resources directly, call 301/444-2223. **Corporate headquarters location:** This location. **International locations:** Worldwide. **Listed on:** NASDAQ. **Stock exchange symbol:** OPTC. **President/CEO:** Edmund D. Ludwig.

PATTON ELECTRONICS COMPANY
7622 Rickenbacker Drive, Gaithersburg MD 20879. 301/975-1000. **Contact:** Human Resources. **E-mail address:** employment@patton.com. **World Wide Web address:** http://www.patton.com. **Description:** Manufactures computer hardware including modems, surge protectors, and interface converters. Founded in 1984. **Positions advertised include:** National Account Representative; Regional Account Representative; Outside Sales; Nuclear Medicine Technician; Respiratory Monitor; Buyer; Respiratory Therapist; Mortgage Banker; Purchasing Assistant; Human Resource Manager. **Corporate headquarters location:** This location. **International locations:** Worldwide. **Listed on:** Privately held. **Annual sales/revenues:** $11 - $20 million. **CEO:** Robert E. Patton. **Number of employees worldwide:** Over 170.

THE PRESIDIO CORPORATION
7601 Ora Glen Drive, Suite 100, Greenbelt MD 20770. 301/459-2200. **Fax:** 301/955-3554. **Contact:** Human Resources. **E-mail address:** jobs@presido.com. **World Wide Web address:** http://www.presidio.com. **Description:** Provides applications and systems integration that enable electronic mail, file exchanges, shared peripherals, and a wide range of group applications. **NOTE:** Mail resumes to 7601 Ora Glen

Drive, Suite 100, Greenbelt MD 20770. Resumes sent via e-mail must be formatted in ASCII text. **Company slogan:** Delivering unified solutions. **Corporate headquarters location:** This location. **Other U.S. locations:** CA; FL; GA; VA; TX; NC. **CEO/Chairperson:** Kristine Cruikshank. **Listed on:** Privately held.

REYNOLDS & REYNOLDS
14600 York Road, Suite E, Sparks MD 21152. 410/771-9211. **Contact:** Human Resources. **E-mail address:** hr@reyrey.com. **World Wide Web address:** http://www.reyrey.com. **Description:** Provides systems integration and analysis for the automotive and health care industries. The company also supplies these industries with business forms. **NOTE:** Apply online. **Special programs:** Internships; Co-ops. **Corporate headquarters location:** Dayton OH. **Other U.S. locations:** Nationwide. **International locations:** Worldwide. **Operations at this facility include:** Manufacturing; Sales; Service. **Listed on:** New York Stock Exchange. **Stock exchange symbol:** REY. **President/CEO/Chairman:** Lloyd G. Waterhouse. **Sales/revenue:** Over $990 million. **Number of employees worldwide:** Over 5,000.

SFA, INC.
2200 Defense Highway, Suite 405, Crofton MD 21114. 301/858-1230. **Fax:** 301/858-1233. **Contact:** Lisa Broome, Human Resources. **E-mail address:** lbroome@sfa.com. **World Wide Web address:** http://www.sfa.com. **Description:** A diversified international supplier of products and services aimed at helping clients capitalize on leading edge systems and technologies. SFA conducts advanced research studies; designs and develops state-of-the-art prototypes; and produces customized hardware and software systems for defense, communications, and other commercial applications. **NOTE:** Fax resume or apply online. **Corporate headquarters location:** This location. **Other area locations:** Virginia Beach VA; Frederick MD; Easton MD. **Subsidiaries include:** SFA DataComm, Incorporated; SFA SACOM. **Listed on:** Privately held. **President/CEO:** Jerry D. Robinson. **Number of employees at this location:** 300.

SI INTERNATIONAL
2099 Gaither Road, 3rd Floor, Rockville MD 20850. 240/778-1200. **Fax:** 240/778-1400. **Contact:** Human Resources. **E-mail address:** jobs@si-intl.com. **World Wide Web address:** http://www.si-intl.com. **Description:** Provides computer systems engineering consulting services and information technology network solutions. The company's primary customer is the federal government. **Positions advertised include:** Application Designer; EPSS Developer; Project Manager; Technical Manager; Material Handler; Requirement Analyst. **Special programs:** Tuition Reimbursement Program. **Corporate headquarters location:** Reston VA. **Other area locations:** Hanover MD. **Other U.S. locations:** Denver CO; Colorado Springs CO; Arlington VA; Bakersville CA. **Listed on:** NASDAQ. **Stock exchange symbol:** SINT. **CEO/Chairman:** Ray J. Oleson.

SABA
300 East Lombard Street, 15th Floor, Baltimore MD 21202. 410/727-5112. **Fax:** 410/837-7903. **Contact:** Human Resources. **World Wide Web address:** http://www.saba.com. **Description:** A leading provider of integrated Human Capital Management (HCM) solutions. **Positions advertised include:** Technical Support Engineer. **Listed on:** NASDAQ. **Stock exchange symbol:** SABA.

SAFENET, INC.
4690 Millenium Drive, Belcamp MD 21017. 410/931-7500. **Fax:** 410/931-7524. **Contact:** Human Resources. **E-mail address:** humanresources@safenet-inc.com. **World Wide Web address:** http://www.safenet-inc.com. **Description:** Develops encryption software to ensure secure transactions. **Positions advertised include:** Software Engineer; Product Line Manager; Contracts Administrator; Corporate Tax Manager; Accountant; Corporate Tax Manager; OEM Sales & Hardware Channel Manager; Sales Director; Account Manager; Marketing Manager; Quality Manager; Configuration Analyst; Purchasing Manager; Trainer; Desktop Support Technologists. **Corporate headquarters location:** This location. **Other U.S. locations:** Los Gatos CA; Danvers MA. **International locations:** The Netherlands; Switzerland. **Listed on:** NASDAQ. **Stock exchange symbol:** SFNT.

STORAGE TECHNOLOGY CORPORATION (STORAGETEK)
6095 Marshalee Lane, Elkridge MD 21075. 410/564-5300. **Fax:** 888/775-2899. **Contact:** Human Resources. stkjobs@storagetek.com. **World Wide Web address:** http://www.stortek.com. **Description:** Manufactures high-performance computer information storage and retrieval systems for mainframe and mid-frame computers and networks. Products include automated cartridge systems, random access subsystems, and fault-tolerant disk arrays. The company also distributes equipment; sells new peripherals, software, and hardware; and offers support services. **Positions advertised include:** Financial Sales Manager; Product Sales Specialist; Sales Executive; Strategic Executive; Systems Engineer. **Special programs:** Internships. **Corporate headquarters location:** Louisville CO. **Other area locations:** Elkridge MD; Hunt Valley MD; Baltimore MD. **Other U.S. locations:** Nationwide. **International locations:** Worldwide. **Listed on:** New York Stock Exchange. **Stock exchange symbol:** STK. **Sales/revenue:** $2.04 billion. **Number of employees worldwide:** Over 7,000.

SYBASE, INC.
6550 Rock Spring Drive, Suite 800, Bethesda MD 20817. 301/896-1800. **Fax:** 301/896-1111. **Contact:** Human Resources. **E-mail address:** mdresumes@sybase.com. **World Wide Web address:** http://www.sybase.com. **Description:** Develops, markets, and supports a full line of relational database management software products and services for integrated, enterprise-wide information management systems. **NOTE:** Resumes should be mailed to Sybase, Incorporated, 5000 Hacienda Drive, Dublin CA 94568 or faxed to 301/896-1774. **Positions advertised include:** Federal Security Specialist; Federal Security Operations Manager; Practice Manager; Consultant; Channel Account Manager; Strategic Account Manager. **Corporate headquarters location:** Dublin CA. **Other U.S. locations:** Nationwide. **International locations:** Worldwide. **Operations at this facility include:** This location is a sales office that also provides education services. **Listed on:** New York Stock Exchange. **Stock exchange symbol:** SY.

SYMANTEC CORPORATION
6750 Alexander Bell Drive, Columbia MD 21046-2166. 410/872-0063. **Contact:** Human Resources. **World Wide Web address:** http://www.symantec.com. **Description:** Provides content and network security software and appliance solutions to individual, corporate, and computer service customers. Founded in 1984. **Positions advertised include:** Agency Account Manager; National Account Manager; Systems Engineer; Sales Manager. **Corporate headquarters:** Cupertino CA. **International locations:** Worldwide. **Listed on:** NASDAQ. **Stock exchange symbol:** SYMC. **CEO/Chairman:** John W. Thompson. **Sales/revenue:** $1,071 million. **Number of employees worldwide:** Over 4,000.

SYSTEMS ALLIANCE, INC.
34 Loveton Circle, Suite 102, Sparks MD 21152. 410/584-0595. **Toll-free phone:** 877/797-2554. **Fax:** 410/584-0594. **Contact:** Human Resources: **E-mail address:** bambrose@systemsalliance.com. **World Wide Web address:** http://www.systemsalliance.com. **Description:** An information technology solutions company. **Positions advertised include:** Business Analyst; Network Administrator; Network/LAN

Administrator; Product Support Technician.

SYTEL, INC.
6430 Rockledge Drive, Suite 400, Bethesda MD 20817. 301/530-1000. **Contact:** Matt Smith, Human Resources. **E-mail address:** resumes@sytel.com. **World Wide Web address:** http://www.sytel.com. **Description:** An information technology consulting firm with specializations in the areas of e-business and network infrastructure support and solutions. **Positions advertised include:** LAN Support Technician; Network Security Analyst; Web Developer. **Special programs:** Educational Assistance Program. **Other U.S. locations:** Herndon VA. **President/CEO:** Jeannette Lee White.

TECTURA CORPORATION
11350 McCormick Road, Suite 801, Hunt Valley MD 21031. 410/229-9898. **Contact:** Human Resources. **World Wide Web address:** http://www.us.tectura.com. **Description:** Tectura provides software, consulting, and IT implementation services to clients in the distribution, manufacturing, healthcare, and service-based industries. **Positions advertised include:** Account Executive; Great Plains Consultant I. **Corporate headquarters location:** Redwood City CA. **Other U.S. locations:** Nationwide. **International locations:** Worldwide.

TRI-COR INDUSTRIES, INC.
4600 Forbes Boulevard, Suite 205, Lanham MD 20706. 301/731-6140. **Fax:** 301/306-6742. **Contact:** Stafford DeWitt, Personnel. **E-mail address:** resumes@tricorind.com. **World Wide Web address:** http://www.tricorind.com. **Description:** Provides contractual computer services to the federal government. Services include networking, software development, operations, and security. Founded in 1983. **Note:** Can download employment applications on website. **Positions advertised include:** Proposal Manager. **Corporate headquarters location:** This location. **Other U.S. locations:** Nationwide. **President/CEO:** Louis Gonzalez. **Sales/revenue:** Over $50 million. **Number of employees nationwide:** Over 350.

VIPS, INC.
One West Pennsylvania Avenue, Suite 700, Baltimore MD 21204. 410/832-8300. **Fax:** 410/832-8315. **Contact:** Human Resources Specialist. **E-mail address:** career@vips.com. **World Wide Web address:** http://www.vips.com. **Description:** Offers computer consulting services and business solutions for the health care industry. **Positions advertised include:** A Web Applications Programmer; Unix System Administrator; Clinical Analyst; System Analyst; Programming Analyst. **Corporate headquarters location:** This location. **Other U.S. locations:** Washington DC; Minneapolis MN; Los Angeles CA. **CEO:** Jenny Morgan.

Massachusetts

ACI WORLDWIDE
492 Old Connecticut Path, Suite 600, Framingham MA 01701. 508/424-5300. **Fax:** 508/424-5305. **Contact:** Human Resources. **World Wide Web address:** http://www.aciworldwide.com. **Description:** Develops networking software. **Positions advertised include:** Senior Technical Writer. **NOTE:** Search and apply for open positions online. **Parent company:** Transaction Systems Architects, Inc.

ASA INTERNATIONAL LTD.
10 Speen Street, Framingham MA 01701. 508/626-2727. **Fax:** 508/626-0645. **Contact:** Human Resources. **World Wide Web address:** http://www.asaint.com. **Description:** Designs, develops, and installs proprietary vertical market software. **Special programs:** Internships. **Corporate headquarters location:** This location. **Other U.S. locations:** Nashua NH; Blue Bell PA. **Subsidiaries include:** RainMaker Software; Khameleon Software; ASA Tire Systems; Verticent.

ABERDEEN GROUP
260 Franklin Street Suite 260, Boston MA 02110. 617/723-7890. **Toll-free phone:** 800/577-7897. **Contact:** Human Resources. **E-mail address:** inquiry@Aberdeen.com. **World Wide Web address:** http://www.aberdeen.com. **Description:** A computer systems, software, and communications consulting and research firm. Aberdeen Group provides strategic management solutions for domestic and international clients. **Positions advertised include:** Sales Account Manager; Product Marketing Manager; Curriculum Director.

ACCENTURE
100 William Street, Wellesley MA 02481. 617/454-4000. **Fax:** 617/454-4001. **Contact:** Human Resources. **World Wide Web address:** http://www.accenture.com. **Description:** A management and technology consulting firm. Accenture offers a wide range of services including business re-engineering, customer service system consulting, data system design and implementation, Internet sales systems research and design, and strategic planning. **Positions advertised include:** Oracle Operations Consultant; PeopleSoft Financials Functional Consultant; SAP Technical Architect; Credit & Collections Solutions Consultant; Service Attendant; Transaction Attorneys; Finance Professional; Executive Assistant; Project Administrator. **Corporate headquarters location:** Chicago IL. **Other area locations:** Boston MA. **Other U.S. locations:** Nationwide. **International locations:** Worldwide. **Listed on:** New York Stock Exchange. **Stock exchange symbol:** ACN.

ADOBE SYSTEMS INCORPORATED
275 Grove Street, Newton MA 02466. 617/219-2000. **Fax:** 617/219-2100. **Contact:** Human Resources. **World Wide Web address:** http://www.adobe.com. **Description:** Develops and supports application development and server software that allow businesses to develop e-commerce systems. **Positions advertised include:** Architect; Computer Scientist; Sr. Product Marketing Manager; Sr. Quality Engineer. **Corporate headquarters location:** San Jose CA.

ADVIZEX TECHNOLOGIES
128 Wheeler Road, Burlington MA 01803. 781/229-2419. **Toll-free phone:** 800/366-6096. **Fax:** 781/229-9991. **Contact:** Human Resources. **E-mail address:** jobs@advizex.com. **World Wide Web address:** http://www.advizex.com. **Description:** Provides open systems technology integration along with other business services including IT planning and developing, and computer reselling. **Positions advertised include:** Oracle Apps Data Base Administrator; Project Manager; Storage Consultant; Oracle Solution Architect; Unix Consultant; Account Executive.

AEGIS ASSOCIATES, INC.
1440 Main Street, Waltham MA 02451. 781/895-5200. **Fax:** 781/895-5100. **Contact:** Marie Stefanik, Human Resources Coordinator. **E-mail address:** hr2@aegis-inc.com. **World Wide Web address:** http://www.aegis-inc.com. **Description:** A computer reseller and network integrator that provides custom computer systems, networks, and related services. This location also hires seasonally. Founded in 1989. **NOTE:** Entry-level positions are offered. **Positions advertised include:** Sr. Security Consultant; Sr. Systems Engineer; Technical Project Manager; Inside sales Representative. **Special programs:** Training. **Office hours:** Monday - Friday, 8:30 a.m. - 5:00 p.m. **Corporate headquarters location:** This location. **Annual sales/revenues:** $5 - $10 million.

AIRVANA, INC.
19 Alpha Road, Chelmsford MA 01824. 866/344-7437. **Fax:** 978/250-3910. **Contact:** Human Resources. **E-mail address:** information@airvananet.com. **World Wide Web address:** http://www.arivananet.com. **Description:** Develops All-IP 3G Radio Access

Network infrastructure equipment for wireless carriers and global infrastructure suppliers such as Nortel Networks and Ericsson. **Positions advertised include:** Business Development; Customer Network Engineer; Director of Marketing Communications; IP Network Security Architect; Principal Release Engineer Principal Software Engineer; Principal Systems Engineer; SQA Manager.

AKAMAI
8 Cambridge Center, Cambridge MA 02142. 617/444-3000. **Toll-free phone:** 877/425-2624. **Fax:** 617/444-3001. **Contact:** Human Resources. **E-mail address:** jobs@akamai.com. **World Wide Web address:** http://www.akamai.com. **Description:** Provides distributed computing solutions and services. The company created the world's largest and most widely used on-demand distributed computing platform, with more than 14,000 servers in 1,100 networks in 65+ countries. Akamai delivers on average 10-20% of daily Web traffic. **Positions advertised include:** Customer Integration Consultant; Sr. Product Manager; Revenue Accountant; Financial Analyst; Application Support Engineer; Software Engineer; Marketing Program Specialist; Server Operations Engineer; Principal Technical Consultant; Network Infrastructure Engineer. **Other U.S. locations:** CA; VA; NY; TX; IL; WA; GA.

ALPHA SOFTWARE CORPORATION
83 Cambridge Street, Suite 3B, Burlington MA 01803. 781/229-4500. **Fax:** 781/272-4876. **Contact:** Human Resources. **E-mail address:** jobs@alphasoftware.com. **World Wide Web address:** http://www.alphasoftware.com. **Description:** Develops and markets business software for IBM personal computers and compatibles. The company distributes its products to Canada and Europe. **Positions advertised include:** Customer Service Representatives.

APOGEE TECHNOLOGY INC.
129 Morgan Drive, Norwood MA 02062. 781/551-9450. **Fax:** 781/440-9528. **Contact:** Human Resources. **World Wide Web address:** http://www.apogeemems.com. **Description:** A silicon based semiconductor manufacturer specializing in audio technology.

APPLIX, INC.
289 Turnpike Road, Westborough MA 01581. 508/870-0300. **Contact:** Human Resources. **E-mail address:** jobs@applix.com. **World Wide Web address:** http://www.applix.com. **Description:** Develops and markets software applications for the UNIX market. **Positions advertised include:** Quality Assurance Engineer; Sr. Application Engineer; Product Manager. **Corporate headquarters location:** This location. **Other U.S. locations:** Warren NJ; Vienna VA. **International locations:** Worldwide. **Listed on:** NASDAQ. **Stock exchange symbol:** APLX.

ARBOR NETWORKS
430 Bedford Street, Suite 160, Lexington MA 02420. 781/684-0900. **Toll-free phone:** 866/212-7267. **Fax:** 781/768-3299. **Contact:** Human Resources. **World Wide Web address:** http://www.arbornetworks.com. **Description:** Develops network integrity systems for enterprises and service providers. **Positions advertised include:** SOC Engineer; Sr. Accountant; Federal Consulting Engineer; Director of Product Marketing. **Corporate headquarters location:** This location. **Other U.S. locations:** Ann Arbor MI.

ARTESYN TECHNOLOGIES
125 Newbury Street, Suite 100, Framingham MA 01701. 508/628-5600. **Fax:** 508/424-2752. **Contact:** Human Resources. **E-mail address:** Jackie.kallman@artsesyn.com. **World Wide Web address:** http://www.artesyn.com. **Description:** Designs, manufactures, and markets advanced power conversion equipment and board-level computing solutions for infrastructure applications in telecommunication and data-communication systems. **Positions advertised include:** SAP Sales & Distribution Lead; Tactical Marketing Engineer. **Other international locations:** Worldwide. **Listed on:** NASDAQ. **Stock exchange symbol:** ATSN.

ASPEN TECHNOLOGY, INC.
10 Canal Park, Cambridge MA 02141-2201. 617/949-1000. **Fax:** 617/949-1030. **Contact:** Human Resources. **E-mail address:** info@aspentech.com. **World Wide Web address:** http://www.aspentech.com. **Description:** Supplies chemical engineering software to the chemicals, petroleum, pharmaceuticals, metals, minerals, food products, consumer products, and utilities industries. **Positions advertised include:** Human Resources Coordinator; Manager Payroll; Marketing Communications Specialist; Sr. Tax Analyst; Accountant; Software Engineer; Development Engineer. **Corporate headquarters location:** This location. **Other U.S. locations:** Nationwide. **International locations:** Worldwide. **Listed on:** NASDAQ. **Stock exchange symbol:** AZPN.

ATEX MEDIA SOLUTIONS
5 Burlington Woods Drive, Suite 100, Burlington MA 01803. 781/685-3240. **Contact:** Human Resources. **World Wide Web address:** http://www.atex.com. **Description:** Designs, develops, and sells computer software products for the newspaper, magazine, and prepress publishing markets worldwide. **Positions advertised include:** Vice President of Customer Support Services. **Other U.S. locations:** Tampa FL. **Operations at this facility include:** Administration; Research and Development; Sales; Service. **Listed on:** Privately held. **Number of employees at this location:** 240. **Number of employees nationwide:** 400.

ATLANTIC DATA SERVICES
One Batterymarch Park, Quincy MA 02169. 617/770-3333. **Contact:** Director of Human Resources. **E-mail address:** joinourteam@adsfs.com. **World Wide Web address:** http://www.atlanticdataservices.com. **Description:** A professional services firm providing computer consulting and project management services to the banking and financial industries. **Positions advertised include:** Project Consultant; Business Development Manager. **Corporate headquarters location:** This location. **Other U.S. locations:** Nationwide. **Listed on:** NASDAQ. **Stock exchange symbol:** ADSC. **Annual sales/revenues:** $21 - $50 million. **Number of employees nationwide:** 200.

AVID TECHNOLOGY, INC.
Avid Technology Park, One Park West, Tewksbury MA 01876. 978/640-6789. **Contact:** Human Resources. **World Wide Web address:** http://www.avid.com. **Description:** A leading provider of digital audio and video tools. Products include digital editing systems and networking and shared storage systems. The company's products are used for various media and entertainment applications. Founded in 1987. **Positions advertised include:** Customer Service & Technical Support Representative; Broadcast Engineer; Post Engineer; Workgroup & Storage Engineer; Finance & Accounting Representative; Human Resources Representative; Information Systems Representative; Manufacturing Representative; Marketing Representative; Product Marketing Representative. **Corporate headquarters location:** This location. **International locations:** Worldwide. **Listed on:** NASDAQ. **Stock exchange symbol:** AVID.

AVOCENT CORPORATION
4 Meeting House Road, Chelmsford MA 01824. 978/244-2000. **Toll-free phone:** 800/264-9443. **Fax:** 978/244-0351. **Contact:** Human Resources. **World Wide Web address:** http://www.avocent.com. **Description:** Develops and markets connectivity solutions for businesses, data centers, service providers, and financial institutions. Avocent Corporation's products include KVM switching, remote access, and video display solutions. **Positions advertised include:** Software Engineer. **NOTE:** Search and apply for positions online. **Corporate headquarters location:** Huntsville AL. **Other U.S. locations:** Sunrise FL; Austin TX; Redmond WA. **International locations:**

Canada; Germany; Hong Kong; Ireland. **Listed on:** NASDAQ. **Stock exchange symbol:** AVCT.

AWARE INC.
40 Middlesex Turnpike, Bedford MA 01730. 781/276-4000. **Fax:** 781/276-4001. **Contact:** Human Resources. **E-mail address:** jobs2006@aware.com. **World Wide Web address:** http://www.aware.com. **Description:** A world leader in the development of xDSL technology for high-speed, broadband modems. Founded in 1986. **Positions advertised include:** Analog IC Design Engineer; Sr. DSP Engineer; Sr. Firmware Engineer. **Other U.S. locations:** Lafayette CA. **Listed on:** NASDAQ. **Stock exchange symbol:** AWRE. **Annual sales/revenues:** $5 - $10 million. **Number of employees at this location:** 80.

AXIS COMPUTER SYSTEMS
293 Boston Post Road West, Marlborough MA 01752-4615. 508/481-9600. **Toll-free phone:** 800/370-2947. **Fax:** 508/481-7234. **Contact:** Human Resources. **E-mail address:** hr@axiscomp.com. **World Wide Web address:** http://www.axiscomp.com. **Description:** Develops software for manufacturing facilities in the metals industry. **Positions advertised include:** Software Developer; Development Manager; Software Quality Assurance Manager; Customer Service Consultant; Product Support Specialist; Sales Professional; Support Specialist.

BMC SOFTWARE
400-2 Totten Pond Road, Waltham MA 02451. 781/891-0000. **Contact:** Human Resources. **World Wide Web address:** http://www.bmc.com. **Description:** Manufactures, sells, and supports software used for MIS and business productivity. The integrated software is written for IBM, IBM compatible VAX/VMS mainframes and RS/6000 workstations, new applications, and network performance management. The company distributes its products across North America, South America, Europe, the Middle East, and the Pacific Rim. **Positions advertised include:** Principal Solution Consultant; solutions Architect; Desktop Support Analyst. **Other U.S. locations:** Nationwide. **International locations:** Worldwide. **Listed on:** New York Stock Exchange. **Stock exchange symbol:** BMC. **Number of employees at this location:** 180.

BITSTREAM, INC.
245 First Street 17th Floor, Cambridge MA 02142. 617/497-6222. **Fax:** 617/868-4732. **Contact:** Human Resources. **E-mail address:** careers@bitstream.com. **World Wide Web address:** http://www.bitstream.com. **Description:** Develops and markets digital font software packages for original equipment manufacturers and end users. Products include fonts used in graphic arts image setters, printers, and screen displays for both personal computer and Macintosh platforms. Founded in 1981. **Positions advertised include:** Applications Specialist; Network Administrator; Product Marketing Manager; Sr. Training Specialist.

BROADVISION
400 Fifth Avenue, Waltham MA 02451. 781/290-0710. **Contact:** Human Resources. **World Wide Web address:** http://www.broadvision.com. **Description:** BroadVision creates communications and marketing applications for business and governmental entities. **Positions advertised include:** Sales Representative. **Special programs:** Internships. **Corporate headquarters location:** Redwood City CA. **Other U.S. locations:** Nationwide. **International locations:** Brazil; Canada; Mexico. **Operations at this facility include:** This location develops document management systems and solutions software. **Listed on:** NASDAQ. **Stock exchange symbol:** BVSN.

BRYLEY SYSTEMS INC.
12 Main Street, Hudson MA 01749. 978/562-6077. **Fax:** 978/562-5680. **Contact:** Human Resources. **E-mail address:** humanresources@bryley.com. **World Wide Web address:** http://www.bryley.com. **Description:** A network systems integrator that provides computer network/telephone solutions to businesses throughout New England. The company provides analysts, consulting, design, and installation services. **Positions advertised include:** Account Executives.

BULL HN INFORMATION SYSTEMS INC.
300 Concord Road, Billerica MA 01821-4199. 978/294-6000. **Fax:** 978/294-6601. **Contact:** Human Resources. **E-mail address:** job.opportunities@bull.com. **World Wide Web address:** http://www.bull.com/us. **Description:** Bull HN Information Systems is a major systems and technologies integrator with a comprehensive range of solutions, services, and support capabilities. Bull's strategy, the Distributed Computing Model, allows users to integrate multivendor systems in a flexible, open environment. **Corporate headquarters location:** This location. **International locations:** Worldwide. **Parent company:** Groupe Bull (France).

BYTEX CORPORATION
495 Commerce Park, 113 Cedar Street, Suite 2, Milford MA 01757. 508/422-9422. **Fax:** 508/422-9410. **Contact:** Personnel. **E-mail address:** personnel@bytex.com. **World Wide Web address:** http://www.bytex.com. **Description:** A data communications and internetworking company providing manufacturing, sales, and service of an intelligent switching hub used in both local and wide area computer networks. **Other U.S. locations:** Columbia MD; Minnetonka MI. **Operations at this facility include:** Engineering and Design; Manufacturing; Marketing; Service. **Number of employees at this location:** 200.

CGI-AMS
600 Federal Street, Andover MA 01810. 978/946-3000. **Fax:** 978/686-0130. **Contact:** Human Resources. **World Wide Web address:** http://www.cgi.ca. **Description:** Provides systems integration, outsourcing, consulting, and business solutions to the financial, telecommunications, manufacturing, government, health care, and utilities industries. **Positions advertised include:** Project Manager. **Other area locations:** Boston MA; Canton MA. **Other U.S. locations:** Nationwide. **International locations:** Worldwide. **Listed on:** New York Stock Exchange. **Stock exchange symbol:** GIB.

CMGI
1100 Winter Street, Suite 4600, Waltham MA 02451. 781/663-5001. **Contact:** Human Resources. **World Wide Web address:** http://www.cmgi.com. **Description:** Develops and integrates a variety of advanced Internet and database management technologies. **Corporate headquarters location:** This location. **Other area locations:** Wilmington MA. **International locations:** Worldwide. **Subsidiaries Include:** ModusLink; SalesLink. **Listed on:** NASDAQ. **Stock exchange symbol:** CMGI.

CSC CONSULTING & SYSTEMS
275 Second Avenue, Waltham MA 02451. 781/890-7446. **Fax:** 781/890-1208. **Contact:** Human Resources. **World Wide Web address:** http://www.csc.com. **Description:** A consulting firm specializing in systems integration, systems design, and applications development for the commercial and private sectors. Founded in 1959. **Positions advertised include:** Application Architect; Business Analyst; Project Leader; Project Manager; Accounting Specialist; Data Architect; System Administrator; Programmer Analyst. **Corporate headquarters location:** El Segundo CA. **Other U.S. locations:** Nationwide. **Parent company:** Computer Sciences Corporation. **Listed on:** New York Stock Exchange. **Stock exchange symbol:** CSC. **Number of employees at this location:** 300. **Number of employees worldwide:** 44,000.

CSPI
43 Manning Road, Billerica MA 01821. 978/663-7598. **Toll-free phone:** 800/325-3110. **Fax:** 978/663-0150.

Contact: Human Resources Director. **E-mail address:** hr@cspi.com. **World Wide Web address:** http://www.cspi.com. **Description:** CSPI designs, manufactures, and markets digital signal processing, high-performance, multiprocessing systems for real-time applications. These low-power, special purpose computers enhance a system's ability to perform high-speed arithmetic and are primarily used for defense, medical, industrial, and real-time applications. **Special programs:** Co-ops. **Corporate headquarters location:** This location. **Other U.S. locations:** CA; FL; MD; VA. **Subsidiaries include:** MODCOMP, Inc. sells real-time process control systems and legacy solutions; Scanalytics, Inc. is focused on hardware and software products for scientific imaging. **Listed on:** NASDAQ. **Stock exchange symbol:** CSPI. **Number of employees at this location:** 60. **Number of employees nationwide:** 150.

CADENCE DESIGN SYSTEMS, INC.
270 Billerica Road, Chelmsford MA 01824. 978/667-8811. **Fax:** 978/262-6777. **Contact:** Human Resources. **World Wide Web address:** http://www.cadence.com. **Description:** Develops automation software for wireless computers and telecommunication devices. **Positions advertised include:** Sales Rep; Sales Technical Leader. **Corporate headquarters location:** San Jose CA. **Other U.S. locations:** Nationwide. **International locations:** Worldwide. **Listed on:** New York Stock Exchange. **Stock exchange symbol:** CDN.

CAMBEX CORPORATION
115 Flanders Road, Westborough MA 01581. 508/983-1200. **Toll-free phone:** 800/325-5565. **Fax:** 508/983-0255. **Contact:** Human Resources. **World Wide Web address:** http://www.cambex.com. **Description:** Cambex Corporation develops, manufactures, and markets a variety of direct access storage products that improve the performance of large- and mid-size IBM computers. These products include central and expanded memory, controller cache memory, disk array systems, disk and tape subsystems, and related software products. **Positions advertised include:** Sales Executive; Sales Development Representative. **Corporate headquarters location:** This location. **Other U.S. locations:** Scottsdale AZ; Thousand Oaks CA; Walnut Creek CA; Westport CT; Clearwater FL; Roswell GA; Schaumburg IL; Troy MI; Chesterfield MO; Charlotte NC; Clark NJ; Cincinnati OH; Blue Bell PA; Dallas TX; Reston VA. **Operations at this facility include:** Administration; Manufacturing; Research and Development; Sales; Service.

CAMBRIDGE TECHNOLOGY PARTNERS
8 Cambridge Center, Cambridge MA 02142. 617/613-2000. **Contact:** Human Resources. **World Wide Web address:** http://www.ctp.com. **Description:** Provides information technology consulting and software development services to organizations with large-scale information processing and distribution needs that are utilizing or migrating to open systems computing environments. **Positions advertised include:** Technical Account Manager. **Other U.S. locations:** Nationwide. **International locations:** Worldwide. **Parent company:** Novell, Inc.

CANTATA TECHNOLOGY, INC.
410 First Avenue, Needham MA 02494. 781/449-4100. **Fax:** 781/433-9009. **Contact:** Human Resources. **E-mail address:** hr@brooktout.com. **World Wide Web address:** http://www.brooktrout.com. **Description:** Designs, manufactures, and markets software, hardware, and systems solutions for electronic messaging applications in telecommunications and networking environments worldwide. These products help integrate voice, fax, and data communications across networks. **Positions advertised include:** Principal Software Engineer; Firmware Engineer; Sr. Oracle Developer; Technical Support Engineer. **Corporate headquarters location:** This location. **Other U.S. locations:** NH; CA; NC; GA; IL. **International locations:** Worldwide. **Listed on:** NASDAQ. **Stock exchange symbol:** BRKT. **Number of employees worldwide:** 357.

CHANNEL 1 INTERNET
P.O. Box 338, Cambridge MA 02238. 617/864-0100. **Fax:** 617/354-3100. **Physical address:** 14 Arrow Street, Cambridge MA 02138. **Contact:** Human Resources. **World Wide Web address:** http://www.channel1.com. **Description:** Designs Websites and virtual stores.

COGNEX CORPORATION
One Vision Drive, Department W3, Natick MA 01760-2059. 508/650-3000. **Fax:** 508/650-3340. **Recorded jobline:** 508/650-3232. **Contact:** Human Resources. **E-mail address:** human.resources@cognex.com. **World Wide Web address:** http://www.cognex.com. **Description:** Designs, develops, manufactures, and markets machine vision systems used to automate a wide range of manufacturing processes. Cognex machine vision systems are used in the electronics, semiconductor, pharmaceutical, health care, aerospace, automotive, packaging, and graphic arts industries to gauge, guide, inspect, and identify products in manufacturing operations. Founded in 1981. **NOTE:** Entry-level positions and part-time jobs are offered. **Company slogan:** To preserve and enhance vision. **Positions advertised include:** PeopleSoft Administrator; HR Generalist; Text Engineer; Manufacturing Engineer; Sr. Revenue Analyst; Principal Programmer/Analyst; Engineering Change Control Specialist. **Special programs:** Internships; Training; Co-ops; Summer Jobs. **Office hours:** Monday - Friday, 8:00 a.m. - 5:00 p.m. **Corporate headquarters location:** This location. **Other U.S. locations:** Alameda CA; Mountain View CA; Naperville IL; Novi MI; Portland OR; Wayne PA; Austin TX; West Allis WI. **International locations:** Worldwide. **Listed on:** NASDAQ. **Stock exchange symbol:** CGNX. **President/CEO:** Dr. Robert Shillman. **Number of employees at this location:** 300. **Number of employees nationwide:** 450. **Number of employees worldwide:** 600.

COGNOS CORPORATION
15 Wayside Road, Burlington MA 01803. 781/229-6600. **Toll-free phone:** 800/426-4667. **Fax:** 781/229-9844. **Contact:** Human Resources. **World Wide Web address:** http://www.cognos.com. **Description:** Develops a line of business management software. **Positions advertised include:** Account Executive; Database Marketing Manager; Engagement Manager; Sr. Manager, Marketing Programs; Consulting Resource Coordinator; Sr. Financial Analyst. **Corporate headquarters location:** This location. **Other U.S. locations:** Nationwide. **International locations:** Worldwide. **Listed on:** NASDAQ. **Stock exchange symbol:** COGN.

COMPUREX SYSTEMS
35 Eastman Street, South Easton MA 02375-1279. 508/230-3700. **Toll-free phone:** 800/426-5499. **Fax:** 508/238-8250. **Contact:** Human Resources. **World Wide Web address:** http://www.compurex.com. **Description:** Provides IT solutions for small to mid-size businesses. **Positions advertised include:** Cisco Sales Rep.

COMPUTER ASSOCIATES INTERNATIONAL, INC.
100 Staples Drive, Framingham MA 01702. 508/628-8000. **Contact:** Human Resources. **World Wide Web address:** http://www.cai.com. **Description:** Computer Associates International, Inc. is one of the world's leading developers of client/server and distributed computing software. The company develops, markets, and supports enterprise management, database and applications development, business applications, and consumer software products for a broad range of mainframe, midrange, and desktop computers. The company serves major business, government, research, and educational organizations. **Positions advertised include:** Communications Specialist; Director, Product Management; Principal Software Engineer; Product Manager; Sr. Consultant; Quality Assurance Engineer. **Corporate headquarters location:** Islandia NY. **Other U.S. locations:** Nationwide. **International**

locations: Worldwide. **Operations at this facility include:** This location develops software. **Listed on:** New York Stock Exchange. **Stock exchange symbol:** CA.

COMPUTER CORPORATION OF AMERICA, INC.
500 Old Connecticut Path, Framingham MA 01701. 508/270-6666. **Fax:** 508/270-6688. **Contact:** Human Resources. **World Wide Web address:** http://www.cca-int.com. **Description:** Develops high-speed database software. **Corporate headquarters location:** This location. **International locations:** Canada; England.

THE COMPUTER MERCHANT, LTD.
95 Longwater Circle, Norwell MA 02061. 781/878-1070. **Toll-free phone:** 800/617-6172. **Fax:** 781/878-4712. **Contact:** Human Resources. **World Wide Web address:** http://www.tcml.com. **Description:** Provides IT staffing and software consulting services. **NOTE:** Part-time jobs are offered. **Positions advertised include:** Tester; Engineer; Project Manager; Business Analyst; Programmer; Database Administrator; Network Service Support Technician. **Special programs:** Internships; Summer Jobs. **Listed on:** Privately held. **CEO:** John Danieli. **Information Systems Manager:** Donna Cash. **Annual sales/revenues:** More than $100 million. **Number of employees at this location:** 80.

CONTINENTAL RESOURCES, INC.
175 Middlesex Turnpike, P.O. Box 9137, Bedford MA 01730-9137. 781/275-0850. **Toll-free phone:** 800/937-4688. **Fax:** 781/533-0212. **Contact:** Human Resources. **World Wide Web address:** http://www.conres.com. **Description:** Configures, integrates, sells, services, and supports computer systems and electronic test equipment. **NOTE:** Entry-level positions are offered. **Special programs:** Internships. **Corporate headquarters location:** This location. **Other U.S. locations:** Milpitas CA; Torrance CA; Orlando FL; Wood Dale IL; Silver Spring MD; Mount Laurel NJ; Somerset NJ; New York NY. **Subsidiaries include:** Wall Industries manufactures AC/DC power sources and DC/DC converters; Continental Leasing is a lease financing company. **Operations at this facility include:** Administration; Manufacturing; Sales; Service. **Annual sales/revenues:** More than $100 million. **Number of employees at this location:** 120. **Number of employees nationwide:** 275.

D&B SALES AND MARKETING SOLUTIONS
460 Totten Pond Road, 7th Floor, Waltham MA 02451. 781/672-9200. **Toll-free phone:** 800/590-0085. **Fax:** 781/672-9290. **Contact:** Personnel. **World Wide Web address:** http://www.b2bsalesandmarketing.com. **Description:** Develops desktop marketing software that allows companies to computerize their marketing efforts. Products include MarketPlace, which gives the user desktop access to the Dun & Bradstreet marketing database.

DATA DIRECT, INC.
27 Charles Street, Needham Heights MA 02494. 781/444-9290. **Contact:** Human Resources. **Description:** Distributes products and services for the software manufacturing industry including software duplication systems, data recording media, and CD-ROMs. The company offers data recording products from suppliers including 3M, Maxell, and Sony.

DATA SET CABLE COMPANY
ADD-ON DATA
323 Andover Street, Wilmington MA 01887. 978/988-1900. **Contact:** Human Resources. **Description:** Data Set Cable Company manufactures custom computer cable assemblies. Add-On Data (also at this location) resells computers.

DATA TRANSLATION
100 Locke Drive, Marlborough MA 01752-1192. 508/481-3700. **Contact:** Human Resources. **E-mail address:** hresources@datx.com. **World Wide Web address:** http://www.datatranslation.com. **Description:** Designs, develops, and manufactures high-performance digital media, data acquisition, and imaging products. The company's principal products are digital signal processing boards and software, which use personal computers to receive analog signals, convert them to digital form, and process the digital data. One product, Media 100, enables video producers to produce broadcast quality videos on a Macintosh computer. **Positions advertised include:** Inside Sales Rep. **Corporate headquarters location:** This location. **Subsidiaries include:** Data Translation, GmbH (Germany); Data Translation Ltd. (England). **Listed on:** NASDAQ. **Stock exchange symbol:** DATX.

DATACUBE, INC.
300 Rosewood Drive, Danvers MA 01923. 978/777-4200. **Fax:** 978/777-3117. **Contact:** Human Resources. **World Wide Web address:** http://www.datacube.com. **Description:** A manufacturer of board- and system-level hardware for image processing. **NOTE:** Entry-level positions are offered. **Corporate headquarters location:** This location. **Listed on:** Privately held. **Annual sales/revenues:** $11 - $20 million. **Number of employees at this location:** 140.

DATAWATCH CORPORATION
271 Mill Road, Chelmsford MA 01824. 978/441-2200. **Fax:** 978/441-1114. **Contact:** Human Resources. **World Wide Web address:** http://www.datawatch.com. **Description:** Designs, manufactures, markets, and supports personal computer software including Monarch, which provides data access, translation, and reporting capability to users of network PCs, and VIREX, which detects, repairs, and monitors virus infections for Macintosh computers. **Positions advertised include:** Sales Executive; Business Process Technical Consultant; Public Relations Manager. **Subsidiaries include:** Datawatch Europe Ltd. (England); Datawatch GmbH (Germany); Datawatch International Ltd. (England); Datawatch Pty Ltd. (Australia); Datawatch Sarl (France). **Listed on:** NASDAQ. **Stock exchange symbol:** DWCH.

DELPHI FORUMS INC.
25 Porter Road, Littleton MA 01460. 978/698-6599. **Fax:** 978/698-6515. **Contact:** Human Resources. **E-mail address:** jobs@delphi.com. **World Wide Web address:** http://www.delphiforums.com. **Description:** Manages a Website that hosts online forums and supports thousands of special interest communities including free do-it-yourself message boards, chat rooms, and personal home pages. Delphi Forums has more than 2 million registered users of approximately 80,000 forums. **Corporate headquarters location:** This location. **Parent company:** Prospero Technologies.

DIGI INTERNATIONAL
411 Waverley Oaks Road, Suite 304, Waltham MA 02452. 781/647-1234. **Toll-free phone:** 800/243-2333. **Fax:** 781/893-1338. **Contact:** Human Resources. **World Wide Web address:** http://www.digi.com. **Description:** Develops and markets hardware and software that allows copiers, fax machines, printers, and scanners to communicate over internal and external networks. **Positions advertised include:** Applications Support Engineer. **Corporate headquarters location:** Minnetonka MN. **Listed on:** NASDAQ. **Stock exchange symbol:** DGII.

EAD SYSTEMS CORPORATION
300 Congress Street #304, Quincy MA 02169. 617/328-5258. **Fax:** 617/328-4941. **Contact:** Human Resources. **World Wide Web address:** http://www.ead.com. **Description:** Provides product and customer support outsourcing services for the technology industry. **Other U.S. locations:** Fremont CA.

EMC CORPORATION
176 South Street, P.O. Box 9103, Hopkinton MA 01748-9103. 508/435-1000. **Fax:** 508/435-8884. **Contact:** Human Resources. **E-mail address:** resumes@emc.com. **World Wide Web address:**

http://www.emc.com. **Description:** EMC designs, manufactures, markets, and supports high-performance data storage products. The company also provides related services for selected mainframe and mid-range computer systems primarily manufactured by IBM and Unisys. **Positions advertised include:** District Administration; Functional Program Manager; Software Release Administrator; Speechwriter; PR Specialist; Corporate Systems Engineer; Lead Corporation Systems Engineer; Product Manager; Controller; Financial Analyst; Cost Accounting Supervisor; Global Solutions; Mechanical Engineer; Materials Quality Engineer; HR Operation Manager; IT Program Research; Paralegal. **Corporate headquarters location:** This location. **Listed on:** New York Stock Exchange. **Stock exchange symbol:** EMC. **Annual sales/revenues:** More than $100 million. **Number of employees at this location:** 1,500.

EASTMAN KODAK COMPANY
900 Chelmsford Street, Lowell MA 01851. 978/323-7600. **Contact:** Human Resources. **World Wide Web address:** http://www.kodak.com. **Description:** Develops color management software. **Subsidiaries include:** Eastman Software (Billerica MA).

ELCOM INTERNATIONAL INC.
10 Oceana Way, Norwood MA 02062. 781/440-3333. **Contact:** Human Resources. **E-mail address:** hr@elcon.com. **World Wide Web address:** http://www.elcom.com. **Description:** Elcom International Inc. produces products for the electronic commerce software market. The company's software is designed to support the sales of computer products, as well as aid companies in the production of electronic catalogs and ordering systems. **Corporate headquarters location:** This location. **Other U.S. locations:** San Diego CA; Washington DC; Tampa FL; Chicago IL; New York NY. **International locations:** Brazil; England; India; South Africa. **Operations at this facility include:** This location resells computers.

ENDECA
55 Cambridge Parkway, Cambridge MA 02142. 617/577-7999. **Fax:** 617/577-7766. **Contact:** Human Resources. **World Wide Web address:** http://www.endeca.com. **Description:** Endeca offers a variety of search, navigation, and analysis solutions. Founded in 1999. **Positions advertised include:** Sr. Systems Engineer; Sales Engineer; Project Manager; Product Manager; Sr. Account Development Rep; Principal Software Engineer; Business Operations Analyst; Corporate Counsel; Technical Support Engineer.

EPSILON
601 Edgewater Drive, Wakefield MA 01880. 781/685-6000. **Fax:** 781/685-0830. **Contact:** Human Resources. **E-mail address:** jobs@epsilon.com. **World Wide Web address:** http://www.epsilon.com. **Description:** Designs, implements, and supports database marketing programs in a variety of industries including financial services, retail, health care, technology, telecommunications, and nonprofit. Founded in 1970. **NOTE:** Entry-level positions and second and third shifts are offered. **Special programs:** Internships; Summer Jobs. **Office hours:** Monday - Friday, 8:30 a.m. - 5:30 p.m. **Corporate headquarters location:** This location. **Other U.S. locations:** Earth City MO; Irving TX; Arlington VA. **Operations at this facility include:** Administration; Divisional Headquarters; Research and Development; Sales; Service. **Parent company:** Alliance Data.

GCC PRINTERS, INC.
209 Burlington Road, Bedford MA 01730. 781/275-5800. **Contact:** Human Resources. **E-mail address:** jobs@gccprinters.com. **World Wide Web address:** http://www.gcctech.com. **Description:** Manufactures printers for use with personal computers. GCC also does research in the areas of computer graphics, VLSI design, consumer robotics, and digital sound generation. **Positions advertised include:** Direct Sales Representative; Education Account Manager; Administrative Assistant; PCB Repair & Test Technician; Hardware Engineer; Software Engineer; Networking Software Engineer. **Corporate headquarters location:** This location. **Operations at this facility include:** Administration; Manufacturing; Research and Development; Sales; Service. **Number of employees at this location:** 150.

GE HEALTHCARE
116 Huntington Avenue, Boston MA 02116. 617/424-6800. **Fax:** 617/266-5676. **Contact:** Human Resources. **World Wide Web address:** http://www.idx.com. **Description:** Develops medical software for hospitals. IDX Systems Corporation provides health care information to physician groups and academic medical centers across the country. **Corporate headquarters location:** Barrington IL. **Other U.S. locations:** Burlington VT; Seattle WA.

GALAXY INTERNET SERVICES
188 Needham Street, Suite 110R, Newton MA 02164. 617/558-0909. **Contact:** Human Resources. **World Wide Web address:** http://www.gis.net. **Description:** Offers services including Web page design, technical support, and business connectivity. **Positions advertised include:** Customer Care Assisant.

GE FANUC AUTOMATION
325 Foxboro Boulevard, Foxboro MA 02035. 508/698-3322. **Contact:** Human Resources. **World Wide Web address:** http://www.gefanucautomation.com. **Description:** Develops industrial automation solutions software. **Positions advertised include:** Software Developer; Sustaining Software Developer; Tier 3 Support Engineer.

GLOBALWARE SOLUTIONS
200 Ward Hill Avenue, Haverhill MA 01835. 978/469-7500. **Fax:** 978/521-7229. **Contact:** Personnel. **E-mail address:** hr@gwsmail.com. **World Wide Web address:** http://www.globalwaresolutions.com. **Description:** Provider of supply-chain management, fulfillment, e-commerce, and reverse logistics services. for hardware and software OEMs as well as the EMS, broadband, medical devices and retail industries. **Positions advertised include:** Marketing Manager.

HARTE-HANKS DATA TECHNOLOGIES
25 Linnell Circle, Billerica MA 01821. 978/436-8981. **Fax:** 978/663-3576. **Contact:** David Lobley, Human Resources Representative. **World Wide Web address:** http://www.harte-hanks.com. **Description:** A leading provider of database marketing services and software for database marketing uses. Harte-Hanks Data Technologies supports corporations in banking, insurance, retail, and technology. Founded in 1968. **Company slogan:** Directly ahead. **Positions advertised include:** Account Executive; Customer Support Engineer; Director, Lists and Data; Software Engineer; Technical Architect; Sales Engineer; Principal Analyst; VP, Database Marketing. **Special programs:** Internships; Training. **Corporate headquarters location:** San Antonio TX. **Other U.S. locations:** Nationwide. **International locations:** Asia; Australia; Canada; South America; United Kingdom. **Parent company:** Harte-Hanks Communications. **Listed on:** New York Stock Exchange. **Stock exchange symbol:** HHS. **Annual sales/revenues:** More than $100 million. **Number of employees at this location:** 550. **Number of employees nationwide:** 6,000. **Number of employees worldwide:** 7,000.

HEWLETT PACKARD
200 Forest Street, Marlborough MA 01752. 978/493-5111. **Contact:** Human Resources. **World Wide Web address:** http://www.hp.com. **Description:** Designs, manufactures, sells, and services computers and associated peripheral equipment, and related software and supplies. Applications and programs include scientific research, computation, communications, education, data analysis, industrial control, time sharing, commercial data processing, graphic arts, word processing, health care, instrumentation, engineering, and simulation. **Positions advertised include:** Sales

Representative; Direct Deployment Specialist; Pre Sales Consultant; Director Client Manager; Lead Solutions Architect; Inbound Operation Manager; Web Manager; End User Sales Representative; Director Client Manager; Business Systems Analyst; Information Technology Technical Lead; Logistics Individual Contributor; Market Researcher; HP Services Tax Manager. **Corporate headquarters location:** Palo Alto CA. **Other U.S. locations:** Nationwide.

HITACHI COMPUTER PRODUCTS
1601 Trapelo Road, 3rd Floor, Waltham MA 02451. 781/890-0444. **Toll-free phone:** 800/745-4056. **Fax:** 781/890-4998. **Contact:** Human Resources. **E-mail address:** cssc@hitachisoftware.com. **World Wide Web address:** http://www.hi.com. **Description:** Develops electronic commerce software. **International locations:** England; Japan.

IBM INFORMATION INTEGRATION SOLUTIONS
50 Washington Street, Westborough MA 01581. 508/366-3888. **Fax:** 508/389-3669. **Contact:** Human Resources Manager. **World Wide Web address:** http://www.ibm.ascential.com. **Description:** Manufactures a wide range of software products including database systems and warehouse development tools. Ascential serves government and business customers in the manufacturing, health care, telecommunications, aerospace, defense, financial services, and utilities industries. **Positions advertised include:** Solutions Architect; SQA Engineer; Software Engineering Web Services; Software Engineer; Tax Analyst; Manager of Marketing Communication & Services; Account Development Representative; Help Desk Analyst; Account Executive; District Sales Manager. **Other U.S. locations:** CA; CO; GA; IL; NC; NJ; TX; WA. **International locations:** Australia; Brazil; Canada; France; Germany; Hong Kong; Japan; South Africa; United Kingdom. **Parent company:** IBM.

ITG INC.
44 Farnsworth Street, 9th Floor, Boston MA 02210. 617/728-2800. **Toll-free phone:** 800/983-4484. **Contact:** Human Resources. **E-mail address:** itg_hr@itginc.com. **World Wide Web address:** http://www.itginc.com. **Description:** Provides automated securities trade execution and analysis services to institutional equity investors. ITG's main service technologies are POSIT, ITG Algorithms, and Transaction Cost Analysis (TCS). **Corporate headquarters location:** New York NY. **Other U.S. locations:** Los Angeles CA. **International locations:** London, England. **Parent company:** Investment Technology Group. **Listed on:** New York Stock Exchange. **Stock exchange symbol:** ITG.

INTEGRATED IT SOLUTIONS
290 Vanderbilt Avenue, Norwood MA 02494. 781/453-5100. **Fax:** 781/453-5110. **Contact:** Human Resources. **E-mail address:** jobs@integratedit.com. **World Wide Web address:** http://www.integratedit.com. **Description:** A full-service consulting firm. Integrated IT Solutions offers information and consultation on system choice, network configurations, the Internet, and e-business solutions. **Positions advertised include:** Sales Engineer; Field Service Engineer; Account Executive. **Corporate headquarters location:** This location.

INTEL NETWORK SYSTEMS
75 Reed Road, Hudson MA 01749. 978/553-4000. **Contact:** Human Resources. **World Wide Web address:** http://www.intel.com. **Description:** Produces a line of direct-dial products and remote access servers. **NOTE:** Apply online. **Positions advertised include:** Engineering Group Leader; Manufacturing Rotation Engineer; Manufacturing Excellence Engineer; Windows/UNIX Systems Administrator; Software Engineer. **Other area locations:** Boston MA; Framingham MA; Lowell MA; Shrewsbury MA; Waltham MA; Springfield MA. **Other U.S. location:** Nationwide. **International locations:** Worldwide.

JUNIPER NETWORKS, INC.
10 Technology Park Drive, Westford MA 01886-3146. 978/589-5800. **Fax:** 978/589-0800. **Contact:** Human Resources. **World Wide Web address:** http://www.juniper.net. **Description:** Builds IP platforms that enable service providers, enterprises, governments and research and education institutions communications over a single IP network. **Positions advertised include:** Sr. Collection Analyst; Sr. Premier Engineer; Multicast-Development Engineer; Staff Engineer. **Corporate headquarters location:** Sunnyvale CA. **Listed on:** NASDAQ. **Stock exchange symbol:** JNPR.

KEANE, INC.
100 City Square, Boston MA 02129. 617/241-9200. **Contact:** Human Resources. **World Wide Web address:** http://www.keane.com. **Description:** Develops application and business process services, including application development and integration services, architectural services, application outsourcing, program management, and testing, as well as business process improvement and business process outsourcing. Founded in 1965. **Positions advertised include:** Web Developer; Web Applications Developer; Technical Recruiter; Project Manager; Proposal Writer; Technical Support Manager; Business Analyst; Client Server Developer; Recruiting Associate; Quality Assurance Analyst; Business Analyst. **Corporate headquarters location:** This location. **Other U.S. locations:** Nationwide. **Listed on:** American Stock Exchange. **Stock exchange symbol:** KEA. **Number of employees at this location:** 100.

KEMA
67 South Bedford Street, Suite 201, Burlington MA 01803-5177. 781/273-5700. **Fax:** 781/229-4867. **Contact:** Human Resources Department. **E-mail address:** recruitus@kema.com. **World Wide Web address:** http://www.kema.com. **Description:** Develops software products for utilities and energy companies. **Positions advertised include:** Director of Corporate Marketing.

KRONOS INC.
297 Billerica Road, Chelmsford MA 01824. 978/250-9800. **Fax:** 978/367-5900. **Contact:** Human Resources. **World Wide Web address:** http://www.kronos.com. **Description:** Designs, develops, and markets labor management software and computerized systems that measure employee attendance and schedules. Founded in 1977. **Positions advertised include:** Information Systems Manager; Software Quality Assurance Engineer; Software Engineer; Prospect Marketing Representative; Marketing Writer; Solutions Consultant; Financial Analyst; Enterprise Account Manager; Vice President of Marketing; Network Security Officer; Technical Support Engineer; Events Specialist; Software Product Manager. **Special programs:** Internships. **Corporate headquarters location:** This location. **Other U.S. locations:** Nationwide. **International locations:** Worldwide. **Operations at this facility include:** Administration; Research and Development; Sales; Service. **Listed on:** NASDAQ. **Stock exchange symbol:** KRON. **Annual sales/revenues:** More than $100 million. **Number of employees at this location:** 900.

KUBOTEK USA
100 Locke Drive, Marlborough MA 01752. 508/229-2020. **Fax:** 508/229-2121. **Contact:** Human Resources. **World Wide Web address:** http://www.kubotekusa.com. **Description:** A developer of 3-D mechanical design software for CAD systems. **Corporate headquarters location:** This location.

L-3 COMMUNICATIONS TITAN CORPORATION
300 Concord Road, 4th Floor, Billerica MA 01821. 978/663-6600. **Contact:** Human Resources. **World Wide Web address:** http://www.titan.com. **Description:**

Provides information and communications products, solutions, and services for national security, serving the Department of Defense, intelligence agencies, and other government customers.

LANGUAGE ENGINEERING CORPORATION
215 Washington Street, Belmont MA 02478. 781/489-4000. **Fax:** 617/489-3850. **Contact:** Human Resources. **E-mail address:** info@hq.lec.com. **World Wide Web address:** http://www.lec.com. **Description:** Develops translation software and services.

LIANT SOFTWARE CORPORATION
354 Waverly Street, Framingham MA 01702. 508/626-0006. **Fax:** 508/626-2221. **Contact:** Human Resources. **World Wide Web address:** http://www.liant.com. **Description:** A developer of network-based programming and software development tools that enhance client/server systems and architectures. **Corporate headquarters location:** This location. **Other U.S. locations:** Austin TX. **International locations:** London, England. **Listed on:** Privately held. **Number of employees worldwide:** 60.

LOGICA NORTH AMERICA, INC.
32 Hartwell Avenue, Lexington MA 02421. 617/476-8000. **Fax:** 617/476-8010. **Contact:** Andrea Merurio, Human Resources. **World Wide Web address:** http://www.logicacmg.com. **Description:** Provides business consultancy, IT and value-added business process outsourcing, systems integration, and telecom products and solutions. **Other U.S. locations:** New York NY; Southfield MI; Plano TX; Houston TX; Kirkland WA; Atlanta GA; Glen Allen VA. **International locations:** Worldwide.

LOTUS DEVELOPMENT CORPORATION
55 Cambridge Parkway, Cambridge MA 02142. 617/577-8500. **Toll-free phone:** 800/796-9876. **Contact:** Personnel. **World Wide Web address:** http://www.lotus.com/jobs. **Description:** Lotus develops, manufactures, and markets applications software and services that meet the evolving technology and business application needs for individuals, work groups, and entire organizations. Products include Lotus Notes, a software application that provides groupware links allowing workers to share information. **Positions advertised include:** Associate Project Manager; Lead Consultant. **NOTE:** Visit: http://www-1.ibm.com/employment/ for current positions. **Corporate headquarters location:** This location. **Parent company:** IBM. **Number of employees nationwide:** 4,400.

LUCENT TECHNOLOGIES INTERNETWORKING SYSTEMS
One Robbins Road, Westford MA 01886. 978/952-1600. **Fax:** 978/392-9682. **Contact:** Human Resources. **World Wide Web address:** http://www.lucent.com. **Description:** Develops, manufactures, markets, and supports a family of high performance, multiservice wide area network (WAN) switches that enable public carrier providers and private network managers to provide cost-effective, high-speed, enhanced data communications services. These products direct and manage data communications across wide area networks that utilize different network architectures and services, and are designed to support, on a single platform, the major high-speed packet data communications services. These services include frame relay, switched multimegabit data service, and asynchronous transfer mode. The company markets its products to public network providers, including interexchange carriers, local exchange carriers, competitive access providers, other public network providers, and private network managers. **NOTE:** Lucent and Alcatel are merging. **Positions advertised include:** Security Consultant; Logistics Strategy Manager; EMEA Regional PEC Leader; CALA Regional PEC Leader. **Corporate headquarters location:** Murray Hill NJ. **Other U.S. locations:** Nationwide. **Listed on:** New York Stock Exchange. **Stock exchange symbol:** LU. **Number of employees at this location:** 650.

LYCOS, INC.
100 5th Avenue, Waltham MA 02451. 781/370-2700. **Fax:** 781/370-3415. **Contact:** Human Resources. **World Wide Web address:** http://www.lycos.com. **Description:** An Internet search engine that finds, indexes, and filters information from the World Wide Web. **Positions advertised include:** Product Manager; Program Manager; Sr. Production Support Analyst; **Corporate headquarters location:** This location. **Other U.S. locations:** New York NY; San Francisco CA. **Listed on:** NASDAQ. **Stock exchange symbol:** LCOS.

MRO SOFTWARE, INC.
100 Crosby Drive, Bedford MA 01730. 781/280-2000. **Fax:** 781/280-0207. **Contact:** Human Resources. **World Wide Web address:** http://www.mro.com. **Description:** Develops, markets, and supports enterprisewide client/server applications software used to assist in maintaining and developing high-value capital assets such as facilities, systems, and production equipment. The company's products enable customers to reduce downtime, control maintenance expenses, cut spare parts inventories, improve purchasing efficiency, shorten product development cycles, and deploy productive assets and personnel more effectively. **Positions advertised include:** Sr. Technical Writer; Tax Manager; PeopleSoft Business Systems Analyst; Marketing Projects Coordinator; Web Marketing Manager; Sr. Software Engineer. **Corporate headquarters location:** This location. **International locations:** Worldwide. **Listed on:** NASDAQ. **Stock exchange symbol:** MROI.

MRV COMMUNICATIONS
295 Foster Street, Littleton MA 01460. 978/952-4700. **Contact:** Human Resources. **E-mail address:** hr@mrv.com. **World Wide Web address:** http://www.mrv.com. **Description:** Designs, manufactures, markets, and supports high-performance data communications network systems. **Positions advertised include:** Inside Sales Rep. **Corporate headquarters location:** Chatsworth CA. **Listed on:** NASDAQ. **Stock exchange symbol:** MRVC.

MATH WORKS
3 Apple Hill Drive, Natick MA 01760. 508/647-7000. **Fax:** 508/647-7001. **Contact:** Human Resources. **World Wide Web address:** http://www.mathworks.com. **Description:** Develops mathematical software packages. **Positions advertised include:** Applications Support Engineer; FPC Manager; MATLAB Software Developer; Software Engineer; Release Engineer; Principal Tools Engineer; Business Systems Administration; Physical Modeling Developer; Communications Quality Engineer; Applications Engineer.

MATHSOFT ENGINEERING & EDUCATION, INC.
101 Main Street, 16th Floor, Cambridge MA 02142. 617/444-8000. **Fax:** 617/444-8001. **Contact:** Human Resources. **E-mail address:** hrjobs@mathsoft.com. **World Wide Web address:** http://www.mathsoft.com. **Description:** A leading developer of mathematical software and electronic books for desktop computers. Products include Mathcad, a live interactive environment for mathematics work in a wide variety of fields including engineering, science, and education. MathSoft also publishes the Mathcad Library of Electronic Books, Maple V symbolic computation software, and other third-party mathematical software. Founded in 1984. **Positions advertised include:** Math CAD Author; Math CAD Reviewer. **Corporate headquarters location:** This location. **International locations:** England; Germany. **Annual sales/revenues:** $11 - $20 million. **Number of employees at this location:** 60. **Number of employees nationwide:** 150.

MCKESSON HEALTH SOLUTIONS
275 Grove Street, Suite 1-110, Newton MA 02466. 17/273-2800. **Contact:** Human Resources. **World Wide Web address:** http://healthsolutions.mckesson.com. **Description:** McKesson Health Solutions offers a

comprehensive suite of medical management products and services to help providers and payers better manage the cost and quality of care. **Positions advertised include:** Sr. Marketing Manager; Sr. Account Manager; AVP Clinical Content; Software Engineer; Product Manager; Sr. Database Architect.

MEDITECH (MEDICAL INFORMATION TECHNOLOGY, INC.)
One MEDITECH Circle, Westwood MA 02090. 781/821-3000. **Fax:** 508/626-0337. **Contact:** Recruiting Specialist. **E-mail address:** jobs@meditech.com. **World Wide Web address:** http://www.meditech.com. **Description:** Develops, sells, installs, and supports computer software designed to help the medical community share critical information. **NOTE:** Entry-level positions are offered. **Positions advertised include:** Client Training Specialist; Programmer; Development Analyst; Programmer Development. **Office hours:** Monday - Friday, 9:00 a.m. - 5:30 p.m. **Corporate headquarters location:** This location. **Other U.S. locations:** Canton MA; Framingham MA; Norwood MA. **Operations at this facility include:** Administration; Research and Development; Sales; Service. **Number of employees nationwide:** 1,900.

MENTOR GRAPHICS
300 Nickerson Road, Suite 200, Marlborough MA 01752. 508/480-0881. **Toll-free phone:** 800/592-2210. **Contact:** Human Resources. **World Wide Web address:** http://www.mentor.com. **Description:** A leader in electronic hardware and software design solutions, providing products, consulting services and support for electronics and semiconductor companies. **Positions advertised include:** Corporate Application Engineer. **Special programs:** Internships. **Other area locations:** Billerica MA; Waltham MA.

MERCURY COMPUTER SYSTEMS, INC.
199 Riverneck Road, Chelmsford MA 01824. 978/967-1401. **Contact:** Human Resources. **World Wide Web address:** http://www.mc.com. **Description:** A leading provider of high-performance, real-time, embedded solutions for diverse applications including medical imaging, defense electronics, and shared storage configurations. **NOTE:** Entry-level positions are offered. **Positions advertised include:** Tax Director; Sr. Software Engineer; Sr. Business Systems Analyst; Staff Systems Engineer; Sr. Product Operations Manager. **Special programs:** Internships; Co-ops; Summer Jobs. **Corporate headquarters location:** This location. **Listed on:** NASDAQ. **Stock exchange symbol:** MRCY. **Annual sales/revenues:** $51 - $100 million. **Number of employees nationwide:** 370.

MERCURY INTERACTIVE CORPORATION
25 Burlington Mall Road, 3rd Floor, Burlington MA 01803. 800/837-8911. **Contact:** Personnel. **World Wide Web address:** http://www.mercuryinteractive.com. **Description:** Mercury Interactive Corporation is a developer of automated software quality (ASQ) tools for enterprise applications testing. The company's products are used to isolate software and system errors prior to application deployment. **Positions advertised include:** Product Marketing Manager; Product Manager; Brand Manager; ITG Applications Engineer; Technical Support Application Engineer; Commercial Counsel; Contract Negotiation; Stock Administrator; Financial Analyst; Treasury Operations Manager; Accountant. **NOTE:** Resumes should be sent to: Human Resources, 1325 Borregas Avenue, Sunnyvale CA 94089. **Corporate headquarters location:** Sunnyvale CA. **Operations at this facility include:** This location is a sales office. **Listed on:** NASDAQ. **Stock exchange symbol:** MERQ. **Annual sales/revenues:** More than $100 million.

META SOFTWARE CORPORATION
125 Cambridge Park Drive, Cambridge MA 02140. 617/576-6920. **Toll-free phone** 800/227-4106. **Fax:** 617/661-2008. **Contact:** Human Resources. **E-mail address:** resumes@metasoft.com. **World Wide Web address:** http://www.metasoftware.com. **Description:** Develops business process re-engineering software and provides consulting services. Founded in 1985. **Positions advertised include:** Senior Consultant; Technical Support Specialist; Programmer/Analyst. **Corporate headquarters location:** This location. **President/CEO:** Robert Seltzer.

METRATECH CORP.
330 Bear Hill Road, Waltham MA 02451. 781/839-8300. **Fax:** 781/839-8301. **Contact:** Human Resources. **E-mail address:** jobs@metratech.com. **World Wide Web address:** http://www.metratech.com. **Description:** Provides a Web Services-based solution for billing, customer self-care, and partner management. Founded in 1998. **Positions advertised include:** Principal Technical Consultant; Technical Support Engineer; Technical Sales Engineer; Senior Accountant/Accounting Supervisor. **Corporate headquarters location:** This location. **Other U.S. locations:** San Francisco.

MICROTIME COMPUTER DISTRIBUTION, INC.
300 Wildwood Avenue, Woburn MA 01801. 781/938-6699. **Contact:** Human Resources. **World Wide Web address:** http://www.microtime.rite2u.com. **Description:** Wholesales and distributes computer peripherals and components to the reseller market. The company also assembles custom-built PCs.

MICROWAY, INC.
Plymouth Industrial Park 12 Richards Road, Plymouth MA 02360. 508/746-7341. **Fax:** 508/746-4678. **Contact:** Human Resources. **E-mail address:** info@microway.com. **World Wide Web address:** http://www.microway.com. **Description:** Designs state-of-the-art, high quality Linux clusters, servers, and RAID storage solutions for universities, life sciences, Fortune 500 companies and research agencies worldwide. **NOTE:** Check http://www.monster.com for latest job postings.

MOLECULAR, INC.
343 Arsenal Street, Watertown MA 02472. 617/218-6500. **Fax:** 617/218.6700. **Contact:** Human Resources. **E-mail address:** careers@molecular.com. **World Wide Web address:** http://www.molecular.com. **Description:** A technology consulting firm that designs and builds Internet-based solutions to help companies increase revenues and decrease operating costs. Founded in 1994. **Positions advertised include:** Managing Director; Information Systems Manager.

NATIONAL DATACOMPUTER, INC.
900 Middlesex Turnpike, Building 5, Billerica MA 01821. 978/663-7677. **Fax:** 978/663-6043. **Contact:** Human Resources. **E-mail address:** tferra@ndcomputer.com. **World Wide Web address:** http://www.ndcomputer.com. **Description:** Designs, manufactures, and markets computerized systems used to automate the collection, processing, and communication of information related to product sales, distribution, and inventory control. The company's products and services include data communication networks, application-specific software, hand-held computers and related peripherals, and associated training and support services. The company's products facilitate rapid and accurate data collection, data processing, and two-way communication of information with a customer's host information system.

NAVISITE, INC.
400 Minuteman Road, Andover MA 01810. 978/682-8300. **Fax:** 978/688-8100. **Contact:** Human Resources. **World Wide Web address:** http://www.navisite.com. **Description:** NaviSite provides IT hosting, outsourcing, and professional services for mid- to large-sized organizations. **Positions advertised include:** Director, Delivery, Outsourcing Services; Director, Professional Services; Director, Technology, Outsourcing Services; Functional Client Manager; PeopleSoft Technical Client Manager; Oracle Project Manager. **Corporate headquarters location:** This location. **Other U.S. locations:** Atlanta GA; Chicago

IL; Houston TX; New York NY; San Jose CA; Syracuse NY; Vienna VA.

NETEZZA CORPORATION
200 Crossing Boulevard, 5th Floor, Framingham MA 01702. 508/665-6800. **Fax:** 508/665-6811. **Contact:** Human Resources. **World Wide Web address:** http://www.netezza.com. **Description:** A provider of enterprise-class data warehouse solutions that integrate database, server, and storage in one appliance. **Positions advertised include:** Software Engineer, Storage Manager; Sr. Software Engineer, Project Leader; Sr. Customer Service Engineer; System Product Manager; Sr. Software Quality Engineer; Channels Manager.

NORTEL NETWORKS
600 Technology Park Drive, Billerica MA 01821. 978/670-8888. **Contact:** Human Resources. **World Wide Web address:** http://www.nortel.com. **Description:** Designs, produces, and supports multimedia access devices for use in building corporate, public and Internet networks. The primary focus of the company's services is the consolidation of voice, fax, video, and data and multimedia traffic into a single network link. **Positions advertised include:** Software Engineer; Technical Support Engineer; Account Manager; Product Line Manager; Solution Architect; Enterprise Supply Planner; Power Design Engineer. **Other U.S. locations:** Nationwide. **International locations:** Worldwide. **Listed on:** New York Stock Exchange. **Stock exchange symbol:** NT.

NUANCE COMMUNICATIONS, INC.
1 Wayside Road, Burlington MA 01803. 781/565-5000. **Fax:** 781/565-5001. **Contact:** Human Resources Department. **E-mail address:** nuance@agents.icims.com. **World Wide Web address:** http://www.nuance.com. **Description:** Provides speech and imaging software. **Positions advertised include:** Sr. Research Engineer; Licensing Attorney; Program Manager; Sr. Payroll Administrator; Compensation Specialist; HRIS Administrator; Public Relations Manager; Tax Accountant; Sr. Account Manager; PDF Product Manager; Marketing Database Administrator. **Corporate headquarters location:** This location. **Listed on:** NASDAQ. **Stock exchange symbol:** NUAN.

ORACLE CORPORATION
10 Van De Graaff Drive, Burlington MA 01803. 781/744-0000. **Contact:** Human Resources. **World Wide Web address:** http://www.oracle.com. **Description:** Designs and manufactures database and information management software for businesses. The company also provides consulting services. **Positions advertised include:** Consulting Project Manager; Contracts Administrator; Product Manager; Telesales Representative; Contracts Manager; Field Support Sales; Applications Developer; Technical Writer; Quality Assurance Engineer; Manager Business Development. **Corporate headquarters location:** Redwood Shores CA. **Other U.S. locations:** Nationwide. **Listed on:** NASDAQ. **Stock exchange symbol:** ORCL.

OVID TECHNOLOGIES
100 River Ridge Drive, Norwood MA 02062. 781/769-2599. **Fax:** 781/769-8763. **Contact:** Amy Narcotta, Human Resources. **E-mail address:** resumes@ovid.com. **World Wide Web address:** http://www.ovid.com. **Description:** Publishes and distributes over 225 authoritative databases. Ovid Technologies also publishes CD-ROMs and develops software systems for data retrieval and full text linking. Founded in 1985. **NOTE:** Entry-level positions are offered. **Positions advertised include:** Database Design Analyst; Database Production Analyst; Royalties Administrator. **Corporate headquarters location:** New York NY. **Other U.S. locations:** New York NY; Salt Lake City UT. **International locations:** Berlin, Germany; Bologna, Italy; Hong Kong; London, England; Paris, France; Sydney, Australia. **Listed on:** Privately held. **Annual sales/revenues:** $51 - $100 million. **Number of employees at this location:** 200. **Number of employees nationwide:** 240.

PARAMETRIC TECHNOLOGY CORPORATION
140 Kendrick Street, Needham MA 02494. 781/370-5000. **Fax:** 781/370-6000. **Contact:** Human Resources. **World Wide Web address:** http://www.ptc.com. **Description:** Designs and develops fully integrated software products for mechanical engineering and automated manufacturing based upon a parametric solids modeling system. **Positions advertised include:** Associate Programmer Analyst; Revenue Accountant; Technical Consultant; Sr. Product Definition Engineer; QA Engineer; Principal Software Engineer; Localization Specialist; Controller. **Corporate headquarters location:** This location. **International locations:** Worldwide. **Listed on:** NASDAQ. **Number of employees at this location:** 500. **Number of employees nationwide:** 1,600.

PASSKEY INTERNATIONAL INC.
180 Old Colony Avenue, Quincy MA 02170. 617/238-8200. **Fax:** 617/328-1212. **Contact:** Human Resources. **E-mail address:** hr@passkey.com. **World Wide Web address:** http://www.passkey.com. **Description:** Provides web-based solutions for processing group hotel reservations. **Positions advertised include:** Direct Marketing Manger; Sr. Product Manager; Oracle Database Administrator; Quality Assurance Engineer. **Corporate headquarters location:** This location.

PEGASYSTEMS INC.
101 Main Street, Cambridge MA 02142-1590. 617/374-9600. **Fax:** 617/374-9620. **Contact:** Personnel. **World Wide Web address:** http://www.pegasystems.com. **Description:** Develops business process software for financial, insurance, healthcare, manufacturing, and government markets. **Positions advertised include:** Product Manager; Software Engineer; System Architect; Engagement Leader. **Listed on:** NASDAQ. **Stock exchange symbol:** PEGA.

PERCUSSION SOFTWARE, INC.
600 Unicorn Park Drive, Woburn MA 01801. 781/438-9900. **Toll-free phone:** 800/283-0800. **Fax:** 781/438-9955. **Contact:** Human Resources. **World Wide Web address:** http://www.percussion.com. **Description:** Develops enterprise content management software. **NOTE:** See website for positions and contact information. **Positions advertised include:** Marketing Communications Manager; Software Engineer; Sr. Technical Writer; Notes/Domino consultant; Sr. Consultant.

PHOENIX TECHNOLOGIES LTD.
320 Norwood Park South, Norwood MA 02062. 781/551-5000. **Fax:** 781/551-5001. **Contact:** Human Resources. **World Wide Web address:** http://www.phoenix.com. **Description:** Designs, develops, and markets systems software and end user software products. The Peripherals Division designs, develops, and supplies printer emulation software, page distribution languages, and controller hardware designs for the printing industry. The PhoenixPage imaging software architecture enables printer manufacturers to offer products that are compatible with the PostScript language, the PCL printer language, and other imaging standards. Phoenix Technologies' PC Division works with leading vendors and standards committees to ensure that Phoenix products enable manufacturers to develop and deploy next-generation PCs quickly and cost effectively. The company's Package Products Division is a single-source publisher of MS-DOS, Windows, and other software packages. **Corporate headquarters location:** Milpitas CA. **Listed on:** NASDAQ. **Stock exchange symbol:** PTEC. **Number of employees at this location:** 330.

PRIMUS MANAGED HOSTING SOLUTIONS
330 Lynnway, Lynn MA 01901. 781/586-6100. **Fax:** 781/593-6858. **Contact:** Human Resources. **World Wide Web address:** http://www.primustel.net. **Description:** Provides Internet access and other online services including dial-up networking, Web design, and

scripting. **Positions advertised include:** Customer Account Manager; Agent Channel Marketing; Help Desk Technician; Inside Accounting Representative; Internal Auditor; Legal Secretary; Manager Training Quality Assistant.

PROGRESS SOFTWARE CORPORATION
14 Oak Park Drive, Bedford MA 01730. 781/280-4000. **Contact:** Human Resources. **World Wide Web address:** http://www.progress.com. **Description:** Manufactures and supplies application development software to business and government customers worldwide. Products include Progress OpenEdge, an integrated environment for developing, deploying, integrating, and managing business applications. **Positions advertised include:** Developmental Editor; Principal Graphic Designer; Product Marketing manager; System Engineer; Web Marketing Specialist. **Listed on:** NASDAQ. **Stock exchange symbol:** PRGS. **Number of employees nationwide:** 630.

RSA SECURITY, INC.
174 Middlesex Turnpike, Bedford MA 01730. 781/515-5000. **Contact:** Human Resources. **World Wide Web address:** http://www.rsasecurity.com. **Description:** Develops and markets software for security applications. **Positions advertised include:** Systems Engineer; Inside Sales Representative; Account Manager; Executive Assistant; Accountant; Business Analyst; Administrative Assistant; Quality Assurance Performance Test Engineer; Product Manager; Financial Analyst; Strategic Web Manager; Programming Analyst. **Corporate headquarters location:** This location. **Listed on:** NASDAQ. **Stock exchange symbol:** RSAS.

RATIONAL IBM SOFTWARE
20 Maguire Road, Lexington MA 02421. 781/676-2400. **Contact:** Human Resources. **World Wide Web address:** http://www.rational.com. **Description:** Rational Software develops, markets, and supports embedded software products for Web and e-commerce applications. The company's products operate on both Windows and UNIX systems. **Positions advertised include:** Unix Administrator; Advisory software Engineer; Build/Test Engineer; Financial Analyst; Software Engineer. **International locations:** Worldwide. **Operations at this facility include:** This location is the North American sales center.

SAP AMERICA, INC.
950 Winter Street, Suite 3800, Waltham MA 02451. 781/672-6500. **Fax:** 781/672-6683. **Contact:** Human Resources. **World Wide Web address:** http://www.sap.com. **Description:** Develops a variety of client/server computer software packages including programs for finance, human resources, and materials management applications. Founded in 1972. **Positions advertised include:** Manager Channel Marketing. **Special programs:** Internships; Summer Jobs. **Corporate headquarters location:** Newtown Square PA. **Other U.S. locations:** Nationwide. **International locations:** Germany. **Parent company:** SAP AG. **Annual sales/revenues:** More than $100 million. **Number of employees at this location:** 200. **Number of employees nationwide:** 3,000. **Number of employees worldwide:** 13,000.

SPSS INC.
One Alewife Center, Cambridge MA 02140. 617/996-5500. **Fax:** 617/996-5601. **Contact:** Human Resources. **World Wide Web address:** http://www.spss.com. **Description:** Develops software that allows businesses to analyze and predict online consumer behavior. **NOTE:** Apply online. **Other U.S. locations:** San Francisco CA; Miami FL; Newton MA; New York NY; Cincinnati OH; Arlington VA.

SSA INFINIUM SOFTWARE
25 Communication Way, P.O. Box 6000, Hyannis MA 02601. 508/778-2000. **Contact:** Human Resources. **World Wide Web address:** http://www.infinium.com. **Description:** Provides enterprise business software for mid-sized and large organizations, primarily in select manufacturing, consumer and services industries. **Other area locations:** Framingham MA. **Listed on:** NASDAQ. **Stock exchange symbol:** SSAG.

SAPIENT CORPORATION
25 First Street, Cambridge MA 02141. 617/621-0200. **Contact:** Director of Hiring. **World Wide Web address:** http://www.sapient.com. **Description:** Provides systems integration, consulting, and software integration services. Founded in 1991. **Positions advertised include:** IT Associate; Office Services Associate; Sr. Technology Associate; Technology Manager. **Corporate headquarters location:** This location. **Other U.S. locations:** Los Angeles CA; San Francisco CA; Denver CO; Washington DC; Atlanta GA; Chicago IL; Portland ME; Minneapolis MN; Jersey City NJ; Austin TX; Dallas TX. **International locations:** Australia; England; Germany; India; Italy; Japan. **Listed on:** NASDAQ. **Stock exchange symbol:** SAPE. **Annual sales/revenues:** More than $100 million.

SEAPORT GRAPHICS
12 Channel Street, Suite 802, Boston MA 02210. 617/330-1200. **Contact:** Human Resources. **E-mail address:** employment@seaportgraphics.com. **World Wide Web address:** http://www.seaportgraphics.com. **Description:** Manufactures presentation graphics software and workstation products. Seaport Graphics also creates imaging systems for personal computers and Macintosh desktop packages, color electronic prepress systems, and overnight slide services. **Positions advertised include:** Sales Representative; Account Manager.

SELECT, INC.
31 Dartmouth Street, Westwood MA 02090. 781/326-8600. **Toll-free phone:** 800/634-1806. **Contact:** Human Resources. **World Wide Web address:** http://www.select.com. **Description:** Manufactures and sells network servers.

SIEBEL SYSTEMS, INC.
One Apple Hill, Suite 301, Natick MA 01760. 508/652-8600. **Fax:** 508/652-8601. **Contact:** Human Resources. **World Wide Web address:** http://www.siebel.com. **Description:** Siebel Systems is a leading provider of customer relationship management (CRM) solutions and applications for business intelligence and standards-based integration. **Parent company:** Oracle Corporation.

SIEMENS BUSINESS SERVICES
45 Shawmut Road, Canton MA 02021-1408. 781/830-2200. **Contact:** Human Resources. **World Wide Web address:** http://www.sbs-usa.siemens.com. **Description:** A manufacturer of computer systems, software, and peripherals. The company also offers consulting, planning, and implementation services. **Positions advertised include:** Program Director. **Corporate headquarters location:** Rye Brook NY. **Other U.S. locations:** Nationwide. **International locations:** Worldwide.

SKY COMPUTERS INC.
8 Centennial Drive, M/S A-14, Peabody MA 01960. 978/977-3000. **Fax:** 978/978-6968. **Contact:** Human Resources Department. **E-mail address:** SKYemployment@skycomputers.com. **World Wide Web address:** http://www.skycomputers.com. **Description:** Manufactures high-speed processing computer components including compilers, daughterboards, and accelerators.

SMART MODULAR TECHNOLOGIES, INC.
3 Highwood Drive, Suite 103E, Tewksbury MA 01876. 978/805-2100. **Fax:** 978/805-2357. **Contact:** Human Resources. **World Wide Web address:** http://www.smartm.com. **Description:** Designs, manufactures, and sells personal computer cards used in portable computers and industrial applications and font cartridges used in laser printers. The PC cards enhance the utility of portable computers and electronic equipment by adding memory, data/fax capabilities,

and custom applications. The company's laser printer font cartridges broaden the capabilities of laser printers with applications in desktop publishing, word processing, and spreadsheet preparation. **Corporate headquarters location:** Fremont CA.

SOFTECH, INC.
2 Highwood Drive, Tewksbury MA 01876. 978/640-6222. **Fax:** 978/858-0440. **Contact:** Human Resources. **E-mail address:** hr-tewks@softech.com. **World Wide Web address:** http://www.softech.com. **Description:** Manufacturers, markets, and maintains product life-cycle software. Founded in 1969. **Positions advertised include:** Senior Account Manager. **NOTE:** Apply online.

SOFTRAX CORPORATION
45 Shawmut Road, 3rd Floor, Canton MA 02021. 781/830-9200. **Fax:** 781/830-9345. **Contact:** Maryann Jordan, Director of Human Resources. **E-mail address:** jobs@softrax.com. **World Wide Web address:** http://www.softrax.com. **Description:** A provider of enterprise billing and revenue management software solutions. **Positions advertised include:** Technical Services Manager; Release Engineer; Technical Writer; Quality Assurance Engineer; Financial Analyst; Account Manager.

SOFTRICITY, INC.
27 Melcher Street, 3rd Floor, Boston MA 02210. 617/695-0336. Toll-free phone: 877/763-8737. **Fax:** 617/338-7769. **Contact:** Human Resources. **World Wide Web address:** http://www.softricity.com. **Description:** A software developer. The company's main product, SoftGrid, allows organizations to install Microsoft Windows applications to numerous computer desktops from a central location. SoftGrid enables application virtualization, where IT administrators can provide desktop software on an on-demand basis to multiple users, without installing the software on each individual desktop. Founded in 1999. **Positions advertised include:** Sr. Software Engineer; Sr. Engineer; Sr. QA Engineer.

SOFTSCAPE, INC.
526 Boston Post Road, Wayland MA 01778. 508/358-1072. **Fax:** 508/358-3072. **Contact:** Human Resources. **E-mail address:** careers@softscape.com. **World Wide Web address:** http://www.softscape.com. **Description:** Develops human capital management and case management software for companies and government agencies. **Positions advertised include:** Project Manager; Business Analyst; Sr. Technical Consultant; Project Accountant; Quality Assurance Engineer; Software Engineer; Product Manager; Sales Engineer; Paralegal. **Other U.S. locations:** Chicago IL; San Francisco CA; Hartford CT; Washington DC; New York NY.

SOFTWARE PUNDITS, INC.
67 South Bedford Street, Suite 202W, Burlington MA 01803. 781/229-6655. **Fax:** 781/229-6660. **Contact:** Human Resources. **E-mail address:** techjobs@pundits.com. **World Wide Web address:** http://www.pundits.com. **Description:** Provides development consulting support services. **Positions advertised include:** Market Research Analyst; Business Objects/SAS Developer; Informatica Lead Developer; Software QA Tester.

SPOTFIRE, INC.
212 Elm Street, Somerville MA 02144. 617/702-1600. **Toll-free phone:** 800/245-4211.**Fax:** 617/702-1700. **Contact:** Human Resources. **E-mail address:** hr@spotfire.com. **World Wide Web address:** http://www.spotfire.com. **Description:** Provides interactive, visual data analysis applications and services that enable enterprises and their end-users to improve operational performance. Founded in 1996. **Positions advertised include:** Sales Administrator; Solutions Developer; Sr. Financial Analyst; Clinical Development Solution Marketing Manager; Life Science Industry Marketing Program Manager; Software Applications Marketing Engineer.

SPRINGBOARD TECHNOLOGY CORPORATION
1 Federal Street, Lincoln Street Gate, Springfield MA 01105. Toll-free phone: 800/397-6759. **Fax:** 413/272-4114. **Contact:** Human Resource Director. **E-mail address:** humanresources@springboard.com. **World Wide Web address:** http://www.springboard.com. **Description:** Provides reverse supply chain services and is a repair, warranty, logistics management, and order fulfillment service provider for original device manufacturers, service providers, and enterprise clients. **Positions advertised include:** Operator/Assembler; Technician; Customer Service Representative; Buyer/Planner; Production/Inventory Controller; Logistics Associate.

STORAGETEK
230 Third Avenue, 3rd Floor, Waltham MA 02451. 781/890-2650. **Fax:** 781/890-9106. **Contact:** Human Resources. **World Wide Web address:** http://www.stortek.com. **Description:** Storage Technology Corporation manufactures high-performance computer information storage and retrieval systems for mainframe and mid-frame computers and networks. Products include automated cartridge systems, random access subsystems, and fault-tolerant disk arrays. The company also distributes equipment; sells new peripherals, software, and hardware; and offers support services. **Corporate headquarters location:** Louisville CO. **Operations at this facility include:** This location sells computer data storage systems.

STRATUS TECHNOLOGIES
111 Powdermill Road, Maynard MA 01754. 978/461-7000. **Contact:** Human Resources. **World Wide Web address:** http://www.stratus.com. **Description:** Stratus Technologies offers a broad range of computer systems, application solutions, middleware, and professional services for critical online operations. **Corporate headquarters location:** This location. **Positions advertised include:** Cost Accountant; Director, Compensation and Benefits; Hardware Engineer; Linux Engineer; Linux Project Lead; Manufacturing Segment Marketing Manager; Product Manager; Quality Assurance Manager; Sr. Financial Analyst; Sr. QA Engineer; Sr. Software Engineer; Sr. Compensation Analyst.

STREAM INTERNATIONAL
85 Dan Road, Canton MA 02021. 781/575-6800. **Contact:** Human Resources. **World Wide Web address:** http://www.stream.com. **Description:** Resells computer software and offers support services. **Positions advertised include:** Oracle Applications Developer; Data Central Representative; Java Programmer. **Other locations:** Beaverton Oregon, Watertown New York.

SUN MICROSYSTEMS, INC.
One Network Drive, Burlington MA 01803. 978/442-6200. **Contact:** Human Resources. **World Wide Web address:** http://www.sun.com. **Description:** Produces high-performance computer systems, workstations, servers, CPUs, peripherals, and operating system software. The company developed its own microprocessor called SPARC. **Positions advertised include:** Programming Analyst; Web Design Administration; Mission Critical Technical Support; Technical Training Development & Delivery; Customer Services; Application Development; GUI Design; Test Engineer; Product Engineer; Product Management. **Corporate headquarters location:** Santa Clara CA. **Subsidiaries include:** Forte Software Inc. manufactures enterprise application integration software. **Listed on:** NASDAQ. **Stock exchange symbol:** SUNW.

SYBASE, INC.
561 Virginia Road, Concord MA 01742. 978/287-1975. **Fax:** 978/369-3175. **Contact:** Human Resources. **World Wide Web address:** http://www.sybase.com. **Description:** Develops, markets, and supports a full line of relational database management software

products and services for integrated, enterprisewide information management systems. Founded in 1984. **Positions advertised include:** Systems Consultant; Sr. Marketing Manager; Software Engineer; Telesales Rep. **Special programs:** Internships; Co-ops. **Corporate headquarters location:** Dublin CA. **Other U.S. locations:** Nationwide. **Operations at this facility include:** Divisional Headquarters. **Listed on:** NASDAQ. **Stock exchange symbol:** SYBS. **President/CEO:** Michael Kietzman. **Annual sales/revenues:** More than $100 million. **Number of employees at this location:** 800. **Number of employees worldwide:** 5,600.

SYMANTEC
275 Second Avenue, Waltham MA 02451. 781/487-3300. **Fax:** 781/487-3301. **Contact:** Human Resources. **World Wide Web address:** http://www.symantec.com. **Description:** Symantec provides solutions to help individuals and enterprises assure the security, availability, and integrity of their information. Founded in 1982. **Positions advertised include:** Sr. Learning Consultant; Sr. Software Engineer; Principal Engineer; SQA Engineer; Tech Support Engineer; Sr. Information Developer; Business Development Sales Rep; Principal Systems Engineer; Sr. Solutions Specialist. **Number of employees worldwide:** 15,500.

SYSTEMS ENGINEERING, INC.
657 Main Street, Waltham MA 02451-0602. 781/736-9100. **Fax:** 781/736-6969. **Contact:** Human Resources. **E-mail address:** info@sengi.com. **World Wide Web address:** http://www.sengi.com. **Description:** A computer consulting firm. **Positions advertised include:** Microsoft Software Designer/Developer; Sales Professional.

THE SYSTEMS GROUP, INC.
281 Winter Street, Suite 380, Waltham MA 02451. 617/243-0220. **Toll-free phone:** 800/501-5863. **Fax:** 860/657-4503. **Contact:** Human Resources. **World Wide Web address:** http://www.thesystemsgroup.com. **Description:** Provides local, regional and national clients with consulting services ranging from on-site, short-term and long-term staff augmentation and special projects to off-site turnkey system development, as well as e-commerce and e-business support services. **Positions advertised include:** Consultant, Various Technologies and Skills. **Corporate headquarters location:** Hartford CT.

SYSTEMSOFT CORPORATION
275 Grove Street, Suite 1-300, Newton MA 02466-2273. 617/614-4315. **Fax:** 508/614-4601. **Contact:** Recruiter. **World Wide Web address:** http://www.systemsoft.com. **Description:** Supplies PCMCIA (Personal Computer Memory Card International Association) and other system-level software to the rapidly growing market of mobile computers, comprised of laptops, notebooks, subnotebooks, and personal computing devices. System-level software provides both a connectivity layer, which facilitates the addition, configuration, and use of peripheral devices; and a hardware adaptation layer including the communication link between a computer operating system and hardware. **Corporate headquarters location:** This location. **Parent company:** Rocket Software. **Number of employees nationwide:** 250.

TATARA SYSTEMS
35 Nagog Park, Acton MA 01720. 978/206-0800. **Fax:** 978-206-0888. **Contact:** Human Resources. **E-mail address:** jobs@tatarasystems.com. **World Wide Web address:** http://www.tatarasystems.com. **Description:** Develops and deploys solutions for service and content providers wanting to deliver converged mobile offerings to their customers across networks and devices. Tatara's products make it possible to deliver services and content over multiple IP access networks and across secure client connections to laptops, PDAs, and smartphones. Founded in 2001. **Positions advertised include:** Consulting/Senior Customer Support Engineer; Principal Engineer, Windows Application Developer; Contract Principal/Consulting Software Developer; Pre-Sales/Senior Systems Engineer.

TAXWARE INTERNATIONAL, INC.
401 Edgewater Place, Suite 260, Wakefield MA 01880-6210. 781/557-2600. **Fax:** 781/557-2606. **Contact:** Lisa Burns, Human Resources Manager. **E-mail address:** careers@taxware.com. **World Wide Web address:** http://www.taxware.com. **Description:** Develops a line of tax software. **Positions advertised include:** Business Development Director; Sr. Application Developer; Product manager; Tax Research Associate; Development Manager; Sr. Software Engineer; Sr. QA Analyst.

TECHNICAL COMMUNICATIONS CORPORATION (TCC)
100 Domino Drive, Concord MA 01742. 978/287-5100. **Fax:** 978/371-1280. **Contact:** Personnel. **E-mail address:** tccjobs@tccsecure.com. **World Wide Web address:** http://www.tccsecure.com. **Description:** Technical Communications Corporation designs, manufactures, and sells communications security devices and systems. Products include the Cipher family of encryption devices, which protect computer terminals with an encryption key that needs to be changed on a regular basis; and KEYNET key management system, which is an advanced system that permits geographically dispersed data networks to be managed economically and safely from a single secured site. The KEYNET system provides an electronic courier to distribute the keys automatically, securely, cost effectively, and invisibly. KEYNET protects and manages the sensitive data traveling between U.S. government agencies on government networks. **Positions advertised include:** Sr. Software Engineer; Quality Assurance Engineer. **Corporate headquarters location:** This location. **Annual sales/revenues:** $11 - $20 million. **Number of employees at this location:** 65.

TELCO SYSTEMS
2 Hampshire Street, Suite 3A, Foxboro MA 02035-2897. 781/551-0300. **Fax:** 781/551-0538. **Contact:** Human Resources. **World Wide Web address:** http://www.telco.com. **Description:** Develops, manufactures, and markets fiber-optic transmission products, customer premises network access products, and LAN/WAN internetworking products. Applications include voice, data, and video communication networks. Primary customers are independent telephone companies, resellers, competitive access providers, interexchange carriers, and corporate end users. **Corporate headquarters location:** This location.

TELELOGIC
3 Riverside Drive, Andover MA 01810. 978/682-2100. **Toll-free phone:** 888/245-6449. **Fax:** 978/645-3173. **Contact:** Human Resources. **World Wide Web address:** http://www.ilogix.com. **Description:** Manufactures software for high-technology applications. **Positions advertised include:** Operations Specialist; Rhapsody Developer; Rhapsody Application Engineer. **International locations:** England; France; Germany; Israel.

3COM CORPORATION
350 Campus Drive, Marlborough MA 01752. 508/323-5000. **Contact:** Human Resources. **World Wide Web address:** http://www.3com.com. **Description:** 3Com is a *Fortune* 500 company delivering global data networking solutions to organizations around the world. 3Com designs, manufactures, markets, and supports a broad range of ISO 9000-compliant global data networking solutions including routers, hubs, remote access servers, switches, and adapters for Ethernet, Token Ring, and high-speed networks. **Positions advertised include:** Web Developer; SEC Reporting Manager; SAP Analyst; Product Manager; LAN Administrator. **Corporate headquarters location:** This location. **Listed on:** NASDAQ. **Stock exchange**

symbol: COMS. **Annual sales/revenues:** More than $100 million. **Number of employees worldwide:** 1,800.

3M TOUCH SYSTEMS
501 Griffin Brook Park Drive, Methuen MA 01844. 978/659-9000. **Fax:** 978/659-9100. **Contact:** Human Resources Manager. **World Wide Web address:** http://www.3mtouch.com. **Description:** 3M Touch Systems is a manufacturer of touch-screen systems. Products are used in a broad range of applications including point-of-sale terminals, self-service kiosks, gaming machines, industrial systems, ATMs, multimedia applications, and many other computer-based systems. MicroTouch also manufactures and markets TouchPen, a touch- and pen-sensitive digitizer used for pen-based and whiteboarding applications; TouchMate, a pressure-sensitive pad that makes any monitor placed on it touch-sensitive; and ThruGlass, a product that can sense a touch through up to two inches of glass, allowing kiosks to be placed behind store windows for 24-hour access. **Listed on:** New York Stock Exchange. **Stock exchange symbol:** MMM.

TOP LAYER NETWORKS
2400 Computer Drive, Westboro MA 01581. 508/870-1300. **Fax:** 508/870-9797. **Contact:** Recruiting. **E-mail address:** recruiting@toplayer.com. **World Wide Web address:** http://www.toplayer.com. **Description:** Develops security infrastructure solutions that help commercial and government organizations protect their on-line assets from the losses and risks associated with cyber threats. **Positions advertised include:** Director of North American channel Sales, Regional Account Manager; Sr. Text Automation Engineer; Software Engineer.

TURBINE INC.
60 Glazier Drive, Westwood MA 02090. 781/320-8222. **Fax:** 781/329-5463. **Contact:** Human Resources. **World Wide Web address:** http://www.turbine.com. **Description:** A leading producer and publisher of multiplayer online games. **Positions advertised include:** Corporate Controller; Human Resources Director; Director of Game Systems; Principal Engineer; Software Architect; Software Engineer; Technical Writer. **Other U.S. locations:** Santa Monica CA.

UNICA CORPORATION
Reservoir Place North, 170 Tracer Lane, Waltham MA 02451-1379. 781/839-8000. **Fax:** 781/890-0012. **Contact:** Human Resources. **E-mail address:** careers@unica.com. **World Wide Web address:** http://www.unica.com. **Description:** A provider of Enterprise Marketing Management (EMM) software, focusing exclusively on the needs of marketing organizations. **Positions advertised include:** Technical Project Manager; Sr. Software Development Engineer; Director, Financial Planning and Analysis; Quality Assurance Engineer. **Other U.S. locations:** Chicago IL; Dallas TX; San Francisco CA.

UNISYS CORPORATION
154 Middlesex Turnpike, Burlington MA 01803. 781/238-1300. **Contact:** Human Resources. **World Wide Web address:** http://www.unisys.com. **Description:** Provides technology services and solutions in consulting, systems integration, outsourcing, infrastructure, and server technology. **Positions advertised include:** System Architect. **Corporate headquarters location:** Blue Bell PA. **Other U.S. locations:** Nationwide. **Listed on:** New York Stock Exchange. **Stock exchange symbol:** UIS.

UNIVERSAL SOFTWARE CORPORATION
100 Apollo Drive, Chelmsford MA 01824. 978/677-2600. **Fax:** 978/244-9511. **Contact:** Human Resources. **World Wide Web address:** http://www.universal-sw.com. **Description:** A provider of global software engineering, customization, and integration services. **Positions advertised include:** Systems Administrator; Database Administrator; Programmer/Analyst; J2EE, EJB Architect.

VFA, INC.
266 Summer Street, Boston MA 02210-1112. 617/451-5100. **Toll-free phone:** 800/693-3132. **Fax:** 617/350-7087. **Contact:** Human Resources. **E-mail address:** hr@vfa.com. **World Wide Web address:** http://www.vfa.com. **Description:** Provides software and services for facilities management and capital planning. VFA provides Web-based software and consulting services to nearly 300 organizations to strategically manage over two billion square feet of real estate. **Positions advertised include:** Facilities Assessment Consultant; Project Manager; Project Assistant; Systems Administrator.

VERTICAL COMMUNICATIONS, INC.
One Memorial Drive, Cambridge MA 02142. 617/354-0600. **Fax:** 617/452-9159. **Contact:** Personnel. **E-mail address:** jobs@vertical.com. **World Wide Web address:** http://www.vertical.com. **Description:** A provider of IP-based voice and data communications systems for business. **Positions advertised include:** Public Relations Manager; Sr. Product Manager. **Corporate headquarters location:** This location. **Listed on:** NASDAQ. **Stock exchange symbol:** ASFT.

VIISAGE
296 Concord Road, Third Floor, Billerica MA 01821. 978/932-2200. **Fax:** 978/932-2225. **Contact:** Human Resources. **E-mail address:** hr@viisage.com. **World Wide Web address:** http://www.viisage.com. **Description:** Delivers advanced technology identity solutions for governments, law enforcement agencies and businesses concerned with enhancing security, reducing identity theft, and protecting personal privacy. Viisage solutions include secure credentials such as passports and drivers' licenses, biometric technologies for uniquely linking individuals to those credentials, and credential authentication technologies to ensure the documents are valid before individuals are allowed to cross borders, gain access to finances, or granted other privileges. **Positions advertised include:** Division Counsel; Sr. Project Manager; Sr. Revenue Analyst.

VIRYANET
2 Willow Street, Southborough MA 01745. 508/490-5600. **Contact:** Human Resources Department. **E-mail address:** jobs@viryanet.com. **World Wide Web address:** http://www.viryanet.com. **Description:** Develops field management system software for large organizations. **Positions advertised include:** Sales; Pre Sales; Sales Engineering; Product Management; Project Management; Software Engineer; Product Marketer.

WEBHIRE, INC.
91 Hartwell Avenue, Lexington MA 02421. 781/869-5000. **Fax:** 781/869-5050. **Contact:** Human Resources. **World Wide Web address:** http://www.webhire.com. **Description:** Manufactures and sells software that sorts and ranks resumes by criteria selected by the resume screener. **Positions advertised include:** Staff Accountant; Strategic Process Consultant; Vice President Client Services & Operations; Lead Development Representative. **Corporate headquarters location:** This location. **Listed on:** Privately held.

WIND RIVER
120 Royall Street, Canton MA 02021. 781/828-5588. **Fax:** 781/821-2268. **Contact:** Human Resources. **World Wide Web address:** http://www.windriver.com. **Description:** A producer of software that enables companies to develop and run device software better, faster, at lower cost, and more reliably through device software optimization. **Positions advertised include:** Sr. Product Manager; Sr. Product Support Engineer; System Test Engineer; Technical Staff; Sr. Analyst, Systems Administration; Field Marketing Manager. **Corporate headquarters location:** Alameda CA. **Listed on:** NASDAQ. **Stock exchange symbol:** WIND.

XYVISION ENTERPRISE SOLUTIONS, INC.
101 Edgewater Drive, Wakefield MA 01880-1296. 781/756-4400. **Fax:** 781/756-4330. **Contact:** Diane

Lambas, Human Resources. **E-mail address:** careers@xyenterprise.com. **World Wide Web address:** http://www.xyvision.com. **Description:** Develops and supports software for document management, publishing, and prepress applications worldwide. The company combines its software with standard computer hardware, selected third-party software, and support services to create integrated systems that improve productivity and strategic position. Xyvision's color electronic prepress applications are marketed to commercial trade shops, printers, prepress service organizations, consumer goods companies, advanced design firms, and packaging manufacturers. **Positions advertised include:** IT Manager; Sr. Software Engineer. **Corporate headquarters location:** This location.

YANTRA CORPORATION
One Park West, Tewksbury MA 01876. 978/513-6000. **Toll-free phone:** 888/292-6872. **Fax:** 978/513-6006. **Contact:** Human Resources. **World Wide Web address:** http://www.yantra.com. **Description:** Provides industry-specific synchronized fulfillment solutions for the retail, wholesale distribution, logistics, communications and manufacturing industries, enabling intelligent execution between customers, operations and partners. **Positions advertised include:** Yantra Senior Consultant; Software Systems Test Engineer, Quality Assurance; Senior Customer Service Engineer; Quality Assurance, Software Test Engineer; Technical Writer; Software Engineer; Customer Service Engineer.

ZAIQ TECHNOLOGIES, INC.
78 Dragon Court, Woburn MA 01801. 781/932-2442. **Fax:** 781/932-7488. **Contact:** Human Resources. **E-mail address:** info@zaiqtech.com. **World Wide Web address:** http://www.zaiqtech.com. **Description:** Provides verification solutions for companies that develop complex telecommunications, networking and computer products. **Positions advertised include:** Northeast Account Executive; Verification Engineer; FPGA Design Engineer; Technical Recruiter.

ZOOM TELEPHONICS INC.
207 South Street, Boston MA 02111. 617/423-1072. **Fax:** 617/423-2836. **Contact:** Karen Player, Director of Human Resources. **E-mail address:** hr@zoom.com. **World Wide Web address:** http://www.zoomtel.com. **Description:** Designs and produces Voice over IP Gateways, DSL modems, cable modems, dial-up modems, Bluetooth products, and other communications products. **Corporate headquarters location:** This location. **Listed on:** NASDAQ. **Stock exchange symbol:** ZOOM. **Annual sales/revenues:** $51 - $100 million. **Number of employees at this location:** 320.

Michigan

ABL ELECTRONIC SERVICE, INC.
314 East 14 Mile Road, Madison Heights MI 48071. 248/588-6663. **Fax:** 248/588-0851. **Contact:** Personnel. **E-mail address:** ablserv@htdconnect.com. **World Wide Web address:** http://www.ablserv.com. **Description:** Services computer hardware for individuals and businesses. ABL Electronic Service repairs CPUs, monitors, printers, and other peripherals for IBM, IBM compatibles, and some Apple units. **Positions advertised include:** T.V. Repair Bench Technician; T.V. Repair Road Technician. **Corporate headquarters location:** This location. **Other area locations:** Southfield MI.

ADVANTAGE COMPUTING SYSTEMS, INC.
3850 Ranchero Drive, Ann Arbor MI 48108. 734/327-3600. **Fax:** 734/327-3620. **Contact:** Glenda Stegenga, Human Resources Manager. **E-mail address:** jobs@advantagecs.com. **World Wide Web address:** http://www.advantagecs.com. **Description:** Markets Publisher's Advantage Computing System brand software to special interest publishers. The company also resells a wide range of hardware options. Founded in 1980. **Corporate headquarters location:** This location. **Operations at this facility include:** Administration; Manufacturing; Research and Development; Sales; Service. **Listed on:** Privately held. **Annual sales/revenues:** $5 - $10 million. **Number of employees at this location:** 75.

AIR GAGE COMPANY
12170 Globe Road, Livonia MI 48150. 734/853-9220. **Fax:** 734/853-2435. **Contact:** Human Resources. **World Wide Web address:** http://www.airgage.com. **Description:** Develops and manufactures air gages and statistical process control software that allow manufacturers to monitor, regulate, and collect data on their manufacturing processes. **Corporate headquarters location:** This location. **Parent company:** SPX Corporation. **Listed on:** New York Stock Exchange. **Stock exchange symbol:** SPW.

ANALYSTS INTERNATIONAL CORPORATION (AIC)
3252 University Drive, Suite 200, Auburn Hills MI 48326. 248/299-2660. **Fax:** 248/299-4830. **Contact:** Human Resources. **E-mail address:** jobs@analysts.com. **World Wide Web address:** http://www.analysts.com. **Description:** An international computer consulting firm. The company assists clients in developing systems in a variety of industries using different programming languages and software. **Corporate headquarters location:** Minneapolis MN. **Other U.S. locations:** Nationwide. **International locations:** Canada; United Kingdom. **Listed on:** NASDAQ. **Stock exchange symbol:** ANLY. **Number of employees worldwide:** 3,000.

ANN ARBOR COMPUTER
34375 West Twelve Mile Road, Farmington Hills MI 48331-5624. 248/553-5200. **Fax:** 248/553-5292. **Contact:** Human Resources. **E-mail address:** info@jerviswebb.com. **World Wide Web address:** http://www.annarborcomputer.com. **Description:** Designs software for automated inventory systems used by warehouses. Founded in 1965. **Corporate headquarters location:** This location. **Parent company:** Jervis B. Webb Company.

AUTODESK INC.
26200 Town Center Drive, Suite 300, Novi MI 48375. 248/347-9650. **World Wide Web address:** http://www.autodesk.com. **Description:** Offers software and related services for the building, manufacturing, infrastructure, digital media, and wireless data services fields to help create, manage, and share their digital assets more efficiently. **Positions available include:** Software Development Intern. **Corporate headquarters location:** San Rafael CA. **Listed on:** NASDAQ. **Stock exchange symbol:** ADSK.

CIBER, INC.
30 Oak Hollow, Suite 340, Southfield MI 48034. 248/352-8650. **Toll-free phone:** 800/324-6001. **Fax:** 248/352-3010. **Contact:** Human Resources. **E-mail address:** jobs@ciber.com. **World Wide Web address:** http://www.ciber.com. **Description:** Provides consulting for client/server development, mainframe and legacy systems, industry-specific analysis, application-specific analysis, and network development. Founded in 1974. **Corporate headquarters location:** Greenwood Village CO. **Other U.S. locations:** Nationwide. **International locations:** Canada; the Netherlands. **Listed on:** New York Stock Exchange. **Stock exchange symbol:** CBR. **Number of employees worldwide:** 5,750.

COMPUTER DECISIONS INTERNATIONAL INC.
23933 Research Drive, Farmington Hills MI 48355. 248/347-4600. **Fax:** 248/478-3445. **Contact:** Human Resources. **World Wide Web address:** http://www.cdi-usa.com. **Description:** A computer hardware and software reseller. Founded in 1981. **Corporate headquarters location:** This location.

COMPUWARE CORPORATION
One Campus Martius, Detroit MI 48226. 313/227-7300. **Toll-free phone:** 800/521-9353. **Fax:** 877/873-6784.

Contact: Corporate Recruiting. **E-mail address:** compuware.recruiting@compuware.com. **World Wide Web address:** http://www.compuware.com. **Description:** Develops, markets, and supports an integrated line of systems software products that improve the productivity of programmers and analysts in application program testing, test data preparation, error analysis, and maintenance. Compuware also provides a broad range of professional data processing services including business systems analysis, design, and programming, and systems planning and consulting. **Positions advertised include:** Software Developer; Product Consultant; Services Account Manager; Customer Support Analyst; System Administrator; Global Channel Manager; Director of Marketing. **Special programs:** Training; Continued Career Development Program. **Corporate headquarters location:** This location. **Other U.S. locations:** Nationwide. **International locations:** Worldwide. **Listed on:** NASDAQ. **Stock exchange symbol:** CPWR. **Number of employees worldwide:** Approximately 10,000.

CORE TECHNOLOGY CORPORATION
7435 Westshire Drive, Lansing MI 48917. 517/627-1521. **Toll-free phone:** 800/338-2117. **Fax:** 517/627-8944. **Contact:** Human Resources. **E-mail address:** jobs@ctc-core.com. **World Wide Web address:** http://www.ctc-core.com. **Description:** Provides connectivity solutions for companies in a variety of markets. **Positions advertised include:** Sales Representative; Software Developer; Software Support Representative; Marketing Representative. **Corporate headquarters location:** This location.

COVANSYS
32605 West Twelve Mile Road, Suite 250, Farmington Hills MI 48334. 248/488-2088. **Toll-free phone:** 800/688-2088. **Fax:** 248/488-2089. **Contact:** Faye Silva, Personnel Department. **E-mail address:** fsilva@covansys.com. **World Wide Web address:** http://www.cbsinc.com. **Description:** An international systems integration consulting firm specializing in strategic systems development, systems integration, software application development, projects, contracts, and business process/system re-engineering. **Corporate headquarters location:** This location. **Other area locations:** Detroit MI; Lansing MI; Okemos MI. **Other U.S. locations:** Nationwide. **International locations:** Worldwide. **Listed on:** NASDAQ. **Stock exchange symbol:** CVNS. **Number of employees worldwide:** 4,700.

CREATIVE SOLUTIONS
7322 Newman Boulevard, Dexter MI 48130. 734/426-5860. **Contact:** Human Resources Department. **E-mail address:** recruiting@creativesolutions.com. **World Wide Web address:** http://www.creativesolutions.com. **Description:** Develops, markets, and supports accounting and tax software. **Positions advertised include:** Project Support Representative; Account Representative; Associate Account Representative; Tax Development Analyst. **Special programs:** Internships; Co-ops. **Corporate headquarters location:** This location. **Other area locations:** Ann Arbor MI. **Parent company:** Thomson.

EDS (ELECTRONIC DATA SYSTEMS CORPORATION)
River East Centre, 500 Renaissance Center, 3rd – 21st Floors, Detroit MI 48243. 313/230-2664. **Contact:** Human Resources. **E-mail address:** careers@eds.com. **World Wide Web address:** http://www.eds.com. **Description:** Provides business services in the area of information technology to clients in the communications, consumer, retail, energy, financial, healthcare, and transportation industries, as well as governments. **Special programs:** Internships. **Corporate headquarters location:** Plano TX. **Other U.S. locations:** Nationwide. **International locations:** Worldwide. **Operations at this facility include:** Administration. **Listed on:** New York Stock Exchange. **Stock exchange symbol:** EDS. **Sales/revenue:** $21.5 billion. **Number of employees worldwide:** Over 130,000.

EXTENSITY
555 Briarwood Circle, Ann Arbor MI 48108. 734/994-4800. **Toll-free phone:** 800/922-7979. **Fax:** 734/994-0341. **Contact:** Human Resources. **World Wide Web address:** http://www.extensity.com. **Description:** Develops financial applications software for mid-sized companies and international enterprises. **Positions advertised include:** Media Writer. **Corporate headquarters location:** Atlanta GA. **Other U.S. locations:** Nationwide. **International locations:** Worldwide.

FEDERAL APD, INC.
42775 Nine Mile Road, Novi MI 48375. 248/374-9600. **Fax:** 248/374-9610. **Contact:** Human Resources Administrator. **E-mail address:** hr@federalapd.com. **World Wide Web address:** http://www.federalapd.com. **Description:** Manufactures facility management system software used for parking, access, and revenue control. Products include the self-park, microprocessor-based barrier gate. **Positions advertised include:** Marketing Coordinator. **Corporate headquarters location:** This location. **Other U.S. locations:** Nationwide. **International locations:** Hong Kong; Brazil. **Parent company:** Federal Signal Corporation.

FISHER/UNITECH INC.
1150 Stevenson Highway, Troy MI 48083. 248/577-5100. **Toll-free phone:** 800/816-8314. **Fax:** 248/577-8524. **Contact:** Human Resources Department. **E-mail address:** info@funtech.com. **World Wide Web address:** http://www.funtech.com. **Description:** An engineering technologies firm. **Corporate headquarters location:** This location. **Other area locations:** Grand Rapids MI. **Other U.S. locations:** Chicago IL; Cleveland OH; Milwaukee WI; Fort Wayne IN; St. Peters MO; Riverside MO.

FOREST COMPUTER INC.
1749 Hamilton Road, Okemos MI 48864. 517/349-4700. **Toll-free phone:** 800/951-3135. **Fax:** 517/349-2947. **Contact:** Human Resources. **E-mail address:** info@forest.com. **World Wide Web address:** http://www.forest.com. **Description:** Develops network software. Founded in 1981. **Corporate headquarters location:** This location.

GEDAS, INC.
3499 Hamlin Road, Rochester Hills MI 48309. 248/754-3100. **Fax:** 248/273-8130. **Contact:** Karen Raleigh, Human Resources. **E-mail address:** careers@gedas.com. **World Wide Web address:** http://www.gedasusa.com. **Description:** A worldwide information technology company. **Positions advertised include:** Web Operations Cyclone Specialist. **Corporate headquarters location:** Berlin, Germany. **International locations:** Worldwide.

GREAT LAKES COMPUTER CORPORATION
5555 Corporate Exchange Court SE, Grand Rapids MI 49512. 616/698-1100. **Toll-free phone:** 800/488-2587. **Fax:** 616/565-2005. **Contact:** Lonna Blair, Human Resources. **E-mail address:** lblair@glcomp.com. **World Wide Web address:** http://www.glcomp.com. **Description:** Refurbishes and sells computer and information technology equipment. **Positions advertised include:** Account Representative; Technical Engineer; IT Solutions Account Representative. **Corporate headquarters location:** This location.

INFOR GLOBAL SOLUTIONS
41780 Six Mile Road, Northville MI 48168. 248/697-3332. **Toll-free phone:** 800/442-2488. **Fax:** 248/697-3201. **Contact:** Human Resources. **E-mail address:** hr@infor.com. **World Wide Web address:** http://www.infor.com. **Description:** Develops software for the automotive industry. **Corporate headquarters location:** Alpharetta GA. **Other area locations:** Grand Rapids MI. **Operations at this facility include:** This location is the North American Headquarters of the

company's Automotive Division. **Number of employees worldwide:** 800.

MANATRON INC.
510 East Milham Avenue, Portage MI 49002. 269/567-2900. **Toll-free phone:** 800/666-5300. **Fax:** 269/567-2912. **Contact:** Human Resources. **E-mail address:** recruiter@manatron.com. **World Wide Web address:** http://www.manatron.com. **Description:** Develops software for government agencies. **Positions advertised include:** Sales Executive. **Corporate headquarters location:** This location. **Other U.S. locations:** Beavercreek OH; Miamisburg OH; Springfield OH; Canton OH; Indianapolis IN; Greenville NC; Excelsior Springs MO; Tampa FL. **Listed on:** NASDAQ. **Stock exchange symbol:** MANA.

THE MEDSTAT GROUP, INC.
777 East Eisenhower Parkway, 10th Floor, Ann Arbor MI 48108. 734/913-3000. **Contact:** Human Resources. **World Wide Web address:** http://www.medstat.com. **Description:** A health care information, software, and consulting firm that designs and builds database systems for use in analyzing health care claims and benefits for large employers, insurance companies, and the research industry. **Positions advertised include:** Collections Accountant; Data Management Analyst; Data Management Consultant; Marketing Director; Sales Director; Project Manager; Sales Support Consultant. **Corporate headquarters location:** This location. **Other U.S. locations:** San Francisco CA; Sacramento CA; Rocklin CA; Santa Barbara CA; Atlanta GA; Boston MA; Franklin TN; Cambridge MA; Washington DC. **Parent company:** The Thomson Corporation. **Operations at this facility include:** Administration; Research and Development; Sales; Service.

MIRACLE SOFTWARE SYSTEMS, INC.
23800 West Ten Mile Road, Suite 260, Southfield MI 48034. 248/350-1515, extension 31178. **Fax:** 248/350-2575. **Contact:** Siva Ratnala, Human Resources. **E-mail address:** jobs@miraclesoft.com. **World Wide Web address:** http://www.miraclesoft.com. **Description:** A worldwide business consulting company. **Positions advertised include:** Java/J2EE Consultants; WBI/MB/ICS Consultants. **Corporate headquarters location:** This location. **Other U.S. locations:** CA; GA; MA; OH. **International locations:** Worldwide. **Number of employees worldwide:** 1,200.

NEMATRON CORPORATION
5840 Interface Drive, Ann Arbor MI 48103. 734/214-2000. **Fax:** 734/994-8074. **Contact:** Human Resources. **E-mail address:** jobs@nematron.com. **World Wide Web address:** http://www.nematron.com. **Description:** Manufactures rugged computers with touch screen interfaces. **Positions advertised include:** Software Technical Designer; Technical Writer; Shipping Clerk. **Corporate headquarters location:** This location. **Other area locations:** Auburn Hills MI. **Other U.S. locations:** Huntsville AL. **International locations:** United Kingdom. **Listed on:** American Stock Exchange. **Stock exchange symbol:** NMN. **Annual sales/revenues:** Approximately $3.3 million.

PARAMETRIC TECHNOLOGY CORPORATION
3310 West Big Beaver Road, Suite 100, Troy MI 48084. 248/458-7700. **Contact:** Human Resources. **World Wide Web address:** http://www.ptc.com. **Description:** Parametric Technology Corporation is engaged in the design and development of fully integrated software products for mechanical engineering and automated manufacturing based upon a parametric solids modeling system. **Positions advertised include:** Implementation Consultant; Strategic Account Sales Representative. **Special programs:** Training; Tuition Reimbursement Program. **Corporate headquarters location:** Needham MA. **Other area locations:** Grand Rapids MI. **Other U.S. locations:** Nationwide. **International locations:** Worldwide. **Operations at this facility include:** This location is a sales and technical support office. **Listed on:** NASDAQ. **Stock exchange symbol:** PMTC. **Number of employees worldwide:** 3,200.

PRINTEK, INC.
1517 Townline Road, Benton Harbor MI 49022. 616/925-3200. **Fax:** 616/934-6567. **Contact:** Human Resources. **E-mail address:** hr@printek.com. **World Wide Web address:** http://www.printek.com. **Description:** Designs and manufactures mobile and desktop printers. Founded in 1980. **Positions advertised include:** Software/Application Engineer; Engineering Clerk; Engineering Technician; National Sales Manager. **Corporate headquarters location:** This location. **Other U.S. locations:** Wheaton IL. **Listed on:** Privately held. **Number of employees at this location:** 100.

QAD INC.
34405 West Twelve Mile Road, Farmington Hills MI 48331. 248/324-3150. **Contact:** Irene Solovij, Corporate Recruiter. **E-mail address:** ijs@qad.com. **World Wide Web address:** http://www.qad.com. **Description:** QAD develops software including MFG/PRO, a software package designed to aid in supply and distribution management for large companies. **Corporate headquarters location:** Carpinteria CA. **Other U.S. locations:** Hoffman Estates IL; Mt. Laurel NJ. **International locations:** Worldwide. **Operations at this facility include:** This location develops software for the automotive industry. **Listed on:** NASDAQ. **Stock exchange symbol:** QADI.

RJ NETWORKING
31700 West 12 Mile Road, Suite 202, Farmington Hills MI 48334. 248/553-9111. **Contact:** Human Resources. **Description:** Provides data management systems and computer network integration services. **Corporate headquarters location:** This location.

SER SOLUTIONS, INC.
811 South Boulevard East, Suite 220, Rochester Hills MI 48307. 248/293-0332. **Fax:** 248/293-0340. **Contact:** Human Resources. **E-mail address:** jobs@ser.com. **World Wide Web address:** http://www.ser.com. **Description:** A systems integrator offering both hardware and software solutions. SER Solutions assembles tape and disk storage subsystems for mainframe and open systems. The company also develops computer imaging systems. **Corporate headquarters location:** Dulles VA. **Other U.S. locations:** Norfolk CT. **International locations:** United Kingdom.

SOFTECH
755 West Big Beaver Road, Suite 410, Troy MI 48084. 248/269-8380. **Toll-free phone:** 888/294-9450. **Fax:** 248/269-8355. **Contact:** Human Resources. **E-mail address:** careers@softech.com. **World Wide Web address:** http://www.softech.com. **Description:** Designs customized, automated, engineering software that assists in a variety of industrial process. Clients include tool and die companies and molding companies. **Corporate headquarters location:** Tewksbury MA. **Other area locations:** Troy MI. **International locations:** France; Germany; Italy.

SYSTEMS INTEGRATION SPECIALISTS COMPANY, INC. (SISCO)
6605 19½ Mile Road, Sterling Heights MI 48314-1408. 586/254-0020. **Fax:** 586/254-0053. **Contact:** Human Resources. **World Wide Web address:** http://www.sisconet.com. **Description:** A privately held company founded in 1983 that is dedicated to applying standards to address real-world problems in the electric utility, manufacturing, and automation industries. SISCO offers communications and application integration products and services that are used by leading OEMs, system integrators, and end users. **Positions advertised include:** Software Engineer. **Other U.S. locations:** Hartselle AL.

TECHSMITH CORPORATION
2405 Woodlake Drive, Okemos MI 48864-5910. 517/381-2300. **Toll-free phone:** 800/517-3001. **Fax:**

517/913-6121. **Contact:** Human Resources. **E-mail address:** personnel@techsmith.com. **World Wide Web address:** http://www.techsmith.com. **Positions advertised include:** Corporate Sales Consultant; C++ Programmer. **Special programs:** Internships. **Description:** Develops SnagIt screen capture software; Camtasia, a desktop camcorder and DubIt, an audio editing utility. Founded in 1988. **Corporate headquarters location:** This location. **Listed on:** Privately held. **Number of employees at this location:** Over 70.

TECHTEAM GLOBAL, INC.
27335 West Eleven Mile Road, Southfield MI 48034. 248/357-2866. **Toll-free phone:** 800/522-4451. **Fax:** 248/357-2570. **Contact:** Human Resources. **E-mail address:** jobs@techteam.com. **World Wide Web address:** http://www.techteam.com. **Description:** Provides computer network design, programming, and training services. **Positions advertised include:** Support Technician. **Special programs:** Training. **Corporate headquarters location:** This location. **Other area locations:** Dearborn MI. **Other U.S. locations:** Davenport IA. **International locations:** Germany; Sweden; Belgium; United Kingdom. **Listed on:** NASDAQ. **Stock exchange symbol:** TEAM. **Annual sales/revenues:** $88 million. **Number of employees worldwide:** 1,600.

UNISYS CORPORATION
41100 Plymouth Road, Plymouth MI 48170. 734/737-4000. **Fax:** 734/737-4616. **Contact:** Human Resources Department. **World Wide Web address:** http://www.unisys.com. **Description:** Provides technology services and solutions in consulting, systems integration, outsourcing, infrastructure, and server technology. **Corporate headquarters location:** Blue Bell PA. **Other area locations:** Grand Rapids MI; Okemos MI. **Other U.S. locations:** Nationwide. **International locations:** Worldwide. **Operations at this facility include:** Engineering assembly and marketing. **Listed on:** New York Stock Exchange. **Stock exchange symbol:** UIS. **Number of employees worldwide:** 37,000.

VIRTUAL SERVICES
25307 Dequindre Road, Madison Heights MI 48071. 248/545-3100. **Fax:** 248/546-8404. **Contact:** Carol Taylor, Human Resources Coordinator. **E-mail address:** info@virtualgrp.com. **World Wide Web address:** http://www.virtualc3p.com. **Description:** Sells, leases, repairs, and services various types of computer hardware and software. Founded in 1983. **Positions advertised include:** Computer Field Service Engineer; Sales Account Manager. **Corporate headquarters location:** This location. **Other area locations:** Troy MI. **Number of employees at this location:** 60.

XYCOM AUTOMATION
750 North Maple Road, Saline MI 48176-1292. 734/429-4971. **Fax:** 734/492-8206. **Contact:** Human Resources. **E-mail address:** hrdept@xycom.com. **World Wide Web address:** http://www.xycom.com. **Description:** Develops, manufactures, and sells industrial microcomputers. Applications include the regulation and monitoring of continuous batch processes, and the control and monitoring of material handling equipment. **Positions advertised include:** National Channel Partner Manager; Area Sales Manager; Application Engineer. **Corporate headquarters location:** This location. **International locations:** Worldwide.

ZENACOMP INCORPORATED
17187 North Laurel Park Drive, Suite 351, Livonia MI 48152. 734/464-3700. **Toll-free phone:** 800/639-5967. **Fax:** 734/464-3730. **Contact:** Consulting Manager. **E-mail address:** recruiter@zenacomp.com. **World Wide Web address:** http://www.zenacomp.com. **Description:** Provides computer consulting services. **Corporate headquarters location:** This location.

Minnesota

APA CABLES & NETWORKS
5480 Nathan Lane, Plymouth MN 55442. 763/476-6866. **Fax:** 763/475-8457. **Contact:** Human Resources. **E-mail address:** apacn-hr@apacn.com. **World Wide Web address:** http://www.apacn.com. **Description:** Designs and manufactures a complete line of passive fiber optic connectivity solutions. **Positions advertised include:** Program Manager, Copper. **Parent company:** APA Enterprises.

ASI DATAMYTE, INC.
2800 Campus Drive, Suite 60, Plymouth MN 55441. 763/553-1040. **Toll-free phone:** 800/207-5631. **Fax:** 763/553-1041. **Contact:** Human Resources. **E-mail address:** asijobs@asidatamyte.com. **World Wide Web address:** http://www.asidatamyte.com. **Description:** Develops products for quality planning and control, data collection, precision measurement, analysis and reporting, and gage management for the manufacturing marketplace. **Positions advertised include:** Software Engineer. **Corporate headquarters location:** This location. **Listed on:** Privately held. **Annual sales/revenues:** $5 - $10 million. **Number of employees at this location:** 50.

AFFILIATED COMPUTER SERVICES, INC. (ACS)
2901 Third Street South, Waite Park MN 56387. 320/253-2170. **Fax:** 320/255-9986. **Contact:** Human Resources. **World Wide Web address:** http://www.acs-inc.com. **Description:** Provides diversified business process and information technology outsourcing solutions to commercial and government clients worldwide. **Description:** Develops business process and assessment software for commercial and government clients. **Corporate headquarters location:** Dallas TX. **Other area locations:** Eagan MN; Mankato MN; Minneapolis MN. **Other U.S. locations:** Nationwide. **International locations:** Worldwide. **Listed on:** New York Stock Exchange. **Stock exchange symbol:** ACS.

ANALYSTS INTERNATIONAL CORPORATION (AIC)
3601 West 76th Street, Minneapolis MN 55435-3000. 952/835-5900. **Toll-free phone:** 800/800-5044. **Fax:** 952/897-4555. **Contact:** Senior Staffing Assistant. **E-mail address:** jobs@analysts.com. **World Wide Web address:** http://www.analysts.com. **Description:** Analysts International is an international computer consulting and staffing firm. The company assists clients in analyzing, designing, and developing systems using different programming languages and software. **NOTE:** Search and apply for jobs online at http://www.jobsatanalysts.com. A minimum of one to two years of programming experience is required. **Corporate headquarters location:** This location. **Other U.S. locations:** Nationwide. **Listed on:** NASDAQ. **Stock exchange symbol:** ANLY. **Annual sales/revenues:** More than $100 million. **Number of employees at this location:** 400.

BLM TECHNOLOGIES INC.
14755 27th Avenue North, Minneapolis MN 55447. 763/559-5100. **Fax:** 763/551-4319. **Contact:** Katy Bentrott, Operations Manager. **World Wide Web address:** http://www.blmtechnology.com. **Description:** Provides information technology products and services to corporate and government entities. **NOTE:** Entry-level positions are offered.

BT CONSULTING & SYSTEM INTEGRATION
4201 Lexington Avenue North, Arden Hills MN 55126. 651/415-4737. Fax: 651/415-4891. **Contact:** Katy Adams, Human Resources. **World Wide Web address:** http://www.btconsulting.com. **Description:** The company's consultants offer analysis and implementation in the areas of information and IT infrastructure management, messaging, mobility, network security and services, and provisioning. Formerly known as Control Data Systems. **Parent company:** BT PLC.

BANKERS SYSTEMS, INC.
P.O. Box 1457, St. Cloud MN 56302-1457. 320/251-3060. **Physical address:** 6815 Saukview Drive, St. Cloud MN 56303-0811. **Toll-free phone:** 800/397-2341. **Contact:** Human Resources. **E-mail address:** hr@bankerssystems.com. **World Wide Web address:** http://www.bankerssystems.com. **Description:** Develops marketing, operations, regulatory compliance, and training software for the financial services industry. **Positions advertised include:** Program Manager; SQA Engineer; Financial Accountant. **Parent company:** Wolters Kluwer.

CA, INC.
7760 France Avenue, Suite 810, Bloomington MN 55435. 952/835-4200. **Contact:** Human Resources. **World Wide Web address:** http://www.ca.com. **Description:** A leading international provider of computer services for businesses. **Positions advertised include:** Attorney; Sales Executive; Senior Consultant; Software Engineer; Solution Manager. **Corporate headquarters location:** Islandia NY. **Other U.S. locations:** Nationwide. **International locations:** Worldwide. **Listed on:** New York Stock Exchange. **Stock exchange symbol:** CA.

CERIDIAN CORPORATION
3311 East Old Shakopee Road, Minneapolis MN 55425. 952/853-8100. **World Wide Web address:** http://www.ceridian.com. **Contact:** Human Resources. **Description:** Provides information services for human resources, transportation, and retailing. **Positions advertised include:** Account Services Representative; Channel Development Manager; Financial Analyst; Network Analyst; Sales Contract Analyst; Tax Specialist. **Listed on:** New York Stock Exchange. **Stock exchange symbol:** CEN.

CIBER, INC.
2222 18th Avenue NW, Suite 100, Rochester MN 55901. 507/280-9267. **Toll-free phone:** 888/232-4237. **Fax:** 507/280-0833. **Contact:** Human Resources. **E-mail address:** RochesterMNJobs@ciber.com. **World Wide Web address:** http://www.ciber.com. **Description:** Provides consulting for client/server development, mainframe and legacy systems, industry-specific analysis, application-specific analysis, and network development. **Corporate headquarters location:** Greenwood Village CO. **Other area locations:** Minneapolis MN.

CIM SOFTWARE CORPORATION
5735 Lindsay Street, Minneapolis MN 55422. 763/544-1752. **Fax:** 763/543-9449. **Contact:** Human Resources. **E-mail address:** employment@cimsoftware.com. **World Wide Web address:** http://www.cimsoftware.com. **Description:** Develops networking software for systems integration. **NOTE:** See website for current job openings, or contact the office directly. **Other area locations:** Rochester MN. **Parent company:** Lakeland Companies.

COMPUWARE CORPORATION
11095 Viking Drive, Suite 430, Eden Prairie MN 55344. 612/851-2200. **Fax:** 612/851-2300. **Contact:** Clara Shmyel, Human Resources. **E-mail address:** compuware.recruiting@compuware.com. **World Wide Web address:** http://www.compuware.com. **Description:** Provides technology-based consulting solutions in the areas of software engineering, business applications development, and network architecture and security. **Positions advertised include:** .Net Developer; Sales Representative; Product Account Manager.

COREL CORPORATION
7905 Fuller Road, Eden Prairie MN 55344. 952/934-8888. **Toll-free phone:** 888/267-3548. **Fax:** 952/937-1732. **Contact:** Human Resources. **World Wide Web address:** http://www.corel.com. **Description:** Develops Windows-based graphics and multimedia software. **Special programs:** Internships. **Number of employees at this location:** 25.

CRAY INC.
1340 Mendota Heights Road, Mendota Heights MN 55120. 651/605-9000. **Fax:** 651/605-9001. **Contact:** Human Resources. **World Wide Web address:** http://www.cray.com. **Description:** Cray designs, develops, markets, and services high-performance computer systems, commonly known as supercomputers. **Corporate headquarters location:** Seattle WA. **Other U.S. locations:** WI. **Number of employees nationwide:** 900.

DIGI INTERNATIONAL INC.
11001 Bren Road East, Minnetonka MN 55343. 952/912-3444. **Contact:** Human Resources. **World Wide Web address:** http://www.dgii.com. **Description:** Provides data communications hardware and software that enable connectivity solutions for multi-user environments, remote access, and LAN connectivity markets. Digi International also provides cross-platform compatibility and software and technical support services. The company's products are marketed to a broad range of worldwide distributors, system integrators, value-added resellers, and OEMs. **Positions advertised include:** Administrative Assistant; Applications Support Engineer; Business Development Manager; Business Development Representative; Manager of External Financial Reporting and SOX Compliance; Marketing Internship; Product Management Internship; Programmer Analyst. **Corporate headquarters location:** This location. **International locations:** Worldwide. **Listed on:** NASDAQ. **Stock exchange symbol:** DGII.

EFI
1340 Corporate Center Curve, Eagan MN 55121. 651/365-5200. **Fax:** 651/365-5346. **Contact:** Human Resources. **E-mail address:** careers@efi.com. **World Wide Web address:** http://www.efi.com. **Description:** Develops management software for the graphic arts industry. **Corporate headquarters locations:** Foster City CA. **Other U.S. locations:** Nationwide.

EPICOR SOFTWARE CORPORATION
2000 Interchange Tower, 600 South Highway 169, Minneapolis MN 55426. 952/417-5000. **Fax:** 952/544-8253, **Contact:** Human Resources. **World Wide Web address:** http://www.epicor.com. **Description:** Provides integrated enterprise software to mid-market companies. Founded in 1984. **Positions advertised include:** Technical Support Analyst. **Corporate headquarters location:** Irvine CA. **Number of employees worldwide:** 950.

HUTCHINSON TECHNOLOGY INC.
40 West Highland Park, Hutchinson MN 55350. 320/587-3797. **Fax:** 320/587-1290. **Contact:** Human Resources. **E-mail address:** HUT.HR@hti.htch.com. **World Wide Web address:** http://www.htch.com. **Description:** Manufactures suspension assemblies for disk drives. **Positions advertised include:** Sr. Instructional Designer; Materials Contract Analyst; Process Engineer; Machine Design Engineer; Data Architect; Systems Integration Architect; Engineering Supervisor. **Special programs:** Internships. **Corporate headquarters location:** This location. **Other area locations:** Plymouth MN. **Other U.S. locations:** Sioux Falls SD; Eau Claire WI. **Operations at this facility include:** Administration; Manufacturing; Research and Development; Sales. **Listed on:** NASDAQ. **Stock exchange symbol:** HTCH.

IBM CORPORATION
3605 Highway 52 North, Rochester MN 55901-7829. 507/253-4011. **Toll-free phone:** 800/796-9876. **Contact:** IBM Staffing Services. **World Wide Web address:** http://www.ibm.com. **Description:** IBM is a developer, manufacturer, and marketer of advanced information processing products including computers and microelectronic technology, software, networking systems, and information technology-related services. **Positions advertised include:** Facility Management/Construction; Physical Design Integrator; Software Developer; Software Engineer. **Corporate headquarters location:** Armonk NY. **Operations at**

this facility include: This location is a manufacturing facility. **Subsidiaries include:** IBM Credit Corporation; IBM Instruments, Inc.; IBM World Trade Corporation. **Number of employees worldwide:** 319,000.

IMAGE SYSTEMS CORPORATION
6103 Blue Circle Drive, Minnetonka MN 55343. 952/935-1171. **Contact:** Human Resources. **E-mail address:** daves@imagesystemscorp.com. **World Wide Web address:** http://www.imagesystemscorp.com. **Description:** Develops, markets, and supports LCD and CRT displays, controllers, calibration, and display accessory products. **NOTE:** Second and third shifts are offered. **Special programs:** Internships. **Corporate headquarters location:** This location. **Parent company:** Richardson Electronics. **Listed on:** NASDAQ. **Stock exchange symbol:** RELL. **Annual sales/revenues:** $5 - $10 million. **Number of employees at this location:** 40.

IMATION CORPORATION
One Imation Place, Oakdale MN 55128-3414. 651/704-4000. **Toll-free phone:** 888/466-3456. **Fax:** 651/704-4171. **Contact:** Human Resources. **E-mail address:** info@imation.com. **World Wide Web address:** http://www.imation.com. **Description:** Develops and manufactures magnetic and optical removable data storage media. **Special programs:** Internships. **Corporate headquarters location:** This location. **Listed on:** New York Stock Exchange. **Stock exchange symbol:** IMN. **Annual sales/revenues:** More than $100 million. **Number of employees worldwide:** 2,100.

INTERNATIONAL ASSESSMENT NETWORK
7400 Metro Boulevard, Suite 350, Edina MN 55439. 952/921-9368. **Fax:** 952/844-9025. **Contact:** Human Resources. **World Wide Web address:** http://www.assessment.com. **Description:** Develops software and assessment products for jobseekers, career counselors, coaches, students, and companies.

KROLL ONTRACK INC
9023 Columbine Road, Eden Prairie MN 55347. 952/937-1107. **Toll-free phone:** 800/347-6105. **Fax:** 952/937-5750. **Contact:** Human Resources. **E-mail address:** hr@krollontrack.com. **World Wide Web address:** http://www.krollontrack.com. **Description:** Kroll Ontrack provides computer software and services to help companies and computer users worldwide manage, recover, and discover their valuable data. **Corporate headquarters location:** This location. **Parent company:** Marsh & McLennan.

LASER DESIGN INC.
9401 James Avenue South, Suite 132, Bloomington MN 55431. 952/884-9648. **Fax:** 952/884-9653. **Contact:** Personnel. **E-mail address:** sales@laserdesign.com. **World Wide Web address:** http://www.laserdesign.com. **Description:** Designs and manufactures three-dimensional laser scanners. **Positions advertised include:** Application Engineer.

LAWSON SOFTWARE
380 St. Peter Street, St. Paul MN 55102-1302. 651/767-7000. **Contact:** Human Resources. **World Wide Web address:** http://www.lawson.com. **Description:** Provides business application software and consulting services. **Positions advertised include:** Sr. Project Manager; Strategic Finance Analyst; Sr. Accountant; PSA Application Consultant; Engagement Manager; Database Administrator; Sr. Emerging Technology Web Developer; Manager, Marketing Operations; Sr. Application Development Manager. **Corporate headquarters location:** This location. **Listed on:** NASDAQ. **Stock exchange symbol:** LWSN.

LOCKHEED MARTIN MARITIME SYSTEMS & SENSORS
3333 Pilot Knob Road, Eagan MN 55121. 651/456-2222. **Contact:** Human Resources. **World Wide Web address:** http://www.lockheedmartin.com. **Description:** Maritime Systems & Sensors (MS2) provides surface, air, and undersea applications on more than 460 programs for U.S. military and international customers. **Positions advertised include:** Business Development Analysis Manager; Computer System Design Engineer; Cost-Schedule Analysis. **Corporate headquarters location:** Bethesda MD. **Operations at this facility include:** This location designs computer systems for the defense industry. **Parent company:** Lockheed Martin Corporation.

McDATA
6000 Nathan Lane North, Plymouth MN 55442. 763/268-6000. **Fax:** 763/268-6800. **Contact:** Human Resources. **World Wide Web address:** http://www.mcdata.com. **Description:** Provides storage networking solutions that help customers build, connect, optimize, and centrally manage data infrastructures across SAN, MAN, and WAN environments. **Positions advertised include:** Executive Admin; Contracts Analyst; Call Management Technician; Technical Support Engineer; Strategic Account Manager.

McKESSON PROVIDER TECHNOLOGIES
2700 Snelling Avenue North, Roseville MN 55113. 651/697-5900. **Contact:** Human Resources. **Email address:** jobs.infosolutions@mckesson.com. **World Wide Web address:** http://www.mckesson.com. **Description:** Provides information system solutions for the healthcare industry. **Positions advertised include:** Product Manager/Development Manager. **Parent company:** McKesson Corp.

METAFILE INFORMATION SYSTEMS INC.
2900 43rd Street Northwest, Rochester MN 55901-5895. 507/286-9232. **Fax:** 507/286-9065. **Contact:** Human Resources. **E-mail address:** jobs@metafile.com. **World Wide Web address:** http://www.metafileweb.com. **Description:** A software and systems integration company. Founded in 1979. **Special programs:** Internships.

MULTI-TECH SYSTEMS INC.
2205 Woodale Drive, Mounds View MN 55112. 763/785-3500. **Toll-free phone:** 800/328-9717. **Fax:** 763/785-9874. **Contact:** Human Resources. **World Wide Web address:** http://www.multitech.com. **Description:** Manufactures telephony, Internet, remote access, and device networking products.

NETASPX
1200 Washington Avenue South, Minneapolis MN 55415. 612/337-0200. **Fax:** 612/337-3400. **Contact:** Personnel Department. **E-mail address:** employment@netaspx.com **World Wide Web address:** http://www.netaspx.com. **Description:** Provides Lawson-managed applications for finance, human resources, accounting, payroll, and supply chain management. **Positions advertised include:** Windows Application Administrator. **Corporate headquarters location:** Herndon VA.

ORACLE
950 Nicollet Mall, Minneapolis MN 55403. 612/587-5000. **Toll-free phone:** 877/517-3835. **Fax:** 612/587-5100. **Contact:** Human Resources. **World Wide Web address:** http://www.oracle.com. **Description:** Retek is a worldwide provider of mission-critical software and services to the retail industry. Founded in 1986. **NOTE:** Do not submit resumes via e-mail. **Positions advertised include:** Software Engineer; Business Consultant; Technical Consultant; Revenue Recognition Director. **Corporate headquarters location:** Redwood Shores CA. **Other area locations:** Bloomington MN. **Other U.S. locations:** Nationwide. **Listed on:** NASDAQ. **Stock exchange symbol:** ORCL. **Number of employees worldwide:** 49,872.

PC SOLUTIONS
5155 East River Road, Suite 409, Minneapolis MN 55421. 763/852-1600. **Fax:** 763/852-1603. **Contact:** Human Resources. **E-mail address:** info@pcstechnology.com. **World Wide Web address:** http://www.pcstechnology.com. **Description:** Provides

security, networking, consulting, support, web development, and IT staffing services to local companies. **NOTE:** See website for current job openings. Submit resume by e-mail or fax. **Positions advertised include:** Network Engineer; Sales Engineer; Sales Associate.

PC WHOLESALE
1295 Bandana Boulevard, Suite 310, St. Paul MN 55108-5116. 651/632-5600. **Toll-free phone:** 800/801-6285. **Fax:** 651/632-5601. **Contact:** Human Resources. **World Wide Web address:** http://www.pcwholesale.com. **Description:** Distributes computer systems, peripherals, supplies, and services to an international client base. Founded in 1989. **Corporate headquarters location:** Bloomingdale IL. **Other U.S. locations:** MA; NJ.

PEARSON ASSESSMENTS
5601 Green Valley Drive, Bloomington MN 55437. 952/681-3000. **Toll-free phone:** 800/328-6172. **Contact:** Human Resources. **E-mail address:** pearsonassessments@pearson.com. **World Wide Web address:** http://www.pearsonncs.com. **Description:** A global information services company providing software, service, and systems for the collection, management, and interpretation of data. **Positions advertised include:** Director, Scanning Products. **Special programs:** Internships. **Corporate headquarters location:** This location. **Other U.S. locations:** Nationwide. **Parent company:** Pearson Education, Inc. (Pearson Plc). **Annual sales/revenues:** More than $100 million. **Number of employees nationwide:** 3,000.

QUALITY BUSINESS SOLUTIONS (QBS)
1250 Northland Drive, Suite 155, Mendota Heights MN 55120. 651/646-7154. **Contact:** Deborah Besch, Human Resources. **E-mail address:** dbesch@qbs.com. **World Wide Web address:** http://www.qbs.com. **Description:** QBS provides technology and project management services to corporations in the Twin Cities. The company's primary focus is on software and consulting services for health care, retail, and commercial businesses.

RIMAGE CORPORATION
7725 Washington Avenue South, Minneapolis MN 55439. 952/944-8144. **Fax:** 952/946-4576. **Contact:** Human Resources. **E-mail address:** hr@rimage.com. **World Wide Web address:** http://www.rimage.com. **Description:** Designs and manufactures CD-R/DVD-R duplication equipment. **NOTE:** See website for current job openings. Submit resume by mail, fax, or e-mail. **Positions advertised include:** Manufacturing Engineer; Program Manager. **Listed on:** NASDAQ. **Stock exchange symbol:** RIMG.

SPSS INC.
4115 Highway 52 North, Suite 300, Rochester MN 55901. 507/288-5922. **Contact:** Human Resources. **World Wide Web address:** http://www.showcasecorp.com. **Description:** Provides predictive analytics software and solutions. **NOTE:** Search and apply for positions online. **Positions advertised include:** Customer Support Representative; Product Manager; Product Support Specialist. **Corporate headquarters location:** Chicago IL.

SAGEBRUSH CORPORATION
7900 Xerxes Avenue South, Suite 600, Edina MN 55431. 952/656-2999. **Toll-free phone:** 800/328-2923. **Fax:** 952/656-2993. **Contact:** Human Resources. **E-mail address:** hr@sagebrushcorp.com. **World Wide Web address:** http://www.sagebrushcorp.com. **Description:** A developer of software for libraries. Products are used by librarians as well as by library patrons. **NOTE:** Search for positions online. Submit resume by e-mail.

SEAGATE TECHNOLOGY
7801 Computer Avenue South, Bloomington MN 55435-5412. 952/844-8000. **Fax:** 952/402-7008. **Contact:** Human Resources. **World Wide Web address:** http://www.seagate.com. **Description:** Seagate Technology is a designer and manufacturer of data storage devices and related products including hard disk drives, tape drives, software, and systems for many different computer-related applications and operating systems. These products include 2.5 and 3.5 inch drives with memory storage capacity between 150 megabytes and one gigabyte. **Special programs:** Training. **Corporate headquarters location:** George Town, Cayman Islands. **Other area locations:** Shakopee MN. **Other U.S. locations:** CA; CO; OK; PA. **Operations at this facility include:** This location is a manufacturing and R&D facility for Seagate's recording heads operation. **Annual sales/revenues:** More than $100 million. **Number of employees at this location:** 3,500. **Number of employees nationwide:** 89,000.

SOFTBRANDS, INC.
Two Meridian Crossings, Suite 800, Minneapolis MN 55423. 612/851-1500. **Fax:** 612/851-1560. **Contact:** Human Resources. **World Wide Web address:** http://www.fs.com. **Description:** An international company that provides enterprise software and support solutions for small to medium-sized businesses worldwide. The company operates through two segments, Manufacturing and Hospitality. **International locations:** Worldwide.

SOFTWARE AG AMERICAS
1650 West 82nd Street, Suite 750, Bloomington MN 55431. 952/948-3500. **Contact:** Recruiting. **E-mail address:** jobs@softwareagusa.com. **World Wide Web address:** http://www.softwareagusa.com. **Description:** Provides system software and high-performance databases to allow customers to run cross-platform applications, and to simplify the exchange of data between systems. **Corporate headquarters location:** Reston VA. **International locations:** Germany. **Parent company:** Software AG (Germany). **Operations at this facility include:** This location develops software products and serves as a regional sales office for Software AG Americas.

SUN MICROSYSTEMS
33 South Sixth Street, 4130 Multifoods Tower, Suite 4130, Minneapolis MN 55402. 612/339-6161. **Fax:** 612/321-5718. **World Wide Web address:** http://www.sun.com. **Description:** Provides products and services for network computing that consist of computer systems, network storage systems, support services, and professional and knowledge services. **Corporate headquarters location:** Santa Clara CA. **Other U.S. locations:** Nationwide. **International locations:** Worldwide. **Listed on:** NASDAQ. **Stock exchange symbol:** SUNW.

TRANSITION NETWORKS
6475 City West Parkway, Eden Prairie MN 55344. 952/941-7600. **Fax:** 952/941-2322. **Contact:** Human Resources. **E-mail address:** hr@transition.com. **World Wide Web address:** http://www.transition.com. **Description:** Provides network connectivity solutions that allow for the conversion of different media types. **Positions advertised include:** Inside Sales Account Manager; International Account Manager (Latin America & Asia); Field Applications/Sales Engineer; Outside Sales Manager, Mid-Atlantic Region; Assembly & Test Technician I. **Corporate headquarters location:** This location. **Parent company:** Communications Systems, Inc.

TREEFORT.NET, INC.
4317 Upton Ave South, Minneapolis MN 55410. 612/285-5625. **Fax:** 800/728-2967. **Contact:** Staffing. **E-mail address:** solutions@treefort.net. **World Wide Web address:** http://www.treefort.net. **Description:** A web development firm primarily serving small-and medium-sized businesses and organizations across the United States. **NOTE:** Submit resume by e-mail.

TREEV LLC
6 Pine Tree Drive, Suite 150, Arden Hills MN 55112. 651/486-7901. **Toll-free phone:** 800/229-5430. **Fax:**

651/486-7911. **Contact:** Human Resources. **E-mail address:** jobs@treev.com. **World Wide Web address:** http://www.treev.com. **Description:** Provides software and consulting services to financial institutions. **NOTE:** Search and apply for positions online. **Corporate headquarters location:** Herndon VA. **Parent company:** Metavante Corp.

TRIMIN SYSTEMS, INC.
2277 Highway 36 West, Suite 101E, Roseville MN 55113. 651/636-7667. **Fax:** 651/636-9932. **Contact:** Staffing. **World Wide Web address:** http://www.triminsystems.com. **Description:** Engaged in the implementation of information systems and technology for manufacturing companies and government organizations. Founded in 1986.

XATA CORPORATION
151 East Cliff Road, Suite 10, Burnsville MN 55337. 952/707-5600. **Fax:** 952/894-2463. **Contact:** Human Resources. **E-mail address:** hr@xata.com. **World Wide Web address:** http://www.xata.com. **Description:** Manufactures onboard computers and software for the transportation and logistics segments of the fleet trucking industry. Founded in 1985. **Corporate headquarters location:** This location. **Listed on:** NASDAQ. **Stock exchange symbol:** XATA.

ZOMAX INCORPORATED
5353 Nathan Lane, Plymouth MN 55442. 763/553-9300. **Fax:** 763/553-0826. **Contact:** Human Resources. **E-mail address:** jobs@zomax.com. **World Wide Web address:** http://www.zomax.com. **Description:** A supply chain outsourcing services company. The company offers various supply chain services principally comprising customer contact services, including inbound/outbound telecommunication services, order processing, billing services, and e-commerce; sourcing services, such as print, packaging, and hardware procurement services to support customers' businesses; media requirements in the production of CD and DVD; assembly and kitting services to handle various products; and various retail and end-customer distribution models and integrated returns management services. **NOTE:** To view current listings and apply for an open position, visit Hotjobs.com and Monster.com. **Corporate headquarters location:** This location. **Other U.S. locations:** Brooklyn Park MN. **Other U.S. locations:** CA; TN. **International locations:** Canada; Germany; Ireland. **Listed on:** NASDAQ. **Stock exchange symbol:** ZOMX. **Annual sales/revenues:** $100 million.

Mississippi

CREATIVE CONTROLLERS INC.
128 Kendrick Lane, Picayune MS 39466. 601/798-0577. **Toll-free phone:** 800/950-6224. **Fax:** 601/798-0656. **Contact:** General Manager. **E-mail address:** cci@datastar.net. **Description:** Manufactures boards that interface with IBM computers, enabling their compatibility to all types of printers.

DIVERSIFIED TECHNOLOGY, INC.
P.O. Box 748, Ridgeland MS 39158. 601/856-4121. **Physical address:** 476 Highland Colony Parkway, Ridgeland MS 39157. **Toll-free phone:** 800/443-2667. **Fax:** 601/898-4157. **Contact:** Human Resources Department. **E-mail address:** personnel@dtims.com. **World Wide Web address:** http://www.dtims.com. **Description:** Manufactures passive backplane, PC compatible single board computers and blades that are used in a wide array of industrial applications. Founded in 1971. **Positions advertised include:** Manufacturing/Industrial Engineer; Electronic Repair Specialist. **Corporate headquarters location:** This location. **Parent company:** Ergon, Inc. **Listed on:** Privately held.

Missouri

ACS
229 North 7th Street, St. Louis MO 63101. 314/450-2825. **Contact:** Human Resources. **World Wide Web address:** http://www.acs-inc.com. **Description:** A provider of diversified business process and information technology outsourcing solutions to commercial and government clients. **NOTE:** Search and apply for positions online. **Positions advertised include:** Parking Consultant. **Corporate headquarters location:** Dallas TX. **Listed on:** New York Stock Exchange. **Stock exchange symbol:** ACS. **Number of employees worldwide:** 40,000.

AOS, L.L.C.
403 Axminister Drive, Fenton MO 63026. 636/680-1000. **Contact:** Thatcher Alexander, Human Resources. **E-mail address:** thatchera@aos5.com **World Wide Web address:** http://www.globalsolutionsgroup.com. **Description:** Develops IT solutions through consultation, design, and implementation. **Positions advertised include:** Sr. Microsoft Systems Engineer; Account Manager; Scheduler; Web Developer; Computer Operator.

ACCENTURE
1010 Market Street, St. Louis, Missouri 63101. 314/345-3000. **Fax:** 314/345-3505. **Contact:** Human Resources. **World Wide Web address:** http://www.accenture.com. **Description:** Accenture is a global management consulting, technology services, and outsourcing company. The company helps clients identify and enter new markets, increase revenues in existing markets, improve operational performance, and deliver their products and services more effectively and efficiently. Founded in 1989. **NOTE:** Search and apply for positions online. **Positions advertised include:** JAVA/J2EE Sr. Programmer/Analyst Programmer; Cobol Sr. Programmer; Cobol Systems Analyst.

AJILON SERVICES INC.
425 South Woodsmill Road, Suite 110, Town & Country MO 63017-3441. 314/434-5003. **Fax:** 314/434-7441. **Contact:** Human Resources Department. **E-mail address:** recruit@stlouis.ajilon.com. **World Wide Web address:** http://www.ajilon.com. **Description:** Offers computer consulting services, project support, and end user services. **Other U.S. locations:** Nationwide. **Parent company:** Adecco

ANALYSTS INTERNATIONAL CORPORATION (AIC)
Broadway Summit, 3101 Broadway, Suite 550, Kansas City MO 64111-2416. 816/531-5050. **Toll-free phone:** 800/530-5259. **Fax:** 888/442-4122. **Contact:** Human Resources Department. **E-mail address:** kc.jobs@analysts.com. **World Wide Web address:** http://www.analysts.com. **Description:** AiC is an international computer consulting firm. The company assists clients in developing systems in a variety of industries using different programming languages and software. **NOTE:** Search and apply for positions online. **Positions advertised include:** Natural Adabase Programmer. **Corporate headquarters location:** Minneapolis MN. **Other area locations:** St. Louis MO. **Other U.S. locations:** Nationwide. **Listed on:** NASDAQ. **Stock exchange symbol:** ANALY. **Annual sales/revenues:** More than $100 million.

BRICK NETWORK
1000 Macklind Avenue, Lower Level, St. Louis MO 63100. 314/645-5550. **Fax:** 314/638-7814. **Toll-free phone:** 888/999-7540. **Contact:** Human Resources. **E-mail address:** job@brick.net. **World Wide Web address:** http://www.brick.net. **Description:** A local network service provider for St. Louis area businesses.

CERNER CORPORATION
2800 Rockcreek Parkway, Kansas City MO 64117. 816/221-1024. **Fax:** 816/474-1742. **Contact:** Human Resources. **World Wide Web address:** http://www.cerner.com. **Description:** Cerner designs, installs, and supports software systems for the health care industry including hospitals, HMOs, clinics, physicians' offices, and integrated health organizations. **NOTE:** Search and apply for positions online. **Positions advertised include:** Business Analyst;

Human Resources Operations Support; Graphic Designer; Sr. Software Engineer; Legal Specialist; Technology Engineer; Operations Analyst; Java Architect. **Corporate headquarters location:** This location. **Other U.S. locations:** Nationwide. **Operations at this facility include:** This location develops software. **Listed on:** NASDAQ. **Stock exchange symbol:** CERN. **Annual sales/revenues:** More than $100 million. **Number of employees worldwide:** 5,100.

CIBER INFORMATION SERVICES
12312 Olive Boulevard, Suite 175, St. Louis MO 63141. 314/434-7900. **Toll-free phone:** 800/878-1596. **Fax:** 314/434-1117. **Contact:** Recruiter. **World Wide Web address:** http://www.ciber.com. **Description:** Provides consulting for client/server development, mainframe and legacy systems, industry-specific analysis, application-specific analysis, and network development. Founded in 1974. **NOTE:** Search and apply for positions online. **Positions advertised include:** Java Middleware Developer; Information Architect; JAVA Developer; Sr. ABAP Programmer/Analyst; QA Software Tester. **Corporate headquarters location:** Greenwood Village CO. **Other U.S. locations:** Nationwide. **Listed on:** New York Stock Exchange. **Stock exchange symbol:** CBR. **Number of employees at this location:** 115. **Number of employees nationwide:** 4,000.

CITATION COMPUTER SYSTEMS, INC.
424 South Woods Mill Road, Suite 200, Chesterfield MO 63017. 314/579-7900. **Contact:** Vice President of Human Resources. **World Wide Web address:** http://www.cita.com. **Description:** Designs, develops, markets, and services cost-effective proprietary networking systems for laboratories, financial/administrative departments, and order communications/results reporting areas. These systems are marketed to hospitals, group practices, clinics, reference laboratories, and nursing homes. **Positions advertised include:** Test Analyst. **NOTE:** Search and apply for positions online. **Parent Company:** Cerner Corporation. **Listed on:** NASDAQ. **Stock exchange symbol:** CERN. **Number of employees at this location:** 110. **Number of employees nationwide:** 185.

DST SYSTEMS, INC.
333 West 11th Street, Kansas City MO 64105. 816/435-1000. **Contact:** Human Resources. **World Wide Web address:** http://www.dstsystems.com. **Description:** A software developer and transfer agent for the financial industry. **NOTE:** Entry-level positions are offered. **Special programs:** Internships. **Corporate headquarters location:** This location. **Subsidiaries include:** Argus Health Systems, Inc.; NFDS. **Number of employees at this location:** 6,000.

DAUGHERTY SYSTEMS
Three City Place Drive, Suite 400, St. Louis MO 63141. 314/432-8200. **Fax:** 314/432-8217. **Contact:** Human Resources. **E-mail address:** staffingstl@daugherty.com. **World Wide Web address:** http://www.daugherty.com. **Description:** A computer consulting firm. **Special programs:** Training. **Corporate headquarters location:** This location. **Other U.S. locations:** Atlanta GA; Chicago IL; Baltimore MD; Dallas TX. **Listed on:** Privately held. **Annual sales/revenues:** $21 - $50 million. **Number of employees at this location:** 190. **Number of employees nationwide:** 300.

DIAGRAPH CORPORATION
One Missouri Research Park Drive, St. Charles MO 63304-5685. 636/300-2000. **Toll-free phone:** 800/526-2531. **Contact:** Human Resources. **E-mail address:** hr@diagraph.com. **World Wide Web address:** http://www.diagraph.com. **Description:** A manufacturer of ink-jet printers.

FAIRCOM
6300 West Sugar Creek Drive, Columbia MO 65203-0100. 573/445-6833. **Fax:** 573/445-9698. **Contact:** Human Resources Department. **World Wide Web address:** http://www.faircom.com. **Description:** Develops database file handler software. Founded in 1979. **NOTE:** Entry-level positions are offered. **Office hours:** Monday - Friday, 9:00 a.m. - 5:00 p.m. **Corporate headquarters location:** This location. **International locations:** Brazil; Italy; Japan. **Listed on:** Privately held. **Number of employees worldwide:** 35.

FINANCIAL INFORMATION TECHNOLOGY INC.
P.O. Box 1058, Blue Springs MO 64013-1058. 816/229-8225. **Physical address:** 1504 NW Mock, Blue Springs MO 64013. **Contact:** Al Opsal, Recruiting. **Description:** Develops policy administration software packages for insurance agencies.

HEARTLAND TECHNOLOGY SOLUTIONS
526 South Main Street, Joplin MO 64801. 417/623-5553. **Contact:** Human Resources. **World Wide Web address:** http://www.cpoint-joplin.com. **Description:** Provides IT solutions for small and medium-sized businesses. **Other U.S. locations:** Harlan IA; Ames IA.

JACK HENRY AND ASSOCIATES, INC.
663 West Highway 60, P.O. Box 807, Monett MO 65708-0807. 417/235-6652. **Fax:** 972/359-5609. **Contact:** Anne Puddister, Human Resources. **E-mail address:** hr@jackhenry.com. **World Wide Web address:** http://www.jackhenry.com. **Description:** Provides integrated computer systems to banks and other financial institutions for in-house data processing. The company also provides data conversion, software installation, and software customization services for the implementation of its systems, as well as customer maintenance and support services. Founded in 1976. **NOTE:** Search and apply for positions online. **Positions advertised include:** Development Programmer; Business Analyst; Programmer Analyst; Corporate Disaster Recovery Manager. **Special programs:** Internships. **Corporate headquarters location:** This location. **Other U.S. locations:** St. Paul MN; Charlotte NC; Houston TX. **Subsidiaries include:** Bankvision Software, Ltd.; Commlink Corporation; Jack Henry International, Ltd. **President/CEO:** Michael E. Henry. **Annual sales/revenues:** $51 - $100 million. **Number of employees at this location:** 340. **Number of employees nationwide:** 500.

IBM CORPORATION
325 James S Mcdonnell Boulevard, Hazelwood MO 63042. 314/731-2328. **Toll-free phone:** 800/796-9876. **Contact:** IBM Staffing Services. **World Wide Web address:** http://www.ibm.com. **Description:** IBM Corporation is a developer, manufacturer, and marketer of advanced information processing products including computers and microelectronic technology, software, networking systems, and information technology-related services. **NOTE:** Search and apply for positions online. Positions advertised include: IT Architect/Specialist. **Corporate headquarters location:** Armonk NY. **International locations:** Africa; Asia Pacific; Canada; Europe; Latin America; Middle East. **Operations at this facility include:** This location is a sales office. **Subsidiaries include:** IBM Credit Corporation; IBM Instruments, Inc.; IBM World Trade Corporation.

IMPACT TECHNOLOGIES, INC.
16647 Chesterfield Grove, Suite 200, Chesterfield MO 63005. 314/743-1400. **Fax:** 314/763-1401. **Contact:** Human Resources. **E-mail address:** HR@impacttech.com. **World Wide Web address:** http://www.impacttech.com. **Description:** Develops software for telecommunications applications. Founded in 1990. **NOTE:** Search and apply for positions online. **Positions advertised include:** Network Engineer.

JBM ELECTRONICS COMPANY
4645 Laguardia Drive, St. Louis MO 63134-3100. 314/426-7781. **Toll-free phone:** 800/489-7781. **Fax:** 314/426-0007. **Contact:** Human Resources. **World**

Wide Web address: http://www.jbmelectronics.com. **Description:** Manufactures network connectivity products including TC/IP, ethernet and token ring, frame relays, and ISDNs. Founded in 1975.

MISSOURI INFORMATION SOLUTIONS
8333 East State Route 350, Kansas City MO 64133. 816/358-5545. **Fax:** 816/358-5546. **Contact:** Human Resources. **World Wide Web address:** http://www.moinfo.com. **Description:** A provider of hardware, software, voice, data, and video networking that also provides service and support. **NOTE:** Apply online.

MULTIDATA SYSTEMS INTERNATIONAL CORPORATION
9801 Manchester Road, St. Louis MO 63119. 314/968-6880. **Contact:** Human Resources. **E-mail address:** jobs@multidata-systems.com. **World Wide Web address:** http://www.multidata-systems.com. **Description:** Provider of radiation oncology products and systems. Founded in 1979. **NOTE:** Search and apply for positions online. **Positions advertised include:** Sr. Delphi Programmer; Product Design Engineer; Application Support Specialist.

THE NEWBERRY GROUP
2440 Executive Drive, Suite 208, St. Charles MO 63303. 636/928-9944. **Fax:** 636/928-8899. **Contact:** Human Resources. **World Wide Web address:** http://thenewberrygroup.com. **Description:** Specializes in IT and systems consulting services. **NOTE:** Search and apply for positions online. **Positions advertised include:** Sr. Data Security Analyst; Sr. IT Client/Server Developer/Programmer. **Other U.S. locations:** Stroudsburg PA; Arlington VA.

QUALITY SOFTWARE ENGINEERING, INC.
10820 Sunset Office Drive, Suite 302, St. Louis MO 63127-1037. 314/965-7800. **Fax:** 314/965-7802. **Contact:** Human Resources. **E-mail address:** resumes@qse.com. **World Wide Web address:** http://www.qse.com. **Description:** An information technology consulting and services firm. The Information Systems Consulting Division provides services to professionals including application system development and maintenance, database administration, system installation and management, network installation and management, technical writing, training, quality assurance, project management, and management consulting. The Information Technologies Division provides services for clients who outsource those functions, including hardware and software evaluation and selection, installation, systems integration, project development services, training, and end user support. **NOTE:** Search and apply for positions online. **Positions advertised include:** Technical Resource Planner; Process Improvement Specialist; Project Managers; Business Objects Developer; Client/Server Programmer/Analyst; Java Application Team Lead/Developer. **Corporate headquarters location:** This location.

SAVVIS COMMUNICATIONS INC.
1 Savvis Parkway, Town & Country MO 63017. 314/628-7000. **Contact:** Human Resources. **World Wide Web address:** http://www.savvis.net. **Description:** An IT utility provider that delivers secure and reliable hosting, network, and application services. **Positions advertised include:** Billing Analyst; Revenue Assurance Analyst; Collection Analyst; Fixed Asset Accountant; Sr. Analyst Carrier Management; Metrics Sr. Analyst; Sr. Procurement Manager. **Other U.S. locations:** Atlanta GA; Waltham MA; Chicago IL; Dallas TX; Denver CO; Santa Clara CA; Miami FL; New York NY; San Francisco CA.

SIRSI CORPORATION
1276 North Warson Road, St. Louis MO 63132-1806. 314/432-1100. **Toll-free phone:** 800/325-0888. **Fax:** 314/993-8927. **Contact:** Human Resources. **E-mail address:** hr-stl@sirsi.com. **World Wide Web address:** http://www.sirsi.com. **Description:** An automation systems integrator for libraries and other information providers. Sirsi's products and services improve efficiency in traditional library operations and give libraries networking capabilities. Sirsi's automation systems and networking services are adaptable for use in libraries of various sizes. Sirsi's customer base includes more than 10,000 libraries worldwide. Founded in 1975. **Positions advertised include:** Data Conversion Specialist; JAVA Developer; Software Trainer. **Corporate headquarters location:** Huntsville AL.

SKYWALKER COMMUNICATIONS
9390 Veterans Memorial Parkway, O'Fallon MO 63366. 636/272-8025. **Toll-free phone:** 800/844-9555. **Contact:** Human Resources. **E-mail address:** jobs@skywalker.com. **World Wide Web address:** http://www.skywalker.com. **Description:** Distributes satellite systems and computer products including mice, modems, and scanners. **Corporate headquarters location:** This location.

SOCKET INTERNET
810 Cherry Street, Columbia MO 65201. 573/817-0000. **Fax:** 573/875-5812. **Toll-free phone:** 800/762-5383. **Contact:** Human Resources. **E-mail address:** joinsocket@socket.net. **World Wide Web address:** http://www.socket.net. **Description:** An internet service provider for homes and businesses. **Positions advertised include:** Major Account Representative; Sales Representative; Customer Service Representative; Technical Support Agent.

TALX CORPORATION
11432 Lackland Road, Saint Louis MO 63146. 314/214-7000. **Toll-free phone:** 800/888-8277. **Fax:** 314/214-7588. **Contact:** Human Resources Manager. **E-mail address:** hr@talx.com. **World Wide Web address:** http://www.talx.com. **Description:** A business process outsourcer of payroll and HR functions. **NOTE:** Search and apply for positions online. **Positions advertised include:** Claims Service Representative; Director of Training; Equipment Technician; Payroll Data Analyst. **Other U.S. locations:** Hilliard OH; Richardson TX. **Listed on:** NASDAQ. **Stock exchange symbol:** TALX. **Number of employees nationwide:** 1,000.

TRIPOS INC.
1699 South Hanley Road, St. Louis MO 63144. 314/647-1099. **Toll-free phone:** 800/323-2960. **Fax:** 314/647-9241. **Contact:** Human Resources Manager. **E-mail address:** hr@tripos.com. **World Wide Web address:** http://www.tripos.com. **Description:** A provider of discovery chemistry, integrated discovery software products, software consulting services, and discovery research services to the pharmaceutical, biotechnology, agrochemical, and other life sciences industries. **NOTE:** Search and apply for positions online. **Positions advertised include:** Controller; Database Application Developer. **Corporate headquarters location:** This location. **Listed on:** NASDAQ. **Stock exchange symbol:** TRPS.

WORLD WIDE TECHNOLOGY INC.
62 Weldon Parkway, Maryland Heights MO 63043. 314/569-7000. **Fax:** 314/919-1441. **Contact:** Human Resources. **E-mail address:** careers@wwt.com. **World Wide Web address:** http://www.wwt.com. **Description:** Provides information technology solutions for e-commerce supply chains. **Positions advertised include:** Contract Administrator; Maintenance Coordinator; Price Analyst; Business Systems Analyst; Lab Manager. **Other U.S. locations:** Phoenix AZ; Livermore CA; Los Angeles CA; Detroit MI; Reno NV; Nashville TN; Austin TX; Plano TX; San Antonio TX; Mclean VA.

XYQUAD INC.
2921 South Brentwood Boulevard, St. Louis MO 63144-2700. 314/961-5995. **Toll-free phone:** 800/228-3168. **Fax:** 314/961-8094. **Contact:** Human Resources. **World Wide Web address:** http://www.xyquad.com. **Description:** A computer integration firm, specializing in systems automation and providing a variety of

computer related services to financial, industrial and government clients nationwide. **Corporate headquarters location:** This location.

Montana

5 STAR BUSINESS TECHNOLOGY GROUP
1515 Wyoming Street, Missoula MT 59801. 406/532-5454. **Fax:** 406/532-5451. **Contact:** Human Resources. **Description:** Provides networking services for a variety of systems including Compaq and Hewlett-Packard. **Corporate headquarters location:** This location. **Annual sales/revenues:** Less than $5 million.

LOGISTICS SYSTEMS INC.
3000 Palmer Street, Missoula MT 59808. 406/728-0921. **Fax:** 406/728-8754. **Contact:** Human Resources. **E-mail address:** careers@logistic-systems.com. **World Wide Web address:** http://www.logistic-systems.com. **Description:** Develops logistics and inventory management software used by police and fire departments. **Positions advertised include:** Project Manager; Programmer; UNIX Trainer; Technical Support Troubleshooter; Software Tester; Information Technology Specialist; Network Administrator.

MSE TECHNOLOGY APPLICATIONS, INC.
P.O. Box 4078, Butte MT 59702. 406/494-7385. **Physical address:** 200 Technology Way, Butte MT 59701. **Fax:** 406/494-7230. **Contact:** Leslie Clark, Human Resources Manager. **E-mail address:** jobs@mse-ta.com. **World Wide Web address:** http://www.mse-ta.com. **Description:** An advanced technology development firm that manages federal government technology research and development. The company develops, tests, evaluates, and deploys technologies for the energy and aerospace sector. The company maintains a Tetragenics Division, which manufactures communications software and hardware for monitoring and control systems used in hydroelectric plants. **Corporate headquarters location:** Montana Economic Revitalization and Development Institute, MERI, 65 East Broadway, Butte, MT. **Other area locations:** Bozeman MT. **Other U.S. locations:** Sacramento CA; Washington DC; Idaho Falls ID; Fort Bragg NC; Pittsburgh PA; Richland WA; Morgantown WV. **Subsidiaries include:** Tetragenics Division. **Number of employees nationwide:** 206.

NORTHROP GRUMMAN MISSION SYSTEMS
2401 Colonial Drive, Helena MT 59601. 406/443-8600. **Contact:** Human Resources. **World Wide Web address:** http://www.Northropgrumman.com. **Description:** This is the former TRW Systems location that develops software. Overall, the company is an information technology services firm whose operating subsidiaries provide research and development and contract support to clients in the following industries: aerospace, automotive markets, national defense, communications, energy, transportation, environmental, and other areas. **NOTE:** Due to high volume of applicants – search postings and apply online only. No paper accepted. **Positions advertised include:** Systems Engineer; IS Technologist. **Corporate headquarters:** Los Angeles CA. **Other U.S. locations:** Nationwide. **International locations:** Worldwide. **Parent company:** TRW/Mission Systems remains a wholly owned subsidiary of the Northrop Grumman Corporation. **Listed on:** New York Stock Exchange. **Stock exchange symbol:** NOC. **Number of employees nationwide:** 15,000.

RIGHTNOW TECHNOLOGIES, INC.
40 Enterprise Boulevard, P.O. Box 9300, Bozeman MT 59718. 406/522-2942. **Toll-free phone:** 877/363-5678. **Fax:** 406/522-4227. **Contact:** Phyllis Wernikowski, Human Resources. **World Wide Web address:** http://www.rightnow.com. **Description:** A provider of customer service solutions offering unified, online customer service operations, plus tools for online surveys, data analysis, call center management and marketing. Products feature quick installation, Web hosting, and professional support services. Founded in 1997. **NOTE:** Online application available on company Website. **Positions advertised include:** Linux System Administrator; Marketing Project Manager; Senior Quality Assurance Engineer; Software Developer; Technical Writer; Implementation Specialist; Pro Services Integration Architect; Direct Response Rep. **Corporate headquarters location:** This location. **Other U.S. locations:** Dallas TX. **International locations:** Australia; Germany; Japan; United Kingdom. **Number of employees worldwide:** 260.

Nebraska

ACI WORLDWIDE
330 South 108th Avenue, Omaha NE 68154-2602. 402/390-7600. **Fax:** 402/330-1528. **Contact:** Lauralee Neubauer, Personnel. **World Wide Web address:** http://www.aciworldwide.com. **Description:** Manufactures the BASE24 family of software. Products include electronic payment, wire transfer, and clearing software solutions. ACI supports customers operating over 900 systems in more than 71 countries on six continents including some of the world's largest financial institutions, retailers, petroleum companies, and data processing service bureaus. The company also offers a suite of networking, connectivity, transaction delivery, and system software tools that help customers maximize the value of their operations. Founded in 1975. **Positions advertised include:** Division Controller; Engineer/Sr.; Engineer; Executive Assistant; Sr./Pre-Sales Support Analyst; Sr./Tax Analyst; Sr./Product Manager; Sr. Manager of Finance. **Corporate headquarters location:** This location. **Parent company:** Transaction Systems Architects, Inc. **Listed on:** NASDAQ. **Stock exchange symbol:** TSAI. **Annual sales/revenues:** More than $100 million. More than $100 million. **Number of employees at this location:** 600. **Number of employees nationwide:** 650. **Number of employees worldwide:** 1,000.

ACHALA CREATIVE SOLUTIONS
3141 North 93rd Street, Omaha NE 68134. 402/343-0920. **Fax:** 402/343-1004. **Contact:** Recruitment. **E-mail address:** jobs@achala.com. **World Wide Web address:** http://www.achala.com. **Description:** Provides IT consulting, Internet development, and website creation.

ANALYSTS INTERNATIONAL CORPORATION (AIC)
6610 So. 118th Street, Omaha NE 68137. 402/861-0061. **Toll-free phone:** 800/735-3300. **Fax:** 402/861-0064. **Contact:** Human Resources. **E-mail address:** jobs@analysts.com. **World Wide Web address:** http://www.analysts.com. **Description:** AIC is an international computer consulting firm. The company assists clients in developing systems in a variety of industries using different programming languages and software. **Positions advertised include:** Sr. level data administrator. **Corporate headquarters location:** Minneapolis MN. **Other U.S. locations:** Nationwide. **International locations:** Canada; United Kingdom. **Listed on:** NASDAQ. **Stock exchange symbol:** ANLY.

AUTOMATED SYSTEMS, INC.
P.O. Box 22277, Lincoln NE 68542. 402/420-6000. **Physical address:** 1201 Libra Drive, Lincoln NE 68512. **Fax:** 402/420-6006. **Contact:** Human Resources. **World Wide Web address:** http://www.asiweb.com. **Description:** Automated Systems is engaged in network design, sales, installation, management, training, and support services. Founded in 1981. **Positions advertised include:** Network Engineer; Sales Consultant; Software Support Specialist; Part-time Application Support Specialist; Account Executive; Delphi Developer/Programmer; Application Developer. **Corporate headquarters location:** This location. **Other U.S. locations:** Lenexa KS. **Operations at this facility include:** This location houses administrative offices.

BOOZ ALLEN HAMILTON
1299 Farnam Street, Suite 1230, Omaha NE 68102. 402/522-2800. **Fax:** 308/254-4800. **Contact:** Human

Resources. **World Wide Web address:** http://www.boozallen.com. **Description:** A global strategy and technology consulting firm. **NOTE:** For employment opportunities, visit website, do not call. **Positions advertised include:** Information Operations JMEN CND Analyst; Human Source Intelligence Analyst; Operational Concepts Analyst; Sr. Associate Financial Services. **Other U.S. locations:** Nationwide. **International locations:** Worldwide.

CENTURION WIRELESS TECHNOLOGIES INC.
P.O. Box 82846, Lincoln NE 68501. 402/467-4491. **Physical address:** 3425 North 44th Street, Lincoln NE 68504. **Fax:** 402/465-1338. **Contact:** Human Resources. **E-mail address:** USHR@centurion.com. **World Wide Web address:** http://www.centurion.com. **Description:** A leading designer and manufacturer of antennas and batteries for the wireless communications industry. **Positions advertised include:** Customer Care Representative; Director of Engineering; Manufacturing Engineer; Quality Engineer; Mechanical Design Technician; Mechanical Engineer; RF Engineer.

COMPUTER CABLE CONNECTION, INC.
P.O. Box 1269, Bellevue NE 68005-1269. 402/291-9500. **Physical address:** 2810 Harlan Drive, Bellevue NE 68005. **Toll-free phone:** 800/535-1715. **Fax:** 402/291-0179. **Contact:** Human Resources. **World Wide Web address:** http://www.cccne.com. **Description:** Installs office networking systems and provides various custom cabling services, including technological consulting, design, and installation. **President:** Eric Parks.

EX-CEL SOLUTIONS, INC.
14618 Grover Street, Omaha NE 68144. 402/333-6541. **Fax:** 402/333-3124. **Contact:** Human Resources. **E-mail address:** recruiters@excels.com. **World Wide Web address:** http://www.excels.com. **Description:** Provides customized computer sales, service, and maintenance. Ex-Cel Solutions is a systems integrator for Novell Netware and Windows NT networks. Founded in 1974. **Positions advertised include:** Visual Basic - Oracle Programmer. **NOTE:** Entry-level positions are offered. Please see website for online application form and printable application. **Office hours:** Monday - Friday, 8:00 a.m. - 5:00 p.m. **Corporate headquarters location:** This location. **Listed on:** Privately held. **President:** Glenn J. Stenger. **Annual sales/revenues:** $11 - $20 million. **Number of employees at this location:** 55.

INFORMATION TECHNOLOGY, INC.
P.O. Box 22705, Lincoln NE 68542-2705. 402/423-2682. **Physical address:** 1345 Old Cheney Road, Lincoln NE 68512. 402/423-2682. **Contact:** Human Resources. **NOTE:** Human Resources phone is 402/421-4269. **World Wide Web address:** http://www.itiwnet.com. **Description:** Develops financial software for companies in the banking industry. **Positions advertised include:** Sales Executive; Conversion Programmer; Customer Support Analyst; Software Development Analyst; Technical Writer. **Parent company:** Fiserv, Inc.

MODIS
12829 West Dodge Road, Omaha NE 68154. 402/333-1700. **Fax:** 402/333-2239. **Contact:** Human Resources. **E-mail address:** resume@modisit.com. **World Wide Web address:** http://www.modisit.com. **NOTE:** Please see website for online application form. **Description:** A consulting firm that specializes in software. Founded in 1987. **Corporate headquarters location:** Jacksonville FL. **Other U.S. locations:** Nationwide. **Annual sales/revenues:** $21 - $50 million.

NORTHROP GRUMMAN
1408 Fort Crook Road South, Bellevue NE 68005. 402/291-8300. **Contact:** Human Resources. **World Wide Web address:** http://www.northropgrumman.com. **NOTE:** Please see website for information on how to apply. **Description:** A developer of client/server and distributed computing software. The company develops, markets, and supports enterprise management, database and applications development, business applications, and consumer software products for a broad range of mainframe, midrange, and desktop computers. Northrop Grumman serves major business, government, research, and educational organizations. **Positions advertised include:** Software Test Lead; Contracts Administrator; PR Cis Development; Human Resources Generalist; Systems Software Engineer; Customer Service Analyst; Technical Service Engineer; Lead Engineer; Technical Writer; Software Installer/Maintainer; Software Engineer. **Corporate headquarters location:** Los Angeles, CA. **Other U.S. locations:** Nationwide. **International locations;** UK, Norway, Austria, Japan. **Operations at this facility include:** Information technology, Missions systems. **Listed on:** New York Stock Exchange. **Stock exchange symbol:** NOC. **Number of employees worldwide:** 120,000.

Nevada
ACUITY SOLUTIONS
7881 West Charleston Boulevard, Suite 165, Las Vegas NV 89117. 702/966-2000. **Contact:** Diana Miller, Office Manager. **E-mail address:** dmiller@acuitynv.com. **World Wide Web address:** http://www.acuitynv.com. **Description:** A technology consulting firm that designs accounting and business management software solutions. **Corporate headquarters location:** This location.

ARCATA ASSOCIATES, INC.
2588 Fire Mesa Street, Suite 110, Las Vegas NV 89128. 702/642-9500. **Fax:** 702/968-2238. **Contact:** Director of Human Resources. **E-mail address:** resumes@arcataassoc.com. **World Wide Web address:** http://www.arcataassoc.com. **Description:** Provides computer engineering and systems manufacturing services. **Positions advertised include:** Quality Assurance Engineer II; Computer Operator IV. **Corporate headquarters location:** This location. **Other area locations:** Fallon NV. **Other U.S. locations:** Huntsville AL; Barstow CA; Greenbelt MD; Las Cruces NM; Wallops Island VA.

COMGLOBAL SYSTEMS INC.
7385 Prairie Falcon Road, Suite 150, Las Vegas NV 89128. 702/856-3363. **Fax:** 702/869-9530. **Contact:** Human Resources. **E-mail address:** apply@comglobal.com. **World Wide Web address:** http://www.comglobal.com. **Description:** Provides information technology solutions for federal agencies, including defense. **Positions advertised include:** Software Engineer. **Corporate headquarters location:** San Diego CA. **Other U.S. locations:** Norfolk VA; Arlington VA; San Jose CA. **Parent company:** Analex Corporation.

CUBIX CORPORATION
2800 Lockheed Way, Carson City NV 89706-0719. 775/888-1000. **Toll-free phone:** 800/829-0550. **Fax:** 775/888-1001. **Contact:** Human Resources Department. **E-mail address:** personnel@cubix.com. **World Wide Web address:** http://www.cubix.com. **Description:** Designs and manufactures computer networking products for use as mission-critical communication, specialty, and file servers. **Corporate headquarters location:** This location. **Other U.S. locations:** Tampa FL.

INFOSCIENTIFIC.COM
2240 Village Walk Drive, Suite 2310, Henderson NV 89052. 702/368-5577. **Fax:** 702/368-5575. **Contact:** Human Resources. **E-mail address:** info@infoscientific.com. **World Wide Web address:** http://infoscientific.com. **Description:** Designs software applications for the collection of scientific data. **Other U.S. locations:** Manassas VA; Carmichael CA.

LAHEY COMPUTER SYSTEMS, INC.
P.O. Box 6091, Incline Village NV 89450. 775/831-2500. **Physical address:** 865 Tahoe Boulevard, Incline Village NV 89451. **Toll-free phone:** 800/548-4778.

Fax: 775/831-8123. **Contact:** Human Resources Department. **World Wide Web address:** http://www.lahey.com. **Description:** Develops and markets high-performance compilers and productivity tools. **Corporate headquarters location:** This location.

PERFECT COMMERCE, INC.
3301 North Buffalo Avenue, Suite 180, Las Vegas NV 89129. 816/448-4869. **Fax:** 702/396-4735. **Contact:** Human Resources. **E-mail address:** jobs@perfect.com. **World Wide Web address:** http://www.perfect.com. **Description:** Develops internet-based purchasing software, as well as providing related services and expertise. **Corporate headquarters location:** Kansas City MO. **Other U.S. locations:** Cupertino CA; San Diego CA.

New Hampshire
ASA TIRE SYSTEMS
615 Amherst Street, Nashua NH 03063-1017. 603/889-8700. **Fax:** 603/880-3438. **Contact:** Human Resources. **E-mail address:** webmaster@asaint.com. **World Wide Web address:** http://www.asatire.com/index.htm. **Description:** Designs and develops software for tire retailers. **NOTE:** Search posted listings on-line and respond via e-mail. Telephone contact is discouraged. **Positions advertised include:** Receptionist; Territory Manager; Account Manager; Software Support Analyst. **Corporate headquarters location:** Framingham MA. **Subsidiaries include:** ASA Legal Systems Company, Inc.; ASA, Inc. **Parent company:** ASA International Ltd. designs and develops proprietary vertical market software and installs software on a variety of computers and networks. **Listed on:** NASDAQ. **Stock exchange symbol:** ASAA.

BOTTOMLINE TECHNOLOGIES
325 Corporate Drive, Portsmouth NH 03801. 603/436-0700. **Toll-free phone:** 800/243-2528. **Fax:** 603/427-6556. **Contact:** Human Resources. **E-mail address:** humanresources@bottomline.com. **World Wide Web address:** http://www.bottomline.com. **Description:** Designs and manufactures software that allows users to print checks from a laser printer. **Positions advertised include:** Internships; Account Manager; Customer Support Specialist; Application Developer; Java Programmer; Lotus Notes Script Programmer; Senior Software Developer; Quality Assurance Analyst; Human Resources Director; Application Support Specialist; Account Executive. **NOTE:** Search posted listings and apply on-line only. Telephone contact is discouraged and paper resume are not accepted. **Corporate headquarters location:** This location. **Other U.S. locations:** San Francisco CA; Lakewood CO; Charlestown MA. **Listed on:** NASDAQ. **Stock exchange symbol:** EPAY. **President and CEO:** Joseph L. Mullen. **Number of employees worldwide:** 450.

CADEC CORPORATION
8 East Perimeter Road, Londonderry NH 03053. 603/668-1010. **Toll-free phone**: 800/252-2332. **Fax:** 603/623-0604. **Contact:** Human Resources. **E-mail address:** hr@cadec.com. **World Wide Web address:** http://www.cadecsystems.com. **Description:** A manufacturer of on-board computer systems for the trucking industry. **Positions advertised include:** Regional Sales Manager.

CITADEL COMPUTER CORPORATION
29 Armory Road, Milford NH 03055. 603/672-5500. **Fax:** 603/672-5590. **Contact:** Human Resources. **E-mail address:** careers@citadelcomputer.com. **World Wide Web address:** http://www.citadelcomputer.com. **Description:** A manufacturer of durable computers for use in warehouses and on loading docks. **NOTE:** E-mailed resumes are invited by this company. **Office hours:** Monday – Friday, 8:00 a.m. – 5:00 p.m.

RJ COLE SOLUTIONS
250 Commercial Street, Suite 4002A, Manchester NH 03101. 603/606-5585. **Fax:** 603/606-5586. **Contact:** Human Resources. **E-mail address**: mheiman@rjcolesolutions.com. **World Wide Web address:** http://www.rjcolesolutions.com. **Description:** Provides Information Technology services for the medical and dental practice market. **Positions advertised include:** Administrative Assistant.

COMPUWARE CORPORATION
9 Townsend West, Nashua NH 03063. 603/578-8400. **Fax:** 603/578-8401. **Contact:** Recruiting. E-mail address: compuware.recruiting@compuware.com. **World Wide Web address:** http://www.compuware.com. **Description:** A technology and market leader in the development of Windows-based advanced error detection and debugging tools. **NOTE**: Search posted openings nationwide at corporate website and apply on-line. Resumes may be submitted on-line, by mail or by fax. **Positions advertised include:** Software Developer; QA Testing Analyst Lead; Release Engineer; Software Developer; Products Telesales Representative. **Corporate headquarters location:** Detroit MI. **Other U.S. locations:** Nationwide. **International locations:** Worldwide. **Listed on:** NASDAQ. **Stock exchange symbol:** CPWR. **Number of employees at this location:** 85.

IMAGIC, INC.
235 West Road, Unit 7, Portsmouth NH 03801. 603/427-5544. **Toll-free phone:** 800/953-2459. **Fax**: 603/427-5644. **Contact:** Human Resources. E-mail address: sales@imagic-inc.com. **World Wide Web address:** http://www.imagic-inc.com. **Description:** A software and hardware engineering firm that develops products for factory automation, data acquisition, and microprocessor-based applications.

INFOR GLOBAL SOLUTIONS
500 Lafayette Road, Hampton NH 03842. 603/926-9696. **Fax:** 603/926-9698. **Contact:** Corporate human resources in Atlanta, GE, 678/319-8000. **E-mail address:** infor.careers@infor.com. **World Wide Web address:** http://www.infor.com. **Description:** Develops materials requirement planning (MRP) client/server software, called Visual Manufacturing, which allows managers to track all phases of production. **NOTE:** Search posted openings nationwide and respond with resume via e-mail. **Positions advertised include:** Maintenance Programmer; Lead Generation Representative; Account Representative; Field Sales Representative. **Office hours:** Monday - Friday, 8:00 a.m. - 6:00 p.m. **Corporate headquarters location:** This location. **Other U.S. locations:** Miami FL; Minnetonka MN; Concord NC; Farmington NY; Bay Shore NY; Cuyahoga Falls OH; West Chester PA; Pleasant Grove UT. **International locations:** Worldwide. **President:** Richard T. Lilly.

KANA COMMUNICATIONS
50 Phillipe Cote Street, Manchester NH 03101. 603/625-0070. **Toll-free phone**: 800/437-8738. **Fax:** 603/625-0428. **Contact:** Human Resources. **E-mail address:** jobs@kana.com. **World Wide Web address:** http://www.kana.com. **Description:** Develops and manufactures customer support software. **Positions advertised include:** Engineering Manager; Product Designer/Architect; Financial Services Industry Solutions Product Manager. **Corporate headquarters location:** Menlo Park CA. **Other U.S. locations:** Atlanta GA; Framingham MA; New York NY; Plano TX. **International locations:** Worldwide. **Listed on:** NASDAQ. **Stock exchange symbol:** KANA. **CEO:** Chuck Bay.

NTP SOFTWARE
427 Amherst Street, Unit 381, Nashua NH 03063. 603/641-6937. **Toll-free phone:** 800/ 226-2755. **Fax:** 603/263-2375. **Contact:** Jeff Truesdale, Human Resources. **E-mail address:** jtruesdale@ntpsoftware.com. **World Wide Web address:** http://www.ntpsoftware.com. **Description:** Develops software products for Windows NT and UNIX add-ons, and also provides technology consulting and training. **Note**: Search posted openings

online. **Positions advertised include:** Inside Sales Representative. **Office hours:** Monday – Friday, 8:30 a.m. – 5:00 p.m.

OASIS IMAGING PRODUCTS
460 Amherst Street, Nashua NH 03063. 603/880-3991. **Toll-free phone:** 888/627-6555. **Fax:** 603/598-4277. **Contact:** Nancy Boisvert, Human Resources. **E-mail address:** nlb@oasis-imaging.com. **World Wide Web address:** http://www.oasis-imaging.com. **Description:** Repairs Canon and IBM bubble-jet printers. **Corporate headquarters location:** This location. **Other U.S. locations:** Orange CA; Oak Brook IL; Sanford NC; Memphis TN; Richardson TX. **International locations:** Netherlands; Canada.

OMTOOL
8A Industrial Way, Salem NH 03079. 603/303-8098. **Fax:** 603/890-1919. **Contact:** Human Resources. **E-mail address:** jobs@omtool.com. **World Wide Web address:** http://www.omtool.com. **Description:** Develops client/server software solutions serving the network fax, document management, and workgroup markets. **Positions advertised include:** Territory Sales Manager; Business Manager for Account Services and Support; Inside Sale Representative; Inside Sales Representative for Legal Vertical; Renewal Sales Representative. **Corporate headquarters location:** This location. **Other U.S. locations:** Beaverton OR. **International locations:** England. **Listed on:** NASDAQ. **Stock exchange symbol:** OMTL.

ORACLE
One Oracle Drive, Nashua NH 03062. 603/897-3000. **Fax:** 603/897-3300. **Contact:** Personnel. **World Wide Web address:** http://www.oracle.com. **Description:** Oracle is a global IT organization, providing databases, applications, and development tools to business throughout the world. **NOTE:** Search posted openings and apply on-line. Do not fax or e-mail resumes. **Positions advertised include:** Software Development Manager; Corporate Development Manager; Technology Sales Representative; Applications Sales Representative; Market Analyst; QA Engineer; Applications Development Engineer. **Other U.S. locations:** Nationwide. **International locations:** Worldwide.

PROFITKEY INTERNATIONAL, INC.
2 Keywaydin Drive, Salem NH 03079. 603/898-9800. **Fax:** 603/898-7554. **Contact:** Sandra Arnold, Human Resources. **E-mail address:** pkjobs@profitkey.com. **World Wide Web address:** http://www.profitkey.com. **Description:** A leader in the advanced planning and scheduling industry, providing manufacturers with real-time ERP systems. ProfitKey International markets Rapid Response Manufacturing Client/Server, a graphical 32-bit application. **NOTE:** Part-time jobs are offered. **Special programs:** Co-ops. **Corporate headquarters location:** This location. **Other U.S. locations:** Nationwide. **Parent company:** Platinum Equity Holdings. **Listed on:** Privately held. **Number of employees at this location:** 45.

SERIF, INC.
10 Columbia Drive, Amherst NH 03031. 603/889-8650. **Fax:** 603/889-1127. **Contact:** Human Resources. **World Wide Web address:** http://www.serif.com. **Description:** Develops and supports software products for the desktop publishing and graphics markets. **Positions advertised include:** Outbound Sales. **International locations:** England. **Number of employees worldwide:** 150.

TELCORDIA
228 Elm Street, 1st Floor, Manchester NH 03101-1115. 603/625-0100. **Contact:** Human Resources, corporate office, 732/699-2000. **World Wide Web address:** http://www.telcordia.com. **Description:** Develops network operations software including Xper. **NOTE:** Search posted openings nationwide and apply online only. **Corporate headquarters location:** New Jersey. **Other U.S. locations:** Denver CO; Miami FL. **International locations:** France; Germany; Italy; Singapore; United Kingdom. **Listed on:** Privately held. **President/CEO:** Jay Borden.

ZETA ELECTRONIC DESIGN, INC
1461 Hooksett Road, Hooksett NH 03106. 603/644-3239. **Fax:** 603/644-3413. **E-mail address:** pierre@zetainc.com. **World Wide Web Address:** http://www.zetainc.com. **Description:** Develops electronic hardware and software for a range of clients. **NOTE:** Provides job listings online and a form to submit your resume. No paper resumes are accepted. **Corporate Headquarters:** This location.

New Jersey

ACI
90 Woodbridge Center Drive, Suite 400, Woodbridge NJ 07095. 732/602-0200. **Contact:** Personnel. **World Wide Web address:** http://www.aci.com. **Description:** Provides systems integration services. **Positions advertised include:** Analyst; Help Desk Associate; Unix Administrator; DBA; Project Manager; Technical Writer; Quality Assurance Tester; Developer; Java Programmer.

ADP
1 ADP Boulevard, Roseland NJ 07068. 973/974-5000. **Contact:** Human Resources. **World Wide Web address:** http://www.adp.com. **Description:** Develops trade-processing software for the financial services industry. **Positions advertised include:** Accounting Project Specialist; Applications Design Consultant; Associate Mainframe Programmer; Business Application Manager; Corporate Compensation Manager; Director of Usability Engineering; Lead Consultant; Operational Audit Manager. **Corporate headquarters location:** This location.

AM BEST COMPANY
Ambest Road, Oldwick NJ 08858. 908/439-2200. **Fax:** 908/439-3027. **Contact:** Human Resources. **E-mail address:** hr@ambest.com. **World Wide Web address:** http://www.ambest.com. **Description:** Manufactures products including software, CD-ROMs, and diskette support products for the insurance industry. **Positions advertised include:** Tax Analyst; Customer Service; Financial Analyst; Editorial Assistant; Sales Analyst. **Corporate headquarters location:** This location.

AXS-ONE INC.
301 Route 17 North, 12th Floor, Rutherford NJ 07070. 201/935-3400. **Toll-free phone:** 800/828-7660. **Fax:** 201/935-5431. **Contact:** Human Resources. **E-mail address:** hr@axsone.com. **World Wide Web address:** http://www.axsone.com. **Description:** Develops and markets various financial software products. **Positions advertised include:** QA Team Lead; Technology Architect.

ACCENTURE
300 Campus Drive, Florham Park NJ 07932. 973/301-1000. **Contact:** Human Resources. **World Wide Web address:** http://www.accenture.com. **Description:** A management and technology consulting firm. Accenture offers a wide range of services including business re-engineering; customer service system consulting; data system design and implementation; Internet sales systems research and design; and strategic planning. **Number of employees nationwide:** 5,600.

AFFINITI GROUP
16 Portland Road, 2nd Floor, Highlands NJ 07732. 732-747-9600. **Fax:** 732/747-9960. **Contact:** Human Resources. **E-mail address:** careers@affinitigroup.com. **World Wide Web address:** http://www.affinitigroup.com. **Description:** Provides systems integration and software development services. **Positions advertised include:** Sales Representative; Programmer; Unix System Administrator; Technical Support Representative; Network Engineer; Traffic Coordinator.

ANALYSTS INTERNATIONAL CORPORATION (AIC)
111 Wood Avenue South, Iselin NJ 08830. 732/906-0100. **Fax:** 732/906-8808. **Contact:** Human Resources.

World Wide Web address: http://www.analysts.com. **Description:** AiC is an international computer consulting firm. The company assists clients in analyzing, designing, and developing systems in a variety of industries using different programming languages and software. **Corporate headquarters location:** Minneapolis MN.

ANSOFT CORPORATION
1287 Tudor Court, Hillsborough NJ 08844. 908/874-8556. **Contact:** Human Resources. **E-mail address:** jobs@ansoft.com. **World Wide Web address:** http://www.ansoft.com. **Description:** Develops and distributes circuit design software. **Corporate headquarters location:** Pittsburgh PA.

ASPECT COMPUTER CORPORATION
19 World's Fair Drive, Somerset NJ 08873. 732/563-1304. **Contact:** Human Resources. **World Wide Web address:** http://www.aspectcomputer.com. **Description:** Manufactures computers. **Positions advertised include:** Business Systems Analyst.

BLUEBIRD AUTO RENTAL SYSTEMS INC.
200 Mineral Springs Drive, Dover NJ 07801. 973/989-2423. **Contact:** Human Resources. **E-mail address:** info@barsnet.com. **World Wide Web address:** http://www.barsnet.com. **Description:** Designs computer applications for automobile rental agencies.

CANTERBURY CONSULTING GROUP, INC.
352 Stokes Road, Suite 200, Medford NJ 08055. 609/953-0044. **Toll-free phone:** 800/873-2040. **Fax:** 609/953-0062. **Contact:** Nancy Rose, Manager of Human Resources Department **E-mail address:** careers@canterburyconsultinggroup.com. **World Wide Web address:** http://www.canterburyconsultinggroup.com. **Description:** A corporate training company providing information technology services. Training covers entry-level vocational, managerial, executive, and technical areas. **Corporate headquarters location:** This location. **Subsidiaries include:** ATM/Canterbury Corp. is a software development and consulting firm. CALC/Canterbury Corp. is a computer software training company. MSI/Canterbury Corp. is a management, sales, and communication training company. ProSoft/Canterbury Corp. is a provider of technical staffing, applications development, and corporate training.

CAPGEMINI U.S.
400 Broadacres Drive, 4th Floor, Bloomfield NJ 07003. 973/337-2700. **Fax:** 973/337-2701. **Contact:** Human Resources. **World Wide Web address:** http://www.us.capgemini.com. **Description:** A provider of information technology consulting services with offices nationwide. **Positions advertised include:** Human Resources Manager; Administrative Assistant; Government Solutions Manager; Sales Executive; Sales Associate; Pharmacist Manager. **Other U.S. locations:** Nationwide.

CHERRYROAD TECHNOLOGIES INC.
199 Cherry Hill Road, Parsippany NJ 07054. 973/402-7802. **Contact:** Human Resources. **E-mail address:** careers@cherryroad.com. **World Wide Web address:** http://www.cherryroad.com. **Description:** A computer information technology company that provides comprehensive systems integration and consulting services that maximize enterprise performance for private and public sector as well as federal clients. **NOTE:** Search and apply for positions online. **Positions advertised include:** PeopleSoft Consultant. **Corporate headquarters location:** This location. **Other U.S. locations:** Chicago IL; Vienna VA; Irvine CA.

CIBER, INC.
5 Marineview Plaza, Suite 214, Hoboken NJ 07030. 201/795-3601. **Fax:** 201/795-5355. **Contact:** Human Resources. **World Wide Web address:** http://www.ciber.com. **Description:** A leading systems integrator. The company's services include computer network design, installation, and administration; helpdesk support; technical education; cabling and telecommunications sales and service; computer product sales and services; and Internet services. Clients include many small and mid-range companies, national and global *Fortune* 1000 companies, and large government agencies. Founded in 1984. **Corporate headquarters location:** Greenwood Village CO. **Other U.S. locations:** Nationwide. **Listed on:** New York Stock Exchange. **Stock exchange symbol:** CBR. **Annual sales/revenues:** More than $100 million.

CLARION OFFICE SUPPLIES INC.
101 East Main Street, Little Falls NJ 07424. 973/785-8383. **Contact:** Human Resources. **World Wide Web address:** http://www.clarionofficesupply.com. **Description:** Distributes a wide variety of office supplies including computer hardware. Clarion Office Supplies provides individuals and businesses with most major brands of CPUs and monitors.

COMMVAULT SYSTEMS
2 Crescent Place, P.O. Box 900, Oceanport NJ 07757-0900. 732/870-4000. **Contact:** Human Resources. **E-mail address:** employment@commvault.com. **World Wide Web address:** http://www.commvault.com. **Description:** Develops and sells software for businesses with computer backup systems. **Positions advertised include:** Customer Engineer; Technical Account Manager; Technical Writer; Staff Accountant; Systems Development Leader; Creative Services and eMarketing Manager. **Corporate headquarters location:** This location.

COMPUTER ASSOCIATES INTERNATIONAL, INC.
2000 Midlantic Drive, Suite 300, Mount Laurel NJ 08054. 856/273-9100. **Contact:** Human Resources. **E-mail address:** joinCA@ca.com. **World Wide Web address:** http://www.cai.com. **Description:** Computer Associates International is one of the world's leading developers of client/server and distributed computing software. The company develops, markets, and supports enterprise management, database and applications development, business applications, and consumer software products for a broad range of mainframe, midrange, and desktop computers. Computer Associates International serves major business, government, research, and educational organizations. Founded in 1976. **NOTE:** Mail resumes to: CAI Inc., One Computer Associates Plaza, Islandia NY 11749. **Special programs:** Internships. **Corporate headquarters location:** Islandia NY. **Operations at this facility include:** This location sells software and offers technical support. **Other U.S. locations:** Nationwide. **Listed on:** New York Stock Exchange. **Stock exchange symbol:** CA. **Annual sales/revenues:** More than $100 million.

COMPUTER HORIZONS CORPORATION
49 Old Bloomfield Avenue, Mountain Lakes NJ 07046-1495. 973/299-4000. **Toll-free phone:** 800/321-2421. **Fax:** 973/402-7986. **Contact:** Human Resources. **E-mail address:** info@computerhorizons.com. **World Wide Web address:** http://www.computerhorizons.com. **Description:** A full-service technology solutions company offering contract staffing, outsourcing, re-engineering, migration, downsizing support, and network management. Founded in 1969. **Corporate headquarters location:** This location. **Other U.S. locations:** Nationwide. **Subsidiaries include:** Birla Horizons International Ltd.; Horizons Consulting, Inc.; Strategic Outsourcing Services, Inc.; Unified Systems Solutions, Inc. **Listed on:** NASDAQ. **Stock exchange symbol:** CHRZ. **Number of employees nationwide:** 1,500.

COMPUTER SCIENCES CORPORATION
304 West Route 38, P.O. Box 1038, Moorestown NJ 08057-0902. 856/234-1166. **Contact:** Human Resources. **World Wide Web address:** http://www.csc.com. **Description:** An information technology services company offering systems design and integration; IT and business process outsourcing; applications software development; Web and

application hosting; and management consulting. **Positions advertised include:** Technology Architect; Programmer Analyst; Knowledge Management Specialist. **Corporate headquarters location:** El Segundo CA. **Other U.S. locations:** Nationwide. **Operations at this facility include:** This location develops software.

COMTREX SYSTEMS CORPORATION
1247 North Church Street, Suite 7, Moorestown NJ 08057. 856/778-0090. **Fax:** 856/778-9322. **Contact:** Personnel. **World Wide Web address:** http://www.comtrex.com. **Description:** Designs, develops, assembles, and markets computer software electronics terminals, which provide retailers with transaction processing, in-store controls, and management information capabilities. The company primarily serves the food service and hospitality industries. Founded in 1981. **Corporate headquarters location:** This location. **Listed on:** NASDAQ. **Stock exchange symbol:** COMX.

CORPORATE DISK COMPANY
1800 Bloomsbury Avenue, Ocean City NJ 07712. 732/431-5300. **Contact:** Controller. **World Wide Web address:** http://www.disk.com. **Description:** Provides a broad range of integrated software and information distribution options in multiple formats on disk, in print, and online to many industries including the technology, insurance, financial services, pharmaceutical, publishing, government, and transportation communities. **NOTE:** Resumes should be sent to Human Resources, Corporate Disk Company, 1226 Michael Drive, Wood Dale IL 60191.

CRADEN PERIPHERALS CORPORATION
7860 Airport Highway, Pennsauken NJ 08109. 856/488-0700. **Fax:** 856/488-0925. **Contact:** Human Resources. **E-mail address:** info@craden.com. **World Wide Web address:** http://www.craden.com. **Description:** Manufactures and markets printers under the Craden brand name.

DRS TECHNOLOGIES
5 Sylvan Way, Suite 60, Parsippany NJ 07054. 973/898-1500. **Fax:** 973/898-4730. **Contact:** Ann Carcione, Human Resources. **World Wide Web address:** http://www.drs.com. **Description:** A producer of magnetic recording heads for the information processing industry. **Positions advertised include:** Sr. Internal Control Analyst; Director, Contracts and Compliance; Technical design Supervisor; Benefits Coordinator. **Corporate headquarters location:** This location.

DATA SYSTEMS & SOFTWARE INC.
200 Route 17, Mahwah NJ 07430. 201/529-8050. **Fax:** 201/529-4564. **Contact:** Human Resources. **E-mail address:** ir@dssinc.com. **World Wide Web address:** http://www.dssiinc.com. **Description:** A leading provider of consulting and development services for computer software and systems to high-technology companies in Israel and the United States, principally in the area of embedded real-time systems.

DATARAM CORPORATION
P.O. Box 7528, Princeton NJ 08543-7528. 609/750-0475. **Physical address:** 186 Princeton Road, West Windsor NJ 08550. **Toll-free phone:** 800/DAT-ARAM. **Fax:** 609/897-7021. **Contact:** Dawn Craft, Human Resources Administrator. **E-mail address:** hr@dataram.com. **World Wide Web address:** http://www.dataram.com. **Description:** Designs and manufactures memory products that improve the performance of computer systems. Dataram primarily serves HP, DEC, Sun, and IBM users in the manufacturing, finance, government, telecommunications, utilities, research, and education industries. **Positions advertised include:** Sales Professional. **Corporate headquarters location:** This location. **Listed on:** American Stock Exchange. **Stock exchange symbol:** DTM. **Number of employees at this location:** 100. **Number of employees nationwide:** 150.

DENDRITE INTERNATIONAL, INC.
1405 U.S. Highway 206, Bedminster NJ 07921. 908/443-2000. **Fax:** 908/470-9900. **Contact:** Personnel. **World Wide Web address:** http://www.dendrite.com. **Description:** Develops software and provides consulting services aimed at optimizing the sales force effectiveness of pharmaceutical and consumer packaged goods companies. **Positions advertised include:** Production Control Programmer; Staff Accountant; Sr. Human Resource Manager; Project Manager; VP Client Services. **Corporate headquarters location:** This location. **International locations:** Worldwide. **Listed on:** NASDAQ. **Stock exchange symbol:** DRTE. **Annual sales/revenues:** More than $100 million.

DESKTOP ENGINEERING INTERNATIONAL, INC.
172 Broadway, Woodcliff Lake NJ 07677. 201/505-9200. **Toll-free phone:** 800/888-8680. **Fax:** 201/505-1566. **Contact:** Human Resources. **E-mail address:** information@deiusa.com. **World Wide Web address:** http://www.deiusa.com. **Description:** Designs and manufactures software for use in mechanical and structural engineering industries.

DOUBLE-TAKE SOFTWARE
Baker Waterfront Plaza, 2 Hudson Place, Suite 700, Hoboken NJ 07030. 201/656-2121. **Toll-free phone:** 800/775-4674. **Fax:** 201/610-9501. **Contact:** Human Resources. **E-mail address:** info@nsisoftware.com. **World Wide Web address:** http://www.doubletake.com. **Description:** Develops network performance and fault-tolerant software tools. Products are compatible with Novell NetWare, Microsoft Windows NT, and UNIX. **Corporate headquarters location:** Southborough MA. **Other U.S. locations:** Indianapolis IN.

EDS
25 Hanover Road, 3rd Floor, Florham Park NJ 07932-1424. 973/301-7502. **Contact:** Human Resources. **World Wide Web address:** http://www.eds.com. **Description:** Provides integrated hardware, software, and network solutions to *Fortune* 500 companies. EDS focuses primarily on international corporations in the service, wholesale, distribution, and transportation industries. **Corporate headquarters location:** Plano TX. **Listed on:** New York Stock Exchange. **Stock exchange symbol:** EDS.

EDUNEERING, INC.
202 Carnegie Center, Princeton NJ 08540. 609/627-5300. **Fax:** 609/627-5316. **Contact:** Human Resources. **E-mail address:** careers@eduneering.com. **World Wide Web address:** http://www.eduneering.com. **Description:** Develops technology-enabled knowledge solutions for improving business performance and assuring regulatory compliance. The company serves corporate and government clients in the life sciences, healthcare, energy and industrial sectors using proprietary platforms that integrate business, learning and technology. **Other U.S. locations:** Houston TX; Bloomsburg PA.

EXECUTIVE IMAGING SYSTEMS INC.
1 Allison Drive, Cherry Hill NJ 08043. 856/424-5898. **Fax:** 856/424-7848. **Contact:** Human Resources Department. **World Wide Web address:** http://www.executiveimaging.com. **Description:** Resells computers, facsimiles, printers, and peripherals.

FDS INTERNATIONAL
18 West Ridgewood Avenue, Paramus NJ 07652. 201/670-1300. **Fax:** 201/670-0400. **Contact:** Human Resources Department. **E-mail address:** jobs@fdsinternational.com. **World Wide Web address:** http://www.fdsinternational.com. **Description:** Develops transportation and custom brokerage software.

FORMATION, INC.
121 Whittendale Drive, Moorestown NJ 08057. 856/234-5020. **Toll-free phone:** 800/220-1209. **Fax:**

856/234-8543. **Contact:** Human Resources. **E-mail address:** resume@formation.com. **World Wide Web address:** http://www.formation.com. **Description:** Designs and manufactures communications products and real-time, high-performance storage and retrieval systems. The company's products are capable of integrating a number of inputs including video, audio, data/text, and radar, and can employ a variety of communications protocols. The company supplies an open systems storage system using Redundant Array of Independent Disks (RAID) technology. Formation also supplies plug-compatible data storage systems for IBM AS/400 computers, as well as data storage systems to open systems computer manufacturers and systems integrators. **Corporate headquarters location:** This location. **Operations at this facility include:** Administration; Manufacturing; Research and Development; Sales; Service. **Number of employees at this location:** 75.

FUJITSU COMPUTER SYSTEMS
41 Vreeland Avenue, Suite 36, Totowa NJ 07512. 973/837-0444. **Fax:** 973/837-0446. **Contact:** Human Resources. **World Wide Web address:** http://www.computers.us.fujitsu.com. **Description:** Offers a wide range of enterprise hardware and software products and services. **Positions advertised include:** Field Operations Installer; Field Operations Engineer; Area Sales Manager. **NOTE:** Search and apply for positions online. **Corporate headquarters location:** Sunnyvale CA.

FUJITSU CONSULTING
333 Thornall Street, Edison NJ 08837. 732/549-4100. **Fax:** 732/549-2375. **Contact:** Recruiting Administrator. **World Wide Web address:** http://consulting.fujitsu.com. **Description:** Provides computer consulting services including outsourcing solutions and systems integration. **Positions advertised include:** Consultant. **Corporate headquarters location:** This location. **Parent company:** Fujitsu Limited. **Number of employees worldwide:** 8,000.

GLOBE MANUFACTURING SALES, INC.
1159 U.S. Route 22, Mountainside NJ 07092. 908/232-7301. **Fax:** 908/232-0179. **Contact:** Personnel. **World Wide Web address:** http://www.globebrackets.com. **Description:** Manufactures computer brackets that hold computer chips and other plastic parts. **Parent company:** AK Stamping Company, Inc.

HEWLETT-PACKARD MIDDLEWARE
6000 Irwin Road, Mount Laurel NJ 08054-4128. 856/638-6000. **Toll-free phone:** 866/452-2318. **Fax:** 856/638-6170. **Contact:** Monique McLaughlin, Recruiter. **World Wide Web address:** http://www.hpmiddleware.com. **Description:** Develops computer technology programs and provides user training. Offers Web-based software including dynamic Web applications and GUIs. **NOTE:** Entry-level positions are offered. **Special programs:** Training. **Corporate headquarters location:** Palo Alto CA. **Other U.S. locations:** Nationwide. **Listed on:** New York Stock Exchange. **Stock exchange symbol:** HWP.

IBM CORPORATION
1551 South Washington Avenue, 3rd Floor, Piscataway NJ 08854. 732/968-1900. **Recorded jobline:** 800/964-4473. **Contact:** IBM Staffing Services Center. **World Wide Web address:** http://www.ibm.com. **Description:** IBM develops, manufactures, and markets advanced information processing products including computers and microelectronic technology, software, networking systems, and information technology-related services. IBM operates in the United States, Canada, Europe, Middle East, Africa, Latin America, and Asia Pacific. **NOTE:** Jobseekers should send a resume to IBM Staffing Services Center, 1DPA/051, 3808 Six Forks Road, Raleigh NC 27609. **Corporate headquarters location:** Armonk NY. **Operations at this facility include:** This location is a marketing office. **Subsidiaries include:** IBM Credit Corporation; IBM Instruments, Inc.; IBM World Trade Corporation. **Number of employees at this location:** 100.

IDT CORPORATION
520 Broad Street, Newark NJ 07102. 973/438-1000. **Toll-free phone:** 800/CAL-LIDT. **Contact:** Human Resources Manager. **World Wide Web address:** http://www.idt.net. **Description:** An Internet access provider that offers dial-up services, Web hosting, and e-mail by phone. Founded in 1990. **NOTE:** Entry-level positions, part-time jobs, and second and third shifts are offered. **Positions advertised include:** Accounts Receivable Analyst; Product Manager; Internal Reporting Manager; Business Development Director; EDP Auditor. **Corporate headquarters location:** This location. **Other U.S. locations:** Nationwide. **International locations:** London, England; Mexico City, Mexico. **Subsidiaries include:** Amerimax; Net2Phone; Union Telecard Alliances. **Listed on:** NASDAQ. **Stock exchange symbol:** IDTC. **Founder:** Howard Jonas. **Annual sales/revenues:** More than $100 million. **Number of employees at this location:** 1,000. **Number of employees nationwide:** 1,200. **Number of employees worldwide:** 4,000.

ITT INDUSTRIES AEROSPACE/COMMUNICATIONS DIVISION
100 Kingsland Road, Clifton NJ 07014. 973/284-0123. **Contact:** Human Resources. **World Wide Web address:** http://www.ittind.com. **Description:** Designs and engineers software for satellite communications under government contracts. **Positions advertised include:** Commodity Team Manager; Manager, Internal Control Compliance; Manager, Operations; Marketing Manager, Specialty Products.

IKEGAMI ELECTRONICS INC.
37 Brook Avenue, Maywood NJ 07607. 201/368-9171. **Fax:** 201/569-1626. **Contact:** Human Resources. **World Wide Web address:** http://www.ikegami.com. **Description:** Manufactures and sells computer and broadcast monitors. **Positions advertised include:** MIS Department Tech Support.

INNODATA ISOGEN, INC.
3 University Plaza, Hackensack NJ 07601. 201/488-1200. **Contact:** Human Resources. **E-mail address:** hr-department@innodata-isogen.com. **World Wide Web address:** http://www.innodata.com. **Description:** A worldwide electronic publishing company specializing in data conversion for CD-ROM, print, and online database publishers. The company also offers medical transcription services to health care providers through its Statline Division. **Positions advertised include:** Business Development Executive. **Corporate headquarters location:** Brooklyn NY. **Listed on:** NASDAQ. **Stock exchange symbol:** INOD.

INSTRUCTIVISION, INC.
16 Chapin Road, P.O. Box 2004, Pine Brook NJ 07058. 973/575-9992. **Toll-free phone:** 888/551-5144. **Fax:** 973/575-9134. **Contact:** Human Resources. **World Wide Web address:** http://www.instructivision.com. **Description:** Develops video production and education software. Instructivision also operates a full-service video production facility encompassing a production stage, an interformat digital editing suite, offline editing, 3-D animation, and audio recording equipment.

ION NETWORKS INC.
120 Corporate Boulevard, South Plainfield NJ 07080. 908/546-3900. **Contact:** Human Resources. **E-mail address:** resumes@ion-networks.com. **World Wide Web address:** http://www.ion-networks.com. **Description:** Develops and markets software and hardware for computer security. **Corporate headquarters location:** This location. **International locations:** Belgium; United Kingdom. **Listed on:** NASDAQ. **Stock exchange symbol:** IONN.

ITOX
8 Elkins Road, East Brunswick NJ 08816. 732/390-2815. **Toll-free phone:** 888/200-4869. **Fax:** 732/390-2817. **Contact:** Human Resources. **E-mail address:** sales@itox.com. **World Wide Web address:** http://www.itox.com. **Description:** Manufactures computer components including graphics accelerator

boards, motherboards, and sound cards for commercial and industrial systems.

KEANE, INC.
36 Washington Road, Princeton Junction NJ 08550. 609/750-5260. **Fax:** 609/750-5287. **Contact:** Human Resources. **World Wide Web address:** http://www.keane.com. **Description:** Keane offers businesses a variety of computer consulting services. Keane also develops, markets, and manages software for its clients and assists in project management. **Positions advertised include:** Systems Administrator; Programmer/Analyst; Technical Support Analyst; Project Manager; Web Developer; Database Administrator. **Corporate headquarters location:** Boston MA. **Other U.S. locations:** Nationwide. **Listed on:** American Stock Exchange. **Stock exchange symbol:** KEA. **Number of employees worldwide:** 7,800.

LUMETA CORPORATION
220 Davidson Avenue, Suite 401, Somerset NJ 08873-4146. 732/357-3500. **Toll-free phone:** 866/586-3827. **Fax:** 732/564-0731. **Contact:** Human Resources. **E-mail address:** careers@lumeta.com. **World Wide Web address:** http://www.lumeta.com. **Description:** Lumeta is a provider of network intelligence solutions. Lumeta's IPsonar product suite permits IT security and operations managers to audit, protect, and secure network assets to ensure continuous compliance with internal and external regulations. **Positions advertised include:** Software Engineer; Sr. QA/QC Engineer.

MDY ADVANCED TECHNOLOGIES
21-00 Route 208 South, Fair Lawn NJ 07410. 201/797-6676. **Fax:** 201/797-6852. **Contact:** Human Resources. **E-mail address:** jobs@mdy.com. **World Wide Web address:** http://www.mdy.com. **Description:** Provides computer networking and record management services. **Positions advertised include:** New York Account Executive; Sales Accountant Executive Inside Sales; Telemarketing Representative.

MAINTECH
39 Paterson Avenue, Wallington NJ 07057. 973/614-1700. **Toll-free phone:** 800/426-8324. **Contact:** Personnel. **World Wide Web address:** http://www.maintech.com. **Description:** Provides on-site computer maintenance services.

MCDATA
100 Mount Holly Bypass, P.O. 440, Lumberton NJ 08048. 609/518-4000. **Fax:** 609/518-4019. **Contact:** Human Resources. **World Wide Web address:** http://www.inrange.com. **Description:** Produces proprietary switching and control equipment used to increase the performance of online data communications, data processing, and information systems. The company's products help anticipate system failures. **Special programs:** Internships. **Corporate headquarters location:** Broomfield CO. **Other U.S. locations:** Santa Clara CA; Minneapolis MN.

McKESSON
220 Davidson Avenue, Ste 732, Somerset NJ 08873-4149. 732/764-9898. **Contact:** Human Resources. **E-mail address:** job.infosolutions@mckesson.com. **World Wide Web address:** http://www.mckesson.com. **Description:** McKesson provides networking solutions and software by supplying physicians, hospitals, and other health care facilities with network service and support. **NOTE:** Search and apply for positions online. **Positions advertised include:** Route Sales Representative. **Corporate headquarters location:** San Francisco CA. **Operations at this facility include:** This location offers sales and technical support. **Listed on:** New York Stock Exchange. **Stock exchange symbol:** MCK.

MOTOROLA, INC.
85 Harristown Road, Glen Rock NJ 07452. 201/447-7500. **Contact:** Human Resources. **World Wide Web address:** http://www.motorola.com. **Description:** A leading supplier of corporate networking solutions including data, voice, and video interfaces. Motorola also provides platform software and Internet connectivity services.

OKI DATA AMERICAS, INC.
2000 Bishops Gate Boulevard, Mount Laurel NJ 08054. 856/235-2600. **Contact:** Human Resources. **World Wide Web address:** http://www.okidata.com. **Description:** Manufactures computer printers and fax machines. **Positions advertised include:** Human Resources Business Partner. **Corporate headquarters location:** This location. **International locations:** Worldwide.

ORACLE CORPORATION
517 Route 1 South, Suite 4000, Iselin NJ 08830. 732/636-2000. **Fax:** 732/636-5915. **Contact:** Human Resources. **World Wide Web address:** http://www.oracle.com. **Description:** Oracle Corporation designs and manufactures database and information management software for businesses and provides consulting services. **Corporate headquarters location:** Redwood Shores CA. **Other U.S. locations:** Nationwide. **Operations at this facility include:** This location designs and manufactures business software programs for small companies. **Listed on:** NASDAQ. **Stock exchange symbol:** ORCL. **Number of employees worldwide:** 42,000.

PNY TECHNOLOGIES, INC.
299 Webro Road, Parsippany NJ 07054. 973/515-9700. **Toll-free phone:** 800/234-4597. **Fax:** 973/560-5590. **Contact:** Human Resources. **E-mail address:** hr@pny.com. **World Wide Web address:** http://www.pny.com. **Description:** Manufactures and designs computer memory products. Founded in 1985. **NOTE:** Entry-level positions are offered. **Positions advertised include:** Buyer; End of the Line Inspector; Memory Marketing Manager; Test Technician; Traffic Coordinator. **Corporate headquarters location:** This location. **Listed on:** Privately held. **Annual sales/revenues:** More than $100 million. **Number of employees at this location:** 250. **Number of employees nationwide:** 320. **Number of employees worldwide:** 420.

PARAGON COMPUTER PROFESSIONALS INC.
20 Commerce Drive, 2nd Floor, Cranford NJ 07016. 908/709-6767. **Toll-free phone:** 800/462-5582. **Contact:** Human Resources Administrative Assistant. **World Wide Web address:** http://www.paracomp.com. **Description:** Offers computer consulting services to a variety of businesses. **Positions advertised include:** E-business Strategist; E-business Architect; Infrastructure Architect; Project Manager; Lead Developer; Interface Developer; Client Side Developer; Server Side Developer; Legacy Integration; Database Administrator; Business Systems Analyst; Systems Analyst; Quality Analyst. **Corporate headquarters location:** This location.

PRINCETON FINANCIAL SYSTEMS INC.
600 College Road East, Princeton NJ 08540. 609/987-2400. **Fax:** 609/987-9320. **Contact:** Human Resources. **World Wide Web address:** http://www.pfs.com. **Description:** Develops and supports investment management software. Founded in 1969. **NOTE:** Entry-level positions are offered. **Positions advertised include:** Client Support Analyst; Applications Developer; Implementation Manager. **Special programs:** Apprenticeships. **Corporate headquarters location:** This location. **International locations:** London; Toronto. **Parent company:** State Street Boston Corporation. **Number of employees at this location:** 150. **Number of employees nationwide:** 185. **Number of employees worldwide:** 200.

PRINCETON INFORMATION
399 Thornall Street, 4th Floor, Edison NJ 08837-2246. 732/906-5660. **Contact:** Human Resources. **World Wide Web address:** http://www.princetoninformation.com. **Description:** Offers computer consulting services. **Positions advertised include:** Developer.

PRINCETON SOFTECH
111 Campus Drive, Princeton NJ 08540. 609/627-5500. **Toll-free phone:** 800/457-7060. **Fax:** 609/457-7060. **Contact:** Human Resources. **World Wide Web address:** http://www.princetonsoftech.com. **Description:** Provides IT professionals with software solutions. Develops, researches, sells, and markets software products that are focused on intelligent data migration and database synchronization. The company offers data and program synchronization tools to solve application development and database problems. Founded in 1989. **Positions advertised include:** Oracle Application Representative. **Corporate headquarters location:** This location. **International locations:** Worldwide. **Parent company:** Computer Horizons Corporation.

QAD INC.
10000 Midlantic Drive, Suite 100 East, Mount Laurel NJ 08054. 856/273-1717. **Contact:** Human Resources. **World Wide Web address:** http://www.qad.com. **Description:** QAD develops MFG/PRO, a software package designed to aid in supply and distribution management for large companies. **Positions advertised include:** Customer Service Regional Director. **Corporate headquarters location:** Carpinteria CA. **Operations at this facility include:** This location serves as a technical support branch and regional sales office. **Listed on:** NASDAQ. **Stock exchange symbol:** QADI.

QUADRIX SOLUTIONS, INC.
1982 Washington Valley Road, Suite 195, P.O. Box 309, Martinsville NJ 08836-0309. 908/252-9635. **Fax:** 309/404-7749. **Contact:** Human Resources. **E-mail address:** info@quadrix.com. **World Wide Web address:** http://www.quadrix.com. **Description:** Quadrix Solutions is a systems integrator and managed colocation services provider. The company designs, implements, and supports eBusiness solutions.

QUALITY SOFTWARE SYSTEMS INC.
200 Centennial Avenue, Suite 110, Piscataway NJ 08854. 732/885-1919. **Fax:** 732-885-1872. **Contact:** Human Resources. **E-mail address:** emtrojanello@qssi-wns.com. **World Wide Web address:** http://www.qssi-wms.com. **Description:** Develops software to aid in warehouse management and development. **Positions advertised include:** Sales; Implementation Consultant.

QUINTUM TECHNOLOGIES, INC.
71 James Way, Eatontown NJ 07724. **Toll-free phone:** 877/773-2547. 732/460-9000. **Fax:** 732/544-9119. **Contact:** Human Resources. **World Wide Web address:** http://www.quintum.com. **Description:** Develops voice-over IP technologies. **Positions advertised include:** Inside Sales Account Manager.

RARITAN COMPUTER INC.
400 Cottontail Lane, Somerset NJ 08873. 732/764-8886. **Fax:** 732/764-8887. **Contact:** Human Resources. **E-mail address:** hr@raritan.com. **World Wide Web address:** http://www.raritan.com. **Description:** Designs and manufactures a line of products for sharing PCs and peripherals. Products include MasterConsole, a keyboard/video/mouse switch; CompuSwitch, a KVM switch allowing central control for up to four PCs; and Guardian, a virtual keyboard and mouse device that emulates keyboard and mouse signals. Founded in 1985. **Positions advertised include:** Software Group Consultant; System Tester; Software Engineer; Assistant Controller; Network Communication Director; Marketing Communication Launch Manager; Material Planner; Product Marketing Manager; Product Manager; Sales Engineer; Business Marketing Manager; Technical Support Representative; National Account Manager; Territory Sales Manager. **Corporate headquarters location:** This location. **Number of employees at this location:** 40. **Number of employees nationwide:** 100.

SPHERION
400 Interpace Parkway, Parsippany NJ 07054. 973/909-2807. **Contact:** Human Resources. **World Wide Web address:** http://www.spherion.com. **Description:** A nationwide computer outsourcing service company, providing short-run supplemental and long-term contractual support for computer operations, communications operations, PC help desks, local area networks, computer programming, and technology training. The company's computer services are provided from offices strategically located throughout the United States. The company also provides the expertise for meeting applications and systems development objectives within information systems organizations. Capabilities extend beyond evaluating computer software and hardware to providing technically qualified professionals for any task in the systems development life cycle -- from conception through feasibility analysis, system design, programming, testing, implementation, and full systems maintenance and support. **Positions advertised include:** Dispatcher. **Corporate headquarters location:** Fort Lauderdale FL. **Other U.S. locations:** Nationwide. **International locations:** Worldwide. **Listed on:** New York Stock Exchange. **Stock exchange symbol:** SFN.

STORAGE ENGINE, INC.
One Sheila Drive, Tinton Falls NJ 07724. 732/747-6995. **Fax:** 732/747-6542. **Contact:** Human Resources. **E-mail address:** hr@storageengine.com. **World Wide Web address:** http://www.eccs.com. **Description:** Designs and configures computer systems. Storage Engine's mass storage enhancement products include RAID (Redundant Array of Independent Disks) products and technology; external disk, optical, and tape systems; internal disk and tape storage devices; and RAM. The company also provides related technical services. **Corporate headquarters location:** This location.

SUN MICROSYSTEMS, INC.
400 Atrium Drive, Somerset NJ 08873. 732/469-1000. **Contact:** Human Resources. **World Wide Web address:** http://www.sun.com. **Description:** Sun Microsystems produces high-performance computer systems, workstations, servers, CPUs, peripherals, and operating systems software. The company developed its own microprocessor called SPARC. **Positions advertised include;** Systems Engineer. **Note:** Submit resume online. **Corporate headquarters location:** Santa Clara CA. **Operations at this facility include:** This location is a sales office. **Subsidiaries include:** Forte Software Inc. manufactures enterprise application integration software. **Listed on:** NASDAQ. **Stock exchange symbol:** SUNW.

SYNCSORT
50 Tice Boulevard, Woodcliff Lake NJ 07677. 201/930-8200. **Fax:** 201/930-8281. **Contact:** Human Resources. **World Wide Web address:** http://www.syncsort.com. **Description:** Develops operating systems software for businesses. **NOTE:** Submit resume online. **Positions advertised include:** Software Designer; Software Developer; Sales Representative.

ULTICOM INC.
1020 Briggs Road, Mount Laurel NJ 08054. 856/787-2700. **Toll-free phone:** 888/295-6664. **Fax:** 856/866-2033. **Contact:** Human Resources. **E-mail address:** hr@ulticom.com. **World Wide Web address:** http://www.ulticom.com. **Description:** Ulticom provides service-enabling, signaling software for wireless, wireline, and Internet communications. Ulticom's products are used by telecommunication equipment and service providers worldwide to deploy mobility, location, payment, switching, and messaging services. **NOTE:** Search and apply for positions online. **Positions advertised include:** Oracle CRM Project Lead; Customer Manager; Software Support Engineer; Technical Instructor; Sr. Product Manager; Software Quality Assurance Engineer System Test Engineer. **Listed on:** NASDAQ. **Stock exchange symbol:** ULCM.

New Mexico

AEROTEK
6700 Jefferson, Building E, Albuquerque NM 87109. 505/342-5000. **Toll-free phone:** 800/298-0534. **Fax:** 505/342-5052. **Contact:** Angelo Turiciano. **E-mail address:** aturicia@aerotek.com. **World Wide Web address:** http://www.aerotek.com. **Description:** Provides commercial, industrial, and technical recruiting and staffing services. **Positions advertised include:** Senior Piping Process Engineer; Test Engineer; Process Engineer; Software Engineer; Systems Test Engineer.

AFFILIATED COMPUTER SERVICES, INC.
14820 Central Avenue SE, Albuquerque NM 87123. 505/242-3443. **Contact:** Human Resources. **World Wide Web address:** http://www.acsonline.com. **Description:** Provides business process outsourcing and information technology solutions to commercial and government clients. **NOTE:** See website for current job openings and application instructions. **Positions advertised include:** Provider Help Desk Dental Specialist; Programmer Analyst III.

COMPUTER ASSETS
805 South Riverside Drive, Espanola NM 87532. 877/448-9386. **Fax:** 505/753-6347. **Contact:** Human Resources. **World Wide Web address:** http://www.computerassets.com. **Description:** Provides communications solutions for state agencies and schools. **NOTE:** See website for current job openings and application instructions. **Positions advertised include:** Server Engineer; Design Engineer; Director of NocNett; HR Generalist/Recruiter; Accounts Payable Clerk.

GREAT RIVER TECHNOLOGY
6121 Indian School Road NE, Suite 141, Albuquerque NM 87110. 505/881-6262. **Contact:** Human Resources. **E-mail address:** jalexand@greatrivertech.com. **World Wide Web address:** http://www.greatrivertech.com. **Description:** Specializes in high performance digital video solutions for aerospace and the military.

HOLMAN'S
6201 Jefferson Street NE, Albuquerque NM 87109. 505/343-0007. **Contact:** Human Resources. **E-mail address:** jobs@holmans.com. **World Wide Web address:** http://www.holmans.com. **Description:** Provides advanced solution-oriented technologies for professionals in the fields of GIS, engineering, surveying, construction, government, education, and business.

IBM CORPORATION
2155 Louisiana Boulevard NE, Suite 10500, Albuquerque NM 87110. **Toll-free phone:** 800/426-4968. **Contact:** Human Resources. **World Wide Web address:** http://www.ibm.com. **Description:** A developer, manufacturer, and marketer of advanced information processing products including computers and microelectronic technology, software, networking systems, and information technology-related services. **NOTE:** Search and apply for positions online. **Corporate headquarters location:** Armonk NY. **Other area locations:** Farmington NM; Santa Fe NM. **Subsidiaries include:** IBM Rational Software Corporation; IBM Instruments, Inc.; IBM World Trade Corporation.

NORSAM TECHNOLOGIES, INC.
852 Gilmore, Santa Fe NM 87501. 505/984-1133. **Fax:** 815/550-1394. **Contact:** Human Resources. **World Wide Web address:** http://www.norsam.com. **Description:** Provides services and products in the fields of nanotechnology, micro tooling, archival preservation, and gemstone marking.

OSOGRANDE TECHNOLOGIES INC.
5921 Jefferson Avenue NE, Albuquerque NM 87109. 505/345-6555. **Contact:** Human Resources. **E-mail address:** jobs@osogrande.com. **World Wide Web address:** http://www.osogrande.com. **Description:** A locally owned and operated Internet/telecommunications company. Founded in 1984. **NOTE:** Search and apply for positions online. **Positions advertised include:** Network Engineer III. **Number of employees at this location:** 45.

POD INC.
5971 Jefferson NE, Suite 101, Albuquerque NM 87109. 505/243-2287. **Fax:** 505/243-4677. **Contact:** James Geisler. **E-mail address:** jageisl@respec.com. **World Wide Web address:** http://www.podassoc.com. **Description:** Provides solutions for the development, maintenance, and support of information systems. POD specializes in network setup and support, database creation and support, and Web development and support. Founded in 1988. **Special programs:** Internships; Apprenticeships; Co-ops. **Other U.S. locations:** Phoenix AZ. **Parent company:** RESPEC.

RHINOCORPS
1128 Pennsylvania Avenue, Suite 100, Albuquerque NM 87110. 505/323-9836. **Fax:** 505/323-9863. **Contact:** Human Resources. **E-mail address:** hr@rhinocorps.com. **World Wide Web address:** http://www.rhinocorps.com. **Description:** Provides specialized professional engineering and software services with an emphasis in Modeling and Simulation, Software Development, Web-based Application Development, and Specialized Scientific and Engineering services. **Positions advertised include:** Programmer.

WIRED NATION
3600 Cerillos Road, Suite 711, Santa Fe NM 87507. 505/471-2820. **Fax:** 866/260-0795. **Contact:** Human Resources. **E-mail address:** info@wirednation.com. **World Wide Web Address:** http://www.wirednation.com. **Description:** Provides computer consulting services. **NOTE:** Please apply for positions through company website.

New York

AMI (ADVANCED MEDIA INC.)
80 Orville Drive, Bohemia NY 11716. 631/244-1616. **Fax:** 631/244-3209. **Contact:** Office Manager. **World Wide Web address:** http://www.advancedmedia.net. **Description:** Provides professional multimedia development products, services, and proprietary technologies to corporate accounts. AMI's services include Website designing and redesigning. **Listed on:** Over The Counter. **Stock exchange symbol:** AVMJ. **Annual sales/revenues:** $1.26 million. **Number of employees:** 7.

A2IA CORPORATION
584 Broadway, Suite 810, New York NY 10012-3229. 917/237-0390. **Fax:** 917/237-0391. **Contact:** Human Resources. **E-mail address:** career@a2ia.com. **World Wide Web address:** http://www.a2ia.com. **Description:** Develops natural handwriting recognition, intelligent word recognition, and intelligent character recognition technologies and products for the payment, mail, document, and forms processing markets. A2iA's products are used in banking and finance, insurance and healthcare, retail and direct merchants, government, telecommunications, mail, and other paper-intensive industries. **Positions advertised include:** Technical Support Engineer. **Corporate headquarters location:** Paris France.

ADVANCE CIRCUIT TECHNOLOGY, INC.
19 Jet View Drive, Rochester NY 14624. 585/328-2000. **Fax:** 585/328-2019. **Contact:** Human Resources Department. **World Wide Web address:** http://www.advcircuit.com. **Description:** A contract manufacturer of hybrid circuits and printed circuit board assemblies. **Positions advertised include:** Quality Engineer.

AJILON SERVICES INC.
317 Madison Avenue, Suite 500, New York NY 10017. 212/661-8235. **Fax:** 212/867-3583. **Contact:** Human Resources. **World Wide Web address:** http://www.ajilon.com. **Description:** Offers computer consulting services, staffing services, project support, and end user services with 450 offices in 17 countries.

Corporate headquarters location: Towson MD. **Other U.S. locations:** Worldwide.

ANALYSTS INTERNATIONAL CORPORATION
7 Penn Plaza, Suite 300, New York NY 10001. 212/465-1660. **Fax:** 212/465-1724. **Contact:** Recruiter. **World Wide Web address:** http://www.analysts.com. **Description:** AIC is an international computer consulting firm. The company assists clients in developing systems in a variety of industries using different programming languages and software. **Corporate headquarters location:** Minneapolis MN. **Other U.S. locations:** Nationwide. **International locations:** Cambridge, England; Toronto, Canada. **Listed on:** NASDAQ. **Stock exchange symbol:** ANLY. **Annual sales/revenues:** $426 million. **Number of employees:** 3,200.

ANSEN CORPORATION
100 Chimney Point Drive, Ogdensburg NY 13669-2289. 315/393-3573. **Fax:** 315/393-7638. **Contact:** Human Resources. **E-mail address:** info@ansencorp.com. **World Wide Web address:** http://www.ansencorp.com. **Description:** Formerly Aimtronics, Ansen manufactures electronic products and componets for the microelectronic and computer industry including computer parts and hybrid circuits. The company provides services including printed circuit board surface mounting and assembles chip-on board and multi-chip modules. **Corporate headquarters location:** This location. **International locations:** Kanata, Ontario, Canada. **Parent company:** Ansen Group (Kanata, Ontario, Canada).

AUTHENTIDATE HOLDING CORPORATION
811 10th Avenue, New York NY 10019. 212/459-0416. **Contact:** Human Resources. **World Wide Web address:** http://www.authentidate.com. **Description:** The company's main subsidiary, AuthentiDate, Inc., is engaged in the manufacture and distribution of document imaging systems, computer systems and related peripheral equipment, components, and accessories and network and Internet services. **Corporate headquarters location:** Berkeley Heights NJ. **Subsidiaries include:** AuthentiDate, Inc.; Computer Professionals International; DocSTAR; Authentidate Sports Edition; Trac Medical Solutions, Inc.; DJS Marketing Group, Inc.; WebCMN, Inc. **Listed on:** NASDAQ. **Stock exchange symbol:** ADAT. **President/CEO:** Suren Pai. **Annual sales/revenues:** $16 million. **Number of employees:** 41.

BANCTEC SYSTEMS, INC.
888 Veterans Memorial Highway, Suite 515, Hauppauge NY 11788. 631/234-5353. **Contact:** Human Resources. **E-mail address:** jobs@banctec.com. **World Wide Web address:** http://www.banctec.com. **Description:** BancTec is engaged in systems integration and specializes in document management solutions. The company also provides network support services and develops image management software. Founded in 1972. **NOTE:** Resumes should be sent to P.O. Box 660204, Dallas TX 75266-0204. **Corporate headquarters location:** Dallas TX. **Other locations:** Worldwide. **Number of employees worldwide:** 3,000.

BARRISTER GLOBAL SERVICES NETWORK, INC.
186 Exchange Street, Buffalo NY 14204-2026. 716/845-5033. **Toll-free phone:** 800/786-2472. **Fax:** 716/845-1867. **Contact:** Human Resources. **World Wide Web address:** http://www.barrister.com. **Description:** Barrister Global Services Network provides multivendor computer equipment maintenance services. Founded in 1972. **Positions advertised include:** Technical Support Specialist. **Corporate headquarters location:** New Orleans LA. **Subsidiaries include:** Barrister Advantage Services LLC. **Listed on:** American Stock Exchange. **Stock exchange symbol:** BIS. **President/CEO:** Henry (Hank) P. Semmelhack. **Annual sales/revenues:** $12.8 million. **Number of employees:** 122.

BIDNET
20A Railroad Avenue, Albany NY 12205. **Toll-free phone:** 800/677-1997. **Contact:** Human Resources. **E-mail address:** info@bidnet.com. **World Wide Web address:** http://www.bidnet.com. **Description:** Provides a centralized bid distribution and notification service to both government purchasing agencies and the companies who sell to them. The E-Procurement Division provides online procurement systems servicing state and local government agencies throughout the U.S. Founded in 1985. **Positions advertised include:** Quality Assurance Analyst; Web Developer/Programmer.

BIGVAULT
47 Mall Drive, Commack NY 11725-5717. 631/864-3636. **Contact:** Human Resources. **E-mail address:** jobs@bigvault.com. **World Wide Web address:** http://www.bigvault.com. **Description:** Offers online file storage, remote backup, and recovery services to individuals, small- to medium-sized businesses, and resellers as a privately labeled online service. **Positions advertised include:** Software Developer. **Parent company:** Digi-Data Corporation.

CAM GRAPHICS COMPANY INC.
166 New Highway, Amityville NY 11701. 631/842-3400. **Fax:** 631/842-1005. **Contact:** Human Resources. **E-mail address:** info@camgraphics.com. **World Wide Web address:** http://www.camgraphics.com. **Description:** CAM Graphics Company supplies businesses and manufacturers with assorted memory-related devices.

CAPGEMINI U.S.
750 7th Avenue, Suite 1800, New York NY 10019. 212/314-8000. **Fax:** 212/314-8001. **Contact:** Human Resources. **World Wide Web address:** http://www.us.capgemini.com. **Description:** Provider of management consulting services including business strategy, operations, and people and information management. Services include systems integration; application design, development, and documentation; systems conversions and migrations; and information technology consulting. **NOTE:** Jobseekers are encouraged to apply online. **Positions advertised include:** Oracle Planner; Graphic Designer; JD Edwards Planner; Patient Financial Services Manager; Supply Chain Health Manager; Health Information Manager; Health Revenue Manager; Tech Direct Sales Executive; Business Transformation Manager; Campus Health Providers Consultant; Clinical Health Integrator. **Corporate headquarters location:** This location. **Other U.S. locations:** Nationwide. **International locations:** Worldwide. **Parent company:** Cap Gemini Ernst & Young (Paris, France). **Number of employees:** 10,000.

CENTRIS GROUP
100 Merrick Road, Suite 418E, Rockville Centre NY 11570. 516/766-4448. **Fax:** 516/766-4896. **Contact:** Human Resources. **E-mail address:** centrisresumes@centrisgroup.com. **World Wide Web address:** http://www.centrisgroup.com. **Description:** Develops web-based products for the educational market. Founded in 1984. **Positions advertised include:** Crystal Reports Developer.

CLICK COMMERCE SPO, INC.
500 Willow Brook Office Park, Suite 500, Fairport NY 14450. 716/248-9600. **Toll-free phone:** 800/248-9602. **Fax:** 585/258-9199. **Contact:** Human Resources Department. **World Wide Web address:** http://www.clickcommerce.com. **Description:** Develops supply chain management software for large corporations. **Corporate headquarters location:** Chicago IL. **Other U.S. locations:** San Francisco CA; Portland OR; Costa Mesa CA; Fremont CA; Houston TX. **International locations:** United Kingdom. **Listed on:** NASDAQ. **Stock exchange symbol:** CKCM.

CLIENTLOGIC
640 Ellicott Street, Suite 390, Buffalo NY 14203. 716/871-6400. **Fax:** 716/871-2157. **Contact:** Human

Resources. **E-mail address:** buffalojobs@clientlogic.com. **World Wide Web address:** http://www.clientlogic.com. **Description:** Provides outsourcing services to a variety of Fortune 2000 companies. **Positions advertised include:** Customer Service Representative; Telesales Representative. **Corporate headquarters location:** Nashville TN. **Other U.S. locations:** Nationwide. **International locations:** Austria; France; Germany; Ireland; Spain; United Kingdom. **Number of employees:** 12,000.

COMPUTER ASSOCIATES INTERNATIONAL, INC.
One Computer Associates Plaza, Islandia NY 11749. 631/342-6000. **Fax:** 631/342-6800. **Contact:** Global Recruiting Department. **E-mail address:** joinca@ca.com. **World Wide Web address:** http://www.ca.com. **Description:** A developer of client/server and computer software, the company develops, markets, and supports enterprise management, database and applications development, business applications, and consumer software products for a broad range of mainframe, midrange, and desktop computers. Computer Associates International serves major business, government, research, and educational organizations. Founded in 1976. **Positions advertised include:** Business Development Owner; Business Manager; Channel Marketing Manager; Channel Program Manager; Collections Representative; Contract Representative; Database Manager; Product Management Director; Project Manager; Proposal Specialist; Quality Assurance Engineer; Regional Legal Manager; Sales Specialist; Software Engineer. **Special programs:** Internships. **Corporate headquarters location:** This location. **Other U.S. locations:** Nationwide. **Subsidiaries include:** ACCPAC International, Inc. **Operations at this facility include:** Administration; Research and Development; Sales. **Listed on:** New York Stock Exchange. **Stock exchange symbol:** CA. **Chairman/President/CEO:** Sanjay Kumar. **Annual sales/revenues:** $3 billion. **Number of employees at this location:** 2,500. **Number of employees worldwide:** 16,600.

COMPUTER HORIZONS CORPORATION
845 Third Avenue, 6th Floor, New York NY 10022. 212/371-9600. **Toll-free phone:** 800/847-4097. **Fax:** 212/980-4676. **Contact:** Recruiting. **E-mail address:** info@computerhorizons.com. **World Wide Web address:** http://www.computerhorizons.com. **Description:** A full-service technology solutions company offering contract staffing, outsourcing, re-engineering, migration, downsizing support, and network management. The company has a worldwide network of 33 offices. Founded in 1969. **Positions advertised include:** Systems Analyst. **Corporate headquarters location:** Mountain Lakes NJ. **Other U.S. locations:** Nationwide. **Subsidiaries include:** Birla Horizons International Ltd.; Horizons Consulting, Inc.; Strategic Outsourcing Services, Inc.; Unified Systems Solutions, Inc. **Listed on:** NASDAQ. **Stock exchange symbol:** CHRZ. **Annual sales/revenues:** $279 million. **Number of employees nationwide:** 1,400. **Number of employees worldwide:** 2,800

COMPUTER SCIENCES CORPORATION (CSC)
1 CSC Way, Rensselaer NY 12144. 518/447-9200. **Contact:** Human Resources. **World Wide Web address:** http://www.csc.com. **Description:** An information technology services company offering systems design and integration; IT and business process outsourcing; applications software development; Web and application hosting; and management consulting. **Description: Positions advertised include:** Application Developer; Network Administrator; Technician. **Corporate headquarters location:** El Segundo CA. **Listed on:** New York Stock Exchange. **Stock exchange symbol:** CSC. **Number of employees worldwide:** 79,000.

CURAM SOFTWARE INC.
595 New Loudon Road, Suite 275, Latham NY 12110. **Contact:** Human Resources. **E-mail address:** USjobs@CuramSoftware.com. **World Wide Web address:** http://www.curamsoftware.com. **Description:** Provides social enterprise management software for social agencies including health, human services, labor, workers' compensation, and social security programs. Founded in 1990. **Positions advertised include:** Technical Project Manager. **Corporate headquarters location:** Dublin Ireland. **Other U.S. locations:** Herndon VA.

CYBER DIGITAL, INC.
400 Oser Avenue, Suite 1650, Hauppauge NY 11788-3641. 631/231-1200. **Fax:** 631/231-1446. **Contact:** Human Resources. **E-mail address:** cybd@cyberdigitalinc.com. **World Wide Web address:** http://www.cyberdigitalinc.com. **Description:** Cyber Digital designs, develops, manufactures, and markets digital switching and networking systems that enable simultaneous communication of voice and data to a large number of users. The company's systems are based on its proprietary software technology that permits the modem-less transmission of data between a variety of incompatible and dissimilar end user equipment including computers, printers, workstations, and data terminals over standard telephone lines. **Corporate headquarters location:** This location. **Listed on:** Over The Counter. **Stock exchange symbol:** CYBD.

CYBERCHRON CORPORATION
2700 Route 9, P.O. Box 160, Cold Spring NY 10516. 845/265-3700 ext. 243. **Fax:** 845/265-2909. **Contact:** Ms. Gerry Maroulis, Human Resources. **E-mail address:** gmaroulis@cyberchron.com. **World Wide Web address:** http://www.cyberchron.com. **Description:** Cyberchron manufactures computers that are made to withstand environmental extremes. The U.S. military is one user of Cyberchron's products as well as foreign defense departments. **NOTE:** Human Resources telephone extension: x243. **Positions advertised include:** Regional Sales Representative.

DESIGN STRATEGY CORPORATION
600 Third Avenue, 25th Floor, New York NY 10016. 212/370-0000. **Fax:** 212/949-3648. **Contact:** Human Resources. **World Wide Web address:** http://www.designstrategy.com. **Description:** Develops and markets inventory control software. **Positions advertised include:** SAS Programmer/Analyst; Network Engineer; Egenera Systems Administrator. **Corporate headquarters location:** This location. **Other locations:** Upper Marlboro MD; Cranford NJ.

DIRECT INSITE CORPORATION
80 Orville Drive, Suite 100, Bohemia NY 11716. 631/244-1500. **Fax:** 631/563-8085. **Contact:** Human Resources. **World Wide Web address:** http://www.directinsite.com. **Description:** Direct Insite Corp. designs, markets, and supports information delivery software products including end user data access tools for personal computers and client/server environments, and systems management software products for corporate mainframe data centers. Products include dbExpress, which offers methods of searching, organizing, analyzing, and utilizing information contained in databases; systems management software products, which improve mainframe system performance, reduce hardware expenditures, and enhance the reliability and availability of the data processing environment; client/server products, which develop client/server relational database administration and programmer productivity tools. **Corporate headquarters location:** This location. **Subsidiaries include:** d.b.Express; Account Management Systems. **Listed on:** NASDAQ. **Stock exchange symbol:** DIRI. **Chairman/CEO:** James A. Cannavino. **Annual sales/revenues:** $4 million. **Number of employees:** 65.

E.F.L.S.
545 Eighth Avenue, Suite 401, New York NY 10018. 212/868-1121. **Fax:** 212/714-1453. **Contact:** Human Resources. **World Wide Web address:** http://www.efls.net. **Description:** Provides telephone

and messaging services as well as computer consulting services for Macintosh systems.

ELECTROGRAPH SYSTEMS INC.
50 Marcus Boulevard, Hauppauge NY 11788. 631/951-7065. **Fax:** 631/951-8892. **Contact:** Carol Dinow, Recruitment Manager. **World Wide Web address:** http://www.electrograph.com. **Description:** Distributes microcomputer peripherals, components, and accessories throughout the East Coast of the United States. Electrograph Systems distributes national brand names such as Mitsubishi, Sony, Hitachi, Magnavox, Toshiba, and Idex. The company's products include monitors, printers, large-screen televisions, CD-ROMs, computer video products, optical storage products, notebook computers, and personal computers. Founded in 1982. **Other U.S. locations:** Garden Grove CA; Madeira Beach FL; Woodridge IL; Olathe KS; Timonium MD; Plano TX. **Parent company:** Manchester Technologies, Inc. (also at this location).

ENSCO INC.
3 Holiday Hill Road, Endicott NY 13760. 607/786-9000. **Contact:** Human Resources. **World Wide Web address:** http://www.ensco.com. **Description:** The company provides engineering, science, and advanced information technologies software for the defense, security, transportation, environmental, and aerospace industries. Founded in 1969. **Positions advertised include:** Electrical Design Engineer; Technical Writer. **Corporate headquarters location:** Springfield VA. **Other locations:** Melbourne FL; Cocoa Beach FL; Beijing, China. **Number of employees:** 800.

FALCONSTOR SOFTWARE, INC.
2 Huntington Quadrangle, Suite 2S01, Melville NY 11747. 631/777-5188. **Fax:** 631/501-7633. **Contact:** Human Resources. **E-mail address:** careers@falconstor.com. **World Wide Web address:** http://www.falconstor.com. **Description:** Develops data storage and protection software and related services such as consulting, engineering, implementation, and maintenance. **Positions advertised include:** Product Manager; Technical Marketing Manager; Marketing Writer; Application Developer; Java Programmer; System Software Engineer; Quality Assurance Engineer; Senior Technical Project Manager; Storage Architect. **Listed on:** NASDAQ. **Stock exchange symbol:** FALC.

HAUPPAUGE DIGITAL INC.
dba HAUPPAUGE COMPUTER WORKS INC.
91 Cabot Court, Hauppauge NY 11788. 631/434-1600. **Fax:** 631/434-3198. **Contact:** Cheryl Willins, Human Resources Manager. **World Wide Web address:** http://www.hauppauge.com. **Description:** Manufactures PC circuit boards that allow viewers to use computers to watch TV, videoconference, and watch VCRs or camcorders as well as boards that allow for radio and Internet broadcasting. **Corporate headquarters location:** This location. **Other locations:** Worldwide. **Listed on:** NASDAQ. **Stock exchange symbol:** HAUP. **Chairman/CEO:** Kenneth H. Plotkin. **Annual sales/revenues:** $43 million. **Number of employees:** 107.

HAZLOW ELECTRONICS INC.
49 Saint Bridget's Drive, Rochester NY 14605. 585/325-5323. **Fax:** 585/325-4308. **Contact:** Human Resources. **E-mail address:** info@hazlow.com. **World Wide Web address:** http://www.hazlow.com. **Description:** Manufactures cables for computers and other electronic devices. Founded in 1971.

IPC INFORMATION SYSTEMS
Wall Street Plaza, 88 Pine Street, New York NY 10005. 212/825-9060. **Fax:** 212/344-5106. **Contact:** Human Resources. **World Wide Web address:** http://www.ipc.com. **Description:** Provides network communications solutions for the financial industry. Through its Information Transport Systems (ITS) business, the company provides its customers with voice, data, and video solutions through the design, integration, implementation, and support of local and wide area networks. ITS solutions incorporate the latest technology and are supported by a team of systems engineers. Founded in 1973. **Corporate headquarters location:** This location. **International locations:** Asia; Europe. **Number of employees nationwide:** 775.

ITT INDUSTRIES
4 West Red Oak Lane, White Plains NY 10604. 914/641-2000. **Fax:** 914/696-2965. **Contact:** Katherine Campbell, Human Resources. **E-mail address:** Katherine.Campbell@itt.com. **World Wide Web address:** http://www.ittind.com. **Description:** A multinational company with operations divided into four business segments: fluid technology; defense electronics; motion and flow control; and electronic components; as well as providing maintenance services for its products. **Corporate headquarters location:** This location. **Other locations:** Worldwide. **Listed on:** New York Stock Exchange. **Stock exchange symbol:** ITT. **Subsidiaries include:** ITT Defense Electronics & Services. **Chairman/President/CEO:** Louis J. Giuliano. **Annual sales/revenues:** $5 billion. **Number of employees:** 38,000.

INFORMATION BUILDERS INC.
Two Penn Plaza, New York NY 10121-2898. 212/736-4433. **Fax:** 212/239-6674. **Contact:** Lila Goldberg, Human Resources Director. **E-mail address:** employment_opportunities@ibi.com. **World Wide Web address:** http://www.ibi.com. **Description:** A software development firm. Products include FOCUS, EDA, and SmartMart software for various platforms. **NOTE:** Jobseekers may see http://www.hotjobs.com for a listing of current openings with detailed application information. **Positions advertised include:** WebFOCUS Technical Specialist; MVS Systems Programmer; Network Operating Systems Analyst; XML Programmer; Sales Engineer; Software Engineer; Inside Sales Representative; Software Sales Representative; Direct Marketing Manager; Administrator; Senior Administratorp Business Development Analyst; Senior Implementation Manager; Project Manager; WebFOCUS Team Leader. **Corporate headquarters location:** This location. **Other U.S. locations:** Nationwide. **President:** Gerald D. Cohen. **Annual sales/revenues:** $300 million. **Number of employees:** 1,800.

INTERCON ASSOCIATES INCORPORATED
95 Allens Creek Road, Building 2, Suite 200, Rochester NY 14618. 585/244-1250. **Toll-free phone:** 800/422-3880. **Fax:** 585/473-4387. **Contact:** Personnel. **World Wide Web address:** http://www.interconweb.com. **Description:** Develops document assembly software and font cartridges.

INTERNATIONAL BUSINESS MACHINES CORPORATION (IBM)
New Orchard Road, Armonk NY 10504. 914/499-1900. **Fax:** 914/765-7382. **Recorded jobline:** 800/796-9876. **Contact:** IBM Staffing Services Center. **World Wide Web address:** http://www.ibm.com. **Description:** A developer, manufacturer, and marketer of advanced information processing products including computers and microelectronic technology, software, networking systems, and information technology-related services. **Positions advertised include:** Executive Assistant; Business Controls Advisor; EOL Administrator Analyst; Human Capital Analyst; Sales Operation Specialist; SAP Conversion Analyst; SAP Security Analyst; Senior Tax Specialist; Tax Supplemental Specialist; Treasury Operations Manager. **Corporate headquarters location:** This location. **Other locations:** Worldwide. **Subsidiaries include:** Hitachi Global Storage Technologies; IBM Canada Ltd.; IBM Credit Corporation; IBM Global Services; IBM Instruments, Inc.; IBM Software; IBM World Trade Corporation; International Business Machines – Microelectronics; Lotus Development Corporation; Tivoli Software. **Listed on:** New York Stock Exchange. **Stock exchange symbol:** IBM. **Chairman/President/CEO:** Samuel J. Palmisano. **Annual sales/revenues:** $81.2 billion. **Number of employees:** 315,889.

INTERNET COMMERCE CORPORATION
45 Research Way, Suite 210, East Setauket NY 11733. 631/590-1010. **Fax:** 212/271-8580. **Contact:** Claire Schank, Human Resources Manager. **E-mail address:** hr@icc.net. **World Wide Web address:** http://www.icc.net. **Description:** Manufactures computer systems that enable protection, retrieval, and monitoring of digital information use. **Corporate headquarters location:** Norcross GA. **Listed on:** NASDAQ. **Stock exchange symbol:** ICCA. **Chairman:** Charles C. Johnston. **Number of employees:** 115.

INVESTMENT TECHNOLOGY GROUP, INC.
380 Madison Avenue, 4th Floor, New York NY 10017. 212/588-4000. **Toll-free phone:** 800/215-4484. **Fax:** 212/444-6295. **Contact:** Human Resources. **E-mail address:** itg_hr@itginc.com. **World Wide Web address:** http://www.itginc.com. **Description:** Provides automated securities trade execution and analysis services to institutional equity investors. ITG's two main services are POSIT, one of the largest automated stock crossing systems operated during trading hours, and QuantEX, a proprietary software to enhance customers' trading efficiencies, access to market liquidity, and portfolio analysis capabilities. **NOTE:** Human resources phone number is 617/692-6700. **Corporate headquarters location:** This location. **Other U.S. locations:** Los Angeles CA; Boston MA. **International locations:** Dublin, Ireland; Toronto, Canada; Melbourne, Australia; Hong Kong, China. **Subsidiaries include:** Hoenig Group Inc. **Listed on:** New York Stock Exchange. **Stock exchange symbol:** ITG. **Chairman:** Raymond L. Killian Jr. **Annual sales/revenues:** $388 million. **Number of employees:** 635.

JUNO ONLINE SERVICES, INC.
120 West 45th Street, New York NY 10036. 212/597-9000. **Contact:** Human Resources. **World Wide Web address:** http://www.juno.com. **Description:** A leading Internet access provider offering a variety of online services. Founded in 1996. **Positions advertised include:** Corporate Systems Administrator; Project Manager, Quality Assurance Engineer. **Special programs:** Internships. **Office hours:** Monday - Friday, 9:00 a.m. - 6:00 p.m. **Parent company:** United Online, Inc. **Corporate headquarters location:** Westlake Village CA. **Listed on:** NASDAQ. **Stock exchange symbol:** UNTD.

KANTEK INC.
3460 Hampton Road, Oceanside NY 11572. 516/594-4600. **Fax:** 516/594-1555. **Contact:** Human Resources Department. **E-mail address:** info@kantek.com. **World Wide Web address:** http://www.kantek.com. **Description:** Manufactures glare reduction screens for computer monitors as well as other computer and desk accessories. Founded in 1982. **NOTE:** Human Resources phone: 516/593-3212.

KEANE, INC.
525 Seventh Avenue, 4th Flloor, New York NY 10018-4901. 212/677-8800. **Fax:** 212/677-9654. **Contact:** Human Resources. **E-mail address:** careers.nyc@keane.com. **World Wide Web address:** http://www.keane.com. **Description:** Keane develops, markets, and manages software for its clients and assists in project management as well as offering computer consulting services. Founded in 1965. **Company slogan:** We Get IT Done. **Positions advertised include:** Programmer Analyst; Systems Analyst; Service Delivery Manager; Application Specialist; Database Administrator; Project Manager; Business Analyst. **Corporate headquarters location:** Boston MA. **Other U.S. locations:** Nationwide. **Operations at this facility include:** Divisional Headquarters **Listed on:** American Stock Exchange. **Stock exchange symbol:** KEA. **Number of employees:** 7,331.

LSI COMPUTER SYSTEMS INC.
1235 Walt Whitman Road, Melville NY 11747-3010. 631/271-0400. **Fax:** 631/271-0405. **Contact:** Human Resources. **E-mail address:** hr@lsicsi.com. **World Wide Web address:** http://www.lsicsi.com. **Description:** Manufactures integrated circuits and microchips. Founded in 1969. **Positions advertised include:** Integrated Circuit Design Engineer; Integrated Circuit Layout Designer; Test Engineer.

MAINTECH
560 Lexington Avenue, 15th Floor, New York NY 10020. 212/704-2400. **Fax:** 212/944-1639. **Contact:** Jan Ferrer or Louise Ross. **E-mail address:** jferrer@voltdelta.com or lross@voltdelta.com. **World Wide Web address:** http://www.maintech.com. **Description:** Provides on-site computer maintenance services. **Corporate headquarters location:** Wallington NJ. **Other locations:** Orange CA. **Parent company:** Volt Delta Resources (also at this location).

MANCHESTER TECHNOLOGIES, INC.
160 Oser Avenue, Hauppauge NY 11788-3711. 631/435-1199. **Fax:** 631/951-7913. **Contact:** Human Resources. **Description:** A network integrator and reseller of computer systems, software, and peripherals. Manchester also services and maintains computer systems, manages networks, distributes peripherals, and offers temporary IT staffing. Founded in 1973. **NOTE:** Human Resources phone: 631/951-7065. **Positions advertised include:** Purchasing Clerk; Customer Service Representative. **Subsidiaries include:** Coastal Office Products; Electrograph Systems; ManTech Computer Services; Donovan Consulting Group; eTrack Solutions. **Listed on:** NASDAQ. **Stock exchange symbol:** MANC. **Chairman/President/CEO:** Barry R. Steinberg. **Annual sales/revenues:** $262 million. **Number of employees:** 348.

MAPINFO CORPORATION
One Global View, Troy NY 12180-8371. 518/285-6000. **Fax:** 518/285-6070. **Contact:** Human Resources. **E-mail address:** jobs@mapinfo.com. **World Wide Web address:** http://www.mapinfo.com. **Description:** Develops geography software and databases used in business intelligence, analysis, and forecasting by commercial and public sector clients for emergency response and planning. The company operates offices in 60 countries providing geography software in 20 languages as well as offering consulting, training, and support services. **Positions advertised include:** Channel Marketing & Events Specialist; International Quality Engineer; Quality Assurance Engineer. **Corporate headquarters location:** This location. **Other locations:** Worldwide. **Listed on:** NASDAQ. **Stock exchange symbol:** MAPS. **Chairman:** John C. Cavalier. **Annual sales/revenues:** $93 million. **Number of employees:** 681.

MERCURY INTERACTIVE CORPORATION
One Penn Plaza, Suite 1721, New York NY 10019. 212/613-0800. **Contact:** Jeff Loehr, Director of Human Resources. **World Wide Web address:** http://www.mercury.com/us. **Description:** Mercury Interactive is a provider of automated software quality tools for enterprise applications testing. The company's products are used to isolate software and system errors prior to application deployment. **Corporate headquarters location:** Mountain View CA. **Other U.S. locations:** Nationwide. **International locations:** Worldwide. **Subsidiaries include:** Freshwater Software, Inc. **Listed on:** NASDAQ. **Stock exchange symbol:** MERQ. **Chairman/President/CEO:** Amnon Landon. **Annual sales/revenue:** $400 million. **Number of employees:** 1,822.

MOBIUS MANAGEMENT SYSTEMS, INC.
120 Old Post Road, Rye NY 10580. 914/921-7200. **Fax:** 914/921-1360. **Contact:** Human Resources. **E-mail address:** staffing@mobius.com. **World Wide Web address:** http://www.mobius.com. **Description:** Develops and sells business-related software products including a report distribution program and an automated balance program. **Positions advertised include:** Customer Support Representative; Quality Assurance Analyst; Quality Assurance Software

Developer; Software Engineer; Project Manager; Business Systems Analyst; Senior Technical Writer. **Other U.S. locations:** Nationwide. **Listed on:** NASDAQ. **Stock exchange symbol:** MOBI. **Chairman/President/CEO:** Mitchell Gross. **Annual sales/revenues:** $68 million. **Number of employees:** 408.

MUZE INC.
304 Hudson Street, 8th Floor, New York NY 10013. 212/824-0300. **Fax:** 212/741-1246. **Contact:** Jeanne Petras, Director of Personnel. **E-mail address:** humanresource@muze.com. **World Wide Web address:** http://www.muze.com. **Description:** Muze is a multimedia company that develops software for touch-screen, point-of-sales terminals that allow users access to a musical database. **Positions advertised include:** MS Access Database Coordinator; In-house Legal Counsel; E-Commerce Developer; Java/XML Developer. **Special programs:** Internships. **Corporate headquarters location:** This location. **International locations:** United Kingdom. **Parent company:** MetroMedia. **Operations at this facility include:** Administration; Manufacturing; Research and Development; Sales; Service. **Number of employees at this location:** 120.

NEXTSOURCE
120 East 56th Street, 12th Floor, New York NY 10022. 212/736-5870. **Toll-free phone:** 800/727-6583. **Fax:** 212/736-9046. **Contact:** Human Resources. **World Wide Web address:** http://www.nextsource.com. **Description:** Develops and offers instructor-led and computer-based personal computer training programs and provides consulting services, primarily to large businesses and public sector organizations. The company's instructor-led training programs include a wide range of introductory and advanced classes in operating systems including MS/DOS, Microsoft Windows, and Macintosh systems; word processing; spreadsheets; databases; communications; executive overviews; integrated software packages; computer graphics; and desktop publishing. The company's computer-based training programs include offerings on Lotus Notes, CC Mail, Microsoft Office, and Lotus Smartsuite. The consulting division provides computer personnel on a temporary basis. **Parent company:** Formula Systems, Limited. **Listed on:** NASDAQ. **Stock exchange symbol:** FORTY. **President/CEO:** Joseph Musacchio. **Sales/revenue:** Over $700 million.

OMX
140 Broadway, 25th Floor, New York NY 10005. 646/428-2800. **Contact:** Human Resources. **World Wide Web address:** http://www.om.com. **Description:** OM Technologies develops software for the securities and brokerage industries. **Corporate headquarters location:** Stockholm, Sweden. **International locations:** Worldwide. **Listed on:** Stockholmsborsen. **Stock exchange symbol:** OM. **Number of employees worldwide:** Over 16,000.

ORACLE CORPORATION
560 White Plains Road, Suite 315, Tarrytown NY 10591. 914/524-1600. **Contact:** Human Resources. **E-mail address:** resumes_us@oracle.com. **World Wide Web address:** http://www.oracle.com. **Description:** Designs and manufactures database and information management software for business and provides consulting services. **NOTE:** Resumes should be submitted online or sent to Human Resources, 500 Oracle Parkway, Redwood Shores CA 94065. **Corporate headquarters location:** Redwood Shores CA. **Other U.S. locations:** Nationwide. **International locations:** Worldwide. **Listed on:** NASDAQ. **Stock exchange symbol:** ORCL. **CEO/Chairman:** Lawrence J. Ellison. **Number of employees worldwide:** 43,000.

PENCOM SYSTEMS INC.
40 Fulton Street, 18th Floor, New York NY 10038-1850. 212/513-7777. **Fax:** 212/227-1854. **Contact:** Tom Morgan, Recruiting. **E-mail address:** career@pencom.com. **World Wide Web address:** http://www.pencom.com. **Description:** Provides computer consulting services including open systems management and software consulting. **NOTE:** Resumes submitted via e-mail must be formatted in HTML, Microsoft Word, or plain text. **Positions advertised include:** Research Associate; Toxicologist; Regulatory Affairs Associate; Quality Assurance Engineer; Project Manager; Pharmacist; Pharmaceutical Sales Representative; Microbiologist; Clinical Researcher; Clinical Database Designer; Biostatistician; **Corporate headquarters location:** This location. **Other U.S. locations:** Santa Clara CA; Boston MA; Ruston VA; Chicago IL; Livingston NJ.

PERFORMANCE TECHNOLOGIES
205 Indigo Creek Drive, Rochester NY 14626-5100. 585/256-0200. **Contact:** K. Mikityansky, Human Resources. **E-mail address:** km@pt.com. **World Wide Web address:** http://www.pt.com. **Description:** Develops systems, platforms, components, and software for communications infrastructure in commercial and military markets. Principal Software Engineer, Embedded Real-Time; IS Operations, Group Leader; Electronic Technician; Technical Support Engineer; Software Product Manager.

PRAXAIR MRC
542 Route 303, Orangeburg NY 10962. 845/398-8307. **Contact:** Human Resources Department. **World Wide Web address:** http://www.praxairmrc.com. **Description:** Designs and manufactures thin-film coating and etching systems used in the manufacture of integrated circuits for sale to the semiconductor, computer, and telecommunications industries. The company also processes and fabricates ultra-high-purity metals and metal alloys, principally for thin-film purposes. Praxair MRC's thin-film technology products are also used in nonelectronic applications such as protective coatings for corrosion and wear resistance in razor blades and various automotive products. The company operates in three segments: Sputtering Equipment, Associated Target Materials, and Other High-Purity Materials. **Special programs:** Internships. **Corporate headquarters location:** This location. **International locations:** France; Korea; Taiwan. **Parent company:** Praxair, Incorporated. **Listed on:** New York Stock Exchange. **Stock exchange symbol:** PX. **Number of employees at this worldwide:** Over 250.

ROYALBLUE TECHNOLOGIES INC.
17 State Street, New York NY 10004-1501. 212/269-9000. **Contact:** Human Resources. **E-mail address:** resumes@royalblue.com. **World Wide Web address:** http://www.royalblue.com. **Description:** Develops software for the NASDAQ stock exchange. **Positions advertised include:** Technical Support Supervisor; Visual Basic Developer; Software Designer/Developer; Graduate Developer; Data Implementation Consultant; First-line Support Analyst. **International locations:** China; France; Japan; United Kingdom. **Number of employees worldwide:** Over 400.

SCJ ASSOCIATES INC.
60 Commerce Drive, Rochester NY 14623. 585/359-0600. **Fax:** 585/359-0856. **Contact:** Human Resources. **World Wide Web address:** http://www.scjassociates.com. **Description:** Assembles printed circuit boards. SCJ Associates also tests products and wraps cable. Founded in 1971.

SECTOR, INC.
90 Broad Street, Third Floor, New York NY 10004. 212/383-2000. **Toll-free phone:** 866/383-3315. **Fax:** 212/809-4978. **Contact:** Human Resources. **World Wide Web address:** http://www.sectorinc.com. **Description:** Provides a range of communications, networking, and managed services, which include archival compliance, outsourcing, facilities management, business continuity and disaster recovery compliance, E solutions, enterprise services, network, market data, and data distribution services. **Corporate headquarters location:** This location. **Other U.S. locations:** Chicago IL; San Francisco CA.

SECURITIES INDUSTRY AUTOMATION CORPORATION (SIAC)
2 Metrotech Center, Brooklyn NY 11201. 212/383-4800. **Contact:** Human Resources. **World Wide Web address:** http://www.siac.com. **Description:** SIAC is the technology subsidiary of the New York Stock Exchange and the American Stock Exchange, with responsibility for the design, development, implementation and operation of the exchanges' computer systems and communications networks. SIAC is responsible for disseminating U.S. market data worldwide. **Positions advertised include:** Lead Design Analyst/Web Application Development; Sr. Oracle Database Administrator; Systems Support Analyst. **Parent company:** New York Stock Exchange and American Stock Exchange.

STANDARD MICROSYSTEMS CORPORATION
80 Arkay Drive, P.O. Box 18047, Hauppauge NY 11788. 631/435-6000. **Fax:** 631/435-0373. **Contact:** Human Resources. **E-mail address:** jobsny@smsc.com. **World Wide Web address:** http://www.smsc.com. **Description:** This location houses the VLSI circuit design and LAN hub and switch engineering centers, marketing, customer support, and wafer fabrication, as well as operations and administrative staff. The company's Component Products Division supplies MOS/VLSI circuits for personal computers and embedded control systems. The System Products Division provides a range of networking solutions for scaling, managing, and controlling LANs. Founded in 1971. **Positions advertised include:** Design Engineer; Product Engineer; Design Automation Engineer. **Special programs:** Internships. **Corporate headquarters location:** This location. **Other U.S. locations:** Irvine CA; San Jose CA; Danvers MA; Austin TX. **International locations:** Worldwide. **Listed on:** NASDAQ. **Stock exchange symbol:** SMSC. **Annual sales/revenues:** More than $100 million. **Number of employees at this location:** 500. **Number of employees worldwide:** 800.

SUNBURST TECHNOLOGY
400 Columbus Avenue Suite 160E, Valhalla NY 10595-1349. 914/747-3310. **Fax:** 914/747-4109. **Contact:** Human Resources. **E-mail address:** hr-us@sunburst.com. **World Wide Web address:** http://www.sunburst.com. **Description:** Develops and markets educational videos and software. **Special programs:** Internships. **Office hours:** Monday - Friday, 8:00 a.m. - 5:00 p.m. **Corporate headquarters location:** This location. **Annual sales/revenues:** $21 - $50 million. **Number of employees at this location:** 150.

SYMBOL TECHNOLOGIES INC.
One Symbol Plaza, Holtsville NY 11742-1300. 631/738-2400. **Contact:** Human Resources. **E-mail address:** jobopps@symbol.com. **World Wide Web address:** http://www.symbol.com. **Description:** Symbol Technologies designs, manufactures, and markets integrated products based on barcode laser scanning, hand-held computing, and wireless LANs. **Positions advertised include:** Senior Manager. **Corporate headquarters location:** Costa Mesa CA. **Operations at this facility include:** This location manufactures barcode and data capture equipment. **Listed on:** New York Stock Exchange. **Stock exchange symbol:** SBL.

SYSTEMAX INC.
11 Harbor Park Drive, Port Washington NY 11050. 516/625-4300. **Fax:** 516/625-4072. **Contact:** Human Resources. **E-mail address:** recruiting@systemax.com. **World Wide Web address:** http://www.systemax.com. **Description:** A direct marketer of brand-name and private-label computer, office, and industrial products targeting mid-range and major corporate accounts, small office/home customers, and value-added resellers. Founded in 1949. **Positions advertised include:** Inside Sales Representative. **Special programs:** Internships; Summer Jobs. **Corporate headquarters location:** This location. **Other U.S. locations:** CA; FL; GA; IL; NJ; NC; OH. **Subsidiaries include:** Global Computer Supplies; Midwest Micro Corp.; Misco America, Inc.; Misco Canada Inc.; TigerDirect Inc. **Listed on:** New York Stock Exchange. **Stock exchange symbol:** SYX. **Annual sales/revenues:** More than $100 million. **Number of employees at this location:** 500. **Number of employees nationwide:** 2,000. **Number of employees worldwide:** 4,000.

TSR INC.
400 Oser Avenue, Suite 150, Hauppauge NY 11788. 631/231-0333. **Contact:** Recruiter. **World Wide Web address:** http://www.tsrconsulting.com. **Description:** Provides computer consulting services. **Positions advertised include:** Data Analyst; Senior Developer Programmer/Analyst; Senior Business Analyst; Rational Administrator; Centura/Oracle Developer. **Corporate headquarters location:** This location. **Listed on:** NASDAQ. **Stock exchange symbol:** TSRI.

TRACK DATA
95 Rockwell Place, Brooklyn NY 11217. 718/522-7373. **Contact:** Human Resources. **World Wide Web address:** http://www.trackdata.com. **Description:** Electronically provides trading information, news, and third-party database services on stocks, bonds, commodities, and other securities through its Dial/Data service. The company's AIQ Systems division produces expert systems software for individual and professional investors. **Listed on:** NASDAQ. **Stock exchange symbol:** TRAC.

VESON INC.
29 Broadway, Suite 1002, New York NY 10006. 212/422-0300. **Contact:** Michael Veson, Manager. **World Wide Web address:** http://www.veson.com. **Description:** Develops computer software for the shipping industry. **Corporate headquarters location:** Boston MA.

WEN TECHNOLOGY CORPORATION
22 Saw Mill River Road, Hawthorne NY 10532. 914/592-1145. **Fax:** 914/345-1147. **Contact:** Human Resources. **E-mail address:** info@wentech.com. **World Wide Web address:** http://www.wentech.com. **Description:** Manufactures computer monitors and displays. **Corporate headquarters location:** This location. **Annual sales/revenues:** $51 - $100 million. **Number of employees at this location:** 40.

North Carolina

AMT DATASOUTH CORPORATION
4216 Stuart Andrew Boulevard, Charlotte NC 28217. 704/523-8500. **Contact:** Human Resources. **E-mail address:** humanresources@amtdatasouth.com. **World Wide Web address:** http://www.amtdatasouth.com. **Description:** Designs, manufactures, and markets heavy-duty dot matrix and thermal printers used for high-volume print applications. The company's product lines include the XL series for medium-volume dot matrix printing applications and Documax, which has high-speed dot matrix printing capabilities. The company also manufactures a portable thermal printer, Freeliner, which is used primarily for printing one packing or shipping label at a time. **Corporate headquarters location:** Camarillo CA. **International locations:** Northampton, England. **Number of employees nationwide:** 125.

A4 HEALTH SYSTEMS
5501 Dillard Drive, Cary NC 27511. 919/851-6177. **Toll-free phone:** 888/672-3282. **Fax:** 919/851-5991. **Contact:** Human Resources. **E-mail address:** hr@A4healthsystems.com. **World Wide Web address:** http://www.a4healthsys.com. **Description:** Develops software and related hardware for hospitals to manage clinical, financial and administrative patient information. Founded in 1970. **Positions advertised include:** Regional Sales Manager/Sales Representative; HealthMatics ED Project Manager; EMR Implementation Specialist. **Corporate headquarters:** This location. **Other U.S. locations:** Novi MI; Austin TX; Nashua NH. **Parent company:** Allscripts.

AGILYSYS, INC.
7512 East Independence Boulevard, Suite 106, Charlotte NC 28227. 704/567-8203. **Toll-free phone:** 888/833-2106. **Fax:** 704/567-9468. **Contact:** Human Resources. **World Wide Web address:** http://www.agilysys.net. **Description:** Writes computer programs, resells computer hardware and software, and offers technical support. Founded 1974. **Corporate headquarters location:** Mayfield Heights OH. **Other area locations:** Greenville NC. **Other U.S. locations:** Nationwide. **Operations at this facility include:** Retail Solutions. **Listed on:** NASDAQ. **Stock exchange symbol:** AGYS.

AJILON CONSULTING
6000 Fairview Road, Suite 410, Charlotte NC 28210. 704/552-0868. **Toll-free phone:** 877/293-2342. **Fax:** 704/556-5902. **Contact:** Human Resources. **E-mail address:** recruit.charlotte@ajilon.com. **World Wide Web address:** http://www.ajilonconsulting.com. **Description:** Offers personalized IT solutions to Fortune 1000, mid-tier, government and private organizations in every industry. **Corporate headquarters location:** Towson MD. **Other U.S. locations:** Nationwide. **International locations:** Worldwide. **Parent company:** Adecco Group. **Number of employees worldwide:** 10,000.

AMDOCS
9401 Arrowpoint Boulevard, Charlotte NC 28273. 704/559-4900. **Fax:** 704/559-4949. **Contact:** Human Resources. **World Wide Web address:** http://www.amdocs.com. **Description:** Supplies operations support software used by telecommunications service providers to deliver voice, data, and wireless services to their customers. Amdocs also provides software to automate customer relationship management, sales, and billing operations, as well as publishing software for creating print and online directories. In addition, the company offers outsourced customer service and data center operations. **Positions advertised include:** Business Analyst; Conversion Developer; Customization Developer; Development Manager; Infrastructure Expert; Oracle Database Administrator; Quality Assurance Expert; Senior Testing Engineer; Software Developer; Senior Billing Analyst. **Corporate headquarters location:** St. Louis MO. **Other U.S. locations:** Jersey City NJ; El Dorado Hills CA; Alpharetta GA; San Jose CA; Champaign IL. **Listed on:** New York Stock Exchange. **Stock exchange symbol:** DOX. **Number of employees worldwide:** 13,000.

AVAYA INC.
ViViD Program Office C1D19, 5440 Millstream Road, McLeansville NC 27301. 336/574-7401. **Contact:** Human Resources. **World Wide Web address:** http://www.avaya.com. **Description:** Develops computer software and IT solutions. **Positions advertised include:** Purchasing Supervisor. **Corporate headquarters location:** Basking Ridge NJ. **Operations at this facility include:** ViViD Program Office provides management of the implementation and support of worldwide DoD Telecommunications and solutions.

COMPUTER TASK GROUP
6501 Weston Parkway, Suite 175, Cary NC 27513. 919/677-1313. **Fax:** 919/677-1910. **Contact:** Human Resources. **World Wide Web address:** http://www.ctg.com. **Description:** An IT company that develops software for project management and system enhancement, conversion, upgrade, implementation, testing, and maintenance. **Positions advertised include:** Unix Systems Administrator. **Corporate headquarters location:** Buffalo NY.

DATALINK CORPORATION
201 Shannon Oaks Circle, Suite 200, Cary NC 27511-5570. 919/654-4585. **Toll-free phone:** 800/771-9636. **Contact:** Human Resources. **E-mail address:** humanresources@datalink.com. **World Wide Web address:** http://www.datalink.com. **Description:** Datalink analyzes, designs, implements, and supports information storage infrastructures that store, protect, and provide continuous access to information. Datalink's capabilities and solutions span storage area networks, network-attached storage, direct-attached storage and IP-based storage, using hardware, software and technical services. **Positions advertised include:** Account Executive; Storage Engineer. **Corporate headquarters location:** Chanhassen MN. **Other U.S. locations:** Nationwide. **Listed on:** NASDAQ. **Stock exchange symbol:** DTLK.

FUJITSU TRANSACTIONS SOLUTIONS INC.
14101 Capitol Boulevard, Youngsville NC 27596. 919/556-6721. **Fax:** 919/556-7566. **Contact:** Personnel. **E-mail address:** careers@ftxs.fujitsu.com. **World Wide Web address:** http://www.ftxs.fujitsu.com. **Description:** Designs software for the banking, food, and retail industries. **Corporate headquarters location:** Frisco TX. **Other area locations:** Statewide. **Other U.S. locations:** Carrolton TX. **International locations:** Canada; Caribbean. **Parent company:** Fujitsu Limited. **Number of employee worldwide:** 1,000.

IBM EXECUTIVE BRIEFING CENTER
3039 Cornwallis Road, Building 002, Research Triangle Park NC 27707. 919/543-5221. **Contact:** Staffing Services. **World Wide Web address:** http://www-1.ibm.com/servers/eserver/briefingcenter/rtpbc. **Description:** Provides products and services to IBM Systems Group (IBM eServer and IBM Storage) and the IBM Personal Computing Division. The Briefing Center offers IBM Business Partners the opportunity to understand and view IBM's current and future solutions in a professional demonstration environment. **Positions advertised include:** Array Circuit Designer; Array Designer Engineer; Communications Professional; CSS Specialist; Engineer; Fulfillment Coordinator; Hardware Engineer; Licensing Technical Team Leader; Logic Design Engineer; Mechanical Engineer; Network Analyst; Network Management Professional; PeopleSoft Consultant; Physical Design Engineer; Program Manager; Scheduler; Software Engineer. **Special programs:** Internships; Co-ops. **Corporate headquarters location:** White Plains NY. **Other area locations:** Statewide. **Other U.S. locations:** Nationwide. **International locations:** Worldwide. **Parent company:** IBM Corporation. **Listed on:** New York Stock Exchange. **Stock exchange symbol:** IBM.

IENTERTAINMENT NETWORK
124 Quade Drive, Cary NC 27513. 919/678-8301. **Fax:** 919/678-8302. **Contact:** Human Resources. **E-mail address:** cwall@ient.com. **World Wide Web address:** http://www.ient.com. **Description:** Develops and produces strategy and simulation computer games and online entertainment communities. **Corporate headquarters location:** This location. **Listed on:** NASDAQ. **Stock exchange symbol:** IENT.

KNOWLEDGE SYSTEMS CORPORATION
1143 Executive Circle, Suite G, Cary NC 27511. 919/789-8549. **Toll-free phone:** 800/348-8323. **Fax:** 919/789-8615. **Contact:** Recruiting Manager. **E-mail address:** jemerson@ksc.com. **World Wide Web address:** http://www.ksc.com. **Description:** Develops educational software and provides computer consulting services. Founded in 1985.

LEAD TECHNOLOGIES, INC.
1201 Greenwood Cliff, Suite 400, Charlotte NC 28204. 704/332-5532. **Toll-free phone:** 800/637-4699. **Fax:** 704/372-8161. **Contact:** Human Resources. **E-mail address:** hr@leadtools.com. **World Wide Web address:** http://www.leadtools.com. **Description:** Develops image file format, processing, and compression tool kits. **Positions advertised include:** Technical Writer; Senior Programmer. **Corporate headquarters location:** This location.

LEVEL 8 SYSTEMS
8000 Regency Parkway, Suite 542, Cary NC 27511. 919/380-5000. **Fax:** 919/380-5121. **Contact:**

Personnel. **E-mail address:** careers@level8.com. **World Wide Web address:** http://www.level8.com. **Description:** Develops business applications software. **Corporate headquarters location:** Farmingdale NJ. **Other U.S. locations:** Wilmington DE, Dulles VA. **International locations:** London, England; Paris, France; Milan, Italy. **Listed on:** NASDAQ. **Stock exchange symbol:** LVEL.

MANAGEMENT INFORMATION SYSTEMS GROUP, INC.
10 Laboratory Drive, P.O. Box 13966, Research Triangle Park NC 27709-3966. 919/406-8829. **Fax:** 919/549-8733. **Contact:** Human Resources. **E-mail address:** techjobs@misg.com. **World Wide Web address:** http://www.misg.com. **Description:** Offers EDI (Electronic Data Interchange) services that help process business documents over networks. **Corporate headquarters location:** This location.

McKESSON PROVIDER TECHNOLOGIES
10735 David Taylor Drive, Charlotte NC 28262. 704/549-7000. **Contact:** Tracy Schweikert, Human Resources. **World Wide Web address:** http://mpt.mckesson.com. **Description:** McKesson Information Solutions provides technology to health care enterprises including hospitals, integrated delivery networks, and managed care organizations. McKessonHBOC's primary products are Pathways 2000, a family of client/server-based applications that allow the integration and uniting of health care providers; STAR, Series, and HealthQuest transaction systems; and TRENDSTAR decision support system. The company also offers outsourcing services that include strategic information systems planning, data center operations, receivables management, business office administration, and major system conversions. **Positions advertised include:** Receptionist; Route Sales Representative; Enterprise Vice President of New Business; Regional Vice President; Account Manager. **Corporate headquarters location:** Alpharetta GA. **Other U.S. locations:** Nationwide. **International locations:** Canada; France; Netherlands; United Kingdom; Puerto Rico. **Operations at this facility include:** This location offers sales and technical support.

MISYS HEALTHCARE SYSTEMS
8529 Six Forks Road, Suite 300, Raleigh NC 27615. 919/847-8102. **Contact:** Human Resources. **E-mail address:** recruiter@misyshealthcare.com. **World Wide Web address:** http://www.misyshealthcare.com. **Description:** Misys develops health care management software. Products include +Medic Vision, +Medic PM, Auto Chart, AutoImage, and FasTracker. **Positions advertised include:** Administrative Assistant; Application Product Specialist; Client Support Analyst; Corporate Receptionist; Director of the Customer Call Center; EMR Template Care Analyst; Human Factors Engineer; Inside Sales Representative; Internal Auditor; Manager of Client Implementation Services; Product Line Director; Sales Development Executive; Sales Executive Assistant; Test Engineer. **Corporate headquarters location:** This location. **Other U.S. locations:** Nationwide. **International locations:** United Kingdom; Denmark; Ireland; Middle East. **Operations at this facility include:** This location provides sales, training, and support. **Parent company:** Misys Group.

NETIQ CORPORATION
4825 Creekstone Drive, Suite 400, Durham NC 27703. 919/767-0200. **Toll-free phone:** 888/426-9633. **Fax:** 919/767-0201. **Contact:** Human Resources. **World Wide Web address:** http://www.netiq.com. **Description:** Develops software for integrated systems and security management. **Positions advertised include:** Nortel Alliance Manager. **Corporate headquarters location:** San Jose CA. **Operations at this facility include:** Research and Development.

NEXUS SOFTWARE, INC.
8024 Glenwood Road, Suite 305, Raleigh NC 27612-1912. 919/788-8665. **Fax:** 919/788-8733. **Contact:** Human Resources. **World Wide Web address:** http://www.nexussoft.com. **Description:** Manufactures vendor-neutral, standards-based middleware and related services for the retail and financial services industries. **Positions advertised include:** Software Developer; EMEA Executive Account Manager. **Corporate headquarters location:** This location. **Operations at this facility include:** Administration; Research & Development; Sales; Service. **International locations:** Hampshire, United Kingdom.

OASYS MOBILE, INC.
434 Fayetteville Street Mall, Suite 600, Raleigh NC 27601. 919/807-5600. **Fax:** 919/807-5601. **Contact:** Human Resources. **E-mail address:** info@oasysmobile.com. **World Wide Web address:** http://www.oasysmobileinc.com. **Description:** Oasys Mobile develops, publishes and distributes more than 30 branded mobile applications in all major categories, from personalization and games to messaging and entertainment. The White Label Service gives carriers and content companies access to a venue that will extend their mobile offerings off-deck and reach new customers. **Corporate headquarters location:** This location. **Listed on:** Over-The-Counter. **Stock exchange symbol:** OYSM.

OPSWARE, INC.
11000 Regency Parkway, Suite 301, Cary NC 27511. 919/653-6000. **Contact:** Human Resources. **E-mail address:** jobs@opsware.com. **World Wide Web address:** http://www.opsware.com. **Description:** Manufactures information center automation software. **Special programs:** Internships. **Corporate headquarters location:** Sunnyvale CA. **Other U.S. locations:** Novi MI; New York NY; Bethesda MD. **International locations:** United Kingdom. **Listed on:** NASDAQ. **Stock exchange symbol:** OPSW.

ORACLE
2550 West Tyvola, Suite 200, Charlotte NC 28217. 704/357-3155. **Fax:** 704/423-1307. **World Wide Web address:** http://www.oracle.com. **Description:** Provides technology for managing database systems. **Positions advertised include:** Technology Sales Representative. **Corporate headquarters location:** Redwood Shores CA. **Other area locations:** Morrisville NC. **Other U.S. locations:** Nationwide. **International locations:** Worldwide. **Number of employees worldwide:** 40,000.

PROGRESSIVE COMPUTER SYSTEMS, INC.
615 Eastowne Drive, Chapel Hill NC 27514. 919/929-3087. **Fax:** 919/929-3087. **Contact:** Lisa Mitchell, Chief Executive Officer. **Description:** A computer firm providing hardware assembly, sales, and service. **Corporate headquarters location:** This location.

RTI MCNC CAMPUS
3021 Cornwallis Road, Research Triangle Park NC 27709-3910. 919/990/2000. **Fax:** 919/248-1923. **Contact:** Personnel. **World Wide Web address:** http://www.rti.org. **Description:** An independent, nonprofit corporation with research activities that support diverse commercial, industrial, and academic endeavors in health and pharmaceuticals, economic and social development, advanced technology, education and training, surveys and statistics, international development, and the environment. **Positions advertised include:** Research Engineer. **Special programs:** Internships. **Corporate headquarters location:** This location. **Parent company:** RTI International.

RED HAT SOFTWARE, INC.
1801 Varsity Drive, Raleigh NC 27606. 919/754-3700. **Fax:** 919/754-3701. **Contact:** Personnel. **E-mail address:** careers@redhat.com. **World Wide Web address:** http://www.redhat.com. **Description:** Develops software for Linux systems and offers technical support. **Positions advertised include:** Lead Generation Representative; Programmer/Analyst; Database Administrator; Web Engineer; Technical Writer; Senior Corporate Communications Specialist;

Legal Administrative Assistant; Product Marketing Manager; Global Account Director; Telephony Engineer; Financial Analyst; Order Entry Administrator. **Corporate headquarters location:** This location. **Other U.S. locations:** Nationwide. **International locations:** Worldwide. **Listed on:** NASDAQ. **Stock exchange symbol:** RHAT. **Number of employees worldwide:** 600.

SAS INSTITUTE INC.
100 SAS Campus Drive, Cary NC 27513-2414. 919/677-8000. **Toll-free phone:** 800/727-0025. **Fax:** 919/677-4444. **Contact:** Human Resources. **World Wide Web address:** http://www.sas.com. **Description:** Designs a variety of software programs including those used for warehouse management, statistics, and inventory control. **Positions advertised include:** Account Executive; Analytical Consultant; Applications Developer; Administrative Support Student; Data Architect; Development Tester; Food Service Associate; Human Factors Engineer; Industry Strategist; Java Development Applications Engineer; Pricing Optimization Tester; Research Statistician; Staff Assistant; Technical Writer. **Corporate headquarters location:** This location. **Other U.S. locations:** Nationwide. **International locations:** Worldwide. **Number of employees at this location:** 3,989. **Number of employees nationwide:** 5,085. **Number of employees worldwide:** 9,227.

SIMCLAR NORTH AMERICA INC.
176 Laurie Ellis Road, P.O. Box 1369, Winterville NC 28950. 252/355-3443. **Fax:** 252/355-3144. **Contact:** Kevin Jamieson, Plant Manager. **E-mail address:** kevin.jamieson@simclar.com. **World Wide Web address:** http://www.simclar.com. **Description:** Manufactures parts for the large appliances industries, including makers of photocopiers, and ATMs. **NOTE:** Entry-level positions and second and third shifts are offered. **Corporate headquarters location:** Scotland. **Other U.S. locations:** Hialeah FL; Dayton OH; North Attleboro MA; Kenosha WI; Round Rock TX. **International locations:** Tianjin, China; Tamps, Mexico. **Parent company:** Simclar Group. **Operations at this facility include:** The plants manufactures metal bases components and products. **Listed on:** NASDAQ. **Stock exchange symbol:** SIMC. **Number of employees at this location:** 70. **Number of employees worldwide:** 2,500.

SLICKEDIT, INC.
3000 Aerial Center Parkway, Suite 120, Morrisville NC 27560. 919/473-0070. **Toll-free phone:** 800/934-EDIT. **Fax:** 919/473-0080. **Contact:** Personnel. **E-mail address:** careers@slickedit.com. **World Wide Web address:** http://www.slickedit.com. **Description:** Develops graphical programmers' editing software including Visual SlickEdit and SlickEdit text-mode version. **Positions advertised include:** Software Engineer. **Corporate headquarters location:** This location.

SOURCE TECHNOLOGIES, INC.
2910 Whitehall Park Drive, Charlotte NC 28273. 704/969-7500. **Toll-free phone:** 800/922-8501. **Contact:** Human Resources Department. **World Wide Web address:** http://www.sourcetech.com. **Description:** A reseller of computer printers and printer equipment. Source Technologies also offers a wide variety of printing solutions. **Corporate headquarters location:** This location. **Other U.S. locations:** GA; SC; MN; WA; CA; NY.

STRATEGIC TECHNOLOGIES
301 Gregson Drive, Cary NC 27511. 919/379-8000. **Fax:** 919/379-8100. **Contact:** Human Resources. **E-mail address:** info@stratech.com. **World Wide Web address:** http://www.stratech.com. **Description:** Provides network integration services. **Positions advertised include:** Oracle Technical Trainer. **Corporate headquarters location:** This location. **Other area locations:** Charlotte NC; Greensboro NC. **Other U.S. locations:** Atlanta GA; Birmingham AL; Fort Lauderdale FL; Hartford CT. **Listed on:** Privately held.

SYNOPSYS, INC.
1101 Slater Road, Brighton Hall, Suite 300, Durham NC 27703. 919/425-7300. **Fax:** 919/941-6700. **Contact:** Director of Human Resources. **World Wide Web address:** http://www.synopsys.com. **Description:** Develops, markets, and supports software products that assist integrated circuit design engineers in performing automated design, layout, physical verification, and analysis of advanced integrated circuits. **Corporate headquarters location:** Mountain View CA. **Other U.S. locations:** Nationwide. **International locations:** Worldwide. **Listed on:** NASDAQ. **Stock exchange symbol:** SNPS. **Number of employees at this location:** 4,362.

THALES COMPUTERS
3100 Spring Forest Road, Raleigh NC 27616. 919/231-8000. **Toll-free phone:** 800/848-2330. **Fax:** 919/231-8001. **Contact:** Personnel. **World Wide Web address:** http://www.thalescomputers.com. **Description:** A designer and manufacturer of computer boards for use in harsh environments. **Corporate headquarters location:** France. **Other U.S. locations:** Addison TX. **International locations:** France; United Kingdom. **Operations at this facility include:** This location serves as the USA Headquarters.

TRANSBOTICS CORPORATION
3400 Latrobe Drive, Charlotte NC 28211. 704/362-1115. **Fax:** 704/364-4039. **Contact:** Human Resources. **E-mail address:** careers@transbotics.com. **World Wide Web address:** http://www.transbotics.com. **Description:** Supplies hardware and software that are incorporated into and used to control automatic guided vehicle systems (AGVS), which are used by customers to transport materials between various locations within a manufacturing or distribution facility. **Corporate headquarters location:** This location. **Other U.S. locations:** Fraser MI.

ULTIMUS
15200 Weston Parkway, Suite 106, Cary NC 27513. 919/678-0900. **Fax:** 919/678-0901. **Contact:** Office Manager. **E-mail address:** admin@ultimus.com. **World Wide Web address:** http://www.ultimus.com. **Description:** Offers workflow automation software through client/server Windows applications, allowing users to design, simulate, implement, monitor, and measure workflow for various administrative business processes. Founded in 1994. **Positions advertised include:** Regional Sales Manager; Senior Workflow Consultant; Technical Support Specialist; Technical Trainer; Technical Training Manager; Workflow Consultant. **Corporate headquarters location:** This location. **International locations:** Worldwide. **Listed on:** Privately held.

VERBATIM CORPORATION
1200 West W.T. Harris Boulevard, Charlotte NC 28262. 704/547-6500. **Contact:** Human Resources Manager. **World Wide Web address:** http://www.verbatimcorp.com. **Description:** Develops data storage products including computer disks and CD ROMs. **Corporate headquarters location:** This location. **Parent company:** Mitsubishi Chemical Corporation.

WILDON SOFTWARE CORPORATION
301 Trimble Avenue, P.O. Box 1565, Cary NC 27512. 919/835-1514. **Contact:** Human Resources. **E-mail address:** jobs@wildon.com. **World Wide Web Address:** http://www.wildon.com. **Description:** Provides IT professionals to business and government organizations in North Carolina. **Positions advertised include:** Computer Programmer; Technical Writer. **Corporate Headquarters:** This location.

XEROX
5900 Greenville Boulevard NE, Greenville NC 27834 252/695-0055. **Fax:** 252/353-0690. **Contact:** Personnel. **World Wide Web address:**

http://www.xerox.com. **Description:** Provides printing and publishing services as well as network printer, copiers, and fax machines. **Corporate headquarters location:** Stamford CT. **Other area locations:** Winston-Salem NC; Charlotte NC; Greensboro NC; Matthews NC; Rocky Mount NC. **Other U.S. locations:** Nationwide. **International locations:** Worldwide. **Operations at this facility include:** Sales. **Listed on:** New York Stock Exchange. **Stock exchange symbol:** XRX.

North Dakota

ATLAS BUSINESS SOLUTIONS, INC.
P.O. Box 9013, Fargo ND 58106-9013. 701/235-5226. **Physical address:** 3330 Fiechtner Drive SW, Suite 200, Fargo ND 58103. **Toll-free phone:** 800/874-8801. **Fax:** 701/280-0842. **Contact:** Jay Forknell. **E-mail address:** hr@abs-usa.com. **World Wide Web address:** http://www.abs-usa.com. **Description:** Develops business software. **Positions advertised include:** Technical Support Specialist; Marketing Manager; Customer Service Associate. **Corporate headquarters location:** This location.

IMATION CORPORATION
2100 15th Street North, Wahpeton ND 58075. 701/642-8711. **Fax:** 701/642-8206. **Contact:** Marilee Tischer, Human Resources. **E-mail address:** info@imation.com. **World Wide Web address:** http://www.imation.com. **Description:** Imation provides systems, products, and services for the handling, storage, transmission, and use of information. The company develops data storage products, medical imaging and photo products, printing and publishing systems, and customer support technologies and document imaging, and markets them under the trademark names Dry View laser imagers, Matchprint and Rainbow color proofing systems, Travan data cartridges, and LS-120 diskette technology. **NOTE:** Imation requests that jobseekers apply using its online form. No paper resumes will be accepted. If interested in a production job opening, applications may be submitted via Jobservice (phone: 701/671-1500.) **Positions advertised include:** Maintenance Technician. **Special Programs:** Internships; Internal Courses. **Other U.S. locations:** Tuscon AZ; Camarillo CA; Miami FL; Oakdale MN; Weatherford OK; Nekoosa WI. **International locations:** Worldwide. **Operations at this facility include:** The manufacturing of diskettes. **Listed on:** New York Stock Exchange and Chicago Stock Exchange. **Stock exchange symbol:** IMN. **Number of employees worldwide:** 10,000.

MICROSOFT DYNAMICS
One Lone Tree Road, Fargo ND 58104-3911. 701/281-6500. **Toll-free phone:** 800/477-7989. **Fax:** 701/281-3752. **Contact:** Human Resources. **World Wide Web address:** http://www.microsoft.com/dynamics. **Description:** A developer of integrated and modular accounting and financial management software. The company offers solutions for customers ranging from small businesses to mid-range corporations. **NOTE:** This is a sub entity of Microsoft Corporation; applicants must register online with Microsoft Careers. **Positions advertised include:** New Product Development Manager; Product Planner; Query Services Program Manager; Software Design Engineer; Application Framework PM; Program Manager; Application Developer; Program Manager – Financial Design; Systems Administrator. **Special programs:** Educational Training; Internships. **Corporate headquarters:** Redmond WA. **Other area locations:** Nationwide. **International locations:** Worldwide. **Operations at this location include:** Business software production. **Listed on:** NASDAQ. **Stock exchange symbol:** MSFT. **Number of employees at this location:** 550. **Number of employees worldwide:** Over 50,000.

NAVIGATION TECHNOLOGIES CORPORATION
1715 Gold Drive, Fargo ND 58102-6400. 701/476-6032. **Fax:** 312/894-7263. **Contact:** Dail Hassler, Human resources Manager. **E-mail address:** career@navtech.com. **World Wide Web address:** http://www.navtech.com. **Description:** Provides digital map information, software, and services for numerous applications, such as vehicle navigation, mapping and geographic information systems. Areas of specialization include Internet/wireless applications and business solutions. Founded in 1985 in Silicon Valley CA. **Corporate headquarters location:** Chicago IL. **Other U.S. locations:** Nationwide. **International locations:** The United Kingdom; France; Spain; Portugal; Italy; Czech Republic; Switzerland; Austria; Germany; Benelux; the Nordics. **Operations at this facility include:** This location is the company's worldwide production facility. **President/CEO:** Judson Green. **Number of employees worldwide:** Over 1,100.

PEMSTAR CORPORATION
P.O. Box 940, Dunseith ND 58329. 701/242-2519. **Physical address:** First Street South, Dunseith ND 58329. **Contact:** Lona Davis, Human Resources. **E-mail address:** chad.ihla@pemstar.com. **World Wide Web address:** http://www.pemstar.com. **Description:** Develops and manufactures electronic circuit boards for IBM and other computer companies. **Other U.S. locations include:** St. Paul MN. **Operations at this facility include:** Production. **Number of employees at this location:** 260.

Ohio

ADPI
P.O. Box 499, Troy OH 45373-0499. 937/339-2241. **Physical address:** 312 Walnut Street, Cincinnati OH 45202. **Toll-free phone:** 800/758-1041. **Fax:** 937/339-0070. **Contact:** Human Resources. **E-mail address:** info@adpi.com. **World Wide Web address:** http://www.adpi.com. **Description:** Designs, manufactures, and markets data acquisition and transfer products for engineers, manufacturers, plant operators, and field technicians. Founded in 1978. **President/CEO:** Jerry Davis.

AOL COLUMBUS COMPUSERVE INC.
5000 Arlington Center Boulevard, Columbus OH 43220. 614/457-8600. **Fax:** 614/538-1780. **Contact:** Human Resources. **World Wide Web address:** http://www.compuserve.com. **Description:** An Internet access and online services provider. Founded in 1969. **Positions advertised include:** Direct Sales Associate; Installer; Technical Project Manager; Supervisor; Design Intern; Associate Space Planner; Senior Programming Manager; Senior Software Engineer; Finance and Planning Senior Manager. **Special programs:** Internships. **Corporate headquarters location:** This location. **Other area locations:** Statewide. **Other U.S. locations:** Nationwide. **Parent company:** AOL Time Warner, Inc. **Operations at this facility include:** Administration; Research and Development; Service. **Number of employees nationwide:** 2,200.

AJILON SERVICES INC.
6055 Rockside Woods Boulevard, Suite 390, Independence OH 44131. 216/573-2370. **Toll-free phone:** 888/381-6970. **Fax:** 410/828-0106. **Contact:** Human Resources. **E-mail address:** recruit.cleveland@ajilon.com. **World Wide Web address:** http://www.ajilon.com. **Description:** Provides information technology services including functional outsourcing, IT management, systems security, systems transformation, managed maintenance, and Internet commerce enabling services to the communications, finance, manufacturing, transportation, and insurance industries. Founded in 1969. **Positions advertised include:** MVS Systems Programmer; Lotus Notes Administrator; Data Warehouse Analyst; Application Developer. **Corporate headquarters location:** Towson MD. **Other U.S. locations:** Nationwide. **Parent company:** Adecco SA.

ANALYSTS INTERNATIONAL CORPORATION (AIC)
9365 Allen Road, Cincinnati OH 45069. 513/772-6080. **Toll-free phone:** 800/960-9682. **Fax:** 330/725-4133.

Contact: Human Resources Department. **E-mail address:** jobs@analysts.com. **World Wide Web address:** http://www.analysts.com. **Description:** An international computer consulting firm. The company assists clients in analyzing, designing, and developing systems using different programming languages and software. Founded in 1966. **NOTE:** Apply online. **Corporate headquarters location:** Minneapolis MN. **Listed on:** NASDAQ. **Stock exchange symbol:** ANLY. **Annual sales/revenues:** More than $100 million. **Number of employees at this location:** 130.

ATTACHMATE CORPORATION
424 Wards Corner Road, Loveland OH 45140. 513/965-8030. **Toll-free phone:** 800/872-2829. **Fax:** 513/794-8108. **Contact:** Human Resources. **World Wide Web address:** http://www.attachmate.com. **Description:** Manufactures and supplies enterprise information access and management software and services to government agencies and major businesses worldwide. The company's products include authoring tools, desktop-to-host and web-to-enterprise business solutions, management software, and hardware adapters that offer secure access and management of business information. **Corporate headquarters location:** Bellevue WA. **Other U.S. locations:** Nationwide. **International locations:** Worldwide.

BELCAN CORPORATION
10200 Anderson Way, Cincinnati OH 45242. 513/891-0972. **Toll-free phone**: 800/423-5226. **Contact:** Human Resources. **E-mail address:** tech@tech.belcan.com. **World Wide Web address:** http://www.belcan.com. **Description:** Provides IT specialists to companies in need of programming, help desk, and system administration support. **Positions advertised include:** Lab Technician; Software Engineer. **Corporate Headquarters:** This location.

CACI NTL SYSTEMS, INC.
3481 Dayton-Xenia Road, Dayton OH 45432-2796. 937/426-3111. **Fax:** 937/426-8301. **Contact:** Sue App, Human Resources. **E-mail address:** sapp@mtl.com. **World Wide Web address:** http://www.mtl.com. **Description:** Engaged in electronic products systems, image exploitation, imaging technology, modeling and simulation, networking, and web-based business solutions for commercial clients and government agencies. MTL Systems specializes in computer engineering, electronic and sensor technology, and reconnaissance and intelligence activities. **Positions advertised include:** Darkroom/Production Technician; Photographic Engineer; Computer Engineer; Remote Sensing Scientist; Senior Remote Sensing Engineer. **Corporate headquarters location:** This location.

CTC PARKER AUTOMATION
50 West TechneCenter Drive, Milford OH 45150. 513/831-2340. **Fax:** 513/831-5042. **Contact:** Human Resources. **World Wide Web address:** http://www.ctcusa.com. **Description:** Designs, develops, and manufactures computer hardware and software for industrial applications. **Corporate headquarters location:** This location. **Parent company:** Parker Hannifin Corporation.

CABLES TO GO
1501 Webster Street, Dayton OH 45404. 937/224-8646. **Contact:** Human Resources Administrator. **E-mail address:** hr@cablestogo.com. **World Wide Web address:** http://www.cablestogo.com. **Description:** Manufactures and distributes computer connection equipment including adapters, cables, connectors, and networking equipment. **Corporate headquarters location:** This location.

CAP GEMINI ERNST & YOUNG
1000 Skylight Office Tower, 1660 West Second Street, Cleveland OH 44113. 216/583-3300. **Fax:** 216/583-8319. **Contact:** Recruiting Manager. **World Wide Web address:** http://www.capgemini.com. **Description:** Provides management consulting services including business strategy, operations, and people and information management. Services include systems integration; application design, development, and documentation; systems conversions and migrations; and information technology consulting. **Other U.S. locations:** Nationwide.

CHAMPION COMPUTER TECHNOLOGIES
23400 Mercantile Road, Suite 7, Beachwood OH 44122. 216/831-1800. **Toll-free phone:** 800/860-7466. **Fax:** 216/831-2541. **Contact:** Personnel. **E-mail address:** hr@cctupgrades.com. **World Wide Web address:** http://www.cctupgrades.com. **Description:** Manufactures computer memory upgrades for desktops, servers, printers, and notebooks, as well as high-performance PCMCIA notebook computer adapters for communications, network connectivity, and storage. Founded in 1992.

CINCOM SYSTEMS, INC.
55 Merchant Street, Cincinnati OH 45246. 513/612-2300. **Toll-free phone:** 800/224-6266. **Fax:** 513/612-2000. **Contact:** Human Resources. **World Wide Web address:** http://www.cincom.com. **Description:** Develops business software for manufacturing companies, solutions for object-oriented and fourth-generation language application development, client/server and relational object-oriented databases, workflow automation, and document solutions. Founded in 1968. **Positions advertised include:** Financial Services Consultant; Payroll Assistant; Marketing Communications Specialist. **Corporate headquarters location:** This location. **Other area locations:** Columbus OH. **Other U.S. locations:** Nationwide. **International locations:** Worldwide. **Listed on:** Privately held. **Annual sales/revenues:** More than $100 million. **Number of employees at this location:** 500. **Number of employees nationwide:** 1,000.

COLE-LAYER-TRUMBLE COMPANY
3199 Klepinger Road, Dayton OH 45406. 937/276-5261. **Fax:** 937/278-3711. **Contact:** Christel Brooks, Human Resources Manager. **E-mail address:** cbrooks@cltco.com. **World Wide Web address:** http://www.cltco.com. **Description:** One of the nation's largest mass appraisal firms offering both manual and computer-assisted appraisals. The company also offers consulting services for appraisals, data processing, training, and systems design. Founded in 1938. **Positions advertised include:** Real Estate Appraiser. **Corporate headquarters location:** This location. **Parent company:** Tyler Technologies Inc. provides data products, software, technology, and electronic document management systems to local governments and other enterprises. **Listed on:** Privately held.

COMPUTER ASSOCIATES INTERNATIONAL, INC.
7965 North High Street, Suite 200, Columbus OH 43235. 614/888-1775. **Contact:** Human Resources. **World Wide Web address:** http://www.ca.com. **Description:** Computer Associates International is one of the world's leading developers of client/server and distributed computing software. The company develops, markets, and supports enterprise management, database and applications development, business applications, and consumer software products for a broad range of mainframe, midrange, and desktop computers. Founded in 1976. **NOTE:** Send resumes online. **Corporate headquarters location:** Islandia NY. **Other area locations:** Beavercreek OH; Independence OH; Mason OH. **Other U.S. locations:** Nationwide. **International locations:** Worldwide. **Operations at this facility include:** This location develops software. **Listed on:** New York Stock Exchange. **Stock exchange symbol:** CA. **Annual sales/revenues:** More than $100 million. **Number of employees nationwide:** 4,000. **Number of employees worldwide:** 9,000.

COMPUTER HORIZONS CORPORATION
6450 Rockside Woods Boulevard South, Suite 270, Independence OH 44131. 216/524-8816. **Fax:** 216/524-9015. **Contact:** Recruiting. **E-mail address:** recruiting@computerhorizons.com. **World Wide Web**

address: http://www.computerhorizons.com. **Description:** A full-service global technology services firm providing IT products and services across a full range of industries. Computer Horizons Corporation specializes in e-Business, enterprise solutions, ERP implementation, financial services, global staffing, network services, software products, and training and education. Founded in 1969. **Corporate headquarters location:** Mountain Lakes NJ. **Other area locations:** Centerville OH; Cincinnati OH. **Other U.S. locations:** Nationwide. **Operations at this facility include:** Regional Headquarters. **Listed on:** NASDAQ. **Stock exchange symbol:** CHRZ. **President/CEO:** John Cassese. **Annual sales/revenues:** More than $100 million.

COMPUTER SCIENCES CORPORATION (CSC)
5900 Landerbrook Drive, Suite 380, Cleveland OH 44124. 440/449-3600. **Fax:** 440/442-3050. **Contact:** Human Resources. **World Wide Web address:** http://www.csc.com. **Description:** Provides information technology solutions and services to commercial and government markets. CSC Consulting specializes in information systems consulting and integration; management consulting; and outsourcing and e-business solutions. Founded in 1959. **Corporate headquarters location:** El Segundo CA. **International locations:** Worldwide. **Annual sales/revenues:** More than $100 million. **Number of employees worldwide:** 52,000.

COMPUWARE CORPORATION
6480 Rockside Woods Boulevard, Suite 200, Independence OH 44131. 216/986-8500. **Fax:** 887/220-5529. **Contact:** Human Resources. **World Wide Web address:** http://www.compuware.com. **Description:** Develops, markets, and supports an integrated line of systems software products. Compuware also provides a range of professional data processing services including business systems analysis, design, and programming, as well as systems planning and consulting. **Positions advertised include:** Testing Specialist; Software Sales Manager. **Corporate headquarters:** Farmington Hills MI. **Other area locations:** Cincinnati OH; Cleveland OH; Columbus OH. **Other U.S. locations:** Nationwide. **International locations:** Worldwide. **Listed on:** NASDAQ. **Stock exchange symbol:** CPWR.

CONVERGYS INFORMATION SYSTEMS, INC.
201 East Fourth Street, Cincinnati OH 45202. 513/723-7000. **Contact:** Human Resources. **World Wide Web address:** http://www.convergys.com. **Description:** Designs and markets information systems and provides consulting and technical services for telecommunications companies. **Positions advertised include:** Systems Analyst; Data Collection Supervisor; Senior Finance Manager; Client Support Associate; Sales Support Manager. **Parent company:** Convergys. **Other area locations:** Norwood OH; Toledo OH. **Other U.S. locations:** Nationwide. **International locations:** Worldwide.

CRANEL, INC.
8999 Gemini Parkway, Columbus OH 43240. 614/431-8000. **Fax:** 614/431-8388. **Contact:** Employment. **E-mail address:** employment@cranel.com. **World Wide Web address:** http://www.cranel.com. **Description:** Provides document imaging distribution, enterprise storage solutions, and maintenance and repair services nationwide. Founded in 1985. **Positions advertised include:** Accounts Payable Clerk; Inside Sales Consultant; Receptionist; Renewal Support Specialist; Software Engineer. **Office hours:** Monday - Friday, 8:00 a.m. - 6:00 p.m. **Corporate headquarters location:** Columbus OH. **Other area locations:** Cleveland OH. **Other U.S. locations:** Nationwide. **International locations:** Toronto Ontario. **Number of employees nationwide:** Over 200.

DATA-BASICS INC.
9450 Midwest Avenue, Garfield Heights OH 44125. 216/663-5600. **Toll-free phone:** 800/837-7574. **Fax:** 216/663-5454. **Contact:** Human Resources Department. **E-mail address:** hr@databasics.com. **World Wide Web address:** http://www.databasic.com. **Description:** Develops job cost accounting software and service-account management software for the construction and architecture industries.

EXACT MACOLA SOFTWARE
8800 Lyra Drive, Columbus OH 43240. 614/410-2650. **Toll-free phone:** 800/468-0834. **Fax:** 740/382-0239. **Contact:** Human Resources. **World Wide Web address:** http://www.macola.com. **Description:** Develops client/server-based accounting, distribution, and manufacturing business software solutions. Founded in 1971. **NOTE:** Entry-level positions are offered. **Special programs:** Internships. **Office hours:** Monday - Friday, 8:30 a.m. - 5:30 p.m. **Corporate headquarters location:** This location. **Other U.S. locations:** Nationwide. **International locations:** Canada; China; Malaysia; Thailand. **Parent company:** Exact Software North America. **Listed on:** Privately held. **Number of employees at this location:** 280.

HARRIS INFOSOURCE
2057 East Aurora Road, Twinsburg OH 44087-1999. 330/425-9000. **Toll-free phone:** 800/888-5900. **Fax:** 330/963-3839. **Contact:** Human Resources. **E-mail address:** hr@harrisinfo.com. **World Wide Web address:** http://www.harrisinfo.com. **Description:** Publishes magazine directories and software containing lists of manufacturers nationwide. Founded in 1972. **NOTE:** Resumes are accepted on a continuous basis, and may be submitted by mail, fax, or e-mail. **Special programs:** Training. **Corporate headquarters location:** This location. **Listed on:** Privately held. **Number of employees at this location:** 100.

INFOR
2800 Corporate Exchange Drive, Columbus OH 43231. 678/319-8000. **Toll-free phone**: 866/244-8000. **Fax:** 614/895-2504. **Contact:** Personnel. **World Wide Web address:** http://www.infor.com. **Description:** A developer and manufacturer of open client/server software. **Positions advertised include:** Director of Customer Contacts; Collections Specialist. **Corporate headquarters location:** This location.

INTUIT REAL ESTATE SOLUTIONS
20800 Harvard Road, Highland Hills OH 44122. 216/464-3225. **Contact:** Human Resources. **World Wide Web address:** http://www.intuit.com. **Description:** Provides money management and tax filing software to consumers and businesses. **NOTE:** Applications many be submitted at company website. **Positions advertised include:** Business Development Representative; Consulting Product Development Manager; Strategic Solutions Specialist; Senior Software Engineer; Software Engineer; Software Quality Engineer; Strategic Sales Manager; Internal Sales Representative. **Corporate headquarters location:** Mountain View CA

IOTECH, INC.
25971 Cannon Road, Cleveland OH 44146. 440/439-4091. **Toll-free phone:** 888/714-3272. **Fax:** 440/439-4093. **Contact:** Human Resources. **World Wide Web address:** http://www.iotech.com. **Description:** Develops, manufactures, and markets interfaces and data acquisition instruments. The company's hardware and software products are used primarily to support personal computers and engineering workstations. **Corporate headquarters location:** This location. **Other U.S. locations:** Nationwide. **International locations:** Worldwide. **Listed on:** Privately held. **Number of employees at this location:** 90.

LEXIS-NEXIS
P.O. Box 933, Dayton OH 45401. 937/865-6800. **Physical address:** 9443 Springboro Pike, Miamisburg OH 45342. **Toll-free phone:** 800/227-9597. **Fax:** 937/865-7476. **Contact:** Staffing Department. **E-mail address:** employment.hr@lexisnexis.com. **World Wide Web address:** http://www.lexisnexis.com. **Description:** An online, full-text database service including legal, news, business, and general information. The service enables lawyers, business

professionals, and government agencies to electronically research thousands of resources from their own computers. **Positions advertised include:** Regional Sales Executive; Senior Software Engineer; Data Analyst; Web Designer; Product Manager; Systems Engineer; Employee Benefits Specialist; Telephone Sales Executive; Senior Human Resources Generalist; Market Planner; Architect; Customer Service Research Associate. **Special programs:** Internships; Co-ops. **Corporate headquarters location:** This location. **Parent company:** Reed Elsevier Group (United Kingdom).

LIEBERT CORPORATION
1050 Dearborn Drive, P.O. Box 29186, Columbus OH 43229. 614/888-0246. **Fax:** 614/841-5890. **Contact:** Human Resources. **E-mail address:** careers@liebert.com. **World Wide Web address:** http://www.liebert.com. **Description:** A leading worldwide manufacturer of computer support equipment and related applications. **NOTE:** Entry-level positions are offered. **Positions advertised included:** Service Operations Manager; Systems Analyst; Business Development Manager. **Special programs:** Internships; Training; Co-ops; Summer Jobs. **Corporate headquarters location:** This location. **Other area locations:** Westerville OH; **Other U.S. locations:** Nationwide. **Parent company:** Emerson Electric. **Number of employees at this location:** 950.

LOGTEC
1825 Commerce Center Boulevard, Fairborn OH 45324. 937/878-8450. **Fax:** 937/429-3483. **Contact:** Human Resources. **E-mail address:** hr@logtec.com. **World Wide Web address:** http://www.logtec.com. **Description:** A computer services company. LOGTEC specializes in acquisition, data management, enterprise services, functional processes, logistics processes, network services, product data, and software development. Founded in 1985. **Positions advertised include:** Contracts Administrator; Acquisitions Manager; Logistician; Configuration Manager; Program Manager. **Corporate headquarters location:** This location. **Other area locations:** Columbus OH; Dayton OH. **Other U.S. locations:** Nationwide.

MCSI
6175 Shamrock Court, Suite J, Dublin OH 43016. 614/792-3903. **Fax:** 937/291-7741. **Contact:** Marta Cash, Human Resources Department. **World Wide Web address:** http://www.mcsinet.com. **Description:** Distributes computer equipment, supplies, and accessories to corporate and government clients. MCSI also distributes office automation equipment. Founded in 1981. **Corporate headquarters location:** This location. **Listed on:** NASDAQ. **Stock exchange symbol:** MCSI. **Annual sales/revenues:** More than $100 million.

MTC TECHNOLOGIES
4032 Linden Avenue, Dayton OH 45432. 937/252-9199. **Fax:** 937/258-3863. **Contact:** Human Resources. **E-mail address:** mctjobs@mcttechnologies.com. **World Wide Web address:** http://www.modtechcorp.com. **Description:** Provides a range of sophisticated system engineering, intelligence, information technology, and program management solutions, primarily to the Department of Defense. **Positions advertised include:** Quality Controller; Group Controller; Senior Contracts Administrator. **Corporate headquarters location:** This location. **Listed on:** NASDAQ. **Stock exchanges symbol:** MTCT. **Number of employees nationwide:** 2,000.

MACAULAY-BROWN, INC.
4021 Executive Drive, Dayton OH 45430. 937/426-3421. **Fax:** 937/426-5364. **Contact:** Human Resources. **World Wide Web address:** http://www.macb.com. **Description:** A technical firm specializing in intelligence/threat analysis; systems engineering; digital system model development; technique development; test and evaluation of hardware in the loop; software engineering; instrumentation system design and development; computer system/LAN development; facility modification and operation; and management support. Founded in 1978. **Corporate headquarters location:** This location. **Other U.S. locations:** CA; FL; GA; IL; MD; NM; TX. **Parent company:** SYTEX Group. **Operations at this facility include:** Analysis; Computer Modeling; Management Support; Testing. **Listed on:** Privately held. **Annual Sales/Revenues:** $45 million. **Number of employees nationwide:** 460.

METASYSTEMS
6 Corporation Center Drive, Broadview Heights OH 44147. 440/526-1454. **Toll-free phone:** 800/788-5253. **Fax:** 440/526-1406. **Contact:** Personnel. **E-mail address:** careers@metasystems.com. **World Wide Web address:** http://www.metasystems.com. **Description:** Develops and implements computer systems and provides network and infrastructure consulting services in partnership with Berish & Associates, which operates in the areas of client/server development, Internet/intranet development, Microsoft Office integration, LAN and WAN services, and installation and implementation. Founded in 1985. **Listed on:** Privately held. **President/Owner:** Joseph Berish. **Number of employees at this location:** 60.

MICROSOFT GREAT PLAINS BUSINESS SOLUTIONS
4605 Duke Drive, Mason OH 45040. 513/339-2800. **Contact:** Human Resources. **World Wide Web address:** http://www.greatplains.com. **Description:** Develops accounting software. **NOTE:** Mail all resumes to: Human Resources, One Lone Tree Road, Fargo ND 58104.

NCR SYSTEMEDIA GROUP
9095 Washington Church Road, Miamisburg OH 45342-4428. 937/439-8200. **Contact:** Human Resources. **World Wide Web address:** http://www.ncr.com. **Description:** Develops, produces, and markets a complete line of information technology products including transaction processing media, auto identification media, business form communication products, managing documents and media, and a full line of integrated equipment solutions. **Special programs:** Internships. **Corporate headquarters location:** Dayton OH. **Other U.S. locations:** El Segundo CA; San Diego CA; Atlanta GA; Columbia SC; Washington DC. **International locations:** Worldwide. **Parent company:** NCR Corporation. **Listed on:** New York Stock Exchange. **Stock exchange symbol:** NCR.

NEWCOME CORPORATION
9005 Antares Avenue, Columbus OH 43240. 614/848-5688. **Fax:** 614/848-9921. **Contact:** Human Resources. **World Wide Web address:** http://www.newcome.com. **Description:** Designs and installs voice and data distribution systems, primarily to support the communications needs of commercial enterprises in LAN- and WAN-based environments. Founded in 1978. **NOTE:** Entry-level positions are offered. **Positions advertised include:** Audio/Video Lead Technician. **Special programs:** Internships; Apprenticeships; Training. **Internship information:** Newcome Corporation hires interns interested in the areas of LAN/WAN environments and the design, installation, and marketing of audio/video systems. **Corporate headquarters location:** This location. **Other U.S. locations:** Somerville NJ. **Listed on:** Privately held. **President:** Tim Newcome.

NORTHROP GRUMMAN TASC INC.
2555 University Boulevard, Fairborn OH 45410. 937/426-1040. **Fax:** 937/426-8888. **Contact:** Human Resources. **World Wide Web address:** http://www.tasc.com. **Description:** Offers computer consulting services to businesses and the government. **Parent company:** Northrop Grumman Corporation. **Listed on:** New York Stock Exchange. **Stock exchange symbol:** NOC.

PATIENT FOCUS SYSTEMS (PFS)
PASCO GROUP
2096 Ravenna Street, Hudson OH 44236-4400. 330/655-2907. **Toll-free phone:** 800/787-3477. **Fax:** 330/650-0613. **Contact:** Director of Business Support. **World Wide Web address:** http://www.pasco-group.com. **Description:** PFS provides software products and services for the medical industry. **Parent company:** PASCO Group (also at this location) is a holding company with interests in a variety of information processing services: Automated Tracking Systems (also at this location) is the country's largest provider of insurance follow-up services; Quality Data Solutions (QDS) provides telemarketing, mail fulfillment, and data capture services; Customer Management Systems offers consulting products and services to automobile sales professionals; Information Management Group (also at this location) is a provider of fully-integrated information systems for the retail industry.

PINNACLE DATA SYSTEMS, INC.
6600 Port Road, Groveport OH 43125. 614/748-1150. **Fax:** 614/748-1209. **Contact:** Human Resources. **E-mail address:** jobs@pinnacle.com. **World Wide Web address:** http://www.pinnacle.com. **Description:** Builds custom computers and provides computer repair services. **Positions advertised include:** Program Manager.

QUATECH
5675 Hudson Industrial Parkway, Hudson OH 44236. 330/434-1409. **Toll-free phone:** 800/553-1170. **Fax:** 330/655-9010. **Contact:** Human Resources. **E-mail address:** resumes@quatech.com. **World Wide Web address:** http://www.quatech.com. **Description:** A manufacturer of a line of communication, data acquisition, PCMCIA, and control products for IBM PC/XT, PC/AT, PS/2, and compatible systems. **Positions advertised include:** Customer Support Engineer; Inside Sales Engineer; Field Sales Engineer; Hardware Engineer. **Corporate headquarters location:** This location. **Other area locations:** Akron OH.

SARCOM
8337 Green Meadows Drive North, Lewis Center OH 43035. 614/854-1002. **Contact:** Human Resources Department. **E-mail address:** hr@sarcom.com. **World Wide Web address:** http://www.sarcom.com. **Description:** A computer and software retailer. SARCOM also provides service and repairs for its commercial and residential customers. **Positions advertised include:** Inventory Supervisor. **Corporate headquarters location:** This location.

SARCOM COMPUTER RENTALS
600 Lakeview Plaza Boulevard, Columbus OH 43085. 614/854-1200. **Toll-free phone:** 800/589-2052. **Contact:** Glenn Orr, Executive Vice President. **World Wide Web address:** http://www.accessrentals.net. **Description:** A computer rental company. **Other area locations:** Columbus OH.

STERLING COMMERCE
P.O. Box 8000, 4600 Lakehurst Court, Dublin OH 43016. 614/793-7000. **Fax:** 614/793-7092. **Contact:** Human Resources. **World Wide Web address:** http://www.sterlingcommerce.com. **Description:** Develops and markets a suite of client/server systems development software tools used to automate time-sensitive information delivery processes such as order entry, inventory query, and price list and product catalog updates. **Positions advertised include:** Attorney; Strategic Programs Manager; Software Developer; Senior Events Specialist; Administrative Assistant; Contract Negotiator. **Parent company:** SBC Communications. **Corporate headquarters location:** This location. **Number of employees worldwide:** 1,800.

SYSTRAN CORPORATION
4126 Linden Avenue, Dayton OH 45432. 937/252-5601. **Fax:** 937/252-1480. **Contact:** Manager of Human Resources. **E-mail address:** careers@systran.com. **World Wide Web address:** http://www.systran.com. **Description:** Manufactures I/O boards, memory systems, and network interface cards. **Positions advertised include:** Sales Manager. **Corporate headquarters location:** This location. **Listed on:** Privately held. **Number of employees at this location:** 135.

UGS
2000 Eastman Drive, Loveland OH 45140. 513/576-2400. **Fax:** 513/576-2734. **Contact:** Human Resources. **E-mail address:** careers@eds.com. **World Wide Web address:** http://www.eds.com. **Description:** An international supplier of mechanical computer-aided engineering (MCAE) software and engineering services. **Corporate headquarters location:** Plano TX. **Other U.S. locations:** Nationwide. **International locations:** Worldwide. **Operations at this facility include:** Administration; Divisional Headquarters; Regional Headquarters; Research and Development; Sales; Service. **Listed on:** New York Stock Exchange. **Stock exchange symbol:** EDS. **Number of employees at this location:** 1,000. **Number of employees worldwide:** 130,000.

WIZARD COMPUTER SERVICES, INC.
21555 Drake Road, Strongsville OH 44149. 440/891-0060. **Fax:** 440/891-0066. **Contact:** Human Resources Department. **E-mail address:** info@wizardcomputer.com. **World Wide Web address:** http://www.wizardcomputer.com. **Description:** Wizard Computer Services provides a variety of computer services including planning networks, providing hardware, integrating operating systems, and continual service and support.

Oklahoma

DECISIONONE
2488 East 81st Street, Suite 1100, Tulsa OK 74137-4275. 918/384-3300. **Contact:** Human Resources. **World Wide Web address:** http://www.decisionone.com. **Description:** A worldwide technology support provider whose operations include planning and consulting, call center services, technical deployment and support, network services, and logistics. **Corporate headquarters location:** Devon PA. **Other U.S. locations:** Nationwide. **International locations:** Canada. **Number of employees worldwide:** 5,000.

ESKER SOFTWARE
100 East 7th Avenue, Stillwater OK 74074. 608/828-6000. **Fax:** 405/624-3010. **Contact:** Personnel. **E-mail address:** recruiting@esker.com. **World Wide Web address:** http://www.esker.com. **Description:** Develops and delivers document management software such as Delivery Ware, Fax Server, and Host Access solutions for use by large corporations. Founded in 1985. **Corporate headquarters location:** Madison WI. **Other U.S. locations:** Lake Forest CA. **International locations:** United Kingdom; Germany; Spain; Italy; Australia. **Subsidiaries include:** Teubner and Associates; Persoft; V-Systems, Incorporated. **Number of employees worldwide:** Over 300.

FRONTIER ELECTRONIC SYSTEMS CORPORATION
4500 West 6th Avenue, Stillwater OK 74075. 405/624-1769. **Fax:** 405/624-7866. **Contact:** Kathy Herwig, Human Resources Division. **E-mail address:** humanresources@fescorp.com. **World Wide Web address:** http://www.fescorp.com. **Description:** Designs, manufactures, and tests electronic products and systems for aerospace, maritime, and other commercial customers. Founded in 1981. **Corporate headquarters location:** This location. **Other area locations:** Midwest City OK. **Annual sales/revenue:** $24 million. **Number of employees nationwide:** 110.

HITACHI COMPUTER PRODUCTS (AMERICA), INC.
OKLAHOMA MANUFACTURING DIVISION
1800 East Imhoff Road, Norman OK 73071. 405/360-5500. **Toll-free phone:** 800/449-6586. **Contact:**

Human Resources. **World Wide Web address:** http://www.hitachiomd.com. **Description:** Involved in the pre-manufacturing, production, distribution, and post-manufacturing support of PCB assemblies, box builds, build-to-order, and configure-to-order electronic products for computing, networking, communications, medical, and security customers. **NOTE:** This location hires through Oasis Employment Services. **Parent Company:** Hitachi, Ltd. **Listed on:** New York Stock Exchange. **Stock exchange symbol:** HIT.

PEGASUS IMAGING CORPORATION
P.O. Box 1358, Stillwater OK 74076. 405/377-0880. **Physical address:** 206 West 6th Avenue, Stillwater OK 74074. **Toll-free phone:** 800/944-7654. **Fax:** 405/742-1710. **Contact:** Personnel. **E-mail address:** jobs@jpg.com. **World Wide Web address:** http://www.pegasusimaging.com. **Description:** Offers imaging technology, digital imaging components, and image compression SDKs for application development. Founded in 1991. **Positions advertised include:** Software Engineer; Program Manager; Software Support Engineer; Component Technical Writer; Technical Lead; Technology Salesperson; Marketing Coordinator. **Special programs:** Tuition Reimbursement Program; Engineering Employee Equipment Purchase Program. **Corporate headquarters location:** Tampa FL. **Listed on:** OTC. **Stock exchange symbol:** TMSS.OB. **Sales/revenue:** Over $1 million.

PER-SE TECHNOLOGIES
One Warren Place, 6100 South Yale Avenue, Suite 1900, Tulsa OK 74136. 918/496-2451. **Contact:** Human Resources. **World Wide Web address:** http://www.per-se.com. **Description:** Develops software and Web-base applications used by physicians, hospitals, and retail pharmacies for electronic billing and other EDI transactions. **Positions advertised include:** Director, Human Resources; Technical Support Analyst; Database Administrator. **Corporate headquarters location:** Alpharetta GA. **Other U.S. locations:** Nationwide. **International locations:** Canada; Germany; United Kingdom. **Listed on:** NASDAQ. **Stock exchange symbol:** PSTI. **Sales/revenue:** $458 million. **Number of employees worldwide:** 6,400.

SEAGATE TECHNOLOGY LLC
10321 West Reno, Oklahoma City OK 73127. 405/324-3379. **Fax:** 405/ 324-3002. **Contact:** Earl Welsh, Staffing Recruiter. **World Wide Web address:** http://www.seagate.com. **Description:** A designer and manufacturer of data storage devices and related products including hard disk drives, tape drives, software, and systems for many different computer-related applications and operating systems. Customers include computer equipment manufacturers such as Dell, IBM, EMC, Hewlett-Packard, and Sun Microsystems. Founded in 1979. **Positions advertised include:** Technical Support Specialist. **Special programs:** Internships; Co-ops. **Corporate headquarters location:** Scotts Valley CA. **International locations:** Worldwide. **Subsidiaries include:** Arcada Holdings, Incorporated, an information protection and storage management software company serving several operating systems. **Operations at this facility include:** Production. **Listed on:** New York Stock Exchange. **Stock exchange symbol:** STX. **Sales/revenues:** $8.1 billion. **Number of employees worldwide:** 45,000.

SEAGULL SOFTWARE.
5601 NW 72nd, Suite 347, Oklahoma City OK 73132. 405/728-1902. **Contact:** Human Resources. **World Wide Web address:** http://www.seagullsoftware.com. **Description:** Specializes in software and technology for IT professionals that transforms "legacy" applications into SOA-compliant Web services. **Positions advertised include:** Terminal Emulation Sales Representative; Enterprise Integration Sales Representative. **Corporate headquarters location:** Atlanta GA. **International locations:** France; Germany; Australia; the Netherlands; the UK. **Listed on:** Euronext Amsterdam Exchange.

STATSOFT, INC.
2300 East 14th Street, Tulsa OK 74104. 918/749-1119. **Fax:** 918/749-2217. **Contact:** Human Resources. **E-mail address:** jobs@statsoft.com. **World Wide Web address:** http://www.statsoft.com. **Description:** A manufacturer of data analysis software utilized at research centers, universities, corporations, and manufacturing facilities. Statsoft's major product line is *STATISTICA*. **Positions advertised include:** Senior Statistician/Developer; System Analyst; Statistical Support/Data Mining Analyst; Software Test Engineer; Application Developer; Statistical Support Specialist; Consultant. **Special programs:** Training. **Corporate headquarters location:** This location. **Operations at this facility include:** Sales; Training; Consulting Services. **International locations:** Worldwide. **Listed on:** Privately held.

WABASH COMPUTER PRODUCTS
4720 West 90th Street, Suite 104, Tulsa OK 74132. 918/447-8977. **Toll-free phone:** 800/323-9868. **Fax:** 918/447-9377. **Contact:** Human Resources. **World Wide Web address:** http://www.wabashcomp.com. **Description:** Manufactures magnetic tapes, cartridges, and flexible diskettes. **Corporate headquarters location:** This location.

OREGON

ADP DEALER SERVICES
2525 SW First Avenue, Suite 450, Portland OR 97201. 503/294-4200. **Toll-free phone:** 800/225-5237. **Fax:** 503/294-4262. **Contact:** Senior Technical Recruiter. **World Wide Web address:** http://www.adp.com. **Description:** One of the largest companies in the world dedicated to providing computerized transaction processing, data communications, and information services. **Positions advertised include:** Tech Support Specialist; Administrative Coordinator; Hardware Client Technical Analyst; Materials Handler; Software Engineer; Columbia Repair Manager; Client Trainer. **Corporate headquarters location:** Roseland NJ. **Other U.S. locations:** Nationwide. **Operations at this facility include:** Research and Development; Sales; Service. **Listed on:** New York Stock Exchange. **Stock exchange symbol:** ADP.

ANALOG DEVICES, INC.
1100 NW Compton Drive, Suite 301, Beaverton OR 97006-1994. 503/690-1333. **Fax:** 503/690-1347. **Contact:** Human Resources Department. **World Wide Web address:** http://www.analog.com. **Description:** Designs, manufactures, and markets a broad line of high-performance linear, mixed-signal, and digital integrated circuits (ICs) that address a wide range of real-world signal processing applications. The company's principal products include system-level, general purpose, and standard linear ICs. Other products include devices manufactured using assembled product technology, such as hybrids, which combine unpackaged IC chips and other chip-level components in a single package. Analog's system-level ICs are used primarily in communications and computer applications. **Corporate headquarters location:** Norwood MA.

APCON, INC.
17938 SW Upper Boones Ferry Road, Portland OR 97224. 503/639-6700. **Toll-free phone:** 800/624-6808. **Fax:** 503/639-6740. **Contact:** Human Resources. **E-mail address:** hire@apcon.com. **World Wide Web address:** http://www.apcon.com. **Description:** Manufactures and markets a line of products for SCSI computer systems. APCON, Inc. manufactures PowerSwitch/NT, a clustering solution for Windows NT, which protects network servers from downtime. The company also offers PowerLink, which provides disaster recovery for RAIDS's and tape backup devices. Founded in 1986. **Positions advertised include:** Hardware Design Engineer; International Sales Representative; Product Marketing Manager. **Office**

hours: Monday - Friday, 7:30 a.m. - 5:00 p.m. **Corporate headquarters location:** This location.

BARCOVIEW INC.
1600 NW Compton Drive, Beaverton OR 97006. 503/690-1550. **Fax:** 503/690-1525. **Contact:** Personnel. **World Wide Web address:** http://www.barcomedical.com. **Description:** Designs, manufactures, and markets high-resolution graphics equipment for medical imaging systems. **Positions advertised include:** Mechanical Design Engineer; Business Applications Analyst; Lead Assembler. **International locations:** Worldwide.

CADENCE DESIGN SYSTEM
13221 SW 68th Parkway, Suite 200, Portland OR 97223. 503/968-5400. **Toll-free phone:** 800/671-9511. **Fax:** 503/968-7888. **Contact:** Human Resources. **World Wide Web address:** http://www.cadence.com. **Description:** Develops desktop electronic design automation (EDA) software. Cadence Design System's Windows-based software aids in the design of field-programmable gate arrays, complex programmable logic devices, and printed circuit boards. **Positions advertised include:** Design Engineer; Applications Engineer; Executive Administrator; Marketing Director. **Corporate headquarters location:** San Jose CA.

CHRISTENSON VELAGIO
1631 NW Thurman Street, Suite 200, Portland OR 97209. 503/419-3600. **Toll-free phone:** 800/234-4115. **Fax:** 503/419-3636. **Contact:** Human Resources. **E-mail address:** info@christenson.com. **World Wide Web address:** http://www.christenson.com. **Description:** An electrical and technology contractor that works in various locations including high-rise buildings and industrial businesses. Christenson Velagio leverages core competencies in electrical services and information technology in the areas of voice, data, video and life-safety into enterprise energy management solutions. Christenson Velagio has the ability to deliver turnkey solutions from energy management solutions to technology infrastructure implementation, including: Enterprise Energy Management Solutions, Electrical and Lighting Services, Electrical Design and Implementation, Digital Video CCTV Systems and Infrastructure, Telecommunications Systems and Infrastructure, Wireless Networking Solutions, IT Network (Voice and Data) Design and Implementation, Enterprise Security and Life–Safety Systems. **Corporate headquarters location:** This location.

COMPVIEW
10035 SW Arctic Drive, Beaverton OR 97005. 503/641-8439. **Fax:** 503/626-8439. **World Wide Web address:** http://www.compview.com. **Description:** CompView is a premier provider of presentation technology and group communication solutions. **Corporate Headquarters:** This location.

CORVALLIS MICROTECHNOLOGY INC.
413 SW Jefferson Avenue, Corvallis OR 97333. 541/752-5456. **Fax:** 541/752-4117. **Contact:** Human Resources Department. **World Wide Web address:** http://www.cmtinc.com. **Description:** Develops, manufactures, and markets handheld computers for the forestry, environmental, wildlife, and utility markets.

EPSON PORTLAND INC.
3950 NW Aloclek Place, Hillsboro OR 97124-7199. 503/645-1118. **Contact:** Human Resources. **World Wide Web address:** http://www.epson.com. **Description:** Epson develops and manufactures computers, electronic and crystal devices, factory automation systems, liquid crystal displays (LCDs), printers, and watches. **Corporate headquarters location:** Torrance CA. **Parent company:** Seiko Epson Corporation. **Operations at this facility include:** This location is a manufacturing facility.

HEWLETT-PACKARD COMPANY
15115 SW Sequoia Parkway, Suite 100, Portland OR 97224. 503/598-8000. **Contact:** Human Resources. **World Wide Web address:** http://www.hp.com. **Description:** Hewlett-Packard is engaged in the design and manufacturing of measurement and computation products and systems used in business, industry, engineering, science, health care, and education. Principal products are integrated instrument and computer systems (including hardware and software), peripheral products, and medical electronic equipment and systems. **NOTE:** Jobseekers are encouraged to apply via the Website: http://www.jobs.hp.com. **Special programs:** Internships. **Corporate headquarters location:** Palo Alto CA. **Other U.S. locations:** Nationwide. **Operations at this facility include:** This location is a sales office. **Listed on:** New York Stock Exchange. **Stock exchange symbol:** HPQ.

INSPIRATION SOFTWARE, INC.
9400 SW Beaverton Hillsdale Highway, Suite 300, Beaverton OR 97005-2167. 503/297-3004. **Toll-free phone:** 800/877-4292. **Fax:** 503/297-4676. **Contact:** Personnel. **E-mail address:** jobs@inspiration.com. **World Wide Web address:** http://www.inspiration.com. **Description:** Develops visual creative learning tools for the education market. **Positions advertised include:** Palm OS Programmer. **Corporate headquarters location:** This location.

INTEGRATED SERVICES
12242 SW Garden Place, Portland OR 97223. 503/968-8100. **Toll-free phone:** 800/922-3099. **Fax:** 503/968-9100. **Contact:** Human Resources Department. **World Wide Web address:** http://www.ints.com. **Description:** Develops management software for automobile lube shops and car washes.

INTEL CORPORATION
5200 NE Elam Young Parkway, Hillsboro OR 97124. 503/696-8080. **Toll-free phone:** 800/238-0486. **Contact:** Personnel. **World Wide Web address:** http://www.intel.com. **Description:** Intel is one of the largest semiconductor manufacturers in the world. Other operations include supercomputers; embedded control chips and flash memories; video technology software; multimedia hardware; personal computer enhancement products; and designing, making, and marketing microcomputer components, modules, and systems. **NOTE:** Jobseekers are encouraged to apply via the Website: http://www.intel.com/jobs. **Positions advertised include:** Administrative Assistant; Administrative Audit Specialist; Cellular Hardware Design Engineer; CAD Specialist; Electronics Engineer; Patent Attorney; Software Engineer; Technical Project Manager. **Operations at this facility include:** This location manufactures computer microprocessors and computer related parts. **Corporate headquarters location:** Santa Clara CA.

KENTROX LLC
20010 NW Tanasbourne Drive, Portland OR 97124. 503/643-1681. **Contact:** Human Resources Department. **World Wide Web address:** http://www.kentrox.com. **Description:** Manufactures standards-based, high-speed digital network access and service internetworking products for connectivity of local area networks (LANs) and customer premises equipment over wide area networks (WANs).

LATTICE SEMICONDUCTOR CORPORATION
5555 NE Moore Court, Hillsboro OR 97124. 503/681-0118. **Fax:** 503/268-8174. **Contact:** Human Resources. **World Wide Web address:** http://www.latticesemi.com. **Description:** A leader in the design, development, and marketing of high-speed Programmable Logic Devices (PLDs) in both low-density and high-density ranges. Lattice products are sold primarily to original equipment manufacturers of microcomputers, graphic systems, workstations, peripherals, telecommunications, military, and industrial controls. CMOS PLDs are assembled in 20 to 207 PIN standard packages and offered with various speed, power, and packaging options in commercial,

industrial, and military temperature versions. **Corporate headquarters location:** This location.

MENTOR GRAPHICS CORPORATION
8005 SW Boeckman Road, Wilsonville OR 97070-7777. 503/685-7000. **Toll-free phone:** 800/592-2210. **Recorded jobline:** 800/554-5259. **Contact:** Manager of Human Resources Department. **World Wide Web address:** http://www.mentor.com/jobs. **Description:** Develops electronic design automation (EDA) software used to automate the design, analysis, and documentation of electronic components and systems. Founded in 1981. **Positions advertised include:** Database Administrator; QA Engineer; Systems Administrator; Assistant Treasurer; Substitute Early Childhood Teacher; Software Engineer; Technical Marketing Engineer. **Special programs:** Internships. **Corporate headquarters location:** This location. **Other U.S. locations:** San Jose CA; Warren NJ; Dallas TX. **Operations at this facility include:** Administration; Research and Development.

MICROSOFT CORPORATION
10260 SW Greenburg Road, Suite 600, Portland OR 97223. 503/452-6400. **Contact:** Lori Colby, Human Resources. **World Wide Web address:** http://www.microsoft.com. **Description:** Microsoft designs, sells, and supports a product line of systems and applications microcomputer software for business, home, and professional use. Microsoft also produces related books and hardware products. Software products include spreadsheet, desktop publishing, project management, graphics, word processing, and database applications as well as operating systems and programming languages. **NOTE:** Resumes can be sent by mail to: Microsoft Corporation, One Microsoft Way, Suite 303, Redmond WA 98052-8303 or sent along with an online application via the Internet **Operations at this facility include:** The primary function of this location is sales and consulting.

NUTECH SOFTWARE SOLUTIONS, INC.
11575 SW Pacific Highway, Suite 109, Tigard OR 97223-8671. 503/443-2000. **Fax:** 503/968-1877. **Contact:** Human Resources. **E-mail address:** resume@nutech.com. **World Wide Web address:** http://www.nutech.com. **Description:** Develops SQL database, Web connectivity software, and Web-based video servers.

PACIFIC SOFTWARE ASSOCIATES
5605 NE Elam Young Parkway, Hillsboro OR 97124. 800/764-8326. **Contact:** Human Resources. **World Wide Web address:** http://www.psateam.com. **Description:** A provider of business solutions including, hardware systems, disaster recovery options, application software, e-commerce business-to-business solutions.

PALO ALTO SOFTWARE, INC.
144 East 14th Avenue, Eugene OR 97401. 541/683-6162. **Fax:** 541/683-6250. **Contact:** Human Resources. **E-mail address:** info@palo-alto.com. **World Wide Web address:** http://www.pasware.com. **Description:** Develops business plan and marketing software including Business Plan Pro, Marketing Plus, and DecisionMaker. **International locations:** London UK, Ireland, Canada.

PLANAR SYSTEMS, INC.
1195 NW Compton Drive, Beaverton OR 97006-1992. 503/748-1100. **Fax:** 503/748-1493. **Contact:** Director of Human Resources Department. **World Wide Web address:** http://www.planar.com. **Description:** A manufacturer of both high-performance flat-panel and CRT-based display products including electroluminescent and taut shadow mask CRT displays. Founded in 1983. **Special programs:** Internships. **Positions advertised include:** Supplier Quality Engineer; Process Engineer; Supply Chain Operations Manager; Regulatory Compliance Engineer. **Subsidiaries include:** Planar Advance, Inc.; Planar International. **Parent company:** Planar Systems, Inc. **Operations at this facility include:** Administration; Divisional Headquarters; Manufacturing; Research and Development; Sales; Service.

THE PORTLAND GROUP, INC. (PGI)
2 Centerpointe Drive, Suite 320, Lake Oswego OR 97035. 503/682-2806. **Fax:** 503/682-2637. **Contact:** Personnel. **World Wide Web address:** http://www.pgroup.com. **Description:** Develops compilers and software development tools for parallel computing. **Corporate headquarters location:** This location. **Parent company:** ST Microelectronics.

RADISYS CORPORATION
5445 NE Dawson Creek Drive, Hillsboro OR 97124. 503/615-1100. **Toll-free phone:** 800/950-0044. **Fax:** 503/615-1115. **Contact:** Personnel. **E-mail address:** info@radisys.com. **World Wide Web address:** http://www.radisys.com. **Description:** Designs and manufactures embedded computer technology used by OEMs in the manufacturing automation, telecommunications, medical devices, transportation, test and measurement, and retail automation industries. RadiSys offers a broad range of embedded computer subsystems, board-level modules, and chip-level products at varying levels of customization from standard products to full custom solutions. **Positions advertised include:** PC Board Designer; Mechanical Engineer; Senior Financial Reporting Analyst. **Corporate headquarters location:** This location. **Listed on:** NASDAQ. **Stock exchange symbol:** RSYS.

RICO BUSINESS SYSTEMS
4000 Kruseway Place, Building 1, Suite 300, Lake Oswego OR 97035. 503/636-7696. **Fax:** 503/697-0234. **Contact:** Human Resources. **World Wide Web address:** http://www.applied-info.com. **Description:** Offers a variety of network integration and computer systems services. Applied Information Services specializes in the development and installation of computer systems for businesses. Founded in 1970. **Positions advertised include:** Field Service Representative. **Parent company:** Savin Corp.

ROGUE WAVE SOFTWARE
815 NW Ninth Street, Suite L145, Corvallis OR 97330. 541/754-4096. **Fax:** 541/753-1912. **Contact:** Human Resources. **E-mail address:** hr@roguewave.com. **World Wide Web address:** http://www.roguewave.com. **Description:** Develops C++ and Java reusable cross-platform software and tools. **NOTE:** Entry-level positions and part-time jobs are offered. **Corporate headquarters location:** Boulder CO. **Other U.S. locations:** Nationwide. **International locations:** Worldwide.

SERENA SOFTWARE
3445 NW 211th Terrace, Hillsboro OR 97124. 503/645-1150. **Fax:** 503/645-4576. **Contact:** Human Resources. **World Wide Web address:** http://www.merant.com. **Description:** Provides computer programming and software services. **Positions advertised include:** Answerline Manager; Customer Marketing Manager; Paralegal; Product Marketing Manager; Staff Software Developer. **International locations:** Worldwide.

SOGETI
1500 SW First Avenue, Suite 890, Portland OR 97201. 503/295-1909. **Contact:** Human Resources Manager. **World Wide Web address:** http://www.sogeti.com. **Description:** A leading provider of information technology consulting services. The company provides its clients with the solutions needed to achieve business and operational goals. CGA's principal focus is on three major activities: consultancy, implementation, and systems integration. **Other U.S. locations:** Nationwide. **Parent company:** The Cap Gemini Sogeti Group is a top-ranked provider of information technology services throughout Europe and its major markets.

TEKTRONIX, INC.
P.O. Box 500, Mail Stop 55-545, Beaverton OR 97077-0001. 503/627-7111. **Contact:** Professional Staffing. **World Wide Web address:** http://www.tek.com.

Description: Tektronix, Inc. produces electronic test and measurement, computer graphics, and communications equipment. Test and measurement products include oscilloscopes, logic analyzers, digitizers, and curve tracers. Computer graphics products include printers and terminals primarily for scientific and engineering uses. Communications equipment includes vectorscopes, waveform monitors, signal generators, cable and fiber-optic testers, demodulators, and television routing and switching items. **Positions advertised include:** Engineering Director; Product Engineer; Security Support Associate; Senior Package Design Engineer; Wireless Regional Marketing Manager; Principal ASIC Engineer; Americas Field Marcom Manager. **Special programs:** Internships. **Corporate headquarters location:** This location. **Other area locations:** Wilsonville OR. **Other U.S. locations:** Nationwide. **Operations at this facility include:** This location manufactures oscilloscopes.

THIN PATH SYSTEMS
26200 SW 95th Avenue, Suite 300, Wilsonville OR 97070. 971/404-3285. **Contact:** Human Resources. **E-mail address:** info@tp-sys.com. **World Wide Web address:** http://www.thinpathsystems.com. **Description:** Provides desktop information access solutions for network computing environments. Thin Path Systems is a worldwide supplier of X Window System terminals and PC-X server software products, which integrate Microsoft Windows- and DOS-based PCs into X/UNIX networks. The company also supplies the Z-Mail family of cross-platform electronic mail and messaging software for open systems environments, as well as Mariner, an Internet access and navigation software tool that provides a unified interface to all Internet resources. **Corporate headquarters location:** This location. **Operations at this facility include:** This location develops and manufactures hardware and software that enables computers to be networked.

TIMBERLINE SOFTWARE CORPORATION
15195 NW Greenbrier Parkway, Beaverton OR 97006-5701. 503/690-6775. **Fax:** 503/439-5819. **Contact:** Personnel. **E-mail address:** jobs@timberline.com. **World Wide Web address:** http://www.timberline.com. **Description:** Timberline Software Corporation develops and markets computer software programs, primarily for the construction and property management industries. **Positions advertised include:** Lead Install Engineer; Payroll Administrator; Senior Accounting Clerk; Technical Support Specialist; Technical Writer; QA Manager; Vice President of Information Technology. **Corporate headquarters location:** This location.

TOSOH QUARTZ INC.
14380 NW Science Park Drive, Portland OR 97229. 503/605-5600. **Fax:** 503/605-5696. **Contact:** Kathy Copeland, Human Resources Manager. **E-mail address:** jobs@tosohquartz.com. **World Wide Web address:** http://www.tosohquartz.com. **Description:** Manufactures quartz semiconductors. Founded in 1957. **Positions advertised include:** Manufacturing Tech; Inspector. **Number of employees worldwide:** 200.

TRIQUINT SEMICONDUCTOR, INC.
2300 NE Brookwood Parkway, Hillsboro OR 97124. 503/615-9000. **Fax:** 503/615-8900. **Contact:** Corporate Staffing. **E-mail address:** info_hr@tqs.com. **World Wide Web address:** http://www.tqs.com. **Description:** TriQuint Semiconductor designs, develops, manufactures, and markets a broad range of high-performance analog and mixed-signal integrated circuits for the wireless communications, telecommunications, and computing markets. **Positions advertised include:** Receptionist; Payroll Specialist; Design Engineer. **Corporate headquarters location:** This location. **Operations at this facility include:** This location houses administrative offices.

VESTA CORPORATION
309 SW Sixth Avenue, Fourth Floor, Portland OR 97204. 503/790-2500. **Fax:** 503/790-2525. **Contact:** Human Resources. **E-mail address:** jobs@trustvesta.com. **World Wide Web address:** http://www.trustvesta.com. **Description:** Vesta Corporation is a provider of stored value commerce solutions such as account recharge, payment processing, risk management, customer service, and program management. **Positions advertised include:** IVR Call Flow Programmer; Chief Operations Officer; Senior NET Engineer; Channel Marketing Manager; Security Specialist; Customer Service Representative.

WACKER SANITATION
13105 SE 197th Street, P.O. Box 83180, Boring OR 97009. 503/658-3347. **Fax:** 503/658-6369. **Recorded jobline:** 503/241-7547. **Contact:** Senior Corporate Recruiter. **E-mail address:** employment@siltronic.com. **World Wide Web address:** http://www.siltronic.com. **Description:** Manufactures polish and epitaxially coated silicon wafers for the semiconductor industry. **Positions advertised include:** Operators; Material Handler. **Corporate headquarters location:** Munich, Germany. **Parent company:** Wacker Siltronic A.G.

Pennsylvania

ACTIVANT SOLUTIONS INC.
19 West College Avenue, Yardley PA 19067. **Toll-free phone:** 800/776-7438. **Contact:** Human Resources. **World Wide Web address:** http://www.activant.com. **Description:** A technology provider of business management solutions serving small and medium-sized retail and wholesale distribution businesses in three primary vertical markets: hardlines and lumber; wholesale distribution; and the automotive parts aftermarket. Founded in 1972. **Positions advertised include:** Business analyst; Customer Account Executive; Events Specialist; Financial Analyst; Sales Engineer. Sales Engineering Manager. **Corporate headquarters location:** Austin TX.

ADONIX
2200 Georgetowne Drive, Sewickley PA 15143. 724/933-1377. **Fax:** 724/933-1379. **Contact:** Human Resources. **E-mail address:** careers@adonix.com. **World Wide Web address:** http://www.adonix.com. **Description:** A provider of business software and consulting services. The company's software products include TOLAS and Baan, which are used for sales, customer service, product distribution, logistics, warehouse management, inventory, and financial control. **Positions advertised include:** ERP Consultant; Financial Consultant; Manufacturing Consultant. **Listed on:** Privately held. **President:** Ronald Book. **Number of employees nationwide:** 200.

AJILON SERVICES INC.
5001 Louise Drive, 2nd Floor, Mechanicsburg PA 17055-6912. 717/790-0729. **Fax:** 717/790-9159. **Contact:** Recruiting. **E-mail address:** recruit.pittsburgh@ajilon.com. **World Wide Web address:** http://www.ajilon.com. **Description:** Provides computer consulting services, project support, and end user services. **Other U.S. locations:** Nationwide.

ALTEC LANSING TECHNOLOGIES, INC.
Route 6 & 209, P.O. Box 277, Milford PA 18337-0277. 570/296-4434. **Toll-free phone:** 866/570-5702. **Fax:** 570/296-6887. **Contact:** Personnel. **E-mail address:** resumes@alteclansing.com. **World Wide Web address:** http://www.altecmm.com. **Description:** Manufactures speakers and surround sound systems for computers. **NOTE:** Entry-level positions are offered. **Positions advertised include:** Sr. Oracle Business Analyst; Product Manager. **Special programs:** Internships; Co-ops. **Office hours:** Monday - Friday, 8:30 a.m. - 5:00 p.m. **Corporate headquarters location:** This location. **Other U.S. locations:** Nationwide. **International locations:** Worldwide. **Listed on:** Privately held. **Number of employees at this location:** 130.

ANALYTICAL GRAPHICS, INC.
220 Valley Creek Boulevard, Exton PA 19341. 610/981-8000. **Fax:** 610/981-8001. **Contact:** Human Resources. **E-mail address:** hr@agi.com. **World Wide**

Web address: http://www.stk.com. **Description:** AGI provides software to more than 30,000 national security and space professionals for integrated analyses of land, sea, air, and space assets. Key applications include: battlespace management, geospatial intelligence initiatives, space systems, and national defense programs. **Positions advertised include:** DBA/Developer; Contracts Specialist; Inside Sales Associate; Application Support Engineer; Aerospace Engineer, Mathematician, Physicist; Training Coordinator.

ANSYS, INC.
275 Technology Drive, Canonsburg PA 15317. 724/514-2991. **Fax:** 724/514-1990. **Contact:** Human Resources. **E-mail address:** jobs@ansys.com. **World Wide Web address:** http://www.ansys.com. **Description:** Develops finite element analysis software for engineering firms. **Positions advertised include:** Sr. System Administrator; Global Tax Manager. **Corporate headquarters location:** This location. **Number of employees at this location:** 600. **Listed on:** NASDAQ. **Stock exchange symbol:** ANSS.

ASTEA INTERNATIONAL INC.
240 Gibraltar Road, Horsham PA 19044-2306. 215/682-2500. **Toll-free phone:** 800/347-7334. **Fax:** 215/682-2515. **Contact:** Kelly Posch, Human Resources. **E-mail address:** kposch@astea.com. **World Wide Web address:** http://www.astea.com. **Description:** Develops, markets, and supports a variety of applications for client/server and host-based environments that permit organizations of various sizes across a wide range of industries to automate and integrate field service and customer support functions. Astea also offers a full range of consulting, training, and customer support services. **NOTE:** Entry-level positions are offered. **Positions advertised include:** QA Analyst; Technical Architect; Support Programmer; Project Manager. **Corporate headquarters location:** This location. **Other U.S. locations:** San Mateo CA; Denver CO; Bedford MA. **Listed on:** NASDAQ. **Stock exchange symbol:** ATEA. **Annual sales/revenues:** $21 - $50 million. **Number of employees at this location:** 200. **Number of employees nationwide:** 450.

AUTOMATED FINANCIAL SYSTEMS
123 Summit Drive, Exton PA 19341. 610/524-9300. **Contact:** Human Resources. **World Wide Web address:** http://www.afsvision.com. **Description:** Develops commercial lending and treasury management software and provides services to U.S. financial institutions. Founded in 1970. **Positions advertised include:** Senior Network Engineer; Programmer/Analyst; Senior Business Analyst; Associate Business Analyst; Visual Basic Programmer/Analyst; Sr. Level Java Programmer; Systems Architect. **Corporate headquarters location:** This location. **Other U.S. locations:** AK; CA; IL; NC; NJ. **Subsidiaries include:** Automated Financial Systems GmbH. **Number of employees worldwide:** 350.

BENTLEY SYSTEMS INC.
685 Stockton Drive, Exton PA 19341. 610/458-5000. **Contact:** Human Resources. **World Wide Web address:** http://www.bentley.com. **Description:** Develops AEC software. **Positions advertised include:** SAP Marketing Functional Analyst; Product eMarketing Manager; Marketing Database Specialist; Systems Analyst.

BLACK BOX CORPORATION
1000 Park Drive, Lawrence PA 15055. 877/877-2269. **Fax:** 724/873-6502. **Contact:** Human Development. **E-mail address:** bbcareers@blackbox.com. **World Wide Web address:** http://www.blackbox.com. **Description:** Manufactures modems and switches. Founded in 1976. **Positions advertised include:** Distribution Center Rep; External Reporting Analyst; Internal Auditor; Marketing Analyst; Publications Designer; Test Technician.

BRODART AUTOMATION
500 Arch Street, Williamsport PA 17701. **Toll-free phone:** 800/474-9802 ext. 6772. **Fax:** 800/999-6799. **Contact:** Human Resources. **E-mail address:** salesmkt@brodart.com. **World Wide Web address:** http://www.brodart.com. **Description:** A leading provider of automated library services including computer-based bibliographic maintenance. Founded in 1975. **Positions advertised include:** Web Application Developer; Project Manager. **Parent company:** Brodart Company.

CAM CO ENTERPRISES, INC.
125 South College Street, Washington PA 15301. 724/222-2315. **Contact:** Human Resources. **World Wide Web address:** http://www.camconet.com. **Description:** Manufactures and sells computer systems and provides networking and Website design services.

CIBER, INC.
701 Lee Road, Suite 100, Wayne PA 19087. 610/993-8100. **Fax:** 610/993-8092. **Contact:** Human Resources. **World Wide Web address:** http://www.ciber.com. **Description:** A systems integration consultancy. The company's services include computer network design, installation, and administration; helpdesk support; technical education; cabling and telecommunications sales and service; computer product sales and services; and Internet services. Clients include many small and mid-range companies, national and global *Fortune* 1000 companies, and large government agencies. The company maintains 60 U.S. offices, 20 European offices, and four offices in Asia. Founded in 1974. **Positions advertised include:** BEA Weblogic Administrator; Sr. Informatica Administrator; Apache Webserver Administrator; Project Manager; SQL Server Developer. **Corporate headquarters location:** Greenwood Village CO. **Other area locations:** Harrisburg PA; Pittsburgh PA. **Other U.S. locations:** Nationwide. **Listed on:** New York Stock Exchange. **Stock exchange symbol:** CBR. **Annual sales/revenues:** More than $950 million. **Number of employees worldwide:** 8,000.

COMPUTER ASSOCIATES INTERNATIONAL (CA)
220 West Germantown Pike, Plymouth Meeting PA 19462. 610/940-9900. **Contact:** Human Resources. **World Wide Web address:** http://www.ca.com. **Description:** One of the world's leading developers of client/server and distributed computing software. The company develops, markets, and supports enterprise management, database and applications development, business applications, and consumer software products for a broad range of mainframe, midrange, and desktop computers. Computer Associates International serves major business, government, research, and educational organizations. Founded in 1976. **Positions advertised include:** Sr. Consultant; Sr. Project Manager. **Corporate headquarters location:** Islandia NY. **Other U.S. locations:** Nationwide. **Listed on:** New York Stock Exchange. **Stock exchange symbol:** CA.

COMPUTER HARDWARE SERVICE COMPANY (CHSC)
48 D Vincent Circle, Ivyland PA 18974. 215/443-9220. **Fax:** 215/443-9024. **Contact:** Human Resources. **E-mail address:** jobs@chscinc.com. **World Wide Web address:** http://www.chscinc.com. **Description:** Provides computer network maintenance and repair services.

COMPUTER SCIENCES CORPORATION
1160 Swedesford Road, Suite 200, Berwyn PA 19312. 856/251-0660. **Contact:** Human Resources. **World Wide Web address:** http://www.csc.com. **Description:** An information technology services company offering systems design and integration; IT and business process outsourcing; applications software development; Web and application hosting; and management consulting. **Positions advertised include:** Application Designer; Application Developer; Application Development Manager. **Corporate headquarters location:** El Segundo CA. **Other U.S. locations:** Nationwide.

CYBERTECH INC.
935 Horsham Road, Suite I, Horsham PA 19044. 215/957-6220. **Fax:** 215/674-8515. **Contact:** Human Resources. **World Wide Web address:** http://www.cbrtech.com. **Description:** Manufactures specialty printers for corporate customers.

DAISY DATA DISPLAYS, INC.
2850 Lewisberry Road, York Haven PA 17370. 717/932-9999. **Fax:** 717/932-8000. **Contact:** Human Resources. **E-mail address:** shefetv@daisydata.com. **World Wide Web address:** http://www.daisydata.com. **Description:** Manufactures rugged computers for industrial environments. **Positions advertised include:** Mechanical Designer.

DATA SCIENCE AUTOMATION, INC.
375 Valley Brook Road, Suite 106, McMurray PA 15317. 724/942-6330. **Fax:** 724/942-8390. **Contact:** Human Resources. **World Wide Web address:** http://www.dsautomation.com. **Description:** An automation engineering firm specializing in developing PC-based solutions to data acquisition, analysis, process, and quality control applications. **Positions advertised include:** Architect; Sr. Architect; Consultant; Sr. Consultant; Engineer; Sr. Engineer.

DATA-CORE SYSTEMS INC.
3700 Market Street, Philadelphia PA 19104. 215/243-1990. **Contact:** Human Resources. **World Wide Web address:** http://www.datacoresystems.com. **Description:** Develops database applications software. **Parent company:** DC Kuljian Group is a diversified holding company engaged in engineering, construction management, software, communications, chemicals, and health care.

DATACAP SYSTEMS, INC.
100 New Britain Boulevard, Chalfont PA 18914. 215/997-8989. **Fax:** 215/997-3919. **Contact:** Human Resources. **World Wide Web address:** http://www.dcap.com. **Description:** Develops software and point-of-sale systems.

DAY-TIMER, INC.
One Willow Lane, East Texas PA 18046. 610/398-1151. **Toll-free phone:** 800/225-5005. **Contact:** Human Resources Manager. **World Wide Web address:** http://www.daytimer.com. **Description:** Designs and manufactures personal and organizational calendars, accessories, and software. **NOTE:** Online application is encouraged at http://www.jobs.acco.icims.com. **Positions advertised include:** Director of Catalog and Web Marketing. **Corporate headquarters location:** This location.

DECISIONONE
426 West Lancaster Avenue, Devon PA 19333. 610/296-6000. **Toll-free phone:** 800/767-2876. **Fax:** 610/296-2910. **Contact:** Human Resources Department. **World Wide Web address:** http://www.decisionone.com. **Description:** An international supplier of plug-compatible computer equipment and accessories. Products include disk and tape storage devices, terminals, intelligent workstations and systems, controllers, printers, airline reservation systems, and a comprehensive range of computer supplies. **Corporate headquarters location:** This location. **International locations:** Nationwide.

DIGITAL SOLUTIONS, INC. (DSI)
4200 Industrial Park Drive, Altoona PA 16602. 814/944-0405. **Contact:** Human Resources. **World Wide Web address:** http://www.dsicdi.com. **Description:** A worldwide criminal justice and public safety automation industry leader.

EBIX.COM, INC.
7 Parkway Center, Suite 655, Pittsburgh PA 15220. 412/920-7025. **Fax:** 412/937-3688. **Contact:** Human Resources. **E-mail address:** jobs@ebix.com. **World Wide Web address:** http://www.ebix.com. **Description:** Ebix.com develops management applications software for insurance agencies. **Corporate headquarters location:** Atlanta GA. **Operations at this facility include:** This location develops software and offers technical support.

EGAMES, INC.
2000 Cabot Boulevard West, Suite 110, Langhorne PA 19047-1811. 215/750-6606. **Fax:** 215/750-3722. **Contact:** Human Resources. **E-mail address:** jobs@egames.com. **World Wide Web address:** http://www.egames.com. **Description:** Publishes and distributes PC software games. Founded in 1992. **Positions advertised include:** Production Developer/Webmaster.

EPLUS, INC.
130 Futura Drive, P.O. Box 479, Pottstown PA 19464. 610/495-7800. **Fax:** 610/495-2800. **Contact:** Darren Raiguel, Human Resources. **E-mail address:** draiguel@eplus.com. **World Wide Web address:** http://www.eplus.com. **Description:** Leases and sells computers and other IT equipment. ePlus also develops online software products that provide supply chain management solutions including electronic procurement, e-financing, and e-asset management. **Positions advertised include:** Sr. Account Executive. **Corporate headquarters location:** Herndon VA. **Other U.S. locations:** Scottsdale AZ; Sacramento CA; San Diego CA; Lenexa KS; Columbia MD; Minneapolis MN; Greenville NC; Raleigh NC; Waxhaw NC; Wilmington NC; West Chester PA; Harrisburg PA; Dallas TX; Austin TX. **Listed on:** NASDAQ. **Stock exchange symbol:** PLUS.

E-TECH SOLUTIONS, INC.
1487 Dunwoody Drive, Suite 100, West Chester PA 19380. 610/408-0722. **Fax:** 610/408-0994. **Contact:** Sarah Holbrook, Human Resources. **E-mail address:** sholbrook@etechsolutions.com. **World Wide Web address:** http://www.etechsolutions.com. **Description:** A technology consultancy that provides solutions to businesses with a focus on business analysis, user experience, e-business solutions, and infrastructure management. **Positions advertised include:** Sr. Business Analyst; Application Developer; Portal Developer; Sr. Project Manager; Sr. Architect; Director; Support Developer Sr. IP Consultant; Security Consultant. **Other U.S. locations:** Houston TX.

EXPEDIENT
810 Parrish Street, Pittsburgh PA 15220. **Toll-free phone:** 877/570-7827. **Contact:** Human Resources. **E-mail address:** resumes@expedient.com. **World Wide Web address:** http://www.expedient.com. **Description:** A national telecommunications company offering services throughout the U.S. **Positions advertised include:** Sr. Network Engineer; Software Developer; Microsoft Windows System Engineer; Network Operations Center Engineer.

FIS EMPOWER
50 South Water Avenue, Sharon PA 16146. 724/981-5087. **Fax:** 724/981-4323. **Contact:** Melissa Thomas, Human Resources. **E-mail address:** carolpe@eastsoft.com. **World Wide Web address:** http://www.fidelityinfoservices.com. **Description:** Develops software for consumer mortgage lending and commercial loans. **Positions advertised include:** Mortgage/Lending Business Analyst; Mortgage Administration Trainer. **Parent company:** Fidelity National Information Services.

FINANCIAL SOFTWARE SYSTEMS
240 Gibraltar Road, Suite 200, Horsham PA 19044. 215/784-1100. **Contact:** Human Resources. **E-mail address:** humanresources@fssnet.com. **World Wide Web address:** http://www.finsoftware.net. **Description:** A financial risk-management software and consulting firm. The company provides foreign exchange and interest rate risk-management software and consulting for banks, corporations, and fund managers. **Positions advertised include:** Client Account Manager; Database Analyst/Administrator; Financial Software Analyst; Quality Assurance;

Software Engineer; Sr. Software Engineer; Technical Writer. **International locations:** London; Singapore.

GE ENERGY SERVICES
2849 Sterling Drive, Hatfield PA 19440. 215/996-9200. **Fax:** 215/996-9201. **Contact:** Human Resources. **World Wide Web address:** http://www.gepower.com. **Description:** Formerly KVB-Enertec Inc., now a division of GE Power Systems. A manufacturer of SNIFFER computerized CEM (continuous emissions monitoring) systems used to test for state and EPA compliance for pollutant-emitting sources such as incinerators, boilers, turbines, and cogeneration plants. **Corporate headquarters location:** Atlanta GA. **Parent company:** General Electric Company. **Listed on:** New York Stock Exchange. **Stock exchange symbol:** GE. **Number of employees worldwide:** 35,000.

GSI COMMERCE, INC.
935 First Avenue, King of Prussia PA 19406. 610/491-7000. **Fax:** 610/265-0736. **Contact:** Melissa Reinish, Human Resources Director. **E-mail address:** jobs@globalsports.com. **World Wide Web address:** http://www.gsicommerce.com. **Description:** Provides e-commerce outsourcing solutions for retailers, manufacturers, media companies, and professional sports organizations. Founded in 1991. **Positions advertised include:** Online Business Manager; Financial Analyst; Senior Cost Analyst; Production Support Analyst. **Special programs:** Internships. **Office hours:** Monday - Friday, 8:30 a.m. - 5:30 p.m. **Corporate headquarters location:** This location. **Listed on:** NASDAQ. **Stock exchange symbol:** GSPT. **CEO:** Michael Rubin. **Annual sales/revenues:** More than $100 million. **Number of employees at this location:** 85. **Number of employees nationwide:** 95. **Number of employees worldwide:** 140.

GATEWAY TICKETING SYSTEMS, INC.
315 East Second Street, Boyertown PA 19512. 610/987-4000. **Toll-free phone:** 800/487-8587. **Fax:** 610/987-4002. **Contact:** Human Resources. **E-mail address:** employment@gatewayticketing.com. **World Wide Web address:** http://www.gatewayticketing.com. **Description:** Provides access control, admission control, and ticketing software for the attraction, amusement, and intercity bus transportation industries. **Positions advertised include:** Account Representative; Field Technician; Implementation Specialist; Information Systems Technician; Product Communication Specialist; Program Manager; Programmer; Sr. Programmer.

HMW ENTERPRISES INC.
207 North Franklin Street, P.O. Box 309, Waynesboro PA 17268. 717/765-4690. **Fax:** 717/765-4660. **Contact:** Human Resources. **World Wide Web address:** http://www.hmwent.com. **Description:** Manufactures industrial computers.

IBM TRANSARC CORPORATION
11 Stanwix Street, Pittsburgh PA 15222. 412/667-4400. **Contact:** Staffing Manager. **World Wide Web address:** http://www.transarc.ibm.com. **Description:** Develops AFS and DCE software. **Parent company:** IBM Corporation.

IGATE CORPORATION
1000 Commerce Drive, Suite 500, Pittsburgh PA 15275. 412/787-2100. **Contact:** Human Resources. **E-mail address:** careers@igate.com. **World Wide Web address:** http://www.igatecorp.com. **Description:** Provides high value information technology services including e-business solutions, enterprise solutions implementation, network services, and supply chain management solutions and applications design. Founded in 1986. **Corporate headquarters location:** This location. **International locations:** Worldwide. **Subsidiaries include:** iGate Global Solutions Ltd.; iGate Professional Services; iGate Virtual University; iGate Clinical Research. **Listed on:** NASDAQ. **Stock exchange symbol:** IGTE. **Number of employees worldwide:** 5,500.

KEANE, INC.
460 Norristown Road, Suite 200, Blue Bell PA 19422. 610/260-0640. **Contact:** Human Resources. **E-mail address:** careers@keane.com. **World Wide Web address:** http://www.keane.com. **Description:** Offers businesses a variety of computer consulting services. Keane also develops, markets, and manages software for its clients and assists in project management. **Positions advertised include:** Engagement Manager; Business Analyst; Project Manager. **Corporate headquarters location:** Boston MA. **Listed on:** American Stock Exchange. **Stock exchange symbol:** KEA.

KEYSTONE COMPUTER ASSOCIATES
1055 Virginia Drive, Fort Washington PA 19034. 215/643-3800. **Fax:** 215/643-0115. **Contact:** Human Resources. **World Wide Web address:** http://www.keystoneca.com. **Description:** A computer consulting firm. **Positions advertised include:** IT Management; Project Management.

LINK COMPUTER CORPORATION
Stadium Drive, P.O. Box 250, Bellwood PA 16617. 814/742-7700. **Fax:** 814/742-7900. **Contact:** Karen Barr, Human Resources. **E-mail address:** kbarr@linkcorp.com. **World Wide Web address:** http://www.linkcorp.com. **Description:** Provides a wide range of information technology solutions including networking services, consulting, programming, Internet development, and systems analysis. Founded in 1980. **NOTE:** Entry-level positions are offered. **Positions advertised include:** Account Manager; Web Developer; Implementation Engineer. **Special programs:** Internships; Co-ops; Summer Jobs. **Corporate headquarters location:** This location. **Other U.S. locations:** Pittsburgh PA. **Listed on:** Privately held. **Annual sales/revenues:** $21 - $50 million. **Number of employees at this location:** 80. **Number of employees nationwide:** 110.

LUGARU SOFTWARE, LTD.
1645 Shady Avenue, Pittsburgh PA 15217. 412/421-5911. **Fax:** 412/421-6371. **Contact:** Human Resources. **World Wide Web address:** http://www.lugaru.com. **Description:** Manufactures an EMACS-style programmer's text editor for Windows, DOS, and OS/2 called Epsilon Programmer's Editor. **Corporate headquarters location:** This location.

MANAGEMENT SCIENCE ASSOCIATES, INC.
6565 Penn Avenue, Pittsburgh PA 15206-4490. 412/362-2000. **Toll-free phone:** 800/MSA-INFO. **Fax:** 412/363-8170. **Contact:** Human Resources Director. **E-mail address:** careers@msa.com. **World Wide Web address:** http://www.msa.com. **Description:** Develops analytical software and related systems. **NOTE:** Part-time jobs are offered. **Positions advertised include:** Controller; Client Service Analyst; Support Technician; Project Planner; Quality Assurance Analyst; Sr. Software Developer; Sr. Software Engineer. **Special programs:** Summer Jobs.

MARCONI
1000 Marconi Drive, Warrendale PA 15086-7502. 866/627-2664. **Fax:** 724/742-6464. **Contact:** Human Resources. **World Wide Web address:** http://www.marconi.com. **Description:** Manufactures LAN and WAN switches. Marconi also develops internetworking software and network management software. **Positions advertised include:** Software Test Engineer; Test Engineer. **Corporate headquarters location:** London UK. **Other U.S. locations:** Nationwide. **International locations:** Worldwide. **Parent company:** Ericsson.

MARKETING & BUSINESS INTEGRATION, LLC (MBI)
379 West Uchwlan Avenue, Suite 202, Exton PA 19335. 610/269-6900. **Fax:** 610/269-7454. **Contact:** Human Resources. **World Wide Web address:** http://www.mbius.net. **Description:** A management consulting and technology services firm that designs, installs, manages, and maintains information

technology infrastructures for clients.

MAXWELL SYSTEMS, INC.
2500 DeKalb Pike, Norristown PA 19401. 610/277-3515. **Contact:** Human Resources. **World Wide Web address:** http://www.maxwellsystems.com. **Description:** Maxwell Systems sells business management software to construction, service, and related industries. **NOTE:** An online request can be done to get employment information sent to your e-mail address. **Corporate headquarters location:** This location. **Operations at this facility include:** This location is a computer training facility.

McKESSON CORPORATION
5 Country View Road, Malvern PA 19355-1421. 610/407-0736. **Contact:** Human Resources. **World Wide Web address:** http://www.mckesson.com. **Description:** Provides information systems and technology to health care enterprises including hospitals, integrated delivery networks, and managed care organizations. McKesson's primary products are Pathways 2000, a family of client/server-based applications that allow the integration and uniting of health care providers; STAR, Series, and HealthQuest transaction systems; TRENDSTAR decision support system; and QUANTUM enterprise information system. The company also offers outsourcing services that include strategic information systems planning, data center operations, receivables management, business office administration, and major system conversions. **Positions advertised include:** Product Manager; Accountant; Software Engineer. **Corporate headquarters location:** San Francisco CA. **Other U.S. locations:** Boston MA. **Operations at this facility include:** Administration; Divisional Headquarters; Research and Development; Sales; Service. **Number of employees at this location:** 155. **Number of employees nationwide:** 175.

MISYS HEALTHCARE SYSTEMS
Foster Plaza #6, 681 Andersen Drive, Pittsburgh PA 15220. 412/937-0690. **Contact:** Human Resources. **World Wide Web address:** http://www.misyshealthcare.com. **Description:** Develops health care management software. **Operations at this facility include:** This location provides sales, training, and support.

NCR CORPORATION
1160 East Main Street, Mount Joy PA 17552-9337. 717/653-1801. **Contact:** Human Resources. **World Wide Web address:** http://www.ncr.com. **Description:** NCR Corporation is a worldwide provider of computer products and services. The company provides computer solutions to three targeted industries: retail, financial, and communications. **Corporate headquarters location:** Dayton OH. **Listed on:** New York Stock Exchange. **Stock exchange symbol:** NCR. **Number of employees nationwide:** 19,000. **Number of employees worldwide:** 29,000.

NEOWARE SYSTEMS, INC.
3200 Horizon Drive, King of Prussia PA 19406. 610/277-8300. **Fax:** 610/275-5739. **Contact:** Human Resources. **E-mail address:** resume@neoware.com. **World Wide Web address:** http://www.neoware.com. **Description:** Provides enterprise software, thin client appliances, and related services. **Positions advertised include:** Director of Product Management; LAN Administrator; Marketing Manager; Sr. Accountant.

PDS INC. (PERSONNEL DATA SYSTEMS)
650 Sentry Parkway, Blue Bell PA 19422. 610/238-4600. **Fax:** 610/238-4550. **Contact:** Human Resources. **E-mail address:** jobs@pdssoftware.com. **World Wide Web address:** http://www.pdssoftware.com. **Description:** PDS designs and develops human resources and payroll systems software for PC networks, IBM mainframes, and operating environments with strong emphasis on client/server technology. **Positions advertised include:** Application Product Support Specialist; HRMS Software Implementation Consultant.

PERIPHERAL DYNAMICS INC. (PDI)
5150 Campus Drive, Plymouth Meeting PA 19462-1197. 610/825-7090. **Contact:** Human Resources. **World Wide Web address:** http://www.pdiscan.com. **Description:** Manufactures scanners, optical readers, and other peripherals used in computer data entry.

PRESCIENT SYSTEMS, INC.
1247 Ward Avenue, Suite 200, West Chester PA 19380. 610/719-1600. **Toll-free phone:** 888/610-1800. **Fax:** 610/719-8575. **Contact:** Human Resources. **E-mail address:** hr@prescientsystems.com. **World Wide Web address:** http://www.prescientsystems.com. **Description:** A developer and supplier of forecasting and logistics software solutions. The company's supply chain management software provides a solution for demand forecasting, inventory planning, and continuous replenishment. This software is used by manufacturers, distributors, and retailers worldwide. **Corporate headquarters location:** This location. **Operations at this facility include:** Administration; Research and Development; Sales; Service. **Annual sales/revenues:** Less than $5 million. **Number of employees at this location:** 30. **Number of employees nationwide:** 45.

PRIMAVERA SYSTEMS INC.
3 Bala Plaza West, Suite 700, Bala-Cynwyd PA 19004. 610/667-8600. **Fax:** 610/949-6761. **Contact:** Joanne McCool, Vice President of Human Resources. **E-mail address:** careers@primavera.com. **World Wide Web address:** http://www.primavera.com. **Description:** Develops and supports an array of project management software for assisting clients in risk analysis, large-scale projects, contract management, team communication, and remote real-time updating. Founded in 1983. **NOTE:** Entry-level positions are offered. **Positions advertised include:** Product & Industry Market Manager; Channel Marketing Manager; Corporate Account Executive. **Special programs:** Internships; Co-ops. **Office hours:** Monday - Friday, 8:00 a.m. - 5:00 p.m. **Corporate headquarters location:** This location. **Other U.S. locations:** Nationwide. **International locations:** Worldwide. **Annual sales/revenues:** $21 - $50 million. **Number of employees at this location:** 180. **Number of employees nationwide:** 230. **Number of employees worldwide:** 260.

RAINMAKER SOFTWARE, INC.
1777 Sentry parkway West, Dublin Hall, Suite 100, Blue Bell PA 19422. 610/567-3400. **Contact:** Human Resources. **E-mail address:** jobs@rainmakerlegal.com. **World Wide Web address:** http://www.rainmakerlegal.com. **Description:** Develops computer applications for the legal industry. **Corporate headquarters location:** Framingham MA. **Parent company:** ASA International Ltd. designs and develops proprietary vertical market software and installs software on a variety of computers and networks.

RAYTHEON COMPANY
P.O. Box 60, 300 Science Park Road, State College PA 16804. 814/238-4311. **Contact:** Nancy Boozer, Human Resources Manager. **World Wide Web address:** http://www.raytheon.com. **Description:** Raytheon Systems designs, manufactures, and installs state-of-the-art communications and integrated command-and-control systems for military and industrial customers worldwide. The company markets its products to the commercial and defense electronics industry. **Positions advertised include:** Configuration Analyst; System Architect; Technical Support Associate; Principal Systems Engineer; UNIX Systems Administrator; Software Engineer II; Management Assistant. **Corporate headquarters location:** Waltham MA. **Operations at this facility include:** This location develops software.

REDSIREN TECHNOLOGIES, INC.
650 Smithfield Street, Suite 910, Pittsburgh PA 15222. 412/281-4427. **Toll-free phone:** 877/360-7602. **Fax:** 412/434-1264. **Contact:** Jim Leindecker, Director of Human Resources. **E-mail address:**

careers@redsiren.com. **World Wide Web address:** http://www.redsiren.com. **Description:** Provides systems management solutions and data processing services. Founded in 1996. **Office hours:** Monday - Friday, 8:30 a.m. - 5:00 p.m. **Corporate headquarters location:** This location. **Parent company:** Getronics. **Annual sales/revenues:** Less than $5 million. **Number of employees at this location:** 35.

SAP AMERICA, INC.
3999 West Chester Pike, Newtown Square PA 19073. 610/661-1000. **Contact:** Human Resources. **World Wide Web address:** http://www.sap.com. **Description:** Develops a variety of client/server computer software packages including programs for finance, human resources, and materials management applications. **Positions advertised include:** Consulting Engagement Manager; Consulting Engagement Manager CRM; Contract Recruiter; Contract Specialist; Contracts-Compliance Analyst; Corporate Real Estate Planner; Corporate Travel Analyst; Customer Engagement Manager; Database Marketing Analyst; Database Marketing Analyst; Developer/Architect, e-Recruiting. **Corporate headquarters location:** This location. **Other U.S. locations:** Nationwide. **International locations:** Germany. **Parent company:** SAP AG. **Number of employees nationwide:** 3,000. **Number of employees worldwide:** 34,000.

SAFEGUARD SCIENTIFICS, INC.
800 Safeguard Building, 435 Devon Park Drive, Wayne PA 19087. 610/293-0600. **Toll-free phone:** 877/506-7371. **Fax:** 610/293-0601. **Contact:** Personnel Department. **World Wide Web address:** http://www.safeguard.com. **Description:** A strategic information systems holding company. **Corporate headquarters location:** This location. **Listed on:** New York Stock Exchange. **Stock exchange symbol:** SFE.

SIEMENS MEDICAL SOLUTIONS HEALTH SERVICES CORPORATION
51 Valley Stream Parkway, Malvern PA 19355. 610/219-6300. **Fax:** 610/219-3124. **Contact:** Human Resources. **World Wide Web address:** http://www.medical.siemens.com. **Description:** A provider of health information and service solutions to hospitals, multi-entity health care corporations, integrated health networks, physician groups, and other health care providers in North America and Europe. Founded in 1969. **NOTE:** Entry-level positions are offered. **Special programs:** Internships. **Corporate headquarters location:** This location. **Other U.S. locations:** Nationwide. **Operations at this facility include:** Administration; Research and Development; Sales; Service. **Listed on:** New York Stock Exchange. **Stock exchange symbol:** SMS. **Annual sales/revenues:** More than $100 million. **Number of employees at this location:** 3,200. **Number of employees worldwide:** 5,000.

SOFTMART, INC.
450 Acorn Lane, Downingtown PA 19335. 610/518-4058. **Fax:** 610/518-3014. **Contact:** Recruiting Manager. **E-mail address:** hresource@softmart.com. **World Wide Web address:** http://www.softmart.com. **Description:** Resells computer software and hardware to government and commercial clients. Founded in 1983. **Positions advertised include:** Marketing Account Executive; Purchasing Agent; Web Developer. **Special programs:** Internships; Training; Summer Jobs. **Office hours:** Monday - Friday, 8:30 a.m. - 5:30 p.m. **Corporate headquarters location:** This location. **President:** Elliot Levine. **Annual sales/revenues:** More than $100 million. **Number of employees at this location:** 490.

STORAGE TECHNOLOGY CORPORATION
6 Tower Bridge, Suite 400, 181 Washington Street, Conshohocken PA 19428. 484/530-4100. **Contact:** Personnel. **E-mail address:** stkjobs@storagetek.com. **World Wide Web address:** http://www.storagetek.com. **Description:** Manufactures, sells, and services data storage devices. Overall, Storage Technology Corporation manufactures high-performance computer information storage and retrieval systems for mainframe and mid-frame computers and networks. **Positions advertised include:** Financial Analyst/Accountant; Intern-Finance/Accounting. **Corporate headquarters location:** Louisville CO.

SUNGARD ASSET MANAGEMENT SYSTEMS, INC.
333 Technology Drive, Malvern PA 19355. 610/251-6500. **Fax:** 610/251-6585. **Contact:** Teresa Urban, Human Resources Coordinator. **World Wide Web address:** http://www.sungard.com. **Description:** Develops, markets, and supports software for the financial industry. **NOTE:** Entry-level positions are offered. **Positions advertised include:** Data Communications Engineer; Resource Analyst; Recovery Specialist; Customer Service Representative. **Special programs:** Internships; Training. **Corporate headquarters location:** This location. **Other U.S. locations:** Nationwide. **Operations at this facility include:** Administration; Sales; Service. **Listed on:** Privately held. **Annual sales/revenues:** $21 - $50 million.

SUNGARD DATA SYSTEMS INC./SUNGARD RECOVERY SERVICES
680 East Swedesford Road, Wayne PA 19087. 484/582-2000. **Contact:** Anne Beeson, Vice President of Human Resources. **World Wide Web address:** http://www.sungard.com. **Description:** Provides specialized computer services including proprietary investment support systems for the financial services industry and computer disaster planning/recovery services. **Corporate headquarters location:** This location. **Number of employees at this location:** 2,100.

SUNGARD HIGHER EDUCATION
4 Country View Road, Malvern PA 19355. 610/647-5930. **Toll-free phone:** 800/223-7036. **Fax:** 610/578-5102. **Contact:** Human Resources. **World Wide Web address:** http://www.sungardsct.com. **Description:** Develops software and offers computer-related services to the higher education, local government, utility, and manufacturing communities. **NOTE:** Entry-level positions are offered. **Positions advertised include:** Market Manager; Sr. Training Consultant; Proposal Manager; Technology Product Manager. **Corporate headquarters location:** This location. **Number of employees nationwide:** 1,600.

SUNGARD PENTAMATION INC.
3 West Broad Street, Suite 1, Bethlehem PA 18018. 610/691-3616. **Fax:** 610/691-1031. **Contact:** Human Resource Manager. **E-mail address:** humanresources@pentamation.com. **World Wide Web address:** http://www.pentamation.com. **Description:** Develops software and computer systems for school districts and government facilities. **Positions advertised include:** Programmer Analyst.

THE SYCAMORE GROUP
580 Virginia Drive, Suite 100, Fort Washington PA 19034. 215/283-4877. **Fax:** 215/283-4942. **Contact:** Human Resources. **E-mail address:** jobs@thesycamoregroup.com. **World Wide Web address:** http://www.thesycamoregroup.com. **Description:** An IT solutions and software integration firm that helps customers connect back-office production data systems and business automation technologies including e-commerce, web services, and wireless devices. **Positions advertised include:** Enterprise Development Architect; Senior Java Developer; Senior Perl Developer; Technical Writer; Project Manager; Quality Assurance/Tester; Systems Engineer/Systems Integrator; Web Developer/User Interface Design.

TENEX SYSTEMS INC.
2011 Renaissance Boulevard, Suite 100, King of Prussia PA 19406-2746. 610/239-9988. **Fax:** 610/239-9995. **Contact:** Minh Hien Le Pham, Human Resources. **E-mail address:** jobs@tenexsys.com. **World Wide Web address:** http://www.tenexsys.com.

Description: Provides administrative software development and support services for school districts. **Positions advertised include:** .Net Software Developer; Business Support Specialist. **Office hours:** Monday - Friday, 7:30 a.m. - 4:30 p.m. **Parent company:** Harris Computer Systems.

TRIVERSITY INC.
311 Sinclair Street, Bristol PA 19007. 215/785-4321. **Toll-free phone:** 888/989-7274. **Fax:** 215/785-5329. **Contact:** Human Resources Manager. **E-mail address:** careers@triversity.com. **World Wide Web address:** http://www.triversity.com. **Description:** Provides transaction processing and customer relationship management solutions for physical, catalog, and online retailers. **Corporate headquarters location:** Toronto, Canada.

UNISYS CORPORATION
Township Line & Union Meeting Roads A, Unisys Way, Blue Bell PA 19424. 215/986-4011. **Fax:** 215/986-6732. **Contact:** Recruiting and Staffing. **E-mail address:** jobs@unisys.com. **World Wide Web address:** http://www.unisys.com. **Description:** Provides information services, technology, and software. **NOTE:** Entry-level positions and part-time jobs are offered. **Positions advertised include:** Sr. Consultant; Security Network Design Engineer; Internal Audit Consultant; SQL Server Database Administrator. **Special programs:** Internships; Training; Co-ops; Summer Jobs. **Corporate headquarters location:** This location. **Other U.S. locations:** Nationwide. **International locations:** Worldwide. **Listed on:** New York Stock Exchange. **Stock exchange symbol:** UIS. **Annual sales/revenues:** More than $100 million. **Number of employees at this location:** 2,500. **Number of employees worldwide:** 37,000.

VERTEX SYSTEMS INC.
1041 Old Cassatt Road, Berwyn PA 19312. 610/640-4200. **Contact:** Human Resources. **E-mail address:** jobs@vertexinc.com. **World Wide Web address:** http://www.vertexinc.com. **Description:** Provides corporate clients with tax manuals and tax reference products and software. **Positions advertised include:** Senior Software Developer; Software Developer; Web Developer; Marketing Communications Project Manager; Tax Consultant; Enterprise Database Architect.

VOCOLLECT INC.
701 Rodi Road, Pittsburgh PA 15235. 412/829-8145. **Fax:** 412/829-0972. **Contact:** Human Resources. **E-mail address:** jobs@vocollect.com. **World Wide Web address:** http://www.vocollect.com. **Description:** Manufactures voice-activated computing systems. **Positions advertised include:** Sr. Financial Analyst.

XEROX GLOBAL SERVICES, INC.
411 Eagleview Boulevard, Exton PA 19341. 610/458-6440. **Toll-free phone:** 800/884-4736. **Contact:** Human Resources. **World Wide Web address:** http://www.xeroxconnect.com. **Description:** Offers systems integration services. The company operates in three service groups: Consulting and Design Services, Systems Integration, and Operations and Support Services. **Parent company:** Xerox Corporation.

Rhode Island
ABAQUS, INC.
166 Valley Street, Providence RI 02909-2499. 401/276-4400. **Fax:** 401/276-4408. **Contact:** Catherine Kelleher, Human Resources. **E-mail address:** info@abaqus.com. **World Wide Web address:** http://www.abaqus.com. **Description:** Develops and sells ABAQUS software, which is used primarily in engineering disciplines as part of the design process. **Positions advertised include:** Development Group Manager; Engineering Specialist; Project Manager; Senior Financial Analyst; Software License Specialist; Senior Development Engineer. **Corporate headquarters location:** This location. **Other area locations:** Warwick RI. **Other U.S. locations:** Nationwide. **International locations:** Worldwide. **Parent company:** Dassault Systèmes. **President and CEO:** Mark Goldstein.

AMERICAN POWER CONVERSION (APC)
132 Fairgrounds Road, West Kingston RI 02892. 401/789-5735. **Toll-free phone:** 800/788-2208. **Fax:** 401/789-3710. **Contact:** Human Resources. **E-mail address:** apcresumes@apcc.com. **World Wide Web address:** http://www.apcc.com. **Description:** Provides products and services that work to improve the availability, manageability and performance of sensitive electronic, network, communication and industrial equipment. These products and services help companies increase the availability and reliability of their IT systems. **NOTE:** See website for current positions and to apply online. **Positions advertised include:** Project Engineer BSEE; Staff Programmer Analyst - Enterprise Architecture; Senior Programmer Analyst; Systems Administrator - Cognos; Director, CTO Order Mgmt & Logistics; Technical Support Engineer; Inside Sales Representative Level 1; Business Process Analyst; Applications Engineering Manager; Marketing Manager. **Special programs:** Internships; entry-level positions. **Corporate headquarters location:** This location. **Other area locations:** East Providence RI; West Warwick RI. **Other U.S. locations:** Billerica MA; St. Louis MO; Austin TX. **International locations:** Worldwide. **Operations at this facility include:** Administration; Manufacturing; Sales; Service. **Listed on:** NASDAQ. **Stock exchange symbol:** APCC. **Number of employees worldwide:** 6,500.

ANTEON CORPORATION
One Corporate Place, Middletown RI 02842. 401/849-5952. **Fax:** 401/846-7811. **Contact:** Human Resources. **E-mail address:** careers@anteon.com. **World Wide Web address:** http://www.anteon.com. **Description:** Anteon provides government clients with the systems integration, strategy and program management, systems engineering, operations services, and simulation and training skills to manage the development and operations of their mission critical systems. **NOTE:** See website for current job openings and to apply online. **Positions advertised include:** Intern; Electronics Technician; Lead Software Engineer; Mechanical Technician; Staff Software Engineer. **Special programs:** Internships; Co-ops. **Office hours:** Monday - Friday, 8:00 a.m. - 5:00 p.m. **Corporate headquarters location:** Fairfax VA. **Other area locations:** Newport RI. **Other U.S. locations:** Nationwide. **International locations:** United Kingdom. **Listed on:** New York Stock Exchange. **Stock exchange symbol:** ANT. **President and CEO:** Joseph M. Kampf. **Number of employees worldwide:** 9,500.

ASTRO-MED, INC.
600 East Greenwich Avenue, West Warwick RI 02893. 401/828-4000. **Fax:** 401/822-0139. **Contact:** Human Resources. **E-mail address:** humanresources@astro-med.com. **World Wide Web address:** http://www.astro-medinc.com. **Description:** Manufactures and supplies specialty printers that display, monitor, analyze and print data for aerospace, industrial and medical applications. Founded in 1969. **Positions advertised include:** Administrative Assistant; Firmware Engineer; Mechanical Engineer; Regional Sales Manager. **Corporate headquarters location:** This location. **International locations:** Worldwide. **Listed on:** NASDAQ. **Stock exchange symbol:** ALOT. **Number of employees worldwide:** 350.

ELECTRO STANDARDS LABORATORIES.
36 Western Industrial Drive, Cranston RI 02921. 401/943-1164. **Toll-free phone:** 887/943-1164. **Fax:** 401/946-5790. **Contact:** Human Resources. **E-mail address:** eslab@electrostandards.com. **World Wide Web address:** http://www.electrostandards.com. **Description:** A privately held company with expertise in electric motor systems, sensor-less motor controls, power electronics, control systems, digital signal processor based electronics, mechanics, software programming, GPS, web-enabled systems, multilevel

inverters and embedded instrumentation. **Special Programs:** Internships. **Positions advertised include:** Dynamic Models and System Simulations Design Engineer; Hardware and Real-Time Control Design Engineer; Instrumentation, Control and Power Electronics Design Engineer; Communication Products Design Engineer; Data Switch and Cable Assembler; Measurement Instrument Assembler; Data Network Installer. **Number of employees at this location:** 75.

NORTHROP GRUMMAN
Metro Center Boulevard, Suite 104, Warwick RI 02886. 401/732-9000. **Fax:** 401/732-9009. **Contact:** Human Resources. **World Wide Web address:** http://www.northropgrumman.com. **Description:** Provides technological products and services in defense and commercial electronics, nuclear and non-nuclear shipbuilding, information technology, mission systems, systems integration and space technology. **NOTE:** See website for current job openings and application instructions. **Corporate headquarters location:** Los Angeles CA. **Other area locations:** Middletown RI; Newport RI. **Other U.S. locations:** Nationwide. **International locations:** United Kingdom. **Operations at this facility include:** IT services.

SAIC ENTERPRISE SOLUTIONS
28 Jacome Way, Middletown RI 02842. 401/849-8900. **Fax:** 401/848-0638. **Contact:** Human Resources. **World Wide Web address:** http://www.saic.com. **Description:** An employee-owned research and engineering company that provides networking, software development and systems integration, as well as technical analysis, research and support, for many federal and state agencies and branches of the military. The company also provides consulting and technology services for some commercial customers. **NOTE:** See website for current job openings and to apply online. **Positions advertised include:** Associate Analyst; Engineering Division Manager; System Administrator; Oracle System Administrator; Programmer Analyst. **Corporate headquarters location:** San Diego CA. **Other area locations:** Newport RI. **Other U.S. locations:** Nationwide. **International locations:** Worldwide

SEA CORP
62 Johnny Cake Hill, Middletown RI 02842. 401/847-2260. **Fax:** 401/841-5860. **Contact:** Bobbi-Jo Sullivan, Human Resources. **E-mail address:** hr@seacorp.com. **World Wide Web address:** http://www.seacorp.com. **Description:** SEA CORP (Systems Engineering Associates Corporation) is a small business focusing on systems engineering, software, and test and evaluation services. This is primarily for the U.S. Navy's submarine electronic systems. Founded in 1981. **NOTE:** See website for current job openings. Mail, fax or e-mail resumes to Human Resources. **Positions advertised include:** Documentation Specialist; Engineering Assistant; Administrative Assistant; Part-Time Machinist; Ship Alteration Engineer; Systems Analyst; Programmer; Electrical Engineer; Computer Engineer. **Special programs:** Internships.

South Carolina
ACUMEN DESIGN AND CONSULTING
3620 Pelham Road, PMB 9, Greenville SC 29615. 864/271-9000. **Contact:** Human Resources. **E-mail address:** employment@acumendesign.net. **World Wide Web address:** http://www.acumendesign.net. **Description:** Provides IT solutions for medium and small businesses. **Positions advertised include:** Help Desk; Programmer. **Corporate headquarters location:** This location.

AVISTA SOLUTIONS, INC.
115 Atrium Way, Suite 218, Columbia SC 29223. 803/788-4936. **Contact:** Human Resources. **E-mail address:** careers@avistasolutions.com. **World Wide Web address:** http://www.avistasolutions.com. **Description:** A financial services software company. Avista's products include software for wholesale lenders, correspondent mortgage lenders, retail mortgage lenders, and consumer direct lending. The company's fully automated web-enabled loan origination and processing system is verified by Fannie Mae and Freddie Mac. **Positions advertised include:** Mortgage Business Analyst; Software Engineer.

BLACKBAUD, INC.
2000 Daniel Island Drive, Charleston SC 29492-7541. 843/216-6200. **Fax:** 843/216-6100. **Contact:** Laura Kennedy, Vice President of Human Resources. **E-mail address:** recruiting@blackbaud.com. **World Wide Web address:** http://www.blackbaud.com. **Description:** Provides computer programming services for nonprofit companies and designs software that helps companies with a wide variety of activities including fundraising, administration, and organization. Founded in 1981. **NOTE:** Submit resumes online through the company Website. **Positions advertised include:** Customer Service Representative; Staff Accountant; Division Controlling Associate; Blackbaud Director; Prospect Researcher; Consulting Representative; Corporate Revenue Analyst; Customer Support Analyst; Application Developer; Software Instructor; High Tech Recruiters; Corporate Paralegal; Product Marketing Manager; Sales Manager; System Administrator. **Special programs:** Internships. **Corporate headquarters location:** This location. **Other locations:** Glasgow, Scotland; Sydney, Australia. **Listed on:** Privately held. **Annual sales/revenues:** $105.2 million. **Number of employees:** 700.

CGI
810 Dutch Square Boulevard, Suite 410, Columbia SC 29210. 803/561-9006. **Fax:** 803/561-0605. **Contact:** Human Resources. **World Wide Web address:** http://www.cgi.com. **Description:** Provides information technology and business process services. GGI services include planning, design, development, implementation, and management of business and IT environments for industries including financial services, government, healthcare, telecommunications, utilities, manufacturing, distribution, and retail. CGI has more than 100 offices in 16 countries. **Positions advertised include:** Sr. Consultant, Technical; Sr. Consultant, Business; Project Manager; Sr. Consultant, Business Trainer; Quality Control Tester; Developer/Consultant Technical Direct Placement and Contract. **Corporate headquarters location:** Montreal Canada. **Other U.S. locations:** Nationwide. **Listed on:** New York Stock Exchange. **Stock exchange symbol:** GIB. **Number of employees worldwide:** 25,000.

CAMBAR SOFTWARE, INC.
2387 Clements Ferry Road, Charleston SC 29492. 843/856-2822. **Toll-free phone:** 800/756-4402. **Fax:** 842/881-4893. **Contact:** Human Resources. **E-mail address:** hr@cambarsoftware.com. **World Wide Web address:** http://www.cambarsoftware.com. **Description:** Develops order and warehouse system software used by large distributors and manufacturers. **Corporate headquarters location:** This location. **Other locations:** Bohemia NY. **Parent company:** Supply Chain Holdings, LLC (Charleston SC).

DATASTREAM SYSTEMS, INC.
50 Datastream Plaza, Greenville SC 29605. 864/422-5305. **Fax:** 864/422-5000. **Contact:** Human Resources. **E-mail address:** infor@datastream.net. **World Wide Web address:** http://www.datastream.net. **Description:** Develops maintenance management software. Datastream serves many major industries including government, health care, hospitality, manufacturing, and transportation. Founded in 1996. **Positions advertised include:** Corporate Accounting Manager; Tax Compliance Manager; Systems Administrator; Account Manager; Technical Writer; Product Engineer; Project Manager; Billable Consultant; Senior Consultant; Software Developer. **Special programs:** Internships. **Corporate headquarters location:** This location. **Other locations:** GA; IL; NJ; PA; TX. **International locations:** Canada; China; Japan; Singapore. **Listed on:** NASDAQ. **Stock exchange symbol:** DSTM. **Annual**

sales/revenues: $90 million. **Number of employees:** 713.

MODIS IT RESOURCE MANAGEMENT
1122 Lady Street, Suite 640, Columbia SC 29201. 803/227-3010. **Toll-free phone:** 800/508-6063. **Fax:** 803/227-3020. **Contact:** Angie Greenwood. **E-mail address:** angie.greenwood@modisit.com. **World Wide Web address:** http://www.modisit.com. **Description:** A provider of information technology resource management services and solutions. **Positions advertised include:** Web Tester; Business Objects Server Administrator. **Corporate headquarters location:** Jacksonville FL. **Other area locations:** Greenville SC. **Other U.S. locations:** Nationwide. **Parent company:** MPS Group.

SOLUTIENCE, INC.
P.O. Box 8876, Greenville SC 29604-8876. 864/242-6302. **Physical address:** 640 South Main Street, Suite 200, Greenville SC 29601-2564. **Fax:** 864/242-6303. **Contact:** Human Resources. **World Wide Web address:** http://www.solutience.com. **E-mail address:** jobs@solutience.com. **Description:** Develops, markets, and supports software for banks and insurance companies. Founded in 1971. **Positions advertised include:** Warehouse Manager; Console Consultant; Quality Management Consultant; Functional Consultant. **Corporate headquarters location:** This location. **Other U.S. locations:** Alpharetta GA; Birmingham AL; Jersey City NJ; Orangeburg SC; Southfield MI. **Parent company:** The BMW Group (Munich, Germany).

SYNNEX INFORMATION TECHNOLOGIES, INC.
39 Pelham Ridge Drive, Greenville SC 29615. 864/289-4000. **Toll-free phone:** 800/756-9888. **Fax:** 864/289-4284. **Contact:** Human Resources. **E-mail address:** hr.gsc@synnex.com. **World Wide Web address:** http://www.synnex.com. **Description:** Formerly Gates Arrow Distributors, Synnex distributes microcomputers, networking software, and computer peripheral equipment including monitors, hard-disk drives, and modems. The company also packages computer systems, offers systems integration services, and provides technical support services. **Positions advertised include:** Computer Operator; Computer Programmer; Customer Service Representative; Services Sales Representative. **Corporate headquarters location:** Fremont CA. **Operations at this facility include:** Administration; Sales.

South Dakota

ALTAIRE ENTERPRISES, INC.
144 East Grant, Spearfish SD 57783. 605/642-1400. **Contact:** Human Resources. **E-mail address:** info@mato.com. **World Wide Web address:** http://www.mato.com. **Description:** Internet service provider in the northern Black Hills of South Dakota. **Corporate headquarters location:** This location.

GATEWAY, INC.
610 Gateway Drive, P.O. Box 2000, North Sioux City SD 57049. 800/846-2000. **Recorded jobline:** 605/232-2222. **Contact:** Human Resources. **World Wide Web address:** http://www.gateway.com. **Description:** Manufactures and sells PCs and related products to consumers, businesses, government agencies and schools. The third largest PC company in the U.S. Founded in 1985. **Positions advertised include:** Accountant II; eSource Web Support; Chief Infrastructure Architect; Manager, Solutions 2; Inside Sales, Account Executive; Program Manager; Specialist, Finance; Senior Engineer; Technical Sales Representative. **Corporate headquarters location:** Irvine CA. **Other area locations:** Sioux Falls. **Other U.S. locations:** Nationwide. **Listed on:** New York Stock Exchange. **Stock exchange symbol:** GTW.

HUTCHINSON TECHNOLOGY INC.
2301 East 60th Street North, Sioux Falls SD 57104. 605/978-2200. **Fax:** 605/978-2210. **Contact:** Human Resources. **World Wide Web address:** http://www.htch.com. **Description:** Designs and manufactures suspension assemblies for hard disk drives. **NOTE:** Hutchinson Technology Inc. does not accept unsolicited resumes. See website for current openings and application instructions. Please specify the job you are applying for when sending your resume. **Positions advertised include:** Toolmaker; Manufacturing Supervisor; Process Specialist; **Corporate headquarters location:** Hutchinson MN. **Other U.S. locations:** Plymouth MN; Eau Claire WI. **International locations:** China; Japan; Korea; Singapore; Thailand. **Operations at this facility include:** Employs production operators, technicians, engineers, toolmakers and support staff in the high-volume production of suspension assemblies. **Listed on:** NASDAQ. **Stock exchange symbol:** HTCH. **Number of employees at this location:** 1,500. **Number of employees nationwide:** 4,000.

PRECISION COMPUTER SYSTEMS
4501 South Technology Drive, Sioux Falls SD 57106. 605/362-1260. **Fax:** 605/362-9442. **Contact:** Human Resources. **E-mail address:** hr@pcsbanking.com. **World Wide Web address:** http://www.pcsbanking.com. **Description:** Develops, markets, and supports software applications for community banking and city governments. **NOTE:** See website for current openings, application instructions and to download an application. **Positions advertised include:** Account Manager; Conversion Programmer/Analyst; Installation Services Representative; Integrated Products Representative; Programmer/Analyst; Research Analyst; Technical Support/Programmer; Training Services Representative. **Parent company:** Fiserv. **Number of employees at this location:** 200.

TOSHIBA AMERICA BUSINESS SOLUTIONS
901 North Foster, Mitchell SD 57301. 605/996-7731. **Fax:** 605/995-2056. **Contact:** Human Resources. **E-mail address:** employment@tabs.toshiba.com. **World Wide Web address:** http://www.toshiba.com. **Description:** Toshiba America Business Solutions, Inc., (TABS) is an independent operating company of Toshiba Corp., a large electronics/electrical equipment company, and is a manufacturer and distributor of office product solutions for businesses in the United States, Latin America and Caribbean. Toshiba Corp. TABS specializes in the digital copier and color markets. **NOTE:** For production positions, contact the local job services office; for management positions, see the Toshiba website or submit a resume by mail. **Corporate headquarters location:** Irvine CA. **Operations at this facility include:** A production facility that manufactures toner for photocopiers.

Tennessee

CELERITY SYSTEMS, INC.
122 Perimeter Park Drive, Knoxville TN 37922. 865/539-3561. **Fax:** 865/539-3502. **Contact:** Human Resources. **World Wide Web address:** http://www.celerity.com. **Description:** Designs, develops and markets advanced digital set-top-boxes and video servers for interactive television and high-speed Internet. Founded in 1993. **Corporate headquarters location:** This location. **Listed on:** OTC Bulletin Board. **Stock exchange symbol:** CESY. **Number of employees at this location:** 80.

CIBER, INC.
1770 Kirby Parkway, Memphis TN 38138. 901/754-6577. **Fax:** 901/754-8463. **Contact:** Recruiting. **World Wide Web address:** http://www.ciber.com. **Description:** A system integration consultancy for private and government clients. **NOTE:** Search and apply for positions or submit resume online. **Positions advertised included:** Business/Technical Architect. **Corporate headquarters location:** Greenwood Village CO. **Number of employees worldwide:** 6,000.

DATA RESEARCH AND APPLICATIONS INC.
10425 Cogdill Road, Suite 450, Knoxville TN 37932. 865/671-4474. **Fax:** 865/671-3533. **Contact:** Human Resources. **E-mail address:** jobs@dra-hq.com. **World**

Wide Web address: http://www.dra-international.com. **Description:** Develops software for data recovery and provides computer hardware.

EAGLE SYSTEMS TECHNOLOGY, INC.
1300 Wolf Park Drive, Germantown TN 38138. 901/683-7851. **Toll-free phone:** 800/845-6471. **Fax:** 901/685-3706. **Contact:** Human Resources. **E-mail address:** eaglem@eaglemphs.com. **World Wide Web address:** http://www.eaglemphs.com. **Description:** Engaged in systems integration and contract programming services. Founded in 1986.

FIDELITY INTEGRATED FINANCIAL SOLUTIONS
202 East Broadway Avenue, Maryville TN 37804-5782. 865/982-0116. **Fax:** 678/982-1879. **Contact:** Human Resources. **World Wide Web address:** http://www.fidelity.com. **Description:** Provides technology products and services to the financial industry, including core processing, check imaging and item processing, electronic funds transfer, debit card processing, communications management and related products and services. Operates 30 processing centers nationwide. **NOTE:** Search and apply for positions online. **Positions advertised include:** Product Specialist. **Other area locations:** Cookeville TN; Nashville TN.

PDS CONSULTING
25 Maple Grove Drive, Suite 101, Crossville TN 38555. 931/456-2999. **Fax:** 931/456-6182. **Contact:** Human Resources. **E-mail address:** crossville@pdsconsulting.com. **World Wide Web address:** http://www.pdsconsulting.com. **Description:** A Hewlett-Packard PC and peripherals reseller. PDS Consulting also custom builds its own line of computers, and is engaged in computer repair, networking, and upgrading. Founded in 1995. **Other area locations:** Knoxville TN; Morristown TN.

PERFORMANCE DEVELOPMENT CORPORATION
109 Jefferson Avenue, Oak Ridge TN 37830. 865/482-9004. **Contact:** Personnel Administrator. **World Wide Web address:** http://www.pdcnet.com. **Description:** An environmental management and information systems consulting firm. Performance Development Corporation (PDC) also offers training programs to corporate clients. Founded in 1987.

SERV-A-COMP INC.
1813 South Market Street, Chattanooga TN 37408. 423/265-8010. **Contact:** Personnel. **Description:** Provides repair service for computers, printers, and monitors. Serv-A-Comp Inc. also sells refurbished hardware.

UNISYS CORPORATION
3150 Lenox Park Boulevard, Suite 200, Memphis TN 38115-4396. 901/368-7600. **Contact:** Human Resources. **World Wide Web address:** http://www.unisys.com. **Description:** Provides technology services and solutions in consulting, systems integration, outsourcing, infrastructure, and server technology. **NOTE:** Search and apply for positions online. **Other area locations:** Knoxville TN; Dyersburg TN; Chattanooga TN; Alcoa TN; Blountville TN. **Other U.S. locations:** Nationwide. **Number of employees worldwide:** 37,000.

Texas

ADS ADAPTIVE SYSTEMS, LLC.
4221 Freidrich Lane, Suite 150, Austin TX 78744. 512/851-2377. **Fax:** 512/851-2379. **Contact:** Human Resources. **World Wide Web address:** http://www.ads-as.com. **Description:** Develops fulfillment and distribution center software. **Positions advertised include:** Technical Support Engineer. **Corporate headquarters location:** This location. **Other U.S. locations:** Berkeley CA.

AT&T GOVERNMENT SOLUTIONS
6100 Bandera Road, Suite 505, San Antonio TX 78238. 210/520-7878. **Fax:** 210/520-7881. **Contact:** Human Resources. **World Wide Web address:** http://www.att.com/hr/gvtsol.html. **Description:** AT&T Business Solutions (formerly GRC International) creates large-scale, decision-support systems and software engineering environments; applies operations research and mathematical modeling to business and management systems; and implements advanced database technology. **NOTE:** Job listings by location can be found at http://www.att.hire.com. **Corporate headquarters location:** Vienna VA. **Other U.S. locations:** Nationwide. **Operations at this facility include:** This location is involved in technical research. **Parent company:** AT&T Corporation. **Listed on:** New York Stock Exchange. **Stock exchange symbol:** T.

ACCENTURE
2929 Allen Parkway, Suite 2000, Houston TX 77019-7107. 713/837-1500. **Fax:** 713/837-1593. **Contact:** Human Resources. **World Wide Web address:** http://www.accenture.com. **Description:** A management and technology consulting firm. Accenture offers a wide range of services including business re-engineering, customer service system consulting, data system design and implementation, Internet sales systems research and design, and strategic planning. **NOTE:** Please visit website to search for jobs and apply online. **Other area locations:** Austin TX; Dallas TX. **Other U.S. locations:** Nationwide. **International locations:** Worldwide. **Listed on:** New York Stock Exchange. **Stock exchange symbol:** ACN. **CEO:** Joe W. Forehand. **Number of employees worldwide:** 90,000.

ANALYSTS INTERNATIONAL CORPORATION (AIC)
7000 North Mopac Expressway, Suite 220, Austin TX 78731. 512/206-2700. **Toll-free phone:** 800/654-8194. **Fax:** 512/206-2720. **Contact:** Human Resources. **World Wide Web address:** http://www.analysts.com. **Description:** An international computer consulting firm. The company assists clients in developing systems in a variety of industries using diverse programming languages and software. Founded in 1966. **NOTE:** Please visit website to register, search for jobs, and apply online. **Positions advertised include:** Cisco Consultant. **Corporate headquarters location:** Minneapolis MN. **Other U.S. locations:** Nationwide. **International locations:** Canada; England. **Listed on:** NASDAQ. **Stock exchange symbol:** ANLY. **President/CEO:** Mike LaVelle.

APPLE COMPUTER, INC.
2420 Ridgepoint Drive, Austin TX 78754. 512/674-2000. **Contact:** Employment. **World Wide Web address:** http://www.apple.com. **Description:** Apple Computer manufactures personal computers and computer-related products for home, business, scientific, industrial, professional, and educational use. **NOTE:** Please visit https://jobs.apple.com to search for jobs and apply online. **Positions advertised include:** Inside Software Sales Account Executive; K12 Education Inside Account Executive; Product Administration Specialist; Professional Video Technical Support Representative; Senior Tax Accountant. **Special programs:** Internships. **Corporate headquarters location:** Cupertino CA. **Operations at this facility include:** This location offers sales and technical support to companies and educational institutions. **Listed on:** NASDAQ. **Stock exchange symbol:** AAPL.

AQUENT
8140 North Mopac Expressway, Building I, Suite 150, Austin TX 78759. 512/442-0992. **Fax:** 512/442-2462. **Contact:** Human Resources. **World Wide Web address:** http://www.aquent.com. **Description:** Engaged in software consulting, training, and staffing. Founded 1986. **Corporate headquarters location:** Boston MA. **Other area locations:** Dallas TX; Houston TX. **Other U.S. locations:** Nationwide. **International locations:** Worldwide. **Operations at**

this facility include: This office is part of the Marketing and Creative Services division.

ASPEN TECHNOLOGY, INC.
1293 Eldridge Parkway, Houston TX 77077. 281/584-1000. **Fax:** 281/584-4329. **Contact:** Human Resources. **World Wide Web address:** http://www.aspentech.com. **Description:** Aspen Technology, Inc. supplies computer-aided chemical engineering software to the chemical, petroleum, pharmaceutical, metal, mineral, food product, consumer product, and utility industries. **NOTE:** Please visit website to search for jobs and apply online. **Positions advertised include:** Director of Oil and Gas Solutions; Human Resources Generalist; Human Resource Manager; Business Operations Manager; Industry Consultant – Petroleum; Marketing Coordinator; Strategic Account Manager; Territory Account Manager. **Corporate headquarters location:** Cambridge MA. **Other U.S. locations:** CA; NJ; OHL CO; DE; MD; WA. **International locations:** Worldwide. **Operations at this facility include:** This location develops software. **Listed on:** NASDAQ. **Stock exchange symbol:** AZPN. **President/CEO:** David L. McQuillin. **Number of employees worldwide:** 1,850.

AVNET, INC.
1130 Rutherford Lane, Building 2 Suite 208, Austin TX 78753. 512/835-1152. **Recorded jobline:** 800/459-1225. **Contact:** Human Resources. **E-mail address:** avnet.staffing@avnet.com. **World Wide Web address:** http://www.avnet.com. **Description:** Avnet is the world's largest distributor of semiconductors, interconnect, passive, and electromechanical components, computer products, and embedded systems from leading manufacturers. **NOTE:** Contact the corporate information line, at 800/882-8638 option 4, for more information on applying for jobs. Please visit website to view job listings and apply online. Online applications are preferred. **Positions advertised include:** Field Application Engineer. **Corporate headquarters location:** Phoenix AZ. **Other U.S. locations:** Nationwide. **International locations:** Worldwide. **Listed on:** New York Stock Exchange. **Stock exchange symbol:** AVT. **Number of employees worldwide:** 10,000.

BMC SOFTWARE, INC.
2101 City West Boulevard, Houston TX 77042-2827. 713/918-8800. **Toll-free phone:** 800/841-2031. **Fax:** 713/918-8000. **Contact:** Human Resources. **E-mail address:** careers@bmc.com. **World Wide Web address:** http://www.bmc.com. **Description:** Develops, markets, and supports standard systems software products to enhance and increase the performance of large-scale (mainframe) computer database management systems and data communications software systems. Founded in 1980. **NOTE:** Please visit website to search for jobs and apply online. **Positions advertised include:** les Representative; Advisory Software Consultant; Disaster Recovery Analyst; Systems Programmer; Accountant; Inside Sales Associate; Recruiting Advisor; Senior Executive Secretary; Administrative Support Assistant. **Corporate headquarters location:** This location. **Listed on:** New York Stock Exchange. **Stock exchange symbol:** BMC. **Annual sales/revenues:** More than $1.5 billion. **President/CEO:** Robert E. Beauchamp. **Number of employees nationwide:** 6,200.

BANCTEC, INC.
P.O. Box 660204, Dallas TX 75266-0204. 972/821-4000. **Physical address:** 2701 East Grauwyler Road, Irving TX 75061. **Toll-free phone:** 800/226-2832. **Fax:** 972/579-5812. **Contact:** Human Resources Manager. **World Wide Web address:** http://www.banctec.com. **Description:** Engaged in systems integration and specializes in document management solutions. The company also provides network support services and develops image management software. **NOTE:** Please visit website to search for jobs and apply online. **Corporate headquarters location:** This location. **Other U.S. locations:** Nationwide. **Listed on:** Privately held. **Number of employees worldwide:** 3,000.

BOXX TECHNOLOGIES, INC.
10435 Burnet Road, Suite 120, Austin TX 78758. 512/835-0400. **Toll-free phone:** 877/877-2699. **Fax:** 512/835-0434. **Contact:** Human Resources. **E-mail address:** jobs@boxxtech.com. **World Wide Web address:** http://www.boxxtech.com. **Description:** A developer and manufacturer of high-performance workstations and render nodes specifically designed to meet the high-performance and reliability requirements of digital content creators working in the 3D, animation, special effects, digital film, game development, and broadcast markets. **Positions advertised include:** Computer Validation Engineer; Product/Manufacturing Engineer.

CALTECH
4152 South Jackson, San Angelo TX 76903. 325/223-6100. **Fax:** 325/223-6101. **Contact:** Human Resources. **World Wide Web address:** http://www.caltech.com. **Description:** Provides consulting, network administration, and helpdesk IT services to clients in Texas. Founded in 1988. **Positions advertised include:** Associate Systems Engineer.

CALYX SOFTWARE
3535 Travis Street, Suite 130, Dallas TX 75204. 214/320-8601. **Contact:** Personnel. **World Wide Web address:** http://www.calyxsoftware.com. **Description:** Designs and markets POINT for Windows, a processing application for mortgage professionals, and POINTMan, a processing application for loan agents. **Corporate headquarters location:** San Jose CA.

CERNER RADIOLOGY INFORMATION SYSTEMS
5 Greenway Plaza, Suite 2000, Houston TX 77046. 832/325-1500. **Contact:** Human Resources. **World Wide Web address:** http://www.cerner.com. **Description:** Engaged in the design, development, and support of hospital information systems for both clinical and business applications. **NOTE:** Please visit website to search for jobs and apply online. **Corporate headquarters location:** Kansas City MO. **Other U.S. locations:** Detroit MI; St Louis MO; Denver CO; Lake Mary FL; Waltham MA; Washington D.C. **International locations:** Worldwide. **Parent company:** Cerner Corporation. **Listed on:** NASDAQ. **Stock exchange symbol:** CERN. **Number of employees worldwide:** 5,105.

CIRRUS LOGIC, INC.
2901 Via Fortuna, Austin TX 78746. 512/851-4000. **Contact:** Human Resources. **World Wide Web address:** http://www.cirrus.com. **Description:** Designs, markets, and tests computer chips for audio, digital, multimedia, and telecommunication products. Cirrus Logic also supplies high-performance analog circuits. **Positions advertised include:** Operations Production Control Planner Product Marketing Manager; Senior Digital Design Engineer; Analog Design Engineer; Applications Engineer; Senior Internal Auditor; Digital Design Engineer; Staff Design Engineer. **Special programs:** Internships. **Corporate headquarters location:** This location. **International locations:** Hong Kong China; Tokyo Japan; Henley-on-Thames United Kingdom.

COMPUCOM SYSTEMS, INC.
7171 Forest Lane, Dallas TX 75230. 972/856-3600. **Toll-free phone:** 800/225-1475. **Contact:** Human Resources. **E-mail address:** easyhr@compucom.com. **World Wide Web address:** http://www.compucom.com. **Description:** A leading PC integration services company providing product procurement, advanced configuration, network integration, and support services. Founded 1987. **Positions advertised include:** Call Center Team Leader; EDI Developer/Programmer. **Corporate headquarters location:** This location. **Other U.S. locations:** Nationwide. **Listed on:** NASDAQ. **Stock**

exchange symbol: CMPC. **President/CEO:** J. Edward Coleman. **Number of employees nationwide:** 3,300.

COMPUTER ASSOCIATES INTERNATIONAL, INC.
5465 Legacy Drive, Plano TX 75024-3109. 214/473-1000. **Contact:** Human Resources Manager. **World Wide Web address:** http://www.cai.com. **Description:** Computer Associates International is one of the world's leading developers of client/server and distributed computing software. The company develops, markets, and supports enterprise management, database and applications development, business applications, and consumer software products for a broad range of mainframe, midrange, and desktop computers. Computer Associates International serves major business, government, research, and educational organizations. Founded in 1976. **Positions advertised include:** Assistant Teacher; Services Specialist; Senior Alliance Program Manager. **Special programs:** Internships; Co-ops. **Corporate headquarters location:** Islandia NY. **Other area locations:** Austin TX; Houston TX. **Other U.S. locations:** Nationwide. **International locations:** Worldwide. **Operations at this facility include:** This location develops and sells software, and offers support services. **Listed on:** New York Stock Exchange. **Stock exchange symbol:** CA. **Number of employees worldwide:** 16,000.

COMPUTER HORIZONS CORPORATION
2900 North Loop West, Suite 1230, Houston TX 77092. 713/688-8005. **Fax:** 713/688-8002. **Contact:** Human Resources. **World Wide Web address:** http://www.computerhorizons.com. **Description:** A full-service technology solutions company offering contract staffing, outsourcing, re-engineering, and network management. **Corporate headquarters location:** Mountain Lakes NJ. **Other U.S. locations:** Nationwide. **International locations:** Canada; India. **Listed on:** NASDAQ. **Stock exchange symbol:** CHRZ. **President/CEO:** William J. Murphy. **Number of employees worldwide:** 3,000.

COMPUTER SCIENCES CORPORATION (CSC)
8616 Freeport Parkway Irving TX 75063. 972/386-0020. **Fax:** 469/499-8180. **Contact:** Human Resources. **World Wide Web address:** http://www.csc.com. **Description:** Computer Sciences Corporation helps clients in industry and government use information technology to achieve strategic and operational objectives. The company tailors solutions from a broad suite of integrated service and technology offerings including e-business strategies and technologies, management and IT consulting, systems development and integration, application software, and IT and business process outsourcing. Founded in 1959. **NOTE:** Please visit http://careers.csc.com to search for jobs and apply online. **Positions advertised include:** Administrative Assistant/Functional Coordinator; Technology Architect; Business Developer; Data Architect; Enterprise Package Solutions Specialist. **Corporate headquarters location:** El Segundo CA. **International locations:** Worldwide. **Operations at this facility include:** This location develops and markets software for financial institutions. **Listed on:** New York Stock Exchange. **Stock exchange symbol:** CSC. **Number of employees worldwide:** 90,000.

CROSSROADS SYSTEMS, INC.
11000 North Mo-Pac Expressway, Austin TX 78759. 512/349-0300. **Contact:** Human Resources. **World Wide Web address:** http://www.crossroads.com. **Description:** Manufactures routers and storage backup and management software. **Positions advertised include:** IT Support Administrator; Sr. Software Development Manager; Test Engineer; Product Marketing Manager; Product Manager; Sr. Account Manager. **Corporate headquarters location:** This location.

CYBERBASIN INTERNET SERVICES
400 West Illinois Avenue, Midland TX 79701. 432/620-0051. **Contact:** Human Resources. **E-mail address:** info@cyberbasin.com. **World Wide Web address:** http://www.cyberbasin.com. **Description:** This company is an Internet Service Provider. Provides Network and hosting services. **NOTE:** E-mail resumes to this company. **Parent company:** Southwest Royalties, Inc. **Listed on:** Privately held.

DELL INC.
One Dell Way, Round Rock TX 78682. 512/338-4400. **Fax:** 800/816-4643. **Contact:** Human Resources. **World Wide Web address:** http://www.dell.com. **Description:** Designs, develops, manufactures, markets, services, and supports personal computer systems and related equipment including servers, workstations, notebooks, and desktop systems. The company also offers over 4,000 software packages and peripherals. **Special programs:** Dell for MBA's; Dell for Undergrad/Masters; Internships. **Corporate headquarters location:** This location. **International locations:** Ireland; United Kingdom. **Listed on:** NASDAQ. **Stock exchange symbol:** DELL. **Number of employees worldwide:** 46,000.

DELTEK SYSTEMS INC.
15990 North Barkers Landing, Suite 350, Houston TX 77079. 281/558-0514. **Fax:** 281/584-7828. **Contact:** Human Resources. **World Wide Web address:** http://www.deltek.com. **Description:** Designs, develops, and markets project- and cost-management software. **NOTE:** Entry-level positions are offered. **Positions advertised include:** Earned Value and Project Management Consultant. **Special programs:** Internships; Training; Summer Jobs. **Corporate headquarters location:** Herndon VA. **International locations:** United Kingdom; France. **Number of employees worldwide:** 800.

EDS (ELECTRONIC DATA SYSTEMS CORPORATION)
5400 Legacy Drive, Plano TX 75024-3199. 972/605-2700. **Fax:** 800/562-6241. **Contact:** Human Resources. **E-mail address:** careers@eds.com. **World Wide Web address:** http://www.eds.com. **Description:** Provides consulting, systems development, systems integration, and systems management services for large-scale and industry-specific applications. Founded in 1962. **NOTE:** Entry-level positions are offered. **Positions advertised include:** Systems Engineering; Technical Delivery; Customer Business Service; Operations; Communications; Marketing; Contractors. **Special programs:** Internships; Training. **Corporate headquarters location:** This location. **Listed on:** New York Stock Exchange. **Stock exchange symbol:** EDS. **Annual revenues:** $21.5 billion.

ECOM ELITE COMPUTER CONSULTANTS
10333 NW Freeway, Suite 414, Houston TX 77092. 713/686-9740. **Toll-free phone:** 800/929-3266. **Fax:** 713/686-1661. **Contact:** Human Resources. **E-mail address:** Ecom@ecom-inc.com. **Corporate headquarters location:** This location. **Other area locations:** Dallas; San Antonio. **Other U.S. locations:** Kansas City; St. Louis. **World Wide Web address:** http://www.ecom-inc.com. **Description:** A computer consulting firm. **NOTE:** Contract and permanent positions offered. **Positions advertised include:** Support; Team Leader; Programmer/Analyst; Software Engineer; Developer; Technology Specialist; PC Coordinator; Global Windows & Messaging Manager.

EPSIIA CORPORATION
901 South Mopac, Building Three, Suite 500, Austin TX 78746. 512/329-0081. **Toll-free phone:** 800/401-4774. Fax: 512/329-0086. **Contact:** Human Resources. **E-mail address:** jobs@EPSIIA.com. **World Wide Web address:** http://www.epsiia.com. **Description:** Develops retrieval and conversion software. **Positions advertised include:** Sales Account Executive. **Corporate headquarters location:** This location. **International locations:** United Kingdom; Brazil. **Parent company:** Fiserv Resources.

EXECUTRAIN OF TEXAS
12201 Merit Drive, Suite 300, Two Forest Plaza, Dallas TX 75251. 972/387-1212. **Fax:** 972/387-0000.

Contact: Human Resources. **World Wide Web address:** http://www.executrain.com/. **Description:** Trains businesses in the use of computer software and offers IT certification. **Corporate headquarters location:** Alpharetta GA. **Other U.S. locations:** Nationwide. **International locations:** Worldwide.

FARSIGHT COMPUTER
1219 West University Boulevard, Odessa TX 79764-7119. 432/335-0879. **Fax:** 915/335-8411. **Contact:** Human Resources. **World Wide Web address:** http://www.farsweb.com. **Description:** A computer wholesaler, specializing in custom-built PCs.

FORGENT NETWORKS
108 Wild Basin Drive, Austin TX 78746. 512/437-2700. **Toll-free phone:** 888/323-8835. **Fax:** 512/437-2365. **Contact:** Human Resources. **World Wide Web address:** http://www.forgent.com. **Description:** Forgent develops and licenses intellectual property related to communication technologies, and provides scheduling software that helps organizations plan and execute meetings. Much of its business activity involves filing lawsuits against organizations that violate its patents. **Subsidiaries include:** Network Simplicity Software, Inc.

FUJITSU
900 One Galleria Tower, 13355 Noel Road, Suite 900, Dallas TX 75240. 972/239-8611. **Contact:** Human Resources. **World Wide Web address:** http://www.us.fujitsu.com. **Description:** Provides computer consulting, including outsourcing and systems integration. **Corporate headquarters location:** Edison NJ.

GB TECH INC.
2200 Space Park Drive, Suite 400, Houston TX 77058. 281/333-3703. **Fax:** 281/333-3745. **Contact:** Human Resources. **E-mail address:** hr@gbtech.net. **World Wide Web address:** http://www.gbtech.net. **Description:** Performs aerospace and computer engineering services. GB Tech contracts with several organizations including NASA. **NOTE:** Job listings may be also obtained by calling the company. **Positions advertised include:** Mechanical Engineer; Fracture Mechanics Engineer; Safety Engineer; Communication Systems Engineer; Chemical Engineer. **Corporate headquarters location:** This location.

GLOBAL SHOP SOLUTIONS
975 Evergreen Circle, The Woodlands TX 77380-3637. 281/681-1959. **Fax:** 281/681-2663. **Contact:** Dick Alexander, President. **World Wide Web address:** http://www.globalshopsolutions.com. **Description:** Designs and sells manufacturing software systems. Founded in 1976.

HAMILTON AND ASSOCIATES
4415 Spring Cypress Road, Spring TX 77388. 281/353-6691. **Contact:** Bill Hamilton, Owner. **World Wide Web address:** http://www.tola.com. **Description:** A re-seller of high-technology products in the areas of OEM, Connectivity, data communications and retail. In addition to sales, the company markets the products and provides technical support. **Positions advertised:** Sales. **Other U.S. locations:** OK; LA; AK.

HEWLETT-PACKARD COMPANY
3000 Waterview Parkway, Richardson TX 75080. 972/497-4000. **Contact:** Human Resources. **World Wide Web address:** http://www.hp.com. **Description:** Hewlett-Packard is engaged in the design and manufacture of measurement and computation products and systems used in business, industry, engineering, science, health care, and education. Principal products are integrated instrument and computer systems (including hardware and software), peripheral products, and electronic medical equipment and systems. This company also manufacturers computer hardware and related equipment for the consumer market. **NOTE:** Jobseekers are encouraged to apply via the Website: http://www.jobs.hp.com. **Positions advertised include:** Financial Specialist; Commodity Manager; Strategic Program Manager; Remote Application Engineer; Client Manager; Pre-sale Consultant. **Special programs:** Internships. **Corporate headquarters location:** Palo Alto CA. **Other U.S. locations:** Nationwide. **International locations:** Worldwide. **Operations at this facility include:** This location builds computer servers. **Listed on:** New York Stock Exchange. **Stock exchange symbol:** HPQ.

I-SECTOR CORPORATION
6401 Southwest Freeway, Houston TX 77074. 713/795-2000. **Fax:** 713/795-2001. **Contact:** Human Resources. **E-mail address:** careers@I-sector.com. **World Wide Web address:** http://www.i-sector.com. **Description:** Owns and operates subsidiary companies that are engaged in various aspects of the information and technology industries. **Corporate headquarters location:** This location. **Listed on:** American Stock Exchange. **Stock exchange symbol:** ISR. **Number of employees nationwide:** 211.

IBM CORPORATION
11400 Burnett Road, Austin TX 78758. 512/823-0000. **Toll-free phone:** 800/796-7876. **Contact:** Human Resources. **World Wide Web address:** http://www.ibm.com. **Description:** IBM Corporation is a developer, manufacturer, and marketer of advanced information processing products including computers and microelectronic technology, software, networking systems, and information technology-related services. **NOTE:** Jobseekers should apply online via the company's website. **Corporate headquarters location:** Armonk NY. **International locations:** Worldwide. **Operations at this facility include:** This location is a sales office. **Subsidiaries include:** IBM Global; IBM Financing; IBM Technology; IBM Personal Servers; IBM Research; IBM Servers; IBM Software. **Listed on:** New York Stock Exchange. **Stock exchange symbol:** IBM.

INSIGHT INTERACTIVE
5601 North MacAuthur Boulevard, Irving TX 75038. 469/524-0116. **Contact:** Human Resources. **E-mail address:** employment@sourcesite.com. **World Wide Web address:** http://www.srcm.com. **Description:** A leader in interactive content and navigation for interactive television. **Corporate headquarters location:** This location. **Parent company:** Insight Communications Company, Inc.

I.T. PARTNERS, INC.
2735 Villa Creek Drive, Suite 175, Dallas TX 75234. 972/484-5300. **Fax:** 972/484-5605. **Contact:** Human Resources. **E-mail address:** employment@itpartners.com. **World Wide Web address:** http://www.itpartners.net. **Description:** Offers computer consulting services, software training, network implementation, and Web services (Web hosting and development).

I2 TECHNOLOGIES
One i2 Place, 11701 Luna Road, Dallas TX 75234. 469/357-1000. **Toll-free phone:** 800/800-3288. **Fax:** 214/860-6060. **Contact:** Human Resources. **World Wide Web address:** http://www.i2.com. **Description:** Develops and provides e-commerce, business-to-business, and open marketplace solutions. Founded in 1988. **Positions advertised include:** Director of Internal Audit; Information Systems Engineer; Senior Training Analyst. **Corporate headquarters location:** This location. **Other U.S. locations:** Nationwide. **International locations:** Worldwide. **Listed on:** NASDAQ. **Stock exchange symbol:** ITWO.

INTERPHASE CORPORATION
2901 North Dallas Parkway, Suite 200, Dallas TX 75093. 214/654-5000. **Toll-free phone:** 800/777-3722. **Fax:** 214/654-5500. **Contact:** Human Resources. **E-mail address:** iphase.resumes@iphase.com. **World Wide Web address:** http://www.interphase.com. **Description:** A developer, manufacturer, and marketer of networking and mass storage controllers, as well as stand-alone networking devices for computer systems. Networking products are primarily sold to original

equipment manufacturers, value-added resellers, systems integrators, and large end users. **Corporate headquarters location:** This location. **Operations at this facility include:** Administration; Manufacturing; Research and Development; Sales. **Listed on:** NASDAQ. **Stock exchange symbol:** INPH.

INTERVOICE-BRITE, INC.
17811 Waterview Parkway, Dallas TX 75252. 972/454-8000. **Fax:** 972/454-8408. **Contact:** Human Resources. **World Wide Web address:** http://www.intervoice-brite.com. **Description:** Develops, sells, and services interactive voice response systems that allow individuals to access a computer database using a telephone keypad, computer keyboard, or human voice. Applications are functioning in industries including insurance, banking, higher education, government, utilities, health care, retail distribution, transportation, and operator services. **Special programs:** Co-ops. **Positions advertised include:** Help Desk Coordinator; Senior Engineer; Engineer; Project Manager; Business Development Manager. **Listed on:** NASDAQ. **Stock exchange symbol:** INTV. **Corporate headquarters location:** This location.

ITAC SYSTEMS, INC.
3113 Benton Street, Garland TX 75042. 972/494-3073. **Toll-free phone:** 800/533-4822. **Fax:** 972/494-4159. **Contact:** Human Resources. **World Wide Web address:** http://www.itacsystems. com. **Description:** Manufactures the mouse-trak trackball, a computer peripheral product. Founded in 1993. **NOTE:** Entry-level positions are offered. **Corporate headquarters location:** This location. **Listed on:** Privately held.

KANEB SERVICES, INC.
2435 North Central Expressway, Suite 700, Richardson TX 75080. 972/699-4000. **Fax:** 972/699-4025. **Contact:** Personnel. **E-mail address:** employment@kaneb.com. **World Wide Web address:** http://www.kaneb.com. **Description:** A holding company with subsidiaries that are engaged in the technical application and refinement of petroleum products. **Corporate headquarters location:** This location. **Listed on:** New York Stock Exchange. **Stock exchange symbol:** KSL. **Annual sales/revenues:** More than $100 million.

LANDMARK GRAPHICS
P.O. Box 42806, Houston TX 77242. 713/839-2000. **Physical address**: 2101 Citywest Boulevard, Houston X 77042. **Fax:** 713/839-2691. **Contact:** Human Resources. **World Wide Web address:** http://www.lgc.com. **Description:** Software developer whose primary market is the oil industry. Products include data management, geophysical technology, and integrated interpretation applications. Other services include reservoir management and drilling and well consulting. **NOTE:** Landmark Graphics has a nearby shipping and receiving location at 2101 City West Boulevard, Building 1, Suite 200, Houston TX 77042; 713/839-2000. Job listings for all locations are available on the company's website. Apply online. **Other area locations:** Austin TX. **Other U.S. locations:** Anchorage, AK; Denver CO. **International locations:** Canada. Parent company: Halliburton (Dallas TX). **Operations at this facility include:** Administration; Sales; Service.

LIANT SOFTWARE CORPORATION
8911 North Capital of Texas Highway, Suite 4300, Austin TX 78759. 512/343-1010. **Toll-free phone:** 800/349-9222. **Fax:** 512/371-7609. **Contact:** Human Resources. **World Wide Web address:** http://www.liant.com. **Description:** Develops software including Relativity, an SQL relational access through ODBC to COBOL managed data for client/server Windows applications, and Open PL/I, which offers transitions of PL/I mainframe and minicomputer applications from legacy systems to open, client/server environments. **Corporate headquarters location:** Framingham MA. **Operations at this facility include:** This location is engaged in software packaging and distribution. **Listed on:** Privately held.

LINX DATA TERMINALS, INC.
625 Digital Drive, Suite 100, Plano TX 75075. 972/964-7090. **Contact:** Human Resources. **World Wide Web address:** http://www.linxdata.com. **Description:** A manufacturer of networked data collection terminals and host connectivity software.

MESQUITE SOFTWARE, INC.
8500 North Mopac, Suite 825, Austin TX 78759. 512/338-9153. **Contact:** Human Resources. **World Wide Web address:** http://www.mesquite.com. **Description:** Develops software and provides support services for the system simulation market. The company's product line includes CSIM18-The Simulation Engine. **Corporate headquarters location:** This location.

METROWERKS INC.
9801 Metric Boulevard, Suite 100, Austin TX 78758. 512/873-4700. **Fax:** 512/996-4910. **Contact:** Human Resources. **World Wide Web address:** http://www.metrowerks.com. **Description:** Develops and markets software development and programming tools for computers, Internet, and wireless applications as well as games. Founded in 1985. **Corporate headquarters location:** This location. **Other U.S. locations:** CA; MA; WA: UT; TX. **International locations:** Worldwide.

MIILLE APPLIED RESEARCH COMPANY
1730 South Richey, Pasadena TX 77502. 713/472-6272. **Fax:** 713/472-0318. **Contact:** Human Resources. **World Wide Web address:** http://www.miille.com. **Description:** Manufactures and distributes modems and protocol converters for computers.

MINDREADY SOLUTIONS
1611 Headway Circle, Building 1, Suite 200, Austin TX 78754. 514/339-1394. **Contact:** Human Resources. **World Wide Web address:** http://www.mindready.com. **Description:** Mindready designs and manufactures complex automated test engineering solutions and built-to-print systems; micro positioning/assembly solutions; and hardware/software solutions for embedded systems. Customers include original equipment manufacturers, electronic manufacturing service providers, and small and medium-size high technology businesses. **Corporate headquarters location:** Quebec Canada. **Other U.S. locations:** Loveland CO; Huntsville AL.

MISYS HEALTHCARE SYSTEMS
2020 North Loop West, Suite 140, Houston TX 77018. 713/688-3182. **Contact:** Human Resources. **World Wide Web address:** http://www.misyshealthcare.com. **Description:** Develops health care management software. Products include +Medic Vision, +Medic PM, Auto Chart, AutoImage, and FasTracker. **NOTE:** Please send resumes to: MISYS Healthcare Systems, Human Resources, 8529 Six Forks Road, Raleigh NC 27615. **Operations at this facility include:** This location is a sales and engineering facility.

MODIS, INC.
1235 North Loop West, Suite 1100, Houston TX 77008. 713/880-0232. **Contact:** Human Resources. **World Wide Web address:** http://www.modisit.com. **Description:** Provides a wide range of computer consulting services. **Corporate headquarters location:** Jacksonville FL. **Parent company:** MPS Group. **Listed on:** New York Stock Exchange. **Stock exchange symbol:** MPS.

MOTIVE COMMUNICATIONS, INC.
12515-5 Research Boulevard, Austin TX 78759. 512/339-8335. **Fax:** 512/339-9040. **Contact:** Human Resources. **World Wide Web address:** http://www.motive.com. **Description:** A provider of broadband management software. Founded in 1997. **Positions advertised include:** Sales Engineer; Java Software Developer; Software Developer; Staff Developer; Staff Software Developer; Test Execution

Engineer; GL Accountant.

NCR CORPORATION
4100 West Royal Lane, Suite 150, Irving TX 75063. 972/650-2100. **Contact:** Human Resources Consultant. **World Wide Web address:** http://www.ncr.com. **Description:** NCR Corporation is a worldwide provider of computer products and services. The company provides computer solutions to three targeted industries: retail, financial, and communication. **Special programs:** Internships. **Corporate headquarters location:** Dayton OH. **Other U.S. locations:** Nationwide. **Operations at this facility include:** This location is a sales and service office. **Listed on:** New York Stock Exchange. **Stock exchange symbol:** NCR. **Number of employees worldwide:** 29,000.

NETIQ
1233 West Loop South, Suite 1800, Houston TX 77027. 713/548-1700. **Toll-free phone:** 888/323-6768. **Fax:** 713/548-1771. **Contact:** Human Resources. **World Wide Web address:** http://www.netiq.com. **Description:** Developer of software that protects servers and databases, website and e-mail applications. NetIQ has partnerships with many of the world's leading computer hardware and software developers. **NOTE:** Apply online. **Positions advertised include:** Business Unit Director of Finance; Facilities Coordinator; Senior Usability Engineer; Senior Software Engineer; Senior Technical Writer; Channel Marketing Manager; Corporate Sales Representative; Project Manager; Services Billing Administrator; Customer Care Representative; Technical Support Engineer. **Corporate headquarters location:** San Jose CA. **Other U.S. locations:** WA; NC; OR. **International locations:** Worldwide. **Listed on:** NASDAQ. **Stock exchange symbol:** NTIQ.

NETQOS
6504 Bridge Point Parkway, Suite 501, Austin TX 78730. **Toll-free phone:** 877/835-9575. **Fax:** 512/407-8629. **Contact:** Human Resources. **E-mail address:** careers@netqos.com. **World Wide Web address:** http://www.netqos.com. **Description:** Develops software and consulting services to manage the performance of enterprise computer networks of Fortune 1000 companies. **NOTE:** Send resume and cover letter to the company. **Positions advertised include:** Software Engineer; Account Manager; WAN Network Engineer; Sales Executive (New York City area).

NETWORK ASSOCIATES, INC.
13465 Midway Road, Dallas TX 75244. 972/308-9960. **Contact:** Human Resources. **World Wide Web address:** http://www.nai.com. **Description:** Designs, manufactures, markets, and supports software-based analysis and monitoring tools primarily for managing enterprisewide computer networks. Products include McAfee antivirus, Gauntlet firewall, PGP encryption, Sniffer network analyzers, and Magic Help Desk applications. Founded in 1989. **Corporate headquarters location:** Santa Clara CA. **Other area locations:** Plano TX. **Other U.S. locations:** Nationwide. **International locations:** Worldwide. **Listed on:** New York Stock Exchange. **Stock exchange symbol:** NET.

NEWDATA STRATEGIES
5339 Alpha Road, Suite 200, Dallas TX 75240. 972/735-0001. **Fax:** 972/735-8008. **Contact:** Human Resources. **E-mail address:** resumes@newdata.com. **World Wide Web address:** http://www.newdata.com. **Description:** Provides customized data technologies to clients. **Positions advertised include:** CIS Programmer/Analyst; CIS Project Manager; C# Architect; Cisco Engineer; Bilingual Enterprise Exchange 2003 Engineer; .NET Developer.

NEWTEK INC.
5131 Beckwith Boulevard, San Antonio TX 78249. 210/370-8000. **Contact:** Human Resources. **World Wide Web address:** http://www.newtek.com. **Description:** Designs and develops software used for animation and graphics. **Positions advertised include:** Video Software Engineer. **Corporate headquarters location:** This location.

OPENCONNECT SYSTEMS, INC.
2711 LBJ Freeway, Suite 700, Dallas TX 75234. 972/484-5200. **Fax:** 972/888-0458. **Contact:** Human Resources. **E-mail address:** hr@oc.com. **World Wide Web address:** http://www.oc.com. **Description:** A leading provider of software for computer servers, desktops and mainframes. Founded in 1981. **NOTE:** Interested jobseekers should NOT include a cover letter with their resumes when applying via e-mail. **Corporate headquarters location:** This location. **Listed on:** Privately held.

ORACLE CORPORATION
111 Congress Street, Austin TX 78701. 512/703-6200. **Fax:** 512/703-6250. **Contact:** Human Resources. **World Wide Web address:** http://www.oracle.com. **Description:** Designs and manufactures database and information management software for businesses. The company also provides consulting services. **Positions advertised include:** Staff Sales Consultant; Contracts Administrator; Product Manager; Telesales Representative; Contracts Manager; Field Support Sales; Applications Developer; Technical Writer; Quality Assurance Engineer; Manager Business Development. **Corporate headquarters location:** Redwood Shores CA. **Other U.S. locations:** Nationwide. **Listed on:** NASDAQ. **Stock exchange symbol:** ORCL.

PER-SE TECHNOLOGIES, INC.
9441 LBJ Freeway, Suite 400, Dallas TX 75243. 972/664-6900. **Contact:** Human Resources. **World Wide Web address:** http://www.per-se.com. **Description:** A leading provider of comprehensive business management services, financial and clinical software, and Internet solutions to physicians and other healthcare professionals. This company has offices throughout Texas and the United States. **NOTE:** Per-Se Technologies only accepts resumes for open positions. Interested jobseekers should check the company's website for positions and contact information. **Corporate headquarters location:** Atlanta GA. **Listed on:** NASDAQ. **Stock exchange symbol:** PSTI.

PERVASIVE SOFTWARE INC.
12365 Riata Trace Parkway, Building Two, Austin TX 78727. 512/231-6000. **Toll-free phone:** 800/287-4383. **Fax:** 512/231-6010. **Contact:** Human Resources. **E-mail address:** greatjobs@pervasive.com. **World Wide Web address:** http://www.pervasive.com. **Description:** Develops embedded database software. **Positions advertised include:** Quality Technician; Engineering Consultant; Senior Marketing Programs Specialist; Senior Developer. **Corporate headquarters location:** This location. **International locations:** Belgium; Canada; England; France; Germany; Hong Kong; Ireland; Japan. **Listed on:** NASDAQ. **Stock exchange symbol:** PVSW.

R2 TECHNOLOGIES
15455 North Dallas Parkway, Suite 475, Addison TX 75001. 469/621-2421. **Fax:** 214/853-5736. **Contact:** Human Resources. **E-mail address:** r2recruiter@r2now.com. **World Wide Web address:** http://www.r2now.com. **Description:** Provides professional consulting and technical services that support clients' information technology business needs. **Positions advertised include:** Business Intelligence Analyst; Consultant, Enterprise Planner; Customer Support Analyst; Data Modeler Data Warehouse; Data Warehouse Data Architect.

RVSI ACUITY CIMATRIX
6311 North O'Connor Road, Suite N50, Irving TX 75039. 972/869-7684. **Contact:** Human Resources. **E-mail address:** hr@rvsi.net. **World Wide Web address:** http://www.rvsi.com. **Description:** RVSI Acuity CiMatrix provides data collection integrators with complete solutions including scanning

components, networking, software tools, and support services. Products and related services fall into four major categories: omnidirectional scanning systems, intelligent fixed position line scanners, data collection terminals, and networking products. RVSI's foreign subsidiaries are located in Canada, Belgium, England, France, and Germany. **NOTE:** Send resumes to Human Resources, 486 Amherst Street, Nashua NH 03063. **Corporate headquarters location:** Canton MA. **Other U.S. locations:** CA; GA; IL; MI; OH. **Operations at this facility include:** This location is a sales office. **Listed on:** NASDAQ. **Stock exchange symbol:** RVSI.

RAYTHEON
P.O. Box 6056, Greenville TX 75403-6056. 903/455-3450. **Contact:** Human Resources. **World Wide Web address:** http://www.raytheon.com. **Description:** Raytheon Systems designs, manufactures, and installs state-of-the-art communications and integrated command-and-control systems for military and industrial customers worldwide. **NOTE:** See website for job listings and application information. **Other area locations:** Dallas TX (High-technology software). **Parent company:** Raytheon Company. **Operations at this facility include:** This location manufactures electronic equipment for the military and commercial electronics industries. **Listed on:** New York Stock Exchange. **Stock exchange symbol:** RTN. **Number of employees worldwide:** 78,000.

REDSALSA TECHNOLOGIES
13800 Montfort Drive, Suite 230, Dallas TX 75240. 972/503-4200. **Fax:** 972/503-7900. **Contact:** Human Resources. **E-mail address:** jobs@redsalsa.com. **World Wide Web address:** http://www.redsalsa.com. **Description:** Provides application development and testing, business process outsourcing, enterprise content and document management, and IT staffing services. **Positions advertised include:** Software Engineer; Programming Analyst.

SAI PEOPLE SOLUTIONS, INC.
2313 Timber Shadows Drive, Suite 200, Kingwood TX 77339. 281/358-1858. **Fax:** 281/358-8952. **Contact:** Human Resources. **World Wide Web address:** http://www.saisoft.com. **Description:** A computer consulting company. Sai People Solutions offers IT staffing expertise and off-site automated software testing services to *Fortune* 500 firms in a wide range of industries including telecommunications, banking, medical, manufacturing, and transportation. **Corporate headquarters location:** This location. **Other U.S. locations:** CA; AZ; CO: MI; IL; OH; PA; NY; GA; NC; SC; Washington D.C.

SCHLUMBERGER INFORMATION SOLUTIONS
5599 San Felipe, Suite 1700, Houston TX 77056. 713/513-2000. **Contact:** Human Resources. **World Wide Web address:** http://www.slb.com. **Description:** Develops and sells advanced scientific and engineering software to major oil companies and governments. The company helps find and produce oil and gas, manage environmental concerns, and plan regional and urban development. **NOTE:** This company does not accept unsolicited resumes. Apply online at the company's website for open positions. **Parent company:** Schlumberger Limited. **Operations at this facility include:** This facility provides consulting services for information technologies. **Listed on:** New York Stock Exchange. **Stock exchange symbol:** SLB.

SIEMENS BUSINESS SERVICES, INC.
2400 Dallas Parkway, Suite 240, Plano TX. 972/535-2100. **Contact:** Human Resources. **World Wide Web address:** http://www.sbs-usa.siemens.com. **Description:** Provides systems integration, help desk, and PC repair services to *Fortune* 1000 companies and federal clients. The company also resells hardware and software products. **NOTE:** Apply online at this company's website. **Corporate headquarters location:** Norwalk CT. **Other area locations:** Austin TX; Houston TX. **Other U.S. locations:** Nationwide. **International locations:** Worldwide. **Parent company:** Siemens Corporation. **Listed on:** New York Stock Exchange. SI.

S2 SYSTEMS, INC.
4965 Preston Park Boulevard, Suite 800, Plano TX 75093. 972/599-5600. **Toll-free phone:** 800/527-4131. **Fax:** 972/599-5611. **Contact:** Human Resources. **World Wide Web address:** http://www.s2systems.com. **Description:** A provider of data communications middleware and related professional services that bridge the gap between open distributed systems and legacy mainframe and midrange systems used for online applications. **NOTE:** Mail or fax resume and cover letter stating salary requirements. **Corporate headquarters location:** This location.

SANZ
715 North Glenville, Suite 450, Richardson TX 75081. 214/210-6269. **Toll-free phone**: 877/955-4357. **Contact:** Human Resources. **World Wide Web address:** http://www.sanz.com. **Description:** The largest vendor-independent data-storage service company in the United States. This company provides technical support to its customers. **NOTE:** See the company's website for job listings and contact information. **Corporate headquarters location:** Castle Rock CO. **Other area locations:** Dallas TX (Sales); Richardson TX (Technical Support). **Operations at this facility include:** This location is a Regional Office. **Listed on:** NASDAQ. **Stock exchange symbol:** SANZ.

SOFTWARE SPECTRUM INC.
3480 Lotus Drive, Plano TX 75075. 469/443-3900. **Toll-free phone**: 800/624-0503. **Fax:** 972/864-3219. **Contact:** Human Resources. **World Wide Web address:** http://www.softwarespectrum.com. **Description:** Resells microcomputer software and services to businesses and government agencies. Software Spectrum also offers technical support and volume software license services. **NOTE:** Apply online for open positions at this company's website. **Corporate headquarters location:** This location. **Other U.S. locations:** Nationwide. **International locations:** Worldwide. **Subsidiaries include:** Spectrum Integrated Services. **Operations at this facility include:** Administration; Sales; Service. **Listed on:** NASDAQ. **Stock exchange symbol:** LVLT.

SUKATASH
4455 Lyndon B Johnson Freeway, Suite 810, Dallas TX 75244. 972/788-2160. **Toll-free phone:** 866/287-2848. **Fax:** 972/788-8151. **Contact:** Human Resources. **World Wide Web address:** http://www.sukatash.com. **Description:** Performs custom computer programming for multilevel marketing firms.

TECHWORKS, INC.
4030 West Braker Lane, Suite 350, Austin TX 78759. 512/794-8533. **Fax:** 512/794-8520. **Contact:** Human Resources. **World Wide Web address:** http://www.techworks.com. **Description:** Manufactures and sells computer memory.

TRILOGY DEVELOPMENT GROUP
6011 West Courtyard Drive, Austin TX 78730. 512/874-3100. **Fax:** 512/874-8900. **Contact:** Human Resources. **E-mail address:** recruit_US@trilogy.com. **World Wide Web address:** http://www.trilogy.com. **Description:** A developer of configuration software for a variety of industries including automotive, utilities, insurance, shipping, and computers.

21ST CENTURY TECHNOLOGIES INC.
4515 Seton Center Parkway, Suite 320, Austin TX 78759. 512/342-0010. **Contact:** Human Resources. **World Wide Web address:** http://www.21technologies.com. **Description:** Develops software solutions for problems in counter-terrorism detection, natural language processing, computer vision and image processing, terrorist network analysis; computer security intrusion detection systems, logistics and maintenance planning and scheduling for federal and military agencies.

NOTE: Applications accepted only through automated online system. **Positions advertised include:** Technical Project/Program Manager; Software Engineer; Product Marketing Manager.

UGS CORPORATION
5800 Granite Parkway, Suite 600, Plano TX 75024. 972/987-3000. **Fax:** 972/669-0563. **Contact:** Human Resources. **E-mail address:** jobs@us.tecnomatix.com. **World Wide Web address:** http://www.ugs.com. **Description:** Develops, markets, and supports application-enabler software products for real-time monitoring, analysis, information management, and control solutions in worldwide industrial automation markets. UGS also develops, markets, and supports integrated hardware, software, and systems solutions for automated identification and data collection applications that are sold to a broad base of customers throughout North America. The company also acts as a full-service distributor and value-added re-marketer for manufacturers of bar code equipment. **Corporate headquarters location:** This location. **Other U.S. locations:** Nationwide. **International locations:** Worldwide.

UNISYS CORPORATION
13105 NW Freeway, Suite 720, Houston TX 77040. 713/744-2666. **Contact:** Human Resources. **World Wide Web address:** http://www.unisys.com. **Description:** Unisys Corporation provides information services, technology, and software. The company's Enabling Software Team creates a variety of software projects that facilitate the building of user applications and the management of distributed systems. The company's Platforms Group is responsible for UNIX Operating Systems running across multiple processor server platforms including all peripheral and communication drivers. The Unisys Commercial Parallel Processing Team develops microkernel-based operating systems, I/O device drivers, ATM hardware, diagnostics, and system architectures. The System Management Group is in charge of the overall management of development programs for UNIX desktop and entry-server products. **NOTE:** Apply online. **Positions advertised include:** Helpdesk Agent; Curriculum Developer; Healthcare Systems Consultant; Information Technology; Call Center Supervisor; Portfolio Sales Executive; Bid Proposal Manager. **Special programs:** Internships. **Office hours:** Monday - Friday, 8:00 a.m. - 5:00 p.m. **Corporate headquarters location:** Blue Bell PA. **Other U.S. locations:** Nationwide. **International locations:** Worldwide. **Operations at this facility include:** This location manufactures and sells computers. **Number of employees nationwide:** 37,000.

UNIVERSAL COMPUTER SYSTEMS, INC. (UCS)
6700 Hollister, Houston TX 77040. 713/718-1800. **Contact:** Human Resources. **E-mail address:** Careers@UniversalComputerSys.com. **World Wide Web address:** http://www.universalcomputersys.com. **Description:** Supplies computer software and hardware systems specifically designed for the business of automobile dealerships. **NOTE:** Entry-level positions, part-time jobs, and second and third shifts are offered. **Positions advertised include:** General Administrative Clerk; Systems Software Development; Windows Development; COBOL Programmers; Dutch Marketing Representative. Service Pricing Guide Installer; Demo Specialist; Network Technician; Systems Network Engineer. **Special programs:** Internships; Co-ops. **Corporate headquarters location:** This location. **Other area locations:** College Station TX. **Other U.S. locations:** Nationwide. **International locations:** Worldwide. **Listed on:** Privately held. **Number of employees nationwide:** 2,600.

VIGNETTE CORPORATION
1301 South Mopac Expressway, Suite 100, Austin TX 78746-5776. 512/741-4300. **Toll-free phone:** 888/608-9900. **Fax:** 512/741-1403. **Contact:** Human Resources. **World Wide Web address:** http://www.vignette.com. **Description:** Supplies e-business applications to online business clients. **NOTE:** Apply online at this company's website. **Positions advertised include:** Customer Support Engineer; Technical Writer; Systems Administrator; Copywriter/Editor; Customer Reference Specialist; Marketing Programs Manager; Financial Analyst. **Corporate headquarters location:** This location. **Listed on:** NASDAQ. **Stock exchange symbol:** VIGN.

Utah

AFFILIATED COMPUTER SERVICES, INC. (ACS)
510 Parkland Drive, Sandy UT 84070. 801/567-5000. **Fax:** 801/567-5003. **Contact:** Human Resources. **World Wide Web address:** http://www.acs-inc.com. **Description:** Provides diversified business process and information technology outsourcing solutions to commercial and government clients worldwide. **NOTE:** See website to search for jobs and apply online. **Positions advertised include:** Technical Project Manager; Quality Assurance Analyst; Customer Care Assistant; Op Excellence Analyst – Healthcare; Customer Care, Data Entry; Transaction Processor Day; Call Center Program Manager; Service Delivery Manager. **Corporate headquarters location:** Dallas TX. **Other U.S. locations:** Nationwide. **International locations:** Worldwide. **Operations at this facility include:** Operations for ACS Business Process Solutions division.

ALLEN COMMUNICATION LEARNING SERVICES
175 West 200 South, Suite 100 - Garden Level, Salt Lake City UT 84101. 801/537-7800. **Toll-free phone:** 866/310-7800. **Fax:** 801/537-7805. **Contact:** Shelley Duggar, Human Resources Manager. **E-mail address:** shellyd@allencomm.com. **World Wide Web address:** http://www.allencomm.com. **Description:** Provides computer-based training (CBT) and Web-based training solutions to businesses. **NOTE:** Entry-level positions and part-time jobs are offered. **Positions advertised include:** Proposals Manager; Multimedia Developer/Programmer; Full-Time Instructional Designer; Contract Instructional Designers; Instructional Designer Intern. **Special programs:** Internships; Apprenticeships; Training; Summer Jobs. **Corporate headquarters location:** This location. **CEO:** Ron Zamir.

ALTIRIS
588 West 400 South, Lindon UT 84042. 801/226-8500. **Toll-free phone:** 888/252-5551. **Fax:** 801/226-8506. **Contact:** Human Resources. **E-mail address:** hr@altiris.com. **World Wide Web address:** http://www.altiris.com. **Description:** A software company. Founded 1998. **Positions advertised include:** Alliance Product Manager; Creative Director; Database Administrator (DBA); Federal Contract Administrator; Field Marketing Project Manager; Human Resource Information Systems Specialist; Human Resource SR Manager; IP and Software Licensing Counsel; Operations Product Manager. **Corporate headquarters location:** This location. **International locations:** Worldwide. **Listed on:** NASDAQ. **Stock exchange symbol:** ATRS. **President/CEO:** Greg Butterfield.

AXONIX CORPORATION
3785 South 700 East, Salt Lake City Utah 84106. 801/685-0900. **Toll-free phone:** 800/866-9797. **Fax:** 801/685-0901. **Contact:** Human Resources. **World Wide Web address:** http://www.axonix.com. **Description:** Manufactures network multimedia and data storage sharing appliances.

BLUE SQUIRREL
686 East 8400 South, Sandy UT 84070. 801/352-1551. **Toll-free phone:** 800/403-0925. **Fax:** 801/912-6032. **Contact:** Human Resources. **E-mail address:** sales@bluesquirrel.com. **World Wide Web address:** http://www.bluesquirrel.com. **Description:** Develops Internet and content management software including WebWhacker, WebSeeker, ClickBook, Grab-a-Site, TechSeeker, and LegalSeeker. **NOTE:** See website for current job openings. Submit resume by e-mail or fax.

CA, INC.
11778 South Election Drive, Suite 100, Draper UT 84020. 801/619-7500. **Contact:** Human Resources. **World Wide Web address:** http://www.ca.com. **Description:** A leading international provider of computer services for businesses. **NOTE:** See website for current job openings and to apply online. **Positions advertised include:** Attorney; Software Engineer; Solution Manager. **Corporate headquarters location:** Islandia NY. **Other U.S. locations:** Nationwide. **International locations:** Worldwide. **Listed on:** New York Stock Exchange. **Stock exchange symbol:** CA.

CASELLE, INC.
1570 North Main Street, P.O. Box 100, Spanish Fork UT 84660-0100. 801/798-9851. **Toll-free phone:** 800/228-9851. **Fax:** 801/798-1764. **Contact:** Human Resources. **E-mail address:** jobs@caselle.com. **World Wide Web address:** http://www.caselle.com. **Description:** Develops specialized accounting software for use by local government offices. **NOTE:** See website for current job openings. Submit resume by fax or e-mail. **Positions advertised include:** Accountant; Utility Billing.

CIMETRIX, INC.
6979 South High Tech Drive, Midvale UT 84047-3757. 801/256-6500. **Toll-free phone:** 800/344-7292. **Fax:** 801/256-6510. **Contact:** Director of Human Resources. **World Wide Web address:** http://www.cimetrix.com. **Description:** Builds open architecture software for SMT equipment, robots, and assembly cells. Founded in 1989. **Corporate headquarters location:** This location. **CEO:** Robert H. Reback.

CIRQUE CORPORATION
2463 South 3850 West, Suite A, Salt Lake City UT 84120. 801/467-1100. **Toll-free phone:** 800/454-3375. **Fax:** 801/467-0208. **Contact:** Human Resources. **World Wide Web address:** http://www.cirque.com. **Description:** Manufactures the GlidePoint brand and other products, including desktop and OEM input devices such as plug-and-play computer touchpads, micro-keyboards, and biometrics devices . **Parent company:** ALPS Electric Co. Ltd.

CONNECTING EDGE, INC.
P.O. Box 95551, Salt Lake City UT 84095-0551. 801/446-4243. **Fax:** 801/446-4244. **Contact:** Personnel. **E-mail address:** info@connecting-edge.com. **World Wide Web address:** http://www.connecting-edge.com. **Description:** Designs and manufactures data communications equipment including multi-protocol switches and fiber-optic networking equipment.

DHI COMPUTING SERVICE, INC.
P.O. Box 51427, Provo UT 84605-1427. 801/373-8518. **Physical address:** 1525 West 820 North, Provo UT 84601. **Toll-free phone:** 800/453-9400. **Fax:** 801/374-5316. **Contact:** Human Resources. **World Wide Web address:** http://www.dhiprovo.com. **Description:** Develops business software and installs hardware that is used mainly by dairies.

DENTRIX DENTAL SYSTEMS
727 East Utah Valley Drive, Suite 500, American Fork UT 84003. 801/763-9300. **Toll-free phone:** 800/DENTRIX. **Fax:** 801/763-9336. **Contact:** Human Resources. **World Wide Web address:** http://www.dentrix.com. **Description:** Develops clinical and practice management software for dentists. Founded 1989. **NOTE:** Visit website for online application form. Online applications are preferred. **Positions advertised include:** Receptionist; Telecom Specialist; Market Research Associate; Corporate Travel Coordinator; Call Center Technical Support Supervisor; Facilities and Security Technician. **Corporate headquarters location:** This location. **Parent company:** Henry Schein, Inc.

DIGISPEC
115 South State Street, Linden UT 84042. 801/785-5000. **Toll-free phone:** 800/755-8218. **Fax:** 801/785-0339. **Contact:** Human Resources. **World Wide Web address:** http://www.datapad.com. **Description:** Manufactures custom mouse pads. Founded 1984.

EMC LEGATO
71 South 1380 West, Lindon UT 84042. 801/922-9101. **Fax:** 801/223-0199. **Contact:** Human Resources. **World Wide Web address:** http://www.legato.com. **Description:** Produces storage management software that allows data to be moved, managed, and protected. **NOTE:** Please visit website to register, search for jobs, and apply online. **Corporate headquarters location:** Mountain View CA. **Other U.S. locations:** Nationwide. **International locations:** Worldwide. **Parent company:** EMC Corporation. **Listed on:** New York Stock Exchange. **Stock exchange symbol:** EMC Corp.

EVANS & SUTHERLAND COMPUTER CORPORATION
600 Komas Drive, Salt Lake City UT 84108. 801/588-1603. **Fax:** 801/588-4500. **Contact:** Human Resources. **E-mail address:** staffing@es.com. **World Wide Web address:** http://www.es.com. **Description:** Designs, manufactures, sells, and services special purpose 3-D computer graphics hardware and software. The products are developed to help people solve complicated problems and to help train people to perform complex tasks. Uses of this equipment include visual simulation systems for pilot training and engineering workstations for molecular modeling or engineering design. The majority of Evans & Sutherland's customers are in the aerospace and defense-related markets. Founded in 1968. **NOTE:** Submit resume by e-mail. **Corporate headquarters location:** This location. **Other U.S. locations:** Orlando FL. **International locations:** England; Germany; China; United Arab Emirates. **Operations at this facility include:** Administration; Manufacturing; Research and Development; Sales; Service. **President/CEO:** James R. Oyler. **Listed on:** NASDAQ. **Stock exchange symbol:** ESCC.

FRAME RATE
P.O. Box 18830, Salt Lake City UT 84118. 801/840-1770. **Fax:** 801/382-1110. **Contact:** Human Resources. **E-mail address:** support@framerate.com. **World Wide Web address:** http://www.framerate.com. **Description:** Provides businesses and individuals with digital and multimedia messaging services. Founded 1993.

BILL GOOD MARKETING
12393 Gateway Park Place, Suite 600, Draper UT 84020. 801/572-1480. **Fax:** 801/572-1496. **Contact:** Human Resources Manager. **World Wide Web address:** http://www.billgood.com. **Description:** Conducts seminars, sells training programs and tapes to registered representatives in the financial services industry, and develops and markets software used by stockbrokers. **Corporate headquarters location:** This location. **Listed on:** Privately held. **Number of employees at this location:** 100.

HK SYSTEMS
515 East 100 South, Salt Lake City UT 84102. 801/530-4000. **Toll-free phone:** 800/453-3550. **Fax:** 801/530-4476. **Contact:** Human Resources. **E-mail address:** hr.mke@hksystems.com. **World Wide Web address:** http://www.hksystems.com. **Description:** HK Systems designs and manufactures computer-controlled machinery for manufacturing and for various warehousing processes. **NOTE:** See website for current job openings and application instructions. **Positions advertised include:** AGV Integration Specialist. **Special programs:** Internships. **Corporate headquarters location:** New Berlin WI. **Other area locations:** Bountiful UT. **Operations at this facility include:** This location develops inventory control and management software.

HEMISPHERE SOFTWARE
2815 East 3300 South, Salt Lake City UT 84109. 801/466-8899. **Toll-free phone:** 800/866-4364. **Fax:**

801/486-1938. **Contact:** Human Resources. **World Wide Web address:** http://www.hemicorp.com. **Description:** Develops accounting software used by contractors.

HEWLETT-PACKARD COMPANY
10619 South Jordan Gateway, South Jordan UT 84095. 800/222-5547. **Contact:** Human Resources. **World Wide Web address:** http://www.hp.com. **Description:** Hewlett-Packard designs and manufactures measurement and computation products and systems used in business, engineering, science, health care, and education. Principal products are integrated instrument and computer systems including hardware and software, computer systems and peripheral products, and medical electronic equipment and systems. **NOTE:** Jobseekers are encouraged to apply via the Website: http://www.jobs.hp.com. **Corporate headquarters location:** Palo Alto CA. **Other U.S. locations:** Nationwide. **International locations:** Worldwide. **Listed on:** New York Stock Exchange. **Stock exchange symbol:** HPQ. **Number of employees worldwide:** 140,000.

I-O CORPORATION
1490 North 2200 West, Suite 100, Salt Lake City UT 84116. 801/973-6767. **Fax:** 801/974-5683. **Contact:** Human Resources. **World Wide Web address:** http://www.iocorp.com. **Description:** Manufactures peripheral equipment for mainframes.

INSURQUOTE SYSTEMS, INC.
620 East Timpanogos Circle, Building H, Orem UT 84097. 801/373-7345. **Toll-free phone:** 800/658-8778. **Fax:** 801/818-6480. **Contact:** Personnel. **World Wide Web address:** http://www.insurquote.com. **Description:** Designs software for the insurance industry. **Corporate headquarters location:** This location. **CEO:** Keith Toney.

INTEL CORPORATION
3740 West 13400 South, Riverton UT 84065. 801/445-8080. **Contact:** Human Resources. **World Wide Web address:** http://www.intel.com. **Description:** Intel is one of the largest semiconductor manufacturers in the world. Other operations include supercomputers; embedded control chips and flash memories; video technology software; multimedia hardware; personal computer enhancement products; and designing, making, and marketing microcomputer components, modules, and systems. Intel sells its products to original equipment manufacturers and other companies that incorporate them into their products. **NOTE:** Please visit website to submit resume electronically. **Corporate headquarters location:** Santa Clara CA. **Other U.S. locations:** Nationwide. **International locations:** Worldwide. **Operations at this facility include:** This location manufactures network hardware for Macintosh and IBM computers. **Listed on:** NASDAQ. **Stock exchange symbol:** INTC. **Number of employees worldwide:** 80,000.

IOMEGA CORPORATION
1821 West Iomega Way, Roy UT 84067. 801/332-1000. **Contact:** Human Resources. **World Wide Web address:** http://www.iomega.com. **Description:** Creates information storage solutions that enhance the usefulness of personal computers and workstations in a variety of applications. Iomega's products help people manage their information storage needs. The company's products include Zip drives which are three drives in one, offering expansion for hard drives, mobile storage with portable convenience, and backup information. Founded in 1980. **Positions advertised include:** Inside Sales Representative; Cost Accountant; Mechanical Engineer – Tribologist; Business Analyst – Sales; Documentation Control Specialist (Temporary). **Corporate headquarters location:** San Diego CA. **Other U.S. locations:** Houston TX. **International locations:** Singapore; Switzerland; Canada. **Listed on:** New York Stock Exchange. **Stock exchange symbol:** IOM. **CEO:** Jonathan Huberman. **Number of employees worldwide:** 309.

MAS COMPUTERS
1005 North State Street, Orem UT 84057. 801/226-1892. **Contact:** Human Resources. **World Wide Web address:** http://www.mascomputersonline.com. **Description:** Resells new and used computers, computer components, and software. **President:** Tim Bird.

NOVELL, INC.
1800 South Novell Place, Provo UT 84606. 801/861-7000. **Toll-free phone:** 800/453-1267. **Contact:** Human Resources. **World Wide Web address:** http://www.novell.com. **Description:** Novell, Inc. develops software tools and systems, works in partnership with other companies, and provides computer network management services. Products include NetWare 5.1, GroupWise 5.5, ManageWise 2.7, and Novell Net Publisher. **NOTE:** Search and apply for positions online. Contact Human Resources toll-free at 888/475-4631. **Positions advertised include:** Applications Engineer; Business Systems Analyst; Contract Manager; Documentation Specialist; Help Desk Support Engineer; Inside Sales Representative; International Tax Accountant; Managed Services Engineer; Marketing Communications Manager; Network Security Administrator; Public Relations Manager; Security Specialist; Senior Auditor; Senior Consultant; Software Engineer Senior; Tax Accountant; Technical Support Engineer; Web Developer. **Corporate headquarters location:** Waltham MA. **Other area locations:** Salt Lake City UT. **Other U.S. locations:** Nationwide. **International locations:** Worldwide. **Operations at this facility include:** This location provides networking services. **Number of employees at this location:** 3,000.

OPEN SOLUTIONS INC.
720 East Timpanogos Parkway, Orem UT 84097-6214. 801/222-0200. **Toll-free phone:** 800/385-5567. **Fax:** 801/222-0250. **Contact:** Human Resources Department. **E-mail address:** resume@so-sys.com. **World Wide Web address:** http://www.opensolutions.com. **Description:** Provides software and services that help financial institutions with data processing and information management functions, including account, transaction, lending, operations, back office, client information, and reporting. **NOTE:** See website for current job openings and application instructions. **Positions advertised include:** Crystal Reports Writer; Technical Support Representative; Trainer. **Corporate headquarters location:** Glastonbury CT. **Operations at this facility include:** SOSystems Group, which develops a software suite for credit unions. **Listed on:** NASDAQ. **Stock exchange symbol:** OPEN. **Number of employees at this location:** 66.

PARK CITY GROUP INC.
333 Main Street, Park City UT 84060. 435/649-2221. **Toll-free phone:** 800/772-4556. **Fax:** 435/645-2010. **Contact:** Human Resources. **E-mail address:** jobs@parkcitygroup.com. **World Wide Web address:** http://www.parkcitygroup.com. **Description:** Develops software for the retail industry. **Positions advertised include:** Software Engineer (Java); Technical Analyst; Account Manager; Business Analyst; Oracle DBA. **CEO:** Randall K. Fields.

PREMIER COMPUTING TECHNOLOGIES
385 West 2880 South, Salt Lake City UT 84115. 801/487-8400. **Contact:** Human Resources. **E-mail address:** dpotter@premiercomputing.com. **World Wide Web Address:** http://www.premiercomputing.com. **Description:** Provides information technology products and services to institutions, governmental agencies, and corporations worldwide. Founded in 1977.

PROMODEL CORPORATION
556 East Technology Avenue, Orem UT 84097. 801/223-4600. **Fax:** 801/226-6046. **Contact:** Human Resources. **E-mail address:** hr@promodel.com. **World Wide Web address:** http://www.promodel.com. **Description:** Develops and sells simulation software that is used in a wide range of industries including health care and manufacturing. **Positions advertised**

include: Pharmaceutical Sales Representative. **Corporate headquarters location:** Bethlehem PA.

RACORE TECHNOLOGY CORPORATION
4125 South 6000 West, West Valley City UT 84128. 801/973-9779. **Toll-free phone:** 877/252-9779. **Fax:** 801/973-2005. **Contact:** Human Resources. **E-mail address:** hrjobs@racore.com. **World Wide Web address:** http://www.racore.com. **Description:** Designs, develops, manufactures, and markets high performance LAN products with an emphasis on fiber optics, Token-Ring and 10/100 ethernet technologies. **Corporate headquarters location:** This location. **Parent company:** CirTran Corporation.

RADIX INTERNATIONAL
4855 Wiley Post Way, Salt Lake City UT 84116. 801/537-1717. **Toll-free phone:** 800/367-9256. **Fax:** 801/328-3401. **Contact:** Human Resources. **E-mail address:** careers@radix-md.co.uk. **World Wide Web address:** http://www.radix-intl.com. **Description:** Manufactures hand-held computer systems used in meter readings and other applications. **Corporate headquarters location:** This location. **International locations:** United Kingdom.

THE SCO GROUP
355 South 520 West, Suite 100, Lindon UT 84042. 801/765-4999. **Fax:** 801/765-1313. **Contact:** Human Resources. **E-mail address:** jobs@sco.com. **World Wide Web address:** http://www.thescogroup.com. **Description:** Provides software, including UNIX, to small businesses. Founded 1994. **Positions advertised include:** Computer Instructor; Senior Software Engineer; Inside Sales Manager. **Corporate headquarters location:** This location. **Other U.S. locations:** CA; NJ. **International locations:** Worldwide. **Lusted on:** NASDAQ. **Stock exchange symbol:** SCOX. **President/CEO:** Darl C. McBride.

SAFFIRE, INC.
10447 South Jordan Gateway, South Jordan UT 84095. 801/495-4900. **Fax:** 801/495-4901. **Contact:** Human Resources. **E-mail address:** jobs@saffire.com. **World Wide Web address:** http://www.saffire.com. **Description:** Develops computer and video game software. Numerous products are licensed for the Super Nintendo and Sega Genesis game systems. **NOTE:** See website for current job openings. Submit resume by e-mail. **Positions advertised include:** Project Manager; Assistant Project Manager; Art Lead; Animation Lead: Game Designer; Game Tester; Animator; Design Lead. **CEO:** Mark Kendall.

SIRSIDYNIX
400 West Dynix Drive, Provo UT 84604. 801/223-5200. **Toll-free phone:** 800/288-8020. **Fax:** 801/223-5438. **Contact:** Human Resources. **World Wide Web address:** http://www.sirsidynix.com. **Description:** Provides technology services for libraries. **NOTE:** Apply online, or submit resume by e-mail or fax. **Positions advertised include:** Associate Market Consultant; Sales Consultant. **Corporate headquarters location:** Huntsville AL. **Other U.S. locations:** St. Louis MO. **International locations:** Worldwide.

SORENSON MEDIA
4393 South Riverboat Road, Suite 300, Salt Lake City UT 84123. 801/287-9400. **Fax:** 801/287-9401. **Contact:** Human Resources. **E-mail address:** jobs@sorenson.com. **World Wide Web address:** http://www.sorenson.com. **Description:** The company, which does business as Sorenson Communications, provides video technology for Internet purposes. Founded 2000. **NOTE:** See website for current job openings. Submit resume by e-mail. **Corporate headquarters location:** This location. **CEO:** James L. Sorenson, Jr.

SUN MICROSYSTEMS
7090 Union Park Center, Midvale UT 84047. 801/322-2880. **Contact:** Human Resources. **World Wide Web address:** http://www.sun.com. **Description:** Provides products and services for network computing that consist of computer systems, network storage systems, support services, and professional and knowledge services. **NOTE:** Please visit website to search for jobs and apply online. **Corporate headquarters location:** Santa Clara CA. **Other U.S. locations:** Nationwide. **International locations:** Worldwide. **Operations at this facility include:** This location is a remote field service office. **Listed on:** NASDAQ. **Stock exchange symbol:** SUNW.

SYMANTEC CORPORATION
796 East Utah Valley Drive, Suite 100, American Fork UT 84003. 801/224-5306. **Fax:** 801/227-3766. **Contact:** Human Resources Department. **World Wide Web address:** http://www.symantec.com. **Description:** Provides Internet security, including virus protection and firewall networks. Develops software for consumers that secures their computer passwords and personal computer files. **NOTE:** See website for current job openings and to apply online. **Positions advertised include:** Senior Software Engineer; Principal Software Engineer; Senior Human Factors Engineer. **Corporate headquarters location:** Cupertino CA. **Other U.S. locations:** Nationwide. **International locations:** Worldwide. **Listed on:** NASDAQ. **Stock exchange symbol:** SYMC. **Number of employees worldwide:** 5,000.

THINK SUBSCRIPTION
250 West Center Street, 2nd Floor, Provo UT 84601. 801/373-2246. **Toll-free phone:** 800/769-7638. **Fax:** 801/373-5066. **Contact:** Personnel. **E-mail address:** employment@thinksubscription.com. **World Wide Web address:** http://www.thinksubscription.com. **Description:** THINK Subscription is engaged in the development of subscription management and fulfillment software for publishers, application service providers (ASPs), and online media vendors.

3M HEALTH INFORMATION SYSTEMS
575 West Murray Boulevard, Murray UT 84123-4611. 801/265-4400. **Fax:** 801/263-3658. **Contact:** Personnel. **World Wide Web address:** http://www.3mhis.com. **Description:** A systems integrator to more than 3,000 hospitals, health networks and enterprises, managed care organizations, outpatient facilities, and medical group practices. The company provides the health care market with clinical information systems that have data integration, total quality management, and expert system technology capabilities. **NOTE:** Entry-level positions are offered. **Positions advertised include:** Data Innovation System Installer; Inpatient Clinical Consultant/Project Leader; Senior Manager of Outpatient Services; Software Quality Assurance Manager; Business Development Analyst; Product Marketing Manager for Coding/Reimbursement Modules; Products Marketing Manager; Product Marketing/Business Development Manager; Deputy Project Manager; Sales Representative Specialist for Home Health; Advanced Software Engineer; Advanced Product Analyst. **Special programs:** Internships; Training; Co-ops; Summer Jobs. **Corporate headquarters location:** This location. **Other U.S. locations:** Atlanta GA; Westchester IL; Wallingford CT; Burtonsville MD; Washington D.C. **Parent company:** 3M (St. Paul MN). **Listed on:** New York Stock Exchange. **Stock exchange symbol:** MMM.

UINTA BUSINESS SYSTEMS INC.
332 West Bugatti Avenue, Salt Lake City UT 84115. 801/461-7600. **Toll-free phone:** 800/735-0234. **Fax:** 801/486-4720. **Contact:** Jeune Ellis. **E-mail address:** jeunee@uinta.com. **World Wide Web address:** http://www.uinta.com. **Description:** One of Utah's largest systems resellers. Uinta Business Systems sells, leases, and services office machinery including computers, fax machines, and photocopiers. **NOTE:** Unita's employment opportunities are filled through TechStaff, an in-house staffing group. Please e-mail your resume to Jeune Ellis, or call her at 801/461-7655. **Positions advertised include:** Microsoft Certified Systems Engineer; Certified Novell Engineer; LAN/WAN; Desktop Support Specialist; Help Desk

Support Specialist; PC Technician; Unix Administrator. **Other U.S. locations:** Las Vegas NV. **Subsidiaries include:** Unita Information Solutions; Unita Document Systems.

UNISYS CORPORATION
480 North 2200 West, P.O. Box 16800, Salt Lake City UT 84116-0800. 801/594-5000. **Fax:** 801/594-5660. **Contact:** Human Resources. **World Wide Web address:** http://www.unisys.com. **Description:** Unisys Corporation provides information services, technology, and software. Unisys specializes in developing critical business solutions based on open information networks. **Corporate headquarters location:** Blue Bell PA. **Other U.S. locations:** Nationwide. **International locations:** Worldwide. **Operations at this facility include:** This location is involved in scaleable commercial transaction processing systems based on distributed computing technologies. **Listed on:** New York Stock Exchange. **Stock exchange symbol:** UIS. **Number of employees worldwide:** 37,000.

UNIVERSAL SYSTEMS, INC. (USI)
1356 East 3300 South, Salt Lake City UT 84106. 801/484-9151. **Contact:** Human Resources. **E-mail address:** employment@usicomputer.com. **World Wide Web address:** http://www.usicomputer.com. **Description:** Develops workflow and document management software and provides systems integration services. The company provides turnkey solutions to *Fortune* 500 and government clients utilizing the latest in client/server platforms and SQL compliant databases. **Corporate headquarters location:** This location.

WESTGATE SOFTWARE INC.
12345 South 300 East, Draper UT 84020. 801/495-1200. **Fax:** 801/495-1208. **Contact:** Human Resources **E-mail address:** info@westgatesoftware.com. **World Wide Web address:** http://www.westgatesoftware.com. **Description:** Develops software for use in film processing and the dry cleaning industry. **Corporate headquarters location:** This location. **International locations:** United Kingdom; New Zealand.

XACTWARE INFORMATION SERVICES
1426 East 750 North, Orem UT 84097. 801/764-5900. **Fax:** 801/224-5218. **Contact:** K.J. Norton, Human Resources. **E-mail address:** xadmin@xactware.com. **World Wide Web address:** http://www.xactware.com. **Description:** Manufactures software for the insurance and construction industries. **Corporate headquarters location:** This location.

Vermont

AMERICAN HEALTH CARE SOFTWARE ENTERPRISES
99 Swift Street, Suite 300, South Burlington VT 05403. 802/872-3484. **Toll-free phone:** 800/336-1776. **Fax:** 802/872-3476. **Contact:** Marcia DeRosia, President. **E-mail address:** derosiam@ahconline.com. **World Wide Web address:** http://www.ahconline.com. **Description:** Develops software for the nursing home industry and home health care agencies. Founded in 1977. **Positions advertised include:** Sales and Marketing Representative; Programmer/Analyst; Installer/Trainer; Customer Service Representative.

HIGH MEADOW BUSINESS SOLUTIONS, INC. dba RETAIL EDGE
P.O. Box 1546, Manchester Center VT 05255. 802/362-2296. **Physical address:** 343 High Meadow Way, Manchester VT 05254. **Toll-free phone:** 800/755-9692. **Fax:** 802/362-2298. **Contact:** Human Resources. **E-mail address:** info@retailedge.com. **World Wide Web address:** http://www.retailedge.com. **Description:** A software development company that specializes in retail point of sale software, database design, custom software development, and point of sale hardware services. Founded in 1989.

IDX SYSTEMS CORPORATION
40 IDX Drive, P.O. Box 1070, South Burlington VT 05402-1070. 802/862-1022. **Fax:** 802/863-9288. **Contact:** Human Resources. **World Wide Web address:** http://www.idx.com. **Description:** Develops medical software for hospitals. Founded in 1969. **NOTE:** The company does not accept hardcopy resumes. **Positions advertised include:** Imaging Executive; Account Executive; Revenue Analyst Associate. **Special programs:** Internships. **Corporate headquarters location:** This location. **Other U.S. locations:** Atlanta GA; Boston MA; Chicago IL; Dallas TX; Louisville KY; San Diego CA; Seattle WA; Winston-Salem NC. **International locations:** London UK. **Subsidiaries include:** EDiX. **Parent company:** GE Healthcare, a unit of General Electric Company. **Number of employees worldwide:** 2,400.

6 DEGREES SOFTWARE & CONSULTING INC.
176 Battery Street, Suite 3, Burlington VT 05401. 802/660-1923. **Fax:** 802/860-2931. **Contact:** Rich Miller, President. **World Wide Web address:** http://www.6degrees.com. **Description:** Builds server systems on Java, XML, and open source server technologies for educational, corporate, governmental, medical, nonprofit, financial, legal, and many other types of organizations. **Positions advertised include:** Java/Database Developer.

Virginia

AC TECHNOLOGIES, INC.
2751 Prosperity Avenue, Suite 500, Fairfax VA 22031. 703/698-4300. Fax: 703/698-4381. **E-mail:** jobs@ac-tech.com. **World Wide Web address:** http://www.ac-tech.com. **Description:** AC Technologies, Inc. provides a range of management and IT services and solutions to government agencies and companies nationwide. Founded in 1993. **NOTE:** Search and apply for positions online. **Positions advertised include:** J2EE Developer; Testing/IV&V configuration Analyst; Principal IV&V Test Engineer; IV&V software Test Technician. **Parent company:** Nortel Government Solutions.

ASG SOFTWARE SOLUTIONS
12700 Sunrise Valley Drive, Reston VA 20191-5804. 703/464-1300. **Toll-free phone:** 800/333.8666. **Fax:** 703/464-4918. **Contact:** Human Resources. **World Wide Web address:** http://www.asg.com. **Description:** ASG provides businesses with services and software solutions for security, applications, operations, information, performance, and infrastructure management. ASG helps mainframe clients mobilize their resources to boost productivity and enhance performance through intelligent use of technology. ASG has more than 40 offices worldwide with 900 employees. Founded in 1986. **NOTE:** Search and apply for positions online. **Positions advertised include:** Proposal Analyst/Technical Writer; Sr. Quality Assurance Analyst; Solutions Engineer. **Corporate headquarters location:** Naples FL.

AT&T GOVERNMENT SOLUTIONS, INC.
1900 Gallows Road, Vienna VA 22182. 703/506-5000. **Contact:** Human Resources. **World Wide Web address:** http://www.att.com. **Description:** Creates large-scale decision support systems and software engineering environments, applies operations research and mathematical modeling to business and management systems, and implements advanced database technology. AT&T Government Solutions, Inc. also provides studies and analysis capabilities for policy development and planning; modeling and simulation of hardware and software used in real-time testing of sensor, weapon, and battlefield management command, control, and communication systems; and testing and evaluation. The company's services are offered primarily to government and commercial customers. **NOTE:** Search and apply for positions or submit resume online. **Positions advertised include:** Pricing Analyst; Sr. Engineer; Oracle Database Administrator; Sr. Software Engineer; Technical Recruiter; Web Designer; Client Business Manager; Program Manager. **Corporate headquarters location:** This location. **Other U.S. locations:** Nationwide. **Parent company:** AT&T Corporation. **Listed on:** New York Stock Exchange. **Stock exchange symbol:** T. **Number of employees worldwide:** 3,000.

ABOUTWEB
2106D Gallows Road, Vienna VA 22182. 703/448-5048. **Fax:** 703/448-5048. **Contact:** Human Resources. **E-mail address:** info@aboutweb.com. **World Wide Web address:** http://www.aboutweb.com. **Description:** Aboutweb offers Staff Augmentation and IT Project solution services. **NOTE:** Search and apply for positions at website. **Positions advertised include:** Internet Advertising Sales; Lead Microsoft Network Engineer; Web Developer; Financial Systems Analysts; System Engineers. **Corporate Headquarters:** Rockville MD

ACCENTURE
11951 Freedom Drive, Reston VA 20190. 703/947-2000. **Fax:** 703/947-2200 **Contact:** Human Resources. **World Wide Web address:** http://www.accenture.com. **Description:** Accenture is a management consulting, technology services, and outsourcing company. **NOTE:** Search and apply for positions online. **Positions advertised include:** Java Production Support Developer; Tech Architect Administrator; Oracle Database Administrator; Client Financial Management Specialist; BSIC Analyst; Federal Pricing Manager. **Number of employees worldwide:** 90,000.

ADVANCED LOGIC INDUSTRIES (ALI)
922 University City Boulevard, Blacksburg VA 24060. 540/552-6108. **Fax:** 540/552-6126. **Contact:** Human Resources. **E-mail address:** employment@ali-inc.com. **World Wide Web address:** http://www.ali-inc.com. **Description:** Provides consulting, software development, Internet services, product procurement, support, and training services. **Other area locations:** Forest VA; Roanoke VA; Virginia Beach VA.

ADVANCED MANAGEMENT TECHNOLOGY, INC.
1515 Wilson Boulevard, Suite 1100, Arlington VA 22209. 703/841-2684. **Fax:** 703/841-1486. **Contact:** Recruiter/Staffing Specialist. **E-Mail Address:** recruiter@amti.com. **World Wide Web address:** http://www.amti.com. **Description:** Provides information systems management, Internet/intranet development; multimedia product design and distribution, system engineering, and aviation services. Founded in 1987. **NOTE:** Entry-level positions are offered. Search and apply for positions online. **Positions advertised include:** Deputy Program manager; Sr. Business Development Manager; Sr. Programmer. **Special programs:** Training. **Office hours:** Monday - Friday, 8:30 a.m. - 5:30 p.m. **Other U.S. locations:** Los Angeles CA; Atlanta GA; Jamaica NY; Fort Worth TX. **International locations:** New Delhi, India. **Parent company:** Tetra Tech, Inc. **President/CEO:** Anita Talwar. **Number of employees at this location:** 50. **Number of employees nationwide:** 415.

ADVANCED RESOURCE TECHNOLOGIES, INC. (ARTI)
1555 King Street, Suite 400, Alexandria VA 22314. 703/682-4740. **Fax:** 703/682-4823. **Contact:** Human Resources. **E-mail address:** recruiter@team-arti.com. **World Wide Web address:** http://www.team-arti.com. **Description:** A diversified, employee-owned information services provider and systems integrator with expertise in providing information systems engineering, IT security services, network engineering services, security services and management, and program management. **NOTE:** Search and apply for positions or submit resume online. **Positions advertised include:** Document Processing Specialist; Records and Database Management Associate; Research Assistant. **Special programs:** Internships. **Other U.S. locations:** Huntsville AL; St. Louis MO; Tridelphia WV. **Listed on:** Privately held. **Number of employees nationwide:** 280.

ALPHAINSIGHT CORPORATION
3130 Fairview Park Drive, Suite 600, Falls Church VA 22042. 703/584-8100. **Fax:** 703/243-8226. **Contact:** Technical Recruiter. **E-mail address:** recruiting@alphainsight.com. **World Wide Web address:** http://www.alphainsight.com. **Description:** Provides e-strategies/web applications development, network engineering support and administration, and information security and assurance. Founded in 1989. **NOTE:** Search and apply for positions or submit resume online. Entry-level positions are offered. **Positions advertised include:** Configuration Manager; Project Manager; J2EE Developer; Principal Information Engineer; Java Software Developer; Sr. Contracts Administrator. **Corporate headquarters location:** This location. **Listed on:** Privately held. **President:** Kwang Kim.

AMERICAN SYSTEMS CORPORATION (ASC)
13990 Park East Circle, Chantilly VA 20151-2272. 703/968-6300. **Toll-free phone:** 800/733-2721. **Fax:** 703/968-5151. **Contact:** Human Resources. **E-mail address:** recruiting@2asc.com. **World Wide Web address:** http://www.2asc.com. **Description:** Provides information technology services to the Department of Defense and other government agencies, the intelligence community, and commercial clients. Core businesses include systems engineering and network integration services; enterprise-wide structured cable plant installations; training services; and outsourcing of technical and administrative services. **NOTE:** Search and apply for positions online. **Positions advertised include:** Software Engineer; Project Manager; Purchasing Manager; Accounting Operations Manager; System Administrator; Vice President. **Corporate headquarters location:** This location. **Other area locations:** Arlington VA; Norfolk VA; /Dumfries VA; Springfield VA. **Other U.S. locations:** GA; LA; MD; CT; CA; DC; RI; FL; PA; WA; SC. **Subsidiaries include:** American Communications Corporation. **Listed on:** Privately held. **Annual sales/revenues:** $175 million. **Number of employees at this location:** 250. **Number of employees nationwide:** 1,350.

ANALEX CORPORATION
2677 Prosperity Drive, Suite 400, Fairfax VA 22031. 703/852-4000. **Fax:** 703/852-2200. **Contact:** Human Resources. **E-mail address:** jobs@analex.com. **World Wide Web address:** http://www.analex.com. **Description:** Provides intelligence, systems engineering and security services in support of our nation's security. Analex focuses on developing innovative technical approaches for the intelligence community, analyzing and supporting defense systems, designing, developing and testing aerospace systems and providing a full range of security support services to the U.S. government. **NOTE:** Search and apply for positions online. **Positions advertised include:** AP Manager; Contracts Manager; Sr. AP Accountant. **Listed on:** American Stock Exchange. **Stock exchange symbol:** NLX.

ANALYSTS INTERNATIONAL
4136 Innslake Drive, Suite A, Glen Allen, VA 23060. 804/217-8490. **Toll-free phone:** 877/840-7860. **Fax:** 804/217-8493. **Contact:** Human Resources. **E-mail address:** jobs@analysts.com. **World Wide Web address:** http://www.analysts.com. **Description:** A diversified IT services company offering staffing, network infrastructure, and outsourcing services. Founded in 1966. **Positions advertised include:** Sr. Datawarehouse Developer; Business Systems Analyst; Application Architect; Project Manager. **Corporate headquarters location:** Minneapolis MN. **Other U.S. locations:** Nationwide.

ANTEON CORPORATION
44427 Airport Road, California MD 20619. 301/863-1290. **Contact:** Human Resources. **World Wide Web address:** http://www.analex.com. **Description:** A systems integration company that provides mission, operational, and IT enterprise support to the U.S. government. Anteon designs, integrates, maintains, and upgrades systems for national defense, intelligence, emergency response, infrastructure and other high-priority government missions. **Positions advertised include:** Financial Analyst; Configuration Management Specialist; Lead Software Engineer; Operations Analyst; Program Manager. **Operations at this facility**

include: Anteon's Air Warfare Systems provides interactive multimedia instructional systems. **Number of employees worldwide:** 9,500.

ANVICOM, INC.
1934 Old Gallows Road, Suite 200, Vienna VA 22182. 703/970-7300. **Fax:** 703/876-6338. **Contact:** Human Resources. **E-mail address:** jobs@anvi.com. **World Wide Web address:** http://www.anvi.com. **Description:** Provides IT engineering and support services to the U.S. Government and Department of Defense. **NOTE:** Search and apply for positions online. **Number of employees at this location:** 200.

BAE SYSTEMS ADVANCED INFORMATION TECHNOLOGIES
3811 North Fairfax Drive, Suite 500, Arlington, VA 22203. 703/524-6263. **Fax:** 703/524-6280. **Contact:** Human Resources. **World Wide Web address:** http://www.alphatech.com. **Description:** Provides information processing, software development, and systems engineering services. Founded in 1979. **NOTE:** Search and apply for positions online. **Positions advertised include:**. Computational Social Scientist; Director; Lead Engineer; Program Manager/Principal Engineer; Sr. Systems Engineer. **Other U.S. locations:** Burlington MA; San Diego CA. **Number of employees nationwide:** 250.

BAE SYSTEMS INFORMATION TECHNOLOGY
2525 Network Place, Herndon VA 20171. 703/563-7500. **Contact:** Human Resources. **World Wide Web address:** http://www.digitalnet.com. **Description:** BAE Systems Information Technology specializes in end-to-end networking computer solutions for the government and civilian agencies. **Positions advertised include:** Business Services Specialist; Sr. Secure Systems Analyst; Sr. Programmer/Analyst; Sr. Computer Systems Engineer. **NOTE:** Search and apply for positions online.

CACI INTERNATIONAL, INC.
1100 North Glebe Road, Arlington VA 22201. 703/841-7800. **Fax:** 703/961-5031. **Contact:** Human Resources. **E-mail address:** jobs@caci.com. **World Wide Web address:** http://www.caci.com. **Description:** Provides IT and network solutions including system integration, knowledge management, engineering, simulation, and information assurance for the government and international commercial customers. CACI maintains 100 offices in the U.S. and overseas. **NOTE:** Search and apply for positions online. **Positions advertised include:** Applications Support Analyst; Web Applications Developer; Strategic Planning Specialist; Portal Services Team Leader; functional Analyst Expert/Mathematician; Database Developer; Senior Portfolio Analyst; System Analyst; Software Engineer. **Corporate headquarters location:** This location. **Other area locations:** Alexandria VA; Chantilly VA; Chesapeake VA; Fairfax VA; Herndon VA; Manassas VA. **Other U.S. locations:** Nationwide. **International locations:** Worldwide. **Operations at this facility include:** Administration. **Listed on:** NASDAQ. **Stock exchange symbol:** CACI. **Number of employees worldwide:** 7,500.

CTI INC.
3951 Pender Drive, Suite 120, Fairfax VA 22030-6035. 703/383-7200. **Toll-free phone:** 800/765-7208. **Fax:** 703/352-6765. **Contact:** Carol Ismer, Human Resources Manager. **World Wide Web address:** http://www.cti.com. **Description:** Provides systems integration services and products and language translation services for the federal government and commercial healthcare markets. Founded in 1980.

THE CENTECH GROUP, INC.
4600 North Fairfax Drive, Suite 400, Arlington VA 22203. 703/525-4444. **Contact:** Personnel. **E-mail address:** recruiting@centechgroup.com. **World Wide Web address:** http://www.centechgroup.com. **Description:** Specializes in providing information technology integration services to the federal government. **NOTE:** Entry-level positions are offered. **Positions advertised include:** Sr. Training Specialist; Corporate Business Growth Executive; System Operator; Business Development Manager; Analyst. **Office hours:** Monday - Friday, 8:00 a.m. - 5:30 p.m. **Corporate headquarters location:** This location. **Other U.S. locations:** Hugo OK; Montgomery AL. **President:** Fernando V. Galaviz.

COMPUTER ASSOCIATES INTERNATIONAL, INC. (CA)
2291 Wood Oak Drive, Herndon VA 20171. 703/708-3000. **Fax:** 703/709-4580. **Contact:** Janet Nguyen, Director of Human Resources. **World Wide Web address:** http://www.ca.com. **Description:** Computer Associates International is a provider of solutions and services for the management of IT infrastructure, business information and application development. The company provides solutions for enterprise management, storage management, security management, application life cycle management, data management and application development, and portal and business intelligence. Computer Associates International serves major business, government, research, and educational organizations. Founded in 1976. **NOTE:** Search and apply for positions or submit resume online. **Positions advertised include:** Project Manager; Contracts Manager; Sr. Consultant; Architect; Sr. Software Engineer; Solution Manager. **Corporate headquarters location:** Islandia NY. **Other U.S. locations:** Nationwide. **International locations:** Worldwide. **Operations at this facility include:** Divisional Headquarters. **Listed on:** New York Stock Exchange. **Stock exchange symbol:** CA. **CEO:** Sanjay Kumar. **Annual sales/revenues:** More than $3 billion. **Number of employees at this location:** 700. **Number of employees nationwide:** 5,000. Number of employees worldwide: 16,000.

COMPUTER SCIENCES CORPORATION (CSC)
3170 Fairview Park Drive, Falls Church VA 22042. 703/876-1000. **Fax:** 703/876-1376. **Contact:** Human Resources. **World Wide Web address:** http://www.csc.com. **Description:** CSC is a leading IT Consulting and outsourcing firm providing: application outsourcing; business process outsourcing, credit services, customer relationship management, enterprise application integration, enterprise solutions, hosting services, IT infrastructure outsourcing, knowledge management, legal solutions, management consulting, research services, risk management and claims, security, and supply chain management. **NOTE:** Search and apply for positions online. **Positions advertised include:** Financial Analyst; Business Developer; System Analyst; Strategic Management Specialist. **Corporate headquarters location:** El Segundo CA. **International locations:** Worldwide. **Listed on:** New York Stock Exchange. **Stock exchange symbol:** CSC. **Number of employees nationwide:** 20,000. Number of employees worldwide: 90,000.

CYBERNETICS
111 Cybernetics Way, Yorktown VA 23693. 757/833-9100. **Contact:** Human Resources. **E-mail address:** careers@cybernetics.com. **World Wide Web address:** http://www.cybernetics.com. **Description:** Designs, manufactures, markets, and services disk and tape storage solutions. Founded in 1978.

DSD LABORATORIES, INC.
INFORMATION TECHNOLOGY SOLUTIONS GROUP
3959 Pender Drive, Suite 305, Fairfax VA 22030. 703/385-5298. **Fax:** 703/385-5299. **Contact:** Human Resources. **World Wide Web address:** http://www.dsditsg.com. **Description:** Provides leading-edge technical services including web-based applications development, and a full-range of network services, to a wide range of customers, both locally and nationally. **Corporate headquarters location:** Sudbury MA. **Other area locations:** Hampton VA; Reston VA.

DATALINE, INC.
2551 Eltham Ave, Suite O, Norfolk VA 23513. 757/858-0600. **Toll-free phone:** 800/666-9858. **Fax:** 757/858-0606. **Contact:** Human Resources. **World Wide Web address:** http://www.dataline.com. **Description:** Dataline is an information technology systems integrator that specializes in delivering customized IT solutions for customers in the commercial and government sectors. Founded in 1990. **Positions advertised include:** Director, Proposal Development; Document Development Specialist; Electronics Technician; Java Developer; Logistics Manager. **Corporate headquarters location:** This location. **Other area locations:** Richmond VA; McLean VA. **Other U.S. locations;** Atlanta GA; Charleston SC; San Diego CA; Tampa FL; Gaithersburg, MD. **Number of employees nationwide:** 360.

DATALUX CORPORATION
155 Aviation Drive, Winchester VA 22602. 540/662-1500. **Toll-free phone:** 800/328-2589. **Contact:** Human Resources. **E-mail address:** info@datalux.com. **World Wide Web address:** http://www.datalux.com. **Description:** A manufacturer of computer products for use in environments that require durable and compact designs. **Corporate headquarters location:** This location. Other U.S. locations: GA; IL; CA.

DATATEL INC.
4375 Fair Lakes Court, Fairfax VA 22033. 703/968-9000. **Contact:** Human Resources. **E-mail address:** datatel@rpc.webhire.com. **World Wide Web address:** http://www.datatel.com. **Description:** Develops and markets software applications for higher education. Founded in 1968. **NOTE:** Internships available. Search and apply for positions online. **Positions advertised include:** Business Practices Manager; Documentation Specialist; Human Resources Solutions Consultant; Instructional Designer/Developer; Financial Aid Consultant; Fundraising Consultant. **Corporate headquarters location:** This location. **Other U.S. locations:** San Francisco CA; Buffalo NY. **Number of employees nationwide:** 470.

DELEX SYSTEMS INC.
1953 Gallows Road, Suite 700, Vienna VA 22182. 703/734-8300. **Fax:** 703/893-5338. **Contact:** Human Resources. **E-mail address:** hr@delex.com. **World Wide Web address:** http://www.delex.com. **Description:** Provides information technology, program management, modeling and simulation, research and analysis, and training solutions for domestic and international customers. Founded in 1968. **Positions advertised include:** A/P Accountant; EP-3E/Naval Flight Officer. **Corporate headquarters location:** This location. **Other area locations:** California MD. **Other U.S. locations:** CA; OK; WA. **Listed on:** Privately held. **Number of employees at this location:** 140. **Number of employees nationwide:** 250.

DELTEK SYSTEMS INC.
13880 Dulles Corner Lane, Herndon VA 20171. 703/734-8606. **Toll-free phone:** 800/456-2009. **Fax:** 703/734-1146. **Contact:** Human Resources. **E-mail address:** jobs@deltek.com. **World Wide Web address:** http://www.deltek.com. **Description:** Designs, develops, and supports advanced enterprise-level software for project-oriented companies. Deltek focuses on the architecture/engineering/construction, IT/systems integration, professional services and government contracting markets. Services include implementation consulting, training, software maintenance, and support. Founded in 1983. **NOTE:** Search and apply for positions online. **Positions advertised include:** Accounting Software Support Analyst; BPM System Consultant; Business Intelligence Instructor; Director, Information Technology: Project Manager; Quality Assurance Analyst. **Corporate headquarters location:** This location. **Other U.S. locations:** Portland OR; St. Petersburg FL; Cambridge MA. **International locations:** Philippines; United Kingdom. **Listed on:** Privately owned. **Number of employees at this worldwide:** 650.

DYNAMICS RESEARCH CORPORATION
MetroPlace 1 Building, Suite 400, 2650 Park Tower Drive, Vienna VA 22180. 571/226-8600. **Contact:** Human Resources. **World Wide Web address:** http://www.drc.com. **Description:** A provider of high technology products and services to a marketplace of various sized commercial enterprises and federal, state, and local government. Founded in 1955. **Positions advertised include:** Director of Information Assurance; Contracts Administrator; Staff Software Testing Analyst; Database Engineer. **Corporate headquarters location:** Andover MA.

EDO PROFESSIONAL SERVICES
2800 Shirlington Road, Suite 1200, Arlington VA 22206. 703/824-5000. **Fax:** 703/824-5023. **Contact:** Human Resources. **E-mail address:** opportunities@edocorp.com. **World Wide Web address:** http://www.edo-services.com. **Description**: EDO's Professional Services is a provider of advanced technology solutions, training and performance aids, acquisition logistics, strategic business solutions, warfare experimentation and analysis and engineering services. **NOTE:** Search and apply for positions online. **Positions advertised include:** Accounts Receivable Specialist; Sr. Accountant; Program Manager. **Corporate headquarters location:** New York NY. **Other U.S. locations:** CA; MD; MA; UT; PA; NJ; LA; FL; GA; NC RI; NE; TX; VT. **Parent company:** EDO Corporation.

EDS (ELECTRONIC DATA SYSTEMS CORPORATION)
13600 EDS Drive, Herndon VA 20171. 703/742-2000. **Fax:** 703/742-2439. **Contact:** Staffing Department. **E-mail address:** careers@eds.com. **World Wide Web address:** http://www.eds.com. **Description:** EDS provides a portfolio of business and technology solutions to help its clients improve their business performance. EDS' core portfolio comprises information-technology, applications and business process services, as well as information-technology transformation services. Founded in 1962. **NOTE:** Search and apply for positions online. **Positions advertised include:** Consultant Architect; Contract Specialist; Telecommunications Analyst; Financial Analyst; Technical Delivery Team Manager; Senior Systems Engineer. **Corporate headquarters location:** Plano TX. **Other U.S. locations:** Nationwide. **International locations:** Worldwide. **Listed on:** New York Stock Exchange. **Stock exchange symbol:** EDS. **Number of employees nationwide:** 64,000. **Number of employees worldwide:** 130,000.

EMC CORPORATION
8444 Westpark Drive, Suite 700, McLean VA 22102. 703/970-5818. **Fax:** 703/893-2562. **Contact:** Human Resources. **E-mail address:** resumes@emc.com. **World Wide Web address:** http://www.emc.com. **Description:** EMC designs, manufactures, markets, and supports high-performance data storage and management products to industry and government customers. **NOTE:** Search and apply for positions online. **Positions advertised include:** Client Solutions Lead; HR Operations Manager; Account Technology Consultant; Sr. Customer Engineer. **Corporate headquarters location:** Hopkinton MA. **Listed on:** New York Stock Exchange. **Stock exchange symbol:** EMC.

EMCOR FACILITIES SERVICES INC.
320 23rd Street S, Arlington VA 22202. 888/467-2756. **Contact:** Human Resources. **World Wide Web address:** http://www.emcorgroup.com. **Description:** Provides operation, maintenance, and support services to building management systems. **NOTE:** Search and apply for positions online. **Positions advertised include**: Production Specialist/Coordinator; Proposal Manager/Writer; Program Development Manager; Proposal Production Manager. **Parent company:**

EMCOR Group Inc. **Listed on:** New York Stock Exchange. **Stock exchange symbol:** EME.

EPLUS, INC.
13595 Dulles Technology Drive, Herndon VA 20171-3413. 703/984-8400. **Toll-free phone:** 888/482-1122. **Fax:** 703/984-8600. **Contact:** Human Resources. **E-mail address:** resumes@eplus.com. **World Wide Web address:** http://www.eplus.com. **Description:** Provides enterprise cost management solutions. EPlus offer expertise in financial services, e-procurement, content management, supplier enablement, document imaging and collaboration and asset management. Founded in 1990. **Positions advertised include:** Director of Telesales; Inventory Associate; Sr. Contracts Specialist. **Corporate headquarters location:** This location. **Other U.S. locations**: CA; CT; FL; GA; IL; MD; MA; MI; NJ; NY; NC; PA; TX; UT. **Listed on:** NASDAQ. **Stock exchange symbol:** PLUS.

GENERAL DYNAMICS ADVANCED INFORMATION SYSTEMS
1421 Jefferson Davis Highway, Suite 600, Arlington VA 22202. 703/271-7300. **Fax:** 703/271-7301. **Contact:** Human Resources. **E-mail address:** careers.info@veridian.com. **World Wide Web address:** http://www.veridian.com. **Description:** A provider of information-based systems, integrated solutions and services with core capabilities in network security and enterprise protection; intelligence, surveillance and reconnaissance; knowledge discovery and decision support; chemical, biological and nuclear detection; network and enterprise management; and systems engineering services. **Positions advertised include:** Director, Strategic Intelligence and Planning. **Number of employees worldwide:** 7,000.

GOVERNMENT TECHNOLOGY SERVICES, INC. (GTSI)
3901 Stonecroft Boulevard, Chantilly VA 20151-1010. 703/502-2000. **Fax:** 703/222-5240. **Toll-free phone:** 800/999-4874. **Contact:** Human Resources. **E-mail address:** careers@gtsi.com. **World Wide Web address:** http://www.gtsi.com. **Description:** Provides IT solutions to government customers in such areas as high performance computing, advanced networking, mobile and wireless, web portals, high availability storage, and information assurance. Founded in 1983. **NOTE:** Search and apply for positions online. **Positions advertised include:** Product Manager; Business Analyst; Manager, Supply Chain Applications; Accounting Manager; Sales Engineer; Director, Network Services. **Special programs:** Internships. **Corporate headquarters location:** This location. **Operations at this facility include:** Administration; Sales; Service. **Listed on:** NASDAQ. **Stock exchange symbol:** GTSI. **Annual sales/revenues:** More than $100 million. **Number of employees at this location:** 400.

HALIFAX CORPORATION
5250 Cherokee Avenue, Alexandria VA 22312. 703/750-2202. **Fax:** 703/658-2444. **Contact:** Human Resources. **E-mail address:** drandles@hxcorp.com. **World Wide Web address:** http://www.hxcorp.com. **Description:** Performs a variety of computer-related services such as systems integration, consulting, computer maintenance and repair, facilities management, and outsourcing. Founded in 1967. **Corporate headquarters location:** This location. **Other U.S. locations:** Nationwide. **Operations at this facility include:** Administration; Sales; Service. **Listed on:** American Stock Exchange. **Stock exchange symbol:** HX. **Annual sales/revenues:** $51 - $100 million. **Number of employees at this location:** 70. **Number of employees nationwide:** 680.

HARRIS TECHNICAL SERVICES CORPORATION
7799 Leesburg Pike, Suite 700 North, Falls Church VA 22043-2499. 703/610-4200. **Fax:** 703/610-4230. **Contact:** Human Resources. **World Wide Web address:** http://www.harris.com. **Description:** Develops information systems under government contracts and for private industry. **NOTE:** Search and apply for positions online. **Positions advertised include:** Rational Administrator; Sr. Security Manager; Sr. Project Engineer; Test Engineer; Systems Engineer; Program Financial Analyst; Systems Analyst; Business Development Manager; Technical Writer/Documentation Specialist.

HITACHI DATA SYSTEMS
951 East Byrd Street, Suite 950, Riverfront Plaza, Richmond VA 23219-4075. 804/644-7200. **Fax:** 804/643-1254. **Contact:** Human Resources. **World Wide Web address:** http://www.hds.com. **Description:** Provides data storage solutions in government and private sectors. **NOTE:** Search and apply for positions or submit resume online. **Positions available include:** District Operations Manager; Federal Investment Rep. **Corporate headquarters location:** Santa Clara CA. **Other area locations:** Reston VA. **Other U.S. locations:** Nationwide. **International locations:** Worldwide. **Parent company:** Hitachi, Ltd. **Operations at this facility include:** This location serves as a sales and marketing office. **Number of employees worldwide:** 2,700.

IPC TECHNOLOGIES, INC.
7200 Glen Forest Drive, Richmond VA 23226. 804/285-9300. **Fax:** 804/285-4492. **Contact:** Human Resources. **World Wide Web address:** http://www.ipctech.com. **Description:** Provides computer-consulting services. The company specializes in GUI application and database design. **NOTE:** Search and apply for positions online. **Positions advertised include:** Scientific Engineer; Designer; Mechanical Engineer/Designer; Telephony Systems Engineer; Developer. **Corporate headquarters location:** This location.

ITC LEARNING CORPORATION
1616 Anderson Road, Suite 109, McLean VA 22102. 703/442-0670. **Toll-free phone:** 800/638-3757. **Fax:** 703/852-7174. **Contact:** Personnel. **E-mail address:** learning@itclearning.com. **World Wide Web address:** http://www.itclearning.com. **Description:** A full-service training company specializing in the development, production, marketing, and sale of both off-the-shelf and custom-designed multimedia training courseware for commercial, educational, and government organizations. The company also markets, sells, and distributes linear training products (primarily videotape and text-based) through its Training Department. Founded in 1977. **Corporate headquarters location:** This location. **Other U.S. locations:** Atlanta GA. **International locations:** Australia; United Kingdom. **Subsidiaries include:** CI Acquisition Corporation. **Annual sales/revenues:** $21 - $50 million. **Number of employees at this location:** 45. **Number of employees nationwide:** 100.

INFORMATION ANALYSIS INC.
11240 Waples Mill Road, Suite 201, Fairfax VA 22030. 703/383-3000. **Fax:** 703/293-7979. **Contact:** Kathy Hommas, Personnel Director. **World Wide Web address:** http://www.infoa.com. **Description:** IAI provides a full range of IT services specializing in e-business solutions, enterprise portals, system migration and modernization, and enterprise application integration. Founded in 1979. **NOTE:** Search and apply for jobs or submit resume online. **Positions advertised include:** Oracle Developer; Java Developer; Forms Technician. **Corporate headquarters location:** This location.

INFORMATION 1ST, INC.
11710 Plaza America Drive, Suite 1200, Reston VA 20190. 703/691-2480. **Fax:** 703/691-4649. **Contact:** Human Resources. **E-mail address:** recruiting@information1st.com. **World Wide Web address:** http://www.information1st.com. **Description:** Develops scalable web-based solutions that enable organizations to effectively capture, track, and manage issues throughout their lifecycle. Their solutions for information management initiatives include knowledge management, document management, workflow

processing, and records management. **Parent company:** STG, Inc.

INFORMATION MANAGEMENT CONSULTANTS, INC. (IMC)
11480 Commerce Park Drive, Reston VA 20191. 703/871-8700. **Fax:** 703/871-8900. **Contact:** Human Resources. **World Wide Web address:** http://www.imc.com. **Description:** Provides a wide range of information systems planning, development, and implementation services to public and private sector clients in the United States and abroad. Services include image and document management, knowledge management, workflow automation, data warehousing, information navigation and retrieval, web-based applications, and Internet-enabled distribution of public information. Founded in 1981. **NOTE:** Entry-level positions are offered. **Positions advertised include:** Business Analyst; Document Specialist; Systems Administrator; Recruiter; Sr. Software Developer. **Special programs:** Training. **Subsidiaries:** KEVRIC; Intrinsic Management Consultants. **Operations at this facility include:** Administration; Regional Headquarters; Sales. **Listed on:** Privately held. **Annual sales/revenues:** $21 - $50 million. **Number of employees at this location:** 300.

INTEGIC CORPORATION
14585 Avion Parkway, Chantilly VA 20151. 703/222-2840. **Contact:** Human Resources. **World Wide Web address:** http://www.integic.com. **E-mail address:** careers@integic.com. **Description:** Targeting the health care and life sciences industries as well as government agencies, Integic develops enterprise application integration software and provides e-business systems integration services for connecting legacy computer systems and applications to the Internet and other networks. **Positions advertised include:** Technical Project Manager; Sr. Network Engineer. **Other U.S. locations:** CA; MD; MA; NJ; NY; NC; OH; PA. **Parent company:** Northrop Grumman Corporation.

INTEGRATED SYSTEMS ANALYSTS, INC.
2001 North Beauregard Street, Suite 600, Alexandria VA 22311. 703/578-2586. **Fax:** 313/317-5009. **Contact:** Human Resources. **World Wide Web address:** http://www.isa.com. **Description:** Provides systems engineering and computer systems support to government agencies and commercial clients. Founded in 1980. **NOTE:** Search and apply for positions online. **Other U.S. locations:** Detroit MI; Dallas TX; San Diego CA. **Number of employees nationwide:** 600.

JC COMPUTER SERVICES, INC.
4705 Eisenhower Avenue, Alexandria VA 22304. 703/461-0860. **Fax:** 703/370-4017. **Contact:** Dianne Lamb, Vice President of Administration. **E-mail address:** info@jccs.com. **World Wide Web address:** http://www.jccs.com. **Description:** Provides network support, software development, management consulting, training, and other IT related services. Founded in 1985. **NOTE:** Entry-level positions are offered. **Corporate headquarters location:** This location. **Listed on:** Privately held. **Number of employees at this location:** 50.

L-3 COMMUNICATIONS TITAN
11955 Freedom Drive, Reston VA 20190. 703/434-4000. **Contact:** Human Resources. **World Wide Web address:** http://www.titan.com. **Description:** An information technology company providing networking services, systems integration, and systems engineering to the government and other customers. **NOTE:** Search and apply for positions online. **Positions advertised include:** Accounts Payable Specialist; Analyst; Contracts Manager; Director, Business Development; Intelligence Analyst; Sr. Software Engineer; Recruiter. **Corporate headquarters location:** New York NY **Other U.S. locations:** Nationwide. **Listed on:** New York Stock Exchange. **Stock exchange symbol:** LLL.

MKS INC.
12701 Fair Lakes Circle, Suite 350, Fairfax VA 22033. 703/803-3343. **Fax:** 703/803-3344. **Contact:** Human Resources. **World Wide Web address:** http://www.mks.com. **Description:** Provides enterprise software configuration management products to enable companies to better manage and control the process of software development. Founded in 1984. **Corporate headquarters location:** Waterloo, Canada. Other U.S. locations: Lombard IL; Burlington MA.

THE MITRE CORPORATION
7515 Colshire Drive, McLean VA 22102-7539. 703/983-6000. **Contact:** Human Resources. **World Wide Web address:** http://www.mitre.org. **Description:** A not-for-profit organization chartered to work in the public interest, with expertise in systems engineering, information technology, operational concepts, and enterprise modernization. **Positions advertised include:** Business Reporting Manager; Ops Research Analyst; Human Resources Generalist; Systems Engineer; Counterterrorism Intelligence Analyst; Principal Infrastructure Engineer; Data Engineer; Systems Engineer; Information Systems Assurance; Chief Health Sector Engineer. **Corporate headquarters location:** Bedford MA. **Number of employees worldwide:** 5,700.

MODIS
2809 Emerywood Parkway, Suite 380, Richmond VA 23294. 804/672-7558. **Fax:** 804/672-1386. **Contact:** Human Resources. **E-mail address:** resume@modisit.com. **World Wide Web address:** http://www.modisit.com. **Description:** Provides information technology resource management in the areas of staff augmentation, direct placement, and project management. **NOTE:** Search and apply for positions online. **Positions advertised include:** Windows Systems Administrator; Program Manager; Tech Writer; Project Management Office Director; Decision Support Analyst; SAP Configuration Analyst; Computer Operator. **Corporate headquarters location:** Jacksonville FL. **Other U.S. locations:** Nationwide. **Parent company:** MPS Group, Inc.

NCI INFORMATION SYSTEMS, INC.
11730 Plaza America Drive, Reston VA 20190. 703/707-6900. **Toll-free phone:** 888/409-5457. **Fax:** 703/707-6901. **Contact:** Human Resources. **E-mail address:** contactus@nciinc.com. **World Wide Web address:** http://www.nciinc.com. **Description:** Provides both government agencies and commercial clients with IT solutions and services. NCI Information Systems is comprised of six business units: Enterprise Management and Support; Systems Development and Integration; Systems Engineering; Risk Management; Electronic Data Management; and Facilities Management. Founded in 1986. **NOTE:** Search and apply for positions online. **Positions advertised include:** Capture Manager; Operations Director; Financial Reporting Manager; Principal Contracts Administrator. **Corporate headquarters location:** This location. Other U.S. locations: AL; AZ; CO; MI; NJ; GA; IL; MD; OH; TN.

NEC AMERICA INC.
14040 Park Center Road, Herndon VA 22071. 703/834-4000. **Fax:** 703/437-7178. **Contact:** Human Resources. **E-mail address:** resumes@hn.va.nec.com. **World Wide Web address:** http://www.nec.com. **Description:** Provides solutions for broadband networking and mobile Internet with focus on IT-network integrated solutions and semiconductors. **NOTE:** Search and apply for positions online. **Positions advertised include:** Product Manager; Sr. Software Developer; Sr. Planning Analyst; Project Administrator. **Operations at this facility include:** Headquarters for the Optical Network Systems Division, which oversees the development, sales, installation, and service of optical telecommunications products.

NORTEL GOVERNMENT SOLUTIONS
12730 Fair Lakes Circle, Fairfax VA 22033. 703/679-4900. **Fax:** 703/679-4901. **Contact:** Tricia Giannetta, Recruiting Coordinator. **World Wide Web address:**

http://www.nortelgov.com. **Description:** A professional services firm that helps Government clients use information technology to improve mission performance. The company provides customized solutions for Homeland Security, criminal justice and intelligence, defense, and civilian agencies within the Federal Government and first responders and other components at state and local levels. **NOTE:** Search and apply for positions online. **Positions advertised include:** Contracts Specialist; Database Developer; Electro-Mechanical Engineer; J2EE Software Engineer; Lotus Notes Developer; Implementation Manager.

NORTHROP GRUMMAN INFORMATION TECHNOLOGY
7575 Colshire Drive, McLean VA 22102. 703/713-4000. **Contact:** Human Resources. **World Wide Web address:** http://www.northropgrumman.com. **Description**: A provider of IT, systems engineering, and systems integration for the Department of Defense, national intelligence, federal civilian and state/local agencies and commercial customers, with solutions that support simulation and training, information assurance, combat systems, software engineering, weather systems, military intelligence, enterprise systems, secure communications, and space systems. **NOTE:** Search and apply for positions online. **Positions advertised include:** Multimedia Design Engineer; Information Assurance Engineer; Systems Engineer; Network Engineer. **Corporate headquarters location:** Los Angeles CA. **Parent company:** Northrop Grumman Corporation manufactures military aircraft, commercial aircraft parts, radar equipment, and electronic systems. Northrop Grumman has developed the B-2 Stealth Bomber, as well as parts for the F/A-18 and the Boeing 747. Other operations include computer systems development for management and scientific applications. **Listed on:** New York Stock Exchange. **Stock exchange symbol:** NOC. **Number of employees worldwide:** 22,500.

ORACLE CORPORATION
1900 Oracle Way, Reston VA 20190-4735. 703/478-9000. **Fax:** 703/318-6340. **Contact:** Clancy Bucy, Human Resources. **World Wide Web address:** http://www.oracle.com. **Description:** Designs and manufactures database and information management software for businesses and provides consulting services. **Special programs:** Training. **NOTE:** Search and apply for positions online. **Corporate headquarters location:** Redwood Shores CA. **Other area locations:** Chesapeake VA; Richmond VA. **Other U.S. locations:** Nationwide. **Listed on:** NASDAQ. **Stock exchange symbol:** ORCL.

PSI INTERNATIONAL, INC.
10306 Eaton Place, Suite 400, Fairfax VA 22030. 703/352-8700. **Fax:** 703/352-8236. **Contact:** Human Resources Representative. **E-mail address:** jobs@psiint.com. **World Wide Web address:** http://www.psiint.com. **Description:** Provides information technology solutions to government and private sectors, focusing on scientific, pharmaceutical, biotech and regulatory industries worldwide. The company specializes in integrating information technology services with subject matter expertise in health and social sciences. Founded in 1977. **Positions advertised include:** Business Development Manager; Program Director; Technical Writer. **Corporate headquarters location:** This location. **Listed on:** Privately held. **Number of employees at this location:** 25. **Number of employees nationwide:** 175.

PRAGMATICS, INC.
7926 Jones Branch Drive, Suite 711, McLean VA 22102. 703/761-4033. **Fax:** 703/761-4089. **Contact:** Corporate Recruiter. **E-mail address:** Recruiter@pragmatics.com. **World Wide Web address:** http://www.pragmatics.com. **Description:** Offers services in software and system engineering, information assurance, and program management acquisition and consulting. Founded in 1985. **NOTE:** Search and apply for positions online. Most positions require an active security clearance. **Positions advertised include:** Oracle DBA/Developer; Security Engineer; Sr. Functional Analyst; Enterprise Data Architect; Program Manager; Sr. System Architect; Director Business Development.

QUADRAMED
12110 Sunset Hills Road, Suite 600, Reston VA 20190-3224. 703/709-2300. **Toll-free phone:** 800/393-0278. **Fax:** 703/371-1700. **Contact:** Personnel. **E-mail address:** resume@quadramed.com. **World Wide Web address:** http://www.quadramed.com. **Description:** Develops and markets specialized decision support software designed to improve the organizational and clinical effectiveness of hospitals, academic medical centers, managed care providers, large physician groups, and other health care providers. **NOTE:** Search and apply for positions online. **Positions advertised include:** Accountant; Inside Sales Associate. **Corporate headquarters location:** This location. **Listed on:** NASDAQ. **Stock exchange symbol:** QMDC.

STG, INC.
11710 Plaza America Drive, Suite 1200, Reston VA 20190. 703/691-2480. **Fax:** 703/691-3467. **Contact:** Recruiting. **E-mail address:** recruiting@stginc.com. **World Wide Web address:** http://www.stginc.com. **Description:** A full-service information technology, engineering, and scientific services firm. STG provides high-tech consulting services to the federal government and commercial sector. Founded in 1986. **NOTE:** Search and apply for positions online. **Positions advertised include:** Linguists; Director, Info Assurance; Benefits Administrator. **Special programs:** Training. **Corporate headquarters location:** This location. **Other U.S. locations:** MD; PA; CO. **Subsidiaries include:** Information 1st; DSTI. **Listed on:** Privately held. **Annual sales/revenues:** $11 - $20 million. **Number of employees worldwide:** 1,700.

SCIENCE APPLICATIONS INTERNATIONAL CORPORATION (SAIC)
1710 SAIC Drive, P.O. Box 1303, McLean VA 22102. 703/821-4300. **Contact:** Human Resources. **World Wide Web address:** http://www.saic.com. **Description:** A research and engineering firm offering information technology, systems integration and eSolutions to commercial and government customers in the areas of national and homeland security, energy, the environment, space, telecommunications, health care, and logistics. Founded in 1969. **NOTE:** Internships offered. Search and apply for positions online. **Positions advertised include:** Business Development Manager; Senior Contract Representative; Pricing Analyst; Policy Analyst; Business and Information Analyst; Military Historian; Intelligence Analyst; Senior Engineer/Scientist; Senior Systems Engineer; Project Control Analyst; Project Administrator; Enterprise Architect; Application Developer; Systems Engineer; NCI Biophotographer; Subcontracts Administrator. **Corporate headquarters location:** San Diego CA. **Other U.S. locations:** Nationwide. **Number of employees worldwide:** 43,000.

SETA CORPORATION
6862 Elm Street, 6th Floor, McLean VA 22101-3833. 703/821-8178. **Fax:** 703/821-8274. **Contact:** Human Resources Director. **E-mail address:** resume@seta.com. **World Wide Web address:** http://www.seta.com. **Description:** A government contractor providing information technology services primarily in the area of systems engineering support of telecommunication networks essential to national defense, homeland security, and benefits programs. **NOTE:** Search and apply for positions online. **Positions advertised include:** Sr. Java Software Developer; QoS MPLS Network Engineer; Systems Administrator, UNIX/Win2000. **Other area locations:** Norfolk VA; Baltimore MD. **Other U.S. locations:** CA; WA; MO; IL; OH; AL; NY; PA; HI.

SENET INTERNATIONAL CORPORATION
3040 Williams Drive, Suite 510 Fairfax VA 22031. 703/206-9383. **Fax:** 703/206-9666. **Contact:** Human

Resources. **E-mail address:** careers@senet-int.com. **World Wide Web address:** http://www.senet-int.com. **Description:** An Information and network e-security consulting firm. **Positions advertised include:** Security Engineer; Information Security Analyst; Network Engineer; Server Engineer; Network Security Specialist.

SIGNAL CORPORATION
3040 Williams Drive, Suite 200, Fairfax VA 22031. 703/205-0500. **Fax:** 703/560-0463. **Contact:** Human Resources. **World Wide Web address:** http://www.signalcorp.com. **Description**: Provides information technology and engineering & management products and services to industry and Government. Signal Solutions' information technology services include design, installation, and administration of LAN/WANs; help desk services; software development; system design and engineering; facility operations; and system and database administration. Engineering & management services consist of system, hardware and software engineering; in-service engineering; acquisition management; logistics planning and engineering; training; technical and financial planning; and administrative support. **NOTE:** Search and apply for positions online. **Positions advertised include:** Accounts Payable Supervisor; Transit Safety and Security Analyst; Sr. Director of Business Development; Project Manager; Sr. Systems Analyst. **Other area locations:** Arlington VA; Alexandria VA; Norfolk VA. **Parent company:** General Dynamics.

STANDARD TECHNOLOGY INC.
5109 Leesburg Pike, Suite 208, Falls Church VA 22041. 703/933-3183. **Contact:** Human Resources. **World Wide Web address:** http://www.stic2.com. **Description:** Provides information technology solutions, engineering, and technical support to various businesses. Founded in 1985.

STEEL CLOUD
14040 Park Center Road, Suite 210, Herndon VA 20171. 703/674-5500. **Fax:** 703/674-5506. **Contact:** Human Resources. **E-mail address:** jobs@steelcloud.com. **World Wide Web address:** http://www.steelcloud.com. **Description:** Steel Cloud provides custom-configured computer systems and professional services to government and commercial customers. **Positions advertised include:** Account executive; Business Development Manager; Appliance Server Product Manager; Network Engineer. **Listed on:** NASDAQ. **Exchange symbol:** SCLD.

SYSTEMS RESEARCH & APPLICATION (SRA)
4300 Fair Lakes Court, Fairfax VA 22033. 703/803-1500. **Fax:** 703/803-1509. **Contact:** Human Resources. **World Wide Web address:** http://www.sra.com. **Description:** SRA provides information technology services and solutions, including strategic consulting, systems design, development and integration, and outsourcing and operations management, to clients in national security, civil government, and health care and public health. **NOTE:** Search and apply for positions online. **Positions advertised include:** Sr. Web Engineer; Systems Engineer; Technical Recruiter. **Listed on:** New York Stock Exchange. **Stock exchange symbol:** SRX.

TELOS CORPORATION
19886 Ashburn Road, Ashburn VA 20147-2358. 703/724-3800. **Toll-free phone: 800/444-9628. Fax:** 703/724-3860. **Contact:** Human Resources. **World Wide Web address:** http://www.telos.com. **Description**: Provides solutions in the areas of information assurance, secure wireless networking, secure message handling, secure local area networks ("LAN") data integration, and enterprise risk management. Founded in 1968. **NOTE:** Search and apply for positions online. **Positions advertised include:** AMHS Engineer; Assistant Program Manager; Contract Recruiter; Deputy director Security Programs; Logistics Manager; Network Administrator; Security Analyst; Technical Program Manager; Wireless LAN Sustainment Engineer. **Corporate headquarters location:** This location. **Subsidiaries include:** Xacta. **Operations at this facility include:** Administration; Manufacturing; Research and Development; Sales; Service. **Number of employees at this location:** 280. **Number of employees nationwide:** 345.

TREEV
13454 Sunrise Valley Dr., Fourth Floor, Herndon VA 20171. 703/478-2260. **Toll-free phone:** 800/254-0994. **Fax:** 703/481-6920. **Contact:** Human Resources. **E-mail address:** jobs@treev.com. **World Wide Web address:** http://www.treev.com. **Description:** TREEV provides software solutions and consulting services that enable financial institutions to transform paper-intensive operations into more efficient digital and automated processes. Founded in 1986. **NOTE:** Search and apply for positions online. **Positions advertised include:** Software Quality Assurance Analyst. **Parent company:** Metavante Corporation.

UNISYS CORPORATION
11720 Plaza America Drive, Tower III, Reston VA 20190. 703/439-5000. **Fax:** 703/439-5172. **Contact:** Human Resources. **World Wide Web address:** http://www.unisys.com. **Description:** Provides technology services and solutions in consulting, systems integration, outsourcing, infrastructure, and server technology. **NOTE:** Search and apply for positions online. **Positions advertised include:** Sr. Proposal Manager; Program Controller; Project Controller Consultant; Engagement Manager; Director, Marketing Communications; Architect; Financial Analyst; Enterprise Architect. **Corporate headquarters location:** Blue Bell PA. **Other U.S. locations:** Nationwide. **Operations at this facility include:** This location offers various computer services to the federal government. **Listed on:** New York Stock Exchange. **Stock exchange symbol:** UIS. **Number of employees worldwide:** 37,000.

UNIVERSAL SYSTEMS & TECHNOLOGY, INC. (UNITECH)
5870 Trinity Parkway, 4th Floor, Centreville VA 20120. 703/502-9600. **Fax:** 703/502-9300. **Contact:** Staffing. **E-mail address:** careers@unitech1.com. **World Wide Web address:** http://www.unitech1.com. **Description:** A professional services and solutions company concentrating in the areas of training and simulation, government and aviation solutions, sustaining operations, and homeland security for federal, state and local, and commercial customers. **NOTE:** Search and apply for positions online. **Positions advertised include:** Business Development Account Manager; Instructional Systems Designer. **Special programs:** Internships; Training. **Corporate headquarters location:** This location. **Other U.S. locations:** FL; NM; IA; SC; OK; DC. **Operations at this facility include:** Regional Headquarters. **Annual sales/revenues:** $21 - $50 million.

Washington

ADOBE SYSTEMS, INC.
801 North 34th Street, Seattle WA 98103. 206/675-7000. **Contact:** Personnel Department. **World Wide Web address:** http://www.adobe.com. **Description:** Adobe Systems develops, markets, and supports computer software products and technologies for Macintosh, Windows, and OS/2 platforms that enable users to create, display, print, and communicate electronic documents. The company distributes its products through a network of original equipment manufacturer customers, distributors and dealers, and value-added resellers and system integrators. The company has operations in the Americas, Europe, and the Pacific Rim. **Corporate headquarters location:** San Jose CA. **Operations at this facility include:** This location develops several of the company's software products and provides sales and support services. **Listed on:** NASDAQ. **Stock exchange symbol:** ADBE.

ADVANCED BUSINESSLINK CORPORATION
5808 Lake Washington Boulevard NE, Suite 100,

Kirkland WA 98033. 425/602-4777. **Contact:** Human Resources. **E-mail address:** jobs@businesslink.com. **World Wide Web address:** http://www.businesslink.com. **Description:** Develops web-to-host and remote access software for IBM AS/400 servers. **Positions advertised include:** Account Executive; Outside Sales Representative; Marketing Director; Media Relations Manager. **Corporate headquarters location:** San Jose CA.

ADVANCED DIGITAL INFORMATION CORPORATION
11431 Willows Road NE, Redmond WA 98052. 425/881-8004. **Toll-free phone:** 800/336-1233. **Fax:** 425/881-2296. **Contact:** Human Resources. **E-mail address:** jobs@adic.com. **World Wide Web address:** http://www.adic.com. **Description:** Designs, manufactures, and markets hardware and software products for data storage and protection. Founded in 1983. **Positions advertised include:** Mechanical Engineer; Product Test Engineer. **Corporate headquarters location:** This location. **Parent company:** Lockheed Martin Corporation. **Listed on:** NASDAQ. **Stock exchange symbol:** ADIC. **Annual sales/revenues:** $51 - $100 million.

AJILON CONSULTING
11711 SE 8th, Suite 303, Bellevue WA 98005. 425/455-1004. **Fax:** 425/455-5098. **Contact:** Human Resources. **E-mail address:** recruit.seattle@ajilon.com. **World Wide Web address:** http://www.ajilonconsulting.com. **Description:** Offers computer consulting services, project support, and end user services. **Positions advertised include:** Seibel/Genesys Architect; Senior Reports Analyst. **Other U.S. locations:** Nationwide.

ANALYSTS INTERNATIONAL CORPORATION (AIC)
10655 NE Fourth Street, Suite 800, Bellevue WA 98004-5022. 425/454-2500. **Toll-free phone:** 800/698-9411. **Contact:** Human Resources Department. **E-mail address:** jobs@analysts.com. **World Wide Web address:** http://www.analysts.com. **Description:** An international computer consulting firm. The company assists clients in developing systems in a variety of industries using different programming languages and software. Founded in 1966. **Office hours:** Monday - Friday, 8:00 a.m. - 5:00 p.m. **Corporate headquarters location:** Minneapolis MN. **Other U.S. locations:** Nationwide. **International locations:** Cambridge, England; Toronto, Canada. **Listed on:** NASDAQ. **Stock exchange symbol:** ANLY. **Annual sales/revenues:** More than $100 million. **Number of employees at this location:** 250.

ASIX
10900 NE Eighth Avenue, Suite 700, Bellevue WA 98004. 425/635-0709. **Toll-free phone:** 800/335-2525. **Contact:** Personnel. **E-mail address:** resumes@asix.com. **World Wide Web address:** http://www.asix.com. **Description:** Provides computer consulting services.

ATTACHMATE CORPORATION
1500 Dexter Avenue North, Seattle WA 98109. 425/644-4010. **Toll-free phone:** 800/426-6283. **Contact:** Recruiter. **E-mail address:** cooljobs@attachmate.com. **World Wide Web address:** http://www.attachmate.com. **Description:** Designs, manufactures, and markets personal computer to mainframe data communications products worldwide. Products are marketed under the IRMA, Crosstalk, and Quickappbrand names. Founded in 1982. **Positions advertised include:** Software Test Engineer; Senior Database Engineer; Technical Architect; Senior Administrative Assistant; User Interface Developer. **Special programs:** Internships. **Office hours:** Monday - Friday, 9:00 a.m. - 5:00 p.m. **Corporate headquarters location:** This location. **Other U.S. locations:** Nationwide. **International locations:** Worldwide. **Listed on:** Privately held. **Number of employees nationwide:** 1,000.

AVOCENT CORPORATION
9911 Willows Road NE, Redmond WA 98052. 425/861-5858. **Contact:** Human Resources Department. **E-mail address:** hr@avocent.com. **World Wide Web address:** http://www.avocent.com. **Description:** Manufactures a variety of computer components such as concentrated switches. **Positions advertised include:** Auditor; Quality Engineer; Business Analyst; Help Desk Technician; Product Manager; Web Developer. **Listed on:** NASDAQ. **Stock exchange symbol:** AVCT.

AVTECH CORPORATION
3400 Wallingford Avenue North, Seattle WA 98103. 206/634-2540. **Contact:** Personnel Director. **E-mail address:** hr@avtcorp.com. **World Wide Web address:** http://www.avtcorp.com. **Description:** Manufactures a variety of electronic equipment products including interior lighting and flight deck audio control panels. **Positions advertised include:** QA Supervisor. **Corporate headquarters location:** This location.

CAP GEMINI ERNST & YOUNG
105000 NE Eight Street. Suite 1400, Bellevue WA 98004. 425/818-3300. **Fax:** 425/818-3301. **Contact:** Human Resources. **World Wide Web address:** http://www.us.capgemini.com. **Description:** A leading provider of information technology consulting services with over 40 branch offices worldwide. The company provides its clients with the solutions needed to achieve business and operational goals. CapGemini focuses on three major activities: consultancy, implementation, and systems integration. **Corporate headquarters location:** New York NY.

CAPTARIS
10885 NE 4th Street, Suite 400, Bellevue WA 98004. 425/455-6000. **Contact:** Human Resources. **World Wide Web address:** http://www.captaris.com. **Description:** Develops, manufactures, markets, and supports a broad line of open systems-based, computer technology software products and systems that automate call answering. **Positions advertised include:** Financial Analyst; Configuration Management Engineer. **Corporate headquarters location:** This location. **Listed on:** NASDAQ. **Stock exchange symbol:** CAPA.

CELLULAR TECHNICAL SERVICES COMPANY (CTS)
11100 Northeast 8th Streetm Suite 510, Bellevue WA 98004. 425/451-0051. **Fax:** 425/451-0052. **Contact:** Bruce York, Manager. **E-mail address:** hr@celtech.com. **World Wide Web address:** http://www.cellulartech.com. **Description:** Develops and markets real-time information management software systems used for fraud detection, billing, and customer service. Cellular Technical Services Company serves clients in the wireless communications industry. **Corporate headquarters location:** This location. **Listed on:** New York Stock Exchange. **Stock exchange symbol:** CTSC.

COMPUTER ASSOCIATES INTERNATIONAL, INC.
13810 SE Eastgate Way, Suite 500, Bellevue WA 98005. 425/825-2600. **Contact:** Human Resources. **World Wide Web address:** http://www.cai.com. **Description:** Computer Associates International is one of the world's leading developers of client/server and distributed computing software. The company develops, markets, and supports enterprise management, database and applications development, business applications, and consumer software products for a broad range of mainframe, midrange, and desktop computers. Computer Associates serves major business, government, research, and educational organizations. Founded in 1976. **Office hours:** Monday - Friday, 8:00 a.m. - 5:00 p.m. **Corporate headquarters location:** Islandia NY. **Other U.S. locations:** Nationwide. **Operations at this facility include:** This location develops software. **Listed on:** New York Stock Exchange. **Stock exchange symbol:** CA. **Annual**

sales/revenues: More than $100 million. **Number of employees nationwide:** 4,000. **Number of employees worldwide:** 9,000.

CORBIS CORPORATION
710 Second Avenue, Suite 200 Seattle WA 98104. 206/373-8792. **Contact:** Human Resources. **World Wide Web address:** http://www.corbis.com. **Description:** Develops and sells digital images to businesses. **Positions advertised include:** Assistant to General Counsel; Staff Accountant; Client Services Technician; Account Executive. **Corporate headquarters location:** This location.

CRAY INC.
Merrill Place, 411 First Avenue South, Suite 600, Seattle WA 98104-2860. 206/701-2000. **Fax:** 206/701-2500. **Contact:** Corporate Recruiter. **E-mail address:** resumes@cray.com. **World Wide Web address:** http://www.cray.com. **Description:** Develops high-end supercomputers. **Positions advertised include:** Floor Plan Engineer; Release Engineer; Platform Manager; Program Manager. **Corporate headquarters location:** This location. **Listed on:** NASDAQ. **Stock exchange symbol:** CRAY.

DEALER INFORMATION SYSTEMS CORPORATION (DIS)
1315 Cornwall Avenue, Bellingham WA 98225. 360/733-7610. **Contact:** Human Resources. **World Wide Web address:** http://www.discorp.com. **Description:** Develops management software for agricultural, construction, and automobile dealerships throughout the United State and Canada. DIS Corporation also offers its customers communications equipment and technical support. **Corporate headquarters location:** This location.

EDS (ELECTRONIC DATA SYSTEMS CORPORATION)
2405 Carillon Point, Kirkland WA 98033. 425/828-7425. **Contact:** Human Resources. **E-mail address:** careers@eds.com. **World Wide Web address:** http://www.eds.com. **Description:** Provides consulting, systems development, systems integration, and systems management services for large-scale and industry-specific applications. Founded in 1962. **Corporate headquarters location:** Plano TX. **Other U.S. locations:** Nationwide. **International locations:** Worldwide. **Listed on:** New York Stock Exchange. **Stock exchange symbol:** EDS. **Number of employees worldwide:** 115,000.

EXCELL DATA
1756 114th Avenue SE, Suite 220, Bellevue WA 98004. 425/974-2000. **Toll-free phone:** 800/5-EXCELL. **Fax:** 425/974-2001. **E-mail address:** info@excell.com. **World Wide Web address:** http://www.excell.com. **Description:** Excell Data delivers value-add services: Systems Integration; IT Outsourcing; Technology Procurement Services; Contract Consulting; Custom Application Development; Infrastructure Services; Event Technical Support. **Positions advertised include:** Access/Excel Project Manager; Access/Excel VBA Developer; API Tester with C# Skills; Software Designer; NET Developer for User Interfaces; NET Developer with Server Technologies; NET Developers; NET Web Applications Developer. **Corporate headquarters location:** This location. **Other U.S. locations:** Nationwide. **President and COO:** Rick Jorgensen. **Number of employees nationwide:** 3,500 employees.

FILENET CORPORATION
720 Fourth Avenue, Suite 100, Kirkland WA 98033. 425/893-7000. **Contact:** Human Resources. **E-mail address:** cooljobs@filenet.com. **World Wide Web address:** http://www.filenet.com. **Description:** FileNET develops and markets electronic content management software and e-business solutions. Products and services are used to help corporations and organizations build intranets, create electronic portals to streamline information management, and to create, process, edit, organize, and store all forms of digital content for Internet applications. Founded in 1983. **Company slogan:** Putting documents to work. **Special programs:** Internships. **Corporate headquarters location:** Costa Mesa CA. **Other U.S. locations:** Nationwide. **International locations:** Worldwide. **Listed on:** NASDAQ. **Stock exchange symbol:** FILE. **Facilities Manager:** Jennifer Shepherel. **Number of employees nationwide:** 1,700.

GETRONICS
585 Industry Drive, Suite 5, Tukwita WA 98188. 206/575-2566. **Contact:** Human Resources. **World Wide Web address:** http://www.getronics.com . **Description:** Provides information and communication technology solutions and support services worldwide. Getronics conducts its business through two major sectors: Systems Integration and Networked Technology Services includes enterprise system integration, managed services and infrastructure outsourcing, and network integration; and Business Solutions and Consulting includes software services, consulting, industry business solutions, and financial business solutions. **Corporate headquarters location:** Billerica MA. **International locations:** Worldwide.

HEWLETT-PACKARD COMPANY
15815 Southeast 37th Street, Bellevue WA 98006. 425/643-4000. **Contact:** Human Resources. **World Wide Web address:** http://www.hp.com. **Description:** Hewlett-Packard is engaged in the design and manufacture of measurement and computation products and systems used in business, industry, engineering, science, health care, and education. Principal products are integrated instrument and computer systems including hardware and software, peripheral products, and medical electronic equipment and systems. **NOTE:** Jobseekers should send resumes to Employment Response Center, Hewlett-Packard Company, Mail Stop 20-APP, 3000 Hanover Street, Palo Alto CA 94304-1181. **Corporate headquarters location:** Palo Alto CA. **Other U.S. locations:** Nationwide. **Operations at this facility include:** This location is engaged in the sale of electronic measurement and computing products. **Listed on:** New York Stock Exchange. **Stock exchange symbol:** HPQ. **Number of employees at this location:** 225.

IBM CORPORATION
3600 Carillon Point, Kirkland WA 98033. 425/803-0600. **Toll-free phone:** 800/796-9876. **Contact:** Human Resources. **World Wide Web address:** http://www.ibm.com. **Description:** IBM is a developer, manufacturer, and marketer of advanced information processing products including computers and microelectronic technology, software, networking systems, and information technology-related services. **NOTE:** Jobseekers should send a resume to IBM Staffing Services, 1DPA/051, 3808 Six Forks Road, Raleigh NC 27609. **Corporate headquarters location:** Armonk NY. **Other U.S. locations:** Nationwide. **Operations at this facility include:** This location is a programming center. **Subsidiaries include:** IBM Credit Corporation; IBM Instruments, Inc.; IBM World Trade Corporation.

INFORMATION BUILDERS INC.
520 Pike Street, Suite 2900, Seattle WA 98101. 206/624-9055. **Contact:** Human Resources. **E-mail address:** employment_opportunities@ibi.com. **World Wide Web address:** http://www.informationbuilders.com. **Description:** Develops software for client/server technology and application development. **Corporate headquarters location:** New York NY. **Other U.S. locations:** Nationwide. **Number of employees nationwide:** 1,500.

INTEL CORPORATION
2800 Center Drive, DuPont WA 98327-5050. 253/371-8080. **Toll-free phone:** 800/628-8686. **Contact:** Human Resources. **E-mail address:** resumes@intel.com. **World Wide Web address:** http://www.intel.com. **Description:** Intel Corporation is a manufacturer of computer microprocessors and computer related parts. **NOTE:** Resumes should be sent

to Intel Corporation, Staffing Department, P.O. Box 549263, Suite 281, Waltham MA 02454. **Corporate headquarters location:** Santa Clara CA. **Operations at this facility include:** This location manufactures PCs for original equipment manufacturers who market the computers under their own brand names. **Subsidiaries include:** Shiva Corporation produces a line of direct-dial products and remote access servers. **Listed on:** NASDAQ. **Stock exchange symbol:** INTC. **Number of employees worldwide:** 78,000.

INTERLINQ SOFTWARE CORPORATION
11980 NE 24th Street, Bellevue WA 98005. 425/827-1112. **Fax:** 425/827-0927. **Contact:** Human Resources. **E-mail address:** talent@interlinq.com. **World Wide Web address:** http://www.interlinq.com. **Description:** A leading provider of PC-based software solutions for the residential mortgage lending industry. The company's MortgageWare Enterprise product line is sold to banks, savings institutions, mortgage banks, mortgage brokers, and credit unions. The MortgageWare Enterprise product line is a complete PC-based software system that automates all aspects of the loan origination and secondary marketing processes, from qualifying a borrower to processing, settling, closing, and selling loans. MortgageWare Enterprise also includes tools to help lenders track and manage loans in their system, as well as a proprietary electronic communications system that enables data to be transferred via modem between headquarters, branch offices, and laptop origination systems. **Corporate headquarters location:** This location. **Listed on:** NASDAQ. **Stock exchange symbol:** INLQ. **Number of employees at this location:** 180.

IOLINE CORPORATION
14140 200th Street NE, Woodinville WA 98072. 425/398-8282. **Fax:** 425/398-8383. **Contact:** Human Resources. **E-mail address:** resume@ioline.com. **World Wide Web address:** http://www.ioline.com. **Description:** Manufactures plotters for computers. **Positions advertised include:** Apparel Systems Specialist; Sales/Marketing Director. **Corporate headquarters location:** This location.

KEANE, INC.
636 120th Avenue NE, Bellevue WA 98005. 425/451-8272. **Contact:** Human Resources. **E-mail address:** careers@keane.com. **World Wide Web address:** http://www.keane.com. **Description:** Keane offers businesses a variety of computer consulting services. Keane also develops, markets, and manages software for its clients and assists in project management. Founded in 1965. **NOTE:** Mail resume to Ms. Chris Miller, 383 Collins Road NE, Suite 200, Cedar Rapids IA 52402. **Corporate headquarters location:** Boston MA. **Other U.S. locations:** Nationwide. **Operations at this facility include:** This location is an office of the healthcare solutions division. **Listed on:** American Stock Exchange. **Stock exchange symbol:** KEA. **Number of employees nationwide:** 4,500.

KEY TRONIC CORPORATION
4424 North Sullivan Road, Spokane WA 99216. 509/928-8000. **Fax:** 509/927-5383. **Contact:** Personnel. **E-mail address:** jobs@keytronic.com. **World Wide Web address:** http://www.keytronic.com. **Description:** One of the world's largest independent manufacturers of computer keyboards and input devices. Founded in 1969. **Positions advertised include:** Buyer/Planner. **Special programs:** Internships. **Internship information:** Internships are offered on an as needed basis. The company has year-round internships, but primarily has openings in the summer and recruits through local colleges. Please call this location for more information. **Corporate headquarters location:** This location. **Other U.S. locations:** Las Cruces NM; El Paso TX. **International locations:** Dundalk, Ireland; Juarez, Mexico. **Listed on:** NASDAQ. **Stock exchange symbol:** KTCC. **Annual sales/revenues:** More than $100 million. **Number of employees at this location:** 550. **Number of employees nationwide:** 650. **Number of employees worldwide:** 3,000.

LAPLINK.COM, INC.
10210 NE Points Drive, Suite 400, Kirkland WA 98033. 425/952-6000. **Fax:** 425/952-6002. **Contact:** Human Resources. **E-mail address:** hotjobs@laplink.com. **World Wide Web address:** http://www.laplink.com. **Description:** Develops software for businesses and individuals enabling access to private and public computer networks, the Internet, and individual PCs. Founded in 1982. **Company slogan:** The remote access champion. **Office hours:** Monday - Friday, 8:00 a.m. - 5:00 p.m. **Corporate headquarters location:** This location. **Annual sales/revenues:** $21 - $50 million. **Number of employees at this location:** 80. **Number of employees worldwide:** 90.

LOCKDOWN NETWORKS, INC.
100 West Harrison, North Tower, Suite 300, Seattle WA 98119. 206/285-8080. **Fax:** 206/285-8081. **Contact:** Human Resources. **E-mail address:** careers@lockdownnetworks.com. **World Wide Web address:** http://www.lockdownnetworks.com. **Description:** A provider of appliance-based vulnerability management for securing wired and wireless enterprise networks. Their appliances audit, prioritize, remediate, report, and eliminate network security vulnerabilities. **Positions advertised include:** Senior Software Engineer. **Corporate headquarters location:** This location.

MTS
12600 SE 38th Street, Suite 250, Bellevue WA 98006. 425/401-1000. **Toll-free phone:** 800/900-8725. **Fax:** 425/401-1700. **Contact:** Human Resource Department. **E-mail address:** employment@mtsint.com. **World Wide Web address:** http://www.mtsint.com. **Description:** Develops software for the telecommunications industry. **Corporate headquarters location:** This location. **Other U.S. locations:** Piscataway NJ. **Listed on:** NASDAQ. **Stock exchange symbol:** MTSL.

MICROSOFT CORPORATION
One Microsoft Way, Redmond WA 98052-6399. 425/882-8080. **Contact:** Recruiting Department. **World Wide Web address:** http://www.microsoft.com. **Description:** Designs, sells, and supports a product line of systems and applications software for business, home, and professional use. Microsoft also produces related books and hardware products. Software products include spreadsheet, desktop publishing, project management, graphics, word processing, and database applications, as well as operating systems and programming languages. **Corporate headquarters location:** This location. **Listed on:** NASDAQ. **Stock exchange symbol:** MSFT. **Annual sales/revenues:** More than $100 million.

MODIS, INC.
2101 4th Avenue, Suite 220, Seattle WA 98121. 206/441-0707. **Contact:** Human Resources. **E-mail address:** resume@modisit.com. **World Wide Web address:** http://www.modisit.com. **Description:** An IT consulting firm. Founded in 1986. **Corporate headquarters location:** Jacksonville FL. **Parent company:** MPS.

NETMANAGE, INC.
12020 113th Avenue NE, Suite 210, Kirkland WA 98034. 425/814-9255. **Contact:** Human Resources. **World Wide Web address:** http://www.netmanage.com. **Description:** Develops, markets, and supports Windows-based connectivity software and associated applications tools. The company's software products provide PC users easy access to computer applications and data residing on multiple host mainframes and minicomputers in enterprisewide information systems networks. **NOTE:** Job seekers may search for and apply for positions online. **Corporate headquarters location:** Cupertino CA. **Listed on:** NASDAQ. **Stock exchange symbol:** NETM.

ONYX SOFTWARE CORPORATION
1100 112th Avenue NE, Suite 100, Bellevue WA 98004. 425/451-8060. **Fax:** 425/990-3343. **Contact:** Recruiting Department. **E-mail address:** recruiting@onyxcorp.com. **World Wide Web address:** http://www.onyx.com. **Description:** Develops customer management software.

ORACLE CORPORATION
500 108th Avenue NE, Suite 1300, Bellevue WA 98004. 425/646-0200. **Contact:** Human Resources. **World Wide Web address:** http://www.oracle.com. **Description:** Oracle Corporation designs and manufactures database and information management software for business and provides consulting services. **NOTE:** For commercial consultant positions, address resumes to Tammy Yeager. For sales positions, address resumes to Virginia Wagner. **Corporate headquarters location:** Redwood Shores CA. **Other U.S. locations:** Nationwide. **International locations:** Worldwide. **Operations at this facility include:** Administration; Regional Headquarters; Sales. **Listed on:** NASDAQ. **Stock exchange symbol:** ORCL. **Annual sales/revenues:** More than $100 million. **Number of employees at this location:** 230. **Number of employees nationwide:** 41,000.

OUTPUT TECHNOLOGY CORPORATION
3808 North Sullivan Road, Building 3, Spokane WA 99216. 509/536-0468. **Contact:** Personnel Administration. **Email address:** hr@output.com. **World Wide Web address:** http://www.output.com. **Description:** Manufactures and distributes printers and related products. **Corporate headquarters location:** This location. **Number of employees at this location:** 130.

PRECISION DIGITAL IMAGES CORPORATION
Woodville WA 98072. 425/483-1778. **Fax:** 425/867-9177. **Contact:** Human Resources. **World Wide Web address:** http://www.precisionimages.com. **Description:** Designs image processing and image collection subsystems for computers. Products are sold to original equipment manufacturers primarily for such applications as machine vision, desktop video conferencing and medical imaging. Founded in 1992.

RAF TECHNOLOGY, INC.
15400 NE 90th Street, Suite 300, Redmond WA 98052. 425/867-0700. **Contact:** Human Resources. **World Wide Web address:** http://www.raf.com. **Description:** A provider of advanced recognition, verification and identity authentication solutions for government and commercial clients. **Positions advertised include:** QA Engineer; System Quality Assurance and Program Management; Technical Services Consultant. **Corporate headquarters location:** This location.

REALNETWORKS
P.O. Box 91123, Seattle WA 98111-9223. 206/674-2700. **Physical address:** 2601 Elliot Avenue, Suite 1000, Seattle WA 98121. **Fax:** 206/674-2699. **Contact:** Human Resources. **World Wide Web address:** http://www.realnetworks.com. **Description:** Develops software that allows users to listen to audio applications over the Internet. **NOTE:** Jobseekers may submit applications online. **Listed on:** NASDAQ. **Stock exchange symbol:** RNWK.

SHARP MICROELECTRONICS USA
5700 NW Pacific Rim Boulevard, Camas WA 98607. 360/834-8700. **Fax:** 360/817-7544. **Contact:** Human Resources. **World Wide Web address:** http://www.sharp-usa.com. **Description:** Sharp Corporation develops business products, consumer electronics, and electronic components. **Corporate headquarters location:** Mahwah NJ. **Operations at this facility include:** This location is a sales and marketing facility. **Parent company:** Sharp Corporation.

SIERRA, INC.
3060 139th Avenue SE, Suite 500, Bellevue WA 98005. 425/649-9800. **Fax:** 425/641-7617. **Contact:** Human Resources. **E-mail address:** recruit@sierra.com. **World Wide Web address:** http://www.sierra.com. **Description:** Develops and distributes entertainment and educational software. The company's products are designed for IBM compatible and Macintosh systems. Founded in 1979. **NOTE:** Jobseekers may apply for positions online. **Positions advertised include:** Game Designer; Associate Producer; Production Assistant. **Corporate headquarters location:** Oakhurst CA. **Other U.S. locations:** Nationwide. **International locations:** France; Germany. **Annual sales/revenues:** More than $100 million. **Number of employees at this location:** 450.

TALLYGENICOM
6020 S. 190th Street, Kent WA 98032. 425/251-5500. **Fax:** 425/251-5520. **Toll-free phone:** 800/843-1347. **Contact:** Personnel. **E-mail address:** hrd@tally.com. **World Wide Web address:** http://www.tallygenicom.com. **Description:** Manufactures laser, serial, and line matrix printers. **Office hours:** Monday - Friday, 7:45 a.m. - 4:15 p.m.

VYKOR, INC.
200 Mill Avenue South, Suite 100, Renton WA 98055. 425/264-2600. **Fax:** 425/264-2601. **Contact:** Human Resources. **E-mail address:** jobs@vykor.com. **World Wide Web address:** http://www.vykor.com. **Description:** Provides engineered parts management sourcing solutions to industrial manufacturing companies. **Positions advertised include:** Senior Test Engineer. **Corporate headquarters location:** This location.

WACOM TECHNOLOGY COMPANY
1311 SE Cardinal Court, Vancouver WA 98683. 360/896-9833. **Fax:** 360/896-9724. **Contact:** Human Resources. **World Wide Web address:** http://www.wacom.com. **Description:** Manufactures image-enhancing software, animation software, and graphic digitizing equipment.

ZONES, INC.
1102 15th Street SW, Suite 102, Auburn WA 98001-6509. 253/205-3000. **Fax:** 253/205-3450. **Contact:** Human Resources. **E-mail address:** resumes@zones.com. **World Wide Web address:** http://www.zones.com. **Description:** Zones, Inc. and its subsidiaries are single-source, multi-vendor direct marketing resellers of name-brand information technology products. Zones serve the small- to medium-sized business market, as well as enterprise and public sector accounts. **Positions advertised include:** Account Executive; Manager In Training. **Corporate headquarters location:** This location. **Listed on:** NASDAQ. **Stock exchange symbol:** ZONS.

West Virginia

LABYRINTH SOLUTIONS, INCORPORATED
235 High Street, Suite 416, Morgantown WV 26505. 304/292-7700. **Contact:** Human Resources. **World Wide Web address:** http://www.labyrinth.net. **Description:** A local provider of Internet access, web hosting, and colocation. **NOTE:** Send resumes to PO. Box 573, Morgantown WV 26507-0434. Resumes accepted for open positions only.

THE LIBRARY CORPORATION
Research Park, Inwood WV 25428-9733. 304/229-0100. **Toll-free phone:** 800/325-7759. **Fax:** 304/229-0295. **Contact:** Human Resources. **E-mail address:** hr@tlcdelivers.com. **World Wide Web address:** http://www.tlcdelivers.com. **Description:** Develops, manufactures, and markets software that allows libraries to automate their cataloguing systems. **Note**: Prefers applications through their website. **Positions advertised include:** ASP.NET Developer. **Other U.S. locations:** Denver CO. **International locations:** Singapore.

MOUNTAIN CAD
339 Sixth Avenue SW, South Charleston WV 25303. 304/744-7911. **Fax:** 304/744-8049. **Contact:** Human

Resources. **E-mail address:** info@mtncad.com. **World Wide Web address:** http://www.mtncad.com. **Description:** An AutoCAD dealer specializing in mapping and GIS solutions.

Wisconsin

AQS, INC.
1325 Walnut Ridge Drive, Hartland WI 53029-8894. 262/369-7500. **Fax:** 262/369-7501. **Contact:** Human Resources. **E-mail address:** aqs@aqssys.com. **World Wide Web address:** http://www.aqssys.com. **Description:** Develops software for the insurance industry. **Positions advertised include:** Sales Support Specialist; Database Administration Technician; Program Manager; Business Analyst; Director of Marketing.

ASI (ANALYTICAL SURVEYS INCORPORATED)
741 North Grand Avenue, Waukesha WI 53186. 262/574-9000. **Fax:** 262/574-9090. **Contact:** Human Resources. **World Wide Web address:** http://www.anlt.com. **Description:** Provides utility and telecommunications companies with asset data management and maintenance outsourcing services. **Corporate headquarters location:** San Antonio TX.

CATALYST INTERNATIONAL
8989 North Deerwood Drive, Milwaukee WI 53223. 414/362-6800. **Toll-free phone:** 800/236-4600. **Fax:** 414/362-6794. **Contact:** Human Resources. **E-mail address:** catalystcareers@catalystinternational.com. **World Wide Web address:** http://www.catalystinternational.com. **Description:** Manufactures software for supply chain systems. **Positions advertised include:** Project Consultant; System Analyst; Sales Administrator; Manager, Internal Support. **Corporate headquarters location:** This location. **Other U.S. locations:** Newtown PA. **International locations:** England; France; Italy; Mexico; South America.

DEDICATED COMPUTING
N26 W23880 Commerce Circle, Waukesha WI, 53188. 262/951-7200. **Toll-free phone:** 877/523-3301. **Fax:** 262/523-2266. **Contact:** Human Resources. **E-mail address:** hr@dedicatedcomputing.com. **World Wide Web address:** http://www.dedicatedcomputing.com. **Description:** Dedicated Computing is a manufacturer and integrator of OEM computer engines. **Positions advertised include:** Cell Member; Project Engineer; Server Cell Member; Account Manager. **Corporate headquarters location:** This location. **Other area locations:** Pewaukee WI. **Parent company:** Omni Tech Corporation.

EPIC SYSTEMS CORPORATION
1979 Milky Way, Verona WI 53593. 608/271-9000. **Fax:** 608/271-7237. **Contact:** Human Resources. **E-mail address:** jobs@epicsystems.com. **World Wide Web address:** http://www.epicsystems.com. **Description:** A healthcare software company. **Positions advertised include:** Clinical Informatics; Consultant; Pharmacy Software Advocate; Problem Solver; Software Developer; UNIX or VMS Systems Engineer.

ESKER SOFTWARE
465 Science Drive, Madison WI 53711. 608/273-2724. **Toll-free phone:** 800/368-5283. **Fax:** 608/273-8227. **Contact:** Personnel. **E-mail address:** recruiting@esker.com. **World Wide Web address:** http://www.esker.com. **Description:** Develops communications software to help users automate document creation and delivery. Founded in 1982. **Positions advertised include:** Software Product Manager; Technical Support Manager; Technical Support Specialist. **Corporate headquarters location:** France. **Other U.S. locations:** Stillwater OK; Lake Forest CA. **International locations:** Worldwide.

EXPRESS TECHNOLOGIES CORPORATION
400 Reid Street, Suite 0, De Pere WI 54115. 920/337-1640. **Toll-free phone:** 800/654-9548. **Fax:** 920-337-1643. **Contact:** Human Resources. **World Wide Web address:** http://www.exptech.com. **Description:** A developer of software called World Watch, displaying real time geographical locations throughout the world, as well as illuminated patterns that delineate regions currently experiencing daylight. Express products are also available as World Watch screen savers.

FIRSTLOGIC, INC.
100 Harborview Plaza, La Crosse WI 54601-4071. 608/782-5000. **Toll-free phone:** 888/215-6442. **Fax:** 608/788-1188. **Contact:** Employment Specialist. **E-mail address:** hr@firstlogic.com. **World Wide Web address:** http://www.firstlogic.com. **Description:** Develops and manufactures software for postal automation, document processing, and database management. Founded in 1984. **NOTE:** Entry-level positions are offered. **Positions advertised include:** Product Test Engineer; Instructor/Consultant; Senior Consultant; Software Engineer. **Corporate headquarters location:** This location. **Other U.S. locations:** Chicago IL; Denver CO. **International locations:** Belgium; Canada; Denmark; Brazil; Mexico; Norway; Sweden; United Kingdom. **Number of employees at this location:** 200. **Number of employees nationwide:** 400.

FRONTIER TECHNOLOGIES CORPORATION
10201 North Port Washington Road, Mequon WI 53092. 414/241-4555. **Fax:** 414/241-7084. **Contact:** Human Resources. **World Wide Web address:** http://www.frontiertech.com. **Description:** Develops network software solutions and digital signature software. **Corporate headquarters location:** This location.

GRANITE MICROSYSTEMS
10202 North Enterprise Drive, Mequon WI 53092. 262/242-8800. **Toll-free phone:** 800/822-2983. **Fax:** 22/242-8825. **Contact:** Human Resources. **E-mail address:** quality-jobs@granitem.com. **World Wide Web address:** http://www.granitem.com. **Description:** Develops, customizes, and manufactures hardware. In addition, the company develops software and offers research and development, consulting, and technical support services.

HK SYSTEMS
2855 South James Drive, New Berlin WI 53151-3662. 262/860-7000. **Fax:** 262/860-7013. **Contact:** Human Resources. **E-mail address:** hr.mke@hksystems.com. **World Wide Web address:** http://www.hksystems.com. **Description:** HK Systems designs and manufactures computer-controlled machinery for manufacturing and various warehousing processes. **Positions advertised include:** Account Executives; Proposal Manager; Pharmaceutical Industry Account Executive. **Corporate headquarters location:** This location. **Other U.S. locations:** UT; KY; AL. **International locations:** Canada. **Operations at this facility include:** This location houses the corporate offices only.

HARRISDATA
13555 Bishop's Court, Suite 300, Brookfield WI 53005-6277. 262/784-9099. **Toll-free phone:** 800/225-0585. **Fax:** 262/784-5994. **Contact:** Human Resources. **E-mail address:** hr@harrisdata.com. **World Wide Web address:** http://www.harrisdata.com. **Description:** Manufactures software that facilitates a variety of operations including human resources, financial services, and distribution. **Corporate headquarters location:** This location.

HEARTLAND BUSINESS SYSTEMS
1700 Stephen Street, P.O. Box 347, Little Chute WI 54140. 920/788-7720. **Toll-free phone:** 800/236-7914. **Fax:** 920/788-7739. **Contact:** Human Resources. **E-mail address:** klevanetz@hbs.net. **World Wide Web address:** http://www.hbs.net. **Description:** Heartland Business Systems is a provider of value added integration services and networking technologies. Heartland has developed services and support programs for commercial, industrial, government, and education

clients throughout Wisconsin. **Positions advertised include:** Computer Engineer and Trainer; Receiving and Purchasing Associate; Senior System Engineer. **Corporate headquarters location:** This location. **Other area locations:** Milwaukee WI.

IFS
12000 West Park Place, Milwaukee WI 53224. 414/359-9800. **Fax:** 414/359-9011. **Contact:** Human Resources. **E-mail address:** info@ifsna.com. **World Wide Web address:** http://www.ifsworld.com. **Description:** Develops enterprise application components used in manufacturing, supply chain management, customer relationship management, service provision, financials, product development, maintenance, and human resource administration. Founded in 1983. **Other U.S. locations:** AZ; CA; IL; MN; NC; OH. **Parent company:** Industrial & Financial Systems. **Number of employees worldwide:** 3,200.

IDEXX LABORATORIES
2536 Alpine Road, Eau Claire WI 54703. 715/855-5800. **Fax:** 715/855-5981. **Contact:** Human Resources. **World Wide Web address:** http://www.idexx.com. **Description:** Develops and sells software for veterinarians. **Positions advertised include:** Senior Call Center Specialist; Trainer; National Sales Manager, Computer Systems; Programmer/Analyst. **Corporate headquarters location:** Westbrook ME. **Other U.S. locations:** Statewide. **International locations:** Worldwide. **Operations at this facility include:** This location specializes in computer services for the company. **Number of employees worldwide:** 2,400.

INACOM INFORMATION SYSTEMS
3001 West Beltline Highway, Madison WI 53713. 608-661-7700. **Toll-free phone:** 877-462-2664. **Fax:** 608-661-7701. **Contact:** Corporate Recruiter. **E-mail address:** jobs@inacom.com. **World Wide Web address:** http://www.inacom.com. **Description:** A locally owned and operated information technology consulting and training firm, offering business solutions in the areas of application development, education, networking, product procurement, project management, security, storage, and voice, video, and data convergence. **Positions advertised include:** Outbound Sales Position; Microsoft Certified Instructor; Microsoft Networking Specialist. **Other area locations:** Brookfield WI; Appleton WI; Holmen WI.

INTERNETWORX SYSTEMS, INC.
325 North Corporate Drive, Suite 280, Brookfield WI 53045. 262/792-0050. **Fax:** 262/792-0620. **Contact:** Human Resources Department. **E-mail address:** careers@internetworxsystems.com. **World Wide Web address:** http://www.internetworxsystems.com. **Description:** Designs enterprise resource planning software for manufacturing facilities. **Corporate headquarters location:** This location. **Other U.S. locations:** Chicago IL.

KEANE, INC.
11925 West Lake Park Drive, Suite 190, Milwaukee WI 53224. 414/410-2000. **Toll-free phone:** 800/442-9902. **Fax:** 414/359-1703. **Contact:** Senior Recruiter. **E-mail address:** info.milw@keane.com. **World Wide Web address:** http://www.keane.com. **Description:** Designs, develops, and manages software for corporations and health care facilities. Keane, Inc.'s services enable clients to leverage existing information systems and develop and manage new software applications more rapidly and proficiently. Founded in 1965. **Positions advertised include:** Programmer/Analyst; Web Application Developer; Application Specialist. **Corporate headquarters location:** Boston MA. **Other U.S. locations:** Nationwide. **Listed on:** American Stock Exchange. **Stock exchange symbol:** KEA. **Number of employees at this location:** 200.

KONICA MINOLTA BUSINESS SOLUTIONS U.S.A., INC.
5133 W. Terrace Drive, Suite 101, Madison WI 53718. 608/257-6315. **Contact:** Human Resources. **World Wide Web address:** http://www.kmbs.konicaminolta.us. **Description:** KMBS is a leader in document imaging, providing its customers with solutions for document creation, production and management. The company provides the essentials of imaging to companies and organizations ranging from small office/home office to workgroups and departments and to large production operations with its technologically advanced line products and services. **Positions advertised include:** Account Executive; Copier/Printer Technician; Digital Product Specialist; Major Account Print Production Specialist; Sales Representative. **Corporate headquarters location:** Ramsey NJ.

NETRION CORPORATION
250 North Sunny Slope Road, Brookfield WI 53005. **Contact:** Human Resources. **E-mail address:** milwaukee@netrion.com. **World Wide Web address:** http://www.netrion.com. **Description:** Provides IT consulting services. **Corporate headquarters location:** Chicago IL. **Other U.S. locations:** Cupertino CA; Detroit MI. **Listed on:** Privately held.

OMNI RESOURCES INC.
155 South Executive Drive, Suite 216, Brookfield WI 53005. 262/797-0600. **Fax:** 262/797-8866. **Contact:** Human Resources. **E-mail address:** resumes@omniresources.com. **World Wide Web address:** http://www.omniresource.com. **Description:** An information systems consulting firm. Founded in 1984. **Positions advertised include:** BW Analyst; SMS Engineer; SAP SD Functional Consultant; Software Testing Technician; Consultant, CCAT; Senior AIX UNIX System Administrator; Java Developer; Oracle Financials Developer/Analyst. **Corporate headquarters location:** This location. **Other area locations:** Statewide. **Other U.S. locations:** Carrollton TX; Tampa FL; Minneapolis MN; Denver CO. **Listed on:** Privately held. **Number of employees at this location:** 100. **Number of employees nationwide:** 500.

OMNI TECH CORPORATION
N27 W2367 Paul Road, Pewaukee WI 53072. 262/951-2046. **Contact:** Human Resources. **World Wide Web address:** http://www.otcwi.com. **Description:** A telecommunications and computer company. **Subsidiaries include:** Dedicated Computing. **Listed on:** Privately held.

PKWARE, INC.
9025 North Deerwood Drive, Brown Deer WI 53223-2480. 414/354-8699. **Fax:** 414/354-8559. **Contact:** Human Resources. **E-mail address:** hr@pkware.com. **World Wide Web address:** http://www.pkware.com. **Description:** Develops data compression software including PKZIP. **Positions advertised include:** Senior Software Sales; Webmaster; Financial Analyst. **Corporate headquarters location:** This location. **Other U.S. locations:** Miamisburg OH; Redwood Shores CA.

PTC (PARAMETRIC TECHNOLOGY CORPORATION)
Crossroads Corporate Center II, 20800 Swenson Drive, Suite 250, Waukesha WI 53186. 262/798-9494. **Fax:** 262/798-9467. **Contact:** Office Manager. **World Wide Web address:** http://www.ptc.com. **Description:** Parametric Technology Corporation designs and develops fully-integrated software products for mechanical engineering and automated manufacturing. The company has offices in 23 countries. **Corporate headquarters location:** Needham MA. **Other U.S. locations:** WA. **Operations at this facility include:** This location serves as a regional sales office. **Listed on:** NASDAQ. **Stock exchange symbol:** PMTC.

PARAGON DEVELOPMENT SYSTEMS, INC.
1823 Executive Drive, P.O. Box 128, Oconomowoc WI 53066. 262/569-5300. **Toll-free phone:** 800/966-6090. **Fax:** 262/569-5390. **Contact:** Human Resources. **E-mail address:** info@pdspc.com. **World Wide Web address:** http://www.pdspc.com. **Description:** Assists

medium- to large-sized organizations plan for, procure, deploy, manage, support, and retire IT assets. **Corporate headquarters location:** This location. **Other area locations:** Brookfield WI; Madison WI.

RENAISSANCE LEARNING INC.
2911 Peach Street, P.O. box 8036, Wisconsin Rapids WI 54494. 715/424-3636. **Toll-free phone:** 800/565-6740. **Fax:** 715/424-3414. **Contact:** Human Resources. **E-mail address:** jobs@renlearn.com. **World Wide Web address:** http://www.renlearn.com. **Description:** Provides assessment and progress-monitoring software for pre K-12 schools and districts. **Positions available:** Software Engineer. **Corporate headquarters location:** This location. **Other area locations:** Madison WI.

SIERRA INCORPORATED
566 State Street, Racine WI 53402. 262/638-1851. **Toll-free phone:** 800/644-7267. **Fax:** 262/638-1852. **Contact:** Human Resources Department. **World Wide Web address:** http://www.sierrainc.com. **Description:** Sells and services computers for large retailers. **Corporate headquarters location:** This location.

SILICON GRAPHICS, INC.
890 Industrial Boulevard, Chippewa Falls WI 54729. 715/726-8000. **Fax:** 715/726-7110. **Contact:** Staffing. **World Wide Web address:** http://www.sgi.com. **Description:** SGI manufactures a family of workstation and server systems that are used by engineers, scientists, and other creative professionals to develop, analyze, and simulate complex, three-dimensional objects. **Positions advertised include:** Director, Strategic Tech Initiatives. **Corporate headquarters location:** Mountain View CA. **Operations at this facility include:** This location manufactures supercomputers.

SKYWARD, INC.
5233 Coye Drive, Stevens Point WI 54481. **Toll-free phone:** 800/236-7274. **Fax:** 715/341-1370. **Contact:** Human Resources Department. **World Wide Web address:** http://www.skyward.com. **Description:** Develops student, budgetary, and human resources administrative data processing software for K-12 school districts. Founded in 1980. **NOTE:** Entry-level positions are offered. **Positions advertised include:** Programmer. **Corporate headquarters location:** This location. **Other U.S. locations:** WA; ID; UT; SD; KS; MN; MI; IL; IN; PA; MO; TX. **Listed on:** Privately held. **Annual sales/revenues:** $5 - $10 million. **Number of employees at this location:** 110.

SONIC FOUNDRY, INC.
222 West Washington Avenue, Suite 775, Madison WI 53703. 608/443-1600. **Fax:** 608/443-1601. **Contact:** Personnel. **World Wide Web address:** http://www.sfoundry.com. **Description:** Develops enterprise media communications technology. Founded in 1991. **Positions advertised include:** Inside Sales Representative. **Other U.S. locations:** Pittsburgh PA. **Listed on:** NASDAQ. **Stock exchange symbol:** SOFO.

SPHERION
790 North Milwaukee Street, Milwaukee WI 53202. 414/276-2345. **Contact:** Staffing. **World Wide Web address:** http://www.spherion.com. **Description:** Provides staffing, recruiting, and workforce solutions nationwide from 750 locations. **Positions advertised include:** Account Manager; Forklift Driver; Customer Service Supervisor; Benefits Coordinator; Director of Sales. **Corporate headquarters location:** Fort Lauderdale FL. **Other U.S. locations:** Nationwide. **Parent company:** Spherion Pacific Enterprises LLC. **Listed on:** New York Stock Exchange. **Stock exchange symbol:** SFN.

STRATAGEM, INC.
200 Woodland Prime, Suite 300, Menomonee Falls WI 53051. 262/532-2700. **Fax:** 262/532-2701. **Contact:** Human Resources. **E-mail address:** careers@stratagemnet.com. **World Wide Web address:** http://www.stratagemconsulting.com. **Description:** Offers comprehensive information technology consulting services. Founded in 1986. **Positions advertised include:** Project Manager; Systems Analyst; Design Architect; Developer. **Corporate headquarters location:** This location. **Other area locations:** Appleton WI; Madison WI. **Listed on:** Privately held. **Annual sales/revenues:** $21 - $50 million. **Number of employees at this location:** 250. **Number of employees nationwide:** 450.

SYSTEMS & PROGRAMMING SOLUTIONS
530 North 108th Place, Suite 100, Wauwatosa WI 53226. 414/302-2929. **Toll-free phone:** 800/353-7774. **Fax:** 414/302-2930. **Contact:** Human Resources. **E-mail address:** hr@spsinet.com. **World Wide Web address:** http://www.spsinet.com. **Description:** Provides software and hardware consulting services for AS/400, Internet PC, and network systems including systems planning, design and development, project management, capacity planning, hardware configuration and procurement, hardware/software installations and conversions. Founded in 1987. **Corporate headquarters location:** This location. **Other area locations:** Madison WI. **Number of employees at this location:** 40.

TDS INFORMATION SERVICES
8401 Greenway Boulevard, Suite 230, Middleton WI 53562-0980. 608/664-8600. **Contact:** Human Resources. **E-mail address:** careers@teldta.com. **World Wide Web address:** http://www.tds.net. **Description:** TDS Computing Services offers system integration, development, support, and processing. The company also provides bill printing and mailing services for customers. **Positions advertised include:** Accountant; Financial Analyst; Applications Systems Analyst; SAP Business Systems Analyst. **Corporate headquarters location:** Chicago IL. **Other area locations:** Statewide. **Other U.S. locations:** Nationwide. **Parent company:** Telephone & Data Systems, Inc. **Number of employees at this location:** 320.

TEKLYNX
1529 Continental Drive, Eau Claire WI 5470. 414/535-6200. **Fax:** 715/833-1995. **Contact:** Human Resources. **E-mail address:** info@teklynx.com. **World Wide Web address:** http://www.teklynx.com. **Description:** A developer and marketer of bar code labeling software. **Corporate headquarters location:** This location. **International locations:** Worldwide.

WINGRA TECHNOLOGIES, INC.
525 Junction Road, Suite 2500, Madison WI 53717. 608/662-4400. **Fax:** 608/662-0545. **Contact:** Personnel. **E-mail address:** personnel@wingra.com. **World Wide Web address:** http://www.wingra.com. **Description:** Provides enterprise messaging integration and migration solutions. **Corporate headquarters location:** This location.

ZYWAVE, INC.
2323 North Mayfair Road, Suite 320, Milwaukee WI 53226. 414/475-1591. **Fax:** 414/475-0739. **Contact:** Human Resources. **E-mail address:** hr@zywave.com. **World Wide Web address:** http://www.zywave.com. **Description:** Zywave provides a line of Web-based employee benefits and property and casualty communication, administration, and claims data analysis systems designed to help insurance brokers gain profitable market share. Servicing over 500 partners and over half of the top 100 insurance agencies, Zywave applications help brokers secure and retain business by differentiating them from their competitors, and allow them to compete on a high-capabilities basis. **Positions advertised include:** Implementation Consultant; partner Consultant, Property and Casualty; .NET Applications Developer; BrokerageBuilder/HRconnection Specialist; Partner Consultant, Employee Benefits; Claims Data Analyst; Project Manager, Benefits Initiatives; Team Lead, Partner Services; Quality Assurance Analyst.

Wyoming

PERTECH RESOURCES, INC.
860 College View Drive, Riverton WY 82501. 307/856-4821. **Fax:** 307/856-0412. **Contact:** Ryan Harrison, Human Resources. **E-mail address:** hr@pertechresources.com. **World Wide Web address:** http://www.pertechresources.com. **Description:** Pertech Resources specializes in best-in-class custom printing solutions for the banking, gaming, money order, kiosk and other markets. Also offers contract manufacturing, consumables, technical support, repair, refurbishment and machine shop services. **Positions advertised include:** Network Administrator; Product Manager.

TETON DATA SYSTEMS
dba STAT!REF
125 South King Street, P.O. Box 4798, Jackson WY 83001. 307/733-5494. **Toll-free phone:** 800/901-5494. **Fax:** 307/739-1229. **Contact:** Human Resources Department. **E-mail address:** info@statref.com. **World Wide Web address:** http://www.statref.com. **Description:** STAT!Ref is a product of Teton Data Systems (TDS). Provides electronic publishing products to medical professionals. A small, tight-knit company, **Positions advertised include:** Vice President of Technology; Data Conversion Programmer. **Office hours:** Monday - Friday, 8:00 a.m. - 5:00 p.m. **Number of employees at this location:** 30.

EDUCATIONAL SERVICES

You can expect to find the following types of companies in this section:
Business/Secretarial/Data Processing Schools • Colleges/Universities/Professional Schools • Community Colleges/Technical Schools/Vocational Schools • Elementary and Secondary Schools • Preschool and Child Daycare Services

Educational services employ 8,171,000 workers and are expected to increase by 20.3% or 1,662,000 new jobs. Job opportunities for teachers over the next 10 years will vary from good to excellent, depending on the locality, grade level, and subject taught. The total number of job openings, 3,357,000, is attributable to the expected retirement of a large number of teachers. Through 2014, overall preschool to secondary student enrollments, a key factor in the demand for teachers, are expected to rise more slowly than in the past. Overall, employment of postsecondary teachers is expected to grow much faster than the average due to an expected increase in the population of 18- to 24-year-olds, as a larger percentage of high school graduates attend college, and as more adults return to college to enhance their career prospects or update their skills. The 67,000 child daycare service jobs are expected to increase by 38.5% or 295,000 new jobs. The number of women in the labor force with children young enough to require child daycare will increase steadily. Also, the number of children under age 5 is expected to increase during this period. An unusually large number of job openings also will result each year from the need to replace experienced workers who leave this industry.

Alabama

AUBURN UNIVERSITY
Langdon Hall, Auburn AL 36849. 334/844-4145. **Contact:** Human Resources. **E-mail address:** working@auburn.edu. **World Wide Web address:** http://www.auburn.edu. **Description:** A public university with approximately 22,000 students. **Positions advertised include:** Agri Technician; Audit Manager; Civil Engineer; Energy Manager; Financial Assistant; Information Technology Specialist; Research Assistant; Research Fellow; Security Technician; Veterinary Technician.

JACKSONVILLE STATE UNIVERSITY
700 Pelham Road North, Jacksonville AL 36265. 256/218-3536. **Contact:** Director of Personnel. **World Wide Web address:** http://www.jsu.edu. **Description:** A four-year state university offering bachelor's and master's (including MBA) degrees. Approximately 7,400 undergraduate and 1,000 graduate students attend Jacksonville State University. **Positions advertised include:** Nursing Clinic Coordinator; Disability Specialist; Department Head, Health, Physical Education & Recreation; Assistant Director, English Language Institute; Instructors, Various Departments.

MOBILE COUNTY PUBLIC SCHOOLS
P.O. Box 1327, Mobile AL 36633. 251/221-4543. **Fax:** 251/221-4546. **Contact:** Human Resources. **E-mail address:** humanresources@mcpss.com. **World Wide Web address:** http://www.mcpss.com. **Description:** Provides public education through city and county schools. **NOTE:** Entry-level positions are offered. **Positions advertised include:** Principal; Assistant Principal; Teacher; High School Counselor; Diagnostician. **Corporate headquarters location:** This location. **Number of employees at this location:** 7,800.

UNIVERSITY OF ALABAMA
P.O. Box 870126, Tuscaloosa AL 35487-0126. 205/348-6690. **Recorded jobline:** 205/348-7780. **Contact:** Human Resources. **E-mail address:** uaemploy@bama.ua.edu. **World Wide Web address:**. **Description:** A university with an enrollment of nearly 21,000, offering more than 200 bachelor's, master's, and doctoral degrees. **NOTE:** See website for application information. **Positions advertised include:** Admissions Counselor; Assistant Director Business Administration Facilities; Assistant Director for Conference Services; Associate Vice President for Administration; Benefits Specialist; Communications Specialist; Associate/Full Professor; Assistant Professor; Instructor. **Corporate headquarters location:** This location. **Number of employees at this location:** 3,700.

UNIVERSITY OF ALABAMA AT BIRMINGHAM
1530 Third Avenue South, Birmingham AL 35294. 205/934-5248. **Contact:** Patricia Robinson, Director of Employment. **World Wide Web address:** http://www.uab.edu. **Description:** A branch of the university with approximately 17,000 students. This location also operates a medical center. **NOTE:** Search for available positions online.

UNIVERSITY OF MONTEVALLO
Station 6055, Montevallo AL 35115. 205/665-6055. **Recorded jobline:** 205/665-8050. **Contact:** Human Resources. **World Wide Web address:** http://www.montevallo.edu. **Description:** A four-year, public university with an undergraduate enrollment of approximately 3,200 students and a graduate enrollment of approximately 360. Areas of study include biology, communications, English, foreign languages, international studies, math and physics, behavioral and social sciences, business, fine arts, counseling, and education. **NOTE:** See website for application information. **Positions advertised include:** Assistant Professor; Professor.

UNIVERSITY OF SOUTH ALABAMA
Administration Building, Room 286, Mobile AL 36688. 251/460-6133. **Contact:** Human Resources. **World Wide Web address:** http://www.southalabama.edu. **Description:** A university enrolling more than 13,000 students in its extensive allied health, nursing, arts and sciences, business, computer, and engineering disciplines. **NOTE:** Search for positions and application information online. **Number of employees at this location:** 5,800.

Alaska

ANCHORAGE SCHOOL DISTRICT
P.O. Box 196614, Anchorage AK 99519. 907/742-4116. **Fax:** 907/742-4176. **Contact:** Human Resource Department. **World Wide Web address:** http://www.asdk12.org. **Description:** Administration for the Anchorage School District that includes 59 elementary, nine middle, seven high, one vocational, 10 specialized, and five charter schools. **Positions advertised include:** Administrative Assistant; Senior Budget Analyst; Accountant; Bilingual Tutor; Teacher Assistant.

UNIVERSITY OF ALASKA ANCHORAGE
3211 Providence Drive, Anchorage AK 99508. 907/786-4608. **Fax:** 907/786-4727. **Contact:** Human Resource Services. **World Wide Web address:** http://www.uaa.alaska.edu. **Description:** A university with over 20,000 students. **Positions advertised include:** Fiscal. Technician; Special Events Manager; Project Manager/Designer; Program Assistant; Dental Hygienist; Networks/Systems Operations Technician; Assistant Professor; Various Departments. **Office hours:** Monday - Friday, 8:00 a.m. - 5:00 p.m.

UNIVERSITY OF ALASKA SOUTHEAST
11120 Glacier Highway, Juneau AK 99801. 907/465-6263. **Toll-free phone:** 877/465-4827. **Fax:** 907/465-6365. **Contact:** Human Resources. **World Wide Web address:** http://www.jun.alaska.edu. **Description:** A regional unit of the University of Alaska statewide system of higher education. The university was established in 1987 with the restructuring of the former University of Alaska Juneau, Ketchikan Community College, and Islands Community College. The university offers certificate programs and associate's degrees in vocational/technical and business-related areas; Associate of Arts degrees; bachelor's degrees in liberal arts, sciences, education, business, and public administration; and master's degrees in education and public administration. **Positions advertised include:** Assistant/Associate Professor, Various Departments; Student Employment Coordinator; Accounting Professional; Assistant to the Dean. **Other area locations:** Ketchikan AK; Sitka AK.

Arizona

ARIZONA STATE UNIVERSITY (ASU)
1551 South Rural Road, P.O. Box 875612, Tempe AZ 85287-5612. 480/965-2701. **Fax:** 480/965-0554. **Recorded jobline:** 480/965-5627. **Contact:** Human Resources. **E-mail address:** resumes@asu.edu. **World Wide Web address:** http://www.asu.edu/hr/jobs. **Description:** A four-year state university offering bachelor's, master's (including MBAs), and doctoral degrees. Approximately 30,000 undergraduate and 10,500 graduate students attend ASU. **NOTE:** Interested jobseekers are asked to call the jobline before sending a resume. Please only respond to advertised openings. **Positions advertised include:** Accountant; Administrative Assistant; Applications System Analyst; Business Manager; Computer Programmer; Development Officer; Editor/Publisher; Financial Analyst; Instructional Specialist; Management Research Analyst; Program Coordinator; Research Technician; Sales Assistant; Security Officer; Technology Support Analyst.

ARIZONA STATE UNIVERSITY/WEST (ASU)
P.O. Box 37100, Phoenix AZ 85069-7100. 602/543-8400. **Physical address:** 4701 West Thunderbird Road, Glendale AZ 85306. **Fax:** 602/543-8412. **Contact:** Human Resources. **World Wide Web address:** http://www.west.asu.edu. **Description:** A four-year state university with an enrollment of nearly 8,000, offering bachelor's, master's, and doctoral degrees. **Positions advertised include:** Business Manager; Director of Public Relations; Program Coordinator; Student Support Specialist.

ARIZONA WESTERN COLLEGE
P.O. Box 929, Yuma AZ 85366-0929. 928/317-6000. **Physical address:** 9500 South Avenue 8E, Yuma AZ 85365-8834. **Fax:** 928/317-6001. **Contact:** Department of Human Resources. **E-mail address:** human.resources@azwestern.edu. **World Wide Web address:** http://www.awc.cc.az.us. **Description:** Arizona Western College is a two-year community college offering associate of arts and associate of applied sciences degrees. The college provides occupational programs in technical, vocational, and paraprofessional fields. Certificate programs are also available. **Positions advertised include:** Coordinator of Residence Life; Human Resources Coordinator; Director of Financial Aid; Vice President for Learning Services; System and Network Manager.

CENTRAL ARIZONA COLLEGE
8470 North Overfield Road, Coolidge AZ 85228. 520/723-4141. **Fax:** 520/876-1908. **Contact:** Office of Human Resources. **E-mail address:** human_resources@python.cac.cc.az.us. **World Wide Web address:** http://www.cac.cc.az.us. **Description:** A public, two-year community college offering a variety of programs. **Positions advertised include:** Assistant Director, Advising and Testing; Director of Auxiliary Financial Services; Executive Director, Foundation. **Special programs:** Internships. **Corporate headquarters location:** This location. **Other area locations:** Apache Jct AZ; Winkelman AZ.

COCONINO COMMUNITY COLLEGE
2800 South Lonetree Road, Flagstaff AZ 86001. 928/226-4280. **Toll-free phone:** 800/350-7122. **Fax:** 928/226-4114. **Contact:** Human Resources. **World Wide Web address:** http://www.coco.cc.az.us. **Description:** A community college offering 14 associate degrees and 22 certificate programs. Approximately 3,000 students are enrolled at the college. Founded in 1991. **NOTE:** The Human Resources Department only accepts a completed application, including a resume, a cover letter, and a completed CCC application form. **Positions advertised include:** Foundation/Development Director; Accounts Payable Specialist; Network Engineer. **Other U.S. locations:** Fredonia AZ; Grand Canyon AZ; Page AZ; Williams AZ.

DYNAMIC EDUCATIONAL SYSTEMS, INC. (DESI)
8433 North Black Canyon Highway, Suite 188, Phoenix AZ 85021. **Fax:** 602-995-4091 **Contact:** HR Director. **E-mail address:** corphr@exodyne.com. **World Wide Web address:** http://www.exodyne.com. **Description:** Provides career training and job placement. **Positions advertised include:** Accounting Clerk; HR Director. **Parent company:** Exodyne, Inc.

EMBRY-RIDDLE AERONAUTICAL UNIVERSITY
3700 Willow Creek Road, Prescott AZ 86301. 928/777-3710. **Toll-free phone:** 800/888-3728. **Contact:** Department of Human Resources. **E-mail address:** eraujobs@erau.edu. **World Wide Web address:** http://www.erau.edu/pr. **Description:** A private, four-year, coeducational, undergraduate institution committed to studies in aviation, aerospace, and engineering. The university's engineering program has been recognized by *U.S. News and World Report* as one of the 10 best engineering programs in the nation and has been approved by the Accreditation Board of Engineering and Technology. The university has approximately 1,500 students enrolled. **Positions advertised include:** Adult Education Program Manager.

GUIDANCE INVESTORS, INC.
dba AMERICAN GRADE SCHOOLS/AMERICAN CHILD CARE CENTERS
4040 East McDowell Road, Suite 501, Phoenix AZ 85008. 602/993-6070. **Contact:** Human Resources. **Description:** Operates 25 child-care centers in Arizona, Oklahoma, and California that provide daycare and preschool services. **Special programs:** Internships. **Office hours:** Monday - Friday, 7:30 a.m. - 4:30 p.m. **Corporate headquarters location:** This location. **Operations at this facility include:** Administration. **Listed on:** Privately held.

MARICOPA COUNTY COMMUNITY COLLEGE DISTRICT
2411 West 14th Street, Tempe AZ 85281. 480/731-8000. **Contact:** Employee Services. **World Wide Web address:** http://www.maricopa.edu. **Description:** A college district that consists of ten colleges and two skill centers. Founded in 1962. **NOTE:** Search for positions online. Completed application (available online) required.

MOHAVE COMMUNITY COLLEGE (MCC)
1971 Jagerson Avenue, Kingman AZ 86401. 928/757-0835. **Fax:** 928/757-0875. **Contact:** Human Resources. **World Wide Web address:** http://www.mohave.edu. **Description:** Mohave Community College (MCC) uses a microwave communications system to link the three campus sites in Bullhead, Kingman, and Lake Havasu City. MCC offers three associate's degrees and more than 45 certificates, including an associate of arts degree for students planning to transfer to a four-year institution; an associate of applied science degree designed to prepare students for employment; and an associate of science degree for students pursuing a

career in the life sciences, nursing, and paramedic fields. Founded in 1971. **NOTE:** Part-time jobs are offered. **Corporate headquarters location:** This location. **Operations at this facility include:** Regional Headquarters. **Number of employees at this location:** 575.

NORTHERN ARIZONA UNIVERSITY
P.O. Box 4113, South San Francisco Street, Flagstaff AZ 86011-4113. 928/523-2222. **Fax:** 928/523-2220. **Contact:** Human Resources. **E-mail address:** human.resources@nau.edu. **World Wide Web address:** http://www.nau.edu. **Description:** A state university with an enrollment of 13,000 undergraduate and 5,800 graduate students. **NOTE:** Application form and instructions available online. **Positions advertised include:** Curator of Visual Materials; Academic Advisor; Assistant Clinical Professor, Various Departments; Assistant Professor, Various Departments; Development Officer; Director of Annual Giving; Instructor; Library Specialist. **Number of employees at this location:** 3,650.

NORTHLAND PIONEER COLLEGE
P.O. Box 610, Holbrook AZ 86025. 928/524-7670. **Fax:** 928/524-7612. **Contact:** Personnel Office. **World Wide Web address:** http://www.northland.cc.az.us. **Description:** Northland Pioneer College is a comprehensive, multicampus community college. Northland Pioneer College has four campuses in Navajo County: the Painted Desert Campus at this location, the Little Colorado Campus in Winslow, the Silver Creek Campus in Snowflake/Taylor, and the White Mountain Campus in Show Low. **Positions advertised include:** Pre-Nursing Advisor; Faculty in Mathematics; Faculty in Software Quality Assurance.

OTTAWA UNIVERSITY
10020 North 25th Avenue, Phoenix AZ 85021. 602/371-1188. **Contact:** Human Resources. **World Wide Web address:** http://www.ottawa.edu. **Description:** A university offering programs in business administration, education, psychology, human services, human resources, and public administration. Graduate programs include human resources management, human resources and organizational development, and counseling. Founded in 1865. **Positions advertised include:** Registration Representative; Enrollment Specialist; Adjunct Instructors. **Corporate headquarters location:** Ottawa KS. **Other area locations:** Scottsdale AZ; Mesa AZ.

PHOENIX COLLEGE
1202 West Thomas Road, Phoenix AZ 85013. 602/264-2492. **Contact:** Human Resources. **World Wide Web address:** http://www.pc.maricopa.edu. **Description:** A two-year community college enrolling over 14,000 students. Degrees include an associate of arts, an associate of general studies, and an associate of applied science. Phoenix College also offers 45 occupational programs, several of which are the only ones of their type in the country or state, and also offers 175 computer courses for both the novice and the professional. Founded in 1920. **Positions advertised include:** Faculty, Various Departments; Director, Grants Development and Management.

RIO SALADO COLLEGE
2323 West 14th Street, Tempe AZ 85281-6950. 480/517-8560. **Contact:** Human Resources. **World Wide Web address:** http://www.rio.maricopa.edu. **Description:** A comprehensive community college, with an enrollment of 20,000. Rio Salado is an innovative network of over 250 locations serving Maricopa County. The college does not have a traditional campus, but instead offers classes in schools, churches, businesses, and shopping malls throughout Maricopa County. Founded in 1978. **Positions advertised include:** Adjunct Faculty.

THUNDERBIRD
THE GARVIN SCHOOL OF INTERNATIONAL MANAGEMENT
15249 North 59th Avenue, Glendale AZ 85306-6000. 602/978-7101. **Fax:** 602/978-8305. **Contact:** Human Resources. **E-mail address:** HRResumes@t-bird.edu. **World Wide Web address:** http://www.t-bird.edu. **Description:** A graduate school of business management with approximately 1,450 students enrolled. Founded in 1946. **Positions advertised include:** Writing Technology Specialist; Admissions Coordinator; Assistant Director Leadership Annual Giving; Marketing Communications Editor; Director Of Internet Marketing.

UNIVERSITY OF ARIZONA
888 North Euclid Avenue, Suite 114, P.O. Box 210158, Tucson AZ 85721-1058. 520/621-3662. **Contact:** Human Resources Department. **E-mail address:** HRInfo@email.arizona.edu. **World Wide Web address:** http://www.arizona.edu. **Description:** A four-year state university offering bachelor's, master's (including MBAs), first professional, and doctoral degrees. Approximately 34,000 students attend the University of Arizona. **Positions advertised include:** Senior Accountant; Adjunct Assistant Professor, Various Departments; Adjunct Instructor, Various Departments; Applications Systems Analyst; Assistant Vice President for Admissions and Financial Aid; Professor, Various Departments.

UNIVERSITY OF PHOENIX
4615 East Elwood Street, MS AA-D103, Phoenix AZ 85040. 480/966-7400. **Contact:** Human Resources Department. **World Wide Web address:** http://www.phoenix.edu. **Description:** A private university enrolling 200,000 students online and at 140 campuses in 29 states, Puerto Rico, and Canada. Founded in 1976. **Positions advertised include:** Sr. Tax Accountant; Business Development Specialist. **Parent company:** Apollo Group, Inc.

Arkansas
ARKANSAS STATE UNIVERSITY
P.O. Box 1500, State University AR 72467. 870/972-3454. **Fax:** 870/972-3337. **Contact:** Human Resources. **E-mail address:** HR@astate.edu. **World Wide Web address:** http://www.astate.edu. **Description:** A state university. **Positions advertised include:** Assistant/Associate Professor, Various Departments; College Dean; Instructor; Assistant/Associate Registrar; Computer Technician.

California
ALLIANT INTERNATIONAL UNIVERSITY
10455 Pomerado Road, San Diego CA 92131-1799. 858/635-4772. **Fax:** 858/635-4739. **Contact:** Human Resources. **E-mail address:** jobs@alliant.edu. **World Wide Web address:** http://www.alliant.edu. **Description:** Offers undergraduate and graduate degree programs in liberal arts, education, business, and behavioral and social sciences. **Positions advertised include:** Lecturer; Assistant Professor. **Corporate headquarters location:** This location. **Other area locations:** Fresno CA; Irvine CA; Los Angeles CA; Sacramento CA; San Francisco CA. **International locations:** Nairobi, Kenya; Mexico City, Mexico. **Number of employees nationwide:** 1,100.

CALIFORNIA CULINARY ACADEMY, INC.
625 Polk Street, San Francisco CA 94102. 415/771-3536. **Toll-free phone:** 800/739-9700. **Contact:** Human Resources. **World Wide Web address:** http://www.baychef.com. **Description:** One of the largest accredited schools for professional chef training in the United States. The academy offers instruction in classic and modern methods of food preparation in its core degree program, specialized baking and pastry certificate programs, and a full range of classes for cooking and wine enthusiasts. Founded in 1977. **Corporate headquarters location:** This location. **Listed on:** NASDAQ. **Stock exchange symbol:** COOK.

CALIFORNIA INSTITUTE OF TECHNOLOGY
399 South Holliston Avenue, Pasadena CA 91125. 626/395-3300. **Fax:** 626/405-9842. **Contact:** Human Resources. **E-mail address:** employment@caltech.edu.

World Wide Web address: http://www.caltech.edu. **Description:** A university offering BS, MS, and PhD degrees, with an enrollment of 2,100 undergraduate and graduate students. **Positions advertised include:** Accountant; Assistant Animal Lab Technician; Director of Corporate and Foundation Relations; Director of Protein Expression Center; Laboratory Research Engineer; Mechanical Engineer; Optical Engineer; Purchasing Administrator; Research Engineer, Mechanical; Sr. Analyst; Sr. Communications Coordinator; Staff Scientist.

CALIFORNIA POLYTECHNIC STATE UNIVERSITY
One Grand Avenue, Administration Building, Room 110, San Luis Obispo CA 93407. 805/756-2236. **Fax:** 805/756-5483. **Recorded jobline:** 805/756-1533. **Contact:** Human Resources. **E-mail address:** humanresources@calpoly.edu. **World Wide Web address:** http://www.calpoly.edu. **Description:** A university specializing in the field of engineering. **Positions advertised include:** Administrative Support Coordinator; Director of Donor Relations; Lecturer, Agribusiness; Full-time Lecturer, Aerospace Engineering; Medical Microbiologist; Project Manager; Provost and Vice President for Academic Affairs.

CALIFORNIA SCHOOL OF PODIATRIC MEDICINE AT SAMUEL MERRITT COLLEGE
370 Hawthorne Avenue, Oakland CA 94609. 510/869-6856. **Fax:** 510/869-6115. **Contact:** Human Resources. **E-mail address:** hr@samuelmerritt.edu. **World Wide Web address:** http://www.samuelmerritt.edu. **Description:** A college/teaching hospital offering postgraduate programs in the field of podiatry. One of only seven podiatry schools in the U.S. **Positions advertised include:** Academic Coordinator; Assistant Director of Admissions.

CALIFORNIA STATE UNIVERSITY, EAST BAY
25800 Carlos Bee Boulevard, Warren Hall Room 615, Hayward CA 94542-3026. 510/885-3634. **Fax:** 510/885-2951. **Contact:** Human Resources. **E-mail address:** applycsh@csuhayward.com. **World Wide Web address:** http://www.csuhayward.edu. **Description:** One of 23 campuses of the California State University System. California State University, East Bay offers 37 bachelor's degree programs and 26 master's degree programs. **NOTE:** A CSU Hayward Employment Application must be submitted for each job. Faxed applications are not accepted. **Positions advertised include:** Part-time Lecturer, Various Disciplines; Pharmacist; Speech Pathologist; Student Services Professional; Police Officer. **Other area locations:** Concord CA.

CALIFORNIA STATE UNIVERSITY, FULLERTON
2600 East Nutwood Avenue, Suite 700, P.O. Box 34080, Fullerton CA 92834-6806. 714/278-2425. **Fax:** 714/278-4163. **Recorded jobline:** 714/278-3385. **Contact:** Employment Coordinator. **E-mail address:** csuf-hr@fullerton.edu. **World Wide Web address:** http://www.fullerton.edu. **Description:** A four-year state university with an enrollment of over 32,000 students. **NOTE:** Resumes are no longer accepted in hard copy form. **Parent company:** California State University System. **Operations at this facility include:** Administration. **Number of employees at this location:** 3,400.

CALIFORNIA STATE UNIVERSITY, STANISLAUS
801 West Monte Vista Avenue, Turlock CA 95382. 209/667-3351. **Recorded jobline:** 209/667-3354. **Fax:** 209/664-7011. **Contact:** Human Resources. **E-mail address:** hr_department@csustan.edu. **World Wide Web address:** http://www.csustan.edu. **Description:** A four-year state university offering undergraduate and graduate programs of study. California State University, Stanislaus is one of 23 campuses of the California State University System. **Positions advertised include:** Dean, College of Education; Dean, College of Business Administration; Assistant Professor, Various Departments. **Other area locations:** Stockton CA.

CALIFORNIA TEACHERS ASSOCIATION
P.O. Box 2153, Santa Fe Springs CA 90670-0053. 562/942-7979. **Physical address:** 11745 East Telegraph Road, Santa Fe Springs CA 90670. **Fax:** 562/949-9438. **Contact:** Human Resources Department. **E-mail address:** employment@cta.org. **World Wide Web address:** http://www.cta.org. **Description:** An affiliate of the National Education Association, California Teachers Association represents over 175,000 public school teachers throughout the state of California. **Corporate headquarters location:** Burlingame CA. **Other area locations:** Citrus Heights CA; Los Angeles CA; Foster City CA; Norco CA.

COLLEGE OF THE DESERT
43-500 Monterey Avenue, Palm Desert CA 92260. 760/773-2529. **Contact:** Human Resources. **E-mail address:** humanresources@collegeofthedesert.edu. **World Wide Web address:** http://www.collegeofthedesert.edu. **Description:** A community college offering degrees in over 70 majors. **Positions advertised include:** Dean, Communications; Dean, Social Science & Arts; Instructor, Various Departments; Part-time Instructor, Various Departments.

EAST LOS ANGELES COLLEGE
1301 Cesar Chavez Avenue, Monterey Park CA 91754. 323/265-8650. **Recorded jobline:** 213/419-5122. **Contact:** Human Resources. **World Wide Web address:** http://www.elac.cc.ca.us. **Description:** A two-year, community college. Part of the Los Angeles Community College District. **Positions advertised include:** Mathematics Faculty; History Faculty; Respiratory Therapy Instructor. **Corporate headquarters location:** This location. **Number of employees at this location:** 600.

FOOTHILL - DE ANZA COMMUNITY COLLEGE DISTRICT
12345 El Monte Road, Los Altos Hills CA 94022. 650/949-6217. **Recorded jobline:** 650/949-6218. **Contact:** Employment Services. **E-mail address:** employment@fhda.edu. **World Wide Web address:** http://www.fhda.edu. **Description:** A nonprofit community college district composed of Foothill College (also at this location) and De Anza College (Cupertino CA). Foothill College offers associate in arts, associate in science, certificate, and transfer programs in over 80 areas of study. De Anza Community College offers two-year degrees and certificate programs in approximately 100 areas of study. **NOTE:** Entry-level positions and part-time jobs are offered. **Positions advertised include:** Dean, Business and Social Sciences; Math Instructor; Physics Instructor; ESL Composition Instructor; English Instructor; Music Instructor; Drama Instructor; History Instructor; Administrative Assistant; Nurse Practitioner. **Corporate headquarters location:** This location. **Number of employees at this location:** 2,500.

FREMONT UNIFIED SCHOOL DISTRICT (FUSD)
4210 Technology Drive, Fremont CA 94538. 510/659-2545. **Toll-free phone:** 800/883-0180. **Fax:** 510/659-2507. **Contact:** Human Resources. **World Wide Web address:** http://www.fremont.k12.ca.us. **Description:** A school district comprised of 31 elementary schools, 6 junior high schools, and 12 high schools. **Number of employees nationwide:** 1,250.

GLENDALE COMMUNITY COLLEGE
P.O. Box 10477, Glendale CA 91209-3477. 818/240-1000, extension 5921. **Physical address:** 1500 North Verdugo Road, SM 265, Glendale CA 91208. **Fax:** 818/551-5169. **Recorded jobline:** 818/291-6655. **Contact:** Office of Human Resources. **World Wide Web address:** http://www.glendale.cc.ca.us. **Description:** A two-year community college with an enrollment of over 20,000 students.

KNOWLEDGE LEARNING CORPORATION (KLC)
1485 North McDowell Boulevard, Petaluma CA 04054. 707/794-0211. **Contact:** Human Resources. **E-mail address:** familyservices@klcorp.com. **World Wide Web address:** http://www.knowledgelearning.com. **Description:** Operates one of the largest chains of childcare centers in the United States with more than 150 childcare centers in 15 states. KLC's community schools operate under the names Children's Discovery Centers, Magic Years, Learning Universe, and Hildebrandt Learning Centers. **Positions advertised include:** District Manager; Teacher; Assistant Teacher; Center Director; Assistant Center Director. **Corporate headquarters location:** Portland OR. **Parent company:** Knowledge Universe.

THE LOS ANGELES COMMUNITY COLLEGES DISTRICT OFFICE
770 Wilshire Boulevard, Los Angeles CA 90017. 213/891-2000. **Fax:** 213/891-2411. **Contact:** Human Resources. **E-mail address:** jobs@laccd.cc.ca.us. **World Wide Web address:** http://www.laccd.edu. **Description:** Encompasses nine community colleges. **Positions advertised include:** English Instructor; Associate Vice Chancellor; Executive Assistant; Physical Sciences Laboratory Technician; Executive Legal Secretary; Registration Assistant.

LOYOLA MARYMOUNT UNIVERSITY
One LMU Drive, Suite 1900, Los Angeles CA 90045. 310/338-2723. **Fax:** 310/338-7711. **Recorded jobline:** 310/338-4488. **Contact:** Human Resources. **E-mail address:** jobs@lmu.edu. **World Wide Web address:** http://www.lmu.edu. **Description:** A private, four-year college offering certificates, bachelor's degrees, and master's degrees including a Master's in Business Administration. Approximately 3,800 undergraduate and 1,000 graduate students attend Loyola Marymount University. **Positions advertised include:** Assistant Director, Campus Recreation; Assistant Director, Judicial Affairs; Student Life Coordinator; Development Director; Financial Aid Counselor; Nurse Practitioner; Sports Medicine Assistant; Technology Coordinator; Therapist; Web Editor; Administrative Assistant; Lead Teacher; Teacher Assistant; Custodian.

MARIN COMMUNITY COLLEGE (COLLEGE OF MARIN)
835 College Avenue, Kentfield CA 94904. 415/485-9340. **Fax:** 415/485-0135. **Recorded jobline:** 415/485-9693. **E-mail address:** hrjobs@marin.cc.ca.us. **World Wide Web address:** http://www.marin.cc.ca.us. **Description:** A community college. **Positions advertised include:** Financial Aid Assistant; Instructor, Various Departments.

MILLS COLLEGE
5000 MacArthur Boulevard, Oakland CA 94613. 510/430-2282. **Fax:** 510/430-3311. **Recorded jobline:** 510/430-2012. **Contact:** Personnel Department. **E-mail address:** hire@mills.edu. **World Wide Web address:** http://www.mills.edu. **Description:** An independent liberal arts college for women offering bachelor's and master's degrees. Founded in 1852. **Positions advertised include:** Administrative Assistant; Maintenance Technician; Director of Human Resources; Food Service Worker; Art Instructor; Dance Instructor.

OHLONE COLLEGE
43600 Mission Boulevard, P.O. Box 3909, Fremont CA 94539-0390. 510/659-6088. **Fax:** 510/659-6025. **Recorded jobline:** 510/656-8295. **Contact:** Human Resources. **E-mail address:** hr@ohlone.edu. **World Wide Web address:** http://www.ohlone.cc.ca.us. **Description:** A college offering both undergraduate and graduate degrees. **Positions advertised include:** Instructors, Various Disciplines; Director of Grants Development; Director of Institutional Research. **Other area locations:** Newark CA. **Number of employees at this location:** 550.

POMONA COLLEGE
550 North College Avenue, Alexander Hall, Room 129, Claremont CA 91711-6318. 909/621-8175. **Contact:** Anne Johnson, Personnel. **E-mail address:** anne.johnson@pomona.edu. **World Wide Web address:** http://www.pomona.edu. **Description:** A private, four-year, liberal arts college. **NOTE:** Search for positions and download application form online.

SAN DIEGO COMMUNITY COLLEGE DISTRICT
3375 Camino Del Rio South, Suite 330, San Diego CA 92108. 619/388-6579. **Fax:** 619/388-6897. **Recorded jobline:** 619/388-6850. **Contact:** Beverly Dean, Employment Manager. **E-mail address:** jobs@sdccd.net. **World Wide Web address:** http://www.sdccd.cc.ca.us. **Description:** A community college district comprised of San Diego City College, San Diego Mesa College, and San Diego Miramar College. **Positions advertised include:** Adjunct Instructors, Various Disciplines; Assistant Professor, Biology; Assistant Professor, Chemistry; Assistant Professor, English; Assistant Professor, Mathematics. **Office hours:** Monday – Friday, 8:00 a.m. – 5:00 p.m. **Number of employees at this location:** 5,000.

SAN DIEGO STATE UNIVERSITY
5500 Campanile Drive, San Diego CA 92182-1625. 619/594-6404. **Fax:** 619/594-1147. **Contact:** Sue Blair, Director of Personnel. **E-mail address:** employ@mail.sdsu.edu. **World Wide Web address:** http://www.sdsu.edu. **Description:** An undergraduate and graduate state university. **Positions advertised include:** Administrative Support Coordinator; Nutritionist; Developmental Counselor; Assistant Coach, Women's Basketball; Research Technician; Accountant; Physician; Part-time Lecturers, Various Disciplines.

SAN FRANCISCO CONSERVATORY OF MUSIC
1201 Ortega Street, San Francisco CA 94122-4498. 415/759-3437. **Fax:** 415/759-3499. **Contact:** Karen Heather, Human Resources Manager. **E-mail address:** kjh@sfcm.edu. **World Wide Web address:** http://www.sfcm.edu. **Description:** A music conservatory with an enrollment of 270 students. **Positions advertised include:** Associate Dean for Student Life; Director of Communications.

SAN FRANCISCO STATE UNIVERSITY
1600 Holloway Avenue, Administration Building, Room 252, San Francisco CA 94132. 415/338-1871. **Contact:** Human Resources. **E-mail address:** hrwww@sfsu.edu. **World Wide Web address:** http://www.sfsu.edu. **Description:** A four-year, state university. San Francisco State University offers 115 bachelor's degree programs, 93 master's degree programs, a Ph.D. and Ed.D. in education with University of California Berkeley, a master's of science in physical therapy with University of California San Francisco, 28 credential programs, and 22 certificate programs. **Positions advertised include:** Director, Undergraduate Admissions; Administrative Analyst/Specialist; Police Officer. **NOTE:** Entry-level positions are offered. **Special programs:** Internships. **Parent company:** California State University System. **Number of employees at this location:** 3,000.

SANTA CLARA UNIVERSITY
500 El Camino Real, Santa Clara CA 95053-0850. 408/554-4392. **Fax:** 408/554-5488. **Contact:** Human Resources Department. **E-mail address:** hrservicedesk@scu.edu. **World Wide Web address:** http://www.scu.edu. **Description:** A four-year independent Jesuit university offering undergraduate programs through its schools of Arts and Sciences, Business, Engineering, and Education. The university also offers graduate programs through its schools of Law, Engineering, Business, Agricultural Business, and Counseling Psychology. **Positions advertised include:** Administrative Assistant; Associate Director, Planned Giving; Network Engineer; Senior Information Specialist; Lecturer, Various Disciplines. **Corporate headquarters location:** This location.

SIERRA COMMUNITY COLLEGE
5000 Rocklin Road, Rocklin CA 95677. 916/624-3333. **Toll-free phone:** 800/242-4004. **Recorded jobline:** 916/781-0424. **Contact:** Peter Kolster, Associate Vice President of Human Resources. **World Wide Web address:** http://www.sierracollege.edu. **Description:** A community college. **Positions advertised include:** Instructor, Various Disciplines. **Operations at this facility include:** Administration; Divisional Headquarters. **Number of employees at this location:** 450.

STANFORD UNIVERSITY
655 Serra Street, Stanford CA 94305-6110. 650/723-1888. **Contact:** Human Resources. **E-mail address:** empwebsite@lists.stanford.edu. **World Wide Web address:** http://www.stanford.edu. **Description:** A private university offering undergraduate programs through its schools of Humanities and Sciences, Engineering, and Earth Sciences. Stanford University also offers graduate programs through its professional schools of Law, Medicine, Business, and Education. Founded in 1885. **Positions advertised include:** Benefits Associate; Administrative Associate; Life Science Research Assistant; Development Associate.

UNIVERSITY OF CALIFORNIA, BERKELEY
247 University Hall, #3544, Berkeley CA 94720-3544. 510/642-9046. **Contact:** Office of Human Resources. **E-mail address:** hrweb@berkeley.edu. **World Wide Web address:** http://www.berkeley.edu. **Description:** A university offering undergraduate and graduate programs in various liberal arts and professional fields. The university is a leader in teaching, research, and public service. Undergraduate divisions include the colleges of Chemistry, Engineering, Environmental Design, Letters and Science, and Natural Resources. Founded in 1868. **NOTE:** Apply online. To contact Human Resources call: 510/643-4443. **Positions advertised include:** Lecturer, Women's Studies; Scholarship Assistant; Programmer Analyst; Executive Assistant; Academic Affairs Coordinator; Prospect Development Director; Staff Research Associate; Human Resources Manager. **Operations at this facility include:** Administration; Research and Development.

UNIVERSITY OF CALIFORNIA, DAVIS
Employment Office, One Shields Avenue, Davis CA 95616. 530/752-0530. **Recorded jobline:** 530/752-1760. **Contact:** Personnel. **E-mail address:** apply@ucdavis.edu. **World Wide Web address:** http://www.ucdavis.edu. **Description:** A university offering various degrees through its colleges of Agricultural and Environmental Sciences, Engineering, and Letters and Science; Graduate School of Management; School of Law; School of Medicine; and School of Veterinary Medicine. **Positions advertised include:** Local Government Relations Director; Federal Government Relations Director; Director of Corporate Relations; Nursery Technician; Laboratory Assistant; Database Programmer.

UNIVERSITY OF CALIFORNIA, IRVINE
Berkeley Place, Suite 1000, Irvine CA 92697-4600. 949/824-5210. **Fax:** 949/824-4065. **Contact:** Human Resources. **E-mail address:** hrquestions@uci.edu. **World Wide Web address:** http://www.uci.edu. **Description:** A research university that is part of the University of California system. University of California, Irvine offers bachelors, masters, and doctoral degrees. **NOTE:** Part-time positions are offered. **Positions advertised include:** Custodian; Student Affairs Director; Fire Safety Program Manager; Laboratory Assistant; Counseling Psychologist. **Special programs:** Summer Jobs. **Operations at this facility include:** Administration; Research and Development; Service. **Number of employees at this location:** 5,000.

UNIVERSITY OF CALIFORNIA, LOS ANGELES
10920 Wilshire Boulevard, Suite 205, Los Angeles CA 90024-6504. 310/794-0890. **Fax:** 310/794-0895. **Recorded jobline:** 310/825-9151. **Contact:** Employment Services. **E-mail address:** mycareer@ucla.edu. **World Wide Web address:** http://www.chr.ucla.edu. **Description:** A campus of the state university system offering undergraduate and graduate degree programs. **NOTE:** Part-time positions are offered. **Company slogan:** UCLA - The University of Big Ideas. **Positions advertised include:** Database Developer; Programmer Analyst; Senior Custodian; Auditor; Police Officer; Laboratory Assistant; Student Affairs Officer. **Special programs:** Internships. **Corporate headquarters location:** This location. **Number of employees at this location:** 18,000.

UNIVERSITY OF CALIFORNIA, SAN DIEGO
9500 Gilman Drive, Mail Code 0922, La Jolla CA 92093-0922. 858/534-2812. **Physical address:** 10280 North Torrey Pines Road, Suite 265A, La Jolla CA 92093. **Contact:** Human Resources. **World Wide Web address:** http://www.ucsd.edu. **Description:** A campus of the state university system offering undergraduate and graduate programs. **Positions advertised include:** Cosmos Program Manager; Administrative Specialist; Laboratory Assistant; Fund Manager; Human Resources Specialist; Dean of Student Affairs.

UNIVERSITY OF CALIFORNIA, SAN FRANCISCO
3333 California Street, Suite 305, San Francisco CA 94143. 415/476-1645. **Fax:** 415/476-4672. **Contact:** Human Resources. **World Wide Web address:** http://www.ucsf.edu. **Description:** A medical teaching university and hospital offering degrees in dentistry, general medicine, nursing; pharmacology and research. **NOTE:** See website for job listings and application procedures. Interested jobseekers must apply online. **Special programs:** Internship. **Office hours:** Monday – Friday, 8:00 a.m. – 5:00 p.m.

UNIVERSITY OF CALIFORNIA, SANTA BARBARA
Human Resources Office, 3101 Student Affairs & Administrative Services Building, Santa Barbara CA 93106-3160. 805/893-7261. **Fax:** 805/893-8645. **Contact:** Employment Manager. **E-mail address:** hr.webcontact@hr.ucsb.edu. **World Wide Web address:** http://www.ucsb.edu. **Description:** A campus of the state university system offering undergraduate and graduate degree programs. **NOTE:** Apply online. Paper applications are no longer accepted. **Positions advertised include:** Senior Cook; Information Systems Manager; Graduate Program Assistant; Computer Resource Specialist.

UNIVERSITY OF CALIFORNIA, SANTA CRUZ
1156 High Street, Santa Cruz CA 95064. 831/459-2009. **Recorded jobline:** 831/459-2011. **Contact:** Personnel Office. **World Wide Web address:** http://www.ucsc.edu. **Description:** This campus of the University of California emphasizes undergraduate education in the arts and sciences. The university has an undergraduate enrollment of approximately 11,000 and a graduate enrollment of approximately 1,000. **Positions advertised include:** Programmer Analyst; Administrative Assistant; Financial/Purchasing Assistant; Assistant Department Manager, Engineering; Academic Counselor.

UNIVERSITY OF SAN FRANCISCO
2130 Fulton Street, Campion Hall, Room C-7, San Francisco CA 94117-1080. 415/422-2988. **Fax:** 415/386-1074. **Contact:** Human Resources. **E-mail address:** resumes@usfca.edu. **World Wide Web address:** http://www.usfca.edu. **Description:** Established as one of San Francisco's first universities, the University of San Francisco serves approximately 8,000 students in the schools of arts and sciences, business, education, nursing, law, and professional studies. The university is a nonprofit, private, Catholic and Jesuit institution. Founded in 1855. **Positions advertised include:** Associate Director, Research; Assistant Women's Track Coach; Assistant Registrar; Financial Analyst; First Assistant Athletic Trainer; Library Assistant. **Corporate headquarters location:** This location. **Other area locations:** Cupertino CA; Sacramento CA; San Ramon CA; Santa Rosa CA. **Operations at this facility include:** Administration.

President: Father Stephen A. Privett, S.J. **Number of employees at this location:** 1,100.

UNIVERSITY OF SOUTHERN CALIFORNIA
3535 South Figueroa Street, Suite 100, Los Angeles CA 90089-1260. 213/740-7252. **Contact:** Employment Manager. **World Wide Web address:** http://www.usc.edu. **Description:** A private university offering bachelor's, master's, doctoral, and professional degrees to approximately 28,000 students. **NOTE:** Candidates must apply online. **Positions advertised include:** Account Representative; Administrative Assistant; Administrative Services Coordinator; Biller; Child Care Teacher; Community Service Officer; Computer Scientist; Office Assistant; Research Associate; Receptionist. **Office hours:** Monday – Friday, 9:30 a.m. – 3:00 p.m. **Corporate headquarters location:** This location. **Operations at this facility include:** Administration; Research and Development; Service.

UNIVERSITY OF THE PACIFIC
3601 Pacific Avenue, Stockton CA 95211. 209/946-2124. **Fax:** 209/946-2835. **Contact:** Human Resources. **E-mail address:** jobs@pacific.edu. **World Wide Web address:** http://www.uop.edu. **Description:** A four-year university offering undergraduate and graduate degree programs. **Positions advertised include:** Community Service Officer; Dental Assistant; Assistant Baseball Coach; University Budget Manager; Development Research Analyst; Financial Aid Technician; Archivist; Staff Psychologist; Systems Administrator; Police Officer. **Office hours:** Monday – Friday, 8:30 a.m. – 5:00 p.m.

WESTED
730 Harrison Street, San Francisco CA 94107. 415/565-3000. **Toll-free phone:** 877/493-7833. **Fax:** 415/565-3012. **Contact:** Personnel Manager. **E-mail address:** jobs@wested.org. **World Wide Web address:** http://www.wested.org. **Description:** WestEd is a nonprofit educational agency focused on improving the quality of education by helping policy makers and practitioners apply knowledge from research, development, and practice. Founded in 1966. **Positions advertised include:** Director, New Business Development; Contracts Assistant; Financial Assistant; Manager of Organizational Branding and Visibility; Program Assistant. **Corporate headquarters location:** This location. **Other U.S. locations:** Tucson AZ; Boston MA; Burlington VT; Washington DC. **Number of employees at this location:** 145. **Number of employees nationwide:** 165.

WHITTIER COLLEGE
13406 Philadelphia Street, P.O. Box 634, Whittier CA 90608. 562/907-4208. **Fax:** 562/907-4884. **Recorded jobline:** 562/907-4850. **Contact:** Human Resources. **World Wide Web address:** http://www.whittier.edu. **Description:** A four year liberal arts college. Whittier was founded in 1887 by members of the Religious Society of Friends. The college was named in honor of the Quaker poet and abolitionist, John Greenleaf Whittier. **Office hours:** Monday – Friday, 8:00 a.m. – 5:00 p.m.

Colorado

ADAMS STATE COLLEGE
208 Edgemont Boulevard, Alamosa CO 81102. 719/587-7990. **Fax:** 719/587-7938. **Contact:** Human Resources. **World Wide Web address:** http://www.adams.edu. **Description:** A state college with approximately 2,500 students. **Positions advertised include:** Assistant/Associate Professor, Various Departments; Web Application Developer; title V Cooperative Grant Project Specialist. **Number of employees at this location:** 310.

AMERICAN EDUCATIONAL PRODUCTS INC.
401 West Hickory Street, P.O. Box 2121, Fort Collins CO 80522. 970/484-7445. **Contact:** Human Resources. **World Wide Web address:** http://www.amep.com. **Description:** Manufactures and markets a wide variety of educational products including pattern blocks, cubes, geological oddities, puzzles, and arts and crafts supplies. The company also designs, develops, manufactures, markets, and services supplementary educational products including filmstrips and anatomical systems. **Number of employees at this location:** 135.

COLORADO MOUNTAIN COLLEGE
831 Grand Avenue, P.O. Box 10001, Glenwood Springs CO 81602. 970/945-8691. **Fax:** 970/947-8324. **Contact:** Director of Human Resources. **World Wide Web address:** http://www.coloradomtn.edu. **Description:** A two-year college. The school's Associate of Arts and Associate of Science degrees are academic programs designed for students who plan to transfer to a four-year college or university. Colorado Mountain College includes seven campuses in western Colorado. **NOTE:** Applications available online. Resumes accepted only for posted positions. **Positions advertised include:** Dean of Arts and Sciences; Chief Information Officer; Director of Marketing and Communications.

COLORADO MOUNTAIN COLLEGE/EAST
901 South U.S. Highway 24, Leadville CO 80461-9724. 719/486-2015. **Contact:** Human Resources. **World Wide Web address:** http://www.coloradomtn.edu. **Description:** A two-year college. The school's Associate of Arts and Associate of Science degrees are academic programs designed for students who plan to transfer to a four-year college or university. Colorado Mountain College includes seven campuses in western Colorado. **NOTE:** All hiring is done by the Glenwood campus.

COLORADO SCHOOL OF MINES
1500 Illinois Street, Golden CO 80401. 303/273-3250. **Fax:** 303/384-2025. **Contact:** Human Resources. **World Wide Web address:** http://www.mines.edu. **Description:** Colorado School of Mines is a public research university devoted to engineering and applied science. Founded in 1874. **Positions advertised include:** Assistant/Associate Professor, Various Departments; Program Assistant.

COLORADO STATE UNIVERSITY
Human Resource Services, Fort Collins CO 80523-6004. 970/491-1794. **Fax:** 970/491-2548. **Recorded jobline:** 970/491-3941. **Contact:** Human Resource Services. **World Wide Web address:** http://www.colostate.edu. **Description:** A state university offering undergraduate, graduate, and doctorate programs. **Positions advertised include:** Research Associate; Assistant/Associate Professor; Vice President for Research.

COLORADO STATE UNIVERSITY AT PUEBLO
2200 Bonforte Boulevard, Pueblo CO 81001-4901. 719/549-2100. **Contact:** Human Resources Department. **World Wide Web address:** http://www.colostate-pueblo.edu. **Description:** Colorado State/Pueblo has an enrollment of approximately 4,600 students. The university operates through five divisions: The College of Applied Science & Engineering, The School of Business, The College of Humanities and Social Science, The College of Science and Mathematics, and The Center for Teaching and Learning.

EMILY GRIFFITH OPPORTUNITY SCHOOL
1250 Welton Street, Denver CO 80204. 303/575-4700. **Contact:** Human Resources. **World Wide Web address:** http://www.egos-school.com. **Description:** A trade school offering continuing education (high school diploma, G.E.D.), as well as classes in areas such as medicine, art, aviation, and automotive mechanics.

MESA STATE COLLEGE
1100 North Avenue, Lowell Heiny Hall, Room 237, Grand Junction CO 81502. 970/248-1820. **Contact:** Jan Purin, Human Resources. **E-mail address:** jpurin@mesastate.edu. **World Wide Web address:** http://www.mesastate.edu. **Description:** Mesa State College grants the Bachelor of Business

Administration, Bachelor of Science in Nursing, Bachelor of Arts, and Bachelor of Science degrees. The college awards Associate of Arts and Associate of Science degrees, as well as Associate of Applied Science degrees and certificates of proficiency in occupational (vocational-technical) areas. Over 4,500 students are enrolled at the college. Founded in 1925. **Positions advertised include:** Assistant VP for Academic Affairs; Director of Admissions; Grants Specialist; Assistant/Associate Professor, Various Departments.

REGIS UNIVERSITY
3333 Regis Boulevard, Mail Code K-4, Denver CO 80221-1099. 303/458-4161. **Fax:** 303/964-5498. **Recorded jobline:** 303/458-4386. **Contact:** Human Resources. **E-mail address:** resumes@regis.edu. **World Wide Web address:** http://www.regis.edu. **Description:** A four-year, liberal arts/preprofessional, Jesuit university. Six academic divisions offer more than 30 programs of study. Approximately 1,400 students attend Regis University. **Positions advertised include:** Assistant Professor, Various Departments; Programmer/Analyst; Sr. Accountant. **Special programs:** Internships. **Other U.S. locations:** WY. **Number of employees at this location:** 550.

U.S. AIR FORCE ACADEMY
8034 Edgerton Drive, Suite 100, Colorado Springs CO 80840. 719/333-1110. **Contact:** Civilian Personnel Office. **Recorded jobline:** 719/333-2222. **World Wide Web address:** http://www.usafa.af.mil. **Description:** An undergraduate educational institution offering the bachelor of science degree and military training leading to commission in the U.S. Air Force. **NOTE:** Instructions for application for positions are available at the Air Force Personnel Center website: https://ww2.afpc.randolph.af.mil/resweb. **Positions advertised include:** Architect; Budget Technician; Operations Research Analyst.

UNIVERSITY OF COLORADO AT BOULDER
3100 Marine Street, Campus Box 565, Boulder CO 80309. 303/492-6475. **Contact:** Human Resources. **World Wide Web address:** http://www.colorado.edu. **Description:** A four-year state university offering undergraduate and graduate degree programs. Founded in 1876. **Positions advertised include:** Assistant Director for Budget Services; Software System Architect; Education Coordinator; Manager of Information Technology; Director of Operations; Faculty Positions, Various Departments.

UNIVERSITY OF COLORADO AT DENVER
P.O. Box 173364, Campus Box 130, Denver CO 80217-3364. 303/556-2868. **Contact:** Kevin Jacobs, Human Resources. **World Wide Web address:** http://www.ucdhsc.edu. **Description:** A four-year state university offering undergraduate and graduate degree programs. **Positions advertised include:** Computer Technology Coordinator; Grant Specialist Manager; Fiscal Manager; Manager, Academic Technology; Dean, College of Liberal Arts and Sciences; Dean School of Dentistry.

UNIVERSITY OF DENVER
2199 South University Boulevard, Denver CO 80208. 303/871-7420. **Fax:** 303/871-3656. **Contact:** Human Resources. **E-mail address:** hr-postings@du.edu. **World Wide Web address:** http://www.du.edu. **Description:** A four-year university offering undergraduate, graduate, and continuing education programs to more than 8,500 students. **Positions advertised include:** Assistant Professor, Various Departments; Program Counselor; Reference Librarian. **Special programs:** Internships. **Corporate headquarters location:** This location. **Operations at this facility include:** Administration; Research and Development; Service.

UNIVERSITY OF NORTHERN COLORADO
501 20th Street, Carter Hall, Room 2002, Greeley CO 80639. 970/351-2718. **Contact:** Debbi Rees, Human Resources. **World Wide Web address:** http://www.unco.edu. **Description:** A four-year university offering undergraduate and graduate degree programs to more than 12,000 students. **Positions advertised include:** Director, Center for the Enhancement of Teaching and Learning; Director, Various Schools; Assistant Professor, Various Departments

Connecticut

ALBERTUS MAGNUS COLLEGE
700 Prospect Street, New Haven CT 06511. 203/773-8550. **Fax:** 203/773-8984. **Contact:** Human Resources. **World Wide Web address:** http://www.albertus.edu. **Description:** A four-year, liberal arts and sciences college. Founded in 1925.

AMERICAN INSTITUTE FOR FOREIGN STUDY (AIFS)
River Plaza, 9 West Broad Street, Stamford CT 06902. 203/399-5000. **Toll-free phone:** 800/727-2437. **Contact:** Human Resources. **World Wide Web address:** http://www.aifs.org. **Description:** Engaged in the placement of au pairs in American homes, as well as the placement of American students in study programs abroad.

CENTRAL CONNECTICUT STATE UNIVERSITY
1615 Stanley Street, New Britain CT 06050. 860/832-2278. **Contact:** Human Resources. **World Wide Web address:** http://www.ccsu.edu. **Description:** A four-year state university offering undergraduate and graduate degree programs. **Positions advertised include:** Associate Dean, School of Education and Professional Studies; Director of the Doctoral Program in Educational Leadership; Assistant Professor in Educational Leadership; Accountant; Sociologist.

FAIRFIELD UNIVERSITY
1073 North Benson Road, Fairfield CT 06430. 203/254-4000, Ext.: 4080. **Fax:** 203/254-4295. **Contact:** Office of Human Resources. **World Wide Web address:** http:// www.fairfield.edu. **Description:** A four-year Jesuit university providing both undergraduate and graduate programs. Founded in 1942. **NOTE:** Entry-level positions, part-time jobs, and second and third shifts are offered. **Special programs:** Internships. **Corporate headquarters location:** This location. **Number of employees at this location:** 800.

LINDAMOOD-BELL
1574 Post Road, Darien CT 06820. 203/656-0771. **Toll-free phone:** 800/300-1818. **Contact:** Human Resources. **World Wide Web address:** http:// www.lindamoodbell.com. **Description:** A learning-enhancing organization. Runs process-based educational programs. Reaches students from those with severe learning disabilities to those who are extremely gifted. **NOTE:** Part time positions offered. **Positions advertised include:** Clinician. **Special programs:** Seasonal work. **Corporate headquarters location:** San Luis Obispo CA. **Other U.S. locations:** Nationwide. **International locations:** London, England.

MITCHELL COLLEGE
437 Pequot Avenue, New London CT 06320. 860/701-5000. **Fax:** 860/701-5090. **Contact:** Human Resources. **World Wide Web address:** http://www.mitchell.edu. **Description:** A private college offering two- and four-year programs. The college has approximately 650 students enrolled.

NEW TECHNOLOGY SOLUTIONS, INC.
432 Washington Avenue, North Haven CT 06473. 203/234-1404. **Fax:** 203/239-7230. **Contact:** Human Resources. **World Wide Web address:** http://www.newtechusa.com. **Description:** Provides Microsoft Windows and VB developer training. The company offers seminars, on-site training programs, videos, and other related services. Founded in 1993. **Positions advertised include:** Systems Engineer; Senior Systems Engineer; Systems Architect; Practice Manager; Business Development Manager; Technical

Services Director. **Corporate headquarters location:** This location. **Other U.S. locations:** Waltham MA; Providence RI.

PRINCETON REVIEW INC.
1246 Post Road East, Westport CT 06880. 203/226-2662. **Contact:** Human Resources. **World Wide Web address:** http://www.princetonreview.com. **Description:** Offers a variety of review and test preparation courses for students taking exams such as the SAT, GRE, LMAT, LSAT, and GMAT. **Corporate headquarters location:** New York NY. **Listed on:** NASDAQ. **Stock exchange symbol:** REVU.

QUINNIPIAC UNIVERSITY
275 Mount Carmel Avenue, Hamden CT 06518. 203/582-8200. **Contact:** Human Resources. **World Wide Web address:** http://www.quinnipiac.edu. **Description:** A private university with an enrollment of 6,000 students. The university offers undergraduate degrees in business, health sciences, and liberal arts; and graduate degree programs in business, education, health sciences, mass communications, journalism, and law.

SACRED HEART UNIVERSITY
5151 Park Avenue, Fairfield CT 06825-1000. 203/371-7999. **Fax:** 203/365-7527. **Contact:** Human Resources. **E-mail address:** resumehr@sacredheart.edu. **World Wide Web address:** http://www.sacredheart.edu. **Description:** One of the largest Catholic universities in the New England area. Sacred Heart University offers programs through the College of Arts & Sciences, the College of Business, the College of Education & Health Professions, and the University College. Founded in 1963. **Positions advertised include:** Cleaning Supervisor; Director of Bands; Director of Major and Planned Gifts; Graduate Residence Hall Director; Programmer Analyst; Public Safety Officer.

SCORE! LEARNING, INC.
Goodwives Shopping Center, 25 Old Kings Highway North, Suite 43, Darien CT 06820. 203/656-1455. **Toll-free phone:** 800/49SCORE. **Contact:** Human Resources. **E-mail address:** score@trm.brassring.com. **World Wide Web address:** http://www.escore.com. **Description:** Provides learning programs for children. Founded in 1992. **NOTE:** Apply online or send resume to SCORE! Recruiting, 343 Winter Street, Waltham MA 02451. **Positions advertised include:** Assistant Director. **Corporate headquarters location:** Oakland CA. **Other area locations:** Westport CT. **Other U.S. locations:** Nationwide. **Parent company:** Kaplan Inc., The Washington Post Company.

SOUTHERN CONNECTICUT STATE UNIVERSITY
501 Crescent Street, New Haven CT 06515-1355. 203/392-5200. **Fax:** 203/392-5571. **Contact:** Personnel Department. **World Wide Web address:** http://www.southernct.edu. **Description:** A four-year state university offering a variety of undergraduate, graduate, and doctoral degree programs.

UNIVERSITY OF BRIDGEPORT
126 Park Avenue, 7th Floor, Bridgeport CT 06604. 203/576-4000. **Fax:** 203/576-4601. **Contact:** Human Resources. **World Wide Web address:** http://www.bridgeport.edu. **Description:** A four-year, liberal arts university offering over 30 undergraduate and 14 graduate degree programs. **Corporate headquarters location:** This location.

UNIVERSITY OF CONNECTICUT
Brown Building, Mansfield Depot Campus, 9 Walters Avenue, Unit 5075, Storrs CT 06269-5075. 860/486-3034. **Toll-free phone:** 860/486-2000. **Fax:** 860/486-0378. **Contact:** Human Resources. **World Wide Web address:** http://www.hr.uconn.edu. **Description:** This location is the main campus. University of Connecticut is a four-year, state university offering several undergraduate, graduate, and doctoral degrees. **Other area locations:** Hartford CT; Stamford CT; Waterbury CT.

UNIVERSITY OF NEW HAVEN
300 Boston Post Road, West Haven CT 06516. 203/932-7240. **Contact:** Human Resources. **World Wide Web address:** http://www.newhaven.edu. **Description:** An independent, four-year university. Founded in 1920. **NOTE:** Resumes sent via fax or e-mail will not be accepted. **Corporate headquarters location:** This location.

WESTERN CONNECTICUT STATE UNIVERSITY
181 White Street, Danbury CT 06810. 203/837-8210. **Contact:** Human Resources. **World Wide Web address:** http://www.wcsu.edu. **Description:** A four-year state university offering the Ancell School of Business, the School of Arts & Sciences, and the School of Professional Studies.

YALE UNIVERSITY
155 Whitney Avenue, New Haven CT 06510. 203/432-5775. **Contact:** Human Resources. **World Wide Web address:** http://www.yale.edu. **Description:** One of the country's oldest universities. Yale University is a private, nonprofit institution that offers bachelor's, master's, and doctoral degrees. Founded in 1801. **Number of employees at this location:** 8,000.

Delaware

DELAWARE STATE UNIVERSITY
1200 DuPont Highway, Dover DE 19901. 302/857-6261. **Fax:** 302/857-6264. **Contact:** Human Resources. **E-mail address:** hr@desu.edu. **World Wide Web address:** http://www.desu.edu. **Description:** A state university offering bachelor's, master's and professional degrees. **NOTE:** See website for current job openings and application instructions. **Positions advertised include:** Maintenance Mechanic II; Maintenance Craftsman Mechanic III; Construction Field Manager; Post Doctoral Research Fellow; Grants Officer; Assistant Professor of Psychology; Assistant/Associate Professor of Sport Management; Computer Analyst. **Other area locations:** Georgetown DE; Wilmington DE.

DELAWARE TECHNICAL AND COMMUNITY COLLEGE
Terry Campus, 100 Campus Drive, Dover DE 19904-1383. 302/857-1290. **Recorded jobline:** 302/857-1994. **Fax:** 302/857-1297. **Contact:** Human Resources. **E-mail address:** terry-jobs@dtcc.edu. **World Wide Web address:** http://www.dtcc.edu. **Description:** A statewide institution of higher education, providing academic, technical, continuing education and industrial training at four campuses. **NOTE:** See website for current job openings and application instructions. **Positions advertised include:** Student Records Technician; Custodian; Nursing Instructor. **Other area locations:** Georgetown DE; Newark DE; Stanton DE; Wilmington DE.

GOLDEY-BEACOM COLLEGE
4701 Limestone Road, Wilmington DE 19808. 302/998-8814. **Fax:** 302/998-0539. **Contact:** Director of Human Resources. **E-mail address:** hr@gbc.edu. **World Wide Web address:** http://www.gbc.edu. **Description:** Private, coeducational college offering bachelor's and master's degrees in all areas of business. **NOTE:** See website for current job openings and to download an application. **Positions advertised include:** Security Guard.

CAESAR RODNEY SCHOOL DISTRICT
219 Old North Road, Wyoming DE 19934. 302/697-2173. **Fax:** 302/697-3406. **Contact:** Human Resources. **World Wide Web address:** http://www.k12.de.us/cr. **Description:** A school district comprised of eight elementary schools, one junior high school, one high school and one special education school. Serves nearly 7,000 students whose families are spread over more than 140 square miles. **NOTE:** See website for current job openings and application instructions. **Positions advertised include:** Substitute Teacher; Speech Language Pathologist.

UNIVERSITY OF DELAWARE
43 Academy Street, Newark DE 19716. 302/831-2171. **Recorded jobline:** 302/831-6612. **Contact:** Human Resources. **World Wide Web address:** http://www.udel.edu. **Description:** A four-year, state university offering bachelor's, master's (including MBAs) and doctoral degrees. Approximately 16,000 undergraduate and 2,600 graduate students attend the University of Delaware. **Positions advertised include:** Department of Art Chair; Assistant/Associate Professor, Various Departments. **President:** David P. Roselle. **Number of employees at this location:** 4,500.

WILMINGTON COLLEGE
Pratt Student Center, 320 North DuPont Highway, New Castle DE 19720. 302/328-9401. **Fax:** 302/328-7918. **Contact:** Gloria Johnson, Human Resources Director. **E-mail address:** humanresources@wilmcoll.edu **World Wide Web address:** http://www.wilmcoll.edu. **Description:** A private, career-oriented institution offering undergraduate and graduate degrees. Undergraduate enrollment is approximately 3,000.

District Of Columbia
AMERICAN ASSOCIATION OF UNIVERSITY WOMEN
1111 16th Street NW, Washington DC 20036. 202/785-7795. **Fax:** 202/872-1425. **Contact:** Beverly McCalop, Human Resources. **E-mail address:** aauwjobs@aauw.org. **World Wide Web address:** http://www.aauw.org. **Description:** An organization targeting the needs of women in the college community. **NOTE:** Resumes are accepted by mail, e-mail, or fax. **Positions advertised include:** Field Associate; Helpline Representative; Fellows Alumnae Network Officer; Administrative Assistant; Controller. **Internship information:** A variety of internships are offered. See website for more information regarding specific requirements and application deadlines. **Other U.S. locations:** Nationwide. **Executive Director:** Jacqueline E. Woods.

AMERICAN UNIVERSITY
4400 Massachusetts Avenue NW, Washington DC 20016-8054. 202/885-2591. **Fax:** 202/885-2558. **Contact:** Human Resources. **E-mail address:** careers@American.edu. **World Wide Web address:** http://www.american.edu. **Description:** An independent, four-year university. American University has program offerings within the School of Public Affairs, the School of Communications, the College of Arts and Sciences, the Washington College of Law, the Kogod College of Business Administration, and the School of International Services. The university also offers return-to-school programs. **NOTE:** Please check the Website for a listing of available positions. **Number of employees at this location:** 1,100.

BLACKBOARD INC.
1899 L Street NW, 11th Floor, Washington DC 20036. 202/463-4860. **Toll-free phone:** 800/424-9299. **Fax:** 202/463-4863. **Contact:** Human Resources. **E-mail address:** jobs@blackboard.com. **World Wide Web address:** http://www.blackboard.com. **Description:** An education software provider. Founded in 1997. **Positions advertised include:** Account Manager; Developer; Administrative Assistant; Budget Analyst; Channel Sales Manager; Contracts Manager; Database Administrator; Director, Higher Education Marketing; International Developer; Software Engineer; Technical Consultant; Trademark Paralegal. **Other U.S. locations:** Phoenix AZ. **Listed on:** Privately held. **Number of employees nationwide:** 400.

THE CATHOLIC UNIVERSITY OF AMERICA
620 Michigan Avenue NE, Room 170, Leahy Hall, Washington DC 20064. 202/319-5050. **Fax:** 202/319-5802. **Contact:** Gigi R. Washington, Employment Manager. **E-mail address:** resumes@cua.edu. **World Wide Web address:** http://www.cua.edu. **NOTE:** See website for updated position listings. **Description:** A four-year, Catholic university offering bachelor's, master's, first professional, and doctoral degrees. Approximately 2,800 undergraduate and 3,700 graduate students attend the university. **Corporate headquarters location:** This location.

GALLAUDET UNIVERSITY
800 Florida Avenue NE, College Hall, Room 106, Washington DC 20002. 202/651-5000. **Recorded jobline:** 202/651-5358. **Fax:** 202/651-5344. **Contact:** Human Resources Services. **E-mail address:** personnel.office@gallaudet.edu. **World Wide Web address:** http://www.gallaudet.edu. **Description:** A liberal arts school for deaf and hearing-impaired students. Graduate programs admit both hearing and non-hearing students. Gallaudet University has an enrollment of approximately 1,500 students. **NOTE:** Please call the jobline for a listing of available positions. Unsolicited applications are not accepted. **Positions advertised include:** Staff Interpreter; Occupational Therapist; Speech/Language Pathologist; Social Worker; Manager, Data Center; Residential Educator.

GEORGE WASHINGTON UNIVERSITY
2033 K Street NW, Suite 220, Washington DC 20052. 202/994-9600. **Fax:** 202/994-9619. **Contact:** Human Resources Department. **E-mail address:** hrweb@gwu.edu. **World Wide Web address:** http://www.gwu.edu. **Description:** A four-year, liberal arts university offering certificates, associate's, bachelor's, master's (including MBA), and doctoral degrees. Approximately 6,000 undergraduate and 8,700 graduate students attend George Washington University. **Positions advertised include:** Library Specialist; Campus community Director; Director of Alumni Programming; Sr. Budget Analyst; Sr. Programming Analyst.

HOWARD UNIVERSITY
400 Bryant Street NW, Washington DC 20059. 202/806-7714. **Fax:** 202/806-5315. **Contact:** Office of Human Resource Management, Department of Employment. **E-mail address:** huemploymentapplic@howard.edu. **World Wide Web address:** http://www.howard.edu. **Description:** A private research university with law, dental, and medical schools. Approximately 9,500 undergraduate and 3,100 graduate students attend Howard University. **Positions advertised include:** Director of Development; Librarian; Director of Engineering; Compensation Analyst; Sr. Benefit Analyst; Academic Resource Manager. **President:** H. Patrick Swygert.

NATIONAL EDUCATION ASSOCIATION (NEA)
1201 16th Street NW, Washington DC 20036-3290. 202/822-7613. **Fax:** 202/822-7619. **Contact:** Human Resources. **World Wide Web address:** http://www.nea.org. **Description:** A national, nonprofit membership organization that represents teachers, the teaching profession, and education support personnel. Major programs and functions include organizing and membership, education policy, government relations, communications, publishing, research, human and civil rights, negotiations, and administration. **Positions advertised include:** Sr. Program/Policy Specialist; Sr. Accountant; Sr. Systems Administrator; Sr. Government Relations Specialist. **Corporate headquarters location:** This location. **Other U.S. locations:** Nationwide. **Number of employees at this location:** 500.

STRAYER UNIVERSITY
1025 15th Street NW, Washington DC 20005. 202/408-2400. **Contact:** Human Resources. **World Wide Web address:** http://www.strayer.edu. **Description:** A four-year university offering business and information technology programs both on-campus and online. Its 27 campuses are located throughout Maryland, North Carolina, South Carolina, Tennessee, Virginia, and Washington DC. **Positions advertised include:** Learning Resource Center Assistant.

UNIVERSITY OF THE DISTRICT OF COLUMBIA
4200 Connecticut Avenue NW, Building 38, Room 301, Washington DC 20008. 202/274-5020. **Contact:**

Human Resources. **World Wide Web address:** http://www.udc.edu. **Description:** Offers programs through the College of Professional Studies, which includes the School of Business and Public Administration and the School of Engineering and Applied Science; and the College of Arts and Sciences, encompassing the School of Arts and Education and the School of Science and Mathematics. Each year, 800 to 900 graduates receive one-year certificates, two-year Associate in Applied Science and Associate of Arts degrees, four-year Bachelor of Arts and Bachelor of Science degrees, and master's degrees. Founded in 1976. **Positions advertised include:** Assistant/Associate Professor, Various Departments; Head Soccer Coach; Financial Aid Counselor.

Florida

EDISON COMMUNITY COLLEGE
8099 College Parkway, Fort Myers 33919. 239/489-9300. **Fax:** 941/489-9041. **Recorded jobline:** 941/489-9120. **Contact:** Leslie Rider, Human Resources Specialist. **World Wide Web address:** http://www.edison.edu. **Description:** A two-year college offering associate's degrees, certification programs, and noncredit continuing education courses. **NOTE:** Part-time jobs are offered. **Positions advertised include:** Spanish Professor; Mathematics Professor; Humanities Professor; Nursing Professor; Campus Dean; Business & Technology Coordinator; Faculty Planner; Construction Manager; Student Services Specialist; Clerk Specialist; Adjunct Services Coordinator. **Other area locations:** Naples FL; Port Charlotte FL. **Number of employees at this location:** 300.

EMBRY-RIDDLE AERONAUTICAL UNIVERSITY
600 South Clyde Morris Boulevard, Daytona Beach FL 32114-3900. 386/226-6145. **Contact:** Human Resources. **World Wide Web address:** http://www.db.erau.edu. **Description:** A private, four-year, coeducational, undergraduate university offering studies in aviation, aerospace, and engineering. **Positions advertised include:** Department Chair Mathematics; Dean of the College of Career Education; Assistant Provost; Office Associate; Assistant Professor of Mathematics; Interactive Designer; Assistant Director Sports and Marketing and Promotions; Accounting Clerk; Assistant Center Director; Mailroom Clerk; Resident Director; Administrative Assistant; Shift Safety Officer; Serials Librarian; Data Entry Operator; Vice President Chief Financial Officer. **Special programs:** Internships. **Other U.S. locations:** Prescott AZ. **Number of employees nationwide:** 1,200.

EVERGLADES UNIVERSITY
5002 T Rex Avenue, Suite 100, Boca Raton FL 33431. 954/772-2655. **Toll-free phone:** 888/772-6077. **Fax:** 954/772-2695. **World Wide Web address:** http://www.evergladesuniversity.edu. **Description:** A private four-year university with graduate and undergraduate students. **Positions advertised include:** Admission Coordinator; Dean; Administrative Assistant; Financial Aide Officer; Aviation Adjunct Faculty.

FLORIDA ATLANTIC UNIVERSITY
777 Glades Road, P.O. Box 3091, Boca Raton FL 33431. 461/297-3057. **Recorded jobline:** 561/297-3506. **Contact:** Human Resources. **World Wide Web address:** http://www.fau.edu. **Description:** A four-year liberal arts university offering bachelor's, master's (including MBA), and doctoral degrees. Approximately 11,500 undergraduate and 3,000 graduate students attend Florida Atlantic University. **Positions advertised include:** Assistant Director Student Affairs; Medical Curriculum Coordinator; Admissions Coordinator; Media Coordinator; Communications Supervisor; Facility Planning Coordinator; Athletic Academic Advisor; Student Affairs Coordinator; Chief of Police; Director Student Affairs; Program Assistant; Secretary College of Business; Registration Clerk; Secretary Women's Studies; Ocean Engineering Clerk; Office Support Specialist Admissions; Police Service Technician; Medical Research Assistant.

FLORIDA COMMUNITY COLLEGE AT JACKSONVILLE
501 West State Street, Jacksonville FL 32202. 904/632-3210. **Recorded jobline:** 904/632-3161. **Contact:** Employment Manager, Human Resources Department. **World Wide Web address:** http://www.fccj.org. **Description:** An accredited institution offering associate's degrees, corporate and technical training, and special and continuing education programs. Total enrollment is approximately 28,000. Founded in 1966. **Positions advertised include:** Administrative Assistant; Administrative Specialist; Plant Service Manager; Plant Service Worker; Security Officer; Student Offices Advisor; Student Learning Specialist; Business Development Officer; Database Administrator; Dean of Virtual College; Network System Specialist; System Programmer; Counseling Coordinator; Administrative Specialist; Audio Visual Specialist; Security Officer. **NOTE:** Entry-level positions and part-time jobs are offered. **President:** Dr. Steven Wallace. **Number of employees at this location:** 2,700.

FLORIDA INTERNATIONAL UNIVERSITY
University Park, 11200 South West 8th Street PC 224, Miami FL 33199-0001. 305/348-2181. **Contact:** Human Resources. **World Wide Web address:** http://www.fiu.edu. **E-mail address:** hr@fiu.edu. **Description:** A multi-campus, accredited university. **Positions advertised include:** Production Manager; University Controller; Admissions Coordinator; Account Manager; PR Writer; Word Processing Operator; Inventory Clerk; Office Assistant; Engineer; Technical Writer; Librarian Technical Assistant.

FLORIDA MEMORIAL COLLEGE
15800 NW 42nd Avenue, Miami FL 33054. 305/626-3622. **Fax:** 305/626-3109. **Contact:** Human Resources. **World Wide Web address:** http://www.fmc.edu. **Description:** A private, four-year, liberal arts college with an enrollment of approximately 1,500 students. **Positions advertised include:** Assistant Professor Biology; Assistant Professor Broadcasting; Assistant Professor Criminology; Assistant Professor Elementary Education; Assistant Professor Environmental Science; Assistant Professor Finance; Assistant Professor Physical Education; Assistant Professor Psychology. **Special programs:** Internships. **Operations at this facility include:** Administration. **Listed on:** Privately held. **Number of employees at this location:** 220.

FLORIDA STATE UNIVERSITY
6200-A University Center, Tallahassee FL 32306-2410. 850/644-6035. **Contact:** Phaedra Harris, Coordinator of Human Resources. **World Wide Web address:** http://www.fsu.edu. **Description:** A four-year state university offering certificates, bachelor's, master's (including MBA), and doctoral degrees. Approximately 21,500 undergraduate and 5,500 graduate students attend Florida State University. **Positions advertised include:** Assistant Director; Multi Purpose Faculty; Assistant Director University Housing; Assistant in Accounting; Assistant in Communication; Assistant Professor; Office Assistant; Office Manager; Professor & Dean; Program Assistant; Psychologist; Broadcast Specialist; Fiscal Assistant; Telecom Technician; University School Instructor. **Operations at this facility include:** Administration; Research and Development. **Number of employees at this location:** 2,500.

HILLSBOROUGH COMMUNITY COLLEGE
P.O. Box 31127, Tampa FL 33631-3127. 813/253-7000. **Physical address:** 39 Columbia Drive, Davis Island, Tampa FL 33601. **Fax:** 813/253-7034. **Recorded jobline:** 813/253-7185. **Contact:** Human Resources Department. **E-mail address:** employ@hccfl.com. **World Wide Web address:** http://www.hcc.cc.fl.us. **Description:** Hillsborough Community College is a multicampus, state-run

community college accredited by the Southern Association of Colleges and Schools. **Positions advertised include:** Staff Assistant; Accountant; Aqua Culture Instructor; Dean of Health & Wellness & Sports Technician; Cashier Clerk; Lab Assistant; Shipping & Receiving Specialist; Learning Resources Technician; Nursing Instructor; Trade Worker; Child Development Associate; HVAC Station Operator. **Corporate headquarters location:** This location. **Operations at this facility include:** This location offers programs specializing in computer programming, business management, fire science, and criminal justice training. **Number of employees at this location:** 1,500.

JACKSONVILLE UNIVERSITY
2800 University Boulevard North, Jacksonville FL 32211. 904/256-8000. **Fax:** 904/256-7553. **Contact:** Career Services. **E-mail address:** careerservices@ju.edu. **World Wide Web address:** http://www.ju.edu. **Description:** A private four year liberal arts college on 260 acres in North Western Florida offering undergraduate and graduate programs. **Positions advertised include:** Assistant Professor of Art Ceramics; Assistant Professor of Biology Marine Science; Office Coordinator; Public Safety Officer; Accounting Associate.

LYNN UNIVERSITY
3601 North Military Trail, Boca Raton FL 33431-5598. 561/237-7853. **Fax:** 561/237-7926. **Contact:** Angela Juiliano, Human Resources. **E-mail address:** resumes@lynn.edu. **World Wide Web address:** http://www.lynn.edu. **Description:** An accredited, private university offering 38 associate's, bachelor's, master's, and doctoral degree programs. Program areas include Arts and Sciences, Business, and Education. Founded in 1962.

MIAMI-DADE COMMUNITY COLLEGE KENDALL CAMPUS
11011 SW 104th Street, Miami FL 33176. 305/237-2051. **Toll-free phone:** 800/955-8771. **Fax:** 305/237-0961. **Recorded jobline:** 305/237-2050. **Contact:** Human Resources. **World Wide Web address:** http://www.mdcc.edu. **Description:** A two-year state college offering an Associate in Science degree, Associate in Arts degree, and Vocational Credit Certificates. **NOTE:** Entry-level positions and second and third shifts are offered. **Positions advertised include:** Mathematics Faculty; Foreign Language Faculty; Physician Assistant Program Faculty; Emergency Medical Services Faculty; Veteran Technology Faculty; Department Chair; School of Nursing Director; Department Chair Person; Provost for Education; Director of Publications; Instructional Development Coordinator. **Corporate headquarters location:** This location. **Operations at this facility include:** Administration. **Number of employees at this location:** 2,300.

MIAMI-DADE COMMUNITY COLLEGE MEDICAL CENTER CAMPUS
950 NW 20th Street, Miami FL 33127. 305/237-4247. **Contact:** Human Resources. **World Wide Web address:** http://www.mdcc.edu. **Description:** A two-year state college offering programs through the School of Allied Health, School of Nursing, Physical Assistant Program, and Continuing Education. **Positions advertised include:** Mathematics Faculty; Foreign Language Faculty; Physician Assistant Program Faculty; Emergency Medical Services Faculty; Veteran Technology Faculty; Department Chair; School of Nursing Director; Department Chair Person; Provost for Education; Director of Publications; Instructional Development Coordinator

MIAMI-DADE COMMUNITY COLLEGE MITCHELL WOLFSON CAMPUS
300 NE Second Avenue, Miami FL 33132. 305/237-3000. **Contact:** Human Resources. **World Wide Web address:** http://www.mdcc.edu. **Description:** A two-year state college offering programs through the School of Allied Health, School of Nursing, Physical Assistant Program, and Continuing Education. **Positions advertised include:** Mathematics Faculty; Foreign Language Faculty; Physician Assistant Program Faculty; Emergency Medical Services Faculty; Veteran Technology Faculty; Department Chair; School of Nursing Director; Department Chair Person; Provost for Education; Director of Publications; Instructional Development Coordinator.

MIAMI-DADE COMMUNITY COLLEGE NORTH CAMPUS
11380 NW 27th Avenue, Miami FL 33167. 305/237-1000. **Contact:** Human Resources. **World Wide Web address:** http://www.mdcc.edu. **Description:** A two-year state college offering programs through the School of Allied Health, School of Nursing, Physical Assistant Program, and Continuing Education. **Positions advertised include:** Mathematics Faculty; Foreign Language Faculty; Physician Assistant Program Faculty; Emergency Medical Services Faculty; Veteran Technology Faculty; Department Chair; School of Nursing Director; Department Chair Person; Provost for Education; Director of Publications; Instructional Development Coordinator.

NOVA SOUTHEASTERN UNIVERSITY
3301 College Avenue, Fort Lauderdale FL 33314. 954/262-7870. **Contact:** Human Resources. **World Wide Web address:** http://www.nova.edu. **Description:** A university offering undergraduate and graduate programs to approximately 18,000 students. **Positions advertised include:** Reference Librarian; Acquisitions Librarian; Reference Instructor Librarian; Medical Assistant; Customer Service Representative; Library Network Specialist; Buyer; Mail / Sort Clerk; Mail Researcher; Executive Assistant.

PALM BEACH ATLANTIC UNIVERSITY
P.O Box 24708, West Palm Beach FL 33401. 561/803-2000. **Physical address:** 901 South Flagler Drive, West Palm Beach FL 33401 **Contact;** Cindi Lewis, faculty or Mona Hicks, staff. **E-mail address;** cindy_lewis@pba.edu; mona_hicks@pba.edu. **World Wide Web address:** http://www.pba.edu. **Description:** A four year private college in West Palm Beach with undergraduate and graduate programs with approximately 3000 students. **Positions advertised include:** Secretary; Academic Advisor; Administrative Assistant; Help Desk Specialist; Network Administrator; Assistant Professor; Reference Librarian.

PALM BEACH COMMUNITY COLLEGE
4200 Congress Avenue, Lake Worth FL 33461. 561/868-3114. **Fax:** 561/439-8202. **Contact:** Human Resources. **World Wide Web address:** http://www.pbcc.cc.fl.us. **Description:** A community college offering associate's degrees in the arts and sciences. **Positions advertised include:** Early Learning Coach; Learning Specialist; Program Coordinator; Program Specialist; Business Analyst; Student Services Specialist; Accounting Associate; Groundskeeper; Media Assistant; Office Assistant; Security Guard; Student Ambassador; Teacher Assistant; Nursing Tutor.

ROLLINS COLLEGE
1000 Holt Avenue, Campus Box 2718, Winter Park FL 32789. 407/646-2320. **Contact:** Personnel. **World Wide Web address:** http://www.rollins.edu/hr/jobindex.htm. **Description:** A private, liberal arts college offering bachelor's and master's degrees to approximately 1,400 students. **NOTE:** Jobseekers may apply in person at the Warren Administration Building, Monday - Thursday, 9:00 a.m. - 4:00 p.m. **Positions advertised include:** Athletic Training Assistant; Director of Career Services; Assistant Professor of Acting; Assistant Professor of Elementary Secondary Education; Dispatcher; Head Provost Advisor; Integrated Past Management Technology; Marketing Assistant; Math Teacher; Project Custodian; Resident Advisor; Safety Officer; Summer Day Camp Counselor; Summer Day Camp Instructor; Facilities Management; Visiting Assistant; Professor of Economics. **Operations at this facility include:** Administration. **Listed on:** Privately

held. **President:** Rita Bornstein. **Number of employees at this location:** 530.

ST. PETERSBURG JUNIOR COLLEGE
14025 58th Street, Clearwater FL 33760. 727/341-3081. **Contact:** Mae Widit, Human Resources. **World Wide Web address:** http://www.spjc.cc.fl.us. **Description:** A junior college serving Pinellas County. The school offers associate's degrees in the arts and sciences and prepares students for transferring to other institutions. **NOTE:** To apply for a position you must complete the on-line application. **Positions advertised include:** Programming Analyst; Assistant Director of Center for Teaching and Transportation Principals Program; Assistant Vice President of Financial Aide & Management; Development Coordinator Fundraising; Project Coordinator; Industrial Development Coordinator; Instructional Development Coordinator; Curriculum Designer; Curriculum Development Specialist; Orthotics & Prosthetics; Educational Technologist; Program Director; Project Technologist; Allstate Campus Provost; Scholarships & Student Financial Assistant Officer; Student Financial Assistant Officer. **Operations at this facility include:** Administration; Service. **Number of employees at this location:** 940.

UNIVERSITY OF CENTRAL FLORIDA
12565 Research Parkway, Suite 360, Orlando FL 32826-2912. 407/823-2771. **Contact:** Mark Roberts, Human Resources Director. **World Wide Web address:** http://www.ucf.edu. **Description:** A university offering bachelor's, master's, and doctoral degrees to approximately 31,000 students. **Positions advertised include:** Assistant Vice President; Coordinator of Information Public Services; Assistant Director; Academic Support Services; Associate Director; Administrative Services Coordinator; Human Resources Coordinator; High School Coordinator; Human Resources Coordinator; Intercollegiate Athletics Coordinator; Student Affairs Coordinator; University Counseling Services Director; Academic Support Services Director; Associate Professor – School of Nursing; Student Affairs Director; Custodial Worker.

UNIVERSITY OF FLORIDA
4th Floor Stadium, P.O. Box 115002, Gainesville FL 32611. 352/392-4621. **Fax:** 352/392-7094. **Contact:** Human Resources. **World Wide Web address:** http://www.hr.ufl.edu. **Description:** A state university offering graduate, undergraduate, and professional programs to approximately 43,000 students. **NOTE:** Entry-level positions are offered. **Positions advertised include:** Registered Nurse; Laboratory Technician; Clerk; Dental Assistant; Office Manager; Library Technical Assistant; Motor Vehicle Operator; Locksmith; Custodial Worker; Clerical Aide; Accountant; Vet Care Technician; Vet Hospital Technician; Administrative Assistant; Assistant Carpenter; Secretary; Law Enforcement Officer; Program Assistant; Fiscal Assistant. **Number of employees at this location:** 11,500.

UNIVERSITY OF MIAMI
1507 Levante Avenue, Coral Gables FL 33124. 305/284-2211. **Contact:** Human Resources. **World Wide Web address:** http://www.miami.edu. **Description:** A university offering bachelor's, master's, doctoral, and professional degrees. **Positions advertised include:** Research Associate; Senior Research Associate; Postdoctoral Associate; Nurse Specialist; Pathology Program Specialist; Audiologist; Hospital Division Manager; Executive Assistant; Associate Professor of Clinical Obstetrics; Associate Professor of Clinical Surgery. **NOTE:** Jobseekers are advised to obtain a copy of the university's job bulletin through the Website for information about employment opportunities. **Number of employees at this location:** More than 9,000.

UNIVERSITY OF NORTH FLORIDA
4567 St. John's Bluff Road South, Jacksonville FL 32224. 904/620-2903. **Contact:** Human Resources. **World Wide Web address:** http://www.unf.edu. **Description:** A university offering graduate and undergraduate programs to approximately 12,000 students. **Positions advertised include:** Maintenance Mechanic; Accountant; Custodial Worker; Office Assistant; Data Entry Clerk; OPS Receptionist; Administrative Assistant; Coordinator Computer Applications; Intercollegiate Athletics Coordinator; Research Program Coordinator; Special Events Coordinator; Associate General Counsel; Research Coordinator. **President:** Annie H. Hopkins.

UNIVERSITY OF SOUTH FLORIDA (USF)
4202 East Fowler Avenue, SVC 2172, Tampa FL 33620-6980. 813/974-2974. **Contact:** Human Resources. **World Wide Web address:** http://www.usf.edu. **Description:** A state university serving approximately 37,000 undergraduate, graduate, and doctoral students. **Positions advertised include:** Advancement Coordinator; Broadcasting Coordinator; Human Services Coordinator; Student Affairs Coordinator; University Housing Coordinator.

UNIVERSITY OF WEST FLORIDA
11000 University Parkway, Pensacola FL 32514-5750. 850/474-2694. **Recorded jobline:** 850/474-2842. **Contact:** Human Resources. **World Wide Web address:** http://www.uwf.edu. **Description:** A university offering associate's, bachelor's, master's, and doctoral degrees to approximately 8,000 students. **Positions advertised include:** HVAC Operator; Police Communications Operator; Senior Fiscal Assistant; Maintenance Superintendent; Clerk Typist; Vocational Counselor/Teacher; Rehabilitative Technician; Camp Counselor; Coordinator, Educational/Trainee Programs; Coordinator, Facilities Planning; Assistant Professor; Lecturer. **President:** Dr. Morris L. Marx.

Georgia

AGNES SCOTT COLLEGE
141 East College Avenue, Decatur GA 30030-3797. 404/471-6384. **Toll-free phone:** 800/868-8602 Ext. 6384. **Fax:** 404/471-6682. **Recorded jobline:** 404/471-6383. **Contact:** Karen Gilbert, Human Resources Director. **E-mail address:** hrjobs@agnesscott.edu; kgilbert@agnesscott.edu. **World Wide Web address:** http://www.agnesscott.edu. **Description:** A four-year private college offering bachelor's and master's degrees. **Positions advertised include:** Assistant Professor of English; Visiting Assistant Professor; Director of Assessment; Director of the Science Center; Director of the Dalton Gallery; Laboratory Specialist.

THE AMERICAN INTERCONTINENTAL UNIVERSITY
3330 Peachtree Road NE, Atlanta GA 30326. 888/999-4248. **Fax:** 404/965-5701. **Contact:** Human Resources. **World Wide Web address:** http://www.houseofedu.com/aiuat/index.jsp. **Description:** A college offering associate's and bachelor's degrees in international business, interior and fashion design, information technology, and multimedia communication. **Corporate headquarters location:** This location. **Other area locations:** Dunwoody GA. **Other U.S. locations:** Los Angeles CA; Fort Lauderdale FL; Houston TX. **International locations:** London England.

THE ART INSTITUTE OF ATLANTA
6600 Peachtree Dunwoody Road, 100 Embassy Row, Atlanta GA 30328-1649. 770/394-8300. **Toll-free phone:** 800/275-4242. **Fax:** 770/394-9949. **Contact:** Joselyn Cassidy, Director of Human Resources. **E-mail address:** cassidyj@aii.edu. **World Wide Web address:** http://www.aia.artinstitutes.edu. **Description:** A two- and four-year art college specializing in visual communications, culinary arts, interior design, photographic imaging, video production, computer animation, multimedia, and fashion marketing. **NOTE:** Entry-level positions are offered. Direct contact phone is 770/689-4813. **Positions advertised include:** Department Chair – Media Arts and Animation. **Corporate headquarters location:** Pittsburgh PA. **Other U.S. locations:** Nationwide. **Operations at this

facility include: Administration; Sales. **Listed on:** Privately held. **Number of employees at this location:** 225. **Number of employees nationwide:** 5,000.

ATKINSON COUNTY SCHOOLS
506 East Roberts Avenue, Pearson GA 31642. 912/422-7373. **Fax:** 912/422-7369. **World Wide Web address:** http://www.atkinson.k12.ga.us. **Description:** Office of the Superintendent of Atkinson County Schools.

ATLANTA METROPOLITAN COLLEGE
1630 Metropolitan Parkway SW, Atlanta GA 30310-4498. 404/756-4000. **Fax:** 404/756-4777. **Contact:** Regina Ray Simmons, Human Resources. **E-mail address:** hr@amcmail.atlm.peachnet.edu. **World Wide Web address:** http://www.atlm.edu. **Description:** A two-year college with an enrollment of approximately 2,000. **Positions advertised include:** Reference Librarian; Financial Aid Counselor. **Offices hours:** Monday – Friday, 8:30 a.m. – 5:15 p.m.

ATLANTA TECHNICAL COLLEGE
1560 Metropolitan Parkway SW, Atlanta GA 30310. 404/756-3700. **Contact:** Human Resources. **World Wide Web address:** http://www.atlantatech.org. **Description:** A technical college whose programs of study include business and media technology, human services, health occupations, and information technology. **President:** Dr. Brenda Watts Jones.

BAUDER COLLEGE
384 Northyards Boulevard NW, Suite 190 and 400, Atlanta GA 30313. 404/237-7573. **Toll-free phone:** 800/241-3797. **Contact:** Human Resources. **World Wide Web address:** http://www.bauder.edu. **Description:** A two-year college offering associate's degrees in business administration, fashion design, merchandising, and interior design.

CLAYTON COLLEGE & STATE UNIVERSITY
5900 North Lee Street, Morrow GA 30260. 770/961-3400. **Contact:** Human Resources. **World Wide Web address:** http://www.clayton.edu. **Description:** A four-year state university enrolling nearly 6,000 students. **NOTE:** Human Resources phone is 770/961-3540. Please visit website to see job listings and to download application form. A separate application must be submitted for each position applied for. **Positions advertised include:** Head Women's Basketball Coach; Head Men's Soccer Coach; Instructor – Various Departments; Faculty – Various Departments.

DEKALB TECHNICAL COLLEGE
1085 Montreal Road Center, Clarkston GA 30021-1360. 404/297-9522, Ext.: 2106. **Fax:** 404/298-3601. **Contact:** Gale Belton, Personnel Services. **E-mail address:** employment@dekalbtech.org. **World Wide Web address:** http://www.dekalb.tec.ga.us. **Description:** A technical college offering associate's degrees in a broad range of studies. **NOTE:** Please visit website to search for jobs, find more specific contact information, and to download employment application. **Positions advertised include:** Adjunct Instructor of English; Adjunct Instructor of Psychology; Adjunct Instructor of Speech. **Office hours:** Monday – Friday, 8:00 a.m. – 5:00 p.m. **Other area locations:** Covington GA.

EMANUEL COUNTY SCHOOLS
201 North Main, P.O. Box 130, Swainsboro GA 30401. 478/237-6674. **Fax:** 478/237-3404. **World Wide Web address:** http://www.emanuel.k12.ga.us. **Description:** Runs the schools in Emanuel County. **NOTE:** Please visit website to see job listings.

EMORY UNIVERSITY
OXFORD COLLEGE OF EMORY UNIVERSITY
1762 Clifton Road, Room 103, Atlanta GA 30322. 404/727-7613. **Contact:** Employment Division, Human Resources. **World Wide Web address:** http://www.emory.edu. **Description:** An independent, four-year university offering bachelor's, master's, and doctoral degrees in a variety of disciplines. Oxford College was established as an alternative schooling option for freshmen entering Emory University. Oxford College students matriculate into Emory University after one year. **NOTE:** Visit http://emory.hr.emory.edu/careers.nsf to register, search for jobs, and apply online. **Positions advertised include:** Senior Accountant; Administrative Assistant; Applications Developer; Assistant/Associate Professor – Various Departments; Assistant Director of Student Life; Clinical Administrator; Cytogen Technologist; Director – Business and Finance; Genetics Counselor; Post-Doctorate Fellow; Research Specialist- Various Departments; Tumor Registrar.

GEORGIA HIGHLANDS COLLEGE
3175 Cedartown Highway SE, Roma GA 30161. 706/802-5000. **Toll-free phone:** 800/332-2406. **Fax:** 706/295-6610. **Contact:** Human Resources. **E-mail address:** hr@floyd.edu. **World Wide Web address:** http://www.floyd.edu. **Description:** A two-year state college with an enrollment of approximately 3,000 students. Founded in 1970. **NOTE:** Human Resources phone is 706/802-5136. Please visit website to search for jobs and apply online. **Positions advertised include:** Director of College Relations; Enrollment Management Registrar; Assistant Professor – Accounting; Assistant Professor – Dental Hygiene; Instructor – Physical Education – Part-time; Student Financial Aid Counselor. **President:** J. Randy Pierce.

GEORGIA HIGHLANDS COLLEGE
NORTH METRO CAMPUS
5198 Ross Road, Acworth GA 30102. 770/975-4088. **Fax:** 770/975-4119. **Contact:** Human Resources. **E-mail address:** hr@floyd.edu. **World Wide Web address:** http://www.floyd.edu. **Description:** A two-year state college. Founded in 1970. **NOTE:** Please send resumes to the main campus: Human Resources, P.O. Box 1864, Rome GA 30162-1864. **Positions advertised include:** Director of College Relations; Enrollment Management Registrar; Assistant Professor – Accounting; Instructor – Physical Education – Part-time; Student Financial Aid Counselor

GEORGIA INSTITUTE OF TECHNOLOGY
GEORGIA TECH RESEARCH INSTITUTE
500 Tech Parkway, Atlanta GA 30332-0435. 404/894-9765. **Fax:** 404/894-1235. **Contact:** Human Resources. **World Wide Web address:** http://www.gatech.edu. **Description:** A public technical institute with approximately 12,000 students enrolled in its undergraduate, graduate, and doctoral programs. Georgia Tech Research Institute is a nonprofit, client-oriented, applied research and development organization. The majority of the institute's research is sponsored by the U.S. Department of Defense. Founded in 1885. **NOTE:** Please visit website to search for jobs and apply online. **Positions advertised include:** Security Guard; Air Conditioning Mechanic; Contracting Officer; Accounting Personnel; Research Technician; Administrative Assistant; Director of the Language Institute; Public Safety Officer; Retail Manager; Electrical Engineer. **Number of employees at this location:** 4,000.

GEORGIA PERIMETER COLLEGE
3251 Panthersville Road, Decatur GA 30034-3897. 678/891-2300. **Fax:** 404/244-5774. **Recorded jobline:** 404/244-2376. **Contact:** Human Resources. **E-mail address:** gpchrapp@gpc.edu. **World Wide Web address:** http://www.gpc.edu. **Description:** A community college offering a variety of classes in business, fire science, foreign languages, health care, humanities, physical education, and the social sciences. Founded in 1972. **Positions advertised include:** Electronics Technician; Skills Lab Coordinator; Coordinator of Instructional Support Services; Dean of Student Services; Director of Student Life; Photographic Supervisor; Nursing Coordinator; Instructor – Various Departments – Part-time. **Other area locations:** Clarkston GA; Dunwoody GA; Alpharetta GA; Conyers GA; Lawrenceville GA.

GEORGIA SOUTHERN UNIVERSITY
P.O. Box 8104, Statesboro GA 30460-8104. 912/681-5468. **Fax:** 912/681-0325. **Recorded jobline:** 912/681-

0629. **Contact:** Personnel Director. **World Wide Web address:** http://www.jobs.georgiasouthern.edu **Description:** A regional state university. Georgia Southern enrolls over 11,000 students in its undergraduate and graduate degree programs. Founded in 1906. **NOTE:** Applications are accepted Monday – Friday, 8:00 to 3:00 p.m. Please visit website to search for jobs. For faculty positions, please contact your department of interest. **Positions advertised include:** Assistant director for Health Education and Promotion; Counseling Psychologist; Director of Major Gifts; Assistant Athletics Media Relations Director; Instructional Services Coordinator; Hall Director; Academic Advisor Assistant Director of Design Services; Research Associate; Custodial Foreman; Vice President for Business and Finance; Educational Program Specialist; Conference Facilitator; Public Safety Officer; Accounting Assistant; AC Mechanic; Delivery Worker; Trades Helper. **Special programs:** Internships. **Parent company:** Board of Regents, University System of Georgia.

GEORGIA STATE DEPARTMENT OF EDUCATION PUBLIC SCHOOL RECRUITMENT SERVICES
2 Peachtree Street, Suite 6000, Atlanta GA 30303. 404/232-2603. **Contact:** Human Resources. **World Wide Web address:** http://www.teachgeorgia.org. **Description:** Assists 180 Georgia public school systems in locating qualified teachers, administrators, and related service personnel. **Office hours:** Monday - Friday, 8:00 a.m. - 4:30 p.m.

GEORGIA STATE DEPARTMENT OF EDUCATION
2052 Twin Towers East, Atlanta GA 30334. 404/656-2510. **Fax:** 404/657-7840. **World Wide Web address:** http://www.doe.k12.ga.us. **Description:** Serves as the office for the Superintendent of Schools. Organizes educational programs and methods in the state of Georgia. **NOTE:** please visit website to search for jobs and download application form. **Positions advertised include:** Education Program Specialist; Legal Secretary; School Director; Education Facilities; Accountant; Program Associate; Education Program Specialist; Custodian; Residential Advisor; Teacher; School Social Worker; School Clinic Nurse; Speech Language Pathologist; Vocational Teacher; Teacher – Blind/Deaf; Assistant Director for Administrative Operations.

HERZING COLLEGE OF BUSINESS AND TECHNOLOGY
3393 Peachtree Road NE, Atlanta GA 30326. 404/816-4533. **Fax:** 404/816-4533. **Contact:** Director. **World Wide Web address:** http://www.herzing.edu/atlanta. **Description:** A business and technical college offering Associate's and Bachelor's degrees. **NOTE:** Visit website for online application form. **Corporate headquarters location:** Milwaukee WI. **Other U.S. locations:** Birmingham AL; Madison WI; Minneapolis MN; New Orleans LA; Orlando FL. **International locations:** Canada. **Parent company:** Herzing Institutes. **Operations at this facility include:** Administration; Sales; Service. **Listed on:** Privately held.

INSTITUTE OF PAPER SCIENCE AND TECHNOLOGY
500 10th Street NW, Atlanta GA 30332-0620. 404/894-5700. **Toll-free phone:** 800/558-6611. **Fax:** 404/894-4778. **Contact:** Human Resources Manager. **World Wide Web address:** http://www.ipst.gatech.edu. **Description:** A graduate school offering master's and doctoral degrees in paper science engineering. **NOTE:** IPST recently merged with Georgia Institute of Technology. Please contact their employment office for information on open positions.

KENNESAW STATE UNIVERSITY
1000 Chastain Road, Mail Box 3504, Campus Services Building, Room 143, Kennesaw GA 30144-5591. 770/423-6030. **Contact:** Office of Personnel Services. **E-mail address:** personel@kennesaw.edu. **World Wide Web address:** http://www.kennesaw.edu. **Description:** A four-year state institution of higher education within the university system of Georgia. Kennesaw State University offers certificates, bachelor's, and master's degrees including a Master's of Business Administration. Approximately 12,000 undergraduate and 1,100 graduate students attend the university. **NOTE:** Please call listed number and dial 1 for the employment jobline. **Office hours:** Monday – Friday, 8:00 a.m. – 5:00 p.m.

LIFE UNIVERSITY
1269 Barclay Circle, Marietta GA 30060. 770/426-2884. **Toll-free phone:** 800/543-3202. **Fax:** 770/426-2987. **Contact:** Human Resources. **World Wide Web address:** http://www.life.edu. **Description:** A four-year university that offers undergraduate and graduate degrees. Life University operates an outpatient clinic and a School of Chiropractics. **NOTE:** Human Resources phone is 770/426-2930. **Positions advertised include:** Vice President of Academic Affairs; Chief Financial Officer/Vice President of Financial Affairs; Director of Institutional Effectiveness, Planning and Assessment; Assistant Director of Post-Graduate Education; Administrative Assistant – Executive Office.

MERCER UNIVERSITY
3001 Mercer University Drive, Atlanta GA 30341-4155. 678/547-6000. **Fax:** 678/547-6157. **Recorded jobline:** 678/547-6015. **Contact:** Human Resources. **E-mail address:** jobinfo@mercer.edu. **World Wide Web address:** http://www.mercer.edu. **Description:** The Atlanta location of the independent four-year university. Mercer University offers undergraduate and graduate degrees and enrolls approximately 1,000 students at this location. **NOTE:** Human Resources phone is 678/547-6155. If interested in a position, you must complete an online application. Please visit website to register, search for jobs, and apply online. Online applications are the only accepted format. You may submit a resume with your application. **Positions advertised include:** Assistant Professor – Various Departments; Director of Media Center; Faculty – Nursing; Maintenance Technician; Police Officer; Tenure Track Faculty – Pharmaceutical Sciences. **Office hours:** Monday, Wednesday, Friday, 7:30 a.m. – 3:30 p.m. **Other area locations:** Macon GA.

MITCHELL COUNTY BOARD OF EDUCATION
108 South Harney Street, Camilla GA 31730. 229/336-4543. **Fax:** 229/336-1615. **World Wide Web address:** http://www.mitchell.k12.ga.us. **Description:** Runs the schools in Mitchell County.

MOREHOUSE COLLEGE
830 Westview Drive SW, Suite 207, Gloster Hall, Atlanta GA 30314. 404/681-2800. **Recorded jobline:** 404/614-6048. **Contact:** Human Resources. **World Wide Web address:** http://www.morehouse.edu. **Description:** A four-year liberal arts college. Morehouse College also offers medical studies through the Morehouse School of Medicine. For more information about the medical school please call 404/752-1500 or visit the Website. **NOTE:** Entry-level positions are offered. Interested jobseekers should place inquiries between 10:00 a.m. and 12:00 p.m. or 2:00 p.m. and 4:00 p.m., Tuesdays through Thursdays only. When applying for faculty positions, please contact the specific department. **President:** Dr. Walter E. Massey. **Annual sales/revenues:** $51 - $100 million.

MORRIS BROWN COLLEGE
643 Martin Luther King, Jr. Drive NW, Atlanta GA 30314. 404/739-1000. **Contact:** Human Resources. **World Wide Web address:** http://www.morrisbrown.edu. **Description:** A four-year college offering bachelor of arts and bachelor of science degrees. Founded 1881. **President:** Dolores E. Cross, PhD.

OGLETHORPE UNIVERSITY
4484 Peachtree Road NE, Atlanta GA 30319. 404/261-1441. **Toll-free phone:** 800/428-4484. **Contact:**

Human Resources. **World Wide Web address:** http://www.oglethorpe.edu. **Description:** A four-year university offering bachelor of arts, bachelor of science, and master's degrees; total enrollment is approximately 1,200. Founded in 1835. **NOTE:** Please visit website to search for jobs, and for more details on applying for specific jobs. Human Resources phone is 404/364-8325. **Positions advertised include:** University College Administration Operations Coordinator; Assistant Professor – Management; Assistant Professor – Social Psychology; Director of Admissions.

REINHARDT COLLEGE
7300 Reinhardt College Circle, Waleska GA 30183-2981. 770/720-5600. **Fax:** 770/720-9215. **Contact:** Tammy Edge, Human Resources Specialist. **E-mail address:** TJE@reinhardt.edu. **World Wide Web address:** http://www.reinhardt.edu. **Description:** An undergraduate college offering two- and four-year degrees in the liberal arts. Approximately 1,100 students are enrolled at the college. Founded 1883. **NOTE:** Please visit website for a listing of jobs. Contact Human Resources directly at 770/720-5661. **Positions advertised include:** Vice President for Academic Affairs; Dean of College; Assistant Professor – Communication; Assistant Professor – History, Western Civilization; Adjunct Instructor – Various Departments; Assistant Director of Admissions; College Chaplain; Head Softball Coach.

SHORTER COLLEGE
315 Shorter Avenue, P.O. Box 2119, Rome GA 30165. 706/291-2121. **Toll-free phone:** 800/868-6980. **Fax:** 706/236-1514. **Contact:** Brenda Newman, Human Resources. **E-mail address:** bnewman@shorter.edu. **World Wide Web address:** http://www.shorter.edu. **Description:** A liberal arts college. **NOTE:** Please visit website to search for jobs, download application form, and for more details about applying to specific positions. **Positions advertised include:** Adjunct Teacher – School of Professional Programs; Assistant Professor of Music. **President:** Ed L. Schrader.

SOUTHERN POLYTECHNIC STATE UNIVERSITY
Building V, Norton Dormitory, 1100 South Marietta Parkway, Marietta GA 30060-2896. 678/915-7778. **Toll-free phone:** 800/635-3204. **Fax:** 770/528-3535. **E-mail address:** human_resources@spsu.edu. **World Wide Web address:** http://www.spsu.edu. **Description:** A state university specializing in technology and enrolling 4,000 students. Founded 1948. **NOTE:** Human Resources phone is 770/528-7331. Please visit website to search for jobs and download application form. **Positions advertised include:** Tenure Track Professor – Apparel/Textile; Catalog/Serials Librarian; Dean – School of Engineering, Technology, and Management; Adjunct Professor – Various Departments; Area Program Coordinator – Residential Life; Assistant Director of Budget; Loan Specialist; Public Safety Officer.

SPELMAN COLLEGE
350 Spelman Lane SW, Box 1133, Atlanta GA 30314-4399. 404/681-3643. **Fax:** 866/289-0968. **Contact:** Human Resources. **E-mail address:** resumes@spelmancareers.net. **World Wide Web address:** http://www.spelman.edu. **Description:** A women's four-year liberal arts college offering bachelor of arts and bachelor of science degrees. **NOTE:** Human resources phone is 866/289-0968. **Positions advertised include:** Groundsperson; Police Officer/Public Safety Officer; Associate Coordinator of Student Accounts; Director of Research Resources; Vice Provost for Academic Affairs; LPN. **President:** Dr. Beverly Daniel Tatum.

STATE UNIVERSITY OF WEST GEORGIA
1601 Maple Street, Carrollton GA 30118. 678/839-5000. **Recorded jobline:** 770/830-2280. **Contact:** Human Resources Department. **E-mail address:** personnel@westga.edu. **World Wide Web address:** http://www.westga.edu. **Description:** A four-year college offering associate's, bachelor's, and master's degrees including MBAs. **NOTE:** Human Resources phone is 770/836-6403; fax: 770/836-4637. Please visit website to search for jobs, for more specific details on applying for positions, and to access the online application form. . **Positions advertised include:** Public Safety Officer; Assistant to the Registrar; Assistant Director of Greek Life and Community Outreach; Assistant Director of Residence Life; Academy Residential Coordinator. **Number of employees at this location:** 900.

SUMTER COUNTY SCHOOLS
100 Learning Lane, Americus GA 31719. 229/931-8500. **Fax:** 229/931-8555. **World Wide Web address:** http://www.sumter.k12.ga.us. **Contact:** Dr. James Drew, Assistant Superintendent. **NOTE:** Please visit http://www.teachgeorgia.org to search for jobs.

UNIVERSITY OF GEORGIA
215 South Jackson Street, Human Resources Building, Athens GA 30602-4135. 706/542-2623. **Fax:** 706/542-7321. **Contact:** Employment Department. **World Wide Web address:** http://www.uga.edu. **Description:** The University of Georgia offers a broad range of studies at the undergraduate, graduate, and doctoral levels. The university enrolls more than 30,000 students. **NOTE:** Please visit website to search for jobs and apply online. **Positions advertised include:** Accounting Assistant; Management Information Specialist; Academic Advisor; Art Coordinator; Assistant Director of Housing; Assistant to the Dean; Program Coordinator; Laboratory Technician; Clinical Nurse; Medical Records Technician; Agricultural Specialist; Research Technician.

VALDOSTA STATE UNIVERSITY
1500 North Patterson Street, Valdosta GA 31698. 229/333-5800. **Toll-free phone:** 800/618-1878. **Fax:** 229/259-5030. **Contact:** Amy Reed, Employment Manager. **World Wide Web address:** http://www.valdosta.edu. **Description:** A state university with 9,700 students enrolled. **NOTE:** Human Resources is located at 1205 North Patterson, Valdosta GA. Contact them at 229/333-5709. Please visit website to download an employment application, or pick one up at the Business and Finance offices at the University Center. **Positions advertised include:** Maintenance Worker; Trades Helper; Public Safety Officer; Nursing Supervisor; Library Assistant; Computer Service Specialist; House Director; Bus Operator.

Hawaii

CHAMINADE UNIVERSITY
3140 Waialae Avenue, Honolulu HI 96816-1578. 808/735-4730. **Toll-free phone:** 800/735-3733. **Contact:** Personnel Director. **E-mail address:** hr@chaminade.edu. **World Wide Web address:** http://www.chaminade.edu. **Description:** An independent, teaching university conducted in the Catholic-Marianist tradition that offers undergraduate and graduate programs. **NOTE:** Include a statement of interest with resume. **Positions advertised include:** Lecturer; Dean of Division of Education; Registrar; Financial Aid Counselor.

HAWAII PACIFIC UNIVERSITY
1164 Bishop Street, Honolulu HI 96813. 808/544-0200. **Toll-free phone:** 866/CALL-HPU. **Fax:** 808/544-1192. **Contact:** Linda Kawamura, Associate Vice President of Human Resources. **E-mail address:** hr@hpu.edu. **World Wide Web address:** http://www.hpu.edu. **Description:** A nonprofit, coeducational university with approximately 8,900 undergraduate and graduate students and 1,400 faculty and staff. **NOTE:** For faculty positions, mail resume, cover letter, transcripts and letters of reference to Hawaii Pacific University, Human Resources Associate Vice President, 1166 Fort Street, Suite 201, Honolulu HI 96813. **Positions advertised include:** Adjunct Professors in Various Departments; Head of Library Reference Services; Residence Life Coordinator; Telecommunication Engineer; University Marine Technician. **Special programs:** Internships; Co-ops.

KAMEHAMEHA SCHOOLS
567 South King Street, Suite 200, Honolulu HI 96813. 808/523-6200. **Fax:** 808/541-5305. **Contact:** Human Resources. **E-mail address:** recruit@ksbe.edu. **World Wide Web address:** http://www.ksbe.edu. **Description:** As an independent, statewide educational system, Kamehameha Schools includes K-12 campuses on Oahu, Hawaii, and Maui, and 31 preschools statewide. Total enrollement is almost 7,000 K-12 students. **Note:** No phone inquiries. **Positions advertised include:** Kindergarten Test Administrator; Assistant Coach, Various Sports; Lifeguard; Clerk; Brand management Administrator; Dormitory Leader; Driver/Aide; Program Aide; Instructor.

LEEWARD COMMUNITY COLLEGE
96-045 Ala Ike, Pearl City HI 96782-3393. 808/455-0237. **Contact:** Human Resources. **E-mail address:** lcccdc@hawaii.edu. **World Wide Web address:** http://www.lcc.hawaii.edu. **Description:** One of several community colleges in the University of Hawaii System. Many of its programs and classes coordinate with those at the University of Hawaii campuses at Manoa, Hilo, and West Oahu. The college offers approximately 500 courses in four academic divisions and two vocational divisions, as well as short-term courses through the Office of Special Programs and Community Services. Degrees and certificates include an associate of arts degree, an associate of science degree, a certificate of achievement, and a certificate of completion. Over 5,000 students attend the college. **NOTE:** Search http://workatuh.Hawaii.edu for job postings.

UNIVERSITY OF HAWAII AT HILO
200 West Kawili Street, Hilo HI 96720-4091. 808/974-7687. **Fax:** 808/974-7689. **Contact:** Human Resources. **World Wide Web address:** http://www.uhh.hawaii.edu. **Description:** A public liberal arts and science university that offers the following degrees: BA, BS, BBA, BSN, MA, MEd, MS. The university offers 33 undergraduate majors and 5 graduate majors to its 3,000 students. **NOTE:** Search for current job openings and apply online. All correspondence should include the position number of the desired job positing. **Positions advertised include:** Chancellor; Vice Chair for Academic Affairs; Vice Chair for Administrative Affairs; Vice Chair for Student Affairs; Head of Technical Services; Assistant Professors in Various Departments.

UNIVERSITY OF HAWAII AT MANOA
2500 Campus Road, Hawai'i Hall 202, Honolulu HI 96822. 808/956-8111. **Fax:** 808/956-3952. **Recorded jobline:** 808/587-0977 (Civil Service only). **Contact:** Evelyn Nowaki, Director of Faculty Human Resources. **World Wide Web address:** http://www.uhm.hawaii.edu. **Description:** As the flagship for the University of Hawaii System, Manoa is a research university that offers undergraduate, graduate, professional, and postdoctoral studies. The university's Hawaiian, Asian, and Pacific orientation and unique location provides ample advantages in the studies of tropical agriculture, tropical medicine, oceanography, astronomy, volcanology, evolutionary biology, urban planning, and international trade. **NOTE:** Search current job opportunities online. For Executive/Managerial, Faculty, and Administrative job listings, refer to the specific posting for information regarding the application process. For all other listings, search online at http://www.ehawaiigov.org/statejobs, and send applications to Department of Human Resources Development, State Recruiting Office, Leiopapa Kamehameha Building, 235 South Beretania Street – Room 1100, Honolulu HI 96813. **Positions advertised include:** Associate Dean for Academic Affairs' Chancellor; Director of Student Housing; Vice President for Academic Planning and Policy.

Idaho

BOISE STATE UNIVERSITY
Human Resources Services, Administration Building Room 218, 1910 University Drive, Boise ID 83725. 208/426-1616. **Fax:** 208/426-3100. **Contact:** Viola Boman, Employment Manager. **E-mail address:** vboman@boisestate.edu. **World Wide Web address:** http://www.idbsu.edu. **Description:** Boise State University has one of the largest student enrollments in Idaho with approximately 18,500 students. Founded in 1932. **NOTE:** Applicants for classified jobs must fill out a state employment application or apply online at http://www.dhr.state.id.us. See Boise State University's website for non-classified and faculty positions and application instructions. **Positions advertised include:** Assistant Professor - Organic Chemistry; Customer Service Representative; Maintenance Craftsman; Program Information Coordinator; Technical Records Specialist; Budget Analyst; Systems Engineer; Payroll Manager. **Number of employees at this location:** 1,500.

IDAHO STATE UNIVERSITY
Campus Box 8107, Pocatello ID 83209. 208/282-2517. **Physical address:** 741 South Seventh Avenue, Pocatello ID 83209. **Fax:** 208/282-4976. **Contact:** David Miller, Director of Personnel. **E-mail address:** hr@isu.edu **World Wide Web address:** http://www.isu.edu. **Description:** Provides undergraduate and graduate educational services in Pocatello, Idaho Falls, Twin Falls and Boise, as well as in outlying communities via audio/video technology. **NOTE:** Applicants for classified jobs must fill out a state employment application or apply online at http://www.dhr.state.id.us. See Idaho State University's website for non-classified and faculty positions and application instructions. **Positions advertised include:** Building Facility Foreman; Custodian; IT Information Services Technician; Technical Records Specialist; Administrative Assistant; Post-Doctoral Researcher; Men's Basketball Head Coach; Assistant Professor in Chemistry; Instructor in Sign Language Studies.

LEWIS-CLARK STATE COLLEGE
500 Eighth Avenue, Lewiston ID 83501. 208/792-2269. **Fax:** 208/792-2872. **Contact:** Lori Gaskill, Director of Human Resources. **E-mail address:** lgaskill@lcsc.edu. **World Wide Web address:** http://www.lcsc.edu. **Description:** Founded in 1893, Lewis-Clark State is a public undergraduate college with more than 3,300 students. The college offers instruction in the liberal arts and sciences, as well as in professional and applied technical programs. **NOTE:** Applicants for classified jobs must fill out a state employment application or apply online at http://www.dhr.state.id.us. See Lewis-Clark State's website for non-classified and faculty positions and application instructions. **Positions advertised include:** Assistant Professor of Philosophy; Director of Student Support Services; PC Support Specialist. **Office hours:** Monday-Friday, 8:00 a.m. - 5:00 p.m. **President:** Dene Kay Thomas, Ph. D.

NORTHWEST NAZARENE UNIVERSITY
623 Holly Street, Nampa ID 83686. 208/467-8011. **Toll-free phone:** 800/NNU-4YOU. **Fax:** 208/467-8597. **Contact:** Human Resources. **World Wide Web address:** http://www.nnu.edu. **Description:** A Christian liberal arts university that is an institution of the Church of the Nazarene. Founded in 1913. **NOTE:** See Website for contact information and application instructions for specific positions. **Positions advertised include:** Administrative Assistant; Secretary; Bookstore Head Cashier and Operations Assistant; Director of Admissions; Professor of Art; Professor of Business; Professor of Counselor Education; Professor of Music; Professor of Psychology; Registrar.

UNIVERSITY OF IDAHO
415 West Sixth Street, P.O. Box 444332, Moscow ID 83844-4332. 208/885-3609. **Fax:** 208/885-3602. **Contact:** Human Resources. **E-mail address:** employment@uidaho.edu. **World Wide Web address:** http://www.hr.uidaho.edu. **Description:** The University of Idaho is a land-grant research institution committed to undergraduate and graduate-research education, as well as extension services. **NOTE:** See the website to search and apply for open positions. **Positions advertised include:** Administrative Assistant; Apprentice Steam Plant Operator; DFA Programmer

Analyst; Financial Technician; Program Coordinator; Scientific Aide.

Illinois

AURORA UNIVERSITY
347 South Gladstone Avenue, Aurora IL 60506. 630/844-5493. **Fax:** 630/844-5650. **Contact:** Human Resources. **E-mail address:** jobs@aurora.edu. **World Wide Web address:** http://www.aurora.edu. **Description:** A private university with an enrollment of approximately 2,000 graduate and undergraduate students. **NOTE:** Resumes and cover letters may be faxed, e-mailed, or mailed. Interested jobseekers may also apply online at the university's website. **Positions advertised include:** Assistant Professor (Various); Adjunct Faculty (Various);.

BRADLEY UNIVERSITY
239 Sisson Hall, Elmwood Avenue, Peoria IL 61625. 309/677-3223. **Fax:** 309/677-3867. **Contact:** Human Resources. **World Wide Web address:** http://www.bradley.edu. **Description:** A private, four-year university offering both undergraduate and graduate degrees. Founded in 1897. **NOTE:** See website for job listings and to download an application. **Office hours:** Monday – Friday, 8:00 a.m. – 5:00 p.m. (closed between noon and 1:00 p.m.) **Corporate headquarters location:** This location.

CHICAGO STATE UNIVERSITY
9501 South King Drive, Chicago IL 60628. 773/995-2000. **Contact:** Human Resources. **World Wide Web address:** http://www.csu.edu. **Description:** A four-year, state university offering undergraduate and graduate degree programs through its colleges of Arts and Sciences, Business, Education, and Health Sciences. **NOTE:** See website for job listings and contact information. **Office hours:** Monday – Friday, 8:30 a.m. – 5:00 p.m.

COLLEGE OF LAKE COUNTY
19351 West Washington Street, Grayslake IL 60030. 847/543-2065. **Fax:** 847/223-0824. 223-6601. **Contact:** Human Resources. **E-mail address:** personnel@clcillinois.edu. **World Wide Web address:** http://www.clcillinois.edu. **Description:** A two-year community college. College of Lake County offers a variety of transfer and career preparation programs to over 14,000 students. The college is a nonresidential institution. **NOTE:** See website for job listings, contact information, and application procedures. **Positions advertised include:** Instructor (Various); Bookstore Buyer; Director of Financial Aid; Financial Aid Veterans and Student Employment Representative. **Office hours:** Monday – Friday, 8:00 a.m. – 4:30 p.m.

COLUMBIA COLLEGE CHICAGO
600 South Michigan Avenue, Chicago IL 60605-1996. 312/344-8215. **Contact:** Human Resources. **World Wide Web address:** http://www.colum.edu. **Description:** A college offering bachelor's and master's degrees and specializing in communications, media, applied and fine arts, theatrical and performing arts, and management and marketing. Columbia College's enrollment is approximately 7,300 students. **NOTE:** See website for job listings, contact information and application procedures. The address of the Office of Recruitment and Development is 33 East Congress Street, Suite 532, Chicago IL 60605.

DEVRY UNIVERSITY
3300 North Campbell Avenue, Chicago IL 60618. 773/929-8500. **Fax:** 773/348-1780. **Contact:** Human Resources. **World Wide Web address:** http://www.chi.devry.edu. **Description:** A technical training institute that provides courses in electronics technology, computer information systems, business operations, telecommunications management, accounting, and technical management. Founded in 1931. **NOTE:** Search and apply for open positions online at http://www.devryinc.com/careers. **Corporate headquarters location:** Oakbrook Terrace IL. **International locations:** Canada. **Listed on:** New York Stock Exchange. **Stock exchange symbol:** DV.

EASTERN ILLINOIS UNIVERSITY
600 West Lincoln Avenue, Old Main, Room 2010, Charleston IL 61920-3099. 217/581-3514. **Fax:** 217/581-3614. **Contact:** Human Resources. **E-mail address:** humanres@eiu.edu. **World Wide Web address:** http://www.eiu.edu. **Description:** A four-year, state university offering a variety of degree programs to approximately 9,200 undergraduate and 1,400 graduate students. **NOTE:** See website to download applications and other forms, view current job openings, and review application procedures.

ELMHURST COLLEGE
190 Prospect Avenue, Elmhurst IL 60126. 630/617-3016. **Fax:** 630/617-3746. **Recorded jobline:** 630/617-3779. **Contact:** Human Resources. **E-mail address:** hr@elmhurst.edu. **World Wide Web address:** http://www.elmhurst.edu. **Description:** A private liberal arts college affiliated with the United Church of Christ. The college has 22 academic departments and offers 48 majors. Pre-professional studies in dentistry, medicine, law, engineering, and theology are also offered. Founded in 1871. **NOTE:** See website for current job openings and application instructions. Entry-level positions and second and third shifts are offered. **Special programs:** Internships; Apprenticeships; Summer Jobs. **Office hours:** Monday - Friday, 8:30 a.m. - 5:00 p.m.

GOVERNORS STATE UNIVERSITY
One University Parkway, University Park IL 60466. 708/534-5000. **Contact:** Human Resources. **World Wide Web address:** http://www.govst.edu. **Description:** A state university offering 42 degree programs to juniors, seniors, and master's candidates. **NOTE:** See website for job listings and contact and application information.

HAROLD WASHINGTON COLLEGE
30 East Lake Street, Chicago IL 60601. 312/553-5600. **Contact:** Steve Crosby, Director of Personnel. **World Wide Web address:** http://www.hwashington.ccc.edu. **Description:** A four-year college operating as part of the City Colleges of Chicago system. The college offers associate's degrees and certificates to approximately 9,400 students. **NOTE:** Apply online at the college's website or visit the Human Resources Office during regular business hours. **Office hours:** Monday – Friday, 9:00 a.m. – 4:30 p.m.

HARPER COLLEGE
1200 West Algonquin Road, Palatine IL 60067. 847/925-6000. **Contact:** Human Resources. **World Wide Web address:** http://www.harpercollege.edu. **Description:** A community college offering associate's degrees and certificates to approximately 23,000 students. **NOTE:** Harper College no longer will accept mailed or faxed resumes. Apply online at its website. **Positions advertised include:** Counselor; Instructors (Various); Professors (Various); Student Development Specialist; Coordinator of Accommodations; Secretary; Custodian; Career Mentor; Computer Support and Training.

ILLINOIS INSTITUTE OF TECHNOLOGY
3300 South Federal Street, Main Building, Room 302, Chicago IL 60616. 312/567-3318. **Fax:** 312/567-3450. **Contact:** Human Resources. **E-mail address:** hr@iit.edu. **World Wide Web address:** http://www.iit.edu. **Description:** A four-year college offering bachelor's, master's (including MBA), and doctoral degrees. Approximately 2,500 undergraduate and 2,500 graduate students attend Illinois Institute of Technology. **NOTE:** The Human Resources Office prefers resumes to be sent via e-mail. **Positions advertised include:** Assistant to the Director; Service Coordinator; Administrative Assistant; Career Specialist; International Student Advisor; Web Programmer; Help Desk Supervisor.

ILLINOIS STATE UNIVERSITY
Campus Box 1300, Normal IL 61790. 309/438-8311. **Fax:** 309/438-7421. **Contact:** Office of Human Resources. **World Wide Web address:**

http://www.ilstu.edu. **Description:** A four-year, state university offering bachelor's, master's, and doctoral degrees to approximately 20,000 students. **NOTE:** To apply for administrative and professional positions, see website for job listings and contact information. To apply for civil service positions, an application is required and can be obtained on the website or in person at the Human Resources Office in the Nelson Smith Building, Room 101 Applications may also be faxed to Human Resources at 309/438-7421. **Office hours:** Monday – Friday, 7:30 a.m. – 4:30 p.m.

JOLIET JUNIOR COLLEGE
1215 Houbolt Road, Joliet IL 60431-8938. 815/280-2266. **Fax:** 815/729-3331. **Contact:** Human Resources. **E-mail address:** hr@jjc.edu. **World Wide Web address:** http://www.jjc.cc.il.us. **Description:** A community college offering associate degrees and career and technical degrees and certificates. Founded in 1901. **NOTE:** An application is required. See website to download a copy or contact the Human Resources Office to have one mailed or faxed. Entry-level positions and second and third shifts are offered. **Positions advertised include:** Office Systems Instructor; Pastry and Baking Instructor; Adjunct Faculty (Various).

KAPLAN UNIVERSITY
550 West Van Buren, 7th Floor, Chicago IL 60607. 312/777-6333. **Contact:** Human Resources. **E-mail address:** kaplaninc@trm.brassring.com. **World Wide Web address:** http://www.kaplan.edu. **Description:** Kaplan is an online university offering Associates, Bachelors, Masters, and Certificate programs to students who wish to learn over the Internet. **NOTE:** Search and apply for positions online. **Positions advertised include:** Editorial Assistant; Faculty; Advanced Website Design Technicians. **Corporate headquarters location:** Fort Lauderdale FL.

LEWIS & CLARK COMMUNITY COLLEGE
5800 Godfrey Road, Godfrey IL 62035. 618/468-3010. **Fax:** 618/468-3105. **Recorded jobline:** 618/468-5627. **Contact:** Human Resources. **World Wide Web address:** http://www.lc.cc.il.us. **Description:** A two-year junior college. **NOTE:** See website for job listings. An application is required. Complete online or download and fax it to the Human Resources Office. Interested jobseekers may also apply in person at the Human Resources Office in Erickson Hall, Room 107.

LOYOLA UNIVERSITY OF CHICAGO
820 North Michigan Avenue, Chicago IL 60611. 312/915-6175. **Contact:** Human Resources. **E-mail address:** hr-wtc@luc.edu. **World Wide Web address:** http://www.luc.edu. **Description:** A private university and medical center. Loyola University operates four additional campuses in the greater Chicago area including Loyola University Medical Center in Maywood, Lake Shore and Water Tower campuses in Chicago, and Mallinckrodt campus in Wilmette. **NOTE:** See website for staff and faculty job listings and application and resume submission procedures. The Human Resources Office is located at 820 North Michigan Avenue.

McKENDREE COLLEGE
701 College Road, Lebanon IL 62254. 618/537-6533. **Fax:** 618/537-6960. **Contact:** Shirley Jacob, Human Resources Director. **E-mail address:** HR@McKendree.edu. **World Wide Web address:** http://www.mckendree.edu. **Description:** A four-year college offering 28 academic majors to an enrollment of over 1,000. **NOTE:** Mail, fax or e-mail resumes to Mr. Place. Entry-level and part-time positions are offered. **Positions advertised include:** Adjunct Faculty (Various); Assistant Men and Women's Soccer Coach; Residence Hall Director; Student Services Specialist. **Corporate headquarters location:** This location. **Other U.S. locations:** Louisville KY; Radcliff KY.

MILLIKIN UNIVERSITY
1184 West Main Street, Decatur IL 62522-2084. 217/362-6416. **Fax:** 217/424-6468. **Contact:** Human Resources. **World Wide Web address:** http://www.millikin.edu. **Description:** A liberal arts university affiliated with the Presbyterian Church. Approximately 2,000 students are enrolled at Millikin University. **NOTE:** See website for job listings and application. Interested jobseekers may apply to open positions by mailing or faxing resumes. Interested jobseekers may also apply in person at the Human Resources Office, Room 212 of Shilling Hall. **Office hours:** Monday – Friday, 8:00 a.m. – 5:00 p.m. **Positions advertised include:** Continuing Education Services Coordinator and Research/Instruction Librarian; Instructor of Nursing; Assistant Professor; Acting Department Chair; Hall Director; Database Analyst; Team Coach (Various); Executive Secretary. **Special programs:** Internships. **Corporate headquarters location:** This location. **Operations at this facility include:** Administration. **Listed on:** Privately held.

MORAINE VALLEY COMMUNITY COLLEGE
9000 West College Parkway, Building L, Room 167, Palos Hills IL 60465. 708/974-5704. **Fax:** 708/974-3374. **Contact:** Director of Human Resources. **World Wide Web address:** http://www.moraine.cc.il.us. **Description:** A community college offering programs for students who are planning to transfer to a four-year institution. Founded in 1967.

NATIONAL EDUCATION TRAINING GROUP (NETG)
2651 Warrenville Road, Suite 550, Downers Grove IL 60515. 480/315-4000. **Toll-free phone:** 888/577-5779. **Contact:** Human Resources. **World Wide Web address:** http://www.netg.com. **Description:** A source of products and services for training and education in the areas of advanced technologies. **NOTE:** Apply online. **Positions advertised include:** Corporate/Financial Analyst; Senior Systems Specialist; Lead Product Development Manager; Contract Analyst; Senior Software Engineer. **Corporate headquarters location:** This location. **Parent company:** Thomson Corporation.

NATIONAL-LOUIS UNIVERSITY
1000 Capitol Drive, Wheeling IL 60090. 847/465-0575. **Fax:** 847/465-5610. **Recorded jobline:** 847/465-5400. **Contact:** Human Resources. **E-mail address:** resumes@nl.edu. **World Wide Web address:** http://www.nl.edu. **Description:** A university offering undergraduate and graduate programs to approximately 1,600 students. **NOTE:** See website for job postings and contact information. Entry-level positions, part-time jobs, and second and third shifts are offered. **Positions advertised include:** Administrative Assistant; Enrollment Representative; Associate Director of Alumni Relations; Director of School-College Relations; Construction Manager. **Office hours:** Monday - Friday, 8:30 a.m. - 4:30 p.m. **Corporate headquarters location:** This location. **Other area locations:** Chicago IL; Evanston IL. **Other U.S. locations:** Washington DC; Orlando FL; Tampa FL; Atlanta GA; St. Louis MO; Milwaukee WI.

NORTHEASTERN ILLINOIS UNIVERSITY
5500 North St. Louis Avenue, Chicago IL 60625. 773/583-4050. **Contact:** Human Resources. **World Wide Web address:** http://www.neiu.edu. **Description:** A state university serving more than 10,000 commuter students with over 80 graduate and undergraduate programs. **NOTE:** See website for job listings and contact information and application requirements. **Positions advertised include:** Associate Director of Admissions; Clinical Psychologist of Counseling Office; Director of Public Safety; Professor (Various); Assistant Professor (Various); Secretary.

NORTHERN ILLINOIS UNIVERSITY
1515 West Lincoln Highway, De Kalb IL 60115. 815/753-6000. **Fax:** 815/753-2335. **Contact:** Human Resources. **World Wide Web address:** http://www.niu.edu. **Description:** A university comprised of seven colleges offering more than 100 graduate and undergraduate programs to approximately

23,000 students. **NOTE:** See web site for job listings, contact information and application procedures. **Positions advertised include:** Assistant Area Coordinator; Professor (Various); Assistant Professor (Various); Information Technology Associate; Route Driver; Secretary.

NORTHWESTERN UNIVERSITY
720 University Place, Evanston IL 60208. 847/491-7507. **Contact:** Human Resources. **E-mail address:** resume@northwestern.edu. **World Wide Web address:** http://www.northwestern.edu. **Description:** One of the country's largest private research universities. The university offers academic specialties in 12 colleges to its 17,700 students. **NOTE:** See website for job listings and contact information. **Positions advertised include:** Administrative Secretary; Animal Care Technician; Group Leader; Library Assistant; Research Technologist; Program Assistant.

OAKTON COMMUNITY COLLEGE
1600 East Golf Road, Des Plaines IL 60016. 847/635-1675 **Fax:** 847/635-1764. **Contact:** Human Resources. **E-mail address:** hr@oakton.edu. **World Wide Web address:** http://www.oakton.edu. **Description:** A community college offering programs for students who are planning to transfer to a four-year institution. The college also offers training courses and career programs. **NOTE:** See website for job listings, contact information and application form. **Positions advertised include:** Director of Resource Development; Admission Specialist; Health Services Manager; Learning Center Specialist; Faculty (Various); System Director.

ROOSEVELT UNIVERSITY
430 South Michigan Avenue, Chicago IL 60605. 312/341-3500. **Contact:** Human Resources. **World Wide Web address:** http://www.roosevelt.edu. **Description:** A university offering graduate and undergraduate programs through its colleges of Arts and Sciences, Business, Education, and Performing Arts. **NOTE:** See website for job listings and application procedures.

SOUTHERN ILLINOIS UNIVERSITY AT CARBONDALE
805 South Elizabeth Street, Carbondale IL 62901. 618/453-6689. **Recorded jobline:** 618/536-2116. **Fax:** 618/453-1353. **Contact:** Employment Manager. **World Wide Web address:** http://www.siu.edu. **Description:** A four-year public university offering both undergraduate and graduate degree programs. **NOTE:** See website for job listings and contact information.

SOUTHERN ILLINOIS UNIVERSITY AT EDWARDSVILLE
Campus Box 1040, Edwardsville IL 62026. 618/650-2190. **Fax:** 618/650-2696. **Contact:** Human Resources. **World Wide Web address:** http://www.siue.edu. **Description:** A state university offering both undergraduate and graduate programs. **NOTE:** See website for administrative, faculty, professional staff, and civil service positions and related contact and application procedure information. Interested jobseekers may also visit the Human Resources office located at Rendleman Hall, Room 3210.

SOUTHWESTERN ILLINOIS COLLEGE
2500 Carlyle Avenue, Belleville IL 62221. 618/235-2700. **Fax:** 618/277-7346. **Contact:** Human Resources. **E-mail address:** humanresources@swic.edu. **World Wide Web address:** http://www.southwestern.cc.il.us. **Description:** A public, two-year community college. **NOTE:** Mail resumes to Mr. Friederich's attention. **Positions advertised include:** Americorps Field Coordinator; Public Safety Officers; Assistant Professor (Various); Adjunct Instructors (Various); Systems Analyst-Programmer.

TRUMAN COLLEGE
1145 West Wilson Avenue, Chicago IL 60640. 773/878-1700. **Contact:** Human Resources. **World Wide Web address:** http://www.trumancollege.cc. **Description:** A community college offering automotive, cosmetology, ESL, and continuing education classes. **NOTE:** See website for job listings and contact information. Positions advertised include: Faculty (Various); Nursing Laboratory Coordinator.

UNIVERSITY OF CHICAGO
956 East 58th Street, Chicago IL 60637. 773/702-8900. **Contact:** Human Resources. **World Wide Web address:** http://www.uchicago.edu. **Description:** A university with a total enrollment of over 12,000 students. Founded in 1892. **NOTE:** Apply online.

UNIVERSITY OF ILLINOIS AT CHICAGO
715 South Wood Street, Mail Code 862, Chicago IL 60612. 312/996-9305. **Fax:** 312/413-1190. **Contact:** Associate Director of Employment. **World Wide Web address:** http://www.uic.edu. **Description:** One location of the state university offering graduate and undergraduate programs of study to approximately 25,000 students. **NOTE:** Applicants must apply online. **Operations at this facility include:** Administration; Research and Development; Service.

UNIVERSITY OF ILLINOIS AT SPRINGFIELD
One University Plaza, HRB 30, Springfield IL 62703-5704. 217/206-6652. **Contact:** Human Resources. **World Wide Web address:** http://www.uis.edu. **Description:** One location of the state university specializing in liberal arts and professional studies. The university offers undergraduate and graduate programs of study. Founded in 1969.

UNIVERSITY OF ILLINOIS AT URBANA-CHAMPAIGN
52 East Gregory Drive, Champaign IL 61820. 217/333-2137. **Contact:** Human Resources. **World Wide Web address:** http://www.uiuc.edu. **Description:** The main campus of the state university. Graduate and undergraduate programs are offered through the colleges of Communications; Liberal Arts and Sciences; Fine and Applied Arts; Agriculture, Consumer, and Environmental Sciences; Commerce and Business Administration; Applied Life Sciences; Library and Information Science; Law; Social Work; Medicine; and Veterinary Medicine.

WAUBONSEE COMMUNITY COLLEGE
Route 47 at Waubonsee Drive, Building A, Sugar Grove IL 60554. 630/466-4811. **Contact:** Office of Human Resources. **World Wide Web address:** http://www.wcc.cc.il.us. **Description:** A community college offering occupational programs and programs to students who are planning to transfer to a four-year institution. **Positions advertised include:** Adult Education Student Records Clerk; Bookstore Clerk; Child Care Center Aide; ESL Secretary; Public Safety Cadet; Fitness Center Technical Assistant; Site Manager.

WESTERN ILLINOIS UNIVERSITY
One University Circle, 105 Sherman Hall, Macomb IL 61455. 309/298-1971. **Fax:** 309/298-2300. **Contact:** Pam Bowman, Director Human Resources. **World Wide Web address:** http://www.wiu.edu. **Description:** A university offering over 80 graduate and undergraduate programs of study.

WHEATON COLLEGE
501 College Avenue, Wheaton IL 60187. 630/752-5060. **Contact:** Human Resources. **E-mail address:** hr@wheaton.edu. **World Wide Web address:** http://www.wheaton.edu. **Description:** A private, coeducational, Christian college with an undergraduate enrollment of 2,300.

Indiana

BROWN MACKIE COLLEGE
3000 Coliseum Boulevard, Suite 100, Fort Wayne IN 46805. 260/484-4400. **Fax:** 260/484-2678. **Contact:** Human Resources. **World Wide Web address:** http://www.brownmackie.edu. **Description:** A system of schools that offers associate's degrees and/or

diplomas, and certificate programs in business, health sciences, legal studies, information technology, and electronic fields to over 7,000 students in 21 locations in eight states. **Positions advertised include:** Admission Recruiter; Certified Surgical Technologist; Financial Aid Officer. **Parent company:** Education Management Corporation.

DEPAUW UNIVERSITY
Office of Human Resources, 313 South Locust Street, Greencastle IN 46135. 765/658-4181. **Contact:** Susan Hacker, Human Resources Specialist. **E-mail address:** susanhacker@depauw.edu. **World Wide Web address:** http://www.depauw.edu. **Description:** A selective undergraduate liberal arts college with a separate school of music. DePauw offers a variety of academic programs and educational opportunities. Special programs for students include: The Honor Scholar Program; The Management Fellows Program; The Media Fellows Program; The Science Research Fellows Program. DePauw has an enrollment of approximately 2,300 students. Founded in 1837 by the Methodist Episcopal Church. **Positions advertised include:** Professor, Latin American History; Professor, English; Choral Director. **President:** Robert G. Bottoms.

ITT EDUCATIONAL SERVICES, INC. (ESI)
9511 Angola Court, Indianapolis IN 46268. 317/875-8640 **Toll-free phone:** 800/937-4488. **Fax:** 317/594-4327. **Contact:** Human Resources. **World Wide Web address:** http://www.itttech.edu. **Description:** A leading private college system providing associate's and bachelor's degrees in technology-based disciplines. ESI operates 67 ITT Technical Institutes in 27 states. **Company slogan:** We teach technology. **Corporate headquarters location:** This location. **Listed on:** New York Stock Exchange. **Stock exchange symbol:** ESI.

INDIANA STATE UNIVERSITY/TERRE HAUTE
210 North Seventh Street, Rankin Hall, Terre Haute IN 47809. 812/237-4371. **Fax:** 812/237-8331. **Contact:** Human Resources. **E-mail address:** jobs@ind.state.edu. **World Wide Web address:** http://www.indstate.edu. **Description:** A four-year state university offering associate's, bachelor's, master's (including MBA), and doctoral degrees. Approximately 10,200 undergraduate and 1,500 graduate students attend Indiana State University. **NOTE:** Jobseekers must obtain an application from the university before sending a resume. Resumes without applications will be returned. Candidates for faculty positions should consult the website for departmental contacts and requirements. **Positions advertised include:** Graphic Designer; Student Services Assistant; Custodial Worker; Public Safety Officer; Director of Admissions; Assistant Professor, Creative Writing; Assistant Professor, Music Education; Assistant Professor, American Politics. **Office hours:** Monday – Friday, 8:00 a.m. – 4:30 p.m.

INDIANA UNIVERSITY BLOOMINGTON
Poplars Building, 400 East Seventh Street, Bloomington IN 47405-3085. 812/855-2172. **Recorded jobline:** 812/855-9102. **Contact:** Human Resources. **World Wide Web address:** http://www.indiana.edu. **Description:** A branch of the state university offering bachelor's, master's (including MBA), first professional, and doctoral degrees. The School of Business and the School of Public and Environmental Affairs are also at this location. **NOTE:** Application procedures vary according to the type of position. See website for specific instructions. **Office hours:** Monday – Friday, 8:00 a.m. – 5:00 p.m. **Other area locations:** Kokomo IN; Gary IN; South Bend IN; New Albany IN.

INDIANA UNIVERSITY/PURDUE UNIVERSITY AT FORT WAYNE
2101 Coliseum Boulevard East, Fort Wayne IN 46805-1499. 260/481-6840. **Contact:** Human Resources. **E-mail address:** jobs@ipfw.edu. **World Wide Web address:** http://www.ipfw.edu. **Description:** Branches of the two state universities. **Office hours:** Monday – Friday, 8:00 a.m. – 5:00 p.m.

INDIANA UNIVERSITY/PURDUE UNIVERSITY AT INDIANAPOLIS
620 Union Drive, Student Union Building, Room 340, Indianapolis IN 46202-5168. 317/274-7617. **Fax:** 317/274-5481. **Contact:** Human Resources Administration. **E-mail address:** hra@iupui.edu. **World Wide Web address:** http://www.iupui.edu. **Description:** A four-year state university with professional schools, teaching hospitals, and schools of medicine and dentistry. IUPUI offers degrees from both Indiana University and Purdue University.

PURDUE UNIVERSITY
Freehafer Hall of Administrative Services, 401 South Grant Street, West Lafayette IN 47907. 765/494-9687. **Fax:** 765/494-6138. **Recorded jobline:** 765/496-5627. **Contact:** Human Resources. **E-mail address:** resumes@purdue.edu. **World Wide Web address:** http://www.purdue.edu. **Description:** Purdue has an enrollment of approximately 64,000 students across five campuses with numerous teaching and research sites statewide. Degrees are offered in agriculture, consumer and family sciences, education, engineering, health sciences, liberal arts, management, nursing, pharmacy and pharmaceutical sciences, science, technology, and veterinary medicine. **Positions advertised include:** Web Development Manager; Office Manager; Career Services Consultant; Editor; Computer Systems Administrator; NMR Applications Scientist; Research Assistant; Research Associate; Laboratory Technician; Secretary; Library Assistant; Account Clerk. **Special programs:** Internships. **Office hours:** Monday – Friday, 8:00 a.m. – 5:00 p.m. **Corporate headquarters location:** This location.

PURDUE UNIVERSITY/CALUMET
2200 169th Street, Hammond IN 46323-2094. 219/989-2251. **Fax:** 219/989-2185. **Contact:** Personnel. **E-mail address:** jobs@calumet.purdue.edu. **World Wide Web address:** http://www.calumet.purdue.edu. **Description:** A regional campus of the university. **Positions advertised include:** Information Clerk; Accounting Clerk; Secretary; Coordinator, Northwest Indiana Writing Project.

UNIVERSITY OF EVANSVILLE
1800 Lincoln Avenue, Evansville IN 47722. 812/479-2943. **Fax:** 812/479-2320. **Contact:** Director of Human Resources. **World Wide Web address:** http://www.evansville.edu. **Description:** A nonprofit, four-year university offering bachelor's and master's degrees. Approximately 2,600 undergraduate and 500 graduate students attend the University of Evansville. Founded in 1854. **NOTE:** Entry-level positions and second and third shifts are offered. **Positions advertised include:** Administrative Assistant; University Chaplain; Assistant Professor, Physics; Assistant Professor, Political Science; Assistant Professor, Nursing. **Corporate headquarters location:** This location. **Operations at this facility include:** Administration. **Listed on:** Privately held.

UNIVERSITY OF INDIANAPOLIS
1400 East Hanna Avenue, Indianapolis IN 46227. 317/788-3368. **Fax:** 317/788-3468. **Contact:** Human Resources. **E-mail address:** sclark@uindy.edu. **World Wide Web address:** http://www.uindy.edu. **Description:** A four-year university offering associate's, bachelor's, and master's degrees including MBAs. Enrollment is approximately 1,900 undergraduate and 460 graduate students. **Positions advertised include:** Assistant Professor, Art; Assistant Football Coach; Coaching Coordinator.

UNIVERSITY OF NOTRE DAME
Office of Human Resources, 100 Grace Hall, Notre Dame IN 46556-5612. 574/631-5900. **Fax:** 574/631-6790. **Contact:** Human Resources. **E-mail address:** hr@nd.edu. **World Wide Web address:** http://www.nd.edu. **Description:** An independent Catholic university offering undergraduate, graduate, and professional degree programs. The university's graduate school offers 44 master's degree programs, and 22 doctoral degree programs. The campus is

located in Notre Dame, adjacent to the city of South Bend, Indiana. Founded in 1842. **Positions advertised include:** Operations Manager; Writer/Editor; Assistant Director, Non-Degree Programs; Banquet Server; Senior Research Technician. **President:** Rev. Edward A. Malloy, C.S.C.

UNIVERSITY OF SOUTHERN INDIANA
8600 University Boulevard, Evansville IN 47712-3596. 812/464-1844. **Recorded jobline:** 812/465-7117. **Contact:** Human Resources. **E-mail address:** humanres@usi.edu. **World Wide Web address:** http://www.usi.edu. **Description:** A public university offering both undergraduate and graduate degrees in a broad range of disciplines. Approximately 8,700 students are enrolled at the university. Founded in 1965. **Positions advertised include:** English Instructor; Assistant Professor, Chemistry; Residence Life Coordinator; Special Funds Accountant; Benefits Supervisor. **Office hours:** Monday – Friday, 8:00 a.m. – 4:30 p.m.

Iowa
DES MOINES AREA COMMUNITY COLLEGE
2006 South Ankeny Boulevard, Building 1, Ankeny IA 50023. 515/964-6200. **Fax:** 515/965-7316. **Contact:** Human Resources. **E-mail address:** jobs@dmacc.org. **World Wide Web address:** http://www.dmacc.cc.ia.us. **Description:** A publicly supported, two-year institution serving the Des Moines metropolitan area and surrounding counties. **NOTE:** Search current postings and apply on-line. **Positions advertised include:** Student Activities and Housing Coordinator; Volleyball Coach; Industrial Outreach Specialist; Training Consultant; Counselor; Math Instructor. **President:** David C. England.

IOWA STATE UNIVERSITY
Recruitment and Employment Office, 3810 Beardshear Hall, Ames IA 50011-2033. 515/294-2936. **Contact:** Cindy Manning, Human Resources Services. **World Wide Web address:** http://www.iastate.edu/jobs. **Description:** A four-year university offering bachelor's, master's (including MBA), and doctoral degrees. Approximately 24,000 students attend Iowa State University. **NOTE:** Search posted openings and apply on-line only. **Positions advertised include:** Education Lecturer; Sociology Lecturer; Veterinary Microbiology Assistant Professor; Zoology & Microbiology Lecturer; Administrative Specialist; Program Coordinator; Biomedical Research Associate; Kitchen Helper; Athletic Equipment Manager; Post-Doctoral Botany Researcher. **President:** Gregory L. Geoffroy. **Annual revenues:** $743 million. **Number of employees:** 6,157.

UNIVERSITY OF IOWA
102 University Services Building, Suite 21, Iowa City IA 52242-1911. 319/335-3558. **Fax:** 319/335-2384. **Recorded jobline:** 319/335-2682. **Contact:** Susan Lee, Human Resources. **E-mail address:** Jobs@UIowa. **World Wide Web address:** http://www.uiowa.edu/jobs. **Description:** A university with 27,900 students enrolled in over 150 areas of study. **NOTE:** Entry-level positions, part-time jobs, and second and third shifts are offered. Search posted openings and apply on-line. **Positions advertised include:** Clerk; Library Assistant; Nursing Unit Clerk; Patient Account Representative; Pharmacy Technician; Secretary; Custodian; Nursing Assistant; Psychiatric Nursing Assistant; Dental Assistant; Radiographer; Steamfitter; Surgical Technologist. **Number of employees at this location:** 15,000.

Kansas
KANSAS WESLEYAN UNIVERSITY
100 East Claflin Avenue, Salina KS 67401-6196. 785/827-5541. **Fax:** 785/227-0927. **Toll-free phone**: 800/874-1154. **Contact:** Human Resources. **World Wide Web address:** http://www.kwu.edu. **Description:** A university affiliated with the United Methodist Church with an enrollment of 800 students. Founded in 1886. **Positions advertised include:** Faculty; Controller; Communications Faculty; Sociology Faculty; Resident Director.

PITTSBURG STATE UNIVERSITY
1701 South Broadway, Pittsburg KS 66762. 620/235-4191. **Contact:** Budget & Human Resource Services Staff. **E-mail address:** hrs@pittstate.edu. **World Wide Web address:** http://www.pittstate.edu. **Description:** A state university offering over 50 degree programs in four colleges: College of Arts and Sciences; The Kelce College of Business; College of Education; College of Technology. **Positions advertised include:** Staff Attorney; Applications Programmer; Analyst III; Corrections Manager; Office Assistant; Plumber. **Number of employees at this location:** 675.

FRED PRYOR SEMINARS
A DIVISION OF PRYOR RESOURCES, INC.
9757 Metcalf Avenue, Overland Park KS 66212. 913/967-8599. **Fax:** 913/967-8580. **Contact:** Human Resources. **E-mail address:** careeropportunities@pryor.com. **World Wide Web address:** http://www.pryor.com. **Description:** Fred Pryor Seminars and CareerTrack Seminars provide motivational and professional training for individuals and corporations. **NOTE**: Applicants are requested not to contact company by telephone or fax. **Positions advertised include:** On-Site Training Consultant; Inside Sales Representative; Contract Trainer.

SKILLPATH SEMINARS
P.O. Box 2768, Shawnee Mission KS 66201-2768. 913/362-3900. **Physical address:** 6900 Squibb Road, Shawnee Mission KS 66202. **Fax:** 913/362-4241. **Toll-free phone:** 800/873-7545. **Contact:** Personnel Department. **E-mail address:** opportunities@skillpath.net. **World Wide Web address:** http://www.skillpath.com. **Description:** A training company that conducts educational seminars targeted to professionals from a variety of businesses and organizations. **NOTE:** Contact Human Resources at extension 129. For contract trainer positions contact Christy Gaddis: cgaddis@skillpath.net. **Positions advertised include:** Contract Trainer; (Canada-based) Business and Management Skills Trainer. **Parent company:** The Graceland College Center for Professional Development and Lifelong Learning, Inc.

TELECOMMMUNICATIONS RESEARCH ASSOCIATES (TRA)
P.O. Box A, St. Marys KS 66536-0016. 785/437-2000. **Physical address:** 505 West Bertrand Avenue, St. Marys KS 66536. **Toll-free phone:** 800/872-4736. **Fax:** 785/437-2600. **Contact:** Human Resources. **E-mail address:** HumanResources@tra.com. **World Wide Web address:** http://www.tra.com. **Description:** A technology training vendor for the communications industry. TRA also offers on-site training and some material on CD.

UNIVERSITY OF KANSAS
1246 West Campus Road, Room 103, Lawrence KS 66045-7505. 785/864-4946. **Contact:** Human Resources. **World Wide Web address:** http://www.ku.edu. **Description:** A four-year university serving as a comprehensive research and teaching institution. Founded in 1864. **NOTE:** HR staff prefer that resumes are submitted via web site; paper resumes are not accepted. **Positions advertised include:** Accounting Specialist; Administration Assistant; Assistant Professor; Associate Dean; Design Chair Person; Director of Laboratory; Financial Analyst; Information Technology Manager; Instructor Education / Chemistry; Lecturer; Network Manager; Research Aide; Vice Provost for Research.

WASHBURN UNIVERSITY
1700 SW College Avenue, Topeka KS 66621. 785/670-1538. **Physical address**: 135 Morgan Hall, Room 135, Topeka KS 66621. **Contact:** Personnel Office. **World Wide Web address:** http://www.washburn.edu. **Description:** A public, four-year university offering undergraduate and graduate degrees in Arts & Sciences, Business, and Law with a Nursing School and a continuing education program. **NOTE:** Search postings and apply online.

WICHITA AREA TECHNICAL COLLEGE
301 South Grove Street, Wichita KS 67211-2099. 316/677-9471. **Contact:** Heather Perkins, Dir. Human Resources. **World Wide Web address:** http://www.watc.edu/employment/index.html. **Description:** A nonprofit technical college. **NOTE:** Entry-level positions are offered. All employment inquiries are redirected to www.hrepartners.com, which posts openings throughout the state. **Positions advertised include:** CATIA Instructor; Geriatric Aide.

WICHITA STATE UNIVERSITY
1845 Fairmount Street, Box 15, Wichita KS 67260-0015. 316/978-3106. **Contact:** Mike Turner, Human Resources. **World Wide Web address:** http://www.wichita.edu. **Description:** A state university with an enrollment of approximately 13,000 part-time students who are predominantly beyond the traditional college age. The university offers undergraduate, graduate, and continuing education courses. **NOTE:** Search postings on www.hrepartners.com and apply on-line only. No paper resumes are accepted. **Positions advertised include:** Custodial Specialist; Seasonal Grounds Worker; Administrative Assistant; Equipment Operator Trainee-Greenhouse; Assistant Director Financial Aid; Registered Nurse; Administrative Representative. **Number of employees:** 3,000.

Kentucky

BELLARMINE UNIVERSITY
2001 Newburg Road, Louisville KY 40205. 502/452-8435. **Toll-free phone:** 800/274-4723. **Fax:** 502/452-8293. **Contact:** Human Resources. **E-mail address:** humanresources@bellarmine.edu. **World Wide Web address:** http://www.bellarmine.edu. **Description:** A Catholic liberal arts university that supplies undergraduate and graduate degree programs through its central college, the Rubel School of Business, the Lansing School of Nursing and Health Sciences, and the Thornton School of Education. **NOTE:** For faculty positions, contact the appropriate department chair or search committee member. **Positions advertised include:** Press Operator; Dean of the Thornton School of Education; Assistant Professor, Various Departments.

GEORGETOWN COLLEGE
400 East College Street, Highbaugh Hall Room 102, Georgetown KY 40324. 502/863-8069. **Fax:** 502/868-7737. **Contact:** Human Resources. **E-mail address:** humanresources@georgetowncollege.edu. **World Wide Web address:** http://www.georgetowncollege.edu. **Description:** A private, four-year, Christian liberal arts college, which also offers several pre-professional academic programs. The student body is made up of approximately 1,200 undergraduates. **NOTE:** Those applying for faculty positions must contact Dr. Rosemary Allen, Provost, by phone at 502/863-8146, or by e-mail at rosemary)allen@georgetowncollege.edu. **Positions advertised include:** Building Services Technician; Grounds Crew; Campus Safety Officer Assistant Professor, Various Departments.

KENTUCKY STATE UNIVERSITY
400 East Main Street, Frankfort KY 40601. 502/597-5837. **Contact:** Human Resources. **E-mail address:** jobs@kysu.edu. **World Wide Web address:** http://www.kysu.edu. **Description:** A liberal arts university that offers undergraduate degrees through its College of Arts, Social Sciences, and Interdisciplinary Studies, College of Mathematics, Sciences, Technology and Health, and the College of Professional Studies. **Positions advertised include:** Administrative Assistant; Payroll manager; Research Assistant for Human Nutrition; Lab Assistant; Food Specialist; Lead Teacher; Records Manager; Substitute Teacher; Assistant Football Coach; Comptroller; Director of Auxiliary Enterprises; Payroll Analyst.

MOREHEAD STATE UNIVERSITY
150 University Boulevard ,101 Howell-McDowell Administration Building, Morehead KY 40351. 606/783-2097. **Fax:** 606/783-5028. **Contact:** Roger Barker, Director of Human Resources. **E-mail address:** humanresources@moreheadstate.edu. **World Wide Web address:** http://www.morehead-st.edu. **Description:** A state university that offers its 9,000 undergraduate and graduate students nearly 80 degree programs. **Positions advertised include:** Assistant Professor of Health Education; Coordinator of Baccalaureate Nursing Program; Consortium Training Coordinator; Associate Provost for Research; Building Services Technician; Enrollment Services Counselor; Head Men's Basketball Coach; Traffic Control Assistant. **Other area locations:** Ashland KY; Jackson KY; Mount Sterling KY; Prestonburg KY; West Liberty KY. **Number of employees at this location:** 920.

MURRAY STATE UNIVERSITY
404 Sparks Hall, Murray KY 42071-3312. 270/762-2147. **Fax:** 270/762-3464. **Contact:** Rita Culver, Human Resources. **E-mail address:** human.resources@murraystate.edu. **World Wide Web address:** http://www.murraystate.edu. **Description:** A state university comprised of five academic colleges: Business and Public Affairs, Humanities and Fine Arts, Health Sciences and Human Resources, Engineering and Technology, and a School of Agriculture. The school enrolls 9,000 students. **NOTE:** For faculty positions, contact appropriate department or search committee member. **Positions advertised include:** Patrol Officer; Parking Enforcement/Communications Operator; Bookkeeper of Student Refunds; Freshman Admissions Clerk; Sanitation Truck Driver; Building Services Technician; Grants Proposal Manager. **Number of employees at this location:** 1200.

NORTHERN KENTUCKY UNIVERSITY (NKU)
708 Lucas Administrative Center, Highland Heights KY 41099-8125. 859/572-6385. **Toll-free phone:** 800/637-9948. **Fax:** 859/572-6998. **Contact:** Human Resources. **E-mail address:** jobs@nku.edu. **World Wide Web address:** http://www.nku.edu. **Description:** NKU is a diverse, metropolitan university offering 19 associate's degree programs, 51 bachelor's degree programs, five graduate degree programs, and a joint JD/MBA program. **Positions advertised include:** Adjunct Faculty; Budget Positions; Costume Shop manager; Director of the Student Union; Institutional Research Position; Planning & Performance Position. **Number of employees at this location:** 1,200.

UNIVERSITY OF THE CUMBERLANDS
6184 College Station Drive, Williamsburg KY 40769. 606/539-4211. **Toll-free phone:** 800/343-1609, extension 4211. **Fax:** 606/549-2828. **Contact:** Human Resources. **E-mail address:** hr@ucumberlands.edu. **World Wide Web address:** http://www.ucumberlands.edu. **Description:** A four-year liberal arts college associated with the Southern Baptist Church. Degrees offered include Bachelors of Arts, Science, General Studies, and Music and a Master of Arts in Education. Preprofessional degrees include medical technology, ministry and religious vocations, pre-engineering, premedicine, pre-veterinary science, predentistry, prepharmacy, and prenursing. Founded in 1889. **Positions advertised include:** Supply Center Coordinator; Part-time Faculty in All Academic Areas; Mountain Outreach Director.

UNIVERSITY OF KENTUCKY
112 Scovell Hall, Lexington KY 40506-0064. 859/257-9555, extension 2. **Fax:** 859/323-8512. **Contact:** Human Resources. **E-mail address:** ukjobs@email.uky.edu. **World Wide Web address:** http://www.uky.edu. **Description:** A state university with an enrollment of over 24,000, which is composed of a graduate school and 16 academic colleges. UK Hospital, a 473-bed facility at this location, cares for more than 21,000 inpatients yearly and is ranked as one of the top 100 hospitals by Modern Healthcare magazine. The university is designated a Research University of the First Class by the Carnegie Foundation, one of 59 public universities in the country to have earned this distinction. Founded in 1865. **NOTE:** Part-time and temporary positions are offered.

Positions advertised include: Accounting Manager; Administrative Staff Officer; Administrative Support; Administrative Coordinator; Cardiac Catheter Technician; Obstetrician Case Manager; Clinical Research Executive; Data Center Analyst; Dental Assistant; Registered Dietitian; Psychiatric Director; Image Management Specialist; Lab Animal Technician; Laboratory Technician; Multimedia Specialist; Nursing Care Worker; Research Analyst; Scientist. **Number of employees at this location:** 7,500. **Number of employees nationwide:** 11,500.

UNIVERSITY OF LOUISVILLE
1900 Arthur Street, Louisville KY 40208-2776. 502/852-6258. **Toll-free phone:** 800/334-8635. **Fax:** 502/852-5665. **Contact:** Stacy Gardner. **E-mail address:** employ@Louisville.edu. **World Wide Web address:** http://www.louisville.edu. **Description:** The University of Louisville is run by the state of Kentucky and is in the largest metropolitan area in the state. It has three campuses, enrolls 27,000 students, and offers many different courses including undergraduate and graduate school programs. **Positions advertised include:** Accounting Clerk; Administrative Assistant; Human Resources Assistant; Nurse Practitioner; Research Technologist.

WESTERN KENTUCKY UNIVERSITY
One Big Red Way, Weatherby Administrative Building 42, Bowling Green KY 42101. 270/745-5360. **Fax:** 270/745-5582. **Contact:** Patty Booth, Human Resources. **E-mail address:** human.resources@wku.edu. **World Wide Web address:** http://www.wku.edu. **Description:** A liberal arts university that offers 88 academic majors and variety of professional and pre-professional programs. **NOTE:** Part-time positions are offered. Job seekers may submit applications online. **Positions advertised include** Accounting Associate; Office Associate; Lab Technician; Teachers; Assistant Farm Manager; Building Services Attendant. **Special programs:** Tuition Scholarship Program; Wellness Program.

Louisiana

LOUISIANA TECH UNIVERSITY
305 Wisteria Street, Ruston LA 71272. 318/257-2235. **Toll-free phone:** 800/LATECH-1. **Fax:** 318/257-2482. **Contact:** Personnel. **World Wide Web address:** http://www.latech.edu. **Description:** A technical university that offers a broad range of fully-accredited undergraduate degrees, master's degrees in a variety of areas, and doctoral programs in business administration and engineering. Approximately 10,000 students are enrolled. Founded in 1894. **NOTE:** Search for current job openings online. Application material should be e-mailed to specific job-related e-mail address. Refer to the job posting for more information. **Positions advertised include:** Assistant Professor; Technology Coordinator; Custodian; Football Coach; Administrative Coordinator; Video Coordinator; UNIX Network Specialist; Senior Writer. **President:** Dr. Daniel D. Reneau.

LOYOLA UNIVERSITY NEW ORLEANS
Box 16, 6363 St. Charles Avenue, New Orleans LA 70118. 504/864-7757. **Fax:** 504/864-7100. **Recorded jobline:** 504/864-7700. **Contact:** Sue Metzner, Director of Human Resources. **E-mail address:** resumes@loyno.edu. **World Wide Web address:** http://www.loyno.edu. **Description:** A large Catholic University that offers graduate and undergraduate programs and is composed of a College of Arts and Sciences, Business Administration, and Music, as well as a School of Law, the Loyola Institute for Ministry, and the Loyola Intensive English Program. The school has a total enrollment of 5,500 students, including 3,500 undergraduates. It was founded by a group of Jesuits in 1912. **NOTE:** Staff Positions are recruited through Human Resources, while Faculty Positions are recruited through the specific academic departments. Job seekers may apply in person at 2020 Calhoun Street, Mercy Hall, Room 102. **Positions advertised include:** Administration; Professional; Information Technology; Physical Plant; University Police. **Special programs:** Training; Tuition Remission Program; Student Assistant Program. **President:** The Reverend Kevin William Wildes, S.J.

SOUTHEASTERN LOUISIANA UNIVERSITY
SLU 10799, Hammond LA 70402. 985/549-2001. **Fax:** 985/549-2308. **Recorded jobline:** 985/549-5065. **Contact:** Jessie R. Roberts, Human Resources Director. **E-mail address:** jessie.roberts@selu.edu. **World Wide Web address:** http://www.selu.edu. **Description:** A state university offering a variety of academic programs. Founded in 1925. **NOTE:** For faculty positions and unclassified staff positions, do not e-mail or send resumes to the Human Resources Office. Contact the appropriate search committee. For classified positions, the Civil Service Application, SLU Pre-Employment Application Form and a copy of the Civil Service test score must reach the Human Resources Office by 4:30pm on the closing day. **Positions advertised include:** Custodian; Parking Lot Attendant; Police Officer; Assistant/Associate Professor – Various Departments; Academic Career Specialist; Director, University Counseling Center. **President:** Dr. Randy Moffett. **Number of employees at this location:** 1,500.

TULANE UNIVERSITY
Uptown Square, 200 Broadway, Suite 120, New Orleans LA 70118-5680. 504/865-5280. **Fax:** 504/865-6727. **Contact:** Human Resources – Judy Payne or Cassandra Manning. **E-mail address:** jpayne@tulane.edu or upthrapp@tulane.edu. **World Wide Web address:** http://www2.tulane.edu. **Description:** A university comprised of several academic schools including a business school. **NOTE:** Search for current job opportunities and apply online at http://www.profilesams.com/tulane. For further information about job openings, contact Cassandra Manning at 504/865-5280 for positions at the Uptown Campus or Judy Payne at 504/588-5425 for the Health Sciences Center. **Positions advertised include:** Academic Advisor; Associate General Counsel; Development Officer; Driver; Executive House Manager; FEMA Grant Administrator; Field Assistant; General Maintenance Worker; Instrumentation Assistant; Locksmith; Police Officer; Refrigeration Technician. **President:** Scott S. Cowen. **Number of employees at this location:** Over 5,000.

UNIVERSITY OF LOUISIANA
104 University Circle, Lafayette LA 70504. 337/482-6242. **Contact:** Human Resources. **World Wide Web address:** http://www.louisiana.edu. **Description:** A university that offers 108 majors in 11 colleges and schools and provides both undergraduate and graduate programs of study. **NOTE:** For faculty positions, contact appropriate search committee member. For all other positions, search current job openings on the website, then mail resumes to Martin Hall, Room 175, P.O. Box 40196, Lafayette LA 70504 or e-mail to gbj3997@louisiana.edu. **Positions advertised include:** Accounting Specialist; Mobile Equipment Operator; Administrative Assistant; Painter; **President:** Dr. Ray Authement.

UNIVERSITY OF NEW ORLEANS
2000 Lakeshore Drive, New Orleans LA 70148. 504/280-7418. **Toll-free phone:** 888/514-4275. **Fax:** 504/280-6390. **Contact:** Myron Angel, Director of Human Resources. **E-mail address:** mangel@uno.edu. **World Wide Web address:** http://www.uno.edu. **Description:** A university with an enrollment of approximately 16,000 students, that offers both graduate and undergraduate programs of study. **NOTE:** The majority of applicants must complete the Civil Service Test. Information about the test may be obtained at the Department of Civil Service – Room 411, State Office Building, 325 Loyola Avenue, or from the UNO Office of Human Resource Management, Room 213 in the Administration Building. Non-classified, administrative, and faculty positions are advertised in newspapers, magazines, professional journals, and/or on the UNO web page at http://hrm.uno.edu/unoemployment.htm. **Special**

programs: Training and Development Program. **Chancellor:** Dr. Timothy P. Ryan.

Maine

ANDOVER COLLEGE
901 Washington Avenue, Portland ME 04103. 207/774-6126. **Toll-free phone:** 800/639-3110. **Fax:** 207/774-1715. **Contact:** Mike Davis, Human resources. **E-mail address:** mdavis@andovercollege.com. **World Wide Web address:** http://www.andovercollege.com. **Description:** A two-year college offering associate's degrees and certificate programs in the fields of accounting, business administration, computer technology, criminal justice, legal studies, medical assisting, office administration, travel and tourism, and childhood education. Founded in 1966. **NOTE:** Entry-level positions and part-time jobs are offered. College posts most openings at www.JobsInME.com. **Company slogan:** Skills for success in a changing work place. **Positions advertised include:** Adjunct Instructor – Various Departments; Adjunct Instructor – Early Childhood Education Program; Certified Nurse's Assistant Instructor. **Special programs:** Internships; Co-ops. **Corporate headquarters location:** This location. **Listed on:** Privately held. **CEO/President:** Stephen K. Ingram. **Annual sales/revenues:** Less than $5 million. **Number of employees at this location:** 60.

AUGUSTA SCHOOL DEPARTMENT
40 Pierce Drive, Suite 3, Augusta ME 04330. 207/626-2468. **Fax:** 207/626-2444. **Contact:** Lisa Boucher, Director of Human Resources. **E-mail address:** lboucher@augustaschools.org. **World Wide Web address:** http://www.augustaschools.org. **Description:** Manages and staffs all public schools in Augusta, including one high, two middle, four elementary, and one secondary technical school. **NOTE**: Download application but must submit by fax or mail.

BANGOR SCHOOL DEPARTMENT
73 Harlow Street, Bangor ME 04401. 207/992-4152. **Fax:** 207/992-4163. **Contact:** Human Resources. **E-mail address**: sbestes@bangorschools.net. **World Wide Web address:** http://www.bangorschools.net. **Description:** Responsible for the management and staffing of 10 local schools including Bangor High School, two middle schools (grades 6-7), two intermediate level schools (grades 4-5), and five elementary level schools (K-3). **NOTE:** Request an application on-line and search posted openings. **Positions advertised include:** Custodian; Educational Technician; Secretary; Substitute Teacher – Various Positions; Tutor – Various Grades/Positions.

BATES COLLEGE
215 College Street, Lewiston ME 04240. 207/786-6140. **Contact:** Sue, Human Resources. **Fax:** 207/786-6170. **E-mail address:** hrdept@bates.edu. **World Wide Web address:** http://www.bates.edu. **Description:** A four-year, liberal arts college offering 32 bachelor's degree programs. Approximately 1,600 students attend Bates College. Founded in 1855. **NOTE**: Search posted openings and apply on-line. **Positions advertised include:** Lecturer – Various Departments; Assistant Professor – Various Departments; Behavioral/Cognitive Neuroscientist; Tenure-track Position – Various Departments; Dean of Students; Life Model; Leadership Gifts Officer; Operations Coordinator for Planned Giving; Director – Archives.

BOWDOIN COLLEGE
3501 College Station, Brunswick ME 04011-8426. 207/725-3837. **Fax:** 207/725-3976. **Recorded jobline:** 207/725-3923. **Contact:** Kimberly Bonsey, Manager of Employment. **E-mail address:** kbonsey@bowdoin.edu; hr@bowdoin.edu. **World Wide Web address:** http://www.bowdoin.edu. **Description:** A private, four-year, liberal arts college with approximately 1,500 students. **NOTE:** Recorded jobline provides current listing of available positions. Human Resources address is McLellan Building, 85 Union Street, Brunswick. Faculty applicants need not fill out application. **Positions advertised include:** Visiting Fellow in Education; Groundskeeper; Coordinator of Multicultural Student Programs; Academic Department Coordinator; Administrative Coordinator; Associate Director of Academic Communications; Assistant Director of Residential Life; Capital Gifts Officer; Secretary; Substitute Teacher; Communication Officer. **Number of employees at this location:** 1,000.

BREWER SCHOOL DEPARTMENT
49 Capri Street, Brewer ME 04412. 207/989-3160. **Fax:** 207/989-8622. **Contact:** Betsy Webb, Superintendent. **E-mail address:** bwebb@breweredu.org. **World Wide Web address:** http://www.breweredu.org. **Description:** Responsible for the management and staffing of the area's schools. Brewer School Department consists of Brewer High School, Brewer Middle School, and four elementary schools. **Positions advertised include:** Head Football Coach; Assistant Tennis Coach; JV Softball Coach; "B" Softball Coach.

COLBY COLLEGE
5500 Mayflower Hill Drive, Waterville ME 04901. 207/872-3406. **Contact:** Office of Personnel. **E-mail address**: personnel@colby.edu. **World Wide Web address:** http://www.colby.edu/personnel. **Description:** A four-year, liberal arts college serving approximately 1,800 undergraduate students. Colby College offers a variety of bachelor's degree programs and gives students the option to establish their own unique degree program. **NOTE:** College personnel department provides web access to search posted openings and apply on-line. **Positions advertised include:** Visiting Assistant Professor – Various Departments; Faculty Fellow – Various Departments; Tenure-track Assistant Professor – Various Departments; Chair – Psychology; Interim Assistant Coach of Football; Dean of Students; Director of Donor Relations; RN.

HUSSON COLLEGE
One College Circle, Bangor ME 04401-2999. 207/941-7000. **Toll-free phone**: 800/448-7766. **Fax:** 207/941-7905. **Contact:** Jody Vale, Human Resources. **E-mail address**: admin@husson. **World Wide Web address:** http://www.husson.edu. **Description:** A four-year college with certificate, associate, bachelor, and graduate degree programs. Approximately 1,800 students attend Husson College.

MAINE MARITIME ACADEMY
Co-op Administration, Pleasant Street, Castine ME 04421. 207/326-2231. **Fax:** 207/326-2268. **Toll-free phone:** 800/277-8465. **Contact:** Human Resources. **E-mail address**: career@mma.edu. **World Wide Web address:** http://www.mma.edu. **Description:** A four-year college with associate, bachelor's, and master's degree programs in engineering, science, and management. **Positions advertised include:** Master, Small Craft Waterfront; Assistant/Associate Professor – Various Departments; Foundation Officer; STCW Auditor; Summer Sea Session Residential Counselor; Adjunct Instructor – Various Departments; Assistant Men's Basketball Coach; Head Men's Lacrosse Coach; Instructor – Continuing Education; Technical Reader. **Special programs:** Internships.

ST. JOSEPH'S COLLEGE
278 Whites Bridge Road, Standish ME 04084-5263. 207/893-7755. **Contact:** Human Resources. **E-mail address:** jlaflemme@sjcme.edu. **World Wide Web address:** http://www.sjcme.edu. **Description:** A four-year college with associate and bachelor's degree programs, as well as master's degrees in health care administration. **NOTE:** Please visit website to search posted openings online and download application form. **Positions advertised include:** Assistant Professor of Nursing; Assistant Professor Elementary Education; Adjunct Professor – Various Departments; Library Assistant; Area Coordinator; Campus Services Assistant; Volleyball Coach; Field Hockey Coach; Van/Mini Bus Driver; HVAC Technician; Peer

Reviewer for Master in Health Administrative Program; Security Officer.

THOMAS COLLEGE
180 West River Road, Waterville ME 04901. 207/859-1111. **Fax:** 207/859-1114. **Contact:** Human Resources. **E-mail address:** hr@thomas.edu. **World Wide Web address:** http://www.thomas.edu. **Description:** A four-year college with associate, bachelor's, and master's degree programs. **NOTE:** Thomas College accepts letters of interest for adjunct faculty positions. Search posted openings on-line. **Positions advertised include:** Adjunct Faculty – Various Departments; Security Officer; Student Financial Services Counselor; Custodian.

UNIVERSITY OF MAINE AT FARMINGTON
224 Main Street, Farmington ME 04938. 207/778-7272. **Fax:** 207/778-7247. **Contact:** Laurie Gardner, Director of Personnel. **E-mail address:** lgardner@maine.edu. **World Wide Web address:** http://www.umf.maine.edu. **Description:** One location of the state university. University of Maine is a four-year, undergraduate, public university with an emphasis on education and liberal arts. **Positions advertised include:** Assistant English Professor; Assistant/Associate Professor of Computer Science; Assistant Director of Facilities Management; Administrative Assistant; Plumber. **Operations at this facility include:** Administration; Service. **Number of employees at this location:** 330.

UNIVERSITY OF MAINE AT MACHIAS
9 O'Brien Avenue, Machias ME 04654. 207/255-1200. **Contact:** Personnel. **E-mail address:** ummjobs@maine.edu. **World Wide Web address:** http://www. umm.maine.edu. **Description:** One location of the state university. The University of Maine is a four-year, undergraduate, public university with an emphasis on education and liberal arts. **NOTE:** Search posted openings on-line and respond via e-mail. **Positions advertised include:** Part-time teaching positions for the following disciplines: Mathematics, Psychology, History, Humanities, and Art.

UNIVERSITY OF MAINE AT ORONO
124 Corbett Hall, Orono ME 04469-5717. 207/581-2362. **Contact:** Katherine Pease, Human Resources. **World Wide Web address:** http://www.umaine.edu/hr. **Description:** One location of the state university. The University of Maine is a four-year, undergraduate, public university with an emphasis on education and liberal arts. **NOTE:** Search posted listings and apply on-line. Paper resumes must be accompanied by completed application form and a cover letter.

UNIVERSITY OF MAINE AT PRESQUE ISLE
181 Main Street, Presque Isle ME 04769-2888. 207/768-9551. **Fax:** 207/768-9552. **Contact:** Carolyn Cheney, Personnel. **E-mail address**: cheney@umpi.maine.edu. **World Wide Web address:** http://www.umpi.maine.edu. **Description:** One location of the state university. The University of Maine is a four-year, undergraduate, public university with an emphasis on education and liberal arts. **Positions advertised include:** Faculty tenure positions for the following disciplines: Educational Computing; Pedagogy/Adapted Physical Education; Recreation and Leisure Services; Director of Instructional Technology and Support Services; Administrative Assistant.

UNIVERSITY OF MAINE COOPERATIVE EXTENSION
5741 Libby Hall, Room 106 Orono ME 04469-5741. 207/581-3191. **Contact:** Sandy Vaillancourt, Human Resources. **World Wide Web address:** http://www.umext.maine.edu. **Description:** Loosely affiliated with University of Maine at Orono. University of Maine Cooperative Extension provides community-based, noncredit workshops in four main areas: agriculture; backyard landscape for wildlife; family matters (nutrition, parenting, and other programs); and kids at risk. **NOTE:** Completed application packet is required. No e-mailed or faxed resumes will be accepted.

UNIVERSITY OF NEW ENGLAND
11 Hills Beach Road, Biddeford ME 04005. 207/602-2394. **Contact:** Tammy Louko, Human Resources. **E-mail address**: tlouko@une.edu. **World Wide Web address:** http://www.une.edu. **Description:** A four-year college offering associate, bachelor, and master degree programs, with a total student enrollment of 2,800. Founded in 1831. **NOTE:** Search posted openings and apply on line. Entry-level positions and part-time jobs are offered. **Positions advertised include:** Visiting Biology Instructor; Associate Education Professor; Assistant Professor of Political Science; Computer Purchasing and Support Specialist; Veterinarian; Staff Physician; Director of Marine Science Center; Payroll Manager. **Number of employees at this location:** 525.

UNIVERSITY OF SOUTHERN MAINE (USM)
37 College Avenue, Gorham ME 04038. 207/780-4141. **Toll-free phone:** 800/800-4USM. **Contact:** Employment Manager. **World Wide Web address:** http://www.usm.maine.edu/hrs/jobs/. **Description:** University of Southern Maine has an enrollment of approximately 10,500. The university is a comprehensive public institution comprised of eight academic units including applied science, arts and sciences, business, education and human development, law, Lewiston-Auburn College, Muskie School of Public Service, and nursing and health professions. **NOTE:** Search posted listings and apply on-line only. No paper resumes are accepted. Part-time jobs and second and third shifts are offered. **Positions advertised include:** Administrative Assistant; Plumber Coordinator; Police Officer; Refrigeration Mechanic; Teacher Assistant; Truck Driver; Database Applications Developer; Project Assistant; Project Specialist; Research Associate; Senior Policy Analyst; Woman's Volleyball Coach. **Number of employees at this location:** 1,200.

Maryland

BOWIE STATE UNIVERSITY
14000 Jericho Park Road, Bowie MD 20715. 301/860-3450. **Fax:** 301/860-3454. **Recorded jobline:** 301/860-3449. **Contact:** Human Resources. **E-mail address:** hr@bowiestate.edu. **World Wide Web address:** http://www.bowiestate.edu. **Description:** A four-year, state university offering bachelor's and master's degrees. Approximately 3,200 undergraduate and 1,600 graduate students attend Bowie State. **Positions advertised include:** University Police Officer; Assistant Men's Basketball Coach; Application Software Developer; Software Systems Analyst; Administrative Assistant; Professor of Sociology/Criminal Justice; Nursing Department Chair; Mass Communications/Public Relations Professor; English Lecturer; Theatre/Dance Teacher.

COMMUNITY COLLEGE OF BALTIMORE COUNTY
800 South Rolling Road, Baltimore MD 21228. 410/869-7137. **Fax:** 410/869-7149. **Contact:** Galye D. Slowe, Employment and Recruitment Administrator. **E-mail address:** recruitment@ccbcmd.edu. **World Wide Web address:** http://www.ccbcmd.edu. **Description:** One location of the community college that offers more than 60 degree and certificate programs. **NOTE:** Online applications are available. **Positions advertised include:** Assistant Director; Director Public Safety; Evening Receptionist; Grants Revenue Coordinator; Information Assistant Instructor; Registration Information Specialist; Switchboard Operator; Video Production Assistant. **President:** Dr. Andrew C. Jones.

COPPIN STATE COLLEGE
2500 West North Avenue, Baltimore MD 21216. 410/951-3666. **Fax:** 410/951-3667. **Contact:** Human Resources. **E-mail address:** careers@coppin.edu. **World Wide Web address:** http://www.coppin.edu. **Description:** A four-year, liberal arts college offering both bachelor's and master's degrees. Approximately 2,500 undergraduate and 275 graduate students attend the college. **Positions advertised include:** Counselor; Assistant Professor; Assistant Director. **NOTE:**

Applications are available online. **Special programs:** Internships; Training. **Office hours:** Monday – Friday, 8:00 a.m. – 5:30 p.m. **Corporate headquarters location:** This location. **President:** Dr. Stanley F. Battle. **Number of employees at this location:** 530.

FROSTBURG STATE UNIVERSITY
101 Braddock Road, 3rd Floor, Hitchins Building, Frostburg MD 21532-1099. 301/687-4105. **Fax:** 301/687-4118. **Contact:** Office of Human Resources. **E-mail address:** humanresources@frostburg.edu. **World Wide Web address:** http://www.frostburg.edu. **Description:** A four year state university focusing in liberal arts, business and education with graduate and undergraduate student body. **Positions advertised include:** Consulting Psychologist; University Police Officer.

HOOD COLLEGE
401 Rosemont Avenue, Frederick MD 21701-8575. 301/696-3592. **Fax:** 301/696-3880. **Contact:** Human Resources. **E-mail address:** humanresources@hood.edu. **World Wide Web address:** http://www.hood.edu. **Description:** A liberal arts college that specializes in science programs. The school offers both undergraduate and graduate programs with residential housing available for undergraduate and graduate women; male students are day students only. Hood College has approximately 1,100 undergraduate students and 900 graduate students. **NOTE:** Part-time positions are offered. **Positions advertised include:** Assistant Biology Professor; Building Services Manager; Set-up and Delivery Technician; Library Technician; Floor-Care Specialist; Director of Graduate School Marketing and Recruitment; Accounting Clerk. **Special programs:** Tuition Exchange Program. **President:** Ronald J. Volpe.

LOYOLA COLLEGE
4501 North Charles Street, Baltimore MD 21210-2699. 410/617-2354. **Toll-free phone:** 800/221-9107. **E-mail address:** humanresources@loyola.edu. **World Wide Web address:** http://www.loyola.edu. **Description:** A Jesuit Catholic University. **Note:** Human resources phone: 410/617-2354. **Positions advertised include:** Information Systems Assistant Professor; Reading Education Assistant Professor; Operations Management Assistant Professor; Art History Assistant Professor; Computer Science Visiting Faculty; Education Administrative Associate Professor; Economics Instructor; Special Gifts Assistant Director; Capital Program Director; Annual Giving Assistant; Account Affairs Vice President; Student Life Director; Alumni Relations Office Manager; Alumni Relations Administrative Assistant.

MARYLAND COLLEGE OF ART AND DESIGN
10500 Georgia Avenue, Silver Spring MD 20902-4111. 301/649-4454. **Contact:** Human Resources. **World Wide Web address:** http://www.mcadmd.org. **Description:** A two-year college focusing on fine arts, visual communications, and studio arts. Founded in 1954. **President:** Donald J. Smith.

MARYLAND INSTITUTE COLLEGE OF ART
1300 Mount Royal Avenue, Baltimore MD 21217-4191. 410/225-2420. **Fax:** 410/225-2557. **Contact:** Human Resources. **E-mail address:** jobs@mica.edu. **World Wide Web address:** http://www.mica.edu. **Description:** An art school that offers undergraduate, graduate, continuing education, and summer programs in various areas of art studies. Full-time undergraduate enrollment is approximately 900 students. **Positions advertised include:** Director of Annual Fund; Associate Dean of Continuing Studies; Data Processor; Assistant Director of Academics; Artist-in-Residence; Department of Environmental Design Chair; Art History Professor. **Special programs:** Tuition Remission Program.

MCDANIEL COLLEGE
2 College Hill, Westminster MD 21157-4390. 410/857-2229. **Contact:** Thomas G. Steback, Human Resources. **E-mail address:** tsteback@mcdaniel.edu. **World Wide Web address:** http://www.mcdaniel.edu. **Description:** A private, coeducational institution offering both undergraduate and graduate programs. The college has a full-time enrollment of approximately 1,500 students. **NOTE:** To contact Human Resources directly, call 410/857-2229. **Positions advertised include:** Residential Life Coordinator; Assistant Woman's Volley Ball Coach; PC Support Technician; Administrative Secretary; Housekeeper; Grounds Maintenance Worker. **Office hours:** Monday – Friday, 8:30 a.m. – 4:30 p.m.

MORGAN STATE UNIVERSITY
1700 East Cold Spring Lane, Baltimore MD 21251. 443/885-3195. **Fax:** 443/885-8209. **Contact:** Human Resources. **E-mail address:** jobs@moac.morgan.edu. **World Wide Web address:** http://www.morgan.edu. **Description:** Morgan State University is an African-American institution conferring degrees to the doctoral level. The university offers programs through the College of Arts and Sciences; the School of Education and Urban Studies; and the School of Engineering. **NOTE:** To contact Human Resources directly, call 443/885-3195. Applications are available online. **Positions advertised include:** Program Contract Manager; Grants Associate; Assistant to Assistant Vice President; Administrative Assistant; Office Secretary; Architecture CADD Technician; Broadcast Engineer; Director of Financial Aide. **Special programs:** Internships. **President:** Earl Richardson.

SALISBURY UNIVERSITY
1101 Camden Avenue, Holloway Hall, Salisbury MD 21801. 410/543-6000. **Contact:** Human Resources. **World Wide Web address:** http://www.salisbury.edu. **Description:** Offers a traditional liberal arts curriculum and a variety of preprofessional and professional programs on both the graduate and undergraduate levels. The university's 5,200 full-time undergraduates can also earn their degrees from the Franklin P. Perdue School of Business, the Richard A. Henson School of Science and Technology, the School of Education and Professional Studies, or the Charles R. and Martha N. Fulton School of Liberal Arts. **NOTE:** To reach Human Resources directly, call 410/543-6035. **Positions advertised include:** Electronic Resources Librarian; Spanish Associate Professor; Developing Psychology Associate Professor; Film and Literature Associate Professor; Health Psychology Associate Professor; Medieval Associate Professor; Executive Chief; University Registrar; Business Consultant.

TOWSON UNIVERSITY
8000 York Road, Towson MD 21252-0001. 410/704-2162. **Fax:** 410/704-2603. **Recorded jobline:** 410/704-2161. **Contact:** Philip Ross III, Human Resources. **World Wide Web address:** http://www.towson.edu. **Description:** Offers undergraduate programs of study through the College of Allied Health Sciences and Physical Education, the College of Education, the College of Fine Arts and Communication, the College of Liberal Arts, the College of Natural and Mathematical Sciences, and the School of Business and Economics. Founded in 1866. **NOTE:** To contact Human Resources directly, call 410/704-2162. **Positions advertised include:** Administrative Assistant; Executive Assistant; Finisher- Bindery Assistant; Geographical Information Systems Student Coordinator; Geographical Information Systems Technician; Program Director; Consultant Trainer; Athletic Director; Admission Director; Event Planning Director; Field Work Director; Business Counselor; Admissions Recruitment; Parking Director; Service Worker; Campus Police Officer. **Office hours:** Monday – Friday, 8:00 a.m. – 4:30 p.m.

UNIVERSITY OF BALTIMORE
1420 North Charles Street, Baltimore MD 21201. 410/837-5410. **Contact:** Human Resources. **E-mail address:** hrresume@ubalt.edu. **World Wide Web address:** http://www.ubalt.edu. **Description:** A state university composed of a School of Business, a School of Law, and a Liberal Arts School. The university offers both graduate and undergraduate programs. Full-

time enrollment is approximately 5,000 students. **Positions advertised include** Law Library Director; People Soft Systems Administrator; Cabinet Maker; Golf Driving Range Manager; Golf Driving Range Attendants; Admissions Counselor; Campus Web Master; Executive Administrative Assistant; Academic Program Specialist. **Special programs:** Tuition Waiver Program. **Office hours:** Monday – Friday, 8:30 a.m. – 4:30 p.m. **Parent company:** University System of Maryland. **President:** Robert L. Bogomolny.

UNIVERSITY OF MARYLAND AT BALTIMORE COUNTY
1000 Hilltop Circle, 532 Administration Building, Baltimore MD 21250. 410/455-2337. **Recorded jobline:** 410/455-1100. **Contact:** Human Resources. **World Wide Web address:** http://www.umbc.edu. **Description:** A research university with an enrollment of more than 10,500 students, serving the Baltimore metropolitan region. The university places special emphasis on its undergraduate programs, offering 30 majors. Founded in 1966. **Note:** http://www.umbc.edu/hr/employment is the University's employment web page. **Positions advertised include:** HVAC Mechanic; Accounting Associate; Librarian Technician. **Special programs:** Tuition Remission Program. **Office hours:** Monday – Friday, 8:00 a.m. – 5:00 p.m. **Parent company:** University System of Maryland. **Operations at this facility include:** Administration; Research and Development; Service. **President:** Freeman A. Hrabowski III. **Number of employees at this location:** 1,800.

UNIVERSITY OF MARYLAND AT COLLEGE PARK
COOPERATIVE EXTENSION SERVICE
Symons Hall, Room 2119, College Park MD 20742. 301/405-5679. **Contact:** Personnel Services Department. **E-mail address:** personnel@accmail.umd.edu. **World Wide Web address:** http://www.umd.edu. **Description:** A university offering 117 undergraduate and 84 graduate programs. **Positions advertised include:** Assistant Director of Special Events; Information Technology Coordinator; Web Communications Manager; Assistant Director; Registrar Analyst; Admissions Coordinator; Auditor; Business Manager; Program Coordinator; Registered Nurse; Resident Director; Science Editor. **President:** C.D. Mote, Junior. **Number of employees at this location:** 12,478.

UNIVERSITY OF MARYLAND BALTIMORE
111 South Greene Street, Second Floor, Baltimore MD 21201. 410/706-7171. **Recorded jobline:** 410/706-5562. **Contact:** Human Resources. **E-mail address:** resume@hr.umaryland.edu. **World Wide Web address:** http://www.umaryland.edu. **Description:** The University of Maryland Baltimore specializes in health and human service programs. The 32-acre campus is a leader in medical research and education and is affiliated with the University of Maryland Medical System. **NOTE:** Applications are available online. **Positions advertised include:** Database Engineer; People Soft Functional Specialist; Information Systems Engineer; Information Technology Specialist; People Soft Functional Analyst. **Office hours:** Monday – Friday, 8:30 a.m. – 4:30 p.m. **Parent company:** University System of Maryland. **Operations at this facility include:** Administration; Research and Development. **Number of employees at this location:** 4,500.

Massachusetts
AMERICAN INTERNATIONAL COLLEGE
1000 State Street, Springfield MA 01109. 413/737-7000. **Contact:** Human Resources. **World Wide Web address:** http://www.aic.edu. **Description:** A private, independent, coeducational college with approximately 1,200 undergraduate and 800 graduate and part-time students. The college offers more than 35 majors within the schools of Arts and Sciences, Business Administration, Psychology and Education, and Health Sciences. **Positions advertised include:** Non Credit Program Manager; Student Activities Director; Political Science Assistant Professor.

ANNA MARIA COLLEGE
50 Sunset Lane, Paxton MA 01612-1198. 508/849-3398. **Toll-free phone:** 800/344-4586. **Fax:** 508/849-3319. **Contact:** Human Resources. **E-mail address:** ldriscoll@annamaria.edu. **World Wide Web address:** http://www.annamaria.edu. **Description:** A nonprofit, private, liberal arts college for women offering both undergraduate and graduate degrees. Founded in 1947. **NOTE:** Entry-level positions and part-time jobs are offered. **Special programs:** Internships; Summer Jobs. **Office hours:** Monday - Friday, 8:30 a.m. - 4:30 p.m. **President:** William McGarry. **Facilities Manager:** Paul Chenevert. **Information Systems Manager:** John Price. **Purchasing Manager:** Susan Lynch. **Number of employees at this location:** 165.

ASSUMPTION COLLEGE
P.O. Box 15005, Worcester MA 01615-0005. 508/767-7000. **Fax:** 508/756-1780. **Contact:** Human Resources. **E-mail address:** resumes@assumption.edu. **World Wide Web address:** http://www.assumption.edu. **Description:** A Catholic college with an undergraduate enrollment of approximately 1,600 students. Approximately 1,200 students are enrolled in graduate and continuing education programs. The college also offers a Center for Continuing and Professional Education, which grants associate's and bachelor's degrees on a part-time basis; The French Institute, an academic research facility and a center for French cultural activities; and the Institute for Social and Rehabilitation Services. Founded in 1904. **Positions advertised include:** Annual Giving Director; Graduate Assistant for Student Activities; Resident Director; Area Coordinator; Assistant Director of Athletics for Sports Medicine. **Corporate headquarters location:** This location.

BABSON COLLEGE
Nichols Hall, Babson Park MA 02457. 781/239-4121. **Contact:** Human Resources. **E-mail address:** jobs@babson.edu. **World Wide Web address:** http://www.babson.edu. **Description:** A four-year business college with an enrollment of approximately 1,700 undergraduate students and 1,730 graduate students. **Positions advertised include:** Undergraduate Student Accounts Coordinator; Financial Accounting Coordinator; Corporate Outreach Manager; Reserve Librarian.

BAY STATE SCHOOL OF TECHNOLOGY
225 Turnpike Street, Canton MA 02021. 781/828-3434. **Toll-free phone:** 888/828-3434. **Fax:** 781/575-0089. **Contact:** Human Resources. **E-mail address:** bssanet@ultranet.com. **World Wide Web address:** http://users.rcn.com/bssanet. **Description:** A technical institute offering programs in electronics, HVAC, and computers. **Positions advertised include:** Electronics Instructor; Major Appliance Instructor.

BECKER COLLEGE
61 Sever Street, Box 15071, Worcester MA 01609-2195. 508/791-9241. **Toll-free phone:** 877/5BECKER. **Fax:** 508/849-5275. **Contact:** Kathy Garvey, Director of Human Resources. **E-mail address:** kgarvey@becker.edu. **World Wide Web address:** http://www.beckercollege.com. **Description:** Offers a variety of associate's and bachelor's degrees, and certificate programs in business, law, computers, health, education, and social sciences. **Positions advertised include:** Nursing Faculty; Library Supervisor; Adjunct Faculty.

BENTLEY COLLEGE
175 Forest Street, Waltham MA 02452-4705. 781/891-3427. **Fax:** 781/891-2494. **Contact:** Joseph Salvucci, Senior Human Resources Business Partner. **World Wide Web address:** http://www.bentley.edu. **Description:** A business college offering undergraduate and graduate programs, as well as professional development certificates. The college offers associate's, bachelor's, and master's (including MBAs) degrees. **Positions advertised include:** Associate Director of

Corporate Relations; Communication Designer; Assistant Director of Development; Receptionist; Campus Police Officer; Dispatcher; Records Coordinator; Work Order Control Assistant; Behavioral & Political Sciences Faculty; CIS Faculty; English Faculty; History Faculty; International Studies Faculty; Media Studies Faculty; Philosophy Faculty.

BERKLEE COLLEGE OF MUSIC
1140 Boylston Street, Boston MA 02215. 617/266-1400. **Fax:** 617/247-0166. **Contact:** Employee Relations Manager. **World Wide Web address:** http://www.berklee.edu. **Description:** An independent music college offering four-year programs of study in composition, film scoring, music business/management, music education, music production and engineering, music synthesis, music therapy, and performance. The college enrolls 3,000 students. **Positions advertised include:** Assistant Chair; Stage Manager; Assistant Vice President for Berklee Media; Course Developer; Continuing Education Registrar; Lab Monitor; Harmony Department Chair; Front Desk Supervisor. **Corporate headquarters location:** This location. **Number of employees at this location:** 170.

BOSTON COLLEGE
140 Commonwealth Avenue, More Hall, Room 315, Chestnut Hill MA 02467. 617/552-3330. **Contact:** Human Resources. **World Wide Web address:** http://www.bc.edu/. **Description:** A private, four-year, Jesuit college offering bachelor's and master's degree programs. **Positions advertised include:** Administrative Secretary; Administrative Coordinator; General Service Worker; Development Secretary; Staff Assistant; Research Director; Sales Assistant; Second Cook; Digital Media Producer; Associate Dean; Gate Attendant; Classroom Technology Specialist.

BOSTON UNIVERSITY
25 Buick Street, Boston MA 02215. 617/353-2380. **Contact:** Human Resources. **World Wide Web address:** http://www.bu.edu/. **Description:** A private, four-year university offering both undergraduate and graduate degrees. **Positions advertised include:** Administrative Assistant; Patient Coordinator; Research Administrative Assistant; Data Technician; Admissions Officer; Clinical Operations Manager; Program Manager; Research Administrator; Community Liaison; Project Coordinator; Data Manager; Executive Secretary; Program Coordinator. **Corporate headquarters location:** This location.

BRANDEIS UNIVERSITY
Mail Stop 118, P.O. Box 9110, Waltham MA 02454-9110. 781/736-4473. **Fax:** 781/736-4466. **Contact:** Employment Administrator. **World Wide Web address:** http://www.brandeis.edu. **Description:** A four-year university offering both undergraduate and graduate programs of study. **Positions advertised include:** Assistant Controller; Executive Director of Intellectual Properties; Director of Athletics; Advancement Services Director; Research Analyst; Lab Coordinator; Lab Technician; Administrative Assistant; Cashier; University Police Officer. **Corporate headquarters location:** This location. **Number of employees at this location:** 1,300.

BRIDGEWATER STATE COLLEGE
Boyden Hall, Room 103, Offices of Human Resources, Bridgewater MA 02325. 508/697-1324. **Fax:** 508/531-1725. **Contact:** Human Resources. **E-mail address:** humres@bridgew.edu. **World Wide Web address:** http://www.bridgew.edu. **Description:** A four-year state college offering a variety of undergraduate and graduate degree programs. **Positions advertised include:** Vice President Student Affairs; Head Women's Tennis Coach; Bookkeeper; Clerk. **Special programs:** Internships. **Number of employees at this location:** 900.

CAMBRIDGE COLLEGE
1000 Massachusetts Avenue, Cambridge MA 02138. 617/873-0100. **Toll-free phone:** 888/868-1002. **Contact:** Human Resources. **World Wide Web address:** http://www.cambridgecollege.edu. **Description:** A college offering bachelor's and master's degrees for adult psychology students.

CAPE COD COMMUNITY COLLEGE
2240 Iyanough Road, West Barnstable MA 02668. 508/362-2131. **Toll-free phone:** 877/846-3672. **Fax:** 508/362-3988. **Contact:** Human Resources. **E-mail address:** info@capecod.mass.edu. **World Wide Web address:** http:///www.capecod.mass.edu. **Description:** A two-year college offering associate degrees. **Positions advertised include:** Program Assistant; Special Program Coordinator; Part Time Faculty; Associate Academic Dean.

CATHOLIC CHARITIES
EL CENTRO DEL CARDENAL
76 Union Park Street, Boston MA 02118. 617/542-9292. **Contact:** Human Resources. **Description:** A social service agency. Services include career counseling, alternative education, immigration refugee services and relief, family guidance, shelter and ministry programs, substance abuse services, and English-as-a-Second-Language (ESL) programs.

CLARK UNIVERSITY
950 Main Street, Worcester MA 01610. 508/793-7294. **Fax:** 508/793-8809. **Contact:** Human Resources Department. **E-mail address:** resumes@clarku.edu. **World Wide Web address:** http://www.clarku.edu. **Description:** A four-year research university offering bachelor's, master's, and doctoral degrees. The student body consists of approximately 2,200 graduate and undergraduate students. During the summer the College of Professional and Continuing Education (C.O.P.A.C.E.) program offers select classes for credit or personal enrichment. **NOTE:** Entry-level positions and part-time jobs are offered. **Positions advertised include:** Assistant Director of Admissions; Office Assistant; Assistant Director; Area Coordinator; Director of Major Gifts. **Office hours:** Monday - Friday, 8:30 a.m. - 4:30 p.m. **Other area locations:** Framingham MA.

CLARK UNIVERSITY
COMPUTER CAREER INSTITUTE
10 California Avenue, Framingham MA 01701. 508/620-5904. **Toll-free phone:** 800/568-1776. **Fax:** 508/875-7285. **Contact:** Human Resources. **Description:** Offers a variety of computer-related courses designed to help people reentering the workforce. Certificates are awarded at the end of 9 to 12 week daytime class sessions, or 6 to 7 month evening class sessions.

CURRY COLLEGE
1071 Blue Hill Avenue, Milton MA 02186. 617/333-0500. **Contact:** Human Resources. **World Wide Web address:** http://www.curry.edu. **Description:** A four-year liberal arts college with programs for undergraduate and graduate students. **Positions advertised include:** Graduate Education Faculty; Assistant Director Financial Aide; Enrollment Representative; Assistant Director Admissions; Public Safety Officer

EMERSON COLLEGE
120 Boylston Street, Boston MA 02116. 617/824-8500. **Contact:** Human Resources. **World Wide Web address:** http://www.emerson.edu. **E-mail address:** employment@emerson.edu. **Description:** A four-year communications college offering both undergraduate and graduate degrees to approximately 2,000 students. **Positions advertised include:** Associate Vice President; College Counsel; Assistant Director; Head Women's Soccer Coach; Social Worker; Education Technologist; Loading Dock Supervisor; Public Safety Officer; Journalism Technology Manager; Student Service Advisor; Multi-cultural Student Affairs Director. **Special programs:** Internships. **Corporate headquarters location:** This location. **Operations at this facility include:** Administration. **Number of employees at this location:** 350.

EMMANUEL COLLEGE
400 The Fenway, Boston MA 02115. 617/735-9991. **Fax:** 617/735-9877. **Contact:** Human Resources. **E-mail address:** jobs@emaunuel.edu. **World Wide Web address:** http://www.emmanuel.edu. **Description:** A four-year undergraduate college. **Positions advertised include:** Site Coordinator; Director of the Annual Fund; Assistant Director of Corporate; Development Assistant; Web Designer; Graphic Designer; Assistant Professor.

FISHER COLLEGE
118 Beacon Street, Boston MA 02116. 617/536-4647. **Contact:** Human Resources. **World Wide Web address:** http://www.fisher.edu. **Description:** A private junior college. **Positions advertised include:** Administrative Assistant; Associate Registrar; Dean of Student Affairs; Campus Safety Officer; Director for Annual Giving. **Other in-state locations:** Fall River; New Bedford; Attleboro Falls.

FITCHBURG STATE COLLEGE
160 Pearl Street, Fitchburg MA 01420. 978/345-2151. **Contact:** Human Resources. **E-mail address:** resumes@fsc.edu. **World Wide Web address:** http://www.fsc.edu. **Description:** A state college offering bachelor's and master's degrees. **Positions advertised include:** Assistant Professor, Special Education; Assistant/Associate Professor, Criminal Justice; Assistant Professor, Industrial Technology.

FRAMINGHAM STATE COLLEGE
100 State Street, Framingham MA 01701-9101. 508/626-4530. **Fax:** 508/626-4592. **Contact:** Human Resources. **World Wide Web address:** http://www.framingham.edu. **Description:** Founded as the first public teacher's college in the country, Framingham State has grown to include 28 majors in undergraduate, graduate, and continuing education programs with an emphasis on business administration, and elementary and early childhood education. Framingham State's nationally recognized faculty is involved in many community and professional organizations. Learning resources include an advising center, the MetroWest Economic Research Center, modern computer facilities, and a planetarium. Founded in 1839. **Positions advertised include:** Director of Health Services; Distance Education Program Clerical; Office of Residential Life Maintainer; Office of Residential Life Trade Worker; Steam Firemen; Skilled Laborer; HVAC Mechanic; Communications Dispatcher.

GORDON COLLEGE
255 Grapevine Road, Wenham MA 01984. 978/927-2300. **Contact:** Human Resources. **World Wide Web address:** http://www.gordon.edu. **Description:** A four-year liberal arts college offering Bachelor of Science, Bachelor of Arts, Bachelor of Music, and Master of Education degrees. **Positions advertised include:** Head Women's Soccer Coach; Director of Communications; Public Safety Officer.

HARVARD UNIVERSITY
11 Holyoke Street, Harvard Square, Cambridge MA 02138. 617/495-2771. **Contact:** Personnel. **World Wide Web address:** http://www.hr.harvard.edu/employment. **Description:** A private, four-year, Ivy League university. Harvard University collaborates with nearby Radcliffe College, allowing graduate and undergraduate students to take certain classes at Radcliffe and vice versa. **Positions advertised include:** Special Assistant to the President; Facility Manager; Payroll Accountant; Staff Assistant. **NOTE:** Harvard University posts listings for all support and professional job openings. Please check these listings in the employment office or on Harvard University's website and respond directly to the department that is hiring. **Office hours:** Monday, Tuesday, Wednesday, Friday, 11:00 a.m. - 4:00 p.m.; Thursday, 8:30 a.m. - 6:00 p.m.

HEBREW COLLEGE
160 Herrick Street, Newton Centre MA 02459. 617/559-8600. **Toll-free phone:** 800/866-4814. **Fax:** 617/559-8601. **Contact:** Human Resources Department. **E-mail address:** hr@hebrewcollege.edu. **World Wide Web address:** http://www.hebrewcollege.edu. **Description:** A college offering courses in the Hebrew language and literature, Rabbinics, and Jewish music and culture. The college offers courses in cooperation with Boston University, Northeastern University, Simmons College, Boston College, Brandeis University, and University of Massachusetts Boston. **Positions advertised include:** Vice President of Institutional Achievement; Database Depart Writer.

COLLEGE OF THE HOLY CROSS
One College Street, Worcester MA 01610. 508/793-3756. **Fax:** 508/793-3575. **Contact:** Director of Personnel. **E-mail address:** resumes@holycross.edu. **World Wide Web address:** http://www.holycross.edu. **Description:** A private, four-year college offering bachelor's and master's degree programs. **Positions advertised include:** Dining Room Manager; Assistant Director; Community Development Coordinator; Applications Administrator; Vice President Administrative & Finance. **Special programs:** Internships. **Operations at this facility include:** Administration; Sales; Service. **Number of employees at this location:** 800.

GIBBS COLLEGE
126 Newbury Street, Boston MA 02116. 617/578-7100. **Toll-free phone:** 800/6SK-ILLS. **Contact:** Human Resources. **World Wide Web address:** http://www.katharinegibbs.com. **Description:** A business instruction school. Founded in 1911. **Other U.S. locations:** Nationwide.

LESLEY UNIVERSITY
29 Everett Street, Cambridge MA 02138-2890. 617/349-8787. **Toll-free phone:** 800/999-1959. **Contact:** Maryanne Gallagher, Associate Director of Human Resources. **World Wide Web address:** http://www.lesley.edu. **Description:** A private, four-year university offering an undergraduate liberal arts program and a variety of graduate and doctoral degree programs including arts, education, management, and social sciences. **Positions advertised include:** Assistant Director of Financial Aide; Assistant Professor of Mathematics; Conference Assistant; Administrative Assistant; Director of Health Services; Certification Officer; Graphic Design Faculty; Customer Care Coordinator; Administrative Assistant. **Listed on:** Privately held. **Number of employees at this location:** 400. **Number of employees nationwide:** 450.

MIT (MASSACHUSETTS INSTITUTE OF TECHNOLOGY)
400 Main Street, 2nd Floor, Cambridge MA 02142. 617/253-4251. **Contact:** Human Resources. **World Wide Web address:** http://web.mit.edu/personnel. **Description:** A private, four-year academic and research institution with an enrollment of approximately 4,300 undergraduate students and 5,600 graduate students. **Positions advertised include:** Administrative Assistant; Associate Counsel; Chief Radiological Technician; Circulation Assistant; Computational Biologist; Departmental Liaison; Mechanic; Member Relations Representative; Post Doctoral Associate; Research Scientist; Software Engineer; Staff Accountant; Technical Assistant. **Office hours:** Monday - Friday, 9:00 a.m. - 5:00 p.m. **NOTE:** Send resumes to P.O. Box 391229, Cambridge MA 02139.

MASSACHUSETTS COLLEGE OF ART
621 Huntington Avenue, Boston MA 02115. 617/232-1555. **Fax:** 617/879-7911. **Contact:** Human Resources. **World Wide Web address:** http://www.massart.edu. **Description:** An art school offering multimedia courses in a variety of disciplines including photography and painting.

MASSASOIT COMMUNITY COLLEGE
One Massasoit Boulevard, Brockton MA 02302. 508/588-9100. **Toll-free phone:** 800/CAR-EERS.

Contact: Personnel. **World Wide Web address:** http://www.massasoit.mass.edu. **Description:** A community college offering a variety of two-year programs. **Other area locations:** Canton MA, **NOTE:** Call 781/821-2222 for Canton Campus.

MOUNT HOLYOKE COLLEGE
50 College Street, South Hadley MA 01075. **Contact:** Human Resources. **World Wide Web address:** http://www.mtholyoke.edu. **Description:** A private, four-year college offering a variety of programs for undergraduate and graduate students. **Positions advertised include:** Director of Administrative Computing; Public Safety Officer; Director of Financial Assistance; Class Dean; Administrative Assistant; Coordinator of Educational Opportunities Abroad; Academic Computer Support Specialist; Director of Residential Life; Counseling Service Postdoctoral Clinician; Research Assistant in Educational Psychology; Laboratory Director Introductory Physics; Coordinator of Multicultural Affairs; Director of Equestrian Center; Payroll Specialist.

NATIONAL EVALUATION SYSTEMS
30 Gatehouse Road, Amherst MA 01002. 413/256-0444. **Contact:** Personnel Director. **E-mail address:** personnel@nesinc.com. **World Wide Web address:** http://www.nesinc.com. **Description:** A contract-based company providing educational products and services in a variety of areas including professional licensing and certification testing programs, large-scale pupil assessment, and print-based educational materials. Clients include state departments of education and professional licensing boards. **Positions advertised include:** Project Director; Statistical Programmer/Analyst; Project Assistant. **Corporate headquarters location:** This location. **Other U.S. locations:** Sacramento CA; Austin TX. **Operations at this facility include:** Administration; Research and Development; Service.

NEW ENGLAND COLLEGE OF FINANCE
One Lincoln Plaza, 89 South Street, Boston MA 02111. 617/951-2350. **Fax:** 617/951-2533. **Contact:** Personnel. **E-mail address:** info@finance.edu. **World Wide Web address:** http://www.finance.edu. **Description:** A college offering associate's degrees, bachelor's degrees, and certificate courses in the areas of finance, banking, and insurance. Founded in 1909.

NEW ENGLAND CONSERVATORY OF MUSIC
290 Huntington Avenue, Boston MA 02115. 617/585-1230. **Contact:** Human Resources. **World Wide Web address:** http://www.newenglandconservatory.edu. **Description:** A music school. New England Conservatory of Music also operates a preparatory school and offers continuing education classes for students of all levels. **Positions advertised include:** Composition Faculty; Music Theory Faculty; Academic Training; Executive Director of Development; Office Manager; Major Gifts Officer; Technology Support Specialist.

NICHOLS COLLEGE
P.O. Box 5000, Dudley MA 01571-5000. 508/943-2055. **Toll-free phone:** 800/470-3379. **Contact:** Rick Woods, Director of Human Resources. **E-mail address:** rick.woods@nichols.edu. **World Wide Web address:** http://www.nichols.edu. **Description:** A private, coeducational, liberal arts college known for business education with an enrollment of 700 undergraduates. Founded in 1815. **Positions advertised include:** Office Assistant.

NORTHEASTERN UNIVERSITY
360 Huntington Avenue, 250 Columbus Place, Boston MA 02115. 617/373-2230. **Contact:** Human Resources. **World Wide Web address:** http://www.neu.edu. **Description:** A university operating through several colleges and programs including the College of Arts and Science, the Boston Bouve College of Pharmacy and Health Professions, the Graduate School of Business Administration, a law school, part-time evening programs, and graduate, professional, and continuing education courses. **Positions advertised include:** Spanish Instructor; Math Instructor; Science Instructor; Math SAT Instructor; Decision Making Instructor; Recreational Coordinator; Current Events Instructor; English SAT Instructor; English Instructor; Assistant Residential Director; Administration Coordinator; Grants & Contract Specialist; Carpentry & Lockshop Supervisor. **Corporate headquarters location:** This location. **Other area locations:** Burlington MA; Dedham MA.

QUINCY COLLEGE
34 Coddington Street, Quincy MA 02169. 617/984-1600. **Contact:** Steve McGrath, Human Resources. **E-mail address:** smcgrath@quincycollege.edu. **World Wide Web address:** http://www.quincycollege.edu. **Description:** A two-year commuter college. Quincy College's combined full-time and part-time student enrollment is 5,000.

RADCLIFFE INSTITUTE FOR ADVANCED STUDY
10 Garden Street, Faye House, Room 106, Cambridge MA 02138. 617/495-8608. **Fax:** 617/496-0255. **Contact:** Human Resources. **E-mail address:** info@radcliffe.edu. **World Wide Web address:** http://www.radcliffe.edu. **Description:** A college offering both graduate and undergraduate programs. Radcliffe Institute for Advanced Study was established as a result of the merger of Radcliffe College with Harvard University.

REGIS COLLEGE
Box 4, 235 Wellesley Street, Weston MA 02493. 781/768-7210. **Contact:** Human Resources. **World Wide Web address:** http://www.regiscollege.edu. **Description:** A private liberal arts and sciences college for women. Founded in 1927.

SALEM STATE COLLEGE
352 Lafayette Street, Salem MA 01970. 978/542-6000. **Contact:** Human Resources. **E-mail address:** eo-hr@salemstate.edu. **World Wide Web address:** http://www.salemstate.edu. **Description:** A state college.

SIMMONS COLLEGE
300 The Fenway, Boston MA 02115-5898. 617/521-2000. **Contact:** Human Resources. **World Wide Web address:** http://www.simmons.edu. **Description:** A private, four-year, liberal arts and sciences college for women. The college also offers 12 graduate programs for both men and women. The total graduate enrollment is approximately 2,000.

SINNOTT SCHOOL
210 Winter Street, Suite 204, Weymouth MA 02188. 781/331-6769. **Contact:** Human Resources. **World Wide Web address:** http://www.sinnottschool.com. **Description:** A computer training school offering classes in Microsoft Office and other applications. Clients are both individuals and corporations. The Microsoft Office curriculum includes Windows, NT, Microsoft Word, Excel, Access, and PowerPoint. Classes are held both on-site as well as at corporate locations. Sinnott School offers long-term day courses as well as half- and full-day courses.

STONEHILL COLLEGE
320 Washington Street, Easton MA 02357. 508/565-1000. **Contact:** Human Resources. **E-mail address:** employment_ervices@stonehill.edu. **World Wide Web address:** http://www.stonehill.edu. **Description:** A private, four-year, Catholic college. Stonehill offers liberal arts programs to approximately 2,000 undergraduate students.

SUFFOLK UNIVERSITY
8 Ashburton Place, Boston MA 02108. 617/573-8415. **Fax:** 617/367-2250. **Contact:** Judy Minardi, Director of Human Resources. **E-mail address:** jobs@suffolk.edu. **World Wide Web address:** http://www.suffolk.edu. **Description:** A four-year university. Suffolk University's Frank Sawyer School

of Management offers an Executive MBA program. Suffolk University also houses a law school. **Positions advertised include:** Assistant Director; Leadership Giving Officer.

TERC
2067 Massachusetts Avenue, Cambridge MA 02140. 617/547-0430. **Fax:** 617/349-3535. **Contact:** Human Resources. **E-mail address:** communications@terc.edu. **World Wide Web address:** http://www.terc.edu. **Description:** A not-for-profit education research and development organization dedicated to improving math, science, and technology education. TERC contributes to the understanding of teaching and learning through research, fosters professional development, develops applications of new technologies, creates curricula and other products, and supports school reform. Founded in 1965. **Positions advertised include:** Desktop Support Specialist; Development Officer; Investigations Workshops Intern; Senior Investigator/Program Leader.

TUFTS UNIVERSITY
169 Holland Street, Somerville MA 02144. 617/627-3272. **Fax:** 617/627-3725. **Contact:** Human Resources. **World Wide Web address:** http://www.tufts.edu. **Description:** Offers both undergraduate and graduate programs through the schools of arts and sciences; Fletcher School of Law and Diplomacy; medical, dental, and veterinary schools; and a human nutrition research center. **Other area locations:** Boston MA.

UNIVERSITY OF MASSACHUSETTS/AMHERST
167 Whitmore Administration Building, Amherst MA 01003. 413/545-1396. **Contact:** Employment Office. **World Wide Web address:** http://www.umass.edu. **Description:** The main campus of the four-year, state university. **Other U.S. locations:** Boston MA; North Dartmouth MA; Lowell MA.

UNIVERSITY OF MASSACHUSETTS/BOSTON
100 Morrissey Boulevard, Boston MA 02125-3393. 617/287-5150. **Fax:** 617/287-5179. **Contact:** Human Resources. **World Wide Web address:** http://www.umb.edu. **Description:** A campus of the four-year, state university offering approximately 90 fields of study to over 12,000 students. **Other area locations:** Amherst MA; North Dartmouth MA; Lowell MA. **Number of employees at this location:** 1,800.

UNIVERSITY OF MASSACHUSETTS/DARTMOUTH
285 Old Westport Road, North Dartmouth MA 02747-2300. 508/999-8060. **Contact:** Todd Swarts, Director of Human Resources. **World Wide Web address:** http://www.umassd.edu. **Description:** A campus of the four-year, state university offering graduate and undergraduate programs to approximately 6,000 students. **Other area locations:** Amherst MA; Boston MA; Lowell MA.

UNIVERSITY OF MASSACHUSETTS/LOWELL
883 Broadway Street, Room 101, Lowell MA 01854. 978/934-3555. **Contact:** Human Resources. **World Wide Web address:** http://www.uml.edu. **Description:** A campus of the four-year, state university. University of Massachusetts/Lowell offers undergraduate majors in a variety of disciplines including engineering, computer technology, sales, business, sciences, education, health professions, human services, liberal arts, and music. The college also offers post-graduate certificate programs in paralegal studies, electronics technology, packaging, data/telecommunications, technical writing, purchasing management, quality assurance, and wastewater treatment. **NOTE:** Each fall (and sometimes in the spring) UMass/Lowell hosts a business and technology career fair. For more information, visit the UMass/Lowell Career Services Website at http://ocs.uml.edu. **Other area locations:** Amherst MA; Boston MA; North Dartmouth MA.

WELLESLEY COLLEGE
106 Central Street, Wellesley MA 02481. 781/235-0320. **Contact:** Human Resources. **World Wide Web address:** http://www.wellesley.edu. **Description:** A private liberal arts college for women. **Positions advertised include:** Vice President for Finance Treasurer; Director of Admission; Campus Police Office; Science Librarian; Director of International Studies; Residential Director.

WENTWORTH INSTITUTE OF TECHNOLOGY
550 Huntington Avenue, Boston MA 02115-5998. 617/989-4590. **Fax:** 617/989-4195. **Contact:** Anne Gill, Associate Vice President of Human Resources. **World Wide Web address:** http://www.wit.edu. **Description:** A technical university noted for its strengths in engineering, science, technology, and design. Total student enrollment is approximately 3,000. Founded in 1904. **Positions advertised include:** Student Services Representative; Assistant Director of Alumni Relations; Provost; Architecture Faculty; Laboratory Technician; Academic Department Head; Career Planning Coordinator; Co-op Coordinator; Assistant Director of Student Undergraduate Program HVAC B Level Mechanic. **Special programs:** Internships. **Corporate headquarters location:** This location. **Number of employees at this location:** 380.

WHEATON COLLEGE
26 East Main Street, Norton MA 02766. 508/285-7722. **Fax:** 508/286-8262. **Recorded jobline:** 508/286-3547. **Contact:** Barbara Lema. Director of Human Resources. **E-mail address:** hr@wheatoncollege.edu. **World Wide Web address:** http://www.wheatonma.edu. **Description:** A private, coed, four-year college. **Positions advertised include:** Program Coordinator; Communications Officer; Grounds Helper; Writing Teacher; Quantitative Analysis Instructor.

WHEELOCK COLLEGE
200 The Riverway, Boston MA 02215. 617/734-5200. **Fax:** 6177/879-2000. **Contact:** Human Resources. **E-mail address:** opportunities@wheelock.edu. **World Wide Web address:** http://www.wheelock.edu. **Description:** A small liberal arts college offering both graduate and undergraduate courses of study. **Positions advertised include:** Assistant Professor of Human Development; Associate Professor in Juvenile Justice; Department Chair; Head Field Coach; HVAC Maintenance Mechanic.

WORCESTER POLYTECHNIC INSTITUTE
100 Institute Road, Worcester MA 01609. 508/831-5000. **Fax:** 508/831-5715. **Contact:** Human Resources. **E-mail address:** human-resources@wpi.edu. **World Wide Web address:** http://www.wpi.edu. **Description:** A technical college offering both undergraduate and graduate programs. Founded in 1865. **Positions advertised include:** Instructional Technologist; Accounting Manager; Assistant Director of Annual Giving; Web Applications Director; Assistant Football Coach; Magazine Editor.

WORLDTEACH
Center for International Development, Harvard University, 79 JFK Street, Cambridge MA 02138. 617/495-5527. **Toll-free phone:** 800/4TE-ACH0. **Fax:** 617/495-1599. **Contact:** Director of Recruiting. **E-mail address:** info@worldteach.org. **World Wide Web address:** http://www.worldteach.org. **Description:** A nonprofit organization, based at Harvard University, which places volunteers overseas as teachers in developing countries. Volunteers have served in Asia, Africa, Central America, and Central Europe. Volunteers make a commitment of either six months or one year and pay a program fee of approximately $4,800. Volunteers must have a bachelor's degree, but no previous teaching or foreign language is required. WorldTeach also runs a summer teaching program in China for undergraduate and graduate students. **Positions advertised include:** Ecuador Summer Field Director.

Michigan

ABB UNIVERSITY
1250 Brown Road, Auburn Hills MI 48326. 248/393-4800. **Fax:** 248/393-4602. **Contact:** Alison Worsely, Human Resources Professional. **E-mail address:**

alison.m.worsely@us.abb.com. **World Wide Web address:** http://www.abb.com. **Description:** A training center for ABB Group, an engineering company that helps customers use electrical power effectively and increase industrial productivity in a sustainable manner. The training center offers 40 robotics and flexible automation courses. **Positions advertised include:** Account Executive. **Special programs:** Training; Internships. **Corporate headquarters location:** This location. **International locations:** Worldwide. **Parent company:** ABB Group (Zurich, Switzerland). **Listed on:** New York Stock Exchange. **Stock exchange symbol:** ABB. **Annual sales/revenues:** Approximately $5 billion. **Number of employees worldwide:** 33,343.

ANN ARBOR PUBLIC SCHOOLS
2555 South State Street, Ann Arbor MI 48104. 734/994-2240. **Fax:** 734/994-1792. **Contact:** Human Resources. **World Wide Web address:** http://www.aaps.k12.mi.us. **Description:** Coordinates information, resources, and services for the Ann Arbor public school district. The district serves over 16,000 students and employs over 3,000 full and part-time staff members. **Positions advertised include:** Speech Therapist; Behavioral Specialist; Early Childhood Special Education Teacher; Substitute Teacher; Bus Mechanic; Communications Classroom Assistant; Varsity Girl's Lacrosse Coach; Substitute Teacher Assistant.

AQUINAS COLLEGE
1607 Robinson Road SE, Grand Rapids MI 49506-1799. 616/459-8281. **Fax:** 616/459-2563. **Contact:** Human Resources. **E-mail address:** humanresources@aquinas.edu. **World Wide Web address:** http://www.aquinas.edu. **Description:** A Catholic liberal arts college offering undergraduate and graduate programs in over 40 majors. Founded by the Dominican Sisters of Grand Rapids in 1886. **Positions advertised include:** Associate Professor, Business Management.

BAKER COLLEGE
1050 West Bristol Road, Flint MI 48507. 810/766-4028. **Fax:** 810/766-4279 **Contact:** Rosemary Zawacki, Vice President of Human Resources. **E-mail address:** hr@baker.edu. **World Wide Web address:** http://www.baker.edu. **Description:** A business college offering both graduate and undergraduate programs of study. **Positions advertised include:** Financial Aid Officer; Residence Life Director.

CENTRAL MICHIGAN UNIVERSITY
109 Rowe Hall, Mount Pleasant MI 48859. 989/774-3753. **Fax:** 989/774-3256. **Recorded jobline:** 989/774-7195. **Contact:** Human Resources. **E-mail address:** http://www.cmu.jobs@cmich.edu. **World Wide Web address:** http://www.cmich.edu. **Description:** A four-year university with an enrollment of approximately 28,000 undergraduate and graduate students. **Positions advertised include:** Assistant Professor, Broadcast and Cinematic Arts; Adjunct Professor, Business; Assistant Professor, Community Health/Health Administration; Assistant Football Coach; Head Women's Volleyball Coach; Academic Advisor; Assistant Manager, Bookstore; Communications Coordinator; Graphic Designer; Residence Hall Director; Writer/Editor; Radio Producer.

COLLEGE FOR CREATIVE STUDIES
201 East Kirby Street, Detroit MI 48202-4034. 313/872-3118. **Fax:** 313/872-7505. **Contact:** Human Resources. **E-mail address:** hr@ccscad.edu. **World Wide Web address:** http://www.ccscad.edu. **Description:** A four-year college specializing in professional .arts programs. **Positions advertised include:** Chairperson, Interior Design; Professor, Graphic Design/Interactive Design; Professor, Transportation Design; Adjunct Professor, Various Disciplines; Director, Marketing and Communications

DAVENPORT UNIVERSITY
415 East Fulton Street, Grand Rapids MI 49503-5926. 616/451-3511. **Toll-free phone:** 800/632-9569. **Fax:** 616/732-1145. **Contact:** Human Resources. **E-mail address:** personnel@davenport.edu. **World Wide Web address:** http://www.davenport.edu. **Description:** A four-year college specializing in business. Davenport College also offers programs in medical, travel, and paralegal studies. **Positions advertised include:** Accounts Receivable Clerk. **Corporate headquarters location:** This location. **Other area locations:** Statewide. **Other U.S. locations:** TN.

EASTERN MICHIGAN UNIVERSITY
202 Bowen, Ypsilanti MI 48197. 734/487-3431. **Fax:** 734/487-7995. **Recorded jobline:** 734/487-0016. **Contact:** Human resources. **E-mail address:** emu.employment@emich.edu. **World Wide Web address:** http://www.emich.edu. **Description:** A public, comprehensive university with an enrollment of 25,000 students. Founded in 1849. **Positions advertised include:** Area Complex Director; Academic Advisor; Principal Plant Engineer; Mathematics Professor; Business Librarian. **Number of employees at this location:** 2,000.

FERRIS STATE UNIVERSITY
420 Oak Street, Prakken 150, Big Rapids MI 49307-2031. 231/591-2150. **Fax:** 231/591-2978. **Recorded jobline:** 231/591-JOBS. **Contact:** Human Resources. **E-mail address:** hr@ferris.edu. **World Wide Web address:** http://www.ferris.edu. **Description:** A university with approximately 9,500 students offering a wide range of educational programs, including doctoral, master's, bachelor's and associate's degrees. **NOTE:** Part-time and temporary positions are offered. **Positions advertised include:** Assistant Secretary; Biology Professor; Dental Hygienist; Database Administrator; History Professor; Educational Counselor; Residence Hall Director; Nuclear Medicine Technology Instructor. **Number of employees at this location:** Approximately 1,800.

KALAMAZOO PUBLIC SCHOOLS
1220 Howard Street, Kalamazoo MI 49008. 269/337-0177. **Fax:** 269/377-0185. **Contact:** Kathy Thompson, Administrative Personnel Officer. **E-mail address:** thompsonkj@kalamazoo.k12.mi.us. **World Wide Web address:** http://www.kalamazoopublicschools.com. **Description:** Coordinates information, resources, and services for the Kalamazoo public school district. Kalamazoo Public Schools serve over 11,000 students. **Positions advertised include:** Head Football Coach; Substitute Teacher; Substitute Paraprofessional; Substitute Secretary; Bus Driver.

LAKE SUPERIOR STATE UNIVERSITY
650 West Easterday Avenue, Sault Ste. Marie MI 49783. 906/635-2213. **Fax:** 906/635-2111. **Contact:** Human Resources Office. **E-mail address:** humanresources@lssu.edu. **World Wide Web address:** http://www.lssu.edu. **Description:** A four-year, comprehensive state university with an enrollment of approximately 3,400 students. **Positions advertised include:** Professor, Marketing; Professor, Electrical and Computer Engineering; Electrician; Director, University Safety; Director, Admissions; Webmaster.

LAWRENCE TECHNOLOGICAL UNIVERSITY
21000 West Ten Mile Road, Southfield MI 48075-1058. 248/204-2151. **Fax:** 248/204-2118. **Contact:** Lorana Stewart, Human Resources Generalist. **E-mail address:** lstewart@ltu.edu. **World Wide Web address:** http://www.ltu.edu. **Description:** An independent university specializing in technology and management. Approximately 5,000 students are enrolled in the university. **Positions advertised include:** Business Services Director; Program Manager; Internal Auditor; Research Assistant; Help Desk Technician; Admissions Counselor; Recruitment Coordinator; Clerical Assistant; Campus Safety Officer; Senior Lecturer, Developmental Mathematics; Management Professor.

MICHIGAN STATE UNIVERSITY
1407 South Harrison Road, Nisbet Building Room 110, East Lansing MI 48823-5294. 517/353-3720. **Contact:**

Human Resources. **World Wide Web address:** http://www.msu.edu. **Description:** A state university offering more than 200 programs of study. MSU is comprised of 14 degree-granting colleges as well as an affiliated law college. MSU has an enrollment of approximately 44,500 students. **Positions advertised include:** Accountant; Development Officer; Information Technologist; Research Assistant, Genomic Technology; Instructor, Linguistics and Languages; Lecturer, Chemistry; Police Officer.

MICHIGAN TECHNOLOGICAL UNIVERSITY
1400 Townsend Drive, Houghton MI 49931-1295. 906/487-2280. **Fax:** 906/487-3220. **Contact:** Human Resources. **E-mail address:** jobs@mtu.edu. **World Wide Web address:** http://www.mtu.edu. **Description:** A university offering undergraduate and graduate degree programs. MTU is divided into two colleges and three schools: The College of Engineering; The College of Sciences and Arts; The School of Business and Economics; The School of Forest Resources and Environmental Science; and The School of Technology. **Positions advertised include:** Administrative Assistant; Office Assistant; Executive Secretary; Alumni Outreach Coordinator; Contract Analyst; Coordinator, Student Orientation and Parent Programs; System Administrator.

MUSKEGON COMMUNITY COLLEGE
221 South Quarterline Road, Muskegon MI 49442. 231/777-0407. **Fax:** 231/777-0601. **Contact:** Human Resources. **E-mail address:** hr@muskegoncc.edu. **World Wide Web address:** http://www.muskegoncc.edu. **Description:** A community college. **Positions advertised include:** Adjunct Instructors, Various Disciplines; Machining Technology Instructor; Psychology Instructor; Associate Director of Financial Aid.

NORTHERN MICHIGAN UNIVERSITY
1401 Presque Isle Avenue, Marquette MI 49855. 906/227-2330. **Fax:** 906/227-2334. **Recorded jobline:** 906/227-2562. **Contact:** Lynne D. Sundblad, Assistant Director of Human Resources. **World Wide Web address:** http://www.nmu.edu. **Description:** A four-year public university offering undergraduate and graduate degrees in 180 academic programs. NMU has an enrollment of 9,300 students. Founded in 1899. **Positions advertised include:** Gifts Officer; Director, Development Fund Operations; Political Science Instructor; Assistant Professor, Nursing; Professor, Secondary Education; Assistant Professor, Sociology.

OAKLAND UNIVERSITY
140 North Foundation Hall, Rochester MI 48309-4401. 248/370-3840. **Fax:** 248/370-3044. **Recorded jobline:** 248/370-4500. **Contact:** Human Resources. **E-mail address:** uhr@oakland.edu. **World Wide Web address:** http://www.oakland.edu. **Description:** A university with approximately 14,000 students that offers 114 bachelor degrees and graduate and certificate programs in 72 academic areas. **NOTE:** Faculty hiring is handled by the Office of the Vice President of Academic Affairs and Provost: 205 Wilson Hall, Rochester MI 48309-4401. Phone: 248/370-2190. Fax: 248/370-4475. E-mail: provost@oakland.edu. **Positions advertised include:** Visiting Assistant Professor, Music Education; Senior Accountant; Academic Advisor, Health Sciences; Publicist; Information Technology Specialist.

UNIVERSITY OF DETROIT MERCY
8200 West Outer Drive, Administrative Building, Room 104, Detroit MI 48219-0900. 313/993-1036. **Fax:** 313/993-1015. **Contact:** Netina Anding, Assistant Director of Human Resources. **E-mail address:** andingnv@udmercy.edu. **World Wide Web address:** http://www.udmercy.edu. **Description:** A Catholic university with an enrollment of approximately 6,900 students. UDM was formed in 1990 when the University of Detroit and Mercy College of Detroit consolidated. **Positions advertised include:** Director, Gift Planning; Head Women's Golf Coach; Patient Care Coordinator; Faculty Legal Secretary; Director, International Programs; Library Technician.

UNIVERSITY OF MICHIGAN
3003 South State Street, Room G250 Wolverine Tower, Ann Arbor MI 48109. 734/764-6580. **Recorded jobline:** 734/647-0976 (Office/Technical positions) and 734/764-7292 (Professional/Administrative positions). **Contact:** Employment Services. **World Wide Web address:** http://www.umich.edu. **Description:** A public university consisting of 19 schools and colleges, a comprehensive health system, and various affiliated research institutes. The University of Michigan serves approximately 50,000 students, and has 5,000 faculty and 30,000 staff members. This location is the main campus; regional campuses are located in Dearborn and Flint. Founded in 1817. **Positions advertised include:** Chair, Microbiology and Immunology; Chair and Professor, Neurosurgery; Financial Clerk; Research Secretary; Administrative Assistant; Associate Hall Director; Student Services Assistant; Director of Sales; Editor; Business Analyst; Data Analyst; Treasury Manager; Clinical Professor, Urology; Clinical Professor, General Medicine; Clinical Professor, Emergency Medicine; Lecturer, Romance Languages. **Special programs:** Apprenticeships; Summer Jobs. **Number of employees at this location:** 21,000.

WALSH COLLEGE
3838 Livernois Road, P.O. Box 7006, Troy MI 48007-7006. 248/689-8282. **Contact:** Human Resources. **E-mail address:** hr@walshcollege.edu. **World Wide Web address:** http://www.walshcollege.edu. **Description:** A business college with approximately 4,000 undergraduate and graduate students. **NOTE:** For adjunct faculty positions, e-mail resume to rliebe@walshcollege.edu. **Corporate headquarters location:** This location. **Other area locations:** Novi MI. **Number of employees at this location:** 200.

WAYNE COUNTY COMMUNITY COLLEGE DISTRICT
801 West Fort Street, Detroit MI 48226. 313/496-2765. **Fax:** 313/963-5816. **Contact:** Gail Arnold, Senior Associate Vice Chancellor for Human Resources. **E-mail address:** jobs@wcccd.edu. **World Wide Web address:** http://www.wcccd.edu. **Description:** A multi-campus community college offering liberal arts and occupational courses and programs. **Positions advertised include:** Learning Resource Center Assistant; General Clerk; Math Instructor; Nursing Instructor; English Instructor; Surgical Technology Instructor; Welding Instructor. **Corporate headquarters location:** This location. **Other area locations:** Taylor MI; Belleville MI.

WAYNE STATE UNIVERSITY
5700 Cass Avenue, Suite 1900 A/AB, Detroit, MI 48202. 313/577-2010. **Fax:** 313/577-7508. **Contact:** Department of Employment Services. **E-mail address:** jobs@wayne.edu. **World Wide Web address:** http://www.wayne.edu. **Description:** A university with 14 colleges and schools offering 128 bachelor's, 136 master's, and 61 doctoral degrees. WSU has an enrollment of 33,000 undergraduate and graduate students. **Positions advertised include:** Research Assistant, Various Disciplines; Lecturer, Communications; Associate Professor, Computer Science; Associate Dean, Science; Academic Services Officer; Development Officer; Research Scientist, Neurology; Professor, Internal Medicine; University Counselor; Information Officer; Assistant Professor, Music.

WESTERN MICHIGAN UNIVERSITY
1300 Seibert Administration Building, 1903 Western Michigan Avenue, Kalamazoo MI 49008-5217. 269/387-3441. **Fax:** 269/387-3441. **Contact:** Human Resources. **E-mail address:** hr-jobs@wmich.edu. **World Wide Web address:** http://www.wmichedu. **Description:** A four-year university offering undergraduate and graduate programs of study. **Positions advertised include:** Fitness Programs Coordinator; Director, Marketing and Communications; Medical Office Assistant; Research Fellow, Chemistry. **Operations at this facility include:** Administration. **Number of employees at this location:** 3,000.

Minnesota

AUGSBURG COLLEGE
2211 Riverside Avenue, CB #79, Minneapolis MN 55454. 612/330-1058. **Contact:** Human Resources Department. **E-mail address:** jobs@augsburg.edu. **World Wide Web address:** http://www.augsburg.edu. **Description:** A private, four-year college, affiliated with the Evangelical Lutheran Church in America, offering undergraduate degrees in 50 areas of study and five graduate programs. Enrollment is approximately 3,000 students.

CARLETON COLLEGE
One North College Street, Northfield MN 55057. 507/646-7471. **Contact:** Human Resources. **World Wide Web address:** http://www.carleton.edu. **Description:** A private, four-year, liberal arts college. **NOTE:** See website for current job openings and to download application. **Positions advertised include:** Prospect Research Officer; Library Reference/Instruction Educational Associate; Library Evening Supervisor; Art/Exhibitions Educational Associate; Project Librarian, Cooperative Collection Development Project; Chief Operating Engineer; Assistant Coach of Football and Defensive Coordinator; Media Relations Assistant

CENTURY COLLEGE
3300 Century Avenue North, White Bear Lake MN 55110. 651/779-5804. **Fax:** 651/779-5757. **Contact:** Betty Mayer, Human Resources Director. **World Wide Web address:** http://www.century.cc.mn.us. **Description:** A community college offering associate's degrees, as well as diplomas and certificates. **NOTE:** See website for current job openings and application instructions. **Positions advertised include:** Nursing Instructor.

COLLEGE OF SAINT BENEDICT
37 College Avenue South, St. Joseph MN 56374. 320/363-5500. **Fax:** 320/363-2115. **Contact:** Herb Trenz, Director of Human Resources. **E-mail address:** employment@csbsju.edu. **World Wide Web address:** http://www. csbsju.edu. **Description:** A private, four-year, Catholic liberal arts college for women.

CONCORDIA COLLEGE
Outreach Center, Suite 208, 901 8th Street South, Moorhead MN 56562. 218/299-3339. **Fax:** 218/299-4456. **Contact:** Phyllis Murray, Human Resources. **E-mail address:** murray@cord.edu. **World Wide Web address:** http://www.cord.edu. **Description:** A private, four-year liberal arts college of the Evangelical Lutheran Church in America. **NOTE:** See website for current job openings, application instructions, and to download an application.

CONCORDIA UNIVERSITY – ST. PAUL
275 Syndicate Street North, St. Paul MN 55104-5494. 651/641-8846. **Fax:** 651/659-0207. **Contact:** Human Resources. **E-mail address:** humanresources@csp.edu. **World Wide Web address:** http://www.csp.edu. **Description:** A Lutheran liberal arts university offering undergraduate and graduate degrees. **NOTE:** See website for current job openings, application instructions, and to download an application.

GUSTAVUS ADOLPHUS COLLEGE
800 West College Avenue, St. Peter MN 56082. 507/933-8000. **Contact:** Human Resources Department. **E-mail address:** nhaukoos@gustavus.edu. **World Wide Web address:** http://www.gustavus.edu. **Description:** Gustavus Adolphus College is a church-related, residential liberal arts college rooted in its Swedish and Lutheran heritage. Offers 75 majors and 15 pre-professional programs in 27 departments. **NOTE:** See website for current job openings, application instructions, and to download an application.

HAMLINE UNIVERSITY
1536 Hewitt Avenue, St. Paul MN 55104-1284. 651/523-2210. **Recorded jobline:** 651/523-3046. **Contact:** Dixie Lindsley, Director of Human Resources. **World Wide Web address:** http://www.hamline.edu. **Description:** A private, Methodist university with an enrollment of 4,000. **NOTE:** See website for current job openings. Submit resume and references by mail. **Positions advertised include:** Admissions Coordinator – Law School; Assistant Dean for Student and Multicultural Affairs – Law School.

INVER HILLS COMMUNITY COLLEGE
2500 80th Street East, Inver Grove Heights MN 55076. 651/450-8670. **Fax:** 651/450-8399. **Contact:** Human Resources Representative. **World Wide Web address:** http://www.inverhills.mnscu.edu. **Description:** A state community college offering two-year associate degrees, as well as vocational certificates and professional development certificates. **NOTE:** Applicants for open positions must submit an employment application, which may be downloaded online. Search for positions online.

MACALESTER COLLEGE
1600 Grand Avenue, St. Paul MN 55105. 651/696-6000. **Fax:** 651/696-6612. **Contact:** Human Resources Representative. **E-mail address:** hr@macalester.edu. **World Wide Web address:** http://www.macalester.edu. **Description:** A private, four-year, liberal arts college with an enrollment of 1,850. Founded in 1874. **Positions advertised include:** Telemarketer; Oracle Database Administrator; Director of Principal Gifts; Assistant Director of Campus Programs for Multicultural Life; Associate Director of Major Gifts; Associate Director for Residential Life; Assistant Dean of Students; Hall Director; Career Counselor.

MINNESOTA STATE UNIVERSITY MANKATO
336 Wigley Administration Center, Minnesota State University Mankato, Mankato MN 56001. 507/389-2015. **Fax:** 507/389-2960. **Contact:** Johanna Simpson, Human Resources. **E-mail address:** johanna.simpson@mnsu.edu. **World Wide Web address:** http://www.mnsu.edu. **Description:** A four-year, state university offering undergraduate and graduate degrees in arts and humanities; business; education; allied health and nursing; science, engineering, and technology; and social and behavioral sciences. Approximately 14,000 students attend Minnesota State University Mankato. **Number of employees at this location:** 1,300.

MINNESOTA STATE UNIVERSITY MOORHEAD
Box 95, 1104 Seventh Avenue South, Moorhead MN 56563. 218/477-2157. **Fax:** 218/477-2123. **Contact:** Human Resources. **E-mail address:** employ@mnstate.edu. **World Wide Web address:** http://www.mnstate.edu. **Description:** A four-year, state university offering bachelor's and master's degrees in over 100 majors, as well as preprofessional programs in 20 disciplines. Approximately 7,800 students attend Moorhead State University. **Positions advertised include:** Alumni foundation Executive Director; Assistant Professor, Various Disciplines. **Number of employees at this location:** 790.

ST. CLOUD STATE UNIVERSITY
204 Administrative Services, 720 Fourth Avenue South, St. Cloud MN 56301-4498. 320/308-3203. **Fax:** 320/308-1607. **Contact:** Human Resources. **E-mail address:** humanresources@stcloudstate.edu. **World Wide Web address:** http://www.stcloudstate.edu. **Description:** A four-year state university offering 175 programs of study, with an enrollment of 16,000. **Positions advertised include:** Director of Affirmative Action and Social Equity; University Assessment Director; Dean of Undergraduate Studies; Alumni Director; Alumni Communications Specialist; Coordinator of Business Operations/Marketing; Various Faculty Positions. **Number of employees at this location:** 1,450.

SOUTHWEST STATE UNIVERSITY
1501 State Street, Marshall MN 56258. 507/537-7021. **Fax:** 507/537-6812. **Contact:** Office of Human

Resources. **E-mail address:** hr@southwestmsu.edu. **World Wide Web address:** http://www.southwestmsu.edu. **Description:** A four-year, state university with approximately 2,400 students. The university offers graduate programs in education and management. **Positions advertised include:** Assistant/Associate Professor, Various Disciplines; Building Maintenance Supervisor; Network Specialist.

UNIVERSITY OF MINNESOTA CROOKSTON
121 Selvig Hall, 2900 University Avenue, Crookston MN 56716-5001. 218/281-8346. **Fax:** 218/281-8050. **Contact:** Jackie Normandin, Human Resources. **E-mail address:** normand@mail.crk.umn.edu. **World Wide Web address:** http://www.crk.umn.edu. **Description:** One of five regional campuses that comprise the University of Minnesota land-grand system, a public liberal arts university offering undergraduate and graduate degrees as well as professional programs, and the state's primary research university. Enrollment at UMD is 2,100 students. **NOTE:** Entry-level positions offered. **Positions advertised include:** Principal Office and Administrative Assistant; Community Program Specialist; Vice Chancellor for Finance and University Services. **Corporate headquarters location:** Minneapolis MN.

UNIVERSITY OF MINNESOTA DULUTH
255 Darland Administration Building, 1049 University Drive, Duluth MN 55812-3011. 218/726-7161. **Recorded jobline:** 218/726-6506. **Contact:** Human Resources. **E-mail address:** umdhr@d.umn.edu. **World Wide Web address:** http://www.d.umn.edu. **Description:** One of five regional campuses that comprise the University of Minnesota land-grand system, a public liberal arts university offering undergraduate and graduate degrees as well as professional programs, and the state's primary research university. Enrollment at UMD is 10,500 students. **NOTE:** Entry-level positions offered. **Positions advertised include:** Development Assistant; Student Activities Advisor; Recreational Sports Specialist; Coordinator; Teaching Specialist. **Corporate headquarters location:** Minneapolis MN. **Number of employees at this location:** 1,700.

UNIVERSITY OF MINNESOTA MORRIS
306 Behmler Hall, 600 East Fourth Street, Morris MN 56267. 320/589-6024. **Fax:** 218/589-6399. **Contact:** Sarah Mattson, Human Resource Director. **E-mail address:** mattsosj@morris.umn.edu. **World Wide Web address:** http://www.morris.umn.edu. **Description:** One of five regional campuses that comprise the University of Minnesota land-grand system, a public liberal arts university offering undergraduate and graduate degrees as well as professional programs, and the state's primary research university. Enrollment at UMM is 1,900 students. **NOTE:** Entry-level positions offered. **Positions advertised include:** Professor, Various Disciplines; Associate Professor, Various Disciplines. **Corporate headquarters location:** Minneapolis MN. **Number of employees at this location:** 380.

UNIVERSITY OF MINNESOTA ROCHESTER
851 30th Avenue Southeast, Rochester MN 55904. 507/292-5113. **Fax:** 507/280-2820. **Contact:** Jade Rowland, Recruiter. **E-mail address:** jrowland@umn.edu. **World Wide Web address:** http://www.r.umn.edu. **Description:** One of five regional campuses that comprise the University of Minnesota land-grand system, a public liberal arts university offering undergraduate and graduate degrees as well as professional programs, and the state's primary research university. The University of Minnesota Rochester (UMR), through a partnership with the Minnesota State Colleges and Universities, extends upper division undergraduate and post-baccalaureate degree programs to people in southeastern Minnesota. **NOTE:** See website for current job openings and application instructions. **Corporate headquarters location:** Minneapolis MN.

UNIVERSITY OF MINNESOTA TWIN CITIES
170 Donhowe Building, 319 15th Avenue Southeast, Minneapolis MN 55455. 612/625-2000. **Fax:** 612/626-7911. **Contact:** Human Resources. **E-mail address:** jobctr@umn.edu. **World Wide Web address:** http://www.umn.edu/twincities. **Description:** The main campus of five regional campuses that comprise the University of Minnesota land-grand system, a public liberal arts university offering undergraduate and graduate degrees as well as professional programs, and the state's primary research university. The Twin Cities campus offers 161 bachelor's degrees, 218 master's degrees, 114 doctoral degrees, and five professional degrees. **NOTE:** Entry-level positions offered. Local staffing agencies, such as Adecco, recruit for administrative and service positions at this campus. **Positions advertised include:** Professor, Various Disciplines; Associate Professor, Various Disciplines. **Corporate headquarters location:** This location. **Operations at this facility include:** Administration; Research and Development; Service.

UNIVERSITY OF ST. THOMAS
Mail Number AQU217, 2115 Summit Avenue, St. Paul MN 55105. 651/962-6510. **Fax:** 651/962-6905. **Contact:** Human Resources Department. **E-mail address:** employment@stthomas.edu. **World Wide Web address:** http://www.stthomas.edu. **Description:** A Catholic, four-year, liberal arts college with 11,000 undergraduate and graduate students. **Positions advertised include:** Business Process Analyst; Editor; Senior Researcher; Program Manager; Assistant Director, Law Admissions; Senior Gift Officer; Graduate Residence Hall Director; Research Librarian; Application Analyst; Coordinator. **Other area locations:** Minneapolis MN.

WINONA STATE UNIVERSITY
P.O. Box 5838, Winona MN 55987-5838. 507/457-5008. **Fax:** 507/457-5054. **Contact:** Human Resources. **E-mail address:** rdelong@winona.edu. **World Wide Web address:** http://www.winona.edu. **Description:** A state university offering undergraduate, graduate, and pre-professional programs through Winona State University's five colleges: business, education, liberal arts, nursing and health sciences, and science and engineering. Approximately 8,000 students attend the university. **NOTE:** See website for current job openings and application instructions.

Mississippi

JACKSON STATE UNIVERSITY
1400 Lynch Street, P.O. Box 17028, Jackson MS 39217. 601/979-2015. **Toll-free phone:** 800/848-6817. **Fax:** 601/968-8644. **Contact:** Lester Pourciau, Director of Human Resources. **E-mail address:** l.pourciau@jsums.edu. **World Wide Web address:** http://www.jsums.edu. **Description:** A state university. Founded in 1877. **NOTE:** For faculty positions, contact specific department. **Positions advertised include:** Activity Coordinator; Assistant Controller; Clinical and Community Coordinator; Migrant Recruiter; Doctoral Research Associate; Clinic Secretary; Community Safety Monitor; Receptionist. **Special programs:** Internships. **Number of employees at this location:** 1,165.

MISSISSIPPI STATE UNIVERSITY
P.O. Box 9603, Starkville MS 39762. 662/325-3713. **Physical address:** 150 McArthur Hall, Barr Avenue, Mississippi State MS 39762. **Fax:** 662/325-8395. **Contact:** Julie Rester, Senior Human Resources Generalist. **E-mail address:** rester@hrm.msstate.edu. **World Wide Web address:** http://www.msstate.edu. **Description:** One of Mississippi's largest universities, with over 16,000 students and 840 faculty members. The university offers a wide range of bachelor's degrees and pre-professional programs, as well as master's and doctoral degree programs. **NOTE:** Applicants must apply online at http://www.jobs.msstate.edu. **Positions advertised include:** Forest Technician; Communication Operator; Marketing Coordinator; Systems Engineer; Programmer Analyst; Custodial Supervisor; Resource Technician; Clinical Instructor;

Agricultural Technician; Professor, Various Departments; Associate Professor, Various Departments. **Number of employees at this location:** 4,240.

UNIVERSITY OF MISSISSIPPI AT OXFORD
P.O. Box 1848, University MS 38677-1848. 662/915-5690. **Fax:** 662/915-5836. **Recorded jobline:** 662/915-7666. **Contact:** Rebecca Harvey, Human Resources. **E-mail address:** employ@olemiss.edu. **World Wide Web address:** http://www.olemiss.edu. **Description:** A state university with an undergraduate and graduate enrollment of approximately 16,500 students. The University of Mississippi offers more than 100 programs of study through the College of Liberal Arts, Medical Center, School of Accountancy, School of Business Administration, School of Education, School of Engineering, School of Law, and School of Pharmacy. Founded in 1848. **Positions advertised include:** Airport Line Service Technician; Assistant Director for Technology Management; Assistant or Associate Professor, Various Departments; Chair of Medicinal Chemistry; Communications Officer; Computer Operator; Custodian; Director, Mississippi Judicial College; Language Instructor; Manager of Parking Services; Microcomputer Consultant. **Special programs:** Internships; Apprenticeships. **Other area locations:** Jackson MS; Southaven MS; Tupelo MS. **Number of employees at this location:** 2,800.

UNIVERSITY OF SOUTHERN MISSISSIPPI
118 College Drive, Box 5111, Hattiesburg MS 39406. 601/266-4050. **Physical location:** Room 317, Forest County Hall. **Fax:** 601/266-4541. **Contact:** Wanda Naylor, Employment Coordinator. **E-mail address:** wanda.naylor@usm.edu. **World Wide Web address:** http://www.usm.edu. **Description:** A state university offering undergraduate degrees to 12,000 students. The university is comprised of five colleges: the College of Arts and Letters; the College of Business; the College of Education and Psychology; the College of Health; and the College of Science and Technology. Founded in 1910. **NOTE:** Applications accepted for open positions only. **Positions advertised include:** Assistant/Associate Professor, Various Departments; Bioinformatics Network Engineer; Child Care Provider; Concrete Finisher; Database Administrator; Director of Admissions; Early Intervention Training Specialist; Mechanical Engineer; Master Black Belt; Partnership Coordinator; Security Officer. **Other area locations:** Long Beach MS. **Number of employees at this location:** 1,900.

Missouri
CENTRAL INSTITUTE FOR THE DEAF
4560 Clayton Avenue, St. Louis MO 63110. 314/977-0000. **Fax:** 314/977-0025. **Contact:** Personnel Manager. **World Wide Web address:** http://www.cid.wustl.edu. **Description:** A specialized educational agency that operates speech and hearing clinics, professional education programs, research facilities, and an elementary school for deaf children. **Corporate headquarters location:** This location.

CENTRAL MISSOURI STATE UNIVERSITY
P.O. Box 800, Warrensburg MO 64093. 660/543-4255. **Recorded jobline:** 660/543-8300. **Contact:** Office of Human Resources. **World Wide Web address:** http://www.cmsu.edu. **Description:** Offers over 150 undergraduate and graduate programs and has an enrollment of approximately 11,000 students. Founded in 1871. **NOTE:** Search and apply for positions online.

COLUMBIA COLLEGE OF MISSOURI
1001 Rogers Street, Room 14, Columbia MO 65216. 573/875-7260. **Toll-free phone:** 800/231-2391. **Fax:** 573/875-7379. **Contact:** Patty Fisher, Director of Human Resources. **World Wide Web address:** http://www.ccis.edu. **Description:** A post-secondary educational institution offering both undergraduate and graduate programs of study. Founded in 1851. **NOTE:** Search and apply for positions online. **Positions advertised include:** Nursing Instructor; Adjunct Faculty, Computer Information Systems; Visiting Professor, Biology. **Corporate headquarters location:** This location. **Number of employees at this location:** 200.

CONCORDIA SEMINARY
801 De Mun Avenue, St. Louis MO 63105. 314/505-7000. **Fax:** 314/505-7001. **Contact:** Employment. **E-mail address:** sumoskip@csl.edu. **World Wide Web address:** http://www.csl.edu. **Description:** A four-year seminary college that also offers a variety of graduate programs in theology. **Positions advertised include:** Director of Alumni Activities.

EAST CENTRAL COLLEGE
1964 Prairie Dell Road, Union MO 63084. 636/583-5195. **Contact:** Beth Watts, Human Resources. **E-mail address:** wattsb@eastcentral.edu. **World Wide Web address:** http://www.eastcentral.edu. **Description:** A two-year college with an enrollment of approximately 3,000 students. Founded in 1968. **Number of employees at this location:** 100.

FONTBONNE COLLEGE
6800 Wydown Boulevard, St. Louis MO 63105. 314/889-1493. **Fax:** 314/719-8023. **Contact:** Sandy Davis, Human Resources. **E-mail address:** sdavis@fontbonne.edu. **World Wide Web address:** http://www.fontbonne.edu. **Description:** A four-year, liberal arts college. **Number of employees at this location:** 200.

JEFFERSON COLLEGE
1000 Viking Drive, Hillsboro MO 63050. 636/797-3000. **Fax:** 636/789-4012. **Contact:** Director of Human Resources. **World Wide Web address:** http://www.jeffco.edu. **Description:** A two-year community college. **NOTE:** Search and apply for positions online. **Positions advertised include:** Registrar; Director of Student Development. **Corporate headquarters location:** This location. **Number of employees at this location:** 220.

KENRICK GLENNON SEMINARY
5200 Glennon Drive, St. Louis MO 63119-4399. 314/792-6100. **Fax:** 314/792-6500. **Contact:** Human Resources. **World Wide Web address:** http://www.kenrick.edu. **Description:** A men's seminary specializing in a four-year undergraduate college program and a five-year graduate program that prepares men for the priesthood.

LINDENWOOD UNIVERSITY
209 South Kingshighway, St. Charles MO 63301. 636/949-2000. **Contact:** Dr. James D. Evans, Provost and Dean of Faculty. **World Wide Web address:** http://www.lindenwood.edu. **Description:** A four-year university offering 80 undergraduate and graduate degrees with an enrollment of 12,000. **NOTE:** Address resumes for teaching and administrative positions to above contact; address resumes for staff or management positions to: Ms. Julie Mueller, Chief Operating Officer.

MARYVILLE UNIVERSITY
13550 Conway Road, St. Louis MO 63141. 314/529-9398. **Contact:** Jacqueline Plunkett, Director of Personnel. **World Wide Web address:** http://www.maryville.edu. **Description:** A four-year university with and enrollment of 1,450 undergraduate and 500 graduate students. Founded in 1872. **NOTE:** Search and apply for positions and download application forms online. Only resumes received for a specific opening will be accepted. **Positions advertised include:** Adjunct Instructors; Assistant director of Residential Life; Director of Multicultural Programs; Personal Counselor.

MISSOURI BAPTIST COLLEGE
One College Park Drive, St. Louis MO 63141. 314/434-1115. **Contact:** Human Resources. **World Wide Web address:** http://www.mobap.edu. **Description:** A four-year Baptist college with an enrollment of approximately 3,600 at four locations around St. Louis.

NORTHWEST MISSOURI STATE UNIVERSITY
800 University Drive, Maryville MO 64468-6001. 660/562-1127. **Fax:** 660/562-1034. **Contact:** Michelle Drake, Personnel. **E-mail address:** mmattso@mail.nwmissouri.edu. **World Wide Web address:** http://www.nwmissouri.edu. **Description:** A four-year, state university offering bachelor's, master's, and specialist in education degrees with an enrollment of 6,500. Founded in 1905. **NOTE:** Search and apply for positions online. **Positions advertised include:** Assistant Professor; Teaching Assistant; Accounting Manager; Counselor. **Number of employees at this location:** 855.

PARK UNIVERSITY
8700 North West River Park Drive, Parkville MO 64152-3795. 816/741-2000. **Contact:** Director of Human Resources. **E-mail address:** careers@park.edu. **World Wide Web address:** http://www.park.edu. **Description:** An independent, four-year liberal arts college with an enrollment of 21,000 on 40 campus centers in 20 states, 34 of which are located on military bases. Founded in 1875. **NOTE:** Search and apply for positions online. **Positions advertised online:** Multimedia Application Developer; Assistant VP for Academic Affairs; Dean, College of Liberal Arts and Sciences; Visiting Assistant Professor of Spanish; Adjunct Faculty; Online Instructor.

ST. LOUIS CHRISTIAN COLLEGE
1360 Grandview Drive, Florissant MO 63033. 314/837-6777. **Fax:** 314/837-8291. **Contact:** Manager of Human Resources Department. **World Wide Web address:** http://www.slcconline.edu. **Description:** A college offering two- and four-year undergraduate degrees.

ST. LOUIS COLLEGE OF PHARMACY
4588 Parkview Place, St. Louis MO 63110-1088. 314/367-8700. **Toll-free phone:** 800/278-5267. **Contact:** Human Resources. **E-mail address:** HR@stlcop.edu. **World Wide Web address:** http://www.stlcop.edu. **Description:** A private, nonsectarian college of pharmaceutical study. Degrees offered are Bachelor of Science in Pharmacy, Master of Science in Pharmacy Administration, and Doctor of Pharmacy. Founded in 1864.

SAINT LOUIS UNIVERSITY
221 North Grand Boulevard, St. Louis MO 63103. 314/977-2222. **Toll-free phone:** 800/758-3678. **Fax:** 314/977-8598. **Recorded jobline:** 314/977-2265. **Contact:** Sandy Cox, Human Resources. **World Wide Web address:** http://www.slu.edu. **Description:** Saint Louis University is a Catholic, Jesuit university and leading research institution, offering undergraduate, graduate and professional degree programs. Founded in 1818. Enrollment is 11,000 students on campuses in St. Louis and Madrid, Spain. **Number of employees at this location:** 6,237.

SAINT LOUIS UNIVERSITY SCHOOL OF MEDICINE
1402 South Grand Blvd, St. Louis MO 63104. 314/977-9853. **Contact:** Human Resources. **World Wide Web address:** http://medschool.slu.edu. **Description:** Saint Louis University School of Medicine trains physicians and biomedical scientists, conducts medical research, and provides health services on a local, national and international level. Founded in 1836. The School of Medicine is a pioneer in geriatric medicine, organ transplantation, chronic disease prevention, cardiovascular disease, neurosciences and vaccine research, among others. **NOTE:** Search for positions online.

SOUTHEAST MISSOURI STATE UNIVERSITY
One University Plaza, Cape Girardeau MO 63701. 573/651-2206. **Contact:** Personnel Director. **World Wide Web address:** http://www.semo.edu. **Description:** A state university offering 150 areas of study. Founded in 1873.

SOUTHWEST MISSOURI STATE UNIVERSITY
901 South National Avenue, Springfield MO 65897. 417/836-5000. **Contact:** Human Resources. **World Wide Web address:** http://www.smsu.edu. **Description:** A state university offering 150 undergraduate and 43 graduate academic programs. **NOTE:** Search and apply for positions online. **Positions advertised include:** Assistant/Associate Professors; Associate Dean of Agricultural Sciences; Lecturers; Distance Learning Media Production Specialist; Financial and System Administrator; Videographer/Editor.

TRUMAN STATE UNIVERSITY
106 McClain Hall, 100 East Normal Street, Kirksville MO 63501. 660/785-4000. **Fax:** 660/785-7520. **Contact:** Human Resources Department. **E-mail address:** hrstaff@truman.edu. **World Wide Web address:** http://www.truman.edu. **Description:** A liberal-arts university with an undergraduate enrollment of 5,500 and 200 graduate students. Founded in 1867. **NOTE:** Search for positions online.

UNIVERSITY OF MISSOURI/COLUMBIA
201 South Seventh Street, 130 Heinkel Building, Columbia MO 65201. 573/882-7976. **Recorded jobline:** 573/884-9675. **Contact:** Human Resources. **World Wide Web address:** http://www.missouri.edu. **Description:** A university offering 278 degree programs with an enrollment of 20,000 undergraduate and 6,300 graduate students. Founded in 1839. **NOTE:** Search and apply for positions online. **Positions advertised include:** Assistant Manager, University Club; Manager, Business/Fiscal Operations; Manager, Network Security; Project Director; Academic Advisor; Director of Development; Database Administrator; Programmer/Analyst; Health Physicist; Research Specialist; Sr. Veterinary Technician. **Special programs:** Internships. **Corporate headquarters location:** This location. **Number of employees nationwide:** 11,000.

UNIVERSITY OF MISSOURI/ST. LOUIS
211 General Services Building, One University Drive, St. Louis MO 63121-4499. 314/516-5804. **Fax:** 314/516-6463. **Recorded jobline:** 314/516-5926. **Contact:** Human Resource Services. **World Wide Web address:** http://www.umsl.edu. **Description:** A university offering 88 degree programs with an enrollment of 16,000 students. **NOTE:** Search and apply for positions online. **Positions advertised include:** Admissions counselor; Associate Vice Chancellor for Information Technology; System Administrator Specialist;

WASHINGTON UNIVERSITY IN ST. LOUIS
7425 Forsyth Boulevard, Box 1178, St. Louis MO 63105. 314/935-5906. **Fax:** 314/935-9780. **Contact:** Personnel. **E-mail address:** human_resources@aismail.wustl.edu. **World Wide Web address:** http://www.wustl.edu. **Description:** A four-year university that offers 90 programs and has an enrollment of 6,500 undergraduate and 5,500 graduate students. Founded in 1853. **NOTE:** Search and apply for positions online. **Positions advertised include:** Associate Director of Development; Contract Manager; Director, donor Relations and Major Gifts; Hazardous Materials Manager; LAN Engineer; Research Statistician; Summer School and Special Sessions Coordinator. **Number of employees at this location:** 10,500.

WEBSTER UNIVERSITY
470 East Lockwood Avenue, St. Louis MO 63119. 314/968-7192. **Recorded jobline:** 314/968-7114. **Contact:** Julie Dreiling, Human Resources. **E-mail address**: dreilija@webster.edu. **World Wide Web address:** http://www.webster.edu. **Description:** A four-year university offering undergraduate and graduate programs. **NOTE:** Search and apply for positions online. **Positions advertised include:** Assistant Director, Employment Services; Development Officer for Alumni Programs; Network Coordinator; Director of Academic Assessment.

Montana

MONTANA STATE UNIVERSITY/BILLINGS
1500 University Drive, Billings MT 59101-0298. 406/657-2278. **Fax:** 406/657-2120. **Toll-free phone:** 800/565-6782. **Contact:** Human Resources. **E-mail address:** employment@msubillings.edu. **World Wide Web address:** http://www.msubillings.edu. **Description:** Montana State University/Billings consists of a graduate studies program and four undergraduate programs: Arts and Sciences; Business; Education; and Human Services; and a separately located two-year College of Technology. Unique within the university system are undergraduate and graduate programs in special education, human services, and rehabilitation counseling. The Center for Continuing Education, Summer Session, and Community Services provides a wide variety of professional courses, workshops, seminars, and conferences across the state. A faculty of about 190 serves a student body of approximately 4,000. Founded in 1927. **Positions advertised include:** Administrative Associate; Assistant Professor; Associate Professor; Full Professor; University Lecturer; Instructor. **Chancellor:** Dr. Ronald P. Sexton. **Number of employees at this location:** 500.

MONTANA STATE UNIVERSITY - NORTHERN
P.O. Box 7751, Havre MT 59501. 406/265-3710. **Toll-free phone:** 800/662-6132. **Fax:** 406/265-3777. **Contact:** Employee Relations Specialist. **E-mail address:** hr@msun.edu. **World Wide Web address:** http://www.msun.edu. **Description:** Montana State University - Northern is a comprehensive university serving approximately 1,640 students seeking technical and liberal arts educations. The university offers certificate, associate's, bachelor's, and master's degrees. **Other area locations:** Great Falls MT; Lewistown MT. **Chancellor:** Alexander Capdeville.

MONTANA TECH OF THE UNIVERSITY OF MONTANA
1300 West Park, Butte MT 59701. 406/496-4280. **Toll-free phone:** 800/445-TECH. **Contact:** Personnel Office. **E-mail address:** kvandaveere@mtech.edu. **World Wide Web address:** http://www. mtech.edu. **Description:** Montana Tech of the University of Montana is an engineering, science, and computer science institution offering degrees that specialize in mineral and energy-related engineering education and in related areas in the arts and sciences. Montana Tech offers 13 undergraduate degree programs (with 18 concentrations available) and 11 graduate degree programs. Founded in 1900. **Positions advertised include:** Director of Nursing Programs; Assistant Professor; Team Leader; Training Specialist; Research Assistant.

UNIVERSITY OF MONTANA - MISSOULA
Emma B. Lommasson Center, Room 252, Missoula MT 59812. 406/243-6766. **Fax:** 406/243-6095. **Recorded jobline:** 406/243-6760. **Contact:** Rob Gannon, Human Resource Services. E-mail address: Kristina.cashella.mso.umt.edu. **World Wide Web address:** http://www.umt.edu. **Description:** A university offering undergraduate and graduate degrees in a variety of disciplines as well as continuing education and summer programs. The university maintains schools of law, business and journalism, and offers Arts and Sciences degrees in technology, education, fine arts, forestry, and pharmacy. **Company slogan:** The discovery continues. **Positions advertised include:** Assistant Professor; Professor; Associate Dean; Director; Lecturer; Fiscal Officer; Administrative Associate; Research Assistant.

Nebraska

CREIGHTON UNIVERSITY
2500 California Plaza, Omaha NE 68178. 402/280-2700. **Fax:** 402/280-5516. **Recorded jobline:** 402/280-2943. **Contact:** William Hill, Director of Human Resources. **E-mail address:** resume@creighton.edu. **World Wide Web address:** http://www.creighton.edu. **Description:** A Jesuit university. In addition to the College of Arts and Sciences, Creighton has a College of Business Administration; University College; Schools of Dentistry, Medicine, Law, Nursing, and Pharmacy and Allied Health Professions; and a Graduate School offering master's and doctoral degrees. The university has an enrollment of approximately 6,340. **NOTE:** Human Resources phone is 402/280-2709. **Positions advertised include:** Administrative Assistant Cardiology; Cardiac Technician; Coordinator of Multicultural Student Affairs; Director of the Magis Program; Medical Assistant; Office Manager, Registered Sonographer; Research Fellow; Research Nurse; Senior Laboratory Technician; Staff Assistant.

UNIVERSITY OF NEBRASKA AT KEARNEY
905 West 25th Street, Kearney NE 68849. 308/865-8441. **Fax:** 308/865-8630. **Contact:** Human Resources. **World Wide Web address:** http://www.unk.edu. **NOTE:** See website for available positions and corresponding direct contacts. **Description:** A state university.

UNIVERSITY OF NEBRASKA AT LINCOLN
P.O. Box 880438, Lincoln NE 68588-0438. 402/472-3101. **Physical address:** 407 Canfield Administration Building, 501 North 10th Street, Room 128, Lincoln NE 68588. **Contact:** Department of Human Resources. **World Wide Web address:** http://www.unl.edu. **Description:** A state university

UNIVERSITY OF NEBRASKA AT OMAHA
6001 Dodge Street, EAB 205, Omaha NE 68182-0263. 402/554-2321. **Fax:** 402/554--3777. **Recorded jobline:** 402/554-2959. **Contact:** Employment Manager. **E-mail address:** msweaney@mail.unomaha.edu **World Wide Web address:** http://www.unomaha.edu. **Description:** A university. **Positions advertised include:** Computer Systems Specialist; Associate Vice President and Director of Budget; Assistant Vice President and Director of Institutional Research. **Special programs:** Internships. **Number of employees at this location:** 1,200.

Nevada

GREAT BASIN COLLEGE
1500 College Parkway, Elko NV 89801. 775/753-2914. **Contact:** R. Erik Seastedt, Director of Human Resources. **E-mail address:** hr@gwmail.gbcnv.edu. **World Wide Web address:** http://www.gbcnv.edu. **Description:** A two-year community college with an enrollment of approximately 5,000 students. The college offers certificates and associate's degrees. **Positions advertised include:** Recruiter; Development Coordinator; Instructor; Library Director.

LA PETITE ACADEMY
76 North Pecos Road, Henderson NV 89074-3380. 702/897-0171. **Contact:** Personnel. **World Wide Web address:** http://www.lapetite.com. **Description:** Owns and operates a group of proprietary child care and preschool education centers. **Corporate headquarters:** Chicago IL. **Other U.S. locations:** Nationwide. **Number of employees nationwide:** 12,800.

TRUCKEE MEADOWS COMMUNITY COLLEGE (TMCC)
7000 Dandini Boulevard, Sierra Building LIB 200, Reno NV 89512-3999. 775/673-7168. **Fax:** 775/674-7560. **Contact:** Human Resources. **World Wide Web address:** http://www.tmcc.edu. **Description:** A community college with an enrollment of approximately 11,000 students. TMCC offers more than 50 degree and certificate programs in 40 academic and occupational areas. The community college is accredited by the Northwest Association of Schools and Colleges. Founded in 1971. **NOTE:** Part-time positions are offered. **Positions advertised include:** Director of Nursing; Employment Specialist; Vice President of Student Services; Dental Hygiene Instructor; Nursing Instructor.

UNIVERSITY OF NEVADA, LAS VEGAS
4505 South Maryland Parkway, Box 451026, Las Vegas NV 89154. 702/895-3504. **Fax:** 702/895-1545. **Contact:** Human Resources. **World Wide Web**

address: http://www.unlv.edu. **Description:** A university offering more than 180 undergraduate, master's, and doctoral degree programs to 24,000 students. UNLV has 11 academic colleges and two schools: Architecture, Construction Management, and Planning; Business and Economics; Education; Engineering; Fine and Performing Arts; Graduate College; Health Sciences; Hotel Administration; Human Performance and Development; Liberal Arts; Science and Mathematics; the Greenspun School of Communication; and the School of Social Work. More than 700 full-time instructional faculty are involved in teaching, research, and community service. Founded in 1957. **Positions advertised include:** Accountant; Assistant Professor; Associate Professors; Full Professor; Program Coordinator; Career Counselor; Computer Application Developer; Technical Administrator; Director of Annual Giving; Liberal Arts Dean.

WESTERN NEVADA COMMUNITY COLLEGE
2201 West College Parkway, Bristlecone Building, Room 104, Carson City NV 89703. 775/445-4237. **Fax:** 775/445-3183. **Contact:** Human Resources. **E-mail address:** personnel@wncc.edu. **World Wide Web address:** http://www.wncc.edu. **Description:** A two-year, general community college with 6000 students offering 50 academic degrees and certificates. **Positions advertised include:** Coordinator of Counseling; Dean of Instruction; Student Services Programmer/Analyst; Academic Skills Coordinator; Instructors. **Other area locations:** Douglas NV; Fallon NV.

New Hampshire

COLBY-SAWYER COLLEGE
541 Main Street, New London NH 03257. 603/526-3740. **Contact:** Andrea, Human Resources. **E-mail address:** welcome@colby-sawyer.edu/people-offices/hr/current. **World Wide Web address:** http://www.colby-sawyer.edu. **Description:** A four-year, coeducational liberal arts college. Major programs offered include business administration, nursing, psychology, sports science, communication studies, and graphic design. **NOTE:** Electronic submissions are preferred but may contact by mail. **Positions advertised include:** Assistant Professor – Various Departments; Teaching Faculty – Various Departments; Head Coach – Tennis; Assistant Athletic Trainer/Instructor; Assistant Coach – Various Sports. **Number of employees at this location:** 250.

DANIEL WEBSTER COLLEGE
20 University Drive, Nashua NH 03063-1300. 603/577-6481. **Fax:** 603/577-6001. **Contact:** Becky McLennon, Personnel Office. **E-mail address:** hr@dwb.edu. **World Wide Web address:** http://www.dwc.edu. **Description:** A small, private, four-year college specializing in aviation, computer science, business, and sports management. Daniel Webster College offers both bachelor's and associate's degrees. **Positions advertised include:** Database/Information Technology Manager; Director of Annual Fund; Director of Flight Operations; Assistant/Associate Professor; Campus Safety Officer; Assistant Professor - Business and Management; Assistant Professor- Sports Management; Director of Academic Resources; Assistant Registrar. **President:** Hannah McCarthy. **Number of employees at this location:** 100.

DARTMOUTH COLLEGE
7 Lebanon Street, Suite 203, Hanover NH 03755. 603/646-3411. **E-mail address**: jobs@dartmouth.com. **World Wide Web address:** http://jobs.dartmouth.edu. **Description:** Founded in 1769, Dartmouth is a four-year, coeducational college and graduate school of business, engineering, and medicine and sixteen graduate programs in the arts and sciences. **NOTE:** Search posted openings and apply on-line. **Positions advertised include:** Research Assistant, Faculty positions, Librarian, Budget Planner/Analyst; IC Coordinator Athletics; Assistant to the Director Tuck School; System Administrator.

FRANKLIN PIERCE COLLEGE
20 College Road, Rindge NH 03461-0060. 603/899-4000. **Toll-free phone:** 800/437-0048. **Fax:** 603/899-4326. **Contact:** John Mims, Director of Human Resources. **E-mail address:** hr@fpc.edu. **World Wide Web address:** http://www.fpc.edu. **Description:** A private college offering bachelor of arts and bachelor of science degrees, as well as MBAs. Associate of arts degrees are awarded in the continuing education programs. **NOTE:** Entry-level positions are offered. Please visit website to search posted openings and apply on-line. **Positions advertised include:** Administrative Assistant; Network Analyst; Head Women's Golf Coach; Head Cheerleading Coach; Assistant Softball Coach; Dean of Undergraduate Studies; Director of Recreation; Adjunct Faculty – Various Locations; Assistant Professor – Various Departments; Application Analyst; Experience Director; Campus Safety Officer. **Operations at this facility include:** Administration; Education. **Annual sales/revenues:** $21 - $50 million. **Number of employees at this location:** 475.

GRANITE STATE COLLEGE
8 Old Suncook Road, Concord NH 03301. 603/228-3000. **Fax:** 603/229-0964. **Contact:** Human Resources. **World Wide Web address:** http://www.granite.edu. **Description:** A part of the University System of New Hampshire, offers a bachelor's of professional studies in management, behavioral science, criminal justice, and early childhood education; bachelor's of general studies; associate's degrees in general studies, microcomputer applications, business studies, early childhood education, and behavioral sciences; certificate programs in child care, library techniques, computer applications, adult learning and development, leadership in the workplace, and paralegal studies; and professional continuing education with teacher education courses, management development training, real estate recertification, real estate appraisal, certified nurses assistant, administrative assistant programs, and computer training workshops. Accredited by the New England Association of Schools and Colleges. **Positions advertised include:** Adjunct Faculty. **Corporate headquarters location:** This location. **Other area locations:** Statewide.

KEENE STATE COLLEGE
229 Main Street, Keene NH 03435. 603/358-2496. **Toll-free phone:** 800/572-1909. **Contact:** Kimberly Harkness, Director Human Resources. **E-mail address:** kharknes@keene.edu. **World Wide Web address:** http://www.keene.edu/hr/vacancies.cfm. **Description:** A four-year state college offering certificates, associate's, bachelor's, and master's degrees including an MBA. Approximately 3,500 undergraduate and 500 graduate students attend Keene State College. **NOTE:** Search posted openings online. **Positions advertised include:** Administrative Assistant; Accreditation and Assessment Coordinator; Demographic Data Processor; Funds and Stewardship Coordinator; Divisional Dean; Bursar; Tenure-track Positions – Various Departments.

NEW HAMPSHIRE CORRECTIONAL INDUSTRIES
P.O. Box 14, Concord NH 03302-0014. 603/271-5650. **Physical address:** 281 North State Street, Concord NH 03302. **Fax:** 603/271-1116. **Contact:** Cheryl Harrison, New Hampshire Dept. of Corrections Human Resources. **World Wide Web address:** http://www.state.nh.us/nhci. **Description:** Located at New Hampshire State Prison, New Hampshire Correctional Industries educates and trains inmates. It offers a number of school and vocational training courses to prepare inmates for work upon release. **NOTE:** Search posted openings online. **Positions advertised include:** Corrections Officer Trainee; Dental Assistant; Dental Hygienist; Nurse Practitioner; Program Specialist; Psychological Associate. **Number of employees at this location:** 500.

NEW HAMPSHIRE TECHNICAL INSTITUTE
31 College Drive, Concord NH 03301-7412. 603/271-7731. **Fax:** 603/271-7734. **Contact:** Alissa Labelle,

Human Resources. **E-mail address:** alabelle@nhctc.edu. **World Wide Web address:** http://www.nhti.net. **Description:** A technical college. The largest programs at NHTI include nursing and engineering. Other courses of study include computer science, early childhood education, human services, and criminal justice. **NOTE:** The state of New Hampshire requires an application to be filled out for any of these positions; a resume cannot be submitted instead of an application. Please visit website to download the application and to see more details on applying. **Positions advertised include:** Part-time Instructors – Various Departments; Adjunct Instructor – Various Departments; Tutor – Various Departments. **Special programs:** Internships. **Number of employees at this location:** 150.

PINKERTON ACADEMY
5 Pinkerton Street, Derry NH 03038. 603/437-5200, Ext.: 3110. **Contact:** Director of Human Resources. **E-mail address:** marierogers@pinkertonacademy.org. **World Wide Web address:** http://www.pinkertonacademy.net. **Description:** A private, regional high school serving students from the towns of Derry, Hampstead, and Chester. **NOTE:** Search posted openings online. Download application for mailing. No faxed resumes or applications will be accepted. Must submit completed application with your resume by mail only. State certification is required for all teaching positions. **Positions advertised include**: Grounds Worker; Coach; Teacher; Substitute Teacher; Special Education Reimbursable Aid; Custodian; Food Service Worker. **Number of employees at this location:** 175.

RIVIER COLLEGE
420 Main Street, Nashua NH 03060-5086. 603/897-8211. **Toll-free phone:** 800/44-RIVIER. **Fax:** 603/897-8883. **Contact:** Gail M. Galipeau, Human Resources Coordinator. **E-mail address:** hr@rivier.edu. **World Wide Web address:** http://www.rivier.edu. **Description:** A college. **NOTE:** Search posted openings online. **Positions advertised include:** Assistant Professor, Various Departments; Chairperson, Nursing and Health Sciences; Clinical Adjunct, Nursing Faculty; Controller; Database Administrator; Director of Library; Human Resource Administrator; Public Relations/ Web Writer.

RMC RESEARCH CORPORATION
1000 Market Street, Portsmouth NH 03801. 603/422-8888. **Toll-free phone:** 800/258-0802. **Fax:** 603/436-9166. **Contact:** Human Research. **E-mail address:** rmc@rmcres.com. **World Wide Web address:** http://www.rmcres.com. **Description:** An educational research firm. RMC works with Chapter 1, Title 1, Head Start, and Even Start programs. **Other U.S. locations:** Denver CO; Portland OR; Arlington VA.

ST. ANSELM COLLEGE
100 Saint Anselm Drive, Manchester NH 03102. 603/641-7020. **Fax:** 603/222-4014. **Contact:** Human Resources Director. **E-mail address:** hr@anselm.edu. **World Wide Web address:** http://www.anselm.edu. **Description:** A four-year, coeducational, Catholic, liberal arts college. Approximately 1,850 full-time students are enrolled in 27 majors offered, in addition to professional and cooperative engineering programs. In recent years, *U.S. News and World Report* has ranked Saint Anselm among the top 10 liberal arts colleges in the Northeast. Founded in 1889. **NOTE:** Search posted openings online. **Positions advertised include:** Administrative Assistant; Chair/Director – Department of Nursing; Assistant Head Reference Librarian; Director of Development Operations; Director, Student Activities & Leadership Program; Systems Administrator.

ST. PAUL'S SCHOOL
325 Pleasant Street, Concord NH 03301. 603/229-4641. **Fax:** 603/229-4761. **Contact:** Steven Smith, Human Resources. **E-mail address:** allhr@sps.edu. **World Wide Web address:** http://www.sps.edu. **Description:** A private, college preparatory school. **NOTE:** Search posted openings online. **Positions advertised include:** Humanities Teacher; Biology Teacher; Classroom Assistant/Long-term Substitute, Infant/Toddler Classroom.

SOUTHERN NEW HAMPSHIRE UNIVERSITY
2500 North River Road, Manchester NH 03106. 603/644-3125. **Fax:** 603/645-9661. **Recorded jobline:** 603/629-INFO. **Contact:** Human Resources. **World Wide Web address:** http://www.snhu.edu. **Description:** Southern New Hampshire University is a private, independent college offering undergraduate, graduate, and doctoral academic programs. SNHU has a day college enrollment of over 1,000 students, 1,500 in the graduate school of business, and nearly 4,000 in the division of continuing education. Founded in 1932. **NOTE:** Search posted openings online but must mail a hard copy of resume and cover letter. Part-time positions are offered. **Positions advertised include:** Assistant/Associate Professor – Various Departments; Teacher Education Faculty; Vice President of Academic Affairs; Vice President of Student Affairs; Development Coordinator; Men's Head Soccer Coach; Academic Advisor; Computer Lab Assistant. **Office hours:** Monday – Friday, 8:00 a.m. – 4:30 p.m. **Other U.S. locations:** ME; VT. **Number of employees worldwide:** 1,500.

UNIVERSITY OF NEW HAMPSHIRE
2 Leavitt Lane, Durham NH 03824. 603/862-0501. **Fax:** 603/862-0077. **Contact:** Human Resources. **World Wide Web address:** http://www.unhjobs.com. **Description:** A four-year state university. Originally founded as an agricultural school, the University of New Hampshire now encompasses a wide variety of disciplines, including the Whittemore School of Business & Economics, which provides one of the oldest Executive MBA programs in New England. Founded in 1866. **NOTE:** Search posted openings online only. No paper resumes are accepted. **Positions advertised include:** Accountant; Assistant Professor, Various Departments; Athletic Coach; Chairperson, Nursing; Clinical Coordinator; Executive Director for Alumni Affairs; Information Support Assistant; Information Technologist; Instructor, Various Departments; Lecturer, Various Departments; Manager of Research Administration; Nutritionist; Research Faculty; Residence Hall Director; Sedimentary Geologist; Television Producer/Director. **Office hours:** Monday – Friday, 8:00 a.m. – 4:30 p.m. **Operations at this facility include:** Administration; Research and Development. **Number of employees at this location:** 2,500.

New Jersey

BERGEN COMMUNITY COLLEGE
400 Paramus Road, Room A-316, Paramus NJ 07652-1595. 201/447-7442. **Fax:** 201/251-4987. **Contact:** Department of Human Resources. **E-mail address:** employment@bergen.edu. **World Wide Web address:** http://www.bergen.cc.nj.us. **Description:** A community college enrolling over 12,000 students. The college offers associate degrees in arts, sciences, and applied sciences. **Positions advertised include:** Vice President of Student Services; Central Records Manager; Resource Accommodations Specialist.

BERLITZ INTERNATIONAL, INC.
400 Alexander Park, Princeton NJ 08540. 609/514-3400. **Contact:** Human Resources. **World Wide Web address:** http://www.berlitz.com. **Description:** A language services firm providing instruction and translation services through 298 language centers in 28 countries around the world. The company also publishes travel guides, foreign language phrase books, and home study materials. **Corporate headquarters location:** This location. **Operations at this facility include:** Administration. **Number of employees nationwide:** 3,500.

BLOOMFIELD COLLEGE
467 Franklin Street, Bloomfield NJ 07003. 973/748-9000. **Fax:** 973/743-3998. **Contact:** Human Resources. **World Wide Web address:** http://www.bloomfield.edu. **Description:** A private four-year college with ties to the

Presbyterian Church offering bachelors and bachelor of science degrees. **Positions advertised include:** Director of Alumni Relations; Vice President for Enrollment Management.

CAMDEN COUNTY COLLEGE
College Road, P.O. Box 200, Blackwood NJ 08012. 856/227-7200. **Contact:** Human Resources. **E-mail address:** hr@camdencc.edu. **World Wide Web address:** http://www.camdencc.edu. **Description:** A community college with more than 11,500 students enrolled in over 80 academic areas.

THE COLLEGE OF NEW JERSEY
P.O. Box 7718, Ewing NJ 08628-0718. 609/771-1855. **Contact:** Human Resources. **World Wide Web address:** http://www.tcnj.edu. **Description:** A four-year state college offering bachelor's and master's degrees to approximately 6,000 undergraduate and 1,000 graduate students. **Positions advertised include:** Assistant Professor; Psychologist; Music Media Librarian; Instructional Technology Coordinator.

EDUCATIONAL TESTING SERVICE (ETS)
Rosedale Road, Princeton NJ 08541. 609/921-9000. **Fax:** 609/734-5410. **Contact:** Human Resources. **World Wide Web address:** http://www.ets.org. **Description:** An educational research and evaluation service that administers many aptitude and achievement tests including the SAT, CLEP, TOEFL, GRE, GMAT, and AP. **Positions advertised include:** Client Service Coordinator; Assessment Specialist; Associate Research Scientist; Audio Visual Specialist; Information Technology Auditor; Business Systems Analyst; Call Center Telephone Analyst; Group Manager; Media Planner; Information Security; SAT Mentor; GRE Mentor

KEAN UNIVERSITY
1000 Morris Avenue, Union NJ 07083. 908/527-2150. **Contact:** Human Resources. **World Wide Web address:** http://www.kean.edu. **Description:** A university offering more than 60 programs of study for graduates and undergraduates. The university has an enrollment of over 12,000 students. Founded in 1855.

MONMOUTH UNIVERSITY
400 Cedar Avenue, West Long Branch NJ 07764-1898. 732/571-3470. **Recorded jobline:** 732/571-3513. **Contact:** Human Resources. **E-mail address:** mujobs@monmouth.edu. World **Wide Web address:** http://www.monmouth.edu. **Description:** A private four-year university offering 26 undergraduate programs & many graduate & certificate degrees. **Positions advertised include:** Assistant Dean of Advising; Head Coach; Director of Tennis; Assistant Director of Residential Life; Assistant to the Dean; Electrician.

MONTCLAIR STATE UNIVERSITY
One Normal Avenue, Box CO 316, Upper Montclair NJ 07043. 973/655-4398. **Fax:** 973/655-7210. **Contact:** Division of Human Resources. **E-mail address:** hr@mail.monclair.edu. **World Wide Web address:** http://www.montclair.edu. **Description:** A state university with an enrollment of 13,500. The university offers over 70 programs of study. The university is located about 30 minutes south of New York City **Positions advertised include:** Adjunct Instructor; Admissions Counselor; Assistant Director; Assistant Professor; Contract Administrator; Project Coordinator; Project Director; Department Chair Person; Mail Clerk; Head Coach; Pro Award Officer. **NOTE:** E-mail applications can only be accepted in text format in Microsoft Word or Adobe Acrobat.

NEW JERSEY CITY UNIVERSITY
2039 Kennedy Boulevard, Hepburn Hall 105, Jersey City NJ 07305. 201/200-2335. **Fax:** 201/200-2219. **Contact:** Robert Piaskowsky, Director of Human Resources. **E-mail address:** hr@njcu.edu. **World Wide Web address:** http://www.njcu.edu. **Description:** A state university with approximately 8,000 students enrolled in undergraduate, graduate, and continuing education programs. **Positions advertised include:** Director; Dean of Students; Assistant Dean; Nurse; Criminal Justice Professor; Fitness Exercise Specialist; Information Technology Specialist; Health Science Professor; Business Administration; Special Education; Learning Disabilities Teachers Consultant; Early Childhood Education; Education Technology; Elementary Technology; Literacy Education; Speech Language Specialist; Therapeutic Services Supervisor; Typist Clerk.

NEW JERSEY INSTITUTE OF TECHNOLOGY
University Heights, Fenster Hall, Room 500, Newark NJ 07102. 973/596-3140. **Fax:** 973/642-4066. **Contact:** Department of Human Resources. **E-mail address:** hr@njit.edu. **World Wide Web address:** http://www.njit.edu. **Description:** A technical institute of higher learning offering undergraduate and graduate degrees in engineering, architecture, liberal arts/sciences, management, and education. **Positions advertised include:** Academic Advisor; Academic Coordinator; Accounts Payable Clerk; Administrative Assistant; Assistant Physical Education Specialist; Assistant Theatre Technician; Assistant Trainer; Associate Dean; Control Specialist; Academic Computing Director; University Information Systems Director; University Learning Director; Facility Engineer; HVAC Mechanic; Library Assistant; Provost; Receptionist; Security Officer; Recycler.

PRINCETON UNIVERSITY
One New South, Princeton NJ 08544. 609/258-3300. **Contact:** Office of Human Resources. **E-mail address:** jobs@princeton.edu. **World Wide Web address:** http://www.princeton.edu/hr. **Description:** A private, four-year university offering bachelor of arts and science degrees, as well as master's and doctoral degrees. Approximately 4,500 undergraduate and 1,800 graduate students attend Princeton. **NOTE:** Current lists of positions can be found online. **Positions advertised include:** Administrative Support; Data Management Support; Departmental Office Support; Field Electrician; Production Supervisor; Retail Food Service Worker; Planner; Shift Supervisor.

ROWAN UNIVERSITY
201 Mullica Hill Road, Linden Hall, 1st Floor, Glassboro NJ 08028. 856/256-4134. **Fax:** 856/256-4714. **Contact:** Human Resources. **World Wide Web address:** http://www.rowan.edu. **Description:** A four-year, state college offering bachelor's and master's degrees (including MBAs). Approximately 9,000 students attend Rowan University. **Positions advertised include:** Assistant Dean of Students; Director of Judicial Affairs; Assistant Director, Graduate Assistantships.

RUTGERS STATE UNIVERSITY OF NEW JERSEY
56 Bevier Road, Piscataway NJ 08854. 732/445-3020. **Fax:** 732/445-3087. **Contact:** Personnel Department. **E-mail address:** info@hr.Rutgers.edu. **World Wide Web address:** http://www.rutgers.edu. **Description:** A four-year, state university offering undergraduate and graduate programs in a wide variety of disciplines. **Positions advertised include:** Administrative Director; Administrative Assistant; Area Director; Assistant to the Dean; Director Athletics; Editorial Media Specialist; Unit Computing Specialist. **Other U.S. locations:** Camden NJ; Newark NJ.

RUTGERS STATE UNIVERSITY OF NEW JERSEY
UNIVERSITY COLLEGE-NEWARK
249 University Avenue, Room 202, Newark NJ 07102. 973/353-5500. **Contact:** Human Resources. **E-mail address:** angelis@newark.rutgers.edu. **World Wide Web address:** http://www.rutgers.edu. **Description:** A campus of the state university. **Positions advertised include:** Administrative Director; Administrative Assistant; Area Director; Assistant to the Dean; Director Athletics; Editorial Media Specialist; Unit Computing Specialist. **Other U.S. locations:** Brunswick NJ; Camden NJ.

SETON HALL UNIVERSITY
400 South Orange Avenue, Stafford Hall, South Orange NJ 07079. 973/761-9177. **Fax:** 973/761-9007. **Contact:** Human Resources. **E-mail address:** humanres@shu.edu. **World Wide Web address:** http://www.shu.edu. **Description:** A Catholic university offering a wide range of undergraduate and graduate programs. **Positions advertised include:** Secretary; Assistant Psychology Professor; Assistant Professor of Philosophy; Assistant Professor of Spanish; Physiologist; Web Services Applications Developer; Technology Budget Manager.

THOMAS EDISON STATE COLLEGE
315 West State Street, Trenton NJ 08608. 609/292-5629. **Fax:** 609/984-1115. **Contact:** Human Resources. **E-mail address:** hr@tesc.edu. **World Wide Web address:** http://www.tesc.edu. **Description:** An adult education college offering associate's, bachelor's, and master's degree programs. **Positions advertised include:** Assistant Director of Financial Aide; Assistant To Prior Learning Assessment Specialist; Dean; Director of Learning Assessment; Information Center Representative; Program Assistant. **Corporate headquarters location:** This location.

WILLIAM PATERSON UNIVERSITY OF NEW JERSEY
358 Hamburg Turnpike, College Hall-Room 150, Wayne NJ 07470. 973/720-2605. **Fax:** 973/720-2090. **Contact:** Human Resources. **E-mail address:** humanresources@wpunj.edu. **World Wide Web address:** http://www.wpunj.edu. **Description:** A public university with approximately 9,000 students. Programs include liberal arts, nursing, sciences, English, history, and music. **Positions advertised include:** Assistant Director of Financial Aide; Assistant Director of Counsel; Associate Director Career Development Center; Director of the Honors College; Grant Writer; Accounting Manager.

New Mexico

ALBUQUERQUE ACADEMY
6400 Wyoming Boulevard NE, Albuquerque NM 87109-3899. 505/858-8801. **Fax:** 505/858-8809. **Contact:** Mary Jo Carrier, Human Resources. **E-mail address:** carrier@aa.edu. **World Wide Web address:** http://www.aa.edu. **Description:** A private school serving approximately 1,000 students from the sixth through twelfth grades. Founded in 1955. **NOTE:** For faculty positions contact: Andrew T. Watson, Head of School. For Staff Positions contact: Mary Jo Carrier, Head of Human Resources.

ALBUQUERQUE PUBLIC SCHOOLS
725 University Boulevard SE, Albuquerque NM 87106. 505/842-3581. **Recorded jobline:** 505/842-3737. **Contact:** Human Resources. **World Wide Web address:** http://ww2.aps.edu. **Description:** The administrative offices of the Albuquerque school district, which includes 80 elementary, 26 middle, 10 alternative, and 11 high schools with more than 86,000 students. **Positions advertised include:** Coaches; Clerks; Counselors; Educational Assistants; Instructional Manager; Librarian; Principal; Secretaries; Plumbers; Speech Language Pathologists; Teachers.

ALBUQUERQUE TECHNICAL VOCATIONAL INSTITUTE
525 Buena Vista Drive SE, Albuquerque NM 87106. 505/224-4600. **Recorded jobline:** 505/224-4601. **Contact:** Robert Brown, Human Resources. **E-mail address:** tvicareers@tvi.edu. **World Wide Web address:** http://www.tvi.edu. **Description:** A two-year community college offering certificates, associate degrees, college transfer credit, and development education to approximately 20,000 students on four campuses. **NOTE:** Search and apply for positions online. **Positions advertised include:** Quality Assurance Analyst; Business Development Manager; Instructional Technician; Tutor; Security Dispatcher; Clerical Specialist; Instructor; Program Director; Security Officer.

AZTEC MUNICIPAL SCHOOL DISTRICT
1118 West Aztec Boulevard, Aztec NM 87410. 505/334-9474. **Fax:** 505/334-9861. **Contact:** Dr. Linda Paul, Associate Superintendent. **E-mail address:** aztecpersonnel@yahoo.com. **World Wide Web address:** http://www.aztecschools.com. **Description:** Administrative office of the Aztec public school system. **NOTE:** Entry-level positions are offered. Search and apply for positions online. **Positions advertised include:** Technology Educational Assistant; Speech Language Pathologist; Head Football Coach; Physical Ed Teacher.

CLOVIS MUNICIPAL SCHOOLS
1009 Main Street, Clovis NM 88101 505/769-4300. **Fax:** 505/769-4333. **Contact:** Jim McDaniel, Assistant Superintendent for Personnel. **World Wide Web address:** http://www.cms.k12.nm.us. **Description:** Houses the administrative offices for the Clovis public school system, which serves 8,500 students with one high school, three junior high schools, 13 elementary schools, one pre-school, and one evening high school. **NOTE:** Part-time jobs are offered. Applications may be downloaded. **Positions advertised include:** Administrative Intern; Assistant Director of Finance; Swim Coach; Custodian; Elementary Principal; Secretary; Special Ed Teacher; Speech Language Pathologist.

COLLEGE OF SANTA FE
1600 Saint Michael's Drive, Santa Fe NM 87505-7634. 505/473-6335. **Toll-free phone:** 800/456-2673. **Fax:** 505/473-6251. **Contact:** Human Resources Manager. **E-mail address:** rdinkel@csf.edu. **World Wide Web address:** http://www.csf.edu. **Description:** A four-year liberal arts college with 900 traditional and 1000 evening students. Operates degree-granting programs at Albuquerque campus. **NOTE:** See website for current job openings and application instructions. **Positions advertised include:** Art Historian – Native-American Art; Director – Anne and John Marion Center for Photographic Arts; Executive Assistant – Development Office. **Number of employees at this location:** 200.

COLLEGE OF THE SOUTHWEST
6610 Lovington Highway, Hobbs NM 88240. 505/392-6561. **Toll-free phone:** 800/530-4400. **Fax:** 505/392-6006. **Contact:** Connie Gray, Personnel Services Coordinator. **E-mail address:** cgray@csw.edu. **World Wide Web address:** http://www.csw.edu. **Description:** An independent, Christian, five-year, liberal arts college that also offers master's programs in education and education administration. Approximately 700 students attend College of the Southwest. **NOTE:** See website for current job openings and application instructions. **Positions advertised include:** Admission Specialist; Webmaster

COOPERATIVE EDUCATIONAL SERVICES
4216 Balloon Park Road NE, Albuquerque NM 87109. 505/344-5470. **Contact:** Human Resources Department. **World Wide Web address:** http://www.ces.org. **Description:** A cooperative of school districts that provide a variety of educational services. **NOTE:** Search and apply for positions in New Mexico public schools through website link to New Mexico Regional Education Applicant and Placement Program (http://www.nmreap.net).

DEMING PUBLIC SCHOOL DISTRICT
400 Cody Road, Deming NM 88030. 505/546-8841. **World Wide Web address:** http://www.demingps.org. **Contact:** Human Resources. **Description:** This location serves as the administrative offices of the Deming school system, which includes seven elementary, one middle, one middle high, and one high school. The office is responsible for staffing municipal schools. **NOTE:** See website for current job openings and application instructions. **Positions advertised include:** Health Assistant; Speech Language Pathologist; Track Coach; Special Education Bilingual EA; Crossing Guard; Custodian.

EASTERN NEW MEXICO UNIVERSITY
ENMU Station 21, 1500 South Avenue K, Portales NM 88130. 505/562-2115. **Contact:** Personnel Office. **World Wide Web address:** http://www.enmu.edu. **Description:** A university offering 50 undergraduate major and several pre-professional programs as well as 19 masters degree programs. ENMU has campuses in Roswell and Ruidoso. **NOTE:** Support, professional, and administrative positions are listed online; call the Personnel Office at 505/562-2115 concerning faculty positions. **Positions advertised include:** Nurse; Admissions Manager; Webmaster; Broadcast Engineer; Coordinator for Prospective Students.

FARMINGTON MUNICIPAL SCHOOL DISTRICT
2001 North Dustin, P.O. Box 5850, Farmington NM 87401. 505/324-9840. **Contact:** Human Resources. **World Wide Web address:** http://www.fms.k12.nm.us. **Description:** The administrative offices of the Farmington school system, which includes 11 elementary, four middle, and three high schools. The office is responsible for staffing at all municipal schools. **NOTE:** Search and apply for positions online. **Positions advertised include:** Speech Language Pathologist; Indian Education Counselor; Spanish Bilingual Instructor; Coach; Secretary.

GALLUP-MCKINLEY COUNTY PUBLIC SCHOOLS
700 South Boardman Avenue, P.O. Box 1318, Gallup NM 87305-1318. 505/722-7711. **Toll-free phone:** 800/842-5587. **Fax:** 505/721-1134. **Contact:** Karl Herr, Director of Personnel. **World Wide Web address:** http://www.gmcs.k12.nm.us. **Description:** A public school district serving 14,500 students in grades K-12 in northwestern New Mexico. **NOTE:** Resumes must be in regards to a specific position. Search for positions online. **Positions advertised include:** Principal; Special Education Director; Food Services Director; Assistant Principal; Social Worker; Office Assistant; Educational Interpreter; Nurse; Teacher; Counselor; Coach; Librarian.

LA PETITE ACADEMY
1361 Rufina Circle, Santa Fe NM 87505. 505/473-9525. **Contact:** Human Resources. **World Wide Web address:** http://www.lapetite.com. **Description:** A preschool and daycare center for children ages six weeks to 12 years. The chain includes 673 early childhood education centers in 36 states. **NOTE:** Search for positions online. Submit application online. **Positions advertised include:** Maintenance Technician. **Corporate headquarters location:** Chicago IL. **Other area locations:** Rio Rancho NM; Albuquerque NM; Bernalillo NM.

LAS CRUCES PUBLIC SCHOOLS
505 South Main, Suite 249, Las Cruces NM 88001. 505/527-5973. **Fax:** 505/527-6658. **Contact:** Charles W. White, Associate Superintendent for Human Resources. **World Wide Web address:** http://www.lcps.k12.nm.us. **Description:** The administrative offices for the Las Cruces public school system, which includes 22,700 students, 23 elementary, seven middle, four high schools, and a special education training center. The office is responsible for staffing all municipal schools. **NOTE:** Search for positions online. Application packet may be requested online. **Positions advertised include:** Bilingual Teacher; Special Education Teacher; Physical Therapist; Speech Language Pathologist; Sign Language Interpreter; Professional Development Teacher; Coach; Assistant Comptroller; Campus Security Guard; Educational Assistant; Kitchen Staff Member; Food Service Cashier.

NEW MEXICO INSTITUTE OF MINING & TECHNOLOGY
801 Leroy Place, Wells Hall, Socorro NM 87801-4796. 505/835-6962. **Fax:** 505/835-5337. **Contact:** Salina A. Lopez, Human Resources. **World Wide Web address:** http://www.nmt.edu. **Description:** An undergraduate and graduate university with an enrollment of 1800 specializing in science and engineering education and research. **NOTE:** E-mail applications are not accepted. See website for current job openings and application instructions. **Positions advertised include:** Lab Associate; Assistant/Associate Professor; Community College Lecturer; Ordnance Technician; Petroleum Geologist; Admission Counselor; Senior Engineer; Postdoctoral Researcher; Seismological Staff Scientist; Data Specialist; Distance Education Administrator; Heavy Equipment Operators; Accounting Technician.

NEW MEXICO MILITARY INSTITUTE
101 West College, Roswell NM 88201-5173. 505/624-8078. **Contact:** MAJ David W. Gray, Comptroller. **E-mail address:** david@nmmi.edu. **World Wide Web address:** http://www.nmmi.edu. **Description:** A co-ed residential, college preparatory high school and two-year junior college in a military setting with a total enrollment of 970. Founded in 1891.

NEW MEXICO STATE UNIVERSITY
P.O. Box 30001, MSC Department 5273, Las Cruces NM 8800. 505/646-2420. **Contact:** Diana Quintana, Human Resources Director. **E-mail address:** diquinta@nmsu.edu. **World Wide Web address:** http://www.nmsu.edu. **Description:** The state university's main campus with an enrollment of 16,000 offers 73 bachelor's, 51 master's, three Specialist, and 24 doctoral programs. Founded in 1888. **NOTE:** Open positions and application instructions available online. **Positions advertised include:** Electrical Technician; Assistant Conference Coordinator; Director of Financial Aid and Scholarship Services; Sr. Electrical Engineer; Director of Black Programs; Director of Campus Activities; Assistant Professor; Instructor; Animal Nutritionist; Electrician; Research Assistant; Teacher Assistant; Secretary; Program Facilitator.

POJOAQUE VALLEY SCHOOL DISTRICT
P.O. Box 3468, Pojoaque Station, Santa Fe NM 87501-0468. 505/455-2284. **Contact:** Human Resources. **E-mail address:** vta@pvs.k12.nm.us. **World Wide Web address:** http://pvs.k12.nm.us. **Description:** Personnel offices for the Pojoaque Valley School District. The office is responsible for staffing at all public schools, grades K-12. **Positions advertised include:** Health Assistant; Elementary Instructional Assistant; Library Assistant; Substitute Teachers; Custodian; Coach. **Number of employees at this location:** 200.

ROSWELL INDEPENDENT SCHOOL DISTRICT
300 North Kentucky Street, P.O. Box 1437, Roswell NM 88202-1437. 505/627-2500. **Fax:** 505/627-2524. **Contact:** Alma Aguilar, Human Resources Specialist. **World Wide Web address:** http://www.risd.k12.nm.us. **Description:** The administrative offices of the Roswell school system, responsible for staffing municipal schools, which includes 15 elementary, four middle, and three high schools. **NOTE:** See website for current job openings and application instructions. **Positions advertised include:** Special Education Teacher; Speech Language Pathologist; Band Director; Math Instructor.

ST. JOHN'S COLLEGE
1160 Camino De La Cruz Blanca, Santa Fe NM 87505. 505/984-6141. **Contact:** Ted Gonzales, Director of Human Resources. **E-mail address:** ted.gonzales@sjcsf.edu. **World Wide Web address:** http://www.sjcsf.edu. **Description:** A co-ed, four-year liberal arts college with approximately 500 undergraduate students. St. John's College also has a graduate program. **Positions advertised include:** Associate Director of Alumni Activities. **Other U.S. locations:** Annapolis MD.

SAN JUAN COLLEGE
4601 College Boulevard, Farmington NM 87402. 505/326-3311. **Fax:** 505/566-3521. **Contact:** Director of Human Resources. **World Wide Web address:** http://www.sjc.cc.nm.us. **Description:** A comprehensive community college offering vocational, industrial, and academic transfer programs. Enrollment at San Juan College is approximately 7,300. **NOTE:**

See website for current job openings and application instructions. **Positions advertised include:** Dental Hygiene Instructor; Assistant Custodial Supervisor Physical Plant; Assistant Vice President for Business Services/Controller; Clerical Aid; Coordinator of Fitness & Conditioning; Dean of School of Energy; Grants Compliance Specialist; Health Information Technologies Instructor; Nursing Faculty.

SANTA FE INDIAN SCHOOL
1501 Cerrillos Road, P.O. Box 5340, Santa Fe NM 87502. 505/989-6309. **Fax:** 505/989-6304. **Contact:** Roni Johnson, Director of Personnel. **World Wide Web address:** http://www.sfis.k12.nm.us. **Description:** A private educational institution consisting of a secondary school, with grades seven and eight, and a high school. **NOTE:** See website for current job openings and application instructions. **Positions advertised include:** Computer Assisted Drafting/Keyboarding Instructor; Spanish II Instructor; Special Education Teacher/Transition Specialist; Language Arts Instructor.

SANTA FE PUBLIC SCHOOLS
610 Altavista Street, Santa Fe NM 87505. 505/467-2017. **Fax:** 505/995-3302. **Contact:** Human Resources. **World Wide Web address:** http://www.sfps.k12.nm.us. **Description:** Administrative offices of the Santa Fe public school system, which includes 29 schools with 13,000 students. **NOTE:** See website for current job openings and application instructions. **Positions advertised include:** Bilingual Educational Assistants; Speech and Language Pathologist; School Counselor; Manager for Extended School Year Program; Director of Technology; Library Media Specialist; Coaches/Assistant Coaches; Occupational Therapist; Plumber; Welder; High School Principal; Elementary School Principal.

SILVER CITY SCHOOLS
2810 North Swan Street, Silver City NM 88061. 505/388-1527. **Fax:** 505/956-2039. **Contact:** Frances Vazquez, Human Resources. **Description:** The administrative offices of the Silver City school system, responsible for staffing municipal schools. **NOTE:** Visit the office to see postings of current job openings.

TAOS MUNICIPAL SCHOOLS
213 Paseo del Canon, Taos NM 87571. 505/758-5205. **Fax:** 505/758-5205. **Contact**: Ester Winter, Human Resources. **E-mail address:** esther@taosschools.org. **World Wide Web address:** http://www.taosschools.org. **Description:** The administrative office of the Taos school system, which is responsible for staffing municipal schools. **NOTE:** See website for current job openings and to download application. Part-time jobs are offered. **Positions advertised include:** Math Teacher; Language Arts Teacher; Purchasing Agent/Fixed Assets Manager; Indian Education Program Manager; Student Nutrition Custodian; Campus Security; Baseball Coach. **Special programs:** Internships; Summer Jobs.

UNIVERSITY OF NEW MEXICO
MSC01 1220, 1 University of New Mexico, Albuquerque NM 87131-0001. 505/277-6947. **Physical address:** 730 Lomas Boulevard NE, Albuquerque, NM 87131. **Fax:** 505/277-2278. **Contact:** Human Resources. **World Wide Web address:** http://www.unm.edu. **Description:** A four-year university offering associate's, bachelor's, master's, certificate, professional, and doctoral degree programs to nearly 25,000 students on the main campus and 7,000 on branch campuses and education centers. Founded in 1889. **NOTE:** Search and apply for positions online. **Positions advertised include:** Systems Analyst; Case Manager; Library Info Specialist; Enrollment Representative; Editor; Administrative Assistant; Director, Employee Assistance Programs; Dean; Visiting Professor; Lecturer.

UNIVERSITY OF PHOENIX
7471 Pan American Freeway NE, Albuquerque NM 87109. 505/821-4800. **Contact:** Human Resources. **World Wide Web address:** http://www.phoenix.edu. **Description:** This location of the university offers undergraduate and graduate programs. **NOTE:** Search and apply for positions online at http://www.apollogrp.edu/Careers. **Parent company:** Apollo Group, Inc.

WESTERN NEW MEXICO UNIVERSITY
Room 103, Juan Chacon Building, P.O. Box 680, Silver City NM 88062. 505/538-6328. **Fax:** 505/538-6294. **Contact:** Human Resources Manager. **World Wide Web address:** http://www.wnmu.edu. **Description:** A four-year university that offers graduate and undergraduate programs to approximately 2,500 students. Founded in 1893. **NOTE:** Search and apply for positions online. **Positions advertised include:** University Librarian; Teacher, Early Childhood Program; Faculty Positions.

ZUNI PUBLIC SCHOOL DISTRICT
PO Drawer A, Zuni NM 87327. 505/782-5511 ext 20045. Fax: 505/782-5870. **Contact:** Human Resources Department. **World Wide Web address:** http://www.zuni.k12.nm.us. **Description:** A public school district serving more than 2,000 students. **NOTE:** See website for current job openings and to download application packets. **Positions advertised include:** Superintendent of Schools; Certified Teacher; Educational Assistant.

New York

AFS INTERCULTURAL PROGRAMS, INC.
71 West 23rd Street, 17th Floor, New York NY 10010. 212/807-8686. **Fax:** 212/807-1001. **Contact:** Human Resources. **E-mail address:** jobs@afs.org. **World Wide Web address:** http://www.afs.org. **Description:** An international exchange organization that provides intercultural learning opportunities for high school students, families, and teachers. The agency operates programs in approximately 55 countries via an international network of volunteers. **Positions advertised include:** Youth Ambassadors Program Coordinator; Development Associate; Admissions Advisor; Administrative Assistant; Regional Coordinator. **Other locations:** Worldwide.

ALS INTERNATIONAL
18 John Street, Suite 300, New York NY 10038. 212/766-4111. **Toll-free phone:** 800/788-0450. **Fax:** 212/349-0964. **Contact:** Human Resources Supervisor. **E-mail address:** hr@alsintl.com. **World Wide Web address:** http://www.alsintl.com. **Description:** A translation and interpreting company serving a worldwide, diversified clientele. **Positions advertised include:** Language Specialist; On-site Technician; Studio Engineer; Software Engineer/Programmer.

ADELPHI UNIVERSITY
One South Avenue, P.O. Box 701, Levermore Hall, Room 203, Garden City NY 11530. 516/877-3220. **Toll-free phone:** 800/ADELPHI. **Fax:** 516/877-4970. **Contact:** Office of Human Resources. **E-mail address:** humanres@adelphi.edu. **World Wide Web address:** http://www.adelphi.edu. **Description:** A private university with approximately 7,000 undergraduate and graduate students enrolled. Founded in 1896. **NOTE:** Entry-level positions are offered. Human Resources phone: 516/877-3224. **Positions advertised include:** Administrative Assistant; Secretary; Teacher/Professor. **Corporate headquarters location:** This location. **Number of employees at this location:** 1,300.

ALFRED UNIVERSITY
Saxon Drive, Greene Hall, Alfred NY 14802. 607/871-2118. **Fax:** 607/871-2318. **Contact:** Patrice Beadle, Director of Human Resources. **E-mail address:** humanresources@alfred.edu. **World Wide Web address:** http://www.alfred.edu. **Description:** This nonsectarian university consists of the privately endowed College of Business, the College of Engineering and Professional Studies, the College of Liberal Arts and Sciences, and the New York State College of Ceramics (School of Ceramic Engineering and Sciences) and School of Art and Design. Bachelors,

masters, and doctoral degrees are offered. Approximately 2,350 undergraduate and graduate students attend Alfred University. Founded in 1836. **NOTE:** Human Resources phone: 607/871-2118. **Positions advertised include:** College of Business Dean; School of Engineering Dean; Museum of Ceramic Art Director; Raw Materials Technician; Biomedical Materials Engineering Science Professor; Photonic Materials Professor.

BARNARD COLLEGE
3009 Broadway, New York NY 10027-6598. 212/854-2551. **Fax:** 212/854-2454. **Contact:** Employment Manager. **World Wide Web address:** http://www.barnard.edu. **Description:** An independent college of liberal arts and sciences for women, affiliated with Columbia University. Barnard College has an enrollment of approximately 2,200 undergraduates from more than 40 countries. Founded in 1889. **Positions advertised include:** Psychological Counselor; Web/Oracle Programmer; Teacher; Student Assistant to the Director; English Poetry Lecturer; Philosophy Lecturer; Migration and Diaspora Studies Lecturer; Dance Department Chairperson; Anthropology Lecturer; Asian and Middle Eastern Cultures Lecturer; Biology Lab Associate; Biology Lecturer; Economics Lecturer; Assistant Physics Professor; Architecture & Urban Studies Lecturer; Art History Lecturer; Sociology Lecturer; Slavic Professor; Spanish Professor; Theater Professor.

BARUCH COLLEGE
THE CITY UNIVERSITY OF NEW YORK (CUNY)
135 East 22nd Street, Room 200, New York NY 10010. 646/660-6590. **Fax:** 646/660-6591. **Contact:** Human Resources. **World Wide Web address:** http://www.baruch.cuny.edu. **Description:** A college offering undergraduate and graduate programs through its School of Business, School of Liberal Arts and Sciences, and School of Public Affairs. **Positions advertised include:** Accountancy Instructor; Black & Hispanic Studies Instructor; Career Counseling Instructor; Communication Studies Instructor; Computer Information Systems Instructor; Economics & Finance Instructor; English Instructor; Fine and Performing Arts Instructor; History Instructor; Law Instructor; Management Instructor; Marketing Instructor. **Other area locations:** Bronx NY; Brooklyn NY; Flushing NY; Jamaica NY; Staten Island NY. **Operations at this facility include:** Administration; Research and Development; Service. **Number of employees at this location:** 1,800.

BINGHAMTON UNIVERSITY
STATE UNIVERSITY OF NEW YORK
P.O. Box 6000, Binghamton NY 13902-6000. 607/777-2186. **Contact:** Human Resources. **World Wide Web address:** http://www.binghamton.edu. **Description:** A four-year undergraduate and graduate university. SUNY at Binghamton offers the following degree programs: Bachelor of Arts, Bachelor of Science, master's, MBA, and doctoral. Enrollment is approximately 11,000 undergraduate and 3,000 graduate students.

BROOME COMMUNITY COLLEGE
103 Wales Administration Building, P.O. Box 1017, Binghamton NY 13902-1017. 607/778-5319. **Fax:** 607/778-5482. **Contact:** Elizabeth Wood, Human Resources. **E-mail address:** jobs@mail.sunybroome.edu. **World Wide Web address:** http://www.sunybroome.edu. **Description:** A two-year community college. **Positions advertised include:** Financial Aid Staff Assistant.

THE CITY COLLEGE OF NEW YORK
THE CITY UNIVERSITY OF NEW YORK (CUNY)
160 Convent Avenue, Shepard Hall, Room 50, New York NY 10031. 212/650-7226. **Contact:** Human Resources Department. **World Wide Web address:** http://www.ccny.cuny.edu. **Description:** A public, coeducational college offering both undergraduate and graduate programs of study in a wide variety of disciplines. **Positions advertised include:** Associate Architecture Professor; Education Teacher; Assistant Physics Professor; Economics Professor; Medical Lecturer; Associate Film & Video Production Professor; Advertising & Public Relations Professor; Film & Video Full Professor. **Other area locations:** Bronx NY; Brooklyn NY; Flushing NY; Jamaica NY; Staten Island NY.

CLARKSON UNIVERSITY
8 Clarkson Avenue, P.O. Box 5542, Potsdam NY 13699. 315/268-6497. **Fax:** 315/268-4437. **Contact:** Human Resources. **World Wide Web address:** http://www.clarkson.edu. **Description:** A four-year, liberal arts college of 3,000 undergraduates and 350 graduate students with specialization in engineering sciences. **Positions advertised include:** Assistant Civil and Environmental Engineering Professor; Bioengineering/Rehabilitation Engineering Director; Assistant Chemistry Professor; Assistant Physics Professor; Assistant Cardiopulmonary Physical Therapy Professor; Safety Manager; Analytical Laboratory Director; Women's Ice Hockey Assistant Coach; Director of Gift Planning; Maintenance Mechanic.

COLGATE UNIVERSITY
13 Oak Drive, Hamilton NY 13346. 315/228-7411. **Fax:** 315/228-7171. **Contact:** Amy Barnes, Associate Vice President of Human Resources. **E-mail address:** humres@mail.colgate.edu. **World Wide Web address:** http://www.colgate.edu. **Description:** A four-year, liberal arts college located in central New York with 2,700 students. Founded in 1819. **NOTE:** Human Resources phone: 315/228-7411. **Positions advertised include:** Art History Professor; Assistant Football Coach; Fitness Center Coach; Greek & Latin Professor; Computer Science Lecturer; Geography Lecturer; East Asian History Lecturer; Music Composition Professor; Peace Studies Chairperson; Sociology/Anthropology Lecturer; Admissions Counselor; Career Services Assistant Director; Leadership Center Assistant Director. **Special programs:** Apprenticeships. **Number of employees at this location:** 700.

COLLEGE OF SAINT ROSE
432 Western Avenue, Albany NY 12203-1419. 518/454-5111. **Contact:** Human Resources. **World Wide Web address:** http://www.strose.edu. **Description:** A four-year college with 4,500 students offering 41 undergraduate and 28 masters degrees as well as six graduate certificates. **Positions advertised include:** Alumni Relations Assistant Director: Building Maintenance Mechanic; Building Maintenance Worker; Educational Technologist; Registered Nurse; Art History Lecturer; Biology Lecturer; Computer Information Systems Lecturer; Counseling Lecturer.

COLUMBIA UNIVERSITY
475 Riverside Drive, 1901 Interchurch Center, New York NY 10015. 212/870-3074. **Contact:** Department of Human Resources. **World Wide Web address:** http://www.columbia.edu. **Description:** A private university comprised of 15 schools and 71 academic departments and divisions. The university is affiliated with Barnard College, Teachers College, and Union Theological Seminary. There are approximately 20,000 students enrolled at the university including 11,800 graduate and professional, 5,600 undergraduate, and 2,500 nondegree students. Founded in 1754. **NOTE:** Interested jobseekers are strongly encouraged to apply online via the company Website, but may send Scannable resumes to: Columbia University, P.O. Box 920, Burlington MA 01803. **Positions advertised include:** Facilities Porter; Computer Science Technology Director; Library Assistant; Financial Services Assistant; Earth Institute Associate Director; Facilities Handy Person; Real Estate Building Superintendent.

CORNELL UNIVERSITY
337 Pine Tree Road, Ithaca NY 14850. 607/254-8370. **Fax:** 607/255-4943. **Contact:** Recruitment and

Employment Center. **E-mail address:** employment_svcs@cornell.edu. **World Wide Web address:** http://www.cornell.edu. **Description:** An Ivy-league university offering both undergraduate and graduate degree programs through 13 colleges and schools. The university enrolls approximately 13,600 undergraduates and over 5,000 graduate students. Founded in 1865. **Positions advertised include:** Earth & Atmospheric Sciences Assistant Professor; Associate Population Medicine & Diagnostic Sciences Professor; Research Aide; Technical Services Supervisor; Administrative Assistant; Administrative Manager; Director of Rooms/Operations. **Number of employees:** 9,200.

DAEMEN COLLEGE
4380 Main Street, Amherst NY 14226-3592. 716/839-8325. **Fax:** 716/839-8362. **Contact:** Pamela R. Neumann, Personnel Director. **E-mail address:** personnel@daemen.edu or personnel@deamen.edu. **World Wide Web address:** http://www.daemen.edu. **Description:** A four-year, private college primarily offering undergraduate courses. As a liberal arts school, Daemen College offers majors including education, nursing, psychology, business and commerce, physical therapy, and physician's assistant. Graduate programs are offered in physical therapy and nursing. Founded in 1947. **NOTE:** Part-time positions offered. Human Resources phone: 716/839-8325. **Positions advertised include:** Assistant Biology Professor; Assistant English Professor; Assistant Spanish Professor; Assistant History Professor.

DOWLING COLLEGE
150 Idle Hour Boulevard, Oakdale NY 11769-1999. 631/244-3020. **Fax:** 631/589-6123. **Contact:** Bridget Carroll, Human Resources. **E-mail address:** carrollb@dowling.edu. **World Wide Web address:** http://www.dowling.edu. **Description:** Dowling College is an independent, comprehensive, coeducational college. The college serves approximately 6,000 full- and part-time students, offering undergraduate programs leading to bachelor of arts, bachelor of science, and bachelor of business administration degrees. Graduate program degrees include master of science in reading and special education, master of business administration, and master of education with the following concentrations: elementary education, secondary education, special education, life-span special services, and reading. Founded in 1968. **Number of employees at this location:** 900.

D'YOUVILLE COLLEGE
320 Porter Avenue, Buffalo NY 14201. 716/881-3200. **Contact:** Human Resources. **World Wide Web address:** http://www.dyc.edu. **Description:** A four-year liberal arts college that offers graduate and undergraduate programs. D'Youville College offers majors including business, education, and nursing. The physical therapy and occupational therapy programs both entail five years of study.

ELMIRA COLLEGE
One Park Place, Elmira NY 14901. 607/735-1800. **Toll-free phone:** 800/935-6472. **Contact:** Personnel Department. **World Wide Web address:** http://www.elmira.edu. **Description:** A four-year, private undergraduate and graduate university. Degree programs include associate's, bachelor of arts, bachelor of science, master of business administration, and master of science. Enrollment is approximately 1,100. **Positions advertised include:** Human Services Professor; Physical Chemistry/Physics Professor; Teacher Education Professor; Psychology Professor; Graduate Assistant; Director of English as a Second Language; Executive Secretary to the President; Health Center Head Nurse; Coordinator of Performing Arts Programming and Student Activities; Director of Major Gifts.

ERIE COMMUNITY COLLEGE
4041 Southwestern Boulevard, Orchard Park NY 14127-2199. 716/851-1840. **Contact:** Human Resources. **World Wide Web address:** http://www.ecc.edu. **Description:** A two-year community college that offers both certificates and associate degrees. Classes are held at three campuses. **Other U.S. locations:** Williamsville NY; Orchard Park NY.

FASHION INSTITUTE OF TECHNOLOGY
7th Avenue at 27th Street, New York NY 10001-5992. 212/217-7999. **Contact:** Human Resources. **World Wide Web address:** http://www.fitnyc.edu. **Description:** A fashion institute offering degrees in art and design or business and technology.

FLIGHTSAFETY INTERNATIONAL, INC.
Marine Air Terminal, LaGuardia Airport, Flushing NY 11371-1061. 718/565-4100. **Toll-free phone:** 800/749-8818. **Fax:** 718/565-4169. **Contact:** Personnel. **E-mail address:** jobs@flightsafety.com. **World Wide Web address:** http://www.flightsafety.com. **Description:** FlightSafety International provides training to operators of aircraft and ships from 42 training centers in North America and Europe. Total training systems are used including the company's 200 simulators and training devices, computer-based training, and professional instructors. Founded in 1951. **Positions advertised include:** Pilot Simulator Instructor; Flight Engineer Instructor. **Corporate headquarters location:** This location. **Other U.S. locations:** Nationwide. **International locations:** Canada; France; United Kingdom. **Subsidiaries include:** FlightSafety Boeing Training International; MarineSafety International. **Parent company:** Berkshire Hathaway (Omaha NE). **Number of employees worldwide:** 2,000.

FORDHAM UNIVERSITY
441 East Fordham Road, Bronx NY 10458. 718/817-1000. **Contact:** Human Resources Department. **E-mail address:** hr@fordham.edu. **World Wide Web address:** http://www.fordham.edu. **Description:** A private, Jesuit university offering bachelor's and master's degrees from three campuses and 11 schools. **Positions advertised include:** Public Affairs Assistant; Assistant Director of Student Financial Services; Media Relations Specialist; Custodial Services Supervisor; Security Duty Supervisor; Resident Director; Wellness Center Coordinator. **Special programs:** Internships.

HOFSTRA UNIVERSITY
205 Hofstra University, Human Resources Center, Hempstead NY 11549-1000. 516/463-6060. **Contact:** Human Resources Department. **World Wide Web address:** http://www.hofstra.edu. **Description:** A private, four-year university offering both undergraduate and graduate degree programs. The university enrolls over 12,800 students. **Positions advertised include:** Financial Aid Counselor; Assistant Cheerleading Coach; Assistant Director for the Annual Fund; Manager of Telecommunications; Director of Financial Aid.

HUNTER COLLEGE
THE CITY UNIVERSITY OF NEW YORK (CUNY)
695 Park Avenue, East Building, 1502, New York NY 10021. 212/772-4451. **Fax:** 212/650-3889. **Contact:** Robert McGarry, Director of Human Resources. **E-mail address:** jobs@hccs.hunter.cuny.edu. **World Wide Web address:** http://www.hunter.cuny.edu. **Description:** One of the largest coeducational colleges of CUNY. Hunter College offers undergraduate and graduate programs in arts and sciences, education, health sciences, nursing, and social work. Founded in 1870. **NOTE:** Resumes can be mailed to 71 East 94th Street, New York NY 10128. **Positions advertised include:** Associate Nursing Professor; Associate Special Education Professor; Associate Education Professor; Head Librarian. **Other area locations:** Bronx NY; Brooklyn NY; Flushing NY; Jamaica NY; Staten Island NY.

IONA COLLEGE
715 North Avenue, New Rochelle NY 10801. 914/633-2000. **Contact:** Rosemary Bartolomeo, Manager of

Employment. **E-mail address:** rbartolomeo@iona.edu. **World Wide Web address:** http://www.iona.edu. **Description:** A four-year Catholic college offering bachelor's and master's degree programs. Founded in 1940. **NOTE:** Employment Manager phone: 914/633-2496, fax: 914/637-7732. Faculty applicants should contact the Dean's Office in the School of Arts & Sciences or the Hagan School of Business. **Positions advertised include:** Facilities Custodian; Library Document Delivery Assistant; Career Services Associate Director; Business School Academic Advisor; Director of Libraries.

ITHACA COLLEGE
240 Job Hall, Ithaca NY 14850-7018. 607/274-1207. **Contact:** Martha Turnbull, Director of Human Resources. **E-mail address:** employment@ithaca.edu. **World Wide Web address:** http://www.ithaca.edu. **Description:** A four-year liberal arts college specializing in physical therapy and communications programs. Approximately 5,000 students are enrolled at Ithaca college. **NOTE:** Human Resources phone: 607/274-3245. **Positions advertised include:** Anthropology Lecturer; Art Lecturer; Art History Lecturer; Biology Lecturer; Economics Lecturer; English Lecturer; History Lecturer; Math & Computer Science Lecturer; Philosophy & Religion Lecturer; Physics Lecturer. **Number of employees:** 1,300.

JOHN JAY COLLEGE OF CRIMINAL JUSTICE THE CITY UNIVERSITY OF NEW YORK (CUNY)
899 Tenth Avenue, New York NY 10019. 212/237-8000. **Contact:** Donald J. Gray, Director of Human Resources Department. **E-mail address:** dgray@jjay.cuny.edu. **World Wide Web address:** http://www.jjay.cuny.edu. **Description:** A college with undergraduate and graduate programs of study concentrating in criminal justice. **Positions advertised include:** Assistant Organic Chemistry Professor; Associate African-American Studies Professor.

KATHARINE GIBBS SCHOOLS INC.
50 West 40th Street, 1st Floor, New York NY 10018. 212/867-9300. **Contact:** President. **World Wide Web address:** http://www.katharinegibbs.com. **Description:** One of the nation's foremost business instruction schools. **Corporate headquarters location:** Piscataway NJ. **Other U.S. locations:** MA; CT; PA; RI; VA.

LE MOYNE COLLEGE
1419 Salt Springs Road, Grewen Hall, Room 209-E, Syracuse NY 13214. 315/445-4155. **Fax:** 315/445-6023. **Contact:** Human Resources. **E-mail address:** lemoynehr@lemoyne.edu. **World Wide Web address:** http://www.lemoyne.edu. **Description:** A four-year, co-ed, Jesuit college. Le Moyne offers bachelor of arts and bachelor of science undergraduate degrees in approximately 30 majors. Graduate programs include master's degrees in business administration and education. **Positions advertised include:** Coordinator of Housing; Residential Director; Graduate Student Residential Hall Director; Associate Professor for Special Education; Education Department Chairperson; Physician Assistant Program Director.

LEHMAN COLLEGE THE CITY UNIVERSITY OF NEW YORK (CUNY)
250 Bedford Park Boulevard West, Shuster Hall, Room 230, Bronx NY 10468. 718/960-8181. **Contact:** Personnel Office. **World Wide Web address:** http://www.lehman.cuny.edu. **Description:** A public coeducational liberal arts college offering over 90 undergraduate and graduate programs. **NOTE:** Personnel phone: 718/960-8181.

LONG ISLAND UNIVERSITY
C.W. Post Campus, 720 Northern Boulevard, Brookville NY 11548-1300. 516/299-2000. **Contact:** Human Resources. **World Wide Web address:** http://www.liunet.edu. **Description:** A university offering undergraduate and graduate programs of study. The university's programs of study are offered through its six schools: College of Liberal Arts & Sciences; School of Education; College of Management; School of Health Professions; School of Visual & Performing Arts; and the Palmer School of Library & Information Sciences. **Positions advertised include:** Assistant Mathematics Professor. **Special programs:** Internships. **Corporate headquarters location:** This location. **Other area locations:** Brentwood NY; Brooklyn NY; Greenvale NY; Southampton NY. **Operations at this facility include:** Administration. **Number of employees:** 4,328.

MARIST COLLEGE
3399 North Road, 120 Donelly Hall, Poughkeepsie NY 12601-1387. 845/575-3349. **Fax:** 845/575-3348. **Contact:** Bruce Wagner, Assistant Vice President. **E-mail address:** human.resources@marist.edu. **World Wide Web address:** http://www.marist.edu. **Description:** A liberal arts college with an enrollment of 3,300 undergraduate and 600 graduate students. Marist College offers a variety of academic programs including business management, communication, computer science and information systems, behavioral sciences, science, and the humanities. **Positions advertised include:** Emerging Technology Adjunct Instructor; First Year Programs Director; Judicial Affairs Director; Organizational Leadership & Communication Program Director; Teacher Education Director; Alumni Relations Executive Director; Network Security Support Analyst; Programmer; Information Technology Analyst.

MERCY COLLEGE
Verrazzano Hall, 555 Broadway, Dobbs Ferry NY 10522. 914/674-7318. **Fax:** 914/674-7578. **Contact:** Theresa Morgan, Human Resources Director. **E-mail address:** hr@mercy.edu. **World Wide Web address:** http://www.mercy.edu. **Description:** A private commuter college offering a wide range of undergraduate, graduate, associate, and certificate programs. **Other area locations:** Bronx NY; Manhattan NY; White Plains NY; Yorktown Heights NY.

MOHAWK VALLEY COMMUNITY COLLEGE
1101 Sherman Drive, Utica NY 13501-5394. 315/792-5636. **Fax:** 315/731-5858. **Contact:** Jerome Brown, Dean of Human Resources. **E-mail address:** humanresources@mvcc.edu. **World Wide Web address:** http://www.mvcc.edu. **Description:** A two-year community college with an enrollment of approximately 6,500 full- and part-time students. Certificates and degrees offered include accounting, banking and insurance, chef training, chemical technology, criminal justice, drafting technology, engineering drawing, food service, graphic arts, human services, international studies, media marketing and management, photography, and respiratory care. Founded in 1946.

MOUNT ST. MARY COLLEGE
330 Powell Avenue, Newburgh NY 12550. 845/561-0800. **Contact:** Human Resources. **World Wide Web address:** http://www.msmc.edu. **Description:** A Judeo-Christian liberal arts college. Mount St. Mary College is an independent and coeducational institution with approximately 1,800 students. Founded in 1960.

NASSAU COMMUNITY COLLEGE
One Education Drive, 8th Floor, Room 820,, Garden City NY 11530. 516/572-7211. **Contact:** Beverly Harrison, Associate Vice President Human Resources. **E-mail address:** harrisb@ncc.edu. **World Wide Web address:** http://www.sunynassau.edu. **Description:** A two-year college that is part of the State University of New York educational system. **Special programs:** Internships. **Number of employees at this location:** 2,500.

NAZARETH COLLEGE OF ROCHESTER
4245 East Avenue, Smith Hall, Room 183, Rochester NY 14618. 585/389-2065. **Fax:** 585/389-2063. **Contact:** Carol O'Neill, Director of Personnel. **E-mail**

address: humanresources@naz.edu. **World Wide Web address:** http://www.naz.edu. **Description:** A four-year college that offers undergraduate and graduate programs in a wide variety of disciplines. Founded in 1924. **NOTE:** Entry-level positions and part-time jobs are offered. For faculty positions contact Dr. Dennis Silva, Vice President for Academic Affairs, or the appropriate search committee member. **Positions advertised include:** Vice President for Finance and Treasurer; Gift Processing Coordinator; Protestant Chaplain; Coordinator of Partners for Learning; Assistant Men's Lacrosse Coach. **Special programs:** Internships. **Number of employees at this location:** 300.

NEW YORK INSTITUTE OF TECHNOLOGY
P.O. Box 8000, Old Westbury NY 11568-8000. 516/686-7667. **Fax:** 516/686-7929. **Contact:** Human Resources. **E-mail address:** humanresources@nyit.edu. **World Wide Web address:** http://www.nyit.edu. **Description:** A technical university offering associate, bachelor's, and master's degree programs in health and life sciences, architecture, arts/sciences, education, technology, and management. **Positions advertised include:** Senior Technician; Assistant to the Dean; Office Assistant; Refund Coordinator; Cleaner; Assistant Fine Arts Professor; Academic Clinical Coordinator; Director of Major Gifts; Associate Director of Admissions and Operations; Associate Registrar; Dean of Students.

NEW YORK UNIVERSITY
7 East 12th Street, Main Floor, New York NY 10003-4475. 212/998-1250. **Fax:** 212/995-4229. **Contact:** Personnel Department. **E-mail address:** empinfo@nyu.edu. **World Wide Web address:** http://www.nyu.edu/hr. **Description:** A state university. **NOTE:** Interested job seekers may apply online. The University no longer accepts faxed or e-mailed resumes. **Positions advertised include:** Math Department Manager; Associate Director of Career Counseling and Placement; Chief Information Officer.

PACE UNIVERSITY
One Pace Plaza, New York NY 10038-1598. 212/346-1200. **Contact:** Human Resources. **World Wide Web address:** http://www.pace.edu. **Description:** A university with three campus locations and an enrollment of nearly 14,000 students. Founded in 1906. **Positions advertised include:** Secretary; Administrative Assistant; Admissions Recruiter; Evening Program Coordinator; Assistant Vice-President of Marketing and Communications; Tutor; International Student Advisor; Coordinator of Support Services for Online Teaching and Learning; Courseware Designer; Director of Funded Research Administration; Assistant Dean of Students. **Other area locations:** Pleasantville NY; White Plains NY.

QUEENS COLLEGE
THE CITY UNIVERSITY OF NEW YORK (CUNY)
65-30 Kissena Boulevard, Flushing NY 11367-1597. 718/997-4455. **Fax:** 718/997-5799. **Contact:** Human Resources Department. **World Wide Web address:** http://www.qc.edu. **Description:** A liberal arts commuter college. Founded in 1937. **Special programs:** Tuition Assistance Program.

RENSSELAER POLYTECHNIC INSTITUTE (RPI)
110 8th Street, Troy NY 12180-3590. 518/276-6302. **Fax:** 518/276-6370. **Contact:** Human Resources Department. **E-mail address:** jobs@rpi.edu. **World Wide Web address:** http://www.rpi.edu. **Description:** A private, four-year research university specializing in science and technology. **NOTE:** Interested job seekers may apply online. **Positions advertised include:** Materials Science and Engineering Assistant; Assistant Dean; Assistant Director of Research and Assessment; Assistant Director of Financial Aid, Student Records, and Financial Services. **Number of employees at this location:** 1,700.

ROCHESTER INSTITUTE OF TECHNOLOGY
8 Lomb Memorial Drive, Rochester NY 14623-5604. 716/475-2424. **Fax:** 585/475-7170. **Recorded jobline:** 585/475-7095. **Contact:** Department of Human Resources. **E-mail address:** resumes@rit.edu. **World Wide Web address:** http://www.rit.edu. **Description:** A four-year technical institute offering bachelor's and master's degrees, as well as Ph.D.s in imaging science. **Positions advertised include:** Assistant Engineering Professor; Director of North Star Center; C-Print Captionist; College of Applied Science and Technology Chairperson. **Special programs:** Internships.

ST. JOHN'S UNIVERSITY
8000 Utopia Parkway, Queens NY 11439. 718/990-2787. **Fax:** 719/990-5887. **Contact:** Human Resources. **E-mail address:** employment@stjohns.edu. **World Wide Web address:** http://www.stjohns.edu. **Description:** A private, four-year university. St. John's University offers bachelor's and master's degrees. Founded in 1870.

SARAH LAWRENCE COLLEGE
One Mead Way, Bronxville NY 10708. 914/395-2315. **Fax:** 914/395-2669. **Contact:** Human Resources. **E-mail address:** admin@slc.edu. **World Wide Web address:** http://www.slc.edu. **Description:** Sarah Lawrence College is a four-year, liberal arts college that emphasizes independent study through undergraduate and graduate programs. Founded in 1926. **Positions advertised include:** Assistant to the Dean of Graduate Studies; Center for Continuing Education Director; Planned Giving Officer; Cognitive Developmental Psychology Professor; Digital Imaging Faculty Member; Director of the Theatre Program; Islamic Studies Professor; Painting Instructor.

SIENA COLLEGE
515 Loudon Road, Loudonville NY 12211-1462. 518/783-2420. **Contact:** Human Resources. **E-mail address:** humanresources@siena.edu. **World Wide Web address:** http://www.siena.edu. **Description:** A private, co-ed, four-year, liberal arts university. Siena offers several undergraduate degrees in arts, sciences, and business, as well as an MBA in Accounting. **Positions advertised include:** Criminology Professor; Assistant Spanish Professor; Assistant Professor of Marketing and Management; Journalism Faculty Member; Assistant Director of Development.

SKIDMORE COLLEGE
815 North Broadway, Saratoga Springs NY 12866-1632. 518/580-5800. **Fax:** 518/580-5805. **Contact:** Human Resources. **E-mail address:** jobs@skidmore.edu. **World Wide Web address:** http://www.skidmore.edu. **Description:** A private, four-year liberal arts college that offers both bachelor's and master's degrees. Founded in 1903. **Positions advertised include:** Director of Multicultural Student Affairs; Community Coordinator; Visiting Assistant Professor; Postdoctoral Fellow; Teaching Associate; Biology Instructor; History Lecturer; Trustee Visiting Scholar; Assistant Professor of Philosophy; Head Women's Soccer Coach.

STATE UNIVERSITY OF NEW YORK
1215 Western Avenue, UAB Room 300, Albany NY 12222. 518/437-4700. **Fax:** 518/437-4731. **Contact:** Human Resources. **World Wide Web address:** http://www.albany.edu. **Description:** A four-year university, offering a bachelor of arts degree, a bachelor of science degree, as well as master's and doctoral programs. Enrollment is approximately 12,000 undergraduate and 5,000 graduate students. **Other area locations:** Brockport NY; Cortland NY; Fredonia NY; Geneseo NY; New Paltz NY; Oswego NY; Stony Brook NY.

STATE UNIVERSITY OF NEW YORK COLLEGE OF ENVIRONMENTAL SCIENCE AND FORESTRY
One Forestry Drive, 217 Bray Hall, Syracuse NY 13210. 315/470-6611. **Contact:** Elaine Irvin, Personnel Department Manager. **World Wide Web address:**

http://www.esf.edu. **Description:** One of 13 four-year colleges in the SUNY system with an enrollment of approximately 1,800 students. The college offers the following areas of study: engineering, forest resources, chemistry, environmental and forest biology, environmental studies, environmental science, forest engineering, forestry, landscape architecture, and wood products engineering. Founded in 1911.

SYRACUSE UNIVERSITY
Skytop Office Building, Syracuse NY 13244. 315/443-4042. **Contact:** Human Resources. **World Wide Web address:** http://www.syr.edu. **Description:** A university with an enrollment of approximately 12,000 undergraduate and 5,000 graduate students. Syracuse University offers bachelor's and master's degrees, J.D.s, and Ph.D.s.

TASA (TOUCHSTONE APPLIED SCIENCE ASSOCIATES, INC.)
4 Hardscrabble Heights, P.O. Box 382, Brewster NY 10509-0382. 845/277-8100. **Fax:** 845/277-8115. **Contact:** Human Resources. **E-mail address:** tasa@tasa.com. **World Wide Web address:** http://www.tasa.com. **Description:** TASA designs, develops, publishes, and distributes educational tests, instructional materials, and microcomputer software to elementary and secondary schools, colleges, and universities. The educational tests, known as Primary, Standard, and Advanced Degrees of Reading Power tests and Degrees of Word Meaning tests, are components on the company's Degrees of Literacy Power program. **Corporate headquarters location:** This location.

UNION COLLEGE
807 Union Street, Schenectady NY 12308. 518/388-6108. **Contact:** Human Resources. **World Wide Web address:** http://www.union.edu. **Description:** An independent, four-year liberal arts college with an engineering program. Founded in 1795.

UNIVERSITY OF ROCHESTER
601 Elmwood Avenue, Rochester NY 14627. 585/275-2815. **Contact:** Human Resources. **World Wide Web address:** http://www.rochester.edu. **Description:** A private, coeducational university offering bachelor's, master's, and doctoral degree programs. Founded in 1850. **NOTE:** Interested jobseekers should send resumes to Employment Center, 1325 Mount Hope Avenue, Suite 202, Rochester NY 14620.

UTICA COLLEGE OF SYRACUSE UNIVERSITY
1600 Burrstone Road, Utica NY 13502. 315/792-3276. **Fax:** 315/792-3386. **Contact:** Human Resources. **E-mail address:** hr@utica.edu. **World Wide Web address:** http://www.utica.edu. **Description:** A four-year, undergraduate, liberal arts college. Utica College of Syracuse University offers 35 majors.

VASSAR COLLEGE
124 Raymond Avenue, Poughkeepsie NY 12604. 845/437-5820. **Fax:** 845/437-7729. **Contact:** Human Resources. **E-mail address:** careers@vassar.edu. **World Wide Web address:** http://www.vassar.edu. **Description:** Vassar College is a four-year undergraduate college focusing on the liberal arts. Student enrollment is approximately 2,250. Founded in 1860. **Number of employees at this location:** 1,000.

WATERTOWN CITY SCHOOL DISTRICT
376 Butterfield Avenue, Watertown NY 13601. 315/785-3700. **Contact:** Director of Personnel. **World Wide Web address:** http://www.watertowncsd.org. **Description:** Provides educational services that serve Jefferson County. Schooling ranges from elementary schools to high schools. **Number of employees at this location:** 630.

North Carolina

APPALACHIAN STATE UNIVERSITY
504 Dauph Blan Street, Founder's Hall, First Floor, Boone NC 28608. 828/262-3186. **Fax:** 828/262-6489. **Recorded jobline:** 828/262-6488. **Contact:** Human Resources. **World Wide Web address:** http://www.appstate.edu. **Description:** A four-year state university. **NOTE:** An application form is required. **Positions advertised include:** Student Center Technical Director; Sales Manager; Chairperson, Various Departments; Assistant Professor, Various Departments; Dean, College of Arts and Sciences; GIS Lab Supervisor; Adjunct Faculty, Various Departments; Collection Development Librarian. **Special programs:** Internships. **Number of employees at this location:** 2,034.

ASHEBORO CITY SCHOOLS
P.O. Box 1103, Asheboro NC 27204-1103. 336/625-5104. **Physical address:** 1126 South Park Street, Asheboro NC 27203. **Fax:** 336/625-9238. **Contact:** Timothy Allgood, Assistant Superintendent of Human Resources Department. **E-mail address:** tallgood@asheboro.k12.nc.us. **World Wide Web address:** http://www.asheboro.k12.nc.us. **Description:** Operates the public school system in Asheboro for students in kindergarten through grade 12. The curriculum includes both a vocational and college preparatory program. **NOTE:** Entry-level positions are offered. **Positions advertised include:** Custodian; Teacher Assistant; Bus Driver; Occupational Therapist; School Psychologist; Speech/Language Pathologist; Pre-Kindergarten Teacher; ESL Teacher; Technology Education Teacher; Elementary Teacher; Media Personnel. **Number of employees at this location:** 592.

BREVARD COLLEGE
400 North Broad Street, Brevard NC 28712. 828/883-8292. **Fax:** 828/884-3790. **Contact:** Employment. **World Wide Web address:** http://www.brevard.edu. **Description:** A four-year liberal arts college with an enrollment of 650 students. Founded 1853. **Positions advertised include:** Director of the Center for Career, Service, and Learning; Director of Student Activities; Director of First Year Programs; Admissions Counselor; Director of the Academic Enrichment Center; Head Women's Soccer Coach; Assistant Professor; Athletic Director.

CHARLOTTE-MECKLENBURG SCHOOL SYSTEM
P.O. Box 30035, Charlotte NC 28230-0035. 980/343-7132. **Physical address:** 701 East Second Street, Charlotte NC 28202. **Fax:** 704/343-3124. **Recorded jobline:** 980/343-5384. **Contact:** John Brady, Director of Employment. **E-mail address:** hr@cms.k12.nc.us. **World Wide Web address:** http://www.cms.k12.nc.us. **Description:** Administrative offices of the public school system. **Positions advertised include:** Bus Driver; ASEP Associate; Site Coordinator; Science/Chemistry Teacher; Office Coordinator; Preschool Psychologist; Administrative Secretary; HVAC Mechanic; Grounds Worker; ISS Assistant; Early Reading First Coach; Custodian; Administrative Student Intervention Assistant; Bilingual Resource Assistant; Senior Administrative Secretary; Band Teacher; Keyboarding Teacher; Business Analyst; Technician; Talent Development Compliance Teacher. **Corporate headquarters location:** This location.

DAVIDSON COLLEGE
431 Concord Road, #11 Jackson Court, Box 7163, Davidson NC 28035-7163. 704/894-2212. **Fax:** 704/894-2638. **Recorded jobline:** 704/894-2693. **Contact:** Human Resources. **E-mail address:** jobs@davidson.edu. **World Wide Web address:** http://www2.davidson.edu. **Description:** An independent liberal arts college enrolling more than 1,500 students. Founded 1837. **Positions advertised include:** Assistant Professor, Biology; ITS Widows System Administrator; Prospect Researcher.

DUKE UNIVERSITY
P.O. Box 90496 Durham NC 27708. 919/684-5600. **Physical address:** 705 Broad Street, Durham NC 27705. **Contact:** Human Resources Center. **Fax:** 919/668-0386. **E-mail address:** hr@mc.duke.edu. **World Wide Web address:** http://www.duke.edu.

Description: A research university operating four campuses. Duke enrolls 5,300 undergraduates in its Trinity College of Arts and Sciences; 1,000 students in its School of Engineering; and 4,500 graduate and professional students in a variety of other programs. The university also operates the Duke University Art Museum, the Duke University Marine Laboratory, and the Duke Primate Center. Duke University Community Service Center (CSC) provides support to various groups including the Duke Cancer Patient Support Group and the Durham County Youth Home. Founded in 1892. **Positions advertised include:** Associate Dean of External Affairs; Musician; Administrative Secretary; Utility Worker; Research and Development Engineer; Departmental Business Manager; Veterinary Technician; General Maintenance Mechanic.

DURHAM PUBLIC SCHOOLS
511 Cleveland Street, P.O. Box 30002, Durham NC 27701. 919/560-2548. **Fax:** 919/560-3625. **Contact:** Human Resources. **World Wide Web address:** http://www.dpsnc.net. **Description:** Operators of the public schools in Durham. **Positions advertised include:** Child Nutrition Assistant; School Bus Driver; Lead Translator; Painter; Elementary Literacy Specialist; Energy Management Coordinator; Group Leader, Various Schools; Assistant Manager, Before School Care; Internal Control and Risk Manager; Heavy Equipment Operator; Electrician; Computer Programmer; Preschool Facilitator; Plumber; Wellness Specialist; Coordinator of Arts Education.

EAST CAROLINA UNIVERSITY
210 East 1st Street, Greenville NC 27858-4353. 252/328-6352. **Fax:** 252/328-4191. **Contact:** Human Resources. **World Wide Web address:** http://www.ecu.edu. **Description:** A university offering undergraduate, graduate, and medical programs. **Positions advertised include:** Administrative Assistant; Office Assistant; Accounting Clerk; Clinical Pharmacist; ECU Staff Nurse; Nursing Assistant; Research Technician; Facility Architect; Enrollment Services Officer; Electronics Technician; Laboratories Mechanic; Housekeeper; Computing Consultant; Research Assistant; Assistant Professor, Various Departments; Student Employment Administrator; Faculty Position, Various Departments. **Corporate headquarters location:** This location.

FORSYTH TECHNICAL COMMUNITY COLLEGE
2100 Silas Creek Parkway, Winston-Salem NC 27103-5197. 336/734-7246. **Fax:** 336/761-2309. **Contact:** Gregory M. Chase, Director of Human Resources. **World Wide Web address:** http://www.forsyth.tec.nc.us. **Description:** A community college with five office locations in Winston-Salem, and campuses in Kernersville NC and Danbury NC. **NOTE:** Faxed and e-mailed applications are no longer accepted. Job seekers must apply online. **Positions advertised include:** Program Coordinator, Emergency Medical Science; Program Coordinator BLET & Instructor of Criminal Justice; Dean of Business Information Technologies. **Number of employees at this location:** 310.

MEREDITH COLLEGE
3800 Hillsborough Street, Johnson Hall, 3rd Floor, Raleigh NC 27607. 919/760-8898. **Fax:** 919/760-8164. **Contact:** Pamela Davis, Director of Human Resources. **E-mail address:** davispam@meredith.edu. **World Wide Web address:** http://www.meredith.edu. **Description:** As the largest private women's college in the southeast, Meredith offers undergraduate students more than 35 majors. **Positions advertised include:** Director of Financial Assistance; French Instructor; Latin Instructor; Assistant Director of the Learning Center; Director of Human Resources; Italian Instructor; Spanish Instructor.

NORTH CAROLINA AGRICULTURAL & TECHNICAL STATE UNIVERSITY
1601 East Market Street, Greensboro NC 27411. 336/334-7862. **Fax:** 336/334-7477. **Recorded jobline:** 336/334-7292. **Contact:** Personnel. **World Wide Web address:** http://www.ncat.edu. **Description:** A state university offering graduate and undergraduate programs in agriculture, business, engineering, and other disciplines. **NOTE:** Applicants must complete a North Carolina State Government Application for Employment, available at http://www.osp.state.nc.us/jobs/gnrlinfo.htm#app. Mail applications to 1020 East Wendover Avenue, Greensboro NC 27411. **Positions advertised include:** Director of Development for Athletics; Professor, Various Departments; Tenure Tract Position, Various Departments; University Physician; Assistant/Associate Professor, Various Departments; Staff Psychiatrist. **Corporate headquarters location:** This location.

NORTH CAROLINA CENTRAL UNIVERSITY
1801 Fayetteville Street, 12 William Jones Building, Durham NC 27707. 919/530-6334. **Fax:** 919/530-6670. **Contact:** Audrey L. Crawford-Turner, Associate Vice Chair of Human Resources. **E-mail address:** acturner@nccu.edu. **World Wide Web address:** http://www.nccu.edu. **Description:** A university offering graduate and undergraduate programs in business, education, law, library science, and other disciplines. **Positions advertised include:** Administrative Officer; Attorney; Official Court Reporter; Reimbursement Officer.

NORTH CAROLINA SCHOOL OF THE ARTS
1533 South Main Street, Administrative Building Room 105, P.O. Box 12189, Winston-Salem NC 27117-2189. 336/770-1428. **Fax:** 336/770-1462. **Contact:** Earla Burren, Human Resources Coordinator. **E-mail address:** burrene@ncarts.edu. **World Wide Web address:** http://www.ncarts.edu. **Description:** A college offering specialized programs in the fine arts, including dance, drama, filmmaking, music, design and production, and visual arts. **Positions advertised include:** Program Assistant; Assistant Manager of Fitness Center; Faculty, Various Departments; Vice Chancellor of Development and Public Relations; Dean of School of Music. **Number of employees at this location:** 500.

NORTH CAROLINA STATE UNIVERSITY
2711 Sullivan Drive, Box 7210, Raleigh NC 27695-7210. 919/515-4424. **Fax:** 919/515-7543. **Contact:** Rick Williams, Employment Manager. **E-mail address:** rick.williams@ncsu.edu. **World Wide Web address:** http://www.ncstate.edu. **Description:** A state university offering graduate and undergraduate programs in agriculture, design, engineering, and other disciplines. **Positions advertised include:** Associate Dean for Academic Affairs and Interdisciplinary Program; Associate General Counsel; Director of Centennial Campus Development; Executive Director of Development; Career Counselor; Costume Designer; Director of Software Systems; Grant Proposal Developer; Research Assistant; Assistant Professor, Various Departments; Lecturer, Various Departments; Housekeeper; Accountant; Groundskeeper; Laboratory Mechanic; Veterinary Technician. **Number of employees at this location:** 7,000.

OMEGA PERFORMANCE INC.
8701 Red Oak Boulevard, Suite 450, Charlotte NC 28217-3972. 704/672-1400. **Fax:** 704/672-1417. **Contact:** Vice President of Human Resources. **E-mail address:** abury@omega-performance.com. **World Wide Web address:** http://www.omega-performance.com. **Description:** Trains personnel in financial services, telecommunications, transportation, and other industries using interactive, multimedia teaching methods along with traditional classroom instruction. **Positions advertised include:** Product Development/Instructional Designer; Executive Consultant; Regional Sales Manager; Account Manager; Relationship Manager. **Corporate headquarters location:** This location. **International locations:** Sydney, Australia; Toronto, Canada; London, England; Wellington, New Zealand; Singapore.

SALEM COLLEGE
SALEM ACADEMY
P.O. Box 10548, Winston-Salem NC 27108-0548. 336/721-2600. **Physical address:** 601 South Church Street, Main Hall, Winston-Salem NC 27101. **Fax:** 336/721-2785. **Recorded jobline:** 336/917-5522. **Contact:** Human Resources. **World Wide Web address:** http://www.salem.edu. **Description:** A women's liberal arts college offering both undergraduate and graduate programs of study. Salem Academy (also at this location) is a private, college preparatory boarding and day school for girls in grades 9 through 12. **Positions advertised include:** Assistant Dean of Continuing Studies; Faculty, Various Departments. **Operations at this facility include:** Administration; Service. **Listed on:** Privately held.

UNIVERSITY OF NORTH CAROLINA AT CHAPEL HILL
104 Airport Road, Suite 1200, Campus Box 1040, Chapel Hill NC 27599-1045. 919/843-2300. **Fax:** 919/962-5926. **Contact:** Human Resources. **E-mail address:** employment@unc.edu. **World Wide Web address:** http://www.unc.edu. **Description:** A campus of the state university which offers graduate and undergraduate programs in education, dentistry, law, public health, journalism, nursing, and other disciplines. **Positions advertised include:** Dean, Various Schools/Departments; Vice Chancellor of Student Affairs; University Librarian; Professor, Various Departments; Assistant Professor, Various Departments; Tenure-track Faculty, Various Departments; Clinical Instructor. **Number of employees at this location:** 8,000.

UNIVERSITY OF NORTH CAROLINA AT CHARLOTTE
9201 University City Boulevard, King Building, Room 222, Charlotte NC 28223. 704/687-2276. **Fax:** 704/687-3239. **Contact:** Human Resources. **E-mail address:** employment@email.uncc.edu. **World Wide Web address:** http://www.uncc.edu. **Description:** A campus of the state university. The university has an enrollment of approximately 15,600 students. **Positions advertised include:** Faculty Engineering Specialist; Director of Purchasing; Manuscript Librarian; Senior Program Manager. **Number of employees at this location:** 2,500.

UNIVERSITY OF NORTH CAROLINA AT WILMINGTON
601 South College Road, Wilmington NC 28403-5960. 910/962-3160. **Physical address:** 5051 New Centre Drive, Suite 200, Wilmington NC 28403. **Fax:** 910/962-3840. **Recorded jobline:** 910/962-3791. **Contact:** Janice Dickey, Employment Assistant. **E-mail address:** hrsearch@uncw.edu. **World Wide Web address:** http://www.uncwil.edu. **Description:** A campus of the state university enrolling approximately 9,200 students. **Positions advertised include:** Dean of the College of Arts and Sciences; Art Historian; Director of Student Life Assessment.

WATTS NURSING SCHOOL
3643 North Roxboro Road, Durham NC 27704. 919/470-7348. **Contact:** Human Resources. **E-mail address:** wattsson@mc.duke.edu. **World Wide Web address:** http://www.wattsschoolofnursing.org. **Description:** The oldest nursing school in North Carolina. **Parent company:** Duke University Health System.

WAYNE COUNTY PUBLIC SCHOOLS
2001 East Royall Avenue, P.O. Drawer 1797, Goldsboro NC 27533-1797. 919/705-6179. **Contact:** Human Resources. **E-mail address:** ecromartie@wcps.org. **World Wide Web address:** http://www.waynecountyschools.org. **Description:** Offices of the Wayne County public school district. **Positions advertised include:** Director of Summer Focus Intervention Program.

WELDON CITY SCHOOL DISTRICT
301 Mulberry Street, Weldon NC 27890. 252/536-4821. **Fax:** 252/538-4247. **Contact:** Executive Director of Human Resources. **E-mail address:** edwardsk@weldoncityschools.k12.nc.us. **World Wide Web address:** http://www.weldoncityschools.k12.nc.us. **Description:** Operates the public schools of Weldon. **Special programs:** Training. **Number of employees at this location:** 225.

WESTERN CAROLINA UNIVERSITY
220 HFR Administration, Western Carolina University, Cullowhee NC 28723. 828/227-7218. **Fax:** 828/227-7007. **Contact:** Human Resources. **E-mail address:** hr@email.wcu.edu. **World Wide Web address:** http://www.wcu.edu. **Description:** A university offering programs in business, education, and other disciplines. **Positions advertised include:** Assistant Professor, Various Departments; Assistant Women's Basketball Coach; Director of Enrollment Support; Professor, Various Departments.

North Dakota

DICKINSON STATE UNIVERSITY
291 Campus Drive, Dickinson ND 58601-4896. 701/483-2507. **Toll-free phone:** 800/279-HAWK. **Fax:** 701/483-2177. **Contact:** Gail Ebeltoft, Personnel Services. **World Wide Web address:** http://www.dsu.nodak.edu. **Description:** A public liberal arts university with approximately 1,600 students and over 80 faculty members, which offers a wide range of baccalaureate, associate, and certificate programs. **Positions advertised include:** University Bookstore Assistant; Accounting Faculty Member.

FARGO PUBLIC SCHOOLS
415 North 4th Street, Fargo ND 58102. 701/446-1037. **Fax:** 701/446-1201. **Recorded jobline:** 701/446-1099. **Contact:** Becky Ganze, Human Resources. **World Wide Web address:** http://www.fargo.k12.nd.us. **Description:** Administrative offices for the Fargo public school district. The district includes two high schools, an alternative community high school, three middle schools, thirteen elementary schools, one kindergarten center, and the Trollwood Performing Arts School. **NOTE**: Search posted openings and apply online. **Positions advertised include:** Special Education Paraprofessional; Trollwood Program Coordinator; Substitute Teacher.

MINOT STATE UNIVERSITY
500 University Avenue West, Minot ND 58707. 701/858-3361. **Toll-free phone:** 800/777-0750. **Fax:** 701/858-3396. **Contact:** Ron Rogelstad, Human Resources. **E-mail address:** msujobs@minotstateu.edu. **World Wide Web address:** http://www.minotstateu.edu. **Description:** A small university comprised of four undergraduate colleges, including a College of Arts and Sciences, of Business, of Education and Health Services, and a graduate school. Minot State offers over forty majors, fourteen master's degrees, and several pre-professional programs. **NOTE:** Resumes can be sent to MSU Career Services Office; Second Floor, Student Union. **Office Hours:** Monday – Friday, 8:00 a.m. – 4:30 p.m. **Positions advertised include:** Small Business Development Region Director; Small Business Development Center Consultant; Scheduling Coordinator; Dean of the College of Education and Health Sciences. **Number of employees at this location:** 850.

NORTH DAKOTA STATE UNIVERSITY
P.O. Box 5345 – University Station, Old Main Room 205, Fargo ND 58105. 701/231-8525. **Toll-free phone:** 800/366-6888. **Fax:** 710/231-9686. **Contact:** Colette Erickson, Assistant Director of Personnel. **E-mail address:** colette.hr@ndsu.nodak.edu. **World Wide Web address:** http://www.ndsu.nodak.edu. **Description:** A four-year state university offering undergraduate and graduate degree programs. **NOTE:** NSDU lists its open faculty positions and professional staff positions at Higher Education Jobs Online: http://www.higherjobs.com. **Positions advertised include:** Microbiologist; Research Specialist; Ruminant Nutrition Technician; Hall Director; Sign Language

Interpreter; Director of Student Financial Services; Head Soccer Coach; Head Football Coach. **Number of employees at this location:** 2,000.

UNIVERSITY OF NORTH DAKOTA (UND)
Box 8010, Grand Forks ND 58202. 701/777-4361. **Fax:** 701/777-4857. **Recorded jobline:** 701/777-6200. **Contact:** Diane Nelson, Personnel Director. **E-mail address:** human.resources@mail.und.nodak.edu. **World Wide Web address:** http://www.und.edu. **Description:** A liberal arts University offering 150 programs of graduate and undergraduate study, including special programs in humanities, integrated studies, honors, and cooperative education. Founded in 1883. **NOTE**: Search posted openings and apply online. Completed application card required. **Positions advertised include:** Project Coordinator; Assistant Athletic Director; Staff Psychologist; Research Scientist/Engineer; Administrative Assistant; Building Services Technician. **University President:** Dr. Charles E. Kupchella.

WILLISTON STATE COLLEGE
P.O. Box 1326, Williston ND 58802. 701/774-4200, ext.: 4240. **Physical address:** 1410 University Ave, Williston ND 58802. **Toll-free phone:** 888/863-9455. **Contact:** Brenda Wigness, Personnel Director. **World Wide Web address:** http://www.wsc.nodak.edu. **Description:** A two-year community college with an enrollment of 800 undergraduate students. **Positions advertised include:** Massage Therapy Instructor; Chemistry Instructor. **President:** Joe McCann. **Number of employees at this location:** Over 100.

Ohio

AKRON PUBLIC SCHOOLS
70 North Broadway, Akron OH 44308. 330/761-2945. **Contact:** Jeanette Hintz, Human Resources. **Fax:** 330/761-3225. **E-mail address:** mdeshane@akron.k12.oh.us. **World Wide Web address:** http://www.akronschools.com. **Description:** This location houses the administrative offices of the Akron public school system. **Positions advertised include:** Diagnostic Writing Specialist; Substitute Teacher.

ANTIOCH COLLEGE
795 Livermore Street, Yellow Springs OH 45387. 937/769-1000. **Contact:** Lisa Lowery, Employment Specialist. **E-mail address:** llowery@antioch.edu. **World Wide Web address:** http://www.antioch-college.edu. **Description:** A private, independent liberal arts college offering baccalaureate programs in a variety of disciplines. Antioch College has an enrollment of approximately 650 students. Founded in 1852 by the Christian Church, Antioch was later reorganized as an independent, nonsectarian college. Antioch's first president was Horace Mann. **NOTE:** Mail resumes to: Antioch College, Human Resources Office, 150 E.S. College Street, Yellow Springs OH 45387. Unsolicited resumes are not accepted.

ASHLAND UNIVERSITY
Room 106 Founders Hall, 401 College Avenue, Ashland OH 44805-3799. 419/289-4142. **Fax:** 419/289-5993. **Contact:** Personnel Office. **World Wide Web address:** http://www.ashland.edu. **Description:** A private liberal arts and sciences institution offering undergraduate, graduate, and professional programs to approximately 6,000 students. Founded in 1878. **Positions advertised include:** Assistant Professor, Microbiology; Assistant Professor, Educational Administration; Adjunct Instructor, Art; Adjunct Instructor, Composition; Project Engineer.

BALDWIN-WALLACE COLLEGE
275 Eastland Road, Berea OH 44017-2088. 440/826-2900. **Contact:** Hilary B. Wilson, Human Resources Department. **E-mail address:** hwilson@bw.edu. **World Wide Web address:** http://www.bw.edu. **Description:** A private liberal arts college offering undergraduate, graduate, and pre-professional programs. Baldwin-Wallace College has an enrollment of 2,750 undergraduates, 600 graduate students, and 1,300 evening and weekend students. Founded in 1845. **Positions advertised include:** Secretary; Human Resources Director; Collection Specialist; Assistant Professor, Mathematics and Computer Science.

BOWLING GREEN STATE UNIVERSITY
100 College Park Office Building, Bowling Green OH 43403. 419/372-8421. **Fax:** 419/372-2920. **Contact:** Human Resources. **E-mail address:** ohr@bgnet.bgsu.edu. **World Wide Web address:** http://www.bgsu.edu. **Description:** A four-year university offering bachelor's, master's, and doctoral degree programs to approximately 18,500 students. **NOTE:** Classified staff jobline: 419/372-8669. Administrative staff jobline: 419/372-8522. Faculty hiring is done through Academic Affairs. **Positions advertised include:** Residence Hall Director; Assistant Football Coach; Food Service Worker; Personnel Technician.

CAPITAL UNIVERSITY
One College and Main Street, 116 Yochum Hall, Columbus OH 43209-2394. 614/236-6168. **Fax:** 614/236-6820. **Contact:** Theresa Feldmeier, Personnel. **E-mail address:** tfeldmei@capital.edu. **World Wide Web address:** http://www.capital.edu. **Description:** A private university affiliated with the Evangelical Lutheran Church in America. The university offers six undergraduate degrees and more than 70 majors, as well as six graduate degrees to its approximately 3,820 students. Founded in 1830. **Positions advertised include:** Assistant Professor, Rhetoric and Composition; Director of Residence Life; Director of Student Activities; Records Management Assistant; Public Safety Officer.

JOHN CARROLL UNIVERSITY
20700 North Park Boulevard, University Heights OH 44118. 216/397-4976. **Fax:** 216/397-4933. **Contact:** Lisa Mencini, Director of Human Resources. **World Wide Web address:** http://www.jcu.edu. **Description:** A university with an enrollment of approximately 4,382 undergraduate and graduate students. John Carroll University offers 58 bachelor's and master's degree programs. Founded in 1886. **Positions advertised include:** Director of Athletics and Recreation; Area Coordinator, Residential Life; Dean, College of Arts and Sciences; Hockey Coach; Technical Assistant; Gate Attendant; Bus/Van Driver. **Number of employees at this location:** 500.

CLEVELAND INSTITUTE OF MUSIC
11021 East Boulevard, Cleveland OH 44106. 216/791-5000 ext. 219. **Fax:** 216/791-1530. **Contact:** Janice Snyder, Director of Human Resources. **E-mail address:** jms46@cwru.edu. **World Wide Web address:** http://www.cim.edu. **Description:** A leading international conservatory offering baccalaureate, graduate, and doctoral programs in Music and Musical Arts. CIM offers a joint music program with Case Western University. Founded in 1920. **Positions advertised include:** Director of the Sato Center of Suzuki Studies; Director of Opera Program.

CLEVELAND MUNICIPAL SCHOOL DISTRICT
Employee Services Department, 1380 East 6th Street, Room 500N, Cleveland OH 44114. 216/574-8175. **Contact:** Human Resources. **E-mail address:** hr@cmsdnet.net. **World Wide Web address:** http://www.cmsdnet.net/jobs. **Description:** Coordinates resources and information for Cleveland area public schools. **NOTE:** Teacher recruitment information is available at: http://www.teachcleveland.com. **Positions advertised include:** Substitute Cleaner; Food Supervisor; Parent Mentor; Speech Language Pathologist.

DAYTON PUBLIC SCHOOLS
115 South Ludlow Street, Dayton OH 45402. 937/542-3000. **Contact:** Human Resources. **World Wide Web address:** http://www.dps.k12.oh.us. **Description:** Coordinates resources and information for the public schools of Dayton. **Positions advertised include:** Speech Language Pathologist; School Counselor;

Middle School Math Teacher; High School Social Studies Teacher; High School Science Teacher; High School Music Teacher; Bus Driver.

FRANKLIN UNIVERSITY
201 South Grant Avenue, Columbus OH 43215. 614/797-4700. **Toll-free phone:** 877/341-6300. **Fax:** 614/341-6422. **Contact:** Human Resources. **E-mail address:** resume@franklin.edu. **World Wide Web address:** http://www.franklin.edu. **Description:** A four-year independent university with a focus on adult education. Franklin University has an enrollment of approximately 8,000 students. Founded in 1902. **Positions advertised include:** Adjunct Instructor, Accounting; Program Chair, Business Administration; Professor, Computer Sciences; Director, Academic Software; Administrative Assistant; Student Services Liaison; Facilities Assistant; Computer Science Lab Assistant.

KENT STATE UNIVERSITY
P.O. Box 5190, Kent OH 44242. 330/672-2901. **Physical address:** Route 59, Kent OH 44242. **Contact:** Employment Services. **E-mail address:** employment@kent.edu. **World Wide Web address:** http://www.kent.edu. **Description:** A four-year state university offering bachelor's, master's (including MBAs), and doctoral degrees. Approximately 26,000 undergraduate and 3,500 graduate students attend Kent State University. **Positions advertised include:** Spanish Instructor; Assistant Professor, Communication Studies; Instructor, College of Nursing. **Other area locations:** Ashtabula OH; East Liverpool OH; Geauga OH; Salem OH; Stark OH; Trumbull OH; Tuscarawas OH.

KENYON COLLEGE
Human Resources, 209 Chase Avenue, The Eaton Center, Gambier OH 43022-9623. 740/427-5173. **Fax:** 740/427-5901. **Recorded jobline:** 740/427-5900. **Contact:** Jennifer Cabral, Director of Human Resources. **E-mail address:** cabral@kenyon.edu. **World Wide Web address:** http://www.kenyon.edu. **Description:** A selective private liberal arts college with an enrollment of 1,500 students. **Positions advertised include:** Director, Student Activities; Associate Director, Career Development; Visiting Assistant Professor, Russian; Visiting Assistant Professor, Classics; Assistant Professor, French and Italian; Accounts Receivable Coordinator.

LAKELAND COMMUNITY COLLEGE
7700 Clocktower Drive, Kirtland OH 44094-5198. 440/953-7078. **Fax:** 440/525-7606. **Recorded jobline:** 440/975-4701. **Contact:** Manager of Recruiting. **E-mail address:** bhenderson@lakelandcc.edu. **World Wide Web address:** http://www.lakelandcc.edu. **Description:** A two-year community college. **NOTE:** Resumes are accepted for current openings only. Please consult the website for available positions. **Positions advertised include:** Psychology Professor; Environmental Biology Instructor; Early Childhood Education Instructor; Summer Camp Instructor.

MALONE COLLEGE
515 25th Street NW, Canton OH 44709-3897. 330/471-8100. **Fax:** 330/454-6977. **Contact:** Human Resources. **E-mail address:** careerservices@malone.edu. **World Wide Web address:** http://www.malone.edu. **Description:** A Christian liberal arts college. Malone College is affiliated with the Evangelical Friends Church. Founded in 1957.

OBERLIN COLLEGE
173 West Lorain Street, Oberlin OH 44074. 440/775-8121. **Fax:** 440/775-8683. **Contact:** Human Resources. **World Wide Web address:** http://www.oberlin.edu. **Description:** A four-year, liberal arts college with approximately 2,800 students. **NOTE:** To contact human resources directly call: 440/775-8430. **Positions advertised include:** Assistant Administrative Technician; Assistant Professor, Classics; Professor, Musicology; Professor, American Literature; Professor, Mathematics. **Special Programs:** Internships. **Office hours:** Monday – Friday, 8:30 a.m. – 4:30 p.m.

OHIO NORTHERN UNIVERSITY
525 South Main Street, Ada OH 45810. 419/772-2000. **Fax:** 419/772-1932. **Contact:** Personnel. **E-mail address:** personnel@onu.edu. **World Wide Web address:** http://www.onu.edu. **Description:** Ohio Northern University is organized into five colleges. The Getty College of Arts and Sciences is organized into 15 different departments. The T.J. Smull College of Engineering is organized into the departments of civil, electrical, and mechanical engineering. The Raabe College of Pharmacy is organized into the departments of pharmacy practice and pharmaceutical and biomedical sciences. The College of Business Administration offers majors in accounting, international business and economics, and management. The Pettit College of Law awards the Juris Doctor degree. **NOTE:** Contact the Academic Affairs Office for faculty positions. **Positions advertised include:** Admissions Counselor.

OHIO STATE UNIVERSITY
Northwood/High Building, 2231 North High Street, Suite 250, Columbus OH 43201. 614/292-9380. **Contact:** Employment Services. **E-mail address:** employment@hr.osu.edu. **World Wide Web address:** http://www.osu.edu. **Description:** A leading teaching and researching university offering more than 170 undergraduate programs and more than 200 graduate areas of study. Ohio State University has an enrollment of 48,000 students at its main campus in Columbus. Established in 1870. **Positions advertised include:** Administrative Associate; Research Assistant; Office Associate; Food Services Manager; Dental Assistant; Academic Studies Coordinator; Librarian; Senior Lecturer, English; TV Producer; Videographer. **Other area locations:** Lima; Mansfield; Marion; Newark; Wooster. **Number of employees at this location:** 18,000.

OHIO UNIVERSITY
McKee House, 169 West Union Street, Athens OH 45701-2979. 740/593-1636. **Fax:** 740/593-0386. **Recorded jobline:** 740/593-4080. **Contact:** Human Resources. **World Wide Web address:** http://www.uhr.ohiou.edu. **Description:** A four-year university. 16,350 undergraduate students, with 276 majors and 775 full-time faculty. Established in 1804. **Positions advertised include:** Assistant Resident Director; Molecular Biology Technician; Assistant Manager, Dining Services; Assistant Professor, Nursing; Visiting Assistant Professor, Psychology; Assistant Professor, English; Assistant Professor, Economics; Visiting Assistant Professor, Chemistry.

SHAWNEE STATE UNIVERSITY
940 Second Street, Portsmouth OH 45662-4344. 740/354-3205. **Contact:** Human Resources. **World Wide Web address:** http://www.shawnee.edu. **Description:** A university offering a variety of programs through the College of Arts and Sciences, the College of Business, the College of Engineering Technologies, the College of Health Sciences, and the Center for Teacher Education. **Positions advertised include:** Adjunct Instructors, Various Disciplines; Occupational Therapy Instructor.

SINCLAIR COMMUNITY COLLEGE
Building 7, Room 7430, 444 West Third Street, Dayton OH 45402. 937/512-2514. **Fax:** 937/512-2777. **Contact:** Director of Human Resources. **E-mail address:** hrdept@sinclair.edu. **World Wide Web address:** http://www.sinclair.edu. **Description:** A community college. **NOTE:** No paper resumes accepted, please apply online. **Positions advertised include:** Executive Director, Project READ; Nursing Professor; Student Services Application Coordinator; Project Manager; Groundskeeper.

TOLEDO PUBLIC SCHOOLS
Office of Human Resources, Room 105, 420 East Manhattan Boulevard, Toledo OH 43608. 419/729-

8231. **Recorded jobline:** 419/729-8355. **Contact:** Human Resources. **World Wide Web address:** http://www.tps.org. **Description:** Coordinates resources and information for the public schools of Toledo. **Positions advertised include:** Contract Teacher; Substitute Teacher; Substitute Bus Driver; Substitute Food Service Worker; Substitute Secretary.

UNIVERSITY OF AKRON
Human Resources, 277 South Broadway Street, Second Floor, Akron OH 44325-4704. 330/972-5988. **Recorded jobline:** 330/972-7091. **Contact:** Employment Services. **E-mail address:** univofakron_employment@uakron.edu. **Description:** A public university serving approximately 24,000 students. The University of Akron offers 200 undergraduate majors and areas of study, as well as 100 master's degree programs, 17 doctoral degree programs, and four law degree programs. Founded in 1870 as Buchtel College. **NOTE:** Apply to posted positions only. Contact information and application procedures vary for Faculty and Professional positions. Consult website or contact Employment Services for further information regarding procedure and deadlines. **Positions advertised include:** Visiting Instructor, Mathematics; Assistant Professor, Voice; Assistant Professor, Biomedical Engineering; Spanish Instructor; Institutional Research Analyst; Residence Life Coordinator. **President:** Dr. Luis M. Proenza

UNIVERSITY OF CINCINNATI
51 Goodman Drive, P.O. Box 210117, Cincinnati OH 45221-0117. 513/556-3702. **Fax:** 513/556-9652. **Contact:** Employment Services. **E-mail address:** hrempl@ucmail.uc.edu. **World Wide Web address:** http://www.hr.uc.edu. **Description:** A university offering over 200 undergraduate and 125 graduate programs. The university is comprised of 16 colleges, a medical center, and a library with 1.8 million volumes. Founded in 1819. **NOTE:** Entry-level positions and second and third shifts are offered. **Positions advertised include:** Law Enforcement Officer; Laborer; Apprentice Stationary Engineer; Assistant Dean; Assistant Preschool Teacher; Grant Manager; Inventory Control Specialist; Training Specialist; Assistant Librarian. **Special programs:** Internships.

UNIVERSITY OF FINDLAY
1000 North Main Street, Findlay OH 45840-3695. 419/434-6964. **Toll-free phone:** 800/548-0932. **Fax:** 419/434-5976. **Contact:** Karen A. (Powell) Lieb, Human Resources. **E-mail address:** powell@findlay.edu. **World Wide Web address:** http://www.findlay.edu. **Description:** A private, coeducational university. Programs include Bilingual Business Education, Criminal Justice, Environmental and Hazardous Materials Management, Equestrian Studies, Japanese, Nuclear Medicine Technology, and Theatre Production. Founded in 1882. **Positions advertised include:** Professor, Art History; Assistant Professor, Accounting and Finance; Assistant Professor, Marketing; Instructor, Biology and Anatomy.

WRIGHT STATE UNIVERSITY
3640 Colonel Glenn Highway, 280 University Hall, Dayton OH 45435. 937/775-2120. **Recorded jobline:** 937/775-4562. **Contact:** Human Resources. **E-mail address:** human_resources@wright.edu. **World Wide Web address:** http://www.wright.edu. **Description:** A university engaged in teaching, research, and service. **NOTE:** Resumes only accepted for posted positions. **Positions advertised include:** Research Assistant; University Engineer; Adjunct Mathematics Instructor, Assistant Professor, Obstetrics and Gynecology; Faculty Associate, Modern Languages. **Operations at this facility include:** Education. **Number of employees at this location:** 2,300.

XAVIER UNIVERSITY
3800 Victory Parkway, Cincinnati OH 45207-4641. 513/745-3638. **Fax:** 513/745-3644. **Contact:** Kathleen Riga, Assistant Vice President of Human Resources. **E-mail address:** hr@xu.edu. **World Wide Web address:** http://www.xu.edu. **Description:** A private, coeducational, liberal arts, Jesuit university. **NOTE:** Candidates interested in Adjunct Faculty positions should forward a resume to the Chair of the appropriate department. **Positions advertised include:** Assistant Professor, Psychology; Visiting Assistant Professor, Economics and Human Resources.

YOUNGSTOWN STATE UNIVERSITY
One University Plaza, Youngstown OH 44555. 330/941-3122. **Fax:** 330/941-3716. **Contact:** Human Resources Department. **World Wide Web address:** http://www.ysu.edu. **Description:** A state university offering a wide range of associate, baccalaureate, and graduate degrees and certificate programs. **Positions advertised include:** Assistant Professor, Geography; Assistant Professor, Center for Working Class Studies; Assistant Professor, Psychology; Assistant Professor, Social Work; Electronic Services Librarian; Bursar.

Oklahoma

LANGSTON UNIVERSITY
Highway 33 East, Langston OK 73050. 405/466-3203. **Fax:** 405/466-6002. **Contact:** Beverly H. Smith, Personnel Director. **World Wide Web address:** http://www.lunet.edu. **Description:** A four-year, liberal arts university that offers both undergraduate and graduate programs. **NOTE:** To apply for open positions advertised online, submit materials to the Human Resources Office, P.O. Box 1205, Langston OK 73050. **Positions advertised include:** Upward Bound Counselor; Administrative Assistant. **Other area locations:** Oklahoma City OK. **Number of employees at this location:** 450.

OKLAHOMA STATE UNIVERSITY
106 Whitehurst Hall, Stillwater OK 74078-1037. 405/744-5373. **Fax:** 405/744-8345. **Contact:** Personnel Services. **E-mail address:** osu-hr@okstate.edu. **World Wide Web address:** http://www.okstate.edu. **Description:** A four-campus state university with an enrollment of approximately 26,000 students that offers bachelor's, master's, and doctor's degrees in a wide range of fields. **NOTE:** For faculty positions, contact individual departments. **Positions advertised include:** Support Specialist; Research Specialist; Communications Specialist; Microbiologist; TV Studio Operations Supervisor; Building Controls Technician; Roofer; Refuse Worker; Financial Assistant; Stock Clerk; Research Engineer; Academic Counselor; Database Administrator. **Special programs:** Staff Development Program. **Other area locations:** Oklahoma City OK; Okmulgee OK; Tulsa OK. **Number of employees at this location:** 6,000. **Number of employees nationwide:** 10,000.

UNIVERSITY OF CENTRAL OKLAHOMA
Lilliard Administration Building, Room 204, 100 North University Drive, Edmond OK 73034. 405/974-2366. **Recorded jobline:** 405/974-3089. **Contact:** Human Resources. **E-mail:** jobs@ucok.edu. **World Wide Web address:** http://www.ucok.edu. **Description:** A state university with five undergraduate colleges and an office of graduate studies and research. Founded in 1890. **NOTE:** For academic positions, contact appropriate department. **Positions advertised include:** Data Entry; Student Receptionist; Employer Relations Coordinator; Accountant; Technology Support Specialist; Fitness Student Worker; Electrician; Audio/Visual Night Host; Web Application Developer; Chemistry Laboratory Assistant.

UNIVERSITY OF OKLAHOMA
905 Asp Avenue, Room 205, Norman OK 73019-6043. 405/325-1826. **Fax:** 405/325-7627. **Recorded jobline:** 405/325-1826. **Contact:** Personnel Services. **E-mail address:** ohr@ou.edu. **World Wide Web address:** http://www.ou.edu/. **Description:** A doctoral-degree granting state university that is composed of nineteen colleges and offers 154 majors. **Positions advertised include:** Director of Technical Services; Executive Director of UO Hillel; Lecturer for Freshman Writing Seminars; Cataloger, Special Collections. **Number of employees at this location:** 9,000.

Oregon

BEAVERTON SCHOOL DISTRICT
16550 SW Merlo Road, Beaverton OR 97006. 503/591-8000. **Recorded jobline:** 503/591-4397. **Contact:** Human Resources. **World Wide Web address:** http://www.beavton.k12.or.us. **Description:** A state school district comprised of 29 elementary schools, seven middle schools, four high schools, and two alternative high schools (with programs such as continuing education for young parents and an evening academy). **Positions advertised include:** Custodian; Satellite Leader; Cafeteria Manager.

CHEMEKETA COMMUNITY COLLEGE
4000 Lancaster Drive NE, P.O. Box 14007, Salem OR 97309. 503/589-7691. **Recorded jobline:** 503/399-5228. **Contact:** Human Resources. **E-mail address:** humanresources@chemeketa.edu. **World Wide Web address:** http://www.chemeketa.edu. **Description:** A community college with an enrollment of approximately 44,000 students including full-time, part-time, and noncredit students.

CLACKAMAS COMMUNITY COLLEGE
19600 South Molalla Avenue, Oregon City OR 97045-7998. 503/657-6958 ext. 2318. **Fax:** 503/650-7348. **Recorded jobline:** 503/650-6655. **Contact:** Human Resources. **E-mail address:** debbiej@clackamas.edu. **World Wide Web address:** http://www.clackamas.edu. **Description:** A community college offering associate's degrees to approximately 27,000 students. **Positions advertised include:** Project Management Instructor; Skills Development Department Instructor; Faculty.

EUGENE SCHOOL DISTRICT 4J
200 North Monroe Street, Eugene OR 97402. 541/687-3123. **Recorded jobline:** 541/687-3344. **Contact:** Human Resources Department. **World Wide Web address:** http://www.4j.lane.edu. **Description:** A state school district comprised of 23 elementary schools, 11 middle schools, and 4 high schools. **Positions advertised include:** Teacher; School Nurse; Occupational/Physical Therapist; Driver.

KNOWLEDGE LEARNING CORPORATION
650 NE Holladay Street, Portland OR 97232. 503/872-1300. **Toll-free phone:** 800/633-1488. **Contact:** Human Resources. **World Wide Web address:** http://www.kindercare.com. **Description:** A leading provider of early childhood care and educational services to children ages six weeks to five years old. KinderCare operates approximately 1,130 facilities.

LANE COMMUNITY COLLEGE
4000 East 30th Avenue, Eugene OR 97405. 541/463-5211. **Fax:** 541/463-3970. **Contact:** Human Resources Director. **World Wide Web address:** http://www.lanecc.edu. **Description:** A community college with an enrollment of approximately 40,000 students per year. Founded in 1964. **Positions advertised include:** Executive Chef. **Number of employees at this location:** 1,000.

MOUNT HOOD COMMUNITY COLLEGE
26000 SE Stark Street, Gresham OR 97030. 503/491-6422. **Fax:** 503/491-7257. **Recorded jobline:** 503/491-7645. **Contact:** Human Resources. **E-mail address:** hr@mhcc.edu. **World Wide Web address:** http://www.mhcc.cc.or.us. **Description:** A community college offering associate's degrees in applied science and arts to approximately 26,000 students. Founded in 1966. **Positions advertised include:** Instructor of Respiratory Care; Instructor of Mathematics; Instructor-Automotive Program; Director of Library Resources; Financial Aid Coordinator; KMHD Development Coordinator; Center Assistant/Driver; Teacher/Home Visitor.

MULTNOMAH EDUCATIONAL SERVICE DISTRICT
P.O. Box 301039, Portland OR 97294. 503/255-1841. **Physical address:** 11611 NE Ainsworth Circle, Portland OR 97220. **Fax:** 503/257-1519. **Recorded jobline:** 503/257-1510. **Contact:** Human Resources Department. **World Wide Web address:** http://w3.mesd.k12.or.us. **Description:** Provides services and programs for the Multnomah School District including early intervention, environmental education, job training, functional living skills, and substitute teacher call-in systems. **Positions advertised include:** Autism Specialist; Supervisor of Special Education; Teacher of Special Education; Occupational Therapist; Physical Therapist; Communications Assistant; Office Assistant; Translator. **Office hours:** Monday - Friday, 8:00 a.m. - 5:00 p.m.

OREGON CITY SCHOOL DISTRICT
1417 12th Street, P.O. Box 2110, Oregon City OR 97045. 503/785-8427. **Recorded jobline:** 503/785-8449. **Contact:** Linda Matsies, Human Resources Director. **E-mail address:** matsiesl@orecity.k12.or.us. **World Wide Web address:** http://www.orecity.k12.or.us. **Description:** A state school district comprised of ten elementary schools, two middle schools, and one high school. **Positions advertised include:** Assistant Transportation Supervisor.

OREGON GRADUATE INSTITUTE OF SCIENCE & TECHNOLOGY
20000 NW Walker Road, Beaverton OR 97006. 503/748-1121. **Contact:** Director of Personnel. **World Wide Web address:** http://www.ohsu.edu/hr/sum.htm. **Description:** A private graduate institute offering master's and Ph.D. programs in five areas: computer science and engineering; management in science and technology; biochemistry and molecular biology; environmental science and engineering; and electrical and computer engineering. Founded in 1963. **Positions advertised include:** Financial Analyst; Administrative Assistant; Management Analyst; Program Technician; Emergency Department Technician; Photographer; Medical Laboratory Technician.

OREGON HEALTH SCIENCES UNIVERSITY
2525 SW 3rd Avenue, Suite 110, Portland OR 97239-3098. 503/494-8060. **Recorded jobline:** 503/494-6478. **Fax:** 503/494-6469. **Contact:** Human Resources. **World Wide Web address:** http://www.ohsu.edu. **Description:** A university comprised of the Schools of Dentistry, Medicine, and Nursing; Biomedical Information Communication Center; Center for Research on Occupational and Environmental Toxicology; University Hospital; Doernbecher Children's Hospital; and the Oregon Regional Primate Research Center. The Oregon Health Sciences University also includes the Vollum Institute, a neurological research center at this location, Mail Code L474, and can be reached at 503/494-5042. **NOTE:** The nursing jobline may be reached by dialing 503/494-6546. **Positions advertised include:** Assistant Hospital Director of Information; Laboratory Animal Technician; MRI Technician; Pharmacist; Physical Therapist.

OREGON INSTITUTE OF TECHNOLOGY
3201 Campus Drive, Klamath Falls OR 97601. 541/885-1120. **Recorded jobline:** 541/885-1500. **Contact:** Human Resources. **E-mail address:** oithr@oit.edu. **World Wide Web address:** http://www.oit.edu. **Description:** A college that offers associate's and bachelor's degrees in a variety of engineering fields and a master's program in engineering technology to approximately 2,800 students. **Positions advertised include:** Assistant Professor of Physics; Communication Faculty Member; Manufacturing Consultant; Computer Systems Laboratory Manager.

OREGON STATE UNIVERSITY
122 & 204 Kerr Administration, Corvallis OR 97331-2132. 541/737-3103. **Contact:** Stephanie Taylor, Employment Services Supervisor. **Toll-free phone:** 800/735-2900. **Fax:** 541/737-0553. **World Wide Web address:** http://www.oregonstate.edu/jobs. **Description:** A state university offering bachelor's, master's, and doctoral degrees to approximately 15,100 students.

PACIFIC UNIVERSITY
2043 College Way, Forest Grove OR 97116-1797. 503/357-6151. **Contact:** Human Resources. **World Wide Web address:** http://www.pacificu.edu. **Description:** A university offering graduate and undergraduate programs to approximately 2,000 students. Areas of study include liberal arts, education, and health care. Founded in 1849. **NOTE:** The faculty is hired through the Dean's Office, while administration is hired through Human Resources. **Positions advertised include:** Faculty Position-School of Occupational Therapy; Campus Public Safety Officer; Certified Medical Assistant; Resident Director-Student Life.

PORTLAND COMMUNITY COLLEGE
705 N Killingsworth, Student Services Building, 3rd Floor,, Portland OR 97217-0990. 503/978-5857. **Fax:** 503/286-0410. **Recorded jobline:** 503/978-5858. **Contact:** Human Resources. **E-mail address:** pccjobs@pcc.edu. **World Wide Web address:** http://www.pcc.edu. **Description:** A community college with an enrollment of approximately 8,000 full-time students. **Positions advertised include:** Accounting Clerk; Division Assistant, English and Modern Languages; Division Dean, Business and Humanities; Instructor/Clinic Dentist, Dental Hygiene; Manager, Campus Computer and Facilities Resources; Project Assistant; Senior Accountant.

REED COLLEGE
3203 SE Woodstock Boulevard, Portland OR 97202-8199. 503/771-1112. **Fax:** 503/777-7769. **Recorded jobline:** 503/777-7706. **Contact:** Human Resources. **E-mail address:** mary.sullivan@reed.edu. **World Wide Web address:** http://www.reed.edu. **Description:** A liberal arts college with an enrollment of approximately 1,350 students. **Positions advertised include:** Assistant Director of the Annual Fund; Research Associate, Chemistry.

SPRINGFIELD SCHOOL DISTRICT
525 Mill Street, Springfield OR 97477. 541/747-3331. **Contact:** Human Resources. **World Wide Web address:** http://www.sps.lane.edu. **Description:** A state school district comprised of 16 elementary schools, 5 middle schools, 2 high schools, and an alternative education program. **Positions advertised include:** High School Principal; School Psychologist; Accountant; Head Men's Basketball Coach; Head Women's Basketball Coach; Head Wrestling Coach. **Number of employees at this location:** 1,500.

UNIVERSITY OF OREGON
5210 University of Oregon, Eugene OR 97403-5210. 541/346-3159. **Fax:** 5641/346-2548. **Contact:** Linda King, Director of Personnel. **World Wide Web address:** http://www.uoregon.edu. **Description:** A state university offering graduate and undergraduate programs to approximately 16,700 students. **NOTE:** Unsolicited resumes are not accepted. **Positions advertised include:** Office Specialist; Education Project Assistant; Custodian; Food Service Worker; Analyst Programmer; Complex Director; Program Coordinator; Director of Development; Head Scientific Instrument Researcher; Visiting Instructor of Norwegian; Assistant Professor; Tenure Track Faculty Member.

UNIVERSITY OF PORTLAND
5000 North Willamette Boulevard, Portland OR 97203. 503/943-7331. **Fax:** 503/943-7399. **Recorded jobline:** 503/943-7536. **Contact:** James Kuffner, Human Resources Director. **E-mail address:** kuffner@up.edu. **World Wide Web address:** http://www.up.edu. **Description:** A Catholic university offering graduate and undergraduate programs in sciences, engineering, education, business, arts, humanities, and nursing. The University of Portland has an enrollment of approximately 2,600 students. Founded in 1901. **NOTE:** The university also hires through the Oregon State Employment Office. **Positions advertised include:** Assistant Director of Student Media and Adult Programs Coordinator. **Employees at this location:** 700.

WESTERN OREGON UNIVERSITY
345 North Monmouth Avenue, Monmouth OR 97361. 503/838-8490. **Toll-free phone:** 877/877-1593. **Fax:** 503/838-8144. **Contact:** Personnel. **World Wide Web address:** http://www.wou.edu. **Description:** A state university with an enrollment of approximately 4,500 students. **NOTE:** All jobs other than faculty positions are filled through the Oregon State Employment Office. **Positions advertised include:** Director of Public Safety; Registrar; Administrative Assistant to the Dean; Visiting Art Gallery Director; Assistant Professor of Special Education; Assistant Professor of Criminal Justice; Adjunct Faculty of Spanish.

Pennsylvania

ALLEGHENY COLLEGE
520 North Main Street, Meadville PA 16335. 814/332-2312. **Contact:** Human Resources. **E-mail address:** info@allegheny.edu. **World Wide Web address:** http://www.alleg.edu. **Description:** A four-year college awarding B.A. and B.S. degrees. Allegheny College has an undergraduate enrollment of approximately 1,950 students.

ART INSTITUTE OF PITTSBURGH
420 Boulevard of the Allies, Pittsburgh PA 15219. 412/263-6600. **Toll-free phone:** 800/275-2470. **Contact:** Melinda Hallett, Personnel Director. **World Wide Web address:** http://www.aip.aii.edu. **Description:** A two-year art school with an enrollment of approximately 2,500. The Art Institute of Pittsburgh also offers four-year Bachelor of Science degree programs in computer animation, interior design, industrial design, and graphic design.

BRYN MAWR COLLEGE
101 North Merion Avenue, Bryn Mawr PA 19010-2899. 610/526-5000. **Fax:** 610/526-7478. **Contact:** Human Resources. **E-mail address:** jobs@brynmawr.edu. **World Wide Web address:** http://www.brynmawr.edu. **Description:** A women's liberal arts college with an enrollment of 1,700 offering undergraduate, master's and Ph.D. programs. **Positions advertised include:** Faculty, Various Departments; Associate Comptroller.

BUCKS COUNTY COMMUNITY COLLEGE
Tyler Hall, Room 130, 275 Swamp Road, Newtown PA 18940. 215/968-8000. **Fax:** 215/504-8506. **Contact:** Human Resources Office. **World Wide Web address:** http://www.bucks.edu. **Description:** A public, two-year community college offering certificates and associate's degrees in more than 50 academic disciplines. **Positions advertised include:** Coordinator, Healthcare Programs; Director, Facility Operations; Director of Advising and Counseling; Assistant Director, Budget and Internal Audit; Director, Library Services.

CALIFORNIA UNIVERSITY OF PENNSYLVANIA
Dixon Hall, Room 408, 250 University Avenue, California PA 15419. 724/938-4427. **Contact:** Office of Human Resources. **E-mail address:** cupjobs@cup.edu. **World Wide Web address:** http://www.cup.edu. **Description:** A university offering two-year, four-year, and graduate programs leading to associate's, bachelor's, and master's degrees. Enrollment includes approximately 6,000 undergraduates and 700 graduate students. **Positions advertised include:** Director of Major Gifts; Management Technician.

CARLOW COLLEGE
FWH 2nd Floor, 3333 Fifth Avenue, Pittsburgh PA 15213. 412/578-8897. **Recorded jobline:** 412/578-6054. **Fax:** 412/578-6265. **Contact:** Andra Tokarsky, Human Resources. **E-mail address:** atokarsky@carlow.edu. **World Wide Web address:** http://www.carlow.edu. **Description:** Carlow College is a Catholic four-year college offering certificate, B.A., B.S., and master's degree programs. Undergraduate enrollment is approximately 1,600 students.

CARNEGIE MELLON UNIVERSITY
143 North Craig Street, Whitfield Hall, Pittsburgh PA 15213-3890. 412/268-4747. **Recorded jobline:** 412/268-8545. **Contact:** Human Resources. **E-mail address:** hrhelp@andrew.cmu.edu. **World Wide Web address:** http://www.cmu.edu. **Description:** A university offering certificate, associate's, B.A., B.S., master's, M.B.A., and doctoral programs. Enrollment is approximately 4,300 undergraduates and 2,600 graduate students. **NOTE:** Please see website for online application details. **Positions advertised include:** Network Engineer; Research Assistant; Research Programmer; Sr. Writer/Editor for University Publications; Associate Director of Class Programs.

CHATHAM COLLEGE
Woodland Road, Pittsburgh PA 15232. 412/365-1847. **Contact:** Personnel. **E-mail address:** chathr@chatham.edu. **World Wide Web address:** http://www.chatham.edu. **Description:** A four-year women's college offering certificate, bachelor's, and master's degree programs. At the undergraduate level, the school has an all-women enrollment. Graduate programs are coed. The combined undergraduate and graduate enrollment is approximately 1,000 students. **Positions advertised include:** Assistant Professor, Various Departments; Director of Institutional Research; Admissions Counselor.

CLARION UNIVERSITY OF PENNSYLVANIA
B29, Carrier Administration Building, Clarion PA 16214. 814/393-2000. **Toll-free phone:** 800/672-7171. **Contact:** Human Resources. **E-mail address:** info@clarion.edu. **World Wide Web address:** http://www.clarion.edu. **Description:** A university offering two-year, four-year, and graduate degree programs. Degrees awarded include associate's, bachelor's, master's, and MBAs. Enrollment includes approximately 5,700 undergraduates and 450 graduate students. **NOTE:** Faculty and staff openings are posted on www.higheredjobs.com.

COMMUNITY COLLEGE OF ALLEGHENY COUNTY
808 Ridge Avenue Pittsburgh PA 15212. 412/237-3000. **Contact:** Human Resources. **E-mail address:** humanresources@ccac.edu. **World Wide Web address:** http://www.ccac.edu. **Description:** A two-year community college with an enrollment of approximately 4,500. **NOTE:** Online application preferred. **Positions advertised include:** Dean of Academic Affairs; Dean of Enrollment Management; Director of Marketing; Employment Specialist; Nursing Adjunct Faculty.

COMMUNITY COLLEGE OF BEAVER COUNTY
One Campus Drive, Monaca PA 15061. 724/775-8561. **Contact:** Human Resources. **World Wide Web address:** http://www.ccbc.edu. **Description:** A two-year community college, with an enrollment of approximately 3,000.

COMMUNITY COLLEGE OF PHILADELPHIA
1700 Spring Garden Street, Room M2-3, Philadelphia PA 19130. 215/751-8035. **Fax:** 215/972-6307. **Contact:** Human Resources. **E-mail address:** jobs@ccp.edu. **World Wide Web address:** http://www.ccp.edu. **Description:** A two-year community college offering certificates and associate's degrees. Approximately 40,000 students attend Community College of Philadelphia. **NOTE:** Please see the website for a complete listing of current openings. Online application is preferred.

DREXEL UNIVERSITY
3201 Arch Street, 4th Floor, Suite 430, Philadelphia PA 19104. 215/895-2850. **Recorded jobline:** 215/895-2562. **Fax:** 215/895-5813. **Contact:** Human Resources. **E-mail address:** hrdept@drexel.edu. **World Wide Web address:** http://www.drexel.edu. **Description:** A four-year university offering bachelor's and master's degrees including MBAs. Approximately 8,000 undergraduate and 3,700 graduate students attend Drexel University. **NOTE:** Search for positions online.

DUQUESNE UNIVERSITY
200 Fisher Hall, 600 Forbes Avenue, Pittsburgh PA 15282. 412/396-6575. **Contact:** Human Resources. **E-mail address:** hr.office@duq.edu. **World Wide Web address:** http://www.duq.edu. **Description:** A private university offering programs up to the doctoral level. Approximately 9,000 students attend Duquesne University. **NOTE:** See the website for a listing of staff and faculty positions and online application information.

EDINBORO UNIVERSITY OF PENNSYLVANIA
Reeder Hall, 2nd Floor, Edinboro PA 16444. 814/732-2810. **Fax:** 814/732-2885. **Contact:** Ms. Janet Dean, Associate Vice President of Human Resources. **World Wide Web address:** http://www.edinboro.edu. **Description:** A four-year state university offering graduate and doctoral programs. Approximately 7,000 students attend Edinboro University. **NOTE:** See website for a list of current openings, however online applications are discouraged unless otherwise stated. **Number of employees at this location:** 840.

ERIE SCHOOL DISTRICT
148th West 21st, Erie PA 16502. 814/874-6001. **Fax:** 814/874-6010. **Contact:** Mary Blucas, Personnel Director. **E-mail address:** mblucas@eriesd.iu5.org. **World Wide Web address:** http://esd.iu5.org. **Description:** Administrative offices for the Erie school district. The office is responsible for staffing 19 area schools including three high schools, three middle schools, and 13 elementary schools.

FRANKLIN AND MARSHALL COLLEGE
P.O. Box 3003, Lancaster PA 17604-3003. 717/291-3911. **Fax:** 717/291-3969. **Contact:** Human Resources. **World Wide Web address:** http://www.fandm.edu. **Description:** A private, four-year college with approximately 2,000 students enrolled. **NOTE:** Job opportunities are posted on the above Website. No phone calls or walk-ins. **Positions advertised include:** Director of Career Partnerships; Associate Vice President for Facilities Planning and Capital Projects; Magazine Editor.

GENEVA COLLEGE
3200 College Avenue, Beaver Falls PA 15010. 724/847-6560. **Contact:** Donald McBurney, Human Resources Director. **World Wide Web address:** http://www.geneva.edu. **Description:** A four-year college offering associate's, bachelor's, and master's degree programs. Enrollment includes 1,200 undergraduates and 250 graduate students. **Positions advertised include:** Counseling Center Director; Assistant/Associate Professor of Education; Communication Disorders Faculty Position; Reference/Instruction Librarian; Political Science Faculty Position.

GROVE CITY COLLEGE
100 Campus Drive, Grove City PA 16127-2104. 724/458-2200. **Contact:** Human Resources. **Description:** A four-year Christian-based college.

INDIANA UNIVERSITY OF PENNSYLVANIA (IUP)
Sutton Hall G-1, 1011 South Drive, Indiana PA 15705. 724/357-2431. **Fax:** 724/357-2685. **Recorded jobline:** 724/357-7536. **Contact:** Human Resources Representative. **World Wide Web address:** http://www.iup.edu/humanresources. **Description:** One of the largest schools of the Pennsylvania State System of Higher Education, IUP is approximately 50 miles northeast of Pittsburgh. **Positions advertised include:** Assistant Physics Professor; Assistant Chemistry Professor; Assistant Poetry Professor; Director of Admissions; Director of Corporate & Foundation Relations. **Special programs:** Internships.

THOMAS JEFFERSON UNIVERSITY
201 South 11th Street, The Martin Building, Philadelphia PA 19107. 215/955-6000. **Fax:** 215/503-2183. **Contact:** Office of Employee Selection & Placement. **Recorded jobline:** 215/503-8313. **World**

Wide Web address: http://www.tju.edu. **Description:** An academic medical university. Thomas Jefferson University includes one of the largest private medical schools in the United States, a hospital, and graduate programs in the biomedical sciences. **Positions advertised include:** Administrator (CFO); Associate Director for Decision Support; Claims and Litigation Manager; Grants Administrator; Director of Finance; Project Director, Health Policy; Research Coordinator.

JUNIATA COLLEGE
1700 Moore Street, Huntingdon PA 16652. 814/641-3195. **Fax:** 814/641-3199. **Contact:** Gail Ulrich, Director of Human Resources. **E-mail address:** ulrichg@juniata.edu. **World Wide Web address:** http://www.juniata.edu. **Description:** A four-year college offering B.A. and B.S. degrees. Juniata's enrollment is approximately 1,100 students. **Positions advertised include:** Assistant Professor, Various Departments; Telecommunications Assistant.

KUTZTOWN UNIVERSITY
P.O. Box 730, Kutztown PA 19530-0730. 610/683-1353. **Physical address:** Personnel Office, Stratton Administration Center, Room 109, Kutztown PA 19530. **Fax:** 610/683-4641. **Contact:** Personnel Department. **World Wide Web address:** http://www.kutztown.edu. **Description:** A four-year university offering bachelor's and master's degrees including MBAs. Approximately 9,000 undergraduate and 800 graduate students attend Kutztown University.

LA SALLE UNIVERSITY
1900 West Olney Avenue, Philadelphia PA 19141. 215/951-1013. **Contact:** Human Resources. **World Wide Web address:** http://www.lasalle.edu. **Description:** A four-year Catholic university offering bachelor's and master's degrees including MBAs. Approximately 3,600 undergraduate and 900 graduate students attend La Salle University.

LACKAWANNA COLLEGE
501 Vine Street, Scranton PA 18509. 570/961-7841. **Contact:** Personnel Office. **World Wide Web address:** http://www.lackawanna.edu. **Description:** A college offering associate degrees.

LEHIGH UNIVERSITY
428 Brodhead Avenue, Bethlehem PA 18015-1687. 610/758-3900. **Fax:** 610/758-6226. **Recorded jobline:** 610/758-5627. **Contact:** Human Resources. **E-mail address:** inhro@lehigh.edu. **World Wide Web address:** http://www.lehigh.edu. **Description:** A four-year university offering bachelor's, master's (including MBAs), and doctoral degrees. Approximately 4,400 undergraduate and 2,000 graduate students attend Lehigh University. Founded in 1865. **NOTE:** Positions posted at http://www.higheredjobs.com.

MERCYHURST COLLEGE
501 East 38th Street, Erie PA 16546-0001. 814/824-2279. **Toll-free phone:** 800/825-1926. **Contact:** Human Resources. **World Wide Web address:** http://www.mercyhurst.edu. **Description:** A college offering four-year, two-year, and graduate programs. Degrees awarded include certificate, associate's, bachelor's, and master's degrees. Enrollment is approximately 2,000 undergraduates and 100 graduate students.

MILLERSVILLE UNIVERSITY
Dilworth Building, P.O. Box 1002, Millersville PA 17551-0302. 717/872-3011. **Contact:** Human Resources. **World Wide Web address:** http://muweb.millersville.edu. **Description:** A four-year university offering associate's, bachelor's, and master's degrees to approximately 7,500 students. **NOTE:** Unsolicited resumes are not accepted. Applications/resumes must be mailed or hand delivered to the above address. **Positions advertised include:** Associate Provost for Academic Administration; Vice President for Finance and Administration; Faculty, Various Departments.

MORAVIAN COLLEGE
MORAVIAN THEOLOGICAL SEMINARY
1200 Main Street, Bethlehem PA 18018. 610/861-1527. **Fax:** 610/625-7883. **Contact:** Human Resources. **E-mail address:** employment@moravian.edu. **World Wide Web address:** http://www.moravian.edu. **Description:** A four-year college offering bachelor's degrees and MBAs to approximately 1,200 students. Moravian Theological Seminary (also at this location) is a graduate-professional school of theology. **Positions advertised include:** Director of Career Development; Director of Leadership Giving; Moravian Fund Director; Assistant Professor, Various Departments. **Operations at this facility include:** Administration; Service. **Number of employees at this location:** 400.

MUHLENBERG COLLEGE
2400 Chew Street, Allentown PA 18104-5586. 484/664-3166. **Fax:** 484/664-3107. **Contact:** Anne W. Hochella, Vice President Human Resources. **E-mail address:** hocella@muhlenberg.edu. **World Wide Web address:** http://www.muhlenberg.edu. **Description:** A four-year, undergraduate, liberal arts college. Founded in 1848. **Positions advertised include:** Athletics Director; Adjunct Communications Professor; Network Administrator; Visiting Psychology Professor; Residence Coordinator. **President:** Arthur R. Taylor. **Number of employees at this location:** 500.

NOBEL LEARNING COMMUNITIES
1615 West Chester Pike, West Chester PA 19382. 484/947-2000. **Contact:** Human Resources. **World Wide Web address:** http://www.nobellearning.com. **Description:** Operates 147 nonsectarian private schools, including preschools, elementary schools, and middle schools in 13 states. Founded in 1982. **NOTE:** Teachers interested in employment opportunities may apply through website. The job postings for administrative/executive positions are listed on http://www.monster.com. **Positions advertised include:** Executive Director; Principal.

PENNSYLVANIA STATE HARRISBURG
777 West Harrisburg Pike, Middletown PA 17057. 814/865-1387. **Fax:** 814/865-3750. **Recorded jobline:** 814/865-JOBS. **Contact:** Employment Division. **World Wide Web address:** http://www.hbg.psu.edu. **Description:** A state university offering undergraduate and graduate programs. Approximately 3,500 students attend Penn State Harrisburg. **NOTE:** Application instructions are provided online. **Special programs:** Internships. **Corporate headquarters location:** University Park PA. **Number of employees at this location:** 350. **Number of employees nationwide:** 16,000.

PENNSYLVANIA STATE NEW KENSINGTON
3550 Seventh Street, New Kensington PA 15068. 724/334-6025. **Contact:** Human Resources. **World Wide Web address:** http://www.nk.psu.edu. **Description:** The New Kensington location of the state university system. This campus offers a four-year program and awards associate degrees. Enrollment is 1,100 undergraduates. **NOTE:** Application instructions are provided online.

PENNSYLVANIA STATE UNIVERSITY
THE BEHREND COLLEGE
5091 Station Road, Erie PA 16563-0103. 814/898-6000. **Fax:** 814/865-3750. **Recorded jobline:** 814/865-JOBS. **Contact:** Employment Division. **World Wide Web address:** http://www.pserie.psu.edu. **Description:** A location of the Penn State University system. The Behrend College, with an enrollment of 2,800 undergraduates and 200 graduate students, offers four-year undergraduate as well as graduate programs. Penn State awards associate, bachelor's, and master's degrees including MBAs. **NOTE:** Application instructions are provided online.

PHILADELPHIA UNIVERSITY
School House & Henry Avenue, Philadelphia PA 19144. 215/951-2965. **Contact:** Kathryn Flannery, Director Human Resources. **E-mail address:**

humanresources@philau.edu. **World Wide Web address:** http://www.philau.edu. **Description:** A four-year college offering bachelor's and master's degrees including MBAs. Approximately 3,100 undergraduate and graduate students attend Philadelphia University. **Positions advertised include:** Assistant/Associate Professor, Various Departments; Director of Institutional Research; Sr. Accountant; Systems Administrator & Developer.

SHIPPENSBURG UNIVERSITY
1871 Old Main Drive, Shippensburg PA 17257-2299. 717/477-1124. **Fax:** 717/477-4037. **Contact:** Office of Human Resources. **E-mail address:** hr@ship.edu. **World Wide Web address:** http://www.ship.edu. **Description:** A four-year university offering bachelor's and master's degrees. Approximately 5,200 undergraduates and 1,200 graduate students attend Shippensburg University. **Positions advertised include:** Assistant Professor, Various Departments; Assistant Woman's Basketball Coach; Custodial Worker.

SLIPPERY ROCK UNIVERSITY
1 Morrow Way, 205 Old Main, Slippery Rock PA 16057. 724/738-2070. **Fax:** 724/738-4475. **Contact:** Human Resources. **World Wide Web address:** http://www.sru.edu. **Description:** A four-year university offering several undergraduate, graduate, and doctoral programs. Enrollment at Slippery Rock University is approximately 7,500.

STATE COLLEGE AREA SCHOOL DISTRICT
131 West Nittany Avenue, State College PA 16801. 814/231-1051. **Contact:** Dennis Guthe, Personnel Director. **World Wide Web address:** http://www.scasd.k12.pa.us. **Description:** Administrative offices of the State College public school district. The district includes 11 elementary schools, two middle schools, and one high school.

SWARTHMORE COLLEGE
500 College Avenue, Swarthmore PA 19081. 610/328-7797. **Fax:** 610/690-2040. **Recorded jobline:** 610/328-8494. **Contact:** Human Resources. **E-mail address:** jobapps@swarthmore.edu. **World Wide Web address:** http://www.swarthmore.edu. **Description:** Swarthmore College is a private, liberal arts college with an enrollment of 1,500. Founded in 1864. **Positions advertised include:** Dean of Students; Social Sciences Librarian; Electronic Resources Coordinator.

TEMPLE UNIVERSITY
University Services Building, 1601 North Broad Street, USB Room 202, Philadelphia PA 19122. 215/204-7174. **Contact:** Personnel Department. **World Wide Web address:** http://www.temple.edu. **Description:** A four-year university offering bachelor's, master's (including MBAs), first professional, and doctoral degrees. Approximately 22,000 undergraduate and 9,400 graduate students attend Temple University. **Positions advertised include:** Accounts Payable Clerk; Administrative Assistant; Assistant Area Manager; Assistant Director of Residential Life; Bibliographic Assistant; Carpenter; Claims Manager; Coding Specialist; Director of Development; General Mechanic; Laboratory Technician. **Corporate headquarters location:** This location. **Number of employees at this location:** 9,000.

UNIVERSITY OF PENNSYLVANIA
3401 Walnut Street, Suite 527A, Philadelphia PA 19104-6228. 215/898-7284. **Contact:** Human Resources. **E-mail address:** recruitment@hr.upenn.com. **World Wide Web address:** http://www.upenn.edu. **Description:** An Ivy League university offering undergraduate and graduate degrees. **NOTE:** Search and apply for positions online. Current Penn staff can forward resumes to recruitment@hr.upenn.edu. **Positions advertised include:** Accountant; Administrative Assistant; Assistant Director of Operations; Business Manager; Caseworker; Clinic Clerk; Data Entry Clerk; Driver/Escort; Electrician. **Special programs:** Internships; Training.

UNIVERSITY OF PITTSBURGH
200 South Craig Street, 100 Craig Hall, Pittsburgh PA 15260. 412/624-8150. **Fax:** 412/624-8720. **Contact:** Human Resources. **World Wide Web address:** http://www.pitt.edu. **Description:** A university. **Corporate headquarters location:** This location. **Operations at this facility include:** Administration; Research and Development; Service. **Number of employees at this location:** 10,700.

UNIVERSITY OF PITTSBURGH AT BRADFORD
300 Campus Drive, 220 Hanley Library, Bradford PA 16701. 814/362-7531. **Fax:** 814/362-5079. **Contact:** Laurel Retzer, Human Resources Manager. **E-mail address:** leb2@pitt.edu. **World Wide Web address:** http://www.upb.pitt.edu. **Description:** As part of the University of Pittsburgh system, the University of Pittsburgh at Bradford offers 39 baccalaureate and professional programs. **NOTE:** Teaching positions are filled through the Academic Affairs Department. **Number of employees at this location:** 200.

UNIVERSITY OF PITTSBURGH AT GREENSBURG
1150 Mount Pleasant Road, Room 103, Lynch Hall, Greensburg PA 15601. 724/836-9902. **Contact:** Human Resources. **World Wide Web address:** http://www.upg.pitt.edu. **Description:** The Greensburg location of the University of Pittsburgh. **NOTE:** Hiring is conducted through the Pittsburgh campus Human Resources Office.

UNIVERSITY OF SCRANTON
St. Thomas Hall, Room 104, Scranton PA 18510. 570/941-7452. **Fax:** 570/941-4636. **Contact:** Darrell Frederick, Director Human Resources. **World Wide Web address:** http://www.uofs.edu. **Description:** A four-year Jesuit university offering certificates, associate's, bachelor's, and master's degrees (including MBAs). Approximately 3,950 undergraduate and 700 graduate students attend the University of Scranton.

VILLANOVA UNIVERSITY
800 Lancaster Avenue, Villanova PA 19085-1699. 610/519-7900. **Fax:** 610/519-6667. **Recorded jobline:** 610/519-5900. **Contact:** Barbara Kearns, Employment Coordinator. **E-mail address:** hr@villanova.edu. **World Wide Web address:** http://www.villanova.edu. **Description:** A Catholic university serving approximately 6,000 full-time undergraduates and 4,000 graduate and part-time students in the Colleges of Arts & Sciences, Engineering, Commerce & Finance, Nursing, and Law, as well as an MBA program. Founded in 1842. **Corporate headquarters location:** This location. **Number of employees at this location:** 1,500.

WEST CHESTER UNIVERSITY
201 Carter Drive, Suite 100, West Chester PA 19383. 610/436-2800. **Fax:** 610/436-3464. **Recorded jobline:** 610/436-3464. **Contact:** Office of Human Resources. **World Wide Web address:** http://www.wcupa.edu. **Description:** A four-year university offering certificates, associate's, bachelor's, and master's degrees. Approximately 9,300 undergraduate and 1,800 graduate students attend West Chester University.

WIDENER UNIVERSITY
One University Place, Chester PA 19013-5792. 610/499-4278. **Fax:** 610/499-4386. **Contact:** Office of Human Resources. **World Wide Web address:** http://www.widener.edu. **Description:** A four-year university offering bachelor's, master's (including MBAs), and doctoral degrees. Approximately 4,900 undergraduate and 3,000 graduate students attend Widener.

WILKES UNIVERSITY
256 South Franklin Street, Wilkes-Barre PA 18766. 570/408-4630. **Fax:** 570/408-7863. **Contact:** Mary Lorusso, Manager Human Resources. **World Wide Web address:** http://www.wilkes.edu. **Description:** A four-year university offering bachelor's and master's

degrees. Approximately 2,000 undergraduate and 2,000 graduate students attend Wilkes University.

YORK COLLEGE OF PENNSYLVANIA
Country Club Road, York PA 17405-7199. 717/846-7788. **Contact:** Human Resources. **E-mail address:** kgood@ycp.edu. **World Wide Web address:** http://www.ycp.edu. **Description:** A four-year college offering associate's, bachelor's, and master's degrees including MBAs. Approximately 4,900 undergraduate and 50 graduate students attend York College. **NOTE:** Unsolicited resumes not accepted. **Positions advertised include:** Assistant Dean of Athletics and Recreation; Adjunct Instructor; Academic Advisor; Laboratory Coordinator; Administrative Support.

Rhode Island
BROWN UNIVERSITY
P.O. Box 1879, 164 Angell Street, Providence RI 02912. 401/863-3175. **Fax:** 401/863-1833. **Contact:** Human Resources. **E-mail address:** hrweb@brown.edu. **World Wide Web address:** http://www.brown.edu. **Description:** An Ivy League university with over 7,500 students in undergraduate, graduate and medical programs. **NOTE:** See website to search and apply for open positions. **Positions advertised include:** Project Coordinator; Radiation Safety Officer; Registered Nurse; Research Assistant; Secretary; Science Media Specialist; International Advancement Officer; Investment Analyst; Financial Office Assistant; Help Desk Coordinator; Executive Coordinator; Development Associate; Custodian; University Archivist; Assistant Food Service Worker.

COMMUNITY COLLEGE OF RHODE ISLAND (CCRI)
400 East Avenue, Warwick RI 02886-1807. 401/825-2311. **Fax:** 401/825-2345. **Contact:** Human Resources. **E-mail address:** personnel@ccri.edu. **World Wide Web address:** http://www.ccri.edu. **Description:** Community College of Rhode Island (CCRI) provides a career, technical, and academic programs. CCRI enrolls more than 16,000 students in credit courses each semester. The college offers associate degrees in arts, science, applied science, applied science in technical studies, and fine arts degrees. **NOTE:** See website for current job openings and application instructions. **Positions advertised include:** Adjunct Faculty (various departments); Staff Assistant; Part-Time Athletic Trainer; Part-time Database Manager. **Other area locations:** Lincoln RI; Providence RI; Newport RI; North Kingstown RI; Westerly RI.

JOHNSON & WALES UNIVERSITY
8 Abbott Park Place, Providence RI 02903. 401/598-1000. **Contact:** Human Resources. **E-mail address:** work@jwu.edu. **World Wide Web address:** http://work.jwu.edu. **Description:** A university concentrating in the culinary arts and hospitality, with additional programs in business and technology. Degree programs are offered at the undergraduate, graduate and doctoral level. **NOTE:** Applications are only accepted online. **Positions advertised include:** Finance Faculty; IT Study Abroad Communications & Database Coordinator; Assistant Director; Administrative Assistant; Billing Representative; Head Women's Soccer Coach; HVAC Master Adjunct Faculty (various departments). **Other U.S. locations:** NC; SC; VA; FL; CO.

NEW ENGLAND INSTITUTE OF TECHNOLOGY (NEW ENGLAND TECH)
2500 Post Road, Warwick RI 02886. 401/467-7744. **Toll-free phone:** 800/736-7744. **Contact:** Human Resources. **World Wide Web address:** http://www.neit.edu. **Description:** A technical school offering associate's degrees and bachelor's degrees in a variety of fields. New England Institute of Technology's career services office is available to graduates for the duration of their careers.

PROVIDENCE COLLEGE
Harkins Hall, Room 407, Providence RI 02918. 401/865-2341. **Fax:** 401/865-1341. **Contact:** Kathleen Alvino, Director of Human Resources. **E-mail address:** hr@providence.edu. **World Wide Web address:** http://www.providence.edu. **Description:** The only college in the United States under the stewardship of the Dominican Friars. The college offers bachelor's, master's and doctoral degrees in arts and sciences. Founded in 1917. **NOTE:** See website for current job openings and application instructions. **Positions advertised include:** Academic/Life Skills Coordinator for Student Athletes; Associate Dean of SCE/Director of Summer School; Assistant Director of Annual Giving; Environmental Compliance Officer; Associate Director of Financial Aid; Major Gifts Officer; Senior Hall Director; Adjunct Assistant Professor in Psychology; Cataloging and Digital Projects Librarian/Assistant Professor.

RHODE ISLAND COLLEGE
600 Mount Pleasant Avenue, Providence RI 02908. 401/456-8216. **Fax:** 401/456-8217. **Contact:** Robert G. Tetreault, Office of Human Resources. **E-mail address:** rtetreault@ric.edu. **World Wide Web address:** http://www.ric.edu. **Description:** A liberal arts college offering undergraduate and graduate degrees. The college has 1,000 employees and 8,500 students. It operates 40 buildings and has a budget of nearly $90 million. **NOTE:** See website for current job openings and application instructions. **Positions advertised include:** Associate Professor, School of Social Work; Assistant Professor, Cell Biology; Assistant Director of Security and Safety; Cook's Helper; Substitute Teacher; Substitute Nurse.

RHODE ISLAND SCHOOL OF DESIGN
2 College Street, Providence RI 02903-2784. 401/454-6606. **Recorded jobline:** 888/816-7473. **Fax:** 401/454-6565. **Contact:** Human Resources. **World Wide Web address:** http://www.risd.edu. **Description:** A preeminent art and design college with roughly 1,900 undergraduates and 400 graduate students. Included within the college is The RISD Museum of Art, which houses a world-class collection of art. **Positions advertised include: Positions advertised include:** Account Coordinator; Assistant Professor (various departments); Controller; Curator; Department Coordinator; Department Buyer – RISD Store; Network Engineer; Special Events Assistant.

ROGER WILLIAMS UNIVERSITY
One Old Ferry Road, Bristol RI 02809. 401/254-3028. **Fax:** 401/254-3370. **Contact:** Human Resources. **E-mail address:** human_resources@rwu.edu. **World Wide Web address:** http://www.rwu.edu. **Description:** An independent, coeducational university of liberal arts and selected professional programs. It enrolls approximately 3,800 students in 31 majors. **NOTE:** See website for current job openings. Send resume and cover letter by mail or e-mail. **Positions advertised include:** Financial Analyst; Energy Manager; Career Services Coordinator; Public Services Librarian; Web and Electronic Communication Coordinator; Career Services Coordinator; Curator of Visual Resources; Development Officer.

SALVE REGINA UNIVERSITY
100 Ochre Point Avenue, Newport RI 02840-4192. 401/847-6650. **Fax:** 401/341-2921. **Contact:** Diane Blanchette, Director of Human Resources. **E-mail address:** resumes@salve.edu. **World Wide Web address:** http://www.salve.edu. **Description:** A coeducational university of arts and sciences founded by the Sisters of Mercy with an enrollment of more than 2,200. The university offers more than 40 concentrations leading to associate's and bachelor's degrees and offers master's degrees in 15 majors. **NOTE:** See website for current job openings and application instructions. Positions classified as Administrative & Staff; Dining & Custodial; and Faculty. **Positions advertised include:** Training and Special Events Manager; Executive Director, Pell Center for International Relations and Public Policy; Information Security Advisor.

UNIVERSITY OF RHODE ISLAND
80 Lower College Road, Kingston RI 02881. 401/874-2416. **Fax:** 401/874-5741. **Recorded jobline:** 401/874-7117. **Contact:** Human Resources. **E-mail address:** humanres@etal.uri.edu. **World Wide Web address:** http://www.uri.edu. **Description:** A public university with an enrollment of over 10,000 undergraduates and over 3,000 graduate students. URI offers undergraduate and graduate programs in the Liberal Arts and Sciences as well as focus programs in areas such as: marine and environmental studies; health; children, families, and communities; and enterprise and advanced technology. **NOTE:** Applicants for academic and professional positions should consult website for individual contacts and requirements. Classified positions fall under Rhode Island's Civil Service System, and primarily include the University's service/maintenance/dining positions, clerical support positions, nurses and various technical/para-professional positions. **Positions advertised include:** Assistant Professor (various departments); Coordinator - Student Leadership Programs/Student Life; Dean, University Libraries; Director, Compliance, Research Office; Marine Research Specialist I; Senior Associate Director, Enrollment Services; Specialist, Major Donor Research/Development. **Special programs:** Tuition Waivers for employees, their spouses and dependents. **Office hours:** Monday – Friday, 8:30 a.m. – 4:30 p.m. **Other area locations:** Providence RI; West Greenwich RI. **President:** Robert L. Carothers.

South Carolina
ANDERSON COUNTY SCHOOL DISTRICT 1
P.O. Box 99, Williamston SC 29697. 864/847-7344. **Fax:** 864/847-3543. **Contact:** David Havird, Associate Superintendent. **E-mail address:** jobopportunities@.anderson1.k12.sc.us. **World Wide Web address:** http://www.anderson1.k12.sc.us. **Description:** Administrative offices for the public school district. **Positions advertised include:** Elementary Education Director; Bus Driver Assistant; Custodian; School Nurse.

COASTAL CAROLINA UNIVERSITY
P.O. Box 261954, Conway SC 29528-6054. 843/349-2036. **Fax:** 843/349-6432. **Contact:** Jeniffer Silver, Employment Manager. **E-mail address:** jobs@coastal.edu. **World Wide Web address:** http://www.coastal.edu. **Description:** A private four-year university offering both graduate and undergraduate programs that currently enrolls 6,780 students. **Positions advertised include:** Athletic Training Instructor; Director of Counseling Services; Security Officer.

ORANGEBURG CONSOLIDATED SCHOOL DISTRICT 5
578 Ellis Avenue, Orangeburg SC 29115. 803/534-7936. **Contact:** Assistant Superintendent of Human Resources/Support Services. **World Wide Web address:** http://www.orangeburg5.k12.sc.us. **Description:** A public school district comprised of eight elementary schools, five middle schools, and three high schools. **Positions advertised include:** Elementary School Principal; Educable Mentally Disabled Learning Teacher; Emotionally Disabled Teacher; Social Studies Teacher; Occupational Therapist; Registered Nurse; Building Fund Management Specialist; Guidance Counselor.

UNIVERSITY OF SOUTH CAROLINA
1600 Hampton Street, Columbia SC 29208. 803/777-3821. **Fax:** 803/777-0302. **Contact:** Ella Marshall, Employment Manager. **E-mail address:** uscjobs@sc.edu. **World Wide Web address:** http://www.sc.edu. **Description:** A four-year, state university. The university awards bachelors, masters, and doctoral degrees and enrolls over 25,000 students per year. The University of South Carolina also has campuses in Spartanburg and Aiken. Founded in 1801. **Positions advertised include:** Administrative Coordinator; Lab Technician; Technical Medical Associate; Administrative Specialist; Research Technician; Public Information Coordinator; Data Entry & Control Clerk. **Corporate headquarters location:** This location. **Operations at this facility include:** Administration; Research and Development; Service.

WILLIAMSBURG COUNTY SCHOOL DISTRICT
423 School Street, P.O. Box 1067, Kingstree SC 29556. 843/355-5571. **Fax:** 843/355-0804. **Contact:** Director of Personnel. **E-mail address:** wcsd@hotmail.com. **World Wide Web address:** http://www.wcsd.k12.sc.us. **Description:** Early Childhood Education Teacher; Family Consulting Services; Music Teacher; Language Arts Teacher; Mathematics Teacher; Physical Education Teacher; Science Teacher; Special Education Teacher. **Number of employees:** 450.

South Dakota
AUGUSTANA COLLEGE
2001 South Summit Avenue, Sioux Falls SD 57197. 605/274-4110. **Toll-free phone:** 800/727-2844. **Fax:** 605/274-5547. **Contact:** Human Resources. **E-mail address:** humanresources@augie.edu. **World Wide Web address:** http://www.augie.edu. **Description:** A liberal arts college of the Evangelical Lutheran Church in America that offers associate's, bachelor's, and master's degrees. **NOTE:** See website for current openings, application instructions and to download an application. Jobs classified as faculty, administrative and staff. **Positions advertised include:** Assistant Professor – Physics; Research/Teaching Postdoctoral - Plant Genetics; Assistant Professor of English/American Literature; Substitute Teacher.

BLACK HILLS SPECIAL SERVICES COOPERATIVE
P.O. Box 218, Sturgis SD 57785. 605/423-4444. **Fax:** 605/347-5223. **Contact:** Human Resources. **World Wide Web address:** http://www.bhssc.org. **Description:** A direct extension of 12 South Dakota public school districts. It provides a wide range of services, many statewide, which schools cannot establish independently. **NOTE:** See website for current openings and application instructions. **Positions advertised include:** PLANS Coordinator; Residential Assistant. **Number of employees at this location:** 450.

BLACK HILLS STATE UNIVERSITY
1200 University Street, Unit 9568, Spearfish SD 57799. 605/642-6545. **Fax:** 605/642-6254. **Contact:** Anita Haeder, Human Resource Officer. **E-mail address:** anitahaeder@bhsu.edu. **World Wide Web address:** http://www.bhsu.edu. **Description:** A university offering associate's, bachelor's, and master's degrees. Founded in 1885. **NOTE:** See website for current positions and to download application form. **Positions advertised include:** Head Women's Softball Coach; Assistant Professor – Various Departments; Career Counselor; Custodial Worker. **Special programs:** Internships; Volunteer positions. **Number of employees at this location:** 305.

DAKOTA STATE UNIVERSITY
820 North Washington Avenue, Madison SD 57042. 605/256-5127. **Toll-free phone:** 800/DSU-9988. **Fax:** 605/256-5197. **Contact:** Nancy Grassel, Director of Human Resources. **E-mail address:** Nancy.Grassel@dsu.edu. **World Wide Web address:** http://www.dsu.edu. **Description:** A public university that offers undergraduate majors in education, arts and sciences, and business and information systems, as well as graduate degrees in information systems, educational technology and information assurance. **Positions advertised include:** Accounting Faculty; Information Systems Faculty; Offensive Coordinator/Instructor – Football; Physics Faculty. **President:** Douglas Knowlton. **Number of employees at this location:** 220.

NORTHERN STATE UNIVERSITY
1200 South Jay Street, Aberdeen SD 57401-7198. 605/626-2520. **Fax:** 605/626-3022. **Contact:** Mary Ellen Lehr, Human Resources. **E-mail address:** lehrme@northern.edu. **World Wide Web address:** http://www.northern.edu. **Description:** Offers pre-professional and professional programs leading to the

Bachelor of Arts, Bachelor of Science, and Bachelor of Science in education and bachelor of music education degrees. The school also provides undergraduate and graduate professional programs in education for the preparation of teachers, guidance counselors and principals. **NOTE:** See website for current job openings and to download application. **Positions advertised include:** Dean; Provost/Vice President for Academic Affairs; Accounting Professor; Assistant; Professor of Biology; Banking & Financial Services Faculty. **Number of employees at this location:** 300.

SOUTH DAKOTA SCHOOL OF MINES & TECHNOLOGY
501 East St. Joseph Street, Rapid City SD 57701. 605/394-1203. **Toll-free phone:** 800/544-8162. **Fax:** 605/394-6131. **Contact:** Director of Human Resources. **E-mail address:** deborah.sloat@sdsmt.edu. **World Wide Web address:** http://sdmines.sdsmt.edu. **Description:** A university of engineering and science offering bachelor's, master's and doctoral degrees. The school has approximately 2,500 undergraduate and graduate students. Founded in 1885. **NOTE:** Please visit website for current job openings and to download an application form. **Positions advertised include:** Budget Analyst; Hall Director; Dean, College of Engineering; Director of Admissions; Program Assistant; Assistant Professor (various departments); Associate Professor (various departments).

SOUTH DAKOTA STATE UNIVERSITY
P.O. Box 2201, Brookings SD 57007. 605/688-4128. **Toll-free phone:** 800/952-3541. **Fax:** 605/688-5822. **Contact:** Mary Larson, Human Resources Generalist. **E-mail address:** mary.larson@sdstate.edu. **World Wide Web address:** http://www.sdstate.edu. **Description:** A state university offering bachelor's, master's, and doctoral degrees in agriculture and biological sciences; arts and sciences; education and counseling; engineering; family and consumer sciences; general registration; nursing; pharmacy; and graduate school studies. Founded in 1881. **NOTE:** See website for current job openings and application instructions. **Positions advertised include:** Temporary Secretary; Temporary Pilot; Custodial Worker; Senior Agricultural Research Technician; Laboratory Technician; Microbiologist; Building Maintenance Worker. **President:** Peggy Miller. **Number of employees at this location:** 1,700.
University of South Dakota

Tennessee
BELMONT UNIVERSITY
CHRISTIAN BROTHERS UNIVERSITY
650 East Parkway South, Memphis TN 38104. 901/321-3000. **Contact:** Human Resources. **World Wide Web address:** http://www.cbu.edu. **Description:** A Catholic university with an enrollment of 1,900 students offering bachelor of arts, bachelor of science, master's, and M.B.A. degrees. Founded in 1871.

EAST TENNESSEE STATE UNIVERSITY
ETSU Box 70564, Johnson City TN 37614-1707. 423/439-4457. **Fax:** 423/439-8354. **Contact:** Human Resources. **World Wide Web address:** http://www.etsu.edu. **Description:** A state university with an enrollment of approximately 11,000 students. The university offers over 100 academic programs including two-year, four-year, and graduate degrees. **NOTE:** E-mailed applications and resumes are not accepted. Search for positions and download application form online. **Positions advertised include:** Instructor, Various Departments; Assistant/Associate Professor, Various Departments; Research Analyst; Assistant Athletic Director; Associate Vice President for University Advancement Capital Campaign.

MIDDLE TENNESSEE STATE UNIVERSITY
Cope Administration Building, Room 215, Murfreesboro TN 37132. 615/898-2928. **Fax:** 615/898-5444. **Recorded jobline:** 615/898-5353. **Contact:** Human Resource Services. **E-mail address:** hrs@mtsu.edu. **World Wide Web address:** http://www.mtsu.edu. **Description:** A state university with a total student enrollment of approximately 21,000 students. Founded in 1911. **Positions advertised include:** Director of Alumni Relations; Director of Records; Assistant Dean for Judicial Affairs and Mediation Services; Psychologist; Coordinator of Field Placements; Coordinator, College of Liberal Arts; Academic Advisor; Faculty Positions. **Number of employees at this location:** 1,400.

MONTGOMERY BELL ACADEMY
4001 Harding Road, Nashville TN 37205. 615/298-5514. **Fax:** 615/297-0271. **Contact:** Headmaster. **World Wide Web address:** http://www.montgomerybell.com. **Description:** An all-male, private high school with a total enrollment of 660. Founded in 1867.

NASHVILLE STATE COMMUNITY COLLEGE
120 White Bridge Road, Nashville TN 37209. 615/353-3304. **Contact:** Human Resources. **E-mail address:** hr@nscc.edu. **World Wide Web address:** http://www.nscc.edu. **Description:** A two-year college offering associate's degree programs in science, applied science, and arts, as well as one-year certificates. The Tennessee Technology Center, which offers vocational programs, is also at this location. **NOTE:** Search and apply for positions online.

OAK RIDGE ASSOCIATED UNIVERSITIES
130 Badger Avenue, P.O. Box 117, Oak Ridge TN 37831-0117. 865/576-3000. **Contact:** Employment Department. **E-mail address:** empdept@orau.gov. **World Wide Web address:** http://www.orau.org. **Description:** A nonprofit association of more than 50 colleges and universities acting as prime contractor for research, training, education, and information activities. **NOTE:** Search and apply for positions online. **Positions advertised include:** Health Physicist; Operations Planner; Proposal Analyst; Contracts Specialist; Engineering Technician; System Support Specialist.

RHODES COLLEGE
2000 North Parkway, Memphis TN 38112-1690. 901/843-3750. **Recorded jobline:** 901/843-3759. **Contact:** Human Resources. **E-mail address:** hr@rhodes.edu. **World Wide Web address:** http://www.rhodes.edu. **Description:** A four-year liberal arts college with an enrollment of 1,500. Founded in 1848.

SOUTHWEST TENNESSEE COMMUNITY COLLEGE
5983 Macon Cove, Memphis TN 38134-7693. 901/333-4226. **Fax:** 901/333-5264. **Contact:** Human Resources Department. **World Wide Web address:** http://www.southwest.tn.edu. **Description:** A two-year technical institute offering associate's degrees with an enrollment of 12,000. **NOTE:** Search and apply for positions online. **Positions advertised include:** Instructor, Radiologic Technology; Program Coordinator; Instructor, Biology; Instructor, Mathematics.

TENNESSEE STATE UNIVERSITY
3500 John A. Merritt Boulevard, Campus Box 9628, Nashville TN 37209. 615/963-5281. **Contact:** Human Resources Office. **World Wide Web address:** http://www.tnstate.edu. **Description:** A state university with an enrollment of approximately 8,750 students. Founded in 1912. **NOTE:** Search for positions online. **Positions advertised include:** Director, School of Nursing; Assistant/Associate Professor, Health Sciences; Assistant/Associate Professor, Criminal Justice.

TENNESSEE TECHNOLOGICAL UNIVERSITY
Derryberry Hall, One William Jones Drive, Room 146, P.O. Box 5132, Cookeville TN 38505. 931/372-3713. **Fax:** 931/372-3898. **Recorded jobline:** 931/372-3048. **Contact:** Tammy Reynolds, Employment Manager. **E-mail address:** treynolds@ tntech.edu. **World Wide Web address:** http://www.tntech.edu. **Description:** A technical university with a total enrollment of approximately 9,100 graduate and undergraduate

students. The school offers 44 bachelor's degree and 20 graduate programs. **NOTE:** Search for positions online. **Positions advertised include:** Network Support Specialist; Assistant Professor (several disciplines); Chairperson, civil and Environmental Engineering; Chairperson, English Department; Chairperson, Mechanical Engineering Department.

UNIVERSITY OF TENNESSEE, CHATTANOOGA
615 McCallie Avenue, Department 3603, Chattanooga TN 37403-2598. 423/755-4221. **Contact:** Personnel Services Department. **E-mail address:** personnel@utc.edu. **World Wide Web address:** http://www.utc.edu. **Description:** A campus of the state university. **NOTE:** Search and apply for positions or download employment application (for non-faculty positions) online. **Positions advertised include:** Assistant Professor, Various Disciplines;

UNIVERSITY OF TENNESSEE, KNOXVILLE
221 Conference Center Building, Knoxville TN 37996-4125. 865/974-6642. **Fax:** 865/974-0659. **Recorded jobline:** 865/974-6644. **Contact:** Office of Human Resources. **E-mail address:** rgresshoff@utk.edu. **World Wide Web address:** http://www.utk.edu. **Description:** A university and research institution with a total enrollment of 27,300 students. **NOTE:** Search for positions online. **Positions advertised include:** Accounting Specialist; Financial Systems Analyst; IT Specialist; Research Assistant; Assistant/Associate Professor, Various Disciplines; Dean, Education, Health and Human Sciences. **Special programs:** Training. **Operations at this facility include:** Administration. **Number of employees at this location:** 4,500.

Texas

AMARILLO COLLEGE
P.O. Box 447, Amarillo TX 79178-0001. 806/371-5040. **Contact:** Human Resources. **World Wide Web address:** http://www.actx.edu/hr. **Description:** A two-year community college. Approximately 7,300 students are enrolled at this location. Amarillo College has three other campuses in Amarillo. **NOTE:** Please visit website to view job listings and to download application forms. Resumes are not accepted online; you must mail your resume. The Human Resources office is located at the Washington Street Campus, on the second floor of the Student Service Center, Suite 280. **Positions advertised include:** Instructor – Various Departments; Director of Human Resources; Director of Broadcasting Operations; Associate Director – Center for Continuing Healthcare Education; Dean of Student Services; Staff Assistant; Student Services and Outreach Representative; Senior Programmer/Analyst.

ANGELO STATE UNIVERSITY
P.O. Box 11009, ASU Station, San Angelo TX 76909. 325/942-2555. **Physical address:** 2601 West Avenue North, San Angelo TX 76909. **Contact:** Office of Human Resources. **E-mail address:** laura.billings@angelo.edu. **World Wide Web address:** http://www.angelo.edu. **Description:** A state university offering 45 bachelor's degree and 21 master's degree programs. Angelo State University has an enrollment of approximately 6,300 students. Founded in 1976. **NOTE:** Please visit website to view job listings and access application forms. **Positions advertised include:** Assistant Professor – Various Departments; Head – Department of Computer Science; Head, Department of Physical Therapy; Physical Therapy Faculty; Director of Institutional Effectiveness; Assistant Manager of Infrastructure Services; Area Coordinator.

THE ART INSTITUTE OF DALLAS
2 North Park East, 8080 Park Lane, Suite 100, Dallas TX 75231. 214/692-8080. **Toll-free phone:** 800/275-4243. **Fax:** 214/361-0178. **Contact:** Human Resources. **E-mail address:** aidjobs@aii.edu. **World Wide Web address:** http://www.aid.aii.edu. **Description:** A two-year accredited institute with associate degree programs in art, fashion, photography, interior design, and music and video production. **NOTE:** Please visit website to view job listings and apply online. **Positions advertised include:** Animation Instructor; Assistant Director of Admissions; Custodian/Porter; Digital Audio Instructor; Director of Residential Life and Housing. **Parent company:** Art Institutes International.

AUSTIN COMMUNITY COLLEGE
5930 Middle Fiskville Road, Austin TX 78752. 512/223-7534. Recorded jobline: 512/223-5621. **Contact:** Human Resources. **World Wide Web address:** http://www.austin.cc.tx.us. **Description:** A two-year community college. **NOTE:** Please visit website to search for jobs and download employment application. **Positions advertised include:** Coordinator, Internal Audit; Coordinator, Texas Success Initiative Program; Associate Vice President for Institutional Effectiveness; Web Development Specialist; Internal Programs Manager; Technical Office Assistant; Specialist, Student Recruitment; Senior Computer Support Technician; Online Application Software Administrator; Account Executive; Instructor, Various Departments; Faculty, Various Departments.

AUSTIN INDEPENDENT SCHOOL DISTRICT
1111 West Sixth Street, Austin TX 78703. 512/414-1700. **Contact:** Human Resources. **World Wide Web address:** http://www.austin.isd.tenet.edu. **Description:** This location serves as the administrative offices for the entire Austin K-12 school system. **NOTE:** This website has job listings for all of the schools in the Austin district. See website and apply online. **Positions advertised include:** Accounting Clerk; Art Teacher; Assistant Band Director; Bilingual Behavior Specialist; Biology/Athletics Teacher; Elementary Special Education Teacher; Geography Teacher; French Teacher; High School Librarian; History Teacher; Housekeeping Services Specialist.

BAYLOR UNIVERSITY
700 University Parks Drive, Clifton Robinson Tower, 2nd Floor, Waco TX 76706. 254/710-2219. **Fax:** 254/710-3819. **Contact:** Human Resources. **World Wide Web address:** http://www.baylor.edu. **Description:** One of the largest Baptist universities in the nation. Baylor University has over 13,000 students enrolled in a wide range of undergraduate and graduate programs. Founded in 1845. **NOTE:** Please visit website to search for jobs and to find more specific contact information. Applications are only accepted for open positions. Applications are kept on file for six months. Contact a Human Resources Specialist at 254/710-8539.

BROOKHAVEN COLLEGE
3939 Valley View Lane, Farmers Branch TX 75244. 972/860-4813. **Fax:** 972/860-4897. **Recorded jobline:** 214/860-243.8. **Contact:** Human Resources Department. **E-mail address:** bhcresume@dcccd.edu. **World Wide Web address:** http://www.dcccd.edu/bhc. **Description:** A two-year community college offering a full range of transferable, freshman- and sophomore-level college courses. The college serves the northern portion of Dallas County, including North Dallas, Carrollton, Farmers Branch, Addison, Lewisville, Flower Mound, and The Colony. Founded in 1978. **NOTE:** Please visit website to view job listings. **Positions advertised include:** Instructional Dean; Dispatcher; **Corporate headquarters location:** This location. **Parent company:** Dallas County Community College District.

THE BROWN SCHOOLS DALLAS COUNTY JUVENILE JUSTICE CHARTER SCHOOLS
2525 Murworth Drive, Suite 100, Houston TX 77054. 214/752-5976. **Contact:** Human Resources. **E-mail address:** educationcareers@cedu.com. **World Wide Web address:** http://www.brownschools.com. **Description:** Provides specialty services including psychiatric and behavioral services, rehabilitation services, educational services, home health services,

outpatient services, residential treatment, and adoption and foster care. The Brown Schools operate more than 25 facilities in ten states. **Corporate headquarters location:** North Palm Beach FL. **Operations at this facility include:** This school provides a Juvenile Justice Education program in a day school setting for children from age 10 – 17. The school also provides services for those placed with the Dallas County Juvenile Probation Department.

CISCO JUNIOR COLLEGE
101 College Heights, Cisco TX 76437. 254/442-2567. **Contact:** Personnel. **World Wide Web address:** http://www.cisco.cc.tx.us. **Description:** A junior college. **NOTE:** Please visit website to view job listings and download application form. Contact Personnel directly at 254/442-5121. **Positions advertised include:** Assistant Director of Financial Aid. **Other area locations:** Abilene TX.

COLLIN COUNTY COMMUNITY COLLEGE DISTRICT
P.O. Box 869055, Plano TX 75086. 972/985-3781. **Physical address:** 4800 Preston Park Boulevard, Suite B303, Plano TX 75093. . **Fax:** 972/985-3778. **Recorded jobline:** 972/881-5627. **Contact:** Vicki York, Human Resources. **E-mail address:** vyork@ccccd.edu. **World Wide Web address:** http://www.ccccd.edu. **Description:** A community college offering courses in computer science, humanities, international studies, fine arts, mathematics/natural science, health sciences, education, and engineering. **NOTE:** Please visit website to search for jobs and apply online. **Positions advertised include:** Associate Professor, Various Departments; Classroom Assistant; Natatorium Facilities Operator; Professor, Various Departments; Lab Assistant; Reference Librarian; Program Coordinator for Student Life and Student Organizations; Counselor Instructional Associate; Corporate Trainer; Financial Aid/Veterans Affairs Advisor; Accounts Payable Supervisor; Grant Coordinator. **Special programs:** Internships. **Corporate headquarters location:** This location. **Other area locations:** Allen TX; McKinney TX; Frisco TX; Rockwall TX.

DALLAS COUNTY COMMUNITY COLLEGE DISTRICT
701 Elm Street, Suite 600, Dallas TX 75202. 214/860-2431. **Recorded job line:** 214/860-2438. **Contact:** Human Resources. **World Wide Web address:** http://www.dcccd.edu. **Description:** A consortium of seven community colleges. **NOTE:** Online job listings for each of the community colleges in the district. **Positions advertised include:** Administrative, Full-time and part-time faculty, Information and Technology; Professional Support Staff.

DALLAS INDEPENDENT SCHOOL DISTRICT
3700 Ross Avenue, Dallas TX 750204. 972/925-3700. **Contact:** Human Resources. **World Wide Web address:** http://www.dallasisd.org. **Description:** The administrative offices for the Dallas school district. **NOTE:** This website provides job listings for all the schools in the Dallas area. An application is required for any position. Apply online. **Positions advertised include:** Band/Orchestra Teacher; ESL Elementary Teacher; Bilingual Elementary Teacher; Food and Child Nutrition Division Manager.

DEVRY INSTITUTE OF TECHNOLOGY
4800 Regent Boulevard, Irving TX 75063. 972/929-5777. **Contact:** Ms. Amy Rhodes, Human Resources Manager. **E-mail address:** gwilliams@dal.devry.edu. **World Wide Web address:** http://www.dal.devry.edu. **Description:** Devry Institute of Technology is a fully accredited college offering baccalaureate degrees in business and technology. **Corporate headquarters location:** Oakbrook Terrace IL. **Listed on:** New York Stock Exchange. **Stock exchange symbol:** DV.

EASTFIELD COLLEGE
3737 Motley Drive, Mesquite TX 75150. 972/860-7630. **Contact:** Kate Kelley, College Director, Human Resources. **World Wide Web address:** http://www.efc.dcccd.edu. **Description:** A community college.

EL CENTRO COLLEGE
801 Main Street, Dallas TX 75212. 214/860-2064. **Contact:** Human Resources. **World Wide Web address:** http://www.dcccd.edu. **Description:** A two-year community college. El Centro College operates as part of the Dallas County Community College District, which is comprised of seven area colleges.

FLIGHT SAFETY INTERNATIONAL, INC.
8900 Trinity Boulevard, Hurst TX 76102. 817/276-7500. **Fax:** 817/276-7501. **Contact:** Phyllis Lovelace, Manager of Human Resources. **World Wide Web address:** http://www.flightsafety.com. **Description:** Provides high-technology training to operators of aircraft and ships. Total training systems are used including sophisticated simulators and training devices, computer-based training, and professional instructors. **Corporate headquarters location:** Flushing NY. **Other U.S. locations:** Nationwide. **Listed on:** New York Stock Exchange. **Number of employees nationwide:** 2,000.

GALVESTON COLLEGE
4015 Avenue Q, Galveston TX 77550-7496. 409/763-6551. **Fax:** 409/762-0973. **Contact:** Human Resources. **E-mail address:** hrmail@gc.edu. **World Wide Web address:** http://www.gc.edu. **Description:** A community college with an enrollment of 2,500. **NOTE:** Some positions require an application and proof of credentials. See website for specific requirements. **Positions advertised include:** Full-time faculty; Adjunct Faculty; Administrative; Classified; Part-Time.

HARCOURT ASSESSMENT, INC.
19500 Bulverde, San Antonio TX 78259. 800/872-1726. **Contact:** Human Resources. **World Wide Web address:** http://www.marketplace.psychcorp.com. **Description:** One of the oldest and largest commercial test publishers in the nation. The company provides tests (e.g. the Stanford Achievement Test Series, the Metropolitan Achievement Tests, and Wechsler Intelligence Scales for Children and Adults) and related services to schools and colleges, clinicians and professional organizations, businesses, and public entities. **NOTE:** This company also seeks people test administrators and test writers. See website for contact information. **Positions advertised include:** Production Coordinator-Planning; Senior Associate, Sampling; Psychometrician; Test Development Manager; Senior Programmer Analyst.

HOUSTON INDEPENDENT SCHOOL DISTRICT
4400 West 18th Street, 1-SW, Houston TX 77092. 713/556-7383. **Toll-free phone:** 800/446-2821. **Contact:** Human Resources. **E-mail address:** jobs@houstonisd.org. **World Wide Web address:** http://www.houstonisd.org. **Description:** The administrative offices for Houston's schools. **NOTE:** The job listings for all the schools in the district are available on this website. Apply online. **Positions advertised include:** Instructional Coordinator; Early Childhood Specialist; Evaluation Specialist; Itinerant Teacher; Librarian; Counselor.

HUMBLE INDEPENDENT SCHOOL DISTRICT
P.O. Box 2000, Humble TX 77346. 281/641-1000. **Physical address**: 20200 Eastway Village Drive, Humble TX 77346. **Fax**: 281/641-1050. **Contact:** Guy Sconzo, Superintendent. **World Wide Web address:** http://www.humble.k12.tx.us. **Description:** Offices for the Humble school district, which comprises fifteen elementary schools, six middle schools, and five high schools. **NOTE:** Applications are available online for all positions. **Positions advertised include:** Attendance Specialist; Library Aide; Special Education Aide.

LAMAR UNIVERSITY
P.O. Box 11127, Beaumont TX 77710. 409/880-8375. **Physical address**: 1030 East Florida, Beaumont TX

77710. **Recorded jobline:** 409/880-8371. **Contact:** Human Resources. **World Wide Web address:** http://www.dept.lamar.edu/humanresources. **Description:** A university offering associate's, bachelor's, master's, and doctoral degrees. Both two- and four-year programs are available. Approximately 7,300 undergraduate and 700 graduate students attend Lamar University. **NOTE:** An application must be submitted with a resume. The application can be found at the company's website. Applications and resumes may be submitted online or hand-delivered to the Human Resources Office located at 1030 E. Florida, Beaumont TX. **Positions advertised include:** Faculty; Staff. **Corporate headquarters location:** This location.

LAREDO COMMUNITY COLLEGE
West End Washington Street, Laredo TX 78040. 956/721-5138. **Fax:** 956/721-5367. **Contact:** Human Resources. **World Wide Web address:** http://www.laredo.cc.tx.us. **Description:** Offers Associate's degrees in programs including business, computers, electronics, and nursing. Approximately 6,900 students attend the college. Founded in 1947. **NOTE:** An application must be submitted via mail for any position. The application can be downloaded on the college's website. **Positions advertised include:** Catalog Librarian; Chemistry Instructor; ENSL Spanish Instructor; Government Instructor; Mathematics Instructor; Music/Strings; Speech/Theater.

McMURRY UNIVERSITY
14th and Sayles, Abilene TX 79601. 325/793-3800. **Contact:** Human Resources. **World Wide Web address:** http://www.mcm.edu. **Description:** A four-year university offering undergraduate degrees. Approximately 1,425 students attend McMurry University **NOTE:** This company lists all job listings and specific contact information on its website. **Positions advertised include:** Instructor; Night Custodian; Assistant Professor.

MIDWESTERN STATE UNIVERSITY
3410 Taft Boulevard, Wichita Falls TX 76308. 940/397-4221. **Fax:** 940/397-4780. **Contact:** Jane Wolf, Human Resources. **E-mail address:** jane.wolf@mwsu.edu. **World Wide Web address:** http://www.mwsu.edu. **Description:** A state university with approximately 6,000 students enrolled in its undergraduate and graduate degree programs. **NOTE:** Interested jobseekers should see the university's website for listings and specific contact information. **Positions advertised include:** Admissions Assistant II; Custodian I; Intensive English Language Institute.

THE NATIONAL ALLIANCE FOR INSURANCE EDUCATION & RESEARCH
P.O. Box 27027, Austin TX 78755-1027. 512/345-7932. **Fax:** 512/343-2167. **Contact:** Amy Schott, Human Resources Director. **World Wide Web address:** http://www.scic.com. **Description:** A nonprofit insurance education organization offering the Certified Insurance Counselors (CIC) designation, the Certified Insurance Service Representatives (CISR) designation, and the Certified Risk Manager (CRM) designation. The Academy of Producers Insurance Studies is the research arm of The National Alliance.

NATIONAL FLUID POWER INSTITUTE
8305 New England, Amarillo TX 79119. 806/351-2841. **Toll-free phone:** 800/704-1066. **Fax:** 806/467-8026. **Contact:** Human Resources. **World Wide Web address:** http://www.nfpitraining.com. **Description:** Conducts nationwide troubleshooting classes for maintenance, mechanic, and engineering personnel. **Positions advertised include:** Inside Sales.

NORTH LAKE COLLEGE
5001 North MacArthur Boulevard, Irving TX 75038. 972/273-3000. **Contact:** Human Resources. **World Wide Web address:** http://www.northlakecollege.edu. **Description:** A two-year community college offering technical occupational courses as well as general studies. Approximately 6,200 students are enrolled. North Lake College operates as part of the Dallas County Community College District. **NOTE:** Interested jobseekers may apply at the college's Human Resources Office, Third Floor of the Administration Building Monday – Friday, 8:00 a.m. – 5:00 p.m.; Friday, 8:00 a.m. – 4:30 p.m. Job listings and applications are located also on the Dallas County Community College District's website: http://www.dcccd.edu.

RICE UNIVERSITY
Employment Office -- MS-56, P.O. Box 1892, Houston TX 77251-1892. 713/348-4074. **Physical address**: 6100 Main Street, Allen Center, Room 111, Houston TX 77251. **Fax:** 713/348-5496. **Recorded jobline:** 713/348-6080. **Contact:** Human Resources. **E-mail address:** careers@rice.edu. **World Wide Web address:** http://employment.rice.edu. **Description:** An independent, co-educational, private university for undergraduate and graduate studies, research, and professional training in selected disciplines. Rice University has an undergraduate and graduate enrollment of approximately 4,100. **NOTE:** An application is required for any position. It can be located on the website. Jobseekers may apply in person. **Positions advertised include:** Assistant Director; Research Analyst; Internal Auditor; Bookkeeper; Office Assistant; Program Coordinator; Staff Assistant.

RICHLAND COLLEGE
12800 Abrams Road, Dallas TX 75243-2199. 972/238-6240. Recorded jobline: 214/860-2438. **Contact:** Human Resources Director. **World Wide Web address:** http://www.rlc.dcccd.edu. **Description:** A junior college offering one- and two-year associate's degrees and certificates to approximately 12,500 students. Richland College operates as part of the Dallas County Community College District. **NOTE:** See the Dallas County's Community College District's website for job listings: http://www.dccd.edu. An application is required for any open position. It can be found on the District's website. **Positions advertised include:** Program Administrator; Dance Instructor; English Instructor; Department Assistant; Instructional Associate.

ST. EDWARD'S UNIVERSITY
Campus Mailbox 1042, 3001 South Congress Avenue, Austin TX 78748. 512/448-8587. **Fax:** 512/464-8813. **Recorded jobline:** 512/448-8541. **Contact:** Human Resources. **World Wide Web address:** http://www.stedwards.edu/humr/jobs.htm. **Description:** A private university affiliated with the Catholic Church. St. Edward's University offers a liberal arts program to undergraduate and graduate students interested in business or human services. **NOTE:** See website for job listings and contact information. **Positions advertised include:** Dean, School of Business; Assistant Professor, Finance; Assistant Professor, Bioinformatics; Library Instruction Coordinator; Adjunct Faculty; Residence Hall Director; Senior Secretary; Public Relations Assistant; Groundskeeper; Graduate Internship; Office Specialist. **Corporate headquarters location:** This location. **Operations at this facility include:** Administration. **Listed on:** Privately held.

SAM HOUSTON STATE UNIVERSITY
P.O. Box 2356, Huntsville TX 77341. 936/294-1069. **Physical address:** 1903 University Avenue, Estill Building #334, Huntsville TX 77341. **Fax:** 936/294-3611. **Recorded jobline:** 936/294-1067. **Contact:** Human Resources. **World Wide Web address:** http://www.shsu.edu. **Description:** A four-year state university offering programs through its four colleges: Arts & Sciences, Business Administration, Criminal Justice, and Educational and Applied Sciences. **NOTE:** Application forms must be submitted for any position. See website for forms, job listings and contact information. **Positions advertised include:** Assistant Professor; Lecturer; Full Professor; Staff Assistant; Computer Systems Technician; Staff Associate.

SAN ANTONIO INDEPENDENT SCHOOL DISTRICT
141 Lavaca Street, San Antonio TX 78210. 210/299-5606. **Contact:** Human Resources. **World Wide Web address:** http://www.saisd.net. **Description:** Administrative offices for the K-12 school system in San Antonio. **NOTE:** See the district's website for job listings for all schools in San Antonio and apply online. **Positions advertised include:** Librarian; Food Service Accounting Director; Assistant Principal; Special Education/Educational Diagnostician; Curriculum Lead Teacher; Technology Grant Specialist; Campus Social Worker; Data Clerk; Head Golf Coach; Head Soccer Coach; General Assistant Coach; Scheduler; Bus Driver; Head Custodian; Electrician; Police Officer.

SAN JACINTO COLLEGE DISTRICT
4624 Fairmont Parkway, Suite 106, Pasadena TX 77504. 281/998-6115. **Toll-free phone:** 800/825-5069. **Recorded jobline:** 281/998-6399. **Contact:** Human Resources. **World Wide Web address:** http://www.sjcd.cc.tx.us. **Description:** This location houses the administrative offices for the community college. Campuses are located in Pasadena and Houston. **NOTE:** See website for job listings and application requirements. **Positions advertised include:** Administrative Assistant; Accounting Assistant; Biology Professor; Graphic Artist Instructor; Adjunct Professor; Part-time Professor.

SOUTH PLAINS COLLEGE
1401 South College Avenue, Levelland TX 79336. 806/894-9611. **Fax:** 806/894-6880. **Contact:** Human Resources. **World Wide Web address:** http://www.spc.cc.tx.us. **Description:** A two-year, state-funded college. South Plains College offers majors in education, arts and sciences, nursing, and continuing education. The college has an enrollment of approximately 5,400 students. **NOTE:** An application is required for any position. See website for job listings and application information.

SOUTH TEXAS COLLEGE OF LAW
1303 San Jacinto Street, Houston TX 77002-7000. 713/646-1812. **Fax:** 713/646-1833. **Contact:** Human Resources. **World Wide Web address:** http://www.stcl.edu713/646-1812. **Description:** A private law school with an enrollment of approximately 1,250 students. Founded in 1923. **NOTE:** An application is required for any position. See website for job listings and application information. **Corporate headquarters location:** This location. **Operations at this facility include:** Administration. **Listed on:** Privately held.

SOUTHWEST COLLEGIATE INSTITUTE FOR THE DEAF
3200 Avenue Centre, Big Spring TX 79720-9960. 432/264-3700. **Fax:** 432/264-3707. **Contact:** Dr. Ron Brasel, Provost. **World Wide Web address:** http://www.hc.cc.tx.us. **Description:** A college for the deaf with an enrollment of approximately 105 students. The institute offers courses in liberal arts, technical, vocational/occupational, and developmental studies. Founded in 1980. **NOTE:** An application must be submitted for any position. See website for job listings and applications. **Positions advertised include:** Men's Residence Hall Supervisor; Preparatory English Instructor; Fitness Center Director; Utility Maintenance Technician; Speech Instructor. **Parent company:** Howard County Junior College.

STEPHEN F. AUSTIN STATE UNIVERSITY
P.O. Box 13039, SFA Station, Nacogdoches TX 75962. 936/468-2304. **Recorded jobline:** 936/468-3003. **Contact:** Human Resources. **World Wide Web address:** http://www.sfasu.edu. **Description:** A four-year college offering bachelor's and master's degrees. **NOTE:** Job listings and requirements are available online. A complete application is required for any position. Some positions may require an assessment test or documentation of credentials. To apply in person, visit the Human Resources Office in Room 201 of the Austin Building. Applications can be downloaded also from the university's website and mailed.

TARLETON STATE UNIVERSITY
Mail Stop T-510, Tarleton Station, Stephenville TX 76402. 817/965-5078. **Fax:** 254/968-9590. **Recorded jobline:** 254/968-9750. **Contact:** Mary Chenault, Employment Specialist. **World Wide Web address:** http://www.tarleton.edu. **Description:** A four-year state university offering bachelor's and master's degrees to approximately 6,300 students. Tarleton State University operates as part of the Texas A&M University System. **NOTE:** See the university's website for job listings, skill assessment test and application procedures. **Corporate headquarters location:** College Station TX.

TARRANT COUNTY JUNIOR COLLEGE
1500 Houston Street, Fort Worth TX 76102. 817/515-5250. **Contact:** Human Resources. **E-mail address:** jobs@tccd.edu. **World Wide Web address:** http://www.tcjc.cc.tx.us. **Description:** A two-year college offering associate's degrees and certificates. **NOTE:** This college requires jobseekers to complete a test online at its website. See website for additional information. **Positions advertised include:** Adjunct Instructor. **Operations at this facility include:** Administration.

TEXAS A&M UNIVERSITY
700 East University Drive, Suite 110C, College Station TX 77840. 979/845-5154. **Fax:** 979/847-8877. **Contact:** Human Resources. **E-mail address:** emploffice@tamu.edu. **World Wide Web address:** http://www.tamujobs.tamu.edu. **Description:** A university that offers a wide range of bachelor's, master's, doctoral and professional programs. Texas A&M also provides continuing education programs that serve the needs of area businesses and professionals. **NOTE:** Texas A&M University has 17 locations throughout the state. Its website provides a job listings for all locations. Apply online at the university's website or visit the Human Resources Office in Suite 101A.

TEXAS CHIROPRACTIC COLLEGE
5912 Spencer Highway, Pasadena TX 77505. 281/998-6003. **Toll-free phone:** 800/468-6839. **Fax:** 281/991-5237. **Contact:** Human Resources Director. **E-mail address:** HR@txchiro.edu. **World Wide Web address:** http://www.txchiro.edu. **Description:** Offers Doctor of Chiropractic and Bachelor of Science in Human Biology degrees. **Positions advertised include**: Moody Health Center Director.

TEXAS SOUTHERN UNIVERSITY
3100 Cleburne Avenue, Houston TX 77004. 713/313-7011. **Contact:** Human Resources. **World Wide Web address:** http://www.tsu.edu. **Description:** A four-year university offering both undergraduate and graduate degree programs. **NOTE:** See this university's website for job listings and application. **Positions advertised include:** Security Officer; Assistant Band Director; Program Director; Archivist; Professor (Various).

TEXAS STATE UNIVERSITY/SAN MARCOS
601 University Drive, J.C. Kellam Building, Suite 340, San Marcos TX 78666. 512/245-2557. **Fax:** 512/245-3911. **Contact:** Human Resources. **E-mail address:** hr@txstate.edu. **World Wide Web address:** http://www.humanresources.swt.edu. **Description:** A college offering undergraduate, graduate and doctoral degrees. **NOTE:** To apply for staff positions, a completed application must accompany a resume. Download application at the website. For faculty and other positions, see website for application procedures. **Positions advertised include:** Administrative Assistant; Grant Secretary; Data Entry Operator; Business Manager, Microcomputer Lab Assistant; Professor (Various).

TEXAS TECH UNIVERSITY
P.O. Box 41093, Lubbock TX 79409-1093. 806/742-3851. **Physical address**: West Hall 136, Lubbock TX

79401. **Contact:** James A. Brown, Managing Director. **E-mail address:** employment@ttu.edu. **World Wide Web address:** http://www.ttu.edu. **Description:** A state university. The university offers undergraduate and graduate degrees in liberal arts, law, applied health, and medicine. **NOTE:** Texas Tech University has campus locations throughout Texas. See website for locations, job listings and application requirements. **Positions advertised include:** Administrative Assistant; Analyst; Professor (Various); Chief Accountant; Chief of Police; Coordinator; Custodian; Development Officer; Lead Advisor; Medical Lab Technician; Patient Services Supervisor; Proposal Writer; Section Manager. **Corporate headquarters location:** This location.

TEXAS WESLEYAN UNIVERSITY
1201 Wesleyan Street, Fort Worth TX 76105. 817/531-4403. **Fax:** 817/531-4402. **Contact:** Human Resources. **E-mail address:** hr@txwes.edu. **World Wide Web address:** http://www.txwesleyan.edu. **Description:** A small, private university affiliated with the United Methodist Church. Texas Wesleyan University offers a variety of undergraduate and graduate degrees to approximately 3,000 students. Founded in 1890. **NOTE:** To apply, submit cover letter, resume and references. **Positions advertised include:** Benefactor/Colleague Data Base Administrator; module Support Specialist; Associate Dean; Provost and Senior Vice President; Assistant Professor (Various); Dean. **Corporate headquarters location:** This location.

360TRAINING
200 Academy Drive, Suite 260, Austin TX 78704. 512/441-1097. **Toll-free phone:** 800/442-1149. Fax: 512/441-1811. **Contact:** Human Resources. **E-mail address:** hr@360training.com. **World Wide Web address:** http://www.360training.com. **Description:** A provider of compliance and workforce e-learning solutions, serving organizations in the real estate, hospitality, power, insurance/financial services and safety industries. Founded in 1997. **Positions advertised include:** Computer System Analyst; Subject Matter Expert; Content Writer; Computer Analyst; Sr. Developer.

TRINITY UNIVERSITY
One Trinity Place, Box 91, San Antonio TX 78212-7200. 210/999-7507. **Fax:** 210/999-7542. **Recorded jobline:** 210/999-7510. **Contact:** Human Resources. **E-mail address:** humanresources@trinity.edu. **World Wide Web address:** http://www.trinity.edu. **Description:** A four-year college with majors including education, biology, communications, business administration, and engineering. The current enrollment is approximately 2,400. Founded in 1869. **NOTE:** See website for job listings and application information. **Positions advertised include:** Senior Data Entry Clerk; Degree Audit Coordinator; Associate Director of Development; Information Resources Communications Officer; Assistant Director of Financial Aid; Assistant Director of Admissions, Professor (Various); Molecular Biologist.

UNIVERSITY OF HOUSTON/DOWNTOWN
One Main Street, Suite 910 South, Houston TX 77002. 713/221-8427. **Recorded jobline:** 713/221-8609. **Contact:** Human Resources. **World Wide Web address:** http://www.dt.uh.edu. **Description:** The main campus of the University of Houston. **NOTE:** A complete application must accompany a resume. Resumes and applications are only accepted for current openings. For more information, an application and job listings, see the university's website. **Positions advertised include:** Professors (Various); Vice President of Student Affairs; Reference Librarian; Scholarship Counselor; Student Loan Coordinator; Staff Nurses; Dean.

UNIVERSITY OF NORTH TEXAS
P.O. Box 311010, Denton TX 76203-1010. 940/565-2281. **Fax:** 940/565-4382. **Recorded jobline:** 940/565-4070. **Contact:** Human Resources. **World Wide Web address:** http://www.unt.edu. **Description:** A university offering undergraduate and graduate programs of study in numerous fields. Enrollment at the university is approximately 25,000. **NOTE:** This university also has a Dallas campus called the System Center. See website for both locations' job listings and application information. **Special programs:** Internship; Work-Study.

UNIVERSITY OF NORTH TEXAS HEALTH SCIENCE AT FORT WORTH
3500 Camp Bowie Boulevard, Fort Worth TX 76107-2699. 817/735-2000. **Fax:** 817/735-0107. **Recorded jobline:** 817/735-2675. **Contact:** Human Resources. **E-mail address:** careers@hsc.unt.edu. **World Wide Web address:** http://www.hsc.unt.edu. **Description:** A health science education center. **NOTE:** See website for job listings and specific contact information. Apply online for open positions. **Positions advertised include:** Certified Coder; Clinical Services Representative; Senior Administrative Clerk; Associate Director of Development and Alumni Relations; Communications Coordinator; Compliance Analyst; Financial Aid Counselor.

UNIVERSITY OF ST. THOMAS
3800 Montrose Boulevard, Houston TX 77006. 713/522-7911. **Fax:** 713/525-3896. **Contact:** Human Resources. **World Wide Web address:** http://www.stthom.edu. **E-mail address:** hr@stthom.edu. **Description:** A liberal arts university affiliated with the Catholic Church. The university has an enrollment of 2,700 students. **NOTE:** Entry-level positions and part-time jobs are offered. See website for job listings and contact information. **Positions advertised include:** Vice President for Student Affairs; Dean of Scholarships & Financial Aid; Registrar; Records Clerk; Professor (Various). **Corporate headquarters location:** This location.

UNIVERSITY OF TEXAS AT ARLINGTON
1225 West Mitchell Street, Suite 112, Box 19176, Arlington TX 76019. 817/272-3461. **Fax:** 817/272-5798. **Contact:** Human Resources. **E-mail address:** employment@uta.edu. **World Wide Web address:** http://www.uta.edu. **Description:** A state university offering 55 bachelor's, 60 master's, and 19 doctoral degrees to approximately 20,000 students. Founded in 1895. **NOTE:** This university posts its staff and support job listings on its website. Apply online. Resumes for general consideration are not accepted. Jobseekers interested in faculty positions should visit the departments' separate web pages for openings. **Positions advertised include:** Continuing Education Director; Associate Registrar; Associate Director; Public Service Librarian; Software Systems Specialist; **Special programs:** Internships. **Office hours:** Monday – Friday, 8:00 a.m. – 5:00 p.m. **Corporate headquarters location:** Austin TX. **Operations at this facility include:** Administration; Research and Development; Sales; Service.

UNIVERSITY OF TEXAS AT AUSTIN
P.O. Box Drawer V, Austin TX 78713-8922. 512/471-3656. **Physical address:** University of Texas at Austin, Austin TX 78712. **Toll-free phone:** 800/687-8086. **Contact:** Jim DeWitt, Human Resources. **World Wide Web address:** http://www.utexas.edu. **Description:** One location of the state university. **NOTE:** Interested jobseekers can mail their applications; apply online at the school's website, or visit the Human Resources. See the website for staff job listings, additional application procedures and requirements. **Office hours:** Monday, Tuesday, Thursday, and Friday, 8:00 a.m. – 5:00 p.m. Wednesday, 9:00 a.m. – 5:00 p.m. **Operations at this facility include:** Administration; Research and Development; Service.

UNIVERSITY OF TEXAS AT BROWNSVILLE
80 Fort Brown Street, Cortez Building, Suite 129, Brownsville TX 78520. 956/882-8205. **Fax:** 956/882-7476. **Contact:** Human Resources. **World Wide Web address:** http://www.utb.edu. **Description:** University of Texas at Brownsville and Texas Southmost College are partner institutions offering the following programs

of study: College of Liberal Arts, College of Science, Mathematics & Technology, School of Business, School of Education, and School of Health Sciences. Founded in 1973. **NOTE:** A completed application is required for any position. See website for job listings and application procedures. Applications and resumes may be mailed, faxed or delivered to the Human Resources Office located in the Cortez Building, Suite 129. **Positions advertised include:** Accounting Clerk; Accounting Group Supervisor; Chemistry Lab Coordinator; Librarian; Staff Nurse; Lecturer (Various); Professor (Various).

UNIVERSITY OF TEXAS AT DALLAS
Mail Station AD 35, P.O. Box 830688, Richardson TX 75083-0688. 972/883-2221. **Fax:** 972/883-2156. **Contact:** Human Resources. **E-mail address:** jobs@utdalla.edu. **World Wide Web address:** http://www.utdallas.edu. **Description:** A state university offering programs at the undergraduate, graduate, and doctoral levels. Enrollment at the university is approximately 10,000. There is also a campus in the Dallas TX area. **NOTE:** Apply online at the university's website. Part-time jobs are offered. **Positions advertised include:** Academic Advisor; Child Development Specialist; Admissions Counselor; Research Associate; Program Coordinator; Professor (Various).

UNIVERSITY OF TEXAS AT EL PASO
Administration Building, Room 216, El Paso TX 79968-0507. 915/747-5202. **Recorded jobline:** 915/747-8837. **Contact:** Human Resource Services. **World Wide Web address:** http://www.utep.edu. **Description:** One location of the state university with more than two-thirds of the student population representing the area's strong Mexican-American community. Bachelors, masters, and doctoral degrees offered in liberal arts and science fields. **NOTE:** See website for job listings, contact information and application requirements and procedures. **Positions advertised include:** Horticulturist; Coach (Various); Special Projects Manager; Database Administrator; Professor (Various); Lecturer (Various); Literacy Coordinator; Research Associate.

UNIVERSITY OF TEXAS AT TYLER
3900 University Boulevard, Administration Building 108, Tyler TX 75799. 903/566-7358. **Fax:** 903/566-5690. **Contact:** Human Resources. **E-mail address:** humanresources@mail.uttyl.edu. **World Wide Web address:** http://www.uttyl.edu. **Description:** A state university offering undergraduate and graduate programs of study. **NOTE:** A completed application is required for any position. Apply online at the website. **Positions advertised include:** Police Cadet; Guard; Tennis Coach. **Office hours:** Monday – Friday, 8:00 a.m. – 5:00 p.m.

UNIVERSITY OF TEXAS-PAN AMERICAN
1201 West University Drive, Edinburg TX 78541. 956/381-2551. **Fax:** 956/381-2340. **Recorded jobline:** 956/381-2551. **Contact:** Human Resources. **World Wide Web address:** http://www.panam.edu. **Description:** One location of the state university. **NOTE:** A complete application is required for any position. To apply, visit the website or Human Resources. Jobseekers may also call for an application. See website for job listings, contact information, and application procedures and requirements. **Positions advertised include:** Orientation Coordinator; Business/Economic Research Assistant; Coordinator of Student Development; Library Clerk; Duplicating Equipment Operator; Staff Nurse; Student Development Specialist. **Corporate headquarters location:** Austin TX.

WINDHAM SCHOOL DISTRICT
P.O. Box 40, Huntsville TX 77342-0040. 936/291-5321. **Fax:** 936/291-4622. **Contact:** Minnie Madison, Human Resources. **E-mail address:** personnel@wsdtx.org. **World Wide Web address:** http://www.windhamschooldistrict.org. **Description:** Responsible for correctional education for the Texas Department of Criminal Justice. **NOTE:** Windham School District is governed by the Texas Education Agency and hires only certified teachers and administrators, some positions requiring a degree, and clerical positions. See the district's website for job listings for all locations.

Utah

ALPINE SCHOOL DISTRICT
575 North 100 East, American Fork UT 84003. 801/756-8400. **Contact:** Human Resources. **World Wide Web address:** http://www.alpine.k12.ut.us. **Description:** Operates 33 elementary schools, 8 junior high schools, and 7 senior high schools. **NOTE:** Jobs classified as teaching and non-teaching. See website for current job openings and application instructions. **Positions advertised include:** Elementary Library Media Specialist; Elementary Teacher; Lead Secretary Elementary; Secondary Teacher; Special Education Para-Educator; Special Education Teacher; Teacher's Assistant.

BRIGHAM YOUNG UNIVERSITY
D-70 ASB, Provo UT 84602. 801/422-3563. **Fax:** 801/422-0209. **Contact:** Employment Services. **E-mail address:** staff_employment@byu.edu. **World Wide Web address:** http://www.byu.edu. **Description:** A private, coeducational university with approximately 32,000 students enrolled. **NOTE:** For faculty positions, please visit website to download BYU employment application online. For other positions, please visit website to register and apply online. Administrative and staff applications are kept on file for one year; those for full-time employees are kept on file for three years. **Positions advertised include:** Academic Advisor; University Photography Manager; Service Engineer; Donor Liaison; Faculty, Various Departments; Radiology Technician; **Special programs:** Internships.

DAVIS COUNTY SCHOOL DISTRICT
45 East State Street, P.O. Box 588, Farmington UT 84025. 801/402-5261. **Fax:** 801/402-5354. **Contact:** Human Resources. **World Wide Web address:** http://www.davis.k12.ut.us. **Description:** Operates the public schools in Davis County. **NOTE:** Entry-level positions are offered. See website for current job openings and to download application. **Positions advertised include:** Custodian – Part-time; Transition Assistant; Educational Interpreter; Certified Occupational Therapy Assistant. **Special programs:** Internships; Training. **Corporate headquarters location:** This location. **Other area locations:** Salt Lake City; Ogden.

GRANITE SCHOOL DISTRICT
Administration Building, 2500 South State Street, Salt Lake City UT 84115-3110. 801/646-4511. **Fax:** 801/801-6464204. **Contact:** Human Resources. **World Wide Web address:** http://www.graniteschools.org. **Description:** Operates 89 public schools with an enrollment of 76,000 students. **NOTE:** See website for current job openings and to apply online.

JORDAN SCHOOL DISTRICT
9361 South 300 East, Sandy UT 84070. 801/567-81050. **Fax:** 801/567-8056. **Contact:** Human Resources. **World Wide Web address:** http://www.jordan.k12.ut.us. **Description:** Operates the public schools in southern Salt Lake County, servicing more than 73,000 students. **NOTE:** When applying for a general position, please be sure to include a resume, cover letter, application form (available on the website, or in the Human Resource Department), and a typing test (which should be certified by Job Services). For licensed positions, please complete an online application at http://careers.utah.edu/teacher. **Positions advertised include:** District Delivery Driver; Assistant Custodians; Part-time Assistants; Substitute Nutrition Workers; Nutrition Manager; Language Arts Instructor; Adult ESL Instructor; Itinerant Guidance Specialist.

SALT LAKE COMMUNITY COLLEGE
4600 South Redwood Road, Salt Lake City UT 84123. 801/957-4210. **Fax:** 801/957-4721. **Recorded jobline:**

801/957-4133. **Contact:** Human Resources. **E-mail address:** HR@slcc.edu. **World Wide Web address:** http://www.slcc.edu. **Description:** A two-year community college with over 16,000 students. **NOTE:** Please visit website for current job openings and to apply online. **Positions advertised include:** Facilities Lead; Faculty in History; Courtesy Desk Clerk; Counselor; Employment Technician.

SNOW COLLEGE
150 East College Avenue, Ephraim UT 84627. 435/283-7057. **Fax:** 435/ 283-6285. **Contact:** Claudia Jarrett, Assistant Director of Human Resources. **E-mail address:** bonnie.edwards@snow.edu. **World Wide Web address:** http://www.snow.edu. **Description:** A two-year community college. **NOTE:** Please visit website to download application form, view current job openings, and review application instructions. **Positions advertised include:** Adjunct German Instructor; Faculty Nursing Instructor; Theatre Scenic Designer/Instructor; Assistant Director of High School Relations; Computer Lab Supervisor; Welcome Center Receptionist.

SOUTHERN UTAH UNIVERSITY
351 West University Boulevard, Cedar City UT 84720. 435/586-7754. **Fax:** 435/586-7948. **Contact:** Human Resources Department. **World Wide Web address:** http://www.suu.edu. **Description:** A public, state-assisted university. The university offers programs in over 80 fields including arts, letters, and humanities; business, technology, and communication; and education. The university has approximately 6,000 students enrolled. Founded in 1897. **Positions advertised include:** Assistant Professor, Various Departments; Adjunct Instructor, Various Departments; Associate Provost for Undergraduate Programs; Director of Marketing and Promotions, Athletics. **Special programs:** Internships. **Corporate headquarters location:** Salt Lake City UT.

UNIVERSITY OF UTAH
420 Wakara Way, Suite 105, Salt Lake City UT 84108. 801/581-2169. **Fax:** 801/581-4579. **Contact:** Human Resources. **E-mail address:** employment@hr.utah.edu. **World Wide Web address:** http://www.hr.utah.edu. **Description:** A state university offering more than 70 undergraduate degree programs and more than 90 graduate majors. **Positions advertised include:** Clerk; Dispatcher; Executive Secretary; Academic Coordinator; Community Liaison; Education Specialist; Academic Advisor; Lab Technician.

UTAH STATE UNIVERSITY
9510 Old Main Hill, Logan UT 84322. 435/797-0124. **Fax;** 435/797-1816. **Contact:** Human Resources. **E-mail address:** job@hrmail.usu.edu. **World Wide Web address:** http://www.usu.edu. **Description:** A four-year state university with an enrollment of approximately 20,000 students. **NOTE:** Please visit website to search for jobs, apply online, and review certain application instructions. **Positions advertised include:** Department Head – Various Departments; Assistant Professor – Various Departments; Senior Lecturer & Executive in Residence – Business Administration; Early Childhood Teacher; Research Assistant – Special Education and Rehabilitation; Faculty – Music; Research Associate; Extension Educator; Medical Laboratory Technologist; Cataloger; Clinical Instructor. **Special programs:** Internships.

WEBER STATE UNIVERSITY
Miller Administration Building, Room 111, 1016 University Circle, Ogden UT 84408-1016. 801/626-6032. **Fax:** 801/626-6925. **Contact:** Human Resources. **E-mail address:** hr@weber.edu. **World Wide Web address:** http://www.weber.edu. **Description:** A state university with approximately 14,000 students enrolled. **NOTE:** Please visit website to search for jobs and apply online. **Positions advertised include:** Loan Officer; Assistant Professor – Various Departments; Automotive Technology Faculty; Faculty – First Year Coordinator; Nursing Lab Coordinator; Employee Wellness Program Coordinator; Financial Aid Counselor; Web Administrator; Secretary. **Corporate headquarters location:** This location.

WESTMINSTER COLLEGE
106 Bamberger Hall, 1840 South 1300 East, Salt Lake City UT 84105. 801/832-2570. **Fax:** 801/832-3107. **Contact:** Human Resources. **E-mail address:** jobs@westminstercollege.edu. **World Wide Web address:** http://www.wcslc.edu. **Description:** A small, private, four-year college offering bachelor's and master's degree programs. **NOTE:** See website for current job openings and to apply online. **Positions advertised include:** Administrative Assistant; Associate Director of Admissions; Campus Patrol Officer; Executive Director of Communications; Graduate Program Marketing/Recruitment Specialist; Seasonal Groundskeeper; Dean of Nursing; Faculty, Various Departments.

Vermont

BENNINGTON COLLEGE
One College Drive, Bennington VT 05201-6003. 802/440-4423. **Fax:** 802/440-4424. **Contact:** Heather Faley, Director of Human Resources. **E-mail address:** hroffice@bennington.edu. **World Wide Web address:** http://www.bennington.edu. **Description:** A four-year private college with 725 students in southern Vermont offering bachelor's and master's degrees. **Positions advertised include:** Professor, Various Departments; Instructional Technology Manager; Technology Resources Librarian; President's Office Coordinator; Records Assistant; Psychotherapist; Associate Director for Information; Soccer Coach.

CASTLETON STATE COLLEGE
62 Alumni Drive, Castleton VT 05735. 802/468-1207. **Contact:** Lyn Sawyer, Director of Human Resources. **E-mail address:** lyn.sawyer@castleton.edu. **World Wide Web address:** http://www.castleton.edu. **Description:** A four-year state college serving 1700 students. Castleton offers more than 30 undergraduate programs of study, as well as graduate programs in Education and Forensic Psychology. Founded in 1787. **NOTE:** For faculty positions, contact Joseph T. Mark, Academic Dean, at 802/468-1200. **Positions advertised include:** Professor, Various Faculties.

COMMUNITY COLLEGE OF VERMONT
Wasson Hall, P.O. Box 120, Waterbury VT 05676-0120. 802/241-3535. **Fax:** 802/241-3526. **Contact:** Barbara Martin, Dean of Administration. **World Wide Web address:** http://www.ccv.vsc.edu. **Description:** The Community College of Vermont is a non-campus, community college offering courses and degree programs at twelve locations throughout the state and online. **NOTE:** For faculty positions contact the Site Coordinator at each location. **Other area locations:** Bennington VT; Brattleboro VT; Burlington VT; Middlebury VT; Montpelier VT; Morrisville VT; Newport VT; Rutland VT; St. Albans VT; St. Johnsbury VT; Springfield VT; Upper Valley VT. **Operations at this facility include:** Administrative Offices; Financial Aid; Registrar. **Number of employees statewide:** 125 staff employees and 750 Part-time instructors.

LANDMARK COLLEGE
River Road South, P.O. Box 820, Putney VT 05346. 802/387-6871. **Fax:** 802/387-7111. **Contact:** Thomas R. Brown, Director of Human Resources. **E-mail address:** tbrown@landmark.edu. **World Wide Web address:** http://www.landmark.edu. **Description:** A two-year liberal arts college designed specifically for students with Dyslexia, Attention Deficit Hyperactivity Disorder, and other learning disabilities and differences. **Positions advertised include:** Assistant Registrar; Director of Transfer Services; Business Faculty; Manager of Web Services; Vice President of Student Affairs.

MIDDLEBURY COLLEGE
84 Self Service Road, Middlebury VT 05753. 802/443-5465. **Fax:** 802/443-2058. **Contact:** Melissa Nicklaw, Employment Assistant. **E-mail address:**

hr@middlebury.edu. **World Wide Web address:** http://www.middlebury.edu. **Description:** A small, independent, liberal arts college with approximately 2,200 undergraduates enrolled. Founded in 1800. **NOTE:** Send resumes and applications materials to: Human Resources, Middlebury College, Service Building, Second Floor, Middlebury VT 05753. **Positions advertised include:** Public Safety Officer; Human Resources Generalist.

NEW ENGLAND CULINARY INSTITUTE
250 Main Street, Montpelier VT 05602. 802/225-3230. **Fax:** 802/225-3281. **Contact:** Jennifer Zetarski, Recruiting and Staffing Manager. **E-mail address:** greatjobs@neci.edu. **World Wide Web address:** http://www.neci.edu. **Description:** A culinary school offering certificate programs, associate's degrees, and bachelor's degrees in various culinary-related programs. **Positions advertised include:** Executive Sous Chef, Décor Culinary Theatre; Garde Manger Chef Instructor; Pastry Chef Instructor. **Other area locations:** Burlington VT; Essex VT; Essex Junction VT. **International locations:** Tortola, British Virgin Islands. **Number of employees worldwide:** 509.

NORWICH UNIVERSITY
158 Harmon Drive, Northfield VT 05663. 802/485-2075. **Fax:** 802/485-2090. **Contact:** Ellen Danahy Liptak, Human Resources Assistant. **E-mail address:** jobs@norwich.edu. **World Wide Web address:** http://www.norwich.edu. **Description:** A private military college founded in 1819. Norwich University is a diversified academic institution that educates students in a Corps of Cadets or as civilians. **Positions advertised include:** Bookkeeper; Web Editor; Human resources Generalist; Flash Developer; University Music Director; Professor, Various Departments. **Number of employees:** 492.

UNIVERSITY OF VERMONT
85 South Prospect Street, 228 Waterman Building, Burlington VT 05405. 802/656-3494. **Fax:** 802/656-3476. **Recorded jobline:** 802/656-2248. **Contact:** Lynn Budnick, Human Resources Manager - Employment. **E-mail address:** employment@uvm.edu. **World Wide Web address:** http://www.uvm.edu. **Description:** A state university offering a liberal arts curriculum with over 90 undergraduate majors, 72 master's and 20 PhD programs. Colleges at the University of Vermont include Agriculture and Life Sciences, Allied Health Sciences, Business Administration, Education, Engineering, and Nursing. Founded in 1791. **Positions advertised include:** Assistant/Associate Professor, Various Departments; Associate Dean; Business Support Assistant; Clinical Researcher; Database Administrator; Deputy Director; Gift Records Assistant; Media Advisor; Program Administrator; Provost; Psychiatrist; Spine Surgeon. **Number of employees:** 3,000.

Virginia

AVERETT UNIVERSITY
420 West Main Street, Danville VA 24541. 434/791-5600. **Contact:** Faye Dix, Human Resources. **World Wide Web address:** http://www.averett.edu. **Description:** A private, co-ed, four-year, liberal arts college. Averett offers bachelor of arts and bachelor of science degrees in 30 undergraduate programs, as well as a master of business administration, a master of arts and teaching, and a master of education. Total enrollment is 2,800.

CHRISTOPHER NEWPORT UNIVERSITY
One University Place, Newport News VA 23606. 757/594-7000. **Contact:** Human Resources. **World Wide Web address:** http://www.cnu.edu. **Description:** A four-year comprehensive, coeducational, state-supported institution within Virginia's public university system. The university has an enrollment of approximately 5,000 students and offers 115 academic majors and programs. **NOTE:** Search for positions online. **Positions advertised include:** Vice President for Administration; Assistant Director of Financial Aid; Manager of Records and Research; Assistant Professor, Various Departments. **Number of employees at this location:** 932.

COLLEGE OF WILLIAM AND MARY
P.O. Box 8795, Thiemes House, Williamsburg VA 23187-8795. 757/221-3169. **Fax:** 757/221-3156. **Recorded jobline:** 757/221-3167. **Contact:** Office of Personnel Services. **World Wide Web address:** http://www.wm.edu. **Description:** A four-year college offering bachelor's, master's (including MBAs), first professional, and doctoral degrees. Approximately 5,250 undergraduate and 2,400 graduate students attend the College of William and Mary. **NOTE:** Search for positions online. Applications must be submitted online; paper applications will not be accepted. **Positions advertised include:** Assistant Professor, Various Departments; Director of Development; Assessment Coordinator; Assistant Dean of Students. **Number of employees nationwide:** 2,000.

GEORGE MASON UNIVERSITY
4400 University Drive, Fairfax VA 22030-4444. 703/993-1000. **Fax:** 703/993-2601. **Recorded jobline:** 703/993-4000. **Contact:** Human Resources. **World Wide Web address:** http://www.gmu.edu. **Description:** A four-year university offering bachelor's, master's (including MBAs), first professional, and doctoral degrees. Approximately 29,000 students attend George Mason University. **NOTE:** Search for positions online. **Other area locations:** Arlington VA; Manassas VA.

HAMPTON UNIVERSITY
Office of Human Resources, Armstrong-Slater Hall, Room 110, Hampton VA 23668. 757/727-5250. **Contact:** Office of Human Resources. **World Wide Web address:** http://www.hamptonu.edu. **Description:** A four-year university offering bachelor's and master's degrees, including MBAs. Approximately 5,700 students attend Hampton University. **NOTE:** Search for openings online; specific application instructions provided.

JAMES MADISON UNIVERSITY
800 South Main Street, Harrisonburg VA 22807. 540/568-3825. **Fax:** 540/568-1796. **Contact:** Human Resources Department. **E-mail address:** jobs@jmu.edu. **World Wide Web address:** http://www.jmu.edu/humanresources. **Description:** A four-year university offering bachelor's and master's degrees. Approximately 15,000 students attend James Madison University. **NOTE:** Search and apply for positions online. **Positions advertised include:** HelpDesk Consultant; Security Engineer; Instructor; Lecturer; Visiting Assistant Professor; Clinical Instructor; Assistant Professor; Management Lecturer; Coordinator of Information Technology; Capital Gifts Officer; Grant Writer; Director of Development. **Corporate headquarters location:** This location. **Number of employees at this location:** 1,400.

MARYMOUNT UNIVERSITY
2807 North Glebe Road, Arlington VA 22207-4299. 703/284-1680. **Contact:** Human Resource Services. **World Wide Web address:** http://www.marymount.edu. **Description:** A coeducational university affiliated with the Catholic Church, enrolling approximately 2,200 students in undergraduate studies and 1,600 students in graduate studies. Marymount University offers associate's, bachelor's, and master's degrees. The university's various degrees are offered in the schools of Arts and Sciences, Business Administration, Education and Human Services, and Nursing. **NOTE:** Search and apply for positions online. **Positions advertised include:** Associate Registrar; Assistant/Associate Professor, Various Departments; Director, Physical Plant Operations.

NORFOLK STATE UNIVERSITY
700 Park Avenue, Suite 210, Norfolk VA 23504. 757/823-8160. **Fax:** 757/823-2805. **Contact:** Human Resources. **E-mail address:** humanresources@nsu.edu. **World Wide Web address:** http://www.nsu.edu.

Description: A university offering undergraduate and graduate programs. The university has an enrollment of approximately 8,000. Founded in 1979. **NOTE:** Search for positions online.

NORTHERN VIRGINIA COMMUNITY COLLEGE
4001 Wakefield Chapel Road, Annandale VA 22003-3796. 703/323-3110. **Fax:** 703/323-3155. **Contact:** Myrtho Blanchard, Human Resources Director. **E-mail address:** resumes@nvcc.edu. **World Wide Web address:** http://www.nv.cc.va.us/hr. **Description:** A two-year, nonprofit college offering transfer and occupational/technical programs. Northern Virginia Community College has five campuses and an Extended Learning Institute. **NOTE:** Second and third shifts are offered. A Virginia State Employment Application is required to apply for all positions. Search for positions online. **Special programs:** Training. **Office hours:** Monday - Friday, 8:30 a.m. - 5:00 p.m. **Corporate headquarters location:** This location. **Number of employees nationwide:** 600.

OLD DOMINION UNIVERSITY
1510 West 48th Street, Norfolk VA 23529. 757/683-3042. **Fax:** 757/683-3047. **Contact:** Human Resources. **World Wide Web address:** http://www.odu.edu. **Description:** A four-year university offering bachelor's, master's, and doctoral degree programs. Approximately 21,000 students are enrolled. Founded in 1930. **NOTE:** Search and apply for positions online. Only online applications accepted. **Positions advertised include:** Architect/Engineer; Info Tech Specialist.

ROANOKE COLLEGE
221 College Lane, Salem VA 24153. 540/375-2500. **Contact:** Kathy Page, Human Resources Manager. **World Wide Web address:** http://www.roanoke.edu. **Description:** One of the oldest Lutheran colleges in the nation. This four-year liberal arts undergraduate college offers 29 majors, 28 minors, and 13 concentrations. Roanoke College has an enrollment of 1,750 students. Founded in 1842. **Positions advertised include:** Assistant Professor of Philosophy; Community Programs and Special Events Coordinator.

J. SERGEANT REYNOLDS COMMUNITY COLLEGE
P.O. Box 85622, Richmond VA 23285-5622. 804/371-3249. **Contact:** Human Resources. Department **World Wide Web address:** http://www.jsr.cc.va.us. **Description:** A community college offering one- and two-year programs of study in business, liberal arts, community service, education, and science. **NOTE:** Search for positions online. **Positions advertised include:** Director of Financial Aid; Dean, School of Nursing and Allied Health; Reference Librarian; Vice President, Community College Workforce Alliance; Mathematics Instructor. **Corporate headquarters location:** This location. **Operations at this facility include:** Administration. **Number of employees at this location:** 1,000.

SHENANDOAH UNIVERSITY
1460 University Drive, Winchester VA 22601. 540/665-4500. **Contact:** Human Resources. **World Wide Web address:** http://www.su.edu. **Description:** A private, coeducational university offering over 60 programs of study at the undergraduate, graduate, doctorate and professional. Shenandoah University is affiliated with the United Methodist Church. There are about 2,500 students enrolled at the university. Founded in 1875. **NOTE:** Search for positions online. **Positions advertised include:** Associate/Assistant Professor of OT; Director of the Leadership Circle; Director of Residence Life; Pharmacy Faculty; Director of Clinical Education; Education Faculty.

THE UNIVERSITY OF MARY WASHINGTON
1301 College Avenue, Fairfax House, Fredericksburg VA 22401. 540/654-1046. **Fax:** 540/654-1078. **Contact:** Personnel Office. **World Wide Web address:** http://www.mwc.edu. **Description:** The university includes a four-year, coeducational, state-supported, residential college of the liberal arts and sciences with an enrollment of approximately 3,500 students, and a College of Graduate and Professional Studies. **NOTE:** Search for positions online. **Positions advertised include:** Director of User Services.

UNIVERSITY OF VIRGINIA
914 Emmett Street, Charlottesville VA 22904. 434/924-4598. **Fax:** 434/924-6911. **Recorded jobline:** 434/924-4400. **Contact:** Human Resources. **E-mail address:** hrdept@virginia.edu. **World Wide Web address:** http://www.hrs.virginia.edu. **Description:** A state university with 19,000 undergraduate and graduate students enrolled. **NOTE:** Search for positions online. **Special programs:** Internships. **Corporate headquarters location:** This location. **Operations at this facility include:** Administration; Research and Development; Service. **Number of employees at this location:** 11,000.

VIRGINIA COMMONWEALTH UNIVERSITY
P.O. Box 842511, Richmond VA 23284-2511. 804/828-0177. **Contact:** Human Resource Division. **World Wide Web address:** http://www.vcu.edu. **Description:** The largest university in Virginia, with more than 31,000 students. The school is recognized for its nationally ranked art, social work, health administration, and medical degree programs. Established in 1838. **Positions advertised include:** Special Collections Assistant; Research Coordinator; Laboratory Specialist; Cardiac Sonographer; Payroll Director; RN Manager; Editor; Sr. Laboratory Technician.

VIRGINIA POLYTECHNICAL INSTITUTE (VIRGINIA TECH)
Southgate Center, 1st Floor, Blacksburg VA 24061-0318. 540/231-9331. **Fax:** 540/231-3830. **Contact:** Personnel Services. **E-mail address:** perserv@vt.edu. **World Wide Web address:** http://www.vt.edu. **Description:** A land grant university that provides advanced instruction, research, and outreach programs. Continuing education is also offered at Roanoke Graduate Center, Northern Virginia Graduate Center, and Tidewater Graduate Center. **NOTE:** Search for positions online. **Corporate headquarters location:** This location. **Operations at this facility include:** Administration; Education; Research and Development. **Number of employees at this location:** 6,000.

Washington

BAINBRIDGE ISLAND SCHOOL DISTRICT
8489 Madison Avenue NE, Bainbridge Island WA 98110. 206/842-4714. **Contact:** Personnel Specialist. **E-mail address:** dbrown@bainbridge.wednet.edu. **World Wide Web address:** http://www.bainbridge.wednet.edu. **Description:** A public school district that is comprised of one high school, one middle school, three elementary schools, and an alternative learning program. **Operations at this facility include:** Administration. **Number of employees at this location:** 400.

BELLEVUE COMMUNITY COLLEGE
3000 Landerholm Circle SE, Bellevue WA 98007-6484. 425/564-2247. **Recorded jobline:** 425/564-2082. **Contact:** Human Resources. **World Wide Web address:** http://www.bcc.ctc.edu. **Description:** A community college operating as part of the Washington State Community College System. Over 18,000 students are enrolled each quarter.

CENTRAL KITSAP SCHOOL DISTRICT
P.O. Box 8, Silverdale WA 98383. 360/662-1680. **Physical address:** 9210 Silverdale Way NW, Silverdale WA 98383. **Fax:** 360/662-1611. **Recorded jobline:** 360/662-1699. **Contact:** Personnel Department. **E-mail address:** tiffanyw@cksd.wednet.edu. **World Wide Web address:** http://www.cksd.wednet.edu. **Description:** Administrative offices for the school district. **Positions advertised include:** Executive Director of Secondary Teaching & Learning; Assistant Superintendent of Human Resources; Director of Special Services. **Corporate headquarters location:** This location. **Number of employees at this location:** 1,500.

CENTRAL WASHINGTON UNIVERSITY
400 East University Way, Ellensburg WA 98926. 509/963-1202. **Recorded jobline:** 509/963-1562. **Contact:** Human Resources. **E-mail address:** humanres@cwu.edu. **World Wide Web address:** http://www.cwu.edu. **Description:** A regional university offering baccalaureate and graduate degrees in more than 90 academic programs serving nearly 8,000 students. **Number of employees at this location:** 1,000.

CLOVER PARK SCHOOL DISTRICT
10903 Gravelly Lake Drive SW, Lakewood WA 98499. 253/583-5095. **Recorded jobline:** 253/583-5003. **Fax:** 253/589-7440. **Contact:** Lori Liedes, Recruitment Coordinator. **E-mail address:** Lliedes@cloverpark.k12.wa.us. **World Wide Web address:** http://cpsd.cloverpark.k12.wa.us. **Description:** Administrative offices of the Clover Park school district. **Positions advertised include:** Counselor; Math Teacher; Science Teacher; English Teacher; Social Studies Teacher. **Number of employees at this location:** 1,800.

COMMUNITY COLLEGE OF SPOKANE
P.O. Box 6000, Spokane WA 99217-6000. 509/434-5040. **Physical address:** 501 North Riverpoint Boulevard, Spokane WA 992170. **Fax:** 509/434-5055. **Recorded jobline:** 509/533-2013. **Contact:** Manager of Human Resources Department. **E-mail address:** hr@ccs.spokane.edu. **World Wide Web address:** http://www.ccs.spokane.edu. **Description:** Provides academic and vocational education and training to more than 22,000 full- and part-time students in six northeastern Washington counties. **Number of employees at this location:** 1,900.

EASTERN WASHINGTON UNIVERSITY
314 Showalter Hall, Cheney WA 99004-2431. 509/359-2381. **Fax:** 509/359-2874. **Recorded jobline:** 509/359-4390. **Contact:** Human Resources Department. **E-mail address:** hr@mail.ewu.edu. **World Wide Web address:** http://www.ewu.edu. **Description:** A four-year university offering undergraduate and graduate degrees to approximately 8,500 students. **Corporate headquarters location:** This location. **Operations at this facility include:** Administration. **Number of employees at this location:** 1,100.

EDMONDS COMMUNITY COLLEGE
20000 68th Avenue West, Lynnwood WA 98036. 425/640-1400. **Recorded jobline:** 425/640-1510. **Contact:** Human Resources. **E-mail address:** jobs@edcc.edu. **World Wide Web address:** http://www.edcc.edu. **Description:** A community college that operates as part of the Washington State Public Higher Education System. **NOTE:** Please call the jobline for a listing of available positions. **Positions advertised include:** Media Maintenance Technician; ESL Instructor; Mathematics Instructor; Chemistry Instructor. **Number of employees at this location:** 1,000.

FRANKLIN PIERCE SCHOOL DISTRICT
315 129th Street South, Tacoma WA 98444. 253/537-0211. **Fax:** 253/536-0797. **Contact:** Mrs. Jamie Siegel, Executive Director of Personnel. **E-mail address:** jamies@fp.k12.wa.us. **World Wide Web address:** http://www.midland.fp.k12.wa.us. **Description:** Public school district for the Tacoma area. **Positions advertised include:** Special Education Teacher; Physical Therapist; Elementary School Counselor; Music/Movement Teacher. **Operations at this facility include:** Administration.

GONZAGA UNIVERSITY
502 East Boone, Spokane WA 99258-0080. 509/328-4220. **Physical address:** 414 East Sharp, Spokane WA 99258-0080. **Fax:** 509/323-5813. **Recorded jobline:** 509/323-5916. **Contact:** Tracy Kelly, Employment and HR Specialist. **E-mail address:** kelly@gonzaga.edu. **World Wide Web address:** http://www.gonzaga.edu. **Description:** A university offering coursework in a number of fields including arts and sciences, business administration, education, engineering, law, nursing, and military science. Gonzaga University enrolls approximately 3,000 undergraduate and 2,000 graduate students.

HIGHLINE COMMUNITY COLLEGE
P.O. Box 98000, Des Moines WA 98198-9800. 206/878-3710. **Physical address:** 2400 South 240th Street, Des Moines WA 98198. **Fax:** 206/870-4853. **Contact:** Human Resources. **World Wide Web address:** http://www.highline.ctc.edu. **Description:** A community college with an enrollment of approximately 10,000 students. Founded in 1961.

OLYMPIC COLLEGE
1600 Chester Avenue, 5th Floor, College Service Center, Bremerton WA 98337-1699. 360/475-7300. **Fax:** 360/475-7302. **Contact:** Linda Yerger, Personnel Director. **E-mail:** jobs@oc.ctc.edu. **World Wide Web address:** http://www.oc.ctc.edu. **Description:** A two-year community college that offers associate degrees in arts and science, transfer programs, and various technical degrees. **Corporate headquarters location:** This location.

RENTON TECHNICAL COLLEGE
3000 NE Fourth Street, Renton WA 98056. 425/235-2352. **Fax:** 425/235-7832. **Recorded jobline:** 425/235-2354. **Contact:** Human Resources. **World Wide Web address:** http://www.renton-tc.ctc.edu. **Description:** A technical college operated by the State Board for Community and Technical Colleges.

SEATTLE PACIFIC UNIVERSITY
330 West Nickerson, Suite 302, Seattle WA 98119. 206/281-2809. **Fax:** 206/281-2846. **Recorded jobline:** 206/281-2065. **Contact:** Kathleen Abbott, Employment Manager. **World Wide Web address:** http://www.spu.edu. **Description:** A Christian university of arts and sciences with an enrollment of approximately 3,400. **NOTE:** Jobseekers are encouraged to submit both the SPU Employment Application and the specific application for the position. **Positions advertised include:** Assistant Professor of Accounting; Physical Education Instructor; Residence Life Coordinator; Senior Administrative Assistant.

SKAGIT VALLEY COLLEGE
11042 State Route 525, #138, Clinton WA 98236. 360/341-2324. **Fax:** 360/416-7878. **Recorded jobline:** 360/416-7800. **Contact:** Human Resources. **E-mail address:** employ@skagit.edu. **World Wide Web address:** http://www.skagit.edu. **Description:** A community college offering degrees in more than 20 disciplines.

SOUTH PUGET SOUND COMMUNITY COLLEGE
2011 Mottman Road SW, Olympia WA 98512-6218. 360/754-7711. **Recorded jobline:** 360/754-7711 ext. 7. **Contact:** Human Resources. **World Wide Web address:** http://www.spscc.ctc.edu. **Description:** A two-year, community college with over 5,000 full- and part-time students enrolled.

UNIVERSITY OF PUGET SOUND
1500 North Warner Street, Camp Murray WA 98430. 253/879-3100. **Recorded jobline:** 253/879-3368. **Contact:** Human Resources Department. **World Wide Web address:** http://www.ups.edu. **Description:** A four-year, liberal arts college.

UNIVERSITY OF WASHINGTON
4045 Brooklyn Avenue NE, Seattle WA 98105. 206/543-2354. **Fax:** 206/685-0636. **Contact:** Lisa Anderson, HR Employment Specialist. **E-mail address:** lindaa@u.washington.edu. **World Wide Web address:** http://www.washington.edu. **Description:** The oldest public university on the west coast, offering 140 majors, 90 minors, and numerous graduate programs.

WASHINGTON STATE UNIVERSITY
P.O. Box 641014, Pullman WA 99164-1014. 509/335-4521. **Fax:** 509/335-1259. **Recorded jobline:** 509/335-7637. **Contact:** Human Resources. **E-mail address:** hrs@wsu.edu. **World Wide Web address:** http://www.wsu.edu. **Description:** A state university. Approximately 15,000 undergraduate and 2,000 graduate students are enrolled in almost 100 programs of study. **Special programs:** Summer Jobs. **Office hours:** Monday - Friday, 8:00 a.m. - 5:00 p.m. **President:** V. Lane Rawlins, President.

WESTERN WASHINGTON UNIVERSITY
Mail Stop 5221, Bellingham WA 98225. 360/650-3774. **Physical address**: 516 High Street, Bellingham WA 98225. **Fax:** 360/650-2810. **Contact:** Human Resources. **World Wide Web address:** http://www.wwu.edu. **Description:** A four-year university.

WHITMAN COLLEGE
345 Boyer Avenue, Walla Walla WA 99362. 509/527-5172. **Fax:** 509/527-5859. **Contact:** Personnel Director. **E-mail address:** luckstd@whitman.edu. **World Wide Web address:** http://www.whitman.edu. **Description:** A four-year, liberal arts college with an enrollment of approximately 1,300. Founded in 1859. **Positions advertised include:** Director of Admission; Director of Foundation & Corporate Relations; Executive Director of Development; Physics Technician and Laboratory Coordinator.

WHITWORTH COLLEGE
300 West Hawthorne Road, Spokane WA 99251. 509/777-1000. **Fax:** 509/777-3773. **Recorded jobline:** 509/777-3202. **Contact:** Human Resources. **World Wide Web address:** http://www.whitworth.edu. **Description:** A private, liberal arts college affiliated with the Presbyterian Church.

West Virginia
BLUEFIELD STATE COLLEGE
219 Rock Street, Bluefield WV 24701-2198. 304/327-4049. **Fax:** 304/325-7747. **Contact:** David Lord, Human Resources. **E-mail address:** dlord@bluefieldstate.edu. **World Wide Web address:** http://www.bluefield.wvnet.edu. **Description:** An open admissions, state-supported institution that offers undergraduate liberal arts and professional programs in applied sciences, business, education, humanities, social sciences, engineering technologies, and allied health sciences. The college grants baccalaureate and associate degrees, as well as the nontraditional Regents Bachelor of Arts degree. **Other area locations:** Beckley; Lewisburg. **Number of employees at this location:** 200.

CONCORD COLLEGE
Vermillion Street, P.O. Box 1000, Athens WV 24712-1000. 304/384-5121. **Toll-free phone:** 800/344-6679. **Contact:** Human Resources. **World Wide Web address:** http://www.concord.wvnet.edu. **Description:** A four-year public college with a student enrollment of over 3,000. **Positions advertised include:** Assistant Athletic Trainer; Assistant Professor of Education; History/Philosophy; Assistant Professor of Health and Physical Education. **Number of employees at this location:** 300.

MARSHALL UNIVERSITY
One John Marshall Drive, Huntington WV 25755. 304/696-6455. **Fax:** 304/696-6844. **Contact:** Jim Stephens, Director of Human Resource Services. **E-mail address:** recruiting@marshall.edu. **World Wide Web address:** http://www.marshall.edu. **Description:** A state-supported, interactive university with 2-year and 4-year undergraduate and graduate programs. **NOTE:** Follow specific application instructions for each job posting. **Positions advertised include:** Assistant Athletic Trainer; Assistant/Associate Professor, Various Departments; Broadcast Engineer; Culinary Coordinator; Data Technician; Hospitality Program Coordinator; Trades Specialist.

UNIVERSITY OF CHARLESTON
2300 MacCorkle Avenue SE, Charleston WV 25304-9954. 304/357-4736. **Toll-free phone:** 800/995-4682. **Fax:** 304/357-4831. **Contact:** Roy Howell, Department of Human Resources. **Email address:** hr@ucwv.edu. **World Wide Web address:** http://www.ucwv.edu. **Description:** A private, undergraduate university with an enrollment of 1,000 students that offers Baccalaureate programs, Associate degrees, and Master's degrees. **Positions advertised include:** Assistant to the President; Systems Administrator; Mathematics Professor.

WEST VIRGINIA UNIVERSITY
P.O. Box 6640, One Waterfront Place, Second Floor, Morgantown WV 26506. 304/293-5700. **Fax:** 304/293-7532. **Recorded jobline:** 304/293-7234. **Contact:** James A. Morris, Director of Employment and Employee Relations. **World Wide Web address:** http://www.wvu.edu. **Description:** A state university that offers 171 majors. **NOTE:** Go to http://www.hr.wvu.edu/apply.cfm for an employment application. **Positions advertised include:** Area Advisor/Night Staff Supervisor; Information Systems Specialist; Web Developer; Systems Programmer; Accountant.

Wisconsin
BELOIT COLLEGE
762 Church Street, Beloit WI 53511. 608/363-2630. **Fax:** 608/363-2221. **Contact:** Tammy Few, Employment/Safety Coordinator. **E-mail address:** fewt@beloit.edu. **World Wide Web address:** http://www.beloit.edu. **Description:** A four-year college offering a liberal arts curriculum. Founded in 1847. **Positions advertised include:** Area Hall Director; Assistant Director of Admissions; Assistant Director for Computing Infrastructure; Assistant Professor, Spanish.

BELOIT SCHOOL DISTRICT
Kolak Education Center, 1633 Keeler Avenue, Beloit WI 53511. 608/361-4018. **Fax:** 608/361-4123. **Contact:** Personnel Office. **E-mail address:** mereynol@sdb.k12.wi.us. **World Wide Web address:** http://www.sdb.k12.wi.us. **Description:** A public school district with 12 elementary, two middle, one high, and one charter school.

MARQUETTE UNIVERSITY
915 West Wisconsin Avenue, David Straz Tower, Room 185, P.O. Box 1881, Milwaukee WI 53201-1881. 414/288-7305. **Fax:** 414/288-7425. **Recorded jobline:** 414/288-7000. **Contact:** Human Resources. **E-mail address:** resume@marquette.edu. **World Wide Web address:** http://www.marquette.edu. **Description:** A four-year, Jesuit-affiliated university with approximately 7,600 undergraduate and 3,400 graduate students. Founded in 1881. **NOTE:** E-mail applications for non-exempt or entry level positions to: jobs@margette.edu.

MEDICAL COLLEGE OF WISCONSIN
8701 Watertown Plank Road, Milwaukee WI 53226. 414/456-8296. **Fax:** 414/456-6502. **Recorded jobline:** 414/456-8193. **Contact:** Human Resources. **E-mail address:** mcw_emp@mcw.edu. **World Wide Web address:** http://www.mcw.edu. **Description:** A medical school offering a four-year M.D. program prior to residency. Medical College of Wisconsin enrolls approximately 1,200 students. Founded in 1893. **Positions advertised include:** Research Scientist; Medical Education Coordinator; Accountant; Biostatistician; Case Manager; Nurse Practitioner; Systems Analyst; Assistant/Associate Professor. **Number of employees at this location:** 4,370.

MILWAUKEE PUBLIC SCHOOLS
5225 West Villet Street, Room 124, P.O. Box 2181, Milwaukee WI 53201-2182. 414/475-8227. **Fax:** 414/475-8722. **Contact:** Division of Staffing Services, Human Resources Department. **World Wide Web address:** http://www.milwaukee.k12.wi.us. **Description:**

Manages the public school system for the city of Milwaukee, which includes 21 high schools, 24 middle schools, 119 elementary schools, 36 community schools, and 10 early childhood contract sites with 105,000 students. Founded in 1836. **Positions advertised include:** Certified Teacher; Substitute; Secretary. **Special programs:** Internships; Training; Co-ops; Summer Jobs. **Corporate headquarters location:** This location. **Annual sales/revenues:** Less than $5 million. **Number of employees at this location:** 12,000.

MILWAUKEE SCHOOL OF ENGINEERING
1025 North Broadway Street, Milwaukee WI 53202-3109. 414/277-7132. **Toll-free phone:** 800/332-6763. **Fax:** 414/277-2233. **Recorded jobline:** 414/277-4546. **Contact:** Kevin Morin, Director of Human Resources. **E-mail address:** hr@msoe.edu. **World Wide Web address:** http://www.msoe.edu. **Description:** A technical university that offers bachelor's and master's degrees and certificate programs in the areas of engineering, engineering technology, technical communication, and business. **Corporate headquarters location:** This location. **Operations at this facility include:** Administration; Service.

UNIVERSITY OF WISCONSIN/MADISON
500 Lincoln Drive, 166 Bascom Hall, Madison WI 53706. 608/263-6561. **Fax:** 608/262-5203. **Contact:** Human Resources. **World Wide Web address:** http://www.wisc.edu/ohr. **Description:** A campus of the state university with an enrollment of 42,000. UW Madison is a research university. **Positions advertised include:** Microbiologist; IS Systems Development Services Professional; Licensed Practical Nurse; Assistant Professor; Director of Research and Sponsored Programs; Associate Dean. **Operations at this facility include:** Administration; Research and Development; Sales; Service. **Number of employees nationwide:** 16,000.

Wyoming

UNIVERSITY OF WYOMING
1000 East Wyoming Avenue, Department 3422, Laramie WY 82071. 307/766-2215. **Fax:** 307/766-5607. **Contact:** Human Resources. **E-mail address:** jobapps@uwyo.edu. **World Wide Web address:** http://www.uwyo.edu/hr. **Description:** A state university offering bachelor's, master's, and doctoral degree programs. **NOTE:** Part-time jobs are offered. **NOTE:** See website for current openings and application instructions. Positions are classified as benefited, academic, administrative and non-benefited temporary. **Positions advertised include:** Accounting Associate; Office Assistant; Assistant Professor; Associate Professor; Director of International Programs; Development Associate; Archives Aide. **Special programs:** Internships; Summer Jobs. **Operations at this facility include:** Administration; Education; Regional Headquarters. **Number of employees at this location:** 2,600.

ENVIRONMENTAL & WASTE MANAGEMENT SERVICES

You can expect to find the following types of companies in this section:

Environmental Engineering Firms • Sanitary Services

Occupations including environmental engineers, technicians, scientists and geoscientists, as well as waste treatment operators should grow by 19% or 58,000 jobs, from 303,000 to 361,000. Employment will be stimulated by a need to meet environmental regulations, develop methods of cleaning up existing hazards, and, more generally, respond to increasing public concern for a safe and clean environment.

Alabama

RUST CONSTRUCTORS, INC.
500 Corporate Parkway, Suite 100, Birmingham AL 35242-2928. 205/995-7171. **Fax:** 205/995-6691. **Contact:** Charlotte Lewis, Human Resources. **E-mail address:** charlotte.lewis @wgint.com. **World Wide Web address:** http://www.rustconstructors.com. **Description:** Provides construction and maintenance services to industrial customers. **Other U.S. locations:** CO; SC.

Alaska

ENSR CORPORATION
1835 South Bragaw Street, Suite 490, Anchorage AK 99508. 907/561-5700. **Fax:** 907/273-4555. **Contact:** Human Resources. **World Wide Web address:** http://www.ensr.com. **Description:** Engaged in arctic engineering, soil engineering, petroleum engineering, geology, geophysics, seismology, surface and groundwater hydrology, meteorology, oceanography, environmental impact assessment, air and water quality, and biological sciences. ENSR Corporation has 70 offices in 17 countries. **Positions advertised include:** Sr. Project Manager. **Corporate headquarters location:** Westford MA. **Other area locations:** Fairbanks AK. **Other U.S. locations:** Nationwide. **International locations:** Worldwide.

SHANNON & WILSON
2355 Hill Road, Fairbanks AK 99709-5326. 907/479-0600. **Fax:** 907/479-5691. **Contact:** Human Resources. **E-mail address:** jobs@shanwil.com. **World Wide Web address:** http://www.shannonwilson.com. **Description:** Engaged in a variety of geotechnical, environmental, and construction materials engineering activities, including permafrost engineering, foundation engineering, engineering geology, hydrology, hydrogeology, and the design of environmental remediation projects. **Positions advertised include:** Geotechnical Engineer (Multiple positions). **Corporate headquarters location:** Seattle WA. **Other area locations:** Anchorage AK. **Other U.S. locations:** CO; IL; MA; MI; OR; WA. **Subsidiaries include:** S&W Construction Services, Inc.; Shannon & Wilson International, Inc. **Number of employees at this location:** 170.

UNITECH OF ALASKA, INC.
P.O. Box 240167, Anchorage AK 99524-0167. 907/349-5142. **Physical address:** 2401 Cinnabar Loop, Anchorage AK 99507. **Fax:** 907/349-2733. **Contact:** Human Resources. **E-mail address:** unitech@alaska.net. **Description:** Offers environmental services, products, and equipment to the Alaskan marketplace. Founded in 1985. **Other U.S. locations:** Portland OR; Seattle WA. **Number of employees at this location:** 20.

Arizona

ALLIED WASTE INDUSTRIES, INC.
15880 North Greenway-Hayden Loop, Suite 100, Scottsdale AZ 85260. 480/627-2700. **Contact:** Human Resources. **World Wide Web address:** http://www.awin.com. **Description:** One of the world's largest waste services company. Allied Waste provides collection, disposal, and recycling services to residential, commercial, and industrial customers. **Corporate headquarters location:** This location. **Listed on:** New York Stock Exchange. **Stock exchange symbol:** AW.

AMEC
2001 West Camelback Road, Suite 300, Phoenix AZ 85015. 602/343-2400. **Fax:** 602/343-2499. **Contact:** Human Resources. **E-mail address:** careers.ee.krk@amec.com. **World Wide Web address:** http://www.amec.com. **Description:** One of North America's largest full-service, environmental engineering consulting firms. There are over 250 AMEC offices worldwide. **Positions advertised include:** Billing Revenue Accountant; Field Working Supervisor. **Corporate headquarters location:** London, England. **Number of employees nationwide:** 1,300.

URS
7720 North 16th Street, Suite 100, Phoenix AZ 85020. 602/371-1100. **Fax:** 602/371-1615. **Contact:** Human Resources. **World Wide Web address:** http://www.urscorp.com. **Description:** An architectural, engineering, and environmental consulting firm that specializes in air transportation, environmental solutions, surface transportation, and industrial environmental and engineering concerns. **Positions advertised include:** Archaeologist; Biologist; CADD Technician; Civil Engineer; Environmental Planner. **Corporate headquarters location:** San Francisco CA. **Other area locations:** Tucson AZ. **Parent company:** URS Corporation. **Listed on:** New York Stock Exchange. **Stock exchange symbol:** URS.

WASTE MANAGEMENT, INC.
7025 North Scottsdale Road, Suite 200, Scottsdale AZ 85253. 480/624-8400. **Fax:** 480/951-5280. **Contact:** Human Resources. **World Wide Web address:** http://www.wm.com. **Description:** An international provider of comprehensive waste management services, as well as engineering, construction, industrial, and related services. Waste Management has operations in 19 countries. **Positions advertised include:** Data Entry Coordinator; Sr. Internal Auditor; HR Coordinator. **Corporate headquarters location:** Houston TX. **Listed on:** New York Stock Exchange. **Stock exchange symbol:** WMI.

WESTERN TECHNOLOGIES, INC.
3737 East Broadway Road, Phoenix AZ 85040. 602/437-3737. **Fax:** 602/470-1341. **Contact:** Human Resources. **World Wide Web address:** http://www.wt-us.com. **Description:** Provides engineering, consulting, and testing of environmental, geotechnical, and construction materials. Environmental services include site assessments, investigations, feasibility studies, problem solving, and remedial services. Geotechnical services are provided with use of a wide variety of exploration equipment including highly mobile drilling rigs. Materials Engineering and Testing provides analysis and quality assurance of materials and methods for clients. Materials Research develops methods of improving the strength and durability of conventional construction materials through research into the feasibility of using waste and less expensive or more available materials. Construction Quality Control provides interpretation of geotechnical reports, observation and testing of reinforced steel and concrete, visual and nondestructive evaluation of bolted and welded structural steel components, preparing concrete and asphalt mix designs, as well as sampling and testing many other architectural and structural components. Founded in 1955. **Positions advertised include:** Senior Geotechnical Engineer; Geotechnical

Engineer; Environmental Scientist; Geologist; Industrial Hygienist; Senior Engineering Technician. **Corporate headquarters location:** This location. **Listed on:** Privately held. **Annual sales/revenues:** $21 - $50 million. **Number of employees at this location:** 285.

California

ATC ASSOCIATES
50 East Foothill Boulevard, Arcadia CA 91006. 626/447-5216. **Fax:** 626/447-7593. **Contact:** Human Resources Manager. **E-mail address:** recruiter@atcassociates.com. **World Wide Web address:** http://www.atc-enviro.com. **Description:** Performs comprehensive environmental consulting, engineering, and on-site remediation services throughout the United States for a variety of clients including federal, state, and local government agencies. **Positions advertised include:** Project Geologist; Staff Scientist; Sales Representative; Group Leader/Manager. **Corporate headquarters location:** Woburn MA. **Other area locations:** Statewide. **Other U.S. locations:** Nationwide.

ARCADIS
1400 North Harbor Boulevard, Suite 700, Fullerton CA 92835-4127. 714/278-0992. **Fax:** 714/278-0051. **Contact:** Human Resources. **E-mail address:** arcadisgm@arcadis-us.com. **World Wide Web address:** http://www.arcadis-us.com. **Description:** A consulting firm that provides environmental and engineering services. The company focuses on the environmental, building, and infrastructure markets. Founded in 1888. **Positions advertised include:** Scientist/Engineer; Scientist. **Corporate headquarters:** Highlands Ranch CO. **Other U.S. locations:** Nationwide. **International locations:** The Netherlands; United Kingdom. **Subsidiaries include:** JSA Environmental Inc. (Long Beach CA) provides environmental assessment and analysis services. **Listed on:** NASDAQ. **Stock exchange symbol:** ARCAF. **Number of employees worldwide:** 9,000.

ALLIED WASTE OF SAN MATEO COUNTY
225 Shoreway Road, P.O. Box 1068, San Carlos CA 94070. 650/592-2411. **Contact:** Human Resources. **World Wide Web address:** http://www.alliedwastesanmateocounty.com. **Description:** Engaged primarily in the collection and disposal of solid waste for commercial, industrial, and residential customers. Services include landfill services, waste-to-energy programs, hazardous waste removal, and liquid waste removal. The company has worldwide operations at more than 500 facilities. **Corporate headquarters location:** Houston TX. **Parent company:** Allied Waste Industries. **Listed on:** New York Stock Exchange. **Stock exchange symbol:** AW.

BROWN & CALDWELL
201 North Civic Drive, Suite 115, Walnut Creek CA 94596. 925/937-9010. **Toll-free phone:** 800/727-2224. **Fax:** 925/937-9026. **Contact:** Professional Staffing. **E-mail address:** resumes@brwncald.com. **World Wide Web address:** http://www.brwncald.com. **Description:** An employee-owned environmental engineering and consulting firm. Brown & Caldwell specializes in the planning, engineering, and design of waste management systems. The company is also engaged in construction management and environmental analytical testing. **Positions advertised include:** Supervising Engineer; Health and Safety risk Manager; Senior Electronic Media Specialist; Graphic Designer; Managing Scientist. **Corporate headquarters location:** This location. **Other U.S. locations:** Nationwide. **Number of employees nationwide:** 1,000.

CATALYTICA ENERGY SYSTEMS, INC.
430 Ferguson Drive, Building 3, Mountain View CA 94043. 650/960-3000. **Contact:** Human Resources. **E-mail address:** hr@catalyticaenergy.com. **World Wide Web address:** http://www.catalyticaenergy.com. **Description:** Develops catalytic technologies for the prevention of pollution in combustion systems, advanced process technologies, and chemical products. The company also develops an ultraslow emission-combustion system for natural gas turbines. **Positions advertised include:** Process Development Engineer. **Corporate headquarters location:** Gilbert AZ. **Operations at this facility include:** Research and Development. **Subsidiaries include:** Advanced Sensor Devices. **Listed on:** NASDAQ. **Stock exchange symbol:** CESI.

ENSR INTERNATIONAL
1420 Harbor Bay Parkway, Suite 120, Alameda CA 94502-7059. 510/748-6700. **Fax:** 510/748-6799. **Contact:** Human Resources. **E-mail address:** askensr@ensr.aecom.com. **World Wide Web address:** http://www.ensr.aecom.com. **Description:** A full-service environmental consulting firm specializing in regulatory compliance management, risk assessment, and remediation. **Positions advertised include:** Senior Program Manager; Senior Water Resources Specialist. **Corporate headquarters location:** Westford MA. **Other area locations:** Camarillo CA; Orange CA; Sacramento CA. **Other U.S. locations:** Nationwide. **Parent company:** AECOM.

EARTH TECH
2101 Webster Street, Suite 1000, Oakland CA 94612-3060. 510/419-6000. **Fax:** 510/419-5355. **Contact:** Personnel Department. **E-mail address:** oaklandjobs@earthtech.com. **World Wide Web address:** http://www.earthtech.com. **Description:** Provides global water management, environmental, and transportation services. **Positions advertised include:** Electrical Engineer. **Corporate headquarters location:** Long Beach CA. **Other area locations:** Statewide. **Other U.S. locations:** Nationwide. **Parent company:** Tyco International Ltd. **Listed on:** New York Stock Exchange. **Stock exchange symbol:** TYC.

EBERLINE SERVICES
2030 Wright Avenue, P.O. Box 4040, Richmond CA 94804-3823. 510/235-2633. **Fax:** 510/235-0438. **Contact:** Human Resources Administrator. **E-mail address:** hr@eberlineservices.com. **World Wide Web address:** http://www.eberlineservices.com. **Description:** Engaged in hazardous, radiological, and mixed-waste testing of soil and water. The company's work is related to regulatory compliance, and each of their laboratories is extensively licensed and qualified to accept radioactive samples. **Positions advertised include:** Radiochemistry Laboratory Manager. **Corporate headquarters location:** Albuquerque NM. **Other U.S. locations:** Los Alamos NM; Denver CO; Lionville PA; Oak Ridge TN; Richland WA.

ENVIRON CORPORATION
6001 Shellmound Street, Suite 700, Emeryville CA 94608. 510/655-7400. **Fax:** 510/655-9517. **Contact:** Director of Human Resources. **E-mail address:** hremeryville@environcorp.com. **World Wide Web address:** http://www.environcorp.com. **Description:** A multidisciplinary environmental and health sciences consulting firm that provides a broad range of services relating to the presence of hazardous substances in the environment, consumer products, and the workplace. Services provided by ENVIRON are concentrated in the assessment and management of chemical risk. **Positions advertised include:** Associate, Due Diligence; Associate, Human Health Risk Assessment; Senior Manager, Hydrogeology; Senior Ecological Risk Assessor. **Corporate headquarters location:** Arlington VA. **Other area locations:** Statewide. **Other U.S. locations:** Nationwide. **Parent company:** Applied BioScience International Inc.

LOCUS TECHNOLOGIES
1333 North California Boulevard, Suite 350, Walnut Creek CA 94596. 925/906-8100. **Fax:** 925/906-8101. **Contact:** Human Resources Department. **E-mail address:** humanresources@locustec.com. **World Wide Web address:** http://www.locustec.com. **Description:** A leading environmental consulting, engineering, and remediation services provider. **NOTE:** Candidates should send a resume with salary requirements and

references. **Positions advertised include:** Project Scientist; Project Engineer. **Corporate headquarters location:** This location. **Other area locations:** Mountain View CA; Middletown CA; Sacramento CA; Los Angeles CA. **Listed on:** Privately held.

MWH LABORATORIES
750 Royal Oaks Drive, Suite 100, Monrovia CA 91016. 626/386-1100. **Fax:** 626/386-1101. **Contact:** Corporate Human Resources. **E-mail address:** Damian J Guerin@mwhglobal.com. **World Wide Web address:** http://www.mwlaboratories.com. **Description:** Offers engineering consulting services for water, wastewater, and hazardous waste facilities. **Positions advertised include:** Staff Chemist; Administrative Assistant. **Special programs:** Internships. **Corporate headquarters location:** This location. **Other U.S. locations:** Nationwide. **Parent company:** MWH Americas, Inc. **Annual sales/revenues:** More than $100 million.

NORCAL WASTE SYSTEMS INC.
160 Pacific Avenue, Suite 200, San Francisco CA 94111. 415/875-1000. **Fax:** 415/875-1134. **Contact:** Human Resources Department. **World Wide Web address:** http://www.norcalwaste.com. **Description:** Engaged in waste management and recycling services. **Corporate headquarters location:** This location. **Number of employees at this location:** 1,375.

PARSONS CORPORATION
100 West Walnut Street, Pasadena CA 91124. 626/440-2000. **Fax:** 626/440-2630. **Contact:** Staffing Department. **World Wide Web address:** http://www.parsons.com. **Description:** Parsons Corporation provides engineering, planning, design, project management, and related services for a variety of projects including rail systems, highways, bridges, hazardous waste management, aviation facilities, environmental engineering, resorts, power generation and delivery systems, natural resources development, defense systems, industrial and institutional facilities, and community planning and development. **NOTE:** Apply online. **Positions advertised include:** Senior Engineer; Business Development Manager; Project Manager; Operations Manager; Associate Engineer; Principal Process Engineer; Senior Transportation Engineer. **Corporate headquarters location:** This location. **Other U.S. locations:** Nationwide. **Number of employees nationwide:** 2,000.

SAFETY-KLEEN CORPORATION
10651 Hickson Street, El Monte CA 91731. 626/575-4685. **Fax:** 626/575-1927. **Contact:** Human Resources. **World Wide Web address:** http://www.safety-kleen.com. **Description:** A chemical waste recycler. **Corporate headquarters location:** Plano TX.

SEVERN TRENT LABORATORIES, INC.
1721 South Grand Avenue, Santa Ana CA 92705. 714/258-8610. **Fax:** 714/258-0921. **Contact:** Human Resources. **World Wide Web address:** http://www.stl-inc.com. **Description:** Provides a complete range of environmental testing services to private industry, engineering consultants, and government agencies in support of federal and state environmental regulations. The company also possesses analytical capabilities in the fields of air toxins, field analytical services, radiochemistry/mixed waste, and advanced technology. **Corporate headquarters location:** North Canton OH. **Other U.S. locations:** FL; MO; NC; OH; TN; TX; WA.

SHAW ENVIRONMENTAL & INFRASTRUCTURE
3347 Michelson Drive, Suite 200, Irvine CA 92612. 949/261-6441. **Fax:** 949/474-8309. **Contact:** Human Resources. **World Wide Web address:** http://www.shawgrp.com. **Description:** Applies engineering, analytical, remediation, and pollution control expertise to meet the environmental needs of its clients from site assessment to remediation. **Corporate headquarters location:** Baton Rouge LA. **Number of employees worldwide:** 6,000.

J.F. SHEA COMPANY, INC.
655 Brea Canyon Road, Walnut CA 91789. 909/594-9500. **Contact:** Chief Estimator. **World Wide Web address:** http://www.jfshea.com. **Description:** Engaged in the construction of water resource, water, and wastewater treatment systems. **Corporate headquarters location:** This location. **Parent company:** Zurn Industries, Inc. (Erie PA) also has operations in three other industry segments. The Power Systems segment designs, constructs, and operates small to medium-sized alternate energy and combined-cycle power plants; designs steam generators and waste heat energy recovery and incineration systems; and produces equipment and fans to control emissions of solid particulate and gaseous pollutants. The Mechanical Power Transmission segment manufactures and markets clutches, couplings, and universal joints in the United States and Europe. The last segment, Lynx Golf, manufactures golf clubs in Nevada, which are finished and assembled in California, Mexico, and Scotland for distribution worldwide. **Operations at this facility include:** Administration; Divisional Headquarters. **Listed on:** New York Stock Exchange. **Annual sales/revenues:** $51 - $100 million. **Number of employees at this location:** 250.

SIMSMETAL AMERICA
600 South Fourth Street, Richmond CA 94804-3504. 510/412-5300. **Contact:** Human Resources. **World Wide Web address:** http://www.sims-group.com. **Description:** A multifaceted company involved in metals recycling and related ventures. **Corporate headquarters location:** This location. **Parent company:** Simsmetal Limited (Australia).

SMITH-EMERY COMPANY
791 East Washington Boulevard, Los Angeles CA 90021. 213/749-3411. **Contact:** Human Resources. **World Wide Webb address:** http://www.smithemery.com. **Description:** A testing and inspection laboratory for concrete, soil, and chemical samples. **Corporate headquarters location:** This location.

TETRA TECH, INC.
3475 East Foothill Boulevard, Pasadena CA 91107. 626/351-4664. **Fax:** 626/470-2694. **Contact:** Human Resources Manager. **E-mail address:** jobs@tetratech.com. **World Wide Web address:** http://www.tetratech.com. **Description:** Tetra Tech is a leading provider of specialized management consulting and technical services in resource management, infrastructure, and communications. Founded in 1966. **NOTE:** Entry-level positions and part-time jobs are offered. **Positions adverties include:** Human Resource Assistant; Oracle Programmer; Financial Analyst; Construction Manager; Senior Accountant. **Special programs:** Internships. **Office hours:** Monday - Friday, 8:00 a.m. - 5:00 p.m. **Corporate headquarters location:** This location. **Other U.S. locations:** Nationwide. **Subsidiaries include:** Environmental Management, Inc.; FLO Engineering; HSI GeoTrans; IWA Engineers; KCM Inc.; Simons, Li & Associates. **Listed on:** NASDAQ. **Stock exchange symbol:** TTEK. **Number of employees at this location:** 95. **Number of employees nationwide:** 8,900.

URS CORPORATION
600 Montgomery Street, 26th Floor, San Francisco CA 94111-2728. 415/774-2700. **Fax:** 415/398-1905. **Contact:** Personnel Department. **World Wide Web address:** http://www.urscorp.com. **Description:** An international professional services organization with substantial engineering, training, architectural planning, environmental, and construction management capabilities. **Positions advertised include:** Project Manager; Internal Auditor; Vice President. **Corporate headquarters location:** This location. **Listed on:** New York Stock Exchange. **Stock exchange symbol:** URS. **Number of employees worldwide:** 26,000.

USA BIOMASS CORPORATION
1912 North Batavia Street, Unit C, Orange CA 92865. 714/921-2886. **Contact:** Human Resources. **World**

Wide Web address: http://www.usabiomasscorp.com. **Description:** USA Biomass provides waste removal and recycling services for green waste. The company is a vertically integrated green waste management business that services both corporate customers and municipalities. **Corporate headquarters location:** Lampasas TX.

WASTE MANAGEMENT, INC.
1970 East 213th Street, Long Beach CA 90249. 310/605-6000. **Contact:** Human Resources. **E-mail address:** careers@wm.com. **World Wide Web address:** http://www.wastemanagement.com. **Description:** Engaged in commercial and residential refuse removal. **NOTE:** Search and apply for positions online. **Corporate headquarters location:** Oak Brook IL. **Other U.S. locations:** Nationwide. **Listed on:** New York Stock Exchange. **Stock exchange symbol:** WMI.

ZYMAX ENVIROTECHNOLOGY INC.
71 Zaca Lane, San Luis Obispo CA 93401-7300. 805/544-4696. **Contact:** Human Resources. **E-mail address:** employment@zymaxusa.com. **World Wide Web address:** http://www.zymaxusa.com. **Description:** A high tech environmental testing company. **Advertised positions:** Inorganics Laboratory Technician; Volatiles Laboratory Specialist; Geochemist.

Colorado
ACURA ENGINEERING
13276 East Fremont Place, Centennial CO 80112. 303/799-8378. **Fax:** 303/799-8392. **Contact:** Human Resources. **E-mail address:** potential@acurageo.com. **World Wide Web address:** http://www.acurageo.com. **Description:** Provides geotechnical engineering and construction materials testing services, Phase 1 environmental site assessments, and forensic investigation services. **Positions advertised include:** GEO and CMT Field Tech.

ALLIED WASTE SERVICE OF DENVER
5075 East 74th Avenue, Denver CO 80022. 303/287-8043. **Contact:** Human Resources. **World Wide Web address:** http://www.awin.com. **Description:** Engaged primarily in the collection and disposal of solid wastes for commercial, industrial, and residential customers. Services provided include landfill services, waste-to-energy programs, hazardous waste removal, and liquid waste removal. The company has worldwide operations at more than 500 facilities. **Corporate headquarters location:** Scottsdale AZ. **Other U.S. locations:** Nationwide. **Listed on:** New York Stock Exchange. **Stock exchange symbol:** AW.

ARCADIS
630 Plaza Drive, Suite 200, Highlands Ranch CO 80129. 720/344-3500. **Contact:** Corporate Technical Recruiter. **World Wide Web address:** http://www.arcadis-us.com. **Description:** A consulting firm that provides environmental and engineering services. The company focuses on the environmental, building, and infrastructure markets. Founded in 1888. **Positions advertised include:** Communications Manager; Regional Recruiter; Purchasing Assistant. **Other U.S. locations:** Nationwide. **International locations:** The Netherlands; United Kingdom. **Parent company:** Arcadis NV. **Listed on:** NASDAQ. **Stock exchange symbol:** ARCAF.

COMMODORE ADVANCED SCIENCES, INC.
4251 Kipling Street, Suite 575, Wheat Ridge CO 80033. 303/421-1511. **Contact:** Human Resources. **World Wide Web address:** http://www.commodore.com. **Description:** A technical services consulting firm that provides waste management, environmental sciences, advanced technologies, and remediation. Founded in 1977. **NOTE:** Entry-level positions are offered. **Corporate headquarters location:** Alexandria VA. **Other U.S. locations:** Idaho Falls ID; Carlsbad NM; Los Alamos NM; Oak Ridge TN. **Parent company:** Commodore Applied Technologies, Inc. **Listed on:** OTC BB. **Stock exchange symbol:** CXIA.

GEOTRANS INC.
363 Centennial Parkway, Suite 210, Louisville CO 80027. 303/665-4390. **Contact:** Human Resources. **World Wide Web address:** http://www.geotransinc.com. **Description:** Provides environmental consulting services. **NOTE:** search and apply for positions online. **Parent company:** Tetra-Tech. **Listed on:** NASDAQ. **Stock exchange symbol:** TTEK.

METRO WASTEWATER RECLAMATION DISTRICT
6450 York Street, Denver CO 80229-7407. 303/286-3000. **Fax:** 303/286-3034. **Contact:** Human Resources. **E-mail address:** resume@mwrd.dst.co.us. **World Wide Web address:** http://www.metrowastewater.com. **Description:** A regional government agency that provides wastewater transmission and treatment services to local governments. **NOTE:** Application required. **Positions advertised include:** Staff Engineer.

SEVERN TRENT LABORATORIES, INC.
4955 Yarrow Street, Arvada CO 80002. 303/736-0100. **Fax:** 303/431-7171. **Contact:** Human Resources. **World Wide Web address:** http://www.stl-inc.com. **Description:** Provides a complete range of environmental testing services to private industry, engineering consultants, and government agencies in support of federal and state environmental regulations. The company also possesses analytical capabilities in the fields of air toxins, field analytical services, radiochemistry/mixed waste, and advanced technology. **NOTE:** Resumes accepted only for open positions. Search and apply for positions online. **Parent company:** Severn Trent Services.

SIEMENS WATER TECHNOLOGIES
1335 Ford Street, Colorado Springs CO 80915-2934. 719/570-5600. **Contact:** Human Resources. **World Wide Web address:** http://www.usfilter.com. **Description:** Siemens Water Technologies provides products, systems, services and automation for water and wastewater treatment. **Positions advertised include:** Drafter/Designer; Engineer; Engineering Director; Manufacturing Supervisor; Project Manager. **Corporate headquarters location:** Warrendale PA. **Parent company:** Siemens.

URS CORPORATION
8181 East Tufts Avenue, Denver CO 80237. 303/694-2770. **Fax:** 303/694-3946. **Contact:** Human Resources. **World Wide Web address:** http://www.urscorp.com. **Description:** Provides regulatory compliance support, site investigation and remediation, air pollution controls, VOC and air toxins control, biotreatment, waste management, ambient and source monitoring, risk management, information management, project chemistry, specialty chemicals, remote sensing services, materials and machinery analysis, and electronic services. Founded in 1969. **Positions advertised include:** Project CADD Designer; Civil Designer; Contracts Manager; Development Engineer Manager; Electrical Engineer; Geologist; Geotechnical Engineer; Industrial Hygienist; Mechanical Engineer. **Corporate headquarters location:** San Francisco CA. **International locations:** Worldwide. **Listed on:** New York Stock Exchange. **Stock exchange symbol:** URS.

WASTE MANAGEMENT COLORADO
2400 West Union Avenue, Englewood CO 80110-5354. 303/797-1600. **Contact:** Human Resources. **World Wide Web address:** http://www.wmcolorado.com. **Description:** A waste disposal company specializing in the hauling of waste materials. **Parent company:** Waste Management, Inc. is an international provider of comprehensive waste management services, as well as engineering and construction, industrial, and related services, with operations in 19 countries. **Listed on:** New York Stock Exchange. **Stock exchange symbol:** WMI.

WASTE MANAGEMENT, INC.
6091 Brighton Boulevard, Commerce City CO 80022. 303/288-5115. **Contact:** Human Resources. **World**

Wide Web address: http://www.wm.com. **Description:** A community provider of waste hauling, dumping, and recycling services. **Corporate headquarters location:** Houston TX. **Listed on:** New York Stock Exchange. **Stock exchange symbol:** WMI.

Connecticut

BROOKS LABORATORIES
9 Isaac Street, Norwalk CT 06850. 203/853-9792. **Contact:** Human Resources. **World Wide Web address:** http://www.brookslabs.com. **Description:** An environmental consulting firm and laboratory engaged in water testing, lead inspection, and air quality testing. **Positions advertised include:** Chemist.

CLEAN HARBORS ENVIRONMENTAL SERVICES
761 Middle Street, Bristol CT 06010. 860/583-8917. **Contact:** Human Resources. **World Wide Web address:** http://www.cleanharbors.com. **Description:** Clean Harbors, Inc., through its subsidiaries, provides a wide range of hazardous waste management and environmental support services to a diversified customer base. The company's services include treatment, storage, recycling, transportation, risk analysis, site assessment, laboratory analysis, site closure, and disposal of hazardous materials through environmentally sound methods including incineration. Environmental remediation services include emergency response, surface remediation, groundwater restoration, industrial maintenance, and facility decontamination. **Positions advertised include:** Field Service Foreman; Class A Driver; Field Technician. **Corporate headquarters location:** Braintree MA. **Other U.S. locations:** Nationwide. **Listed on:** NASDAQ. **Stock exchange symbol:** CLHB. **Number of employees nationwide:** 1,400.

EEW MANAGEMENT
P.O. Box 1548, Torrington CT 06790. 860/489-7575. **Physical address:** 715 Main Street, Torrington CT 06790. **Contact:** Human Resources. **World Wide Web address:** http://www.eewm.com. **Description:** Engaged in the removal and disposal of hazardous waste material.

ENVIROMED SERVICES
470 Murdock Avenue, Box 13, Meriden CT 06450. 203/786-5580. **Contact:** Personnel. **World Wide Web address:** http://www.enviromedservices.com. **Description:** Provides environmental consulting services.

SCHOONER INC.
60 South Water Street, New Haven CT 06519. 203/865-1737. **Contact:** Human Resources. **World Wide Web address:** http://www.schoonersoundlearning.org. **Description:** A marine science company engaged in preserving the marine life of Long Island Sound and promoting environmental educational awareness.

TRC COMPANY
5 Waterside Crossing, Windsor CT 06095. 860/289-8631. **Fax:** 860/298-6385. **Contact:** Krystal Lechsit, Human Resources. **World Wide Web address:** http://www.trcsolutions.com. **Description:** TRC Company provides a wide range of services including environmental engineering and consulting, site and traffic engineering, weather modification, and specialized pollution control measurement instrumentation to the private sector and government markets. **Other U.S. locations:** Nationwide.

USA HAULING & RECYCLING, INC
184 Municipal Road, Waterbury CT 06708. 203/757-3659. **Contact:** Human Resources. **Description:** Provides residential and commercial waste disposal services.

WASTE MANAGEMENT, INC.
209 Pickering Street, Portland CT 06480. 860/342-0667. **Contact:** Human Resources. **E-mail address:** careers@wm.com. **World Wide Web address:** http://www.wm.com. **Description:** Provides waste removal services. **Corporate headquarters location:** Houston TX. **Other U.S. locations:** Nationwide. **Listed on:** New York Stock Exchange. **Stock exchange symbol:** WMI.

YORK ANALYTICAL LABORATORIES
120 Research Drive, Stratford CT 06615. 203/325-1371. **Contact:** Human Resources. **Description:** A laboratory engaged in soil, water, and air quality testing.

Delaware

ASHLAND NATURE CENTER
P.O. Box 700, Hockessin DE 19707. 302/239-2334. **Fax:** 302/239-2473. **Contact:** Helen Fischel, Associate Director Education. **E-mail address:** helen@dnsashland.org. **World Wide Web address:** http://www.delawarenaturesociety.org. **Description:** A private, nonprofit, membership organization dedicated to environmental education and the preservation of natural areas. **Positions advertised include:** Teacher-Naturalists. **Special Programs:** Internships; Volunteer Opportunities; Seasonal Programs; School Programs. **Parent company:** Delaware Nature Society operates Ashland Nature Center and Abbott's Mill, offering year-round programming for all age groups.

District Of Columbia

CH2M HILL
555 11th Street NW, Suite 525, Washington DC 20004. 202/393-2426. **Fax:** 202/783-8410. **Contact:** Human Resources. **E-mail address:** hr@ch2m.com. **World Wide Web address:** http://www.ch2m.com. **Description:** An environmental engineering company specializing in water and remediation projects. **Positions advertised include:** Program Services Specialist. **Other U.S. locations:** Nationwide. **International locations:** Worldwide.

OCEANA
2501 M Street NW, Suite 300, Washington DC 20037-1311. 202/833-3900. **Fax:** 202/833-2070. **Contact:** Human Resources. **E-mail address:** resumes@oceana.org. **World Wide Web address:** http://www.oceana.org. **Description:** An international, non-profit ocean protection and advocacy agency. **NOTE:** Does not accept calls regarding status of resumes or applications. **Positions advertised include:** Communications Manager; Chief Scientist; Database and IT Administrator; Director, E-Activism/Marketing. **Special programs:** Seasonal Internships available. **Corporate headquarters location:** This location. **Other U.S. locations:** Los Angeles CA; Juneau AK.

Florida

AJT & ASSOCIATES, INC.
8910 Astronaut Boulevard, Cape Canaveral FL 32920-4225. 321/783-7989. **Contact:** Karen Yorio, Human Resources Representative. **E-mail address:** kareny@ajt-assoc.com. **World Wide Web address:** http://www.ajt-assoc.com. **Description:** Provides environmental science and architectural engineering services.

ATC ASSOCIATES
9955 NW 116 Way, Suite 1, Miami FL 33178. 305/882-8200. **Fax:** 305/882-1200. **Contact:** Human Resources. **World Wide Web address:** http://www.atc-enviro.com. **Description:** Performs comprehensive environmental consulting, engineering, and on-site remediation services. Services include assessment of environmental regulations, investigation of contaminated sites, and the design and engineering of methods to correct or prevent the contamination. The company also performs remedial actions, and emergency response actions in cases of spills and accidental releases of hazardous waste. ATC Associates addresses hazardous and nonhazardous contaminants in municipal and industrial water supplies; in wastewater and storm water from municipal, industrial, and military installations; and in groundwater, soils, and air space. Customers include federal, state, and local government agencies. **Positions advertised include:** NDT Technician.

BROWNING-FERRIS INDUSTRIES, INC. (BFI)
1475 SW 4th Avenue, Delray Beach FL 33444. 561/278-1717. **Contact:** Human Resources. **Description:** Engaged in the collection and disposal of solid waste for commercial, industrial, and residential customers. Services provided by Browning-Ferris Industries include landfill services, waste-to-energy programs, hazardous waste removal, and liquid waste removal. The company has worldwide operations at more than 500 facilities. **Parent company:** Allied Waste Industries, Inc.

EVANS ENVIRONMENTAL CORPORATION
14505 Commerce Way, Suite 400, Miami Lakes FL 33016. 305/374-8300. **Contact:** Human Resources. **Description:** Engaged in environmental testing and consulting, and in the manufacture and distribution of remote control cable television units. **Subsidiaries include:** ABC Cable Products, Inc.; Enviropact Consultants, Inc.; Evans Environmental & Geological Sciences & Management, Inc.; Evans Management Co.; Geos Inc.

MUNTERS CORPORATION
P.O. Box 6428, Fort Myers FL 33911. 239/936-1555. **Fax:** 239/936-8858. **Physical address:** 108 Sixth Street, Fort Myers Fl 33911. **Contact:** Human Resources. **World Wide Web address:** http://www.munters-fl.com. **Description:** An environmental technology and pollution control company. **Positions advertised include:** District Manager; Industrial Account Manager; Regional Water Damage Sales Manager; Water Damage Recovery Account. **Operations at this facility include:** Administration; Manufacturing; Research and Development; Sales. **Number of employees at this location:** 120. **Number of employees nationwide:** 420.

SEVERN TRENT LABORATORIES, INC.
3355 Meclemore Drive, Pensacola FL 32514. 850/474-1001. **Fax:** 850/478-2671. **Contact:** Human Resources. **World Wide Web address:** http://www.stl-inc.com. **Description:** Provides a complete range of environmental testing services to private industry, engineering consultants, and government agencies in support of federal and state environmental regulations. The company also possesses analytical capabilities in the fields of air toxins, field analytical services, radiochemistry/mixed waste, and advanced technology. **Positions advertised include:** Operations Manager; Field Service Technician. **Other area locations:** Tampa FL. **Other U.S. locations:** Nationwide. **Parent Company:** Severn Trent plc. **Number of employees nationwide:** Over 2,000.

Georgia

BFI WASTE SYSTEMS
3045 Bankhead Highway NW, Atlanta GA 30318-4405. 404/792-2660. **Contact:** Human Resources. **World Wide Web address:** http://www.alliedwaste.com. **Description:** BFI is engaged primarily in the collection and disposal of solid wastes for commercial, industrial, and residential customers, landfill services, waste-to-energy programs, hazardous waste removal, and liquid waste removal. The company has worldwide operations at more than 500 facilities. **Corporate headquarters location:** Scottsdale AZ. **Parent company:** Allied Waste Industries, Inc. **Operations at this facility include:** This location hauls waste and provides waste services such as portable toilets for commercial and residential markets. **Listed on:** New York Stock Exchange. **Stock exchanges symbol:** AW. **CEO:** Thomas H. Van Weelden.

GEORGIA FORESTRY COMMISSION
P.O. Box 819, Macon GA 31202-0819. 478/751-3500. **Physical address:** 5645 Riggins Mill Road, Dry Branch GA 31020. **Fax:** 478/751-3465. **Contact:** Human Resources Department. **E-mail address:** gfchrpersonnel@gfc.state.ga.us. **World Wide Web address:** http://www.gfc.state.ga.us. **Description:** Protects Georgia's forests resources, and provides education in the protection and management of those resources. **NOTE:** Mail resumes to Human Resources at 6835 James B. Rivers/Memorial Drive, Stone Mountain GA 30083. Phone is 678/476-6220, fax is 678/476-6230. **Positions advertised include:** Ranger; Forester. **Other area locations:** Statewide.

URS CORPORATION
400 Northpark Town Center, 1000 Abernathy Road NE, Suite 900, Atlanta GA 30328. 678/808-8800. **Fax:** 678/808-8400. **Contact:** Human Resources. **World Wide Web address:** http://www.urscorp.com. **Description:** Develops and alters transportation systems, buildings, and industrial facilities. URS Corporation is also involved in environmental reconstruction and preservation services. Founded in 1969. **Positions advertised include:** Civil Engineer; Graduate Civil Engineer; Graduate Water Resources Engineer; MIS Coordinator; Project Accountant/Accounting Manager; Project Civil Engineer; Project Environmental Scientist; Project Transportation Engineer; Senior Accountant; Senior CADD Designer; Senior Civil-Bridge Engineer; Water Resources Engineer. **Special programs:** Internships; Co-ops. **Corporate headquarters location:** San Francisco CA. **Other U.S. locations:** Nationwide. **International locations:** Worldwide. **Listed on:** New York Stock Exchange. **Stock exchange symbol:** URS. **Number of employees worldwide:** 26,000.

Idaho

GEOENGINEERS
802 West Bannock Street, Suite 700, Boise ID 83702. 208/433-8098. **Fax:** 208/433-8092. **Contact:** Human Resources. **E-mail address:** employment@geoengineers.com. **World Wide Web address:** http://www.geoengineers.com. **NOTE:** Apply online. **Description:** Provides earth science, environmental, and technology consulting services focusing on the areas of transportation, energy, development, government services, and water and natural resources. **Positions advertised include:** Senior Geotechnical Engineer; Project 2 Geotechnical Engineer. **Corporate headquarters location:** Redmond WA. **Other locations:** AK; HI; MO; OR; TX.

NORTH WIND INC.
P.O. Box 51174, 1425 Hingham Street, Idaho Falls ID 83405. 208/528-8718. **Fax:** 208/528-8714. **Contact:** Human Resources. **World Wide Web address:** http://www.nwindenv.com. **Description:** An engineering consulting firm. Focus on environmental restoration, engineering, program management, geosciences, waste management and civil construction services. **NOTE:** Search and apply for positions online. **Positions advertised include:** Accounting System Supervisor; Archaeologist; Chemist; Engineer; Quality Representative; Seasonal Construction Laborer; Environmental Engineer; Industrial Hygienist; Waste Shipper. **Corporate office location:** This location. **Other area locations:** Kellogg ID; Salmon ID. **Other U.S. Locations:** AK; AL; CO; FL; GA; KS; MD; MS; NM; SC; TN; TX; UT; WA; WY.

WASHINGTON GROUP INTERNATIONAL
P.O. Box 73, Boise ID 83729. 208/386-5000. **Physical address:** 720 Park Boulevard, Boise ID 83712 **Fax:** 208/386-7186. **Recorded jobline:** 208/386-6966. **Contact:** Corporate Staffing. **E-mail address:** jobs@wgjobs.com. **World Wide Web address:** http://www.wgint.com. **Description:** Provides integrated engineering, construction and management solutions for businesses and governments worldwide in more than two-dozen major markets. **NOTE:** Entry-level positions are offered. For craft/labor positions, contact the local job services office. **Positions advertised include:** Payroll Specialist; Human Resource Representative; Construction Engineer; Design Engineer; Project Control Manager; Structural Supervisor. **Special programs:** Internships; Co-ops; Summer Jobs. **Corporate headquarters location:** This location. **Other U.S. locations:** Nationwide. **International locations:** Worldwide. **Listed on:**

NASDAQ. **Stock exchange symbol:** WGII. **Number of employees worldwide:** 25,000.

Illinois

AB&H, A DONOHUE GROUP
20 North Wacker Drive, Suite 1401, Chicago IL 60606. 312/236-9147. **Fax:** 312/236-0692. **Contact:** Human Resources. **E-mail address:** info@abh-donohue.com. **World Wide Web address:** http://www.abh-donohue.com. **Description:** An employee-owned firm that provides water, wastewater, and transportation engineering services. **NOTE:** Contact the office directly, or see website http://www.dohohue-associates.com.

ATC
419 Eisenhower Lane South, Lombard IL 60148-5706. 630/916-7272. **Fax:** 630/916-7013. **Contact:** Human Resources. **World Wide Web address:** http://www.atc-enviro.com. **Description:** Provides comprehensive environmental consulting, engineering, and on-site remediation services throughout the United States for clients including federal, state, and local government agencies. ATC's services include assessment of environmental regulations, investigation of contaminated sites, and the design and engineering of methods to correct or prevent contamination. The company addresses hazardous and non-hazardous contaminants in municipal and industrial water supplies; wastewater and storm water from municipal, industrial, and military installations; groundwater, soils, and air space surrounding these types of complexes; and contaminants in buildings and facilities such as asbestos, lead paint, and radioactive contamination. **NOTE:** Apply online. **Positions advertised include:** Project Scientist; Group Leader/Manager.

ARCADIS GERAGHTY & MILLER, INC.
35 East Wacker Drive, Suite 1000, Chicago IL 60601. 312/263-6703. **Fax:** 317/231-6514. **Contact:** Phil Hutton, Office Administrator. **World Wide Web address:** http://www.arcadis-us.com. **Description:** A consulting firm that provides environmental and engineering services. The company focuses on the environmental, building, and infrastructure markets. Founded in 1888. **NOTE:** Apply online at the company's website. **Positions advertised include:** Principal Scientist; Engineer. **Corporate headquarters location:** Denver CO. **International locations:** Worldwide. **Listed on:** NASDAQ. **Stock exchange symbol:** ARCAF.

BLOOM ENGINEERING COMPANY, INC.
18161 Morris Avenue, Homewood IL 60430. 412/760-8737. **Contact:** Human Resources. **E-mail address:** tfennell@bloomeng.com. **World Wide Web address:** http://www.bloomeng.com. **Description:** Provides innovative energy and environmental solutions to industry. **Positions advertised include:** Combustion Technician; Boiler Technician; Controls Technician. **Corporate headquarters location:** Pittsburgh PA.

CH2M HILL
8501 West Higgins Road, Suite 300,Chicago IL 60631-2801. 773/693-3809. **Contact:** Human Resources. **World Wide Web address:** http://www.ch2m.com. **Description:** CH2M Hill is a group of employee-owned companies operating under the names CH2M Hill, Inc., Industrial Design Corporation, Operations Management International, CH2M Hill International, and CH2M Hill Engineering. The professional staff includes specialists in environmental engineering, waste management, water management, transportation, industrial facilities, and a broad spectrum of infrastructure systems. **NOTE:** This company has offices throughout Chicago, Illinois and the United States. See website for job listings and apply online. **Operations at this facility include:** This location provides transportation and environmental engineering services.

CLAYTON GROUP SERVICES, INC.
3140 Finley Road, Downers Grove IL 60515. 630/795-3200. **Fax:** 630/795-1130. **Contact:** Human Resources. **E-mail address:** hr@claytongrp.com. **World Wide Web address:** http://www.claytongrp.com. **Description:** An environmental consulting firm that also offers occupational health and safety, strategic environmental management, environmental risk management, and laboratory services. **NOTE:** Resumes may be sent to Human Resources, 45525 Grand River Avenue, Suite 200, Novi, MI 48374; or, they may be faxed to 248/344-0229. Indicate job code in cover letter.

CLEAN HARBORS, INC.
11800 South Stony Island Avenue, Chicago IL 60617. 773/646-6202. **Fax:** 773/646-6381. **Contact:** Human Resources. **World Wide Web address:** http://www.cleanharbors.com. **Description:** Clean Harbors, Inc., through its subsidiaries, provides comprehensive environmental services in 35 states in the Northeast, Midwest, Central, and Mid-Atlantic regions. Clean Harbors provides a wide range of hazardous waste management and environmental support services to a diversified customer base from over 40 locations. The company's hazardous waste management services include treatment, storage, recycling, transportation, risk analysis, site assessment, laboratory analysis, site closure, and disposal of hazardous materials through environmentally sound methods including incineration. Environmental remediation services include emergency response, surface remediation, groundwater restoration, industrial maintenance, and facility decontamination. **NOTE:** See website for job listings and contact information. **Positions advertised include:** Field Technician. **Corporate headquarters location:** Braintree MA. **Other U.S. locations:** Nationwide.

CONESTOGA ROVERS & ASSOCIATES
8615 West Bryn Mawr, Chicago IL 60631. 773/380-9933. **Contact:** Human Resources. **World Wide Web address:** http://www.craworld.com. **Description:** An environmental engineering and consulting firm. Founded in 1976. Apply online at this company's website.

CONSOER TOWNSEND ENVIRODYNE ENGINEERS, INC.
303 East Wacker Drive, Suite 600, Chicago IL 60601. 312/938-0300. **Fax:** 312/938-1109. **Contact:** Director of Human Resources. **E-mail address:** jobs@cte-eng.com. **World Wide Web address:** http://www.cte-eng.com. **Description:** Provides engineering consulting for highways, airports, and waste management projects. **NOTE:** Apply online at the company's website or e-mail resumes.

GABRIEL ENVIRONMENTAL SERVICES
1421 North Elston Avenue, Chicago IL 60622. 773/486-2123. **Fax:** 773/486-0004. **Contact:** Human Resources. **World Wide Web address:** http://www.gabrielenvironmental.com. **Description:** Provides environmental consulting, fieldwork, and laboratory services. **Special programs:** Internships. **Corporate headquarters location:** This location.

GREELEY AND HANSEN
100 South Wacker Drive, Suite 1400, Chicago IL 60606. 312/558-9000. **Contact:** Human Resources. **E-mail address:** careers@greeley-hansen.com. **World Wide Web address:** http://www.greeley-hansen.com. **Description:** A consulting engineering firm specializing in water and wastewater treatment. The company also provides construction management, design engineering, and operations assistance. **Positions advertised include:** Civil Engineer; Management Consultant; Administrative Support. **Listed on:** Privately held.

HANDEX OF ILLINOIS
1701 West Quincy Avenue, Naperville IL 60540. 630/527-1666. **Contact:** Human Resources. **World Wide Web address:** http://www.handex.com. **Description:** Provides environmental services including overseeing the installation and removal of underground storage tanks, as well as groundwater and

soil sampling. **NOTE:** To apply for a position, contact Paula Griffin, Human Resources Director, Handex Group, Inc., 30914 Suneagle Drive, Mt. Dora FL 32757; 800/989-3753 (phone); 352/735-1904 (fax). **Corporate headquarters location:** Dora FL.

LANDAUER, INC.
2 Science Road, Glenwood IL 60425. 708/755-7000. **Toll-free phone:** 800/323-8830. **Fax:** 708/755-7016. **Contact:** Lana Gowen, Human Resources. **World Wide Web address:** http://www.landauerinc.com. **Description:** Provides environmental testing services that determine exposure to occupational and environmental radiation hazards. The company also provides radiation dosimetry services to a number of industries in which radiation is a threat to employees. Founded in 1954.

MACTEC
8901 North Industrial Road, Peoria IL 61615. 309/692-4422. **Toll-free phone:** 800/373-1999. **Fax:** 309/692-9364. **Contact:** Human Resources. **World Wide Web address:** http://www.mactec.com. **Description:** An engineering and consulting company providing environmental and infrastructure services to commercial and municipal clients, as well as to state and federal government agencies. Founded in 1965. **NOTE:** Search and apply for positions online. **Positions advertised include:** Mechanical Drafter/Designer. **Special programs:** Internships; Co-ops. **Office hours:** Monday - Friday, 8:00 a.m. - 5:00 p.m. **Other U.S. locations:** Nationwide. **Listed on:** Privately held.

TEST AMERICA
1090 Rock Road Lane, Suite 11, East Dundee IL 60118. 847/783-4960. **Fax:** 847/783-4969. **Contact:** Human Resources. **World Wide Web address:** http://www. testamericainc.com. **Description:** Performs testing of wastewater, hazardous waste, and food. **NOTE:** See website for job listings and contact information. **Operations at this facility include:** Service; Sales.

WASTE MANAGEMENT, INC.
720 East Butterfield Road, Lombard IL 60148. 630/572-8800. **Contact:** Human Resources Manager. **World Wide Web address:** http://www.wm.com. **Description:** An international provider of comprehensive waste management services as well as engineering, construction, industrial, and related service. **Corporate headquarters location:** Houston TX. **International locations:** Worldwide. **Listed on:** New York Stock Exchange. **Stock exchange symbol:** WMI.

Indiana
ATC ASSOCIATES INC.
7988 Centerpoint Drive, Suite 100, Indianapolis IN 46256. 317/849-4990. **Fax:** 317/849-4278. **Contact:** Human Resources Department. **E-mail address:** atcjobs@atc-enviro.com. **World Wide Web address:** http://www.atc-enviro.com. **Description:** An environmental consulting services firm. **Positions advertised include:** Industrial Hygienist.

ALLIED WASTE
2017 North Fares Avenue, Evansville IN 47711-3967. 812/424-3345. **Contact:** Human Resources. **World Wide Web address:** http://www.awin.com. **Description:** Specializes in residential, medical, and commercial solid waste collection, processing, and disposal. **Other U.S. locations:** Nationwide. **Parent company:** Allied Waste Industries, Inc. **Listed on:** New York Stock Exchange. **Stock exchange symbol:** AW.

JAMAX CORPORATION
12820 Cumminsville Road, Pimento, IN 47866. 812/298-2100. **Contact:** Human Resources. **Description:** Offers commercial and residential trash removal services and roll-off containers for businesses.

LANGSDALE RECYCLING
832 Langsdale Avenue, Indianapolis IN 46206. 317/926-5492. **Contact:** Human Resources. **World Wide Web address:** http://www.therecyclinggroup.com. **Description:** Specializes in paper recycling and processing. Langsdale Recycling purchases recyclable paper products, provides recycling containers, and offers pick-up services for businesses. Founded in 1979.

NATIONAL SERVE-ALL
P.O. Box 2234, Fort Wayne IN 46801. 260/747-4117. **Physical address:** 6231 Macbeth Road, Fort Wayne IN 46809. **Contact:** Human Resources. **Description:** A full-service waste management company that offers corporate and residential waste removal, recycling services, and waste chemical handling and disposal.

POLLUTION CONTROL INDUSTRIES
4343 Kennedy Avenue, East Chicago IN 46312. 219/397-3951. **Contact:** Human Resources. **E-mail address:** nsanders@pollutioncontrol.com. **World Wide Web address:** http://www.pollutioncontrol.com. **Description:** Engaged in the handling and disposal of hazardous materials. Pollution Control Industries provides assessments of waste chemicals and operates remote control units and secure containment equipment to handle and remove the material safely.

REPUBLIC SERVICES
832 Langsdale Drive, Indianapolis IN 46202. 317/823-6881. **Contact:** Human Resources. **World Wide Web address:** http://www.republicservices.com. **Description:** Specializes in residential and commercial solid waste collection, processing, and disposal as well as medical waste collection and recycling. **NOTE:** Entry-level positions are offered. **Corporate headquarters location:** Houston TX. **Other U.S. locations:** Nationwide. **Parent companies:** Allied Waste Industries.

WASTE MANAGEMENT, INC.
3200 West Bertha Street, Indianapolis IN 46222. 317/635-2491. **Contact:** Human Resources. **E-mail address:** careers@wm.com. **World Wide Web address:** http://www.wm.com. **Description:** Provides waste collection, removal, and disposal services to its residential, commercial, and industrial customers. **Other U.S. locations:** Nationwide.

Kansas
TERRACON COMPANIES, INC.
16000 College Boulevard, Lenexa KS 66219. 913/599-6886. **Toll-free phone:** 800/593-7777. **Fax:** 913/599-0574. **Contact:** Human Resources Director. **E-mail address:** careers@terracon.com. **World Wide Web address:** http://www.terracon.com. **Description:** An employee-owned engineering and consulting company providing geotechnical, environmental, construction, and facilities management services with 55 offices in 23 states. Founded in 1965. **NOTE:** Please submit resumes online. **Positions advertised include:** Administrative Assistant; Environmental Scientist; Industrial Hygiene Professional; Asbestos Air Quality Control Technician; Microsoft Applications Programmer; Construction Services Assistant; Secretary; Environmental Project Engineer; Constructions Materials Technician; Geotechnical Engineer. **Corporate headquarters location:** This location. **Other area locations:** Garden City KS; Kansas City KS; Topeka KS; Wichita KS; **Other U.S. locations:** Nationwide. **Subsidiaries include:** HBC/Terracon; Titan Atlantic Group, Inc.; Infrastructure Management Services, Inc.; The Terra Group of Chicago, Inc. **President/CEO:** David Gaboury. **Number of employees nationwide:** 1,400.

Kentucky
REPUBLIC SERVICES
2343 Alexandria Drive, Suite 400, Lexington KY 40504. 859/885-5138. **Contact:** Human Resources. **World Wide Web address:** http://www.republicservices.com. **Description:** Provides environmental services such as waste collection, recycling, and disposal, as well as mining. **NOTE:** All employment inquiries should be

directed to the corporate office at 110 Southeast 6th Street, Suite 2100, Fort Lauderdale FL 33301. **Corporate headquarters location:** Fort Lauderdale FL. **Operations at this facility include:** Administration; Sales. **Other U.S. locations:** Nationwide. **Listed on:** New York Stock Exchange. **Stock exchange symbol:** RSG. **Number of employees at this location:** 50. **Number of employees nationwide:** 12,700.

Louisiana

SHAW ENVIRONMENTAL & INFRASTRUCTURE

4171 Essen Lane, Baton Rouge LA 70809. 225/932-2500. **Fax:** 225/932-2661. **Contact:** Human Resources. **E-mail address:** jobssouth@shawgrp.com. **World Wide Web address:** http://www.shawgrp.com. **Description:** Provides engineering, design, construction, and maintenance services to government and private-sector clients in industries such as energy, environment, infrastructure, and emergency response. **NOTE:** Resumes may be submitted online as specified on the company Website, or via mail. **Positions advertised include:** Project Control Cost Scheduler; Scientist; Construction Engineer manager; Project Accountant. **Corporate headquarters location:** This location. **Other U.S. locations:** Nationwide. **Subsidiaries:** Fronek Company, Incorporated; Word Industries Fabricators, Incorporated; Naptech, incorporated; United Crafts, Incorporated; Merit Industrial Constructors, Incorporated; EntergyShaw LLC; Stone & Webster, Incorporated; The IT Group, Incorporated; Envirogen, Incorporated; MWR, Incorporated. **Parent company:** The Shaw Group Incorporated. **Listed on:** New York Stock Exchange. **Stock exchange symbol:** SGR. **President/CEO:** J.M. Bernard, Jr. **Number of employees worldwide:** 20,000.

Maine

CLEAN HARBORS ENVIRONMENTAL SERVICES

17 Main Street, South Portland ME 04106. 207/799-8111. **Toll-free phone:** 800/282-0058, ext.: 4244. **Fax:** 781/356-1363. **Contact:** Human Resources. **E-mail address**: fowler.timothy@cleanharbors.com, **World Wide Web address:** http://www.cleanharbors.com. **Description:** Clean Harbors, Inc., through its subsidiaries, provides comprehensive environmental services in 35 states in the Northeast, Midwest, Central, and Mid-Atlantic regions. **NOTE**: Search posted openings on-line; respond by e-mail only. **Positions advertised include:** Field Service Foreman; Class A Driver; Field Technician. **Corporate headquarters location:** Braintree MA. **Other area locations:** Newburgh ME. **Other U.S. locations:** Nationwide. **Number of employees nationwide:** 1,400.

GZA GEOENVIRONMENTAL SERVICES

4 Free Street, Portland ME 04101-3926. 207/879-9190. **Fax:** 207/879-0099. **Contact:** Tom Lawless, Office Manager. **World Wide Web address:** http://www.gza.net. **Description:** Provides consulting and remediation services, as well as geotechnical services, principally in the Northeast and the Midwest. The company also maintains its own drilling, laboratory, and instrumentation facilities to support environmental and geotechnical activities. **Corporate headquarters location:** Norwood MA. **Other U.S. locations:** MA; NY; MI; CT; NH; NJ; WI; RI; PA. . **Subsidiaries include:** GZA Drilling, Inc.; Soil and Rock Instrumental Division. **Number of employees nationwide:** 500.

WRIGHT-PIERCE ENGINEERS

99 Main Street, Topsham ME 04086. 207/725-8721. **Fax:** 947/729-8414. **Contact:** Human Resources. **E-mail address:** dma@wright-pierce.com. **World Wide Web address:** http://www.wright-pierce.com. **Description:** A full-service civil and environmental engineering firm. The company specializes in civil and transportation engineering; structural engineering; environmental laboratory services; and water, wastewater, and solid waste treatment. **NOTE:** Search posted listings and apply on-line. **Positions advertised include**: Internship; Civil CAD Technician. **Corporate headquarters location:** This location. **Other area locations:** Portland ME. **Other U.S. locations:** Middletown CT; Portsmouth NH. **Number of employees at this location:** 95.

Maryland

CLEAN HARBORS ENVIRONMENTAL SERVICES, INC.

3527 Whisky Bottom Road, Laurel MD 20724. 301/939-6000. **Fax:** 301/939-6076. **Contact:** Human Resources. **World Wide Web address:** http://www.cleanharbors.com. **Description:** Provides comprehensive environmental services in 35 states in the northeast, midwest, central, and mid-Atlantic regions through its subsidiaries. Clean Harbors provides a wide range of hazardous waste management and environmental support services to a diversified customer base from over 40 locations. The company's hazardous waste management services include treatment, storage, recycling, transportation, risk analysis, site assessment, laboratory analysis, site closure, and disposal of hazardous materials through environmentally sound methods including incineration. Environmental remediation services include emergency response, surface remediation, groundwater restoration, industrial maintenance, and facility decontamination. Customers include nearly 300 of the *Fortune* 500 companies, regional utilities, oil, pharmaceutical, and chemical companies, small businesses, and the high-tech and biotech industries. **Positions advertised include:** Field Technician; Class A Driver; Field Service Technician. **Corporate headquarters location:** Braintree MA. **Other U.S. locations:** Nationwide. **International locations:** Canada; Mexico; Puerto Rico. **Listed on:** NASDAQ. **Stock exchange symbol:** CLHB. **CEO:** Alan S. McKim. **Number of employees nationwide:** 1,400.

DURATEK, INC.

10100 Old Columbia Road, Columbia MD 21044. 410/312-5100. **Contact:** Human Resources. **E-mail address:** corprec@duratekinc.com. **World Wide Web address:** http://www.duratekinc.com. **Description:** An environmental and technology services company specializing in the process of solidifying nuclear waste into glass (vitrification). The Department of Energy and other companies employ Duratek to vitrify and dispose of their radioactive and nuclear wastes. **Positions advertised include:** Environmental Health Associate; Safety Director. **Corporate headquarters location:** This location. **Other U.S. locations:** Oak Ridge TN; Memphis TN; Kingston TN; Lakewood CO; Barnwell SC; Richland WA; Los Alamos NM. **Subsidiaries include:** Waste Management Nuclear Services. **Listed on:** NASDAQ. **Stock exchange symbol:** DRTK. **Sales/revenue:** $300 million.

EA ENGINEERING, SCIENCE, AND TECHNOLOGY, INC.

11019 McCormick Road, Hunt Valley MD 21031. 410/584-7000. **Fax:** 410/771-1625. **Contact:** Human Resources. **E-mail address:** careers@eaest.com. **World Wide Web address:** http://www.eaest.com. **Description:** An engineering firm that operates ecological and environmental testing laboratories. Founded in 1973. **NOTE:** Online applications are available. **Positions advertised include:** Administrative Assistant; Engineer; Geologist; Technician; Scientist; Natural Resource Management. **Special programs:** Internships; Tuition Reimbursement Program. **Other area locations:** Baltimore MD; Sparks MD. **Other U.S. locations:** Nationwide.

ENVIRONMENTAL ELEMENTS CORPORATION

3700 Koppers Street, Baltimore MD 21227. 410/368-7000. **Toll-free phone:** 800/333-4331. **Fax:** 410/368-7344. **Contact:** Human Resources. **E-mail address:** hr@eec1.com. **World Wide Web address:** http://www.eec1.com. **Description:** Designs and engineers air pollution control systems and equipment, and offers related services. Founded in 1946. **NOTE:** Entry-level positions and part-time jobs are offered. Resumes submitted via e-mail must be formatted in Microsoft or ASCII text. **Positions advertised include:** Regional Sales Manager; Service Engineer/Manager. **Company slogan:** A breath of fresh air. **Special programs:** Internships; Co-ops; Summer Jobs. **Office hours:** Monday - Friday, 8:00 a.m. - 5:00 p.m. **Corporate headquarters location:** This location. **Listed on:** American Stock Exchange. **Stock exchange symbol:** EEC. **President/CEO:** John L. Sams. **Sales/revenues:** Approximately $70 million. **Number of employees at this location:** 130. **Number of employees nationwide:** 160.

TETRA TECH NUS, INC.
20251 Century Boulevard, Suite 200, Germantown MD 20874-7114. 301/528-5552. **Fax:** 301.528-2000. **Contact:** Human Resources **World Wide Web address:** http://www.tetratech.com. **Description:** Provides engineering and environmental waste services. **Corporate headquarters location:** Pasadena CA. **Other area locations:** Bel Air MD; Annapolis MD; Edgewater MD; Laurel MD; Owings Mills MD. **Other U.S. locations:** Nationwide. **Parent company:** Tetra Tech, Incorporated is an environmental management, consulting, and technical services group. **Listed on:** NASDAQ. **Stock exchange symbol:** TTEK. **President:** James M. Jaska. **Sales/revenue:** $740 million. **Number of employees worldwide:** Over 7,000.

WASTE MANAGEMENT, INC.
8101 Beechcraft Avenue, Gaithersburg MD 20879. 301/340-0774. **Contact:** Human Resources. **World Wide Web address:** http://www.wastemanagement.com. **Description:** An international provider of comprehensive waste management services, as well as engineering and construction, industrial, and related services. **Positions advertised include:** Safety Quality Specialist; Sales Representative; Outside Sales Representative. **Corporate headquarters location:** Houston TX. **Other U.S. locations:** Nationwide. **Listed on:** New York Stock Exchange. **Stock exchange symbol:** WMI.

Massachusetts

BETA GROUP, INC.
1420 Providence Highway, Suite 117, Norwood MA 02062. 781/255-1982. **Contact:** Human Resources. **E-mail address:** tgarro@beta-inc.com. **World Wide Web address:** http://www.beta-inc.com. **Description:** An engineering firm specializing in environmental engineering and site remediation; highway engineering; water/wastewater engineering; and landfill closures. **Positions advertised include:** Civil Transportation Engineer; Structural Engineer; Geographic Information Systems Project Manager.

BLACK & VEATCH
230 Congress Street, Suite 802, Boston MA 02110. 617/451-6900. **Contact:** Human Resources. **World Wide Web address:** http://www.bv.com. **Description:** An environmental/civil engineering and construction firm serving utilities, commerce, and government agencies in more than 40 countries worldwide. Black & Veatch provides a broad range of study, design, construction management, and turnkey capabilities to clients in the water and wastewater fields **Positions advertised include:** Communication Specialist; Document Associate; Civil Engineer; Consultant; Electrical Engineer; Engineering Technician; Associate Estimator; Programming Analyst; Human Resources Division Director; Mechanical Engineer; Planning Specialist; Engineer; Procurement Specialist. **Special programs:** Co-ops. **Corporate headquarters location:** Kansas City MO. **Other U.S. locations:** Nationwide. **International locations:** Worldwide. **Listed on:** Privately held. **Number of employees worldwide:** 10,000.

C.E.A. (CORPORATE ENVIRONMENTAL ADVISORS)
127 Hartwell Street, West Boylston MA 01583. 508/835-8822. **Contact:** Human Resources **Description:** An environmental consulting firm engaged in contract consulting projects.

CH2M HILL
25 New Chardon Street, Suite 500, Boston MA 02114. 617/523-2260. **Fax:** 617/723-9036. **Contact:** Human Resources. **World Wide Web address:** http://www.ch2m.com. **Description:** An environmental engineering company specializing in water and remediation projects. **Positions advertised include:** NEPA Expert; Process Engineer; Air Water Process Project Manager; Construction Manager. **NOTE:** Jobseekers should address resumes to the attention of the manager of the group to which they are applying. Please contact this location for further information. **Corporate headquarters location:** Greenwood Village CO. **Other U.S. locations:** Nationwide. **International locations:** Worldwide.

THE CADMUS GROUP, INC.
57 Water Street, Watertown MA 02472. 617/673-7000. **Contact:** Human Resources. **World Wide Web address:** http://www.cadmusgroup.com. **Description:** An environmental consulting and engineering firm. **Positions advertised include:** Analyst; Environmental Professional; Research Analyst.

CAMP DRESSER & McKEE, INC. (CDM)
One Cambridge Place, 50 Hampshire Street, Cambridge MA 02139. 617/452-6000. **Contact:** Human Resources. **World Wide Web address:** http://www.cdm.com. **Description:** A worldwide provider of environmental engineering, scientific, planning, and management services. The company focuses on professional activities for the management of wastewater, drinking water, water resources, hazardous waste, solid waste, infrastructure, and environmental systems. **Positions advertised include:** Geotechnical Engineer; Environmental Scientist; Environmental Engineer; Instrumentation Control Engineer; O&M Specialist; Marketing Coordinator; Planner; Air Quality Scientist or Engineer; Administrative Assistant. **Special programs:** Internships. **Corporate headquarters location:** This location. **Other U.S. locations:** Nationwide. **International locations:** Worldwide.

CHECKPOINT ENVIRONMENTAL, INC.
12 Linden Street, Hudson MA 01749. 978/562-4300. **Contact:** Personnel. **Description:** An environmental engineering firm specializing in the drilling of small diameter wells.

CLEAN HARBORS, INC.
P.O. Box 859048, Braintree MA 02185-9048. 781/849-1800. **Fax:** 781/356-1363. **Contact:** Personnel. **World Wide Web address:** http://www.cleanharbors.com. **Description:** Through its subsidiaries, Clean Harbors, Inc. provides comprehensive environmental services in 35 states in the Northeast, Midwest, Central, and Mid-Atlantic regions. Clean Harbors provides a wide range of hazardous waste management and environmental support services. **Positions advertised include:** Accountant; Transportation Compliance Manager; Container Business Development Manager; Web Developer; Technician Services Representative; Purchase Order Administrator; Billing Clerk; Credit Request Check; T&D Order Placement Representative Billing Supervisor; Tech Services. **NOTE:** Interested jobseekers should direct resumes to: Human Resources, 1501 Washington Street, Braintree MA 02184. **Corporate headquarters location:** This location. **Other area locations:** Kingston MA; Natick MA; North Grafton MA: West Springfield MA; Weymouth MA; Woburn MA. **Other U.S. locations:** Nationwide. **Listed on:** NASDAQ. **Stock exchange symbol:** CLHB. **Number of employees nationwide:** 1,400.

COLER & COLANTONIO
101 Accord Park Drive, Norwell MA 02061. 781/982-5400. **Contact:** Human Resources. **World Wide Web address:** http://www.col-col.com. **Description:** A civil and environmental engineering firm. Coler &

Colantonio specializes in a variety of engineering projects including pipeline, transportation, and water projects. **Positions advertised include:** Waste Water Treatment Operator; Project Engineer; Drafter; Civil Engineer. **Other area locations:** South Deerfield MA; South Easton MA. **Other U.S. locations:** Houston TX.

COVANTA ENERGY
141 Cranberry Highway, Wareham MA 02576-1504. 508/291-4400. **Contact:** Human Resources. **World Wide Web address:** http://www.covantaholding.com. **Description:** Incinerates solid waste. **Positions advertised include:** Business Manager. **Corporate headquarters location:** Fairfield NJ.

CYN ENVIRONMENTAL
P.O. Box 119, Stoughton MA 02072. 781/341-1777. **Toll-free phone:** 800/242-5818. **Fax:** 781/341-6246. **Physical address:** 100 Tosca Drive, Stoughton MA 02072. **Contact:** Chuck Klinger, Human Resources. **E-mail address:** cklinger@cynenv.com. **World Wide Web address:** http://www.cynenv.com. **Description:** Provides hazardous waste removal and remediation. **Positions advertised include:** Environmental Project Manager. **Other area locations:** Wilbraham MA. **Other U.S. locations:** Dover NH; Johnston RI.

DEC-TAM CORPORATION
50 Concord Street, North Reading MA 01864. 978/470-2860. **Contact:** Human Resources. **World Wide Web address:** http://www.dectam.com. **Description:** Provides lead paint and asbestos removal.

DEER ISLAND TREATMENT PLANT
P.O. Box 100, Winthrop MA 02152. 617/846-5800. **Contact:** Human Resources. **Description:** A wastewater treatment facility run by the Massachusetts Water Resources Authority (MWRA).

ENSR INTERNATIONAL
2 Technology Park Drive, Westford MA 01886-3140. 978/589-3000. **Toll-free phone:** 800/722-2440. **Contact:** Human Resources. **World Wide Web address:** http://www.ensr.com. **Description:** An environmental consulting and engineering services firm. Services include pollution prevention, risk assessment, property transfer assessment, environmental permitting, environmental communication, remedial design, and engineering and construction management. ENSR has over 1,000 scientists, engineers, communications professionals, construction managers, regulatory specialists, and health and safety experts nationwide. **Positions advertised include:** Proposal Coordinator; Staff Specialist; Technician; Project Specialist; Engineer; Administrative Assistant; Training Specialist; Project Manager; Program Manager; Fisheries Biologist. **Corporate headquarters location:** This location. **Other U.S. locations:** Nationwide. **International locations:** Worldwide.

EARTHTECH
196 Baker Avenue, Concord MA 01742. 978/371-4000. **Contact:** Human Resources. **World Wide Web address:** http://www.earthtech.com. **Description:** An environmental engineering compliance firm. **Positions advertised include:** Administrative Assistant; Project Professional. **Corporate headquarters location:** Long Beach CA. **Other area locations:** Middleboro MA. **Other U.S. locations:** Nationwide. **International locations:** Worldwide.

ENVIRONMENTAL SCIENCE SERVICES, INC.
888 Worcester Street, Suite 240, Wellesley MA 02482. 781/431-0500. **Contact:** Human Resources. **World Wide Web address:** http://www.essgroup.com. **Description:** An environmental consulting and engineering firm offering a variety of services including soil sampling, water sampling, and hazardous materials services. **Other U.S. locations:** Providence RI. **Positions advertised include:** Environmental Engineer; Engineer; Geologist; Civil Engineer.

ENVIRONMENTAL STRATEGIES CORPORATION
1740 Massachusetts Avenue, Boxborough MA 01719. 978/635-9600. **Contact:** Human Resources. **E-mail address:** envtl-recruit@escva.com. **World Wide Web address:** http://www.envstratcorp.com. **Description:** An environmental engineering firm. **Positions advertised include:** Environmental Engineer; Geologist; Environmental Professional; Environmental Compliance Auditor; Industrial Hygienist Safety Specialist. **Corporate headquarters location:** Reston VA. **Other U.S. locations:** San Jose CA; Denver CO; Minneapolis MN; Somerset NJ; Albany NY; Cazenovia NY; Durham NC; Pittsburgh PA; Houston TX.

GEI CONSULTANTS, INC.
1021 Main Street, Winchester MA 01890. 781/721-4000. **Contact:** Human Resources. **World Wide Web address:** http://www.geiconsultants.com. **Description:** An environmental and geo-technical engineering firm. **Positions advertised include:** Accounting Assistant; Geotechnical Engineer; Civil Engineer; Drafter; Environmental Engineer; Geologist; Human Resources Generalist; Laboratory & Field Technician; Project Manager; Staff Engineer; Technician. **Corporate headquarters location:** This location. **Other U.S. locations:** Carlsbad CA; Oakland CA; Colchester CT; Englewood CO; Concord NH; St. Louis MO.

GZA GEOENVIRONMENTAL TECHNOLOGIES
One Edgewater Drive, Norwood MA 02062. 781/278-3700. **Contact:** Human Resources. **World Wide Web address:** http://www.gza.com. **Description:** Provides consulting, remediation, and geo-technical services, principally in the Northeast and the Midwest. The company also maintains its own drilling, laboratory, and instrumentation facilities to support environmental and geo-technical activities. Environmental services range from initial assessment and evaluation of contaminated sites to design, construction, and operation of remediation systems. **Corporate headquarters location:** This location. **Other U.S. locations:** CT; ME; MA; MI; NH; NJ; NY; PA; RI; VT; WI. **Subsidiaries include:** Environmental Real Estate Investors, Inc. (EREI); GZA Drilling, Inc. provides drilling services; GZA GeoEnvironmental, Inc. provides environmental consulting and geo-technical services; Soil and Rock Instrumentation Division (SRI). **Number of employees nationwide:** 450.

GANNETT FLEMING
150 Wood Road, Braintree MA 02184. 781/380-7750. **Contact:** Donald B. Nicholas, Human Resources. **E-mail address:** dnicholas@gfnet.com. **World Wide Web address:** http://www.gannettfleming.com. **Description:** An engineering firm offering a wide variety of services including structural, geo-technical, environmental, hazardous waste, bridge design, and tunnel design. **Positions advertised include:** Environmental Engineer; Resident Engineer. **Other U.S. locations:** Nationwide.

GEOLABS, INC.
45 Johnson Lane, Braintree MA 02184. 781/848-7844. **Toll/free phone:** 800/298-7060. **Fax:** 781/848-7811. **Contact:** Human Resources. **E-mail address:** geolabs@attbi.net. **World Wide Web address:** http://www.geolabs.com. **Description:** Provides analytical environmental testing of soil, ground water, wastewater, and air. Founded in 1995. **NOTE:** Entry-level positions are offered. **Company slogan:** Quick service without sacrificing. **Special programs:** Internships; Training; Co-ops; Summer Jobs. **Office hours:** Monday - Friday, 8:00 a.m. - 5:00 p.m. **Corporate headquarters location:** This location. **Listed on:** Privately held. **President/Owner:** David J. Kahler. **Annual sales/revenues:** Less than $5 million. **Number of employees at this location:** 20.

GEOLOGIC SERVICES CORPORATION
15 Robert Bonazzoli Avenue, Hudson MA 01749. 978/568-8740. **Contact:** Human Resources. **Description:** Provides underground storage tank

evaluation services.

GRADIENT CORPORATION
238 Main Street, Cambridge MA 02142. 617/395-5000. **Contact:** Laura Gordon, Human Resources. **E-mail address:** lgordon@gradientcorp.com. **World Wide Web address:** http://www.gradcorp.com. **Description:** An environmental consulting firm. **Positions advertised include:** Technologist; Environmental Engineer. **Other U.S. locations:** Mercer Island WA. **Annual sales/revenues:** $5 - $10 million. **Number of employees at this location:** 50.

GROUNDWATER & ENVIRONMENTAL SERVICES, INC.
364 Littleton Road, Suite 4, Westford MA 01886. 978/392-0090. **Contact:** Human Resources. **World Wide Web address:** http://www.gesonline.com. **Description:** An environmental engineering firm specializing in groundwater and remediation. **Corporate headquarters location:** Wall NJ. **Other U.S. locations:** CT; IL; MD; MI; NJ; NY; OH; PA; TN; VA; WV. **Listed on:** Privately held.

GULF OF MAINE RESEARCH CENTER
204 Lafayette Street, Salem MA 01970. 978/745-6618. **Contact:** Human Resources. **Description:** An environmental consulting firm specializing in a variety of areas including wetlands projects and hazardous waste remediation.

HALEY & ALDRICH INC.
465 Medford Street, Suite 2200, Charlestown MA 02129. 617/886-7300. **Contact:** Human Resources. **E-mail address:** info@haleyaldrich.com. **World Wide Web address:** http://www.haleyaldrich.com. **Description:** An environmental and geotechnical engineering firm. **Positions advertised include:** Geotechnical Engineer; Tunnel Engineer; Structural Engineer; Environmental Scientist; Environmental Engineer; Chemical Engineer; Environmental Health & Safety Specialist; Industrial Hygienist; Geologist; Information Technology Specialist; Scientific Visualization Specialist.

LOCKHEED ENVIRONMENTAL SYSTEMS
175 Cabot Street, Suite 415, Lowell MA 01854. 978/275-9730. **Contact:** Personnel. **Description:** Engaged in contract environmental analysis work for the Environmental Protection Agency (EPA).

MWH
12 Farnsworth Street, Boston MA 02110. 617/338-7100. **Contact:** Human Resources. **World Wide Web address:** http://www.mw.com. **Description:** An environmental engineering firm specializing in water and wastewater projects. **Corporate headquarters location:** Broomfield CO. **Other U.S. locations:** Nationwide.

MWRA (MASSACHUSETTS WATER RESOURCES AUTHORITY)
100 First Avenue, Charlestown Navy Yard, Boston MA 02129. 617/242-6000. **Contact:** Human Resources. **World Wide Web address:** http://www.mwra.com. **Description:** Manages the quality of water throughout Massachusetts, including the cleanup of Boston Harbor and other large projects.

META ENVIRONMENTAL, INC.
49 Clarendon Street, Watertown MA 02472. 617/923-4662. **Fax:** 617/923-4610. **Contact:** Human Resources. **Description:** An environmental engineering firm. This location also houses a research laboratory. **NOTE:** Entry-level positions are offered. **Special programs:** Co-ops. **Corporate headquarters location:** This location. **Listed on:** Privately held. **Annual sales/revenues:** Less than $5 million. **Number of employees at this location:** 15.

METCALF & EDDY, INC.
30 Harvard Mill Square, P.O. Box 4071, Wakefield MA 01880-5371. 781/246-5200. **Fax:** 781/245-6293. **Contact:** Human Resources. **World Wide Web address:** http://www.m-e.com. **Description:** An environmental engineering firm offering professional consulting services for water, wastewater, hazardous waste, and landfills. Metcalf & Eddy, Inc. specializes in design engineering. The firm's projects include wastewater treatment facilities, waterworks projects, industrial and hazardous waste treatment, environmental modeling, and solid waste treatment. **Positions advertised include:** Human Resources Generalist; Production Architect; Librarian; Project Director. **Other U.S. locations:** Nationwide. **Parent company:** AECOM.

NORFOLK RAM GROUP
One Roberts Road, Plymouth MA 02360. 508/822-5500. **Contact:** Human Resources. **World Wide Web address:** http://www.norfolkenvironmental.com. **Description:** An environmental and civil engineering firm. **Positions advertised include:** Civil Engineer.

RANSOM ENVIRONMENTAL CONSULTANTS, INC.
Brown's Wharf, Newburyport MA 01950. 978/465-1822. **Fax:** 978/465-2986. **Contact:** Human Resources. **World Wide Web address:** http://www.ransomenv.com. **Description:** An environmental consulting firm specializing in remediation design and environmental risk assessment. **Positions advertised include:** Project Geologist; Project Manager; Engineer Geologist; Manager Engineer. **Corporate headquarters location:** This location. **Other U.S. locations:** Bristol RI.

RIZZO ASSOCIATES, INC.
P.O. Box 9005, One Grant Street, Framingham MA 01701-9005. 508/903-2401. **Fax:** 508/903-2000. **Contact:** Human Resources. **E-mail address:** hr@rizzo.com. **World Wide Web address:** http://www.rizzo.com. **Description:** An engineering and environmental consulting firm. The company provides engineering, environmental compliance, hazardous waste management, transportation, and water/wastewater services. **NOTE:** Entry-level positions and part-time jobs are offered. **Positions advertised include:** Civil Engineer; Site Engineer; Engineer. **Special programs:** Internships; Co-ops. **Office hours:** Monday - Friday, 9:00 a.m. - 5:30 p.m. **Parent company:** Tetra Tech, Inc. **Listed on:** Privately held. **Annual sales/revenues:** $21 - $50 million.

SEA CONSULTANTS, INC.
485 Massachusetts Avenue, Cambridge MA 02139. 617/497-7800. **Contact:** Human Resources. **World Wide Web address:** http://www.seacon.com. **Description:** A multifunctional engineering firm offering a wide variety of engineering services including civil, structural, scientific, and environmental engineering. **Positions advertised include:** Accounts Payable Coordinator.

SHAW ENVIRONMENTAL & INFRASTRUCTURE
88C Elm Street, Hopkinton MA 01748-1656. 508/435-9561. **Contact:** Human Resources. **World Wide Web address:** http://www.shawgrp.com. **Description:** Develops advanced technologies for the environmental restoration of contaminated sites. One of the largest environmental consulting, engineering, and remediation firms in the world, the company operates 70 locations worldwide. **Positions advertised include:** Engineer Technician.

TELLUS INSTITUTE
11 Arlington Street, Boston MA 02116. 617/266-5400. **Fax:** 617/266-8303. **Contact:** David McAnulty, Human Resources. **E-mail address:** dmac@tellus.org. **World Wide Web address:** http://www.tellus.org. **Description:** An environmental research and consulting agency. Much of the Tellus Institute's work is under government contract in the fields of energy, gas, and solid waste. **Corporate headquarters location:** This location.

TETRA TECH, INC.
55 Jonstin Road, Wilmington MA 01887. 978/658-

7500. **Contact:** Human Resources. **World Wide Web address:** http://www.tetratech.com. **Description:** An environmental engineering firm.

WTE CORPORATION
7 Alfred Circle, Bedford MA 01730. 781/275-6400. **Contact:** Human Resources. **World Wide Web address:** http://www.wte.com. **Description:** Recycles plastics and metals. **Corporate headquarters location:** This location.

WASTE MANAGEMENT, INC.
256 New Lancaster Road, Leominster MA 01453. 978/840-9557. **Contact:** Human Resources. **World Wide Web address:** http://www.wastemanagement.com. **Description:** Engaged in hauling trash and waste.

WESTON & SAMPSON ENGINEERS INC.
5 Centennial Drive, Peabody MA 01960. 978/532-1900. **Toll-free phone:** 800/SAM-PSON. **Fax:** 978/977-0100. **Contact:** Colleen Manning, Human Resources Manager. **World Wide Web address:** http://www.wseinc.com. **Description:** Specializes in infrastructure and environmental engineering. The company provides services in the areas of water, wastewater, transportation, solid waste, and geotechnical. Founded in 1899. **Positions advertised include:** Construction Inspector; Project Manager; Environmental Scientist; Engineer; Waste Water Treatment Operator; Water Operator.

Michigan
PM ENVIRONMENTAL
3340 Ranger Road, Lansing MI 48906. 517/485-3333. **Toll-free phone:** 800/485-0090. **Fax:** 517/323-7228. **Contact:** Human Resources. **E-mail address:** pme@pmenv.com. **World Wide Web address:** http://www.pmenv.com. **Description:** An environmental consulting firm. **Other area locations:** Hazel Park MI; Grand Rapids MI. **Other U.S. locations:** Decatur AL.

SECOR INTERNATIONAL
2321 Club Meridian Drive, Suite E, Okemos MI 48864. 517/349-9499. **Contact:** Marguerite Shuffleton, Human Resources. **E-mail address:** mshuffleton@secor.com. **World Wide Web address:** http://www.secor.com. **Description:** An environmental engineering firm. **Corporate headquarters location:** Redmond WA. **Other area locations:** Detroit MI. **Other U.S. locations:** Nationwide. **International locations:** Canada; United Kingdom. **Listed on:** Privately held. **Annual sales/revenues:** $100 million. **Number of employees worldwide:** 700.

STERICYCLE, INC.
1040 Market Avenue SW, Grand Rapids MI 49503. 616/454-9405. **Contact:** Human Resources. **E-mail address:** careers@stericycle.com. **World Wide Web address:** http://www.stericycle.com. **Description:** The largest provider of medical waste management services in the United States. **Positions advertised include:** Driver. **Corporate headquarters location:** Lake Forest IL. **Other U.S. locations:** Nationwide. **Listed on:** NASDAQ. **Stock exchange symbol:** SRCL. **Number of employees nationwide:** Approximately 2,900.

SUPERIOR ENVIRONMENTAL
1128 Franklin Street, Marne MI 49435. 616/667-4000. **Toll-free phone:** 800/669-0699. **Fax:** 616/667-3668. **Contact:** Human Resources. **E-mail address:** resumes@superiorenvironmental.com. **World Wide Web address:** http://www.superiorenvironmental.com. **Description:** Provides environmental assessment, soil testing, remediation, underground storage tank removal, and other environmental services. **Positions advertised include:** Environmental Driller. **Corporate headquarters location:** This location. **Other area locations:** Detroit MI; Bay City MI. **Other U.S. locations:** Indianapolis IN; Rochelle IL; Springfield IL; Hartford CT.

Minnesota
AERATION INDUSTRIES INTERNATIONAL
P.O. Box 59144, Minneapolis MN 55459-0144. 952/448-6789. **Physical address:** 4100 Peavey Road, Chaska MN 55318-2353. **Toll-free phone:** 800/328-8287. **Fax:** 952/448-7293. **Contact:** Personnel. **E-mail address:** aiii@aireo2.com. **World Wide Web address:** http://www.aireo2.com. **Description:** Provides products and systems to treat industrial and municipal wastewater, restore lakes, rivers and harbors, increase production yields in aquaculture, and improve water quality on golf courses and recreational water areas. **Positions advertised include:** Eastern Regional Sales Manager.

ALLIED WASTE SERVICES
9813 Flying Cloud Drive, Eden Prairie MN 55347. 952/946-5214. **Contact:** Human Resources. **World Wide Web address:** http://www.alliedwaste.com. **Description:** Engaged primarily in the collection and disposal of solid waste for commercial, industrial, and residential customers. Services provided by BFI include landfill services, waste-to-energy programs, hazardous waste removal, and liquid waste removal. The company has operations at more than 500 facilities worldwide. **NOTE:** Apply in person. **Parent company:** Allied Waste Industries. **Listed on:** New York Stock Exchange. **Stock exchange symbol:** AW.

APPLIANCE RECYCLING CENTER OF AMERICA, INC.
7400 Excelsior Boulevard, Minneapolis MN 55426. 952/930-9000. **Contact:** Human Resources Manager. **World Wide Web address:** http://www.arcainc.com. **Description:** Provides a full range of environmentally sound appliance collection, processing, and recycling services and reclaims hazardous substances for reuse. **NOTE:** Call to inquire about current job openings. **Number of employees at this location:** 280.

LEGGETTE, BRASHEARS & GRAHAM
Northpark Corporate Center, 8 Pine Tree Drive, Suite 250, St. Paul MN 55112. 651/490-1405. **Fax:** 651/490-1006. **Contact:** J. Kevin Powers, Principal. **E-mail address:** kevin.powers@lbgmn.com. **World Wide Web address:** http://www.lbgweb.com. **Description:** A consulting company that tests soil and groundwater samples and recommends environmentally sound cleanup procedures. **Positions advertised include:** Environmental Remediation Engineer.

STORK TWIN CITY TESTING
662 Cromwell Avenue, St. Paul MN 55114-1776. 651/645-3601. **Toll-free phone:** 888/645-8378. **Fax:** 651/659-7348. **Contact:** Vivian Kreger, Human Resources Manager. **E-mail address:** vivian.kreger@stork.com. **World Wide Web address:** http://www.twincitytesting.com. **Description:** Provides environmental consulting, geotechnical engineering, specialty testing, and chemistry services. **Corporate headquarters location:** This location. **Parent company:** Stork NV (The Netherlands).

URS CORPORATION
Thresher Square, 700 Third Street South, Minneapolis MN 55415-1199. 612/370-0700. **Fax:** 612/370-1378. **Contact:** Personnel. **World Wide Web address:** http://www.urscorp.com. **Description:** A fully-integrated engineering and architectural organization that specializes in the project management, design, and construction management of industrial, private, and government facilities. URS Corporation also provides process and environmental engineering, architectural design, and total support services. **Positions advertised include:** Administrative Intern; CADD Technician; Project Administrator; Project Architect/Designer; Project Environmental Engineer; Regional Controller. **Corporate headquarters location:** San Francisco CA. **Other U.S. locations:** Nationwide. **International locations:** Worldwide. **Listed on:** New York Stock Exchange. **Stock exchange symbol:** URS.

WESTERN LAKE SUPERIOR SANITARY DISTRICT
2626 Courtland Street, Duluth MN 55806. 218/722-3336. **Fax:** 218/727-7471. **Contact:** Personnel. **World Wide Web address:** http://www.wlssd.com. **Description:** Provides regional solid waste services for northeastern Minnesota and operates a wastewater treatment plant. **NOTE:** See website for current job openings and to download application.

Mississippi
ECO SYSTEMS, INC.
6360 I-55 North, Suite 330, Jackson MS 39211. 601/936-4440. **Fax:** 601/936-4463. **Contact:** Operations Manager. **World Wide Web address:** http://www.eco-systemsinc.com. **Description:** An environmental engineering and consulting firm providing consulting services to large and small companies seeking assistance with complex environmental problems. Founded in 1993. **Other U.S. locations:** Little Rock AR; Houston TX. **Number of employees at this location:** 15.

HAZCLEAN ENVIRONMENTAL CONSULTANTS, INC.
160 Upton Drive, P.O. Box 16485, Jackson MS 39236-6485. 601/922-0766. **Fax:** 601/922-7927. **Contact:** E. Corbin McGriff, Director of Operations. **E-mail address:** corbin.mcgriff@hazclean.com. **World Wide Web address:** http://www.hazclean.com. **Description:** A multi-disciplined environmental engineering and hazardous waste management consulting firm. **Corporate headquarters location:** This location. **Other U.S. locations:** Birmingham AL.

SEVERN TRENT SERVICES
3810 I-55 South, P.O. Box 7578, Jackson MS 39212. 601/372-3439. **Contact:** Bob Maines. **E-mail address:** bmaines@stes.com. **World Wide Web address:** http://www.severntrentservices.com. **Description:** A leading supplier of water and wastewater purification products and services. **Corporate headquarters location:** Fort Washington PA. **Other area locations:** Cleveland MS; Clinton MS; Laurel MS. **Other U.S. locations:** Nationwide. **International locations:** Worldwide. **Parent company:** Severn Trent PLC. **Operations at this facility include:** Regional Office; Operating Services. **Annual sales/revenues:** $2.4 billion. **Number of employees worldwide:** 14,000.

Missouri
GEOENGINEERS
5051 South National Avenue, Suites 4-10, Springfield MO 65810. 417/831-9700. **Fax:** 417/831-9777. **Contact:** Human Resources. **E-mail address:** employment@geoengineers.com. **World Wide Web address:** http://www.geoengineers.com. **Description:** Provides earth science, environmental, and technology consulting services focusing on the areas of transportation, energy, development, government services, and water and natural resources. **NOTE:** Apply online. **Positions advertised include:** Design Engineer; HDD Design Engineer. **Other locations:** Anchorage AK; Honolulu HI; Boise ID; Portland OR; Redmond WA.

SEVERN TRENT LABORATORIES, INC.
13715 Rider Trail North, Earth City MO 63045. 314/298-8566. **Fax:** 314/298-8757. **Contact:** Personnel Department. **World Wide Web address:** http://www.stl-inc.com. **Description:** Provides a complete range of environmental testing services to private industry, engineering consultants, and government agencies in support of federal and state environmental regulations. The company also possesses analytical capabilities in the fields of air toxins, field analytical services, radiochemistry/mixed waste, and advanced technology. **Positions advertised include:** Project Manager; Analyst; **Other U.S. locations:** Nationwide.

URS CORPORATION
1001 Highlands Plaza Drive West, Suite 300, St. Louis MO 63110. 314/429-0100. **Fax:** 314/429-0462. **Contact:** Human Resources. **World Wide Web address:** http://www.urscorp.com. **Description:** An architectural, engineering, and environmental consulting firm that specializes in air transportation, environmental solutions, surface transportation, and industrial environmental and engineering concerns. URS operates 300 offices in 20 countries. **NOTE:** Search and apply for positions online. **Positions advertised include:** Graduate Civil-Geotechnical Engineer; Inspector/Field Technician. **Corporate headquarters location:** San Francisco CA. **Number of employees worldwide:** 26,000.

Montana
HKM ENGINEERING INC.
P.O. Box 31318, Billings, MT 59107. 406/869-6307. **Physical Address:** 222 N 32nd Street, Suite 700, Billings MT 59101. **Fax:** 406/656-6398. **Contact:** Personnel Director. **E-mail address:** hr@hkminc.com. **World Wide Web address:** http://www.hkminc.com. **Description:** Provides technology development, demonstration, and fabrication services to government agencies. The company operates in a variety of areas including plasma-based systems for the treatment of hazardous materials and waste; civil engineering design and project management; biological treatment, thermal spraying technologies; and specialized technology development and research services. **Positions advertised include:** Civil CAD Technician; Water Resources Project Manager; Senior Water/Wastewater Treatment Engineer; Transportation Engineer; Water Engineer. **Special programs:** Internships. **Corporate headquarters location:** This location. **Other area locations:** Bozeman MT; Butte MT; Miles City MT. **Other U.S. locations:** Rapid City SD; Sheridan WY. **Operations at this facility include:** Administration; Divisional Headquarters; Regional Headquarters; Research and Development. **Listed on:** Privately held. **Number of employees at this location:** 250. **Number of employees nationwide:** 360.

MONTANA DEPARTMENT OF ENVIRONMENTAL QUALITY
P.O. Box 200901, Helena MT 59620. 406/444-6717. **Physical address:** 1520 East Sixth Avenue, Helena MT 59601. **Fax:** 406/444-4386. **Contact:** Virginia Cameron, Personnel Department. **E-mail address:** Vcameron@mt.us. **World Wide Web address:** http://www.deq.state.mt.us. **Description:** The environmental management agency for the state of Montana with divisions for enforcing water quality regulations, issuing permits, and assessing environmental impact compliance. **NOTE:** Application materials can be found on http://www.employmontana.com. **Positions advertised include:** Contracts Officer; Data Management Section Supervisor; Project Manager; Special Projects Manager; Systems Analyst; Water Quality Specialist. **Other area locations:** Billings; Kalispell; Ronan; Missoula.

Nevada
CONVERSE CONSULTANTS
731 Pilot Road, Suite H, Las Vegas NV 89119. 702/269-8336. **Contact:** Personnel. **E-mail address:** lasvegas@converseconsultants.com. **World Wide Web address:** http://www.converseconsultants.com. **Description:** An environmental engineering consulting firm. Founded in 1946. **Positions advertised include:** Environmental Technician; Geotechnical Technician; Soils Technician; Environmental Professional; Geologist; Geotechnical Engineer; Construction Materials Engineer. **Other U.S. locations:** CA; NJ; PA. **Number of employees nationwide:** 275.

GREELEY & HANSEN
6236 West Desert Inn Road, Las Vegas NV 89146. 702/736-7062. **Contact:** Human Resources. **E-mail address:** careers@greeleyhansen.com. **World Wide Web address:** http://www.greeleyhansen.com. **Description:** A national engineering consulting company specializing in water, wastewater, and solid waste management. The firm's services include technical and feasibility reports, facility design, engineering services during construction, operations

assistance, and performance evaluation. **Positions advertised include:** Project Managers; Civil Engineers; Management Consultants; Construction Engineers. **Corporate headquarters location:** Chicago IL. **Other U.S. locations:** Nationwide. **Number of employees nationwide:** 300.

New Hampshire

CLEAN HARBORS, INC.
20 Dunklee Road, Bow NH 03304. 603/224-6626. **Toll-free phone:** 800/645-8265. **Fax:** 603/224-6778. **Contact:** Timothy Fowler, Human Resources. **E-mail address:** fowler.timothy@cleanharbors.com. **World Wide Web address:** http://www.cleanharbors.com. **Description:** Clean Harbors, Inc., through its subsidiaries, provides comprehensive environmental services in 35 states in the Northeast, Midwest, Central, and Mid-Atlantic regions. Clean Harbors provides a wide range of hazardous waste management and environmental support services to a diversified customer base from over 40 locations. **NOTE:** Search posted openings nationwide on corporate website and respond by e-mail only. **Positions advertised include:** Field Technician. **Corporate headquarters location:** Braintree MA. **Other U.S. locations:** Nationwide. **Listed on:** NASDAQ. **Stock exchange symbol:** CLHB. **CEO:** Alan S. McKim. **Number of employees nationwide:** 3,775.

THE DUMPSTER DEPOT
8051 S. Willow Road, Manchester NH 03103. 603/222-9066. **Toll-free phone:** 866/99-DEPOT. **Fax:** 603/222-9077. **E-mail address:** dumpsterdepot@aol.com. **World Wide Web address:** http://www.dumpsterdepot.com. **Description:** The Dumpster Depot removes waste from businesses, homes, contract sites, and commercial locations. They specialize in construction material. The company is in the process of expanding business and finding new locations. **Other area locations:** Andover NH. **Other U.S. locations:** Hull MA.

MOUNT WASHINGTON OBSERVATORY
P.O. Box 2310, North Conway NH 03860. 603/356-2137. **Fax:** 603/356-0307. **Contact:** Human Resources. **World Wide Web address:** http://www.mountwashington.org. **Description:** A non-profit institution that maintains a permanently staffed observatory at the top of Mount Washington. Environmental and scientific research is continually conducted. **NOTE:** Staff openings posted online as available. Internships are available, details online. Volunteer positions are available, details online. E-mailed applications are preferred.

NORMANDEAU ASSOCIATES, INC.
25 Nashua Road, Bedford NH 03110-5500. 603/472-5191. **Fax:** 603/472-0874. **Contact:** HR Manager. **E-mail address:** rchadwick@normandeau.com. **World Wide Web address:** http://www.normandeau.com. **Description:** An environmental consulting company specializing in wetland studies, air quality control, and hydrogeology. Founded in 1970. **NOTE:** Search posted openings online as available. **Corporate headquarters location:** This location. **Other area locations:** Hampton NH; Westmoreland NH. **Other U.S. locations:** Norfolk CT; Yarmouth ME; Plymouth MA; Point Pleasant Beach NJ; Peekskill NY; Spring City PA; Aiken SC; Lewes DE; Stevenson WA; WI. **Number of employees at this location:** 180.

WHEELABRATOR TECHNOLOGIES INC.
4 Liberty Lane West, Hampton NH 03842. 603/929-3000. **Toll-free phone:** 800/682-0026. **Fax:** 207/221-1322. **Contact:** Human Resources Department. **E-mail address:** jen@talentfusion.com. **World Wide Web address:** http://www.wheelabratortechnologies.com. **Description:** Engineers, fabricates, operates, and maintains clean air systems. The company's pollution control and measurement equipment, and oxidation and carbon systems operate at hundreds of power plants, industries, and water and wastewater treatment facilities. **NOTE:** Search posted openings online and respond by e-mail only. **Positions advertised include:** Assistant Utility Operator; Scalehouse Operator; Plant Maintenance Mechanic; Assistant Control Room Operator; Mobile Equipment Operator/Fuel Handler; Electrical and Instrumentation Technician. **Parent company:** Waste Management, Inc.

New Jersey

CLEAN HARBORS, INC.
3 Sutton Place, Edison NJ 08817. 732/248-1997. **Toll-free phone:** 800/782-8805. **Fax:** 732/248-4414. **Contact:** Human Resources. **World Wide Web address:** http://www.cleanharbors.com. **Description:** Clean Harbors, Inc., through its subsidiaries, provides comprehensive environmental services in 35 states in the Northeast, Midwest, Central, and Mid-Atlantic regions. Clean Harbors provides a wide range of hazardous waste management and environmental support services to a diversified customer base from over 40 locations. **Positions advertised include:** Class B Driver; Field Technician; Class A Driver; Field Service Foreman; Pack Chemist; Apollo Chemist. **NOTE:** See Website for current job opportunities and contact information. **Corporate headquarters location:** Braintree MA. **Other U.S. locations:** Nationwide. **Number of employees nationwide:** 1,400.

COVANTA ENERGY GROUP
40 Lane Road, Fairfield NJ 07007. 973/882-9000. **Contact:** Human Resources. **World Wide Web address:** http://www.covantaenergy.com. **Description:** Develops waste-to-energy facilities nationwide through its subsidiaries and provides hazardous waste disposal and recycling services. **Positions advertised include:** Auxiliary Operator; Maintenance Mechanic. **Number of employees at this location:** 310.

ENVIRON INTERNATIONAL CORPORATION
214 Carnegie Center, Princeton NJ 08540. 609/452-9000. **Fax:** 609/452-0284. **Contact:** Margaret Breyer, Human Resources. **E-mail address:** mbreyer@environcorp.com. **World Wide Web address:** http://www.environcorp.com. **Description:** A multidisciplinary environmental and health sciences consulting firm that provides a broad range of services relating to the presence of hazardous substances found in the environment, consumer products, and the workplace. ENVIRON International provides assessment and management of chemical risk and supports private sector clients with complex, potentially high-liability concerns. **Positions advertised include:** Associate Engineer; Associate Geologist. **Corporate headquarters location:** Arlington VA. **Other U.S. locations:** Nationwide.

GROUNDWATER AND ENVIRONMENTAL SERVICES, INC. (GES)
P.O. Box 1750, Wall NJ 07719. 732/919-0100. **Physical address:** 1340 Campus Parkway, Wall NJ 07719. **Fax:** 732/919-0916. **Contact:** Human Resources. **E-mail address:** resume@gesonline.com. **World Wide Web address:** http://www.gesonline.com. **Description:** An environmental engineering firm specializing in groundwater remediation. Founded in 1985. **Positions advertised include:** Business Developmental Manager; Geologist; Scientist; Hydrogeologist; Environmental Engineer; Project Manager; Well Driller.

HAMON RESEARCH-COTTRELL
58 East Main Street, Somerville NJ 08876. 908/685-4000. **Contact:** Human Resources. **E-mail address:** info.hcorp@hamonusa.com. **World Wide Web address:** http://www.hamon-researchcottrell.com. **Description:** An environmental treatment and services company that provides a comprehensive range of services and technologies directed at controlling air pollution; protecting the integrity of the nation's water resources; providing services in support of the management and remediation of hazardous waste; and providing services for the operations, maintenance, and management of treatment facilities. **Parent company:** Hamon Group.

HANDEX ENVIRONMENTAL
500 Campus Drive, Morganville NJ 07751. 732/536-8500. **Contact:** Human Resources. **World Wide Web**

address: http://www.handex.com. **Description:** Provides environmental remediation and educational services including comprehensive solutions to contamination of groundwater and soil resulting from leaking underground storage tanks; petroleum distribution systems; refineries; heavy industrial plants; chemical, aerospace, and pharmaceutical facilities; airports; auto and truck fleet facilities; and related contamination sources. **Positions advertised include:** Professional Engineer; Filler Press Field Engineer; Permits Coordinator; Staff Hydrologist; General Manager.

HATCH MOTT MACDONALD, INC.
27 Bleeker Street, Millburn NJ 07041. 973/379-3400. **Toll-free phone:** 800/832-3272. **Fax:** 973/912-3354. **Contact:** Personnel. **E-mail address:** hr@hatchmott.com. **World Wide Web address:** http://www.killam.com. **Description:** An infrastructure engineering, environmental, and industrial process consulting firm that serves both public and private sectors. The company operates within a wide range of areas providing architectural, environmental, outsourcing, transportation engineering, and water resource management services. Founded in 1937. **Positions advertised include:** Asbestos Inspector; Assistant Resident Engineer; Business Development Manager, Environment; Civil Engineer, Water; Civil Engineer, Environmental; Environmental Geologist; Project Manager. **Special programs:** Internships. **Internship information:** Internships are offered May through September, as well as during December and January. **Corporate headquarters location:** This location. **Other area locations:** Cape May Court House NJ; Freehold NJ; Hackensack NJ; Randolph NJ; Toms River NJ; Whitehouse NJ. **Other U.S. locations:** Nationwide.

MIDCO RESIDENTIAL SERVICES
11 Harmich Road, South Plainfield NJ 07080. 908/561-8380. **Contact:** Human Resources. **Description:** Provides integrated solid waste management services to residential customers concentrated in the Midwestern and mid-South regions of the United States and in Costa Rica.

MORETRENCH AMERICAN CORPORATION
P.O. Box 316, 100 Stickle Avenue, Rockaway NJ 07866. 973/627-2100. **Fax:** 973/627-3950. **Contact:** Personnel. **E-mail address:** lobrzut@mtac.com. **NOTE:** E-mail resume for current information about positions available. **World Wide Web address:** http://www.moretrench.com. **Description:** A nationwide engineering and contracting firm specializing in groundwater control and hazardous waste removal. **Corporate headquarters location:** This location.

RECOVERY TECHNOLOGIES GROUP
7000 Boulevard East, Guttenberg NJ 07093. 201/854-7777. **Fax:** 201/854-1771. **Contact:** Office Manager. **E-mail address:** contactus@rtginc.com. **World Wide Web address:** http://www.rtginc.com. **Description:** Develops and owns waste-to-energy facilities that provide a means of disposal of nonhazardous municipal solid waste. **Corporate headquarters location:** This location.

THE SHAW GROUP
200 Horizon Center Boulevard, Trenton NJ 08691. 609/584-8900. **Contact:** Recruiter. **World Wide Web address:** http://www.shawgrp.com. **Description:** Provides environmental engineering, consulting, and construction services to a variety of public and private sector clients. Shaw Group is a leader in the design and remediation of solid and hazardous waste, transfer, storage, and disposal facilities. The company's waste facility services include site selection and evaluation, facility design, development of preprocessing and operating plans, assistance in regulatory compliance and permitting, final closures, and end use planning and design. Services also include the development of programs dealing with environmental assessments and remediation of contaminated sites, as well as services related to applied sciences such as marine fate-and-effect studies and fuel spill and natural resource damage assessments. **Positions advertised include:** Cost Schedule Engineer; Field Technician; Project Director.

TRIANGULAR WAVE TECHNOLOGIES, INC.
85 Chestnut Ridge Road, Montvale NJ 07645. 201/573-0030. **Toll-free phone:** 800/728-3420. **Fax:** 201/573-8710. **Contact:** Human Resources, **E-mail address:** info@triangularwave.com. **World Wide Web address:** http://www.triangularwave.com. **Description:** Provides fluid management solutions for residential, commercial, and industrial customers.

New Mexico

WASTE MANAGEMENT OF NEW MEXICO, INC.
402 Industrial Park Loop NE, Rio Rancho NM 87124. 505/892-1200. **Contact:** Human Resources. **World Wide Web address:** http://www.wm.com. **Description:** One of the nation's largest waste management companies. Waste Management of New Mexico provides hazardous waste management services and recycling and waste collection for residential customers and businesses. The company operates land disposal sites, collection facilities, transfer stations, and trash-to-energy plants. **NOTE:** Search and apply for positions online. **Corporate headquarters location:** Houston TX.

New York

ATC ASSOCIATES INC.
104 East 25th Street, 10th Floor, New York NY 10010-2917. 212/353-8280. **Fax:** 212/353-8306. **E-mail address:** atcjobs@atc-enviro.com. **Contact:** Human Resources. **World Wide Web address:** http://www.atc-enviro.com. **Description:** An environmental consulting firm operating 65 offices in the U.S. providing asbestos, lead, water, and soil testing. Founded in 1985. **Positions advertised include:** Project Manager. **Corporate headquarters location:** Woburn MA. **Other locations:** Nationwide. **Number of employees nationwide:** 1,800.

ARCADIS G&M, INC.
88 Duryea Road, Melville NY 11747. 631/249-7600. **Contact:** Human Resources. **World Wide Web address:** http://www.arcadis-us.com. **Description:** A consulting firm that provides environmental and engineering services. The company focuses on the environmental, building, and infrastructure markets. Founded in 1888. **NOTE:** Interested jobseekers are encouraged to apply online. **Positions advertised include:** Engineering Technician. **Special programs:** Internships. **Corporate headquarters location:** Arnhem, Netherlands. **Other U.S. locations:** Nationwide. **Listed on:** NASDAQ. **Stock exchange symbol:** ARCAF. **Annual sales/revenues:** $502 million. **Number of employees worldwide:** 8,000.

CAMP DRESSER & McKEE, INC. (CDM)
15 British American Boulevard, Latham NY 12110. 518/782-4500. **Fax:** 518/786-3810. **Contact:** Human Resources Department. **E-mail address:** hr@cdm.com. **World Wide Web address:** http://www.cdm.com. **Description:** Camp Dresser & McKee, Inc. is a worldwide provider of environmental engineering, scientific, planning, and management services. The company focuses on professional activities for the management of water resources, hazardous and solid wastes, wastewater, infrastructure, and environmental systems for industry and government. **NOTE:** Resumes should be sent to CDM, One Cambridge Place, 50 Hampshire Street, Cambridge MA 02139. **Positions advertised include:** Geotechnical Engineer; Electrical Engineer; Project Manager; Environmental Engineer; Senior Project Manager. **Corporate headquarters location:** Cambridge MA. **Other area locations:** Massena NY; New York NY; Syracuse NY; Rochester NY; Woodbury NY; Troy NY. **Other U.S. locations:** Nationwide. **International locations:** Worldwide.

CLEAN HARBORS, INC.
32 Bask Road, Glenmont NY 12077. 518/434-0149. **Fax:** 518/434-9118. **Contact:** Human Resources. **World Wide Web address:** http://www.cleanharbors.com. **Description:** Clean Harbors, Inc., through its subsidiaries, provides comprehensive environmental services in 35 states in the Northeast, Midwest, Central, and Mid-Atlantic regions. Clean Harbors provides a wide range of hazardous waste management and environmental support services to a diversified customer base from over 40 locations. **Positions advertised include:** Class A Driver; Field Technician; Field Service Foreman; Class B Driver. **Corporate headquarters location:** Braintree MA. **Other U.S. locations:** Nationwide. **Listed on:** NASDAQ. **Stock exchange symbol:** CLHB. **Annual sales/revenues:** $252 million. **Number of employees nationwide:** 1,500.

COMMODORE APPLIED TECHNOLOGIES, INC.
150 East 58th Street, Suite 3238, New York NY 10155-0035. 212/308-5800. **Fax:** 212/753-0731. **Contact:** Human Resources. **World Wide Web address:** http://www.commodore.com. **Description:** Develops technologies to destroy PCBs, chemical weapons, dioxins, and pesticides. Commodore Applied Technologies also salvages and resells cross-contaminated CFCs, and acquires and cleans up environmentally distressed properties. **Corporate headquarters location:** Alexandria VA. **Subsidiaries include:** Commodore Advanced Sciences, Inc.; Commodore Separation Technologies, Inc.; Commodore Solution Technologies, Inc.; Teledyne-Commodore LLC. **Listed on:** Over The Counter. **Stock exchange symbol:** CXII. **Annual sales/revenues:** $10 million.

EARTH TECH
One World Financial Center, New York NY 10281. 212/798-8500. **Fax:** 212/798-8501. **Contact:** Human Resources. **World Wide Web address:** http://www.earthtech.com. **Description:** An engineering consulting firm specializing in water, environmental, transportation, and construction. **Parent company:** Tyco International Ltd.

ECOLOGY AND ENVIRONMENT, INC.
Buffalo Corporate Center, 368 Pleasant View Drive, Lancaster NY 14086-1397. 716/684-8060. **Fax:** 716/684-0844. **Contact:** Human Resources. **E-mail address:** resumes@ene.com. **World Wide Web address:** http://www.ene.com. **Description:** Ecology and Environment, Inc. is an environmental consulting firm operating 27 offices worldwide. The company offers a broad range of environmental consulting services including biological baseline and biodiversity studies; environmental audits; environmental impact assessments; terrestrial, aquatic, and marine surveys; air quality management and air pollution control; environmental engineering; noise pollution evaluations; wastewater analyses; water pollution control; industrial hygiene and occupational health studies; archaeological and cultural resource studies; and environmental infrastructure planning. Founded in 1970. **NOTE:** Word format is preferred for resumes. **Positions advertised include:** Environmental Chemist; Emergency Planner; Human Resources Recruiter; Technical Services Sales Representative. **Listed on:** American Stock Exchange. **Stock exchange symbol:** EEI. **Annual sales/revenues:** $74 million. **Number of employees:** 770.

ENVIRONMENT ONE CORPORATION (E/ONE)
2773 Balltown Road, Niskayuna NY 12309-1090. 518/346-6161. **Fax:** 518/346-6188. **Contact:** Human Resources. **E-mail address:** eone@eone.com. **World Wide Web address:** http://www.eone.com. **Description:** Environment One Corporation is an environment-oriented product and service company that operates in two business segments: sewer systems and detection systems. Detection products include Generator Overheat Monitors and The Generator Gas Analyzer. **Parent company:** Precision Castparts Corp. (Portland OR).

HUDSON TECHNOLOGIES, INC.
275 North Middletown Road, Pearl River NY 10965. 845/735-6000. **Fax:** 845/512-6070. **Contact:** Michele Chazen, Human Resources Manager. **World Wide Web address:** http://www.hudsontech.com. **Description:** Hudson provides services for the recovery and reclamation of refrigerants in response to the requirements of the United States Clean Air Act from 13 locations. The company's services consist of removing used refrigerants from air conditioning and refrigeration systems and transferring them into cylinders for collection. Hudson's reclamation services consist of cleaning used refrigerants to remove impurities and contaminants and returning them to their original purity standards. Founded in 1991. **Corporate headquarters location:** This location. **Other locations:** Nationwide. **Listed on:** NASDAQ. **Stock exchange symbol:** HDSN. **Chairman/CEO:** Kevin J. Zugibe. **Annual sales/revenues:** $20 million. **Number of employees:** 102.

SEVENSON ENVIRONMENTAL SERVICES, INC.
2749 Lockport Road, Niagara Falls NY 14305-0396. 716/284-0431. **Fax:** 716/284-7645. **Contact:** Joyce Oswald, Human Resources. **World Wide Web address:** http://www.sevenson.com. **Description:** Provides a range of services for the remediation of sites and facilities contaminated by hazardous materials. **Positions advertised include:** Laboratory Technician; Heavy Truck Mechanic. **Corporate headquarters location:** This location. **Other area locations:** Buffalo NY. **Other U.S. locations:** Chadds Ford PA; Delmont PA; Merrillville IN; Long Beach CA. **Subsidiaries include:** Sevenson Environmental, Limited (also at this location); Sevenson Industrial Services, Incorporated (also at this location); Waste Stream Technology Incorporated. **Sales/revenue:** $1.2 billion.

WASTE STREAM TECHNOLOGY
302 Grote Street, Buffalo NY 14207. 716/876-5290. **Contact:** Human Resources. **World Wide Web address:** http://www.wastestream.com. **Description:** Provides a range of services for the remediation of sites and facilities contaminated by hazardous materials. **Corporate headquarters location:** This location.

North Carolina

MANTECH ENVIRONMENTAL TECHNOLOGY, INC.
2 Triangle Drive, P.O. Box 12313, Research Triangle Park NC 27709. 919/549-0611. **Fax:** 919/549-9058. **Contact:** Human Resources. **E-mail address:** jobs@mantech.com. **World Wide Web address:** http://www.mantech.com. **Description:** An environmental engineering firm offering analytical research services and environmental information services. **Positions advertised include:** Secretary/Administrative Assistant; Environmental Scientist. **Corporate headquarters location:** Fairfax VA. **Other area locations:** Fort Bragg NC; Havelock NC. **Other U.S. locations:** Nationwide. **International locations:** Worldwide. **Listed on:** NASDAQ. **Stock exchange symbol:** MANT. **Number of employees worldwide:** 5,000.

QORE PROPERTY SCIENCES
2521 Schieffelin Road, Suite 128, Apex NC 27502. 919/363-9899. **Fax:** 919/363-7916. **Contact:** Human Resources. **E-mail address:** raleigh@qore.net. **World Wide Web address:** http://www.qore.net. **Description:** Specializes in geotechnical engineering, environmental consulting, environmental studies and permitting. **Positions advertised include:** Engineering Field Technician. **Corporate headquarters location:** Duluth GA.

SHAMROCK ENVIRONMENTAL SERVICES
P.O. Box 14987, Greensboro NC 27415. 336/375-1989. **Physical address:** 503 Patton Aevnue, Greensboro NC 27406. **Toll-free phone:** 800/881-1098. **Fax:** 336/375-

1801. **Contact:** Human Resources. **World Wide Web address:** http://www.shamrockenviro.com. **Description:** Provides hazardous and nonhazardous material collection and disposal services. **NOTE:** In addition to advertising positions on their website, Shamrock Environmental Services uses the North Carolina Employment Security Commission to find qualified applicants. **Positions advertised include:** Project Manager; Site Supervisor; Field Technician; Equipment Operator; CDL Driver.

URS CORPORATION
1600 Perimeter Park Drive, Suite 400, Morrisville NC 27560. 919/461-1100. **Fax:** 919/461-1415. **Contact:** Human Resources. **E-mail address:** nc_recruiter@urscorp.com. **World Wide Web address:** http://www.urscorp.com. **Description:** Provides technical solutions and services such as regulatory compliance support, site investigation and remediation, air pollution controls, VOC and air toxin control, biotreatment, waste management, ambient and source monitoring, risk management, information management, project chemistry, specialty chemicals, remote sensing services, materials and machinery analysis, and electronic services. **Positions advertised include:** Geologist; Project Environmental Engineer; Senior Geologist; Assistant Programmer; Civil Engineer; Environmental Scientist; Graduate Environmental Engineer; Project Civil Engineer; Structural/Facility/Foundation Engineer. **Corporate headquarters location:** San Francisco CA. **Other area locations:** Charlotte NC. **Other U.S. locations:** Nationwide. **International locations:** Worldwide. **Listed on:** New York Stock Exchange. **Stock exchange symbol:** URS.

WASTE MANAGEMENT, INC.
P.O. Box 16148, Winston-Salem NC 27115. 336/723-5744. **Physical address:** 3303 North Glenn Avenue, Winston-Salem NC 27105. **Toll-free phone:** 800/422-2315. **Fax:** 336/725-3113. **Contact:** Human Resources. **World Wide Web address:** http://www.wm.com. **Description:** Provides garbage removal services for residential and commercial locations. **Corporate headquarters location:** Houston TX. **Other U.S. locations:** Nationwide. **International locations:** Canada. **Listed on:** New York Stock Exchange. **Stock exchange symbol:** WMI. **Number of employees worldwide:** 51,700.

Ohio

CLEAN HARBORS, INC.
4879 Spring Grove Avenue, Cincinnati OH 45232. 513/681-6242. **Toll-free phone:** 800/805-4582. **Contact:** Human Resources Department. **World Wide Web address:** http://www.cleanharbors.com. **Description:** Provides comprehensive environmental services in 35 states in the Northeast, Midwest, Central, and Mid-Atlantic regions. Clean Harbors provides a wide range of hazardous waste management and environmental support services to a diversified customer base. **Positions advertised include:** Facility Technician; Field Technician; Compliance Specialist; Compliance Guard; Class A Driver. **Corporate headquarters location:** Braintree MA. **Other U.S. locations:** Nationwide. **Listed on:** NASDAQ. **Stock exchange symbol:** CLHB. **Chairman/CEO:** Alan S. McKim. **Number of employees nationwide:** 1,400.

ENVIRONMENTAL ENTERPRISES
10163 Cincinnati-Dayton Road, Cincinnati OH 45241. 513/772-2818. **Contact:** Human Resources. **World Wide Web address:** http://www.eeienv.com. **Description:** Operates a hazardous waste treatment and storage facility. Environmental Enterprises also offers asbestos monitoring and transportation, emergency response, household hazardous waste, laboratory, and remediation services.

MONTGOMERY WATSON HARZA
1300 East Ninth Street, Suite 2000, Cleveland OH 44114. 216/621-2407. **Contact:** Human Resources. **World Wide Web address:** http://www.mwhglobal.com. **Description:** An environmental engineering, construction, and consulting firm. Montgomery Watson also specializes in applied research, construction and construction management, environmental engineering and remediation, financing, government relations, and information technology. **Positions advertised include:** Data Conversion Technician. **Special programs:** Internships. **Operations at this facility include:** Regional Headquarters.

RMT INC.
655 Metro Place South, Dublin OH 43017-1591. 614/793-0026. **Fax:** 614/793-0151. **Contact:** Human Resources. **E-mail address:** rmthr@rmtinc.com. **World Wide Web address:** http://www.rmtinc.com. **Description:** An environmental management firm that builds landfills and tests soil, land, and groundwater. **NOTE:** Resumes are accepted by mail, fax, or e-mail. Unsolicited resumes are not accepted. **Positions advertised include:** Senior Engineer. **Corporate headquarters location:** Madison WI. **Other U.S. locations:** Nationwide.

SEVERN TRENT LABORATORIES, INC.
4101 Shuffel Drive NW, North Canton OH 44720. 330/497-9396. **Fax:** 330/497-0772. **Contact:** Human Resources. **World Wide Web address:** http://www.stl-inc.com. **Description:** Provides a complete range of environmental testing services to private industry, engineering consultants, and government agencies in support of federal and state environmental regulations. The company also possesses analytical capabilities in the fields of air toxins, field analytical services, radiochemistry/mixed waste, and advanced technology. **Other U.S. locations:** CA; CO; FL; MO; TN; TX; WA.

WASTE MANAGEMENT, INC.
1006 Walnut Street, Canal Winchester OH 43110. 614/833-9155. **Fax:** 614/833-5280. **Contact:** Tim Turner, Personnel. **E-mail address:** tturner@wm.com. **World Wide Web address:** http://www.wm.com. **Description:** A non-hazardous solid waste management business. **Positions advertised include:** Commercial Driver; Customer Service Representative; Laborer; Mechanic. **Corporate headquarters location:** Houston TX. **Other U.S. locations:** Nationwide. **Listed on:** New York Stock Exchange. **Stock exchange symbol:** WMI. **Number of employees nationwide:** 51,700.

Oklahoma

THE BEARD COMPANY
5600 North May Avenue, Suite 320, Oklahoma City OK 73112. 405/842-2333. **Fax:** 405/842-9901. **Contact:** Linda Shrum or Rebecca Witcher, Human Resources. **E-mail address:** lshrum@beardco.com, or rwitcher@beardco.com. **World Wide Web address:** http://www.beardco.com. **Description:** Primary operations include carbon dioxide production, coal reclamation projects, the construction of fertilizer plants in China, and the pursuit of e-commerce activities related to starpay, an Internet payments and security technologies company. Founded in 1921. **Subsidiaries include:** Beard Sino-American Resources Co., Inc. (Beijing, China); Beard Technologies (Pittsburgh PA); starpay.com (Oklahoma City OK). **Listed on:** OTC. **Stock exchange symbol:** BRCO.

Oregon

AGGREGATE MACHINERY INC. (AMI)
3575 Blossom Drive NE, Salem OR 97305. 503/390-6284. **Fax:** 503/390-6342. **Contact:** Personnel. **World Wide Web address:** http://www.thunderbird2.com. **Description:** Manufactures crushing and recycling equipment and machinery for the construction and mining industries.

BFI
6161 NW 61st Avenue, Portland OR 97210. 503/226-6161. **Contact:** Human Resources. **World Wide Web address:** http://www.awin.com. **Description:** Engaged primarily in the collection, disposal, and recycling of solid wastes for commercial, industrial, and residential customers. Services include landfill services, waste-to-

energy programs, hazardous waste removal, and liquid waste removal. **Corporate headquarters location:** Scottsdale AZ. **Parent company:** Allied Waste Industries, Inc. **Listed on:** New York Stock Exchange. **Stock exchange symbol:** AW.

BROWN & CALDWELL
9620 SW Barbur Boulevard, Suite 200, Portland OR 97219. 503/244-7005. **Contact:** Bryan Paulson, Human Resources Manager. **World Wide Web address:** http://www.brownandcaldwell.com. **Description:** An employee-owned environmental engineering and consulting firm. Brown & Caldwell specializes in the planning, engineering, and design of waste management systems. The company is also engaged in construction management and environmental analytical testing. **Positions advertised include:** Principal Engineer; Business Development; Geologist/Hydrologist. **Corporate headquarters location:** Pleasant Hill CA. **Operations at this facility include:** Regional Headquarters.

DESCHUTES NATIONAL FOREST
CRESCENT RANGER DISTRICT
136471 Highway 97 North, P.O. Box 208, Crescent OR 97733. 541/433-3200. **Contact:** Human Resources. **World Wide Web address:** http://www.fs.fed.us/r6/deschutes. **Description:** Manages public forestlands. **NOTE:** Online application process preferred. **Special programs:** Summer Jobs.

SAFETY-KLEEN CORPORATION
16540 SE 130th Avenue, Clackamas OR 97015. 503/655-5798. **Fax:** 503/655-3952. **Contact:** Human Resources. **E-mail address:** info@safety-kleen. **World Wide Web address:** http://www.safety-kleen.com. **Description:** An environmental services company providing the collection, recycling, and disposal of both hazardous and nonhazardous waste. **Corporate headquarters location:** Plano TX.

SANIPAC
P.O. Box 10928, Eugene OR 97440. 541/736-3600. **Physical Address:** 1650 Glenwood Boulevard, Eugene OR 97403. **Fax:** 541/736-3650. **Contact:** Human Resources. **E-mail address:** info@sanipac.com. **World Wide Web address:** http://www.sanipac.com. **Description:** Collects and recycles garbage.

THERMO FLUIDS INC.
6400 SE 101st Avenue, Portland OR 97266-5130. 503/788-4612. **Toll-free phone:** 800/350-7565. **Contact:** Human Resources. **World Wide Web address:** http;//www.thermofluids.com. **Description:** Recycles antifreeze, oil and oil filters and provides some oil clean-up services. The company also offers environmental consulting services. Founded in 1978. **Parent company:** HIG Capital.

WASTE MANAGEMENT OF PORTLAND
7227 NE 55th Avenue, Portland OR 97218. 503/249-8078. **Contact:** Human Resources. **World Wide Web address:** http://www.wm,com. **Description:** A waste disposal company specializing in the hauling of waste materials. **Parent company:** WMX Technologies is an international provider of comprehensive waste management services, as well as engineering and construction, industrial, and related services, with operations in 19 countries.

Pennsylvania

ADVANCED GEOSERVICES CORP.
1055 Andrew Drive, Suite A, West Chester PA 19380-4293. 610/840-9100. **Fax:** 610/840-9199. **Contact:** Human Resources Department. **E-mail address:** agc@agcinfo.com. **World Wide Web address:** http://www.advancedgeoservices.com. **Description:** A technical services company that provides environmental remediation and geotechnical services. **Positions advertised include:** Graduate Landscape Architect; Professional Land Surveyor; Graduate Engineer; Sr. Geologist/Hydrogeologist; Sr. Civil Engineer/Project Manager; Geotechnical Engineer; Environmental Field Technician.

CAMP DRESSER & McKEE, INC. (CDM)
205 Granite Run Drive, Suite 350, Lancaster PA 17601. 717/560-7500. **Fax:** 717/560-7525. **Contact:** Human Resources. **World Wide Web address:** http://www.cdm.com. **Description:** Camp Dresser & McKee is a worldwide provider of environmental engineering, scientific, planning, and management services. The company focuses on professional activities for the management of water resources, hazardous and solid wastes, wastewater, infrastructure, and environmental systems for industry and government. **Positions advertised include:** Environmental Engineer. **Corporate headquarters location:** Cambridge MA.

CLEAN HARBORS, INC.
4105 Whitaker Avenue, Philadelphia PA 19124. 215/425-5144. **Contact:** Human Resources. **World Wide Web address:** http://www.cleanharbors.com. **Description:** Clean Harbors, Inc., through its subsidiaries, provides comprehensive environmental services in 35 states in the Northeast, Midwest, Central, and Mid-Atlantic regions. Clean Harbors provides a wide range of hazardous waste management and environmental support services to a diversified customer base from over 40 locations. **NOTE:** Please send resumes to the appropriate party as shown on the website. **Corporate headquarters location:** Braintree MA. **Other U.S. locations:** Nationwide. **Listed on:** NASDAQ. **Stock exchange symbol:** CLHB. **Number of employees nationwide:** 1,400.

HATCH
Gateway View Plaza, 1600 West Carson Street, Pittsburgh PA 15219-1031. 412/497-2000. **Fax:** 412/497-2212. **Contact:** Ms. Geri Rupert, Human Resources Director. **E-mail address:** hr@hatch.ca. **World Wide Web address:** http://www.hatch.ca. **Description:** One of the nation's largest engineering, construction, and consulting services companies. Hatch provides fully integrated capabilities to clients worldwide in four related market areas: environment, infrastructure, industry, and energy. **Corporate headquarters location:** Ontario Canada. **International locations:** Worldwide. **Number of employees worldwide:** 5,700.

MACTEC
5205 Militia Hill Road, Plymouth Meeting PA 19462. 610/941-9700. **Fax:** 610/941-9707. **Contact:** Personnel Director. **World Wide Web address:** http://www.mactec.com. **Description:** Offers a full range of services in environmental and engineering consulting, laboratory analysis, asbestos management, industrial hygiene, engineering, and architecture for governmental, industrial, and commercial clients. **NOTE:** Search and apply for positions online. **Positions advertised include:** Sr. Geotechnical Engineer; Project Geologist; Project Engineer. **Corporate headquarters location:** Alpharetta GA. **Other U.S. locations:** Nationwide.

PDG ENVIRONMENTAL, INC.
1386 Beulah Road, Building 801, Churchill 15235. 412/856-2200. **Toll-free phone:** 800/972-7341. **Fax:** 412/243-4900. **Contact:** Human Resources. **World Wide Web address:** http://www.pdge.com. **Description:** Provides asbestos and lead abatement services, environmental hazard clean-up services, and building demolition.

SHAW ENVIRONMENTAL &
INFRASTRUCTURE CORPORATION
2790 Mosside Boulevard, Monroeville PA 15146. 412/372-7701. **Toll-free phone:** 877/869-9269. **Contact:** Human Resources. **E-mail address:** jobnorth@theitgroup.com. **World Wide Web address:** http://www.theitgroup.com. **Description:** Delivers a full range of environmental management services. The company applies engineering, analytical, remediation, and pollution control expertise to meet the environmental needs of its clients, from site assessment to remediation. **Positions advertised include:** Engineer; Scientist; Financial Analyst; Transaction

Processing Administrator. **Corporate headquarters location:** Baton Rouge LA. **Parent company:** Shaw Group Inc. **Listed on:** New York Stock Exchange. **Stock exchange symbol:** SGR. **Number of employees worldwide:** 4,000.

Rhode Island

CLEAN HARBORS, INC.
8 Dexter Road, East Providence RI 02914. 401/431-1847. **Toll-free phone:** 800/645-8265. **Contact:** Tim Fowler. **E-mail address:** fowler.timothy@cleanharbors.com. **World Wide Web address:** http://www.cleanharbors.com. **Description:** Clean Harbors, Inc., through its subsidiaries, provides comprehensive environmental services in 35 states in the Northeast, Midwest, Central and Mid-Atlantic regions. Clean Harbors provides a wide range of hazardous waste management and environmental support services to a diversified customer base from over 40 locations. **NOTE:** See website for current job openings. Submit resume via e-mail, referencing the position you are applying for and the location. **Positions advertised include:** Field Service Specialist; Field Technician. **Corporate headquarters location:** Braintree MA. **Other U.S. locations:** Nationwide. **Number of employees nationwide:** 1,400.

ESS GROUP, INC.
401 Wampanoag Trail, Suite 400, East Providence RI 02915. 401/434-5560. **Fax:** 401/434-8158. **Contact:** Human Resources. **E-mail address:** recruitment@essgroup.com. **World Wide Web address:** http://www.essgroup.com. **Description:** Environmental Science Services is an environmental consulting engineering firm offering a variety of services throughout the Northeast, including soil sampling, water sampling and hazardous materials services. Established in 1979. **NOTE:** See website for current job openings. Send resumes by e-mail, fax or mail, identifying the position for which you are applying. **Positions advertised include:** Senior Project Manager, Energy & Industrial Services; Environmental Compliance Engineer, Energy & Industrial Services; Group Manager, Site Assessment & Remediation; Remediation Engineer; Geologist/Hydro Geologist; Engineer/Scientist, Environmental Geosciences & Engineering; Director of Land Development & Engineering Services; Civil/Site Project Engineers, Land Development & Engineering; GIS Analyst. **Other U.S. locations:** Wellesley MA.

South Carolina

GENERAL ENGINEERING LABORATORIES, LLC
2040 Savage Road, Charleston SC 29407. 843/556-8171. **Fax:** 843/766-1178. **Recorded jobline:** 843/769-7376, extension 4798. **Contact:** Human Resources Director. **E-mail address:** bch@gel.com. **World Wide Web address:** http://www.gel.com. **Description:** Provides environmental testing on soil, air, water, and sludge for private industry and the government. Founded in 1981. **NOTE:** Entry-level positions, part-time jobs, and second and third shifts are offered. This location also hires seasonally. **Positions advertised include:** Laboratory Technician; Senior Civil Engineer; Chemical Engineer; Computer Support Technician; Draftsperson; Environmental Engineer; Industrial Engineer; Project Manager. **Special programs:** Internships. **Affiliates include:** General Engineering & Environmental, LLC; General Engineering Geophysics, LLC. **Parent company:** The GEL Group, Inc.

SAFETY-KLEEN CORPORATION
164 Frontage Road, Lexington SC 29073. 803/356-1250. **Fax:** 803/356-4447. **Contact:** Human Resources. **World Wide Web address:** http://www.safety-kleen.com. **E-mail address:** info@safety-kleen.com. **Description:** A landfill company that accepts mainly nonhazardous waste from companies. **NOTE:** All available positions are posted online at http://www.monster.com. **Corporate headquarters location:** Plano TX. **Other locations:** Nationwide. **Number of employees nationwide:** 4,500.

Tennessee

BFI
700 Murfreesboro Road, Nashville TN 37210. 615/244-6250. **Fax:** 615/256-5219. **Contact:** Human Resources. **World Wide Web address:** http://www.disposal.com. **Description:** Engaged primarily in the collection and disposal of solid wastes for commercial, industrial, and residential customers. Services provided include landfills, waste-to-energy programs, hazardous waste removal, and liquid waste removal. **Other U.S. locations:** Nationwide. **International locations:** Worldwide. **Parent Company:** Allied Waste Industries, Inc. **Annual sales/revenues:** More than $100 million.

BECHTEL JACOBS COMPANY LLC,
Highway 58, P. O. Box 4699, Oak Ridge, Tennessee 37831-7020. 865/576-4006. **Toll-free phone:** 800/382-6938. **Fax:** 865-241-1379. **E-mail address:** bcf@bechteljacobs.com. **World Wide Web address:** http://www.bechteljacobs.com. **Description:** Bechtel Jacobs is the environmental management contractor for the U. S. Department of Energy's Oak Ridge Operations Office, located in Oak Ridge, Tennessee. **NOTE:** Resumes accepted only for posted positions. **Positions advertised include:** Engineering Supervisor; Sr. Engineering Specialist; Purchasing Specialist; Project QA Manager; Health Physicist.

CH2M HILL
151 Lafayette Drive, Suite 110, Oak Ridge TN 37830. 865/483-9032. **Fax:** 865/481-3541. **Contact:** Human Resources. **World Wide Web address:** http://www.ch2m.com. **Description:** CH2M Hill is a group of employee-owned companies operating under the names CH2M Hill, Inc.; Industrial Design Corporation; Operations Management International; CH2M Hill International; and CH2M Hill Engineering. The company provides planning, engineering design, and operation and construction management services to help clients apply technology, safeguard the environment, and develop infrastructure. **NOTE:** Search and apply for positions or submit resume online. **Positions advertised included:** Staff Engineer; Security Escort. **Corporate headquarters location:** Denver CO. **Operations at this facility include:** This location provides environmental consulting services and subcontracts to Bechtel National, Inc. **Number of employees nationwide:** 5,000.

COMMODORE APPLIED TECHNOLOGIES, INC
800 Oak Ridge Turnpike, Suite C-260, Oak Ridge TN 37830. 865/483-1274. **Contact:** Human Resources. **World Wide Web address:** http://www.commodore.com. **Description:** A technical services consulting firm that provides innovative, multidisciplinary solutions to a wide range of environmental challenges. A staff of environmental professionals provides services in waste management, environmental sciences, advanced technologies, and bioremediation. **Corporate headquarters location:** New York NY.

ENVIRONMENTAL SYSTEMS CORPORATION
200 Tech Center Drive, Knoxville TN 37912. 865/688-7900. **Fax:** 865/219-0992. **Contact:** Human Resources. **E-mail address:** hr@envirosys.com. **World Wide Web address:** http://www.envirosys.com. **Description:** Manufactures custom-designed environmental and engineering systems and provides services for air quality monitoring, hazardous waste management, and ground water management for the coal and nuclear energy industry. **NOTE:** Search and apply for positions online. **Positions advertised include:** Customer Service Supervisor; Engineer; Software Support; Project Engineer; Regulations Specialist; Director, Manufacturing; Sr. Engineer; Technical Manager; Calibration Technologist; Configuration Manager; Programmer Analyst; Database Administrator.

GTS DURATEK
1009 Commerce Park Drive, Suite 100, Oak Ridge TN 37830. 865/425-4600. **Fax:** 865/481-2087. **Contact:**

Human Resources. **E-mail address:** oakrec@duratekinc.com. **World Wide Web address:** http://www.duratekinc.com. **Description:** Processes low-level radioactive waste. **NOTE:** Search and apply for positions online. **Positions advertised include:** Senior Radiological Engineer; Waste Engineer; Waste Handler/Project Technician. **Corporate headquarters location:** Columbia MD. **Other area locations:** Memphis TN. Other U.S. locations: Lakewood CO; Barnwell SC. **Listed on:** NASDAQ. **Stock exchange symbol:** DRTK.

NUCLEAR FUEL SERVICE
1205 Banner Hill Road, Erwin TN 37650. 423/743-1755. **Fax:** 423/743-9025. **Contact:** Personnel Resources Specialist. **E-mail address:** rvbishop@nuclearfuelservices.com. **World Wide Web address:** http://www.nuclearfuelservices.com. **Description:** Provides advanced nuclear technology, manufacturing, and management services to both government and commercial clients. Founded in 1957. **Office hours:** Monday - Friday, 8:00 a.m. - 5:00 p.m. **Listed on:** Privately held. **Number of employees at this location:** 500.

PAI CORPORATION
116 Milan Way, Oak Ridge TN 37830-6913. 865/483-0666. **Fax:** 865/481-0003. **Contact:** Office Manager. **E-mail address:** hr.dept@paicorp.com. **World Wide Web address:** http://www.paicorp.com. **Description:** PAI Corporation provides services to commercial and government programs that require expertise in science, technology, and regulations. **Corporate headquarters location:** This location. **Other U.S. locations:** Moffet Field CA; Las Vegas NV. **Operations at this facility include:** This location provides technical and environmental support services to the Department of Energy; engineering, environmental, research, and development services to Lockheed Martin Energy Systems, Inc.; and environmental restoration and management support to DOE/OR through Jacobs Engineering Group.

PRECIPITATOR SERVICES GROUP
P.O. Box 339, Elizabethton TN 37644-0339. 423/543-7331. **Physical address:** 1625 Broad Street, Elisabethton TN 37643. **Toll-free phone:** 800/345-0484. **Fax:** 423/543-8737. **Contact:** Human Resources. **World Wide Web address:** http://www.psgtn.net. **Description:** A manufacturer of air pollution control equipment, replacement parts, and upgrade components. Replacement components and services include discharge electrodes, bottle weights, collecting plates, plate repair, rappers, and rapper accessories. Accessory components include high-voltage components and bus ducts, high-voltage frames and hanger assemblies, rapper trains, collecting plate support beams, spacer bars and assemblies, access doors, and antisway assemblies.

SCIENCE APPLICATIONS INTERNATIONAL CORPORATION (SAIC)
P.O. Box 2501, Oak Ridge TN 37831-2501. 865/482-9031. **Physical Address:** 151 Lafayette Drive, Oak Ridge TN 37831-2501. **Contact:** Kathy Phillips, Human Resources Manager. **World Wide Web address:** http://www.saic.com. **Description:** Offers engineering services, nuclear fuel cycle and waste storage analysis, technical information services, information systems, environmental analysis and modeling, program management, and document preparation. **NOTE:** Search and apply for positions online. **Positions advertised include:** Project Control Analyst; Sr. Financial Controller; Project Controls Analyst; Sr. Programmer/Analyst; WNP Fallout Specialist; Subcontract Administrator. **Corporate headquarters locations:** San Diego. **Number of employees worldwide:** 43,000.

SEVERN TRENT LABORATORIES, INC.
5815 Middlebrook Pike, Knoxville TN 37921. 865/291-3000. **Fax:** 865/584-4315. **Contact:** Human Resources. **World Wide Web address:** http://www.stl-inc.com. **Description:** Provides a complete range of environmental testing services to private industry, engineering consultants, and government agencies in support of federal and state environmental regulations. The company also possesses analytical capabilities in the fields of air toxins, field analytical services, radiochemistry/mixed waste, and advanced technology. **NOTE:** Search and apply for positions online. **Other U.S. locations:** Nationwide. **Parent company:** Severn Trent Plc (London). **Number of employees nationwide:** 2,100.

SMURFIT-STONE CONTAINER CORPORATION
700 Cawan Street, Nashville TN 37207. 615/256-8965. **Contact:** Lance Greenwalt, Controller. **World Wide Web address:** http://www.smurfit-stone.com. **Description:** One of the world's leading paper-based packaging companies. The company's main products include corrugated containers, folding cartons, and multiwall industrial bags. The company is also one of the world's largest collectors and processors of recycled products that are then sold to a worldwide customer base. Smurfit-Stone Container Corporation also operates several paper tube, market pulp, and newsprint production facilities. **Corporate headquarters location:** Chicago IL. **Other U.S. locations:** Nationwide. **International locations:** Dublin, Ireland. **Listed on:** NASDAQ. **Stock exchange symbol:** SSCC. **Annual sales/revenues:** More than $100 million. **Number of employees worldwide:** 35,000.

TENNESSEE WILDLIFE RESOURCES AGENCY
Ellington Agricultural Center, P.O. Box 40747, Nashville TN 37204. 615/781-6622. **Personnel phone:** 615/781-6594. **Contact:** Personnel. **World Wide Web address:** http://www.state.tn.us/twra. **Description:** Dedicated to the preservation and conservation on native wildlife. The Tennessee Wildlife Resources Agency also issues fishing and hunting licenses statewide. Founded in 1949. **Office hours:** Monday - Friday, 8:00 a.m. - 4:30 p.m. **Corporate headquarters location:** This location. **Other U.S. locations:** Crossville TN; Morristown TN; Jackson TN.

TETRA TECH NUS
800 Oak Ridge Turnpike, Suite A600, Oak Ridge TN 37830. 865/483-9900. **Fax:** 865/483-2014. **Contact:** Norma Gillespie, Human Resources Representative. **World Wide Web address:** http://www.tetratech.com. **Description:** Provides environmental services, water/wastewater management, infrastructure services, communications support, and outsourcing services. **NOTE:** Search and apply for positions online. **Corporate headquarters location:** Pasadena CA. **Number of employees worldwide:** 9,000.

TOXCO
109 Flint Road, Oak Ridge TN 37830. 865/482-5532. **Contact:** Human Resources. **World Wide Web address:** http://www.toxco.com. **Description:** A battery recycling company. **Corporate headquarters location:** Anaheim CA. **Operations at this facility include:** Administration; Service. **President:** Terry Adams.

URS CORPORATION
1093 Commerce Park Drive, Suite 100, Oak Ridge TN 37830-8029. 865/483-9870. **Fax:** 865/483-9061. **Contact:** Human Resource Manager. **World Wide Web address:** http://www.urscorp.com. **Description:** Offers professional planning and design, systems engineering and technical assistance, program and construction management, and operations and maintenance services for surface transportation, air transportation, rail transportation, industrial process, facilities and logistics support, water/wastewater treatment, hazardous waste management and military platforms support. **NOTE:** Search and apply for positions online. **Positions advertised include:** IS Manager; Inspector; Project Manager; Sr. Environmental Engineer; Staff Programmer. **Corporate headquarters location:** San Francisco CA. **Other U.S. locations:** Nationwide. **International locations:** Worldwide. **Listed on:** New York Stock Exchange.

Stock exchange symbol: URS. **Number of employees worldwide:** 26,000.

Texas

ADS ENVIRONMENTAL SERVICES INC.
10450 Stancliff Road, Suite 115, Houston 77099. 281/933-0951. **Contact:** Human Resources Department. **E-mail address:** careers@adsenv.com. **World Wide Web address:** http://www.adsenv.com. **Description:** Provides diagnostic testing services of water and wastewater, flow monitoring, and sewer system evaluation. Founded in 1974. **NOTE:** Send resumes to: ADS Corporation, 5030 Bradford Drive, Building One, Suite 210, Huntsville AL 35805; phone is 256/430-3366. **Corporate headquarters location:** Huntsville AL. **Parent company:** ADS Corporation. **President/CEO:** Karl Boone.

ENSR INC.
4888 Loop Central Drive, Loop Central One, Suite 600, Houston TX 77081-2214. 713/520-9900. **Contact:** Human Resources. **E-mail address:** hrcentral@ensr.com. **World Wide Web address:** http://www.ensr.com. **Description:** Offers comprehensive environmental services including consulting, engineering, and remediation. **NOTE:** Entry-level opportunities available. **Other area locations include:** Plano; Austin. **Positions advertised include:** Staff Specialist; Project Manager. **Corporate headquarters location:** Westford MA.

GEO-MARINE, INC.
550 East 15th Street, Plano TX 75074. 972/423-5480. **Contact:** Human Resources. **Fax:** 972/422-2736. **World Wide Web address:** http://www.geo-marine.com. **Description:** An environmental, engineering, consulting firm that provides services to government, business, and industry. Geo-Marine specializes in hazardous materials/waste management, natural resources management, energy management, and utility privatization, and NEPA Consulting. **Positions advertised include:** Senior Project Manager; Wetlands Specialist; Architectural Historian. **Corporate headquarters location:** This location. **Other area locations:** El Paso TX; San Antonio TX. **Other U.S. locations:** CA; FL; NV; OK; TX; VA.

HVJ ASSOCIATES
6120 South Dairy Ashford Road, Houston TX 77072. 281/933-7388. **Contact:** Human Resources. **World Wide Web address:** http://www.hvj.com. **Description:** An engineering consulting firm specializing in geotechnology, construction materials; pavement; and facilities and environmental management. Founded in 1985. **Other area locations:** Austin TX; San Antonio TX.

NATIONAL MARINE FISHERIES SERVICE
4700 Avenue U, Galveston TX 77551. 409/766-3500. **Contact:** Human Resources. **World Wide Web address:** http://galveston.ssp.nmfs.gov/galv/. **Description:** A laboratory that researches the management processes of commercial and recreational shellfish and works to protect coastal habitats. **NOTE:** Applicants are asked to forward resumes, college transcripts, and a list of references. **Positions advertised include:** Biological Science Technician. **Special programs:** Internships.

ONYX ENVIRONMENTAL
1800 South Highway 146, Baytown TX 77520. 281/427-4099. **Contact:** Human Resources. **World Wide Web address:** http://www.onyxes.com. **Description:** A provider of comprehensive waste management services, as well as engineering and construction, industrial, and related services, with operations in 19 countries. **NOTE:** Resumes should be faxed to: 626/334-4563. **Positions advertised include:** National Accounts Manager; Project Manager. **Other U.S. locations:** Nationwide. **Operations at this facility include:** Sales.

SAFETY-KLEEN CORPORATION
1722 Cooper Creek Road, Denton TX 76208. 940/483-5200. **Contact:** Human Resources. **World Wide Web address:** http://www.safety-kleen.com. **Description:** The company offers treatment, recycling, and disposal services. **NOTE:** This company has administrative and sales offices throughout Texas. See the company's website for job listings and application information. **Corporate headquarters location:** Plano TX. **Other U.S. locations:** Nationwide. **Operations at this facility include:** This location is a recycling center for hazardous waste.

SEVERN TRENT LABORATORIES, INC.
14046 Summit Drive, Suite 111, Austin TX 78728. 512/244-0855. **Fax:** 512/244-0160. **Contact:** Human Resources. **World Wide Web address:** http://www.stl-inc.com. **Description:** Provides a complete range of environmental testing services to private industry, engineering consultants, and government agencies in support of federal and state environmental regulations. The company also possesses analytical capabilities in the fields of air toxins, field analytical services, radiochemistry/mixed waste, and advanced technology. **Corporate headquarters location:** United Kingdom. **Other area locations:** Corpus Christi TX; Houston TX; Baytown TX. **Other U.S. locations:** Nationwide. **Number of employees worldwide:** 2,800.

TANKNOLOGY-NDE INTERNATIONAL, INC.
8900 Shoal Creek Boulevard, Building 200, Austin TX 78757. 512/451-6334. **Toll-free phone:** 800/964-0010x119. **Contact:** Human Resources Department. **E-mail address:** thebestjobsare@tankology.com. **World Wide Web address:** http://www.tanknde.com. **Description:** Through its subsidiaries, Tanknology-NDE provides environmental compliance, information, and management services to owners and operators of underground storage tanks. The company has three principal lines of business: domestic underground storage tank testing; domestic tank management; and international underground storage tank testing. The company's primary service is tank tightness testing, tank integrity testing, or precision testing. This service involves testing underground storage tanks and associated piping to determine if they are leaking. **NOTE:** See company's website for job listings and contact information.

TEAM INDUSTRIAL SERVICES, INC.
P.O. Box 123, Alvin TX 77512. 281/331-6154. **Physical address:** 200 Hermann Drive, Alvin TX 77511. **Contact:** Human Resources. **World Wide Web address:** http://www.teamindustrialservices.com. **Description:** Provides a wide variety of environmental services for industrial corporations including consulting, engineering, monitoring, and leak repair. Founded in 1973. **NOTE:** This company has 10 locations throughout Texas. See website for job listings, addresses and application. **Positions advertised include:** Field Machining Manager. **Corporate headquarters location:** This location. **Other U.S. locations:** Nationwide. **International locations:** Worldwide. **Listed on:** American Stock Exchange. **Stock exchange symbol:** TMI. **Number of employees worldwide:** 800.

URS CORPORATION
P.O. Box 201088, Austin TX 78720-1088. 512/454-4797. **Contact:** Human Resources. **World Wide Web address:** http://www.urscorp.com. **Description:** An architectural, engineering, and environmental consulting firm that specializes in air transportation, environmental solutions, surface transportation, and industrial environmental and engineering concerns. Founded in 1969. **NOTE**: See this company's website for all job listings in Texas. Apply online. **Positions advertised include:** Accounting Clerk; Contract Administrator; Environmental Engineer; Geologist; Scientist; Senior Chemical Engineer; Technical Assistant. **Corporate headquarters location:** This location. **Other area locations:** Dallas TX; Freeport TX; Houston TX; San Antonio TX. **Listed on:** New York Stock Exchange. **Stock exchange symbol:** URS.

WAID AND ASSOCIATES
14205 Burnet Road, Suite 600, Austin TX 78728. 512/255-9999. **Fax:** 512/255-8780. **Contact:** Human Resources. **E-mail address:** waid@waid.com. **World Wide Web address:** http://www.waid.com. **Description:** An engineering and environmental services firm. The company specializes in air quality services for industrial clients, particularly involving emissions control; permitting and compliance. Waid and Associates also provides services in waste and wastewater management, environmental management, and environmental information systems. Founded in 1978. **NOTE:** Entry-level positions are offered. **Office hours:** Monday - Friday, 8:00 a.m. - 5:00 p.m. **Corporate headquarters location:** This location. **Other area locations:** Houston TX; Midland TX. **Parent company:** Waid Corporation. **Listed on:** Privately held.

WASTE MANAGEMENT, INC.
1001 Fannin Street, Suite 4000, Houston TX 77002. 713/512-6200. **Contact:** Human Resources. **World Wide Web address:** http://www.wm.com. **Description:** An international provider of comprehensive waste management services as well as engineering, construction, industrial, and related service. **NOTE:** This company has several locations throughout Texas and the U.S. For corporate positions, apply online. For positions at specific locations, see website for addresses and contact information. **Positions advertised include:** ETL Programmer; Strategic Sourcing Manager; Toxic Tort Manager; Administrative Assistant; Training Manager; Senior Internal Auditor. **Corporate headquarters location:** This location. **Other U.S. locations:** Nationwide. **Operations at this facility include:** Administration. **Listed on:** New York Stock Exchange. **Stock exchange symbol:** WMI.

Vermont
ARD, INC.
159 Bank Street, Suite 300, Burlington VT 05401. 802/658-3890. **Contact:** Human Resources. **E-mail address:** homeofficejobs@ardinc.com. **World Wide Web address:** http://www.ardinc.com. **Description:** ARD is an international development and consulting firm that works mainly with the U.S. Agency for International Development (USAID) and other multilateral development agencies specializing in issues relating to agriculture, rural development, energy conservation, the environment, local governance, and organizational development. Founded in 1977. **NOTE:** The company offers overseas opportunities. Phone calls are not accepted. **Positions advertised include:** Home Office Professional Roster Data Entry Assistant; Home Office Assistant Project Manager; Home Office Program Manager for Transition Initiative; Home Office Democracy and Governance Analytical Services Specialist; Home Office AgriBusiness Associate. **Other locations:** Washington DC. **International locations:** Worldwide.

SEVERN TRENT LABORATORIES, INC.
208 South Park Drive, Suite 1, Colchester VT 05446. 802/655-1203. **Fax:** 802/655-1248. **Contact:** Human Resources. **World Wide Web address:** http://www.stl-inc.com. **Description:** Provides a complete range of environmental testing services to private industry, engineering consultants, and government agencies in support of federal and state environmental regulations. The company also possesses analytical capabilities in the fields of air toxins, field analytical services, radiochemistry/mixed waste, and advanced technology. **NOTE:** Unsolicited resumes are not accepted. **Other U.S. locations:** Nationwide. **Operations at this facility include:** This location is an environmental analytical laboratory that performs EPA and SW846 methods. It also has an air toxic department. **Number of employees nationwide:** 2,000.

Virginia
CLEAN HARBORS ENVIRONMENTAL SERVICES, INC.
7515 Harvest Road, Prince George VA 23875. 804/452-1800. **Contact:** Human Resources. **World Wide Web address:** http://www.cleanharbors.com. **Description:** This location is a regional environmental service center. Clean Harbors, Inc., through its subsidiaries, provides environmental and waste management services in 36 states, Canada, Mexico, and Puerto Rico. The company's hazardous waste management services include treatment, storage, recycling, transportation, risk analysis, site assessment, laboratory analysis, site closure, and disposal of hazardous materials through environmentally sound methods including incineration. Environmental remediation services include emergency response, surface remediation, groundwater restoration, industrial maintenance, and facility decontamination. **NOTE:** Search and apply for positions online. **Positions advertised include:** Field Service Foreman; field Technician; Field Service Supervisor; Field Operations Manager. **Corporate headquarters location:** Braintree MA. **Other U.S. locations:** Nationwide. **Listed on:** NASDAQ. **Stock exchange symbol:** CLHB. **Number of employees nationwide:** 1,400.

ETS, INC.
1401 Municipal Road NW, Roanoke VA 24012-1309. 540/265-0004. **Fax:** 540/265-0131. **Contact:** Personnel. **E-mail address:** etsi@infionline.net. **World Wide Web address:** http://www.etsi-inc.com. **Description:** ETS is an environmental service firm specializing in air emissions control, testing, training, troubleshooting, and testimony. **Corporate headquarters location:** This location. **Other U.S. locations:** Sanford FL.

EARTH TECH INC.
675 North Washington Street, Suite 300, Alexandria VA 22314. 703/549-8728. **Fax:** 703/549-9134. **Contact:** Human Resources. **World Wide Web address:** http://www.earthtech.com. **Description:** Earth Tech provides a full suite of engineering, construction and operations services to the global water/wastewater, environmental, transportation, and facilities marketsFounded in 1970. **Positions advertised include:** Chemist; Civil/Environmental Engineer; Contract Administrator; Document Control Administrator; Electrical Inspector; Environmental Engineer; Environmental Professional; Project Controls Specialist. **Corporate headquarters location:** Long Beach CA. **Other area locations:** Norfolk VA; Richmond VA. **Other U.S. locations:** Nationwide. **Parent company:** Tyco International. **Number of employees worldwide:** 8,500.

TETRA TECH, INC.
10306 Eaton Place, Suite 340, Fairfax VA 22030. 703/385-6000. **Fax:** 703/385-6007. **Contact:** Human Resources. **World Wide Web address:** http://www.tetratech.com. **Description:** Provides consulting, engineering, and technical services to commercial and government clients. **NOTE:** Search and apply for positions online. **Corporate headquarters location:** Pasadena CA. **Listed on:** NASDAQ. **Stock exchange symbol:** TTEK. **Number of employees worldwide:** 7,500.

UXB INTERNATIONAL, INC.
1715 Pratt Drive, Suite 1300, Blacksburg VA 24060. 540/443-3700. **Fax:** 540/443-3790. **Contact:** Human Resources. **E-mail address:** HR@uxb.com. **World Wide Web address:** http://www.uxb.com. **Description:** Provides ordnance and explosive waste services for the United States Army. The company specializes in chemical warfare identification, recovery, and disposal; extraction and transportation of reactive materials; geophysical studies; metal detection; seismic refraction; and humanitarian remining. **Positions advertised include:** UXO Supervisor; Technician; UXO Safety Officer; Quality Control Specialist. **Corporate headquarters location:** Ashburn VA.

VERSAR, INC.
6850 Versar Center, Springfield VA 22151. 703/750-3000. **Fax:** 703/642-6807. **Contact:** Human Resources. **World Wide Web address:** http://www.versar.com.

Description: Versar is a professional services firm working in the areas of environment, energy, architecture/engineering/construction, defense, information technology, and management and policy consulting. Founded in 1969. **Positions advertised include:** Civil Engineer; Environmental Analyst; Principal Mechanical Engineer. **Other U.S. locations:** Tempe AZ; Sacramento CA; Northglenn CO; Lombard IL; Columbia MD; Eden Beaver Creek OH; Oklahoma City OK; Horsham PA; San Antonio TX. **Subsidiaries include:** GEOMET Technologies, Inc., 8577 Atlas Drive, Gaithersburg MD. **Listed on:** American Stock Exchange. **Stock exchange symbol:** VSR. **Number of employees nationwide:** 495.

Washington

ABSORPTION CORPORATION
2011 Young Street, Bellingham WA 98225. 360/734-7415. **Fax:** 360/671-1588. **Contact:** Human Resources. **World Wide Web address:** http://www.absorbent.com. **Description:** Develops, produces, and markets absorbent products for use in the marine spill clean-up, general industrial, oil/water filtration, animal litter/bedding, and commercial markets. **Corporate headquarters location:** This location. **Subsidiaries include:** Absorption Corp. **Operations at this facility include:** Manufacturing; Sales.

BROWN & CALDWELL
701 Pike Place, Suite 1200, Seattle WA 98101. 206/624-0100. **Contact:** Personnel. **E-mail address:** resumes@brwncald.com. **World Wide Web address:** http://www.brownandcaldwell.com. **Description:** An employee-owned environmental engineering and consulting firm specializing in the planning, engineering, and design of waste management systems. The company is also engaged in construction management and analytical environmental testing. **Positions advertised include:** Engineer; Office Support Associate. **Corporate headquarters location:** Walnut Creek CA.

CAMP DRESSER & McKEE INC. (CDM)
P.O. Box 3885, Bellevue WA 98009. 425/453-8383. **Physical address:** 11811 NE First Street, Suite 201, Bellevue WA 98005. **Fax:** 425/646-9523. **Contact:** Human Resources Department. **E-mail address:** hr@cdm.com. **World Wide Web address:** http://www.cdm.com. **Description:** A worldwide provider of environmental engineering, scientific, planning, and management services. The company focuses on professional activities for the management of water resources, hazardous and solid wastes, wastewater, infrastructure, and environmental systems for industry and government. **Positions advertised include:** Senior Wastewater Engineer; Senior O&M Technician; Assistant Project Manager. **Other U.S. locations:** Nationwide. **International locations:** Worldwide.

DOWL ENGINEERS
8320 154th Avenue NE, Redmond WA 98052. 425/869-2670. **Fax:** 425/869-2679. **Contact:** Linda Finch, Human Resources. **E-mail address:** lfinch@dowl.com. **World Wide Web address:** http://www.dowl.com. **Description:** Offers specialized environmental engineering services to a variety of clients in government and industry. The company also provides civil engineering and surveying services to municipal and private development clients. **Positions advertised include:** Civil Engineer; Transportation/Traffic Engineer; Auto CAD Technician; Construction Inspector; Licensed Surveyor; Geologist.

HART CROWSER
1910 Fairview Avenue East, Suite 100, Seattle WA 98102. 206/324-9530. **Contact:** Human Resources. **E-mail address:** staffing@hartcrowser.com. **World Wide Web address:** http://www.hartcrowser.com. **Description:** An environmental consulting firm offering site development, remediation, and waste management services. Founded in 1974. **Corporate headquarters location:** This location. **Other U.S. locations:** AK; CA; CO; IL; NJ; OR.

PARAMETRIX, INC.
P.O. Box 460, Sumner WA 98390. 253/863-5128. **Contact:** Human Resources. **World Wide Web address:** http://www.parametrix.com. **Description:** An environmental and engineering consulting firm. The company is also engaged in environmental surveying. Founded in 1969. **Positions advertised include:** Structural Design Engineer; Bridge Design Engineer; Senior Word Processor; Marketing Database Coordinator. **Corporate headquarters location:** This location.

PHILIP SERVICES CORPORATION
20245 77th Avenue South, Kent WA 98032. 253/872-8030. **Contact:** Human Resources. **World Wide Web address:** http://www.contactpsc.com. **Description:** Philip Services Corporation is divided into three groups: Northwest By-Products Management; Metals Recovery; and Industrial Services. Founded in 1970. **Operations at this facility include:** This location is a hazardous-waste treatment facility. **Annual sales/revenues:** More than $100 million.

SEVERN TRENT LABORATORIES, INC.
5755 8th Street East, Tacoma WA 98033. 425/576-5040. **Fax:** 253/922-5047. **Contact:** Human Resources. **World Wide Web address:** http://www.stlinc.com. **Description:** Provides a complete range of environmental testing services to private industry, engineering consultants, and government agencies in support of federal and state environmental regulations. **Corporate headquarters location:** St. Louis MO.

SHANNON & WILSON, INC.
P.O. Box 300303, Seattle WA 98103. 206/632-8020. **Physical address:** 400 North 34th Street, Suite 100, Seattle WA 98103. **Fax:** 206/633-6777. **Contact:** Human Resources. **E-mail address:** jobs@shanwil.com. **World Wide Web address:** http://www.shannonwilson.com. **Description:** Provides geotechnical consulting services to a variety of industrial and government clients. Services include foundation engineering studies, waste management, and construction monitoring. **Positions advertised include:** Office Support Clerk. **Corporate headquarters location:** This location.

URS CORPORATION
Century Square, 1501 Fourth Avenue, Suite 1440, Seattle WA 98101-1616. 206/438-2700. **Contact:** Human Resources. **World Wide Web address:** http://www.urscorp.com. **Description:** An architectural, engineering, and environmental consulting firm that specializes in air transportation, environmental solutions, surface transportation, and industrial environmental and engineering concerns. **Positions advertised include:** Civil Geotechnical Engineer; Electrical Senior Designer; Environmental Technician; Graduate Civil Engineer; Graduate Geologist; Marketing Services Manager; Mechanical Engineer; Principal Environmental Scientist; Project Toxicologist; CADD Designer; Senior Estimator.

West Virginia

ALLIANCE CONSULTING, INCORPORATED
124 Philpott Lane, Beckley WV 25813. 304/255-0491. **Fax:** 304/255-4232. **Contact:** Jody Lilly. **Email:** jlilly@aci-wbv.com. **World Wide Web address:** http://www.aci-ecs.com. **Description:** Provides environmental consulting and engineering services. **Positions advertised include:** Civil Engineer.

ALLIED WASTE SERVICES OF WHEELING
404 Glenns Run Road, Wheeling WV 26003. 304/277-2088. **Toll free phone:** 800/696-3173. **Contact:** Human Resources. **E-mail address:** careers@alliedwaste.com. **World Wide Web address:** http://www.alliedwaste.com. **Description:** Engaged primarily in the collection and disposal of solid waste for commercial, industrial, and residential customers. Services include landfill services, waste-to-energy

programs, hazardous waste removal, and liquid waste removal. **Positions advertised include:** Major Accounts Sales Representative; Maintenance Manager/Truck Shop; Truck Mechanic. **Corporate headquarters location:** Scottsdale AZ. **Parent company:** Allied Waste, Incorporated. **Listed on:** New York Stock Exchange. **Stock exchange symbol:** AW.

Wisconsin

COOPER ENVIRONMENTAL & ENGINEERING RESOURCES, INC.
5569 Peters Drive, West Bend WI 53095. 262/338-9697. **Fax:** 262/338-9645. **Contact:** Human Resources. **Description:** An environmental services firm with risk assessment and cleanup-level determination, site development and remedial strategies, site investigations, remediation design, and construction monitoring.

GRAEF, ANHALT, SCHLOEMER & ASSOCIATES, INC.
125 South 84th Street, Suite 401, Milwaukee WI 53214-1470. 414/259-1500. **Fax:** 414/259-0037. **Contact:** Carrie Kopischkie, Recruiter. **World Wide Web address:** http://www.gasai.com. **Description:** A full-service civil engineering and consulting firm. Founded in 1961. **NOTE:** Entry-level positions are offered. **Positions advertised include:** Accounting Manager; Architect; Architectural Technician; Electrical Engineer; Environmental Scientist; Human Resources Assistant; Hydrologist; Municipal Project Manager. **Special programs:** Co-ops. **Corporate headquarters location:** This location. **Other area locations:** Green Bay WI; Madison WI. **Other U.S. locations:** Chicago IL; Davenport IA; Naples FL. **Number of employees at this location:** 175. **Number of employees nationwide:** 230.

LEGGETTE, BRASHEARS & GRAHAM, INC.
6525 Grand Teton Plaza, Madison WI 53719. 608/833-5555. **Fax:** 608/833-5551. **Contact:** Human Resources. **E-mail address:** wisconsin@lbgweb.com. **World Wide Web address:** http://www.lbgweb.com. **Description:** A professional groundwater and environmental engineering services company. **Corporate headquarters location:** Shelton CT. **Other U.S. locations:** Nationwide.

MILLER ENGINEERS & SCIENTISTS
5308 South 12th Street, Sheboygan WI 53081. 920/458-6164. **Toll-free phone:** 800/969-7013. **Fax:** 920/458-0369. **Contact:** Tracy Taylor, Human Resources. **E-mal address:** ttaylor@startwithmiller.com. **World Wide Web address:** http://www.startwithmiller.com. **Description:** An environmental consulting firm that also performs land surveying and materials testing. **Corporate headquarters location:** This location.

NORTHERN LAKE SERVICE, INC.
400 North Lake Avenue, Crandon WI 54520-1298. 715/478-2777. **Toll-free phone:** 800/278-1254. **Fax:** 715/478-3060. **Contact:** Personnel. **E-mail address:** norlake@northernlakeservice.com. **World Wide Web address:** http://www.northernlakeservice.com. **Description:** An environmental analytical laboratory that conducts a wide range of tests on soil and water samples to determine whether contaminants are present.

FINANCIAL SERVICES

You can expect to find the following types of companies in this section:

Consumer Financing and Credit Agencies • Investment Specialists • Mortgage Bankers and Loan Brokers • Security and Commodity Brokers, Dealers, and Exchanges

---

The number of new securities, commodities, and investment openings will increase by 15.7% or 121,000 to 888,000. As people's incomes continue to climb, they will increasingly seek the advice and services of securities, commodities, and financial services sales agents to realize their financial goals. Growth in the volume of trade in stocks over the Internet will reduce the need for brokers for many transactions. Nevertheless, the overall increase in investment is expected to spur employment growth among these workers, with a majority of transactions still requiring the advice and services of securities, commodities, and financial services sales agents. Within this industry, personal financial advisor jobs are projected to increase by 25.9%, adding 41,000 new jobs. Increased investment by businesses and individuals is expected to result in faster-than-average employment growth of financial analysts and personal financial advisors through 2014. Both occupations will benefit as baby boomers save for retirement and as a generally better educated and wealthier population requires investment advice.

Alabama

ALABAMA CENTRAL CREDIT UNION

3601 4th Avenue South, Birmingham AL 35222. 205/591-2228. **Toll-free phone:** 800/223-2415. **Fax:** 205/595-8078. **Contact:** Human Resources. **World Wide Web address:** http://www.alabamacentral.org. **Description:** A Credit Union servicing Birmingham and the surrounding communities. **Other area locations:** Creola, Decatur, Demopolis, Florence, Homewood, Mobile, Muscle Shoals, Russellville, Tuscaloosa.

ALABAMA CREDIT UNION

220 Paul Bryant Drive East, P.O. Box 862998, Tuscaloosa AL 35486-0027. 205/348-5944. **Fax:** 205/348-7456. **Contact:** Jon Garner. **E-mail address:** jgarner@alabamacu.com. **World Wide Web address:** http://www.alabamacu.com. **Description:** A financial institution providing its members with personal financial management services. **Positions advertised include:** Teller. **Office hours:** Monday – Thursday, 9:00 a.m. to 5:00 a.m. Friday, 9:00 a.m. to 5:30. **Corporate headquarters location:** This location. **Other area locations:** Huntsville; Madison, Decatur, Hartselle, Moulton, Tuscaloosa, Birmingham, Mobile.

HARBERT MANAGEMENT CORPORATION

One Riverchase Parkway South, Birmingham AL 35244. 205/987-5500. **Contact:** Cathy Sinclair, Human Resources. **World Wide Web address:** http://www.harbert.net. **Description:** Provides financial management services. **Corporate headquarters location:** This location. **Other U.S. locations:** New York NY; Richmond VA; Nashville TN. **International locations:** London UK.

Alaska

ALASKA USA TRUST COMPANY

P/O Box 196613, Anchorage AK 99519-6613. 907/562-6544. **Toll-free phone:** 888/628-4567. **Fax:** 907/786-2546. **Physical address:** 4000 Credit Union Drive, Suite 600, Anchorage AK 99503. **Contact:** Human Resources. **E-mail address:** employment@alaskausa.org. **World Wide Web address:** http://www.alaskausatrust.com. **Description:** Provides a wide range of financial services. **NOTE:** Employment application available online. **Positions advertised include:** Trust Assistant.

Arizona

AIG FINANCIAL ADVISORS

2800 North Central Avenue, Suite 2100, Phoenix AZ 85004. 619/471-3700. **Contact:** Human Resources. **World Wide Web address:** http://www.aigfinancialadvisors.com. **Description:** A financial services company specializing in retirement planning. **Positions advertised include:** Advertising Compliance Analyst; Branch Office Examiner; Claim Investigator; Operations Specialist. **Corporate headquarters location:** This location. **Parent company:** American International Group, Inc.

AXA ADVISORS

14851 North Scottsdale Road, Suite 103, Scottsdale AZ 85254. 480/444-3734. **Contact:** Human Resources. **World Wide Web address:** http://www.axaonline.com. **Description:** A major life insurance company offering a variety of life insurance and annuity products and services through 8,200 career agents.

CHARLES SCHWAB & CO., INC.

2423 East Lincoln Drive, Phoenix AZ 85016. 800/435-4000. **Contact:** Human Resources. **World Wide Web address:** http://www.schwab.com. **Description:** With more than 325 offices and 7.1 million client accounts, provides a full range of securities brokerage, banking, money management and financial advisory services to individual investors and independent investment advisors. **NOTE:** Search and apply for positions online. **Positions advertised include:** Systems Administrator; Data Security Officer; Capacity Planner; Internal Applications Product Manager; Sr. Operations Specialist; Trading Analyst; Traffic Analyst. **Corporate headquarters location:** San Francisco CA. **Operations at this facility include:** This is a retail operations center.

CONSECO FINANCE

7360 South Kyrene Road, Suite 106, Tempe AZ 85283. 480/361-0034. **Contact:** Human Resources. **World Wide Web address:** http://www.conseco.com. **Description:** Aggregates and secures conventional manufactured home and home improvement loans and sells securities through public offerings and private placements.

FIRST INVESTORS CORPORATION

5125 North 16th Street, Suite B123, Phoenix AZ 85016. 602/841-2627. **Fax:** 602/841-2565. **Contact:** Personnel. **World Wide Web address:** http://www.firstinvestors.com. **Description:** Specializes in the distribution and management of investment programs for individuals and corporations including retirement plans. **Corporate headquarters location:** New York NY. **Operations at this facility include:** Sales; Service. **Number of employees at this location:** 20. **Number of employees nationwide:** 2,000.

KHIMETRICS

4343 North Scottsdale Road, Suite 345, Scottsdale AZ 85251. 480/609-2833. **Contact:** Judy Weiler, Human Resources Director. **E-mail address:** hr@khimetrics.com. **World Wide Web address:** http://www.khimetrics.com. **Description:** Provides revenue management services to retailers. **Positions advertised include:** Sr. Consultant; Account Manger; Product Consultant; Business Consultant; Technical Consultant. **President/CEO:** Brent W. Lippman.

MERRILL LYNCH
2555 East Camelback Road, Suite 900, Phoenix AZ 85016. 602/954-5000. **Fax:** 602/954-5089. **Contact:** Personnel. **World Wide Web address:** http://www.ml.com. **Description:** A diversified financial service organization. Merrill Lynch is a major broker in securities, option contracts, commodities and financial futures contracts, and insurance. The company also deals with corporate and municipal securities and investment banking. **Positions advertised include:** Finance Manager; Senior Underwriter. **Corporate headquarters location:** New York NY.

MORGAN STANLEY
8601 North Scottsdale Road, Suite 335, Scottsdale AZ 85253. 480/624-5700. **Contact:** Human Resources. **World Wide Web address:** http://www.morganstanley.com. **Description:** Offers diversified financial services including equities, fixed income securities, commodities, money market instruments, and investment banking services. **Positions advertised include:** Financial Advisor Trainee; Sales Assistant. **Corporate headquarters location:** New York NY. **Operations at this facility include:** Sales. **Number of employees at this location:** 85. **Number of employees nationwide:** 5,000.

PRUDENTIAL RELOCATION
16260 North Scottsdale Road, Scottsdale AZ 85254. 800/210-0299 **Contact:** Human Resources. **World Wide Web address:** http://www.prudential.com. **Description:** A full-service global mobility management firm supporting recruitment, retention, and relocation of personnel. **Positions advertised include:** Accounting Associate; International Operations Compensation Analyst; Relocation Associate; System Analysis and Development Associate; Team Lead, Database. **Corporate headquarters location:** New York NY. **Parent company:** Prudential Financial.

RBC DAIN RAUSCHER
16150 North Arrowhead Fountains Center Drive, Suite 300, Peoria AZ 85382. 623/334-9033. **Fax:** 623/334-2633. **Contact:** Personnel. **World Wide Web address:** http://www.rbcdain.com. **Description:** Offers investment banking and brokerage services including mutual funds, money market funds, options, commodities, tax shelters, financial futures, municipal bonds, life insurance deferred annuities, and IRA and Keogh plans. Founded in 1909. **Corporate headquarters location:** Minneapolis MN. **Other area locations:** Phoenix AZ; Scottsdale AZ; Tucson AZ. **Parent company:** Royal Bank of Canada.

SMITH BARNEY
6710 North Scottsdale Road, Suite 250, Scottsdale AZ 85253. 480/368-6500. **Contact:** Human Resources. **World Wide Web address:** http://www.smithbarney.com. **Description:** An international investment banking firm. Smith Barney offers a wide range of financial services through more than 100 locations worldwide. **Corporate headquarters location:** New York NY. **Parent company:** Citigroup, Inc. **Listed on:** New York Stock Exchange. **Stock exchange symbol:** C.

UBS FINANCIAL SERVICES INC.
2555 East Camelback Road, Suite 600, Phoenix AZ 85016. 602/957-5100. **Contact:** James Van Steenhuyse, Division Vice President & Branch Manager. **World Wide Web address:** http://www.ubspainewebber.com. **Description:** A full-service securities firm with over 300 offices nationwide. Services include investment banking, asset management, merger and acquisition consulting, municipal securities underwriting, estate planning, retirement programs, and transaction management. UBS PaineWebber offers its services to corporations, governments, institutions, and individuals. **Corporate headquarters location:** New York NY. **Other U.S. locations:** Nationwide. **Number of employees nationwide:** 26,000.

Arkansas

STEPHENS, INC.
P.O. Box 3507, Little Rock AR 72203-3507. 501/377-2000. **Physical address:** 111 Center Street, Little Rock AR 72201. **Toll-free phone:** 800/643-9691. **Fax:** 501/377-2111. **Contact:** Ellen Gray, Human Resources. **E-mail address:** hr@stephens.com. **World Wide Web address:** http://www.stephens.com. **Description:** An investment banking firm. Founded in 1933. **Positions advertised include:** Financial Consultants. **Corporate headquarters location:** This location. **Operations at this facility include:** Administration; Research and Development; Sales. **Listed on:** NYSE. **Stock exchange symbol:** SIPC.

California

AIG SUNAMERICA INC.
One SunAmerica Center, Los Angeles CA 90067-6022. 310/772-6000. **Contact:** Human Resources. **World Wide Web address:** http://www.aigsunamerica.com. **Description:** SunAmerica Inc. is a large financial services company specializing in long-term, tax-deferred, investment-oriented savings products. **NOTE:** Search and apply for positions online. **Corporate headquarters location:** This location. **Operations at this facility include:** Administration; Divisional Headquarters; Service. **Number of employees at this location:** 450. **Number of employees nationwide:** 1,000.

AAMES FINANCIAL CORPORATION
350 South Grand Avenue, 43rd Floor, Los Angeles CA 90071. 323/210-5000. **Fax:** 323/210-4535. **Contact:** Human Resources. **World Wide Web address:** http://www.aamesfinancial.com. **Description:** Offers mortgage loans to homeowners. Aames Financial Corporation also functions as an insurance agent and mortgage trustee through some of its subsidiaries. Services include originating (brokering and funding), purchasing, selling, and servicing first and junior trust deed loans primarily for single-family residences in the western United States. **Positions advertised include:** Business Systems Analyst; Collections Officer. **Corporate headquarters location:** This location. **Other U.S. locations:** Nationwide.

ACS EDUCATION SERVICES
One World Trade Center, Suite 2200, Long Beach CA 90831-2200. 310/513-2700. **Contact:** Human Resources. **World Wide Web address:** http://www.acs-education.com. **Description:** Administers, bills, and processes student loans acquired by individuals attending higher education institutions. **Corporate headquarters:** Dallas TX. **Other area locations:** Statewide. **Other U.S. locations:** Nationwide. **Parent company:** ACS Inc. **Listed on:** New York Stock Exchange. **Stock exchange symbol:** ACS.

AMERICAN EXPRESS COMPANY
455 Market Street, San Francisco CA 94105. 415/536-2600. **Toll-free phone:** 800/554-AMEX. **Contact:** Human Resources Department. **World Wide Web address:** http://www.americanexpress.com. **Description:** A diversified travel and financial services company operating in 160 countries around the world. American Express Travel Related Services offers charge cards as well as American Express Traveler's Cheques and travel services including trip planning, reservations, ticketing, and management information. American Express Financial Advisors offers financial planning, annuities, mutual funds, insurance, investment certificates, institutional investment advisory trust services, tax preparation, and retail securities brokerage services. Founded in 1850. **Positions advertised include:** Tax Accountant; Financial Advisor. **Corporate headquarters location:** New York NY. **Other U.S. locations:** Nationwide. **International locations:** Worldwide. **Listed on:** New York Stock Exchange. **Stock exchange symbol:** AXP. **Annual sales/revenues:** $25.9 billion. **Number of employees worldwide:** 78,200.

AMERICAN GENERAL FINANCE
400 South Citrus Avenue, Covina CA 91723-2989. 626/966-0501. **Fax:** 626/332-5021. **Contact:** Branch Manager. **World Wide Web address:** http://www.agfinance.com. **Description:** American General Finance offers wholesale and retail financing to business and industry, as well as direct consumer loans to individuals through 1,400 offices in 44 states. **Positions advertised include:** Management Trainee; Customer Account Administrator; Customer Account Specialist. **Corporate headquarters location:** Evansville. IN. **Other U.S. locations:** Nationwide. **Operations at this facility include:** Sales; Service.

BARCLAYS GLOBAL INVESTORS
45 Fremont Street, San Francisco CA 94105. 415/597-2000. **Fax:** 415/597-2492. **Contact:** Human Resources Staffing. **E-mail address:** staffing@barclaysglobal.com. **World Wide Web address:** http://www.barclaysglobal.com. **Description:** An investment banking company. **Positions advertised include:** Systems Developer; Research Analyst; Research Officer; Derivatives Trading Analyst; Business Analyst; Solutions Strategist; Portfolio Analyst; Portfolio Manager; Currency Trader; Investment Process Supervisor. **Corporate headquarters locations:** This location. **Other U.S. locations:** Chicago IL; Boston MA. **International locations:** China; India; Indonesia; Korea; Malaysia; Mexico; New Zealand; Philippines; Taiwan; Thailand. **Parent company:** Barclays (London).

BEAR, STEARNS & COMPANY, INC.
1999 Avenue of the Stars, 32nd Floor, Los Angeles CA 90067-6100. 310/201-2600. **Toll-free phone:** 800/777-1234. **Fax:** 310/201-2755. **Contact:** Human Resources. **E-mail address:** hresources_internet@bear.com. **World Wide Web address:** http://www.bearstearns.com. **Description:** Bear, Stearns & Company, Inc. is a leading worldwide investment banking, securities trading, and brokerage firm. The firm's business includes corporate finance, mergers and acquisitions, public finance, institutional equities, fixed-income sales and trading, private client services, foreign exchange, future sales and trading, derivatives, and asset management. **Internship information:** The company offers internships year-round. Applicants should mail or fax a resume to the Personnel Department. **Corporate headquarters location:** New York NY. **Other U.S. locations:** Nationwide. **International locations:** Worldwide. **Parent company:** The Bear Stearns Companies Inc. other subsidiaries include Bear, Stearns Securities Corporation, providing professional and correspondent clearing services including securities lending, and Custodial Trust Company, providing master trust, custody, and government securities services. **Listed on:** New York Stock Exchange. **Stock exchange symbol:** BSC. **Annual sales/revenues:** $789 million. **Number of employees nationwide:** 7,800.

CALIFORNIA FIRST LEASING CORPORATION (CALFIRST LEASING)
18201 Von Karmen Avenue, Suite 800, Irvine CA 92612. 714/751-7551. **Toll-free phone:** 800/496-4640. **Fax:** 949/255-0501. **Contact:** Human Resources Department. **E-mail address:** recruiter@cfnbc.com. **World Wide Web address:** http://www.calfirstbancorp.com. **Description:** A lessor of capital assets including high-technology equipment and systems. Founded in 1977. **Positions advertised include:** Account Executive; Account Representative. **Corporate headquarters location:** This location. **Parent company:** California First National Bancorp. **Listed on:** NASDAQ. **Stock exchange symbol:** CFNB.

CALIFORNIA FRINGE BENEFIT
2185 North California Boulevard, Suite 590, Walnut Creek CA 94596. 925/817-1628. **Fax:** 925/817-1698. **Contact:** Director of Recruiting. **E-mail address:** info@cfbretirement.com. **World Wide Web address:** http://www.cfbretirement.com. **Description:** Markets financial services and products to high-net-worth individuals and business owners. **Corporate headquarters location:** Bloomfield CT. **Parent company:** Lincoln Financial Group. **Operations at this facility include:** Administration; Sales; Service. **Listed on:** New York Stock Exchange. **Number of employees at this location:** 55.

THE CAPITAL GROUP COMPANIES AMERICAN FUNDS DISTRIBUTORS
333 South Hope Street, 53rd Floor, Los Angeles CA 90071-1406. 310/996-6000. **Contact:** Recruiting Department. **World Wide Web address:** http://www.capgroup.com. **Description:** An investment management company with 15 mutual funds and 10 companies. American Funds Distributors (http://www.americanfunds.com) is also at this location. The company provides financial advisement services including 28 mutual funds, variable annuities, and retirement planning. **Positions advertised include:** Research Associate; Economist; Investment Group Assistant; Project Manager; Portfolio Control Assistant; Programmer Analyst; Java Technologist; Web Copy Editor. **Corporate headquarters location:** This location. **Other area locations:** Brea CA; San Francisco CA. **Other U.S. locations:** Washington DC; Atlanta GA; Chicago IL; Indianapolis IN; New York NY; Reno NV; San Antonio TX. **International locations:** Canada; England; Hong Kong; Japan; Singapore.

CHARLES SCHWAB & CO., INC.
101 Montgomery Street, San Francisco CA 94104. 415/627-7000. **Fax:** 415/636-8018. **Recorded jobline:** 415/636-2077. **Contact:** Human Resources. **World Wide Web address:** http://www.schwab.com. **Description:** One of the largest discount brokerage companies in the United States. The firm has more than 200 branches and over 2.5 million active customer accounts. **Positions advertised include:** Director, Credit Risk Management; Finance Manager; Business Strategy Project Specialist; Technology Consultant; Compliance Analyst. **Special programs:** Internships. **Corporate headquarters location:** This location. **Other U.S. locations:** Nationwide. **International locations:** Worldwide. **Parent company:** Charles Schwab Corporation. **Operations at this facility include:** Administration; Sales; Service. **Listed on:** New York Stock Exchange. **Stock exchange symbol:** SCH. **Number of employees at this location:** 2,200.

CITIBANK
135 Main Street, San Francisco CA 94105. 415/904-1100. **Contact:** Human Resources. **World Wide Web address:** http://www.citibank.com. **Description:** Provides investment and financial services to individuals, businesses, governments, and financial institutions through approximately 3,000 locations. **Corporate headquarters location:** New York NY. **Parent company:** Citigroup. **Listed on:** New York Stock Exchange. **Stock exchange symbol:** C. **Annual sales/revenues:** $45.8 billion.

COMMONWEALTH FINANCIAL CORPORATION
524 Escondido Avenue, Vista CA 92084. 760/519-7090. **Toll-free phone:** 888/686-7090. **Fax:** 760/945-4991. **Contact:** Human Resources. **E-mail address:** cjwiggins@verizon.net. **World Wide Web address:** http://www.cfchomeloan.com. **Description:** Provides a wide range of mortgages, home loans, and debt consolidation services. **Corporate headquarters location:** This location.

CONSUMER PORTFOLIO SERVICES, INC.
13655 Laguna Canyon Road, Irvine CA 92618. 949/753-6800. **Contact:** Human Resources. **E-mail address:** humanr@consumerportfolio.com. **World Wide Web address:** http://www.consumerportfolio.com. **Description:** Consumer Portfolio Services, Inc. and its subsidiaries purchase, sell, and service retail automobile installment sales contracts originated by dealers located primarily in California. The company purchases contracts to resell them to institutional investors either as bulk sales or in the form of securities backed by the contracts. **Positions advertised include:**

Underwriter; Collector; Credit Analyst; Customer Service Rep. **Corporate headquarters location:** This location. **Number of employees at this location:** 65. **Number of employees nationwide:** 692.

ELKINS PROPERTY MANAGEMENT
3130 Wilshire Boulevard, Second Floor, Santa Monica CA 90403. 310/862-1000. **Fax:** 310/862-1050. **Contact:** Monica Ponce. **E-mail address:** mponce@elkinsmanagement.com. **World Wide Web address:** http://www.elkinsmanagement.com. **Description:** Provides commercial and residential property management services for family trusts, financial institutions, investment groups and high net worth individuals. **Corporate headquarters location:** This location. **Other area locations:** San Francisco CA. **Number of employees at this location:** 50.

E*TRADE FINANCIAL CORPORATION
532 Market Street, San Francisco CA 94104. 415/445-0101. **Contact:** Human Resources. **E-mail address:** recruiting@etrade.com. **World Wide Web address:** http://www.etrade.com. **Description:** Operates a website that provides online investing services. **Special programs:** Internships. **Corporate headquarters location:** New York NY. **International locations:** Worldwide. **Listed on:** New York Stock Exchange. **Stock exchange symbol:** ET.

FIRST AMERICAN TITLE COMPANY OF LOS ANGELES
520 North Central Avenue, Glendale CA 91203. 818/242-5800. **Toll-free phone:** 800/328-2652. **Fax:** 818/242-0196. **Contact:** Terry Hampton, Human Resources Manager. **World Wide Web address:** http://www.fatcola.com. **Description:** Provides escrow and mortgage services for real estate transactions. **Corporate headquarters location:** This location. **Parent company:** The First American Financial Corporation. **Listed on:** New York Stock Exchange. **Stock exchange symbol:** FAF.

FIRST MORTGAGE CORPORATION
3230 Fallow Field Drive, Diamond Bar CA 91765. 909/595-1996. **Fax:** 909/598-1574. **Contact:** Tammy Russ, Vice President of Human Resources. **E-mail address:** rhogan@firstmortgage.com. **World Wide Web address:** http://www.firstmortgage.com. **Description:** Originates, purchases, sells, and services first deed of trust loans (mortgage loans) for the purchase or refinance of owner-occupied one- to four-family residences. Founded in 1975. **Positions advertised include:** Mortgage Loan Processor. **Corporate headquarters location:** This location. **Other U.S. locations:** NV; OR; WA.

FRANKLIN RESOURCES, INC.
dba FRANKLIN TEMPLETON INVSTMENTS
One Franklin Parkway, San Mateo CA 94403. 650/312-2000. **Toll-free phone:** 800/632-2350. **Fax:** 650/312-3655. **Contact:** Human Resources. **E-mail address:** careers@frk.com. **World Wide Web address:** http://www.franklin-templeton.com. **Description:** Provides mutual fund and money market services. **Positions advertised include:** Senior Financial Systems Analyst; IT Manager; Controller; software Asset Manager; Senior Business Analyst; Marketing Research Analyst. **Special programs:** Internships. **Corporate headquarters location:** This location. **Other area locations:** Rancho Cordova CA. **Other U.S. locations:** Fort Lauderdale FL; New York NY; St. Petersburg FL. **Listed on:** New York Stock Exchange. **Stock exchange symbol:** BEN.

GATX CORPORATION
Four Embarcadero Center, Suite 2200, San Francisco CA 94111. 415/955-3200. **Fax:** 415/955-3416. **Contact:** Human Resources. **E-mail address:** sfjobs@gatx.com. **World Wide Web address:** http://www.gatx.com. **Description:** GATX is a diversified, international financial services company providing asset-based financing for transportation and industrial equipment. The company arranges full payout financing leases, secured loans, operating leases, and other structured financing both as an investing principal and with institutional partners. **Positions advertised include:** Senior Internal Auditor. **Corporate headquarters location:** This location. **Listed on:** New York Stock Exchange. **Stock exchange symbol:** GMT. **Number of employees at this location:** 190.

GE COMMERCIAL FINANCE
4 Park Plaza, Irvine CA 92614-8560. 949/225-2000. **Contact:** Human Resources. **World Wide Web address:** http://www.gecommercialfinance.com. **Description:** GE Commercial Finance provides lending products, growth capital, revolving lines of credit, equipment leasing of every kind, cash flow programs, and asset financing for the healthcare, manufacturing, fleet management, communications, construction, energy, aviation, infrastructure and equipment industries. **Parent company:** General Electric.

GOLDEN GATE CAPITAL
One Embarcadero Center, 33rd Floor, San Francisco CA 94111. 415/627-4500. **Fax:** 415/627-4501. **Contact:** Human Resources. **World Wide Web address:** http://www.goldengatecap.com. **Description:** A private equity firm with over $2.6 billion in capital under management. **Corporate headquarters location:** This location.

HOUSEHOLD FINANCE CORPORATION
388 Market Street, Suite 850, San Francisco CA 94111. 415/362-4542. **Fax:** 415/362-4548. **Contact:** Branch Manager. **World Wide Web address:** http://www.hfc.com. **Description:** Offers real estate, home equity, and personal loans. **Corporate headquarters location:** Prospect Heights IL. **Parent company:** Household International. **Operations at this facility include:** Sales; Service. **Listed on:** New York Stock Exchange. **Stock exchange symbol:** HI. **Number of employees nationwide:** 5,000.

IMPAC COMPANIES
1401 Dove Street, Suite 100, Newport Beach CA 92660. 714/556-0122. **Toll-free phone:** 800/597-4101. **Fax:** 949/475-3969. **Contact:** Sheralee Urano, Vice President, Human Resources. **World Wide Web address:** http://www.impaccompanies.com. **Description:** Provides mortgage banking services. **Corporate headquarters location:** This location. **Listed on:** American Stock Exchange. **Stock exchange symbol:** IMH.

ITEX CORPORATION
DIRECT BUSINESS EXCHANGE OF CALIFORNIA, INC.
3400 Cottage Way, Sacramento CA 95825. 916/679-1111. **Contact:** Human Resources. **World Wide Web address:** http://www.itex.com. **Description:** ITEX Corporation operates one of the nation's largest barter exchanges with over 130 franchises nationwide. ITEX operates an internationally accessible electronic trading and communications system known as BarterWire, which allows ITEX members coast-to-coast to market and purchase goods and services. The company publishes *alt.finance*, which focuses on the barter industry. All goods and services advertised within its pages are sold for ITEX trade dollars. The company also has the ITEX Express Card, the first debit/credit card in the barter industry. **Corporate headquarters location:** Bellevue WA. **Other area locations:** Statewide. **Other U.S. locations:** Nationwide.

JEFFERIES & COMPANY, INC.
11100 Santa Monica Boulevard, 11th Floor, Los Angeles CA 90025. 310/445-1199. **Fax:** 310/914-1270. **Contact:** Human Resources. **E-mail address:** westcoastrecruiting@jefco.com. **World Wide Web address:** http://www.jefco.com. **Description:** Jefferies & Company is engaged in equity, convertible debt and taxable fixed income securities brokerage and trading, and corporate finance. Jefferies & Company is one of the leading national firms engaged in the distribution and trading of blocks of equity securities primarily in the third market. Founded in 1962. **NOTE:** For opportunities in IT, HR, Marketing, and Finance,

contact Mel Locke, Director of People Services. E-mail: mlocke@jefco.com. Fax: 310/914-1066. **Corporate headquarters location:** This location. **Parent company:** Jefferies Group, Inc. is a holding company that, through Investment Technology Group, Inc., Jeffries & Company, Inc., Jefferies International Limited, and Jefferies Pacific Limited, is engaged in securities brokerage and trading, corporate finance, and other financial services. **Listed on:** New York Stock Exchange. **Stock exchange symbol:** JEF.

MERRILL LYNCH
101 California Street, Suite 1400, San Francisco CA 94111. 415/274-7000. **Fax:** 415/986-3196. **Contact:** Human Resources. **World Wide Web address:** http://www.ml.com. **Description:** Merrill Lynch provides financial services in the following areas: securities, extensive insurance, and real estate. One of the largest securities brokerage firms in the United States, the company also brokers commodity futures and options and corporate and municipal securities and is engaged in investment banking activities. The company operates three offices in San Francisco. **Positions advertised include:** Business Retirement Manager; Client Service Officer; Commercial Banking Professional. **Corporate headquarters location:** New York NY. **Operations at this facility include:** Sales. **Listed on:** New York Stock Exchange. **Stock exchange symbol:** MITT.

MORGAN STANLEY
101 California Street, 3rd Floor, San Francisco CA 94111. 415/693-6000. **Contact:** Human Resources. **World Wide Web address:** http://www.morganstanley.com. **Description:** Offers diversified financial services including equities, fixed income securities, commodities, money market instruments, and investment banking services. **NOTE:** Positions within the firm are organized by four main divisions: Institutional Securities, the Individual Investor Group, Investment Management, and Discover Financial Services. Search and apply for positions online. **Corporate headquarters location:** New York NY. **Operations at this facility include:** This location is an individual/retail branch office. **Listed on:** New York Stock Exchange. **Stock exchange symbol:** MWD.

PACIFIC LIFE INSURANCE
P.O. Box 9000, Newport Beach CA 92658-9030. 949/640-3011. **Physical address:** 700 Newport Center Drive, Newport Beach CA 92660. **Fax:** 949/640-7614. **Contact:** Human Resources. **E-mail address:** plemploy@pacificlife.com. **World Wide Web address:** http://www.pacificlife.com. **Description:** Provides insurance services including group health, life, and pensions. Pacific Life Insurance also provides financial services including annuities, mutual funds, and investments. **Positions advertised include:** Accounting Manager; Reporting Representative; Business Systems Analyst; Business Service Specialist; Executive Administrative Specialist; Senior Database Administrator; Software Engineer; Securities Accounting Analyst; Benefits Plan Analyst; Contracting Specialist; Actuarial Intern; Marketing Intern; Risk Management Intern. **Special programs:** Internships. **Corporate headquarters location:** This location.

PROMINENT USA
777 South Figueroa Street, Suite 4500, Los Angeles CA 90017. 213/623-4001. **Contact:** Human Resources. **Description:** An international, multibusiness trading and investment company. Prominent USA specializes in developing and sponsoring profitable opportunities in international and domestic commerce, industry, and finance, either as a principal or as an agent. **Corporate headquarters location:** New York NY.

PROVIDIAN FINANCIAL
201 Mission Street, San Francisco CA 94105. 415/543-0404. **Contact:** Human Resources. **World Wide Web address:** http://www.providian.com. **Description:** Provides lending, deposit, bankcard issuing, and other related financial services. **NOTE:** Search and apply for positions online. **Positions advertised include:** Accountant; Accounting Manager; Credit Analyst; Project Manager; Marketing Director; Marketing Analyst; Human Resources Compliance Officer; Online Product Manager. **Corporate headquarters location:** This location. **Listed on:** New York Stock Exchange. **Stock exchange symbol:** PVN.

PRUDENTIAL FINANCIAL
1731 Technology Drive, Suite 600, San Jose CA 95110-1017. 408/452-1300. **Contact:** Personnel. **World Wide Web address:** http://www.prudential.com. **Description:** An international securities brokerage and investment firm. The company offers clients investment products including stocks, options, bonds, commodities, tax-favored investments, and insurance, as well as several specialized financial services. **Corporate headquarters location:** New York NY. **Listed on:** New York Stock Exchange. **Stock exchange symbol:** PRU.

RBC DAIN RAUCHER
345 California Street, Suite 2900, San Francisco CA 94104. 415/445-8500. **Fax:** 415/391-9586. **Contact:** Tony Schultz, Manager of Human Resources. **World Wide Web address:** http://www.rbcdain.com. **Description:** A full-service, regional investment brokerage firm. Founded in 1858. **Positions advertised include:** Regional Administrative Assistant; Research Associate; Financial Consultant. **Special programs:** Financial Consultant Program. **Corporate headquarters location:** Minneapolis MN. **Parent company:** Royal Bank of Canada. **Operations at this facility include:** Administration; Research and Development; Sales; Service. **Listed on:** New York Stock Exchange. **Stock exchange symbol:** RY. **Number of employees nationwide:** 5,000.

TRANSAMERICA CORPORATION
1150 South Olive Street, Los Angeles CA 90015. 213/742-4141. **Contact:** Human Resources. **World Wide Web address:** http://www.transamerica.com. **Description:** Operates diversified financial services and insurance companies. **Corporate headquarters location:** This location. **Parent company:** AEGON N.V. (The Netherlands). **Operations at this facility include:** Administration. **Listed on:** New York Stock Exchange. **Stock exchange symbol:** TFD.

UBS FINANCIAL SERVICES, INC.
555 California Street, Suite 3200, San Francisco CA 94104-1501. 415/398-6400. **Contact:** Mr. Shawn Macfarlan, Branch Manager. **World Wide Web address:** http://financialservices.ubs.com. **Description:** A full-service securities firm with over 300 offices nationwide. Services include investment banking, asset management, merger and acquisition consulting, municipal securities underwriting, estate planning, retirement programs, and transaction management. UBS offers its services to corporations, governments, institutions, and individuals. **Corporate headquarters location:** New York NY. **Other U.S. locations:** Nationwide.

VISA U.S.A. INC.
P.O. Box 8999. San Francisco CA 94128-8999. 415/693-0330. **Contact:** Human Resources. **World Wide Web address:** http://www.usa.visa.com. **Description:** One of the largest credit card companies in the world. Founded in 1976. **NOTE:** See website for job listings and apply online. **Other U.S. locations:** Nationwide. **International locations:** Worldwide. **Listed on:** Privately held. **Number of employees worldwide:** 6,000.

WFS FINANCIAL
15750 Alton Parkway, Irvine CA 92618. 949/727-1000. **Contact:** Human Resources. **E-mail address:** employment@wfsfinancial.com. **World Wide Web address:** http://www.wfb.com. **Description:** A financial services holding company that operates throughout the West Coast. **Positions advertised include:** Special Activities Associate; Compensation

Coordinator; IRA Specialist; Senior Product Development Manager. **Corporate headquarters location:** This location. **Parent company:** Wachovia. **Listed on:** NASDAQ. **Stock exchange symbol:** WFSI. **Number of employees at this location:** 350. **Number of employees nationwide:** 1,200.

WASHINGTON MUTUAL
3701 Wilshire Boulevard, Los Angeles CA 90010-2810. 213/252-4320. **Contact:** Human Resources. **World Wide Web address:** http://www.wamuhomeloans.com. **Description:** Originates, acquires, sells, and services mortgage loans, principally first lien mortgage loans secured by single-family residences. North American Mortgage also sells servicing rights associated with a portion of such loans. The company operates through a network of 50 loan origination offices in 14 states, primarily in California and Texas. **Parent company:** Washington Mutual Bank. **Listed on:** New York Stock Exchange. **Stock exchange symbol:** WM.

WAUSAU MORTGAGE CORPORATION
3600 Sisk Road, Suite 4A, Modesto CA 95356-0532. 209/545-7738. **Contact:** Human Resources. **World Wide Web address:** http://www.wausau.com. **Description:** Sells casualty, property, and other commercial insurance products to medium- and large-sized companies. **Corporate headquarters location:** Wausau WI.

WEDBUSH MORGAN SECURITIES
P.O. Box 30014, Los Angeles CA 90030. 213/688-8000. **Physical address:** 1000 Wilshire Boulevard, 9th Floor, Los Angeles CA 90017. **Contact:** Human Resources Department. **E-mail address:** hrd@wedbush.com. **World Wide Web address:** http://www.wedbush.com. **Description:** An investment banking securities brokerage. **NOTE:** Search and apply for positions online. **Positions advertised include:** Equity Research Analyst; Senior Associate, Financial Services; Director of Research; Institutional Equity Sales. **Special programs:** Internships. **Corporate headquarters location:** This location. **Listed on:** Privately held. **Number of employees at this location:** 270. **Number of employees nationwide:** 510.

WELLS FARGO FOOTHILL
2450 Colorado Avenue, Suite 300W, Santa Monica CA 90404. 310/453-7300. **Toll-free phone:** 800/535-1811. **Contact:** Human Resources. **World Wide Web address:** http://www.wffoothill.com. **Description:** One of the largest publicly owned commercial lenders in the nation. The company operates two businesses: commercial lending and money management. **NOTE:** Search and apply for positions online. **Positions advertised include:** Loan Portfolio Manager; Financial Analyst; Treasury Analyst; Communications Administrative Coordinator; Loan Closer; Senior Account Executive. **Corporate headquarters location:** This location. **Parent company:** Wells Fargo & Company.

Colorado

AMERICAN CENTURY INVESTMENTS
8300 Fairmount Drive, Denver CO 80247. 303/329-0230. **Contact:** Human Resources Manager. **World Wide Web address:** http://www.americancentury.com. **Description:** Provides mutual fund investment services. Founded in 1958. **Corporate headquarters location:** Kansas City MO. **Listed on:** Privately held. **Number of employees at this location:** 350. **Number of employees nationwide:** 2,000. **Number of employees worldwide:** 2,100.

COLUMBIA MANAGEMENT ADVISORS, LLC
12100 East Iliff Avenue, Suite 300, Aurora CO 80014. 303/337-6555. **Fax:** 303/743-6341. **Contact:** Personnel. **World Wide Web address:** http://www.columbiafunds.com. **Description:** Provides investment products. **Special programs:** Training. **Office hours:** Monday - Friday, 6:00 a.m. - 6:00 p.m. **Corporate headquarters location:** Boston MA. **Parent company:** Banc of America Capital Management, LLC.

COUNTRYWIDE FUNDING CORPORATION
8433 Church Ranch Boulevard, Suite 300, Broomfield CO 80021. 303/410-9100. **Fax:** 303/410-9900. **World Wide Web address:** http://www.countrywide.com. **Contact:** Human Resources. **Description:** Originates, purchases, sells, and services mortgage loans. The company's mortgage loans are principally first-lien mortgage loans secured by single-family residences. **Other U.S. locations:** Nationwide. **Parent company:** Countrywide Credit Industries. **Listed on:** New York Stock Exchange. **Stock exchange symbol:** CCR.

FOUNDERS ASSET MANAGEMENT, LLC
201 University Boulevard, Suite 800, Denver CO 80206. 303/394-4404. **Fax:** 303/394-7840. **Contact:** Human Resources. **E-mail address:** employment@founders.com. **World Wide Web address:** http://www.founders.com. **Description:** Offers mutual funds including small-stock, international funds and conservative bond funds. The company services approximately 125,000 account holders worldwide and manages assets of approximately $2 billion. Founded in 1938. **Corporate headquarters location:** This location. **Parent company:** Mellon Financial Company.

JANUS CAPITAL GROUP
100 Fillmore Street, Denver CO 80206. 303/333-3863. **Contact:** Recruiting Manager. **World Wide Web address:** http://www.janus.com. **Description:** Manages mutual funds and offers a wide variety of account options and investment services. **Positions advertised include:** Solution Services Specialist; External Wholesaler; Director, Investment Writing; Institutional Marketing Manager; Sr. Audit Manager; Product Manager. **Corporate headquarters location:** This location. **Listed on:** Privately held. **Number of employees at this location:** 700.

SMITH BARNEY
370 17th Street, Suite 2800, Denver CO 80202-1370. 303/572-4025. **Contact:** Human Resources. **World Wide Web address:** http://www.smithbarney.com. **Description:** An investment banking and securities broker. Smith Barney also provides related financial services. **Parent company:** Citigroup, Inc. **Listed on:** New York Stock Exchange. **Stock exchange symbol:** C.

STIFEL NICOLAUS
1125 17th Street, Suite 1500, Denver CO 80202-2032. 303/534-1180. **Contact:** Human Resources. **World Wide Web address:** http://www.stifel.com. **Description:** A securities brokerage firm. **Corporate headquarters location:** St. Louis MO.

UBS FINANCIAL SERVICES INC.
370 17th Street, Suite 4100, Denver CO 80202. 303/436-9000. **Contact:** Human Resources Department. **World Wide Web address:** http://www.financialservicesinc.ubs.com. **Description:** A full-service securities firm with over 300 offices nationwide. Services include investment banking, asset management, merger and acquisition consulting, municipal securities underwriting, estate planning, retirement programs, and transaction management. Clients include corporations, governments, institutions, and individuals. Founded in 1879. **Corporate headquarters location:** New York NY. **Other U.S. locations:** Nationwide. **Annual sales/revenues:** More than $100 million.

WELLS FARGO BUSINESS CREDIT
1700 Lincoln Street, Suite 21, Denver CO 80203. 303/864-6593. **Contact:** Human Resources. **World Wide Web address:** http://www.wellsfargo.com. **Description:** A diversified financial institution with over $234 billion in assets. Wells Fargo serves over 17 million customers through 5,300 independent locations worldwide. The company also maintains several stand-alone ATMs and branches within retail outlets. Services include community banking, credit and debit cards, home equity and mortgage loans, online banking, student loans, and insurance. Wells Fargo also offers a

complete line of commercial and institutional financial services. Founded in 1852. **Positions advertised include:** Sr. Business Relationship Manager; Lending Manager; Business Associate. **Corporate headquarters location:** San Francisco CA. **Other U.S. locations:** Nationwide. **International locations:** Worldwide. **Operations at this facility include:** Regional Headquarters; Sales; Service. **Parent company:** Wells Fargo & Company. **Listed on:** New York Stock Exchange. **Stock exchange symbol:** WFC. **Annual sales/revenues:** More than $100 million. **Number of employees worldwide:** 104,000.

Connecticut

THE ADVEST GROUP, INC.
90 State House Square, Hartford CT 06103. 860/509-1000. **Fax:** 860/509-3849. **Contact:** Ralph J. Presutti, Human Resources. **World Wide Web address:** http://www.advest.com. **Description:** Provides diversified financial services including securities brokerage, trading, investment banking, commercial and consumer lending, and asset management. **Positions advertised include:** Compensation Consultant; Due Diligence Analyst; Internal Auditor; Margin Specialist; Mutual Fund Operations Consultant. **Corporate headquarters location:** This location. **Other U.S. locations:** Nationwide. **Number of employees nationwide:** 1,525.

AG EDWARDS & SONS
2960 Post Road, Southport CT 06890. 203/255-6881. **Contact:** Human Resources. **World Wide Web address:** http://www.agedwards.com. **Description:** An investment firm offering bonds, money market accounts, mutual funds, IRAs, annuities, estate planning, and related services. **Corporate headquarters location:** St. Louis MO. **Other U.S. locations:** Nationwide. **Listed on:** New York Stock Exchange. **Stock exchange symbol:** AGE. **CEO:** Robert L. Bagby. **Number of employees nationwide:** 15,400.

AMERICAN PAYMENT SYSTEMS
15 Sterling Drive, P.O. Box 504415, Wallingford CT 06492. 203/679-4400. **Toll-free phone:** 800/309-7668. **Contact:** Human Resources. **E-mail address:** jobs@apsnet.com. **World Wide Web address:** http://www.apsnet.com. **Description:** Specializes in walk-in bill payments. Processes payments in person for various billers. Founded in 1990. **Positions advertised include:** Marketing Project Manager. **Corporate headquarters location:** This location.

GE CAPITAL CORPORATION
260 Long Ridge Road, Stamford CT 06927. 203/357-4000. **Contact:** Human Resources. **World Wide Web address:** http://www.gecapital.com. **Description:** GE Capital Corporation is one of the largest leasing companies in the United States and Canada, providing financing and related management services to corporate clients through 27 divisions. **NOTE:** Fill out online application at www.gecareers.com. **Corporate headquarters location:** This location. **Parent company:** General Electric Company.

JEFFERIES & COMPANY, INC.
Metro Center, One Station Place, 3 North, Stamford CT 06902. 203/708-5800. **Contact:** Human Resources. **E-mail address:** Eastcoastrecruiting@jefco.com. **World Wide Web address:** http://www.jefco.com. **Description:** Jefferies & Company is engaged in equity, convertible debt and taxable fixed income securities brokerage and trading, and corporate finance. Jefferies is one of the leading national firms engaged in the distribution and trading of blocks of equity securities and conducts such activities primarily in the third market, which refers to transactions in listed equity securities taking place away from national securities exchanges. Founded in 1962. **Corporate headquarters location:** New York NY. **Other U.S. locations:** Nationwide. **International locations:** Worldwide. **Listed on:** New York Stock Exchange. **Stock exchange symbol:** JEF. **Number of employees worldwide:** 1,600.

LOUIS DREYFUS CORPORATION
20 Westport Road, Wilton CT 06897. 203/761-2000. **Fax:** 203/761-8380. **Contact:** Human Resources. **World Wide Web address:** http://www.louisdreyfus.com. **Description:** A financial company involved in the worldwide trade of agricultural and energy-related commodities. **Special programs:** Internships. **Office hours:** Monday - Friday, 9:00 a.m. - 5:00 p.m. **Other U.S. locations:** Nationwide. **International locations:** Worldwide. **Number of employees nationwide:** 1,200. **Number of employees worldwide:** 7,000.

MERRILL LYNCH
City Place II, 185 Asylum Street, Hartford CT 06103. 860/728-3511. **Contact:** Human Resources. **World Wide Web address:** http://www.ml.com. **Description:** A diversified financial services organization. Merrill Lynch is a major broker in securities, option contracts, commodities and financial futures contracts, and insurance. The company also deals with corporate and municipal securities and investment banking. **NOTE:** Call this location for specific information on where to mail a resume. **Corporate headquarters location:** New York NY. **Other U.S. locations:** Nationwide.

MORGAN STANLEY DEAN WITTER & COMPANY
One Pickwick Plaza, Greenwich CT 06830. 203/625-4600. **Contact:** Human Resources. **World Wide Web address:** http://www.msdw.com. **Description:** One of the largest investment banking firms in the United States. Services include financing; financial advisory services; real estate services; corporate bond services; equity services; government and money market services; merger and acquisition services; investment research services; investment management services; and individual investor services. **Corporate headquarters location:** New York NY. **Other U.S. locations:** Nationwide.

PHIBRO INC.
500 Nyala Farms Road, Westport CT 06880. 203/221-5800. **Contact:** Human Resources. **World Wide Web address:** http://www.phibro.com. **Description:** A commodities trading group that deals with oil, gas, grain, wheat, and cocoa.

WARWICK GROUP, INC.
70 Main Street, 2nd Floor, New Canaan CT 06840. 203/966-7447. **Contact:** Human Resources. **World Wide Web address:** http://www.warwickgroup.com. **Description:** An investment bank.

Delaware

ACCESS GROUP
P.O. Box 7430, Wilmington DE 19803-0430. 302/477-4000. **Physical address:** 5500 Brandywine Parkway, Wilmington DE 19803. **Fax:** 302/477-4067. **Contact:** Human Resources. **E-mail address:** recruitingservices@accessgroup.org. **World Wide Web address:** http://www.accessgroup.org. **Description:** A loan broker whose programs, materials and services are designed for graduate/professional student borrowers. **NOTE:** See website for current job openings. Submit resume by mail or fax. **Positions advertised include:** Director - School Services & Sales; Internal Account Executive; Database Administrator; Business Analyst; Manager - Consumer Marketing; System Architect; Risk Management Analyst.

AMERIPRISE FINANCIAL
200 Bellevue Parkway, Suite 250, Wilmington DE 19809. 302/798-3199. **Contact:** Amy Levithan, Human Resources. **E-mail address:** amy.l.levithan@ampf.com. **World Wide Web address:** http://www.ameriprise.com. **Description:** A financial planning and services company that provides solutions for clients' asset accumulation, income management and insurance protection needs. **NOTE:** See website for current job openings and to apply online. **Corporate headquarters location:** Minneapolis MN. **Listed on:** New York Stock Exchange. **Stock exchange symbol:** AMP.

BANK OF AMERICA
655 Bay Road, Dover DE 19901. 302/741-1133. **World Wide Web address:** http://www.bankofamerica.com. **Description:** A large financial institution serving individual consumers, small and middle market businesses and large corporations with banking, investing, asset management and other financial and risk-management products and services. **NOTE:** Bank of America acquired MBNA (www.mbna.com). It is recommended to search both companies' job databases for a complete picture of career opportunities. Must apply for current job openings online. **Special programs:** Internships. **Corporate headquarter locations:** Charlotte NC. **Other area locations:** Greenville DE; Wilmington DE. **Other U.S. locations:** Nationwide. **Operations at this facility include:** Call center. **Listed on:** New York Stock Exchange. **Stock exchange symbol:** BAC.

CITIBANK DELAWARE
One Penn's Way, New Castle DE 19720. 302/421-2228. **Contact:** Human Resources. **World Wide Web address:** http://www.citigroup.com. **Description:** Citibank Delaware's primary businesses are Corporate Cash Management Operations and Customer Service. Other groups include: Global Loans, Implementation, Technology Services, Data Center and other support services. Other Citigroup operations in Delaware include Citicorp Trust Bank, fsb, Citicorp Credit Services, Inc. and CitiFinancial. **NOTE:** See website for all available positions and to apply online. **Other U.S. locations:** Nationwide. **Parent company:** Citigroup Inc.

HSBC NORTH AMERICA HOLDINGS INC.
1105 North Market Street, Suite 1, Wilmington DE 19801. 302/652-4673. **Toll-free number:** 800/975-4722. **Contact:** Human Resources. **World Wide Web address:** http://www.hsbcusa.com. **Description:** HSBC North America offers personal and commercial banking services, mortgage services, consumer finance, private banking, insurance and corporate investment banking under the HSBC, HFC and Beneficial brands to some 60 million customers. **NOTE:** See website for current job openings and to apply online. **Parent company:** HSBC Holdings.

J.P. MORGAN CHASE & COMPANY
500 Stanton Christiana Road, Newark DE 19713-2107. 302/634-1000. **Fax:** 302/634-4090. **Contact:** Human Resources. **World Wide Web address:** http://www.jpmorganchase.com. **Description:** Specializes in global financial services and retail banking. J.P. Morgan Chase and Company's services include asset management, card-member services, community development, commercial banking for middle market companies, diversified consumer lending, global markets, home finance, investment banking, private banking, private equity, regional consumer and small business banking, and treasury and securities services. **Positions advertised include:** Margin Analyst; Private Banking Income Specialist; Business Analyst; Program Coordinator; Portfolio Servicing Specialist. **Special programs:** Internships. **Number of employees at this location:** 1,000.

PFPC WORLDWIDE INC.
301 Bellevue Parkway, Wilmington DE 19809. 302/791-2000. **Contact:** Human Resources. **World Wide Web address:** http://www.pfpc.com. **Description:** PFPC provides fund administration services to the investment management industry. Services include fund accounting and record keeping, trust and custody, and mutual fund transfer agency services. It also performs administrative services related to hedge funds and other alternative investments. **Parent company:** PNC Financial Services Group.

District Of Columbia
FEDERAL NATIONAL MORTGAGE ASSOCIATION (FANNIE MAE)
3900 Wisconsin Avenue NW, Washington DC 20016. 202/752-7000. **Recorded jobline:** 202/752-JOBS. **Contact:** Human Resources. **World Wide Web address:** http://www.fanniemae.com. **Description:** A stockholder-owned corporation chartered by Congress for the purpose of helping to finance housing by supplementing the supply of mortgage funds. Fannie Mae purchases a variety of mortgage plans including adjustable rate mortgages, conventional fixed rate home mortgages, and second mortgages. The company also participates in pools of conventional first and second mortgages and guarantees conventional mortgage-based securities. **Positions advertised include:** Senior Developer; Credit Risk Manager; Senior Financial Engineer; Director, Finance; Senior Database Administrator; Senior Investor Relations Manager; Senior Technology Risk Specialist. **Special programs:** Internships. **Corporate headquarters location:** This location. **Other U.S. locations:** Atlanta GA; Chicago IL; Philadelphia PA; Dallas TX; Pasadena CA. **Operations at this facility include:** Administration; Divisional Headquarters; Regional Headquarters; Sales; Service. **Listed on:** New York Stock Exchange. **Stock exchange symbol:** FNM. **Number of employees at this location:** 3,800.

JOHNSTON, LEMON & COMPANY
1101 Vermont Avenue NW, Washington DC 20005. 202/842-5500. **Toll-free phone:** 800/424-5158. **Contact:** John Clardy, Sales Manager. **E-mail address:** john_clardy@johnstonlemon.com. **World Wide Web address:** http://www.johnstonlemon.com. **Description:** Underwrites, distributes, and deals in corporate and municipal securities, revenue bonds, and mutual funds, and provides business management services.

MERRILL LYNCH
1850 K Street NW, Suite 700, Washington DC 20006. 202/659-7333. **Contact:** Staff Supervisor: **World Wide Web address:** http://www.ml.com. **Description:** Provides financial services in the following areas: securities, extensive insurance, and real estate and related services. Merrill Lynch, which is one of the largest securities brokerage firms in the United States, also brokers commodity futures and options; corporate and municipal securities; and is engaged in investment banking activities. **Positions advertised include:** Client Associate. **Corporate headquarters location:** New York NY. **Operations at this facility include:** Sales. **Listed on:** New York Stock Exchange. **Stock exchange symbol:** MER.

Florida
EVERBANK OF FLORIDA
8100 Nations Way, Jacksonville FL 32256. 904/281-2400. **Fax:** 904/281-6165. **Contact:** Human Resources. **World Wide Web address:** http://www.everhomemortgage.com. **Description:** Engaged in the origination, purchase, sale, and servicing of residential first mortgages. Founded in 1962. **Positions advertised include:** Report & Business Analyst; Accounts Payable Supervisor; Customer Service Lead; Reconciliation Coordinator; Marketing Analyst; Loan Office Assistant; Closer; Sales Team Manager; Loss Mitigation Processor; Internet Processor; Telemarketer. **Corporate headquarters location:** This location. **Operations at this facility include:** Administration; Production; Service. **Listed on:** Privately held. **Number of employees at this location:** 250. **Number of employees nationwide:** 350

FISERV INC.
1250 Grumman Place, Suite A, Titusville FL 32780. 321/268-2622. **Contact:** Human Resources. **World Wide Web address:** http://www.fiserv.com. **Description:** Conducts online data processing for credit unions. **Positions advertised include:** Internet Network Architect. **Listed on:** NASDAQ. **Stock exchange symbol:** FISV.

FRANKLIN TEMPLETON INVESTMENTS
500 East Broward Boulevard, Suite 2100, Ft. Lauderdale FL 33394. 954/527-7500. **Contact:** Human Resources. **World Wide Web address:** http://www.franklintempleton.com. **Description:** A

global investment management company. **Positions advertised include:** Proposal Specialist; Research Librarian; Settlements Assistant; Trading Settlements Analyst; Performance Consultant Trainer; Mail Room Clerk; Investment Operations Manager; Financial Accounting Auditor; Administrative Assistant; Investment Operations Supervisor; Futures Program; Information Technology Manager. **Corporate headquarters location:** San Mateo CA.

RAYMOND JAMES AND ASSOCIATES
P.O. Box 12749, St. Petersburg FL 33733-2749. 727/573-3800. **Physical address:** 880 Carillon Parkway, St. Petersburg FL 33716. **Fax:** 727/573-8420. **Recorded jobline:** 727/573-8490. **Contact:** Human Resources. **E-mail address:** employment@hr.rjf.com. **World Wide Web address:** http://www.rjf.com. **Description:** An investment brokerage firm. Founded in 1962. **Positions advertised include:** Account Maintenance Associate; Acquisitions Analyst; Administrative Assistant; Agency Trader; Assessment Specialist. **Parent company:** Raymond James Financial, Inc. **Operations at this facility include:** Administration; Divisional Headquarters; Regional Headquarters; Research and Development; Sales; Service. **Listed on:** New York Stock Exchange. **Stock exchange symbol:** RJF.

EDWARD JONES
1736 Thomasville Road, Tallahassee FL 32303. 850/224-1736. **Contact:** Don McClelland. **World Wide Web address:** http://www.edwardjones.com. **Description:** An investment trading company. **Positions advertised include:** Investment Representative.

J.I. KISLAK MORTGAGE CORPORATION
7900 Miami Lakes Drive West, Miami Lakes FL 33016. 305/364-4116. **Contact:** Human Resources. **Description:** A mortgage banking and real estate firm. **Positions advertised include:** Production. **Office Hours:** Monday – Friday, 8:30 a.m. – 5:00 p.m. **Corporate headquarters location:** This location.

LBS CAPITAL MANAGEMENT, INC.
311 Park Place Boulevard, Suite 330, Clearwater FL 33759. 727/726-5656. **Toll-free phone:** 800/477-1296. **Fax:** 727/725-9173. **Contact:** Human Resources. **World Wide Web address:** http://www.lbs.com. **Description:** A financial consulting firm.

MARSHALL & ILSLEY TRUST COMPANY OF FLORIDA
800 Laurel Oak Drive, Suite 101, Naples FL 34108. 941/597-2933. **Contact:** William Wade, President. **World Wide Web address:** http://www.mitrust.com. **Description:** Provides trust and custodial services for corporate, institutional, and individual clients in the Southeast. **Parent company:** Marshall & Ilsley Corporation (Milwaukee WI) is a diversified, interstate bank holding company.

MERRILL LYNCH
50 P.O. Box 1918, Jacksonville FL 32201. 904/634-6000. **Physical address:** 50 North Laura Street, Suite 3700, Jacksonville FL 32202. **Contact:** Human Resources. **World Wide Web address:** http://www.ml.com. **Description:** A diversified financial service organization. Merrill Lynch is a major broker in securities, option contracts, commodities and financial futures contracts, and insurance. The company also deals with corporate and municipal securities and investment banking. **Positions advertised include:** Conversion Administrator; Commercial Banking Professional; Annuity Product Specialist; Controller; Correspondent Account Executive; Mortgage Underwriter; Regional Manager; Clearing Specialist; Financial Advisor. **NOTE:** Call for specific information on where to mail a resume. **Corporate headquarters location:** New York NY. **Listed on:** New York Stock Exchange. **Stock exchange symbol:** MER.

PRUDENTIAL SECURITIES, INC.
P.O. Box 45049, Jacksonville FL 32232-5049. 904/391-3400. **Physical address:** 701 San Marcos Boulevard, 19th Floor, Jacksonville FL 32207. **Contact:** Branch Manager. **World Wide Web address:** http://www.prufn.com. **Description:** An international securities brokerage and investment firm. The company offers clients more than 70 investment products including stocks, options, bonds, commodities, tax-favored investments, and insurance. Prudential Securities also offers specialized financial services. **Corporate headquarters location:** New York NY.

QUICK AND REILLY, INC.
420 Royal Palm Way, Palm Beach FL 33480. 561/655-8000. **Contact:** Human Resources. **World Wide Web address:** http://www.quick-reilly.com. **Description:** Quick and Reilly is a holding company that, through its subsidiaries, provides discount brokerage services primarily to retail customers throughout the United States. The company also clears securities transactions for its own customers and for other brokerage firms and banks and acts as a specialist on the floor of the New York Stock Exchange. **Number of employees nationwide:** 850.

SCOTT TRADE
1425 West Granada Boulevard, Ormond Beach FL 32174-5900. 386/671-9303. **Toll-free phone:** 877/602-1980. **Contact:** Human Resources. **E-mail address:** support@scottrade.com. **World Wide Web address:** http://www.scottrade.com. **Description:** A stock trading investment company allowing individuals to trade online. **Positions advertised include:** Customer Service; Office Assistant.

UBS FINANCIAL INC.
One Independent Drive, 2nd Floor, Jacksonville FL 32202. 904/354-6000. **Contact:** Human Resources. **World Wide Web address:** http://www.ubspainewebber.com. **Description:** A full-service securities firm with over 300 offices nationwide. Services include investment banking, asset management, merger and acquisition consulting, municipal securities underwriting, estate planning, retirement programs, and transaction management. UBS Financial offers its services to corporations, governments, institutions, and individuals. Founded in 1879. **Special programs:** Internships. **Corporate headquarters location:** New York NY. **Other U.S. locations:** Nationwide. **Operations at this facility include:** Sales; Service. **Listed on:** New York Stock Exchange. **Stock exchange symbol:** UBS. **Annual sales/revenues:** More than $100 million.

WACHOVIA
1000 Tyrone Boulevard, Saint Petersburg FL 33710. 727/892-7441. **Contact:** Human Resources. **World Wide Web address:** http://www.wachovia.com. **Description:** Wachovia Securities is one of the nation's largest bank holding companies with subsidiaries operating over 1,330 full-service bank branches in the south Atlantic states. These subsidiaries provide retail banking, retail investment, and commercial banking services. Wachovia Securities provides other financial services including mortgage banking, home equity lending, leasing, insurance, and securities brokerage services from more than 220 branch locations. The company also operates one of the nation's largest ATM networks. **Listed on:** New York Stock Exchange. **Stock exchange symbol:** WB. **Number of employees nationwide:** 32,000.

Georgia

APPLIED FINANCIAL GROUP
6065 Rosswell Road NE, Suite 215, Atlanta GA 30328. 770/992-0955. **Toll-free phone:** 800/298-9904. **Fax:** 770/594-9631. **World Wide Web address:** http://www.afg-online.com. **Description:** Provides financial planning and investment management services. **Corporate headquarters location:** This location.

BEAR, STEARNS & COMPANY, INC.
3424 Peachtree Road NE, Suite 1700, Atlanta GA 30326. 404/842-4000. **Fax:** 404/842-4523. **Toll-free phone:** 800/444-2327. **Contact:** Human Resources. **World Wide Web address:** http://www.bearstearns.com. **Description:** An investment banking, securities trading, and brokerage firm. Bear, Stearns & Company, Inc. serves corporations, governments, institutions, and private investors worldwide. **NOTE:** Not accepting hard copy resumes for the foreseeable future. Please visit website to search for employment opportunities. **Corporate headquarters location:** New York NY. **Other U.S. locations:** Boston MA; Chicago IL; Dallas TX; Denver CO; Los Angeles CA; San Francisco CA. **International locations:** Worldwide. **Listed on:** New York Stock Exchange. **Stock exchange symbol:** BSC. **Annual sales/revenues:** More than $100 million. **Number of employees nationwide:** 10,500.

CITIFINANCIAL
8420 Abercom Street, Savannah GA 31406. 912/927-4295. **Contact:** Human Resources. **E-mail address:** jobs@citifinancial.com. **World Wide Web address:** http://www.citifinancial.com. **Description:** CitiFinancial offers loans including: bill consolidation, home equity, home improvement, and student. Citifinancial has more than 21,000 offices in the United States and Canada. Founded in 1912. **NOTE:** Please visit website to register, search for jobs, and apply online. **Positions advertised include:** Customer Service Representative. **Parent company:** Citigroup. **Other area locations:** Statewide. **Other U.S locations:** Nationwide. **International locations:** Canada. **Listed on:** New York Stock Exchange. **Stock exchange symbol:** C. **Number of employees worldwide:** 13,000.

EQUIFAX, INC.
P.O. Box 4081, Atlanta GA 30302. 404/885-8000. **Physical address:** 1550 Peachtree Street NE, Atlanta GA 30309. **Contact:** Human Resources. **World Wide Web address:** http://www.equifax.com. **Description:** Provides a range of financial and information management services, enabling global commerce between buyers and sellers. Founded in 1899. **NOTE:** Please visit website to search for jobs and to apply online. **Positions advertised include:** Customer Service Consultant; Telephone Sales Representative; Vice President – Solution Shaping and Pricing; Director of Budget and Financial Analysis; Financial Analyst Senior; Director of Product Innovation; Director of Marketing; Systems Analyst; Associate Consultant; Senior Project Manager; Econometrician. **Corporate headquarters location:** This location. **Other U.S. locations:** Nationwide. **Operations at this facility include:** Administration. **Listed on:** New York Stock Exchange. **Stock exchange symbol:** EFX. **CEO:** Thomas F. Chapman. **Number of employees worldwide:** 4,800.

HOMEBANC MORTGAGE CORPORATION
2002 Summit Boulevard, Suite 100, Atlanta GA 30319. 404/303-4113. **Fax:** 404/303-4116. **Contact:** Human Resources. **E-mail address:** careers@homebanc.com. **World Wide Web address:** http://www.homebanc.com. **Description:** A full-service mortgage lender. **Office hours:** Monday – Friday, 8:00 a.m. – 5:00 p.m. **Corporate headquarters location:** This location. **Operations at this facility include:** Administration; Sales; Service. **CEO:** Patrick Flood.

JEFFERIES & COMPANY, INC.
3414 Peachtree Road NE, Suite 810, Atlanta GA 30326. 404/264-5000. **Contact:** Human Resources. **World Wide Web address:** http://www.jefco.com. **Description:** Engaged in equity, convertible debt and taxable fixed income securities brokerage and trading, and corporate finance. Founded in 1962. **NOTE:** Please visit website for more specific contact information. **Corporate headquarters location:** New York NY. **Other U.S. locations:** Nationwide. **International locations:** London England; Paris France; Zurich Switzerland; Tokyo Japan; Sydney Australia; Melbourne Australia. **Parent company:** Jefferies Group, Inc. **Listed on:** New York Stock Exchange. **Stock exchange symbol:** JEF. **Number of employees worldwide:** 1,400.

PEACHTREE PLANNING CORPORATION
5040 Roswell Road, Atlanta GA 30342. 404/260/1600. 231-0839. **Toll-free phone:** 800/366-0839. **Fax:** 404/260-1700. **Contact:** Sarah Brannon, Director of Manpower Development. **E-mail address:** sarah.brannon@glic.com. **World Wide Web address:** http://www.peachtreeplanning.com. **Description:** Specializes in estate planning (wealth creation and wealth conservation). Product lines include stocks, bonds, mutual funds, life insurance, disability insurance, and annuities. **NOTE:** Contact Director of Manpower Development at 404/260-1627 or at listed toll-free number, ext. 1627; fax is 404/260-1727. Please visit website to complete online employment form. **Corporate headquarters location:** This location. **Other area locations:** Statewide. **Number of employees at this location:** 45.

PRIMERICA FINANCIAL SERVICES
3120 Breckinridge Boulevard, Duluth GA 30099. 770/381-1000. **Fax:** 770/564-6110. **Contact:** Human Resources. **Wide Web address:** http://www.primerica.com. **Description:** Provides financial services including insurance and securities. **Corporate headquarters location:** This location. **Parent company:** Citigroup. **Other U.S. locations:** Nationwide. **International locations:** Asia; Europe. **Number of employees worldwide:** 100,000.

PRUDENTIAL PREFERRED FINANCIAL SERVICES
3500 Lenox Road NE, Suite 1200, Atlanta GA 30326. 404/262-2600. **Fax:** 404/262-1835. **Contact:** Andy Gentile, Human Resources. **World Wide Web address:** http://www.prudential.com. **Description:** Markets a complete portfolio of insurance (group life and health) and financial services products to business owners, professionals, and upper-income individuals. Founded in 1875. **NOTE:** Please visit website to search for jobs and apply online. **Positions advertised include:** Annuities Wholesaler; Investment Associate Manager of Financial Services. **Special programs:** Training. **Office hours:** Monday - Friday, 8:00 a.m. - 5:00 p.m. **Corporate headquarters location:** Newark NJ. **Other area locations:** Statewide. **Other U.S. locations:** Nationwide. **International locations:** Worldwide. **Listed on:** New York Stock Exchange. **Stock exchange symbol:** PRU. **Parent company:** Prudential Insurance Company of America. **Operations at this facility include:** Administration; Sales; Service. **Annual sales/revenues:** More than $100 million. **Number of employees worldwide:** 39,400.

SMITH BARNEY
3455 Peachtree Road NE, Suite 1400, The Pinnacle Building, Atlanta GA 30326. 404/266-0090. **Toll-free phone:** 800/241-4277. **Fax:** 404/842-2393. **Contact:** Human Resources. **World Wide Web address:** http://www.smithbarney.com. **Description:** An international investment banking, market making, and research firm serving corporations, state and local governments, sovereign and provincial governments and their agencies, central banks, and other financial institutions. **Office hours:** Monday – Friday, 8:00 a.m. – 5;00 p.m. **Corporate headquarters location:** New York NY. **Other U.S. locations:** Nationwide. **Parent company:** Citigroup. **Listed on:** New York Stock Exchange. **Stock exchange symbol:** C.

SYNOVUS FINANCIAL CORPORATION
P.O. Box 120, Columbus GA 31902. 706/649-2311. **Physical address:** 1111 Bay Avenue, Columbus GA 31901. **Fax:** 706/641-6555. **Recorded jobline:** 706/649-4758. **Contact:** Human Resources. **E-mail address:** careers@sfcts.com. **World Wide Web address:** http://www.synovus.com. **Description:** A multiservice financial company. **NOTE:** Search for jobs and apply online. All applicants should contact the jobline for available positions. Entry-level positions and second and third shifts are offered. If applying for more than one position, please submit a separate resume for

each position. **Positions advertised include:** Commercial Sales Trainer; Teller; Accounting Manager; Marketing Project Coordinator; Operations Associate; Operations Associate Adjustments; Receptionist; Database Administrator; Assistant Financial Reporting Manager; Balancing Clerk; Manager – Security Applications; Call Support Analyst. **Corporate headquarters location:** This location. **Other U.S. locations:** AL; FL; SC. **Special programs:** Internships; Training; Summer Jobs. **Listed on:** New York Stock Exchange. **Stock exchange symbol:** SNV. **Annual sales/revenues:** $21 - $50 million. **Number of employees nationwide:** 11,000.

WELLS FARGO FINANCIAL
975 Dawsonville Highway, Suite 18, Gainesville GA 30501. 770/536-5070. **Contact:** Human Resources. **World Wide Web address:** http://www.financial.wellsfargo.com. **Description:** Wells Fargo Financial offers real estate and automobile loans and financing solutions. They also provide credit cards to retailers through private labels and co-brands, and also directly to customers. Founded in 1897. **NOTE:** Please visit website to explore career opportunities. **Corporate headquarters location:** Des Moines IA. **Other U.S. locations:** Nationwide. **International locations:** Worldwide. **Parent company:** Wells Fargo. **Operations at this facility include:** This location provides loans to small businesses and individuals. **Annual sales/revenues:** More than $100 million. **Number of employees worldwide:** 16,500.

Hawaii
BANK OF HAWAII
P.O. Box 2900, Honolulu HI 96846-2900. 808/537-8844. **Toll-free phone:** 888/643.3888. **Contact:** Kimberly Treehill. **World Wide Web address:** http://www.boh.com. **Description:** A bank holding company that provides a variety of financial services. **NOTE:** Above address is the human resources address, not the address for a branch location. Search available job openings and apply online. **Positions advertised include:** Administrative Assistant; Auditor; CIS Specialist; Compliance Analyst; Consumer Lending Associate; Sales Manager; Mortgage Banker; Banking Officer; Service Representative. **Other area locations:** Statewide. **International locations:** American Somoa; Saipan, Marianas Islands; Guam; Palau. **Listed on:** New York Stock Exchange. **Stock exchange symbol:** BOH.

Illinois
BEAR, STEARNS & COMPANY, INC.
3 First National Plaza, Chicago IL 60602. 800/753-2327. **Contact:** Human Resources. **World Wide Web address:** http://www.bearstearns.com. **Description:** A leading investment banking and securities trading and brokerage firm serving governments, corporations, institutions, and individuals worldwide. The company offers services in corporate finance, mergers, acquisitions, institutional equities, fixed income sales and trading, derivatives, futures sales and trading, asset management, and custody. **NOTE:** This company provides job listings for all its lo locations on its website. See website and apply online. **Corporate headquarters location:** New York NY. **Other U.S. locations:** Nationwide **International locations:** Worldwide. **Parent company:** The Bear Stearns Companies Inc. **Listed on:** NASDAQ. **Stock exchange symbol:** BSC. **Number of employees nationwide:** 10,500.

THE CHICAGO BOARD OF TRADE
141 West Jackson Boulevard, Suite 2080, Chicago IL 60604. 312/435-3494. **Fax:** 312/435-7150. **Contact:** Employment Office. **World Wide Web address:** http://www.cbot.com. **Description:** A commodities, futures, and options exchange. **Positions advertised include:** Trading Systems Analyst; e-CBOT Senior Systems Administrator; Program Office Administrator; Revenue Auditor; Senior Programmer Analyst; Systems Integration Specialist. **Corporate headquarters location:** This location.

THE CHICAGO BOARD OPTIONS EXCHANGE
400 South LaSalle Street, Chicago IL 60605. 312/786-7800. **Toll-free phone:** 877/THE-CODE. **Fax:** 312/786-7808. **Contact:** Human Resources. **World Wide Web address:** http://www.cboe.com. **Description:** A nonprofit financial institution engaged in options trading. **NOTE:** Entry-level positions are offered. **Positions advertised include:** Senior Business Analyst; VIP Help Desk Director; Examiner; Investigator; Engineer. **Corporate headquarters location:** This location.

CHICAGO MERCANTILE EXCHANGE
20 South Wacker Drive, Chicago IL 60606. 312/930-8240. **Fax:** 312/930-2036. **Contact:** Human Resources. **World Wide Web address:** http://www.cme.com. **Description:** One of the world's largest commodities, futures, and options exchanges. **Positions advertised include:** Associate Director of Product Communication; Senior Internal Auditor; Business Analyst; Market Reporter; Assistant General Counsel. **Special programs:** Internships. **Corporate headquarters location:** This location. **Other U.S. locations:** Washington DC; New York NY. **Listed on:** American Stock Exchange. **Stock exchange symbol:** CME.

CHICAGO STOCK EXCHANGE INC.
440 South LaSalle Street, Chicago IL 60657. 312/663-2526. **Contact:** Human Resources. **E-mail address:** hrrecruiting@chx.com. **World Wide Web address:** http://www.chx.com. **Description:** A stock exchange offering securities trading and depository services. **NOTE:** Send resumes by fax or e-mail only. **Positions advertised include:** Surveillance Investigator; Enforcement Attorney; Senior Programmer Analyst. **Corporate headquarters location:** This location. **Other U.S. locations:** New York NY.

HOUSEHOLD FINANCE CORPORATION
961 Weigel Drive, Elmhurst IL 60126. 630/617-7000. **Contact:** Human Resources. **World Wide Web address:** http://www.householdfinance.com. **Description:** Household Finance Corporation is one of the oldest and largest independent consumer finance companies in the United States, providing secured and unsecured loans for home improvement, education, bill consolidation, and leisure activities to 1.7 million customers through 400 branches and two regional headquarters. **NOTE:** Apply to job listings found on the company's website. **Positions advertised include:** Underwriter; Sales Assistant Beneficial; Bankruptcy Specialist; Collection Representative; Operations Systems Associate. **Special programs:** Internships. **Other U.S. locations:** San Francisco CA; Wood Dale IL. **Parent company:** Household International (Prospect Heights IL).

JEFFERIES & COMPANY, INC.
DERIVATIVES DIRECT
55 West Monroe Street, Suite 3500, Chicago IL 60603. 312/750-4700. **Contact:** Human Resources. **World Wide Web address:** http://www.jefco.com. **Description:** Jefferies & Company is engaged in equity, convertible debt, and taxable fixed income securities brokerage and trading, and corporate finance. Jefferies & Company is one of the leading national firms engaged in the distribution and trading of blocks of equity securities and conducts such activities primarily in the third market. Founded in 1962. **NOTE:** To apply for investment banking positions, contact Dee Dee Bird, Recruiting Coordinator, at dbird@jefco.com or by fax at 310/575-5165. To apply for other positions, contact Mel Locke, Director of People Services at mlocke@jefco.com or via fax at 310/914-1066. **Corporate headquarters location:** Los Angeles CA. **Parent company:** Jefferies Group, Inc. is a holding company that operates several subsidiaries in the securities brokerage and trading, corporate finance, and financial services markets.

LINCOLN FINANCIAL ADVISORS
8755 West Higgins Road, Suite 550, Chicago IL 60631. 773/380-8518. **Fax:** 773/693-2531. **Contact:** Linda Proskurniak, Vice President of Professional

Development. **E-mail address:** Lsproskurniak@LNC.com. **World Wide Web address:** http://www.lfachicago.com. **Description:** Lincoln Financial Advisors markets financial planning, permanent and term life insurance, annuities, disability coverage, and investment products to business owners and professionals. The company also provides complex estate planning and business planning advice. Founded in 1905. **Corporate headquarters location:** Fort Wayne IN. **Other U.S. locations:** Nationwide. **International locations:** Argentina; China; United Kingdom. **Parent company:** Lincoln Financial Group. **Operations at this facility include:** Regional Headquarters; Sales. **Listed on:** New York Stock Exchange. **Stock exchange symbol:** LNC.

MERRILL LYNCH
33 West Monroe Street, Suite 2200, Chicago IL 60603. 312/269-5100. **Fax:** 312/269-5092. **Contact:** Human Resources. **World Wide Web address:** http://www.ml.com. **Description:** One of the largest securities brokerage firms in the world, Merrill Lynch provides financial services in securities, financial planning, insurance, estate planning, mortgages, and related areas. The company also brokers commodity futures and options, is a major underwriter of new securities issues, and is a dealer in corporate and municipal securities. **NOTE:** This company has other locations throughout Chicago, Illinois and the United States. See website for additional locations and job listings. Apply online. **Special programs:** Internships. **Corporate headquarters location:** New York NY. **Operations at this facility include:** Sales; Service.

JOHN NUVEEN & COMPANY, INC.
333 West Wacker Drive, 34th Floor, Chicago IL 60606. 312/917-7700. **Toll-free phone:** 800/257-8787. **Fax:** 312/917-8049. **Contact:** Wendy Lindquist, Human Resources Assistant. **World Wide Web address:** http://www.nuveen.com. **Description:** An investment banking company. **Positions advertised include:** Advisor Support Manager; Internal Adviser Services Representative; Data Specialist; Sales; Administrative Assistant.

STEIN ROE INVESTMENT COUNSEL
One South Wacker Drive, Chicago IL 60606. 312/368-7700. **Fax:** 312/368-8129. **Contact:** Human Resources. **World Wide Web address:** http://www.sric.net. **Description:** An investment counseling firm offering professional advice and services to individuals, institutions, and other organizations. Stein Roe & Farnham also manages 20 no-load mutual funds. **NOTE:** Apply online. **Corporate headquarters location:** This location. **Other U.S. locations:** San Francisco CA; New York NY; Cleveland OH. **International locations:** San Juan, Puerto Rico.

UNITRIN, INC.
One East Wacker Drive, Chicago IL 60601. 312/661-4600. **Toll-free phone:** 800/999-0546. **Contact:** Personnel. **World Wide Web address:** http://www.unitrin.com. **Description:** A financial services company with subsidiaries engaged in three business areas: life and health insurance, property and casualty insurance, and consumer finance. Founded in 1990. **Positions advertised include:** Actuarial Services Manager; Product Technician; Territory Sales Manager; Regional Claims Manager. **Special programs:** Internships; Summer Jobs. **Office hours:** Monday - Friday, 8:00 a.m. - 4:30 p.m. **Corporate headquarters location:** This location. **Listed on:** NASDAQ. **Stock exchange symbol:** UTR.

VAN KAMPEN INVESTMENTS
One Parkview Plaza, P.O. Box 5555, Oakbrook Terrace IL 60181. 630/684-6000. **Contact:** Human Resources. **World Wide Web address:** http://www.vankampen.com. **Description:** An investment management firm.

WASHINGTON MUTUAL HOMELOANS
75 North Fairway Drive, Vernon Hills IL 60061. 847/549-6500. **Fax:** 847/549-2568. **Contact:** Human Resources. **World Wide Web address:** http://www.wamumortgage.com. **Description:** A full-service mortgage banking company that originates, acquires, and services residential mortgage loans. **Operations at this facility include:** Administration; Divisional Headquarters; Service.

WELLS FARGO HOME MORTGAGE
4800 West Wallbash Road, Springfield IL 62711. 217/547-7500. **Contact:** Human Resources. **World Wide Web address:** http://www.wellsfargo.com. **Description**: Wells Fargo is a diversified financial institution with over $234 billion in assets. Wells Fargo serves over 17 million customers through 5,300 independent locations worldwide. The company also maintains several stand-alone ATMs and branches within retail outlets. Services include community banking, credit and debit cards, home equity and mortgage loans, online banking, student loans, and insurance. Wells Fargo also offers a complete line of commercial and institutional financial services. Founded in 1852. **Corporate headquarters location:** San Francisco CA. **Other U.S. locations:** Nationwide. **International locations:** Worldwide. **Operations at this facility include:** This location offers home equity and mortgage services. **Listed on:** New York Stock Exchange. **Stock exchange symbol:** WFC.

Indiana

AMERICAN GENERAL FINANCE
P.O. Box 59, Evansville IN 47708. 812/468-5677. **Physical address:** 601 North West Second Street, Unit 2, Evansville IN 47708. **Fax:** 812/468-5119. **Recorded jobline:** 812/468-5600. **Contact:** Human Resources. **World Wide Web address:** http://www.agfinance.com. **Description:** One of the country's largest public insurance companies. American General Finance also provides financial services including mortgage loans, real estate investment and development, investment counseling, and management and distribution of mutual funds. Founded in 1920. **Positions advertised include:** Accounting Analyst; Business/Financial Analyst; Collector; Senior Mail Clerk; Design Specialist; Quality Assurance Supervisor; Retail Credit Analyst; Specialist Programmer. **Corporate headquarters location:** This location. **Other U.S. locations:** Nationwide. **Subsidiaries include:** MorEquity. **Parent company:** American General Corporation.

FORETHOUGHT FINANCIAL SERVICES
One Forethought Center, Highway 46 East, Batesville IN 47006. 812/933-6600. **Contact:** Human Resources. **World Wide Web address:** http://www.forethought.com. **Description:** Provides financial services for the planning of funeral arrangements. **Corporate headquarters location:** This location.

HILLENBRAND INDUSTRIES, INC.
1069 State Route 46 East, Mail Code J-18, Batesville IN 47006. 812/934-7771. **Fax:** 812/934-1998. **Contact:** Director, Administrative Services **E-mail address:** resume_admin@Hillenbrand.com. **World Wide Web address:** http://www.hillenbrand.com. **Description:** A holding company. **Corporate headquarters location:** This location. **Subsidiaries include:** Batesville Casket Company, Inc. (Batesville IN) manufactures funeral-related products including caskets and urns. Forethought Financial Services (Batesville IN) provides financial services for the purpose of planning funeral arrangements. Hill-Rom Company, Inc. (Batesville IN) manufactures and rents a variety of health care products including birthing beds, hospital beds, and stretchers.

HILLIARD-LYONS INC.
P.O. Box 98, Evansville IN 47701. 812/426-1481. **Fax:** 812/428-8697. **Contact:** Human Resources. **E-mail address:** careers@hilliard.com. **World Wide Web address:** http://www.hilliard.com. **Description:** A security broker and dealer offering stocks, bonds, mutual funds, and other financial services. **Corporate headquarters location:** Louisville KY.

IRWIN MORTGAGE CORPORATION
105000 Kincaid Drive, Fishers, Indianapolis IN 46037. 317/844-7788. **Contact:** Human Resources. **World**

Wide Web address: http://www.irwinmortgage.com. **Description:** A financial services company specializing in the refinancing of loans.

IRWIN UNION BANK
P.O. Box 929, Columbus IN 47202-0929. 812/376-1020. **Physical address:** 500 Washington Street, Columbus IN 47201. **Contact:** Human Resources. **E-mail address:** human.resources@irwinunion.com. **World Wide Web address:** http://www.irwinunion.com. **Description:** A diversified financial services company that offers commercial banking, credit card services, insurance services, mortgage banking, investment services, and other financial activities. **Positions advertised include:** Teller; Administrative Assistant; Vice President, Bank Operations.

MERRILL LYNCH
130 West Main Street, Fort Wayne IN 46802. 260/424-2424. **Fax:** 219/423-3493. **Contact:** Human Resources. **World Wide Web address:** http://www. ml.com. **Description:** One of the largest securities brokerage firms in the world, Merrill Lynch provides financial services in corporate and municipal securities, financial planning, insurance, estate planning, mortgages, and related areas. The company also provides investment banking services. **Positions advertised include:** Consulting Relationship Manager; Client Associate; Financial Advisor. **Other U.S. locations:** Nationwide.

OXFORD FINANCIAL GROUP LTD.
11711 North Meridian Street, P.O. Box 80238, Indianapolis IN 46280-0238. 317/843-5678. **Fax:** 317/843-5679. **Contact:** Human Resources. **World Wide Web address:** http://www. ofac.com. **Description:** Specializes in financial and investment advising for wealthy individuals and institutions.

SMITH BARNEY
111 Monument Circle, Indianapolis IN 46204. 317/263-8700. **Contact:** Human Resources. **World Wide Web address:** http://www. salomonsmithbarney.com. **Description:** An international investment banking, market making, and research firm serving corporations, state, local, and foreign governments, central banks, and other financial institutions. **Corporate headquarters location:** New York NY. **Other U.S. locations:** Nationwide.

UBS FINANCIAL SERVICES INC.
8888 Keystone Crossing, 10th Floor, Indianapolis IN 46240-4613. 317/816-0800. **Contact:** Human Resources. **World Wide Web address:** http://www.ubs.com/financialservicesinc. **Description:** A full-service securities firm with over 300 offices nationwide. Services include investment banking, asset management, merger and acquisition consulting, municipal securities underwriting, estate planning, retirement programs, and transaction management. UBS PaineWebber offers its services to corporations, governments, institutions, and individuals. Founded in 1879. **Corporate headquarters location:** New York NY. **Other U.S. locations:** Nationwide.

Iowa

CUNA MUTUAL LIFE INSURANCE COMPANY
2000 Heritage Way, Waverly IA 50677. 319/352-1000. **Fax:** 319/352-1272. **Contact:** Manager of Human Resources. **World Wide Web address:** http://www.cunamutual.com. **Description:** The company, part of the Cuna Mutual Group, designs markets and administers individual investments, life insurance plans, long term care insurance and annuity products. Founded in 1935. **NOTE:** Applicants are requested to register and apply for positions through the company's Online Response Form. **Positions advertised include:** Mail Clerk; Imaging & Retrieval Specialist; HVAC Mechanic; Service Representative; Financial Services Sales Assistant. **Corporate headquarters location:** Madison WI. **Other are locations:** Dubuque IA. **Parent company:** Cuna Mutual Group. **Chairman:** James L. Bryan. **Annual sales/revenues:** $2 billion. **Number of employees nationwide:** 5,000.

PRINCIPAL FINANCIAL GROUP, INC.
711 High Street, Des Moines IA 50392-0001. 515/247-5111. **Toll-free phone:** 800/986-3343. **Fax:** 515/246-5475. **Contact:** Cherise, Human Resources. **World Wide Web address:** http://www.principal/careers.com. **Description:** Provides financial services including annuities, home mortgages, mutual funds, and retirement plans. The Principal Financial Group also offers dental, disability, health, life, and vision insurance policies. **Positions advertised include:** Associate Technician Consultant; Senior Product Manager; Sales Support Leader; Underwriter; Communications Specialist. **NOTE:** Human Resources phone: 515/248-3476. **Corporate headquarters location:** This location. **Subsidiaries include:** Principal Bank; Principal Capital; Principal Life Insurance Company; Principal Residential Mortgage, Inc. **Listed on:** New York Stock Exchange. **Stock exchange symbol:** PFG. **Annual sales/revenues:** $9.2 billion. **Number of employees:** 17,600.

Kansas

WADDELL & REED INC.
P.O. Box 29217, Shawnee Mission KS 66201-9217. 913/236-2000. **Physical address:** 6301 Glennwood Avenue, Shawnee Mission KS 66201. **Toll-free phone:** 888/923-3355. **Fax:** 913/236-1909. **Contact:** Human Resources. **E-mail address:** jobs@waddell.com. **World Wide Web address:** http://www.waddell.com. **Description**: The company and its affiliates administer over 45 mutual funds and manage accounts for institutional investors and individual clients, as well as selling annuities and insurance. Founded in 1937. **NOTE**: Applicants encouraged to apply via web site. **Positions advertised include:** Administrative Assistant; IT Administration Specialist; Fund Pricing Manager; Investor Departmental Operations; Siebel Business Analyst; Siebel Configuration; IT Administrative Support; Senior Systems Administrator. **Corporate headquarters location:** This location. **Other area locations:** Statewide. **Other U.S. locations:** Nationwide. **Parent company:** Waddell & Reed Financial, Inc. **Listed on:** New York Stock Exchange. **Stock exchange symbol:** WDR. **Annual sales/revenues:** $435 million. **Number of employees at this location:** 400. **Number of employees worldwide:** 1,430.

Kentucky

A.G. EDWARDS
130 Thompson Poynter Road, First Floor, London KY 40741-7238. 606/864-8400. **World Wide Web address:** http://www.agedwards.com. **Description:** A financial consulting company with over 700 offices nationwide. A.G. Edwards offers informative investment information for planning for the future. **Positions advertised include:** Financial Sales Consultant. **Corporate headquarters location:** St. Louis MO. **Other area locations:** Statewide. **Other U.S. locations:** Nationwide. **Number of employees worldwide:** 15,000.

Louisiana

AEGIS MORTGAGE CORPORATION
10049 North Reiger Road, Baton Rouge LA 70809-4559. **Toll-free phone:** 800/988-8252. **Fax:** 225/215-7346. **Contact:** Human Resources. **World Wide Web address:** http://www.aegismtg.com. **Description:** A mortgage production company that offers new home mortgages, refinancing of existing mortgages, home equity loans, and mortgage loan servicing. **Positions advertised include:** Application Support Administrator; E-Commerce Business Analyst; IT Desktop Technician; IT Help Desk Technician; IT Network Engineer; Mortgage Loan Originator/Sales Professional; Mortgage Purchase Specialist; Operations Director; Post Closing Reviewer; SQL Database Administrator. **Corporate headquarters location:** Houston TX. **Other U.S. locations:** Nationwide. **Number of employees nationwide:** 3,200.

JEFFERIES & COMPANY, INC.
650 Poydras Street, Suite 2215, New Orleans LA 70130. 504/681-5700. **Contact:** Human Resources.

World Wide Web address: http://www.jefco.com. **Description:** A global investment bank and institutional securities firm that provides its customers with advisory services, institutional brokerage, securities research and asset management. **Corporate headquarters location:** New York NY. **Other U.S. locations:** Nationwide. **International locations:** Worldwide. **Parent company:** Jefferies Group, Incorporated. **Listed on:** New York Stock Exchange. **Stock exchange symbol:** JEF. **Annual Revenues:** $1.2 billion. **Number of employees worldwide:** Nearly 2,000.

Maine

CITIGROUP GLOBAL TRANSACTION SERVICES

2 Portland Square, Portland ME 04101. 207/879-1900. **Fax:** 207/874-2159. **Contact:** Human Resources Department. **World Wide Web address:** http://www.citibank.com. **Description:** A financial services firm. **NOTE:** Search posted openings and apply on-line only at www.jobinme.com. Each branch posts openings locally. **Positions advertised include:** Cash Management Analyst; Shareholder Services Representative.

Maryland

THE AMERITAS/ACACIA COMPANY

7315 Wisconsin Avenue, Bethesda MD 20814. 301/280-1000. **Toll-free phone:** 800/444-1889. **Fax:** 301/280-1261. **Contact:** Human Resources. **E-mail address:** hr@acaciagroup.com. **World Wide Web address:** http://www.acaciagroup.com. **Description:** Provides diversified financial and insurance services through its operating companies. **NOTE:** Resumes for advertised positions may be submitted online. **Positions advertised include:** Executive Assistant; Telecommunications Analyst; Compliance Director; Administrative Assistant; Investor Relations Representative. **Corporate headquarters location:** This location. **Other U.S. locations:** Nationwide. **Parent company:** Ameritas Acacia Mutual Holding Company. **Operations at this facility include:** Administration; Service. **Number of employees at this location:** 300. **Number of employees nationwide:** 1,000.

THE CALVERT GROUP, LTD.

4550 Montgomery Avenue, Suite 1000N, Bethesda MD 20814. 301/951-4800. **Toll-free phone:** 800/369-2748. **Fax:** 301/657-7000. **Contact:** Personnel. **E-mail address:** calvertjobs@calvert.com. **World Wide Web address:** http://www.calvertgroup.com. **Description:** Offers mutual fund management services. Founded in 1976. **Note:** Apply via email. **Positions advertised include:** Performance Analytics Supervisor; Senior Technical Support Specialist; Institutional Coordinator. **Special programs:** Education Program; Tuition Reimbursement Program. **Subsidiaries include:** Calvert Asset Management Company, Incorporated; Calvert Shareholder Services, Incorporated; Calvert Administrative Services Company, Incorporated; Calvert Distributors, Incorporated. **Parent company:** The Acacia Group (Bethesda MD).

DEUTSCHE BANC ALEX. BROWN

One South Street, Baltimore MD 21202. 410/727-1700. **Toll-free phone:** 800/ 638-2596. **Fax:** 410/895-3450. **Recorded jobline:** 410/895-5350. **Contact:** Human Resources. **World Wide Web address:** http://www.alexbrown.db.com. **Description:** A financial services, investment advisory, and investment banking firm. Founded in 1800. **Corporate headquarters location:** This location. **Other U.S. locations:** Atlanta GA; Boston MA; Winston-Salem NC; Chicago IL; Greenwich CT; Los Angeles CA; San Francisco CA; Philadelphia PA; Houston TX; Dallas TX; New York NY. **Parent Company:** Deutsche Bank Securities, Incorporated. **Listed on:** New York Stock Exchange. **Stock exchange symbol:** DB. **CEO:** Tom Hughes.

LEGG MASON, INC.

100 Light Street, Baltimore MD 21202-1099. 410/539-3400. **Contact:** Human Resources. **World Wide Web address:** http://www.leggmason.com. **Description:** A full-service broker-dealer that also offers investment banking services. **Parent company:** Legg Mason, Incorporated (Baltimore MD) is a holding company with subsidiaries engaged in securities brokerage and trading; investment management of mutual funds and individual and institutional accounts; underwriting of corporate and municipal securities and other investment banking activities; sales of annuities and banking services; and the provision of other financial services. The company serves its brokerage clients through 128 offices and manages $82 billion in assets for individual and institutional accounts and mutual funds. **Positions advertised include:** Accountant; Account Administrator; Administrative Assistant; Administrative Manager; Administrative Assistant; Business Analyst; Compliance Officer; Corporate Technical College; Developer Analyst; Graphic Designer; Operations Trainee; Proposal Writer; Research Associate. **Special programs include:** Internships. **Corporate headquarters location:** This location. **Listed on:** New York Stock Exchange. **Stock exchange symbol:** LM. **Chairman:** Raymond A. Mason. **Number of employees nationwide:** 4,200.

THOMSON FINANCIAL

1455 Research Boulevard, Rockville MD 20850. 301/545-4000. **Contact:** Human Resources. **World Wide Web address:** http://www.thomsonfinancial.com. **Description:** Provides financial information to the investment industry through its four business units: the Investment Banking Group, the Investment Management Group, the Sales and Trading Group, and the Corporate Group. **Positions advertised include:** Administrative Assistant; Database Engineer; FDR Research Specialist; Financial Data Analyst; Inside Sales Representative; Product Manager; Senior Product Specialist; SQL Systems Administrator; Systems Operator; Technical Account Specialist. **Corporate headquarters location:** New York NY. **Other U.S. locations:** San Francisco CA; Chicago IL; Boston MA. **International locations:** Worldwide. **Parent company:** The Thomson Corporation. **CEO:** David H. Shaffer.

Massachusetts

ACADIAN ASSET MANAGEMENT INC.

1 Post Office Square, Boston MA 02109. 617/850-3500. **Fax:** 617/850-3501. **Contact:** Human Resources. **World Wide Web address:** http://www.acadian-asset.com. **Description:** A money management firm specializing in international stocks. **Positions advertised include:** Accountant; Business Systems Analyst; Corporate Controller; Data Analyst; Data Architect; Development Manager; Performance Developer. **NOTE:** Summer internships available. Search for current positions on website.

ADVEST

100 Federal Street, 29th Floor, Boston MA 02110. 617/348-2200. **Contact:** Human Resources. **World Wide Web address:** http://www.advest.com. **Description:** Provides stock brokerage services. **Positions advertised include:** Financial Analyst. **Parent company:** Merrill Lynch.

BEAR, STEARNS & COMPANY, INC.

One Federal Street, 29th Floor, Boston MA 02110. 617/654-2800. **Toll-free phone:** 800/333-2327. **Fax:** 617/654-2329. **Contact:** Human Resources. **World Wide Web address:** http://www.bearstearns.com. **Description:** An investment banking, securities trading, and brokerage firm. The firm's business includes corporate finance, mergers and acquisitions, public finance, institutional equities, fixed income sales and trading, private client services, foreign exchange, future sales and trading, derivatives, and asset management. **Corporate headquarters location:** New York NY. **Other U.S. locations:** Nationwide. **International locations:** Worldwide. **Parent company:** The Bear Stearns Companies Inc. also operates Bear, Stearns Securities Corporation, providing professional and correspondent clearing services, including securities lending; and Custodial Trust Company, providing master trust, custody, and government securities services. **Listed on:** New York Stock Exchange. **Stock exchange symbol:** BSC. **Annual sales/revenues:** More than $100 million. **Number of employees nationwide:** 7,800.

BLACKROCK
One Financial Center, Boston MA 02111. 617/357-1200. **Contact:** Human Resources. **World Wide Web address:** http://www.blackrock.com. **Description:** A provider of investment management products; offering alternatives, equity, fixed income, liquidity, and risk management.

THE BOSTON COMPANY
One Boston Place, 14th Floor, Boston MA 02108. 617/722-7029. **Contact:** Human Resources. **World Wide Web address:** http://www.thebostoncompany.com. **Description:** Manages equity and balanced portfolios for institutional clients. **NOTE:** Search and apply for positions at: http://www.careers.mellon.com. **Parent company:** Mellon Bank Corporation. **Listed on:** New York Stock Exchange. **Stock exchange symbol:** MEL.

BOSTON FINANCIAL DATA SERVICES, INC.
2 Heritage Drive, North Quincy MA 02171. 617/483-5000. **Toll-free phone:** 888/772-BFDS. **Contact:** Human Resources. **E-mail address:** jobs@bostonfinancial.com. **World Wide Web address:** http://www.bostonfinancial.com. **Description:** A service agent for State Street Bank & Trust Company specializing in the mutual fund, corporate stock transfer, and insurance services industries. **Positions advertised include:** Fund Liaison; Customer Support Representative; Marketing Communications Specialist. **Special programs:** Internships. **Parent company:** State Street Bank & Trust and DST Systems. **Operations at this facility include:** Administration; Service.

BOSTON 128 COMPANIES, INC.
42 Fairview Road, Weston MA 02493. 781/642-0777. **Fax:** 781/899-8030. **Contact:** Human Resources. **World Wide Web address:** http://www.boston128companies.com. **Description:** A full-service financial company. Boston 128 Companies specializes in deferred compensation plans for corporate and individual clients. **Positions advertised include:** Account Manager; Brokerage Relationship Manager.

BOSTON STOCK EXCHANGE
100 Franklin Street, Boston MA 02110. 617/235-2000. **Fax:** 617/235-2200. **Contact:** Human Resources. **World Wide Web address:** http://www.bostonstock.com. **Description:** A stock exchange. **Positions advertised include:** System Administrator; Network Engineer; Production Control Manager; Staff Accountant.

CDC IXIS ASSET MANAGEMENT NORTH AMERICA
399 Boylston Street, Boston MA 02116. 617/449-2100. **Contact:** Human Resources. **World Wide Web address:** http://www.ixis-amgroup.com. **Description:** An investment management company. **Parent company:** CDC IXIS Asset Management (France). **Corporate headquarters location:** This location.

CGM FUNDS
P.O. Box 8511, Boston MA 02266 **Physical address:** 222 Berkeley Street, Suite 1013, Boston MA 02116. 617/859-7714. **Toll-free phone:** 800/345-4048. **Fax:** 617/226-1838. **Contact:** Tony Figueiredo, Human Resources. **World Wide Web address:** http://www.cgmfunds.com. **Description:** Manages mutual funds for investors.

CHARLES SCHWAB & CO., INC.
127 Congress Street, Boston MA 02110. 617/210-7400. **Fax:** 617/210-7418. **Contact:** Branch Manager. **World Wide Web address:** http://www.schwab.com. **Description:** A leading provider of discount brokerage services and no-transaction fee mutual funds. The company provides a wide range of services for individuals, institutions, financial advisors, and retirement plans, and has over 4 million investor accounts. Charles Schwab & Co., Inc. also provides online brokerage services. **Positions advertised include:** Account Representative; Branch Manager. **Corporate headquarters location:** San Francisco CA. **Other U.S. locations:** Nationwide. **Operations at this facility include:** Sales; Service. **Listed on:** New York Stock Exchange. **Stock exchange symbol:** SCH. **Number of employees worldwide:** 10,400.

COMPUTERSHARE
250 Royall Street, Canton MA, 02021. 781/575-2508. **Contact:** Human Resources. **World Wide Web address:** http://www.equiserve.com. **Description:** A stock trading transfer agency. **Positions advertised include:** eLearning Project Specialist; Communications Engineer; Sr. Web Developer; Reconcilement Accountant; Production Database Administrator.

CONTRAVISORY RESEARCH & MANAGEMENT CORPORATION
99 Derby Street, Suite 302, Hingham MA 02043. 781/740-1786. **Contact:** Human Resources. **E-mail address:** info@contravisory.com. **World Wide Web address:** http://www.contravisory.com. **Description:** An investment advisory firm whose services include mutual funds.

THE CREDIT NETWORK
59 Howard Street, Framingham MA 01702. 508/626-1368. **Fax:** 508/766-5611. **Contact:** Human Resources. **E-mail address:** resumes@tcnlink.com. **World Wide Web address:** http://www.tcnlink.com. **Description:** A credit reporting service catering to the mortgage industry. **Positions advertised include:** National Account Manager.

EATON VANCE CORPORATION
255 State Street, Boston MA 02109. 617/482-8260. **Toll-free phone:** 800/225-6265. **Contact:** Mora O'Brien, Recruiting Manager. **World Wide Web address:** http://www.eatonvance.com. **Description:** An investment firm. **Positions advertised include:** Accountant; Vice President, Investments; Trading Associate; Fund Administration Manager. **CEO/President:** James Hawkes.

FIDELITY INVESTMENTS
82 Devonshire Street, Boston MA 02109. 617/563-7000. **Fax:** 617/476-4262. **Contact:** Human Resources. **World Wide Web address:** http://www.fidelity.com/employment. **Description:** One of the nation's leading investment counseling and mutual fund/discount brokerage firms. **Positions advertised include:** Quantitative Analyst; Report Developer; Business Analyst; Benefits Specialist; Team Manager; Fund Accounting Manager. **Corporate headquarters location:** This location. **Other U.S. locations:** Nationwide. **International locations:** Worldwide. **Listed on:** Privately held. **Number of employees at this location:** 9,000.

FIRST INVESTORS CORPORATION
404 Wyman Street, Suite 385, Waltham MA 02451. 781/890-9201. **Fax:** 781/890-8817. **Contact:** Human Resources. **World Wide Web address:** http://www.firstinvestors.com. **Description:** Offers investment programs, life insurance, retirement planning, and other tax-deferred programs. Founded in 1930. **NOTE:** Entry-level workers begin as Registered Representative/Management Trainees after successfully completing the National Association of Securities Dealers Licensing Course and passing examinations administered by First Investors Corporation. **Corporate headquarters location:** New York NY. **Other U.S. locations:** Nationwide. **Operations at this facility include:** Regional Headquarters.

FREEDOM CAPITAL
One Beacon Street, 5th Floor, Boston MA 02108. 617/725-2300. **Contact:** Human Resources. **Description:** A security brokerage firm.

JEFFERIES & COMPANY, INC.
One Post Office Square, Suite 3400, Boston MA 02109. 617/342-7800. **Contact:** Human Resources. **World Wide Web address:** http://www.jefco.com. **Description:** Engaged in equity, convertible debt, taxable fixed income securities brokerage and trading, and corporate finance. Jefferies is one of the leading national firms engaged in the distribution and trading of blocks of equity securities and conducts such activities primarily in the third market. Founded in 1962. **Corporate headquarters location:** Los Angeles CA. **Other U.S. locations:** San Francisco CA; Stamford CT; Atlanta GA; Chicago IL; New Orleans LA; Jersey City NJ; Short Hills NJ; New York NY; Nashville TN; Dallas TX; Richmond VA. **International locations:** Australia; Hong Kong; London; Paris; Tokyo; Zurich. **Listed on:** New York Stock Exchange. **Stock exchange symbol:** JEF. **Parent company:** Jefferies Group, Inc.

JOHN HANCOCK FINANCIAL SERVICES
John Hancock Place, Box 111, Boston MA 02117. 617/572-4500. **Fax:** 617/572-4539. **Contact:** Human Resources. **E-mail address:** employment@jhancock.com. **World Wide Web address:** http://www.johnhancock.com. **Description:** An insurance and financial services firm operating through two divisions: The Retail Sector offers protection and investment products to middle- and upper-income markets; The Investment & Pension Group is involved in bond and corporate finance services as well as in real estate and mortgage loans. Founded in 1862. **NOTE:** Entry-level positions are offered. **Special programs:** Internships; Training. **Corporate headquarters location:** This location. **International locations:** Worldwide. **Parent company:** Manulife Financial. **Annual sales/revenues:** More than $100 million. **Number of employees at this location:** 4,100. **Number of employees nationwide:** 11,000.

MFS INVESTMENT MANAGEMENT
500 Boylston Street, Boston MA 02116. 617/954-5000. **Contact:** Human Resources. **E-mail address:** jobs@mfs.com. **World Wide Web address:** http://www.mfs.com. **Description:** A full-service investment management firm. Founded in 1924. **Positions advertised include:** Divisional Director; Administrative Assistant; Regional Vice President; Regional Sales Representative; Office Associate; Lead RFP Writer; Programmer; Financial Systems Analyst; Corporate Tax Manager; Tax Analyst; Equity Trader; Asset Controller; Fund Administrator; Fund Team Manager. **NOTE:** Entry-level positions are offered. **Corporate headquarters location:** This location. **Other U.S. locations:** Phoenix AZ. **Parent company:** Sun Life Assurance. **Operations at this facility include:** Administration; Research and Development; Sales; Service. **Number of employees at this location:** 1,500.

MERRILL LYNCH
2 Batterymarch Park, Quincy MA 02169. 617/745-5500. **Contact:** Human Resources. **World Wide Web address:** http://www.ml.com. **Description:** One of the largest securities brokerage firms in the United States. Merrill Lynch provides securities, extensive insurance, and real estate and related services. The company also brokers commodity futures, commodity options, and corporate and municipal securities. In addition, Merrill Lynch is engaged in investment banking activities. **Positions advertised include:** Manager Assistant; Financial Advisor. **Special programs:** Internships. **Corporate headquarters location:** New York NY. **Other U.S. locations:** Nationwide. **International locations:** Worldwide. **Listed on:** New York Stock Exchange. **Stock exchange symbol:** MER. **Annual sales/revenues:** More than $100 million. **Number of employees worldwide:** 63,800.

MORGAN STANLEY DEAN WITTER & COMPANY
125 High Street, 24th Floor, Boston MA 02110. 617/478-6400. **Contact:** Human Resources. **World Wide Web address:** http://www.msdw.com. **Description:** Offers diversified financial services including equities, fixed income securities, commodities, money market instruments, and investment banking services. **Office hours:** Monday - Friday, 8:30 a.m. - 5:00 p.m. **Corporate headquarters location:** New York NY.

NORTHWESTERN MUTUAL FINANCIAL NETWORK
55 William Street Suite 110, Wellesley MA, 02481. 781/237-7070. **Contact:** Steve Tipton, Director of Training & Development. **World Wide Web address:** http://www.nmfn.com. **Description:** A financing network with home offices in Milwaukee WI.

OLD MUTUAL ASSET MANAGERS (U.S.)
200 Clarendon Street, 53rd Floor, Boston MA 02116. 617/369-7300. **Contact:** Lucy Stinson, Human Resources. **World Wide Web address:** http://www.omam.com. **Description:** Provides investment management services primarily to institutional investors through 42 operating firms. **Positions advertised include:** Sr. Accountant; Sr. Legal Counsel. **Corporate headquarters location:** This location. **Number of employees nationwide:** 1,500.

PFPC
101 Federal Street, Boston MA 02110. 617/535-0300. **Contact:** Human Resources. **World Wide Web address:** http://www.pfpc.com. **Description:** Provides a broad range of financial services including accounting, global fund services, retirement services, securities lending services, and fund custody services.

PNC ADVISORS
99 High Street, Oliver Tower, 27th Floor, Boston MA 02110. 617/334-6030. **Contact:** Human Resources. **World Wide Web address:** http://www.pncadvisors.com. **Description:** An investment firm that provides financial planning, customized credit solutions, brokerage services, mutual funds, and customized investment portfolios. **Positions advertised include:** Sr. Relationship Manager. **NOTE:** Apply online. **Parent company:** PNC Bank Corporation (Pittsburgh, PA).

THE PIONEER GROUP, INC.
60 State Street, 19th Floor, Boston MA 02109. 617/742-7825. **Contact:** Human Resources. **E-mail address:** work@pioneerinvest.com. **World Wide Web address:** http://www.pioneerfunds.com. **Description:** Offers individual investment, institutional investment management, real estate advisory, venture capital, and emerging market services. **Positions advertised include:** Institutional Marketing Specialist; Business Analyst; Manager, Production Support; Group Communications Manager. **Corporate headquarters location:** This location.

PUTNAM INVESTMENTS
859 Willard Street, Boston MA 02169. 617/292-1000. **Contact:** Human Resources. **World Wide Web address:** http://www.putnaminv.com. **Description:** A money management firm. **Positions advertised include:** Business Data Analyst; Strategic Relationship Analyst; Mail Clerk; Investment Reporting Analyst; Portfolio Analyst; Financial Engineer. **Corporate headquarters location:** This location. **Other U.S. locations:** Andover MA; Franklin MA; Quincy MA.

SEACOAST CAPITAL PARTNERS
55 Ferncroft Road, Suite 110, Danvers MA 01923-4001. 978/750-1300. **Fax:** 978/750-1301. **Contact:** Human Resources. **World Wide Web address:** http://www.seacoastcapital.com. **Description:** A personal credit institution. **Other U.S. location:** San Francisco CA.

SMITH BARNEY
53 State Street, 39th Floor, Boston MA 02109. 617/589-3500. **Contact:** Human Resources. **World Wide Web address:** http://www.smithbarney.com.

Description: An international investment banking, market making, and research firm serving corporations, state and local governments, sovereign and provincial governments and their agencies, central banks, and other financial institutions. **Other area locations:** Brockton; Hingham; Pittsfield; Waltham; State Street Boston; Danvers; Hyannis; Springfield; Worcester. **Parent company:** Citigroup Global Markets Inc.

SOVEREIGN BANK
One Harvard Street, Brookline Village MA 02446. 617/232-0467. **Toll-free phone:** 877/768-2265. **Contact:** Human Resources. **World Wide Web address:** http://www.sovereignbank.com. **Description:** A $55 billion financial institution with nearly 600 community banking offices and 1,000 ATMs in Connecticut, Massachusetts, New Hampshire, New Jersey, New York, Pennsylvania, and Rhode Island. **Parent company:** Sovereign Bancorp, Inc. **Listed on:** New York Stock Exchange. **Stock exchange symbol:** SOV. **Number of employees nationwide:** 9,500.

STATE STREET CORPORATION
One Lincoln Street, Boston MA 02111. 617/786-3000. **Contact:** Human Resources. **World Wide Web address:** http://www.statestreet.com. **Description:** Provides securities and recordkeeping services to nearly 2,000 mutual funds and manages a large number of tax-exempt assets. State Street is a major manager of international index assets and provides corporate banking services, specialized lending, and international banking services. **Positions advertised include:** Tax Manager; Account Manager; Sr. Accounting Associate. **Corporate headquarters location:** This location. **Parent company:** State Street Boston Corporation. **Number of employees worldwide:** 17,400.

STOCKCROSS
77 Summer Street, Boston MA 02110. 617/367-5700. **Toll-free phone:** 800/225-6196. **Fax:** 617/367-6399. **Contact:** Human Resources. **E-mail address:** info@stockcross.com. **World Wide Web address:** http://www.stockcross.com. **Description:** A discount stock brokerage.

UBS FINANCIAL SERVICES INC.
100 Federal Street, 27th Floor, Boston MA 02110. 617/261-1000. **Contact:** Human Resources. **World Wide Web address:** http://www.ubspainewebber.com. **Description:** A full-service securities firm with over 300 offices nationwide. Services include investment banking, asset management, merger and acquisition consulting, municipal securities underwriting, estate planning, retirement programs, and transaction management. Clients include corporations, governments, institutions, and individuals. Founded in 1879. **Corporate headquarters location:** New York NY. **Other U.S. locations:** Nationwide. **Listed on:** New York Stock Exchange. **Stock exchange symbol:** UBS. **Annual sales/revenues:** More than $100 million.

UPROMISE
117 Kendrick Street, Suite 200, Needham MA 02494. 781/707-8400. **Contact:** Human Resources. **World Wide Web address:** http://www.upromise.com. **Description:** Offers college savings plans. **Positions advertised include:** Plan Lead; Call Center Rep; Client Service Rep; Director of Compliance; Director of Public Relations; Product Development Manager; Reconciliation and Control Associate; Reporting Manager; Sr. Business Systems Analyst; Sr. Software Engineer; Manager, Member Marketing; Manager, Online Acquisition; Marketing Manager; Director of Partner Analysis; Statistical Analyst; Ops DBA; Sr. Systems Engineer; Sr. Unix System Administrator.

Michigan

AMERIPRISE FINANCIAL
5751 East G Avenue, Kalamazoo MI 49004. 269/349-8006. **Contact:** Human Resources. **World Wide Web address:** http://www.ameriprise.com. **Description:** Provides a variety of financial products and services to help individuals, businesses, and institutions establish and achieve their financial goals. Ameriprise offers financial planning, annuities, mutual funds, insurance, and investment certificates. Other services include institutional investment advisory trust, tax preparation, and retail securities brokerage. **Corporate headquarters location:** Minneapolis MI. **Other area locations:** Statewide. **Other U.S. locations:** Nationwide. **Listed on:** New York Stock Exchange. **Stock exchange symbol:** AXP. **Annual sales/revenues:** $5.6 billion. **Number of employees nationwide:** Approximately 10,000.

FIFTH THIRD BANCORP
19233 Fifteen Mile Road, Clinton Township MI 48035. 586/741-1421. **Recorded jobline:** 800/552-4350. **Contact:** Human Resources. **World Wide Web address:** http://www.53.com. **Description:** A financial services institution that, through its subsidiaries, provides mortgage loans and traditional banking services. Founded in 1853. **NOTE:** Entry-level positions, part-time jobs, and second and third shifts are offered. **Positions advertised include:** Securities Retail Investment Consultant; Credit Analyst. **Corporate headquarters location:** Cincinnati OH. **Other area locations:** Statewide. **Other U.S. locations:** Nationwide. **Subsidiaries include:** Fifth Third Bank Processing Solutions; Fifth Third Securities, Incorporated; Fifth Third Leasing Company. **Listed on:** NASDAQ. **Stock exchange symbol:** FITB. **Number of employees nationwide:** Over 19,000.

OPPENHEIMER
300 River Place, Suite 4000, Detroit MI 48207. 313/259-2600. **Toll-free phone:** 800/795-4366. **Contact:** Human Resources Director. **E-mail address:** humanresources@opco.com. **World Wide Web address:** http://www.opco.com. **Description:** An investment banking corporation and one of Michigan's leading brokerage firms. **Corporate headquarters location:** New York NY. **Other area locations:** Statewide. **Other U.S. locations:** Nationwide. **International locations:** Worldwide. **Subsidiaries include:** Freedom Investments, Incorporated. **Operations at this facility include:** Administration; Sales. **Listed on:** New York Stock Exchange; Toronto Stock Exchange. **Stock exchange symbol:** OPY. **Number of employees nationwide:** 3,000.

RAYMOND JAMES INVESTMENT BANK
One Griswold Street, Detroit MI 48226. 313/963-6700. **Fax:** 313/442-1600. **Recorded jobline:** 727/567-1490. **Contact:** Director of Human Resources. **E-mail address:** employment@raymondjames.com. **World Wide Web address:** http://www.raymondjames.com. **Description:** A regional, full-service investment banking and securities brokerage firm. Products and services include mutual funds, insurance, corporate bonds, investment management services, and retirement planning. **Positions advertised include:** Support Analyst; Supervisor. **Special programs:** Internships; Co-ops. **Corporate headquarters location:** St. Petersburg FL. **Other U.S. locations:** FL; TX; IL; NY; GA; TN; CA. **International locations:** Worldwide. **Parent company:** Raymond James Financial, Inc. **Listed on:** New York Stock Exchange. **Stock exchange symbol:** RJF. **Annual sales/revenues:** Over $1 billion.

STANDARD FEDERAL BANK
2600 West Big Beaver Road, Troy MI 48084-3275. 800/643-9600. **Fax:** 248/637-2759. **Contact:** Human Resources. **World Wide Web address:** http://www.lasallebankmidwest.com. **Description:** One of the largest banks in the Midwest with assets of over $50.5 billion and 273 branch locations in Michigan and Indiana. **Corporate headquarters location:** This location. **Other area locations:** Statewide. **Other U.S. locations:** IL; IN. **Parent company:** LaSalle Bank Corporation. (Chicago IL) **Number of employees nationwide:** Over 4,000.

Minnesota

AFFINITY PLUS FEDERAL CREDIT UNION
175 West Lafayette Road, St. Paul MN 55107. 651-312-9342. **Toll-free phone:** 800/322-7228. **Contact:**

Human Resources. **E-mail address:** hr@affinityplus.org. **World Wide Web address:** http://www.affinityplus.org. **Description:** Affinity Plus is a not-for-profit member-owned financial institution/credit union. **Positions advertised include:** Accounting Manager; Assistant Manager; Branch Manager; Financial Service Officer; IT Help Desk Associate; Member Relations Specialist; Member Service Representative; Mortgage Specialist; Operations Service Representative; Records Service Representative; Systems Administrator. **Corporate headquarters location:** This location. **Other area locations:** Statewide.

AMERIPRISE FINANCIAL
707 2nd Avenue South, Minneapolis MN 55474. 612/671-3131. **Contact:** Human Resources. **World Wide Web address:** http://www.ameriprise.com. **Description:** A financial planning and services company that provides solutions for clients' asset accumulation, income management and insurance protection needs. The company specializes in meeting the retirement-related financial needs of the mass affluent. **Corporate headquarters location:** This location. **Listed on:** New York Stock Exchange. **Stock exchange symbol:** AMP.

GMAC-RFC
8400 Normandale Boulevard, Suite 250, Minneapolis MN 55437. 952/832-7000. **Contact:** Human Resources. **World Wide Web address:** http://www.rfc.com. **Description:** A secondary mortgage provider. **Positions advertised include:** Account Executive; Accounts Receivable Senior Associate; Administrative Assistant; Associate Counsel; Business Continuity Program Manager. **Special programs:** Internships. **Corporate headquarters location:** This location. **Parent company:** GMAC Mortgage Corporation. **Operations at this facility include:** Administration; Sales; Service. **Number of employees nationwide:** 500.

GREEN TREE SERVICING, LLC
345 St. Peter Street, St. Paul MN 55102. 651/293-3400. **Fax:** 651/293-3622. **Recorded jobline:** 651/293-5825. **Contact:** Human Resources. **World Wide Web address:** http://www.gtservicing.com. **Description:** Services manufactured home loans; it also services home equity, home improvement, and consumer installment loans. In addition, the company originates manufactured home loans and sells insurance. **Corporate headquarters location:** This location.

MARSHALL BANKFIRST CORP.
150 South Fifth Street, Suite 3000, Minneapolis MN 55402. 612/376-1500. **Fax:** 612/692-5150. **Contact:** Kathy Jeong, Human Resources. **E-mail address:** kjeong@marshallbankfirst.com. **World Wide Web address:** http://www.marshallbankfirst.com. **Description:** A financial services company specializing commercial lending and loan participations, residential mortgage services, and stored value card services. **Number of employees at this location:** 280.

MINNEAPOLIS GRAIN EXCHANGE
400 South Fourth Street, Suite 111, Minneapolis MN 55415. 612/321-7101. **Fax:** 612/321-7196. **Contact:** Human Resources. **E-mail address:** resumes@mgex.com. **World Wide Web address:** http://www.mgex.com. **Description:** The Minneapolis Grain Exchange trades on futures and options contracts. **Positions advertised include:** Part-Time Exchange Room Clerk; Marketing/Public Relations Professional; Operations/IT Division Staff.

MONEYGRAM INTERNATIONAL, INC.
1550 Utica Avenue South, St Louis Park MN 55416-5301. 952/591-3000. **Toll-free phone:** 800/328-5678. **Fax:** 952/591-3121. **Contact:** Human Resources. **Description:** MoneyGram International, Inc. and its subsidiaries provide payment services in the United States and internationally. It operates through two segments, Global Funds Transfer and Payment Systems. **Positions advertised include:** Legal Specialist – Regulatory; Senior Network Analyst; Buyer; Compliance Telephone Trainer; Manager, Systems Development; Service Request Center Analyst. **Other area locations:** Brooklyn Center MN.

PIPER JAFFRAY COMPANIES
800 Nicollet Mall, Suite 800, Minneapolis MN 55402. 612/303-6000. **Toll-free phone:** 800/333-6000. **Fax:** 612/303-1311. **Contact:** Human Resources. **World Wide Web address:** http://www.piperjaffray.com. **Description:** A securities firm that serves middle-market companies, government, nonprofit entities, and institutional and individual investors through 73 branch offices in 17 states.

RBC DAIN RAUSCHER
Dain Rauscher Plaza, 60 South Sixth Street, Minneapolis MN 55402-4422. 612/371-2711. **Toll-free phone:** 800/678-3246. **Contact:** Human Resources. **World Wide Web address:** http://www.rbcdain.com. **Description:** A full-service investment firm. The company also provides real estate syndication and property investment services, as well as data processing services. **Positions advertised include:** Sr. Associate, Margins; Sr. Associate, Annuity Operations; Supervisor, Margins; Associate General Counsel; Sr. Compliance Officer. **Corporate headquarters location:** This location. **Parent company:** Royal Bank of Canada.

WELLS FARGO HOME MORTGAGE
3601 Minnesota Drive, Suite 100, Bloomington MN 55435. 952/844-2200. **Contact:** Personnel Department. **World Wide Web address:** http://www.wellsfargo.com/mortgage. **Description:** A diversified financial services company with $482 billion in assets, providing banking, insurance, investments, mortgage and consumer finance to more than 23 million customers from more than 6,200 stores and wellsfargo.com across North America and elsewhere internationally. Founded in 1852. **Corporate headquarters location:** San Francisco CA. **Other area locations:** Statewide. **Other U.S. locations:** Nationwide. **International locations:** Worldwide. **Operations at this facility include:** This location offers home equity and mortgage services. **Listed on:** New York Stock Exchange. **Stock exchange symbol:** WFC. **Annual sales/revenues:** More than $100 million. **Number of employees worldwide:** 120,000.

Mississippi
MS DIVERSIFIED CORPORATION
1501 Lakeland Drive, Jackson MS 39216. 601/420-4909. **Contact:** Human Resources. **World Wide Web address:** http://www.assurantsolutions.com. **Description:** An insurance group with primary dealings in the selling and servicing of extended vehicle service contracts, consumer financing, credit and casualty insurance, and other financial services to automobile dealers and financial institutions. **Corporate headquarters location:** New York NY. **Parent company:** Assurant Solutions, a business division of Assurant Group. **Listed on:** New York Stock Exchange. **Stock exchange symbol:** AIZ. **Annual sales/revenues:** $7.4 billion. **Number of employees at this location:** 100.

Missouri
EDWARD JONES
201 Progress Parkway, Maryland Heights MO 63043. 314/515-2000. **Fax:** 866/860-4094. **Contact:** Personnel. **World Wide Web address:** http://www.edwardjones.com. **Description:** A securities brokerage firm. **Corporate headquarters location:** This location. **Listed on:** Privately held. **Number of employees nationwide:** 7,000.

GENERAL AMERICAN LIFE INSURANCE CORPORATION
13045 Tesson Ferry Road, St. Louis MO 63128. 314/843-8700. **Contact:** Human Resources. **World Wide Web address:** http://www.genamerica.com. **Description:** Offers life insurance, securities, and other related financial services to corporate and individual

clients. **Corporate headquarters location:** This location.

MERRILL LYNCH
8235 Forsyth Boulevard, Suite 1500, Saint Louis MO 63105. 314/290-4900. **Contact:** Personnel. **World Wide Web address:** http://www.ml.com. **Description:** Merrill Lynch is a worldwide financial firm. The company provides both traditional and innovative products and services to a broad range of individual and institutional customers. Merrill Lynch operates primarily through functional units that include individual services; capital markets; assets management; futures; international; real estate; and insurance. **NOTE:** Search and apply for positions online. **Positions advertised include:** Commercial Banking Professional; Sr. Regional Manager. **Special programs:** Internships. **Corporate headquarters location:** New York NY. **Listed on:** New York Stock Exchange. **Stock exchange symbol:** MER.

STIFEL, NICOLAUS & COMPANY
501 North Broadway, St. Louis MO 63102. 314/342-2000. **Fax:** 314/342-2051. **Recorded jobline:** 314/342-2900. **Contact:** Human Resources. **World Wide Web address:** http://www.stifel.com. **Description:** A full-service regional investment firm. Services include fixed income securities, corporate finance, public finance, syndicate participation, trading, broker-dealer services, options, research, mutual funds, asset management, and estate planning. Founded in 1890. **Corporate headquarters location:** This location. **Parent company:** Stifel Financial Corporation. **Number of employees at this location:** 275. **Number of employees nationwide:** 1,000.

Montana
D.A. DAVIDSON & COMPANY
P.O. Box 5015, Great Falls MT 59403. 406/791-7467. **Toll-free phone:** 800/332-5915. **Physical address:** 8 Third Street North, Great Falls MT 59401. **Contact:** Dan McLaughlin. **E-mail address:** DMcLaughlin@dadco.com. **World Wide Web address:** http://www.dadco.com. **Description:** A financial services holding company, security broker, and travel agency. Founded in 1935. **Positions advertised include:** Account Supervisor; IT Technician. **Corporate headquarters location:** This location. **Other U.S. locations:** ID; OR; UT; WA; WY. **Operations at this facility include:** Full-service investment firm. **Number of employees at this location:** 200. **Number of employees nationwide:** 750.

Nebraska
AMERITRADE HOLDING CORPORATION
4211 South 102nd Street, Omaha NE 68127. 402/331-7856. **Toll-free phone:** 800/237-8692. **Contact:** Human Resources. **World Wide Web address:** http://www.ameritradeholding.com. **Description:** Provides discount brokerage and financial services including electronic trading, market data, and research services. **Positions advertised include:** Quality Assurance Manager; Apex Program Manager; Outbound Sales Associate; Training & Development Specialist; Human Resource Manager; Client Service Representative; Licensed Service Representative; Sr. Manager of Information Technology Sourcing; Enterprise Project Manager; QA Manager. **Corporate headquarters location:** This location. **Listed on:** NASDAQ. **Stock exchange symbol:** AMTD.

Nevada
JOHN DEERE CAPITAL CORPORATION
First Interstate Bank Building, One East 1st Street, Suite 600, Reno NV 89501. 775/786-5527. **Contact:** Human Resources. **World Wide Web address:** http://www.deere.com. **Description:** The US credit subsidiary of Deere & Company. The credit segment primarily finances sales and leases by John Deere dealers of new and used agricultural, commercial, consumer, construction, and forestry equipment. In addition, it provides wholesale financing to dealers, as well as operating loans and retail revolving charge accounts. **Corporate headquarter location:** Moline IL. **Listed on:** New York Stock Exchange. **Stock exchange symbol:** DE.

LAND TITLE OF NEVADA, INC.
3301 North Buffalo Road, Suite 3, Las Vegas NV 89129. 702/474-3300. **Contact:** Personnel. **World Wide Web address:** http://www.landtitlenv.com. **Description:** This location is the main office of the land title and escrow company. **Positions advertised include:** Searcher; Policy Typist; Courier.

MERRILL LYNCH
2300 West Sahara Avenue, Suite 1200, Las Vegas NV 89102. 702/227-7000. **Contact:** Manager. **World Wide Web address:** http://www.ml.com. **Description:** A diversified financial services organization. Merrill Lynch is a major broker in securities, option contracts, commodities and financial futures contracts, and insurance. The company also deals with corporate and municipal securities and investment banking. **NOTE:** Entry-level positions are offered. **Corporate headquarters location:** New York NY. **Other U.S. locations:** Nationwide. **International locations:** Worldwide. **Number of employees worldwide:** Over 49,000.

MORGAN STANLEY DEAN WITTER & COMPANY
3800 Howard Hughes Parkway, Suite 800, Las Vegas NV 89109-0925. 702/737-7275. **Contact:** Manager. **World Wide Web address:** http://www.msdw.com. **Description:** Offers diversified financial services including equities, fixed income securities, commodities, money market instruments, and investment banking services. **Positions advertised include:** Financial Advisor Trainee. **Other U.S. locations:** Nationwide. **International locations:** Worldwide.

NORTH AMERICAN MORTGAGE COMPANY
5300 West Sahara Avenue, Las Vegas NV 89102. 702/365-0476. **Contact:** Human Resources. **World Wide Web address:** http://www.namc.com. **Description:** Originates, acquires, sells, and services mortgage loans, principally first lien mortgage loans secured by single-family residences. North American Mortgage Company also sells servicing rights associated with a portion of such loans. The company operates through a network of 50 loan origination offices in 14 states. Founded in 1948. **Other U.S. locations:** Nationwide. **Parent company:** Washington Mutual Bank, FA.

UBS FINANCIAL SERVICES INC.
3800 Howard Hughes Parkway, Suite 1200, Las Vegas NV 89109. 702/731-1121. **Toll-free phone:** 800/428-7573. **Contact:** David Frieden, Senior Vice President. **World Wide Web address:** http://financialservicesinc.ubs.com. **Description:** A full-service securities firm with offices nationwide. Services include investment banking, asset management, merger and acquisition consulting, municipal securities underwriting, estate planning, retirement programs, and transaction management. UBS Financial Services offers its services to corporations, governments, institutions, and individuals. Founded in 1879. **Corporate headquarters location:** New York NY. **Other U.S. locations:** Nationwide. **Parent company:** UBS AG. **Listed on:** New York Stock Exchange. **Stock exchange symbol:** UBS. **Number of employees nationwide:** Over 8,000. **Number of employees worldwide:** 66,000.

WACHOVIA SECURITIES
3763 Howard Hughes Parkway, Suite 330, Las Vegas NV 89109. 702/836-8200. **Contact:** Human Resources. **World Wide Web address:** http://www.wachovia.com. **Description:** An international securities brokerage and investment firm. The company offers clients more than 70 investment products including stocks, options, bonds, commodities, tax-favored investments, and

insurance. **Special programs:** Financial Advisor in Training Program.

New Hampshire

WHITE MOUNTAINS INSURANCE GROUP

80 Main Street, Hanover NH 03755. 603/640-2200. **Fax:** 603/643-4592. **Contact:** Human Resources. **World Wide Web address:** http://www.whitemountains.com. **Description:** A major financial services holding company specializing in reinsurance, as well as property and casualty insurance. NOTE: All employment is handled out of OneBeacon Group. Contact Jessica Wiley, 617/725-6602. **Corporate headquarters location:** Hamilton Bermuda. **Subsidiaries include:** OneBeacon Insurance Group; Folksamerica Reinsurance Company; Fund American Reinsurance Company, Ltd.; White Mountains Underwriting Limited; Esurance; AutoOne Insurance. **Parent company:** Tuckerman Capital. **Listed on:** New York Stock Exchange. **Stock exchange symbol:** WTM.

New Jersey

BEAR, STEARNS & COMPANY, INC.

115 South Jefferson Road, Whippany NJ 07981. 973/793-2600. **Fax:** 973/793-2040. **Contact:** Managing Director of Personnel. **World Wide Web address:** http://www.bearstearns.com. **Description:** An investment banking, securities trading, and brokerage firm engaged in corporate finance, mergers, and acquisitions; institutional equities and fixed income sales and trading; individual investor services; asset management; and correspondent clearing. **Corporate headquarters location:** New York NY. **Parent company:** The Bear Stearns Companies Inc. is a leading worldwide investment banking, securities trading, and brokerage firm. **Listed on:** New York Stock Exchange. **Stock exchange symbol:** BSC.

CIT GROUP, INC.

1 CIT Drive, Livingston NJ 07039. 973/740-5000. **Contact:** Personnel Officer. **World Wide Web address:** http://www.citgroup.com. **Description:** A diversified financial services organization that provides flexible funding alternatives, secured business lending, and financial advisory services for corporations, manufacturers, and dealers. Founded in 1908. **Positions advertised include:** Asset Management Specialist; Regional Account Manager; Document Administrator; AVP Financial Systems; Executive Assistant; Internal Audit Manager; Risk Management Vice President; Information Security Specialist; Executive Secretary; Night Shift Operator; Manager; Tax Manager; Underwriter; Accounting Manager; Network Analyst; Information Security Specialist. **Corporate headquarters location:** New York NY. **Other U.S. locations:** Nationwide. **International locations:** Worldwide. **Number of employees nationwide:** 2,500.

FIRST MONTAUK FINANCIAL CORPORATION

328 Newman Springs Road, Red Bank NJ 07701. 732/842-4700. **Contact:** Human Resources. **World Wide Web address:** http://www.firstmontauk.com. **Description:** A diversified holding company that provides financial services throughout the United States to individuals, corporations, and institutions. **Subsidiaries include:** First Montauk Securities Corporation is a securities broker/dealer with a nationwide network of more than 300 registered representatives in 90 branch offices serving approximately 25,000 retail and institutional clients. Montauk Insurance Services, Inc. is an insurance agency.

J.B. HANAUER & COMPANY

4 Gatehall Drive, Parsippany NJ 07054. 973/829-1000. **Toll-free phone:** 800/631-1094. **Fax:** 973/829-0565. **Contact:** Human Resources. **World Wide Web address:** http://www.jbh.com. **Description:** A full-service brokerage firm specializing in fixed-income investments. J.B. Hanauer & Company provides a broad range of financial products and services. Founded in 1931. . **Positions advertised include:** Sr. Operations Associate. **Special programs:** Internships; Training. **Corporate headquarters location:** This location. **Other U.S. locations:** North Miami FL; Tampa FL; West Palm Beach FL; Princeton NJ; Rye Brook NY; Philadelphia PA. **Listed on:** Privately held. **Annual sales/revenues:** More than $100 million. **Number of employees at this location:** 250. **Number of employees worldwide:** 600.

JEFFERIES & COMPANY, INC.

51 JFK Parkway, 3rd Floor, Short Hills NJ 07078. 973/912-2900. **Fax:** 310/971-1066. **Contact:** See NOTE. **World Wide Web address:** http://www.jefco.com. **Description:** Engaged in equity, convertible debt and taxable fixed income securities brokerage and trading, and corporate finance. Founded in 1962. **NOTE:** Fax or email resumes for non-banking opportunities to Mel Locke (310/914-1066; mlocke@jefco.com), and for banking opportunities to Eastcoastrecruiting@jefco.com. **Parent company:** Jefferies Group, Inc.

PERSHING

One Pershing Plaza, 9th Floor, Jersey City NJ 07399. 201/413-2000. **Contact:** Personnel Department. **World Wide Web address:** http://www.pershing.com. **Description:** A securities brokerage firm. **Positions advertised include:** Customer Service Associate; Conversion Account Manager; Unit Manager; Workflow Processing Associate. **Parent company:** Donaldson, Lufkin & Jenrette Securities Corporation.

WASHINGTON MUTUAL HOME LOANS CENTER

One Garret Mountain Plaza, 3rd Floor, West Paterson NJ 07424. 973/881-2360. **Contact:** Human Resources. **World Wide Web address:** http://www.wamu.com. **Description:** A full-service mortgage banking company that originates, acquires, and services residential mortgage loans. **Positions advertised include:** Assistant Financial Center Manager; Mortgage Sales Assistant; Financial Center Manager. **Corporate headquarters location:** Pittsburgh PA. **Other U.S. locations:** KY; OH. **Parent company:** PNC Financial Services Group. **Operations at this facility include:** Regional Headquarters. **Listed on:** New York Stock Exchange. **Stock exchange symbol:** WM. **Number of employees nationwide:** 6,000.

New Mexico

AMERICAN GENERAL FINANCE

2500 El Paseo Road, Suite B, Las Cruces NM 88001. 505/527-8539. **Fax:** 505/527-0653. **Contact:** Human Resources. **World Wide Web address:** http://www.agfinance.com. **Description:** One of the country's largest consumer finance companies, focusing on consumer lending, mortgages, home equity lines of credit, retail sales financing, and credit insurance. Operates more than 1400 branches in 44 states, Puerto Rico and the U.S. Virgin Islands. **NOTE:** Submit resume to local branch. **Positions advertised include:** Management Trainee; Customer Account Administrator; Customer Account Specialist. **Corporate headquarters location:** Evansville IN. **Parent company:** American International Group Inc.

EDWARD JONES

One Grand Avenue Plaza, Suite A, Roswell NM 88201. 505/624-2963. **Contact:** Human Resources. **World Wide Web address:** http://www.edwardjones.com. **Description:** A brokerage firm. **NOTE:** Internships and co-ops available. Submit resume or application online. **Corporate headquarters location:** St. Louis Mo. **Other U.S. locations:** Nationwide. **International locations:** Worldwide.

MERRILL LYNCH

P.O. Box 1946, 123 East Marcy Street, Santa Fe NM 87501. 505/982-6500. **Contact:** Elise Davis, Director. **World Wide Web address:** http://www.ml.com. **Description:** Offices for the worldwide financial services company, organized to provide both traditional and innovative products and services to a broad range of individual and institutional customers. Merrill Lynch operates primarily through functional units that include Individual Services; Capital Markets; Assets

Management; Futures; International; and Real Estate and Insurance. Offices are in 35 countries. **NOTE:** Search and apply for positions online.

MORGAN STANLEY
6701 Uptown Boulevard NE, Albuquerque NM 87110. 505/883-6262. **Contact:** Human Resources. **World Wide Web address:** http://www.morganstanley.com. **Description:** With more than 600 offices in 28 countries, Morgan Stanley is a global financial services firm specializing in securities, investment management and credit services. **NOTE:** Must apply online. See website for current job openings and application instructions. **Positions advertised include:** Wealth Management Analyst; Financial Advisor Trainee; Registered Client Service Associate. **Listed on:** New York Stock Exchange. **Stock exchange symbol:** MS.

SOUTHWEST SECURITIES
Two Park Square, 6565 Americas Parkway, Suite 950, Albuquerque NM 87110. 505/889-7777. **Contact:** Branch Manager. **E-mail address:** careers@onlinepreferred.com. **World Wide Web address:** http://www.onlinepreferred.com. **Description:** Provides securities brokerage and other financial management services. **Corporate headquarters location:** Dallas TX. **Other U.S. locations:** Santa Fe NM; Tulsa OK; Kerrville TX; Lufkin TX; San Antonio TX. **Operations at this facility include:** Sales; Service.

THORNBURG INVESTMENT MANAGEMENT
119 East Marcy Street, Santa Fe, NM 87501. 800-847-0200. **Contact:** Human Resources. **E-mail address:** humanresources@thornburg.com. **World Wide Web address:** http://www.thornburginvestments.com. **Description:** Advises four equity funds, eight bond funds, and separately managed portfolios for institutions and individuals. **NOTE:** See http://www.thornburg.jobs for current job openings and to apply online. If submitting resume by mail, address is: Human Resources, Thornburg Companies, 150 Washington Avenue, Suite 201, Santa Fe NM 87501.**Listed on:** New York Stock Exchange. **Stock exchange symbol:** TMA.

THORNBURG MORTGAGE
150 Washington Avenue, Suite 302, Santa Fe NM 87501. 505/989-1900. **Contact:** Human Resources. **E-mail address:** humanresources@thornburg.com. **World Wide Web address:** http://www.thornburgmortgage.com. **Description:** A special purpose financial institution that invests in adjustable-rate mortgage securities and provides capital to the single-family housing market. The company leverages its equity capital using borrowed funds, invests in adjustable-rate mortgage securities, and generates income based on earnings that are greater than what it pays for its borrowings. Thornburg Mortgage is a real estate investment trust and pays out its taxable earnings in the form of dividends. **NOTE:** See http://www.thornburg.jobs for current job openings and to apply online. If submitting resume by mail, address is: Human Resources, Thornburg Companies, 150 Washington Avenue, Suite 201, Santa Fe NM 87501. **Listed on:** New York Stock Exchange. **Stock exchange symbol:** TMA.

UBS FINANCIAL SERVICES INC.
2155 Louisiana Boulevard NE, Suite 3000, Albuquerque NM 87110. 505/881-1700. **Fax:** 505/880-2799. **Contact:** Personnel. **World Wide Web address:** http://www.ubs.com. **Description:** A full-service financial services firm with over 300 offices nationwide. Services include investment banking, asset management, merger and acquisition consulting, municipal securities underwriting, estate planning, retirement programs, and transaction management. Clients include corporations, governments, institutions, and individuals. Founded in 1879. **NOTE:** Search and apply for positions online. **Corporate headquarters location:** Switzerland. **Other U.S. locations:** Nationwide.

WELLS FARGO BANK
241 Washington Avenue, Santa Fe NM 87501. 505/984-0500. **Contact:** Human Resources. **Description:** A financial services company with $482 billion in assets, providing banking, insurance, investments, mortgage, and consumer finance to more than 23 million customers from more than 6,200 stores and the Internet across North America and elsewhere internationally. **NOTE:** Search and apply for positions online. **Corporate headquarters location:** San Francisco CA. **Listed on:** New York Stock Exchange. **Stock exchange symbol:** WFC.

New York

ALLIANCEBERNSTEIN L.P.
1345 Avenue of the Americas, New York NY 10105. 212/969-1000. **Contact:** Human Resources. **E-mail address:** resumes@alliancebernstein.com. **World Wide Web address:** http://www.alliancebernstein.com. **Description:** Alliance Capital Management manages mutual funds for corporations and individual investors operating 36 offices in 19 countries. **Positions advertised include:** Fixed Income Software Developer; Applications Support Specialist. **Corporate headquarters location:** This location. **Other locations:** Worldwide. **Annual sales/revenues:** $2.75 billion. **Number of employees worldwide:** 4,200.

ALLIANCE FINANCIAL CORPORATION dba ALLIANCE BANK
120 Madison Street, Human Resources Tower II, 18th Floor, Syracuse NY 13202. 315/475-2100. **Contact:** Human Resources. **E-mail:** humanresources@alliancebankna.com. **World Wide Web address:** http://www.alliancebankna.com. **Description:** Alliance Financial Corporation, formerly Cortland First Financial and Oneida Valley Bancshares, in the holding company for Alliance Bank, an independent commercial bank delivering financial services from 20 branches in central New York State for individuals and small businesses. **Positions advertised include:** Teller; Residential Mortgage Originator; Director of Trust and Investment Services; Branch Manager; Branch Operations Associate; Sales Program Specialist. **Corporate headquarters location:** This location. **Other locations:** Statewide. **Subsidiaries include:** Alliance Leasing, Inc.; Alliance Bank. **Listed on:** NASDAQ. **Stock exchange symbol:** ALNC. **Chairman/President/CEO:** Jack H. Webb. **Annual sales/revenues:** $50 million. **Number of employees:** 300.

AMBAC FINANCIAL GROUP INC.
One State Street Plaza, 15th Floor, New York NY 10004. 212/668-0340. **Fax:** 212/509-9190. **Contact:** Gregg Bienstock, Human Resources. **World Wide Web address:** http://www.ambac.com. **Description:** AMBAC Inc. is a holding company that provides, through its affiliates, financial guarantee insurance, financial services, and health care information services to both public and private clients worldwide. **Positions advertised include:** Underwriter; Financial Services Specialist; Legal Counselor; Risk Management Associate; Investment Manager; Operations Manager; Internal Auditor; Information Technology Specialist. **Corporate headquarters location:** This location. **Other locations:** London, England; Tokyo, Japan; Sydney, Australia. **Listed on:** New York Stock Exchange. **Stock exchange symbol:** ABK. **Annual sales/revenues:** $740.5 million. **Number of employees:** 370.

AMERICAN CENTURION LIFE ASSURANCE
20 Madison Avenue Extension, P.O. Box 5550, Albany NY 12205. 518/452-4150. **Toll-free phone:** 800/633-3565. **Fax:** 518/452-3857. **Contact:** Human Resources. **Description:** Administers insurance and fixed and variable annuity products in the State of New York on behalf of American Express Financial Advisors. **Office hours:** Monday - Friday, 8:00 a.m. - 4:30 p.m. **Corporate headquarters location:** This location. **Parent company:** American Express Company.

AMERICAN EXPRESS COMPANY
200 Vesey Street, New York NY 10285. 212/640-2000. **Contact:** Human Resources. **World Wide Web address:** http://www.americanexpress.com. **Description:** American Express Company is a diversified travel and financial services company. Founded in 1850. **NOTE:** Applicants are encouraged to use the company's online Resume Builder to create a resume profile account to apply to positions as well as using the automated Job Search Agent. **Positions advertised include:** Travel Support Counselor; Senior Marketing Manager; Corp Services Operations Team Leader; Senior Risk Management Manager; Purchasing/Training Manager; Acquisition Manager; Senior Marketing Manager; Cardmember Cross-Sell Senior Manager; Account Management Representative; Contracts Manager; Treasury Manager. **Corporate headquarters location:** This location. **Other U.S. locations:** Nationwide. **International locations:** Worldwide. **Listed on:** New York Stock Exchange. **Stock exchange symbol:** AXP. **Chairman/CEO:** Kenneth I. Chenault. **Annual sales/revenues:** $24 billion. **Number of employees at this location:** 5,000. **Number of employees nationwide:** 84,400.

AMERICAN STOCK EXCHANGE LLC
86 Trinity Place, New York NY 10006. 212/306-1000. **Fax:** 212/306-1218. **Contact:** Catherine M. Casey, Senior Vice President of Human Resources. **E-mail address:** career@amex.com. **World Wide Web address:** http://www.amex.com. **Description:** One of the nation's largest stock exchanges, the American Stock Exchange is one of the only primary marketplaces for both stocks and derivative securities. The American Stock Exchange also handles surveillance, legal, and regulatory functions that are related to the stock exchange. **NOTE:** Human Resources phone: 212/306-1239. **Positions advertised include:** Assistant General Counsel; Chief Sales Officer; Business Strategy and Equity Order Flow Vice President; Exchange Traded Funds Analyst; Exchange Traded Funds Marketing Specialist; Building Operations Manager; Compliance Analyst; Financial Analyst; Public Relations Specialist. **Special programs:** Internships. **Parent company:** NASD (District of Columbia). **Chairman/CEO:** Salvatore F. Sodano. **Annual sales/revenues:** $287 million. **Number of employees at this location:** 700.

ATALANTA SOSNOFF CAPITAL CORPORATION
101 Park Avenue, 6th Floor, New York NY 10178-0002. 212/867-5000. **Fax:** 212/922-1820. **Contact:** Human Resources Director. **E-mail address:** ksk@atalantasosnoff.com. **World Wide Web address:** http://www.atalantasosnoff.com. **Description:** Atalanta Sosnoff Capital Corporation provides discretionary investment management and brokerage services. **Corporate headquarters location:** This location. **Other locations:** Cardiff CA. **Listed on:** New York Stock Exchange. **Stock exchange symbol:** ATL. **Chairman/CEO:** Martin T. Sosnoff. **Annual sales/revenues:** $15.4 million. **Number of employees:** 46.

THE AYCO COMPANY, L.P.
321 Broadway, P.O. Box 860, Saratoga Springs NY 12866. 518/886-4000. **Fax:** 518/886-4350. **Contact:** Human Resources. **E-mail address:** hresources@lpmaycoedia.com. **World Wide Web address:** http://www.ayco.com. **Description:** Provides financial counseling and education services for corporate executives and employees as well as individuals and families. The firm is organized into five business groups: financial counseling, family office practice, financial related services, wealth strategies group and investment services group. **Positions advertised include:** Information Services Assistant; Web Application Developer. **Corporate headquarters location:** This location. **Other U.S. locations:** Albany NY; Atlanta GA; Chicago IL; Clifton Park NY; Dallas TX; Los Angeles CA; Parsippany NJ; Pittsburgh PA; Troy MI. **Parent company:** The Goldman Sachs Group, Inc. **Number of employees nationwide:** 1,125.

BANK OF AMERICA
69 State Street, Albany, NY 12207. 518/447-4300. **Fax:** 518/626-2554. **Contact:** Human Resources. **World Wide Web address:** http://www.bankofamerica.com. **Description:** The bank provides commercial and consumer banking services to individuals, corporations, institutions, and governments of the Genesee, Finger Lakes, Southern Tier, and western regions of upstate New York. **NOTE:** Applications accepted online through the company Website. **Positions advertised include:** Emerging Markets/Outside Loan Officer; Applications Development Analyst; Infrastructure Specialist; Senior Relation Manager; Large Government Account Officer; Associate Staff Auditor; Technical Project Analyst; Infrastructure Engineer. **Corporate headquarters location:** Charlotte NC. **Other U.S. locations:** Nationwide.

BEAR, STEARNS & COMPANY, INC.
THE BEAR STEARNS COMPANIES INC.
383 Madison Avenue, 30th Floor, New York NY 10179. 212/272-2000. **Fax:** 2212/272-4785. **Contact:** Human Resources. **World Wide Web address:** http://www.bearstearns.com. **Description:** A leading worldwide investment banking, securities trading, and brokerage firm. **NOTE:** The company does not accept hard copy resumes and requests that resumes be submitted online via the company Website. **Corporate headquarters location:** This location. **Other U.S. locations:** Nationwide. **International locations:** Worldwide. **Listed on:** New York Stock Exchange. **Stock exchange symbol:** BSC. **Annual sales/revenues:** $6.9 billion. **Number of employees nationwide:** 10,600.

SANFORD C. BERNSTEIN & CO., LLC
dba BERNSTEIN INVESTMENT RESEARCH & MANAGEMENT
1345 Avenue of the Americas, New York NY 10105. 212/486-5800. **Fax:** 212/756-4455. **Contact:** Human Resources. **E-mail address:** resumes@bernstein.com. **World Wide Web address:** http://www.bernstein.com. **Description:** An investment management research company that conducts research on specific companies and provides investment-banking services for both private and institutional clients. **Positions advertised include:** Financial Advisor. **Corporate headquarters location:** This location. **Other U.S. locations:** Nationwide. **Parent company:** Alliance Capital Management L.P. (also at this location).

BROWN BROTHERS HARRIMAN & COMPANY
140 Broadway, New York NY 10005. 212/483-1818. **Fax:** 212/493-8545. **Contact:** Human Resources. **E-mail address:** jobs@bbh.com. **World Wide Web address:** http://www.bbh.com. **Description:** Operating some 40 partnerships and 16 offices in seven countries worldwide, the company provides commercial banking, brokerage, and investment advisory services. Founded in 1818. **Positions advertised include:** Human Resources Assistant; Domestic Banking Officer; Event Planner; Operations Specialist; Relationship Manager. **Corporate headquarters location:** This location. **Other locations:** Boston MA; Jersey City NJ; Palm Beach FL. **Number of employees:** 3,000.

CIT GROUP, INC.
505 Fifth Avenue, New York NY 10017. 212/382-7000. **Contact:** Human Resources. **World Wide Web address:** http://www.citgroup.com. **Description:** This division provides factoring services to a wide range of customers as a subsidiary of CIT Financial Services. Overall, CIT Group is a diversified financial services organization providing flexible funding alternatives, secured business lending, and financial advisory services for corporations, manufacturers, and dealers. Founded in 1908. **Positions advertised include:** Executive Assistant; Verification Examiner; Collateral Analyst Supervisor; Contracts Associate; Field Examiner; Underwriter; Credit Officer; Attorney; District Sales Manager. **Corporate headquarters location:** This location. **Other locations:** Worldwide. **Subsidiaries include:** Capital Finance; CIT

Commercial Finance Group; CIT Equipment Financing; CIT Specialty Finance Group; CIT Structured Finance. **Listed on:** New York Stock Exchange. **Stock exchange symbol:** CIT. **Annual sales/revenues:** $3.5 billion. **Number of employees nationwide:** 2,500.

CAMERON ASSOCIATES
1370 Avenue of the Americas, Suite 902, New York NY 10019. 212/245-8800. **Fax:** 212/245-4165. **Contact:** Human Resources. **World Wide Web address:** http://www.cameronassoc.com. **Description:** An investor relations firm providing financial services for public companies. Cameron Associates also offers corporate communications services. **Corporate headquarters location:** Toronto, Canada.

CANTOR FITZGERALD SECURITIES CORPORATION
110 East 59th Street, New York NY 10022. 212/938-5000. **Contact:** Human Resources Department. **World Wide Web address:** http://www.cantor.com. **Description:** An institutional brokerage firm dealing in fixed income securities, equities, derivatives, options, eurobonds, and emerging markets. Founded in 1945. **NOTE:** You may see the website for the appropriate web address for forward resumes. **Positions advertised include:** Computer Programmer. **Special programs:** Summer Internships (you may e-mail internshipopportunities@cantor.com). **Corporate headquarters location:** This location. **Other U.S. locations:** Los Angeles CA; Chicago IL; Boston MA; Dallas TX. **International locations:** Germany; China; England; Italy; France; Japan.

CITIGROUP INC.
399 Park Avenue, New York NY 10043. 212/559-1000. **Fax:** 212/793-3946. **Contact:** Human Resources. **World Wide Web address:** http://www.citigroup.com. **Description:** A holding company offering a wide range of financial services through its subsidiaries. **Positions advertised include:** Financial Analyst; Data Privacy/Information Security Specialist; Administrative Assistant; Data Analyst; Area Sales Manager; GI Analyst & Liaison; Event Planner; Senior Reviewer; Senior Contract Recruiter. **Corporate headquarters location:** This location. **Subsidiaries include:** Citibank; CitiFinancial; Global Corporate & Investment Banking; Primerica Financial Services; Smith Barney; SSB Citi Asset Management Group; Travelers Life & Annuity; Travelers Property Casualty Corp. **Listed on:** New York Stock Exchange. **Stock exchange symbol:** C. **Chairman/CEO:** Sanford (Sandy) I. Weill. **Annual sales/revenues:** $92.6 billion. **Number of employees:** 255,000.

CREDIT SUISSE
466 Lexington Avenue, New York NY 10017-3140. 212/875-3500. **Fax:** 212/658-0728. **Contact:** Recruiting. **World Wide Web address:** http://www.credit-suisse.com. **Description:** A diversified financial services firm serving as underwriters, distributors, and investment dealers. **NOTE:** Apply online. **International locations:** Switzerland; United Kingdom. **Parent company:** Credit Suisse Group (Zurich, Switzerland). **Subsidiaries include:** Imagyn Medical Technologies, Inc.; Sprout Group. **CEO:** John J. Mack. **Annual sales/revenues:** $13.7 billion. **Number of employees:** 28,415.

DEUTSCHE BANK AG
31 West 52nd Street, New York NY 10019. 212/250-2500. **Contact:** Human Resources. **World Wide Web address:** http://www.deutsche-bank.com. **Description:** A merchant investment bank. Deutsche Bank also manages index funds. **Corporate headquarters location:** Frankfurt, Germany. **Subsidiaries include:** DWS Group; Deutsche Bank, S.A.E.; Deutsche Financial Services Corporation; BPT Limited; Coral Eurobet plc; Deutsche Banc Alex, Brown Incorporated; The Laurel Pub Company Limited; Piaggio SpA; RREEF; Taunus Corporation. **Listed on:** New York Stock Exchange. **Stock exchange symbol:** DB. **Annual sales/revenues:** $66.5 billion. **Number of employees:** 95,000.

THE DREYFUS CORPORATION
200 Park Avenue, 7th Floor, New York NY 10166. 212/922-6000. **Fax:** 212/922-7533. **Contact:** Human Resources. **World Wide Web address:** http://www.dreyfus.com. **Description:** A nationwide investment corporation managing over 150 mutual funds. **NOTE:** Entry-level positions are offered. **Positions advertised include:** Associate Financial Analyst; Human Resources Consultant; Regional Wholesaler; Secretary; Fund Wholesaler; Broker-Dealer Channel Wholesaler; Financial Advisor Channel Wholesaler; Portfolio Assistant; Risk Manager and Compliance Team Leader; Executive Secretary; Financial Consultant; Mellon Business Advisor. **Corporate headquarters location:** This location. **Parent company:** Mellon Financial Corporation (Pittsburgh PA).

ENCOMPASS INSURANCE
P.O. Box 5000, Glens Falls NY 12801. 518/761-4000. **Fax:** 800/426-3692. **Contact:** Human Resources. **World Wide Web address:** http://www.encompassinsurance.com. **Description:** A property and casualty insurance writer offering commercial and personal policies. **Corporate headquarters location:** Chicago IL. **Parent company:** The Allstate Corporation (Northbrook IL).

FIDUCIARY TRUST INTERNATIONAL
600 Fifth Avenue, New York NY 10020. 212/632-3000. **Contact:** Human Resources. **World Wide Web address:** http://www.ftci.com. **Description:** Provides global investment management and custody services for institutional and individual clients with offices in 35 countries. **Positions advertised include:** Human Resources Analyst; Marketing Administrative Assistant; Credit Research Analyst; Legal Administrative Assistant; Futures Associate; Fixed Income Portfolio Analyst. **Parent company:** Franklin Templeton Investments. **Number of employees:** 6,800.

FINANCIAL FEDERAL CORPORATION
733 Third Avenue, 24th Floor, New York NY 10017. 212/599-8000. **Fax:** 212/286-5885. **Contact:** Human Resources Department. **World Wide Web address:** http://www.financialfederal.com. **Description:** Provides financing of leases and capital loans on industrial, commercial, and professional equipment to middle market customers in a variety of industries. Founded in 1989. **Corporate headquarters location:** This location. **Other U.S. locations:** Irvine CA; Lisle IL; Charlotte NC; Teaneck NJ; Houston TX. **Listed on:** New York Stock Exchange. **Stock exchange symbol:** FIF. **Chairman/President/CEO:** Paul R. Sinsheimer. **Annual sales/revenues:** $139 million. **Number of employees nationwide:** 237.

FIRST ALBANY COMPANIES, INC.
677 Broadway, Albany NY 12207-2990. 518/447-8500. **Fax:** 518/447-8527. **Contact:** Human Resources. **World Wide Web address:** http://www.fac.com. **Description:** First Albany Companies offers a variety of investment and financial services through its three subsidiaries: First Albany Corporation, First Albany Asset Management Corporation, and Northeast Brokerage Services Corporation. Founded in 1953. **Positions advertised include:** Senior LAN Administrator; Network Specialist; Research Associate. **Special programs:** Internships. **Corporate headquarters location:** This location. **Other U.S. locations:** Nationwide. **Subsidiaries include:** First Albany Corporation; First Albany Asset Management; FA Technology Ventures. **Listed on:** NASDAQ. **Stock exchange symbol:** FACT. **Chairman:** George C. McNamee. **Annual sales/revenues:** $182.5 million. **Number of employees:** 382.

FIRST INVESTORS CORPORATION
95 Wall Street, 23rd Floor, New York NY 10005. 212/858-8000. **Fax:** 212/858-8003. **Contact:** Human Resources. **E-mail address:** hr@firstinvestors.com. **World Wide Web address:** http://www.firstinvestors.com.

Description: Specializes in the distribution and management of investment programs for individuals and corporations, as well as retirement plans. First Investors operates nationwide and through several area locations in Westchester County, New Jersey, and Long Island. Founded in 1930. **Corporate headquarters location:** This location. **Other locations:** Nationwide. **Subsidiaries include:** First Investors Life Insurance Company; First Investors Federal Savings Bank; First Investors Management Company, Inc.; Administrative Data Management Corp.; SMART Tuition Management Services. **Number of employees:** 1,000.

FOUR CORNERS ABSTRACT CORPORATION
370 East Avenue, Rochester NY 14604. 716/454-2263. **Contact:** Human Resources. **World Wide Web address:** http://www.fourcornersabstract.com. **Description:** Provides services and products including real estate title searching, preparation of abstracts of title, issuance of title insurance as an agent for certain national underwriting companies, and real estate appraisals, primarily in western and central New York state. **Other area locations:** Albany NY; Binghamton NY; Buffalo NY; Syracuse NY; Utica NY. **Subsidiaries include:** Four Corners Abstract Corporation; Proper Appraisal Specialists, Inc.

GILMAN & CIOCIA INC.
11 Raymond Avenue, Poughkeepsie NY 12603. 845/485-3300. **Contact:** Human Resources Director. **E-mail address:** resumes@gilcio.com. **World Wide Web address:** http://www.gilcio.com. **Description:** Provides income tax and financial planning services including insurance, investments, pensions, and estate planning. **Positions advertised include:** Tax Preparer; Financial Planner; Receptionist. **Corporate headquarters location:** This location. **Listed on:** Over The Counter. **Stock exchange symbol:** GTAX. **Chairman:** James Ciocia. **Annual sales/revenues:** $ 106.5 million. **Number of employees:** 819.

GOLDMAN SACHS & COMPANY
85 Broad Street, New York NY 10004. 212/902-1000. **Contact:** Recruiting Department. **World Wide Web address:** http://www.gs.com. **Description:** An investment banking firm. **NOTE:** Interested jobseekers should send resumes to 180 Maiden Lane, 23rd Floor, New York NY 10038. **Corporate headquarters location:** This location. **Other U.S. locations:** Nationwide. **International locations:** Worldwide.

IDS LIFE OF NEW YORK
P.O. Box 5144, Albany NY 12205-5144. 518/869-8613. **Physical address:** 20 Madison Avenue Extension, Albany NY 12203. **Toll-free phone:** 800/797-9000. **Fax:** 518/869-8753. **Contact:** Human Resources. **Description:** Administers life, disability, long-term care, and annuity products. **Parent company:** American Express Company.

ING INVESTMENT MANAGEMENT AMERICAS
230 Park Avenue, New York NY 10169. 212/309-8200. **Contact:** Human Resources. **World Wide Web address:** http://www.inginvestment.com. **Description:** A global financial institution origin offering banking, insurance and asset management. Manages over $400 billion in assets. **Other U.S. locations:** Hartford CT; Atlanta GA; Scottsdale AZ; Minneapolis MN. **Parent company:** ING Group.

ING AMERICAS
1325 Avenue of the Americas, New York NY 10019. 646/424-6000. **Contact:** Human Resources. **World Wide Web address:** http://www.ing.com. **Description:** A financial services company offering comprehensive financial products and services including life insurance; fixed and variable annuities; defined contribution retirement plans; and mutual funds as well as other investment and banking services. **Positions advertised include:** Internal Wholesaler. **Corporate headquarters location:** Atlanta GA. **Parent company:** ING Groep (Amsterdam, The Netherlands). **Operations at this facility:** ING U.S. Financial Services. **Number of employees:** 30,000.

INVESTEC ERNST & COMPANY
One Battery Park Plaza, 2nd Floor, New York NY 10004. 212/898-6200. **Contact:** Human Resources. **E-mail address:** info@investec.com. **World Wide Web address:** http://www.investec.com. **Description:** A securities brokerage firm. Investec Ernst & Company is one of the largest financial clearinghouses in New York City, with over 80 correspondents. **NOTE:** Human Resources phone: 212/898-6450. **Corporate headquarters location:** This location. **Other locations:** Chicago IL; New York NY; Rhinebeck NY; Stamford CT; Woodbury NY.

J.P. MORGAN CHASE & COMPANY
522 5th Avenue, New York NY 10036. 212/837-2300. **Contact:** Human Resources. **World Wide Web address:** http://www.jpmorganchase.com. **Description:** Specializes in global financial services and retail banking. The company's consumer services include credit card; diversified consumer lending; mortgages and home finance; automobile loans; private banking; and asset management services. The bank offers commercial banking services for middle market companies and small business banking. The company is also engaged in global markets; investment banking operations; mergers and acquisition consulting, risk management; treasury and securities services and debt underwriting. **Positions advertised include:** Home Equity Retention Vice President; Business Systems Analyst; Underwriter; Customer Service Supervisor; Quality Assurance Analyst Underwriter; Subordination Specialist; Consumer Banker; File Reviewer; Direct Channel Manager; Client Associate; Teller; Senior Underwriter. **Corporate headquarters location:** New York NY. **Other locations:** Worldwide. **Subsidiaries include:** J.P. Morgan Private Bank; J.P. Morgan Fleming Asset Management; American Century; Brown & Company Securities Corp.; J.P. Morgan H&Q; J.P. Morgan Partners; Chase. **Listed on:** New York Stock Exchange. **Stock exchange symbol:** JPM. **Chairman/CEO:** William B. Harrison Jr. **Annual sales/revenues:** $43.4 billion. **Number of employees:** 94,335.

J.P. MORGAN PARTNERS
1221 Avenue of the Americas, New York City NY 10020-1080. 212/899-3400. **Fax:** 212/899-3401. **Contact:** Human Resources. **World Wide Web address:** http://www.jpmorganpartners.com. **Description:** Provides equity and other financial services.

JEFFERIES GROUP, INC.
dba JEFFERIES & COMPANY, INC.
520 Madison Avenue, 12th Floor, New York NY 10022. 212/284-2300. **Fax:** 310/914-1066. **Contact:** See NOTE. **World Wide Web address:** http://www.jefco.com. **Description:** An investment banking firm providing banking, research, and merger consulting services to small and mid-sized business. Through the Jefferies & Company subsidiary the firm is engaged in equity, convertible debt, and taxable fixed income securities as well as brokering off-exchange trades for institutional investors and underwrites stock offerings specializing in high-yield junk bonds. **NOTE:** Fax or e-mail resumes for non-banking opportunities to Mel Locke (310/914-1066; mlocke@jefco.com), and for banking opportunities to Eastcoastrecruiting@jeffco.com. **Subsidiaries include:** Jefferies International Limited; Jefferies Pacific Limited; The Europe Company. Founded in 1962. **Corporate headquarters location:** This location. **Other U.S. locations:** Nationwide. **International locations:** Worldwide. **Listed on:** New York Stock Exchange. **Stock exchange symbol:** JEF. **Chairman/CEO:** Richard B. Handler. **Annual sales/revenues:** $755 million. **Number of employees:** 1,600.

LEHMAN BROTHERS HOLDINGS
745 Seventh Avenue, New York NY 10019. 212/526-7000. **Contact:** Stephanie Jacobs, Recruiting. **E-mail address:** invbank.associate.us@lehman.com. **World Wide Web address:** http://www.lehman.com.

Description: An equities trading company engaged in merchant banking and other financial services including underwriting, fixed-income products, and asset management, as well as stock trading, currency, derivatives, and commodities. **Corporate headquarters location:** This location. **Subsidiaries include:** Lehman Brothers Bank, FSB. **Chairman/CEO:** Richard (Dick) S. Fuld Jr. **Annual sales/revenues:** $17 billion. **Number of employees:** 12,343.

MERRILL LYNCH & CO., INC.
250 Vesey Street, 4 World Financial Center, North Tower, New York NY 10080. 212/449-1000. **Contact:** Human Resources. **World Wide Web address:** http://www.merrilllynch.com. **Description:** One of the largest securities brokerage firms in the United States, Merrill Lynch provides financial services in the following areas: securities, extensive insurance, and real estate and related services. The company also brokers commodity futures, commodity options, and corporate and municipal securities. In addition, Merrill Lynch is engaged in investment banking activities. **NOTE:** Jobseekers are asked to call or see website for specific information on where to mail resumes. **Positions advertised include:** Equity Portfolio Trader; Credit Analyst; Equity Financial Analyst; Managing Directors Administrator; Valuation and Documentation Specialist; Corporate Strategy Analyst; Market Data Project and Service Manager; Problem Management Specialist; Equity Control Group Analyst; Policies and Procedures Analyst; Senior Financial Analyst; Senior Executive Assistant; Distressed Loan Closer; Credit Policy Project Manager. **Corporate headquarters location:** This location. **Other U.S. locations:** Nationwide. **International locations:** Worldwide. **Subsidiaries include:** Merrill Lynch Investment Managers Limited. **Listed on:** New York Stock Exchange. **Stock exchange symbol:** MER. **Chairman/CEO:** Stanley (Stan) O'Neil. **Annual sales/revenues:** $28.3 billion. **Number of employees worldwide:** 50,900.

MORGAN STANLEY DEAN WITTER & COMPANY
1211 Avenue of the Americas, New York NY 10020. 212/903-7600. **Contact:** Human Resources Director. **World Wide Web address:** http://www.msdw.com. **Description:** One of the largest investment banking firms in the United States. Services include financing, financial advisory services, real estate services, corporate bond services, equity services, government and money market services, merger and acquisition services, investment research services, investment management services, and individual investor services. **NOTE:** Resumes should be sent to the corporate headquarters: Human Resources, 1585 Broadway, New York NY 10036. 212/761-4000.

NATIONAL ASSOCIATION OF SECURITIES DEALERS, INC. (NASD)
One Liberty Plaza, 165 Broadway, New York NY 10006. 212/858-4000. **Contact:** Human Resources. **E-mail address:** careers.fr@nasd.com. **World Wide Web address:** http://www.nasd.com. **Description:** The self-regulatory organization of the securities industry, overseeing the over-the-counter market. Working closely with the Securities and Exchange Commission, NASD sets the standards for over the counter securities and market makers, and provides ongoing surveillance of trading activities. NASD also provides key services for its membership and companies, particularly through its cooperative efforts with governmental and other agencies on policies and legislation that affect the investment banking and securities business. **Positions advertised include:** Legal Assistant; Human Resources Manager; Regulatory Policy and Oversight Examiner. **Special programs:** Internships. **Corporate headquarters location:** Washington DC. **Other U.S. locations:** Nationwide. **President/CEO/Chairman:** Robert Glauber. **Sales/revenue:** $1.5 billion. **Number of employees at this location:** 350. **Number of employees nationwide:** 2,500.

NEW YORK STOCK EXCHANGE
11 Wall Street, New York NY 10005. 212/656-3000. **Contact:** Ms. Dale Bernstein, Managing Director of Staffing and Training. **World Wide Web address:** http://www.nyse.com. **Description:** The principal securities trading marketplace in the United States, serving a broad range of industries within and outside of the securities industry. More than 2,500 corporations, accounting for approximately 40 percent of American corporate revenues, are listed on the exchange. The New York Stock Exchange is engaged in a wide range of public affairs and economic research programs. **Positions advertised include:** Confidential Secretary; Director of Listings and Client Service; Administrative Secretary. **Corporate headquarters location:** This location. **Number of employees at this location:** 1,550.

OPPENHEIMER
125 Broad Street, 16th Floor, New York NY 10004. 212/668-8000. **Toll-free phone:** 800/221-5588. **Contact:** Human Resources. **E-mail address:** info@opco.com. **World Wide Web address:** http://www.opco.com. **Description:** A stock brokerage firm with 89 offices nationwide serving corporate clients and individual investors. **Subsidiaries include:** Freedom Investments. **Parent company:** Fahnestock Viner Holdings Inc. (Toronto, Canada).

RYAN BECK & CO
650 Madison Avenue, 10th Floor, New York NY 10022. 212/407-0500. **Contact:** Staffing Specialist. **E-mail address:** jobs@ryanbeck.com. **World Wide Web address:** http://www.ryanbeck.com. **Description:** Having recently acquired Gruntal & Co. and The GMS Group, Ryan Beck now operates 35 offices in 12 states offering financial services in three distinct areas: capital markets, investment banking, and the private client group. Founded in 1946. **NOTE:** Jobseekers should contact the human resources department at the company's headquarters: Liz Maynor, Staffing Specialist, 220 South Orange Avenue, Livingston NJ 07039; phone: 973/597-5980; fax: 973-597-6408. **Positions advertised include:** Financial Consultant; Sales Associate; Client Services Representative; Operations Specialist; Investment Analyst; Senior Investment Banker. **Corporate headquarters location:** Livingston NJ. **Other U.S. locations:** Nationwide. **Parent company:** BankAtlantic Bancorp, Inc. (Fort Lauderdale FL). **Annual sales/revenues:** $44 million. **Number of employees:** 400.

SG COWEN SECURITIES CORPORATION
1221 Avenue of the Americas, 9th Floor, New York NY 10020. 646/562-1000. **Contact:** Human Resources. **World Wide Web address:** http://www.cowen.com. **Description:** An investment banking firm. **Special programs:** Training; Tuition Reimbursement Program; Summer Associate Program. **Corporate headquarters location:** This location. **Other area locations:** Albany NY. **Other U.S. locations:** Chicago IL; Boston MA; Cleveland OH; Dayton OH; Philadelphia PA; Dallas TX; Denver CO; San Francisco CA. **International locations:** Canada; France; Switzerland; United Kingdom. **Parent company:** Societe Generale Group (Paris, France). **Number of employees at this location:** 1,000. **Number of employees nationwide:** 2,300.

SMITH BARNEY
1345 6th Avenue, New York NY 10105. 212/586-5505. **Fax:** 212/307-2879. **Contact:** Human Resources. **World Wide Web address:** http://www.smithbarney.com. **Description:** An international investment banking, market making, and research firm serving corporations, state, local, and foreign governments, central banks, and other financial institutions. **Corporate headquarters location:** This location. **Parent company:** Citigroup. **Listed on:** New York Stock Exchange. **Stock exchange symbol:** C. **Number of employees worldwide:** Over 40,000.

SCHONFELD SECURITIES
650 Madison Avenue, 20th Floor, New York NY 10022.

212/832-0900. **Contact:** Human Resources. **World Wide Web address:** http://www.schonfeld.com. **Description:** A securities trading firm. **Corporate headquarters location:** New York, NY. **Other area locations:** Purchase NY; Brooklyn NY. **Other U.S. locations:** Paramus NJ; Miami Beach FL; Boca Raton FL; Chicago IL; Houston TX; Los Angeles CA. **Parent company:** Schonfeld Group.

TD AMERITRADE
100 Wall Street, New York NY 10005. 212/806-3500. **Contact:** Human Resources. **World Wide Web address:** http://www.tdameritrade.com. **Description:** TD Waterhouse Securities, Inc. provides brokerage and banking services for individuals that manage their own investments and financial affairs. **Positions advertised include:** Surveillance Manager; Institutional Sales Representative; Credit Analyst; Investment Consultant. **Corporate headquarters location:** Omaha NB. **Other U.S. locations:** Nationwide. **Parent company:** TD Ameritrade Holding Company. **Listed on:** NASDAQ. **Stock exchange symbol:** AMTD. **Number of employees at this location:** 250.

THOMSON FINANCIAL
195 Broadway, New York NY 10007. 646/822-2000. **Contact:** Personnel Manager. **World Wide Web address:** http://www.thomsonfinancial.com. **Description:** Provides financial information to the investment industry through its many business units. American Banker/Bond Buyer publishes banking and financial industry information in a variety of publications. Rainmaker Information provides software products to help members of the sales and investment industries. **Corporate headquarters location:** This location. **Other U.S. locations:** Boston MA; Rockville MD; Chicago IL; San Francisco CA.

UBS FINANCIAL SERVICES INC.
1285 Avenue of the Americas, 3rd Floor, New York NY 10019. 212/713-2000. **Contact:** Personnel. **World Wide Web address:** http://www.ubs.com. **Description:** A full-service securities firm with over 300 offices nationwide. Services include investment banking, asset management, merger and acquisition consulting, municipal securities underwriting, estate planning, retirement programs, and transaction management. Clients include corporations, governments, institutions, and individuals. Founded in 1879. **Other U.S. locations:** Nationwide. **Annual sales/revenues:** More than $100 million.

UBS
299 Park Avenue, New York NY 10171-0026. 212/821-3000. **Fax:** 212/821-3285. **Contact:** Human Resources. **World Wide Web address:** http://www.ibb.ubs.com. **Description:** A national investment banking firm serving corporate clients. **Parent company:** UBS AG. **Listed on:** New York Stock Exchange. **Stock exchange symbol:** UBS.

UNITED STATES TRUST COMPANY OF NEW YORK
114 West 47th Street, New York NY 10036. 212/852-1000. **Contact:** Human Resources. **World Wide Web address:** http://www.ustrust.com. **Description:** An investment management, private banking, and securities services firm. Service categories include investment management; estate and trust administration; financial planning; and corporate trust. **Corporate headquarters location:** This location.

VALUE LINE
220 East 42nd Street, 6th Floor, New York NY 10017. 212/907-1500. **Contact:** Human Resources. **World Wide Web address:** http://www.valueline.com. **Description:** An investment advisory firm. Founded in 1931. **Positions advertised include:** Junior Security Analyst. **Corporate headquarters location:** This location. **Listed on:** NASDAQ. **Stock exchange symbol:** VALU.

WACHOVIA SECURITIES, LLC
1211 Avenue of the Americas, Suite 2702, New York NY 10036-8701. 212/205-2829. Toll-free phone: 877/239-7187. **Fax:** 212/205-2832. **Contact:** Human Resources. **World Wide Web address:** http://www.wachoviasec.com. **Description:** Provides financial advisory, brokerage, asset management, and other financial services through more than 2,800 locations nationwide. **Corporate headquarters location:** Richmond VA. **Parent company:** Wachovia Corporation.

North Carolina

AMERICAN GENERAL FINANCIAL SERVICES
1724 Winkler Street, Wilkesboro NC 28697-2251. 336/838-5157. **Fax:** 336/838-7881. **Contact:** Human Resources. **World Wide Web address:** http://www.agfinance.com. **Description:** A consumer lending company with over 1,300 branches in 41 states. The company's subsidiaries are engaged in the consumer finance, credit card, and insurance businesses. Founded in 1920. **Positions advertised include:** Management Trainee; Customer Account Administrator; Customer Account Specialist. **Corporate headquarters location:** Evansville IN. **Other area locations:** Statewide. **Other U.S. locations:** Nationwide. **Parent company:** American International Group, Inc. **Number of employees nationwide:** 8,700.

CAROLINA FARM CREDIT
P.O. Box 1827, Statesville NC 28687. 704/873-0276. **Physical address:** 1704 Wilkesboro Highway, Statesville NC 28625. **Toll-free phone:** 800/521-9952. **Fax:** 704/873-6900. **Contact:** Human Resources. **E-mail address:** jobs@carolinafarmcredit.com (for support staff positions and more information). **World Wide Web address:** http://www.carolinafarmcredit.com. **Description:** Farm Credit Services provides financial services through 39 branch offices across the United States. FCS offers long-, intermediate-, and short-term financing to agricultural producers, farm-related businesses, fishermen, part-time farmers, and rural homeowners. **NOTE:** Please visit http://www.agfirst.com and click the 'Employment Opportunities' button to search for job opportunities at Farm Credit institutions. **Positions advertised include:** Appraiser; Credit Analyst. **Corporate headquarters location:** This location. **Other area locations:** Statewide.

SCOTT & STRINGFELLOW, INC.
2626 Glenwood Avenue, Suite 430, Raleigh NC 27608. 919/571-1893. **Toll-free phone:** 800/763-1893. **Contact:** Hiring Manager. **E-mail address:** resume@scottstringfellow.com. **World Wide Web address:** http://www.scottstringfellow.com. **Description:** A full-service regional brokerage and investment banking firm. Services include investment advice and brokerage for individual and institutional clients, investment banking and securities underwriting for corporations and municipalities, and a wide array of other investment-related financial services including investment advisory services through its affiliate, Scott & Stringfellow Capital Management, Inc. Founded 1893. **Corporate headquarters location:** Richmond VA. **Other area locations:** Statewide. **Other U.S. locations:** SC; VA. **Parent company:** BB&T Corporation. **Listed on:** New York Stock Exchange. **Stock exchange symbol:** BBT. **Number of employees nationwide:** 600.

WACHOVIA CORPORATION
301 South College Street, Suite 4000, One Wachovia Center, Charlotte NC 28202. 704/374-6161. **Recorded jobline:** 888/WORK4WB. **Contact:** Human Resources Director. **E-mail address:** firstplace@wachovia.com (for contract employment). **World Wide Web address:** http://www.wachovia.com. **Description:** A full-service financial and banking services firm offering mortgage, credit, and securities services. **Positions advertised include:** Manager of Financial Analysis and Production; Senior Credit Default Swap Trader; CIB Risk Officer; Quality Assurance Analyst; Senior Trader; Finance Senior Consultant; Junior High Yield Trader; Systems Analyst; Loan Market Research Analyst; Client Manager. **Corporate headquarters**

location: This location. **Other area locations:** Statewide. **Other U.S. locations:** Nationwide. **International locations:** Worldwide. **Listed on:** New York Stock Exchange. **Stock exchange symbol:** WB. **Number of employees worldwide:** 87,000.

Ohio

C.H. DEAN & ASSOCIATES, INC.
2480 Kettering Towers, Dayton OH 45423. 937/222-9531. **Toll-free phone:** 800/327-3656. **Fax:** 937/227-9304. **Contact:** Human Resources. **E-mail address:** info@chdean.com. **World Wide Web address:** http://www.chdean.com. **Description:** A private investment management company. Founded in 1972. **Corporate headquarters location:** This location. **Other area locations:** Columbus OH.

KEYCORP
127 Public Square, Cleveland OH 44114. 216/689-3000. **Recorded jobline:** 888/539-7247. **Contact:** Michelle Rochon, Director of Personnel. **World Wide Web address:** http://www.keybank.com. **Description:** A diverse financial services company offering commercial and retail banking, financial management, brokerage services, mortgage banking, and trust services. **Corporate headquarters location:** This location. **Listed on:** New York Stock Exchange. **Stock exchange symbol:** KEY. **Annual sales/revenues:** More than $100 million.

MBNA MARKETING SYSTEMS
388 South Main Street, Suite 303, Akron OH 44311. 330/761-5000. **Recorded jobline:** 800/637-2070. **E-mail address:** central@mbnacareers.com. **Contact:** Human Resources. **World Wide Web address:** http://www.mbnainternational.com. **Description:** Provides credit cards and cross-sells individual loan, deposit, and insurance products. **Positions advertised include:** New Account Specialist; Customer Marketing Account Manager; Customer Satisfaction Account Manager; Customer Assistance Account Manager. **Parent company:** MBNA Corporation (Newark DE). **Operations at this facility include:** Customer Service; Marketing; Regional Headquarters; Sales. **Number of employees at this location:** 600. **Corporate headquarters location:** Wilmington DE. **Other area locations:** Akron OH. **Listed on:** New York Stock Exchange. **Stock exchange symbol:** KRB.

McDONALD & COMPANY INVESTMENTS, INC.
800 Superior Avenue, Cleveland OH 44114. 216/443-2300. **Contact:** Human Resources. **World Wide Web address:** http://www.mcdonaldinvest.com. **Description:** Operates a regional investment banking, brokerage, and investment advisory business. **Corporate headquarters location:** This location. **Subsidiaries include:** McDonald & Company; McDonald & Company Securities, Inc. **Parent company:** KeyCorp. **Number of employees nationwide:** 1,030.

STATE TEACHERS RETIREMENT SYSTEM OF OHIO
275 East Broad Street, Columbus OH 43215-3771. 614/227-2908. **Fax:** 614/227-2952. **Contact:** Staffing Coordinator. **E-mail address:** resumes@strsoh.org. **World Wide Web address:** http://www.strsoh.org/jobs.htm. **Description:** One of the largest pension funds in the United States, serving Ohio's teachers and managing assets totaling $50 billion. The nonprofit fund serves over 375,000 members and retirees. Founded in 1920. **Positions advertised include:** Associate Teacher; General Counsel. **Special programs:** Internships; Co-ops. **Office hours:** Monday - Friday, 8:00 a.m. - 4:30 p.m. **Corporate headquarters location:** This location. **Number of employees at this location:** 675.

WACHOVIA SECURITIES
110 Main Street, Dayton OH 45402. 937/228-2828. **Toll-free phone:** 800/543-9083. **Fax:** 937/226-6767. **Contact:** Human Resources. **World Wide Web address:** http://www.wachovia.com. **Description:** An international securities brokerage and investment firm. The company offers clients more than 70 different investment products including stocks, options, bonds, commodities, tax-favored investments, and insurance, as well as several specialized financial services. **Other U.S. locations:** Nationwide.

Oregon

AMERICONTINENTAL COLLECT COMPANY
P.O. Box 3514, Portland OR 97208. 503/241-1118. **Physical address:** 1500 SW First Street, Suite 885, Portland OR 97209. **Contact:** Human Resources. **World Wide Web address:** http://www.accountsreceivable.com. **Description:** A collection agency. **Corporate headquarters location:** This location.

COLUMBIA MANAGEMENT GROUP
121 SW Morrison, Suite 700, Portland OR 97204. 503/222-3600. **Contact:** Human Resources. **World Wide Web address:** http://www.columbiamanagement.com. **Description:** An investment management firm. **Parent company:** Bank of America.

COUNTRYWIDE HOME LOANS INC.
9738 SE Washington Street, Suite S, Portland OR 97216. 503/255-7584. **Fax:** 503/255-8093. **Contact:** Human Resources. **World Wide Web address:** http://www.countrywide.com. **Description:** Offers consumer home loans. **Positions advertised include:** Home Loans Consultant. **Corporate headquarters location:** Calabasas CA. **Parent company:** Countrywide Financial Corporation.

HARLAND FINANCIAL SOLUTIONS
400 SW Sixth Avenue, Suite 200, Portland OR 97204. 503/274-7280. **Toll-free phone:** 800/274-7280. **Fax:** 503/274-7284. **Contact:** Anne Centis, Employment Manager. **World Wide Web address:** http://www.harlandfinancialsolutions.com. **Description:** A leading provider of integrated, financial software. Founded in 1978. **NOTE:** Unsolicited resumes are not accepted. **Positions advertised include:** Database Administrator; G/L Accountant; Senior Programmer; Network Administrator. **Special programs:** Internships. **Corporate headquarters location:** This location. **Other U.S. locations:** Nationwide. **Parent company:** John H. Harland Company. **Listed on:** New York Stock Exchange. **Stock exchange symbol:** JH.

KPMG
1300 SW Fifth Avenue, Suite 3800, Portland OR 97201. 503/221-6500. **Contact:** Recruiting Coordinator. **World Wide Web address:** http://www.kpmg.com. **Description:** KPMG delivers a wide range of value-added assurance, tax, and consulting services. Founded in 1897. **Corporate headquarters location:** Montvale NJ. **Other U.S. locations:** Nationwide. **International locations:** Worldwide. **Parent company:** The company is a leader among professional services firms engaged in capturing, managing, assessing, and delivering information to create knowledge that will help its clients maximize shareholder value. **Operations at this facility include:** This location houses the offices of the company's legal department as well as the top management staff.

MILLENNIUM FUNDING GROUP
805 Broadway Street, Suite 600, Vancouver WA 98660-3333. 877/771-6566. **Fax:** 877/771-6555. **Contact:** Recruiting Department. **E-mail address:** hr@mfgloans.com. **World Wide Web address:** http://www.mfgloans.com. **Description:** A national mortgage lender offering wholesale non-prime, first, and second loan products to mortgage brokers and the secondary mortgage market. Founded in 1999. **Positions advertised include:** Legal Assistant; Senior Corporate Trainer; Secondary Marketing Analyst. **Corporate headquarters location:** This location.

PAULSON INVESTMENT COMPANY
811 SW Naito Parkway, Suite 200, Portland OR 97204. 503/243-6000. **Fax:** 503/243-6018. **Contact:** Human Resources. **World Wide Web address:** http://www.paulsoninvestment.com. **Description:**

Paulson Investment Company is a full-service brokerage firm engaged in the purchase and sale of securities, trading, market-making, and other investment banking activities. The company has independent branch offices in cities throughout the West, Midwest, and on the East Coast. **Corporate headquarters location:** This location. **Parent company:** Paulson Capital Corporation.

PHILLIPS & COMPANY SECURITIES, INC.
220 NW Second Avenue, Suite 950, Portland OR 97209. 503/224-0858. **Toll-free phone:** 888/667-4114. **Fax:** 503/224-8207. **Contact:** Executive Recruiter. **World Wide Web address:** http://www.phillipsandco.com. **Description:** A brokerage firm specializing in corporate and private client accounts. Founded in 1992. **NOTE:** Entry-level positions are offered. **Special programs:** Training. **Corporate headquarters location:** This location.

UBS FINANCIAL SERVICES
805 SW Broadway, Suite 2600, Portland OR 97205. 503/221-5800. **Contact:** Kerry McHale, Personnel Director. **World Wide Web address:** http://www.financialservicesinc.ubs.com. **Description:** A full-service securities firm with over 300 offices nationwide. Services include investment banking, asset management, merger and acquisition consulting, municipal securities underwriting, estate planning, retirement programs, and transaction management. UBS PaineWebber offers its services to corporations, governments, institutions, and individuals. Founded in 1879. **Corporate headquarters location:** New York NY. **Other U.S. locations:** Nationwide.

Pennsylvania

ADVANTA CORPORATION
Welsh & McKean Roads, P.O. Box 844, Spring House PA 19477-0844. 215/657-4000. **Contact:** Human Resources. **World Wide Web address:** http://www.advanta.com. **Description:** Advanta Corporation is a consumer financial services holding company. The company provides origination and management services for credit cards and mortgages; markets deposit products; and engages in credit insurance, life insurance, disability insurance, and unemployment insurance services. **Positions advertised include:** Business Analyst; Marketing Analyst. **Corporate headquarters location:** This location. **Other U.S. locations:** CA; MD; NJ; NY. **Subsidiaries include:** Advanta Leasing Corporation specializes in small-ticket equipment leasing; Colonial National Bank offers traditional financial services. **Listed on:** NASDAQ. **Stock exchange symbol:** ADVNA; ADVNB. **Number of employees nationwide:** 1,750.

COLLEGE CREDIT CARD CORPORATION
1500 JFK Boulevard, Suite 800, Philadelphia PA 19102. 215/568-1700. **Fax:** 215/568-1701. **Contact:** Edward Soloman, President. **Description:** Markets credit cards and other financial services to college students on-campus and to the general public at special events and venues. **Special programs:** Internships. **Corporate headquarters location:** This location. **Other U.S. locations:** Monroeville PA. **Parent company:** Campus Dimensions Inc. **Listed on:** Privately held. **Number of employees at this location:** 60. **Number of employees nationwide:** 115.

DELAWARE INVESTMENTS
2005 Market Street, Philadelphia PA 19103. 215/255-1200. **Fax:** 215/255-1002. **Contact:** Personnel. **World Wide Web address:** http://www.delawarefunds.com. **Description:** Specializes in mutual funds and investment management. **Positions advertised include:** Business Analyst; Staff Accountant; Accounting Systems Derivative Analyst. **Parent company:** Lincoln Financial Group.

DUN & BRADSTREET INFORMATIONAL RESOURCES
899 Easton Road, Bethlehem PA 18025. 610/882-7000. **Contact:** Human Resources. **E-mail address:** perezd@dnb.com. **World Wide Web address:** http://www.dnb.com. **Description:** Provides business-to-business credit, marketing, and investment management services. **Positions advertised include:** Relationship Manager; Merger and Acquisition Analyst; Quality and Compliance Leader. **Corporate headquarters location:** Short Hills NJ.

FEDERATED INVESTORS
Federated Investors Tower, 1001 Liberty Avenue, Pittsburgh PA 15222-3779. 412/288-1900. **Contact:** Human Resources Department. **E-mail address:** resume@federatedinv.com. **World Wide Web address:** http://www.federatedinvestors.com. **Description:** Sells and manages mutual funds. **NOTE:** Online application is encouraged. **Positions advertised include:** Sr. Investment Analyst; Fund Administrator; Performance Risk Analyst; Technical Specialist.

FIRST CLEARFIELD FUNDS INC.
1801 JFK Boulevard, Suite 1109, Philadelphia PA 19103. 215/557-8620. **Contact:** Human Resources. **Description:** Provides homeowner loans.

FIRST COMMONWEALTH TRUST COMPANY
P.O. Box 400, 614 Philadelphia Street, Indiana PA 15701. 724/465-3282. **Fax:** 724/463-5719. **Contact:** Rose Cogley, Personnel Manager. **World Wide Web address:** http://www.fcfbank.com. **Description:** A state-chartered trust company specializing in estate planning, living trusts, pension plans, and investment management. **Corporate headquarters location:** This location. **Other U.S. locations:** Bridgeville PA; Chambersburg PA; DuBois PA; Hollidaysburg PA; Huntingdon PA; Johnstown PA; New Castle PA. **Parent company:** First Commonwealth Financial Corporation. **Operations at this facility include:** Administration; Divisional Headquarters; Regional Headquarters; Sales; Service. **Listed on:** New York Stock Exchange. **Stock exchange symbol:** FCF. **Number of employees at this location:** 20. **Number of employees nationwide:** 35.

FISERV
2005 Market Street, Philadelphia PA 19103-3212. 215/636-3000. **Contact:** Anna DiDio, Vice President of Human Resources. **World Wide Web address:** http://www.fiserv.com. **Description:** Provides integrated processing and support services to securities brokerage affiliates of its owner institutions. **Positions advertised include:** Facility Control Shift Leader; Network Technician; System Administration Supervisor; Tools Group Analyst. **Corporate headquarters location:** Brookfield WI. **Other area locations:** Valley Forge PA; Pittsburgh PA; Huntingdon Valley PA; Norristown PA; King of Prussia PA. **Listed on:** NASDAQ. **Stock exchange symbol:** FISV.

GMAC MORTGAGE CORPORATION
132 Welsh Road, Suite 130, P.O. Box 2046, Horsham PA 19044. 215/682-4500. **Contact:** Human Resources. **E-mail address:** staffing@gmacm.com. **World Wide Web address:** http://www.gmacmortgage.com. **Description:** Provides a wide range of mortgage banking and related financial services. Founded in 1908. **Special programs:** Internships. **Office hours:** Monday - Friday, 8:30 a.m. - 5:00 p.m. **Corporate headquarters location:** Bloomington MN. **Other U.S. locations:** Nationwide. **Subsidiaries include:** Residential Funding Corporation. **Parent company:** General Motors Corporation. **Operations at this facility include:** Administration; Research and Development; Sales; Service. **Number of employees at this location:** 800. **Number of employees nationwide:** 3,300.

JANNEY MONTGOMERY SCOTT INC. (JMS)
1801 Market Street, 9th Floor, Philadelphia PA 19103. 215/665-6000. **Toll-free phone:** 800/526-6397. **Fax:** 215/587-9623. **Contact:** Human Resources. **E-mail address:** careers@jmsonline.com. **World Wide Web address:** http://www.janneys.com. **Description:** A full-service brokerage firm with 100 branch offices.

Positions advertised include: Receptionist; Mutual Funds Clerk; New Accounts Clerk; Sales Assistant. **Corporate headquarters location:** This location. **Parent company:** Penn Mutual Life Insurance Company. **Operations at this facility include:** Sales.

EDWARD JONES
2550 Mosside Boulevard, Suite 104, Monroeville PA 15146. 412/372-3511. **Contact:** Human Resources. **World Wide Web address:** http://www.edwardjones.com. **Description:** A securities brokerage firm.

MELLON FINANCIAL CORPORATION
500 Grant Street, One Mellon Bank Center, Room 705, Pittsburgh PA 15258-0001. 412/234-5000. **Contact:** Human Resources. **E-mail address:** recruiting@mellon.com. **World Wide Web address:** http://www.mellon.com. **Description:** A global financial services company. Mellon is one of the world's leading providers of financial services for institutions, corporations and high net worth individuals, providing institutional asset management, mutual funds, private wealth management, asset servicing, payment solutions and investor services, and treasury services. Mellon has approximately $4.7 trillion in assets under management, administration or custody, including $781 billion under management. **Positions advertised include:** Buyer; Distributed Application Developer; Operations Specialist; Project Manager; Senior Buyer; Trust Operations Specialist. **Corporate headquarters location:** This location. **Subsidiaries include:** Mellon Mortgage Company. **Listed on:** New York Stock Exchange. **Stock exchange symbol:** MEL. **Annual sales/revenues:** More than $100 million.

MERRILL LYNCH
120 Regent Court, Suite 200, State College PA 16801. 814/238-0100. **Contact:** Office Manager. **World Wide Web address:** http://www.ml.com. **Description:** Provides financial services in the areas of securities, extensive insurance, and real estate and related services. Merrill Lynch, which is one of the largest securities brokerage firms in the United States, also brokers commodity futures and options, and corporate and municipal securities, and is engaged in investment banking activities.

NVR MORTGAGE FINANCE INC.
111 Ryan Court, Pittsburgh PA 15205. 412/276-4225. **Fax:** 412/429-4542. **Contact:** Human Resources. **E-mail address:** kkimberl@nvrinc.com. **World Wide Web address:** http://www.nvrinc.com. **Description:** Provides financial and mortgage services. **NOTE:** Mail resumes to: NVR Inc., Human Resources Department, 7601 Lewinsville Road, Suite 300, McLean VA 22102. 703/761-2000. **Positions advertised include:** Financial Analyst; Management Trainee; Sales and Marketing Associate. **Corporate headquarters location:** McLean VA. **Other U.S. locations:** Nationwide. **Parent company:** NVR. **Number of employees at this location:** 140. **Number of employees nationwide:** 500.

PNC FINANCIAL SERVICES GROUP
USX Tower, 600 Grant Street, Pittsburgh PA 15219. **Fax:** 800/267-3755. **Recorded jobline:** 800/PNC-JOBS. **Contact:** Human Resources Department. **E-mail address:** resumes@pncbank.com. **World Wide Web address:** http://www.pnc.com. **Description:** Offers a complete range of financial services and products to individuals and corporations. Major businesses include corporate banking, consumer banking, PNC Mortgage, and PNC Asset Management Group. **NOTE:** Entry-level positions, part-time jobs, and second and third shifts are offered. Mailed in resumes should be sent in a scannable format, check the Website for further details. **Positions advertised include:** Branch Financial Sale Consultant; Branch Services Manager; Customer Service Associate; Senior Financial Consultant; Teller; Financial Processor. **Special programs:** Training; Co-ops; Summer Jobs. **Corporate headquarters location:** This location. **Other area locations:** Philadelphia PA. **Other U.S. locations:** Nationwide. **Subsidiaries include:** Blackrock Financial Management; PNC Mortgage. **Operations at this facility include:** Administration; Sales. **Listed on:** New York Stock Exchange. **Stock exchange symbol:** PNC. **Annual sales/revenues:** More than $100 million. **Number of employees at this location:** 5,000.

PARENTE RANDOLPH, PC
46 Public Square, Suite 400, Wilkes-Barre PA 18701. 570/820-0100. **Fax:** 570/824-9865. **Contact:** Human Resources. **E-mail address:** hr@parentenet.com. **World Wide Web address:** http://www.parentenet.com. **Description:** Parente Randolph is one of the mid-Atlantic's leading independent accounting and consulting firms. The firm's 400 employees provide accounting, audit, tax, and general business consulting services to corporations and closely held businesses from 10 offices in Pennsylvania, New Jersey, and Delaware. Industry expertise includes healthcare, senior living services, financial services, education, government/nonprofit, manufacturing, construction, real estate, retail, wholesale, and distribution. Specialty services include corporate finance, business reorganization, forensic accounting, and litigation support. Parente Randolph affiliates provide technology consulting, energy consulting, HR consulting, leadership development and training, and executive search services. Founded in 1970. **Positions advertised include:** Accountant; Tax Accountant. **Special programs:** Internship.

PHILADELPHIA STOCK EXCHANGE INC.
1900 Market Street, Philadelphia PA 19103. 215/496-5000. **Fax:** 215/496-1196. **Contact:** Human Resources. **World Wide Web address:** http://www.phlx.com. **Description:** A stock exchange. **Positions advertised include:** Chief Enforcement Counsel; Corporate Counsel; Manager, Financial Reporting & Compliance; Lead Programmer/Analyst; Lead J2EE Developer; Business Analyst; Testing Analyst.

PUBLIC FINANCIAL MANAGEMENT, INC.
2 Logan Square, Suite 1600, Philadelphia PA 19103. 215/567-6100. **Fax:** 215/567-4180. **Contact:** Marie Biggans, Human Resources Associate. **E-mail address:** recruit@publicfm.com. **World Wide Web address:** http://www.pfm.com. **Description:** A leading financial advisory firm serving the public sector. Public Financial Management oversees $7.5 billion in public sector funds. **Corporate headquarters location:** This location. **Other area locations:** Harrisburg PA. **Other U.S. locations:** Newport Beach CA; San Francisco CA; Washington DC; Miami FL; Fort Myers FL; Orlando FL; Sarasota FL; Atlanta GA; Des Moines IA; Boston MA; Trenton NJ; New York NY; Harrisburg PA; Pittsburgh PA; Memphis TN; Dallas TX; Austin TX; Houston TX. **Parent company:** Marine Midland Bank. **CEO:** F. John White. **Number of employees at this location:** 50.

RITTENHOUSE FINANCIAL SERVICES
100 Matsonford Road, 5 Radnor Corporate Center, Suite 300, Radnor PA 19087-4541. **Toll-free phone:** 800/847-6369. **Contact:** Human Resources. **E-mail address:** Rittenhouse.HR@nuveen.com. **World Wide Web address:** http://www.rittenhousefinancial.com. **Description:** A money management firm. **Positions advertised include:** Investment Portfolio Specialist; Manager, Internal Audit; Operations Analyst. **Parent company:** Nuveen.

SEI INVESTMENTS COMPANY
One Freedom Valley Drive, Oaks PA 19456. 610/676-1000. **Contact:** Human Resources. **E-mail address:** careers@seic.com. **World Wide Web address:** http://www.seic.com. **Description:** SEI Investments operates primarily in two business markets: Trust and Banking and Fund Sponsor/Investment Advisory. The company invests for clients worldwide in both public and private markets. SEI Investments also provides investment and business solutions to those who serve their own investor clients. SEI Investments provides direct investment solutions for $100 billion of investable capital and delivers systems and business

solutions to organizations investing nearly $1 trillion. SEI Investments is one of the largest providers of trust systems in the world. **NOTE:** Jobseekers should indicate area of interest when applying. **Positions advertised include:** Private Equity Accountant; Hedge Fund Accountant; Fund Accounting Supervisor; Investor Services Representative. **Operations at this facility include:** Administration; Research and Development; Sales; Service. **Listed on:** NASDAQ. **Stock exchange symbol:** SEIC. **CEO:** Alfred West. **Annual sales/revenues:** More than $100 million. **Number of employees nationwide:** 1,300. **Number of employees worldwide:** 1,400.

UBS FINANCIAL SERVICES
1735 Market Street, Mellon Bank Center, Philadelphia PA 19103. 215/496-2000. **Contact:** Human Resources. **World Wide Web address:** http://www.ubs.com. **Description:** A full-service securities firm with over 300 offices nationwide. Services include investment banking, asset management, merger and acquisition consulting, municipal securities underwriting, estate planning, retirement programs, and transaction management. Services are offered to corporations, governments, institutions, and individuals. Founded in 1879. **Corporate headquarters location:** New York NY. **Other U.S. locations:** Nationwide. **Annual sales/revenues:** More than $100 million.

THE VANGUARD GROUP, INC.
P.O. Box 2900, Valley Forge PA 19482. 610/669-1000. **Contact:** Human Resources. **E-mail address:** careers@vanguard.com. **World Wide Web address:** http://www.vanguard.com. **Description:** A mutual funds company that also offers assistance in educational financing, retirement planning, and trust services. **Corporate headquarters location:** This location. **Positions advertised include:** Planning and Reporting Coordinator; Tax Administrator; Business Reporting Analyst; Compliance Administrator.

WADDELL & REED
2 Meridian Boulevard, Wyomissing PA 19610. 610/374-6249. **Fax:** 610/374-6293. **Contact:** Human Resources. **World Wide Web address:** http://www.waddell.com. **Description:** Waddell and Reed is a mutual fund and financial planning company that also offers a multitude of insurance plans. **Positions advertised include:** Financial Planners. **Corporate headquarters location:** Overland Park KS.

Rhode Island
BANK OF AMERICA
111 Westminster Street, Providence RI 02903. 401/865-7996. **Fax:** 401/865-7997. **Contact:** Human Resources. **E-mail address:** jennifer.m.ranaldi@bankofamerica.com. **World Wide Web address:** http://www.bankofamerica.com. **Description:** A large financial institution serving individual consumers, small and middle market businesses and large corporations with banking, investing, asset management and other financial and risk-management products and services. The company has 5,800 retail banking offices, more than 16,700 ATMs and a major online banking presence with more than 14 million active users. **NOTE:** Must apply for current job openings online. **Positions advertised include:** Trust Assistant; Credit Support Associate; Operations Representative; Trust Officer I; Intermediate Financial Analyst; Private Client Advisor II; Teller; Change Manager; Control Administrator; Senior Legal Admin Assistant; Program Development Manager; Sales Assistant; Trust Officer II; Document Administrator II. **Special programs:** Internships. **Corporate headquarter locations:** Charlotte NC. **Other area locations:** Statewide. **Other U.S. locations:** Nationwide. **Listed on:** New York Stock Exchange. **Stock exchange symbol:** BAC.

FIDELITY INVESTMENTS
100 Salem Street, Smithfield RI 02917. 401/292-5050. **Toll-free phone:** 800/FIDELITY. **Fax:** 401/275-3029. **Contact:** Human Resources. **World Wide Web address:** http://www.fidelity.com. **Description:** A financial services conglomerate that is the world's #1 mutual fund company. Serving more than 19 million individual and institutional clients, Fidelity manages approximately 360 funds and has more than $1 trillion of assets under management. It also operates a leading online discount brokerage and has investor centers in about 100 cities throughout the US and Canada, as well in Europe and Asia. **NOTE:** See website for current job openings and to apply online. **Positions advertised include:** Senior Training Administrator; Consultant Software Engineer; Helpdesk Specialist; Project Manager; Executive Secretary; Business Analyst; Communications Analyst; Inside Wholesaler. **Special programs:** Entry-level jobs; Internships; Temporary jobs. **Corporate headquarters location:** Boston MA. **Other U.S. locations:** Covington KY; Jersey City NJ; Marlborough MA; Merrimack NH; New York City NY; Raleigh NC; Salt Lake City UT; Westlake TX. **International locations:** Canada; Hong Kong; Japan; France; India; United Kingdom; Germany; Ireland. **Operations at this facility include**: Regional operating center for Fidelity Investments Institutional Services Company and Fidelity Personal Investments phone site. **Number of employees at this location:** 1,600.

MORGAN STANLEY
1900 Financial Plaza, 19th Floor, Providence RI 02903. 401/863-8400. **Contact:** Human Resources. **World Wide Web address:** http://www.morganstanley.com. **Description:** With more than 600 offices in 28 countries, Morgan Stanley is a global financial services firm specializing in securities, investment management and credit services. **NOTE:** Must apply online. See website for current job openings and application instructions. **Positions advertised include:** Wealth Management Analyst; Financial Advisor Trainee; Registered Client Service Associate. **Listed on:** New York Stock Exchange. **Stock exchange symbol:** MS.

PROVIDENCE FINANCIAL NETWORK
1 Richmond Square, 1st Floor Suite 330-D, Providence RI 02906. 888/359-8260. **Fax:** 206/495-6504. **Contact:** Vicki Moore. **E-mail address:** vmoore@pnfdirect.com. **World Wide Web address:** http://www.pfndirect.com. **Description:** Provides financial services in the residential, commercial, business and personal finance markets. **NOTE:** Send resumes via e-mail. Entry-level positions available. **Positions advertised include:** Consultant Liaison/Account Representative; Residential Services Consultant/Executive; Commercial Services Consultant/Executive; Liquidation Services Consultant/Executive; Real Estate Consultant/Investor. **Corporate headquarters location:** This location.

South Carolina
AMERICAN GENERAL FINANCIAL SERVICES
412 Bells Highway, Walterboro SC 29488. 843/549-5536. **Fax:** 843/549-6543. **Contact:** Human Resources. **World Wide Web address:** http://www.agfinance.com. **Description:** A large consumer lending company with over 1,300 branches nationwide. The company's subsidiaries are engaged in the consumer finance, credit card, and insurance businesses. Founded in 1920. **Positions advertised include:** Management Trainee; Customer Account Administrator; Customer Account Specialist. **Corporate headquarters location:** Evansville IN. **Parent company:** American International Group, Inc. (New York NY).

HAWTHORNE CORPORATION
6543 Fair Street, P.O. Box 61000, Charleston SC 29419. 843/797-8484. **Fax:** 843/797-5258. **Contact:** David Bush, Vice President of Operations. **E-mail address:** dave.bush@hawthornecorp.com. **World Wide Web address:** http://www.hawthornecorp.com. **Description:** A holding company whose subsidiaries are engaged in a wide variety of industries including aviation (operating airports); real estate operations that develop land for fixed base operations; and financial services (investor services). **Corporate headquarters location:** This location.

MERRILL LYNCH & CO., INC.
One Chamber of Commerce Drive, P.O. Box 5607, Hilton Head SC 29938. 843/785-9620. **Contact:**

Human Resources. **World Wide Web address:** http://www.ml.com. **Description:** One of the largest securities brokerage firms in the world, Merrill Lynch provides financial services in securities, financial planning, insurance, estate planning, mortgages, and related areas. The company also brokers commodity futures and options, is a major underwriter of new securities issues, and is a dealer in corporate and municipal securities. **Positions advertised include:** Financial Advisor; Underwriter; Investment Officer; Auditor; Cash Flow Director; Real Estate Team Leader; Account Executive; Credit Officer. **Corporate headquarters location:** New York NY. **Other locations:** Worldwide. **Listed on:** New York Stock Exchange. **Stock exchange symbol:** MER. **Annual sales/revenues:** $28.3 billion. **Number of employees worldwide:** 50,900.

SMITH BARNEY
551 East Main Street, P.O. Box 2628, Spartanburg SC 29302. 864/585-7761. **Contact:** Human Resources. **World Wide Web address:** http://www.smithbarney.com. **Description:** An investment banking and securities broker. Smith Barney also provides related financial services including stocks, bonds, and money market accounts. **Parent company:** Citigroup.

SECURITY FINANCE
P.O. Drawer 811, Spartanburg SC 29304. 864/582-8193. **Physical address:** 181 Security Place, Spartanburg SC 29307. **Fax:** 864/582-2532. **Contact:** Human Resources. **E-mail address:** careers@security-finance.com. **World Wide Web address:** http://www.securityfinancecorp.com. **Description:** A consumer loan company. **Corporate headquarters location:** This location.

WASHINGTON MUTUAL HOME LOANS
1333 Main Street, Columbia SC 29201. 803/929-7900. **Contact:** Human Resources. **World Wide Web address:** http://www.wamuhomeloans.com. **Description:** A provider of single-family residential mortgages and one of the nation's largest originators of home loans. **Positions advertised include:** Loan Specialist; Home Loan Manager; Support Specialist; Mortgage Underwriter. **Other area locations:** Florence SC; Greenville SC. **Parent company:** Washington Mutual, Inc.

South Dakota

CNA SURETY CORPORATION
101 South Phillips Avenue, Sioux Falls SD 57104-6703. 605/336-0850. **Toll-free phone:** 888/736-9704. **Fax:** 605/335-0357. **Contact:** Human Resources. **E-mail address:** employment@cnasurety.com. **World Wide Web address:** http://www.cnasurety.com. **Description:** CNA Surety Corporation is the largest publicly traded surety company in the country. Through its principal subsidiary, Western Surety Company, CNA Surety provides surety and fidelity bonds in all 50 states through a combined network of approximately 35,000 independent agencies. **Positions advertised include:** Citrix/Middleware Administrator; Licensing Associate - CNA Insurance; Office Supply Clerk; Underwriting Associate I. **Special programs:** Internships. **Corporate headquarters location:** Chicago IL. **Other U.S. locations:** Nationwide. **Listed on:** New York Stock Exchange. **Stock exchange symbol:** SUR.

CITIGROUP, INC.
701 East 60th Street North, MC 3105, Sioux Falls SD 57117. 605/331-1876. **Fax:** 605/331-1185. **Contact:** Heidi Anderson, Human Resources. **E-mail address:** Heidi.Anderson@citigroup.com. **World Wide Web address:** http://www.careers.citigroup.com. **Description:** A global financial services company that provides consumers, corporations, governments and institutions with a broad range of financial products and services, including consumer banking and credit, corporate and investment banking, insurance, securities brokerage and asset management. **NOTE:** See website for current openings and to apply online; open positions also listed on www.careerbuilder.com. **Positions advertised include:** Risk Analyst; Clerk; Project Analyst; Project Leader; Trial Manager; Technical Advisor; Account Executive; VP/Associate Manager – Policy Risk. **Corporate headquarters location:** New York NY. **Operations at this facility include:** All aspects of processing for Citibank credit cards and student loan products. **Listed on:** New York Stock Exchange. **Stock exchange symbol:** C. **Number of employees at this location:** 3,200.

EDWARD JONES
3001 South Phillips Avenue, Sioux Falls SD 57105. 605/330-0090. **Toll-free phone:** 800/999-5650. **Contact:** Human Resources. **World Wide Web address:** http://www.edwardjones.com. **Description:** An investment firm. **NOTE:** Please see website to search for jobs and apply online. **Corporate headquarters:** St. Louis MO. **Other U.S. locations:** Nationwide. **International locations:** Canada; United Kingdom.

PREMIER BANKCARD
900 West Delaware, Sioux Falls SD 57104. 605/357-3440. **Recorded jobline:** 800/501-5091. **Contact:** Human Resources. **E-mail address:** jobs@firstpremier.com. **World Wide Web address:** http://www.firstpremier.com. **Description:** A credit card provider. First PREMIER Bank owns the credit card accounts and credit card loans of PREMIER Bankcard; PREMIER Bankcard is the service provider for those accounts. Founded in 1989. Serves over 3.1 million customers nationwide. **NOTE:** Search and apply for positions online. **Positions advertised include:** Bilingual Retention Sales Agent; Collections Representative; Retention Representative; Senior Business Analyst; Workforce Specialist; Director of Networking. **Special programs:** Internships; Jobs for recent graduates. **Corporate headquarters location:** This location. **Other area locations:** Dakota Dunes SD; Spearfish SD; Watertown SD.

Tennessee

CATERPILLAR FINANCIAL SERVICES CORPORATION
2120 West End Avenue, Nashville TN 37203-0001. 615/341-1000. **Contact:** Human Resources. **World Wide Web address:** http://www.cat.com. **Description:** Provides financing for Caterpillar brand equipment. **NOTE:** Search and apply for positions or submit resume online. **Positions advertised included:** Credit Manager; Associate Tax Accountant; Accountant. **Corporate headquarters location:** This location. **Other U.S. locations:** Nationwide. **International locations:** Worldwide.

CHARLES SCHWAB
320 North Cedar Bluff Road, The Stokely Building, Suite 101, Knoxville TN 37923. 800/435-4000. **Contact:** Human Resources. **World Wide Web address:** http://www.schwab.com. **Description:** Provides investment services. **NOTE:** Submitting your resume online is the fastest and most efficient way to express interest in job opportunities at Charles Schwab. **Positions advertised include:** Investment Specialist. **Corporate headquarters location:** San Francisco CA. **Other area locations:** Memphis TN; Brentwood TN.

FIRST DATA
2525 Horizon Lake Drive, Suite 120, Memphis TN 38133. 901/371-8000. **Toll-free phone:** 800/238-7675. **Contact:** Human Resources Department. **World Wide Web address:** http://www.firstdata.com . **Description:** Engaged in debit and credit card authorization and processing, check authorization, ATM transaction processing, Internet transaction processing, and the development of new payment methods. **Parent company:** First Data. **Listed on:** New York Stock Exchange. **Stock exchange symbol:** FDC. **Annual sales/revenues:** More than $100 million. **Number of employees worldwide:** 30,000.

MERRILL LYNCH
101 South Highland Avenue, Jackson TN 38301. 731/422-6600. **Contact:** Personnel. **World Wide Web**

address: http://www.ml.com. **Description:** One of the largest securities brokerage firms in the United States. Merrill Lynch provides financial services in securities, insurance, real estate, and related services. The company also brokers commodity futures, commodity options, and corporate and municipal securities. In addition, Merrill Lynch is engaged in investment banking activities. **NOTE:** Search and apply for positions online. **Corporate headquarters location:** New York NY. **Other area locations:** Memphis TN; Chattanooga TN; Nashville TN. **Other U.S. locations:** Nationwide.

MORGAN KEEGAN & COMPANY
Morgan Keegan Tower, 50 North Front Street, Memphis TN 38103. 901/524-4100. **Fax:** 901/579-4833. **Contact:** Personnel. **E-mail address:** jobs@morgankeegan.com. **World Wide Web address:** http://www.morgankeegan.com. **Description:** A regional investment firm serving individual investors throughout the southeastern United States. Morgan Keegan & Company also serves institutional clients nationwide and abroad. **NOTE:** Search and apply for positions online. **Positions advertised include:** Associate Analyst; Editor, Equity Research; Annuity Processor; Technical Analyst. **Listed on:** New York Stock Exchange. **Stock exchange symbol:** MOR. **Corporate headquarters location:** This location. **Other U.S. locations:** Nationwide. **Parent company:** Regions Financial Corporation.

PERSHING YOAKLEY & ASSOCIATES
One Perkins Place, 525 Portland Street, Knoxville TN 37919. 865/673-0844. **Fax:** 865/673-0173. **Contact:** Deanna Sexton, Director of Human Resources. **E-mail address:** recruiter@pyapc.com. **World Wide Web address:** http://www.pyapc.com. **Description:** An accounting firm offering tax services, business consulting, strategic planning, health care management, audit services, real estate and strategic facilities planning, and other professional and health care consulting services. Founded in 1983. **NOTE:** Search and apply for positions online. **Positions advertised include:** Audit Manager; Managed Care Executive; Sr. Coding & Compliance Consulting Staff; Physician Services Coding Consultant. **Other U.S. locations:** Atlanta GA; Tampa FL; Charlotte NC.

UBS FINANCIAL SERVICES.
3102 West End Avenue, Suite 500, Nashville TN 37203. 615/750-8000. **Contact:** Human Resources. **World Wide Web address:** http://www.ubs.com. **Description:** A full-service securities firm with over 300 offices nationwide. Services include investment banking, asset management, merger and acquisition consulting, municipal securities underwriting, estate planning, retirement programs, and transaction management. UBS PaineWebber offers its services to corporations, governments, institutions, and individuals. Founded in 1879. **Corporate headquarters location:** New York NY. **Other area locations:** Chattanooga TN; Cookeville TN; Jackson TN; Kingsport TN; Knoxville TN; Memphis TN; Oak Ridge TN. **Other U.S. locations:** Nationwide. **Annual sales/revenues:** More than $100 million.

WACHOVIA SECURITIES
10 Cadillac Drive, Suite 300, Brentwood TN 37027. 931/552-1300. **Toll-free phone:** 800/736-1300. **Fax:** 931/551-8031. **Contact:** Human Resources. **World Wide Web address:** http://www.wachoviasec.com. **Description:** Provides a broad range of financial services including asset management, lending, trust services, and investment banking. **Corporate headquarters location:** Richmond VA.

Texas

AIM MANAGEMENT GROUP INC.
301 Congress Avenue, Suite 1700, Austin TX 78701. 512/424-3100. **Contact:** Human Resources. **World Wide Web address:** http://www.aiminvestments.com. **Description:** Manages mutual funds. **Positions advertised include:** Analyst/Automation Specialist; Financial Reporting Accountant; Administrative Assistant; Senior Financial Writer; Project Event Coordinator; Internal Wholesaler; Accounting Clerk; Fund Accountant; HR Business Partner; Quantitative Research Associate; Compliance Specialist; Multimedia Specialist; Manager – Competitive Research. **Corporate headquarters location:** This location. **Other U.S. locations:** Denver CO; San Francisco CA. **Listed on:** Privately held. **President/CEO:** Mark Williamson. **Number of employees nationwide:** 2,368.

AMERICAN EXPRESS FINANCIAL ADVISORS
9442 Capital of Texas Highway North, Plaza One Suite 800, Austin TX 78759. 512/346-5400. **Fax:** 512/338-1705. **Contact:** Katie Froelich. **E-mail address:** advisor.resumes@aexp.com. **World Wide Web address:** http://www.americanexpress.com/advisors. **Description:** Offers financial planning, annuities, mutual funds, insurance, investment certificates, and institutional investment advisory trust, tax preparation, and retail securities brokerage services. **Corporate headquarters location:** Minneapolis MN. **Other U.S. locations:** Nationwide. **Parent company:** American Express Company (New York NY).

AMERICAN PHYSICIANS SERVICE GROUP, INC. (APS)
1301 South Capital of Texas Highway, Suite C-300, Austin TX 78746. 512/328-0888. **Fax:** 512/314-4398. **Contact:** Human Resources. **World Wide Web address:** http://www.amph.com. **Description:** A management and financial services firm with subsidiaries and affiliates that provide medical malpractice insurance services for doctors, brokerage and investment services to institutions and individuals, lithotripsy services in 34 states, refractive vision surgery, and dedicated care facilities for Alzheimer's patients. **Corporate headquarters location:** This location. **Subsidiaries include:** APS Financial Corporation; AMPC Insurance Services; American Physicians Insurance Exchange. **Listed on:** NASDAQ. **Stock exchange symbol:** AMPH.

AMERICREDIT CORPORATION
801 Cherry Street, Suite 3900, Fort Worth TX 76102. 817/302-7000. **Toll-free phone:** 866/411-HR4U. **Fax:** 817/302-7878. **Contact:** Personnel. **World Wide Web address:** http://www.americredit.com. **Description:** A national consumer finance company specializing in the purchasing, securitizing, and servicing of automobile loans. **Position advertised include:** Centralized Funding Analyst; Credit Risk Analyst. **Corporate headquarters location:** This location. **Other U.S. locations:** Nationwide. **Listed on:** New York Stock Exchange. **Stock exchange symbol:** ACF.

BANK ONE TEXAS
202 West Main Street, Dallas TX 75220. 214/290-2000. **Toll-free phone:** 877/226-5663. **Contact:** Human Resources. **World Wide Web address:** http://www.bankone.com. **Description:** Provides financial services in the areas of stocks, bonds, and mutual funds. **NOTE:** Please visit website to search for jobs and apply online. **Corporate headquarters location:** Chicago IL. **Other area locations:** Statewide. **Other U.S. locations:** Nationwide. **International locations:** Worldwide. **Parent company:** Bank One Corporation. **Listed on:** New York Stock Exchange. **Stock exchange symbol:** ONE.

BEAR, STEARNS & COMPANY, INC.
300 Crescent Court, Suite 200, Dallas TX 75201. 214/979-7900. **Fax:** 214/979-7911. **Contact:** Human Resources. **World Wide Web address:** http://www.bearstearns.com. **Description:** A leading worldwide investment banking, securities trading, and brokerage firm. The firm's business includes corporate finance, mergers and acquisitions, public finance, institutional equities, fixed income sales and trading, private client services, foreign exchange, future sales and trading, derivatives, and asset management. **Corporate headquarters location:** New York NY. **Other U.S. locations:** Nationwide. **Parent company:** The Bear Stearns Companies Inc. **Listed on:** New York

Stock Exchange. **Stock exchange symbol:** BSC. **Number of employees nationwide:** 10,500.

CENTEX CORPORATION
P.O. Box 199000, Dallas TX 75219. 214/981-5000. **Physical address:** 2728 North Harwood Street, Suite 200, Dallas TX 75201. **Contact:** Human Resources. **E-mail address:** human.resources@checmail.com. **World Wide Web address:** http://www.centex.com. **Description:** Provides home building, mortgage banking, contracting, and construction products and services. **Positions advertised include:** Loan Officer. **Corporate headquarters location:** This location. **Other U.S. locations:** Nationwide. **International locations:** United Kingdom. **Listed on:** New York Stock Exchange. **Stock exchange symbol:** CTX. **Number of employees worldwide:** 18,000.

CHARLES SCHWAB
100 Congress Street, Austin TX 78701. 512/370-3880. **Toll-free phone:** 877/729-2379. **Contact:** Human Resources. **World Wide Web address:** http://www.schwab.com. **Description:** Founded in 1974, this company is a large financial firm marketing its services to individuals, institutions, and financial professionals. This location manages the operations for its online trading subsidiary, Cybertrader. **NOTE:** To read more about Cybertrader, visit its website at http://www.cybertrader.com. Apply online. **Positions advertised include:** Technology Solutions Staff; Staff Software Developer; Reporter Developer; Associate Web Application Developer. **Listed on:** New York Stock Exchange. **Stock exchange symbol:** SCH. **Number of employees worldwide:** 19,000.

CITIGROUP
1301 Fannin Street, Suite 2300, Houston TX 77002. 713/752-5200. **Fax:** 972/653-8154. **Contact:** Jim Price, Human Resources. **World Wide Web address:** http://www.citigroup.com. **Description:** Citigroup offers financial solutions with home mortgages, credit cards, personal loans, insurance, business financing, banking and investments. **NOTE:** Please visit website to search for jobs and apply online. **Positions advertised include:** Citified Loan Processor, Marketing Administrator; Credit Specialist; Senior Underwriter; Mortgage Processor; Senior Lead Analyst; QC Analyst; Associate Finance Director; Vice President of Financial Planning. Corporate headquarters location: New York NY. **Other U.S. locations:** Nationwide. **Listed on:** New York Stock Exchange. **Stock exchange symbol:** C.

CONSELIUM
14221 Dallas Parkway, Suite 1500, Dallas TX 75254. 214/540-8428. **Contact:** Maurice Gilbert, Managing Director. **E-mail address:** maurice@conselium.com. **World Wide Web address:** http://www.conselium.com. **Description:** Provides auditing services. Specialty areas are high-tech, financial and operations services for Fortune 500 companies. **Positions advertised include:** IT Auditors; Auditor Senior. **Other area locations include:** Houston TX. **Other U.S. locations:** NY; CA. **Listed on:** Privately held.

A.G. EDWARDS & SONS
2305 Cedars Spring Road, Suite 300, Dallas TX 75201. 214/954-1999. **Contact:** Human Resources. **E-mail address:** employment@agedwards.com. **World Wide Web address:** http://www.agedwards.com. **Description:** An investment firm offering bonds, money market accounts, mutual funds, IRAs, annuities, estate planning, and related services. Founded in 1887. **NOTE:** Mail resume to A.G. Edwards Employment Department; One North Jefferson; St. Louis MO 63103; or, complete online resume. **Corporate headquarters location:** St. Louis MO.

FIDELITY INVESTMENTS
1576 East Southlake Boulevard, Southlake TX 76092. 817/310-3656. **Contact:** Human Resources. **World Wide Web address:** http://www.fidelity.com. **Description:** One of the nation's leading investment counseling and mutual fund/discount brokerage firms. **NOTE:** Entry-level positions and second and third shifts are offered. **Positions advertised include:** Principal Operating Systems Consultant. **Special programs:** Internships. **Internship information:** The company has an MIS internship program. Applications must be submitted by March 1st via e-mail or in writing. **Corporate headquarters location:** Boston MA. **Other U.S. locations:** Nationwide. **Listed on:** Privately held.

FIRST SOUTHWEST COMPANY
325 North Saint Paul Street, Suite 800, Dallas TX 75201-4652. 214/953-4000. **Fax:** 214/953-8790. **Contact:** Human Resources. **World Wide Web address:** http://www.firstsw.com. **Description:** Offers a full line of investment services including public, private, and corporate banking; funds management; trading of debt and equity securities; institutional sales; and clearing. **Corporate headquarters location:** This location. **Other area locations:** Abilene TX; Austin TX; Fort Worth TX; Houston TX; Lubbock TX; San Antonio TX. **Other U.S. locations:** AR; FL; CA; NY; AL.

FORESTERS
10333 Richmond Avenue, Suite 700, Houston TX 77042. 713/266-3463. **Contact:** Human Resources. **E-mail address:** recruitsoft@foresters.biz. **World Wide Web address:** http://www.forester.com. **Description:** A financial services company specializing in life insurance and annuities. **NOTE:** This company has several sales offices throughout Texas and the U.S. See website for job listings and locations. Apply online. **Positions advertised include:** Financial Representative. **Corporate headquarters location:** Toronto Canada. **Other area locations:** Amarillo TX; Austin TX; Bedford TX; San Antonio TX. **International locations:** United Kingdom.

INVESTOOLS INC.
5959 Corporate Drive, Suite LL250, Houston TX 77036. 281/588-9700. **Fax:** 281/588-9797. **Contact:** Human Resources. **World Wide Web address:** http://www.investools.com. **Description:** Develops and provides proprietary analytics and content to investors. **Corporate headquarters location:** This location. **Listed on:** American Stock Exchange. **Stock exchange symbol:** IED.

J.P. MORGAN CHASE & COMPANY
1717 Main Street, Suite 4300, Dallas TX 75201. 214/290-5350. **Contact:** Human Resources. **World Wide Web address:** http://www.jpmorganchase.com. **Description:** Specializes in global financial services and retail banking. J.P. Morgan Chase and Company's services include asset management, card member services, community development, commercial banking for middle market companies, diversified consumer lending, global markets, home finance, investment banking, private banking, private equity, regional consumer and small business banking, and treasury and securities services. **NOTE:** Job seekers are encouraged to apply via the company's website: http://careers.jpmorganchase.com. **Other U.S. locations:** Nationwide. **International locations:** Worldwide. **Listed on:** New York Stock Exchange. **Stock exchange symbol:** JPM.

JEFFERIES & COMPANY, INC.
13355 Noel Road, Suite 1400, Dallas TX 75240. 972/701-3000. **Contact:** Human Resources. **World Wide Web address:** http://www.jefco.com. **Description:** Engaged in equity, convertible debt and taxable fixed income securities brokerage and trading, and corporate finance. Jefferies & Company is one of the leading national firms engaged in the distribution and trading of blocks of equity securities primarily in the third market. Founded in 1962. **NOTE:** This company has positions in investment banking and in office support. For investment banking, jobseekers should e-mail their resumes to Westcoastrecruiting@jefco.com. Office support inquires should be faxed to Mel Locke, Director of People Services, at 310/914-1066 or via e-

mail at mlocke@jefco.com. **Corporate headquarters location:** New York NY. **Other area locations:** Houston TX. **Parent company:** Jefferies Group, Inc.

MARSH USA, INC.
1000 Main Street, Suite 3000, Houston TX 77002. 713/276-8000. **Contact:** Human Resources. **World Wide Web address:** http://www.marsh.com. **Description:** Provides advice and services worldwide to clients concerned with the management of assets and risks. Specific services include insurance and risk management services, reinsurance, consulting and financial services, merchandising, and investment management. The company has subsidiaries and affiliates in 57 countries, with correspondents in 20 other countries. **NOTE:** This company has offices throughout Texas and the United States. See its website for a complete list. Resumes must be submitted online. **Corporate headquarters location:** New York NY. **Parent company:** Marsh & McLennan Companies (MMC). **Listed on:** New York Stock Exchange. **Stock exchange symbol:** MMC.

MCDONALD FINANCIAL CORPORATION
1616 South Voss Road, Suite 870, Houston TX 77207. 713/977-2113. **Fax:** 713/977-4055. **Contact:** Human Resources. **World Wide Web address:** http://www.mcdonaldfinancial.com. **Description:** MFC Finance Company provides financing for construction.

MERRILL LYNCH
701 South Taylor Street, Suite 100, Amarillo TX 79101. 806/376-4861. **Contact:** Human Resources. **World Wide Web address:** http://www.ml.com. **Description:** Brokers in securities, option contracts, commodities, financial futures contracts, and insurance. **NOTE:** Interested jobseekers must apply online at the corporate website. **Positions advertised include:** Commercial Banking Professionals; Financial Advisor. **Other U.S. locations:** Nationwide. **Listed on:** New York Stock Exchange. **Stock exchange symbol:** MER.

RBC DAIN RAUSCHER
2711 North Haskell Avenue, Suite 2400, Dallas TX 75204. 214/989-1000. **Contact:** Jamie Tiland, Office Administrator. **World Wide Web address:** http://www.rbcdain.com. **Description:** A financial consulting and securities firm. The company also provides real estate syndication and property investment services, as well as data processing services. **Corporate headquarters location:** Minneapolis MN. **Parent company:** Royal Bank of Canada. **Operations at this location:** This office specializes in personal investing. **Listed on:** New York Stock Exchange. **Stock exchange symbol:** RY. **Number of employees worldwide:** 6,000.

RAYMOND JAMES & ASSOCIATES
6034 West Courtyard Drive, Suite 305, Austin TX 78730. 512/418-1700. **Contact:** Human Resources. **World Wide Web address:** http://www.raymondjames.com. **Description:** An investment brokerage firm offering financial planning, investment banking, asset management, and trust services. Founded in 1962. **NOTE:** This company has 10 other locations in the Austin area. See website for additional addresses and contact information.

SOUTHWEST SECURITIES PRIVATE CLIENT GROUP, INC.
1201 Elm Street, Suite 3500, Dallas TX 75270-2180. 214/651-1800. **Contact:** Human Resources. **E-mail address:** careers@onlinepreferred.com. **World Wide Web address:** http://www.onlinepreferred.com. **Description:** Southwest Securities Group, Inc. is a holding company with subsidiaries engaged in providing securities brokerage, investment banking, and investment advisory services. The company also offers online banking and stock trading services. Founded in 1972. **Corporate headquarters location:** This location. **Other area locations:** Longview TX: Lufkin TX; Georgetown TX; San Antonio TX; Austin TX; Houston TX. **Other U.S. locations:** Chicago IL; Albuquerque NM; Santa Fe NM; Oklahoma City, OK. **Listed on:** New York Stock Exchange. **Stock exchange symbol:** SWS. **Number of employees worldwide:** 1,100.

TRADESTAR INVESTMENTS
1900 St. James Place, Suite 120. Houston TX 77056. 713/350-3700. **Fax:** 713/350-3838. **Contact:** Human Resources. **Wide Web address:** http://www.selecttrade.com. **Description:** A regional brokerage firm. **NOTE:** Apply online at this company's website. **Corporate headquarters location:** This location. **Other area locations:** Dallas TX.

UBS FINANCIAL SERVICES INC.
100 Crescent Court, Suite 600, Dallas TX 75201. 214/220-0400. **Contact:** Branch Manager. **World Wide Web address:** http://www.ubs.com. **Description:** A full-service securities firm with over 300 offices nationwide. Services include investment banking, asset management, merger and acquisition consulting, municipal securities underwriting, estate planning, retirement programs, and transaction management. Clients include corporations, governments, institutions, and individuals. Founded in 1879. **NOTE:** This company has more than 30 locations throughout Texas. See website for job listings, locations and application information. **Positions advertised include:** Experienced Financial Advisor. **Special programs:** Internships; MBA Training. **Corporate headquarters location:** New York NY. **Other U.S. locations:** Nationwide.

WACHOVIA SECURITIES
200 Crescent Court, Suite 1080, Dallas TX 75201. 214/740-3200. **Toll-free phone:** 800/327-6861. **Fax:** 214/740-3250. **Contact:** Human Resources. **World Wide Web address:** http://www.wachoviasec.com. **Description:** Provides a broad range of financial services, including asset management, lending, trust services, and investment banking. **Corporate headquarters location:** Richmond VA. **Other area locations:** Major metropolitan cities in TX. **Other U.S. locations:** Nationwide.

WORLD FINANCIAL GROUP
2600 Via Fortuna, Suite 220, Austin TX 78746. 512/328-4220. **Contact:** Human Resources. **World Wide Web address:** http://www.wfg-online.com. **Description:** Offers a wide variety of financial services including mutual funds, debt consolidation, securities, mortgages, health insurance, and life insurance. **Parent company:** AEGON.

WUKASCH COMPANY
1810 Guadalupe Street, Austin TX 78701. 512/472-4700. **Contact:** Don C. Wukasch, President. **Description:** A diversified real estate and securities investment company providing real estate property management and securities portfolio management. **Special programs:** Internships. **Corporate headquarters location:** This location. **Listed on:** Privately held.

Utah

CITI COMMERCE SOLUTIONS
2195 University Park Boulevard, Layton UT 84041. 801/779-7000. **Fax:** 801/779-7011. **Contact:** Employment Manager. **World Wide Web address:** http://www.citicommercesolutions.citi.com. **Description:** Provides private-label credit programs and operational outsourcing services. **NOTE:** Please visit website http://careers.citigroup.com to search for current job openings and apply online. **Parent company:** Citigroup Inc.

DIRECT MORTGAGE CORPORATION
6995 South Union Park Center, Suite 540, Salt Lake City UT 84047. 801/924-2300. **Fax:** 801/924-2394. **Contact:** Human Resources. **World Wide Web address:** http://www.directmortgagewholesale.com. **Description:** A wholesale mortgage company. **NOTE:** See website for current job openings. Submit resume by e-mail or fax. **Positions advertised include:** Account Executive; Broker Coordinator; Underwriting. **Other area**

locations: Midvale UT. **Other U.S. locations:** Sacramento CA.

DISCOVER CARD SERVICES
8475 South Sandy Parkway, Sandy UT 84070. 801/542-5440. **Contact:** Human Resources. **World Wide Web address:** http://www.discovercard.com. **Description:** Provides customer service for Discover credit card holders and also engages in payment collection. **NOTE:** Please visit website for online application form. **Corporate headquarters location:** Riverwoods IL. **Other area locations:** Salt Lake City UT; West Valley City UT. **Other U.S. locations:** Nationwide. **International locations:** United Kingdom. **Number of employees nationwide:** 18,000.

GE CAPITAL FINANCIAL
4246 South Riverboat Road, Salt Lake City UT 84123. 801/517-5000. **Contact:** Human Resources. **World Wide Web address:** http://www.ge.com. **Description:** Provides second mortgage and home equity loans as well as corporate credit cards. **NOTE:** Please visit website to search for jobs and apply online. **Positions advertised include:** General Counsel. **Listed on:** New York Stock Exchange. **Stock exchange symbol:** GE. **Number of employees worldwide:** 315,000.

MERRILL LYNCH
Eagle Gate Tower, 60 East South Temple Street, Suite 200-61, Salt Lake City UT 84111. 801/535-1300. **Fax:** 801/355-3410. **Contact:** Human Resources. **World Wide Web address:** http://www.ml.com. **Description:** A diversified financial service organization. The company is a major broker in securities, option contracts, commodities and financial futures contracts, and insurance. Merrill Lynch also deals with corporate and municipal securities and investment banking. **NOTE:** Please visit website to search for jobs and apply online. **Positions advertised include:** Loan Accountant; Consulting Relationship Manager; Receptionist. **Corporate headquarters location:** New York NY. **Other area locations:** Statewide. **Other U.S. locations:** Nationwide. **International locations:** Worldwide.

PRESTIGE FINANCIAL
1420 South 500 West, Salt Lake City UT 84115. 866/PFS-CREDIT. **Fax:** 801/844-2626. **Contact:** Human Resources. **E-mail address:** jobs@gopfs.com. **World Wide Web address:** http://www.prestige-financial.com. **Description:** Provides consumer vehicle financing through a nationwide dealership network. **Corporate headquarters location:** This location. **Parent company:** Larry H. Miller Group.

SELECT PORTFOLIO SERVICING
P.O. Box 65250, Salt Lake City UT 84165-0250. 801/293-1883. **Contact:** Human Resources. **E-mail address:** Pam.Gurmankin@spservicing.com. **World Wide Web address:** http://www.spservicing.com. **Description:** A financial services company that engages in the servicing of single-family residential mortgage loans. It also services impaired credit loans and non-performing loans for a variety of clients. Founded in 1989. **NOTE:** Please visit website to search for jobs and apply online. **Positions advertised include:** Accounts Payable Specialist; Administrative Assistant; Bankruptcy Supervisor; Bankruptcy Specialist; Entry Level Office Position; Manager, Investor Reporting; Mortgage Collections Certified Real Estate Appraiser; Programmer Analyst. **Corporate headquarters location:** This location. **Other U.S. locations:** Jacksonville FL.

Virginia

CAPITAL ONE FINANCIAL CORPORATION
1680 Capital One Drive, McLean VA 22102. 703/720-1000. **Contact:** Management Recruiter. **E-mail address:** jobs@capitalone.com. **World Wide Web address:** http://www.capitalone.com. **Description:** A holding company. Its principal subsidiaries, Capital One Bank and Capital One, F.S.B., offer consumer lending products and are among the largest providers of MasterCard and Visa credit cards in the world. **Positions advertised include:** Transactions Attorney; Financial Analyst; Product Manager; Bilingual Relationship Manager; Statistician; State Tax Reporting Manager. **Corporate headquarters location:** This location. **Other U.S. locations:** CA; FL; ID; MA; TX; WA. **Listed on:** New York Stock Exchange. **Stock exchange symbol:** COF. **Number of employees at this location:** 1,000. **Number of employees nationwide:** 2,600.

CAPITAL GROUP COMPANIES
5300 Robin Hood Road, Norfolk VA 23513-2407. 757/461-2210. **Contact:** Human Resources. **Description:** Provides investment management services. **Positions advertised include:** Sr. Mutual Fund Accountant; Trainer; Retirement Plan Coordinator; HR Manager; Team Manager; Business Analyst.

CONSUMER PORTFOLIO SERVICES
860 Greenbrier Circle, Suite 600, Chesapeake VA 23320-2640. 757/420-3650. **Fax:** 757/413-5374. **Contact:** Human Resources. **World Wide Web address:** http://www.consumerportfolio.com. **Description:** Consumer Portfolio Services, Inc. is a specialty finance company that provides indirect automobile financing to vehicle purchasers with past credit problems, low incomes, or limited credit histories by purchasing retail installment sales contracts from factory franchised automobile dealers, securing them, accumulating the contracts into pools, and selling the pooled contracts to investors in the form of "AAA" rated asset-backed securities. Founded in 1991. Purchases contracts in 41 states from approximately 3,800 dealers. **Corporate headquarters location:** Irvine CA. **Listed on:** NASDAQ. **Stock exchange symbol:** CPSS.

DYNEX CAPITAL
4551 Cox Road, Suite 300, Glen Allen VA 23060. 804/217-5800. **Contact:** Human Resources. **E-mail address:** askdx@dynexcapital.com. **World Wide Web address:** http://www.dynexcapital.com. **Description:** A financial services company, which invests in loans and securities consisting of or secured by, single-family mortgage loans, commercial mortgage loans, manufactured housing installment loans and delinquent property tax receivables. **Corporate headquarters location:** This location. **Listed on:** New York Stock Exchange. **Stock exchange symbol:** DX.

FREDDIE MAC
8200 Jones Branch Drive, McLean VA 22102. 703/903-2000. **Contact:** Director of Employment. **World Wide Web address:** http://www.freddiemac.com. **Description:** Provides mortgage credit services and secondary mortgages. Founded in 1970. **NOTE:** Second and third shifts are offered. Search and apply for positions online. **Positions advertised include:** Collections Specialist; Control Manager; Business Planning and Development Manager; Marketing Communication Specialist; Business Applications Analyst; Financial Analyst; Senior Economist; Examiner; Operational Management Director; Website Production Manager; Research Analyst. **Special programs:** Internships; Co-ops. **Corporate headquarters location:** This location. **Other U.S. locations:** Woodland Hills CA; Washington DC; Atlanta GA; Chicago IL; New York NY; Carrollton TX. **Listed on:** New York Stock Exchange. **Stock exchange symbol:** FRE. **Number of employees nationwide:** 3,500.

LEGG MASON, INC.
8444 Westpark Drive, Suite 100, McLean VA 22102. 703/821-9100. **Fax:** 703/821-7597. **Contact:** Human Resources. **World Wide Web address:** http://www.leggmason.com. **Description:** Legg Mason is a holding company with subsidiaries engaged in securities brokerage and trading; investment management of mutual funds and individual and institutional accounts; underwriting of corporate and municipal securities and other investment banking activities; sales of annuities and banking services; and the provision of other financial services. The company

serves its brokerage clients through 128 offices. **NOTE:** Search and apply for positions online. **Positions advertised include:** Client Services Representative. **Corporate headquarters location:** Baltimore MD. **Subsidiaries include:** Legg Mason Wood Walker, Inc. (Baltimore MD) and Howard, Weil, Labouisse, Friedrichs, Inc. (New Orleans LA). Founded in 1899. **Listed on:** New York Stock Exchange. **Stock exchange symbol:** LM. **Number of employees nationwide:** 4,200.

NVR, INC.
11700 Plaza America Drive, Suite 500, Reston VA 20190. 703/956-4000. **Fax:** 703/956-4750. **Contact:** Human Resources. **E-mail address:** info@nvrinc.com. **World Wide Web address:** http://www.nvrinc.com. **Description:** A national homebuilder and mortgage company. Founded in 1948. **NOTE:** Entry-level positions and part-time jobs are offered. Search and apply for positions online. **Positions advertised include:** Mortgage Accountant; Network Engineer; Programmer/Analyst; Risk Management Analyst; Tax Accountant. **Special programs:** Internships; Training; Co-ops; Summer Jobs. **Corporate headquarters location:** This location. **Other U.S. locations:** DE; MD; NC; NJ; NY; OH; PA; SC; TN. **Listed on:** American Stock Exchange. **Stock exchange symbol:** NVR. **Annual sales/revenues:** More than $100 million. **Number of employees at this location:** 75. **Number of employees nationwide:** 3,500.

NATIONAL RURAL UTILITIES COOPERATIVE FINANCE CORPORATION
2201 Cooperative Way, Herndon VA 20171. 703/709-6700. **Fax:** 703/709-6773. **Contact:** Human Resources. **World Wide Web address:** http://www.nrucfc.org. **Description:** A nonprofit financial institution owned by more than 1,000 rural electric systems and related organizations. National Rural Utilities Cooperative Finance Corporation offers its members/owners a variety of loan, investment, service, and specialized financing options to supplement the loan programs of the Rural Utilities Service of the United States Department of Agriculture. **NOTE:** Search and apply for positions or submit resume online. **Positions advertised include:** AVP/Credit Analyst; Corporate Communications Specialist; corporate counsel; Corporate Paralegal. **Corporate headquarters location:** This location. **Number of employees nationwide:** 1,040.

SCOTT & STRINGFELLOW INC.
909 East Main Street, Richmond VA 23219. 804/643-1811. **Toll-free phone:** 800/552-7757. **Fax:** 804/643-3786. **Contact:** Jordan Ball, Manager. **World Wide Web address:** http://www.scottstringfellow.com. **Description:** A full-service regional brokerage and investment banking firm serving individual, institutional, corporate, and municipal clients in Virginia, North Carolina, and South Carolina. **NOTE:** Search and apply for positions online. **Positions advertised include:** Public Finance Assistant; Marketing Assistant; Administrative Assistant. **Corporate headquarters location:** This location. **Parent company:** BB&T Corporation. **Listed on:** New York Stock Exchange. **Stock exchange symbol:** BBT. **Number of employees nationwide:** 600.

STUDENT LOAN MARKETING ASSOCIATION (SALLIE MAE)
12061 Bluemont Way, Reston VA 20190. 703/810-3000. **Contact:** Employment. **World Wide Web address:** http://www.salliemae.com. **Description:** A major financial intermediary to the educational financing market in the U.S. The company provides student loan services, as well as other financial and management services to loan originators. The association also provides financing for academic equipment. Founded in 1972. **NOTE:** Search and apply for positions online. **Positions advertised include:** Accounts Payable Specialist; Web Solutions Manager; Litigation Paralegal; Mortgage Consultant; Collection Manager; Underwriter; Team Supervisor; Risk Analyst. **Corporate headquarters location:** This location. **Parent company:** SLM Corporation (also at this location.) **Number of employees nationwide:** 3,275.

Washington

CORUM GROUP LTD.
10500 NE Eighth Street, Suite 1500, Bellevue WA 98004. 425/455-8281. **Fax:** 425/455-1415. **Contact:** Gina Stanhope, Human Resources. **World Wide Web address:** http://www.corumgroup.com. **Description:** Assists software companies to successfully execute company mergers and alliances. **Corporate headquarters location:** This location.

INTERPACIFIC INVESTORS SERVICES, INC.
2623 Second Avenue, Seattle WA 98121-1294. 206/269-5050. **Fax:** 206/269-5055. **Contact:** Human Resources. **World Wide Web address:** http://www.iisbonds.com. **Description:** A regional securities broker/dealer specializing in conservative investments such as corporate and municipal bonds, mutual funds, stocks, and life insurance. **Sales Manager:** Bill Shultheis.

MERRILL LYNCH
601 108th Avenue NE, Suite 2100, Bellevue WA 98004. 425/462-8158. **Contact:** Human Resources. **World Wide Web address:** http://www.ml.com. **Description:** One of the largest securities brokerage firms in the United States, Merrill Lynch provides financial services in the following areas: securities, extensive insurance, and real estate and related services. The company also brokers commodity futures, commodity options, and corporate and municipal securities. In addition, Merrill Lynch is engaged in investment banking activities. **Positions advertised include:** Senior Underwriter; Investment Officer; Cash Flow Associate. **Corporate headquarters location:** New York NY. **Listed on:** NASDAQ. **Stock exchange symbol:** MITT.

NATIONAL SECURITIES CORPORATION
1001 Fourth Avenue, Suite 2200, Seattle WA 98154. 206/622-7200. **Contact:** Human Resources. **World Wide Web address:** http://www.nationalsecurities.com. **Description:** A securities brokerage providing services such as asset management, investment banking, and institutional sales and research. **Corporate headquarters location:** This location.

NORTHWEST FARM CREDIT SERVICES
P.O. Box 2515, Spokane WA 99224. 509/340-5300. **Physical address:** 1700 South Assembly Street, Spokane WA 99224. **Toll-free phone:** 800/743-2125. **Fax:** 800/255-1789. **Contact:** Human Resources. **E-mail address:** hrdept@farm-credit.com. **World Wide Web address:** http://www.farm-credit.com. **Description:** Provides long-, intermediate-, and short-term financing to agricultural producers, farm-related businesses, fisherman, part-time farmers, and country homeowners. The banks and related associations provide credit and credit-related services to eligible borrowers for qualified agricultural purposes. **Positions advertised include:** Mortgage Loan Officer. **Corporate headquarters location:** This location. **Other U.S. locations:** AK; ID; MT.

RAGEN MACKENZIE INCORPORATED
999 Third Avenue, Suite 4000, Seattle WA 98104. 206/343-5000. **Fax:** 206/389-8245. **Contact:** Personnel Department. **World Wide Web address:** http://www.ragen-mackenzie.com. **Description:** Engaged in investment banking. Founded in 1982.

FRANK RUSSELL COMPANY
909 A Street, Tacoma WA 98402. 253/572-9500. **Fax:** 253/594-1727. **Recorded jobline:** 253/596-5454. **Contact:** Personnel. **E-mail address:** empsvc@russell.com. **World Wide Web address:** http://www.russell.com. **Description:** Provides a variety of financial services such as investment management, mutual funds, and investment consulting. Founded in 1936. **NOTE:** Jobseekers may submit applications and resumes online. **Corporate headquarters location:** This location. **Other U.S.**

locations: Boston MA; New York NY. **International locations:** Australia; Canada; France; Italy; New Zealand; Singapore; South Africa; United Kingdom. **Number of employees at this location:** 1,000. **Number of employees nationwide:** 1,200.

SIRACH CAPITAL MANAGEMENT INC.
520 Pike Street, Suite 2800, Seattle WA 98101-1389. 206/624-3800. **Fax:** 206/626-5410. **Contact:** Personnel. **World Wide Web address:** http://www.sirachcap.com. **Description:** An investment advisory firm specializing in managing the assets of institutions and high-worth individuals. Services include mutual funds, 401(k) plan, investment, and trust fund management. **Number of employees at this location:** 45.

Wisconsin

AMERICAN APPRAISAL ASSOCIATES
411 East Wisconsin Avenue, Suite 1900, Milwaukee WI 53202. 414/271-7240. **Toll-free phone:** 800/558-8650. **Fax:** 414/221-7065. **Contact:** Colleen Stoltmann, Human Resources Manager. **E-mail address:** careers@american-appraisal.com. **World Wide Web address:** http://www.american-appraisal.com. **Description:** An independent international valuation consulting organization specializing in tangible and intangible assets; closely held securities; insurance services; and merger, acquisition, and investment services. Founded in 1896. **Positions advertised include:** Associate Appraiser/Valuation Consultant. **Corporate headquarters location:** This location. **Operations at this facility include:** Administration; Regional Headquarters; Sales. **Listed on:** Privately held. **Number of employees worldwide:** 900.

AMERICAN EXPRESS FINANCIAL ADVISORS
1400 Lombardi Avenue, Suite 201, IDS Center, Green Bay WI 54304. 920/499-2141. **Fax:** 920/498/9588. **Contact:** Human Resources Department. **World Wide Web address:** http://www.amercianexpress.com. **Description:** Provides a variety of financial products and services to help individuals, businesses, and institutions establish and achieve their financial goals. American Express Financial Advisors has a field of more than 10,000 financial advisors in the United States and offers financial planning, annuities, mutual funds, insurance, investment certificates, and institutional investment advisory trust, tax preparation, and retail securities brokerage services.

ROBERT W. BAIRD & COMPANY
777 East Wisconsin Avenue, P.O. Box 672, Milwaukee WI 53201-0672. 414/765-3500. **Toll-free phone:** 800/792-2473. **Fax:** 414/765-7303. **Contact:** Human Resources. **World Wide Web address:** http://www.rwbaird.com. **Description:** A full-service investment firm. Founded in 1919. **NOTE:** Entry-level positions and part-time jobs are offered. **Positions advertised include:** Trading Support Specialist; Equity Research Associate; Branch Registered Sales Associate; Computer Operations Analyst; Retirement Plans Field Consultant; Experience Financial Advisor. **Corporate headquarters location:** This location. **Number of employees at this location:** 1,200. **Number of employees nationwide:** 2,300.

BRADY CORPORATION
BRADY FINANCIAL COMPANY
P.O. Box 571, Milwaukee WI 53201-0571. 414/358-6600. **Physical address:** 6555 West Good Hope Road, Milwaukee WI 53223. **Fax:** 800/292-2289. **Contact:** Human Resources. **World Wide Web address:** http://www.bradycorp.com. **Description:** Develops, manufactures, and markets industrial identification products and coated materials. Brady Financial Company (also at this location) provides treasury, insurance, credit, collection, and other services to Brady Corporation operations. **Positions advertised include:** Flow Process Engineer; Benefits Supervisor; collection Coordinator; Internal Auditor; Senior Tax Analyst; Senior Organizational Effectiveness Consultant. **Special programs:** Internships. **Corporate headquarters locations:** This location. **Number of employees worldwide:** 3,100.

DOVER DIVERSIFIED
2607 North Grandview Boulevard, Suite 105, Waukesha WI 53188. 262/548-6060. **Fax:** 262/548-6069. **Contact:** Human Resources Department. **World Wide Web address:** http://www.dovercorporation.com. **Description:** Dover Diversified consists of eight companies organized into two groups: Industrial Equipment and Process Equipment. **Parent company:** Dover Corporation (New York NY).

EDWARD JONES
200 East Main Street, Sun Prairie WI 53590. 608/837-2700. **Fax:** 888/672-2353. **Contact:** Personnel. **World Wide Web address:** http://www.edwardjones.com. **Description:** A securities brokerage firm. **Corporate headquarters location:** Maryland Heights MD. **Listed on:** Privately held. **Number of employees at this location:** 5. **Number of employees nationwide:** 7,000.

GREAT LAKES EDUCATIONAL LOAN SERVICES, INC.
2401 International Lane, Madison WI 53704-3192. 608/246-1800. **Fax:** 608/246-1600. **Contact:** Human Resources Department. **E-mail address:** hr@mygreatlakes.com. **World Wide Web address:** http://www.mygreatlakes.com. **Description:** A leading guarantor and servicer of student loans. **NOTE:** Entry-level positions are offered. **Positions advertised include:** Loan Counselor; Senior Data Administrator; IT Project Manager; Project Engineering Deployment Specialist. **Special programs:** Internships. **Corporate headquarters location:** This location. **Other area locations:** Eau Claire WI. **Other U.S. locations:** Oak Brook IL; St. Paul MN; Columbus OH. **Parent company:** Great Lakes Higher Education Corporation. **Number of employees at this location:** 550. **Number of employees nationwide:** 700.

RBC DAIN RAUSCHER INC.
4010 West Spencer Street, Appleton WI 54914-4064. 920/739-6311. **Toll-free phone:** 800/365-0050. **Fax:** 920/739-9447. **Contact:** Human Resources. **World Wide Web address:** http://www.rbcdain.com. **Description:** A financial consulting and securities firm. **Other area locations:** Brookfield WI; Eau Claire WI; Madison WI; Mequon WI; Milwaukee WI; Sturgeon Bay WI. **Other U.S. locations:** Nationwide. **Parent company:** Royal Bank of Canada. **Number of employees worldwide:** 6,000.

WASHINGTON MUTUAL HOME LOANS
11200 West Parkland Avenue, Milwaukee WI 53224. 414/359-9300. **Contact:** Human Resources. **World Wide Web address:** http://www.wamuhomeloans.com. **Description:** Provides single-family residential mortgages. **Other U.S. locations:** Jacksonville FL. **Parent company:** Washington Mutual, Inc. **Operations at this facility include:** This locations provides customer service to those customers with existing home loans.

WELLS FARGO ADVANTAGE FUNDS
100 Heritage Reserve, Menomonee Falls WI 53051. 414/359-1400. **Contact:** Human Resources Department. **World Wide Web address:** http://www.wellsfargoadvantagefunds.com. **Description:** A mutual fund retailer and investment firm. **Positions advertised include:** Senior Marketing and Database Analyst; Compliance Manager. **Other U.S. locations:** Nationwide. **Number of employees at this location:** 800.

HEALTH CARE SERVICES, EQUIPMENT, AND PRODUCTS

You can expect to find the following types of companies in this section:
Dental Labs and Equipment • Home Health Care Agencies • Hospitals and Medical Centers • Medical Equipment Manufacturers and Wholesalers • Offices and Clinics of Health Practitioners • Residential Treatment Centers/Nursing Homes • Veterinary Services

---

The number of openings in healthcare practitioners and technical operations and healthcare support occupations will grow 28.3% or 3,000,000 new jobs, from 10,619,000 to 13,625,000 jobs. Rapid growth among health-related occupations reflects an aging population that requires more healthcare, a wealthier population that can afford better healthcare, and advances in medical technology that permit more health problems to be treated more aggressively.

Alabama

BAPTIST MEDICAL CENTER OF PRINCETON
701 Princeton Avenue SW, Birmingham AL 35211. 205/783-3000. **Contact:** Human Resources. **World Wide Web address:** http://www.baptistmedical.org. **Description:** A 400-bed acute care hospital whose services include general medical and surgical procedures, heart and cancer programs, and a birthing center. **Positions advertised include:** Clinical Pharmacy Specialist; Registered Nurse (Multiple Departments); Physical Therapist; Medical Technologist; Radiology Technologist. **NOTE:** Search and apply for positions online. **Parent company:** Baptist Health System.

BROOKWOOD MEDICAL CENTER
2010 Brookwood Medical Center Drive, Birmingham AL 35209. 205/877-1467. **Fax:** 205/877-2279. **Contact:** Human Resources. **World Wide Web address:** http://www.bwmc.com. **Description:** A 586-bed tertiary care medical center. **Positions advertised include:** Acute Care Physical Therapist; Surgical Support Associate; RN; LPN; OR Assistant; Insurance Associate; Respiratory Therapist. **Parent company:** Tenet Healthcare Corporation.

CAREMARK RX
3000 Riverchase Galleria, Birmingham AL 35244. 205/733-8996. **Contact:** Human Resources. **World Wide Web address:** http://www.caremark.com. **Description:** A pharmaceutical company that provides pharmacy benefit management and therapeutic pharmaceutical services. Caremark Rx also offers pharmaceutical services that target chronic conditions and genetic disorders. **NOTE:** Search and apply for positions online. **Corporate headquarters location:** Nashville TN. **Listed on:** New York Stock Exchange. **Stock exchange symbol:** CMX.

CHILDREN'S HEALTH SYSTEM
1600 7th Avenue South, Birmingham AL 35233. 205/939-9100. **Fax:** 205/939-5111. **Contact:** Human Resources. **World Wide Web address:** http://www.chsys.org. **Description:** A pediatric healthcare system that includes Children's Hospital, a 225-bed pediatric hospital, and a statewide network of primary and specialty care offices. **Positions advertised include:** RT Technician; Coordinator, Inpatient Facility; CT/MRI Technologist; Medical Lab Technician; Imaging Center Assistant; Nursing Unit Director; Occupational Therapist; Operating Room Technician; Respiratory Therapist; RN.

ENOVATION GRAPHIC SYSTEMS, INC.
100 Centerview Drive, Suite 100, Birmingham AL 35216. 205/824-7699. **World Wide Web address:** http://www.enovationgraphics.com. **Contact:** Human Resources. **Description:** A worldwide distributor of plastic surgery instruments and equipment. **Corporate headquarters location:** Valhalla NY. **Parent Company:** Fuji Film.

GADSDEN REGIONAL MEDICAL CENTER
1007 Goodyear Avenue, Gadsden AL 35903. 256/494-4553. **Fax:** 256/494-4579. **Contact:** Human Resources. **World Wide Web address:** http://www.gadsdenregional.com. **Description:** A full-service medical center. **Positions advertised include:** Licensed Physical Therapist; Occupational Therapist; Registered Nurse; Ultrasound Tech; Respiratory Therapist; Radiology Technologist. **NOTE:** Entry-level positions and second and third shifts are offered. Search and apply for positions online.

HEALTHSOUTH CORPORATION
One HealthSouth Parkway, Birmingham AL 35243. 205/967-7116. **Fax:** 205/969-6884. **Contact:** Human Resources. **E-mail address:** employmentcoordinator@healthsouth.com. **World Wide Web address:** http://www.healthsouth.com. **Description:** Provides rehabilitative health care services through approximately 250 outpatient and 40 inpatient rehabilitation facilities, and several medical centers. Services offered include rehabilitation, occupational therapy, physical therapy, head injury therapy, respiratory therapy, speech-language pathology, surgery, laser treatment of tumors, and rehabilitation nursing. **Positions advertised include:** Systems Engineer; Project Manager; Sr. Accountant; Revenue Reporting Manager; Market Accountant. **Corporate headquarters location:** This location. **Other U.S. locations:** Nationwide. **International locations:** Australia; Puerto Rico.

HOWARD INSTRUMENTS
4749 Appletree Street, Tuscaloosa AL 35405. 205/553-4453. **Fax:** 205/569-9267. **Contact:** Human Resources. **E-mail address:** howard@howardinstruments.com. **World Wide Web address:** http://www.howardinstruments.com. **Description:** A wholesaler of ophthalmic equipment and supplies. Howard Instruments also offers repair services.

JACKSON COUNTY HEALTHCARE AUTHORITY
P.O. Box 1050, Scottsboro AL 35768. 256/259-4444. **Fax:** 256/218-3656. **Contact:** Human Resources. **E-mail address:** ssivley@jcha.org. **World Wide Web address:** http://www.jacksoncountyhospital.com. **Description:** Operates Jackson County Hospital and North Jackson Hospital. **Positions advertised include:** RN, Emergency Department; Patient Accounts Rep; Paramedic; Certified Athletic Trainer; Physical Therapist; Certified Respiratory Therapist. **Corporate headquarters location:** This location. **Operations at this facility include:** Administration; Service.

SEARCY HOSPITAL
P.O. Box 1090, Mount Vernon AL 36560. 251/829-9411. **Fax:** 251/829-9075. **Contact:** Human Resources. **Description:** A psychiatric hospital within the state of Alabama's Department of Mental Health/Mental Retardation. The hospital provides inpatient services to individuals with serious mental illnesses while promoting the individual's quality of life, human worth, and dignity. **Positions advertised include:** RN. **Corporate headquarters location:** Montgomery AL. **Operations at this facility include:** Administration; Service. **Number of employees at this location:** 750.

THREE SPRINGS, INC.
1131 Eagletree Lane, Huntsville AL 35801. 256/880-3339. **Toll-free phone:** 888/758-4356. **Fax:** 256/880-3082. **Contact:** Recruitment Officer. **E-mail:** employment@ threespings.com. **World Wide Web address:** http://www.threesprings.com. **Description:** Provides mental health counseling geared toward troubled teens and their families. **Positions advertised**

include: Counselor. **Other U.S. locations include:** FL, GA, NC, TN, MD. **President:** Thomas M. Watson.

L.V. STABLER MEMORIAL HOSPITAL
29 L.V. Stabler Drive, Greenville AL 36037. 334/383-2245. **Contact:** Human Resources. **World Wide Web address:** http://www.lvstabler.com. **Description:** A 72-bed hospital. **Positions advertised include:** CCU Registered Nurse; LPN; Medical Technologist; Registered Nurse (Multiple Positions). **Listed on:** Privately held. **Annual sales/revenues:** Less than $5 million. **Number of employees at this location:** 225.

Alaska

A.P.I. (ALASKA PSYCHIATRIC INSTITUTE)
2900 Providence Drive, Anchorage AK 99508. 907/269-7100. **Contact:** Cynthia Keyes, Personnel Officer. **World Wide Web address:** http://www.hss.state.ak.us/dbh/api. **Description:** A comprehensive, public, mental health treatment facility that is one of the only state-run institutions of its kind in Alaska. API provides treatment to more than 1,000 patients each year through the following units: the Youth Treatment Program for children and adolescents; the Security Treatment Program for forensic patients and short-term admissions for adults in crisis; the Third Floor Unit and Denali Treatment Unit for longer term adult patients; and the Intermediate Care Program for geriatric patients and patients who are developmentally disabled or suffer long-term medical problems with accompanying psychiatric difficulties. Founded in 1962. **NOTE:** Interested jobseekers should request an application through the Department of Administration, Division of Personnel, P.O. Box 110201, Juneau AK 99811-0201. Some positions are available only to state residents; this information is available on the state Website (http://www.state.ak.us). **Positions advertised include:** Nurse I/Nurse II (Psychiatric)

ALASKA REGIONAL HOSPITAL
P.O. Box 143889, Anchorage AK 99514-3889. 907/276-1131. **Physical address:** 2801 Debarr Road, Anchorage AK 99508. **Fax:** 907/264-1143. **Contact:** Human Resources. **World Wide Web address:** http://www.akreg.com. **Description:** A 238-bed, acute care hospital. The hospital has critical care units, emergency services, rehabilitation services, a maternity center, and a diagnostic imaging department. The hospital offers specialized neurosurgery, spinal surgery, and orthopedic surgery. As one of the only acute care hospitals in the state with direct airplane access, Alaska Regional Hospital serves as a medical referral center for the state. The hospital also has a referral center for cancer treatment. **Positions advertised include:** Clinical Exercise Physiologist; RN's; Occupational Therapist; Pharmacist; Physical Therapist. **Parent company:** Columbia/HCA Health Care Corporation is one of the largest health care services providers in the world, with more than 190 acute care and specialty hospitals in 26 states and two foreign countries.

FAIRBANKS MEMORIAL HOSPITAL/DENALI CENTER
1650 Cowles Street, Fairbanks AK 99701. 907/452-8181. **Contact:** Human Resources. **Description:** A non-profit, 162-bed hospital owned by the Greater Fairbanks Community Hospital Foundation and managed by Banner Health. **NOTE:** Search and apply for positions online. **Positions advertised include:** Area Healthcare Education Center (AHEC) Director; Certified Nursing Assistant; Clinical Informatics Spec; Critical Care CNS; Financial Counselor; HIRS Analyst; LPN II; Med Lab Tech; Medical Technologist; Network Analyst; Network Support Specialist; Nuclear Medicine Tech; Patient Care Coordinator; Phlebotomist; Radiology Technologist; RN; Respiratory Therapist; Senior Programmer/Analyst; Sexual Assault Nurse Examiner; Supervisor Clinical Informatics; Ultrasound Tech.

HOPE COMMUNITY RESOURCES, INC.
540 West International Airport Road, Anchorage AK 99518. 907/561-5335. **Toll-free phone:** 800/478-0078. **Fax:** 907/564-7429. **Recorded jobline:** 907/562-6226. **Contact:** Eva Jo Henning, Hiring Specialist. **E-mail address:** jobs@hopealaska.com. **World Wide Web address:** http://www.hopealaska.org. **Description:** A private, nonprofit organization providing support to people with developmental disabilities. Services focus on adults and children, community building, mental health, family support, consumer rights, employment, and cultural relevance. This location also hires seasonally. Founded in 1968. **Positions advertised include:** Behavioral Health Services Clinician; Care Coordinator; Home Alliance Coordinator; Individual Support Specialist; Mental Health Associate; Accountant. **Special programs:** Internships; Training; Summer Jobs. **Internship information:** Summer practicums are offered for students from New York, Oregon, and Ireland. **Office hours:** Monday - Friday, 8:00 a.m. - 5:00 p.m. **Corporate headquarters location:** This location. **Other area locations:** Barrow AK; Dillingham AK; Juneau AK; Kodiak AK; Seward AK; Wasilla AK. **Listed on:** Privately held. **Executive Director:** Stephen Lesko. **Annual sales/revenues:** $11 - $20 million.

KANAKANAK HOSPITAL
BRISTOL BAY AREA HEALTH CORPORATION
P.O. Box 130, Dillingham AK 99576. 907/842-5201. **Contact:** Victor Sifof, Personnel Director. **World Wide Web address:** http://www.ihs.gov. **Description:** A regional hospital providing a wide range of health services including radiology, a pharmacy, outpatient services, a mental health program, maternal/child health services, a clinical laboratory, and an alcohol and drug abuse recovery program. The staff travels to over 20 villages two months out of the year. Bristol Bay Area Health Corporation (BBAHC) in 1980 became one of the first tribal organizations in the nation to assume control of a Native American hospital/service unit under the Indian Self-Determination and Education Assistance Act. Kanakanak Hospital became the centerpiece of BBAHC's range of acute, preventive, and educational services for the rest of the Bristol Bay Region. **Number of employees at this location:** 300.

KODIAK AREA NATIVE ASSOCIATION
3449 East Rezanof Drive, Kodiak AK 99615. 907/486-9800. **Fax:** 907/486-9898. **Contact:** Norma Peterson, Director of Human Resources. **World Wide Web address:** http://www.kanaweb.org. **Description:** A private, nonprofit organization providing health care and social services to Alaskan Native and Native American individuals. **Positions advertised include:** Community Health Aid. **Note:** The Kodiak Area Native Association is an equal opportunity employer, however, in accordance with P.L. 93-638, preference in filling vacancies is given Alaska Natives/Native American Indian candidates. **Positions advertised include:** Community Health Aid; Physician.

PROVIDENCE ALASKA MEDICAL CENTER
3200 Providence Drive, Anchorage AK 99508. 907/562-2211. **Contact:** Human Resources. **World Wide Web address:** http://www.providence.org/alaska. **Description:** An acute care hospital with 341 beds. **NOTE:** For more information about employment opportunities, contact the Providence Human Resources Service Center, 701 East Tudor Road, Suite 135, Anchorage AK 99503, 907/565-6400 or 800/478-9940. **Positions advertised include:** Analyst-Database Reporting; Assistant Clinical Manager; Certified Nurse Assistant; Dietitian; Registered Nurse; Pharmacy Intern; LPN; Medical Technologist; Occupational Therapist; Phlebotomist.

PROVIDENCE EXTENDED CARE CENTER
4900 Eagle Street, Anchorage AK 99503-7490. 907/562-2281. **Contact:** Human Resources. **World Wide Web address:** http://www.providence.org/alaska. **Description:** A 224-bed, long-term care facility for children, adolescents, adults, and the elderly. Services are for people with mental and physical disabilities due to accidents, paralysis, advanced age, Alzheimer's disease, or any other condition that has made self-care difficult. **Positions advertised include:** Accountant; Analyst-Health Information; Assistant Physical

Therapist. **NOTE:** For more information about employment opportunities, contact the Providence Human Resources Service Center, 701 East Tudor Road, Suite 135, Anchorage AK 99503, 907/565-6400 or 800/478-9940.

Arizona

BANNER HEALTH
BANNER BEHAVIORAL HEALTH CENTER
7575 East Earll Drive, Scottsdale AZ 85251. 602/254-4357. **Fax:** 480/941-8494. **Contact:** Kathleen McFarland, Human Resources. **World Wide Web address:** http://www.bannerhealthaz.com. **Description:** A nonprofit, residential facility for the treatment of psychiatric and addiction disorders in adolescents and adults. **NOTE:** Entry-level positions and second and third shifts are offered. Search and apply for positions online. **Positions advertised include:** Clinical Nurse; Pharmacist; RN; Staff Psychiatrist. **Special programs:** Internships. **Corporate headquarters location:** Phoenix AZ. **Operations at this facility include:** Service. **Number of employees at this location:** 225. **Number of employees nationwide:** 11,000.

BANNER HEALTH
BANNER DESERT MEDICAL CENTER
1400 South Dobson Road, Mesa AZ 85202. 480/512-3246. **Fax:** 480/512-8734. **Recorded jobline:** 480/512-3180. **Contact:** Human Resources. **World Wide Web address:** http://www.bannerhealthaz.com. **Description:** A 600-bed, full-service community hospital. The hospital has clinical specialties in cardiac care, emergency medicine, dialysis, labor and delivery, lithotripsy, special care nursery, pediatrics, oncology, orthopedics, pulmonary medicine, neurology, rehabilitation, and surgery. The hospital has 64 critical care and intermediate beds dedicated to intensive nursing care. **Positions advertised include:** Biomedical Technician; Certified Occupational Therapy Assistant; Child Life Specialist; Clinical Care Manager; Clinical Nurse Specialist; Coordinator Respiratory Therapist; Director of Nursing; Licensed Practical Nurse; Medical Claim Approver; Medical Sonographer; MRI Technologist. **Parent company:** Banner Health System.

BANNER HEALTH
BANNER GOOD SAMARITAN MEDICAL CENTER
1111 East McDowell Road, Phoenix AZ 85006. 602/239-2350. **Fax:** 602/239-5160. **Recorded jobline:** 602/239-3200. **Contact:** Human Resources. **World Wide Web address:** http://www.bannerhealthaz.com. **Description:** One of Arizona's largest hospitals with 642 licensed beds. Good Samaritan's medical staff numbers 1,800 physicians, representing 50 specialties. Founded in 1911. **Positions advertised include:** Health Information Clerk; Charging Clerk; Diet Technician; Film Librarian; LPN; Medical Transcriptionist; MRI Technologist; Nurse Extern.

BANNER HEALTH
BANNER MESA MEDICAL CENTER
1010 North Country Club Drive, Mesa AZ 85201. 480/461-2562. **Fax:** 480/461-2939. **Recorded jobline:** 480/461-2562. **Contact:** Human Resources. **World Wide Web address:** http://www.bannerhealthaz.com. **Description:** A 320-bed full-service community medical center. **Positions advertised include:** Care Coordinator; Clinical Lab Assistant; LPN; Radiographer; Sonographer; MRI Technologist; RN.

BANNER THUNDERBIRD MEDICAL CENTER
5555 West Thunderbird Road, Glendale AZ 85306. 602/865-5555. **Contact:** Human Resources. **World Wide Web address:** http://www.bannerhealthaz.com. **Description:** A 352-bed, not-for-profit, general medical and surgical hospital. **Positions advertised include:** Assistant Director, NICU; Clinical Case Manager; Clinical Dietitian; Director of Nursing; MRI Technologist; Physical Therapist; RN, Various Departments; Ultrasound Technologist. **Number of employees at this location:** 2,000.

CARONDELET HEALTH NETWORK
1601 West St. Mary's Road, Tucson AZ 85745. 520/872-3000. **Fax:** 520/872-6067. **Contact:** Employment Office. **World Wide Web address:** http://www.carondelet.org. **Description:** One of the area's top 15 employers, and southern Arizona's oldest and largest not-for-profit health care provider with more than 3,000 employees and 1,200 physicians. A member of Ascension Health, the nation's largest religious-sponsored not-for-profit health care system. Facilities in Arizona include: St. Mary's Hospital, St. Joseph's Hospital, Holy Cross Hospital, the Cerelle Center for Mammography, Carondelet Imaging Services Central, the Medical Mall of Green Valley, and Carondelet Medical Group offices. **NOTE:** One of AARP's 50 Best Employers for Workers Over 50. Recipient of the Arizona Nurses Association "2005 Employer Excellence Award."

CARONDELET HOLY CROSS HOSPITAL
1171 West Target Range Road, Nogales AZ 85621-2497. 520/285-3000. **Toll-free phone:** 800/669-4979. **Contact:** Employment Office. **E-mail address:** chncareers@carondelet.org. **World Wide Web address:** http://www.carondelet.org. **Description:** An 80-bed facility, Holy Cross Hospital is part of the Carondelet Health Network, the largest and oldest not-for-profit health care provider in southern Arizona. **NOTE:** Entry-level positions and second and third shifts are offered. **Positions advertised include:** Certified Nursing Assistant; Imaging Specialist; Medical Technologist; Nuclear Medical Technologist; Nurse Assistant; Occupational Therapist; Patient Care Technician; Pharmacist; Physical Therapist; Registered Nurse; Sonographer. **Special programs:** Internships; Training.

CARONDELET MEDICAL MALL OF GREEN VALLEY
1055 North La Cañada Drive, Green Valley AZ 85614. 520/625-6469. **Toll-free phone:** 800/669-4979. **Contact:** Employment Office. **E-mail address:** chncareers@carondelet.org. **World Wide Web address:** http://www.carondelet.org. **Description:** Carondelet Medical Mall, a part of the Carondelet Health Network, provides primary, specialty and preventive care services. **NOTE:** Entry-level positions and second and third shifts are offered. **Special programs:** Internships; Training. **Positions advertised include:** Certified Nursing Assistant; Imaging Specialist; Medical Technologist; Nuclear Medical Technologist; Nurse Assistant; Occupational Therapist; Patient Care Technician; Pharmacist; Physical Therapist Registered Nurse; Sonographer. **Special programs:** Internships; Training.

CARONDELET ST. JOSEPH'S HOSPITAL
Wilmot Road, Tucson AZ 85711. 520/873-3000. **Toll-free phone:** 800/669-4979. **Contact:** Employment Office. **E-mail address:** chncareers@carondelet.org. **World Wide Web address:** http://www.carondelet.org. **Description:** A 301-bed facility, St. Joseph's Hospital is part of the Carondelet Health Network, the largest and oldest not-for-profit health care provider in southern Arizona. **NOTE:** Entry-level positions and second and third shifts are offered. **Positions advertised include:** Certified Nursing Assistant; Imaging Specialist; Medical Technologist; Nuclear Medical Technologist; Nurse Assistant; Occupational Therapist; Patient Care Technician; Pharmacist; Physical Therapist; Registered Nurse; Sonographer. **Special programs:** Internships; Training.

CASA GRANDE REGIONAL MEDICAL CENTER
1800 East Florence Boulevard, Casa Grande AZ 85222. 520/381-6300. **Fax:** 520/381-6615. **Contact:** Human Resources. **E-mail address:** recruiter@cgrmc.org. **World Wide Web address:** http://www.casagrandehospital.com. **Description:** Casa Grande Regional Medical Center is served by a 24-hour, physician-staffed emergency room. Services available at Casa Grande include maternity and newborn care, day surgery, nutritional counseling,

laboratory service, pediatric care, intensive care, medical and surgical care, pharmacy services, physical therapy, respiratory therapy, radiology (CAT scans, MRIs, and mammograms), and nuclear medicine. Founded in 1984. **Positions advertised include:** Registered Nurse; Physical Therapist; Nurse Technician; Stores Clerk; Director, Intensive Care Unit; Human Resources Manager.

CHANDLER REGIONAL HOSPITAL
475 South Dobson Road, Chandler AZ 85224. 480/821-3112. **Contact:** Human Resources. **World Wide Web address:** http://www.chandlerregional.com. **Description:** A 210-bed, nonprofit hospital. Facilities include the Family Birth Center including state-of-the-art fetal monitoring equipment, seven labor and delivery rooms, eighteen postpartum rooms, a surgery suite for Cesarean deliveries, and two nurseries; an emergency and Level II trauma center providing around-the-clock physician- and nurse-staffed emergency care; a diagnostic imaging services department providing comprehensive, state-of-the-art X-ray and diagnostic imaging services; a 12-bed intensive care unit and a 20-bed telemetry unit; inpatient and outpatient surgery; a 10-bed pediatric unit; physical rehabilitation including physical and occupational therapy, and speech pathology; cardiology services; and outpatient services. **Positions advertised include:** Anesthesia Technician; Business Office Supervisor; Charge RN; Collection Specialist; CT Technologist; EEG Technician; Financial Counselor; Housekeeper; LPN; Phlebotomist; Registrar; Site Manager. **Corporate headquarters location:** San Francisco CA. **Parent company:** Catholic Healthcare West.

FLAGSTAFF MEDICAL CENTER
1200 North Beaver Street, P.O. Box 1268, Flagstaff AZ 86001. 928/779-3366. **Toll-free phone:** 800/446-2324. **Fax:** 928/773-2579. **Recorded jobline:** 928/773-2067. **Contact:** Human Resources. **World Wide Web address:** http://www.nahealth.com. **Description:** A 238-bed acute care facility. Services include cardiology, critical care, endoscopy, imaging, pediatrics, pharmacy, cancer research and care, and cardiology. Founded in 1936. **Positions advertised include:** Neonatal Nurse Practitioner; Registered Nurse; LPN; Clinical Coordinator; Certified Nursing Assistant; Allied Health Professional; Mental Health Technician; Pharmacy Operations Manager; Echo Technician; Housekeeper. **Corporate headquarters location:** This location. **Parent company:** Northern Arizona Health Care. **Operations at this facility include:** Administration. **Number of employees at this location:** 1,800.

W.L. GORE & ASSOCIATES, INC.
1500 North Fourth Street, Flagstaff AZ 86004. 928/526-3030. **Contact:** Human Resources. **World Wide Web address:** http://www.gore.com. **Description:** W.L. Gore & Associates is a research-based organization that manufactures high-technology electronic, industrial, and medical products, as well as specialty fabric products including GORE-TEX fabric. **Positions advertised include:** Sterilization Quality Engineer; Oracle Database Administrator; Mechanical Engineer; Clinical Study Manager; Product Specialist Coordinator; MPD Material Inspector. **Operations at this facility include:** This location manufactures a variety of medical devices used in vascular, cardiology, and facial procedures.

HAVASU REGIONAL MEDICAL CENTER
101 Civic Center Lane, Lake Havasu City AZ 86403. 928/855-8185. **Fax:** 928/453-0810. **Contact:** Human Resources Department. **E-mail address:** humanresources@havasuregional.com. **World Wide Web address:** http://www.havasuregional.com. **Description:** A 138-bed, acute care facility providing comprehensive medical services. **Positions advertised include:** ACU Registered Nurse; Certified Nursing Assistant; Clinical Nurse; LPN; MRI Tech; Pharmacist; Ultrasound Technologist.

KINDRED HOSPITAL/PHOENIX
40 East Indianola Avenue, Phoenix AZ 85012. 602/280-7000. **Fax:** 602/280-7299. **Contact:** Personnel. **World Wide Web address:** http://www.khphoenix.com. **Description:** Kindred Hospital/Phoenix is a 58-bed acute care hospital. Approximately 80 percent of the hospital's patients are transferred from the intensive care units of short-term, acute care hospitals. Services provided at Kindred include some surgical procedures and full-service renal dialysis on both the general floor and the intensive care unit. Technology services include a full-service laboratory, radiology department, and pharmacy. The hospital employs approximately 200 physicians in all medical specialties. **Positions advertised include:** Controller; Nursing Supervisor; RN. **Corporate headquarters location:** Louisville KY. **Parent company:** Kindred Healthcare, Inc. **Listed on:** NASDAQ. **Stock exchange symbol:** KIND.

KINGMAN REGIONAL MEDICAL CENTER
3269 Stockton Hill Road, Kingman AZ 86409. 928/757-2101. **Contact:** Human Resources. **World Wide Web address:** http://www.azkrmc.com. **Description:** A non-profit, 213-bed medical center. The surgery department offers preoperative, intraoperative, and postoperative care for adults and children. Founded in 1992. **Positions advertised include:** Certified Nursing Assistant; Pharmacist; Pharmacy Clinical Coordinator; Radiologic Technologist; Respiratory Therapist; Registered Nurse, Various Departments; Ultrasound Technician; Unit Coordinator.

JOHN C. LINCOLN HOSPITAL DEER VALLEY
19829 North 27th Avenue, Phoenix AZ 85027. 623/879-6100. **Contact:** Human Resources. **World Wide Web address:** http://www.jcl.com/deervalley. **Description:** A 149-bed, not-for-profit community hospital. **Positions advertised include:** Charge RN; Clinical Dietician; CVOR Tech; Medical Technologist; Radiology Supervisor; RN, Various Departments. **Number of employees at this location:** 800.

JOHN C. LINCOLN HOSPITAL NORTH MOUNTAIN
250 East Dunlap Road, Phoenix AZ 85020. 602/943-2381. **Contact:** Human Resources. **World Wide Web address:** http://www.jcl.com/northmountain. **Description:** A 262-bed, not-for-profit community hospital. **Positions advertised include:** Charge RN; Clinical Nurse Specialist; Lab Assistant; OR Tech; Radiology Tech; Pharmacist; Respiratory Clinical Specialist. **Number of employees at this location:** 2,500.

MACHINE SOLUTIONS, INC.
2951 West Shamrell Boulevard, Flagstaff AZ 86001. 928/556-3109. **Fax:** 928/556-3084. **Contact:** Human Resources. **E-mail address:** careers@machinesolutions.org. **World Wide Web address:** http://www.machinesolutions.org. **Description:** Provides proprietary mechanical solutions to a variety of complex process and device design challenges. MSI has been instrumental in automating or semi-automating several manual processes within catheter manufacturing organizations. Founded in 1999. **Positions advertised include:** Director of Engineering; Mechanical Engineer; Software/Electrical Engineer. **Corporate headquarters location:** This location.

MARYVALE HOSPITAL MEDICAL CENTER
5102 West Campbell Avenue, Phoenix AZ 85031. 623/848-5050. **Toll-free phone:** 800/581-9393. **Fax:** 623/848-5959. **Recorded jobline:** 623/848-5675. **Contact:** Human Resources. **World Wide Web address:** http://www.maryvalehospital.com. **Description:** Maryvale Hospital Medical Center is a 239-bed medical facility staffed by over 400 physicians. The medical facility's services include an emergency department; women and children's services, which offer each patient a private labor, delivery, recovery, and postpartum room; special and intermediate care units; surgery; cardiology services

including EKGs, echocardiograms, cardiac dopplers, and treadmill tests; magnetic resonance imaging; oncology, radiation therapy, and other types of treatments and consultations; and rehabilitation services including physical therapy, occupational therapy, and speech-language pathology. **NOTE:** Entry-level positions, part-time jobs, and second and third shifts are offered. **Positions advertised include:** Director of Business Development; Director of Medical Imaging, RN, Various Departments; Staff Pharmacist. **Special programs:** Internships; Training; Co-ops; Summer Jobs. **Corporate headquarters location:** Nashville TN. **Parent company:** Vanguard Health. **Listed on:** Privately held. **Annual sales/revenues:** $51 - $100 million. **Number of employees at this location:** 1,100.

MAYO CLINIC HOSPITAL
5777 East Mayo Boulevard, Phoenix AZ 85054. 480/515-6296. **Contact:** Human Resources. **World Wide Web address:** http://www.mayoclinic.org. **Description:** Mayo Clinic Hospital has 208 licensed beds including 172 medical/surgical beds, 20 intensive/critical care beds, and 7 rehabilitation beds. The hospital provides inpatient care to support the 65 medical and surgical specialties and programs of Mayo Clinic. Full emergency room services and urgent care are also provided at the hospital. **NOTE:** Search and apply for positions online. **Positions advertised include:** IT Sr. Systems Analyst; Advanced Cardiac Sonographer; Contract Portfolio Manager; E-Commerce Coordinator; Manager, Human Resources; Medical Technologist.

MAYO CLINIC SCOTTSDALE
13400 East Shea Boulevard, Scottsdale AZ 85259. 480/301-8000. **Recorded jobline:** 480/301-7678. **Contact:** Human Resources. **World Wide Web address:** http://www.mayoclinic.org/scottsdale. **Description:** Operates an outpatient, multispecialty, group practice providing clinical care, laboratory and diagnostic radiological services, graduate medical education, and basic medical research. **Positions advertised include:** Revenue Analyst; Architect Designer CADD; Cardiac Sonographer; Clinical Dietitian; Facilities Manager: Histotechnologist. **Corporate headquarters location:** Rochester MN. **Other U.S. locations:** Jacksonville FL. **Number of employees nationwide:** 18,000.

MESA GENERAL HOSPITAL MEDICAL CENTER
515 North Mesa Drive, Mesa AZ 85201. 480/969-9111. **Contact:** Human Resources. **World Wide Web address:** http://www.mesageneralhospital.com. **Description:** A medical center staffed by over 200 physicians. Mesa General Hospital's medical services include cardiac catheterization and angiography; critical care/intensive care units; a telemetry unit; an emergency department; a maternity unit offering a birthing room, labor, delivery, and recovery rooms, childbirth education classes, and a specially trained obstetrical nursing staff; a pediatrics/youth care unit; and a pharmacy. Mesa General Hospital offers inpatient and outpatient diagnostic services. **Positions advertised include:** RN; Medical Technologist; Vascular Ultrasound Technologist; Physical Therapist; Respiratory Therapist. **Parent company:** IASIS Healthcare.

NAVAJO AREA INDIAN HEALTH SERVICE
P.O. Box 9020, Window Rock AZ 86515-9020. 928/871-5880. **Contact:** Recruiting. **World Wide Web address:** http://www.navajohealthjobs.ihs.gov. **Description:** Provides direct clinical care to 230,000 Native Americans at six hospitals and seven 24-hour health centers in the Four Corners area. **NOTE:** Clerkships and residency rotations for medical students and engineers are offered. **Positions advertised include:** IT Specialist; Civil Engineering Technician. **Special programs:** Internships. **Corporate headquarters location:** This location. **Parent company:** U.S. Public Health Service. **Operations at this facility include:** Administration. **Annual sales/revenues:** More than $100 million. **Number of employees at this location:** 250. **Number of employees nationwide:** 12,000.

NORTHWEST MEDICAL CENTER
6200 North La Cholla Boulevard, Tucson AZ 85741. 520/742-9000. **Toll-free phone:** 800/280-3963. **Contact:** Human Resources. **World Wide Web address:** http://www.northwestmedicalcenter.com. **Description:** Offers cardiopulmonary services including a cardiac catheterization lab, nuclear imaging, and a complete open heart program. The hospital also offers an emergency department; obstetrics/neonatology care; a cancer treatment center; around-the-clock ask-a-nurse, physician referral, and medical information; and a pediatric urgent care center. The hospital, serving as a medical base for several rural areas, operates clinics in Kearney and Catalina, and is a base station for several of the ambulance companies that operate in northwest Tucson. Founded in 1983. **Positions advertised include:** Registered Nurse, Various Departments; Physical Therapist; Radiology Specialist; Occupational Therapist; Licensed Practical Nurse; Cardiothoracic Case Manager.

ORTHOLOGIC
1275 West Washington Street, Tempe AZ 85281-1210. 602/286-5520. **Contact:** Human Resources. **E-mail address:** recruiter@olgc.com. **World Wide Web address:** http://www.orthologic.com. **Description:** A orthobiologics drug-development company focused on commercializing several potential therapeutics. **Positions advertised include:** Clinical Operations Manager; Research Scientist; Regulatory Affairs Specialist; Toxicology Pharmacology Manager. **Corporate headquarters location:** This location. **Listed on:** NASDAQ. **Stock exchange symbol:** OLGC.

PARADISE VALLEY HOSPITAL
3929 East Bell Road, Phoenix AZ 85032. 602/923-5000. **Contact:** Human Resources. **World Wide Web address:** http://www.paradisevalleyhospital.com. **Description:** A 140-bed facility. The hospital's services include the Northeast Valley's only hospital-based, 24-hour, emergency department; the Women's Center, designed for obstetrical and gynecological patients; the nursing unit; a diagnostic imaging department; and inpatient and outpatient rehabilitation services including physical, speech, and occupational therapy. The hospital also provides comprehensive mental health services. **Positions advertised include:** Pharmacy Director; Case Manager; Chief Nursing Officer; ER Tech; RN, Various Departments.

PHOENIX MEMORIAL HEALTH SYSTEM
1201 South Seventh Avenue, Phoenix AZ 85007. 602/258-5111. **Fax:** 602/824-3420. **Contact:** Human Resources Department. **World Wide Web address:** http://www.phxmemorialhospital.com. **Description:** A general acute care hospital and health services network. Phoenix Memorial's specialties include total joint replacement and cardiovascular services. **Positions advertised include:** Director of Materials Management; Director of Physician Relations; RN, Various Departments; Physical Therapist. **Corporate headquarters location:** This location. **Operations at this facility include:** Administration. **Number of employees at this location:** 1,100.

REMUDA RANCH CENTER
One East Apache Street, Suite A, Wickenburg AZ 85390. 928/684-3913. **Fax:** 928/684-4247. **Recorded jobline:** 800/315-3883. **Contact:** Human Resources. **E-mail address:** jobs@remudaranch.com. **World Wide Web address:** http://www.remuda-ranch.com. **Description:** A treatment center for women and adolescent girls suffering from anorexia, bulimia, and related disorders. **Positions advertised include:** Director of Human Resources; LPN; Program Therapist; RN.

ST. JOSEPH'S HOSPITAL & MEDICAL CENTER
350 West Thomas Road, Phoenix AZ 85013. 602/406-3000. **Contact:** Human Resources Department. **World**

Wide Web address: http://www.ichosestjoes.com. **Description:** A 517-bed, not-for-profit hospital and medical center. **Positions advertised include:** Certified Nurse Assistant; Clerk; Community Outreach Program Coordinator; Customer Service Representative; Dietary Aide; Faculty Physician; Nursing Services Manager; Monitor Technician; Occupational Therapist; Physical Therapist; Plumber; Registrar; Research Assistant; Speech Pathologist; Staff Nurse; Clinical Supervisor. **Office hours:** Monday - Friday, 7:00 a.m. - 5:00 p.m. **Parent company:** Catholic Healthcare West.

ST. MARY'S HOSPITAL
1601 West St. Mary's Road, Tucson AZ 85745. 520/872-3000. **Toll-free phone:** 800/669-4979. **Contact:** Personnel. **E-mail address:** chncareers@carondelet.org. **World Wide Web address:** http://www.carondelet.org. **Description:** A 393-bed hospital, St. Mary's is part of the Carondelet Health Network, the largest and oldest not-for-profit health care provider in Southern Arizona. **NOTE:** Entry-level positions and second and third shifts are offered. **Positions advertised include:** Certified Nursing Assistant; Mammographer; Nuclear Medical Technologist; Occupational Therapist; Pharmacist; Physical Therapist; RN. **Special programs:** Internships; Training.

SCHALLER ANDERSON
4645 East Cotton Center Boulevard, Phoenix AZ 85040. 602/659-1100. **Contact:** Human Resources Generalist. **E-mail:** hr@schalleranderson.com. **World Wide Web address:** http://www.schalleranderson.com. **Description:** Manages privately funded health benefit plans for employers. Founded in 1984. **Positions advertised include:** Accounting Specialist; Sr. Actuarial Financial Analyst; Business Analyst; Claims Analyst; Quality Review Analyst; Claims Supervisor; Research and Adjustment Analyst; HR Recruiter.

SCOTTSDALE HEALTHCARE CORPORATION
5111 North Scottsdale Road, Suite 143, Scottsdale AZ 85250. 480/882-6950. **Contact:** Human Resources. **World Wide Web address:** http://www.shc.org. **Description:** A nonprofit health care organization that operates hospitals, home health care centers, outpatient centers, a primary health care network, and community outreach programs. **NOTE:** One of AARP's 50 Best Employers for Workers Over 50. **Positions advertised include:** Phlebotomist; Pharmacy Tech; Respiratory Therapist; RN; Clinical Lab Tech; Nuclear Medicine Tech; Telemetry Tech; Director, Patient Services; Physical Therapist. **Corporate headquarters location:** This location.

SCOTTSDALE HEALTHCARE OSBORN
7400 East Osborn, Scottsdale AZ 85251. 480/882-4000. **Contact:** Employment. **World Wide Web address:** http://www.shc.org. **Description:** A 305-bed, full-service hospital. **NOTE:** Search and apply for positions online. **Positions advertised include:** RN; Respiratory Therapist; Clinical Lab Tech. **Parent company:** Scottsdale Healthcare Corporation. **Number of employees at this location:** 1,900.

SOUTHERN ARIZONA VA HEALTH CARE SYSTEM
3601 South Sixth Avenue, Tucson AZ 85723. 520/792-1450. **Contact:** Human Resources. **World Wide Web address:** http://www.va.gov/678savahcs. **Description:** A 325-bed medical center with accredited general medical, surgical, and psychiatric facilities. The Tucson VA Medical Center provides a full-range of medical and surgical services, including open heart and kidney transplantation. Due to its strong and active affiliation with the University of Arizona Colleges of Medicine, Nursing, and Pharmacy, a great deal of emphasis has been on education and research. Residency programs in medicine, surgery, anesthesiology, psychiatry, radiology, nuclear medicine, neurology, and pathology promote the delivery of clinical care. **Positions advertised include:** Civilian Pay Technician; Medical Instrument Technician; Medical Supply Technician; Physical Therapist; RN. **Parent company:** U.S. Department of Veterans Affairs (Washington DC.)

SOUTHWEST AMBULANCE SERVICE
222 East Main Street, Mesa AZ 85021. 480/655-7234. **Toll-free phone:** 800/341-7454. **Fax:** 480/649-7752. **Contact:** Human Resources. **E-mail address:** humanresources@swambulance.com. **World Wide Web address:** http://www.swambulance.com. **Description:** An ambulance service provider. **Positions advertised include:** Mechanic; Refurbishing Tech. **Other area locations:** Tucson AZ.

SUN HEALTH
WALTER O. BOSWELL MEMORIAL HOSPITAL
10401 West Thunderbird Boulevard, Sun City AZ 85351. 623/977-7211. **Contact:** Human Resources. **World Wide Web address:** http://www.sunhealth.org. **Description:** A nonprofit health organization that operates Walter O. Boswell Memorial Hospital (also at this location), an acute care, 325-bed facility. **Positions advertised include:** CNA; Coordinator, Medical Staff; Manager Medical Records; Medical Technologist; Physical Therapist; RN; Staffing Resource Coordinator.

TRIWEST HEALTHCARE ALLIANCE
15451 North 28th Avenue, Phoenix AZ 85053. 602/564-2000. **Contact:** Human Resources. **World Wide Web address:** http://www.triwest.com. **Description:** TriWest partners with the Department of Defense to provide access to health care for active and retired uniformed services members and their families in a 21-state area. **Positions advertised include:** Director, Field Operations; Enrollment Specialist; Project Manager; Hub Clinical Director; Quality Management Specialist.

TUBA CITY INDIAN MEDICAL CENTER
167 North Main Street & East Elm Avenue, P.O. Box 600, Tuba City AZ 86045-0600. 928/283-2432. **Contact:** Ferlin Begay, Personnel. **E-mail address:** ferlin.begay@tcimc.ihs.gov. **World Wide Web address:** http://www.navajohealthjobs.ihs.gov. **Description:** A medical center serving the area's Native American population. **Parent company:** Indian Health Service (IHS) agency of the U.S. Department of Health and Human Services in the Phoenix area operates eight hospitals, six health centers, one school health center, and seven health stations. In the Tucson area, Indian Health Services operates one hospital, two health centers, and one health station. Overall, IHS provides a health service delivery system to approximately 1.3 million people and acts as the principal federal health advocate for Native American population.

UPH HOSPITAL AT KINO
2800 East Ajo Way, Tucson AZ 85713. 520/573-2815. **Fax:** 520/407-2817. **Recorded jobline:** 520/874-7240. **Contact:** Human Resources. **E-mail address:** kinojobs@upiaz.org. **World Wide Web address:** http://www.uphkino.org. **Description:** A 200-bed, full-service hospital serving southern Tucson. **NOTE:** One of AARP's 50 Best Employers for Workers Over 50. **Positions advertised include:** Registration Coordinator; Registered Nurse; Certified Nursing Assistant; Educator Med/Surg; MRI Technologist; Medical Technologist; RN Case Manager. **Parent company:** University Physicians Healthcare.

U.S. DEPARTMENT OF VETERANS AFFAIRS
CARL T. HAYDEN VA MEDICAL CENTER
650 East Indian School Road, Phoenix AZ 85012. 602/277-5551. **Recorded jobline:** 602/222-2703. **Contact:** Human Resources. **World Wide Web address:** http://www.va.gov. **Description:** A 590-bed hospital. The medical center's teaching programs include residencies in internal medicine, family practice, ophthalmology, dermatology, and general surgery; and fellowships in gastroenterology, cardiology and pulmonology. The outpatient program includes a mental hygiene clinic, day hospital, and treatment center. Founded in 1951. **Positions**

advertised include: Registered Respiratory Therapist; Clinical Pharmacist; Vascular Lab Technician.

UNIVERSITY MEDICAL CENTER (UMC) ARIZONA HEALTH SCIENCES CENTER
1501 North Campbell Avenue, Tucson AZ 85724. 520/694-0111. **Fax:** 520/694-2531. **Recorded jobline:** 520/694-7227. **Contact:** Human Resources. **World Wide Web address:** http://www.azumc.com. **Description:** A 312-bed, tertiary care, teaching facility. UMC serves as the teaching hospital for the University of Arizona's Colleges of Nursing and Pharmacy and the School of Health Professions, providing a training opportunity for nurses, pharmacists, medical technologists, and allied health professionals. **Positions advertised include:** Business Office Coordinator; Cardiac Specialist Tech; Cardiologist; Clinical Staff Pharmacist; Compensation/HRIS Specialist; Director, Information System Services; Echo Tech; IT Services Specialist; Medical Lab Tech; Medical Tech; RN, Various Departments.

WESTCHESTER CARE CENTER - VOA
6100 South Rural Road, Tempe AZ 85283. 480/831-8660. **Fax:** 480/820-7663. **Contact:** Jan Hamsen, Director of Personnel. **Description:** A nonprofit center that provides long-term care, assisted living, and independent living/retirement services. **Other U.S. locations:** Nationwide. **Parent company:** Volunteers of America. **Number of employees at this location:** 145.

Arkansas

ARKANSAS CHILDREN'S HOSPITAL
800 Marshall Street, Slot 602, Little Rock AR 72202-3591. 501/364-4120. **Toll-free phone:** 800/844-1891. **Fax:** 501/364-3499. **Contact:** Employment Office. **E-mail address:** employment@archildrens.org. **World Wide Web address:** http://www.archildrens.org. **Description:** One of the largest pediatric medical centers in the United States. The private, non-profit hospital also supports the Arkansas Children's Hospital Research Institute, a nutrition research center. Through a partnership with the University of Arkansas for Medical Sciences, the hospital is the site of pediatric training for medical and nursing students, post-doctoral residents, and paramedical professionals. **NOTE**: No paper resumes accepted – apply on-line only. **Positions advertised include:** Account Analyst; Anesthesia Technician; Biochemist; Control Programmer/Analyst; Clinical Nurse Specialist; Director Radiology; Housekeeper; HRIS Analyst; Radiology Technician; RN, Various Departments; Sr. VP, Medical Services; Staff Pharmacist. **Number of employees at this location:** 2,800.

BEVERLY ENTERPRISES, INC.
1000 Beverly Way, Fort Smith AR 72919. 479/201-2000. **Fax:** 479/201-3803. **Contact:** Susan McBride, Human Resources. **E-mail address:** recruit@beverlycorp.com. **World Wide Web address:** http://www.beverlycorp.com. **Description:** Operates acute care hospitals, assisted living centers, hospices, home health centers, institutional and mail services pharmacies, and nursing and rehabilitation facilities in 25 states and the District of Columbia. Founded in 1963. **Positions advertised include:** Billing Analyst; HR Director; Regional Business Development Director; Regional Sales Manager. **Corporate headquarters location:** This location. **Other U.S. locations:** Nationwide. **Operations at this facility include:** Administration. **Listed on:** New York Stock Exchange. **Stock exchange symbol:** BEV. **Number of employees nationwide:** 35,000.

GREEN DENTAL LABORATORIES INC.
1099 Wilburn Road, Heber Springs AR 72543. **Toll-free phone:** 800/247-1365. **Contact**: Teresa Philips, Human Resources. **World Wide Web address:** http://www.greendentallabs.com. **Description:** A dental laboratory that manufactures crowns, bridges, dentures, and other dental products.

PROFESSIONAL DENTAL TECHNOLOGIES, INC.
P.O. Box 4129, Batesville AR 72503. 870/698-2300. **Fax:** 870/698-2390. **Physical address:** 267 East Main Street, Batesville AR 72501. **Contact:** Michelle Ireland/sales, Ernestine Doucet/staff. **World Wide Web address:** http://www.prodentec.com. **Description:** Designs and manufactures products that assist dental professionals in diagnosing, treating, and preventing periodontal and other dental diseases. Products include the Rota-dent plaque removal instrument, the Prism intra-oral camera, the Periocheck in-office enzyme test, and the PerfectByte Practice Management Software System. **Positions advertised include:** Staff Accountant; Professional Sales Representative. **Corporate headquarters location:** This location.

ST. JOSEPH'S MERCY HEALTH CENTER
300 Werner Street, P.O. Box 29001, Hot Springs AR 71903. 501/622-1000. **Fax:** 501/622-2047. **Recorded jobline:** 501/622-4606. **Contact:** Lori Wozniak, Employment Supervisor. **E-mail address:** hr@saintjoesphs.com **World Wide Web address:** http://www.saintjosephs.com. **Description:** A full-service, nonprofit medical center. **NOTE:** Entry-level positions and second and third shifts are offered. **Positions advertised include:** Cardiologist; Charge RN; Dosimetrist; Family Medicine Physician; General Surgeon; Internal Medicine Physician; Licensed Practical Nurse; Neurologist; OB/GYN; Staff RN; Financial Analyst. **Special programs:** Internships; Apprenticeships; Training; Summer Jobs. **Corporate headquarters location:** St. Louis MO. **CEO:** Randy Fale. **Facilities Manager:** Randy Fortner. **Annual sales/revenues:** $5 - $10 million. **Number of employees at this location:** 1,500.

UNIVERSITY OF ARKANSAS FOR MEDICAL SCIENCES
4301 West Markham Street, Little Rock AR 72205. 501/686-5650. **Fax:** 501/296-1825. **Recorded jobline:** 501/686-5009. **Contact:** Betty Coller, Employment Manager. **World Wide Web address:** http://www.uams.edu. **Description:** An academic medical center providing patient care, health care education, and biomedical research. **Positions advertised include:** Account Follow-up Specialist; Administrative Assistant; Administrative Secretary; Ambulatory Technician; Cashier; Chart Technician; Hospital Operator; Medical Diagnostic Analyst; Medical/Legal Secretary; Shipping and Receiving Clerk; Fire Safety Systems Supervisor; Journeymen Electrician; Skilled Trades Helper; Fiscal Manager; Mental health Professional; Occupational Therapist. **Operations at this facility include:** Administration; Research and Development.

California

ADOBE ANIMAL HOSPITAL
396 First Street, Los Altos CA 94022. 650/948-9661. **Fax:** 650/948-1465. **Contact:** Human Resources. **E-mail address:** srbryce10@sbcglobal.net. **World Wide Web address:** http://www.adobe-animal.com. **Description:** A fully equipped animal hospital that provides surgical, pharmaceutical, intensive care, laboratory, and radiology services. The hospital also provides regular checkups and puppy training classes. **Positions advertised include:** Registered Animal Health Technician.

ACCURAY INCORPORATED
1310 Chesapeake Terrace, Sunnyvale CA 94089. 408/716-4600. **Fax:** 408/716-4605. **Contact:** Human Resources. **E-mail address:** jobs@accuracy.com. **World Wide Web address:** http://www.accuray.com. **Description:** A global leader in the field of robotic radiosurgery. Accuray develops and markets the CyberKnife Robotic Radiosurgery System, which treats tumors anywhere in the body with sub-millimeter accuracy. **Corporate headquarters location:** This location. **International locations:** France; Hong Kong.

ADVANCED STERILIZATION PRODUCTS
33 Technology Drive, Irvine CA 92618. 949/581-5799. **Toll-free phone:** 800/595-0200. **Fax:** 949/450-6889. **Contact:** Human Resources. **E-mail address:** resumes@aspus.jnj.com. **World Wide Web address:** http://www.sterrad.com. **Description:** Manufactures sterilization equipment that is used on surgical instruments in hospitals. **Parent company:** Johnson & Johnson (New Brunswick NJ). **International locations:** Worldwide.

ALAMEDA COUNTY MEDICAL CENTER
1411 East 31st Street, Department 470, Oakland CA 94602. 510/437-4108. **Fax:** 510/437-5197. **Contact:** Human Resources. **E-mail address:** resumes@acmedctr.org. **World Wide Web address:** http://www.acmedctr.org. **Description:** A 300-bed, adult, acute care teaching hospital. **Positions advertised include:** RN, Various Departments; Electrocardiograph Technician; Clinical Lab Scientist; Chief Information Officer; Physician; HRIS Analyst; EEG Technologist. **Corporate headquarters location:** Oakland CA. **Other area locations:** San Leandro CA. **Operations at this facility include:** Service.

ALARIS MEDICAL SYSTEMS INC.
P.O. Box 85335, San Diego CA 92186-5335. 858/458-7000. **Physical address:** 10221 Wateridge Circle, San Diego CA 92121-2772. **Toll-free phone:** 800/854-7128. **Fax:** 858/458-6196. **Contact:** Human Resources. **World Wide Web address:** http://www.alarismed.com. **Description:** Designs, manufactures, and markets instruments used to monitor patients and products for intravenous infusion therapy. **Positions advertised include:** Director, Infusion Information; Associate Product Manager; Senior Product Manager; Network Support Engineer. **Corporate headquarters location:** This location. **Other U.S. locations:** Creedmoor NC. **International locations:** Mexico; United Kingdom. **Parent company:** Cardinal Health.

ALL-CARE ANIMAL REFERRAL CENTER
18440 Amistad Street, Fountain Valley CA 92708. 714/963-0909. **Toll-free phone:** 800/944-7387. **Fax:** 714/962-1905. **Contact:** Human Resources. **World Wide Web address:** http://www.acarc.com. **Description:** An animal hospital with a 24-hour critical care facility. **Corporate headquarters location:** This location.

ALLIANCE IMAGING, INC.
1900 South State College Boulevard, Suite 600, Anaheim CA 92806. 714/688-7100. **Toll-free phone:** 800/544-3215. **Fax:** 714/688-3333. **Contact:** Human Resources Department. **E-mail address:** info@allianceimaging.com. **World Wide Web address:** http://www.allianceimaging.com. **Description:** Provides medical diagnostic imaging services to hospitals, physicians, and patients. Services include MRI, Open MRI, computer tomography (CT), ultrasound, and position emission tomography (PET). **Positions advertised include:** Patient Coordinator; PET Technologist. **Corporate headquarters location:** This location. **Other U.S. locations:** Nationwide. **Listed on:** NASDAQ. **Stock exchange symbol:** SCAN.

AMERICAN ACADEMY OF OPHTHALMOLOGY
P.O. Box 7274, San Francisco CA 94120-7424. 415/561-8500. **Physical address:** 655 Beach Street, San Francisco CA 94109. **Fax:** 415/561-8533. **Contact:** Human Resources. **E-mail address:** job@aao.org. **World Wide Web address:** http://www.aao.org. **Description:** A lobbying group that focuses on all government legislation affecting the ophthalmology community. **Corporate headquarters location:** This location.

AMERICAN MEDICAL RESPONSE INC.
20101 Hamilton Avenue, Suite 300, Torrance CA 90502. 310/851-7000. **Fax:** 925/454-6296. **Contact:** Employment Coordinator. **E-mail address:** westresumes2@amr.net. **World Wide Web address:** http://www.amr.net. **Description:** Operates an ambulance service. **Corporate headquarters location:** Greenwood Village CO. **Other area locations:** Statewide. **Other U.S. locations:** Nationwide.

AMERICAN SHARED HOSPITAL SERVICES
Four Embarcadero Center, Suite 3700, San Francisco CA 94111-3823. 415/788-5300. **Toll-free phone:** 800/735-0641. **Fax:** 415/788-5660. **Contact:** Human Resources. **World Wide Web address:** http://www.ashs.com. **Description:** Primarily outsources Gamma Knife stereotactic radiosurgery equipment and services to medical centers. **Corporate headquarters location:** This location. **Other U.S. locations:** AR; CT; IL; MA; MS; NV; NJ; TX; WI. **Subsidiaries include:** GK Financing, LLC.

AMERISOURCEBERGEN
4000 Metropolitan Drive, Orange CA 92868-3502. 714/385-4000. **Toll-free phone:** 800/442-3040. **Fax:** 714/385-1442. **Contact:** Human Resources Recruiting. **E-mail address:** techcareers@amerisourcebergen.com. **World Wide Web address:** http://www.amerisourcebergen.com. **Description:** Distributes pharmaceuticals and medical-surgical supplies. **Positions advertised include:** Project Manager, Systems Assurance; Technical Support Rep; Computer Operator. **Corporate headquarters location:** Valley Forge PA. **Other U.S. locations:** Nationwide (Distribution Centers). **Listed on:** New York Stock Exchange. **Stock exchange symbol:** ABC. **Number of employees nationwide:** 13,000.

ANESTHESIA PLUS, INC.
9255 Survey Road, Suite 1, Elk Grove CA 95624. 916/686-4480. **Toll-free phone:** 800/887-8161. **Fax:** 916/686-4311. **Contact:** Human Resources. **World Wide Web address:** http://www.anesplus.com. **Description:** Manufactures and markets new and refurbished operating room equipment. The company specializes in anesthesia and related products. **Corporate headquarters location:** This location.

APRIA HEALTHCARE GROUP INC.
26220 Enterprise Court, Lake Forest CA 92630. **Toll-free phone:** 800/277-4288. **Fax:** 949/639-6258. **Contact:** Diane Cottrell, Human Resources. **E-mail address:** contact_us@apria.com. **World Wide Web address:** http://www.apria.com. **Description:** Provides a broad range of respiratory therapy services, home medical equipment, and infusion therapy services. Apria Healthcare Group's home health care services are provided to patients who have been discharged from hospitals, skilled nursing facilities, or convalescent homes and are being treated at home. **Positions advertised include:** Internal Auditor; Business Development Manager; Senior Financial Analyst; National Nursing Manager; Vice President, Technology. **Corporate headquarters location:** This location. **Other U.S. locations:** Nationwide. **International locations:** United Kingdom. **Operations at this facility include:** Administration. **Listed on:** New York Stock Exchange. **Stock exchange symbol:** AHG. **Annual sales/revenues:** $1.4 billion. **Number of employees at this location:** 750. **Number of employees nationwide:** 9,000.

AXELGAARD MANUFACTURING COMPANY, LTD.
1667 South Mission Road, Fallbrook CA 92028. 760/723-7554. **Fax:** 760/723-2356. **Contact:** Human Resources. **E-mail address:** hr@axelgaard.com. **World Wide Web address:** http://www.axelgaard.com. **Description:** Manufactures electrodes for neurostimulation. **Corporate headquarters location:** This location.

BAYSHORE ANIMAL HOSPITAL
233 North Amphlette Boulevard, San Mateo CA 94401. 650/342-7022. **Contact:** Human Resources. **Description:** A full-service animal hospital that provides several specialty services including eye and tooth care, in-hospital consultation with outside

specialists, pharmacy, and x-ray. The hospital also provides boarding facilities when required. **Corporate headquarters location:** This location.

BIOLASE TECHNOLOGY, INC.
981 Calle Amanecer, San Clemente CA 92673. 949/361-1200. **Toll-free phone:** 888/424-6527. **Fax:** 949/361-0207. **Contact:** Viviana Jenkins, Corporate Recruiter, (for sales and management positions) or Jodie Saunderson, Human Resources Manager (for all other positions). **E-mail address:** vjenkins@biolase.com or jsaunderson@biolase.com. **World Wide Web address:** http://www.biolase.com. **Description:** Manufactures and markets a full range of advanced dental and medical laser products. **Positions advertised include:** Western Regional Sales Manager. **Listed on:** NASDAQ. **Stock exchange symbol:** BLTI.

BIRD PRODUCTS CORPORATION
22745 Savi Ranch Parkway, Yorba Linda CA 92887-4668. 760/778-7200. **Toll-free phone:** 800/232-7633. **Fax:** 760/778-7346. **Contact:** Human Resources. **E-mail address:** human.resources@viasyshc.com. **World Wide Web address:** http://www.viasyshealthcare.com. **Description:** Manufactures respiratory care and infection control products. **Corporate headquarters location:** This location. **Parent company:** Viasys Healthcare.

BOSTON SCIENTIFIC EP TECHNOLOGIES
2710 Orchard Parkway, San Jose CA 95134. 408/895-3500. **Fax:** 408/895-2203. **Contact:** Human Resources. **World Wide Web address:** http://www.bostonscientific.com. **Description:** A worldwide developer, manufacturer, and marketer of medical devices used in a broad range of interventional procedures including the fields of cardiology, gastroenterology, pulmonary medicine, and vascular surgery. **Special programs:** Internships. **Corporate headquarters location:** Natick MA. **Other area locations:** Fremont CA; Mountain View CA; Santa Clara CA; San Diego CA. **International locations:** Worldwide. **Operations at this facility include:** This location designs and manufactures electrophysiology catheters and cardiac ablation systems. **Listed on:** New York Stock Exchange. **Stock exchange symbol:** BSX. **Number of employees at this location:** 450.

BOSTON SCIENTIFIC TARGET
47900 Bayside Parkway, Fremont CA 94538-6515. 510/440-7700. **Contact:** Human Resources Manager. **World Wide Web address:** http://www.bostonscientific.com. **Description:** Manufactures specialized disposable microcatheters, guidewires, microcoils, and angioplasty products. **Positions advertised include:** Technician; Repair Operations Supervisor. **Corporate headquarters location:** Natick MA. **Parent company:** Boston Scientific Corporation. **Listed on:** New York Stock Exchange. **Stock exchange symbol:** BSX.

BURTON MEDICAL PRODUCTS
21100 Lassen Street, Chatsworth CA 91311. 818/701-8700. **Fax:** 818/701-8725. **Contact:** Bonnie Tharp, Human Resource Manager. **World Wide Web address:** http://www.burtonmedical.com. **Description:** A wholesale distributor of surgical lights. **Corporate headquarters location:** This location. **Parent company:** LUXO ASA.

CALIFORNIA DENTAL ASSOCIATION
1201 K Street, Sacramento CA 95814. 916/443-3382. **Toll-free phone:** 800/736-7071. **Fax:** 916/443-2943. **Contact:** Human Resources Director. **E-mail address:** contactcda@cda.org. **World Wide Web address:** http://www.cda.org. **Description:** A nonprofit dental association providing membership programs and services for California dentists. **Positions advertised include:** Associate. **Corporate headquarters location:** This location. **Operations at this facility include:** Administration; Sales; Service. **Number of employees at this location:** 200.

CASA DE LAS CAMPANAS
18655 West Bernardo Drive, San Diego CA 92127. 858/592-1870. **Toll-free phone:** 800/554-6403. **Fax:** 858/592-1853. **Recorded jobline:** 858/592-1865. **Contact:** Jane Munson, Human Resources Manager. **E-mail address:** info@casadelascampanas.com. **World Wide Web address:** http://www.casadelascampanas.com. **Description:** A nonprofit, continuing care retirement facility with more than 500 residents. **NOTE:** Entry-level positions and second and third shifts are offered. **Positions advertised include:** Certified Nursing Assistant; Registered Nurse; Unit Clerk; Licensed Vocational Nurse; Housekeeper; Resident Helper; Lead Line Cook. **Special programs:** Internships. **Parent company:** Life Care Services LLC. **Number of employees at this location:** 300.

CEDARS-SINAI HEALTH SYSTEM
8723 Alden Drive, Room 110, Los Angeles CA 90048. 310/423-5521. **Recorded jobline:** 310/423-8230. **Fax:** 310/423-8400. **Contact:** Personnel. **E-mail address:** hr.web@cshs.org (for inquiries); jobs@cshs.org (for resume submission). **World Wide Web address:** http://www.csmc.edu. **Description:** A nonprofit health care delivery system that operates through Cedar-Sinai Medical Center, as well as a network of primary care physicians. Cedars-Sinai specializes in acute, subacute, and home patient care; biomedical research; community service; and continuing medical education. **Positions advertised include:** Registered Nurse; Health System Manager; Cytogenetic Technologist; Coder Specialist; Project Coordinator; Accounting Assistant; Chief Exercise Physiologist; Clinical Dietitian; Marketing Representative; Management Assistant. **Corporate headquarters location:** This location. **Operations at this facility include:** Administration; Research and Development; Service.

CENTINELA FREEMAN REGIONAL MEDICAL CENTER
333 North Prairie Avenue, Inglewood CA 90301. 310/674-7050. **Contact:** Recruitment Coordinator. **World Wide Web address:** http://www.centinelafreeman.com/memorial. **Description:** A nonprofit hospital that offers a variety of services including behavioral health, heart care, women's and children's services, and rehabilitation. The hospital also offers a variety of specialty programs such as the Center for Heart and Health, complimentary medicine, and emergency services. **Positions advertised include:** Occupational Therapist; Physical Therapist; Dietitian; Respiratory Care Practitioner; Licensed Vocational Nurse; Registered Nurse; Pharmacist; Human Resources Recruiter; Speech Therapist. **Corporate headquarters location:** This location. **Parent company:** Centinela Freeman HealthSystem.

CHAD THERAPEUTICS, INC.
21622 Plummer Street, Chatsworth CA 91311. 818/882-0883. **Toll-free phone:** 800/426-8870. **Fax:** 818/407-8148. **Contact:** Barbara Muskin, Human Resources Manager. **E-mail address:** bmuskin@chadtherapeutics.com. **World Wide Web address:** http://www.chadtherapeutics.com. **Description:** Designs, manufactures, and markets respiratory care devices. Product names include Oxylite, Oxymatic, and Oxymizer. **Corporate headquarters location:** This location. **Listed on:** American Stock Exchange. **Stock exchange symbol:** CTU.

CITY OF HOPE NATIONAL MEDICAL CENTER
1500 East Duarte Road, Duarte CA 91010. 626/359-8111. **Toll-free phone:** 800/423-7119. **Fax:** 626/256-8601. **Recorded jobline:** 626/301-8200. **Contact:** Human Resources. **E-mail address:** jobs@coh.org. **World Wide Web address:** http://www.coh.org. **Description:** A medical center that incorporates treatment for AIDS, cancer, and diabetes with counseling and helps pay patient expenses based on need. **Positions advertised include:** Research Associate; Flow Cytometry Technologist; Clinical

Trials Monitor; Occupational Therapist. **Corporate headquarters location:** This location. **Other area locations:** Irvine CA; Palm Desert CA; San Diego CA; San Francisco CA. **Other U.S. locations:** AZ; FL; GA; IL; MI; MN; NV; NY; PA; WA.

COMMUNITY HOSPITAL OF SAN BERNARDINO
1805 Medical Center Drive, San Bernardino CA 92411. 909/887-6333. **Recorded jobline:** 909/806-1870. **Fax:** 909/887-6814. **Contact:** Human Resources. **E-mail address:** brehome@chw.edu. **World Wide Web address:** http://www.chsb.org. **Description:** A nonprofit, 321-bed community hospital whose facilities include a convalescent home and rehabilitation center. Founded in 1908. **Positions advertised include:** RN, Various Departments; Respiratory Therapist; Case Manager; Pharmacist. **Parent company:** Catholic Healthcare West. **Number of employees at this location:** 1,600.

COMMUNITY MEDICAL CENTERS
1925 East Dakota Avenue, Suite 110, Fresno CA 93726. 559/459-1919. **Fax:** 559/459-1594. **Contact:** Human Resources. **World Wide Web address:** http://www.communitymedical.org. **Description:** A nonprofit medical system with several acute care hospitals, long-term care facilities, and a variety of home care services. Specialties include cancer, cardiology, emergency services, rehabilitation, and family birthing centers. **Positions advertised include:** Anesthesia Technician; Cardiovascular Radiologic Technologist; Case Manager; Clinical Coordinator; Clinical Nurse Specialist; Cytotechnologist; Licensed Vocational Nurse; Medical Technologist; Occupational Therapist; Registered Nurse; Pharmacist; Sonographer; Respiratory Care Practitioner. **Corporate headquarters location:** This location. **Other U.S. locations:** Clovis CA. **Number of employees at this location:** 4,200.

DEL MAR REYNOLDS MEDICAL, INC.
13 Whatney, Irvine CA 92618-2837. 949/699-3300. **Fax:** 949/699-3380. **Contact:** Personnel Manager. **E-mail address:** usa@dmr.ferrarisgroup.com. **World Wide Web address:** http://www.delmarreynolds.com. **Description:** Develops, manufactures, and markets a wide range of medical monitoring and testing equipment. Products include stress tests, ambulatory blood pressure monitors, ambulatory transesophagael testing devices, and the AVESP (Audiovisual Superimposed Electrocardiographic Presentation). **Corporate headquarters location:** This location. **Parent company:** Ferraris Group (London).

DOCTORS MEDICAL CENTER
2000 Vale Road, San Pablo CA 94806. 510/970-5000. **Fax:** 510/970-5730. **Contact:** Human Resources. **World Wide Web address:** http://www.doctorsmedicalcenter.org. **Description:** A 232-bed acute care hospital serving the East Bay area of Northern California. **Positions advertised include:** Pharmacist; Laboratory Manager; Respiratory Technician; Speech Therapist; Mammography Technician; Clinical Nursing Manager; Registered Dietitian. **Parent company:** West Contra Costa Healthcare District. **Number of employees at this location:** 900.

EDWARDS LIFESCIENCES
One Edwards Way, Irvine CA 92614. 949/250-2500. **Toll-free phone:** 800/428-3278. **Contact:** Human Resources. **E-mail address:** eweb@edwards.com. **World Wide Web address:** http://www.edwards.com. **Description:** Designs, develops, manufactures, and markets disposable medical devices used in the handling, processing, and purifying of blood during surgical and medical procedures. **Positions advertised include:** Catheter Design Engineer; Clinical Research Associate; Compensation Analyst; Director, Clinical Marketing; Engineering Technician; International Tax Manager; Manager, Human Resources. **Corporate headquarters location:** This location. **Other area locations:** Sausalito CA. **International locations:** Worldwide. **Listed on:** New York Stock Exchange. **Stock exchange symbol:** EW. **Annual sales/revenues:** $860 million. **Number of employees at this location:** 1,400. **Number of employees worldwide:** 5,000.

ENLOE MEDICAL CENTER
1531 Esplanade, Chico CA 95926. 530/332-7300. **Toll-free phone:** 800/822-8102x7352. **Fax:** 530/899-2010. **Recorded jobline:** 530/892-6711. **Contact:** Charlene Davis, Recruiting Manager. **E-mail address:** recruiter@enloe.org. **World Wide Web address:** http://www.enloe.org. **Description:** A nonprofit, 203-bed, regional, Level II trauma center. Founded in 1913. **NOTE:** Entry-level positions and second and third shifts are offered. **Positions advertised include:** Registered Nurse; Licensed Vocational Nurse; Certified Nursing Assistant; Unit Secretary; Admissions Representative; Chief Radiology Technologist; Clinical Dietitian; Computer Operator; Emergency Medical Technician; Laboratory Assistant; Occupational Therapist; Patient Support Clerk; Pharmacist; Physical Therapist; Social Worker; Speech Therapist; Surgical Technologist. **Special programs:** Internships; Training. **Number of employees at this location:** 1,800.

EXAMINETICS, INC.
10920 Via Frontera, San Diego CA 92127-1704. 858/485-0933. **Fax:** 858/485-8133. **Contact:** Field Recruiting. **E-mail address:** recruiter@examinetics.com. **World Wide Web address:** http://www.examinetics.com. **Description:** A nationwide mobile health testing service for unions, major corporations, public utilities, and other public and private organizations. **NOTE:** Entry-level positions are offered. **Positions advertised include:** Clerk; Medical Screening Assistant; Licensed Practical Nurse; Licensed Vocational Nurse; Registered Nurse; Occupational Health Specialist; Driver Maintenance Technician. **Corporate headquarters location:** Overland Park KS.

FS PRECISION TECH CO.
3025 East Victoria Street, Rancho Dominguez CA 90221. 310/638-0595. **Fax:** 310/631-2884. **Contact:** Anna Leonard, Human Resources Manager. **E-mail address:** careers@fs-precision.com. **World Wide Web address:** http://www.fs-precision.com. **Description:** Manufactures precision castings for a number of specialty products including medical implants, golf clubs, hand tools, and automotive parts. **Corporate headquarters location:** This location.

FACEY MEDICAL FOUNDATION
15451 San Fernando Mission Boulevard, Suite 300, Mission Hills CA 91345. 818/837-5695. **Fax:** 818/365-5706. **Recorded jobline:** 818/837-5695. **Contact:** Human Resources Department. **E-mail address:** careers@facey.com. **World Wide Web address:** http://www.facey.com. **Description:** A nonprofit, multi-specialty health care clinic and medical group. Founded in 1922. **NOTE:** Entry-level positions, externships, and second and third shifts are offered. **Positions advertised include:** Administrative Director, Managed Care. **Corporate headquarters location:** This location.

4-D NEUROIMAGING
9727 Pacific Heights Boulevard, San Diego CA 92121. 858/453-6300. **Fax:** 858/453-4913. **Contact:** Human Resources. **E-mail address:** info@4dneuroimaging.com. **World Wide Web address:** http://www.4dneuroimaging.com. **Description:** Manufactures specialized instruments for ultrasensitive magnetic field and low-temperature measurements. The company incorporates its core magnetic sensing technologies into its magnetic source imaging (MSI) system, an instrument designed to assist in the noninvasive diagnosis of a broad range of medical disorders. The MSI system developed by the company uses advanced superconducting technology to measure and locate the source of magnetic fields generated by the human body. The company is focusing the development of its technology on market applications such as brain surgery and the diagnosis and

surgical planning for treatment of epilepsy and life-threatening cardiac arrhythmias. Founded in 1970. **Corporate headquarters location:** This location.

FREMONT HOSPITAL
39001 Sundale Drive, Fremont CA 94538. 510/796-1100. **Fax:** 510/574-4877. **Contact:** Human Resources. **World Wide Web address:** http://www.fremonthospital.com. **Description:** A psychiatric and chemical dependency treatment hospital. **Positions advertised include:** Case Manager; Mental Health Technician; Child Psychiatrist; Registered Nurse. **Special programs:** Internships. **Parent company:** Psychiatric Solutions, Inc. **Listed on:** Privately held.

FRESENIUS MEDICAL CARE NORTH AMERICA
2637 Shadelands Drive, Walnut Creek CA 94598. 925/295-0200. **Contact:** Human Resources Manager. **E-mail address:** resumes@fmc-na.com. **World Wide Web address:** http://www.fmcna.com. **Description:** Manufactures, sells, and distributes systems and supplies for hemodialysis and peritoneal dialysis. Products include machines, dialyzers, equipment solutions in bio-compatible flexible plastic bags, and associated disposable tubing assemblies that serve the entire range of end-stage renal disease patients. **NOTE:** Entry-level positions are offered. **Special programs:** Training. **Corporate headquarters location:** Lexington MA. **Other U.S. locations:** Nationwide. **Parent company:** Fresenius Medical Care AG (Germany). **Operations at this facility include:** This location is a training center. **Listed on:** New York Stock Exchange. **Stock exchange symbol:** FMS. **Number of employees at this location:** 375.

GE IMATRON
389 Oyster Point Boulevard, South San Francisco CA 94080. 650/583-9964. **Fax:** 650/827-7706. **Contact:** Human Resources. **World Wide Web address:** http://www.imatron.com. **Description:** Designs, develops, manufactures, and markets electron beam tomography scanners. **Positions advertised include:** Nuclear Sales Representative; Field Engineer. **Corporate headquarters location:** Milwaukee WI. **Parent company:** GE Healthcare, a division of General Electric. **Listed on:** New York Stock Exchange. **Stock exchange symbol:** GE.

GARFIELD MEDICAL CENTER
525 North Garfield Avenue, Monterey Park CA 91754. 626/307-2050. **Fax:** 626/573-9057. **Contact:** Jeanette Auth, Director of Human Resources. **E-mail address:** jeanette.auth@ahmchealth.com. **World Wide Web address:** http://www.garfieldmedicalcenter.com. **Description:** A full-service hospital that provides acute care, emergency care, and a neonatal intensive care unit. **Positions advertised include:** Registered Nurse; Case Manager; Physical Therapist; Licensed Vocational Nurse; Surgical Technician; Pharmacist; Radiology Technologist. **Parent company:** Alhambra Hospital Medical Center.

GEN-PROBE INCORPORATED
10210 Genetic Center Drive, San Diego CA 92121. 858/410-8000. **Fax:** 800/288-3141. **Contact:** Human Resources. **E-mail address:** hr@gen-probe.com. **World Wide Web address:** http://www.gen-probe.com. **Description:** Develops and manufactures products for clinical blood testing. **Corporate headquarters location:** This location.

GENZYME GENETICS
5300 McConnell Avenue, Los Angeles CA 90066. 310/482-5000. **Fax:** 310/482-5001. **Contact:** Human Resources. **World Wide Web address:** http://www.genzymegenetics.com. **Description:** A leading provider of genetic testing and counseling. **Corporate headquarters location:** Westborough MA. **Other area locations:** Monrovia CA; Orange CA. **Other U.S. locations:** Nationwide. **Parent company:** Genzyme Corporation (Cambridge MA). **Operations at this facility include:** Clinical trials; testing services.

GISH BIOMEDICAL, INC.
22942 Arroyo Vista, Rancho Santa Margarita CA 92688. 949/635-6200. **Toll-free phone:** 800/938-0531. **Fax:** 949/635-6291. **Contact:** Human Resources. **E-mail address:** gish@gishbiomedical.com. **World Wide Web address:** http://www.gishbiomedical.com. **Description:** Designs, produces, and markets innovative specialty surgical devices. Gish Biomedical specializes in blood handling and fluid delivery as well as blood management systems for cardiovascular surgery, oncology, and orthopedics. **Corporate headquarters location:** This location. **Parent company:** CardioTech International. **Listed on:** American Stock Exchange. **Stock exchange symbol:** CTE.

GRIFOLS
2410 Lillyvale Avenue, Los Angeles CA 90032-3514. 800/421-0008. **Contact:** Human Resources. **World Wide Web address:** http://www.grifolsusa.com. **Description:** Supplies plasma products, diagnostic reagents, automated analyzers, and dosing machines.

HILLVIEW MENTAL HEALTH CENTER, INC.
11500 Eldridge Avenue, Suite 206, Lake View Terrace CA 91342. 818/896-1161. **Contact:** Human Resources. **Description:** An outpatient and residential mental health services facility for individuals with persistent mental disabilities. Founded in 1985. **NOTE:** Entry-level positions and second and third shifts are offered. **Corporate headquarters location:** This location. **Number of employees at this location:** 80.

HOSPITAL SYSTEMS, INC.
750 Garcia Avenue, Pittsburg CA 94565. 925/427-7800. **Fax:** 925/427-0800. **Contact:** Human Resources. **E-mail address:** info@hospitalsystems.com. **World Wide Web address:** http://www.hospitalsystems.com. **Description:** Manufactures respiratory products that are used for a broad range of health services. Product lines include respiratory therapy equipment, emergency medical products, and medical gas equipment. **Corporate headquarters location:** This location.

INSIGHT HEALTH SERVICES CORPORATION
26250 Enterprise Court, Suite 100, Lake Forest CA 92630. 949/282-6000. **Fax:** 949/452-0203. **Contact:** Human Resources. **E-mail address:** employment@insighthealth.com. **World Wide Web address:** http://www.insighthealthcorp.com. **Description:** Engaged in the establishment and operation of outpatient diagnostic and treatment centers utilizing magnetic resonance imaging systems (MRI), computerized tomography systems (CT), multimodality radiologic imaging systems, cardiovascular diagnostic imaging systems, medical linear accelerators, and Leksell Stereotactic Gamma Units (Gamma Knife). **Positions advertised include:** Accounts Payable Representative; Collector; Director, Government Claims; Enterprise Operations Manager. **Corporate headquarters location:** This location. **Other U.S. locations:** Nationwide. **Listed on:** NASDAQ. **Stock exchange symbol:** IHSC. **Number of employees at this location:** 60. **Number of employees nationwide:** 800.

INTUITIVE SURGICAL, INC.
950 Kifer Road, Sunnyvale CA 94086. 408/523-2100. **Fax:** 408/523-1390. **Contact:** Human Resources. **World Wide Web address:** http://www.intusurg.com. **Description:** Designs, manufactures and markets the *da Vinci* Surgical System, which offers surgeons superior visualization, enhanced dexterity, greater precision and ergonomic comfort for the optimal performance of minimally invasive surgery. **Positions advertised include:** Vision Project Manager; Marketing Manager. **Corporate headquarters location:** This location.

JENNY CRAIG INTERNATIONAL
5770 Fleet Street, Carlsbad CA 92008. 760/696-4000. **Fax:** 760/696-4608. **Contact:** Human Resources. **E-mail address:** kkilburn@jennycraig.com. **World Wide Web address:** http://www.jennycraig.com.

Description: Provides a comprehensive weight-loss program. Jenny Craig International sells protein- and calorie-controlled food items to program participants throughout the United States and in four other countries. **Positions advertised include:** Registered Dietitian. **Corporate headquarters location:** This location. **Number of employees nationwide:** 5,370.

KELLY HOME CARE SERVICES
2900 Bristol Street, Suite J102, Costa Mesa CA 92626. 714/979-7413. **Fax:** 714/979-6895. **Contact:** Human Resources Department. **World Wide Web address:** http://www.kellyhomecare.com. **Description:** Provides home health care aides for senior citizens. **Corporate headquarters location:** Troy MI.

KIMBERLY-CLARK CORPORATION
2001 East Orangethorpe Avenue, Fullerton CA 92831-5396. 714/773-7500. **Contact:** Human Resources. **World Wide Web address:** http://www.kimberly-clark.com. **Description:** A major manufacturer and marketer of fiber-based products for consumer and industrial customers. Kimberly-Clark does business in three primary product classes: Consumer and Service, offering a broad range of paper-based goods such as facial tissue, table napkins, and disposable gowns for medical applications; Newsprint, Pulp, and Forest Products, providing a variety of goods to industrial clients; and Paper and Specialties, producing adhesive-coated paper for commercial printing customers. **Corporate headquarters location:** Neenah WI. **Listed on:** New York Stock Exchange. **Stock exchange symbol:** KMB.

KYPHON INC.
1221 Crossman Avenue, Sunnyvale CA 94089. 408/548-6500. **Fax:** 408/548-6501. **Contact:** Human Resources. **World Wide Web address:** http://www.kyphon.com. **Description:** Designs, manufactures and markets surgical devices used in balloon kyphoplasty that restore spinal function with minimally invasive therapies. **Positions advertised include:** Clinical Research Coordinator; Assembler. **Corporate headquarters location:** This location.

LASERSCOPE
3070 Orchard Drive, San Jose CA 95134-2011. 408/943-0636. **Fax:** 408/943-9630. **Contact:** Human Resources. **E-mail address:** staffing@laserscope.com. **World Wide Web address:** http://www.laserscope.com. **Description:** Designs and markets an advanced line of medical laser systems and related energy delivery products. The company markets its products to hospitals, outpatient surgical centers, and physicians' offices worldwide. **Positions advertised include:** Accounting Manager; Regional Surgical Sales Manager. **Corporate headquarters location:** This location. **Operations at this facility include:** Administration; Manufacturing; Research and Development; Sales; Service. **Listed on:** NASDAQ. **Stock exchange symbol:** LSCP. **President/CEO:** Eric Reuter. **Annual sales/revenues:** $21 - $50 million. **Number of employees at this location:** 170. **Number of employees nationwide:** 220.

LIFESCAN, INC.
1000 Gibraltar Drive, Milpitas CA 95035. 408/263-9789. **Contact:** Human Resources. **World Wide Web address:** http://www.lifescan.com. **Description:** Manufactures and markets a wide variety of diabetic devices designed to improve the lifestyles of people with diabetes. **NOTE:** Search and apply for positions online. **Positions advertised include:** Quality Software Engineer; ELDP Associate Engineer. **Corporate headquarters location:** This location. **Parent company:** Johnson & Johnson (New Brunswick NJ). **Listed on:** New York Stock Exchange. **Stock exchange symbol:** JNJ.

LODI MEMORIAL HOSPITAL
975 South Fairmont Avenue, P.O. Box 3004, Lodi CA 95240-1908. 209/334-3411. **Fax:** 209/339-7687. **Recorded jobline:** 209/339-7562. **Contact:** Mark Wallace, Manager of Human Resources Department. **E-mail address:** humanresources@lodihealth.org. **World Wide Web address:** http://www.lodihealth.org. **Description:** A 172-bed, nonprofit, acute-care hospital. Services include acute physical rehabilitation, subacute services, long-term care, home health care, and adult daycare. **NOTE:** Search and apply for positions online. **Positions advertised include:** Aide; Clerk; Clinical Dietician; Clinical Laboratory Scientist; Certified Nursing Assistant; Licensed Vocational Nurse; Pharmacist; Registered Nurse; Sonographer; Physical Therapist; Occupational Therapist. **Corporate headquarters location:** This location. **Number of employees at this location:** 1,000.

LOGAN HEIGHTS FAMILY HEALTH CENTER
1809 National Avenue, San Diego CA 92113. 619/515-2300. **Fax:** 619/232-1360. **Recorded jobline:** 619/515-2572. **Contact:** Human Resources Manager. **World Wide Web address:** http://www.fhcsd.org. **Description:** A nonprofit, community health center. Services include audiology, counseling, dental, dermatology, early intervention, family planning, health promotion, hearing, internal medicine, laboratory, language, OB/GYN, optometry, pediatric cardiology, pediatrics, pharmacy, radiology, social services, and speech. **Special programs:** Internships. **Other U.S. locations:** Mission Beach CA. **Operations at this facility include:** Administration. **Number of employees at this location:** 250.

LONGWOOD MANOR SANITARIUM
4853 West Washington Boulevard, Los Angeles CA 90001. 323/935-1157. **Fax:** 323/935-3140. **Contact:** Personnel Department. **Description:** A skilled nursing home. Founded in 1970. **NOTE:** Entry-level positions and second and third shifts are offered. **Office hours:** Monday - Friday, 9:00 a.m. - 4:30 p.m.

LOS ANGELES COUNTY DEPARTMENT OF HEALTH SERVICES
5555 Ferguson Drive, Room 200-01, City of Commerce CA 90022. **Recorded jobline:** 800/970-5478. **Contact:** Human Resources. **E-mail address:** hr@adhs.org. **World Wide Web address:** http://www.ladhs.org. **Description:** An organization that encompasses all the county's health offices including those facilities in Acton, Torrance, Lancaster and Sylmar CA. **NOTE:** See website for job listings for all the county's health services facilities. A completed application is required for any position. See website for additional application submission procedures.

LUMENIS
2400 Condensa Street, Santa Clara CA 95051. 408/764-3000. **Toll-free phone:** 800/635-1313. **Fax:** 408/764-3999. **Contact:** Human Resources. **World Wide Web address:** http://www.lumenis.com. **Description:** Manufactures and markets a wide variety of specialty lasers for the medical, scientific, and commercial fields. **NOTE:** Search and apply for positions online. **Positions advertised include:** Senior Development Engineer; Service Contract Specialist; Administrative Assistant; Program Specialist; Area Sales Manager; Customer Relations Representative; Commissions Analyst. **Corporate headquarters location:** Yokneam Israel. **Other U.S. locations:** New York NY. **International locations:** Worldwide. **Operations at this facility include:** Administration; Research and Development; Sales; Service. **Listed on:** NASDAQ. **Stock exchange symbol:** LUME.

MATRIA HEALTHCARE
17701 Cowan Avenue, Suite 150, Irvine CA 92614. 949/794-6500. **Toll-free phone:** 800/456-4060. **Contact:** Human Resources. **E-mail address:** matriahr@matria.com. **World Wide Web address:** http://www.matria.com. **Description:** Offers medical services for pregnant women via 24-hour hotlines. Matria Healthcare is subcontracted through insurance companies. **Corporate headquarters location:** Marietta GA. **Listed on:** NASDAQ. **Stock exchange symbol:** MATR.

McKESSON
One Post Street, 31st Floor, San Francisco CA 94104. 415/983-8300. **Fax:** 415/983-8900. **Contact:** Personnel. **E-mail address:** jobs.infosolutions@mckesson.com. **World Wide Web address:** http://www.mckesson.com. **Description:** Provides information systems and technology to health care enterprises including hospitals, integrated delivery networks, and managed care organizations. McKessonHBOC's primary products are Pathways 2000, a family of client/server-based applications that allow the integration and uniting of health care providers; STAR, Series, and HealthQuest transaction systems; TRENDSTAR decision support system; and QUANTUM enterprise information system. The company also offers outsourcing services that include strategic information systems planning, data center operations, receivables management, business office administration, and major system conversions. Founded in 1833. **Positions advertised include:** EBIS Technical Architect; Marketing Manager; QA Analyst; Senior EAI Specialist; Senior Developer/Analyst. **Corporate headquarters location:** This location. **Other U.S. locations:** Nationwide. **Subsidiaries include:** Automated Healthcare Inc.; Healthcare Delivery Systems, Inc.; McKesson BioServices Corporation; McKesson Pharmacy Systems; Medis Health and Pharmaceutical Services, Inc.; MedPath; U.S. Healthcare; Zee Medical, Inc. **Operations at this facility include:** Administration. **Listed on:** New York Stock Exchange. **Stock exchange symbol:** MCK. **Number of employees at this location:** 700. **Number of employees nationwide:** 24,500.

McKESSON MEDICAL SURGICAL
30497 Canwood Street, Suite 201, Agoura Hills CA 91301. 818/879-0649. **Contact:** Personnel. **World Wide Web address:** http://www.mckesson.com. **Description:** Provides personal health management services to members and consumers through broadcast, telephone, and computer-based programs. Programs include health counseling and prevention services. **Corporate headquarters location:** San Francisco CA.

MED-DESIGN CORPORATION
2810 Bunsen Avenue, Ventura CA 93003. 805/339-0375. **Fax:** 805/339-9751. **Contact:** Human Resources. **E-mail address:** hr@med-design.com. **World Wide Web address:** http://www.med-design.com. **Description:** Designs and develops medical safety devices intended to reduce the incidence of needle accidents that primarily occur in health care settings. Products developed by the company include the retractable needle hypodermic syringe, the retractable vacuum tube phlebotomy set, and the retractable intravenous catheter insertion device. **Corporate headquarters location:** This location. **Listed on:** NASDAQ. **Stock exchange symbol:** MEDC.

MEDLINE INDUSTRIES, INC.
14650 Meyer Canyon Road, Fontana CA 92336. 909/349-6000. **Contact:** Human Resources. **World Wide Web address:** http://www.medline.com. **Description:** Medline Industries manufactures and sells a broad line of health care products used by hospitals, laboratories, pharmaceutical companies, medical schools, dentists, and the general public. **Positions advertised include:** Warehouse Operator. **Corporate headquarters location:** Mundelein IL. **Operations at this facility include:** This location primarily manufactures disposable medical gloves for use in hospitals and laboratories.

MEDTRONIC MINIMED
18000 Devonshire Street, Northridge CA 91325-1219. 818/362-5958. **Toll-free phone:** 800/MIN-IMED. **Fax:** 818/576-6232. **Contact:** Human Resources. **E-mail address:** hr@minimed.com. **World Wide Web address:** http://www.minimed.com. **Description:** Develops and manufactures insulin pumps and other products for the treatment of diabetes. Founded in 1980. **Positions advertised include:** Administrative Assistant; Clinical Research Director; Clinical Services Technician. **Corporate headquarters location:** This location. **Other U.S. locations:** Hollywood FL. **International locations:** Asia; Australia; Europe; South America. **Listed on:** New York Stock Exchange. **Stock exchange symbol:** MDT. **Annual sales/revenues:** More than $100 million.

MENTOR CORPORATION
201 Mentor Drive, Santa Barbara CA 93111. 805/879-6000. **Fax:** 805/964-2712. **Contact:** Human Resources. **World Wide Web address:** http://www.mentorcorp.com. **Description:** Develops, manufactures, and markets a broad range of products for plastic and reconstructive surgery, urology, and ophthalmology. Mentor Corporation's products include surgically implantable devices, diagnostic and surgical instruments, disposable instruments, and disposable products for hospitals and home health care. **NOTE:** Search and apply for positions online. **Positions advertised include:** Senior SEC Accountant; Tax Accountant; International Product Manager. **Corporate headquarters location:** This location. **Other U.S. locations:** Irving TX; Minneapolis MN. **Listed on:** NASDAQ. **Stock exchange symbol:** MNTR. **Number of employees nationwide:** 1,900.

MERCY MEDICAL CENTER MT. SHASTA
914 Pine Street, Mt. Shasta CA 96067. 530/926-6111. **Contact:** Employment Coordinator. **E-mail address:** hr@mercymerced@chw.edu. **World Wide Web address:** http://www.mercymercedcares.org. **Description:** A medical facility that includes acute care beds, a long-term care skilled nursing unit, and ancillary services. **NOTE:** Entry-level positions and second and third shifts are offered. Search and apply for positions online. **Positions advertised include:** Business Services Director; Emergency Services Director; Occupational Therapist; Physical Therapist; Pharmacist; Patient Registrar. **Special programs:** Internships; Training. **Office hours:** Monday - Friday, 8:00 a.m. - 5:00 p.m. **Parent company:** Catholic Healthcare West. **Operations at this facility include:** Administration; Service.

MERCY MEDICAL CENTER REDDING
2175 Rosaline Avenue, Redding CA 96001. 530/225-6000. **Fax:** 530/225-6858. **Contact:** Human Resources Department. **World Wide Web address:** http://www.mercy.org. **Description:** A 273-bed hospital that provides comprehensive health care, acute care, and a variety of special programs to a six-county region. **NOTE:** Search and apply for positions online. **Positions advertised include:** Air Ambulance Communication Specialist; Clinical Laboratory Scientist; Critical Care Specialist; Cardiac Nurse Practitioner; Registered Nurse. **Corporate headquarters location:** This location. **Parent company:** Catholic Healthcare West. **Number of employees at this location:** 1,600.

METROPOLITAN STATE HOSPITAL
11401 South Bloomfield Avenue, Norwalk CA 90650. 562/863-7011. **Fax:** 562/929-3131. **Contact:** Human Resources. **World Wide Web address:** http://www.dmh.cahwnet.gov/statehospitals/metro/default.asp. **Description:** A psychiatric hospital that is part of the California Mental Health Department. **Positions advertised include:** Clinical Dietician; Hospital Police Officer; Registered Nurse; Rehabilitation Therapist; Psychiatric Social Worker.

MICRODENTAL LABORATORIES
5601 Arnold Road, Dublin CA 94568. 925/829-3611. **Toll-free phone:** 800/229-0936. **Fax:** 925/828-0866. **Contact:** Human Resources Department. **E-mail address:** careers@microdental.com. **World Wide Web address:** http://www.microdental.com. **Description:** A dental laboratory that manufactures crowns, bridges, dentures, and other dental products. **Corporate headquarters location:** This location.

OPHTHALMIC IMAGING SYSTEMS
221 Lathrop Way, Suite I, Sacramento CA 95815. 916/646-2020. **Toll-free phone:** 800/338-8436. **Fax:** 916/646-0207. **Contact:** Human Resources. **World**

Wide Web address: http://www.oisi.com. Description: Designs, manufactures, and markets ophthalmic digital imaging systems and other diagnostic imaging equipment used by eye care professionals. Ophthalmic Imaging Systems also develops image enhancement and analysis software. **Corporate headquarters location:** This location. **Parent company:** MediVision Medical Imaging Ltd. (Israel). **Number of employees at this location:** 25.

ORMCO CORPORATION
1717 West Collins Avenue, Orange CA 92867. 714/516-7400. **Fax:** 714/516-7564. **Contact:** Human Resources Manager. **E-mail address:** careers@sybrondental.com. **World Wide Web address:** http://www.ormco.com. **Description:** Manufactures and markets orthodontic appliances and supplies. **NOTE:** Search and apply for positions online. **Positions advertised include:** Account Management Center Representative. **Office hours:** Monday - Friday, 8:00 a.m. - 5:00 p.m. **Corporate headquarters location:** This location. **Parent company:** Sybron Dental Specialties. **Number of employees at this location:** 110.

PALL CORPORATION
1630 Industrial Park Street, Covina CA 91722. 626/339-7388. **Toll-free phone:** 800/288-8377. **Fax:** 626/332-2518. **Contact:** Human Resources. **World Wide Web address:** http://www.pall.com. **Description:** Manufactures filtration, separation, and purification technologies. Founded in 1946. **Company slogan:** Quality flows through our system. **Corporate headquarters location:** East Hills NY. **Other area locations:** San Diego CA. **U.S. locations:** FL; MA; MI. **International locations:** Asia; Canada; Europe; South America. **Listed on:** New York Stock Exchange. **Stock exchange symbol:** PLL. **President:** Eric Krasnoff. **Annual sales/revenues:** $1.6 billion. **Number of employees at this location:** 420. **Number of employees nationwide:** 7,000. **Number of employees worldwide:** 11,000.

PHILIPS MEDICAL SYSTEMS
6400 Oak Canyon Road, Suite 250, Irvine CA 92618-5205. 949/726-3452. **Fax:** 949/726-0928. **Contact:** Vice President of Human Resources. **E-mail address:** recruit@medical.philips.com. **World Wide Web address:** http://www.medical.philips.com. **Description:** Produces medical diagnostic computer systems and components including state-of-the-art digital radiography image processing, nuclear medicine image processing, and radiation therapy planning systems. **NOTE:** Search and apply for positions online. **Positions advertised include:** Expediter; Material Handler; Product Marketing Specialist; Research Scientist; Software Development Manager. **Corporate headquarters location:** This location. **Other U.S. locations:** Washington DC; Philadelphia PA.

POMONA VALLEY HOSPITAL MEDICAL CENTER
1798 North Garey Avenue, Pomona CA 91767. 909/865-9500. **Fax:** 909/623-3253. **Recorded jobline:** 909/865-9840. **Contact:** Rolanda Bradshaw, Employment Specialist. **World Wide Web address:** http://www.pvhmc.com. **Description:** A 449-bed, nonprofit, acute care, teaching hospital. The hospital offers medical services through the Robert and Beverly Lewis Cancer Care Center; the Stead Heart Center; and the Women's Center. Founded in 1903. **Positions advertised include:** Registered Nurse; Admitting Representative; Claims Examiner; Phlebotomist; Patient Account Coordinator; Food Services Associate; Sous Chef; Occupational Therapist; Radiology Technologist; Sonographer; Respiratory Therapist; Medical Social Worker; Speech Therapist. **Office hours:** Monday – Friday. 7:30 a.m. – 5:00 p.m. **Operations at this facility include:** Administration; Service. **Number of employees at this location:** 2,700.

PRACTICEWARES DENTAL SUPPLY
11291 Sunrise Park Drive, Rancho Cordova CA 95742. 916/638-8147. **Contact:** Human Resources. **World Wide Web address:** http://www.practicewares.com. **Description:** Distributes professional and consumer dental products. Practicewares Dental Supply is also an authorized dealer for approximately 120 companies including 3M Dental Products, Eastman Kodak, and Premier. **Corporate headquarters location:** This location.

PROTEIN POLYMER TECHNOLOGIES, INC.
10655 Sorrento Valley Road, San Diego CA 92121. 858/558-6064. **Fax:** 858/558-6477. **Contact:** Human Resources. **World Wide Web address:** http://www.ppti.com. **Description:** Engaged in research and development of products for surgical repair procedures including tissue adhesives and sealants, adhesion barriers, and drug delivery devices. The company also markets a line of polymer-activated cell culture products. **Corporate headquarters location:** This location.

RANCHO LOS AMIGOS NATIONAL REHABILITATION CENTER
7601 East Imperial Highway, Downey CA 90242. 562/401-7511. **Recorded jobline:** 800/970-5478. **Contact:** Human Resources. **World Wide Web address:** http://www.rancho.org. **Description:** A rehabilitation center providing care to patients who suffer from strokes, spinal cord injuries, brain injuries, or other disabling illnesses. **NOTE:** Please consult website for more specific application instructions. **Positions advertised include:** Audiologist; Speech-Language Pathologist; Clinical Instructor, RN; Critical Care Nurse; Licensed Vocational Nurse; Nursing Attendant; Relief Nurse; Staff Nurse; Supervising Staff Nurse; Senior Student Worker; Unit Support Assistant; Occupational Therapist; Occupational Therapist Assistant; Physical Therapist; Physical Therapist Assistant.

RESMED
14040 Danielson Street, Poway CA 92064-6857. 858/746-2400. **Toll-free phone:** 800/424-0737. **Fax:** 858/746-2900. **Contact:** Human Resources Manager. **E-mail address:** usjobs@resmed.com. **World Wide Web address:** http://www.resmed.com. **Description:** Develops, manufactures, and markets respiratory devices. ResMed specializes in respiratory products relating to sleep disordered breathing (SBD) including sleep apnea. Founded in 1989. **Positions advertised include:** HR Generalist; eBusiness Operations Analyst; Director, Occupational Health Marketing. **Corporate headquarters location:** This location. **International locations:** Worldwide. **Listed on:** New York Stock Exchange. **Stock exchange symbol:** RMD. **Annual sales/revenues:** $273 million. **Number of employees worldwide:** Over 1,400.

RIDEOUT MEMORIAL HOSPITAL
726 Fourth Street, Marysville CA 95901. 530/749-4300. **Contact:** Rose Alexander, Personnel. **E-mail address:** ralexander@frhg.org. **World Wide Web address:** http://www.frhg.org. **Description:** A 113-bed full-service hospital. **Positions advertised include:** Registered Nurse; Billing Technician. **Parent company:** Fremont-Rideout Health Group. **Operations at this facility include:** Administration; Service. **Listed on:** Privately held.

ST. JOHN'S HEALTH CENTER
1328 Twenty-Second Street, 6th Floor, Santa Monica CA 90404. 310/829-5511. **Toll-free phone:** 800/359-9003. **Recorded jobline:** 310/829-8323. **Contact:** Penny Bresky, Recruitment and Retention Manager. **World Wide Web address:** http://www.stjohns.org. **Description:** A private, nonprofit, 317-bed, acute health care facility. Founded in 1939. **NOTE:** Unsolicited resumes are not accepted. Search and apply for positions online. **Positions advertised include:** Administrative Specialist; Patient Care Associate; Medical Records Specialist; Case Manager; Licensed Clinical Psychologist; Physical Therapist: Respiratory Specialist; Registered Nurse; Clinical Nurse Educator; Surgical Technician. **Corporate headquarters location:** Leavenworth KS. **Other U.S. locations:** CO;

KS; MT. **Parent company:** Sisters of Charity of Leavenworth. **Operations at this facility include:** Administration; Service. **Listed on:** Privately held. **Number of employees at this location:** 1,000.

ST. JUDE MEDICAL
15900 Valley View Court, Sylmar CA 91342-3577. 818/362-6822. **Toll-free phone:** 800/423-5611. **Contact:** Human Resources. **World Wide Web address:** http://www.sjm.com. **Description:** Manufactures cardiac arrhythmia management devices including pacemakers and defibrillators. **NOTE:** Search and apply for positions online. **Positions advertised include:** Senior Claims Administrator; Clinical Research Associate; Senior Cost Analyst; Accounting Director; Program Management Director; Software Engineer. **Special programs:** Internships; Co-ops. **Corporate headquarters location:** St. Paul MN. **Listed on:** New York Stock Exchange. **Stock exchange symbol:** STJ.

SANTA CLARA PET HOSPITAL
830 Kiely Boulevard, Santa Clara CA 95051. 408/296-5857. **Fax:** 408/243-5434. **Contact:** Human Resources Department. **World Wide Web address:** http://www.santaclarapethospital.com. **Description:** Provides general medical, surgical, dental, and radiological services to domestic and exotic animals. The hospital also provides cardiology services and avian intensive care. **Corporate headquarters location:** This location.

SENECA DISTRICT HOSPITAL
130 Brentwood Drive, P.O. Box 737, Chester CA 96020. 530/258-2159. **Fax:** 530/258-3595. **Contact:** Doreen Turner, Director of Human Resources. **World Wide Web address:** http://www.senecahospital.org. **Description:** Provides a variety of medical services including family centered birthing, obstetrical clinic, outpatient laboratory and X-ray services including mammography and sonography, in-house pharmacy, hospice, anesthesia, inpatient and outpatient surgical services, stress testing, respiratory care, nutritional counseling, EKG, Lifeline, and patient education. Founded in 1952. **NOTE:** Entry-level positions are offered. **Positions advertised include:** Dietary Services Supervisor; CNA. **Corporate headquarters location:** This location. **CEO:** Raymond Marks. **Annual sales/revenues:** Less than $5 million. **Number of employees at this location:** 140.

SHARP HEALTHCARE
8695 Spectrum Center Boulevard, San Diego CA 92123. 858/499-4000. **Fax:** 858/499-5938. **Recorded jobline:** 858/499-5627. **Contact:** Human Resources. **E-mail address:** sharpjob@sharp.com. **World Wide Web address:** http://www.sharp.com. **Description:** A nonprofit organization consisting of six acute care hospitals, one specialty women's hospital, three medical groups, medical clinics, urgent care centers, skilled nursing facilities, and a variety of other community health education programs and related services. Founded in 1954. **NOTE:** Second and third shifts are offered. Apply by mail, fax, or in person. **Positions advertised include:** Account Analyst; Chaplain. **Office hours:** Monday - Friday, 7:00 a.m. - 7:00 p.m. **Corporate headquarters location:** This location. **Operations at this facility include:** Administration; Service. **Listed on:** Privately held. **CEO:** Michael Murphy.

SHASTA REGIONAL MEDICAL CENTER
1100 Butte Street, Redding CA 96001. 530/244-5150. **Contact:** Human Resources. **E-mail address:** srmc-employment@hospitalpartners.com. **World Wide Web address:** http://www.reddingmedicalcenter.com. **Description:** Shasta Regional Medical Center is a regional health care provider operating the California Heart Institute, the Center for Neuroscience, the Cancer Care Professionals oncology unit, the Joint Care Center for knee and hip replacement, and the Baby Place for child birthing. **NOTE:** Second and third shifts are offered. **Positions advertised include:** Pharmacist; Registered Nurse; Respiratory Therapist; Plant Maintenance Engineer. **Parent company:** Hospital Partners of America (Charlotte NC). **Number of employees at this location:** 1,400.

SIEMENS MEDICAL SOLUTIONS
4040 Nelson Avenue, Concord CA 94520. 925/246-8200. **Contact:** Employment Representative. **World Wide Web address:** http://www.siemensmedical.com. **Description:** Engaged in the design and manufacture of medical linear accelerators for use in radiation therapy. **Positions advertised include:** Director, Strategic Purchasing; Lead Test Engineer; Installation Service Engineer; Executive Assistant; Medical Physicist; Staff Technical Writer. **Corporate headquarters location:** Malvern PA. **Parent company:** Siemens A.G. (Berlin, Germany). **Operations at this facility include:** Administration; Manufacturing; Research and Development; Sales; Service. **Listed on:** New York Stock Exchange. **Stock exchange symbol:** SI.

SKILLED HEALTHCARE, LLC
27442 Portola Parkway, Suite 200, Foothill Ranch CA 92610. 949/282-5977. **Fax:** 949/282-5857. **Contact:** Human Resources Director. **E-mail address:** hrjobs-calif@skilledhealthcare.com. **World Wide Web address:** http://www.skilledhealthcare.com. **Description:** Provides long-term care through the operation of skilled nursing centers and nursing homes. **Corporate headquarters location:** This location. **Number of employees nationwide:** 6,500.

STAAR SURGICAL COMPANY
1911 Walker Avenue, Monrovia CA 91016. 626/303-7902. **Fax:** 626/359-8402. **Contact:** Human Resources. **E-mail address:** receptionist@staar.com. **World Wide Web address:** http://www.staar.com. **Description:** Develops, manufactures, and markets ophthalmic medical devices. The company's main product is a foldable lens used in the treatment of cataracts. Founded in 1982. **Corporate headquarters location:** This location. **Listed on:** NASDAQ. **Stock exchange symbol:** STAA.

STANFORD HOSPITAL & CLINICS
300 Pasteur Drive, MC 5513, Stanford CA 94305-5520. 650/723-6155. **Fax:** 650/618-1809. **Contact:** Human Resources. **World Wide Web address:** http://www.stanfordhospital.com. **Description:** The primary teaching hospital for the Stanford University School of Medicine that provides both general acute care services and tertiary medical care. **Positions advertised include:** Staff Nurse; Accelerator Engineer; Administrative Director, Imaging; Administrative Director, Neurosciences; Anesthesia Technician; Audiologist; Business Analyst; Cardiac Sonographer; Cell Therapy Technologist; Chief Compliance Officer; Clinic Manager; CT Technologist. **Number of employees at this location:** 2,400.

SUNRISE MEDICAL MOBILITY PRODUCTS
2382 Faraday Avenue, Suite 200, Carlsbad CA 92008-7220. **Toll-free phone:** 800/333-4000. **Fax:** 760/930-1575. **Contact:** Human Resources Manager. **E-mail address:** resumes@sunmed.com. **World Wide Web address:** http://www.sunrisemedical.com. **Description:** Manufactures and markets assistive technology, patient care products, and rehabilitation products for people with disabilities as well as for use in home-care, hospitals, and nursing homes. **Positions advertised include:** Project Manager. **Corporate headquarters location:** This location.

SUTTER ROSEVILLE MEDICAL CENTER
One Medical Plaza, Roseville CA 95661-3037. 916/781-1000. **Fax:** 916/781-1605. **Contact:** Human Resources. **E-mail address:** employment@sutterhealth.org. **World Wide Web address:** http://www.sutterhealth.org. **Description:** A 205-bed, acute care hospital that serves the health care needs of the Roseville community and its outlying areas. **NOTE:** Search and apply for positions online. **Positions advertised include:** Registered Nurse; Radiological Technologist; Pharmacist. **Corporate headquarters location:** Sacramento CA. **Other U.S.**

locations: Honolulu HI. **Operations at this facility include:** Health Care; Service. **Number of employees at this location:** 1,250.

SYNBIOTICS CORPORATION
11011 Via Frontera, San Diego CA 92127. 858/451-3771. **Contact:** Human Resources. **World Wide Web address:** http://www.synbiotics.com. **Description:** Develops, manufactures, and markets products and services to veterinary specialty markets. Synbiotics provides canine reproduction products and services to purebred dog breeders and their veterinarians. In addition, the company markets a line of life-stage nutritional supplements; and PennHip, a new method for the early diagnosis and evaluation of canine hip dysplasia. **Corporate headquarters location:** This location.

TENDER LOVING CARE/STAFF BUILDERS
3841 North Freeway Boulevard, #130, Sacramento CA 95834. 916/646-4852. **Fax:** 916/648-9650. **Contact:** Human Resources. **World Wide Web address:** http://www.tlcathome.com. **Description:** A home health care agency. **Corporate headquarters location:** Lake Success NY. **Other U.S. locations:** Nationwide. **Number of employees nationwide:** 20,000.

TENET HEALTHCARE CORPORATION
3 Imperial Promenade, Suite 300, Santa Ana CA 92707. 714/428-6800. **Contact:** Human Resources Department. **World Wide Web address:** http://www.tenethealth.com. **Description:** A multibillion-dollar, multihospital corporation that, in conjunction with its subsidiaries, owns or operates approximately 130 acute care facilities nationwide. **Positions advertised include:** Paralegal. **Corporate headquarters location:** Dallas TX. **Listed on:** New York Stock Exchange. **Stock exchange symbol:** THC. **Number of employees nationwide:** 130,000.

TORRANCE MEMORIAL MEDICAL CENTER
3330 Lomita Boulevard, Torrance CA 90505. 310/325-9110. **Recorded jobline:** 310/517-4790. **Contact:** Michele Alarcon, Human Resources Representative. **E-mail address:** michele.alarcon@tmmc.com. **World Wide Web address:** http://www.torrancememorial.org. **Description:** A nonprofit medical center. **Positions advertised include:** Registered Nurse; Emergency Department Technician; Certified Nurse Assistant; Nutrition Assistant; Physical Therapist; Occupational Therapist. **Special programs:** Training. **Corporate headquarters location:** This location.

U.S. DEPARTMENT OF VETERANS AFFAIRS VETERANS ADMINISTRATION SAN DIEGO HEALTHCARE SYSTEM
3350 La Jolla Village Drive, San Diego CA 92161. 858/552-8585. **Contact:** Human Resources. **World Wide Web address:** http://www.san-diego.med.va.gov. **Description:** A medical center operated by the U.S. Department of Veterans Affairs. From 54 hospitals in 1930, the system has grown to include 171 medical centers; more than 364 outpatient, community and outreach clinics; 130 nursing home care units; and 37 domiciliary residences. The VA operates at least one medical center in each of the 48 contiguous states, Puerto Rico, and the District of Columbia. With approximately 76,000 medical center beds, the VA treats nearly 1 million patients in VA hospitals, 75,000 in nursing home care units, and 25,000 in domiciliary residences. The VA's outpatient clinics register approximately 24 million visits a year. The VA is affiliated with 104 medical schools, 48 dental schools, and more than 850 other schools across the country.

USC/NORRIS COMPREHENSIVE CANCER CENTER AND HOSPITAL
1441 Eastlake Avenue, Los Angeles CA 90033. 323/442-2660. **Fax:** 323/442-2442. **Contact:** Human Resources. **E-mail address:** careers@norris.hsc.usc.edu. **World Wide Web address:** http://www.uscnorris.com. **Description:** A 60-bed inpatient and outpatient tertiary care facility. USC Norris Comprehensive Cancer Center and Hospital is a teaching and research hospital located on the Health Sciences campus of the University of Southern California. **Positions advertised include:** Admitting Representative; Cancer Registry Abstractor; Cancer Registry Coordinator; Radiology Department Secretary; Registered Nurse; Mammography Technologist; Medical Transcriptionist. **Corporate headquarters location:** This location. **Operations at this facility include:** Administration; Service. **Number of employees at this location:** 400.

UNIVERSITY COMMUNITY MEDICAL CENTER
5550 University Avenue, San Diego CA 92105. 619/582-3516. **Contact:** Human Resources. **Description:** An acute-care hospital. **Parent company:** Quantum Health Inc. **Number of employees at this location:** 280.

VISTA DEL MAR CHILD & FAMILY SERVICES
3200 Motor Avenue, Los Angeles CA 90034. 310/836-1223. **Fax:** 310/842-9529. **Contact:** Human Resources Director. **E-mail address:** jobs@vistadelmar.org. **World Wide Web address:** http://www.vistadelmar.org. **Description:** A residential treatment facility for children up to 18 years of age. Vista del Mar Child & Family Services offers a variety of programs including chemical dependency treatment, therapeutic schooling, adoption and foster care services, and counseling on both inpatient and outpatient bases. **NOTE:** Second and third shifts are offered. **Positions advertised include:** Youth Counselor; Secretary; Foster Care/Adoptions Coordinator; Data Entry Technician. **Corporate headquarters location:** This location. **Number of employees at this location:** 300.

VISX, INCORPORATED
3400 Central Expressway, Santa Clara CA 95051. 408/773-7321. **Toll-free phone:** 800/246-VISX. **Fax:** 408/773-7200. **Contact:** Human Resources Department. **E-mail address:** greatcareers@visx.com. **World Wide Web address:** http://www.visx.com. **Description:** Designs, manufactures, and markets technologies and systems for laser vision correction. Founded in 1986. **Positions advertised include:** Software Quality Assurance Engineer; Staff Mechanical Engineer; Software Engineer; Optical Engineer. **Corporate headquarters location:** This location. **Listed on:** New York Stock Exchange. **Stock exchange symbol:** EYE. **Annual sales/revenues:** $144 million.

VOLCANO THERAPEUTICS, INC.
2870 Kilgore Road, Rancho Cordova CA 95670. 916/638-8008. **Fax:** 916/638-8239. **Contact:** Human Resources. **E-mail address:** jobs@volcanotherapeutics.com. **World Wide Web address:** http://www.volcanotherapeutics.com. **Description:** Manufactures medical devices that aid in the detection of diseases of the coronary arteries and vascular system. **Positions advertised include:** Signal Processing Engineer; R&D Engineer; Production Planner; Production Supervisor; Manager, Quality Assurance. **Special programs:** Internships. **Corporate headquarters location:** This location. **International locations:** Brussels Belgium.

WASHINGTON HOSPITAL
2000 Mowry Avenue, Fremont CA 94538. 510/797-1111. **Toll-free phone:** 800/963-7070. **Fax:** 510/745-6470. **Contact:** Personnel Services. **E-mail address:** careers@whhs.com. **World Wide Web address:** http://www.whhs.com. **Description:** A general, acute care hospital that offers a community cancer program, health insurance information services, occupational medicine, and joint replacement services. **Positions advertised include:** Cardiac Sonographer; Clinical Laboratory Scientist; Budget Manager; Case Manager; Radiological Technologist; Physical Therapist; Registered Nurse; Licensed Vocational Nurse.

Colorado
ACCREDO THERAPEUTICS INC
361 Inverness Drive South, Suite F, Englewood CO

80112-5816. 303/799-6550. **Fax:** 303/799-6551. **Contact:** Human Resources. **World Wide Web address:** http://www.accredohealth.com. **Description:** Accredo Therapeutics provides specialty biopharmaceuticals and services. **Positions advertised include:** Per Diem Nurse; Per Diem Pharmacist. **Corporate headquarters location:** Memphis TN. **Parent company:** Medco Health Solutions, Inc. **Operations at this facility include:** This location offers infusion therapy services.

AIR METHODS CORPORATION
7301 South Peoria Street, Englewood CO 80112. 303/792-7400. **Fax:** 303/790-0499. **Recorded jobline:** 303/792-7508. **Contact:** Human Resources. **World Wide Web address:** http://www.airmethods.com. **Description:** One of the largest providers of air medical emergency services and systems throughout North America. Air Methods Corporation operates a fleet of 41 aircraft, consisting of 29 helicopters and 12 airplanes. The company provides its services to 54 hospitals located in 14 states. The company designs, services, and installs proprietary medical interiors, allowing each aircraft to be operated as an airborne ICU. Founded in 1982. **NOTE:** Drug screening is a mandatory part of the hiring process. **Positions advertised include:** Assembly/Fabrication Supervisor; Avionics Installation Technician; Quality Assurance Inspector; Stress Analyst. **Number of employees at this location:** 250.

AMERICAN MEDICAL RESPONSE
6200 south Syracuse Way, Suite 200, Greenwood Village CO 80111. 303/495-1200. **Contact:** Human Resources. **World Wide Web address:** http://www.amr-inc.com. **Description:** A medical transportation services company. **Corporate headquarters location:** This location. **Other U.S. locations include:** Nationwide.

ARKANSAS VALLEY REGIONAL MEDICAL CENTER
1100 Carson Avenue, La Junta CO 81050. 719/384-5412. **Fax:** 719/383-6062. **Contact:** Director of Human Resources. **World Wide Web address:** http://www.avrmc.org. **Description:** A nonprofit medical center. **Positions advertised include:** Medical Lab Technician; Occupational Therapist; Physical Therapist; Staff Pharmacist; RN, Various Departments. **Number of employees at this location:** 400.

CSU VETERINARY TEACHING HOSPITAL
300 West Drake Road, Fort Collins CO 80523. 970/221-4535. **Contact:** Human Resources. **World Wide Web address:** http://www.csuvets.colostate.edu. **Description:** A full-service, referral, veterinary, teaching hospital. Departments include cardiology, oncology, ophthalmology, dermatology, neurology, and emergency.

THE CHILDREN'S HOSPITAL
1056 East 19th Street, Denver CO 80218. 303/861-8888. **Fax:** 303/764-8080. **Contact:** Human Resources. **E-mail address:** jobposting@tchden.org. **World Wide Web address:** http://www.childrenshospitalden.org. **Description:** A hospital providing patient care, research, education, and advocacy. **Positions advertised include:** Financial Counselor; Imaging Technician; Patient Service Coordinator; Staff Assistant; Business Systems Analyst; Manager of Accounting; Clinical Nurse Audiologist; Speech Pathologist; Medical Technician; Psychologist.

COLORADO MENTAL HEALTH INSTITUTE AT FORT LOGAN
3550 West Oxford Avenue, Denver CO 80236. 303/866-7100. **Contact:** Human Resources. **World Wide Web address:** http://www.cdhs.state.co.us/ods/mif. **Description:** A 250-bed, state psychiatric hospital. The hospital operates in three divisions: Adolescent; Adult; and Geriatric/Deaf/Aftercare. Treatments include psychotherapy, group therapy, family therapy, behavior modification, occupational and recreational therapy, pastoral counseling, educational services, vocational counseling, and a work therapy program. The hospital is licensed by the Colorado Department of Health and is accredited by the Joint Commission on Accreditation of Hospitals.

CORAM HEALTHCARE CORPORATION
1675 Broadway, Suite 900, Denver CO 80202. 303/672-8745. **Fax:** 303/298-0043. **Contact:** Faye Major, Director, Human Resources. **World Wide Web address:** http://www.coramhc.com. **Description:** One of the largest home health infusion therapy companies in the United States. The company provides a wide range of alternate site delivery services including ambulatory and home infusion therapies, lithotripsy, and institutional pharmacy services. **Corporate headquarters location:** This location. **Other U.S. locations:** Nationwide. **Subsidiaries include:** Coraflex Health Services; HealthInfusion Inc.; Medisys Inc.; T2 Medical. **Listed on:** New York Stock Exchange. **Stock exchange symbol:** CRH. **Annual sales/revenues:** More than $100 million.

CRAIG HOSPITAL
3425 South Clarkson Street, Englewood CO 80113. 303/789-8000. **Recorded jobline:** 303/789-8497. **Contact:** Human Resources. **E-mail address:** humanresources@craighospital.org. **World Wide Web address:** http://www.craighospital.org. **Description:** A hospital for the care and rehabilitation of patients with injuries to the brain and spinal cord. **NOTE:** Entry-level positions are offered. Please check the jobline for available positions before sending a resume. **Positions advertised include:** Nurse Practitioner/Physician Assistant; Occupational Therapist; Speech Pathologist; Pharmacist; Clerical Coordinator; Operations Manager, HIM. **Special programs:** Internships. **Operations at this facility include:** Administration. **Number of employees at this location:** 500.

CROSSROADS MEDICAL CENTER
1000 Alpine Street, Suite 280, Boulder CO 80304. 303/444-6400. **Contact:** Director of Personnel. **Description:** An ambulatory health care and family practice provider. Crossroads Medical Center also provides pharmacological, laboratory, and physical therapy services, as well as specialist physician services through their own group practice. **Operations at this facility include:** Administration; Divisional Headquarters; Sales.

DAVITA INC.
1057 South Wadsworth Boulevard, Suite 100, Lakewood CO 80226-4360. 800/424-6589. **Contact:** Human Resources. **World Wide Web address:** http://www.davita.com. **Description:** A provider of dialysis services in the United States for patients suffering from chronic kidney failure. The company operates more than 1,200 outpatient dialysis centers in 41 states and the District of Columbia. DaVita also provides acute inpatient dialysis services in over 369 hospitals across the country. **Positions advertised include:** Staff RN; Compliance Auditor; HR - Resource Center Specialist; Director of IT Applications; Disability Specialist; PeopleSoft HRMS Developer; HRIS Analyst; Vascular Access Coordinator; Computer Operator. **Corporate headquarters location:** El Segundo CA.

DEVEREUX CLEO WALLACE CENTERS
8405 Church Ranch Boulevard, Westminster CO 80021. 303/438-2251. **Fax:** 303/438-2290. **Contact:** Human Resources. **E-mail address:** hrcolorado@devereux.org. **World Wide Web address:** http://www.devereux.org. **Description:** A nonprofit, psychiatric treatment center offering both inpatient and outpatient treatments for children and adolescents. **NOTE:** Entry-level positions and second and third shifts are offered. **Positions advertised include:** Financial Manager; Human Resources Director. **Special programs:** Internships.

EASTMAN KODAK COMPANY
9952 Eastman Park Drive, Windsor CO 80551-1386.

970/686-7611. **Contact:** Jean Clark, Director of Personnel. **World Wide Web address:** http://www.kodak.com. **Description:** Eastman Kodak Company has four businesses: Digital & Film Imaging Systems; Health; Graphic Communications; and Display & Components. **NOTE:** Search and apply for positions online. **Positions advertised include:** Production Operator; Assembly/Warehouse Worker; IS Systems Administrator. **Special programs:** Internships. **Corporate headquarters location:** Rochester NY. **Operations at this facility include:** This location manufactures photographic and medical X-ray films. **Operations at this facility include:** Manufacturing. **Listed on:** New York Stock Exchange. **Stock exchange symbol:** EK. **Number of employees at this location:** 2,300.

EXEMPLA ST. JOSEPH HOSPITAL
1835 Franklin Street, Denver CO 80218. 303/837-7905. **Contact:** Human Resources. **World Wide Web address:** http://www.saintjosephdenver.org. **Description:** A community hospital providing patient care and education. Founded in 1873. **NOTE:** Search and apply for positions online. **Positions advertised include:** RN, Various Departments; Surgical Tech; Laboratory Supervisor; Respiratory Therapist; Radiology Tech; Director of Marketing; Medical Tech; Neonatal Nurse Practitioner.

FISCHER IMAGING CORPORATION
12300 North Grant Street, Denver CO 80241. 303/452-6800. **Fax:** 303/450-4335. **Contact:** Human Resources. **World Wide Web address:** http://www.fischerimaging.com. **Description:** Develops, manufactures, and markets medical imaging systems. Fischer Imaging Corporation provides medical systems for the electrophysiology, fluoroscopic, mammography, and radiographic markets. **NOTE:** Applications accepted only for open positions. **Corporate headquarters location:** This location. **Listed on:** NASDAQ. **Stock exchange symbol:** FIMG. **Number of employees at this location:** 350. **Number of employees nationwide:** 540.

GAMBRO RENAL PRODUCTS, USA
10810 West Collins Avenue, Lakewood CO 80215. **Toll-free phone:** 800/525-2623. **Contact:** Human Resources. **World Wide Web address:** http://www.usa-gambro.com. **Description:** Develops and supplies products, therapies, and services for both in-center and home dialysis, as well as for blood purification in intensive care units. **Positions advertised include:** Accounting Manager; Marketing Manager; Marketing Manager-Water Systems; Vice President of Human Resources GRP Americas.

HEI ADVANCED MEDICAL OPERATIONS
4801 North 63rd Street, Boulder CO 80301. 720/622-4100. **Fax:** 303/530-8291. **Contact:** Human Resources. **World Wide Web address:** http://www.heii.com. **Description:** Manufactures electro-mechanical medical devices, catheters, respiratory diagnostic instruments, MRI (Magnetic Resonance Imaging) systems, and similar medical devices. **Corporate headquarters location:** Victoria MN.

LITTLETON ADVENTIST HOSPITAL
7700 South Broadway, Littleton CO 80122. 303/730-8900. **Fax:** 303/738-2688. **Recorded jobline:** 888/808-8828. **Contact:** Human Resources. **World Wide Web address:** http://www.littletonhosp.org. **Description:** A full service hospital serving Littleton and the surrounding areas. Founded 1989. **Positions advertised include:** Clinical Charge Auditor; Clinical Coordinator; Certified Nurse Assistant; Nursing Unit Secretary; OR Technician; Pharmacy Technician; Radiology Technician; Respiratory Therapist; Transcriptionist; Ultrasound Technician. **Parent company:** Centura Health.

LONGMONT UNITED HOSPITAL
1950 Mountain View Avenue, Longmont CO 80501. 303/485-4136. **Fax:** 303/485-4137. **Recorded jobline:** 303/651-5241. **Contact:** Human Resources. **World Wide Web address:** http://www.luhcares.org. **Description:** A 143-bed general, acute care, nonprofit, community hospital. Longmont United Hospital offers a cancer care center, a cardiac lab, cardiopulmonary services, a sports rehabilitation center, complimentary medicine, cardiovascular rehabilitation, trauma/emergency center, and behavioral health services. **NOTE:** Second and third shifts are offered. **Positions advertised include:** RN, Various Departments; Respiratory Therapist; CAN; Med Tech; MRI Tech. **Special programs:** Training. **Corporate headquarters location:** This location. **Annual sales/revenues:** $51 - $100 million. **Number of employees at this location:** 930.

THE MEDICAL CENTER OF AURORA
1501 South Potomac Street, Aurora CO 80012. 303/695-2600. **Contact:** Human Resources. **Description:** A medical center with two campuses, and 346 licensed beds. **Positions advertised include:** Sr. Accountant; Clinical Nurse Manager; Director, EMS, Trauma & Disaster; RN; Surgical Tech; Director, Surgical Services. **Parent company:** HealthONE.

MEDTRONIC INC.
826 Coal Creek Circle, Louisville CO 80027. 720/890-3200. **Contact:** Human Resources. **World Wide Web address:** http://www.medtronic.com. **Description:** Develops, manufactures, and markets products, therapies and services used to treat conditions such as diabetes, heart disease, neurological disorders, and vascular illnesses. **Positions advertised include:** Associate Product Manager; Corporate Account Director; Customer Service Rep; Financial Systems Analyst. **Corporate headquarters location:** Minneapolis MN. **Parent company:** Medtronic Inc. **Listed on:** New York Stock Exchange. **Stock exchange symbol:** MOT.

MOUNT SAN RAFAEL HOSPITAL
410 Benedicta Avenue, Trinidad CO 81082. 719/846-9213. **Fax:** 719/846-2752. **Contact:** Human Resources. **World Wide Web address:** http://www.msrhc.org. **Description:** A nonprofit, JCAHO-accredited, acute care hospital with 70 beds offering 24-hour physician coverage; an emergency department; a full laboratory; a pharmacy; X-ray facilities; physical, occupational, and speech therapy; diabetic education; home health care; and prenatal education. **NOTE:** Entry-level positions and second and third shifts are offered. **Special programs:** Training. **Office hours:** Monday - Friday, 8:00 a.m. - 4:30 p.m. **Executive Director:** James D'Agostino. **Annual sales/revenues:** Less than $5 million. **Number of employees at this location:** 144.

NATIONAL JEWISH MEDICAL & RESEARCH CENTER
1400 Jackson Street, G113, Denver CO 80206. 303/388-4461. **Fax:** 303/398-1775. **Recorded jobline:** 800/686-9512. **Contact:** Human Resources Director. **E-mail address:** hr@njc.org. **World Wide Web address:** http://www.njc.org. **Description:** A world leader in the research and treatment of respiratory, immune system, and allergic disorders. National Jewish Medical & Research Center is a nonprofit, nonsectarian institution. Founded in 1899. Positions advertised include: Certified Medical Assistant; Clinical Research Coordinator; Database/Operations Coordinator; Executive Director, Business Development.

NICOLET VASCULAR INC.
720 Corporate Circle, Suite A, Golden CO 80401. 608/441-2266. **Toll-free phone:** 800/525-2519. **Fax:** 608/441-2232. **Contact:** Human Resources. **World Wide Web address:** http://www.viasyshealthcare.com. **Description:** Manufactures diagnostic equipment including fetal heart detectors for determining fetal viability, and systems that aid in the diagnosis of cardiovascular disease. The company also manufactures electronic instrumentation for medical applications in neuro-physiological diagnosis and for monitoring the treatment of brain, muscle, nerve, and sleep disorders, and to test for hearing impairment. **Special programs:** Internships; Summer Jobs. **Corporate headquarters**

location: Madison WI. **Parent company:** VIASYS Healthcare. **Listed on:** New York Stock Exchange. **Stock exchange symbol:** VAS. **Annual sales/revenues:** $11 - $20 million. **Number of employees at this location:** 75.

NORTH COLORADO MEDICAL CENTER (NCMC)
BANNER HEALTH COLORADO
1801 16th Street, Greeley CO 80631-5199. 970/352-4121. **Fax:** 970/350-6446. **Recorded jobline:** 970/350-6565. **Contact:** Director of Personnel. **World Wide Web address:** http://www.bannerhealth.com. **Description:** A not-for-profit hospital that serves as the primary full-service tertiary facility for northern and eastern Colorado, southern Wyoming, western Nebraska, and Kansas.. **NOTE:** Apply online. Entry-level positions are offered. **Positions advertised include:** Certified Nursing Assistant; Clinical Nurse Educator; Emergency Department Technician; Infection Control Analyst; Licensed Respiratory Therapist; Medical Technologist; Nuclear Medicine Technologist; Patient Account Representative; Pharmacist; Physical Therapist; Radiology Technologist; RN, Various Departments. **Corporate headquarters location:** Fargo ND. **Other area locations:** Brush CO; Loveland CO; Sterling CO. **Operations at this facility include:** Administration; Regional Headquarters; Service. **Annual sales/revenues:** $21 - $50 million. **Number of employees at this location:** 1,700. **Number of employees nationwide:** 14,000.

NORTH SUBURBAN MEDICAL CENTER (NSMC)
9191 Grant Street, Thornton CO 80229-4341. 303/451-7800. **Contact:** Human Resources. **World Wide Web address:** http://www.northsuburban.com. **Description:** A 157-bed, family-centered health care facility. North Suburban Medical Center offers a full range of services including orthopedics, ICU/CCU, 24-hour emergency coverage, medical and surgical, pediatrics, and oncology. In addition, NSMC also operates a 23-bed Transitional Care Center and a program for inpatient treatment of geriatric, psychiatric disorders. **Positions advertised include:** RN, Various Departments; Cardiovascular Specialist; Clinical Nurse Specialist; Occupational Therapist; Quality Management Coordinator.

PENROSE-ST. FRANCIS HEALTH SERVICES
PENROSE HOSPITAL
2222 North Nevada Avenue, Colorado Springs CO 80907. 719/776-5000. **Contact:** Human Resources. **World Wide Web address:** http://www.centura.org. **Description:** Operates a 300-bed hospital; a cytology laboratory; Huff and Puff, a children's asthma program; The Women's Life Center; ReadyCare clinics; The Penrose Cancer Center; The Namaste Alzheimer Center; The Heart Center at Penrose Hospital; The Center for Health and Nutrition; trauma rehabilitation and comprehensive rehabilitation; and The Clinical Pastoral Education Program. **Positions advertised include:** RN, Various Departments; CNA. **Other area locations:** Green Mountain Falls CO; Woodland Park CO. **Parent company:** Centura Health.

PORTER ADVENTIST HOSPITAL
2525 South Downing Street, Denver CO 80210. 303/778-1955. **Contact:** Human Resources. **World Wide Web address:** http://www.centura.org. **Description:** A 369-bed, nonprofit, acute care hospital. Founded in 1930. **Positions advertised include:** RN, Various Departments; OR Technician; Pharmacy Tech; Physical Therapist; CT Tech. **Parent company:** Centura Health.

POUDRE VALLEY HOSPITAL
1024 South Lemay Avenue, Fort Collins CO 80524. 970/495-7300. **Fax:** 970/495-7629. **Recorded jobline:** 970/495-7310. **Contact:** Patti Oakes, Director of Human Resources. **World Wide Web address:** http://www.pvhs.org. **Description:** A 255-bed hospital providing health care services in northern Colorado, western Nebraska, and southern Wyoming. **NOTE:** Search and apply for positions online. **Positions advertised include:** Clinical Coordinator, Pharmacy; Medical Technologist; Physical Therapist; Supervisor, Clinical Applications **Special programs:** Internships. **Office hours:** Monday - Friday, 7:00 a.m. - 4:30 p.m. **Parent company:** Poudre Valley Health System. **Number of employees at this location:** 1,800.

PRESBYTERIAN/ST. LUKE'S MEDICAL CENTER
1719 East 19th Avenue, Denver CO 80218. 303/839-6000. **Contact:** Human Resources. **World Wide Web address:** http://www.pslmc.com. **Description:** A 680-bed, tertiary care hospital. Presbyterian/St. Luke's Medical Center has comprehensive programs in pediatrics, obstetrics, oncology, cardiology, and orthopedics. The medical center is a leader in tertiary programs such as organ and bone marrow transplantation; high-risk obstetrical care; diabetes management; wound care; and head, neck, and skull surgery. **Positions advertised include:** Patient Care Director; Apheresis Technologist; Nurse Manager; RN Case Manager; Sonographer; Clinical Education Coordinator; Nurse Recuiter: Manager of Communications. **Parent company:** HealthONE facilities include Medical Center of Aurora, Spalding Rehabilitation Hospital, Swedish Medical Center, Rose Medical Center, and North Suburban Medical Center.

ROCKY MOUNTAIN POISON AND DRUG CENTER
777 Bannock Street, Mail Code 0180, Denver CO 80204. 303/739-1100. **Contact:** Human Resources. **World Wide Web address:** http://www.rmpdc.org. **Description:** Provides rapid and accurate treatment recommendations over the telephone to consumers and health professionals, 24 hours a day. Registered nurses and physicians manage over 120,000 cases per year. Rocky Mountain Poison and Drug Center consults in all areas dealing with chemicals, drugs, and plants. The center's public education program focuses on early intervention and prevention education platforms.

ROSE MEDICAL CENTER
4567 East Ninth Avenue, Denver CO 80220. 303/320-2121. **Contact:** Human Resources. **World Wide Web address:** http://www.rosemed.com. **Description:** A 420-bed medical center that provides inpatient and outpatient services. Founded in 1949. **Positions advertised include:** Controller; Contract Administrator; Ambulatory Surgery Manager; Surgical Tech; Director of Case Management; Oncology Coordinator; Operating Room Manager; RN, Various Departments. **Corporate headquarters location:** This location. **Parent company:** HealthONE. **Listed on:** Privately held. **Number of employees at this location:** 1,600.

ST. ANTHONY CENTRAL HOSPITAL
4231 West 16th Avenue, Denver CO 80204. 303/629-3511. **Contact:** Human Resources. **World Wide Web address:** http://www.centura.org. **Description:** A 593-bed, full-service hospital and the only nonprofit, private Level 1 trauma center in Colorado. **Positions advertised include:** Pharmacy Manager; Case Manager; RN, Various Departments; CT Scan Tech; Occupational Therapist; Mammography Tech. **Parent company:** Centura Health.

ST. ANTHONY NORTH HOSPITAL
2551 West 84th Avenue, Westminster CO 80031. 303/426-2151. **Contact:** Human Resources. **World Wide Web address:** http://www.centura.org. **Description:** A 196-bed hospital. Major medical specialties include family practice, pediatrics, neonatology, cardiology, emergency medicine, obstetrics, oncology, and an adult psychiatric unit. **Positions advertised include:** Clinical Nursing Manager; OR Tech; CT Scan Tech; RN, Various Departments; Ultrasound Tech; Physician Business Liaison. **Parent company:** Centura Health.

ST. MARY-CORWIN REGIONAL MEDICAL CENTER
1008 Minnequa Avenue, Pueblo CO 81004. 719/560-4000. **Contact:** Ms. Jackie Armstrong, Human Resources Services Representative. **World Wide Web address:** http://www.centura.org. **Description:** A hospital. **Positions advertised include:** Director Quality Resources; Physical Therapist; Surgical Tech; Speech Language Pathologist; Registered Respiratory Therapist; Radiation Therapist. **Corporate headquarters location:** Denver CO. **Parent company:** Centura Health. **Operations at this facility include:** Administration. **Number of employees at this location:** 1,300.

SKY RIDGE MEDICAL CENTER
10101 RidgeGate Parkway, Lone Tree CO 80124. 720/225-1000. **Fax:** 303/788-2590. **Contact:** Human Resources. **World Wide Web address:** http://www.skyridgemedcenter.com. **Description:** A health care facility whose services include emergency care, surgical services, cardiac services, and diagnostic and imaging services. **Positions advertised include:** RN; CT Tech; HIM Specialist; CNA; Medical Technologist; Assistant Vice President Surgical Services. **Parent company:** HealthONE.

SPALDING REHABILITATION HOSPITAL
900 Potomac Street, Aurora CO 80011. 303/367-1166. **Contact:** Human Resources. **World Wide Web address:** http://www.spaldingrehab.com. **Description:** One of Denver's leading resources for physical rehabilitation services. In partnership with the HealthONE system, Spalding provides rehabilitation services. Spalding's treatment programs target an array of musculoskeletal problems and neurological disorders, including brain injury; head, neck, and spinal injuries; stroke; multiple sclerosis; and chronic pain. Founded in 1914. **Positions advertised include:** Evening Supervisor; Staff RN; Lead Therapist. **Parent company:** HealthONE.

THE SPECTRANETICS CORPORATION
96 Talamine Court, Colorado Springs CO 80907. 719/633-8333. **Toll-free phone:** 800/633-0960. **Fax:** 719/475-7086. **Contact:** Human Resources. **World Wide Web address:** http://www.spectranetics.com. **Description:** Researches, develops, manufactures, services, supports, and sells medical lasers and attendant catheters used in heart surgery. **Positions advertised include:** Sr. Technician; Sr. Laser Scientist; Engineer; Manufacturing Engineer; Clinical Affairs Manager. **Corporate headquarters location:** This location. **Other U.S. locations:** Nationwide. **International locations:** Worldwide. **Listed on:** NASDAQ. **Stock exchange symbol:** SPNC. **Number of employees at this location:** 75. **Number of employees nationwide:** 140.

U.S. DEPARTMENT OF VETERNS AFFAIRS DENVER VETERANS ADMINISTRATION MEDICAL CENTER
1055 Clermont Street, Denver CO 80220-3808. 303/399-8020. **Contact:** Human Resources Management Service. **World Wide Web address:** http://www.va.gov. **Description:** A medical center. VA operates medical centers in each of the 48 contiguous states, Puerto Rico, and the District of Columbia. With approximately 76,000 medical center beds, VA treats nearly 1 million patients in VA hospitals, 75,000 in nursing home care units, and 25,000 in domiciliary residences. **Positions advertised include:** Nurse Manager; Physical Therapist; RN; Chief of Staff. **Corporate headquarters location:** Washington DC. **Parent company:** U.S. Department of Veterans Affairs. **Number of employees at this location:** 1,600.

UNIVERSITY OF COLORADO HOSPITAL UNIVERSITY OF COLORADO HEALTH SCIENCES CENTER
4200 East 9th Avenue, Campus Box A028, Denver CO 80262. 303/372-2121. **Fax:** 303/372-9650. **Contact:** Human Resources. **World Wide Web address:** http://www.uchsc.edu. **Description:** A regional, tertiary health care and academic medical center. University Hospital is the principal teaching hospital for the University of Colorado Health Sciences Center. Founded in 1921. **Positions advertised include:** Research Assistant; Project Manager; Assistant Professor; Instructor; Senior Instructor. **Special programs:** Internships. **Operations at this facility include:** Administration. **Number of employees at this location:** 2,200.

VALLEYLAB, INC.
5920 Longbow Drive, Boulder CO 80301-3299. 303/530-2300. **Toll-free phone:** 800/255-8522. **Fax:** 303/530-6285. **Contact:** Human Resources Department. **World Wide Web address:** http://www.valleylab.com. **Description:** Develops, manufactures, markets, and services medical equipment and accessories used in hospitals and other medical environments. Principal products are electrosurgical generators, ultrasonic surgical aspirators, and associated disposable products used to perform a variety of surgical and medical procedures. **Positions advertised include:** R&D Engineer; Sr. Research Scientist; Sales Analyst; Associate Product Manager; R&D Director; Design Engineer. **Special programs:** Internships. **Corporate headquarters location:** New York NY. **Parent company:** Tyco Healthcare Group. **Operations at this facility include:** Administration; Divisional Headquarters; Manufacturing; Research and Development; Sales; Service.

VITAL SIGNS - COLORADO
11039 East Lansing Circle, Englewood CO 80112. 303/790-4835. **Contact:** Human Resources. **E-mail address:** humanresources@vital-signs.com. **World Wide Web address:** http://www.vital-signs.com. **Description:** Manufactures disposable medical products such as facemasks, manual resuscitators, anesthesia kits, and related products. **Corporate headquarters location:** Totowa NJ. **Operations at this facility include:** Administration; Manufacturing. **Listed on:** NASDAQ. **Stock exchange symbol:** VITL. **Number of employees at this location:** 250.

Connecticut

ACME UNITED CORPORATION
1931 Black Rock Turnpike, Fairfield CT 06432. 203/332-7330. **Fax:** 203/576-0007. **Contact:** Human Resources. **World Wide Web address:** http://www.acmeunited.com. **Description:** A holding company. **NOTE:** Send resumes to Human Resources, P.O. Box 458, Fremont NC 27830. **Corporate headquarters location:** This location. **Subsidiaries include:** Acme United Ltd. (England) manufactures medical scissors, household scissors and shears, nail files, and other manicure items. Acme United Limited (Canada) markets scissors, rulers, and yardsticks. Emil Schlemper GmbH (Germany) and Peter Altenbach and Son (Germany) both manufacture knives, scissors, shears, and manicure products. **Listed on:** American Stock Exchange. **Stock exchange symbol:** ACU. **Number of employees nationwide:** 570.

AMERICAN MEDICAL RESPONSE (AMR)
55 Church Street, 6th Floor, New Haven CT 06510. 203/781-1092. **Fax:** 203/781-1192. **Contact:** Cyndee Knapp, Human Resources. **E-mail address:** Cyndee.Knapp@amr-ems.com. **World Wide Web address: http://www.amr.net. Description:** Provides emergency medical transportation. **Positions advertised include:** Administrative Assistant. **Corporate headquarters location:** Greenwood Village CO. **Other U.S. locations:** Nationwide.

ANTHEM
370 Bassett Road, North Haven CT 06473. 203/239-4911. **Contact:** Human Resources. **World Wide Web address:** http://www.anthem.com. **Description:** Health care benefits company. Provides health care plans, dental plans, visual and behavioral health plans, pharmacy benefits, and life insurance. Anthem is the Blue Cross and Blue Shield licensee in nine different states. **Positions advertised include:** Case Manager; RN-CVD, Diabetes. **Other U.S. locations:** Nationwide.

APRIA HEALTHCARE GROUP INC.
40 Sebethe Drive, Cromwell CT 06416. 860/613-4600. **Fax:** 860/632-9673. **Contact:** Human Resources. **World Wide Web address:** http://www.apria.com. **Description:** Provides a broad range of respiratory therapy services, home medical equipment, and infusion therapy services. Apria Healthcare Group's home health care services are provided to patients who have been discharged from hospitals, skilled nursing facilities, or convalescent homes and are being treated at home. In conjunction with medical professionals, Apria personnel deliver, install, and service medical equipment, as well as provide appropriate therapies and coordinate plans of care for their patients. Apria personnel also instruct patients and care-givers in the correct use of equipment and monitor the equipment's effectiveness. Patients and their families receive training from registered nurses and respiratory therapy professionals concerning the therapy administered including instruction in proper infusion technique and the care and use of equipment and supplies. **Corporate headquarters location:** Lake Forest CA. **Other U.S. locations:** Nationwide. **Listed on:** New York Stock Exchange. **Stock exchange symbol:** AHG. **Number of employees nationwide:** 7,500.

BIO-MED DEVICES
1445 Boston Post Road, Guilford CT 06437. 203/458-0202. **Toll-free phone:** 800/224-6633. **Fax:** 203/458-0440. **Contact:** Human Resources. **World Wide Web address:** http://www.biomeddevices.com. **Description:** Designs, manufactures, and markets a complete line of critical care and transportable respirators/ventilators, air-oxygen blenders, ventilation monitors, oxygen-temperature monitors, disposable and reusable breathing circuits, and accessories.

BRADLEY MEMORIAL HOSPITAL AND HEALTH CENTER
81 Meriden Avenue, Southington CT 06489. 860/276-5000. **Fax:** 860/276-5058. **Contact:** Human Resources. **World Wide Web address:** http://www.bradleymemorial.org. **Description:** An 84-bed acute care hospital and medical center. **Positions advertised include:** Lab Supervisor; Phlebotomist; Radiologic Technologist; Respiratory Care Practitioner; Senior Medical Technologist; Staff Pharmacist; Nursing Supervisor; Maintenance Worker.

BRIDGEPORT HOSPITAL
267 Grant Street, P.O. Box 5000, Bridgeport CT 06610. 203/384-3000. **Contact:** Human Resources. **World Wide Web address:** http://www.bridgeporthospital.org. **Description:** A community hospital providing services through a trauma center, heart center, a women's care center, a joint reconstruction center, and the Norma F. Pfriem Cancer Center. **Positions advertised include:** Administrative Professional Psychiatric Nurse; Administrative Professional Nurse; Ambulatory Support Technician; Billing Analyst; Bloodless Medicine Coordinator; C.A.T. Scan Technician; Care Coordinator; Clinical Care Provider; Department Secretary; Director of Planning; Medical Technologist; Mental Health Consultant; Nurse Case Manager; Professional Nurse; Quality Improvement Nurse; Radiology Technician; Respiratory Therapist; Staff Pharmacist; Surgical Technician; Team Lead.

CARDIUM HEALTH
16 Munson Road, Farmington CT 06032. 860/408-1300. **Fax:** 860/678-1600. **Contact:** Human Resources. **E-mail address:** hr@cardiumhealth.com. **World Wide Web address:** http://www.cardium.com. **Description:** A disease management services company, partners with large employers to promote a healthier workforce. **Positions advertised include:** Health Management Clinician.

FUJI MEDICAL SYSTEMS USA
419 West Avenue, Stamford CT 06902. 203/324-2000. **Contact:** Human Resources. **World Wide Web address:** http://www.fujimed.com. **Description:** Manufactures and distributes X-ray machines, digital imaging systems, and radiography printers for medical offices and hospitals. **Parent company:** Fuji Photo Film Co., Ltd.

GAYLORD HOSPITAL
P.O. Box 400, Wallingford CT 06492. 203/284-2830. **Physical address:** Gaylord Farm Road, Wallingford CT 06492. **Fax:** 203/284-2773. **Contact:** Nancy Ullamn, Manager of Human Resources. **E-mail address:** jobs@gaylord.org. **World Wide Web address:** http://www.gaylord.org. **Description:** Provides medical rehabilitation services for SCI, TBI, MS, chronic pulmonary, and alcohol or chemically dependent patients. **Positions advertised include:** Care Manager; Admissions Representative; Regional Healthcare Associate; Budget and Reimbursement Coordinator; Payroll Coordinator; Food Service Assistant; Certified Occupational Therapy Aide; Nursing Assistant; Certified Occupational Therapy Assistant; Licensed Practical Nurse; Senior Mobility Assistant; Nursing Supervisor; Registered Nurse; Benefit Verification Representative; Respiratory Care Practitioner; Secretary; Audiologist; Speech Pathologist. **Number of employees at this location:** 500.

GERBER COBURN OPTICAL, INC.
55 Gerber Road, South Windsor CT 06074. 860/648-6600. **Toll-free phone:** 800/843-1479. **Fax:** 860/648-6601. **Contact:** Joyce Reynolds, Human Resources. **E-mail address:** joyce.reynolds@gerberoptical.com. **World Wide Web address:** http://www.gerbercoburn.com. **Description:** Designs, manufactures, and markets computer-driven systems for eyeglass lens processing using multiaxis machinery technology. The company produces prescription lenses and edge lenses to fit eyeglass frames. **NOTE:** Entry-level positions are offered. **Positions advertised include:** Controller; Manufacturing Engineer; Materials Test Specialist. **Special programs:** Co-ops; Summer Jobs. **Office hours:** Monday - Friday, 8:00 a.m. - 4:30 p.m. **Corporate headquarters location:** This location. **Other U.S. locations:** San Marcos CA; Miami FL; Muskogee OK. **International locations:** Canada; England; The Netherlands; Singapore; South Australia. **Parent company:** Gerber Scientific, Inc. **Listed on:** New York Stock Exchange. **Stock exchange symbol:** GRB. **President:** Shawn Harrington. **Annual sales/revenues:** \$21 - \$50 million. **Number of employees at this location:** 110.

HARTFORD HOSPITAL
80 Seymour Street, Hartford CT 06102. 860/545-5000. **Contact:** Human Resources Department. **World Wide Web address:** http://www.harthosp.org. **Description:** A hospital specializing in orthopedics and cardiac bypass surgery. **Positions advertised include:** Registered Nurse.

ICU MEDICAL INC.
129 Reservoir Road, Vernon CT 06066. 860/870-6112. **Contact:** Human Resources. **E-mail address:** jr@icumed.com. **World Wide Web address:** http://www.icumed.com. **Description:** Designs, develops, manufactures, and markets safety medical products for hospitals and medical organizations under the Punctur-Guard and Drop-It brand names. The first product was a patented blood collection needle with a mechanism that blunts the needle prior to its removal from the patient, greatly reducing the risk of accidental needle sticks that can spread hepatitis, HIV, and other infectious diseases. Other products include intravenous catheters and winged intravenous sets. **Corporate headquarters location:** San Clemente CA. **Number of employees nationwide:** 75.

JOHNSON MEMORIAL HOSPITAL, INC.
201 Chestnut Hill Road, Stafford Springs CT 06076. 860/684-4251. **Fax:** 860/684-8459. **Recorded jobline:** 860/684-8204. **Contact:** Sue Tanner, Human Resources. **E-mail address:** stanner@jmhosp.org. **World Wide Web address:** http://www.johnsonhealthnetwork.com. **Description:** An 89-bed, general, acute care hospital. **Positions advertised include:** Administrative Assistant;

Development Secretary; Health Information Services Clerk; Per Diem Registered Dietician; Patient Care Technician; Mental Health Worker; Administrative Director of Emergency Services; Quality Managed Care Specialist; Crisis Worker; Mental Health Worker; Maintenance Mechanic; Environmental Technician. **Parent company:** Johnson Health Network is a nonprofit health service organization comprised of several subsidiaries: The Johnson Evergreen Corporation, which includes Evergreen Health Care Center, a 120-bed skilled nursing and rehabilitation facility; Johnson Health Care, Inc., encompassing the free-standing Johnson Surgery Center and Johnson Occupational Medicine Center in Enfield CT; The Enfield Visiting Nurse Association, Inc., which provides comprehensive home health care; Johnson Memorial Hospital Development Fund, Inc.; and Wellcare, Inc., charged with managing Johnson Memorial's construction projects. **Operations at this facility include:** Administration; Service. **Number of employees at this location:** 700.

LA WEIGHTLOSS CENTERS
Radisson Hotel, Danbury CT 06811. 203/778-2501. **Toll-free phone:** 800/331-4035. **Contact:** Human Resources. **World Wide Web address:** http://www.laweightloss.com. **Description:** A weight loss center. **Positions advertised include:** Sales Counselor; Bilingual Sales Counselor.

MIDDLESEX HOSPITAL
28 Crescent Street, Middletown CT 06457. 860/344-6380. **Fax:** 860/344-6973. **Recorded jobline:** 860/344-6055. **Contact:** Human Resources. **World Wide Web address:** http://www.midhosp.org. **Description:** A 275-bed, nonprofit, acute care hospital. Middlesex Hospital is affiliated with The University of Connecticut Health Center School of Medicine. **Positions advertised include:** Dietary Aide; Administrative Director, Cancer Center; Respiratory Therapist; Social Worker; Child Psychiatrist; Crisis Clinician; Registered Nurse. **Special programs:** Internships. **Operations at this facility include:** Administration. **Number of employees at this location:** 1,400.

NEW CANAAN VETERINARY HOSPITAL
7 Vitti Street, New Canaan CT 06840. 203/966-1627. **Contact:** Human Resources. **E-mail address:** ncvhdoc1@aol.com. **Description:** New Canaan Veterinary Hospital is an animal hospital. Services include radiology, dentistry, electrocardiography, surgery, diagnostic ultrasound, boarding, and kennel services.

NOVAMETRIX MEDICAL SYSTEMS INC.
5 Technology Drive, Wallingford CT 06492. 203/265-7701. **Fax:** 203/284-0753. **Contact:** Human Resources. **E-mail address:** hr@novrametrix.com. **World Wide Web address:** http://www.novametrix.com. **Description:** Novametrix Medical Systems Inc. develops, manufactures, and markets noninvasive, critical care blood gas monitors, respiratory monitors, and disposable products. Distributed worldwide, these electronic medical instruments provide continuous patient monitoring capabilities in hospital and nonhospital environments. The company's product line is comprised of capnographs; pulse oximeters; transcutaneous blood gas monitors; respiratory mechanics monitors; and reusable and disposable sensors, adapters, related accessories, and replacement parts. One branch of Novametrix Medical Systems, Cascadia Technology Division, is primarily a research and development group located in Redmond WA. **NOTE:** Apply online at http://www.responics.appone.com. **Corporate headquarters location:** This location. **Other U.S. locations:** Norwell MA; Redmond WA. **Listed on:** NASDAQ. **Stock exchange symbol:** NMTX. **Number of employees nationwide:** 230.

ST. FRANCIS HOSPITAL & MEDICAL CENTER
114 Woodland Street, Hartford CT 06105. 860/714-4160. **Contact:** Human Resources. **World Wide Web address:** http://www.stfranciscare.org. **Description:** A 617-bed Catholic hospital specializing in cardiology, oncology, women's and children's services, behavioral health care, emergency/trauma care, and rehabilitation. **Positions advertised include:** Medical Staff Trainer; Clinical Educator; School Clinician; Crisis Clinician; Primary Therapist; Speech/Language Pathologist; Physical Therapist; Medical Radiation Dosimetrist; Medical Physicist; Audiologist; Certified Theraputic Recreation Specialist; Operations Supervisor; Pharmacist; Catering Supervisor; Chief Medical Physicist; Medical Assistant; Mental Health Worker; Nursing Assistant; Clinical Nursing Supervisor; Assistant Nurse Manager; Nurse Practitioner; Admission Nurse; Neonatal Nurse; Staff Physician; Geriatric Medicine Physician; Rheumatologist; Registered Nurse Endoscopy; Staff RN; Registered Nurse; Occupational Health Nurse; Coding Specialist; Secretary; Counter Aide; Porter; Driver; Food Service Assistant; Teacher Aide; Data Coordinator; Accessioning Clerk. **Special programs:** Internships. **Operations at this facility include:** Administration; Divisional Headquarters.

ST. MARY'S HOSPITAL
56 Franklin Street, Waterbury CT 06706. 203/574-6000. **Fax:** 203/575-7753. **Contact:** Dee Anderson, Human Resources. **E-mail address:** danderson@stmh.org. **World Wide Web address:** http://www.stmh.org. **Description:** A nonprofit, full-service hospital offering behavioral health care, a family health center, a children's health center, a women's center, a Level II trauma center, and pediatric care. **NOTE:** Part-time jobs and second and third shifts are offered. **Positions advertised include:** Registered Nurse; Patient Care Assistant; Secretary; Clerk; Security Officer; Clinical Supervisor; Human Resources Manager; Office Manager; Pharmacist. **CEO:** Sister Marguerite Waite. **Number of employees at this location:** 1,700.

SHARON HOSPITAL, INC.
P.O. Box 789, Sharon CT 06069-0789. 860/364-4080. **Physical address:** 50 Hospital Hill Road, Sharon CT 06069. **Contact:** Personnel. **E-mail:** hr@sharonhospital.org. **World Wide Web address:** http://www.sharon.org. **Description:** A full-service, 78-bed hospital. **NOTE:** Entry-level positions and second and third shifts are offered. **Company slogan:** Quality health care for our community. **Positions advertised include:** Registered Nurse; Manager; Nuclear Medicine Technologist; Radiology Technologist; Surgical Technologist; Patient Biller; Medical Staff Coordinator; Cashier Control Clerk; EVS Supervisor; Sterile Processing Technician. **Special programs:** Internships; Summer Jobs. **Corporate headquarters location:** This location. **President:** James E. Sok. **Number of employees at this location:** 500.

TENDER LOVING CARE/STAFF BUILDERS
1234 Summer Street, 3rd Floor, Stamford CT 06905. 203/327-2680. **Contact:** Office Manager. **World Wide Web address:** http://www.tlcathome.com. **Description:** A home health care agency. **Corporate headquarters location:** Lake Success NY. **Other U.S. locations:** Nationwide. **Number of employees nationwide:** 20,000.

U.S. SURGICAL
150 Glover Avenue, Norwalk CT 06856. 203/845-1000. **Contact:** Human Resources Department. **World Wide Web address:** http://www.ussurg.com. **Description:** A manufacturer of surgical instruments. **Parent company:** Tyco Healthcare Group LP.

Delaware

BAYHEALTH MEDICAL CENTER AT KENT GENERAL HOSPITAL
640 South State Street, Dover DE 19901. 866/305-5627. **Fax:** 866/866-6442. **Recorded jobline:** 888/397-JOBS. **Contact:** Human Resources. **E-mail address:** jobs@bayhealth.org. **World Wide Web address:** http://www.bayhealth.org. **Description:** A full-service, nonprofit, 231-bed medical center. **NOTE:** See website

for current job openings and to apply online. Entry-level positions and second- and third-shifts are offered. **Special programs:** Co-ops. **Other U.S. locations:** Milford DE. **Subsidiaries include:** Middletown Medical Center, Smyrna-Clayton Medical Services, Harrington Outpatient Services Center, Milton Outpatient Services Center, Lifestyles Fitness Centers, HealthWorks, Home Health Services, WalkIn Medical Care. **Annual sales/revenues:** $51 - $100 million. **Number of employees nationwide:** 2,000.

BAYHEALTH MEDICAL CENTER AT MILFORD MEMORIAL HOSPITAL
21 West Clarke Avenue, P.O. Box 199, Milford DE 19963. 866/305-5627. **Fax:** 866/866-6442. **Recorded jobline:** 888/397-JOBS. **Contact:** Human Resources. **E-mail address:** jobs@bayhealth.org. **Contact:** Human Resources. **World Wide Web address:** http://www.bayhealth.org. **Description:** A full-service, nonprofit, 168-bed medical facility.

BEEBE MEDICAL CENTER
424 Savannah Road, Lewes DE 19958-9913. 302/645-3336. **Fax:** 302/645-0965. **Recorded jobline:** 302/856-0676. **Contact:** Human Resources. **E-mail address:** employment@bbmc.org. **World Wide Web address:** http://www.beebemed.org. **Description:** A community-owned, nonprofit, 135-bed acute care, hospital. Founded in 1916. **NOTE:** See website for current job openings and to apply online. Or, submit resume by fax. Entry-level positions and second- and third-shifts are offered. **Positions advertised include:** Billing Representative; Cardiac Cath Tech; CAT Scan Tech; Cath Lab Supervisor; Clinical Laboratory Assistant; Cost Budget Assistant; Diagnostic Imaging Assistant; Director, CCU. **Special programs:** Summer Jobs. **Number of employees at this location:** 1,100.

EMILY P. BISSELL HOSPITAL
3000 Newport Gap Pike, Wilmington DE 19808. 302/995-8400. **Fax:** 302/255-4437. **Contact:** Human Resources. **Description:** A long-term care facility licensed as a nursing home that is operated by Delaware Health and Social Services. Offers skilled and intermediate nursing care to Delaware residents. There are currently 74 residents living at the 102-bed facility. **NOTE:** To inquire about current job openings and submit an online application, visit www.delawarestatejobs.com/postings. Or, contact Delaware Health and Social Services for more information.

CHRISTIANA CARE HEALTH SYSTEM CHRISTIANA HOSPITAL
4755 Ogletown-Stanton Road, Newark DE 19718. 302/733-1000. **Toll-free phone:** 800/999-9169. **Contact:** Human Resources. **World Wide Web address:** http://www.christianacare.org. **Description:** A 780-bed facility that provides a range of care services available in large-scale teaching hospitals. Part of an integrated health care system comprised of acute care hospitals, outpatient services, rehabilitative medicine, a primary care network, transitional/long-term care facilities and home health care agencies. **NOTE:** See website to search and apply for job openings in the following areas: technical, professional, service, craft, clerical, physician, nursing, information services, management and administrative. **Number of employees at this location:** 400.

CHRISTIANA CARE HEALTH SYSTEM WILMINGTON HOSPITAL
501 West 14th Street, Wilmington DE 19801. 302/428-2229. **Toll-free phone:** 800/999-9169. **Fax:** 302/428-5770. **Contact:** Human Resources. **World Wide Web address:** http://www.christianacare.org. **Description:** Offers: 250 licensed beds, plus 41 licensed inpatient-beds. Part of an integrated health care system including acute care hospitals, outpatient services, rehabilitative medicine, a primary care network, transitional/long-term care facilities, and home health care agencies. **NOTE:** See website to search and apply for job openings. **Operations at this facility include:** This location is an acute care hospital. **Number of employees at this location:** 7,000.

CHURCHMAN VILLAGE
4949 Ogletown-Stanton Road, Newark, DE 19713. 302/998-6900. **Fax:** 302/998-1128. **Description:** A 101-bed nursing facility providing skilled, intermediate, custodial and respite care, including physical therapy and inhalation therapy. **NOTE:** Contact Human Resources to inquire about current job openings.

COKESBURY VILLAGE
726 Loveville Road, Suite 3000, Hockessin DE 19707. 302/235-6800. **Fax:** 302/235-6125. **Contact:** Sheronda Patrick, Employee Relations Manager. **E-mail address:** spatrick@pumh.org. **World Wide Web address:** http://www.pumh.org/communities. **Description:** A full-service retirement community offering assisted living care and nursing home care. **Positions advertised include:** Aquatics/Fitness Instructor; Occupational Therapist; Registered Nurse; Certified Nurses Aide; Assistant Regional Dining Director; Utility Cleaner; Housekeeping Aide; Maintenance Person. **Parent company:** Peninsula United Methodist Homes, Inc.

CONCENTRA MEDICAL CENTER
4110 Ogletown-Stanton Road, Newark DE 19713. 302/738-0103. **Fax:** 302/738-6612. **Contact:** Human Resources. **World Wide Web address:** http://www.concentra.com. **Description:** Provides employers, insurers and payors with a series of services that include employment-related injury and occupational healthcare, in-network and out-of-network medical claims review and repricing, access to preferred provider organizations, first notice of loss services, case management and other cost containment services. **NOTE:** See website for current job openings. All applications must be submitted online.

DENTSPLY INTERNATIONAL INC. L.D. CAULK DIVISION
38 West Clarke Avenue, Milford DE 19963. 302/422-4511. **Fax:** 302/424-4385. **Contact:** Leola Roberts, Human Resources. **E-mail address:** lroberts@dentsply.com. **World Wide Web address:** http://www.caulk.com. **Description:** Manufactures a wide variety of dental supplies including cements for orthodontic procedures and materials for making fillings and impressions. **Positions advertised include:** Director of Research and Development; Equipment Engineer; Brand Manager; Merchandise Manager; Associate Product Manager. **Corporate headquarters location:** York PA. **Other U.S. locations:** Carlsbad CA; Encino CA; Los Angeles CA; Lakewood CO; Des Plaines IL; Elgin IL; Burlington NJ; Maumee OH; Tulsa OK; Johnson City TN. **International locations:** Worldwide. **Listed on:** NASDAQ. **Stock exchange symbol:** XRAY.

DODD DENTAL LABORATORIES, INC.
24 Lukens Drive, New Castle DE 19720-7005. 302/661-6000. **Fax:** 302/661-6016. **Contact:** Human Resources. **E-mail address:** Elaine@doddlab.com. **World Wide Web address:** http://www.doddlab.com. **Description:** A dental laboratory providing dental prosthetic devices. **NOTE:** See website for current job openings and to apply online. **Positions advertised include:** Dental Lab Trainee; Driver; Scheduler; Skilled Technician; Shipping & Receiving Clerk; Office Staff. **Parent company:** National Dentex Corporation is one of the largest operators of dental laboratories in the United States.

A. I. DUPONT HOSPITAL FOR CHILDREN & NEMOURS CHILDREN'S CLINIC
P.O. Box 269, Wilmington DE 19899. 302/651-4000. **Physical Address:** 1600 Rockland Road, Wilmington DE 19803. **Fax:** 302/651-6119. **Recorded jobline:** 800/545-0056. **Contact:** Human Resources. **World Wide Web address:** http://www.nemours.org. **Description:** Operates specialty hospital and clinics for children. **Positions advertised include:** Billing Liaison; Clinical Data Abstractor-Neurology; Certified

Ophthalmic Technician; Administrative Secretary; Medical Secretary; Advanced Practice Nurse Cardiac; Advanced Nurse Practitioner; Registered Nurse. **Corporate headquarters location:** Jacksonville FL.

FORWOOD MANOR
1912 Marsh Road, Wilmington DE 19810. 302/529-1600. **Contact:** Human Resources. **World Wide Web address:** http://www.sunriseseniorliving.com. **E-mail address:** forwoodmanor.hrm@sunriseseniorliving.com. **Description:** A full-service retirement community consisting of 140 apartments, 37 assisted-living suites and 66 nursing beds. **NOTE:** See website for current job openings. Submit resume by e-mail or fax. **Positions advertised include:** Registered Nurse; Executive Director. **Listed on:** New York Stock Exchange. **Stock exchange symbol:** SRZ.

ST. FRANCIS HOSPITAL
7th & Clayton Streets, Wilmington DE 19805-0500. 302/575-8260. **Contact:** Human Resources. **E-mail address:** jobs@stfrancishealthcare.org. **World Wide Web address:** http://www.stfrancishealthcare.org. **Description:** A community-based hospital. **NOTE:** See website for current job openings and application instructions. **Positions advertised include:** Cardiac Rehab Nurse; Chaplain; C.A.T. Scan Technician; Chief Surgical Physician Assistant; Courier; Desktop Analyst; Vice President, Human Resources; HVAC Mechanic; Nurse; Nursing Senior Team Leader; RN; LPN; Physical Therapist; Radiographic Technologist; Respiratory Therapist; Surgical Physician Assistant; Ultrasound Technician.

U.S. DEPARTMENT OF VETERANS AFFAIRS WILMINGTON VETERANS ADMINISTRATION MEDICAL CENTER
1601 Kirkwood Highway, Wilmington DE 19805. 302/994-2511. **Contact:** Human Resources. **World Wide Web address:** http://www.va.gov. **Description:** A medical center. From 54 hospitals in 1930, the VA health care system has grown to include more than 170 medical centers; more than 364 outpatient, community and outreach clinics; 130 nursing home care units; and 37 domiciliary facilities. The VA operates at least one medical center in each of the 48 contiguous states, Puerto Rico and the District of Columbia.

District Of Columbia

AMERICAN ACADEMY OF OPHTHALMOLOGY
1101 Vermont Avenue NW, Suite 700, Washington DC 20005. 202/737-6662. **Fax:** 202/737-7061. **Contact:** Human Resources. **E-mail address:** jobs@aao.org. **World Wide Web address:** http://www.aao.org. **Description:** A lobbying group that tracks legislation in all areas of government that may have an effect on the ophthalmology field. **Corporate headquarters location:** San Francisco CA. **President:** Allan D. Jensen, M.D.

AMERICAN HEALTH CARE ASSOCIATION
1201 L Street NW, Washington DC 20005. 202/842-4444. **Fax:** 202/842-3860. **Contact:** Human Resources Manager. **E-mail address:** hr@ahca.org. **World Wide Web address:** http://www.ahca.org. **Description:** A national association of nursing homes and related long-term care facilities. The association promotes an economic and governmental environment within which nursing homes and residential care facilities can provide quality care in safe surroundings. **Positions advertised include:** Vendor Relations Manager.

AMERICAN PSYCHOLOGICAL ASSOCIATION (APA)
750 First Street NE, Washington DC 20002. 202/336-5500. **Toll-free phone:** 800/374-2721. **Contact:** Human Resources. **E-mail address:** jobs@apa.org. **World Wide Web address:** http://www.apa.org. **Description:** Works to advance psychology as a science, a profession, and a means of promoting human welfare. The association has divisions in 49 subfields of psychology and affiliations with 57 state and Canadian provincial associations. Membership includes more than 159,000 researchers, educators, clinicians, and students. **Positions advertised include:** Business Manager; Database Coordinator; Director of Applied Psychological Science; Manager for Budget and Reporting; Manager Journal Operations; Manuscript Editor; Marketing Director. **Corporate headquarters location:** This location. **Number of employees at this location:** 500.

CHILDREN'S HOSPITAL SCOTTISH RITE CENTER FOR CHILDHOOD LANGUAGE DISORDERS
1630 Columbia Road NW, Washington DC 20009. 202/939-4703. **Recorded jobline:** 202/884-2060. **Fax:** 202/939-4717. **Contact:** Human Resources. **NOTE:** Mail resumes to: Department of Human Resources, 111 Michigan Avenue NW, Washington DC 20010. The hospital only accepts resumes for open positions. **Description:** A medical center for children with language disorders. **Corporate headquarters location:** This location.

GEORGE WASHINGTON UNIVERSITY MEDICAL CENTER
2033 K Street, Suite 220 NW, Washington DC 20052. 202/994-9600. **Contact:** Manager of Personnel. **World Wide Web address:** http://www.gwumc.edu. **NOTE:** Job postings are listed on the George Washington University Human Resource Services page. **Description:** An interdisciplinary health care facility that includes the University Hospital, a top-ranked School of Medicine and Health Sciences, a comprehensive basic and clinical research program, and a health maintenance organization (George Washington University Health Plan.) Clinical services are provided through the University Hospital and Medical Faculty Associates, a group of specialists who practice and teach at George Washington. The University Hospital is a center-city facility that is also the health care provider for the president of the United States. The University Hospital is also a certified Level I trauma center. **Positions advertised include:** Library Specialist; Director, Medical Center Alumni Programs.

GREATER SOUTHEAST COMMUNITY HOSPITAL
1310 Southern Avenue SE, Washington DC 20032. 202/574-6641. **Contact:** Human Resources. **World Wide Web address:** http://www.greatersoutheast.org. **Description:** A 450-bed hospital that offers comprehensive medical and surgical care, obstetrics and gynecology services, psychiatry services, pediatric care, 24-hour emergency care, rehabilitation services, and home health care. Greater Southeast Community Hospital addresses the needs of seniors through programs and services offered at the Center for the Aging, which provides long-term care for the elderly. The 183-bed Health Care Institute and the 150-bed Livingston Health Care Center offer intermediate and skilled nursing home care for residents. Founded in 1966. **Positions advertised include:** Infection Control Manager; Sr. Physical Therapist; Sr. Occupational Therapist; Clinical Pharmacy; Respiratory Therapist; Registered Radiographer; Cardiac Sonographer.

NATIONAL REHABILITATION HOSPITAL
102 Irving Street NW, Washington DC 20010-2921. 202/877-1710. **Fax:** 202/726-7701. **Recorded jobline:** 202/877-1700. **Contact:** Human Resources. **E-mail address:** nrhhumanresources@mhg.edu. **World Wide Web address:** http://www.nrhrehab.org. **Description:** Provides rehabilitation services through patient care, assisted technology, research, education and training, and advocacy. The hospital's patient care services include the outpatient center in Bethesda MD, providing musculoskeletal rehabilitation; the Performance Diagnostic Laboratory, offering sophisticated video and computer technology to analyze individual's movements; the Brain Injury Rehabilitation and the Stroke Recovery Program, offering day-treatment programs for those who are re-entering the community; the Department of Obstetrics and Gynecology, offering OB/GYN services for women with disabilities; and multiple sclerosis services.

Positions advertised include: Publications & Productions Coordinator; Clinical Nurse Manager; Pharmacy Technician; Occupational Therapist; Physical Therapist; Staff Psychologist.

PROVIDENCE HOSPITAL
1150 Varnum Street NE, Washington DC 20017-2180. 202/269-7928. **Fax:** 202/269-7662. **Contact:** Employment Office. **World Wide Web address:** http://www.provhosp.org. **Description:** Offers a variety of programs, treatments, and counseling services. The Wellness Institute and Women's Center provides cancer assessments, exercise programs, and classes in nutrition, weight management, hypertension, stress management, and smoking cessation. The Senior Connection Program, Telecare, is a service that performs phone checks for seniors who, due to age, illness, or immobility, spend most of their time home alone. The Fort Lincoln Family Medicine Center provides continuous health care and serves as the outpatient training site for 21 family practice residents. Center for Life helps pregnant women in urban areas who have difficulties with language, money, and transportation. Seton Home provides inpatient and outpatient treatment, inpatient psychiatric care, and a special program for patients with both psychiatric and substance abuse problems. Umoja Treatment Service is a hospital-based alcohol and drug abuse center. **Positions advertised include:** Registered Nurse; Nurse Practitioner; Assistant Vice President; Admitting/Registration Officer; Medical Technologist; Cardiac Diagnostic Technician; Cardiovascular Technologist; Social Worker; Corporate Controller. **Special programs:** Internships available.

SIBLEY MEMORIAL HOSPITAL
5255 Loughboro Road NW, Washington DC 20016. 202/537-4750. **Fax:** 202/363-2677. **Recorded jobline:** 202/364-8665. **Contact:** Queenie Plater, Employment Manager. **E-mail address:** qplater@sibley.org. **World Wide Web address:** http://www.sibley.org. **Description:** A 340-bed, community hospital. This is a nonprofit company. Founded in 1890. **NOTE:** Second and third shifts are offered. **Positions advertised include:** Admissions Representative; Communications Assistant; Sr. Network Engineer; Microsoft systems Security Administrator; Information Technology Specialist; Internal Auditor; Risk Management Specialist; Radiation Oncology Therapist. **Special programs:** Summer Jobs. **Corporate headquarters location:** This location. **Number of employees at this location:** 1,200.

TENDER LOVING CARE/STAFF BUILDERS
1212 New York Avenue, Suite 200, Washington DC 20005. 202/682-2200. **Fax:** 202/682-0822. **Contact:** Human Resources. **World Wide Web address:** http://www.tlcathome.com. **Description:** A home health care agency. **Positions advertised include:** Assistant Director of Clinical Services; Care Team Manager; Home Care Nurse; Physical Therapist; Speech Language Pathologist. **Special programs:** Apprenticeships. **Corporate headquarters location:** Lake Success NY. **Other U.S. locations:** Nationwide. **Number of employees nationwide:** 20,000.

U.S. DEPARTMENT OF VETERANS AFFAIRS WASHINGTON DC VETERANS AFFAIRS MEDICAL CENTER
50 Irving Street NW, Department 05-A, Washington DC 20422. 202/745-8000. **Contact:** Employment Office. **World Wide Web address:** http://www.va.gov. **Description:** A medical center operated by the U.S. Department of Veterans Affairs (VA.) From 54 hospitals in 1930, the VA health care system has grown to include 171 medical centers; more than 364 outpatient, community, and outreach clinics; 130 nursing home care units; and 37 domiciliaries. VA operates at least one medical center in each of the 48 contiguous states, Puerto Rico, and the District of Columbia. **Positions advertised include:** Nurse, Various Departments; Clinical Educator; Supervisory General Engineer.

VISITING NURSE ASSOCIATION OF WASHINGTON DC
6000 New Hampshire Avenue NW, Washington DC 20011. 202/882-6988. **Toll-free phone:** 800/634-5702. **Contact:** Human Resources Director. **World Wide Web address:** http://www.vnaa.org. **Description:** Visiting Nurse Association is a home health care organization providing skilled nursing care to patients in their homes. **Operations at this facility include:** This location serves the District of Columbia, and Montgomery and Prince George's Counties in Maryland.

WASHINGTON HOSPITAL CENTER
110 Irving Street NW, Washington DC 20010-2975. 202/877-7441. **Contact:** Human Resources. **World Wide Web address:** http://www.whcenter.org. **Description:** A nonprofit hospital. Washington Heart at Washington Hospital annually performs almost 1,700 heart operations and more than 10,000 cardiac catheterization procedures. The Washington Cancer Institute provides cancer care including surgery, radiation and chemotherapy treatments, counseling, education, and community outreach. Washington Hospital Center is the home of the MedSTAR trauma unit, whose two helicopters transport more than 3,000 critically ill and injured patients each year. The center also consists of The Institute for Asthma & Allergy, a burn center, women's services, and the Washington National Eye Center. **Positions advertised include:** Chief Perfusionist; Clinical Manager; Clinical Pharmacist; Clinical Specialist; Director of Recruitment; Dosimetrist; Infection Control Practitioner; Manager, Cardiac Catherization Laboratory. **Parent company:** Medlantic Healthcare Group (also at this location.) **Number of employees at this location:** 5,100.

Florida

APRIA HEALTHCARE GROUP INC.
8509 Benjamin Road, Tampa FL 33634. 813/886-6228. **Contact:** Human Resources. **World Wide Web address:** http://www.apria.com. **Description:** One of the largest national providers of home health care products and services including a broad range of respiratory therapy services, home medical equipment, and infusion therapy services. Apria has over 400 branches throughout the United States and two respiratory therapy branches in the United Kingdom. In conjunction with medical professionals, Apria personnel deliver, install, and service medical equipment, as well as provide appropriate therapies and coordinate plans of care for their patients. Apria personnel also instruct patients and caregivers in the correct use of equipment and monitor the equipment's effectiveness. **Positions advertised include:** Collections Representative; Suspended Billing Representative; Cleaning Technician; Respiratory Therapist; Logistics Coordinator; Customer Service Representative; Delivery Technician; Patient Service Technician; Account Executive; Marketing Manager. **Corporate headquarters location:** Costa Mesa CA. **Listed on:** New York Stock Exchange. **Stock exchange symbol:** AHG.

ARTHREX INC.
1370 Creekside Boulevard, Naples FL 34108. 239/643-5553. **Toll-free phone:** 800/933-7001. **Fax:** 239/643-7386. **Contact:** Human Resources. **E-mail address:** hr@arthrex.com. **World Wide Web address:** http://www.arthrex.com. **Description:** Manufactures products used for orthopedic and arthroscopic surgery. Arthrex also offers educational courses through surgical skills training centers in Arizona, California, and Florida. **Positions advertised include:** Telecommunications Manager; Multimedia Developer; Project Engineer; Product Specialist; Buyer/Planner; Graphic Designer; Senior Engineer; Quality Engineer; Product Manager; Medical Illustrator; Cost Accountant; Quality Assurance Engineer; Quality Control Inspector.

ASO CORPORATION
300 Sarasota Center Boulevard, Sarasota FL 34240. 941/379-0300. **Fax:** 941/554-1434. **Contact:** Human

Resources. **E-mail address:** careers@asocorp.com. **World Wide Web address:** http://www.asocorp.com. **Description:** A manufacturer and distributor of wound care products. **NOTE:** Second and third shifts are offered. **Positions advertised include:** Maintenance Mechanic. **Corporate headquarters location:** This location. **Subsidiaries include:** Aso Pharmaceutical Co., Ltd. (Kumamoto, Japan); Aso Seiyaku Philippines, Inc. (Cebu, Philippines); Texas Aso Corporation (El Paso TX). **Parent company:** Aso International. **Listed on:** Privately held. **Number of employees at this location:** 100.

BAPTIST MEDICAL PLAZA AT WEST KENDALL
13001 North Kendall Drive, Miami FL 33186. 786/596-3800. **Fax: Contact:** Human Resources. **E-mail address:** recruitment@baptisthealth.net. **World Wide Web address:** http://www.baptisthealth.net. **Description:** A non-profit health care facility serving south Florida. **Positions advertised include:** Corporate Analyst Manager; Corporate Director; Nurse Department Head; Manager Accreditation Readiness Person; Manager; Admitting Manager; Speech Therapist; Physical Therapist; Occupational Therapist; Pharmacist; Supervisor; Medical Technician; Clerk; Financial Representative; Office Coordinator; Coder; Executive Assistant; Billing Clerk; Research Registered Nurse; Registered Nurse; Assistant Nursing Manager; Certified Nursing Assistant; Licenses Practical Nurse; Case Manager.

BAPTIST ST. VINCENT'S HEALTH SYSTEMS BAPTIST ST. VINCENT MEDICAL CENTER
1800 Barrs Street, Jacksonville FL 32204. 904/308-7307. **Fax:** 904/308-2951. **Contact:** Human Resources. **World Wide Web address:** http://www.jaxhealth.com. **Description:** Operates the Baptist St. Vincent Medical Center (also at this location) and the St. Catherine Laboure Manor nursing home in Jacksonville. Baptist St. Vincent Medical Center is a 711-bed hospital that provides the following services and facilities: acute care, AIDS treatment, behavioral medicine, a cancer center, cardiology, chemical dependency treatment, emergency services, geriatrics, gastroenterology, laser surgery, neonatology, neurosurgery, OB/GYN, occupational health, orthopedics, otolaryngology, otology, pediatrics, plastic surgery, psychiatric, substance abuse, and women's/children's services. Baptist St. Vincent's Health Systems is a member of the Daughters of Charity national health system, which also includes Mercy Hospital (Miami FL), Sacred Heart Hospital (Pensacola FL), and the Haven of Our Lady of Peace nursing home (Pensacola FL). **Positions advertised include:** Patient Accounting Representative; Registration Associate; Office Specialist; Medical Lab Assistant; Registration Associate; Console Operator; Registered Nurse; Licensed Practical Nurse; Nurse Manager; Unit Clerk; Behavioral Health Evaluation; Care Manager; Social Worker; Director Imaging Services; Safety Specialist; Painter. **Corporate headquarters location:** St. Louis MO. **Number of employees at this location:** 4,000.

BAPTIST ST. VINCENT'S VISITING NURSES
3563 Phillips Highway, Suite 202, Jacksonville FL 32207. 904/202-4300. **Contact:** Human Resources. **Description:** Provides home health care services as part of the greater Baptist St. Vincent's medical organization. **Positions advertised include:** Emergency Medical Technician; Paramedic; Technical Assistant; Ultrasound Technologist; CT Technologist; Medical Assistant; Senior Phlebotomist; Pharmacist; Patient Escort; RN; LPN; Certified Nurse Assistant.

BAUSCH & LOMB PHARMACEUTICALS, INC.
8500 Hidden River Parkway, Tampa FL 33637. 813/975-7700. **Fax:** 813/975-7779. **Contact:** Human Resources. **World Wide Web address:** http://www.bausch.com. **Description:** Bausch & Lomb operates in selected segments of global health care and optical markets. The health care segment consists of three sectors: personal health, medical, and biomedical. The personal health sector is comprised of branded products purchased directly by consumers in health and beauty aid sections of pharmacies, food stores, and mass merchandise outlets. Products include contact lens care solutions, oral care, eye and skin care products, and nonprescription medications. The medical sector manufactures contact lenses, ophthalmic pharmaceuticals, hearing aids, dental implants, and other products sold to health care professionals or obtained by consumers through a prescription. The biomedical sector is engaged in the research and development of pharmaceuticals and the production of genetically-engineered materials. These include purpose-bred research animals, bioprocessing services, and products derived from specific pathogen-free eggs. The optics segment consists primarily of premium-priced sunglasses sold under such brand names as Ray-Ban and Revo. The company's manufacturing or marketing organizations have been established in 34 countries and the company's products are distributed in more than 70 other nations. **Positions advertised include:** Aseptic Production Operator; 3rd Shift Compounder. **Operations at this facility include:** This location manufactures contact lenses and related products, ophthalmic drugs, dental plaque removal devices, and optical items. . **Listed on:** New York Stock Exchange. **Stock exchange symbol:** BOL. **Number of employees worldwide:** 14,400.

BAXTER HEALTHCARE CORPORATION
14600 NW 60th Avenue, Miami Lakes FL 33014-2811. 305/823-5240. **Contact:** Human Resources. **World Wide Web address:** http://www.baxter.com. **Description:** An international company that manufactures and markets critical therapies for conditions involving the blood and circulatory system. The company operates within three main areas. The BioScience division manufactures products that collect, separate, and store blood. The Renal products are designed to cleanse the blood. Intravenous products are designed to help infuse drugs and other solutions into the blood stream. **Corporate headquarters location:** Deerfield IL. **Operations at this facility include:** Administration; Manufacturing; Research and Development; Sales. **Listed on:** New York Stock Exchange. **Stock exchange symbol:** BAX.

BAYFRONT MEDICAL CENTER
701 Sixth Street South, St. Petersburg FL 33701. 727/823-1234. **Contact:** Human Resources. **World Wide Web address:** http://www.bayfront.org. **Description:** A nonprofit, 502-bed hospital. **Positions advertised include:** Administrative Assistant; Assistant Operator; Certified Occupational Therapist; Histologist; Clinical Nurse Specialist; Medical Technician; Dietitian; Environmental Services Aide; Flight Nurse; Home Health Assistant. **Parent company:** Bayfront-St. Anthony's Health Care.

BON SECOURS-ST. JOSEPH HOSPITAL
2500 Harbor Boulevard, Port Charlotte FL 33952. 941/766-4122. **Fax:** 941/766-4296. **Contact:** Human Resources. **World Wide Web address:** http://www.bonsecours.org. **Description:** A JCAHO-accredited, 212-bed, acute care facility with an affiliated 104-bed, long-term care facility located on the Gulf Coast of southwestern Florida. Bon Secours-St. Joseph Hospital is part of the Bon Secours Health System. **Positions a advertised include:** Accounting Clerk; Certified Nurse Assistant; Chief Financial Officer; Clinical Coordinator; Employment Coordinator; Laboratory Director; Materials Technician; Chaplain; RN; Social Worker. **Special programs:** Internships. **Corporate headquarters location:** Mariottsville MD. **Other area locations:** Miami FL; St. Petersburg FL. **Other U.S. locations:** St. Clair Shores MI; Charlotte NC; Richmond VA. **Operations at this facility include:** Administration; Service. **Number of employees at this location:** 1,000.

BOVIE MEDICAL CORPORATION
7100 30th Avenue North, St. Petersburg FL 33710-2902. 727/384-2323. **Fax:** 727/347-9144. **Contact:** Human Resources. **World Wide Web address:** http://www.boviemedical.com. **Description:**

Manufactures and markets a variety of electrosurgical medical products including electrodes and electrosurgical pencils, as well as developing related technologies and products.

BROOKS REHABILITATION HOSPITAL
3599 University Boulevard South, Jacksonville FL 32216. 904/858-7600. **Toll-free phone:** 800/487-7342. **Fax: Contact:** Sandra Williamson. **E-mail address:** sandra.williamson@brookshealth.org. **World Wide Web address:** http://www.brookshealth.org. **Description:** Provides medical rehabilitation services to northeast Florida. **NOTE:** Resumes can be sent to: resume@brookshealth.org. **Positions advertised include:** Registered Nurse; Certified Nurses Aide; Physical Therapist; Referral Coordinator; Occupational Therapy Coordinator; Part Time Assistant Occupational Therapy; Rehab Aide; Speech Language Pathologist; Brooks Rehab Network President; University Center Manager. **Other area locations include:** Green Grove Springs FL; Hudson FL; Orange Park FL; Palatka FL; Palm Coast FL.

CALADESI ANIMAL HOSPITAL
903 Curlew Road, Dunedin FL 34698. 813/733-9395. **Contact:** Human Resources. **E-mail address:** caladesivet@caladesi.com. **World Wide Web address:** http://www.caladesi.com. **Description:** Caladesi Animal Hospital offers general surgical and medical care, acupuncture, orthopedic surgery, boarding services, a pet taxi, and travel services.

CARE MEDICAL EQUIPMENT
102 Drennen Road, Suite B-1, Orlando FL 32806. 407/856-2273. **Toll-free phone:** 800/741-2282. **Contact:** Human Resources. **E-mail address:** info@caremedicalequipment.com. **World Wide Web address:** http://www.caremedicalequipment.com. **Description:** Engaged in the short-term rental of wheelchairs, scooters, shower chairs, lifts, hospital beds, and IV stands to hotels, condos, and homes.

CHARLOTTE REGIONAL MEDICAL CENTER
809 East Marion Street, Punta Gorda FL 33950. 941/639-3131. **Toll-free phone:** 800/677-3132. **Fax:** 941/637-2469. **Recorded jobline:** 888/639-3166. **Contact:** Human Resources Department. **World Wide Web address:** http://www.charlotteregional.com. **Description:** A 208-bed, private, acute care hospital with specialized services including cardiac care; a sports medicine/wellness program (physical fitness, aerobics, aquatic programs, and rehabilitative services); a behavioral center (mental health and addictions treatment); sleep disorder programs; a pulmonary rehabilitation program (breathing disorder treatment); home health services; occupational medicine (offered through an outpatient clinic in North Port); an emergency department; an ambulatory care center; a critical care recovery unit (recovery from open heart surgery); a diabetes center; and a lifeline emergency response system. **Positions advertised include:** Registered Nurse; Nursing Supervisor; Case Manager; Home Health Aide; Health Information Specialist; Dietician; Cook; Medical Transcriptionist; Nutritional Services Aide; Administration Secretary Human Resources; Psych Receptionist; Unit Secretary; Respiratory Therapist; Director Material Management; Medical Social Worker; Physical Therapist; Sleep Technician. **Special programs:** Internships. **Office hours:** Monday - Friday, 8:00 a.m. - 5:00 p.m. **Corporate headquarters location:** Naples FL. **Parent company:** Health Management Associates, Inc. operates 29 hospitals in 11 states across the Southeast and Southwest, focusing on acquiring underachieving community health care facilities with solid potential. **Operations at this facility include:** Administration; Service. **Listed on:** New York Stock Exchange. **Stock exchange symbol:** HMA. **Number of employees at this location:** 830.

CLEVELAND CLINIC FLORIDA HOSPITAL
2950 Cleveland Clinic Boulevard, Weston FL 33331. 954/659-5000. **Fax:** 954/978-7487. **Contact:** Human Resources. **World Wide Web address:** http://www.ccf.org. **Description:** Operates an outpatient clinic and outpatient surgery center that specializes in the diagnosis and treatment of complex medical problems that have resisted previous forms of treatment. Founded in 1921. **NOTE:** Entry-level positions are offered. **Positions advertised include:** General Medicine Assistant; Practical Registered Nurse; Licensed Practical Nurse; Assistant Director Inpatient Services; Inpatient Pharmacist; Outpatient Pharmacist; Pediatric Pharmacist; Pharmacy Manager Medical Safety; Pharmacy Case Manager; Pharmacy Technician; Certified Nurse Aide; Registered Nurse; Medical Secretary. **Special programs:** Internships. **Corporate headquarters location:** Cleveland OH. **Number of employees at this location:** 500.

COLUMBIA NEW PORT RICHEY HOSPITAL
5637 Marine Parkway, New Port Richey FL 34656. 727/848-1733. **Fax:** 727/845-9146. **Recorded jobline:** 727/845-4379. **Contact:** Mark Cohen, Director of Human Resources. **World Wide Web address:** http://www.communityhospitalnpr.com. **Description:** A 415-bed, JCAHO-accredited hospital. Services offered to the community include medical/surgical nursing, telemetry, psychiatry, ambulatory surgery, a catheterization lab, an in-house pool, critical care nursing, emergency rooms, and OR/RR. Columbia New Port Richey Hospital also has laboratory, radiology, nuclear medicine, pharmacy, and surgical suites. **NOTE:** Second and third shifts are offered. **Positions advertised include:** Unit Secretary; Certified Nursing Assistant; Cafeteria Aide; Nutrition Services Trayline Aide; Activity Assistant; Speech Therapist; Clinical Dietician; Administrative Assistant; Registered Nurse; Imaging Assistant; Physical Therapy Assistant; Unit Secretary General Position; Informative System General Position. **Corporate headquarters location:** Nashville TN. **CEO:** Andrew Oravec, Jr.

CONMED LINVATEC CORPORATION
11311 Concept Boulevard, Largo FL 33773. 727/392-6464. **Toll-free phone:** 800/237-0169. **Fax:** 727/399-9900. **Contact:** Human Resources. **E-mail address:** cust_serv@linvatec.com. **World Wide Web address:** http://www.linvatec.com. **Description:** Manufactures and markets medical instruments used in orthoscopy and endoscopy for minimally invasive surgery. **Positions advertised include:** Associate Product Manager; Coach / Team Facilitator; Electronic Assembler; CNC Setup Engineer; Production Machine Operator; Manufacturing Engineer; Tooling Engineer. **Corporate headquarters location:** New York NY. **Parent company:** Bristol-Myers Squibb.

CORAM HEALTHCARE CORPORATION
9143 Phillips Highway, Suite 300, Jacksonville FL 32256. 904/363-3089. **Toll-free phone:** 800/365-6275. **Contact:** Human Resources. **World Wide Web address:** http://www.coram-healthcare.com. **Description:** One of the largest home health infusion therapy companies in the United States. The company provides a wide range of alternate site delivery services including ambulatory and home infusion therapies, lithotripsy, and institutional pharmacy services. Coram Healthcare Corporation has a network of more than 85 locations nationwide. **Positions advertised include:** Pharmacy Nurse Case Manager; Delivery Warehouse Technician; Pharmacy Technician; Account Manager; Nurse Manager; Clinical Pharmacist; Purchasing Representative. **NOTE:** Jobseekers should send employment inquiries to Coram Healthcare, Human Resources, 1125 17th Street, Suite 1500, Denver CO 80202. **Corporate headquarters location:** Denver CO. **Number of employees nationwide:** 4,000.

CORDIS CORPORATION
14201 NW 60th Avenue, Miami Lakes FL 33014. 305/824-2000. **Contact:** Human Resources. **World Wide Web address:** http://www.cordis.com. **Description:** Manufactures medical devices including angiographics and neurovascular products. The company also acts as a supplier for hospitals and physicians. **Positions advertised include:** Unit

Manager; PQS Specialist. **Parent company:** Johnson & Johnson.

CYPRESS VILLAGE
4600 Middleton Park Circle East, Jacksonville FL 32224. 904/223-6100. **Toll-free phone:** 800/228-6163. **Fax:** 904/223-6186. **Contact:** Human Resources. **World Wide Web address:** http://www.cypressvillage.com. **E-mail address:** sales@cypressvillage.com. **Description:** A nonprofit, multilevel retirement community consisting of single-family homes, townhouses, and apartments for independent living. There are also 39 assisted living units, a 120-bed skilled nursing facility, and an Alzheimer's facility with 60 beds. Founded in 1991. **NOTE:** Second and third shifts are offered. **Office hours:** Monday - Friday, 8:00 a.m. - 5:00 p.m. **Parent company:** National Benevolent Association (St. Louis MO). **Annual sales/revenues:** $11 - $20 million. **Number of employees at this location:** 300.

DELRAY MEDICAL CENTER
5352 Linton Boulevard, Suite 210, Delray Beach FL 33484. 561/498-4440. **Toll-free phone:** 800/926-8282. **Fax:** 561/637-5357. **Recorded jobline:** 561/495-3459. **Contact:** Human Resources. **World Wide Web address:** http://www. delraymedicalctr.com. **Description:** A 343-bed hospital offering a variety of specialized services including rehabilitation and psychiatric services. Founded in 1982. **Positions advertised include:** Registered Nurse; CT Scan Technician; Case Management Supervisor; Assistant Nurse Manager; Nurse Practitioner; Clinical Pharmacist; Purchasing Warehouse Assistant; Emergency Room Director; Lab Supervisor.

ESSILOR OF AMERICA
4900 Park Street North, St. Petersburg FL 33709. 727/541-5733. **Contact:** Clair Amrhein, Personnel Director. **World Wide Web address:** http://www.essilor.com. **Description:** A manufacturer of optical lenses for eyeglasses.

FLORIDA INFUSION SERVICES
1053 Progress Court, Palm Harbor FL 34683. 727/942-1829. **Fax:** 727/942-6165. **Contact:** Personnel. **World Wide Web address:** http://www.floridainfusion.com. **Description:** A distributor of pharmaceutical and medical supplies. Florida Infusion Services also provides a variety of pharmacy services.

FLORIDA STATE HOSPITAL
P.O. Box 1000, Chattahoochee FL 32324-1000. 850/663-7258. **Contact:** Tom Carpenter, Recruitment Coordinator. **Description:** Florida State Hospital is a rehabilitative mental health institution for persons with mental/addictive illnesses. **Special programs:** Internships. **Corporate headquarters location:** Tallahassee FL. **Operations at this facility include:** Administration. **Number of employees at this location:** 3,000.

FREEDOM SQUARE RETIREMENT CENTER
10801 Johnson Boulevard, Seminole FL 33772. 727/398-0379. **Contact:** Human Resources. **World Wide Web address:** http://www.arclp.com. **Description:** A retirement community providing all levels of nursing care to its clients. **Positions advertised include:** Physical Therapist; LPN; Certified Nurse Assistant. **Listed on:** New York Stock Exchange. **Stock exchange symbol:** ACR.

FREEDOM VILLAGE
6501 17th Avenue West, Bradenton FL 34209. 941/798-8200. **Employment hotline:** 941/798-8143. **Contact:** Sharon Peters, Human Resources Director. **World Wide Web address:** http://www.freedomvillage.com. **Description:** A continuing care retirement center offering skilled nursing, assisted living, and independent living options. **Positions advertised include:** Server; Utility Aide; Security Guard. **Office hours:** Monday - Friday, 8:30 a.m. - 5:00 p.m. **Corporate headquarters location:** This location. **Number of employees at this location:** 550.

GULF COAST CENTER
5820 Buckingham Road, Fort Myers FL 33905. 239/694-2151. **Contact:** Human Resources. **Description:** A state-run residential facility for people with mental disabilities.

HEALTH FIRST/HOLMES REGIONAL MEDICAL CENTER
PALM BAY COMMUNITY HOSPITAL
1350 South Hickory Street, Melbourne FL 32901. 321/434-7110. **Fax:** 321/434-8587. **Contact:** Dennis Voglas, Director of Employment. **World Wide Web address:** http://www.health-first.org. **Description:** A medical center. **Positions advertised include:** Registered Nurse; Advanced Therapist; Clinical Change Nurse; Education Technologist; Health Unit Coordinator; Medical Technologist; Practical Care Technologist; Radiological Technician; Support Technician; Winter Team Registered Nurse. **Operations at this facility include:** Service. **Number of employees at this location:** 2,800.

HEALTH MANAGEMENT ASSOCIATES, INC.
5811 Pelican Bay Boulevard, Suite 500, Naples FL 34108. 239/598-3131. **Contact:** Human Resources. **World Wide Web address:** http://www.hma-corp.com. **Description:** Provides a broad range of general, acute care health services to rural communities through its ownership of several hospitals and medical centers. **Positions advertised include:** Network Systems Engineer; Legal Secretary; Accounts Payable Clerk; Tax Manager; Reimbursement Consultant. **Listed on:** New York Stock Exchange. **Stock exchange symbol:** HMA. **Number of employees nationwide:** 5,300.

HEALTHSOUTH DOCTORS HOSPITAL
5000 University Drive, Coral Gables FL 33146. 305/666-2111. **Contact:** Director of Human Resources. **World Wide Web address:** http://www.healthsouth.com. **Description:** A 218-bed hospital offering a variety of specialized services including orthopedics, radiological imaging, neuroscience, and sports medicine. **Listed on:** New York Stock Exchange. **Stock exchange symbol:** HRC.

HEARTLAND REHABILITATION CENTER
4101 Sawyer Road, Sarasota FL 34233. 941/925-3427. **Contact:** Human Resources. **Description:** A physical therapy facility offering both inpatient and outpatient services.

HOSPICE BY THE SEA, INC.
1531 West Palmetto Park Road, Boca Raton FL 33486. 561/395-5031. **Fax:** 561/395-9897. **Contact:** Human Resources Department. **World Wide Web address:** http://www.hospicebytheseafl.org. **Description:** Provides nonprofit health care services to terminally ill patients and offers bereavement counseling and other services for the families of the patients. **NOTE:** Second and third shifts are offered. **Positions advertised include:** Administration Receptionist; Bilingual Team Certified Nurses Aide; Bilingual Team Physician; Donations Database Specialist; Accounting Assistant; Registered Nurse; Licensed Practical Nurse; Runner; Certified Nurses Aide; Auditor; Data Entry Medical Records; Social Worker; Volunteer Specialist. **Special programs:** Internships; Summer Jobs. **Office hours:** Monday - Friday, 8:30 a.m. - 5:00 p.m. **CEO:** Trudi Webb. **Annual sales/revenues:** $11 - $20 million. **Number of employees at this location:** 350.

HOSPICE OF NORTHEAST FLORIDA
4266 Sunbeam Road, Jacksonville FL 32257. 904/268-5200. **Contact:** Human Resources. **World Wide Web address:** http://www.hospicene.org. **Description:** Provides health care services for terminally ill patients in their homes or in nursing facilities. **Positions advertised include:** Chef; Patient Care Coordinator; Registered Nurse; Systems Specialist; Help Desk

Technician; Social Service Specialist; Medical Director; Chaplain; Clinical Nurse RN; Mail Clerk.

INDIAN RIVER MEMORIAL HOSPITAL
1000 36th Street, Vero Beach FL 32960-6592. 772/567-4311. **Contact:** Human Resources. **World Wide Web address:** http://www.irmh.com. **Description:** A 335-bed community hospital. Founded in 1932. **Positions advertised include:** Coder; Financial Counselor; Patient Care Technician; Nursing Assistant; Accounting Clerk; Mental Health Technician;; Emergency Department Technician; Medical Assistant; Radiation Therapist; Social Worker; Clinical Dietician; Radiation Therapist; Medical Technician; Technical Support; EMT; Registered Nurse; Case Manager; Utility Worker; Environmental Services Aide.

INTERIM HEALTHCARE INC.
32644 Blossom Lane, Leesburg FL 34788. 352/326-0400. **Contact:** Human Resources. **World Wide Web address:** http://www.interimhealthcare.com. **Description:** A home health care agency.

JACKSON MEMORIAL HOSPITAL
1611 NW 12th Avenue, Park Plaza West L-301, Miami FL 33136. 305/585-1111. **Fax:** 305/326-9470. **Recorded jobline:** 305/585-7886. **Contact:** Ruth Francis, Employment Manager. **World Wide Web address:** http://www.um-jmh.org. **Description:** A 1,567-bed, tertiary, teaching hospital offering specialized services in neurology, pediatrics, dermatology, radiology, pathology, and obstetrics and gynecology. Founded in 1952. **Positions advertised include:** Radiological Technician; Nuclear Medical Technologist; Respiratory Therapy Technologist; Physical Therapist; Hospital Billing Clerk; Health Patient Finance Associate; Nurse Educator; Social Worker; Clinical Social Worker; Practice Pharmacist; Pharmacy Technician; Research Analyst; Clinical Staff Nurse; Associate Nurse Manager; Administrative Support Specialist; Clerk; Support Associate; Health Services Associate; Operating Room Technician; Practical Nurse; Nurse Anesthetist; Patient Care Technologist; Nurse Practitioner; Dietician; Environmental Worker; Electrician Attending Physician; Executive Associate. **Operations at this facility include:** Administration.

JOHN KNOX VILLAGE OF CENTRAL FLORIDA
101 Northlake Drive, Orange City FL 32763. 386/775-3840. **Toll-free phone:** 800/978-5669. **Contact:** Human Resources. **E-mail address:** johnknoxvillage@jkvfl.com. **World Wide Web address:** http://www.johnknoxvillage.com. **Description:** A continuing care retirement community offering skilled nursing, assisted living, and independent living.

JOHN KNOX VILLAGE OF FLORIDA
651 SW 6th Street, Pompano Beach FL 33060. 954/783-4000. **Toll-free phone:** 800/978-5669. **Contact:** Human Resources. **E-mail address:** johnknoxvillage@kvfl.com. **World Wide Web address:** http://www.johnknoxvillage.com. **Description:** A continuing care retirement community offering skilled nursing, assisted living, and independent living.

JOHN KNOX VILLAGE OF TAMPA BAY
4100 East Fletcher Avenue, Tampa FL 33613. 813/971-7038. **Toll-free phone:** 800/978-5669. **Contact:** Human Resources. **E-mail address:** johnknoxvillage@kvfl.com. **World Wide Web address:** http://www.johnknoxvillage.com. **Description:** A continuing care retirement community offering skilled nursing, assisted living, and independent living.

KELLY ASSISTED LIVING SERVICES
300 31st Street, Suite 330, St. Petersburg FL 33713. 727/327-5961. **Contact:** Human Resources. **World Wide Web address:** http://www.kellyservices.com. **Description:** Provides home health care services.

KENDALL MEDICAL CENTER
11750 SW 40th Street, Miami FL 33175. 305/223-3000. **Contact:** Human Resources. **World Wide Web address:** http://www.kendallmed.com. **Description:** A full-service hospital that features LDRP Maternity Suites, advanced diagnostic services, and a 24-hour emergency department. **Positions advertised include:** Marketing Specialist; Unit Leader; Clinical Nurse; Clinical Officer; Registered Nurse; Night Shift Staff Pharmacist; Risk Management Coordinator.

KINDRED HEALTHCARE
1859 Van Buren Street, Hollywood FL 33020. 954/920-9000. **Contact:** Human Resources. **World Wide Web address:** http://www.kindredhealthcare.com. **Description:** A hospital that specializes in the long-term critical care of patients suffering from acute-level chronic diseases. Founded in 1985. **Positions advertised include:** RN. **Corporate headquarters:** Louisville, KY. **Other U.S. locations:** Nationwide. **President/CEO:** Paul J. Diaz. **Number of employees nationwide:** 53,000.

KISSIMMEE GOOD SAMARITAN VILLAGE
1550 Aldersgate Drive, Kissimmee FL 34746. 407/933-1999. **Contact:** Human Resources. **World Wide Web address:** http://www.goodsamkiss.com. **Description:** A nursing home licensed for 166 beds. **Positions advertised include:** Staff Coordinator. **Other U.S. locations:** Nationwide.

LA AMISTAD BEHAVIORAL HEALTH SERVICES
1650 Park Avenue North, Maitland FL 32751. 407/647-0660. **Fax:** 407/629-0552. **Contact:** Human Resources. **E-mail address:** laamistadhr@aol.com. **World Wide Web address:** http://www.lamistad.com. **Description:** Operates a 50-bed inpatient facility. La Amistad offers the following: Deaf and Hearing Impaired Program, Child Psychiatric Program, Adolescent Psychiatric Program, Conversion Treatment Programs, a Dual Diagnosis Psychiatric Treatment Program, an Adult Psychiatric Program, and Academic Programs. **Positions advertised include:** RN; Case Manager; Marketing Representative. **Other U.S. locations:** Winter Park FL. **Parent company:** Universal Health Services.

LEE MEMORIAL HEALTH SYSTEM
P.O. Box 2218, Fort Myers FL 33902. 239/334-5333. **Physical address:** 2776 Cleveland Avenue, Fort Myers FL 33901. **Toll-free phone:** 800/642-5267. **Fax:** 941/332-4199. **Contact:** Human Resources. **World Wide Web address:** http://www.leememorial.org. **Description:** A leading provider of health care in southwest Florida. The nonprofit hospital is comprised of three acute care hospitals, a skilled nursing facility, home health services, and physician offices. Founded in 1916. **Positions advertised include:** Certified Nursing Assistant; Nursing Director; Licensed Practical Nurse; Physical Therapist; Case Manager; Child Care Assistant; Cook; Food Service Assistant; Marketing Service Line Representative; Medical Records Representative; Monitor Technician; Registered Nurse. **NOTE:** Entry-level positions and second and third shifts are offered. **Corporate headquarters location:** This location. **Operations at this facility include:** Administration; Service. **Number of employees at this location:** 5,200.

LIFE CARE SERVICES
800 NW 17th Avenue, Delray Beach FL 33445. 561/272-7779. **Contact:** Human Resources. **Description:** Provides home health care services and manages nursing staffs at various facilities.

MP TOTAL CARE PHARMACY
615 South Ware Boulevard, Tampa FL 33619. 813/621-4800. **Toll-free phone:** 800/424-0920. **Fax:** 831/621-1610. **Contact:** Human Resources. **E-mail address:** humanresources@mptotalcare.com. **World Wide Web address:** http://www.mptotalcare.com. **Description:** Distributor of pharmacy and medical supplies. Founded in 1990. **Positions advertised include:** Patient Account

Representatives; Intake Coordinator; Pharmacist; Pharmacy Technician; Customer Service Representative; Compliance Associate; Program Representatives. **Parent Company:** Charterhouse Group International, Inc. **CEO/President:** Kevin Pawlowski.

MANATEE MEMORIAL HOSPITAL
206 Second Street East, Bradenton FL 34208. 941/746-5111. **Contact:** Personnel. **World Wide Web address:** http://www.manateememorial.com. **Description:** A 512-bed, acute care hospital whose departments include emergency, telemetry, ICU, CVSICU, CCU, and surgery. **Positions advertised include:** Accounting Clerk; Administrative Assistant; Emergency Room Admissions Director; Clinical Manager; Customer Service Representative; Echo Technologist; Admissions Registrar; Lab Assistant; Licensed Practical Nurse; Safety Manager; Physical Therapist; Registered Nurse; Security Officer; Unit Assistant. **Parent company:** Universal Health Services. **CEO:** Brian Flynn.

MARTIN MEMORIAL HEALTH SYSTEMS, INC.
P.O. Box 9010, Stuart FL 34995. 772/287-5200. **Physical address:** 300 Hospital Avenue, Stuart FL 34994. **Contact:** Jennifer T. Slaugh, Employment Coordinator. **World Wide Web address:** http://www.mmhs.com. **Description:** A nonprofit, 336-bed, multifacility health care organization. Martin Memorial Health Systems is comprised of Martin Memorial Medical Center and Martin Memorial Hospital South, both accredited facilities. The medical center is a 236-bed, acute care facility providing a range of inpatient and outpatient services including cancer and cardiac care, a 24-hour emergency department, maternity and pediatrics, and a wide variety of laser surgeries. Martin Memorial Hospital South is a 100-bed community hospital providing inpatient and outpatient services with 92 private rooms, an 8-bed intensive care unit, and a 24-hour emergency department. **Positions advertised include:** Access Services Coordinator; Bariatric Surgery; Book Keeper; Cardiovascular Technician; Data Processing Specialist; Department Secretary; Emergency Medical Technician; Data Processing Specialist; Environmental Services Aide; Exercise Leader; Health Unit Coordinator; Imaging Services Representative; Instrument Technician; Licensed Practical Nurse; Medical Assistant; Message Therapist; Materials Data Analyst; Office Coordinator; Patient Care Technician; Pharmacist; Physician; Radiological Technician; Registered Nurse; Systems Analyst. **Corporate headquarters location:** This location. **Annual sales/revenues:** More than $100 million. **Number of employees at this location:** 2,000.

MAYO CLINIC
4500 San Pueblo Road, Jacksonville FL 32224. 904/953-2000. **Toll-free phone:** 800/336-2838. **Fax:** 904/296-4668. **Recorded jobline:** 904/296-5588. **Contact:** Human Resources. **E-mail address:** mcjhr@mayo.edu. **World Wide Web address:** http://www.mayo.edu. **Description:** An outpatient medical and surgical clinic offering a wide variety of specialty care services. Founded in 1986. **Positions advertised include:** Respiratory Care Practitioner; Anesthesia Technologist; Animal Care Technician; Clinical Dietician; Clinical Nurse; Educator; Controls Technologist; Medical Secretary; Medical Assistant; Medical Technician; Patient Care Technician; Phlebotomist; Regional Occupational Therapist; Registered Nurse; Surgical Technician; Telephone Operator; Unit Supervisor. **President/CEO:** Robert M. Walters. **Facilities Manager:** Gary Pezall. **Information Systems Manager:** Barbara Cummings. **Purchasing Manager:** David Johnson.

MEASE HEALTHCARE
601 Main Street, Dunedin FL 34698. 727/734-6435. **Fax:** 727/734-6119. **Recorded jobline:** 727/734-6937. **Contact:** Human Resources. **World Wide Web address:** http://www.mpmhealth.com. **Description:** A nonprofit, full-service hospital. Specialties include cancer treatment, cardiovascular medicine, neurosciences, orthopedics, rehabilitation, and surgery services. **Positions advertised include:** Medical Records Technician; Patient Account Services Representative; Customer Communications Specialist; Executive Assistant; Medical Records Coder; Patient Access Services Representative; Data Entry Clerk; Administrative Associate; Financial Representative; Services Representative; Certified Nursing Aide; Licensed Practical Nurse; Care Technician; Food Service Coordinator; Lab Medical Assistant; Massage Therapist; Registered Dietician; Radiology Therapist; Speech Therapist. **Corporate headquarters location:** This location. **Number of employees at this location:** 6,000.

MEDICAL TECHNOLOGY SYSTEMS
12920 Automobile Boulevard, Clearwater FL 33762. 727/576-6311. **Fax:** 727/579-8067. **Contact:** Peter Benjamin, Vice President of Human Resources. **Description:** Manufactures and markets blister cards for drug packaging and pharmaceutical dispensing systems for use in nursing homes and hospitals. **Listed on:** NASDAQ. **Stock exchange symbol:** MSYS.

MEDTRONIC XOMED SURGICAL PRODUCTS, INC.
6743 Southpoint Drive North, Jacksonville FL 32216. 904/296-9600. **Toll-free phone:** 800/874-5797. **Contact:** Human Resources. **E-mail address:** employment@Medtronic.com. **World Wide Web address:** http://www.xomed.com. **Description:** Manufactures medical devices and products for ear, nose, and throat surgery. **Positions advertised include:** Customer Service Representative; Manufacturing Engineer; Principal Medical Design Engineer; Product Manager; Quality Assurance Technician; Financial Analyst; Quality Assurance Engineer; Regulatory Specialist; Xomed ATM Distributor; Xomed ATM Ophthalmic Disposable Representative. **Corporate headquarters location:** This location. **Operations at this facility include:** Divisional Headquarters; Manufacturing; Research and Development.

MEMORIAL HOSPITAL OF TAMPA
2901 Swann Avenue, Tampa FL 33609. 813/873-6400. **Fax:** 813/873-6494. **Contact:** Cathy Massessa, Director of Human Resources. **World Wide Web address:** http://www.memorialhospitaltampa.com. **Description:** A hospital that provides inpatient and outpatient services. **Positions advertised include:** Registered Nurse; Licensed Practical Nurse; Physical Therapist; Medical Director; Physical Therapist; Home Health Aide; House Keeping; Unit Secretary; Outpatient Coder; Case Manager; Histology Technician; Registered Dietician; Chief Nursing Officer; Medical Technologist; Quality Manager. **Corporate headquarters location:** Dallas TX. **Parent company:** AMI. **Operations at this facility include:** Service. **Number of employees at this location:** 600.

MERCY HOSPITAL
3663 South Miami Avenue, Miami FL 33133. 305/285-2929. **Recorded jobline:** 305/285-2727. **Fax:** 305/285-5015. **Contact:** Human Resources. **E-mail address:** hr@mercymiami.com. **World Wide Web address:** http://www.mercymiami.com. **Description:** A 500 bed hospital serving Miami and south Florida. **Positions advertised include:** Certified Nurse Assistant; Clinical Services Manager; Director of Surgical Services; Home Health Aide; Field RN; Respiratory Therapist; Mammography Technician; Medical Technician; Monitor Technician; Nuclear Medicine Technologist; Financial Services Coordinator; Director of Corporate Integrity; Director of Managed Care; Billing Representative; Clerk/Receptionist; Communications Operator. **Note:** Applications are accepted in person 7:30 a.m. – 4:30 p.m., Monday – Friday. **President/CEO:** John E. Matuska.

THE MIAMI CHILDREN'S HOSPITAL
3100 SW 62nd Avenue, Miami FL 33155-3009. 305/668-5567. **Toll-free phone:** 800/955-6511. **Recorded jobline:** 305/662-8295. **Contact:** Human

Resources. **World Wide Web address:** http://www.mch.com. **Description:** A pediatric medical care facility. **Positions advertised include:** Practical Coordinator; Lead Office Assistant; Data Entry Clerk; Ward Secretary; Billing Analyst; Customer Greeter; Collections Physician Office Registrar; Secretary; Medical Records Clerk; Communications Specialist; Physical Therapist; Speech Pathologist; Pediatric Social Worker; Physician Assistant; Business Operations Manager; Pharmacist; Chaplain; Project Manager; Registered Dietician; Registered Nurse; Care Assistant; Licensed Practical Nurse. **CEO/President:** Thomas M. Rozek.

MIAMI JEWISH HOME & HOSPITAL
5200 NE 2nd Avenue, Miami FL 33137. 305/751-8626. **Contact:** Larry McDonald, Director of Human Resources. **World Wide Web address:** http://www.douglasgardens.com. **Description:** A hospital that also operates a nursing home for senior citizens. **Positions advertised include:** Driver; Therapeutic Recreation Manager; Transporter; Food Service Supervisor; C-bord Systems Coordinator; Sous Chef; Wait Staff; Secretary; Technician Help Desk; Therapist; Nurse Supervisor; Physical Therapy Assistant; Registered Nurse; Licensed Practical Nurse.

MOORINGS PARK
111 Moorings Park Drive, Naples FL 34105. 239/261-1616. **Fax:** 239/262-7040. **Contact:** Human Resources. **E-mail address:** jwallace@mooringspark.com. **World Wide Web address:** http://www.mooringspark.com. **Description:** A continuing care retirement community offering skilled nursing, assisted living, and independent living. **Positions advertised include:** Certified Nursing Assistant; Registered Nurse; Licensed Practical Nurse; Physical Therapist; Occupational Therapist; Staff Development; Coordinator Secretary; Servers; Direct Aides; Janitor; Housekeeping. **Office hours:** Monday – Friday, 8:30 a.m. – 4:00 p.m.

MORTON PLANT HOSPITAL
300 Pinelles Street, Clearwater FL 33756. 727/462-7000. **Contact:** Human Resources. **Description:** A 687-bed community hospital offering a full range of medical/surgical services.

NAPLES MEDICAL CENTER
400 8th Street North, Naples FL 34102. 239/261-5511. **Fax:** 941/649-3301. **Recorded jobline:** 239/213-2275. **Contact:** Kathleen Phelps, Human Resources Director. **World Wide Web address:** http://www.naplesmedicalcenter.com. **Description:** A multispecialty medical center with diagnostic and administrative departments. Founded in 1958. **NOTE:** Entry-level positions are offered. **Positions advertised include:** Licensed Practical Nurse; Medical Records File Clerk; Medical Secretary; Medical Technician; Patient Account Collector; Representative; Phlebotomist; Radiological Therapist. **Parent company:** ProMedCo Management Corporation. **Listed on:** Privately held. **Number of employees at this location:** 230.

ORLANDO REGIONAL HEALTHCARE
1414 South Kuhl Avenue, Orlando FL 32806-2008. 321/841-5111. **Fax:** 407/237-6374. **Contact:** Nancy Dinon, Vice-President. **World Wide Web address:** http://www.orhs.org. **Description:** A comprehensive medical system that operates several health care facilities throughout central Florida. **NOTE:** Entry-level positions, part-time jobs, and second and third shifts are offered. **Positions advertised include:** Orlando Regional Healthcare; Financial Manager. **Special programs:** Internships; Summer Jobs. **Number of employees nationwide:** 9,000.

ORLANDO REGIONAL LUCERNE HOSPITAL
818 Main Lane, Orlando FL 32806. 407/649-6111. **Contact:** Human Resources. **World Wide Web address:** http://www.orlandoregional.org. **Description:** A medical center serving Orlando and its surrounding cities. **Positions advertised include:** Clinical Technician; Discharge Planner; Guest Services Assistant; Medical Technician; Neurotechnologist; Occupational Therapist; Physical Therapist; Pool Physical Therapist; Registered Nurse; Security; Social Worker.

OSCEOLA REGIONAL MEDICAL CENTER
700 West Oak Street, Kissimmee FL 34741. 407/846-2266. **Contact:** Silvia Loillis, Director of Personnel. **World Wide Web address:** http://www.osceolaregional.com. **Description:** A 171-bed hospital offering a full range of services including diagnostic testing, cardiac care, and rehabilitation. **Positions advertised include:** Administrative Support Associate; Registered Nurse; Certified Pharmaceutical Technician; Certified Surgical Technician; Clinical Dietician; Lab Assistant; Nurse Specialist; Licensed Practical Nurse; Monitor Tech; Nurse Manager; Patient Care Technologist; Personal Computer Technician; Registered Nurse; Radiological Technician; Staff Pharmacist; Transcriptionist; Unit Secretary.

PLANTATION GENERAL HOSPITAL
401 NW 42nd Avenue, Plantation FL 33317. 954/587-5010. **Fax:** 954/587-7869. **Recorded jobline:** 954/321-4068. **Contact:** Human Resources. **World Wide Web address:** http://www.plantationgeneral.com. **Description:** A hospital offering a full range of inpatient and outpatient services. **Positions advertised include:** Registered Nurse; Unit Secretary; Women's Services Radiology; Ultra Sound Technology; CT Technologist; Physical Therapist; Case Manager; Environmental Services Aide; Housekeeping; Coding Compliance Manager. **Special programs:** Internships. **CEO:** Anthony M. Degina, Jr.

PRIME CARE HEALTH AGENCY INC.
8405 NW 53rd Street, Building 106, Miami FL 33166. 305/591-7774. **Toll-free phone:** 800/591-7747. **Fax:** 305/594-8951. **Recorded jobline:** 305/591-7774x815. **World Wide Web address:** http://www.primecarehealthagency.com. **E-mail address:** info@primecarehealth.com. **Contact:** Josie Melero, Human Resources Director. **Description:** Provides in-home nursing services. Founded in 1985. **Positions advertised include:** High Tech Registered Nurse; Registered Nurse; Licensed Practical Nurse; Certified Home Health Aide; Companion; Babysitter; Escort; Medical Social Worker. **Office hours:** Monday - Friday, 8:00 a.m. - 5:00 p.m. **President:** Barry G. Shoor. **Number of employees at this location:** 250. **Number of employees nationwide:** 300.

RAMSAY YOUTH SERVICES, INC.
Columbus Center, One Alhambra Plaza, Suite 750, Coral Gables FL 33134. 305/569-6993. **Fax:** 305/569-4647. **Contact:** Human Resources. **World Wide Web address:** http://www.ramsay.com. **Description:** Ramsay Youth Services, Inc. is a provider and manager of juvenile justice and behavioral healthcare treatment programs and services. The programs and services are provided primarily to at-risk and troubled youth in residential and nonresidential settings. **Positions advertised include:** Administrative Assistant. **Other U.S. locations:** Nationwide. **Operations at this facility include:** Administration. **Listed on:** NASDAQ. **Stock exchange symbol:** RYOU.

ROTECH MEDICAL CORPORATION
2600 Technology Drive Suite 300, Orlando FL 32804. 407/822-4600. **Contact:** Human Resources. **E-mail address:** corporate@rotech.com. **World Wide Web address:** http://www.rotech.com. **Description:** RoTech Medical Corporation markets, provides, and delivers outpatient health care products and services to patients in physician offices and at their home. Services and products involve respiratory therapy equipment, convalescent medical equipment, prelabeled and prepackaged pharmaceuticals, and home infusion therapy products. **Other U.S. locations:** Nationwide. **Listed on:** NASDAQ. **Stock exchange symbol:** ROTC. **Number of employees at this location:** 350.

S.H. MEDICAL CORPORATION
3061 NW 82nd Avenue, Miami FL 33122. 305/406-2222. **Fax:** 305/406-2113. **Contact:** Hiring Manager. **E-mail address:** shmedical@shmedical.com. **World Wide Web address:** http://www.shmedical.com. **Description:** A medical equipment distribution and export company that sells new, refurbished, and preowned medical equipment. The company specializes in diagnostic equipment, endoscopy equipment and instruments, fetal monitors, parts, pulse oximeters, surgical instruments, and ultrasounds. **Corporate headquarters location:** This location.

SACRED HEART HEALTH SYSTEMS
5151 North Ninth Avenue, Pensacola FL 32513. 850/416-7175. **Fax:** 850/416-6740. **Contact:** Sue Byrd, Director of Human Resources. **E-mail address:** shmedical@shmedical.com. **World Wide Web address:** http://www.sacred-heart.org. **Description:** A member of the Daughters of Charity national health system. Sacred Heart Health Systems is a 431-bed acute care facility. The hospital offers services in the following areas: cardiology, cardiovascular surgery, emergency, gastroenterology, laser surgery, neonatology, neurology, OB/GYN, oncology, orthopedics, otolaryngology, otology, pediatrics, and plastic surgery. Sacred Heart Health Systems also operates a skilled nursing facility, medical residence programs, and a wellness/health education center. **NOTE:** Job seekers may apply in person at the employment office from 8:00 a.m. to 3:00 p.m. The employment office is located at 5110 Bayou Boulevard, Pensacola FL 32513. **Positions advertised include:** Chief Sonnographer; Ultrasound Technician; Registered Nurse; Licensed Practical Nurse; Medical Office Secretary. **Corporate headquarters location:** St. Louis MO. **Number of employees at this location:** 2,500. **CEO:** Patrick J. Madden.

SEMPER CARE HOSPITAL
615 North Bonita Avenue, Panama City FL 32401. 850/767-3180. **Fax:** 850/767-3190. **Contact:** Human Resources: **Description:** A hospital with 902 beds. **Positions advertised include:** Registered Nurse. **President:** Steve Johnson.

SKYWAY ANIMAL HOSPITAL
3258 Fifth Avenue South, St. Petersburg FL 33712. 727/327-5141. **Fax:** 727/327-3405. **Contact:** Human Resources. **World Wide Web address:** http://www.skywayah.com. **Description:** Provides general medical, surgical, dental, and radiological services to small animals.

SMITH DENTAL LABS
2131 Art Museum Drive, Jacksonville FL 32207. 904/398-6844. **Toll-free phone:** 800/828-9976. **Contact:** Human Resources. **World Wide Web address:** http://www.smithdentallab.com. **Description:** Provides a full range of custom-made dental prosthetic appliances, divided into three main groups: restorative products (crowns and bridges); reconstructive products (partial and full dentures); and cosmetic products (porcelain veneers and ceramic crowns.) **Positions advertised include:** Dental Lab Trainee; Skilled Technician; Department Supervisor. **Corporate headquarters location:** Wayland MA. **Parent company:** National Dentex Corporation is one of the largest operators of dental laboratories in the United States. Each lab is operated as a stand-alone facility under the direction of a local manager. All sales and marketing is done through each lab's own direct sales force. **Other U.S. locations:** Nationwide. **Listed on:** NASDAQ. **Stock exchange symbol:** NADX. **Annual sales/revenues:** Less than $5 million.

STAR MULTICARE SERVICES INC.
2221 North University Drive, Pembroke Pines FL 33024. 954/962-0926. **Contact**: Human Resources. **World Wide Web address:** http://www.starmulticare.com. **Description**: A home health care agency that also provides temporary personnel to health care facilities. **Positions advertised include**: Licensed Practical Nurse; Registered Nurse; Nurses Aide; Home Health Aide. **Corporate headquarters location:** Huntington Station NY. **Other U.S. locations**: NJ; NY; OH; PA. **Listed on**: NASDAQ. **Stock exchange symbol**: SMCS.

SUNRISE COMMUNITY, INC.
22300 SW 162nd Avenue, Miami FL 33170. 305/245-6150. **Contact:** Human Resources. **E-mail address:** info@sunrisegroup.com. **World Wide Web address:** http://www.sunrisegroup.org. **Description:** A residential treatment facility for individuals with developmental disabilities. **Positions advertised include:** Assistant Residential Program Director; Residential Program Director; Secretary; Training Instructor. **Other area locations:** Cape Coral FL; Clewiston FL; Lakeland FL; Naples FL; Panama City FL; St. Petersburg FL; Tallahassee FL. **Other U.S. locations:** AL; CT; GA; TN; VA. **President/CEO:** Les Leech, Jr. **Number of employees nationwide:** 4,000.

TAMPA GENERAL HOSPITAL
P.O. Box 1289, Tampa FL 33601. 813/844-7551. **Fax:** 813/844-4345. **Recorded jobline:** 813/844-4100. **Contact:** Human Resources. **World Wide Web address:** http://www.tgh.org. **Description:** A medical facility providing hospital and ambulatory services. **Positions advertised include:** Aeromed; Anesthesia Care Technician; Cardiac Monitor Technician; Care Coordinator; Clinical Nurse; Clinical Admission Supervisor; Clinician; Epiderm Clinician; Lactation Consultant; Licensed Practical Nurse; Medical Assistant Technician; Registered Nurse; Support Services Aide; Surgical Technician; Unit Coordinator. **Special programs:** Internships. **CEO:** Ron Hytoff. **Operations at this facility include:** Administration. **Number of employees at this location:** 3,000.

TENDER LOVING CARE/STAFF BUILDERS
3225 West Commercial Boulevard, #125,, Fort Lauderdale FL 33309. 954/486-5506. **Fax:** 954/739-5129. **Contact:** Human Resources. **World Wide Web address:** http://www.tlcathome.com. **Description:** A home health care agency. **Positions advertised include:** Home Care Nurse; Licensed Practical Nurse; Physical Therapist. **Corporate headquarters location:** Lake Success NY. **Other U.S. locations:** Nationwide. **CEO:** Stephen Savitsky. **Number of employees nationwide:** 20,000.

3I (IMPLANT INNOVATIONS, INC.)
4555 Riverside Drive, Palm Beach Gardens FL 33410. 561/776-6700. **Fax:** 561/776-6825. **Contact:** Human Resources. **E-mail address:** mfischer@3implant.com. **World Wide Web address:** http://www.3Ionline.com. **Description:** A manufacturer and distributor of dental implants. **Positions advertised include:** New Product Development Coordinator; Clinical Research Manager; CNVC Machinist; Customer Service Technical Representative; Product Marketing Director; Document Control Coordinator; Patient Specific Manager; Product Manager; Regulatory Services Technology Representative; Territory Sales Manager.

TRANSITIONS OPTICAL INC.
9251 Belcher Road, Pinellas Park FL 33782. 727/545-0400. **Contact:** Human Resources. **World Wide Web address:** http://www.transitions.com. **Description:** Manufactures plastic photochromatic ophthalmic lenses. Founded in 1990. **Listed on:** Privately held. **Annual sales/revenues:** More than $100 million.

TYCO HEALTHCARE/KENDALL
P.O. Box 62078, DeLand FL 32721-2078. 386/734-3685. **Contact:** J. Ralph Mills, Human Resources Manager. **World Wide Web address:** http://www.kendallhq.com. **Description:** Manufactures disposable hypodermic needles and syringes. Founded in 1903. **NOTE:** Second and third shifts are offered. **Positions advertised include:** Principal Electrical Engineer; Process Engineer; Project Engineer; Tooling Engineer; Supervising Maintenance. **Corporate headquarters location:** Mansfield MA. **Other U.S. locations:** Nationwide. **International locations:** Worldwide. **Parent company:** Tyco International.

Operations at this facility include: Manufacturing. **Listed on:** New York Stock Exchange. **Stock exchange symbol:** TYC. **President/CEO:** Rich Meelia. **Annual sales/revenues:** More than $100 million.

U.S. DEPARTMENT OF VETERANS AFFAIRS BAY PINES VA MEDICAL CENTER
P.O. Box 5005, 10000 Bay Pines Boulevard, Bay Pines FL 33744. 727/398-6661. **Contact:** Human Resources. **World Wide Web address:** http://www.va.gov. **Description:** A medical center operated by the U.S. Department of Veterans Affairs. The VA health care system includes 171 medical centers; more than 364 outpatient, community, and outreach clinics; 130 nursing home care units; and 37 domiciliaries. **Positions advertised include:** Nursing Assistant; Licensed Practical Nurse. **NOTE:** Applicants must call 800/369-6008 to request application materials, applicants must refer to specific job title and location. Once received applications can be mailed to: Department of Veterans Affairs, Delegated Examining Unit, 1201 Broad Rock Boulevard #507, Richmond VA 23249. **Corporate headquarters location:** Washington DC. **Other U.S. locations:** Nationwide.

U.S. DEPARTMENT OF VETERANS AFFAIRS MIAMI VA MEDICAL CENTER
1201 NW 16th Street, Miami FL 33125. 305/575-4455. **Fax:** 305/575-3374. **Recorded jobline:** 305/324-4455. **Contact:** Human Resources. **World Wide Web address:** http://www.va.gov/546miami. **Description:** A medical center operated by the U.S. Department of Veterans Affairs. From 54 hospitals in 1930, the VA health care system has grown to include 171 medical centers; more than 364 outpatient, community, and outreach clinics; 130 nursing home care units; and 37 domiciliaries. VA operates at least one medical center in each of the 48 contiguous states, Puerto Rico, and the District of Columbia. With approximately 76,000 medical center beds, VA treats nearly 1 million patients in VA hospitals; 75,000 in nursing home care units; and 25,000 in domiciliaries. VA's outpatient clinics register approximately 24 million visits per year. **Positions advertised include:** Certified Respiratory Therapy Technician; Nurse Practitioner; Nurse Researcher; Advanced Registered Nurse Researcher; Dialysis Nurse; Staff Nurse; Optometrist; Physician; Physician Assistant; Podiatrist; Registered Respiratory Therapist. **Corporate headquarters location:** Washington DC. **Other U.S. locations:** Nationwide. **Operations at this facility include:** Administration; Research and Development; Service. **Number of employees at this location:** 2,700.

UNIVERSITY COMMUNITY HOSPITAL
3100 East Fletcher Avenue, Tampa FL 33613. 813/615-7290. **Recorded jobline:** 813/615-7830. **Contact:** Bernadette Stypula, Human Resources Manager. **World Wide Web address:** http://www.uch.org. **Description:** A 431-bed, full-service, acute care hospital. **Positions advertised include:** Occupational Health Services; CT Technologist; Staff Pharmacist; Ultrasound Technologist; Physical Therapist; General Accounting Systems Manager; Ultrasound Supervisor; Speech Therapist; Public Relations Manager; Registered Nurse; Home Health Registered Nurse; Billing Representative; Press Release Manager; Respirator Therapist; Medical Coder; Surgical Technologist. **Office hours:** Monday - Friday, 8:00 a.m. - 5:00 p.m. **Operations at this facility include:** Administration; Service. **President:** Norm Stein. **Number of employees at this location:** 2,500.

UNIVERSITY HOSPITAL & MEDICAL CENTER
7710 NW, 71st Court, Suite 10, Tamarac FL 33321. 954/721-2200. **Physical address:** 7201 North University Drive, Tamarac FL 33321. **Fax:** 954/724-6666. **Recorded jobline:** 954/724-6114. **Contact:** Human Resources. **World Wide Web address:** http://www.uhmchealth.com. **Description:** A 317-bed hospital offering a full range of inpatient and outpatient health care services. Founded in 1974. **Positions advertised include:** Nurse Auditor; Registered Nurse; Nuclear Medicine Technologist; Wound Care Clinical Supervisor. **Number of employees at this location:** 1,550.

VISITING NURSE ASSOCIATION
2400 SE Monterey Road, Suite 300, Stuart FL 34996. 772/286-1844. **Fax:** 772/286-8753. **Contact:** Human Resources. **E-mail address:** resumes@vnaflorida.org. **World Wide Web address:** http://www.visitingnurses.com. **Description:** A nonprofit home health agency that also offers rehabilitation and mental health services, home IV therapies, pre-op visits, private duty nurses, HIV/AIDS care, case management, and oncology care. **Other area locations include:** Bradenton FL; Clearwater FL; Lake Wales FL; Okeechobee FL; Port Richey FL; Sarasota FL; Spring Hill FL; Tampa FL.

VISITING NURSE ASSOCIATION & HOSPICE
1111 36th Street, Vero Beach FL 32960. 772/567-5551. **Contact:** Human Resources. **World Wide Web address:** http://www.vnatc.com. **Description:** A nonprofit home health agency that also offers rehabilitation and mental health services, home IV therapies, pre-op visits, private duty nurses, HIV/AIDS care, case management, and oncology care. **Positions advertised include:** Occupational Therapist; Registered Nurse; Director of Quality Education; Clinical Specialist/Educator.

WESTCHESTER GENERAL HOSPITAL, INC.
2500 SW 75th Avenue, Miami FL 33155. 305/264-5252. **Fax:** 305/264-5958. **Recorded jobline:** 305/558-9700x600. **Contact:** Human Resources. **World Wide Web address:** http://www.westchestergeneral.com. **Description:** A general acute care hospital with 192 beds.

WHITEHALL BOCA NURSING HOME
7300 Del Prado Circle South, Boca Raton FL 33433. 561/392-3000. **Contact:** Human Resources. **Fax:** 561/392-6031. **World Wide Web address:** http://www.whitehallboca.com. **Description:** A skilled nursing home that also offers some assisted living services.

WINDMOOR HEALTH CARE
11300 U.S. 19 North, Clearwater FL 33764. 727/541-2646. **Recorded jobline:** 727/541-2646. **Contact:** Human Resources. **E-mail address:** clearwaterhr@windmoor-healthcare.com. **World Wide Web address:** http://www.windmoorhealthcare.com. **Description:** A full-service hospital specializing in psychiatric treatment and chemical dependency therapy. The hospital provides both inpatient and outpatient services. **Positions advertised include:** Intake Specialist; Staff Psychologist; Case Manager; Therapist; Pool Case Manager.

WINTER PARK MEMORIAL HOSPITAL
200 North Lakemont Avenue, Winter Park FL 32789. 407/646-7000. **Fax:** 407/646-7639. **Contact:** Human Resources Department. **E-mail address:** administrative@winterparkhospital.com. **World Wide Web address:** http://www.winterparkhospital.com. **Description:** A 334-bed medical/surgical hospital offering neonatal intensive care and oncology services. **Parent company:** Adventist Health System.

WINTER PARK TOWERS
1111 South Lakemont Avenue, Winter Park FL 32789. 407/647-4083. **Contact:** Human Resources. **World Wide Web address:** http://www.westminsterretirement.com/ccrc_wpt.html. **Description:** A retirement community offering skilled nursing, assisted living, and independent living.

Georgia

AMEDISYS HOME HEALTH
440 Martin Luther King Jr. Boulevard, Suite 300, Macon GA 31201. 478/738-0807. **Toll-free phone:** 800/675-1073. **Fax:** 478/738-0923. **Contact:** Human Resources. **World Wide Web address:** http://www.healthfield.com. **Description:** Provides

home health care nursing services. **NOTE:** Please visit website to search for jobs and apply online. **Positions advertised include:** Speech Language Pathologist; Nurse Liaison; Medical Social Worker; Clinical Manager; LPN; RN. **Other area locations:** Statewide. **Other U.S. locations:** Southern U.S. **Listed on:** NASDAQ. **Stock exchange symbol:** AMED.

ANCHOR HOSPITAL
5454 Yorktown Drive, Atlanta GA 30349. 770/991-6044. **Toll-free phone:** 866/667-8797. **Fax:** 770/991-3843. **Contact:** Human Resources. **World Wide Web address:** http://www.magellanhealth.com. **Description:** A specialty treatment hospital, helping teens and adults with chemical dependency or behavioral health problems. **NOTE:** Contact Human Resources at 678/251-3339. Please visit website to download employment application. **Special programs:** Internships.

JOHN D. ARCHBOLD MEMORIAL HOSPITAL
P.O. Box 1018, Thomasville GA 31799-1018. 229/228-2000. **Physical address:** 915 Gordon Avenue, Thomasville GA 31792. **Fax:** 229/228-8583. **Contact:** Employment Manager. **World Wide Web address:** http://www.archbold.org. **Description:** A regional trauma center serving the southwest region of Georgia. The hospital also provides some outpatient services. **NOTE:** Human Resources phone is 229/228-2744. Please visit website to search for jobs, and to download employment application. **Positions advertised include:** Administrative Assistant; Secretary – Nursing Administration; Transcriptionist; Unit Secretary Coordinator; Cardiovascular Technician; Director of Quality Improvement; MRI Technician; Pharmacist; Pharmacy Technician; Phlebotomy Technician; Respiratory Therapist; Social Worker – Wound Management; Special Procedures Technician; Speech Language Pathologist; Computer Operator; House Supervisor; Patient Care Technician; RN – Various Departments; Transporter; Cafeteria Aide; Cook; Environmental Services Aide; Floor Technician; Nutrition Services Technician. **Corporate headquarters location:** This location. **Subsidiaries include:** Brooks County Hospital; Grady General Hospital; Mitchell County Hospital. **Operations at this facility include:** Administration; Research and Development. **Listed on:** Privately held.

BJC MEDICAL CENTER
70 Medical Center Drive, Commerce GA 30529. 706/335-1000. **Fax:** 706/335-7701. **Recorded jobline:** 706/335-1114. **Contact:** Human Resources. **E-mail address:** manglin@bjcmc.org. **World Wide Web address:** http://www.bjcmc.org. **Description:** A full-service medical center. BJC Medical Center comprises a 109-bed hospital facility and a 90-bed nursing facility. **NOTE:** Human Resources phone is 706/335-1108. **Positions advertised include:** RN – Various Departments; LPN; Certified Nursing Assistant; ARRT Registered Technician – Radiology; Controller; Housekeeping Technician; Floor Technician; Dietary Aide; Purchaser/Buyer – Materials Management. **Office hours:** Monday – Friday, 8:00 a.m. – 4:30 p.m. **Corporate headquarters location:** This location.

BEST MANUFACTURING COMPANY
P.O. Box 8, Menlo GA 30731-0008. 706/862-2302. **Physical address:** 579 Edison Street, Menlo GA 30731. **Contact:** Human Resources. **World Wide Web address:** http://www.bestglove.com. **Description:** Manufactures protective gloves for medical and industrial use. **Corporate headquarters location:** This location. **Other area locations:** Rome GA. **Other U.S. locations:** Moss Point AL; Fayette AL; Johnson City TN; Fall River MA; Guatemala CA. **International locations:** Canada; Belgium. Number of employees worldwide: 2,000.

BLUE CROSS AND BLUE SHIELD OF GEORGIA
3350 Peachtree Road NE, Atlanta GA 30326. 404/842-8000. **Contact:** Human Resources. **World Wide Web address:** http://www.bcbsga.com. **Description:** Offers healthcare to thousands of individuals in Georgia. **Positions advertised include:** Senior HR Associate; Business Operations Analysis Specialist; Business Data Architecture Manager; Disability Case Manager; Associate Medical Director; Director of Disease Management. **Parent company:** WellPoint owns and operates several healthcare companies, including Blue Cross of California, Blue Cross and Blue Shield of Missouri, Blue Cross and Blue Shield of Wisconsin, HealthLink, Unicare, Golden West Dental & Vision, PrecisionRx, WellPoint Behavioral Health, WellPoint Dental Services, WellPoint Pharmacy Management, and WellPoint Workers' Compensation Managed Care Services. **Corporate headquarters location:** This location. **Other area locations:** Columbus GA. **Listed on:** New York Stock Exchange. **Stock exchange symbol:** WLP.

CANDLER HOSPITAL
ST. JOSEPH'S/CANDLER HEALTH SYSTEM
5353 Reynolds Street,, Savannah GA 31419. 912/819-6000. **Toll-free phone:** 800/569-5463. **Fax:** 912/692-6662. **Contact:** Human Resources. **World Wide Web address:** http://www.stjosephs-candler.org. **Description:** A hospital. **NOTE:** Entry-level positions and second and third shifts are offered. Resumes should be mailed to 11700 Middleground Road, Savannah GA 31419. **Positions advertised include:** Department Secretary; Legal Secretary; Scheduling Specialist; Insurance Representative; Pharmacy Technician; Imaging Transcriptionist; Clinical Manager; Operations Manager; Nurse Manager; Program Director; Health Information Manager; Loss Prevention Manager; House Supervisor; LPN – Various Departments; RN – Various Departments. . **Annual sales/revenues:** $51 - $100 million. **President/CEO:** Paul P. Hinchey.

CHILDREN'S HEALTHCARE OF ATLANTA
1600 Tullie Circle, Atlanta GA 30329. 404/325-6000. **Fax:** 404/929-8615. **Recorded jobline:** 404/929-8640. **Contact:** Human Resources. **E-mail address:** jobapplicants@choa.org. **World Wide Web address:** http://www.choa.org. **Description:** A children's hospital. **NOTE:** Volunteer positions are also available. Please visit website to register, search for jobs, and apply online. **Positions advertised include:** Lead Patients Access Specialist; Diet Clerk/Typist; Patient Care Technician; Bill Editor; Public Relations Coordinator; Writer/Editor; Director of Logistics; Unit Secretary; Customer Service Ambassador. . **Operations at this facility include:** Administration; Service. **Listed on:** Privately held. **Number of employees nationwide:** 5,250.

CHRISTIAN CITY
7290 Lester Road, Union City GA 30291-2317. 770/964-3301. **Fax:** 770/964-7041. **Recorded jobline:** 770/964-3301, Ext. 773. **Contact:** Human Resources Department. **E-mail address:** milliec@christian-city.org. **World Wide Web address:** http://www.christiancity.org. **Description:** A nonprofit company operating a home for children, retirement homes, a convalescent center, and an Alzheimer's care center. Founded in 1964. **NOTE:** Volunteer positions, entry-level positions and second and third shifts are offered. **Company slogan:** Multiple ministries. One mission. **Positions advertised include:** Activity Aids; Administrative Support; Chaplain; Courtesy Officers; Dietary Staff; Foster Parents; Housekeeping; Laundry Worker; Maintenance Worker; LPN; RN; CNA; Social Worker. **Special programs:** Summer Jobs. **Corporate headquarters location:** This location. **Listed on:** Privately held. **President/CEO:** Robert L. Crutchfield. **Number of employees at this location:** 400.

CIBA VISION CORPORATION
11460 Johns Creek Parkway, Duluth GA 30097. 678/415-3937. **Contact:** Staffing Specialist. **World Wide Web address:** http://www.cibavision.com. **Description:** Engaged in the research, development, manufacture, and sale of soft contact lenses and contact lens care products. **NOTE:** Please visit website to search for jobs and apply online. **Positions advertised include:** Business Planning Analyst; Category Manager; Channel Marketing Manager; Consumer

Marketing Manager; Document Management Representative; Global Marketing Director; Manager – North American Credit; Manager – Academic Development; Payroll Administrator; Senior Administrative Assistant; Process Engineer; Patent Attorney. **Corporate headquarters location:** This location. **Other U.S. locations:** IL. **International locations:** Worldwide. **Parent company:** Novartis. **Operations at this facility include:** Administration; Manufacturing; Research and Development; Sales; Service. **Listed on:** New York Stock Exchange. **Stock exchange symbol:** NVS.

CORAM HEALTHCARE CORPORATION
2140 Newmarket Parkway, Suite 106, Marietta GA 30067. 770/952-3021. **Fax:** 770/952-6840. **Contact:** Human Resources. **World Wide Web address:** http://www.coram-healthcare.com. **Description:** One of the nation's largest home health infusion therapy companies. The company provides a wide range of services including ambulatory and home infusion therapies, nutrition services, lithotripsy, hemophilia management, transplant services, and prescription services. **NOTE:** Please send resumes to corporate office at 1675 Broadway, Suite 900, Denver CO 80202, or fax to 303/672-8733. Be sure to mention what job you are applying for. **Positions advertised include:** Clinical Pharmacist; Purchasing Representative. **Corporate headquarters location:** Denver CO. **Other U.S. locations:** Nationwide. **International locations:** Canada. **President/CEO:** Daniel Crowley. **Number of employees worldwide:** 4,000.

DOGWOOD VETERINARY HOSPITAL
COWETA VETERINARY ASSOCIATES, P.C.
24 Hospital Road, Newnan GA 30263. 770/253-3416. **Fax:** 770/683-3416. **Contact:** Donna Robinson, Office Manager. **E-mail address:** dogwoodvet@mail.newnanutilities.org. **World Wide Web address:** http://www.dogwoodvet.com. **Description:** Offers veterinary care for small and large animals. The small animal services include general medicine, surgery, boarding, and in-house clinical and pathological testing. The large animal services include house and farm calls, pathology testing, surgery, reproductive health, and regulatory testing. **Positions advertised include:** Veterinary Technician; Veterinary Office Staff – Full-time; Office Staff – Part-time; Groomer; Kennel Staff. **Office hours:** Monday – Friday, 8:00 a.m. – 6:00 .m.; Saturday, 8::00 a.m. – 12:00 p.m.

DORNIER MEDTECH
1155 Roberts Boulevard, Kennesaw GA 30144. 770/426-1315. **Toll-free phone:** 800/367-6437. **Fax:** 770/426-6115. **Contact:** Human Resources. **E-mail address:** info@dornier.com. **World Wide Web address:** http://www.dornier.com. **Description:** Engaged in the service, sale, and installation of lithotomic, ultrasound, and laser equipment for hospitals and medical facilities. **Corporate headquarters location:** Munich, Germany. **International locations:** Worldwide.

ETHICON, INC.
P.O. Box 70, Cornelia GA 30531. 706/778-2281. **Physical address:** 655 Ethicon Circle, Cornelia GA 30531. **Contact:** Human Resources. **World Wide Web address:** http://www.ethiconinc.com. **Description:** Manufactures products for precise wound closure including sutures, ligatures, mechanical wound closure instruments, and related products. The company makes its own surgical needles and provides thousands of needle-suture combinations to surgeons. **Office hours:** Monday – Friday, 8:00 a.m. – 6:00 p.m. **Corporate headquarters location:** Somerville NJ. **Other U.S. locations:** MA; NJ; TX. **International locations:** Mexico; Argentina. **Parent company:** Johnson & Johnson. **Listed on:** New York Stock Exchange. **Stock exchange symbol:** JNJ. **President:** Cliff Holland. **Number of employees worldwide:** 11,000.

GENESIS HOME CARE
2501 Plant Avenue, Waycross GA 31501. 912/285-5200. **Fax:** 912/285-9378. **Contact:** Human Resources. **E-mail address**: genesisdma@accessate.net. **Description:** Offers home health care and medical equipment and supplies.

GRADY MEMORIAL HOSPITAL
80 Jesse Hill Jr. Drive, Atlanta GA 30303-3050. 404/616-4307. **E-mail address:** gbedford@gmh.edu. **Contact:** Human Resources. **World Wide Web address:** http://www.gradyhealthsystem.org. **Description:** A 1,024-bed, primary care hospital. The hospital is a teaching facility for Emory University and Morehouse College. **NOTE:** Please visit website to search for jobs and apply online. Be sure to include the listed job code when applying. **Positions advertised include:** Pharmacist; Pharmacy Technician; Director of Customer Service; Director of Quality Improvement and Staff Development; Executive Director of Trauma Services; Vice President of Government Relations; Vice President of Patient Care; RN – Various Departments; Advice Nurse; Bionic Nurse; Charge Nurse; Clinical Manager; Clinical Nurse Specialist; LPN; Nurse Case Manager; Nurse Coordinator; Nurse Practitioner; Senior Staff Nurse; Surgical Technician; Coder; Coding Supervisor; Financial Counselor; Medical Transcriptionist; Quality Control Representative. **Parent company:** Grady Health System.

HAMILTON MEDICAL CENTER
P.O. Box 1168, Dalton GA 30722-1168. 706/272-6145. **Physical address:** 1200 Memorial Drive, Dalton GA 30720. **Recorded jobline:** 706/217-2020. **Fax:** 706/272-6285. **E-mail address:** employment@hhcs.org. **Contact:** Employment Services. **World Wide Web address:** http://www.hamiltonhealth.com. **Description:** A 282-bed, acute care medical center. Hamilton Medical Center provides a variety of services including cancer care, diabetes treatment, substance abuse, and psychiatric care. **Positions advertised include:** RN – Various Departments; LPN – Various Departments; Staff Pharmacist; Planning Analyst; Director of Information Services; Director of Surgery; RN Supervisor; Radiologic Technician; Staff Respiratory Therapist; Ultrasound Technologist; Reimbursement Analyst; Transcriptionist – Medical Records; Registration Clerk; CNA. **Office hours:** Monday – Thursday, 8:00 a.m. – 4:00 p.m.; Friday – 7:00 a.m. – 4:00 p.m.

HEALTHFIELD INC.
6666 Powers Ferry Road, Suite 328, Atlanta GA 30339. 770/953-9510. **Fax:** 770/541-3747. **Contact:** Personnel. **World Wide Web address:** http://www.healthfield.com. **Description:** Provides home health care services throughout Georgia and Alabama. **Positions advertised include:** RN; LPN; Physical Therapist; Speech Therapist; Occupational Therapist; Case Manager; Order Manager; Pharmacist; Respiratory Therapist; Service Technician; Care Coordinator; Biller/Collector. **Parent company:** Four Seasons Healthcare Inc.

MEDTRONIC
3225 Cumberland Boulevard SE, Suite 500, Atlanta GA 30339. 770/955-3808. **Contact:** Human Resources. **World Wide Web address:** http://www.medtronic.com. **Description:** The world's leader in medical technology. Medtronic develops technology that treats vascular illnesses, neurological disorders, and heart disease. **NOTE:** Please visit website to search for jobs and apply online. **Positions advertised include:** District Sales Manager; Field Service Representative; Regional Health Care Economics Manager; Senior Human Resources Manager. **Corporate headquarters location:** Minneapolis MN. **Other area locations:** Albany GA; Alpharetta GA; Augusta GA; Cordele GA; Macon GA; Savannah GA; Valdosta GA. **Other U.S. locations:** Nationwide. **International locations:** Worldwide. **Listed on:** New York Stock Exchange. **Stock exchange symbol:** MDT. **Number of employees worldwide:** 29,000.

NORTHLAKE MEDICAL CENTER
1455 Montreal Road, Tucker GA 30084. 770/270-3000. **Fax:** 770/270-3046. **Recorded jobline:** 770/270-3080. **Contact:** Kevin Trameri, Human Resources. **E-mail address:** kevin.trameri@hcahealthcare.com. **World Wide Web address:** http://www.northlakemedical..com. **Description:** A 120-bed general acute care medical center. **NOTE:** Direct contact phone number is 770/270-3118. Please visit website to search for jobs. Part-time jobs, second and third shifts, and volunteer positions are also offered. **Positions advertised include:** Mammography Technician; RN – Various Departments; Occupational Therapist; Physician Assistant; Physical Therapist; CT Technician. **Special programs:** Internships.

OCONEE REGIONAL MEDICAL CENTER
821 North Cobb Street, P.O. Box 690, Milledgeville GA 31061. 478/454-3500. **Recorded jobline:** 478/454-3545. **Contact:** Human Resources. **E-mail address:** jobs@oconeeregional.com. **World Wide Web address:** http://www.oconeeregional.com. **Description:** A medical center. **NOTE:** Human Resources phone is 478/454-3540. Please visit website to search for jobs and download employment application. Volunteer positions are also available. **Positions advertised include:** Accounting Clerk; Accounting Supervisor; Billing Specialist; Conversion Assistant; Director of Foundation and Development; Driver – Non-emergency Transportation; EMT/Paramedic; Maintenance Mechanic - Engineering; Monitor Technician – Radiology; Nuclear Medicine Technologist – Radiology; OB Nurse Manager; PBX Operator; Physical Therapy Assistant; RN; - Various Departments; Registration Representative; Respiratory Care Practitioner; Transcriptionist; Transport/Monitor Technician; Ultrasound Technologist. **Special programs:** Internships. **Operations at this facility include:** Administration. **Listed on:** Privately held. **President/CEO:** Brian Riddle.

PITTMAN DENTAL LABORATORY
2355 Centennial Circle, Gainesville GA 30504. 770/534-4457. **Fax:** 770/503-1173. **World Wide Web address:** http://www.pittmandental.com. **Contact:** Human Resources. **Description:** A dental laboratory that manufactures crowns, bridges, and dentures.

SATILLA CARDIAC AND PULMONARY REHABILITATION CENTER
2004 Pioneer Street, Waycross GA 31501. 912/284-2410. **Contact:** Human Resources. **E-mail address:** recruiting@satilla.org. **World Wide Web address:** http://www.satilla.org. **Description:** An outpatient facility that provides rehabilitation services and instructions on lifestyle changes to patients diagnosed with heart disease. **NOTE:** Human Resources phone is 912/287-2630. Please visit website to search for jobs and apply online. **Positions advertised include:** Cash Control Officer; Cardiac Sonographer; Pharmacist; Occupational Therapist; Ultrasound Radiology Technologist; CRT-RCP; RN – Various Departments; LPN – Various Department; CNA; Dietary Manager. **Parent company:** Satilla Health Services, Inc. **CEO:** Robert M. Trimm.

SATILLA REGIONAL MEDICAL CENTER
SATILLA HEALTH SERVICES, INC.
P.O. Box 139, Waycross GA 31501. 912/283-3030. **Physical address:** 410 Darling Avenue, Waycross GA 31501. 912/283-3030. **Fax:** 912/287-2632. **Recorded jobline:** 912/338-6308.**Contact:** Human Resources. **E-mail address:** recruiting@satilla.org. **World Wide Web address:** http://www.satilla.org. **Description:** A 257-bed acute care hospital. **NOTE:** Human Resources phone is 912/287-2630. Please visit website to search for jobs and apply online, or write to request an application. Applications are accepted Tuesday, Wednesday, and Thursday, from 9:00 a.m. – 3:00 p.m. **Positions advertised include:** Cash Control Officer; Cardiac Sonographer; Pharmacist; Occupational Therapist; Ultrasound Radiology Technologist; CRT-RCP; RN – Various Departments; LPN – Various Department; CNA; Dietary Manager. **Parent company:** Satilla Health Services, Inc. (also at this location). **President/CEO:** Robert M. Trimm.

SOUTH FULTON MEDICAL CENTER
1170 Cleveland Avenue, East Point GA 30344. 404/466-1170. **Fax:** 404/466-1120. **Recorded jobline:** 404/466-1200, Ext. 1. **Contact:** Recruitment. **World Wide Web address:** http://www.southfultonmedicalcenter.com. **Description:** A nonprofit, 392-bed, acute care facility serving the metropolitan Atlanta area. South Fulton Medical Center is affiliated with Emory University System of Health. Founded in 1963. **NOTE:** Please visit website to search for jobs and access online application form. **Positions advertised include:** RN – Various Departments; Case Manager; Secretary; Patient Care Assistant; Emergency Room Technician; Radiology Technician; MRI/CT Scanner Technician; Unit Supervisor – Nursing/SNF Rehabilitation; HVAC Mechanic; Transport/Courier; Accountant; Pharmacy Technician. **Parent company:** Tenet Healthcare Corporation. **Listed on:** New York Stock Exchange. **Stock exchange symbol:** THC.

SOUTHEAST GEORGIA REGIONAL MEDICAL CENTER
2415 Parkwood Drive, Brunswick GA 31520. 912/466-7000. **Fax:** 912/466-3113. **Recorded jobline:** Nursing positions – 912/466-5512; Non-nursing positions – 912/466-5515. **Contact:** Human Resources. **E-mail address:** careers@sghs.org. **World Wide Web address:** http://www.sghs.org/brunswick.php. **Description:** A 316-bed hospital offering full medical service, except open heart surgery. **NOTE:** Please visit website to search for jobs. **Positions advertised include:** **Manager** – Core Laboratory; CT Technologist; CAN; LPN; RN; Physical Therapist; MRI Technologist; Team Coordinator; Unit Coordinator Applications Analyst; Medical Office Assistant; Application Analyst; Director of Development; Family Nurse Practitioner; Occupational Therapist; Operating Room Assistant; Clerical Assistant; Senior Financial analyst; Clinical Auditor; Coding Specialist; HR Generalist; Maintenance Assistant; Infection Control Practitioner. **Special programs:** Internships. **Other area location:** Camden GA. **Parent company:** Southeast Georgia Health System. **Operations at this facility include:** Administration; Service. **Number of employees at this location:** 1,500.

SURGICAL INFORMATION SYSTEMS
3650 Mansell Road, Suite 300, Alpharetta GA 30022. 770/643-5555. **Toll-free phone:** 800/866-0656. **Fax:** 770/643-5777. **Contact:** Human Resources. **E-mail address:** jobs@orsoftware.com. **World Wide Web address:** http://www.orsoftware.com. **Description:** Provides physician management services for hospitals and health care facilities. The company's divisions serve the health care industry by assisting hospitals and physicians in the organization and operation of cost-effective health care, improved productivity and low costs in operating rooms, and physician placement services. **NOTE:** Please visit website for a listing of jobs. **Positions advertised include:** Surgical Software Implementation Consultant.

TENDER LOVING CARE/STAFF BUILDERS
100 Hannover Park Road, Atlanta GA 30350. 678/323-1640. **Fax:** 678/323-1641. **Contact:** Human Resources. **World Wide Web address:** http://www.tlcathome.com. **Description:** A nonprofit home health care agency. **NOTE:** There are two locations in Atlanta. Another office is located at 3401 Norman Berry Drive # 138. Entry-level positions are offered. Please visit website to register, search for jobs, and apply online. **Positions advertised include:** Home Care Nurse; Occupational Therapist; Physical Therapist. **Corporate headquarters location:** Lake Success NY. **Other U.S. locations:** Nationwide. **CEO:** James Happ. **Number of employees nationwide:** 20,000.

THERAGENICS CORPORATION
5203 Bristol Industrial Way, Buford GA 30518. 770/271-0233. **Toll-free phone:** 800/998-8479. **Fax:** 770/831-4369. **Contact:** Human Resources. **E-mail address:** pfeiferk@theragenics.com. **World Wide Web address:** http://www.theragenics.com. **Description:** Develops and manufactures implantable radiation devices for the treatment of prostate cancer. Founded in 1981. **Positions advertised include:** Advanced Process Chemical Development Engineer; Network Systems Administrator. **Corporate headquarters location:** This location. **Other U.S. locations:** Oak Ridge TN. **Listed on:** New York Stock Exchange. **Stock exchange symbol:** TGX.

TY COBB HEALTHCARE SYSTEM, INC.
P.O. Box 589, Royston GA 30662. 706/245-5071. **Physical address:** 521 Franklin Springs Street, Royston GA. **Fax:** 706/245-1831. **Contact:** Personnel. **World Wide Web address:** http://www.tycobbhealthcare.org. **Description:** Operates a 71-bed hospital. Specializations include physical and speech therapy, as well as pediatric and occupational therapy. **NOTE:** Contact Personnel directly at 706/245-1846. Entry-level positions and second and third shifts are offered. Please visit website to search for jobs. **Positions advertised include:** RN; CNA; Dietician; Food Service Worker; Respiratory Therapist; Case Manager; Administrative Assistant; Patient Access Representative; Pharmacist; Custodian; RN Supervisor; Dietary Aide; Radiology Technician. **Special programs:** Training. **CEO:** Chuck Adams.

TYCO HEALTHCARE/ KENDALL
110 Kendall Parklane, Atlanta GA 30336. 404/344-7400. **Contact:** Human Resources. **World Wide Web address:** http://www.tycohealthcare.com. **Description:** Manufactures and distributes adult incontinence products for hospitals and nursing homes. **NOTE:** Please visit http://www.tycohealthcarecareers.com to search for jobs and apply online. **Corporate headquarters location:** Mansfield MA. **Other U.S. locations:** Nationwide. **International locations:** Canada; Mexico. **Parent company:** Tyco Healthcare. **President/CEO:** Rich Meelia.

UNIVERSITY HEALTH CARE SYSTEM
UNIVERSITY HOSPITAL
1350 Walton Way, Augusta GA 30901-2629. 706/774-8982. **Toll-free phone:** 800/338-9599. **Fax:** 706/774-8782. **Recorded jobline:** 706/774-8933. **Contact:** Human Resources. **World Wide Web address:** http://www.universityhealth.org. **Description:** A nonprofit, comprehensive healthcare system. University Hospital (also at this location) is a full-service, 612-bed hospital. Founded in 1818. **NOTE:** Please visit website to search for jobs and apply online. Entry-level positions and second and third shifts are offered. Printed lists of open positions are available for pickup at the Human Resources lobby during office hours. **Special programs:** Internships. **Office hours:** Monday – Friday, 7:00 a.m. – 7:00 p.m. **Corporate headquarters location:** This location. **Operations at this facility include:** Administration; Service. **Listed on:** Privately held.

VISITING NURSE HEALTH SYSTEM
1066 Bay Circle, Norcross GA 30071. 770/454-0900. **Toll-free phone:** 800/800-8647. **Recorded jobline:** 770/451-4044. **Contact:** Human Resources. **World Wide Web address:** http://www.vnhs.org. **Description:** A nonprofit home health care agency. Founded in 1940. **NOTE:** Second and third shifts are offered. Please mail resumes to 6610 Bay Circle Suite A Norcross GA 30071; fax to 770/936-1044. **Positions advertised include:** Health Information Specialist; Medical Collector; Medical Records Coordinator; Pharmacy Billing Clerk; Delivery Technician; Equipment Technician II; Occupational Therapist; Pharmacist; Pharmacy Operations Manager; Respiratory Therapist; Area Nursing Director; Evening Nursing Team Leader; Level II RN; LPN Floater; Weekend Admissions Nurse. **Special programs:** Internships. **Other area locations:** Buford GA.

WAYNE MEMORIAL HOSPITAL
P.O. Box 410, Jesup GA 31598. 912/427-6811. **Physical address:** 865 South First Street, Jesup GA 31545. **Fax:** 912/530-3106. **Contact:** Human Resources. **E-mail address:** sdaniel@wmhweb.com. **World Wide Web address:** http://www.wmhweb.com. **Description:** A short-term health care facility. **NOTE:** Please visit website to see listed jobs. Contact Human Resources at 912/530-3309. **Positions advertised include:** Nuclear Medical Technician; Medical Lab Technologist; Respiratory Therapist; Clinical Pharmacist; Physical Therapist; Physical Therapist Director.

WESLEY WOODS CENTER OF EMORY UNIVERSITY
1817 Clifton Road, Atlanta GA 30329. 404/728-6200. **Contact:** Employment Coordinator. **E-mail address:** careers@emoryhealthcare.org. **World Wide Web address:** http://www.emoryhealthcare.org/departments/WW/index.html. **Description:** A 100-bed geriatric hospital specializing in rehabilitation, psychiatry, and neurology. Wesley Woods is a residential facility providing intermediate health care. **NOTE:** Contact corporate Employment office at 404/712-4938. Please visit website to register, search for jobs, and apply online, **Positions advertised include:** Accounting Assistant; Clinical Nutritionist; Computer Tomography Technologist; Environmental Services Aide; Food Services Attendant; Infection Control Assistant; LPN; Nursing Technician; Occupational Therapist; Occupational Therapy Assistant; Physical Therapist; Receptionist; RN; Respiratory Therapist; Speech Pathologist; Supervisor – Nursing Administration. **Special programs:** Internships. **Parent company:** Emory Heathcare. **Number of employees at this location:** 868.

Hawaii

CASTLE MEDICAL CENTER
640 Ulukahiki Street, Kailua HI 96734-4498. 808/263-5500. **Fax:** 808/266-3617. **Contact:** Human Resources. **World Wide Web address:** http://www.castlemed.com. **Description:** A full-service, acute care hospital offering both inpatient care and outpatient programs. **NOTE:** Search available openings and apply online. **Positions advertised include:** Cardiac Cath Lab Coordinator; Contract/Reimbursement Specialist; Counselor; Medical Technologist; Radiologic Technologist; Security Officer. **Special programs:** Volunteer Opportunities available. Call 808/263-5252, or e-mail kongfk@ah.org. **Parent company:** Adventist Health System/West. **Number of employees at this location:** 800.

HILO MEDICAL CENTER
1190 Waianuenue Avenue, Hilo HI 96720. 808/974-6837. **Fax:** 808/733-4028. **Contact:** Human Resources. **E-mail address:** hmcrecruit@hhsc.org. **World Wide Web address:** http://www.hmc.hhsc.org. **Description:** A 274-bed facility providing acute, long-term care, and psychiatric services to the island's central, eastern, and southern sectors. **Positions advertised include:** Contract Administrator; Regional Director of Radiology; Student Helper; Biomed Engineering Supervisor; Chargemaster Coordinator; Speech Pathologist. **Special programs:** Internships. **Corporate headquarters location:** Honolulu HI. **Parent company:** Hawaii Health Systems Corporation. **Number of employees at this location:** 850.

KAHI MOHALA BEHAVIORAL HEALTH
91-2301 Old Fort Weaver Road, Ewa Beach HI 96706. 808/677-2525. **Toll-free phone:** 800/999-9889. **Fax:** 808/677-2570. **Recorded jobline:** 808/948-2525. **Contact:** Christina Enoka, Director of Human Resources. **World Wide Web address:** http://www.kahimohala.org. **Description:** A freestanding, community-based, non-profit psychiatric hospital. **Positions advertised include:** Clinical Director; Child/Adolescent Specialist; Cook; Clinical Therapist; Purchasing Technician; Unit Clerk; Staff

Pharmacist; Staff Development Coordinator. **Special programs:** Training. **Corporate headquarters location:** Sacramento CA. **Parent company:** Sutter Health. **Number of employees at this location:** 225.

KAPIOLANI HEALTH
55 Merchant Street, 23rd Floor, Honolulu HI 96813. 808/535-7555. **Contact:** Human Resources. **World Wide Web address:** http://www.kapiolani.org. **Description:** Kapiolani Health operates two flagship hospitals, Kapiolani Medical Center for Women and Children and Kapiolani Medical Center at Pali Momi, as well as Kapiolani Health Research institute, Kapiolani Women's Center, and Kapioloani Health Foundation. **NOTE:** Search for available positions and apply online at http://www.hawaiipacifichealth.org. **Positions advertised include:** Child Life Specialist; Clinical Assistant; Genetic Counselor; Information Assistant. **Parent Company:** Hawaii Pacific Health.

THE QUEEN'S MEDICAL CENTER
1301 Punchbowl Street, Honolulu HI 96813. 808/547-4627. **Contact:** Human Resources. **E-mail address:** hr_recruitment@queens.org. **World Wide Web address:** http://www.queens.org. **Description:** A private, non-profit, acute care medical facility. As the largest private hospitals in Hawaii, it operates with 533 beds. **Positions advertised include:** Director of Behavioral Health; Controller; Social Worker; Nurse Manager; Radiologic Technologist. **Special Programs:** Volunteer work available. Contact Queen's Volunteer Services at 808/547-4397. **Parent company:** The Queen's Health Systems. **Operations at this facility include:** Administration and Health Care Services. **Number of employees at this location:** 3,000.

REHABILITATION HOSPITAL OF THE PACIFIC
226 North Kuakini Street, Honolulu HI 96817. 808/544-3334. extension 334. **Fax:** 808/544-3337. **Contact:** Human Resources. **E-mail address:** hr@rehabhospital.org. **World Wide Web address:** http://www.rehabhospital.org. **Description:** A comprehensive physical rehabilitation hospital offering both inpatient and outpatient services to individuals with physical disabilities. The hospital is licensed for 100 acute beds. The outpatient network consists of 7 clinics on the islands of Oahu, Maui, and Hawaii. **NOTE:** Search available positions and apply online. **Positions advertised include:** Physical Therapist; Occupational Therapist; Accountant; Manager of Revenue Cycle; Patient Registrar; Food Service Worker; Housekeeper; Therapy Scheduler; Security Officer. **President/CEO:** Stuart T.K. Ho. **Number of employees at this location:** 400.

ST. FRANCIS HEALTHCARE SYSTEM OF HAWAII
2230 Liliha Street, Honolulu HI 96820. 808/678-7100. **Fax:** 808/547-6352. **Contact:** Recruitment and Employment. **E-mail address:** apply@sfhs-hi.org. **World Wide Web address:** http://www.stfrancishawaii.org. **Description:** A nonprofit, acute care, Catholic hospital sponsored by The Sisters of the Third Franciscan Order of Syracuse NY. Under the system are the Liliha Medical Center, the West Medical Center, Hospice Nuuanu, Hospice West, and Homecare services. **NOTE:** For Physician opportunities, call Susan Hashimoto at 808/547-6290. **Positions advertised include:** Accounting Analyst; Call Center Scheduling Representative; Chaplain; Human Resources Assistant; Mission Educator; Network Engineer; Worker's Compensation Coordinator. **Special programs:** Internships; Training; Summer Jobs. **Number of employees at this location:** 2,400.

STRAUB CLINIC & HOSPITAL
888 South King Street, Honolulu HI 96813. 808/535-7571. **Toll-free phone:** 800/850-8916. **Fax:** 808/522-4060. **Contact:** Human Resources. **World Wide Web address:** http://www.straubhealth.com. **Description:** As an affiliate of Hawaii Pacific Health, Straub is a private, nonprofit hospital and clinic with 200 physician specialists. **NOTE:** For physician positions, contact Ellen Kaye, Physician Recruitment Coordinator by e-mail at ekaye@straub.net, by telephone at 808/522-3006 or 800/578-7282, or by fax at 808/522-4006. For all other positions, search for current openings and apply through the Hawaii Pacific Health website at http://www.hawaiipacifichealth.org/careers/careers-index.html. **Positions advertised include:** Anesthesiologist; Echo Technologist; File Clerk; Medical Assistant; Occupational Therapist; Patient Account Representative.

WILCOX MEMORIAL HOSPITAL
3420 Kuhio Highway, Lihue HI 96766. 808/245-1100. **Fax:** 808/245-1211. **Contact:** Human Resources. **World Wide Web address:** http://www.wilcoxhealth.org. **Description:** An affiliate of Hawaii Pacific Health, Wilcox Memorial Hospital cares for about 70% of the residents on Kauai. Services include 24-hour emergency care, labor and delivery, and surgeries. **NOTE:** Search current job openings and apply through the Hawaii Pacific Health website at http://www.hawaiipacifichealth.org/careers/careers-index.html. **Positions advertised include:** Echo Technologist; Financial Counselor; Patient Account Representative; Registered Nurse; Receptionist; Technical Analyst; Ultrasonographer. **Number of employees at this location:** 600.

Idaho

BENEWAH COMMUNITY HOSPITAL
229 South Seventh Street, Saint Maries ID 83861. 208/245-5551. **Fax:** 208/245-2262. **Contact:** Debbie Kerns, Human Resources Department. **World Wide Web address:** http://www.chmed.org. **Description:** Benewah Community Hospital is a 19-bed Critical Access Hospital that offers diagnostic and therapeutic services. The recent completion of a $1.6 million surgical suite expansion allows for the provision of general, orthopedic and cataract surgeries. **NOTE:** Applications can be completed and printed out online. Return completed applications with a current resume to Human Resources by mail, fax or in person with the hospital front desk. Applications are accepted Monday – Friday, 6:00 am – 6:00 pm. **Number of employees:** 145.

BINGHAM MEMORIAL HOSPITAL
98 Poplar Street, Blackfoot ID 83221-1758. 208/785-3841. **Fax:** 208/785-3842. **Contact:** Tara Preston, Human Resources. **E-mail address:** tpreston@binghammemorial.org. **World Wide Web address:** http://www.binghammemorial.org. **Description:** Bingham Memorial Hospital has a 40-bed acute care division, a birthing center, and a variety of rehabilitative outpatient services including physical therapy. Bingham County Extended Care Facility (also at this location) is a 100-bed long-term care facility. **NOTE:** Applications can be completed or printed out online, or contact human resources to have one mailed to you. **Positions advertised include:** Acute Care Director; House Supervisor; Engineering Tech; Phlebotomist; Registered Nurse, ER. **Number of employees at this location:** 300.

BUSINESS PSYCHOLOGY ASSOCIATES
380 East Parkcenter Boulevard, Suite 300, Boise ID 83706. 208/343-4080. **Toll-free phone:** 800/486-4372. **Fax:** 208/344-7430. **Contact:** Sarah Woodley, Manager of Operations. **World Wide Web address:** http://www.bpahealth.com. **Description:** Business Psychology Associates is both an employee assistance program (EAP) and a managed behavioral healthcare organization (MBHO). BPA serves the behavioral health needs of more than 200,000 members nationwide. **NOTE:** Applicants for counselor positions should address inquiries to the attention of Bruce Wixson, Clinical Supervisor. Applicants for office administrative positions should address inquiries to Sarah Woodley, Manager of Operations.

IDAHO ELKS REHABILITATION HOSPITAL
600 North Robbins Road, Boise ID 83702. 208/489-4444. **Fax:** 208/489-4005. **Contact:** Jim Atkins,

Director-Employee Services. **E-mail address:** jatkins@ierh.org. **World Wide Web address:** http://www.idahoelksrehab.org. **Description:** A rehabilitation hospital providing inpatient and outpatient services. Founded in 1941, this hospital began as a convalescent home for children recovering from polio. A new, state-of-the-art facility was opened in 2001.

WALTER KNOX MEMORIAL HOSPITAL
1202 East Locust Street, Emmett ID 83617-2715. 208/365-3561. **Contact:** Michael Cornell, Human Resources Department. **E-mail address:** cornellm@wkmh.org. **World Wide Web address:** http://www.wkmh.org. **Description:** A 24-bed, acute care hospital that offers a full range of general medical and surgical services as well as specialty services. **NOTE**: Apply online or contact Human Resources. **Positions advertised include:** Medical Assistant; Registered Nurse; LPN. **CEO:** Max Long.

MAGIC VALLEY REGIONAL MEDICAL CENTER
P.O. Box 409, Twin Falls ID 83303. 208/737-2000. **Recorded jobline:** 208/737-2775. **Contact:** Human Resources. **E-mail address:** jessicat@mvrmc.com **World Wide Web address:** http://www.mvrmc.com. **Description:** The medical facility's services include the Southern Idaho Regional Cancer Center, home care services, a same-day surgery center, an intensive care unit, emergency transport services, a 24-hour physician-staffed emergency department, maternity and newborn services, physical therapy, and a pharmacy. **NOTE:** Unsolicited resumes and applications are not accepted. See website for position listings and information on how to apply.

MERCY MEDICAL CENTER
1512 12th Avenue Road, Nampa ID 83686. 208/463-5800. **Recorded jobline:** 208/463-5802. **Contact:** Human Resources. **World Wide Web address:** http://www.mercymedicalnampa.com. **Description:** Mercy Medical Center is a 152-bed community-based, acute care hospital. **NOTE:** See website for open positions, to apply online and to sign up for Career-Mail, an e-mail service that automatically sends an e-mail when new job openings are posted. **Positions advertised include:** Clinical Dietician; Clinical Specialist; Driver; Food Tech; Med Tech; Occupational Therapist; PBX Operator; Physical Therapy Assistant; Phlebotomist; Pharmacist; Registered Nurse. **Parent Company:** Catholic Health Initiatives (CHI.) **Number of employees at this location:** 700.

SAINT LUKE'S REGIONAL MEDICAL CENTER
148 East Jefferson Street, Boise ID 83712. **Toll-free phone:** 800/722-7052. **Fax:** 208/381-4649. **Recorded jobline:** 208/381-1187. **Contact:** Human Resources. **E-mail address:** jobs@slrmc.org. **World Wide Web address:** http://www.stlukesonline.org. **Description:** Idaho's largest healthcare provider with full service hospitals and twenty-five outpatient treatment facilities and clinics. **Positions advertised include:** A variety of clerical, service, technical, professional and management, registered nursing and graduate (registered) nursing positions listed. **Other area locations:** Meridian ID; Ketchum ID.

SALTZER MEDICAL GROUP
215 East Hawaii Avenue, Nampa ID 83686. 208/463-3000. **Contact:** Human Resources. **World Wide Web address:** http://www.saltzermedical.com. **Description:** A multi-specialty medical group whose providers represent such practice areas as pediatrics, orthopedics, family practice, internal medicine, surgery, ENT, urology, OB and gynecology, rheumatology, endocrinology, dermatology, ophthalmology, neurology and pulmonology. Saltzer Medical Group operates five facilities throughout the greater Boise-Nampa metropolitan area. **Positions advertised include:** Physician Assistant/Nurse Practitioner; Registered Nurse; Part-Time Medical Assistant; Customer Service Representative; Full-Time Medical Assistant; Customer Service Representative; Physical Therapist; Coder/Biller; Radiology Clerk and Dark Room Aide; Administrative Clerk.

SHOSHONE MEDICAL CENTER
25 Jacobs Gulch Road, Kellogg ID 83837. 208/784-1221. **Fax:** 208/784-0961. **Contact:** Wanda Groves, Human Resources. **E-mail address:** wgroves@shomed.org. **World Wide Web address:** http://www.shomed.org. **Description:** A 25-bed, community-owned hospital serving the Silver Valley of North Idaho. Offers emergency care, general surgery, orthopedic surgery and a full range of outpatient Services. Founded in 1958. **NOTE**: Shoshone Medical Center only accepts applications for posted positions, with the exception of Registered Nurse, Radiology Technician and Laboratory Technician applicants. Check *The Spokesman Review* classified ads for current openings. **Company slogan:** Excellence in health care. **Positions advertised include:** Peri-Operative Registered Nurse; Therapist. **Corporate headquarters location:** This location. **CEO:** Gary M. Moore.

STATE HOSPITAL NORTH
300 Hospital Drive, Orofino ID 83544. 208/476-4511. **Fax:** 208/476-7898. **Contact:** Quinn Galbraith or Sharon Larson of Human Resources Staff; or Debbie Manfull, Assistant Administrative Director. **World Wide Web address:** http://www.welcome.to/shn. **Description:** A 50-bed residential psychiatric hospital for adults. State Hospital North also has a chemical dependency unit. **NOTE:** Inquiries about employment can be faxed to the hospital. Current positions also listed on the Idaho Hospital Association website: http://www.teamiha.org.

STATE HOSPITAL SOUTH
700 East Alice Street, P.O. Box 400, Blackfoot ID 83221. 208/785-1200. **Fax:** 208-785-8519. **Contact:** Jackie Wieland, Human Resources. **E-mail address:** wielandJ@idhw.state.id.us. **Description:** A 136-bed, JCAHO-accredited, state-owned psychiatric hospital. **NOTE:** Current positions also listed on the Idaho Hospital Association website: http://www.teamiha.org.

WEST VALLEY MEDICAL CENTER
1717 Arlington Avenue, Caldwell ID 83605. 208/455-3835. **Fax:** 208/455-4057. **Recorded jobline:** 208/455-3828. **Contact:** Human Resources. **E-mail address:** hrdept@westvalleymedctr.com. **World Wide Web address:** http://www.westvalleymedctr.com. **Description:** West Valley Medical Center is a 150-bed hospital serving many western Idaho communities as well as eastern Oregon. Founded in 1950. **NOTE:** Apply for positions by downloading a job application from the website. Once completed, send or fax it along with a resume and cover letter to the hospital. **Positions advertised include:** Registered Nurse - Critical Care Unit/Nights; Physical Therapist Assistant; Certified Occupational Therapist; Psych Tech; Speech Therapist; Part-Time HR Assistant; PBX Operator; Director, Skill Nursing; Custodian.

Illinois

ADVOCATE GOOD SAMARITAN HOSPITAL
3815 Highland Avenue, Downers Grove IL 60515. 630/275-5900. **Contact:** Human Resources. **World Wide Web address:** http://www.advocatehealth.com. **Description:** A 300-bed hospital offering a wide range of health services from emergency care to pediatrics. **NOTE:** Apply online. **Positions advertised include:** Central Outpatient Scheduler; Cleaning and Process Technician; Clinical Education Specialist; RN (Various); Physician (Various).

ADVOCATE ILLINOIS MASONIC MEDICAL CENTER
836 West Wellington Avenue, Chicago IL 60657. 773/975-1600. Contact: Human Resources. **World Wide Web address:** http://www.advocatehealth.com/immc. **Description:** A hospital specializing in oncology, cardiology and emergency care. **NOTE:** Apply online.

ALEXIAN BROTHERS MEDICAL CENTER
800 Biesterfield Road, Elk Grove Village IL 60007. 847/437-5500. **Contact:** Human Resources. **World Wide Web address:** http://www.alexian.org. **Description:** A nonprofit, acute care hospital. Alexian Brothers Medical Center offers a wide range of health care services including oncology, radiology, mental health, and obstetrics. Founded in 1972. **NOTE:** This medical center is part of the Alexian Brothers Health System, which includes Alexian Brothers Behavioral Hospital and St. Alexius Medical Center, both in Hoffman Estates IL. Job listings for this hospital and the others can be found at http://www.alexianjobs.org. **Positions advertised include:** Registered Nurse; LPN; Education Coordinator; Critical Care Respiratory Therapist; Staff Chaplains; Administrative Director Perioperative Services, Cardiology Services Director.

ALTON MENTAL HEALTH CENTER
4500 College Avenue, Alton IL 62002. 618/474-3200. **Fax:** 618/465-4800. **Contact:** Human Resources. **Description:** An inpatient medical facility specializing in the treatment of psychiatric developmental disabilities. Part of the Illinois Department of Human Services.

AMERICAN DENTAL ASSOCIATION
211 East Chicago Avenue, Chicago IL 60611. 312/440-2500. **Contact:** Human Resources. **E-mail address:** jobs@ada.org. **World Wide Web address:** http://www.ada.org. **Description:** A professional association serving the dental community. **Positions advertised include:** Senior Manager, Corporate Relations and Marketing; Marketing Communications Director; Operations Specialist; Editorial/Advertising Assistant; Production Associate, Client Services. **Corporate headquarters location:** This location.

AMERICAN OSTEOPATHIC ASSOCIATION
142 East Ontario Street, Chicago IL 60611-2864. 312/202-8000. **Toll-free phone:** 800/621-1773. **Fax:** 312/202-8200. **Contact:** Human Resources. **E-mail address:** recruiter@osteopathic.org. **World Wide Web address:** http://www.osteopathic.org. **Description:** The AOA is a member association representing more than 54,000 osteopathic physicians. The AOA serves as the primary certifying body for osteopathic physicians and is the accrediting agency for all osteopathic medical colleges and health care facilities. The AOA's mission is to advance the philosophy and practice of osteopathic medicine by promoting excellence in education, research, and the delivery of quality, cost-effective healthcare within a distinct, unified profession. **NOTE:** Search for open positions online. **Positions advertised include:** Administrative Assistant; Editorial Assistant; HR Manager; Program Educational Specialist; Research Director. **Corporate headquarters location:** This location.

BAXTER HEALTHCARE CORPORATION
Route 120 and Wilson Road, Round Lake IL 60073. 847/270-5850. **Contact:** Human Resources. **World Wide Web address:** http://www.baxter.com. **Description:** Baxter Healthcare operates four global businesses: Biotechnology develops therapies and products in transfusion medicine; Cardiovascular Medicine develops products and provides services to treat late-stage cardiovascular disease; Renal Therapy develops products and provides services to improve therapies to fight kidney disease; and Intravenous Systems/Medical Products develops technologies and systems to improve intravenous medication delivery and distributes disposable medical products. **NOTE:** Apply online at the company's website. **Corporate headquarters location:** Deerfield IL. **Operations at this facility include:** This location is a research facility. **Listed on:** New York Stock Exchange. **Stock exchange symbol:** BAX. **Number of employees worldwide:** 48,000.

BAXTER INTERNATIONAL, INC.
One Baxter Parkway, Deerfield IL 60015. 847/948-2000. **Toll-free phone:** 800/422-9827. **Fax:** 847/948-2964. **Contact:** Human Resources. **World Wide Web address:** http://www.baxter.com. **Description:** A global medical products and services company that is a leader in technologies related to blood and the circulatory system. The company operates four global businesses: Biotechnology develops therapies and products in transfusion medicine; Cardiovascular Medicine develops products and provides services to treat late-stage cardiovascular disease; Renal Therapy develops products and provides services to improve therapies to fight kidney disease; and Intravenous Systems/Medical Products develops technologies and systems to improve intravenous medication delivery and distributes disposable medical products. **NOTE:** Apply online. **Positions advertised include:** Communications Manager; Senior Paralegal; Training and eLearning. . **Special programs:** Internships. **Corporate headquarters location:** This location. **Operations at this facility include:** Administration. **Listed on:** New York Stock Exchange. **Stock exchange symbol:** BAX. **Number of employees worldwide:** 48,000.

BEVERLY FARM FOUNDATION INC.
6301 Humbert Road, Godfrey IL 62035. 618/466-0367. **Contact:** Peggy Price, Human Resources. **E-mail address:** pprice@beverlyfarm.org. **World Wide Web address:** http://www.beverlyfarm.org. **Description:** A nonprofit residential care facility for developmentally disabled individuals. **Positions advertised include:** Dietary Aide; Client Program Coordinator. **Office hours:** Monday – Friday, 8:00 a.m. – 4:30 p.m.

BROMENN REGIONAL MEDICAL CENTER
Franklin & Virginia Streets, Normal IL 61761. 309/268-5717. **Contact:** Human Resources. **World Wide Web address:** http://www.bromenn.org. **Description:** A 244-bed hospital offering a variety of inpatient, outpatient, rehabilitation, acute, and preventive health care services including women's and children's, emergency and trauma, neurological, cardiac, and pulmonary, and orthopedic. **NOTE:** A completed application is required for any position. Apply online. **Positions advertised include:** Cardiovascular Operating Room Technician; Coder; Cook; Help Desk Operator; Lead Patient Service Representative; Nursing Technician; Physical Therapist. **Parent company:** Bromenn Healthcare. **Operations at this facility include:** Administration; Service.

CGH MEDICAL CENTER
100 East LeFevre Road, Sterling IL 61081-1279. 815/625-0400. **Contact:** Director of Human Resources. **World Wide Web address:** http://www.cghmc.com. **Description:** An acute care trauma center housing a variety of specialty centers including home nursing, home health, sleep disorder, and speech and hearing. **NOTE:** See website for job listings. An application is required for any position. Download an application from the website and mail it or apply online. **Positions advertised include:** Patient Registration Clerk; RN.

CARDINAL HEALTH
1430 Waukegan Road, McGraw Park IL 60085. 847/578-9500. **Contact:** Human Resources. **World Wide Web address:** http://www.cardinal.com. **Description:** Cardinal Health is a producer, developer, and distributor of medical products and technologies for use in hospitals and other health care settings. The company operates through two industry segments: medical specialties, and medical/laboratory products and distribution. **NOTE:** Apply online. **Corporate headquarters location:** Dublin OH. **Operations at this facility include:** This location distributes medical supplies to hospitals and government facilities. Number of employees worldwide: 55,000. **Listed on:** New York Stock Exchange. **Stock exchange symbol:** CAH.

CAREMARK INTERNATIONAL
2211 Sanders Road, Northbrook IL 60062. 847/559-4700. **Contact:** Director of Human Resources. **World Wide Web address:** http://www.caremark.com. **Description:** A leading provider of patient services through health care networks. Divisions include

physician practice management and pharmaceutical services, which includes one of the country's largest independent pharmacy benefit management programs, serving approximately 29 million Americans through a mail-order and retail network of pharmacies. AdvancePCS, a mail-order prescription company, is also part of Caremark. Apply online. **International locations:** Worldwide. **Operations at this facility include:** Administration; Operations. **Listed on:** New York Stock Exchange. **Stock exchange symbol:** CMX.

CARLE FOUNDATION HOSPITAL
611 West Park Street, Urbana IL 61801. 217/383-4000. **Fax:** 217/383-3373. **Contact:** Human Resources. **E-mail address:** Foundation.HR@carle.com. **World Wide Web address:** http://www.carle.com/CFH/about. **Description:** A 295-bed, tertiary care and regional trauma center. Carle Foundation Hospital also includes a 295-bed, long-term care facility, home care agency, retail pharmacy, daycare center, and psychiatric and chemical dependency services. This hospital also provides services for the Carle Medical Clinic, (located in the same building) as well as other healthcare facilities throughout Illinois. **NOTE:** Interested jobseekers may mail or apply online for open positions. Resumes and applications are also accepted in the Human Resources office. **Positions advertised include:** Certified/Registered Coder; Inpatient Coding Coordinator; Therapy Office Coordinator; Health Care Technician; Advanced Practice Nurse; Physical Therapist; Telemedicine and Mobile Clinic Coordinator; Contract Administrator; Physician Services Director. **Office hours:** Monday – Friday, 7:00 a.m. – 5:00 p.m.

CENTRAL DUPAGE HOSPITAL BEHAVIORAL HEALTH SERVICES
25 North Winfield Road, Winfield IL 60190. 630/653-4000. **Fax:** 630/933-2652. **Contact:** Human Resources. **E-mail address:** hr@cdh.org. **World Wide Web address:** http://www.cdh.org. **Description:** A mental health and chemical dependency outpatient and inpatient treatment center. **Positions advertised include:** Purchasing Assistant; Physician Peer Review Clinical Decision Support; RN (Various); Home Health Aide.

CHICAGO ASSOCIATION FOR RETARDED CITIZENS (CARC)
8 South Michigan Avenue, Suite 1700, Chicago IL 60603. 312/346/6230. **Contact:** Recruiting Manager. **E-mail address:** recruiting@chgoarc.org. **Description:** Provides self-help and vocational training skills to people with physical and mental disabilities. Operates 14 education and vocational centers throughout the Chicago area. **NOTE:** See website for center locations. Send all resumes and cover letters to this address. **Positions advertised include:** Special Education Teacher; QMRP/Counselor.

DELNOR COMMUNITY HOSPITAL
300 Randall Road, Geneva IL 60134. 630/208-3000. **Contact:** Human Resources. **World Wide Web address:** http://www.delnor.com. **Description:** A 118-bed hospital offering a variety of specialized services including massage therapy, orthopedics, heart care, pediatrics, and cancer care. **NOTE:** Apply online. **Positions advertised include:** RN (Various); Nursing Coordinator; RN Patient Care Coordinator; Special Procedure Anesthetist; Cardiac Ultrasonographer.

EDWARD HOSPITAL
801 South Washington Street, Naperville IL 60540. 630/527-3401. **Contact:** Human Resources. **World Wide Web address:** http://www.edward.org. **Description:** A 159-bed full-service, nonprofit hospital. Edward Hospital provides a number of health services ranging from preventive education to advanced treatment technology. Its 50-acre campus supports a state-of-the-art, all-private-room inpatient facility; Edward Cardiovascular Institute; Edward Health & Fitness Center; Edward Hospital Cancer Center, affiliated with the Oncology Institute at Loyola University Medical Center; CARE Center, a diagnostic program for sexually abused children; and Linden Oaks Hospital, a private psychiatric facility. The hospital also operates Edward Healthcare Center in Bolingbrook, a satellite health care center with primary and specialty care physicians and a full range of diagnostic services. **NOTE:** Complete the online application located on the hospital's website.

ELGIN MENTAL HEALTH CENTER
750 South State Street, Elgin IL 60123. 847/742-1040. **Contact:** Director of Employee Services. **Description:** An inpatient, psychiatric hospital serving the metropolitan and suburban Chicago areas. Part of the Illinois Department of Human Services. **NOTE:** Download an application at the Department of Human Service's website: http://www.dhs.state.i.us/careers.

EVANSTON HOSPITAL CORPORATION
2650 Ridge Avenue, Evanston IL 60201. 847/570-2600. **Fax:** 847/570-1903. **Contact:** Employment Office. **World Wide Web address:** http://www.enh.org. **Description:** Operates Evanston Hospital (also at this location), as well as Glenbrook Hospital (Glenview IL). **NOTE:** Apply online. **Positions advertised include:** RN (Various); Staff Nurse; Physical Medicine Aide; Research Scientist; Audiologist; Patient Service Representative; Nursing Assistant. **Corporate headquarters location:** This location. **Operations at this facility include:** Administration; Regional Headquarters; Service.

GALENA-STRAUSS HOSPITAL & NURSING CARE FACILITY
215 Summit Street, Galena IL 61036. 815/777-1340. **Contact:** Melissa Kaiser, Human Resources Manager. **E-mail address:** mjkaiser@galenastauss.org. **World Wide Web address:** http://www.galenahealth.org. **Description:** A 25-bed, nonprofit, acute care hospital and 60-bed nursing home. Founded in 1962. **NOTE:** Entry-level positions and second and third shifts are offered. **Positions advertised include:** Exercise Specialist; Certified Nurses' Assistant; Laboratory Manager; Assistant Director of Nursing. **Office hours:** Monday - Friday, 8:00 a.m. - 4:00 p.m. **Corporate headquarters location:** This location.

GLENBROOK HOSPITAL
2100 Pfingsten Road, Glenview IL 60026. 847/657-5800. **Contact:** Human Resources. **World Wide Web address:** http://www.enh.org. **Description:** A 136-bed hospital offering a variety of health services including coronary care, plastic surgery, cancer care, and joint replacement. **NOTE:** Apply online. **Positions advertised include:** Medical Secretary; MRI Technologist; EKG Technician; Ophthalmic Technician; Senior Secretary. **Parent company:** Evanston Northwestern Healthcare.

GLENOAKS HOSPITAL
701 Winthrop Avenue, Glendale Heights IL 60139. 630/545-7300. **Fax:** 630/545-3999. **Contact:** Human Resources. **World Wide Web address:** http://www.ahsmidwest.org. **Description:** A 186-bed, nonprofit, acute care hospital. The hospital is affiliated with the Seventh-Day Adventist Church. Founded in 1980. **NOTE:** Second and third shifts are offered. Apply online. **Positions advertised include:** Case Manager; Certified Nurse Midwife; Charge Nurse; CT Technologist; Quality Management Director. **Special programs:** Training. **Office hours:** Monday - Friday, 7:30 a.m. - 4:30 p.m. **Corporate headquarters location:** Washington DC. **Parent company:** Adventist Health System.

GREAT LAKES NAVAL HOSPITAL
3001A Sixth Street, Great Lakes IL 60088. 847/688-4561. **Contact:** Human Resources. **World Wide Web address:** http://www.greatlakes.med.navy.mil. **Description:** A military hospital serving active and retired military personnel and their families in the Midwest region. **NOTE:** This hospital has jobs for military personnel and civilians. Call the regional Human Resources Office at 847/688-2222 to hear job listings and how application procedures.

HARRISBURG MEDICAL CENTER
100 Dr. Warren Tuttle Drive, P.O. Box 428, Harrisburg IL 62946. 618/253-7671x300. **Fax:** 618/252-2077. **Contact:** Human Resources. **World Wide Web address:** http://www.harrisburgmedicalcenter.com. **Description:** A hospital. **NOTE:** See the center's website for application procedures.

HELP AT HOME INC.
17 North State Street, Suite 1400, Chicago IL 60602. 312/762-9999. **Fax:** 312/704-0022. **Contact:** Human Resources. **World Wide Web address:** http://www.helpathome.com. **Description:** Provides homemaker and nurses aide services for the elderly. **Corporate headquarters location:** This location. **Other area locations:** Danville IL; East Alton IL; Galesburg IL; Joliet IL; Macomb IL; Mount Vernon IL; Oak Forest IL; Ottawa IL; Rock Island IL; Rockford IL; Skokie IL; Springfield IL; St. Charles IL; Waukegan IL. **Other U.S. locations:** IN; MO; MI; AL; MS; TN. **Subsidiaries include:** Oxford Health Care. **Listed on:** NASDAQ. **Stock exchange symbol:** HAHI.

EDWARD HINES JR. VA HOSPITAL
P.O. Box 5000, Hines IL 60141. 708/202-8387. **Contact:** Human Resources. **World Wide Web address:** http://www.vagreatlakes.org. **Description:** A medical center operated by the U.S. Department of Veterans Affairs. **NOTE:** For job listings at this facility, visit http://www.vacareers.com. Mail resumes to this location and indicate which center or job you are applying.

HOLY CROSS HOSPITAL
2701 West 68th Street, Chicago IL 60629. 773/471-9050. **Fax:** 773/884-8013. **Contact:** Human Resources. **E-mail address:** hrd@holycrosshospital.org. **World Wide Web address:** http://www.holycrosshospital.org. **Description:** A 331-bed, nonprofit, community hospital offering a wide range of inpatient and outpatient health services. **NOTE:** See website for job listings. Resumes may be mailed or faxed. Interested jobseekers may also apply in person at the Human Resources Office. **Office hours:** Monday – Friday, 8:00 a.m. – 4:30 p.m.

HUDSON RESPIRATORY CARE INC.
900 West University Drive, Arlington Heights IL 60004. 847/259-7400. **Contact:** Althea J. Schuler, Human Resources Manager. **World Wide Web address:** http://www.hudsonrci.com. **Description:** A specialized manufacturer of sterile disposable products for respiratory therapy. **NOTE:** Apply online or fax resumes for open positions. **Positions advertised include:** Territory Sales Manager; Quality Assurance Compliance Specialist. **Corporate headquarters location:** Temecula CA. **Operations at this facility include:** Administration; Manufacturing. **Listed on:** Privately held.

INTERIM HEALTHCARE
3020 West Willow Knolls Drive, Peoria IL 61614. 309/693-7665. **Fax:** 309/693-7664. **Contact:** Human Resources. **World Wide Web address:** http://www.interimhealthcare.com/peoria_il. **Description:** Provides home health care services. **Positions advertised include:** RN; LPN; Physical Therapist; Occupational Therapist; Dental Hygienists; Dental Assistants.

JACKSON PARK HOSPITAL
7531 Stony Island Avenue, Chicago IL 60649. 773/947-7512. **Contact:** Human Resources. **World Wide Web address:** http://www.jacksonparkhospital.com. **Description:** A 326-bed hospital offering inpatient and outpatient services. **NOTE:** Apply in person at the hospital's Human Resources Office. **Office hours**: Monday – Friday: 8:00 a.m. – 4:30 p.m. **Operations at this facility include:** Administration; Service.

KINDRED HOSPITAL/NORTHLAKE
365 East North Avenue, Northlake IL 60164. 708/345-8100. **Contact:** Human Resources. **World Wide Web address:** http://www.kindrednorthlake.com. **Description:** A hospital specializing in wound care; pulmonary medicine; rehabilitative medicine; and vision care. **NOTE:** Apply online. **Positions advertised include:** RN; LPN; Pharmacist; Occupational Therapist; Monitor Technician; Dietary Aide. **Parent company:** Kindred Healthcare.

LA RABIDA CHILDREN'S HOSPITAL
East 65th Street at Lake Michigan, Chicago IL 60649. 773/363-6700x635. **Fax:** 773/363-7905. **Recorded jobline:** 773/363-6700x500. **Contact:** Recruiter. **E-mail address:** gchurnovic@larabida.org. **World Wide Web address:** http://www.larabida.org. **Description:** A 77-bed pediatric hospital specializing in treating children with chronic illnesses and long-term disabilities. Founded in 1896. **NOTE:** Mail, fax or e-mail resumes or visit the Human Resources Office to fill out an application. **Positions advertised include:** Nutritionist; Senior Physical Therapist; Medical Technologist; Speech Language Pathologist; Respiratory Therapist; RN; LPN; Certified Nurse Assistants.

LINDEN OAKS HOSPITAL
801 South Washington Street, Naperville IL 60540. 630/305-5500. **Contact:** Human Resources. **World Wide Web address:** http://www.edward.org. **Description:** A full-service behavioral health care system meeting the needs of persons with emotional, behavioral, and substance abuse problems, as well as eating disorders. Linden Oaks Hospital is located on 10 acres of the Edward Hospital medical campus. **NOTE:** Interested jobseekers may apply online at the hospital's website or in person at the Human Resources Office. **Positions advertised include:** File Clerk; Customer Service Specialist; ER Physician Coder; Financial Counselor; Float Unit Secretary; Case Manager; Mammography Technician. **Special programs:** Internships. **Corporate headquarters location:** Macon GA. **Other U.S. locations:** Nationwide. **Operations at this facility include:** Service. **Listed on:** Privately held.

LITTLE COMPANY OF MARY HOSPITAL
2800 West 95th Street, Evergreen Park IL 60805. 708/422-6200. **Recorded jobline:** 708/229-5050. **Contact:** Human Resources. **World Wide Web address:** http://www.lcmh.org. **Description:** A nonprofit hospital offering a variety of services including oncology, orthopedics, pediatrics, mother/baby care, home care, senior services, and a full-service emergency room. **NOTE:** Jobseekers are encouraged to apply via the website. **Positions advertised include:** Ultrasound Technologist; RN (Various); Surgical Technician; Nurse Manager; Medical Assistant. **Special programs:** Internships; Summer Jobs.

LOMBART MIDWEST INSTRUMENTS
1312 Marquette Drive, Suite G, Romeoville IL 60446. 630/759-7666. **Toll-free phone:** 800/831-1194. **Fax:** 630/759-1744. **Contact:** Human Resources. **Description:** Lombart Midwest Instruments manufactures nonsurgical, ophthalmic equipment for examinations.

McDONOUGH DISTRICT HOSPITAL
525 East Grant Street, Macomb IL 61455. 309/833-4101. **Fax:** 309/836-1677. **Contact:** Human Resources. **E-mail address:** info@mdh.org. **World Wide Web address:** http://www.mdh.org. **Description:** A 120-bed, nonprofit community hospital. **NOTE:** A completed application is require for any position. See website to download an application and mail or fax it or deliver it in person to the Human Resources Office. **Positions advertised include:** Cardiac Rehabilitation Nurse; Physical Therapist; RN (Various); Staff Dietitian; Nursing Instructor. **Office hours:** Monday – Friday, 7:00 a.m. – 4:30 p.m.

MEDLINE INDUSTRIES, INC.
One Medline Place, Mundelein IL 60060. 847/949-5500. **Toll-free phone:** 800/MED-LINE. **Fax:** 847/949-2109. **Contact:** Human Resources. **E-mail**

address: employment@medline.com. **World Wide Web address:** http://www.medline.net. **Description:** One of the largest privately held manufacturers and distributors of health care products including beds, cots, gowns, and wheelchairs. Founded in 1910. **NOTE:** For sales positions, mail resumes to the Sales Recruiter at this location or send resumes via e-mail to salesrecruiter@medline.com. Entry-level positions and second and third shifts are offered. **Positions advertised include:** Product Manager; Quality Control Inspector; Administrative Assistant; Sales Administration Coordinator; Customer Relations Specialist. **Special programs:** Internships; Co-ops; Summer Jobs. **Office hours:** Monday - Friday, 8:00 a.m. - 5:00 p.m. **Corporate headquarters location:** This location. **Other U.S. locations:** Nationwide. **Operations at this facility include:** Administration; Manufacturing; Sales. **Listed on:** Privately held.

MELMEDICA CHILDREN'S HEALTHCARE
17600 South Pulaski Road, Country Club Hills IL 60478. 708/335-3331. **Toll-free phone:** 800/387-PEDS. **Fax:** 630/357-4696. **Contact:** Human Resources. **World Wide Web address:** http://www.melmedica.com. **Description:** Provides private, in-home nursing care primarily in pediatrics. The company also offers limited obstetric services. **NOTE:** For all RN positions, call 800/387-7337 or fax resumes to 800/434-7337.

MEMORIAL HOSPITAL
4500 Memorial Drive, Belleville IL 62226-5399. 618/257-5230. **Fax:** 618/257-6911. **Recorded jobline:** 618/257-5627. **Contact:** Recruiter. **E-mail address:** personnel@memhosp.com. **World Wide Web address:** http://www.memhosp.com. **Description:** A nonprofit, acute and long-term care hospital, housing 346 adult and pediatric beds, 32 bassinets, and a 108-bed skilled nursing facility. **NOTE:** Entry-level, second and third shifts are offered. See website for online application or e-mail resumes. **Positions advertised include:** RN; LPN; CT Scan Technologist; Phlebotomist; Occupational Therapist; Admitting Supervisor. **Number of employees at this location:** 2,200.

MERCY HOSPITAL & MEDICAL CENTER
2525 South Michigan Avenue, Chicago IL 60616. 312/567-2011. **Fax:** 312/567-5562. **Contact:** Kay Jensen, Human Resources Director. **E-mail address:** employment@mercy-chicago.org. **World Wide Web address:** http://www.mercy-chicago.org. **Description:** A mid-size teaching hospital that is part of a network of satellite clinic facilities. NOTE: An application is required for any position. See website for job listings and application. Part-time and second and third shifts are offered. **Positions advertised include:** RN (Various); LPN; Patient Care Attendant; Clinical Lab Assistant; Physical Therapist; Clinical Educator; Speech Pathologist; Coding and Data Research Manager; Laboratory Supervisor; Application Business Analyst. **Operations at this facility include:** Administration; Research and Development; Service.

METHODIST HOSPITAL OF CHICAGO
5015 North Paulina Street, Chicago IL 60640. 773/271-9040. **Contact:** Human Resources. **World Wide Web address:** http://www.bethanymethodist.org. **Description:** A 235-bed, nonprofit, acute care facility that specializes in geriatrics. The hospital is affiliated with a nursing home, retirement community, and immediate care centers. Founded in 1887. **NOTE:** Fax resume or apply in person at the Human Resources Office. Entry-level positions and second and third shifts are offered. **Positions advertised include:** RN; LPN; Coder; Mental Health Social Worker; Phlebotomist. **Internship information:** Internships in Human Resources are coordinated through area schools. Applications for summer internships must be submitted by mid-April. **Parent company:** Bethany Methodist.

MIDWEST DENTAL PRODUCTS CORPORATION
901 West Oakton Street, Des Plaines IL 60018. 847/640-4800. **Toll-free phone:** 800/800-2888. **Contact:** Human Resources. **World Wide Web address:** http://www.midwestdental.com. **Description:** Designs, develops, manufactures, and markets a full line of medical and dental X-ray equipment. **Parent company:** DENTSPLY International.

MIDWESTERN REGIONAL MEDICAL CENTER
2520 Elisha Avenue, Zion IL 60099. 847/872-4561. **Contact:** Human Resources. **World Wide Web address:** http://www.cancercenter.com. **Description:** A community hospital specializing in treating various forms of cancer. **NOTE:** Apply online at http://www.cancercenter.com/employment. **Positions advertised include:** Assistant Director of Imaging; Bone Marrow Transplant; Case Manager; Clinical Manager Assistant; Housekeeper; Medical Technologist.

MOUNT SINAI HOSPITAL
California Avenue at 15th Street, Chicago IL 60608. 773/542-6236. **Contact:** Human Resources. **World Wide Web address:** http://www.sinai.org. **Description:** A 432-bed, tertiary care hospital. Mount Sinai Hospital also serves as a teaching hospital for The Chicago Medical School. **NOTE:** See website for job listings and contact information. Entry-level, part-time and evening positions offered. Jobseekers interested in nursing positions should call 773/257-6566.

NORTHWESTERN MEMORIAL HOSPITAL
251 East Huron Street, Chicago IL 60611. 312/908-2000. **Contact:** Human Resources. **World Wide Web address:** http://www.nmh.org. **Description:** A hospital offering a variety of specialized services ranging from preventive medicine to organ transplantation. Northwestern Memorial also serves as the teaching hospital for Northwestern University Medical School. **NOTE:** See website for job listings and contact information. **Special programs:** Internship.

OTTAWA DENTAL LABORATORY
1304 Starfire Drive, P.O. Box 771, Ottawa IL 61350. **Toll-free phone:** 800/851-8239. **Fax:** 815/434-0760. **Contact:** Joanie Bretag, Human Resources. **E-mail address:** hrodl@ottawadentallab.com. **World Wide Web address:** http://www.ottawadentallab.com. **Description:** A dental lab that manufactures dentures, crowns, bridges, and other dental products. **NOTE:** See website for application.

OUR LADY OF THE RESURRECTION MEDICAL CENTER
5645 West Addison Street, Chicago IL 60634. 773/282-7000. **Recorded jobline:** 877/737-4636(option 9). **Fax:** 773/794-8467. **Contact:** Human Resources. **World Wide Web address:** http://www.reshealth.org. **Description:** A 288-bed, acute care, community hospital. **NOTE:** The hospital only accepts resumes for open positions. See website for job listings and apply online. Evening and part-time positions offered. **Positions advertised include:** Activities Assistant; Certified Nursing Assistant; Environmental Service Worker; Nurse Practitioner; Occupational Therapist.

PALOS COMMUNITY HOSPITAL
12251 South 80th Avenue, Palos Heights IL 60463. 708/923-4880. **Recorded jobline:** 708/923-8088. **Contact:** Human Resources. **World Wide Web address:** http://www.paloshospital.org. **Description:** A community hospital. For professional positions, e-mail resumes to holly_brasher@paloscommunityhospital.org. For support staff positions, e-mail resumes to diane_jorgensen@paoloscommunityhospital.org. E-mail regina_sibley@paloscommunityhospital.org. for nursing positions. Part-time jobs and second and third shifts are offered. **Special programs:** Volunteers.

PEKIN HOSPITAL
600 South 13th Street, Pekin IL 61554. 309/347-1151. **Fax:** 309/347-1249. **Contact:** Human Resources. **E-mail address:** hr@phs1.org. **World Wide Web address:** http://www.pekinhospital.org. **Description:** A hospital engaged in allied health services. **NOTE:** See website for job listings and online application.

Positions advertised include: Decision Support Analyst; House Supervisor; RN(Various); Surgical Technologist. **Operations at this facility include:** Administration; Service.

PERKINELMER
2200 Warrenville Road, Downers Grove IL 60515. 630/969-6000. **Toll-free phone:** 800/323-5891. **Fax:** 630/969-6511. **Contact:** Human Resources. **World Wide Web address:** http://www.perkinelmer.com. **Description:** Manufactures biomedical instruments that test blood for disease including the scintillation gamma counter. Primary customers are hospitals and universities located worldwide. **NOTE:** Final Acceptance Testing; Electrical Engineering Manager; Technical Services Manager.

PROCTOR HOSPITAL
5409 North Knoxville Avenue, Peoria IL 61614. 309/691-1062. **Fax:** 309/689-6062. **Contact:** Human Resources. **World Wide Web address:** http://www.proctor.org. **Description:** A 200-bed general hospital with a specialty addiction recovery clinic. **NOTE:** Entry-level, second- and third- shifts are offered. See website for job listings and application procedures. For nursing opportunities, contact Sheila Johnson at 309/683-6062. **Positions advertised include:** Linen Handler; Medical Lab Technician; Phlebotomist; RN (Various); LPN (Various).

PROVENA COVENANT MEDICAL CENTER
1400 West Park Street, Urbana IL 61801-2334. 217/337-2224. **Fax:** 217/337-2619. **Contact:** Human Resources. **World Wide Web address:** http://www.provenacovenant.org. **Description:** A 280-bed, nonprofit, acute care hospital. **NOTE:** Apply online. Entry-level positions are offered. **Positions advertised include:** Assistant to the President; Charge RN: Certified Occupational Therapy Assistant; Coder; Communication/Scheduler; Food Service Worker. **Corporate headquarters location:** Mokena IL. **Parent company:** Provena Health.

PROVENA MERCY CENTER FOR HEALTH CARE
1325 North Highland Avenue, Aurora IL 60506. 630/859-2222. **Contact:** Human Resource. **World Wide Web address:** http://www.provenamercy.com. **Description:** A 356-bed hospital offering general health and behavioral services. **NOTE:** Apply online. **Positions advertised include:** Central Scheduling; Clinical Coordinator; Intake Counselor; LPN; Physical Therapist; On-Call Social Worker.

RED BUD REGIONAL HOSPITAL
325 Spring Street, Red Bud IL 62278. 618/282-3831. **Contact:** Human Resources Assistant. **Description:** An acute care hospital and a long-term, rehabilitative care, skilled nursing facility. **NOTE:** See website for job listings, contact information and application procedures. Second and third shifts are offered.

THE REHABILITATION INSTITUTE OF CHICAGO
345 East Superior Street, Chicago IL 60611. 312/238-6290. **Toll-free phone:** 800/782-7342. **Fax:** 312/238-1263. **Recorded jobline:** 312/238-5600. **Contact:** Human Resources. **World Wide Web address:** http://www.rehabchicago.org. **Description:** A comprehensive rehabilitation facility offering inpatient, outpatient, subacute, and day treatment. The Rehabilitation Institute of Chicago also offers at home rehabilitation services. **NOTE:** Part-time, second and third shifts are offered. **Positions advertised include:** Clinical Instructor; Help Desk Specialist; Nurse Manager; Phlebotomist; Occupational Therapist; Fitness Instructor; Director of Development; Financial Clearance Coordinator. **Corporate headquarters location:** This location.

ROCKFORD MEMORIAL HOSPITAL
2400 North Rockton Avenue, Rockford IL 61103. 815/968-6861. **Contact:** Human Resources. **World Wide Web address:** http://www.rhsnet.org. **Description:** A 490-bed hospital. **NOTE:** Apply online at the hospital's website. **Parent company:** Rockford Health System. **Special programs:** Internships.

RUSH UNIVERSITY MEDICAL CENTER
1650 West Harrison, Chicago IL 60612. 312/942-5000. **Contact:** Human Resources. **World Wide Web address:** http://www.rush.edu. **Description:** A 825-bed hospital, specializing in children's medicine. It is the teaching hospital for Rush University. **NOTE:** Apply online. **Positions advertised include:** Dosimetrist; Supervisor of Billing; Applications Analyst; Assistant Professor; Staff Pharmacist; Polysomnographic Technician.

ST. ANTHONY'S HOSPITAL
1 Saint Anthony's Way, P.O. Box 340, St. Anthony's Way, Alton IL 62002-0340. 618/465-2571. **Contact:** Personnel Director. **World Wide Web address:** http://www.sahc.org. **Description:** A general hospital. **NOTE:** Apply online or download the application at the hospital's website and mail it in. **Positions advertised include:** RN; Nurse Assistant; Nuclear Medicine Technologist; Intervention Specialist.

ST. JOHN'S HOSPITAL
800 East Carpenter Street, Springfield IL 62769. 217/525-5644. **Toll-free phone:** 800/419-2296. **Fax:** 217/525-5601. **Recorded jobline:** 217/525-5600. **Contact:** Human Resources. **World Wide Web address:** http://www.st-johns.org. **Description:** A 750-bed, nonprofit, tertiary care, teaching facility affiliated with Southern Illinois University School of Medicine. **Positions advertised include:** File Clerk; Unit Clerk; RN (Various). **NOTE:** Entry-level positions and second and third shifts are offered. **Corporate headquarters location:** This location. **Other U.S. locations:** WI. **Parent company:** Hospital Sisters Health System.

ST. JOSEPH'S HOSPITAL
1515 Main Street, Highland IL 62249. 618/654-7421x2396. **Contact:** Human Resources. **World Wide Web address:** http://www.stjosephs-highland.org. **Description:** A general hospital. **NOTE:** Part-time and weekend shifts offered. Call or visit the Human Resources Office for more information. **Positions advertised include:** RN (Various).

ST. JOSEPH MEDICAL CENTER
77 North Airlite Street, Elgin IL 60123. 847/931-5505. **Contact:** Human Resources. **World Wide Web address:** http://www.provenasaintjoseph.com. **Description:** A 280-bed, acute care hospital with satellite facilities in surrounding communities. **NOTE:** Apply online. **Corporate headquarters location:** Frankfort IL. **Other U.S. locations:** Avilla IN. **Parent company:** Provena Health.

SHAY HEALTH CARE SERVICES
5730 West 159th Street, Oak Forest IL 60452. 708/535-4300. **Fax:** 708/535-7520. **Contact:** Karen Carter, Human Resources Coordinator. **Description:** A home health care agency. Founded in 1981. **NOTE:** Entry-level positions and second and third shifts are offered. **Company slogan:** Beyond business as usual. **Positions advertised include:** Certified Nurses Aide; Daycare Worker; Home Health Aide; Licensed Practical Nurse; Registered Nurse. **Office hours:** Monday - Friday, 8:00 a.m. - 4:00 p.m. **Corporate headquarters location:** Chicago IL. **Listed on:** Privately held.

SOUTH SHORE HOSPITAL
8012 South Crandon Avenue, Chicago IL 60617. 773/768-0810. **Fax:** 773/468-0749. **Contact:** Joe Perez, Human Resources Director. **E-mail address:** jobs@southshorehospital.com. **World Wide Web address:** http://www.southshorehospital.com. **Description:** A 170-bed, acute care hospital offering a full range of inpatient and outpatient health services. **NOTE:** This company prefers that resumes be mailed or faxed; however, there is an online application form available on its website.

SOUTHERN ILLINOIS HEALTHCARE
1239 East Main Street, Carbondale IL 62902. 618/457-5200. **Contact:** Employment Office. **World Wide Web address:** http://www.sih.net. **Description:** A nonprofit health care corporation that operates six hospitals and several rural clinics. Southern Illinois Healthcare also offers home health care and outreach programs. **NOTE:** This company has three hospitals in its network: Herrin Hospital; Memorial Hospital of Carbondale, and St. Joseph Medical Center. It also has other medical facilities. See website for job listings for all locations. An application may also be completed at the Human Resources office for each location. **Corporate headquarters location:** This location.

STERICYCLE, INC.
28161 North Keith Drive, Lake Forest IL 60045. **Toll-free phone:** 800/643-0240. **Fax:** 847/367-9493. **Contact:** Human Resources. **E-mail address:** careers@stericycle.com. **World Wide Web address:** http://www.stericycle.com. **Description:** Provides medical waste management services. Services include regulated medical waste collection, transportation, treatment, disposal, and reduction services. Founded in 1989. **NOTE:** See website for job listings. Entry-level, part-time and temporary positions offered. **Corporate headquarters location:** This location. **Listed on:** NASDAQ. **Stock exchange symbol:** SRCL.

STREAMWOOD BEHAVIORAL HEALTH CENTER
1400 East Irving Park Road, Streamwood IL 60107. 630/837-9000. **Fax:** 630/540-4290. **Contact:** Mark Paladino, Director of Human Resources. **World Wide Web address:** http://www.streamwoodhospital.com. **Description:** A psychiatric hospital for children and adolescents aged 3 through 18. **NOTE:** Apply online. Entry-level positions and second and third shifts are offered. **Special programs:** Internships. **Listed on:** Privately held.

THOREK HOSPITAL AND MEDICAL CENTER
850 West Irving Park Road, Chicago IL 60613. 773/525-6780. **Fax:** 773/975-6839. **Contact:** Human Resources. **E-mail address:** humanresources@thorek.org. **World Wide Web address:** http://www.thorek.org. **Description:** A medical center. Thorek also offers The Center for Male Health. **Positions advertised include:** RN; LPN.

U.S. DEPARTMENT OF VETERANS AFFAIRS JESSE BROWN VA MEDICAL CENTER
820 South Damen Avenue, HRMS, Chicago IL 60612. 312/569-8387. **Contact:** Human Resources. **World Wide Web address:** http://www.vagreatlakes.org. **Description:** A medical center operated by the U.S. Department of Veterans Affairs. From 54 hospitals in 1930, the system has grown to include 171 medical centers; more than 364 outpatient, community and outreach clinics; 130 nursing home care units; and 37 domiciliary residences. The VA operates at least one medical center in each of the 48 contiguous states, Puerto Rico, and the District of Columbia. With approximately 76,000 medical center beds, the VA treats nearly 1 million patients in VA hospitals, 75,000 in nursing home care units, and 25,000 in domiciliary residences. The VA's outpatient clinics register approximately 24 million visits a year. The VA is affiliated with 104 medical schools, 48 dental schools, and more than 850 other schools across the country. **NOTE:** For job listings at this facility, visit http://www.vacareers.com. Send resumes and inquiries to Edward Hines Jr. VA Hospital, Human Resources, Chicago Network, HRMS-05, Hines IL 60141. 708/343-7200. Indicate to which center or for which job you are applying. **Corporate headquarters location:** Washington DC. **Other U.S. locations:** Nationwide. **Operations at this facility include:** Administration; Research and Development; Service.

U.S. DEPARTMENT OF VETERANS AFFAIRS LAKESIDE CLINIC
333 East Huron Street, Chicago IL 60611. 312/569-8387. **Contact:** Human Resources. **World Wide Web address:** http://www.vagreatlakes.org. **Description:** An outpatient center dedicating to serving veterans and their dependents. The hospital is operated by the U.S. Department of Veterans Affairs. **NOTE:** For job listings at this facility, visit http://www.vacareers.com. Send resumes and inquiries to Edward Hines Jr. VA Hospital, Human Resources, Chicago Network, HRMS-05, Hines IL 60141. 708/343-7200. Indicate to which center or for which job you are applying. **Other U.S. locations:** Nationwide.

UNIVERSITY OF CHICAGO HOSPITALS & HEALTH SYSTEM
5841 South Maryland Avenue, Chicago IL 60637. 773/702-0198. **Contact:** Human Resources. **World Wide Web address:** http://www.uchospitals.edu. **Description:** A hospital. **NOTE:** Applicants should send resumes to the Employment Office, 800 East 55th Street, Chicago IL 60615. **Positions advertised include:** Certified Nurses Aide; Certified Occupational Therapy Assistant; Dietician/Nutritionist; EEG Technologist; EKG Technician; Emergency Medical Technician; Home Health Aide; Medical Records Technician; Nuclear Medicine Technologist; Occupational Therapist; Pharmacist; Physical Therapist; Physician; Radiological Technologist; Registered Nurse; Respiratory Therapist; Social Worker; Speech-Language Pathologist. **Operations at this facility include:** Administration.

VICTORY MEMORIAL HOSPITAL
1324 North Sheridan Road, Waukegan IL 60085. 847/360-4170. **Fax:** 847/360-4230. **Contact:** Human Resources. **World Wide Web address:** http://www.vistahealth.com. **Description:** A hospital that provides inpatient, outpatient, and home health care services. **Positions advertised include:** Transcriptionist; Evening & Nights Manager; Medical Technologist; Pharmacist; Senior Environmental Services Aides; Patient Care Technician; Registered Nurse; Transporter. **Other area locations:** Lindenhurst IL. **Parent company:** Vista Health Services.

VISITING NURSE ASSOCIATION
1245 Corporate Boulevard, 5th Floor, Aurora IL 60504. 630/978-2532. **Contact:** Human Resources. **World Wide Web address:** http://www.vnafoxvalley.com. **Description:** Provides home health services to patients. Services include nursing, physical therapy, occupational therapy, speech pathology, nutritional therapy, mental health and enterostomal therapy, medical social services, and hospice care. **Other U.S. locations:** Nationwide.

Indiana

ANCILLA SYSTEMS, INC.
1000 South Lake Park Avenue, Hobart IN 46342. 219/947-8500. **Contact:** Molly Lawlor. **E-mail address:** mlawlor@ancilla.org. **World Wide Web address:** http://www.ancilla.org. **Description:** A multi-institutional, nonprofit health care corporation. Ancilla Systems is sponsored by the Poor Handmaids of Jesus Christ. The company operates seven hospitals in Illinois and Indiana, a home health care affiliate, and a community hospital. Founded in 1857. **Corporate headquarters location:** This location. **Subsidiaries include:** Harbor Health Services, Inc.; Lakeshore Health Systems Incorporated; Michiana Community Hospital, Inc.; St. Elizabeth's Hospital of Chicago, Inc.; St. Joseph Medical Center of Fort Wayne; St. Joseph Mishawaka Health Services, Inc.; St. Mary's Hospital of East St. Louis, Inc. **Listed on:** Privately held.

BALL MEMORIAL HOSPITAL
2401 West University Avenue, Muncie IN 47303-3499. 765/747-3007. **Fax:** 765/747-4476. **Recorded jobline:** 765/747-3636. **Contact:** Human Resources. **World Wide Web address:** http://www.ballhospital.org. **NOTE:** The jobine is updated on the 15th and 30th of every month. For current job listings and descriptions visit the parent company's website: http://www.cardinalhealthsystems.org. **Description:** A 550-bed teaching hospital and medical referral center for east central Indiana. The hospital has

comprehensive rehabilitation services and a full-service laboratory. **Special programs:** Internships. **Parent company:** Cardinal Health System. **Listed on:** Privately held.

BIOMET, INC.
P.O. Box 587, Warsaw IN 46582. 574/267-6639. **Physical address:** 56 East Bell Drive, Warsaw IN 46582. **Fax:** 574/267-8137. **Contact:** Human Resources. **E-mail address:** human.resources@biomet.com. **World Wide Web address:** http://www.biomet.com. **Description:** Designs, manufactures, and markets products used by orthopedic medical specialists in both surgical and non-surgical therapy. Products include reconstructive and trauma devices, electrical bone growth stimulators, orthopedic support devices, operating room supplies, powered surgical instruments, general surgical instruments, arthroscopy products, and oral-maxillofacial implants and instruments. **NOTE:** Resumes that do not adhere to the guidelines indicated on the website will not be considered. **Corporate headquarters location:** This location. **International locations:** Worldwide.

BIVONA MEDICAL TECHNOLOGIES
5700 West 23rd Avenue, Gary IN 46406. 219/989-9150. **Contact:** Human Resources. **Description:** Specializes in the manufacture of silicone catheters. **Parent company:** Smiths Group.

BLOOMINGTON HOSPITAL
P.O. Box 1149, Bloomington IN 47402. 812/336-9535. **Toll-free phone:** 800/354-0561. **Fax:** 812/353-5447. **Contact:** Human Resources Department. **E-mail address:** careers@bloomhealth.org. **World Wide Web address:** http://www.bhhs.org. **Description:** A 314-bed, nonprofit, acute care hospital. **Positions advertised include:** Chief Clinical Microbiologist; Assistant Director of Nursing; Certified Nursing Assistant; Clinical Educator, Oncology; Cook; Dietary Aide; Occupational Therapist; Physical Therapist; Registered Nurse; House Orderly; Patient Services Secretary; Phlebotomist; Respiratory Technician. **Listed on:** Privately held.

BOSTON SCIENTIFIC CORPORATION
780 Brookside Drive, Spencer IN 47460. 812/829-4877. **Contact:** Human Resources Director. **World Wide Web address:** http://www.bsci.com. **Description:** Boston Scientific Corporation is a worldwide developer, manufacturer, and marketer of medical devices used in a broad range of interventional medical procedures including cardiology, gastroenterology, pulmonary medicine, radiology, urology, and vascular surgery. Boston Scientific's products are used by physicians to perform less invasive procedures. **Positions advertised include:** Principal Learning and Development Specialist. **Corporate headquarters location:** Natick MA. **Other U.S. locations:** San Jose CA; Mansfield MA; Milford MA; Redmond WA. **Operations at this facility include:** This location manufactures disposable medical devices such as catheters.

BROAD RIPPLE ANIMAL CLINIC, PC
6225 Broadway Street, Indianapolis IN 46220. 317/257-5334. **Fax:** 317/255-3371. **Contact:** Corry Lampe, Patient Services Coordinator. **E-mail address:** branimal@aol.com. **World Wide Web address:** http://www.bracpet.com. **Description:** A veterinary hospital. **Positions advertised include:** Veterinary Technician.

CLARIAN HEALTH PARTNERS
I-65 at 21st Street, P.O. Box 1367, Indianapolis IN 46206-1367. 317/274-4406. **Contact:** Human Resources. **World Wide Web address:** http://www.clarian.com. **Description:** In 1997, Indiana University Hospital, Methodist Hospital, and Riley Hospital joined to form Clarian Health Partners. **NOTE**: Main HR office is a Methodist **Hospital.** See website for information on how to contact recruiters. **Positions advertised include:** Medical Technologist; Medical Assistant; Patient Care Assistant; Respiratory Therapist; Surgical Technologist; Social Worker; Pharmacy Technician; Registered Nurse; Clinical Educator. **Special programs:** Internships; Externships; Scholarships; Educational Opportunities.

CLARK MEMORIAL HOSPITAL
1220 Missouri Avenue, Jeffersonville IN 47130. 812/282-2216. **Recorded jobline:** 812/283-2213. **Contact:** Human Resources Department. **World Wide Web address:** http://www.clarkmemorial.org. **Description:** Affiliated with Jewish Hospital HealthCare Services since 1992, the hospital provides services including the CompCare occupational medicine program, emergency care, maternal-child health, inpatient psychiatric care, pediatrics, home health, and cardiology. Founded in 1922. **NOTE:** Entry-level positions and second and third shifts are offered. **Positions advertised include:** Cardiac Rehabilitation Specialist; Occupational Therapist; Patient Care Associate; Charge Nurse; Registered Nurse. **Special programs:** Internships; Training; Co-ops; Summer Jobs.

CLARK NURSING & REHABILITATION CENTER
1964 Clark Road, Gary IN 46404. 219/949-5600. **Contact:** Human Resources. **World Wide Web address:** http://www.clarknursinghome.com. **Description:** Offers long-term and respite health care. Clark Nursing & Rehabilitation Center also arranges occupational, speech, and physical therapy.

THE COMMUNITY HOSPITAL
901 MacArthur Boulevard, Munster IN 46321. 219/836-4568. **Fax:** 219/852-6434. **Contact:** Personnel. **E-mail address:** personnel@comhs.org. **World Wide Web address:** http://www.communityhospital.org. **Description:** A 305-bed hospital with a staff of over 1,900 employees, offering a wide range of medical services. The hospital operates one of the area's most advanced neonatal intensive care units, as well as an oncology center. Founded in 1973. **Positions advertised include:** Accountant; Operational Secretary; Massage Therapist; Coder; Microbiologist; Home Care Registered Nurse; Nursing Assistant; Pharmacy Technician; Physical Therapist; Speech/Language Pathologist; Exercise Instructor; Transcriptionist; Cancer Registry Technician. **Office hours:** Monday – Friday, 8:00 a.m. – 4:30 p.m.

DEPUY INC.
P.O. Box 988, Warsaw IN 46581-0988. 574/267-8143. **Physical address:** 700 Orthopedic Drive, Warsaw IN 46582. **Contact:** Human Resources. **World Wide Web address:** http://www.depuy.com. **Description:** A medical device manufacturing company specializing in orthopedic products including total joint replacement and fracture management devices. **Special programs:** Internships. **Corporate headquarters location:** This location. **Other U.S. locations:** Jackson MI; Albuquerque NM. **Parent company:** Johnson & Johnson. **Operations at this facility include:** Administration; Manufacturing; Research and Development; Service.

EDGEWATER SYSTEMS FOR BALANCED LIVING
1100 West Sixth Avenue, Gary IN 46402. 219/885-4264. **Fax:** 219/885-0165. **Contact:** Personnel Recruiter. **World Wide Web address:** http://www.edgewatersystems.org. **Description:** A not-for-profit outpatient facility that offers behavioral health care services, mental health services, alcoholism and addiction treatment, crisis intervention, and counseling. Edgewater Systems for Balanced Living also provides short-term residential care for children and teenagers, and offers an Employee Assistance Program. **Positions advertised include:** Therapist; Addictions Specialist; Childcare Worker; Case Manager; Client Affairs Counselor; Administrative Assistant; Driver.

FLOYD MEMORIAL HOSPITAL AND HEALTH SERVICES
1850 State Street, New Albany IN 47150. 812/944-7701. **Recorded jobline:** 812/949-5660. **Contact:** Personnel. **World Wide Web address:** http://www.floydmemorial.org. **Description:** An acute care hospital offering 24-hour adult and pediatric emergency care. Floyd Memorial Hospital and Health Services also has an oncology unit, a critical care cardiac unit, and a full surgery center. **Positions advertised include:** Case Manager; Certified Nursing Assistant; Director, Rehabilitation Services; Environmental Services Aide; Home Health Aide; Imaging Systems Coordinator; Medical Technologist; Nurse Practitioner; Orderly; Radiation Therapist; Receptionist; Registered Nurse.

FRANKLIN UNITED METHODIST COMMUNITY
1070 West Jefferson Street, Franklin IN 46131. 317/736-7185. **Fax:** 317/736-1150. **Contact:** Kathi Couch, Human Resources Director. **E-mail address:** kcouch@fumeth.com. **World Wide Web address:** http://www.fumeth.com. **Description:** A continuing care retirement community. Founded in 1957. **Positions advertised include:** Activity Director; Certified Nursing Assistant; Dietary Cart Personnel; Dining Room Waitress; Staff Nurse; Unit Charge Nurse; Qualified Medication Aide; Housekeeper; Beauty Shop Operator. **Office hours:** Monday - Friday, 8:00 a.m. - 4:30 p.m.

GOOD SAMARITAN HOSPITAL
GOOD SAMARITAN HEART CENTER
520 South Seventh Street, Vincennes IN 47591. 812/885-3373. **Fax:** 812/885-3961. **Recorded jobline:** 888/866-9356. **Contact:** Human Resources. **World Wide Web address:** http://www.gshvin.org. **Description:** A 262-bed, acute care facility. The hospital provides a full range of services including cardiovascular surgery; neurosurgery; a Women and Infants Center; a cancer program; physical, occupational, and speech therapy; and hemodialysis. Good Samaritan Hospital also provides mental health and home health care services to the community. Good Samaritan Heart Center (also at this location; 812/885-3243) offers prevention, diagnosis, intervention (balloon angioplasty and pacemakers), surgery, and rehabilitation for a variety of heart ailments. **Positions advertised include:** Registered Nurse; Environmental Services Assistant; Case Manager; Clinical Psychologist; Laboratory Assistant; Radiologic Technologist; Staff Nurse; Staff Pharmacist.

GREATER LAFAYETTE HEALTH SERVICES
1301 Hartford Street, Lafayette IN 47903. 765/423-6175. **Fax:** 765/423-6475. **Contact:** Human Resources. **World Wide Web address:** http://www.glhsi.org. **Description:** A 365-bed hospital with surgery facilities, a recovery unit, Ambulatory Surgery Center, Critical Care Center, Neonatal Intensive Care Nursery, and Hook Rehabilitation Center. **Positions advertised include:** Registered Nurse; Social Worker; Nurse Technician; Home Health Aide; Educator; Certified Surgical Technologist; Bereavement Coordinator; Chaplain; Spiritual Counselor; Radiographer; Pharmacist; Speech Pathologist; Paramedic; Phlebotomist; Food Services Worker; Cook; Housekeeper. **Special programs:** Internships; Scholarships. **Office hours:** Monday – Friday, 8:00 a.m. – 5:00 p.m.

GUIDANT CORPORATION
111 Monument Circle, Suite 2900, Indianapolis IN 46204. 317/971-2000. **Fax:** 317/971-2040. **Contact:** Human Resources. **World Wide Web address:** http://www.guidant.com. **Description:** Designs, develops, manufactures, and markets a broad range of products for use in cardiac rhythm management, coronary artery disease intervention, and other forms of minimally invasive surgery. **Corporate headquarters location:** This location. **Listed on:** New York Stock Exchange. **Stock exchange symbol:** GDT.

HILL-ROM COMPANY, INC.
1069 State Route 46 East, Batesville IN 47006. 812/934-7777. **Fax:** 812/934-8329. **Contact:** Human Resources. **E-mail address:** careers@hill-rom.com. **World Wide Web address:** http://www.hill-rom.com. **Description:** Manufactures and rents a variety of health care products including birthing beds, hospital beds, and stretchers. **Positions advertised include:** Project Test Engineer; Quality Engineer; Advanced Electrical Design Engineer; Marketing Manager; Asset Management Analyst. **Corporate headquarters location:** This location. **Parent company:** Hillenbrand Industries, Inc.

HILLENBRAND INDUSTRIES, INC.
1069 State Route 46 East, Mail Code J-18, Batesville IN 47006. 812/934-7771. **Fax:** 812/934-1998. **Contact:** Director, Administrative Services **E-mail address:** resume_admin@Hillenbrand.com. **World Wide Web address:** http://www.hillenbrand.com. **Description:** A holding company. **Corporate headquarters location:** This location. **Subsidiaries include:** Batesville Casket Company, Inc. (Batesville IN) manufactures funeral-related products including caskets and urns. Forethought Financial Services (Batesville IN) provides financial services for the purpose of planning funeral arrangements. Hill-Rom Company, Inc. (Batesville IN) manufactures and rents a variety of health care products including birthing beds, hospital beds, and stretchers.

HOWARD COMMUNITY HOSPITAL
3500 South Lafountain Street, Kokomo IN 46901. 765/453-8560. **Fax:** 765/453-8380. **Recorded jobline:** 765/453-8185. **Contact:** Lee Springer, Human Resources. **E-mail address:** lspringe@hch-kokomo.org. **World Wide Web address:** http://www.howardcommunity.org. **Description:** A nonprofit, 125-bed, community-based medical facility. The hospital also operates as a regional mental health center. Founded in 1961. **Positions advertised include:** Home Health Aide; Registered Nurse; Nuclear Medicine Technologist; Respiratory Therapist; Staff Pharmacist.

JOHNS DENTAL LABORATORY INC.
P.O. Box 606, Terre Haute IN 47808-0606. 812/232-6026. **Physical address:** 423 South 13th Street, Terre Haute IN 47807. **Contact:** Human Resources. **World Wide Web address:** http://www.johnsdental.com. **Description:** A full-service dental laboratory.

KING SYSTEMS
15011 Herriman Boulevard, Noblesville IN 46060. 317/776-6823. **Fax:** 317/776-6827. **Contact:** Bill Stephan, Human Resources Director. **World Wide Web address:** http://www.kingsystems.com. **Description:** Manufactures plastic disposable breathing circuits used for the delivery of anesthesia in the operating room. **NOTE:** Entry-level positions and second and third shifts are offered. **Corporate headquarters location:** This location. **Listed on:** Privately held.

KING'S DAUGHTER'S HOSPITAL
One King's Daughter's Drive, Madison IN 47250. 812/265-5211. **Recorded jobline:** 812/265-0265. **Contact:** Debbie Temple, Human Resources Director. **World Wide Web address:** http://www.kdhhs.org. **Description:** A hospital that offers a surgery unit with outpatient capabilities; an obstetrics unit with several birthing options; specialized areas for pediatrics and geriatrics; laser surgery; emergency services; an ICU; radiology; diagnostic services; oncology; respiratory care; home health care; and physical therapy. Founded in 1915. **Office hours:** Monday – Friday, 8:00 a.m. – 4:30 p.m.

LOGANSPORT STATE HOSPITAL
1098 South State Road 25, Logansport IN 46947. 574/722-4141. **Contact:** Human Resources. **World Wide Web address:** http://www.lshonline.org. **Description:** A district psychiatric hospital serving 24 counties in northwest and north central Indiana. **Parent**

company: Indiana Family and Social Services Administration. **Administrator:** Dr. Jeffrey H. Smith. **Number of employees at this location:** 700.

LUTHERAN HOME OF NORTHWEST INDIANA
1200 East Luther Drive, Crown Point IN 46307. 219/663-3860. **Fax:** 219/662-3070. **Contact:** Human Resources. **Description:** A nursing home. The Lutheran Home of Northwest Indiana also offers assisted living and independent living programs, and arranges for home health care for clients in these programs.

MEMORIAL HOSPITAL
615 North Michigan Street, South Bend IN 46601. 574/234-9041. **Contact:** Human Resources. **World Wide Web address:** http://www.qualityoflife.org. **Description:** A 525-bed, general medical and surgical hospital. **Positions advertised include:** Patient Care Manager; Market Research Analyst; Medical Assistant; Nurse Manager; Coder/Analyst; Occupational Therapist; Physical Therapist; Registered Nurse; Surgical Technologist.

PARKVIEW HOSPITAL
2200 Randallia Drive, Fort Wayne IN 46805. 260/373-4000. **Contact:** Human Resources. **World Wide Web address:** http://www.parkview.com. **Description:** A nonprofit health system comprised of several hospitals, a health plan, a foundation of employed physicians, and a managed services organization. **Positions advertised include:** Registered Nurse; Occupational Therapist; Women's Health Specialist; Lab Technician; Flight Paramedic; Licensed Practical Nurse; Certified Nursing Assistant; Medical Technologist; Pharmacist. **Special programs:** Internships. **Operations at this facility include:** Administration; Divisional Headquarters; Regional Headquarters; Research and Development; Service. **Listed on:** Privately held.

PORTER MEMORIAL HOSPITAL SYSTEM
814 La Porte Avenue, Valparaiso IN 46383. 219/465-4653. **Fax:** 219/531-7017. **Contact:** Human Resources. **World Wide Web address:** http://www.portermemorial.org. **Description:** Offers a growing number of health care services. The hospital's specialties include family practice, obstetrics, pediatrics, and cardiology. **Positions advertised include:** Patient Registrar; Registered Nurse; Certified Nursing Assistant; Special Projects Analyst; Professional Recruiter; Infection Control Coordinator; Medical Technologist; Pharmacist; Emergency Department Director; Administrative Supervisor; Security Officer; Food Service Worker; Housekeeper.

REHABILITATION HOSPITAL OF INDIANA
4141 Shore Drive, Indianapolis IN 46254-2607. 317/329-2233. **Contact:** Human Resources. **E-mail address:** resumes@rhin.com. **World Wide Web address:** http://www.rhin.com. **Description:** An 89-bed, nonprofit, physical rehabilitation facility. Rehabilitation Hospital of Indiana provides specialized care, through both inpatient and outpatient services, for patients who have experienced spinal cord injuries, head injuries, stroke, amputation, orthopedic problems, or neuromuscular disease. **Positions advertised include:** Registered Nurse; Admissions Nurse; House Coordinator; Licensed Practical Nurse; Unit Secretary; Nursing Rehabilitation Technician; Physical Therapist; Occupational Therapist; Fiscal Services Clerk; Radiology Technician. **Operations at this facility include:** Administration; Service.

ST. ANTHONY MEDICAL CENTER
1201 South Main Street, Crown Point IN 46307. 219/663-8120. **Contact:** Personnel. **World Wide Web address:** http://www.stanthonymedicalcenter.com. **Description:** An acute care hospital. **NOTE:** Human Resources phone: 219/757-6451. **Positions advertised include:** Registered Nurse; Receptionist; Scheduling Clerk; Physical Therapist; Speech Pathologist; Receptionist; Medical Staff Coordinator; Respiratory Therapist; Food Service Aide; Environmental Service Attendant.

ST. JOSEPH HOSPITAL & HEALTH CENTER
1907 West Sycamore Street, Kokomo IN 46904. 765/456-5403. **Fax:** 765/456-5823. **Contact:** Human Resources. **World Wide Web address:** http://www.stjhhc.org. **Description:** A nonprofit, acute care medical facility that offers diagnostic and therapeutic services. **NOTE:** Entry-level positions, part-time jobs, and second and third shifts are offered. **Positions advertised include:** Physical Therapist; Respiratory Therapist; Pharmacist; Staff Nurse; Nursing Assistant. **Special programs:** Training. **Operations at this facility include:** Administration.

ST. JOSEPH HOSPITAL
700 Broadway, Fort Wayne IN 46802. 260/425-3016. **Contact:** Human Resources Manager. **World Wide Web address:** http://www.lutheranhealthnetwork.com/stjoe. **Description:** A nonprofit, medical center offering primary and secondary acute care, neighborhood clinics, preventative outreach programs, and a satellite surgery center. Founded in 1869. **NOTE:** Second and third shifts are offered. **Positions advertised include:** Registered Nurse; Home Health Care Nurse; Licensed Practical Nurse; Lead Therapist; Medical Assistant; Nursing Assistant; Medical Transcriptionist; ; Respiratory Care Clinician; Pharmacy Technician. **Corporate headquarters location:** Hobart IN. **Other U.S. locations:** Chicago IL; St. Louis MO. **Parent company:** Lutheran Health Network. **Operations at this facility include:** Administration; Divisional Headquarters; Service.

ST. MARY'S HOSPITAL
3700 Washington Avenue, Evansville IN 47750. 812/485-4000. **Fax:** 812/485-6735. **Contact:** Human Resources. **E-mail address:** llcollins@stmarys.org. **World Wide Web address:** http://www.stmarys.org. **Description:** A general hospital with over 400 beds providing a wide range of medical and surgical services. Founded in 1894. **Positions advertised include:** Speech Language Pathologist; Nuclear Medicine Technologist; Occupational Therapist; Patient Care Technician; Respiratory Therapist; Group Exercise Instructor; Pharmacist; Licensed Practical Nurse; Registered Nurse; Cook; Paramedic.

TENDERLOVINGCARE/STAFF BUILDERS
6100 North Keystone Street, Suite 360, Indianapolis IN 46220. 317/205-6010. **Contact:** Human Resources. **World Wide Web address:** http://www.tlcathome.com. **Description:** A home health care agency. **Corporate headquarters location:** Success NY. **Other U.S. locations:** Nationwide.

TIPTON COUNTY MEMORIAL HOSPITAL
1000 South Main Street, Tipton IN 46072. 765/675-8500. **Contact:** Human Resources. **World Wide Web address:** http://www.tiptonhospital.org. **Description:** A nonprofit, acute-care, community hospital. **NOTE:** Entry-level positions and second and third shifts are offered. **Positions advertised include:** Registered Nurse; Licensed Practical Nurse; Office Nurse; Housekeeping Aide. **Corporate headquarters location:** This location.

TRI-CITY COMMUNITY MENTAL HEALTH CENTER
3903 Indianapolis Boulevard, East Chicago IN 46312. 219/392-6001. **Contact:** Human Resources. **World Wide Web address:** http://www.tricitycenter.org. **Description:** A mental health care facility that primarily provides care on an outpatient basis. Other services offered by Tri-City Community Mental Health Center include a detoxification unit for adults and residential care for adolescent women. **NOTE:** Resumes for Tri-City Community Mental Health Center must be sent to Geminus Corporation, Attention Dee Dee Shoemaker, Human Resources Associate, 5281 Fountain Drive, Crown Point IN 46307. **Positions advertised include:** Therapist; Psychiatric Technician; Case Manager.

UNION HOSPITAL HEALTH GROUP
1606 North Seventh Street, Terre Haute IN 47804. 812/238-7000. **Recorded jobline:** 812/238-7200. **Contact:** Mary Halsted, Employment Manager. **World Wide Web address:** http://www.uhhg.org. **Description:** Owns and operates two hospitals, a physicians/surgeons clinic, and physician office sites. Union Hospital Health Group is a nonprofit, regional referral center. **NOTE:** Entry-level positions, part-time jobs, and second and third shifts are offered. **Positions advertised include:** Occupational Therapist; Respiratory Therapist; Physical Therapist; Pharmacist; Registered Nurse; Licensed Practical Nurse; Psychologist; Speech Language Pathologist; Nutrition Assistant. **Special programs:** Internships. **Office hours:** Monday - Friday, 8:00 a.m. - 4:30 p.m. **Corporate headquarters location:** This location. **Other area locations:** Clinton IN.

ZIMMER INC.
P.O. Box 708, Warsaw IN 46581. 574/267-6131. **Physical address:** 1800 West Center Street, Warsaw IN 46581. 800/613-6131. **Fax:** 574/372-4988. **Contact:** Employment Office. **World Wide Web address:** http://www.zimmer.com. **Description:** Develops, manufactures, and markets orthopedic products for human implant and patient care. Zimmer's primary customers are hospitals. **Positions advertised include:** Inventory Accountant; Process Engineer; Quality Engineer; Tax Manager; Product Manager; Brand Manager. **Corporate headquarters location:** This location. **Operations at this facility include:** Administration; Manufacturing; Research and Development. **Listed on:** New York Stock Exchange. **Stock exchange symbol:** ZMH.

Iowa

ALLEN MEMORIAL HOSPITAL
1825 Logan Avenue, Waterloo IA 50703. 319/235-3605. **Fax:** 319/235-5260. **Contact:** Ken Leibold, Director of Human Resources. **E-mail address**: karrtr@ihs.org. **World Wide Web address:** http://www.allenhospital.org. **Description:** Part of the Iowa Health System, this 240-bed hospital's programs and services include an ambulatory medical center, an ambulatory surgery center, anesthesiology, angiography, angioplasty, audiology, a back injury program, neurology, nuclear medicine, radiology services, senior services, hospice services, home health services, infection control, intensive/coronary care, CT scan, MRI, mental health services, tele-care, trauma center, wellness center, women's health center, oncology, open heart surgery, ophthalmology, orthopedics, nursing school, International Diabetes Center/North Iowa Affiliate, speech pathology, urology, hyperbaric oxygen for extremities, maxillofacial surgery, and an emergency department. **NOTE:** For consideration applicants must submit a resume and a completed application available from the company Website. **Positions advertised include:** Family Practice Physician; Cardiologist; Emergency Medicine Physician; Obstetrics and Gynecology Physician; Nursing Assistant; Admitting Technician; Licensed Practical Nurse; Medical Transcriptionist; Registered Nurse; Physical Therapist; Patient Service Representative; Development Assistant; Diagnostic Radiographer; Respiratory Therapist; Cytotechnologist. **Other clinic locations:** Cedar Falls IA; Eldora IA; Sumner IA. **Affiliates include:** Allen College. **Parent company:** Allen Health System, Inc.

BROADLAWNS MEDICAL CENTER
1801 Hickman Road, Des Moines IA 50314. 515/282-2210. **Fax:** 515-282-2526. **Contact:** Human Resources. **World Wide Web address:** http://www.broadlawns.org. **Description:** A 200-bed general medical and psychiatric hospital serving the residents of Polk County. Founded in 1925. **NOTE:** Apply on-line and search posted openings on company website: http://www.broadlawns.org. **Positions advertised include:** Director of Development; Program Specialist Supervisor; Coder; Medical Lab Technician; Radiology Technician; Residential Treatment Worker; Health Service Technician; Emergency Department Technician; Licensed Practical Nurse; Certified Medical Assistant; Transcriptionist; Communications Clerk; Patient Access Representative; Pre-Registration Clerk; Intensive Care Nurse; Medical/Surgical Nurse; Adult Psychologist.

CENTRAL IOWA HEALTH SYSTEM
1313 High Street, Suite 111, Des Moines IA 50309. 515/241-6313. **Toll-free phone:** 800/843-4522. **Fax:** 515/241-8515. **E-mail address:** careers@ihs.org. **Contact:** Personnel. **World Wide Web address:** http://www.iowahealth.org. **Description:** Iowa Methodist Medical Center, Iowa Lutheran Hospital, and St. Luke's are affiliated hospitals under the Central Iowa Health System. They form one of Iowa's largest nonprofit medical facilities with a combined total of 1,175 beds. Iowa Methodist is central Iowa's only designated trauma center and is also a teaching, regional referral center. Iowa Lutheran is a community hospital that focuses on family medicine and behavioral health sciences. St. Luke's is a general hospital located in Cedar Rapids. **Positions advertised include:** Care Manager; CDTR Community Services; Certified Occupational Therapy Assistant; Chemical Depression Counselor; Clinical Lab Technician; Clinical Education Specialist; Clinical Nurse Specialist; Certified Medical Assistant; Coder/Abstractor; Facilities Manager; Financial Counselor; Housekeeper; Licensed Practical Nurse; Medical Lab Technician; Medical Records Technician; Medical Technologist; Nursing Manager; Health Information Manager; Nuclear Medicine Technologist; Occupational Therapist. **NOTE:** Post resumes on the company Website. **Corporate headquarters location:** This location. **Other area locations:** Knoxville IA. **Subsidiaries include:** Blank Children's Hospital; Iowa Lutheran Hospital; Iowa Methodist Medical Center. **Parent company:** Iowa Health Systems. **Number of employees at this location:** 5,200. **Number of employees statewide:** 7,000.

EVO MEDICAL SOLUTIONS
2636 289th Place, Adel IA 50003-8021. 515/993-5001. **Fax:** 515/993-4172. **Toll-free phone**: 800/759-3038. **Contact:** Human Resources. **World Wide Web address**: http://www.evomedicalsolutions.com. **Description:** Manufactures and distributes a line of home respiratory care equipment.

THE FINLEY HOSPITAL
350 North Grandview Avenue, Dubuque IA 52001. 563/589-2457. **Toll-free phone:** 800/582-1891. **Contact:** Human Resources. **World Wide Web address:** http://www.finleyhospital.org. **Description:** A 158-bed, non-profit, locally owned and controlled, regional hospital serving the tri-state area offering comprehensive health care services. **NOTE**: Search posted openings and apply on-line only. **Positions advertised include:** Certified Nurse Assistant; Mental Health Technician; Nurse Practitioner; Occupational Therapist; Operating Room Technician; Licensed Practical Nurse; Radiographer; Registered Nurse; Speech Language Pathologist; Unit Technician. **Other area locations:** Elkader IA. **Affiliates include:** Cascade Medical Center; Galena Health Clinic; Hazel Green Health Clinic; Home Healthcare; Business Health. **Parent company:** Iowa Health Systems. **President/CEO:** Kevin Rogols. **Number of employees:** 800.

FRIENDSHIP HAVEN, INC.
420 Kenyon Road, Fort Dodge, IA 50501. 515/573-6006. **Toll-free phone:** 800/593-2121. **Fax:** 515/573-6013. **Contact:** Julie Magennis, Human Resources Director. **E-mail address**: jmagennis@friendshiphaven.com. **World Wide Web address:** http://www.friendshiphaven.org. **Description:** A nonprofit retirement community offering continuing care ranging from independent living to 24-hour nursing care. Founded in 1950. **NOTE:** Entry-level positions and second and third shifts are offered. May search posted openings on-line. **Company slogan:** A tradition of caring. **Positions advertised include:** Staff Accountant; Certified Nurses Aide; Licensed Practical

Nurse; Registered Nurse. **Office hours:** Monday - Friday, 8:00 a.m. - 4:30 p.m. **CEO/President:** Craig Johnsen. **Annual sales/revenues:** Less than $5 million. **Number of employees at this location:** 385.

MARSHALLTOWN MEDICAL & SURGICAL CENTER
3 South Fourth Avenue, Marshalltown IA 50158. 641/754-5113. **Fax:** 641/753-2570. **Contact:** Human Resources. **World Wide Web address:** http://www.everydaychampions.org. **Description:** A 176-bed, acute care medical center with a rehabilitation and sports medicine facility. **NOTE:** Search posted listings and apply on-line. **Positions advertised include:** Emergency Department Assistant; Interpreter; Phlebotomist; Medical Registered Nurse; Surgical Registered Nurse; Pediatric Registered Nurse; Respiratory Therapist; Staff Radiographer; Operating Room Surgical Technologist; Physician Assistant. **Number of employees:** 700.

MERCY HOSPITAL MEDICAL CENTER
11116 Sixth Avenue, Des Moines IA 50314. 515/247-3121. **Fax:** 515/643-8831. **Contact:** Human Resources. **World Wide Web address:** http://www.mercydesmoines.org. **Description:** A 917-bed hospital. **NOTE:** Search posted openings and apply on-line only. No paper resumes accepted. **Positions advertised include:** Obstetrician; Allied Health Administrator; Pharmacist; Interpreter/Translator; Clinic Supervisor; Medical Records Supervisor; Physical Therapist; Primary Counselor; Nuclear Medicine Technician; Cytotechnologist; Radiology Technologist; Respiratory Therapist; Surgical Technician; Coder; Certified Medical Assistant. **Corporate headquarters location:** Omaha NE. **Parent company:** Catholic Health Corporation. **Listed on:** Privately held.

MERCY MEDICAL CENTER
801 Fifth Street, Sioux City IA 51102. 712/279-2010. **Fax:** 712/279-5623. **Contact:** Pat Rodriguez, Recruiter. **E-mail address:** mercysiouxcity@mercyhealth.com. **World Wide Web address:** http://www.mercysiouxcity.com. **Description:** A nonprofit, regional medical center. Mercy Medical Center serves as the state-designated trauma center for the region and provides a vital lifesaving link to rural areas via the hospital's helicopter ambulance service. Mercy Medical also provides a full range of comprehensive medical services including balloon angioplasty, atherectomy, full diagnostic capabilities, and open-heart surgery. **NOTE**: Search posted openings and apply on-line only. No paper resumes will be accepted. **Positions advertised include:** Central Processing Technician; Certified Surgical Technologist; Certified Nursing Assistant; Customer Service Technician; Maintenance Worker; Medical Assistant; Medical Records Clerk; Medical Technologist; Medical Transcriptionist; Pharmacy Intern; Physical Therapist; Physical Therapy Assistant; Registered Nurse; Licensed Practical Nurse; Speech Pathologist; Staff Pharmacist.

ST. ANTHONY REGIONAL HOSPITAL
400 South Clark Street, P.O. Box 628, Carroll IA 51401. 712/792-3581. **Fax:** 712/792-2124. **Contact:** Gina Ramaekers, Human Resources Representative. **World Wide Web address:** http://www.stanthonyhospital.org. **Description:** A 99-bed nonprofit, full-service community hospital with a 79-bed nursing home. **NOTE:** Entry-level positions and second and third shifts are offered. May apply in person or on-line. **Company slogan:** People Caring for People. **Positions advertised include:** Certified Registered Anesthesia Nurse; Dietary Aide; Licensed Practical Medical Nurse; Advanced Cardiac Life Support Nurse; Licensed Practical Surgical Nurse; Certified Nursing Assistant; Licensed Practical Pediatric Nurse; Registered Nurse; Registered Mental Health Nurse; Licensed Practical Nursery Nurse; Director of Surgical Services; Surgery Technician; Certified Occupational Therapy Assistant; Certified Nursing Home Assistant; Intensive Care Registered Nurse; Housekeeper; Pharmacy Technician. **President/CEO:** Gary Riedmann. **Number of employees at this location:** 420.

ST. LUKE'S HEALTH CARE SYSTEM
2720 Stone Park Boulevard, Sioux City IA 51104. 712/279-3123. **Fax:** 712/279-3368. **Contact:** Laura Hill, Human Resources. **E-mail address:** hilll@stlukes.org. **World Wide Web address:** http://www.stlukes.org. **Description:** A regional health care system that operates over 20 facilities including outpatient rehabilitation centers, physician clinics, a senior living community, and a charitable foundation. St. Luke's Health Care System is also affiliated with several area hospitals. Founded in 1884. **NOTE:** Search posted openings and apply on-line only. stlukes.org **Positions advertised include:** Computer-aided Tomography Technician; Dietitian; Emergency Room Technician; Respiratory Care Instructor; Clinical Coordinator; Licensed Practical Nurse; Medical Laboratory Technician; Medical Records Clerk; MRI Technologist; Nursing Assistant; Registered Nurse Manager; Surgical Technician; Pharmacist; Pharmacy Technician; Burn Unit Registered Nurse; Respiratory Therapist; Women/Children's Services Director; Staff Histologist. **Other area locations:** Sergeant Bluffs IA. **Number of employees at this location:** 1,450.

SHENANDOAH MEMORIAL HOSPITAL
300 Pershing Avenue, Shenandoah IA 51601. 712/246-7102. **Fax:** 712/246-7357. **Contact:** Linda Braden, Human Resources Director. **E-mail address:** lbraden@shenandoahmedcenter.com. **World Wide Web address:** http://www.shenandoahmedcenter.com. **Description:** A nonprofit hospital offering acute care, outpatient services, skilled nursing, long-term care, and home health services. **NOTE:** Entry-level positions and second and third shifts are offered. **Positions advertised include:** Nurse Manager; Program Director; Physical Therapist; Physical Therapy Assistant; Home Health Aide; Housekeeper; Registered Nurse. **Office hours:** Monday - Friday, 8:00 a.m. - 4:30 p.m. **Corporate headquarters location:** This location. **CEO:** Chuck Millburg. **Annual sales/revenues:** $5 - $10 million. **Number of employees at this location:** 200.

SPENCER MUNICIPAL HOSPITAL
1200 First Avenue East, Spencer IA 51301. 712/264-6205. **Fax:** 712/264-6466. **Contact:** Michael Schauer, Human Resources. **E-mail address:** mschauer@spencerhospital.org. **World Wide Web address:** http://www.spencerhospital.org. **Description:** A 99-bed, nonprofit hospital. **NOTE:** Entry-level positions and second and third shifts are offered. Search posted openings and apply on-line, by fax, email or in person locally. **Positions advertised include:** Registered Nurse; Mental Health Nurse; Medical/Surgical Nurse; Diagnostic Imaging Director; Clinical Nurse Coordinator; Respiratory Therapist; Radiation Therapist; Mental Health Department Manager; Certified Nurse Aide; Certified Occupational Therapy Assistant; Physical Therapist; Radiologic Technologist; Dietitian; Coder; Social Worker; Central Supply Clerk. **Office hours:** Monday - Friday, 8:00 a.m. - 4:30 p.m. **President/CEO:** John W. Allen. **Number of employees:** 500.

U. S. DEPARTMENT OF VETERAN AFFAIRS VETERANS ADMINISTRATION CENTRAL IOWA HEALTH CARE SYSTEM
1515 West Pleasant, Knoxville IA 50138. 641/842-3101. **Contact:** Human Resources. **Description:** Provides a variety of inpatient and outpatient services including acute, long-term, and community-based psychiatric, rehabilitative, and medical care. The center has more than 600 beds. **NOTE**: Administrative staff openings posted on www.usajobs.opm.gov. Healthcare professionals may contact: 515/ 699-5693 to request an application. **Positions advertised include:** Licensed Practical Nurse; Pharmacist; Physical Therapist; Physician; Registered Nurse; Respiratory Therapist. **Corporate headquarters location:** Washington DC. **Other U.S. locations:** Nationwide. **Parent company:** U.S. Department of Veterans Affairs. **Operations at**

this facility include: Administration; Health Care. **Number of employees at this location:** 830.

UNIVERSITY OF IOWA HOSPITALS AND CLINICS
200 Hawkins Drive, Iowa City IA 52242. 319/356-2120. **Toll-free phone:** 800/777-4692. **Recorded jobline:** 319/335-2682. **Contact:** Human resource department at University of Iowa. **E-mail address:** Jobs@UIowa. **World Wide Web address:** http://www.uihealthcare.com. **Description:** A university-affiliated tertiary health care center with 800 beds and a 22-suite perioperative nursing division. **NOTE:** Entry-level positions, part-time jobs, and second and third shifts are offered. Search posted openings and apply on-line. **Positions advertised include:** Research Assistant; Postdoctoral Research Scholar; Postdoctoral Scholar; Assistant Anatomy Professor; Anesthesiologist; Ophthalmology Professor; Clinical Lab Scientist; Social Worker; Stem Cell Biologist; Bone Marrow Transplant Physician; Staff Nurse.

WASHINGTON COUNTY HOSPITAL AND CLINICS
400 East Polk Street, Washington IA 52353. 319/863-3909. **Fax:** 319/653-4271. **Contact:** Tracy Ousey, Human Resources. **E-mail address:** tousey@wchc.org. **World Wide Web address:** http://www.wchc.org. **Description:** A nonprofit, rural health care facility including a 48-bed hospital and 43-bed nursing home with 24-hour emergency care, a family birthing center, medical/surgical care, an intensive care unit, skilled care, home health services, and broad diagnostic capabilities providing inpatient, outpatient, long-term care and emergency services for the Washington County area. Founded in 1912. **NOTE:** Entry-level positions, part-time jobs, and second and third shifts are offered. **Positions advertised include:** Medical/Surgery Registered Nurse; Obstetric Registered Nurse; Operating Room Nurse; Certified Nurses Aide; Radiology Technologist; clinical Dietician; Coder; Lab Technician; Licensed Practical Nurse. **Number of employees at this location:** 230.

Kansas

CENTRAL KANSAS MEDICAL CENTER ST. ROSE HOSPITAL CAMPUS
3515 Broadway, Great Bend KS 67530. 620/786-6186. **Fax:** 620/786-6380. **Contact:** Human Resources. **E-mail address:** deniseschreiber@catholichealth.net. **World Wide Web address:** http://www.ckmc.org. **Description:** A two-campus, 121-bed regional medical center with the main, St. Rose campus in Great Bend and a second, St. Joseph Hospital in Larned. Founded by the Dominican Sisters in 1902. **Positions advertised include:** Registered Nurse; Licensed Practical Nurse; Medical Record File Clerk; Respiratory Therapist; Cook; Plant Mechanic Coder; Nurse Manager; Physician. **Other area locations:** Larned KS (St. Joseph Memorial Hospital). **Operations at this facility include:** St. Rose Hospital; Golden Belt Home Health & Hospice. **Number of employees at this location:** 630.

COFFEYVILLE REGIONAL MEDICAL CENTER
1400 West Fourth Street, Coffeyville KS 67337. 620/252-1500. **Contact:** Human Resources. **E-mail address:** bmccune@crmcinc.com. **World Wide Web address:** http://www.crmcinc.com. **Description:** A 110-bed, not-for-profit, community hospital providing acute care and skilled care services, as well as outpatient health care services to Southeast Kansas and Northeast Oklahoma. **NOTE:** Applicants may apply for positions online. **Positions advertised include:** Registered Nurse; Certified Nurses Aid; Health Information Clerk; Health Information Scanner; Maintenance Worker; Housekeeping Clerk. **Operations at this facility include:** Administration; Service. **Number of employees at this location:** 450.

LAWRENCE MEMORIAL HOSPITAL
325 Maine Street, Lawrence KS 66044. 785/840-3007. **Fax:** 785/840-3006. **Contact:** Human Resources. **E-mail address:** lisa.kutait@lmh.org. **World Wide Web address:** http://www.lmh.org. **Description:** A 177-bed, nonprofit community hospital with a third surgical unit, a 12-bed intensive care unit, a 10-bed rehabilitation unit, an 8-bed pediatric department, a 16-bed mental health unit, and a 13-bed maternity care unit. **NOTE:** Applicants may apply online for current positions via web site. Entry-level positions as well as second and third shifts are offered. **Positions advertised include:** Clinical Associate; Registered Nurse; Licensed Practical Nurse; Systems Engineer; Testing Coordinator; Lab Assistant; Clerk III. **Number of employees at this location:** 850.

Medicalodges, Inc.
P.O. Box 509, Coffeyville KS 67337-0509. 620/251-6700. **Physical address:** 201 West Eighth, Coffeyville KS 67337. **Fax:** 620/251-6427. **Contact:** Director of Training and Resources. **E-mail address:** dsdenton@medicalodges.com. **World Wide Web address:** http://www.medicalodges.com. **Description:** An employee-owned health care company operating 23 skilled nursing facilities, 11 assisted living centers, five residential care units, two resident care facilities for the developmentally disabled, a skilled facility for the mentally handicapped, two geriatric psychiatry units, and several specialized units. Founded in 1961. **Company slogan:** Quality Care with Dignity. **Positions advertised include:** Information Systems Specialist; Nurse Consultant; Regional Business Specialist; Activities Director; Administrative In Training; Certified Medication Aide; Certified Nursing Assistant; Charge Nurse; Directory Service; Housekeeping; Maintenance Plant Supervisor; Marketing Director; Medical Records Clerk; Nurses Aid. **Special programs:** Internships. **Corporate headquarters location:** This location. **Other area locations:** Statewide. **Other U.S. locations:** AR; MO; OK. **Operations at this facility include:** Administration; Service. **Number of employees nationwide:** 2,600.

MT. CARMEL REGIONAL MEDICAL CENTER, INC.
1102 East Centennial, Pittsburg KS 66762. 620/232-0170. **Fax:** 620/232-3586. **Recorded jobline:** 620/235-3535. **Contact:** Human Resources. **E-mail address for nursing:** jhenderson@via-christi.org. **E-mail address for allied health/clerical:** cpuckett@via-christi.org. **World Wide Web address:** http://www.mtcarmel.org. **Description:** A nonprofit medical center with 188 beds offering home health services, inpatient care, emergency care, and a community cancer therapy program. MCRMC is: a member of Via Christi Health System of Wichita; sponsored by the Sisters of St. Joseph of Wichita and the Sisters of the Sorrowful Mother; and accredited by JCAHO. Founded in 1903. Resumes can be submitted through the company's website and applications can be filled out online. **Positions advertised include:** Staff Nurses; Nursing Assistants; CT/MRI Tester; Technologist Nuclear Medicine; Administrative Secretary; Physician Coder; Developmental Coordinator. **Office Hours:** Monday – Friday, 8:00 a.m. – 4:30 p.m. **Special programs:** Nursing Scholarships; Internships. **Subsidiaries include:** Mt. Carmel Medical Center; Mt. Carmel Cancer Center; Mt. Carmel Durable Medical Equipment; Crossroads Counseling Center. **Operations at this facility include:** Administration; Manufacturing; Service. **Annual sales/revenues:** $141 million. **Number of employees at this location:** 1,000.

OLATHE HEALTH SYSTEMS, INC. dba OLATHE MEDICAL CENTER, INC.
20333 West 151st Street, Suite 356, Olathe KS 66061. 913/791-4243. **Fax:** 913/791-4240. **Recorded jobline:** 913/791-4246. **Contact:** Human Resources. **E-mail address:** resumes@ohsi.com. **World Wide Web address:** http://www.ohsi.com. **Description:** Since beginning as the Olathe Health Foundation, this regional hospital has a reputation for its rehabilitation services; hospice and home health; cardiology, emergency services, obstetrics, oncology and women's health. The Olathe Health System operates several

subsidiary corporations including the main Medical Center campus at I-35 and 151st Street, which is one of the largest in the country. Founded in 1948. **Positions advertised include:** Film Librarian Clerk; Radiology Registered Nurse; Registered Nurse; Unit Secretary; Clinical Resource Nurse; Security Officer; Accounts Payable Coder; Medical Records Transcriber; Patient Registration Clerk; Housekeeping Associate; Cashier. **Special programs:** Internships. **Subsidiaries include:** Olathe Medical Center, Inc.; Miami County Medical Center; Olathe Medical Services; Olathe Medical Center Charitable Fund; Olathe Health Development Corporation; Health Access; Cedar Lake Village, Inc. **Operations at this facility include:** Administration. **President/CEO:** Frank H. Devocelle. **Number of employees at this location:** 965.

PRAIRIE VIEW INC.
P.O. Box 467, Newton KS 67114. 316/284-6311. **Physical address:** 1901 East First Street, Newton KS 67114. **Fax:** 316/284-6352. **Contact:** Joy Robb, Personnel. **E-mail address:** robbjh@pvi.org. **World Wide Web address:** http://www.prairieview.com. **Description:** Established by the Mennonite churches, Prairie View is a private, nonprofit regional behavioral and mental health system with eight locations including the 70-acre headquarters in Newton. A 60-bed psychiatric hospital and partial hospitalization program are also available as well as outpatient services. **Positions advertised include:** Administrative Assistant; Registered Nurse; Licensed Practical Nurse; Mental Health Worker; Psychiatrist; Community Case Manager. **Corporate headquarters location:** This location. **Other area locations:** Hutchinson KS; Marion KS; McPherson KS; Newton KS; Salina KS; Wichita KS. **Operations at this facility include:** Administration; Services. **Number of employees at this location:** 250. **Number of employees nationwide:** 375.

SPECIALTY HOSPITAL OF MID AMERICA
6509 West 103rd Street, Overland Park KS 66212. 913/649-3701. **Toll-free phone**: 800/367-5690. **Fax:** 913/649-3701. **Contact:** Darin Enix, Human Resources. **World Wide Web address:** http://thicare.com/SpecHospOfMidAmerica. **Description:** Provides health care services including nursing care, rehabilitation, and other therapies; institutional pharmacy services; specialty care to Alzheimer's patients; and subacute care. The hospital's specialty and subacute care units provide a range of specialized services including post-acute medical care; rehabilitative ventilator care; infusion therapy; stroke, pain, and wound management; and physical rehabilitation.

UNIVERSITY OF KANSAS MEDICAL CENTER
3901 Rainbow Boulevard, Kansas City KS 66160. 913/588-5627. **Fax:** 913/588-5863. **Contact:** Director of Human Resources. **World Wide Web address:** http://www.kumed.com. **Description:** A medical center providing a full range of health care services and offering health education. **NOTE:** Offers applications on website but will accept paper resumes by mail or fax. **Positions advertised include:** Administrative Specialist; Administrative Assistant; Division Director of Nephrology; Research Associate; Medical Billing; Student Financial Aid Advisor; Nurse Manager; Assistant Professor; Post Doctoral Fellow; Senior Coordinator. **Other area locations:** Wichita KS.

WICHITA SPECIALTY HOSPITAL
8080 East Pawnee, Wichita KS 67207. 316/682-0004. **Fax:** 316/682-5790. **Contact:** Human Resources. **World Wide Web address:** http://www.thicare.com. **Toll-free phone:** 800/255-4730. **Description:** Wichita Specialty Hospital is a long-term, acute care hospital. It is a 26-bed long-term JCAHO accredited hospital dedicated to providing high quality care for medically and surgically complex patients who are critically ill and require extend hospitalization.

Kentucky

APPALACHIAN REGIONAL HEALTHCARE (ARH)
100 Medical Center Drive, Hazard KY 41701. 606/439-1331. **Contact:** Marilyn Hamblin, Human Resources. **E-mail address:** humanresources@arh.org. **World Wide Web address:** http://www.arh.org. **Description:** A nonprofit health care system with hospitals, clinics, home health agencies, and other health services in the central Appalachian region of Kentucky, West Virginia, and Virginia. Products and services offered by ARH include hospital care, home health, durable medical equipment, psychiatric care, ambulatory clinics, laboratory, and EEG/EKG/Holter monitoring. **NOTE:** Resumes should be mailed to Marilyn Hamblin, ARH System Professional Recruiter, Appalachian Regional Healthcare, P.O. Box 8086, Lexington KY 40533, or faxed to 859/226-2586. **Positions advertised include:** Family Nurse Practitioner. **Special programs:** Internships. **Other area locations:** Beckley KY; Harlan KY; Lexington KY; McDowell KY; Middlesboro KY; Morgan Country, KY; Summers Country KY; Whitesburg KY; Williamson KY. **Other U.S. locations:** Wise VA; Beckley WV; Hinton WV; Man WV. **Operations at this facility include:** This location is the ARH Regional Medical Center. **Number of employees nationwide:** 5,500.

BAPTIST HEALTHCARE SYSTEM INC.
4007 Kresge Way, Louisville KY 40207. 502/896-5032. **Fax:** 502/896-5097. **Contact:** Human Resources. **E-mail address:** recruiter@bhsi.com. **World Wide Web address:** http://www.bhsi.com. **Note:** Applicants can submit job interest form online. **Description:** A nonprofit health care system with acute care hospitals in Louisville, Paducah, Lexington, Corbin, and La Grange, Kentucky. The system has over 1,500 licensed beds and is comprised of Baptist Hospital East, Western Baptist Hospital, Central Baptist Hospital, Baptist Regional Medical Center, and Tri-County Baptist Hospital. **Positions advertised include:** Charge Master Coordinator; Maxsys Auditor; Accounts Receivable Clerk; Medicare Specialist; Call Center Specialist; Web system Developer; Business Systems Analyst; Network Engineer. **Corporate headquarters location:** This location. **Operations at this facility include:** Administration; Information Services. **Number of employees nationwide:** 8,400.

DRE INCORPORATED
1800 Williamson Court, Louisville KY 40223-4114. 502/244-4444. **Toll-free phone:** 800/462-8195. **Fax:** 502/244-0369. **Contact:** Human Resources. **World Wide Web address:** http://www.dremed.com. **Description:** A distributor of new, preowned, and refurbished medical equipment, including anesthesia machines, surgical tables, patient monitors, and surgery lights. The company has five divisions – DRE International Division; DRE Veterinary Division; Oral & Maxillofacial Surgery Division; Plastic Surgery Division; and Integrated Rental Services. **Corporate headquarters location:** This location. **Number of employees at this location:** 45.

HARLAN APPALACHIAN REGIONAL HEALTHCARE
81 Ball Park Road, Harlan KY 40831. 606/573-8100. **Fax:** 606/573-8200. **Contact:** Marilyn Hamblin, Professional Recruiter. **E-mail address:** mhamblin@arh.org. **World Wide Web address:** http://www.arh.org. **Description:** A 150-bed acute care hospital that provides a full range of primary and secondary health care services. **NOTE:** Send resumes to Marilyn Hamblin, ARH Systems Professional Recruiter, Appalachian Regional Healthcare, P.O. Box 8086, Lexington KY 40533, or fax to 859/226-2586. **Positions advertised include:** Hospital Health Records Analyst; Community Chief Executive Officer; Pharmacy Director. **Special programs:** Internships. **Parent company:** Appalachian Regional Healthcare. **Number of employees at this location:** 450.

KINDRED HEALTHCARE
680 South Fourth Street, Louisville KY 40202. 502/596-7300. **Fax:** 502/596-4052. **Contact:** Human Resources. **World Wide Web address:** http://www.kindredhealthcare.com. **Description:** A healthcare network that operates 61 hospitals and pulmonary units, 315 nursing centers, and contract rehabilitation services in 40 states. **Note:** Job seekers may apply for openings online. Part-time positions are offered. Positions are listed on http://www.monster.com as well as Kindred Health Care's website. **Positions advertised include:** Senior Programming Analyst; C# Developer; Pharmacy Operations Specialist; Implementation Project Manager; Transcriptionist; Program Manager; Outpatient Medical Records Coder; Systems Programmer; Manager of Enterals. **Special programs:** Tuition Reimbursement Program. **Corporate headquarters location:** This location. **Other area locations:** Lexington KY. **Other U.S. locations:** Nationwide. **Listed on:** New York Stock Exchange. **Stock exchange symbol:** KIND. **Number of employees at this location:** 350. **Number of employees nationwide:** 53,000.

KOSAIR CHILDREN'S HOSPITAL
211 East Chestnut Street, Louisville KY 40202. 502/629-5950. **Contact:** Human Resources. **World Wide Web address:** http://www.kosairchildrens.com. **Description:** A free-standing, full-service, tertiary care, 253-bed children's hospital. **NOTE:** All hiring is conducted through the parent company. Resumes should be directed to Norton Healthcare Workforce Development Office, 233 East Broadway, Louisville KY 40202. **Positions advertised include:** LPN Child Psychiatric; Coordinator of Eligibility Services/Financial Counselor. **Parent company:** Norton Healthcare.

NORTON HEALTHCARE
233 East Broadway, Louisville KY 40202. 502/629-3696. **Contact:** Workforce Development Office. **World Wide Web address:** http://www.nortonhealthcare.com. **Description:** A healthcare system that operates seven hospitals including Norton Hospital and Kosair Children's Hospital and provides services throughout Kentucky and southern Indiana. **NOTE:** Hiring for all of Norton Healthcare's hospitals and clinics takes place at this location. Entry-level positions are offered. **Positions advertised include:** Registered Nurse; Radiology Vice President. **Special programs:** Norton Scholar Program; Internships. **Corporate headquarters location:** This location (Norton Hospital). **Number of employees at this location:** 1,913.

OWENSBORO MEDICAL HEALTH SYSTEM
811 East Parrish Avenue, P.O. Box 20007, Owensboro KY 42303. 270/688-2780. **Fax:** 270/688-1610. **Recorded jobline:** 270/688-2790. **Contact:** Recruitment Staff. **World Wide Web address:** http://www.omhs.org. **Description:** A comprehensive health system that operates hospitals and other medical facilities in Kentucky and Indiana. **Positions advertised include:** Physical Therapy Associate; Physical Therapist; Vascular Lab Tech; Certified Surgical Technician; Registered Nurse; Licensed Practical Nurse; Nurses Aide; Financial Counselor. **Number of employees at this location:** 2,400.

ROOD & RIDDLE EQUINE HOSPITAL
2150 Georgetown Road, P.O. Box 12070, Lexington KY 40580. 859/233-0371. **Fax:** 859/255-5367. **Contact:** Personnel. **E-mail address:** rreh@roodandriddle.com. **World Wide Web address:** http://www.roodandriddle.com. **Description:** A full-service equine hospital. Founded in 1986. **Positions advertised include:** Surgery Technician; Nursing Staff. **Special programs:** Internships; Training. **Number of employees at this locations:** 200.

ST. JOSEPH HOSPITAL
One Saint Joseph Drive, Lexington KY 40504. 859/313-1000. **Fax:** 859/313-3100. **Contact:** Laura Solomonson, Employment Coordinator. **E-mail address:** solomonsonl@sjhlex.org. **World Wide Web address:** http://www.sjhlex.org. **Description:** A private, nonprofit hospital that is one of eight divisions of the Sisters of Charity of Nazareth Health Corporation. **Positions advertised include:** Medical Records Specialist; Health Data Analyst; Business Office Registrar; Unit Secretary; Radiology Dispatch; Radiology Secretary; Transcriptionist Supervisor; Technician; Case Manager; Echo Vascular Tech; Endoscopy Tech; Anesthesia Technician; Registered Nurse; Lab Support Specialist; Licenses Practical Nurse; Nurses Aide.

JENNIE STUART MEDICAL CENTER
320 West 18th Street, P.O. Box 2400, Hopkinsville KY 42240-2400. 270/887-0177. **Fax:** 270/887-0178. **Recorded jobline:** 270/887-0654. **Contact:** Austin Moss, Vice President of Human Resources. **World Wide Web address:** http://www.jsmc.org. **Description:** A 195-bed, acute care hospital offering a full range of services. **Positions advertised include:** Physician; Radiology Technician; Operating Room Registered Nurse; Medical Technician; Microbiologist; Medical Surgeon Registered Nurse; Licensed Practical Nurse; Ambulatory Services Licensed Practical Nurse. **Number of employees at this location:** 600.

U.S. DEPARTMENT OF VETERANS AFFAIRS VETERANS ADMINISTRATION MEDICAL CENTER
1101 Veteran's Drive, Lexington KY 40502-2236. 859/281-3939. **Contact:** Katherine Smith. **World Wide Web address:** http://www.va.gov. **Description:** A medical center operated by the U.S. Department of Veterans Affairs that provides acute and extended care services. From 54 hospitals in 1930, the VA health care system has grown to include 171 medical centers; more than 364 outpatient, community, and outreach clinics; 130 nursing home care units; and 37 domiciles. VA operates at least one medical center in each of the 48 contiguous states, Puerto Rico, and the District of Columbia. With approximately 76,000 medical center beds, VA treats nearly 1 million patients in VA hospitals; 75,000 in nursing home care units; and 25,000 in domiciles. VA's outpatient clinics register approximately 24 million visits per year. **Positions advertised include:** Staff Nurse. **Number of employees at this location:** 2,000.

VETERINARY ASSOCIATES STONEFIELD
203 Moser Road, Louisville KY 40223. 502/245-7863. **Fax:** 502/245-2869. **Contact:** Dr. Sam Vaughn. **E-mail address:** drvaughn@vetcity.com. **World Wide Web address:** http://www.vetcity.com. **Description:** A small animal clinic with specialties in bird care, breeding, dental care, and laser surgery, as well as exotic pet care.

Louisiana

AMCOL HEALTH AND BEAUTY SOLUTIONS
301 Laser Lane, Lafayette LA 70507. 337/232-6838. **Toll-free phone:** 866/657-0743. **Fax:** 337/235-8118. **Contact:** Human Resources. **World Wide Web address:** http://www.healthbeautysolutions.com. **Description:** AMCOL Health & Beauty Solutions, Inc. uses technology and a staff of chemists and engineers to provide Personal Care, Cosmetics, Pharmaceutical, and Nutraceutical products. **Corporate headquarters location:** Arlington Heights IL. **Parent company:** AMCOL International Corporation.

AMEDISYS
11100 Mead Road, Suite 300, Baton Rouge LA 70816. 225/292-2031. **Contact:** Human Resources. **E-mail Address:** info@amedisys.com. **World Wide Web address:** http://www.amedisys.com. **Description:** A provider of home health care services operating in 17 states. **Positions advertised include:** Internal Auditor; Programmer; SEC Accountant; Sr. Accountant; Sr. Accounting Manager; Case Manager RN; Director of Operations; Home Health Aide; RN. **Corporate headquarters location:** This location. **Listed on:** NASDAQ. **Stock exchange symbol:** AMED.

BATON ROUGE GENERAL MEDICAL CENTER
3600 Florida Boulevard, Baton Rouge LA 70806. 225/387-7000.**Fax:** 225/381-6825. **Recorded jobline:** 866/800-1126. **Contact:** Human Resources. **E-mail address:** human.resources@brgeneral.org. **World Wide Web address:** http://www.generalhealth.org. **Description:** A community-owned, non-profit, full-service hospital, specializing in Cancer Care, Heart Care and Neonatal Care. **NOTE:** Visit the website for a current listing of all available positions. **Positions advertised include:** Nursing Support; Office/Clerical; Physicians; Registered Nurses. **Other area locations:** Bluebonnet LA. **President/CEO:** William R. Holman. **Number of employees at this location:** Over 2,000.

CHRISTUS ST. PATRICK HOSPITAL
P.O. Box 3401, Lake Charles LA 70602-3401. 337/436-2511. **Physical address:** 524 South Ryan Street, Lake Charles LA 70601. **Toll-free phone:** 888/72B-WELL. **Fax:** 337/491-7157. **Recorded jobline:** 337/491-7519. **Contact:** Joe Anderson, Recruiter. **World Wide Web address:** http://www.stpatrickhospital.org. **Description:** A nonprofit, Catholic hospital that offers a variety of services including cardiovascular care, inpatient and outpatient services, cancer treatment, rehabilitation, physical therapy, and behavioral health services. Founded in 1908. **NOTE:** Job seekers are encouraged to apply in person at 1607 Foster Street, Lake Charles LA, online at http://www.christushealth.org, or by contacting the recruiter, Joe Anderson, at 337/491-7572. **Positions advertised include:** Management; Nursing; Professional, Clinical; Professional, Non-Clinical. **Special programs:** Tuition Reimbursement Program; Continuing Education Program; Internships. **Other U.S. locations:** AR; TX; OK; UT. **Parent company:** Christus Health.

GREEN CLINIC
1200 South Farmerville Street, Ruston LA 71270. 318/255-3690. **Fax:** 318/255-4360. **Contact:** Nita Green, DON, at 318/251-6299 **World Wide Web address:** http://www.green-clinic.com. **Description:** A health clinic consisting of an in-house physical therapy department and an outpatient ambulatory surgical center. Founded in 1948. **NOTE:** Positions are listed on website when they become available. **Positions advertised include:** Licensed Practical Nurse. **Number of employees at this location:** over 200.

LIFECARE HOSPITALS OF SHREVEPORT
9320 Linwood Avenue, Shreveport LA 71106. 318/688-8504. **Toll-free phone:** 800/280-5433. **Fax:** 318/683-4545. **Contact:** Human Resources. **E-mail address:** ShreveportHR@lifecare-hospitals.com. **World Wide Web address:** http://www.lifecare-hospitals.com. **Description:** A long-term, acute care hospital with 130 beds that specializes in individualized, therapy-driven treatment. LifeCare services include respiratory, physical, occupational, speech, and recreational therapy. **Positions advertised include:** RN; LPN; Physical Therapist; Charge Nurse; Rehabilitation Technician; Director of Human Resources. **Corporate headquarters location:** Plano TX. **Other area locations:** New Orleans. **Parent company:** LifeCare Hospitals, Incorporated, with locations nationwide. **Listed on:** Privately held. **CEO:** Doug Parker. **Number of employees at this location:** 160.

OAKDALE COMMUNITY HOSPITAL
130 North Hospital Drive, Oakdale LA 71463. 318/335-3700. **Fax:** 318/215-3024. **Contact:** Human Resources Department at 318/215.3253. **World Wide Web address:** http://www.oakdalecommunityhospital.com. **Description:** A community hospital that provides a wide array of both inpatient and outpatient services. **NOTE:** Search current job openings and apply online. For physician opportunities, contact CEO H.J. Gaspard at 318/335-3700. **Positions advertised include:** Medical Technologist; Patient Care Assistant; Nurse Manager; Orthopaedic Surgeon; General Surgeon; Ear/Nose/Throat Physician; Primary Care Physician. **Special programs:** Summer Jobs. **Parent Company:** Rapides Healthcare System, LLC. **CEO:** H.J. Gaspard. **Number of employees at this location:** over 200.

OCHSNER CLINIC FOUNDATION
1514 Jefferson Highway, New Orleans LA 70121. 504/842-4000. **Toll-free phone:** 800/874-8984. **Fax:** 225/761.5441. **Contact:** Human Resources. **World Wide Web address:** http://www.ochsner.org. **Description:** A nonprofit organization offering patient care, medical education, and clinical research activities. The foundation has 24 clinics located throughout the region. **NOTE:** Search current job openings and apply online. For physician positions, call the Ochsner Clinic Foundation's Department of Professional Recruiting at 800/488-2240, fax 225/761-5441, or e-mail profrecruiting@ochsner.org. Resumes for physician positions can be sent to Ochsner Clinic Foundation, 9001 Summa Avenue, Baton Rouge LA 70809. **Positions advertised include:** Physicians; Registration Receptionist; Medical Records Analyst; Scanner; Customer Service Representative; Collector; Human Resources Assistant; Cancer Registrar; Coder. **Special Programs:** Administrative Fellowship Program. **Corporate headquarters location:** This location. **Other area location:** Statewide.

OUR LADY OF THE LAKE REGIONAL MEDICAL CENTER
5000 Hennessy Boulevard, Baton Rouge LA 70808. 225/765-8803. **Recorded jobline:** 225/765-1004. **Contact:** Human Resources. **World Wide Web address:** http://www.ololrmc.com. **Description:** Established by the Franciscan Missionaries of Our Lady, Our Lady of the Lake is a major medical center located on a 100-acre campus. The hospital has 852 beds and a medical staff with 700 physicians. Services range from emergency room to home health and outpatient programs, and include intermediate care such as skilled nursing. Founded in 1923. **NOTE:** Send resumes to 5311 Dijon, Baton Rouge LA 70808, or search job openings and apply online. **Positions advertised include:** Administrative Assistant; Blood Donor Recruiter; Blood Donor Technician; Caregiver; Case Technician; Certified Respiratory Therapist; Chaplain; Chemical Dependency Counselor; Communications Clerk; Compensation Analyst; COPE Specialist; Director Pastoral Care; Driver. **Special programs:** Tuition Reimbursement; Health Center. **CEO:** Robert C. Davidge. **Number of employees at this location:** over 3,000.

RICHLAND PARISH HOSPITAL
407 Cincinnati Street, Delhi LA 71232. 318/878-6327. **Contact:** Personnel Director. **Description:** A small, short-term, nonprofit hospital of 40 beds with affiliated home care, cardiac rehabilitation programs, KidMed children's services, and outpatient psychiatric care for the elderly. Create a profile at http://www.hospitalsoup.com to be notified by e-mail of future job openings. **Special programs:** Internships. **Administrator:** Michael Carroll. **Number of employees at this location:** 80.

ST. CHARLES PARISH HOSPITAL
1057 Paul Maillard Road, Luling LA 70070. 985/785-3704. **Recorded jobline:** 985/785-4249. **Contact:** Human Resources. **World Wide Web address:** http://www.st.ch.net. **Description:** A non-profit, community-based hospital with a 56 bed facility. Hospital services include emergency medicine, physical therapy, speech therapy, cardiac rehabilitation, outpatient surgeries, dialysis, intensive care, and adult psychiatry. **NOTE:** Applications are accepted for posted positions only during the hours of 9:30-11:30am and 1:00-4:00pm, Monday through Thursday, in the Human Resources Building. **Positions advertised include:** Equipment Technician; Ultrasonographer; Clinical Associate; Case Manager; Medical Transcriptionist.

ST. FRANCIS MEDICAL CENTER
309 Jackson Street, Monroe LA 71201. 318/327-4000. **Fax:** 318/327-4870. **Recorded jobline:** 318/327-4562. **Contact:** Human Resources. **World Wide Web**

address: http://www.stfran.com. **Description:** A modern, 450-bed, private, full-service hospital sponsored by the Franciscan Missionaries of Our Lady. **NOTE:** Submission of resumes online is the recommended manner of application. **Number of employees at this location:** 1,700.

SLIDELL MEMORIAL HOSPITAL
1001 Gause Boulevard, Slidell LA 70458-2939. 985/649-8519. **Contact:** Human Resources. **World Wide Web address:** http://www.slidellmemorial.org. **Description:** A 182 bed, full-service, acute care, non-profit, community hospital that provides health care services to the entire St. Tammany Parish, Pearl River County of Mississippi, and the greater Gulf Coast region. The hospital provides a full spectrum of health care services, community education, and physician referral services. **NOTE:** Submit applications in person at the Human Resources Building at 1111 Gause Boulevard on the east side of the building, or by e-mail to hr@smhplus.org. For physician positions, contact the Physician Recruiter at 985/649-8834. **Positions advertised include:** Respiratory Therapist; Clinical Manager; Transcriptionist; Nurse Extender; Switchboard Operator; Medical Auditor; Physical Therapist. **CEO:** Bob Hawley.

TOURO INFIRMARY
1401 Foucher Street, New Orleans LA 70115. 504/897-7011. **Fax:** 504/897-8719. **Recorded jobline:** 866/710-4183. **Contact:** Lynne Jones, Human Resources Recruiter. **E-mail address:** resumes@touro.com. **World Wide Web address:** http://www.touro.com. **Description:** A nonprofit 350-bed hospital composed of centers for physical medicine and rehabilitation, obstetrics and gynecology, mental health services, and cancer care and treatment. **NOTE:** For information on nursing, call 504/897-8340. **Positions advertised include:** MRI/CT Tech; Patient Care Supervisor; Reimbursement Log Clerk; Home Health Speech Therapist; Exercise Leader; General Mechanic; Temporary Courier; Pathology Clerk; Manager of Reimbursement; Emergency Department Tech; Food Service Worker; Housekeeper; Application Analyst; Trayline Supervisor; Health Record Analyst. **Special programs:** Internships. **President/CEO:** Gary M. Stein.

WEST JEFFERSON MEDICAL CENTER
1101 Medical Center Boulevard, Marrero LA 70072. 504/347-5511. **Contact:** Human Resources. **World Wide Web address:** http://www.wjmc.org. **Description:** A non-profit, community hospital of the West Bank in Jefferson Parish. Comprehensive programs and services include preventative care, fitness and wellness, acute care, skilled nursing, rehabilitation, and home health care. **Positions advertised include:** Coding Specialist; EKG Technician; EMT Paramedic; Fitness Coordinator; Medical Assistant. **NOTE:** Search open positions and apply online. **President/CEO:** A. Gary Muller. **Number of employees at this location:** Over 1,800.

WOMEN'S HOSPITAL
P.O. Box 95009, Baton Rouge LA 70895-9009. 225/924-8655. **Physical address:** 9050 Airline Highway, Baton Rouge LA 70815. **Fax:** 225/928-8850. **Recorded jobline:** 225/924.8655, extension 3. **Contact:** Human Resources. **World Wide Web address:** http://www.womans.com. **Description:** A 225-bed, non-profit women's specialty hospital composed of a Breast Center, Osteoporosis Center, Cosmetic Surgery Center, Urinary Incontinence Center, Genetics Clinic, Woman's Center for Fertility and Advanced Reproductive Medicine, and a Women's Fitness Center. Other services include prenatal and women's health education; gynecologic and prenatal surgery and care; physical, speech, respiratory, and occupational therapy; as well as pediatric subspecialty clinics. **NOTE:** Search current job openings and apply online. **Positions advertised include:** Respiratory Therapist; Communications Operator; Distribution Manager; Financial Analyst; Pharmacist; Grants Administrator. **Special Programs:** Tuition Reimbursement Program; Staff Development Program. **President/CEO:** Teri G. Fontenot. **Number of employees at this location:** 1,500.

<u>Maine</u>

THE AROOSTOOK MEDICAL CENTER
P.O. Box 151, 140 Academy Street, Presque Isle ME 04769. 207/768-4026. **Fax:** 207/768-4045. **Contact:** Pamela, Human Resources. **E-mail address:** bturner@tamc.org. **World Wide Web address:** http://www.tamc.org. **Description:** A 212-bed, tri-campus facility located in northern Maine. The center is a nonprofit organization and offers a wide range of services. Founded in 1912**Positions advertised include:** CPT – Physical Therapist; Food Service Attendant; Medical Assistant; LPN/Office Nurse; Billing Technician; Central Registration Representative; Clinical Coordinator; Clinical Social Worker; CAN; EMT; Nuclear Medical Technician; Nursing Home Administrator; Radiology Technician; Receptionist; RN – OR; Secretary/Receptionist; Transcriptionist; Ultrasound Technician; VP of Nursing Services; Warehouse Receiving Clerk; RN – Labor and Delivery. **Corporate headquarters location:** This location. **Number of employees at this location:** 650.

CENTRAL MAINE MEDICAL CENTER
300 Main Street, Lewiston ME 04240-0305. 207/795-2390. **Fax:** 207/753-2385. **Contact:** Human Resources. **E-mail address:** recruitment@cmhc.org. **World Wide Web address:** http://www.cmmc.org. **Description:** A 250-bed medical center offering a full-range of medical services including cardiac care, emergency services, rehabilitation services, cancer care, and LifeFlight of Maine, a medical helicopter service. **NOTE:** Search posted openings and apply on-line only. Paper resumes not accepted and telephone contact is discouraged. **Positions advertised include:** Aerobic Instructor; Biomedical Equipment Technician; Budget Analyst; Cat Scan Technologist; Clinical Assistant; LPN; Clinical Dietician; Clinical Lab Scientist; Cytotechnologist; Environmental Services Aide; ER Office Manager; Insurance Follow-up Representative; Medical Technologist; Nursing Supervisor; Outpatient Licensed Clinical Social Worker; Pediatric Nurse Practitioner; Phlebotomist; Respiratory Therapist; RN, Various Departments; Staff Therapist – Occupational Therapy and Physical Therapy. **Parent company:** Central Maine Health Care. **Number of employees at this location:** 1,100.

FRANKLIN MEMORIAL HOSPITAL
111 Franklin Health Commons, Farmington ME 04938. 207/779-2363. **Toll-free phone:** 800/398-6031. **Fax:** 207/779-2606. **Contact:** Carol Jackson, Human Resources. **E-mail address:** humanresources@fchn.org. **World Wide Web address:** http://www.fchn.org/fmh. **Description:** A 70-bed, acute care, community hospital serving west central Maine. This is a nonprofit company. **NOTE:** Search posted openings and download application on-line. **Positions advertised include:** Clinician Counselor; Radiologic Technologist; Evening Radiologic Technologist; Ultrasound Sonographer; OR Staff Nurse; ICU RN. **Parent company:** Franklin Community Health Network. **Operations at this facility include:** Administration; Service. **Number of employees at this location:** 465.

HEALTHREACH NETWORK
8 Highwood Street, P.O. Box 829, Waterville ME 04903-0829. 207/872-4660. **Toll-free phone:** 800/427-1127. **Contact:** Human Resources. **World Wide Web address:** http://www.mainegeneral.org. **Description:** Provides a variety of health care services ranging from counseling to home health nursing. **NOTE:** Healthreach Network is a subsidiary of Maine General, applicants will be forwarded to Maine General web site to search posted openings and apply on-line. No paper resumes are accepted and telephone contact is discouraged. **Positions advertised include:** Medical Care Review Coordinator; Medical Physicist; Occupational Therapist; Pharmacist; Physical Therapist; Physical Therapy Assistant; Speech-

Language Pathologist Float; Mental Health/Substance Abuse Clinician; Substance Abuse Counselor; RN – various Departments; Float RN – Various Departments; Dialysis Technician; Nursing Unit Assistant; Phlebotomist; Rehab Technician; Health Information Clerk; Registration Representative; Team Leader. **Other area locations:** Statewide. Parent company: **Parent company:** Maine General. **Number of employees nationwide:** 376.

MERCY HOSPITAL
144 State Street, Portland ME 04101. 207/879-3464. **Toll-free phone:** 800/293-6583. **Recorded jobline:** 207/879-3674. **Contact:** Human Resources Department. **World Wide Web address:** http://www.mercyhospital.org. **Description:** A hospital providing service to Portland ME and surrounding communities. **NOTE:** Search posted openings and apply on-line only. No paper resumes are accepted and telephone contact is discouraged. **Positions advertised include:** Accountant; Cafeteria Service Assistant; Certified Surgical Technologist; Clinical Dietitian; Clinical Nurse Educator; Clinical Nurse – Various Departments; CRNA; Environmental Service Assistant; Food Service Assistant; Lab Assistant; Nuclear Medicine Technologist; Out-Patient Counselor; Physical Therapist; Radiology Client Service Coordinator; Security Officer; Switchboard Operator; Therapist; Ultrasound Technician.

INLAND HOSPITAL
200 Kennedy Memorial Drive, Waterville ME 04901. 207/861-3028. **Fax:** 207/861-3053. **Contact:** Human Resources. **World Wide Web address:** http://www.inlandhospital.org. **Description:** A 78-bed, nonprofit, acute care hospital that uses both osteopathic and allopathic physicians. **NOTE:** Search poste openings and apply on-line. No paper resumes are accepted. Applicants are redirected to www.emh.org and must select search platform 1. Please visit website for online application form. **Positions advertised include:** File Clerk – Radiology; Occupational Therapist; Occupational Therapy Assistant; Physical Therapist; Physical Therapy Assistant; Radiology Technician; RN – Various Departments; Home Health Aide; Anesthesia Technician; Phlebotomist; Housekeeping Aide; Medical Assistant. **Corporate headquarters location:** This location. **Parent company:** Eastern Maine Healthcare. **Number of employees at this location:** 315.

INTELLICARE
500 Southborough Drive, South Portland ME 04106. 207/775-2600. **Fax:** 207/775-0250. **Toll-free phone:** 888/200-1724. **Contact:** Kris Hoelcher, Human Resources. **E-mail address:** jobs@intellicare.com. **World Wide Web address:** http://www.intellicare.com. **Description:** Operates the largest network of medical call centers in the U.S., with over 225 organizations using the company's technology to provide more efficient and effective care. **NOTE:** Search posted openings and apply on-line. No paper resumes are accepted. **Positions advertised include:** Clinical Service Provider Nurse Consultant; Customer Service Representative; Helpline Screener; Software Engineer. **Other U.S. locations:** Williamsville NY; Columbia MD; Dallas TX; Knoxville TN; Earth City MO.

INTERIM HEALTHCARE
Wonderbrook Center, 57 Portland Road, Kennebunk ME 04043. 207/985-8586. **Fax:** 207/985-4581. **Contact:** Human Resources. **World Wide Web address:** http://www.interimhealthcare.com. **Description:** A home health care agency. **NOTE:** Search posted openings and apply online. **Corporate headquarters location:** Sunrise FL. **Other area locations:** Brunswick ME; Lewiston ME; South Portland ME. **Other U.S. locations:** Nationwide.

MAINE GENERAL MEDICAL CENTER
149 North Street, Waterville ME 04901. 207/872-4600. **Contact:** Human Resources. **World Wide Web address:** http://www.mainegeneral.org. **Description:** A hospital serving central Maine. **NOTE:** Please visit website to search posted openings and apply on-line. Applications are kept on record for one year. **Positions advertised include:** Medical Care Review Coordinator; Medical Physicist; Occupational Therapist; Pharmacist; Physical Therapist; Speech-Language Pathologist Float; Mental Health/Substance Abuse Clinician; Substance Abuse Counselor; RN – Various Departments; Dialysis Technician; Nursing Unit Assistant; Phlebotomist; Rehab Technician; Central Scheduler; Health Information Clerk; Registration Representative; Team Leader. **Other area locations:** Augusta ME; Gardiner ME; Manchester ME; Jackman ME; Skowhegan; Winthrop ME. **Number of employees at this location:** 1,738.

MAINE MEDICAL CENTER
7 Bramhall Street, Suite 1, Portland ME 04102-3175. 207/871-2974. **Recorded jobline:** 877/JOBSMMC. **Fax:** 207/871-4999. **Contact:** Human Resources. **E-mail address:** resumes@mmc.org. **World Wide Web address:** http://www.mmc.org. **Description:** A 598-bed teaching and referral hospital serving northern New England. **NOTE**: Search posted openings and apply on-line. **Positions advertised include:** Administrative Secretary; Admitting Representative; Billing Representative; Care Coordinator; Certified Nursing Assistant – Various Departments; Chief Nuclear Medical Tech; Clinical Medical Physicist; Clinical Nurse – Various Departments; Clinical Pharmacist; Diagnostic Medical Sonographer; Employee Relations Manager; Executive Director; Financial Planning Specialist; HR Receptionist; Medical Office Assistant; Medical Transcriptionist; Nurse Manager; Nursing Unit Secretary; Pediatric Clinical Nurse Specialist; Physical Therapist; Research Fellow; Secretary – Various Departments.

MOUNT DESERT ISLAND HOSPITAL
10 Wayman Lane, P.O. Box 8, Bar Harbor ME 04609. 207/288-5082, ext.: 410. **Fax:** 207/288-4861. **Contact:** Human Resources. **E-mail address:** hr@mdihospital.org. **World Wide Web address:** http://www.mdihospital.org. **Description:** A nonprofit hospital with physician practices. Founded in 1897. **NOTE:** Human Resources is Extension 410. Entry-level positions and second and third shifts are offered. Please visit website, call, or email to request an application form. You may also print an application form from the website. **Positions advertised include:** Health Care Systems Trainer; Health Center Clinical Operations Educator; Medical Assistant; Health Center Receptionist; CNA; Environmental Services Aide; RN-OR; X-ray Technician; Ultrasonographer; Radiologic Technologist. **Number of employees at this location:** 310.

NEW ENGLAND HOME HEALTH CARE
P.O. Box 722, Bangor ME 04402-0722. 207/945-3374. **Physical address:** 412 State Street, Bangor ME 04402. **Toll-free phone:** 800/287-0338. **Fax:** 207/942-1022. **Contact:** Jen Ashmore, Human Resources Manager. **E-mail address:** jen@nehhc.com. **World Wide Web address:** http://www.nehhc.com. **Description:** Provides home care services in Penobscot, Piscataquis, and Hancock Counties of Maine. The company also provides temporary staffing services to hospitals, boarding homes, assisted living centers, nursing homes, and other home care agencies. Founded in 1984. **NOTE:** Please visit website for online application form. Second and third shifts are offered. New England Home Health Care also offers a personal care attendant training program three times a year. **Company slogan:** Helping you meet the challenges of today and tomorrow. **Positions advertised include:** CAN – Various Departments. **Special programs:** Summer Jobs. **Listed on:** Privately held. **Other area locations:** Statewide. **President:** Margaret Michaud-Cain. **Number of employees at this location:** 200.

NORDX LABORATORIES
102 Campus Drive, Unit 118, Scarborough ME 04074. 207/885-7877. **Fax:** 207/885-8350. **Contact:** Human Resources. **E-mail address:** hr@nordx.org. **World**

Wide Web address: http://www.nordx.org. **Description:** Provides comprehensive laboratory services for the Northeast medical community. **Positions advertised include:** Cytology Engineer; Per Diem Phlebotomist; Lead Histology Technician; LIS Analyst; Specimen Processor; Medical Lab Technician; Medical Technologist.

REDINGTON-FAIRVIEW GENERAL HOSPITAL
P.O. Box 468, Skowhegan ME 04976. 207/474-5121. **Physical address:** 46 Fariview Avenue, Skowhegan ME. **Fax:** 207/474-7004. **Contact:** Debbie Buckingham, Human Resources Director. **E-mail address:** wbrooks@rfgh.net. **World Wide Web address:** http://www.rfgh.net. **Description:** A nonprofit, acute care hospital. Founded in 1969. **NOTE:** Download application form on-line. Job-posting boards are also available inside hospital. **Positions advertised include:** Clinic/CAN; Endoscopy Aide; General Maintenance Worker/Plumber; Infection Control Practitioner; MT/MLT; Occupational Therapist; Phlebotomist; Physical Therapist; RN – Various Departments. **President/CEO:** Richard Willett. **Number of employees at this location:** 540.

ST. ANDREWS HOSPITAL & HEALTHCARE CENTER
P.O. Box 417, 6 Saint Andrew's Lane, Boothbay Harbor ME 04538. 207/633-2121. **Fax:** 207/633-4209. **Contact:** Human Resources. **World Wide Web address:** http://www.standrewshealthcare.org. **Description:** A nonprofit hospital that offers acute care, long-term care, a family medical practice, home health care, emergency services, and a retirement community center. Founded in 1908. **NOTE:** Search posted openings and apply on-line. May contact by fax, e-mail or phone. Second and third shifts are offered. **Company slogan:** A tradition of caring. **Listed on:** Privately held. **Annual sales/revenues:** $5 - $10 million. **Number of employees at this location:** 185.

ST. MARY'S REGIONAL MEDICAL CENTER
Campus Avenue, Lewiston ME 04243. 207/777-8779. **Fax:** 207/777-8783. **Contact:** Nicole Moran-Scribner, Employee Relations Director. **World Wide Web address:** http://www.stmarysmaine.com. **Description:** A hospital that operates as part of the Sisters of Charity Health System. **NOTE:** Please visit website to search posted openings and access online application form. **Positions advertised include:** Certified Nurse Assistant; Office Secretary; Account Representative; Behavioral Services Technician; Director – Imaging Services; Nurse Practitioner; Respiratory Care Practitioner; RN – Various Departments; Medical Assistant; Cytotechnologist; Phlebotomist; Behavioral Services Technician; Laboratory Technical Assistant; Dental Hygienist; Resident Technician; Occupational Therapist; Social Worker; LPN; Polysomnography – Registered. **Operations at this facility include:** Administration. **Number of employees at this location:** 1,400.

SPRING HARBOR HOSPITAL
123 Andover Road, Westbrook ME 04092. 207/761-2300. **Toll-free phone:** 888/524-0080. **Fax:** 207/761-2388. **Contact:** Wendy Worcester, Employment Specialist. **E-mail address:** recruitment@springharbor.org. **World Wide Web address:** http://www.springharbor.org. **Description:** A psychiatric hospital that offers inpatient treatment and outpatient counseling services to people of all ages. **NOTE:** Online application form not functioning, e-mail contact only. **Positions advertised include:** Payroll Specialist; Psychiatric NP; Psych Tech; RN; Behavioral Psychologist; Discharge Planner; Clinical Nurse Manager; Dietary Aide. **Special programs:** Internships. **Number of employees at this location:** 500.

STEPHENS MEMORIAL HOSPITAL
181 Main Street, Norway ME 04268-1297. 207/743-5933. **Contact:** Human Resources. **E-mail address:** benochl@wmhcc.org. **World Wide Web address:** http://www.wmhcc.com. **Description:** A hospital offering a special care unit, pace paramedic service, and educational programs on health issues. **NOTE:** Please visit website for online application form. **Positions advertised include:** CNA – Various Departments; LPN – Various Departments; RN – Various Departments; CT Technologist; PT or PTA; Ultrasonographer; Pharmacist; Physical Therapist; IT Meditech Support Analyst. **Parent company:** Western Maine Health. **CEO:** Timothy A. Churchill. **Number of employees at this location:** 400

Maryland

AMERICAN RADIOLOGY SERVICES, INC.
1838 Greene Tree Road, Suite 450. Baltimore MD 21208. 410/484-1900. **Toll-free phone:** 877/559-4277. **Fax:** 410/602-9005. **Recorded jobline:** 410/484-7290 ext. 300. **Contact:** Recruiting Department. **E-mail address:** arsrecruit@americanradiology.com. **World Wide Web address:** http://www3.americanradiology.com. **Description:** Owns and operates fixed-site diagnostic imaging centers located throughout Maryland. Founded in 1997. **Positions advertised include:** Marketing Representative; Senior Accountant; Transcription Supervisor. **Corporate headquarters location:** This location.

ANNE ARUNDEL MEDICAL CENTER
Wayson Pavilion, Suite 350, 2001 Medical Parkway, Annapolis MD 21401. 443/481-1950. **Toll-free phone:** 800/242-2262. **Fax:** 443/481-1951. **Contact:** Human Resources. **World Wide Web address:** http://www.aahs.org. **Description:** A 290-bed, nonprofit, acute care hospital serving more than 64,000 people annually. The medical center's family practice and internal medicine physicians provide comprehensive care for family members including diagnosis, treatment, and prevention of illnesses. Other affiliates of the medical center include Anne Arundel Diagnostics, a complete outpatient radiology service that offers general and specialized radiology services; Anne Arundel Magnetic Resonance Imaging, which diagnoses disorders; and Pathways, a 40-bed treatment facility for adolescents and young adults aged 12 to 25 who suffer from substance abuse or chemical dependency. Founded in 1902. **NOTE:** Entry-level positions are offered. Job seekers may view current openings and apply online. To contact Nursing Recruitment, call 443/481-1958, fax 443/481-1321, or e-mail nursingrecruitment@aahs.org. **Special programs:** Tuition Assistance Program. **Positions advertised include:** Certified Orthopedic Technologist; Clinical Escort; Clinical Nurse; Clinical Specialist; Coding Technician; Compliance Auditor; Database Administrator; Nursing Director; Insurance Validation Unit Team Leader; Intake Counselor; Paralegal; Programming Analyst; Social Worker; Staff Pharmacist.

ATLANTIC GENERAL HOSPITAL
9733 Health Way Drive, Berlin MD 21811. 410/641-9612. **Fax:** 410/641-9715. **Toll-free phone:** 877/641-1100. **Contact:** Trish Tanski, Human Resources. **E-mail address:** ttanski@atlanticgeneral.org. **World Wide Web address:** http://www.atlanticgeneral.org. **Description:** 62 Bed Facility with 163 Physician that opened in 1993. **Positions advertised include:** Medical Technician; Medical Licensed Technician; Certified Nursing Assistant; Nurse Technician; Outpatient Services Technician; Respiratory Therapist; Registered Nurse.

BD BIOSCIENCES
P.O. Box 999, 7 Loveton Circle, Sparks MD 21152. 410/316-4000. **Fax:** 410/316-4156. **Contact:** Human Resources. **World Wide Web address:** http://www.bdbiosciences.com. **Description:** Through its four business units: Clontech, Discovery Labware, Immunocyotmetry Systems, and Pharmingen, BD Biosciences manufactures health care products, medical instrumentation, a line of diagnostic products, and industrial safety equipment. Medical equipment includes hypodermics, intravenous equipment, operating room products, thermometers, gloves, and specialty needles. The company also offers contract

packaging services. **Special programs:** Training; Educational Assistance Program. **Corporate headquarters location:** Franklin Lakes NJ. **International locations:** Worldwide. **Parent company:** Becton, Dickinson & Company. **Operations at this facility include:** Divisional Headquarters; Manufacturing; Research and Development; Sales; Service. The Diagnostics and Industrial Products division manufactures and sells a broad range of medical supplies, devices, and diagnostic systems for use by health care professionals, medical research institutions, and the general public. **Listed on:** New York Stock Exchange. **Stock exchange symbol:** BDX. **President:** Deborah J. Neff. **Number of employees worldwide:** Over 3,000.

BALTIMORE WASHINGTON MEDICAL CENTER
301 Hospital Drive, Glen Burnie MD 21061. 410/787-4000. **Fax:** 410/553-0671. **Recorded jobline:** 410/787-4270. **Contact:** Human Resources. **World Wide Web address:** http://www.bwmc.umms.org. **Description:** A full-service hospital that offers care in the ambulatory surgery, cardiology, community health and wellness programs, comprehensive rehabilitation care, emergency, endoscopy, home care, laboratory, nursing, oncology, orthopedic, primary care, pediatrics, psychiatry, radiology, and respiratory and pulmonary fields. **Positions advertised include:** Registered Nurse; Nurse Practitioner; Nurse Manager. **NOTE:** Online applications are available. Part-time positions and second and third shifts are offered. **Parent company:** University of Maryland Medical System.

BAXTER
9000 Virginia Manner Road, Beltsville MD 20705. 301/210-7040. **Contact:** Human Resources. **World Wide Web address:** http://www.baxter.com. **Description:** A global health-care company that, through its subsidiaries, applies expertise in medical devices, pharmaceuticals, and biotechnology to assist health-care professionals and their patients with treatment of complex medical conditions. **Positions advertised include:** IT Project Manager; Marketing Group Manager; Medical Supervisor; Quality Associate. **Corporate headquarters location:** Deerfield IL. **International locations:** Worldwide. **Listed on:** New York Stock Exchange. **Stock exchange symbol:** BAX. **Number of employees worldwide:** 51,000.

BON SECOURS HOSPITAL
2000 West Baltimore Street, Baltimore MD 21223. 410/362-3000. **Fax:** 410/947-3210. **Recorded jobline:** 410/362-3414. **Contact:** Human Resources. **World Wide Web address:** http://www.bonsecours.org. **Description:** An acute care hospital. **Positions advertised include:** Accounts Payable Assistant; Dance Movement Instructor; Addict Counselor; Project Specialist; Administrative Secretary; Registered Nurse; Clinical Nurse; Physical Therapist; Social Worker; Unit Secretary; Communication Support Specialist; Imaging Services Technician; Special Programming Associate; CT Technician; Environmental Services Associate; Licensed Practical Nurse; Medical Technician; Mental Health Assistant; Network Auditor. **Corporate headquarters location:** Marriottsville MD. **Other U.S. locations:** MI; NY; NJ; PA; VA; FL; KY; SC. **Parent company:** Bon Secours Health System, Incorporated.

CARDINAL HEALTH
3737 Old Georgetown Road, Baltimore MD 21227. 410/536-1000. **Fax:** 410/536-1039. **Contact:** Personnel. **World Wide Web address:** http://www.cardinal.com. **Description:** A producer, developer, and distributor of medical products and technologies for use in hospitals and other health care settings. The company also provides consulting services. **NOTE:** Entry-level positions are offered. **Positions advertised include:** Nuclear Medical Technician. **Special programs:** Internships. **Corporate headquarters location:** Dublin OH. **Other U.S. locations:** Nationwide. **International locations:** Worldwide **Operations at this location include:** This location is a nuclear pharmacy. **President/CEO:** George L. Fotiades. **Sales/revenues:** $40 billion. **Number of employees worldwide:** Over 49,000.

CARROLL COUNTY GENERAL HOSPITAL
200 Memorial Avenue, Westminster MD 21157. 410/871-6833. **Fax:** 410/871-6989. **Recorded jobline:** 410/871-7147. **Contact:** Human Resources. **E-mail address:** hrdept@carrollhospitalcenter.org. **World Wide Web address:** http://www.carrollhospitalcenter.org. **Description:** A private, nonprofit, 158-bed hospital governed by a community-based board which offers comprehensive laboratory and radiology services, an ambulatory surgery center, a cardiac catheterization lab and angiography service, and an inpatient psychiatric unit. **Positions advertised include:** Clincal Social Worker; Director; Clinical Representative; Registered Nurse; Licensed Practical Nurse; Applications Coordinator; Team Leader; Clinical Education Coordinator; Unit Secretary; Emergency Room Registrar; Attendant; Nuclear Medical Technician; Environmental Services Associate; Phlebotomist; Representative Therapist. **Special programs:** Internships; Tuition Reimbursement Program. **Office hours:** Monday – Friday, 7:30 a.m. – 3:00 p.m.

CAT HOSPITAL AT TOWSON
6701 York Road, Baltimore MD 21212. 410/377-7900. **Contact:** Human Resources. **E-mail address:** catdoc@catdoc.com. **World Wide Web address:** http://www.catdoc.com. **Description:** Provides general medical and surgical services as well as chemotherapy, electrocardiograms, and dental care for cats. **Office hours:** Monday – Thursday, 8:00 a.m. – 8:00 p.m., Friday, 8:00 a.m. – 6:00 p.m., Saturday, 8:00 a.m. – 4:00 p.m.

CIVISTA MEDICAL CENTER
701 East Charles Street, P.O. Box 1070, La Plata MD 20646. 301/609-4444. **Fax:** 301/609-4417. **Recorded jobline:** 301/638-1805. **Contact:** Human Resources. **E-mail address:** hr@civista.org. **World Wide Web address:** http://www.civista.org. **Description:** A 131-bed, full-service community hospital. Founded in 1939. **Positions advertised include:** Business Associate; Clerical Imaging Technician; CT Technician; Exercise Physiologist; Medical Technician; Practical Registered Nurse; Nuclear Medical Technologist; Patient Account Representative; Pharmacist. **Special programs:** Internships. **Office hours:** Monday - Tuesday, Thursday – Friday, 8:30 a.m. – 4:00 p.m., Wednesday, 8:00 a.m. – 4:00 p.m. **Corporate headquarters location:** Waldorf MD. **Parent company:** Civista Health is a non-profit organization that delivers health care services to southern Maryland. **Operations at this facility include:** Administration; Divisional Headquarters; Regional Headquarters; Service. **Number of employees at this location:** 750.

FRANKLIN SQUARE HOSPITAL CENTER
9000 Franklin Square Drive, Baltimore MD 21237-3998. 443/777-7000. **Fax:** 443/777-7910. **Contact:** Frank Heine, Human Resources Generalist. **E-mail address:** frank.heine@medstar.net. **World Wide Web address:** http://www.franklinsquare.org. **Description:** A 405-bed acute care community hospital in Baltimore County. Franklin Square specializes as a teaching hospital and offers emergency medicine, oncology, cardiology, labor and delivery, and general medicine. Other major programs include family health, neonatology, psychiatry, and pediatrics. **NOTE:** Online applications are available. To contact Human Resources directly, call 443/777-7233. **Positions advertised include:** Care Associate; Case Manager; Clinical Administrator; Clinical Aide; Administrative Coordinator; Diagnostic Technician; Environmental Support Associate; Generalist; Infection Control Practitioner; Lactating Consultant; Linen Handler; Mammographer; Materials Handler; Mechanic; Medical Assistant; Medical Technician; OD Specialist; Patient Care Associate; Plumber; Program Manager; Registered Nurse; Respiratory Therapist; Site Coordinator; Speech Therapist; Materials Management; Sterile Processing Technician; Ultrasound Technician.

Parent company: MedStar Health is a diversified health care system comprised of over 30 businesses, including seven hospitals in the Baltimore/Washington area. **President:** Charles J. Schindelar.

GARRETT COUNTY MEMORIAL HOSPITAL
251 North Fourth Street, Oakland MD 21550. 301/533-4000. **Fax:** 301/533-4328. **Contact:** Human Resources. **World Wide Web address:** http://www.gcmh.com. **Description:** A county hospital offering comprehensive health care services. **NOTE:** To contact Human Resources directly, call 301/533-4325. **Positions advertised include:** Registered Nurse; Staff Registered Nurse; Certified Nursing Aide; Radiographer; Phlebotomist; Admissions Clerk. **Office hours:** Monday – Friday, 9:00 a.m. – 3:00 p.m. **President/CEO:** Donald P. Battista. **Number of employees at this location:** 350.

HANGER PROSTHETICS AND ORTHOPEDICS SOUTHERN MARYLAND BRACE AND LIMB
8329 Leonardtown Road, P.O. Box 588, Hughesville MD 20637. 301/274-4548. **Contact:** Human Resources. **E-mail address:** sking@hanger.com. **World Wide Web address:** http://www.hanger.com. **Description:** Manufactures braces and prosthetic limbs for hospitals and retail stores. **NOTE:** Interested applicants should send resumes to: Hanger Orthopedic Group, Incorporated, 2 Bethesda Metro Center, Suite 1200, Bethesda MD 20814. **Positions advertised include:** Prosthetist; Orthotist. **Corporate headquarters location:** Bethesda MD. **Other U.S. locations:** Nationwide. **Parent company:** Hanger Orthopedic Group, Incorporated, which is comprised of Hanger Prosthetics and Orthopedics, Incorporated, OPNET, Incorporated, and Southern Prosthetic Supply, Incorporated. **Listed on:** New York Stock Exchange. **Stock exchange symbol:** HGR. **CEO/Chairman:** Ivan R. Sabel. **Number of employees nationwide:** Over 1,000.

HOLY CROSS HOSPITAL
1500 Forest Glen Road, Silver Spring MD 20910. 301/754-7050. **Fax:** 301/754-7031. **Recorded jobline:** 301/754-7044. **Contact:** Human Resources. **World Wide Web address:** http://www.holycrosshealth.org. **Description:** A nonprofit, 442-bed, community teaching hospital that provides primary and secondary health care in both Montgomery and Prince George's Counties, serving almost 200,000 patients each year. Holy Cross Hospital has teaching affiliations with George Washington University School of Medicine in obstetrics and gynecology, general medicine, and surgery, and with Children's National Medical Center in pediatrics. Holy Cross Hospital also offers Healthy Side, a program providing health seminars, classes, support groups, and special events. **NOTE:** Entry-level positions and second and third shifts are offered. **Positions advertised include:** Home Health Services Registered Nurse; Nurse Practitioner; Administrative Coordinator; Depart Patient Care Services; Clinical Nurse. **Special programs:** Internships. **Parent company:** Trinity Health (Novi MI).

HOMECALL, INC.
92 Thomas Johnson Drive, Suite 140, Frederick MD 21702-4383. 301/664-3086. **Toll-free phone:** 800/695-7820. **Contact:** Human Resources. **World Wide Web address:** http://www.homecallinc.com. **Description:** HomeCall provides nursing care to patients who are confined to their homes. **Positions advertised include:** Registered Nurse; LPN; Private Duty Case Nursing Assistant; Home Health Aide; Physical Therapist; Occupational Therapist; Speech Therapist; Medical Social Worker; Medical Records Clerk; Nursing Supervisor; MIS Senior Programmer. **Special programs:** Educational Assistance Program; Mileage Reimbursement Program. **Corporate headquarters location:** This location. **Other area locations:** Statewide. **Subsidiaries include:** FirstCall, Incorporated. **Parent company:** Mid-Atlantic Medical Services, Incorporated (MAMSI), a holding company whose subsidiaries also include HomeCall Pharmaceutical Services and HomeCall Hospice Services. Mid-Atlantic is one of the largest managed care companies in its market, which currently includes Maryland, Virginia, Washington DC, and West Virginia.

HOWARD COUNTY GENERAL HOSPITAL
5755 Cedar Lane, Columbia MD 21044. 410/740-7815. **Fax:** 410/740-7542. **Recorded jobline:** 410/884-4567. **Contact:** Personnel. **E-mail address:** careers@hcgh.org. **World Wide Web address:** http://www.hcgh.org. **Description:** A full-service hospital. **Positions advertised include:** Department of Diagnostic Imaging Administrator; Admitting Counselor; Biomedical Engineering Technician; Cardiographic Technician; Cardiovascular Radiologic Technologist; Chaplain Associate; Cross-Sectional Imaging Supervisor; Dietary Assistant; Director of Plant Operations; Environmental Services Technician; Health Information Clerk; Hostess; LPN; MRI Technician; Medical Social Work Associate; Newborn Hearing Screening Technician; Nuclear Medicine Technologist; Occupational Therapist; Operating Room Technician; Patient Care Technician; Physician Assistant; Registered Nurse Case Manager; Psychiatric Assistant. **Special programs:** Internships; Tuition Assistance Program. **Parent company:** Johns Hopkins Medicine. **Operations at this facility include:** Administration. **Listed on:** Privately held. **Number of employees at this location:** 1,600.

JOHNS HOPKINS HOSPITAL
600 North Wolfe Street, Baltimore MD 21287-1454. 410/955-6575. **Fax:** 410/ 614-2960. **Contact:** Human Resources. **E-mail address:** careers@jhmi.edu. **World Wide Web address:** http://www.hopkinshospital.org. **Description:** A 1,036-bed hospital that is a part of Johns Hopkins Health System, which includes Johns Hopkins Bayview Medical Center, an outpatient center, a geriatrics center, and Johns Hopkins Home Care Group. Johns Hopkins offers programs in AIDS and cancer treatment, cardiology, endocrinology, gastroenterology, geriatrics, gynecology, neurology, orthopedics, otolaryngology, rheumatology, urology, ophthalmology, pediatrics, and psychiatry. **NOTE:** Resumes should be mailed to: The Johns Hopkins Hospital, Department of Human Resources, Office of Career Services, 98 North Broadway, 3rd Floor, Baltimore MD 21231. Online applications are also available. **Positions advertised include:** Addiction Therapist; Administrative Coordinator; Assistant Director; Case Manager Nursing Associate; Clinical Social Worker; Clinical Technician; Credentialing Coordinator; Information Receptionist; Lab Technician; Mail Services Support Clerk; Clinical Nurse; Pharmacist; Programs Analyst. **Special programs:** Training; Tuition Reimbursement Program. **Office hours:** Monday – Friday, 9:00 a.m. – 4:00 p.m. **President:** Ronald R. Peterson. **Number of employees at this location:** 8,500.

KENNEDY KRIEGER INSTITUTE
707 North Broadway, Baltimore MD 21205. 443/923-9200. **Recorded jobline:** 443/923-5820. **Contact:** Human Resources. **World Wide Web address:** http://www.kennedykrieger.org. **Description:** Kennedy Krieger Institute began as Children's Rehabilitation Center in 1937 to serve children with cerebral palsy and from there developed in a center for research and treatment of children's neurological diseases. The Kennedy Krieger School for children with physical, emotional, and learning disabilities offers extended day programs for adolescents with severe emotional disabilities. **NOTE:** Interested jobseekers are encouraged to apply online. If submitting resume by mail, send to: KKI Processing Center, 28501-A Ryan Road, A-105, Warren MI 48092. **Positions advertised include:** Aide; Accounting Specialist; Administrative Assistant; Assistant Teacher. **Special program:** Tuition Reimbursement Program. **President:** Gary W. Goldstein, MD.

KESWICK MULTI-CARE CENTER
700 West 40th Street, Baltimore MD 21211. 410/662-4218. **Fax:** 410/662-4263. **Recorded jobline:** 410/662-

4350. **Contact:** Human Resources. **E-mail address:** hr@keswick-multicare.org. **World Wide Web address:** http://www.keswick-multicare.org. **Description:** A nursing home that provides adult daycare and assisted living services. Founded in 1883. **NOTE:** Entry-level positions and second and third shifts are offered. Job seekers may apply online. **Company slogan:** We can make it happen. **Positions advertised include:** Dietitian; Floor Technician; Geriatric Nursing Assistant; Staff Registered Nurse; Licensed Practical Nurse; MDS Coordinator; Adult Day Services Driver; Building Engineer; Security Agent; Nursing Director; 1st Class Mechanic. **Special programs:** Summer Jobs; Tuition Reimbursement Program; Nursing Scholarship Program. **Office hours:** Monday – Friday, 8:00 a.m. – 5:00 p.m. **Corporate headquarters location:** This location. **Listed on:** Privately held. **CEO:** Andrea Braid. **Number of employees at this location:** 435.

McCREADY HEALTH SERVICES FOUNDATION
201 Hall Highway, Crisfield MD 21817. 410/968-1200. **Fax:** 410/968-3005. **Contact:** Human Resources. **E-mail address:** hr@mccreadyfoundation.org. **World Wide Web address:** http://www.mccreadyfoundation.org. **Description:** Operates the Edward W. McCready Memorial Hospital, the Alice Byrd Tawes Nursing Home, and the Peyton Center. Combined, these facilities offer emergency services; inpatient accommodations including acute medical and surgical beds, skilled nursing beds, and a comprehensive care unit; surgical services including inpatient and outpatient general, gynecological, plastic, and dental surgeries; diagnostic services; rehabilitation and extended recovery services; and social services. Founded in 1923. **NOTE:** Entry-level positions and second and third shifts are offered. Applications are available online. **Positions advertised include:** Registered Nurse; Licensed Practical Nurse; Manager Medical Surgical Unit; Patient Care Registered Nurse; Facilitator. **Special programs:** Training; Co-ops; Summer Jobs. **Corporate headquarters location:** This location. **Administrator/CEO:** Novella Bozman. **Number of employees at this location:** 300.

MEDSTAR HEALTH
5565 Sterrett Place, 5th Floor, Columbia MD 21044. 410/772-6500. **Fax:** 410/ 715-3809. **Contact:** Zipporah Williams, Human Resources Generalist. **E-mail address:** zipporah.williams@medstar.net. **World Wide Web address:** http://www.medstarhealth.org. **Description:** A healthcare organization that operates Franklin Square Hospital; Harbor Hospital Center; National Rehabilitation Hospital; Washington Hospital Center; Union Memorial Hospital; Good Samaritan Hospital; nursing centers; Ask-A-Nurse health information and physician referral; home health care services; and rehabilitation services. **NOTE:** To contact Human Resources directly, call 410/772-6751. **Positions advertised include:** Administrative Assistant; Outreach Program Director. **Corporate headquarters location:** This location. **Number of employees nationwide:** 22,000.

MEMORIAL HOSPITAL OF EASTON
219 South Washington Street, Easton MD 21601. 410/822-1000. **Toll-free phone:** 888/463-3150. **Fax:** 410/819-0161. **Contact:** Human Resources. **World Wide Web address:** http://www.shorehealth.org. **Description:** A 137-bed, acute care hospital that offers inpatient and outpatient services. **NOTE:** Entry-level positions and second and third shifts are offered. Job seekers may apply online. **Positions advertised include:** Staff Production Therapist; Clinical Coordinator; Cardiopulmonary Service; Clinical Information Management Specialist; Editorial Specialist; Environmental Technician; Food Production Associate; Food Services Aide; Development & Operations Director; Database Administrator; Materials Management Director; Licensed Practical Nurse; Registered Nurse; Radiological Specialist; Quality Improvement Nurse. **Special programs:** Co-ops. **Other area locations:** Cambridge MD.

MERCY MEDICAL CENTER
301 St. Paul Place, Baltimore MD 21202. 410/332-9000. **Fax:** 410/783-5863. **Recorded jobline:** 866/332-9414. **Contact:** Human Resources. **E-mail address:** edaly@mercymed.com. **World Wide Web address:** http://www.mdmercy.com. **Description:** An acute care general hospital. Specialty services at Mercy Medical Center include eating disorder treatment programs, women's services, detoxification facilities, and a sexual assault and crisis center. **Positions advertised include:** AC Service Technician; Admissions Coordinator; Patient Transport Aide; Anesthesia Technician; Clinical Nurse; Billing Clerk; Director of Facilities Services; Echocardiology Sonographer; Fire Safety Technician; IT Support Technician; Medical Transcriptionist; Medical Assistant; Medical Technologist; Patient Care Coordinator; Pharmacist; Phlebotomy Supervisor; Physical Therapy Assistant; Registrar; Systems Analyst; Security Officer. **Number of employees at this location:** 1,800.

MID-ATLANTIC MEDICAL SERVICES, INC. (MAMSI)
4 Taft Court, Rockville MD 20850. 301/294-5057. **Fax:** 301/545-5389. **Contact:** Human Resources. **E-mail address:** rockvilleresume@mamsi.com. **World Wide Web address:** http://www.mamsi.com. **Description:** A holding company whose subsidiaries are active in managed health care. MAMSI operates two health maintenance organizations: Maryland Individual Practice Association, Incorporated and Optimum Choice, Incorporated, a nonfederally qualified HMO that serves commercial and other specialized markets such as Medicare and Medicaid. Other MAMSI subsidiaries include Alliance PPO, Incorporated, a preferred provider organization marketing its provider network products to self-insured employers, indemnity carriers, and other health care purchasing groups; Mid-Atlantic Psychiatric Services, Incorporated, which provides specialized nonrisk mental health services; and FirstCall and HomeCall, which provide nursing and care to patients who are confined to their homes. **Positions advertised include:** Web Designer; Web Developer; ARS Sales Representative; Actuate; Developer Representative; Sales Analyst; Applications Developer; Programming Analyst; SQV Database Analyst; Staff Accountant; Implementation Specialist; Program Manager; Benefits Consultant. **Corporate headquarters location:** This location. **Listed on:** New York Stock Exchange. **Stock exchange symbol:** MME. **Number of employees nationwide:** 2,025.

MONTGOMERY GENERAL HOSPITAL
18101 Prince Philip Drive, Olney MD 20832. 301/774-8666. **Fax:** 301/774-7389. **Recorded jobline:** 301/774-8787. **Contact:** Human Resources. **World Wide Web address:** http://www.montgomerygeneral.com. **Description:** A 229-bed, nonprofit, acute care, community hospital. **Positions advertised include:** Administrative Supervisor; Addiction and Mental Health Center Counselor; Cardiovascular/Radiology Nurse; Charge Nurse; Director of Performance Improvement Risk Management; Environmental Assistant; Field Psychiatric Registered Nurse; Home Care Aide; LPN; Nursing Technician; Phlebotomy Clerk; Occupational Therapist; Performance Improvement Specialist; Physical Therapist; Radiologic Technologist; Security Officer; Special Procedures Technician; Speech/Language Pathologist; Unit Clerk; Ultrasound Technologist. **Office hours:** Monday - Friday, 9:00 a.m. - 5:00 p.m. **Operations at this facility include:** Administration. **Listed on:** Privately held. **President/CEO:** Peter W. Monge. **Number of employees at this location:** Over 1,000.

MOSAIC COMMUNITY SERVICES, INC.
1925 Greenspring Drive, Timonium MD 21093. 410/453-9553 ext. 1804. **Fax:** 410/308-8926. **Contact:** Human Resources. **World Wide Web address:** http://www.mosaicinc.org. **Description:** A mental health care provider offering a variety of services and community programs. **Positions advertised include:** Accounting Clerks; Accountant; Administrative

Assistants; Licensed Mental Health Professionals; Program Coordinators; Program Specialists; Rehabilitation Counselors; Residential Service Coordinators.

NORTHWEST HOSPITAL CENTER
5401 Old Court Road, Baltimore MD 21133-5103. 410/521-2200. **Contact:** Human Resources. **World Wide Web address:** http://www.lifebridgehealth.org. **Description:** Northwest Hospital Center is a 240-bed, private, nonprofit hospital with more than 500 doctors specializing in a range of fields. The hospital serves the health care needs of the northwest Baltimore metropolitan area. The hospital is accredited by the Joint Commission on Accreditation of Healthcare Organizations, the American Association of Blood Banks, and the College of American Pathologists. Northwest Hospital Center is affiliated with Cherrywood Manor Extended Care Centre, a 161-bed nursing home. Northwest Hospital Center is also a member of the SunHealth Network, the Preferred Health Network of Maryland, and the Maryland Hospital Association. **NOTE:** Online applications are available. **Positions advertised include:** Registered Nurse; Licensed Practical Nurse; Clinical Nurse; Nurse Manager; Nursing Director; Emergency Room Technician; Sitter; CAT Scan Technician; Medical Radiation Technician; Nuclear Medicine Technologist; Physical & Occupational Therapist; Respiratory Therapist. **Special programs:** Tuition Reimbursement Program.

PARADISE PLAZA INN
9th Street, Ocean City Maryland 21842. 410/289-6381. **Fax:** 410/289-1303. **Toll-free phone:** 888/678-4111. **Contact:** Human Resources. **World Wide Web address:** http://www.paradiseplazainn.com. **Description:** An AAA approved hotel on the boardwalk in Ocean City Maryland. **Positions advertised include:** Maintenance Manager.

PENINSULA REGIONAL MEDICAL CENTER
100 East Carroll Street, Salisbury MD 21801 410/546-6400. **Contact:** Human Resources. **World Wide Web address:** http://www.peninsula.org. **Description:** A 106 year old Care facility with 322 acute & 36 sub acute care beds. **Positions advertised include:** Environmental Services Aide; Licensed Practical Nurse; Clinical Technician; Registered Nurse; Personal Care Assistant; Inventory Control Coordinator; Security Police; Nurse Assistant; Health Care Center Manager; Radiology Registered Nurse; Medical Lab Technician; Cat Scan Technician; Console Operator; Clinical Dietitian; Hospitalist.

ROCKY GORGE ANIMAL HOSPITAL
7515 Brooklyn Bridge Road, Laurel MD 20707. 301/776-7744. **Fax:** 301/776-1575. **Contact:** Personnel. **World Wide Web address:** http://www.rockygorgevet.com. **Description:** Provides general medical and surgical services to domestic animals. **NOTE:** Online applications are available. **Positions advertised include:** Veterinary Receptionist/Assistant. **Office hours:** Monday – Friday, 8:00 a.m. – 8:00 p.m., Saturday, 9:00 a.m. – 2:00 p.m.

ST. JOSEPH MEDICAL CENTER
7601 Osler Drive, Towson MD 21204-7582. 410/337-1288. **Fax:** 410/337-1203. **Contact:** Human Resources. **E-mail address:** stjosmedhr@chi-east.org. **World Wide Web address:** http://www.sjmcmd.org. **Description:** A member of the Franciscan Health System and a regional medical center providing comprehensive acute care with diversified specialty services. The medical center is sponsored by the Sisters of St. Francis of Philadelphia. **NOTE:** Interested job seekers may apply online. **Positions advertised include:** Clinical Unit Clerk; Medical Technician; Occupational Therapist; Physical Therapist; Respiratory Therapist; Certified Nurses Aide; Nurse Practitioner; Registered Nurse; Maintenance Engineer; Physical Therapy Assistant; Radiological Technician; Case Management Director; Medical Records Technologist; Phlebotomist; Data Analyst; Social Worker; Data Entry Clerk; Medical Transcriptionist; Executive Assistant; Case Manager. **President/CEO:** John K. Tolmie.

SHEPPARD PRATT HEALTH SYSTEM
6501 North Charles Street, P.O. Box 6815, Baltimore MD 21285-6815. 410/938-3000. **Contact:** Georgia Coleman, Director of Human Resources. **E-mail address:** recruitment@sheppardpratt.org. **World Wide Web address:** http://www.sheppardpratt.org. **Description:** A nonprofit health system, Sheppard Pratt is a provider of managed behavioral health care services. Sheppard Pratt Health System offers integrated EAP/managed mental health programs, case management, claims processing, and at-risk or fee-for-service contracting. **NOTE:** To contact Human Resources directly, call 410/938-3315. **Positions advertised include:** Chemical Dependency Counselor; Quality Director; Educational Aide; Mental Health Worker; Office Assistant; Patient Accounts Representative; Plant Operations Mechanic; Recreation Therapist; Resource Specialist; School Records Technician; Secretary; Teacher Social Studies; Unit Secretary. **Corporate headquarters location:** This location. **President/CEO:** Dr. Steven S. Sharfstein.

SYMPHONY HEALTH SERVICES
11350 McCormick Road, Executive Plaza IV, Suite 600, Hunt Valley MD 21031. 443/886-2200. **Toll-free phone:** 800/359-5971. **Fax:** 443/886-2350. **Contact:** Human Resources. **World Wide Web address:** http://www.symphonyhealth.com. **Description:** Provides physical, occupational, respiratory, and speech therapy services. The company's operates through four divisions: Respiratory Services, Rehabilitation Works, Mobilex, and Consulting Services. **Other U.S. locations:** Nationwide. **Operations at this facility include:** This location is home to the company's Respiratory Services division. Symphony's Respiratory Services offers management and administrative services, as well as equipment and staffing, to hospitals and nursing facilities.

TENDER LOVING CARE/STAFF BUILDERS
4000 Blackburn Lane, Suite 150, Burtonsville MD 20866. 301/421-9091. **Contact:** Human Resources. **World Wide Web address:** http://www.tlcathome.com. **Description:** A home health care agency. **NOTE:** Interested job seekers may submit resumes online for specific positions or for general consideration. **Positions advertised include:** Care Team Manager; Dietitian; Home Care Nurse; Home Health Aide; Performance Improvement Clinician; Physical Therapist; Social Worker; Speech Language Pathologist. **Special programs:** Training; Tuition Assistance Program. **Corporate headquarters location:** Lake Success NY. **Other area locations:** Baltimore MD. **Other U.S. locations:** Nationwide. **CEO:** James Happ. **Number of employees nationwide:** 20,000.

U.S. DEPARTMENT OF VETERANS AFFAIRS BALTIMORE VETERANS ADMINISTRATION MEDICAL CENTER
10 North Greene Street, Baltimore MD 21201-1524. 410/605-7000. **Recorded jobline:** 800/463-6295x7211. **Contact:** Human Resources. **World Wide Web address:** http://www.va.gov. **Description:** A medical center operated by the U.S. Department of Veterans Affairs (VA). From 54 hospitals in 1930, the VA health care system has grown to include 171 medical centers; more than 364 outpatient, community, and outreach clinics; 130 nursing home care units; and 37 domiciliary residences. VA operates at least one medical center in each of the 48 contiguous states, Puerto Rico, and the District of Columbia. With approximately 76,000 medical center beds, VA treats nearly 1 million patients in VA hospitals; 75,000 in nursing home care units; and 25,000 in domiciliary residences. **Positions advertised include:** Social Worker; Diagnostic Technician; Physical Therapist; Physical Account Supervisor; Medical Records Administrator; Medical Support Assistant.

WARWICK MANOR
3680 Warwick Road, East New Market MD 21631. 410/943-8108. **Contact:** Human Resources. **Description:** Provides behavioral health care and substance abuse services.

WASHINGTON COUNTY HOSPITAL
251 East Antietam Street, Hagerstown MD 21740. 301/790-8500. **Contact:** Human Resources. **World Wide Web address:** http://www.wchsys.org. **Description:** An acute care, nonprofit, regional medical center. Washington County Hospital serves a tri-state region including western Maryland, southern Pennsylvania, and northern West Virginia. Washington County Hospital includes facilities totaling 371 beds; intensive care, coronary care, and progressive care units; a cardiac catheterization lab; a family birthing center; a full range of radiologic/diagnostic services; a pediatric unit; inpatient and outpatient mental health units/services; a certified oncology program; extended care facilities; Alzheimer's disease and related disorders programs; cardiac rehabilitation; community education programs; physician practices; and home health care. **NOTE:** To contact Human Resources directly, call 301/790-8500. **Positions advertised include:** Patient Accounts Representative; Washing Machine Assistant; Registered Nurse; Home Health Aide Therapist; Out Patient Speech Therapist; Ortho Physical Therapist; Neuro Physical Therapist; Occupational Physical Therapist; Day House Keeper; Linen Assistant; Environmental Services Assistant; Licensed Practical Nurse; Utilization Revenue Specialist; Certified Nursing Assistant; Pharmaceutical Technician; Ultrasonographer. **Number of employees at this location:** 1,500.

Massachusetts

ABBOTT LABORATORIES
4A Crosby Drive, Bedford MA 01730. 781/276-6000. **Contact:** Human Resources. **World Wide Web address:** http://www.abbott.com. **Description:** Develops, manufactures, and markets blood-glucose monitoring systems that enable diabetics to manage their disease more effectively. **Positions advertised include:** Site Director; Engineer; Program Coordinator; Scientist; Material Handler; Label Editor. **Corporate headquarters location:** Abbott Park IL. **Other U.S. locations:** Nationwide. **International locations:** Worldwide.

ABIOMED, INC.
22 Cherry Hill Drive, Danvers MA 01923. 978/777-5410. **Fax:** 978/777-8411. **Contact:** Human Resources. **E-mail address:** staffing@abiomed.com. **World Wide Web address:** http://www.abiomed.com. **Description:** Develops, manufactures, and markets cardiovascular, medical, and dental products. The company is also engaged in the research and development of heart support systems. **Positions advertised include:** Clinical Manager, Field Operations; Clinical Research Manager; Product Manager; Scientist. **Corporate headquarters location:** This location. **Subsidiaries include:** Abiodent; Abiomed B.V., Abiomed Cardiovascular; Abiomed R&D. **Operations at this facility include:** Administration; Manufacturing; Research and Development; Sales; Service. **Listed on:** NASDAQ. **Stock exchange symbol:** ABMD. **Number of employees at this location:** 140. **Number of employees nationwide:** 170.

ACCELLENT
100 Fordham Road, Wilmington MA 01887. 978/570-6900. **Toll-free phone:** 866/899-1392. **Fax:** 978/657-0878. **Contact:** Human Resources. **World Wide Web address:** http://www.accellent.com. **Description:** Provides contract manufacturing and design services to medical device manufacturers in the cardiology, endoscopy and orthopaedic markets. **Positions advertised include:** Talent Acquisition Manager; Financial Reporting Specialist; Corporate Account Director; Project Development Engineer. **Corporate headquarters location:** This location. **Other U.S. locations:** Nationwide.

ACTON MEDICAL ASSOCIATES, PC
321 Main Street, Acton MA 01720. 978/263-1425. **Fax:** 978/263-1562. **Contact:** Human Resources. **E-mail address:** hr@actonmedical.com. **World Wide Web address:** http://www.actonmedical.com. **Description:** Offices of a primary care medical group that include laboratory and X-ray facilities. Founded in 1958. **NOTE:** Entry-level positions are offered. **Positions advertised include:** Medical Technologist; PA Diabetes Management; Phlebotomist; Registered Nurse; Licensed Practical Nurse; Internal Medicine. **Special programs:** Internships; Summer Jobs. **Listed on:** Privately held. **Number of employees at this location:** 170.

ALL CARE VISITING NURSE ASSOCIATION
16 City Hall Square, Lynn MA 01901. 781/598-2454. **Toll-free phone:** 800/287-2454. **Fax:** 781/586-1636. **Contact:** Ray Felice, Human Resources Representative. **E-mail address:** professional@allcarevna.org. **World Wide Web address:** http://www.allcarevna.org. **Description:** A nonprofit, certified, home health care agency. The agency's services include HIV/AIDS, mental health, pediatric, oncology, rehab nursing, home nursing, and paraprofessional care. **NOTE:** Entry-level positions and second and third shifts are offered. **Company slogan:** A tradition of caring. **Positions advertised include:** Community Health Nurse; Physical Therapist. **Special programs:** Training; Summer Jobs. **Office hours:** Monday - Friday, 8:00 a.m. - 5:00 p.m. **Corporate headquarters location:** This location. **Subsidiaries include:** All Care Resources provides private-duty nurses and companion care to the elderly. **Number of employees nationwide:** 650.

ALLIANCE IMAGING
600 Federal Street, Andover MA 01810. 978/658-5357. **Contact:** Human Resources. **World Wide Web address:** http://www.allianceimaging.com. **Description:** Alliance Imaging provides magnetic resonance imaging systems and services. The company schedules and screens patients; maintains medical and administrative records; and operates both mobile and fixed MRI systems. **Positions advertised include:** Medical Records Clerk; Scheduling Coordinator. **NOTE:** Search and apply for jobs online. **Corporate headquarters location:** Anaheim CA. **Other U.S. locations:** Nationwide. **Listed on:** New York Stock Exchange. **Stock exchange symbol:** AIQ.

AMERICAN MEDICAL RESPONSE (AMR)
4 Tech Circle, P.O. Box 3720, Natick MA 01760. 508/650-5600. **Toll-free phone:** 800/950-9266. **Fax:** 508/650-5656. **Contact:** Human Resources. **E-mail address:** snorton@amr-ems.com. **World Wide Web address:** http://www.amr-inc.com. **Description:** Provides emergency medical transportation. **Other U.S. locations:** Nationwide.

ANGELL MEMORIAL ANIMAL HOSPITAL
350 South Huntington Avenue, Boston MA 02130. 617/522-7400. **Fax:** 617/989-1601. **Contact:** Recruiter/Trainer. **E-mail address:** recruiter@mspca.org. **World Wide Web address:** http://www.angell.org. **Description:** A veterinary hospital that offers general medical care as well as specialized services including heart catheterization facilities, kidney transplant procedures, and radiology treatments. **Parent company:** Massachusetts Society for the Prevention of Cruelty to Animals (MSPCA).

THE ANIMAL CARE CENTER
678 Brookline Avenue, Brookline MA 02445. 617/277-2030. **E-mail address:** careers@healthypet.org. **World Wide Web address:** http://www.healthypet.org. **Contact:** Human Resources. **Description:** An animal hospital providing medical and surgical services. The Animal Care Center also runs a pet adoption service for the city of Boston.

ANIMED PET HOSPITAL
918 Providence Highway, Dedham MA 02026.

781/329-5333. **Contact:** Human Resources. **Description:** A full-service pet hospital.

ARBOUR SENIOR CARE & COUNSELING SERVICES
100 Ledgewood Place, Suite 202, Rockland MA 02370. 781/871-6550. **Contact:** Human Resources. **Description:** Provides behavioral health services delivered by mobile multidisciplinary teams of clinicians at outpatient service sites. The company offers therapeutic, psychiatric, neurological, and diagnostic imaging services. **Corporate headquarters location:** This location. **Number of employees at this location:** 100.

ARROW INTERNATIONAL, INC.
9 Plymouth Street, Everett MA 02149. 617/389-6400. **Contact:** Human Resources. **E-mail address:** staffing.manager@arrowintl.com. **World Wide Web address:** http://www.arrowintl.com. **Description:** Arrow International develops, manufactures, and markets central vascular access catheterization products. The company's products are also used for patient monitoring, diagnosis, pain management, and treating patients with heart and vascular disease. **Corporate headquarters location:** Reading PA. **Operations at this facility include:** This location manufactures intra-aortic balloons. **Listed on:** NASDAQ. **Stock exchange symbol:** ARRO.

ATHOL MEMORIAL HOSPITAL
2033 Main Street, Athol MA 01331. 978/249-3511. **Fax:** 978/249-5658. **E-mail address:** eamparo@atholhospital.org. **Contact:** Human Resources. **World Wide Web address:** http://www.atholhospital.org. **Description:** An acute care hospital. **Positions advertised include:** MLT; Respiratory Therapist; Physical Therapist.

BETH ISRAEL DEACONESS MEDICAL CENTER
330 Brookline Avenue, Boston MA 02215. 617/667-8000. **Contact:** Human Resources. **World Wide Web address:** http://www.bidmc.harvard.edu. **Description:** A hospital that also supports a network of primary care physicians. **NOTE:** Applicants should send resumes to The Talent Bank at: CareGroup, 21 Autumn Street, Boston MA 02215. **Positions advertised include:** Procurement Manager; Food Service Worker; Director of Human Resources Information Systems; Ultrasonographer; Clinical Research Coordinator; Research Student; Customer Service Representative; Administrative Assistant; Financial Analyst; Materials Handler.

BEVERLY HOSPITAL
85 Herrick Street, Beverly MA 01915. 978/922-3000. **Contact:** Human Resources. **World Wide Web address:** http://www.nhs-healthlink.org. **Description:** A hospital. Beverly Hospital is part of the Northeast Health System. **Positions advertised include:** Access Representative; Administrative Associate; Admissions Registered Nurse; Clinical Associates; Coder; Data Manager; Employment Manager; Executive Assistant; Human Resources Clerk; Lab Associate; Registered Nurse; Security Guard.

BOSTON MEDICAL CENTER
88 East Newton Street, Boston MA 02118. 617/638-8585. **Fax:** 617/638-8577. **Contact:** Human Resources. **World Wide Web address:** http://www.bmc.org. **Description:** A private, nonprofit, 277-bed hospital. The center provides a full range of medical services and offers specialty care units that include psychiatric care, coronary care, metabolic care, medical intensive care, surgical intensive care, the Northeast Regional Center for Brain Injury, the New England Regional Spinal Cord Injury Center, the Breast Health Center, the Cancer Center, the Center for Minimal Access Surgery, the Center for Lung Disease, the Voice Center, the Wald Neurological Unit, the New England Male Reproductive Center, and the University Continence Center. As a major teaching hospital, Boston Medical Center ENC specializes in heart care, the neurosciences, emergency medicine and critical care, elderly care, cancer care, and women's health. The center serves approximately 10,000 admissions and 153,000 outpatient and emergency visits annually. Founded in 1855. **NOTE:** Please send resumes to: Human Resources Department, 88 East Newton Street, Boston MA 02118. **Positions advertised include:** Medical Staff Assistant; Medical Technologist; Radiology Technologist; Respiratory Therapist; Certified Nurses Assistant; Nurse Manager; Registered Nurse; Unit Coordinator; Accounts Receivable Clerk; Administrative Assistant; Administrative Coordinator; Billing Assistant; Patient Access Representative; Research Assistant; Medical Staff Assistant; Residency Coordinator; Payment Processor; General Cleaner; Dietary Aide; Central Processing Technician; Lab Support Technician; Clinical Pharmacist; Budget Manager; Dietician; Record Assistant; Team Leader.

BOSTON PUBLIC HEALTH COMMISSION
1010 Massachusetts Avenue, 6th Floor, Boston MA 02118. 617/534-5395. **Fax:** 617/534-2418. **Contact:** Patty Hall, Staffing Specialist. **E-mail address:** patty_hall@bphc.org. **World Wide Web address:** http://www.bphc.org. **Description:** A nonprofit agency whose mission is to protect, preserve, and promote the well-being of all Boston residents. Boston Public Health Commission provides community-based public health programs including tobacco control, domestic violence prevention, environmental health, communicable disease awareness, maternal/child health, addictions services, homeless services, and AIDS services. **NOTE:** All positions with Boston Public Health Commission require residency in the city of Boston or a willingness to move to Boston if hired. Entry-level positions and second and third shifts are offered. **Positions advertised include:** Research Assistant; Administrative Assistant; Project Manager; Head Administrative Clerk; Project Manager; Administrative Assistant; Social Worker; Program Coordinator; Counselor; Staffing Coordinator; Resource Clerk; Medical Director; Custodian; Data Analyst. **Number of employees at this location:** 1,100.

BOSTON SCIENTIFIC CORPORATION
One Boston Scientific Place, Natick MA 01760-1537. 508/650-8000. **Contact:** Human Resources. **World Wide Web address:** http://www.bostonscientific.com. **Description:** A worldwide developer, manufacturer, and marketer of medical devices used in a broad range of interventional procedures including cardiology, gastroenterology, pulmonary medicine, and vascular surgery. **Positions advertised include:** Research Director; Human Resources Manager; Database Administrator; Software Quality Assurance Specialist; Clinical Data Specialist; Principal Engineer; Safety Coordinator; Project Manager; Administrative Assistant; Clinical Counsel; Strategic Sourcing Manager; Associate Scientist; Medical Research Associate; Tax Analyst; Benefits Analyst; Quality Engineer; Human Resource Process Analyst; Database Specialist; Quality Engineer; Assistant Medical Director; Product Manager; Marketing Communication Specialist; Product Manager. **Corporate headquarters location:** This location. **Other area locations:** Quincy MA. **Other U.S. locations:** CA; FL; IN; MN; NJ; NY. **International locations:** Argentina; Brazil; Mexico; Uruguay; Venezuela. **Listed on:** New York Stock Exchange. **Stock exchange symbol:** BSX.

BRIGHAM & WOMEN'S HOSPITAL
75 Francis Street, Boston MA 02115. 617/732-5790. **Fax:** 617/277-1263. **Contact:** Human Resources. **World Wide Web address:** http://www.brighamandwomens.org. **Description:** A 750-bed, nonprofit hospital. Brigham & Women's houses one of New England's largest birthing centers and a regional center for high-risk obstetrics and neonatology. The hospital is nationally recognized for its transplant programs; joint replacement and orthopedic surgery; and the treatment of arthritis, rheumatic disorders, and cardiovascular disease. **Positions advertised include:** Access Facilitator;

Administrative Secretary; Admitting Officer; Nurse Manager; Licensed Practical Nurse; Clinical Dietician; Coding Specialist; Data Coordinator; Environmental Services Aide; Exercise Psychologist; Programmer Analyst; Medical Technologist; Nurse Practitioner; Personal Care Assistant; Processing Technician; Research Assistant; Registered Nurse; Social Worker; Unit Coordinator. **Parent company:** Partners HealthCare System Inc. **Number of employees at this location:** 8,500.

BROCKTON HOSPITAL
680 Centre Street, Brockton MA 02302. 508/941-7000. **Fax:** 508/941-6204. **Contact:** Human Resources. **World Wide Web address:** http://www.brocktonhospital.com. **Description:** A 250-bed, acute care hospital. **Positions advertised include:** Case Manager; Centralized Scheduler; Certified Nurses Assistant; Clerk; Clinical Care Assistant; Mental Health Worker; Physical Therapist; Registered Nurse; Speech Pathologist; Staff Accountant; Switch Board Operator; Unit Secretary.

CAMBRIDGE HEALTH ALLIANCE
1493 Cambridge Street, Cambridge MA 02139. 617/498-1000. **Contact:** Human Resources. **World Wide Web address:** http://www.challiance.org. **Description:** An alliance made up of Cambridge Hospital, Somerville Hospital, a nursing home and several neighborhood health centers. Cambridge Hospital, also at this location, is a 170-bed, full-service hospital owned by the city of Cambridge and affiliated with Harvard and Tufts Medical Schools. **Positions advertised include:** Administrative Assistant; Applications Analyst; Buyer; Clerk; Cardiac Sonographer; Central Processing Department Technician; Clerk & Typist; Computerized Tomography Technologist; Dental Hygienist; Marketing Specialist; Medical Technician; Medical Assistant; Physical Therapist; Dietary Trainee; Case Management Director; General Data Manager; Hospital Aide.

CANDELA CORPORATION
530 Boston Post Road, Wayland MA 01778. 508/358-7400. **Contact:** Human Resources. **World Wide Web address:** http://www.clzr.com. **Description:** Designs, manufactures, markets, and services lasers for a variety of medical applications. The company also licenses medical products and sells them through its worldwide distribution network. Products include Vbeam, which treats vascular lesions; AlexLAZR, which removes tattoos; and GentleLASE Plus, which removes unwanted hairs and also treats vascular lesions. **Corporate headquarters location:** This location. **Number of employees at this location:** 200.

CAPE COD HOSPITAL
27 Park Street, Hyannis MA 02601. 508/771-1800. **Fax:** 508/790-7964. **Contact:** Personnel. **World Wide Web address:** http://www.capecodhealth.org. **Description:** A nonprofit, 258-bed, general acute care, regional hospital. **Positions advertised include:** Assessment Team Clinician; CAT Scan Technologist; Clinical Dietician; Environmental Service Aide; Food Service Assistant; Occupational Therapist. **Number of employees at this location:** 1,400.

CARITAS ST. ELIZABETH'S MEDICAL CENTER
736 Cambridge Street, Brighton MA 02135. 617/789-3000. **Contact:** Human Resources. **World Wide Web address:** http://www.semc.org. **Description:** A hospital. **Positions advertised include:** Nursing Administration; Administrative Assistant; Ambulatory Scheduling Coordinator; Benefits Manager; Billing Coordinator; Care Manager; Counselor; Dietician; Housekeeper; Licensed Practical Nurse; Medical Technician; Nursing Assistant; Secretary; Registered Nurse. **Parent company:** Caritas Christi Health System.

CATHOLIC MEMORIAL HOME
2446 Highland Avenue, Fall River MA 02720-4599. 508/679-0011. **Contact:** Human Resources. **World Wide Web address:** http://www.dhfo.org. **Description:** A 300-bed nursing home with a unit specializing in caring for those with Alzheimer's disease. **Positions advertised include:** Registered Nurse; Certified Nursing Aide; Licensed Practical Nurse. **Parent company:** Diocesan Health Facilities Office (Fall River MA) operates five nursing homes throughout southeastern Massachusetts.

CHILDREN'S HOSPITAL
333 Longwood Avenue, 2nd Floor, Boston MA 02115. 617/355-7780. **Contact:** Human Resources. **Note:** Please send all resumes to: P.O. Box 549252, Suite 227, Waltham MA 02454-9252. **Fax:** 781/663-3722. **World Wide Web address:** http://www.childrenshospital.org/jobs. **Description:** A full-service pediatric hospital. **Positions advertised include:** Research Technician; Speech Language Pathologist; Application Development Specialist; Staff Nurse; Patient Access Representative; Audiologist; Physician Assistant.

COMMONWEALTH HEMATOLOGY-ONCOLOGY
10 Willard Street, Quincy MA 02169. 617/479-3550. **Contact:** Human Resources. **World Wide Web address:** http://www.chomed.com. **Description:** A private practice outpatient facility specializing in the treatment of cancer and blood disorders. **Other area locations:** Brighton MA; Dorchester MA; Lawrence MA; Malden MA; Milton MA; South Weymouth MA.

COMMUNITY HEALTHLINK
72 Jaques Avenue, Worcester MA 01610. 508/860-1000. **Contact:** Human Resources. **World Wide Web address:** http://www.umassmemorial.org. **Description:** A multifaceted community service center whose programs include substance abuse treatment, outpatient services, geriatric services, medical day treatment, and services for the homeless. Community Healthlink is a member of the UMass Memorial Behavioral Health System.

DANA FARBER CANCER INSTITUTE
44 Binney Street, Boston MA 02115. 617/732-3000. **Contact:** Human Resources. **World Wide Web address:** http://www.dfci.havard.edu. **Description:** A cancer research institute and hospital. **Positions advertised include:** Administrative Assistant; Administrative Specialist; Lab Systems Coordinator; Office Support Specialist; Child Life Specialist; Clinic Assistant; Facilitator; Level II Pharmacist; New Patient Coordinator; Human Resources Specialist; Program Administrator; Clinical Research Audit manager; Intranet Specialist; Health Educator; Intervention Coordinator; Survey Assistant; Research Associate; Research Fellow; Credit Collection Officer; Statistician; Transcription Assistant; Application Analyst; Research Scientist; Nurse Practitioner; Registered Nurse; Research Nurse; Social Worker.

DAVOL INC.
160 New Boston Street, Woburn MA 01801. 781/932-5900. **Fax:** 781/932-4125. **Contact:** Human Resources. **E-mail address:** arlene.andreozzi.@crbard.com. **World Wide Web address:** http://www.davol.com. **Description:** Develops, manufactures, and markets specialty medical products for use in surgical and nonsurgical procedures. Davol specializes in products relating to hernia repair, laparascopy, and orthopedics. **Positions advertised include:** Product Manager; Cost Supervisor; Manufacturing Engineer. **Corporate headquarters location:** Cranston RI. **Parent company:** C.R. Bard, Inc. **Number of employees at this location:** 45.

DEPUY SPINE, INC.
325 Paramount Drive, Raynham MA 02767. 508/880-8100. **Toll-free phone:** 800/227-6633. **Contact:** Personnel. **E-mail address:** careers_acromed@dpyus.jnj.com. **World Wide Web address:** http://www.depuyacromed.com. **Description:** Manufactures and supplies a broad line of surgical

products including instruments, equipment, implants, surgical disposables, and electronic pain control stimulators and electrodes. **Positions advertised include:** Financial Analyst; Sr. Marketing Financial Analyst; Sr. Cost Analyst; Sr. Regulatory Affairs Associate/Project Manager. **Parent company:** Johnson & Johnson.

DIELECTRICS INDUSTRIES, INC.
300 Burnett Road, Chicopee MA 01020. 413/594-8111. **Toll-free phone:** 800/472-7286. **Fax:** 413/594-2343. **Contact:** Personnel. **World Wide Web address:** http://www.dielectrics.com. **Description:** As the medical division of Dielectrics Industries, DMC designs and fabricates a variety of sophisticated medical devices for the laparoscopic, orthopedic, and blood fluid delivery markets. Overall, Dielectrics Industries is a leading designer, developer, fabricator, and supplier of air cell and other bladder technologies. Markets served include medical, aerospace, automotive, recreational, and industrial. Products include laparoscopic surgical devices, inflatable vests, in-line skate inserts, and lumbar support systems. **Corporate headquarters location:** This location.

DIOCESAN HEALTH FACILITIES
368 North Main Street, Fall River MA 02720. 508/679-8154. **Contact:** Human Resources. **World Wide Web address:** http://www.dhfo.org. **Description:** Operates nonprofit nursing homes including Catholic Memorial Home (Fall River MA), Our Lady's Haven (Fairhaven MA), Madonna Manor (North Attleboro MA), Sacred Heart (New Bedford MA), and Marian Manor (Taunton MA). **Corporate headquarters location:** This location.

DIVERSIFIED VISITING NURSE ASSOCIATION (DVNA)
316 Nichols Road, Fitchburg MA 01420. 978/342-6013. **Contact:** Human Resources. **Description:** Provides home care to residents of north central Massachusetts and south central New Hampshire. Nursing care services include antibiotic and nutritional infusions, wound care, cardiac care, and care of ventilator patients. Rehabilitation services include physical, occupational, and speech therapy. **Corporate headquarters location:** Leominster MA. **Parent company:** HealthAlliance also operates a number of other subsidiaries, which include Burbank Hospital; Diversified Medical Equipment Services; Leominster Hospital; Fairlawn Nursing Home; The Highlands; and Coordinated Primary Care.

EAST BOSTON NEIGHBORHOOD HEALTH CENTER
10 Gove Street, East Boston MA 02128. 617/569-5800. **Contact:** Human Resources. **Description:** A community health clinic supporting area urgent care, home care, and physician services.

EAST CAMBRIDGE NEIGHBORHOOD HEALTH CENTER
163 Gore Street, Cambridge MA 02141. 617/665-3000. **Contact:** Human Resources. **Description:** A community-based clinic offering general care on an outpatient basis. **Parent company:** Cambridge Hospital is a 170-bed, full-service hospital owned by the city of Cambridge and affiliated with Harvard and Tufts Medical Schools.

EASTWOOD CARE CENTER
1007 East Street, Dedham MA 02026. 781/329-1520. **Contact:** Human Resources. **Description:** A 145-bed medical center focusing on long-term care and rehabilitation.

EPIX MEDICAL INC.
71 Rogers Street, Cambridge MA 02142. 617/250-6000. **Fax:** 617/250-6041. **Contact:** Human Resources. **E-mail address:** careers@epixmed.com. **World Wide Web address:** http://www.epixmed.com. **Description:** Engaged in the development of advanced imaging agents. The company's initial products in development are for magnetic resonance imaging. **Positions advertised include:** Biophysics Intern; Synthetic Organic Chemist; Director of Pharmacology. **Corporate headquarters location:** This location. **Operations at this facility include:** Administration; Research and Development. **Listed on:** NASDAQ. **Stock exchange symbol:** EPIX. **Number of employees at this location:** 30.

FAIRLAWN NURSING HOME
370 West Street, Leominster MA 01453. 978/537-0771. **Fax:** 978/534-0824. **Contact:** Human Resources. **Description:** Offers long-term care services to the elderly and other adults who need 24-hour nursing and personal care. **Parent company:** HealthAlliance operates a number of other subsidiaries, which include Burbank Hospital, Coordinated Primary Care, Diversified Medical Equipment Services, Diversified Visiting Nurse Association, The Highlands, and Leominster Hospital.

FAULKNER HOSPITAL
1153 Centre Street, Boston MA 02130. 617/522-5800. **Recorded jobline:** 617/983-7426. **Contact:** Human Resources Department. **World Wide Web address:** http://www.faulknerhospital.org. **Description:** A hospital. **Positions advertised include:** Registration Office; Community Benefits Associate; Health Information Systems; Receptionist; Rehab Services; Switch Board Operator; Safety Security Shift Operator; Security Officer.

FRANCISCAN CHILDREN'S HOSPITAL AND REHABILITATION CENTER
30 Warren Street, Brighton MA 02135. 617/254-3800. **Contact:** Human Resources. **E-mail address:** aeponte@fchrc.org. **World Wide Web address:** http://www.fchrc.org. **Description:** A hospital and rehabilitation center for children. The hospital also operates the Kennedy Day School for children with special needs. **Positions advertised include:** Certified Nurses Assistant; Care Manager; Home Health Registered Nurse; Nurse Practitioner; Registered Nurse; Family Therapist; Mental Health Specialist; Psychologist; Impatient Clinical Supervisor; Respiratory Therapist; Teaching Assistant; Fiscal Administrative Coordinator; Registration Manager; Admissions Clerk; Dental Assistant; Pediatric Dietician; Van Driver.

FRESENIUS MEDICAL CARE NORTH AMERICA
2 Ledgemont Center, 95 Hayden Avenue, Lexington MA 02420. 781/402-9000. **Toll-free phone:** 800/662-1237. **Fax:** 781/402-9005. **Contact:** Human Resources. **E-mail address:** resumes@fmc-na.com. **World Wide Web address:** http://www.fmcna.com. **Description:** One of the nation's leading manufacturers and distributors of renal dialysis products and services. The company also provides dialysis treatment, diagnostic testing, blood testing, and home health programs. Fresenius Medical Care's dialysis services include outpatient hemodialysis, peritoneal dialysis, and support for home dialysis patients. **Positions advertised include:** Financial Analyst; Staff Auditor; Secretary; Switchboard Operator; Clinical Quality Manager; Documentation Coordinator; Real Estate Specialist; Treasury Analyst; Employment Coordinator; Human Resources Secretary; Research Assistant; Benefits Analyst; Legal Secretary; Regulatory Affairs Specialist; Clinical Applications Programmer; Manager NT Services; Manager or Desktop PC; Network Security; Specialist; Program Analyst. **Special programs:** Co-ops. **Corporate headquarters location:** This location. **Parent company:** Fresenius Medical Care AG (Germany) **Listed on:** New York Stock Exchange. **Stock exchange symbol:** FMS. **Number of employees at this location:** 600. **Number of employees nationwide:** 21,000. **Number of employees worldwide:** 24,000.

FRESH POND ANIMAL HOSPITAL
15 Flanders Road, Belmont MA 02478. 617/484-1555. **Fax:** 617/484-2509. **Contact:** Human Resources. **World Wide Web address:** http://www.fpah.com.

Description: An animal hospital offering surgical, dental, and medical services.

DR. SOLOMON CARTER FULLER MENTAL HEALTH CENTER
85 East Newton Street, Boston MA 02118. 617/626-8700. **Contact:** Human Resources. **Description:** A psychiatric hospital.

GAMBRO HEALTHCARE
660 Harrison Avenue, Boston MA 02118. 617/859-7000. **Contact:** Human Resources. **World Wide Web address:** http://www.usa-gambro.com. **Description:** Provides renal dialysis services to patients suffering from chronic kidney failure, primarily in its freestanding outpatient dialysis centers. The company also provides dialysis in patients' homes or at hospitals on a contractual basis; urine and blood testing at its centers; and independent physicians at its clinical labs. **Positions advertised include:** Center Director; Clinical Nurse Manager; Registered Nurse; Patient Care Technician. **Number of employees nationwide:** 1,240.

HAEMONETICS CORPORATION
400 Wood Road, Braintree MA 02184. 781/848-7100. **Toll-free phone:** 800/225-5242. **Fax:** 781/848-9959. **Contact:** Human Resources. **World Wide Web address:** http://www.haemonetics.com. **Description:** Designs, manufactures, markets, and services blood processing systems and related sterile, disposable items used for the processing of human blood for transfusion and other therapeutic medical purposes. The company sells its products to blood banks, hospitals, and commercial plasma centers. **Positions advertised include:** Contract Agent; Supply Chain Integration Manager; Project Manager; Planning Analyst. **Corporate headquarters location:** This location. **Other U.S. locations:** Leetsdale PA; Union SC. **Operations at this facility include:** Administration; Divisional Headquarters; Manufacturing; Research and Development; Sales; Service. **Listed on:** New York Stock Exchange. **Stock exchange symbol:** HAE. **Number of employees at this location:** 700. **Number of employees nationwide:** 1,000.

HAMMERSMITH HOUSE NURSING CARE CENTER
73 Chestnut Street, Saugus MA 01906. 781/233-8123. **Fax:** 781/231-2918. **Contact:** Human Resources. **Description:** A 103-bed nursing home and rehabilitation center. Hammersmith House also operates a 47-bed special care unit for Alzheimer's patients. **Positions advertised include:** Certified Nurses Aide; Licensed Practical Nurse.

HARVARD PILGRIM HEALTHCARE
1600 Crowne Colony Park, Quincy MA 02169. 617-745-1001. **Contact:** Human Resources. **World Wide Web address:** http://www.harvardpilgrim.org. **Description:** The oldest non-profit healthcare available in New England. **Positions advertised include:** Nurse Care Manager; Account Services Coordinator; Clinical Trainer; Account Services Manager. **NOTE:** Apply online.

HEALTHALLIANCE/BURBANK HOSPITAL
275 Nichols Road, Fitchburg MA 01420. 978/343-5000. **Contact:** Human Resources. **World Wide Web address:** http://www.healthalliance.com. **Description:** An acute care medical facility. The hospital provides inpatient and outpatient services including medical, surgical, and subspecialty care, as well as same-day surgery and 24-hour emergency coverage. The hospital also offers a psychiatric center, speech and hearing center, and regional trauma center. A 25-bed inpatient rehabilitation center affiliated with the Spaulding Rehabilitation Hospital in Boston is also at this location. The center offers a rehabilitation program for patients who have suffered from strokes and patients with arthritis, amputations, neurological disorders, orthopedic conditions, spinal cord injuries, brain injuries, and complex medical conditions. **Corporate headquarters location:** Leominster MA. **Subsidiaries include:** Coordinated Primary Care; Diversified Medical Equipment Services; Diversified Visiting Nurse Association; Fairlawn Nursing Home; The Highlands; and Leominster Hospital.

HEALTHALLIANCE/LEOMINSTER HOSPITAL
60 Hospital Road, Leominster MA 01453. 978/466-2000. **Fax:** 978/466-2189. **Contact:** Human Resources. **World Wide Web address:** http://www.healthalliance.com. **Description:** An acute care medical facility. The hospital provides inpatient and outpatient services including medical, surgical, and subspecialty care, as well as same-day surgery and 24-hour emergency coverage. The hospital also offers the Center for Cancer Care and Blood Disorders, diagnostic services including mobile MRIs, cardiac catheterization labs, and a diagnostic lab for the diagnostic study of sleep disorders. **NOTE:** Entry-level positions are offered. **Positions advertised include:** Certified Nurses Aide; Certified Occupational Therapy Assistant; Clinical Lab Technician; Computer Operator; Computer Programmer; EEG Technologist; EKG Technician; Home Health Aide; Licensed Practical Nurse; Medical Records Technician; Network/Systems Administrator; Nuclear Medicine Technologist; Occupational Therapist; Physical Therapist; Physical Therapy Assistant; Radiological Technologist; Recreational Therapist; Registered Nurse; Respiratory Therapist; Social Worker; Speech-Language Pathologist. **Operations at this facility include:** Administration; Service. **Annual sales/revenues:** More than $100 million. **Number of employees at this location:** 750. **Number of employees nationwide:** 2,000.

HEALTHALLIANCE HOSPITAL
275 Nichols Road, Fitchburg MA 01420. 978/343-5000. **Contact:** Human Resources. **World Wide Web address:** http://www.healthalliance.com. **Description:** A hospital that includes a rehabilitation center. **NOTE:** Entry-level positions are offered. **Positions advertised include:** Accountant/Auditor; Dietician/Nutritionist; Health Services Manager; Licensed Practical Nurse; Occupational Therapist; Physical Therapist; Registered Nurse; Social Worker. **Special programs:** Training. **Corporate headquarters location:** Leominster MA. **Subsidiaries include:** Burbank Hospital; Coordinated Primary Care; Diversified Medical Equipment Services; Diversified Visiting Nurse Association; Fairlawn Nursing Home; Leominster Hospital. **Operations at this facility include:** Service. **Annual sales/revenues:** $5 - $10 million.

HEALTHSOUTH BRAINTREE HOSPITAL
P.O. Box 859020, Braintree MA 02185-9020. 781/848-5353. **Physical address:** 250 Pond Street, Braintree MA 02184. **Contact:** Human Resources. **World Wide Web address:** http://www.healthsouth.com. **Description:** A rehabilitation hospital. Founded in 1984. **Other U.S. locations:** Nationwide. **Listed on:** New York Stock Exchange. **Stock exchange symbol:** HRC.

HOLOGIC INC.
35 Crosby Drive, Bedford MA 01730. 781/999-7300. **Fax:** 781/275-7090. **Contact:** Human Resources. **E-mail address:** hr@hologic.com. **World Wide Web address:** http://www.hologic.com. **Description:** Manufactures quantitative digital radiography X-ray bone densitometers that are used for the precise measurement of bone density to assist in the diagnosis and monitoring of metabolic bone diseases. **Positions advertised include:** Application Support Specialist; Regulatory Affairs Manager. **Corporate headquarters location:** This location. **Other area location:** Littleton MA. **Other U.S. locations:** Danbury CT; Newark DE. **International locations:** Belgium; France. **Listed on:** NASDAQ. **Stock exchange symbol:** HOLX.

HOLYOKE HOSPITAL, INC.
575 Beech Street, Holyoke MA 01040. 413/534-2547. **Fax:** 413/534-2635. **Recorded jobline:** 413/534-2639. **Contact:** Anne Barrett, Human Resources Administrator. **World Wide Web address:** http://www.holyokehealth.com. **Description:** A 225-

bed, acute care, community hospital that serves an aggregate population of 145,000 and admits nearly 7,000 patients annually. **Positions advertised include:** Audiologists; Head Research Processor; Medical Transcriber; Nursing Division; Radiological Technology; Speech Pathologist. **Number of employees at this location:** 1,000.

HOME HEALTH AND CHILDCARE SERVICES
P.O. Box 640, Brockton MA 02303-0640. 508/588-6070. **Fax:** 508/587-3560. **Physical address:** 15 Jonathan Drive, Brockton MA 02301. **Contact:** Human Resources. **E-mail address:** ccrr@hhcc.org. **World Wide Web address:** http://www.hhcc.org. **Description:** A private, nonprofit family care services agency providing in-home health care for the elderly and childcare services.

INSTRUMENTATION LABORATORY
101 Hartwell Avenue, Lexington MA 02421. 781/861-0710. **Contact:** Human Resources. **World Wide Web address:** http://www.ilww.com. **Description:** Manufactures medical instruments used in blood gas analysis. **Positions advertised include:** Administrative Support; Marketing Product Specialist; Principal Software Engineer.

INVACARE SUPPLY GROUP
75 October Hill Road, Holliston MA 01746. 508/429-1000. **Fax:** 508/429-6669. **Contact:** Human Resources. **Description:** A wholesale distributor of medical supplies including ostomy dressings, wound care products, respiratory products, and enteral feeding products. **NOTE:** Entry-level positions and part-time jobs are offered. **Positions advertised include:** Account Representative; Consumer Services Representative; Distribution Center Associate. **Special programs:** Training; Summer Jobs. **Office hours:** Monday - Friday, 8:00 a.m. - 5:30 p.m. **Corporate headquarters location:** Elyria OH. **Parent company:** Invacare Corporation. **Listed on:** New York Stock Exchange. **Stock exchange symbol:** IVC. **Number of employees at this location:** 100.

LAHEY AT ARLINGTON MEDICAL CENTER
Hospital Road, Arlington MA 02474. 781/646-1500. **Contact:** Human Resources. **World Wide Web address:** http://www.lahey.org. **Description:** Part of the Lahey Clinic's network of health care services. This location provides emergency, acute, transitional, subacute, and intensive care. **Positions advertised include:** Clinical Nurse; Medical Office Secretary; Physician.

LAWRENCE MEMORIAL HOSPITAL
170 Governors Avenue, Medford MA 02155. 781/306-6000. **Fax:** 781/306-6573. **Contact:** Human Resources. **World Wide Web address:** http://www.lmh.org. **Description:** A hospital that serves as a teaching facility for Tufts University School of Medicine. **Positions advertised include:** Registered Nurse; Clinical Associate; Licensed Practical Nurse; Clinical Nurse Educator; Medical Transcriptionist; Application Analyst; Desktop Technician; Director; Registered Respiratory Therapist. **Parent company:** Hallmark Health.

LIFELINE SYSTEMS, INC.
111 Lawrence Street, Framingham MA 01702-8156. 508/988-1000. **Fax:** 508/988-1384. **Contact:** Personnel. **World Wide Web address:** http://www.lifelinesys.com. **Description:** Manufactures personal emergency response systems and provides monitoring and related services. The company's services consist of 24-hour, at-home assistance and personalized support for elderly and physically challenged individuals. The company's principal product is LIFELINE, which consists of equipment manufactured by the company combined with a monitoring service. The equipment includes a personal help button, worn or carried by the individual subscriber, and a communicator that connects to the phone line in the subscriber's home. **Positions advertised include:** Marketing Communications Manager; Personal Response Associate; Inside Sales Account; Customer & Referral Sales Manager; Employment Manager; Equipment Product Manager. **Corporate headquarters location:** This location. **Subsidiaries include:** Lifeline Systems Canada. **Listed on:** NASDAQ. **Stock exchange symbol:** LIFE. **Number of employees at this location:** 735.

ERICH LINDEMANN MENTAL HEALTH CENTER
25 Staniford Street, Boston MA 02114. 617/626-8000. **Contact:** Human Resources. **Description:** A residential mental health center. **Number of employees at this location:** 300.

LOWELL GENERAL HOSPITAL INC.
295 Varnum Avenue, Lowell MA 01854. 978/937-6000. **Contact:** Human Resources. **World Wide Web address:** http://www.lowellgeneral.org. **Description:** A 200-bed hospital that offers a variety of specialized services including the Special Care Nursery, the Cancer Center, and the Children's Place. **Positions advertised include:** 2nd Cook; ACR Mechanic; Clinical Manager; CT Technician; Development Assistant; Endoscopy Coordinator; Financial Specialist; Medical Technologist; Registered Nurse.

LUXTEC CORPORATION
99 Hartwell Street, West Boylston MA 01583. 508/856-9454. **Toll-free phone:** 800/325-8966. **Contact:** Human Resources. **World Wide Web address:** http://www.luxtec.com. **Description:** Designs, develops, manufactures, and markets illumination and vision products utilizing fiber-optic technology for the medical and dental industries. These products are designed to produce high-quality light delivered directly to the operative site. Products include fiber-optic headlights and headlight television camera systems for audio/video recordings of surgical procedures; light sources; cables; retractors; loupes; surgical telescopes; and other custom-made surgical specialty instruments. **Corporate headquarters location:** This location. **Subsidiaries include:** Cathtec, Inc.; Fiber Imaging Technologies, Inc.; Luxtec Fiber Optics B.V. **Parent company:** PrimeSource Healthcare (Tuscon AZ). **Number of employees nationwide:** 50.

THE MARINO CENTER FOR PROGRESSIVE HEALTH
2500 Massachusetts Avenue, Cambridge MA 02140. 617/661-6225. **Fax:** 617/492-2002. **Contact:** Human Resources. **E-mail address:** contact@marinocenter.org. **World Wide Web address:** http://www.marinocenter.org. **Description:** A medical center with a full-service health store specializing in family medicine, acupuncture, health education, prevention programs, and complementary therapies. The Marino Center for Progressive Health includes: The Center for Men's Health is devoted to diagnosing and treating sexual dysfunction, prostate disease, and incontinence; The Center for Women's Health is devoted to gynecological care, birth control, sexually transmitted diseases, PMS, menstrual disorders, and menopause; The UroCare Clinic is devoted to addressing the needs of women with urinary incontinence. Also provided are classes, therapy groups, workshops, and free lectures. Areas of specialization include general medicine, psychology, psychotherapy, stress-reduction, urology, neurology, chiropractic, acupuncture, traditional Chinese medicine, nutrition, massage therapy, infusion therapy, chelation therapy, biofeedback, coping with cancer, yoga, meditation, and fitness. **Positions advertised include:** Primary Care Physician; Nurse Practitioner; Physicians Assistant. **Other area locations:** Dedham MA; Wellesley MA.

MASSACHUSETTS GENERAL HOSPITAL
55 Fruit Street, Boston MA 02114. 617/726-2000. **Fax:** 617/724-2266. **Contact:** Human Resources. **World Wide Web address:** http://www.mgh.harvard.edu. **Description:** An 820-bed, nonprofit, teaching hospital. As part of the Harvard Medical School, MGH offers diagnostic and therapeutic care in virtually every

specialty of medicine. This location also hires seasonally. **NOTE:** Please direct resumes to Partners HealthCare System Inc., Human Resources, 101 Merrimac Street, 5th Floor, Boston MA 02114. 617/726-2210. Entry-level positions are offered. **Positions advertised include:** Administrative Assistant; Admissions Coordinator; Admissions Interviewer; Beautician. **Special programs:** Internships; Training; Co-ops; Summer Jobs. **Office hours:** Monday - Friday, 8:30 a.m. - 4:30 p.m. **Parent company:** Partners HealthCare System Inc. **Operations at this facility include:** Administration; Research and Development; Service. **Number of employees at this location:** 10,000.

MASSACHUSETTS HOSPITAL ASSOCIATION
5 New England Executive Park, Burlington MA 01803. 781/272-8000. **Contact:** Lisa Bales, Human Resources. **World Wide Web address:** http://www.mhalink.org. **World Wide Web address:** http://www.mhalink.org. **Description:** A trade association for professionals in the hospital industry, providing such services as continuing education and information on new developments within the industry.

THE MEDSTAT GROUP
125 Cambridge Park Drive, Cambridge MA 02140. 617/576-3237. **Contact:** Human Resources. **E-mail address:** recruiting@medstat.com. **World Wide Web address:** http://www.medstat.com. **Description:** Provides information that helps manage the purchasing and administration of health benefits and services. **Positions advertised include:** Senior Consultant. **Corporate headquarters location:** Ann Harbor MI. **Parent Company:** Thompson Financial.

MEDTRONIC/AVE
37A Cherry Hill Drive, Danvers MA 01923. 978/777-0042. **Contact:** Human Resources Department. **World Wide Web address:** http://www.medtronic.com. **Description:** Manufactures a line of minimally invasive devices for use in treating patients with coronary artery and peripheral vascular disease. **Positions advertised include:** Packaging Engineer; Manufacturing Engineer; RaD Engineer; Production Scheduler; Supplier Quality Manager. **Corporate headquarters location:** Minneapolis MN. **Listed on:** New York Stock Exchange. **Stock exchange symbol:** MDT.

MILTON HOSPITAL
92 Highland Street, Milton MA 02186. 617/696-4600. **Fax:** 617/698-4730. **Contact:** Human Resources. **E-mail address:** humanresources@miltonhospital.org. **World Wide Web address:** http://www.miltonhospital.org. **Description:** A general hospital. Milton Hospital offers free health screenings, support groups, and lectures for the public, as well as free vaccinations for public safety workers. **Positions advertised include:** Admitting Representative; Care Manager; Environmental Services Assistant; Human Resources Manager; PP&D Supervisor; Medical Technician; Records Clerk; Dietary Aide; Secretary; Pharmacist; Radiological Technician; CT Technician; Ultrasound Technician; Physical Therapist; Registered Nurse; Licensed Practical Nurse; Nurse Assistant; Ward Clerk; Nurse Manager. **Special programs:** Internships.

NATIONAL DENTEX CORPORATION
526 Boston Post Road, Suite 207, Wayland MA 01778. 508/358-4422. **Contact:** Human Resources. **World Wide Web address:** http://www.nationaldentex.com. **Description:** National Dentex Corporation is one of the largest operators of dental laboratories in the United States. These dental laboratories provide a full range of custom-made dental prosthetic appliances, divided into three main groups: restorative products including crowns and bridges; reconstructive products including partial and full dentures; and cosmetic products including porcelain veneers and ceramic crowns. **Positions advertised include:** Dental Lab Trainee; Maintenance; Janitorial Associate; Driver; Office Representative; Scheduler Associate; Department Manager; Shipping & Receiving Clerk; Skilled Technician; Corporate Support Specialist. **Corporate headquarters location:** This location. **Other U.S. locations:** Nationwide. **Subsidiaries include:** Dodd Dental Laboratories; H&O Associated Dental Laboratories; H&O Eliason; Lakeland Dental; Massachusetts Dental Associates. **Listed on:** NASDAQ. **Stock exchange symbol:** NADX.

NEW ENGLAND BAPTIST HOSPITAL
125 Parker Hill Avenue, Boston MA 02120. 617/754-5800. **Contact:** Human Resources. **World Wide Web address:** http://www.nebh.org. **Description:** A 150-bed, surgical hospital providing specialty services in cardiology, sports medicine, occupational medicine, and musculoskeletal care. Founded in 1893. **Positions advertised include:** Administrative Assistant; Central Support Operator; Coding Supervisor; File Clerk; Registered Nurse; Groundskeeper; Head Therapist; Quality Manager; Nurse Assistant; Unit Aide; Unit Secretary.

NEW ENGLAND SINAI HOSPITAL AND REHABILITATION CENTER
150 York Street, Stoughton MA 02072. 781/344-0600. **Contact:** Human Resources. **Description:** A hospital and rehabilitation center providing a variety of services including physical therapy, occupational therapy, and pulmonary rehabilitation, as well as special areas dealing specifically with back, feet, vision, and speech problems.

NEWTON-WELLESLEY HOSPITAL
2014 Washington Street, Newton MA 02462. 617/243-6000. **Fax:** 617/243-6876. **Contact:** Human Resources. **World Wide Web address:** http://www.nwh.org. **Description:** A hospital serving as a teaching facility for Tufts School of Medicine. **Positions advertised include:** Administrative Assistant; Assistant Cook; CT Technologist; Clinical Social Worker; Executive Assistant; Food Service Worker; Human Resources Coordinator; Image Service Representative; Medical Lab Assistant; Pharmacist; Registered Nurse; Ultrasound Technologist; Unit Coordinator

NORTH SHORE MEDICAL CENTER SALEM HOSPITAL
81 Highland Avenue, Salem MA 01970. 978/741-1200. **Recorded jobline:** 978/741-1215x4365. **Contact:** Personnel. **World Wide Web address:** http://www.partners.org. **Description:** Salem Hospital is a 322-bed teaching hospital that operates as part of North Shore Medical Center. North Shore Medical Center is a nonprofit health care system consisting of several hospitals and health organizations. Services range from primary, emergency/trauma, and advanced levels of acute care to rehabilitation and long-term care. A program of ambulatory health care includes walk-in medical centers and one of the region's largest occupational and preventative health companies. North Shore Medical Center's facilities include Salem Hospital; Shaughnessy-Kaplan Rehabilitation Hospital, a 160-bed rehabilitation facility; North Shore Children's Hospital; Work Venture, a comprehensive industrial rehabilitation program geared toward returning injured workers to their jobs; and the Visiting Nurse Association of Greater Salem. **Positions advertised include:** Clinical Lab Technician; Dietician/Nutritionist; Medical Records Technician; Nuclear Medicine Technologist; Occupational Therapist; Pharmacist; Physical Therapist; Physician; Registered Nurse. **Parent company:** Partners HealthCare System Inc. **Number of employees at this location:** 3,000.

NORTHEAST SPECIALTY HOSPITAL
2001 Washington Street, Braintree MA 02184. 781/848-2600. **Contact:** Human Resources. **Description:** A hospital specializing in the treatment of respiratory diseases.

NEW ENGLAND SINAI HOSPITAL AND REHABILITATION CENTER
150 York Street, Stoughton MA 02072. 781/344-0600.

Contact: Human Resources. **Description:** A hospital and rehabilitation center providing a variety of services including physical therapy, occupational therapy, and pulmonary rehabilitation, as well as special areas dealing specifically with back, feet, vision, and speech problems.

NEWTON-WELLESLEY HOSPITAL
2014 Washington Street, Newton MA 02462. 617/243-6000. **Fax:** 617/243-6876. **Contact:** Human Resources. **World Wide Web address:** http://www.nwh.org. **Description:** A hospital serving as a teaching facility for Tufts School of Medicine. **Positions advertised include:** Administrative Assistant; Assistant Cook; CT Technologist; Clinical Social Worker; Executive Assistant; Food Service Worker; Human Resources Coordinator; Image Service Representative; Medical Lab Assistant; Pharmacist; Registered Nurse; Ultrasound Technologist; Unit Coordinator

NORTH SHORE MEDICAL CENTER SALEM HOSPITAL
81 Highland Avenue, Salem MA 01970. 978/741-1200. **Recorded jobline:** 978/741-1215x4365. **Contact:** Personnel. **World Wide Web address:** http://www.partners.org. **Description:** Salem Hospital is a 322-bed teaching hospital that operates as part of North Shore Medical Center. North Shore Medical Center is a nonprofit health care system consisting of several hospitals and health organizations. Services range from primary, emergency/trauma, and advanced levels of acute care to rehabilitation and long-term care. A program of ambulatory health care includes walk-in medical centers and one of the region's largest occupational and preventative health companies. North Shore Medical Center's facilities include Salem Hospital; Shaughnessy-Kaplan Rehabilitation Hospital, a 160-bed rehabilitation facility; North Shore Children's Hospital, one of only four pediatric hospitals in the state; Work Venture, a comprehensive industrial rehabilitation program geared toward returning injured workers to their jobs; and the Visiting Nurse Association of Greater Salem, consisting of various private duty services. **Positions advertised include:** Clinical Lab Technician; Dietician/Nutritionist; Medical Records Technician; Nuclear Medicine Technologist; Occupational Therapist; Pharmacist; Physical Therapist; Physician; Registered Nurse. **Parent company:** Partners HealthCare System Inc. **Number of employees at this location:** 3,000.

PLC MEDICAL SYSTEMS, INC.
10 Forge Park, Franklin MA 02038. 508/541-8800. **Fax:** 781/326-6048. **Contact:** Jeanne Watkins, Personnel. **E-mail address:** kpapa@insightperformance.com. **World Wide Web address:** http://www.plcmed.com. **Description:** Develops cardiovascular products used to perform transmocardia revascularization (TMR). **Positions advertised include:** Quality Engineer; Principal Engineer. **Corporate headquarters location:** This location. **Parent company:** PLC Systems Inc. **Listed on:** American Stock Exchange. **Stock exchange symbol:** PLC.

PALOMAR MEDICAL TECHNOLOGIES, INC.
82 Cambridge Street, Burlington MA 01803. 781/993-2300. **Fax:** 781/993-2330. **Contact:** Human Resources. **E-mail address:** hr@palmed.com. **World Wide Web address:** http://www.palmed.com. **Description:** Palomar Medical Technologies designs, manufactures, and markets lasers, delivery systems, and related disposable products for use in medical and surgical procedures. The company operates in two business segments. The Medical Product segment develops and manufactures pulsed dye and diode medical lasers for use in clinical trials and is engaged in the research and development of additional medical and surgical products. The Electronic Products segment manufactures high-density, flexible, electronic circuitry for use in industrial, military, and medical devices. **Positions advertised include:** Clinical Research Manager; Accounting Manager; Programming Specialist; Optical Assembler; Laser Technician. **NOTE:** This company also has distribution opportunities. **Corporate headquarters location:** This location. **Listed on:** NASDAQ. **Stock exchange symbol:** PMTI.

PHILIPS ANALYTICAL
12 Michigan Drive, Natick MA 01760. 508/647-1100. **Contact:** Human Resources. **World Wide Web address:** http://www.philips.com. **Description:** Sells and services analytical X-ray systems. **Positions advertised include:** Applications Engineer; Application Group Leader; Assembly Technician; Technology Group Leader. **Corporate headquarters location:** New York NY. **Other U.S. locations:** Tempe AZ; Fremont CA; Alpharetta GA; Roselle IL; Columbia MD; Bellaire TX. **Parent company:** Philips Electronics North America, one of the larger industrial companies in the United States, is a multimarket manufacturing organization with nationwide locations and various subsidiaries. Philips concentrates its efforts primarily in the fields of consumer electronics, consumer products, electrical and electronics components, and professional equipment.

PHILIPS MEDICAL SYSTEMS
3000 Minuteman Road, Andover MA 01810. 978/687-1501. **Contact:** Human Resources. **World Wide Web address:** http://www.medical.phillips.com. **Description:** Produces stethoscopes, electrolytes, and disposable ECG monitoring electrodes for adults and infants, as well as blood-pressure transducers and disposable transducer domes, chart papers, and disposable pressure kits.

PIONEER BEHAVIORAL HEALTH
200 Lake Street, Suite 102, Peabody MA 01960. 978/536-2777. **Toll-free phone:** 800/543-2447. **Fax:** 978/536-2677. **Contact:** Human Resources. **E-mail address:** info@phc-inc.com. **World Wide Web address:** http://www.phc-inc.com. **Description:** Operates a variety of mental health, chemical dependency, and dual diagnosis programs throughout the country that provide inpatient and outpatient services, partial hospitalization, residential care, aftercare, and employee assistance programs. Founded in 1976. **Subsidiaries include:** Behavioral Stress Center (Elmhurst NY); Harbor Oaks Hospital (New Baltimore MI); Harmony Healthcare (Las Vegas NV); Highland Ridge Hospital (Salt Lake City UT); Mount Regis Center (Salem VA); Pioneer Counseling Centers of Michigan (Farmington Hills MI); Pioneer Counseling of Virginia (Salem VA); Pioneer Development & Support Services (Salt Lake City UT). **President/CEO:** Bruce A. Shear. **Number of employees at this location:** 300.

POLYMEDICA CORPORATION
11 State Street, Woburn MA 01801. 781/933-2020. **Fax:** 781/933-7992. **Contact:** Human Resources. **World Wide Web address:** http://www.polymedica.com. **Description:** A leading provider of targeted medical products and services focusing primarily on the diabetes and consumer health care markets. Founded in 1988. **Special programs:** Co-ops. **Corporate headquarters location:** This location. **Other U.S. locations:** Golden CO; Palm City FL. **Subsidiaries include:** Liberty Medical Supply is one of the largest direct-mail distributors of diabetes supplies covered by Medicare. Liberty distributes more than 200,000 diabetes products to over 70,000 customers. PolyMedica Healthcare, Inc. holds leading positions in the urinary health and over-the-counter medical device markets by distributing a broad range of products to food, drug, and mass retailers nationwide. PolyMedica Pharmaceuticals (USA), Inc. manufactures, distributes, and markets prescription urological and suppository products. **Listed on:** NASDAQ. **Stock exchange symbol:** PLMD. **CEO:** Steven J. Lee. **Annual sales/revenues:** More than $100 million. **Number of employees at this location:** 30. **Number of employees nationwide:** 345.

PRECISION OPTICS CORPORATION
22 East Broadway, Gardner MA 01440. 978/630-1800.

Fax: 978/630-1487. **Contact:** Human Resources. **E-mail address:** info@poci.com. **World Wide Web address:** http://www.poci.com. **Description:** Designs, develops, manufactures, and sells specialized optical systems and components and optical thin film coatings. The products and services are used in the medical and advanced optical systems industries. Medical products include endoscopes and image couplers, beamsplitters, and adapters that are used as accessories to endoscopes. Advanced optical design and developmental services provide advanced lens design, image analysis, optical system design, structural design and analysis, prototype production and evaluation, optics testing, and optical system assembly. **Corporate headquarters location:** This location. **Listed on:** NASDAQ. **Stock exchange symbol:** POCI.

QUINCY MEDICAL CENTER
114 Whitwell Street, Quincy MA 02169. 617/773-6100. **Contact:** Human Resources. **World Wide Web address:** http://www.quincymc.com. **Description:** A hospital offering a variety of services including a 24-hour emergency room, surgery, OB/GYN services, radiology, and a center for women's health. **Positions advertised include:** Cafeteria Helper; CT Technologist; Occupational Therapist; Physical Therapist; Radiological Therapist; Registered Nurse; Respiratory Therapist; Security Officer; Ultrasonographer.

RIVERSIDE HEALTH CENTER
205 Western Avenue, Cambridge MA 02139. 617/498-1109. **Contact:** Human Resources. **Description:** An outpatient clinic providing services that include general medical care for adults, prenatal, family planning, nutrition, psychiatric treatment, and pediatric care. **Parent company:** Cambridge Hospital is a 170-bed, full-service hospital owned by the city of Cambridge and affiliated with Harvard and Tufts Medical Schools.

SMITH & NEPHEW, INC.
ENDOSCOPY DIVISION
150 Minuteman Road, Andover MA 01810. Toll-free phone: 800/343-5717. **Contact:** Human Resources. **E-mail address:** endo.inquiry@smith-nephew.com. **World Wide Web address:** http://www.endo.smith-nephew.com. **Description:** Develops and commercializes endoscopic techniques. **Positions advertised include:** Associate Market Manager; Sr. Technician; Sales Information Analyst; Sr. Development Engineer; Sr. Communications Specialist; Group Director; Clinical Research Associate; PC Analyst; Sr. Network Engineer; Production Support Analyst. **Other area locations:** Mansfield MA.

SOLDIERS' HOME
110 Cherry Street, Holyoke MA 01040. 413/532-9475. **Contact:** Human Resources. **Description:** A hospital and nursing home for veterans offering both inpatient and outpatient care.

SONAMED CORPORATION
1250 Main Street, Waltham MA 02451. 781/899-6499. **Fax:** 781/899-8318. **Contact:** Human Resources. **E-mail address:** sonamed@sonamed.com. **World Wide Web address:** http://www.sonamed.com. **Description:** Sells equipment for detecting long-term hearing problems in infants. **Positions advertised include:** Sales and Marketing Representative.

SPAULDING REHABILITATION HOSPITAL
125 Nashua Street, Boston MA 02114. 617/720-6400. **Contact:** Human Resources. **World Wide Web address:** http://spauldingrehab.org. **Description:** A 296-bed, rehabilitation hospital. Spaulding is one of the largest rehabilitation facilities nationwide. **Positions advertised include:** Case Manager; Clinical Director; Liaison Representative; Registered Nurse; Nurse Practitioner; Occupational Therapist; Paramedic; Speech Pathologist; Physical Therapist.

TLC STAFF BUILDERS HOME HEALTH
175 Cabot Street, Suite 100, Lowell MA 01853. 978/458-4357. **Toll-free phone:** 800/698-1535. **Contact:** Human Resources. **World Wide Web address:** http://www.tlcathome.com. **Description:** A home health care agency. **Positions advertised include:** Assistant Director of Clinical Services; General Manager; Home Care Nurse; Home Health Aide. **Corporate headquarters location:** Lake Success NY. **Other U.S. locations:** Nationwide. **Number of employees nationwide:** 20,000.

TNCO, INC.
15 Colebrook Boulevard, Whitman MA 02382. 781/447-6661. **Fax:** 781/447-2132. **Contact:** Human Resources. **E-mail address:** info@tnco-inc.com. **World Wide Web address:** http://www.tnco-inc.com. **Description:** Manufactures surgical instruments. Founded in 1964. **NOTE:** Part-time jobs are offered. **Company slogan:** Passion for precision. **Special programs:** Co-ops. **Office hours:** Monday - Friday, 7:00 a.m. - 3:30 p.m. **Corporate headquarters location:** This location. **Listed on:** Privately held. **Annual sales/revenues:** $5 - $10 million. **Number of employees at this location:** 65.

TUFTS-NEW ENGLAND MEDICAL CENTER
750 Washington Street, New England Medical Center #795, Boston MA 02111. 617/636-5666. **Fax:** 617/636-4658. **Contact:** Human Resources. **World Wide Web address:** http://www.nemc.org. **Description:** New England Medical Center is the major teaching hospital for Tufts University Medical School. One branch of the New England Medical Center is the Floating Hospital for Children, which provides treatment for children suffering from various kinds of cancer, leukemia, and arthritis. **Positions advertised include:** Administrative Assistant; Audiologist; Business Operations Manager; Clinical Educator; Clinical Pharmacist; Clinical Research Coordinator; Coder; CT Scanner; Lab Technologist; Medical Assistant; Nursing Technologist; Physical Therapist. **Operations at this facility include:** Administration. **Number of employees at this location:** 6,000.

TUFTS NEW ENGLAND VETERINARY MEDICAL CENTER
200 Westborough Road, North Grafton MA 01536. 508/839-5395. **Contact:** Human Resources. **World Wide Web address:** http://www.tufts.edu/vet. **Description:** An animal hospital that offers a broad range of services including cardiology, dermatology, neurology, nutrition, oncology, and surgical procedures.

TYCO HEALTHCARE KENDALL
15 Hampshire Street, Mansfield MA 02048. 508/261-8000. **Toll-free phone:** 800/962-9888. **Fax:** 508/261-8105. **Contact:** Human Resources. **E-mail address:** jobs@kendallhq.com. **World Wide Web address:** http://www.kendallhq.com. **Description:** Manufactures and markets disposable medical supplies and adhesives for general medical and industrial uses. The company sells its products to hospitals and to alternative health care facilities worldwide, and also markets products to pharmacies and retail outlets. Products include wound care, vascular therapy, urological care, incontinence care, anesthetic care, and adhesives and tapes. Founded in 1903. **NOTE:** Entry-level positions are offered. **Positions advertised include:** Accountant; Associate General Counsel; Patent & Trademarks Attorney; Customer Accounts Representative; Marketing Director. **Special programs:** Internships; Co-ops. **Corporate headquarters location:** This location. **Other U.S. locations:** Nationwide. **International locations:** Worldwide. **Parent company:** Tyco International Inc. **Listed on:** New York Stock Exchange. **Stock exchange symbol:** TYC. **CEO/Chairman:** L. Dennis Kozlowski. **Annual sales/revenues:** More than $100 million. **Number of employees at this location:** 600. **Number of employees nationwide:** 5,000. **Number of employees worldwide:** 19,000.

U.S. DEPARTMENT OF VETERANS AFFAIRS BROCKTON VETERANS ADMINISTRATION MEDICAL CENTER
940 Belmont Street, Building 1, Brockton MA 02301.

508/583-4500. **Contact:** Craig Polucha, Human Resources Manager. **World Wide Web address:** http://www.va.gov. **Description:** A medical center operated by the U.S. Department of Veterans Affairs. From 54 hospitals in 1930, the VA health care system has grown to include 171 medical centers; more than 364 outpatient, community, and outreach clinics; 130 nursing home care units; and 37 domiciliaries. The VA operates at least one medical center in each of the 48 contiguous states, Puerto Rico, and the District of Columbia. With approximately 76,000 medical center beds, the VA treats nearly 1 million patients in VA hospitals; 75,000 in nursing home care units; and 25,000 in domiciliaries. The VA's outpatient clinics register approximately 24 million visits per year.

U.S. DEPARTMENT OF VETERANS AFFAIRS EDITH NOURSE ROGERS MEMORIAL VETERANS HOSPITAL
200 Springs Road, Bedford MA 01730-1114. 781/687-2490. **Contact:** Human Resources. **World Wide Web address:** http://www.visn1.med.va.gov/bedford. **Description:** A medical center operated by the U.S. Department of Veterans Affairs. From 54 hospitals in 1930, the VA health care system has grown to include 171 medical centers; more than 364 outpatient, community, and outreach clinics; 130 nursing home care units; and 37 domiciliaries. VA operates at least one medical center in each of the 48 contiguous states, Puerto Rico, and the District of Columbia. With approximately 76,000 medical center beds, VA treats nearly one million patients in VA hospitals; 75,000 in nursing home care units; and 25,000 in domiciliaries. VA's outpatient clinics register approximately 24 million visits per year.

VCA SOUTH SHORE ANIMAL HOSPITAL
595 Columbian Street, South Weymouth MA 02190. 781/337-6622. **Contact:** Human Resources. **World Wide Web address:** http://www.vca.com. **Description:** A full-service pet hospital providing medical, nursing, and surgical services.

VISION-SCIENCES INC.
9 Strathmore Road, Natick MA 01760. 508/650-9971. **Fax:** 508/650-9976. **Contact:** Human Resources. **E-mail address:** info@visionsciences.com. **World Wide Web address:** http://www.visionsciences.com. **Description:** Manufactures a flexible endoscopy system that utilizes single-use protective sheaths designed to reduce reprocessing time and infection concerns. Founded in 1990. **NOTE:** Entry-level positions are offered. **Office hours:** Monday - Friday, 8:00 a.m. - 5:00 p.m. **Corporate headquarters location:** This location. **Other U.S. locations:** Orangeburg NY. **International locations:** Israel. **Listed on:** NASDAQ. **Stock exchange symbol:** VSCI. **President/CEO:** Katsumi Oneda. **Annual sales/revenues:** $5 - $10 million. **Number of employees at this location:** 35. **Number of employees nationwide:** 70.

WAYSIDE YOUTH & FAMILY SUPPORT NETWORK
118 Central Street, Waltham MA 02453. 781/891-0555. **Toll-free phone:** 800/564-4010. **Fax:** 781/647-1432. **Contact:** Human Resources Director. **E-mail address:** wayside_info@waysideyouth.org. **World Wide Web address:** http://www.waysideyouth.org. **Description:** A childcare center and children's mental health clinic. **Positions advertised include:** Classroom Behavioral Assistant; Overnight Counselor; Case Manager; Clinician; Floating Counselor; Day Counselor; Shift Supervisor.

WINCHESTER HOSPITAL
41 Highland Avenue, Winchester MA 01890. 781/729-9000. **Contact:** Personnel. **World Wide Web address:** http://www.winchesterhospital.org. **Description:** A community hospital offering a variety of medical services including emergency, pediatrics, surgery, maternity, intensive care, and telemetry. Winchester Hospital also supports wellness and home health care programs. **Positions advertised include:** Accountant; Administrative Assistant; Billing Representative; Cat Scan Technologist; Child Life Coordinator; Clinical Associate; Diet Technician; Message Therapist; Medical Records Clerk; MRI Technologist; Patient Registrar; Radiology Technologist; Registered Nurse; Sleep Lab Technician; Team leader; Ultrasound Technologist.

THE WINDHOVER VETERINARY CENTER
944-A Main Street, Walpole MA 02081. 508/668-4520. **Contact:** Human Resources. **World Wide Web address:** http://www.windhovervet.com. **Description:** A veterinary center providing basic care for small pets with an emphasis on treating birds.

WINDSOR STREET HEALTH CENTER
119 Windsor Street, Cambridge MA 02139. 617/665-3600. **Contact:** Human Resources. **Description:** A community-based health clinic providing general medicine and care. **Parent company:** Cambridge Hospital is a 170-bed, full-service hospital owned by the city of Cambridge and affiliated with Harvard and Tufts Medical Schools.

YOUVILLE HOSPITAL
1575 Cambridge Street, Cambridge MA 02138-4398. 617/876-4344. **Fax:** 617/234-7996. **Contact:** Jack Carrol, Human Resources Director. **World Wide Web address:** http://www.youville.org. **Description:** A nonprofit hospital and nursing home offering rehabilitation and medical care. **Positions advertised include:** Occupational Therapist; Pharmacist; Physical Therapist; Recreational Therapist; Registered Nurse; Respiratory Therapist.

ZOLL MEDICAL CORPORATION
32 Second Avenue, Burlington MA 01803. 781/229-0020. **Contact:** Human Resources. **World Wide Web address:** http://www.zoll.com. **Description:** Designs, manufactures, and markets an integrated line of proprietary, noninvasive, cardiac resuscitation devices and disposable electrodes. **Positions advertised include:** Hospital Territory Manager; Sales Development Specialist; Administrative Assistant; Clinical Nurse Specialist.

Michigan

AMFAB INC.
1446 South 35th Street, Galesburg MI 49053-9679. 269/665-6703. **Contact:** Alan Anderson, Human Resources. **Description:** Manufactures and sells physical therapy and orthopedic products. **Parent company:** Bissell, Incorporated.

BATTLE CREEK HEALTH SYSTEM
300 North Avenue, Battle Creek MI 49016. 616/966-8060. **Fax:** 616/966-8366. **Contact:** Jill Cardenas, Human Resources. **E-mail address:** cardenaj@trinity-health.org. **World Wide Web address:** http://www.bchealth.com. **Description:** A multi-campus health care provider comprised of two hospitals, which offers a comprehensive range of services. **Positions advertised include:** CT Technologist; Outcomes Specialist; Radiation Therapist; Registered Nurse. **Special programs:** Internships. **Corporate headquarters location:** This location. **Operations at this facility include:** Service. **Number of employees at this location:** 1,800.

BIXBY MEDICAL CENTER
818 Riverside Avenue, Adrian MI 49221. 517/424-3223. **Recorded jobline:** 517/265-0920. **Contact:** Doris Kemner, Recruiter. **World Wide Web address:** http://www.promedica.org. **Description:** A 140-bed, acute care medical center. **Positions advertised include:** Physical Therapist; Switchboard Operator; Registration Clerk. **Parent company:** ProMedica Health System (Toledo OH).

BRONSON HEALTHCARE GROUP BRONSON METHODIST HOSPITAL
601 John Street, Box G, Kalamazoo MI 49007. 269/341-7654. **Fax:** 269/341-7644. **Recorded jobline:** 269/341-6800. **Contact:** Human Resources. **World**

Wide Web address: http://www.bronsonhealth.com. **Description:** Bronson Healthcare Group is a community-owned, nonprofit health care provider. The group operates Bronson Methodist Hospital, a full-service 414-bed medical center that provides both inpatient and outpatient services. **NOTE:** Entry-level positions and second and third shifts are offered. **Positions advertised include:** Clinical Dietician; Ultrasound Technician; CT Technologist; Licensed Practical Nurse; Medical Assistant; MRI Technologist; Occupational Therapist; Occupational Therapy Assistant; Paramedic; Pharmacist; Physical Therapist; Radiologic Technologist; Registered Nurse. **Special programs:** Internships. **Corporate headquarters location:** This location. **Subsidiaries include:** Bronson Health Foundation; Bronson Home Health Care; Bronson Medical Group; Bronson Outpatient Surgery; Bronson Vicksburg Hospital; IBA Health and Life Assurance Company; Physicians Health Plan of Southwest Michigan. **Number of employees at this location:** 2,750.

CHILDREN'S HOSPITAL OF MICHIGAN
3901 Beaubien Street, Detroit MI 48201. 313/5778-3930. **Contact:** Human Resources. **World Wide Web address:** http://www.chmkids.org/chm. **Description:** One of the nation's largest pediatric hospitals. Founded in 1886. **Positions advertised include:** Staff Nurse; Patient Services Clerk; Student Nurse Associate; Pediatrics Administrative Coordinator; Pharmacy Technician; Patient Management Clerical Associate; **Parent company:** The Detroit Medical Center. **Number of employees at this location:** Approximately 1,900.

COMMUNITY MENTAL HEALTH FOR CENTRAL MICHIGAN
2603 West Wackerly Road, Midland MI 48640. 989/631-2320. **Fax:** 989/631-9903. **Contact:** Human Resources. **World Wide Web address:** http://www.cmhcm.org. **Description:** Provides outpatient therapy, case management services, and children's intensive services. **Corporate headquarters location:** This location. **Other area locations:** Gladwin MI; Harrison MI; Mount Pleasant MI; Big Rapids MI; Reed City MI.

COVENANT MEDICAL CENTER HARRISON
1447 North Harrison Street, Saginaw MI 48602. 989/583-4080. **Fax:** 989/583-4816. **Contact:** Human Resources. **World Wide Web address:** http://www.covenanthealthcare.com. **Description:** A 700-bed hospital that offers comprehensive inpatient and outpatient care. **Positions advertised include:** Food Service Worker; HIM Transcriptionist; Clerical Medical Assistant; Clinical Documentation Specialist; Mammographer; Nuclear Medicine Technologist; Office Support Associate; Occupational Therapist; Patient Placement Specialist; Pharmacist; Nursing Care Assistant; Radiographer; Registered Nurse. **Corporate headquarters location:** This location. **Parent company:** Covenant Healthcare. **Number of employees at this location:** 4,000.

DOC OPTICS CORPORATION
19800 West Eight Mile Road, Southfield MI 48075. 248/354-7100. **Contact:** Personnel Director. **World Wide Web address:** http://www.docoptics.com. **Description:** Manufactures prescription glasses and contacts. DOC Optics operates over 100 retail locations in six states offering eye care products and laser eye surgery. Founded in 1946. **Special programs:** Training. **Positions advertised include:** Retail Manager; Assistant Retail Manager; Lab Manager; Assistant Lab Manager; Optician; Service Coordinator; Optometric Technician. **Corporate headquarters location:** This location. **Other area locations:** Statewide. **Other U.S. locations:** FL; MO; OH; WI; IL. **Number of employees at this location:** 800.

DAVIS DENTAL LABORATORY
5830 Crossroads Commerce Parkway, Wyoming MI 49509. 616/261-9191. **Fax:** 616/261-9889. **Recorded jobline:** 800/253-9227. **Contact:** Human Resources. **World Wide Web address:** http://www.dentalservices.net. **Description:** A full-service dental laboratory that manufactures and supplies various restorative dental products. **Corporate headquarters location:** Minneapolis MN. **Special programs:** Internships; Co-ops. **Parent company:** Dental Services Group. **Number of employees at this location:** 130.

FOOTE HEALTH SYSTEM
205 North East Avenue, Jackson MI 49201. 517/796-6400. **Fax:** 517/789-5933. **Contact:** Human Resources Manager. **E-mail address:** hrinfo@wafoote.org. **World Wide Web address:** http://www.footehealth.org. **Description:** A 411-bed hospital offering comprehensive services. **Positions advertised include:** Clinical Nurse Manager; Registered Nurse; Licensed Practical Nurse; Physical Therapist; Respiratory Therapist; Ultrasound Supervisor; Sleep Technologist; MRI Technologist; Human Resources Recruiter. **Operations at this facility include:** Service. **Number of employees at this location:** 1,900.

HARPER UNIVERSITY HOSPITAL
3990 John R. Street, Detroit MI 48201. 313/578-3930. **Contact:** Director of Human Resources. **World Wide Web address:** http://www.dmc.org. **Description:** A hospital affiliated with the Wayne State University School of Medicine that specializes in teaching, cardiology, and oncology. **Positions advertised include:** Transplant Services Director; Surgical Technician; Staff Nurse; Clinical Pharmacist; Radiologic Technologist; Vascular Surgical Technologist; Respiratory Therapist; Ultrasound Technologist; Special Procedures Nurse; MRI Technologist; Adjunct Chaplain; Research Assistant. **Special programs:** Internships. **Parent company:** Detroit Medical Center.

HURLEY MEDICAL CENTER
One Hurley Plaza, Flint MI 48503. 810/257-9140. **Fax:** 810/762-6513. **Contact:** Human Resources. **E-mail address:** resume@hurleymc.com. **World Wide Web address:** http://www.hurleymc.com. **Description:** A 463-bed publicly owned teaching hospital affiliated with Michigan State University's College of Human Medicine, the University of Michigan Medical School, and the Henry Ford Health System. **NOTE:** Entry-level positions are offered. **Positions advertised include:** Assistant Head Nurse; Registered Nurse; Nurse Manager; Licensed Practical Nurse; Certified Hand Therapist; Clinical Nurse Specialist; Clinical Practitioner; Director of Environmental Services; Director of Facilities ManagementRespiratory Therapist; Registered Dietitian; Medical Technologist; Pharmacy Technician; Surgical Technician; Special Procedures Technician; Reimbursement Analyst; Public Safety Officer. **Special programs:** Internships. **Operations at this facility include:** Administration; Research and Development; Service. **Number of employees at this location:** 2,700.

HUTZEL HOSPITAL
4707 St. Antoine Boulevard, Detroit MI 48201. 313/745-7555. **Recorded jobline:** 313/745-JOBS. **Contact:** Employment Center. **E-mail address:** jobs@dmc.org. **World Wide Web address:** http://www.hutzel.org. **Description:** A 244-bed hospital specializing in obstetrics, orthopedics, and ophthalmology. **NOTE:** The hospital is part of the Detroit Medical Center; applicants should contact the Employment Center at One Orchestra Place, 3663 Woodward Avenue, Suite 200, Detroit MI 48201. **Positions advertised include:** Clinical Nurse Manager; Physician Assistant; Nurse Practitioner; Clinical Improvement Specialist; Research Nurse; Lactation Consultant; Staff Nurse. **Parent company:** Detroit Medical Center. **Operations at this facility include:** Service. **Number of employees at this location:** 2,500.

McKESSON SURGICAL
38220 Plymouth Road, Livonia MI 48150. 734/632-6400. **Contact:** Human Resources. **World Wide Web**

address: http://www.mckesson.com. **Description:** A wholesale distributor of medical equipment and supplies. **Positions advertised include:** Account Manager; Marketing Manager; Warehouse Supervisor. **Corporate headquarters locations:** San Francisco CA. **Other U.S. locations:** Nationwide. **Operations at this facility include:** Administration. **Listed on:** New York Stock Exchange. **Stock exchange symbol:** MCK. **Annual sales/revenues:** $50 billion. **Number of employees worldwide:** 24,000.

MIDMICHIGAN MEDICAL CENTER – MIDLAND
4005 Orchard Drive, Midland MI 48670. 989/839-3230. **Contact:** Human Resources. **E-mail address:** recruitment@midmichigan.org. **World Wide Web address:** http://www.midmichigan.org. **Description:** An 250-bed acute care hospital that provides comprehensive health-care services. **Positions advertised include:** Paramedic; Home Care Coordinator; Respiratory Therapist; System Administrator; Transcriptionist. **Special programs:** Tuition Reimbursement Program; Mentorship Program. **Other area locations:** Clare MI; Gladwin MI; Houghton Lake MI; Mount Pleasant MI. **Parent company:** MidMichigan Health. **Number of employees at this location:** 1,670.

MUNSON MEDICAL CENTER
1105 Sixth Street, Traverse City MI 49684-2386. 231/935-6490. **Toll-free phone:** 800/713-3206. **Fax:** 231/935-7191. **Contact:** Gina Ranger, Recruiter. **E-mail address:** employment@mhc.net. **World Wide Web address:** http://www.munsonhealthcare.org. **Description:** A 368-bed, acute care, regional referral center. Founded in 1915. **NOTE:** Second and third shifts are offered. **Company slogan:** Expertise, when and where you need it most. **Positions advertised include:** Admitting Representative; Certified Athletic Trainer; Licensed Practical Nurse; Registered Nurse; Nurse Assistant; Medical Transcriptionist; Human Resources Director; Pharmacist; Radiologic Technologist; Speech Pathologist; Ultrasonographer. **NOTE:** Part-time and Temporary positions are available. **Special programs:** Summer jobs. **Corporate headquarters location:** This location. **Parent company:** Munson Healthcare System. Other subsidiaries of the parent company include Kalkaske Memorial Hospital and Paul Oliver Memorial Hospital. **Operations at this facility include:** Administration; Service. **Number of employees at this location:** 3,000.

OAKWOOD HOSPITAL & MEDICAL CENTER
18101 Oakwood Boulevard, P.O. Box 2500, Dearborn MI 48124. 313/586-4960. **Fax:** 313/436-2038. **Contact:** Human Resources. **E-mail address:** carra@oakwood.org. **World Wide Web address:** http://www.oakwood.org. **Description:** A 615-bed, full-service teaching hospital serving southeast Michigan. **Positions advertised include:** Staff Nurse; Nursing Assistant; Radiology Technologist; Security Officer; Dietary Clerk; Physical Therapist; Staff Attorney; Surgical Technologist; Medical Technologist; Laboratory Support Specialist. **Parent company:** Oakwood Healthcare System operates seven area hospitals and 25 area ambulance services.

POH MEDICAL CENTER
50 North Perry Street, Pontiac MI 48342. 248/338-5662. **Fax:** 248/338-5174. **Contact:** Human Resources. **E-mail address:** poh.hr@pohmedical.org. **World Wide Web address:** http://www.pohmedical.org. **Description:** An osteopathic teaching hospital. **Positions advertised include:** Registered Nurse; Licensed Practical Nurse; Medical Technologist; Patient Care Associate; Financial Analyst; Information Clerk; X-Ray Technologist; Telemetry Technician. **Other U.S. locations:** Oxford MI. **Listed on:** Privately held. **Number of employees at this location:** 1,500.

SAINT JOSEPH MERCY LIVINGSTON HOSPITAL
620 Byron Road, Howell MI 48843. 517/545-6295. **Recorded jobline:** 517/545-6606. **Contact:** Human Resources. **World Wide Web address:** http://www.sjmercyhealth.org. **Description:** A 136-bed full-service hospital. Founded in 1928. **NOTE:** Entry-level positions and second and third shifts are offered. **Positions advertised include:** Physical Therapist; Radiologic Technologist; Registered Nurse; Speech Language Pathologist; Mental Health Clinician; Environmental Aide; Surgical Technician; Nurse Anesthetist; Medical Assistant; Patient Care Assistant. **Corporate headquarters location:** Ann Arbor MI. **Parent company:** Saint Joseph Mercy Health System.

ST. JOSEPH'S HEALTHCARE
15855 Nineteen Mile Road, Clinton Township MI 48038. 586/263-2808. **Toll-free phone:** 866/756-2266. **Fax:** 586/263-2803. **Contact:** Human Resources. **E-mail address:** harringt@trinity-health.org. **World Wide Web address:** http://www.stjoe-macomb.com. **Description:** A full-service hospital. **Positions advertised include:** Certified Occupational Therapy Assistant; Field Service Specialist; Pharmacy Technician; Lead Clinical Pharmacist; Nurse Technician; Respiratory Therapist; Speech and Language Pathologist; Registered Nurse. **Parent company:** Trinity Health. **Operations at this facility include:** Administration. **Number of employees at this location:** 2,600.

SINAI-GRACE HOSPITAL
6071 West Outer Drive, Detroit MI 48235. 313/966-3101. **Contact:** Human Resources. **World Wide Web address:** http://www.sinaigrace.org. **Description:** A 500-bed hospital offering comprehensive patient care. **Positions advertised include:** Patient Care Associate; Staff Nurse; Paramedic; Licensed Practical Nurse; Surgical Physician Assistant; Speech Language Pathologist; Physical Therapist Assistant; Mental Health Associate; Clinical Pharmacist; Radiologic Technologist; Respiratory Therapist; Clinical Social Worker. **Parent company:** Detroit Medical Center. **Number of employees at this location:** Over 3,000.

SPARROW HEALTH SYSTEM
SPARROW HOSPITAL
1200 East Michigan Avenue, Lansing MI 48912. 517/364-5858. **Fax:** 517/364-5818. **Contact:** Human Resources. **E-mail address:** hr@sparrow.org. **World Wide Web address:** http://www.sparrow.org. **Description:** A community hospital engaged in inpatient and outpatient health care services. **Positions advertised include:** Health Unit Coordinator; Patient Care Technician; Registered Nurse; Licensed Practical Nurse; Respiratory Therapist; Health Record Analyst; Paramedic; Clinical Pharmacist; Health Desk Specialist; Customer Service Supervisor; Physical Therapy Assistant; Phlebotomy Technician; Medical Technologist. **Corporate headquarters location:** This location.

STRYKER CORPORATION
2725 Fairfield Road, Kalamazoo MI 49002. 269/385-2600. **Toll-free phone:** 800/726-2725. **Fax:** 269/385-2659. **Contact:** Personnel. **World Wide Web address:** http://www.stryker.com. **Description:** Develops, manufactures, and markets specialty surgical and medical products including endoscopic systems, orthopedic implants, powered surgical instruments, and patient care and handling equipment for the global market. Stryker also provides outpatient physical therapy services in the United States. Founded in 1941. **Special programs:** Internships. **Corporate headquarters location:** This location. **Other U.S. locations:** Nationwide. **International locations:** Worldwide. **Subsidiaries include:** Howmedica Osteonics. **Listed on:** New York Stock Exchange. **Stock exchange symbol:** SYK. **Number of employees worldwide:** Over 14,000.

WAR MEMORIAL HOSPITAL
500 Osborn Boulevard, Sault Ste. Marie MI 49783. 906/635-4421. **Fax:** 906/635-4423. **Contact:** Recruiter. **E-mail address:** toverman@wmhos.org. **World Wide Web address:** http://www.warmemorialhospital.org. **Description:** An 82-bed, full-service hospital that also

offers a long-term care center. **Positions advertised include:** Radiology Technologist; Registered Nurse. **Corporate headquarters location:** This location. **Number of employees at this location:** 400.

Minnesota

ATS MEDICAL, INC.
3905 Annapolis Lane, Suite 105, Minneapolis MN 55447. 763/553-7736. **Toll-free phone:** 800/399-1381. **Contact:** Human Resources. **E-mail address:** human.resources@atsmedical.com. **World Wide Web address:** http://www.atsmedical.com. **Description:** Manufactures and markets medical devices including aortic valve graft prosthesis, mechanical heart valves, and related cardiovascular devices. Founded in 1991. **Corporate headquarters location:** This location. **Subsidiaries include:** ATS Medical, Ltd. (Glasgow, Scotland). **Listed on:** NASDAQ. **Stock exchange symbol:** ATSI.

ABBOTT NORTHWESTERN HOSPITAL
800 East 28th Street, Minneapolis MN 55407. 612/863-4000. **World Wide Web address:** http://www.abbottnorthwestern.com. **Description:** The largest not-for-profit hospital in the Twin Cities area. **Positions advertised include:** Business Analyst; Cardiac Sonographer; Director, Planned Giving; EMT; Film Librarian; Nursing Manager; Practice Manager; Operations Coordinator; Perinatal Ultrasonographer; Physical Therapist; RN's; Speech Pathologist. **Parent company:** Allina Hospitals & Clinics.

ALBANY AREA HOSPITAL & MEDICAL CENTER
300 Third Avenue, Albany MN 56307. 320/845-6104. **Fax:** 320/845-6127. **Contact:** Renee Thelen, Human Resources. Manager **E-mail address:** reneethelen@catholichealth.net. **World Wide Web address:** http://www.albanyareahospital.com. **Description:** A hospital offering acute care services.

ALLINA HOSPITALS & CLINICS
Mail Route 10703, 2925 Chicago Avenue South, Minneapolis MN 55407-1321. 612/262-4590. **Contact:** Human Resources. **World Wide Web address:** http://www.allina.com. **Description:** A not-for-profit system of hospitals, clinics, and other health care services. Patient care facilities include 11 hospitals, 42 Allina Medical Clinic sites, 22 hospital-based clinics, 14 community pharmacies, and 4 ambulatory care centers in Minnesota and western Wisconsin. **Number of employees nationwide:** 23,000.

AMERICAN MEDICAL SYSTEMS, INC.
10700 Bren Road West, Minnetonka MN 55343. 952/933-4666. **Toll-free phone:** 800/328-3881. **Fax:** 952/930-6157. **Contact:** Human Resources. **E-mail address:** careers@americanmedicalsystems.com. **World Wide Web address:** http://www.americanmedicalsystems.com. **Description:** Manufactures and distributes medical devices for the diagnosis and treatment of a variety of illnesses including prostate diseases, severe fecal incontinence, urethral strictures, and urinary incontinence. **Positions advertised include:** Database Administrator; Assistant Treasurer; Financial Business Analyst; Operations Engineer; Scientist/Neuroscientist; Receptionist; Product Manager. **Listed on:** NASDAQ. **Stock exchange symbol:** AMMD.

ARIZANT HEALTHCARE, INC.
10393 West 70th Street, Eden Prairie MN 55344. 952/947-1200. **Fax:** 952/947-1400. **Contact:** Deb McGahey, Human Resources. **World Wide Web address:** www.arizant.com. **Description:** Manufactures convective warming blankets and fluid warmers for the healthcare industry. **Parent company:** Arizant Inc.

BIGFORK VALLEY
258 Pine Tree Drive, Bigfork MN 56628. 218/743-4244. **Fax:** 218/743-3559. **Contact:** Miriam Osborn, Human Resources Manager. **E-mail address:** mosborn@bigforkvalley.org. **World Wide Web address:** http://www.bigforkvalley.org. **Description:** A health care campus consisting of a 20-bed hospital, a long-term care facility, senior living facilities, medical and dental clinics, and rehabilitation and fitness centers. **NOTE:** Entry-level positions and second and third shifts are offered.

BIOSCRIP
10050 Crosstown Circle. Suite 300, Eden Prairie MN 55344. 952/979-3600. **Toll-free phone:** 800/444-5951. **Fax:** 952/979-3713. **Contact:** Human Resources. **E-mail address:** hr@bioscrip.com. **World Wide Web address:** http://www.bioscrip.com. **Description:** Provides specialty pharmacy services, including clinical management and specialty medication distribution, as well as infusion medications for patients with complex health conditions. BioScrip serves patients with a broad range of complex health conditions, including HIV/AIDS, Transplantation, Oncology, Hepatitis C, Arthritis, Multiple Sclerosis and more. **Positions advertised include:** A/R Specialist; Accountant-Retail Revenue & A/R; Director, Customer Service; Traditional Customer Service Representative. **Corporate headquarters location:** Elmsford NY. **Other U.S. locations:** Nationwide. **Operations at this facility include:** Business Headquarters. **Listed on:** NASDAQ. **Stock exchange symbol:** BIOS.

BOSTON SCIENTIFIC CORP.
One Scimed Place, Maple Grove MN 55311-1506. 763/494-1700. **Contact:** Human Resources. **World Wide Web address:** http://www.bostonscientific.com. **Description:** Engages in the development, manufacture, and marketing of medical devices that are used in interventional medical specialties. **Positions advertised include:** Trainer; R&D Technician; Sr. Process Engineer; Patent Attorney; Manufacturing Engineer; Global Director, Design Assurance; Vice President Cardiology; Principal Pharmaceutical Scientist. **Corporate headquarters location:** Natick MA. **Other area locations:** Plymouth MN. **Listed on:** New York Stock Exchange. **Stock exchange symbol:** BSX. **Number of employees worldwide:** 19,800.

CENTER FOR DIAGNOSTIC IMAGING
5775 Wayzata Boulevard, Suite 400, St. Louis Park MN 55416. 952/543-6500. **Toll-free phone:** 877-566-6500. **Fax:** 952/513-6881. **E-mail address:** jobs@cdirad.com. **World Wide Web address:** http://www.cdirad.com. **Description:** A physician-led national radiology practice with 26 centers in six states. **Positions advertised include:** Staff Accountant; Accounts Payable Associate; Scheduling Specialist.

CHILDREN'S HOSPITALS & CLINICS OF MINNESOTA - MINNEAPOLIS
2525 Chicago Avenue South, Minneapolis, MN 55404. 612/813-6000. **Contact:** Human Resources. **World Wide Web address:** http://www.childrensmn.org. **Description:** A children's hospital and medical center with 147 beds. **NOTE:** Search and apply for positions online. Human Resources address is: Mail Stop 80-H190, 2577 Territorial Road, St. Paul MN 55114; Telephone: 612/813-7469. **Other area locations:** Minnetonka MN; Roseville MN; Woodbury MN.

CHILDREN'S HOSPITALS & CLINICS OF MINNESOTA - ST. PAUL
345 North Smith Avenue, St. Paul MN 55102. 651/220-6000. **Contact:** Human Resources. **E-mail address:** hrrecruiting@childrensmn.org. **World Wide Web address:** http://www.childrenshc.org. **Description:** A 105-bed pediatric hospital. Founded in 1920. **NOTE:** Search and apply for positions online. Human Resources address is: Mail Stop 80-H190, 2577 Territorial Road, St. Paul MN 55114; Telephone: 612/813-7469.**Other area locations:** Minnetonka MN; Roseville MN; Woodbury MN.

COMMUNITY MEMORIAL HOSPITAL
855 Mankato Avenue, Winona MN 55987. 507/457-4308. **Fax:** 507/453-3739. **Contact:** Human Resources. **E-mail address:** jobs@winonahealth.org. **World Wide Web address:** http://www.winonahealthonline.org.

Description: A 99-bed accredited, nonprofit, primary care hospital with a 111-year tradition of serving the healthcare needs of the Winona regional community. Part of Winona Health. **Positions advertised include:** Executive Assistant; Health Unit Coordinator; Nursing Assistant; Charge Nurse; Licensed Practical Nurse.

EMPI, INC.
599 Cardigan Road, St. Paul MN 55126-4099. 651/415-9000. **Fax:** 651/415-8406. **Contact:** Human Resources. **E-mail address:** employmentspecialist@empi.com. **World Wide Web address:** http://www.empi.com. **Description:** Manufactures and markets products for incontinence, physical rehabilitation, and orthopedics. Major products include neuromuscular stimulators, braces and splints, drug administering devices, and cervical traction devices. **NOTE:** See website for current job openings. Send resume by fax, e-mail, or mail. **Positions advertised include:** Division Controller; Regional Sales Manager; Patient Account Specialist; Refund Specialist; Clinic Service Representative; Business Analyst – Healthcare; Patient Care Services Rep; Territory Manager (Outside Sales). **Corporate headquarters location:** This location. **Listed on:** NASDAQ. **Stock exchange symbol:** EMPI.

FAIRVIEW HEALTH SERVICES
2450 Riverside Avenue, Minneapolis MN 55454. 612/672-6945. **Fax:** 612/672-6337. **Contact:** Human Resources. **E-mail address:** corpres@fairview.org. **World Wide Web address:** http://www.fairview.org. **Description:** A nonprofit, regionally integrated health care network of primary, specialty, acute, long-term, and home care services. Fairview Health Services consists of seven hospitals, over 96 primary and specialty care clinics, 20 retail pharmacies, and long-term care facilities. **NOTE:** Entry-level positions are offered. **Special programs:** Internships. **Corporate headquarters location:** This location. **Parent company:** Fairview Health Services. **Listed on:** Privately held. **Number of employees nationwide:** 15,000.

GUIDANT CORPORATION
4100 Hamline Avenue North, St. Paul MN 55112-5798. 651/582-4000. **Toll-free phone:** 800/227-3422. **Fax:** 651/582-4166. **Contact:** Human Resources Manager. **World Wide Web address:** http://www.guidant.com. **Description:** Develops, manufactures, and sells a wide range of products used in the treatment of cardiac arrhythmias. The company's products are both implantable and external electronic devices and accessories that are sold to hospitals and other health care providers worldwide. **NOTE:** Guidant was recently acquired by Boston Scientific. See website for current company news and to search and apply for positions online. **Positions advertised include:** Electrical Engineer; Electronic Engineer; Mechanical Engineer; Process/Quality Engineer; Systems Engineer; Business Analyst; Contract Administrator; Clinical Consultant. **Corporate headquarters location:** Indianapolis IN. **Operations at this facility include:** Cardiac Rhythm Management unit.

GYRUS MEDICAL CORPORATION
6655 Wedgwood Road, Suite #105, Osseo MN 55311-3602. 763/416-3000. **Fax:** 763/463-1200. **Contact:** Julie Seurer, Human Resources Department. **E-mail address:** julie.seurer@gyrusmed.com. **World Wide Web address:** http://www.gyrusmedical.com. **Description:** Manufactures tissue management surgical instruments. **NOTE:** See website for current job openings and to download application. **Positions advertised include:** IT Program Manager; Marketing Manager; Quality Engineer; Senior Buyer; Service Technician; Website Development Specialist; **Corporate headquarters location:** This location.

HEARTLAND HOME HEALTH CARE AND HOSPICE
2250 County Road C, Roseville MN 55113. 651/633-6522. **Contact:** Human Resources. **E-mail address:** jobline@hcr-manorcare.com. **World Wide Web address:** http://www.heartlandhomehealth.com. **Description:** Heartland Home Health Care & Hospice provides home health and hospice care through 80 offices in 22 states. **NOTE:** Search and apply for positions online at http://www.hcr-manorcare.com. **Positions advertised include:** Director of Admissions; Hospice Administrator; Patient Care Coordinator; RN. **Corporate headquarters location:** Toledo OH. **Parent company:** HCR Manor Care.

IMMANUEL ST. JOSEPH'S HOSPITAL
1025 Marsh Street, P.O. 8673, Mankato MN 56002-8673. 507/345-2632. **Fax:** 507/389-4750. **Recorded jobline:** 866/488-8736. **Contact:** Human Resources Department. **World Wide Web address:** http://www.isj-mhs.org. **Description:** Immanuel St. Joseph's Hospital serves as south central Minnesota's regional medical center. Specialized care includes birthing suites for expectant mothers; a fully staffed emergency room; the assessment, diagnosis, and treatment of behavioral health problems; a cancer center; home health care; and a hospice for terminally ill patients and their families. **Positions advertised include:** Clinical Coordinator; Clinical Dietitian; Coordinator, New Hire Support; Internist; Lead Registered Nurses; LPN's; Manager, Facilities Project; Medical Oncologist; Polysomnography Technologist; Pulmonologist; RN's. **Subsidiaries include:** Waseca Area Memorial Hospital. **Parent company:** Mayo Health Systems. **Number of employees at this location:** 900.

LIFECORE BIOMEDICAL INC.
3515 Lyman Boulevard, Chaska MN 55318. 952/368-4300. **Fax:** 952/368-3411. **Contact:** Human Resources. **E-mail address:** careers@lifecore.com. **World Wide Web address:** http://www.lifecore.com. **Description:** Manufactures and markets implantable biomaterials and medical devices. Lifecore Biomedical's products are used in the fields of dentistry, drug delivery, general surgery, ophthalmology, and wound care management. **Positions advertised include:** Aseptic Manufacturing Technician; Packaging Technician; Quality Control Analyst II; Sales Representative; Senior Design Engineer; Staff Accountant. **Corporate headquarters location:** This location.

MAICO DIAGNOSTICS
7625 Golden Triangle Drive, Eden Prairie MN 55344. 952/941-4200. **Toll-free phone:** 888/941-4201. **Fax:** 952/903-4200. **Contact:** Human Resources. **E-mail address:** info@maico-diagnostics.com. **World Wide Web address:** http://www.bernafon-us.com. **Description:** Produces and sells hearing aides and audiometer equipment. The company also provides support services and resources for the hearing impaired. Founded in 1936. **Corporate headquarters location:** This location. **Operations at this facility include:** Administration; Manufacturing; Research and Development; Sales; Service.

MALLINCKRODT, INC.
2200 University Avenue West, Suite 170, St Paul MN 55114. 651/646-7229. **Contact:** Human Resources. **World Wide Web address:** http://www.mallinckrodt.com. **Description:** Manufactures and markets health care products through three main specialty groups. The Imaging Group provides contrast media and delivery systems, radiopharmaceuticals, and urology imaging systems for the diagnosis and treatment of disease in many imaging procedures. **Special programs:** Internships; Co-ops. **Corporate headquarters location:** St. Louis MO. **Other U.S. locations:** Nationwide. **International locations:** Worldwide. **Parent company:** Tyco Healthcare. **Number of employees at this location:** 350. **Number of employees worldwide:** 12,000.

McKESSON CORP.
8121 10th Avenue North, Golden Valley MN 55427-9824. 763/595-6000. **Toll-free phone:** 800/328-8111. **Fax:** 763/595-6677. **Contact:** Human Resources. **World Wide Web address:** http://www.mckesson.com. **Description:** Distributes medical equipment to nursing homes and hospitals.

Positions advertised include: Pricing Coordinator; Rebate Coordinator; Business Analyst.

MEDICAL GRAPHICS CORPORATION
350 Oak Grove Parkway, St. Paul MN 55127. 651/484-4874. **Fax:** 651/484-8941. **Contact:** Ms. Sheryl Raphael, Director of Human Resources Department. **E-mail address:** hr@medgraphics.com. **World Wide Web address:** http://www.medgraphics.com. **Description:** A manufacturer of computerized medical testing equipment for the health care industry. Products include diagnostic systems that test and treat lung and heart disorders. **NOTE:** Submit resume by e-mail or mail. **Positions advertised include:** Clinical/National Accounts Manager; Clinical Research Applications Specialists; Bio-Medical Technical Support Specialist

MEDTRONIC ENERGY & COMPONENT CENTER
6700 Shingle Creek Parkway, Brooklyn Center MN 55430. 763/514-1000. **Contact:** Human Resources. **World Wide Web address:** http://www.medtronic.com. **Description:** Researches, designs, and manufactures medical equipment used in cardiac rhythm management, neurological, spinal, ENT, cardiac, and vascular surgery. Founded in 1949. **Positions advertised include:** Manufacturing Engineer; Sr. Manufacturing Engineer; Sr. Project Engineer; Sr. Assembler; Principle Health and Safety Specialist. **Corporate headquarters location:** Minneapolis MN. **Operations at this facility include:** This location manufactures implantable, cardiac pacemakers. **Listed on:** New York Stock Exchange. **Stock exchange symbol:** MDT. **Number of employees worldwide:** 30,000.

MEDTRONIC, INC.
710 Medtronic Parkway, Minneapolis MN 55432-5604. 763/514-4000. **Fax:** 763/514-4879. **Recorded jobline:** 763/505-2222. **Contact:** Human Resources. **E-mail address:** employment@medtronic.com. **World Wide Web address:** http://www.medtronic.com. **Description:** Researches, designs, and manufactures medical equipment used in cardiac rhythm management, neurological, spinal, ENT, cardiac, and vascular surgery. Founded in 1949. **Positions advertised include:** Perfusion Systems Sales Manager; Sr. Manufacturing Engineer; Sr. QA Engineer; Sr. Competitive Intelligence Specialist. **Corporate headquarters location:** This location. **Other U.S. locations:** Nationwide. **International locations:** Worldwide. **Operations at this facility include:** Manufacturing; Research and Development. **Listed on:** New York Stock Exchange. **Stock exchange symbol:** MDT. **Number of employees at this location:** 4,000. **Number of employees worldwide:** 30,000.

METHODIST HOSPITAL
6500 Excelsior Boulevard, Saint Louis Park MN 55426. 952/993-1600. **Fax:** 952/993-1638. **Contact:** Human Resources Representative. **World Wide Web address:** http:// www.parknicollet.com/methodist. **Description:** A 426-bed, full-service hospital. **NOTE:** Search and apply for positions online, or mail resumes to: Human Resources, 3800 Park Nicollet Boulevard, St. Louis Park MN 55416-2699. **Parent company:** Park Nicollet Health Services. **Number of employees at this location:** 4,650.

OPTICAL SENSORS INCORPORATED DBA VÄSAMED
7615 Golden Triangle Drive, Suite C, Eden Prairie MN 55344. 952.944.5857. **Fax:** 952/944-6022. **Contact:** Human Resources. **E-mail address:** hr@vasamed.com. **World Wide Web address:** http://www.vasamed.com. **Description:** Optical Sensors Incorporated (OSI), doing business as väsamed, engages in the design, license, manufacture, and distribution of noninvasive hemodynamic technologies for vascular, wound care, cardiovascular, and emergency medicine diagnostics.

PARK NICOLLET HEALTH SERVICES
3800 Park Nicollet Boulevard, St. Louis Park MN 55416-2699. 952/993-1600. **Fax:** 952/993-1638. **Contact:** Human Resources. **World Wide Web address:** http://www.parknicollet.com. **Description:** Operates Methodist Hospital, a 426-bed, full-service hospital, and Park Nicollet Clinic, one of the largest multi-specialty clinics in the United States, with 25 neighborhood clinics. **NOTE:** Search and apply for positions online. **Number of employees nationwide:** 7,500.

PATTERSON COMPANIES INC.
1031 Mendota Heights Road, St. Paul MN 55120. 651/686-1600. **Toll-free phone:** 800/328-5536. **Fax:** 651/686-9331. **Contact:** Director of Human Resources. **E-mail address:** jobs@pattersondental.com. **World Wide Web address:** http://www.pattersondental.com. **Description**: A distributor serving the dental supply, companion-pet veterinarian supply and rehabilitation supply markets. **Positions advertised include:** Patterson Brand & New Product Manager; Compensation Manager; Internal Auditor; Advertising Project Manager. **Corporate headquarters location:** This location. **Other area locations:** Eagan MN.

PRESBYTERIAN HOMES AND SERVICES
2845 North Hamline Avenue, Roseville MN 55113. 651/631-600. **Fax:** 651/631-6108. **Recorded jobline:** 877/747-4473. **Contact:** Human Resources Representative. **World Wide Web address:** http://www.preshomes.com. **Description:** Offers a broad range of residential and support services to the elderly at facilities throughout the Twin Cities. Services include apartment living, long-term nursing care, and home health respite programs. **NOTE:** Entry-level positions and second and third shifts are offered. **Positions advertised include:** Clinical Coordinator; Physical Therapist; RN. **Special programs:** Internships; Summer Jobs. **Corporate headquarters location:** This location. **CEO:** Daniel Lindh. **Number of employees at this location:** 1,500.

REGIONS HOSPITAL
640 Jackson Street, St. Paul MN 55101. 651/254-4784. **Toll-free phone:** 800/332-5720. **Fax:** 651/254-3450. **Recorded jobline:** 651/254-0855. **Contact:** Alissa A. Fleming, Human Resources. **E-mail address:** Alissa.A.Fleming@healthpartners.com. **World Wide Web address:** http://www.regionshospital.com. **Description:** A full-service private hospital with a Level I trauma center. **NOTE:** Human Resources Department is located at: 690 North Robert Street, St. Paul MN 55101. **Positions advertised include:** Custodial Worker; Patient Care Assistant; Infection Control Manager; Manager of Benefits and Compensation; Orthopedic Practice Manager; Chemical Health Counselor; Cytotechnologist; Neurodiagnostic Technologist; Pharmacists; Polysomnographic Technologist; LPN's; RN's. **Special programs:** Internships. **Corporate headquarters location:** This location. **Parent company:** HealthPartners, Inc. **Number of employees at this location:** 500.

REM, INC.
6921 York Avenue South, Edina MN 55435. 952/925-5067. **Toll-free phone:** 800/896-8814. **Fax:** 952/925-0739. **Contact:** Human Resources Manager. **World Wide Web address:** http://www.reminc.com. **Description:** A provider of community-based health care and related services, with locations in Minnesota and Wisconsin. **Positions advertised include:** RN; LPN; Home Health Aide. **Special programs:** Training; Summer Jobs. **Corporate headquarters location:** This location. **Parent company:** The Mentor Network. **Listed on:** Privately held. **Annual sales/revenues:** $11 - $20 million. **Number of employees at this location:** 1,000.

RESISTANCE TECHNOLOGY INC.
1260 Red Fox Road, Arden Hills MN 55112. 651/636-9770. **Fax:** 651/636-9503. **Contact:** Human Resources. **World Wide Web address:** http://www.rti-corp.com. **Description:** A manufacturer of injection-molded plastic products for the hearing health and medical care industry. **Corporate headquarters location:** This location.

RICE MEMORIAL HOSPITAL
301 Becker Avenue Southwest, Willmar MN 56201. 320/231-4499. **Toll-free phone:** 800/537-4677. **Fax:** 320/231-4940. **Contact:** Nancy Skindelien, Human Resources. **E-mail address:** nski@rice.willmar.mn.us. **World Wide Web address:** http://www.ricehospital.com. **Description:** A 136-bed hospital offering both acute care and outpatient services. **NOTE:** See website for current job openings and submit resume and cover letter by mail or e-mail. **Positions advertised include:** RN's; Security Officer; Dietary Aide. **Number of employees at this location:** 900.

RIDGEVIEW MEDICAL CENTER
500 South Maple Street, Waconia MN 55387-1714. 952/442-2191. **Toll-free phone:** 800/967-4620. **Recorded jobline:** 952/442-2191 ext. 6025. **Contact:** Human Resources. **World Wide Web address:** http://www.ridgeviewmedical.org. **Description:** A medical center with 129 beds offering both acute care and outpatient services. Administers a regional network that includes neighborhood clinics, emergency facilities, and specialty programs and services. With more than 250 physicians in 39 areas of specialization, Ridgeview offers comprehensive medical and surgical services. **Positions advertised include:** Health Unit Coordinator; Pharmacist; Radiology Technologist; Home Medical Equipment Services Director; Clinical Informatics Coordinator; RN's.

ROCHESTER METHODIST HOSPITAL MAYO CLINIC
201 West Center Street, Rochester MN 55902-3003. 507/266-7890. **Contact:** Human Resources. **World Wide Web address:** http://www.mayoclinic.org/methodisthospital. **Description:** Rochester Methodist Hospital is one of two Mayo Foundation hospitals in Rochester. It contains 794 licensed beds and 36 operating rooms. It is a 794-bed hospital offering acute care and outpatient services through its Epilepsy Monitoring Unit; a perinatal care center for high-risk pregnancies; a psoriasis and dermatology program; an intraoperative radiation surgical suite; transplant programs for bone marrow, kidney, liver, and pancreas diseases; and a women's cancer center. Rochester Methodist Hospital is an affiliate of the Mayo Clinic. **NOTE:** Search and apply for positions online. **Positions advertised include:** Administrator; Administrator, health Information Operations; Application Analyst; Biomedical Engineer; Cardiac Monitor Technician; Clinical Nurse Specialist; Contract Manager; Creative Services Director; Cytogenetics Education Specialist.

ST. BENEDICT'S SENIOR COMMUNITY
1810 Minnesota Boulevard Southeast, St. Cloud MN 56304. 320/252-0010. **Fax:** 320/229-8311. **Contact:** Human Resources. **World Wide Web address:** http://www.centracare.com/stben/stben_stcloud.html. **Description:** Offers nonprofit health care and housing for older adults. St. Benedict's Senior Community provides nursing services to over 220 individuals who require 24-hour care. St. Benedict's Senior Community also offers a sub acute care unit, a special care unit, hospice care, and respite care. The center also operates a retirement community, an assisted living facility, income-based senior housing, a residential center for those in the early stages of Alzheimer's disease or memory loss, home care services, and a senior dining program for the residents of southeast St. Cloud. Founded in 1978. **NOTE:** Entry-level positions, part-time jobs, and second and third shifts are offered. **Positions advertised include:** Registered Nurse; Licensed Practical Nurse; Certified Nursing Assistant; Registered Dietician; Recreational Therapist. **Special programs:** Internships; Summer Jobs. **Internship information:** Unpaid internships are offered during the fall and spring. Opportunities are available in Human Resources, working with people suffering from cognitive disorders, and social services. For more information or to volunteer, call the Volunteer Coordinator at 320/252-0010. **Parent company:** CentraCare Health Systems. **Number of employees at this location:** 525.

ST. CLOUD HOSPITAL
1406 Sixth Avenue North, St. Cloud MN 56303. 320/255-5650. **Fax:** 320/255-5711. **Contact:** Employment Department. **E-mail address:** hrs@centracare.com. **World Wide Web address:** http://www.centracare.com/sch/index.html. **Description:** A regional medical center offering a variety of medical specialties. **Positions advertised include:** Community Initiatives Specialist; Diagnostic Medical Sonographer; Disease Management/Wellness Specialist; Pharmacist; Physical Therapist; Recruiter; Staff Psychotherapist; RN's. **Special programs:** Internships. **Operations at this facility include:** Health Care; Service. **Number of employees at this location:** 3,600.

ST. JUDE MEDICAL, INC.
One Lillehei Plaza, St. Paul MN 55117-9983. 651/483-2000. **Fax:** 651/482-8315. **Contact:** Human Resources. **World Wide Web address:** http://www.sjm.com. **Description:** A world leader in the development of cardiovascular medical devices. The company operates through three divisions: Cardiac Surgery, which develops mechanical heart valve devices; the Cardiac Rhythm Management Division, which manufactures cardiac rhythm products; and Daig, which specializes in the manufacture of catheters. **Positions advertised include:** Quality Technician; Manager, R&D; Marketing Manager; Principal Engineer; Senior Business Analyst: Senior Information Technology Security & Control Analyst; Senior Software Developer; Senior Clinical Research Associate. **Corporate headquarters location:** This location. **Other area locations:** Maple Grove MN: Minnetonka MN. **International locations:** Worldwide. **Listed on:** New York Stock Exchange. **Stock exchange symbol:** STJ. **Annual sales/revenues:** More than $100 million. **Number of employees worldwide:** 10,000.

ST. PETER COMMUNITY HOSPITAL
1900 North Sunrise Drive, St. Peter MN 56082. 507/931-2200. **Fax:** 507/934-7651. **Contact:** Human Resources. **World Wide Web address:** http://www.stpeterhealth.org. **Description:** A medical center offering acute care and outpatient services as well as a wide variety of diagnostic testing. **Positions advertised include:** Radiology Technologist; Occupational Therapist; Registered Nurse; Volunteer EMT.

ST. THERESE HOME
8000 Bass Lake Road, New Hope MN 55428. 763/531-5000. **Fax:** 763/531-5004. **Contact:** Rand Brugger, Director of Human Resources. **E-mail address:** jobs@sttheresenh.org. **World Wide Web address:** http://www.sttheresenh.org **Description:** A religious-sponsored nonprofit organization that provides long-term health care to the elderly. The company consists of a 302-bed care center, 220 units of senior housing, home care services, and a rehabilitation agency. **NOTE:** See website for current job openings. Submit resume by e-mail. Entry-level positions and second and third shifts are offered. **Special programs:** Internships; Summer Jobs. **Parent company:** St. Therese Home, Inc. **Number of employees at this location:** 600.

SMITHS MEDICAL MD, INC.
1265 Grey Fox Road, St. Paul MN 55112. 651/633-2556. **Fax:** 651/628-7153. **Contact:** Jean Jacobs, Human Resources. **E-mail address:** jean.jacob@smiths-medical.com. **World Wide Web address:** http://www.smiths-medical.com. **Description:** Manufactures and markets ambulatory infusion systems, large-volume infusion pumps, and vascular access systems. **Corporate headquarters location:** London, United Kingdom. **Parent company:** Smiths Group PLC.

SPECTRUM COMMUNITY HEALTH, INC.
1831 24th Street NW, Rochester MN 55901. 507/282-8052. **Fax:** 507/292-1382. **Contact:** Vickie Thornton.

E-mail address: vthornton@spectrumchealth.com. **World Wide Web address:** http://www.spectrumhomecare.com/locations/rochester. **Description:** A home health care provider that offers nursing, rehabilitation, and personal care assistance to individuals of all ages. **Other U.S. locations:** Brainerd MN; Duluth MN; Ely MN; Faribault MN; Grand Rapids MN; Minneapolis/St. Paul MN; Virginia MN; Willmar MN.

STEN CORPORATION
10275 Wayzata Boulevard, Suite 310, Minnetonka MN 55305. 952/545-2776. **Contact:** Human Resources. **World Wide Web address:** http://www.stencorporation.com. **Description:** A diversified holding company. In Minnesota, STEN Corporation is currently engaged in the operation of fast food restaurants. Its Burger Time Acquisition Corporation operates a chain of fast food, drive-through restaurants under the Burger Time name. As of September 30, 2005, the company operated 13 Burger Time restaurants in Minnesota, North Dakota, South Dakota, and Iowa. **NOTE:** See http://www.itsburgertime.com to apply online for positions with Burger Time. **Corporate headquarters location:** This location. **Listed on:** NASDAQ. **Stock exchange symbol:** STEN. **Annual sales/revenues:** Less than $5 million.

STEVENS COMMUNITY MEDICAL CENTER
400 East First Street, Box 660, Morris MN 56267. 320/589-7646. **Fax:** 320/589-3533. **Contact:** Personnel. **E-mail address:** krlarson@runestone.net. **World Wide Web address:** http://www.scmcmorris.com. **Description:** A nonprofit, multi-specialty clinic and hospital serving the west central Minnesota region. Founded in 1951. **NOTE:** See website to download application, or contact Human Resources for a list of current open positions or to request an application. Submit completed applications by mail, e-mail, or fax. **Company slogan:** Caring is our reason for being. **Corporate headquarters location:** This location.

TIMM MEDICAL TECHNOLOGIES, INC.
6585 City West Parkway, Eden Prairie MN 55344. 952/947-9410. **Fax:** 952/947-9411. **Contact:** Human Resources. **World Wide Web address:** http://www.timmmedical.com. **Description:** Makes erectile dysfunction products. **Parent company:** Plethora Solutions Holdings PLC.

VISION-EASE LENS, INC.
7000 Sunwood Drive, Ramsey MN 55303. 763/576-3930. **Fax:** 763/576-5127. **Contact:** Human Resources. **World Wide Web address:** http://www.vision-ease.com. **Description:** A leading supplier of optical lenses both in North America and in other parts of the world. It is a leading manufacturer of polycarbonate lenses and glass and also distributes plastic lenses. **Positions advertised include:** Coating Scientist. **Other area locations:** Bloomington MN; St. Cloud MN. **Parent company:** Insight Equity.

WALMAN OPTICAL COMPANY
801 12th Avenue North, Minneapolis MN 55411. 612/520-6000. **Fax:** 612/520-6096. **Contact:** Human Resources. **E-mail address:** hr@walman.com. **World Wide Web address:** http://www.walman.com. **Description:** An employee-owned manufacturer of ophthalmic products with 40 offices in 19 states. **Positions advertised include:** Account Manager, Contact Lens Customer Service Representative; Contact Lens Production Technician. **Other U.S. locations:** Nationwide. **Operations at this facility include:** Administration; Manufacturing; Sales; Service.

ZIMMER SPINE
7375 Bush Lake Road, Edina MN 55439. 952/832-5600. **Fax:** 952/832-5620. **Contact:** Human Resources. **World Wide Web address:** http://www.zimmerspine.com. **Description:** Designs, manufactures, and distributes medical devices and surgical tools that aid spine care for patients with back pain, neck pain, degenerative disc conditions, and injuries due to trauma. **Positions advertised include:** Senior Finance Analyst; Clinical Research Associate.

Mississippi

BAXTER HEALTHCARE CORPORATION
911 North Davis Avenue, Cleveland MS 38732. 662/843-9421. **Contact:** Human Resources Manager. **World Wide Web address:** http://www.baxter.com. **Description:** Baxter Healthcare, through its subsidiaries, is a producer, developer, and distributor of medical products and technologies for use in hospitals and other health care settings. **NOTE:** Baxter no longer accepts paper resumes. **Positions advertised include:** Department Specialist; Engineer; Quality Associate; Quality Lab Associate; Superintendent, Maintenance Supervisor, Manufacturing; Warehouse Coordinator. **Special Programs:** Internships. **Corporate headquarters location:** Deerfield IL. **Operations at this facility include:** Administration; Manufacturing. **Listed on:** New York Stock Exchange. **Stock exchange symbol:** BAX. **Annual sales/revenues:** $3.5 billion. **Number of employees at this location:** 1,200. **Number of employees worldwide:** 48,000.

BILOXI REGIONAL MEDICAL CENTER
150 Reynoir Street, Biloxi MS 39530. 228/432-1232. **Recorded jobline:** 228/436-1145. **Contact:** Human Resources. **E-mail address:** human.resources@brmc.hma-corp.com. **World Wide Web address:** http://www.hmabrmc.com. **Description:** A 153-bed, acute care private hospital, with a 24 hour emergency room and patient oriented programs with an emphasis on elderly, women's and children's healthcare. **NOTE:** Applications accepted Monday-Friday, 9am-3pm. For nursing positions, contact nurse.recruiter@brmc.hma-corp.com. **Positions advertised include:** OR Technician; Unit Clerk; Community Liaison; Telemetry Monitor Technician; Physical Therapist; EKG Technician; Housekeeper; Director of Radiology. **Special Programs:** Volunteer Opportunities. **Corporate headquarters location:** Naples FL. **Parent company:** Health Management Associates, Inc. **Operations at this facility include:** Administration; Service. **Number of employees at this location:** 600. **Number of employees nationwide:** 12,000.

HATTIESBURG CLINIC
415 South 28th Avenue, Hattiesburg MS 39401. 601-579-5152. **Fax:** 601/579-5152. **Recorded jobline:** 601/268-5803. **Contact:** Human Resources. **World Wide Web address:** http://www.hattiesburgclinic.com. **Description:** A physician-owned group practice with more than 180 physicians representing almost every medical specialty. **NOTE:** For physician employment, contact William C. Allen, Jr., Senior Assistant Administrator, at 800/844-9355. **Positions advertised include:** Vascular Technician; X-RAY Technician; Pacemaker Technician; Phlebotomist; Manager, Imaging; Insurance Clerk; Medicare Review Team; Contract Accounts Clerk; Data Processor; File Clerk; CT Technician Assistant; Contract Accountant Clerks; Receptionist; Patient Account Representative; Patient Representative. **Number of employees at this location:** 1,100.

MAGNOLIA REGIONAL HEALTH CENTER
611 Alcorn Drive, Corinth MS 38834. 662/293-1300. **Fax:** 662/293-4285. **Contact:** Regenia Brown, Human Resources Coordinator. **E-mail address:** regeniabrown@mrhc.org. **World Wide Web address:** http://www.mrhc.org. **Description:** A 165-bed, full-service medical center. **NOTE:** For physician positions, contact Don Lloyd, Director of Physician Operations, at 662/287-6913, or dlloyd@mrhc@org. **Positions advertised include:** Ancillary Greeter; PBX Operator; Registration Clerk; H.I.M. Inpatient Coder; Food Service Worker; Phlebotomist; Physical Therapist; EMT Paramedic. **Operations at this facility include:** Administration. **Number of employees at this location:** 700.

MAXXIM MEDICAL
549 Yorkville Park Square, Columbus MS 39702. 888/462-9922. **Contact:** Human Resources. **E-mail address:** employment@medline.com. **World Wide Web address:** http://www.medline.com. **Description:** Manufactures and distributes medical products and textiles for the health care industry. Products include clinical and surgical procedure trays, drapes, gowns, and other instruments such as sutures, needles, gloves, tubing, sponges, towels and gauze. Founded in 1976. **Corporate headquarters location:** Clearwater FL. **Parent company:** Medline Industries, Inc. (Mundeleine IL).

RIVER REGION HEALTH SYSTEM
2100 Highway 61 North, Vicksburg MS 39183. 601/883-5900. **Toll-free phone:** 800/548-2419. **Fax:** 601/883-5014. **Recorded jobline:** 601/631-2749. **Contact:** Human Resources. **E-mail address:** human.resources@riverregion.com. **World Wide Web address:** http://www.riverregion.com. **Description:** A health care company comprised of seven area clinics and a 227-bed medical center. **Positions advertised include:** Critical Care Director; Outreach Health Representative; Coding Analyst; Medical Transcriptionist; Pharmacist; Respiratory Care Practitioner. **Number of employees at this location:** 750.

SOUTH CENTRAL REGIONAL MEDICAL CENTER
23 Mason Street, Laurel MS 39440. 601/399-0517. **Fax:** 601/425-7535. **Recorded jobline:** 601/399-0510. **Contact:** Rachel Evans, Personnel. **E-mail address:** revans@scrmc.com. **World Wide Web address:** http://www.scrmc.com. **Description:** A 285-bed medical center. **NOTE:** For Non-Licensed Applicants, apply in person only. **Positions advertised include:** Physical Therapist; Occupational Therapist; Paramedic; ER Technician; Respiratory Practitioner; BioMed Technician; Collector; Dietician; Biller; Coder; Radiation Technician; Carpenter; Security Officer; Dispatcher; Sleep Lab Technician. **Number of employees at this location:** 1,100.

WESLEY MEDICAL CENTER
5001 Hardy Street, Hattiesburg MS 39402. 601/268-8106. **Recorded jobline:** 800/246-1675. **Contact:** Human Resources. **World Wide Web address:** http://www.wesley.com. **Description:** A 211-bed health care facility operated under the Christian tradition. **Positions advertised include:** Admissions Coordinator; Surgical Technician; Phlebotomist; Environmental Services Technician; Coder; Systems Administrator; Customer Service Representative; Team Leader; Pharmacist; Physical Therapist; Rehabilitation Technician; Clinical Dietician; Exercise Physiologist. **Parent company:** Triad Hospitals, Inc. **Number of employees at this location:** 725.

WINSTON MEDICAL CENTER
562 East Main Street, P.O. Box 967, Louisville MS 39339. 662/779-5102. **Fax:** 662/773-6223. **Contact:** Human Resources Department. **E-mail address:** info@winstonmedical.org. **World Wide Web address:** http://www.winstonmedical.org. **Description:** A 65-bed acute care hospital that also operates a 120-bed nursing home and home health care agency. Founded in 1958. **Number of employees at this location:** 250.

Missouri
ALLEGIANCE HEALTHCARE CORPORATION
5 Sunnen Drive, St. Louis MO 63143. 314/647-0700. **Contact:** Human Resources. **World Wide Web address:** http://www.cardinal.com. **Description:** Allegiance Healthcare, through its subsidiaries, produces, develops, and distributes medical products and technologies for use in hospitals and other health care settings. The company operates in two industry segments: medical specialties and medical/laboratory products and distribution. **Parent company:** Cardinal Health Company.

ALLIED HEALTHCARE PRODUCTS, INC.
1720 Sublette Avenue, St. Louis MO 63110-1968. 314/771-2400. **Toll-free phone:** 800/444-3954. **Contact:** Human Resources. **World Wide Web address:** http://www.alliedhpi.com. **Description:** A manufacturer of medical gas construction equipment, respiratory therapy equipment, home health care products, and emergency medical equipment. **Corporate headquarters location:** This location. **Number of employees at this location:** 830.

ALPHA CARE
9312 Olive Street Road, St. Louis MO 63132. 314/993-2273. **Toll-free phone:** 888/758-4200. **Fax:** 314/993-1196. **Contact:** Director of Administration. **Description:** A home health care agency offering private duty nursing services, supplemental staffing, live-in companions, short-term respite, therapy services, social work, and in-home support services. Founded in 1976. **NOTE:** Entry-level positions and second and third shifts are offered. Search and apply for positions online. **Positions advertised include:** CNA; Branch Manager. **Special programs:** Summer Jobs. **Office hours:** Monday - Friday, 8:00 a.m. - 5:30 p.m. **Corporate headquarters location:** This location. **Other area locations:** Hillsboro MO; St. Charles MO. **Parent company:** Auxi Health, Inc.

AUDRAIN MEDICAL CENTER
620 East Monroe Street, Mexico MO 65265. 573/582-5000. **Fax:** 573/582-3725. **Contact:** Manager of Human Resources Department. **World Wide Web address:** http://www.audrainmedicalcenter.com. **Description:** A private, nonprofit health care center providing a nursery, as well as cancer, cardiology, emergency, and home care services. **NOTE:** Search for positions and download application online. **Positions advertised include:** Therapist; Computer Operator; Director of Medical Imaging Services; Registered Nurse; Licensed Practical Nurse. **Special programs:** Internships. **Listed on:** Privately held. **Number of employees at this location:** 830.

BARNES-JEWISH HOSPITAL NORTH
One Barnes-Jewish Hospital Plaza, St. Louis MO 63110. 314/454-7025. **Contact:** Human Resources. **World Wide Web address:** http://www.barnesjewish.org. **Description:** An 887-bed general hospital. **NOTE:** Search and apply for positions online. **Positions advertised include:** Admitting Representative; Assistant Professor; Biomedical Electronic Technician; Cardiac Sonographer; Case Coordinator; Clinical Manager; Nurse Practitioner; Doula; Nursing Practice Manager; Orderly; Pharmacist; Physical Therapist; Registered Respiratory Therapist; Resource Nurse. **Special programs:** Internships. **Parent company:** BJC Health System. **Number of employees at this location:** 9,250.

BARNES-JEWISH ST. PETERS HOSPITAL
10 Hospital Drive, St. Peters MO 63376. 314/278-5900. **Fax:** 636/916-9127. **Recorded jobline:** 636/916-9734. **Contact:** Recruiting Department. **World Wide Web address:** http://www.bjsph.org. **Description:** A 111-bed acute-care community hospital. The hospital offers general care, intensive care, obstetric, and pediatric services. **NOTE:** Search and apply for positions online. **Positions advertised include:** Medical Imaging Technologist; Nuclear Medicine Technologist; Staff Nurse; Phlebotomist; Sonographer; Speech Pathologist; Registered Polysomnographic Technician. **Corporate headquarters location:** St. Louis MO. **Parent company:** BJC Health System. **Number of employees at this location:** 700.

BARNES-JEWISH WEST COUNTY HOSPITAL
12634 Olive Boulevard, St. Louis MO 63141. 314/996-8000. **Fax:** 314/996-8436. **Contact:** Personnel. **World Wide Web address:** http://www.bjc.org/bjwch.html. **Description:** A 113-bed general hospital. The hospital specializes in cosmetic surgery, dermatology, sports medicine, and urology. **NOTE:** Search and apply for positions online. **Positions advertised include:** Medical Imaging Technologist; Charge Nurse;

Occupational Therapist; Staff RN; Patient Care Technician. **Corporate headquarters location:** This location. **Number of employees at this location:** 625.

BAUSCH & LOMB SURGICAL
3365 Tree Court Industrial Boulevard, St. Louis MO 63122. 636/225-5051. **Contact:** Employment Department. **World Wide Web address:** http://www.bausch.com. **Description:** A manufacturer and distributor of micro-surgical instruments and diagnostic medical equipment. **NOTE:** Search and apply for positions online. **Positions advertised include:** Contract Administrator; Associate Product Manager; Marketing Coordinator; Manager, Mechanical Design; Sr. Marketing Coordinator. **Special programs:** Internships. **Corporate headquarters location:** Rochester NY. **Parent company:** Bausch & Lomb, Inc.

BIG BEN WOODS
110 Highland Avenue, Valley Park MO 63088. 636/225-5144. **Fax:** 636/225-8427. **Contact:** Staff Development. **Description:** A nursing home providing rehabilitation, physical, speech, and occupational therapy services. **Operations at this facility include:** Administration. **Number of employees at this location:** 120.

CARDIOVASCULAR CONSULTANTS, PC
4330 Wornall Road, Suite 2000, Kansas City MO 64111. 816/931-1883. **Fax:** 816/931-7714. **Contact:** Human Resources. **World Wide Web address:** http://www.cc-pc.com. **Description:** A 20-physician cardiology practice providing patient care and research services in the fields of nuclear cardiology, preventive cardiology, and EP/rhythm. Offices in Missouri and Kansas. **Positions advertised include:** Clinical Technician; Administrative Assistant; Receptionist; Scheduler; Clinical Technician; Charge Entry Clerk. **Office hours:** Monday - Friday, 8:00 a.m. - 5:00 p.m. **Corporate headquarters location:** This location. **Number of employees at this location:** 125.

THE CATHOLIC HEALTH ASSOCIATION OF THE U.S.
4455 Woodson Road, St. Louis MO 63134-3797. 314/427-2500. **Fax:** 314/427-0029. **Contact:** Personnel Director. **World Wide Web address:** http://www.chausa.org. **Description:** Engaged in a wide variety of administrative services for member hospitals and organizations across the United States. **Other U.S. locations:** Washington DC.

CHATEAU GIRARDEAU
3120 Independence Street, Cape Girardeau MO 63703. 573/335-1281. **Toll-free phone:** 800/428-0069. **Contact:** Administrative Secretary. **World Wide Web address:** http://www.chateaugiradeau.com. **Description:** A retirement center for senior citizens. Chateau Girardeau offers four levels of care: a health center/nursing home providing complete health care services; an assisted living option; apartments providing an opportunity for a more independent lifestyle; and private houses.

COLUMBIA REGIONAL HOSPITAL
404 Keene Street, Columbia MO 65201. 573/875-9000. **Recorded jobline:** 573/499-6499. **Contact:** Human Resources Department. **World Wide Web address:** http://www.muhealth.org/~columbiaregional. **Description:** A 219-bed medical referral center with over 200 staff physicians representing medical specialties including orthopedics, oncology, neurology, and ophthalmology. Columbia Regional Hospital is an American Medical International affiliate. Founded in 1974. **Positions advertised include:** Benefits Specialist; Clinical Dietician; Director of Development; Managed Care Specialist; Pharmacist; Medical Technologist; Radiologic Technologist; Registered Respiratory Therapist; RN's; Clinical Coordinator.

COMPUTERIZED MEDICAL SYSTEMS, INC.
1145 Corporate Lake Drive, Suite 100, St. Louis MO 63132. 314/993-0003. **Toll-free phone:** 800/878-4267. **Fax:** 314/993-0075. **Contact:** Human Resources. **World Wide Web address:** http://www.cms-stl.com. **Description:** A developer of radiation treatment software. **NOTE:** Search and apply for positions online. **Positions advertised include:** Applications Specialist; Database Developer.

CORRECTIONAL MEDICAL SERVICES
12647 Olive Boulevard, St. Louis MO 63141. 314/919-8500. **Toll-free phone:** 800/325-3982. **Fax:** 314/919-8903. **Recorded jobline:** 314/919-9547. **Contact:** Dorothy Henricks, Personnel. **E-mail address:** dhenricks@spectrumhealth.com. **World Wide Web address:** http://www.spectrumhealth.com. **Description:** A leading clinical management company that provides outpatient services in emergency care at over 450 facilities. Spectrum offers health care and administrative management services to hospitals, physicians, clinics, managed care programs, insurers, businesses, and government entities. **NOTE:** Entry-level positions are offered. **Special programs:** Internships; Training. **Corporate headquarters location:** This location. **Other U.S. locations:** Nationwide. **Listed on:** Privately held. **Number of employees at this location:** 500.

COX HEALTH SYSTEM
3801 south National Avenue, Springfield MO 65802. 417/269-3000. **Fax:** 417/269-3548. **Recorded jobline:** 417/269-5525. **Contact:** Human Resources. **World Wide Web address:** http://www.coxhealth.com. **Description:** Operates a multi-facility hospital. **Positions advertised include:** Business Office Representative; Clinic Office Assistant; File Specialist; Information Desk Receptionist; Support Staff Assistant; Accounting Supervisor; Community Support Worker. **Corporate headquarters location:** This location. **Subsidiaries include:** Burrell; Cox Monett; Oxford Health Care. **Operations at this facility include:** Administration; Service. **Number of employees at this location:** 4,500.

ERICSON VETERINARY HOSPITAL
1000 NW South Outer Road, Blue Springs MO 64015. 816/229-8255. **Contact:** Human Resources. **E-mail address:** vetinfo@bluespringsvet.com. **World Wide Web address:** http://www.bluespringsvet.com. **Description:** Ericson Veterinary Hospital provides general medical and surgical care to animals.

FULTON STATE HOSPITAL
600 East Fifth Street, Fulton MO 65251. 573/592-4100. **Fax:** 573/592-3000. **Contact:** Lori Hollinger, Personnel. **World Wide Web address:** http://www.modmh.state.mo.us/fulton. **Description:** A maximum-security psychiatric hospital that provides long-term residential care to mentally ill patients. **Special programs:** Internships. **Office hours:** Monday - Friday, 8:00 a.m. - 4:30 p.m. **Corporate headquarters location:** Jefferson City MO. **Operations at this facility include:** Administration; Service. **CEO:** Felix Vincenz. **Number of employees at this location:** 1,400.

HANNIBAL REGIONAL HOSPITAL
Highway 36 West, Hannibal MO 63401. 573/248-1300. **Fax:** 573/248-5612. **Recorded jobline:** 573/248-5611. **Contact:** Ms. Marcia Davis, Personnel. **E-mail address:** marcia.davis@hrhonline.org. **World Wide Web address:** http://www.hrhonline.org. **Description:** A 105-bed, acute care hospital. **Positions advertised include:** Clinical Educator; Director of Hospital Operations; Monitor Technician; Occupational Therapist; Physical Therapist; Registered Nurse; Licensed Practical Nurse. **Special programs:** Internships. **Number of employees at this location:** 600.

HAWTHORN CHILDREN'S PSYCHIATRIC HOSPITAL
1901 Pennsylvania Avenue, St. Louis MO 63133. 314/512-7800. **Contact:** Department of Human Resources. **Description:** A psychiatric hospital for children ranging in ages from 6 to 17 years old.

JEWISH CENTER FOR AGED
13190 South Outer 40 Road, Chesterfield MO 63017. 314/434-3330. **Fax:** 314/434-9179. **Recorded jobline:** 314/434-8561. **Contact:** Human Resources. **Description:** A skilled nursing facility for the elderly. **NOTE:** Candidates for therapist and nursing positions must have applicable licenses, degrees, and certification. **Operations at this facility include:** Service.

JOHN KNOX VILLAGE
1001 Northwest Chipman Road, Lees Summit MO 64081. 816/251-8000. **Fax:** 816/246-4739. **Contact:** Human Resources. **E-mail address:** jobs@jkv.org. **World Wide Web address:** http://www.johnknoxvillage.org. **Description:** One of the nation's largest continuing care retirement communities that offers various living options and services including support groups, social, nursing, nutritional, rehabilitation, and ambulance services. Founded in 1970. **NOTE:** Entry-level positions and second and third shifts are offered. **Special programs:** Training. **Office hours:** Monday - Friday, 8:00 a.m.-4:30 p.m. **Corporate headquarters location:** This location. **Annual sales/revenues:** $21 - $50 million. **Number of employees at this location:** 950.

MERIDIAN MEDICAL TECHNOLOGIES
2550 Hermelin Drive, St. Louis MO 63144. 314/236-4200. **Fax:** 314/236-4201. **Contact:** Personnel. **World Wide Web address:** http://www.meridianmeds.com. **Description:** Manufactures auto-injectors that are used for injecting medication. The company also develops, manufactures, and markets cardiopulmonary medical devices including noninvasive cardiac arrhythmia management devices. **NOTE:** Search and apply for positions online. **Positions advertised include:** Export Compliance Administrator. **Corporate headquarters location:** Rockville MD. **Parent company:** King Pharmaceuticals, Inc. **Operations at this facility include:** Administration; Manufacturing; Research and Development; Service. **Number of employees at this location:** 235. **Number of employees nationwide:** 275.

MISSOURI BAPTIST MEDICAL CENTER
3015 North Ballas Road, St. Louis MO 63131. 314/996-5525. **Fax:** 314/996-6974. **Contact:** Human Resources. **World Wide Web address:** http://www.missouribaptistmedicalcenter.org. **Description:** A 400-bed, acute care hospital. **NOTE:** Search and apply for positions online. **Positions advertised include:** Pharmacist; Asst. Nurse, PRN; Biomedical Electronic Technician; Coder; Case Coordinator; Director, Oncology and Digestive Disease Service Line; Director, Facility Services; Dosimetrist; DRG Coordinator; Integrated Clinical Specialist Technician; Manager, Financial Services; Medical Technologist; Nurse; Occupational Therapist; Registered Nurse; Nuclear Medicine Technologist. **Special programs:** Internships. **Parent company:** BJC HealthCare. **Operations at this facility include:** Administration; Service. **Number of employees at this location:** 2,000.

NORTH KANSAS CITY HOSPITAL
2800 Clay Edwards Drive, North Kansas City MO 64116. 816/691-2060. **Contact:** Personnel. **E-mail address:** human.resources@nkch.org. **World Wide Web address:** http://www.nkch.org. **Description:** A 360-bed, nonprofit, acute care hospital with a medical staff of over 300 physicians representing 44 medical specialties. **Positions advertised include:** Registered Nurse; Licensed Practical Nurse; CS Technician; Teacher; Environmental Services Worker; Food Service Worker; Health Information Services Clerk; Physical Therapist; Lab Assistant; Unit Secretary; Orderly; Supervisor; Respiratory Therapist. **Number of employees at this location:** 1,400.

OZARKS MEDICAL CENTER
1100 Kentucky Avenue, P.O. Box 1100, West Plains MO 65775. 417/287-6730. **Fax:** 417/257-5804. **Contact:** Joann Blackburn, Personnel Manager. **E-mail address:** omchrdept1@townsqr.com. **World Wide Web address:** http://www.ozarksmedicalcenter.com. **Description:** A 114-bed, not-for-profit medical center. **Positions advertised include:** Cardiologist; Clinic LPN; CRNA; Emergency Dept. Physician; Family Nurse Practitioner; ICU Nurse Manager; LPN; OB/GYN Physician; Occupational Therapist; Phlebotomist; Physical Therapist; Psychiatrist; Radiation Oncologist; Radiation Technologist; RN's. **Number of employees at this location:** 1,100.

SSM CARDINAL GLENNON CHILDREN'S HOSPITAL
1465 South Grand Boulevard, St. Louis MO 63104-1003. 314/577-5600. **Fax:** 314/268-4188. **Contact:** Kathleen A. Morris, Human Resources Services Representative. **E-mail address:** kathleen_a_morris@ssmhc.com. **World Wide Web address:** http://www.cardinalglennon.com. **Description:** A pediatric hospital. **Positions advertised include:** Staff Nurses; LPN's; RN's; Administrative Director; Clinical Dietitian; Cytogenetics Technologist; Emergency Technician; Information Specialist; Medical Technologist. **Number of employees at this location:** 1,600.

SSM REHABILITATION INSTITUTE
St. Mary's Health Center, 6420 Clayton Road, St. Louis MO 63117. 314/768-5207. **Fax:** 314/768-5342. **Contact:** Human Resources. **World Wide Web address:** http://www.ssmrehab.com. **Description:** A specialty hospital providing rehabilitation for persons with head injuries, spinal cord injuries, and general rehabilitation needs. **Positions advertised include:** Occupational Therapist; Physical Therapist; Registered Nurse; Social Worker; Speech-Language Pathologist. **Special programs:** Internships. **Other area locations:** Bridgeton MO; St. Charles MO; Kirkwood MO. **Number of employees nationwide:** 450.

ST. ALEXIUS HOSPITAL, BROADWAY CAMPUS
3933 South Broadway, St. Louis MO 63118. 314/865-7910. **Fax:** 314/865-7934. **Contact:** Human Resources. **E-mail address:** jobs@st-alexius-hospital.com. **World Wide Web address:** http://www.stalexiushospital.com. **Description:** St. Alexius Hospital, Broadway Campus, formerly Alexian Brothers Hospital, is a 203-bed community hospital. Founded in 1869. **NOTE:** Search and apply for positions or submit resume online. **Positions advertised include:** Occupational Therapist; LPN's; Pharmacist; RN's; CNA; Respiratory Tech; Nuclear Med Tech. **Corporate headquarters location:** Dallas TX. **Parent company:** Tenet Healthcare Corporation. **Listed on:** New York Stock Exchange. **Stock exchange symbol:** THC.

ST. ALEXIUS HOSPITAL, JEFFERSON CAMPUS
2639 Miami Street, St. Louis MO 63118. 314/268-6000. **Fax:** 314/577-5805. **Recorded jobline:** 314/268-6262. **Contact:** Manager of Human Resources Department. **World Wide Web address:** http://www.stalexiushospital.com. **Description:** A general, 408-bed acute care medical center. **Positions advertised include:** Registered Nurse; Licensed Practical Nurse; Recreation Therapist; Security Officer; Social Worker; Pharmacist; Chart Auditor. **Corporate headquarters location:** Dallas TX. **Parent company:** Tenet Healthcare Corporation. **Listed on:** New York Stock Exchange. **Stock exchange symbol:** THC.

ST. ANTHONY'S MEDICAL CENTER
10010 Kennerly Road, St. Louis MO 63128. 314/525-1010. **Contact:** Personnel. **World Wide Web address:** http://www.stanthonysmedcenter.com. **Description:** A 292-bed health care facility consisting of St. Anthony's Hospital and St. Clare's Hospital. **NOTE:** Online applications are the preferred method of employment inquiry. **Positions advertised include:** Certified Nursing Assistant; Cardiac Ultrasonographer; Clinical Dietician; Cook; CT/MRI Technologist; Food Service Aide; Housekeeper; Imaging Clerk; Licensed Practical Nurse; Nurse Assistant; Nutrition Services Assistant;

Physical Therapist; Registered Nurse; Rehabilitation Technician; Speech Therapist; Therapy Attendant; Transport Technician; Unit Secretary.

ST. JOSEPH HOSPITAL
525 Couch Avenue, Kirkwood MO 63122. 314/966-1551. **Fax:** 314/822-6340. **Recorded jobline:** 877/916-7300. **Contact:** Human Resources. **World Wide Web address:** http://www.stjosephkirkwood.com. **Description:** An acute-care hospital. **NOTE:** Search and apply for positions online. **Positions advertised include:** Cardiovascular Coordinator; Certified Nurse Assistant; Coding Specialist; Communications Coordinator; Director, Revenue integrity; Director of Health Information Management; Echo Technician; EMS Liaison; Nursing Supervisor; Nuclear Medicine Technologist; Radiologic Technologist; RN's. **Special programs:** Internships; Training. **Corporate headquarters location:** St. Louis MO. **Parent company:** SSM Health Care.

ST. LOUIS CHILDREN'S HOSPITAL
One Children's Place, St. Louis MO 63110. 314/454-6000. **Physical address:** 4444 Forrest Park Avenue, 2nd Floor, St. Louis MO 63178. **Fax:** 314/454-4775. **Recorded jobline:** 314/863-5627. **Contact:** Human Resources Department. **World Wide Web address:** http://www.stlouischildrens.org. **Description:** A 235-bed hospital that specializes in pediatrics. **NOTE:** Only online applications are accepted. Set up profile to search for non-physician positions. **Positions advertised include:** Neonatologist; Pediatric Emergency Medicine Physician; Pediatric Pulmonologist; Pediatric Allergist; **Parent company:** BJC Health Systems. **Operations at this facility include:** Administration; Service. **Number of employees at this location:** 2,000.

ST. LOUIS REHABILITATION CENTER
5300 Arsenal Street, St. Louis MO 63139. 314/877-6500. **Fax:** 314/877-5982. **Contact:** Director of Human Resources. **E-mail address:** hrmail@dmh.mo.gov. **World Wide Web address:** http://www.dmh.missouri.gov. **Description:** A long-term, psychosocial rehabilitation hospital. The facility provides treatment and rehabilitation services to forensic patients committed to the Department of Mental Health as the result of a criminal offense and the diagnosis of a serious mental disorder. Specific rehabilitation programs are available for individuals with severe and persistent mental illnesses, individuals with personality disorders, and individuals requiring restoration of competence to stand trial. **NOTE:** View open positions for DMH facilities at: http://www.dmh.missouri.gov/offices/hr/jobs. Contact facility directly to apply. **Corporate headquarters location:** Jefferson City MO. **Parent company:** Missouri Department of Mental Health.

SAINT LOUIS UNIVERSITY HOSPITAL
3635 Vista Avenue, St. Louis MO 63110. 314/577-8000. **Contact:** Human Resources. **World Wide Web address:** http://www.sluhospital.com. **Description:** A 356-bed, teaching hospital for the Saint Louis University School of Medicine. The hospital is a certified Level I Trauma Center in both Missouri and Illinois. **NOTE:** Search and apply for positions or submit resume online. **Parent company:** Tenet HealthSystem.

SAINT LUKE'S HOSPITAL
232 South Woods Mill Road, Chesterfield MO 63017. 314/434-1500. **Recorded jobline:** 314/205-6677. **Contact:** Human Resources Department. **E-mail address:** jobs@stlukes-stl.com. **World Wide Web address:** http://www.stlukes-stl.com. **Description:** A general hospital. **NOTE:** Search and apply for positions online. **Positions advertised include:** Associate Head Nurse; Certified Nurse Assistant; Occupational Therapist; Perfusionist; Licensed Practical Nurse; Registered Nurse; Pharmacist; Physical Therapist; Speech Language Pathologist.

SHRINERS HOSPITAL FOR CHILDREN
2001 South Lindbergh Boulevard, St. Louis MO 63131. 314/432-3600. **Fax:** 314/872-7873. **Recorded jobline:** 314/872-7852. **Contact:** Jean Anton, Human Resources Manager. **E-mail address:** janton@shrinenet.org. **World Wide Web address:** http://www.shriners.com. **Description:** An 80-bed nonprofit hospital providing free care, inpatient services, and outpatient services for orthopedically handicapped children. **NOTE:** Entry-level positions, part-time jobs, and second and third shifts are offered. Search and apply for positions online. **Positions advertised include:** Nurse Practitioner; RN; Orthotics Technician; Respiratory Therapist. **Corporate headquarters location:** Tampa FL. **Listed on:** Privately held. **Number of employees at this location:** 300. **Number of employees nationwide:** 3,000.

TENET HEALTHCARE
15450 South Outer 40 Drive, Suite 120, Chesterfield MO 63017. 636/537-7950. **Contact:** Human Resources. **World Wide Web address:** http://www.tenethealth.com. **Description:** Tenet Health owns or operates 97 acute care hospitals and medical centers in 14 states. Missouri operations include DePeres Hospital, Forest Park Hospital, St. Alexius Hospital, St. Alexius Hospital Jefferson Campus, and St. Louis University Hospital. **NOTE:** Entry-level positions and second and third shifts are offered. **Positions advertised include:** Regional Director, Managed Care. **Corporate headquarters location:** Dallas TX. **Operations at this facility include:** Regional management.

TRUMAN MEDICAL CENTER HOSPITAL HILL
2301 Holmes Street, Kansas City MO 64108. 816/404-1000. **Fax:** 816/556-4124. **Contact:** Corporate Director of Personnel. **World Wide Web address:** http://www.trumed.org. **Description:** The primary teaching hospital for the University of Missouri-Kansas City School of Health Sciences. Inpatient and outpatient services include the hospital's Level I trauma center; pregnancy and childbirth services; radiology services, which include an on-site MRI and a fully-accredited mammography program; and The Eye Foundation, which provides care for the eye. Truman Medical Center West also provides complete dental care, inpatient services, a skilled nursing unit, and a wide variety of outpatient clinics. **NOTE:** Search and apply for positions online.

U.S. DEPARTMENT OF VETERANS AFFAIRS VETERANS ADMINISTRATION MEDICAL CENTER
IRM Service, 915 North Grand, St. Louis 63106. 314/652-4100. **Physical address:** One Jefferson Barracks Drive, St. Louis MO 63125. **Contact:** Human Resources. **World Wide Web address:** http://www.va.gov/stlouis. **Description:** The VA health care system includes 171 medical centers; more than 364 outpatient, community, and outreach clinics; 130 nursing home care units; and 37 domiciliary residences. VA operates at least one medical center in each of the 48 contiguous states, Puerto Rico, and the District of Columbia. With approximately 76,000 medical center beds, VA treats nearly 1 million patients in VA hospitals, 75,000 in nursing home care units, and 25,000 in domiciliary residences. **Special programs:** Internships. **Corporate headquarters location:** Washington DC. **Operations at this facility include:** This location is a tertiary care, teaching medical center. **Parent company:** U.S. Department of Veterans Affairs.

VISITING NURSE ASSOCIATION OF GREATER ST. LOUIS
9450 Manchester Road, Suite 206, St. Louis MO 63119. 314/918-7171. **Fax:** 314/918-8053. **Contact:** Human Resources Department. **World Wide Web address:** http://www.vnastl.com. **Description:** Provides in-home health services and support to terminally-ill patients and their family. Services include nursing, physical therapy, occupational therapy, speech pathology, nutritional therapy, mental health and

enterostomal therapy, medical social services, and hospice care. **Office hours:** Monday - Friday, 8:00 a.m. - 4:15 p.m. **Operations at this facility include:** Service. **Number of employees at this location:** 45.

WESTERN MISSOURI MEDICAL CENTER
403 Burkarth Road, Warrensburg MO 64093-3101. 660/747-2500. **Fax:** 660/747-8455. **Contact:** Human Resources. **E-mail address:** aowens@wmmconline.org. **World Wide Web address:** http://www.wmmconline.org. **Description:** A 104-bed acute care hospital with a 14-bed skilled nursing facility. **Positions advertised include:** RN's; LPN's; CNA's; Director of Quality/Risk; Compliance Coordinator; Physical Therapist. **Operations at this facility include:** Administration; Service. **Number of employees at this location:** 315.

Montana

BIG HORN COUNTY MEMORIAL HOSPITAL
17 North Miles Avenue, Hardin MT 59034. 406/665-2802. **Fax:** 406/665-9238. **Contact:** Paula Small, Human Resources. **E-mail address:** psmall@bhwi.net. **World Wide Web address:** http://www.bighornhospital.org. **Description:** A not-for-profit general medical and surgical hospital with 16 beds. Big Horn County Memorial Hospital also operates a nursing home with 37 beds. **Annual sales/revenues:** $5 - $10 million. **NOTE:** Openings advertised locally. **Number of employees at this location:** 59

BILLINGS CLINIC HOSPITAL
P.O. Box 37000, Billings MT 59107. 406/238-2595. **Physical address:** 2825 8th Avenue North, Billings MT 59101. **Fax:** 406/238-2355. **Recorded jobline:** 800/332-7156 x4600. **Contact:** Human Resources. **E-mail address:** careers@billingsclinic.org. **World Wide Web address:** http://www.billingsclinic.com. **Description:** A full-service, nonprofit, 272-bed regional medical center. Affiliates include Billings Clinic, a 140-physician multi-specialty medical clinic with six locations; Deaconess Research Institute; Deaconess Foundation; and Deaconess Psychiatric Billings Clinic Services, which includes the Psychiatric Center and Behavioral Health Clinic, providing adults and youth with a continuum of comprehensive mental health care. Long-term care is provided through Aspen Meadows, a skilled nursing facility, and Deaconess Hospital's Transitional Care Unit. Cardiology services are provided at the Deaconess Medical Center and the Billings Clinic. Deaconess also provides a series of educational programs and a women's resource center. Three hundred physicians have hospital privileges. **NOTE:** May search openings online and download application but must mail or fax the completed application to facility. Largest employer in Billings.

FALLON MEDICAL COMPLEX
P.O. Box 820, Baker MT 59313-0820. 406/778-3331. **Toll-free phone:** 800/676-7161. **Fax:** 406/778-2488. **Physical address:** 202 South Fourth Street West, Baker MT 59313. **Contact:** Kathleen Lehti, Human Resources for nursing. **E-mail address:** llmeredi@fallonmedical.org. **Description:** Fallon Medical Complex consists of three main divisions: a 40-bed nursing home; a 12-bed, acute care hospital providing general medical services, cardiac rehabilitation, chemotherapy, and outpatient surgery; and a clinic with two general practitioners and one physician's assistant. **NOTE:** No web site but may apply in person locally.

HOLY ROSARY HEALTH CENTER
2600 Wilson Street, Miles City MT 59301-5094. 406/233-2600. **Fax:** 406/233-2617. **Contact:** Human Resources. **E-mail address:** sheryl.kron@hrh-mt.org. **World Wide Web address:** http://www.hrh-mt.org. **Description:** Holy Rosary Health Center consists of an acute care hospital with 44 beds, offering general medical and surgical services, chemotherapy treatments, and a 5-bed intensive care unit. The health center also operates a nursing home with 120 beds, 18 of which are in the skilled care unit and are devoted to physical rehabilitation. Opened in 1910. **NOTE:** Search openings online and print and complete application to mail or fax with resume to HR office. **Positions advertised include:** Director of Human Resources; Physician (various specialties); Registered Nurse; Surgical Services Nurse Manager. **Number of employees at this location:** 375

KALISPELL REGIONAL MEDICAL CENTER
310 Sunnyview Lane, Kalispell MT 59901. 406/752-1760. **Fax:** 406/257-5430. **Recorded jobline:** 406/756-4405. **Contact:** Human Resources Recruiter. **E-mail address:** human_resources@krmc.org. **World Wide Web address:** http://www.krmc.org. **Description:** A medical center that is also the primary referral center for northwest Montana. Facilities include a 100-bed hospital, a long-term care facility, a cancer center, a medical library, a birthing center, a chemical treatment center, the Brenden House, a nursing and rehabilitation facility, and Pathways Treatment Center, which offers behavioral health, psychiatric, and substance abuse treatment. The Center also offers emergency, home health, diabetes, diagnostic imaging, hospice, private care, nutritional, and helicopter rescue services. **Positions advertised include:** Licensed Practical Nurse; Certified Nurses Aide; Restorative Aide; Operating Room Technician; Home Health Aide; Respiratory Therapist; Registered Nurse; Infection Control; Patient Coordinator; Dietary Aide. **Number of employees at this location:** 1,300.

KIDS BEHAVIORAL HEALTH OF MONTANA, INC.
55 Basin Creek Road, Butte MT 59701-9704. 406/494-4183. **Fax:** 406/494-5889. **Toll-free phone:** 800/447-1067. **Contact:** Kristine Carpenter, Human Resources. **E-mail address:** kcarpenter@kidsbh.com. **World Wide Web address:** http://www.kidsofmontana.com. **Description:** An 85-bed child and adolescent psychiatric hospital that provides services on inpatient, outpatient, and day program bases. **Positions advertised include:** Mental Health Associate. **Number of employees at this location:** 200.

MISSOURI RIVER MANOR
1130 17th Avenue, South Great Falls MT 59405. 406/771-4507. **Fax:** 406/761-6020. **Contact:** Peak Medical Corporation Human Resources, P.O. Box 94060, Albuquerque NM 87199. **World Wide Web address:** http://www.sunh.com. **Description:** A nursing home with 278 beds offering nursing care, restorative programs, and physical rehabilitation. **Positions advertised include:** Facility Administrator; Director of Nursing. **Parent company:** Sun Health Corporation.

MONTANA STATE HOSPITAL
300 Garnet Way, Warm Springs MT 59756. 406/693-7000. **Fax**: 406/693-7069. **E-mail address**: eamberg@mt.gov. **Contact:** Human Resources at http://mt.gov/jobs/. **World Wide Web address:** http://www.msh.mt.gov. **Description:** A state psychiatric hospital with 200 beds that provides inpatient care for adults. **Positions advertised include:** Director of Human Resources; Physician Assistant; Psychiatric Nurse; Licensed Practical Nurse; Recreation Therapist.

ST. PATRICK HOSPITAL & HEALTH SCIENCES CENTER
P.O. Box 4567, Missoula MT 59806. 406/329-5625. **Physical address:** 500 West Broadway, Missoula MT 59802. **Fax:** 406/329-5856. **Recorded jobline:** 406/329-5885. **Contact:** Human Resources. E-mail address: info@saintpatrick.org. **World Wide Web address:** http://www.saintpatrick.org. **Description:** A nonprofit, 213-bed, acute care hospital. Founded in 1873. **NOTE:** Entry-level positions and second and third shifts are offered. Search posted openings and apply online. **Positions advertised include:** Registered Nurse; Radiation Therapist; File Room Tech; Pharmacy Tech. **Special programs:** Internships. **Internship information:** Internships are unpaid. **Corporate headquarters location:** Spokane WA. **Parent**

company: Sisters of Providence. **Operations at this facility include:** Administration; Research and Development. **Number of employees at this location:** 1,400.

ST. PETER'S COMMUNITY HOSPITAL
2475 East Broadway, Helena MT 59601. 406/442-2277. **Fax:** 406/447-2609. **Contact:** Carla Sisk, Human Resources. **E-mail address:** csisk@stpetes.org. **World Wide Web address:** http://www.stpetes.org. **Description:** St. Peter's Community Hospital is a 99-bed, acute-care facility. St. Peter's Community Hospital services include general medical and surgical services, pediatrics, a psychiatric unit, intensive/cardiac care, emergency services, OB/nursery, same-day surgery, a regional dialysis unit, a pharmacy, oncology, respiratory therapy, cardiac catheterization, and neuroscience and physician medicine. **NOTE**: Search posted openings and apply online. Faxed resumes are accepted. **Positions advertised include:** Registered Nurse; Licensed Practical Nurse; MRI Technician; Radiological Technologist; Transcriptionist; Physical Therapist; Accountant; Aide.

Nebraska
BECTON DICKINSON
1329 West Highway 6, P.O. Box 860, Holdrege NE 68949-0860. 308/995-6501. **Recorded jobline:** 800/349-4726. **Contact:** Human Resources. **World Wide Web address:** http://www.bd.com. **Description:** Becton Dickinson is a medical and pharmaceutical company engaged in the manufacture of health care products, medical instrumentation, diagnostic products, and industrial safety equipment. Major medical equipment product lines include hypodermics, intravenous equipment, operating room products, thermometers, gloves, and specialty needles. The company also offers contract packaging services. Founded in 1896. **NOTE:** Entry-level positions and second and third shifts are offered. **Positions advertised include:** Sr. Quality Engineer; Finance Team Leader; Manufacturing Quality Engineer; Engineering Coordinator; Quality Engineer. **Special programs:** Internships; Apprenticeships. **Office hours:** Monday - Friday, 7:30 a.m. - 4:30 p.m. **Corporate headquarters location:** Franklin Lakes NJ. **Other U.S. locations:** Nationwide. **International locations:** Worldwide. **Operations at this facility include:** This location manufactures disposable medical devices such as syringes, pens, lancets, and pen needles for the treatment of diabetes. **Listed on:** New York Stock Exchange. **Stock exchange symbol:** BDX. **Annual sales/revenues:** More than $100 million. **Number of employees at this location:** 750. **Number of employees worldwide:** 25,000.

COMMUNITY HOSPITAL
P.O. Box 1328, McCook NE 69001. 308/345-2650. **Physical address:** 1301 East H Street, McCook NE 69001. **Fax:** 308/345-8358. **Contact:** Human Resources Coordinator. **E-mail address:** sbeiber@chmccook.org. **World Wide Web address:** http://www.chmccook.org. **Description:** An acute care hospital. **NOTE:** Human Resources phone is 308/345-8307. Please visit website for online employment application. **Company slogan:** Better care for the good life. **Positions advertised include:** Home Health Director; Surgery RN and Surgery Tech; Home Health RN/LPN; Licensed Practical Nurse; Registered Nurse. **Annual sales/revenues:** $5 - $10 million.

CREIGHTON UNIVERSITY MEDICAL CENTER
601 North 30th Street, Omaha NE 68131. 402/449-4000. **Recorded jobline:** 402/449-4451. **Contact:** Human Resources Manager. **World Wide Web address:** http:// www.creightonhospital.com. **NOTE:** Please see website for online application form and to search for jobs. **Description:** A hospital. **Parent company:** Tenet HealthSystem.

GREAT PLAINS REGIONAL MEDICAL CENTER
P.O. Box 1167, North Platte NE 69103. 308/696-8000. **Physical address:** 601 West Leota, North Platte NE 69101. **Toll-free phone:** 800/662-0011. **Contact:** Human Resources. **E-mail address:** recruiter@mail.gprmc.com. **World Wide Web address:** http://www.gprmc.com. **Description:** A medical center. **NOTE:** Human Resources phone is 308/535-7437. **Positions advertised include:** Blood Bank Supervisor; Director – Surgery; Histology technician; Licensed Practical Nurse; Occupational Therapist; Physical Therapist; Practitioner; Registered Nurse; Tech Assistant. **Special programs:** Internships. **Listed on:** Privately held. **Number of employees at this location:** 720.

MARY LANNING MEMORIAL HOSPITAL
715 North St. Joseph Avenue, Hastings NE 68901. 402/463-4521. **Contact:** Human Resources. **E-mail address:** lflorian@mlmh.org. **World Wide Web address:** http://www.mlmh.org. **Description:** A general, acute care hospital. **Positions advertised include:** Controller; Director – Patient Accounts; Registered Nurse; Respiratory Therapist; Physical Therapist; Occupational Therapist; Speech Pathologist. **Number of employees at this location:** 770.

MEMORIAL HEALTH CENTER
645 Osage Street, Sidney NE 69162. 308/254-5825. **Fax:** 308/254-2300. **Contact:** Carrie Trost, Director of Human Resources. **E-mail address:** mhchr@hamilton.net. **World Wide Web address:** http://www.memorialhealthcenter.org. **Description:** A nonprofit home health counseling and medical center with a 30-bed acute care unit and a 70-bed extended care unit, as well as physical therapy and surgery departments. **NOTE:** Entry-level positions and second and third shifts are offered. Please see website for downloadable job application. Director of Human Resources phone is 877/642-8326. **Special programs:** Internships; Training; Summer Jobs. **Office Hours:** Monday – Friday 8:00 am – 5:00 pm. **CEO:** Rex Walk. **Annual sales/revenues:** Less than $5 million. **Number of employees at this location:** 240.

U.S. DEPARTMENT OF VETERANS AFFAIRS VA NEBRASKA WESTERN IOWA HEALTH CARE SYSTEM
2201 North Broadwell Avenue, Grand Island NE 68803-2196. 308/382-3660. **Contact:** Human Resources. **World Wide Web address:** http://www.va.gov/index.htm. **Description:** A medical center. From 54 hospitals in 1930, the VA health care system has grown to include 171 medical centers; more than 364 outpatient, community, and outreach clinics; 130 nursing home care units; and 37 domiciliary residences. VA operates at least one medical center in each of the 48 contiguous states, Puerto Rico, and Washington DC. With approximately 76,000 medical center beds, VA treats nearly 1 million patients in VA hospitals; 75,000 in nursing home care units; and 25,000 in domiciliary residences. VA's outpatient clinics register approximately 24 million visits per year. **Positions advertised include:** Dentist; Nurse; Occupational Therapist; Optometrist; Pharmacist; Physical Therapist; Physician; Podiatrist; Registered Therapy Technician. **Other area locations:** Lincoln NE; Omaha NE.

Nevada
NATHAN ADELSON HOSPICE
4141 Swenson Street, Las Vegas NV 89119-6718. 702/796-3131. **Fax**: 702/796-3163. **Contact:** Karen Carnevale, Human Resources. **E-mail address:** kcarnavale@nah.org. **World Wide Web address:** http://www.nah.org. **Description:** A non-profit program that provides care and support for patients who have been diagnosed with a terminal illness and a life expectancy that can be measured in weeks or months. Founded in 1978. **Positions advertised include:** Registered Nurse; Certified Nursing Assistant; Social Worker; Spiritual Care Counselor; Receptionist.

ALERE MEDICAL INC.
595 Double Eagle Court, Suite 1000, Reno NV 89521. 775/829-8885. **Fax:** 775/829-8637. **Contact:** Human Resources. **E-mail address:** jobs@alere.com. **World**

Wide Web address: http://www.alere.com. **Description:** Works to improve home health care of individuals with heart failure through technology and education. **Positions advertised include:** RN; Call Center Director; Software Engineer/Developer. **Corporate headquarters location:** This location.

AMERICAN MEDICAL RESPONSE
1200 South Martin Luther King Boulevard, Las Vegas NV 89102-2303. 702/671-6975. **Contact:** Human Resources. **E-mail address:** westresumes2@amr-ems.com. **World Wide Web address:** http://www.amr.net. **Description:** The nation's leading private medical transportation company. **Positions advertised include:** Paramedic. **Corporate headquarters location:** Aurora CO. **Number of employees nationwide:** 18,000.

CARSON-TAHOE HOSPITAL
P.O. Box 2168, Carson City NV 89702-2168. 775/882-1361. **Physical address:** 775 Fleischmann Way, Carson City NV 89703. **Fax:** 775/885-4500. **Contact:** Human Resources. **World Wide Web address:** http://www.carsontahoe.com. **Description:** A fully-accredited, nonprofit county hospital. Carson-Tahoe maintains a 128-bed, acute care facility, and provides medical, surgical, obstetrical, neonatal, nursery, pediatric, psychiatric, intensive, cardiac, and emergency care services. Founded in 1949. **Positions advertised include:** Certified Nurse Assistant; Cook; Dietitian; Lab Assistant; LPN; RN; Ultrasound Technician. **Number of employees at this location:** 900.

DESERT RADIOLOGISTS
2020 Palomino Lane, Suite 100, Las Vegas NV 89106. 702/384-5210. **Recorded jobline:** 702/759-8792. **Contact:** Human Resources. **E-mail address:** careers@desertrad.com. **World Wide Web address:** http://www.desertrad.com. **Description:** An outpatient group that performs radiology, radiation therapy, and angiography. **NOTE:** Apply in person at 612 South Tonopah, Las Vegas NV 89106. **Positions advertised include:** Billing Representative; Payroll Administrator. **Annual sales/revenues:** $21 - $50 million. **Number of employees at this location:** 180.

HEART INSTITUTE OF NEVADA
653 North Town Center Drive, Suite 400, Las Vegas NV 89144. 702/765-5793. **Fax:** 702/765-5826. **Contact:** Diane Love, Human Resources. **Description:** A medical practice specializing in cardiology. Founded in 1975. **NOTE:** Entry-level positions are offered. **Special programs:** Internships. **Parent company:** Cardiology Associates of Nevada. **Number of employees at this location:** 65.

KINDRED HEALTHCARE
5110 West Sahara Avenue, Las Vegas NV 89146. 702/871-1418. **Contact:** Human Resources Manager. **World Wide Web address:** http://www.kindredhealthcare.com. **Description:** A full-service health care center that specializes in providing long-term, acute care. **Corporate headquarters location:** Louisville KY. **Other U.S. locations:** Nationwide. **Listed on:** NASDAQ. **Stock exchange symbol:** KIND.

NORTHERN NEVADA MEDICAL CENTER
2375 East Prater Way, Sparks NV 89434. 775/356-4085. **Fax:** 775/356-4901. **Contact:** Patricia Downs, Human Resources. **E-mail address:** patricia.downs@uhsinc.com. **World Wide Web address:** http://www.northernnvmed.com. **Description:** A full-service medical center. **Positions advertised include:** Chief Nurse Executive; Critical Care Unit Manager; Registered Nurse; Certified Nursing Assistant; Physical Therapist; Occupational Therapist.

ST. MARY'S REGIONAL MEDICAL CENTER
235 West Sixth Street, Reno NV 89503. 775/770-6318. **Fax:** 775/770-3260. **Contact:** Suellen Bacigalupi, Human Resources. **E-mail address:** suellen.bacigalupi@saintmarysreno.com. **World Wide Web address:** http://www.saintmarysreno.com. **Description:** A private, nonprofit hospital that is a complete medical and surgical facility with 367 beds. **Positions advertised include:** Billing Representative; Administrative Assistant; CT Technologist; Certified Nursing Assistant; Clinical Nurse Specialist; Collector; Health Management Specialist; EMT; Food Service Worker; Intake Representative; LPN; Laboratory Assistant; Manager Cardiac Services; Medical Technologist; New Graduate Nurse; Nurse Practitioner; OB Tech; Occupational Therapist; RN. **Employees at this location:** 2,500.

ST. ROSE DOMINICAN HOSPITALS
3001 St. Rose Parkway, Henderson NV 89052. 702/616-5000. **Recorded jobline:** 702/616-6100. **Contact:** Human Resources Representative. **E-mail address:** srdhnursingcareers@chw.edu (for nursing opportunities); srdhclinicalcareers@chw.edu (for ancillary clinical opportunities); srdhnonclinicalcareers@chw.edu (for ancillary nonclinical opportunities). **World Wide Web address:** http://www.strosehospitals.org. **Description:** A 214-bed hospital affiliated with the 138-bed Rose de Lima hospital. **Positions advertised include:** Assistant Nurse Manager; Case Manager; Certified Nursing Assistant; Charge Registered Nurse; Coder; Customer Service Rep; Echocardiographer; GI Lab Technician; Imaging Technologist; Medical Technologist; Occupational Therapist; RN. **Parent company:** Catholic HealthcareWest.

SUNRISE HOSPITAL & MEDICAL CENTER
SUNRISE CHILDREN'S HOSPITAL
3186 South Maryland Parkway, Las Vegas NV 89109. 702/731-8898. **Toll-free phone:** 800/634-6864. **Fax:** 702/836-3813. **Recorded jobline:** 702/731-8350. **Contact:** Human Resources. **E-mail address:** sunrise.humanresources@hcahealthcare.com. **World Wide Web address:** http://www.sunrisehospital.com. **Description:** An acute care hospital and a children's hospital with over 730 beds. **NOTE:** Entry-level positions and second and third shifts are offered. **Positions advertised include:** Director, Cardiovascular Services; Accessioning Clerk; Medical Lab Tech; Charge Nurse; Clinical Nurse Specialist; Director, Maternal Services; LPN; RN; Director, Critical Care Services; Nurse Manager; Pharmacist; Occupational Therapist; Physical Therapist Assistant; Social Worker. **Corporate headquarters location:** Nashville TN. **Parent company:** HCA Healthcare Corporation. **Listed on:** New York Stock Exchange. **Stock exchange symbol:** HCA. **Number of employees at this location:** 2,500.

U.S. DEPARTMENT OF VETERANS AFFAIRS
VA SOUTHERN NEVADA HEALTHCARE SYSTEM (VASNHS)
P.O. Box 360001, North Las Vegas NV 89036. 702/636-3033. **Fax:** 702/636-4000. **Contact:** Human Resources. **E-mail address:** vhaplacementservice@hq.med.va.gov. **World Wide Web address:** http://www.las-vegas.med.va.gov. **Description:** The Department of Veterans Affairs was established in 1989 to provide federal benefits to veterans and their dependents. The department operates nationwide programs of health care, assistance services, and national cemeteries. The VA's health care system is the largest in the nation. From 54 hospitals in 1930, the system has grown to include 171 medical centers; more than 364 outpatient, community and outreach clinics; 130 nursing home care units; and 37 domiciliary residences. The VA operates at least one medical center in each of the 48 contiguous states, Puerto Rico, and the District of Columbia. With approximately 76,000 medical center beds, the VA treats nearly 1 million patients in VA hospitals, 75,000 in nursing home care units, and 25,000 in domiciliary residences. The VA's outpatient clinics register approximately 24 million visits a year. The VA is affiliated with 104 medical schools, 48 dental schools, and more than 850 other schools across the country. **NOTE:** Search and apply for positions online at http://www.vacareers.com. **Corporate headquarters location:** Washington DC.

U.S. DEPARTMENT OF VETERANS AFFAIRS SIERRA NEVADA HEALTH CARE CENTER
1000 Locust Street, Reno NV 89502. 775/786-7200. **Fax:** 775/328-1464. **Contact:** Human Resources. **E-mail address:** vhaplacementservice@hq.med.va.gov. **Description:** The Reno Veterans Administration Medical Center consists of a fully-accredited, 168-bed, general medical and surgical hospital and a 60-bed nursing home care unit. The medical center has an active affiliation with the University of Nevada School of Medicine and the Orvis School of Nursing, University of Nevada-Reno. **NOTE:** Search and apply for positions online at http://www.vacareers.com. **Special programs:** Internships. **Corporate headquarters location:** Washington DC.

UNIVERSITY MEDICAL CENTER
1815 West Charleston Boulevard, Suite 3, Las Vegas NV 89102-2386. 702/383-2230. **Toll-free phone:** 800/228-2354. **Recorded jobline:** 702/383-2490. **Contact:** Human Resources. **World Wide Web address:** http://www.umc-cares.org. **Description:** A hospital that offers comprehensive health care services and is designated a Level One Trauma Center for southern Nevada. **Positions advertised include:** Applications Programmer; Clinical Laboratory Technologist; Clinical Manager; Data Specialist; MRI Technologist; Pharmacist; Registered Nurse; Staff Physician; Systems Programmer; Ultrasound Technologist. **Number of employees at this location:** Over 3,500.

WEST HILLS HOSPITAL
P.O. Box 30012, Reno NV 89520-0012. 775/323-0478. **Physical address:** 1240 East 9th Street, Reno NV 89512. **Toll-free phone:** 800/242-0478. **Fax:** 775/789-4203. **Recorded jobline:** 775/789-4286. **Contact:** Janet White, Human Resources. **E-mail address:** janetwhite@ardenthealth.com. **World Wide Web address:** http://www.psysolutions.com. **Description:** A medical facility that specializes in the treatment of alcohol and chemical dependency. The hospital also offers psychiatric and mental health services. **NOTE:** Entry-level positions, part-time jobs, and second and third shifts are offered. **Positions advertised include:** Human Resources Director. **Special programs:** Internships; Apprenticeships. **Parent company:** Psychiatric Solutions Inc. **Operations at this facility include:** Administration. **Number of employees at this location:** 300.

New Hampshire

ANDROSCOGGIN VALLEY HOSPITAL
59 Page Hill Road, Berlin NH 03570-3542. 603/752-2200. **Fax:** 603/752-3727. **Contact:** Human Resources Director. **E-mail address:** employment@avhosp.org. **World Wide Web address:** http://www.avhnh.com. **Description:** Androscoggin Valley Hospital provides various medical services including inpatient and outpatient services, clinics, community programs, and emergency services. **NOTE**: Search posted openings on-line. **Positions advertised include:** CT/Radiologist Technologist; Medical Technologist; Ultrasound Technician. **Parent company:** NorthCare (also at this location) is a nonprofit health care corporation.

BEL-AIR NURSING HOME
29 Center Street, Goffstown NH 03045-2936. 603/497-4871. **Contact:** Robert Lenox, Human Resources. **Description:** An intermediate care nursing home. Founded in 1970. **NOTE:** Part-time jobs and second and third shifts are offered. **Special programs:** Internships. **Office hours:** Monday - Friday, 9:00 a.m. - 5:00 p.m. **Facilities Manager:** William Goldthwaite. **Purchasing Manager:** Robert W. Lenox. **Annual sales/revenues:** Less than $5 million. **Number of employees at this location:** 60.

CHESHIRE MEDICAL CENTER
580 Court Street, Keene NH 03431. 603/354-5454 Ext. 3520. **Fax:** 603/354-6519. **Contact:** Maryanne Flemming, Human Resources. **E-mail address:** lsandstrum@Cheshire-Med.com; cstalker@cheshire-med.com. **World Wide Web address:** http://www.cheshire-med.com. **Description:** A nonprofit, 177-bed, regional medical center with medical/surgical, emergency care, women's and children's, rehabilitation, oncology, and mental health services. **NOTE:** Search posted openings and apply on-line. Entry-level positions and second and third shifts are offered. **Positions advertised include:** Housekeeper; RN – Various Departments; Physical Therapist; LPN; Medical Technologist; Laundry Tech; Psychiatric Technician; Cafeteria Representative; Hostess; Vascular Technologist; Optician; Ultrasound Tech. **President/CEO:** Robert Langlais. **Facilities Manager:** Frank Werbinski. **Annual sales/revenues:** $21 - $50 million. **Number of employees at this location:** 800.

CONCORD HOSPITAL
250 Pleasant Street, Concord NH 03301. 603/225-2711. **Fax:** 603/228-7346. **Recorded jobline:** 877/777-8444. **Contact:** Human Resources. **World Wide Web address:** http://www.concordhospital.org. **Description:** A full-service, nonprofit hospital offering both inpatient and outpatient services. **NOTE:** Search posted openings and apply on-line only. **Positions advertised include:** Cafeteria Aide; Call Center Associate; Care Partner; Cashier; Central Sterile Supply Tech; Clerical Partner; Clinical Lab Assistant; Clinical Nurse Specialist; Commercial Claim Representative; Cytotechnologist; Dental Assistant; ED Technician; Exercise Instructor; Food Service Assistant; Heart Gifts Boutique Assistant Manager; Insurance Authorization Assistant; Lead Mammographer; Medical Assistant – Internal Medicine; MT/MLT; Multi-Tech Outpatient; Nurse Practitioner; Pathology Lab Assistant; Phlebotomist; Physical Therapist – Various Departments; Porter Dishwasher; Rehab Secretary; RN – Various Departments; Security Officer; Spiritual Care Counselor; Transporter. **Special programs:** Internships. **Number of employees at this location:** 1,800.

ALICE PECK DAY MEMORIAL HOSPITAL
125 Mascoma Street, Lebanon NH 03766-3205. 603/448-7484. **Fax:** 603/443-9501. **Contact:** Human Resources. **E-mail address:** jobs@alicepeckday.org. **World Wide Web address:** http://www.alicepeckday.org. **Description:** A hospital. **Positions advertised include:** Mammography Technologist; Radiologic Technologist; Manager, Rehab Services; Social Worker; RN – Various Departments; Patient Care Tech; Occupational Therapist; Clinic Coordinator; Housekeeper; Custodian; Public Affairs and Marketing Coordinator; Catering Cook; Wait Staff.

DOVER VETERINARY HOSPITAL
96 Durham Road, Dover NH 03820-4278. 603/742-6438. **Fax:** 603/742-4037. **Contact:** Human Resources. **E-mail address:** resume@dovervet.com. **World Wide Web address:** http://www.dovervet.com. **Description:** Dover Veterinary Hospital offers general medical, surgical, and diagnostic services for dogs and cats. The hospital specializes in orthopedic surgery. **NOTE:** Please visit website to access application form. You may apply online, or print and fax or mail the application. **Positions advertised include:** Small Animal Surgeon; Internist; Part Time Veterinarian; Veterinary Nurse; Animal Care Specialist; Client Care Coordinator. **Office hours:** Monday – Friday, 8:00 a.m. – 6:00 p.m.

ELLIOT HOSPITAL
One Elliot Way, Manchester NH 03103. 603/663-2628. **Contact:** Personnel. **World Wide Web address:** http://www.elliothospital.com. **Description:** A 296-bed acute care hospital serving southern New Hampshire. Established in 1890, Elliot Hospital serves as the trauma center for the Manchester metropolitan area. Facilities include the Max K. Wilscher Urology Center, the Elliot Regional Cancer Center, and a level-three neonatal intensive care unit (NICU). **NOTE:** Search posted openings and apply on-line only. Resumes are forwarded to departments throughout hospital electronic mail system. No paper resumes are accepted.

Positions advertised include: Accounting Clerk; Associate Teacher; Breast Sonographer; CT Technologist; Cardiac Ultrasonographer; Clinical Leader; Clinical Nurse; Clinical Nursing Supervisor; Cytotechnologist; Diet Aide; Director of Pharmacy Services; Environmental Services Technician; LNA – Various Departments; Mailroom Clerk; Non-Invasive Cardiac Tech; Nurse Practitioner; Occupational Therapist; Pharmacy Technician; Physical Therapist; Physician Recruiter; Project Manager; RN – Various Departments; Radiology Technologist; Respiratory Care Practitioner.

EXETER HOSPITAL
5 Alumni Drive, Exeter NH 03833. 603/778-6660. **Toll-free phone:** 800/439-3837. **Fax:** 603/580-6905.. **Contact:** Danielle Hughes, Human Resources Department. **World Wide Web address:** http://www.foreveryday.com/careers. **Description:** An acute care, 100-bed hospital. Founded in 1892. **NOTE:** Search posted listings and apply on-line only. Resumes are forwarded to departments throughout hospital electronic mail system. No paper resumes are accepted. Entry-level positions and second and third shifts are offered. **Positions advertised include:** Yoga Instructor; Vice President; Vascular Technologist; Unit Educator; Social Worker; Respiratory Therapist; Research Coordinator; Radiologic Technologist; Physical Therapist; Pharmacist; Paramedic; Pediatric Dental Receptionist; Occupational Therapist; RN – Various Departments; Medical Lab Technician; LNA – Various Departments; Dietitian; Cook; Biller. **Special programs:** Internships; Summer Jobs. **Corporate headquarters location:** This location. **Parent company:** Exeter Health Resources. **President/CEO:** Kevin Callahan. **Number of employees at this location:** 1,200.

FRANKLIN REGIONAL HOSPITAL
15 Aiken Avenue, Franklin NH 03235. 603/934-2060, ext.: 249. **Fax:** 603/934-4616. **Contact:** Human Resources. **World Wide Web address:** http://www.frh.org. **Description:** A hospital. Established in 1910, Franklin Regional Hospital now employs over 300 employees. **Positions advertised include:** Environmental Services Aide; Clinical Nurse; Medical Transcriptionist; Health Unit Coordinator; Radiologic Technologist; Respiratory Therapist; Speech Language Pathologist. **NOTE:** Search posted openings and apply on-line via multi-facility site. For questions call 603/527-2872, or 603/524-3211 Ext. 3124.

FRISBIE MEMORIAL HOSPITAL
11 Whitehall Road, Rochester NH 03867-3439. 603/335-8191. **Fax:** 603/335-8975. **Contact:** Human Resources Department. **E-mail address:** fmh.resumes@fmhospital.com. **World Wide Web address:** http://www.frisbiehospital.com. **Description:** A 101-bed, acute care hospital. Frisbie is a nonprofit, community hospital that offers a broad range of services. The medical staff includes more than 140 physicians representing 28 specialties in addition to general practice. Founded in 1919. **NOTE:** Search posted openings and apply online via website. **Positions advertised include:** Care Manager; Clinical Coordinator; Director of Radiology; Geriatric Psychiatrist; Medical Assistant; Nursing Care Technician; Office Nurse; Patient Account Clerk; Pharmacist; Phlebotomist; Respiratory Therapist; RN – Various Departments.

GENESIS HEALTHCARE CORPORATION
P.O. Box 441, Lancaster NH 03584. 603/788-4935. **Physical address:** 91 Country Village Road, Lancaster NH 03584. **Contact:** Corporate office human resources at 877/403-JOBS for nursing careers and 800/444-6306 for rehabilitation therapy careers. **World Wide Web address:** http://www.genesishcc.com. **Description:** A nursing home that offers intermediate care and has an assisted-living residential facility. **NOTE:** Search posted openings nationwide via corporate website and apply on-line. **Positions advertised include:** Registered Nurse; Occupational Therapist; Physical Therapist; Speech/Language Pathologist; Rehab Program Manager; Staff Developmental Coordinator. **Corporate Headquarters location**: Kennett Square, PA.

HACKETT HILL HEALTHCARE CENTER
191 Hackett Hill Road, Manchester NH 03102. 603/668-8161. **Fax:** 603/622-2584. **Contact:** Tina Brown, Human Resources. **Description:** The Hackett Hill Healthcare Center is a housing facility for the care of elderly patients that is concerned with providing communities with quality services in the medical and healthcare industries.

HEALTHSOUTH
254 Pleasant Street, Concord NH 03301-2551. 603/226-9800. **Fax:** 603/226-9808. **Contact:** Erika Pouliot, Human Resources. **E-mail address:** Erika.pouliot@healthsouth.com. **World Wide Web address:** http://www.healthsouth.com. **NOTE:** Please visit website for online application form. **Description:** An acute care rehabilitation center offering physical and occupational therapy services. HealthSouth also offers inpatient services. **NOTE:** Search posted openings nationwide and apply online. **Positions advertised include:** Physical Therapist. **Corporate headquarters location:** Birmingham AL. **Other U.S. locations:** Nationwide. **International locations:** Australia; Puerto Rico; United Kingdom. **Listed on:** OTC Pink Sheets. **Stock exchange symbol:** HLSH. **Number of employees at this location:** 200.

INTERIM HEALTHCARE
PO Box 1780, 608 Chestnut Street, Manchester NH 03105. 603/668-6956. **Toll-free phone**: 800/486-3746. **Fax:** 603/668-6959. **Contact:** Human Resources. **World Wide Web address:** http://www.interimhealthcare.com/newhampshire. **Description:** Provider of in-home health care. **NOTE**: Search posted openings online. **Positions advertised include:** RN; LPN/LVN; Certified Nursing Assistants; Home Health Aides; Allied Health Professionals.

NEW LONDON HOSPITAL
273 County Road, New London NH 03257. 603/526-5307. **Fax:** 603/526-5150. **Contact:** Shari Phetteplace, Human Resources Assistant. **E-mail address:** shari.phetteplace@nlh.crhm.org. **World Wide Web address:** http:// newlondonhospital.org. **Description:** A community based, full service hospital. Founded in 1918. **NOTE:** Search posted openings and apply online through website. Volunteer positions are also available. **Positions advertised include:** Central Sterilization Technologist; EMT; LPN; CMA; COTA/Certified Occupational Therapist Assistant; Child Care Assistant; Controller; Courier; Emergency Department Staff RN; Financial Analyst; LNA; Night Nursing Supervisor; Occupational Therapist; Certified Surgical Tech; Physical Therapist; Respiratory Therapist; Staff Radiographer. **CEO:** Bruce King.

NORTHEAST REHABILITATION HEALTH NETWORK
70 Butler Street, Salem NH 03079. 603/893-2900, ext.: 444. **Fax:** 603/893-9625. **Contact:** Human Resources. **E-mail address:** jobs@northeastrehab.com. **World Wide Web address:** http://www.northeastrehab.com. **Description:** A rehabilitation hospital. Northeast Rehabilitation Hospital has both inpatient and outpatient services including acute physical rehabilitation, physical therapy, and occupational therapy. **NOTE:** Search posted openings online. **Positions advertised include:** Certified Hand Therapist; Cold Production Worker; Food and Nutritionist; Housekeeping Associate; Laundry Associate; LNA; Nursing Supervisor; Patients Account Representative; Physical Therapy Assistant; Physical Therapist; Respiratory Therapist; RN; Speech Language Pathologist. **Other U.S. locations:** MA. **Number of employees at this location:** 460.

PARKLAND MEDICAL CENTER
One Parkland Drive, Derry NH 03038. 603/421-2070. **Fax:** 603/421-2074. **Recorded jobline:** 603/432-1500

Ext. 4400. **Contact:** Cynthia King, Human Resources. **World Wide Web address:** http://www.parklandmedicalcenter.com. **Description:** A Hospital. **NOTE:** Search posted openings and apply online. Volunteer positions also available. **Positions advertised include**: Administrative Nursing Supervisor; Admissions Nurse; Case Manager; Floor Tech; Medical Staff Manager; Medical Technologist; Quality Coordinator; Radiology Technologist; Registered Dietician; RN – Various Departments; Speech Pathologist; Staff Physical Therapist; Surgical Tech; Switchboard Operator. **Office hours:** Monday – Friday, 8:00 a.m. – 4:30 p.m. **Number of employees at this location:** 800.

PRESIDENTIAL OAKS
200 Pleasant Street, Concord NH 03301-2599. 603/225-6644. **Toll-free phone:** 800/678-1333. **Contact:** Human Resources. **E-mail address:** jobs@presidentialoaks.com. **World Wide Web address:** http://www.presidentialoaks.org. **Description:** A home for the aged. Presidential Oaks offers three levels of care: independent living, supported residential care, and nursing care. **Positions advertised include:** MDS Coordinator; Recreation Professional. **NOTE:** Employee inquiries dial Ext. 106. **Number of employees at this location:** 200.

SACO RIVER MEDICAL GROUP
7 Greenwood Avenue, P.O. Box 2679, Conway NH 03818. 603/447-3500. **Fax:** 603/447-5568. **Contact:** Human Resources. **World Wide Web address:** http://www.sacodocs.com. **Description:** An independent medical office that provides general practice, pediatrics, walk-in, gynecology, counseling, and acupuncture services. **Office hours:** Monday – Friday, 8:30 a.m. – 4:30 p.m.

ST. VINCENT DE PAUL HEALTH CARE CENTER
29 Providence Avenue, Berlin NH 03570-3199. 603/752-1820. **Fax:** 603/752-7149. **Contact:** Personnel. **E-mail address**: hresource@ncia.net. **Description:** A nursing home licensed for 80 beds. **NOTE**: Advertises openings locally.

SMITHS MEDICAL
10 Bowman Drive, Keene NH 03431. 603/352-3812. **Contact:** Personnel. **E-mail address:** human.resources@portex.com. **World Wide Web address:** http://www.portex.com/index2.asp. **Description:** Manufactures disposable hospital supplies. Brand-name products include Concord Laboratory and Portex. **International locations:** United Kingdom. **Parent company:** Smiths Medical.

U.S. DEPARTMENT OF VETERANS AFFAIRS MEDICAL CENTER
718 Smyth Road, Manchester NH 03104. 603/624-4366, Ext.: 6513. **Toll-free phone:** 800/892-8384. **Fax:** 603/626-6568. **Contact:** Jerri Amplicata, Human Resources Department. **World Wide Web address:** http://www.visn1.med.va.gov/manchester.
Description: A medical center operated by the U.S. Department of Veterans Affairs. From 54 hospitals in 1930, the VA health care system has grown to include 171 medical centers; more than 364 outpatient, community and outreach clinics; 130 nursing home care units; and 37 domiciliaries. VA operates at least one medical center in each of the 48 contiguous states, Puerto Rico, and the District of Columbia. With approximately 76,000 medical center beds, VA treats nearly 1 million patients per year in VA hospitals, 75,000 in nursing home care units, and 25,000 in domiciliaries. **NOTE:** May only respond to posted openings. Visit website for more information on how to search the openings and apply. **Operations at this facility include:** Administration; Service. **Number of employees at this location:** 580.

New Jersey
AMERICAN STANDARD COMPANIES INC.
P.O. Box 6820, Piscataway NJ 08854. 732/980-6000. **Physical address:** One Centennial Avenue, Piscataway NJ 08855. **Contact:** Human Resources. **World Wide Web address:** http://www.americanstandard.com. **Description:** A global, diversified manufacturer. The company's operations are comprised of four segments: air conditioning products, plumbing products, automotive products, and medical systems. The air conditioning products segment (through subsidiary The Trane Company) develops and manufactures Trane and American Standard air conditioning equipment for use in central air conditioning systems for commercial, institutional, and residential buildings. The plumbing products segment develops and manufactures American Standard, Ideal Standard, Porcher, Armitage Shanks, Dolomite, and Standard bathroom and kitchen fixtures and fittings. The automotive products segment develops and manufactures truck, bus, and utility vehicle braking and control systems under the WABCO and Perrot brands. The medical systems segment manufactures Copalis, DiaSorin, and Pylori-Chek medical diagnostic products and systems for a variety of diseases including HIV, osteoporosis, and renal disease. **Corporate headquarters location:** This location. **International locations:** Worldwide. **Listed on:** New York Stock Exchange. **Stock exchange symbol:** ASD. **Chairman/CEO:** Frederic M. Poses. **Number of employees worldwide:** 57,000.

ANCORA HOSPITAL
202 Spring Garden Road, Ancora NJ 08037. 609/561-1700. **Contact:** Human Resources. **Description:** A 500-bed psychiatric hospital that offers inpatient services for adults.

ATLANTIC CITY MEDICAL CENTER
1925 Pacific Avenue, Atlantic City NJ 08401. 609/344-4081. **Contact:** Human Resources Department. **World Wide Web address:** http://www.atlanticare.org. **Description:** A full-service hospital, also providing a cancer center, neonatal intensive care unit, coronary care center, and a Level II Trauma Center. **Positions advertised include:** Patient Access Coordinator; Pool Technician; Group Teacher; Clinical Therapist; Operations Assistant; Lab Assistant; Lab Testing Personnel; Emergency Medical Person; Administrative Associate; Dialysis Technician; Nutritional Counselor; Clinical Nurse Specialist; Registered Nurse. **Other area locations:** Pomona NJ.

C.R. BARD, INC.
730 Central Avenue, Murray Hill NJ 07974. 908/277-8000. **Fax:** 908/277-8412. **Contact:** Human Resources. **World Wide Web address:** http://www.crbard.com. **Description:** Manufactures and distributes disposable medical, surgical, diagnostic, and patient care products. Cardiovascular products include angioplastic recanalization devices such as balloon angioplasty catheters, inflation devices, and developmental atherectomy and laser devices; electrophysiology products such as temporary pacing catheters, diagnostic and therapeutic electrodes, and cardiac mapping systems; a cardiopulmonary system; and blood oxygenators, cardiotomy reservoirs, and other products used in open heart surgery. Urological products include Foley catheters, trays, and related urine contract collection systems used extensively in postoperative bladder drainage. Surgical products include wound and chest drainage systems and implantable blood vessel replacements. **Corporate headquarters location:** This location. **Listed on:** New York Stock Exchange. **Stock exchange symbol:** BCR.

BARNERT HOSPITAL
680 Broadway, Paterson NJ 07514. 973/977-6600. **Fax:** 973/279-2924. **Recorded jobline:** 973/977-6824. **Contact:** Human Resources. **World Wide Web address:** http://www.barnerthosp.com. **Description:** A 280-bed hospital. **Positions advertised include:** Nurse Assistant; Unit Clerk; Medical Assistant; Ultrasonographer; Physical Therapist; Laboratory Technician; Medical Technologist; Pharmacy Tech; Independent Living Specialist; Mental Health Clinic; Outpatient Clinician; Resident Counselor; American Sign Language Associate; Maintenance Supervisor; Operator; Mechanic; Patient Biller; Credit

Representative; House Keeper; Communications Representative; Registrar. **Special programs:** Internships. **Operations at this facility include:** Administration; Service. **Number of employees at this location:** 1,000.

BECTON DICKINSON & COMPANY
One Becton Drive, Franklin Lakes NJ 07417. 201/847-6800. **Contact:** Human Resources. **World Wide Web address:** http://www.bd.com. **Description:** A medical company engaged in the manufacture of health care products, medical instrumentation, diagnostic products, and industrial safety equipment. Major medical equipment product lines include hypodermics, intravenous equipment, operating room products, thermometers, gloves, and specialty needles. The company also offers contract packaging services. Founded in 1896. **Positions advertised include:** Administrative Assistant; Project Leader; Customer Service Associate; Customer Service Representative; Transactional Six Sigma Black Belt; Help Desk Analyst; Product Development Engineer; Cost Analyst; Training Administrator; Project Manager; Rebate Reconciliation Analyst; Corporate Development Manager; Business Analyst; Claims Associate; Data Entry Associate. **Corporate headquarters location:** This location. **Listed on:** New York Stock Exchange. **Stock exchange symbol:** BDX. **Number of employees worldwide:** 18,000.

BIOSEARCH MEDICAL PRODUCTS, INC.
35A Industrial Parkway, Somerville NJ 08876. 908/722-5000. **Toll-free phone:** 800/326-5976. **Fax:** 908/722-5024. **Contact:** Human Resources. **World Wide Web address:** http://www.biosearch.com. **Description:** Manufactures specialty medical devices for the gastroenterology, endoscopy, urology, and enteral feeding markets. The company's products are sold directly to hospitals and alternative care centers through domestic and international specialty dealers. Founded in 1978. **NOTE:** Entry-level positions are offered. **Special programs:** Training. **Parent company:** Hydromer Inc. **Listed on:** NASDAQ. **Stock exchange symbol:** BMPI. **Annual sales/revenues:** $5 - $10 million. **Number of employees at this location:** 30.

BURDETTE TOMLIN MEMORIAL HOSPITAL
2 Stone Harbor Boulevard, Cape May Court House NJ 08210. 609/463-2000. **Fax:** 609/463-2379. **Contact:** Meaghan Sterner, Employment Representative. **E-mail address:** msterner@bthosp.com. **World Wide Web address:** http://www.btmh.com. **Description:** A 242-bed, acute care, community hospital. **Positions advertised include:** Nurse Manager; Registered Nurse; Medical Technologist; Medical Transcriptionist.

CANTEL INDUSTRIES, INC.
Overlook at Great Notch, 150 Clove Road, 9th Floor, Little Falls NJ 07424. 973/890-7220. **Contact:** Human Resources. **World Wide Web address:** http://www.cantelmedical.com. **Description:** A holding company. **Subsidiaries include:** Carson Group Inc. (Canada) markets and distributes medical instruments including flexible and rigid endoscopes; precision instruments including microscopes and image analysis systems; and industrial equipment including remote visual inspection devices, laser distance measurement and thermal imaging products, and online optical inspection and quality assurance systems for specialized industrial applications. Carson also offers a full range of photographic equipment and supplies for amateur and professional photographers. **Listed on:** NASDAQ. **Stock exchange symbol:** CNTL.

CAPITAL HEALTH SYSTEM FULD CAMPUS
750 Brunswick Avenue, Trenton NJ 08638. 609/394-6000. **Fax:** 609/394-4444. **Contact:** Human Resources. **E-mail address:** employment@chsnj.org. **World Wide Web address:** http://www.capitalhealth.org. **Description:** A 589-bed, acute-care, teaching hospital. **NOTE:** Mail resumes to: Human Resources Department, 446 Bellevue Avenue, Trenton NJ 08607. **Corporate headquarters location:** This location.

CAPITAL HEALTH SYSTEM MERCER CAMPUS
446 Bellevue Avenue, Trenton NJ 08607. 609/394-4000. **Fax:** 609/394-4444. **Contact:** Human Resources. **E-mail address:** employment@chsnj.org. **World Wide Web address:** http://www.capitalhealth.org. **Description:** A 318-bed, community-based, acute care facility. **Positions advertised include:** Assistant Store Manager; Cardiac Monitor Technician; Case Manager; Claims Manager; Coder; Cook; Dietary Aide; Emergency Medical Technician; File Clerk; Food Service Worker; Housekeeper; Licensed Practical Nurse; Registered Nurse.

DENTSPLY CERAMCO
6 Terri Lane, Suite 100, Burlington NJ 08016. 609/386-8900. **Toll-free phone:** 800/487-0100. **Fax:** 609/386-5266. **Contact:** Ms. Pat McDade, Office Administrator. **World Wide Web address:** http://www.ceramco.com. **Description:** A leading manufacturer of dental porcelain, raw materials, and equipment. Ceramco distributes these products to dental laboratories for use in preparing crowns, bridges, and restorations. Founded in 1959. **Office hours:** Monday - Friday, 8:00 a.m. - 5:00 p.m. **Corporate headquarters location:** This location. **International locations:** England; Puerto Rico. **Parent company:** Dentsply International, Inc. **Annual sales/revenues:** $21 - $50 million. **Number of employees at this location:** 65. **Number of employees nationwide:** 90. **Number of employees worldwide:** 130.

COMMUNITY MEDICAL CENTER
99 Highway 37 West, Toms River NJ 08755. 732/240-8000. **Contact:** Human Resources. **E-mail address:** info@sbhcs.com. **World Wide Web address:** http://www.sbhcs.com/hospitals/community_medical. **Description:** An affiliate of Saint Barnabus Health Care System, Community Medical Center is a 596-bed, general, short-term care hospital.

COOPER HEALTH
1 Cooper Plaza, Suite 500, Camden NJ 08103. 856/342-2000. **Fax:** 856/968-8319. **Contact:** Human Resources. **World Wide Web address:** http://www.cooperhealth.org. **Description:** A 554-bed, nonprofit, academic medical center. Cooper Health specializes in the care of seriously-ill and critically-injured patients.

CORDIS CORPORATION
45 Technology Drive, Warren NJ 07059. 908/755-8300. **Contact:** Human Resources. **World Wide Web address:** http://www.cordis.com. **Description:** Cordis manufactures medical devices such as catheters to treat cardiovascular diseases. **NOTE:** All hiring is done through the parent company. Resumes should be sent to Johnson & Johnson Recruiting Services, Employment Management Center, Room JH-215, 501 George Street, New Brunswick NJ 08906-6597. **Operations at this facility include:** This location handles administration, research and development, and quality assurance. **Parent company:** Johnson & Johnson (New Brunswick NJ).

DATASCOPE CORPORATION
14 Phillips Parkway, Montvale NJ 07645. 201/391-8100. **Contact:** Human Resources. **E-mail address:** career_opportunities@datascope.com. **World Wide Web address:** http://www.datascope.com. **Description:** Manufactures cardiac assist systems for hospital use in interventional cardiology and cardiac surgery; and patient monitors for use in the operating room, postanesthesia care, and critical care. Datascope's VasoSeal product rapidly seals femoral arterial punctures after catheterization procedures including coronary angioplasty and angiography. Datascope also manufactures a line of collagen hemostats, which are used to control bleeding during surgery. The company's cardiac assist product is an intra-aortic balloon pumping system used for treating cardiac shock, heart failure, and cardiac arrhythmia. The pump can also be used in

various procedures including cardiac surgery and coronary angioplasty. Datascope's patient monitoring products comprise a line of multifunction and stand-alone models that measure a broad range of physiological data including blood oxygen saturation, airway carbon dioxide, ECG, and temperature. **Positions advertised include:** Industrial Engineer; Electro-Mechanical Engineer; Electrical Engineer; Secretary; Lotus Notes Database Developer. **Listed on:** NASDAQ. **Stock exchange symbol:** DSCP.

DEBORAH HEART & LUNG CENTER
200 Trenton Road, Browns Mills NJ 08015. 609/893-6611. **Contact:** Human Resources. **E-mail address:** employment@deborah.org. **World Wide Web address:** http://www.deborah.org. **Description:** A hospital providing a variety of services including cardiac and pulmonary care. **Positions advertised include:** Medical Transcriptionist; Batch Control Representative; Coder; Office Assistant; Nuclear Medical Technician; Pharmacist; Registered Nurse; Licensed Practical Nurse.

EBI MEDICAL SYSTEMS, INC.
100 Interpace Parkway, Parsippany NJ 07054. 973/299-9300. **Toll-free phone:** 800/526-2579. **Fax:** 973/402-1396. **Contact:** Department of Human Resources. **E-mail address:** humanresources@ebimed.com. **World Wide Web address:** http://www.ebimedical.com. **Description:** Designs, develops, manufactures, and markets products used primarily by orthopedic medical specialists in both surgical and nonsurgical therapies. Products include electrical bone growth stimulators, orthopedic support devices, spinal fixation devices for spinal fusion, external fixation devices, and cold temperature therapy. Founded in 1977. **NOTE:** Entry-level positions and part-time jobs are offered. **Special programs:** Internships; Training; Summer Jobs. **Corporate headquarters location:** This location. **Other U.S. locations:** OK. **International locations:** Puerto Rico. **Parent company:** Biomet, Inc. **Listed on:** NASDAQ. **Stock exchange symbol:** BMET. **Number of employees at this location:** 360.

EAST COAST TECHNOLOGIES
301 Pinedge Drive, Pinedge Industrial Park, West Berlin NJ 08091. 856/753-7778. **Contact:** Personnel. **E-mail address:** gwolfe@eastcoasttech.com. World **Wide Web address:** http://www.eastcoasttech.com. **Description:** Wholesales and repairs medical equipment, primarily laser and medical imaging systems.

ETHICON, INC.
U.S. Route 22, P.O. Box 151, Somerville NJ 08876. 908/218-0707. **Contact:** Human Resources. **World Wide Web address:** http://www.ethiconinc.com. **Description:** Manufactures products for precise wound closure including sutures, ligatures, mechanical wound closure instruments, and related products. The company also makes its own surgical needles and provides needle-suture combinations to surgeons. **Corporate headquarters location:** This location. **Parent company:** Johnson & Johnson (New Brunswick NJ).

GLAXOSMITHKLINE CORPORATION
257 Cornelison Avenue, Jersey City NJ 07302. 201/434-3000. **Contact:** Human Resources. **World Wide Web address:** http://www.gsk.com. **Description:** Develops, manufactures, and sells products in four general categories: denture, dental care, oral hygiene, and professional dental products; proprietary products; ethical pharmaceutical products; and household products. Dental-related products include Polident denture cleansers. **Positions advertised include:** Pharmaceutical Sales Representative. **Listed on:** New York Stock Exchange. **Stock exchange symbol:** GSK.

HCR MANOR CARE HEALTH SERVICES
1412 Marlton Pike, Cherry Hill NJ 08034. 856/428-6100. **Contact:** Human Resources. **E-mail address:** jobline@hcr.manorcare.com. **World Wide Web address:** http://www.manorcare.com. **Description:** An inpatient and outpatient rehabilitation center providing physical, occupational, and speech therapies. **Positions advertised include:** Admissions Director; Registered Nurse; Licensed Practical Nurse; Nurses Assistant; Occupational Therapist. **Special programs:** Training. **Corporate headquarters location:** Toledo OH. **Other U.S. locations:** Nationwide. **Subsidiaries include:** Milestone Healthcare. **Listed on:** New York Stock Exchange. **Stock exchange symbol:** HCR. **Number of employees nationwide:** 50,000.

HACKENSACK UNIVERSITY MEDICAL CENTER
30 Prospect Avenue, Hackensack NJ 07601. 201/996-2000. **Contact:** Human Resources. **World Wide Web address:** http://www.humc.net. **Description:** A teaching medical hospital and research center affiliated with the University of Medicine. **Positions advertised include:** Registered Nurse; Licensed Practical Nurse; OB Technician; Case Manager; Social Worker.

HAUSMANN INDUSTRIES
130 Union Street, Northvale NJ 07647. 201/767-0255. **Toll-free phone:** 877/737-3332. **Fax:** 201/767-1369. **Toll-free fax:** 877-737-33322. **Contact:** Human Resources. **E-mail address:** info@hausmann.com. **World Wide Web address:** http://www.hausmann.com. **Description:** Manufactures medical examination tables and physical therapy equipment. **Corporate headquarters location:** This location.

HOOPER HOLMES, INC.
dba PORTAMEDIC
170 Mount Airy Road, Basking Ridge NJ 07920. 908/766-5000. **Contact:** Manager of Human Resources. **E-mail address:** hres@hooperholmes.com. **World Wide Web address:** http://www.hooperholmes.com. **Description:** Performs health exams for insurance companies. Founded in 1899. **Positions advertised include:** Administrative Assistant. **Office hours:** Monday - Friday, 8:30 a.m. - 5:00 p.m. **Corporate headquarters location:** This location. **Other U.S. locations:** Nationwide. **Operations at this facility include:** Administration; Divisional Headquarters; Research and Development; Sales; Service. **Listed on:** American Stock Exchange. **Stock exchange symbol:** HH. **Annual sales/revenues:** More than $100 million. **Number of employees at this location:** 120. **Number of employees nationwide:** 2,500.

HUNTERDON DEVELOPMENTAL CENTER
P.O. Box 4003, Clinton NJ 08809-4003. 908/735-4031. **Physical address:** 40 Pittstown Road, Clinton NJ 08060. **Contact:** Human Resources. **Description:** A state-run residential facility for adults with developmental disabilities.

INTEGRA LIFESCIENCES CORPORATION
311C Enterprise Drive, Plainsboro NJ 08536. 609/275-0500. **Fax:** 609/275-3684. **Contact:** Human Resources. **World Wide Web address:** http://www.integra-ls.com. **Description:** Researches and develops a wide range of medical devices including artificial skin for burn victims; collagen sponges for use in surgery; dental wound and dermal ulcer dressings; and packing agents for ear, nose, and throat surgery. **Positions advertised include:** Associate Product Manager; Accountant; Product Manager; Internal Audit Manager; Project Engineer; Compliant Corporate Coordinator; Marketing Administrative Assistant; Quality Assurance Director; Finance Cost Analyst; Finance Assistant Controller. **Listed on:** NASDAQ. **Stock exchange symbol:** IART.

LOHMANN ANIMAL HEALTH INTERNATIONAL
111 Highland Avenue, Vineland NJ 08361. 856/696-9994. **Fax:** 856/691-4392. **Contact:** Patti Murphy. **E-mail address:** pmurphy@lahinternational.com. **World Wide Web address:** http://www.lah.de. **Description:** Manufacturer of avian vaccines. LAH belongs to the PHW-Group, which today embraces more than 35

companies working in the field of agriculture and nutrition. The PHW-Group focuses on promoting animal and human nutrition and health. **Positions advertised include:** Poultry Veterinarian; Production Coordinator; Production Manager.

THE MATHENY SCHOOL AND HOSPITAL
P.O. Box 339, Peapack NJ 07977. 908/234-0011. **Fax:** 908/234-9496. **Contact:** Human Resources. **World Wide Web address:** http://www.matheny.org. **Description:** A licensed hospital and school for people with severe physical disabilities such as cerebral palsy and spina bifida. **NOTE:** Entry-level positions and second and third shifts are offered. **Positions advertised include:** Nurse; Occupational Therapist; Physical Therapist; Social Worker; Speech Therapist; Research Therapist; Rehab Technologist. **Special programs:** Internships; Apprenticeships; Training. **President:** Robert Schonhorn.

MAXIM HEALTHCARE
622 George's Road, North Brunswick NJ 08902. 732/246-1687. **Toll-free phone:** 800/697-2247. **Contact:** Manager. **World Wide Web address:** http://www.maxhealth.com. **Description:** A home health care agency. **Positions advertised include:** Sales Recruiter. **Corporate headquarters location:** Lake Success NY. **Other U.S. locations:** Nationwide. **Number of employees nationwide:** 20,000.

MEDICAL RESOURCES, INC.
125 State Street, Suite 200, Hackensack NJ 07601. 201/488-6230. **Fax:** 201/488-8455. **Contact:** Human Resources. **World Wide Web address:** http://www.mrii.com. **Description:** Owns and manages medical diagnostic imaging centers nationwide. The centers offer magnetic resonance imaging (MRI), computerized tomography (CT), nuclear medicine, mammography, ultrasound, and X-ray. **Positions advertised include:** Data Analyst; Ultrasound Technologist; MRI Technologist; CT Technologist. **Listed on:** NASDAQ. **Stock exchange symbol:** MRII. **Annual sales/revenues:** More than $100 million.

MONMOUTH-OCEAN HOSPITAL SERVICE CORPORATION
4806 Megill Road, Wall Township, Neptune NJ 07753. 732/919-3045. **Fax:** 732-919-2699. **Contact:** Human Resources. **E-mail address:** http://www.jobs@monoc.org. **World Wide Web address:** http://www.monoc.org. **Description:** The Monmouth Ocean Hospital Service Corporation, is a non-profit company consisting of nineteen acute-care hospitals located in Monmouth, Ocean, Atlantic, Begen, Cape May, Hudson, Essex and Union Counties, New Jersey. **NOTE:** Search for open positions online. **Positions advertised include:** Control Center Supervisor; Emergency Medical Dispatcher; Emergency Medical Technician; EMS Supervisor (Clinical/QA); Medical Collector; Paramedic; Registered Nurse. **Number of employees nationwide:** 850.

OCEAN COUNTY VETERINARY HOSPITAL
838 River Avenue, Lakewood NJ 08701. 732/363-7202. **Fax:** 732/370-4176. **Contact:** Human Resources. **World Wide Web address:** http://www.ocvh.com. **Description:** Provides health care services to dogs, cats, and exotic pets including surgery, hospitalization, and diagnostic testing. **Positions advertised include:** Technician; Receptionist.

OVERLOOK HOSPITAL
P.O. Box 220, Summit NJ 07902-0220. 908/522-2241. **Physical address:** 99 Beauvoir Avenue, Summit NJ 07901. **Contact:** Human Resources. **World Wide Web address:** http://www.overlookfoundation.org. **Description:** A part of Atlantic Health Systems, Overlook Hospital is a 490-bed, public hospital with extensive facilities for pediatrics, oncology, cardiology, and same-day surgery.

P.S.A. HEALTHCARE
4900 Route 33, Suite 100, Neptune NJ 07753-6804. 732/938-5550. **Fax:** 732/938-6535. **Contact:** Human Resources. **World Wide Web address:** http://www.psakids.com. **Description:** Provides infusion therapy, nursing, and other home health care services to clients. **Positions advertised include:** Clinical Care Coordinator; Registered Nurse; Field Nurse Recruiter.

SJ NURSES
850 Hamilton Avenue, Trenton NJ 08629. 609/396-7100. **Toll-free phone:** 800/727-2476. **Fax:** 609/396-7559. **Contact:** Human Resources. **E-mail address:** application@sjnurses.com. **World Wide Web address:** http://www.sjnurses.com. **Description:** Provides home health care services. **Corporate headquarters location:** This location.

SAINT BARNABAS HEALTH CARE SYSTEM
368 Lakehurst Road, Suite 203, Toms River NJ 08755. 888/724-7123. **Contact:** Human Resources. **E-mail address:** info@sbhcs.com. **World Wide Web address:** http://www.sbhcscareers.com. **Description:** A health care delivery system that spans the state of New Jersey and includes eight acute care hospitals, nine nursing and rehabilitation centers, three assisted living facilities, geriatric centers, and ambulatory care centers. **NOTE:** Search and apply for positions online. **Positions advertised include:** Administrative Assistant; Case Coordinator; Certified Nursing Assistant (CNA); CM Director of Nursing; Coder; Compliance Associate; Endo Technician; General Clerical; Housekeeper; Licensed Practical Nurse; Payroll Coordinator; Respiratory Therapist; Respiratory Therapy Coordinator; Staff Registered Nurse. **Other area locations:** Statewide.

SHORE MEMORIAL HOSPITAL
One East New York Avenue, Somers Point NJ 08244-2387. 609/653-3500. **Fax:** 609/926-1987. **Contact:** Human Resources Department **World Wide Web address:** http://www.shorememorial.org. **Description:** A 350-bed, nonprofit medical center providing medical, surgical, pediatric, and obstetrical services. Shore Memorial Hospital joined with Shore Care Home Health Services and Ocean Point Health Care Center to form Shore Memorial Health Care System. **Positions advertised include:** Radiation Therapist; Care Manager; Registered Nurse; Staff Technologist; MRI Technician; Chart Clerk; CT Technologist; Special Procedures Technologist. **Number of employees at this location:** 1,400.

SIEMENS MEDICAL
186 Wood Avenue South, Iselin NJ 08830. 732/321-4500. **Contact:** Personnel Office. **World Wide Web address:** http://www.siemensmedical.com. **Description:** Develops, manufactures, and sells medical systems including digital X-rays and 3-D ultrasound equipment. Products are used in a variety of areas including cardiology, audiology, surgery, critical care, and oncology. **Positions advertised include:** Advanced Consultant; Business & Product Development Manager; Repair Operating Manager; Technical Competence Center Representative; New Units Vice President. **Corporate headquarters location:** This location.

SLACK INCORPORATED
6900 Grove Road, Thorofare NJ 08086-9447. 856/848-1000. **Toll-free phone:** 800/257-8290. **Fax:** 856/848-6091. **Contact:** Human Resources Manager. **E-mail address:** resume@slackinc.com. **World Wide Web address:** http://www.slackinc.com. **Description:** SLACK Incorporated is a provider of information, education, and event management services focusing mainly in the healthcare marketplace. A leader in the healthcare information industry SLACK publishes over 25 journals and medical newspapers distributed worldwide; over 125 medical and allied health books worldwide; conducts major publication-related conferences and trade shows; provides exhibit sales, management services, and advertising sales representation for association clients; produces dozens of periodical special projects each year, including

supplements, monographs, satellite symposia, and industry-sponsored symposia, and customized CD-ROMs; and designs and manages customized Websites for resident training and continuing education. SLACK is certified by the Accreditation Council for Continuing Medical Education to sponsor continuing education events and periodical-based Continuing Medical Education activities. **Positions advertised include:** Advertising Sales Administrator; Assistant Associate Editor; Customer Service Representative; Help Desk Representative; Copywriter; Sales Representative; Inside Sales Representative; Staff Writer; Web Editor **Corporate headquarters location:** This location.

SOUTH JERSEY HEALTH SYSTEM
SOUTH JERSEY HOSPITAL
333 Irving Avenue, Bridgeton NJ 08302-2123. 856/451-6600. **Fax:** 856/575-4500. **Contact:** Personnel. **World Wide Web address:** http://www.sjhs.com. **Description:** Provides extensive medical services throughout southern New Jersey. **NOTE:** Mail employment correspondence to: 65 South State Street, Vineland NJ 08360. **Positions advertised include:** Accountant; Case Manager; Corporate Compliance Specialist; Environmental Services Aide; Food Service Aide; Human Resources Representative; Marketing and Press Release Specialist; Nurse Manager; Pharmacist; Radiological Technician; Registrar; Registered Nurse. **Subsidiaries include:** Elmer Community Hospital has 91 beds. Millville Hospital has 109 beds. Newcomb Medical Center has 235 beds. South Jersey Hospital (also at this location) has 224 beds.

STRYKER ORTHOPAEDICS
325 Corporate Drive, Mahwah NJ 07430. 201/831-5000. **Contact:** Human Resources Department. **World Wide Web address:** http://www.stryker.com. **Description:** Manufactures medical implants including artificial knees, hips, shoulders, and elbows.

TRINITAS HOSPITAL
18-20 South Broad Street, Elizabeth NJ 07201. 908/994-5325. **Fax:** 908/527-0195. **Contact:** Human Resources. **World Wide Web address:** http://www.trinitashospital.org. **Description:** A hospital providing treatments for a variety of illnesses including cardiovascular diseases and cancer. **Positions advertised include:** Telephone Operator; Receptionist; Secretary; Lead Cashier; Registrar Trainee; Registrar; Insurance Bill Representative; Radiation Therapist; Van Driver; Diet Aide; Medical Technologist; Registered Nurse; Licensed Practical Nurse; Certified Nurses Aide; Occupational Therapist; Physical Therapist; Medical Technologist; Physicist; Mental Health Worker; Fitness Aide.

UNDERWOOD MEMORIAL HOSPITAL
509 North Broad Street, Woodbury NJ 08096. 856/845-0100. **Recorded jobline:** 856/853-2050. **Contact:** Personnel. **E-mail address:** humanresources@umhospital.org. **World Wide Web address:** http://www.umhospital.org. **Description:** A hospital.

UNIVERSITY HOSPITAL
30 Bergen Street, Building 8, Newark NJ 07107. 973/972-0012. **Recorded jobline:** 973/972-6740. **Contact:** Human Resources. **World Wide Web address:** http://www.theuniversityhospital.com. **Description:** A 466-bed teaching hospital of the University of Medicine and Dentistry of New Jersey. **Positions advertised include:** Transport Customer Service; Principal Lab Assistant; Food Service Worker; Program Support Specialist; Research Associate; Patient Accounts Clerk; Research Teaching Specialist; Advanced Practical Nurse; Management Assistant; Case Management Coordinator.

VINELAND DEVELOPMENTAL CENTER
1676 East Landis Avenue, P.O. Box 1513, Vineland NJ 08362-1513. 856/696-6000. **Contact:** Human Resources. **Description:** A residential treatment facility for females who have mental retardation.

VISITING NURSE SERVICE SYSTEM, INC.
150 East 9th Avenue, P.O. Box 250, Runnemede NJ 08078. 856/939-9000. **Fax:** 856/939-9010. **Contact:** Human Resources. **E-mail address:** hr@vnss.com. **World Wide Web address:** http://www.vnss.com. **Description:** Provides home-based health care services including nursing, physical therapy, occupational therapy, speech pathology, nutritional therapy, mental health and enterostomal therapy, medical social services, and hospice care. **Other U.S. locations:** Nationwide.

VITAL SIGNS, INC.
20 Campus Road, Totowa NJ 07512. 973/790-1330. **Toll-free phone:** 800/932-0760. **Fax:** 973/790-4271. **Contact:** Human Resources. **E-mail address:** humanresources@vital-signs.com. **World Wide Web address:** http://www.vital-signs.com. **Description:** Manufactures disposable medical products such as face masks, manual resuscitators, anesthesia kits, and other respiratory-related critical care products. **Corporate headquarters location:** This location. **Operations at this facility include:** Administration; Manufacturing; Research and Development; Service. **Number of employees at this location:** 350. **Number of employees nationwide:** 450.

New Mexico

ADDUS HEALTHCARE
1100 Paseo De Onate, Suite C, Espanola NM 87532. 505/753-2284. **Contact:** Human Resources. **E-mail address:** personnel@addus.com. **World Wide Web address:** http://www.addus.com. **Description:** Provides home health care services including respiratory therapy, skilled nursing, medical equipment, and rehabilitation from 127 offices in 23 states. Addus HealthCare also provides disease management programs and supplemental staffing. Founded in 1977. **NOTE:** Send resumes to: Addus Healthcare, Personnel, 2401 South Plum Grove Road, Palatine IL 60067 or to e-mail address. **Corporate headquarters location:** Palatine IL. **Other area locations:** Albuquerque NM.

ALBUQUERQUE REGIONAL MEDICAL CENTER
601 Dr. Martin Luther King Jr. Avenue NE, Albuquerque NM 87102. 505/727-8000. **Contact:** Human Resources. **World Wide Web address:** http://www.lovelace.com. **Description:** A medical center with 254 beds. Part of Lovelace Sandia Health System. **NOTE:** Search and apply for positions online. **Positions advertised include:** Patient Transporter; Scheduler; Director, Case Management; Diet Technician; Nutrition Assistant; Housekeeping Supervisor; Phlebotomist; HIM Coding Manager; Mental Health Tech; RN; Charge Nurse; House Supervisor; Director of Pharmacy; Pharmacist. **Parent company:** Ardent Health Services.

CASA REAL NURSING FACILITY
1650 Galisteo Street, Santa Fe NM 87505. 505/984-8313. **Contact:** Office Manager. **E-mail address:** jobs@peakmedicalcorp.com. **World Wide Web address:** www.peakmedicalcorp.com. **Description:** A 118-room nursing facility. Casa Real has four different units including an Alzheimer's unit. **Parent company:** Peak Medical Corp.

GERALD CHAMPION REGIONAL MEDICAL CENTER
2669 North Scenic Drive, Alamogordo NM 88310. 505/443-7445. **Contact:** Human Resources. **World Wide Web address:** http://www.gcrmc.org. **Description:** A one-story, 95-bed hospital focused on outpatient services. **NOTE:** Search and apply for positions online.

CONCENTRA MEDICAL CENTER
801 Encino Place, Suite E-12, Albuquerque NM 87102. 505/842-5151. **Contact:** Human Resources Department. **World Wide Web address:** http://www.concentra.com. **Description:** Performs drug screenings and physical examinations for corporations. Concentra Medical Center also provides medical

services for individuals collecting workers' compensation. **NOTE:** See website for current job openings and application instructions. **Positions advertised include:** Physical Therapist. **Corporate headquarters location:** Addison TX. **Other area locations:** Santa Fe NM. **Other U.S. locations:** Nationwide.

EASTERN NEW MEXICO MEDICAL CENTER
405 West Country Club Road, Roswell NM 88201. 505/622-8170. **Fax:** 505/624-8797. **Contact:** Beth Irizarry. **E-mail address:** Elvia_Garcia@chs.net. **World Wide Web address:** http://www.enmmc.com. **Description:** A 162-bed acute-care hospital. **NOTE:** See website for current job openings and application instructions. **Positions Advertised Include:** Clinic RN/LPN; Coder; Controller; Patient Account Rep; Transcriptionist. **Number of employees at this location:** 630.

EYE ASSOCIATES OF NEW MEXICO
8801 Horizon Boulevard NE, Suite 360, Albuquerque NM 87113. 505/246-2622. **Contact:** Human Resources. **E-mail address:** info@eyenm.com. **World Wide Web address:** http://www.eyenm.com. **Description:** The largest ophthalmic and optometric physician group in the Southwest. Made up of 35 Ophthalmologists and Optometrists, 14 clinic locations, and 9 optical shops. **NOTE:** Search and apply for positions online. **Other area locations:** Clovis NM; Espanola NM; Farmington NM; Gallup NM; Las Vegas NM; Los Alamos NM; Santa Fe NM.

HOBBS HEALTHCARE CENTER
5715 North Lovington Highway, Hobbs NM 88240-9131. 505/392-6845. **Contact:** Human Resources Department. **Description:** A 118-bed nursing home providing long-term care for elderly residents.

LOVELACE SANTA FE PRIMARY CARE
440 St. Michael's Drive, Santa Fe NM 87505. 505/995-2400. **Contact:** Clinic Manager. **World Wide Web address:** http://www.lovelace.com. **Description:** A walk-in health care clinic. Part of Lovelace Sandia Health System. **NOTE:** See website for current job openings and application instructions. **Parent company:** Ardent Health Services.

MEMORIAL MEDICAL CENTER
2450 Telshor Boulevard, Las Cruces NM 88011-5065. 505/556-5833. **Contact:** Sandra Miramontes, Employment Specialist. **E-mail address:** Sandra.miramontes@lpnt.com. **World Wide Web address:** http://www.mmclc.org. **Description:** Memorial Medical Center is a not-for-profit, 286-bed, acute care hospital, providing health care services to the people of southern New Mexico. Services include a cardiovascular lab for diagnostic procedures, a lithotripsy unit offering a nonsurgical technique for treating kidney stones, and the Ikard/Memorial Cancer Treatment Center, which provides radiation therapy to complement a multidisciplinary approach for the treatment of cancer. Founded in 1950. **NOTE:** Search and apply for positions online. **Positions advertised include:** Business Analyst; Inventory Coordinator; Surgical Tech; RN; Director, Surgical Services; Behavioral Health Therapist; LPN.

MIMBRES MEMORIAL HOSPITAL
900 West Ash Street, Deming NM 88030. 505/546-5806. **Fax:** 505/543-6914. **Contact:** Melanie Alfaro, Human Resources. **World Wide Web address:** http://www.mimbresmemorial.com. **Description:** A full-service, 49-bed acute-care hospital. **Positions advertised include:** Registered Nurse. **NOTE:** See website for current job openings. Entry-level positions and part-time jobs are offered. **Special programs:** Internships; Training. **Corporate headquarters location:** Brentwood TN. **Parent company:** Community Health System.

NEW MEXICO VA HEALTH CARE SYSTEM
1501 San Pedro Drive, SE, Albuquerque NM 87108-5153. 505/265-1711. **Fax:** 505/265-2855. **Contact:** Human Resources. **Description:** A comprehensive health care system consisting of a Level 1 tertiary referral center in Albuquerque with 217 beds, and a system of community based outpatient clinics in 21 locations throughout New Mexico and southwest Colorado. Affiliated with the University of New Mexico School of Medicine. **NOTE:** Search for statewide openings in the Veterans Health Administration at http://www.vacareers.va.gov.

NORTHERN NAVAJO MEDICAL CENTER
P.O. Box 160, Shiprock NM 87420. 505/368-6001. **Fax:** 505/368-6260. **Contact:** Human Resources. **Description:** A 55-bed medical center that also operates specialty outpatient clinics. This is a facility of the Navajo Area Indian Health Service, one of the administrative units of the Indian Health Service, an agency of the U.S. Public Health Service Department of Human Health Services. **NOTE:** Search current job openings on the Indian Health Service website, http://www.ihs.gov.

OCULAR SCIENCES, INC.
6805 Academy Parkway West NE, Albuquerque NM 87109. 505/345-7967. **Fax:** 888/301-0264. **Contact:** Human Resources. **World Wide Web address:** http://www.ocularsciences.com. **Description:** One of the world's largest producers of ophthalmic products, specializing in soft contact lenses including sphericals, multifocals, and torics. **Corporate headquarters location:** Concord CA. **Parent company:** CooperVision Inc. **Number of employees worldwide:** 4,000.

PLAINS REGIONAL MEDICAL CENTER
2100 Dr. Martin Luther King Jr. Boulevard, Clovis NM 88101. 505/761-7159. **Fax:** 505/769-7227. **Recorded jobline:** 505/841-1720. **Contact:** Human Resources. **E-mail address:** vjensen@phs.org. **World Wide Web address:** http://www.phs.org/facilities/clovis/index.shtml. **Description:** A 106-bed general medical center offering both inpatient and outpatient services. Operated by Presbyterian Healthcare Services. **NOTE:** Must apply for positions online. **Positions advertised include:** Administrative Staff Support; LPN; Nursing Tech; Cook; Nursing Supervisor; Patient Services Coordinator; Physical Therapist; Radiation Therapist; Radiographer; RN; Ultrasound Specialist; Transcriptionist.

PRESBYTERIAN MEDICAL SERVICES
P.O. Box 2267, Santa Fe NM 87504. 505/982-5565. **Physical address:** 422 Paseo de Peralta, Building #3, Santa Fe NM 87501. **Contact:** Human Resources. **World Wide Web address:** http://www.pms-inc.org. **Description:** Presbyterian Medical Services operates health care clinics throughout New Mexico. **NOTE:** Search and apply for positions online. **Operations at this facility include:** This location houses administrative offices.

PRINCETON PLACE
500 Louisiana Boulevard Northeast, Albuquerque NM 87108. 505/255-1717. **Contact:** Human Resources. **Description:** One of New Mexico's largest long-term nursing care facilities. Princeton Place has an on-site medical clinic, pharmacy, and rehabilitative care center for physical, occupational, speech, and respiratory therapy. A child development center, which is open to the general public, offers an Intergenerational Program. Founded in 1986. **Positions advertised include:** Nursing Manager; Registered Nurse; Licensed Practical Nurse; Certified Nurses Assistant; Housekeeper. **Internship information:** GN, GPN, and Social Services internships are available on a limited basis. **Listed on:** Privately held.

RANCHO VALMORA
HCR 50 Box 1, Valmora NM 87750. 505/425-6057. **Contact:** Human Resources. **World Wide Web address:** http://www.ranchovalmora.com. **Description:** A non-profit, long-term residential treatment center for

adolescents ages 12 through 18. The facility specializes in the treatment of behavioral and mental disorders.

ST. VINCENT HOSPITAL
455 St. Michael's Drive, Santa Fe NM 87505. 505/820-5730. **Fax:** 505/989-6408. **Contact:** Human Resources. **E-mail address:** HRWebContactUs@stvin.org. **World Wide Web address:** http://www.stvin.org. **Description:** A 268-bed, non-affiliated, nonprofit acute care facility. St. Vincent Hospital is JCAHO-accredited. Founded in 1865. **NOTE:** See website for application instructions. **Office hours:** Monday - Friday, 8:00 a.m. - 4:30 p.m.

SUN HEALTHCARE GROUP, INC.
101 Sun Avenue NE, Albuquerque NM 87109. 505/821-3355. **Contact:** Human Resources. **World Wide Web address:** http://www.sunh.com. **Description:** One of the nation's largest nursing home operators. Sun Healthcare Group is a comprehensive health care system that provides skilled nursing, pharmaceutical services, rehabilitation therapy, home health care services, and medical supplies. Founded in 1993. **NOTE:** Search and apply for positions online. **Corporate headquarters location:** Irvine CA. **Subsidiaries include:** SunAlliance Healthcare Services; SunBridge Healthcare Corporation; SunCare Respiratory Services, Inc.; SunChoice Medical Supply, Inc.; SunDance Rehabilitation Corporation; SunFactors, Inc.; SunPlus Home Health Services; SunScript Pharmacy Corporation. **Number of employees nationwide:** 16,800.

SUNRISE SENIOR LIVING
4910 Tramway Ridge Drive NE, Albuquerque NM 87111. 505/271-9600. **Fax:** 505/271-9966. **Contact:** Human Resources. **World Wide Web address:** http://www.sunriseassistedliving.com. **Description:** Operates 370 senior living communities in 34 states, Canada, and the United Kingdom. Founded in 1981. **NOTE:** Search and apply for positions online. **Number of employees worldwide:** 30,000.

UNIVERSITY OF NEW MEXICO HOSPITALS
1650 University Boulevard NE, Albuquerque NM 87102-1726. 505/272-2325. **Contact:** Human Resources. **World Wide Web address:** http://hospitals.unm.edu. **Description:** Consists of the University of New Mexico (UNM) Health Sciences Center, UNM Carrie Tingley Hospital, UNM Children's Hospital, UNM Children's Psychiatric Center, UNM Hospital, UNM Psychiatric Center, and various clinics and health centers. UNM Hospital is the primary teaching hospital for the University of New Mexico's School of Medicine. **NOTE:** Search and apply for positions online.

WOMEN'S HOSPITAL
4701 Montgomery Boulevard NE, Albuquerque NM 87108. 505/727-7800. **Contact:** Human Resources. **World Wide Web address:** http://www.lovelace.com. **Description:** The first and only hospital in New Mexico devoted entirely to women's health. Features a family birthing center with 16 labor and delivery recovery rooms, 41 postpartum beds, a neonatal intensive care unit, a special care nursery, a pediatric urgent care center and a well-baby nursery. Part of Lovelace Sandia Health System. **NOTE:** See website for current job openings and application instructions. **Parent company:** Ardent Health Services.

New York

AFP IMAGING CORPORATION
250 Clearbrook Road, Elmsford NY 10523. 914/592-6100. **Fax:** 914/592-6148. **Contact:** Human Resources Manager. **E-mail address:** afp@afpimaging.com. **World Wide Web address:** http://www.afpimaging.com. **Description:** Provides medical equipment utilized by radiologists, cardiologists, and other medical professionals for generating, recording, processing, and viewing hard copy diagnostic images. The company's products are applied in medical diagnostics X-ray inspection. Products are marketed under the AFP, DENT-X, and SENS-A-RAY 2000 brand names. **International locations:** Geilenkirchen, Germany. **Listed on:** Over The Counter. **Stock exchange symbol:** AFPC. **Chairman:** David Vozick. **Annual sales/revenues:** $24 million. **Number of employees:** 106.

ACUPATH LABORATORIES, INC.
28 South Terminal Drive, Plainview NY 11803. **Toll-free phone:** 888/228-7284. **Fax:** 516/326-3455. **Contact:** Human Resources. **E-mail address:** resume@acupath.com. **World Wide Web address:** http://www.acupath.com. **Description:** A pathology and cancer genetics lab. **Positions advertised include:** Technical Writer.

ALBANY MEDICAL CENTER
43 New Scotland Avenue, MC-56, Albany NY 12208-3478. 518/262-3125. **Physical address:** 411 Myrtle Avenue, Albany NY 12208. **Fax:** 518/262-4487. **Contact:** Cathy Halakan, Vice President of Human Resources. **World Wide Web address:** http://www.amc.edu. **Description:** An academic health science center. The facility specializes in inpatient and outpatient tertiary and general medical care, biomedical research, and education. **NOTE:** Employment Office phone: 518/262-8414. Resumes may be submitted online. **Positions advertised include:** Registered Nurse; Licensed Practical Nurse; Clinical Dietitian; Organ Procurement Coordinator; Cytogenetic Technologist; Genetic Counselor; Research Associate; Research Technician; Client Services Manager; Practice Operations Director; Research Director; Microbiology Director; Nursing Supervisor; Assistant Nurse Manager; Research Coordinator; Auditor; Administrative Coordinator; Cancer Registrar; Teacher Assistant; Security Officer; Parking Attendant; Driver/Courier; Food Service Worker; Housekeepers; Plant Maintenance Custodian.

ALL METRO HEALTH CARE
50 Broadway, Lynbrook NY 11563. 516/887-1200. **Toll-free phone:** 800/225-1200. **Fax:** 516/593-2848. **Contact:** Human Resources. **E-mail address:** all-metro@aol.com. **Description:** A home health care provider. Plaza Domestic Agency and Caregivers on Call also operate out of this facility. Founded in 1955. **Positions advertised include:** Certified Nurses Aide; Clerical Supervisor; Home Health Aide; Licensed Practical Nurse; Marketing Manager; Occupational Therapist; Physical Therapist; Registered Nurse. **Office hours:** Sunday - Saturday, 8:30 a.m. - 8:30 p.m. **Corporate headquarters location:** This location. **Other area locations:** Statewide. **Other U.S. locations:** FL; MO; NJ. **Parent company:** All Metro Aids Inc. **Annual sales/revenues:** $50 million. **Number of employees at this location:** 2,000. **Number of employees nationwide:** 5,000.

AMERICUS DENTAL LABS LP
150-15 Hillside Avenue, Jamaica NY 11432. 718/658-6655. **Fax:** 718/657-8389. **Contact:** Human Resources. **E-mail address:** info@americuslab.com. **World Wide Web address:** http://www.americuslab.com. **Description:** A dental lab that manufactures crowns, bridges, and other dental products. **Positions advertised include:** Ceramist; Die Trimmer. **Corporate headquarters location:** This location. **Other locations:** New York NY. **Number of employees:** 150.

AMSTERDAM MEMORIAL HEALTH CARE SYSTEM
AMSTERDAM MEMORIAL HOSPITAL
4988 State Highway 30, Amsterdam NY 12010. 518/842-3100. **Fax:** 518/841-3749. **Contact:** Human Resources. **World Wide Web address:** http://www.amsterdammemorial.org. **Description:** A network of community health care programs and facilities providing a full range of services for residents of Fulton, Montgomery, Hamilton, Schoharie, Schenectady, and Saratoga counties which includes primary care centers, a pharmacy, the Wilkinson Center, therapy services, diagnostic imaging, and dozens of other services. Amsterdam Community

Hospital offers a variety of services including primary care, rehabilitation, CT scanning, MRI, hemodialysis, ambulatory surgery, orthopedics, and women's and children's services.

ANIMAL MEDICAL CENTER
THE E&M BOBST HOSPITAL
510 East 62nd Street, New York NY 10021. 212/838-8100. **Fax:** 212/758-8157. **Contact:** Human Resources. **E-mail address:** careers@amcny.org. **World Wide Web address:** http://www.amcny.org. **Description:** A full-service, nonprofit animal hospital with a staff of over 80 veterinarians. Founded in 1910. **Positions advertised include:** Staff Accountant; Stockroom Clerk; Pet Outreach Coordinator; Public Relations Administrative Assistant; Receptionist Medical Records; Veterinary Technician.

AUBURN MEMORIAL HOSPITAL
17 Lansing Street, Auburn NY 13021. 315/255-7225. **Fax:** 315/255-7018. **Contact:** Colleen McLaughlin, Employment Specialist. **E-mail address:** ahmjobs@dreamscape.com. **World Wide Web address:** http://www.auburnhospital.com. **Description:** A 226-bed hospital. **NOTE:** Human Resources phone: 315/255-7225. **Positions advertised include:** Registered Nurse; Nursing Supervisor; Licensed Practical Nurse; Certified Nursing Assistant. **Parent company:** Auburn Hospital System Foundation, Inc. (also at this location).

C.R. BARD, INC.
730 Central Avenue, Murray Hill NJ 07974. 908/277-8000. **Fax:** 908/277-8412. **Contact:** Human Resources. **World Wide Web address:** http://www.crbard.com. **Description:** Manufactures and distributes disposable medical, surgical, diagnostic, and patient care products. Cardiovascular products include angioplastic recanalization devices such as balloon angioplasty catheters, inflation devices, and developmental atherectomy and laser devices; electrophysiology products such as temporary pacing catheters, diagnostic and therapeutic electrodes, and cardiac mapping systems; a cardiopulmonary system; and blood oxygenators, cardiotomy reservoirs, and other products used in open heart surgery. Urological products include Foley catheters, trays, and related urine contract collection systems used extensively in postoperative bladder drainage. Surgical products include wound and chest drainage systems and implantable blood vessel replacements. **Corporate headquarters location:** This location. **Listed on:** New York Stock Exchange. **Stock exchange symbol:** BCR.

BARKSDALE HEALTH CARE SERVICES INC.
BARKSDALE HOME CARE SERVICES CORP.
BARKSDALE SERVICES CORP.
327 Fifth Avenue, Pelham NY 10803. 914/738-5600. **Fax:** 914/738-0658. **Contact:** Rosa K. Barksdale, CEO. **World Wide Web address:** http://www.barksdaleathome.com. **Description:** A home health care agency providing health care services to private homes, hospitals, and institutions in Westchester County and the Bronx NY. **Positions advertised include:** Nurses Aide; Personal Care Aide; Certified Nurses Aide; Medical Social Worker; Live-in Companion; Home Health Aide; Licensed Practical Nurse; Registered Nurse. **Corporate headquarters location:** This location. **Other locations:** Riverdale NY.

BAUSCH & LOMB, INC.
One Bausch & Lomb Place, Rochester NY 14604-2701. 585/338-6000. **Toll-free phone:** 800/344-8815. **Fax:** 585/338-6007. **Contact:** Centralized Staffing. **World Wide Web address:** http://www.bausch.com. **Description:** Manufactures eye care products, pharmaceuticals, and surgical equipment including contact lenses; lens care solutions; premium sunglasses (sold under Ray-Ban and Revo brands) prescription and over-the-counter ophthalmic drugs; and equipment used for cataract and ophthalmic surgery. **NOTE:** You may apply online through the company Website. **Positions advertised include:** Senior Clinical Consultant; Professional Services Manager; Audit Manager; Professional Communications Manager; Procurement Manager. **Special programs:** Summer Internships. **Corporate headquarters location:** Rochester NY. **Other area locations** Pearl River NY. **Other U.S. locations:** Nationwide. **Operations at this facility include:** Manufacturing. **Listed on:** New York Stock Exchange. **Stock exchange symbol:** BOL. **Chairman/CEO:** Ronald L. Zarrella. **Annual sales/revenues:** $1.8 billion. **Number of employees:** 11,600.

BAYER DIAGNOSTICS DIVISION
BAYER HEALTHCARE
511 Benedict Avenue, Tarrytown NY 10591-5097. 914/631-8000. **Fax:** 914/333-6536. **Contact:** Kim MacNeil, Human Resources. **E-mail address:** hr.grp@bayer.com or kim.macneil.b@bayer.com. **World Wide Web address:** http://www.bayerdiag.com. **Description:** Develops, manufactures, and sells clinical diagnostic systems. Bayer Diagnostics specializes in critical care, laboratory, and point-of-care testing. **NOTE:** See http://www.monster.com for current job listings. **Positions advertised include:** Service and Support Engineer; Laboratory Automation Engineer; Health Care Professional/Manager; Research Scientist; Staff System Engineer; Senior Financial Analyst; Sales Trainer; National Advertising Division Marketing Manager; Managed Care Manager; Hemotology Sales Specialist. **Corporate headquarters location:** Pittsburgh PA. **Other area locations:** Middletown NY; Nyack NY. **Other U.S. locations:** IL; LA; MA; OH; PA. **International locations:** Worldwide. **Parent company:** Bayer Corporation (Pittsburgh PA). **Operations at this facility include:** Administration; Divisional Headquarters; Manufacturing; Research and Development; Sales; Service. **Listed on:** New York Stock Exchange. **Stock exchange symbol:** BAY. **Number of employees at this location:** 800. **Number of employees nationwide:** 8,000.

BETH ISRAEL HEALTH CARE SYSTEM
First Avenue at 16th Street, New York NY 10003. 212/420-2000. **Contact:** Human Resources. **World Wide Web address:** http://www.bethisraelny.org. **Description:** An integrated health care system providing a full continuum of primary, acute, tertiary, and long-term care. The system also operates New York HealthCare/Doctors' Walk In, the Japanese Medical Practice, Schnurmacher Nursing Home of Beth Israel Medical Center, Robert Mapplethorpe Residential Treatment Facility, Phillips Beth Israel School of Nursing, Karpas Health Information Center, and D-O-C-S, a multisite, private, group medical practice in the suburbs. **NOTE:** Resumes should be sent to Human Resources, 555 West 57th Street, New York NY 10019; or faxed to: 212/523-7193. **Positions advertised include:** Registered Dietician; Director of Safety; Cathode Laboratory Expiditer; Senior Credentialing Analyst; Patient Advocate; Medical Biller; Medical Administrative Assistant; Senior Systems Analyst; Cardiovascular Technician; Radiological Technician; Registered Nurse; Cardiology Nurse; Nurse Recruiter. **Corporate headquarters location:** This location. **Other locations:** Throughout the New York City metropolitan region. **Subsidiaries include:** Beth Israel Medical Center; St Luke's-Roosevelt Hospital Center. Long Island College Hospital; New York Eye and Ear Infirmary. **Parent company:** Continuum Health Partners Inc.

BROOKS MEMORIAL HOSPITAL
529 Central Avenue, Dunkirk NY 14048. 716/366-1111 ext. 7262. **Fax:** 716/363-7239. **Contact:** Human Resources. **E-mail address:** hrstaffing@brookshospital.org. **World Wide Web address:** http://www.brookshospital.org. **Description:** A nonprofit, 133-bed primary acute care hospital serving the Chautauqua County community. The hospital is JCAHO accredited. Founded in 1898. **NOTE:** Entry-level positions, part-time jobs, and second and third shifts are offered. **Company slogan:** Building a Healthy Community. **Positions advertised**

include: Director of Patient Accounting; Registered Nurse; Nursing Supervisor; Licensed Practical Nurse; Physical Therapist; Respiratory Therapist. **Special programs:** Internships. **President:** Richard Ketcham. **Number of employees:** 500.

CMP INDUSTRIES LLC
413 North Pearl Street, Albany NY 12201. 518/434-3147. **Toll-free phone:** 800/833-2343. **Fax:** 518/434-1288. **Contact:** Phyll Tabone, Director of Administration. **E-mail address:** info@cmpindustries.com. **World Wide Web address:** http://www.cmpindustry.com. **Description:** A manufacturer of dental materials, dental equipment, and other dental supplies. Founded in 1889. **Corporate headquarters location:** This location. **Operations at this facility include:** Manufacturing. **Number of employees at this location:** 65.

CANTON-POTSDAM HOSPITAL
50 Leroy Street, Potsdam NY 13676-1786. 315/265-3300. **Contact:** Human Resources. **E-mail address:** human.resources@cphospital.net. **World Wide Web address:** http://www.cphospital.org. **Description:** CPH provides comprehensive acute medical-surgical care and emergency care, as well as programs in chemical dependency treatment, cardiac care, obstetrics, and physical rehabilitation services. The hospital operates the Warner Cancer Treatment Center with the main hospital campus in Potsdam, and provides services in Canton, Norfolk, and Richville. **Positions advertised include:** Respiratory Therapist; Respiratory Technician; Respiratory Registered Nurse; Allied Health Professional; Building Attendant; Central Supply Aide; Endoscopy Registered Nurse; Nurse Practitioner; Physician Assistant; Medical Technologist; Nurses Aide; Ward Clerk; Certified Nursing Assistant; Licensed Practical Nurse; Patient Representative; Occupational Therapy Assistant; Physical Therapist; Radiologic Technologist; Transcriptionist.

CARDINAL HEALTH
500 Neely Town Road, Montgomery NY 12549. 845/457-2000. **Contact:** Human Resources. **World Wide Web address:** http://www.cardinal.com. **Description:** A producer, developer, and distributor of medical products and technologies for use in hospitals and other health care settings such as surgical apparel, surgical drapes, surgical instruments, and respiratory care products. The company operates through two industry segments: medical specialties, and medical/laboratory products and distribution. **Corporate headquarters location:** Dublin OH. **Operations at this facility include:** Administration; distribution point of medical supplies and equipment to hospitals.

CARDIOVASCULAR RESEARCH FOUNDATION
55 East 59th Street. 6th Floor, New York NY 10022-1122. 212/851-9300. **Fax:** 212/753-7664. **Contact:** Human Resources Department. **E-mail address:** job@crf.org. **World Wide Web address:** http://www.crf.org. **Description:** A not-for-profit research organization dedicated to developing nonsurgical and drug-based treatments of heart and vascular diseases. The Foundation's activities center on the development and investigation of minimally invasive nonsurgical mechanical and pharmacologic treatments of atherosclerotic heart and vascular diseases; the convening of medical thought leaders to develop creative solutions for cardiovascular dysfunction; and the establishment of multidisciplinary collaborative efforts with academics, industry, and government representatives to stimulate new therapies. Founded in 1991. **Positions advertised include:** Clinical Research Associate; Clinical Trials Manager; Director, Regulatory Affairs and Compliance; Senior Clinical Research Associate; Senior Clinical Trials Manager; Medical Proof Reader/Copy Editor; Meeting Planner; Imaging Research Associate; Quality Assurance GLP Specialist.

CATSKILL REGIONAL MEDICAL CENTER
68 Harris Bushville Road, P.O. Box 800, Harris NY 12742-0800. 845/794-3300. **Contact:** Human Resources. **World Wide Web address:** http://www.catskillregional.com. **Description:** A 300-bed hospital. Catskill Regional Medical Center's services include oncology, treatment of biochemical dependence, mental health services, a diabetes unit, a cardiac care unit and a maternity ward. **Number of employees at this location:** 800.

CENTER FOR VETERINARY CARE
236 East 75th Street, New York NY 10021. 212/734-7480. **Contact:** Human Resources. **Description:** A full-service animal hospital offering medical and surgical procedures.

CHILDREN'S HOSPITAL OF BUFFALO
219 Bryant Street, Buffalo NY 14222. 716/878-7000. **Fax:** 716/862-6631. **Contact:** Human Resources. **E-mail address:** kaleidajobs@kaleidahealth.org. **World Wide Web address:** http://www.chob.edu. **Description:** A hospital specializing in the treatment and care of children. **NOTE:** Interested jobseekers should send resumes to 2900 Main Street, Buffalo NY 14214. **Parent company:** Kaleida Health Systems.

CLIFTON SPRINGS HOSPITAL & CLINIC
2 Coulter Road, Clifton Springs NY 14432. 315/462-1327. **Fax:** 716/924-4160. **Contact:** Human Resources. **E-mail address:** humanresources@cshop.com. **World Wide Web address:** http://www.cliftonspringshospital.com. **Description:** A 262-bed hospital with several units including a nursing home, medical/surgical floor, ICU, psychiatry wing, and an alcohol recovery unit. **NOTE:** Human Resources phone: 315/462-1327. **Positions advertised include:** Occupational Therapist; Radiology Technologist; Addictions Counselor; Behavioral Counselor; Psychiatric Technician; Crisis Specialist; Registered Nurse; Licensed Practical Nurse; Certified Nursing Assistant; Hemotologist; Oncologist. **Subsidiaries include:** Finger Lakes Community Cancer Center. **Operations at this facility include:** Administration. **Number of employees at this location:** 800.

COLUMBIA MEMORIAL HOSPITAL
71 Prospect Avenue, Hudson NY 12534. 518/828-7601. **Fax:** 518/828-8243. **Contact:** Human Resources. **World Wide Web address:** http://www.columbiamemorial.com. **Description:** A nonprofit, community-based hospital operating nine satellite facilities serving central New York. **NOTE:** Entry-level positions and second and third shifts are offered. **Company slogan:** Making a Difference! **Positions advertised include:** Certified Nurses Aide; Computer Programmer; Dietician/Nutritionist; Licensed Practical Nurse; Medical Records Technician; Nurse Practitioner; Occupational Therapist; Pharmacist; Physical Therapist; Physician; Project Manager; Radiological Technologist; Registered Nurse; Respiratory Therapist. **Special programs:** Internships. **Number of employees:** 1,000.

COMMUNITY MEMORIAL HOSPITAL
150 Broad Street, Hamilton NY 13346. 315/824-1100. **Contact:** Human Resources. **World Wide Web address:** http://www.communitymemorial.org. **Description:** A regional hospital operating six Family Health Centers and a 120-bed community center and a 40-bed skilled nursing facility all serving the lower Hudson Valley region. **Positions advertised include:** Registered Nurse; Licensed Practical Nurse; Certified Nursing Assistant.

CONIFER PARK
79 Glenridge Road, Glenville NY 12302. 518/399-6446. **Toll-free phone:** 800/989-6446. **Fax:** 518/399-6842. **Contact:** Jenna Bongermino, Human Resources Manager. **E-mail address:** resumes@libertymgt.com. **World Wide Web address:** http://www.libertymgt.com. **Description:** An inpatient and outpatient alcohol and drug abuse rehabilitation

center. **NOTE:** Resumes should be sent to: Liberty Management Corporation, Corporate Human Resources Department, 70 Glenridge Road, Glenville NY 12302; or fax: 518/384-1394. **Positions advertised include:** Accounts Payable Clerk. **Parent company:** Liberty Management Group, Inc. (Ramsey NJ). **Number of employees at this location:** 400.

CONMED CORPORATION
525 French Road, Utica NY 13502. 315/797-8375. **Fax:** 315/735-1523. **Contact:** Human Resources. **E-mail address:** info@conmed.com. **World Wide Web address:** http://www.conmed.com. **Description:** Develops, manufactures, and markets advanced electrosurgical and single-use medical products for surgeons and other critical care providers. The company offers complete electrosurgical systems that include generators and disposable electrosurgical pencils, instruments, and ground pads. Patient care products include disposable electrocardiogram electrodes to monitor the heart, a disposable stabilization device for intravenous therapy, electrodes for neuromuscular stimulation, and various cable and wire products used in medical telemetry. **Positions advertised include:** Machine Operator; Mechanical Engineer; Quality Engineer; Process Technician. **Corporate headquarters location:** This location. **Other area locations:** Rome NY; Utica NY. **Other locations:** CA; CO; FL; TX. **Operations at this facility include:** Administration; Manufacturing; Research and Development. **Listed on:** NASDAQ. **Stock exchange symbol:** CNMD. **Chairman/CEO:** Eugene R. Corasanti. **Annual sales/revenues:** $453 million. **Number of employees at this location:** 200. **Number of employees nationwide:** 2,560.

CORTLAND MEMORIAL HOSPITAL
134 Homer Avenue, P.O. Box 2010, Cortland NY 13045. 607/756-3781. **Fax:** 607/756-3375. **Contact:** Human Resources Department. **E-mail address:** hr@cortlandhospital.org. **World Wide Web address:** http://www.cortlandhospital.org. **Description:** A 180-bed, community-based, nonprofit, acute care hospital. Cortland Memorial Hospital's residential geriatric care facility has 80 beds, offering such services as long-term home health care and a psychiatric unit. Founded in 1891. **NOTE:** Entry-level positions and second and third shifts are offered. **Positions advertised include:** Nuclear Medical Technologist; Registered Nurse; Physical Therapist; Registered Dietician; Medical Technologist. **Subsidiaries include:** CMH Services.

CURATIVE HEALTH SERVICES, INC.
150 Motor Parkway, 4th Floor, Hauppauge NY 11788. 631/232-7000. **Fax:** 631/232-9322. **Contact:** Michelle, LeDell, Director of Human Resources. **World Wide Web address:** http://www.curative.com. **Description:** Curative Health Services primarily manages, on behalf of hospital clients, a nationwide network of wound-care centers. Most of the wound-care centers managed by Curative Health Services are outpatient, although, a small portion are inpatient. The company is also engaged in the research and development of therapeutic products for wound-healing applications. **NOTE:** Jobseekers can see http://www.monster.com for a current the job listing. **Corporate headquarters location:** This location. **Other U.S. locations:** Nationwide. **Listed on:** NASDAQ. **Stock exchange symbol:** CURE. **Chairman:** Joseph L. Feshbach. **Annual sales/revenues:** $139 million. **Number of employees:** 340.

ELLIS HOSPITAL
1101 Nott Street, Schenectady NY 12308. 518/243-4004. **Fax:** 518/243-1402. **Contact:** Human Resources. **World Wide Web address:** http://www.ellishospital.org. **Description:** A regional referral center with 368 beds, an 82-bed nursing home, network of five primary care centers, and a Heart Center providing a variety of services including cardiovascular services, open heart surgery, oncology, neurology, critical care, day surgery, MRI, mental health, and long-term care. **NOTE:** Human Resources phone: 518/243-4004. **Positions advertised include:** Mental Health Assistant; Mental Health Clinical Coordinator; Operating Room Technician; Patient Care Technician; Patient Registrar; Performance Improvement Specialist; Phlebotomist; Physical Therapist; Practice Manager; Project Housekeeper; Psychiatric Social Worker; Radiology Technologist; Patient Registered Nurse; Short Order Cook; Ultrasound Technologist.

ELMIRA PSYCHIATRIC CENTER
100 Washington Street, Elmira NY 14902-2898. 607/737-4711. **Fax:** 607/737-4722. **Contact:** Personnel Office. **World Wide Web address:** http://www.omh.state.ny.us/omhweb/facilities/elpc/facility.htm. **Description:** An inpatient and outpatient psychiatric care facility, the majority of whose patients suffer from chronic mental illness. **NOTE:** Human Resources phone: 607/737-4726. **Positions advertised include:** Residential Program Counselor; Psychiatric Nurse; Psychiatrist; Nurse; Dietitian.

FISHKILL HEALTH CENTER, INC.
130 North Road, Beacon NY 12508-1560. 845/831-8704. **Fax:** 845/831-1124. **Contact:** Human Resources. **Description:** The company operates a 160-bed, skilled care nursing home and the 62-bed Hudson Haven Care Center. Founded in 1973. **NOTE:** Entry-level positions and second and third shifts are offered. **Positions advertised include:** Certified Nurses Aide; Dietician/Nutritionist; Licensed Practical Nurse; Occupational Therapist; Physical Therapist; Registered Nurse; Social Worker. **Special programs:** Internships; Training; Summer Jobs. **Office hours:** Monday - Friday, 8:30 a.m. - 8:00 p.m. **Corporate headquarters location:** This location. **Other U.S. locations:** Wappingers Falls NY. **Owner:** Lynn Kasin. **Number of employees at this location:** 300. **Number of employees nationwide:** 400.

FLUSHING HOSPITAL MEDICAL CENTER
4500 Parsons Boulevard, Flushing NY 11355. 718/670-5000. **Recorded jobline:** 718/670-JOBS. **Contact:** Recruitment Department. **E-mail address:** yng@jhmc.org. **World Wide Web address:** http://www.flushinghospital.org. **Description:** A 428-bed hospital. Flushing Hospital Medical Center is a major teaching affiliate of The Albert Einstein School of Medicine. **NOTE:** Recruitment phone: 718/206-8670. **Number of employees at this location:** 2,400.

FOXCARE NETWORK
dba A.O. FOX HOSPITAL
One Norton Avenue, Oneonta NY 13820. 607/431-5900. **Fax:** 607/431-5160. **Contact:** Keith Valk, Vice President of Human Resources. **E-mail address:** djohnson@foxcarenetwork.com. **World Wide Web address:** http://www.foxcarenetwork.com. **Description:** A hospital and nursing home that provide general medical care to the surrounding community. **NOTE:** Human Resources phone: 607/431-5940. **Positions advertised include:** Anesthesiologist; Environmental Services Aide; Front Desk Coach; General Dentist; Hospitalist; Kitchen Aide; Licensed Practical Nurse; Family Practices Nurse; Pediatrician; Pharmacy Technician; Psychiatrist; Admission Nurse; Radiologist; Registered Nurse. **Special programs:** Internships. **Operations at this facility include:** Administration; Service. **Number of employees at this location:** 740.

GATEWAY COMMUNITY INDUSTRIES, INC.
P.O. Box 5002, Kingston NY 12402-5002. 845/331-1261. **Physical address:** One Amy Kay Parkway, Kingston NY 12401. **Fax:** 845/331-2112. **Contact:** Human Resources Manager. **E-mail address:** humanresources@gatewayindustries.org. **World Wide Web address:** http://www.gatewayindustries.org. **Description:** An independent, non-profit vocational rehabilitation and training center assisting people with mental and physical disabilities to acquire, use, and maintain skills by providing comprehensive employment services including vocational evaluation, job training, job placement, vocational work center employment, supported employment, psychiatric

rehabilitation, continuing day treatment, and residential rehabilitation. **Positions advertised include:** Assistant Residential Director; Nurse Practitioner; Resident Counselor; Senior Counselor; Site Supervisor; Vocational Waiver Counselor.

GENZYME GENETICS
521 West 57th Street, 5th Floor, New York NY 10019. 212/698-0300. **Fax:** 212/258-2137. **Contact:** Human Resources. **World Wide Web address:** http://www.genzymegenetics.com. **Description:** Offers diagnostic testing services for physicians and their patients. **NOTE:** Apply online. **Positions advertised include:** Lead Lab Assistant; Lab Assistant; Histology Technician; Senior A/R Manager; Sales Administration Liaison; Accounts Payable Coordinator; Clinical Research Coordinator; Accounts Payable Supervisor; Sales Representative; Regional Sales Representative; Surgical Pathologist. **Parent company:** Genzyme Corporation.

GERICARE
5 Odell Plaza, Yonkers NY 10701. 914/476-6500. **Contact:** Human Resources. **World Wide Web address:** http://www.gericaremedicalsupply.com. **Description:** A supplier of pharmaceuticals and related products to long-term care facilities, hospitals, and assisted living communities.

GLENS FALLS HOSPITAL
100 Park Street, Glens Falls NY 12801. 518/926-1000. **Contact:** Human Resources. **E-mail address:** humanresources@glensfallshosp.org. **World Wide Web address:** http://www.glensfallshospital.org. **Description:** A full-service, acute care, community hospital providing inpatient and outpatient services. **NOTE:** Human Resources phone: 518/926-1801. **Positions advertised include:** Respite Care Provider; Licensed Practical Nurse; Physical Therapy Assistant; Social Worker; Mammography Technologist; Staff Registered Nurse; Psychiatric Social Worker. **Parent company:** Adirondack Health Services Corporation.

HANGER ORTHOPEDIC GROUP, INC.
151 Hempstead Turnpike, West Hempstead NY 11552. 516/481-9670. **Contact:** Human Resources. **World Wide Web address:** http://www.hanger.com. **Description:** A provider of orthotic and prosthetic rehabilitation services with 600 offices in 43 states. **NOTE:** Send resumes to: Sharon King, Recruitment Manager, P.O. Box 406, Alpharetta GA 30009; phone: 800/303-4969; fax: 800/288-5702; e-mail: sking@hanger.com. **Corporate headquarters location:** Bethesda MD. **Other U.S. locations:** Nationwide. **Operations at this facility include:** Hanger Prosthetics & Orthotics East, Inc. **Listed on:** New York Stock Exchange. **Stock exchange symbol:** HGR. **Number of employees nationwide:** 125. **Annual sales/revenues:** $525.5 million. **Number of employees:** 3,083.

HARMAC MEDICAL PRODUCTS, INC.
2201 Bailey Avenue, Buffalo NY 14211. 716/897-4500. **Fax:** 716/897-0016. **Contact:** Donna Ciulis, Human Resources. **E-mail address:** info@harmac.com. **World Wide Web address:** http://www.harmac.com. **Description:** Manufactures disposable medical devices. **NOTE:** Entry-level positions and second and third shifts are offered. **Special programs:** Internships; Training. **Office hours:** Monday - Friday, 9:00 a.m. - 5:00 p.m. **International locations:** Ireland. **Number of employees at this location:** 450.

HERON HOME & HEALTH CARE AGENCY
168-30 89th Avenue, Jamaica NY 11432. 718/291-8788. **Fax:** 718/291-8852. **E-mail address:** heron@heronhomecare.com. **World Wide Web address:** http://www.heronhomecare.com. **Contact:** Director. **Description:** A home health care agency providing skilled medical professionals to homebound patients and sells surgical and medical equipment. **Corporate headquarters location:** This location. **Other area locations:** Manhattan NY; Long Island NY.

RICHARD H. HUTCHINGS PSYCHIATRIC CENTER
620 Madison Street, Syracuse NY 13210. 315/426-3600. **Fax:** 315/426-3603. **Contact:** Manager of Human Resources Department. **World Wide Web address:** http://www.omh.state.ny.us/omhweb/facilities/hupc/facility.htm. **Description:** The Richard H. Hutchings Psychiatric Center is a comprehensive, community-based mental health system serving the Central New York region specializing in treating individuals with mental illness. The facility offers both inpatient and outpatient services. **Positions advertised include:** Administrative Aide; Social Worker; Recreation Therapist; Housekeeper; Psychiatrist; Food Service Worker; Mental Health Aide; Safety/Security Officer.

ALICE HYDE MEDICAL CENTER
133 Park Street, P.O. Box 729, Malone NY 12953-0729. 518/483-3000. **Fax:** 518/481-2598. **Contact:** Pat Gaglianese, Director of Human Resources. **E-mail address:** pgaglianese@alicehyde.com. **World Wide Web address:** http://www.alicehyde.com. **Description:** A full-service health facility operating a 75-bed medical center and half-a-dozen clinics and medical centers in the central New York region. **Positions advertised include:** Nurse Practitioner; Nuclear Medicine Technologist; X-Ray Technologist; CAT Scan Technician; Respiratory Therapist; Respiratory Technician; Licensed Practical Nurse; Skilled Nurse; Health Center Nurse; Medical Technologist; Concurrent Coder; Ultrasound Technologist; Radiologic Technologist; Registered Nurse.

INTEGRAMED AMERICA, INC.
One Manhattanville Road, 3rd Floor, Purchase NY 10577-2133. 914/253-8000. **Fax:** 914/253-8008. **Contact:** Human Resources. **E-mail address:** info@integramed.com. **World Wide Web address:** http://www.integramed.com. **Description:** Manages and provides services to clinical facilities and physician practices that provide assisted reproductive technology (ART) and infertility services. ART services consist of medical, psychological, and financial consultations and administration of the appropriate ART services and techniques. Infertility services provided include diagnostic testing, fertility drug therapy, tubal surgery, and intrauterine insemination. **Corporate headquarters location:** This location. **Other locations:** Nationwide. **Listed on:** NASDAQ. **Stock exchange symbol:** INMD. **Chairman/President/CEO:** Gerarda Canet. **Annual sales/revenues:** $88 million. **Number of employees:** 660.

J & K HEALTHCARE SERVICES INC.
140 Huguenot Street, New Rochelle NY 10801. 914/633-7810. **Fax:** 914/633-7864. **Contact:** Manager. **Description:** A 24-hour, supplemental staffing, private nursing, and home health care agency offering nursing and personal care services to Westchester County Medicaid recipients.

JACOBI MEDICAL CENTER
1400 Pelham Parkway South, Building 2, Room 101, Bronx NY 10461. 718/918-5000. **Contact:** Barbara Juliano, Manager of Employment & Recruitment. **World Wide Web address:** http://www.ci.nyc.ny.us/html/hhc/jacobi/home.html. **Description:** A major medical center with over 700 beds operating six community-based Family Health Services Clinics and other medical centers throughout New York City. **Special programs:** Internships. **Parent company:** New York Health and Hospitals Corporation. **Operations at this facility include:** Administration; Regional Headquarters; Service. **Annual sales/revenues:** $4.3 billion. **Number of employees at this location:** 5,000. **Number of employees nationwide:** 60,000.

KINGSTON HOSPITAL
396 Broadway, Kingston NY 12401. 845/331-3131. **Fax:** 845/334-2850. **Contact:** Human Resources. **World Wide Web address:** http://www.kingstonhospital.org. **Description:** An 150-bed, acute care hospital. **Parent company:** Kingston Regional Health Care System. **Number of employees at this location:** 680.

MANHATTAN EYE, EAR & THROAT HOSPITAL
210 East 64th Street, New York NY 10021. 212/838-9200. **Fax:** 212/605-3765. **Contact:** Recruitment Manager. **World Wide Web address:** http://www.meeth.org. **Description:** A nonprofit hospital specializing in problems of the eye, ear, and throat. Founded in 1825. **NOTE:** Entry-level positions are offered. Recruitment phone: 212/605-3708. **Number of employees:** 450.

MARY IMMACULATE HOSPITAL SAINT VINCENT CATHOLIC MEDICAL CENTERS
152-11 89th Avenue, Jamaica NY 11432. 718/558-2000. **Fax:** 718/558-2304. **Contact:** M. Caravel, Human Resources. **E-mail address:** mcaravello@svcmcny.org. **World Wide Web address:** http://www.svcmc.org. **Description:** One of the medical centers operated by St. Vincent Catholic Medical Centers in the New York area. **Positions advertised include:** Cat Scan Technician; Chief Physicist; Housekeeping Cleaner; Emergency Department Clerk; Radiology Clerk; Health Information Coordinator; Materials Management Coordinator; Mental Health Psychiatric Technician; Operating Room Technician; Patient Care Associate; Pharmacist; Radiological Technologist; Registered Nurse; Respiratory Therapist; Special Procedures Technician; Staff Nurse; Operating Room Nurse.

MENNEN MEDICAL INC.
10123 Main Street, Clarence NY 14031. 716/759-6921. **Toll-free phone:** 800/223-2201. **Fax:** 215/322-0199. **Contact:** Human Resources Director. **E-mail address:** humanresources_hr@mennenmedical.com. **World Wide Web address:** http://www.mennenmedical.com. **Description:** Mennen Medical Inc. manufactures and sells heart monitors. **Positions advertised include:** Clinical Education Specialist; Clinical Care Registered Nurse; Medical Equipment Sales Representative. **Parent company:** Charterhouse Group International.

MERCY HOSPITAL OF BUFFALO
565 Abbott Road, Buffalo NY 14220. 716/826-7000. **Fax:** 716/828-2700. **Contact:** Human Resources. **World Wide Web address:** http://www.chsbuffalo.org. **Description:** One of the four regional hospitals run by the Catholic Health System. Mercy is a 350-bed community hospital. Mercy's Surgical Services Department has access to multispecialty laser equipment for surgery in ophthalmology, obstetrics and gynecology, otolaryngology, gastroenterology, plastic surgery, and urology. Mercy Hospital of Buffalo also manages the ancillary services of the Mercy Diagnostic & Treatment Center-West Seneca. Founded in 1904. **Parent company:** Catholic Health System.

NATIONAL HOME HEALTH CARE CORPORATION
700 White Plains Road, Suite 275, Scarsdale NY 10583. 914/722-9000. **Fax:** 914/722-9239. **Contact:** Human Resources. **World Wide Web address:** http://www.nhhc.net. **Description:** National Home Health Care, through its subsidiaries, is a national provider of a variety of health related services including home care, general care, nurses, and therapists. **Corporate headquarters location:** This location. **Subsidiaries include:** Health Acquisition Corporation provides home health care services, primarily through certified home health aides and personal care aides in the New York metropolitan area; Brevard Medical Center, Incorporated provides both primary and specialty outpatient medical services in Brevard County FL; First Health, Incorporated provides primary care outpatient medical services in Volusia County FL. **Listed on:** NASDAQ. **Stock exchange symbol:** NHHC. **President/CEO:** Steven Fialkow. **Number of employees nationwide:** 2,200.

THE NEW YORK EYE AND EAR INFIRMARY
310 East 14th Street, Second Avenue, New York NY 10003. 212/979-4000. **Contact:** Human Resources. **World Wide Web address:** http://www.nyee.edu. **Description:** A hospital specializing in ocular and auditory care. Founded in 1820. **NOTE:** To contact Human Resources directly, call 2121/979-4275. **Positions advertised include:** Outpatient Registrar; Medical Records Clerk; Administrative Coordinator; LPN; Registered Nurse; Ancillary Technician; Nursing Assistant; Ophthalmic Technician; Physician Assistant; Social Worker; Security Guard. **Number of employees at this location:** 600.

NEW YORK METHODIST HOSPITAL
506 Sixth Street, Brooklyn NY 11215. 718/768-4305. **Fax:** 718/768-4324. **Contact:** Human Resources. **World Wide Web address:** http://www.nym.org. **Description:** An acute-care teaching hospital affiliated with the Weil Medical College of Cornel University. Founded in 1881. **Positions advertised include:** Food Service Worker; Laundry Worker; Radiation Therapist; Respiratory Therapist; Stationary Engineer; Physician Assistant; Radiologic Technologist; Imaging Technologist; EEG Technician; Lab Supervisor; X-Ray Technician; Senior Accountant; LPN; Registered Nurse; Case Manager; Anesthesia Technician; Nurse Clinical Coordinator. **Operations at this facility include:** Administration; Research and Development. **Number of employees nationwide:** 2,300.

NEW YORK UNIVERSITY MEDICAL CENTER
One Park Avenue, 16th Floor, New York NY 10016. 212/263-1999. **Fax:** 212/404-3897. **Contact:** Recruitment and Staffing Department. **E-mail address:** nyumc-careers@msnyuhealth.org. **World Wide Web address:** http://www.med.nyu.edu. **Description:** A nonprofit medical center engaged in patient care, research, and education. The central component of New York University Medical Center is Tisch Hospital, a 726-bed acute care facility and a major center for specialized procedures in cardiovascular services, neurosurgery, AIDS, cancer treatment, reconstructive surgery, and transplantation. The medical center also includes the Rusk Institute of Rehabilitation Medicine, the Hospital of Joint Diseases, and several medical schools. The Rusk Institute of Rehabilitation Medicine, a 152-bed unit, is one of the world's largest university-affiliated centers for the treatment and training of physically disabled adults and children, as well as for research in rehabilitation medicine. The Hospital of Joint Diseases, with 226 beds, is dedicated solely to neuromusculoskeletal diseases. The School of Medicine, the Post-Graduate Medical School, and the Skirball Institute of Biomolecular Medicine are also part of the medical center. **Positions advertised include:** Assistant Research Scientist; Staff Physical Therapist; Divisional Assistant; Office Assistant; Departmental Assistant; Restricted Funds Manager; Executive Assistant; Assistant Laboratory Technician; Programmer; Receptionist; Network Support Specialist; Nurse Practitioner; Billing Coordinator; Library Assistant; Special Procedure Technician; MRI Specialist; CT Technologist; Business Systems Analyst; Grants Writer. **Special programs:** Internships; Summer Job; Tuition Assistance Program. **Corporate headquarters location:** This location. **Number of employees at this location:** 8,000.

NORTHEAST HEALTH
2212 Burdett Avenue, Troy NY 12180. 518/274-3382. **Contact:** Human Resources. **World Wide Web address:** http://www.nehealth.com. **Description:** A comprehensive network of health care and community services that operates through three hospitals: Albany Memorial Hospital, The Eddy, and Samaritan Hospital. **Positions advertised include:** Home Health Aide; Registered Nurse; LPN; Nursing Assistant; Clinical

Staff Member; Ancillary Staff Member; Support Worker; Manager; Supervisor. **CEO:** Craig Duncan. **Number of employees nationwide:** Over 4,000.

NORTHERN DUTCHESS HOSPITAL
6511 Springbrook Avenue, P.O. Box 5002, Rhinebeck NY 12572-5002. 845/871-3240. **Fax:** 845/871-3252. **Contact:** Human Resources. **World Wide Web address:** http://www.ndhosp.com. **Description:** A hospital. Northern Dutchess Hospital's staff treats the physiological, psychological, social, and spiritual needs of the geriatric and physically challenged by using a multidisciplinary approach. Since 1978, Northern Dutchess Hospital has primary health care centers in five New York communities: Beacon Community Dental (Beacon NY); Germantown Community Dental (Germantown NY); Hyde Park Medical/Dental (Hyde Park NY); Rhinebeck Community Dental (Rhinebeck NY); and Stanfordville Medical/Dental (Stanfordville NY). **NOTE:** Online applications are available. **Positions advertised include:** Food Service Supervisor; Food Service Aide; Billing Representative; Respiratory Therapist; Nurse Practitioner; Physical Therapist; Physical Therapist Aide; Nuclear Medicine Technologist; Registered Nurse Supervisor; LPN; Nurse Aide Coordinator; Surgical Technician; Staff Nurse; Registered Nurse.

NICHOLAS H. NOYES MEMORIAL HOSPITAL
111 Clara Barton Street, Dansville NY 14437. 585/335-6001. **Fax:** 585/335-4250. **Recorded jobline:** 585/335-4233. **Contact:** Human Resources. **E-mail address:** lgriffin@noyes-hospital.org. **World Wide Web address:** http://www.noyes-health.org. **Description:** A nonprofit, 72-bed, full-service health care institution. The hospital provides medical/surgical inpatient services in most medical specialties. Patient care units include emergency room, operating room, obstetrics/gynecology, and intensive care/coronary care. Support services include a clinical laboratory, diagnostic radiology department, electrocardiology, respiratory therapy, physical therapy, and social services. **NOTE:** Resumes submitted via e-mail should be formatted in Microsoft Word or ASCII. **Positions advertised include:** Certified Nursing Aide; Tradesman/Professional Finisher; Registered Nurse Coordinator. **Special programs:** Internships; Summer Jobs. **Number of employees at this location:** 430.

NUTRITION 21
4 Manhattanville Road, Purchase NY 10577-2197. 914/701-4500. **Fax:** 914/696-0860. **Contact:** Human Resources Department. **E-mail address:** mail@nutrition21.com. **World Wide Web address:** http://www.nutrition21.com. **Description:** Develops and markets nutrition products. The company focuses on products with medical value for consumers concerned with cardiovascular health and diabetes. The company is composed of an Ingredients Division, a Consumer Products Division, and Therapeutic Division. Founded in 1982. **Corporate headquarters location:** This location. **Listed on:** NASDAQ. **Stock exchange symbol:** NXXI. **President/CEO/Director:** Gail Montgomery. **Sales/revenue:** $14.7 million. **Number of employees at this location:** 27.

OLEAN GENERAL HOSPITAL
515 Main Street, Olean NY 14760. 716/375-2600. **Fax:** 716/375-6393. **Contact:** Larry Jeffries, Director of Human Resources. **E-mail address:** ljeffries@ogh.org. **World Wide Web address:** http://www.ogh.org. **Description:** A 217-bed, nonprofit, acute care hospital. Supported by over 100 physicians and specialists, Olean General Hospital has a wide range of services such as acute and chronic pain management, allergy immunology, anesthesiology, cardiac rehabilitation, colon and rectal surgery, dermatology, emergency services, endocrinology, family practice, gynecology, lithotripsy, nephrology, obstetrics, occupational medicine, ophthalmology, oral surgery, orthopedic surgery, otolaryngology, pathology, pediatrics, psychiatry, pulmonary medicine, radiology, and urology. Founded in 1912. **NOTE:** To contact Human Resources directly, call 716/375-6152. Interested job seekers may apply online. **Positions advertised include:** Registered Nurse; LPN; Staff Pharmacist; Medical Technologist; Respiratory Therapist.

ONEIDA HEALTHCARE CENTER
321 Genesee Street, Oneida NY 13421. 315/363-6000. **Fax:** 315/361-2240. **Contact:** John G. Margo, Director of Personnel. **E-mail address:** jobs@oneidahealthcare.org. **World Wide Web address:** http://www.oneidahealthcare.org. **Description:** A 101-bed acute care hospital and 160-bed extended care facility adjoining three outpatient clinics serving the health care needs of Madison County in central New York. **Positions advertised include:** Registered Nurse; LPN; Child Care Assistant. **Office hours:** Monday – Friday, 9:00 a.m. – 3:00 p.m. **Corporate headquarters location:** This location. **Operations at this facility include:** Administration; Service. **Number of employees at this location:** 950.

PARK EAST ANIMAL HOSPITAL
52 East 64th Street, New York NY 10021. 212/832-8417. **Fax:** 212/355-3620. **Contact:** Vicki Ungar, Office Manager. **World Wide Web address:** http://www.parkeastanimalhospital.com. **Description:** A 24-hour small animal hospital offering medical, nursing, and surgical services for pets. This location also hires seasonally. Founded in 1961. **Special programs:** Internships; Training; Summer Jobs. **Corporate headquarters location:** This location. **President:** Dr. Lewis Berman. **Number of employees at this location:** 25.

PFIZER
235 East 42nd Street, New York NY 10017. 212/573-2323. **Recorded jobline:** 212/733-4150. **Contact:** Employee Resources. **E-mail address:** resumes@pfizer.com. **World Wide Web address:** http://www.pfizer.com. **Description:** A leading pharmaceutical company that distributes products concerning cardiovascular health, central nervous system disorders, infectious diseases, and women's health worldwide. The company's brand-name products include Benadryl, Ben Gay, Cortizone, Desitin, Halls, Listerine, Sudafed, and Zantac 75. **Company slogan:** We're part of the cure. **NOTE:** Interested job seekers may apply online. **Positions advertised include:** Marketing Manager; Conventions Manager; Corporate Philanthropy Programs Manager; Administrative Assistant; Senior Human Resources Manager; Capacity and Inventory Analysis Manager; Corporate Counsel; Product Manager; Assistant Director of Corporate Media Relations; Regional Medical Research Specialist; Business Technology Manager. **Corporate headquarters location:** This location. **Other U.S. locations:** Nationwide. **International locations:** Worldwide. **Subsidiaries include:** Pfizer Animal Health Group; Pfizer Consumer Products Division; Pfizer Hospital Products Group; Pfizer International; Pfizer Pharmaceutical Group; Pfizer Specialty Chemicals. **Listed on:** New York Stock Exchange. **Stock exchange symbol:** PFE. **Number of employees worldwide:** 46,000.

PHARMACARE
80 Air Park Drive, Ronkonkoma NY 11779. 631/981-0034. **Fax:** 631/981-0722. **Contact:** Human Resources. **World Wide Web address:** http://www.pharmacare.com. **Description:** A national provider of outpatient drug therapies and a broad array of distribution, case management, and support services to meet the ongoing needs of patients with chronic medical conditions, the health professionals who care for them, and the third-party payers responsible for such care. The company's services include distribution of prescription drug therapies, drug utilization review programs, patient compliance monitoring, psychosocial support services, and assistance in insurance investigation, verification, and reimbursement. **Parent company:** CVS Corporation (Woonsocket RI). **Other U.S. locations:** Nationwide.

QUANTRONIX
41 Research Way, East Setauket NY 11733. 631/784-

6100. **Fax:** 631/784-6101. **Contact:** Human Resources. **E-mail address:** hr@quantronixlasers.com. **World Wide Web address:** http://www.quantronixlasers.com. **Description:** Manufactures laser systems for dental and medical uses. The company also manufactures lasers for industrial purposes. **NOTE:** Interested job seekers may apply online. **Positions advertised include:** High Power Industrial Laser Scientist; Diode-Pumped Laser Engineer; Ultrafast Systems Scientist; Applications Technician; Micro-Electronic Technician; Product Manager; Customer Service Representative; Marketing/Graphic Artist; CNC Operator; Optical Inspection Technician; Buyer; Senior Planner; Stockroom Clerk. **Corporate headquarters location:** This location. **International locations:** Germany; Malaysia; France; India; Japan.

RICHMOND CHILDREN'S CENTER
100 Corporate Drive, Yonkers NY 10701. 914/968-7170. **Contact:** Director of Human Resources. **World Wide Web address:** http://www.richmondgroup.org. **Description:** A nonprofit, intermediate care facility (residential to long-term) for individuals with severe to profound physical and developmental disabilities. Services in the main facility include medical care; recreational services; and physical, language, occupational, and speech therapies. Richmond Children's Center offers other services in the community including case management, early intervention, group homes, and respite programs (for children with special needs who are cared for at home). **Number of employees at this location:** 325.

ROCHESTER GENERAL HOSPITAL
1425 Portland Avenue, Rochester NY 14621. 585/922-4000. **Contact:** Human Resources. **World Wide Web address:** http://www.viahealth.org. **Description:** A hospital with approximately 450 beds serving the Rochester area.

SACHEM ANIMAL HOSPITAL
227 Union Avenue, Holbrook NY 11741. 631/467-2121. **Contact:** Human Resources. **World Wide Web address:** http://www.sachemanimalhospital.com. **Description:** Sachem Animal Hospital provides general medical and surgical services, dental services, and boarding for domestic and exotic pets. The hospital also specializes in reproduction and infertility services.

ST. CLARE'S HOSPITAL
600 McClellan Street, Schenectady NY 12304. 518/347-5630. **Toll-free phone:** 800/462-1713. **Fax:** 518/347-5522. **Contact:** Peter Jones, Employment Coordinator. **E-mail address:** jobs@stclares.org. **World Wide Web address:** http://www.stclares.org. **Description:** A 200-bed acute care hospital. Founded in 1949. **Positions advertised include:** Registered Nurse; LPN; Clinical Leader; Nursing Supervisor; Supervisor/Educator; Cardiology Technician; Certified Respiratory Therapy Technician; Chaplain; Diet Technician; Medical Technologist; Patient Care Dietician; Pharmacist; Physical Therapy Assistant; Security Officer; Microbiology Technical Specialist; Ultrasound Technologist; Film Librarian; Receptionist; Unit Secretary; Weekend Clerk. **Office hours:** Monday - Friday, 10:00 a.m. - 2:00 p.m. **Corporate headquarters location:** This location. **Operations at this facility include:** Administration. **President/CEO:** Paul Chodkowski. **Number of employees at this location:** 1,150.

ST. JOSEPH'S HOSPITAL
555 East Market Street, Elmira NY 14901. 607/737-1518. **Fax:** 607/737-7837. **Contact:** Kip Burlew, Human Resources. **E-mail address:** kburlew@jstjosephs.org. **World Wide Web address:** http://www.stjosephs.org. **Description:** A hospital that maintains an acute care center, an emergency care center, and a chemotherapy outpatient center. **NOTE:** Jobseekers may apply online. **Positions advertised include:** Certified Occupational Therapy Assistant; Registered Nurse; Pharmacist. **Special programs:** Internships. **CEO:** Sister Marie Castagnaro. **Number of employees at this location:** 1,100.

ST. LUKE'S CORNWALL HOSPITAL
19 Laurel Avenue, Cornwall NY 12518. 845/534-7711. **Contact:** Human Resources. **E-mail address:** jobs@slh-tch.org. **World Wide Web address:** http://www.stlukeshospital.org. **Description:** A 125-bed acute care, community-based, nonprofit hospital. St. Luke's Cornwall Hospital has 20 additional beds devoted to mental health care. **NOTE:** Resumes may be mailed to the Human Resources Department, 70 Dubois Street, Newburgh NY 12550. **Positions advertised include:** ASA Counselor; Nutritional Services Associate; Environmental Services Associate; Guest Services Associate; HVAC Technician; Maintenance Associate; Methadone Counselor; Registered Nurse; Occupational Therapist; Patient Accounting Associate; Physical Therapist; Programmer; Security and Safety Officer; Switchboard Operator; Valet Parking Attendant. **Office hours:** Monday – Friday, 8:00 a.m. – 5:00 p.m. **Other area locations:** Newburgh NY. **Number of employees at this location:** 500. **Number of employees statewide:** Over 1,700.

ST. LUKE'S-ROOSEVELT HOSPITAL CENTER
1111 Amsterdam Avenue, New York NY 10025. 212/523-4000. **Contact:** Recruitment. **World Wide Web address:** http://www.wehealnewyork.org. **Description:** A 1,315-bed, teaching hospital associated with Columbia University. **NOTE:** Resumes should be sent to Human Resources, 555 West 57th Street, 19th Floor, New York NY 10019 or faxed to: 212/523-7193. **Positions advertised include:** Nurse Practitioner; Neurophysiology Technician; Occupational Therapist; General Accounting Manager; Nurse Supervisor; Registered Dietician; Expeditor; Director of Safety; Patient Advocate; Medical Biller; Medical Administrative Assistant; Senior Systems Analyst; Nurse Recruiter; Medical Office Coordinator; Nurse Educator; EEG Technician; Senior Financial Analyst; Epilepsy Monitoring Technician. **Special programs:** Internships. **Parent company:** Continuum Health Partners, Inc. **Number of employees at this location:** 6,000.

ST. MARY'S HOSPITAL AT AMSTERDAM
427 Guy Park Avenue, Amsterdam NY 12010. 518/841-7152. **Fax:** 518/841-7158. **Recorded jobline:** 518/841-7155. **Contact:** Human Resources. **E-mail address:** hremp@smha.org. **World Wide Web address:** http://www.smha.org. **Description:** A community hospital that provides acute care as well as both inpatient and outpatient services for mental health and alcoholism treatment. **NOTE:** Interested job seekers may apply online. **Positions advertised include:** Alcoholism Counselor; Certified Nurse Aide; Clinical Systems Coordinator; Certified Coder Analyst; Financial Services Manager; LPN; Pharmacist; Psychiatric Social Worker; Psychiatric Assistant; Radiologic Technologist; Registered Nurse; Sterile Processing Technician; Third Party Payor Representative. **Special programs:** Internships. **Parent company:** Carondelet Health System. **Number of employees at this location:** 850.

ST. PETER'S HEALTHCARE SERVICES
310 South Manning Boulevard, Albany NY 12208. 518/525-2300. **Contact:** Human Resources. **E-mail address:** jobs@stpetershealthcare.org. **World Wide Web address:** http://www.stpetershealthcare.org. **Description:** Provides comprehensive health care services including hospital, primary and preventative care, educational services, addiction services, long-term care, childcare, and rehabilitation services as a member of the Eastern Mercy Health System.

ST. PETER'S HOSPITAL
315 South Manning Boulevard, Albany NY 12208. 518/525-1550. **Contact:** Human Resources. **E-mail address:** jobs@stpetershealthcare.org. **World Wide Web address:** http://www.stpetershealthcare.org. **Description:** A nonprofit general hospital. **Positions advertised include:** Accounting Assistant; Administrative Director of Laboratory Services; Audiologist; Birth Registrar; CT Technologist; Cardiovascular Technologist; Certified Home Health

Aide; Clinical Care Coordinator; Clinical Nurse Specialist; Computer Operator; Dietician; Ambulatory Sites Director; Fitness Instructor; Food Service Worker; Hemodialysis Technician; Hospice Patient Care Assistant; Housekeeper; Medical Records Clerk; Laboratory Assistant. **Special programs:** Internships. **Corporate headquarters location:** This location. **Parent company:** St. Peter's Health Care Services.

SAMARITAN HOSPITAL
NORTHEAST HEALTH
2212 Burdett Avenue, Troy NY 12180. 518/274-3382. **Fax:** 518/271-3781. **Contact:** Human Resources. **World Wide Web address:** http://www.nehealth.com. **Description:** A hospital. **Positions advertised include:** Adjunct Instructor; Behavioral Health Unit Assistant; Cardiology/Neurology Technician; Clerical Associate; Clinical Dietician; Coder; Patient Accounting Liaison; Console Attendant; Courier; Environmental Services Technician; Interviewer; Laboratory Client Service Specialist; Behavioral Health Manager; Medical Receptionist; Medical Technologist.

SAMARITAN MEDICAL CENTER
830 Washington Street, Watertown NY 13601. 315/785-4000. **Toll-free phone:** 877/888-6138. **Fax:** 315/786-4939. **Contact:** Human Resources. **World Wide Web address:** http://www.samaritanhealth.com. **Description:** A 319-bed acute care hospital and referral center that offers comprehensive medical services. **Positions advertised include:** Certified Nursing Assistant; LPN; Registered Nurse; Nursing Supervisor; Environmental Service Worker; Critical Care Unit Clerk; Clinical Leader; Staff Development Educator; Food Service Worker; Laboratory Technician; Sleep Technician; Medical Technologist; Activities Aide; Data Quality Supervisor; Dosimetrist; Imaging Services Assistant. **Number of employees at this location:** 1,100.

SARATOGA HOSPITAL
211 Church Street, Saratoga Springs NY 12866. 518/587-3222. **Fax:** 518/583-8428. **Contact:** Human Resources. **World Wide Web address:** http://www.saratogacare.org. **Description:** A community hospital that maintains an acute care and skilled nursing facility. Founded in 1892. **Positions advertised include:** Director of Food Services; Director of Volunteers; Emergency Room Technician; Environmental Services Associate; Medical Technologist; Mental Health Therapy Assistant; Office Assistant; Office Coordinator; Phlebotomist; Registered Nurse; Registrar; Respiratory Therapist; Secretary/Transcriptionist. **Parent company:** Saratoga Care.

HENRY SCHEIN, INC.
135 Duryea Road, Melville NY 11747. 631/843-5500. **Contact:** Human Resources. **World Wide Web address:** http://www.henryschein.com. **Description:** Manufactures and distributes dental and medical instruments. Henry Schein, Incorporated serves the dental, medical, and veterinary markets. **Positions advertised include:** Associate Financial Analyst; Veterinary Division Telesales Representative; Hyperion Senior Systems Analyst; Credit and Collections Representative. **Corporate headquarters location:** This location. **Other U.S. locations:** Nationwide. **International locations:** Worldwide. **Operations at this facility include:** Sales. **Listed on:** NASDAQ. **Stock exchange symbol:** HSIC. **President/CEO/Chairman:** Stanley M. Bergman. **Sales/revenue:** $2.8 billion. **Number of employees at this location:** 1,000. **Number of employees nationwide:** 1,700.

SETON HEALTH SYSTEM
ST. MARY'S HOSPITAL OF TROY
1300 Massachusetts Avenue, Troy NY 12180. 518/268-5525. **Fax:** 518/268-5733. **Contact:** Human Resources. **E-mail address:** jobs@setonhealth.org. **World Wide Web address:** http://www.setonhealth.org. **Description:** A comprehensive health care system serving the tri-county area. St. Mary's Hospital (also at this location) is the anchor hospital in the Seton Health System. **Positions advertised include:** Nuclear Medicine Technologist; Phlebotomist; Registered Nurse; Respiratory Therapist; Multicraftsman/Construction Worker; Patient Service Representative; LPN. **Corporate headquarters location:** This location.

SOUTH BEACH PSYCHIATRIC CENTER
777 Seaview Avenue, Staten Island NY 10305. 718/667-2726. **Fax:** 718/667-2467. **Contact:** Human Resources. **World Wide Web address:** http://www.omh.state.ny.us. **Description:** South Beach Psychiatric Center is a New York State Office of Mental Health outpatient facility that is organized to deliver comprehensive mental health services to people in West Brooklyn, Staten Island, and New York City. **Positions advertised include:** Licensed Psychologist; Mental Health Therapy Aide; Nurse Administrator; Community Mental Health Nurse; Psychiatrist; Director of Nursing. **Corporate headquarters location:** Albany NY. **Operations at this facility include:** Administration. **Number of employees at this location:** 1,100.

TENDER LOVING CARE/STAFF BUILDERS
1983 Marcus Avenue, Suite 200, Lake Success NY 11042. 516/358-1000. **Fax:** 516/358-2465. **Contact:** Human Resources Department. **World Wide Web address:** http://www.tlcathome.com. **Description:** A home health care agency. **Corporate headquarters location:** This location. **Other U.S. locations:** Nationwide. **Operations at this facility include:** Administration. **Number of employees at this location:** 300. **Number of employees nationwide:** 20,000.

TERESIAN HOUSE NURSING HOME
200 Washington Avenue Extension, Albany NY 12203. 518/456-2000. **Fax:** 518/456-1142. **Contact:** Human Resources. **E-mail address:** info@teresianhouse.com. **World Wide Web address:** http://www.teresianhouse.com. **Description:** A nonprofit, 300-bed skilled and health-related nursing home. Teresian House has a dementia care and an Alzheimer's care unit, which provides private rooms for all residents. Founded in 1974. **Company slogan:** Together we are one. **Positions advertised include:** Assistant Director of Nurse; Registered Nurse; Licensed Practical Nurse; Certified Nurse Aide; Ward Clerk; Light Duty Mechanic; Food Service Worker; Activities Coordinator. **Special programs:** Internships; Summer Jobs. **Number of employees at this location:** 385.

THOMPSON HEALTH
350 Parrish Street, Canandaigua NY 14424. 585/396-6000. **Fax:** 585/396-6480. **Contact:** Susan Mahoney, Director of Associates. **E-mail address:** careers@thompsonhealth.com. **World Wide Web address:** http://www.thompsonhealth.com. **Description:** A locally owned, nonprofit, community-based health care facility comprised of a 113-bed hospital, a 188-bed nursing home, and a planned senior living community. Founded in 1904. **NOTE:** Entry-level positions, part-time jobs, and second and third shifts are offered. **Company slogan:** Excellence in health care. **Positions advertised include:** Asthma Educator; Clinical Secretary; EMT; Executive Assistant; Licensed Practical Nurse; Certified Nurse Aide; Nurse Practitioner; Paramedic. **Special programs:** Training; Summer Jobs. **Office hours:** Monday - Friday, 8:00 a.m. - 4:30 p.m. **CEO:** Linda Janczak. **Annual sales/revenues:** $51 - $100 million. **Number of employees at this location:** 1,100.

TRIZETTO GROUP, INC.
1700 Broadway, New York NY 10019. 212/765-8500. **Contact:** Human Resources. **World Wide Web address:** http://www.trizetto.com. **Description:** Develops health management software for insurance agencies and health care providers. **NOTE:** Interested jobseekers should send resumes to 1085 Morris Avenue, Union NJ 07083. **Corporate headquarters**

location: Newport Beach CA. **Listed on:** NASDAQ. **Stock exchange symbol:** TZIX.

TYCO HEALTHCARE KENDALL
5439 State Route 40, Argyle NY 12809. 518/638-6101. **Contact:** Human Resources. **World Wide Web address:** http://www.tycohealthcare.com. **Description:** Engaged in the manufacture of medical tubing and catheters.

UNITED MEMORIAL MEDICAL CENTER
127 North Street, Batavia NY 14020. 585/343-6030. **Contact:** Human Resources Assistant. **Description:** An acute care hospital. St. Jerome Hospital is a member of Mercy Health System of Western New York and Eastern Mercy Health System. **Special programs:** Internships. **Corporate headquarters location:** Buffalo NY. **Operations at this facility include:** Administration; Divisional Headquarters; Service. **Number of employees at this location:** 450.

U.S. DEPARTMENT OF VETERANS AFFAIRS STRATTON VETERANS ADMINISTRATION MEDICAL CENTER
113 Holland Avenue, Albany NY 12208. 518/626-5000. **Contact:** Human Resources. **World Wide Web address:** http://www.va.gov. **Description:** A medical center operated by the U.S. Department of Veterans Affairs. From 54 hospitals in 1930, the VA health care system has grown to include 171 medical centers; more than 364 outpatient, community, and outreach clinics; 130 nursing home care units; and 37 domiciliary residences. VA operates at least one medical center in each of the 48 contiguous states, Puerto Rico, and the District of Columbia. With approximately 76,000 medical center beds, VA treats nearly 1 million patients in VA hospitals; 75,000 in nursing home care units; and 25,000 in domiciliary residences. VA's outpatient clinics register approximately 24 million visits per year. **Number of employees at this location:** 1,765.

WATERVIEW NURSING CARE CENTER
119-15 27th Avenue, Flushing NY 11354. 718/461-5000. **Fax:** 718/321-1984. **Contact:** Personnel. **Description:** A 200-bed facility that offers specialized, long-term nursing care to chronically ill individuals of all ages. Waterview's in-house medical staff provides care in areas that include psychiatry, psychotherapy, dentistry, podiatry, otolaryngology, ophthalmology, hematology, urology, neurology, optometry, portable X-rays, and lab work. **Special programs:** Training; Summer Jobs. **Office hours:** Monday - Friday, 9:00 a.m. - 5:00 p.m. **Number of employees at this location:** 280.

WEIGHT WATCHERS INTERNATIONAL INC.
175 Crossways Park West, Woodbury NY 11797. 516/390-1400. **Contact:** Human Resources. **World Wide Web address:** http://www.weightwatchers.com. **Description:** Conducts and supervises franchised weight-control classes in 21 countries, markets packaged products through its food licensees, and publishes the *Weight Watchers* magazine in three countries. **Corporate headquarters location:** This location. **Listed on:** New York Stock Exchange. **Stock exchange symbol:** WTW.

WELCH ALLYN MEDICAL PRODUCTS
4341 State Street Road, Skaneateles Falls NY 13153-0220. 315/685-4556. **Toll-free phone:** 800-535-6663. **Fax:** 315/685-4091. **Contact:** Human Resources. **World Wide Web address:** http://www.welchallyn.com. **Description:** A leading manufacturer of medical diagnostic and therapeutic devices, cardiac defibrillators, patient monitoring systems, and miniature precision lamps. Founded in 1915. **Positions advertised include:** Director Global Customer Development; Document Control Manager; Engineer II/ PE Automation/Process Engineer; Engineer II/ PE; Electrical/Mfg Engineer; Process Engineer; Regulatory Affairs Engineer; Sales Trace Specialist; Senior Regulatory Affairs Engineer.

WESTSIDE VETERINARY CENTER
220 West 83rd Street, New York NY 10024. 212/580-1800. **Contact:** Human Resources. **Description:** An animal hospital offering medical, surgical, and dental services.

WOMEN'S CHRISTIAN ASSOCIATION HOSPITAL
207 Foote Avenue, Jamestown NY 14702. 716/664-8227. **Fax:** 716/664-8307. **Contact:** Gayle Lutgen, Human Resource. **E-mail address:** Gayle.Lutgen@wcahospital.org. **World Wide Web address:** http://www.wcahospital.org. **Description:** A 342-bed, nonsectarian, nonprofit, regional medical center. Founded in 1885. **Positions advertised include:** Staff Development Clinical Educator; Clinical Dietician; Nurse Manager; Registered Respiratory Therapist; Registered Nurse. **Office hours:** Monday - Friday, 7:00 a.m. - 5:00 p.m. **Number of employees at this location:** 1,300.

North Carolina

ALPHA OMEGA HEALTH INC.
5950 Six Forks Road, Raleigh NC 27609. 919/844-1008. **Toll-free phone:** 800/525-5293. **Fax:** 919/844-0042. **Contact:** Kathryn Ray, Human Resources. **E-mail address:** kray@aohealth.com. **World Wide Web address:** http://www.aohealth.com. **Description:** A home health care agency that also offers nurse-staffing services. Founded 1989. **Positions advertised include:** Residential Habitation Technician; Qualified Professional. **Corporate headquarters location:** This location. **Other area locations:** Boone NC; Burnsville NC; Chapel Hill NC; Greenville NC; Lenoir NC; Smithfield NC; Wilmington NC; Winston-Salem NC.

CENTRAL PRISON HOSPITAL
1300 Western Boulevard, Raleigh NC 27606. 919/733-0800x411. **Fax:** 919/715-2645. **Contact:** Personnel. **World Wide Web address:** http://www.doc.state.nc.us/DOP/prisons/Central.htm. **Description:** A prison hospital. **NOTE:** Job seekers must complete an application to be considered for employment. Specific contact information is available with listed jobs. **Positions advertised include:** Dentist; RN; LPN; Staff Psychologist; Correctional Officer. **Number of employees at this location:** 500.

CHARTER MEDICAL, LTD.
3948-A West Point Boulevard, Winston-Salem NC 27013. 866/458-3116. **Fax:** 336/714-4241. **Contact:** Human Resources. **E-mail address:** info@lydall.com. **World Wide Web address:** http://www.chartermedical.com. **Description:** Provides products to facilitate the collection, separation, manipulation, transportation, storage, and administration of blood and blood components and vital fluids in the biotech and pharmaceutical industries. The company's medical devices include transfusion and cell therapy products such as platelet sampling devices, stem cell/oncology products, and blood transfusion products as well as biopharmaceutical containers. Charter also provides contract manufacturing services. **Positions advertised include:** Manufacturing Engineer. **Parent company:** Lydall Company.

MOSES CONE HEALTH SYSTEM
1200 North Elm Street, Greensboro NC 27401-1020. 336/832-7400. **Toll-free phone:** 800/476-6737. **Fax:** 336/832-2999. **Contact:** Corporate Recruitment. **E-mail address:** recruitment@mosescone.com. **World Wide Web address:** http://www.mosescone.com. **Description:** A nonprofit hospital system with operations at the Moses H. Cone Memorial Hospital (547 beds), the Women's Hospital of Greensboro (130 beds), and Wesley Long Community Hospital. **Positions advertised include:** Certified Medical Assistant; Clinical Nutritionist; CRNA; Development Coordinator; LPN; Physical Therapist Assistant; Physician Practice Administrator; RN. **Corporate headquarters location:** This location. **Operations at this facility include:** Administration. **Number of employees at this location:** 6,800.

DAVIS REGIONAL MEDICAL CENTER
P.O. Box 1823, Statesville NC 28687. 704/873-7110. **Physical address:** 218 Old Marksville Road, Statesville NC 28625. **Fax:** 704/838-7114. **Recorded jobline:** 704/838-7500. **Contact:** Alison Kay, Human Resources. **E-mail address:** alison.kay@drmc.hma-corp.com. **World Wide Web address:** http://www.davisregional.com. **Description:** A 149-bed, state-of-the-art, acute care medical center. **Positions advertised include:** Licensed Physical Therapy Assistant; Medical Technologist; MRI Technologist; RN; Telemetry Technician. **Special programs:** Internships. **Corporate headquarters location:** This location. **Parent company:** Health Trust, Inc. **Operations at this facility include:** Administration; Service. **Number of employees at this location:** 540.

DURHAM REGIONAL HOSPITAL
3643 North Roxboro Road, Durham NC 27704. 919/470-4000. **Toll-free phone:** 888/275-3853. **Fax:** 919/470-7376. **Recorded jobline:** 919/470-JOBS; 800/233-3313. **Contact:** Human Resources. **World Wide Web address:** http://www.durhamregional.org. **Description:** A full-service hospital. **Positions advertised include:** Clerk; Health Unit Coordinator; Chief Operating Officer; Clinical Speech Pathologist; Dietitian Clinician; Director of Radiology; Financial Management Analyst; Laboratory Supervisor; Manager CSR; Occupational Therapist; Physical Therapist; Senior Physicians Assistant; Security Captain; Clinical Nurse, Various Departments; Nurse Practitioner; Nursing Care Assistant; Food Services Supervisor; Patient Transporter; Computer Operator; Interventional Technologist; Pharmacy Technician; Radiologic Technician; Respiratory Care Practitioner; Surgical Technician. **Parent company:** Duke University Health System.

ECKERD YOUTH ALTERNATIVES INC.
4654 High Rock Road, Boomer NC 28606. 336/921-2222. **Contact:** Human Resources. **E-mail address:** recruiting@eckerd.org. **World Wide Web address:** http://www.eckerd.org. **Description:** An alternative treatment program for at-risk youths. Eckerd provides therapeutic treatment in outdoor settings, residential treatment and community-based programs for juvenile offenders, and early intervention and prevention curriculum. **NOTE:** Resumes may be faxed to Renee H. at 727/461-4387. **Positions advertised include:** Registered Nurse. **Corporate headquarters location:** Clearwater FL. **Other area locations:** Statewide. **Other U.S. locations:** TN; GA; OH; VT; NH; RI.

GRACE HOSPITAL
2201 South Sterling Street, Morganton NC 28655. 828/580-5000. **Fax:** 828/580-5609. **Contact:** Human Resources. **World Wide Web address:** http://www.blueridgehealth.org/grace-hospital.html. **Description:** A nonprofit, full-service hospital. **NOTE:** Second and third shifts are offered. **Positions advertised include:** Admitting Nurse; Aerobic/Aquatic/Pilates Instructor; Catering Supervisor; CNA; RN; Chief Radiologic Technologist; Coder; Director of Maternal Child Health Services; Exercise Physiologist; Food Service Assistant; Front Desk Clerk; Housekeeper; LPN; Materials Manager; Psychiatric Technician; Social Worker; Secretary. **Special programs:** Internships; Apprenticeships; Summer Jobs. **Parent company:** BlueRidge HealthCare System. **Number of employees at this location:** 800.

MEDCATH CORPORATION
10720 Sikes Place, Suite 300, Charlotte NC 28277. 704/708-6610. **Contact:** Human Resources. **World Wide Web address:** http://www.medcath.com. **Description:** Develops and manages cardiovascular care hospitals and catheterization laboratories. **Positions advertised include:** Senior Coding Consultant. **Corporate headquarters location:** This location. **Other area locations:** Greensboro NC; Raleigh NC; Wilmington NC. **Other U.S. locations:** Nationwide. **Listed on:** NASDAQ. **Stock exchange symbol:** MDTH.

MISSION ST. JOSEPH'S HOSPITAL
509 Biltmore Avenue, Asheville NC 28801. 828/213-5600. **Recorded jobline:** 828/213-4400. **Contact:** Human Resources. **World Wide Web address:** http://www.missionhospitals.org. **Description:** A hospital licensed for over 800 beds and bassinets. The hospital has been ranked as a top 50 hospital for heart and heart surgery services, and a top 100 for breast cancer research, among other awards. **NOTE:** To apply for clerical temp-to-hire positions, please go through Kelly Services. **Positions advertised include:** Nuclear Medicine Technologist; Lead Physicist; Clinical Trials Manager; Pharmacy Manager; Respiratory Therapist. **Corporate headquarters location:** This location. **Number of employees at this location:** 5,600.

NORTH CAROLINA DEPARTMENT OF HEALTH AND HUMAN SERVICES JOHN UMSTEAD HOSPITAL
1003 12th Street, Butner NC 27509. 919/575-2553. **Fax:** 919/575-7550. **Recorded jobline:** 919/575-7680. **Contact:** Pat Rust, Human Resources. **E-mail address:** pat.rust@ncmail.net. **World Wide Web address:** http://www.dhhs.state.nc.us. **Description:** A psychiatric hospital providing mental health treatment and psycho-educational rehabilitation. The hospital also operates the Butner Adolescent Treatment Center, which is composed of BATC, a locked residential facility, and Oakview Residential Treatment Program, a nonsecure apartment facility. **Positions advertised include:** Health Care Technician; LPN; RN; Clinical Pharmacist; Clinical Social Worker; Cook; Food Service Assistant; Internal Escort; Housekeeper; Occupational Therapist; Painter; Physician; Quality Assurance Specialist; Substance Abuse Counselor; Teacher. **Number of employees at this location:** 1,400.

NORTHERN HOSPITAL OF SURRY COUNTY
830 Rockford Street, Suite 6, P.O. Box 1101, Mount Airy NC 27030. 336/719-7110. **Fax:** 336/719-7473. **Contact:** Human Resources. **E-mail address:** recruiting@nhsc.org. **World Wide Web address:** http://www.northernhospital.com. **Description:** A full-service hospital that offers home health care services in addition to in-hospital services. **Positions advertised include:** Speech Therapist; Occupational Therapist; PRN; CRNA; RN; Coding Specialist; Security Officer; Spanish Interpreter; Project Manager; Patient Registration Representative; HVAC Mechanic; Infection Control/Quality Review Practitioner. **Corporate headquarters location:** This location. **Other U.S. locations:** Cana VA. **Listed on:** Privately held. **Number of employees at this location:** 200.

ONSLOW MEMORIAL HOSPITAL
317 Western Boulevard, Jacksonville NC 28541. 910/577-2345. **Recorded jobline:** 910/577-2250. **Contact:** Human Resources. **E-mail address:** employment@onslowmemorial.org. **World Wide Web address:** http://www.onslowmemorial.org. **Description:** A hospital equipped with 162 beds, treating more than 37,000 patients every year. **Positions advertised include:** Occupational Therapist; Transcriptionist Coordinator; Radiologic Technician; RN, Various Departments; PC Technician; Sterile Processing and Distribution Technician; Speech/Language Pathologist; MRI Technician; Lab Assistant. **Special programs:** Internships. **Number of employees at this location:** 1000.

MARGARET R. PARDEE MEMORIAL HOSPITAL
800 North Justice Street, Hendersonville NC 28791. 828/696-4209. **Fax:** 828/696-1208. **Recorded jobline:** 828/696-4700. **Contact:** Human Resources. **E-mail address:** human.resources@pardeehospital.org. **World Wide Web address:** http://www.pardeehospital.org. **Description:** A 262-bed, acute care hospital. **Positions advertised include:** Director of Rehab Services; ER Registration Clerk; Switchboard Relief; File Room

Receptionist; RN; CNA; Phlebotomist; Clinical Dietician; Certified Surgical Technician; Pharmacist; Radiation Therapist; Registered Respiratory Therapist; Trayline Supervisor; Nutrition Assistant; Supply Technician.

PITT COUNTY MEMORIAL HOSPITAL
UNIVERSITY HEALTH SYSTEMS OF EASTERN CAROLINA
2100 Statonsburg Road, P.O. Box 6028, Greenville NC 27835-6028. 252/847-4130. **Toll-free phone:** 800/346-4307. **Fax:** 252/847-8225. **Contact:** Manager of Employment. **World Wide Web address:** http://www.uhseast.com. **Description:** A 725-bed, Level I, regional medical center and constituent of the University Health Systems of Eastern Carolina. This location also serves as the teaching facility for the East Carolina University School of Medicine, Nursing, and Allied Health. **Positions advertised include:** Advanced Level Practitioner; Annual Fund Coordinator; Assistant Nursing Manager; Call Center Nurse Consultant; Clinical Analyst; Child Life Specialist; Contract Behavioral Health Triage; Exercise Physiologist; Home Health Nurse; Neonatal Nurse Practitioner; Pharmacist; Physical Therapist; Area Technician; Operating Room Assistant; Cytotechnologist; LPN; Paramedic. **Number of employees at this location:** 4,000.

PREMIER, INC.
2320 Cascade Pointe Boulevard, Charlotte NC 28208. 704/357-0022. **Contact:** Human Resources. **World Wide Web address:** http://www.premierinc.com. **Description:** Operates hospitals and provides healthcare. **Positions advertised include:** Clinical Analyst; Manager of Environmentally Preferred Purchasing; Senior Director of Alternate Site HealthCare; Vice President of Clinical Programs; Contract Recruiter; Application Quality Engineer; Clinical Advisor; Director of Analytics & Research; ETL Development and Applications Engineer; Perspective Analyst; Product Manager; Senior Unix Systems Administrator. **Other U.S. locations:** San Diego CA; Chicago IL; Washington D.C.

RANDOLPH HOSPITAL
364 White Oaks Street, P.O. Box 1048, Asheboro NC 27204-1048. 336/629-8857. **Fax:** 336/633-7749. **Recorded jobline:** 336/629-8842. **Contact:** Human Resources. **E-mail address:** resumes@randolphhospital.org. **World Wide Web address:** http://www.randolphhospital.org. **Description:** A 145-bed general hospital. **Positions advertised include:** Registered Respiratory Therapist; Senior Director of Clinical Services; Diabetic Educator; Clinical Educator; ED Patient Representative; ED Technician; Dining Commons Manager; Food Server; Home Health Aide; Occupational Therapist; Physical Therapist; Rehab Coordinator; Unit Secretary; OB Technician; RN. **Number of employees at this location:** 560.

U.S. DEPARTMENT OF VETERANS AFFAIRS
DURHAM VETERANS ADMINISTRATION MEDICAL CENTER
508 Fulton Street, Durham NC 27705. 919/286-0411. **Toll-free phone:** 888/878-6890. **Fax:** 919/286-6825. **Contact:** Human Resources. **World Wide Web address:** http://www1.va.gov/midatlantic/facilities/durham.htm. **Description:** A 274-bed general medical and surgical tertiary facility affiliated with Duke University School and Medicine and the University of North Carolina School of Dentistry. **NOTE:** Job opportunities are posted at http://www.va.gov/jobs. **Corporate headquarters location:** Washington DC. **Other U.S. locations:** Nationwide.

WAKE FOREST UNIVERSITY-BAPTIST MEDICAL CENTER
Medical Center Boulevard, Winston-Salem NC 27157. 336/716-4255. **Toll-free phone:** 800/323-9777. **Fax:** 336/716-5656. **Contact:** Human Resources. **E-mail address:** erecruit@wfubmc.edu. **World Wide Web address:** http://www.wfubmc.edu. **Description:** One of the country's leading hospitals, offering a wide variety of services. The medical center has 20 subsidiary or affiliate hospitals and 87 satellite clinics throughout the surrounding areas. **NOTE:** For nursing positions, call 336/716-3339,or e-mail nrsrecrt@wfubmc.edu. **Positions advertised include:** Assistant Unit Manager; Clinical Documentation Consultant; Manager of Abdominal Transplant Program; Neonatal Nurse Practitioner; OR Service Coordinator; Palliative Care Coordinator; Quality Improvement Coordinator; Dental Assistant; Clinical Nutritionist; Histologic Technician; MRI Technologist; Physical Therapist; Respiratory Therapist; Pharmacist; Database Specialist; Community Health Program Coordinator; Social Worker; Assistant Teacher; Dietetic Clerk; Housekeeping Technician; Carpenter; Electrician. **Corporate headquarters location:** This location. **Number of employees at this location:** 5,500.

WAKEMED
3000 New Bern Avenue, PO Box 14465, Raleigh NC 27620. 919/350-8000. **Contact:** Human Resources. **E-mail address:** recruiting@wakemed.org. **World Wide Web address:** http://www.wakemed.org. **Description:** A network of medical centers, ambulatory care centers, outpatient facilities and other health resources serving the needs of the region. **Positions advertised include:** Bioterrorism Disaster Planner; Client Services Analyst; Nurse Aide, Occupational Therapist. **Corporate Headquarters:** This location. **Other area locations:** North Raleigh NC; Cary NC; Fuquay-Varina NC; Zebulon/Wendell NC; Clayton NC. **Number of employees statewide:** 7,500.

THE WOMEN'S HOSPITAL OF GREENSBORO
801 Green Valley Road, Greensboro NC 27408. 336/832-6500. **Contact:** Human Resources. **E-mail address:** recruitment@mosescone.com. **World Wide Web address:** http://www.mosescone.com. **Description:** A 134-bed full-service hospital dedicated to women and infants. **NOTE:** Resumes should be sent to: Moses Cone Health System Recruitment Department, 1200 Elm Street, Greensboro NC 27401-1020. Phone: 336/832-7400, or 800/476-6737. Fax: 336/832-2999. **Positions advertised include:** Assistant Director, Nursing Leadership; Food Service Technician; Laundry Technician; Nursing Secretary; Nursing Technician; Phlebotomist; RN, Various Departments; Scheduler; Ultrasound Technician. **Parent company:** Moses Cone Health Systems. **Number of employees nationwide:** 6,900.

North Dakota

ALTRU HOSPITAL
ALTRU HEALTH INSTITUTE
1000 South Columbia Road, P.O. Box 6003, Grand Forks ND 58206-6000. 701/780-6596. **Fax:** 701/780-6641. **Contact:** Human Resources. **E-mail address:** hr@altru.org. **World Wide Web address:** http://www.altru.org. **Description:** The hospital is a 277-bed regional facility providing patient care, health-related support services, and preventive services. Altru Health Institute is a 34-bed rehabilitation hospital providing occupational and physical therapies. **NOTE:** Physicians may contact the Physicians Recruiting Department at the above address or e-mail: Jkeller@Altru.org. **Positions advertised include:** Nursing Assistant; Support Service Technician; Billing Specialist; Communication Clerk; Health Unit Coordinator; Budget/Reimbursement and Charge Master Associate; Lab Receptionist; Phlebotomist. **Special programs:** Shadowing program; staff career development programs.

BETHANY HOMES, INC.
201 South University Drive, Fargo ND 58103. 701/239-3522. **Fax:** 701/239-3237. **Contact:** Adam Broers, Employment Coordinator. **E-mail address:** abroers@bethanyhomes.org. **World Wide Web address:** http://www.bethanyhomes.org. **Description:** A 192-bed nursing home and retirement living center. Bethany Homes is a nonprofit corporation affiliated with the Evangelical Lutheran Church of America. **NOTE:** Entry-level positions and second and third

shifts are offered. **Positions advertised include:** Registered Nurse; LPN; Certified Nursing Assistant; Therapeutic Recreation Personnel; Housekeeper; Cook; Cook Helper; Dietary Aide; Home Health Aide; Sitter/Companion. **Special programs:** Training. **Number of employees at this location:** 420.

DAKOTA CLINIC/INNOVIS HEALTH
1701 South University Drive, 58104. 701/364-3462. **Toll-free phone:** 800/437-4054x3432. **Contact:** Human Resources Manager. **E-mail address:** humanr@dakcl.com. **World Wide Web address:** http://www.dakotaclinic.com. **Description:** A chain of approximately 15 multispecialty clinics located throughout North Dakota and Minnesota. The clinics have a network of approximately 200 physicians, 100 of which practice at this location. **NOTE:** Innovis Health employment opportunities located under separate listing. **Positions advertised include:** Medical Receptionist; LPN/Endocrinology; LPN/Neurology; CRNA; Radiation Therapist; Medical Technologist; Bloodbank Supervisor; Nuclear Medicine Technician; Radiology Technician; Ultrasound Supervisor; Ultrasound Technician. **Other area locations:** West Fargo; Medina; Jamestown; Valley City; Lisbon; Casseltor; Wahpeton; Hankinson. **Other U.S. locations:** MN.

MERCY MEDICAL CENTER
1301 15th Avenue West, Williston ND 58801. 701/774-7454. **Fax:** 701/774-7670. **Contact:** Jim Hansel, Human Resources Director. **E-mail address:** JimHansel@CHI-Midwest.org. **World Wide Web address:** http://www.mercy-williston.org. **Description:** A 134-bed acute care facility. Mercy Medical Center is a member of Catholic Health Initiatives. **NOTE:** Friendliest human recourse department ever encountered, prefers applicants apply in person but may apply on-line. **Positions advertised include:** Environmental Service Technician; Licensed Practical Nurse; Licensed Registered Dietician; Medical Technologist; Nurse Assistant (certified and non-certified); Occupational Therapist; Pharmacist; Physical Therapist; Registered Nurse. **Number of employees at this location:** Over 500.

MERITCARE MEDICAL CENTER
P.O. Box MC, Fargo ND 58122. 701/280-4800. **Physical address:** 720 4th Street North, Fargo ND 58122. **Toll-free number:** 800/437-4010. **Fax:** 701/280-4989. **Contact:** Bonnie Green, Human Resources. **E-mail address:** bonniegreen@meritcare.com. or MyJobs@meritcare.com. **World Wide Web address:** http://www.meritcare.com. **Description:** A medical center that is comprised of a regional network of twenty-four primary care clinics. **Positions advertised include:** Clinical Coordinator; Coding Specialist; Insurance Processing/Office Specialist; Office Assistant; Distribution Worker; Cook; Environmental Services Worker. **Special Programs:** Tuition assistance program. **Operations at this facility include:** Administration; Service. **Other area locations:** West Fargo; Hatton; Mayville; Enderlin; Wahpeton; Hillsboro; LaMoure; Edgely; Gackle; Jamestown; Wimbledon. **Other U.S. locations:** MN. **Number of employees at this location:** 2,500.

MISSOURI SLOPE LUTHERAN CARE CENTER
2425 Hillview Avenue, Bismarck ND 58501. 701/223-9407. **Contact:** Patty Tangen, Director of Human Resources. **World Wide Web address:** www.mslcc.com. **Description:** A nonprofit, residential nursing home. Founded in 1967. **NOTE:** Second and third shifts are offered. **Company slogan:** Together enriching life. **Special programs:** Internships; Training; Co-ops; Summer Jobs. **Corporate headquarters location:** This location. **Administrator:** Robert Thompson.

ST. ALEXIUS PRIMECARE
900 East Broadway Avenue, Bismarck ND 58501. 701/530-7175. **Contact:** Jackie Heil, Employment Coordinator. **World Wide Web address:** http://www.st.alexius.org. **Description:** A 302-bed regional Catholic hospital that provides inpatient and outpatient healthcare services. Founded in 1885 by a group of Benedictine nuns. **NOTE:** Must apply online and must complete the online survey to initiate resume consideration. **Positions advertised include:** General Psychiatrist; Child/Adolescent Psychiatrist; Emergency Medicine Physician; Neurosurgeon; Customer Service Representative; Account Representative; Medical Transcriptionist; Messenger Clerk; Certified Nurse Assistant; Communication Clerk; Staff Accountant; Chaplain; Social Worker; Pharmacist; Respiratory Therapist; Speech/Language Pathologist; Surgical Technician; LPN; Registered Nurse; Clinical Coordinator; Perioperative Clinical Educator; Aide; Custodian; Personal Care Attendant; Exercise Physiology Aide; Phlebotomist; Physical Therapy Aide; Psychiatry Technician; Nurse Assistant. **Office hours:** Monday – Friday, 8:00 a.m. – 4:30 p.m.

ST. JOSEPH'S HOSPITAL AND HEALTH CENTER
30 West 7th Street, Dickinson ND 58601. 701/456-4274. **Recorded jobline:** 701/456-4554. **Contact:** Human Resources. **World Wide Web address:** http://www.stjoeshospital.org. **Description:** A 109-bed, community-based hospital with a medical staff comprised of over 30 physicians. The hospital offers an array of services, including diabetes education; obstetrics and gynecology services; a cancer center; various specialized clinics; critical care; mental health services; home care; diagnostics; medical/surgical services; children's services; Medquest Medical Equipment provision; nutrition services, restorative and rehabilitation Services; rural health clinics; a sleep diagnostics program. **Positions advertised include:** Registered Nurse; Charge Nurse; LPN; Respiratory Care Practitioner; Certified Registered Nurse Anesthetist; Certified Medical Assistant; Occupational Therapist; Occupational Therapy Assistant; Director of Radiology; **Subsidiaries include:** St. Joseph LifeCare Foundation coordinates fundraising, outreach education, support groups, and public relations.

TRINITY HOSPITAL
P.O. Box 5020, Minot ND 58702-5020. 701/857-5191. **Physical address:** One West Burdick Expressway West, Minot ND 58701. **Toll-free phone:** 800/862-0005. **Contact:** Human Resources. **E-mail address:** jobs@trinityhealth.org. **World Wide Web address:** http://www.trinityhealth.org. **Description:** A 250-bed hospital that provides inpatient and outpatient medical care. Other services include home care, mental health services, pastoral care, and diagnostics services. **NOTE**: Fill out application online and attach resume to application for fast review. **Positions advertised include:** LPN; Addiction Counselor; Licensed Counselor; Psychologist; Radiation Therapist; Office Assistant; Surgical Technician; Certified Nursing Assistant; Childcare Provider; Registered Nurse; Occupational Therapist; Human Resources Assistant; Nursing Aide; Occupational Therapy Coordinator; Physical Therapy Assistant; Pharmacy Technician; Respiratory Therapist; Social Worker. **Special Programs:** Internships. **President/CEO:** Terry G. Hoff.

Ohio

ADENA REGIONAL MEDICAL CENTER
272 Hospital Road, Chillicothe OH 45601. 740/779-7562. **Fax:** 740/779-7902. **Recorded jobline:** 740/779-7941. **Contact:** Human Resources. **World Wide Web address:** http://www.adena.com. **Description:** A medical center serving more than 100,000 patients annually. **Positions advertised include:** Unit Secretary; Registrar; Billing Specialist; Patient Accounts Manager; Radiologic Technologist; Occupational Therapist; System Analyst; Service Attendant; Mental Health Technician; Patient Care Associate; Surgical Technician; Staff Sonographer. **Number of employees at this location:** 800.

AKRON GENERAL MEDICAL CENTER
400 Wabash Avenue, Akron OH 44307. 330/384-6000.

Fax: 330/344-1845. **Contact:** Division of Recruitment and Retention. **E-mail address:** careers@agmc.org. **World Wide Web address:** http://www.agmc.org. **Description:** A 537-bed, acute care teaching hospital that is affiliated with the Northeastern Ohio Colleges of Medicine. **Positions advertised include:** Clinical Nursing Manager; Coding Technician; Compensation Analyst; Licensed Practical Nurse; Medical Secretary; Nursing Assistant; Pharmacist; Research Assistant; Ultrasound Technologist. **Number of employees at this location:** 3,300.

ALLIANCE COMMUNITY HOSPITAL
264 East Rice Street, Alliance OH 44601-4341. 330/829-4000. **Fax:** 330/829-4122. **Recorded jobline:** 330/829-4101. **Contact:** Trace Pasco, Colleague Relations Specialist. **E-mail address:** jobs@achosp.org. **World Wide Web address:** http://www.achosp.org. **Description:** A full-service, acute care hospital specializing in adolescent and pediatric care, cancer care, cardio-pulmonary services, emergency care, intensive care, progressive care, rehabilitation, and surgical services. The hospital also operates a community care center and a visiting nurse's association and hospice, **Positions advertised include:** Home Health Aide; Registered Nurse; Respiratory Therapist; Physical Therapist. **Parent company:** Alliance VNA IMS. **Operations at this facility include:** Administration.

ALLIED THERAPY ASSOCIATES, INC.
4353-D Tuller Road, Dublin OH 43017-5071. 614/764-7900. **Toll-free phone:** 800/589-8786. **Fax:** 614/764-0715. **Contact:** Mary Jane Hershey, President. **E-mail:** ata@iwaynet.net. **World Wide Web address:** http://www.alliedtherapy.com. **Description:** A service agency that provides physical, occupational, and speech therapy to facilities, agencies, and individuals throughout central Ohio. **Positions advertised include:** Part-Time Therapist; Full-Time Therapist; Occupational Therapist; Pediatric Physical Therapist; Speech Therapist.

AULTMAN HOSPITAL
2600 Sixth Street SW, Canton OH 44710. 330/452-9911. **Contact:** Human Resources. **World Wide Web address:** http://www.aultman.com. **Description:** A full-service, acute care, 682-bed hospital specializing in diabetes, diagnostic and nuclear radiology, rehabilitation, and skilled nursing. The hospital also operates specialized departments for a variety of medical needs including cancer, coronary care, emergency/trauma medicine, maternal/child services, and surgery. Founded in 1892. **Positions advertised include:** Registered Nurse; Radiation Therapist; Neonatal Nurse Practitioner; Occupational Therapist; Clinical Pharmacist; Transcriptionist; Social Worker; Vascular Sonographer.

BARBERTON CITIZENS HOSPITAL
155 Fifth Street NE, Barberton OH 44203. 330/848-7771. **Fax:** 330/848-7833. **Recorded jobline:** 330/848-7777. **Contact:** Human Resources. **World Wide Web address:** http://www.barbhosp.com. **Description:** A 311-bed, full-service, acute care hospital. Barberton Citizens Hospital specializes in a number of inpatient services including coronary care, extended care, intensive care, obstetrics, pediatrics, psychiatry, and surgery. The hospital also offers outpatient services and community outreach programs. Founded in 1915. **NOTE:** Entry-level positions, part-time jobs, and second and third shifts are offered. **Positions advertised include:** Registration Specialist; Computer Operator; Hospital Aide; Porter; Phlebotomist; Medical Transcriptionist; Licensed Practical Nurse; Registered Nurse; Occupational Therapist; Operator. **Special programs:** Internships. **Parent company:** Quorum Health Group, Inc. **Listed on:** NASDAQ. **Number of employees at this location:** 1,000.

BETHESDA NORTH HOSPITAL
10500 Montgomery Road, Cincinnati OH 45242-4402. 513/745-1111. **Contact:** Human Resources. **World Wide Web address:** http://www.trihealth.com. **Description:** A progressive 255 bed hospital and health care organization. Five core areas make up Bethesda North's structure: member acquisition, health status management, health services and physician services, internal services, and integrating services. Bethesda North's regional home care includes American Nursing Care, two adult DayBreak Centers, and Hospice of Cincinnati, which works with more than 30 nursing homes. Bethesda North also operates two group practices that bring primary care physicians, pharmacists, lab, and X-ray technicians together at one site. **Positions advertised include:** Fitness Technician; Receptionist; Donor Relations Officer; Physical Therapist; Rehabilitation Attendant; Lifeguard; Practice Physician; Registered Nurse; Medical Assistant.

BLANCHARD VALLEY REGIONAL HEALTH CENTER
145 West Wallace Street, Findlay OH 45840. 419/423-5229. **Contact:** Connie Walter, Human Resources. **E-mail address:** candidate@bvha.org. **World Wide Web address:** http://www.bvha.org. **Description:** A full-service medical center. Blanchard Valley Regional Health Center specializes in cardiac care, catheterization, cardiopulmonary care, dialysis, emergency medicine, intensive and coronary care units, laboratory services, nuclear medicine, oncology, pathology, pediatrics, pharmacy, radiology, and rehabilitation. **Positions advertised include:** Registered Nurse. **Parent company:** Blanchard Valley Health Association.

CARDINAL HEALTH, INC.
7000 Cardinal Place, Dublin OH 43017. 614/757-5000. **Toll-free phone:** 800/234-8701. **Fax:** 614/757-8602. **Recorded jobline:** 614/757-5627. **Contact:** Human Resources Department. **World Wide Web address:** http://www.cardhealth.com. **Description:** A wholesale distributor of pharmaceuticals, medical and surgical products, and related health supplies. The company also distributes merchandise typically sold in retail drug stores, hospitals, and health care provider facilities. Cardinal Health provides specialized support services to assist clients such as order-entry and confirmation, inventory control, monitoring pricing strategies, and financial reporting. The company has developed an in-pharmacy computer system that provides prices, patient profiles, financial data, and management services. **Positions advertised include:** Senior Programmer Analyst; Graphic Designer; Compensation Analyst; Administrative Assistant; Buyer Assistant; Project Engineer; Credit Collections Specialist; Quality Assurance Analyst; Business Systems Analyst; Financial Analyst; Senior Tax Analyst; Human Resources Manager; Senior Auditor. **Special programs:** Internships. **Corporate headquarters location:** This location. **Subsidiaries include:** Medicine Shoppe International, Inc.; National PharmPak Services, Inc.; PCI Services, Inc.; ScriptLINE. **Listed on:** New York Stock Exchange. **Stock exchange symbol:** CAH. **Annual sales/revenues:** $21 - $50 million. **Number of employees at this location:** 1,300. **Number of employees nationwide:** 30,000. **Number of employees worldwide:** 36,000.

CHRIST HOSPITAL
2139 Auburn Avenue, Cincinnati OH 45219-2989. 513/585-2000. **Fax:** 513/585-3646. **Recorded jobline:** 513/585-2251. **Contact:** Human Resources. **World Wide Web address:** http://www.health-alliance.com/christ.html. **Description:** A nonprofit, 550-bed acute care hospital. The hospital specializes in advanced orthopedics, behavioral medicine, cancer care, cardiac care, geriatric medicine, internal medicine, surgical specialties, and women's health. Founded in 1889. **NOTE:** The hospital is offering a signing bonus of up to $30,000 for Registered Nurses in critical care areas who are able to make a three year commitment. **Positions advertised include:** Pharmacist; Physical Therapist; Radiologic Technologist; Clinical Supervisor; Health Unit Coordinator; Chemical Dependency Therapist; Licensed Practical Nurse; Administrative Secretary; Coder; Nurse Manager; Case

Manager; Safety Security Officer; File Clerk; Ultrasound Technician; Registered Nurse.

CINCINNATI CHILDREN'S HOSPITAL MEDICAL CENTER
Professional Services Building, 2900 Vernon Place, Cincinnati OH 45229-3039. 513/636-4244. **Toll-free phone:** 800/344-2462. **Contact:** Human Resources. **E-mail address:** careers@chmcc.org. **World Wide Web address:** http://www.cincinnatichildrens.org. **Description:** A nationally recognized children's hospital serving the needs of infants, children, and adolescents. Cincinnati Children's Hospital's state-of-the-art facilities include a Heart Center, a Pediatric Liver Care Center, and a Hematology and Oncology Division. The medical center also functions as a research institution and teaching hospital for the University of Cincinnati College of Medicine. Cincinnati Children's Hospital operates several outpatient facilities located within Cincinnati and throughout Ohio. These outpatient sites offer a variety of services to supplement the treatment available at the Medical Center's main campus. **Positions advertised include:** Clinical Nurse; Nurse Practitioner; Surgical Technologist; Research Nurse; Occupational Therapist; Food Service Assistant; Respiratory Therapist; Social Worker; Health Unit Coordinator; Patient Attendant; Assistant Professor, Orthopedic Surgery. **Special programs:** Fellowships; Internships; Residency Programs. **Other area locations:** Fairfield OH; Harrison OH; Mason OH; Middletown OH; Westchester OH. **Other U.S. locations:** Crestview Hills KY. **Operations at this facility include:** Health Care. **Number of employees nationwide:** Approximately 7,200.

CLEVELAND CLINIC FOUNDATION
P.O. Box 606140, Cleveland OH 44106. 216/445-1386. **Physical address:** 9500 Euclid Avenue, Cleveland OH 44195. **Fax:** 216/444-6096. **Contact:** Miriam J. Barton, Director of Human Resources. **E-mail address:** bartonm1@ccf.org. **World Wide Web address:** http://www.cchs.net. **Description:** A national referral center and international health resource center specializing in tertiary care, medical research, and medical education. Founded in 1921. **Positions advertised include:** Registered Nurse Practitioner; Registered Nurse; Licensed Nurse Practitioner. **Corporate headquarters location:** This location. **Other U.S. locations:** Fort Lauderdale FL. **Number of employees nationwide:** 10,000.

COMMUNITY HOSPITALS OF WILLIAMS COUNTY INC.
BRYAN HOSPITAL
433 West High Street, Bryan OH 43506. 419/636-1131. **Fax:** 419/636-3100. **Contact:** Marianne Potts, Human Resources Director. **E-mail address:** personnel@chwchospital.com. **World Wide Web address:** http://www.chwchospital.com. **Description:** An organization of three acute care hospitals offering a variety of services and treatment facilities. This location is the main campus site of Bryan Hospital. Community Hospitals of Williams County also operates Archbold Hospital and Montpelier Hospital. **NOTE:** Personnel phone extension is 1172. **Positions advertised include:** Registered Nurse; Respiratory Therapist; Licensed Occupational Therapist; Radiologic Technologist. **Corporate headquarters location:** This location. **Other area locations:** Archbold OH; Montpelier OH. **Operations at this facility include:** Administration; Service. **Number of employees at this location:** 600.

COMPREHENSIVE CANCER CENTER
OHIO STATE UNIVERSITY MEDICAL CENTER
300 West 10th Street, Columbus OH 43210. 614/293-4995. **Toll-free phone:** 800/293-5066. **Contact:** Personnel. **World Wide Web address:** http://www.jamesline.com. **Description:** A cancer research center engaged in treating patients and developing new drugs to treat the disease. **NOTE:** Please send resumes to Human Resources, 141 Means Hall, 1654 Upham Drive, Columbus OH 43210. **Positions advertised include:** Licensed Radiation Therapist; Rehabilitation Nurse; Patient Care Resource Manager.

CUYAHOGA FALLS GENERAL HOSPITAL
1900 23rd Street, Cuyahoga Falls OH 44223-1499. 330/971-7006. **Contact:** Human Resources. **E-mail address:** summajobs@summa-health.org. **World Wide Web address:** http://www.summahealth.org. **Description:** A 257-bed, acute care hospital offering ambulatory, medical, obstetric, psychiatric, rehabilitative, and surgical services. The hospital also offers several specialized services including Easy Street Environments rehabilitation, Falls Pain Management, and the New Beginnings Maternity Center. **Positions advertised include:** Unit Clerk; Licensed Practical Nurse; Registered Nurse; Information Services Librarian; Environmental Aide. **Parent Company:** Summa Health Systems.

DEACONESS HOSPITAL
311 Straight Street, Cincinnati OH 45219. 513/559-2100. **Fax:** 513/475-5428. **Contact:** Human Resources. **E-mail address:** greatjobs@deaconess-cinti.com. **World Wide Web address:** http://www.deaconess-healthcare.com. **Description:** A 250-bed, nonprofit, acute care hospital. Deaconess Hospital specializes in arthritis, back treatment, cardiac care, care for the elderly, diabetes, emergency services, endoscopy, home health care, mental health, nutrition counseling, joint replacement, occupational therapy, orthopedic care, osteoporosis, physical therapy, rehabilitation, and sports medicine. Founded in 1888. **Positions advertised include:** Registered Nurse; Licensed Practical Nurse; Medical Assistant; Nurse Assistant; Occupational Therapist; Physical Therapist; Respiratory Therapist; Phlebotomist; Radiology Technician.

DOCTORS HOSPITAL
5100 West Broad Street, Columbus OH 43228. 614/429-3200. **Fax:** 614/566-6953. **Contact:** Human Resources. **World Wide Web address:** http://www.ohiohealth.com. **Description:** A 256-bed, nonprofit, acute care, osteopathic hospital. Founded in 1940. **NOTE:** Entry-level positions and second and third shifts are offered. Resumes are accepted by mail or fax. Mail resumes to: Ohio Health, Attention: Human Resources, 3535 Olentangy River Road, Columbus OH 43214. **Positions advertised include:** Emergency Medical Technician; Nurse Administrator; Assistant Nurse Manager; Registered Nurse; Case Manager; Patient Escort; Materials Handler; Social Worker; Cardiac Sonographer; Radiology Technologist. **Special programs:** Medical Residencies; Internships. **Parent company:** D.H. Corporation. **Listed on:** Privately held. **Number of employees at this location:** 2,100.

DRAKE CENTER, INC.
151 West Galbraith Road, Cincinnati OH 45216. 513/948-2500. **Toll-free phone:** 800/948-0003. **Fax:** 513/948-2619. **Contact:** Human Resources. **E-mail address:** info@drakecenter.com. **World Wide Web address:** http://www.drakecenter.com. **Description:** A full-service, 356-bed, rehabilitation and post-acute care facility. The Drake Center specializes in brain injury rehabilitation, cardiac rehabilitation, neurological rehabilitation, orthopedic rehabilitation, pulmonary rehabilitation, skin and wound care, stroke rehabilitation, and ventilator weaning. The Drake Center also provides on-site laboratory, pharmacy, and radiology services. **Positions advertised include:** Care Coordination Leader; Social Worker; Pharmacist; Licensed Practical Nurse; Certified Nursing Assistant; Occupational Therapist; Physical Therapist; Speech Language Pathologist; Lifeguard; Cook; Receptionist. **Operations at this facility include:** Administration. **Number of employees at this location:** 730.

EAST OHIO REGIONAL HOSPITAL
90 North Fourth Street, Martins Ferry OH 43935. 740/633-1100. **Contact:** Human Resources. **World Wide Web address:** http://www.eastohioregionalhospital.com. **Description:**

A 249-bed hospital with two divisions: acute including cancer treatment and general surgical and medical procedures; and skilled including cardiac and other rehabilitation programs. **Positions advertised include:** Staff Nurse; Licensed Practical Nurse; Senior Staff Pharmacist; Speech Language Pathologist; Housekeeper; Dietary Aide; Medical Assistant; Phlebotomist. **Parent company:** Ohio Valley Health Services and Education Corp.

ETHICON ENDO-SURGERY, INC.
4545 Creek Road, Cincinnati OH 45242. 513/786-7000. **Toll-free phone:** 800/USE-ENDO. **Contact:** Personnel. **World Wide Web address:** http://www.ethiconendo.com. **Description:** Develops and manufactures medical devices including instruments for endoscopic surgery. **Positions advertised include:** Medical Director; Regulatory Affairs Associate; Director, Short-Run Manufacturing. **Special programs:** Co-ops. **Parent company:** Johnson & Johnson (New Brunswick NJ).

FAIRFIELD MEDICAL CENTER
401 North Ewing Street, Lancaster OH 43130. 740/687-8017. **Fax:** 740/687-8633. **Recorded jobline:** 740/687-8450. **Contact:** Human Resources. **World Wide Web address:** http://www.fmchealth.org. **Description:** A 222-bed acute care hospital serving southeastern and central Ohio. **Positions advertised include:** Registered Nurse; Coding Supervisor; Community Services Coordinator; Home Health Aide; Infection Control Coordinator; Case Manager; Nursing Assistant; Physical Therapist. **Special programs:** Summer Jobs. **Office hours:** Monday - Friday, 6:30 a.m. - 5:00 p.m. **President:** Creighton Likes, Jr. **Number of employees at this location:** 1,400.

FIDELITY HEALTHCARE INC.
3832 Kettering Boulevard, Dayton OH 45439. 937/208-6400. **Toll-free phone:** 800/946-6344. **Fax:** 937/208-6539. **Contact:** Human Resources Secretary. **World Wide Web address:** http://www.fidelityhealthcare.org. **Description:** A home health care agency that provides nurses and home health aides to clients. **Positions advertised include:** Home Care Registered Nurse; Home Care Nursing Assistant; Physical Therapist; Occupational Therapist. **Office hours:** Monday - Friday, 8:00 a.m. - 5:00 p.m. **Number of employees at this location:** 325.

FIRST COMMUNITY VILLAGE
1800 Riverside Drive, Columbus OH 43212-1814. 614/486-9511. **Toll-free phone:** 888/328-9511. **Fax:** 614/481-7190. **Contact:** Human Resources Department. **E-mail address:** career@firstcommunity.org. **World Wide Web address:** http://www.firstcommunityvillage.org. **Description:** A nonprofit, continuing care retirement community with facilities that include a nursing home, an assisted living center, and an independent living center. 175 beds. Founded in 1963. **NOTE:** Entry-level positions and second and third shifts are offered. **Positions advertised include:** Activities Coordinator; Maintenance Technician; Diet Aide; Registered Nurse; Licensed Practical Nurse; Nursing Assistant. **President/CEO:** Harry Hobson. **Number of employees at this location:** Approximately 400.

FORUM HEALTH
NORTHSIDE MEDICAL CENTER
500 Gypsy Lane, Youngstown OH 44501. 330/884-1000. **Fax:** 330/884-0100. **Contact:** Human Resources. **E-mail address:** aondo@forumhealth.org. **World Wide Web address:** http://www.forumhealth.org. **Description:** Operates three hospitals, an outpatient surgery center, a nursing home, a laboratory, and a home health care agency. **NOTE:** See website for specific contact information regarding nursing, physician, and residency opportunities. **Positions advertised include:** Cardiovascular Care Manager; Emergency Department Coordinator; Director of Pharmacy; Culinary Operations Coordinator; Pediatric Clinical Supervisor; MRI Technologist; Charge Nurse; Gastroenterologist; Head and Neck Surgeon; Vascular Surgeon. **Special Programs:** Internships; Volunteer Opportunities.

FRANCISCAN SERVICES CORPORATION
6832 Convent Boulevard, Sylvania OH 43560. 419/882-8373. **Fax:** 419/882-7360. **Contact:** John W. O'Connell, President. **World Wide Web address:** http://www.fscsylvanian.org/fcc.htm. **Description:** This location's facilities include Providence Corporation, which offers long-term care services; Providence Hospital; Franciscan Center, a performing arts and conference center; and Franciscan Properties, which manages Convert Park Apartments, an independent living complex for senior adults. Franciscan Services Corporation is a nonprofit health care provider. Other facilities include Bethany House (Toledo OH), which serves women and children; St. John Medical Center (Steubenville OH); Trinity Medical Center (Brenham TX); Holy Cross Hospital (Detroit MI); and St. Francis Services Corporation (Bryan TX), a free clinic. **Corporate headquarters location:** This location.

GEAUGA REGIONAL HOSPITAL
13207 Ravenna Road, Chardon OH 44024. 440/285-6000. **Fax:** 440/285-6483. **Contact:** Mark Jepson, Human Resources. **E-mail address:** mark.jepson@uhhs.com. **World Wide Web address:** http://www.uhhsgrh.com. **Description:** A 206-bed hospital offering acute care, oncology, physical therapy, respiratory therapy, cardiac rehabilitation, radiology, and maternity care services. **Positions advertised include:** Cook; Certified Nursing Assistant; Licensed Practical Nurse; Critical Care Nurse; Switchboard Operator. **Parent company:** University Hospitals Health System (UHHS).

GENTIVA HEALTH SERVICES
941 Chatham Lane, Suite 207, Columbus OH 43221. 614/326-7638. **Toll-free phone:** 800/325-6696. **Fax:** 330/644-2823. **Contact:** Human Resources. **World Wide Web address:** http://www.gentiva.com. **Description:** Gentiva Health Services provides home health care services, pharmaceutical support, and supplemental staffing services. **Corporate headquarters location:** Melville NY.

GOOD SAMARITAN HOSPITAL & HEALTH CENTER
2222 Philadelphia Drive, Dayton OH 45406. 937/278-2612 Extension 2532. **Fax:** 937/276-7618. **Recorded jobline:** 937/276-8257. **Contact:** Human Resources. **World Wide Web address:** http://www.goodsamdayton.com. **Description:** A 560-bed, nonprofit medical center specializing in cardiovascular services, mental health, emergency care, obstetrics, physical medicine, and ambulatory care. **Positions advertised include:** Registered Nurse; Nutrition Associate; Senior Data Analyst; Database Coordinator; Dentist; Senior Accountant; Pharmacist; Physical Therapist; Occupational Therapist; Respiratory Therapist; Radiation Therapist; Security Officer; Nuclear Medicine Technician; Ultrasound Technologist; Secretary; Department Assistant. **Special programs:** Internships. **Parent company:** Samaritan Health Partners. **Number of employees at this location:** 2,500.

GREEN MEADOWS HEALTH AND WELLNESS CENTER
7770 Columbus Road NE, Louisville OH 44641. 330/875-1456. **Fax:** 330/875-1459. **Contact:** Human Resources. **Description:** A nonprofit nursing home. **NOTE:** Entry-level positions and second and third shifts are offered. **Special programs:** Internships; Apprenticeships; Training; Summer Jobs. **Office hours:** Monday - Friday, 8:00 a.m. - 4:30 p.m. **Number of employees at this location:** 300.

HEALTH CLEVELAND
FAIRVIEW HOSPITAL
18101 Lorain Avenue, Cleveland OH 44111-5612. 216/476-7000. **Fax:** 216/476-7023. **Contact:** Personnel. **World Wide Web address:**

http://www.fairviewhospital.org. **Description:** A hospital. Services include a birthing.center, pediatrics, a heart center, emergency services, orthopedics, a cancer center, and a hospice support system. The hospital is part of a network that includes 11 locations in 6 communities. **Positions advertised include:** Staff Pharmacist; Mammography Technologist; MRI Technician; Ultra Sound Technician; Registered Radiation Therapist; Coding Manager; Licensed Practical Nurse; Registered Nurse; Senior Operations Project Coordinator; Western Region Finance Director. **Special Programs:** Volunteering Opportunities. **Office hours:** Monday – Friday, 9:00 a.m. – 4:00 p.m. **Number of employees at this location:** 2,600.

HEINZERLING MEMORIAL FOUNDATION
Developmental Center, 1755 Heinzerling Drive, Columbus OH 43223. 614/272-8888. **Fax:** 614/272-0268. **Recorded jobline:** 614/255-3900. **Contact:** N. Christine Rafeld, Director of Human Resources Department. **E-mail address:** online_application@heinzerling.org. **World Wide Web address:** http://www.heinzerling.org. **Description:** A private, nonprofit residential treatment facility for mentally disabled individuals of all ages. The Heinzerling Memorial Foundation provides care, education, and development skills to approximately 220 residents with special needs. **Positions advertised include:** Nursing Shift Coordinator; Nurse; Dish Machine Operator; Physical Therapist; Therapy Assistant; Laundry Aide; Housekeeper; Occupational Therapist.

HILLCREST HOSPITAL
6780 Mayfield Road, Mayfield Heights OH 44124. 440/449-4633. **Contact:** Human Resources. **World Wide Web address:** http://www.hillcresthospital.org. **Description:** Hillcrest Hospital is a 311-bed community hospital providing specialized services such as OB, NICU, critical care, oncology, ambulatory surgery, and digestive health services. **Positions advertised include:** Registered Nurse; Respiratory Therapist; Phlebotomist; Social Worker; Ultrasound Technician; Laboratory Assistant; Staff Pharmacist; Radiology Coordinator; Radiology Technician; Occupational Therapist; Patient Care Coordinator; Staffing Coordinator; Security Officer. **Corporate headquarters location:** Mayfield Village OH. **Parent company:** Cleveland Clinic Health System. **Operations at this facility include:** Service. **Number of employees nationwide:** 1,600.

INVACARE CORPORATION
P.O. Box 4028, Elyria OH 44036. 440/329-6000. **Physical address:** One Invacare Way, Elyria OH 44036. **Fax:** 440/329-6840. **Contact:** Human Resources. **E-mail address:** ivcrjobsrc@invacare.com. **World Wide Web address:** http://www.invacare.com. **Description:** Designs, manufactures, and distributes an extensive line of durable medical equipment for the home health care and extended care markets. Products include standard manual wheelchairs, motorized and lightweight prescription wheelchairs, motorized scooters, patient aids, home care beds, home respiratory products, and seating and positioning products. Invacare is one of the leading home medical equipment manufacturers in the country. **NOTE:** Entry-level positions and second and third shifts are offered. **Special programs:** Internships; Co-ops; Summer Jobs. **Corporate headquarters location:** This location. **Other U.S. locations:** CA; FL; NY; TX. **Operations at this facility include:** Administration; Divisional Headquarters; Manufacturing; Research and Development; Service. **Listed on:** New York Stock Exchange. **Stock exchange symbol:** IVC. **Annual sales/revenues:** More than $100 million. **Number of employees at this location:** 1,700. **Number of employees nationwide:** 6,000.

KINDRED HOSPITAL
2351 East 22nd Street, Cleveland OH 44115. 216/861-1964. **Contact:** Human Resources. **World Wide Web address:** http://www.kindredhealthcare.com. **Description:** Provides health care services for acute care patients. **NOTE:** Please apply for all positions at company website. **Positions advertised include:** Respiratory Therapist; Nurse Practitioner; Registered Nurse Night Shift; Registered Nurse.

LIFEBANC
20600 Chagrin Boulevard, Suite 350, Cleveland OH 44122. 216/751-5433. **Fax:** 216/751-4204. **Contact:** Human Resources. **E-mail address:** hr@lifebanc.org. **World Wide Web address:** http://www.lifebanc.org. **Description:** Responsible for all aspects of the organ and tissue donation process in northeast Ohio. **Positions advertised include:** Advanced Practice Coordinator; Donor Referral Coordinator.

LIFECARE ALLIANCE
1699 West Mound Street, Columbus OH 43223. 614/278-3130. **Fax:** 614/278-3143. **Contact:** Personnel. **E-mail address:** hr@lifecarealliance.org. **World Wide Web address:** http://www.lifecarealliance.org. **Description:** A nonprofit home health care agency. LifeCare Alliance also provides Meals on Wheels. Founded in 1898. **NOTE:** Entry-level, part-time and seasonal positions are offered. **Positions advertised include:** Foodservice Worker; Meals on Wheels Driver; Visiting Nurse. **Special programs:** Internships. **Office hours:** Monday - Friday, 8:00 a.m. - 5:00 p.m. **Corporate headquarters location:** This location. **President and CEO:** Charles Gehring. **Number of employees at this location:** 400.

LUTHERAN HOSPITAL
1730 West 25th Street, Cleveland OH 44113. 216/696-4300. **Fax:** 216/363-5199. **Recorded jobline:** 216/363-2491. **Contact:** Human Resources Department. **World Wide Web address:** http://www.lutheranhospital.org. **Description:** A 200-bed, acute care hospital. Facilities include a muscular/skeletal unit and a general psychiatric unit. **Positions advertised include:** Nuclear Medicine Technician; X-Ray Technician; Occupational Therapist; Physical Therapist; Speech Therapist; Respiratory Therapist; Licensed Practical Nurse; Registered Nurse; Nurse Practitioner; Manager, Food and Nutrition Services. **Office hours:** Monday – Friday, 8:00 a.m. – 4:30 p.m.

MARIETTA MEMORIAL HOSPITAL
401 Matthew Street, Marietta OH 45750-1635. 740/374-1400. **Fax:** 740/376-5045. **Recorded jobline:** 740/374-4997. **Contact:** James Offenberger, Employment Manager. **E-mail address:** jpoffenberger@mmhospital.org. **World Wide Web address:** http://www.mmhospital.org. **Description:** A community-based, acute care hospital. Marietta Memorial Hospital offers a variety of services including behavioral health, cardiac rehabilitation, community outreach, home nursing, mammography, radiology, outpatient surgery, and the Strecker Cancer Center. Founded in 1929. **Company slogan:** The heart of a healthy community. **Positions advertised include:** Ultrasonographer; Speech Language Pathologist; Registered Nurse; Staff Coordinator; Evening Lab Supervisor; Outpatient Services Technician; Orderly; Registration Clerk; Mechanics Assistant; Housekeeper; Food Service Worker; Laundry Aide; Social Worker; Occupational Therapist; Respiratory Therapist; Pharmacist; Home Health Aide. **Office hours:** Monday – Friday, 7:00 a.m. – 5:00 p.m. **Number of employees at this location:** 1,300.

MARION GENERAL HOSPITAL
1000 McKinley Park Drive, Marion OH 43302. 740/383-8690. **Fax:** 740/383-8612. **Recorded jobline:** 740/383-8695. **Contact:** Human Resources. **World Wide Web address:** http://www.mariongeneral.com. **Description:** A hospital offering a variety of specialty areas including heart care, cancer care, emergency care, women's health, mental health care, nursing services, ICU/CCU, step-down/transition, surgical/orthopedic, oncology, Center for New Beginnings (labor and delivery, mother/baby nursery, pediatrics), off-site nursing services (home care, hospice/quality of life, adult daycare, Alzheimer's), pharmacy, clinical

laboratory services, nutrition, rehabilitation, work transitions, pain management, occupational therapy, physical therapy, nuclear medicine, radiology, cardiac catheter, inpatient psychiatric, recreational therapy, and social services. Founded in 1920. **NOTE:** Candidates should apply online. **Positions advertised include:** Respiratory Therapist; Social Worker; Health Unit Coordinator; Clinical Instructor; Paramedic; Licensed Practical Nurse; Registered Nurse; Nurse Assistant; Clinical Dietitian; Director of Safety; Environmental Services Technician; Pharmacist. **Special programs:** Internships. **Corporate headquarters location:** Columbus OH. **Parent company:** U.S. Health Corporation. **Number of employees at this location:** 900.

MEDCENTRAL HEALTH SYSTEM
335 Glessner Avenue, Mansfield OH 44903. 419/526-8000. **Fax:** 419/526-8848. **Contact:** Human Resources. **E-mail address:** careers4u@medcentral.org. **World Wide Web address:** http://www.medcentral.org. **Description:** MedCentral Health System is a leading health care delivery system that operates three acute care hospitals: Crestline Hospital, Mansfield Hospital, and Shelby Hospital. The company also operates a cardiac care center, substance abuse programs, a walk-in medical center, and industrial health and safety services. **NOTE:** Apply online. **Positions advertised include:** Assistant Nurse Manager; Registered Nurse; Licensed Practical Nurse; Speech Language Pathologist; Pharmacy Manager; Respiratory Care Technician. **Other area locations:** Crestline OH; Shelby OH. **Number of employees at this location:** 2,000.

MEDEX INC.
6250 Shier Rings Road, Dublin OH 43016. 614/889-4775. **Contact:** Human Resources. **World Wide Web address:** http://www.medex.com. **Description:** An international manufacturer and supplier of critical care products and infusion systems for medical and surgical applications. These products are sold to hospitals, alternative health care facilities, home health care providers, and original equipment manufacturers. **Positions advertised include:** Internal Audit Manager; Senior Mechanical Engineer; Software Engineer; Accounts Receivable Specialist. **Special programs:** Internships. **Corporate headquarters location:** Carlsbad CA. **Other U.S. locations:** Atlanta GA. **Operations at this facility include:** Administration; Manufacturing; Sales; Service.

MEDINA GENERAL HOSPITAL
1000 East Washington Street, Medina OH 44256. 330/725-1000. **Fax:** 330/721-4925. **Contact:** Human Resources. **E-mail address:** hr@medinahospital.org. **World Wide Web address:** http://www.medinahospital.org. **Description:** An acute care facility with 118 beds. Medina General Hospital offers such services as prenatal care, an oncology unit, pediatrics, and an intensive care unit. **Positions advertised include:** Registered Nurse; Computer Operator; MRI Technologist; Phlebotomist; Physical Therapist; Radiology Technician; Security Supervisor; Housekeeping Assistant; Maintenance Worker; Nursing Assistant.

MEMORIAL HOSPITAL
715 South Taft Avenue, Fremont OH 43420. 419/332-7321. **Fax:** 419/334-6691. **Contact:** Human Resources. **World Wide Web address:** http://www.fremontmemorial.org. **Description:** A community-focused, acute care hospital. Opened in 1918. **Positions advertised include:** Licensed Practical Nurse; Medical Records Technician; Radiological Technologist; Registered Nurse; Respiratory Therapist; Surgical Technician; Account Representative; House Keeper; Cardiovascular Technician. **Operations at this facility include:** Administration; Service. **Number of employees at this location:** 570.

THE METROHEALTH SYSTEM
2500 MetroHealth Drive, Cleveland OH 44109. 216/778-7800. **Toll-free phone:** 800/332-4060. **Fax:** 216/778-8905. **Contact:** Human Resources. **E-mail address:** humres@metrohealth.org. **World Wide Web address:** http://www.metrohealth.org. **Description:** Provides comprehensive health care services through its member facilities and affiliation with Case Western University School of Medicine. The MetroHealth System is comprised of several facilities: MetroHealth Medical Center (also at this location) is one of the nation's most successful publicly owned hospitals. The 728-bed hospital provides a variety of medical services including dentistry, dermatology, ambulatory care, medical aircraft services, obstetrics, gynecology, psychiatry, family practice, substance abuse, and surgery; MetroHealth's Outpatient Plaza houses separate centers for rehabilitation, women and children, specialty services including cardiology and neurology, and cancer care; The Charles H. Rammelkamp, Jr., M.D. Center for Research and Education; MetroHealth Center for Rehabilitation; MetroHealth Clement Center for Family Care; and MetroHealth Center for Skilled Nursing Care. **Positions advertised include:** Occupational Therapist; Physical Therapist; Social Worker; Speech Pathologist; Communication Specialist; Laboratory Processing Clerk; Education Specialist; Coding Specialist; Communication Specialist; Grants Support Specialist; Data Entry Operator; Gift Shop Clerk; Library Aide; Clinical Dietitian; Flight Nurse Specialist; Licensed Practical Nurse; Nurse Practitioner; Registered Nurse. **Special programs:** Internships. **Office hours:** Monday - Friday, 7:30 a.m. - 5:00 p.m. **President/CEO:** John F. Sideras. **Number of employees at this location:** 6,000.

OHIO STATE UNIVERSITY MEDICAL CENTER THE ARTHUR G. JAMES CANCER HOSPITAL & RESEARCH INSTITUTE
164 Doan Hall, 410 West 10th Avenue, Columbus OH 43210. 614/293-4995. **Fax:** 614/293-3080. **Recorded jobline:** 614/293-4900. **Contact:** Human Resources. **E-mail address:** recruitment@medctr.osu.edu. **World Wide Web address:** http://www.jamesline.com. **Description:** An academic medical center. The Arthur G. James Cancer Hospital & Research Institute (also at this location) is a 160-bed treatment and research facility that provides care to oncology patients. **Positions advertised include:** Nurse Manager; Oncology Nurse; Licensed Radiation Therapist; Dosimetrist; Patient Care Associate; Coding Specialist; Research Associate. **Special programs:** Internships. **Number of employees at this location:** 4,500.

OHIO STATE UNIVERSITY VETERINARY HOSPITAL
601 Tharp Street, Columbus OH 43210. 614/292-6661. **Contact:** Human Resources. **World Wide Web address:** http://www.vet.ohio-state.edu. **Description:** A full-service animal hospital with services ranging from vaccinations to major surgery and cancer treatment. The hospital provides treatment for pets and small animals, as well as large farm animals, and also supports an equine center.

PARMA COMMUNITY GENERAL HOSPITAL
7007 Powers Boulevard, Parma OH 44129. 440/743-4900. **Fax:** 440/743-4092. **Recorded jobline:** 440/743-4005. **Contact:** Human Resources Department. **E-mail address:** employment@parmahospital.org. **World Wide Web address:** http://www.parmahospital.org. **Description:** A 339-bed, acute care hospital. **NOTE:** Resumes are accepted by mail, fax, or e-mail. **Positions advertised include:** Radiology Scheduler; Radiology Transcriptionist; Occupational Therapist; Physical Therapist; Pharmacist; Licensed Practical Nurse; Certified Physician Assistant; MRI Technologist; Operating Room Technician; Registered Nurse. **President/CEO:** Patricia A. Ruflin. **Number of employees at this location:** 2,000.

PAULDING COUNTY HOSPITAL
1035 West Wayne Street, Paulding OH 45879. 419/399-4080. **Fax:** 419/399-5560. **Contact:** Amy Lieb, Director of Human Resources. **E-mail address:** pchhr@saa.net. **World Wide Web address:** http://www.pauldingcountyhospital.com. **Description:**

A nonprofit, county-supported hospital offering a wide range of services. **NOTE:** Entry-level positions and second and third shifts are offered. **Special programs:** Internships; Summer Jobs. **Office hours:** Monday - Friday, 8:30 a.m. - 4:30 p.m. **CEO:** Gary W. Adkins. **Number of employees at this location:** 210.

PHILIPS MEDICAL SYSTEMS
595 Miner Road, Highland Heights OH 44143. 440/473-3000. **Fax:** 440/483-6784. **Contact:** Human Resources Coordinator. **World Wide Web address:** http://www.philips.com. **Description:** Specializes in the research, design, development, and manufacture of X-ray equipment for the worldwide medical community. **Positions advertised include:** Administrator; Application Support Specialist; Clinical Scientist; Clinical Education Training Specialist; Field Service Engineer. **Special programs:** Internships.

RELIANCE MEDICAL PRODUCTS
3535 Kings Mills Road, Mason OH 45040-2303. 513/398-3937. **Contact:** Personnel. **World Wide Web address:** http://www.reliance-medical.com. **Description:** A medical equipment manufacturer. The company primarily manufactures floor units and related equipment for optometrists.

RIVERSIDE METHODIST HOSPITAL
3535 Olentangy River Road, Columbus OH 43214. 614/566-4757. **Fax:** 614/566-6953. **Contact:** Human Resources. **World Wide Web address:** http://www.grmh.org. **Description:** An acute care hospital with a medical staff of 1,200 physicians specializing in cardiac, orthopedic, and maternity services. **NOTE:** Human Resources is located at 550 Thomas Lane, Columbus OH. **Positions advertised include:** Coder; Emergency Room Chart Specialist; Ambulatory Coordinator; Administrative Assistant; Senior Medical Records Associate; Unit Coordinator; Reimbursement Specialist; Clinical Receptionist.

ROBINSON MEMORIAL HOSPITAL
6847 North Chestnut Street, Ravenna OH 44266. 330/297-0811. **Fax:** 330/297-4047. **Contact:** Director of Human Resources. **E-mail address:** humanresources@rmh2.org. **World Wide Web address:** http://www.robinsonmemorial.org. **Description:** A 280-bed hospital. **NOTE:** The Human Resources direct line is 330/297-2700. **Positions advertised include:** Director of Physician Services; Front Office Associate; Nutrition Services Aide; Medical Assistant; Telecommunications Operator; Pharmacy Technician; Surgical Technologist; Licensed Practical Nurse; Registered Nurse.

SALEM COMMUNITY HOSPITAL
1995 East State Street, Salem OH 44460. 330/332-7148. **Fax:** 330/332-7592. **Contact:** Human Resources. **E-mail address:** jobs@salemhosp.com. **World Wide Web address:** http://www.salemhosp.com. **Description:** A community hospital. **Positions advertised include:** Radiologic Technologist; Licensed Practical Nurse; Surgical Technologist; Pediatric Registered Nurse. **Special programs:** Internships; Co-ops. **Number of employees at this location:** 800.

SHRINER'S HOSPITAL
3229 Burnet Avenue, Cincinnati OH 45229-3095. 513/872-6000. **Fax:** 513/872-6370. **Contact:** Julia Faehr, Human Resources Specialist. **E-mail address:** jfaehr@shrinenet.org. **World Wide Web address:** http://www.shrinershq.org/shc/cincinnati/index.htm. **Description:** A 30-bed hospital that specializes in the treatment of child burn victims. **NOTE:** To reach Human Resources directly call: 513/872-6242. **Positions advertised include:** Human Resources Specialist; Registered Nurse; Research Specialist; Sterile Processing Technician.

STERIS CORPORATION
5960 Heisley Road, Mentor OH 44060-1834. 440/354-2600. **Toll-free phone:** 800/548-4873. **Fax:** 440/354-7043. **Contact:** Human Resources. **World Wide Web address:** http://www.steris.com. **Description:** A leading provider of infection prevention products, contamination control, and surgical support systems and products to health care, scientific, research, and industrial customers worldwide. Founded in 1987. **NOTE:** Entry-level positions and second and third shifts are offered. Interested candidates can search and apply for positions online. **Positions advertised include:** Administrative Assistant; Internal Auditor; Financial Analyst; Applications Analyst; Chemist; Pathogenic Microbiologist; Electrical Engineer; Hardware Engineer; Project Manager. **Corporate headquarters location:** This location. **Other U.S. locations:** Nationwide. **International locations:** Worldwide. **Subsidiaries include:** Amsco International, Inc.; Iosmedix, Inc. **Listed on:** New York Stock Exchange. **Stock exchange symbol:** STE. **Number of employees worldwide:** 5,100.

TENDER LOVING CARE/STAFF BUILDERS
6100 Rockside Woods Boulevard, Suite 100, Independence OH 44131. 216/642-0202. **Fax:** 216/642-3273. **Contact:** Human Resources. **World Wide Web address:** http://www.tlcathome.com. **Description:** A home health care agency. **Positions advertised include:** Home Health Aide; Licensed Practical Nurse; Registered Nurse; Physical Therapist. **Corporate headquarters location:** Lake Success NY. **Other U.S. locations:** Nationwide. **Number of employees nationwide:** 20,000.

TYCO HEALTHCARE/MALLINCKRODT
2111 East Galbraith Road, Cincinnati OH 45237. 513/761-2700. **Contact:** Manager of Human Resources. **World Wide Web address:** http://www.mallinckrodt.com. **Description:** A producer of medical and surgical electronic equipment including X-ray equipment. **Positions advertised include:** Design Engineer. **Corporate headquarters location:** St. Louis MO. **Other U.S. locations:** Nationwide. **International locations:** Worldwide. **Parent company:** Tyco Healthcare.

U.S. DEPARTMENT OF VETERANS AFFAIRS CHILLICOTHE VETERANS ADMINISTRATION MEDICAL CENTER
17273 State Route 104, Chillicothe OH 45601. 740/773-1141 ext. 7560 or 7079. **Fax:** 740/ 772-7056. **Contact:** Nate Darden, Human Resources. **World Wide Web address:** http://www.chillicothe.med.va.gov. **Description:** A medical center operated by the U.S. Department of Veterans Affairs. From 54 hospitals in 1930, the VA health care system has grown to include 171 medical centers; more than 364 outpatient, community, and outreach clinics; 130 nursing home care units; and 37 domiciliary residences. VA operates at least one medical center in each of the 48 contiguous states, Puerto Rico, and the District of Columbia. With approximately 76,000 medical center beds, VA treats nearly one million patients in VA hospitals; 75,000 in nursing home care units; and 25,000 in domiciliary residences. VA's outpatient clinics register approximately 24 million visits per year. **Positions advertised include:** Registered Nurse; Licensed Practical Nurse; Occupational Therapist; Physical Therapy Assistant; Medical Technician; Physician. **Other area locations:** Athens; Lancaster; Marietta; Portsmouth.

U.S. DEPARTMENT OF VETERANS AFFAIRS CLEVELAND VETERANS ADMINISTRATION MEDICAL CENTER
10000 Brecksville Road, Brecksville OH 44141. 440/526-3030. **Contact:** Human Resources Department. **World Wide Web address:** http://www.cleveland.med.va.gov. **Description:** A medical center operated by the U.S. Department of Veterans Affairs. From 54 hospitals in 1930, the VA health care system has grown to include 171 medical centers; more than 364 outpatient, community, and outreach clinics; 130 nursing home care units; and 37 domiciliary residences. VA operates at least one medical center in each of the 48 contiguous states, Puerto Rico, and the District of Columbia. With

approximately 76,000 medical center beds, VA treats nearly 1 million patients in VA hospitals; 75,000 in nursing home care units; and 25,000 in domiciliary residences. VA's outpatient clinics register approximately 24 million visits per year. **Corporate headquarters location:** Washington DC. **Other area locations:** Akron; Canton; East Liverpool; Mansfield; McCafferty; New Philadelphia; Painesville; Ravenna; Sandusky; Wade Park; Warren; Youngstown.

U.S. DEPARTMENT OF VETERANS AFFAIRS DAYTON VETERANS ADMINISTRATION MEDICAL CENTER
4100 West Third Street, Dayton OH 45428. 937/268-6511. **Contact:** Human Resources. **World Wide Web address:** http://www.dayton.med.va.gov. **Description:** A medical center operated by the U.S. Department of Veterans Affairs. From 54 hospitals in 1930, the VA health care system has grown to include 171 medical centers; more than 364 outpatient, community, and outreach clinics; 130 nursing home care units; and 37 domiciliary residences. VA operates at least one medical center in each of the 48 contiguous states, Puerto Rico, and the District of Columbia. With approximately 76,000 medical center beds, VA treats nearly 1 million patients in VA hospitals; 75,000 in nursing home care units; and 25,000 in domiciliary residences. VA's outpatient clinics register approximately 24 million visits per year.

UNIVERSITY HOSPITAL
234 Goodman Street, Cincinnati OH 45219. 513/584-2279. **Fax:** 513/584-2784. **Contact:** Human Resources. **World Wide Web address:** http://www.health-alliance.com/university.html. **Description:** A hospital specializing in acute and tertiary care. **Positions advertised include:** Radiologic Technologist; Special Procedures Technologist; Coder; Clinical Education Manager; Psychiatry Director; Patient Flow Manager; Health Unit Coordinator; Behavior Management Specialist; Administrative Secretary; Environmental Services Assistant; Paramedic; Licensed Practical Nurse; Pharmacist; Registered Nurse.

UNIVERSITY HOSPITAL BEDFORD MEDICAL CENTER
44 Blaine Avenue, Bedford OH 44146. 440/739-3900. **Recorded jobline:** 216/844-7500. **Fax:** 440/735-3552. **Contact:** Human Resources Manager. **E-mail address:** lashell.smith@uhhs.com. **World Wide Web address:** http://www.uhhsbmc.com. **Description:** A 110-bed nonprofit community hospital. **NOTE:** Second and third shifts are offered. **Positions advertised include:** Rehabilitation Aide; Licensed Practical Nurse; Nurse Practitioner; Registered Nurse; Pharmacist; Patient Registrar; Emergency Services Technician; Laboratory Technologist; Transcriptionist. **Parent company:** University Hospitals Health System (Cleveland OH). **Number of employees at this location:** 450.

UNIVERSITY HOSPITALS OF CLEVELAND
11100 Euclid Avenue, Cleveland OH 44106. 216/844-1000. **Fax:** 216/844-4765. **Recorded jobline:** 216/844-7500. **Contact:** Manager. **World Wide Web address:** http://www.uhhs.com. **Description:** A 947-bed, tertiary medical center. University Hospitals of Cleveland includes Rainbow Babies & Children's Hospital, Ireland Cancer Center, and MacDonald Women's Hospital. **NOTE:** Entry-level positions are offered. **Positions advertised include:** Accountant; Clerical Supervisor; Clinical Lab Technician; Dietician; EEG Technologist; EKG Technician; Emergency Medical Technician; Human Resources Manager; Licensed Practical Nurse; MIS Specialist; Nuclear Medicine Technologist; Occupational Therapist; Pharmacist; Physical Therapist; Psychologist; Registered Nurse; Social Worker; Software Engineer; Speech-Language Pathologist; Systems Analyst.

Oklahoma

HEALTHSOUTH SPORTS MEDICINE & REHABILITATION CENTER
12221 East 51st Street, Tulsa OK 74146. 918/249-0623. **Fax:** 405/624-7557. **Contact:** Joe Ogle, Administrator. **World Wide Web address:** http://www.healthsouth.com. **Description:** Provides general orthopedic and sports medicine treatments. **Special programs:** Continuing Education Program; Tuition Reimbursement Program. **Corporate headquarters location:** Birmingham AL. **Other area locations:** Statewide. **Other U.S. locations:** Nationwide. **International locations:** United Kingdom; Puerto Rico; Australia; Saudi Arabia. **Parent company:** HealthSouth. **Listed on:** New York Stock Exchange. **Stock exchange symbol:** HRC. **Number of employees worldwide:** Over 32,000.

HIGH POINTE
6501 NE 50th Street, Oklahoma City OK 73141-9613. 405/419-1500. **Fax:** 405/424-0729. **Contact:** Human Resources. **Description:** A 36-bed inpatient psychiatric hospital that provides services for children and adolescents. **NOTE:** Create an account and search for current jobs at http://www.okhealthjobs.com. **Positions advertised include:** Lead Film Librarian; Transporter; Financial Counselor; Health Unit Coordinator. **Number of employees at this location:** 43.

HILLCREST MEDICAL CENTER
1120 South Utica, Tulsa OK 74104. 918/579-5257. **Fax:** 918/579-7861. **Contact:** L. Clifton, Recruiter. **E-mail address:** lclifton@hillcrest.com. **World Wide Web address:** http://www.hillcrest.com. **Description:** A 577-bed tertiary hospital that is part of the Hillcrest Healthcare System network and provides a full range of diagnostic and therapeutic services to eastern Oklahoma. Established in 1916. **NOTE:** Online applications are available. For nursing positions, contact the Nurse Recruiter at 918/579-7645 or e-mail skeith@hillcrest.com. **Positions advertised include:** Chief Nursing Officer; Administration Director, Surgical Services; NICU Respiratory Therapist; Speech Pathologist; Pharmacist; Radiation Therapist; Coder; Executive Assistant.

LAUREATE PSYCHIATRIC CLINIC AND HOSPITAL
6655 South Yale Avenue, Tulsa OK 74136. 918/491-3742. **Fax:** 918/481-4080. **Recorded jobline:** 918/491-5662. **Contact:** Human Resources. **World Wide Web address:** http://www.laureate.com. **Description:** A private, non-profit, freestanding psychiatric facility that provides mental health care for adults, adolescents, and children. **NOTE:** For Nursing positions, contact Tricia Way, Nurse Recruiter, by telephone at 918/491-3742, or by fax at 918/481-4080. **Positions advertised include:** Care Worker; Intake Counselor; Psychiatric Technician; Recreational Therapy Specialist; Staff Secretary; Case Manager; Host Technician; Unit Communicator. **Special programs:** Tuition Assistance Plan. **Parent company:** Saint Francis Health System.

OKLAHOMA STATE UNIVERSITY CENTER FOR VETERINARY HEALTH SCIENCES
112 McElroy Hall, Stillwater OK 74078. 405/744-6985. **Contact:** Human Resources. **World Wide Web address:** http://www.cvm.okstate.edu. **Description:** A full-service veterinary teaching hospital for both small and large animals. **NOTE:** Current listings may be obtained from the Job Board at the OSU Human Resources/Staffing Solutions, 106 Whitehurst, Stillwater OK 74078. **Positions advertised include:** Veterinary Anesthesiologist; Postdoctoral Fellow; Postdoctoral Research Associate.

PARKVIEW HOSPITAL
2115 Park View Drive, El Reno OK 73036. 405/262-2640, extension 3023. **Fax:** 405/422-2575. **Contact:** Wendy Finnen. **E-mail address:** wendyfinnen@aol.com. **World Wide Web address:** http://www.parkview-hospital.com. **Description:** A nonprofit hospital that provides inpatient care, inpatient/outpatient surgical care, and outpatient services. **Positions advertised include:** Registered Nurse; Charge Nurse. **Number of employees at this location:** 350.

PLAZA MEDICAL GROUP
3433 NW 56th Street, Suite 400, Oklahoma City OK 73112. 405/951-4325. **Fax:** 405/951-4359. **Contact:** Human Resources. **E-mail address:** hr@plazamed.com. **World Wide Wed address:** http://www.plazamed.com. **Description:** A physician-owned and operated multispecialty medical group. **Positions advertised include:** Patient Accounts Representative; Switchboard Operator; Staff Accountant; Mobile Cardiovascular Sonographer; Cardiovascular Technician; Medical Assistant. **Corporate headquarters location:** This location. **Other area locations:** Statewide. **Listed on:** Privately held. **Number of employees at this location:** 140.

SOUTHWESTERN MEDICAL CENTER
5602 SW Lee Boulevard, Lawton OK 73505. 580/531-4700. **Fax:** 580/510-2816. **Contact:** Human Resources. **E-mail address:** hrdept@swmconline.com. **World Wide Web address:** http://www.swmconline.com. **Description:** A civilian hospital offering inpatient and outpatient services, as well as specialized services through its behavioral health, cancer, rehabilitation, and women's centers. Founded in 1907. **NOTE:** For physician positions, contact the Office of Physician Development at 877/303-3544, or by e-mail at ronnie.shaw@capellahealth.com or nikki.smith@capellahealth.com. **Positions advertised include:** Occupational Therapist; Ultrasonographer; CAT Scan Technologist; Physical Therapist; Staff Pharmacist; Registered Nurse. **Special programs:** Internships. **Parent company:** Capella Health. **Number of employees at this location:** 600.

U.S. DEPARTMENT OF VETERANS AFFAIRS VETERANS ADMINISTRATION MEDICAL CENTER
921 NE 13th Street, Oklahoma City OK 73104. 405/270-0501. **Fax:** 405/270-1560 **Contact:** Linda Oberly, Human Resources Specialist. **World Wide Wed address:** http://www.va.gov. **Description:** A 169-bed facility that serves as a primary, secondary, and tertiary care center for veterans. Founded in 1930, the VA Healthcare System has grown to include 171 medical centers, more than 364 outpatient, community, and outreach clinics, 130 nursing home care units, and 37 domiciliary residences. **NOTE:** Available positions are posted online at http://www.usajobs.opm.gov. Applications must be submitted either via mail or in person. **Positions advertised include:** Psychology Technician; Supervisory Occupational Therapist; Pipefitter; Physician; Occupational Therapist. **Other area locations:** Lawton OK; Ponca City OK; Ardmore OK; Clinton OK; Konawa OK. **Other U.S. locations:** AR; LA; TX; MS.

Oregon
ACUMED LLC
5885 Northwest Cornelius Pass Road, Hillsboro OR 97124. 503/627-9957. **Toll-free phone:** 888/627-9957. **Fax:** 503/643-1909. **Contact:** Human Resources. **E-mail address:** careers@acumed.net. **World Wide Web address:** http://www.acumed.net. **Description:** Designs, manufactures, and markets unique orthopedic trauma and reconstruction products. Products include: screw/pin fixation; elbow plates; modular hand system; intramedullary rods; bone plates; external fixation system; osteoclage cable system; and instruments. Founded in 1988. **Positions advertised include:** Machinist; Network Engineer. **Corporate headquarters location:** This location. **Parent company:** The Marmon Group.

ADVENTIST MEDICAL CENTER
10123 SE Market Street, Portland OR 97216. 503/257-2500. **Recorded jobline:** 503/251-6195. **Contact:** Human Resources. **E-mail address:** hrdept@ah.org. **World Wide Web address:** http://www.adventisthealthnw.com. **Description:** A 300-bed hospital. **NOTE:** The jobline number is for nursing postings only. For all other listings, please call 503/251-6295. **Positions advertised include:** Staff RN; Therapist; Surgical Technologist; Visiting RN; Account Representative; Department Secretary; Receptionist; Imaging Assistant; Cleaning Technician; Patient Service Representative; Plant Services Engineer; Staff Technologist; Security Officer. **Corporate headquarters location:** Rosedale CA. **Parent company:** Advent Health System.

ARTISAN DENTAL LABORATORY
2532 SE Hawthorne Boulevard, Portland OR 97214. 503/238-6006. **Toll-free phone:** 800/222-6721. **Fax:** 503/231-3684. **Contact:** Human Resources. **World Wide Web address:** http://www.addl.com. **Description:** A dental laboratory that manufactures dentures, implants, crowns, bridges, and other ceramic dental products.

ASSISTED LIVING CONCEPTS, INC.
2825 Neff Road, Bend OR 97701. 541/317-8464. **Fax:** 541/317-4147. **Contact:** Personnel. **E-mail address:** hr@alcco.com. **World Wide Web address:** http://www.alcco.com. **Description:** Owns, operates, and develops assisted living facilities for elderly persons. The company also provides personal care and support services. **Positions advertised include:** Regional Nurse Consultant; Assisted Living Administrator; Regional Director of Operations; Community Sales Coordinator; Lead Cook; Cook; Nurse Consultant; Activity Services Coordinator; Lead Personal Services Assistant; Maintenance Technician; Personal Service Assistant. **Corporate headquarters location:** Dallas TX. **Other U.S. locations:** Nationwide. **Operations at this facility include:** Administration; Service. **Listed on:** American Stock Exchange. **Stock exchange symbol:** ALF.

DAHLIN/FERNANDEZ/FRITZ DENTAL LABORATORY
6421 North Cutter Circle, P.O. Box 4755, Portland OR 97217. 503/240-1910. **Toll-free phone:** 800/422-5779. **Fax:** 503/240-1905. **Contact:** Human Resources Department. **E-mail address:** leonetti@dff-dentallab.com. **World Wide Web address:** http://www.dff-dentallab.com. **Description:** Manufactures crowns, prosthetics, and partials.

EASTMORELAND SURGICAL CLINIC
2900 SE Steele Street, Portland OR 97202. 503/232-2163. **Contact:** Manager of Human Resources. A for-profit, acute-care clinic with 100 beds. **Positions advertised include:** District Nurse; Registered Nurse; Certified Nurse Assistant; Nuclear Medical Technician; Case Manager; Respiratory Therapist. **Corporate headquarters location:** Nashville TN. **Parent company:** ORNDA Healthcorp.

GOOD SAMARITAN HOSPITAL CORVALLIS
3600 NW Samaritan Drive, Corvallis OR 97330. 541/768-5111. **Fax:** 541/768-6400. **Contact:** Human Resources Recruiter. **E-mail address:** hrgsrm@goodsam.org. **World Wide Web address:** http://www.samhealth.org . **Description:** A for-profit hospital offering general medical care and 180 beds. **Positions advertised include:** Account Analyst; Cash Specialist; Assistant Department Manager; Engineer; Supervisor; Housekeeper; Blood Bank Assistant; Laboratory Assistant Manager; Certified Nurses Assistant. **Parent company:** Legacy Health System also operates area hospitals Emanuel, Mount Hood, and Meridian Park Medical Center.

GRANDE RONDE HOSPITAL
900 Sunset Drive, La Grande OR 97850-1396. 541/963-8421. **Contact:** Personnel. **World Wide Web address:** http://www.grh.org. **Description:** A hospital with 49 acute care beds, a 14-bed transitional care unit, and a family birthing center. Grande Ronde Hospital also offers home health, hospice, and outpatient services. **Positions advertised include:** Registered Nurse; Respiratory Therapist.

HEALTHNET OF OREGON
13221 SW 68th Parkway, Suite 200, Tigard OR 97223. **Toll-free phone:** 888/802-7001. **Contact:** Human Resources. **E-mail address:** service@health.net. **World Wide Web address:**

http://www.healthnetoregon.com. **Description:** A health maintenance organization serving Oregon and Southwest Washington. **NOTE:** Online applications preferred.

HEALTHSOUTH
2330 Flanders Street, Portland OR 97210. 503/228-8575. **Contact:** Human Resources. **World Wide Web address:** http://www.healthsouth.com. **Description:** Provides comprehensive outpatient rehabilitation services to patients suffering from work-, sports-, and accident-related injuries. **Corporate headquarters location:** Birmingham AL.

HOLY ROSARY MEDICAL CENTER
351 SW Ninth Street, Ontario OR 97914. 541/889-5331. **Toll-free phone:** 877/225-4762. **Contact:** Karen Kosowan, Human Resources Director. **E-mail address:** info@holyrosary-ontario.org. **World Wide Web address:** http://www.holyrosary-ontario.org. **Description:** An 80-bed hospital providing general medical services. **Positions advertised include:** Registered Nurse; Radiology Technician; Registrar; Physical Therapist; Certified Occupational Therapist; Respiratory Care Sleep Technician.

LEGACY EMANUEL CHILDREN'S HOSPITAL
2801 N. Gantenbien Avenue, Portland OR 97227. 503/413-2500. **Toll-free phone:** 866/888-4398. **E-mail address:** employment@lhs.org. **Contact:** Personnel Department. **World Wide Web address:** http://www.legacyhealth.org. **Description:** A for-profit hospital offering children's and general medical services. **NOTE:** Applications are required with resumes. **Positions advertised include:** Benefits Specialist; Clinical Nursing Coordinator; Office Assistant; Registered Nurse. **Parent company:** Legacy Health System also operates the following area hospitals: Good Samaritan, Meridian Park, and Mount Hood Medical Center.

LEGACY HEALTH SYSTEM
1919 NW Lovejoy Street, Portland OR 97209. 503/225-8600. **Fax:** 503/415-5788. **Contact:** Human Resources. **World Wide Web address:** http://www.legacyhealth.org. **Description:** Operates four Portland area hospitals and offers visiting nurse services. **Corporate headquarters location:** This location.

LEGACY LABORATORY SERVICES
1225 NE Second Avenue, Portland OR 97232. 503/413-5000. **Toll-free phone:** 877/270-5566. **Fax:** 503/413-5048. **Contact:** Manager. **Description:** A clinical laboratory that provides a variety of services for area hospitals.

LEGACY MERIDIAN PARK HOSPITAL
19300 SW 65th Avenue, Tualatin OR 97062-9741. 503/692-1212. **Contact:** Human Resources. **World Wide Web address:** http://www.legacyhealth.org. **Description:** A 100-bed hospital providing general medical care. **Parent company:** Legacy Health System (Portland OR).

LEGACY MOUNT HOOD HOSPITAL
24800 SE Stark Street, Gresham OR 97030. 503/667-1122. **Contact:** Human Resources. **World Wide Web address:** http://www.legacyhealth.org. **Description:** A 120-bed for-profit hospital. **Corporate headquarters location:** Portland OR. **Parent company:** Legacy Health System also operates area hospitals Good Samaritan, Meridian Park, and Emanuel.

MACKENZIE WILLAMETTE HOSPITAL
1460 G Street, Springfield OR 97477. 541/726-4400. **Fax:** 541/744-8565. **Contact:** Human Resources Department. **World Wide Web address:** http://www.mckweb.com. **Description:** A hospital with 114 beds. **Positions advertised include:** Special Procedures Technologist; Patient Access Clerk; Home Care Physical Therapist.

MERCY MEDICAL CENTER
2700 Stewart Parkway, Roseburg OR 97470. 541/673-0611. **Toll-free phone:** 800/962-2406. **Fax:** 541/677-2176. **Contact:** Human Resources & Learning Center. **E-mail address:** carriethompson@chiwest.com. **World Wide Web address:** http://www.mercyrose.org. **Description:** A 200-bed hospital providing general medical care. **Number of employees at this location:** 1,400.

MERLE WEST MEDICAL CENTER
2865 Daggett Avenue, Klamath Falls OR 97601. 541/882-6311. **Recorded jobline:** 541/883-6020. **Contact:** Human Resources Department. **World Wide Web address:** http://www.mwmc.org. **Description:** A 176-bed hospital. **Positions advertised include:** Nursing Supervisor; Patient Care Coordinator; RN; Case manager; Radiologic Technologist. **Number of employees at this location:** 1,100.

MICRO SYSTEMS ENGINEERING, INC. (MSEI)
6024 Jean Road, B-4, Lake Oswego OR 97035-5369. **Contact:** Human Resources. **E-mail address:** careers@biotronik.com. **World Wide Web address:** http://www.biotronik.com. **Description:** Researches, develops, and tests microelectronic components used for bradycardia and tachycardia therapy. MSEI's integrated circuit chips are used in pacemakers and defibrillators. Founded in 1979. **Positions advertised include:** Electronics Manufacturing Test Technician. **Other U.S. locations:** Denver CO; Houston TX. **Parent company:** BIOTRONIK CmbH & Co. (Berlin Germany). **Number of employees at this location:** 285.

MURRAYHILL VETERINARY HOSPITAL
14831 SW Teal Boulevard, Beaverton OR 97007. 503/579-3300. **Fax:** 503/579-4645. **Contact:** Human Resources. **E-mail address:** staff@murrayhillvethospital.com. **World Wide Web address:** http://www.murrayhillvethospital.com. **Description:** Murrayhill Veterinary Hospital offers complete animal care including surgery, dentistry, and neuropathic care.

OREGON STATE HOSPITAL
1121 NE 2nd Avenue, Portland OR 97232. 503/731-8620. **Contact:** Human Resources Department. **World Wide Web address:** http://www.dhs.state.or.us/jobs/. **Description:** A 68-bed satellite hospital of Oregon State Hospital in Portland.

PROVIDENCE MEDFORD MEDICAL CENTER
1111 Crater Lake Avenue, Medford OR 97504. 541/732-5078. **Contact:** Director of Human Resources. **World Wide Web address:** http://www.providence.org/medford. **Description:** A 168-bed general hospital. **NOTE:** See website for monthly recruiting events. **Positions advertised include:** Accounting Clerk; Central Service Supply Technician; Home Health Clerk; Emergency Room Technician; Central Point Medical Assistant; Medical Lab Technologist. **Corporate headquarters location:** Seattle WA. **Other U.S. locations:** AL; CA. **Parent company:** Sisters of Providence Health System.

PROVIDENCE MILWAUKIE HOSPITAL
10150 SE 32nd Avenue, Milwaukie OR 97222. 503/652-8300. **Recorded jobline:** 503/513-8488. **Contact:** Human Resources Director. **World Wide Web address:** http://www.providence.org. **Description:** A 56-bed hospital. **NOTE:** It is recommended that employment matters are handled through the website, or the central location at 1235 NE 47th Street, 503/215-5770. **Corporate headquarters location:** Seattle WA. **Parent company:** Providence Health System.

PROVIDENCE PORTLAND MEDICAL CENTER
4805 NE Glisan Street, Portland OR 97213. 503/215-1111. **Recorded jobline:** 503/215-6292. **Contact:** Human Resources. **World Wide Web address:** http://www.providence.org. **Description:** A 483-bed medical center. **Positions advertised include:** Acute

Care Manager; Purchasing Agent; Business Analyst; Bilingual Medical Assistant; Care Manager; Cashier; Cleaning Attendant; Certified Nurses Aide; Collections Representative; Culinary Assistant. **Corporate headquarters location:** Seattle WA. **Parent company:** Providence Health System.

SACRED HEART MEDICAL CENTER
1255 Hilyard Street, Eugene OR 97401. 541/686-7300. **Recorded jobline:** 541/686-6960. **Contact:** Human Resources. **World Wide Web address:** http://www.peacehealth.org. **Description:** A hospital with approximately 432 beds. **NOTE:** Jobseekers are encouraged to apply via the Website. **Positions advertised include:** Charge Nurse; Data Analyst; Diagnostic Technician; Database Systems Analyst; Emergency Room Technician; Licensed Practical Nurse; Patient Access Specialist; Pharmacist; Physical Therapist; Registered Nurse; Surgical Technician. **Parent company:** Peace Health.

ST. CHARLES MEDICAL CENTER
2500 NE Neff Road, Bend OR 97701. 541/388-7770. **Contact:** Human Resources. **E-mail address:** scmc@scmc.org. **World Wide Web address:** http://www.scmc.org. **Description:** A 181-bed community hospital offering general medical care. **Positions advertised include:** RN; Assistant Unit Manager; Care Associate; Dietician; Registered Medical Technologist; Pharmacist; Occupational Therapist; Physical Therapist; Accounting Clerk; Admitting Representative; PC Support Specialist; Patient Account Representative; Refund Analyst; Behavioral Health Clerk; Central Processing Technician; Preparation Cook; Team Leader; Application Analyst; Laboratory Manager; Purchasing Coordinator. **Number of employees at this location:** 1,200.

ST. VINCENT DEPAUL REHABILITATION SERVICE
4660 Portland Road NE, Suite 108, Salem OR 97305. 503/856-9563. **Toll-free phone:** 800/755-5880. **Fax:** 503/856-9848. **Contact:** Human Resources Department. **World Wide Web address:** http://www.stvincentdepaul.org. **Description:** Provides vocational training to disabled individuals. The nonprofit agency also offers job placement services. **Positions advertised include:** Custodian; Certified Flagger. **Corporate headquarters location:** Portland OR. **Other area locations:** Corvallis OR; Hillsboro OR; Springfield OR.

SALEM HOSPITAL
P.O. Box 14001, Salem OR 97309. 503/561-5200. **Physical address**: 665 Winter Street, Salem OR 97301. **Toll-free phone:** 800/825-5199. **Physical address:** 665 Winter Street SE, Salem OR 97301. **Contact:** Employment Office. **E-mail address:** human.resources@salemhospital.org. **World Wide Web address:** http://www.salemhospital.org. **Description:** A nonprofit hospital with approximately 454 beds. **Positions advertised include:** RN; Cancer Registrar; Director of Maternal Child Health; Licensed Physical Therapy Assistant; Nuclear Medical Technician; Occupational Therapist; Radiology Technician; Transcriptionist; Maintenance Helper.

SHRINER'S HOSPITAL
3101 SW Sam Jackson Park Road, Portland OR 97239. 503/241-5090. **Fax:** 503/221-3475. **Recorded jobline:** 503/221-3459. **Contact:** Human Resources. **World Wide Web address:** http://www.shrinershq.org/shc/portland/. **Description:** A children's and general care hospital with approximately 40 beds. **Positions advertised include:** Maintenance Technician; Registered Nurse; House Supervisor; Care Coordinator. **Corporate headquarters location:** Tampa FL.

WILLAMETTE DENTAL GROUP, P.C.
OREGON DENTAL SPECIALISTS, P.C.
14025 SW Farmington Road, Beaverton OR 97005. 503/644-6444. **Recorded jobline:** 503/671-9486. **Contact:** Human Resources. **World Wide Web address:** http://www.denkor.com. **Description:** Willamette Dental Group operates dentist's offices in Oregon and Washington and provides dental insurance plans. **Corporate headquarters location:** This location. **Parent company:** Denkor Dental Management Corporation. **Operations at this facility include:** This location houses administrative offices.

WILLAMETTE VALLEY MEDICAL CENTER
2700 Staratus Avenue, McMinnville OR 97128. 503/472-6131. **Fax:** 503/435-6374. **Recorded jobline:** 503/435-6372. **Contact:** Human Resources Director. **World Wide Web address:** http://www.wvmcweb.com. **Description:** An acute-care inpatient and outpatient medical center. Founded in 1904. **NOTE:** Part-time jobs and second and third shifts are offered. **Positions advertised include:** Charge Nurse; RN Critical Care; Radiology Technologist; RN Emergency; RN Medical/Surgery. **Office hours:** Monday - Friday, 8:00 a.m. - 5:00 p.m. **Corporate headquarters location:** Dallas TX. **Other U.S. locations:** Nationwide. **Parent company:** Triad Hospital, Inc. **Listed on:** NASDAQ. **Stock exchange symbol:** TRIH.

Pennsylvania

ALBERT EINSTEIN MEDICAL CENTER
5501 Old York Road, Philadelphia PA 19141. 215/456-7890. **Contact:** Human Resources. **World Wide Web address:** http://www.einstein.edu. **Description:** A teaching hospital specializing in behavioral health; coronary care; geriatrics; liver, kidney, and pancreas transplants; orthopedics; and women's and children's health. **NOTE:** Search and apply for positions online. **Positions advertised include:** Chief Dosimetrist; RN, Various Departments; Employee Relations/Compliance Specialist; Consultation and Education Specialist; Clinical Manager, Pediatric Clinic; Respiratory Therapist.

ALBRIGHT CARE SERVICES
1700 Normandie Drive, York PA 17404. 717/764-6262. **Toll-free phone:** 888/970-6565. **Contact:** Human Resources. **E-mail address:** normandie@albrightcare.org. **World Wide Web address:** http://www.albrightcare.org. **Description:** Albright Care Services owns and operates senior living communities that offer a range of housing and healthcare options. **Positions advertised include:** CAN; LPN; RN; Director of Environmental Services.

ALLEGHENY VALLEY SCHOOL
1996 Ewings Mill Road, Coraopolis PA 15108. 412/299-7777. **Fax:** 412/299-6701. **Contact:** Richard R. Rizzutto, Director of Human Resources. **World Wide Web address:** http://www.alleghenyvalleyschool.com. **Description:** A nonprofit company that operates residential facilities for individuals with mental disabilities. Founded in 1960. **NOTE:** Entry-level positions, part-time jobs, and second and third shifts are offered. **Positions advertised include:** Program Development Assistant; Assistant House Manager; Direct Care Worker; House Manager Aide; Registered Nurse; Licensed Practical Nurse; Program Instructor. **Corporate headquarters location:** This location. **Executive Director:** Regis G. Champ. **Annual sales/revenues:** $51 - $100 million. **Number of employees at this location:** 1,000.

ALLIANCE IMAGING, INC.
20 Stanwix Street, 11th Floor, Pittsburgh PA 15222. 412/281-5660. **Toll-free phone:** 800/453-8135. **Fax:** 412/281-1767. **Contact:** Human Resources Manager. **E-mail address:** info@allianceimaging.com. **World Wide Web address:** http://www.allianceimaging.com. **Description:** Provides medical diagnostic imaging services to hospitals, physicians, and patients. Services include MRI, Open MRI, computer tomography (CT), ultrasound, and position emission tomography (PET). **Positions advertised include:** MRI/CT Technologist; Driver; **Corporate headquarters location:** Anaheim CA. **Listed on:** New York Stock Exchange. **Stock exchange symbol:** AIQ.

AMERICAN COLLEGE OF PHYSICIANS
190 North Independence Mall West, Philadelphia PA 19106-1572. 215/351-2400. **Toll-free phone:** 800/523-1546. **Contact:** Human Resources. **World Wide Web address:** http://www.acponline.org. **Description:** The American College of Physicians (ACP) is the nation's largest medical specialty society, with 119,000 members. Its mission is to enhance the quality and effectiveness of health care by fostering excellence and professionalism in the practice of medicine. **Positions advertised include:** Administrative/Editorial Coordinator; Statistician; Network Analyst; Council of Associates Coordinator. **Other U.S. locations:** Washington DC.

APRIA HEALTHCARE GROUP INC.
16 Creek Parkway, Boothwyn PA 19061. 610/364-2100. **Fax:** 610/364-2270. **Contact:** Regional Human Resources. **World Wide Web address:** http://www.apria.com. **Description:** One of the largest national providers of home health care products and services, providing a broad range of respiratory therapy services, home medical equipment, and infusion therapy services. Apria has over 500 branches throughout the United States and two respiratory therapy branches in the United Kingdom. Apria's home health care services are provided to patients who have been discharged from hospitals, skilled nursing facilities, or convalescent homes and are being treated at home. In conjunction with medical professionals, Apria personnel deliver, install, and service medical equipment, as well as provide appropriate therapies and coordinate plans of care for their patients. Apria personnel also instruct patients and caregivers in the correct use of equipment and monitor the equipment's effectiveness. **NOTE:** Search and apply for positions online. **Positions advertised include:** Staff Pharmacist; Clinical Coordinator. **Corporate headquarters location:** Costa Mesa CA.

AQUATIC AND FITNESS CENTER AT PENNYPACK
3600 Grant Avenue, Philadelphia PA 19114. 215/677-0400. **Contact:** Human Resources. **World Wide Web address:** http://www.aquahab.com. **Description:** Provides aquatic physical therapy, land therapy, and work conditioning for people recovering from back and neck injuries, industrial injuries, sports-related orthopedic injuries, post-operative arthroscopic surgeries, joint replacement, postfracture recovery and postoperative knee/shoulder recovery. **Positions advertised include:** Medical Collector; Personal Trainer; Physical Therapist.

ARROW INTERNATIONAL INC.
P.O. Box 12888, Reading PA 19612-2888. 610/378-0131. **Fax:** 610/478-3194. **Physical address:** 2400 Bernville Road, Reading PA 19605. **Contact:** Staffing Manager. **E-mail address:** staffing.manager@arrowintl.com. **World Wide Web address:** http://www.arrowintl.com. **Description:** Develops, manufactures, and markets central vascular access catheterization products. Arrow's products are also used for patient monitoring, diagnosis, pain management, and treating patients with heart and vascular disease. **Corporate headquarters location:** This location. **Other U.S. locations:** NJ; NC. **Operations at this facility include:** Administration; Manufacturing; Research and Development. **Listed on:** NASDAQ. **Stock exchange symbol:** ARRO. **Number of employees nationwide:** 1,540.

BARNES-KASSON COUNTY HOSPITAL S.N.F.
400 Turnpike Street, Susquehanna PA 18847. 570/853-3135. **Toll-free phone:** 800/323-2051. **Fax:** 570/853-3223. **Contact:** Human Resources. **World Wide Web address:** http://www.barnes-kasson.org. **Description:** A 50-bed community hospital with an attached 58-bed skilled nursing facility. The hospital also offers home health services and outpatient therapy. **NOTE:** Second and third shifts are offered. **Positions advertised include:** Physician; Physical Therapist; RN; LPN; CPN. **Special programs:** Internships; Summer Jobs. **CEO:** Sara Iveson. **Annual sales/revenues:** $11 - $20 million. **Number of employees at this location:** 350.

BELMONT CENTER FOR COMPREHENSIVE TREATMENT
4200 Monument Road, Philadelphia PA 19131. 215/877-2000. **Contact:** Human Resources Department. **World Wide Web address:** http://www.einstein.edu. **Description:** Offers inpatient and outpatient treatment to adolescents, adults, and families for a range of problems including addictions and eating disorders. **Parent company:** Albert Einstein Healthcare Network.

BENCHMARK MEDICAL, INC.
Valleybrooke Corporate Center, 101 Lindenwood Drive, Suite 420, Malvern PA 19355. 610/644-7824. **Toll-free phone:** 866/786-8482. **Fax:** 610/644-9065. **Contact:** Human Resources. **World Wide Web address:** http://www.keystonerehab.com. **Description:** A provider of musculoskeletal outpatient rehabilitation, with over 402 locations in 22 states. **Positions advertised include:** Human Resource Director. **Corporate headquarters location:** This location.

BENCO DENTAL COMPANY
11 Bear Creek Boulevard, Wilkes-Barre PA 18702. 570/825-7781. **Toll-free phone:** 800/GO-BENCO. **Contact:** Human Resources. **World Wide Web address:** http://www.benco.com. **Description:** Distributes and rents dental equipment to hospitals, schools, and governmental agencies. **Positions advertised include:** Territory Representatives; Service Technicians.

BOEKEL SCIENTIFIC
855 Pennsylvania Boulevard, Feasterville PA 19053. 215/396-8200. **Toll-free phone:** 800/336-6929. **Fax:** 215/396-8264. **Contact:** Human Resources Manager. **World Wide Web address:** http://www.boekelsci.com. **Description:** Manufactures life science and general lab products.

B. BRAUN MEDICAL, INC.
901 Marcon Boulevard, Allentown PA 18109. 610/266-0500. **Fax:** 610/266-5702. **Contact:** Human Resources. **E-mail address:** hr.allentown@bbraunusa.com. **World Wide Web address:** http://www.bbraunusa.com. **Description:** Manufactures intravenous systems and solutions. The company also offers IV accessories, critical care products, epidural anesthesia, and pharmaceutical devices. **Positions advertised include:** Process/Industrial Engineer; Quality Control lab Associate; Sr. Staff Engineer; QA Analyst. **Other area locations:** Bethlehem, PA. **Parent company:** B. Braun of America.

BRYN MAWR HOSPITAL
130 South Bryn Mawr Avenue, Bryn Mawr PA 19010. 610/526-3026. **Fax:** 610/526-3068. **Contact:** Human Resources Department. **World Wide Web address:** http://www.mainlinehealth.org/bmh. **Description:** A teaching hospital that provides medical, psychiatric, and surgical services, and offers the surrounding community the following specialized programs: Primary Care Services, the Arthritis and Orthopaedic Center, Comprehensive Cancer Care Center, Cardiovascular Center, and Women and Children's Health Resources. In addition, the hospital provides a wide array of other community programs including support groups, educational programs, physician referral services, health screenings, and a speakers bureau. **NOTE:** Please see http://www.employment.jefferson.edu/bmh for application details. **Positions advertised include:** Central Intake Coordinator; EAP Consultant; Staff Nurse; Cardiac Cath lab Technologist. **Corporate headquarters location:** Radnor PA. **Parent company:** Main Line Health System.

CJ SYSTEMS AVIATION GROUP
57 Allegheny County Airport, West Mifflin PA 15122. 412/466-2500. **Toll-free phone:** 800/245-0230. **Fax:** 412/469-1556. **Contact:** Dawn Chambers, Director of Human Resources. **E-mail address:**

resumes@cjsystemsaviation.com. **World Wide Web address:** http://www.corpjet.com. **Description:** Provides air medical services in the U.S. with a fleet of 115 helicopters and fixed-wing aircraft. **Positions advertised include:** Director of Standards and Compliance; Director of Training. **Corporate headquarters location:** This location. **Other U.S. locations:** Scottsdale AZ. **International locations:** Naples; Singapore. **Operations at this facility include:** This location houses the company's aircraft maintenance facility. **Parent company:** FSS Airholdings Inc. **Number of employees at this location:** 320. **Number of employees nationwide:** 600.

CATHOLIC HEALTH EAST
14 Campus Boulevard, Suite 300, Newtown Square PA 19073. 610/355-2106. **Fax:** 610/355-2107. **Contact:** Human Resources. **E-mail address:** info@che.org. **World Wide Web address:** http://www.che.org. **Description:** Catholic Health East is a health care system operation 28 regional systems in 10 Eastern states. The health care system includes three behavioral health facilities, 32 hospitals, and 28 skilled nursing centers. **Positions advertised include:** Director, Clinical Transformation and Research; Research Consultant; Sr. Internal Consultant; VP Information Technology and CIO. **Operations at this facility include:** This location houses administrative offices. Number of employees nationwide: 43,000.

CHESTER COUNTY HOSPITAL
701 East Marshall Street, West Chester PA 19380. 610/431-5000. **Recorded jobline:** 610/430-2903. **Fax:** 610/430-2956. **Contact:** Human Resources. **World Wide Web address:** http://www.cchosp.com. **Description:** A hospital. **Positions advertised include:** Case Manager; Social Worker; Registered Nurse, Various Departments; Surgical Tech; Staff Respiratory Therapist; Interpreter. **Number of employees at this location:** 1,400.

CHILDREN'S HOSPITAL OF PITTSBURGH
3705 Fifth Avenue, Pittsburgh PA 15213-2524. 412/692-7500. **Recorded jobline:** 412/692-8000 (non-clinical positions); 412/692-5366 (clinical positions). **Contact:** Human Resources. **E-mail address:** jobs@chp.edu. **World Wide Web address:** http://www.chp.edu. **Description:** A pediatric hospital serving children up to the age of 18. **Positions advertised include:** Behavioral Health Consultant; Chief Research Technician; Sr. Pharmacist; Speech Language Pathologist.

CHILDREN'S INSTITUTE
1405 Shady Avenue, Pittsburgh PA 15217. 412/420-2400. **Contact:** Human Resources. **World Wide Web address:** http://www.amazingkids.org. **Description:** A rehabilitation hospital. **NOTE:** Interested jobseekers should address their resume to the department in which their interest lies. **Positions advertised include:** Director of Pediatric Physical Therapy; Occupational Therapist; Staff Psychologist.

CROZER-CHESTER MEDICAL CENTER
One Medical Center Boulevard, Upland PA 19013-3995. 610/447-2262. **Contact:** Human Resources Department. **World Wide Web address:** http://www.crozer.org. **Description:** This location is a 675-bed teaching hospital. The medical center also offers the Antepartum Assessment Center, Comprehensive Breast Health Program, Crozer Home, Crozer Regional Cancer Center, Heart Surgery/Cardiac Center, John E. DuPont Trauma Center, Maternity Center, and Nathan Speare Burn Center. **Positions advertised include:** CAT Scan Technician; Cardiac Echo Technician; Carpenter; Child Resource Coordinator; Clinical Instructor; Data Quality Supervisor; Director of Purchasing Services; Intensive Case Manager; Lab Services Representative; Paramedic; Registered Nurse; Licensed Practical Nurse. **Parent company:** Crozer-Keystone Health System.

DAVITA, INC.
1180 West Swedesford Road, Suite 300, Berwyn PA 19312. 610/644-4796. **Toll-free phone:** 800/633-9757. **Contact:** Recruiting. **World Wide Web address:** http://www.davita.com. **Description:** Provides dialysis services to patients suffering from chronic kidney disease (CKD) through 1235 outpatient dialysis centers in 41 states. Founded in 1988. **Positions advertised include:** Account Receivables Collections Assistant; Administrative Assistant; Clinical Quality and Education Manager; Collections Representative; Compliance Specialist; Help Desk Analyst. **Special programs:** Internships. **Office hours:** Monday - Friday, 9:00 a.m. - 5:00 p.m. **Corporate headquarters location:** El Segundo CA. **Other U.S. locations:** Nationwide. **International locations:** Argentina. **Subsidiaries include:** Renal Diagnostic Laboratory (Las Vegas NV). **Operations at this facility include:** Divisional Headquarters. **Listed on:** New York Stock Exchange. **Stock exchange symbol:** RXT. **CEO:** Robert Mayer. **Annual sales/revenues:** More than $100 million. **Number of employees at this location:** 250. **Number of employees nationwide:** 3,400.

DENTSPLY INTERNATIONAL INC.
Susquehanna Commerce Center, 221 West Philadelphia Street, P.O. Box 872, York PA 17405-0872. 717/845-7511. **Toll-free phone:** 800/877-0020. **Fax:** 717/849-4762. **Contact:** Human Resources. **E-mail address:** corpjobs@dentsply.com. **World Wide Web address:** http://www.dentsply.com. **Description:** A leading manufacturer of X-ray equipment and other products for the dental field including artificial teeth, prophylaxis paste, ultrasonic sealers, and bone substitute/grafting materials. **Positions advertised include:** Regulatory Manager; Production Supervisor; Sr. Product Manager; HR Generalist; European Business Analyst. **Corporate headquarters location:** This location. **Other U.S. locations:** Carlsbad CA; Encino CA; Los Angeles CA; Lakewood CO; Milford DE; Des Plaines IL; Elgin IL; Burlington NJ; Maumee OH; Tulsa OK; Johnson City TN. **International locations:** Argentina; Australia; Brazil; Canada; China; England; France; Germany; Hong Kong; India; Italy; Japan; Mexico; Philippines; Puerto Rico; Russia; Switzerland; Thailand; Vietnam. **Listed on:** NASDAQ. **Stock exchange symbol:** XRAY.

DOYLESTOWN HOSPITAL
595 West State Street, Doylestown PA 18901. 215/345-2200. **Fax:** 215/345-2827. **Recorded jobline:** 215/345-2538. **Contact:** Human Resources. **E-mail address:** info@dhjobs.org. **World Wide Web address:** http://www.dh.org. **Description:** A 196-bed hospital. **Positions advertised include:** Assistant Teacher; CAT Scan Technician; Chief Information Officer; Chief Financial Officer Development Manager; Registered Nurse; MRI Tech; Pharmacist. **Number of employees at this location:** 1,400.

EASTON HOSPITAL
250 South 21st Street, Easton PA 18042. 610/250-4120. **Fax:** 610/250-4876. **Contact:** Human Resources. **World Wide Web address:** http://www.easton-hospital.com. **Description:** A hospital. **Positions advertised include:** Assistant Chief Executive Officer; Registered Respiratory Therapist; Nuclear Medicine Technologist; Phlebotomist; RN, Various Departments.

ELWYN INC.
111 Elwyn Road, Elwyn PA 19063. 610/891-2414. **Fax:** 610/891-7395. **Contact:** Susan Ladd, Human Resources. **E-mail address:** susan_ladd@elwyn.org. **World Wide Web address:** http://www.elwyn.org. **Description:** A long-term care rehabilitation center for people with physical and mental disabilities.

FLOWERS MILL VETERINARY HOSPITAL P.C.
10 South Flowers Mill Road, Langhorne PA 19047. 215/752-1010. **Fax:** 215/757-2328. **Contact:** Human Resources. **Wide Web address:** http://www.fmvh.com. **Description:** Offers boarding services and general medical and surgical care to small and exotic animals.

FOX CHASE CANCER CENTER
333 Cottman Avenue, Philadelphia PA 19111-2497. 215/728-6900. **Fax:** 215/728-2682. **Contact:** Department of Human Resources. **World Wide Web address:** http://www.fccc.edu. **Description:** A comprehensive cancer center that serves as a national resource for converting research findings into medical applications. Applications are designed to improve cancer detection, treatment, and prevention. **Positions advertised include:** Project Manager; Phlebotomist; Systems Analyst; Data Manager; Pharmacist; Staff RN; Clinical Research Coordinator. **Corporate headquarters location:** This location. **Number of employees at this location:** 1,700.

FRANKFORD HOSPITAL
Knights and Red Lion Roads, Philadelphia PA 19114. 215/612-4000. **Fax:** 215/612-4073. **Contact:** Human Resources Department. **World Wide Web address:** http://www.frankfordhospitals.org. **Description:** Frankford has three hospitals and three outpatient sites that serve patients throughout Northeast Philadelphia and Bucks County. **NOTE:** See website for a listing of current openings with application details. **Positions advertised include:** Certified Nurse Assistant; ER Physician; Home Care Registered Nurse; Medical Technician; Physical Therapist; Speech Pathologist; Emergency Record Coder; Registrar.

FRICK HOSPITAL
508 South Church Street, Mount Pleasant PA 15666-1790. 724/547-1500. **Contact:** Human Resources. **Description:** A 153-bed general hospital with a variety of specialists on staff.

GEISINGER MEDICAL CENTER
100 North Academy Avenue, Danville PA 17822. 570/271-6211. **Toll-free phone:** 877/564-6447. **Fax:** 570/271-5060. **Contact:** Human Resources Department. **E-mail address:** careers@geisinger.edu. **World Wide Web address:** http://www.geisinger.org. **Description:** A tertiary care teaching hospital with 45 regional clinics in central and northeastern Pennsylvania. Geisinger Medical Center is a Level I trauma center. **Positions advertised include:** Cardiologist; Gastroenterologist; Radiologist; Dermatologist; Hematologist; Neurologist. **Operations at this facility include:** Administration; Divisional Headquarters; Research and Development. **Number of employees at this location:** 3,500.

GENESIS HEALTHCARE CORPORATION
101 East State Street, Kennett Square PA 19348. 610/444-6350. **Fax:** 610/925-4352. **Contact:** Recruitment Manager. **World Wide Web address:** http://www.genesishcc.com. **Description:** Provides long term care at 200 skilled nursing centers and assisted living residences in 12 states. **Positions advertised include:** Billing Supervisor; Business Analyst; Certified Nurse Aide; Director, Clinical Practice; Implementation Specialist; Occupational Therapist; Pharmacy Therapist. **Corporate headquarters location:** This location. **Listed on:** NASDAQ. **Stock exchange symbol:** GHCI.

GRADUATE HOSPITAL
1800 Lombard Street, Philadelphia PA 19146. 215/893-2000. **Recorded jobline:** 215/893-4111. **Fax:** 215/892-7506. **Contact:** Sharita Barnett, Human Resources. **E-mail address:** sharita.barnett@tenethealth.com. **World Wide Web address:** http://www.graduatehospital.com. **Description:** A full-service hospital consisting of 240 inpatient beds, four intensive care units, an emergency department, and a variety of inpatient and outpatient diagnostic and treatment facilities. **Positions advertised include:** Phlebotomist; Registered Nurse; Licensed Practical Nurse; Nurse Manager; Financial Counselor; Pharmacist; Case Manager. **Parent company:** Tenet Healthcare.

GREEN COUNTY MEMORIAL HOSPITAL
350 Bonar Avenue, Waynesburg PA 15370. 724/627-3101. **Contact:** Human Resources. **Description:** A general medical and surgical hospital. The hospital's skilled nursing unit has 20 beds; specialty care has five beds; and medical/surgical has 35 beds.

HCR MANORCARE HEALTH SERVICES
600 West Valley Forge Road, King of Prussia PA 19406. 610/337-1775. **Contact:** Human Resources. **E-mail address:** jobline@hcr-manorcare.com. **World Wide Web address:** http://www.hcr-manorcare.com. **Description:** An inpatient and outpatient rehabilitation center providing physical, occupational, and speech therapies. **Positions advertised include:** Admissions Clerk; Business Development Specialist; General Clerk; Activity Assistant; Receptionist; Cook. **Corporate headquarters location:** Toledo OH. **Listed on:** New York Stock Exchange. **Stock exchange symbol:** HCR.

HANOVER HOSPITAL
300 Highland Avenue, Hanover PA 17331. 717/633-2143. **Toll-free phone:** 800/673-2426. **Fax:** 717/633-2217. **Contact:** Jen Walton, Human Resources. **World Wide Web address:** http://www.hanoverhospital.org. **Description:** A 174-bed, acute care hospital. **Positions advertised include:** Licensed Practical Nurse; Nuclear Medicine Technologist; Occupational Therapist; Pharmacist; Physical Therapist; Radiological Technologist; Registered Nurse; Respiratory Therapist; Speech-Language Pathologist; Surgical Technician. **Special programs:** Internships. **Parent company:** Hanover HealthCare Plus Network. **Number of employees at this location:** 800.

HAVEN CONVALESCENT HOME
725 Paul Street, New Castle PA 16101. 724/654-8833. **Contact:** Personnel. **World Wide Web address:** http://www.havenconvalescenthome.com. **Description:** Haven Convalescent Home is a 91-bed long-term, acute care facility for the elderly. **Positions advertised include:** Electrician; Industrial Mechanic.

HEALTHSOUTH REHABILITATION HOSPITAL OF GREATER PITTSBURGH
2380 McGinley Road, Monroeville PA 15146. 412/856-2400. **Contact:** Human Resources. **World Wide Web address:** http://www.healthsouth.com. **Description:** A rehabilitation hospital licensed for 89 beds. **Special programs:** Internships. **Corporate headquarters location:** Birmingham AL. **Listed on:** New York Stock Exchange. **Stock exchange symbol:** HRC. **Number of employees nationwide:** 18,000.

HOLY REDEEMER HOSPITAL
1648 Huntingdon Pike, Meadowbrook PA 19046. 215/947-3000. **Recorded jobline:** 877/499-4473. **Fax:** 215/214-0678. **Contact:** Human Resources. **E-mail address:** recruiter@holyredeemer.com. **World Wide Web address:** http://www.holyredeemer.com. **Description:** A 299-bed community hospital offering a variety of inpatient, outpatient, and emergency services. **Positions advertised include:** Medical Messenger Operator; Operating Room Staff Nurse; Registered Nurse; Hospital Librarian; Occupational Therapist; Physical Therapist; Speech Language Pathologist; Housekeeper; Certified Nurse Assistant; Food Service Worker; Clinical Engineering Technician.

HOLY SPIRIT HEALTH SYSTEM
503 North 21st Street, Camp Hill PA 17011. 717/763-2100. **Fax:** 717/763-2351. **Recorded jobline:** 717/972-4121. **Contact:** Employment Manager. **E-mail address:** resume@hsh.org. **World Wide Web address:** http://www.hsh.org. **Description:** A nonprofit health system that operates a 349-bed hospital as well as several home health, hospice, and family care centers. Holy Spirit Health System also provides ambulance and emergency care services. Founded in 1963. **NOTE:** Entry-level positions, part-time jobs, and second and third shifts are offered. **Positions advertised include:** Administrative Assistant; Certified Nurses Aide; Claim Representative; EEG Technologist; EKG Technician; Emergency Medical Technician; Help-Desk Technician; Home Health Aide; Licensed Practical Nurse; Medical Assistant; Medical Records Technician; Medical Secretary; Network/Systems

Administrator; Nuclear Medicine Technologist; Occupational Therapist; Pharmacist; Physical Therapist; Radiological Technologist; Registered Nurse; Respiratory Therapist; Secretary; Social Worker; Speech-Language Pathologist; Surgical Technician. **Special programs:** Internships. **Office hours:** Monday - Friday, 7:30 a.m. - 4:00 p.m. **Corporate headquarters location:** This location. **Parent company:** Holy Spirit Health System. **Number of employees at this location:** 2,000.

JEFFERSON REGIONAL MEDICAL CENTER
565 Coal Valley Road, P.O. Box 18199, Pittsburgh PA 15236-0119. 412/469-5000. **Fax:** 412/469-5918. **Contact:** Personnel. **E-mail address:** resumes@jeffersonregional.com. **World Wide Web address:** http://www.jeffersonhospital.com. **Description:** A 360-bed hospital. **Parent company:** South Hills Health System. **Positions advertised include:** Case Manager; Clinical Nutritionist; CT Scan Tech; Decision Support Analyst; Manager, Cardio-Pulmonary Rehabilitation; Pharmacist; Physical Therapist; Radiology Tech; RN, Various Departments.

JENNERSVILLE REGIONAL HOSPITAL
1015 West Baltimore Pike, West Grove PA 19390. 610/869-1121. **Fax:** 610/869-1246. **Recorded jobline:** 610/869-1200. **Contact:** Employment Coordinator. **World Wide Web address:** http://www.jennersville.com. **Description:** A 59-bed, nonprofit acute care medical center that offers a surgery/ER center, an intensive care unit, and maternity and outpatient services. Founded in 1920. **NOTE:** Entry-level positions, part-time jobs, and second and third shifts are offered. **Special programs:** Summer Jobs. **Number of employees at this location:** 600.

KANE COMMUNITY HOSPITAL
4372 Route 6, Kane PA 16735. 814/837-8585. **Fax:** 814/837-8139. **Contact:** Director of Employee Services. **E-mail address:** lcole@kanehospital.org. **World Wide Web address:** http://www.kanehosp.com. **Description:** A 53-bed hospital. **Positions advertised include:** Medical Technologist; Physical Therapist; Radiologic Technician; Registered Nurse.

LANKENAU HOSPITAL
100 Lancaster Avenue, Wynnewood PA 19096. 610/645-2000. **Fax:** 610/645-8492. **Contact:** Personnel. **World Wide Web address:** http://www.mainlinehealth.org/lh. **Description:** A hospital. **Parent company:** Mainline Health. **Positions advertised include:** Administrative Coordinator; Charge Pharmacist; Clinical Dietician; Clinical Leader; Site Manager; Social Worker; Pharmacy Supervisor; Certified Registered Nurse; Licensed Practical Nurse; Coding Specialist; Information Clerk.

LUZERNE OPTICAL LABORATORIES, INC.
180 North Wilkes-Barre Boulevard, P.O. Box 998, Wilkes-Barre PA 18703-0998. 570/822-3183. **Toll-free phone:** 800/233-9637. **Fax:** 570/823-4299. **Contact:** Human Resources. **E-mail address:** vision@luzerneoptical.com. **World Wide Web address:** http://www.luzerneoptical.com. **Description:** Manufactures optical products including eyeglasses and contact lenses. Founded in 1973. **NOTE:** Entry-level positions and second and third shifts are offered. **Company slogan:** With an eye on service and quality. **Office hours:** Monday - Friday, 7:00 a.m. - 6:30 p.m. **Corporate headquarters location:** This location. **President:** John Dougherty. **Annual sales/revenues:** $11 - $20 million. **Number of employees at this location:** 110.

MB RESEARCH LABORATORIES
PO Box 178, Spinnerstown PA, 18968. 215/536-4110. **Fax:** 215/536-1816. **Contact:** Human Resources. **E-mail address:** mbweb@mbresearch.com. **World Wide Web address:** http://www.mbresearch.com. **Description:** Research laboratory that conducts acute, chronic, and chronic toxicology and pharmacology studies since 1972. **Positions advertised include:** Senior Quality Assurance Auditor; Marketing Manager/Director of Client Services; Research Assistant; Laboratory Technician; Biological Technician; Maintenance/Cleaning Staff.

MEADVILLE MEDICAL CENTER
751 Liberty Street, Meadville PA 16335. 814/333-5105. **Fax:** 814/333-5471. **Contact:** John Andrews, Assistant Director of Human Resources. **E-mail address:** careers@mmchs.org. **World Wide Web address:** http://www.mmchs.org. **Description:** A medical center. **Positions advertised include:** Certified Occupational Therapy Assistant; Clinical Dietitian; Director of Support Services; LPN, Various Departments; Physical Therapist; RN, Various Departments. **Special programs:** Internships. **Operations at this facility include:** Service. **Number of employees at this location:** 980.

MEDRAD, INC.
One Medrad Drive, Indianola PA 15051-0780. 412/767-2400. **Fax:** 412/767-4128. **Contact:** Corporate Recruiting Manager. **E-mail address:** jobs@medrad.com. **World Wide Web address:** http://www.medrad.com. **Description:** Designs, manufactures, and markets high-tech equipment and disposable products such as CT and angiography injectors, syringes, magnetic resonance coils, and other imaging equipment. **Positions advertised include:** Manager, Customer Support. **Corporate headquarters location:** This location. **International locations:** Brazil; Canada; France; Germany; Italy; Japan; Singapore; the Netherlands; United Kingdom. **Parent company:** Schering AG (Berlin, Germany). **Operations at this facility include:** Administration; Manufacturing; Research and Development; Sales; Service. **Annual sales/revenues:** More than $100 million. **Number of employees at this location:** 670. **Number of employees nationwide:** 780. **Number of employees worldwide:** 870.

MEMORIAL HOSPITAL
325 South Belmont Street, P.O. Box 15118, York PA 17405. 717/849-5479. **Fax:** 717/849-5495. **Contact:** Human Resources Department. **E-mail address:** hrinfo@mhyork.org. **World Wide Web address:** http://www.mhyork.org. **Description:** An acute care, community-based, teaching hospital serving York County. **Positions advertised include:** Cardiovascular Specialist; Certified Occupational Therapy Assistant; Chemistry Technical Coordinator; Clinical Supervisor; Clinical Staff Pharmacist; Director of Emergency Services; Medical Technologist; Paramedic; Registered Nurse; Licensed Practical Nurse. **Parent company:** Memorial Healthcare System. **Operations at this facility include:** Administration; Service. **Annual sales/revenues:** $21 - $50 million. **Number of employees at this location:** 900.

MERCY FITZGERALD HOSPITAL
1500 Lansdowne Avenue, Darby PA 19023. 610/237-4000. **Fax:** 610/853-7030. **Contact:** Central Employment Office. **E-mail address:** mercyjobs@mercyhealth.org. **World Wide Web address:** http://www.mercyhealth.org. **Description:** A 441-bed, acute-care, community hospital that serves southwest Pennsylvania. **NOTE:** Search and apply for positions online. **Positions advertised include:** RN, Various Departments; Respiratory Therapist; Clinical Dietitian; CT Tech; Pharmacist; CRNA. **Parent company:** Mercy Health System.

MERCY HOSPITAL OF PHILADELPHIA
501 South 54th Street, Philadelphia PA 19143. 215/748-9000. **Fax:** 610/853-7030. **Contact:** Central Employment Office. **E-mail address:** mercyjobs@mercyhealth.org. **World Wide Web address:** http://www.mercyhealth.org. **Description:** A 200-bed medical center. **NOTE:** Search and apply for positions online. **Positions advertised include:** RN, Various Departments; Psychiatrist; Staff Pharmacist; ER Tech; Patient Care Manager; Director of Nursing Operations.

METHODIST HOSPITAL
Thomas Jefferson University Hospital, 2301 South Broad Street, Philadelphia PA 19148. 215/952-9000. **Fax:** 215/952-9588. **Contact:** Human Resources. **World Wide Web address:** http://www.jeffersonhospital.org/methodist. **Description:** A hospital licensed for 165 beds. Methodist Hospital is affiliated with Thomas Jefferson University Hospital. **Positions advertised include:** Clinical Dietician; Clinical Pharmacist; Clinical Supervisor; Insurance and Benefit Counselor; Trauma Registrar; Case Manager; Emergency Department Clerk; Endoscopy Nurse; Nurse Manager; Physician Assistant; Security Analyst; Nursing Assistant.

NAZARETH HOSPITAL
2601 Holme Avenue, Philadelphia PA 19152. 215/335-6260. **Fax:** 610/335-6258. **Contact:** Human Resources. **E-mail address:** mercyjobs@mercyhealth.org. **World Wide Web address:** http://www.nazarethhospital.org. **Description:** An acute care hospital serving the northeast Philadelphia community. **NOTE:** Search and apply for positions online. **Positions advertised include:** Occupational Therapist; Director of Information Technology; Physical Therapist; Ultrasound Technician; RN, Various Departments. **Special programs:** Internships. **Parent company:** Mercy Health System. **Number of employees at this location:** 1,400.

NOVACARE REHABILITATION
680 American Avenue, Suite 200, King of Prussia PA 19406. 610/992-7200. **Toll-free phone:** 800/331-8840. **Contact:** Human Resources. **World Wide Web address:** http://www.novacare.com. **Description:** Provides comprehensive medical rehabilitation services to patients with physical disabilities. NovaCare's services include speech-language pathology, occupational therapy, and physical therapy. Services are provided on a contract basis primarily to long-term health care institutions, through inpatient rehabilitation hospitals and community-integrated programs, and through a national network of patient care centers providing orthotic and prosthetic rehabilitation services. **Positions advertised include:** Cash Applications Representative; Medical Collections Representative; Customer Service Representative; Customer Service Supervisor; Athletic Trainer. **Corporate headquarters location:** This location. **Other U.S. locations:** Nationwide. **Parent company:** Select Medical. **Listed on:** New York Stock Exchange. **Stock exchange symbol:** NOV.

NUTRISYSTEM L.P.
202 Welsh Road, Horsham PA 19044. 215/706-5300. **Fax:** 215/706-5388. **Contact:** Human Resources. **World Wide Web address:** http://www.nutrisystem.com. **Description:** A chain of weight loss/weight maintenance centers providing professionally supervised services through a network of 700 company-owned and franchised centers. **Corporate headquarters location:** This location. **Other U.S. locations:** Nationwide. **International locations:** Canada; Saudi Arabia. **Listed on:** NASDAQ. **Stock exchange symbol:** THIN. **Number of employees at this location:** 75. **Number of employees nationwide:** 600.

OHIO VALLEY GENERAL HOSPITAL
25 Heckel Road, Kennedy Township, McKees Rocks PA 15136-1694. 412/777-6218. **Fax:** 412/777-6804. **Recorded jobline:** 412/777-6397. **Contact:** Human Resources Department. **World Wide Web address:** http://www.ohiovalleyhospital.org. **Description:** A 118-bed, nonprofit community hospital serving Pittsburgh's western suburbs and the Pittsburgh International Airport area. **NOTE:** Resumes are accepted in person in the Human Resources office Monday through Friday, from 9:00 a.m. - 4:00 p.m. Entry-level positions, part-time jobs, and second and third shifts are offered. **Positions advertised include:** Registered Nurse; Nursing Supervisor; Cardiology Technician; Physical Therapy Assistant. **Operations at this facility include:** Administration; Health Care; Service. **Number of employees at this location:** 600.

PENN PRESBYTERIAN MEDICAL CENTER
39th & Market Streets, Philadelphia PA 19104. 215/662-8000. **Fax:** 215/662-8936. **Recorded jobline:** 215/662-8222. **Contact:** Human Resources. **World Wide Web address:** http://www.pennhealth.com/presby. **Description:** A teaching hospital specializing in oncology, cardiology, general medicine, and surgery. **Special programs:** Internships. **Operations at this facility include:** Administration; Research and Development; Service. **Number of employees at this location:** 1,500.

PENNSYLVANIA HOSPITAL
800 Spruce Street, Philadelphia PA 19107. 215/829-3000. **Contact:** Human Resources/Employment. **World Wide Web address:** http://www.pahosp.com. **Description:** A 515-bed acute care hospital; part of the University of Pennsylvania Health System. Founded in 1751. **Positions advertised include:** Night Shift Pharmacist; Radiation Therapist; Clinical Pharmacist; Administrative Assistant; Nurse Practitioner; Registered Nurse; Staff Nurse; Medical Technologist; Clinical Information Specialist.

PERFECSEAL
9800 Bustleton Avenue, Philadelphia PA 19115. 215/673-4500. **Fax:** 215/676-1311. **Contact:** Mr. Reno Bianco, Human Resources Manager. **World Wide Web address:** http://www.perfecseal.com. **Description:** Manufactures sterilizable medical packaging for the medical device industry. The company is a world leader in thermoplastic flexible packaging, heat-sealed coated Tyvek, and paper. Products include Perfecseal adhesive coating on Tyvek and paper, film and foil lamination; Breather Bag and linear tear packaging; easy-open and chevron peel pouches; oriented films; custom thermoformed trays and die-cut lids; pharmaceutical labels, cold seal technology, extrusion and saran coating, flexographic and rotogravure printing; and vacuum metallizing. Founded in 1905. **NOTE:** Entry-level positions and second and third shifts are offered. **Special programs:** Internships. **Corporate headquarters location:** Oshkosh WI. **Other U.S. locations:** Mankato MN; New London WI; Oshkosh WI. **International locations:** Carolina, Puerto Rico; Londonderry, Northern Ireland. **Parent company:** Bemis, Inc. **Operations at this facility include:** Administration; Manufacturing; Research and Development; Sales; Service. **Annual sales/revenues:** More than $100 million. **Number of employees at this location:** 200. **Number of employees worldwide:** 700.

PHILHAVEN BEHAVIORAL HEALTH SERVICES
283 South Butler Road, P.O. Box 550, Mount Gretna PA 17064. 717/273-8871. **Fax:** 717/270-2455. **Contact:** Human Resources. **E-mail address:** hr@philhaven.com. **World Wide Web address:** http://www.philhaven.com. **Description:** A psychiatric treatment center offering inpatient, outpatient, residential, and community-based services. **NOTE:** Entry-level positions and second and third shifts are offered. **Positions advertised include:** Clinical Director; Coordinator of Family Based Mental Health Services; Mobile Therapist; Psychiatrist; Licensed Practical Nurse; Registered Nurse. **Corporate headquarters location:** This location. **Operations at this facility include:** Administration; Service. **CEO:** LaVern J. Yutzy. **Annual sales/revenues:** $21 - $50 million. **Number of employees at this location:** 600.

PITTSBURGH MERCY HEALTH SYSTEM
1400 Locust Street, Pittsburgh PA 15219. 412/232-7970. **Recorded jobline:** 412/232-7225. **Fax:** 412/232-7408. **Contact:** Central Employment Office. **E-mail address:** employment@mercy.pmhs.com. **World Wide Web address:** http://www.mercylink.org. **Description:** A nonprofit health care system operating several hospitals in the Pittsburgh area. **Positions advertised include:** Admission Representative; Medical Records Coder; Medical Transcriptionist;

Patient Account Representative; Unit Secretary; Clinical Nurse; Licensed Practical Nurse; Relief Clinical Supervisor; Case Manager; Occupational Therapist. **Corporate headquarters location:** This location. **Subsidiaries include:** Mercy Hospital of Pittsburgh; Mercy Providence Hospital; Mercy Psychiatric Institute; St. Joseph Nursing and Health Care Center. **Operations at this facility include:** Administration; Health Care; Research and Development; Service. **Number of employees at this location:** 2,500. **Number of employees nationwide:** 5,000.

POTTSTOWN MEMORIAL MEDICAL CENTER
1600 East High Street, Pottstown PA 19464. 610/327-7057. **Contact:** Human Resources Department. **E-mail address:** hr@pmmctr.com. **World Wide Web address:** http://www.pottstownmemorial.com. **Description:** A full-service hospital. **NOTE:** Entry-level positions and second and third shifts are offered. **Positions advertised include:** CT Technologist; Respiratory Therapist; X-Ray Technician; Registered Nurse; Licensed Practical Nurse; Nursing Assistant. **Corporate headquarters location:** This location. **Number of employees at this location:** 1,100.

THE POTTSVILLE HOSPITAL AND WARNE CLINIC
420 South Jackson Street, Pottsville PA 17901. 570/621-5000. **Fax:** 570/621-5562. **Contact:** Human Resources. **E-mail address:** phhr@pothosp.com. **World Wide Web address:** http://www.pottsvillehospital.com. **Description:** An acute care facility providing a full range of medical services including the Inpatient Rehabilitation Unit, the Institute for Behavioral Health (an inpatient psychiatric unit), and the Schuylkill Rehabilitation Center (a comprehensive outpatient rehabilitation facility). **Positions advertised include:** Staff Development Coordinator; RN, Various Departments; Occupational Therapist. **Operations at this facility include:** Administration; Service. **Number of employees at this location:** 800.

PREMIER MEDICAL PRODUCTS
1710 Romano Street, Plymouth Meeting PA 19462. 610/239-6000. **Toll-free phone:** 888/670-6100. **Contact:** Karen Giannone, Director of Human Resources. **World Wide Web address:** http://www.premusa.com. **Description:** Manufactures and distributes tracheal and laryngectomy tubes, as well as medical instruments used in gynecology and podiatry.

REGINA NURSING CENTER
550 East Fornance Street, Norristown PA 19401-3561. 610/272-5600. **Fax:** 610/279-0529. **Contact:** Bonnie A. Dudley, RN, Director of Nursing. **E-mail address:** mc@reginanursingcenter.org. **World Wide Web address:** http://www.reginanursingcenter.org. **Description:** A 121-bed nursing care center.

RESPIRONICS INC.
1001 Murry Ridge Lane, Murrysville PA 15668-8550. 724/733-0200. **Fax:** 724/387-4299. **Contact:** Personnel. **World Wide Web address:** http://www.respironics.com. **Description:** Manufactures respiratory medical products. **NOTE:** Entry-level positions are offered. **Positions advertised include** Manufacturing Specialist; Product Assurance Engineer; SAP HR Programmer/Analyst; Director, Human Resources. **Special programs:** Internships. **Corporate headquarters location:** This location. **Operations at this facility include:** Administration; Divisional Headquarters; Manufacturing; Research and Development; Sales; Service. **Listed on:** NASDAQ. **Stock exchange symbol:** RESP. **Annual sales/revenues:** More than $100 million. **Number of employees at this location:** 480. **Number of employees nationwide:** 515. **Number of employees worldwide:** 1,100.

RIDDLE MEMORIAL HOSPITAL
1068 West Baltimore Pike, Media PA 19063. 610/566-9400. **Fax:** 610/891-3644. **Contact:** Human Resources. **E-mail address:** wzaloga@riddlehospital.org. **World Wide Web address:** http://www.riddlehospital.org. **Description:** A short-term, acute care, community hospital and outpatient medical facility. **Number of employees at this location:** 1,300.

SAINT LUKE'S MINERS MEMORIAL MEDICAL CENTER
360 West Ruddle Street, Coaldale PA 18218-0067. 570/645-2131. **Fax:** 570/645-8149. **Contact:** Human Resources. **World Wide Web address:** http://www.slhn-lehighvalley.org. **Description:** A 61-bed, acute care facility with a 53-bed geriatric center. **NOTE:** Entry-level positions and second and third shifts are offered. **Positions advertised include:** Certified Occupational Therapist; Manager of Pharmacy; Pharmacist; Registered Nurse; Vascular Technologist. **Special programs:** Internships. **Operations at this facility include:** Administration; Service. **Number of employees at this location:** 400.

SHAMOKIN AREA COMMUNITY HOSPITAL
4200 Hospital Road, Coal Township PA 17866. 570/644-4200. **Fax:** 570/644-4356. **Contact:** Human Resources Representative. **E-mail address:** l.schoch@shamokinhospital.org. **World Wide Web address:** http://www.shamokinhospital.org. **Description:** A 61-bed nonprofit, community hospital offering acute care, general surgery, subacute and outpatient rehabilitation, inpatient and partial hospitalization care for geriatric-psychiatric patients, 24-hour emergency services, occupational health, specialty clinics and community health programs. Founded in 1912. **NOTE:** Entry-level positions, part-time jobs, and second and third shifts are offered. **Company slogan:** Quality care close to home. **Positions advertised include:** Registered Nurse; Psychiatry Technician; Department Secretary. **Special programs:** Summer Jobs. **Office hours:** Monday - Friday, 8:00 a.m. - 5:00 p.m. **Corporate headquarters location:** This location. **Other U.S. locations:** Elysburg PA. **Subsidiaries include:** Northumberland Health Services. **President/CEO:** John P. Wiercinski. **Annual sales/revenues:** $21 - $50 million. **Number of employees at this location:** 285.

SHARON REGIONAL HEALTH SYSTEM
740 East State Street, Sharon PA 16146. 724/983-3831. **Contact:** Human Resources. **E-mail address:** jobs@srhs-pa.org. **World Wide Web address:** http://www.sharonregional.com. **Description:** A comprehensive health care system that offers a variety of clinical programs and services. **Positions advertised include:** Charge Nurse; Paramedic; Nurse Aide; Licensed Practical Nurse; Registered Nurse; Psychiatrist.

SILVER OAKS NURSING CENTER
715 Harbor Street, New Castle PA 16101. 724/652-3863. **Fax:** 724/652-1756. **Contact:** Human Resources. **Description:** A nursing home specializing in the care of patients with Alzheimer's disease.

SMITHS INDUSTRIES
255 Great Valley Parkway, Malvern PA 19355. 610/296-5000. **Fax:** 610/296-0912. **Contact:** Human Resources. **World Wide Web address:** http://www.smithsind-aerospace.com. **Description:** Develops and manufactures instrumentation and systems for civil and military aircraft. Founded in 1920. **Special programs:** Internships; Co-ops. **Internship information:** Internships are available in Engineering/Manufacturing, Engineering, and Marketing. **Corporate headquarters location:** London, England. **Other U.S. locations:** Nationwide. **International locations:** France; Germany; South America. **Parent company:** Smiths Industries. **Listed on:** European Bourse. **CEO:** Keith Butler-Wheelhouse. **Number of employees at this location:** 165. **Number of employees nationwide:** 2,500. **Number of employees worldwide:** 15,000.

SOUTHWOOD PSYCHIATRIC HOSPITAL
2575 Boyce Plaza Road, Pittsburgh PA 15241. 412/257-2290. **Toll-free phone:** 888/907-5437. **Fax:** 412/257-0374. **Contact:** Jill Yesko, Personnel Manager. **World Wide Web address:** http://www.southwoodhospital.com. **Description:** A psychiatric hospital that offers inpatient and outpatient care to adolescents. **NOTE:** Entry-level positions are offered. **Corporate headquarters location:** This location. **Parent company:** Youth & Family Centered Services. **Number of employees at this location:** 250.

STERIS CORPORATION
2424 West 23rd Street, Erie PA 16506. 814/452-3100. **Contact:** Laurene Bucci, Human Resources. **World Wide Web address:** http://www.steris.com. **Description:** Develops, manufactures, and distributes infection/contamination-preventing devices and surgical supplies, services, and technologies to the health care, scientific, agricultural, and industrial markets. **Positions advertised include:** Lab Technician; Administrative Assistant; Director Environmental Health and Safety; Contract Specialist; Senior Designer. **Corporate headquarters location:** Mentor OH. **Other U.S. locations:** Montgomery AL; Wilson NY; Apex NC. **Listed on:** New York Stock Exchange. **Stock exchange symbol:** STE.

SURGICAL LASER TECHNOLOGIES, INC.
147 Keystone Drive, Montgomeryville PA 18936. 215/619-3600. **Toll-free phone:** 800/366-4758. **Fax:** 215/619-3208. **Contact:** Human Resources. **E-mail address:** hr@slti.com. **World Wide Web address:** http://www.slti.com. **Description:** Develops, manufactures, and sells proprietary laser systems and non-laser surgical devices for otorhinolaryngology, neurosurgery, gynecology, urology and other surgical specialties. **Corporate headquarters location:** This location. **Number of employees at this location:** 160.

TEMPLE CONTINUING CARE CENTER
5301 Old York Road, Philadelphia PA 19141. 215/456-2900. **Fax:** 215/456-2048. **Recorded jobline:** 215/456-2929. **Contact:** Human Resources. **World Wide Web address:** http://www.health.temple.edu. **Description:** A nonprofit nursing home. **NOTE:** Entry-level positions and second and third shifts are offered. **Special programs:** Internships. **Number of employees at this location:** 1,000.

TEMPLE UNIVERSITY HOSPITAL
3401 North Broad Street, GSB Room 107, Philadelphia PA 19140. 215/707-3145. **Contact:** Human Resources Department. **World Wide Web address:** http://www.health.temple.edu/tuhs. **Description:** A hospital that also operates a physicians' information bureau. **Positions advertised include:** Administrative Assistant; Assistant Director of Corporate Accounting; Clinical Pharmacist.

TENDER LOVING CARE & STAFF BUILDERS
1180 Route 315, Wilkes Barre PA 18702. 610/822-9117. **Fax:** 570/829-2551. **Contact:** Human Resources. **World Wide Web address:** http://www.tlcathome.com. **Description:** A home health care agency. **Corporate headquarters location:** Lake Success NY. **Other U.S. locations:** Nationwide. **Number of employees nationwide:** 20,000.

THERAKOS, INC.
437 Creamery Way, Exton PA 19341. 610/280-1000. **Contact:** Human Resources. **World Wide Web address:** http://www.therakos.com. **Description:** Develops and manufactures the UVAR Photopheresis System. The system is used in phototherapy treatment for certain types of cancers. **NOTE:** Search and apply for positions at: http://www.jnj.com/careers. **Positions advertised include:** Scientist; Clinical Trial Leader. **Parent company:** Johnson & Johnson.

TRI-COUNTY MOUNT TREXLER MANOR
5021 St. Joseph's Road, P.O. Box 1001, Limeport PA 18060. 610/965-9021. **Contact:** William Mains, Administrator. **World Wide Web address:** http://www.tcrespite.com. **Description:** A residential psychiatric treatment facility. Tri-County Mount Trexler Manor also runs a nonresident day program for people with mental illnesses. **Special programs:** Internships. **Corporate headquarters location:** Doylestown PA. **Other U.S. locations:** Quakertown PA. **Parent company:** Tri-County Respite operates another subsidiary, Quakertown House. **Operations at this facility include:** Administration; Divisional Headquarters; Service. **Number of employees nationwide:** 60.

UPMC BEDFORD MEMORIAL
10455 Lincoln Highway, Everett PA 15537-7046. 814/623-6161. **Contact:** Human Resources. **World Wide Web address:** http://www.upmc.com. **Description:** An acute care general hospital. **NOTE:** Entry-level positions, part-time jobs, and second and third shifts are offered. See employment information on the website, http://www.jobs.upmc.com. **Positions advertised include:** Clinical Associate; Business Analyst; Clinical Pharmacy Specialist; Customer Service Generalist; Business Analyst; Social Worker; Outreach Representative; Provider Relations Representative; Systems Analyst; Product Manager.

U.S. DEPARTMENT OF VETERANS AFFAIRS BUTLER VETERANS ADMINISTRATION MEDICAL CENTER
325 New Castle Road, Butler PA 16001-2480. 724/287-4781. **Contact:** Human Resources. **E-mail address:** butlervahr@med.va.gov. **World Wide Web address:** http://www.va.gov. **Description:** Provides primary, extended, and behavioral health care for veterans living in western Pennsylvania and eastern Ohio. **NOTE:** The Department of Veterans Affairs Medical Center continually accepts applications for physicians, pharmacists, physical and occupational therapists, registered nurses, licensed practical nurses, and certified/registered respiratory therapists and technicians.

U.S. DEPARTMENT OF VETERANS AFFAIRS PITTSBURGH VETERANS ADMINISTRATION HEALTHCARE SYSTEM
7180 Highland Drive, Pittsburgh PA 15206. 412/365-4900. **Contact:** Human Resources. **Description:** An acute care, tertiary neuropsychiatric facility with 180 beds serving the tri-state area of western Pennsylvania, northern West Virginia, and eastern Ohio. **Corporate headquarters location:** Washington DC.

U.S. DEPARTMENT OF VETERANS AFFAIRS VETERANS ADMINISTRATION MEDICAL CENTER
1111 East End Boulevard, Wilkes-Barre PA 18711. 570/824-3521 ext. 7209. **Contact:** Reese Thomas III, Chief of Human Resources Management Service. **Description:** A general medical and surgical facility consisting of 79 operating hospital beds, 105 operating nursing home beds, and 10 substance abuse residential rehabilitation treatment program beds. The facility serves veterans throughout northeastern and central Pennsylvania and southern New York State. **Special programs:** Internships. **Corporate headquarters location:** Washington DC. **Other U.S. locations:** Nationwide. **Operations at this facility include:** Administration. **Number of employees at this location:** 1,300.

U.S. DEPARTMENT OF VETERANS AFFAIRS VETERANS ADMINISTRATION PITTSBURGH HEALTHCARE SYSTEM
University Drive, Pittsburgh PA 15240. 412/688-6000. **Contact:** Human Resources. **Description:** A major medical/surgical tertiary care facility with 146 general medicine and surgery beds. The facility is a referral center for the following programs: National Liver and Renal Transplant, Cardiac Surgery Center, Oncology, Radiation Therapy and Geriatric Care.

THE UNIONTOWN HOSPITAL
500 West Berkeley Street, Uniontown PA 15401. 724/430-5290. **Fax:** 724/430-5646. **Contact:** Human

Resources Department. **World Wide Web address:** http://www.uniontownhospital.com. **Description:** An acute care hospital. **Positions advertised include:** Registered Nurse; Certified Occupational Therapist Assistant; Medical Technologist; Physical Therapist; MRI Technician; Credit Analyst. **Special programs:** Internships. **Corporate headquarters location:** This location. **Parent company:** UHRI. **Operations at this facility include:** Service. **Number of employees at this location:** 1,000.

UNIVERSAL HEALTH SERVICES, INC.
367 South Gulph Road, P.O. Box 61558, King of Prussia PA 19406. 610/768-3300. **Toll-free phone:** 800/347-7750. **Fax:** 610/768-3466. **Contact:** Coleen Johns, Personnel. **E-mail address:** cjohns@uhsinc.com. **World Wide Web address:** http://www.uhsinc.com. **Description:** Owns and operates acute care hospitals, behavioral health centers, ambulatory surgery centers, and radiation/oncology centers. The company, as a part of its Ambulatory Treatment Centers Division, owns, operates, or manages surgery and radiation therapy centers located in various states. Universal Health Services has also entered into other specialized medical service arrangements including laboratory services, mobile computerized tomography and magnetic imaging services, preferred provider organization agreements, health maintenance organization contracts, medical office building leasing, construction management services, and real estate management and administrative services. **Corporate headquarters location:** This location. **Operations at this facility include:** Administration. **Listed on:** New York Stock Exchange. **Stock exchange symbol:** UHS. **Number of employees at this location:** 145. **Number of employees nationwide:** 35,000.

UNIVERSITY OF PENNSYLVANIA HOSPITAL
3400 Spruce Street, Philadelphia PA 19104. 215/662-4000. **Fax:** 215/662-7835. **Contact:** Human Resources. **World Wide Web address:** http://pennhealth.com/jobs. **Description:** A 722-bed, academic, teaching hospital involved in patient care, education, and research. **Positions advertised include:** Clinical Nurse Specialist; Check Request Processor; Dental Assistant; Clerk; Speech Pathologist; Refund Coordinator; Program Manager; Patient Registration Supervisor; Clinical Pharmacist; Director of Staffing; Customer Service Representative. **Number of employees at this location:** 5,000.

UNIVERSITY OF PENNSYLVANIA VETERINARY HOSPITAL
3800 Spruce Street, Philadelphia PA 19104. 215/746-0398. **Contact:** Amy Shields, Recruiting. **World Wide Web address:** http://www.vet.upenn.edu. **Description:** A full-service animal hospital whose many departments include oncology, radiology, dermatology, internal medicine, and emergency.

VILLA TERESA
1051 Avila Road, Harrisburg PA 17109. 717/652-5900. **Fax:** 717/652-5941. **Contact:** Personnel Director. **Description:** Provides skilled nursing care for the elderly. Founded in 1973. **Office hours:** Monday - Friday, 8:00 a.m. - 4:00 p.m. **Corporate headquarters location:** This location. **Number of employees at this location:** 230.

WARMINSTER HOSPITAL
225 Newtown Road, Warminster PA 18974. 215/441-6691. **Contact:** Human Resources. **World Wide Web address:** http://www.warminsterhospital.com. **Description:** A 145-bed acute care community hospital. **Positions advertised include:** Registered Nurse; CNA; Medical Technologist; Crisis Assessment Counselor; Stress Lab Technician. **Special programs:** Internships. **Parent company:** Tenet Healthcare Corporation.

Rhode Island

ARTIFICIAL KIDNEY CENTER OF RHODE ISLAND
40 Hemingway Drive, East Providence RI 02915. 401/438-5930. **Contact:** Human Resources. **Description:** Provides dialysis services, C.A.P.D. training, and dietary instruction. **NOTE:** Contact Human Resources by phone to inquire about open positions, which are primarily in nursing. **Other area locations:** Providence RI; North Providence RI; Pawtucket RI; Wakefield RI; Westerly RI; Warwick RI. **Other U.S. locations:** Nationwide. **International locations:** Worldwide.

BRADLEY HOSPITAL
1011 Veterans Memorial Parkway, East Providence RI 02915. 401/432-1141. **Fax:** 401/432-1511. **Contact:** Human Resources. **E-mail address:** coliveira@lifespan.org. **World Wide Web address:** http://www.lifespan.org/partners/bh/. **Description:** A private 60-bed, not-for-profit psychiatric hospital devoted exclusively to children and adolescents, as well as a teaching hospital for Brown Medical School. Also operates the Bradley School, a fully certified special education school. Offers a full spectrum of mental health services for children and adolescents ranging from outpatient counseling and therapy to hospitalization. Founded in 1931. **NOTE:** See http://www.lifespancareers.org to search for open positions and apply online. Part-time and per-diem shifts are available. **Positions advertised include:** Clinical Research Assistant; Milieu Therapist; Psychologist; Residential Care Counselor; Classroom Behavior Specialist; Dishwasher; Social Worker; Clinical Staff Nurse. **Number of employees at this location:** 814.

BUTLER HOSPITAL
345 Blackstone Boulevard, Providence RI 02906. 401/455-6245. **Fax:** 401/455-6301. **Contact:** Human Resources. **E-mail address:** jobs@butler.org. **World Wide Web address:** http://www.butler.org. **Description:** Rhode Island's only private, non-profit psychiatric and substance abuse treatment hospital serving children, adolescents and adults. Butler is affiliated with Brown Medical School. **NOTE:** See website for current job openings. Applications are accepted by mail, fax or online. **Positions advertised include:** Intervention Coordinator; Licensed Practical Nurse; Research Assistant; Registered Nurse; Staff Nurse; Nurse Supervisor; Intake Coordinator; Mental Health Worker.

DAVOL INC.
100 Sockanossett Crossroad, P.O. Box 8500, Cranston RI 02920. 401/463-7000. **Fax:** 401/464-9446. **Contact:** Human Resources. **E-mail address:** jobs-crbard.icims.com. **World Wide Web address:** http://www.davol.com. **Description:** Develops, manufactures and markets specialty medical products for use in surgical and nonsurgical procedures. Davol specializes in products relating to hernia repair, laparoscopy and orthopedics. Founded in 1874. **NOTE:** See website for current job openings and to apply online. **Positions advertised include:** Cost Analyst; International Marketing Manager; Advanced Quality Engineer; Regulatory Affairs Associate; Product Manager; Staff Scientist; R&D Lab Technician. **Corporate headquarters location:** Murray Hill NJ. **Parent company:** C.R. Bard, Inc. **Listed on:** New York Stock Exchange. **Stock exchange symbol:** BCR.

THE GRODEN CENTER
610 Manton Avenue, Providence RI 02909. 401/274-6310. **Fax:** 401/421-1161. **Contact:** Mark Hecklinger, Human Resources. **E-mail address:** hiring@grodencenter.org. **World Wide Web address:** http://www.grodencenter.org. **Description:** Provides support to children and adults with autism and other developmental disabilities and behavioral challenges. **Positions advertised include:** Assistant to Director; Residential Director; Speech and Language Pathologist; Vocational Manager; Residential Behavior Specialist;

Home-Based Treatment Worker. **Other area locations:** Warwick RI.

INTERIM HEALTHCARE
245 Waterman Street, Suite 308, Providence RI 02906. 401/272-3520. **Fax:** 401/331-0081. **Contact:** Katie Levin, Human Resources Manager. **E-mail address:** katielevin@interimhealthcarene.com. **World Wide Web address:** http://www.interimhealthcare.com. **Description:** A home health care agency. Founded in 1966. **Positions advertised include:** Therapist; Home Care RN; Pediatric RN/LPN. **Other area locations:** Newport RI. **Corporate headquarters location:** Sunrise FL. **Other U.S. locations:** Nationwide.

KENT HOSPITAL
455 Tollgate Road, Warwick RI 02886. 401/736-4290. **Fax:** 401/736-1030. **Contact:** Human Resources. **World Wide Web address:** http://www.kenthospital.org. **Description:** A 395-bed, nonprofit, acute care hospital offering a comprehensive range of inpatient and outpatient services. The largest community hospital in the state. **NOTE:** See website for current job openings, application instructions and to apply online. **Position advertised include:** Administrative Assistant; Assistant Nurse Manager; Certified Nursing Assistant; Dietary Aide; Director of Finance; EKG Technician; Licensed Practical Nurse; Mammography Technologist; Occupational Therapist; Registered Nurse; Unit Secretary. **Number of employees at this location:** 2,400.

LANDMARK MEDICAL CENTER
115 Cass Avenue, Woonsocket RI 02895. 401/769-4100. **Recorded jobline:** 877/733-8383. **Contact:** Human Resources. **World Wide Web address:** http://www.landmarkmedical.org. **Description:** A 214-bed acute care hospital with 24-hour emergency services, as well as diagnostic, surgical, psychiatric, pediatric, and obstetric care. **NOTE:** See website for current job openings and to apply online. Human Resources phone extension is 2041. **Positions advertised include:** T Tech; CVT Technologist; Lab Generalist; Nurse Manager; Nurse Practitioner; Physician Assistant; Radiology Tech; Staff Pharmacist; Registered Nurse; Ultrasound Technologist. **Special programs:** Internships; Volunteer Opportunities. **Other area locations:** North Smithfield RI. **Operations at this facility include:** Administration; Emergency Care. **President:** Gary J. Gaube. **Number of employees at this location:** 1,100.

MEMORIAL HOSPITAL OF RHODE ISLAND
111 Brewster Street, Pawtucket RI 02860. 401/729-2198. **Fax:** 401/729-3054. **Recorded jobline:** 401/729-2562. **Contact:** Rachel Curtis, Human Resources. **E-mail address:** Rachel_Curtis@mhri.org. **World Wide Web address:** http:7/mhriweb.org. **Description:** A nonprofit hospital that offers a variety of services including adult day care, a birthing center, cardiology, home care, pediatric, primary care, neurology, radiology and rehabilitation. A Brown University teaching and research hospital. **NOTE:** See website for current job openings and application instructions. Entry-level positions, part-time jobs, and second and third shifts are offered. **Positions advertised include:** Receptionist; Home Health Aide; Nursing Assistant; Coder/Abstractor; Certified Surgical Tech; Echocardiography Tech; MRI Technologist; Occupational Therapist; Unit Secretary; Registered Nurse. **Special programs:** Internships; Training. **Office hours:** Monday – Friday, 8:30 a.m. – 5:00 p.m. **Corporate headquarters location:** This location. **President:** Francis R. Dietz.

THE MIRIAM HOSPITAL
164 Summit Avenue, Providence RI 02906. 401/793-2500. **Recorded jobline:** 866/626-JOBS. **Contact:** Human Resources. **World Wide Web address:** http://www.lifespan.org/partners/tmh. **Description:** A private, non-profit, 247-bed acute care hospital founded in 1926 by Rhode Island's Jewish community. It also serves as a primary teaching hospital for Brown Medical School. **NOTE:** See website for current job openings and application instructions. **Positions advertised include:** Pathology Aide; Speech Pathologist; Scheduling Clerk; Phlebotomist; Cardiac Sonographer; Research Assistant; Laboratory Technician; Medical Technologist; MRI Technologist; Research Nurse; Patient Registration Representative; Staff Nurse; Project Director.

NEWPORT HOSPITAL
11 Friendship Street, Newport RI 02840. 401/845-1302. **Toll-free phone:** 866/626-JOBS. **Contact:** Victoria Williams, Human Resources Representative. **World Wide Web address:** http://www.lifespan.org/newport. **Description:** A private, nonprofit, general hospital with 200 beds. The hospital is licensed by the state Department of Health, and accredited by the Joint Commission on Accreditation of Healthcare Organizations and the Commission on Accreditation of Rehabilitation Facilities. Newport Hospital participates in cooperative programs with colleges and universities for the education of nurses, X-ray technicians, physical therapists, and other allied health care personnel. Founded in 1873. **NOTE:** Second- and third-shifts are offered. **Positions advertised include:** Medical Assistant; Clinical Nurse; Nursing Assistant; Mental Health Aide; Environmental Services Attendant; Graduate Nurse; Physical Therapist Assistant; Cardiac Sonographer; Plant Operator; Radiographer; Switchboard Receptionist. **Special programs:** Internships. **Corporate headquarters location:** Providence RI. **Parent company:** Lifespan. **Number of employees at this location:** 850.

REHABILITATION HOSPITAL OF RHODE ISLAND
116 Eddie Dowling Highway, North Smithfield RI 02896. 401/766-0800. **Fax:** 401/766-5037. **Contact:** Michelle Vaillancourt, Human Resources. **E-mail address:** humanresources@rhri.net. **World Wide Web address:** http://www.rhri.net. **Description:** An 82-bed, fully accredited rehabilitation facility. Dedicated exclusively to physical medicine and rehabilitation. The hospital's programs include behavioral neurology, amputee, spinal cord injury, burn recovery, oncology, pulmonary, arthritis, orthopedic and multi-system failure rehabilitation. **NOTE:** See website for current job openings and application instructions. **Positions advertised include:** Physical Therapist; Registered Nurse; LPN; Occupational Therapist; Speech-Language Pathologist.

RHODE ISLAND HOSPITAL
593 Eddy Street, Providence RI 02903. 401/444-4000. **Recorded jobline:** 866/626-JOBS. **Contact:** Human Resources. **World Wide Web address:** http://www.lifespan.org/partners/rih. **Description:** Rhode Island's largest private, non-profit, acute-care hospital, with 719 beds. Provides comprehensive inpatient and outpatient services. Rhode Island Hospital also serves as southeastern New England's only Level One Trauma Center. Rhode Island Hospital's pediatric division, Hasbro Children's Hospital, is world renowned for its level of care and family-friendly environment. A major teaching hospital for Brown Medical School. **NOTE:** Per-Diem and Part-Time positions, as well as second- and third-shifts are available. **NOTE:** See website for current job openings and application instructions. **Positions advertised include:** Interpreter; Lead Secretary; MRI Technologist; Nurse Practitioner; Outpatient Services Representative; Pathology Technologist; Pharmacist; Professional Nurse; Radiation Therapist; Radiologic Technologist; Research Fellow; Social Worker; Secretary; Speech Pathologist; Washroom Attendant; Cafeteria Assistant. **President:** Joseph Amaral, MD.

RHODE ISLAND MEDICAL IMAGING
20 Catamore Boulevard, East Providence RI 02914. 401/432-2520. **Fax:** 401/432-2412. **Contact:** Susan Logan. **E-mail address:** slogan@rimirad.com. **World Wide Web address:** http://www.rimirad.com. **Description:** Provides diagnostic imagery health care services. **NOTE:** See website for current job openings and application instructions. **Positions advertised**

include: Mammography Technologist; Ultrasound Technologist/Sonographer; CT Technologist; PC Network Technician. **Other area locations:** East Greenwich RI; Providence RI; Pawtucket RI; Warren RI.

ROGER WILLIAMS MEDICAL CENTER
825 Chalkstone Avenue, Providence RI 02908-4735. 401/456-2000. **Recorded jobline:** 401/456-2689. **Contact:** Human Resources. **World Wide Web address:** http://www.rwmc.com. **Description:** Roger Williams Medical Center is a major medical complex that provides advanced diagnostic, treatment, education, and support services. The hospital provides treatment for a wide range of medical and surgical conditions as well as advanced cancer care, including the state's only bone marrow transplant unit. Roger Williams Medical Center is also a major teaching and research facility affiliated with Boston University School of Medicine. **NOTE:** See website for current job openings. To apply, send resume by mail. **Positions advertised include:** Assistant HRCC Coordinator; Supervisor, Animal Care Facility; Staff Physicist; Pharmacist; Social Worker; Dietary Technician; Help Desk Analyst; Medical Technologist; Histology Technologist; Research Assistant; Mental Health Worker; Network Administrator; Registered Nurse.

ST. JOSEPH HOSPITAL
21 Peace Street, Providence RI 02907. 401/456-4200. **Fax:** 401/456-4167. **Contact:** Derek Padon, Human Resources. **World Wide Web address:** http://www.saintjosephri.com. **Description:** A specialty hospital focusing on rehabilitation, psychiatric services and clinic/urgent care services. Founded in 1892. **NOTE:** See website for current job openings and to apply online. **Positions advertised include:** Certified Activities Coordinator; Certified Nursing Assistant.

WOMEN & INFANTS HOSPITAL
45 Willard Street, Providence RI 02905. 401/274-1122. **Fax:** 401/453-7976. **Contact:** Human Resources Department. **E-mail address:** wihjobs@carene.org. **World Wide Web address:** http://www.womenandinfants.com. **Description:** One of southeastern New England's premier hospitals for the care of women and newborns. Founded in 1884. **NOTE:** See website for current job openings and to apply online. Entry-level positions and second and third shifts are offered. Applications are accepted online, by fax, or by mail. **Positions advertised include:** Administrative Assistant; Administrative Nursing Supervisor; Campaign Coordinator; Bilingual Patient Services Assistant; Per-Diem Cook; File Retrieval Rep; Phlebotomist; Payroll Analyst; Pharmacist; Registered Nurse; Radiographer/Mammographer.

X-RAY ASSOCIATES
6725 Post Road, North Kingstown RI 02852. 401/886-4830. **Fax:** 401/886-4533. **Contact:** Human Resources. **E-mail address:** hr@xrayassociates.com. **World Wide Web address:** http://www.xrayassociates.com. **Description:** Outpatient imaging center. **NOTE:** Send employment inquiries by fax or e-mail. **Positions advertised include:** Medical Receptionist; Technical Assistant; Site Manager; Supervisor; Ultrasound Technologist; X-ray/Mammography Technologist. **Other area locations:** Cranston R: Johnston RI; Middletown RI; Wakefield RI.

South Carolina

ANMED HEALTH MEDICAL CENTER
800 North Fant Street, Anderson SC 29621. 864/261-1000. **Fax:** 864/261-1952. **Recorded jobline:** 800/423-2172. **Contact:** Human Resources. **World Wide Web address:** http://www.anmed.com. **Description:** A 461-bed, acute care, regional medical center. **Positions advertised include:** Compliance Auditor; Counselor; Certified Registered Nursing Assistant; Nursing Director; Food Service Worker; Histotechnologist; Licensed Practical Nurse; Nurse Assistant; Office Clerk.

BAUSCH & LOMB INCORPORATED
8507 Pelham Road, Greenville SC 29615. 864/297-5500. **Contact:** Human Resources Manager. **World Wide Web address:** http://www.bausch.com. **Description:** Manufactures eye care products, pharmaceuticals, and surgical equipment including contact lenses; lens care solutions; premium sunglasses (sold under Ray-Ban and Revo brands) prescription and over-the-counter ophthalmic drugs; and equipment used for cataract and ophthalmic surgery. **Positions advertised include:** Transportation Specialist; Chemistry Technician III. **Special programs:** Summer Internships. **Corporate headquarters location:** Rochester NY. **Other area locations:** Columbia SC. **Other U.S. locations:** Nationwide. **Operations at this facility include:** Manufacturing; Distribution; Warehousing. **Listed on:** New York Stock Exchange. **Stock exchange symbol:** BOL. **Annual sales/revenues:** $1.8 billion. **Number of employees:** 11,600.

BECTON DICKINSON AND COMPANY (BD)
1575 Airport Road, Sumter SC 29153. 803/469-8010, extension 1610. **Contact:** Human Resources Department. **World Wide Web address:** http://www.bd.com. **Description:** A medical and pharmaceutical company engaged in the manufacture of health care products, medical instrumentation, a line of diagnostic products, and industrial safety equipment. The company also offers contract packaging services. **Positions advertised include:** Project Engineer; Product Development Engineer; Manufacturing Process Engineer; Equipment Technician; Electrical Engineer; Industrial Engineer; Mechanical Engineer; Operations Manager. **Special programs:** Internships; Coops. **Corporate headquarters location:** Franklin Lakes NJ. **Other area locations:** Seneca SC. **Other U.S. locations:** Nationwide. **International locations:** Worldwide. **Operations at this facility include:** Manufacturing of blood collection supplies. **Listed on:** New York Stock Exchange. **Stock exchange symbol:** BDX. **Annual sales/revenues:** $4 billion. **Number of employees:** 25,250.

EAST COOPER MEDICAL CENTER
1200 Johnnie Dodds Boulevard, Mount Pleasant SC 29464. 843/881-0100. **Fax:** 843/881-4396. **Contact:** Human Resources Department. **World Wide Web address:** http://www.eastcoopermedctr.com. **Description:** A full-service hospital. **Positions advertised include:** Registered Nurse; Physical Therapist; Admit Communications Representative; Imaging Assistant; Assistant Nurse. **Parent company:** Tenet Healthcare Corporation.

GE MEDICAL SYSTEMS
3001 West Radio Drive, Florence SC 29501. 843/667-9799. **Contact:** Personnel. **World Wide Web address:** http://www.gemedicalsystems.com. **Description:** Manufactures superconducting magnets for magnetic resonance imaging. **Positions advertised include:** Field Service Engineer; Process Engineer; X-Ray Engineer; Regional Manager; Field Solutions Engineer; Program Coordinator; Electrical Engineer; Mechanical Engineer; Physicist. **Other area locations:** Anderson SC; Charleston SC. **Other U.S. locations:** Nationwide. **Parent company:** General Electric Company (Fairfield CT) is a diversified manufacturer of consumer and industrial products. **Operations at this facility include:** Manufacturing; Research and Development.

GREENVILLE HOSPITAL SYSTEM
701 Grove Road, Greenville SC 29605. 864/455-8976. **Fax:** 864/455-6218. **Recorded jobline:** 864/455-8799. **Contact:** Human Resources. **World Wide Web address:** http://www.ghs.org. **Description:** A multi-hospital system that provides health care services to several communities and major tertiary referral services for the upstate area. **Positions advertised include:** Nurse Supervisor; Registered Nurse; Pediatrician; Chief Technician; Radiology; Physical Therapy. **Number of employees at this location:** 6,500.

KERSHAW COUNTY MEDICAL CENTER
1315 Roberts Street, P.O. Box 7003, Camden SC 29020. 803/432-4311. **Fax:** 803/713-6247. **Contact:** Personnel. **E-mail address:** info@kcmc.org. **World Wide Web address:** http://www.kcmc.org. **Description:** Operates a 121-bed acute care facility, an 88-bed long-term care facility, Health Resource Center, and Home Health/Hospice Agency in Camden. The hospital also has two primary healthcare offices and a medical complex in other satellite locations. **Positions advertised include:** Licensed Practical Nurse; Registered Nurse; Community Health Educator; Physical Therapist; Recruiter; Speech Therapist; CT Scan Diagnostic Technologist; Polysonographer; Respiratory Therapist.

LEXINGTON MEDICAL CENTER
2720 Sunset Boulevard, West Columbia SC 29169. 803/996-6240. **Toll-free phone:** 800/240-7858. **Fax:** 803/359-2267. **Recorded jobline:** 803/739-3562. **Contact:** Betsy Brooks, Employment Coordinator. **E-mail address:** bsbrooks@lexhealth.org. **World Wide Web address:** http://www.lexmed.com. **Description:** A 318-bed metropolitan medical complex, which includes six community medical centers serving Lexington County, an occupational health center and 16 affiliated physician practices. **NOTE:** For physician opportunities contact: Barbara Willm, 2720 Sunset Boulevard, West Columbia SC 29169; Phone: 803/358-6166; E-mail address: willm@lexhealth.org. **Positions advertised include:** Nursing Supervisor; Registered Nurse; Licensed Practical Nurse; Certified Nurses Aide; Ward Clerk; Occupational Manager; Social Worker.

LORIS HEALTHCARE SYSTEM
LORIS COMMUNITY HOSPITAL
3655 Mitchell System Box 690001, Loris SC 29569-9601. 843/716-7196, extension 5360. **Physical address:** 3311 Casey Street, Loris SC 29569. **Fax:** 843/716-7254. **Contact:** Abby Gore, Employment Coordinator. **E-mail address:** agore@lorishealthcaresystem.com. **World Wide Web address:** http://www.lorishealthcaresystem.com. **Description:** A general, acute care hospital. **Positions advertised include:** Carpenter; Cashier; Executive Physiologist; Licensed Practical Nurse; Nuclear Medical Technician; Pharmacist; Physical Therapist; Radiological Technician; Receptionist; Registered Nurse; Transcriptionist; Utility Aide.

PALMETTO HEALTH
P.O. Box 2266, Columbia SC 29202. 803/296-2100. **Physical address:** 5 Richland Medical Park Drive, Columbia SC 29203. **Fax:** 803/296-5928. **Contact:** Human Resources. **E-mail address:** jobs@palmettohealth.org. **World Wide Web address:** http://www.palmettohealth.com. **Description:** A locally-owned, non-profit healthcare system operating several hospitals and medical centers with a total of 1,247 beds. **Positions advertised include:** Administrative Associate; Planning Analyst; Project Manager; Workers Compensation Manager. **Corporate headquarters location:** This location. **Subsidiaries include:** Palmetto Health Baptist; Palmetto Health Richland; Palmetto Health South Carolina Cancer Center; Palmetto Health South Carolina Comprehensive Breast Center; Gamma Knife Center of the Carolinas; CareForce; Palmetto Health Hospice. **Number of employees:** 7,000.

PALMETTO HEALTH RICHLAND
5 Richland Medical Park, Columbia SC 29203. 803/434-7733. **Contact:** Employment Services Department. **E-mail address:** jobs@palmettohealth.org. **World Wide Web address:** http://www.palmettohealth.com. **Description:** A 626-bed, regional, community teaching hospital. Richland Memorial Hospital's facilities include a Children's Hospital; the Center for Cancer Treatment and Research; the Heart Center; the Midlands Trauma Center; and Richland Springs, a free-standing psychiatric hospital. **Positions advertised include:** Data Processor; Dental Assistant; Laboratory Assistant; Linen Technician; Mechanical Engineer; Mental Health Assistant; Emergency Department Nurse; Phlebotomist; Cardiac Care Technician. **Special programs:** Internships. **Parent company:** Palmetto Health. **Number of employees at this location:** 5,100.

SISTERS OF CHARITY PROVIDENCE HOSPITALS
2709 Laurel Street, Columbia SC 29204. 803/256-5410. **Fax:** 803/256-5838. **Recorded jobline:** 803/256-5627. **Contact:** Human Resources. **E-mail address:** prov.hr@providencehospitals.com. **World Wide Web address:** http://www.provhosp.com. **Description:** A non-profit organization operating three facilities with a total of 311 beds: Providence Hospital, Providence Heart Institute, and Providence Hospital Northeast serving the Midlands region of South Carolina. **Positions advertised include:** Office Coordinator; Executive Secretary; Collections Specialist; Environmental Services Technician; Assembly Analyst; Phlebotomist; Registered Nurse; Sleep Lab Technician; Affairs Vice President; Medical Lab Student; Pharmacy Specialist. **Parent company:** Sisters of Charity of Saint Augustine Health System. **Number of employees statewide:** 1,500.

SPAN-AMERICA MEDICAL SYSTEMS, INC.
P.O. Box 5231, Greenville SC 29606. 864/288-8877. **Physical address:** 70 Commerce Centre, Greenville SC 29615. **Toll-free phone:** 800/888-6752. **Fax:** 864/288-8692. **Contact:** Human Resources. **E-mail address:** employment@spanamerica.com. **World Wide Web address:** http://www.spanamerica.com. **Description:** Manufactures and distributes a variety of polyurethane foam products for the health care, consumer, and industrial markets. The company's principal health care products consist of polyurethane foam mattress overlays including its Geo-Matt overlay, therapeutic replacement mattresses, patient positioners, and single-use flexible packaging products. Founded in 1970. **Corporate headquarters location:** This location. **Other locations:** Norwalk CA. **Listed on:** NASDAQ. **Stock exchange symbol:** SPAN. **Number of employees nationwide:** 225.

TUOMEY HEALTHCARE SYSTEM
129 North Washington Street, Sumter SC 29150. 803/778-8760. **Toll-free phone:** 800/648-1195. **Fax:** 803/778-9494. **Contact:** Employment Supervisor. **E-mail address:** ptruluck@tuomey.com. **World Wide Web address:** http://www.tuomey.com. **Description:** A non-profit medical system, which includes the 266-bed Tuomey Regional Medical Center and a staff of over 150 physicians. Facilities include a 36-bed nursery, expanded ICU, 10 operating suites and a satellite medical park as well as diagnostic and treatment capabilities with a Cancer Treatment Center, cardiac catheterization and updated HiSpeed Computed Tomography. **NOTE:** For Nursing and Allied Health positions, call the Recruiter at 803/778-8762. **Positions advertised include:** Echo Vascular Technologist; Licensed Practical Nurse; Mammography Technician; Medical Lab Assistant; Medical Technician; Nurse Technician Extern; Occupational Therapist; Physical Therapist; Registered Nurse; Surgical Technician.

TYCO HEALTHCARE
dba KENDALL HEALTHCARE PRODUCTS COMPANY
525 North Emerald Road, Greenwood SC 29646. 864/223-4281. **Contact:** Human Resources. **World Wide Web address:** http://www.tycohealthcare.com. **Description:** Manufactures and distributes disposable incontinence products. **NOTE:** Entry-level positions and second and third shifts are offered. **Positions advertised include:** Production Superintendent. **Special programs:** Internships. **Corporate headquarters location:** Mansfield MA. **Other area locations:** Camden SC; Seneca SC. **Other U.S. locations:** Nationwide. **International locations:** Worldwide. **Parent company:** Tyco International (Portsmouth NH). **Operations at this facility include:** Administration; Divisional Headquarters; Manufacturing; Sales.

South Dakota

AVERA McKENNAN HOSPITAL & UNIVERSITY HEALTH CENTER
800 East 21st Street, P.O. Box 5045, Sioux Falls SD 57117-5045. 605/322-7850. **Toll-free phone:** 888/677-3222. **Recorded jobline:** 605/322-7880. **Contact:** Human Resources. **E-mail address:** teresa_frederick@mckennan.org. **World Wide Web address:** http://www.mckennan.org. **Description:** Avera McKennan Hospital and University Health Center is a member of Avera Health, a regional healthcare company with more than 100 locations in eastern South Dakota and neighboring states. The McKennan campus includes the 490-bed McKennan Hospital, the Dakota Midwest Cancer Institute, McGreevy Clinic, Sioux Falls Surgical Center, Central Plains Clinic, Midwest Cardiovascular Center, Physician's Office Building, Wee Care, and Center Inn. **NOTE:** Please visit website or current openings and to apply online. **Positions advertised include:** Admitting Representative; Cancer Education Coordinator; Coding Analyst; Dietetic Assistant; Food Service Worker; Housekeeper; Medical Technologist; Medical Transcriber; Nurse Manager. **Special programs:** Internships; Volunteer Opportunities. **Number of employees at this location:** 2,000.

AVERA QUEEN OF PEACE HOSPITAL
525 North Foster, Mitchell SD 57301. 605/995-2496. **Contact:** Chris Nelson, Human Resources. **E-mail address:** chris.nelson@averaqueenofpeace.org. **World Wide Web address**: http://www.averaqueenofpeace.org. **Description:** A 120-bed medical center. Avera Queen of Peace Hospital, a member of Avera Health, consists of several medical facilities providing comprehensive health care in Mitchell, SD and the eleven-county area. **NOTE:** See website for current openings and to apply online. **Positions advertised include:** Nursing Assistant; RAD Tech I. **Corporate headquarters location:** Sioux Falls SD. **Parent company:** Avera Health. **Number of employees at this location:** 650.

AVERA ST. LUKE'S MIDLAND REGIONAL MEDICAL CENTER
305 South State Street, Aberdeen SD 57401. 605/622-5000. **Toll-free phone:** 800/22-LUKES. **Contact:** Human Resources. **World Wide Web address**: http://www.averastlukes.org. **Description:** A regional medical center that offers a comprehensive array of medical and health services to people living in the surrounding ten counties around Aberdeen. In addition to the 137-bed hospital, provides services through Avera Mother Joseph Manor Retirement Community in Aberdeen and Avera Eureka Health Care Center, the long-term care division, and through our clinic division. **NOTE:** See website for current openings and to apply online. **Positions advertised include:** Cath Lab Tech; Critical Care RN; Flight Nurse; Housekeeper; Janitor; Nursing Coordinator; Physical Therapist; Registered Nurse; Ultrasounds Technologist. **Parent company:** Avera Health. **Number of employees at this location:** 1,100.

PRAIRIE LAKES HEALTHCARE SYSTEM
401 9th Avenue Northwest, Watertown SD 57201. 605/882-7716. **Contact:** Kris Munger, **E-mail address:** Kris.Munger@prairielakes.com. **World Wide Web address**: http://www.prairielakes.com. **Description:** A regional health care facility that houses an 83-bed licensed hospital and a 51-bed nursing home. **NOTE:** See website for current openings and to apply online. **Positions advertised include:** Certified Nurse Assistant; Chief CRNA; Physical Therapist; Physical Therapy Assistant; Physician Staff.

SIOUX VALLEY HOSPITAL
1305 West 18th Street, P.O. Box 5039, Sioux Falls SD 57117. 605/333-7000. **Toll-free phone:** 800/258-3333. **Fax:** 605/333-1967. **Contact:** Human Resources. **E-mail address:** hremploy@siouxvalley.org. **World Wide Web address:** http://www.siouxvalley.org. **Description:** A 476-bed, JCHO-accredited comprehensive medical center that is the largest medical facility in the region. In addition to specializing in cardiology, children's, oncology, neuroscience, trauma, orthopedics and women's, provides services in the areas of stroke, neonatal intensive care, air transport, family health, poison control, sports medicine and wellness. **NOTE:** See website for job openings and to apply online. **Positions advertised include:** A variety of positions in nursing, administration, maintenance, housekeeping/food service and physician care. **Special programs:** Summer jobs. **Number of employees at this location:** 3,500.

U.S. DEPARTMENT OF VETERANS AFFAIRS FORT MEADE VETERANS ADMINISTRATION MEDICAL CENTER
113 Comanche Road, Fort Meade SD 57741. 605/347-2511. **Fax:** 605/720-7171. **Contact:** Human Resources. **World Wide Web address:** http://www.va.gov. **Description:** A medical center operated by the U.S. Department of Veterans Affairs. From 54 hospitals in 1930, the VA health care system has grown to include 171 medical centers; more than 364 outpatient, community, and outreach clinics; 130 nursing home care units; and 37 domiciliary residences. VA operates at least one medical center in each of the 48 contiguous states, Puerto Rico, and the District of Columbia. With approximately 76,000 medical center beds, VA treats nearly a million patients in VA hospitals, 75,000 in nursing home care units and 25,000 in domiciliary residences. VA's outpatient clinics register approximately 24 million visits a year. **NOTE:** Please see website for information on how to search and apply for jobs.

U.S. DEPARTMENT OF VETERANS AFFAIRS ROYAL C. JOHNSON VETERANS MEMORIAL HOSPITAL
2501 West 22nd Street, P.O. Box 5046, Sioux Falls SD 57117-5046. 605/336-3230. **Fax:** 605/333-6878. **Contact:** Human Resources. **World Wide Web address:** http://www.va.gov. **Description:** One of eight combined VA Medical and Regional Office Centers throughout the country. A 194-bed teaching facility providing acute medical, surgical, and psychiatric services; intermediate medical inpatient services; and ambulatory care services. In addition, it has a 75-bed extended care unit. The medical center provides medical care to the veteran population in eastern South Dakota, northwestern Iowa, and southwestern Minnesota. The medical center also serves as the primary teaching hospital for the University of South Dakota School of Medicine and also supports 22 additional affiliated training programs from 13 institutions in six states. **NOTE:** Please see website for information on how to search and apply for jobs. **Number of employees at this location:** 780.

U.S. DEPARTMENT OF VETERANS AFFAIRS VETERANS ADMINISTRATION MEDICAL CENTER/HOT SPRINGS
500 North Fifth Street, Hot Springs SD 57747-1497. 605/745-2000. **Fax:** 605/745-2091. **Contact:** Herb Doering, Chief of Human Resources. **World Wide Web address:** http://www.va.gov. **Description:** A medical center operated by the U.S. Department of Veterans Affairs. From 54 hospitals in 1930, the VA health care system has grown to include 171 medical centers; more than 364 outpatient, community, and outreach clinics; 130 nursing home care units; and 37 domiciliary residences. VA operates at least one medical center in each of the 48 contiguous states, Puerto Rico, and the District of Columbia. With approximately 76,000 medical center beds, VA treats nearly 1 million patients in VA hospitals, 75,000 in nursing home care units and 25,000 in domiciliary residences. VA's outpatient clinics register approximately 24 million visits a year. **NOTE:** Please see website for information on how to search and apply for jobs.

Tennessee

ADVOCAT INC.
1621 Galleria Road, Brentwood, Franklin TN 37027. 615/771-7575. **Contact:** Director of Employee and Client Relations. **World Wide Web address:**

http://www.irinfo.com/avc. **Description:** A nursing and social services provider. The company operates assisted living facilities and skilled nursing facilities in 10 states and three Canadian provinces. **Other U.S. locations:** AL; AR; FL; KY; OH; TX; WV. **International locations:** Canada.

AMERICAN HOMEPATIENT, INC.
5200 Maryland Way, Suite 400, Brentwood TN 37027. 615/221-8884. **Fax:** 615/373-9932. **Contact:** Human Resources Department. **E-mail address:** hr@ahom.com. **World Wide Web address:** http://www.ahom.com. **Description:** Provides home health care products and services through 80 locations in 13 states in the southwestern and southeastern United States. The company's main services include respiratory and infusion therapy, enteral and parenteral nutrition, and the rental and sale of medical equipment and related supplies for the home. **Corporate headquarters location:** This location. **Number of employees nationwide:** 3,500.

BAPTIST HEALTH SYSTEM
P.O. Box 1788, Knoxville TN 37901-1788 865/632-5936. **Physical address:** 137 Blount Avenue, Knoxville TN 37920. **Fax:** 865/632-5223. **Recorded jobline:** 865/632-5977. **Contact:** Human Resources. **E-mail address:** hrbaptist@bhset.org. **World Wide Web address:** http://www.bhset.org. **Description:** Operates Baptist Hospital of East Tennessee, Baptist Hospital of Cocke County, Baptist hospital West and Baptist hospital for Women, and eight senior health centers. Founded in 1948. **NOTE:** Search and apply for positions online. **Corporate headquarters location:** This location. **Subsidiaries include:** Home Care East. **Annual sales/revenues:** $5 - $10 million.

BAPTIST HOSPITAL
2000 Church Street, Nashville TN 37236. 615/284-5555. **Fax:** 615/284-5205. **Contact:** Staffing Manager. **World Wide Web address:** http://www.baptisthospital.com. **Description:** A 683-bed, acute care hospital offering services in a variety of specialties including cardiac care, eye care, cancer care, neurosciences, and medical/surgical. Baptist Hospital provides a comprehensive cardiac program that includes angioplasty, open-heart surgery, and cardiac rehabilitation. **NOTE:** Search for positions and download employment application online. **Parent company:** Saint Thomas Health Services. **Number of employees at this location:** 3,300.

BAPTIST MEMORIAL HEALTH CARE SYSTEM
350 North Humphreys Boulevard, Memphis TN 38120. **Toll-free phone:** 800/422-7847. **Fax:** 901/227-5699. **Recorded jobline: 901/227-4515. Contact:** Employment Services. **E-mail address:** employment@bmhcc.org. **World Wide Web address:** http://www.baptistonline.org. **Description:** A health care system that operates 17 hospitals an array of home care and hospice agencies, minor medical clinics, behavioral health programs and a network of surgery, rehabilitation and other outpatient centers. **NOTE:** Physicians may send a CV and cover letter to Lynn Buff, Director of Recruitment at above address or e-mail to: PracticeOpps@bmhcc.org. Resumes for nursing positions may be sent to 6141 Walnut Grove Road, Memphis TN 38120, faxed to 901/226-4501, or e-mailed to: NursingJobs@bmhcc.org. **Positions advertised include:** Contract manager; Director, Baptist Clinical Research Center; Marketing Coordinator; Marketing Specialist; Clinical Resource Nurse; Registered Respiratory Therapist; Staff Development Instructor Specialist; RN's.

BAXTER HEALTHCARE CORPORATION
4835 South Mendenhall Road, Memphis TN 38141. 901/795-7970. **Contact:** Human Resources. **World Wide Web address:** http://www.baxter.com. **Description:** Baxter Healthcare is a global medical products and services company that is a leader in technologies related to blood and the circulatory system. The company has market-leading positions in four global businesses: biotechnology, which develops therapies and products in transfusion medicine; cardiovascular medicine, which develops products and provides services to treat late-stage cardiovascular disease; renal therapy, which develops products and services to improve therapies to fight kidney disease; and intravenous systems/medical products, which develops technologies and systems to improve intravenous medication delivery and distributes disposable medical products. **NOTE:** Search and apply for positions online. **Positions advertised include:** Quality Associate. **Corporate headquarters location:** Deerfield IL. **Operations at this facility include:** This location is a distribution and service center for the medical equipment manufacturer. **Number of employees worldwide:** 35,000.

BLOUNT MEMORIAL HOSPITAL
907 East Lamar Alexander Parkway, Maryville TN 37804-5016. 865/977-5659. **Contact:** Patricia Knight, Director of Human Resources. **World Wide Web address:** http://www.blountmemorial.org. **Description:** A fully accredited, 334-bed, acute care facility. The hospital provides care and education in hospital, outpatient, worksite, and community settings. Blount Memorial Hospital offers a 24-hour physician-staffed emergency department (a designated Level III Trauma Center); comprehensive therapeutic and diagnostic facilities; a state-of-the-art surgery center, same-day surgery, and an intensive care unit; industrial medicine, occupational health, and employee assistance programs for business and industry; a primary care and occupational health clinic network; a family birthing center; and alcohol, drug, and eating disorders treatment. **NOTE:** Entry-level positions are offered. Search and apply for positions online. **Positions advertised include:** Administrative supervisor; CNA's; CT Technologist; Dietitian; Director MSO; HIM Imaging Technician; LPN's; Physical Therapist; Speech Pathologist; Surgical Technician. **Special programs:** Training. **Operations at this facility include:** Administration; Service. **Annual sales/revenues:** $51 - $100 million. **Number of employees at this location:** 1,300.

CHD MERIDIAN HEALTHCARE
40 Burton Hills Boulevard, Suite 200, Nashville TN 37215. 615/665-9500. **Fax:** 615/234-9026. **Contact:** Human Resources. **E-mail address:** HumanResources@CHDMeridian.com. **World Wide Web address:** http://www.chdmeridian.com. **Description:** Provides employer-sponsored healthcare services to large and mid-sized employers. **NOTE:** Search and apply for positions online. **Positions advertised include:** IS Analyst. **Corporate headquarters location:** This location. **Other U.S. locations:** Nationwide.

CTI MOLECULAR IMAGING, INC.
810 Innovation Drive, Knoxville TN 379322571. 865/218-2000. **Fax:** 865/218-3003. **Contact:** Human Resources Manager. **E-mail address:** hr@ctimi.com. **World Wide Web address:** http://www.ctimi.com. **Description:** Develops and manufactures equipment used in Positron Emission Tomography (PET), a noninvasive medical imaging technique that is able to detect abnormal functions of the body in the early stages by imaging biochemical and metabolic changes. **NOTE:** Search and apply for positions online. **Positions advertised included:** Computer Service Engineer; Customer Solutions Specialist; Internal Audit Sr. Manager; Oracle Applications Specialist; Oracle Developer; PET/CT Specialist. **Corporate headquarters location:** This location. **Listed on:** NASDAQ. **Stock exchange symbol:** CTMI. **Number of employees at this location:** 150.

COMMUNITY HEALTH SYSTEMS, INC.
7100 Commerce Way, Suite 100, Brentwood TN 37027-4000. 615/373-9600. **Contact:** Human Resources. **World Wide Web address:** http://www.chs.net. **Description:** Owns and manages 72 hospitals in 22 states. **NOTE:** Search and apply for positions or submit resume online. **Listed on:** New York Stock Exchange. **Stock exchange symbol:** CYH.

COOKEVILLE REGIONAL MEDICAL CENTER
142 West Fifth Street, Cookeville TN 38501. 931/528-2541. **Fax:** 931/646-2635. **Contact:** Human Resources. **E-mail address:** kbailey@crmchealth.org. **World Wide Web address:** http://www.crmchealth.org. **Description:** A nonprofit, acute care medical center with 247 beds. Services offered include general medical and surgical care, a heart catheterization lab, critical care unit, obstetrics, and medical oncology. Founded in 1950. **NOTE:** Entry-level positions and second and third shifts are offered. **Positions advertised include:** Certified Nurses Aide; Pharmacy Technician; Licensed Practical Nurse; Pharmacist; CT Technologist; Registered Nurse; Respiratory Therapist; Secretary; Surgical Technician. **Special programs:** Internships.

CROCKETT HOSPITAL
1607 South Locust Avenue, Highway 43, P.O. Box 847, Lawrenceburg TN 38464. 931/762-6571. **Fax:** 931/766-3248. **Contact:** Bob Augustin, Director of Human Resources. **E-mail address:** robert.augustin@lifepointhospitals.com. **World Wide Web address:** http://www.crocketthospital.com. **Description:** A 107-bed acute-care hospital. Crockett Hospital offers a variety of inpatient and outpatient services including 24-hour emergency care, women's health services, a full range of surgical capabilities, critical care, rehabilitation, diabetes management, and nutrition and dietary counseling. **Positions advertised include:** Respiratory Therapist; Physical Therapist; Registered Nurse.

DELTA MEDICAL CENTER
3000 Getwell Road, Memphis TN 38118. 901/369-8100. **Toll-free phone:** 800/285-9502. **Recorded jobline:** 901/369-4747. **Fax:** 901/369-8527. **Contact:** Human Resources. **World Wide Web address:** http://www.deltamedcenter.com. **Description:** A 243-bed medical/surgical hospital. The center offers a complete range of services including a 24-hour physician-staffed emergency center, inpatient and outpatient health care, mental health services, and treatment for chemical dependency. The hospital's Health Resource Center offers free monthly health seminars and health screenings. **Positions advertised include:** Registered Nurse; House Supervisor; UR Nurse; Speech Therapist; LPN; Nursing Assistant. **Parent company:** Regent Health Group, Inc.

EAST TENNESSEE CHILDREN'S HOSPITAL
P.O. Box 15010, Knoxville TN 37901-5010. 865/541-8000. **Physical address**: 2018 Clinch Avenue, Knoxville TN 37916. **Fax:** 865/541-8340. **Recorded jobline:** 865/541-8565. **Contact:** Human Resources. **E-mail address:** jobs@etch.com. **World Wide Web address:** http://www.etch.com. **Description:** Provides care to 60,000 children from east Tennessee, southeast Kentucky, southwest Virginia, and western North Carolina. Annually, East Tennessee Children's Hospital is one of the region's leading pediatric referral centers. Services include the hospital's Pediatric Intensive Care Unit; the Neonatal Intensive Care Unit; the Pediatric Critical Care Transport Team and the Neonatal Transport Team; the Pediatric Emergency Department and Trauma Center; pediatric medical floors; outpatient clinics; pediatric surgical services; home health; rehabilitation center; hospital intensive psychiatric services; the child life department; pastoral care; nutrition services; and social work. **Positions advertised include:** Registered Nurse; Nursing Director of Critical Care Services; Licensed Practical Nurse; Nursing Supervisor; Pharmacist; Development Phlebotomist; Sonongrapher; CT Technologist; Director of Health Information Management.

ERLANGER MEDICAL CENTER
975 East Third Street, Chattanooga TN 37403-9975. 423/778-7000. **Contact:** Human Resources. **World Wide Web address:** http://www.erlanger.org. **Description:** An 818-bed hospital and teaching facility. Erlanger Medical Center is one of the largest public hospitals in the state. Facilities include a Level I trauma center, the Erlanger Cancer Center, the Miller Eye Center, and T.C. Thompson Children's Hospital. **NOTE:** Search and apply for positions online. **Positions advertised include:** RN's; LPN's; Cytogenetic Lab Director; Surgical Technologist; Phlebotomy Specialist; Medical Technologist; Radiation Therapist; Nuclear Medicine Technologist; Diagnostic Ultrasonographer.

FORT SANDERS PARKWEST MEDICAL CENTER
9352 Park West Boulevard, Knoxville TN 37923. 865/373-1000. **Contact:** Human Resources. **World Wide Web address:** http://www.fsparkwest.com. **Description:** A full-service, acute care hospital. Fort Sanders Parkwest Medical Center specializes in cardiology, critical care, diagnostics, emergency care, gastroenterology, joint replacement, maternity services, oncology, neurosurgery, physical therapy, radiology, and respiratory therapy. **NOTE:** Search and apply for positions online. **Positions advertised include:** RN's; PCA/CNA's; Director, Patient Care Services; LPN's. **Parent company:** Covenant Health.

FORT SANDERS REGIONAL MEDICAL CENTER
1901 Clinch Avenue, Knoxville TN 37916. 865/541-1111. **Contact:** Human Resources. **World Wide Web address:** http://www.fsregional.com. **Description:** A 539-bed, acute care hospital. Fort Sanders Regional Medical Center specializes in cardiology, emergency care, gynecology, pulmonary care, neurology, oncology, orthopedics, and rehabilitation. The medical center also operates The Teddy Bear Hospital, The Hope Center, and The Patricia Neal Rehabilitation Center. Other hospitals and facilities of Covenant Health include Fort Sanders Louden Medical Center, Fort Sanders Parkwest Medical Center, Fort Sanders Sevier Medical Center, Fort Sanders West, Maternity Center of East Tennessee, and Thompson Cancer Survival Center. **NOTE:** Search and apply for positions online. **Positions advertised include:** RN's; Periop Tech; PCA/CNA; Occupational Therapist; Manager of Critical Care; Director, Health Information Management; Physical Therapist; PACS Administrator; Surgical Tech. **Parent company:** Covenant Health.

FORT SANDERS SEVIER MEDICAL CENTER
P.O. Box 8005, Sevierville TN 37864. 865/429-6100. Physical address: 709 Middle Creek Road, Sevierville TN 37862. **Contact:** Human Resources. **World Wide Web address:** http://www.fssevier.com. **Description:** A 79-bed acute care hospital and a 54-bed nursing home. **NOTE:** Search and apply for positions online. **Positions advertised include:** ER Tech; PCA/CNA; RN's; Surgical Tech; Nurse Manager; LPN. **Parent company:** Covenant Health.

GLAXOSMITHKLINE
P.O. Box 868, Bristol TN 37621-0868. **Physical address:** 201 Industrial Drive, Bristol TN 37620-5413. 423/652-3100. **Contact:** Human Resources. **World Wide Web address:** http://www.gsk.com. **Description:** Manufactures penicillin, vitamins, vaccines, cancer treatments, and other pharmaceutical products. **NOTE:** Search and apply for positions online. **Positions advertised include:** Manager, Environmental Affairs. **Corporate headquarters location:** Philadelphia PA. **Other area locations:** Memphis TN. **Parent company:** GlaxoSmithKline Corporation is a health care company engaged in the research, development, manufacture, and marketing of prescription medicines, vaccines, and consumer healthcare products. **Number of employees worldwide:** 100,000.

HCA
One Park Plaza, Nashville TN 37203. 615/344-9551. **Contact:** Human Resources. **E-mail address:** executive.recruitment@hcahealthcare.com. **World Wide Web address:** http://www.hcahealthcare.com. **Description:** A full-service health care system operating approximately 200 hospitals and medical centers in 23 states, England and Switzerland. **NOTE:** Search and apply for positions online. **Corporate headquarters location:** This location. **Annual**

sales/revenues: More than $100 million. **Listed on:** New York Stock Exchange. **Stock exchange symbol:** HCA. **Number of employees at this location:** 2,000.

HEALTHWAYS
3841 Green Hills Village Drive, Nashville TN 37215. 800/327-3822. **Fax:** 615/263-1707. **Recorded jobline:** 800/292-5004 ext. 7575. **Contact:** Human Resources. **E-mail address:** hr@amhealthways.com. **World Wide Web address:** http://www.americanhealthways.com. **Description:** American Healthways provides chronic disease management services to hospitals, physicians, and other health care providers. The company specializes in providing treatment and services relating to diabetes, cardiac care, and respiratory disease. Founded in 1981. **NOTE:** Search and apply for positions online. **Positions advertised include:** Manager, Physician Support Services; Accreditation Director; Corporate Recruiter; Director of Transition Management; Director of CEC Education; Director of Procurement and Facility; Data Analyst; Database Analyst; OLAP Developer; Programmer Analyst. **Corporate headquarters location:** This location. **Listed on:** NASDAQ. **Stock exchange symbol:** AMHC. **Number of employees at this location:** 80. **Number of employees nationwide:** 650.

HENRY COUNTY MEDICAL CENTER
P.O. Box 1030, Paris TN 38242-1030. 731/644-8472. **Physical address:** 301 Tyson Avenue, Paris TN 38242. **Fax:** 731/644-8474. **Recorded jobline:** 731/644-8470. **Contact:** Human Resources. **World Wide Web address:** http://www.hcmc-tn.org. **Description:** A general, acute care hospital and nursing home. Founded in 1952. **NOTE:** Search for positions and download application online. **Positions advertised include:** RN's; CNA's; LPN's; Occupational Therapist; Physical Therapist. **Operations at this facility include:** Administration. **Number of employees at this location:** 600.

JOHN DEERE HEALTH
2033 Meadowview Lane, Kingsport TN 37660. 423/378-5122. **Contact:** Human Resources. **World Wide Web address:** http://www.JohnDeere.com. **Description:** John Deere has four main divisions: agricultural equipment, commercial and consumer equipment, construction and forestry equipment, and John Deere Power Systems. The health care subsidiary provides health-care-management services. **Positions advertised include:** Quality Improvement Coordinator. **Number of employees worldwide:** 43,000.

JOHNSON CITY MEDICAL CENTER
400 North State of Franklin Road, Johnson City TN 37604-6094. 423/431-6111. **Fax:** 423/431-6189. **Contact:** Recruiter/Employment Specialist. **E-mail address:** careers@msha.com. **World Wide Web address:** http://www.msha.com. **Description:** A 410-bed, nonprofit, acute-care teaching hospital, affiliated with the East Tennessee State University College of Medicine. Johnson City Medical Center Hospital is also a major medical referral center serving Tennessee, Virginia, North Carolina, and Kentucky, and includes Level I Trauma Care and the region's only dedicated emergency medical air transport service. **NOTE:** Entry-level positions and second and third shifts are offered. Search and apply for positions online. **Positions advertised include:** Registered Nurses; Licensed Practical Nurses; Corporate Purchasing Manager; CT Tech; Diagnostic Imaging Tech; Director, Marketing; Director, Medical Records; Director, Organizational Development; EEG Technologist; HR Analyst; Phlebotomist; Physical Therapist; Radiation Therapist; Surgical Tech. **Special programs:** Internships; Training. **Parent company:** Mountain States Health Alliance. **Number of employees at this location:** 2,200.

LAKESIDE BEHAVIORAL HEALTH SYSTEM
2911 Brunswick Road, Memphis TN 38133. 901/377-4700. **Fax:** 901/373-0912. **Recorded jobline:** 901/373-0949. **Contact:** Human Resources. **World Wide Web address:** http://www.lakesidebhs.com. **Description:** Lakeside Behavioral Health System offers health services to children, adolescents, and adults for a variety of behavioral and emotional problems. Services provided include treatments for eating disorders, phobias, substance abuse, stress, suicidal tendencies, and adolescent emotional problems. **NOTE:** Entry-level positions and second and third shifts are offered. **Number of employees at this location:** 400.

LAUGHLIN MEMORIAL HOSPITAL
1420 Tusculum Boulevard, Greeneville TN 37745. 423/787-5000. **Fax:** 423/787-5083. **Contact:** Human Resources. **E-mail address:** hr@laughlinmemorial.org. **World Wide Web address:** http://www.laughlinmemorial.org. **Description:** A 140-bed hospital specializing in echo-cardiology, intensive/coronary care, intensive neonatal care, neurology, nuclear medicine, obstetrics, occupational medicine, oncology, outpatient surgery, pediatrics, radiation oncology, and a women's health center. **NOTE:** Search and apply for positions online. **Positions advertised include:** Certified Nursing Assistant; Licensed Practical Nurse; Registered Nurse; Staff Pharmacist.

LE BONHEUR CHILDREN'S MEDICAL CENTER
50 North Dunlap Street, Memphis TN 38103. 901/572-3315. **Recorded jobline:** 901/726-8395. **Fax:** 901/516-0777. **Contact:** Staffing Services. **E-mail address:** employment@methodisthealth.org. **World Wide Web address:** http://www.lebonheur.org. **Description:** A fully accredited, 225-bed medical center. Le Bonheur Children's Medical Center is a pediatric specialty and subspecialty referral center. The center serves more than 105,000 children and adolescents each year through inpatient care, specialty clinics, and a fully staffed emergency department. Facilities include the Crippled Children's Foundation Research Center, a same-day surgery unit, an emergency department, an 18-bed intensive care unit, and a 12-bed transitional care unit. Le Bonheur also serves as the pediatric teaching facility of the University of Tennessee, Memphis. **NOTE:** Search for positions and download application form online. **Positions advertised include:** HIM Supervisor; HR Manager; Medical Technologist; Marketing Strategist; Lead Certified Anesthesia Tech; Pharmacist; Radiology Tech; CT Tech; Ultrasound Tech; Physical Therapist; Occupational Therapist; Speech Therapist; RN's. **Parent company:** Methodist Health.

LUXOTICA OPTICAL GROUP
5780 Shelby Drive East, Memphis TN 38141. 901/375-0015. **Toll-free phone:** 800/336-4535. **Fax:** 901/375-0668. **Contact:** Human Resources. **World Wide Web address:** http://www.colenational.com. **Description:** Manufactures prescription eyewear including contact lenses, eyeglasses, frames, lenses, and sunglasses. **NOTE:** Entry-level positions and second and third shifts are offered. **Special programs:** Summer Jobs. **Office hours:** Monday - Friday, 8:00 a.m. - 5:00 p.m. **Corporate headquarters location:** Twinsburg OH. **Other U.S. locations:** Salt Lake City UT; Richmond VA. **Parent company:** Cole National Corporation. **Annual sales/revenues:** $5 - $10 million.

MAURY REGIONAL HOSPITAL
1224 Trotwood Avenue, Columbia TN 38401. 931/380-4017. **Fax:** 931/540-4306. **Recorded jobline:** 931/380-4111. **Contact:** Employment Coordinator. **E-mail address:** employmentcoordinator@mrhs.com. **World Wide Web address:** http://www.mauryregional.com. **Description:** A 255-bed, nonprofit community hospital that provides specialized services to an eight-county area. Maury provides educational and training services on a regional basis for students through clinical affiliation with Columbia State Community College in the areas of X-ray, respiratory care, and registered nursing. **NOTE:** Search for positions online. **Positions advertised include:** Registered Nurse; Nurse Practitioner; Director, Decision Support – Finance; Pharmacy Manager; Occupational Therapist; Respiratory Therapist; Physical Therapist; Radiation

Therapist. **Number of employees at this location:** 2,000.

MEDTRONIC SOFAMOR DANEK
1800 Pyramid Place, Memphis TN 38132. 901/396-2695. **Contact:** Director of Human Resources. **World Wide Web address:** http://www.medtronic.com. **Description:** Develops, manufactures, and markets spinal implant devices and instruments used in the surgical treatment of spinal degenerative diseases and deformities. **NOTE:** Search and apply for positions online. **Positions advertised include:** Associate Product Development Engineer; Clinical Submissions Writer; Financial Analyst; Manager, Mechanical Testing Lab; Quality Engineer; Regulatory Affairs Associate; Sr. Product Manager; Sr. IT Developer. **Other U.S. locations:** KY; CO; IN. **Number of employees nationwide:** 300.

MEMORIAL NORTH PARK HOSPITAL
2051 Hammill Road, Hixson TN 37343. 423/495-7100. **Contact:** Director of Human Resources. **World Wide Web address:** http://www.memorial.org. **Description:** A fully accredited, 83-bed, acute care facility. Memorial North Park Hospital offers a full range of patient services including cardiopulmonary care, cosmetic surgery, diet counseling, 24-hour emergency treatment, outpatient and home heath care, laser surgery, gastrointestinal/pulmonary care, nuclear medicine, ophthalmology, physical therapy, physician referral, and radiology. As an affiliate of the hospital, Home Health Care provides nursing, physical therapy, speech therapy, and medical social services. **NOTE:** Search and apply for positions online. **Positions advertised include:** Registered Vascular Tech; Medical Technologist; Polysomnographic Tech; Coordinator, Media Relations; Pharmacist; Vascular Tech; Physical Therapist; Registered Nurses; Licensed Practical Nurses. **Number of employees at this location:** 650.

METHODIST HEALTHCARE, INC.
1211 Union Avenue, Memphis TN 38104. 901/516-7000. **Recorded jobline:** 901/726-8394. **Contact:** Personnel. **E-mail address:** employment@methodisthealth.org. **World Wide Web address:** http://www.methodisthealth.org. **Description:** Operates a regional network of health care facilities serving eastern Arkansas, western Tennessee, and northern Mississippi. Methodist Healthcare operates eight hospitals, several rural health clinics, and a home health agency. **Special programs:** Summer Jobs. **Corporate headquarters location:** Memphis TN. **Number of employees nationwide:** 10,250.

METHODIST UNIVERSITY HOSPITAL
1265 Union Avenue, Memphis TN 38104. 901/516-7000. **Contact:** Human Resources. **World Wide Web address:** http://www.methodisthealth.org. **Description:** A 696-bed teaching hospital for the University of Tennessee. **Positions advertised include:** Histology Tech; Surgical Pathology Tech; Sr. Histotechnologist; Nuclear Medicine Technologist; Surgical Tech; Lead Invasive Cardio Tech; Pharmacist; MRI Tech; Radiology Tech; Radiology Systems Coordinator; Mammography Tech; Manager, Special Imaging; Director, Clinical Support Services; RN's PRN's; LPN's.

MIDDLE TENNESSEE MEDICAL CENTER (MTMC)
400 North Highland Avenue, Murfreesboro TN 37130. 615/849-4100. **Contact:** Human Resources. **World Wide Web address:** http://www.mtmc.net. **Description:** A 286-bed private, not-for-profit hospital. MTMC is a member of Saint Thomas Health Services and Ascension Health. Established in 1927, MTMC serves the health care needs of Middle Tennesseans. **NOTE:** Search and apply for positions or submit resume online. **Positions advertised include:** RN's; Chief Radiation Therapist; Director of Compliance; Mammographer; Medical Technologist; Pharmacist; Physical Therapist; Radiation Therapist; Respiratory Therapist; Anesthesia Tech.

NATIONAL HEALTHCARE CORPORATION (NHC)
P.O. Box 1398, Murfreesboro TN 37133-1398. 615/890-2020. **Physical address:** 100 East Vine Street, Murfreesboro TN 37130. **Contact:** Vice President of Personnel. **Description:** Operates 76 long-term health care centers with approximately 9,300 beds, 32 home health care programs, six independent living centers, and 19 assisted living centers. Founded in 1971.

PARTHENON PAVILION
2401 Parman Place, Nashville TN 37203. 615/342-1450. **Contact:** Personnel. **World Wide Web address:** http://parthenonpavilion.com. **Description:** A 158-bed psychiatric hospital that offers a comprehensive program of mental health services for adolescents, adults, and the elderly. Founded in 1971. **Parent company:** Centennial Medical Center.

QHR
105 Continental Place, Brentwood TN 37027-5014. 615/371-7979. **Fax:** 615/221-3206. **Contact:** Recruitment. **E-mail address:** recruitment@qhr.com. **World Wide Web address:** http://www.qhr.com. **Description**: Provides management advisory services, implementation support, education and training programs, consulting and related services to independent hospitals and health systems. QHR manages more than 200 acute care hospitals. **NOTE:** QHR recruits CEO's and CFO's for health care facilities in the Northeast, Southeast, Midwest, and West. **Corporate headquarters location:** Plano TX. **Other U.S. locations:** Dothan AL; Enterprise AL; Gadsen AL; Jacksonville AL; Macon GA; Fort Wayne IN; Frankfort IN; Hattiesburg MS; Vicksburg MS; Las Vegas NV; Barberton OH; Massillon OH; Florence SC; Kingstree SC; Lake City SC; Spartanburg SC; Abilene TX. **Operations at this facility include:** This is a marketing and service center. **Number of employees nationwide:** 8,500.

REGIONAL MEDICAL CENTER AT MEMPHIS
Adams Pavilion Building, 842 Jefferson Avenue, Suite 200, Memphis TN 38103. 901/545-7569. **Fax:** 901/545-8315. **Recorded jobline:** 866/687-8432. **Contact:** Human Resources. **World Wide Web address:** http://www.the-med.org. **Description:** A health care center serving the Mid-South region, with inpatient and outpatient facilities, a trauma center, a burn/wound center, and a neonatal center. **NOTE:** Search and apply for positions online. **Positions advertised include:** Diagnostic Medical Sonographer; Director, Emergency Services; LPN's; Lead Rehab Therapist; Manager, Diagnostic Cardiology Services; Nuclear Medicine Technologist; Nurse Coordinator; Physical Therapist; Radiologic Technologist; RN's. **Operations at this facility include:** Administration; Service.

RENAL CARE GROUP
2525 West End Avenue, Suite 600, Nashville TN 37203. 615/345-5500. **Fax:** 615/345-5505. **Contact:** Human Resources Department. **World Wide Web address:** http://www.renalcaregroup.com. **Description:** Provides care to patients with kidney disease through 390 kidney dialysis centers. Renal Care Group also provides acute dialysis services through approximately 190 hospitals throughout the United States. **NOTE:** Search and apply for positions online. **Positions advertised include:** Director of Contracting; System Developer; Systems Analyst; Network Analyst; Security Analyst. **Corporate headquarters location:** This location. **Listed on:** New York Stock Exchange. **Stock exchange symbol:** RCI. **Annual sales/revenues:** More than $100 million. **Number of employees nationwide:** 8,000.

ST. FRANCIS HOSPITAL
5959 Park Avenue, Memphis TN 38119. 901/765-1000. **Contact:** Human Resources Department. **World Wide Web address:** http://www.saintfrancishosp.com. **Description:** A 611-bed hospital offering a wide range of inpatient, outpatient, and home health services. Founded in 1974. **NOTE:** Search and apply for

positions online. **Positions advertised include:** RN's; Nuclear Medicine Tech; Pharmacist; MRI Tech; LPN's; Respiratory Therapist; Clinical Lab Scientist. **Parent company:** Tenet Healthcare Corporation.

ST. JUDE CHILDREN'S RESEARCH HOSPITAL
332 North Lauderdale Street, Memphis TN 38105. 901/495-2339. **Toll-free phone:** 888/419-5833. **Fax:** 901/495-3123. **Contact:** Human Resources. **World Wide Web address:** http://www.stjude.org. **Description:** A nonprofit, nonsectarian institution that provides care for children with chronic illnesses. The hospital performs laboratory research on the molecular, genetic, and biochemical bases of childhood cancer and other diseases. St. Jude Children's Research Hospital also maintains outreach/consultation programs with other health care providers. **NOTE:** Search and apply for positions online. **Positions advertised include:** Pharmacist; Biostatistician; Research Technologist; Ultrasound Technologist; Sr. Training Analyst; Cytogenetic Technologist; Medical Technologist; Proteomics Analyst; Molecular Interaction Analyst; Sr. Database Architect; Sr. Research Technologist; Manager, Diagnostic Imaging; Pediatric Oncology Nurse; Sr. Internal Auditor.

SKYLINE MEDICAL CENTER
3441 Dickerson Pike, Nashville TN 37207. 615/769-2000. **Contact:** Nurse Manager. **World Wide Web address:** http://www.skylinemedicalcenter.com. **Description:** A 203-bed, full-service medical center serving the middle Tennessee and southern Kentucky areas. Skyline Medical Center specializes in emergency care, neurology, neurosurgery, oncology, orthopedics, and outpatient care. Founded in 1952. **NOTE:** Search and apply for positions online. **Positions advertised include:** RN's; LPN's; Cath Lab Technologist; Internal Relations Coordinator; Medical Technologist; MRI Technologist; Pharmacist; Phlebotomist; Polysomnographic Technologist; Radiation Therapist; **Parent company:** Tri Star Health System.

SMITH & NEPHEW
1450 Brooks Road, Memphis TN 38116. 901/396-2121. **Toll-free phone:** 800/821-5700. **Contact:** Human Resources. **World Wide Web address:** http://www.smith-nephew.com. **Description:** Manufactures and markets medical products used in endoscopy, orthopedics, and wound management. **NOTE:** Search and apply for positions online. **Positions advertised include:** Sr. Product Manager; Team Unit Manager; Sr. Legal Assistant; Sr. Product Development Engineer; Education and Training Administrative Coordinator; Packaging Development Engineer. **Corporate headquarters location:** London. **Listed on:** New York Stock Exchange. **Stock exchange symbol:** SNN. **Number of employees worldwide:** 7,000.

TAKOMA ADVENTIST HOSPITAL
401 Takoma Avenue, Greeneville TN 37743. 423/639-3151. **Fax:** 423/636-0338. **Contact:** Human Resources. **World Wide Web address:** http://www.takoma.org. **Description:** A hospital with services that include patient and family care; a physical therapy unit; a home health agency; specialized care, such as obstetrics/gynecology, urology, orthopedics, ophthalmology, and oral and general surgery; diagnostic care, such as radiology and ultrasound mammography services; emergency care including a 7-bed, 24-hour unit; psychiatric care including an 18-bed inpatient unit; maternal and child health care including two birthing rooms and a nursery; and community care including Takoma's IndustriCare occupational medicine program. **NOTE:** Search and apply for positions online. **Positions advertised include:** Certified Respiratory Technician; RN's; Director of ICU; Physical Therapist; Speech Pathologist.

TENDER LOVING CARE/STAFF BUILDERS
6263 Poplar Avenue, Suite 1000, Memphis TN 38119. 901/388-4663. **Contact:** Human Resources. **E-mail address:** ktoma@tlchhc.com. **World Wide Web address:** http://www.tlcathome.com. **Description:** A home health care agency. **Positions advertised include:** Registered Nurse; Licensed Practical Nurse. **Corporate headquarters location:** Lake Success NY. **Other U.S. locations:** Nationwide. **Number of employees nationwide:** 20,000.

TENNESSEE REHABILITATION CENTER
460 Ninth Avenue, Smyrna TN 37167. 615/459-6811. **Fax:** 615/355-1373. **Contact:** Human Resources. **Description:** A state-operated comprehensive rehabilitation center offering vocational training and physical rehabilitation services to disabled individuals. Founded in 1977. **NOTE:** Second and third shifts are offered. **Company slogan:** Caring for the present. Preparing for the future. **Special programs:** Internships. **Corporate headquarters location:** Nashville TN. **Number of employees at this location:** 125.

U.S. DEPARTMENT OF VETERANS AFFAIRS NASHVILLE VETERANS ADMINISTRATION MEDICAL CENTER
1310 24th Avenue South, Nashville TN 37212-2637. 615/327-4751. **Fax:** 615/321-6350. **Contact:** Human Resources. **World Wide Web address:** http://www.va.gov. **Description:** The Mid South Veterans Healthcare Network, operated by the U.S. Department of Veterans Affairs, serves one million veterans with seven anchor medical centers located in Lexington and Louisville KY; Memphis, Mountain Home, Murfreesboro, and Nashville TN; and Huntington WV. The Network also maintains five nursing home care units, and two long-term psychiatric care programs. **NOTE:** Search and apply for positions at: http://www.vacareers.com. **Corporate headquarters location:** Washington DC.

VANDERBILT UNIVERSITY MEDICAL CENTER
2525 West End Avenue, Station B, Box 357700, Nashville TN 37203. 615/322-8300. **Toll-free phone:** 800/288-6622. **Fax:** 615/343-7143. **Recorded jobline:** 615/322-JOBS. **Contact:** Recruitment and Staffing. **World Wide Web address:** http://www.mc.vanderbilt.edu. **Description:** A comprehensive health care facility that combines the education of health professionals, patient care, and biomedical research. Through its programs, Vanderbilt University Medical Center has become a major referral center for the Southeast and the nation. The medical center consists of The School of Medicine, The School of Nursing, The Vanderbilt Clinic, Children's Hospital, Vanderbilt Psychiatric Hospital, and Vanderbilt Stallworth Rehabilitation Hospital. **Positions advertised include:** Account Reimbursement Specialist; Administrative Assistant; Architect; Assistant Manager Patient Care Services; Audiologist; Care Partner; Case Manager; Coding Specialist; Computer Systems Administrator; Data Coordinator; Echocardiography Technologist; Histotechnologist; LAN Manager; LPN's; MRI Technologist. **Number of employees at this location:** 9,000.

WELLMONT BRISTOL REGIONAL MEDICAL CENTER
One Medical Park Boulevard, Bristol TN 37620. 423/844-3717. **Fax:** 423/844-3720. **Contact:** Employment. **E-mail address:** employment@wellmont.org. **World Wide Web address:** http://www.wellmont.org. **Description:** A 348-bed, nonprofit, regional referral center that provides medical services and resources for patients in northeast Tennessee, southwest Virginia, Kentucky, West Virginia, and North Carolina. The center specializes in acute care, cancer care, diabetes treatment, emergency care, neurosciences, outpatient services, psychiatric care, and women's health. **Positions advertised include:** Assistant Director, Radiology; Diagnostic Technologist; Director, Health Information Services; Physical Therapist; LPN; Radiation Therapist; Registered Nurse. **Parent company:** Wellmont Health System. **Number of employees at this location:** 1,500.

WELLMONT HOLSTON VALLEY MEDICAL CENTER
130 Ravine Road, P.O. Box 238, Kingsport TN 37662-0238. 423/224-6450. **Fax:** 423/224-6419. **Contact:** Human Resources Director. **E-mail address:** employment@wellmont.org. **World Wide Web address:** http://www.wellmont.org. **Description:** A full-service, 540-bed, acute-care medical center. The Holsten Valley Medical Center operates specialty clinics including The Christine LaGuardia Phillips Cancer Center, James H. Quillen Regional Heart Center, and the Regional Children's Center. **NOTE:** Search and apply for positions online. **Positions advertised include:** Cardiac Sonographer; Clinical Manager; Director of Surgical Services; Physical Therapist; Registered Nurses; Licensed Practical Nurses Staff Pharmacist; Surgical Tech. **Parent company:** Wellmont Health System. **Number of employees at this location:** 2,100.

WILLIAMSON MEDICAL CENTER
2021 Carothers Road, Franklin TN 37067. 615/435-5151. **Recorded jobline:** 615/435-5114. **Contact:** Human Resources Director. **E-mail address:** humanresources@williamsonmedicalcenter.org. **World Wide Web address:** http://www.williamsonmedicalcenter.org. **Description:** A hospital offering comprehensive inpatient and outpatient services. **NOTE:** Search or positions and download application form online. **Positions advertised include:** Administrator, Ambulatory Surgery Center; Registered Nurses; CT Technologist.

Texas

ADVANCE PCS
750 West John Carpenter Freeway, Suite 1200, Irving TX 75039. 469/524-4700. **Toll-free phone:** 800/749-6199. **Fax:** 469/524-4702. **Contact:** Human Resources. **World Wide Web address:** http://www.advancepcs.com. **Description:** A mail-order prescription and healthcare supply company. **NOTE:** Apply online. **Parent company:** Caremark Company (Nashville TN.)

AMERIPATH NORTH TEXAS
4300 Alpha Road, Dallas TX 75244. 972/341-5800. **Contact:** Human Resources. **World Wide Web address:** http://www.ameripath.com. **Description:** An outsourcing firm providing diagnostic and medical testing. **NOTE:** Resumes may also be mailed to Ms. Sutton at 7289 Garden Road, Suite 200, Rivera Beach, FL 33404. **Positions advertised include:** Pathologist; Quality Assurance Software Analyst; Dermapathologist; Cytotechnologist; Histotechnologist; Territory Sales Manager. **Corporate headquarters location:** FL. **Other area locations:** San Antonio TX; Lubbock TX. **Other U.S. locations:** FL; WI; CA; NY, OH, AL. **Listed on:** Privately held.

M.D. ANDERSON CANCER CENTER
P.O. Box 301402, Unit 629. Houston TX 77230-1402. **Physical address:** 1515 Holcombe Boulevard, Houston TX 77030. 713/792-6161. **Toll-free phone:** 800/392-1611. **Recorded jobline:** 713/792-8010. **Contact:** Human Resources. **World Wide Web address:** http://www.mdanderson.org. **Description:** Works to eliminate cancer and allied diseases by developing and maintaining integrated quality programs in patient care, research, education, and prevention. **NOTE:** Entry-level positions are offered. The Human Resources office is located at 2450 Holcombe Boulevard, Suite TMC 1.2176. Please visit website to search for jobs and apply online. **Positions advertised include:** Director – Information Security; Director – Chaplaincy & Pastoral Education; Clinical Investigation Technician; Pharmacy Technician; Pathology Assistant; Dispatcher; Bone Marrow Aspiration Technician; Editorial Assistant; Research Administrator; Legal Assistant; Electrician; Animal Technician. **Special programs:** Training. **Corporate headquarters location:** This location. **Parent company:** The University of Texas System. **Operations at this facility include:** Administration; Research and Development; Service. **Number of employees at this location:** 12,000.

ARLINGTON MEMORIAL HOSPITAL
800 West Randol Mill Road, Arlington TX 76012. 817/548-6100. **Contact:** Human Resources. **World Wide Web address:** http://www.texashealth.org. **Description:** A 357-bed acute care hospital with more than 2,500 physician, staff and volunteers. **NOTE:** Apply online at the website. **Parent company:** Texas Health Resources.

ARTHROCARE CORPORATION
111 Congress Avenue, Suite 510, Austin TX 78701-4043. 512/391-3900. **Fax:** 512/391-3901. **Contact:** Human Resources. **World Wide Web address:** http://www.arthrocare.com. **Description:** A medical device company that develops, manufactures and markets minimally invasive surgical products used for sports medicine; spine/neurologic; ear, nose and throat (ENT); cosmetic; urologic; and gynecologic procedures. **Positions advertised include:** Assistant Controller; Credit and Collections Analyst; Director, Reimbursement and Payer Relations; Financial Systems Analyst; Internal Auditor; International Accountant; Patent Attorney; Product Marketing Manager; R&D Manager; R&D Technician; Senior Network Administrator; Senior R&D Engineer; Senior Scientist; Senior/Staff Electrical Compliance Engineer; Senior/Staff Electrical Engineer; Vice President, Legal Affairs. **Other U.S. locations:** Sunnyvale CA.

THE AUSTIN DIAGNOSTIC CENTER
12221 North Mopac Expressway, Austin TX 78701. 512/901-1111. **Toll-free phone:** 800/925-8899. **Recorded jobline:** 512/901-4050. **Contact:** Human Resources. **E-mail address:** jobs@adclinic.com. **World Wide Web address:** http://www.adclinic.com. **Description:** A physician-owned clinic with approximately 120 doctors in various specialties., such audiology, cosmetic laser surgery, diabetes management, menopause management, and optometry. Founded in 1995. **NOTE:** The center has several health facilities throughout Texas. The website lists jobs for all locations. All resumes must accompany an application which can be downloaded at the website or picked up at this location. **Positions advertised include**: LVN; Orthopedic Cast Technician; Business Associate Coordinator; IMX Data Entry; Cardiologist; Adult and Child Psychiatrist; Endocrinologist; Internal Medicine Physician.

AUSTIN REGIONAL CLINIC
2000 S. Mays Street, Suite 202, Round Rock, TX 78664. 512/244-9024. **Fax:** 512/407-6464. **Contact:** Human Resources. **E-mail address:** jobs@covenantmso.com. **World Wide Web address:** http://www.austinregionalclinic.com. **Description:** An acute care, outpatient, multispecialty facility that offers primary care for adults and children, OB/GYN, occupational medicine, mental health services, dermatology, surgery, optometry, allergy treatment, and immunology. **Positions advertised include:** Accounts Payable Technician; Coding Specialist; Patient Registration Representative; Accounts Receivable Clerk; Medical Lab Technician; LVN; Medical Assistant; Patient Services Representative; HIM Technician; Patient Services Representative; RN Team Leader.

AUSTIN STATE HOSPITAL
4110 Guadalupe Street, Austin TX 78751. 512/452-0381. **Fax:** 512/419-2306. **Contact:** Human Resources. **World Wide Web address:** http://www.mhmr.state.tx.us/hospitals/austinsh/austinsh.html. **Description:** A 350-bed, acute psychiatric hospital. Austin State Hospital has many services to offer including a Deaf Unit, Children's Unit, and the Trinity Treatment Center, which aids people with mental retardation. **NOTE:** Please visit website to search for jobs and to download application forms. You may subscribe to have job postings e-mailed to you: Send an e-mail to hiring.services@mhmr.state.tx.us with the word "Subscribe" in the subject; do not send resumes or applications to this e-mail address. **Positions advertised include:** Psychiatrist; Clerk; MHMR Services Assistant; Custodian; Clinical Social

Worker; Interpreter; Nurse; Nurse RN; LVN.

AVANCE
2816 Swiss Avenue Dallas TX 75204. 214/887-9907. **Contact:** Human Resources. **E-mail address:** avance-dallas@avance.org. **World Wide Web address:** http://www.avance-dallas.org. **Description:** A nonprofit company that provides educational programs aimed at Hispanic at-risk children and their families. **Other area locations:** Austin TX; Corpus Christi TX; El Paso TX; Houston TX; Laredo TX; San Antonio TX; Waco TX; Texas Rio Grand Valley area; Texas Middle Rio Grande Valley. **Other U.S. locations:** Los Angeles, CA.

BAPTIST MEDICAL CENTER
111 Dallas Street, San Antonio TX 78205-1230. 210/297-7000. **Contact:** Annette Dunlap, Recruiter. **E-mail address:** amdunlap@baptisthealthsystem.com. **World Wide Web address:** http://www.baptisthealthsystem.org/bmc.asp. **Description:** A 689-bed, nonprofit, acute care hospital offering complete medical facilities for cardiac care, intensive care, emergency services, maternity, surgery, and other specialized services. **NOTE:** Please visit website to view job listings, apply online, or download application form. You may submit your resume or application directly to the hospital, or you can contact the Human Resources Center at 417 Camden, San Antonio TX 78215, fax is 210/297-0093. Volunteer positions are also available. **Positions advertised include:** Certified Occupational Therapy Assistant; LVN; Physical Therapist; RN. . **Parent company:** Baptist Memorial Hospital System is a health care system that is comprised of five acute care, nonprofit hospitals: Baptist Medical Center, Northeast Baptist Hospital, Southeast Baptist Hospital, North Center Baptist Hospital, and St. Luke's Baptist Hospital. In total, these hospitals contain 1,700 beds.

BAPTIST ST. ANTHONY HEALTH SYSTEM
1600 Wallace Boulevard, Amarillo TX 79106. 806/212-2000. **Contact:** Human Resources Manager. **World Wide Web address:** http://www.bsahs.com. **Description:** A 255-bed general hospital. Baptist St. Anthony Health System also offers home health services, a hospice program, a rehabilitation/skilled nursing facility, a senior health center and a sports and occupational health center. **NOTE:** Please visit website to search for jobs and apply online. **Positions advertised include:** Area Technician; Administrative Assistant; Facility Technician; Billing Clerk; Cook; Office Clerk; RN; Nursing Technician; CNA; Paramedic; Biomedical Technician; Radiology Equipment Specialist; Nurse Practitioner; Physical Therapist; Respiratory Therapist; Speech Therapist.

BAYLOR MEDICAL CENTER AT GARLAND
2300 Marie Curie Boulevard, Garland TX 75042. 972/487-5000. **Contact:** Human Resources. **World Wide Web address:** http://www.baylorhealth.com. **Description:** A 206-bed acute care medical and surgical center. **NOTE:** Please visit website to search for jobs and apply online. **Positions advertised include:** RN; Radiologic Technologist; Physical Therapist; PRN; Medical Assistant; OR Technician; Medical Technologist; Director of Radiology; Ultrasound Technologist; Patient Care Assistant; Coding Auditor; Administrative Assistant. **Parent company:** Baylor Health Care System. **Number of employees nationwide:** 14,000.

BAYLOR MEDICAL CENTER AT IRVING
1901 North MacArthur Boulevard, Irving TX 75061. 972/579-8100. **Contact:** Human Resources Department. **World Wide Web address:** http://www.baylorhealth.com. **Description:** A 288-bed, full-service hospital. The hospital employs specialists in the areas of oncology, neurosurgery, neurology, cardiology, and gastroenterology. **NOTE:** Please visit website to search for jobs and apply online. **Positions advertised include:** RN – Various Departments; Physical Therapist; OR Technician; Oncology Care Coordinator; Unite Secretary; Sterile Processing Technician; Senior Anesthesia Technician; Patient Care Assistant; LVN; Nurse Extern; Scheduling Clerk; HIM Associate; Laboratory Director. **Parent company:** Baylor Health Care System. **Number of employees nationwide:** 14,000.

BAYLOR SENIOR HEALTH CENTER
4500 Mansell Road, Richardson TX 75080. 972/498-4500. **Contact:** Human Resources. **World Wide Web address:** http://www.baylorhealth.com. **Description:** An outpatient facility that offers comprehensive primary care services to senior citizens. Founded in 1995. **Parent company:** Baylor Health Care System.

BAYLOR UNIVERSITY MEDICAL CENTER
3500 Gaston Avenue, Roberts Building, 1st Floor, Dallas TX 75246. 214/820-2525. **Contact:** Human Resources. **World Wide Web address:** http://www.baylorhealth.com. **Description:** A full-service, tertiary, teaching hospital. As the flagship hospital of the Baylor Health Care System, Baylor University Medical Center is comprised of five connecting hospitals. Hospital departments include family medicine, neurosurgery, obstetrics, gynecology, oncology, ophthalmology, orthopedic surgery, pathology, pediatrics, physical rehabilitation, plastic and reconstructive surgery, psychiatry, radiology, urology, and anesthesiology. **Positions advertised include:** Medical Technologist; Physical Therapist; Medical Physicist; GN/RN; RN – Various Departments; Nutrition Educator; Utility Aide; Nutrition Services Retail Supervisor; Nutrition Attendant; Certified Respiratory Therapist; Clinical Dietitian; Licensed Vocational Nurse; Clinical Pharmacist; Medical Assistant; Director – Core Laboratory; Health Care Representative; BMET; Social Worker; Ultrasound Supervisor; Access Services Coordinator; Phone Scheduler; Trauma Registrar; Font Desk Registration Representative. **Operations at this facility include:** Administration; Research and Development.

BAYLOR/RICHARDSON MEDICAL CENTER
401 West Campbell Road, Richardson TX 75080. 972/498-4000. **Fax:** 972/498-4978. **Contact:** Human Resources. **World Wide Web address:** http://www.baylorhealth.com. **Description:** A 174-bed, nonprofit medical, surgical, and psychiatric hospital. Hospital specialties include family medicine, pediatrics, women's services, oncology, emergency medicine, cardiology, radiology and imaging, chemical dependency, skilled nursing, respiratory therapy, and home health.

BELLAIRE MEDICAL CENTER
5314 Dashwood Drive, Houston TX 77081-4689. 713/512-1200. **Fax:** 713/512-1577. **Recorded jobline:** 713/512-1580. **Contact:** Director of Human Resources. **World Wide Web address:** http://www.bellairemedicalcenter.com. **Description:** A 350-bed medical center offering a range of inpatient and outpatient care including a diabetes center, an intensive care psychiatric unit, and a women's services center. Bellaire Medical Center also provides geriatric day programs and support groups for chemical dependency. **NOTE:** Applications are only accepted for advertised positions. **Positions advertised include:** RN; Therapist; Distribution/Supply Specialist; LVN; EVS Technician; Recreation Therapist; LPTA. **Operations at this facility include:** Administration; Divisional Headquarters; Regional Headquarters; Service.

BELLVILLE GENERAL HOSPITAL
P.O. Box 977, Bellville TX 77418. 979/865-3141. **Physical address:** 235 West Palm Street, Suite 105, Bellville TX 77418. **Fax:** 979/865-9631. **Contact:** Jackie McEuen, Human Resources. **World Wide Web address:** http://www.bellvillehospital.com. **Description:** A nonprofit, rural hospital with 32 beds. Services at Bellville General Hospital include emergency room care, a nursery, obstetrics, outpatient care, and surgical procedures. Bellville General Hospital is accredited by the Joint Commission on

Accreditation of Healthcare Organizations (JCAHO). **NOTE:** Contact Human Resources at Ext. 135. Second and third shifts are offered. **Positions advertised include:** Registered Nurse. **CEO:** Michael Morris.

BIG SPRING STATE HOSPITAL
1901 North Highway 87, Big Spring TX 79720. 432/267-8216. **Fax:** 432/268-7263. **Contact:** Dennis Warrington, Director of Human Resources. **E-mail address:** dennis.warrington@mhmr.state.tx.us. **World Wide Web address:** http://www.dshs.state.tx.us. **Description:** A nonprofit, state-governed facility that specializes in the treatment of patients with mental illness. **NOTE:** Entry-level positions and second and third shifts are offered. **Special programs:** Internships. **Corporate headquarters location:** Austin TX. **Parent company:** Department of State Health Services. **Operations at this facility include:** Administration. **Number of employees at this location:** 650.

BLOOD AND TISSUE CENTER OF CENTRAL TEXAS
P.O. Box 4679, Austin TX 78765-4679. 512/206-1266. **Physical address:** 4300 North Lamar Boulevard, Austin TX 78756. **Fax:** 512/206-1261. **Recorded jobline:** 512/467-53416. **Contact:** Human Resources. **E-mail address:** resumes@tcms.com. **World Wide Web address:** http://www.bloodandtissue.org. **Description:** The blood bank for 100 Central Texas-area hospitals. It also provides human tissue and organs for 66 area hospitals. **NOTE:** Part-time positions offered. Resumes may be faxed, e-mailed or mailed. Interested jobseekers may also apply in person at the Human Resources office. **Positions advertised include:** Apheresis Technician; Technical Services Director; Donor Coordinator; Medical History Interviewer; Mobile Staff Training Coordinator. **Office hours:** Monday – Friday, 9:00 a.m. – 4:00 p.m.

THE BROWN SCHOOLS
HARRIS COUNTY JUVENILE JUSTICE CHARTER SCHOOLS
2525 Murworth Street, Suite 100, Houston TX 77054. 713/669-0799. **Contact:** Human Resources. **E-mail address:** educationcareers@cedu.com. **World Wide Web address:** http://www.brownschools.com/harriscounty.html. **Description:** Provides specialty services including psychiatric and behavioral services, rehabilitation services, educational services, home health services, outpatient services, residential treatment, and adoption and foster care. The Brown Schools operate more than 25 facilities in ten states. **Corporate headquarters location:** North Palm Beach FL. **Operations at this facility include:** This school provides a Juvenile Justice Education program in a day school setting for children from age 10 – 17. The school also provides services for those placed with the Harris County Juvenile Probation Department.

CARBOMEDICS, INC.
1300 East Anderson Lane, Austin TX 78752-1799. 512/435-3200. **Fax:** 512/435-3350. **Recorded jobline:** 512/435-3413. **Contact:** Human Resources. **E-mail address:** employment@carbomedics.com. **World Wide Web address:** http://www.carbomedics.com. **Description:** A manufacturer of heart valve replacement products. **Parent company:** Sorin Group.

CARDINAL HEALTH
One Butterfield Trail Boulevard, El Paso TX 79906. 915/779-3681. **Fax:** 915/775-9125. **Contact:** Human Resources. **World Wide Web address:** http://www.cardinal.net. **Description:** Cardinal Health is a producer, developer, and distributor of medical products and technologies for use in hospitals and other health care settings. **NOTE:** Please visit website to register, search for jobs, and apply online. **Positions advertised include:** Distribution Expeditor; Inventory Cycle Counter; Technical Associate; Maintenance Supervisor; Sterilization Superintendent; Human Resources Manager; Raw Material Wholesale Supervisor; Group Plant Controller; Drafter; Production Supervisor; Programmer Analyst. **Corporate headquarters location:** Dublin OH. **Operations at this facility include:** This location manufactures disposable hospital gowns and drapes. **Listed on:** New York Stock Exchange. **Stock exchange symbol:** CAH. **Number of employees worldwide:** 55,000.

CHILDREN'S MEDICAL CENTER OF DALLAS
1935 Motor Street, Dallas TX 75235. 214/456-7000. **Contact:** Human Resources. **World Wide Web address:** http://www.childrens.com. **Description:** A private, 322-bed children's medical center operating through 50 specialty clinics. **NOTE:** Please visit website to view job listings and apply online. Contact Human Resources directly at 214/456-2895. **Positions advertised include:** Advanced Practice Nurse; Licensed Vocational Nurse; Management; Nursing Support; RN; Associate Diagnostic Imaging Technician; Cancer Registrar; Child Life Assistant; Clinical Pharmacist; Clinical Research Associate; Dental Hygienist; Lab Support Specialist; Nutrition Technician; Pharmacist; Speech Pathologist; Manager – Clinical Research; Respiratory Care Practitioner; Financial Counselor; Events Specialist; Guest Relations Representative; Payroll Specialist; Volunteer Coordinator; Office Support – Various Departments.

CHRISTUS ST. JOSEPH HOSPITAL
1404 Saint Joseph's Parkway, Houston TX 77002. 713/756-5604. **Contact:** Human Resources. **E-mail address:** careers.stjoseph@christushealth.org. **World Wide Web address:** http://www.christusstjoseph.org. **Description:** A 834-bed, nonprofit medical center. Founded in 1887. **NOTE:** Entry-level positions and second and third shifts are offered. Please visit https://jobs.christushealth.org to search for jobs and apply online. **Positions advertised include:** Buyer; Case Manager; Certified Respiratory Therapist; Clinical Nurse – Various Departments; Coder; Coding Coordinator; Cook; Customer Service Representative; Director of Emergency Department; ER Room Lab Supervisor; Financial Counselor; House Supervisor; Lab Assistant; Maintenance Mechanic; Medical Technologist; Mental Health Technician; Patient Care Technician; Physical Therapist; Reimbursement Specialist; Security Officer; Staff Accountant; Sterile Processing Technician. **Special programs:** Internships; Training; Co-ops. **Parent company:** CHRISTUS Health. **Operations at this facility include:** Service. **Listed on:** Privately held.

CHRISTUS SANTA ROSA HOSPITAL
333 North Santa Rosa Street, San Antonio TX 78207. 210/704-2011. **Contact:** Human Resources. **World Wide Web address:** http://www.christussantarosa.org. **Description:** Santa Rosa Hospital is an acute care hospital with 500 beds. **NOTE:** Contact Human Resources at 210/704-2067. Visit http://heavenlycareers.com to search for jobs. **Positions advertised include:** Registered Nurse; Pre Access Nurse; Licensed Vocational Nurse; Nurse Liaison; Respiratory Therapist; Medical Technologist; Physical Therapist; Registered Nuclear Medicine Technologist; Histology Technician; Medical Lab Technician; Radiology Technician; Laboratory Section Supervisor; OR Technician; Physical Therapy Assistant; Pharmacist; Case Manager; Social Worker; Enterstomal Therapy Nurse; PAL Supervisor; Speech Pathologist; Recreation Therapist; Occupational Therapist; Radiology Director; Senior Financial Analyst; Clerk Phlebotomist. **Parent company:** CHRISTUS Health.

CHRISTUS SPOHN HOSPITAL SHORELINE
600 Elizabeth Street, Corpus Christi TX 78404. 361/881-3000. **Contact:** Human Resources. **World Wide Web address:** http://www.christusspohn.org. **Description:** A 432-bed acute care medical facility. **NOTE:** Please visit website to search for jobs and apply online. **Positions advertised include:** Vice President of Strategic Planning and Business Development; Clinical Dietitian; CRT; LVN; OR Technician; Radiology Technologist; RN – Various Departments; Registered Respiratory Therapist; Ultrasound Technician. **Corporate headquarters location:** San Antonio TX. **Parent company:** CHRISTUS Health. **Operations at this facility**

include: Service.

CITIZENS MEDICAL CENTER
P.O. Box 2024, Victoria TX 77902. 361/573-9181. **Physical address:** 2701 Hospital Drive, Victoria TX 77901. **Fax:** 361/573-0611. **Contact:** Human Resources. **E-mail address:** sfrank@cmcvtx.org. **World Wide Web address:** http://www.citizensmedicalcenter.com. **Description:** A 368-bed acute care medical center. Citizens Medical Center provides many services including a Women's Pavilion and a cancer treatment floor. Founded in 1956. **NOTE:** Contact Employment directly at 361/572-5066. **Positions advertised include:** Fitness Specialist; Physical Therapist; Physical Therapy Assistant; RN – Various Departments. **Number of employees at this location:** 1,300.

COOK CHILDREN'S MEDICAL CENTER
801 Seventh Avenue, Fort Worth TX 76104-2733. 682/885-4000. **Fax:** 817/885-3947. **Recorded jobline:** 682/885-4414. **Contact:** Human Resources. **World Wide Web address:** http://www.cookchildrens.org. **Description:** A pediatric health care center. Founded in 1985. **NOTE:** Entry-level positions and second and third shifts are offered. Apply online or in person at 617 Seventh St., Fort Worth TX. **Positions advertised include:** Surgery Center Director; Diet Aide; Controller; Radiographer; Medical Records Technician; Nurse Manager; Patient Access Specialist; Physical Therapist; Medical Receptionist; Director of Pharmacy Services.

CYPRESS FAIRBANKS MEDICAL CENTER HOSPITAL
10655 Steepletop Drive, Houston TX 77065-4222. 281/897-3500. **Fax:** 281/890-0236. **Recorded jobline:** 281/897-3530. **Contact:** Human Resources. **World Wide Web address:** http://www.cyfairhospital.com. **Description:** A 146-bed acute care hospital offering diagnostic services on both outpatient and inpatient bases. Founded in 1983. **NOTE:** Entry-level positions, part-time jobs, and second and third shifts are offered. **Positions advertised include:** Therapist; Secretary; Registered Nurse; Nurse Manager; Coder; Case Manager; CT Scanner Technician. **Parent company:** Tenet Houston Health System.

DE SOTO ANIMAL HOSPITAL
200 North Hampton, De Soto TX 75115. 972/223-4840. **Contact:** Human Resources. **Description:** Provides general medical and surgical services to domestic animals. Other services include radiology, dentistry, behavior counseling, allergy testing, and boarding.

DOCTORS HOSPITAL
9440 Poppy Drive, Professional Building One, Suite 107, Dallas TX 75218. 214/324-6297. **Fax:** 214/324-6547. **Recorded jobline:** 214/324-6700. **Contact:** Human Resources. **World Wide Web address:** http://www.doctorshospitaldallas.com. **Description:** A hospital specializing in coronary, wound and hospice care. Founded in 1959. **Positions advertised include:** Registered Nurse; LPN; Controller; Pharmacist; Technician. **Other U.S. locations:** Nationwide. **Parent company:** Tenet Healthcare Corporation owns and operates a network of hospitals and related businesses nationwide. **Operations at this facility include:** Administration. **Listed on:** New York Stock Exchange. **Stock exchange symbol:** THC.

EAST TEXAS MEDICAL CENTER
1000 South Beckham, Tyler TX 75701. 903/597-0351. **Recorded jobline:** 903/531-8016. **Contact:** Human Resources. **World Wide Web address:** http://www.etmc.org. **Description:** A 454-bed general hospital. Services include acute care rehabilitation, cardiovascular care, neurological services, obstetrical services, and a level-one trauma center. **NOTE:** Full-time and part-time, weekdays and weekend positions available. **Positions advertised include:** Department Secretary; File Clerk; LPN; Physical Therapist; Speech Pathologist; Housekeeper; Phlebotomist; Technician; Dietary Aide. **Parent company:** East Texas Medical Center Regional Healthcare System.

EDINBURG REGIONAL MEDICAL CENTER
1102 West Trenton Road, P.O. Box 2000, Edinburg TX 78539. 956/388-6000. **Contact:** Human Resources. **World Wide Web address:** http://www.edinburgregional.com. **Description:** A 130-bed medical center offering a wide variety of medical and diagnostic services. **NOTE:** Job listings found on UHS website: uhsinc.com. **Corporate headquarters location:** King of Prussia PA. **Parent company:** Universal Health Services, Inc. **Listed on:** New York Stock Exchange. **Stock exchange symbol:** UHS.

ENCORE MEDICAL CORPORATION
9800 Metric Boulevard, Austin TX 78758. 512/832-9500. **Toll-free phone:** 800/456-8696. **Fax:** 512/834-6300. **Contact:** Human Resources. **World Wide Web address:** http://www.encoremed.com. **Description:** The company develops, manufactures, and distributes a comprehensive range of orthopedic devices, including surgical implants, sports medicine equipment, and products for orthopedic rehabilitation, pain management, and physical therapy. Encore's products are used by orthopedic surgeons, physicians, physical and occupational therapists and other health care professionals to treat patients with musculoskeletal conditions resulting from degenerative diseases, deformities, and acute injuries. **Positions advertised include:** Product Development Engineer; Independent Sales Agent; Production/Setup Machinist.

ESSILOR GROUP
13515 North Stemmons Freeway, Dallas TX 75234. 972/241-4141. **Contact:** Human Resources. **World Wide Web address:** http://www.essilor.com. **Description:** A manufacturer of prescription optical lenses and ophthalmic products. **Corporate headquarters location:** France.

ETHICON, INC.
3348 Pulliam Street, San Angelo TX 76905-4430. 325/482-5200. **Contact:** Human Resources. **World Wide Web address:** http://www.ethicon.com. **Description:** Manufactures products for precise wound closure including sutures, ligatures, mechanical wound closure instruments, and related products. The company makes its own surgical needles and provides thousands of needle-suture combinations to surgeons. Ethicon also provides women's health products under the trade name Gynecare. **Parent company:** Johnson & Johnson (New Brunswick NJ). **Listed on:** New York Stock Exchange. **Stock exchange symbol:** JNJ.

HCA - THE HEALTHCARE COMPANY
7400 Fannin, Suite 650, Houston TX 77054. 713/852-1500. **Contact:** Human Resources. **World Wide Web address:** http://www.hcahouston.com. **Description:** HCA owns several hundred surgical centers and hospitals. Founded in 1992. **NOTE:** This location recruits for 10 hospitals in the Houston area. See company's website for more information. **Other U.S. locations:** Nationwide. **Operations at this facility include:** This location is a regional administrative office.

HCA LONESTAR
10030 North MacArthur Boulevard, Suite 100, Irving TX 75063. 469/420-4928. **Contact:** Human Resources. **World Wide Web address:** http://www.dallassharedservices.com. **Description:** HCA owns more than 200 surgical centers and hospitals. Local HCA medical facilities are located throughout northern Texas. **NOTE:** Applicants can also contact the All About Staffing Group at 972/556-6470. List of affiliated hospitals, job listings and volunteer opportunities available on company's website. **Corporate headquarters location:** Nashville TN. **Other area locations:** Statewide. **Other U.S. locations:** Nationwide. **Operations at this facility include:** This location is a regional administrative office for northern Texas. **Number of employees at this location:** 5,000.

HARBOR VIEW CARE CENTER
1314 Third Street, Corpus Christi TX 78404. 361/888-5511. **Contact:** Jill Doire, Divisional Recruiter. **World Wide Web address:** http://www.tricare.com. **Description:** A 116-bed hospital. Founded in 1993. **Parent company:** Trans Healthcare.

HARRINGTON CANCER CENTER
1500 Wallace Boulevard, Amarillo TX 79106. 806/359-4673. **Toll-free phone:** 800/274-HOPE. **Fax:** 806/354-5881. **Contact:** Lynda McCarty, Human Resources Manager. **World Wide Web address:** http://www.harringtoncc.org. **Description:** Provides various services to cancer patients who formerly had to travel hundreds of miles for treatment. Medical specialties include radiation services, medical oncology, blood diseases and hematology, supportive care, a women's center, and cancer prevention and education. Volunteer opportunities are available. **NOTE:** All interested jobseekers must fill out a job application to be considered for employment. Applications can be picked up in the Human Resources Department or obtained online.

HARRIS METHODIST FORT WORTH HOSPITAL
1301 Pennsylvania Avenue, Fort Worth TX 76104. 817/882-2882. **Fax:** 817/882-2865. **Contact:** Human Resources. **World Wide Web address:** http://www.texashealth.org. **Description:** A member of the Texas Health Resources, a consortium of 13 hospitals. **NOTE:** Entry-level positions, part-time jobs, and second and third shifts are offered. Interested jobseekers can apply in person at the hospital or on the corporate website at http://www.texashealth.org. **Special programs:** Internships; Administrative Fellowship Program **Office hours:** Monday - Friday, 8:00 a.m. - 5:00 p.m. **Parent company:** Texas Health Resources.

HEALTHSMART PREFERRED CARE
P.O. Box 53010, Lubbock TX 79453-3010. **Toll-free phone:** 800/687-0500. **Physical address:** 2002 West Loop 289, Suite 103, Lubbock TX 79407. **Fax:** 281/265-2397. **Contact:** Human Resources. **World Wide Web address:** http://www.healthsmart.net. **Description:** A nationwide preferred provider organization (PPO). Founded in 1993. **Positions advertised include:** Account Executive; Account Manager; Claims Resolution Coordinator; Director of Marketing; Legal Assistant; Nurse. **Corporate headquarters location:** This location. **Other area locations:** Irving TX. **Other U.S. locations:** Edmond OK. **Parent company:** The Parker Group.

HEALTHSOUTH
3340 Plaza 10 Boulevard, Beaumont TX 77707. 409/835-0835. **Fax:** 409/835-1401. **Contact:** Ellen Zimmerman, Human Resources Director. **World Wide Web address:** http://www.healthsouth.com. **Description:** A physical rehabilitation hospital that also offers outpatient and home care services. **NOTE:** Part-time jobs and second and third shifts are offered. **Other U.S. locations:** Nationwide. **International locations:** Worldwide. **Listed on:** New York Stock Exchange. **Stock exchange symbol:** HRC. **Number of employees worldwide:** 33,700.

HENDERSON MEMORIAL HOSPITAL
300 Wilson Street, Henderson TX 75652. 903/657-7541. **Toll-free phone:** 800/329-7541. **Fax:** 903/655-3661. **Recorded jobline:** 903/655-3773. **Contact:** Human Resources. **World Wide Web address:** http://www.hmhnet.org. **Description:** A private, nonprofit, acute care hospital. **NOTE:** Applications are required for all positions and can be found on the company's website. Entry-level positions and second and third shifts are offered. **Positions advertised include:** Physical Therapist; Transcriptionist; Executive Director of HMH Foundation; Relief Cook/Food Service Worker. **Office hours:** Monday – Friday, 8:00 a.m. – 5:00 p.m. **Corporate headquarters location:** This location. **Operations at this facility include:** Administration; Service. **Listed on:** Privately held.

HENDRICK HEALTH SYSTEM
1900 Pine Street, Abilene TX 79601-2316. 325/670-2258. **Fax:** 325/670-4417. **Recorded jobline:** 325/670-3300. **Contact:** Human Resources. **E-mail address:** hrdept@ehendrick.org. **World Wide Web address:** http://www.hendrickhealth.org. **Description:** Operates a 525-bed, general hospital. Founded in 1924. **Positions advertised include:** Admitting Representative; Attendant; Audiologist; Cafeteria Aide; Certified Surgical Technician; Clinical Coordinator/Educator; Construction Technician; Cook; Customer Service Representative; Environmental Services Technician; File Technician; Financial Analyst; General Supervisor; Home Health Aide; LVN; Medical Office Specialist; Medical Technologist; Nurse Aide; Nurse Practitioner; Physical Therapist; Registered Nurse; Security Officer; Specialty Technician; Storage/Retrieval Technician; Trayline Aide. **Parent company:** Baptist General Convention of Texas.

HILL COUNTRY MEMORIAL HOSPITAL
P.O. Box 835, Fredericksburg TX 78624-0835. 830/997-4353. **Physical address:** 1020 South State Highway 16, Fredericksburg TX 78624. **Contact:** Human Resources. **World Wide Web address:** http://www.hillcountrymemorial.com. **E-mail address:** hr@hillcountrymemorial.com. **Description:** A 77-bed, acute care hospital. Hill County Memorial Hospital offers a skilled nursing unit, medical surgery, OB/GYN, urology, and orthopedics. The hospital also has a Wellness Center that offers preventative care. Founded in 1971. **NOTE:** Applications for positions can be found at the company's website. **Positions advertised include:** RN; LVN; Physical Therapist; Nurse Aide; Thrift Shop Helper; Computer Technician; Staffing Clerk; Staffing Clerk.

HOSPIRA
3900 Howard Lane, Austin TX 78728. 512/255-2000. **Contact:** Human Resources. **World Wide Web address:** http://www.abbott.com. **Description:** This location manufactures intravenous bags for the medical industry. Overall, Abbott Laboratories manufactures a wide range of health care products including pharmaceuticals, hospital products, diagnostic products, chemical products, and nutritional products. **NOTE:** Please visit website to search for jobs and apply online. **Positions advertised include:** Quality Assurance and Regulatory Affairs Specialist; Sales and Marketing Specialist. **Special programs:** Internships; Co-ops; Summer programs. **Corporate headquarters location:** Abbott Park IL. **Other U.S. locations:** Nationwide. **International locations:** Worldwide. **Parent company:** Abbott Laboratories is an international manufacturer of a wide range of health care products including pharmaceuticals, hospital products, diagnostic products, chemical products, and nutritional products. **Listed on:** New York Stock Exchange. **Stock exchange symbol:** ABT. **Number of employees worldwide:** 70,000.

HUGULEY MEMORIAL MEDICAL CENTER
P.O. Box 6337, South Fort Worth TX 76115. 817/293-9110. **Physical address**: 11801 South Freeway, Burlison TX 76028. **Fax:** 817/568-1296. **Contact:** Human Resources. **E-mail address:** huguleyresumes@ahss.org. **World Wide Web address:** http://www.huguley.org. **Description:** A 213-bed acute care facility. Huguley Memorial Medical Center also owns Willow Creek (Arlington TX), a mental health facility. **NOTE:** Send resumes to P.O. Box only. **Positions advertised include:** Nurse Practitioner; Educator; RN: LVN: Central Services Technician; Kids Klub Attendant; Swim Instructor; Respiratory Therapist; Exercise Physiologist. **Special programs:** Internships. **Operations at this facility include:** Administration; Service.

HUNTSVILLE MEMORIAL HOSPITAL
P.O. Box 4001, Huntsville TX 77342-4001. 936/291-

4521. **Physical address**: 110 Memorial Hospital Drive, Huntsville TX 77340. **Recorded jobline:** 936/291-4216. **Fax:** 936/291-4241. **Contact:** Dick Hoolahan, Human Resources Director. **E-mail address:** dickh@huntsvillememorial.com. **World Wide Web address:** http://www.huntsvillememorial.com. **Description:** A full-service hospital offering specialized outpatient facilities. **Positions advertised include:** Ultrasonographer; RN; Physician Assistant; Transcriptionist; Histotechnician. **Office hours:** Monday – Friday, 8:00 a.m. – 4:30 p.m.

INTERNATIONAL BIOMEDICAL, INC.
8508 Cross Park Drive, Austin TX 78754. 512/873-0033. **Contact:** Human Resources. **World Wide Web address:** http://www.int-bio.com. **Description:** A manufacturer of high-technology medical instruments including infant incubators and radiation gloves. International Biomedical also manufactures electronic equipment used in research, testing, and teaching. **Corporate headquarters location:** Cleburne TX. **Operations at this facility include:** Manufacturing.

JOHNSON & JOHNSON MEDICAL, INC.
2500 East Arbrook Boulevard, Arlington TX 76014. 817/262-3900. **Contact:** Human Resources. **World Wide Web address:** http://www.jnj.com/careers. **Description:** Manufactures and markets an extensive line of disposable packs and gowns, surgical products, decontamination and disposal systems, latex gloves, and surgical antiseptics. **NOTE:** Jobseekers should apply online at the website for open positions. **Positions advertised include:** Sales Representative. **Special programs:** Internships. **Corporate headquarters location:** This location. **Other U.S. locations:** CA; CT; FL. **Parent company:** Johnson & Johnson (New Brunswick NJ). **Operations at this facility include:** Administration; Manufacturing; Research and Development; Sales. **Listed on:** New York Stock Exchange. **Stock exchange symbol:** JNJ. **Number of employees worldwide:** 109,500.

JORDAN HEALTH SERVICES
P.O. Box 840, Mount Vernon TX 75457. 903/537-7612x311. **Physical address**: 412 Highway 37 South, Mount Vernon TX 75457. **Toll-free:** 800/665-0639. **Fax:** 903/537-4565. **Contact:** John McAuley, Human Resources Manager. **E-mail address:** jmcauley@jhsi.com. **World Wide Web address:** http://www.jhsi.com. **Description:** A diversified home health care agency. **Positions advertised include:** Accounts Payable Specialist; Administrator; PC Technician; Assistant Administrator; Assistant Controller; Benefits Specialist; Billing Specialist; Case Manager; Clerical Specialist; Data Entry Specialist; Director of Nursing; Intake Coordinator; Licensed Vocational Nurse; Registered Nurse; Information System Manager; Payroll Specialist. **Operations at this facility include:** Administration. **Listed on:** Privately held.

KCI (KINECTIC CONCEPTS, INC.)
14th Floor, KCI Tower, 8023 Vantage Drive, San Antonio TX 78230. 210/255-6000. **Toll-free phone:** 210/275-4524. **Fax:** 210/255-6998. **Contact:** Human Resources. **World Wide Web address:** http://www.kci1.com. **Description:** Manufactures, sells, services, and rents hospital beds for the critically ill. **NOTE:** This company provides job listings and specific contact information on its website. **Corporate headquarters location:** This location. **Listed on:** New York Stock Exchange. **Stock exchange symbol:** KCI.

KERRVILLE STATE HOSPITAL
721 Thompson Drive, Kerrville TX 78028. 830/896-2211. **Contact:** Human Resources. **Description:** A psychiatric hospital with 200 inpatient beds and 33 medical unit beds. Founded in 1951. **World Wide Web address:** http://www.mhmr.state.tx.us/hospitals/kerrvillesh. **NOTE:** A completed application must be submitted with each resume. The application can be found on the website. **Positions advertised include:** RN; LVN. **Corporate headquarters location:** Austin TX.

KIMBERLY-CLARK AVENT
14 Finnegan Drive, Del Rio TX 78840. 830/774-7482. **Contact:** Human Resources. **World Wide Web address:** http://www.kchealthcare.com. **Description:** A warehouse that distributes medical products. **Parent company:** Kimberly-Clark Corporation. **Listed on:** New York Stock Exchange. **Stock exchange symbol:** KMB.

LELAND MEDICAL CENTERS
P.O. Box 251548, Plano TX 75075. 972/540-1422. **Contact:** Human Resources. **World Wide Web address:** http://www.lelandmedical.com. **Description:** A 113-bed hospital specializing in industrial, behavioral, orthopedic, plastic surgery, and surgical weight loss programs.

LONGVIEW REGIONAL MEDICAL CENTER
2901 North 4th Street, Longview TX 75605. 903/758-1818. **Fax:** 903/232-3888. **Recorded jobline:** 903/232-3726. **Contact:** Human Resources. **World Wide Web address:** http://www.longviewregional.com. **Description:** A 164-bed, acute care, medical center providing cardiovascular, pediatric, dialysis, intensive care, intermediate care, outpatient care, and laboratory services. Founded in 1980. **NOTE:** Entry-level positions, part-time jobs, and second and third shifts are offered. An application is required for any position. An application can be completed or downloaded at the company's website. **Positions advertised include:** Registered Nurse; LPN; Nursing Assistant; Mid-level Provider; Clinical Nutrition Manager; Respiratory Therapist; Emergency Room Technician; Certified Diabetes Educator; Accounting Clerk; Housekeeper; Speech Therapist. **Office hours:** Monday – Thursday, 8:30 a.m. – 4:00 p.m. **Corporate headquarters location:** Dallas TX. **Other U.S. locations:** Nationwide.

LUMINEX CORPORATION
12212 Technology Boulevard, Austin TX. 78727-6115. 512/219-8020. **Toll-free phone:** 888/219-8020. **Fax:** 512/219-5195. **Contact:** Human Resources. **World Wide Web address:** http://www.luminexcorp.com. **Description:** Manufacturer of sensor and measurement equipment for biotechnology companies. **NOTE:** Apply online. **Positions advertised include:** Software Quality Assurance Engineer. **Listed on:** NASDAQ. **Stock exchange symbol:** LMNX.

MATAGORDA GENERAL HOSPITAL
1115 Avenue G, Bay City TX 77414. 979/241-6690. **Recorded jobline:** 979/241-6695. **Contact:** Human Resources. **Description:** A full-service hospital offering outpatient diagnostic service facilities. This hospital is part of Matagorda County Hospital District, which includes an assisted living facility; an independent living facility; a women's health center, a public clinic and a clinic for low-income mothers and babies. **Positions advertised include:** RN; Certified Respiratory Therapy Technician; Radiologist Technologist; Medical Staff Coordinator.

MCALLEN MEDICAL CENTER
301 West Expressway 83, McAllen TX 78503. 956/632-4000. **Contact:** Human Resources. **World Wide Web address:** http://www.mcallenmedicalcenter.com. **Description:** Part of the South Texas Health System, a full-service acute care hospital. The medical center has a well-known heart hospital, too. **NOTE:** Apply online for open positions. **Parent company:** Universal Health Network.

McKENNA MEMORIAL HOSPITAL
600 North Union Avenue, New Braunfels TX 78130. 830/606-9111. **Recorded jobline:** 830/606-2151. **Contact:** Human Resources Coordinator. **E-mail address:** hr@mckenna.org. **World Wide Web address:** http://www.mckenna.org. **Description:** A 116-bed, short-term care hospital. McKenna Memorial Hospital also offers an occupational health department. **NOTE:** An application must submitted for any position. The application can be obtained at the

company's website. **Positions advertised include:** Coder; Care Coordinator; Parenting Instructor; Medical Technologist; Clinical Recruiter; Occupational Therapist; Monitor Technician; RN; LVN; Ultrasound Technician; Radiology Technician; Respiratory Therapist.

MEDICAL CENTER HOSPITAL/ODESSA
500 West Fourth Street, Odessa TX 79761. 432/640-4000. **Fax:** 915/640-1245. **Contact:** Candy Powell RN, Recruitment/Retention Coordinator. **E-mail address:** lmelson@echd.org. **World Wide Web address:** http://www.odessamch.org. **Description:** A 396-bed, acute care hospital. Medical Center Hospital provides various services including a neonatal care nursery, skilled nursing facility, Intensive Care Unit, Critical Care Unit, and 24-hour emergency care. **NOTE:** An application must be submitted for any position. See company's website for application **Positions advertised include:** Charge RN; Unit Clerk; Divisional Director; Paramedic.

THE MEDICAL CENTER OF MESQUITE
1011 North Galloway Street, Mesquite TX 75149. 214/320-7000. **Fax:** 324/889-7970. **Contact:** Human Resources. **World Wide Web address:** http://www.hma-corp.com/tx1.html. **Description:** Full-service acute care 176-bed hospital operated by Health Management Associates, Inc. **NOTE:** Search for positions online.

MEDICAL CENTER OF PLANO
3901 West 15th Street, Plano TX 75075. 972/596-6800. **Contact:** Human Resources. **World Wide Web address:** http://www.medicalcenterofplano.com. **Description:** A 400-bed medical center providing acute and residential care. **NOTE:** Interested jobseekers must apply online at the company's website.

MEDICAL CITY DALLAS HOSPITAL
7777 Forest Lane, Building B, Suite D-250, Dallas TX 75201. 972/566-7070. **Toll-free phone:** 800/224-4733. **Contact:** Human Resources. **World Wide Web address:** http://www.medicalcityhospital.com. **Description:** A full-service hospital. **NOTE:** Interested jobseekers must apply online at the company's website.

MEMORIAL HERMANN/MEMORIAL CITY HOSPITAL
921 Gessner Road, Houston TX 77024. 713/932-3000. **Fax:** 713/932-3627. **Contact:** Human Resources. **World Wide Web address:** http://www.mhhs.org. **Description:** An acute care general hospital. This hospital is part of a group of 11 medical facilities in the Houston area. **Positions advertised include:** Coding Manager; Dietician; Medical Technologist; OR Attendant; Pharmacist; Radiology Technologist.

MERIT MEDICAL
1111 South Velasco Street, Angleton TX 77515. 979/848-5000. **Contact:** Human Resources. **E-mail address:** recruiting@merit.com. **World Wide Web address:** http://www.merit.com. **Description:** Provides technologically advanced, cost-effective products and services to five medical specialties: anesthesiology, cardiology, critical care, nuclear medicine, and radiology. **Positions advertised include:** Engineer; Senior Process Engineer; Senior Manufacturing Engineer. **Listed on:** NASDAQ. **Stock exchange symbol:** MMSI.

MESA HILLS SPECIALTY HOSPITAL
2311 North Oregon Street, Fifth Floor, El Paso TX 79902. 915/545-1823. **Contact:** Jill Doire, Divisional Recruiter. **World Wide Web address:** http://www.tricare.com. **Description:** A 181-bed long-term, acute care hospital. Parent company: Trans Healthcare.

MESQUITE COMMUNITY HOSPITAL
3500 Interstate 30, Mesquite TX 75150. 972/698-3300. **Fax:** 972/698-2580. **Recorded jobline:** 972/698-2463. **Contact:** Human Resources. **World Wide Web address:** http://www.mchtx.com. **Description:** A hospital with 172 beds. Founded in 1978. **Positions advertised include:** RN; Buyer; Radiologist; Respiratory Therapist; Risk Manager.

THE METHODIST HOSPITAL
6560 Fannin, Scurlock Tower, Houston TX 77030. 713/394-6614. **Fax:** 713/793-7128. **Contact:** Human Resources. **World Wide Web address:** http://www.methodisthealth.com. **Description:** A full-service hospital. It is part of a group of three other hospitals in the Houston area. The Methodist Hospital is also the primary teaching hospital for the Baylor College of Medicine. **NOTE:** All resumes must be submitted with a completed application which can be found online at the hospital's website. **Positions advertised include:** Unit Secretary; Program Development Specialist; Orthopedic Technician; Patient Care Assistant; Physical Therapist; Blood Donor; RN; Service Line Marketing Director. **Corporate headquarters location:** This location. **Parent company:** Methodist Health Care System.

METHODIST DALLAS MEDICAL CENTER
1441 North Beckley Avenue, Dallas TX 75203. 214/947-6510. **Contact:** Human Resources. **World Wide Web address:** http://www.methodisthealthsystem.com. **Description:** An acute care medical center licensed for 478 beds. This medical center has units for organ transplants and trauma. **Positions advertised include:** Assistant Director; Audit Specialist; Capital Project Coordinator; Community-Based Case Manager; Director; Echo Technician; Nurse Manager; Pharmacy Technician, Quality Coordinator, RN.

METHODIST SPECIALTY AND TRANSPLANT HOSPITAL
8026 Floyd Curl Drive, San Antonio TX 78229. 210/575-8110. **Recorded jobline:** 210/575-4562. **Contact:** Human Resources. **World Wide Web address:** http://www.mhshealth.com. **Description:** A 382-bed, licensed medical facility specializing in organ and tissue transplants, impotency treatments, incontinence treatments, gastroenteric procedures, and laparoscopic surgery. **NOTE:** Interested jobseekers may apply online at the company's website. **Positions advertised include:** Activity Therapist; Ancillary Support Technician; Diet Clerk; Echo Technician; LVN; RN: Physical Therapist.

METROPOLITAN METHODIST HOSPITAL
1310 McCullough Avenue, San Antonio TX 78212. 210/208-2200. **Fax:** 210/208-2924. **Recorded jobline:** 210/575-4562. **Contact:** Human Resources. **World Wide Web address:** http://www.metro.sahealth.com. **Description:** A 263-bed hospital that offers both long-term and short-term care. This hospital is part of the Methodist Healthcare System. **NOTE:** Interested jobseekers must complete an application which can be found on the company's website. **Positions advertised include:** Coding/Compliance Manager; Data Entry Clerk; Decentralized Pediatric Pharmacist; Histology Technician; Radiologist.

MIDLAND MEMORIAL HOSPITAL
2200 West Illinois Avenue, Midland TX 79701. 432/685-1111. **Contact:** Maria McAllister, Human Resources Director. **World Wide Web address:** http://www.midland-memorial.com. **Description:** A full-service, 300-bed health facility. Midland Memorial is part of a group of three hospitals serving the Midland area. The other hospitals are Memorial West and Memorial Rehabilitation **NOTE:** Interested jobseekers must complete an application for all positions. The application can be found on the company's website. **Positions advertised include:** RN; Respiratory Care Technician; Human Resources Assistant; Paramedic; Nuclear Medicine Technician; Physical Therapist.

MISSION HOSPITAL, INC.
900 South Bryan Road, Mission TX 78572. 956/580-9188. **Contact:** Marissa Aldrete, Hospital Recruiter at 956/584-4683. **E-mail address:** maldrete@missionhospital.org. **World Wide Web**

address: http://www.missionhospital.org. **Description:** A 138-bed acute care facility. **Positions advertised include:** Respiratory Therapist; Registered Nurse; Radiology Technician; Registration Representative. **Operations at this facility include:** Health Care; Service.

NIX HEALTH CARE SYSTEM
414 Navarro Street, San Antonio TX 78205. 210/271-1800. **Fax:** 210/271-2167. **Contact:** Human Resources. **World Wide Web address:** http://www.nixhealth.com. **Description:** Operates a 150-bed hospital. Nix Health Care offers such services as prenatal care, a geriatric psychiatry unit, and a skilled nursing unit. **Positions advertised include:** Financial Analyst; Needs Assessment Clinician; Community Education Coordinator; Commercial/Managed Care Collector; Medicare Collector; Patient Access Specialist; RN; LVN; Food Service Aide; Food Service Supervisor.

NORTHEAST BAPTIST MRI CENTER
8815 Village Drive, San Antonio TX 78217. 210/297-2870. **Contact:** Human Resources. **World Wide Web address:** http://www.baptisthealth.org. **Description:** A medical center that performs MRIs. The center is part of Baptist Hospital.

NORTHWEST TEXAS HEALTHCARE SYSTEM
1506 Coulter Street, Amarillo TX 79106. 806/354-1000. **Recorded jobline:** 806/354-1905. **Contact:** Human Resources. **World Wide Web address:** http://www.nwtexashealthcare.com. **Description:** Operates Northwest Texas Hospital and The Pavilion. Northwest Texas Hospital offers more than 35 medical specialties and subspecialties. The Pavilion is a full-service mental health facility that provides a comprehensive range of services to people of all ages. **NOTE:** Applications are only accepted in the office for current positions. Application is available online. **Positions advertised include:** RN; LVN. **Parent company:** Universal Health Services. **Office hours:** Monday – Friday, 7:00 a.m. – 5:00 p.m.

NURSEFINDERS
1341 W. Mockingbird, Suite 245 W, Dallas TX 75247. 214/520-8770. **Toll-free phone:** 888/338-0572. **Fax:** 214/520-8675. **Contact:** Human Resources. **World Wide Web address:** http://www.nursefinders.com. **Description:** A home health care agency. Nursefinders has staffing offices throughout Texas. **NOTE:** This company offers per diem, contract, home care, permanent, managed care and travel positions. Interested jobseekers can apply online for positions or visit the nearest staffing location. **Positions advertised include:** Registered Nurse; Home Health Care Nurse; Case Manager. **Corporate headquarters location:** Arlington TX. **Other U.S. locations:** Nationwide.

NURSES TODAY INCORPORATED
4230 LBJ Freeway, Suite 110, Dallas TX 75244. 972/233-9966. **Toll-free phone:** 800/830-7616. **Fax:** 972/233-5354. **Contact:** Anita Porco, Human Resources Manager. **World Wide Web address:** http://www.nursestoday.com. **Description:** Provides home health care and case management services. Founded in 1982. **NOTE:** Permanent, contract, temporary and part-time jobs are offered. **Positions advertised include:** Licensed Vocational Nurse; Registered Nurse; Certified Nurse Assistant; Medical Transcriptionist. **Office hours:** Monday - Friday, 8:00 a.m. - 5:00 p.m. **Corporate headquarters location:** This location.

OAK BEND MEDICAL CENTER
1705 Jackson Street, Richmond TX 77469. 281/341-4831. **Fax:** 281/341-2883. **Recorded jobline:** 281/341-2852. **Contact:** Human Resources. **E-mail address:** jobs@pollyron.org. **World Wide Web address:** http://www.pollyryon.org. **Description:** A nonprofit, acute care medical facility with 185 beds. In addition to general medical and surgical procedures, Polly Ryon offers a wide range of services including active health education in the community; PROMISE, the birthing center; imaging services such as CT scanning, mammography, and MRIs; hospice care; and STAR, the Sports Therapy and Rehabilitation service. Founded in 1949. **NOTE:** Second and third shifts are offered as well as on-call positions. **Positions advertised include:** Microbiologist; Clinical Educator; Radiology Technologist; Ultrasound Technologist; Executive Secretary; Cook; Account Representative; RN; LVN. **Office hours:** Monday – Friday, 7:30 a.m. – 4:30 p.m. **Corporate headquarters location:** This location. **Operations at this facility include:** Administration; Service.

ODESSA REGIONAL HOSPITAL
520 East Sixth Street, Odessa TX 79760. 915/334-8397. **Contact:** Human Resources. **World Wide Web address:** http://www.odessaregionalhospital.com. **Description:** A hospital offering specialized labor/delivery services, pediatrics, family care, and surgical services. **NOTE:** An application is required for any position. The application can be found online at the hospital's website. **Positions advertised include:** RN; Respiratory Therapist; Medical Auditor. **Parent company:** IASIS Healthcare. **Listed on:** Privately held.

ODYSSEY HEALTHCARE
14205 Burnet Road, Suite 400, Austin TX 78728. 512/310-0214. **Contact:** Human Resources. **E-mail address:** resume@odyshealth.com. **World Wide Web address:** http://www.odyshealth.com. **Description:** Hospice provider for end of life care patients. **Positions advertised include:** Certified Nurse, Patient Secretary.

183 ANIMAL HOSPITAL
1010 West Airport Freeway, Irving TX 75062. 972/579-0115. **Contact:** Human Resources. **Description:** Provides general medical and surgical services along with diagnostic testing, radiography, and dentistry for small animals.

ORTHOFIX INC.
1720 Bray Central Drive, McKinney TX 75069. 469/742-2500. **Contact:** Human Resources. **World Wide Web address:** http://www.orthofix.com. **Description:** Orthofix Inc. develops, manufactures, markets, and distributes medical devices to promote bone healing. Products are primarily used by orthopedic surgeons. **Positions advertised include:** Accountant; Marketing Coordinator; Mechanical Engineer; Associate Territory Manager; Customer Service Representative. **Operations at this facility include:** Administration; Divisional Headquarters; Manufacturing; Research and Development; Sales; Service.

PALO PINTO GENERAL HOSPITAL
400 SW 25th Avenue, Mineral Wells TX 76067. 940/328-6229. **Fax:** 940/328-6230. **Recorded jobline:** 940/328-6298. **Contact:** Human Resources. **World Wide Web address:** http://www.ppgh.com. **Description:** A 99-bed, nonprofit, acute care hospital. **NOTE:** Entry-level positions, part-time jobs, and second and third shifts are offered. **Positions advertised include:** Client Care Coordinator; RN; LVN.

PARIS REGIONAL MEDICAL CENTER
820 Clarksville Street, Paris TX 75460. 903/785-4521. **Fax:** 903/737-3887. **Contact:** Human Resources. **World Wide Web address:** http://www.stjosephs.com. **Description:** A nonprofit, 216-bed, acute care hospital that provides comprehensive heart programs, inpatient and outpatient dialysis, rehabilitation services, oncology, radiation therapy, and nuclear medicine services. **NOTE:** Contact Human Resources at 903/737-3943. Please visit website to search for jobs or to download application form. **Positions advertised include:** Director of Cardiology; Registrar; Phlebotomist; Certified Scrub Technologist; Licensed Vocational Nurse; Nurse's Aide; RN; Director of Surgical Services; House Supervisor; Pulmonary Rehab Coordinator; Director of Radiology; Mammography Coordinator; Radiographer; Registered Ultra Sonographer; Kids Klub Attendant.

PARK PLACE MEDICAL CENTER
3050 Thirty-Ninth Street, Port Arthur TX 77642. 409/985-0303. **Contact:** Human Resources. **World Wide Web address:** http://www.parkplacemedicalcenter.com. **Description:** A full-service hospital with 244 beds. Its medical specialties are: cardiology, orthopedics, women's health, infant intensive care, and long-term acute care. Founded in 1958. **NOTE:** Apply online at this hospital's website. Park Place Medical Center has a nearby sister facility called Mid-Jefferson Hospital. To apply for positions at Mid-Jefferson, visit its website at http://www.midjeffersonhospital.com. **Positions advertised include:** RN; Scheduler; Physical Therapist; Pharmacy Technician. **Corporate headquarters location:** Franklin TN. **Parent company:** IASIS Healthcare. **Listed on:** Privately held.

PARK PLAZA HOSPITAL
1313 Hermann Drive, Houston TX 77004. 713/527-5090. **Recorded jobline:** 713/527-5091. **Contact:** Human Resources. **World Wide Web address:** http://www.parkplazahospital.com. **Description:** A full-service hospital with 446 beds. **NOTE:** A completed application is required for any position. Apply online. **Positions advertised include:** Case Manager; Occupational Therapist; Surgical Technician; RN (Various), Dialysis Technician; Radiology Technician; Physical Therapy Assistant. **Parent company:** Tenet Healthcare.

PARKLAND HEALTH AND HOSPITAL SYSTEM
5201 Harry Hines Boulevard, Dallas TX 75235. 214/590-8000. **Contact:** Employment Services. **World Wide Web address:** http://www.pmh.org. **Description:** A Level I trauma center, and a 900-bed teaching hospital. The system operates also neighborhood health centers throughout the Dallas area. Parkland manages also the Parkland Foundation and a North Texas Poison Center. **NOTE:** The system has three types of employment positions: Nursing, Physicians and Employment Service, which includes clerical and support. All job postings and contact information is provided on the website and applicants are encouraged to apply electronically. Nursing resumes may be faxed to 214/590-8991. Employment Service resumes may be faxed to 214/590-2767. Physician resumes may be faxed to 214/590-0024. The Human Resources Office accepts walk-in resumes during certain time periods. See the website for specific days and times. **Number of employees nationwide:** 6,500.

PLAZA SPECIALTY HOSPITAL
1300 Binz Street, Houston TX 77004. 713/285-1000. **Contact:** Human Resources. **World Wide Web address:** http://www.plazaspecialtyhospital.com. **Description:** This hospital provides acute care, including special services for patients with infectious diseases, kidney ailments, cancer, and chronic pain. The hospital is noted for its physical and pulmonary rehabilitation and wound care services. **NOTE:** A completed application is required for any position. Apply online. **Positions advertised include:** Pharmacy Clinical Coordinator; Occupational Therapist; Wound Care Coordinator; RN (Various); LVN (Various); Physical Therapy Assistant. **Parent company:** Tenet Healthcare.

PEARLE VISION, INC.
2534 Royal Lane, Dallas TX 75229. 972/277-5000. **Fax:** 972/277-6415. **Contact:** Human Resources. **World Wide Web address:** http://www.pearlevision.com. **Description:** Manufactures and retails prescription eyewear. **Corporate headquarters location:** Twinsburg OH. **Other U.S. locations:** Nationwide. **Parent company:** Cole National Corporation. **Operations at this facility include:** Administration; Manufacturing. **Listed on:** New York Stock Exchange. **Stock exchange symbol:** CNJ.

SID PETERSON MEMORIAL HOSPITAL
710 Water Street, Kerrville TX 78028. 830/258-7440. **Recorded jobline:** 830/258-7562. **Contact:** Human Resources. **E-mail address:** jobs@spmh.com. **World Wide Web address:** http://www.spmh.com. **Description:** A long-term care general hospital offering centers for cardiac rehabilitation, osteoporosis, and cancer treatment. **NOTE:** This hospital requires interested jobseekers to complete an application. Applications can be downloaded at the website. Full-time and part-time positions are available. **Positions advertised include:** Floor Technician; Housekeeper; Clinical Coordinator; LVN; RN; Administrative Assistant; Speech Language Pathologist; Rehabilitation Aide; Case Manager; Coder; Communications Operator.

PRIME MEDICAL SERVICES, INC.
1301 Capital of Texas Highway South, Suite C-300, Austin TX 78746. 512/328-2892. **Contact:** Human Resources. **World Wide Web address:** http://www.primemedical.com. **Description:** Through its subsidiaries, Prime Medical Services provides non-medical management services to lithotripsy and cardiac rehabilitation centers. Prime Medical Services operates 67 lithotripters. **Listed on:** NASDAQ. **Stock exchange symbol:** PMSI.

PROVIDENCE HEALTH CENTER
6901 Medical Parkway, Waco TX 76712. 254/751-4000. **Fax:** 254/751-4909. **Recorded jobline:** 254/751-4477. **Contact:** Human Resources. **World Wide Web address:** http://www.providence.net. **Description:** A 170-bed, acute care hospital. Founded in 1905. **NOTE:** An application is required for any position. It is available online at the website. Jobseekers may mail or fax their resumes. When applying for RN, LVN, CAN, PT, OT or Speech Therapy positions, send resume and cover letter to: rgoforth@phn-waco.org. For all other positions, send e-mail to: kwest@phn-waco.org. Jobseekers may also complete an application at the Human Resources Office. **Office hours:** Monday -- Friday, 8:00 a.m. – 4:30 p.m. **Corporate headquarters location:** This location. **Parent company:** Providence Healthcare Network (also at this location). **Positions advertised include:** RN; Patient Care Coordinator; Dietician; Receptionist/File Clerk; Environmental Service Technician; Revenue Integrity Value Analyst.

QUEST MEDICAL, INC./ATRION CORPORATION
One Allentown Parkway, Allen TX 75002-4211. 972/390-9800. **Toll-free phone:** 800/627-0226. **Fax:** 972/390-2881. **Contact:** Human Resources. **E-mail address:** hrstaffing@atrioncorp.com. **World Wide Web address:** http://www.questmedical.com. **Description:** Develops, manufactures, markets, sells, and distributes proprietary products to the healthcare industry. **NOTE:** Jobseekers should send resumes to the parent company, Atrion, at the same address. **Corporate headquarters location:** This location. **Parent company:** Atrion Corporation (also at this location) is a holding company that designs, develops, manufactures, markets, sells, and distributes proprietary products and components for the healthcare industry. Other subsidiaries of Atrion Corporation include Atrion Medical Products and Halkey-Roberts. **Listed on:** NASDAQ. **Stock exchange symbol:** ATRI.

RHD MEMORIAL MEDICAL CENTER
7 Medical Parkway, Dallas TX 75234. 972/888-7259. **Recorded jobline:** 972/888-7159. **Contact:** Human Resources. **E-mail address:** RHDRecruiting@tenethealth.com. **World Wide Web address:** http://www.rhdmemorial.com. **Description:** A 160-bed, acute care community hospital. **NOTE:** A completed application must be completed for any position. See website for application. **Parent company:** Tenet Health System. **Positions advertised include:** RN; Nurse Manager; Laboratory Medical Technician; Medical Staff Services Director; Pharmacy Technician.

RIO VISTA REHABILITATION HOSPITAL
1740 Curie Drive, El Paso TX 79902. 915/544-3399. **Contact:** Human Resources. **World Wide Web**

address: http://www.sphn.com. **Description:** An inpatient and outpatient rehabilitation facility that assists patients experiencing orthopedic problems, joint replacement, trauma, arthritis, or amputation. **NOTE:** Apply online at this hospital's website. **Positions advertised include:** RN; LVN; Endoscopy Technician; Case Manager; Surgery Coordinator; Laboratory Assistant; Administrative Director. **Parent company:** Tenet Health System.

ROUND ROCK MEDICAL CENTER
2400 Round Rock Avenue, Round Rock TX 78681. 512/341-5156. **Contact:** Human Resources. **World Wide Web address:** http://www.roundrockhospital.com. **Description:** A 109-bed general hospital. Services include a 24-hour emergency room, Family Birthing Center, medical/surgical unit, six-bed intensive care unit, and a nine-bed skilled nursing unit. Founded in 1983. This hospital is part of the HealthCare Partnership with three other hospitals in Austin TX. **NOTE:** Submit resume online for open positions. **Positions advertised include:** Clinical Dietitian; RN; Supervisor; Pharmacy Technician; Food Services Associate; Security Guard; Mammographer; Speech Language Pathologist.

ST. DAVID'S MEDICAL CENTER
98 San Jacinto Boulevard, Suite 1800, Austin TX, 78701. 512/708-9700. **Contact:** Human Resources. **World Wide Web address:** http://www.stdavids.com. **Description:** A 400-bed hospital specializing in all types of adult medical care. **Positions advertised include:** Patient Care Technician; Phlebotomist; Pharmacy Technician; RN; Physical Therapist; Radiology Technician; Physical Therapist; Diet Clerk.

ST. LUKE'S EPISCOPAL HOSPITAL
P.O. Box 20269, Houston TX 77225-0269. 713/785-8537. **Physical address:** 6720 Bertner Street, Houston TX 77030. **Recorded jobline:** 800/231-1000. **Contact:** Human Resources. **World Wide Web address:** http://www.sleh.com. **Description:** A full-service hospital specializing in pulmonary care in its Texas Heart Institute. This hospital is the flagship for the St. Luke's Health System, which includes three additional healthcare facilities: Kelsey-Seybold, Community Medical Center (The Woodlands) and the Episcopal Health Charities. **NOTE:** Jobseekers may apply online at the hospital's website; apply in person at the Human Resources Department, or mail their resumes. **Positions advertised include:** RN; Home Health Aides; Patient Care Assistant; Unit Secretary; Physical Therapist; Staff Pharmacist; Surgical Technicians; Provider Relations Coordinator; Infection Control Practitioner; Senior Information Protection Analyst; Administrative Secretary; Employment Representative; Senior Admitting Interviewer. **Special programs:** Residencies. **Office hours:** Monday – Friday, 8:00 a.m. – 4:00 p.m.

SAN MARCOS TREATMENT CENTER
120 Bert Brown Road, San Marcos TX 78666. 512/396-8500. **Fax:** 512/754-3883. **Contact:** Human Resources. **World Wide Web address:** http://www.psysolutions.com. **Description:** A 186-bed neuropsychiatric hospital that specializes in treating adolescents and young adults who have not had success in other settings. The center's patients are primarily those who experience emotional disturbances, severe impulses, aggressive behavior patterns, unprovoked mood swings, known neurological or organic disorders, seizure disorders, language problems, or severe learning complications due to substance abuse and sexual trauma. Founded in 1940. **NOTE:** Jobseekers should visit the center to complete an application. **Office hours:** Monday – Friday, 7:00 a.m. – 11:00 p.m. **Parent company:** Psychiatric Solutions, Inc.

SETON HEALTHCARE NETWORK
1201 West 38th Street, Austin TX 78705. 512/324-4000. **Toll-free phone:** 800/880-0038. **Fax:** 512/324-1672. **Recorded jobline:** 512/324-1679. **Contact:** Human Resources Recruiters. **World Wide Web address:** http://www.seton.net. **Description:** A nonprofit, multi-facility health care network. Facilities include four acute care hospitals, community clinics, home care providers, outreach programs, and physicians' offices. **NOTE:** Entry-level positions and second and third shifts are offered. See the company's website for application information and job listings or visit the Human Resources office. **Company slogan:** Health.Care.Made Simpler. **Office hours:** Monday – Friday, 8:00 a.m. – 4:30 p.m. **Corporate headquarters location:** St. Louis MO. **Parent company:** Daughters of Charity.

SHANNON CLINIC
120 East Beauregard, San Angelo TX 76903. 325/658-1511x3159. **Fax:** 325/481-2181. **Contact:** Human Resources. **World Wide Web address:** http://www.shannonhealth.com. **Description:** Part Of The Shannon Health System, this clinic is composed of specialty physicians in Cardiology, Vision, OB/GYN, and Pediatrics. **NOTE:** See website for job listings and applications. **Other area locations:** Del Angelo TX; Big Lake TX.

SHANNON MEDICAL CENTER
206 North Main Street, San Angelo TX 76903. 325/657-5243. **Fax:** 325/481-8521. **Recorded jobline:** 325/657-5298. **Contact:** Human Resources. **E-mail address:** jobs@shannonhealthorg. **World Wide Web address:** http://www.shannonhealth.com. **Description:** A 400-bed, non-profit hospital offering surgery, intensive care, orthopedic, oncology, telemetry, skilled nursing, and cardiac services. Shannon Medical Center also operates a Level III trauma and sleep disorder center. Founded in 1932. This medical center is affiliated with three other healthcare facilities. **NOTE:** Entry-level positions and second and third shifts are offered. **Positions advertised include:** Cashier; Surgery Assistant; Registration Assistant; Dietitian; Medical Technologist; Occupational Therapist; Recreational Therapist; RN; Food Service Worker; Monitor Technician. **Special programs:** Training. **Office hours:** Monday - Friday, 8:00 a.m. - 5:00 p.m. **Corporate headquarters location:** This location.

SHELBY REGIONAL MEDICAL CENTER
602 Hurst Street, Center TX 75935. 936/598-2781. **Contact:** Human Resources. **World Wide Web address:** http://www.shelbyregional.com. **Description:** A 54-bed community hospital. Specialty areas include centers for the treatment of allergies, asthma, and diabetes. Also provides cardiopulmonary and emergency care. **Positions advertised include:** Radiology Technician; RN; Plant Operations Supervisor. **Corporate headquarters location: Parent company:** Tenet Healthcare. **Listed on:** New York Stock Exchange. **Stock exchange symbol:** THC.

SHRINER'S HOSPITAL BURN INSTITUTE
815 Market Street, Galveston TX 77550. 409/770-6600. **Contact:** Human Resources. **World Wide Web address:** http://www.shrinershq.org/shc/galveston. **Description:** A 31-bed, children's burn treatment facility and research center. **NOTE:** There is another Shriner's Hospital in Houston TX. **Positions advertised include:** Medical Technologist.

SIERRA PROVIDENCE HEALTH NETWORK
2001 North Oregon Street, El Paso 79902. 915/577-6000. **Contact:** Human Resources. **World Wide Web address:** http://www.sphn.com. **Description:** The network consists of three hospitals in the area: The Sierra Medical Center, Providence Memorial Hospital, and Rio Vista, a rehab hospital. Combined the network has nearly 900 beds and provides comprehensive acute care medical services. Rio Vista provides services to those patients with brain injuries. **NOTE:** A completed application is required for any position at any of the three hospitals. The website provides job listings for all three facilities. Apply online. **Positions advertised include:** EKG Technician; ECHO Technician; Assistant Security Director; Medical Transcriptionist; RN (Various); LVN (Various); Plant Maintenance; Insurance Verifier; Secretary; Admitting Representative; Speech Therapist; Ultrasound

Technician; Pharmacist; Medical Records Coder. **Parent company:** Tenet Healthcare.

SOUTH AUSTIN HOSPITAL
901 West Ben White Boulevard, Austin TX 78704. 512/448-7110. **Toll-free phone:** 800/568-3297. **Contact:** Human Resources. **World Wide Web address:** http://www.southaustinhospital.com. **Description:** An acute care, 162-bed hospital that provides basic care for the region. **NOTE:** Apply online at this hospital's website. **Positions advertised include:** Health Information Management Director; Food Service Supervisor; Pharmacy Technician; Medical Technician; Patient Care Technician; Anesthesia Technician; RN; Food Services Associate.

SOUTHWEST GENERAL HOSPITAL
7400 Barlite Boulevard, San Antonio TX 78224. 210/921-3439. **Fax:** 210/921-3450. **Recorded jobline:** 210/921-3439. **Contact:** Recruiter. **World Wide Web address:** http://www.swgeneralhospital.com. **Description:** A 319-bed, acute care hospital. Southwest General Hospital offers multiple diagnostic treatment and services in the following medical specialties: general and orthopedic surgery; physical therapy and rehabilitation, the treatment of strokes and complications resulting from diabetes; plastic and oral surgery; pediatrics; cardiac and pulmonary services; treatment of infectious diseases; and diabetes treatment. Southwest General Hospital offers a full range of psychiatric services including adult inpatient, adolescent inpatient, and partial hospitalization for adults. Founded in 1979. Southwest General has three sister facilities in Texas: Mid-Jefferson Hospital (Nederland TX); Odessa Regional Hospital (Odessa TX); and, Park Place Medical Center (Port Arthur TX). **NOTE:** Apply online at this hospital's website. **Positions advertised include:** RN; Biomedical Technician; Case Manager; LVN; Medical Technologist; Coder; Dietician. **Corporate headquarters location:** Franklin TN. **Other U.S. locations:** Nationwide. **Parent company:** IASIS Healthcare. **Operations at this facility include:** Administration; Service.

SOUTHWEST TEXAS METHODIST HOSPITAL METHODIST WOMEN'S & CHILDREN'S HOSPITAL
7700 Floyd Curl Drive, San Antonio TX 78229. 210/575-4000. **Recorded jobline:** 210/57-4562. **Contact:** Human Resources. **World Wide Web address:** http://www.sahealth.com. **Description:** A 626-bed hospital that offers both short- and long-term care. Methodist Women's & Children's Hospital is a 150-bed hospital that specializes in labor, delivery, and pediatrics. **NOTE:** Apply online at the hospital's website for open positions.

SPECIALTY HOSPITAL OF SAN ANTONIO
7310 Oak Manor Drive, San Antonio 78229. 210/308-0261. **Contact:** Jill Doire, Divisional Recruiter. **World Wide Web address:** http://www.tricare.com. **Description:** A long-Term, acute Care hospital. **Note:** Entry-level positions and part-time jobs are offered. **Positions advertised include:** Administrator. **Parent company:** Trans Healthcare.

STARLITE RECOVERY CENTER
2030 Mesa Verde Drive East, Center Point TX 78010-0317. 830/634-2212. **Contact:** Human Resources. **World Wide Web address:** http://www.starliterecovery.com. **Description:** A residential treatment center for adults and adolescents, offering specialized care for substance abusers. **Parent company:** CRC Health Corporation.

TENET HEALTHCARE CORPORATION TENET DALLAS
13737 Noel Road, Dallas TX 75240. 469/893-2200. **Contact:** Manager of Recruitment. **World Wide Web address:** http://www.tenethealth.com. **Description:** A multibillion-dollar, multi-hospital corporation that, with its subsidiaries, owns or operates approximately 100 acute care facilities nationwide. In Texas, it operates 13 hospitals. **NOTE:** Apply online at this company's website for corporate positions. This company also provides hyperlinks to its hospitals' job listings. **Positions advertised include:** RN; Employee Performance Analyst; Quality Control Representative; Corporate Recruiter; Financial Analyst; Managed Care Regional Director;; Clinical Manager. **Corporate headquarters location:** Santa Monica CA. **Other U.S. locations:** Nationwide. **Operations at this facility include:** Administration; Regional Headquarters. **Listed on:** New York Stock Exchange. **Stock exchange symbol:** THC. **Number of employees nationwide:** 106,900.

TEXAS CENTER FOR INFECTIOUS DISEASE
2303 SE Military Drive, San Antonio TX 78223. 210/534-8857x2255. **Fax:** 210/531-4504. **Contact:** Human Resources Director. **World Wide Web address:** http://www.tdh.state.tx.us/tcid. **Description:** A hospital that provides acute and chronic care to all patients referred for evaluation. **NOTE:** Texas Center for Infectious Disease offers career opportunities in the following areas: Chronic Respiratory Disease Services, which allows individuals to work with inpatient respiratory disease patients with a concentration on physical rehabilitation, patient education, and lifestyle adaptations; Diabetic Services, in which care includes medical evaluation and patient teaching; Chest Disease Services, through which the hospital treats diseases such as lung cancer, fungal disease, and tuberculosis; and Ambulatory Services, which offers an opportunity to work in a variety of clinics to include chest, Hansen's Disease, diabetes, and infectious diseases. The Texas Center for Infectious Disease also has a Tuberculosis Education Center. **NOTE:** Apply online at this organization's website. **Special programs:** Internships. **Corporate headquarters location:** Austin TX. **Operations at this facility include:** Administration; Research and Development; Service.

TEXAS CHILDREN'S HOSPITAL
Wells Fargo Building, Second Floor, 6631 South Main Street, MC 404230, Houston TX 77030. 832/824-2020. **Recorded jobline:** 832/824-2022. **Contact:** Human Resources. **World Wide Web address:** http://www.texaschildrenshospital.org. **Description:** A pediatric hospital. **NOTE:** A completed application is required for any position. Apply online only via hospital's website. **Positions advertised include:** RN; Account Representative; Clinical Nurse; Case Manager; Business Analyst; Financial Counselor; Education Coordinator; Medical Auditor Patient Care Assistant; Receptionist; Radiographer; Transplant Coordinator. **Office hours:** Monday – Friday, 8:00 a.m. – 4:00 p.m. **Operations at this facility include:** Administration; Research and Development; Service.

TEXAS HEALTH RESOURCES
611 Ryan Plaza Drive, Suite 900, Arlington TX 76011. 817/462-7900. **Toll-free phone:** 800/749-6877. **Fax:** 866/889-8975. **Contact:** Human Resources. **E-mail address:** thrjobpostings@texashealth.org. **World Wide Web address:** http://www.texashealth.org. **Description:** One of the largest nonprofit health care systems in Texas including a nursing home, 13 acute care hospitals, clinics, and home health services. **NOTE:** Part-time jobs and second and third shifts are offered. This company's website provides job listings for all its facilities. Apply online. **Corporate headquarters location:** This location. **Other area locations:** Greenville TX; Kaufman TX; Plano TX; Winnsboro TX.

TEXAS MEDICAL AND SURGICAL ASSOCIATES
8440 Walnut Hill Lane, Suite 400, Dallas TX 75231. 214/345-1400. **Contact:** Trey Schroeder, Human Resources. **World Wide Web address:** http://www.texasmedicalandsurgical.com. **Description:** A private clinic. **Office hours:** Monday - Friday, 8:30 a.m. - 5:00 p.m. **Other area locations:** Garland TX.

TEXAS MEDICAL CENTER
2151 West Holcombe Boulevard, Houston TX 77021.

713/791-6400. **Contact:** Christy Clark, Associate Vice President of Human Resources. **Fax:** 713/791-6402. **World Wide Web address:** http://www.tmc.edu. **Description:** A private, non-profit medical center.

TEXAS ORTHOPEDIC HOSPITAL
7401 South Main, Houston TX 77030. 713/799-8600. **Toll-free phone:** 800/678-4501. **Contact:** Human Resources. **World Wide Web address:** http://www.texasorthopedic.com. **Description:** An orthopedic hospital offering specialty surgery, sports medicine, and rehabilitation services. Texas Orthopedic Hospital is an affiliate of Columbia/HCA Healthcare Corporation. Founded in 1995. **NOTE:** Part-time and volunteer positions offered. Apply online at this hospital's website. **Positions advertised include:** House Supervisor; Medical Technologist; Occupational Therapist; Pharmacist; RN; Security Representative; Surgical Technician.

TEXAS SPECIALTY HOSPITAL
7955 Harry Heinz Boulevard, Dallas TX 75235. 214/637-0000. **Fax:** 214/905-0566. **Contact:** Jill Doire, Divisional Recruiter. **World Wide Web address:** http://www.tricare.com. **Description:** A long-term, acute care hospital. **NOTE:** Entry-level and part-time positions are available. **Parent company:** Trans Healthcare.

TEXOMA MEDICAL CENTER (TMC)
1000 Memorial Drive, Denison TX 75020. 903/416-4000. **Fax:** 903/416-4087. **Recorded jobline:** 800/566-1211. **Contact:** Joni Horn, Human Resources. **World Wide Web address:** http://www.thcs.org. **Description:** Texoma Medical Center (TMC) is an acute care hospital with 300 beds. TMC offers general medical and surgical services, intensive care, and pediatric care. Founded in 1965. **NOTE:** Second and third shifts are offered. This hospital provides job listings on its website. **Office hours:** Monday, 8:00 a.m. – 4:00 p.m.; Tuesday – Friday, 8:00 a.m. – 5:00 p.m. **Positions advertised include:** LVN; Preoperative Core Technician; Training Service Specialist; Medical Assistant; Cleaning Technician; Floor Technician; Dietitian; Building Maintenance Operator. **Special programs:** Co-ops; Summer Jobs. **Corporate headquarters location:** This location. **Other U.S. locations:** OK. **Subsidiaries include:** Times Medical Equipment. **Parent company:** Texoma Healthcare Systems, Inc. (also at this location). **Operations at this facility include:** Administration; Support Services.

TOMBALL REGIONAL HOSPITAL
605 Holderrieth Road, P.O. Box 889, Tomball TX 77375. 281/401-7780. **Fax:** 281/357-2223. **Jobline:** 281/401-7739. **Contact:** Human Resources. **E-mail address:** jobs@tomballhospital.org. **World Wide Web address:** http://www.tomballhospital.org. **Description:** A full-service hospital employing over 300 physicians. Founded in 1976. **NOTE:** Full-time and part-time shifts are available. An application is required for any position. For job listings and application, see this hospital's website. This company offers RN internships. For information, contact Carol Adolph at 281/401-7990 or via e-mail at cadolph@tomballhospital.org. **Positions advertised include:** Echo/Vascular Technician; Physical Therapist; Psychology Technician; Respiratory Therapist; RN; Aerobic Instructor; Cafeteria Worker; Clinical Dietitian; Cook. **Office hours:** Monday – Friday, 8:00 a.m. – 4:30 p.m.

TRANS HEALTHCARE, INC.
7310 Oak Manor Drive, San Antonio TX 78229. 210/308-0261. **Contact:** Jill Doire, Divisional Recruiter. **E-mail address:** jill.doire@his-inc.com. **World Wide Web address:** http://www.thicare.com. **Description:** A 138-bed acute care hospital offering a wide range of long- and short-term care services. **NOTE:** This company operates several hospitals in Dallas, Corpus Christi and El Paso TX. See company's website for information and job listings for these locations. Jill Doire is the contact for all the hospitals.

TRINITY MEDICAL CENTER
4343 North Josey Lane, Carrollton TX 75010. 972/492-1010. **Contact:** Human Resources. **World Wide Web address:** http://www.trinitymedicalcenter.com. **Description:** A 137-bed acute care hospital that includes a neonatal intensive care unit. **NOTE:** A completed application is required for any position. Apply online. **Positions advertised include:** Scheduling Lead Coordinator; RN (Various); Mammography Technician; Admitting Director; Admitting Representative; Surgery Technician; Hospital Compliance Officer; Medical Records Coordinator. **Parent company:** Tenet Healthcare.

TWELVE OAKS MEDICAL CENTER
4200 Twelve oaks Drive, Houston TX 77027. 713/623-2500. **Contact:** Human Resources. **E-mail address:** employment@twelveoaksmedicalcenter.com. **World Wide Web address:** http://www.twelveoaksmedicalcenter.com. **Description:** A general hospital. **NOTE:** E-mail or fax resumes. **Positions advertised include:** RN; Speech Therapist; Phlebotomist; Speech Therapist; Anesthesia Technician.

UMC HEALTH SYSTEM
602 Indiana Avenue, Lubbock TX 79415. 806/775-9222. **Recorded jobline:** 806/775-9215. **Contact:** Human Resources Manager. **World Wide Web address:** http://www.teamumc.org. **Description:** A 354-bed facility that includes The Children's Hospital, The Southwest Cancer and Research Center, Level I Trauma Center, a Pre-Hospital Emergency Service, a Burn Intensive Care Unit, and Community Outreach Programs. **NOTE:** For nursing opportunities, call 806/775-8912. A complete application is required for any position. Visit the website to print an application or apply online. **Positions advertised include:** Accountant; Cafeteria Aide; Cardiac Sonographer; Health Unit Coordinator; RN, LVN, Patient/Staff Educator; Renovation Technician. **Special programs:** Volunteer.

U.S. DEPARTMENT OF VETERANS AFFAIRS CENTRAL TEXAS VETERANS HEALTH CARE SYSTEM
1901 Veterans Memorial Drive, Temple TX 76504-7451. 254/778-4811ext.4048. **Toll-free phone:** 800/423-2111. **Contact:** Human Resources. **World Wide Web address:** http://www.central-texas.med.va.gov. **Description:** This system consists of two medical centers and several outpatient and community-based clinics. A full-service and teaching hospital with approximately 300 beds. It provides medical, nursing, and hospice care. **NOTE:** See website for additional locations in this system and for job listings. A complete application is required for any position. Apply online. **Positions advertised include:** Physicians; Medical Technicians; Pharmacists; RN; LVN; Nuclear Medicine Technician; Physical Therapist. **Other area locations:** Waco TX (Medical Center); Austin TX (Outpatient Clinic.)

US ONCOLOGY
16825 Northchase, Suite 1300, Houston TX. 77060. 832/601-8766. **Contact**: Human Resources. **World Wide Web address:** http://www.usoncology.com. **Description:** One of the world's largest companies devoted to providing outpatient care to treating cancer patients. US Oncology has cancer research facilities. It has more than 70 cancer centers across 27 states. **Positions advertised include:** Financial Systems Implementation Specialist; Application Engineer; Radiation Therapist. Marketing Director; Project Manager; Regulatory Coordinator; Medical Oncologist; Radiation Oncologist. **Other area locations:** Statewide. **Other U.S. locations:** Nationwide. **Listed on:** NASDAQ. **Stock exchange symbol:** USON.

UNITED REGIONAL HEALTHCARE SYSTEMS
1700 Seventh Street, Wichita Falls TX 76301. 940/764-7800. **Toll-free phone:** 800/301-3879. **Fax:** 940/764-7820. **Recorded jobline:** 940/764-7802. **Contact:** Kim Horton, Recruitment Specialist. **World Wide Web**

address: http://www.urhcs.org. **Description:** A licensed, 300-bed, acute care facility. **NOTE:** Full-time and part-time positions offered. This organization's website provides job listings and contact information on its website. Apply online. **Positions advertised include:** Floor Care Technician; Health Information Resource Nurse; Patient Care Associate; Certified Scrub Technician; Diagnostic Radiological Technician; Emergency Department Services Technician; Phlebotomist; LVN;; Occupational Therapist; Patient Care Associate; Pharmacist; RN.

UNIVERSITY OF TEXAS HEALTH CENTER AT TYLER
11937 U.S. Highway 271, Tyler TX 75708-3154. 903/877-7740. **Fax:** 903/877-7729. **Recorded jobline:** 903/877-7071 (Staff and Support Services); 800/297-3799 (Physician). **Contact:** Human Resources. **E-mail address:** jobs@uthct.edu. **World Wide Web address:** http://www.uthct.edu. **Description:** A non-profit hospital engaged in patient care, education, and research. **NOTE:** A completed application is required for any position. To apply in person, visit the Human Resources Office in Room 179B. **Positions advertised include:** Nurse Clinician; Staff Nurse; Attorney; Exercise Technician; Staff Pharmacist; Research Associate; Respiratory Therapist; Laboratory Technician. **Office hours:** Monday – Friday, 7:00 a.m. – 5:00 p.m.

UNIVERSITY OF TEXAS MEDICAL BRANCH
301 University Boulevard, Galveston TX 77555. 409/772-2758. **Fax:** 409/772-8698. **Contact:** Employment Office. **World Wide Web address:** http://www.hr.utmb.edu. **Description:** Educates health professionals and offers extensive medical services through a network of hospitals and health clinics. Founded in 1891. **NOTE:** Part-time, hourly and temporary positions offered. Apply online at the university's website. This location does not accept walk-in applicants. **Positions advertised include:** Nurse Researcher; Simulator Technician; Librarian; Psychiatrist; Dentist; Professors (Various); Speech Pathologist; RN; Auditor. **Special programs:** Volunteer.

UNIVERSITY OF TEXAS SOUTHWESTERN MEDICAL CENTER AT DALLAS
5323 Harry Hines Boulevard, Mail Code 9023, Dallas TX 75390-9023. 214/648-9865. **Fax:** 214/648-9875. **Recorded jobline:** 214/648-5627. **Contact:** Office of Human Resources. **World Wide Web address:** http://www.swmed.edu. **Description:** An academic medical center affiliated with Southwestern Medical School, Southwestern Graduate School of Biomedical Sciences, and Southwestern Allied Health Sciences School. **NOTE:** Entry-level, part-time and temporary positions are offered. Apply online at the website for all positions. **Positions advertised include:** RN: LVN, Medical Technologist; Dentist; Dental Hygienist; Research Technician; Administrative Staff Assistant; Clinical Staff Assistant; Accountant; Financial Accountant; Budgeter; Billing; Animal Technician; Plumber, Groundskeeper, Electrician. **Special programs:** Internships. **Operations at this facility include:** Administration; Research and Development.

VALLEY BAPTIST MEDICAL CENTER
P.O. Drawer 2588, Harlingen TX 78550. 956/389-4703. **Physical address:** 2101 Pease Street, Harlingen TX 78550. **Toll-free phone:** 800/828-8262. **Recorded jobline:** 956/389-2330. **Contact:** Human Resources. **E-mail address:** humanresources@valleybaptist.net. **World Wide Web address:** http://www.vbmc.org. **Description:** A 588-bed, nonprofit, acute care, medical center. **NOTE:** Part-time, second and third shifts are offered. A completed application is required for any position. Apply online or fax or mail application. Walk-in applicants are also accepted in Human Resources during regular office hours. **Positions advertised include:** Accounting; Speech Language Pathologist; Electro-Physiology Technologist; Corporate Communications Coordinator; Licensed Physical Therapist; Bereavement Coordinator; Nurse Recruiter; RN; LVN; Medication Aide; Buyer—Project Coordinator. **Special programs:** Internships; Co-ops; Summer Jobs. **Corporate headquarters location:** This location.

VALLEY REGIONAL MEDICAL CENTER
100A East Alton Gloor Boulevard, Brownsville TX 78526. 956/350-7000. **Contact:** Human Resources. **World Wide Web address:** http://www.valleyregionalmedicalcenter.com. **Description:** This 171-bed, acute care medical center offers services such as skilled nursing, rehabilitation, and various medical specialties. **NOTE:** Part-time, weekend, flex-time positions offered. Apply online at the center's website. **Positions advertised include:** Director of Imaging; Case Manager; RN; Director of Therapeutic Services; Speech Therapist. **Special programs:** Volunteers.

VISITING NURSE ASSOCIATION
1440 West Mockingbird Lane, Dallas TX 75247. 214/689-0000. **Fax:** 214/689-2977. **Contact:** Human Resources. **E-mail address:** hr@vnatexas.org. **World Wide Web address:** http://www.vnatexas.org. **Description:** A home health care agency that provides intermittent in-home visits. **NOTE:** This website has job listings for all the association's Texas locations. Apply online. **Positions advertised include:** Pediatric Physical Therapist; Home Care RN; Pediatric Occupational Therapist; Child Life Specialist. **Other area locations:** Collins TX; Kaufman TX; Tarrant TX; Denton TX. **Office hours:** Monday – Friday, 8:00 a.m. – 4:00 p.m. **Other U.S. locations:** Nationwide.

WADLEY REGIONAL MEDICAL CENTER
1000 Pine Street, Texarkana TX 75501. 903/798-7160. **Fax:** 903/798-7177. **Recorded jobline:** 903/798-7161. **Contact:** Human Resources. **E-mail address:** resumes@wadleyrmc.com. **World Wide Web address:** http://www.wadleyrmc.com. **Description:** A nonprofit, acute care hospital with 448 beds. The services offered at Wadley Regional Medical Center include a skilled nursing facility, a Cancer Treatment & Diagnostic Imaging Center, a day surgery center, and a Community Oriented Medical Plan Clinic. Founded in 1959. **NOTE:** Second and third shifts are offered. A completed application is required for any position. Apply online. **Positions advertised include:** LVN; Respiratory Therapist; Nursing Technician; Radiology Clerk. **Special programs:** Summer Jobs; Volunteer.

WEST OAKS HOSPITAL
6500 Hornwood Drive, Houston TX 77074. 713/995-0909. **Fax:** 713/778-5253. **Contact:** Human Resources. **World Wide Web address:** http://www.psysolutions.com. **Description:** A 144-bed psychiatric hospital that provides care on inpatient, day treatment, residential treatment, and outpatient bases to children, adolescents, and adults. **NOTE:** Apply online at the hospital's website. **Special programs:** Summer Jobs. **Corporate headquarters location:** Austin TX. **Parent company:** Psychiatric Solutions Inc. **Listed on:** NASDAQ. **Stock exchange symbol:** PSYS.

WICHITA FALLS STATE HOSPITAL
P.O. Box 300, Wichita Falls TX 76307. 940/552-9901. **Fax:** 940/689-5735. **Contact:** Staffing. **Description:** A nonprofit, forensic and mental health hospital. **Special programs:** Internships. **Corporate headquarters location:** Austin TX. **Other area locations:** Vernon TX. **Parent company:** Texas Department of Mental Health. **Operations at this facility include:** Administration.

ZALE LIPSHY UNIVERSITY HOSPITAL UNIVERSITY OF TEXAS SOUTHWESTERN MEDICAL CENTER CAMPUS
5151 Harry Hines Boulevard, Dallas TX 75235-7786. 214/590-3000. **Fax:** 214/879-2652. **Recorded jobline:** 214/590-3484. **Contact:** Human Resources. **World Wide Web address:** http://www.zluh.org. **Description:** Zale Lipshy University Hospital at Southwestern Medical Center was built to serve University of Texas Southwestern Medical Center at

Dallas as its private, nonprofit, adult referral hospital for specialized tertiary care. The facilities consist of 152 hospital beds (20 intensive care unit beds, 89 medical/surgical beds, 22 rehabilitation beds, and 21 psychiatric beds) and 12 operating room suites for specialized surgical care in the areas of neurological surgery, orthopedics, urology, gynecology, otorhinolaryngology (ear, nose, and throat), ophthalmology, cardiothoracic surgery, oral and maxillofacial surgery, vascular surgery, and plastic and reconstructive surgery. Founded in 1989. **NOTE:** Second and third shifts are offered. A complete application is required for any position. Applications and resumes may be faxed, mailed or delivered in person. Interested jobseekers may also apply online at the website. **Positions advertised include:** Lead Medical Therapist; Phlebotomist; Business Systems Manager; Lab Manager; RN; Assistant Nursing Manager; Systems Analyst; Billing Supervisor; Buyer II; Performance Improvement Analyst. **Office hours:** Monday – Friday, 8:00 a.m. – 4:30 p.m. **Operations at this facility include:** Administration; Service.

Utah

ABBOTT LABORATORIES
4455 Atherton Drive, Salt Lake City UT 84124. 801/262-2688. **Contact:** Human Resources Department. **World Wide Web address:** http://www.abbott.com. **Description:** A *Fortune* 500 company engaged in the design and manufacture of disposable medical devices for hemodynamic monitoring and fluid collection. **NOTE:** Please visit website to search for jobs and apply online. **Positions advertised include:** District Manager. **Corporate headquarters location:** Abbott Park IL. **Other U.S. locations:** Nationwide. **International locations:** Worldwide. **Listed on:** New York Stock Exchange. **Stock exchange symbol:** ABT. **Number of employees worldwide:** 70,000.

ARROWHEAD DENTAL LABORATORIES
11170 South State Street, Sandy UT 84070. 801/572-7200. **Toll-free phone:** 800/800-7200. **Fax:** 801/572-7290. **Contact:** Brent Burge, Human Resources. **E-mail address:** resumes@arrowheaddental.com. **World Wide Web address:** http://www.arrowheaddental.com. **Description:** A laboratory that manufactures dental prosthetics such as dentures, crowns, and bridges. **NOTE:** See website for current job openings and to download application.

BD MEDICAL
9450 South State Street, Sandy UT 84070. 801/565-2300. **Toll-free phone:** 888/237-2762. **Fax:** 800/847-2220. **Contact:** Human Resources. **World Wide Web address:** http://www.bd.com. **Description:** BD (Becton, Dickinson and Company) is a medical technology company that serves healthcare institutions, life science researchers, clinical laboratories, industry and the general public. BD manufactures and sells a broad range of medical supplies, devices, laboratory equipment and diagnostic products.. **NOTE:** Please visit website to search for jobs and apply online. **Positions advertised include:** Material Development Manager; Manager of Capability Systems; Senior Process Engineer. **Special programs:** Internships; Co-ops. **Corporate headquarters location:** Franklin Lakes NJ. **Other U.S. locations:** Nationwide. **Parent company:** Becton Dickinson & Company **Operations at this facility include:** This location manufactures a variety of products including peripheral venous access, central venous access, site maintenance, fluid maintenance, and EKG-related equipment.

C.R. BARD ACCESS SYSTEMS
5425 West Amelia Earhart Drive, Salt Lake City UT 84116. 801/595-0700. **Toll-free phone:** 800/443-5505. **Fax:** 801/595-4975. **Contact:** Human Resources. **E-mail address:** zach.farley@crbard.com. **World Wide Web address:** http://www.crbard.com. **Description:** Develops, manufactures, and markets medical devices that focus on oncology, urology, and vascular disease. C.R. Bard Access Systems also offers specialty products that focus on hemostasis, hernia repair, and performance irrigation. **NOTE:** Entry-level positions and second- and third-shifts are offered. See also http://www.bardaccess.com. **Positions advertised include:** Customer Service Representative; Financial Analyst; Technical Support Representative; Product Manager; Paralegal; Materials Manager. **Special programs:** Internships; Training. **Corporate headquarters location:** Murray Hill NJ. **Other U.S. locations:** Pittsburgh PA; Lowell MA; Billerica MA; Covington GA; Tempe AZ; Cranston RI. **International locations:** Worldwide. **Operations at this facility include:** Divisional Headquarters. **Stock exchange symbol:** BCR. **Number of employees at this location:** 275.

DAVIS BEHAVIORAL HEALTH
P.O. Box 689, Farmington UT 84025. 801/451-7799. **Physical address:** 291 South 200 West, Farmington UT 84025. **Fax:** 801/451-6331. **Contact:** Personnel Director. **World Wide Web address:** http://www.dbhutah.org. **Description:** Provides mental health and alcohol and drug services for adults and children. Services include inpatient, outpatient, residential, prevention, day treatment, 24-hour emergency response, evaluation, and therapeutic foster care. **NOTE:** Entry-level positions are offered. **Other area locations:** Clearfield UT; Layton UT; Bountiful UT; Ogden UT.

GE OEC MEDICAL SYSTEMS, INC.
384 Wright Brothers Drive, Salt Lake City UT 84116. 801/328-9300. **Contact:** Human Resources. **World Wide Web address:** http://www.gemedicalsystems.com. **Description:** Part of the GE Healthcare division, the company develops computer-based X-ray and fluoroscopic imaging systems for hospitals, outpatient clinics, and surgical centers. **NOTE:** Please visit website to search for jobs and apply online. **Parent company:** General Electric Company.

INFINIA AT GRANITE HILLS
950 East 3300 South, Salt Lake City UT 84106. 801/486-5121. **Fax:** 801/486-5146. **Contact:** Vicki Nelson, Human Resources. **World Wide Web address:** http://www.infiniahealth.com. **Description:** A 65-bed facility specializing in medical rehabilitation, traumatic brain injury, special needs, and Alzheimer's patients. **NOTE:** See website for current job openings and application instructions. **Other area locations:** Ogden UT; Alta UT.

KIMBERLY-CLARK HEALTHCARE
12050 Lone Peak Parkway, Draper UT 84020. 801/572-6800. **Fax:** 801/572-6999. **Contact:** Human Resources. **E-mail address:** ballardhr@kcc.com. **World Wide Web address:** http://www.kchealthcare.com. **Description:** Manufactures a wide variety of medical products used in intensive care units, emergency rooms, gastrointestinal and radiology procedure rooms, main operating rooms, burn units, and outpatient/satellite surgical centers. **NOTE:** Please visit corporate website to submit resume. **Special programs:** Internships; Co-ops. **Corporate headquarters location:** Roswell GA. **Parent company:** Kimberly-Clark. **Listed on:** New York Stock Exchange. **Stock exchange symbol:** KMB.

LDS HOSPITAL
8th Avenue and C Street, Salt Lake City UT 84143-0001. 801/408-1100. **Contact:** Human Resources. **World Wide Web address:** http://www.ihc.com/ldsh. **Description:** A hospital with 520 beds and various units including a women's health center, cardiac unit, and organ transplant unit. **NOTE:** Applications and resumes are only accepted online. **Positions advertised include:** Food Service Worker; LPN; Medical Technologist/MLT; Patient Service Representative; Imaging Clerk; RN – Various Departments; Medical Director – IHC Community and School Clinics; HR Consultant; Nurse Practitioner; Ultrasonographer; Lead Medical Student; Occupational Therapist Assistant; Echocardiographer; Nurse Educator. **Parent company:** Intermountain Health Care.

LAKEVIEW HOSPITAL
630 East Medical Drive, Bountiful UT 84010. 801/299-2200. **Fax:** 801/299-2511. **Recorded jobline:** 801/299-2563. **Contact:** Human Resources. **World Wide Web address:** http://www.lakeviewhospital.com. **Description:** A hospital with services that include cardiac rehabilitation, trauma, Alzheimer's assessment, and oncology. **NOTE:** Human Resources phone is 801/299-2566. Please visit website for details on contacts for specific positions. Volunteer positions are also available. **Positions advertised include:** RN – Various Departments; Director – Surgical Services; Pharmacist; Occupational Therapist; Physical Therapist; Respiratory Therapist. **Corporate headquarters location:** Nashville TN. **Parent company:** Columbia/HCA.

McKAY-DEE HOSPITAL CENTER
4401 Harrison Boulevard, Ogden UT 84403. 801/627-2800. **Contact:** Human Resources. **World Wide Web address:** http://www.ihc.com/xp/ihc/mckaydee. **Description:** A private, nonprofit, full-service, 415-bed, community hospital owned and administered by Intermountain Health Care, Inc. McKay-Dee's services include The Heart Institute, Women and Children's Services, Northern Utah's high-risk birthing center; prenatal testing and treatment facilities; an around-the-clock trauma team; the Community Health Information Center, offering information on health issues to men, women, children, and seniors; and a chemical dependency treatment program. **NOTE:** Please visit website to search for jobs and to apply online. Human Resources phone is 801/387-7700. **Positions advertised include:** Ultrasonographer; Central Processing Technician; RN – Various Departments; Food Service Worker/Dishwasher; Cook; Cashier; Dietary Technician; Licensed Counselor; Pharmacist. **Special programs:** Internships. **Parent company:** Intermountain Health Care – IHC.

MERIT MEDICAL SYSTEMS, INC.
1600 West Merit Parkway, South Jordan UT 84095. 801/253-1600. **Fax:** 801/253-1687. **Contact:** Robin Nielsen, Employment Supervisor. **E-mail address:** recruit@merit.com. **World Wide Web address:** http://www.merit.com. **Description:** Develops, manufactures, and distributes disposable proprietary medical products used in interventional diagnostic procedures, primarily in cardiology and radiology. The company serves client hospitals worldwide. Founded in 1987. **NOTE:** See website for current job openings. Submit resume by e-mail. **Corporate headquarters location:** This location. **Other U.S. locations:** Santa Clara CA; Angleton TX. **International locations:** Ireland; Netherlands; France. **Subsidiaries include:** Merit Sensor Systems. **Listed on:** NASDAQ. **Stock exchange symbol:** MMSI. **President/CEO:** Fred P. Lampropoulos.

OGDEN REGIONAL MEDICAL CENTER
5475 South 500 East, Ogden UT 84405. 801/479-2111. **Fax:** 801/479.2285. **Recorded jobline:** 801/479.2073. **Contact:** Human Resources Department. **World Wide Web address:** http://www.ogdenregional.com. **Description:** A 239-bed hospital. Ogden Regional Medical Center's services include women's and children's health services, cardiac care, cancer treatment, orthopedics, physical medicine and rehabilitation, behavioral health services, alcohol and chemical dependency treatment, and health education and wellness services. **NOTE:** Please visit website for online application form. Contact Human Resources directly at 801/479-2089. Volunteer positions are also available. **Positions advertised include:** Clinical Dietician; Food and Nutrition Culinary Coordinator; Medical Lab Technician; Mobile Team Supervisor; RN, Various Departments; Pharmacist; COTA; Occupational Therapist; Physical Therapist; Physical Therapy Assistant; Radiology Technician; Sonographer; Special Procedures Technician.

PRIMARY CHILDREN'S MEDICAL CENTER
100 North Medical Drive, Salt Lake City UT 84113-1100. 801/588-2203. **Contact:** Human Resources. **World Wide Web address:** http://www.ihc.com/xp/ihc/primary/. **Description:** A 232-bed facility equipped and staffed to treat children with complex illnesses and injuries. The pediatric center serves five states in the Intermountain West. The hospital is affiliated with the Department of Pediatrics at the University of Utah. Specialized services for children include cancer treatment, a cardiology unit, child abuse/neglect counseling, infant special care, pediatric surgery, and trauma treatment. Founded in 1922. **NOTE:** Please visit website to search for jobs and apply online. **Positions advertised include:** Pediatric Technician; ED Health Unit Coordinator; Pharmacist; Occupational Therapist; Medical Technologist; EGG Technician; Director of Pediatric Education Services; Human Resources Consultant; Surgical Technologist. **Parent company:** Intermountain Health Care.

ST. MARK'S HOSPITAL
1200 East 3900 South, Salt Lake City UT 84124. 801/268-7072. **Toll-free phone:** 800/965-7778. **Fax:** 801/270-3393. **Recorded jobline:** 801/268-7127. **Contact:** Human Resources. **E-mail address:** employment@mountainstarhealth.com. **World Wide Web address:** http://www.stmarkshospital.com. **Description:** A 300-bed, acute care hospital that specializes in cardiology, women's health services, orthopedics, and oncology services. **NOTE:** Please visit website for current job openings and application instructions. **Positions advertised include:** Exercise Specialist; RN Case Manager; Clinical Dietician; Food Service Aide; Childbirth Educator; Clinical Resource Manager; Housekeeper; Medical Assistant; RN – Various Departments; Occupational Therapist; Pharmacist; Mammography Technician; Respiratory Therapist.

SOUTH VALLEY HEALTH CENTER
3706 West 9000 South, West Jordan UT 84088-8866. 801/280-2273. **Contact:** Human Resources. **Description:** A nursing home with 120 beds. The center also provides rehabilitation services and physical and speech therapy.

U.S. DEPARTMENT OF VETERANS AFFAIRS VETERANS ADMINISTRATION MEDICAL CENTER
500 Foothill Drive, Salt Lake City UT 84148. 801/582-1565. **Fax:** 801/584-1289. **Contact:** Human Resources. **World Wide Web address:** http://www.va.gov. **Description:** A medical center. From 54 hospitals in 1930, the VA health care system has grown to include more than 170 medical centers; more than 364 outpatient, community, and outreach clinics; 130 nursing home care units; and 37 domiciliary residences. VA operates at least one medical center in each of the 48 contiguous states, Puerto Rico, and the District of Columbia. With approximately 76,000 medical center beds, VA treats nearly 1 million patients in VA hospitals; 75,000 in nursing home care units; and 25,000 in domiciliary residences. VA's outpatient clinics register approximately 24 million visits per year. **NOTE:** Human Resources phone is 801/584-1284. Fax is 801/584-2588. Visit the USAJOBS website to search for positions and apply online. **Other area locations:** Fountain Green UT; Nephi UT; Orem UT; Roosevelt UT; South Ogden UT; St. George UT. **Other U.S. locations:** Nationwide. **Parent company:** U.S. Department of Veterans Affairs.

ULTRADENT PRODUCTS INC.
505 West 10200 South, South Jordan UT 84095. 801/572-4200. **Toll-free phone:** 800/496-8337. **Fax:** 801/553-4642. **Recorded jobline:** 801/553-4233. **Contact:** Human Resources. **E-mail address:** hr@ultradent.com. **World Wide Web address:** http://www.ultradent.com. **Description:** Manufactures products for use by dentists including syringes and opalescent whitening gel. **Positions advertised include:** Special Events Coordinator; Product Documentation Coordinator; Oracle e-Business Suite Business Analyst; Territory Account Manger.

Corporate headquarters location: This location. **Number of employees at this location:** 600.

UNIVERSITY HOSPITALS & CLINICS
420 Wakara Way, Suite 105, Salt Lake City UT 84108. 801/581-2169. **Fax:** 801/581-4579. **Contact:** Human Resources. **E-mail address:** employment@hr.utah.edu. **World Wide Web address:** http://uuhsc.utah.edu. **Description:** University Hospitals & Clinics is comprised of University of Utah Hospital, a 392-bed tertiary and acute care facility. University Hospitals serves as the clinical arm for the medical school and the college of health, nursing, and pharmacy. **NOTE:** See website http://www.hr.utah.edu to search and apply for jobs at University Health Care. Entry-level and volunteer positions are offered. **Positions advertised include:** Coordinator of Special Events; Executive Secretary; Production Manager; Survey Clerk; Senior Laboratory Specialist; Lab Technician; Outpatient Clinical Representative; Research Nurse; Medical Storekeeper; RN – Various Departments; Compensation Analyst; Medical Assistant; Education Specialist; Accounting Specialist; Computer Operator; Customer Service Representative; Nutrition Care Aide; Library Aide; EMT; Insurance Account Representative; Psychiatric Technician; Drug/Alcohol Counselor; Pharmacist; Clinical Nurse – Various Departments; LPN. **Corporate headquarters location:** This location. **Other area locations:** Park City UT; Sugarhouse UT; Wendover UT.

UTAH MEDICAL PRODUCTS, INC.
7043 South 300 West, Midvale UT 84047. 801/566-1200. **Toll-free phone:** 800/533-4984. **Fax:** 801/566-2062. **E-mail address:** careers@utahmed.com. **Contact:** Human Resources. **World Wide Web address:** http://www.utahmed.com. **Description:** Utah Medical Products, Inc. develops, manufactures, assembles, and markets a broad range of products serving the critical care and obstetrics/gynecology markets. Products include a line of transducers and catheters used in monitoring blood pressure and uterine contraction pressure, an electrosurgery generator and disposable electrodes used in a new treatment to remove precancerous cervical tissue, a line of disposable infant oxygen therapy products, and female incontinence therapy products. Founded in 1978. **NOTE:** See website for current job openings and application instructions. **Positions advertised include:** Accounts Receivable Assistant; Mechanical Engineer. **Corporate headquarters location:** This location. **Other U.S. locations:** Redmond OR. **International locations:** Athlone, Ireland. **Operations at this facility include:** Administration; Divisional Headquarters; Manufacturing; Regional Headquarters; Research and Development; Sales; Service. **Listed on:** NASDAQ. **Stock exchange symbol:** UTMD.

UTAH STATE HOSPITAL
1300 East Center Street, Provo UT 84606. 801/344-4400. **Contact:** Human Resources. **World Wide Web address:** http://www.hsush.state.ut.us. **Description:** A hospital. Specialized programs include a children's unit, an adolescent unit, four adult units, a geriatric unit, and a forensic unit. The children's unit has a capacity of 22 patients, serving children between the ages of 6 and 13 who have psychiatric and/or behavioral disorders. The adolescent unit has a capacity of 50 patients and serves as a residential treatment center for emotionally disturbed youth between the ages of 13 and 18. The adult programs, treating chronically ill patients, are broken down into four units with a total capacity for 149 patients. The geriatric unit, for patients age 55 and over, has a 60-bed patient capacity. The Forensic Unit has a capacity of 54 people. **NOTE:** All current employment opportunities with the Utah State Hospital are posted on the website http://statejobs.utah.gov. **Positions advertised include:** Registered Nurse; Custodian.

UTAH VALLEY REGIONAL MEDICAL CENTER
1034 North 500 West, Provo UT 84604-3337. 801/373-7850. **Contact:** Human Resources. **World Wide Web address:** http://www.ihc.com/xp/ihc/uvrmc. **Description:** With 350 beds, Utah Valley Regional is one of the largest hospitals in the nonprofit Intermountain Healthcare system. The hospital is a tertiary referral center for Utah County and the south and central counties of the state. The center includes an open-heart program, dialysis center, two MRIs, trauma care, newborn intensive care, three heart catheter labs, and a radiation oncology center. **NOTE:** Human Resources phone is 801/357-7035. Please visit website to register, search for jobs, and apply online. **Positions advertised include:** RN – Various Departments; Ultrasonographer; Health Unit Coordinator; Media Manager; Medical Technologist; Cook; Housekeeper; Pharmacy Manager; Radiology Technician; Mammography Technologist; Licensed Psychologist; CT Technologist.

ZEVEX INTERNATIONAL INC.
4314 Zevex Park Lane, Salt Lake City UT 84123. 801/264-1001. **Toll-free phone:** 800/970-2337. **Fax:** 801/293-9018. **Contact:** Human Resources. **E-mail address:** hr@zevex.com. **World Wide Web address:** http://www.zevex.com. **Description:** A research and development, design, and manufacturing facility for ultrasonic medical equipment. **NOTE:** See website for current job openings, to download applications, and to review application instructions. **Positions advertised include:** Corporate Account Representative; Senior Buyer; Mechanical Engineer (Ultrasonics); Manufacturing/Engineering Support Technician; Independent Clinical Coordinator. **Corporate headquarters location:** This location.

Vermont

BURLINGTON HEALTH AND REHABILITATION CENTER
300 Pearl Street, Burlington VT 05401. 802/658-4200. **Fax:** 802/863-8016. **Contact:** Human Resources. **World Wide Web address:** http://www.burlingtonhealthandrehabilitationcenter.com. **Description:** A 168-bed, for-profit, nursing home that provides long-term and subacute care, including IV and antibiotic therapy, pain management, wound care, rehabilitation and pulmonary/ventilator care, social services and respite care. **Positions advertised include:** Transportation Aide; Registered Nurse; Physical Therapy Assistant; Occupational Therapist; Nursing Supervisor; Licensed Practical Nurse; Certified/Licensed Nursing Assistant. **Special programs:** Training. **Parent company:** CPL Long Term Care Real Estate Investment Trust (Toronto, Canada).

CENTRAL VERMONT MEDICAL CENTER
130 Fisher Road, P.O. Box 547, Barre VT 05641. 802/371-4194. **Fax:** 802/371-4700. **Recorded jobline:** 802/371-4562. **Contact:** Human Resources. **World Wide Web address:** http://www.cvmc.hitchcock.org. **Description:** A community medical center that includes Central Vermont Hospital, Central Vermont Medical Center Management, Central Vermont Physician Practice Corporation, CVMC Medical Group Practices, and Woodridge Nursing Home. **Positions advertised include:** Nuclear Technologist; Clinical Coordinator; Clinical Nurse Specialist; Diabetic Nurse Educator; Director of Medical Records; Financial Counselor; Lead Physical Therapist; Manager of Building Services; Medical Office Secretary; Scanning Clerk; Transcriptionist; Vice President of Human Resources. **Parent company:** Dartmouth-Hitchcock Alliance. **Number of employees at this location:** 1,200.

FLETCHER ALLEN HEALTHCARE
111 Colchester Avenue, Burlington VT 05401. 802/847-2825. **Toll-free phone:** 800/722-9922. **Recorded jobline:** 802/847-2722. **Contact:** Employment Office. **E-mail address:** fahcjobs@vtmednet.org. **World Wide Web address:** http://www.fahc.org. **Description:** Operates a full-service, acute care, community hospital with 500 beds. In partnership with the University of Vermont, Fletcher Allen Health Care is also the state's academic health

center. **NOTE:** Applicants are requested to submit information through the company's Website using the Online Resume. For physician opportunities, contact Michelle Sacco at michelle.sacco@vtmednet.org. **Positions advertised include:** Administrative Nurse Coordinator; Clinical Auditor; Director, Various Departments; Senior Staff Accountant; Therapy Supervisor; Angiography Technologist; Child Life Specialist; Financial Counselor; Registration Coordinator; Plant Operator; Security Officer.

NORTHEASTERN VERMONT REGIONAL HOSPITAL
1315 Hospital Drive, P.O. Box 905, St. Johnsbury VT 05819. 802/748-7415. **Fax:** 802/748-7398. **Contact:** Katrina Meigs, Human Resources Representative. **E-mail address:** k.meigs@nvrh.org. **World Wide Web address:** http://www.nvrh.org. **Description:** A full-service, community-based, non-profit, 75-bed acute care facility. **Positions advertised include:** Facility Technician; General Application; Human Resources Manager; Multi-Modality Imaging Technologist; Nuclear Medicine Technician. **Parent company:** Dartmouth-Hitchcock Alliance.

RETREAT HEALTHCARE
Anna Marsh Lane, P.O. Box 803, Brattleboro VT 05302. 802/258-3703. **Fax:** 802/258-3797. **Contact:** Susan Dorais. **E-mail address:** sdorais@retreathealthcare.org. **World Wide Web address:** http://www.retreathealthcare.org. **Description:** A non-profit, regional specialty psychiatric hospital and addictions treatment center, providing a full range of diagnostic, therapeutic and rehabilitation services for individuals and their families. Founded in 1834. **Positions advertised include:** Child Care Assistant; Clinical Manager; Electrical Fire Safety Coordinator; Registered Nurse; Mental Health Worker; Paraprofessional; Power Plant Technician; Social Worker/Therapist; Activity Therapist. **Number of employees at this location:** 650.

RUTLAND REGIONAL MEDICAL CENTER
160 Allen Street, Rutland VT 05701. 802/747-3668. **Fax:** 802/747-6248. **Contact:** Anna White, Recruiter. **E-mail address:** jobs@rrmc.org. **World Wide Web address:** http://www.rrmc.org. **Description:** A 188-bed hospital providing educational, preventive, ambulatory, emergency, secondary, and selected tertiary and long-term care services to Rutland County, central and southern Vermont, and bordering communities in New York. Founded in 1896. **NOTE:** Unsolicited resumes are not accepted. **Positions advertised include:** Compliance Officer; PeopleSoft Supply Chain Management Analyst; Health Information Transcription Application Analyst. **Number of employees at this location:** 1,500.

SPRINGFIELD HOSPITAL
25 Ridgewood Road, P.O. Box 2003, Springfield VT 05156. 802/885-7641. **Fax:** 802/885-7628. **Contact:** Janet Laraway, Human Resources Director. **E-mail address:** jlaraway@springfieldhospital.org. **World Wide Web address:** http://www.springfieldhospital.org. **Description:** A full-service, nonprofit, voluntary hospital with 69 beds. **Positions advertised include:** Director of Patient Financial Services. **Special programs:** Apprenticeships; Summer Jobs.

VERMED, INC.
9 Lowell Drive, P.O. Box 556, Bellows Falls VT 05101-1556. 802/463-9976, extension 222. **Fax:** 802/463-1377. **Contact:** Kristina Utton, Sales Manager. **E-mail address:** employment@vermed.com. **World Wide Web address:** http://www.vermed.com. **Description:** Designs, manufactures, and sells disposable medical monitoring electrodes and other special purpose medical electrodes. Vermed also distributes medical monitoring accessories. Angiolaz (also at this location) is a research and development company specializing in visual enhancement products. Founded in 1978. **Positions available include:** Telesales Regional Manager. **Subsidiaries include:** Angiolaz (also at this location). **Parent company:** CardioDynamics. **Listed on:** Privately held. **Number of employees at this location:** 90.

VERMONT STATE HOSPITAL
103 South Main Street, Weeks Building, Waterbury VT 05671-1601. 802/241-3100. **Fax:** 802/241-3001. **Contact:** Administration. **World Wide Web address:** http://www.healthyvermonters.info. **Description:** Offers health services to mentally ill Vermonters who are unable to receive treatment and care in other settings. The hospital is run by the State of Vermont's Department of Developmental and Mental Health Services.

WASHINGTON COUNTY MENTAL HEALTH SERVICES, INC.
P.O. Box 647, Montpelier VT 05601-0647. 802/229-0591. **Fax:** 802/223-6423. **Contact:** Susan Loynd, Human Resources. **E-mail address:** personnel@wcmhs.org. **World Wide Web address:** http://www.wcmhs.org. **Description:** Provides comprehensive, community-based services to adults with serious and persistent mental illness; developmental disabilities, mental retardation and autism; children with severe emotional disturbances and their families; children and adults with acute behavioral problems; and a wide range of other challenging behaviors. Their services include individualized residential and day treatment. **NOTE:** Search for open positions at http://www.jobsinvt.com. **Positions advertised include:** DTL and Social Skills Interventionist; Community Support Specialist; Community-Based Case Manager. **Other area locations:** Statewide. **Number of employees statewide:** Over 650.

Virginia

ALEXANDRIA ANIMAL HOSPITAL
2660 Duke Street, Alexandria VA 22314. 703/751-2022. **Contact:** Manager. **World Wide Web address:** http://www.alexandriaanimalhospital.com. **Description:** An animal hospital for pets providing medical, dental, and surgical services. **Positions advertised include:** Licensed Veterinary Technician; Veterinary Assistant. **Number of employees at this location:** 100.

AMERIGROUP CORPORATION
4425 Corporation Lane, Virginia Beach, VA 23462. 757/490-6900. **Contact:** Human Resources. **E-mail address:** hrvacorp@amerigroupcorp.com. **World Wide Web address:** http://www.amerigroupcorp.com. **Description:** A multi-state managed health care company serving people who receive health care benefits through publicly sponsored programs. **Positions advertised include:** Pharmacy Technician; AVP, Sr. counsel; Operations Analyst; Technical Reports Analyst; Director, Project Management. **Corporate headquarters location:** This location. **Other U.S. locations:** TX; NJ; MD; IL; FL; Washington DC.

CARILION BEDFORD MEMORIAL HOSPITAL
1613 Oakwood Street, Bedford VA 24523-0688. 540/586-2441. **Recorded jobline:** 800/816-1090. **Contact:** Human Resources. **World Wide Web address:** http://www.bmhva.com. **Description:** A nonprofit, JCAHO-accredited medical facility. Carilion Bedford Memorial Hospital serves as a 110-bed nursing home and a 55-bed hospital. **NOTE:** Search and apply for positions online. **Positions advertised include:** Certified Nursing Assistant; Licensed Practical Nurse; Registered Nurse; Respiratory Care Therapist; Radiologic Technologist. **Parent company:** Carilion Health Systems. **Number of employees at this location:** 400.

CARILION NEW RIVER VALLEY MEDICAL CENTER
2900 Lamb Circle, Christianburg VA 24073. 540/731-2000. **Recorded jobline:** 800/816-1090. **Contact:** Human Resources. **World Wide Web address:** http://www.carilion.com. **Description:** An acute care facility with 175 licensed beds. The hospital offers the following community services: Lifeline, a personal

emergency response system; Meals on Wheels; Viva Club, a health club for people 55 and older; and Home Health Plus, a home health agency that provides nursing and other in-home services. The hospital also offers critical care, dietary services, emergency care, emergency medical services, extended care, endoscopic services, intravenous therapy, neurology, obstetrics, pediatric care, patient education, patient financial services, physical therapy, progressive care, radiology, respiratory care services, same-day surgery, and a sleep disorder center. **Positions advertised include:** Certified Registered Nurse Anesthetist; Licensed Practical Nurse; Multi-Skilled Technologist; Nuclear Medicine Technologist; Nurse Manager; Pharmacist; Radiologic Technologist; Registered Nurse; Sonographer. **Parent company:** Carilion Health Systems.

CATAWBA HOSPITAL
P.O. Box 200, Catawba VA 24070-0200. 540/375-4200. **Fax:** 540/375-4359. **Physical address:** 5525 Catawba Hospital Drive, Catawba VA 24070. **Contact:** Human Resources. **World Wide Web address:** http://www.catawba.dmhmrsas.virginia.gov. **Description:** A 270-bed, state operated, mental health hospital for adults and geriatrics. Affiliated with the University of Virginia School of Medicine. **NOTE:** Search for positions online. All applications require a State Employment Application available online. **Positions advertised include:** Registered Nurse; Nursing Assistant; Adult Psychiatrist; Therapist; Licensed Practical Nurse.

CENTRA HEALTH INC.
1920 Atherholt Road, Lynchburg VA 24501. 434/947-4738. **Contact:** Employment Coordinator. **World Wide Web address:** http://www.centrahealth.com. **Description:** A regional, nonprofit health care system that operates through two hospitals in central Virginia. **NOTE:** Search for positions online. **Positions advertised include:** Case manager; social Worker; Education Specialist; Business Informatics Analyst; Reimbursement Manager; Recuiter. **Corporate headquarters location:** This location. **Number of employees at this location:** 3,300.

CENTRAL VIRGINIA TRAINING CENTER
P.O. Box 1098, Lynchburg VA 24505. 434/947-6000. **Fax:** 434/947-2140. **Toll-free phone:** 866/897-6095. **Contact:** Human Resources. **World Wide Web address:** http://www. cvtc.dmhmrsas.virginia.gov. **Description:** A state residential facility for individuals with mental retardation. **NOTE:** Search for positions online. A state application, which may be downloaded online, must accompany any resumes. **Positions advertised include:** RN; LPN; Therapist. **Number of employees at this location:** 1,400.

CHILDREN'S HOSPITAL OF THE KING'S DAUGHTERS
601 Children's Lane, Norfolk VA 23507-1910. 757/668-7128. **Fax:** 757/668-7745. **Recorded jobline:** 757/668-9123. **Contact:** Human Resources. **E-mail address:** jobs@chkd.org. **World Wide Web address:** http://www.chkd.org. **Description:** A 186-bed, nonprofit medical center, treating children from birth to age 21. This location also serves as a regional pediatric referral center. **NOTE:** Search and apply for positions online. **Positions advertised include:** Clinical Practice and Education Specialist; Neonatal Nurse Practitioner; Sleep Lab Tech; Surgical Tech; Radiology Tech; Occupational Health Nurse; Respiratory Care Practitioner; Respiratory Operations Coordinator; ER Technician; Occupational Therapist; Medical Transcriptionist; Data Quality Manager; Lead Teacher; Patient Interviewer; Licensed Clinical Psychologist; RN; Nurse Manager; Director of Operating Room.

COMMUNITY MEMORIAL HEALTHCENTER
125 Buena Vista Circle, P.O. Box 90, South Hill VA 23970. 434/447-3151. **Fax:** 434/774-2519. **Contact:** Human Resources. **World Wide Web address:** http://www.cmh-sh.org. **Description:** A not-for-profit 144-bed hospital and 140-bed nursing home, offering both emergency and skilled care. Founded in 1954. **NOTE:** Search for positions online. **Positions advertised include:** RN's; CNA's; LPN's; Speech Therapist; Physical Therapist; Occupational Therapist; Social Worker. **Number of employees at this location:** 700.

CORNING INC.
265 Corning Drive, Danville VA 24541-6262. 434/793-9511. **Fax:** 434/797-6323. **Contact:** Human Resources. **World Wide Web address:** http://www.corning.com. **Description:** Corning Inc. is a diverse manufacturer of specialty glass and glass ceramic products. Products include fiber optic and copper cables, frequency control devices, coaxial interconnects and microwave connectors, glass for LCD displays, emissions controls, laboratory products, eyeglass lenses, optical fiber products, photonic materials, semiconductor optics, and technical materials. Brand names include Corning and Pyrex. The company produces over 60,000 products through 70 manufacturing locations. **NOTE:** Search and apply for positions or submit resume online. **Corporate headquarters location:** Corning NY. **Operations at this facility include**: This location is a manufacturing plant that primarily produces eyeglass lenses. **Listed on:** New York Stock Exchange. **Stock exchange symbol:** GLW. Number of employees worldwide: 26,000.

CUMBERLAND HOSPITAL FOR CHILDREN & ADOLESCENTS
9407 Cumberland Road, New Kent VA 23124. 804/966-2242. **Toll-free phone:** 800/368-3472. **Fax:** 804/966-5639. **Contact:** Lee Byrd, Human Resources Manager. **World Wide Web address:** http://www.cumberlandhospital.com. **Description:** An 84-bed pediatric hospital. **NOTE:** Second and third shifts are offered. **Positions advertised include:** Behavioral Psychologist; Physical Therapist. **Office hours:** Monday - Friday, 9:00 a.m. - 5:00 p.m. **Parent company:** Psychiatric Solutions, Inc. **Number of employees at this location:** 250.

DEPAUL MEDICAL CENTER
150 Kingsley Lane, Norfolk VA 23505. 757/489-5000. **Contact:** Human Resources. **World Wide Web address:** http://www.bonsecourshamptonroads.com. **Description:** A 366-bed, nonprofit medical center. DePaul Medical Center is both an inpatient and outpatient acute care teaching hospital, offering residencies in medicine, obstetrics/gynecology, pediatrics, urology, radiology, surgery, and ENT. Specialized treatment centers include The Cancer Center, The Center for Birth, The Laser Center, The Diabetes Center, and the Elise and Henry Clay Hofheimer II Gerontology Center. **NOTE:** Search and apply for positions online. **Positions advertised include:** Cardiovascular Tech; Certified Registered Nurse Anesthetist; Clinical Coordinator; Clinical Instructor; CNA's; Credentialing Analyst; Director of Laboratory Applications Development and Support; LPN's; Phlebotomist; RN's; Registered Vascular Technologist. **Parent company:** Bon Secours Hampton Roads Health System.

DOMINION HOSPITAL
2960 Sleepy Hollow Road, Falls Church VA 22044. 703/536-2000. **Fax:** 703/533-9650. **Contact:** Human Resources. **E-mail address:** dominionhr@hcahealthcare.com. **World Wide Web address:** http://www.dominionhospital.com. **Description:** A short-term psychiatric hospital offering inpatient services covering a wide range of problems including substance abuse, eating disorders, sleep disorders, sexual abuse, emotional trauma, and depression. **NOTE:** Search and apply for positions online. **Parent company:** Columbia/HCA Healthcare Corporation.

FAUQUIER HOSPITAL
500 Hospital Drive, Warrenton VA 20186-3099. 540/347-2550. **Fax:** 540/341-0823. **Recorded jobline:** 800/960-5351. **Contact:** Human Resources Department. **E-mail address:**

humanresources@fauquierhospital.org. **World Wide Web address:** http://www.fauquierhospital.org. **Description:** An 84-bed, acute care, nonprofit hospital providing inpatient, outpatient, and emergency care. The hospital is also affiliated with Warrenton Overlook Health and Rehabilitation Center, a 115-bed long-term and rehabilitative care facility. **Positions advertised include:** Assistant Director of Patient Accounts; Director of Applications; OR Technician; Radiology Technologist; RN; Speech Therapist; Staff Occupational Therapist. **Number of employees at this location:** 600.

INOVA ALEXANDRIA HOSPITAL
4320 Seminary Road, Alexandria VA 22304. 703/504-3000. **Contact:** Director of Human Resources. **E-mail address:** jobs@inova.com. **World Wide Web address:** http://www.inova.com. **Description:** A 339-bed general medical and surgical hospital. Special departments of Alexandria Hospital include a Level II trauma center, a cancer center, a cardiac surgery unit, radiology, pediatrics, a women's specialty unit, and a mental health and behavioral center. **Positions advertised include:** Management Coordinator; Respiratory Therapist; Radiologic Technologist; Medical Technologist; Sonographer; Education Coordinator; Physical Therapist; Computed Tomography Tech; Nuclear Medicine Tech; Registered Nurse. **Parent company:** Inova Health System.

INOVA EMERGENCY CARE CENTER
4315 Chain Bridge Road, Fairfax VA 22030. 703/591-9322. **Contact:** Human Resources. **E-mail address:** jobs@inova.com. **World Wide Web address:** http://www.inova.com. **Description:** A 24-hour emergency care center with laboratory and X-ray services. **Positions advertised include:** Emergency Medical Technician; Registered Nurse; Security Officer. **Other area locations:** Reston VA. **Parent company:** Inova Health System.

INOVA FAIR OAKS HOSPITAL
3600 Joseph Siewick Drive, Fairfax VA 22033. 703/391-3600. **Contact:** Human Resources. **E-mail address:** jobs@inova.com. **World Wide Web address:** http://www.inova.com. **Description:** A 160-bed full-service hospital that provides maternal and infant health care. **Positions advertised include:** Emergency Medical Technician; Care Team Assistant; Pharmacy Technician; Business Manager; Radiologic Technologist; Medical Technologist; Pharmacist; Registered Nurse. **Parent company:** Inova Health System.

INOVA FAIRFAX HOSPITAL
3300 Gallows Road, Falls Church VA 22042-3300. 703/776-4001. **Contact:** Human Resources. **E-mail address:** jobs@inova.com. **World Wide Web address:** http://www.inova.com. **Description:** A full-service, 656-bed, inpatient and outpatient care hospital. Inova Fairfax Hospital provides cancer treatment services, 24-hour emergency services, newborn intensive care, and general medical and surgical care. **Positions advertised include:** Management Coordinator; Registered Nurse; Medical Technologist; Physician; Radiologic Technologist; Sonographer; Phlebotomist; Physical Therapist; Surgical Physician Assistant. **Parent company:** Inova Health System.

INOVA MOUNT VERNON HOSPITAL
2501 Parker's Lane, Alexandria VA 22306. 703/664-7000. **Contact:** Human Resources. **E-mail address:** jobs@inova.com. **World Wide Web address:** http://www.inova.com. **Description:** A full-service hospital. The hospital has emergency, cardiac, rehabilitation, and psychiatry units; the Mount Vernon Cancer Institute; and outpatient surgery. **Positions advertised include:** Speech Pathologist; Medical Records Supervisor; Occupational Therapist; Physical Therapist; Pharmacist; Registered Nurse; Medical Technologist. **Parent company:** Inova Health System.

LIFECARE MEDICAL TRANSPORTS, INC.
1170 International Parkway, Fredericksburg VA 22406. 540/752-7721. **Fax:** 540/752-5194. **Contact:** Human Resources. **World Wide Web address:** http://www.lifecare94.com. **Description:** An ambulance service. **NOTE:** Application form available online. **Positions advertised include:** ALS/BLS Field Technician; Administrative Assistant; Billing Coordinator; Service Technician; Wheelchair Van Driver.

LOUDOUN HOSPITAL CENTER
44045 Riverside Parkway, Leesburg VA 20176. 703/858-6000. **Toll-free phone:** 888/542-8477. **Contact:** Human Resources. **World Wide Web address:** http://www.loudounhospital.org. **Description:** A full-service, general care hospital. **NOTE:** Search and apply for positions online. **Positions advertised include:** Biomedical Technician; Clinical Nurse Specialist; Clinical Systems Analyst; Communication Associate; Lab Assistant; LPN's; Medical Records Specialist; Medical Technologist; Patient Care Tech; Pharmacist; RN's; Radiology Technologist; Security Officer. **Parent company:** Inova Health System.

LUMENOS
1801 North Beauregard Street, Suite 10, Alexandria VA 22311. 888/339-7950. **Contact:** Human Resources. **E-mail address:** jobs@lumenos.com. **World Wide Web address:** http://www.lumenos.com. **Description:** A consumer health care benefits company. **Positions advertised include:** Account Coordinator; Claims Coordinator; Health Care Reporting Analyst; Marketing Manager; Sr. PL/SQL Developer.

LYNCHBURG GENERAL HOSPITAL
1901 Tate Springs Road, Lynchburg VA 24501. 434/947-3000. **Contact:** Human Resources. **World Wide Web address:** http://www.centrahealth.com. **Description:** A 270-bed emergency and critical care center specializing in cardiology, emergency medicine, orthopedics, neurology, and neurosurgery. **NOTE:** Search and apply for positions online. **Positions advertised include:** Radiologic Technologist; Cardiac Sonographer; Phlebotomist II; EEG Tech; Environmental Services Tech; RN; Pharmacist; Pharmacy Tech; Speech Pathologist. **Parent company:** Centra Health.

MHM SERVICES
1593 Spring Hill Road, Suite 610, Vienna VA 22182. 703/749-4600. **Toll-free phone:** 800/416-3649. **Fax:** 703/749-4604. **Contact:** Human Resources. **E-mail address:** jobs@mhm-services.com. **World Wide Web address:** http://www.mhm-services.com. **Description:** Provides behavioral health services. MHM Corrections provides on-site mental health services to private and government agencies including correctional facilities. MHM Solutions specializes in long-term contract staffing for healthcare facilities. MHM Community Care manages behavioral health programs. **NOTE:** Search and apply for positions online. **Positions advertised include:** Recruiter; Writer. **Corporate headquarters location:** This location. **Other U.S. locations:** Montgomery AL; Atlanta GA; Nashville TN; Monticello FL. **Number of employees nationwide:** 510.

MARY IMMACULATE HOSPITAL
2 Bernadine Drive, Newport News VA 23602. 757/886-6000. **Contact:** Human Resources. **World Wide Web address:** http://www.bonsecours.org. **Description:** A 110-bed, acute care, general hospital. Mary Immaculate Hospital offers a Discovery Care Center (child care facility) and two MedCare centers providing walk-in general care. This hospital has three centers to aid its community: St. Francis Nursing Center, which provides 10 beds for skilled care and 105 beds for intermediate care; Kiosk, which provides free weekly blood pressure screenings; and Family Focus, which provides support for parents and families. Founded in 1952. **NOTE:** Search and apply for positions online. **Positions advertised include:** Admissions Nurse; Clinical Coordinator; CNA's; Critical Care Educator; Histotechnologist; LPN's; Nurse Manager; Radiology Therapist; Respiratory Therapist. **Parent company:**

Bon Secours Health System.

MARYVIEW MEDICAL CENTER
3636 High Street, Portsmouth VA 23707. 757/398-2200. **Contact:** Human Resources Manager. **World Wide Web address:** http://www.bonsecours.org. **Description:** A 346-bed acute care hospital, which includes a 54-bed Behavioral Medicine Center. **NOTE:** Search and apply for positions online. **Positions advertised include:** Admission Nurse; CNA's; Education Coordinator; Executive Director, Foundation; HR Assistant; Insurance Verifier; Manager of Staffing and Administrative Services; Radiation Therapist; Radiology Technologist; RN's; Respiratory Therapist. **Parent company:** Bon Secours Health System.

McKESSON MEDICAL GROUP
8741 Landmark Road, Richmond VA 23228. 804/264-7500. **Fax:** 804/264-7679. **Contact:** Human Resources. **E-mail address:** webmail@mckgenmed.com. **World Wide Web address:** http://www.mckgenmed.com. **Description:** A medical equipment wholesaler with distribution and service centers in 24 states. **NOTE:** Search and apply for positions online. **Positions advertised include:** Director of Regulatory Affairs; Financial Business Analyst; Marketing Specialist; Inventory Analyst; Collection Associate; Project Manager, Systems; Category Manager. **Corporate headquarters location:** This location. **Parent company:** McKesson Corporation. **Listed on:** New York Stock Exchange. **Stock exchange symbol:** MCK. **Number of employees nationwide:** 4,000.

MOUNT REGIS CENTER
405 Kimball Avenue, Salem VA 24153. 540/389-4761. **Toll-free phone:** 800/477-3447. **Contact:** Human Resources. **World Wide Web address:** http://www.mtregis.com. **Description:** A drug and alcohol treatment facility. Mount Regis Center has a 25-bed residential treatment center; day and outpatient services are available. Founded in 1947.

NORTHERN VIRGINIA COMMUNITY HOSPITAL
601 South Carlin Springs Road, Arlington VA 22204-1096. 703/671-1200. **Fax:** 703/578-2281. **Contact:** Human Resources. **World Wide Web address:** http://www.nvchospital.com. **Description:** A 164-bed hospital with emergency, intensive care, and long-term acute care facilities. The hospital's services include an outpatient surgery center offering eye laser treatment, a gastroenterology and GI endoscopic lab, a pain management center, and a urodynamics lab; a wide range of urological services; MRI and CAT scans; a cardiac catheterization lab; a sleep disorders lab; and inpatient and partial-day psychiatric programs. Founded in 1961. **NOTE:** Search and apply for positions online. **Number of employees at this location:** 550. **Parent company:** Columbia/HCA Healthcare.

OLD DOMINION ANIMAL HEALTH CENTER
6719 Lowell Avenue, McLean VA 22101. 703/356-5582. **Contact:** Human Resources. **World Wide Web address:** http://www.odahcenter.com. **Description:** An animal hospital offering both routine and emergency care.

OWENS & MINOR
4800 Cox Road, Glen Allen VA 23060-6292. 804/747-9794. **Fax:** 804/270-7281. **Contact:** Erika Davis, Vice President of Human Resources. **World Wide Web address:** http://www.owens-minor.com. **Description:** One of the nation's largest wholesale distributors of national branded medical, surgical, and nontraditional supplies. The distribution centers of Owens & Minor serve hospitals, integrated health care systems, primary care facilities, and group purchasing organizations throughout the United States. The company also helps customers control health care costs and improve inventory management through services in supply chain management, logistics, and technology. **NOTE:** Search and apply for positions online. **Positions advertised include:** OMS Consulting Associate; Consultant; Product Development Analyst; Manager, External Financial Reporting; Director Brand Strategy and Communications. **Special programs:** Internships. **Corporate headquarters location:** This location. **Other U.S. locations:** Nationwide. **Listed on:** New York Stock Exchange. **Stock exchange symbol:** OMI. **Annual sales/revenues:** More than $100 million. **Number of employees at this location:** 3,000.

PENDER VETERINARY CLINIC
4001 Legato Road, Fairfax VA 22033. 703/591-3304. **Fax:** 703/591-6936. **Contact:** Human Resources. **World Wide Web address:** http://www.pendervet.com. **Description:** An animal clinic providing both routine and emergency care. Founded in 1971.

PIEDMONT BEHAVIORAL HEALTH CENTER
P.O. Box 2547, Leesburg VA 20177. **Physical address:** 42009 Victory lane, Leesburg VA 20176. **Toll-free phone:** 800/777-8855. **Contact:** Human Resources. **Description:** A psychiatric medical center offering both inpatient and outpatient treatment in the areas of alcohol and drug dependency, depression, and marital problems.

PIEDMONT GERIATRIC HOSPITAL
5001 East Patrick Henry Highway, P.O. Box 427, Burkeville VA 23922. 434/767-4401. **Contact:** Human Resources. **E-mail address:** aroberts@pgh.state.va.us. **World Wide Web address:** http://www.dmhmrsas.virginia.gov. **Description:** A Virginia state facility that provides inpatient treatment to elderly patients with mental illnesses. **Special programs:** Internships. **Corporate headquarters location:** Richmond VA. **Parent company:** Department of Mental Health. **Number of employees at this location:** 450.

POTOMAC HOSPITAL
2300 Opitz Boulevard, Woodbridge VA 22191. 703/670-1313. **Recorded jobline:** 703/670-1836. **Contact:** Human Resources. **E-mail address:** employment@potomachospital.com. **World Wide Web address:** http://www.potomachospital.com. **Description:** A 153-bed nonprofit general hospital. Potomac Hospital offers clinical services including a 24-hour emergency room, critical care, progressive care, maternal and infant care, neonatology, LDRs, pediatrics, Lamaze/expectant parent classes, an operating room, ambulatory care surgery, post anesthesia care, surgery, medicine/oncology, hospice care, mental health-adult/adolescent care, cardiology services, physical medicine and rehabilitation services, radiation oncology, respiratory services, radiology/angiography, ultrasound, nuclear medicine, a CT scanner, MRI, laboratory, occupational therapy, and an inpatient/retail pharmacy service. **NOTE:** Search and apply for positions online. **Parent company:** Inova Health System. **Number of employees at this location:** 1,000.

PRINCE WILLIAM HOSPITAL
8700 Sudley Road, Manassas VA 20110. 703/369-8000. **Contact:** Susan Barrett, Employment Coordinator. **World Wide Web address:** http://www.pwhs.org. **Description:** A nonprofit, 170-bed, community hospital. Founded in 1964. **NOTE:** Search and apply for positions online. **Positions advertised include:** Coding Manager; Director, Emergency Services Department; Director, Radiology; Manager, Engineering; Manager, Customer Service and Billing; Registered Nurses; Oncology Technician; Surgical Technician; Licensed Practical Nurse; Cardiopulmonary Technician; Clinical Dietitian; Medical Librarian/CME Coordinator. **Number of employees at this location:** 1,000.

PULASKI COMMUNITY HOSPITAL
2400 Lee Highway, P.O. Box 759, Pulaski VA 24301. 540/994-8414. **Fax:** 540/994-8423. **Recorded jobline:** 540/994-8522. **Contact:** Human Resources Director. **E-mail address:** pulaskihrdept@healthcare.com. **World Wide Web address:** http://www.pch-va.com.

Description: A 147-bed acute care hospital. The hospital has various services and units including home health, cardiac rehabilitation, family birthing center, intensive care unit, cardiac care unit, progressive care unit, oncology, emergency center, physical therapy, and orthopedic care. Founded in 1973. **Positions advertised include:** CRNA; Director, Health Information Management; LPN; Registered Nurse; Occupational Therapist; Physical Therapist; Nuclear Medicine Tech; Radiology Tech. **Number of employees at this location:** 400.

RAPPAHANNOCK GENERAL HOSPITAL
101 Harris Road, P.O. Box 1449, Kilmarnock VA 22482. 804/435-8565. **Contact:** Human Resources department. **World Wide Web address:** http://www.rgh-hospital.com. **Description:** An acute care, community-owned, nonprofit hospital with 76 beds. Rappahannock General Hospital offers an array of services including a 24-hour emergency room, a stationary MRI, Rappahannock Home Health Agency, physical therapy, a maternity center, diagnostic X-ray, mammography, and ultrasonography. **Positions advertised include:** Registered Nurse; Physical Therapist; CNA; Exercise Physiologist; Licensed Practical Nurse; Occupational Therapist; Respiratory Therapist. **Number of employees at this location:** 425.

RESTON HOSPITAL CENTER
1850 Town Center Parkway, Reston VA 20190. 703/689-9000. **Fax:** 703/689-0840. **Contact:** Human Resources. **World Wide Web address:** http://www.restonhospital.net. **Description:** A 127-bed general hospital offering 24-hour emergency, critical, and progressive care services. **Positions advertised include:** PBX Operator; Case Manager; HR Assistant; Medical Transcriptionist; DRG Coder; RN; LPN; Sterile Processing Technician; Pharmacist; Scheduling Representative.

RIVERSIDE HEALTH SYSTEM
Fountain Plaza One, Suite 1000, 701 Town Center Drive, Newport News VA 23606. 757/534-7000. **Contact:** Larry Boyles, Vice President of Human Resources. **World Wide Web address:** http://www.riverside-online.com. **Description:** An integrated health care provider operating three acute-care hospitals, a physical rehabilitation hospital, ambulatory centers, seven long-term care facilities, two continuing care retirement communities, home health care services, and five wellness and fitness centers. **NOTE:** Search and apply for positions online.

ROCKINGHAM MEMORIAL HOSPITAL
235 Cantrell Avenue, Harrisonburg VA 22801. 540/433-4100. **Fax:** 540/564-5446. **Contact:** Recruitment/Employment Manager. **World Wide Web address:** http://www.rmhonline.com. **Description:** A 330-bed, nonprofit, community hospital. **NOTE:** Download application and mail to: Human Resources Department at above address. Search for positions online. **Positions advertised include:** LPN; RN; Compliance Review Coordinator; Clinical Resource Specialist; Staff Physical Therapist; Clinical Pharmacist; Polysomnographic Technologist; Nuclear Med Staff Technologist. **Operations at this facility include:** Service. **Number of employees at this location:** 1,500.

SENTARA CAREPLEX HOSPITAL
3000 Coliseum Drive, Hampton VA 23666. 757/736-1000. **Contact:** Human Resources. **World Wide Web address:** http://www.sentara.com. **Description:** Opened in December 2002, Sentara CarePlex Hospital is an acute care facility with 194 private patient rooms and advanced operating, diagnostic, and monitoring systems. **NOTE:** Search and apply for positions online. **Positions advertised include:** Cardiovascular Invasive Specialist; Clinical Nurse; Laboratory Manager; Physical Therapist; RN's; Respiratory Therapist; Staff Development Educator; Team Leader, SPD.

SENTARA HEALTHCARE
6015 Poplar Hall Drive, Norfolk VA 23502. 757/455-7000. **Contact:** Human Resources. **E-mail address:** jobs@sentara.com. **World Wide Web address:** http://www.sentara.com. **Description:** A nonprofit, regional health management organization. Sentara Health System operates six acute care hospitals, one extended care hospital, more than 70 sites of care, 25 primary care practices, a full range of health coverage plans, home health and hospice services, physical therapy and rehabilitation services, urgent care facilities, ground medical transport services, mobile diagnostic vans and two health and fitness facilities. Presently there are more than 312,000 people covered by Sentara. **NOTE:** Search and apply for positions online. **Positions advertised include:** Benefits Consultant. **Number of employees nationwide:** 15,000.

SENTARA NORFOLK GENERAL HOSPITAL
600 Gresham Drive, Norfolk VA 23507. 757/668-3000. **Contact:** Human Resources. **World Wide Web address:** http://www.sentara.com. **Description:** A 569-bed, tertiary care hospital with the area's only Level I Trauma Center and burn trauma unit. **NOTE:** Search and apply for positions online. **Positions advertised include:** Cardiac Tech II; Cardiovascular Invasive Specialist; Clinical Manager, Nursing Unit; Laboratory Technician; MRI Technologist; Marketing/Public Relation Specialist; RN's; Physical Therapist; Occupational Therapist; Transplant Coordinator; Vascular Lab Tech. **Number of employees at this location:** 3,300.

SHELTERING ARMS REHABILITATION HOSPITAL
8254 Atlee Road, Mechanicsville VA 23116. 804/342-4350. **Fax:** 804/342-4316. **Contact:** Human Resources. **E-mail address:** jobs@shelteringarms.com. **World Wide Web address:** http://www.shelteringarms.com. **Description:** A nonprofit hospital providing comprehensive services to individuals with physical and cognitive disabilities. **Positions advertised include:** Occupational Therapist; Physical Therapist; Rehabilitation Technician; Aquatic Specialist; Fitness Specialist; Patient Access Representative; LPN; RN. **Office hours:** Monday - Friday, 8:00 a.m. - 4:30 p.m. **Corporate headquarters location:** This location. **Operations at this facility include:** Administration. **Number of employees at this location:** 350.

SOUTHSIDE COMMUNITY HOSPITAL
800 Oak Street, Farmville VA 23901. 434/315-2570. **Fax:** 434/315-2439. **Contact:** Judy Black, Director of Human Resources. **World Wide Web address:** http://www.sch-farmville.org. **Description:** A nonprofit hospital. Joining the Medical College of Virginia's Massey Cancer Center, the hospital offers an Oncology Clinic to area cancer patients. Southside Community Hospital also offers the following services: dialysis, pharmacy, respiratory therapy, Home Health, Lifeline (personal emergency response system), social services, Anatomical & Clinical Laboratory, radiology, nuclear medicine, Cardiac Diagnostic Unit, surgery, outpatient surgery, anesthesiology, Mobile Lithostar System (state-of-the-art technology to remove kidney stones), physical therapy, patient teaching, speech therapy, pain management, obstetrics, nursery, pediatrics, Residency Program, organ donation, Mobile Health Fair Program (free medical screening to area businesses and their employees), and a speakers bureau. Founded in 1927. **NOTE:** Search and apply for jobs online. **Positions advertised include:** RN's; Patient Registration Supervisor; Staff Pharmacist.

SUNRISE ASSISTED LIVING, INC.
7902 Westpark Drive, McLean VA 22102. 703/273-7500. **Fax:** 703/744-1601. **Recorded jobline:** 888/686-8830. **Contact:** Human Resources. **E-mail address:** careers@mail.sunrise-al.com. **World Wide Web address:** http://www.sunrise-al.com. **Description:** Operates assisted living communities for seniors. Founded in 1981. **Corporate headquarters location:** This location. **Other U.S. locations:** Nationwide. **Listed on:** New York Stock Exchange. **Stock exchange symbol:** SRZ. **Annual sales/revenues:** More

than $100 million.

U.S. DEPARTMENT OF VETERANS AFFAIRS MEDICAL CENTER
1201 Broad Rock Road, Building 507, Richmond VA 23249. 804/675-5000x4784. **Toll-free phone:** 800/368-6008. **Fax:** 804/675-5585. **Contact:** Personnel Office. **World Wide Web address:** http://www.va.gov. **Description:** The Hunter Holmes McGuire VA Medical Center is a 427-bed facility offering primary, secondary, and tertiary health care in medicine, surgery, neurology, rehabilitation medicine, intermediate care, acute and sustaining spinal cord injury, skilled nursing home care, and palliative care. Primary and secondary levels of care are provided in psychiatry beds, along with a substance abuse rehabilitation program. Affiliated with the Medical College of Virginia. **NOTE:** Search and apply for jobs at http://www.usajobs.opm.gov.

URGENT MEDICAL CARE LAKERIDGE
12449 Hedges Run Drive, Lake Ridge VA 22192. 703/494-6160. **Contact:** Human Resources. **World Wide Web address:** http://urgentmedicalcareva.com. **Description:** A walk-in medical facility specializing in the treatment of minor illnesses and injuries. The center also has on-site X-ray and laboratory facilities.

VALUEMARK WEST END BEHAVIORAL HEALTH CARE SYSTEM
12800 West Creek Parkway, Richmond VA 23238. 804/784-2200. **Contact:** Human Resources. **Description:** An acute care psychiatric facility that houses 84 beds that serve children, adolescents, adults, and geriatrics. Founded in 1964.

VIRGINIA BAPTIST HOSPITAL
3300 Rivermont Avenue, Lynchburg VA 24503. 434/947-4000. **Contact:** Human Resources. **World Wide Web address:** http://www.centrahealth.com. **Description:** A 317-bed hospital serving Central Virginia as the regional hospital for cancer care, women's and children's care, mental health and chemical dependency treatment, outpatient surgery, physical rehabilitation, and home health. **NOTE:** Search and apply for positions online. **Positions advertised include:** C-Section Technician; Educator; Radiologic Technologist; LPN; RN; Shift Manager, Nursing; Certified Nursing Assistant; Health Information Analyst; Counselor II; Health Unit Coordinator. **Parent company:** Centra Health.

VIRGINIA HOSPITAL CENTER-ARLINGTON
1701 North George Mason Drive, Arlington VA 22205-3698. 703/558-5000. **Contact:** Human Resources. **World Wide Web address:** http://www.virginiahospitalcenter.net. **Description:** A full-service, nonprofit tertiary care facility. Arlington Hospital operates outpatient clinics, a cancer center, and a cardiac unit. **Positions advertised include:** Assistant Director of Radiography; Assistant Patient Care Director; Case Manager; Clinical Specialist; Manager of Systems Administration; Public Relations Director; RN; LPN; Physical Therapist.

MARY WASHINGTON HOSPITAL
2300 Fall Hill Avenue, Suite 401, Fredericksburg VA 22401. 540/741-1561. **Fax:** 540/741-2571. **Recorded jobline:** 866/860-0946. **Contact:** Employment Office. **World Wide Web address:** http://www.medicorp.org/mwh. **Description:** An acute care hospital with 318 beds. Services also include a nursing home, an assisted living center, a retirement center, a free-standing psychiatric hospital, a same-day surgery center, and an urgent care center. **NOTE:** Search and apply for positions online. **Positions advertised include:** Physical therapist; Diagnostic Technologist; Orthopedic Specialty Coordinator; RN's; LPN; Respiratory Therapist; Radiation Therapist; Ultrasonographer; Network/System Analyst. **Parent company:** MediCorp Health System.

WESTERN STATE HOSPITAL
1301 Richmond Avenue, P.O. Box 2500, Staunton VA 24402. 540/332-8300. **Fax:** 540/332-8305. **Recorded jobline:** 540/332-8315. **Contact:** Human Resources Management and Development. **E-mail address:** donna.brown@wsh.dmhmrsas.virginia.gov. **World Wide Web address:** http://www.wsh.dmhmrsas.virginia.gov. **Description:** A 465-bed hospital operated by the Commonwealth of Virginia, Department of Mental Health, Mental Retardation, and Substance Abuse **NOTE:** Search for positions online. **Number of employees at this location:** 870.

Washington

ADDUS HEALTHCARE, INC.
1010 North Normandie Street, Suite 303, Spokane WA 99202. 509/326-1090. **Fax:** 847/303-5376. **Contact:** Human Resources. **E-mail address:** personnel@addus.com. **World Wide Web address:** http://www.addus.com. **Description:** Provides home health care services for the elderly and disabled. Services include skilled nursing, respiratory therapy, rehabilitation, and home medical equipment. **Corporate headquarters location:** Palatine IL.

APRIA HEALTHCARE GROUP INC.
P.O. Box 3039, Redmond WA 98073-3039. 425/881-8500. **Physical address:** 14945 NE 87th Street, Redmond WA 98052. **Contact:** Human Resources. **World Wide Web address:** http://www.apria.com. **Description:** One of the largest national providers of home health care products and services including a broad range of respiratory therapy services, home medical equipment, and infusion therapy services. Apria's home health care services are provided to patients who have been discharged from hospitals, skilled nursing facilities, or convalescent homes and are being treated at home. In conjunction with medical professionals, Apria personnel deliver, install, and service medical equipment, as well as provide appropriate therapies and coordinate plans of care for their patients. Apria personnel also instruct patients and caregivers in the correct use of equipment and monitor the equipment's effectiveness. **Positions advertised include:** Staff Pharmacist; Branch Pharmacy Manager; Regional Respiratory Therapy Manager. **Corporate headquarters location:** Costa Mesa CA. **Listed on:** New York Stock Exchange. **Stock exchange symbol:** AHG.

CARDIAC SCIENCE CORPORATION
3303 Monte Villa Parkway, Bothell WA 98021-8906. 425/402-2000. **Contact:** Human Resources. **E-mail address:** employment@quinton.com. **World Wide Web address:** http://www.cardiacscience.com. **Description:** Manufactures, markets, and distributes cardiopulmonary instrumentation and devices such as cardiac stress test systems, electrocardiographs, and treadmills. **Positions advertised include:** Accounts Payable Clerk; Contract Administrator. **Corporate headquarters location:** This location.

CHILDREN'S HOSPITAL AND MEDICAL CENTER
4800 Sand Point Way NE, Seattle WA 98105-0371. 206/987-2000. **Toll-free phone:** 866/987-2000. **Recorded jobline:** 206/987-2230. **Contact:** Human Resources. **E-mail address:** jobs@chmc.org. **World Wide Web address:** http://www.chmc.org. **Description:** A tertiary pediatric hospital and medical center that serves Washington, Alaska, Idaho, and Montana. Children's Hospital also provides research and educational facilities. **Positions advertised include:** Lab Aide; Equipment and Logistics Technician; Food Service Worker; Nurse Technician. **Operations at this facility include:** Service. **Number of employees at this location:** 2,400.

EVERETT CLINIC
3901 Hoyt Avenue, Everett WA 98201. 425/259-0966. **Contact:** Human Resources Department. **E-mail address:** hr@everettclinic.com. **World Wide Web address:** http://www.everettclinic.com. **Description:** A multispecialty group medical clinic operating through eight sites in Snohomish County. **Positions advertised include:** Behavioral Health Technician; Staff

Registered Nurse; Nursing Supervisor.

EVERGREEN COMMUNITY HOME HEALTH CARE
12910 Totem Lake Boulevard, Suite 3204, Kirkland WA 98034. 425/899-3300. **Contact:** Human Resources Department. **World Wide Web address:** http://www.evergreenhealthcare.com. **Description:** Offers health services including nursing care, physical therapy, speech therapy, occupational therapy, home health aides, and social work, with specializations in oncology, pediatrics, and diabetic management. Evergreen Community Home Health Care staff help with the transition from the hospital or nursing home back to the primary residence. **Positions advertised include:** Registered Nurse; Licensed Practical Nurse; Certified Nursing Assistant; Housekeeper.

EVERGREEN HOSPITAL MEDICAL CENTER
12040 NE 128th Street, Kirkland WA 98034. 425/899-1000. **Fax:** 425/899-2510. **Contact:** Human Resources. **E-mail address:** jobs@evergreenhealthcare.org. **World Wide Web address:** http://www.evergreenhealthcare.org. **Description:** A medical center housing an acute care hospital, a surgery center, a hospice center, a head injury rehabilitation center, a telemarketing center, and a home health department. **Positions advertised include:** Clinical Nurse Specialist. **Operations at this facility include:** Administration. **Number of employees at this location:** 1,500.

FOSS HOME & VILLAGE
13023 Greenwood Avenue North, Seattle WA 98133. 206/364-1300. **Contact:** Human Resources. **World Wide Web address:** http://www.fosscare.org. **Description:** A long-term care facility that offers skilled nursing and assisted living services.

GROUP HEALTH COOPERATIVE
Human Resources, ASB 1, P.O. Box 34586, Seattle WA 98124-1586. 206/988-7718. **Physical address:** 12501 East Marginal Way, Tukwila WA 98168. **Toll-free phone:** 800/848-4255. **Contact:** Human Resources. **World Wide Web address:** http://www.ghc.org. **Description:** A health maintenance organization and hospital operator. **Corporate headquarters location:** This location. **Number of employees at this location:** 9,000.

GROUP HEALTH EASTSIDE HOSPITAL
2700 152nd Avenue NE, Redmond WA 98052. 425/883-5151. **Contact:** Human Resources. **E-mail address:** recruiters.i@ghc.org. **World Wide Web address:** http://www.ghc.org. **Description:** An acute care hospital that also offers physical therapy and pediatric care.

GUIDANT CORPORATION
6645 185th Avenue NE, Suite 100, Redmond WA 98052. 425/376-1300. **Fax:** 425/376-1426. **Contact:** Human Resources. **World Wide Web address:** http://www.guidant.com. **Description:** Guidant Corporation designs, develops, manufactures, and markets a wide range of products for use in cardiac rhythm management, coronary artery disease intervention, and other forms of minimally invasive surgery. **Corporate headquarters location:** Indianapolis IN. **Operations at this facility include:** This location is engaged in research and development. **Listed on:** New York Stock Exchange. **Stock exchange symbol:** GDT. **Annual sales/revenues:** More than $100 million.

HARBORVIEW MEDICAL CENTER
325 Ninth Avenue, Seattle WA 98104. 206/223-3000. **Contact:** Human Resources. **World Wide Web address:** http://www.uwmedicine.org. **Description:** A unit of the University of Washington Academic Medical Center. The Harborview Medical Center contains an adult and pediatric trauma center and a regional burn center.

HARRISON MEMORIAL HOSPITAL
2520 Cherry Avenue, Bremerton WA 98310. 360/792-6720. **Fax:** 360/792-6724. **Recorded jobline:** 360/792-6729. **Contact:** Sue Wallace, Recruiter. **E-mail address:** suewallace@hmh.westsound.net. **World Wide Web address:** http://www.harrisonhospital.org. **Description:** A 297-bed, full-service hospital specializing in cardiology care, diagnostic imaging, emergency and urgent care, oncology, radiation therapy, and retinal and laparoscopic surgery. Founded in 1918. **Positions advertised include:** Radiologic Technologist; Medical Imaging Aide; Surgical Technician; Supply Support Technician; Speech Language Pathologist; Physical Therapist; Occupational Therapist. **Number of employees at this location:** 1,400.

HOLY FAMILY HOSPITAL
5633 North Lidgerwood Street, Spokane WA 99207. 509/482-2111. **Fax:** 509/482-2178. **Contact:** Human Resources. **World Wide Web address:** http://www.holy-family.org. **Description:** A 272-bed acute care hospital that offers a full range of medical, outpatient, and surgical care. **Positions advertised include:** Registered Nurse; Speech Pathologist; Pharmacist; Social Worker; Lab Assistant.

LAKELAND VILLAGE
P.O. Box 200, Medical Lake WA 99022. 509/299-1800. **Contact:** Human Resources. **Description:** A state residential habilitation facility for individuals with developmental disabilities.

MARTHA & MARY NURSING HOME
P.O. Box 127, Poulsbo WA 98370. 360/779-7500. **Physical address:** 19160 Front Street NE, Poulsbo WA 98370. **Fax:** 360/779-8400. **Contact:** Human Resources. **E-mail address:** healthsvc@mmhc.org. **World Wide Web address:** http://www.marthaandmary.org. **Description:** A 180-bed nursing home that provides activities, horticulture therapy, intergenerational programs, pet therapy, and rehabilitation. **Positions advertised include:** Licensed Practical Nurse; Registered Nurse; Certified Nursing Assistant.

VIRGINIA MASON MEDICAL CENTER
1100 Ninth Avenue, Seattle WA 98101. 206/223-6600. **Contact:** Human Resources. **World Wide Web address:** http://www.vmmc.org. **Description:** A complete health care system that operates a 336-bed, acute care hospital, 16 regional clinics, an AIDS facility, and research laboratories. Founded in 1920. **Positions advertised include:** Administrative Assistant; Biomedical Equipment Technician; Clinic Service Representative; Orthopedics Coordinator; File Clerk; Customer Service Representative. **Special programs:** Internships.

MEDICAL CENTER OF TACOMA
P.O. Box 34586, Seattle WA 98124. 253/596-3300. **Physical address:** 209 Martin Luther King Jr. Way, Tacoma WA 98405. **Contact:** Human Resources. **World Wide Web address:** http://www.ghc.org. **Description:** A full-service medical center that also offers optometry and women's health care services. **Positions advertised include:** Administrative Assistant III; Medical Center Manager; Registered Nurse; Patient Care Representative; Office Assistant III; Vehicle Operator; Analyst/Programmer; Manager Accounting.

MEDTRONIC PHYSIO-CONTROL INC.
P.O. Box 97006, Redmond WA 98073-9706. 425/867-4000. **Physical address:** 11811 Willows Road NE, Redmond WA 98052. **Contact:** Human Resources. **World Wide Web address:** http://www.physiocontrol.com. **Description:** Manufactures, sells, and services defibrillators, monitors, and pacemakers. **Positions advertised include:** Administrative Assistant; Business Director; Commercial Sales Consultant; Commercial Segment Manager; Data Communications Systems Manager. **Parent company:** Medtronic, Inc. **Operations at this facility include:** Administration; Manufacturing;

Research and Development; Sales; Service. **Listed on:** New York Stock Exchange. **Stock exchange symbol:** MDT.

NORTHWEST HOSPITAL
1550 North 115th Street, Suite 1, Seattle WA 98133. 206/368-1785. **Recorded jobline:** 206/368-1791. **Contact:** Human Resources Department. **World Wide Web address:** http://www.nwhospital.org. **Description:** A full-service nonprofit hospital that specializes in brain, breast, and prostate cancer; treatment and rehabilitation for diabetes and vascular disease; radioactive seed implantation; neurological disorders; and rehabilitation therapy. Founded in 1960. **Positions advertised include:** Authorization Referral Representative; Nursing Assistant; Exercise Specialist; Inventory Coordinator; Lab Assistant; EKG Technician.

OVERLAKE HOSPITAL MEDICAL CENTER
1035 116th Avenue NE, Bellevue WA 98004. 425/688-5201. **Fax:** 425/688-5758. **Contact:** Human Resources Department. **World Wide Web address:** http://www.overlakehospital.org. **Description:** A 227-bed, nonprofit, acute care medical center. Overlake Hospital specializes in open-heart surgery and offers a comprehensive cardiac program. **Special programs:** Internships. **Annual sales/revenues:** $5 - $10 million. **Number of employees at this location:** 1,900.

PACMED CLINIC
1200 12th Avenue South, Seattle WA 98144. 206/621-4111. **Fax:** 206/621-4031. **Contact:** Human Resources. **World Wide Web address:** http://www.pacmed.org. **Description:** A nonprofit medical center operating clinics throughout the Seattle area. **Positions advertised include:** Coding Manager; Senior Supervisor of Health Data Services; Clinical RN; Medical Assistant; Physical Therapist; Healthcare Application Analyst. **Office hours:** Monday - Friday, 8:00 a.m. - 4:00 p.m. **Number of employees at this location:** 1,200.

PHILIPS MEDICAL SYSTEMS
P.O. Box 3003, Bothell WA 98041-3003. 425/487-7000. **Physical address:** 22100 Bothell Everett Highway, Bothell WA 98021-3003. **Toll-free phone:** 800/722-7900. **Fax:** 425/485-6080. **Contact:** Personnel. **World Wide Web address:** http://www.medical.philips.com. **Description:** Engaged in the development and manufacture of medical diagnostic ultrasound systems. These systems serve a variety of uses in radiology, cardiology, obstetrics/gynecology, vascular, musculoskeletal, and intraoperative applications. Founded in 1969. **Company slogan:** We are ultrasound. **Special programs:** Internships; Training. **Corporate headquarters location:** This location.

PROCYTE CORPORATION
8511 154th Avenue NE, Building A, Redmond WA 98052. 425/869-1239. **Contact:** Human Resources. **World Wide Web address:** http://www.procyte.com. **Description:** Develops copper peptide complex-based products designed for hair care, skin care, and tissue repair. The company also offers contract manufacturing services to biotech and pharmaceutical companies. **Corporate headquarters location:** This location.

PROVIDENCE EVERETT MEDICAL CENTER
1321 Colby Avenue, Everett WA 98206. 425/261-4460. **Fax:** 425/261-4470. **Contact:** Human Resources. **World Wide Web address:** http://www.providence.org. **Description:** A full-service, acute care hospital. The Center also specializes in advanced cancer treatment and heart surgery.

PROVIDENCE HOSPICE OF SEATTLE
425 Pontius Avenue North, Suite 300, Seattle WA 98109-5452. 206/320-4000. **Fax:** 206/320-2280. **Contact:** Human Resources. **Description:** Provides skilled nursing and other home and hospice services.

PROVIDENCE MOTHER JOSEPH CARE CENTER
3333 Ensign Road NE, Olympia WA 98506. 360/493-4900. **Fax:** 360/493-4000. **Contact:** Human Resources. **World Wide Web address:** http://www.providence.org. **Description:** A 152-bed skilled nursing home that also operates a special care facility for Alzheimer's residents.

PROVIDENCE MOUNT ST. VINCENT
4831 35th Avenue SW, Seattle WA 98126. 206/937-3700. **Fax:** 206/938-8999. **Contact:** Human Resources. **World Wide Web address:** http://www.providence.org. **Description:** A long-term care facility that offers assisted living and skilled nursing services, an intergenerational learning center, and rehabilitation programs.

REGENCE BLUESHIELD
1800 Ninth Avenue, Seattle WA 98101. 206/464-3600. **Contact:** Human Resources. **World Wide Web address:** http://www.wa.regence.com. **Description:** A health care service contractor that has been providing health care coverage to Washington residents for more than 86 years. Regence BlueShield has a roster of more than 19,000 physicians, dentists, and other providers serving more than 1 million members. **Positions advertised include:** Actuary Assistant, Business System Analyst; Director of Sales and Service. **Number of employees:** 2,300 employees.

ST. JOSEPH HOSPITAL
2901 Squalicum Parkway, Bellingham WA 98225. 360/734-5400. **Contact:** Personnel Office. **World Wide Web address:** http://www.peacehealth.org. **Description:** A 253-bed medical center and trauma center that provides a full range of inpatient and outpatient care including cancer care, emergency and trauma care, heart surgery, and neurosurgery. **Positions advertised include:** Registered Nurse; Certified Nurse Manger; Clinical Manager; Coder; Database System Administrator; Internal Auditor; Medical Technologist; Pharmacist; Speech Pathologist; Surgical Technologist.

SIEMENS ULTRASOUND
P.O. Box 7002, Issaquah WA 98027-7002. 425/392-9180. **Physical address:** 22010 SE 51st Street, Issaquah WA 98029. **Contact:** Human Resources. **World Wide Web address:** http://www.siemensultrasound.com. **Description:** Develops and manufactures ultrasound systems. **Positions advertised include:** Technical Instructor. **Corporate headquarters location:** This location.

SKAGIT VALLEY HOSPITAL
1415 East Kincaid, P.O. Box 1376, Mount Vernon WA 98273-1376. 360/428-8228. **Fax:** 360/428-2416. **Recorded jobline:** 360/416-8345. **Contact:** Human Resources. **World Wide Web address:** http://www.skagitvalleyhospital.org. **Description:** A nonprofit, regional health system offering a full line of medical services. **Positions advertised include:** Patient Services Secretary; Monitor Telemetry Technician; Unit Assistant; Imaging Manager; Certified Nursing Assistant; Registered Nurse. **Corporate headquarters location:** This location. **Operations at this facility include:** Administration. **Number of employees at this location:** 1,200.

SPACELABS MEDICAL, INC.
P.O. Box 7018, Issaquah WA 98027-7018. 425/657-7200. **Fax:** 425/657-7211. **Contact:** Human Resources Department. **E-mail address:** resumes@slmd.com. **World Wide Web address:** http://www.spacelabs.com. **Description:** Manufactures patient monitoring equipment, clinical information systems, ambulatory monitoring products, and monitoring supplies. **Positions advertised include:** Product Evaluation Specialist; CV Technologist. **Corporate headquarters location:** This location. **Other U.S. locations:** AZ; CA; CO; FL; NY; NC; OR. **Operations at this facility include:** Administration; Manufacturing; Research and Development. **Number of employees at this location:** 1,200. **Number of**

employees nationwide: 1,700.

STEVENS MEMORIAL HOSPITAL
21727 76th Avenue West, #102, Edmonds WA 98026. 425/640-4190. **Fax:** 425/640-4449. **Contact:** Human Resources Department. **World Wide Web address:** http://www.stevenshealthcare.org. **Description:** A 217-bed, acute care medical center offering a full range of health care services including emergency care, critical care, surgery, a birthing center, orthopedic care, comprehensive cancer care, mental health services, diagnostic imaging, and outpatient services. Founded in 1964.

SWEDISH MEDICAL CENTER
747 Broadway, Seattle WA 98122. 206/386-2141. **Recorded jobline:** 206/386-2888. **Fax:** 206/386-2145. **Contact:** Human Resources. **World Wide Web address:** http://www.swedish.org. **Description:** An 860-bed, full-service, acute care medical center that also provides a wide range of specialty services. **Positions advertised include:** Administrative Assistant; Medical Records Clerk; Nurse Manager; Registered Nurse; Accountant; Revenue Analyst. **Number of employees at this location:** 4,000.

TACOMA LUTHERAN HOME
1301 North Highlands Parkway, Tacoma WA 98406. 253/752-7112. **Contact:** Human Resources. **World Wide Web address:** http://www.tacomalutheran.com. **Description:** A retirement community providing skilled nursing, assisted living, and independent living services.

U.S. DEPARTMENT OF VETERANS AFFAIRS VA PUGET SOUND HEALTHCARE SYSTEM
1660 South Columbian Way, Seattle WA 98108. 206/764-2135. **Contact:** Human Resources. **World Wide Web address:** http://www.puget-sound.med.va.gov. **Description:** A 488-bed, critical care hospital affiliated with the University of Washington Medical School. The VA health care system includes 171 medical centers; more than 364 outpatient, community, and outreach clinics; 130 nursing home care units; and 37 domiciliary residences nationwide. **NOTE:** Employment forms may be downloaded from website. **Office hours:** Monday - Friday, 8:00 a.m. - 4:30 p.m. **Parent company:** U.S. Department of Veterans Affairs. **Number of employees at this location:** 1,800.

U.S. DEPARTMENT OF VETERANS AFFAIRS JONATHAN M. WAINWRIGHT MEMORIAL VA MEDICAL CENTER
77 Wainwright Drive, Walla Walla WA 99362. 509/525-5200. Fax: 509/527-3452. **Contact:** Human Resources. **Description:** A 66-bed facility providing traditional primary and secondary care plus psychiatry and substance abuse residential rehabilitation and CWT programs.

VISITING NURSE PERSONAL SERVICES
600 Birchwood Avenue, Suite 100, Bellingham WA 98225. 360/734-9662. **Contact:** Human Resources. **World Wide Web address:** http://www.vnaa.org. **Description:** Provides home health care and hospice services.

West Virginia

CHARLESTON AREA MEDICAL CENTER
P.O. Box 1574, Charleston WV 25326. 304/388-7458. **Physical address:** 511 Brooks Street, Charleston WV 25301. **Toll-free phone:** 800/323-5157. **Contact:** Employment Services. **World Wide Web address:** http://www.camc.org. **Description:** As the flagship of CAMC Health, the Medical Center is a 893-bed, non-profit, full-service, regional referral center. **NOTE:** For physician positions, fax 304/388-6297 or e-mail Diane Stanley, Physician Recruiter, at diane.stanley@camc.org. **Positions advertised include:** Dental Assistant; Pharmacy Technician; Phlebotomist; Vascular Technologist; Accountant Senior; Medical Records Supervisor; Cook; Housekeeper; Laundry Technician. **Number of employees at this location:** 5,000.

HEALTHSOUTH MOUNTAIN VIEW REGIONAL REHABILITATION HOSPITAL
1160 Van Voorhis Road, Morgantown WV 26505. 304/285-1034. **Fax:** 304/592-1103. **Contact:** Joy Bender, Human Resources. **E-mail address:** joy.bender@healthsouth.com. **World Wide Web address:** http://www.healthsouth.com. **Description:** An acute care, rehabilitation hospital with 80 beds that also offers outpatient services. **Positions advertised include:** Director of Business Operations; Occupational Therapist; Respiratory Therapist; Speech Pathologist; Physical Therapist; Pharmacist. **Corporate headquarters location:** Birmingham AL. **Other area locations:** Beckley; Bluefield; Fairmont; Huntington; Parkersburg; Princeton; Vienna. **Other U.S. Locations:** Nationwide. **Parent company:** HealthSouth Corporation. **Listed on:** New York Stock Exchange. **Stock exchange symbol:** HRC. **Number of employees nationwide:** 40,000.

HUNTINGTON INTERNAL MEDICINE GROUP
1115 20th Street, Huntington WV 25703. 304/528-4600. **Contact:** Human Resources. **E-mail address:** hr@uhswv.com. **World Wide Web address:** http://www.uhswv.com. **Description:** A multi-specialty group of 51 physician staff and 13 midlevel providers who treat clients at the HIMG Regional Medical Center as well as two satellite locations. **NOTE:** For physician positions contact Sarah Christy in the Physician Recruitment Office at 304/528-4657 or e-mail schristy@uhswv.com. **Positions advertised include:** Physician Openings in Various Departments. **Other area locations:** Putnam County; Westmoreland.

OHIO VALLEY MEDICAL CENTER
2000 Eoff Street, Wheeling WV 26003. 304/234-8615. **Contact:** Human Resources. **World Wide Web address:** http://www.ohiovalleymedicalcenter.com. **Description:** An acute care, full-service facility with 200 beds. **Positions advertised include:** Staff Development Educator; Phlebotomist/Registrar; Staff Nuclear Medical Technician; Senior Staff Pharmacist; Physical Therapist; Staff Technologist; Psychiatrist; Pharmacy Intern. **Number of employees at this location:** 844.

PETERSON REHABILITATION HOSPITAL AND GERIATRIC CENTER
20 Homestead Avenue, Wheeling WV 26003. 304/234-0500. **Contact:** Human Resources. **World Wide Web address:** http://www.ohiovalleymedicalcenter.com. **Description:** A 172-bed hospital divided into 3 divisions: skilled care; long-term care; and rehabilitation. Both inpatient and outpatient services are offered. **NOTE:** All resumes should be sent to the parent company at 2000 Eoff Street, Wheeling WV 26003. **Parent company:** Ohio Valley Health Services and Education Corp.

PRESTERA CENTER
3375 U.S. Route 60 East, Huntington WV 25705. 304/525-7851, extension 1006. **Fax:** 304/525-1504. **Contact:** Emily Fitzwater. **E-mail address:** emily.fitzwater@prestera.com. **World Wide Web address:** http://www.prestera.org. **Description:** A nonprofit, community-based, mental health center that offers outpatient and residential treatment for children, adolescents, and adults with behavioral problems, mental illness, or substance addictions. Operates 24 mental health sites in West Virginia. **Positions advertised include:** Cook; Office Assistant; IT Programmer; Contract Supervisor; Case Manager; Residential Assistant. **Special programs:** Internships; Summer Jobs. **Number of employees at this location:** 400.

WEST VIRGINIA UNIVERSITY HOSPITALS
1 Medical Center Drive, P.O. Box 8121, Morgantown WV 26506-8121. 304/598-4075. **Toll-free phone:** 800/453-5708. **Fax:** 304/598-4264. **Contact:** Human Resources. **E-mail address:** wvuhjobs@rcbhsc.wvu.edu.

World Wide Web address: http://www.health.wvu.edu. **Description:** A 450-bed teaching institution that includes Ruby Memorial Hospital, WVU Children's Hospital, Chestnut Ridge Hospital for Behavioral Medicine, the Jon Michael Moore Trauma Center, and Rosenbaum Family House. **Positions advertised include:** Chaplain Resident; Clinical Associate; Manager, Materials Distribution; Client Services Representative; Manager, Inpatient Pharmacy; Support Associate; Lead Dietetic Assistant; Financial Analyst; Phlebotomist; Director, Family House; Vice President for Quality and Patient Safety. **Number of employees at this location:** 3,600.

Wisconsin

A.N.S. HOME HEALTH SERVICES
2711 South 84th Street, West Allis WI 53227. 414/481-9800. **Toll-free phone:** 866/880-5042. **Fax:** 414/481-9808. **Contact:** Human Resources Department. **World Wide Web address:** http://www.anshomecare.com. **Description:** An agency that provides home health care services. **Corporate headquarters location:** This location.

AURORA HEALTH CARE
3000 West Mountain Street, Milwaukee WI 53215. 414/647-3000. **Fax:** 414/671-8111. **Contact:** Human Resources Department. **World Wide Web address:** http://www.aurorahealthcare.org. **Description:** Owns and operates several hospitals, medical groups, and walk-in clinics. Aurora Health Care is one of the largest not-for-profit health care corporations in Wisconsin. **Corporate headquarters location:** This location.

AURORA LAKELAND MEDICAL CENTER
W3985 County Road NN, P.O. Box 1002, Elkhorn WI 53121. 262/741-2000. **Fax:** 262/741-2482. **Recorded jobline:** 262/741-2833. **Contact:** Human Resources Supervisor. **World Wide Web address:** http://www.aurorahealthcare.org. **Description:** A 99-bed hospital. **Positions advertised include:** CNA; Occupational Therapist; Medical Transcriptionist; Radiology Technologist; Certified Nursing Assistant; Respiratory Therapist; Anesthesia Technician. **Corporate headquarters location:** Milwaukee WI. **Annual sales/revenues:** $21 - $50 million. **Number of employees at this location:** 500.

AURORA ST. LUKE'S MEDICAL CENTER
2900 West Oklahoma Avenue, Milwaukee WI 53215. 414/649-6000. **Fax:** 414/649-7982. **Contact:** Human Resources. **World Wide Web address:** http://www.aurorahealthcare.org. **Description:** A medical center providing a full range of health services. **Positions advertised include:** Phlebotomist; Supervisor, Endocrine Center; Radiologic Technologist; Coordinator, Research RN; Reimbursement Analyst; Pharmacist; Instructional Designer; Senior Medical Imaging Technician; Registered Nurse. **Corporate headquarters location:** This location. **Parent company:** Aurora Health Care.

BEACON HEALTH RESOURCE GROUP, INC.
12308 North Corporate Parkway, Suite 100, Mequon WI 53092-3380. 262/243-6100. **Fax:** 262/243-1207. **Contact:** Richard Omdahl, Human Resources Department. **World Wide Web address:** http://www.beaconhealth.org. **Description:** Provides services and distributes instructional literature, pamphlets, and videos to a variety of home care providers.

BEAVER DAM COMMUNITY HOSPITAL
707 South University Avenue, Beaver Dam WI 53916. 920/887-4100. **Fax:** 920/887-4101. **Recorded jobline:** 920/887-4102. **Contact:** Human Resources Department. **E-mail address:** jkrueger@bdch.org. **World Wide Web address:** http://www.bdch.com. **Description:** A nonprofit hospital offering a 125-bed acute care facility, a 123-bed skilled nursing facility, as well as home health services. **NOTE:** Entry-level positions as well as second and third shifts are offered. **Positions advertised include:** Registered Nurse; Licensed Practical Nurse. **Special programs:** Internships; Training. **Annual sales/revenues:** $21 - $50 million. **Number of employees at this location:** 750.

BELLIN MEMORIAL HOSPITAL
2020 Webster Avenue, P.O. Box 23400, Green Bay WI 54305-3400. 920/445-7240. **Fax:** 920/445-7249. **Recorded jobline:** 920/433-3559. **Contact:** Human Resources Specialist. **World Wide Web address:** http://www.bellin.org. **Description:** A 167-bed acute care hospital. **Positions advertised include:** AODA Therapist; Certified Registered Nurse Anesthetist; Counselor; Nuclear Medicine Technologist; Registered Nurse; Surgical Technologist; Ultrasonographer. **Number of employees at this location:** 2,300.

CAMTRONICS MEDICAL SYSTEMS
900 Walnut Ridge Drive, P.O. Box 950, Hartland WI 53029. 262/367-0700. **Fax:** 262/369-3192. **Contact:** Human Resources. **E-mail address:** employment@camtronics.com. **World Wide Web address:** http://www.camtronics.com. **Description:** Camtronics Medical Systems manufactures diagnostic imaging equipment for cardiology and radiology procedures. Founded in 1986. **Positions advertised include:** Customer Service Operations Analyst; Technical Instructor. **Corporate headquarters location:** This location. **Operations at this facility include:** Administration; Manufacturing.

CAPESIDE COVE GOOD SAMARITAN CENTER
23926 4th Avenue South, Siren WI 54872. 715/349-2292. **Fax:** 715/349-7218. **Contact:** Administrator. **World Wide Web address:** http://www.good-sam.com. **Description:** A nonprofit company providing long-term, short-term, and respite care services to adults. The center also has an outpatient therapy clinic that provides services for physical and occupational therapy, pain management, wound care, ostomy care, incontinence, podiatry, and behavioral management. **NOTE:** Entry-level positions and second and third shifts are offered. **Special programs:** Apprenticeships; Training. **Corporate headquarters location:** Sioux Falls SD. **Other area locations:** Fennimore WI; Lodi WI; Siren WI; Sister Bay WI; St. Croix Falls WI. **Other U.S. locations:** Nationwide. **Parent company:** Evangelical Lutheran Good Samaritan Society.

CHILDREN'S HOSPITAL OF WISCONSIN
P.O. Box 1997, Milwaukee WI 53201-1997. 414/266-2000. **Physical address:** 9000 West Wisconsin Avenue, Wauwatosa WI 53226. **Fax:** 414/266-6138. **Contact:** Human Resources. **World Wide Web address:** http://www.chw.org. **Description:** A hospital specializing in pediatric care. **Positions advertised include:** Senior Benefits Analyst; Clinical Dietitian; Pharmacy Technician; Utilization Management Specialist; Outcomes Statistical Analyst; Human Resources Recruiter; Health Unit Coordinator.

THEDA CLARK MEDICAL CENTER
130 2nd Street, P.O. Box 2021, Neenah WI 54956. 920/729-3100. **Fax:** 920/720-7290. **Recorded jobline:** 920/729-2024. **Contact:** Employment Coordinator. **E-mail address:** humanresources@thedacare.org. **World Wide Web address:** http://www.thedacare.org. **Description:** A 250-bed hospital located on Neenah's Doty Island. Specialized services include emergency department and trauma services including a Chest Pain Center; ThedaStar, a medical helicopter service; and Theda Clark Regional Birth Center, which offers single-room maternity care, high-risk obstetrical services, and neonatal intensive care. **Positions advertised include:** Physical Therapist; Licensed Practical Nurse; Registered Nurse; CNA. **Corporate headquarters location:** Appleton WI. **Parent company:** ThedaCare. **Number of employees at this location:** 1,400.

COLUMBIA ST. MARY'S COLUMBIA HOPSITAL
2025 East Newport Avenue, Milwaukee WI 53211. 414/326-2600. **Contact:** Human Resources. **World Wide Web address:** http://www.columbia-stmarys.org.

Description: A hospital affiliated with Columbia St. Mary's. **Positions advertised include:** Case Manager; Director of Performance Improvement and Accreditation; RN Clinical Instructor.

COLUMBIA ST. MARY'S HOSPITAL OZAUKEE
13111 North Port Washington Road, Mequon WI 53097. 414/326-2600. **Fax:** 262/243-7532. **Contact:** Human Resources. **World Wide Web address:** http://www.columbia-stmarys.org. **Description:** A nonprofit, acute care hospital with affiliated clinics. **NOTE:** Entry-level positions, part-time jobs, and second and third shifts are offered. **Advertised positions include:** Cardiovascular Tech; Clinical Nurse Specialist; Emergency Care Technician; Registered Nurse; Speech Language Pathologist. **Parent company:** Columbia St. Mary's. **Listed on:** Privately held. **Number of employees at this location:** 850.

CORE PRODUCTS
1505 Parker Avenue, Chetek WI 54728-0627. 715/924-4525. **Physical address:** 625 Fourth Street, Chetek WI 54728. **Fax:** 715/924-2662. **Contact:** Human Resources. **Description:** Manufactures orthopedic softgoods including medical and athletic braces.

CRITICARE SYSTEMS, INC.
20925 Crossroads Circle, Suite 100, Waukesha WI 53186-4054. 262/798-8282. **Fax:** 262/-798-8290. **Contact:** Human Resources. **World Wide Web address:** http://www.csiusa.com. **Description:** Designs, manufactures, and markets patient monitoring systems and noninvasive sensors. Founded in 1984. **Corporate headquarters location:** This location. **International locations:** Australia; Denmark; Japan; Singapore; Spain. **Listed on:** NASDAQ. **Stock exchange symbol:** CXIM.

DEAN MEDICAL CENTER
1808 West Beltline Highway, Madison WI 53713. 608/250-1500. **Fax:** 608/250-1441. **Recorded jobline:** 608/250-3326. **Contact:** Human Resources. **E-mail address:** deancareers@deancare.com. **World Wide Web address:** http://www.deancare.com. **Description:** A multispecialty group practice with over 30 locations in southwestern Wisconsin. **Positions advertised include:** Certified Nursing Assistant; Certified Medical Assistant; Database Administrator; Licensed Practical Nurse; Registered Nurse; Supervisor of Clinic Services; Drug Information Pharmacist. **Corporate headquarters location:** This location.

ENCORE SENIOR VILLAGE
5555 Burke Road, Madison WI 53704. 608/829-0909. **Fax:** 608/829-3040. **Contact:** Human Resources Department. **World Wide Web address:** http://www.encoresl.com. **Description:** A facility that specializes in caring for individuals with Alzheimer's disease. **Corporate headquarters location:** Portland OR.

EXTENDICARE HEALTH SERVICES
111 West Michigan Street, Milwaukee WI 53203-2903. 414/908-8000. **Toll-free phone:** 800/395-5000. **Fax:** 414/908-8143. **Contact:** Angela Komarek. **E-mail address:** akomarek@extendicare.com. **World Wide Web address:** http://www.extendicare.com. **Description:** Operates 148 long-term care facilities in North America. Services include medical rehabilitation, respiratory services, cardiac rehabilitation, infusion therapy, and wound care. **Positions advertised include:** Nursing Home Administrator; Community Care Branch Manager; Director of Nursing/Care; Nurse Consultant; Registered Nurse; Registered Dietician. **Corporate headquarters location:** This location. **Other U.S. locations:** Nationwide. **Parent company:** Extendicare, Inc. **Operations at this facility include:** Administration.

FRANCISCAN SKEMP MEDICAL CENTER
700 West Avenue South, La Crosse WI 54601. 608/791-9756. **Toll-free phone:** 800/246-6499. **Fax:** 608/791-9504. **Contact:** Human Resources Department. **World Wide Web address:** http://www.franciscanskemp.org. **Description:** A Mayo Health System affiliate providing health services to the tri-state communities of Iowa, Minnesota, and Wisconsin. The system includes hospitals, clinics, elderly care services, behavioral health, and services for women. **NOTE:** Entry-level positions are offered. **Positions advertised include:** Anesthesiologist; Dermatologist; Diabetes Nurse Educator; Hematologist/Oncologist; Invasive Cardiovascular Technologist; Mammography Technologist; Occupational Therapist; Neurosurgeon. **Corporate headquarters location:** This location. **Other area locations:** Statewide. **Other U.S. locations:** IA; MN. **Operations at this facility include:** Administration. **Number of employees at this location:** 2,900.

GE HEALTHCARE TECHNOLOGIES
3000 North Grandview Boulevard, Waukesha WI 53188. 262/544-3011. **Toll-free phone:** 800/643-6439. **Fax:** 414/355-3790. **Contact:** Human Resources. **World Wide Web address:** http://www.gehealthcare.com. **Description:** As a branch of GE Healthcare, GE Healthcare Technologies designs and manufactures medical electronic equipment, software, and systems for the diagnosis, monitoring, and computerized charting of patients. Major product lines include electrocardiographic equipment, patient monitors, clinical information systems, defibrillators, and instruments for respiratory and anesthetic gas analysis. **Positions advertised include:** GEHC Technology Security Director; Development Engineer; X-RAY Downstream Marketing Manager; Financial Analyst. **Corporate headquarters location:** This location. **Parent company:** General Electric.

GENTIVA HEALTH SERVICES
10909 West Greenfield, Suite 201, West Allis WI 53214. 414/257-1156. **Fax:** 414/257-1733. **Contact:** Human Resources. **World Wide Web address:** http://www.gentiva.com. **Description:** Gentiva Health Services provides home health care services, pharmaceutical support, and supplemental staffing services. **Positions advertised include:** Registered Nurse; Nurse Manager/Pediatrics; Branch Director; Physical Therapist. **Corporate headquarters location:** Melville NY. **Other area locations:** Racine WI. **Operations at this facility include:** This location is a home health care agency.

GUNDERSEN LUTHERAN MEDICAL CENTER
1900 South Avenue, H02-011, La Crosse WI 54601-5467. 608/782-7300. **Toll-free phone:** 800/362-9567, extension 54743. **Recorded jobline:** 866/651-1942. **Contact:** Human Resource Services. **E-mail address:** careers@gundluth.org. **World Wide Web address:** http://www.gundluth.org. **Description:** A not-for-profit healthcare system that includes a 325-bed teaching hospital with a Level II Trauma and Emergency Center, 26 medical clinics, seven behavioral health clinics, four reproductive care clinics, 11 vision centers, two affiliated hospitals, and four affiliated nursing homes. **Positions advertised include:** Administrative Director, Orthopaedics; Advanced Practice Nurse; Allergist; Budget Analyst; Cardiologist; Data Specialist; Dermatologist; Echocardiographer; Financial Analyst; Gastroenterologist; Coding Specialist; Medical Assistant; Pediatrician; Pharmacist; Radiologist. **Corporate headquarters location:** This location. **Other area locations:** Statewide. **Other U.S. locations:** IA; MN. **Number of employees at this location:** 5,500.

MARKESAN RESIDENT HOME, INC.
1130 North Margaret Street, P.O. Box 130, Markesan WI 53946. 920/398-2751. **Fax:** 920/398-3937. **Contact:** Business Office Manager. **Description:** A nonprofit nursing home with residential assisted living and Alzheimer's units. **NOTE:** Second and third shifts are offered. **Special programs:** Internships; Training. **Corporate headquarters location:** This location. **Listed on:** Privately held. **Number of employees at this location:** 90.

MARSHFIELD CLINIC
1000 North Oak Avenue, Marshfield WI 54449. 715/387-5511. **Toll-free phone:** 800/782-8581. **Fax:** 715/387-5240. **Contact:** Human Resources. **World Wide Web address:** http://www.marshfieldclinic.org. **Description:** Marshfield Clinic is the largest private group medical practice in Wisconsin and one of the largest in the United States, with 724 physicians representing 86 different medical specialties, 5,696 additional employees, and 41 regional centers/sites in 34 Wisconsin communities. **Corporate headquarters location:** This location. **Other area locations:** Statewide. **Number of employees at this location:** 450.

MEDA-CARE AMBULANCE SERVICE
2515 West Vliet Street, Milwaukee WI 53205. 414/342-1148. **Fax:** 414/342-0888. **Contact:** Linda Wiedmann, Director of Operations. **World Wide Web address:** http://www.meda-care.com. **Description:** Provides both emergency and non-emergency transportation via ambulance. **NOTE:** Second and third shifts are offered. **Positions advertised include:** Emergency Medical Technician; Paramedic; Registered Nurse; Respiratory Therapist. **Special programs:** Training. **Corporate headquarters location:** This location. **Listed on:** Privately held. **Annual sales/revenues:** $5 - $10 million. **Number of employees at this location:** 140.

MERCY HEALTH SYSTEM
MERCY HOSPITAL
1000 Mineral Point Avenue, P.O. Box 5003, Janesville WI 53547. 608/756-6721. **Fax:** 608/756-5627. **Recorded jobline:** 608/741-6979. **Contact:** Human Resources. **E-mail address:** hr@mhsjvl.org. **World Wide Web address:** http://www.mercyhealthsystem.org. **Description:** A health care system with 50 facilities in 21 communities that includes acute-care hospitals, skilled nursing centers, an independent living facility, and several ambulatory care centers. **NOTE:** Entry-level positions and second and third shifts are offered. **Positions advertised include:** Physical Therapist; Speech Therapist; Staff Pharmacist; CT Technician; MRI Technician; Radiology Technician; Respiratory Therapist; Ultrasound Technician; Radiation Therapist; RN; LPN. **Special programs:** Internships; Training; Summer Jobs. **Corporate headquarters location:** This location. **Other area locations:** Statewide. **Other U.S. locations:** IL. **Operations at this facility include:** Administration; Service. **Number of employees at this location:** 2,300.

MERITER HEALTH SERVICES INC.
202 South Park Street, Madison WI 53715. 608/267-6134. **Fax:** 608/267-6568. **Recorded jobline:** 608/267-6055. **Contact:** Michelle Burmester, Employment Coordinator. **E-mail address:** employment@meriter.com. **World Wide Web address:** http://www.meriter.com. **Description:** A full-service health care provider that includes Meriter Hospital, a 448-bed, nonprofit, acute care hospital; Meriter Retirement Services; Meriter Home Health; General Medical Laboratories; and The Meriter Foundation. **Positions advertised include:** Director, Medical Records; Patient Safety Administrator; Epic Support Analyst; Programmer Analyst; Registered Nurse; Nurse Manager; Pharmacy Technician; Phlebotomist; Clinical Nurse Educator. **Special programs:** Internships. **Corporate headquarters location:** This location.

MIDWEST DENTAL MANAGEMENT
680 Hehli Way, P.O. Box 69, Mondovi WI 54755. 715/926-5050. **Toll-free phone:** 800/782-7186. **Fax:** 715/926-5405. **Contact:** Human Resources. **E-mail address:** info@midwest-dental.com. **World Wide Web address:** http://www.midwest-dental.com. **Description:** Midwest Dental Management is a statewide dental practice management company providing dental services through 28 offices in Wisconsin, three offices in Minnesota, and three offices in Illinois. Founded in 1968. **NOTE:** Entry-level positions are offered. **Special programs:** Internships. **Corporate headquarters location:** This location. **Other area locations:** Statewide. **Operations at this facility include:** Administration; Service. **Annual sales/revenues:** $11 - $20 million. **Number of employees at this location:** 250.

THE MILWAUKEE CENTER FOR INDEPENDENCE
2020 West Wells Street, Milwaukee WI 53233. 414/937-2020. **Fax:** 414/937-2021. **Contact:** Human Resources. **E-mail address:** hr@mcfi.net. **World Wide Web address:** http://www.mcfi.net. **Description:** A non-profit, community-based rehabilitation facility that offers more than 50 programs and services to individuals and families with special needs. **NOTE:** Entry-level positions are offered. **Special programs:** Internships. **Number of employees at this location:** 250.

THE MONROE CLINIC
515 22nd Avenue, Monroe WI 53566. 608/324-1458. **Fax:** 608/324-2499. **Contact:** Sharon Mitchell, Human Resources Department. **E-mail address:** sharon_mitchell@monroeclinic.org. **World Wide Web address:** http://www.themonroeclinic.org. **Description:** A nonprofit, multispecialty, 100-bed general hospital with outpatient facilities. Founded in 1939. **NOTE:** Second and third shifts are offered. **Positions advertised include:** Registered Nurse; Licensed Practical Nurse; Respiratory Therapist; Medical Laboratory Technician; Phlebotomist; Interface Programmer. **Special programs:** Internships. **Corporate headquarters location:** This location. **Annual sales/revenues:** $21 - $50 million. **Number of employees at this location:** 920.

MORROW MEMORIAL HOME FOR THE AGED, INC.
331 South Water Street, Sparta WI 54656. 608/269-3168. **Fax:** 608/269-7642. **Contact:** Human Resources Director. **E-mail address:** info@morrowhome.org. **World Wide Web address:** http://www.morrowhome.org. **Description:** A nonprofit nursing home offering long-term care. Founded in 1917. **NOTE:** Entry-level positions, part-time jobs, and second and third shifts are offered. **Special programs:** Internships; Apprenticeships; Training; Co-ops; Summer Jobs. **Corporate headquarters location:** This location. **Number of employees at this location:** 130.

NEW GLARUS HOME INC.
600 Second Avenue, New Glarus WI 53574. 608/527-2126, extension 725. **Fax:** 608/527-5365. **Contact:** Sara Fredickson, Human Resources. **E-mail address:** slfredrickson@nghome.org. **World Wide Web address:** http://www.nghome.org. **Description:** A nursing and retirement home. **Annual sales/revenues:** Less than $5 million. **Number of employees at this location:** 100.

NORTH CENTRAL HEALTH CARE FACILITIES
1100 Lake View Drive, Wausau WI 54403. 715/848-4600. **Fax:** 715/845-5398. **Contact:** Human Resources. **World Wide Web address:** http://www.norcen.org. **Description:** A psychiatric hospital that provides diagnostic treatment of mental health disorders, alcohol and drug abuse, and developmental disabilities. **Corporate headquarters location:** This location. **Other area locations include:** Antigo WI; Merrill WI; Tomahawk WI. **Number of employees at this location:** 850.

NORTHWOODS MEDICAL CENTER
2383 State Highway 17, Phelps WI 54554. 715/545-2313. **Contact:** Human Resources. **Description:** A hospital with numerous facilities that offer a full range of medical services.

ST. CAMILLUS CAMPUS
10100 West Bluemound Road, Wauwatosa WI 53226. 414/259-6333. **Toll-free phone:** 800/317-9422. **Fax:** 414/259-7739. **Contact:** Pam Loveless, Human

Resources Director. **E-mail address:** hrd@stcam.com. **World Wide Web address:** http://www.stcam.com. **Description:** A nonprofit health care center offering home health care services, supportive living, adult day services, and a subacute unit. **NOTE:** Entry-level positions and second and third shifts are offered. **Positions advertised include:** Registered Nurse; Licensed Practical Nurse; Registered Nurse Case Manager; Home Health Aide. **Special programs:** Training. **Corporate headquarters location:** This location. **Number of employees at this location:** 625.

ST. JOSEPH'S HOSPITAL
611 Saint Joseph's Avenue, Marshfield WI 54449. 715/387-7880. **Toll-free phone:** 800/221-3733, extension 77880. **Fax:** 715/387-7001. **Contact:** Human Resource Services. **E-mail address:** sjhjobs@stjosephs-marshfield.org. **World Wide Web address:** http://www.ministryhealth.org. **Description:** A 504-bed, tertiary referral center and teaching hospital. **Positions advertised include:** Certified Nursing Assistant; Communication Specialist; EMS Coordinator; General Practice Pharmacy Resident; Physical Therapist; Respiratory Therapist; Radiology Technologist; Registered Nurse. **Corporate headquarters location:** This location. **Parent company:** Ministry Health Care. **Operations at this facility include:** Administration; Service. **Number of employees at this location:** 2,100.

ST. VINCENT HOSPITAL
835 South Van Buren Avenue, P.O. Box 13508, Green Bay WI 54307-3508. 920/433-8141. **Toll-free phone:** 800/236-3030. **Fax:** 920/431-3151. **Recorded jobline:** 920/431-3279. **Contact:** Human Resources Department. **World Wide Web address:** http://www.stvincenthospital.org. **Description:** A 547-bed, acute care hospital offering a wide variety of medical and diagnostic services. **Positions advertised include:** CT Tech, Radiology; Cancer Registrar; Cath Lab Registered Nurse; Certified Nursing Assistant; Director, Pediatrics; Director, Radiology; Echocardiographer; Medical Technologist; Medical Transcriptionist; Pharmacist. **Parent company:** The Hospital Sisters Health Systems. **Number of employees at this location:** 1,700.

SANNES SKOGDALEN
101 Sunshine Boulevard, P.O. Box 177, Soldiers Grove WI 54655. 608/624-5244. **Fax:** 608/624-3478. **Contact:** Donald A. Sannes, Administrator. **Description:** A nursing home. **Corporate headquarters location:** This location. **Parent company:** Milarn Inc. **Listed on:** Privately held. **Annual sales/revenues:** Less than $5 million. **Number of employees at this location:** 90.

SEVEN OAKS
6263 North Green Bay Road, Glendale WI 53209. 414/351-0543. **Fax:** 414/351-0239. **Contact:** Minnie Harris, Human Resources Director. **Description:** A 94-bed nursing home. **NOTE:** Entry-level positions are offered. **Corporate headquarters location:** This location. **Parent company:** Laureate Group. **Number of employees at this location:** 150.

SKAALEN RETIREMENT SERVICES
400 North Morris Street, Stoughton WI 53589. 608/873-5651, extension 308. **Fax:** 608/873-0696. **Contact:** Assistant Administrator/Human Resource Director. **E-mail address:** khorton@skaalen.com. **World Wide Web address:** http://www.skaalen.com. **Description:** Offers a skilled nursing care facility, assisted living, two residences with support services for independent adults, and a retirement apartment and condominium community. **NOTE:** Entry-level positions are offered. **Positions advertised include:** Registered Nurse; Licensed Practical Nurse; Certified Nursing Assistant. **Annual sales/revenues:** $5 - $10 million. **Number of employees at this location:** 300.

SMITHS MEDICAL PM, INC.
N7 W22025 Johnson Road, Waukesha WI 53186-1856. 262/542-3100. **Toll-free phone:** 800/558-2345. **Fax:** 262/542-2301. **Contact:** Human Resources. **E-mail address:** hr@smiths-bci.com. **World Wide Web address:** http://www.smiths-medical.com. **Description:** Manufactures noninvasive patient equipment that monitors respiration, exhaled gases, anesthetic agents, blood pressure, and temperature. **Corporate headquarters locations:** This location. **Parent company:** Smiths Group plc. **Numbers of employees at this location:** 100.

SUNRISE MEDICAL
5001 Joerns Drive, Stevens Point WI 54481-5040. 715/341-3600. **Toll-free phone:** 800/826-0270. **Fax:** 303/928-5759. **Contact:** Human Resources. **World Wide Web address:** http://www.sunrisemedical.com. **Description:** Manufactures homecare and extended care products Founded in 1983. **NOTE:** Entry-level positions are offered. **Special programs:** Training. **Corporate headquarters location:** Carlsbad CA. **Listed on:** New York Stock Exchange. **Stock exchange symbol:** SMD. **Annual sales/revenues:** $11 - $20 million. **Number of employees at this location:** 70. **Number of employees nationwide:** 2,000. **Number of employees worldwide:** 3,200.

TOMAH MEMORIAL HOSPITAL
321 Butts Avenue, Tomah WI 54660. 608/372-2181. **Fax:** 608/374-6615. **Contact:** Human Resources. **E-mail address:** breinert@tomahhospital.org. **World Wide Web address:** http://www.tomahhospital.org. **Description:** A nonprofit, 49-bed general hospital. **NOTE:** Part-time jobs and second and third shifts are offered. **Positions advertised include:** Certified Occupational Therapy Assistant. **Number of employees at this location:** 200.

TOUCHPOINT HEALTH PLAN
5 Innovation Court, Appleton WI 54914. 920/735-6300. **Toll-free phone:** 800/735-6305. **Fax:** 920/831-6886. **Contact:** Human Resources. **World Wide Web address:** http://www.touchpointhealth.com. **Description:** A health plan with 145,000 members. **Corporate headquarters location:** This location. **Other area locations:** Green Bay WI; Sheboygan WI.

U.S. DEPARTMENT OF VETERANS AFFAIRS TOMAH VA MEDICAL CENTER
500 East Veterans Street, Tomah WI 54660. 608/372-1638. **Toll-free phone:** 800/872-8662, extension 61632. **Contact:** Linda O'Neil, Recruitment/Staffing. **World Wide Web address:** http://www.visn12.med.va.gov/tomah. **Description:** A 271-bed medical facility that offers primary care, mental health services and nursing home care to eligible veterans. **Positions available include:** Motor Vehicle Operator.

VERNON MANOR
E7404A, County Road BB, Viroqua WI 54665. 608/637-5400. **Fax:** 608/637-5441. **Contact:** Administrator. **Description:** A nursing home. Founded in 1981. **NOTE:** Entry-level positions are offered. **Special programs:** Internships. **Corporate headquarters location:** This location. **Parent company:** Vernon County. **Annual sales/revenues:** Less than $5 million. **Number of employees at this location:** 120.

VISITING NURSE ASSOCIATION
520 North 32nd Avenue, Wausau WI 54401. 715/847-2600. **Fax:** 715/847-2607. **Contact:** Human Resources. **Description:** Provides health services to patients in their home or place of residence. Services include nursing, physical therapy, occupational therapy, speech pathology, nutritional therapy, mental health and enterostomal therapy, medical social services, and hospice care.

WALGREEN HEALTH INITIATIVES
1435 North 113th Street, Milwaukee WI 53226. 414/256-7234. **Fax:** 414/908-2530. **Contact:** Human Resources. **E-mail address:** corporate.opportunities@walgreens.com. **World Wide Web address:** http://www.walgreenshealth.com.

Description: Sells medical supplies and equipment to nursing homes, operates institutional pharmacies for long-term care facilities, and provides home health care services. Founded in 1986. **Corporate headquarters location:** Deerfield IL. **Other area locations:** Eau Claire WI; Green Bay WI; Madison WI; Wauwatosa WI; Windsor WI. **Other U.S. locations:** Nationwide.

WAUKESHA MEMORIAL HOSPITAL
725 American Avenue, Waukesha WI 53188. 262/928-7969. **Toll-free phone:** 800/326-2011. **Fax:** 262/544-6437. **Contact:** Barb Dyer, Human Resources Coordinator. **E-mail address:** careers@phci.org. **World Wide Web address:** http://www.waukeshamemorial.org. **Description:** A 300-bed acute care hospital. The hospital operates as part of Waukesha Hospital System, Inc. Founded in 1914. **NOTE:** Entry-level positions and second and third shifts are offered. **Positions advertised include:** Accountant; CT Technologist; Registered Nurse; Clinical Dietician; Echo Lab Coordinator; Licensed Practical Nurse; Information Systems Clinical Specialist. **Parent company:** ProHealth Care, Inc. **Listed on:** Privately held. **Annual sales/revenues:** More than $100 million. **Number of employees at this location:** 2,600.

Wyoming

CAMPBELL COUNTY MEMORIAL HOSPITAL
P.O. Box 3011, Gillette WY 82717. 307/682-8811. **Physical address:** 501 South Burma Avenue, Gillette WY 82716. **Toll-free phone:** 800/208-2043. **Contact:** Human Resources. **E-mail address:** hr@ccmh.net. **World Wide Web address:** http://www.ccmh.net. **Description:** A 90-bed community and area trauma hospital. Designated as a Level II Trauma Center and a Level II Intensive Care Nursery. The hospital also has a Special Care Nursery for older infants who require hospital care. The hospital also offers outpatient care services, intensive and critical care services, home health services, radiology and imaging services, emergency services, rehabilitation services, laboratory services, cardiopulmonary services, and mental and behavioral health services. **NOTE:** See website for current openings, to download an application and apply for positions. If the specific position you are interested in is not listed, please e-mail the Human Resources department. Positions are always available for RNs, LPNs and CNAs. **Positions advertised include:** Counselor III, Mental Health; Registered Respiratory Therapist; Information Systems Analyst; Physical Therapist/Physical Therapist Assistant; Radiology Tech III; Ultrasonographer; Surgical Tech; Childcare Supervisor; Childcare Tech; Wellness Intern.

MEMORIAL HOSPITAL OF CONVERSE COUNTY
111 South Fifth Street, Douglas WY 82433. 307/358-2122. **Fax:** 307/358-3630. **Contact:** Linda York, Human Resources Officer. **E-mail address:** lyork@mhccwyo.org. **World Wide Web address:** http://www.conversehospital.com. **Description:** A nonprofit, 44-bed county hospital. **NOTE:** See website to download an application, submit an online resume and browse current openings. Job categories include Administration; Physician Opportunities; Ambulance/Emergency Medical Services; Certified Nursing Assistant; Dietary; Lab Tech; LPN; Materials management; Medical Assistant; Nuclear Medicine; Radiology; Registered Nurse. **Office hours:** Monday - Friday, 8:30 a.m. - 5:00 p.m.

MEMORIAL HOSPITAL OF SWEETWATER COUNTY
200 College Drive, Rock Springs WY 82901. 307/362-3711. **Fax:** 307/362-8391. **Contact:** Human Resources. **E-mail address:** mhschr@mineralhospital.com. **World Wide Web address:** http://www.minershospital.com. **Description:** A 99-bed, acute care hospital. Services include anesthesiology, emergency care, general surgery, internal medicine, obstetrics, ophthalmology, plastic surgery, radiology, and urology. **NOTE:** See website for current openings and download an application. Employment application and release form must be submitted together. **Positions advertised include:** C.N.A./N.U.S.; Collections Clerk; Data/Filing Clerk; Dietary Aide; Director of Clinical Lab; Director of Health Information Management; Foundation Director; Housekeeper/Custodian; Marketing & Public Relations Manager; P.C. Specialist; P.C./ Network Specialist; Physician positions; Quality Analyst; Registered Nurse. **Number of employees at this location:** 365.

U.S. DEPARTMENT OF VETERANS AFFAIRS VETERANS ADMINISTRATION MEDICAL CENTER
2360 East Pershing Boulevard, Mail Stop 05, Cheyenne WY 82001. 307/778-7331. **Fax:** 307/778-7336. **Contact:** Human Resources. **World Wide Web address:** http://www.va.gov. **Description:** The Cheyenne VA Medical Center and regional office center provide veterans with primary and secondary inpatient services in medicine and surgery as well as outpatient services in medicine, surgery and psychiatry. Presently, there is an operating bed level of 21 hospital beds; 12 general medical beds, 5 intermediate beds and 4 general surgical beds. The Medical Center also supports a 50-bed Nursing Home Care Unit located within the main hospital building. Cheyenne also maintains Community Based Outpatient Clinics (CBOCs) in Fort Collins and Greeley, Colorado and Sidney, Nebraska. **NOTE:** See VA website for current positions and application instructions.

UNITED MEDICAL CENTER
UMC West, 214 East 23rd Street, Cheyenne WY 82001. 307/633-7761. **Fax:** 307/633-7714. **Recorded jobline:** 800/477-4520. **Contact:** Lesley Rider, Human Resources. **E-mail address:** rdagenhart@umcwy.org. **World Wide Web address:** http://www.umcwy.org. **Description:** A 219-bed medical center providing a wide range of medical services including cardiac services that covers acute cardiac care; emergency care for trauma, coronary, adult, and pediatric cases; a 17-bed oncology unit with a low patient to nurse ratio; a short-term, 16-bed, behavioral health unit; maternal/child services with six labor and delivery rooms, a general nursery, and post-partum care; a 15-bed rehabilitation unit operated by Spalding Rehabilitation Hospital; and a series of surgical procedures. **NOTE:** See website for current positions and to apply online. **Positions advertised include:** Numerous positions available in the areas of clerical/administrative support; information technology; management/professional; nursing; nursing support; service/trade.

WEST PARK HOSPITAL
707 Sheridan Avenue, Cody WY 82414. 307/578-2299. **Toll-free phone:** 800/654-9447. **Contact:** Kim Sommers, Human Resources. **E-mail address:** hrdept@wphcody.org. **World Wide Web address:** http://www.westparkhospital.org. **Description:** The hospital is under management contract with Quorum Health Resources. It is a facility licensed for 25 beds, with an adjacent 128-bed long-term care center and a 20-bed chemical dependency center. Some of the regional services provided are acute hospital care, 24-hour emergency/ambulance, outpatient services, dialysis, home health and hospice, cardiac and physical rehabilitation, chemical dependency treatment and urgent care. Thirty-nine physicians on staff provide specialty as well as primary medical care. **NOTE:** See website for current positions and to apply online. **Positions advertised include:** RN/LPN; Physical Therapy Tech; Speech Therapist; Occupational Therapist; Surgical Technician; Certified Nursing Assistant; Director of Nursing; Counselor. Substance Abuse & Mental Health; Receptionist/Insurance Assistant; Massage Therapist Coordinator; Housekeeper. **Number of employees at this location:** 300.

WYOMING MEDICAL CENTER
1233 East Second Street, Casper WY 82601. 307/577-2406. **Toll-free phone:** 800/822-7201. **Fax:** 307/577-2579. **Contact:** Human Resources. **World Wide Web**

address: http://www.wmcnet.org. **Description:** A community-owned, not-for-profit licensed 206-bed regional medical center, which is the state's largest medical facility and regional trauma center. **NOTE:** Applications accepted for open positions only. See website for current openings. Applicants are encouraged to apply online; contact the HR office if this is not possible. **Positions advertised include:** Numerous positions available in the areas of clerical/administrative support; information technology; management/professional; nursing; nursing support; service/trade. **Number of employees at this location:** 1,000.

WYOMING STATE HOSPITAL
P.O. Box 177, Evanston WY 82931-0177. 307/789-3464. **Fax:** 307/789-7373. **Contact:** Human Resources. **World Wide Web address:** http://mentalhealth.state.wy.us/hospital/index.html. **Description:** A 122-bed facility that offers several treatment program services, including adult and adolescent services, a co-occurring diagnosis/substance abuse program, forensic treatment services, behavioral health residential services, a therapeutic learning center and outpatient programs. **Special programs:** Internships. **Number of employees at this location:** 450.

HOTELS AND RESTAURANTS

You can expect to find the following types of companies in this section:

Casinos • Dinner Theaters • Hotel/Motel Operators • Resorts • Restaurants

---

Accommodation occupations numbered 1,796,000 in 2004, and should increase by 16.9% or 304,000 jobs over the next decade. Food preparation and serving related occupations – including chefs, cooks, food preparation workers, food service managers, food and beverage serving workers and related workers – employed 8,850,000 and is expected to grow by 1,451,000 new jobs to 10,301,000, a 16.4% increase. Job growth reflects increases in population, dual-income families, and dining sophistication. While job growth will create new positions, the overwhelming majority of job openings will stem from the need to replace workers who leave this large occupational group.

Alabama

SHERATON BIRMINGHAM

2101 Richard Arrington Junior Boulevard North, Birmingham AL 35203. 205/324-5000. **Fax:** 205/307-3079. **Contact:** Jean Pruiet, Employment Manager. **World Wide Web address:** http://www.sheraton.com. **Description:** A hotel and convention center. **Other U.S. locations:** Nationwide. **International locations:** Worldwide. **Operations at this facility include:** Administration; Sales; Service. **Annual sales/revenues:** $11 - $20 million. **Number of employees at this location:** 400. **Number of employees nationwide:** 60,000. **Number of employees worldwide:** 100,000.

WALL STREET DELI SYSTEMS, INC.

2001 Park Place, Birmingham AL 35203. 205/252-7258. **Contact:** Human Resources. **E-mail address:** jobs@wallstreetdeli.com. **World Wide Web Address:** http://www.wallstreetdeli.com. **Description:** One location of a chain of delicatessen-style restaurants operating in office buildings, business centers, and high-volume retail districts. Through an agreement with Host Marriott, the company also franchises in airports, shopping malls, and roadside service areas. **Corporate headquarters location:** Lake Success NY. **Other U.S. locations:** Nationwide.

Alaska

THE HOTEL CAPTAIN COOK

4th and K Street, Anchorage AK 99501. 907/276-6000. **Toll-free phone:** 800/843-1950. **Fax:** 907/343-2441. **Contact:** Raquel Edelen, Human Resources Director. **World Wide Web address:** http://www.captaincook.com. **Description:** A 565-room, luxury hotel. Founded in 1966. **NOTE:** Resumes should be sent to: 939 West Fifth Avenue, Anchorage AK 99501. **Special programs:** Summer Jobs. **Corporate headquarters location:** This location. **Listed on:** Privately held. **President:** Walter Hickel, Jr. **Number of employees at this location:** 450.

Arizona

ARAMARK/LAKE POWELL RESORTS AND MARINAS

P.O. Box 1597, Page AZ 86040. 928/645-1081. 928/645-2433. **Fax:** 928/645-1031. **Contact:** Human Resources. **E-mail address:** lprm-hr@aramark.com. **World Wide Web address:** http://www.aramark.com. **Description:** Operates five marinas on Lake Powell and owns resorts located throughout the Glen Canyon recreation area. **Special programs:** Internships. **Corporate headquarters location:** Philadelphia PA. **Other U.S. locations:** Nationwide. **Parent company:** ARAMARK is one of the world's leading providers of managed services. The company operates in all 50 states and 10 foreign countries, offering a broad range of services to businesses of all sizes, including most *Fortune* 500 companies and thousands of universities; hospitals; and municipal, state, and federal government facilities. ARAMARK's businesses include Food, Leisure, and Support Services including Campus Dining Services, School Nutrition Services, Business Dining Services, International Services, Health Care Support Services, Conference Center Management, and Refreshment Services; Facility Services; Correctional Services; Industrial Services; Uniform Services, which include Uniform Services and Wearguard, a direct marketer of work clothing; Health and Education Services, including Spectrum Healthcare Services and Children's World Learning Centers; and Book and Magazine Services. **Listed on:** New York Stock Exchange. **Stock exchange symbol:** RMK. **Number of employees at this location:** 1,200.

ARIZONA BILTMORE RESORT & SPA

2400 East Missouri Avenue, Phoenix AZ 85016. 602/955-6600. **Fax:** 602/954-2571. **Recorded jobline:** 602/954-2547. **Contact:** Director of Human Resources. **E-mail address:** resume@arizonabiltmore.com. **World Wide Web address:** http://www.arizonabiltmore.com. **Description:** A resort offering extensive lodging and dining facilities. Founded in 1929. **NOTE:** Entry-level positions and second and third shifts are offered. **Positions advertised include**: On-Call Banquet Servers; Concierge; Laundry Manager; Pool Attendant; Purchasing Storeroom Clerk; Director of Engineering; Banquet Manager. **Special programs:** Internships. **Listed on:** Privately held. **Number of employees at this location:** 900.

AZTAR CORPORATION

2390 East Camelback Road, Suite 400, Phoenix AZ 85016. 602/381-4100. **Contact:** Human Resources. **World Wide Web address:** http://www.aztar.com. **Description:** Operates casino hotel facilities including Tropicana Casino and Resort (Atlantic City NJ), Tropicana Resort and Casino (Las Vegas NV), Ramada Express Hotel and Casino (Laughlin NV), Casino Aztar (Evansville IN), and Casino Aztar (Caruthersville MO). **Listed on:** New York Stock Exchange. **Stock exchange symbol:** AZR.

BEST WESTERN COTTONWOOD INN

993 South Main Street, Cottonwood AZ 86326. 928/634-5575. **Contact:** Personnel. **World Wide Web address:** http://www.cottonwoodinn-az.com. **Description:** A full-service hotel and resort. **Other U.S. locations:** Nationwide.

BEST WESTERN INTERNATIONAL

6201 North 24th Parkway, Phoenix, AZ 85016. 602/957-4200. **Contact:** Human Resources. **World Wide Web address:** http://www.bestwestern.com. **Description:** The world's largest hotel chain with over 4,200 hotels in 80 countries including over 1,000 in Europe. Best Western has over 1,900 meeting facilities worldwide including 900 in the United States. **NOTE:** Resumes accepted only for open positions. **Positions advertised include:** Design Consultant; Sales Service Representative; Manager, Travel Agent Accounts; Marketing Project Specialist; Sales Director, Canada. **Corporate headquarters location:** This location.

BILL JOHNSON'S RESTAURANTS INC.

2906 West Fairmount Avenue, Phoenix AZ 85017. 602/264-5565. **Contact:** Diane Perkins, Personnel Director. **World Wide Web address:** http://www.billjohnsons.com. **Description:** Operates the Bill Johnson's chain of family-style BBQ restaurants. **Corporate headquarters location:** This location.

THE BOULDERS RESORT
34631 North Tom Darlington Drive, P.O. Box 2090, Carefree AZ 85377. 480/488-9009. **Recorded jobline:** 480/488-0992. **Contact:** Human Resources. **World Wide Web address:** http://www.wyndham.com. **Description:** A 160-casita, luxury resort and spa that offers a variety of activities including 36 holes of golf and six tennis courts. **NOTE:** Entry-level positions, second and third shifts, and part-time jobs are offered. **Positions advertised include:** Executive Chef. **Special programs:** Internships; Apprenticeships; Training. **Corporate headquarters location:** Dallas TX. **Parent company:** Wyndham International, Inc. **Listed on:** New York Stock Exchange. **Stock exchange symbol:** WYN. **Number of employees at this location:** 650.

CROWNE PLAZA
2532 West Peoria Avenue, Phoenix AZ 85029. 602/943-2341. **Recorded jobline:** 480/545-3668. **Contact:** Human Resources. **World Wide Web address:** http://www.ichotelsgroup.com. **Description:** A full-service hotel. **NOTE:** Interested jobseekers may apply in person Monday - Friday, 9:00 a.m. - 4:00 p.m. **Corporate headquarters location:** London, England. **Parent company:** InterContinental hotels Group. **Number of employees at this location:** 250.

ED DEBEVIC'S RESTAURANT
2102 East Highland Avenue, Phoenix AZ 85016. 602/956-2760. **Contact:** Human Resources. **World Wide Web address:** http://www.eddebevics.com. **Description:** One location of the casual dining restaurant chain. Ed Debevic's serves American cuisine and operates a gift shop. **Corporate headquarters location:** Chicago IL. **Parent company:** Ed Debevic's Restaurant Corp.

DOUBLETREE GUEST SUITES HOTEL
320 North 44th Street, Phoenix AZ 85008. 602/225-0500. **Fax:** 602/231-0561. **Recorded jobline:** 602/225-0328. **Contact:** Human Resources. **World Wide Web address:** http://www.doubletree.com. **Description:** An independent franchise, this location of Doubletree Guest Suites Hotel has 242 rooms and conference center facilities. **NOTE:** Entry-level positions and second and third shifts are offered. **Special programs:** Internships; Training. **Corporate headquarters location:** Beverly Hills CA. **Other U.S. locations:** Nationwide. **Parent company:** Hilton Hotels Corporation. **Listed on:** New York Stock Exchange. **Stock exchange symbol:** HLT. **Annual sales/revenues:** $5 - $10 million. **Number of employees at this location:** 200.

ECONO LODGE UNIVERSITY
914 South Milton Road, Flagstaff AZ 86001-6386. 928/774-7326. **Contact:** Human Resources. **World Wide Web address:** http://www.comfortinn.com. **Description:** A 67-room economy hotel. **Corporate headquarters location:** Silver Spring MD. **Other U.S. locations:** Nationwide. **International locations:** Worldwide. **Parent company:** Choice Hotels International. **Listed on:** New York Stock Exchange. **Stock exchange symbol:** CHH.

EEGEE'S
3360 East Ajo Way, Tucson AZ 85713-5228. 520/294-3333. **Contact:** Human Resources. **World Wide Web address:** http://www.eegees.com. **Description:** Operates 21 fast-food restaurants in Tucson. The company has its own bakery on the premises and makes rolls and cookies on a daily basis.

EMBASSY SUITES AIRPORT WEST
2333 East Thomas Road, Phoenix AZ 85016. 602/957-1910. **Fax:** 602/955-2861. **Contact:** Personnel. **World Wide Web address:** http://www.embassysuites.com. **Description:** An all-suites hotel and conference facility. **Office hours:** Monday through Friday, 8:00 a.m. - 5:00 p.m. **Corporate headquarters location:** Beverly Hills CA. **Parent company:** Hilton Hotels Corporation. **Listed on:** New York Stock Exchange. **Stock exchange symbol:** HLT.

EMBASSY SUITES FLAGSTAFF
706 South Milton Road, Flagstaff AZ 86001. 928/774-4333. **Contact:** Personnel. **World Wide Web address:** http://www.embassyflagstaff.com. **Description:** An all-suites hotel. **Corporate headquarters location:** Beverly Hills CA. **Parent company:** Hilton Hotels Corporation. **Listed on:** New York Stock Exchange. **Stock exchange symbol:** HLT.

FAIRFIELD FLAGSTAFF RESORT
1900 North Country Club Drive, Flagstaff AZ 86004. 928/526-3232. **Contact:** Human Resources. **World Wide Web address:** http://www.efairfield.com. **Description:** A golf resort and country club. **Parent company:** Cendant Corporation.

HIDDEN PALMS ALL SUITE INN
2100 Swanson Avenue, Lake Havasu City AZ 86403. 928/855-7144. **Toll-free phone:** 800/254-5611. **Fax:** 928/855-2620. **Contact:** Human Resources. **World Wide Web address:** http://www.hiddenpalms.com. **Description:** A full-service hotel offering guest suites that include kitchens and dining areas. **Office hours:** Monday - Friday, 8:00 a.m. - 8:00 p.m.

HILTON GARDEN INN FLAGSTAFF
350 West Forest Meadows Street, Flagstaff AZ 86001. 928/226-8888. **Contact:** Human Resources. **World Wide Web address:** http://www.hilton.com. **Description:** A 90-room, full-service hotel for business and leisure travelers. **Parent company:** Hilton Hotels Corporation. **Listed on:** New York Stock Exchange. **Stock exchange symbol:** HLT.

HILTON PHOENIX EAST/MESA
1011 West Holmes Avenue, Mesa AZ 85210. 480/833-5555. **Fax:** 480/649-1886. **Recorded jobline:** 480/844-6044. **Contact:** Human Resources. **World Wide Web address:** http://www.hilton.com. **Description:** A 263-room hotel. **NOTE:** Entry-level positions and second and third shifts are offered. **Positions advertised include:** Line Cook; Desk Clerk; Engineer; Room Attendant; Business Center Attendant. **Special programs:** Internships. **Corporate headquarters location:** Beverly Hills CA. **Parent company:** Hilton Hotels Corporation. **Listed on:** New York Stock Exchange. **Stock exchange symbol:** HLT. **Number of employees at this location:** 200. **Number of employees nationwide:** 800.

HYATT REGENCY PHOENIX
122 North Second Street, Phoenix AZ 85004. 602/252-1234. **Toll-free phone:** 800/223-1234. **Fax:** 602/440-3124. **Recorded jobline:** 602/440-3154. **Contact:** Valerie Saito, Director of Human Resources. **World Wide Web address:** http://www.hyatt.com. **Description:** A full-service hotel with 712 guest rooms including 45 suites. The Hyatt Regency Phoenix also features 42,000 square feet of meeting space as well as several restaurants and lounges. This location also hires seasonally. **NOTE:** Entry-level positions, part-time jobs, and second and third shifts are offered. **Positions advertised include:** Assistant Engineering Director; Assistant Restaurant Manager; Banquet Captain. **Corporate headquarters location:** Chicago IL. **Other U.S. locations:** Nationwide. **International locations:** Worldwide. **Number of employees at this location:** 500. **Number of employees worldwide:** 45,000.

KFC
4515 South McClintock Drive, Suite 206, Tempe AZ 85282-7382. 480/491-5511. **Contact:** Human Resources. **World Wide Web address:** http://www.kfc.com. **Description:** KFC is a fast-food restaurant chain specializing in chicken dinners. **Corporate headquarters location:** Louisville KY. **Operations at this facility include:** This location houses administrative offices. **Parent company:** Yum! Brands, Inc. **Listed on:** New York Stock Exchange. **Stock exchange symbol:** YUM. **Number of employees at this location:** 8,500.

LA QUINTA INN AND SUITES FLAGSTAFF
2015 South Beulah Boulevard, Flagstaff AZ 86001. 928/556-8666. **Contact:** Human Resources. **World Wide Web address:** http://www.laquinta.com. **Description:** A full-service hotel. **Corporate headquarters location:** Irving TX. **Parent company:** La Quinta Inns operates a nationwide chain of lodging inns. The company has more than 280 locations in 28 states. **Listed on:** New York Stock Exchange. **Stock exchange symbol:** LQI.

LITTLE AMERICA HOTEL
2515 East Butler Avenue, Flagstaff AZ 86004. 928/779-2741. **Fax:** 928/779-7983. **Contact:** Human Resources. **World Wide Web address:** http://www.littleamerica.com/flagstaff. **Description:** A full-service hotel and convention center.

LONDON BRIDGE RESORT
1477 Queens Bay Road, Lake Havasu City AZ 86403. 928/855-0880. **Contact:** Manager. **World Wide Web address:** http://www.londonbridgeresort.com. **Description:** A full-service hotel and resort featuring 120 studios and suites, a restaurant, a dance club, an off-track betting facility, and a nine-hole executive golf course. **Positions advertised include:** Sales Manager; Assistant Manager. **Parent company:** Epic Resorts.

MAIN STREET RESTAURANT GROUP, INC.
5050 North 40th Street, Suite 200, Phoenix AZ 85018. 602/852-9000. **Fax:** 602/852-9086. **Contact:** Personnel. **World Wide Web address:** http://www.mainandmain.com. **Description:** A casual dining and family entertainment company that operates four restaurant brands including TGI Friday's. **NOTE:** Entry-level positions are offered. **Positions advertised include:** Store Manager; Server; Busser; Door Person; Line Cook; Dishwasher; Prep Cook. **Corporate headquarters location:** This location. **Operations at this facility include:** Sales; Service. **Listed on:** NASDAQ. **Stock exchange symbol:** MAIN. **Annual sales/revenues:** $51 - $100 million. **Number of employees nationwide:** 4,500.

MARRIOTT CAMELBACK INN
5402 East Lincoln Drive, Scottsdale AZ 85253. 480/948-1700. **Contact:** Manager of Human Resources. **World Wide Web address:** http://www.marriott.com. **Description:** A full-service, 453-room hotel and resort facility. **Corporate headquarters location:** Bethesda MD. **Parent company:** Marriott International Inc. **Listed on:** New York Stock Exchange. **Stock exchange symbol:** MAR.

McDUFFY'S SPORTS BAR & OFF-TRACK BETTING
P.O. Box 1570, Tempe AZ 85281. 480/966-5600. **Physical address:** 230 West Fifth Street, Tempe AZ 85281. **Fax:** 480/966-6582. **Contact:** Hiring Manager. **World Wide Web address:** http://www.mcduffys.com. **Description:** Operates a full-service restaurant and bar and offers pool tables, games, and live entertainment. McDuffy's also houses off-track betting facilities. **Other area locations:** Peoria AZ.

NAUTICAL INN RESORT & CONFERENCE CENTER
1000 McCulloch Boulevard, Lake Havasu City AZ 86403. 928/855-2141. **Toll-free phone:** 800/892-2141. **Fax:** 928/453-5808. **Contact:** Human Resources. **E-mail address:** careers@nauticalinn.com. **World Wide Web address:** http://www.nauticalinn.com. **Description:** A hotel with 150 beachfront room and condos. The resort features a private beach and waterfront restaurants.

PETER PIPER PIZZA, INC.
14635 North Kierland Boulevard, Suite 160, Scottsdale AZ 85254. 480/609-6400. **Toll-free phone:** 800/899-3425. **Fax:** 480/609-6520. **Contact:** Kenny Holmes, Director of Human Resources. **E-mail address:** recruiting@peterpiperpizza.com. **World Wide Web address:** http://www.peterpiperpizza.com. **Description:** Operates a chain of family-style pizza restaurants with 130 locations in six states and Mexico. Founded in 1973. **NOTE:** Entry-level positions and second and third shifts are offered. **Company slogan:** The pizza people pick. **Special programs:** Training; Summer Jobs. **Corporate headquarters location:** This location. **Other U.S. locations:** CA; NV; TX; UT. **Operations at this facility include:** Administration. **Annual sales/revenues:** $51 - $100 million. **Number of employees at this location:** 65. **Number of employees nationwide:** 1,600.

THE PHOENICIAN
6000 East Camelback Road, Scottsdale AZ 85251. 480/423-2595. **Fax:** 480/423-2543. **Recorded jobline:** 480/423-2555. **Contact:** Alison Rodriguez, Employment Manager. **E-mail address:** career@thephoenician.com. **World Wide Web address:** http://www.thephoenician.com. **Description:** Operates a chain of hotels and resorts. **NOTE:** Entry-level positions, part-time jobs, and second and third shifts are offered. Applications can be obtained and submitted Monday through Friday from 8:00 a.m. until 5:00 p.m. **Positions advertised include:** Human Resources Manager; Banquet Assistant Manager; Chief Engineer; Resort Manager; Spa Director. **Special programs:** Internships. **Parent company:** Starwood Hotels & Resorts Worldwide, Inc. **Listed on:** New York Stock Exchange. **Stock exchange symbol:** HOT. **Number of employees at this location:** 1,700.

THE POINTE HILTON AT SQUAW PEAK
7677 North 16th Street, Phoenix AZ 85020. 602/906-3880. **Fax:** 602/906-3885. **Contact:** Human Resources. **E-mail address:** pointe_sp@hilton.com. **World Wide Web address:** http://www.pointehilton.com. **Description:** A resort offering guest accommodations, five dining establishments, and recreational activities including an eight-acre water park. **Positions advertised include:** Chef de Cuisine. **Corporate headquarters location:** Beverly Hills CA. **Parent company:** Hilton Hotels Corporation is a hospitality, gaming, and lodging company. With its Hilton and Conrad brands, the company develops, owns, manages, and franchises hotel-casinos, resorts, vacation ownership, and hotel properties throughout the world. Other subsidiaries of Hilton Hotels Corporation include Conrad International, Hilton Equipment Corporation, Hilton Grand Vacation Company, and Hilton Inns, Inc. **Operations at this facility include:** Administration; Sales. **Listed on:** New York Stock Exchange. **Stock exchange symbol:** HLT. **Number of employees at this location:** 700.

THE POINTE HILTON AT TAPATIO CLIFFS
11111 North Seventh Street, Phoenix AZ 85020. 602/866-7500. **Fax:** 602/375-4660. **Contact:** Human Resources. **E-mail address:** PHXTC-Tapatio_Jobs@hilton.com. **World Wide Web address:** http://www.pointehilton.com. **Description:** A resort offering several dining establishments and recreational activities including a PGA 18-hole championship golf course. **NOTE:** Entry-level positions and second and third shifts are offered. **Positions advertised include:** Auditor; Executive Chef; Engineer. **Corporate headquarters location:** Beverly Hills CA. **Parent company:** Hilton Hotels Corporation is a hospitality, gaming, and lodging company. With its Hilton and Conrad brands, the company develops, owns, manages, and franchises hotel-casinos, resorts, vacation ownership, and hotel properties throughout the world. Other subsidiaries of Hilton Hotels Corporation include Conrad International, Hilton Equipment Corporation, Hilton Grand Vacation Company, and Hilton Inns, Inc. **Listed on:** New York Stock Exchange. **Stock exchange symbol:** HLT.

POINTE SOUTH MOUNTAIN RESORT
7777 South Pointe Parkway, Phoenix AZ 85044. 602/438-9000. **Contact:** Human Resources. **World Wide Web address:** http://www.pointesouthmtn.com. **Description:** A resort offering guest accommodations, five dining establishments, and recreational activities,

including an 18-hole championship golf course. **Positions advertised include:** Food & Beverage Director; Director Group Sales; National Sales Manager. **Parent company:** Destination Hotels & Resorts.

QUALITY HOTEL & RESORT
3600 North Second Avenue, Phoenix AZ 85013. 602/248-0222. **Contact:** Human Resources. **Description:** A 280-room hotel.

QUALITY SUITES
3101 North 32nd Street, Phoenix AZ 85018. 602/956-4900. **Contact:** Sonal Shah, General Manager. **Description:** A hotel with 76 suites. **Special programs:** Internships. **Corporate headquarters location:** El Cajon CA. **Operations at this facility include:** Service. **Listed on:** Privately held. **Number of employees at this location:** 40.

RADISSON SUITES TUCSON
6555 East Speedway Boulevard, Tucson AZ 85710. 520/721-7100. **Contact:** Human Resources. **World Wide Web address:** http://www.radisson.com. **Description:** A full-service hotel. **NOTE:** Job applicants should contact the Human Resources Department or General Manager at the property. **Corporate headquarters location:** Minneapolis MN. **Parent company:** Carlson Hotels Worldwide.

RADISSON WOODLANDS HOTEL
1175 West Route 66, Flagstaff AZ 86001. 928/773-8888. **Contact:** Human Resources. **World Wide Web address:** http://www.radisson.com. **Description:** A 183-room, full-service hotel operating as part of the national chain. **NOTE:** Job applicants should contact the Human Resources Department or General Manager at the property. **Parent company:** Carlson Hotels Worldwide.

RESIDENCE INN FLAGSTAFF
3440 North Country Club Drive, Flagstaff AZ 86004. 928/526-5555. **Fax:** 928/527-0328. **Contact:** Human Resources. **World Wide Web address:** http://www.marriott.com/residenceinn. **Description:** An extended-stay hotel with meeting facilities. **NOTE:** Search and apply for positions online. **Corporate headquarters location:** Bethesda MD. **Other U.S. locations:** Nationwide. **Parent company:** Marriott International, Inc. **Listed on:** New York Stock Exchange. **Stock exchange symbol:** MAR.

SCOTTSDALE CONFERENCE CENTER & RESORT
7700 East McCormick Parkway, Scottsdale AZ 85258. 480/991-9000. **Contact:** Human Resources. **World Wide Web address:** http://www.thescottsdaleresort.com. **Description:** A 326-room hotel with conference facilities. **Positions advertised include:** PM Engineering; Director of Human Resources; PM Housekeeping Supervisor. **Parent company:** Benchmark Hospitality.

SCOTTSDALE HILTON RESORT & VILLAS
6333 North Scottsdale Road, Scottsdale AZ 85250. 480/948-7750. **Contact:** Human Resources. **World Wide Web address:** http://www.hilton.com. **Description:** A 233-room hotel. **Number of employees at this location:** 230.

WHATABURGER
4610 South 48th Street, Phoenix AZ 85040. 602/454-6453. **Contact:** Human Resources. **World Wide Web address:** http://www.whataburger.com. **Description:** A franchise location of Whataburger, a fast-food restaurant chain. Founded in 1950. **NOTE:** Entry-level positions, second and third shifts, and part-time jobs are offered. **Positions advertised include:** Assistant Manager. **Special programs:** Training; Summer Jobs. **Corporate headquarters location:** Corpus Christi TX. **Other area locations:** Statewide.

WIGWAM RESORT
300 Wigwam Boulevard, Litchfield Park AZ 85340. 623/935-3811. **Recorded jobline:** 623/856-1048. **Contact:** Human Resources. **World Wide Web address:** http://www.wigwamresort.com. **Description:** A resort and country club.

California

ACAPULCO RESTAURANTS
5660 Katella Avenue, Cypress CA 90630. 800/216-9068. **Contact:** Human Resources. **World Wide Web address:** http://www.acapulcorestaurants.com. **Description:** Operates a chain of over 40 Mexican restaurants, primarily in Southern California. **Corporate headquarters location:** This location. **Other area locations:** Statewide. **Parent company:** Real Mex Restaurants.

ANTHONY'S SEAFOOD GROUP
5232 Lovelock Street, San Diego CA 92110. 619/291-7254. **Fax:** 619/298-1212. **Contact:** Constance DeHaven, Director of Human Resources. **World Wide Web address:** http://www.gofishanthonys.com. **Description:** A family-owned restaurant chain specializing in seafood. Anthony's Fish Grotto also sells seafood to the public. **Corporate headquarters location:** This location. **Other area locations:** Chula Vista CA; Kearny Mesa CA; La Mesa CA; Mission Valley CA; Rancho Bernardo CA.

ARAMARK SPORTS AND ENTERTAINMENT SERVICES
3900 West Manchester Boulevard, Inglewood CA 90305. 310/674-2010. **Contact:** Human Resources. **World Wide Web address:** http://www.aramarkentertainment.com. **Description:** Provides food and beverage services; operates large-format films, theaters, and casinos; and offers venue management services. **Operations at this facility include:** This location is a food service provider for the Forum. **Listed on:** New York Stock Exchange. **Stock exchange symbol:** RMK.

BUFFETS, INC.
3007 Clairemont Drive, San Diego CA 92117. 619/275-4622. **Toll-free phone:** 877/560-4084. **Recorded jobline:** 877/7BUFFET. **Contact:** Leota Johnson-Rivera, Human Resources. **E-mail address:** leota.johnson-rivera@buffetsinc.com. **World Wide Web address:** http://www.buffet.com. **Description:** Operates and franchises buffet restaurants. In addition to more than 400 buffet style restaurants throughout the country, Buffets, Inc. and its subsidiaries also operate Tahoe Joe's, a steakhouse restaurant chain with four locations in California. **Corporate headquarters location:** Eagan MN. **Operations at this facility include:** This location is a Hometown Buffet Restaurant.

CKE RESTAURANTS, INC.
401 West Carl Karcher Way, P.O. Box 4349, Anaheim CA 92803-4349. 714/774-5332. **Fax:** 714/490-3630. **Recorded jobline:** 800/227-5757. **Contact:** Human Resources. **World Wide Web address:** http://www.ckr.com. **Description:** Through its subsidiaries, franchisees and licensees, CKE Restaurants operates Carl's Jr., Hardee's, La Salso Fresh Mexican grill and Green Burrito restaurant brands. **Corporate headquarters location:** This location. **Listed on:** New York Stock Exchange. **Stock exchange symbol:** CKR.

THE CHEESECAKE FACTORY INC.
26901 Malibu Hills Road, Calabasas Hills CA 91301. 818/871-3000. **Fax:** 818/871-3100. **Contact:** Recruiting Department. **E-mail address:** careers@thecheesecakefactory.com. **World Wide Web address:** http://www.thecheesecakefactory.com. **Description:** The Cheesecake Factory operates a group of restaurants featuring an extensive menu and moderate prices. The company also operates a production facility that manufactures over 50 varieties of its signature cheesecakes and other baked goods for sale both in its restaurants and through wholesale accounts. **Positions advertised include:** Bilingual

Injury Counselor; Capital Projects Specialist; director of Interactive Sales; Director Purchasing; Senior Benefits Administrator. **Corporate headquarters location:** This location. **Other area locations:** Statewide. **Other U.S. locations:** Nationwide. **Listed on:** NASDAQ. **Stock exchange symbol:** CAKE.

COMMERCE CASINO
6131 East Telegraph Road, Commerce CA 90040. 323/38-3351. **Fax:** 323/838-3475. **Recorded jobline:** 323/838-3399. **Contact:** Human Resources. **World Wide Web address:** http://www.commercecasino.com. **Description:** A casino that hosts poker tournaments and offers a variety of gaming facilities. **Positions advertised include:** Banquet Captain; Bartender; Cashier; Cook; Food Server; Houseperson; Lead Cook; Pan Dealer; Security Advisor; Security Officer; Steward; Station Attendant; Stock Clerk; Surveillance Clerk. **Corporate headquarters location:** This location.

ED DEBEVIC'S RESTAURANT
134 North La Cienega Boulevard, Beverly Hills CA 90211. 310/659-1952. **Contact:** Hiring Manager. **World Wide Web address:** http://www.eddebevics.com. **Description:** One location of the casual dining restaurant chain. Ed Debevic's serves American cuisine and operates a gift shop. **NOTE:** Send or fax application and resume to: Ed Debevic's, Inc., 640 North Wells Street, Chicago IL 60610. Fax: 312/664-7444. **Positions advertised include:** Assistant General Manager. **Corporate headquarters location:** Chicago IL. **Parent company:** Bravo Restaurants, Inc.

THE FAIRMONT HOTEL
650 California Street, 12th Floor, San Francisco CA 94108. 415/772-7800. **Fax:** 415/772-7805. **Contact:** Employment Manager. **E-mail address:** pathfinder@fairmont.com. **World Wide Web address:** http://www.fairmont.com. **Description:** A 591-room hotel. Founded in 1907. **NOTE:** Entry-level positions are offered. **Corporate headquarters location:** This location. **Other U.S. locations:** Los Angeles CA; San Jose CA; Chicago IL; New Orleans LA; Boston MA; Kansas City MO; New York NY; Dallas TX. **Operations at this facility include:** Regional Headquarters; Service. **Listed on:** New York Stock Exchange. **Stock exchange symbol:** FHR. **Number of employees at this location:** 800.

FAIRMONT NEWPORT BEACH
4500 MacArthur Boulevard, Newport Beach CA 92660. 949/476-2001. **Contact:** Human Resources. **World Wide Web address:** http://www.fairmont.com. **Description:** A 444-room hotel, also offering conference facilities.

FARRELL'S ICE CREAM PARLOURS
10606 Camino Ruiz, Miramesa CA 92126. 858/578-9895. **Contact:** Store Supervisor. **World Wide Web address:** http://www.farrellsusa.com. **Description:** A restaurant franchise specializing in ice cream and ice cream products. The restaurants also sell novelties and candy. **Corporate headquarters location:** This location.

FOUR SEASONS HOTEL LOS ANGELES AT BEVERLY HILLS
300 South Doheny Drive, Los Angeles CA 90048. 310/273-2222. **Contact:** Personnel. **E-mail address:** jobs.losangeles@fourseasons.com. **World Wide Web address:** http://www.fourseasons.com/losangeles. **Description:** This location of Four Seasons Hotels & Resorts is a hotel with 285 guest rooms and two restaurants. The hotel also has a pool, whirlpool, fitness facilities, private cabanas, and approximately 10,000 square feet of meeting and function space. Four Seasons Hotels & Resorts operates approximately 50 luxury hotels and resorts in 22 countries. Founded in 1960. **Corporate headquarters location:** Toronto, Canada. **Parent company:** Four Seasons Hotels & Resorts. **Listed on:** New York Stock Exchange. **Stock exchange symbol:** FS.

FRESH CHOICE RESTAURANTS, LLC
485 Cochrane Circle, Morgan Hill CA 95037. 408/776-0799. **Fax:** 408/776-0798. **Contact:** Human Resources. **E-mail address:** employment@freshchoice.com. **World Wide Web address:** http://www.freshchoice.com. **Description:** Operates 36 casual, self-service restaurants in Northern California, Washington, Texas, and Washington DC. **Special programs:** Internships. **Corporate headquarters location:** This location. **Listed on:** NASDAQ. **Stock exchange symbol:** SALD. **Number of employees at this location:** 60. **Number of employees nationwide:** 3,000.

GLADSTONE'S OF MALIBU
17300 Pacific Coast Highway, Pacific Palisades, CA 90272. 310/454-3474. **Fax:** 310/459-9356. **Contact:** Human Resources. **World Wide Web address:** http://www.gladstones.com. **Description:** A seafood restaurant. **Corporate headquarters location:** This location. **Parent company:** Sea View Restaurants, Inc.

HILTON AT FISHERMAN'S WHARF
2620 Jones Street, San Francisco CA 94133. 415/885-4700. **Fax:** 415/771-8945. **Contact:** Personnel Department. **World Wide Web address:** http://www.hiltonfishermanswharf.com. **Description:** A 232-room hotel with a restaurant and lounge. **Corporate headquarters location:** Beverly Hills CA. **Other U.S. locations:** Nationwide. **Parent company:** Hilton Hotels Corporation. **Listed on:** New York Stock Exchange. **Stock exchange symbol:** HLT.

HILTON SAN FRANCISCO & TOWERS
333 O'Farrell Street, San Francisco CA 94102. 415/771-1400. **Fax:** 415/673-6490. **Contact:** Human Resources. **World Wide Web address:** http://www.hilton.com. **Description:** A 2,000-room hotel. **NOTE:** Resumes may be submitted via mail or fax. **Positions advertised include:** Area Director, Purchasing; Assistant Director, Banquets; Assistant Director, Housekeeping; Assistant Executive Steward; Meetings and Conventions Manager; Sales Manager. **Special programs:** Internships. **Corporate headquarters location:** Beverly Hills CA. **Other U.S. locations:** Nationwide. **Parent company:** Hilton Hotels Corporation. **Listed on:** New York Stock Exchange. **Stock exchange symbol:** HLT. **Number of employees at this location:** 1,200.

HOLIDAY INN CIVIC CENTER
50 Eighth Street, San Francisco CA 94103. 415/626-6103. **Contact:** Director of Personnel. **World Wide Web address:** http://www.holiday-inn.com. **Description:** One location of the international hotel chain. Operations include the management of more than 1,750 company-owned and franchised hotels, gaming operations, restaurants, and a sea transportation subsidiary. **Corporate headquarters location:** Memphis TN. **Parent company:** InterContinental Hotels Group.

HOTEL DEL CORONADO
1500 Orange Avenue, Coronado CA 92118. 619/435-6611. **Toll-free phone:** 800/HOTELDEL. **Fax:** 619/522-8160. **Recorded jobline:** 619/522-8158. **Contact:** Employment. **E-mail address:** deljobs@hoteldel.com. **World Wide Web address:** http://www.hoteldel.com. **Description:** A 691-room oceanside resort with seven restaurants, five lounges/bars, two swimming pools, and six tennis courts. **Positions advertised include:** Manager; Concessions Manager. **Special programs:** Internships. **Corporate headquarters location:** This location. **Listed on:** Privately held.

HYATT REGENCY LOS ANGELES
711 South Hope Street, Los Angeles CA 90017. 213/683-1234. **Contact:** Human Resources. **World Wide Web address:** http://www.hyatt.com. **Description:** A hotel and restaurant facility with 485 rooms. **NOTE:** Entry-level positions are offered. **Special programs:** Internships. **Corporate headquarters location:** Chicago IL. **Other U.S.**

locations: Nationwide. **International locations:** Worldwide. **Listed on:** Privately held. **Number of employees at this location:** 300. **Number of employees nationwide:** 40,000.

HYATT REGENCY MONTEREY HOTEL CONFERENCE CENTER
One Old Golf Course Road, Monterey CA 93940-4908. 831/372-1234. **Contact:** Joe Krings, Director of Human Resources Department. **World Wide Web address:** http://www.hyatt.com. **Description:** One location of the nationwide chain of hotels. **Corporate headquarters location:** Chicago IL. **Parent company:** Hyatt Corporation. **Operations at this facility include:** Administration; Sales; Service. **Number of employees at this location:** 430. **Number of employees nationwide:** 40,000.

HYATT REGENCY SAN FRANCISCO
5 Embarcadero Center, San Francisco CA 94111. 415/788-1234. **Fax:** 415/291-6615. **Contact:** Human Resources. **World Wide Web address:** http://www.hyatt.com. **Description:** One location of the Hyatt chain of hotels, which operates hotel and recreational facilities throughout the world. **Corporate headquarters location:** Chicago IL.

HYATT REGENCY SAN FRANCISCO AIRPORT
1333 Bayshore Highway, Burlingame CA 94010. 650/347-1234. **Fax:** 650/348-2541. **Recorded jobline:** 650/696-2625. **Contact:** Human Resources. **World Wide Web address:** http://www.hyatt.com. **Description:** Operates a full-service, four-star hotel complex offering restaurants, banquet rooms, and recreational and convention facilities. **Special programs:** Training. **Corporate headquarters location:** Chicago IL. **Other U.S. locations:** Nationwide. **Parent company:** Hyatt Corporation. **Listed on:** Privately held. **Number of employees at this location:** 500. **Number of employees nationwide:** 40,000.

IHOP CORPORATION
450 North Brand Boulevard, 7th Floor, Glendale CA 91203-1903. 818/240-6055. **Fax:** 818/637-3131. **Contact:** Human Resources. **E-mail address:** jobs@ihopcorp.com. **World Wide Web address:** http://www.ihop.com. **Description:** Operates the International House of Pancakes restaurant chain. **Corporate headquarters location:** This location. **Listed on:** New York Stock Exchange. **Stock exchange symbol:** IHP.

JS FOODS
4250 Executive Square, Suite 500, La Jolla CA 92037. 858/642-0071. **Contact:** Human Resources. **Description:** Manages Burger King, Tony Roma's, and Pacific Bagels franchises. **Corporate headquarters location:** This location.

JACK IN THE BOX INC.
9330 Balboa Avenue, San Diego CA 92123-1516. 858/571-2121. **Fax:** 858/694-1570. **Contact:** Human Resources. **E-mail address:** resumes@jackinthebox.com. **World Wide Web address:** http://www.jackinthebox.com. **Description:** Operates and franchises Jack in the Box restaurants, one of the nation's largest quick-serve hamburger chains. Jack in the Box restaurants are primarily located in the western and southwestern United States. International operations currently include restaurants in Hong Kong and Mexico. **Positions advertised include:** Accounting Representative; Information Systems/Budget Administrator; Regional Marketing Manager; Senior Project Manager; Financial Analyst; Restaurant Auditor. **Corporate headquarters location:** This location. **Listed on:** New York Stock Exchange. **Stock exchange symbol:** JBX.

MARRIOTT SANTA CLARA
2700 Mission College Boulevard, Santa Clara CA 95054. 408/988-1500. **Fax:** 408/352-4353. **Contact:** Recruiter. **World Wide Web address:** http://www.marriott.com. **Description:** Operates a hotel with complete dining and recreational facilities. **Corporate headquarters location:** Washington DC. **Parent company:** Marriott International, Inc. **Listed on:** New York Stock Exchange. **Stock exchange symbol:** MAR.

MICHAEL J'S RESTAURANT
201 North Vineyard Street, Ontario CA 91764. 909/937-6860. **Contact:** Human Resources. **Description:** The management office for the chain of Michael J's restaurants.

MILLENNIUM BILTMORE HOTEL
506 South Grand Avenue, Los Angeles CA 90071. 213/624-1011. **Contact:** Human Resources. **World Wide Web address:** http://www.millenniumhotels.com. **Description:** A luxury hotel. **Corporate headquarters location:** This location. **Operations at this facility include:** Administration; Sales. **Parent company:** CDL Group.

OAKLAND MARRIOTT CITY CENTER
1001 Broadway, Oakland CA 94607. 510/451-4000. **Fax:** 510/835-3460. **Recorded jobline:** 510/466-6440. **Contact:** Human Resources. **World Wide Web address:** http://www.marriott.com. **Description:** A full-service hotel and restaurant with over 400 rooms. Oakland Marriott City Center also has conference rooms and meeting space. This location also hires seasonally. **NOTE:** Entry-level positions and part-time jobs are offered. **Special programs:** Internships. **Office hours:** Monday - Friday, 9:00 a.m. - 5:00 p.m. **Corporate headquarters location:** San Francisco CA. **Parent company:** Park Lane Hotels International. **Listed on:** New York Stock Exchange. **Stock exchange symbol:** HMT. **Number of employees at this location:** 400.

ONE PICO RESTAURANT
One Pico Boulevard, Santa Monica CA 90405-1062. 310/587-1717. **Contact:** Manager. **World Wide Web address:** http://www.shuttersonthebeach.com. **Description:** A restaurant serving New American cuisine. The restaurant is located in Shutters Hotel.

PRANDIUM, INC.
2701 Alton Parkway, Irvine CA 92606. 949/863-8500. **Fax:** 949/863-8855. **Contact:** Ken Gowen, Human Resources. **E-mail address:** careers@prandium.com. **World Wide Web address:** http://www.prandium.com. **Description:** Manages and operates Chi-Chi's restaurants in 13 states. **Corporate headquarters location:** This location. **Annual sales/revenues:** $257 million. **Number of employees at this location:** 200. **Number of employees nationwide:** 15,000.

RADISSON WILSHIRE PLAZA HOTEL
3515 Wilshire Boulevard, Los Angeles CA 90010. 213/381-7411. **Toll-free phone:** 800/333-3333. **Fax:** 213/368-3015. **Contact:** Mr. Otho Boggs, Human Resources Director. **World Wide Web address:** http://www.radisson.com. **Description:** A 393-room hotel, restaurant, and entertainment facility. **NOTE:** Entry-level positions, part-time jobs, and second and third shifts are offered. **Special programs:** Internships; Training; Summer Jobs. **Internship information:** Unpaid internships are available in the fields of rooms; sales and marketing; food and beverage; accounting; and human resources. **Corporate headquarters location:** Minneapolis MN. **President:** Young Sun Kim.

RAMADA PLAZA HOTEL
1231 Market Street, San Francisco CA 94103. 415/626-8000. **Toll-free phone:** 800/272-6232. **Contact:** Personnel Manager. **World Wide Web address:** http://www.ramada.com. **Description:** Operates a 458-room hotel with a variety of facilities including meeting rooms and restaurants.

REGENT BEVERLY WILSHIRE HOTEL
9500 Wilshire Boulevard, Beverly Hills CA 90212. 310/275-5200. **Toll-free phone:** 888/201-1806. **Fax:** 310/274-2851. **Contact:** Sharon Nixon, Director of Human Resources. **World Wide Web address:**

http://www.regenthotels.com. **Description:** A hotel with over 290 rooms. **Corporate headquarters location:** Hong Kong. **Parent company:** Carlson Hotels Worldwide. **Listed on:** New York Stock Exchange. **Stock exchange symbol:** FS. **Number of employees at this location:** 650.

SHERATON FISHERMAN'S WHARF
2500 Mason Street, San Francisco CA 94133. 415/362-5500. **Fax:** 415/627-6529. **Recorded jobline:** 415/627-6567. **Contact:** Lisa Lucas-Yap, Human Resources Director. **World Wide Web address:** http://www.sheraton.com. **Description:** A 525-room hotel. Founded in 1998. **NOTE:** Part-time jobs are offered. To contact Human Resources call: 415/627-6526. **Corporate headquarters location:** Washington DC. **Parent company:** Starwood Hotels & Resorts Worldwide, Inc. **Listed on:** New York Stock Exchange. **Stock exchange symbol:** HOT. **Chairman and CEO:** Paul Whetsell. **Number of employees at this location:** 260. **Number of employees nationwide:** 27,000.

SIZZLER INTERNATIONAL INC.
6101 W. Centinela Avenue, Garden Office Building, Building B, Suite 300, Culver City CA 90230. 310/846-8750. **Contact:** Personnel. **E-mail address:** crogers@wrconcepts.com. **World Wide Web address:** http://www.sizzler.com. **Description:** One of the largest franchises of the KFC Corporation and the majority stockholder for the Sizzler restaurant chain. **NOTE:** Resumes may be sent to the above e-mail address. **Corporate headquarters location:** This location. **Listed on:** New York Stock Exchange. **Stock exchange symbol:** SZ.

VAGABOND INNS CORPORATION
5933 West Century Boulevard, Suite 200, Los Angeles CA 90045. 310/410-5700. **Fax:** 310/410-5771. **Contact:** Personnel. **E-mail address:** svalentino@vagabondinns.com. **World Wide Web address:** http://www.vagabondinns.com. **Description:** Owns and operates hotels. **Corporate headquarters location:** This location. **Operations at this facility include:** Administration; Sales; Service.

WYNDHAM HOTEL SAN JOSE
1350 North First Street, San Jose CA 95112. 408/453-6200. **Contact:** Personnel Assistant. **World Wide Web address:** http://www.wyndham.com. **Description:** Operates a full-service hotel with a wide range of facilities including convention facilities, meeting rooms, suites, three lounges, two restaurants and an exercise room. **Corporate headquarters location:** Dallas TX. **Parent company:** Wyndham International. **Listed on:** New York Stock Exchange. **Stock exchange symbol:** WYN.

Colorado
ADAM'S MARK HOTEL
1550 Court Place, Denver CO 80202. 303/893-3333. **Contact:** Director of Human Resources. **World Wide Web address:** http://www.adamsmark.com. **Description:** A 1,225-room hotel with restaurant and meeting facilities. **Positions advertised include:** Assistant Banquet Manager; Director of Advertising and Promotions; Sales Manager. **Corporate headquarters location:** Minneapolis MN. **Parent company:** Ash and Associates, Inc. **Number of employees at this location:** 375.

BEST WESTERN CENTRAL DENVER
200 West 48th Avenue, Denver CO 80216-1802. 303/296-4000. **Fax:** 303/296-4000. **Contact:** Human Resources Administrator. **World Wide Web address:** http://www.bestwestern.com. **Description:** A 176-room hotel. **Corporate headquarters location:** Phoenix AZ. **Listed on:** Privately held.

BOSTON MARKET, INC.
14103 Denver West Parkway, Golden CO 80401. 303/278-9500. **Fax:** 303/216-5678. **Contact:** Human Resources. **E-mail address:** SC_Recruiting@bost.com. **World Wide Web address:** http://www.bostonmarket.com. **Description:** Operates and franchises food service stores that specialize in fresh, convenient meals. Boston Market's menu features home-style entrees, fresh vegetables, salads, and other side dishes. **Corporate headquarters location:** This location.

THE BROADMOOR HOTEL
1 Lake Avenue, Colorado Springs CO 80906. 719/577-5780. **Fax:** 719/577-5700. **Contact:** Human Resources Office. **World Wide Web address:** http://www.broadmoor.com. **Description:** A 700-room, five-star, five-diamond resort. Facilities include 3 championship golf courses, 15 retail outlets, 9 restaurants, 12 tennis courts, and conference rooms. Founded in 1918. **NOTE:** Entry-level positions, part-time jobs, and second and third shifts are offered. This location also hires seasonally. Send resumes to: 15 Lake Circle, Colorado Springs CO 80906. **Special programs:** Internships; Apprenticeships; Training. **Office hours:** Monday - Friday, 8:00 a.m. - 5:00 p.m. **Corporate headquarters location:** This location. **Parent company:** Oklahoma Publishing Company. **Annual sales/revenues:** \$51 - \$100 million. **Number of employees at this location:** 1,500.

BROWN PALACE HOTEL
321 17th Street, Denver CO 80202. 303/297-3111. **Fax:** 303/312-5940. **Contact:** Human Resources. **World Wide Web address:** http://www.brownpalace.com. **Description:** A full-service hotel. **NOTE:** All positions require experience in four- or five-star properties. **Special programs:** Internships. **Corporate headquarters location:** Dallas TX. **Parent company:** Quorum Hotels and Resorts. **Number of employees at this location:** 400.

COLOMEX, INC.
dba TACO BELL
717 North Tejon Street, Colorado Springs CO 80903. 719/633-2500. **Fax:** 719/633-9610. **Contact:** Human Resources. **Description:** Colomex, Inc. owns the largest Taco Bell franchise in Colorado, operating over 30 restaurants. Taco Bell is a leader in the Mexican, fast-food restaurant industry. **Corporate headquarters location:** This location. **Listed on:** Privately held. **Number of employees at this location:** 1,000.

COPPER MOUNTAIN RESORTS, INC.
209 Ten Mile Circle, P.O. Box 3001, Copper Mountain CO 80443. 970/968-2318. **Contact:** Human Resources Department. **World Wide Web address:** http://www.coppersummer.com. **Description:** Operates a resort with ski facilities and a wide range of warm-weather activities. Founded in 1972. **Positions advertised include:** Call Center Sales Agent; Manager of Research and Development; Homeowner Experience Coordinator; IT Business Analyst. **Office hours:** Sunday - Saturday, 8:00 a.m. - 5:00 p.m. **Corporate headquarters location:** This location. **Other area locations:** Dillon CO; Frisco CO; Leadville CO. **COO:** David Barry. **Facilities Manager:** Becky Yessak. **Information Systems Manager:** Doug Feeley. **Purchasing Manager:** Don Jones. **Sales Manager:** Carol Schmidt.

DENVER MARRIOTT TECH CENTER
4900 South Syracuse Street, Denver CO 80237. 303/779-1100. **Recorded jobline:** 303/782-3214. **Contact:** Human Resources Department. **World Wide Web address:** http://www.marriott.com. **Description:** A 625-room hotel. **NOTE:** Entry-level positions, part-time jobs, and second and third shifts are offered. This location also hires seasonally. **Special programs:** Internships; Training; Summer Jobs. **Corporate headquarters location:** Bethesda MD. **Other U.S. locations:** Nationwide. **International locations:** Worldwide. **Parent company:** Marriot International, Inc. **Listed on:** New York Stock Exchange. **Stock exchange symbol:** MAR. **Annual sales/revenues:** More than \$100 million. **Number of employees at this location:** 375. **Number of employees nationwide:** 100,000. **Number of employees worldwide:** 150,000.

DOUBLETREE HOTEL DURANGO
501 Camino Del Rio, Durango CO 81301. 970/259-6580. **Fax:** 970/259-4398. **Contact:** Human Resources. **World Wide Web address:** www.durango.doubletree.com. **Description:** Luxury hotel within walking distance of downtown Durango and restaurants. **Parent Company:** Hilton.

HOLIDAY INN DENVER DOWNTOWN
1450 Glenarm Place, Denver CO 80202. 303/573-1450. **Contact:** Human Resources. **World Wide Web address:** http://www.holiday-inn.com. **Description:** One location of the nationwide hotel chain. **Corporate headquarters location:** Atlanta GA. **Parent company:** Six Continents Hotels, Inc. **Listed on:** New York Stock Exchange. **Stock exchange symbol:** SXC.

HOTEL JEROME
333 East Main Street, Aspen CO 81611. 970/920-1000. **Fax:** 970/925-3112. **Toll-free phone:** 800/331-7213. **Contact:** Human Resources. **E-mail address:** hr@hjerome.com. **World Wide Web address:** www.hoteljerome.com. **Description:** A 91-room landmark hotel located in downtown Aspen with an award winning restaurant.

KEYSTONE RESORT
P.O. Box 38, Keystone CO 80435. 970/496-4157. **Fax:** 970/496-3260. **Contact:** Director of Human Resources. **E-mail address:** keyjobs@vailresorts.com. **World Wide Web address:** http://www.keystoneresort.com. **Description:** A ski resort. **Positions advertised include:** Accountant; Steward; Cook; Front Desk Agent; Lift Mechanic; Lift Electronics Tech. **Parent company:** Vail Resorts Inc. **Listed on:** New York Stock Exchange. **Stock exchange symbol:** MTN.

LIONSHEAD INN
705 West Lionshead Circle, Vail CO 81657. 970/476-2050. **Fax:** 970/476-9265. **Toll-free phone:** 800/283-8245. **Contact:** Human Resources. **World Wide Web address:** www.lionsheadinn.com. **Description:** Luxury inn located minutes from the Eagle Bay Gondola, shops, and restaurants.

MARRIOTT'S MOUNTAIN VALLEY LODGE AT BRECKENRIDGE
655 Columbine Drive, Breckenridge CO 80424. 970/453-8500. **Fax:** 970/453-8110. **Contact:** Human Resources. **World Wide Web address:** http://www.marriott.com. **Description:** A location of the hotel chain. A 111-room hotel within walking distance of shops, restaurants, and golf.

MILLENNIUM HARVEST HOUSE
1345 28th Street, Boulder CO 80302-6899. 303/443-3850. **Toll-free phone:** 800/545-6285. **Fax:** 303/443-1480. **Contact:** Human Resources Department. **E-mail address:** boulder@mhrmail.com. **World Wide Web address:** http://www.millennium-hotels.com. **Description:** A 270-room corporate and leisure hotel with meeting facilities. Founded in 1959. **Special programs:** Internships. **Positions advertised include:** Group Sales Manager; Executive Chef. **Corporate headquarters location:** Denver CO. **Other U.S. locations:** Nationwide. **International locations:** Worldwide. **Parent company:** Millennium & Copthorne Hotels plc. **Operations at this facility include:** Administration; Sales; Service. **Listed on:** Privately held. **Annual sales/revenues:** $11 - $20 million. **Number of employees at this location:** 200.

RADISSON HOTELS
3200 South Parker Road, Aurora CO 80014. 303/695-1700. **Contact:** Human Resources. **World Wide Web address:** http://www.radisson.com. **Description:** One location of the nationwide hotel chain.

RADISSON STAPLETON PLAZA HOTEL
3333 Quebec Street, Denver CO 80207. 303/321-3500. **Contact:** Human Resources. **World Wide Web address:** http://www.radisson.com. **Description:** A 300-room hotel whose facilities include a fitness center and a restaurant. **NOTE:** Entry-level positions, part-time jobs, and second and third shifts are offered.

RICHFIELD HOSPITALITY, INC.
7600 East Orchard Road, Suite 230 South, Greenwood Village CO 80111. 303/220-2185. **Contact:** Human Resources. **World Wide Web address:** http://www.swanhost.com. **Description:** A company involved in hotel management and ownership. **Positions advertised include:** Payroll Manager; Director of Revenue Management; Corporate Accounting Manager. **Special programs:** Internships; Co-ops. **Office hours:** Monday - Friday, 8:00 a.m. - 5:00 p.m. **Annual sales/revenues:** More than $100 million. **Number of employees at this location:** 50. **Number of employees nationwide:** 7,000.

ROCK BOTTOM RESTAURANTS, INC.
248 Centennial Parkway, Suite 100, Louisville CO 80027. 303/664-4000. **Fax:** 303/664-4199. **Contact:** Human Resources Department. **World Wide Web address:** http://www.rockbottom.com. **Description:** Owns and operates 29 restaurants and breweries. **NOTE:** Entry-level positions and part-time jobs are offered. **Company slogan:** To run great restaurants with great people. **Positions advertised include:** Restaurant Manager; Sous Chef. **Special programs:** Internships; Training; Summer Jobs. **Corporate headquarters location:** This location. **Other U.S. locations:** Nationwide. **Annual sales/revenues:** More than $100 million. **Number of employees at this location:** 70.

VAIL RESORTS
P.O. Box 7, Vail CO 81658. 970/845-2460. **Fax:** 970/845-2465. **Recorded jobline:** 888/SKI-JOB1. **Contact:** Human Resources. **World Wide Web address:** http://www.vailresorts.com. **Description:** Operates the Vail, Breckenridge, Beaver Creek, Keystone, Heavenly, and other resorts. Founded in 1962. **NOTE:** Entry-level positions and second and third shifts are offered. **Special programs:** Internships; Training; Summer Jobs. **Office hours:** Monday - Friday, 8:00 a.m. - 5:00 p.m. **Corporate headquarters location:** This location. **Listed on:** New York Stock Exchange. **Stock exchange symbol:** MTN.

VICORP RESTAURANTS INC.
400 West 48th Avenue, Denver CO 80216. 303/296-2121. **Contact:** Human Resources. **E-mail address:** h.resources@vicorpinc.com. **World Wide Web address:** http://www.vicorpinc.com. **Description:** Operates Bakers Square and Village Inn restaurant chains and franchises restaurants under the Village Inn name. **Positions advertised include:** Architectural Designer/Sr. Drafter; Site Development Coordinator; Construction Coordinator; Purchasing Specialist; Financial Analyst. **Corporate headquarters location:** This location.

WENDY'S INTERNATIONAL, INC.
6695 West Alameda Avenue, Denver CO 80214. 303/238-9721. **Contact:** Staffing Specialist. **World Wide Web address:** http://www.wendysintl.com. **Description:** One of the world's largest restaurant franchising companies. Wendy's International includes Wendy's, a fast-food restaurant chain, and Tim Hortons, a coffee and baked goods restaurant chain. **Corporate headquarters location:** Dublin OH. **Other U.S. locations:** Nationwide. **Operations at this facility include:** Administration; Divisional Headquarters. **Listed on:** New York Stock Exchange. **Stock exchange symbol:** WEN.

Connecticut

BEST WESTERN SOVEREIGN HOTEL
9 Whitehall Avenue, Mystic CT 06355. 860/536-4281. **Contact:** Human Resources. **World Wide Web address:** http://www.bestwestern.com. **Description:** A hotel with 150 rooms. Best Western Sovereign Hotel is part of the national hotel chain. **Other U.S. locations:** Nationwide. **International locations:** Worldwide.

CLUB HOTEL BY DOUBLETREE
789 Connecticut Avenue, Norwalk CT 06854. 203/853-

3477. **Contact:** Human Resources. **World Wide Web address:** http://www.doubletree.com. **Description:** A 268-room business hotel operating as part of the Doubletree chain.

COURTYARD BY MARRIOTT
63 Grand Street, Waterbury CT 06702. 203/596-1000. **Contact:** Human Resources. **World Wide Web address:** http://www.courtyard.com. **Description:** One location of the hotel chain offering 200 rooms, a business center, and four restaurants. **Positions advertised include:** Banquet Chef. **Other U.S. locations:** Nationwide.

FOXWOODS RESORT CASINO
39 Norwich Westerly Road, Mashantucket CT 06339. 860/312-4170. **Contact:** Human Resources. **World Wide Web address:** http://www.foxwoods.com. **Description:** A casino. Foxwoods also offers concerts and entertainment, as well as lodging facilities. The casino is operated by the Mashantucket Pequot Indians. **NOTE:** Send resumes to: Human Resources-Employment and Staffing Division, Route 2, P.O. Box 3777, Mashantucket CT 06339.

HILTON MYSTIC
20 Coogan Boulevard, Mystic CT 06355. 860/572-0731. **Fax:** 860/572-0328. **Contact:** Human Resources. **Description:** Located across from the Mystic Aquarium, the hotel also offers a dining option.

HOLIDAY INN
1070 Main Street, Bridgeport CT 06604. 203/334-1234. **Contact:** Human Resources. **World Wide Web address:** www.ichotelsgroup.com. **Description:** A 234-room hotel located in the heart of downtown offering a restaurant and business amenities.

MOHEGAN SUN CASINO
One Mohegan Sun Boulevard, Uncasville CT 06382. 860/862-8000. **Toll-free phone:** 888/226-7711. **Contact:** Human Resources. **World Wide Web address:** http://www.mohegansun.com. **Description:** A casino and resort facility offering 2,500 slot machines, a wide variety of games, a night club, numerous restaurants, and a 1,500-room hotel. **Positions advertised include:** Surveillance Officer; Front Office Supervisor; Coat Room Attendant; Restaurant Host; Shuttle Driver; Valet Dispatcher; Hvac Mechanic; Retail Shift Manager; Stationary Engineer; Network Technician; Executive Housekeeper; Front Office Assistant Manager; VIP Recreation Supervisor; Voice Services Technician; Support Analyst; Retail Salesperson; Security Officer; Racebook/Keno Mechanic.

SHERATON DANBURY
18 Old Ridgebury Road, Danbury CT 06810. 203/794-0600. **Contact:** Human Resources. **World Wide Web address:** http://www.starwood.com/sheraton. **Description:** One location of the hotel chain, offering meeting facilities, a business center, two restaurants, and a fitness center. **Positions advertised include:** Catering Sales Manager. **Other U.S. locations:** Nationwide.

SHERATON HOTEL AT BRADLEY
One Bradley International Airport, Windsor Locks CT 06096. 860/627-5311. **Contact:** Human Resources. **World Wide Web address:** http://www.sheraton.com. **Description:** A 237-room hotel. Located near Bradley International Airport, the hotel also houses numerous conference and convention facilities.

Delaware
ACW CORPORATION
110 South Poplar Street, Suite 102, Wilmington DE 19801. 302/427-1776. **Fax:** 302/427-1775. **Contact:** Anna Crawford, Director of Human Resources. **Description:** A franchise of Arby's restaurants**Special programs:** Internships. **Corporate headquarters location:** This location. **Operations at this facility include:** Administration; Sales; Service. **Listed on:** Privately held. **Number of employees at this location:** 300.

HOTEL DUPONT
11th and Market Streets, Wilmington DE 19801. 302/594-3100. **Toll-free number:** 800/941-9019. **Contact:** Human Resources. **World Wide Web address:** http://www.dupont.com/hotel. **Description:** A luxury hotel and conference center. **NOTE:** Must apply online. **Parent company:** E.I. DuPont de Nemours & Company.

OLIVE GARDEN RESTAURANT
305 Rocky Run Parkway, Tallyville DE 19803. 302/477-0870. **Contact:** Human Resources. **World Wide Web address:** http://www.olivegarden.com. **Description:** Family-style Italian restaurant chain. **Positions advertised include:** Manager; Host; Server; Line Cook; Preparation Cook; Alley Coordinator; Server Assistant/ Busser; Utility/Dish Machine Operator. **Parent company:** Darden Corporation. **Listed on:** New York Stock Exchange. **Stock exchange symbol:** DRI.

District Of Columbia
CAPITAL HILTON
1001 16th Street NW, Washington DC 20036. 202/393-1000. **Fax:** 202/942-1393. **Recorded jobline:** 202/639-5745. **Contact:** Melissa G. Storino, Employment Manager. **World Wide Web address:** http://www.hilton.com. **Description:** A full-service hotel with two restaurants. **Corporate headquarters location:** Los Angeles CA. **Parent company:** Hilton Hotels Corporation is a hospitality, gaming, and lodging company. With its Hilton and Conrad brands, the company develops, owns, manages, and franchises hotel-casinos, resorts, and hotel properties throughout the world. Other subsidiaries of Hilton Hotels Corporation include Conrad International, Hilton Equipment Corporation, Hilton Grand Vacation Company, and Hilton Inns, Inc. **Operations at this facility include:** Administration; Sales; Service. **Number of employees at this location:** 400.

FOUR SEASONS HOTEL
2800 Pennsylvania Avenue NW, Washington DC 20007. 202/342-0444. **Fax:** 202/944-2072. **Contact:** Human Resources. **E-mail address:** jobs.washingtondc@fourseasons.com. **World Wide Web address:** http://www.fourseasons.com. **Description:** A luxury hotel.

HOTEL HARRINGTON
436 11th Street NW, Washington DC 20004-4389. 202/628-8140. **Contact:** Ann Terry, Personnel Manager. **World Wide Web address:** http://www.hotel-harrington.com. **Description:** A 300-room hotel.

HOTEL WASHINGTON
515 15th Street NW, Washington DC 20004. 202/638-5900. **Fax:** 202/638-1594. **Contact:** Human Resources. **World Wide Web address:** http://www.hotelwashington.com. **Description:** Operates a 350-room hotel with three dining rooms. **Corporate headquarters location:** Galveston TX.

HYATT REGENCY WASHINGTON DC ON CAPITOL HILL
400 New Jersey Avenue NW, Washington DC 20001. 202/737-1234. **Fax:** 202/942-1552. **Recorded jobline:** 202/942-1586. **Contact:** Human Resources. **World Wide Web address:** http://www.hyatt.com. **Description:** An 834-room, full-service hotel. **NOTE:** Entry-level positions, part-time jobs, and second and third shifts are offered. **Positions advertised include:** Security Officer; Cashier; Cook; Housekeeper; Server; Concierge; Bartender; Human Resources Manager; Sous Chef; Catering Administrative Assistant. **Special programs:** Internships; Training; Summer Jobs. **Corporate headquarters location:** Chicago IL. **Other U.S. locations:** Nationwide. **International locations:** Worldwide. **Parent company:** Hyatt Hotels Corporation. **Operations at this facility include:**

Administration; Sales; Service. **Listed on:** Privately held. **Number of employees at this location:** 550. **Number of employees nationwide:** 40,000.

MARRIOTT AT METRO CENTER
775 12th Street NW, Washington DC 20005. 202/737-2200. **Contact:** Human Resources. **World Wide Web address:** http://www.marriott.com. **Description:** A 456-room hotel catering to business travelers. **NOTE:** See website for current listings in the DC area.

MARRIOTT WARDMAN PARK HOTEL
2660 Woodley Road NW, Washington DC 20008. 202/328-2000. **Fax:** 202/234-0015. **Contact:** Lombar Martinez. **E-mail address:** lombar.martinez@marriott.com. **World Wide Web address:** http://www.marriott.com. **Description:** A 1,500-room hotel with a lobby lounge, media spaces, and conference facilities. **Positions advertised include:** Stewarding Supervisor; Room Service Supervisor.

OMNI SHOREHAM HOTEL
2500 Calvert Street NW, Washington DC 20008. 202/756-5148. **Fax:** 202/756-5155. **Contact:** Charlotte Zupancic, Recruitment/Employment Manager. **World Wide Web address:** http://www.omnihotels.com. **Description:** A historic landmark hotel with over 700 rooms and 100,000 square feet of meeting space. **Positions advertised include:** Sales Manager; Reservation Sales Coordinator; Housekeeping Supervisor; Bartender; Beverage Porter; Room Service Supervisor; Front Desk Supervisor; Laundry Manager; Banquet Manager; Front Desk Agent; Message Therapist; Room Attendant; Catering Manager. **Special programs:** Internships. **Number of employees at this location:** 535.

PALM MANAGEMENT CORPORATION
1225 19th Street NW, Washington DC 20036. 202/293-9091. **Fax:** 202/775-1468. **Contact:** Human Resources. **E-mail address:** careers@thepalm.com. **World Wide Web address:** http://www.thepalm.com. **Description:** Owns and operates Palm Restaurants. **Positions advertised include:** Staff Accountant.

WASHINGTON HILTON AND TOWERS
1919 Connecticut Avenue NW, Washington DC 20009. 202/483-3000. **Fax:** 202/797-5750. **Contact:** Human Resources. **World Wide Web address:** http://www.hilton.com. **Description:** Operates a hotel with over 1,000 rooms and extensive meeting and function space. The hotel features complete dining and lounge facilities. **Corporate headquarters location:** Beverly Hills CA. **Parent company:** Hilton Hotels Corporation. **Listed on:** New York Stock Exchange. **Stock exchange symbol:** HLT. **Number of employees nationwide:** 40,000.

WASHINGTON PLAZA HOTEL
10 Thomas Circle NW, Washington DC 20005. 202/842-1300. **Fax:** 202/408-6158. **Contact:** Human Resources. **World Wide Web address:** http://www.washingtonplazahotel.com. **Description:** A hotel and meeting facility catering to business travelers. **Positions advertised include:** Front Office Manager; Chief Engineer.

Florida

ADAMS MARK HOTEL
225 Coast Line Drive East, Jacksonville FL 32202. 904/633-9095. **Fax:** 904/634-4566. **Contact:** Teri Borowski. **E-mail address:** tborowski@adamsmark.com. **World Wide Web address:** http://www.adamsmark.com. **Description:** A hotel, convention, and meeting facility. **Positions advertised include:** Assistant Executive Steward; Assistant Restaurant Manager; Catering Sales Manager; Convention Services Manager; Sales Manager. **Other U.S. locations include:** Nationwide.

ATLANTIC COAST MANAGEMENT
P.O. Box 2066, Winter Park FL 32790. 407/647-4300. **Fax:** 407/647-5306. **Contact:** Joe Hayes, Vice President of Human Resources. **Description:** A restaurant management company. **Positions advertised include:** Management Trainee. **Corporate headquarters location:** This location. **Listed on:** Privately held.

BENIHANA INC.
8685 NW 53rd Terrace, Suite 201, Miami FL 33166. 305/593-0770. **Fax:** 305/592-6371. **Contact:** Human Resources. **E-mail address:** contact@benihana.com. **World Wide Web address:** http://www.benihana.com. **Description:** Owns and operates more than 60 Japanese steakhouses. Additional restaurants are operated by licensees. **Corporate headquarters location:** This location. **Other U.S. locations:** Nationwide. **Subsidiaries include:** Rudy's Restaurant Group, Inc. **Listed on:** NASDAQ. **Stock exchange symbol:** BNHN. **Annual sales/revenues:** $21 - $50 million. **Number of employees nationwide:** 1,650.

CASA GRANDE SUITE HOTEL
834 Ocean Drive, Miami Beach FL 33139. 305/672-7003. **Fax:** 305/673-3669. **E-mail address:** info@casagrandesuitehotel.com. **Contact:** Human Resources. **World Wide Web address:** http://www.casagrandehotel.com. **Description:** A European-style luxury hotel.

CHECKERS DRIVE-IN RESTAURANTS, INC.
3300 West Cypress Street, Suite 600, Tampa FL 33607. 813/283-7000. **Contact:** Human Resources. **E-mail address:** hr@checkers.com. **World Wide Web address:** http://www.checkers.com. **Description:** Develops, owns, operates, and franchises quick-service, drive-thru restaurants under the Checkers name. **Corporate headquarters location:** This location. **Listed on:** NASDAQ. **Stock exchange symbol:** CHKR. **Number of employees at this location:** 130. **Number of employees nationwide:** 12,000.

DARDEN RESTAURANTS, INC.
P.O. Box 593330, Orlando FL 32859-3330. 407/245-4000. **Contact:** Human Resources. **World Wide Web address:** http://www.darden.com. **Description:** Operates the Red Lobster, Olive Garden, and Bahama Breeze restaurant chains. **Corporate headquarters location:** This location. **Listed on:** New York Stock Exchange. **Stock exchange symbol:** DRI. **Annual sales/revenues:** More than $100 million. **Number of employees nationwide:** 122,000.

FMS MANAGEMENT SYSTEMS, INC.
dba INTERNATIONAL HOUSE OF PANCAKES
2655 NE 189th Street, North Miami Beach FL 33180. 305/931-5454. **Fax:** 305/933-3300. **Contact:** Carol Boettcher, Director of Human Resources. **World Wide Web address:** http://www.ihop.com. **Description:** Operates International House of Pancakes (IHOP) restaurants. **Positions advertised include:** General Manager. **Other U.S. locations:** Nationwide. **International locations:** Canada. **Listed on:** New York Stock Exchange. **Stock exchange symbol:** IHP.

FAMOUS AMOS RESTAURANTS, INC.
2765 Clydo Road, Jacksonville FL 32207. 904/731-3396. **Contact:** Human Resources. **Description:** Operates a chain of 10 area restaurants. **Corporate headquarters location:** This location.

H.I. DEVELOPMENT, INC.
111 West Fortune Street, Tampa FL 33602. 813/229-6686. **Fax:** 813/223-9734. **Contact:** David Callen, President. **E-mail address:** mailbox@hidevelopment.com. **World Wide Web address:** http://www.hidevelopment.com. **Description:** A hotel management and consulting firm. **Corporate headquarters location:** This location. **Operations at this facility include:** Regional Headquarters.

HYATT REGENCY ORLANDO INTERNATIONAL AIRPORT
9300 Airport Boulevard, Orlando FL 32827. 407/825-1310. **Fax:** 407/825-1341. **Contact:** Human Resources. **World Wide Web address:** http://www.hyatt.com. **Description:** A full-service hotel that offers two

restaurants, recreational facilities, air line tickets, car rental services, and meeting and banquet facilities. **Positions advertised include:** Front Desk Clerk; Housekeeper; Custodian; Security Officer. **Corporate headquarters location:** Chicago IL. **Other U.S. locations:** Nationwide. **International locations:** Worldwide. **Parent company:** Hyatt Hotel Corporation. **Operations at this facility include:** Service. **Listed on:** Privately held. **Number of employees at this location:** 400. **Number of employees nationwide:** 40,000.

HYATT REGENCY PIER SIXTY-SIX
2301 SE 17th Street Causeway, Fort Lauderdale FL 33316. 954/728-3580. **Fax:** 954/728-3509. **Contact:** Human Resources. **World Wide Web address:** http://www.hyatt.com. **Description:** A full-service hotel that offers six restaurants, multiple recreational facilities, and extensive meeting and banquet facilities. **Special programs:** Internships. **Operations at this facility include:** Administration; Divisional Headquarters; Sales. **Listed on:** Privately held. **Number of employees at this location:** 500.

KING PROVISION CORPORATION
P.O. Drawer U, Jacksonville FL 32203. 904/725-4122. **Contact:** Human Resources. **World Wide Web address:** http://www.kingprovision.com. **Description:** A distributor that provides food and supplies to Burger King Restaurants. **Positions advertised include:** General Manager; Management Trainee; Restaurant/Food Service Manager. **Corporate headquarters location:** This location.

LA CRUISE CASINO
4738 Ocean Street, Jacksonville FL 32233. 904/241-7200. **Contact:** Human Resources. **World Wide Web address:** http://www.lacruise.com. **Description:** A 24-hour casino cruise ship. La Cruise Dockside (also at this location) is a family-style restaurant.

MARRIOT-EXECUSTAY, INC.
5601 Ponlin Park, Suite 303, Forte Lauderdale FL 33309. 866/771-5773. **Fax:** 954/975-0411. **Contact:** Human Resources Department. **World Wide Web address:** http://www.execustay.com. **Description:** Specializes in providing corporations and executives with interim housing throughout south Florida. **Corporate headquarters location:** This location. **Parent company:** Marriott International, Inc.

OUTBACK STEAKHOUSE, INC.
2202 North West Shore Boulevard, 5th Floor, Tampa FL 33607. 813/282-1225. **Fax:** 813/282-1209. **Contact:** Trudy Cooper, Vice President of Training and Development. **World Wide Web address:** http://www.outbacksteakhouse.com. **Description:** The company operates Outback Steakhouse Restaurants. Outback Steakhouses, Inc. also owns and operates several Carraba's Italian Grill and Fleming's Prime Steakhouse and Wine Bar restaurants. **Listed on:** New York Stock Exchange. **Stock exchange symbol:** OSI. **Number of employees nationwide:** 8,800.

POPEYE'S
906 Lee Road, Orlando FL 32810. 407/628-0393. **Fax:** 407/628-8311. **Contact:** Human Resources. **World Wide Web address:** http://www.popeyes.com. **Description:** One location of national restaurant franchise. **Positions advertised include:** Assistant Restaurant Manager. **Corporate headquarters location:** Macon GA. **Listed on:** Privately held. **Number of employees nationwide:** 2,500.

RADISSON RIVERWALK HOTEL
1515 Prudential Drive, Jacksonville FL 32207. 904/396-5100. **Fax:** 904/398-7154. **Contact:** Human Resources. **E-mail address:** sales@radjax.com. **World Wide Web address:** http://www.radjax.com. **Description:** A hotel and conference center. **Positions advertised include:** General Maintenance Worker; Restaurant Server; Restaurant Busser; Lobby Attendant; Floor Technician; Cashier; Bartender.

RENAISSANCE MIAMI BISCAYNE BAY HOTEL
1601 Biscayne Boulevard, Miami FL 33132. 305/374-0000. **Fax:** 305/374-8065. **Contact:** Human Resources. **World Wide Web address:** http://www.marriott.com. **Description:** A 528-room hotel that is located atop a shopping mall. **Positions advertised include:** Sales Administrative Assistant; Assistant Restaurant Manager; Catering Sales Manager; Cook.

RESTAURANT ADMINISTRATION SERVICES
2699 Lee Road, Suite 200, Winter Park FL 32789. 407/645-4811. **Fax:** 407/629-0641. **Contact:** Dale Lucas, Director of Personnel and Training. **Description:** Operates quick-service restaurants. **Corporate headquarters location:** This location. **Listed on:** Privately held. **Number of employees at this location:** 1,200.

RITZ CARLTON GRANDE LAKES
4012 Central Florida Parkway, Orlando FL 32837. 407/200/2400. **Fax:** 407/206-2401. **Contact:** Human Resources, Employment Specialist. **E-mail address:** hrorlando@ritzcarlton.com. **World Wide Web address:** http://www.ritzcarlton.com. **Description:** A five star hotel located in Orlando. **Positions advertised include:** Audio Visual Technician; Houseperson Banquets.

THE WESTIN INNISBROOK RESORT
36750 U.S. Highway 19 North, Palm Harbor FL 34684. 727/942-2000. **Fax:** 727/942-5268. **Contact:** Human Resources. **World Wide Web address:** http://www.westin-innisbrook.com. **Description:** A 221-room hotel and resort that offers four golf courses, six restaurants, full-service recreational facilities, and three convention centers. **NOTE:** Entry-level positions and second and third shifts are offered. **Company slogan:** People make the difference. **Special programs:** Internships; Training; Summer Jobs. **Corporate headquarters location:** Seattle WA. **Other U.S. locations:** Nationwide. **International locations:** Worldwide. **Listed on:** Privately held. **Number of employees at this location:** 1,600. **Number of employees worldwide:** 22,000.

WYNDHAM ORLANDO RESORT
8001 International Drive, Orlando FL 32819. 407/351-2420. **Fax:** 407/352-7054. **Contact:** Human Resources Department. **World Wide Web address:** http://www.wyndham.com/hotels/MCOWD/main.wnt. **Description:** A full-service hotel that offers five restaurants, recreational facilities, and business and meeting accommodations. **Positions advertised include:** Catering Manager; Sales Manager; Housekeeping Manager; Restaurant Manager; Convention Services Manager; Director of Human Resources. **Corporate headquarters location:** Washington DC. **Parent company:** Wyndham International. **Operations at this facility include:** Administration; Sales. **Listed on:** New York Stock Exchange. **Stock exchange symbol:** WYN.

Georgia

AMERICA'S BEST FRANCHISING
50 Glenlake Parkway, NE, Suite 350, Atlanta GA 30328. 770/393-2662. **Toll-free phone:** 800/432-7992. **Contact:** Human Resources. **E-mail address:** celbers@buckheadamerica.com. **World Wide Web address:** http://www.buckheadamerica.com. **Description:** Engaged in hotel franchising, hotel management, settlement, and mortgage services. **Corporate headquarters location:** This location. **Subsidiaries include:** Country Hearth Inn is a mid-sized hotel chain.

ARAMARK HEALTHCARE SUPPORT SERVICES
5775 Peachtree Dunwoody Road, Building C, Suite 500, Atlanta GA 30342. 404/851-1805. **Fax:** 404/851-1911. **Contact:** Human Resources. **World Wide Web address:** http://www.aramark.com. **Description:** Serves 115 million meals annually for health care customers nationwide and offers food service, clinical

nutrition management, facility services, and engineering support to health care administrators. **NOTE:** Please visit website to search for jobs and apply online. **Positions advertised include:** Assistant Director of Patient Services. **Special programs:** Internship. **Parent company:** ARAMARK. **Corporate headquarters location:** Philadelphia PA. **Other U.S. locations:** Nationwide. **Operations at this facility include:** Regional Headquarters. **Listed on:** New York Stock Exchange. **Stock exchange symbol:** RMK. **Number of employees nationwide:** 124,000.

ARBY'S RESTAURANT GROUP
1155 Perimeter Center West, Suite 1200, Atlanta GA 30338. 404/256-4900. **Contact:** Human Resources. **World Wide Web address:** http://www.rtminc.com. **Description:** Operates and franchises national restaurant chains including Arby's, Lee's Famous Recipe Chicken, Mrs. Winner's Chicken & Biscuits, Del Taco Mexican Restaurants, Pasta Connection, Sbarro, and T.J. Cinnamons. **Positions advertised include:** Assistant Manager; General Manager; Operating Partner; Area Supervisor; Director of Operations; Region Vice President of Operations. **Corporate headquarters location:** This location. **Other U.S. locations:** Nationwide. **Operations at this facility include:** Administration; Research and Development. **CEO:** Russ Umphenour. **Number of employees nationwide:** 20,000.

ATLANTA MARRIOTT MARQUIS
265 Peachtree Center Avenue, Atlanta GA 30303. 404/521-0000. **Toll-free phone:** 800/228-9290. **Fax:** 404/586-6299. **Contact:** Ericka Qualls, Director of Personnel. **World Wide Web address:** http://www.marriott.com. **Description:** A 1,675-room hotel with 69 suites, 48 meeting rooms, four restaurants, indoor and outdoor swimming pools, a solarium, a health club, a whirlpool, a sauna, and three golf courses. **Positions advertised include:** Director of Group Sales; Director of Loss Prevention; Executive Sous Chef. **Parent company:** Marriott International. **Corporate headquarters location:** Washington D.C. **Other U.S. locations:** Nationwide. **International locations:** Worldwide. **Listed on:** New York Stock Exchange. **Stock exchange symbol:** MAR. **CEO:** J.W. Marriott, Jr. **Number of employees worldwide:** 154,000.

BUCKHEAD AMERICA CORPORATION
Northpark Town Center, Building 500, 1100 Abernathy Road NE, Suite 1210, Atlanta GA 30328. 770/393-2662. **Toll-free phone:** 800/432-7992. **Contact:** Human Resources. **E-mail address:** celbers@buckheadamerica.com. **World Wide Web address:** http://www.buckheadamerica.com. **Description:** Engaged in hotel franchising, hotel management, settlement, and mortgage services. **Corporate headquarters location:** This location. **Subsidiaries include:** Country Hearth Inn is a mid-sized hotel chain.

CROWNE PLAZA HOTEL
1325 Virginia Avenue, Atlanta GA 30344. 404/768-6660. **Fax:** 404/766-6121. **Contact:** Judith Kruzich, Director of Human Resources. **World Wide Web address:** http://www.crowneplaza.com. **Description:** A 379-room hotel with several conference and meeting facilities. **NOTE:** Visit http://www.ichotelsgroup.new-jobs.com to search for jobs and apply online. **Positions advertised include:** Corporate Group Sales Manager; Loss Prevention Manager; Controller; Assistant Banquet Manager; Director of Catering/Senior Catering Sales Manager. **Parent company:** InterContinental Hotels Group. **Listed on:** New York Stock Exchange. **Stock exchange symbol:** IHG. **Number of employees at this location:** 200.

HOMESTEAD VILLAGE INC.
2239 Powers Ferry Road, Marietta GA 30067. 770/303-0043. **Toll-free phone:** 888/782-9473. **Fax:** 770/303-0063. **Contact:** Human Resources. **World Wide Web address:** http://www.homesteadvillage.com. **Description:** An extended-stay hotel chain. Guests are typically business travelers who are on extended-stay assignments, attending seminars, or in the process of relocating to a new city. The company owns and operates 112 properties. Founded in 1992. **NOTE:** Please visit website to search for jobs and apply online. **Corporate headquarters location:** This location. **Other U.S. locations:** Nationwide. **Listed on:** American Stock Exchange. **Stock exchange symbol:** HSD. **President/CEO:** Gary A. DeLapp. **Annual sales/revenues:** $51 - $100 million. **Number of employees nationwide:** 1,800.

HYATT REGENCY ATLANTA
265 Peachtree Street NE, Atlanta GA 30303. 404/577-1234. **Fax:** 404/588-4137. **Contact:** Human Resources. **World Wide Web address:** http://atlantaregency.hyatt.com. **Description:** Operates a luxury hotel with complete dining and entertainment facilities. **NOTE:** Please visit website to search for jobs and apply online. **Positions advertised include:** Associate Catering Director; Banquet Sous Chef; Bartender; Convention Services Manager; Culinary Lead Cook; Food Server; Greeter; HVAC Engineer; Intermediate Line Cook; Room Attendant/Housekeeper; Sales Manager; Security Officer – On-Call. **Special programs:** Internships. **Corporate headquarters location:** Chicago IL. **Other U.S. locations:** Nationwide. **Parent company:** Hyatt Hotels Corporation. **International locations:** Worldwide. **Operations at this facility include:** Administration; Regional Headquarters; Sales; Service.

INTERCONTINENTAL HOTELS GROUP
3 Ravinia Drive, Suite 2900, Atlanta GA 30346-2149. 770/604-2000. **Fax:** 770/604-2371. **Contact:** Human Resources. **World Wide Web address:** http://www.ihgplc.com. **Description:** Six Continents Hotels owns and operates over 3,200 hotels across 100 countries. **NOTE:** Please visit http://www.ichotelsgroup.new-jobs.com to search for jobs and apply online. **Positions advertised include:** Loyalty Marketing Manager; Director of Finance and Business Support; Analytics Analyst; Senior Market Research Consultant; Software Engineer; Global Alliances Manager; Project Manager – Investment Analysis; Lead Analyst – Technical Services; Specialist – Reporting; Director of Global Consumer Marketing; Revenue Manager. **Corporate headquarters location:** Berkshire England. **International locations:** Worldwide. **Operations at this facility include:** This location houses administrative offices. **Listed on:** New York Stock Exchange. **Stock exchange symbol:** IHG. **CEO:** Richard North. **Number of employees worldwide:** 69,953. Finance Group. **President/CEO:** Jill Jinks.

KFC
675 Mansell Road, Suite 200, Roswell GA 30076. 770/990-4000. **Fax:** 770/552-1739. **Contact:** Human Resources. **World Wide Web address:** http://www.kfc.com. **Description:** A worldwide fast-food chain specializing in chicken. Founded 1939. **Parent company:** Yum! Brands, Inc. **Office hours:** Monday – Friday, 8:00 a.m. – 5:00 p.m. **Corporate headquarters location:** Louisville KY. **Operations at this location include:** This location serves as a regional office. **Number of employees nationwide:** 84,000.

LODGIAN, INC.
3445 Peachtree Road NE, Suite 700, Atlanta GA 30326. 404/364-9400. **Fax:** 404/364-0088. 800/862-5789. **Contact:** Personnel. **E-mail address:** hr@lodgian.com. **World Wide Web address:** http://www.lodgian.com. **Description:** Owns or manages 107 hotels located in North America. These hotels are primarily full service, providing food and beverage service as well as lodging and meeting facilities. Most of the company's hotels are affiliated with nationally recognized hospitality franchises including Holiday Inn, Best Western, Hilton, Doubletree Club Hotel, Radisson, Crowne Plaza, Comfort Inn, and Westin. Lodgian, Inc. was created through a merger between Servico, Inc. and Impac Hotel Group. **Positions advertised include:** Controller;

Housekeeping Instructor; Director of Food and Beverage; Night Auditor. **Corporate headquarters location:** This location. **Other U.S. locations:** Nationwide. **International locations:** Canada. **President/CEO:** W. Thomas Parrington.

McDONALD'S CORPORATION
5901 Peachtree Dunwoody Road NE, Suite C-500, Atlanta GA 30328. 770/698-7498. **Fax:** 770/885-4100. **Contact:** Human Resources. **World Wide Web address:** http://www.mcdonalds.com. **Description:** McDonald's is one of the largest restaurant chains and food service organizations in the world, operating more than 30,000 restaurants in all 50 states and in more than 121 countries. **NOTE:** Please visit http://www.monster.com to search for jobs. **Positions advertised include:** Finance Manager. **Corporate headquarters location:** Oakbrook IL. **Other U.S. locations:** Nationwide. **International locations:** Worldwide. **Operations at this facility include:** Area administrative offices for the worldwide developer, operator, franchiser, and servicer of a system of restaurants that process, package, and sell fast foods. **Listed on:** New York Stock Exchange. **Stock exchange symbol:** MCD. **CEO:** Jim Cantalupo. **Number of employees worldwide:** 418,000.

OMNI HOTEL AT CNN CENTER
100 CNN Center, Atlanta GA 30303. 404/659-0000. **Fax:** 404/525-5050. **Contact:** Human Resources Manager. **World Wide Web address:** http://www.omnihotels.com. **Description:** A luxury hotel offering lodging, dining, lounge, and meeting facilities. **NOTE:** Please visit website to search for jobs and apply online. **Positions advertised include:** Senior Convention Services Manager; Business Travel Sales Manager; Omni Express Sales Manager. **Corporate headquarters location:** Irving TX. **Other U.S. locations:** Nationwide. **International locations:** Canada; Mexico. **Parent company:** Omni Hotels. **Operations at this facility include:** Sales; Service. **President:** James D. Caldwell. **Number of employees worldwide:** 10,000.

PIZZA HUT, INC.
675 Mansell Road, Suite 200, Roswell GA 30076. 770/990-2000. **Contact:** Human Resources. **World Wide Web address:** http://www.pizzahut.com. **Description:** Pizza Hut is a worldwide operator of family restaurants, with more than 12,000 locations. **NOTE:** Entry-level positions are offered. Please visit http://www.yumcareers.com to search for jobs. **Office hours: Monday – Friday,** 8:00 a.m. – 5:00 p.m. **Corporate headquarters location:** Dallas TX. **Other U.S. locations:** Nationwide. **International locations:** Worldwide. **Operations at this facility include:** Home to the administrative offices for the southern region. **Parent company:** Yum! Brands Inc.

RARE HOSPITALITY INTERNATIONAL, INC.
8215 Roswell Road, Building 600, Atlanta GA 30350. 770/399-9595. **Contact:** Director of Employment. **E-mail address:** careeropportunities@rarehospitality.com. **World Wide Web address:** http://www.rarehospitality.com. **Description:** Franchises 193 restaurants and operates 190 LongHorn Steakhouses (located in the southeastern and midwestern United States), 25 Bugaboo Creek Steak Houses, 17 Capital Grille Restaurants (nationwide), Hemenway's Seafood Grill And Oyster Bar, and The Old Grist Mill Tavern. Founded in 1981. **NOTE:** Contact Employment directly at 770/551-5464. **Corporate headquarters location:** This location. **Listed on:** NASDAQ. **Stock exchange symbol:** RARE. **President/CEO:** Philip Hickey, Jr. **Annual sales/revenues:** More than $100 million. **Number of employees nationwide:** 11,200.

SAVANNAH DESOTO HILTON
15 East Liberty Street, Savannah GA 31401. 912/232-9000. **Fax:** 912/232-3089. **Contact:** Human Resources. **World Wide Web address:** http://www.hilton.com. **Description:** A 250-room hotel. **Special programs:** Internships. **Parent company:** Hilton Hotels Corporation is engaged in the operation and management of hotels and inns throughout the world including more than 1,800 franchised hotels operating in the United States. **Corporate headquarters location:** Beverly Hills CA. **Other U.S. locations:** Nationwide. **Listed on:** New York Stock Exchange. **Stock exchange symbol:** HLT. **President/CEO:** Stephen F. Bollenbach.

WAFFLE HOUSE, INC.
P.O. Box 6450, Norcross GA 30091. 770/729-5700. **Physical address:** 5986 Financial Drive, Norcross GA 30071. **Fax:** 770/729-5834. **Contact:** Recruiting. **E-mail address:** info@wafflehouse.com. **World Wide Web address:** http://www.wafflehouse.com. **Description:** One of the largest 24-hour restaurant chains in the country, with more than 1,200 restaurants in 20 states. Founded in 1955. **NOTE:** Contact Recruiting at 770/729-5825. **Corporate headquarters location:** This location. **Listed on:** Privately held.

WELLESLEY INN HOTEL
1377 Virginia Avenue, Atlanta GA 30344. 404/762-5111. **Contact:** Human Resources. **World Wide Web address:** http://www.wellesleyonline.com. **Description:** Operates a full-service hotel with complete lodging facilities.

Hawaii

HILTON HAWAIIAN VILLAGE BEACH RESORT & SPA
2005 Kalia Road, Honolulu HI 96815. 808/949-4321. **Fax:** 808/947-7904. **Recorded jobline:** 808/948-7742. **Contact:** Human Resources. **World Wide Web address:** http://www.hiltonhawaiianvillage.com. **Description:** A resort complex offering a hotel, 22 restaurant and lounges, a spa, and over 90 shops. **Positions advertised include:** Administrative Assistant; Secretary; Safety and Security Officer; Beverage Manager; Restaurant Manager; Pastry Chef; Banquet Porter; Tea Attendant; Door Attendant; Executive Lounge Concierge; Guest Services Linguist. **Special programs:** Internships; Apprenticeships. **Corporate headquarters location:** Beverly Hills CA. **Parent company:** Hilton Hospitality, Incorporated. **Listed on:** New York Stock Exchange. **Stock exchange symbol:** HLT. **Number of employees at this location:** 1,800.

HYATT REGENCY WAIKIKI RESORT & SPA
2424 Kalakaua Avenue, Honolulu HI 96815. 808/923-1234. **Fax:** 808/841-4384. **Contact:** Carla Thomas, Director of Human Resources. **World Wide Web address:** http://waikiki.hyatt.com. **Description:** A hotel/restaurant facility. **Positions advertised include:** Restaurant Manager; Spa Attendant; Pool Attendant; Telephone Operator, Japanese; Concierge; Utility Steward; Houseperson. **Corporate headquarters location:** Chicago IL. **Parent company:** Hyatt Hotels Corporation. **Number of employees at this location:** 850.

THE MAUNA LANI BAY HOTEL & BUNGALOWS
68-1400 Mauna Lani Drive, Kohala Coast HI 96743-9796. 808/885-6622. **Fax:** 808/885-1442. **Recorded Job Line:** 808/881-7973. **Contact:** Human Resources. **World Wide Web address:** http://www.maunalani.com. **Description:** A resort with hotel rooms; one, two, and three-bedroom villas; and five private bungalows. The resort offers golf, tennis, spa services and water sports activities. **NOTE:** Apply in person Mondays, Wednesdays, and Fridays between 9am and 12pm. **Positions advertised include:** Banquet Staff, Wait, Bus, Porter, Bartender; Food Runner; Host/Hostess; Beach/Pool Concierge; Cook; General Maintenance; Florist; Kitchen Utility.

PARK SHORE WAIKIKI HOTEL
2586 Kalakaua Avenue, Honolulu HI 96815. 808/921-7644. **Fax:** 808/921-7645. **Contact:** Elizabeth Uniatowski, Human Resources Manager. **E-mail address:** euniatowski@parkshorewaikiki.com. **World Wide Web address:** http://www.parkshorewaikiki.com.

Description: A full-service hotel of 226 guest rooms offering two restaurants, a shopping plaza, and a car rental service.

SHERATON WAIKIKI HOTEL
2255 Kalakaua Avenue, Honolulu HI 96815. 808/922-4422. **Toll-free phone:** 866/716-8109. **Fax:** 808/931-8785. **Recorded jobline:** 808/931-8294. **Contact:** Human Resources. **E-mail address:** resume.waikiki@sheraton.com. **World Wide Web address:** http://www.sheraton-waikiki.com. **Description:** A hotel with over 4,000 guest rooms located on Oahu's Waikiki Beach. **NOTE:** Search for current job openings and apply online at http://www.starwoodhawaiijobs.com. **Positions advertised include:** Electrician Journeyman; Executive Banquet Sous Chef.

Idaho
DOUBLETREE HOTEL BOISE-RIVERSIDE
2900 Chinden Boulevard, Boise ID 83714. 208/343-1871. **Fax:** 208/344-1079. **Contact:** Director of Human Resources. **World Wide Web address:** http://www.doubletree.com. **Description:** A mountain resort-style hotel. **NOTE:** For management jobs at Hilton Hotels Corporation owned and managed properties, search the Hilton's jobs website. For non-management positions, please contact the hotel directly. **Parent company:** Hilton Hotels Corporation.

THE GROVE HOTEL
245 South Capital Boulevard, Boise ID 83702. 208/333-8000. **Fax:** 208/333-8800. **Recorded jobline:** 208/424-2188. **Contact:** Accounting Department. **World Wide Web address:** http://www.grovehotelboise.com. **Description:** A luxury hotel with 250 rooms and suites, executive boardrooms and a full-service athletic facility. **Positions advertised include:** Suite Server; Banquet Server; Dishwasher; Relief Auditor; Front Desk Agent; Housekeeper. **Corporate headquarters location:** Vancouver, Canada. **Parent company:** Coast Hotels & Resorts.

SUN VALLEY COMPANY
P.O. Box 10, Sun Valley ID 83353. 208/622-2078. **Toll-free phone:** 800/894/9946. **Fax:** 208/622-2082. **Contact:** Human Resources. **E-mail address:** svpersonnel@sunvalley.com. **World Wide Web address:** http://www.sunvalley.com. **Description:** Operates a hotel and ski resort on 4,000 acres in the Idaho Rockies. **NOTE:** See website for current positions and application instructions. **Positions advertised include:** Cook; Baker; Journeymen Electrician; Journeymen Plumber; Diesel Mechanic; Laundry Attendant; Housekeeper; Hairstylist; Manicurist; Audio Visual Technician; Movie Theater Assistant Manager; Reservation Clerk. **Corporate headquarters location:** This location.

Illinois
ARAMARK CORRECTIONAL SERVICES
1801 South Meyers Road, Suite 300, Oakbrook Terrace IL 60181. 630/568-2500. **Contact:** Human Resources. **World Wide Web address:** http://www.aramark.com. **Description:** ARAMARK Correctional Services provides food to more than 125,000 inmates at 175 prisons and jail facilities in 27 states and Puerto Rico. The company also offers facility management services. **Parent company:** ARAMARK. **NOTE:** Apply online, or contact the office directly.

CHICAGO MARRIOTT DOWNTOWN
540 North Michigan Avenue, Chicago IL 60611-3822. 312/836-0100. **Contact:** Human Resources. **World Wide Web address:** http://www.marriott.com. **Description:** A full-service hotel chain offering 1,172 rooms and 20 meeting facilities. **NOTE:** Apply online. **Other U.S. locations:** Nationwide. **Listed on:** New York Stock Exchange. **Stock exchange symbol:** MAR.

CROWNE PLAZA CHICAGO O'HARE
5440 North River Road, Rosemont IL 60018. 847/671-6350. **Contact:** Staffing. **World Wide Web address:** http://chi-ohare.crowneplaza.com. **Description:** A 503-room hotel. **Parent company:** MeriStar Hospitality Corporation.

ED DEBEVIC'S RESTAURANT
640 North Wells Street, Chicago IL 60610. 312/664-1707. **Fax:** 312/664-7444. **Contact:** Human Resources. **World Wide Web address:** http://www.eddebevics.com. **Description:** A casual dining restaurant chain. Ed Debevic's serves American cuisine and operates a gift shop. **NOTE:** Submit resume by mail or fax. **Positions advertised include:** Servers; Bussers; Hosts, Bartenders; Line Cooks; Prep Cooks; Dishwasher. **Parent company:** Bravo Restaurants, Inc.

THE DRAKE HOTEL
140 East Walton Place, Chicago IL 60611. 312/787-2200. **Fax:** 312/475-0523. **Contact:** Human Resources. **World Wide Web address:** http://www.thedrakehotel.com. **Description:** A 535-room hotel and restaurant.

EAGLEWOOD RESORT & SPA
1401 Nordic Road, Itasca IL 60143. 630/773-1400. **Toll-free phone:** 877/285-6150. **Fax:** 630/773-1709. **Contact:** Human Resources. **World Wide Web address:** http://www.eaglewoodresort.com. **Description:** A luxury resort offering accommodations, dining, a golf course, spa, and meeting rooms. **NOTE:** Search and apply for positions at: http://www.benchmark.hospitalityonline.com. **Positions advertised include:** Conference Services Floor Manager; Director of Rooms Division; Banquet Steward; Security Officer; Loss Prevention Agent; Landscaper. **Parent company:** Benchmark Hospitality International.

HOLIDAY INN CITY CENTRE
500 Hamilton Boulevard, Peoria IL 61602. 309/674-2500. **Fax:** 309/674-8705. **Contact:** Human Resources. **World Wide Web address:** http://www.holidayinnpeoria.com. **Description:** A 300-room hotel. The Holiday Inn City Centre also houses one of Illinois' largest convention centers. **NOTE:** To apply, visit the company's website. Positions advertised include: Bennigan's Bar Manager; Sales Manager; Catering Assistant; Sales Assistant.

HOLIDAY INN COLLINSVILLE/ST. LOUIS
1000 Eastport Plaza Drive, Collinsville IL 62234. 618/345-2800. **Fax:** 618/345-9804. **Contact:** Human Resources. **World Wide Web address:** http://www.hicollinsville.com. **Description:** A hotel with full-service banquet and conference facilities located near St. Louis MO. **NOTE:** Call to inquire about current job openings. **Parent company:** Intercontinental Hotels Group.

HOLLYWOOD CASINO AURORA
49 West Galena Boulevard, Aurora IL 60506. 630/801-7000. **Contact:** Human Resources. **World Wide Web address:** http://www.pngaming.com. **Description:** Operates a fixed riverboat casino featuring movie memorabilia. **NOTE:** Apply online at the website. **Positions advertised include:** Bartender; Casino Cashier; Casino Scheduler Internal Auditor. **Parent company:** Penn National Gaming.

HOSTMARK HOSPITALITY GROUP
1111 Plaza Drive, Suite 200, Schaumburg IL 60173. 847/517-9100. **Fax:** 847/517-9797. **Contact:** Human Resources. **World Wide Web address:** http://www.hostmark.com. **Description:** HostMark Hospitality Group is a hotel property management company. **Positions advertised include:** Director of Sales.

HOTEL 71
71 East Wacker Drive, Chicago IL 60601. 312/346-7100. **Toll-free phone:** 800/621-4005. **Fax:** 312/346-1721. **Contact:** Recruitment Manager. **E-mail address:** jobs@hotel71.com. **World Wide Web address:** http://www.hotel71.com. **Description:** A 417-room full-service hotel. Founded in 1958.

HYATT REGENCY CHICAGO
151 East Wacker Drive, Chicago IL 60601. 312/565-1234. **Contact:** Human Resources. **World Wide Web address:** http://www.chicagohyatt.com. **Description:** A hotel with over 2,000 rooms. **NOTE:** Apply online at the website. **Positions advertised include:** Deli Attendant; Food Server Assistant; Front Office Supervisor; Master Accounts Coordinator; Off-Premises Catering Driver.

LETTUCE ENTERTAIN YOU ENTERPRISES INC.
5419 North Sheridan Road, Suite 104, Chicago IL 60640. 773/878-7340. **Fax:** 773/878-0113. **Contact:** Human Resources. **E-mail address:** resumes@leye.com. **World Wide Web address:** http://www.leye.com. **Description:** A restaurant management company operating casual, moderately priced dining establishments. **NOTE:** Call the Recruiting Office at 773/878-5588 for current job listings. Fax or e-mail resumes.

LUNAN CORPORATION
414 North Orleans Street, Suite 402, Chicago IL 60610. 312/645-9898. **Contact:** Human Resources. **World Wide Web address:** http://www.arbysrestaurants.com. **Description:** The restaurant management company of the fast food chain Arby's. **Corporate headquarters location:** This location.

McDONALD'S CORPORATION
2111 McDonald's Drive, Oak Brook IL 60523. 630/623-3000. **Contact:** Human Resources. **World Wide Web address:** http://www.mcdonalds.com. **Description:** McDonald's is one of the largest restaurant chains and food service organizations in the world, operating more than 26,000 restaurants in 119 countries. **NOTE:** For corporate positions, see the website. For restaurant jobs, see http://www.McState.com or apply in person at the nearest location. **Corporate headquarters location:** This location. **Other U.S. locations:** Nationwide. **International locations:** Worldwide. **Listed on:** New York Stock Exchange. **Stock exchange symbol:** MCD.

PHEASANT RUN RESORT & CONVENTION CENTER
4051 East Main Street, St. Charles IL 60174-5200. 630/584-6300. **Contact:** Human Resources. **E-mail address:** lbabusch@pheasantrun.com. **World Wide Web address:** http://www.pheasantrun.com. **Description:** A hotel and convention center. **NOTE:** Fax or e-mail resumes. Interested jobseekers may also apply in person at the Human Resources Office. **Positions advertise include:** Administrative Assistant; Cook; Bartender; Front Desk Agent; Rooms Director; Security. **Corporate headquarters location:** This location. **Operations at this facility include:** Sales; Service.

PIZZA HUT OF AMERICA, INC.
4575 Weaver Parkway, Suite 200, Warrenville IL 60555. 630/791-1000. **Fax:** 630/955-0577. **Contact:** Human Resources. **World Wide Web address:** http://www.pizzahut.com. **Description:** Part of the large, worldwide restaurant chain. **NOTE:** Apply in person at this location or online at http://www.yum.com. **Positions advertised include:** Assistant Manager; Management Trainee. **Special programs:** Internships. **Other U.S. locations:** Nationwide. **Parent company:** Yum Brands.

RAMADA PLAZA SUITES AND CONFERENCE CENTER
200 South Bell School Road, Rockford IL, 61108. 815/226-2100. **Contact:** Human Resources. **World Wide Web address:** http://www.ramada.com. **Description:** A hotel and conference facility. Ramada has locations nationwide, including Stouffers/Renaissance Hotel Properties. **NOTE:** Entry-level positions are offered. **Special programs:** Internships; Training. **Corporate headquarters location:** Solon OH. **Other U.S. locations:** Nationwide. **Parent company:** Cendant Corporation. **Operations at this facility include:** Sales; Service.

SPRINGFIELD HILTON
700 East Adams Street, Springfield IL 62701-1601. 217/789-1530. **Fax:** 217/789-0709. **Contact:** Human Resources. **World Wide Web address:** http://www.hilton.com. **Description:** A 30-story hotel with 368 guest rooms. The hotel also offers long-term guest services. **Parent company:** Hilton Hotels Corporation. **Listed on:** New York Stock Exchange. **Stock exchange symbol:** HLT.

Indiana

GRAND VICTORIA CASINO & RESORT BY HYATT
600 Grand Victoria Drive, Rising Sun IN 47040. 812/438-1234. **Toll-free phone:** 800/GRA-ND11. **Contact:** Human Resources. **World Wide Web address:** http://www.hyatt.com. **Description:** A 200-room hotel and resort featuring an 18-hole golf course, a casino, and multiple banquet facilities.

HAMPTON INN
105 South Meridian Street, Indianapolis IN 46225. 317/261-1200. **Contact:** Human Resources. **World Wide Web address:** www.hamptoninn.com. **Description:** Located downtown within walking distance of Conseco Field House, the RCA Dome, and numerous restaurants. **Other U.S. locations:** Nationwide. **Parent Company:** Hilton.

HILTON FORT WAYNE
1020 South Calhoun Street, Fort Wayne IN 46802-3005. 260/420-1100. **Fax:** 260/424-7775. **Contact:** Human Resources. **World Wide Web address:** www.hilton.com. **Description:** A 246-room hotel attached to the Grand Wayne Convention Center offering downtown conveniences and business amenities.

LEE'S INNS OF AMERICA
5011 North Lafayette Road, Indianapolis IN 46259. 317/297-8880. **Physical address:** 130 North State Street, North Vernon IN 47265. **Fax:** 812/346-7521. **Contact:** Becky Hook, Human Resources. **World Wide Web address:** http://www.leesinn.com. **Description:** Owns and operates 21 limited-service hotels throughout Indiana, Illinois, Michigan, and Ohio. **NOTE:** Entry-level positions are offered. **Special programs:** Internships; Training. **Corporate headquarters location:** This location. **Listed on:** Privately held.

MARRIOTT
123 North Saint Joseph Street, South Bend IN 46601. 574/234-2000. **Fax:** 574/234-2252. **Contact:** Human Resources. **World Wide Web address:** www.marriott.com. **Description:** A 298 room hotel located in downtown South Bend, across from the College Football Hall of Fame. **Other area locations:** Statewide. **Other U.S. locations:** Nationwide.

McDONALD'S CORPORATION D&J PARTNERSHIP
3042 State Street, Columbus IN 47201. 812/376-0552. **Contact:** Human Resources. **World Wide Web address:** http://www.mcdonalds.com. **Description:** A franchisee of McDonald's Restaurants that operates 11 restaurants in Indiana. McDonald's Corporation develops, operates, franchises, and services a worldwide system of restaurants that process, package, and sell a variety of fast foods. McDonald's is one of the largest restaurant operations in the world. The company operates more than 26,000 McDonald's restaurants in all 50 states and in 119 foreign countries.

QUALITY DINING, INC.
4220 Edison Lakes Parkway, Mishawaka IN 46545. 574/271-4600. **Fax:** 574/271-4612. **Contact:** Human Resources Manager. **World Wide Web address:** http://www.qdi.com. **Description:** A franchiser of restaurants. The company operates 71 quick-service Burger King Restaurants, 29 restaurants under the name

Chili's Bar & Grill, five casual dining restaurants under the name Papa Vino's, three casual dining restaurants under the name Spageddie's, and 36 casual dining restaurants under the name Grady's American Grill. **Special programs:** Internships; Summer Jobs. **Corporate headquarters location:** This location. **Other U.S. locations:** Nationwide. **Listed on:** NASDAQ. **Stock exchange symbol:** QDIN.

STEAK N SHAKE
36 South Pennsylvania Street, 500 Century Building, Indianapolis IN 46204. 317/633-4100. **Fax:** 317/633-4105. **Contact:** Human Resources Manager. **E-mail address:** careers@steaknshake.com. **World Wide Web address:** http://www.steaknshake.com. **Description:** Owns and operates a chain of casual-dining restaurants. Steak n Shake operates over 370 locations throughout the Midwest and Southeast. Founded in 1934. **NOTE:** Resumes are accepted by e-mail or regular mail. **Special programs:** Internships. **Internship information:** Corporate and Management internships are offered. **Other U.S. locations:** Nationwide. **Listed on:** New York Stock Exchange. **Stock exchange symbol:** SNS.

UNIVERSITY PLACE
850 West Michigan Street, Indianapolis IN 46202-5198. 317/269-9000. **Toll-free phone:** 800/410-MEET. **Fax:** 317/231-5050. **Contact:** Human Resources Director. **E-mail address:** iuplace@iupui.edu. **NOTE:** Fill out application or apply through www.careerbuilder.com. **World Wide Web address:** http://www.universityplace.iupui.edu. **Description:** A conference center and hotel. University Place offers 28 meeting rooms and a 340-seat auditorium.

Iowa
HAPPY JOE'S PIZZA AND ICE CREAM
2705 Happy Joe Drive, Bettendorf IA 52722. 563/332-8811. **Fax:** 563/332-5822. **Contact:** Stacy Drezek, Human Resources. **E-mail address:** staceed@happyjoes.com. **World Wide Web address:** http://www.happyjoes.com. **Description:** A restaurant chain that serves pizza, pasta, and ice cream. **Positions advertised include:** General Manager; Restaurant Worker Positions. **Operations at this facility include:** Administration; Divisional Headquarters; Research and Development. **Number of employees at this location:** 30.

Kansas
AMERICAN RESTAURANT PARTNERS RESTAURANT MANAGEMENT COMPANY
3020 North Cypress Road, Suite 100, Wichita KS 67226. 316/634-1190. **Fax:** 316/634-1662. **Contact:** Gina Eustice, Human Resources. **Description:** A limited partnership operating more than 120 restaurants and delivery/carry-out facilities (including Kentucky Fried Chicken, Pizza Hut, and Long John Silvers) located primarily in Texas, Montana, Oklahoma, Georgia, Louisiana, and Wyoming. **NOTE:** Entry-level positions are offered. **Positions advertised include:** Assistant Manager; Manager Trainee; Restaurant General Manager; Shift Manager; Food Service Manager. **Special programs:** Training. **Corporate headquarters location:** This location. **Other area locations:** Dodge City KS; El Dorado KS; Newton KS; Park City KS. **Operations at this facility include:** Administration. **Chairman/CEO:** Hal W. McCoy. **Annual sales/revenues:** $64 million. **Number of employees nationwide:** 3,000.

LONE STAR STEAKHOUSE & SALOON, INC.
P.O. Box 12726, Wichita KS 67277-2726. 316/264-8899. **Physical address:** 224 East Douglas, Suite 700, Wichita KS 67202. **Fax:** 316/264-5988. **Contact:** Kim Niswiender, Human Resources. **World Wide Web address:** http://www.lonestarsteakhouse.com. **Description:** Owner/operator of chain of 250 U.S. restaurants offering mid-priced, full-service, casual dining as well as 20 restaurants worldwide. It also operates 15 upscale Sullivan's Steakhouses and five Del Frisco's Double Eagle Steak Houses. **Positions advertised include:** General Manager; Regional Manager; Management Trainee; Restaurant/Food Service Manager Assistant Manager. **Special programs:** Internships. **Corporate headquarters location:** This location. **Other area locations:** Garden City KS; Shawnee Mission KS. **Other U.S. locations:** Nationwide. **Listed on:** NASDAQ. **Stock exchange symbol:** STAR. **Annual sales/revenues:** $598 million. **Number of employees nationwide:** 18,425.

NPC INTERNATIONAL
720 West 20th Street, Pittsburg KS 66762. 620/231-3390. **Fax:** 620/231-5115. **Contact:** Skip Allen, Corporate Recruitment Department. **World Wide Web address:** http://www.npcinternational.com. **Description:** NPC, formerly National Pizza Company, owns and operates 840 Pizza Hut restaurants in 27 states. Founded in 1962. **NOTE:** For restaurant positions, see manager. For management positions, apply online via web site. **Positions advertised include:** Dough Master; Customer Service Representative; Restaurant Shift Manager; Assistant Restaurant Manager; Restaurant Manager; Area Manager. **Special programs:** Internships. **Corporate headquarters location:** This location. **Restaurant locations:** Chanute KS; Emporia KS; Fort Scott KS; Frontenac KS; Girard KS; Parsons KS; Pittsburg KS; Topeka KS. **Listed on:** Privately held. **Annual sales/revenues:** $536 million. **Number of employees nationwide:** 18,000.

Kentucky
EXECUTIVE INN RIVERMONT
One Executive Boulevard, Owensboro KY 42301. 270/926-8000. **Toll-free phone:** 800/626-1936. **Fax:** 270/926-9047. **Contact:** Human Resources. **E-mail address:** bige@executiveinnrivermont.com. **World Wide Web Address:** http://www.executiveinnrivermont.com. **Description:** A hotel/convention center featuring 650 guest rooms and suites, 22 meeting rooms, and an exposition center. **Positions available include:** Security Officer.

GRIFFIN GATE MARRIOTT RESORT
1800 Newtown Pike, Lexington KY 40511. 859/231-5100. **Toll-free phone:** 800/228-9290. **Fax:** 859/255-9944. **Contact:** Angela Brown, Director of Human Resources. **World Wide Web address:** http://www.marriott.com. **Description:** A full-service hotel that also includes a swimming pool, a gift shop, convention and banquet facilities, restaurant and lounge, tennis courts, and a golf course. **Positions advertised include:** Housekeeper; Front Desk Clerk; Night Auditor. **Corporate headquarters location:** Washington DC. **Other U.S. locations:** Nationwide. **Parent company:** Marriott International. **Listed on:** New York Stock Exchange. **Stock exchange symbol:** MAR. **Sales/revenues:** $20 billion. **Number of employees at this location:** 600. **Number of employees nationwide:** 145,000.

HYATT REGENCY LOUISVILLE
320West Jefferson Street, Louisville KY 40202. 502/587-3434. **Fax:** 502/581-0133. **Contact:** Human Resources. **World Wide Web address:** http://louisville.hyatt.com. **Description:** A full-service hotel, centrally located to many attractions in Louisville KY. **Positions advertised include:** General Maintenance; Room Service. **Parent company:** Hyatt Hotels Corporation.

YUM! BRANDS, INC.
1441 Gardiner Lane, P.O. Box 32220, Louisville KY 40213. 502/874-8300. **Fax:** 502/874-2452. **Contact:** Human Resources. **World Wide Web address:** http://www.yum.com. **Description:** Operates and franchises fast food restaurants including KFC, Pizza Hut, Long John Silver's, A&W All-American Food, Yum! Restaurants International, and Taco Bell. **Positions advertised include:** General Manager; Shift Supervisor; Assistant Manager. **Corporate headquarters location:** This location. **Listed on:** New York Stock Exchange. **Stock exchange symbol:** YUM.

Louisiana

BOOMTOWN CASINO WEST BANK
4132 Peters Road, Harvey LA 70058-1805. 504/366-7711. **Toll-free phone:** 800/366-7711. **Fax:** 504/364-8796. **Contact:** Human Resources. **World Wide Web address:** http://www.boomtownneworleans.com. **Description:** A 50-acre complex whose primary operations include the Boomtown Belle Casino, a replica of a paddle-wheel riverboat. It accommodates 1,400 passengers and a crew of 200. The complex's dockside facility offers such amenities as the 200-seat Boomer's Cabaret entertainment lounge, the Mossy Horn Cafe, and a family entertainment center. **NOTE:** Online applications are available. Please visit website to download application. **Positions advertised include:** Restaurant Staff; Revenue Auditor; Financial Analyst; Shift Manager; Shift Supervisor; Cashier, Main Banker; Groundskeeper; Engineer; Dealer; Pit Clerk; Retail Clerk; Buyer; Players Club Representative. **Special programs:** Tuition Reimbursement Program; G.E.D. Program; Computer Classes. **Other U.S. locations:** Biloxi MS; Reno NV. **Parent company:** Boomtown, Incorporated, a subsidiary of Pinnacle Entertainment.

BRENT HOUSE HOTEL
1512 Jefferson Highway, New Orleans LA 70121. 504/842-4140. **Toll-free phone:** 800/535-3986. **Fax:** 504/842-4160. **Contact:** Shelly Williams, Human Resources Coordinator. **E-mail address:** info@brenthouse.com. **World Wide Web address:** http://www.brenthouse.com. **Description:** Located adjacent to the patient care facilities at Ochsner Clinic and Ochsner Foundation Hospital in New Orleans, this hotel provides lodging to the general public with an emphasis on ambulatory and convalescent patients and their families. **NOTE:** Resumes should be sent via fax.

AL COPELAND INVESTMENTS
P.O. Box 277, Metairie LA 70001. 504/830-1000. **Physical Address:** 1405 Airline Drive, Metairie LA 70001. **Fax:** 504/830-1038. **Contact:** Human Resources. **World Wide Web address:** http://www.alcopeland.com. **Description:** Owns and operates several franchises, including Popeye's Famous Fried Chicken restaurants, Copeland's of New Orleans restaurants, and Copeland's Cheesecake Bistro. The company also owns a Diversified Food and Seasonings manufacturing company, an improv comedy club, a hotel and a Cajun diner. **NOTE:** Fill out an online application to be considered for all available positions. **Positions advertised include:** Management; Hourly help. **Corporate headquarters location:** This location. **Listed on:** Private.

PICCADILLY RESTAURANTS, LLC
P.O. Box 2467, Baton Rouge LA 70821-2467. 225/293-9440. **Physical address:** 3232 Sherwood Forest Boulevard, Baton Rouge LA 70816. **Toll-free phone:** 800/552-7422. **Contact:** Sarah Washington or Rob Cooperman. **World Wide Web address:** http://www.piccadilly.com. **Description:** Operates over 150 restaurants located in 14 states. **NOTE:** For management positions, call Sarah Washington at 800/942.7422, extension 8, or Rob Cooperman at 800/942.7422, extension 2. Apply in person for Hourly Team Member positions. **Positions advertised include:** Manager; Team Member. **Special programs:** Training. **Corporate headquarters location:** This location.

Maine

EASTLAND PARK HOTEL
157 High Street, Portland ME 04101. 207/775-5411. **Toll-free phone:** 888/671-8008. **Fax:** 207/775-2872. **Contact:** Personnel. **E-mail address:** info@eastlandparkhotel.com. **World Wide Web address:** http://www.eastlandparkhotel.com. **Description:** A 200-room hotel. Founded 1927.

GRITTY McDUFF'S
396 Fore Street, Portland ME 04101. 207/772-2739. **Fax:** 207/772-6204. **Contact:** Richard Seffer, Manager. **E-mail address:** grittys@grittys.com. **World Wide Web address:** http://www.grittys.com. **Description:** A brew pub in the Old Port section of Portland. **Other area locations:** Freeport ME.

HARRASEEKET INN
162 Main Street, Freeport ME 04032. 207/865-9377. **Toll-free phone:** 800/342-6423. **Fax:** 207/865-1684. **Contact:** John Jacobs, Business Office. **World Wide Web address:** http://www.harraseeketinn.com. **Description:** An 84-room inn featuring two restaurants and an indoor pool. **Positions advertised include:** Banquet Server.

MARRIOTT HOTEL
200 Sable Oaks Drive, South Portland ME 04106-3212. 207/871-8000. **Fax:** 207/871-7971. **Toll-free phone:** 800/752-8810. **Contact:** Human Resources. **World Wide Web address:** http://marriotthotels.com/pwmap. **Description:** A 227-room hotel offering both lodging and restaurant services. **NOTE:** Search posted listings and apply on-line. **Special programs:** Internships. **Corporate headquarters location:** Washington D.C. **Other area locations:** Statewide. **Other U.S. locations:** Nationwide. **Listed on:** New York Stock Exchange. **Stock exchange symbol:** MAR. **Number of employees at this location:** 150. **Number of employees worldwide:** 128,000.

OLIVE GARDEN ITALIAN RESTAURANT
741 Hogan Road, Bangor ME 04401-3625. 207/942-6209. **Fax:** 207/947-6575. **Contact:** General Manager. **World Wide Web address:** http://www.olivegarden.com. **Description:** One location of the nationwide restaurant chain. **NOTE:** Search posted openings and apply on-line. Do not fax or e-mail resumes. May contact manager at local restaurants for information.

SUGARLOAF/USA
5092 Access Road, Carrabasset Valley ME 04947. 207/237-6932. **Toll-free phone:** 800/843-5623. **Fax:** 207/237-6778. **Contact:** Marilyn Curry, Human Resources Director. **World Wide Web address:** http://www.sugarloaf.com. **Description:** An operator of a ski mountain and resort. Features at Sugarloaf include a number of cross-country trails, an Olympic-size ice-skating rink, and an 18-hole golf course. **NOTE:** Search posted openings and apply on-line. **Positions advertised include:** Certified Massage Therapist; Costume Character; Hotel Housekeeper; Lift Dispatcher; Lift Operator; Marketing Services and Interactive Manager; Nordic Pro/Shop Sales; Owner Services Secretary; Race and Event Crew; Security Dispatcher; Security Officer; Snow Shoveler; Sugarloaf Food Service Provider; Water Utilities Technician. **Special programs:** Internships. **Corporate headquarters location:** This location. **Parent company:** American Skiing Company. **Operations at this facility include:** Administration; Sales; Service. **Number of employees at this location:** 750.

Maryland

BETHESDA MARRIOTT HOTEL
5151 Pooks Hill Road, Bethesda MD 20814. 301/897-9400. **Fax:** 301/897-0192. **Contact:** Human Resources. **World Wide Web address:** http://www.marriott.com. **Description:** A 407-room hotel with three restaurants, 23 meeting rooms, and a business center. **Corporate headquarters location:** Washington, D.C. **Other U.S. locations:** Nationwide. **International locations:** Worldwide. **Parent company:** Marriott International, Incorporated. **Listed on:** New York Stock Exchange. **Stock exchange symbol:** MAR. **Sales/revenue:** Over $20 billion. **Number of employees worldwide:** Approximately 145,000.

CHOICE HOTELS INTERNATIONAL
10750 Columbia Pike, Silver Spring MD 20901. 301/592-5000. **Contact:** Human Resources. **E-mail address:** choicehotels@hiresystems.com. **World Wide Web address:** http://www.choicehotels.com. **Description:** An internationally franchised hotel company. **NOTE:** Resumes may be submitted online for advertised positions. **Positions advertised include:** Database Administrator; Strategic Planner;

Coordinating Marketer; Director FRAN – Operations Mexico; Marketing Analyst; Marketing Communications Specialist; Administrative Assistant; Database Marketing Specialist; Revenue Coordinator; People Soft Financial Programmer. **Corporate headquarters location:** This location. **Other U.S. locations:** Nationwide. **International locations:** Worldwide. **Subsidiaries include:** Clarion Hotels; Comfort Inns; Econo Lodge; Main Stay Suites; Quality Inns; Rodeway; Sleep Inns. **Operations at this facility include:** Sales. **Listed on:** New York Stock Exchange. **Stock exchange symbol:** CHH. **President/CEO:** Charles A. Ledsinger, Junior. **Sales/revenue:** $365 million. **Number of employees worldwide:** Approximately 2,000.

INN AT THE COLONNADE
4 West University Parkway, Baltimore MD 21218. 410/235-5400. **Contact:** Human Resources. **World Wide Web address:** http://www.colonnadebaltimore.com. **Description:** A 125 room hotel located across the street from Johns Hopkins University and a short distance to the harbor that offers dining, banquet, and meeting facilities.

THE MARRIOTT GAITHERSBURG
9751 Washingtonian Boulevard, Gaithersburg MD 20878. 301/590-0044. **Recorded jobline:** 888/462-7746. **Contact:** Human Resources. **E-mail address:** staffing@marriott.com. **World Wide Web address:** http://www.marriott.com. **Description:** A hotel. **Positions advertised include:** Sales Manager. **NOTE:** Entry-level positions are offered. Resumes should be sent to: Marriott International, One Marriott Drive, Washington DC 20058. **Special programs:** Internships. **Corporate headquarters location:** Washington, D.C. **Other U.S. locations:** Nationwide. **International locations:** Worldwide. **Parent company:** Marriott International, Incorporated operates and franchises hotels and related lodgings. **Listed on:** New York Stock Exchange. **Stock exchange symbol:** MAR. **Sales/revenue:** $8.4 billion. **Number of employees at this location:** 4,000. **Number of employees worldwide:** 180,000.

Massachusetts

ANTHONY'S PIER FOUR
140 Northern Avenue, Boston MA 02210. 617/482-6262. **Contact:** Anthony Athanas, Owner. **E-mail address:** pier4@pier4.com. **World Wide Web address:** http://www.pier4.com. **Description:** A restaurant. **NOTE:** Jobseekers must apply in person at the restaurant.

AU BON PAIN CORPORATION
19 Fid Kennedy Avenue, Boston MA 02210-2497. 617/423-2100. **Contact:** Human Resources. **E-mail address:** kris_broe@aubonpain.com. **World Wide Web address:** http://www.aubonpain.com. **Description:** Owns and operates a chain of 280 French bakery cafes worldwide. **NOTE:** Entry-level positions are offered. **Company slogan:** The French Bakery Cafe. **Positions advertised include:** General Manager; Baker; Customer Service Representative; Catering Call Center Representative; Shift Supervisor; Associate Manager; District Manager. **Special programs:** Internships. **Corporate headquarters location:** This location. **Other U.S. locations:** Nationwide. **Parent company:** Compass plc. **Listed on:** Privately held. **Number of employees nationwide:** 3,500.

BACK BAY RESTAURANT GROUP, INC.
284 Newbury Street, Boston MA 02115. 617/536-2800. **Fax:** 617/236-4175. **Contact:** Human Resources. **E-mail address:** cbradley@bbrginc.com. **World Wide Web address:** http://www.backbayrestaurantgroup.com. **Description:** Owns several Boston-based restaurant chains including Joe's American Bar & Grill, PapaRazzi, Atlantic Fish Company, and Charlie's Saloon. The company also owns a racetrack in New Hampshire. **Special programs:** Internships. **Corporate headquarters location:** This location. **Parent company:** Westwood Group. **Operations at this facility include:** Administration. **Listed on:** NASDAQ. **Number of employees at this location:** 60. **Number of employees nationwide:** 4,500.

BICKFORD'S FAMILY RESTAURANTS
1330 Soldiers Field Road, Boston MA 02135. 617/782-4010. **Contact:** Human Resources. **World Wide Web address:** http://www.bickfordsrestaurants.com. **Description:** Operates the Bickford's Family Restaurants chain in the New England area. **Positions advertised include:** Waiter; Hostess; Utility Person. **Corporate headquarters location:** This location. **Other area locations:** Statewide. **Other U.S. locations:** CT; RI; VT. **Operations at this facility include:** Administration.

BORDER CAFE
32 Church Street, Cambridge MA 02138. 617/864-6100. **Contact:** Manager. **Description:** A restaurant and bar specializing in Mexican and Cajun food.

BOSTON BEER WORKS
61 Brookline Avenue, Boston MA 02215. 617/536-2337. **Contact:** Manager. **Description:** A restaurant and brewery with a diverse menu serving the area near Fenway Park.

BOSTON CULINARY GROUP
55 Cambridge Parkway, Suite 200, Cambridge MA 02142. 617/499-2700. **Fax:** 617/679-0800. **Contact:** Human Resources. **E-mail address:** inquires@bcginc.com. **World Wide Web address:** http://www.bostonculinarygroup.com. **Description:** Provides food services and related products to a wide range of customers. Boston Concessions operates in 15 states. **Corporate headquarters location:** This location.

BOSTON MARRIOTT NEWTON
2345 Commonwealth Avenue, Newton MA 02466. 617/969-1000. **Fax:** 617/630-3578. **Contact:** Human Resources. **World Wide Web address:** http://www.marriott.com. **Description:** A 430-room hotel. **Positions advertised include:** Director of Housekeeping; Night Manager; Business Transient Sales Manager; Marketing Executive. **Special programs:** Internships. **Corporate headquarters location:** Washington DC. **Parent company:** Marriott International. **Operations at this facility include:** Administration; Sales; Service. **Listed on:** New York Stock Exchange. **Stock exchange symbol:** MAR. **Number of employees at this location:** 400.

BOSTON RESTAURANT ASSOCIATES, INC.
999 Broadway, Suite 400, Saugus MA 01906. 781/231-7575. **Contact:** Human Resources. **World Wide Web address:** http://www.pizzariaregina.com. **Description:** Boston Restaurant Associates owns and operates a chain of seven pizzerias under the name Pizzeria Regina; two Italian/American, family style restaurants under the name Polcari's North End; and three full-service, Italian restaurants under the names Bel Canto and Cappuccino's.

BRIGHAM'S INC.
30 Mill Street, Arlington MA 02476. 781/648-9000. **Fax:** 781/646-0509. **Contact:** Jessica Olson, Human Resources. **E-mail address:** jolson@brighams.com. **World Wide Web address:** http://www.brighams.com. **Description:** Operates a chain of more than 60 restaurants and ice cream parlors throughout New England, New York, and New Jersey. **Positions advertised include:** Sundae Party Coordinator; On Site Special Events Manager; Special Events Staff. **Corporate headquarters location:** This location. **Operations at this facility include:** Administration; Manufacturing; Regional Headquarters; Sales.

THE CACTUS CLUB
939 Boylston Street, Boston MA 02115. 617/236-0200. **Fax:** 617/236-0419. **Contact:** Manager. **E-mail address:** resumes@bestmarguitas.com. **World Wide Web address:** http://www.cactusclubboston.com. **Description:** A restaurant and bar with a diverse menu including Mexican, South American, and Cuban entrees.

THE COLONNADE HOTEL
120 Huntington Avenue, Boston MA 02116. 617/424-7000. **Fax:** 617/424-1717. **Contact:** Human Resources. **E-mail address:** careers@colonnadehotel.com. **World Wide Web address:** http://www.colonnadehotel.com. **Description:** An independently-owned, luxury hotel featuring dining and on-premise parking facilities. **Positions advertised include:** Banquet Line Cook; Line Cook; Lifeguard; Server; Bell Attendant; Turn Down Attendant.

D'ANGELO SANDWICH SHOPS
49 River Street, Waltham MA 02154. 781/893-0034. **Contact:** Human Resources. **World Wide Web address:** http://www.dangelos.com/. **Description:** One location of a chain of 200 quick-service sandwich shops. **Parent company:** Papa Gino's of America Inc. **Positions advertised include:** Assistant Manager; General Manager; District Manager; Shift Leader; Cashier; Server; Cook.

EAT WELL, INC.
19 North Street, Hingham MA 02043. 781/741-5100. **Contact:** Human Resources. **World Wide Web address:** http://www.eatwellinc.com. **Description:** Operates 13 dining and recreational facilities including Waterworks, a large outdoor bar overlooking the ocean with a volleyball court, pool tables, a TV/bar, a mixed drink bar, concert area and dance floor, and a sit-down food court.

FAIRMONT COPLEY PLAZA HOTEL
138 St. James Avenue, Boston MA 02116. 617/267-5300. **Fax:** 617/859-8836. **Recorded jobline:** 617/867-8500. **Contact:** Human Resources. **E-mail address:** fcphr@aol.com. **World Wide Web address:** http://www.fairmont.com. **Description:** A 376-room, four-star, luxury hotel. Founded in 1907. **Positions advertised include:** Staff Accountant; Banquet Manager; Fairmont Gold Manager; Front Office; Guest Service Manager; Housekeeping; Room Attendant; PT Turn Down Attendant; Refreshment Order Taker; Kitchen Cook. **NOTE:** Entry-level positions and second and third shifts are offered. **Office hours:** Monday - Friday, 8:00 a.m. - 6:00 p.m. **Corporate headquarters location:** San Francisco CA. **Other U.S. locations:** Nationwide. **Parent company:** Fairmont. **Operations at this facility include:** Administration; Sales; Service. **Listed on:** New York Stock Exchange. **Stock exchange symbol:** FHR. **CEO:** Robert Small. **Facilities Manager:** John Unwin. **Number of employees at this location:** 440.

FRIENDLY'S ICE CREAM CORPORATION
1855 Boston Road, Wilbraham MA 01095. 413/543-2400. **Contact:** Human Resources. **World Wide Web address:** http://www.friendlys.com. **Description:** Operates approximately 535 Friendly's restaurants serving hamburgers, sandwiches, salads, and ice cream. **Corporate headquarters location:** This location. **Listed on:** American Stock Exchange. **Stock exchange symbol:** FRN. **Number of employees nationwide:** 35,000.

HARD ROCK CAFE
131 Clarendon Street, Boston MA 02116. 617/353-1400. **Contact:** Manager. **World Wide Web address:** http://www.hardrock.com. **Description:** A casual dining restaurant decorated with rock and roll memorabilia. Hard Rock Cafe serves American cuisine and operates a gift shop. **Other U.S. locations:** Nationwide. **International locations:** Worldwide.

HOLIDAY INN
55 Ariadne Road, Dedham MA 02026. 781/329-1000. **Contact:** Human Resources. **World Wide Web address:** http://www.holiday-inn.com. **Description:** One location of the hotel chain. **Other U.S. locations:** Nationwide.

HOLIDAY INN LOGAN AIRPORT
225 McClellan Highway, East Boston MA 02128. 617/569-5250. **Contact:** Human Resources. **Description:** Operates a hotel, restaurant, and entertainment facility, primarily for the business traveler.

HYATT REGENCY BOSTON
One Avenue de Lafayette, Boston MA 02111. 617/422-5414. **Fax:** 617/422-5416. **Contact:** Human Resources. **World Wide Web address:** http://www.hyatt.com. **Description:** Operates a 500-room luxury hotel with full convention and dining services. **Positions advertised include:** Customer Service Representative; Services Sales Representative. **Other U.S. locations:** Nationwide.

HYATT REGENCY CAMBRIDGE
575 Memorial Drive, Cambridge MA 02139. 617/492-1234. **Fax:** 617/491-6906. **Contact:** Human Resources. **World Wide Web address:** http://www.hyatt.com. **Description:** A 460-room hotel and function facility. **NOTE:** Entry-level positions and second and third shifts are offered. **Corporate headquarters location:** Chicago IL. **Other U.S. locations:** Nationwide. **International locations:** Worldwide. **Parent company:** Hyatt Hotels Corporation. **Number of employees at this location:** 480. **Number of employees nationwide:** 40,000.

LANTANA
43 Scanlon Drive, Randolph MA 02368. 781/961-4660. **Contact:** Human Resources. **World Wide Web address:** http://www.thelantana.com. **Description:** A restaurant and meeting facility. **NOTE:** Interested jobseekers must apply in person.

LEGAL SEAFOODS, INC.
1 Seafood Way, Boston MA 02210. 617/783-8084. **Fax:** 617/782-4479. **Contact:** Human Resources. **E-mail address:** careers@legalseafoods.com. **World Wide Web address:** http://www.legalseafoods.com. **Description:** Operates a chain of seafood restaurants. **Special programs:** Internships. **Corporate headquarters location:** This location. **Operations at this facility include:** Administration; Research and Development; Sales.

THE LENOX HOTEL
61 Exeter Street at Boylston Back Bay, Boston MA 02116. 617/536-5300. **Fax:** 617/267-1237. **Contact:** Human Resources. **World Wide Web address:** http://www.lenoxhotel.com. **Description:** A 222-room, full-service hotel.

McDONALD'S CORPORATION
690 Canton Street, Suite 310, Westwood MA 02090. 781/329-1450. **Contact:** Personnel Manager. **World Wide Web address:** http://www.mcdonalds.com. **Description:** McDonald's develops, operates, franchises, and services a worldwide system of restaurants that process, package, and sell a limited menu of fast foods. One of the largest restaurant operations in the United States and one of the largest food service organizations in the world, McDonald's operates more than 30,000 McDonald's restaurants in all 50 states and in 119 countries. **NOTE:** Entry-level positions are offered. **Positions advertised include:** Management Trainee. **Corporate headquarters location:** Oak Brook IL. **Other U.S. locations:** Nationwide. **Operations at this facility include:** This location houses regional management offices for the international fast food chain. **Listed on:** New York Stock Exchange. **Stock exchange symbol:** MCD.

OMNI PARKER HOUSE HOTEL
60 School Street, Boston MA 02108. 617/227-8600. **Fax:** 617/725-1645. **Recorded jobline:** 617/725-1627. **Contact:** Human Resources. **World Wide Web address:** http://www.omnihotels.com. **Description:** A four-star hotel with 550 rooms. **NOTE:** Entry-level positions are offered. **Positions advertised include:** Night Auditor; Housekeeping Manager. **Special programs:** Internships; Summer Jobs. **Corporate headquarters location:** Irving TX. **Other U.S. locations:** Nationwide. **International locations:** Canada; Mexico. **Operations at this facility include:** Service. **Number of employees at this location:** 300.

PAPA GINO'S OF AMERICA INC.
600 Providence Highway, Dedham MA 02026. 781/461-1200. **Toll-free phone:** 800/PAPA-GINO. **Fax:** 781/461-1896. **Contact:** Human Resources. **E-mail address:** hr@papaginos.com. **World Wide Web address:** http://www.papaginos.com. **Description:** Operates an Italian restaurant chain with over 200 restaurants in New England specializing in pizza and pasta. **Positions advertised include:** Restaurant/Food Service Manager. **Operations at this facility include:** Regional Headquarters. **Number of employees nationwide:** 5,500.

ROYAL SONESTA HOTEL
5 Cambridge Parkway, Cambridge MA 02142. 617/491-3600. **Fax:** 617/806-4183. **Contact:** June Oppedisano, Employment Manager. **E-mail address:** joppedisano@sonesta-boston.com. **World Wide Web address:** http://www.sonesta.com. **Description:** Royal Sonesta Hotel offers 400 guest rooms, 15 function rooms, and dining in the Gallery Cafe. **Positions advertised include:** Catering Sales Manager; Shift Engineer; Engineering Office Coordinator; Front Desk Agent. **NOTE:** Entry-level positions are offered. **Corporate headquarters location:** Boston MA. **Other U.S. locations:** Key Biscayne FL; New Orleans LA. **Parent company:** Sonesta International Hotels Corporation. **Operations at this facility include:** Administration; Sales; Service. **Listed on:** NASDAQ. **Stock exchange symbol:** SNSTA. **Number of employees at this location:** 300.

SHERATON COLONIAL HOTEL
One Audubon Road, Wakefield MA 01880. 781/245-9300. **Contact:** Human Resources. **World Wide Web address:** http://www.sheraton.com. **Description:** A full-service hotel complete with restaurant and entertainment facilities, an 18-hole PGA golf course, and a health club. **Corporate headquarters location:** White Plains NY. **Parent company:** Starwood Hotels & Resorts Worldwide, Inc. **Number of employees at this location:** 300.

SHERATON FERNCROFT RESORT
50 Ferncroft Road, Danvers MA 01923. 978/777-2500. **Fax:** 978/750-7959. **Contact:** Joanne Sweeney, Human Resources. **World Wide Web address:** http://www.sheraton.com. **Description:** Operates a 367-room luxury hotel with a wide range of recreational services including a PGA tour country club, USTA tour tennis courts, and a full-service health club. **Special programs:** Internships. **Corporate headquarters location:** White Plains NY. **Parent company:** Starwood Hotels & Resorts Worldwide, Inc. **Operations at this facility include:** Sales; Service. **Number of employees at this location:** 300. **Number of employees nationwide:** 5,000.

SODEXHO
45 Hayden Avenue, Lexington MA 02420. 781/372-6000. **Contact:** Human Resources. **World Wide Web address:** http://www.sodexhousa.com. **Description:** A contract service management company that provides food services to health care facilities, schools and colleges, and corporate dining areas. **Number of employees at this location:** 200. **Number of employees nationwide:** 6,350.

SONESTA INTERNATIONAL HOTELS CORPORATION
116 Huntington Avenue, Boston MA 02116. 617/421-5400. **Fax:** 617/421-5402. **Contact:** Human Resources. **World Wide Web address:** http://www.sonesta.com. **Description:** Operates hotels including the Royal Sonesta Hotels in Cambridge MA and New Orleans LA. **Corporate headquarters location:** This location. **Listed on:** NASDAQ. **Stock exchange symbol:** SNSTA.

UNO RESTAURANT CORPORATION
100 Charles Park Road, Boston MA 02132. 617/323-9200. **Fax:** 617/469-3949. **Contact:** Human Resources. **E-mail address:** resume@unos.com. **World Wide Web address:** http://www.pizzeriauno.com. **Description:** Uno Restaurant Corporation operates and franchises a chain of casual dining, full-service restaurants under the name Pizzeria Uno. **NOTE:** Entry-level positions are offered. **Positions advertised include:** Restaurant/Food Service Manager. **Special programs:** Training. **Corporate headquarters location:** This location. **Other area locations:** Statewide. **Other U.S. locations:** Nationwide. **Operations at this facility include:** Administration. **Listed on:** New York Stock Exchange. **Stock exchange symbol:** UNORST. **Annual sales/revenues:** More than $100 million. **Number of employees at this location:** 100. **Number of employees nationwide:** 5,000.

THE WESTIN COPLEY PLACE
10 Huntington Avenue, Boston MA 02116. 617/262-9600. **Fax:** 617/424-7483. **Contact:** Human Resources. **World Wide Web address:** http://www.starwood.com. **Description:** An 800-room luxury hotel. **Positions advertised include:** Catering Sales Manager; Director of Catering; Engineering Coordinator; Manager of Information Technology; Restaurant Manager; Sales Manager; Stewarding Supervisor.

WESTIN WALTHAM-BOSTON
70 Third Avenue, Waltham MA 02451. 781/290-5600. **Fax:** 781/290-5626. **Contact:** Director of Human Resources. **World Wide Web address:** http://www.starwood.com. **Description:** A Four Star/Four Diamond, 346-room hotel. **Positions advertised include:** Assistant Controller; Director of Group Sales. **NOTE:** Entry-level positions, part-time jobs, and second and third shifts are offered. **Special programs:** Internships. **Office hours:** Monday - Friday, 9:00 a.m. - 5:00 p.m. **Corporate headquarters location:** White Plains NY. **Other area locations:** Boston MA; Cambridge MA; Providence RI. **Parent company:** Starwood Hotels and Resorts. **Listed on:** New York Stock Exchange. **Stock exchange symbol:** HOT. **CEO:** Barry Sternlicht. **Number of employees at this location:** 250. **Number of employees nationwide:** 80,000. **Number of employees worldwide:** 135,000.

Michigan

DOMINO'S PIZZA, INC.
30 Frank Lloyd Wright Drive, P.O. Box 997, Ann Arbor MI 48106-0997. 734/930-3030. **Contact:** Human Resources. **E-mail address:** recruiter1@dominos.com. **World Wide Web address:** http://www.dominos.com. **Description:** Operates a franchised home-delivery pizza chain. Founded in 1960. **NOTE:** Part-time positions are offered. **Positions advertised include:** Cash Accountant; Executive Assistant; Senior Graphic Designer; Print Marketing Manager. **Special programs:** Education Assistance Program; Internships. **Corporate headquarters location:** This location. **Other U.S. locations:** Worldwide. **Number of employees at this location:** 525. **Number of employees worldwide:** Over 140,000.

GRAND HOTEL
P.O. Box 286, Mackinac Island MI 49797. 906/847-3331. **Fax:** 906/847-3259. **Contact:** Human Resources. **E-mail address:** email@grandhotel.com. **World Wide Web address:** http://www.grandhotel.com. **Description:** A summer resort hotel. **NOTE:** Seasonal positions are open from mid-May until late October. **Positions advertised include:** Pantry Cook; Pastry Cook; Dishwasher; Bar Porter; Cocktail Server; Waiter/Waitress; Storeroom Clerk; Cashier; Recreation Attendant; Pool Attendant; Desk Clerk; Convention Porter; Maintenance Worker; Laundry Attendant; Uniform Valet Attendant. **Corporate headquarters location:** This location.

HOLIDAY INN ANN ARBOR HOTEL
3600 Plymouth Road, Ann Arbor MI 48105. 734/769-9800, extension 6290. **Toll-free phone:** 800/800-5560. **Fax:** 734/761-1290. **Contact:** Tracy Prebish, Director of Human Resources. **E-mail address:** tprebish@hiannarbor.com. **World Wide Web address:** http://www.hiannarbor.com. **Description:** A full-

service hotel with meeting and banquet facilities and an on site restaurant and lounge. **Corporate headquarters location:** Cincinnati OH. **Other U.S. locations:** Nationwide. **International locations:** Worldwide. **Parent company:** L.E.T. Group, Inc.

INDIANHEAD MOUNTAIN RESORT
500 Indianhead Road, Wakefield MI 49968. 906/229-5181. **Contact:** Human Resources. **E-mail address:** info@indianheadmtn.com. **World Wide Web address:** http://www.indianheadmtn.com. **Description:** A full-service year-round resort. The resort offers skiing with 18 trails, as well as a health and racquet club. **NOTE:** Seasonal positions are offered. **Parent company:** Indianhead Mountain Enterprises LLC.

LITTLE CAESAR'S
2211 Woodward Avenue, Detroit MI 48201. 313/983-6000. **Fax:** 313/983-6428. **Contact:** Human Resources. **E-mail address:** hrresume@lcecorp.com. **World Wide Web address:** http://www.littlecaesars.com. **Description:** Little Caesar's is a pizza restaurant chain. **Positions advertised include:** Cash Management Coordinator. **Corporate headquarters location:** This location. **Other area locations:** Statewide. **Other U.S. locations:** Nationwide. **Parent company:** Little Caesar Enterprises, Inc. **Operations at this facility include:** Administration.

Minnesota

BUFFETS, INC.
1460 Buffet Way, Eagan MN 55121. 651/994-8608. **Fax:** 651/365-2356. **Contact:** Human Resources. **World Wide Web address:** http://www.buffet.com. **Description:** Operates the Old Country Buffet, Hometown Buffet, Country Buffet, and Tahoe Joe's restaurant chains throughout the United States. **Positions advertised include:** Project Planning Manager; Manager of Application Development; Employee Relations Representative; Market Research Specialist; Restaurant Operations (Various). **Corporate headquarters location:** This location. **Other U.S. locations:** Nationwide. **Number of employees at this location:** 150. **Number of employees nationwide:** 23,000.

DOUBLETREE GUEST SUITES HOTEL
1101 LaSalle Avenue South, Minneapolis MN 55403. 612/332-6800. **Contact:** Human Resources. **World Wide Web address:** http://www.doubletree.com. **Description:** An all-suite hotel.

HOLIDAY INN HOTEL & SUITES
200 West First Street, Duluth MN 55802. 218/722-1202. **Fax:** 218/722-0233. **Contact:** Cheryl Dunbar, Human Resources. **E-mail address:** Cheryl.dunbar@hiduluth.com. **World Wide Web address:** http://www.hiduluth.com. **Description:** A 353-room, full-service hotel with three restaurants, conference facilities, and meeting space. **NOTE:** Entry-level positions, part-time jobs, and second and third shifts are offered. **Annual sales/revenues:** Less than $5 million. **Number of employees at this location:** 240.

HYATT REGENCY MINNEAPOLIS
1300 Nicollet Mall, Minneapolis MN 55403. 612/370-1234. **Fax:** 612/370-1463. **Recorded jobline:** 612/370-1202. **Contact:** Employment Manager. **World Wide Web address:** http://minneapolis.hyatt.com. **Description:** A downtown hotel with over 500 rooms and suites. The hotel's restaurants include Spike's Sports Bar and Grille, and Taxxi, an American bistro. **Special programs:** Internships. **Corporate headquarters location:** Chicago IL. **Other U.S. locations:** Nationwide. **Parent company:** Hyatt Hotels Corporation. **Operations at this facility include:** Administration; Sales; Service. **Listed on:** Privately held. **Number of employees at this location:** 335. **Number of employees nationwide:** 40,000.

INTERNATIONAL DAIRY QUEEN INC.
P.O. Box 39286, 7505 Metro Boulevard, Edina MN 55439-0286. 952/830-0200. **Fax:** 952/830-0498. **Contact:** Human Resources. **E-mail address:** resume@idq.com. **World Wide Web address:** http://www.idq.com. **Description:** A restaurant chain with 5,900 restaurants in 22 countries, specializing in burgers and ice cream. International Dairy Queen operates 11 regional offices. **NOTE:** See website for current job openings. Submit resume by e-mail. For positions at restaurants, contact the restaurant directly. **Corporate headquarters location:** This location. **Subsidiaries include:** Dairy Queen; Karmelkorn Shoppes, Inc.; Orange Julius of America. **Parent company:** Berkshire Hathaway Inc. **Number of employees at this location:** 330. **Number of employees nationwide:** 2,450.

MARRIOTT CITY CENTER HOTEL
30 South Seventh Street, Minneapolis MN 55402. 612/349-4000. **Fax:** 612/332-7165. **Contact:** Susan Mattson, Personnel Director. **World Wide Web address:** http://www.marriott.com. **Description:** A 31-floor glass tower hotel, linked to the city's skyway system. **NOTE:** Call to inquire about current job openings. Can also search and apply for positions online.

MINNEAPOLIS HILTON & TOWERS
1001 Marquette Avenue South, Minneapolis MN 55403-2440. 612/397-4830. **Fax:** 612/397-4872. **Recorded jobline:** 612/397-4870. **Contact:** Adam Welch, Human Resources. **World Wide Web address:** http://www.hilton.com. **Description:** An 814-room convention hotel with both full-service and fine-dining restaurants. **NOTE:** Apply in person or fax resumes to above number. **Special programs:** Internships. **Corporate headquarters location:** Beverly Hills CA. **Other U.S. locations:** Nationwide. **Number of employees at this location:** 600.

RADISSON HOTEL DULUTH HARBORVIEW
505 West Superior Street, Duluth MN 55802. 218/727-8981. **Fax:** 218/727-0162. **Contact:** Human Resources. **World Wide Web address:** http://www.radisson.com/duluthmn. **Description:** A 268-room hotel.

SOFITEL HOTEL
5601 West 78th Street, Bloomington MN 55439. 952/835-1900. **Fax:** 952/835-2696. **Recorded jobline:** 952/835-1900 ext. 5959. **Contact:** Human Resources Director. **World Wide Web address:** http://www.sofitel.com. **Description:** The first North American location of the French hotel chain, offering 282 rooms. **NOTE:** Contact Human Resources to inquire about current job openings, or apply in person. **Parent company:** Accor Hotels & Resorts.

TAHER, INC.
5570 Smetana Drive, Minnetonka, MN 55343-9022. 952/945-0505. **Fax:** 952/945-0444 **Contact:** Human Resources. **E-mail address:** jobs@taher.com. **World Wide Web address:** http://www.taher.com. **Description:** Provides food service management and vending machine services in 12 states. Clients include schools, colleges, businesses, and institutions. **Positions advertised include:** Driver; Cook; Bookkeeper/Accounts Payable. **Corporate headquarters location:** This location. **Operations at this facility include:** Administration; Sales; Service.

Mississippi

AMERISTAR CASINO VICKSBURG
4116 South Washington Street, Vicksburg MS 39180. 601/638-1000. **Toll-free phone:** 800/700-7770. **Recorded Jobline:** 601/630-3696. **Contact:** Human Resources. **World Wide Web address:** http://www.ameristarcasinos.com. **Description:** Operates a riverboat casino that features 1,003 slot machines, 53 table games, and the three-tiered Delta Grand Showroom which hosts nationally-known entertainers. **Positions advertised include:** Bar Steward; Beverage Server; EVS Attendant; Engineer; Restaurant Manager; Count Room Clerk; Dealer; Marketing Ambassador; Security Officer; Slot Supervisor; Employment Supervisor; Risk Manager; Shuttle Driver; Valet Attendant; Desk Clerk.

Corporate headquarters location: Las Vegas NV. **Other U.S. locations:** St. Charles MO; Kansas City MO; Council Bluffs IA; Jackpot NV. **Parent company:** Ameristar Casinos, Inc.

EDISON WALTHALL HOTEL
225 East Capitol Street, Jackson MS 39201. 601/948-6161. **Toll-free phone:** 800/932-6161. **Fax:** 601/948-0088. **Contact:** Personnel. **World Wide Web address:** http://www.edisonwalthallhotel.com. **Description:** A full-service hotel with 208 guest rooms, dining room and bar, recreation center, and meeting and banquet space. Founded in 1928. **Parent company:** Edison Hotels and Resorts Company.

GRAND CASINO TUNICA
13615 Old Highway 61 North, Robinsonville MS 38664. 800/39-GRAND. **Contact:** Human Resources. **World Wide Web address:** http://www.caesars.com/corporate/tunica. **Description:** As the largest gaming resort between Las Vegas and Atlantic City, the Grand Tunica features three hotels, a casino, a golf course, swimming pools, a spa and salon, an RV resort, various recreational activities, an event center, and banquet facilities. **NOTE:** Search available positions and apply online at http://www.harrahs.com. **Positions advertised include:** Cage Cashier; Security Shift Supervisor; Credit Executive; Credit Clerk; Lead PBX Operator; NCM Greeter; Promotions Associate; Dual Rate Dealer; Sous Chef; Maintenance Engineer; Senior Financial Analyst; Slot/Training Supervisor. **Corporate headquarters location:** Las Vegas NV. **Parent company:** Caesars Entertainment. **Listed on:** New York Stock Exchange. **Stock exchange symbol:** CZR. **Annual sales/revenues:** $4.2 billion. **Number of employees nationwide:** 50,000.

THE ISLE OF CAPRI CASINOS, INC.
1641 Popps Ferry Road, Suite B-1, Biloxi MS 39532. 228/396-7000. **Toll-free phone:** 800/843-4753. **Fax:** 228/396-2634. **Contact:** Angela Hubbard, Human Resources Department. **E-mail address:** angie_hubbard@islecorp.com. **World Wide Web address:** http://www.theislecorp.com. **Description:** Develops, owns, and operates riverboat, dockside, and land-based casinos, plus Pompano Park Harness Track. **Positions advertised include:** Staff Accountant; Senior Staff Accountant. **Corporate headquarters location:** This location. **Other area locations:** Lula MS; Natchez MS; Vicksburg MS. **Other U.S. locations:** Bettendorf IA; Blackhawk CO; Boonville MO; Bossier City LA; Kansas City KS; Lake Charles LA; Marquette IA; Pompano Beach FL; Davenport IA. **Listed on:** NASDAQ. **Stock exchange symbol:** ISLE.

VALLEY INNOVATIVE SERVICES
P.O. Box 5454, Jackson MS 39288-5454. 800/541-3805, extension 168. **Fax:** 601/664-3368. **Contact:** Heather Bean, Recruiting. **E-mail address:** jobs@valleyservicesi.com. **World Wide Web address:** http://www.valleyservicesi.com. **Description:** A contract food service management and consulting firm. Primary customers include health care facilities, schools, country clubs, and large businesses. Founded in 1960. **Special programs:** Internships; Training. **Annual sales/revenues:** More than $100 million. **Number of employees nationwide:** 2,750.

Missouri

CMP (CENTRAL MISSOURI PIZZA, INC.) dba DOMINO'S PIZZA
201 Chesterfield Business Parkway, Chesterfield MO 63017. 63005. **Fax:** 636/537-1265. **Contact:** Human Resources Manager. **World Wide Web address:** http://www.dominos.com. **Description:** CMP is one of the largest franchisees of Domino's Pizza, with locations in Missouri and Kentucky. **Corporate headquarters location:** This location. **Number of employees at this location:** 600.

JOHN Q. HAMMONS HOTELS, INC.
300 John Q. Hammons Parkway, Suite 900, Springfield MO 65806. 417/864-4300. **Fax:** 417/873-3593. **Contact:** Human Resources. **World Wide Web address:** http://www.jqhhotels.com. **Description:** A leading owner, manager, and developer of affordable upscale hotels in secondary, tertiary, and airport market areas. The company owns and manages 31 hotels located in 16 states, and also manages six additional hotels located in four states, containing 1,345 guest rooms. The company's existing hotels operate primarily under the Holiday Inn and Embassy Suites trade names.

HOLIDAY INN SELECT
9th and Washington Street, St. Louis MO 63101. 314/421-4000. **Contact:** Personnel Manager. **World Wide Web address:** http://www.holiday-inn.com. **Description:** A hotel. **Special programs:** Internships. **Parent company:** Intercontinental Hotels Group. **Number of employees at this location:** 130.

HOLIDAY INN NORTH
4545 North Lindbergh Boulevard, St. Louis MO 63044. 314/731-2100. **Contact:** Personnel. **World Wide Web address:** http://www.holiday-inn.com. **Description:** Operates a full-service hotel.

HOULIHAN'S RESTAURANT GROUP, INC.
384 Crestwood Plaza, St. Louis MO 63126. 314/963-9994. **Contact:** Thuan Nguyen, Director of Recruiting. **E-mail address:** tnguyen@houlihans.com. **World Wide Web address:** http://www.houlihans.com. **Description:** Houlihan's Restaurant Group owns, operates, and franchises 78 full-service, casual dining restaurants. **Corporate headquarters location:** Leawood KS. **Other U.S. locations:** Nationwide. **Number of employees nationwide:** 3,500.

HOWARD JOHNSON
4530 North Lindbergh Boulevard, Bridgeton MO 63044. 314/731-1652. **Fax:** 314/731-1534. **Contact:** Human Resources. **World Wide Web address:** http://www.hojo.com. **Description:** A hotel with a restaurant and bar. **Operations at this facility include:** Administration; Sales; Service. **Number of employees at this location:** 200.

LION'S CHOICE
12015 Manchester Road, Suite 118, St. Louis MO 63131. 314/821-8665, ext.: 244. **Fax:** 314/822-7144. **Contact:** Human Resources. **E-mail address:** mgadell@lionschoice. com. **World Wide Web address:** http://www.lionschoice.com. **Description:** Owns and operates a chain of 19 fast-food restaurants in Missouri and Illinois. **Corporate headquarters location:** This location.

McDONALD'S CORPORATION
502 Keswick Drive, Lake Saint Louis MO 63367. 636/625-2475. **Contact:** Human Resources. **World Wide Web address:** http://www.mcdonalds.com. **Description:** Develops, operates, franchises, and services a worldwide system of restaurants that process, package, and sell fast foods. One of the largest restaurant operations in the U.S. and one of the largest food service organizations in the world, McDonald's operates more than 30,000 McDonald's restaurants in all 50 states and in 119 other countries. **Positions advertised include:** Marketing Manager; Senior Database Analyst. **Special programs:** Internships. **Corporate headquarters location:** Oak Brook IL. **Other U.S. locations:** Nationwide. **Operations at this facility include:** Regional Headquarters. **Number of employees at this location:** 300.

MOTEL 6
6500 South Lindbergh Boulevard, St. Louis MO 63123. 314/892-3664. **Contact:** Human Resources. **World Wide Web address:** http://www.motel6.com. **Description:** One location of the motel chain. Overall, the company operates more than 800 motels in the U.S. and Canada. **Corporate headquarters location:** Carrollton TX. **Parent company:** Accor (Paris, France).

PRESIDENT CASINO LACLEDE'S LANDING
800 North First Street, St. Louis MO 63102. 314/622-3000. **Fax:** 314/622-3029. **Recorded jobline:** 314/622-

3159. **Contact:** Human Resources. **E-mail address:** careers@presidentcasino.com. **World Wide Web address:** http://www.presidentcasino.com. **Description:** A riverboat casino with over 1,200 slots and 46 table games. Founded in 1907. **Positions advertised include:** Assistant Engineer; Dealer. **Other U.S. locations:** Biloxi MS. **Parent company:** President Casinos, Inc. (St. Louis MO) operates President Casino & Blackhawk Hotel, President Casino Laclede's Landing, and President Casino Broadwater Resort. **Number of employees nationwide:** 2,000.

RAMADA INN BRANSON
1700 West 76 Country Boulevard, Branson MO 65616. 417/334-1000. **Fax:** 417/339-3046. **Toll-free:** 800/641-4106. **Contact:** Human Resources. **World Wide Web address:** www.ramada.com. **Description:** A 296-room hotel on 22 acres in the Ozark Mountains. **Other U.S. locations:** Nationwide.

REGAL RIVERFRONT HOTEL
200 South Fourth Street, St. Louis MO 63102. 314/241-9500. **Fax:** 314/516-8156. **Contact:** Director of Human Resources. **Description:** A downtown convention hotel with 780 rooms, extensive banquet facilities, and two restaurants. **Corporate headquarters location:** Denver CO. **Parent company:** Richfield Hotel Management. **Listed on:** Privately held. **Number of employees at this location:** 600. **Number of employees nationwide:** 18,000.

ST. LOUIS MARRIOTT PAVILION HOTEL
One South Broadway, St. Louis MO 63102. 314/421-1776. **Fax:** 314/331-9029. **Contact:** Rhonda Ross, Human Resources. **World Wide Web address:** http://www.marriotthotels.com. **Description:** A hotel with 672 guest rooms and 11 suites. The hotel offers a variety of recreation facilities, restaurants, and lounges. **NOTE:** Search and apply for positions online. **Special programs:** Internships. **Corporate headquarters location:** Bethesda MD. **Other U.S. locations:** Nationwide. **Number of employees at this location:** 400. **Number of employees nationwide:** 128,000.

SCHNEITHORST'S
1600 South Lindbergh Boulevard, St. Louis MO 63131. 314/993-4100. **Fax:** 314/993-1069. **Contact:** Jim Schneithorst, Jr., Owner. **E-mail address:** info@schneithorst.com. **World Wide Web address:** http://www.schneithorst.com. **Description:** Owns and operates restaurants and catering services. **Annual sales/revenues:** $5 - $10 million. **Number of employees at this location:** 175.

SHERATON WESTPORT CHALET HOTEL ST LOUIS
191 Westport Plaza Tower Drive, St. Louis MO 63146. 314/878-1500. **Fax:** 314/434-0140. **Contact:** Jim Grant, Personnel Department. **World Wide Web address:** http://www.startwoodhotels.com. **Description:** One of several area locations of the international hotel chain, specializing in accommodations for business travelers. **Corporate headquarters location:** Boston MA. **Parent company:** Starwood Hotels and Resorts Worldwide, Inc.

TONY'S INC.
410 Market Street, St. Louis MO 63102. 314/231-7007. **Fax:** 314/231-4740. **Contact:** Human Resources. **World Wide Web address:** http://www.tonysstlouis.com. **Description:** Owners and operators of a restaurant specializing in continental Italian cuisine. **Number of employees at this location:** 90.

Montana
THE BIG MOUNTAIN SKI & SUMMER RESORT WINTER SPORTS, INC. (WSI)
3910 Big Mountain Road, P.O. Box 1400, White Fish, MT 59937. 406/862-1920. **Toll-free phone:** 800/858-3930. **Fax:** 406/862-1998. **Contact:** Director of Human Resources. **E-mail address:** hr wsi@bigmtn.com. **World Wide Web address:** http://www.bigmtn.com. **Description:** A full-service resort featuring 3000 acres of "ski-able" terrain, 11 ski lifts, 11 food and beverage operations, nine retail shops, child care, ski and snowboard school, and slope-side lodging for over 1600 guests. **NOTE:** Entry-level positions are offered. **Special programs:** Internships. **Corporate headquarters location:** This location. **Subsidiaries include:** Big Mountain Water Company furnishes the domestic water supply to the resort and adjacent properties. Big Mountain Development Corporation oversees and coordinates the planning and development of certain parcels owned by Winter Sports, Inc. **Operations at this facility include:** Administration; Sales; Service. **Annual sales/revenues:** $11 - $20 million. **Number of employees at this location:** 450.

ST. MARY LODGE & RESORT
Browning MT 59417. 406/732-4431. **Physical address:** East Gateway to Glacier National Park, St Mary MT 59417. **Fax:** 406/732-9265. **Contact:** Human Resources. **E-mail address:** jobs@glcpark.com. **World Wide Web address:** http://www.glcpark.com. **Description:** A full service, family owned, guest facility located at the East Gateway of Glacier National Park with a wide variety of accommodations in the lodge and cottages as well as a 250-seat dining room. Founded in 1932. **NOTE:** Search posted openings and apply online. **Positions advertised include:** Resort Manager; Chef; Restaurant Manager; Assistant Controller; Retail Manager; Assistant General Manager; Front Office/Reservations Manager; Executive Secretary/ Administrative Assistant. **Internship information:** Those studying hotel-restaurant, accounting, business and retail management may be eligible to receive summer credit for business related experience. **Winter address:** The Resort at Glacier, P.O. Box 1808, Sun Valley ID 83353 (Oct. 15 – April 15) 800/368/3689. **Number of employees:** 200.

Nebraska
GODFATHER'S PIZZA, INC.
9140 West Dodge Road, Suite 300, Omaha NE 68114. 402/391-1452. **Toll-free phone:** 800/456-8347. **Fax:** 402/255-2687. **Contact:** Human Resources. **World Wide Web address:** http://www.godfathers.com. **NOTE:** Please see website for online application form. **Description:** A chain of pizza restaurants offering performance-based compensation. **Corporate headquarters location:** This location. **Other U.S. locations:** Nationwide.

Nevada
AMERISTAR CASINOS, INC.
3773 Howard Hughes Parkway, Suite 490 South, Las Vegas NV 89109. 702/567-7000. **Fax:** 702/866-6416. **Contact:** Recruiter. **E-mail address:** corporaterecruiting@ameristarcasinos.com. **World Wide Web address:** http://www.ameristarcasinos.com. **Description:** A casino holding company. **Positions advertised include:** Administrative Assistant; Assistant VP of Administration; VP of Procurement and QA; Webmaster. **Corporate headquarters location:** This location. **Subsidiaries include:** Ameristar Casino St. Charles (St. Charles MO): Ameristar Casino Hotel Council Bluffs (Council Bluffs IA); Ameristar Casino Hotel Kansas City (Kansas City MO); Ameristar Casino Hotel Vicksburg (Vicksburg MS); Cactus Pete's Resort Casino (Jackpot NV). **Listed on:** NASDAQ. **Stock exchange symbol:** ASCA.

ARAMARK LEISURE SERVICES
3150 Paradise Road, Las Vegas NV 89109. 702/791-8182. **Toll-free phone:** 800/228-3711. **Contact:** Human Resources. **World Wide Web address:** http://www.aramark.com. **Description:** This location provides all food and catering services for Cashman Field, a minor league baseball park. **Corporate headquarters location:** Philadelphia PA. **Parent company:** ARAMARK.

ARIZONA CHARLIE'S DECATUR CASINO & HOTEL
740 South Decatur Boulevard, Las Vegas NV 89107. 702/258-5200. **Contact:** Human Resources. **World Wide Web address:** http://www.arizonacharliesdecatur.com. **Description:** A full-service gaming, entertainment, and

dining facility. **Positions advertised include:** Front Desk Clerk; Night Auditor; Security Officer; Room Attendant; Food Server; Cook; Ultimate Rewards Representative. **Parent company:** Arizona Charlie's Las Vegas, Inc.

BALLY'S LAS VEGAS
3645 Las Vegas Boulevard South, Las Vegas NV 89109. 702/739-4111. **Fax:** 702/967-4405. **Contact:** Human Resources. **World Wide Web address:** http://www.caesars.com/ballys/lasvegas. **Description:** A resort featuring a convention center, a casino and hotel facilities. The hotel features 2,800 rooms. **Parent company:** Caesars Entertainment.

BELLAGIO HOTEL AND CASINO
P.O. Box 7700, Las Vegas NV 89177-7700. 702/693-8279. **Physical address:** 3600 Las Vegas Boulevard South, Las Vegas NV 89109. **Fax:** 702-693-8577. **Contact:** Employment Office. **E-mail address:** employment@bellagioresort.com. **Description:** A luxury resort featuring hotel accommodations, shopping, meeting space, fine dining, gaming, and Cirque du Soleil's "O" theatre production. **Parent company:** MGM Mirage.

BEST WESTERN AIRPORT PLAZA HOTEL
1981 Terminal Way, Reno NV 89502-3215. 775/348-6370. **Contact:** Employment. **World Wide Web address:** http://www.bestwestern.com. **Description:** A hotel operated by Best Western International, the mid-priced hotel chain with over 3,400 hotels in 60 countries including over 1,000 in Europe. Best Western has over 1,900 meeting facilities worldwide with 900 in the United States.

BOYD GAMING CORPORATION
2950 South Industrial Road, Las Vegas NV 89109-1150. 702/792-7200. **Toll-free phone:** 866/JOB-BOYD. **Fax:** 702/792-7354. **Contact:** Human Resources. **World Wide Web address:** http://www.boydgaming.com. **Description:** An owner and operator of casino entertainment properties. Boyd Gaming Corporation owns and operates seven properties in Las Vegas: California Hotel & Casino; Eldorado Casino; Fremont Hotel & Casino; Jokers Wild Casino; Main Street Station Casino, Brewery, & Hotel; Sam's Town Hotel & Gambling Hall; and Stardust Resort & Casino. In addition, the company owns and operates Blue Chip Casino & Hotel (Michigan City IN), Par-A-Dice Hotel & Casino (East Peoria IL), Sam's Town Motel & Gambling Hall (Robinson MS), and Treasure Chest Casino (Kenner LA). **Positions advertised include:** Media Coordinator; Database Manager; Slot Floor Person; Custodian; Food Server; Cocktail Waitress; Maintenance Engineer; Specialty Room Supervisor. **Corporate headquarters location:** This location. **Other U.S. locations:** IL; LA; MO; MS. **Listed on:** New York Stock Exchange. **Stock exchange symbol:** BYD.

CAESARS ENTERTAINMENT, INC
3930 Howard Hughes Parkway, Las Vegas NV 89109. 702/699-5000. **Contact:** Human Resources Manager. **World Wide Web address:** http://www.caesars.com. **Description:** Operates 29 properties including Grand Casinos, Flamingo Casinos, Bally's, and Hilton Gaming Resorts & Casinos. **NOTE:** Search and apply for positions online. **Corporate headquarters location:** This location. **Listed on:** New York Stock Exchange. **Stock exchange symbol:** CZR. **Number of employees worldwide:** 54,000.

CALIFORNIA HOTEL & CASINO
12 East Ogden Avenue, Las Vegas NV 89101. 702/388-2669. **Contact:** Human Resources. **World Wide Web address:** http://www.thecal.com. **Description:** A hotel and casino. **Positions advertised include:** Prep Cook; Database Manager; Security Guard. **Parent company:** Boyd Gaming Corporation.

CIRCUS CIRCUS
2880 Las Vegas Boulevard South, Las Vegas NV 89109. 702/794-3732. **Fax:** 709/734-2051. **Contact:** Vivian Hudson, Personnel. **World Wide Web address:** http://www.circuscircus.com. **Description:** A casino and hotel with over 2,700 rooms. **Positions advertised include:** Gaming Audit Supervisor; Slot Promotions Host; Cooks Helper; Fry Cook; Guest Room Attendant; Housekeeper; Security Guard; Booth Cashier; Floor Person; Money Runner; Investigator. **Parent Company:** MGM Mirage.

ELDORADO HOTEL/CASINO
375 North Virginia Street, P.O. Box 3399, Reno NV 89505-3399. 775/348-9278. **Recorded jobline:** 775/348-9278, extension 4. **Contact:** Human Resources. **E-mail address:** jobinfo@eldoradoreno.com. **World Wide Web address:** http://www.eldoradoreno.com. **Description:** A privately-owned and family-operated hotel/casino featuring a 25-story hotel tower, a 60,000 square-foot casino, eight restaurants, live cabaret entertainment, 24-hour room service, and a heated outdoor pool and spa. **Positions advertised include:** A/P Clerk; Assistant Front Desk Manager; Cage Cashier; Computer Operator; Dealer; Food Server; Restaurant Manager; Retail Sales Associate; Security Officer.

ELSINORE CORPORATION
FOUR QUEENS HOTEL & CASINO
202 Fremont Street, P.O. Box 370, Las Vegas NV 89101-0370. 702/385-4011. **Fax:** 702/387-5125. **Recorded jobline:** 702/385-4011, extension 3126. **Contact:** Linda Yard, Director of Human Resources. **E-mail address:** employment@fourqueens.com. **World Wide Web address:** http://www.fourqueens.com. **Description:** A publicly-held casino management company that develops and operates gaming facilities throughout the country. In addition to its Las Vegas-based Four Queens Hotel & Casino, Elsinore Corporation is working with Native American tribes to develop, construct, and manage casinos on tribal lands. **Positions advertised include:** Multi-Game Dealer; Pit Clerk; Keno Writer; Reservations Clerk; Soft Count Clerk; Armed Security Guard; Casino Porter; Slot Club Supervisor. **Special programs:** Internships. **Corporate headquarters location:** This location. **Subsidiaries include:** Pinnacle Gaming. **Operations at this facility include:** Administration; Sales. **Number of employees at this location:** 1,150.

EXCALIBUR HOTEL
3850 Las Vegas Boulevard South, Las Vegas NV 89109. 702/597-7777. **Fax:** 702/597-7009. **Contact:** Human Resources Department. **World Wide Web address:** http://www.excaliburcasino.com. **Description:** A hotel and casino with over 4,000 rooms. **NOTE:** Search and apply for positions online at http://www.mrgjobs.com. **Positions advertised include:** Assistant Restaurant Manager; Courtesy Host; Game Operator; Lifeguard; Microfilm Clerk; Race and Sports Writer; Surveillance Investigator. **Parent company:** MGM Mirage.

FLAMINGO LAS VEGAS
3555 Las Vegas Boulevard South, Las Vegas NV 89109. 888/308-8899. **Contact:** Human Resources. **World Wide Web address:** http://www.caesars.com/flamingo/lasvegas. **Description:** A gaming resort featuring over 3,600 hotel rooms, gaming facilities, and live entertainment. **Positions advertised include:** Retail Supervisor; Porter; Ticket Writer; Poker Dealer; Booth Cashier; Food Server; Payroll Clerk; Hotel Audit Clerk; Advertising Coordinator; Assistant Chef; Fry Cook; Bartender; Spa Masseur; Valet Attendant. **Parent company:** Caesars Entertainment.

GOLD COAST HOTEL
4000 West Flamingo Road, Las Vegas NV 89103. 702/367-7111. **Toll-free phone:** 800/331-5334. **Fax:** 702/367-1897. **Contact:** Human Resources Manager. **World Wide Web address:** http://www.goldcoastcasino.com. **Description:** A hotel and casino featuring 750 rooms, a heated swimming pool, five restaurants, two show lounges, a 72-lane

bowling center, free child care, and one of Nevada's largest dance halls.

GOLDEN NUGGET HOTEL AND CASINO
129 East Fremont Street, Las Vegas NV 89101. 702/386-8245. **Fax:** 702/388-2238. **Recorded jobline:** 702/386-8181. **Contact:** Employment Manager. **E-mail address:** hr@goldennugget.com. **World Wide Web address:** http://www.goldennugget.com. **Description:** A four-star, four-diamond hotel and casino. Founded in 1950. **NOTE:** Entry-level positions, part-time jobs, and second and third shifts are offered. This location also hires seasonally. **Positions advertised include:** Accounts Receivable Clerk; Assistant Front Desk Manager; Assistant Pastry Chef; Cocktail Server; Employee Relations Coordinator; Room Attendant; Guest Service Representative; Retail Cashier; Security Secretary; Revenue Audit Clerk; Security Officer; Ticket Cashier; Usher. **Special programs:** Internships; Training; Summer Jobs. **Internship information:** Internships are available to University of Las Vegas Nevada students only. **Corporate headquarters location:** This location. **Other U.S. locations:** Biloxi MS; Laughlin NV. **Parent company:** Mirage Resorts, Inc. **Listed on:** New York Stock Exchange. **Stock exchange symbol:** MIR. **Number of employees at this location:** 3,000. **Number of employees nationwide:** 30,000.

HARD ROCK CAFE
4475 Paradise Road, Las Vegas NV 89109-6574. 702/733-7625. **Fax:** 702/733-1027. **Contact:** General Manager. **World Wide Web address:** http://www.hardrock.com. **Description:** A restaurant decorated with rock and roll memorabilia. The Hard Rock Cafe serves American cuisine and operates a gift shop. **Other U.S. locations:** Nationwide. **International locations:** Worldwide.

HARRAH'S LAS VEGAS
3475 Las Vegas Boulevard South, Las Vegas NV 89109. 702/369-5287. **Fax:** 702/369-5108. **Contact:** Human Resources. **World Wide Web address:** http://www.harrahs.com/our_casinos/las/. **Description:** A casino featuring 2,711 tower rooms, six restaurants, convention space, a wedding chapel, five cocktail lounges, the Commander's Theatre featuring nightly entertainment, a health club and Olympic-sized pool, a game room and video arcade, gift shops, and a beauty salon. **Positions advertised include:** Security Officer. **Parent company:** Harrah's Entertainment Inc. (Memphis TN). **Listed on:** New York Stock Exchange. **Stock exchange symbol:** HET. **Number of employees at this location:** 3,000. **Number of employees nationwide:** 10,000.

HARRAH'S RENO
P.O. Box 10, Reno NV 89504-0010. 775/786-3232. **Physical address:** 219 North Center Street, Reno NV 89501. **Contact:** Human Resources Director. **World Wide Web address:** http://www.harrahs.com/our_casinos/ren/. **Description:** Operates hotels and casinos. **Parent company:** Harrah's Entertainment Inc. (Memphis TN). **Listed on:** New York Stock Exchange. **Stock exchange symbol:** HET. **Number of employees nationwide:** 10,000.

HOLIDAY INN EMERALD SPRINGS
325 East Flamingo Road, Las Vegas NV 89109. 702/732-9100. **Contact:** Human Resources. **World Wide Web address:** http://www.holiday-inn.com. **Description:** A quiet non-gaming hotel. **Parent company:** Intercontinental Hotels.

HOST INTERNATIONAL
2000 East Plumb Lane, Reno NV 89502-3250. 775/785-2587. **Fax:** 775/785-2590. **Contact:** Human Resources. **Description:** Provides food, beverage, and merchandise concessions to the travel and leisure industries.

IMPERIAL PALACE, INC.
3535 Las Vegas Boulevard South, Las Vegas NV 89109. 702/731-3311. **Toll-free phone:** 800/634-6441. **Fax:** 702/794-3356. **Recorded jobline:** 702/794-3191. **Contact:** Richard Danzak, Human Resources Director. **E-mail address:** hr@imperialpalace.com. **World Wide Web address:** http://www.imperialpalace.com. **Description:** A hotel and casino. **NOTE:** Part-time positions and second and third shifts are offered. **Positions advertised include:** Lead Cook; Bar Back; Graphic Artist; Front Desk Clerk; Security; Palace Princess; Gift Shop Sales Associate; Counter Person; Grounds Keeper; Medical Claims Processor; Maintenance Laborer; Promotions Model. **Listed on:** Privately held. **Number of employees at this location:** 2,500.

JACK IN THE BOX
3703 East Flamingo Road, Las Vegas NV 89121. 702/451-0950. **Contact:** Manager. **World Wide Web address:** http://www.jackinthebox.com. **Description:** A restaurant with over 1600 locations throughout the western United States. **Listed on:** New York Stock Exchange. **Stock exchange symbol:** JBX.

LAS VEGAS HILTON
3000 Paradise Road, Las Vegas NV 89109. 702/732-5111. **Contact:** Human Resources. **World Wide Web address:** http://www.lvhilton.com. **Description:** A 3,100-room hotel and casino.

LONE STAR STEAKHOUSE & SALOON
1611 South Decatur Boulevard, Las Vegas NV 89102. 702/259-0105. **Contact:** General Manager. **E-mail address:** team@thesteakcompany.com. **World Wide Web address:** http://www.lonestarsteakhouse.com. **Description:** Lone Star Steakhouse & Saloon owns and operates a chain of 265 full-service, casual dining restaurants. **NOTE:** Apply for management positions online. **Corporate headquarters location:** Wichita KS. **Other U.S. locations:** Nationwide. **Listed on:** NASDAQ. **Stock exchange symbol:** STAR.

LUXOR LAS VEGAS RESORT HOTEL & CASINO
3900 Las Vegas Boulevard South, Las Vegas NV 89119-1000. 702/262-4000. **Contact:** Doug McCombs, Human Resources Director. **World Wide Web address:** http://www.luxor.com. **Description:** A resort hotel and casino offering over 2,500 rooms. **Parent company:** MGM Mirage.

MGM GRAND HOTEL AND CASINO
3799 Las Vegas Boulevard South, Las Vegas NV 89109. 702/891-1111. **Contact:** Casting Center. **World Wide Web address:** http://www.mgmgrand.com. **Description:** A hotel that includes over 5,000 guest rooms and suites, one of the world's largest casinos divided into areas with different themes, eight restaurants, a fast-food court, three entertainment lounges, and two showrooms. The complex also includes a youth center for younger guests and the Oz Midway & Arcade. The complex's theme park, MGM Grand Adventures, is set on 33 acres and features seven major rides and five shows in four theaters. **Positions advertised include:** Food and Beverage Service Worker; Hotel/Motel Clerk; Retail Sales Worker. **Corporate headquarters location:** This location. **Parent company:** MGM Grand, Inc.

MONARCH CASINO & RESORT, INC.
dba ATLANTIS RESORT AND CASINO
1175 West Moana Lane, Suite 200, Reno NV 89509. 775/825-3355. **Contact:** Human Resources Department. **World Wide Web address:** http://www.monarchcasino.com. **Description:** Monarch Casino & Resort, Incorporated, through its wholly-owned subsidiary, Golden Road Motor Inn, Incorporated, owns and operates Atlantis Resort Casino in Reno, which caters primarily to area residents and leisure travelers. Atlantis offers approximately 51,000 square feet of casino area, a hotel, seven restaurants, seven public bars, a nightclub, swimming pools and health club. The casino offers 965 slot machines and 34 table games. **Subsidiaries include:** Golden Road Motor Inn, Incorporated. **Listed on:** NASDAQ. **Stock exchange symbol:** MCRI.

OLIVE GARDEN ITALIAN RESTAURANT
6850 West Cheyenne Avenue, Las Vegas NV 89108-4590. 702/658-2144. **Contact:** Manager. **World Wide Web address:** http://www.olivegarden.com. **Description:** One location of the chain of family-style Italian restaurants. **NOTE:** Job application available for download on the company Website. **Other U.S. locations:** Nationwide. **International locations:** Canada.

PALACE STATION HOTEL AND CASINO
2411 West Sahara Avenue, Las Vegas NV 89102. 702/367-2411. **Recorded jobline:** 702/221-6789. **Contact:** Human Resources Director. **World Wide Web address:** http://www.palacestation.com. **Description:** Owns and operates a hotel and casino and provides slot machine route management, vending, and payphone services to numerous food and beverage establishments, commercial businesses, and major hotels and casinos. **Parent company:** Station Casinos. **Listed on:** New York Stock Exchange. **Stock exchange symbol:** STN.

THE PALMS CASINO RESORT
4321 West Flamingo Road, Las Vegas NV 89103. 702/942-6868. **Toll-free phone:** 866/562-3527. **Contact:** Human Resources. **World Wide Web address:** http://www.palms.com. **Description:** A one-stop resort destination that offers 605 hotel rooms, a diverse mix of bars and restaurants and a 95,000 square foot casino. Amenities include the Palms Spa and AMP salon, Brenden Theatres, Rain Night Club, ghostbar, Hart and Huntington Tattoo Company, a recording studio, and over 60,000 square feet of meeting and banquet space. **Positions advertised include:** Banquet Manager.

PORT OF SUBS, INC.
5365 Mae Anne Avenue, Suite A-29, Reno NV 89523. 775/747-0555. **Fax:** 775/747-1510. **Contact:** Personnel. **E-mail address:** kaquino@portofsubs.com. **World Wide Web address:** http://www.portofsubs.com. **Description:** Operates a 125-unit chain of sandwich shops. **Positions advertised include:** IT Manager; Field Marketing Assistant; Accounts Payable Clerk; Payroll Clerk. **Corporate headquarters location:** This location. **Other U.S. locations:** CA; AZ; ID; UT; WA, OR, HI.

PRIMM VALLEY RESORTS
31900 South Las Vegas Boulevard, Primm NV 89019. 702/382-1212. **Fax:** 702/679-5633. **Recorded jobline:** 702/679-5627. **Contact:** Human Resources. **E-mail address:** positions@primm.mgmgrand.com. **World Wide Web address:** http://www.primmvalleyresorts.com. **Description:** Owns and operates hotels and casinos. **Positions advertised include:** Assistant Casino Controller; Audit Clerk; Hard Count Clerk; Ride Associate; Cage Cashier; Assistant Payroll Manager; Payroll Clerk; Purchasing Agent; Staff Accountant; Fry Cook; Busperson; Host/Cashier; Director of Food and Beverage; Application Specialist; Convention Services Manager; EMT Officer; Slot Booth Cashier.

RIO ALL-SUITE HOTEL & CASINO, INC.
3700 West Flamingo Road, Las Vegas NV 89103. 702/777-7777. **Contact:** Human Resources. **E-mail address:** jobs@harrahs.com. **World Wide Web address:** http://www.playrio.com. **Description:** Owns and operates the Rio All-Suites Hotel & Casino in Las Vegas. The Rio is a 21-story hotel containing over 860 suites, 79,000 square feet of casino space, 10 restaurants and food outlets, and other related amenities. The casino has 1,950 slot machines, craps, 21, roulette, pai gow poker, minibaccarat; Keno, poker, and a race and sports book. **NOTE:** Part-time positions are offered. **Positions advertised include:** Pit Clerk; Hard Count Attendant; Showroom Cocktail Server; Cage Cashier; Total Rewards Host; Special Events Coordinator; Food Runner; Spa Receptionist; Massage Therapist; Graphic Artist; Aesthetician; Table Games Supervisor/Dealer; Data Entry Clerk; Keno Writer/Runner; Lifeguard; Utility Cleaner; Security Secretary. **Parent company:** Harrah's Entertainment, Incorporated.

RIVERSIDE RESORT & CASINO
1650 Casino Drive, Laughlin NV 89029. 702/298-2535. **Contact:** Human Resources. **World Wide Web address:** http://www.riversideresort.com. **Description:** A resort featuring an hotel, casino, dining, events, activities, and an RV park. **NOTE:** All applicants must apply in person. **Other U.S. locations:** AZ.

RIVIERA HOTEL & CASINO
2901 Las Vegas Boulevard South, Las Vegas NV 89109. 702/794-9651. **Fax:** 702/794-9668. **Contact:** Human Resources Department. **World Wide Web address:** http://www.theriviera.com. **Description:** The Riviera offers 2,075 rooms, including 158 suites and 35 rooms specially equipped to accommodate wheelchair patrons. The facility also features six restaurants, three cocktail lounges, shopping, meeting and convention facilities, a wedding chapel, award-winning entertainment, and a 100,000 square-foot casino. **Parent company:** Riviera Holdings. **Listed on:** American Stock Exchange. **Stock exchange symbol:** RIV.

SANDS REGENCY HOTEL & CASINO
345 North Arlington Avenue, Reno NV 89501-1132. 775/348-2200.: Human Resources. **E-mail address:** cnorcross@sandsregency.com. **World Wide Web address:** http://www.sandsregency.com. **Description:** Owns and operates an 800-room hotel and casino. **Listed on:** NASDAQ. **Stock exchange symbol:** SNDS.

SILVER LEGACY RESORT/CASINO
P.O. Box 3920, Reno NV 89505. 775/329-4777. **Physical address:** 407 North Virginia Street, Reno NV 89501. **Contact:** Human Resources. **World Wide Web address:** http://www.silverlegacy.com. **Description:** Silver Legacy Resort/Casino is one of the largest casinos in Reno. The hotel features 1,600 rooms and five restaurants including the Sweetwater Cafe. **Positions advertised include:** Reservation Agent; PBX Operator; Spokesmodel; Food Server; Saute Cook; Security Officer; National Sales Manager; Maintenance Person. **Number of employees at this location:** 2,800.

SILVERTON HOTEL AND CASINO
3333 Blue Diamond Road, Las Vegas NV 89139. 702/263-7777. **Toll-free phone:** 866/946-4373. **Recorded jobline:** 702/914-8696. **Contact:** Human Resources. **World Wide Web address:** http://www.silvertoncasino.com. **Description:** A resort facility featuring a 30,000 square-foot casino with 1,100 slot and video gaming machines and 28 table games. There is 24-hour dining in the Comstock Coffee Shop, buffets in the Chuckwagon, a 300-seat combination restaurant-theater called the Opera House, and a lounge called Rattlesnake Ricky's. **Positions advertised include:** Inventory Control Clerk; Revenue Audit Clerk; Cage Cashier; Assistant Director of Food and Beverages; Food Server; Busperson; Kitchen Cleaner; Dealer; Retail Clerk/Cashier; Lifeguard; Vault Cashier; Coin Runner; Housekeeper. **Special programs:** Tuition Reimbursement Program.

STARDUST RESORT & CASINO
3000 Las Vegas Boulevard South, Las Vegas NV 89109. 702/732-6364. **Contact:** Human Resources. **E-mail address:** stardustemployment@boydgaming.com. **World Wide Web address:** http://www.stardustlv.com. **Description:** A 2,335-room hotel and casino. **Positions advertised include:** Security Officer; Assistant Custodial Services Manager; Revenue Audit Clerk; Slot Floor Person; Catering Coordinator. **Parent company:** Boyd Gaming Corporation. **Listed on:** New York Stock Exchange. **Stock exchange symbol:** BYD.

STRATOSPHERE HOTEL & CASINO
2000 South Las Vegas Boulevard, Las Vegas NV 89104-2507. 702/380-7777. **Fax:** 702/383-5349. **Recorded jobline:** 702/383-4800. **Contact:** Manager of Human Resources Department. **E-mail address:** jobs@stratospherehotel.com. **World Wide Web address:** http://www.stratospherehotel.com. **Description:** Operates a free-standing observation tower casino hotel. **Positions advertised include:**

Wedding Chapel Sales Manager; Cook; Host; Revenue Audit Clerk; F&B Supervisor; Food Server; Bus/Runner; Security Officer; Utility Lead Porter; Dealer; Bartender. **Parent company:** American Casino & Entertainment Properties, LLC.

TACO BELL
1210 S Valley View Blvd, Las Vegas NV 89102. 702/880-5818. **Contact:** Sandra Bowen, Director of Human Resources. **World Wide Web address:** http://www.tacobell.com. **Description:** Taco Bell is a global franchise specializing in Mexican style fast food. **NOTE:** Recruitment events are held periodically. **Corporate headquarters location:** Irvine CA. **Parent company:** Yum! Brands, Incorporated operates KFC, Taco Bell, Pizza Hut, Long John Silvers, and A&W restaurants worldwide. **Operations at this facility include:** This location is a business office that manages Taco Bell restaurant franchises.

TREASURE ISLAND HOTEL AND CASINO
3300 Las Vegas Boulevard South, Las Vegas NV 89109. 702/894-7111. **Recorded jobline:** 702/792-JOBS. **Contact:** Personnel. **World Wide Web address:** http://www.treasureislandlasvegas.com. **Description:** A 2,900-room hotel and casino. **NOTE:** Interested job seekers must apply in person at the Employment Center. Search for positions online at: http://www.mgmmirage.com. **Positions advertised include:** Accounts Payable Clerk; Accounts Receivable Clerk; Administrative Clerk; Apprentice Bartender; Assistant Room Service Manager; Assistant Spa Manager; Assistant Lobby Store Manager; Busperson. **Parent company:** Mirage Resorts Incorporated owns 12 properties. **Number of employees nationwide:** 45,000.

TROPICANA RESORT & CASINO
3801 Las Vegas Boulevard South, Las Vegas NV 89109. 702/739-2222. **Fax:** 702/739-2719. **Recorded jobline:** 702/739-2473. **Contact:** Human Resources. **E-mail address:** employment@tropicanalv.com. **World Wide Web address:** http://www.tropicanalv.com. **Description:** A hotel and casino. **Parent company:** Aztar Corporation. **Listed on:** New York Stock Exchange. **Stock exchange symbol:** AZR. **Positions advertised include:** Employee Development Assistant; Security Officer; Claim Examiner; Casino Analyst; Promotions Representative; Paralegal.

WYNN LAS VEGAS
3131 Las Vegas Boulevard South, Las Vegas NV 89109. 702/770-5627. **Contact:** Staff Recruiting Center. **E-mail address:** wynnjobs@wynnlasvegas.com. **World Wide Web address:** http://www.wynnlasvegas.com. **Description:** A grand-scale hotel in Las Vegas, complete with shopping, dining, and golf. **NOTE:** Paper applications are not accepted. Apply online at http://www.wynnjobs.com. **Positions advertised include:** Cook; Concierge; Guest Services Representative; IT Business Systems Analyst; Pit Clerk. **Parent company:** Wynn Resorts, Limited.

New Hampshire

APPLEBEE'S NEIGHBORHOOD GRILL & BAR
40 Key Road, Keene NH 03431-3925. 603/355-6300. **Fax:** 603/358-5122. **Contact:** Manager. **World Wide Web address:** http://www.discoverapplebees.com. **Description:** One franchise location of the national casual dining restaurant chain. Applebee's Neighborhood Grill & Bar offers mainly American fare. **NOTE**: Search posted openings and apply on-line only. **Corporate headquarters location:** Overland Park KA. **Other U.S. locations:** Nationwide. **Other area locations:** Statewide. **Operations at this location include:** This location is a restaurant. **President/CEO:** Lloyd L. Hill. **Listed on:** NASDAQ. **Stock exchange symbol:** APPB.

CHRISTMAS FARM INN AND SPA
P.O. Box CC, Route 16B, Jackson Village NH 03846. 603/383-4313. **Toll-free phone:** 800/443-5837. **Fax:** 603/383-6495. **Contact:** General Manager. **E-mail address:** innkeeper@christmasfarminn.com. **World Wide Web address:** http://www.christmasfarminn.com. **Description:** Privately owned, traditional style inn, restaurant and spa.

MUDDY MOOSE RESTAURANT AND PUB
2344 White Mountain Highway, North Conway NH 03860. 603/356-7696. **Fax:** 603/356-7702. **Contact:** Human Resources. **World Wide Web address:** http://www.muddymoose.com. **Description:** A rustic themed tourist restaurant.

NINETY-NINE RESTAURANT AND PUB
1308 Hooksett Road, Hooksett NH 03106. 603/641-2999. **Fax:** 603/641-2263. **Contact:** Brian Fahle, Human Resources Manager. E-mail address: BFahle@99restaurants.com. **World Wide Web address:** http://www.99restaurants.com. **Description:** A chain restaurant serving moderately priced American food. **Positions advertised include:** Assistant Kitchen Manager; Kitchen Manager; Assistant Manager; General Managing Partner; Dishwasher; Food Server; Prep Cook; Host; Line Cook; Bartender; First Cook; Busser. **NOTE:** Search posted openings online but may contact locally to access information concerning immediate openings. **Corporate headquarters location:** Woburn MA.

OLIVE GARDEN ITALIAN RESTAURANT
219 Loudon Road, Concord NH 03301. 603/228-6886. **Fax:** 603/223-0871. **Contact:** Mark Connelly, General Manager. **World Wide Web address:** http://www.olivegarden.com. **Description:** One location of the nationwide restaurant chain. **NOTE:** Search posted openings and apply on-line. Do not fax or e-mail resumes. May contact manager at local restaurants for information. **Positions advertised include:** Host; Server; Bartender; Line Cook; Preparation Cook; Alley Coordinator; Busser; Dishwasher. **Parent company:** Darden Restaurants.

New Jersey

ATLANTIC CITY HILTON CASINO RESORT
P.O. Box 1737, Boston and Pacific Avenues, Atlantic City NJ 08401. 609/347-7111. **Contact:** Human Resources. **World Wide Web address:** http://www.hiltonac.com. **Description:** An 804-room hotel and casino. Atlantic City Hilton Casino Resort also features gourmet restaurants, live theater, a shopping center, and convention rooms. **Positions advertised include:** Director of Labor Relations; Dealer; Security Officer; Accounting Representative; Financial Analyst.

ATLANTIC CITY SHOWBOAT INC.
801 Boardwalk, P.O. Box 840, Atlantic City NJ 08401. 609/343-4000. **Contact:** Personnel. **World Wide Web address:** http://www.harrahs.com. **Description:** A hotel and casino. **Parent company:** Harrah's.

BALLY'S ATLANTIC CITY
Park Place and Boardwalk, Atlantic City NJ 08401. 609/340-2000. **Contact:** Human Resources. **World Wide Web address:** http://www.ballysac.com. **Description:** A resort hotel and casino with 1,254 rooms, nine restaurants, a theater, retail space and convention facilities. **Subsidiaries include:** Bally's Wild Wild West casino is connected to Bally's Park Place, though it maintains separate gaming, dining and retail facilities. **Parent company:** Harrah's.

CAESARS ATLANTIC CITY HOTEL CASINO
2100 Pacific Avenue, Atlantic City NJ 08401. 609/348-4411. **Fax:** 609/236-4522. **Contact:** Personnel. **World Wide Web address:** http://www.caesars.com. **Description:** A 1,100-room hotel and casino. **Parent company:** Harrah's.

CHEFS INTERNATIONAL, INC.
62 Broadway, P.O. Box 1332, Point Pleasant Beach NJ 08742. 732/295-0350. **Contact:** Office Manager. **World Wide Web address:** http://www.jackbakerslobstershanty.com. **Description:** Operates eight Lobster Shanty restaurants in New

Jersey and Florida. **Corporate headquarters location:** This location.

COURTYARD PRINCETON
3815 US Route 1 at Mapleton Road, Princeton NJ 08540. 609/716-9100. **Fax:** 609/716-8745. **Contact:** Human Resources. **World Wide Web address:** http://www.marriott.com. **Description:** A location of the hotel chain close to numerous shops and restaurants offering 144 rooms. **Other U.S. locations;** Nationwide.

HARRAH'S ATLANTIC CITY
777 Harrah's Boulevard, Atlantic City NJ 08401. 609/441-5000. **Contact:** Human Resources. **E-mail address:** jobs@harrahs.com. **World Wide Web address:** http://www.harrahs.com. **Description:** A hotel and casino providing 1,174 rooms, theaters, retail space, and seven restaurants.

HILTON OF HASBROUCK HEIGHTS
650 Terrace Avenue, Hasbrouck Heights NJ 07604. 201/288-6100. **Contact:** Human Resources. **World Wide Web address:** http://www.hilton.com. **Description:** A hotel that provides a wide range of lodging, restaurant, lounge, meeting, and banquet facilities as part of an international chain. **Positions advertised include:** Customer Service Representative; Food and Beverage Service Worker; Hotel/Motel Clerk; Housekeeper. **Operations at this facility include:** Administration.

HILTON PARSIPPANY
One Hilton Court, Parsippany NJ 07054. 973/267-7373. **Fax:** 973/984-6853. **Contact:** Human Resources. **World Wide Web address:** http://www.hilton.com. **Description:** Recently renovated location of the hotel chain. Features a Ruth's Chris Steak House and accessibility to various area attractions.

PRIME HOSPITALITY CORPORATION
700 Route 46 East, Fairfield NJ 07007. 973/882-1010. **Contact:** Human Resources. **E-mail address:** recruiter@primehospitality.com. **World Wide Web address:** http://www.primehospitality.com. **Description:** An independent hotel operating company with ownership and management of 86 full- and limited-service hotels in 19 states and one resort hotel in the U.S. Virgin Islands. Hotels typically contain 100 to 200 guest rooms or suites and operate under franchise agreements with national hotel chains or under the company's Wellesley Inns or AmeriSuites trade names. Founded in 1961. **Corporate headquarters location:** This location. **Other U.S. locations:** Nationwide. **Operations at this facility include:** Administration. **Listed on:** New York Stock Exchange. **Stock exchange symbol:** PDQ. **Annual sales/revenues:** More than $100 million. **Number of employees at this location:** 190. **Number of employees nationwide:** 6,050.

RESORTS CASINO HOTEL
1133 Boardwalk, Atlantic City NJ 08401. 609/344-6000. **Fax:** 609/340-7751. **Recorded jobline:** 609/340-6756. **Contact:** Employment Office. **E-mail address:** employment@resortsinc.com. **World Wide Web address:** http://www.resortsac.com. **Description:** Atlantic City's first casino hotel, with more than 800 deluxe rooms and suites. The hotel also houses a fine dining restaurant, a full-service beauty salon, and several shops and boutiques. **Positions advertised include:** Beverage Manager; Environmental Services Supervisor; PC Programmer; Cashier; Surveillance Supervisor.

SANDS CASINO & HOTEL
136 South Kentucky Avenue, Atlantic City NJ 08401. 609/441-4000. **Fax:** 609/441-4470. **Recorded jobline:** 609/441-4524. **Contact:** Personnel. **World Wide Web address:** http://www.acsands.com. **Description:** A 532-room resort hotel with extensive gaming facilities, five restaurants, and live entertainment. **Positions advertised include:** Security Officer; Casino Host; Casino Cage Supervisor; Shift Manager; Dealer; Slot Attendant Supervisor; Security Manager; Food Server; Bartender; Bus Person; Heavy Porter; Bus Porter; EMT; Valet Parking Attendant; Warehouse Supervisor; Showroom Captain; General Ledger Accountant.

SHERATON CROSSROADS
1 International Boulevard, Rt. 17 North, Mahwah NJ 07495. 201/529-1660. **Fax:** 201/529-4709. **Contact:** Human Resources. **World Wide Web address:** http://www.starwoodhotels.com. **Description:** A 227-room hotel, 40 minutes from New York City, offering a view of the Ramapo Valley and 23,000 ft of meeting space capable of accommodating 1,200 people. **Other U.S. locations:** Nationwide.

TROPICANA CASINO AND RESORT
2831 Brighton Avenue and the Boardwalk, Atlantic City NJ 08401. 609/340-4000. **Toll-free phone:** 800/843-8767. **Fax:** 609/340-4457. **Contact:** Donald Hoover, Director of Recruiting. **World Wide Web address:** http://www.tropicana.net. **Description:** A large casino and hotel that offers casino gaming, gourmet dining, hotel facilities, and an indoor amusement park. **Positions advertised include:** Security Officer; Poker Dealer; Slot Technician; Marketing Operation Supervisor; Beverage Server; Public Area Attendants; Public Area Manager; Front Desk Clerk; Cook; Food Services Attendant; Housekeeper; Hotel Cashier; Limo Dispatcher; Fleet Dispatcher; Valet Parking Attendant. **Special programs:** Internships. **Corporate headquarters location:** Phoenix AZ. **Other U.S. locations:** Las Vegas NV; Laughlin NV. **Parent company:** Aztar. **Operations at this facility include:** Administration; Service. **Number of employees at this location:** 5,000.

TRUMP ENTERTAINMENT RESORTS. INC.
151 South Pennsylvania Avenue, Atlantic City NJ 08401. 609/441-6500. **Toll-free phone:** 877TRUMPJOB. **Fax:** 609/441-6067. **Contact:** Employment Office. **World Wide Web address:** http://www.trumpemployment.com. **Description:** Operates the Trump Marina, Trump's Taj Mahal, and Trump Plaza casino hotels. **NOTE:** Search and apply for positions online. **Positions advertised include:** Banquet Server; Bar Porter; Beverage Meter Room Technician; Beverage Service Shift Manager; Bus Person; Cook; Food Server; Coin Bank Cashier; Security Officer; Slot Cashier; Compliance Accounting Clerk; Hotel Accounting Clerk; National Marketing Director; Staff Internal Auditor.

New Mexico
ALBUQUERQUE MARRIOTT HOTEL
2101 Louisiana Boulevard NE, Albuquerque NM 87110. 505/881-6800. **Contact:** Human Resources Department. **World Wide Web address:** http://www.marriott.com. **Description:** A 411-room, full-service hotel featuring 18 meeting rooms, an onsite restaurant, and a full business center. **Parent company:** Marriott International has more than 2,600 lodging properties, with operations and franchises in 50 states and 68 countries. The company operates lodging facilities and is the franchiser under 17 separate brand names, including: Marriott Hotels, Resorts, and Suites, Courtyard Inns, Residence Inn, Ritz-Carlton Hotels, and Fairfield Inn. **Number of employees worldwide:** 128,000.

ARBY'S ROAST BEEF RESTAURANT
1711 Seventh Street, Las Vegas NM 87701. 505/425-5448. **Contact:** Manager. **World Wide Web address:** http://www.arbys.com. **Description:** One of the 3000 fast-food restaurants in the national chain. Founded in 1964. **NOTE:** Contact local restaurant for job information. **Other area locations:** Statewide.

BEST WESTERN ADOBE INN
1501 East Will Rogers Drive, P.O. Drawer 410, Santa Rosa NM 88435. 505/472-3446. **Fax:** 505/472-5759. **Contact:** Human Resources Department. **World Wide Web address:** http://www.bestwestern.com. **Description:** A 58-room hotel featuring an outdoor heated pool, queen-sized beds in all rooms, a restaurant, and free parking.

BEST WESTERN ROYAL HOLIDAY
1903 West Highway 66, Gallup NM 87301. 505/722-4900. **Fax:** 505/863-9952. **Contact:** Human Resources. **World Wide Web address:** http://www.bestwestern.com. **Description:** A 50-room, full-service hotel featuring a pool, sauna, Jacuzzi, restaurant and lounge, and fitness center and spa. One of Best Western International's 4,000 hotels in 80 countries. **Corporate headquarters location:** Phoenix AZ.

CARLISLE HOTEL & CONFERENCE CENTER
2500 Carlisle Boulevard NE, Albuquerque NM 87110. 505/888-3311. **Contact:** Human Resources. **Description:** A 366-room, full-service hotel featuring an amphitheatre, meeting and exhibition facilities, a restaurant, and catering services. **Corporate headquarters location:** This location.

DAYS INN
1310 North Main Street, Roswell NM 88201. 505/623-4021. **Fax:** 505/623-0079. **Contact:** General Manager. **World Wide Web address:** http://www.daysinn.com. **Description:** A 62-room hotel featuring meeting and banquet facilities, outdoor pool, restaurant, and room service. There are 1900 hotels worldwide.

DOUBLETREE HOTEL
201 Marquette Avenue NW, Albuquerque NM 87102. 505/247-3344. **Contact:** Human Resources. **World Wide Web address:** http://www.doubletreehotels.com. **Description:** A hotel and convention center. Chain includes 160 hotels. **NOTE:** Search and apply for positions online. **Parent company:** Hilton Hotels.

ELDORADO HOTEL
309 West San Francisco Street, Santa Fe NM 87501. 505/988-4455. **Contact:** Personnel. **E-mail address:** employment@eldoradohotel.com. **World Wide Web address:** http://www.eldoradohotel.com. **Description:** A four-star/four-diamond, 219-room hotel. This location also hires seasonally. Founded in 1986. **NOTE:** Apply in person. Entry-level positions, part-time jobs, and second and third shifts are offered. **Positions advertised include:** Front Desk Agent; Garage Parking Valet; Host/Cashier; Human Resources Clerk; Line Cook; Sales Administration Assistant; Banquet Manager; Catering Sales Manager; Executive Steward; Property Controller; Rooms Division Manager. **Special programs:** Summer Jobs. **Office hours:** Monday - Friday, 7:00 a.m. - 6:00 p.m. **Corporate headquarters location:** Englewood CO. **Parent company:** Richfield Hospitality Services.

GARDUNO'S RESTAURANTS
10555 Montgomery Boulevard NE, Suite 90, Albuquerque, NM 87111. 505/298-5514. **Fax:** 505/323-4445. **Contact:** Human Resources. **E-mail address:** employment@gardunosrestaurants.com. **World Wide Web address:** http://www.gardunosrestaurants.com. **Description:** One location in a chain of 14 Mexican restaurants in New Mexico, Arizona, and Nevada. **NOTE:** Apply in person at area restaurants, or contact Human Resources. **Corporate headquarters:** This location.

GLORIETA CONFERENCE CENTER
P.O. Box 8, Glorieta NM 87535. 505/757-4265. **Contact:** Administrative Services. **World Wide Web address:** http://www.lifeway.com/glorieta. **E-mail address:** glorietaemployment@lifeway.com. **Description:** A full-service Christian conference center that provides accommodations for up to 2,000 guests.

HILTON LAS CRUCES
705 South Telshor Boulevard, Las Cruces NM 88011. 505/522-4300. **Contact:** Human Resources. **World Wide Web address:** http://www.hilton.com. **Description:** Hilton Las Cruces is a luxury hotel located near the White Sands National Monument. The hotel offers exercise facilities, a Jacuzzi, and a pool. **NOTE:** Entry-level positions and second and third shifts are offered. **Special programs:** Internships. **Other U.S. locations:** Nationwide. **International locations:** Worldwide. **Parent company:** American Property. **Operations at this facility include:** Divisional Headquarters; Regional Headquarters.

HOLIDAY INN
4048 Cerrillos Road, Santa Fe NM 87507. 505/473-4646. **Contact:** Human Resources Department. **E-mail address:** gmsfe@lodgian.com. **World Wide Web address:** http://www.ichotelsgroup.com. **Description:** A 116-room, 14-suite hotel with dining room and swimming pool available. **Corporate headquarters location:** United Kingdom. **Other U.S. locations:** Nationwide. **International locations:** Worldwide.

HYATT REGENCY ALBUQUERQUE HOTEL
330 Tijeras Avenue NW, Albuquerque NM 87102. 505/842-1234. **Contact:** Human Resources Director. **World Wide Web address:** http://www.hyatt.com. **Description:** Operates a 395-room luxury hotel with complete dining and entertainment facilities. Hyatt Regency Albuquerque Hotel is part of the international hospitality firm that operates hotels and recreational facilities throughout the world. **NOTE:** Apply online.

INN AND SPA AT LORETTO
211 Old Santa Fe Trail, Santa Fe NM 87501. 505/988-5531. **Toll-free phone:** 800/727-5531. **Fax:** 505/984-7961. **Contact:** Human Resources. **E-mail address:** careers@innatloretto.com. **World Wide Web address:** http://www.innatloretto.com. **Description:** A 140-room, full-service hotel located in historic Santa Fe. Founded in 1996. **NOTE:** Entry-level positions are offered. **Positions advertised include:** Catering Manager; Sales Manager; Line Cook; Host Person; Busperson; Guest Service Agent; Reservation Sales Agent; Transient Sales Manager. **Corporate headquarters location:** Bellevue WA. **Other U.S. locations:** Scottsdale AZ; Daytona FL; Dallas TX. **Parent company:** Noble House. **Listed on:** Privately held.

KFC
2424 North Main Street, Las Cruces NM 88001-1135. 505/523-0662. **Contact:** Manager. **World Wide Web address:** http://www.kfc.com. **Description:** A worldwide fast-food chain specializing in chicken. **NOTE:** Search and apply for positions at http://www.yumcareers.com. **Parent company:** Yum! Brands.

LIFTSWEST CONDOMINIUM RESORT HOTEL
P.O. Box 330, Red River NM 87558. 505/754-2778. **Contact:** Bob Bullington, General Manager. **E-mail address:** lifts@redriver.org. **World Wide Web address:** http://www.liftswest.com. **Description:** Houses 75 condominium units that can be rented nightly. Units are complete with kitchen, living room, and variety of bedrooms. Laundry facilities are also available.

LODGE AT SANTA FE
750 North St. Francis Drive, Santa Fe NM 87501. 505/992-5800. **Fax:** 505/842-9863. **Contact:** Human Resources. **World Wide Web address:** http://www.lodgeatsantafe.com. **Description:** A hotel with 128 rooms, suites, and condos. Featuring meeting and banquet facilities, a restaurant and bar, and catering services. **Corporate headquarters location:** Albuquerque NM. **Parent company:** New Mexico Heritage Hotels.

MCM ELEGANTE HOTEL AND EVENT CENTER
2020 Menaul Boulevard, Albuquerque NM 87107. 505/884-2511. **Contact:** Human Resources. **E-mail address:** shannongriffo@mcmelegante.com. **World Wide Web address:** http://www.mcmelegantealbuquerque.com. **Description:** A 363-room hotel. **NOTE:** Entry-level positions are offered. **Other U.S. locations:** TX.

OLIVE GARDEN ITALIAN RESTAURANT
601 Juan Tabo Boulevard NE, Albuquerque NM 87123. 505/275-9948. **Contact:** Manager. **World Wide Web address:** http://www.olivegarden.com. **Description:** One location of the chain of family-style Italian

restaurants. **NOTE:** Applicants should apply in person. Application forms are available online. **Parent company:** Darden Restaurants.

PIZZA HUT
111 Coors Boulevard NW, Suite E9, Albuquerque NM 87121. 505/831-1133. **Contact:** Store Manager. **World Wide Web address:** http://www.pizzahut.com. **Description:** A casual pizza restaurant. There are 6,600 restaurants in the U.S. and more than 4,000 in 100 other countries. **NOTE:** Apply in person, or search and apply for positions online. **Parent company:** Yum! Brands, Inc.

RAMADA INN
2803 West Second, Roswell NM 88201. 505/623-9440. **Fax:** 505/622-9708. **Contact:** Manager. **World Wide Web address:** http://www.ramada.com. **Description:** A 58-room hotel featuring meeting and banquet facilities, heated and outdoor pools, and a restaurant. Ramada operates 1,000 hotels nationwide. **Other area locations:** Albuquerque, Farmington, Gallup, Rio Rancho, Santa Fe, Taos NM.

SAN FELIPE'S CASINO HOLLYWOOD
25 Hagan Road, San Felipe NM 87001. 505/867-6700. **Toll-free phone:** 877/529-2946. **Fax:** 505/867-6627. **Contact:** Dennis Garcia, Manager. **World Wide Web address:** http://www.sanfelipecasino.com. **Description:** A Las Vegas-style casino featuring a variety of games including slots, craps, black jack, and roulette. Founded in 1995. **NOTE:** Search and apply for positions online. Positions advertised include: Buffet Cashier; Dishwasher; Surveillance Officer; Maintenance Technician.

WENDY'S INTERNATIONAL, INC.
4900 Central Avenue SE, Albuquerque NM 87109. 505/268-8017. **Contact:** Personnel. **World Wide Web address:** http://www.wendysintl.com. **Description:** One of the world's largest restaurant franchising companies with 6,000 restaurants worldwide. Wendy's International includes Wendy's, a fast-food restaurant chain, and Tim Horton's, a coffee and baked goods restaurant chain. **NOTE:** Search and apply for corporate, field office, and restaurant operator jobs online. For crew member positions, apply in person. **Corporate headquarters location:** Columbus OH. **Listed on:** New York Stock Exchange. **Stock exchange symbol:** WEN.

WHITES CITY, INC.
P.O. Box 128, Whites City NM 88268. 505/785-2291. **Contact:** Personnel. **World Wide Web address:** http://www.whitescity.com. **Description:** Owns and operates several hotels, restaurants, gas stations, grocery stores, RV parks, and gift shops catering to tourists in the Whites City NM area.

New York

ARK RESTAURANTS CORPORATION
85 Fifth Avenue, 14th Floor, New York NY 10003. 212/206-8800. **Fax:** 212/206-8845. **Contact:** Marilyn Guy, Personnel Manager. **World Wide Web address:** http://www.arkrestaurants.com. **Description:** Ark Restaurants Corporation and its subsidiaries own, operate, or manage 27 restaurants nationwide. **Corporate headquarters location:** This location. **Listed on:** NASDAQ. **Stock exchange symbol:** ARKR. **Chairman:** Ernest Bogen. **Annual sales/revenues:** $115 million. **Number of employees:** 2,000.

THE CARLYLE HOTEL
35 East 76th Street, New York NY 10021. 212/744-1600. **Fax:** 212/717-4682. **Contact:** Human Resources. **E-mail address:** carlylejobs@rosewoodhotels.com. **World Wide Web address:** http://www.rosewoodhotels.com. **Description:** A luxury hotel offering 180-rooms, three restaurants, and banquet/meeting facilities. **Corporate headquarters location:** This location. **Parent company:** Rosewood Hotels & Resorts.

CARROLS CORPORATION
P.O. Box 6969, Syracuse NY 13217. 315/424-0513. **Physical address:** 968 James Street, Syracuse NY 13203. **Fax:** 315/479-8018. **Contact:** Judy Rosello, Human Resource Manager. **E-mail address:** jrosello@carrols.com. **World Wide Web address:** http://www.carrols.com. **Description:** Owns and operates fast-food restaurants and franchises including 350 Burger King restaurants, 126 Taco Caban restaurants, and 82 Pollo Tropical restaurants. Founded in 1968. **NOTE:** Applicants must fill out the standard application form to be considered. **Positions advertised include:** Lease Accounting Manager; Assistant Manager. **Corporate headquarters location:** This location. **Other U.S. locations:** Nationwide. **Chairman/CEO:** Alan Vituli. **Annual sales/revenues:** $657 million. **Number of employees nationwide:** 16,100

COURTYARD BY MARRIOTT
475 White Plains Road, Tarrytown NY 10591. 914/631-1122. **Contact:** General Manager. **World Wide Web address:** http://www.courtyard.com. **Description:** A hotel with 139 guest rooms and two meeting rooms. **Positions advertised include:** Senior Account Executive. **Parent company:** Marriott International, Inc. (Washington DC).

CROWNE PLAZA
66 Hale Avenue, White Plains NY 10601. 914/682-0050. **Toll-free phone:** 800/752-4672. **Fax:** 914/682-0405. **Contact:** Human Resources. **World Wide Web address:** http://www.crowneplaza.com. **Description:** A 401-room hotel with 13 meeting rooms. **Parent company:** Six Continents PLC (London, United Kingdom).

E.J. DEL MONTE CORPORATION
909 Linden Avenue, Rochester NY 14625. 716/586-3121. **Contact:** Human Resources. **Description:** E.J. Del Monte Corporation builds, owns, and operates 18 Marriott hotels as a franchisee in the greater Rochester area. In addition to hotels, the company is engaged in construction and develops patented equipment used in the production of pre-cast concrete rooms. Originally a generator manufacturer for military aircraft and guided missiles, the company specializes in building systems incorporating precision, monolithic concrete room castings. Founded in 1953. **Chairman:** Ernest J. Del Monte.

DOMINO'S PIZZA, INC.
2024 West Henrietta Road, Suite 5A, Rochester NY 14623-1397. 585/427-8468. **Contact:** Director of Operations. **World Wide Web address:** http://www.dominos.com. **Description:** One location of the home-delivery pizza chain. **Positions advertised include:** General Manager; Restaurant/Food Service Manager. Founded in 1960. **Special programs:** Training. **Corporate headquarters location:** Ann Arbor MI. **Operations at this facility include:** Divisional Headquarters. **Number of employees at this location:** 200.

DORAL ARROWWOOD
975 Anderson Hill Road, Rye Brook NY 10573. 914/935-6651. **Contact:** Human Resources. **E-mail address:** sgarbo@doralarrowwood.com. **World Wide Web address:** http://www.arrowwood.com. **Description:** A hotel and conference center with 272 guest rooms and 36 meeting rooms.

GURNEY'S INN
290 Old Montauk Highway, Montauk NY 11954. 631/668-2345. **Fax:** 631/668-1881. **Contact:** Human Resources. **E-mail address:** hr@gurneys-inn.com. **World Wide Web address:** http://www.gurneys-inn.com. **Description:** Gurney's resort, spa, and convention center offers fine-dining and a full-service, 109-room hotel. **NOTE:** Entry-level positions are offered. Human Resources phone: 631/668-1770. **Positions advertised include:** Hair Stylist; Front Desk Receptionist; Message Therapist; Lifeguard; Weight Room Attendant; Spa Attendant; Porter; Fitness

Instructor; Service Desk Attendant; Counter Server. **Special programs:** Internships; Apprenticeships; Summer Jobs. **Office hours:** Monday - Friday, 9:00 a.m. - 5:00 p.m. **Corporate headquarters location:** This location. **Number of employees at this location:** 250.

THE HELMSLEY PARK LANE HOTEL
36 Central Park South, New York NY 10019. 212/371-4000. **Fax:** 212/935-5489. **Contact:** Personnel. **World Wide Web address:** http://www.helmsleyhotels.com. **Description:** Operates a 650-room, luxury hotel with a wide range of lodging, lounge, dining, and meeting rooms. **Parent company:** Helmsley Hotels Group.

HILTONS OF WESTCHESTER
699 Westchester Avenue, Rye Brook NY 10573. 914/939-6300. **Fax:** 914/939-7374. **Contact:** Human Resources. **World Wide Web address:** http://www.hilton.com. **Description:** A 444-room hotel. **NOTE:** Entry-level positions, part-time jobs, and second and third shifts are offered. **Positions advertised include:** Assistant Director of Human Resources. **Corporate headquarters location:** Beverly Hills CA. **Other U.S. locations:** Nationwide. **International locations:** Worldwide. **Parent company:** Hilton Hotels Corp. (Beverly Hills CA). **Number of employees at this location:** 500.

HOTEL INTER-CONTINENTAL NEW YORK
111 East 48th Street, New York NY 10017. 212/755-5900. **Contact:** Human Resources. **World Wide Web address:** http://www.interconti.com. **Description:** A hotel with 682 rooms. **Special programs:** Internships. **Number of employees at this location:** 500.

HUNTER MOUNTAIN
P.O. Box 295, Hunter NY 12442. 518/263-3800. **Toll-free phone:** 800/486-8376. **Contact:** Human Resources. **World Wide Web address:** http://www.huntermtn.com. **Description:** A full feature ski resort.

JUMEIRAH ESSEX HOUSE
160 Central Park South, New York NY 10019. 212/247-0300. **Fax:** 212/315-1839. **Contact:** Human Resources. **World Wide Web address:** http://www.essexhouse.com. **Description:** Operates a hotel with 597 guest rooms and 150 condominiums. **Parent company:** Jumeirah (Dubai UAE).

LOEWS CORPORATION
655 Madison Avenue, 7th Floor, New York NY 10021-8087. 212/521-2000. **Fax:** 212/521-2466. **Contact:** Margorie Kouroupos, Human Resources. **E-mail address:** hrrep@newposition.com. **World Wide Web address:** http://www.loews.com. **Description:** A holding company and one of the largest diversified financial corporations in the U.S. with interests in the financial, tobacco, hotel, drilling, and watch industries. **Positions advertised include:** Graphic Designer; Digital Image Librarian; Information Technology Security Specialist; Internal Auditor Assistant; Internal Hotel Auditor Assistant. **Corporate headquarters location:** This location. **Listed on:** New York Stock Exchange. **Stock exchange symbol:** LTR. **Co-Chairmen:** Lawrence A. Tisch and Preston (Bob) R. Tisch. **Annual sales/revenues:** $17.5 billion. **Number of employees:** 25,800.

MARRIOTT EASTSIDE
525 Lexington Avenue, New York NY 10017. 212/755-4000. **Toll-free phone:** 800/228-9290. **Fax:** 212/751-3440. **Contact:** Director of Personnel. **World Wide Web address:** http://www.marriotthotels.com. **Description:** Operates a luxury hotel with 652 guest rooms and dining, meeting, and sales function facilities. **Parent company:** Marriott International, Inc. (Washington DC).

THE NEW YORK HELMSLEY HOTEL
212 East 42nd Street, New York NY 10017. 212/490-8900. **Fax:** 212/986-4792. **Contact:** Marilyn O'Brien, Personnel Director. **E-mail address:** general_info@helmsleyhotels.com. **World Wide Web address:** http://www.helmsleyhotels.com. **Description:** Operates a 793-room luxury hotel facility with a wide range of lodging, dining, meeting, and other facilities. **Parent company:** Helmsley Hotels Group.

PARK CENTRAL HOTEL
870 Seventh Avenue, New York NY 10019-4038. 212/247-8000. **Toll-free phone:** 800/346-1359. **Contact:** Human Resources. **World Wide Web address:** http://www.parkcentralny.com. **Description:** A 1,260-room hotel with restaurant, lounge, banquet, convention, and meeting facilities. **Corporate headquarters location:** Hampton NH. **Parent company:** Omni/Donley Hotel Group. **Operations at this facility include:** Sales; Service.

RENAISSANCE WESTCHESTER HOTEL
80 West Red Oak Lane, White Plains NY 10604. 914/694-5400. **Contact:** Human Resources. **World Wide Web address:** http://www.renaissancehotels.com. **Description:** A hotel with 364 guest rooms and 18 meeting rooms. **Parent company:** Marriott International, Incorporated. **Listed on:** New York Stock Exchange. **Stock exchange symbol:** MAR.

RESTAURANT ASSOCIATES CORPORATION
120 West 45th Street, 16th Floor, New York NY 10036. 212/789-8201. **Fax:** 212/613-4695. **Contact:** Manager of Recruitment. **E-mail address:** careers@restaurantassociates.com. **World Wide Web address:** http://www.restaurantassociates.com. **Description:** A broad-based company that operates 60 restaurants in major cities, cultural centers, and leisure attractions along the East Coast. Private food service facilities are also offered to corporations, institutions, and clubs. **NOTE:** To contact Human Resources directly, call 212/789-8201. **Positions advertised include:** Director; Assistant Director; Restaurant Manager; Bar Manager; Beverage Manager; Sous Chef; Controller; Catering Director; Catering Sales Director. **Special programs:** Internships. **Corporate headquarters location:** This location. **Parent company:** Compass Group. **Operations at this facility include:** Divisional Headquarters.

SARA LEE COFFEE AND TEA
500 Mamaroneck Avenue, 5th floor, Harrison NY 10528. 914/670-3300. **Contact:** Personnel. **E-mail address:** recruiting@saralee.com. **World Wide Web address:** http://www.saralee.com. **Description:** Produces a nationally distributed brand of premium coffee. The company also operates a chain of cafes and drive-thru restaurants. **Corporate headquarters location:** Chicago IL. **Other U.S. locations:** Nationwide. **Subsidiaries include:** Cain's Coffee Company; Greenwich Mills Company. **Parent company:** Sara Lee Corporation. **Operations at this facility include:** Administration; Divisional Headquarters; Sales. **Listed on:** New York Stock Exchange. **Stock exchange symbol:** SLE.

SHERATON SYRACUSE UNIVERSITY HOTEL
801 University Avenue, Syracuse NY 13210. 315/475-3000. **Fax:** 315/475-2266. **Contact:** Human Resources. **E-mail address:** hr@sheratonsyracuse.com. **World Wide Web address:** http://www.sheratonsyracuse.com. **Description:** A 236-room hotel located on the Syracuse University campus with convenient access to the Carrier Dome and convention center.

STARBUCKS COFFEE
757 Third Avenue, New York NY 10017. 212/715-9884. **Contact:** Human resources. **World Wide Web address:** http://www.starbucks.com. **Description:** A worldwide retail gourmet coffee chain **NOTE:** Retail and corporate positions are available. **Corporate headquarters location:** Seattle WA **Listed on:** NASDAQ. **Stock exchange symbol:** SBUX.

STARWOOD HOTELS & RESORTS WORLDWIDE, INC.
1111 Westchester Avenue, White Plains NY 10604. 914/640-8100. **Fax:** 914/640-8310. **Contact:**

Personnel. **World Wide Web address:** http://www.starwoodhotels.com. **Description:** Manages and operates hotels under the names Westin, Sheraton, Four Points, St. Regis, and others. **Corporate headquarters location:** This location. **Listed on:** New York Stock Exchange. **Stock exchange symbol:** HOT.

TARRYTOWN HOUSE
East Sunnyside Lane, Tarrytown NY 10591. 914/591-8200. **Contact:** Human Resources. **Description:** A historic hotel and conference center with 148 guest rooms, 30 meeting rooms, and eight private dining areas. Founded in 1981. **Special programs:** Internships; Training. **Internship information:** Internships are available year round in sales/marketing, accounting, human resources, operations, and the culinary arts. **Corporate headquarters location:** This location. **Other U.S. locations:** CT; NJ; OR; TX; WA. **International locations:** Canada; France. **Parent company:** Dolce International. **Number of employees at this location:** 235. **Number of employees worldwide:** 2,500.

North Carolina

BLOCKADE RUNNER BEACH RESORT HOTEL & CONFERENCE CENTER
275 Waynick Boulevard, Wrightsville Beach NC 28480. 910/256-2251. **Contact:** Personnel. **E-mail address:** blockade@bellsouth.net. **World Wide Web address:** http://www.blockade-runner.com. **Description:** A full-service hotel with 150 rooms.

CAROLINA INN
211 Pittsboro Street, Chapel Hill NC 27516. 919/933-2001. **Fax:** 919/918-2763. **Recorded jobline:** 919/918-2769. **Contact:** Cheryl Wendel, Human Resources Director. **E-mail address:** hr@carolinainn.com. **World Wide Web address:** http://www.carolinainn.com. **Description:** A 194-room hotel with conference facilities and banquet staff. The hotel has been rated with Four Diamonds on the National Register of Historic Places. **NOTE:** For management positions, please visit http://www.aramarkcareers.com to search for jobs and apply online.

CHARLOTTE MARRIOTT CITY CENTER
100 West Trade Street, Charlotte NC 28202. 704/333-9000. **Fax:** 704/342-3419. **Contact:** Director of Human Resources. **World Wide Web address:** http://www.marriottcitycenter.com. **Description:** A 421-guest room hotel featuring an indoor pool, a health club, and two restaurants. **Positions advertised include:** Director of Sales; Chief Engineer. **Corporate headquarters location:** Washington D.C. **Other U.S. locations:** Nationwide. **Parent company:** Noble Investment Group owns and operates over 25 resorts and hotels in the United States. **Listed on:** New York Stock Exchange. **Stock exchange symbol:** MAR. **Number of employees worldwide:** 128,000.

GOLDEN CORRAL CORPORATION
P.O. Box 29502, Raleigh NC 27626-0502. 919/781-9310. **Physical address:** 5151 Glenwood Avenue, Raleigh NC 27612. **Toll-free phone:** 800/284-5673. **Fax:** 919/881-4577. **Contact:** Human Resources. **World Wide Web address:** http://www.goldencorralrest.com. **Description:** Operates a chain of family steakhouses. Founded in 1973. **NOTE:** Entry-level positions are offered. **Corporate headquarters location:** This location. **Other U.S. locations:** Nationwide. **Operations at this facility include:** Administration; Research and Development; Service. **Listed on:** Privately held. **Annual sales/revenues:** More than $100 million. **Number of employees at this location:** 170. **Number of employees nationwide:** 3,700.

WINSTON HOTELS, INC.
2626 Glenwood Avenue, Suite 200, Raleigh NC 27608. 919/510-6010. **Fax:** 919/510-6832. **Contact:** Human Resources. **World Wide Web address:** http://www.winstonhotels.com. **Description:** A real estate development trust that owns 16 hotels, including 11 Hampton Inns in Georgia, North Carolina, South Carolina, and Virginia; and five Comfort Inns in North Carolina and Virginia. **Corporate headquarters location:** This location. **Listed on:** New York Stock Exchange. **Stock exchange symbol:** WXH.

North Dakota

RADISSON HOTEL FARGO
201 5th Street North, Fargo ND 58102. 701/232-7363. **Fax:** 701/298-9134. **Contact:** Sandy Adams, Human Resources. **E-mail address**: sadams@radissonfargo.com. **World Wide Web address:** http://www.radisson.com. **Description:** A 151-room hotel offering seven meeting rooms. **Other U.S. locations:** Nationwide. **International locations:** Worldwide.

Ohio

BENNETT ENTERPRISES, INC.
P.O. Box 670, Perrysburg OH 43552. 419/874-1933. **Physical address:** 27476 Holiday Lane, Perrysburg OH 43552. **Fax:** 419/874-2615. **Contact:** Susan Baer, Director of Human Resources. **World Wide Web address:** http://www.bennett-enterprises.com. **Description:** Operates several restaurants and hotels including three Holiday Inns, one Hampton Inn, six Ralphie's Sports Bars, and nineteen Big Boy Family Restaurants. **NOTE:** Entry-level positions and second and third shifts are offered. **Special programs:** Internships. **Corporate headquarters location:** This location. **Operations at this facility include:** Administration; Research and Development; Sales; Service. **Listed on:** Privately held. **Annual sales/revenues:** $5 - $10 million. **Number of employees nationwide:** 1,500.

BOB EVANS FARMS, INC.
3776 South High Street, Columbus OH 43207. 614/491-2225. **Toll-free phone:** 800/272-7675. **Fax:** 614/497-4318. **Contact:** Personnel Director. **E-mail address:** employment@bobevans.com. **World Wide Web address:** http://www.bobevans.com. **Description:** Owns and operates 448 family restaurants in 21 states including Bob Evans Restaurants and Owens Family Restaurants. The company also produces sausage products and deli-style salads, which are distributed primarily through grocery stores in the Midwest, Southwest, and Southeast. **NOTE:** Part-time jobs are offered. **Positions advertised include:** Restaurant Manager; Product Development Secretary. **Special programs:** Scholarship Opportunities. **Corporate headquarters location:** This location. **Listed on:** NASDAQ. **Stock exchange symbol:** BOBE.

BOYKIN LODGING COMPANY
45 West Prospect Avenue, Suite 1500, Guildhall Building, Cleveland OH 44115-1039. 216/241-6375. **Fax:** 216/241-1329. **Contact:** Human Resources. **World Wide Web address:** http://www.boykinlodging.com. **Description:** A Marriott franchisee engaged in the development and management of upscale, full-service hotels. **Special programs:** Internships. **Corporate headquarters location:** This location. **Listed on:** New York Stock Exchange. **Stock exchange symbol:** BOY.

FRISCH'S RESTAURANTS, INC.
2800 Gilbert Avenue, Cincinnati OH 45206. 513/961-2660. **Toll-free phone:** 888/824-4268. **Contact:** Personnel. **World Wide Web address:** http://www.frischs.com. **Description:** Operates and licenses family restaurants with drive-through service under the names Frisch's Big Boy, Kip's Big Boy, and Hardee's. The company also operates two hotels with restaurants in metropolitan Cincinnati. **NOTE:** Human Resources direct line is 888/824-4269. **Corporate headquarters location:** This location. **Other U.S. locations:** FL; IN; KY; OK; TX.

MAX & ERMA'S RESTAURANTS INC.
4849 Evanswood Drive, Columbus OH 43229-6206. 614/431-5800. **Fax:** 614/431-4100. **Contact:** Human Resources. **World Wide Web address:** http://www.max-ermas.com. **Description:** Operates a chain of approximately 30 restaurants. Founded in 1972. **Positions advertised include:** Server; Cook; Host/Hostess; Carryout Person; Bus Person. **Corporate**

headquarters location: This location. **Other U.S. locations:** IL; IN; KY; MI; PA.

SELECT RESTAURANT COMPANY
One Chagrin Highlands, 2000 Auburn Drive, Suite 410, Beechwood OH 44122. 216/464-6606. **Fax:** 216/464-8565. **Contact:** Joan Lewis, Vice President of Human Resources Department. **E-mail address:** info@selectrestaurants.com. **World Wide Web address:** http://www.selectrestaurants.com. **Description:** A national chain of 60 full-service specialty restaurants offering everything from casual to fine dining. **NOTE:** Call or visit local restaurant for hourly positions.

STRANG CORPORATION
8905 Lake Avenue, Cleveland OH 44102. 216/961-6767. **Contact:** Human Resources. **World Wide Web address:** http://www.strangcorp.com. **Description:** A restaurant and hotel management company. **Corporate headquarters location:** This location.

TRAVEL CENTERS OF AMERICA, INC.
24601 Center Ridge Road, Suite 200, Westlake OH 44145-5677. 440/808-9100. **Contact:** Personnel. **World Wide Web address:** http://www.tatravelcenters.com. **Description:** Operates refueling and refreshment stops for motorists. **Corporate headquarters location:** This location. **Other U.S. locations:** Nationwide. **Annual sales/revenues:** More than $100 million. **Number of employees nationwide:** 10,500.

WENDY'S INTERNATIONAL, INC.
4288 West Dublin Granville Road, Dublin OH 43017. 614/764-3100. **Contact:** Human Resources. **World Wide Web address:** http://www.wendysintl.com. **Description:** One of the world's largest restaurant franchising companies. Wendy's International is comprised of Wendy's, a fast-food restaurant chain, and Tim Horton's, a coffee and baked goods restaurant chain. **Positions advertised include:** Marketing Research Manager; Administrative Assistant; Advertising Production Supervisor; Director, Investor Communications; Director, Construction Planning; Equipment Specialist; Treasury Analyst. **Corporate headquarters location:** This location. **Other U.S. locations:** Nationwide. **Listed on:** New York Stock Exchange. **Stock exchange symbol:** WEN.

WHITE CASTLE SYSTEM INC.
555 West Goodale Street, Columbus OH 43215. 614/228-5781. **Contact:** Human Resources Manager. **World Wide Web address:** http://www.whitecastle.com. **Description:** White Castle owns and operates 380 hamburger restaurants, primarily in the Midwest. **Positions advertised include:** Accountant. **Corporate headquarters location:** This location. **Number of employees nationwide:** 13,000.

Oklahoma
RENAISSANCE HOTEL
10 North Broadway, Oklahoma City OK 73102. 405/228-8000. **Fax:** 405/228-2574. **Contact:** Human Resources. **E-mail address:** iwantajob@jqh.com. **World Wide Web address:** http://www.jqhhotels.com. **Description:** A hotel and convention center. John Q. Hammons Hotels also owns and operates resorts and hotels under such trade names as Embassy Suites, Holiday Inn, Sheraton, and the Marriott. **Positions advertised include:** Banquet Manager; Front Office Manager. **Special programs:** Training. **Corporate Headquarters location:** Springfield MO. **Other U.S. locations:** Nationwide. **Parent Company:** John Q. Hammons Hotels, Incorporated. **Listed on:** American Stock Exchange. **Stock exchange symbol:** JQH.

SONIC CORPORATION
300 Johnny Bench Drive, Oklahoma City OK 73104. 405/280-7654. **Contact:** Molly Scalf, Personnel Director. **E-mail address:** soniccorphr@sonicdrivein.com. **Recorded jobline:** 405/225-5004. **World Wide Web address:** http://www.sonicdrivein.com. **Description:** Operates and franchises more than 2,400 drive-in restaurants, which specialize in made-to-order fast food. There are also 149 company-owned Sonic restaurants, which are located principally in the south central region of the United States. **NOTE:** See current job openings at www.jobsok.com. **Positions advertised include:** Payroll Support Team Leader; Retail Technology Analyst; Service and Support Analyst. **Special programs:** Tuition Assistance Program; Internships. **Corporate headquarters location:** This location. **Other U.S. locations:** Sonic Drive-Ins exist nationwide. **Listed on:** NASDAQ. **Subsidiaries include:** SONIC Industries, Incorporated; SONIC Restaurants, Incorporated. **Stock exchange symbol:** SONC. **Sales/revenue:** $3 billion. **Number of employees at this location:** 300.

Oregon
ASTORIA RED LION INN
400 Industry Street, Astoria OR 97103. 503/325-7373. **Fax:** 503/325-8727. **Contact:** Human Resources. **World Wide Web address:** http://www.redlion.com. **Description:** A full-service, 124-room hotel offering a variety of business services and tourist information. **Positions advertised include:** Night Auditor; Room Attendant.

BEAVERTON COURTYARD INN
8500 SW Nimbus Drive, Beaverton OR 97008. 503/641-3200. **Contact:** Manager. **World Wide Web address:** http://www.courtyard.com. **Description:** A 149-room hotel that offers a restaurant, meeting facilities, recreational facilities, and business services. **Corporate headquarters location:** Washington DC. **Parent company:** Marriott International Inc.

THE BENSON HOTEL
309 Southwest Broadway, Portland OR 97205. 503/228-2000. **Fax:** 503/471-3920. **Contact:** Human Resources. **World Wide Web address:** http://www.bensonhotel.com. **Description:** A luxury hotel and conference facility. Founded in 1912. **Parent company:** WestCoast Hotels.

COURTYARD INN-PORTLAND AIRPORT
11550 NE Airport Way, Portland OR 97220. 503/252-3200. **Contact:** Manager. **World Wide Web address:** http://www.courtyard.com. **Description:** A full-service hotel offering a restaurant, exercise facilities, conference rooms, and business services. **Corporate headquarters location:** Washington DC. **Parent company:** Marriott International.

DOUBLETREE HOTEL PORTLAND LLOYD CENTER
1000 NE Multnomah, Portland OR 97232. 503/281-6111. **Recorded jobline:** 503/296-3384. **Contact:** Personnel. **World Wide Web address:** http://www.doubletree.com. **Description:** A full-service 493-room hotel offering three restaurants, meeting facilities, exercise facilities, and business services. **Positions advertised include:** Assistant Restaurant Manager; Kitchen Supervisor. **Parent company:** Hilton Hotels Corporation is a hospitality, gaming, and lodging company. With its Hilton and Conrad brands, the company develops, owns, manages, and franchises hotel-casinos, resorts, vacation ownership, and hotel properties throughout the world. Other subsidiaries of Hilton Hotel Corporation include Conrad International, Hilton Equipment Corporation, Hilton Grand Vacation Company, and Hilton Inns, Inc.

ELMER'S RESTAURANTS, INC.
P.O. Box 16938, Portland OR 97292. 503/252-1485. **Physical address**: 11802 SE Stark Street, Portland OR 97216. **Fax:** 503/257-7448. **Contact:** President. **E-mail address:** employment@elmers-restaurants.com. **World Wide Web address:** http://www.elmers-restaurants.com. **Description:** Owns and operates 11 Elmer's Pancake & Steakhouse restaurants and sells franchises. Franchises and company-owned stores are located throughout the western United States. **Positions advertised include:** General Manager; Kitchen Manager; Assistant Manager; Supervisor; Server; Cashier; Host; Busser; Dishwasher; Cook. **Corporate headquarters location:** This location. **Listed on:** NASDAQ. **Stock exchange symbol:** ELMS.

HILTON EUGENE & CONFERENCE CENTER
66 East Sixth Avenue, Eugene OR 97401. 541/342-2000. **Fax:** 541/349-8610. **Contact:** Human Resources Manager. **World Wide Web address:** http://www.hilton.com. **Description:** A 270-room hotel that offers extensive conference, convention and banquet facilities, two restaurants, exercise facilities, and business services. **Corporate headquarters location:** Beverly Hills CA. **Parent company:** Hilton Hotels Corporation is a hospitality, gaming, and lodging company. With its Hilton and Conrad brands, the company develops, owns, manages, and franchises hotel-casinos,. resorts, vacation ownership, and hotel properties throughout the world. Other subsidiaries of Hilton Hotel Corporation include Conrad International, Hilton Equipment Corporation, Hilton Grand Vacation Company, and Hilton Inns, Inc.

HILTON PORTLAND HOTEL
921 SW Sixth Avenue, Portland OR 97204. 503/226-1611. **Recorded jobline:** 503/220-2560. **Contact:** Human Resources. **World Wide Web address:** http://www.hilton.com. **Description:** A 455-room hotel. **Positions advertised include:** Assistant Financial Director; Room Service Server; Valet; Cafeteria Cook; Host. **Corporate headquarters location:** Beverly Hills CA. **Parent company:** Hilton Hotels Corporation is a hospitality, gaming, and lodging company. With its Hilton and Conrad brands, the company develops, owns, manages, and franchises hotel-casinos, resorts, vacation ownership, and hotel properties throughout the world. Other subsidiaries of Hilton Hotel Corporation include Conrad International, Hilton Equipment Corporation, Hilton Grand Vacation Company, and Hilton Inns, Inc.

MACHEEZMO MOUSE RESTAURANTS INC.
2920 SW Dolph Court, Suite 4, Portland OR 97205. 503/221-4900. **Fax:** 503/274-4369. **Contact:** Human Resources. **Description:** Operates a chain of 15 quick-service restaurants that offer Mexican-style food. Macheezmo Mouse restaurants offer dine-in and take-out lunch and dinner service in the Portland OR and Seattle WA metropolitan areas. **Corporate headquarters location:** This location.

McCORMICK & SCHMICK MANAGEMENT GROUP
720 SW Washington Street, Suite 550, Portland OR 97205. 503/226-3440. **Fax:** 503/228-7729. **Contact:** Senior Personnel Coordinator. **World Wide Web address:** http://www.mccormickandschmicks.com. **Description:** A management company that operates a chain of seafood restaurants. The restaurants operate as Jake's Grill, Jake's Famous Crawfish, McCormick & Schmicks Seafood Restaurant, Spenger's Fresh Fish Grotto, M & S Grill, and McCormick's Fish House & Bar. **Corporate headquarters location:** This location. **Other U.S. locations:** Nationwide.

PORTLAND MARRIOTT HOTEL DOWNTOWN
1401 SW Naito Parkway, Portland OR 97201. 503/226-7600. **Recorded jobline:** 503/499-6334. **Contact:** Jim Coull, Director of Human Resources. **World Wide Web address:** http://www.marriott.com. **Description:** A 503-room, full-service hotel that offers a restaurant and lounge, a fitness club, 18 meeting rooms, and business services. **Positions advertised include:** Guest Service Agent; Host/Cashier. **Corporate headquarters location:** Washington DC.

RESIDENCE INN PORTLAND SOUTH
15200 SW Bangy Road, Lake Oswego OR 97035. 503/684-2603. **Contact:** General Manager. **World Wide Web address:** http://www.residenceinn.com. **Description:** A 112-room hotel that offers two conference rooms, dinner delivery services, and business services. **Corporate headquarters location:** Washington DC. **Parent company:** Marriott International.

RESIDENCE INN PORTLAND WEST
18855 NW Tanasbourne Drive, Hillsboro OR 97124. 503/531-3200. **Contact:** General Manager. **World Wide Web address:** http://www.residenceinn.com. **Description:** A 122-room hotel that offers two conference rooms, exercise facilities, and business services. **Corporate headquarters location:** Washington DC. **Parent company:** Marriott International.

THE RIVERPLACE HOTEL
1510 SW Harbor Way, Portland OR 97201. 503/228-3233. **Fax:** 503/295-6190. **Contact:** Personnel. **World Wide Web address:** http://www.riverplacehotel.com. **Description:** A European-style hotel and waterfront resort offering 84 rooms, banquet and conference facilities, a fitness center, and several dining areas. **Parent company:** WestCoast Hotels.

SALISHAN SPA AND GOLF RESORT
7760 Highway 101, Gleneden Beach OR 97388. 541/764-2371. **Contact:** Human Resources. **World Wide Web address:** http://www.salishan.com. **Description:** A resort hotel offering three restaurants, a wine cellar, an 18-hole golf course, a driving range, guest activities, exercise facilities, banquet and conference rooms, and business services. **NOTE:** Staffing is reduced during the off-season to approximately 280. **Corporate headquarters location:** Portland OR. **Parent company:** Westin.

STARBUCKS COFFEE
7737 SW Capitol Highway, Portland OR 97219. 503/245-1961. **Contact:** Manager. **World Wide Web address:** http://www.starbucks.com. **Description:** Starbucks Coffee sells whole-bean coffees, along with hot coffees and Italian-style espresso beverages through more than 2,500 retail stores worldwide. The company purchases green coffee beans for its coffee varieties from coffee-producing regions throughout the world and custom roasts them In addition to coffee beans and beverages, the company's stores offer a selection of coffee-making equipment, accessories, pastries, and confections. Also, the company sells whole-bean coffees through a specialty sales group and a national mail-order operation. **Corporate headquarters location:** Seattle WA. **Operations at this facility include:** This location is one location of a national chain of cafes.

TIGARD COURTYARD INN
15686 SW Sequoia Parkway, Tigard OR 97224. 503/684-7900. **Contact:** Manager. **World Wide Web address:** http://www.courtyard.com. **Description:** A moderately priced, 110-room hotel offering a restaurant, meeting center, exercise facilities, and business services. **Parent company:** Marriott International.

VALLEY RIVER INN
1000 Valley River Way, Eugene OR 97401. 541/681-5077. **Fax:** 541/681-5064. **Recorded jobline:** 541/686-2803. **Contact:** Sandra de Jonge, Human Resources Director. **E-mail address:** sandrad@valleyriverinn.com. **World Wide Web address:** http://www.valleyriverinn.com. **Description:** A 257-room hotel offering meeting facilities, Sweetwaters restaurant, airport transportation, exercise facilities, and business services. **Positions advertised include:** Assistant Baker; Banquet Server; Front Desk Agent; Restaurant Supervisor. **Corporate headquarters location:** Seattle WA. **Parent company:** Westcoast Hotels.

Pennsylvania

ARAMARK BUSINESS SERVICES GROUP
ARAMARK Tower, 1101 Market Street, Philadelphia PA 19107. 215/238-3591. **Fax:** 215/238-8195. **Contact:** Human Resources. **E-mail address:** resumes@aramark.com. **World Wide Web address:** http://www.aramark.com. **Description:** ARAMARK Business Services consists of Business Dining Services and Conference Center Management. Business Dining Services serves over 3 million people every business day at over 7,000 locations and offers a wide range of operations, marketing, and merchandising programs for executive dining rooms, plant cafeterias, and fully

catered functions. ARAMARK's Conference Center Management provides comprehensive specialized services, ranging from food and beverage to total hospitality and property management. Services are provided in both residential and nonresidential centers such as executive retreats, corporate training complexes, resorts, and continuing education centers. **Parent company:** ARAMARK. **Listed on:** New York Stock Exchange. **Stock exchange symbol:** RMK. **Number of employees worldwide:** 240,000.

ARAMARK CAMPUS DINING SERVICES
ARAMARK Tower, 1101 Market Street, Philadelphia PA 19106. 215/238-3085. **Contact:** Human Resources. **World Wide Web address:** http://www.aramark.com. **Description:** ARAMARK's Campus Dining Services serve more than 200 million meals a year at over 300 college and university campuses. **Parent company:** ARAMARK. **Listed on:** New York Stock Exchange. **Stock exchange symbol:** RMK. **Number of employees worldwide:** 240,000.

ARAMARK HEALTHCARE SUPPORT SERVICES
ARAMARK Tower, 1101 Market Street, Philadelphia PA 19107. 215/238-3541. **Contact:** Human Resources. **World Wide Web address:** http://www.aramark.com. **Description:** ARAMARK Healthcare Support Services serves 115 million meals annually for over 300 health care customers nationwide and also provides food service, clinical nutrition management, facility services, and engineering support to assist health care administrators. **Parent company:** ARAMARK. **Listed on:** New York Stock Exchange. **Stock exchange symbol:** RMK. **Number of employees worldwide:** 240,000.

ARAMARK INTERNATIONAL SERVICES
ARAMARK Tower, 1101 Market Street, Philadelphia PA 19107. 215/238-3077. **Contact:** Human Resources. **World Wide Web address:** http://www.aramark.com. **Description:** ARAMARK International Services provides a broad range of food and related services for customers worldwide. **Parent company:** ARAMARK. **Listed on:** New York Stock Exchange. **Stock exchange symbol:** RMK. **Number of employees worldwide:** 240,000.

ARAMARK REFRESHMENT SERVICES
ARAMARK Tower, 1101 Market Street, Philadelphia PA 19107. 215/238-3525. **Contact:** Human Resources. **World Wide Web address:** http://www.aramark.com. **Description:** ARAMARK Refreshment Services serves more than 1 billion cups of coffee, 400 million cans and cups of soda, and 200 million snacks annually. Over 70 market centers across the country provide service to customers. **Parent company:** ARAMARK. **Listed on:** New York Stock Exchange. **Stock exchange symbol:** RMK. **Number of employees worldwide:** 240,000.

ARAMARK SCHOOL SUPPORT SERVICES
ARAMARK Tower, 1101 Market Street, Philadelphia PA 19107. 215/238-3526. **Contact:** Human Resources. **World Wide Web address:** http://www.aramark.com. **Description:** ARAMARK School Support Services provides professional food service management for more than 1 million students in over 280 school districts. The company offers comprehensive services including menu management to food-handling safety, marketing, merchandising, nutrition education, and recycling programs. **Parent company:** ARAMARK. **Listed on:** New York Stock Exchange. **Stock exchange symbol:** RMK. **Number of employees worldwide:** 240,000.

BROCK AND COMPANY, INC.
257 Great Valley Parkway, Malvern PA 19355. 610/647-5656. **Fax:** 610/647-0867. **Contact:** Human Resources. **E-mail address:** hr@brockco.com. **World Wide Web address:** http://www.brockco.com. **Description:** A contract food service company offering corporate dining, vending, and office coffee services. **Positions advertised include:** General Manager; Executive Chef; Chef Manager; Director of Food Service; Assistant Director; Catering Manager; Culinary Manager in Training. **Special programs:** Apprenticeships; Co-ops. **Corporate headquarters location:** This location. **Annual sales/revenues:** $11 - $20 million. **Number of employees at this location:** 300.

NUTRITION MANAGEMENT SERVICES COMPANY
2071 Kimberton Road, P.O. Box 725, Kimberton PA 19442. 610/935-2050. **Fax:** 610/935-8287. **Contact:** Personnel Department. **World Wide Web address:** http://www.nmsc.com. **Description:** A food service management company specializing in food service programs for health care, retirement, and acute care facilities. **Positions advertised include:** District Manager; Food Service Director; Assistant Food Service Director. **Corporate headquarters location:** This location.

OLIVE GARDEN RESTAURANT
6000 Oxford Drive, Bethel Park PA 15102-1826. 412/835-6353. **Fax:** 412/835-6047. **Contact:** Human Resources. **World Wide Web address:** http://www.olivegarden.com. **Description:** One location in a chain of family-style Italian restaurants. **Positions advertised include:** Service Manager; Sales Manager; Culinary Manager; Server. **Parent Company:** Darden Restaurants.

RADISSON HOTEL GREENTREE
101 Radisson Drive, Pittsburgh PA 15205. 412/922-8400. **Contact:** Human Resources. **Description:** A 500-room hotel, featuring a swimming pool, a putting green, a whirlpool bath, a sauna, and an exercise room.

RADISSON VALLEY FORGE HOTEL & CONVENTION CENTER
1160 First Avenue, King of Prussia PA 19406. 610/337-2000. **Fax:** 610/354-8214. **Contact:** Human Resources. **World Wide Web address:** http://www.Radisson.com/kingofprussia. **Description:** A 488-room hotel and tri-level convention center featuring three full-service restaurants, and Lily Langtry's, a Las Vegas-style dinner theater facility. **NOTE:** Entry-level positions are offered. **Special programs:** Internships. **Parent company:** GF Management. **Number of employees at this location:** 600.

SODEXHO INC.
1000 Liberty Avenue, 2nd Floor, Pittsburgh PA 15222. 412/261-3660. **Contact:** Human Resources. **World Wide Web address:** http://www.sodexhousa.com. **Description:** Manages the food service facility at a Pittsburgh federal office building. **Parent company:** Sodexho Alliance.

South Carolina

THE CARAVELLE GOLD & FAMILY RESORT
6900 North Ocean Boulevard, Myrtle Beach SC 29572. 843/918-8000. **Toll-free phone:** 800/785-4460. **Fax:** 843/626-6276. **Contact:** Personnel. **World Wide Web address:** http://www.thecaravelle.com. **Description:** A resort with 590 rooms and villas. **Parent company:** Caravelle Properties Ltd Partnership (also at this location). **Affiliates include:** Santa Maria Restaurant; Saint Johns.

THE CLUB GROUP, LTD.
71 Lighthouse Road, Suite 300, Hilton Head SC 29938. 843/363-5699. **Contact:** Christiana G. Martin, Controller. **Description:** Operates a resort. **Positions advertised include:** Cook; Hotel Manager; Food Service Manager. **Subsidiaries include:** Harbour Town Resorts; National Liability & Fire Insurance Company.

CROWNE PLAZA RESORT
130 Shipyard Drive, Hilton Head Island SC 29928. 843/842-2400. **Fax:** 843/785-4879. **Contact:** Human Resources. **World Wide Web address:** http://www.crowneplazaresort.com. **Description:** A 340-room hotel located in Shipyard Plantation. **NOTE:** Entry-level positions, part-time jobs, seasonal jobs, and

second and third shifts are offered. **Positions advertised include:** Part Time PM Line Cook; Loss Preventing Associate; Part Time Night Auditor; Mini Bar Attendant; Bartender; Restaurant Servers; Restaurant Supervisor. **Special programs:** Internships; Training; Summer Jobs. **International locations:** Worldwide. **Parent company:** Six Continents PLC (London, United Kingdom).

RYAN'S FAMILY STEAK HOUSES, INC.
405 Lancaster Avenue, Greer SC 29650. 864/879-1011, extension 3572. **Fax:** 864/894-0256. **Contact:** Kim Lynch, Regional Recruiter. **E-mail address:** klynch@ryans.com. **World Wide Web address:** http://www.ryansinc.com. **Description:** Owns and franchises over 250 restaurants in 21 states. **Positions advertised include:** Manager Trainee; Cook; Server; Cashier; Host/Hostess; Utility Worker; Restaurant/Food Service Manager. **Corporate headquarters location:** This location. **Listed on:** NASDAQ. **Stock exchange symbol:** RYAN. **Annual sales/revenues:** $774 million. **Number of employees nationwide:** 21,300.

SANDS RESORTS
201 74th North Avenue, Myrtle Beach SC 25978. 843/692-5233. **Fax:** 843/692-5234. **Contact:** Director of Human Resources. **E-mail address:** hr@sandsresorts.com. **World Wide Web address:** http://www.sandsresorts.com. **Description:** Owns and manages several resorts in Myrtle Beach and one resort in North Carolina. **Positions advertised include:** Customer Service Representative; Human Resources Manager. **Corporate headquarters location:** This location. **Listed on:** Privately held.

THE SEA PINES RESORT
32 Greenwood Drive, Hilton Head Island SC 29928. 843/842-1882. **Fax:** 843/842-1412. **Contact:** Monika Nash, Director of Human Resources. **E-mail address:** monika@seapines.com. **World Wide Web address:** http://www.seapines.com. **Description:** A 5,200 acre resort featuring luxury accommodations, golf and tennis, shopping, and meeting space. **Special programs:** Internships. **Corporate headquarters location:** This location. **Parent company:** Sea Pines Associates, Inc.

South Dakota
SUPER 8 MOTELS, INC.
1910 Eighth Avenue Northeast, Aberdeen SD 57401. 605/229-8981. **Fax:** 605/229-8910. **Contact:** Melanie Johnson, Human Resources. **E-mail address:** melanie.johnson@cendant.com. **World Wide Web address:** http://www.super8.com. **Description:** Provides office support for the Super 8 Motels lodging chain. Super 8 Motels is part of Cendant, the world's largest lodging franchisor. **NOTE:** Super 8 Motels are independently owned and operated. Please inquire about positions with individual hotels by contacting the property directly. For employment in the Aberdeen corporate offices, contact Human Resources or apply online at www.cendant.com. **Corporate headquarters location:** Parsippany NJ. **Parent company:** Cendant Corp.

Tennessee
BACK YARD BURGERS, INC.
1657 North Shelby Oaks Drive, Suite 105, Memphis TN 38134. 901/367-0888. **Fax:** 901/367-0999. **Contact:** Ms. Coy Cella, Human Resources Department. **E-mail address:** ccella@backyardburgers.com. **World Wide Web address:** http://www.backyardburgers.com. **Description:** Operates and franchises a 132-unit chain of fast-food restaurants in 17 states. **Corporate headquarters location:** This location. **Listed on:** NASDAQ. **Stock exchange symbol:** BYBI.

EMBASSY SUITES-MEMPHIS
1022 South Shady Grove Road, Memphis TN 38120. 901/684-1777. **Contact:** General Manager. **World Wide Web address:** http://www.embassy-suites.com. **Description:** A 200-suite hotel. Features include Frank Grisanti's Restaurant and six conference suites. **NOTE:** Search for positions online.

FAMILY INNS OF AMERICA
P.O. Box 10, Pigeon Forge TN 37868-0010. 865/453-4988. **Physical address**: 3124 Tammy King Drive, Pigeon Forge TN 37868. **Contact:** Dian Robertson, Human Resources. **World Wide Web address:** http://www.familyinnsofamerica.com. **Description:** Operates a nationwide motel chain. **Special programs:** Internships. **Corporate headquarters location:** This location. **Parent company:** KMS Enterprises, Inc.

HARRAH'S ENTERTAINMENT
1023 Cherry Road, Memphis TN 38117. 901/762-8600. **Toll-free phone**: 800/467-4278. **Contact:** Human Resources. **World Wide Web address:** http://www.harrahs.com. **Description:** Owns and operates 26 casinos in 13 states under the Harrah's, Harveys, Rio, and Showboat names. **NOTE:** Search and apply for positions online. **Positions advertised include:** Associate Contract Manager; Programmer Analyst; Director Strategic Sourcing; Associate Systems Analyst; Computer Operations specialist; Unix Engineer; Network Engineer; Network Architect; Systems Analyst, CMS; Property marketing Advisor. **Corporate headquarters location:** Las Vegas NV. **Operations at this facility:** Corporate services. **Number of employees nationwide:** 26,000.

THE HILTON HOTEL CORPORATION
755 Crossover Lane, Memphis TN 38117. 901/374-5000. **Contact:** Human Resources. **World Wide Web address:** http://www.hilton.com. **Description:** Owns, operates, and franchises several hotel chains including Hilton, Hampton Inn, Doubletree, Embassy Suites, Homewood Suites by Hilton, Conrad International. **NOTE:** Search for positions online. **Positions advertised include:** Sr. Customer Support Specialist; Accounting Specialist; Financial Analyst; Manager, Loss Prevention; Manager, Brand Distribution; Product Manager; Programmer, Corporate Systems; Sr. Regional Revenue Manager. **Operations at this facility include:** Corporate regional office.

HOLIDAY INN CHATTANOOGA CHOO CHOO
1400 Market Street, Chattanooga TN 37402. 423/266-5000. **Fax:** 423/267-5261. **Contact:** Human Resources. **World Wide Web address:** http://www.choochoo.com. **Description:** A hotel and tourist attraction. **Special programs:** Internships. **Corporate headquarters location:** Atlanta GA. **Operations at this facility include:** Sales; Service. **Number of employees at this location:** 400.

THE KRYSTAL COMPANY
The Krystal Building, One Union Square, Chattanooga TN 37402. 423/757-1500. **Toll-free phone:** 800/458-5841. **Fax:** 423/757-5610. **Contact:** Human Resources. **World Wide Web address:** http://www.krystalco.com. **Description:** Develops, owns and operates, or franchises 428 full-size Krystal and drive-through Krystal Kwik fast-food hamburger restaurants in 12 states. Founded in 1932. **NOTE:** Apply online for corporate positions. For restaurant management positions, forward resume to: Marlene Cole, Regional Recruiter, mcole@crystalco.com or via fax: 800/835-0429. **Parent company:** Port Royal Holdings, Inc.

LOGAN'S ROADHOUSE, INC.
3011 Armory Drive, Suite 300, Nashville TN 37204. 615/885-9056. **Fax:** 615/884-5490. **Contact:** Recruiting Department. **World Wide Web address:** http://www.logansroadhouse.com. **Description:** Operates 106 company-owned and 18 franchised Logan's Roadhouse restaurants in 17 states. Founded in 1991. **Positions advertised include:** Assistant Manager; Management Trainee. **Corporate headquarters location:** This location. **Other U.S. locations:** Nationwide. **Parent company:** CBRL Group, Inc. **Listed on:** NASDAQ. **Stock exchange symbol:** RDHS. **Annual sales/revenues:** $51 - $100 million. **Number of employees nationwide:** 1,600.

O'CHARLEY'S INC.
3038 Sidco Drive, Nashville TN 37204. 615/256-8500. **Fax:** 615/782-5043. **Contact:** Human Resources. **E-**

mail address: resumes@ocharleys.com. **World Wide Web address:** http://www.ocharleys.com. **Description:** Operates and franchises over 214 full-service restaurants in the southern and midwestern United States. **Corporate headquarters location:** This location. **Listed on:** NASDAQ. **Number of employees at this location:** 175.

OPRYLAND HOTEL CONVENTION CENTER
2800 Opryland Drive, Nashville TN 37214. 615/889-1000. **Recorded jobline:** 800/899-6779. **Contact:** Employment Manager. **World Wide Web address:** http://www.gaylordhotels.com/gaylordopryland. **Description:** Operates entertainment attractions including Opryland Hotel, a 3,000-room convention center; General Jackson Showboat; Springhouse Golf Club; Opryland River Taxis; Grand Ole Opry Tours; and the Opryland USA/KOA Campground. **NOTE:** Search and apply for positions online. Online applications preferred. **Corporate headquarters location:** This location. **Parent company:** Gaylord Entertainment Company. **Operations at this facility include:** Administration. **Annual sales/revenues:** More than $100 million.

PERKINS FAMILY RESTAURANTS, L.P.
6075 Poplar Avenue, Suite 800, Memphis TN 38119. 901/766-6400. **Toll-free phone:** 800/877-7375. **Fax:** 901/766-6482. **Contact:** Human Resources. **E-mail address:** jobs@perkinsrestaurants.com. **World Wide Web address:** http://www.perkinsrestaurants.com. **Description:** Operates a restaurant chain with approximately 500 locations in 35 states and Canada. Most of the restaurant locations also include a retail bakery. **NOTE:** Search and apply for positions online. **Positions advertised include:** Financial Planning Manager. **Corporate headquarters location:** This location. **Number of employees worldwide:** 25,000.

RUBY TUESDAY INC.
150 West Church Avenue, Maryville TN 37801. 865/379-5737. **Fax:** 865/379-6826. **Contact:** Human Resources. **World Wide Web address:** http://www.rubytuesday.com. **Description:** The Ruby Tuesday Group operates low-priced, casual restaurants under the name Ruby Tuesday. There are more than 700 company-owned and franchised restaurants worldwide. **NOTE:** Download application online. **Special programs:** Internships. **Corporate headquarters location:** This location. **Listed on:** New York Stock Exchange. **Stock exchanges symbol:** RI. **Number of employees at this location:** 300. **Number of employees nationwide:** 15,000.

SHOLODGE, INC.
130 Maple Drive North, Hendersonville TN 37075. 615/264-8000. **Contact:** Jim Grout, Executive Vice President of Human Resources. **World Wide Web address:** http://www.sholodge.com. **Description:** ShoLodge is the exclusive franchiser of Shoney's Inns, a chain of motels located throughout the Southeast, and GuestHouse International Inns and Suites. **Corporate headquarters location:** This location. **Other U.S. locations:** Nationwide. **Listed on:** NASDAQ. **Stock exchange symbol:** LODG.

SOUTHERN HOSPITALITY CORPORATION
1101 Kermit Road, Suite 310, Nashville TN 37217. 615/399-9700. **Fax:** 615/399-3373. **Contact:** Human Resources. **Description:** Operates Wendy's fast-food franchises. **Other U.S. locations:** Nationwide. **Parent company:** Davco Restaurants Inc. **Number of employees at this location:** 1,000.

TBA GLOBAL EVENTS
210 12th Avenue South, Nashville TN 37203. 615/742-9000. **Fax:** 615/742-9199. **Contact:** Human Resources. **E-mail address:** personnel@tbaent.com. **World Wide Web address:** http://www.tbaglobalevents.com. **Description:** A strategic communications and entertainment company. **Other U.S. locations:** Nationwide.

Texas

ACCOR HOTELS
4001 International Parkway, Carrollton TX 75007. 972/360-9000. **Fax:** 972/360-5996.**Contact:** Human Resources. **E-mail address:** careers@accor-na.com. **World Wide Web address:** http://www.accor.com. **Description:** Accor Hotels operates over 4,000 hotels, including Motel 6 and Red Roof Inn, in 90 countries. **NOTE:** Please visit website to search for jobs and apply online. **Special programs:** Internships. **International locations:** Worldwide. **Operations at this facility include:** This location houses the administrative offices for the U.S. **Number of employees nationwide:** 18,800. **Number of employees worldwide:** 158,000.

ALAMO CAFE
P.O. BOX 790721, San Antonio TX 78279-0721. 210/341-1336. **Physical address**: 754 Isom Road, San Antonio TX 78216. **Fax:** 210/341-3036. **Contact:** Human Resources. **World Wide Web address:** http://www.alamocafe.com. **Description:** A family-style restaurant that serves both American and Mexican foods. **Corporate headquarters location:** This location. **Parent company:** Alamo Restaurants Inc.

BEST VALUE INN & SUITES
2525 Interstate Highway 35 South, Austin TX 78752. 512/441-0143. **Contact:** Human Resources. **World Wide Web address:** http://www.bestvalueinn.com. **Description:** One location of the nationwide hotel chain. **Other area locations:** Buda TX.

BRINKER INTERNATIONAL INC.
6820 LBJ Freeway, Dallas TX 75240. 972/980-9917. **Contact:** Corporate Recruiting. **World Wide Web address:** http://www.brinker.com. **Description:** Operates full-service, casual dining restaurants including Chili's Grill & Bar, Corner Bakery Café, Maggiano's Little Italy, On the Border, Romano's Macaroni Grill, Big Bowl Asian Kitchen, Rockfish Seafood Grill, and Spageddie's Italian Foods. **NOTE:** Please visit website to search for jobs and apply online. **Positions advertised include:** Project Coordinator; Project Manager; Quality Assurance; Real Estate Manager; Regional Training Specialist; Restaurant Accountant; Senior Concept Compensation Analyst; Vice President – Investor Relations. **Corporate headquarters location:** This location. **Other U.S. locations:** Nationwide. **Listed on:** New York Stock Exchange. **Stock exchange symbol:** EAT. **Number of employees nationwide:** 90,000.

CEC ENTERTAINMENT INC.
dba CHUCK E. CHEESE
P.O. Box 152077, Irving TX 75015. 972/258-8507. **Physical address:** 4441 West Airport Freeway, Irving TX 75062. **Contact:** Human Resources. **E-mail address:** careers@cecentertainment.com. **World Wide Web address:** http://www.chuckecheese.com. **Description:** Operates over 400 Chuck E. Cheese's pizza and amusement franchises throughout the United States and Canada. **NOTE:** No phone calls regarding employment. Please visit website to search for jobs and apply online. **Positions advertised include:** Manager of Loss Prevention. **Corporate headquarters location:** This location. **Listed on:** New York Stock Exchange. **Stock exchange symbol:** CEC.

CARLSON RESTAURANTS WORLDWIDE INC.
4201 Marsh Lane, Carrollton TX 75007. 972/662-5400. **Fax:** 972/776-5468. **Contact:** Employee Relations. **World Wide Web address:** http://www.tgifridays.com. **Description:** Operates the TGI Friday's chain of casual-dining restaurants, which has 825 restaurants that can be found in55 countries. **NOTE:** Please visit http://www.carlson.com to search for jobs. **Corporate headquarters location:** This location. **Subsidiaries include:** T.G.I. Friday's U.S.A.; T.G.I. Friday's International; Pick Up Stix. **Parent company:** Carlson Companies, Inc. (Minneapolis MN). **President/CEO:** Richard Snead.

CULINAIRE INTERNATIONAL, INC.
2121 San Jacinto Street, Suite 3100, Dallas TX 75201. 214/754-1880. **Fax:** 214/754-1894. **Contact:** Human Resources. **E-mail address:** recruit@culinaireintl.com. **World Wide Web address:** http://www.culinaireintl.com. **Description:** Provides the food and beverage services for a wide range of corporate clients. **Positions advertised include:** Chef/Catering. **Corporate headquarters location:** This location.

DAVE & BUSTER'S, INC.
2481 Manana Drive, Dallas TX 75220. 214/357-9588. **Fax:** 214/904-2532. **Contact:** Recruiting Department. **World Wide Web address:** http://www.daveandbusters.com. **Description:** An operator of 20 restaurant/entertainment complexes. Each location houses eating venues and amusement facilities including billiards, video games, and virtual reality games. Founded in 1982. **Corporate headquarters location:** This location. **Internship information:** College junior majoring in hospitality, culinary or related field. Two-year minimum field experience. **NOTE:** Management, hourly, and worldwide positions available. Hourly positions must apply at respective local location between 1 p.m. and 5 p.m. All other positions can apply on-line at website; via fax; or by mail. **Other U.S. locations:** Nationwide. **International locations:** Canada; Taiwan. **Listed on:** New York Stock Exchange. **Stock exchange symbol:** DAB.

DOUBLETREE GUEST SUITES HOTEL
303 West 15th Street, Austin TX 78701. 512/478-7000. **Fax:** 512/478-3562. **Contact:** Monica D'Richards, Human Resources Director. **NOTE:** Applications only on Mondays and Tuesdays from 9:00 a.m.-noon. **World Wide Web address:** http://www.doubletree.com. **Description:** A 189-room hotel. **Parent company:** Hilton.

EL CHICO RESTAURANTS, INC.
12200 Stemmons Freeway, Suite 100, Dallas TX 75234. 972/888-8146. **Contact:** Human Resources. **E-mail address:** recruiting@croinc.com. **World Wide Web address:** http://www.elchico.com. **Description:** Operates a chain of full-service restaurants. **NOTE:** Management candidates must have two or more years of experience in casual dining or related experience; good leadership and communication skills. **Corporate headquarters location:** This location. **Parent company:** Consolidated Restaurants Inc. (also at this location). **Operations at this facility include:** Administration; Manufacturing; Research and Development.

EMBASSY SUITES HOTEL
300 South Congress Avenue, Austin TX 78704. 512/469-9000. **Contact:** Human Resources Department. **World Wide Web address:** http://www.embassy-suites.com. **Description:** A 262-room hotel.

FLAGSHIP HOTEL OVER THE WATER
2501 Seawall Boulevard, Galveston TX 77550. 409/762-9000. **Toll-free phone:** 800/392-6542. **Fax:** 409/762-1619. **Contact:** Human Resources. **World Wide Web address:** http://www.galveston.com/flagship. **Description:** A hotel and resort.

FOUR SEASONS HOTEL HOUSTON
1300 Lamar Street, Houston TX 77017. 713/650-1300. **Fax:** 713/650-0434. **Recorded jobline:** 713/652-6240. **E-mail address:** jobs.Houston@fourseasons.com. **Contact:** Human Resources. **World Wide Web address:** http://www.fourseasons.com/employment.com. **Description:** A 399-room hotel that also houses the DeVille Restaurant. Four Seasons Hotels & Resorts operates approximately 55 luxury hotels and resorts in 25 countries. Founded in 1960. **Corporate headquarters location:** Toronto, Canada. **Other area locations:** Austin TX. **Other U.S. locations:** Nationwide. **International locations:** Worldwide.

FOUR SEASONS RESORT AND CLUB
4150 North MacArthur Boulevard, Irving TX 75038. 972/717-0700. **Fax:** 972-717-2578. **Recorded jobline:** 972/717-2544. **Contact:** Human Resources. **E-mail address:** jobs.dalls@fourseasons.com. **World Wide Web address:** http://www.fourseasons.com. **Description:** A 357-room resort offering two championship golf courses, 12 tennis courts, a spa, and a conference center. Founded in 1960. **NOTE:** Entry-level positions, part-time jobs, and second and third shifts are offered. **Special programs:** Training; Summer Jobs. **Corporate headquarters location:** Toronto, Canada. **Other U.S. locations:** Nationwide. **International locations:** Worldwide.

FRONTIER ENTERPRISES
8520 Crownhill Boulevard, San Antonio TX 78209-1199. 210/828-1493. **Contact:** Wendi Scarborough, Human Resources. **World Wide Web address:** http://www.jimsrestaurants.com. **Description:** Owns and operates Jim's Family Restaurants, Magic Time Machine Restaurants, and Towers of America Restaurants. Magic Time Machine Restaurants are seafood and steak dining establishments and the Towers of America Restaurants are family-style restaurants set approximately 6,000 feet in the air. **NOTE:** Online applications available at company's website for all Texas locations. **Positions advertised include:** Manager; Assistant Manager; Waitstaff; Cook; Busperson; Cashier. **Corporate headquarters location:** This location. **Other area locations**: Austin TX; San Antonio TX; Waco TX.

GOLDEN CORRAL
4610 Garth Road, Baytown TX 77521. 281/422-3455. **Contact:** Human Resources. **World Wide Web address:** http://www.goldencorralrest.com. **Description:** One location of a chain of family steakhouses. **Corporate headquarters location:** Raleigh NC. **Other U.S. locations:** Nationwide.

HILTON ANATOLE
2201 Stemmons Freeway, Dallas TX 75207. 214/748-1200. **Contact:** Human Resources. **World Wide Web address:** http://www.hilton.com. **Description:** A luxury convention hotel with more than 1,600 rooms. **NOTE:** Apply online at this company's website. **Positions advertised include:** Assistant Telecommunications Manager. **Operations at this facility include:** Service.

HOLIDAY INN BEAUMONT PLAZA
3950 Interstate 10 South, Beaumont TX 77705. 409/842-5995. **Fax:** 409/842-0315. **Contact:** Human Resources Department. **World Wide Web address:** http://www.ichotelsgroup.com. **Description:** This is a franchise location of the national hotel chain. Holiday Inn Beaumont Plaza offers 235 guest rooms and has one of the largest hotel conference centers in Texas. **NOTE:** Holiday Inn has another location in Beaumont and throughout Texas. See its website for additional locations. **Other U.S. locations:** Nationwide. **Parent company:** Six Continents Hotels.

HOLIDAY INN EXPRESS
5222 Interstate 10 East, Baytown TX 77521. 281/421-7200. **Fax:** 281/421-7209. **Contact:** Human Resources Department. **World Wide Web address:** http://www.ichotelsgroup.com. **Description:** One location of the national hotel chain. **NOTE:** Holiday Inn has several locations throughout Texas. See its website for additional locations. **Other U.S. locations:** Nationwide. **Parent company:** Six Continents Hotels.

HOTELS.COM
10440 North Central Expressway, Suite 400, Dallas TX 75231. 214/361-7311. **Toll-free phone:** 800/964-6835. **Fax:** 214/361-7299. **Contact:** Human Resources. **E-mail address:** careers@hotels.com. **World Wide Web address:** http://www.hotels.com. **Description:** An Internet hotel booking service that offers travelers discounts. Hotels.com has partnerships with large, global hotel chains. **Positions advertised include:** Senior Financial Planning Analyst; Java Programmer

Analyst. Senior Staff Accountant; Senior Java Programmer/Analyst; Group Sales Account Manager; Strategic Corporate Account Manager; Senior Director of Brand Marketing; HRIS Analyst. **NOTE:** Apply online. **Other U.S. locations:** FL; VA. **Parent company:** InterActiveCorp (New York NY). **Listed on:** NASDAQ. **Stock exchange symbol:** IACI.

HYATT REGENCY DALLAS AT REUNION
300 Reunion Boulevard East, Dallas TX 75207. 214/651-1234. **Contact:** Human Resources. **World Wide Web address:** http://www.hyatt.com. **Description:** A luxury hotel offering an 18-story atrium that houses dining and entertainment facilities including a pool, a fully equipped fitness center, tennis and basketball courts, three restaurants, and a revolving rooftop lounge. **Positions advertised include:** Assistant Restaurant Manager; Cocktail Server; Front Office Agent; On-Call Bartender; On-call Banquet Server; Restaurant Server. **Corporate headquarters location:** Chicago IL. **Other U.S. locations:** Nationwide. **Parent company:** Hyatt Hotel Corporation.

HYATT REGENCY HILL COUNTRY RESORT AND SPA
9800 Hyatt Resort Drive, San Antonio TX 78251. 210/647-1234. **Contact:** Penny Nichols Bowden, Human Resources Director. **World Wide Web address:** http://www.hyatt.com. **Description:** Operates as a unit of the nationwide chain of hotels. Hyatt Regency Hill Country Resort has six locations throughout Texas. **Positions advertised include:** Banquet Server; Bartender; Bell Attendant; Cocktail Server; Food Runner; Deli Attendant; Massage Therapist; Nail Technician; Spa Attendant; Retail Clerk; Sales Manager; Room Service Server; Valet Attendant; Yoga Instructor. **Parent company:** Hyatt Hotels Corporation.

HYATT REGENCY HOUSTON
1200 Louisiana Street, Houston TX 77002. 713/654-1234. **Contact:** Human Resources. **World Wide Web address:** http://houstonregency.hyatt.com. **Description:** A 963-room hotel with meeting and banquet facilities. **Positions advertised include:** Cocktail Server; Culinary Lead; Food Server Assistant; Housekeeper. **Corporate headquarters location:** Chicago IL. **Other U.S. locations:** Nationwide. **International locations:** Worldwide. **Parent company:** Hyatt Hotels Corporation.

JACK IN THE BOX
1111 North Loop West, Suite 600, Houston TX 77008. 713/293-6200. **Contact:** Human Resources. **E-mail address:** careers@jackinthebox.com. **World Wide Web address:** http://www.jackinthebox.com. **Description:** Operates and franchises more than 1,600 Jack in the Box restaurants, which are primarily in the western and southwestern United States. International operations currently include restaurants in Hong Kong and Mexico. **Positions advertised include:** Assistant Manager. **Listed on:** New York Stock Exchange. **Stock exchange symbol:** JBX.

LA QUINTA INNS, INC.
909 Hidden Ridge, Suite 600, Irving TX 75038. 210/302-6000. **Contact:** Human Resources. **World Wide Web address:** http://www.lq.com. **Description:** Develops, owns, and operates a nationwide chain of lodging inns. La Quinta Inns has more than 330 locations in 32 states. Founded in 1964. **NOTE:** To apply for hotel positions, see company's website for job listings. **Positions advertised include:** PeopleSoft Administrator. **Corporate headquarters location:** This location. **Parent company:** Meditrust. **Listed on:** New York Stock Exchange. **Stock exchange symbol:** LQI. **Number of employees nationwide:** More than 7,000.

LABATT FOOD SERVICE
P.O. Box 2140, San Antonio TX 78297-2140. 210/661-4216. **Physical address:** 4500 Industry Park, San Antonio TX 78218. **Fax:** 210/661-0973. **Contact:** Human Resources Department. **World Wide Web address:** http://www.labattfood.com. **Description:** A food distributor for restaurants, hospitals, military bases, schools, and other institutions. **NOTE:** Jobseekers interested in positions at this location can fax or mail their resumes. See website for other locations, positions and mailing addresses. **Other area locations:** Corpus Christi TX; Austin TX; Harlingen TX; Houston TX. **Operations at this facility include:** Office; Warehouse.

LANDRY'S RESTAURANTS, INC.
1510 West Loop South, Houston TX 77027. 713/850-1010. **Contact:** Human Resources. **World Wide Web address:** http://www.landrysseafood.com. **Description:** Operates a chain of seafood restaurants. **Positions advertised include:** Front Manager; Accounts Payable Manager; Administrative Assistant; Assistant Building Engineer' Benefits Administrator; Brand Marketing Manager; Cash Analyst; Director of Training; Inventory Control; Loss Prevention Analyst; Marketing Assistant. **Corporate headquarters location:** This location. **Operations at this facility include:** Administration; Sales.

LUBY'S CAFETERIAS
P.O. Box 33069, San Antonio TX 78265. 210/654-9000. **Fax:** 210/225-5750. **Physical address:** 2211 NE Loop 410, San Antonio TX 78217. **Contact:** Human Resources. **E-mail address:** careers@lubys.com. **World Wide Web address:** http://www.lubys.com. **Description:** A national chain restaurant that serves cafeteria-style food. **NOTE:** Hourly positions available. **Positions advertised include:** Restaurant Manager. **Special programs:** Management Training. **Corporate headquarters location:** This location. **Listed on:** New York Stock Exchange. **Stock exchange symbol:** LUB. **Number of employees nationwide:** 11,000.

MARRIOTT SOUTH CENTRAL REGIONAL OFFICE
7200 Bishop Road, Suite 200, Plano TX 75024. 972/244-5500. **Contact:** Regional Director. **World Wide Web address:** http://www.marriott.com713/365-1000. **Description:** Marriott Corporation is a nationwide, diversified food service, retail merchandising, and hospitality company, doing business in more than 25 U.S. airports, as well as operating restaurants under various names nationwide. **NOTE:** This company's website has job listings for all its Texas locations. Interested jobseekers should apply online. **Special programs:** Internships. **Corporate headquarters location:** Washington DC. **Operations at this facility include:** This location houses the regional office for the hotel chain. **Listed on:** New York Stock Exchange. **Stock exchange symbol:** MAR.

METROMEDIA RESTAURANT GROUP
6500 International Parkway, Suite 1000, Plano TX 75093. 972/588-5000. **Fax:** 972/588-5467. **Contact:** Human Resources Manager. **World Wide Web address:** http://www.metromediarestaurants.com. **Description:** One of the largest, full-service, restaurant chain operators in the nation. The company operates nearly 1,000 restaurants in 45 states and two countries including Bennigan's, Bonanza, Ponderosa, And Steak and Ale. **NOTE:** Jobseekers interested in management or hourly positions at specific restaurants should contact the locations or see the chains' separate websites. **Corporate headquarters location:** This location. **Operations at this facility include:** Accounting; Sales; Guest Relations; Public Relations. **Listed on:** Privately held.

OMNI HOTELS
420 Decker Drive, Suite 200, Irving TX 75062-3952. 972/730-6664. **Fax:** 972/871-5669. **Contact:** Bethany Senger, Corporate Recruiting Manager. **World Wide Web address:** http://www.omnihotels.com. **Description:** Operates an international chain of hotels, motels, and resorts. **NOTE:** Entry-level positions are offered. The corporate website lists all open positions throughout the chain's operations, including the corporate office. **Special programs:** Internships; Training. **Corporate headquarters location:** This location. **Other U.S. locations:** Nationwide. **Parent**

company: TRT. **Operations at this facility include:** Administration. **Listed on:** Privately held. **Number of employees worldwide:** 8,000.

PANCHO'S MEXICAN BUFFET, INC.
P.O. Box 7407, Fort Worth TX 76111-0407. 817/831-0081. **Physical address:** 3500 Noble Street, Fort Worth TX 76111. **Contact:** Human Resources. **World Wide Web address:** http://www.panchosmexicanbuffet.com. **Description:** Pancho's Mexican Buffet operates a chain of Mexican restaurants with a buffet-style format. Pancho's Mexican Buffet operates 40 restaurants in Texas, Arizona, Louisiana, New Mexico, and Oklahoma. Founded in 1966. **NOTE:** This chain offers management and hourly positions. Jobseekers interested in management positions should request an application packet online at the company's website. Jobseekers interested in hourly positions should apply at the nearest location. **Corporate headquarters location:** This location. **Operations at this facility include:** This location houses administrative offices.

PIZZA HUT, INC.
14841 Dallas Parkway, Dallas TX 75254. 972/338-7700. **Contact:** Human Resources. **World Wide Web address:** http://www.pizzahut.com. **Description:** An international chain of pizza restaurants. **Positions offered include:** Administrative Assistant; Network Analyst; Director Design and Standards; Sourcing Specialist; Business Financial Analyst; Paralegal; Senior Manager Equipment Engineering; Director of Aviation. **Corporate headquarters location:** This location. **Parent company:** Yum Brands. **Listed on:** New York Stock Exchange. **Stock exchange symbol:** YUM.

PIZZA INN INC.
3551 Plano Parkway, The Colony TX 75056. 469/384-5000. **Fax:** 469/384-5058. **Contact:** Human Resources. **E-mail address:** jobs@pizzainn.com. **World Wide Web address:** http://www.pizzainn.com. **Description:** Engaged primarily in operating and franchising restaurants serving pizza and complimentary foods and beverages. Pizza Inn operates more than 430 restaurants in 20 states. **NOTE:** Jobseekers interested in Assistant Manager and Delivery Driver positions should apply at the nearest location. All other positions should be e-mailed or faxed. **Positions advertised include:** Training Systems Manager; Corporate Restaurant General Manager; Over the Road Truck Driver; Field Training Specialist. **Operations at this facility include:** Administration; Sales. **Listed on:** NASDAQ. **Stock exchange symbol:** PZZI.

QUALITY INN BAYTOWN
300 South Highway 146 Business Road, Baytown TX 77520. 281/427-7481. **Contact:** Human Resources. **World Wide Web address:** http://www.qualityinn.com. **Description:** A full-service hotel, operating as part of the national chain. **Other U.S. locations:** Nationwide. **Parent company:** Choice Hotels International. **Listed on:** NYSE. **Stock exchange symbol:** CHH.

THE RICHARDSON HOTEL
701 East Campbell Road, Richardson TX 75081. 972/231-9600. **Contact:** Human Resources. **World Wide Web address:** http://www.therichardshotel.com. **Description:** A 342-room hotel with two restaurants, meeting facilities, and a fitness center. **Listed on:** Privately held.

SULLINS & ASSOCIATES, INC.
McDONALD'S CORPORATION
122 South 12th Street, Suite 105, Corsicana TX 75110. 903/872-5611. **Contact:** Human Resources. **E-mail address:** personnel@sullinsandassociates.com. **Description:** A franchise owner of McDonald's restaurants in Texas. A leader in the fast-food industry, McDonald's offers quick-service meals, specializing in hamburgers. **NOTE:** Jobseekers may also apply in person in one of the franchises restaurants. **World Wide Web address:** http://www.sulliansandassociates.com. **Special programs:** Internships. **Other area locations:** Ennis TX; Greenville TX; Palestine TX; Terrell TX; Waxahachie TX.

TACO CABANA, INC.
15925 San Pedro Avenue, San Antonio TX 78232. 210/490-1107. **Fax:** 210/804-2425. **Recorded jobline:** 800/357-9924x326. **Contact:** Human Resources. **E-mail address:** recruiting@tacocabana.com. **World Wide Web address:** http://www.tacocabana.com. **Description:** Taco Cabana operates a chain of Mexican restaurants. Founded in 1978. **NOTE:** Jobseekers may also apply at the nearest Taco Cabana restaurant. See the company's website for locations. **Corporate headquarters location:** This location. **Parent company:** Carrols Corporation.

TEXAS COUNTRY COOKIN'
5075 Garth Road, Baytown TX 77520. 281/421-1998. **Contact:** Human Resources. **World Wide Web address:** http://www.hoffbrausteaks.com. **Description:** A casual-dining steak house and beer garden. Hoffbrau Steaks operates through 26 locations. Founded in 1939. **Corporate headquarters location:** Austin TX.

VICTORIAN CONDO HOTEL & CONFERENCE CENTER
6300 Seawall Boulevard, Galveston TX 77551. 409/740-3555. **Toll-free phone:** 800/231-6363. **Contact:** Human Resources. **World Wide Web address:** http://www.galveston.com/victorian. **Description:** A full-service hotel and conference center.

WESTIN HOTEL
4545 West John Carpenter Freeway, Irving TX 75063. 972/929-4500. **Contact:** Human Resources. **World Wide Web address:** http://www.starwoodhotels.com. **Description:** A traditional hotel with 500-rooms. Features guest services and amenities such as typing, copying, fax, car rental information, travel agency information, and word processing services. **Corporate headquarters location:** White Plains NY. **Parent company:** Starwood Hotels and Resorts Worldwide, Inc.

WESTIN PARK CENTRAL HOTEL
12720 Merit Drive, Dallas TX 75251. 972/385-3000. **Fax:** 324/889-7970. **World Wide Web address:** http://www.starwoodhotels.com. **Description:** Provides centrally located accommodations in the city of Dallas. **Positions advertised include:** Accounts Payable Clerk; Accounts Receivable Clerk. **Corporate headquarters location:** White Plains NY. **Parent company:** Starwood Hotels and Resorts Worldwide, Inc.

WHATABURGER, INC.
One Whataburger Way, Corpus Christi TX 78411. 361/878-0650. **Fax:** 361/878-0473. **Contact:** Director of Human Resources. **World Wide Web address:** http://www.whataburger.com. **Description:** Operates 500 restaurants in the Sunbelt area. Founded in 1950. **NOTE:** This website has job listings for all of its locations. Apply online. **Positions advertised include:** General Manager; Manager; Help Desk Support; Purchasing Manager. **Corporate headquarters location:** This location. **Other U.S. locations:** AZ.

WYNDHAM GREENSPOINT
12400 Greenspoint Drive, Houston TX 77060. 281/875-2222. **Contact:** Human Resources. **World Wide Web address:** http://www.wyndham.com. **Description:** A large upscale, luxury hotel chain with locations throughout the world. **NOTE:** Search and apply for positions online. **Listed on:** American Stock Exchange. **Stock exchange symbol:** WBR.

WYNDHAM LAS COLINAS
110 John Carpenter Freeway, Irving TX 75039 972/650-1600. **Contact:** Human Resources. **World Wide Web address:** http://www.wyndham.com. **Description:** A large upscale, luxury hotel chain with locations throughout the world. **NOTE:** Search and apply for positions online. **Listed on:** American Stock Exchange. **Stock exchange symbol:** WBR.

Utah

ARCTIC CIRCLE RESTAURANTS
P.O. Box 339, Midvale UT 84047. 801/561-3620. **Physical address:** 411 West 7200 South, Suite 200, Midvale UT 84047. **Contact:** Human Resources. **World Wide Web address:** http://www.arcticcirclerest.com. **Description:** Owns and operates the Arctic Circle restaurant chain. **NOTE:** Visit website to download application or apply in person at a local restaurant. **Corporate headquarters location:** This location. **Other U.S. locations:** ID; CA; WA; OR; WY; NE; MT.

BRYCE CANYON LODGE
P.O. Box 640079, Bryce Canyon National Park, UT 84717. 435/834-5361. **Fax:** 435/834-5464. **Contact:** Human Resources. **E-mail address:** jobs-bryce@xanterra.com. **World Wide Web address:** http://www.brycecanyonlodge.com. **Description:** A resort affiliated with one of Utah's National Parks. **NOTE:** Please visit website for current job openings and to apply online. Hiring begins in December and continues throughout the season. **Positions advertised include:** Accounting Clerk; Night Auditor; Kitchen Utility; Cook; Food & Beverage Server; Bus Person; Hostess/Host; Bartender; Storekeeper; Guest Room Attendant. **Corporate headquarters location:** Aurora CO. **Parent company:** Xanterra Parks and Resorts.

OGDEN MARRIOTT
247 24th Street, Ogden UT 84401. 801/627-1190. **Fax:** 801/394-6312. **Contact:** Sales Manager. **World Wide Web address:** http://www.marriott.com. **Description:** One location of the Marriott chain. The hotel has a private club and a full-service restaurant. **Corporate headquarters location:** Washington D.C. **Other U.S. locations:** Nationwide. **International locations:** Worldwide. **Listed on:** New York Stock Exchange. **Stock exchange symbol:** MAR.

INTERCONTINENTAL HOTELS GROUP
1275 West 2240 South, Salt Lake City UT 84119. 801/975-3053. **Fax:** 801/975-3040. **Contact:** Human Resources. **World Wide Web address:** http://www.ichotelsgroup.com. **Description:** A reservation center receiving calls from the United States and Canada for the Intercontinental Hotels Group, which includes the Holiday Inn, Staybridge Suites, Crowne Plaza, and Candlewood Suites hotel chains.

Vermont

BASIN HARBOR CLUB
4800 Basin Harbor Road, Vergennes VT 05491. 802/475-7846. **Fax:** 802/475-6547. **Contact:** Rachel Novak, Director of Human Resources. **E-mail address:** employment@basinharbor.com. **World Wide Web address:** http://www.basinharborjobs.com. **Description:** A resort on Lake Champlain that is open from mid-May to mid-October. Amenities include dining, kids activities, golf, conference areas, and recreational activities. **Positions advertised include:** Main Dining Room Captain; Main Dining Room Server; Head Gardener; Bartender; Dining Room Server Assistant; Line Cook. **Number of employees at this location:** 300.

HOLIDAY INN EXPRESS
818 Charlestown Road, Springfield VT 05156. 802/885-4516. **Fax:** 802/885-4595. **Contact:** Cheryl Howes, General Manager. **E-mail address:** hixpressjob@aol.com. **World Wide Web address:** http://www.vermonthi.com. **Description:** An 88-room hotel, which is part of the worldwide hotel chain.

HOLIDAY INN RUTLAND/KILLINGTON
476 US Route 7 South, Rutland VT 05701. 802/775-1911. **Toll-free phone:** 800/462-4810. **Fax:** 802/775-0113. **Contact:** Larry Mckirryher, Controller. **World Wide Web address:** www.holidayinn-vermont.com. **Description:** A full-service, independently-owned franchise of the international hotel chain, with 150 rooms offering complete amenities and close to several area ski resorts. **Positions advertised include:** Assistant General Manager.

MOUNT SNOW LTD
Pisgah Road, P.O. Box 2810, West Dover VT 05356. 802/464-4223. **Fax:** 802/464-4135. **Contact:** Jessi Whidden, Recruiter. **E-mail address:** jobs@mountsnow.com. **World Wide Web address:** http://www.mountsnow.com. **Description:** Owns and operates one of the largest ski resorts in the east. **Positions advertised include:** Vice President Brand Management; Director, Alpine Training Center and Events; Condominium Securer; Purchasing Agent/Stockroom Supervisor; Food & Beverage Accounting Clerk; Risk Manager; Lift Operations Manager; Front Desk Supervisor; Electrician; Plumber; Building Maintenance Foreman.

SHERATON BURLINGTON HOTEL AND CONFERENCE CENTER
870 Williston Road, South Burlington VT 05403. 802/865-6677. **Fax:** 802/865-6696. **Contact:** Amy Murray, Human Resources Manager. **E-mail address:** burlingtonvt.hr@sheraton.com. **World Wide Web address:** http://www.sheratonburlington.com. **Description:** Vermont's largest hotel and conference center featuring 309 guest rooms, a conference space, and an exhibition hall. **Positions advertised include:** Banquet Attendant; Front Office Agent; Housekeeping.

STRATTON CORPORATION
RR1 Box 145, Stratton Mountain VT 05155. 802/297-4107. **Fax:** 802/297-4238. **Contact:** Katie Westbrook, Recruiting Manager. **E-mail address:** kwestbrook@intrawest.com. **World Wide Web address:** http://www.stratton.com. **Description:** Operates Stratton Mountain Resort, with 92 trails serviced by 12 lifts. The resort covers 178 acres and also features cross-country skiing in two areas, as well as a golf course. **Positions advertised include:** Activities Attendant; Cashier; Child Caregiver; Conference Services Coordinator; Front Desk Agent; Group Reservation Specialist; Magic Carpet Operator; Property Caretaker; Scanner. **Parent company:** Intrawest. **Number of employees at this location:** 280.

TRAPP FAMILY LODGE
700 Trapp Hill Road, P.O. Box 1428, Stowe VT 05672. 802/253-5789. **Fax:** 802/253-5757. **Contact:** Kathi Kiernan, Director of Human Resources. **E-mail address:** hr@trappfamily.com. **World Wide Web address:** http://www.trappfamily.com. **Description:** A 2,700 acre cross country ski lodge and resort owned and operated by the von Trapp family. **Positions advertised include:** Reservation Sales Agent; Guest Services Agent; Fitness Center Attendant; Marketing Coordinator; Director of Group Sales. **Special Programs:** Internships.

Virginia

CHESAPEAKE RESTAURANT GROUP
1960 Gallows Road, Suite 200, Vienna VA 22182. 703/827-0320. **Fax:** 703/893-1536. **Contact:** Connie Ohm, Director of Human Resources. **E-mail address:** cohm@chesapeakerestaurants.com. **World Wide Web address:** http://www.chesapeakerestaurants.com. **Description:** Operates 8 Chesapeake Bay Seafood Houses, 23 Chili's, and 3 On the Border, restaurants. **Positions advertised include:** Restaurant Manager. **Special programs:** Internships. **Corporate headquarters location:** This location. **Operations at this facility include:** Administration; Research and Development. **Listed on:** Privately held. **Annual sales/revenues:** Less than $5 million. **Number of employees nationwide:** 3,000.

GUEST SERVICES
3055 Prosperity Avenue, Fairfax VA 22031. 703/849-9300. **Toll-free phone:** 800/345-7534. **Contact:** Human Resources Department. **E-mail address:** biondif@guestservices.com. **World Wide Web address:** http://www.guestservices.com. **Description:** Manages a variety of contract food and hospitality services. Founded in 1917. **NOTE:** Apply for positions online. **Corporate headquarters location:** This location. **Operations at this facility include:** Regional Headquarters. **Number of employees at this location:**

80. **Number of employees nationwide:** 3,500.

RWS ENTERPRISES
dba COUNTRY COOKING
4335 Brambleton Avenue, Roanoke VA 24018. 540/774-0613. **Contact:** Human Resources. **Description:** Operates the Country Cooking restaurant chain with locations throughout Virginia. **Corporate headquarters location:** This location.

Washington

AZTECA RESTAURANTS
133 SW 158th Street, Burien WA 98166. 206/243-7021. **Contact:** Human Resources. **World Wide Web address:** http://www.aztecamex.com. **Description:** Owns and operates a chain of Mexican restaurants. **Corporate headquarters location:** This location.

CRYSTAL MOUNTAIN RESORT
33914 Crystal Mountain Boulevard, Crystal Mountain WA 98022. 360/663-2265. **Contact:** Human Resources. **World Wide Web address:** http://www.crystalmt.com. **Description:** A ski resort and lodge.

FOUR SEASONS OLYMPIC HOTEL
411 University Street, Seattle WA 98101. 206/621-1700. **Recorded jobline:** 206/287-4047. **Contact:** Personnel. **World Wide Web address:** http://www.fourseasons.com. **Description:** A 450-room hotel with 20,000 square feet of meeting and function space, three restaurants, a health club, and a retail arcade with 14 international shops. Four Seasons Hotels & Resorts operates approximately 50 luxury hotels and resorts in 22 countries. **Corporate headquarters location:** Ontario, Canada. **Other U.S. locations:** Nationwide. **International locations:** Worldwide. **Listed on:** New York Stock Exchange. **Stock exchange symbol:** FS. **Number of employees at this location:** 585.

HOTEL LUSSO
One North Post Street, Spokane WA 99201. 509/747-9750. **Fax:** 509/363-2389. **Contact:** Personnel. **World Wide Web address:** http://www.westcoasthotels.com. **Description:** A boutique-style, luxury hotel offering reception and conference rooms. **Parent company:** Westcoast Hotels.

THE PARAMOUNT HOTEL
724 Pine Street, Seattle WA 98101. 206/292-9500. **Fax:** 206/292-8610. **Contact:** Human Resources. **World Wide Web address:** http://www.westcoasthotels.com. **Description:** A 146-room, chateau-style hotel featuring the Blowfish Asian Cafe and two meeting rooms. **Parent company:** Westcoast Hotels.

RED LION BELLEVUE INN
11211 Main Street, Bellevue WA 98004. 425/455-5240. **Fax:** 425/455-0654. **Contact:** Human Resources. **World Wide Web address:** http://www.bestwestern.com. **Description:** A 180-room hotel franchise offering rental car services, restaurants, and meeting facilities. **Corporate headquarters location:** Phoenix AZ.

RESTAURANTS UNLIMITED INC.
1818 North Northlake Way, Seattle WA 98103-9097. 206/634-0550. **Fax:** 206/547-4829. **Contact:** Director of Staffing. **World Wide Web address:** http://www.restaurants-unlimited.com. **Description:** Owns and operates a chain of full-service dinner houses. Founded in 1969. **Corporate headquarters location:** This location. **Operations at this facility include:** Administration.

S&W/CENTERFOODS MANAGEMENT COMPANY
20300 19th Avenue NE, Seattle WA 98155. 206/362-2255. **Fax:** 206/362-8850. **Contact:** Human Resources. **World Wide Web address:** http://www.centerfoods.com. **Description:** Owns and operates several fast-food restaurants located in malls, which are part of the national chains Orange Julius, A&W, Dairy Queen, and Auntie Anne's. Founded in 1971. **Special programs:** Internships; Training. **Internship information:** The company has a paid internship program for hotel/restaurant or business management students. To apply, submit a letter of application and include goals, schedule, and time frame. Call for more information. **Corporate headquarters location:** This location. **Number of employees at this location:** 300.

SEA-TAC MARRIOTT
3201 South 176th Street, Seattle WA 98188. 206/241-2000. **Fax:** 206/241-2235. **Contact:** Personnel Office. **World Wide Web address:** http://www.marriott.com. **Description:** A 465-room, full-service hotel featuring convention and banquet facilities and a restaurant. **Other U.S. locations:** Nationwide.

SEATTLE DAYS INN TOWN CENTER
2205 Seventh Avenue, Seattle WA 98121. 206/448-3434. **Contact:** Personnel. **World Wide Web address:** http://www.daysinn.com. **Description:** A 91-room hotel. This location also houses a restaurant and lounge.

STARBUCKS COFFEE CORPORATION
P.O. Box 34067, Seattle WA 98124. 206/447-1575. **Physical address:** 2401 Utah Avenue South, Seattle WA 98134. **Fax:** 206/447-0828. **Recorded jobline:** 206/447-4123. **Contact:** Human Resources. **World Wide Web address:** http://www.starbucks.com. **Description:** Sells whole-bean coffees, along with hot coffees and Italian-style espresso beverages through more than 2,500 retail stores worldwide. In addition to coffee beans and beverages, the company's stores offer a selection of coffee-making equipment, accessories, pastries, and confections. **Corporate headquarters location:** This location. **Other U.S. locations:** Nationwide. **International locations:** Worldwide. **Number of employees worldwide:** 37,000.

UNIVERSAL SODEXHO
1113 A Street, Tacoma WA 98402. 253/383-9200. **Contact:** Personnel Department. **World Wide Web address:** http://www.universalsodexho.com. **Description:** A catering service specializing in providing services to remote locations.

WESTCOAST VANCE HOTEL
620 Stewart Street, Seattle WA 98101. 206/441-4200. **Fax:** 206/441-8612. **Contact:** Human Resources. **World Wide Web address:** http://www.westcoasthotels.com. **Description:** A 165-room, boutique style, luxury hotel featuring the Yakima Grill Restaurant. **Parent company:** Westcoast Hotels.

West Virginia

OGLEBAY RESORT & CONFERENCE CENTER
Route 88 North, Wheeling WV 26003. 304/243-4000. **Toll-free phone:** 800/624-6988. **Contact:** Human Resources. **World Wide Web address:** http://www.oglebay-resort.com. **Description:** A resort and conference center with 49 cottages for families and large groups that offers two golf course, a zoo, gardens, and specialty shops. **NOTE:** Entry level applications are accepted on a continual basis and kept on file for three months. **Positions advertised include:** Conference Services Coordinator; Golf Maintenance Mechanic; Greenskeeper; Banquet Server; Horticulture Technician; Player Assistant; Golf Starter; Banquet Captain; Pool Supervisor. **Internship information:** Internships available in all departments and at all facilities. Submit a resume to the Human Resources Department, located between the Visitor Center and the Greenhouse.

Wisconsin

BAYMONT INN & SUITES
100 East Wisconsin Avenue, Suite 1800, Milwaukee WI 53202-4119. 414/905-2000. **Fax:** 414/905-2415. **Contact:** Corporate Recruiter. **E-mail address:** recruiter@baymontinns.com. **World Wide Web address:** http://www.baymontinns.com. **Description:** A hospitality company operating a wide variety of hotels, theaters, entertainment centers, and restaurants. Lodging operations are partly comprised of 190 limited-service hotels located in 31 states. Founded in 1973. **Positions advertised include:** General Manager;

Assistant General Manager; Front Desk Clerk. **Special programs:** Internships. **Corporate headquarters location:** San Antonio TX. **Parent company:** La Quinta Corporation. **Number of employees at this location:** 170. **Number of employees nationwide:** 4,000.

ED DEBEVIC'S RESTAURANT
780 North Jefferson Street, Milwaukee WI 53202. 414/226-2200. **Fax:** 414/226-2456. **Contact:** Human Resources. **World Wide Web address:** http://www.eddebevics.com. **Description:** One location of the casual dining restaurant chain. Ed Debevic's serves American cuisine and operates a gift shop. **NOTE:** Send resumes to: Ed Debevic's, Inc., Attn: Hiring Manager, 640 North Wells Street, Chicago IL 60610. Fax: 312/664-7444. **Corporate headquarters location:** Chicago, IL. **Other U.S. locations:** Beverly Hills CA; Chicago IL; Phoenix AZ.

EXEL INNS OF AMERICA, INC.
4706 East Washington Avenue, Madison WI 53704. 608/241-5271. **Fax:** 608/241-3224. **Contact:** Human Resources. **E-mail address:** hrdir@excelinns.com. **World Wide Web address:** http://www.exelinns.com. **Description:** A limited-service motel chain with 35 locations, primarily in the Midwest. Founded in 1973. **Corporate headquarters location:** This location. **Other U.S. locations:** MN; IA; IL; MI; TX; ND. **Listed on:** Privately held. **Annual sales/revenues:** $21 - $50 million. **Number of employees nationwide:** 750.

OLYMPIA RESORT & CONFERENCE CENTER
1350 Royale Mile Road, Oconomowoc WI 53066. 262/369-4976, extension 4976. **Toll-free phone:** 800/558-9573. **Fax:** 262/369-4998. **Contact:** Kim Munro, Human Resources Director. **E-mail address:** kmunro@olympiaresort.com. **World Wide Web address:** http://www.olympiaresort.com. **Description:** A hotel with a health spa, indoor and outdoor pools, child care facility, restaurant, and golf course. **Positions advertised include:** Engineer; Fitness Supervisor.

ONEIDA BINGO & CASINO
P.O. Box 365, Oneida WI 54155. 920/494-7900. **Physical address:** 2630 West Mason Street, Green Bay WI 54313. **Toll-free phone:** 800/238-4263. **Recorded jobline:** 800/236-7050. **Contact:** Human Resources. **E-mail address:** casino@oneidanation.org. **World Wide Web address:** http://www.oneidabingoandcasino.net. **Description:** A casino. **Corporate headquarters location:** This location. **Parent company:** The Oneida Tribe of Wisconsin. **Number of employees at this location:** 3,500.

Wyoming

DORNAN'S
200 Moose Street, P.O. Box 39, Moose WY 83012. 307/733-2415. **Fax:** 307-733-3544. **Contact:** Tim Mowrey. **E-mail address:** timm@dornans.com. **World Wide Web address:** http://www.dornans.com. **Description:** Year round, Dornan's operates cabins, a gourmet grocery store with a full-service deli and gas, wine shop, bar and restaurant. In the summer, it runs an outdoor restaurant, gift shop, rentals for adventure sports and a fly fishing shop. During the winter, it rents cross-country skis and snowshoes. The summer season runs from May through October. **Note:** See website for current positions and to print out an application. Send in completed applications by mail or fax. **Positions advertised include:** Dishwasher; Cook; Baker; Front Desk Agent; Server; Cashier; Janitor; Retail Associate; Manager, Chuck Wagon restaurant; Sauté Cook; Housekeeper; Bartender; Night Auditor.

TETON PINES RESORT & COUNTRY CLUB
P.O. Box 14090, Jackson WY 83002. 307/733-1005. **Physical address:** 3450 North Clubhouse Drive, Wilson WY 83014. **Toll-free phone:** 800/238-2223. **Fax:** 307-733-2860. **Contact:** Human Resources. **E-mail address:** info@tetonpines.com. **World Wide Web address:** http://www.tetonpines.com. **Description:** A vacation resort offering lodging, dinning, golf, hiking, hunting/fishing, skiing, and swimming. **NOTE:** To request an application, please phone, fax, e-mail or stop by. Submit resumes by mail. Summer season runs approximately from May 1st - October 20th; winter season runs approximately from December 1st - April 5th. **Positions advertised include:** Beverage Server; Food Server; Line Cook.

LEGAL SERVICES

You can expect to find the following types of companies in this section:

Law Firms • Legal Service Agencies

Legal occupations, including lawyers, judges and related workers as well as support staff, employ 1,220,000 workers, and will add 194,000 new jobs, an increase of 15.9%. Employment of lawyers is expected to grow about as fast as the average through 2014, primarily as a result of growth in the population and in the general level of business activities. Budgetary pressures at all levels of government will hold down the hiring of judges, despite rising caseloads, particularly in Federal courts. Paralegal employment, currently 224,000 jobs, is expected to increase much faster than average as organizations presently employing paralegals assign them a growing range of tasks, some of which were formerly performed by lawyers, and as paralegals are increasingly employed in small and medium-sized establishments. The number of self-employed workers in this group is projected to remain unchanged, reflecting the difficulty in establishing new legal practices.

Arizona

THE CAVANAGH LAW FIRM
1850 North Central Avenue, Suite 2400, Phoenix AZ 85004. 602/322-4000. **Toll-free phone:** 888/824-3476. **Fax:** 602/322-4100. **Contact:** Kristine McElhaney, Executive Director. **E-mail address:** KMcelhaney@CavanaghLaw.com. **World Wide Web address:** http://www.cavanaghlaw.com. **Description:** A law firm specializing in estate planning and administration. **Other area locations:** Sun City AZ.

ETHERTON LAW GROUP
5555 East Van Buren Street, Suite 100, Phoenix AZ 85008. 602/681-3331. **Fax:** 602/681-3339. **Contact:** Human Resources. **E-mail address:** careers@ethertonlaw.com. **World Wide Web address:** http://www.ethertonlaw.com. **Description:** A full service law firm providing a wide range of legal services including patent, tax, and securities issues. **Positions advertised include:** Intellectual Property Attorney.

INDATA CORPORATION
1325 North Fiesta Boulevard, Suite 4, Gilbert AZ 85233. 480/497-8595. **Fax:** 480/497-1833. **Contact:** Personnel. **World Wide Web address:** http://www.indatacorp.com. **Description:** Provides a variety of imaging, video production, software development, and consulting services to trial lawyers. **Positions advertised include:** Scan/Code/Edit Personnel; Software Developer; Trial Consultant/Trainer. **Other U.S. locations:** Washington D.C.

JENNINGS, STROUSS, AND SALMON
The Collier Center, 11th Floor, 201 East Washington Street, Phoenix AZ 85004. 602/262-5911. **Fax:** 602/253-3255. **Contact:** Janice K. Baker, Director of Attorney Recruitment. **E-mail address:** jbaker@jsslaw.com. **World Wide Web address:** http://www.jsslaw.com. **Description:** A law firm practicing in over 35 legal disciplines including antitrust, corporate, environmental, franchising, government, and tax. **Other area locations:** Scottsdale AZ; Peoria AZ. **Other U.S. locations:** Washington, DC.

MARISCAL, WEEKS, McINTYRE, AND FRIEDLANDER
2901 North Central Avenue, Suite 200, Phoenix AZ 85012. 602/285-5000. **Fax:** 602/285-5100. **Contact:** Human Resources. **World Wide Web address:** http://www.mwmf.com. **Description:** A law firm specializing in a variety of disciplines including corporate, personal injury, commercial, bankruptcy, intellectual property, and entertainment law.

PERKINS COIE LLP
2901 North Central Avenue, Suite 2000, Phoenix AZ 85012. 602/351-8000. **Fax:** 602/648-7074. **Contact:** Human Resources. **World Wide Web address:** http://www.perkinscoie.com. **Description:** A law firm specializing in a variety of legal disciplines including banking, corporate, intellectual property, nonprofit, and tax law. **Positions advertised include:** Patent Litigation Associate; Real Estate Associate.

THE RABB PENNY LAW FIRM
3320 North Campbell Avenue, Suite 150, Tucson AZ 85719. 520/888-6740. **World Wide Web address:** http://www.rabbpenny.com. **Contact:** Human Resources. **Description:** A law firm specializing in personal injury. **Other area locations include:** Tempe AZ; Flagstaff AZ.

RYLEY, CARLOCK, AND APPLEWHITE
One North Central Avenue, Suite 1200, Phoenix AZ 85004-4417. 602/258-7701. **Fax:** 602/257-9582. **Contact:** Shannon Bryant, Human Resources Director. **E-mail address:** sbryant@rcalaw.com. **World Wide Web address:** http://www.rcalaw.com. **Description:** A law firm specializing in antitrust, corporate, estate, and environmental law. Founded in 1948. **Other U.S. locations:** Denver CO.

TREON, STRICK, LUCIA, AND AGUIRRE
2700 North Central Avenue, Suite 1400, Phoenix AZ 85004. 602/285-4407. **Contact:** Human Resources. **Description:** A law firm specializing in personal injury, medical malpractice, and workers' compensation.

California

BAKER & McKENZIE LLP
Two Embarcadero Center, 24th Floor, San Francisco CA 94111-3909. 415/576-3000. **Fax:** 415/576-3099. **Contact:** Andrea Carr, Recruitment. **E-mail address:** andrea.l.carr@bakernet.com. **World Wide Web address:** http://www.bakerinfo.com. **Description:** An international law firm with more than 10 practice areas including banking and finance, e-commerce, intellectual property, labor and employment, tax, and U.S. litigation. **Corporate headquarters location:** Chicago IL. **Other area locations:** Palo Alto CA; San Diego CA. **Other U.S. locations:** DC; FL; IL; NY; TX. **International locations:** Worldwide.

BINGHAM MCCUTCHEN LLP
355 South Grand Avenue, 44th Floor, Los Angeles CA 90071-3106. 213/680-6400. **Fax:** 213/680-6499. **Contact:** Heather Beatty, Hiring Committee. **E-mail address:** lalegalrecruit@bingham.com. **World Wide Web address:** http://www.bingham.com. **Description:** A law firm specializing in corporate law. **Corporate headquarters location:** Boston MA. **Other area locations:** Costa Mesa CA; East Palo Alto CA; San Francisco CA; Walnut Creek CA.

BUCHALTER NEMER
1000 Wilshire Boulevard, Suite 1500, Los Angeles CA 90017-2457. 213/891-0700. **Fax:** 213/896-0400. **Contact:** Recruiting Coordinator. **E-mail address:** rkennedy@buchalter.com. **World Wide Web address:** http://www.buchalter.com. **Description:** A law firm

specializing in the area of business. Practice areas include corporate, real estate, real estate finance, general litigations, labor, financial institution litigation, and multimedia entertainment and communications. **Corporate headquarters location:** This location. **Other area locations:** San Francisco CA; Irvine CA.

CARLSMITH BALL LLP
444 South Flower Street, 9th Floor, Los Angeles CA 90071-2901. 213/955-1200. **Fax:** 213/623-0032. **Contact:** Recruiting Coordinator. **E-mail address:** execdirector@carlsmith.com. **World Wide Web address:** http://www.carlsmith.com. **Description:** A law firm that specializes in civil law. **NOTE:** Send resumes to: Recruiting Coordinator, 1001 Bishop Street, ASB Tower, Suite 2200, Honolulu HI 96813. **Special programs:** Internships. **Corporate headquarters location:** Honolulu HI **Other U.S. locations:** Washington DC; Hilo HI; Kapolei HI; Kona HI; Maui HI. **International locations:** Guam; Saipan.

CHRISTIE, PARKER & HALE
P.O. Box 7068, Pasadena CA 91109-7068. 626/795-9900. **Physical address:** 350 W. Colorado Boulevard. Suite 500, Pasadena CA 91105-1836. **Fax:** 626/577-8800. **Contact:** Human Resources. **E-mail address:** info@cph.com. **World Wide Web address:** http://www.cph.com. **Description:** A law firm specializing in intellectual property law. **Positions advertised include:** Biotech Partner. **Other area locations:** Newport Beach CA.

DEWEY BALLANTINE
333 South Grand Avenue, Suite 2600, Los Angeles CA 90071-1530. 213/621-6288. **Fax:** 213/621-6100. **Contact:** Manager of Legal Recruitment. **E-mail address:** agleeson@deweyballantine.com. **World Wide Web address:** http://www.deweyballantine.com. **Description:** An international law firm specializing in corporate, litigation, tax, ERISA/pension, bankruptcy, and real estate law. **Other area locations:** East Palo Alto CA. **Other U.S. locations:** New York NY; Washington DC; Austin TX; Houston TX. **International locations:** The Czech Republic; England; Germany; Hungary; Italy; Poland.

GREENBERG GLUSKER
1900 Avenue of the Stars, 21st Floor, Los Angeles CA 90067. 310/201-7431. **Fax:** 310/553-0687. **Contact:** Patricia Patrick, Recruitment Administrator. **E-mail address:** ppatrick@ggfirm.com. **World Wide Web address:** http://www.ggfirm.com. **Description:** A law firm practicing bankruptcy, business and tax, entertainment, labor and employment, litigation, and probate and estate planning law.

JAMS
1920 Main Street, Suite 300, Irvine CA 92614. 949/224-1810. **Fax:** 949/224-1818. **Contact:** Human Resources. **World Wide Web address:** http://www.jamsadr.com. **Description:** Provides alternative dispute resolution (ADR) judicial services, which is a means of scheduling and processing cases outside the public court system. **Corporate headquarters location:** This location.

JEFFER, MANGELS, BUTLER, & MARMARO LLP
1900 Avenue of the Stars, 7th Floor, Los Angeles CA 90067. 310/203-8080. **Fax:** 310/203-0567. **Contact:** Amy Frechette, Recruiting Manager. **E-mail address:** afl@jmbm.com. **World Wide Web address:** http://www.jmbm.com. **Description:** A law firm practicing litigation, corporate, entertainment, tax, bankruptcy, health, environment, and international law. **Special programs:** Summer Associate Program for law students. **Corporate headquarters location:** This location. **Other U.S. locations:** San Francisco CA.

GUY KORNBLUM & ASSOCIATES
1388 Sutter Street, Suite 820, San Francisco CA 94109. 415/440-7800. **Toll-free phone:** 888/249-7800. **Fax:** 415/440-7898. **Contact:** Human Resources. **World Wide Web address:** http://www.kornblumlaw.com. **Description:** A law firm specializing in personal injury, wrongful death, malpractice, and class action suits. **Corporate headquarters location:** This location. **Other area locations:** Los Angeles CA. **U.S. locations:** Denver CO; Indianapolis IN.

LATHAM & WATKINS LLP
600 West Broadway, Suite 1800, San Diego CA 92101-3375. 619/236-1234. **Contact:** Cindy D. Edson, Recruitment. **E-mail address:** cindy.edson@lw.com. **World Wide Web address:** http://www.lw.com. **Description:** A law firm practicing corporate, environmental, and real estate law. **NOTE:** For paralegal and staff positions, contact Diana L. Clarke, Human Resources Manager at: diana.clarke@lw.com or the above address. **Special programs:** Public interest fellowships for recent law graduates. **International locations:** Worldwide.

LUCE FORWARD
600 West Broadway, Suite 2600, San Diego CA 92101-3372. 619/236-1414. **Fax:** 619/232-8311. **Contact:** Kathryn Karpinksi, Human Resources. **E-mail address:** legalrecruiting@luce.com. **World Wide Web address:** http://www.luce.com. **Description:** A law firm specializing in corporate, environmental, immigration, and real estate law. **NOTE:** For inquiries regarding staff positions contact: staffrecruiting@luce.com. Candidates may also apply for positions online. Unsolicited resumes not accepted. **Positions advertised include:** Insurance Litigation Associate; Real Estate Associate. **Special programs:** Summer Associate Program. **Corporate headquarters location:** This location.

MORRISON & FOERSTER LLP
425 Market Street, San Francisco CA 94105-2482. 415/268-7000. **Fax:** 415/268-7522. **Contact:** Staff Recruiting Coordinator. **E-mail address:** jobs@mofo.com. **World Wide Web address:** http://www.mofo.com. **Description:** An international law firm specializing in corporate, financial, intellectual property, real estate, and tax law. **NOTE:** Candidates interested in Attorney positions should address resumes to: Mireille Butler, Attorney Recruiting Manager. Fax: 415/268-7522. E-mail: mbutler@mofo.com. **Positions advertised include:** Securities Litigation Associate; Patent Prosecution Associate; Financial Transactions Associate; Tax Associate; Corporate Associate; Real Estate Associate. **Corporate headquarters location:** This location. **Other area locations:** Los Angeles CA; Orange County CA; Palo Alto CA; Sacramento CA; Walnut Creek CA. **Other U.S. locations:** Denver CO; Washington DC; New York NY. **International locations:** Beijing; Brussels; Hong Kong; London; Singapore; Tokyo.

PILLSBURY WINTHROP
101 West Broadway, Suite 1800, San Diego CA 92101. 619/234-5000. **Contact:** Marcia Hommel, Recruiter. **E-mail address:** recruit_sd@pillsburywinthrop.com. **World Wide Web address:** http://www.pillsburywinthrop.com. **Description:** A law firm specializing in bankruptcy, corporate, employment, environmental, intellectual property, and real estate law. **Positions advertised include:** Associate Attorney; It Manager; Trainer. **Corporate headquarters location:** San Francisco CA.

PROCOPIO, CORY, HARGRAVES, & SAVITCH
530 B Street, 21st Floor, San Diego CA 92101. 619/238-1900. **Fax:** 619/235-0398. **Contact:** Human Resources Manager. **E-mail address:** bae@procopio.com. **World Wide Web address:** http://www.procopio.com. **Description:** A law firm specializing in real estate, bankruptcy, litigation, and corporate law. **Positions advertised include:** Corporate/Securities Associate; Intellectual Property Attorney; Real Estate Attorney. **Corporate headquarters location:** This location. **Operations at this facility include:** Administration. **Listed on:** Privately held. **Number of employees at this location:** 100.

ROSENFELD, MEYER & SUSMAN
9601 Wilshire Boulevard, Suite 700, Beverly Hills CA 90210-5288. 310/858-7700. **Fax:** 310/860-2430. **Contact:** Human Resource Director. **E-mail address:** rms@rmslaw.com. **World Wide Web address:** http://www.rmslaw.com. **Description:** A law firm specializing in litigation and entertainment law. **Corporate headquarters location:** This location.

SACK, MILLER & ROSENDIN LLP
One Kaiser Plaza, Suite 340, Oakland CA 94612. 510/286-2200. **Contact:** Human Resources. **World Wide Web address:** http://www.smrlaw.com. **Description:** A law firm specializing in a number of legal disciplines including personal and business injury, real estate, tax, and bankruptcy. **Office hours:** Monday - Friday, 9:00 a.m. - 5:00 p.m. **Corporate headquarters location:** This location.

SALTZBURG, RAY & BERGMAN
12121 Wilshire Boulevard, Suite 600, Los Angeles CA 90025. 310/481-6700. **Fax:** 310/481-6720. **Contact:** Hiring Partner. **World Wide Web address:** http://www.srblaw.com. **Description:** A law firm specializing in bankruptcy, real estate, and corporate law. **Corporate headquarters location:** This location.

SPRAY, GOULD & BOWERS
15139 Woodlawn Avenue, Tustin CA 92780. 714/258-1550. **Fax:** 714/258-1555. **Contact:** Director of Finance and Administration. **E-mail address:** info@sgblaw.com. **World Wide Web address:** http://www.sgblaw.com. **Description:** A law firm specializing in insurance, defense, and entertainment law. **Office hours:** Monday - Friday, 8:30 a.m. - 5:00 p.m. **Corporate headquarters location:** This location. **Operations at this facility include:** Administration; Divisional Headquarters. **Listed on:** Privately held. **Number of employees at this location:** 75. **Number of employees nationwide:** 105.

STRADLING, YOCCA, CARLSON & RAUTH
660 Newport Center Drive, Suite 1600, Newport Beach CA 92660. 949/725-4000. **Fax:** 949/725-4100. **Contact:** Human Resources. **E-mail address:** recruiting@sycr.com. **World Wide Web address:** http://www.sycr.com. **Description:** A law firm specializing in corporate, business, estate planning, and labor law. **Corporate headquarters location:** This location.

Colorado

HOLLAND & HART LLP
P.O. Box 8749, Denver CO 80201-8749. 303/295-8000. **Physical Address:** 555 17th Street, Suite 3200, Denver CO 80202. **Fax:** 303/295-8261. **Contact:** Julie Carroll, Director of Attorney Recruitment. **E-mail address:** jcarroll@hollandhart.com. **World Wide Web address:** http://www.hollandhart.com. **Description:** A law firm. **Other area locations:** Aspen CO; Boulder CO; Colorado Springs CO; Greenwood Village CO. **Other U.S. locations:** MT; ID; WY; UT; NM; DC.

KUTAK ROCK LLP
1801 California Street, Suite 3100, Denver CO 80202-2658. 303/297-2400. **Contact:** Recruitment. **World Wide Web address:** http://www.kutakrock.com. **Description:** A legal services firm specializing in corporate law, public and corporate finance, and litigation. **Positions advertised include:** Attorney. **Other U.S. locations:** Nationwide.

NATIVE AMERICAN RIGHTS FUND
1506 Broadway, Boulder CO 80302. 303/447-8760. **Contact:** Rose Cuny, Office Manager. **World Wide Web address:** http://www.narf.org. **Description:** A national legal defense fund for Native American tribes, villages, groups, and individuals throughout the United States. Founded in 1970. **Special programs:** Internships. **Other U.S. locations:** Anchorage AK; Washington DC.

ROTHGERBER JOHNSON & LYONS LLP
1200 17th Street, Suite 3000, Denver CO 80202-5855. 303/623-9000. **Fax:** 303/623-9222. **Contact:** Beth Martinez, Recruiting Coordinator. **World Wide Web address:** http://www.rothgerber.com. **Description:** A law firm specializing in all aspects of corporate and government law including general representation and litigation. Founded in 1903. **Corporate headquarters location:** This location. **Other area locations:** Colorado Springs CO. **Other U.S. locations:** Cheyenne WY.

Connecticut

COHEN & WOLF
1115 Broad Street, Bridgeport CT 06604. 203/368-0211. **Contact:** Hiring Partner. **World Wide Web address:** http://www.cohenandwolf.com. **Description:** A law firm with 25 attorneys on staff. Cohen & Wolf offers corporate and personal legal services in a variety of disciplines. **Special programs:** Summer jobs. **Other area locations:** Danbury CT; Stamford CT; Westport CT.

KELLEY DRYE & WARREN LLP
2 Stamford Plaza, 281 Tresser Boulevard, 14th Floor, Stamford CT 06901. 203/324-1400. **Contact:** Personnel. **World Wide Web address:** http://www.kelleydrye.com. **Description:** An international law firm specializing in litigation, banking, labor and employment, employee benefits, bankruptcy, tax, real estate, and personal services. **Corporate headquarters location:** New York NY. **Other U.S. locations:** Los Angeles CA; Washington DC; Chicago IL; Parsippany NJ; Vienna VA. **International locations:** Belgium; Hong Kong; India; Indonesia; Japan, Thailand. **Number of employees worldwide:** 300.

O'CONNELL, FLAHERTY & ATTMORE
280 Trumbull Street, Hartford CT 06103. 860/548-1300. **Contact:** Firm Administrator. **World Wide Web address:** http://www.ofalaw.com. **Description:** A law firm specializing in real estate, insurance, probate, and general litigation.

PAUL, HASTINGS, JANOFSKY & WALKER LLP
1055 Washington Boulevard, Stamford CT 06901. 203/961-7400. **Contact:** Human Resources. **World Wide Web address:** http://www.paulhastings.com. **Description:** A law firm specializing in real estate, tax, litigation, and corporate law. Founded in 1951. **Corporate headquarters location:** San Francisco CA. **Other U.S. locations:** Los Angeles CA; Orange County CA; Washington DC; Atlanta GA; New York City NY. **International locations:** London, England; Tokyo, Japan.

ZELDES NEEDLE & COOPER PC
P.O. Box 1740, Bridgeport CT 06601. 203/333-9441. **Physical address:** 1000 Lafayette Boulevard, Bridgeport CT 06604. **Contact:** Hiring Manager. **World Wide Web address:** http://www.znclaw.com. **Description:** A law firm with attorneys specializing in all areas of practice. **Number of employees at this location:** 20.

Delaware

POTTER ANDERSON & CORROON LLP
Hercules Plaza, 1313 North Market Street, Wilmington DE 19801. 302/984-6000. **Fax:** 302/658-1192. **Contact:** Joyce Shtofman, Legal Recruiting Coordinator. **E-mail address:** jshtofman@potteranderson.com. **World Wide Web address:** http://www.pacdelaware.com. **Description:** A law firm comprised of three practice groups: Corporate, Business and Litigation.

PRICKETT, JONES & ELLIOTT
P.O. Box 1328, 1310 King Street, Wilmington DE 19899. 302/888-6500. **Fax:** 302/658-8111. **Contact:** Joanne Hamill, Personnel Manager. **E-mail address:** jchamill@prickett.com. **World Wide Web address:** http://www.prickett.com. **Description:** A legal services firm specializing in insurance law and corporate law. **Other area locations:** Dover DE.

RICHARDS, LAYTON & FINGER, P.A.
One Rodney Square, 20 North King Street, Wilmington DE 19801. 302/658-6541. **Contact:** Joni L. Peet, Human Resources. **E-mail:** peet@rlf.com. **World Wide Web address:** http://www.rlf.com. **Description:** A large law firm with over 120 lawyers that specializes in corporate law.

SCHMITTINGER & RODRIGUEZ, P.A.
414 South State Street, Dover DE 19903-0497. 302/674-0140. **Contact:** Bill Thomas, Personnel Manager. **E-mail address:** bthomas@schmittrod.com. **World Wide Web address:** http://www.schmittrod.com. **Description:** A law firm. **Other area locations:** Odessa DE; Rehoboth DE; Wilmington DE.

YOUNG CONAWAY STARGATT & TAYLOR, LLP
The Brandywine Building, 1000 West Street, 17th Floor, Wilmington DE 19801. 302/571-6600. **Fax:** 302/576-3355. **Contact:** Polina F. Snitkovsky, Human Resources Administrator. **E-mail address:** psnitkovsky@ycst.com. **World Wide Web address:** http://www.ycst.com. **Description:** One of Delaware's largest law firms. Founded in 1959. **NOTE:** E-mail or fax resume to Human Resources.

District Of Columbia
ARNOLD & PORTER
555 12th Street NW, Washington DC 20004. 202/942-5000. **Fax:** 202/942-5999. **Contact:** Stephanie Heeg, Recruiter. **E-mail address:** stephanie_heeg@aporter.com. **World Wide Web address:** http://www.aporter.com. **NOTE:** Candidates for Associate positions in the Washington Office should contact Diane Moore, Hiring Coordinator. Phone: 202/942-5943. E-mail address: Diane_Moore@aporter.com. **Description:** A law firm specializing in commercial law and public policy. **Positions advertised include:** Application Developer; Billing Editor; Business Development Coordinator; Client Analysis Manager; Media Relations Coordinator; SQL Engineer; Sr. Accountant. **Special programs:** Summer Associate Program.

COVINGTON & BURLING
1201 Pennsylvania Avenue NW, Washington DC 20004-2401. 202/662-6000. **Fax:** 202/662-6291. **Contact:** Tiffany L. Comey, Recruitment. **E-mail address:** humanresources@cov.com. **World Wide Web address:** http://www.cov.com. **Description:** A law firm specializing in company, commercial, intellectual property, and international tax law, and food and drug regulation. Founded in 1919. **Other U.S. locations:** New York NY; San Francisco CA.

JONES, DAY, REAVIS & POGUE
51 Louisiana Avenue NW, Washington DC 20001-2113. 202/879-3939. **Fax:** 202/626-1700. **Contact:** Human Resources Coordinator. **World Wide Web address:** http://www.jonesday.com. **Description:** A law firm specializing in business practice law, government regulation, litigation, and tax law. **Positions advertised include:** Paralegal. **Corporate headquarters location:** Cleveland OH.

REEDSMITH LLP
1301 K Street NW, Suite 1100, East Tower, Washington DC 20005. 202/414-9200. **Fax:** 202/414-9299. **Contact:** Cindy Schuler. **E-mail address:** dcjobs@reedsmith.com. **World Wide Web address:** http://www.reedsmith.com. **Description:** A law firm. Founded in 1877. **Positions advertised include:** Business Development Coordinator; Billing Specialist; Life Science Transactions Associate. **Other U.S. locations:** Harrisburg PA; Los Angeles CA; New York NY; Newark NJ; San Francisco CA; Wilmington DE. **International locations:** London.

WILEY REIN & FIELDING
1776 K Street NW, Washington DC 20006. 202/719-7000. **Fax:** 202/719-7049. **Contact:** Irena McGrath. **E-mail Address:** wrfrecruit@wrf.com. **World Wide Web Address:** http://www.wrf.com. **Description:** A leading national law firm. **Positions advertised Include:** Communications Associate; Employment & Labor Associate; Insurance Coverage Litigation Associate. **Number of employees worldwide:** 2,500.

WILMERHALE
2445 M Street NW, Washington DC 20037. 202/663-6000. **Fax:** 202/663-6363. **Contact:** Human Resources. **World Wide Web address:** http://www.wilmer.com. **Description:** A law firm specializing in international and corporate law. **Positions advertised include:** Bankruptcy Associate; Communications Associate; Corporate Finance Associate; Litigation Associate; Securities Associate. **Special programs:** Summer Associates Program.

Florida
CARLTON FIELDS
P.O. Box 3239, Tampa FL 33601. 813/223-7000. **Physical address:** 4221 West Boy Scout Boulevard, Suite 1000, Tampa FL 33607. **Contact:** Catherine Witherspoon, Human Resources. **E-mail address:** cwitherspoon@carltonfields.com. **World Wide Web address:** http://www.carltonfields.com. **Description:** A law firm specializing in real estate and construction. **Positions advertised include:** Practicing Attorney; Judicial Clerks; Legal Administration Assistant; Paralegal; Messenger; File Clerk. **Corporate headquarters location:** This location. **Operations at this facility include:** Administration; Service. **Number of employees at this location:** 420.

FOLEY & LARDNER
One Independent Drive, Suite 1300, Jacksonville FL 32202. 904/359-2000. **Contact:** Human Resources. **World Wide Web address:** http://www.foley.com. **Description:** A law firm specializing in real estate, tax, corporate, securities, and individual planning. Founded in 1842.

FOWLER WHITE BOGGS BANKER
P.O. Box 1438, Tampa FL 33601. 813/228-7411. **Physical address:** 501 East Kennedy Boulevard, Suite 1700, Tampa FL 33602. **Contact:** Human Resources. **World Wide Web address:** http://www.fowlerwhite.com. **Description:** A law firm specializing in corporate, business, and real estate law. **Positions advertised include:** Estate Planning Lawyer; Bankruptcy Creditor; Rights Litigator; Commercial Real Estate Transactions Coverage Litigation Associate; Estate Planning Associate; Products Liability Litigator; Securities Litigation Associate.

GREENBERG TRAURIG
1221 Brickell Avenue, 21st Floor, Miami FL 33131. 305/579-0500. **Fax:** 305/579-0717. **Contact:** Rosalyn Friedman, Human Resources Director. **World Wide Web address:** http://www.gtlaw.com. **Description:** A business law firm specializing in corporate and securities, entertainment, information technology, litigation, real estate, and telecommunications. **Positions advertised include:** Litigation Associate; Health Business Associate; Litigation Associate; Real Estate Associate; Reorganization Bankruptcy & Restructuring Associate; Trust & Real Estate Associate.

MARKS, GRAY, CONROY & GIBBS
P.O. Box 447, Jacksonville FL 32201. 904/398-0900. **Physical address:** 1200 Riverplace Boulevard, Jacksonville FL 32207. **Contact:** Office Administrator. **Description:** A law firm. **Corporate headquarters location:** This location. **Number of employees at this location:** 60.

McGUIREWOODS
50 North Laura Street, Suite 3300, Jacksonville FL 32202. 904/798-3200. **Fax:** 904/798-3207. **Contact:** Human Resources. **World Wide Web address:** http://www.mcguirewoods.com. **Description:** A law firm specializing in environmental, estate trust, and labor law.

Georgia

HAWKINS & PARNELL
303 Peachtree Street NE, 40th Floor, Atlanta GA 30308-3243. 404/614-7400. **Fax:** 404/614-7500. **Contact:** Human Resources. **World Wide Web address:** http://www.hawkinsparnell.com. **Description:** A 54-attorney law firm specializing in civil and appellate litigation. Founded in 1963. **Corporate headquarters location:** This location. **Other U.S. locations:** Charleston WV; Dallas TX. **Number of employees at this location:** 60.

HOLLAND & KNIGHT LLP
1201 West Peachtree Street NE, One Atlantic Center, Suite 2000, Atlanta GA 30309-3400. 404/817-8500. **Fax:** 404/881-0470. **Contact:** Human Resources. **E-mail address:** atl.careers@hklaw.com. **World Wide Web address:** http://www.hklaw.com. **Description:** An international law firm. **NOTE:** Please visit website to search for jobs. **Positions advertised include:** Paralegal. **Special programs:** Summer Associate Program.

HUNTON & WILLIAMS
600 Peachtree Street NE, Suite 4100, Atlanta GA 30308-2216. 404/888-4000. **Fax:** 404/888-4190. **Contact:** Wanda W. Boyd, Human Resources Administrator. **E-mail address:** wboyd@hunton.com. **World Wide Web address:** http://www.hunton.com. **Description:** A law firm specializing in corporate law and securities, energy and environmental issues, international law, litigation, real estate law, and taxes. Founded in 1901. **NOTE:** Contact Theresa Kimble, Recruiter – phone is 404/888-4164, e-mail is tkimble@hunton.com – for potential lawyer positions, and Wanda W. Boyd, Human Resources Administrator – phone is 404/888-4101 –for potential staff positions. Please visit website to search for open positions. **Other U.S. locations:** Nationwide. **International locations:** Thailand, Belgium; China; London; Singapore.

FREEMAN, MATHIS, & GARY, LLP
100 Galleria Parkway, Suite 1600, Atlanta GA 30339-5948. 770/818-0000. **Fax:** 770/937-9960. **Contact:** Human Resources. **E-mail address:** pcovington@fmglaw.com. **World Wide Web address:** http://www.fmglaw.com. **Description:** A law firm servicing national corporate and government agencies. Founded in 1997. **Positions advertised include:** Litigation Associate.

PAUL, HASTINGS, JANOFSKY & WALKER
600 Peachtree Street NE, Suite 2400, Atlanta GA 30308. 404/815-2400. **Fax:** 404/815-2424. **Contact:** Hiring Attorney. **E-mail address:** recruitatl@paulhastings.com. **World Wide Web address:** http://www.paulhastings.com. **Description:** A law firm specializing in corporate, employment, immigration, litigation, and real estate. **NOTE:** Please visit website to see job listings. **Positions advertised include:** Immigration Administrative Case Manager. **Special programs:** Summer Associate program. **Other U.S. locations:** Costa Mesa CA; Los Angeles CA; New York NY; San Diego CA; San Francisco CA; Stamford CT; Washington D.C. **International locations:** Beijing China; Hong Kong China; London England; Shanghai China; Tokyo Japan. **Number of employees at this location:** 83. **Number of employees worldwide:** 900.

SAVELL & WILLIAMS
100 Peachtree Street, Suite 1500, The Equitable Building, Atlanta GA 30303. 404/521-1282. **Fax:** 404/584-0026. **Contact:** Jennifer Chapin, Hiring Partner. **E-mail address:** jhc@savellwilliams.com. **World Wide Web address:** http://www.savellwilliams.com. **Description:** A law firm specializing in insurance, litigation, liability, adoption, and worker's compensation law.

SWIFT, CURIE, McGHEE & HIERS
1355 Peachtree Street NE, Suite 300, Atlanta GA 30309. 404/874-8800. **Fax:** 404/888-6199. **Contact:** Human Resources. **World Wide Web address:** http://www.scmhlaw.com. **Description:** A legal services firm specializing in worker's compensation law. **NOTE:** Please visit website to see job listings and to submit resume online. For those interested in attorney jobs, contact Patricia L. Young, Attorney Recruiting Manager at 404/888-6199. **Positions advertised include:** Paralegal. **Special programs:** Summer Associate Program. **Corporate headquarters location:** This location.

Hawaii

CADES SCHUTTE
1000 Bishop Street, Suite 1200, Honolulu HI 96813. 808/544-3893. **Fax:** 808/521-9210. **Contact:** Grace Nihei Kido, Human Resources. **E-mail address:** gkido@cades.com. **World Wide Web address:** http://www.cades.com. **Description:** A full-service law firm that specializes in business counseling. **Special programs:** Summer Associate Program. **NOTE:** For the Summer Associate Program, contact Michele S. Loudermilk by telephone at 808/544.3837 or by e-mail at mloudermilk@cades.com. **Corporate headquarters location:** This location. **Other area locations:** Kailua-Kona.

CARLSMITH BALL LLP
ASB Tower, 1001 Bishop Street, Pacific Tower, Suite 2200, Honolulu HI 96813. 808/523-2500. **Fax:** 808/523-0842. **Contact:** Recruiting Coordinator. **E-mail address:** execdirector@carlsmith. com. **World Wide Web address:** http://www.carlsmith.com. **Description:** A law firm that specializes in U.S. investment overseas, Asian investment in the U.S., admiralty & maritime, banking & finance, energy development and regulation, environmental compliance and structuring, foreign sales corporations, government contracting, health care, and retail. **Special programs:** Summer Associate Program. **Other area locations:** Kapolei, Hilo, Kona, Maui. **Other U.S. locations:** Los Angeles CA. **International locations:** Guam; Saipan.

Idaho

HOLLAND & HART LLP
P.O. Box 2527, Boise ID 83701. 208/342-5000. **Physical address**: U.S. Bank Plaza, 101 South Capitol Boulevard Suite 1400, Boise ID 83702. **Contact:** Kelly Andrus. **World Wide Web address:** http://www.hollandhart.com. **Description:** A law firm with a wide range of practice areas. **NOTE:** Go to http://www.hhjobs.com for information on how to apply. **Special Programs:** Summer Clerkship. **Other U.S. locations:** CO; DC; MT; NM; UT; WY. **Number of employees nationwide:** 300.

Illinois

AMERICAN BAR ASSOCIATION
321 North Clark Street, Chicago IL 60610. 312/988-5000. **Contact:** Human Resources. **E-mail address:** abajobs@abanet.org. **World Wide Web address:** http://www.abanet.org. **Description:** A professional association serving the legal profession. **NOTE:** Search and apply for positions online. **Corporate headquarters location:** This location.

ARNSTEIN & LEHR
120 South Riverside Plaza, Suite 1200, Chicago IL 60606. 312/876-7100. **Fax:** 312/803-0250. **Contact:** Jennifer Rogalski, Human Resources. **E-mail address:** jlrogalski@arnstein.com. **World Wide Web address:** http://www.arnstein.com. **Description:** A law firm specializing in antitrust, corporate, environmental, insurance, real estate, and tax law. **Positions advertised include:** Word Processor; Network Administrator. **Corporate headquarters location:** This location. **Other area locations:** Hoffman Estates IL. **Other U.S. locations:** WI; FL. **Operations at this facility include:** Administration. **Listed on:** Privately held.

BAKER & McKENZIE
One Prudential Plaza, 130 East Randolph Drive, Chicago IL 60601. 312/861-8000. **Fax:** 312/861-2899. **Contact:** Recruiter. **E-mail address:** chicago-hr@bakernet.com **World Wide Web address:** http://www.bakernet.com. **Description:** A general

practice law firm. **Corporate headquarters location:** This location.

CHAPMAN AND CUTLER
111 West Monroe Street, Chicago IL 60603-4080. 312/845-3898. **Fax:** 312/701-2361. **Contact:** Human Resources. **World Wide Web address:** http://www.chapman.com. **Description:** A law firm specializing in corporate financing, litigation, and tax law. **NOTE**: To apply for attorney positions, submit cover letter and resume to resumes@chapman.com, or fax to 312/516-1488. For corporate and support positions, send resumes to resumes@chapman.com, or fax to 312/516-1488. **Special programs:** Summer Associates. **Corporate headquarters location:** This location. **Operations at this facility include:** Administration; Service. **Listed on:** Privately held.

DLA PIPER RUDNICK GRAY CARY
203 North LaSalle Street, Suite 1900, Chicago IL 60601. 312/368-4000. **Fax:** 312/236-7516. **Contact:** Marguerite E. Strubing, Legal Recruiting Manager. **E-mail address:** marguerite.strubing@piperrudnick.com. **World Wide Web address:** http://www.piperrudnick.com. **Description:** A law firm specializing in bankruptcy, corporate, labor, insurance, and tax law. **Special programs:** Summer employment. **Other U.S. locations:** Nationwide.

VEDDER, PRICE, KAUFMAN, & KAMMHOLZ
222 North LaSalle Street, Suite 2600, Chicago IL 60601. 312/609-7500. **Fax:** 312/609-5005. **Contact:** Gina Grunloh, Human Resources. **E-mail address:** ggrunloh@vedderprice.com. **World Wide Web address:** http://www.vedderprice.com. **Description:** A law firm engaged in a variety of legal services including labor, litigation, corporate, health, and pro bono law. **Other U.S. locations:** New York NY; Roseland NJ.

WILDMAN HARROLD
225 West Wacker Drive, Suite 3000, Chicago IL 60606-1229. 312/201-2000. **Contact:** Human Resources. **World Wide Web address:** http://www.whad.com. **Description:** A law firm specializing in corporate, divorce, medical malpractice, real estate, and wills and trusts law. **Special programs:** Summer Internship. **Office hours:** Monday - Friday, 8:00 a.m. - 6:00 p.m. **Corporate headquarters location:** This location.

Indiana
BAKER & DANIELS
300 North Meridian Street, Suite 2700, Indianapolis IN 46204. 317/237-1299. **Fax:** 317/237-1000. **Contact:** Julie Abowers, Legal Recruiting Administrator. **E-mail address:** Kristin.givens@bakerd.com. **World Wide Web address:** http://www.bakerdaniels.com. **Description:** A legal services firm specializing in corporate, environmental, and international law. Baker & Daniels employs 20 practice teams to serve its clients. **Positions advertised include:** Legal Secretary. **Special programs:** Summer Associate Programs.

BARNES & THORNBURG
11 South Meridian Street, Indianapolis IN 46204. 317/236-1313. **Fax:** 317/231-7433. **Contact:** Joseph Eaton, Chair of Recruiting Committee. **World Wide Web address:** http://www.btlaw.com. **Description:** A legal firm specializing in international, trade, business, utility, taxes, and real estate law.

HARRIS & HARRIS
222 North Buffalo Street, Warsaw IN 46580. 574/267-2111. **Contact:** Recruitment. **Description:** A law firm specializing in diverse areas including corporate, banking, taxation, real estate, environmental, family/domestic, bankruptcy, and estate planning law.

Kansas
WALLACE, SAUNDERS, AUSTIN, BROWN & ENOCHS
10111 West 87th Street, Overland Park KS 66282. 913/888-1000. **Fax:** 913/888-1065. **Contact:** Julie Cramm, Human Resources Director. **World Wide Web address:** http://www.wsabe.com. **Description:** A law firm of 60 attorneys handling a variety of cases involving insurance claims, child custody, divorce, and automobile accidents. Founded in 1963. **Other locations:** Kansas City MO; Wichita KS; Springfield MO.

Maine
VERRILL AND DANA
P.O. Box 586, Portland ME 04112-0586. 207/774-4000. **Fax:** 207/774-7499. **Physical address:** One Portland Square, Portland ME. **Contact:** David Bois, Director of Administration. **E-mail address:** mpattenaude@verrilldana.com. **World Wide Web address:** http://www.verrilldana.com. **Description:** A law firm with a wide variety of specialties. **Positions advertised include:** Legal Secretary; Summer Associate. **Other area locations:** Portland ME; Kennebunk ME; Augusta ME. **Other U.S. locations:** Kansas City KA; Washington DC.

Maryland
GOODELL, DEVRIES, LEECH & DANN, LLP
One South Street, 20th Floor, Baltimore MD 21202. 410/783-4000. **Fax:** 410/783-4040. **Contact:** Human Resources. **E-mail address:** info@gdldlaw.com. **World Wide Web address:** http://www.gdldlaw.com. **Description:** A law firm specializing in litigation. Founded in 1988. **NOTE:** Entry-level positions are offered. **Positions advertised include:** Entry level Associates; Lateral Entry Attorney.

MILES & STOCKBRIDGE
10 Light Street, Baltimore MD 21202-1487. 410/727-6464. **Fax:** 410/385-3700. **Contact:** Randi Lewis, Director of Diversity and Professional Development. **E-mail address:** lewis@milesstockbridge.com. **World Wide Web address:** http://www.milesstockbridge.com. **Description:** A law firm that operates on a regional level in the practice areas of business, litigation, and commercial law. Founded in 1932. **NOTE:** To contact Human Resources directly, call 410/385-3563. **Positions advertised include:** Senior Business Lawyer; Senior Estate Planning and Probate Lawyer; Corporate Lawyer; Litigation Associate; Paralegal. **Special programs:** Summer Associate Program. **Other area locations:** Cambridge MD; Columbia MD; Easton MD; Frederick MD; Rockville MD; Towson MD. **Other U.S. locations:** Tysons Corner VA; Washington DC.

SAUL EWING LLP
500 East Pratt Street, Suite 900, Baltimore MD 21202-3171. 410/332-8600. **Fax:** 410/332-8862. **Contact:** Human Resources. **World Wide Web address:** http://www.saul.com. **Description:** A general practice law firm with over 222 lawyers nationwide in more than 12 fields including business, contracts, employment, estates and trusts, intellectual property, and real estate. **Special programs:** Summer Program. **Other U.S. locations:** Wilmington DE; Princeton NJ; New York NY; Berwyn PA; Harrisburg PA; Philadelphia PA.

SEMMES, BOWEN & SEMMES
250 West Pratt Street, 16th Floor, Baltimore MD 21201. 410/539-5040. **Fax:** 410/576-4868. **Contact:** Human Resources. **E-mail address:** semmes@mail.semmes.com. **World Wide Web address:** http://www.semmes.com. **Description:** A general civil law firm. Founded in 1887. **Special programs:** Summer Jobs. **Corporate headquarters location:** This location. **Other area locations:** Hagerstown MD; Salisbury MD; Towson MD. **Other U.S. locations:** Washington DC; McLean VA.

TYDINGS & ROSENBERG LLP
100 East Pratt Street, 26th Floor, Baltimore MD 21202. 410/752-9700. **Fax:** 410/727-5460. **Contact:** Diane Castello, Hiring Coordinator. **E-mail address:** dcastello@tydingslaw.com. **World Wide Web address:** http://www.tydingslaw.com. **Description:** A general practice law firm with over 60 lawyers in fields including corporate law, commercial and business

litigation, family law, employment law, and environmental litigation. **NOTE:** To reach Human Resources directly, call 410/752-9816. **Special programs:** Summer Associate Program. **Other U.S. locations:** Washington DC.

VENABLE ATTORNEYS AT LAW
2 Hopkins Plaza, Suite 1800, Baltimore MD 21201. 410/244-7400. **Fax:** 410/244-7742. **Contact:** Human Resources. **E-mail address:** careeropp@venable.com. **World Wide Web address:** http://www.venable.com. **Description:** A law firm with over 25 practice areas including corporate law and litigation. **NOTE:** Part-time and temporary positions are offered. **Positions advertised include:** Bankruptcy Associate; Staff Attorney; Para-legal; Employment Associate; Products Paralegal. **Other area locations:** Rockville MD; Towson MD. **Other U.S. locations:** Washington DC; McLean VA.

Massachusetts

ALTMAN & ALTMAN
675 Massachusetts Avenue, 11th Floor, Cambridge MA 02139. 617/492-3000. **Contact:** Human Resources. **World Wide Web address:** http://www.altmanllp.com. **Description:** A law firm specializing in personal injury, divorce and family, and criminal defense law.

BOWDITCH & DEWEY
311 Main Street, P.O. Box 15156, Worcester MA 01615-0156. 508/791-3511. **Fax:** 508/929-3195. **Contact:** Human Resources. **E-mail address:** recruiting@bowditch.com. **World Wide Web address:** http://www.bowditch.com. **Description:** A 50-attorney law firm practicing a variety of law disciplines including environmental, labor, real estate, and litigation. **Other area locations:** Framingham MA.

BROWN, RUDNICK, FREED & GESMER
One Financial Center, Boston MA 02111. 617/856-8200. **Contact:** Human Resources. **World Wide Web address:** http://www.brownrudnick.com. **Description:** A 150-attorney law firm specializing in a variety of legal disciplines including bankruptcy, corporate, international, tax, government, and estate law. **Positions advertised include:** Audio Visual Specialist; Support Specialist; Financial Analyst; Intellectual Property & Litigation Partner. **Corporate headquarters location:** This location. **Other U.S. locations:** Hartford CT; Providence RI. **International locations:** London, England. **Number of employees at this location:** 300.

BULKLEY, RICHARDSON AND GELINAS, LLP
1500 Main Street, Suite 2700, Springfield MA 01115-5507. 413/781-2820. **Fax:** 413/785-5060. **Contact:** Michael Burke, Hiring Partner. **World Wide Web address:** http://www.bulkley.com. **Description:** A law firm specializing in a variety of legal disciplines including environmental, employment, health, and intellectual property law. **Other area locations:** Boston MA.

CHOATE, HALL & STEWART
Two International Place, Boston MA 02110. 617/248-5000. **Fax:** 617/248-4000. **Contact:** Human Resources. **World Wide Web address:** http://www.choate.com. **Description:** A law firm whose legal specialties include business, energy and telecommunications, government enforcement and compliance, health care, real estate, and trusts and estates. **Positions advertised include:** Team Leader; Tax Attorney; Bankruptcy Associate; Probate Paralegal.

DAY, BERRY & HOWARD LLP
One International Place, Boston MA 02110. 617/345-4600. **Contact:** Jill E. Little, Recruitment Coordinator. **E-mail address:** jlittle@dbh.com. **World Wide Web address:** http://www.dbh.com. **Description:** One of New England's largest law firms. Day, Berry & Howard LLP specializes in more than 60 legal disciplines including banking, construction, insurance, torts, and venture capital. **Positions advertised include:** Trust & Estate Paralegal; Paralegal; Associate Employment Litigator; Attorney. **Other U.S. locations:** Greenwich CT; Hartford CT; Stamford CT; New York NY.

DECHERT
200 Clarendon Street, 27th Floor, Boston MA 02116-5021. 617/728-7100. **Fax:** 617/426-6567. **Contact:** Human Resources Department. **World Wide Web address:** http://www.dechert.com. **Description:** A law firm specializing in intellectual property, taxation, and litigation. The firm operates 18 offices throughout the United States and Europe. **Other U.S. locations:** Nationwide. **International locations:** Belgium; England; France; Luxembourg.

EDWARDS ANGELL PALMER AND DODGE LLP
101 Federal Street, Boston MA 02110. 617/439-4444. **Contact:** Human Resources. **World Wide Web address:** http://www.eapdlaw.com. **Description:** A law firm specializing in intellectual property law. **Positions advertised include:** Litigation Legal Secretary; support Staff Supervisor. **Corporate headquarters location:** Providence RI. **Listed on:** Privately held. **Number of employees at this location:** 50.

FISH & RICHARDSON, P.C.
225 Franklin Street, Boston MA 02110-2804. 617/542-5070. **Fax:** 617/542-8906. **Contact:** Betsy Butler, Office Manager. **E-mail address:** work@fr.com. **World Wide Web address:** http://www.fr.com. **Description:** A law firm with various areas of practice including patents, copyrights, and trademarks. **Other U.S. locations:** Redwood City CA; San Diego CA; Wilmington DE; Washington DC; Minneapolis MN; New York NY; Dallas TX.

FOLEY, HOAG & ELIOT, L.L.P.
155 Seaport Boulevard, Boston MA 02210. 617/832-1000. **Contact:** Dina Wreede, Director of Legal Recruiting. **E-mail address:** hiring@foleyhoag,com. **World Wide Web address:** http://www.fhe.com. **Description:** A law firm covering a broad range of practice areas including litigation, labor, business, international, and intellectual property. **Positions advertised include:** Legal Secretary. **Other U.S. locations:** Washington DC.

GOODWIN PROCTER, LLP
53 State Street, Boston MA 02109. 617/570-1000. **Contact:** Human Resources. **World Wide Web address:** http://www.gph.com. **Description:** A general practice law firm. **Corporate headquarters location:** This location. **Other U.S. locations:** Washington DC; Roseland NJ; New York NY.

GOULSTON & STORRS, P.C.
400 Atlantic Avenue, Boston MA 02110-3333. 617/482-1776. **Contact:** Nancy Needle, Recruiting Director. **World Wide Web address:** http://www.goulstorrs.com. **Description:** A law firm with a variety of practice areas including corporate law and litigation. **Other U.S. locations:** Washington DC.

HOLLAND & KNIGHT
10 St. James Avenue, Boston MA 02116. 617/523-2700. **Fax:** 617/523-6850. **Contact:** Hiring Partner. **World Wide Web address:** http://www.hklaw.com. **Description:** A general practice law firm. **Other U.S. locations:** Nationwide. **International locations:** Worldwide.

KIRKPATRICK & LOCKHART LLP
One Lincoln Street, Boston MA 02111-2950. 617/261-3100. **Fax:** 617/261-3175. **Contact:** Jeffrey King, Hiring Partner. **E-mail address:** bmorrissey@kl.com. **World Wide Web address:** http://www.kl.com. **Description:** A law firm with a broad range of practice areas including international law and intellectual property. **Positions advertised include:** Legal Assistant; Clerk; Legal Secretary; Administration. **Other U.S. locations:** Los Angeles CA; San Francisco CA; Washington DC; Miami FL; Newark NJ; New York NY; Harrisburg PA; Pittsburgh PA; Dallas TX.

LOURIE & CUTLER
60 State Street, Boston MA 02109. 617/742-6720. **Contact:** David Andelman, Esq., Hiring Partner. **Description:** A law firm specializing in estate planning and taxation.

McDERMOTT, WILL & EMERY
28 State Street, Boston MA 02109-1775. 617/535-4000. **Contact:** Human Resources. **World Wide Web address:** http://www.mwe.com. **Description:** A law firm with concentrations in health care, corporate law, and litigation. **Number of employees worldwide:** 1,000.

MELICK PORTER & SHEA
28 State Street, 22nd Floor, Boston MA 02109-1775. 617/523-6200. **Fax:** 617/523-8130. **Contact:** Human Resources. **E-mail address:** jobs@melicklaw.com. **World Wide Web address:** http://www.melicklaw.com. **Description:** A law firm consisting mainly of defense attorneys. **Positions advertised include:** Associate; Summer Intern; Legal Secretary; Paralegal.

MINTZ, LEVIN, COHN, FERRIS, GLOVSKY & POPEO
One Financial Center, 40th Floor, Boston MA 02111. 617/542-6000. **Contact:** Julie Zammuto, Manager of Attorney Recruiting & Training. **World Wide Web address:** http://www.mintz.com. **Description:** A law firm with a range of practice areas including trade regulation, real estate, and technology. **Other U.S. locations:** Los Angeles CA; Stamford CT; Washington DC; New York NY; Reston VA.

MIRICK, O'CONNELL, DEMALLIE & LOUGEE
100 Front Street, 17th Floor, Worcester MA 01608. 508/791-8500. **Fax:** 508/791-8502. **Contact:** Human Resources. **World Wide Web address:** http://www.modl.com. **Description:** A law firm with many areas of practice including intellectual property, banking and commercial lending, labor and employment, and biotechnology. **Other area locations:** Westborough MA; Boston MA.

NIXON PEABODY LLP
100 Summer Street, Boston MA 02110. 617/345-1000. **Fax:** 617/345-1300. **Contact:** Claire N. Suchecki. **E-mail address:** csuchecki@nixonpeabody.com. **Wide Web address:** http://www.nixonpeabody.com. **Description:** A law firm covering several areas of practice through its commercial, corporate, estate, litigation, real estate, and syndication groups. **Positions advertised include:** Financial Services Associate; Real Estate Associate.

NUTTER, McCLENNEN & FISH, LLP
155 Seaport Boulevard, Boston MA 02210. 617/439-2000. **Fax:** 617/310-9000. **Contact:** Human Resources. **E-mail address:** tcunningham@nutter.com. **World Wide Web address:** http://www.nutter.com. **Description:** A law firm offering a variety of legal specialties including litigation, intellectual property, environmental, labor and employment, and trusts and estates. **Other area locations:** Hyannis MA.

PEABODY & ARNOLD LLP
30 Rowes Wharf, Boston MA 02110-3342. 617/951-2100. **Fax:** 617/951-2125. **Contact:** Human Resources. **World Wide Web address:** http://www.peabodyarnold.com. **Description:** A law firm that operates through three legal groups: The Personal Law Group provides tax and estate planning services; The Business Law Group specializes in securities, corporate, banking and finance, and health care; and The Litigation Group specializes in antitrust and trade regulation, employment, environmental, surety, and workers' compensation.

ROBINS, KAPLAN, MILLER & CIRESI LLP
800 Boylston Street, 25th Floor, Boston MA 02199. 617/267-2300. **Fax:** 617/267-8288. **Contact:** Human Resources. **World Wide Web address:** http://www.rkmc.com. **Description:** A law firm covering many practice areas including insurance law, business and commercial litigation, and intellectual property law. Founded in 1938. **Corporate headquarters location:** Minneapolis MN. **Other U.S. locations:** Los Angeles CA; San Francisco CA; Washington DC; Atlanta GA; Chicago IL. **Number of employees at this location:** 37. **Number of employees nationwide:** 650.

ROPES & GRAY
One International Place, Boston MA 02110-2624. 617/951-7000. **Fax:** 617/951-7050. **Contact:** Human Resources. **World Wide Web address:** http://www.ropesgray.com. **Description:** A law firm specializing in corporate law.

SKADDEN, ARPS, SLATE, MEAGHER & FLOM
One Beacon Street, 31st Floor, Boston MA 02108. 617/573-4800. **Fax:** 617/573-4822. **Contact:** Human Resources. **World Wide Web address:** http://www.skadden.com. **Description:** One of the world's largest law firms. Skadden, Arps, Slate, Meagher & Flom specializes in more than 40 practice areas through 21 worldwide offices.

SULLIVAN & WORCESTER
One Post Office Square, Boston MA 02109. 617/338-2800. **Fax:** 617/338-2880. **Contact:** Janet Brussard, Legal Recruiting. **E-mail address:** hrdepartment@sandw.com. **World Wide Web address:** http://www.sandw.com. **Description:** A law firm that practices all areas of law including intellectual property and international law.

WOLF, GREENFIELD & SACKS
600 Atlantic Avenue, Boston MA 02210-2206. 617/646-8000. **Fax:** 617/646-8846. **Contact:** Sheila LeDuc, Director of Human Resources. **E-mail address:** sleduc@wolfgreenfield.com. **World Wide Web address:** http://www.wolfgreenfield.com. **Description:** A leading intellectual property law firm. Areas of specialization include patent, trademark, and copyright law.

Michigan

BERRY MOORMAN P.C.
900 Victors Way, Suite 300, Ann Arbor MI 48103. 734/668-4100. **Fax:** 734/668-4101. **Contact:** Thomas E. Dew, Human Resources. **E-mail address:** tdew@berrymoorman.com. **World Wide Web address:** http://www.berrymoorman.com. **Description:** A law firm specializing in corporate law, taxation, securities regulations, estate planning, and labor law. **Corporate headquarters location:** Detroit MI. **Other area locations:** Birmingham MI. **International locations:** St. Petersburg, Russia.

BUTZEL LONG
150 West Jefferson Avenue, Suite 100, Detroit MI 48226. 313/225-7000. **Fax:** 313/225-7080. **Contact:** Mary Ann Walter, Recruiting Coordinator. **E-mail address:** walter@butzel.com. **World Wide Web address:** http://www.butzel.com. **Description:** A law firm specializing in corporate law. **Positions advertised include:** Legal Records Clerk; Research and Intranet Librarian; Library Clerk. **Special programs:** Summer Associate Program. **Corporate headquarters location:** This location. **Other area locations:** Holland MI; Lansing MI; Bloomfield Hills MI; Ann Arbor MI. **Other U.S. locations:** Boca Raton FL; Washington DC.

DYKEMA & GOSSETT
400 Renaissance Center, Detroit MI 48243-1668. 313/568-6800. **Fax:** 313/568-6691. **Contact:** Sarah Staup, Human Resources. **E-mail address:** hr@dykema.com. **World Wide Web address:** http://www.dykema.com. **Description:** A law firm specializing in corporate law. Dykema & Gossett is one of the largest law firms in the Midwest. **Positions advertised include:** Legal Specialist; Floating Administrative Assistant. **Special programs:** Summer jobs. **Corporate headquarters location:** This location. **Other area locations:** Ann Arbor MI; Bloomfield Hills MI; Lansing MI; Grand Rapids MI. **Other U.S.**

locations: Washington DC; Chicago IL. **Number of employees nationwide:** 600.

FIEGER, FIEGER, KENNEY AND JOHNSON P.C.
19390 West Ten Mile Road, Southfield MI 48075-2463. 248/355-5555. **Fax:** 248/355-5148. **Contact:** Human Resources. **E-mail address:** info@fiegerlaw.com. **World Wide Web address:** http://www.fiegerlaw.com. **Description:** A law firm specializing in medical malpractice and complex litigation. Geoffrey Fieger's list of well-known clients includes Dr. Jack Kevorkian. **Corporate headquarters location:** This location. **Operations at this facility include:** Service. **Number of employees at this location:** 50.

Minnesota

ARTHUR, CHAPMAN, KETTERING, SMETAK & PIKALA, P.A.
500 Young Quinlan Building, 81 South Ninth Street, Minneapolis MN 55402. 612/339-3500. **Fax:** 612/339-7655. **Contact:** Human Resources Manager. **E-mail address:** info@arthurchapman.com. **World Wide Web address:** http://www.arthurchapman.com. **Description:** A law firm specializing in insurance, liability, product liability, and workers' compensation cases. Founded in 1974.

BARNA, GUZY & STEFFEN LTD.
400 Northtown Financial Center, 200 Coon Rapids Boulevard, Coon Rapids MN 55433-5894. 763/780-8500. **Toll-free phone:** 800/422-3486. **Fax:** 763/780-1777. **Contact:** Human Resources. **World Wide Web address:** http://www.bgslaw.com. **Description:** A law firm covering a variety of areas.

BASSFORD REMELE
33 South Sixth Street, Suite 3800, Minneapolis MN 55402-3707. 612/333-3000. **Fax:** 612/333-8829. **Contact:** Administrator. **E-mail address:** info@bassford.com. **World Wide Web address:** http://www.bassford.com. **Description:** A law firm specializing in litigation. Founded in 1882. **Positions advertised include:** Attorney. **Number of employees at this location:** 70.

BRIGGS & MORGAN, PROFESSIONAL ASSOCIATION
2200 IDS Center, 80 South Eighth Street, Minneapolis MN 55402. 612/977-8400. **Fax:** 612/977-8650. **Contact:** Human Resources. **World Wide Web address:** http://www.briggs.com. **Description:** A business law and trial law firm. Founded in 1882. **Corporate headquarters location:** This location. **Other U.S. locations:** St. Paul MN. **Listed on:** Privately held. **Number of employees at this location:** 165. **Number of employees nationwide:** 330. **Positions advertised include:** Employee Benefits Attorney; Franchise Attorney; Litigation Associate Attorney.

DORSEY & WHITNEY LLP
50 South Sixth Street, Suite 1500, Minneapolis MN 55402-1498. 612/340-2600. **Fax:** 612/340-2868. **Contact:** Joan Oyaff, Director of Human Resources. **World Wide Web address:** http://www.dorseylaw.com. **Description:** A law firm. Founded in 1912. **NOTE:** Attorney, legal staff, and support positions available. See website for current job openings and application instructions.

FAEGRE & BENSON LLP
2200 Wells Fargo Center, 90 South Seventh Street, Minneapolis MN 55402-3901. 612/766-7000. **Fax:** 612/766-1763. **Contact:** Human Resources. **World Wide Web address:** http://www.faegre.com. **Description:** A Minneapolis-based law firm and consultancy.

FREDRIKSON & BYRON, P.A.
200 South Sixth Street, Suite 4000, Minneapolis MN 55402-1425. 612/492-7000. **Fax:** 612/492-7077. **Contact:** Personnel. **World Wide Web address:** http://www.fredlaw.com. **Description:** A business and trial law firm with 140 attorneys. **Corporate headquarters location:** This location. **Number of employees at this location:** 275.

KINNEY & LANGE, P.A.
312 South Third Street, Minneapolis MN 55415-1002. 612/339-1863. **Fax:** 612/339-6580. **Contact:** Recruitment. **E-mail address:** info@kinney.com. **World Wide Web address:** http://www.kinney.com. **Description:** A full-service intellectual property law firm. **Corporate headquarters location:** This location. **Number of employees at this location:** 55.

LARKIN, HOFFMAN, DALY & LINDGREN
1500 Wells Fargo Plaza, 7900 Xerxes Avenue South, Bloomington MN 55431. 952/835-3800. **Fax:** 952/896-3333. **Contact:** Human Resources. **E-mail address:** hr@larkinhoffman.com. **World Wide Web address:** http://www.lhdl.com. **Description:** A law firm specializing in a wide variety of areas including corporate, franchise, international, and tax law. **Special programs:** Internships. **Corporate headquarters location:** This location.

LINDQUIST & VENNUM PLLP
4200 IDS Center, 80 South Eighth Street, Minneapolis MN 55402. 612/371-3211. **Fax:** 612/371-3207. **Contact:** Lisanne Weisz, Director of Legal Recruiting. **E-mail address:** lweisz@lindquist.com. **World Wide Web address:** http://www.lindquist.com. **Description:** A general practice law firm specializing in a variety of areas including banking, bankruptcy, corporate, employee benefits, family, and real estate. **Other U.S. locations** Denver CO.

MOSS & BARNETT, P.A.
4800 Wells Fargo Center, 90 South Seventh Street, Minneapolis MN 55402-4129. 612/347-0394. **Fax:** 612/339-6686. **Contact:** Julie Donaldson, Hiring Coordinator. **World Wide Web address:** http://www.moss-barnett.com. **Description:** A law firm specializing in a variety of areas, excluding criminal law.

OPPENHEIMER WOLFF & DONNELLY LLP
Plaza VII, Suite 3300, 45 South Seventh Street, Minneapolis MN 55402-1609. 612/607-7000. **Fax:** 612/607-7100. **Contact:** Jackie Gunstad, Recruiting Coordinator. **E-mail address:** jgunstad@oppenheimer.com. **World Wide Web address:** http://www.oppenheimer.com. **Description:** A law firm specializing in a variety of areas including commercial, health care, intellectual property, and tax law. **Positions advertised include:** Real Estate Paralegal; Receptionist; Attorney (Various). **Special programs:** Internships. **Number of employees at this location:** 400.

ROBINS, KAPLAN, MILLER & CIRESI LLP
2800 LaSalle Plaza, 800 LaSalle Avenue, Minneapolis MN 55402. 612/349-8500. **Fax:** 612/339-4181. **Contact:** Human Resources. **World Wide Web address:** http://www.rkmc.com. **Description:** A law firm specializing in medical malpractice, product liability, and similar areas. **Positions advertised include:** Graphics Designer; Records Specialist; Corporate Associate; Intellectual Property Litigation Associate. **Special programs:** Internships. **Corporate headquarters location:** This location. **Other U.S. locations:** Atlanta GA; Boston MA; Los Angeles CA; Naples FL; Washington DC. **Number of employees nationwide:** 600.

ZELLE, HOFMANN, VOELBEL, MASON & GETTE LLP
500 Washington Avenue South, Suite 4000, Minneapolis MN 55415. **Toll-free phone:** 800/899-5291. **Fax:** 612/336-9100. **Contact:** Human Resources. **E-mail address:** zelleweb@zelle.com. **World Wide Web address:** http://www.zelle.com. **Description:** A law firm that specializes in insurance litigation.

Mississippi

WATKINS LUDLAM WINTER & STENNIS, P.A.
P.O. Box 427, Jackson MS 39205-0427. 601/949-4900. **Physical address:** 633 North State Street, Jackson MS 39202. **Fax:** 601/949-4804. **Contact:** Angie Artman, Recruiting Coordinator. **E-mail address:** aartman@watkinsludlam.com. **World Wide Web address:** http://www.wlwslaw.com. **Description:** A legal services firm. Founded in 1905. **Special programs:** Internships; Summer Associate Programs. **Other area locations:** Gulfport MS. **Other U.S. locations:** Memphis TN; New Orleans LA. **Number of employees at this location:** 140.

Missouri

ARMSTRONG TEASDALE LLP
One Metropolitan Square, Suite 2600, 211 North Broadway, St. Louis MO 63102-2740. 314/621-5070. **Contact:** Personnel. **World Wide Web address:** http://www.armstrongteasdale.com. **Description:** A general practice law firm. **Other area locations:** Kansas City MO; Jefferson City MO. **Number of employees at this location:** 290.

BRYAN CAVE LLP
One Metropolitan Square, 211 North Broadway, Suite 3600, St. Louis MO 63102-2750. 314/259-2000. **Fax:** 314/259-2020. **Recorded jobline:** 314/259-2022. **Contact:** Mary B. Featherstone, Recruiter. **E-mail address:** mbfeatherstone@bryancave.com. **World Wide Web address:** http://www.bryancavellp.com. **Description:** An international law firm. **NOTE:** Entry-level positions are offered. **Positions advertised include:** Corporate Associate; Legal Assistant. **Special programs:** Internships; Training; Summer Jobs. **Corporate headquarters location:** This location. **Other U.S. locations:** Phoenix AZ; Los Angeles CA; Washington DC; Kansas City MO; New York NY. **International locations:** China; Kuwait; England; Saudi Arabia; United Arab Emirates. **Number of employees at this location:** 675. **Number of employees worldwide:** 1,380.

GREENSFELDER, HEMKER & GALE, P.C.
2000 Equitable Building, 10 South Broadway, St. Louis MO 63102. 314/241-9090. **Fax:** 314/241-8624. **Contact:** Angela Schaefer, Personnel Director. **E-mail address:** ads@greensfelder.com. **World Wide Web address:** http://www.greensfelder.com. **Description:** A general practice law firm specializing in bankruptcy, construction, corporate, employee benefits, environmental, estate planning, health care, immigration, intellectual property, labor, litigation, real estate, and tax law. Founded in 1895. **Number of employees at this location:** 170.

THOMPSON COBURN LLP
One U.S. Bank Plaza, St. Louis MO 63101-1693. 314/552-6000. **Fax:** 314/552-7000. **Contact:** Personnel. **World Wide Web address:** http://www.thompsoncoburn.com. **Description:** A corporate law firm. **NOTE:** Search and apply for positions online. **Special programs:** Summer Associate Program. **Corporate headquarters location:** This location. **Other U.S. locations:** Washington DC; Belleville IL. **Number of employees nationwide:** 300.

Nevada

AMERICAN VANTAGE COMPANIES
4735 South Durango Drive #105, Las Vegas NV 89147. 702/227-9800. **Fax:** 702/227-8525. **Contact:** Human Resources. **Description:** Provides consulting services to tribal gaming organizations.

HALE LANE PEEK DENNISON AND HOWARD
2300 West Sahara Avenue, Suite 800, Las Vegas NV 89102. 702/222-2500. **Fax:** 702/365-6940. **Contact:** Recruiting Department. **E-mail address:** recruitinghr@halelane.com. **World Wide Web address:** http://www.halelane.com. **Description:** A legal services firm specializing in transactional law and offering a wide range of other legal services. **Positions advertised include:** Commercial Litigation Lawyer. **Special Programs:** Mentoring; Internships; Summer Associate Programs. **Other area locations:** Carson City NV; Reno NV.

JONES VARGAS
3773 Howard Hughes Parkway, 3rd Floor South, Las Vegas NV 89109. 702/734-2220. **Contact:** Lynda Soper, Recruiting Cooridnator. **E-mail address:** lws@jonesvargas.com. **World Wide Web address:** http://www.jonesvargas.com. **Description**: Represents local, national, and international clients in business, litigation, government relations, gaming, corporate, municipal finance, real estate, bankruptcy, estate and probate, tax, zoning, healthcare, and domestic matters. **Other area locations:** Reno NV.

LIONEL, SAWYER & COLLINS
50 West Liberty Street, Suite 1100, Reno NV 89501. 775/788-8666. **Contact:** Rebecca Pamias-Sellers, Human Resources Manager. **World Wide Web address:** http://www.lionelsawyer.com. **Description:** Lionel, Sawyer & Collins is a legal services firm specializing in corporate law. The firm's three areas of focus are commercial, administrative, and litigation. **Other area locations:** Carson City NV; Las Vegas NV. **Other U.S. locations:** Washington DC.

New Hampshire

DEVINE, MILLIMET & BRANCH
111 Amherst Street, Manchester NH 03101. 603/669-1000. **Fax:** 603/669-8547. **Contact:** Alex Walker, Human Resources. **E-mail address:** awalker@dmb.com. **World Wide Web address:** http://www.dmb.com. **Description:** A law firm operating through two groups. The Corporate Group's areas of focus include intellectual property/patent law, estate planning, real estate, and business and tax planning. The Litigation Group's services include insurance defense, business litigation, and commercial litigation. **NOTE:** Openings posted on-line as available. **Positions advertised include:** Summer Associate; First Year Associate; Lateral Associate; Lateral Shareholder; Paralegal; Secretary/Staff. **Corporate headquarters location:** This location. **Other area locations:** Concord NH; North Hampton NH. **Other U.S. locations:** Andover MA. **Number of employees at this location:** 180.

LAW OFFICES OF WM. HOWARD DUNN
221 Broad Street, PO Box 676, Claremont NH 03743. 603/543-0111. **Fax:** 603/543-0604. **Contact:** Lisa Farley. **Description:** Provides local legal services. **Positions advertised include:** Legal Assistant/Secretary; Paralegal.

McLANE, GRAF, RAULERSON & MIDDLETON, P.A.
P.O. Box 326, Manchester NH 03105-0326. 603/625-6464. **Fax:** 603/625-5650. **Physical address:** 900 Elm Street, Manchester NH 03105. **Contact:** Bettina Caminati, Recruitment Coordinator and Director of Human Resources. **E-mail address:** Bettina.caminati@mclane.com. **World Wide Web address:** http://www.mclane.com. **Description:** Provides statewide legal services. Founded in 1920. **NOTE:** Entry-level positions are offered. **Positions advertised include:** Litigation Attorney; Tax Attorney. **Other area locations:** Concord NH; Portsmouth NH. **Special programs:** Summer jobs. **Office hours:** Monday - Friday, 8:30 a.m. - 5:00 p.m. **Corporate headquarters location:** This location. **Number of employees at this location:** 150. **Number of employees nationwide:** 170.

NIXON PEABODY LLP
900 Elm Street, Manchester NH 03101. 603/628-4000. **Fax**: 603/628-4040. **Contact**: Richard Gibson, Office Manager. **World Wide Web Address**: www.nixonpeabody.com. **Description**: Nixon Peabody is one of the largest multi-practice law firms in the United States, with offices in fourteen cities and more than six hundred attorneys collaborating across fifteen major practice areas. **Positions Advertised Include**: Attorneys, Collections Clerk, Paralegal

New Jersey
DECHERT LLP
P.O. Box 5218, Princeton NJ 08543-5218. 609/620-3200. **Physical address:** 997 Lenox Drive, Princeton Pike Corporate Center, Building 3, Suite 210, Lawrenceville NJ 08648-2317. **Fax:** 609/620-3259. **Contact:** Human Resources. **E-mail address:** legal.recruiting@dechert.com. **World Wide Web address:** http://www.dechert.com. **Description:** Dechert is an international law firm with practices in corporate and securities, complex litigation, finance and real estate, and financial services and asset management.

GREENBAUM, ROWE, SMITH, RAVIN, DAVIS & HIMMEL LLP
Metro Corporate Campus One, 99 Wood Avenue South, P.O. Box 5600, Woodbridge NJ 07095. 732/549-5600. **Fax:** 732/549-1881. **Contact:** Victoria Martignetti, Recruitment Coordinator. **E-mail address:** vmartignetti@greenbaumlaw.com. **World Wide Web address:** http://www.greenbaumlaw.com. **Description:** A law firm with practice areas including environmental, product liability, employment, white collar criminal, real estate, corporate, tax, and estate law.

LEBOEUF, LAMB, GREENE & MACRAE LLP
One Riverfront Plaza, Newark NJ 07102. 973/643-8000. **Contact:** Recruiting. **World Wide Web address:** http://www.llgm.com. **Description:** A law firm specializing in corporate law, international law, and litigation. The firm primarily serves the insurance and utilities industries.

LOWENSTEIN SANDLER PC
65 Livingston Avenue, Roseland NJ 07068-1791. 973/597-2500. **Fax:** 973/597-2400. **Contact:** Jane E. Thieberger, Director of Legal Personnel. **E-mail address:** counsel@lowenstein.com. **World Wide Web address:** http://www.lowenstein.com. **Description:** A law firm that represents public and private companies, financial institutions, investors, entrepreneurs, governmental agencies and universities. Issues Management LLC, the firm's lobbying and governmental relations subsidiary, is a lawyer-lobbying firm. **Other area locations:** Somerville NJ. **Other U.S. locations:** New York NY.

SMITH, STRATTON, WISE, HEHER & BRENNAN
2 Research Way, Princeton NJ 08540. 609/924-6000. **Contact:** Karen N. Byrnes, Director of Administrative Services. **E-mail address:** kbyrnes@smithstratton.com. **World Wide Web address:** http://www.sswhb.com. **Description:** A law firm serving businesses, the investment community, and entrepreneurs. Founded in 1948.

WILENTZ, GOLDMAN & SPITZER
90 Woodbridge Center Drive, Suite 900, Woodbridge NJ 07095. 732/636-8000. **Contact:** Kimberly Curtis, Director of Legal Services. **E-mail address:** kcurtis@wilentz.com. **World Wide Web address:** http://www.wilentz.com. **Description:** A law firm specializing in corporate, employment, environmental, and tax law.

New Mexico
HINKLE, HENSLEY, SHANOR & MARTIN
400 Penn Plaza, Suite 700, P.O. Box 10, Roswell NM 88202. 505/622-6510. **Fax:** 505/623-9332. **Contact:** Joel Carson III, Recruiting Partner. **E-mail address:** jcarson@hinklelaw.com. **World Wide Web address:** http://www.hinklelaw.com. **Description:** A law firm specializing in a wide range of areas including oil and gas, and probate law.

SANDERS, BRUIN, COLL & WORLEY
P.O. Box 550, Roswell NM 88202-0550. 505/622-5440. **Fax:** 505/622-5853. **Physical address:** 701 West Country Club Road, Roswell NM 88201. **Contact:** Office Manager. **World Wide Web address:** http://www.sbcw-law.com. **Description:** A law firm offering a wide range of legal specialties including agriculture, bankruptcy, commercial law, criminal law, family law, wills, and workers' compensation. Founded in 1945.

New York
AMERICAN ARBITRATION ASSOCIATION
335 Madison Avenue, 10th Floor, New York NY 10017-4605. 212/716-5800. **Fax:** 212/716-5905. **Contact:** Human Resources. **World Wide Web address:** http://www.adr.org. **Description:** A private, nonprofit organization dedicated to establishing and maintaining fair and impartial procedures of dispute resolution as an effective alternative to the court system. The association helps parties with disputes by encouraging them to settle differences through friendly negotiations, mediation, or arbitration. Founded in 1926. **Other U.S. locations:** Nationwide.

CADWALADER WICKERSHAM & TAFT LLP
One World Financial Center, New York NY 10281. 212/504-6000. **Fax:** 212/504-6666. **Contact:** Human Resources. **E-mail address:** cwtinfo@cwt.com. **World Wide Web address:** http://www.cwt.com. **Description:** A law firm specializing in corporate law, tax, real estate, trusts, and estates. **NOTE:** Lateral Hiring phone: 212/504-5650. **Positions advertised include:** Banking Regulatory Associate; Financial Products Associate; Commercial Mortgage Backed Securities Associate; Residential Mortgage Backed Securities Attorney; Financial Restructuring Attorney; Corporate Healthcare Associate; Healthcare Litigator; General Litigator; Reinsurance Litigator; Real Estate Associate; Tax Associate. **Other U.S. locations:** Washington DC; Charlotte NC. **International locations:** London, England.

CAHILL GORDON & REINDEL
80 Pine Street, 17th Floor, New York NY 10005-1702. 212/701-3000. **Contact:** Joyce Hilly, Hiring Coordinator. **E-mail address:** jhilly@cahill.com. **World Wide Web address:** http://www.cahill.com. **Description:** A corporate law firm also specializing in real estate, trusts, and estates. **Corporate headquarters location:** This location.

CARTER, LEDYARD & MILBURN LLP
2 Wall Street, New York NY 10005. 212/732-3200. **Fax:** 212/732-3232. **Contact:** June Chotoo, Recruitment Manager & Attorney Development. **E-mail address:** recruit@clm.com. **World Wide Web address:** http://www.clm.com. **Description:** A law firm specializing in business, litigation, real estate, tax, and trust and estate law. Founded in 1854. **NOTE:** Recruitment Manager phone: 212/238-8744. **Positions advertised include:** Attorney; Paralegal. **Other U.S. locations:** Washington DC; New York NY. **Number of employees:** 250.

CERTILMAN BALIN ADLER & HYMAN, LLP
90 Merrick Avenue, East Meadow NY 11554. 516/296-7000. **Fax:** 516/296-7111. **Contact:** Laura Gole, Human Resources. **World Wide Web address:** http://www.certilmanbalin.com. **Description:** A law firm with over 100 attorneys practicing in all areas of law. **Positions advertised include:** Litigation Secretary; Foreclosure Attorney; Legal Secretary. **Corporate headquarters location:** This location. **Other locations:** Hauppauge NY.

CLEARY GOTTLIEB STEEN & HAMILTON
One Liberty Plaza, New York NY 10006. 212/225-2000. **Fax:** 212/225-3999. **Contact:** Nancy Roberts, Director of Administration & Personnel. **E-mail address:** nyrecruit@cgsh.com. **World Wide Web address:** http://www.cgsh.com. **Description:** One of the nation's largest law firms, focusing on a variety of different practice areas. **Corporate headquarters location:** This location. **Other U.S. locations:** Nationwide. **International locations:** Worldwide.

COUCH WHITE, LLP
540 Broadway, P.O. Box 22222, Albany NY 12201-2222. 518/426-4600. **Fax:** 518/426-0376. **Contact:** Linda M. Haskell, Hiring Manager. **E-mail address:**

lhaskell@couchwhite.com. **World Wide Web address:** http://www.couchwhite.com. **Description:** A law firm specializing in the areas of electricity and natural gas, health care, public utility regulation, and real estate. **Corporate headquarters location:** This location. **Other locations:** Washington DC.

COUDERT BROTHERS LLP
1114 Avenue of the Americas, New York NY 10036-7794. 212/626-4400. **Fax:** 212/626-4120. **Contact:** Mary Simpson, Director of Legal Personnel. **E-mail address:** simpsonm@coudert.com. **World Wide Web address:** http://www.coudert.com. **Description:** A law firm with 650 lawyers at 30 offices in 18 countries specializing in international business transactions and dispute resolution. **Corporate headquarters location:** This location. **International locations:** Worldwide.

CRAVATH, SWAINE & MOORE
825 Eighth Avenue, New York NY 10019-7475. 212/474-1000. **Fax:** 212/474-3095. **Contact:** Employment Manager. **World Wide Web address:** http://www.cravath.com. **Description:** A corporate law firm specializing in litigation, trusts and estates, and taxation. **Positions advertised include:** Attorney; Legal Assistant; Legal Secretary. **Corporate headquarters location:** This location. **Other locations:** London, United Kingdom. **Number of employees at this location:** 1,200.

DOAR, INC.
170 Earle Avenue, Lynbrook NY 11563. 516/823-4000. **Fax:** 516/823-4400. **Contact:** Human Resources. **E-mail address:** careers@doar.com. **World Wide Web address:** http://www.doar.com. **Description:** Provides litigation consulting services including document management, electronic discovery, jury consulting, trial graphics, and trial presentations. Founded in 1988. **Positions advertised include:** Electronic Data Discovery Data Analyst; Electronic Data Discovery Production Supervisor; Electronic Data Discovery Technical Supervisor; Java Developer; Repository Database Administrator; Software Quality Assurance Engineer; Trial Technologist. **Corporate headquarters location:** This location. **Other U.S. locations:** New York NY; Washington DC.

DAVIS POLK & WARDELL
450 Lexington Avenue, New York NY 10017. 212/450-4000. **Fax:** 212/450-3800. **Contact:** Recruiting Manager. **World Wide Web address:** http://www.dpw.com. **Description:** One of the nation's largest law firms, focusing in a variety of different practice areas. **Special programs:** Summer Internships.

DEBEVOISE & PLIMPTON
919 Third Avenue, New York NY 10022. 212/909-6000. **Fax:** 212/909-6836. **Contact:** Sandra Herbst, Director of Legal Recruitment. **E-mail address:** recruit@debevoise.com. **World Wide Web address:** http://www.debevoise.com. **Description:** An international law partnership specializing in corporate litigation, tax, trust, estates, and real estate law with over 500 lawyers in two U.S. offices and five overseas offices. Founded in 1931. **Corporate headquarters location:** This location. **Other locations:** Washington DC; London, United Kingdom; Paris, France; Frankfurt, Germany; Moscow, Russia; Hong Kong, China; Shanghai, China. **Presiding Partner:** Martin (Rick) F. Evans. **Annual sales/revenues:** $326 million.

DEWEY BALLANTINE LLP
1301 Avenue of the Americas, New York NY 10019. 212/259-8000. **Fax:** 212/259-6333. **Contact:** Recruiting Manager. **E-mail address:** nyrecruitment@deweyballantine.com. **World Wide Web address:** http://www.deweyballantine.com. **Description:** An international law partnership with a range of law specialties including corporate, estates groups, litigation, real estate, tax, and trust with 500 lawyers in a dozen offices worldwide. **Positions advertised include:** Attorney; Paralegal. **Special programs:** Internships; Summer Jobs. **Corporate headquarters location:** This location. **Other U.S. locations:** Los Angeles CA; Washington DC. **International locations:** Budapest, Hungary; Hong Kong, China; London, United Kingdom; Prague, Czech Republic; Warsaw, Poland. **Annual sales/revenues:** $328 million. **Number of employees at this location:** 645. **Number of employees nationwide:** 920. **Number of employees worldwide:** 950.

FRIED, FRANK, HARRIS, SHRIVER & JACOBSON
One New York Plaza, New York NY 10004. 212/859-8000. **Fax:** 212/859-4000. **Contact:** Anwara Khanam, Human Resources Coordinator. **E-mail address:** resumes@friedfrank.com. **World Wide Web address:** http://www.ffhsj.com. **Description:** A law firm specializing in corporate law, litigation, real estate, estates, trusts, and pension. **Positions advertised include:** Attorney; Paralegal. **Corporate headquarters location:** This location. **Other U.S. locations:** Washington DC. **International locations:** London, England.

KAYE SCHOLER LLP
425 Park Avenue, 12th Floor, New York NY 10022-3598. 212/836-8000. **Fax:** 212/836-8689. **Contact:** Human Resources Representative. **E-mail address:** jobs@kayescholer.com. **World Wide Web address:** http://www.kayescholer.com. **Description:** A law partnership engaged in a variety of areas including corporate, finance, real estate, and tax law specializing in anti-trust and white collar crimes from nine offices worldwide. Founded in 1917. **NOTE:** Entry-level positions, part-time jobs, and second and third shifts are offered. **Corporate headquarters location:** This location. **Other U.S. locations:** Los Angeles CA; Washington DC; West Palm Beach FL; Chicago IL. **International locations:** China; Germany; United Kingdom. **Chairman:** David Klingsberg. **Annual sales/revenues:** $272 million. **Number of employees at this location:** 600. **Number of employees nationwide:** 825.

LEBOEUF, LAMB, GREENE & MACRAE LLP
125 West 55th Street, New York NY 10019. 212/424-8000. **Contact:** Jill A. Cameron, Manager of Legal Recruiting. **E-mail address:** jcameron@llgm.com. **World Wide Web address:** http://www.llgm.com. **Description:** One of the nation's largest law firms, focusing in a number of different practice areas. **Corporate headquarters location:** This location. **Special programs:** Summer Associates; Summer Internships.

MILBANK, TWEED, HADLEY & McCLOY LLP
One Chase Manhattan Plaza, 56th Floor, New York NY 10005. 212/530-5000. **Fax:** 212/530-5219. **Contact:** Personnel. **E-mail address:** info@milbank.com. **World Wide Web address:** http://www.milbank.com. **Description:** A law firm specializing in litigation, corporate law, trusts and estates, and tax law. **Corporate headquarters location:** This location. **Other U.S. locations:** Los Angeles CA; Washington DC. **Chairman:** Mel Immergut. **Annual sales/revenues:** $360 million. **Number of employees at this location:** 600.

MORGAN LEWIS & BOCKIUS
101 Park Avenue, New York City NY 10178-0060. 212/309-6000. **Fax:** 212/309-6001. **Contact:** Michele A. Coffey, Hiring Partner. **World Wide Web address:** http://www.morganlewis.com. **Description:** One of the nation's largest law firms, focusing in various practice areas. **Number of employees worldwide:** 1200.

PATTERSON, BELKNAP, WEBB & TYLER LLP
1133 Avenue of the Americas, New York NY 10036. 212/336-2000. **Fax:** 212/336-2222. **Contact:** Donna M. Abramo, Director of Human Resources and Operations. **E-mail address:** dmabramo@pbwt.com. **World Wide Web address:** http://www.pbwt.com. **Description:** A law firm offering services in a variety of practice areas.

PILLSBURY WINTHROP LLP
1540 Broadway, New York NY 10036-4039. 212/858-

1000. **Contact:** Human Resources. **E-mail address:** staff_ny@pillsburywinthrop.com. **World Wide Web address:** http://www.pillsburywinthrop.com. **Description:** An international law firm with a broad-based practice including corporate law, litigation, real estate, and tax law. **Positions advertised include:** Word Processing Operator; Marketing and Practice Support Manager; Paralegal; Help Desk Analyst; Technical Services Specialist; **Corporate headquarters location:** This location. **Other U.S. locations:** CA; CT; VA; DC. **International locations:** Australia; Tokyo; England; Singapore.

PROSKAUER ROSE
1585 Broadway New York NY 10036-8299. 212/969-3000. **Fax:** 212/969-2900. **Contact:** Diane M. Kolnik, Recruiting Manager. **E-mail address:** dkolnik@proskauer.com. **World Wide Web address:** http://www.proskauer.com. **Description:** One of the nation's largest law firms, focusing in a variety of different practice areas. **Special programs:** Summer Associate Program.

SHEARMAN & STERLING LLP
599 Lexington Avenue, New York NY 10022-6069. 212/848-4000. **Fax:** 212/848-7179. **Contact:** Suzanne Ryan, Professional Recruiting Manager. **E-mail address:** sryann@shearman.com. **World Wide Web address:** http://www.shearman.com. **Description:** One of the nation's largest law firms, focusing in a variety of different practice areas. **Corporate headquarters location:** This location.

SIMPSON THATCHER & BARTLETT LLP
425 Lexington Avenue, New York NY 10017-3954. 212/455-2000. **Fax:** 212/455-2502. **Contact:** Dee Pifer, Director Legal Employment. **E-mail address:** dpifer@stblaw.com. **World Wide Web address:** http://www.stblaw.com. **Description:** One of the nation's largest law firms, focusing in a number of different practice areas. **Corporate headquarters location:** This location. **Other U.S. locations:** Palo Alto CA; Los Angeles CA. **International locations:** England; China; Japan.

SKADDEN, ARPS, SLATE, MEAGHER, & FLOM, LLP
Four Times Square, New York NY 10036. 212/735-3000. **Fax:** 212/735-2000. **Contact:** Wallace Schwartz. **World Wide Web address:** http://www.skadden.com. **Description:** One of the nation's largest law firms, focusing in many different areas of practice. **Corporate headquarters location:** This location

SQUIRE SANDERS & DEMPSEY
350 Park Avenue, 15th Floor, New York NY 10022-6022. 212/872-9800. **Fax:** 212/872-9815. **Contact:** Nancy Christopher, Office Manager. **World Wide Web address:** http://www.ssd.com. **Description:** A law firm whose areas of practice include corporate, environmental, and tax law.

WEIL GOTSHAL & MANGES
767 Fifth Avenue, New York NY 10153. 212/310-8000. **Fax:** 212/310-8007. **Contact:** Pat Bowers, Human Resources Director. **World Wide Web address:** http://www.weil.com. **Description:** A law firm specializing in corporate, real estate, and tax law. **Other U.S. locations:** DC; FL; TX. **International locations:** London, England.

WHITE & CASE LLP
1155 Avenue of the Americas, New York NY 10036-2787. 212/819-8200. **Fax:** 212/354-8113. **Contact:** Human Resources Director. **World Wide Web address:** http://www.whitecase.com. **Description:** A general law firm specializing in international law, as well as 30 other practice areas.

WILSON ELSER MOSKOWITZ EDELMAN & DICKER LLP
150 East 42nd Street, New York NY 10017-5639. 212/490-3000. **Fax:** 212/490-3038. **Contact:** Recruiting Manager. **World Wide Web address:** http://www.wemed.com. **Description:** One of the nation's largest law firms, focusing in a number of different practice areas. **Special programs:** Summer Internships.

North Carolina

BROOKS, PIERCE, McLENDON, HUMPHREY & LEONARD, L.L.P.
P.O. Box 26000, Greensboro NC 27420. 336/373-8850. **Physical address:** 2000 Renaissance Plaza, 230 North Elm Street, Greensboro NC 27401. **Fax:** 336/378-1001. **Contact:** Ms. Mary Beth McCausland, Recruiting Coordinator. **E-mail address:** mmccausland@brookspierce.com **World Wide Web address:** http://www.brookspierce.com. **Description:** A corporate law firm. Founded 1897. **NOTE:** For service and administrative positions, contact Ms. Cathy Bennet, Personnel & Facilities Manager, by e-mail: cbennett@brookspierce.com. **Positions advertised include:** Attorney. **Special programs:** Summer Associate Program. **Other area locations:** Raleigh NC. **Other U.S. locations:** Washington D.C. **Number of employees at this location:** 135.

KENNEDY COVINGTON LOBDELL & HICKMAN
Hearst Tower, 47th Floor, 214 North Tryon Street, Charlotte NC 28202. 704/331-7400. **Fax:** 704/331-7598. **Contact:** Sally Brown, Recruiting. **E-mail address:** sebrown@kennedycovington.com. **World Wide Web address:** http://www.kennedycovington.com. **Description:** A law firm that specializes in employee benefits, estate litigation, real estate, taxes, and wills for corporate clients. **Special programs:** Summer Associate Program. **Other area locations:** Raleigh NC; Morrisville NC; Research Triangle Park NC. **Other U.S. locations:** Rock Hill SC; Columbia SC.

PARKER POE ADAMS & BERNSTEIN LLP
Three Wachovia Center, 401 South Tryon Street, Suite 3000, Charlotte NC 28202. 704/372-9000. **Fax:** 704/334-4706. **Contact:** Joann L. Enos, Director of Human Resources (for Staff positions), or John E. Grupp, Recruiting Committee Chairman (for Attorney/Law Student Hiring). **E-mail address:** joannenos@parkerpoe.com, or johngrupp@parkerpoe.com. **World Wide Web address:** http://www.parkerpoe.com. **Description:** A law firm with 140 attorneys that primarily serves corporate clients. **Corporate headquarters location:** This location. **Other area locations:** Raleigh NC. **Other U.S. locations:** Columbia SC; Spartanburg SC; Charleston SC.

PERRY, PERRY & PERRY
518 Plaza Boulevard, P.O. Drawer 1475, Kinston NC 28501. 252/523-5107. **Fax:** 252/523-8858. **Contact:** Office Manager. **Description:** A law firm with five attorneys who specialize in criminal, social security and disability, and real estate law.

WOMBLE CARLYLE SANDRIDGE & RICE, PLLC
P.O. Box 831, Raleigh NC 27602. 919/755-2100. **Physical address:** 150 Fayetteville Street Mall, Suite 2100, Raleigh NC 27601. **Fax:** 919/755-2150. **Contact:** Professional Development and Recruiting. **World Wide Web address:** http://www.wcsr.com. **Description:** One of the largest law firms in the Southeastern and mid-Atlantic U.S. Founded 1876. **NOTE:** For staff positions, contact John Turlington at 919/755-2117. **Special programs:** Summer Associate Program. **Other area locations:** Charlotte NC; Greensboro NC; Research Triangle Park NC; Winston-Salem NC. **Other U.S. locations:** Washington D.C.; Tyson's Corner VA; Atlanta GA.

Ohio

BAKER & HOSTETLER LLP
65 East State Street, Suite 2100, Columbus OH 43215. 614/228-1541. **Fax:** 614/462-2616. **Contact:** Cynthia L. Wesney, Human Resources Manager. **E-mail address:** cwesney@bakerlaw.com. **World Wide Web address:** http://www.bakerlaw.com. **NOTE:**

Candidates for Attorney or Summer Associate positions should contact Jeanie Fulton, Recruiting Coordinator. Phone: 614/462-4703. E-mail address: jfulton@bakerlaw.com. . **Description:** A general practice law firm. Baker & Hostetler specializes in business, employee benefits, employment and labor, intellectual property, litigation, personal planning, and tax law. Founded in 1916. **Other area locations:** Cincinnati OH; Cleveland OH. **Other U.S. locations:** Costa Mesa CA; Los Angeles CA; Denver CO; Washington DC; Orlando FL; New York NY; Houston TX.

BLAUGRUND HERBERT & MARTIN
5455 Rings Road, Suite 500, Dublin OH 43017. 614/764-0681. **Fax:** 614/764-0774. **Contact:** Human Resources. **E-mail address:** bhm@bhmlaw.net. **World Wide Web address:** http://www.bhmlaw.net. **Description:** A general practice law firm representing businesses, corporations, families, government, independent agencies, individuals, and nonprofit organizations. **NOTE:** Contact David Blaugrund regarding Attorney positions. All other inquiries should be directed to Human Resources. **Corporate headquarters location:** This location.

GRAYDON HEAD & RITCHEY
1900 Fifth Third Center, 511 Walnut Street, Suite 1900, Cincinnati OH 45202. 513/621-6464. **Fax:** 513/651-3836. **Contact:** Alexandra Walters, Director of Professional Development. **E-mail address:** awalters@graydon.com. **World Wide Web address:** http://www.graydon.com. **Description:** A corporate law firm. Graydon Head and Ritchey specializes in business and finance, commercial litigation, commercial real estate, computer and high technology, employee benefits, human resources, international issues, and Internet commerce law. Founded in 1871. **NOTE:** People interested in Paralegal, Secretary or Staff Positions should contact Emily Cole at ecole@graydon.com. **Positions advertised include:** Employee Benefits Attorney.

KEATING MUETHING AND KLEKAMP
1400 Provident Tower, One East Fourth Street, Cincinnati OH 45202. 513/579-6400. **Fax:** 513/579-6457. **Contact:** Lori S. Moser, Director of Human Resources. **E-mail address:** lmoser@kmklaw.com. **World Wide Web address:** http://www. kmklaw.com. **Description:** A general practice law firm. Founded in 1954. **NOTE:** Candidates for attorney positions should send resumes to: James M. Jansing, Director of the Hiring Committee. E-mail: jjansing@kmklaw.com. **Positions advertised include:** Bankruptcy Associate; Commercial Finance Associate; Corporate Associate; Employee Benefits Associate; Environmental Associate; Litigation Associate; Legal Secretary; Paralegal; Administrative Assistant; Messenger Clerk.

SQUIRES SANDERS & DEMPSEY LLP
Administration Center, 1500 West Third Street, Suite 450, Cleveland OH 44113. 216/687-3400. **Fax:** 216/687-3401. **Contact:** Jane C. Koehl, Legal Personnel and Professional Development Manager. **World Wide Web address:** http://www.ssd.com. **Description:** A law firm. Squires Sanders & Dempsey specializes in cases pertaining to advocacy, business consulting, capital markets, industry, regulatory, taxation, and technology. Founded in 1890. **Positions advertised include:** Bankruptcy/Corporate Transactions Associate; Labor and Employment Associate; Litigation Associate. **Special Programs:** Summer Associate Programs.

Oregon

ATER WYNNE LLP
222 SW Columbia Street, Suite 1800, Portland OR 97201. 503/226-1191. **Contact:** Randy Johnson for attorney employment matters. **E-mail address:** raj@aterwynne.com. **World Wide Web address:** http://www.aterwynne.com. **Description:** A general practice law firm providing a variety of legal services to regional, national, and international businesses and clients. **NOTE:** Contact Traci Quiroz for staff employment matters, taq@aterwynne.com. **Other area locations:** Seattle WA.

BENNETT, HARTMAN & REYNOLDS
111 SW Fifth Avenue, Suite 1650, Portland OR 97204. 503/227-4600. **Contact:** Human Resources. **Description:** Practices labor, domestic relations, and personal injury law.

BROWNSTEIN, RASK, ARENZ, SWEENY, KERR & GRIM
1200 SW Main, Portland OR 97205-2039. 503/221-1772. **Fax:** 503/221-1074. **Contact:** Human Resources. **World Wide Web address:** http://www.brownrask.com. **Description:** A general practice law firm.

HARRANG LONG GARY RUDNICK P.C.
360 E 10th Avenue, Suite 300, Eugene OR 97401-3248. 541/485-0220. **Toll-free phone:** 800/315-4172. **Fax:** 541/686-6564. **Contact:** Joanne Austin. **World Wide Web address:** http://www.harrang.com. **Description:** A regional law firm that offers experience in a variety of practice areas. **Other area locations:** Portland OR, Salem OR.

KEATING, JONES, STEIN, AND HUGHES, PC
One SW Columbia, Suite 800, Portland OR 97258. 503/222-9955. **Fax:** 503/796-0699. **Contact:** Human Resources. **World Wide Web address:** http://www.keatingjones.com. **Description:** A law firm.

MILLER & NASH
3400 U.S. Bancorp Tower, 111 SW Fifth Avenue, Portland OR 97204-3699. 503/224-5858. **Toll-free phone:** 877-220-5858. **Fax:** 503/224-0155. **Contact:** Katie McCoy, Director of Legal Recruitment. **E-mail address:** katie.mccoy@millernash.com. **World Wide Web address:** http://www.millernash.com. **Description:** A law firm specializing in corporate law.

SCHWABE, WILLIAMSON & WYATT, PC
1211 SW Fifth Avenue, Parkwest Center, Suite 1600-1900, Portland OR 97204. 503/222-9981. **Contact:** Karen Kervin, Director of Legal Recruiting. **E-mail address:** kkervin@schwabe.com. **World Wide Web address:** http://www.schwabe.com. **Description:** A law firm operating through two departments: Transactions and Litigation. The Transactions Department provides a wide range of legal services to area businesses, specializing in general business, corporate tax, energy, environment, natural resources, and real estate. The Litigation Department specializes in admiralty, commercial litigation, intellectual property, product liability, workers' compensation, and insurance. Founded in 1892. **Positions advertised include:** Patent Attorney; Litigation Associate; Business/Corporate Paralegal. **Corporate headquarters location:** This location. **Other U.S. locations:** Seattle WA; Vancouver WA.

STOEL RIVES LLP
900 SW Fifth Avenue, Suite 2600, Portland OR 97204-1268. 503/224-3380. **Fax:** 503/220-2480. **Contact:** Human Resources. **World Wide Web address:** http://www.stoel.com. **Description:** A law firm specializing in corporate law. **NOTE:** Recruiting is done separately for attorneys and staff. **Corporate headquarters:** This location.

Pennsylvania

BARBIERI & ASSOCIATES
1542 McDaniel Drive, West Chester PA 19380. 610/431-4102. **Fax:** 215/546-4848. **Contact:** Pietro Barbieri. **E-mail address:** peterlaw@icdc.com. **Description:** A law firm that offers a range of services in a number of practice areas.

BARLEY SNYDER LLC.
126 East King Street, Lancaster PA 17602-2893. 717/299-5201. **Fax:** 717/291-4660. **Contact:** Mr. David Keller. **E-mail address:** dkeller@barley.com. **World Wide Web address:** http://www.barley.com.

Description: A Pennsylvania law firm that offers a range of civil law services in a number practice areas. **Other area locations:** Berwyn; Chambersburg; Hanover; Harrisburg; Lancaster; Reading; York.

BLANK ROME LLP
One Logan Square, Philadelphia PA 19103-6998. 215/569-5500. **Fax:** 215/569-5555. **Contact:** Marilyn Mason, Personnel Director. **World Wide Web address:** http://www.blankrome.com. **Description:** A law firm, specializing in bankruptcy law.

BUCHANAN INGERSOLL, P.C.
One Oxford Centre, 301 Grant Street, 20th Floor, Pittsburgh PA 15219-1410. 412/562-8800. **Fax:** 412/562-1041. **Contact:** Laurie S. Lenigan, Director of Legal Recruiting. **E-mail address:** info@bipc.com. **World Wide Web address:** http://www.bipc.com. **Description:** A law firm specializing in commercial litigation. Clients include individuals, start-up companies, privately and publicly held institutions, and multinational conglomerates. Founded in 1850. **NOTE:** Contact Stephen M. Ferber, Director of Human Resources, for non-legal staff positions. **Special programs:** Summer Associate Program.

DRINKER BIDDLE AND REATH LLP
One Logan Square, 18th & Cherry Streets, Philadelphia PA 19103-6996. 215/988-2700. **Fax:** 215/988-2757. **Contact:** Personnel Recruiter. **World Wide Web address:** http://www.dbr.com. **Description:** A full service law firm founded in 1849.

DUANE, MORRIS & HECKSCHER LLP
30 South 17th Street, Philadelphia PA 19103-4196. 215/979-1000. **Fax:** 215/979-1020. **Contact:** Patricia Stacey, Director, Legal Hiring. **E-mail address:** recruiting@duanemorris.com. **World Wide Web address:** http://www.duanemorris.com. **Description:** A law firm practicing in over 50 disciplines including administrative and regulatory law, employment, energy, medical malpractice, real estate, and taxation. Founded in 1904. **Positions advertised include:** Attorney; Paralegal. **Special programs include:** Summer Program. **Operations at this facility include:** Service.

JONES DAY REAVIS & POGUE
One Mellon Center, 31st Floor, 500 Grant Street, Pittsburgh PA 15219. 412/391-3939. **Fax:** 412/394-7959. **Contact:** Human Resources. **World Wide Web address:** http://www.jonesday.com. **Description:** Jones Day Reavis & Pogue is an international law firm with specialists in all areas. **Corporate headquarters location:** Cleveland OH. **International locations:** China; France; Germany; India; Japan; Switzerland. **Operations at this facility include:** This location specializes in almost all types of law except personal injury and divorce.

KNOX McLAUGHLIN GORNALL & SENNETT
120 West 10th Street, Erie PA 16501-1461. 814/459-2800. **Fax:** 814/453-4530. **Contact:** Human Resources. **World Wide Web address:** http://www.kmgslaw.com. **Description:** A law firm specializing in business and corporate law. **NOTE:** Attorneys and Summer clerks are recruited by Mark Wassell, mwassell@kmgslaw.com.

KREISHER & GREGOROWICZ
401 Market Street, Bloomsburg PA 17815. 570/784-5211. **Fax:** 570/387-1477. **Contact:** Human Resources. **E-mail address:** info@columbiacountylaw.com. **World Wide Web address:** http://www.columbiacountylaw.com. **Description:** A small, local law firm that provides services in a wide range of practice areas.

LAW OFFICES OF HERBERT S. WOLFSON
Lewis Tower, Suite 701, 225 South Fifteenth Street, Philadelphia PA 19102. 215/545-5428. **Fax:** 215/545-5429. **Contact:** Recruiting. **Description:** A law firm offering a wide range of services to clients doing business in the Middle East. The firm is operated in association with a network of lawyers in a variety of other Middle Eastern countries. **International locations:** Dubai.

LAW OFFICE OF T.M. PEELER
350 South River Road, Suite D4, New Hope PA 18938. 215/575-1108. **Fax:** 215/862-1274. **Contact:** Ms. Theresa Parker. **E-mail address:** tmpjd@home.com. **Description:** A law firm that provides service in a range of practice areas.

MICHAEL BEST & FRIEDRICH LLP (LEHIGH VALLEY OFFICE)
Stabler Corporate Center, 3773 Corporate Parkway, Suite 360, Center Valley PA 18034. 610/798-2170. **Fax:** 610/798-2180. **Contact:** Human Resources. **E-mail address:** info@mbf-law.com. **World Wide Web address:** http://www.mbf-law.com. **Description:** A broad based business law firm with clients ranging from small businesses to Fortune 500 companies. **NOTE:** Attorneys are also licensed to practice in most other states. **Other U.S. locations:** WI; PA; IL. **Number of employees worldwide:** 346.

PEPPER HAMILTON LLP
3000 Two Logan Square, 18th & Arch Streets, Philadelphia PA 19103-2799. 215/981-4000. **Fax:** 215/981-4750. **Contact:** Ms. Meg Urbanski, Director of Recruitment. **E-mail address:** urbanskim@pepperlaw.com. **World Wide Web address:** http://www.pepperlaw.com. **Description:** An international law firm. **NOTE:** Part-time jobs are offered. **Positions advertised include:** Health Affects Litigation Associate; Insurance/Reinsurance Associate; Commercial Litigation Associate. **Corporate headquarters location:** This location. **Operations at this facility include:** Administration. **Number of employees at this location:** 560. **Number of employees nationwide:** 910.

PIPER RUDNICK LLP
One liberty Place, 1650 Market Street, Suite 4900, Philadelphia PA 19103. 215/656-3300. **Fax:** 215/656-3301. **Contact:** James M. Brogan., Managing Partner. **World Wide Web address:** http://www.piperrudnick.com. **Description:** A business law firm, focusing on litigation, real estate, business & technology, government affairs, and international law. Founded 1999. **Corporate headquarters:** Baltimore MD. **Other U.S. locations:** MD; MA; IL; TX; NV; CA; NY; FL; WA. **Number of employees nationwide:** 975

REED SMITH SHAW & McCLAY LLP
2500 One Liberty Place, 1650 Market Street, Philadelphia PA 19103. 215/851-8100. **Fax:** 215/851-1420. **Contact:** Denise Papanier, Human Resources Manager. **World Wide Web address:** http://www.rssm.com. **Description:** A business-oriented law firm specializing in financial and corporate law. **Positions advertised include:** Litigation Associate; Trust and Estates Associate; Intellectual Property Legal Secretary; Library Technical Services Assistant; Litigation Clerk; Litigation Support Analyst; Litigation Support Manager; Serials Assistant. **Other U.S. locations:** Washington DC; Princeton NJ; Harrisburg PA; Pittsburgh PA; McLean VA.

SCHNADER HARRISON SEGAL & LEWIS LLP
1600 Market Street, Suite 3600, Philadelphia PA 19103-7286. 215/751-2000. **Fax:** 215/751-2205. **Contact:** Colleen France, Manager of Legal Recruitment. **E-mail address:** legalopportunities@schnader.com. **World Wide Web address:** http://www.schnader.com. **Description:** A law firm.

WILLIG WILLIAMS & DAVIDSON
1845 Walnut Street, 24th Floor, Philadelphia PA 19103-4708. 215/656-3600. **Fax:** 215/561-5135. **Contact:** Personnel. **World Wide Web address:** http://www.willigwilliamsdavidson.com. **Description:** A law firm. **Other area locations:** Harrisburg PA; Jenkintown PA.

WOLF BLOCK SCHORR AND SOLIS-COHEN
One West Main Street, Suite 500, Norristown PA 19401. 610/272-5555. **Fax:** 610/272-6976. **Contact:** Ms. Lynne Gold-Bikin. **E-mail address:** lgoldbikin@wolfblock.com. **World Wide Web address:** http://www.wolfblock.com. **Description:** A regional law firm offering a variety of services in business transactions, legal matters and litigation in the Mid-Atlantic area. **Other U.S. locations:** PA; NY; NJ; DE; Washington D.C. **Number of employees nationwide:** 300.

Rhode Island
HOLLAND & KNIGHT
One Financial Plaza, Suite 1800, Providence RI 02903. 401/751-8500. **Fax:** 401/553-6850. **Contact:** Bronagh Fay. **E-mail address:** bronagh.fay@hklaw.com. **World Wide Web address:** http://www.hklaw.com. **Description:** A law firm with a broad variety of specialties. The Providence office's main practice areas include environmental law, litigation, bankruptcy, trust and estates, government relations, real estate, corporate and labor/employment. The client base is diverse and includes many Fortune 500 companies. **NOTE:** See website for current positions and application instructions. **Special programs:** Summer opportunities for law students. **Other U.S. locations:** Nationwide.

South Carolina
HAYNSWORTH SINKLER BOYD, P.A.
P.O. Box 2048, Greenville SC 29602. 864/240-3200. **Fax:** 864/240-3300. **Physical address:** 75 Beattie Place, Two Liberty Square, 11th Floor, Greenville SC 29601. **Contact:** Ms. Gantt-Sorenson. **E-mail address:** csorenson@hsblawfirm.com. **World Wide Web address:** http://www.hsblawfirm.com **Description:** A law firm with approximately 50 attorneys that specializes in different areas of the law including bond, corporate, insurance, and real estate. **Special programs:** Summer Associate Program.

LEATHERWOOD WALKER TODD & MANN P.C.
P.O. Box 87, Greenville SC 29602. 864/242-6440. **Physical address:** The Leatherwood Plaza, 300 East McBee Avenue, Suite 500, Greenville SC 29601. **Contact:** Gayle McCall, Recruiting Coordinator. **E-mail address:** gmccall@lwtm.com. **World Wide Web address:** http://www.lwtmlaw.com. **Description:** A law firm with over 50 lawyers that has a variety of specialties including tax and bankruptcy litigation.

MCANGUS, GOUDELOCK & COURIE
PO Box 12519, Columbia SC 29211. 803/779-2300. **Physical address:** 700 Gervais Street, Suite 300, Columbia SC 29201. **Fax:** 803/748-0526. **Contact:** Steve Bates, Recruiting Committee Chairman. **E-mail address:** sbates@mgclaw.com. **World Wide Web address:** http://www.mgclaw.com. **Description:** A law firm that specializes in the areas of Administrative Law and Governmental Relations, Arson/Fraud, Captive Insurance, Commercial Litigation and Bankruptcy, Employment Law, Estate Planning, Probate, and Business Law Practice, General Liability, and Workers' Compensation. **Positions advertised Include:** Human Resources Manager; Associates; Summer Associates. **Other area Locations:** Charleston SC; Greenville SC.

McNAIR LAW FIRM
P.O. Box 11390, Columbia SC 29211. 803/799-9800. **Physical address:** Bank of America Tower, 1301 Gervais Street, Columbia SC 29201. **Fax:** 803/799-9804. **Contact:** Bonnie Nelson, Recruiting Coordinator. **E-mail address:** bnelson@mcnair.net. **World Wide Web address:** http://www.mcnair.net. **Description:** A law firm with approximately 55 attorneys who have broad ranges of specializations in the fields of corporate and civil law. Founded in 1971. **Positions advertised include:** Associate Lawyer; Law Clerk; Summer Associate. **Special programs:** Summer Associate program. **Corporate headquarters location:** This location. **Other locations:** Anderson SC; Charleston SC; Charlotte NC; Georgetown SC; Greenville SC; Hilton Head Island SC; Myrtle Beach SC; Raleigh NC.

NEXSEN PRUET ADAMS KLEEMEIER
P.O. Drawer 2426, Columbia SC 29202-2426. 803/771-8900. **Physical address:** 1441 Main Street, Suite 1500, Columbia SC 29201. **Fax:** 803/253-8277. **Contact:** Human Resources Director. **World Wide Web address:** http://www.nexsenpruet.com. **Description:** A law firm with a wide variety of specialties including real estate, corporate law, banking and finance, securities, tax and estate planning, health care, employee benefits, construction, labor and employment, environmental law, communications, patents and intellectual property, international, regulatory, administrative and legislative law. **Positions advertised include:** Attorney; Litigation Software Support Specialist; File Clerk; Paralegal; Litigation Paralegal; Legal Secretary; Records Clerk. **Corporate headquarters location:** This location. **Other locations:** Charleston SC; Greenville SC; Hilton Head SC; Myrtle Beach SC; Charlotte NC.

STEINBERG LAW FIRM
61 Broad Street, P.O. Box 9, Charleston SC 29402. 843/720-2800. **Fax:** 843/722-1190. **Contact:** Human Resources Director. **E-mail address:** dhardy@steinberglawfirm.com. **World Wide Web address:** http://www.steinberglawfirm.com. **Description:** A law firm specializing in job-related injuries. **Positions advertised include:** Runners.

TURNER PADGET GRAHAM & LANEY
P.O. Box 1473, Columbia SC 29202. 803/227-4211. **Physical address:** Bank of America Plaza, 17th Floor, 1901 Main Street, Columbia SC 29201. **Fax:** 803/799-3957. **Contact:** Mimi Love, Human Resources Manager. **E-mail address:** mwl@tpgl.com. **World Wide Web address:** http://www.tpgl.com. **Description:** A law firm specializing in a variety of legal areas including corporate, insurance defense, medical malpractice, and tax. **NOTE:** For summer internships contact Drew Williams, Recruitment Committee Chairman, by e-mail: daw@tpgl.com. **Positions advertised include:** Attorney; Law Clerk; Paralegal; Secretary; Administrative Assistant. **Corporate headquarters location:** This location. **Other locations:** Charleston SC; Florence SC.

Tennessee
BAKER, DONELSON, BEARMAN AND CALDWELL
211 Commerce Street, Suite 1000, Nashville TN 37201. 615/726-5600. **Fax:** 615/774-5563. **Contact:** Human Resources. **World Wide Web address:** http://www.bdbc.com. **Description:** A corporate law firm representing local, national, and international clients in a number of industries including aerospace, banking, construction, defense, energy, engineering, insurance, pharmaceuticals, restaurant chains, securities, technology, and telecommunications. **Other area locations:** Memphis TN; Knoxville TN; Chattanooga TN; Johnson City TN. **Other U.S. locations:** Jackson MS; Washington DC; Atlanta GA; Birmingham AL; New Orleans; LA.

BOULT, CUMMINGS, CONNERS & BERRY
1600 Division Street, Suite 700, Nashville TN 37203-1744. 615/244-2582. **Fax:** 615/252-3035. **Contact:** Ms. Tara Boosey, Recruiting Manager. **E-mail address:** tboosey@boultcummings.com. **World Wide Web address:** http://www.bccb.com. **Description:** A law firm specializing in real estate, commercial finance, taxation, litigation, corporate, and health care law.

GIBSON, GREGORY AND GWYN
201 Fourth Avenue North, Suite 1900, Nashville TN 37219. 615/242-7700. **Contact:** Office Manager. **Description:** A law firm specializing in general law, excluding divorce and criminal defense.

MILLER & MARTIN
Volunteer Building, Suite 1000, 832 Georgia Avenue, Chattanooga TN 37402-2289. 423/756-6600. **Fax:**

423/785-8480. **Contact:** Allison Lee, Recruiting Director for Tennessee. **E-mail address:** alee@millermartin.com. **World Wide Web address:** http://www.millermartin.com. **Description:** A full-service law firm specializing in bankruptcy, corporate securities, environmental law, estate planning, e-commerce and technology, financial institutions, immigration, international law, labor and employment, litigation, and mergers and acquisitions. Founded in 1867. **Other area locations:** Nashville TN. **Other U.S. locations:** Atlanta GA.

ORTALE, KELLEY, HERBERT AND CRAWFORD
P.O. Box 198985, Nashville TN 37219-8985. 615/256-9999. **Physical address:** Noel Place, 200 Fourth Avenue North, 3rd Floor, Nashville TN 37219. **Fax:** 615/726-1494. **Contact:** Office Manager. **World Wide Web address:** http://www.ortalekelley.com. **Description:** A full-service law firm specializing in bankruptcy, civil rights, corporate law, domestic law, estate planning, litigation, real estate, and taxation. Founded in 1971. **Other area locations:** Franklin TN.

WALLER LANSDEN DORTCH & DAVIS
P.O. Box 198966, Nashville TN 37219-8966. 615/244-6380. **Physical address:** 511 Union Street, Suite 2700, Nashville TN 37219. **Fax:** 615/244-6804. **Contact:** Melissa McKinney, Director of Professional Recruiting and Practice Support Services. **E-mail address:** mmckinney@wallerlaw.com. **World Wide Web address:** http://www.wallerlaw.com. **Description:** A general practice law firm covering a variety of disciplines including bankruptcy, real estate, and tax law. **Positions advertised include:** Corporate Attorney; Healthcare Attorney. **Other area locations:** Columbia TN; Brentwood TN. **Other U.S. locations:** Los Angeles CA.

Texas

ACKELS & ACKELS LLP
2777 North Stemmons Freeway, Suite 879, Dallas TX 75207. 214/267-8600. **Fax:** 214/267-8605. **Contact:** Office Manager. **Description:** A law firm that specializes in civil, criminal, and commercial litigation, and also practices personal injury, juvenile, and entertainment law.

ANDREWS & KURTH L.L.P.
600 Travis Street, Suite 4200, Houston TX 77002. 713/220-4200. **Fax:** 713/220-4285. **Contact:** Deborah Ganjavi, Human Resources Director. **E-mail address:** debbieganjavi@akllp.com. **World Wide Web address:** http://www.andrews-kurth.com. **Description:** A law firm. **NOTE:** Please visit website to search for jobs by category and apply online. Contact Human Resources at this location at 713/220-4174. **Positions advertised include:** Litigation Legal Secretary. **Special programs:** Summer Clerkship Programs. **Corporate headquarters location:** This location. **Other area locations:** Austin TX; Dallas TX; The Woodlands TX. **Other U.S. locations:** Los Angeles CA; Washington DC; New York NY. **International locations:** London England. **Operations at this facility include:** Administration.

ARMBRUST & BROWN L.L.P.
100 Congress Avenue, Suite 1300, Austin TX 78701-2744. 512/435-2300. **Fax:** 512/435-2360. **Contact:** Human Resources Department. **World Wide Web address:** http://www.abaustin.com. **Description:** A law firm specializing in real estate and product liability law.

JOHN ATWOOD LAW OFFICE
3500 Oak Lawn Avenue Suite 400, Dallas TX 75219. 214/523-9520. **Contact:** Personnel Department. **Description:** A law firm that specializes in corporate, real estate, administrative, and taxation law.

BAKER BOTTS LLP
One Shell Plaza, 910 Louisiana Street, Houston TX 77002. 713/229-1234. **Fax:** 713/229-1522. **Contact:** Recruiting. **World Wide Web address:** http://www.bakerbotts.com. **Description:** A law firm providing services in almost all areas of civil law. Baker Botts, LLP is one of the nation's oldest and largest law firms. **NOTE:** Please visit website for more specific contact information for individual areas of interest and locations. **Positions advertised include:** Real Estate Associate; Legal Assistant. **Special programs:** Summer Associate Program. **Corporate headquarters location:** This location. **Other area locations:** Austin TX; Dallas TX. **Other U.S. locations:** Washington DC; New York NY. **International locations:** Azerbaijan; England; Russia; Saudi Arabia. **Operations at this facility include:** Service.

BARON & BUDD, P.C.
3102 Oak Lawn Avenue, Suite 1100, Dallas TX 75219-4281. 214/521-3605. **Toll-free phone:** 800/946-9646. **Fax:** 888/822-2766. **E-mail address:** work@baronbudd.com. **Contact:** Recruiting. **World Wide Web address:** http://www.baronbudd.com. **Description:** A plaintiffs' law firm specializing in environmental and toxic tort litigation. Founded 1977. NOTE: Please visit website to specific contact details. **Special programs:** Summer Associate Program. **Corporate headquarters location:** This location. **Other U.S. locations:** Glen Carbon IL; Cleveland OH; Baton Rouge LA; Canton NY.

BICKEL & BREWER
4800 Bank One Center, 1717 Main Street, Dallas TX 75201. 214/653-4000. **Fax:** 214/653-1015. **Contact:** Human Resources. **E-mail address:** counsel@bickelbrewer.com. **World Wide Web address:** http://www.bickelbrewer.com. **Description:** A law firm specializing in corporate litigation including bankruptcy. **Other U.S. locations:** New York NY.

BRACEWELL AND PATTERSON LLP
711 Louisiana Street, Suite 2900, Houston TX 77002-2781. 713/223-2900. **Fax:** 713/221-1212. **Contact:** Jean Lenzner, Director of Attorney Employment. **E-mail address:** jlenzner@bracepatt.com. **World Wide Web address:** http://www.bracepatt.com. **Description:** A law firm divided into a litigation group and a business group. The litigation group specialties include trial, bankruptcy, and appellate law. The business group specialties include corporate, energy, and real estate law. **Other area locations:** Austin TX; Dallas TX; Corpus Christi TX; Fort Worth TX. **Other U.S. locations:** Reston VA; Washington D.C. **International locations:** Kazakhstan; London England.

CANTEY & HANGER, LLP
801 Cherry Street, Suite 2100, Burnett Plaza, Fort Worth TX 76102-6881. 817/877-2800. **Fax:** 817/877-2807. **Contact:** Personnel. **World Wide Web address:** http://www.canteyhanger.com. **Description:** A law firm specializing in corporate law. Founded 1882. **NOTE:** Please visit website under "Recruitment" for more information on employment. **Special programs:** Summer Associate Program. **Other area locations:** Dallas TX; Austin TX. **Other U.S. locations:** Washington D.C.

DAVIS MUNCK
13155 Noel Road, Suite 900, Dallas TX 75240. 972/628-3600. Fax: 972/628-3616. **Email address:** hr@davismunck.com. **Contact:** Recruiting. **World Wide Web address:** http://www.davismunck.com. **Description:** A law firm specializing in corporate, IPO, estate, and real estate law.

FULBRIGHT AND JAWORSKI LLP
1301 McKinney Street, Suite 5100, Houston TX 77010-3095. 713/651-5151. **Contact:** Human Resources. **World Wide Web address:** http://www.fulbright.com. **Description:** An international legal firm specializing in all areas of law. **Positions advertised include:** Project Manager; Legal Assistant; Project Assistant; Contract Technical Writer. **Special programs:** Internships. **Corporate headquarters location:** This location. **Other area locations:** Austin TX; San Antonio TX. **Other U.S. locations:** Los Angeles CA; Minneapolis MN; New York NY; Washington DC. Nationwide.

International locations: United Kingdom; Germany. **Operations at this facility include:** Administration.

HOWREY, SIMON, ARNOLD & WHITE
1111 Louisiana Boulevard, 25th Floor, Houston TX 77002. 713/787-1400. **Contact:** Human Resources. **World Wide Web address:** http://www.howrey.com. **Description:** A law firm specializing in antitrust matters. **NOTE:** Jobseekers interested in applying for open attorney positions should refer to the company's website for contact names. **Positions advertised include:** Legal; Consultant; Staff. **Other U.S. locations:** Nationwide. **International locations:** Worldwide.

JACKSON WALKER L.L.P.
1401 McKinney Street, Suite 1900, Houston TX 77010. 713/752-4347. **Fax:** 713/752-4435. **Contact:** Bette Avante, Administrator. **E-mail address:** bavante@iw.com. **World Wide Web address:** http://www.jw.com. **Description:** A full-service law firm with a worldwide client base. Jackson Walker specializes in corporate, trust, and estate law. **Special programs:** Internships. **Other area locations:** Dallas TX; Fort Worth TX; Richardson TX; San Antonio TX. **Corporate headquarters location:** Dallas TX.

NATHAN, SOMMERS, LIPPMAN, JACOBS & GORMAN
2800 Post Oak Boulevard, 61st Floor, Houston TX 77056. 713/960-0303. **Contact:** Kristie Ratliff, Financial Administrator. **Description:** A corporate law firm specializing in bankruptcy law, litigation, and real estate law. **Special programs:** Internships. **Corporate headquarters location:** This location.

SUSMAN GODFREY L.L.P.
1000 Louisiana Street, Suite 5100, Houston TX 77002-5096. 713/651-9366. **Contact:** Human Resources. **World Wide Web address:** http://www.susmangodfrey.com. **Description:** A law firm specializing in antitrust, energy and natural resources, libel, negligence, litigation, intellectual property, and product liability law. **Special programs:** Internships. **Other area locations:** Dallas TX. **Other U.S. locations:** CA; WA.

THOMPSON & KNIGHT LLP
1700 Pacific Avenue, Suite 3300, Dallas TX 75201. 214/969-1700. **Contact:** Human Resources. **World Wide Web address:** http://www.tklaw.com. **Description:** A law firm specializing in a wide variety of law disciplines including bankruptcy, corporate, intellectual property, real estate, and environmental. **NOTE:** This law firm has recruiters for each of its location. See its website for contact names and information. **Special programs:** Internships. **Other area locations:** Austin TX; Houston TX; San Antonio TX. **Other U.S. locations:** Monterrey CA. **International locations:** Algiers; Paris; Rio de Janeiro.

U.S. LEGAL SUPPORT, INC.
519 North Sam Houston Parkway East, Houston TX 77060. 713/653-7100. **Toll-free phone:** 800/567-8757. **Fax:** 713/653-7171. **Contact:** Human Resources. **World Wide Web address:** http://www.uslegalsupport.com. **Description:** Provides support services in the areas of certified depositions, trial reporters, specialized video services, records retrieval, and other legal services. **NOTE:** This agency offers temporary and permanent positions within the legal field. **Corporate headquarters location:** This location. **Other area locations:** Dallas TX; Austin TX; San Antonio TX; Corpus Christi TX.

WINSTEAD SECHREST & MINICK P.C.
5400 Renaissance Tower, 1201 Elm Street, Dallas TX 75270. 214/745-5400. **Contact:** Patty Stewart, Recruiting. **World Wide Web address:** http://www.winstead.com. **Description:** A law firm offering services in a variety of practice areas including environmental, insurance, real estate, and tax. **NOTE:** This company offers attorney, staff, and student positions. See website for job listings and contact and application information. **Other area locations:** Austin TX; Fort Worth TX; Houston TX; San Antonio TX; The Woodlands TX. **Other U.S. locations:** Washington D.C. **International locations:** Mexico City. **Number of employees worldwide:** 700.

OFFICES OF NORMAN A. ZABLE, P.C.
5757 Alpha Road, Suite 504, Dallas TX 75240. 972/386-6900. **Contact:** Human Resources Department. **Description:** A civil law practice specializing in business and bankruptcy law.

Utah

CALLISTER, NEBEKER & MCCULLOUGH
Gateway Tower East, Suite 900, Salt Lake City UT 84133. 801/530-7300. **Fax:** 801/364-9127. **Contact:** Michael C. Walch. **World Wide Web address:** http://www.cnmlaw.com. **Description:** A law firm with a wide range of practice areas excluding criminal law. **NOTE:** Please visit website to fill out recruiting form.

HOLME, ROBERTS & OWEN
299 South Main Street, Suite 1800, Salt Lake City UT 84111-2263. 801/521-5800. **Fax:** 801/521-9639. **Contact:** Human Resources. **World Wide Web address:** http://www.hro.com. **Description:** A law firm specializing in corporate and tax law. **NOTE:** Please visit website for current job openings and to apply online. **Positions advertised include:** Corporate Associate; Legal Opportunities; Staff Opportunities. **Corporate headquarters location:** Denver CO.

JONES, WALDO, HOLBROOK & McDONOUGH
170 South Main Street, Suite 1500, Salt Lake City UT 84101-1644. 801/521-3200. **Fax:** 801/328-0537. **Contact:** Kyle V. Leishman, Recruitment Committee Coordinator. **E-mail address:** kleishman@joneswaldo.com. **World Wide Web address:** http://www.joneswaldo.com. **Description:** A law firm specializing in corporate law, litigation, and real estate law. **NOTE:** Please visit website for information on who to contact for more specific employment information. **Corporate headquarters location:** This location. **Other area locations:** Park City UT; St. George UT.

PARSONS, BEHLE & LATIMER
201 South Main Street, Suite 1800, Salt Lake City UT 84111. 801/532-1234. **Fax:** 801/536-6111. **Contact:** Darcie Koski, Human Resources Director. **E-mail address:** dkoski@pblutah.com. **World Wide Web address:** http://www.pblutah.com. **Description:** A law firm with a wide variety of specialties including corporate, environmental, litigation, and tax law. **Special programs:** Internships; Summer Associate Training. **Other area locations:** Lindon UT. **Other U.S. locations:** NV.

Vermont

LEGUS & BISSON PLLC
107 State Street, Montpelier VT 05601. 802/223-1771. **Fax:** 802/223-9922. **Contact:** Human Resources. **Description:** A civil litigation law firm. **NOTE:** Open positions are listed in the *Burlington Free Press*. **Positions advertised include:** Attorney.

MURPHY SULLIVAN KRONK
275 College Street, P.O. Box 4485, Burlington VT 054606-4485. 802/861-7000. **Fax:** 802/861-7007. **Contact:** Debroah J. Sabourin. **E-mail address:** dsabourin@mskvt.com. **World Wide Web address:** http://www.mskvt.com. **Description:** A law firm specializing in transactions, permitting and litigation in real estate, land development, and commercial law. **Positions advertised include:** Legal Assistant.

Virginia

HUNTON & WILLIAMS
1751 Pinnacle Drive, Suite 1700, McLean VA 22102. 703/714-7400. **Fax:** 703/714-7410. **Contact:** Trish McClendon, Human Resources. **E-mail address:** pmcclendon@hunton.com. **World Wide Web address:** http://www.hunton.com. **Description:** A law firm specializing in a wide variety of areas including

constitutional, corporate, patent, and real estate law. Founded in 1901. Maintains 17 offices with 850 attorneys. **Corporate headquarters location:** Richmond VA.

OLIFF & BERRIDGE, PLC
277 South Washington Street, Suite 500, Alexandria VA 22314. 703/836-6400. **Fax:** 703/836-2787. **Contact:** Human Resources. **E-mail address:** hr@oliff.com. **World Wide Web address:** http://www.oliff.com. **Description:** An intellectual property law firm. Founded in 1983. **Positions advertised include:** Floater Patent Secretary; Paralegal. **Corporate headquarters location:** This location. **Other U.S. locations:** St. Louis MO.

Washington

AIKEN, ST. LOUIS & SILJEG, P.S.
801 Second Avenue, Suite 1200, Seattle WA 98104. 206/624-2650. **Contact:** Personnel. **World Wide Web address:** http://www.aiken.com. **Description:** A law firm specializing in corporate, tax, insurance, and environmental law. **Corporate headquarters location:** This location.

FOSTER PEPPER & SHEFELMAN PLLC
1111 Third Avenue, Suite 3400, Seattle WA 98101. 206/447-7296. **Contact:** Meg Clara, Director of Human Resources. **E-mail address:** claram@foster.com. **World Wide Web address:** http://www.foster.com. **Description:** A law firm specializing in corporate and environmental law. Founded in 1904. **Other area locations:** Bellevue WA; Spokane WA. **Other U.S. locations:** Anchorage AK; Portland OR. **Number of employees at this location:** 350.

SCHWABE, WILLIAMSON & WYATT, P.C.
1420 Fifth Avenue, Suite 3010, Seattle WA 98101-2339. 206/622-1711. **Contact:** Recruitment. **World Wide Web address:** http://www.schwabe.com. **Description:** A law firm operating through two departments: Transactions and Litigation. The Transactions Department provides a wide range of legal services to area businesses, specializing in general business, corporate tax, energy, environment, natural resources, and real estate. The Litigation Department specializes in admiralty, commercial litigation, intellectual property, product liability, workers' compensation, and insurance. Founded in 1892. **Corporate headquarters location:** Portland OR. **Other area locations:** Vancouver WA.

STANISLAW ASHBAUGH, LLP
4400 Bank of America Tower, 701 Fifth Avenue, Seattle WA 98104-7012. 206/386-5900. **Fax:** 206/344-7400. **Contact:** Francine Wright, Administrator. **World Wide Web address:** http://www.stanislaw.com. **Description:** A law firm specializing in business, construction, employment, and insurance law. **Number of employees at this location:** 40.

WELLS, ST. JOHN, ROBERTS, GREGORY & MATKIN P.S.
601 West First Avenue, Suite 1300, Spokane WA 99201. 509/624-4276. **Contact:** Recruitment. **World Wide Web address:** http://www.wellsstjohn.com. **Description:** A law firm specializing in copyrights, patents, and trademarks.

West Virginia

BOWLES RICE MCDAVID GRAFF & LOVE, LLP
600 Quarrier Street, Charleston WV 25301. 304/347-1100. **Fax:** 304/343-2867. **Contact:** Elizabeth D. Harter, Recruiting Chairman. **Email address:** bharter@bowlesrice.com. **World Wide Web address:** http://www.bowlesrice.com. **Description:** A full-service, corporate law firm. **Special Programs:** Summer Clerkship Program. **Other area locations:** Fairmont; Martinsburg; Morgantown; Parkersburg. **Other U.S. locations:** Lexington KY; Winchester VA.

Wisconsin

MICHAEL, BEST & FRIEDRICH
100 East Wisconsin Avenue, Suite 3300, Milwaukee WI 53202-4108. 414/271-6560. **Fax:** 414/277-0656. **Contact:** Human Resources Director. **E-mail address:** tamccormack@michaelbest.com. **World Wide Web address:** http://www.mbf-law.com. **Description:** A legal services firm specializing in all types of corporate law. **Positions advertised include:** Business/Corporate Partner; Land and Resources Partner; Tax Partner. **Corporate headquarters location:** This location. **Other area locations:** Manitowoc WI; Waukesha WI; Madison WI. **Other U.S. locations:** Chicago IL; Center Valley PA.

REINHART, BOERNER, VAN DEUREN
1000 North Water Street, Suite 2100, Milwaukee WI 53202. 414/298-1000. **Fax:** 414/298-8097. **Contact:** Human Resources. **World Wide Web address:** http://www.reinhartlaw.com. **Description:** A law firm that specializes in real estate, corporate, banking, and tax law. **Other area locations:** Madison WI; Waukesha WI.

RUDER WARE
500 3rd Street, Suite 700, P.O. Box 8050, Wausau WI 54402-8050. 715/845-4336. **Fax:** 715/845-2718. **Contact:** John J. Kuiken, Human Resources Manager. **E-mail address:** jkuiken@ruderware.com. **World Wide Web address:** http://www.ruder.com. **Description:** A law firm. Primary clients are government and industrial businesses. Founded in 1921. **Corporate headquarters location:** This location. **Other area locations:** Eau Claire WI.

VON BRIESEN & ROPER
P.O. Box 3262, Milwaukee WI 53201-3262. 414/276-1122. **Physical address:** 411 East Wisconsin Avenue, Suite 700, Milwaukee WI 53202. **Toll-free phone:** 800/622-0607. **Fax:** 414/276-6281. **Contact:** Human Resources. **World Wide Web address:** http://www.vonbriesen.com. **Description:** A law firm specializing in corporate, divorce, and environmental law. **Positions advertised include:** Experienced Health Care Associate; Law Clerk; Experienced Estate Planning Attorney; Accounting Manager. **Corporate headquarters location:** This location. **Other area locations:** Madison WI; Racine WI; Kenosha WI; Mequon WI; Brookfield WI.

Wyoming

HOLLAND & HART LLP
2515 Warren Avenue, Suite 450, Cheyenne WY 82001-3162. 307/778-4200. **Fax:** 307/778-8175. **Contact:** Brad Cave, Hiring Partner. **E-mail address:** bcave@hollandhart.com. **World Wide Web address:** http://www.hollandhart.com. **Description:** A full-service law firm. Founded in 1978. The attorneys of the Cheyenne office provide expertise in environmental and natural resources law, general corporate law and litigation of all sorts. They are highly informed about the laws that govern mineral resources, environmental regulation, commercial law, public utilities, construction, labor and employment, taxes, banking, insurance, bankruptcy, real estate, and local securities and municipal bonds. Cheyenne's clients include companies that deal in all phases of coal, oil, gas, water, trona and uranium exploration, development and production. The firm represents mine, milling, processing and refining operations; water development projects; pipeline interests; and a wide range of other banking, commercial, industrial and agricultural enterprises. **NOTE:** Go to http://www.hhjobs.com for information on how to apply. **Special Programs:** Summer Clerkship. **Other U.S. locations:** CO; DC; MT; NM; UT. **Number of employees nationwide:** 300.

REAL ESTATE

You can expect to find the following types of companies in this section:

Land Subdividers and Developers • Real Estate Agents, Managers, and Operators • Real Estate Investment Trusts

Combined real estate and rental and leasing occupations are expected to grow by 18.2%, adding 258,000 jobs by 2014, for a total of 1,675,000 jobs. The bulk of these jobs, 200,000, will come from rental and leasing occupations, representing a 20.7% growth, while real estate brokers and sales agent jobs will grow by just 13%. Growth will be due, in part, to increased demand for housing as the population grows, although increasing use of information technology by agents and customers will tend to limit this growth.

Arizona

BABBITT BROTHERS TRADING COMPANY
P.O. Box 1328, Flagstaff AZ 86002. 928/774-8711. **Physical address:** 1515 East Cedar Road, Flagstaff AZ 86001. **Contact:** Human Resources. **Description:** A holding company involved in a variety of activities including commercial real estate rentals, the operation of hotels and restaurants, and concession services for the Grand Canyon. **Office hours:** Monday - Friday, 8:00 a.m. - 5:00 p.m. **Corporate headquarters location:** This location.

CENTURY 21 ANDERSON GROUP
13771 North Fountain Hills Boulevard, Suite 117, Fountain Hills AZ 85268. 480/837-1331. **Toll-free phone:** 888/678-7901. **Fax:** 480/837-7069. **Contact:** Personnel. **World Wide Web address:** http://www.andersongroup.com. **Description:** A real estate agency. Founded in 1981. **Other area locations:** Lake Havasu City AZ. **Number of employees at this location:** 60.

CUSHMAN & WAKEFIELD OF ARIZONA
2525 East Camelback Road, Suite 1000, Phoenix AZ 85016. 602/253-7900. **Contact:** Human Resources. **World Wide Web address:** http://www.cushmanwakefield.com. **Description:** A commercial and industrial real estate firm, engaged in the management and leasing of commercial office space, appraisals, project development, and related services. **Corporate headquarters location:** New York NY.

EXODYNE PROPERTIES, INC. (EPI)
8433 North Black Canyon Highway, Suite 100, Phoenix AZ 85021. 602/995-0919. Fax: 602/995-8469. **Contact:** HR Director. **E-mail address:** corphr@exodyne.com. **Description:** EPI manages Exodyne's real estate holdings, including commercial office and industrial income-producing properties. EPI provides office and manufacturing facilities for approximately 30 businesses. **Parent company:** Exodyne, Inc.

GOLDEN WEST & ASSOCIATES
4711 East Falcon Drive, Suite 222, Mesa AZ 85215. 480/396-4653. **Contact:** Human Resources. **Description:** A real estate firm. **Corporate headquarters location:** This location.

GRUBB & ELLIS COMMERCIAL REAL ESTATE SERVICES
2375 East Camelback Road, Suite 300, Phoenix AZ 85016. 602/954-9000. **Contact:** Bryon Carney, Sales Manager. **World Wide Web address:** http://www.grubb-ellis.com. **Description:** Office of the commercial and industrial real estate brokerage. Grubb & Ellis also specializes in property management, and institutional and individual investment. **Corporate headquarters location:** Northbrook IL. **Listed on:** New York Stock Exchange. **Stock exchange symbol:** GBE. **Number of employees at this location:** 90.

LEGACY PARTNERS
5333 North Seventh Street, Suite C225, Phoenix AZ 85014. 602/248-0112. **Contact:** Human Resources. **World Wide Web address:** http://www.legacypartners.com. **Description:** A property management and development company. **Positions advertised include:** Business Manager; Service Technician. **Corporate headquarters location:** Foster City CA.

LONG REALTY
900 East River Road, Suite 100, Tucson AZ 85718. 520/888-8844. **Contact:** Tricia Hooper, Manager of Career Development. http://www.longrealty.com **E-mail address:** careers@LognRealty.com. **World Wide Web address:** http://www.longrealty.com. **Description:** A real estate sales and management firm. **Special programs:** Internships. **Corporate headquarters location:** This location. **Number of employees at this location:** 250.

MERITAGE CORPORATION
MONTEREY HOMES
6613 North Scottsdale Road, Suite 200, Scottsdale AZ 85250. 480/998-8700. **Contact:** Human Resources. **World Wide Web address:** http://www.meritagecorp.com. **Description:** Designs, builds, and sells mid-priced single-family homes in Arizona, Northern California, and Texas. **Office hours:** Monday - Friday, 8:00 a.m. - 5:00 p.m. **Corporate headquarters location:** This location. **Other U.S. locations:** San Francisco CA; Plano TX. **Listed on:** New York Stock Exchange. **Stock exchange symbol:** MTH. **Annual sales/revenues:** More than $100 million.

RE/MAX DISCOVER
4234 North Craftsman Court #2, Scottsdale AZ 85251. 480/941-3779. **Fax:** 480/419-5428. **Contact:** Stephen Proski. **World Wide Web address:** http://www.az-homes4u.com. **Description:** A real estate agency.

SUNCOR DEVELOPMENT COMPANY
80 East Rio Salado Parkway, Suite 410, Tempe AZ 85281. 480/317-6800. **Fax:** 480/317-6934. **Contact:** Human Resources. **World Wide Web address:** http://www.suncoraz.com. **Description:** Develops commercial, industrial, and residential properties primarily in Arizona. **Parent company:** Pinnacle West Corporation (Phoenix AZ.) **Listed on:** New York Stock Exchange. **Stock exchange symbol:** PNW.

DEL WEBB CORPORATION
P.O. Box 29040, Phoenix AZ 85038. 602/808-8000. **Physical address:** 6001 North 24th Street, Phoenix AZ 85016. **Recorded jobline:** 602/808-7970. **Contact:** Human Resources. **World Wide Web address:** http://www.delwebb.com. **Description:** A real estate company involved in the planning, development, and construction of active adult communities in the Sun Belt. **Number of employees at this location:** 900.

California

BRE PROPERTIES, INC.
525 Market Street, 4th Floor, San Francisco CA 94105. 415/445-6530. **Fax:** 949/250-5905. **Contact:** Recruiting Department. **E-mail address:** careers@breproperties.com. **World Wide Web address:** http://www.breproperties.com. **Description:** A real estate investment trust. **Positions advertised include:** Development Administrative Assistant; Executive Assistant; Field Systems Support Technician. **Corporate headquarters location:** This location.

Other area locations: Statewide. **Listed on:** New York Stock Exchange. **Stock exchange symbol:** BRE.

BAY MEADOWS COMPANY
P.O. Box 5050, San Mateo CA 94402. 650/573-4540. **Physical address:** 2600 South Delaware Street, San Mateo CA 94403. **Fax:** 650/573-4671. **Contact:** Human Resources. **World Wide Web address:** http://www.baymeadows.com. **Description:** Operates Bay Meadows Race Track on the San Francisco Peninsula, and California Jockey Club, an equity real estate investment trust whose principal asset is Bay Meadows Race Track. **Corporate headquarters location:** This location.

BURNHAM REAL ESTATE SERVICE
4435 East Gate Mall, Suite 200, San Diego CA 92121. 858/452-6500. **Fax:** 858/452-3206. **Contact:** Human Resources Department. **E-mail address:** jobs@burnhamrealestate.com. **World Wide Web address:** http://www.burnhamrealestate.com. **Description:** A real estate investor and syndicate. The firm serves as the general partner or investor in a number of real estate ventures including two public partnerships. **Corporate headquarters location:** This location. **Other area locations:** Carlsbad CA; Newport Beach CA. **Other U.S. locations:** Las Vegas NV.

CB RICHARD ELLIS
100 North Sepulveda Boulevard, Suite 1050, El Segundo CA 90245. 310/524-9413. **Toll-free phone:** 866/225-3099. **Contact:** Human Resources. **E-mail address:** cbrejobs@cbre.com. **World Wide Web address:** http://www.cbre.com. **Description:** A fully integrated commercial real estate services company offering property sales and leasing, property and facility management, mortgage banking, and investment management services. **Positions advertised include:** Coordinator, Senior Information Management; Director, Load Production Officer. **Corporate headquarters location:** This location. **Other U.S. locations:** Nationwide. **International locations:** Worldwide. **Number of employees worldwide:** 13,500.

CASTLE & COOKE, INC.
10000 Stockdale Highway, Suite 300, Bakersfield CA 93311. 661/664-6500. **Contact:** Human Resources. **E-mail address:** human-resources@castlecooke.com. **World Wide Web address:** http://www.castlecooke.com. **Description:** A holding company for firms involved in construction and real estate. Castle & Cooke also owns country clubs, private membership clubs, and a horse farm. **Corporate headquarters location:** This location.

CENTURY 21 AWARD
5640 Baltimore Drive, La Mesa CA 91942. 619/463-5000. **Contact:** Human Resources Representative. **E-mail address:** opportunities@century21award.com. **World Wide Web address:** http://www.century21award.com. **Description:** A real estate agency. **Special programs:** Career seminars held weekly for potential agents. **Other area locations:** Bonita CA; Carlsbad CA; Del Mar CA; El Cajon CA; Escondido CA; Fallbrook CA; San Diego CA.

COLDWELL BANKER RESIDENTIAL BROKERAGE – GREENBRAE
350 Bon Air Center, Suite 100, Greenbrae CA 94904. 415/461-3220. **Toll-free phone:** 800/464-4292. **Fax:** 415/461-5105. **Contact:** Kevin Patsel, Office Manager. **E-mail address:** kevin@coldwellbanker.com. **World Wide Web address:** http://www.californiamoves.com. **Description:** A real estate company specializing in luxury properties and new homes. **Corporate headquarters location:** Parsippany NJ. **Other area locations:** Statewide. **Other U.S. locations:** Nationwide. **Parent company:** Cendant Corporation. **Listed on:** New York Stock Exchange. **Stock exchange symbol:** CD.

CUSHMAN & WAKEFIELD
One Maritime Plaza, Suite 900, San Francisco CA 94111. 415/773-3511. **Contact:** Jill Campbell, Human Resources. **E-mail address:** jill.campbell@cushwake.com. **World Wide Web address:** http://www.cushwake.com. **Description:** An international commercial and industrial real estate services firm. The company is engaged in appraisals, financial services, project development, research services, and the management and leasing of commercial office space. **Positions advertised include:** Financial Accountant; Project Coordinator. **Corporate headquarters location:** New York NY. **Other U.S. locations:** Nationwide. **International locations:** Worldwide.

E&Y KENNETH LEVENTHAL REAL ESTATE GROUP
2049 Century Park East, Suite 1800, Los Angeles CA 90067. 310/277-0880. **Contact:** Human Resources. **World Wide Web address:** http://www.ey.com. **Description:** A full-service real estate agency providing real estate, tax, and audit advice to developers, builders, lenders, owners, and users of real estate. **Positions advertised include:** Assurance Manager; Tax Consulting Manager; Corporate Finance Analyst; Business Risk Services Auditor; Senior Manager, Real Estate Advisory Services. **Parent company:** Ernst & Young.

FOUNTAINGLEN PROPERTIES, LP
320 Commerce, Suite 100, Irvine CA 92602. 714/734-1400. **Fax:** 714/734-1401. **Contact:** Pam Laipple, Human Resources. **E-mail address:** plaipple@fountainglen.com. **World Wide Web address:** http://www.fountainglen.com. **Description:** Designs and constructs active adult living communities. **Corporate headquarters location:** This location.

KB HOME
10990 Wilshire Boulevard, 7th Floor, Los Angeles CA 90024. 310/231-4000. **Fax:** 310/231-4222. **Contact:** Gary Ray, Vice President of Human Resources. **World Wide Web address:** http://www.kbhome.com. **Description:** Kaufman & Broad builds and markets single-family homes; provides mortgage banking services; develops commercial projects and high-density residential properties; and acquires and develops land. **Positions advertised include:** Senior Developer; Payroll Coordinator; Public Relations Coordinator; Web Content Administrator; Paralegal; Merchandise Manager. **Corporate headquarters location:** This location. **Other U.S. locations:** Nationwide. **Listed on:** New York Stock Exchange. **Stock exchange symbol:** KBH. **Number of employees nationwide:** 5,000.

KOLL COMPANY
4343 Von Karman Avenue, Newport Beach CA 92660. 949/833-3030. **Fax:** 949/250-4344. **Contact:** Corporate Recruiting. **E-mail address:** info@koll.com. **World Wide Web address:** http://www.koll.com. **Description:** A real estate development, acquisition, management, and construction firm. The company leases and manages property, operating regional divisions along the West Coast. **Corporate headquarters location:** This location.

LINCOLN PROPERTY COMPANY
601 California Street, Suite 700, San Francisco CA 94108. 415/981-7878. **Fax:** 415/981-6331. **Contact:** Human Resources. **E-mail address:** humanresources@lpc.com. **World Wide Web address:** http://www.lpc.com. **Description:** A property management and development company. Founded in 1965. **Corporate headquarters location:** Dallas TX.

PROLOGIS
47775 Fremont Boulevard, Fremont CA 94538. 510/656-1900. **Fax:** 510/656-4320. **Contact:** Human Resources. **E-mail address:** hr@prologis.com. **World Wide Web address:** http://www.prologis.com. **Description:** Provides distribution facilities and services. **Corporate headquarters location:** Denver CO. **Other area locations:** Statewide. **Other U.S. locations:** Nationwide. **International locations:**

Worldwide. **Listed on:** New York Stock Exchange. **Stock exchange symbol:** PLD.

WILLIAM LYON COMPANY
4490 Von Karman Avenue, Newport Beach CA 92660. 949/833-3600. **Fax:** 949/252-2520. **Contact:** Personnel. **World Wide Web address:** http://www.lyonhomes.com. **Description:** Engaged in home building, financing, and land development. Assets include apartments and commercial real estate that the Hughes Investment Company and Koll Company assist in developing. Lyon also finances residential development through companies such as Warmington Homes, the Aikens Development Company, and the Lusk Company. **NOTE:** Contact information may vary. See job postings on website for more specific instructions on how to apply. **Corporate headquarters location:** This location. **Listed on:** New York Stock Exchange. **Stock exchange symbol:** WLS.

TRIZEC PROPERTIES
725 South Figueroa Street, Suite 2650, Los Angeles CA 90017. 213/624-9100. **Contact:** Human Resources. **World Wide Web address:** http://www.trz.com. **Description:** Trizec is a real estate development/property management company focusing on office buildings and technology complexes with properties across the United States, Canada, and Europe. **Corporate headquarters location:** Chicago IL. **Listed:** New York Stock Exchange. **Stock exchange symbol:** TRZ.

Colorado
BURNS REALTY & TRUST
1625 Broadway, World Trade Center, Penthouse Suite, Denver CO 80202. 303/629-1899. **Contact:** Mark Gritz, Treasurer/Controller. **Description:** Engaged in real estate and investments, as well as owning and operating apartments and nonresidential buildings.

GRUBB & ELLIS COMPANY
One Tabor Center, 1200 17th Street, Suite 2000, Denver CO 80202-5841. 303/572-7700. **Contact:** Administrative Manager. **World Wide Web address:** http://www.grubb-ellis.com. **Description:** A commercial real estate brokerage firm offering a full range of services including transaction, management, and consulting services. Founded in 1973. **Positions advertised include:** Administrative Assistant. **Special programs:** Internships. **Corporate headquarters location:** Northbrook IL. **Other area locations:** Colorado Springs CO. **Other U.S. locations:** Nationwide. **Listed on:** New York Stock Exchange. **Stock exchange symbol:** GBE.

PRUDENTIAL COLORADO REAL ESTATE
9635 Maroon Circle, Suite 400, Englewood CO 80112. 303/750-3475. **Fax:** 303/369-3455. **Contact:** Human Resources. **Description:** Markets residential and commercial real estate throughout metropolitan Denver.

ROSENBERG MANAGEMENT INC.
3400 East Bayaud Avenue, Suite 390, Denver CO 80209. 303/320-6067. **Contact:** Manager. **Description:** A real estate investment company involved in operating apartment buildings.

FREDERICK ROSS COMPANY
717 17th Street, Suite 2000, Denver CO 80202. 303/892-1111. **Contact:** Human Resources. **World Wide Web address:** http://www.frederickross.com. **Description:** A full-service commercial real estate firm. **Corporate headquarters location:** This location. **Parent company:** Oncor International. **Operations at this facility include:** Administration; Research and Development; Sales; Service. **Listed on:** Privately held. **Number of employees at this location:** 150.

WALKER ASSOCIATES
420 East 58th Avenue, Denver CO 80216. 303/292-5537. **Contact:** Human Resources. **Description:** A real estate agency whose dealings include electronic component distributor banks, ranches, and commercial properties.

Connecticut
ASHFORTH COMPANY
707 Summer Street, 4th Floor, Stamford CT 06901. 203/359-8500. **Contact:** Human Resources. **E-mail address:** humanresources@ashforthcompany.com. **World Wide Web address:** http://www.ashforthcompany.com. **Description:** A property management and commercial real estate construction company. **Positions advertised include:** Tax Accountant.

AVALONBAY COMMUNITIES, INC.
220 Elm Street, Suite 200, New Canaan CT 06840. 203/801-3300. **Fax:** 203/762-1240. **Contact:** Human Resources. **World Wide Web address:** http://www.avalonbay.com. **Description:** A self-administered and self-managed equity real estate investment trust that specializes in the development, construction, acquisition, and management of apartment communities in the Mid-Atlantic and Northeastern United States. AvalonBay Communities' real estate consists of approximately 10,000 apartment homes in 33 communities located in six states and Washington DC. **Positions advertised include:** Assistant Superintendent; Financial Analyst. **Corporate headquarters location:** Washington DC. **Other U.S. locations:** Nationwide. **Listed on:** New York Stock Exchange. **Stock exchange symbol:** AVB.

WILLIAM RAVEIS HOME-LINK
7 Trap Falls Road, Shelton CT 06484. 203/926-1090. **Fax:** 203/929-6523. **Contact:** Human Resources. **World Wide Web address:** http://www.raveis.com. **Description:** A commercial real estate agency. Founded in 1974. **Corporate headquarters location:** This location.

District Of Columbia
AKRIDGE
601 Thirteenth Street, NW, Suite 300 North, Washington DC 20005. 202/638-3000. **Fax:** 202/347-8043. **Contact:** Human Resources. **E-mail address:** careers@akridge.com. **World Wide Web address:** http://www.akridge.com. **Description:** A full-service real estate firm, with experience developing, repositioning, managing, and leasing real estate.

CARRAMERICA
1850 K Street NW, Suite 500, Washington DC 20006. 202/729-1700. **Fax:** 202/729-1150. **Contact:** Lynn Millar, Director of Human Resources. **E-mail address:** hr@carramerica.com. **World Wide Web address:** http://www.carramerica.com. **Description:** A real estate, architectural, and construction management firm. The company specializes in the construction and/or renovation of mixed-use developments. **Positions advertised include:** Assistant Records Manager; Special Assistant to General Counsel. **Corporate headquarters location:** This location. **Listed on:** New York Stock Exchange. **Stock exchange symbol:** CRE.

THE DONOHOE COMPANIES, INC.
2101 Wisconsin Avenue NW, Washington DC 20007. 202/333-0880. **Fax:** 202/478-5104. **Contact:** Human Resources Manager. **E-mail address:** employment@donohoe.com. **World Wide Web address:** http://www.donohoe.com. **Description:** A real estate development company. **Positions advertised include:** Senior Project Manager; Safety Supervisor; Construction Superintendent; Project Engineer. **Corporate headquarters location:** This location. **Number of employees at this location:** 300.

Florida
AVATAR HOLDINGS INC.
201 Alhambra Circle, 12th Floor, Coral Gables FL 33134. 305/442-7000. **Contact:** Human Resources, Juanita Kerrigan **E-mail address:** juanita.kerrigan@avatarholdings.com. **World Wide Web address:** http://www.avatarhomes.com. **Description:** A real estate company that develops residential, resort, and recreational properties. **Listed on:** NASDAQ. **Stock exchange symbol:** AVTR.

BLUEGREEN CORPORATION
4960 Blue Lake Drive, Boca Raton FL 33431. 561/912-8000. **Contact:** Human Resources. **E-mail address:** recruit@bxgcorp.com. **World Wide Web address:** http://www.bluegreen-corp.com. **Description:** A national real estate company specializing in rural land acquisitions and sales. Bluegreen Corporation also serves as a mortgage broker **Positions advertised include:** Marketing Support Specialist; Junior Graphic Designer; Production Assistant; Customer Service Associate; Payment Processor. **Corporate headquarters location:** This location. **Other U.S. locations:** Nationwide. **Listed on:** New York Stock Exchange. **Stock exchange symbol:** BXG. **Number of employees at this location:** 70. **Number of employees nationwide:** 400.

COLDWELL BANKER
423 St. Armands Circle, Sarasota FL 34236-1483. 941/388-3966. **Contact:** Sharon Krueger, Manager of Human Resources. **World Wide Web address:** http://www.coldwellbanker.com. **Description:** One of the largest residential real estate companies in the United States and Canada. Coldwell Banker also provides relocation services to businesses worldwide. **Corporate headquarters location:** Mission Viejo CA. **Other U.S. locations:** Nationwide. **Parent company:** Cendant Corporation. **Listed on:** New York Stock Exchange. **Stock exchange symbol:** CD.

DELTONA CORPORATION
999 Brickell Avenue, Suite 700, Miami FL 33131. 305/579-0999. **Toll-free phone:** 800/9935-6378. **Fax:** 305/358-0999. **Contact:** Human Resources. **E-mail address:** corporate@deltona.com. **World Wide Web address:** http://www.deltona.com. **Description:** Develops community housing. Founded in 1962.

FIRST AMERICAN REAL ESTATE SOLUTIONS
1800 NW 66th Avenue, Fort Lauderdale FL 33313. 954/792-2000. **Contact:** Human Resources. **World Wide Web address:** http://www.firstamres.com. **Description:** Maintains credit reports and provides information services for the real estate industry. **Positions advertised include:** Account Executive; Development Territory Manager. **NOTE:** Please send resumes to: Human Resources, 5601 East La Palma Avenue, Anaheim CA 92802. **Operations at this facility include:** Administration; Manufacturing; Regional Headquarters; Research and Development; Sales; Service. **Number of employees at this location:** 320. **Number of employees nationwide:** 1,200.

J.I. KISLAK MORTGAGE CORPORATION
7900 Miami Lakes Drive West, Miami Lakes FL 33016. 305/364-4116. **Contact:** Human Resources. **Description:** A mortgage banking and real estate firm. **Positions advertised include:** Production. **Office Hours:** Monday – Friday, 8:30 a.m. – 5:00 p.m. **Corporate headquarters location:** This location.

LENNAR CORPORATION
700 NW 107th Avenue, Miami FL 33172. 305/559-4000. **Contact:** Carol Burgin, Personnel Manager. **World Wide Web address:** http://www.lennar.com. **Description:** Builds and sells homes, develops and manages commercial and residential properties, and provides real estate-related financial services. **Positions advertised include:** Corporate Accountant; Joint Venture Assistant Controller; Staff Accountant. **Corporate headquarters location:** This location. **Listed on:** New York Stock Exchange. **Stock exchange symbol:** LEN. **Number of employees nationwide:** 1,300.

THE ST. JOE COMPANY
245 Riverside Avenue Suite 500, Jacksonville FL 32202. 904/301-4200. **Fax:** 904/301-4201. **Contact:** Human Resources. **World Wide Web address:** http://www.joe.com. **Description:** A full-service real estate company engaged in the development, building, operation, and sale of commercial and residential real estate. The company also offers real estate financial services including brokerage, financial management, and representation. **Positions advertised include:** Sales Representative; Marketing Manager; Vice President of Land Sales & Development. **Corporate headquarters location:** This location. **Listed on:** New York Stock Exchange. **Stock exchange symbol:** JOE.

WATERMARK COMMUNITIES, INC. (WCI)
P.O. Box 5698, Sun City Center FL 33571. 813/634-3311. **Physical address**: 2020 Clubhouse Drive, Sun City Center FL 33573. **Contact:** Sharon May, Director of Human Resources Department. **World Wide Web address:** http://www.wcicommunities.com. **Description:** Develops, builds, and manages resort communities. **Positions advertised include:** Community Representative; Processor; Community Specialist; Senior Project Manager; Administrative Assistant; Senior Construction Manager; Weekend Receptionist; Landscape Architect; Senior Designer; Golf Course Superintendent. **Corporate headquarters location:** This location. **Operations at this facility include:** Resort/Support Functions. **Number of employees at this location:** 3,600.

Georgia

CB RICHARD ELLIS
3340 Peachtree Road, Suite 1050, Atlanta GA 30326. 404/923-1200. **Fax:** 404/923-1550. **Contact:** Human Resources. **E-mail address:** cbrejobs@cbre.com. **World Wide Web address:** http://www.cbrichardellis.com. **Description:** A real estate services company offering property sales and leasing; property and facility management; mortgage banking; and investment management services. **NOTE:** The company has three other Atlanta offices. Please visit website to register, search for jobs, and apply online. **Positions advertised include:** Senior Real Estate Analyst; Administrative Assistant; Marketing Assistant; Research Assistant; Transaction Coordinator; Building Engineer; Transaction Manager; Sales Professional. **Corporate headquarters location:** Los Angeles CA. **Other U.S. locations:** Nationwide. **Listed on:** New York Stock Exchange. **Stock exchange symbol:** CBG. **CEO:** Raymond Wirta. **Number of employees worldwide:** 13,500.

CARTER & ASSOCIATES INC.
171 17th Street, Atlanta GA 30363. 404/888-3000. **Fax:** 404/888-3006. **Contact:** Barbara Jones. **E-mail address:** bjones@carterusa.com. **World Wide Web address:** http://www.carterusa.com. **Description:** Engaged in the development, management, and sale of commercial real estate. **NOTE:** For employment information, call 404/888-3158. **Corporate headquarters location:** This location. **Other U.S. locations:** AL; FL: NC; TN. **CEO:** Bob Peterson.

COLLIERS, CAUBLE & COMPANY
1349 West Peachtree Street, NE, Two Midtown Plaza, Suite 1100, Atlanta GA 30309. 404/888-9000. **Fax:** 404/870-2845. **Contact:** Human Resources. **World Wide Web address:** http://www.colliers.com. **Description:** Provides services and consultation to users and owners of commercial real estate. Maintains more than 250 offices in 51 countries. Founded in 1967. **Corporate headquarters location:** Boston MA. **Other U.S. locations:** Nationwide. **International locations:** Worldwide. **Parent company:** Colliers International.

THE FRANK M. DARBY COMPANY
100 Ashford Center North, Suite 412, Atlanta GA 30338. 770/901-9100. **Fax:** 404/812-5901. **Contact:** Human Resources. **E-mail address:** amontgomery@fmdarby.com. **World Wide Web address:** http://www.fmdarby.com. **Description:** Specializes in the management and leasing of office, industrial, and investment properties in Atlanta. Founded in 1982. **Company slogan:** Signature service. **Corporate headquarters location:** This location. **Listed on:** Privately held. **President:** Frank M. Darby. **Number of employees at this location:** 30.

DUKE-WEEKS REALTY CORPORATION
3950 Shackleford Road, Suite 300, Duluth GA 30096-8268. 770/717-3200. **Fax:** 707/717-3310. **Contact:**

Human Resources. **E-mail address:** hr@dukerealty.com. **World Wide Web address:** http://www.dukereit.com. **Description:** A developer and owner of industrial buildings and parks. The company also provides a full range of leasing, management, and construction services for its properties and industrial real estate owned by other parties. **NOTE:** Mail resumes to corporate office, at 600 East 96th Street, Suite 100, Indianapolis IN 46240, or fax to 317/808-6791. **Positions advertised include:** Lease Analyst. **Corporate headquarters location:** Indianapolis IN. **Other U.S. locations:** Eastern U.S. **Listed on:** New York Stock Exchange. **Stock exchange symbol:** DRE. **CEO:** Thomas L. Hefner. **Number of employees worldwide:** 1,050.

FOCUS DEVELOPMENT, INC.
3423 Piedmont Road, Suite 325, Atlanta GA 30305. 404/816-6300. **Fax:** 404/816-6622. **Contact:** Human Resources. **World Wide Web address:** http://www.apartmentsbyfocus.com. **Description:** Develops, constructs, and manages residential real estate properties. **Corporate headquarters location:** This location. **President:** Michael Blonder.

INTERPARK
549 Peachtree Street, Suite 1500, Atlanta GA 30308. 404/658-9053. **Fax:** 404/817-3617. **Contact:** Human Resources. **World Wide Web address:** http://www.interparkholdings.com. **Description:** Owns and manages a parking facility and offers consulting services in the design, construction, and operation of other such facilities. **Corporate headquarters location:** Chicago IL. **Other U.S. locations:** Nationwide.

POST PROPERTIES, INC.
One Riverside, 4401 Northside Parkway, Suite 800, Atlanta GA 30327-3057. 404/846-5000. **Fax:** 404/504-9369. **Contact:** Human Resources. **E-mail address:** careers@postproperties.com. **World Wide Web address:** http://www.postproperties.com. **Description:** Operates a real estate investment trust. Post Properties is one of the largest owners and operators of multifamily apartment communities in the southeastern United States. Founded 1971. **NOTE:** Search and apply for jobs online. Contact Human Resources directly at 404/846-6171. **Special programs:** Internships. **Positions advertised include:** Leasing Consultant; Housekeeper; Property Monitor; Property Engineer; Assistant Property Engineer; Preventative Maintenance Engineer; Floriculture Groundsperson; Maintenance Assistant-in-Training. **Corporate headquarters location:** This location. **Listed on:** New York Stock Exchange. **Stock exchange symbol:** PPS. **President/CEO:** David Stockert.

WATKINS ASSOCIATED INDUSTRIES
1958 Monroe Drive NE, Atlanta GA 30324. 404/872-3841. **Fax:** 404/872-2812. **Contact:** Human Resources. **Description:** Operates a variety of companies, including trucking company, real estate development, door and window manufacturing, and seafood processing. **Corporate headquarters location:** This location. **Other U.S. locations:** Nationwide. **International locations:** Canada; Mexico; Puerto Rico. **President/CEO:** Mike Watkins. **Number of employees nationwide:** 9,000.

Hawaii
D.R. HORTON, SCHULER DIVISION
828 Fort Street Mall, 4th Floor, Honolulu HI 96813. 808/548-0087. **Fax:** 808/548-0087. **Contact:** Human Resources. **World Wide Web address:** http://www.schulerhawaii.com. **Description:** Constructs and sells homes designed for the entry-level and first-time markets. **NOTE:** Search for available positions online and complete application form. **Positions advertised include:** Mortgage Underwriter.

Illinois
BAIRD & WARNER
120 South LaSalle Street, Suite 2000, Chicago IL 60603. 312/368-1855. **Toll-free phone:** 800/644-1855. **Fax:** 302/368-1490. **Contact:** Human Resources Director. **E-mail address:** jobs@bairdwarner.com. **World Wide Web address:** http://www.bairdwarner.com. **Description:** A full-service, residential real estate broker operating 30 offices in the Chicago area. **NOTE:** Part-time positions offered. See website for all job listings. **Positions advertised include:** Administrative Assistant; Mortgage Underwriter; Loan Officer. **Corporate headquarters location:** This location.

COLDWELL BANKER RESIDENTIAL BROKERAGE
875 North Michigan Avenue, Suite 3500, Chicago IL 60611. 312/751-9100. **Fax:** 312/751-9293. **Contact:** Human Resources. **World Wide Web address:** http://www.coldwellbanker.com. **Description:** A residential real estate brokerage in downtown Chicago. Coldwell Banker is one of the largest residential real estate companies in the United States and Canada. **Corporate headquarters location:** Parsippany NJ.

GENERAL GROWTH PROPERTIES, INC.
110 North Wacker Drive, Chicago IL 60606. 312/960-5000. **Fax:** 312/960-5475. **Contact:** Human Resources. **E-mail address:** careers@generalgrowth.com. **World Wide Web address:** http://www.generalgrowth.com. **Description:** Owns, operates, develops, and renovates shopping malls. Mail or e-mail resume and cover letters, stating interest in a specific type of position. Special programs: Internships. **Positions advertised include:** CAD Specialist; Director of Grocery Store Leasing; Director of Operations; Group Vice President of Marketing. **Corporate headquarters location:** This location. **Parent company:** Sears, Roebuck & Co. **Listed on:** New York Stock Exchange. **Stock exchange symbol:** GGP.

JMB REALTY CORPORATION
J&V URBAN RETAIL PROPERTIES COMPANY
900 North Michigan Avenue, Chicago IL 60611. 312/440-4800. **Fax:** 312/915-2310. **Contact:** Human Resources. **Description:** Owns and manages shopping malls and strip malls nationwide. **Corporate headquarters location:** This location. **Other U.S. locations:** Nationwide. **Listed on:** Privately held.

MERCHANDISE MART PROPERTIES, INC.
200 World Trade Center, Suite 470, Chicago IL 60654. 312/527-7792. **Fax:** 312/527-7905. **Contact:** Tom Fitzpatrick, Director of Human Resources. **E-mail address:** careers@mmart.com. **World Wide Web address:** http://www.merchandisemart.com. **Description:** The management and leasing agent for prominent wholesale showroom facilities, which include the Merchandise Mart and Apparel Center (Chicago), the Decorators and Designers Building (New York), and the Washington Design Center (Washington DC). **Positions advertised include:** Concierge; Administrative Assistant. **Special programs:** Internships. **Corporate headquarters location:** This location. **Other U.S. locations:** Washington DC; High Point NC. **Parent company:** Vornado Realty Trust. **Operations at this facility include:** Administration; Research and Development; Sales; Service. **Listed on:** Privately held.

RE/MAX TEAM 2000
7130 West 127th Street, Palos Heights IL 60463. 708/361-5950. **Contact:** Human Resources. **World Wide Web address:** http://www.chicago-area-homes.com. **Description:** A residential and commercial real estate agency.

Indiana
CB RICHARD ELLIS
202 South Michigan, Suite 900, South Bend IN 46601. 574/237-6000. **Fax:** 574/237-6001. **Contact:** Personnel. **E-mail address:** cbrejobs@cbre.com. **World Wide Web address:** http://www.cbrichardellis.com. **Description:** A real estate services company offering property sales and leasing; property and facility management; mortgage banking; and investment management services.

Corporate headquarters location: Los Angeles CA. **Listed on:** New York Stock Exchange. **Stock exchange symbol:** CBG.

DUKE-WEEKS REALTY CORPORATION
600 East 96th Street, Suite 100, Indianapolis IN 46240. 317/846-4700. **Fax:** 317/808-6791. **Contact:** Human Resources. **E-mail address:** hr@ dukerealty.com. **World Wide Web address:** http://www.dukereit.com. **Description:** Duke-Weeks Realty Corporation is a self-administered real estate investment trust that provides leasing, management, development, construction, and other tenant-related services for its properties and for about 12 million square feet of properties owned by third parties. **NOTE:** Resumes may be submitted via e-mail, fax, or mail. **Positions advertised include:** Staff Internal Auditor; Systems Administrator; Project Manager. **Corporate headquarters location:** This location. **Operations at this facility include:** Administration; Sales.

Kansas
REECE & NICHOLS REALTORS
11500 Granada, Leawood KS 66211. 913/491-1001. **Fax:** 913/345-0014. **Contact:** Director of Human Resources. **World Wide Web address:** http://www.reeceandnichols.com. **Description:** Engaged in residential real estate, new home developments, resale, property management, and corporate relocation. **NOTE:** In addition to the company's Director of Human Resources, the company also uses an outside employment agency; check the careers page of the company website. **Positions advertised include:** Home Mortgage Consultant; Home Mortgage Associate. **Other area locations:** Twenty branches in the greater Kansas City area. **Number of employees:** 1,400.

Louisiana
SIZELER PROPERTY INVESTORS, INC.
2542 Williams Boulevard, Kenner LA 70062. 504/471-6200. **Fax:** 504/471-6291. **Contact:** Human Resources. **World Wide Web address:** http://www.sizeler.net. **Description:** A self-administered equity real estate investment trust that invests in shopping center and apartment properties in the southern United States. The company's investment portfolio includes interests in three enclosed regional shopping malls, two shopping centers, 11 community shopping centers, and 12 apartment complexes. **Listed on:** New York Stock Exchange. **Stock exchange symbol:** SIZ. **CEO:** Sidney W. Lassen. **Annual sales/revenues:** $52.8 million.

STEWART ENTERPRISES, INC
110 Veterans Memorial Boulevard, Metairie LA 70005. 504/837-5880. **Toll-free phone:** 800/535-6017. **Contact:** Human Resources. **E-mail address:** hrinfo@stei.com. **World Wide Web address:** http://www.stewartenterprises.com. **Description:** A funeral home and cemetery services provider. Through its subsidiaries, the company operates 134 funeral homes and 95 cemeteries in 16 states, as well as Puerto Rico. **NOTE:** Visit the website for possible positions, then call the Human Resources Department at 800/553-8736 for current opportunities. **Positions advertised include:** Sales Representative; Manager; Accounts Payable; Treasurer. **Special programs:** Educational Assistance Program; Internships. **Corporate headquarters location:** This location. **Other U.S. locations:** Nationwide. **Listed on:** NASDAQ. **Stock exchange symbol:** STEI. **Number of employees worldwide:** 6,500.

Maine
COLDWELL BANKER THOMAS AGENCY
75 Main Street, Winthrop ME 04364. 207/377-2121. **Fax:** 207/377-8015. **Contact:** Human Resources. E-mail address: refg.jobs@cendant.com. **World Wide Web address:** http://www.coldwellbanker.com. **Description:** A real estate agency specializing in residential waterfront properties. **NOTE:** Search local posted openings and apply on-line via corporate web site. May respond by e-mail. **Corporate headquarters location:** Parsippany NJ. **Other area locations:** Statewide. **Other U.S. locations:** Nationwide. **Listed on:** New York Stock Exchange. **Stock exchange symbol:** CD. **President/CEO:** Alex Perriello.

MORGAN BAYSIDE MORGAN REAL ESTATE INC.
711 Bayside Road, Ellsworth ME 04605. 207/667-3845. **Toll-free phone:** 800/660-3845. **Fax:** 207/667-7383. **Contact:** Human Resources. **E-mail address:** sold@mbre.net. **World Wide Web address:** http://www.mbre.net. **Description:** Engaged in residential and commercial property sales and rental.

Maryland
FEDERAL REALTY INVESTMENT TRUST
1626 East Jefferson Street, Rockville MD 20852-4041. 301/998-8100. **Toll-free phone:** 800/658-8980. **Contact:** Human Resources. **World Wide Web address:** http://www.federalrealty.com. **Description:** An equity real estate investment firm that acquires and develops prime retail properties. **Positions advertised include:** Accounting Manager; Administrative Assistant; Executive Assistant; Human Resource Training Coordinator; Lease Administration Associate; Network Administration Associate; Programmer; Director of Acquisition. **Special programs:** Training. **Corporate headquarters location:** This location. **Operations at this facility include:** Administration; Sales; Service. **Listed on:** New York Stock Exchange. **Stock exchange symbol:** FRT. **President/CEO:** Donald C. Wood.

GENERAL GROWTH PROPERTIES
10275 Little Patuxent Parkway, Columbia MD 21044. 410/992-6000. **Fax:** 410/ 964-3436. **Contact:** Human Resources. **World Wide Web address:** http://www.generalgrowth.com. **Description:** Develops, acquires, owns, and manages commercial real estate projects, primarily large regional retail centers. The Rouse Company manages approximately 250 properties across the United States including Faneuil Hall Marketplace (Boston MA), South Street Seaport (New York NY), Harborplace (Baltimore MD), Bayside Marketplace (Miami FL), Arizona Center (Phoenix AZ), Pioneer Place (Portland OR), and Westlake Center (Seattle WA). Founded in 1939. **NOTE:** Online applications are available. **Positions advertised include:** Group Secretary; Retail Marketing Manager. **Corporate headquarters location:** Chicago IL. **Listed on:** New York Stock Exchange. **Stock exchange symbol:** GGP.

MONTGOMERY VILLAGE FOUNDATION
10120 Apple Ridge Road, Montgomery Village MD 20886. 301/948-0110. **Toll-free phone:** 800/215-1784. **Fax:** 301//990-7071. **Contact:** William Koarid, Human Resources. **E-mail address:** mvinfo@mvf.org. **World Wide Web address:** http://www.mvf.org. **Description:** A planned living community with 35,000 residents living in Montgomery County. **Positions advertised include:** Aquatics Assistant; Facilities Manager; Part Time Receptionist; Seasonal Receptionist.

ORFG OPERATIONS
7200 Wisconsin Avenue, Suite 1100, Bethesda MD 20814. 301/654-3100. **Contact:** Human Resources. **Description:** Manages apartment complexes.

STEWART ENTERPRISES, INC.
7800 Park Heights Avenue, Baltimore MD 21208. 410/486-5300. **Contact:** Human Resources. **E-mail address:** hrinfo@stei.com. **World Wide Web address:** http://www.stewartenterprises.com. **Description:** A funeral service provider. The company is one of the first in the industry to integrate funeral home and cemetery operations through combined facilities. Through its subsidiaries, the company operates 134 funeral homes and 95 cemeteries worldwide. **Positions advertised include:** Sales Associate; Management Assistants. **Special programs:** Educational Assistance Program; Internships. **Corporate headquarters location:** Metairie LA. **Other U.S. locations:** Nationwide. **International**

locations: Australia; Mexico. **Listed on:** NASDAQ. **Stock exchange symbol:** STEI. **President/CEO:** William E. Rowe. **Sales/revenue:** $581 million. **Number of employees worldwide:** 6,500.

Massachusetts

ACS DEVELOPMENT
80 Everett Avenue, Suite 319, Chelsea MA 02150. 617/889-6900. **Fax:** 617/889-6255. **Contact:** Patricia Simboli, Principal. **Description:** A real estate corporation with assets in the metropolitan Boston and Florida markets. Properties include retail, office, and industrial locations. **Corporate headquarters location:** This location. **Operations at this facility include:** Administration; Sales.

AYRE REAL ESTATE COMPANY, INC.
701 Main Street, Agawam MA 01001. 413/789-0812. **Fax:** 413/789-2427. **Contact:** Human Resources. **E-mail address:** ayrerealestate@ayrerealestate.com. **World Wide Web address:** http://www.ayrerealestate.com. **Description:** A commercial and residential real estate company serving the greater Springfield area.

CB RICHARD ELLIS INVESTORS
600 Atlantic Avenue, Federal Reserve Plaza, 22nd Floor, Boston MA 02210. 617/912-7000. **Fax:** 617/912-7001. **Contact:** Personnel. **World Wide Web address:** http://www.cbre.com/boston. **Description:** Provides real estate services. **Positions advertised include:** Production Analyst. **Corporate headquarters location:** Los Angeles CA. **Other U.S. locations:** Nationwide. **International locations:** Worldwide. **Listed on:** New York Stock Exchange. **Stock exchange symbol:** CBG.

CENTURY 21 CAPE SAILS, INC.
133 Main Street 6A, Sandwich MA 02563. 508/888-2121. **Contact:** Human Resources. **World Wide Web address:** http://www.c21capesails.com. **Description:** A residential real estate company serving the Cape Cod area.

COLDWELL BANKER
326 Washington Street, Wellesley Hills MA 02481. 781/235-6885. **Contact:** Human Resources. **World Wide Web address:** http://www.coldwellbanker.com. **Description:** An integrated residential real estate service company that provides sales and marketing services to residential real estate consumers. In addition, the company originates, processes, and closes residential mortgage loans; provides corporate and employee relocation services; and provides asset management services to a variety of clients. In residential real estate and marketing, the company acts as a broker or agent in transactions through independent sales associates. **Parent company:** Cendant Corporation. **Listed on:** American Stock Exchange. **Stock exchange symbol:** DWL. **Number of employees worldwide:** 120,000.

EQUITY OFFICE PROPERTIES
100 Summer Street, 2nd Floor, Boston MA 02110. 617/425-7500. **Contact:** Human Resources. **World Wide Web address:** http://www.equityoffice.com. **Description:** Operates as a self-administered and self-managed real estate investment trust (REIT). The company specializes in property acquisitions, management, leasing, design, construction, and development. In addition to its own locations, the company manages properties for several third-party property owners. **Corporate headquarters location:** Chicago IL. **Other U.S. locations:** Atlanta GA. **Operations at this facility include:** Administration. **Listed on:** New York Stock Exchange. **Stock exchange symbol:** EOP.

FIRST WINTHROP CORPORATION
P.O. Box 9507, Boston MA 02114. 617/234-3000. **Contact:** Human Resources. **Description:** A real estate agency specializing in commercial properties. Founded in 1978. **Corporate headquarters location:** This location. **Listed on:** Privately held. **Number of employees at this location:** 30. **Number of employees nationwide:** 110.

FOREST CITY DEVELOPMENT
38 Sidney Street, Cambridge MA 02139. 617/225-0310. **Contact:** Human Resources. **World Wide Web address:** http://www.fceboston.com. **Description:** A real estate developer.

HEALTH AND RETIREMENT PROPERTIES TRUST
400 Centre Street, Newton MA 02458. 617/332-3990. **Fax:** 617/332-2261. **E-mail address:** hr@hrpreit.com. **World Wide Web address:** http://www.hrpreit.com. **Contact:** Joyce Silver, Human Resources. **Description:** A real estate investment trust that invests primarily in retirement communities, assisted living centers, nursing homes, and other long-term care facilities. **Corporate headquarters location:** This location.

SPAULDING & SLYE
255 State Street, 4th Floor, Boston MA 02109. 617/523-8000. **Fax:** 617/531-4281. **Contact:** Catherine Spritca, Human Resources. **World Wide Web address:** http://www.spauldslye.com. **Description:** Corporate offices of a national, full-service real estate development firm. Services include development, construction, brokerage and property management, and advisory services. **Positions advertised include:** Project Manager; Property Manager; Associate; Administrative Assistant; Assistant Construction Manager; Graphic Designer; Tenant Coordinator; Superintendent; Construction Manager; Marketing Associate. **Other area locations:** Burlington MA. **Other U.S. locations:** Washington DC. **Operations at this facility include:** Administration; Sales. **Listed on:** Privately held. **Number of employees at this location:** 170. **Number of employees nationwide:** 235.

TORTO WHEATON RESEARCH
200 High Street, 3rd Floor, Boston MA 02110. 617/912-5200. **Fax:** 617/912-5240. **Contact:** Human Resources. **E-mail address:** fmoyniham@tortowheatonresearch.com. **World Wide Web address:** http://www.twr.com. **Description:** Provides real estate services. **Positions advertised include:** Real Estate Analyst; Data Analyst/Programmer. **Corporate headquarters location:** Los Angeles CA. **Parent company:** CB Richard Ellis. **Stock exchange symbol:** CBG.

Michigan

MIDWEST MANAGEMENT
950 Corporate Office Drive, Suite 100, Milford MI 48381. 248/529-2020. **Fax:** 248/529-2001. **Contact:** Human Resources. **World Wide Web address:** http://www.midwest-mgmt.com. **Description:** A property management company. Founded in 1973. **Positions advertised include:** Regional Property Manager; Property Manager; Leasing Consultant; Financial Manager; Office Manager; Maintenance Technician; Janitorial Worker. **Corporate headquarters location:** This location. **Other area locations:** Lansing MI; Kentwood MI; Milford MI. **Other U.S. locations:** Chicago IL; Hamilton OH. **Number of employees nationwide:** 1,400.

SCOTT MANAGEMENT COMPANY
26100 Northwestern Highway, Suite 1913, Southfield MI 48076. 248/354-9900. **Fax:** 248/351-4887. **Contact:** Personnel. **World Wide Web address:** http://www.smcliving.com. **Description:** A real estate brokerage firm specializing in apartment rentals. **Corporate headquarters location:** This location.

Minnesota

BRUTGER EQUITIES, INC.
100 4th Avenue South, Third Floor, P.O. Box 399, St. Cloud MN 56302-0399. 320/529-2837. **Fax:** 320/529-2808. **Contact:** Bev Albright, Human Resources. **E-mail address:** balbright@brutgerequities.com. **Description:** Engaged in real estate development and management of properties, including hotels and apartments. **NOTE:** Most positions are based offsite at

individual properties. Submit resume by mail, fax, or e-mail. **Special programs:** Internships. **Corporate headquarters location:** This location. **Other area locations:** Statewide. **Other U.S. locations:** AZ; CO; ID; MT; ND; SD; WY. **Operations at this facility include:** Administration; Sales. **Listed on:** Privately held. **Number of employees at this location:** 25. **Number of employees nationwide:** 325.

COLDWELL BANKER BURNET
7550 France Avenue South, Suite 300, Edina MN 55435. 952/844-6000. **Fax:** 952/844-6330. **Contact:** Human Resources. **World Wide Web address:** http://www.cbburnet.com. **Description:** A real estate agency. Also offers home financing through Burnet Home Loans, title insurance and closing through Burnet Title, and the services of Burnet Insurance, Burnet Relocation, and Burnet Property & Rental Resources.

WELSH COMPANIES
7807 Creekridge Circle, Minneapolis MN 55439. 952/897-7797. **Fax:** 952/842-7797. **Contact:** Human Resources. **E-mail address:** jobs@welshco.com. **World Wide Web address:** http://www.welshco.com. **Description:** A full-service commercial real estate company. Operations include office, industrial, and retail brokerage; corporate services; property and facility management; construction; community development services; architecture; development; mortgage banking; and investment services. Part of the NAI Global commercial real estate network. **NOTE:** Search for positions online. Submit resume by e-mail or fax. **Special programs:** Internships. **Corporate headquarters location:** This location. **Other area locations:** Statewide. **Other U.S. locations:** IL; CO; MO; FL.

Missouri
EDWARD L. BAKEWELL, INC.
7716 Forsyth Boulevard, St. Louis MO 63105. 314/721-5555. **Toll-free phone:** 800/341-4791. **Contact:** Human Resources Department. **E-mail address:** info@bakewellinc.com. **World Wide Web address:** http://www.bakewellinc.com. **Description:** A real estate agency. **Number of employees at this location:** 100.

COLDWELL BANKER
1505 South Big Bend Boulevard, St. Louis MO 63117. 314/647-0002. **Contact:** Human Resources. **World Wide Web address:** http://www.coldwellbanker.com. **Description:** Coldwell Banker is one of the largest residential real estate companies in the United States and Canada in terms of total home sales transactions. Coldwell Banker is also a leader in meeting corporate America's specialized relocation needs on a worldwide basis. Coldwell Banker operates Coldwell Banker Relocation Services, a corporate relocation management company. Coldwell Banker also launched Coldwell Banker Residential Affiliates, Inc., aimed at franchising select brokers who served small to medium-sized markets. **Corporate headquarters location:** Mission Viejo CA. **Parent company:** Cendant Corporation. **Number of employees at this location:** 800.

FOLLMAN PROPERTIES
ONCOR INTERNATIONAL
13545 Barrett Parkway Drive, Suite 330, Ballwin, MO 63021. 314/966-6966. **Contact:** Gary Follman, President. **World Wide Web address:** http://www.follman.com. **Description:** A full-service, commercial real estate services firm. Follman Properties is part of Oncor International, serving office, industrial, retail, and investment brokerage requirements. The company is also involved in asset and property management, consulting, appraisal, and information services. **Corporate headquarters location:** This location. **Listed on:** Privately held. **Number of employees at this location:** 40.

JOHNSON GROUP, INC.
8860 Ladue Road, Suite 200, St. Louis MO 63124. 314/862-3000. **Fax:** 314/862-1307. **Contact:** Human Resources. **World Wide Web address:** http://www.j-group.com. **Description:** A real estate and office building management firm.

THE MICHELSON ORGANIZATION
7701 Forsyth Boulevard, Suite 900, St. Louis MO 63105. 314/862-7080. **Contact:** Mike Casey, Controller. **World Wide Web address:** http://www.michelson-realty.com. **Description:** Develops, acquires, and manages real estate investments. **Corporate headquarters location:** This location. **Subsidiaries include:** Michelson Commercial Realty and Development Company assists corporate clients with a wide range of services. **Number of employees at this location:** 40.

Nevada
CAMDEN
4041 East Sunset Road, Henderson NV 89014. 702/435-9800. **Fax:** 702/435-6815. **Recorded jobline:** 866/524-3592. **Recorded jobline:** 866/524-3592. **Contact:** Human Resources. **E-mail address:** jobs@camdenliving.com. **World Wide Web address:** http://www.camdenliving.com. **Description:** A self-administered and self-managed real estate investment trust, engaged in the acquisition, development, and operation of multifamily properties. **Corporate headquarters location:** Houston TX. **Listed on:** New York Stock Exchange. **Stock exchange symbol:** CPT.

New Hampshire
THE CORRIGAN COMPANY, INC.
Hills Court, 6-C Hills Avenue, Concord NH 03301. 603/225-3801. **Fax:** 603/225-0436. **E-mail address:** jwctcc.jwc@verizon.net. **World Wide Web address:** http:// www.thecorrigancompany.com. **Description:** A real estate firm that specializes in the leasing/selling of land and property for commercial purposes.

New Jersey
CB RICHARD ELLIS
Park 80 West, Plaza 2, Saddle Brook NJ 07663. 201/712-98056000. **Fax:** 201/712-5650. **Contact:** Human Resources. **E-mail address:** opps@cbre.com. **World Wide Web address:** http://www.cbrichardellis.com. **Description:** A real estate services company offering property sales and leasing, property and facility management, mortgage banking, and investment management services. **Positions advertised include:** Marketing Coordinator; Property Administrator; Manager/Research. **Corporate headquarters location:** Los Angeles CA. **Number of employees worldwide:** 9,000.

CHELSEA PROPERTY GROUP, INC.
105 Eisenhower Parkway, Roseland NJ 07068. 973/228-6111. **Contact:** Human Resources. **E-mail address:** jobs@cpgi.com. **World Wide Web address:** http://www.cpgi.com. **Description:** A self-administered and self-managed real estate investment trust engaged in the development, leasing, marketing, and management of upscale and fashion-oriented manufacturers' outlet centers. **Positions advertised include:** Security Supervisor; Assistant General Manager. **Parent company:** Simon. **Listed on:** New York Stock Exchange. **Stock exchange symbol:** CPG.

K. HOVNANIAN COMPANIES
10 Highway 35, Red Bank NJ 07701. 732/747-7800. **Contact:** Human Resources. **World Wide Web address:** http://www.khov.com. **Description:** Designs, constructs, and sells condominium apartments, townhouses, and single-family homes in residential communities. The company is also engaged in mortgage banking. Founded in 1959. **Positions advertised include:** Training and Development Specialist; Sr. Information Systems Auditor; Jr. HRIS Analyst; Financial Analyst; Programmer Analyst; Methodology Manager. **Corporate headquarters location:** This location. **Other U.S. locations:** CA; FL; NC; NY; PA; VA. **Subsidiaries include:** New Fortis Homes. **Listed on:** New York Stock Exchange. **Stock exchange symbol:** HOV. **Number of employees at**

this location: 90. **Number of employees nationwide:** 1,150.

WEICHERT REALTORS
1625 Route 10 East, Morris Plains NJ 07950. 973/267-7777. **Contact:** Human Resources. **World Wide Web address:** http://www.weichert.com. **Description:** A commercial real estate agency. **NOTE:** Jobseekers should specify a department of interest when applying. **Corporate headquarters location:** This location.

New Mexico
BARKER REALTY, INC.
530 South Guadalupe Street, Santa Fe NM 87501. 505/982-9836. **Contact:** David Barker, Broker/Owner. **E-mail address:** barker@barkerrealty.net. **World Wide Web address:** http://www.barkerrealty.net. **Description:** A full-service realty firm specializing in commercial, residential, and income property, as well as vacant land. Coverage area includes Northern New Mexico.

COLDWELL BANKER TRAILS WEST
2000 Old Pecos Trail, Santa Fe NM 87505. 505/988-7285. **Contact:** Human Resources. **E-mail address:** broker@cbsantafe.com. **World Wide Web address:** http://www.cbsantafe.com. **Description:** Coldwell Banker is one of the largest residential real estate companies in the United States and Canada. Coldwell Banker is also a leader in meeting Corporate America's specialized relocation needs on a worldwide basis. **Corporate headquarters location:** Mission Viejo CA. **Subsidiaries include**: Coldwell Banker Relocation Services provides corporate relocation services; Coldwell Banker Residential Affiliates, Inc. franchises select brokers who serve small to medium-sized markets.

QUAIL RUN ASSOCIATION
3101 Old Pecos Trail, Santa Fe NM 87505. 505/986-2200. **Fax:** 505/986-2257. **Contact:** Human Resources. **E-mail address:** info@qrsf.com. **World Wide Web address:** http://www.quailrunsantafe.com. **Description:** A residential community and resort. Quail Run has 260 residential units. The resort facilities include an indoor pool, weight room, sauna, massage therapy, executive golf course, and tennis courts. **Positions advertised include:** Clubhouse Manager; Human Resources Assistant; Housekeeper; Evening Line Cook; Waitstaff; Table Busser; Banquet Captain.

SANTA FE PROPERTIES
1000 Paseo de Peralta, Santa Fe NM 87501. 505/984-7347. **Fax:** 505/984-1003. **Contact:** Edward Sargent, Principal Broker. **E-mail address:** info@santafeproperties.com. **World Wide Web address:** http://www.santafeproperties.com. **Description:** A locally owned real-estate company.

SOTHEBY'S INTERNATIONAL REALTY
216 Washington Avenue, Santa Fe NM 87501. 866/988-8858. **Contact:** Office Manager. **E-mail address:** santafe@sothebysinternationalrealty.com. **World Wide Web address:** http://www.santafesir.com. **Description:** A real estate agency.

PRUDENTIAL SANTA FE REAL ESTATE
505 Don Gaspar Avenue, Santa Fe NM 87505. 505/988-3700. **Fax:** 505/988-7443. **Contact:** Julia Gelbart, Vice President – Business Development. **World Wide Web address:** http://www.prudentialsantafe.com. **Description:** An independently owned and operated member of the Prudential Real Estate Affiliates, Inc.

New York
CENTRAL PARKING SYSTEMS
360 West 31st Street, 12th Floor, New York NY 10001. 212/502-5075. **Contact:** Human Resources. **World Wide Web address:** http://www.parking.com. **Description:** Operates parking garages and lots throughout New York. **Positions advertised include:** Area Manager; Field Auditor; Night Area Manager; Project Manager; Paralegal; Staff Accountant. **Corporate headquarters location:** Nashville TN. **Other U.S. locations:** Nationwide. **Parent company:** Central Parking Corporation (Nashville TN).

COLDWELL BANKER
151 North Main Street, New City NY 10956. 845/634-0400. **Contact:** Human Resources. **World Wide Web address:** http://www.coldwellbanker.com. **Description:** This location is one of the 3,500 independently owned and operated franchised brokerages engaged in residential and commercial real estate transactions with 106,000 Sales Associates worldwide. **Corporate headquarters location:** Parsippany NJ. **Other locations:** Worldwide. **Parent company:** Cendant Corporation (New York NY). **Operations at this facility include:** Sales.

CUSHMAN & WAKEFIELD, INC.
51 West 52nd Street, 8th Floor, New York NY 10019-6178. 212/841-7500. **Fax:** 212/841-5039. **Contact:** Human Resources. **E-mail address:** recruiting@cushwake.com. **World Wide Web address:** http://www.cushmanwakefield.com. **Description:** An international commercial and industrial real estate services firm with 44 offices in 20 states. The company is engaged in appraisals, financial services, project development, research services, and the management and leasing of commercial office space, as well as providing assessment services, corporate services, brokerage services, financial and general administration, research, sales, and valuation advisory services. **Positions advertised include:** Asset Services Administrator; Executive Assistant; Marketing Coordinator; Accounting Supervisor; Payroll Coordinator; Purchasing Assistant; Broker Compensation Supervisor; New York Area Operations Manager; Administrative Assistant; Hospitality Valuation Professional. **Office hours:** Monday - Friday, 8:30 a.m. - 5:30 p.m. **Corporate headquarters location:** This location. **Other U.S. locations:** Los Angeles CA; San Francisco CA; Chicago IL. **International locations:** Worldwide. **Parent company:** The Rockefeller Group Inc. **Chairman:** John C. Cushman. **Annual sales/revenues:** $870 million. **Number of employees at this location:** 500. **Number of employees nationwide:** 11,000.

DVL INC.
70 East 55th Street, 7th Floor, New York NY 10022. 212/350-9900. **Fax:** 212/350-9911. **Contact:** Human Resources. **Description:** Acquires and develops retirement and resort properties; purchases, collects, and services installment sales contacts originated by national tool companies for automobile mechanics' tools; and manages and services existing real estate properties. **Listed on:** Over The Counter. **Stock exchange symbol:** DVLN. **Chairman:** Frederick E. Smithline. **Annual sales/revenues:** $9.1 million. **Number of employees:** 11.

FIRST ALLIED CORPORATION
270 Commerce Drive, Rochester NY 14623. 585/359-3000. **Toll-free phone:** 800/421-5327. **Fax:** 585/359-4690. **Contact:** Human Resources. **World Wide Web address:** http://www.firstalliedcorp.com. **Description:** Manages several properties including plazas, mobile homes, and nursing homes. **Corporate headquarters location:** This location. **Other locations:** CA; FL; NY. **Number of employees at this location:** 25.

HELMSLEY ENTERPRISES, INC.
dba HELMSLEY-NOYES COMPANY INC.
230 Park Avenue, Suite 659, New York NY 10169-0399. 212/679-3600. **Fax:** 212/953-2810. **Contact:** Human Resources. **Description:** A commercial real estate agency engaged in the management of office buildings and a wide range of other institutional buildings including department stores, hotels, and corporate office buildings. **Corporate headquarters location:** This location. **Subsidiaries include:** Helmsley Hotels. **Chairperson/CEO:** Leona Helmsley. **Annual sales/revenues:** $1 billion. **Number of employees:** 3,000.

HELMSLEY-SPEAR, INC.
60 East 42nd Street, 53rd Floor, New York NY 10165. 212/687-6400. **Contact:** Human Resources Department. **World Wide Web address:** http://www.helmsleyspear.com. **Description:** One of the largest real estate service companies in the nation offering leasing (including industrial leasing, and retail and store leasing divisions); sales and brokerage; management; development; appraisals; and financing services. Founded in 1866. **Corporate headquarters location:** This location. **Parent company:** Helmsley Enterprises, Inc. (New York NY).

INSIGNIA DOUGLAS ELLIMAN
575 Madison Avenue, New York NY 10022. 212/832-0083. **Toll-free phone:** 800/355-4626. **Fax:** 212/891-7239. **Contact:** Human Resources. **E-mail address:** inquiry@elliman.com. **Description:** A real estate firm engaged in apartment sales, rentals, and insurance. **Subsidiaries include:** Insignia/ESG, Inc.; Insignia Richard Ellis; Insignia Residential Group. **Operations at this facility include:** Administration; Sales; Service.

KABLE MEDIA SERVICES
505 Park Avenue, New York NY 10022. 212/705-4624. **Contact:** Human Resources. **World Wide Web address:** http://www.kable.com. **Description:** Kable Media Services is a major landholder and real estate developer in New Mexico. Through Kable Fulfillment Services, Inc., it provides magazine subscription services and product merchandise fulfillment for publishers and direct marketers. Kable Distribution Services, Inc., another subsidiary, is an international distributor of periodicals for 200 publishing clients. **Other U.S. locations:** Mt. Morris IL; Marion OH; Louisville CO. **Parent company:** AMREP Corporation.

LEXINGTON CORPORATE PROPERTIES TRUST
One Penn Plaza, Suite 4015, New York NY 10119-4015. 212/692-7200. **Fax:** 212/594-6600. **Contact:** Human Resources. **E-mail address:** info@lxp.com. **World Wide Web address:** http://www.lxp.com. **Description:** A real estate investment trust that owns and manages office, industrial, and retail properties located in 30 states. Founded in 1993. **Corporate headquarters location:** This location. **Subsidiaries include:** Lexington Realty Advisors. **Listed on:** New York Stock Exchange. **Stock exchange symbol:** LXP. **Number of employees:** 25.

J.W. MAYS, INC.
9 Bond Street, Brooklyn NY 11201-5805. 718/624-7400. **Fax:** 718/935-0378. **Contact:** Frank Mollo, Personnel Director. **World Wide Web address:** http://www.jwmays.com. **Description:** A real estate company operating seven commercial properties in Brooklyn, Jamaica, Levittown, Fishkill, and Dutchess County NY, as well as a warehouse in Circleville OH, all of which were former department store locations, which the company liquidated in 1989. Since 1924. **Corporate headquarters location:** This location. **Listed on:** NASDAQ. **Stock exchange symbol:** MAYS. **Number of employees:** 31.

UNITED CAPITAL CORPORATION
United Capital Building, 9 Park Place, 4th Floor, Great Neck NY 11021. 516/466-6464. **Contact:** Human Resources. **Description:** United Capital Corporation invests in and manages real estate properties. **Subsidiaries include:** Metex Corporation provides antenna systems and knitted wire products to aviation and automotive markets worldwide. **Corporate headquarters location:** This location. **Listed on:** AMEX. **Stock exchange symbol:** AFP.

North Carolina
CB RICHARD ELLIS
201 South College Street, Suite 1900, Charlotte NC 28244. 704/376-7979. **Fax:** 704/331-1259. **Contact:** Steven H. Gassaway, Managing Director. **E-mail address:** steven.gassaway@cbre.com. **World Wide Web address:** http://www.cbre.com. **Description:** A real estate services company offering property sales and leasing, property and facility management, mortgage banking, and investment management services. **Corporate headquarters location:** Los Angeles CA. **Other area locations:** Greensboro NC; Raleigh NC; Research Triangle Park NC. **Other U.S. locations:** Nationwide. **International locations:** Worldwide. **Number of employees nationwide:** 9,600. **Number of employees worldwide:** 13,500.

K. HOVNANIAN HOMES
4310 Regency Drive, Suite 100, Greensboro NC 27265. 336/375-6200. **Fax:** 336/375-6355. **Contact:** Human Resources. **World Wide Web address:** http://www.khov.com. **Description:** A real estate and construction company. Founded in 1959. **Positions advertised include:** Assistant Community Construction Manager; Mortgage Account Manager. **Other area locations:** Cary NC; Charlotte NC; High Point NC. **Other U.S. locations:** Nationwide.

PRUDENTIAL CAROLINAS REALTY
380 Knollwood Street, Suite 420, Winston-Salem NC 27103. 336/721-4700. **Contact:** Director of Recruiting. **World Wide Web address:** http://www.prudential-carolinas.com. **Description:** A real estate company specializing in residential properties. **Corporate headquarters location:** This location. **Other area locations:** Statewide. **Other U.S. locations:** Rock Hill SC.

Ohio
CENTURY 21
JOE WALKER & ASSOCIATES
2965 East Dublin-Granville Road, Westerville OH 43081. 614/899-1400. **Fax:** 614/899-0955. **Contact:** Craig Barone, Recruiting and Career Development. **E-mail address:** craig.barone@aol.com. **World Wide Web address:** http://www.c21joewalker.com. **Description:** A real estate company serving nine counties in central Ohio. **Corporate headquarters location:** This location. **Other area locations:** Columbus OH; Delaware OH; Reynoldsburg OH; Sunbury OH.

CONTINENTAL REAL ESTATE COMPANY
150 East Broad Street, 3rd Floor, Columbus OH 43215. 614/221-1800. **Fax:** 614/221-6365. **Contact:** Human Resources. **E-mail address:** info@continental-realestate.com. **World Wide Web address:** http://www.continental-realestate.com. **Description:** Leases, buys, develops, and manages property.

FOREST CITY ENTERPRISES INC.
50 Public Square, Terminal Tower, Suite 1300, Cleveland OH 44113-2203. 216/621-6060. **Fax:** 216/263-6208. **Contact:** Human Resources. **E-mail address:** humanresources@forestcity.net. **World Wide Web address:** http://www.fceinc.com. **Description:** A real estate investment trust that acquires, develops, and operates commercial, residential, urban entertainment, and land development properties. **NOTE:** Submit resumes to: Forest City Enterprises, Inc., Human Resources Department; 50 Public Square, Suite 1026, Cleveland OH 44113. **Positions advertised include:** Project Manager; Property Analyst; Secretary; Senior Accountant; Senior Auditor; Technical Support Specialist. **Listed on:** New York Stock Exchange. **Stock exchange symbol:** FCEA.

WINEGARDNER AND HAMMONS INC.
4243 Hunt Road, 4th Floor, Cincinnati OH 45242. 513/891-1066. **Fax:** 513/794-2595. **Contact:** Dave Gordon, Human Resources. **E-mail address:** dave.gordon@whihotels.com. **World Wide Web address:** http://www.whihotels.com. **Description:** A hotel managing agency. **Positions advertised include:** Business Development Account Manager.

Oregon
COLDWELL BANKER
BARBARA SUE SEAL PROPERTIES, INC.
2275 W. Burnside Road, Portland OR 97210. 503/224-7325. **Toll-free phone:** 800/342-7767. **Contact:**

Personnel. **E-mail address:** recruiting@cbseal.com. **World Wide Web address:** http://www.cbportland.com. **Description:** A residential real estate company with 15 sales offices. Founded in 1983.

THE HASSON COMPANY REALTORS
15400 SW Boones Ferry Road, Lake Oswego OR 97035. 503/635-9801. **Contact:** Human Resources. **World Wide Web address:** http://www.hasson.com. **Description:** Specializes in the buying and selling of residential property. **NOTE:** Human Resources mailing address is 4500 Cruz Way, Suite 170, Lake Oswego OR 97035. **Corporate headquarters location:** This location. **Other U.S. locations:** Portland OR.

NORRIS, BEGGS & SIMPSON REALTORS
121 SW Morrison Street, Suite 200, Portland OR 97204. 503/223-7181. **Fax:** 503/273-0256. **Contact:** Human Resources. **World Wide Web address:** http://www.nbsrealtors.com. **Description:** A realty company specializing in consulting, sales, leasing, investments, asset management, property management, and real estate finance. Founded in 1932. **Other U.S. locations:** WA.

PACTRUST
15350 SW Sequoia Parkway, Suite 300, Portland OR 97224. 503/624-6300. **Fax:** 503/624-7755. **Contact:** Human Resources Department. **World Wide Web address:** http://www.pactrust.com. **Description:** A real estate investment trust, founded in 1972, with both developed and un-developed properties in its portfolio.

THE PRUDENTIAL NORTHWEST PROPERTIES
14945 SW Sequoia Parkway, Suite 150, Portland OR 97224. 503/646-7826. **Contact:** Human Resources. **E-mail address:** careers@pru-nw.com. **World Wide Web address:** http://www.pru-nw.com. **Description:** Provides a wide range of real estate services to corporate and residential clients. **Corporate headquarters location:** This location.

Pennsylvania

BINSWANGER
2 Logan Square, 4th Floor, Philadelphia PA 19103. 215/448-6200. **Contact:** Frank G. Binswanger III. **E-mail address:** fgbiii@binswanger.com. **World Wide Web address:** http://www.cbbi.com. **Description:** Sells commercial and industrial real estate. **Corporate headquarters location:** This location. **Other U.S. locations:** Nationwide. **International locations:** Worldwide.

CB RICHARD ELLIS
1800 JFK Boulevard, Philadelphia PA 19103-3272. 215/561-8900. **Fax:** 215/557-6719. **Contact:** Human Resources Manager. **World Wide Web address:** http://www.cbrichardellis.com. **Description:** A real estate services company offering property sales and leasing, property management, corporate facilities management, mortgage banking, and market research. **NOTE:** Please see the website for current job openings in each division. **Positions advertised include:** Sr. Project Manager. **Corporate headquarters location:** Los Angeles CA. **Other U.S. locations:** Nationwide. **Number of employees worldwide:** 13,500.

GRUBB & ELLIS COMPANY
600 Six PPG Place, Pittsburgh PA 15222. 412/281-0100. **Fax:** 412/281-8814. **Contact:** Property Management Department. **E-mail address:** jobs@grubb-ellis.com. **World Wide Web address:** http://www.grubb-ellis.com. **Description:** A commercial and industrial real estate brokerage. Grubb & Ellis also specializes in property management, and institutional and individual investment. **Positions advertised include:** Property Accountant. **Other U.S. locations:** Nationwide. **Listed on:** New York Stock Exchange. **Stock exchange symbol:** GBE.

PENNSYLVANIA REAL ESTATE INVESTMENT TRUST
200 South Broad Street, 3rd Floor, Philadelphia PA 19102-3803. 215/875-0700. **Fax:** 215/546-7311. **Contact:** Human Resources. **World Wide Web address:** http://www.preit.com. **Description:** An equity real estate investment trust engaged in the business of managing, acquiring, and holding for investment real estate and interests in real estate. The trust's principal real estate assets consist of 48 properties, 20 of which are wholly-owned and 28 of which are owned by partnerships or joint ventures. **Positions advertised include:** Marketing Director; Tenant Coordinator; Lease Administrator; Director of Corporate Communications; Corporate Accountant; Treasury Analyst. **Listed on:** New York Stock Exchange. **Stock exchange symbol:** PEI.

South Carolina

AMERICAN INVESTMENT AND MANAGEMENT COMPANY (AIMCO)
P.O. Box 1089, Greenville SC 29602. 864/239-2678. **Physical address:** 55 Beattie Place, Third Floor, Greenville SC 29601. **Fax:** 864/239-5819. **Contact:** Martin Haider, Human Resources. **E-mail address:** martin.haider@aimco.com. **World Wide Web address:** http://www.aimco.com. **Description:** A real estate investment trust, management and mortgage banking company managing over 300,000 apartments nationwide. **Positions advertised include:** Real Estate Accountant; Programmer/Analyst. **Corporate headquarters location:** Denver CO. **Other area locations:** Statewide. **Other U.S. locations:** Nationwide. **Listed on:** New York Stock Exchange. **Stock exchange symbol:** AIV. **Annual sales/revenues:** $1.6 billion. **Number of employees nationwide:** 7,800.

DUNES PROPERTIES OF CHARLESTON, INC.
1400 Palm Boulevard. P.O. Box 524, Isle of Palms SC 29451. 843/886-5600. **Toll-free phone:** 800/476-8444. **Fax:** 843/886-4953. **Contact:** Human Resources. **World Wide Web address:** http://www.dunesproperties.com. **Description:** A rental agency for resort and vacation properties. **Positions available include:** Administrative Assistant; Front Desk Sales Agent; Property and Real Estate Manager. **Corporate headquarters location:** This location. **Other area locations:** Folley Beach SC; Johns Island SC; Mount Pleasant SC. **Listed on:** Privately held.

KIAWAH ISLAND REAL ESTATE
P.O. Box 12001, Charleston SC 29422. 843/768-3400. **Physical address:** 7 Beachwalker Drive, Kiawah Island SC 29455. **Toll-free phone:** 888/559-9024. **Contact:** Corporate Recruiter. **E-mail address:** employment@kiawahisland.com. **World Wide Web address:** http://www.kiawahisland.com. **Description:** A real estate company specializing in residential properties. **Positions advertised include:** Real Estate Communications Coordinator; Marketing Production Coordinator.

SOUTHEASTERN COMMERCIAL SERVICES
22 New Orleans Road, Suite 2, P.O. Box 6958, Hilton Head Island SC 29938. 843/686-6660. **Fax:** 843/342-3428. **Contact:** Office Manager. **Description:** A commercial property real estate company.

ZIFF PROPERTIES, INC.
701 East Bay Street, Charleston SC 29403. 843/724-3500. **Contact:** Human Resources. **E-mail address:** email@zpi.net. **World Wide Web address:** http://www.zpi.net. **Description:** A real estate company that specializes in the acquisition of shopping centers, office buildings and light industrial properties in the South East. **Positions advertised include:** Accountant; Accounts Payable Supervisor. **Number of employees:** 30.

Tennessee

BELZ ENTERPRISES
100 Peabody Place, Suite 1400, Memphis TN 38103. 901/260-7348. **Fax:** 901/260-7378. **Contact:** Irvin Scopp, Director of Human Resources. **E-mail address:** info@belz.com. **World Wide Web address:** http://www.belz.com. **Description:** A real estate development and property management company. Belz

Enterprises specializes in hotel, industrial, office, residential, retail, warehouse, and underdeveloped land properties. **Corporate headquarters location:** This location.

COOPER COMPANIES
1407 Union Avenue, Suite 400, Memphis TN 38104. 901/725-9631. **Contact:** Pace Cooper, President. **World Wide Web address:** http://www.cooperhotels.com. **Description:** Provides property management and real estate services and operates several hotels.

CRYE-LEIKE REALTORS
5111 Maryland Way, Brentwood TN 37027. 615/373-2044. **Contact:** Human Resources. **World Wide Web address:** http://www.crye-leike.com. **Description:** A full-service real estate firm with 10 offices across the state. **Positions advertised include:** Relocation Consultant.

KEMMONS WILSON, INC.
8700 Trail Lake Drive West, Suite 300, Memphis TN 38125. 901/346-8808. **Fax:** 901/396-8807. **Contact:** Human Resources. **World Wide Web address:** http://www.kwilson.com. **Description:** Involved in the development and management of hotels, real estate, banking, and manufacturing. **Listed on:** Privately held. **Number of employees at this location:** 600. **Number of employees nationwide:** 2,700.

NATIONAL HEALTH INVESTORS, INC. (NHI)
100 Vine Street, Suite 1402, Murfreesboro TN 37130. 615/890-9100. **Fax:** 615/890-0123. **Contact:** Human Resources. **World Wide Web address:** http://www.nhinvestors.com. **Description:** A real estate investment trust that specializes in the purchase and leaseback of health care real estate, as well as the creation of mortgage loans for health care operators. NHI owns or mortgages 167 properties in 20 states. **Listed on:** New York Stock Exchange. **Stock exchange symbol:** NHI.

SCHATTEN PROPERTIES MANAGEMENT COMPANY, INC.
1514 South Street, Nashville TN 37212. 615/329-3011. **Contact:** Controller. **World Wide Web address:** http://www.schattenproperties.com. **Description:** A property management firm. Founded in 1940. **Positions advertised include:** Maintenance Technician; Leasing Agent. **Corporate headquarters location:** This location.

Texas
BRADFIELD PROPERTIES INC.
Fair Oaks Ranch, San Antonio TX 78201. 210/340-6500. **Fax:** 210/340-7130. **Contact:** Boyd Bradfield, Human Resources. **World Wide Web address:** http://www.bradfieldproperties.com. **Description:** A real estate company specializing in residential, commercial, and multifamily property management. Founded 1982. **NOTE:** There are seven locations in San Antonio in addition to the corporate office. **Corporate headquarters location:** This location. **Other area locations:** Boerne TX; Bulverde TX; New Braunfels TX.

CAMDEN PROPERTY TRUST
3 Greenway Plaza, Suite 1300, Houston TX 77060. 713/354-2500. **Recorded jobline:** 866/524-3592. **Toll-free phone:** 800/9-CAMDEN. **Contact:** Recruiting Manager. **E-mail address:** jobs@camdenliving.com. **World Wide Web address:** http://www.camdenliving.com. **Description:** A real estate investment trust that buys, sells, builds, and manages apartment communities throughout the Southwest. **NOTE:** Entry-level positions are offered. Please visit website to search for jobs. **Positions advertised include:** Director of Internal Audit; Financial Analyst. **Corporate headquarters location:** This location. **Other area locations:** Austin TX; Corpus Christi TX; Dallas TX; El Paso TX; Fort Worth TX; San Antonio TX. **Other U.S. locations:** AZ; CA; CO; FL; KY; MO; NC; NV. **Operations at this facility include:** Administration. **Listed on:** New York Stock Exchange. **Stock exchange symbol:** CPT. **Number of employees nationwide:** 1,750.

CAPSTONE REAL ESTATE SERVICES
210 Barton 512/646-6700Springs Road, Suite 300, Austin TX 78704. 512/646-6700. **Fax:** 512/646-6798. **Contact:** Human Resources. **E-mail address:** info@capstonemanagement.com. **World Wide Web address:** http://www.capstonerealestate.com. **Description:** Sells, rents, and leases apartments and commercial properties. **Corporate headquarters location:** This location. **Other area locations:** Houston TX; Dallas/Fort Worth TX; San Antonio TX. **Other U.S. locations:** FL. **President:** James W. Berkey. **Number of employees nationwide:** 550.

COLDWELL BANKER
7447 North MacArthur Boulevard, Suite 190, Irving TX 75063. 469/420-3900. **Fax:** 972/373-0853. **Contact:** Personnel. **World Wide Web address:** http://www.coldwellbanker.com. **Description:** One of the largest residential real estate companies in the United States and Canada in terms of total home sales transactions. Coldwell Banker is also a leader in corporate relocation services. **NOTE:** This office hires agents only. Please visit website to search for jobs. **Corporate headquarters location:** Parsippany NJ. **Other U.S. locations:** Nationwide. **Parent company:** Cendant Corporation. **Listed on:** New York Stock Exchange. **Stock exchange symbol:** CD. **Number of employees worldwide:** 112,000.

GRUBB & ELLIS
Three Lincoln Center, 5430 LBJ Freeway, No.: 1400, Dallas TX 75240. 972/450-3300. **Contact:** Human Resources. **World Wide Web address:** http://www.grubbellis.com. **Description:** A real estate services firm dealing primarily with commercial properties including shopping centers, office buildings, and similar complexes. Founded in 1958. **Corporate headquarters location:** Northbrook IL.

HINES PROPERTIES INC.
Williams Tower, 2800 Post Oak Boulevard, 48th Floor, Houston TX 77056. 713/966-2629. **Fax:** 713/621-8000. **Contact:** Human Resources. **E-mail address:** Hines_HR@hines.com. **World Wide Web address:** http://www.hines.com. **Description:** Engaged in commercial real estate development and property management. The company has properties in 39 U.S. cities. **NOTE:** Resumes must be submitted online via the company's website or via e-mail. **Corporate headquarters location:** This location. **Other U.S. locations:** Nationwide. **International locations:** Worldwide. **Operations at this facility include:** Administration.

KELLER WILLIAMS REALTORS (LAKE CITIES)
405 Mayfield Avenue, Garland TX 75041. 972/240-4416. **Contact:** Human Resources. **World Wide Web address:** http://www.mc.kw.com. **Description:** A realty company offering both residential and commercial properties. **NOTE:** This is one location of this company. See the corporate website at http://www.kw.com for additional locations throughout Texas and the United States. All interested jobseekers must apply online. **Positions advertised include:** Team Leader; Market Center Administrator; Administrative Assistant; Listing Specialist/Coordinator; Buyer Specialist.

LINCOLN PROPERTY COMPANY
3300 Lincoln Plaza, 500 North Akard Street, Suite 3300, Dallas TX 75201. 214/740-3300. **Contact:** Human Resources. **World Wide Web address:** http://www.lincolnproperty.com. **Description:** A property management company with commercial, residential, and industrial properties. **Positions advertised include:** Tenant Service Coordinator.

MACFARLAN REAL ESTATE
10100 North Central Expressway, Suite 200, Dallas TX 75231. 214/932-3100. **Fax:** 214/932-3199. **Contact:**

Human Resources. **E-mail address:** careers@macfarlan.com. **World Wide Web address:** http://www.macfarlan.com. **Description:** A commercial real estate agency. **Corporate headquarters location:** This location.

POSTON PROPERTIES
300 Crescent Court, Dallas TX 75201. 214/696-0900. **Fax:** 214/369-6996. **Contact:** Personnel. **World Wide Web address:** http://www.adletaposton.com. **Description:** A residential real estate brokerage specializing in the luxury housing and corporate relocation markets. **Positions advertised include:** Real Estate Agent; Receptionist; Secretary. **Special programs:** Internships. **Corporate headquarters location:** This location. **Operations at this facility include:** Administration; Sales. **Number of employees at this location:** 10.

TRAMMELL CROW COMPANY
2001 Ross Avenue, Suite 3400, Dallas TX 75201-2997. 214/863-3000. **Fax:** 214/863-3125. **Contact:** Human Resources. **World Wide Web address:** http://www.trammellcrow.com. **Description:** A national real estate development and brokerage agency. Founded in 1948. **NOTE:** This company has other Texas locations. See its website for addresses, job listings and contact information. **Positions advertised include:** Accounting Associate; CPU Coordinator; Executive Assistant; Lead Operating Engineer; Local Marketing Services Engineer; Security Staff. **Special programs:** Internships. **Other area locations:** Carrolton, TX; Fort Worth, TX; Houston TX; Irving TX; Plano, TX; Richardson TX; San Antonio TX. **Listed on:** New York Stock Exchange. **Stock exchange symbol:** TCC.

USAA REAL ESTATE COMPANY
9800 Fredericksburg Road, San Antonio TX 78288. 210/498-1289. **Toll-free phone:** 800/531-8022. **Fax:** 210/498-1489. **Contact:** Human Resources. **World Wide Web address:** http://www.usaa.com. **Description:** Engaged in commercial real estate services for corporate, institutional, and private investors. **NOTE:** On its website, this company provides job listings, addresses, and contact information for its other locations. **Positions advertised include:** Senior Financial Advisor; Financial Analyst; Commercial Strategy Advisor; Managing Editor; Marketing Director; Teller; Shipper; Consumer Loan Processing; Legal Secretary; Employee Communications Writer; Credit Card Specialist. **Other U.S. locations:** AZ; VA; CO; FL; CA. **International locations:** London; Frankfurt.

WEINGARTEN REALTY INVESTORS
P.O. Box 924133, Houston TX 77292-4133. 713/866-6000. **Physical address:** 2600 Citadel Plaza Drive, Suite 300, Houston TX 77008. **Fax:** 713/866-6049. **Contact:** Human Resources. **E-mail address:** jobs@weingarten.com. **World Wide Web address:** http://www.weingarten.com. **Description:** Buys, sells, and manages shopping centers and industrial properties. **Positions advertised include:** Accounting Assistant; Regional Property Manager; Leasing Representative; Senior Leasing Executive; Regional Director of New Developer. **Stock exchange symbol:** WRI.

WILDWOOD MANAGEMENT GROUP
18585 Sigma Road, Suite 101, San Antonio TX 78258. 210/403-9785. **Contact:** Human Resources. **Description:** Engaged in property management for apartments and condominiums.

WUKASCH COMPANY
1810 Guadalupe Street, Austin TX 78701. 512/472-4700. **Contact:** Don C. Wukasch, President. **Description:** A diversified real estate and securities investment company providing real estate property management and securities portfolio management. **Special programs:** Internships. **Corporate headquarters location:** This location. **Listed on:** Privately held.

WYNNE/JACKSON, INC.
600 North Pearl Street, Suite 650, Dallas TX 75201. 214/880-8600. **Fax:** 214/880-8709. **Contact:** Frank Murphy, Senior Vice President and Chief Financial Officer. **World Wide Web address:** http://www.wynnejackson.com. **Description:** A commercial real estate development and property management company. **Corporate headquarters location:** This location.

Utah

COLDWELL BANKER RESIDENTIAL BROKERAGE
2733 East Parleys Way, Suite 202, Salt Lake City UT 84109. 801/467-9000. **Fax:** 801/486-2777. **Contact:** Karen Sitton, Human Resources. **E-mail address:** karen.sitton@utahhomes.com. **World Wide Web address:** http://www.utahhomes.com. **Description:** One of the largest Utah-based real estate companies with over 1,000 full-time agents and 16 offices located along the Wasatch Front. **Other area locations:** Statewide. **Parent company:** Coldwell Banker. **Listed on:** New York Stock Exchange. **Stock exchange symbol:** CD. **Number of employees worldwide:** 112,000.

DEER VALLEY LODGING
1375 Deer Valley Drive South, P.O. Box 3000, Park City UT 84060. 435/649-4040. **Toll-free phone:** 800/782-4813. **Fax:** 435/655-4816. **Contact:** Human Resources. **E-mail address:** hrdept@deervalleylodging.com. **World Wide Web address:** http://www.deervalleylodging.com. **Description:** Rents condominium-style accommodations to visitors in the Deer Valley area. **NOTE:** Seasonal and full-time positions available. See website for current job openings and to apply online. **Positions advertised include:** Accounts Payable & Receivable; Area Manager; Assistant Area Mgr/Housekeeping; Maintenance Tech.

Vermont

COLDWELL BANKER HICKOK & BOARDMAN REALTY
345 Shelburne Road, P.O. Box 1064, Burlington VT 05402. 802/863-1500. **Toll-free phone:** 800/639-5520. **Fax:** 802/658-7616. **Contact:** Annemarie Daniels. **E-mail address:** careers@hickokandboardman.com. **World Wide Web address:** http://www.hickokandboardman.com. **Description:** Provides residential and commercial real estate services. **Positions advertised include:** Real Estate Sales Associate. **Number of employees at this location:** Over 50.

Virginia

AVALONBAY COMMUNITIES, INC.
2900 Eisenhower Avenue, Suite 300, Alexandria VA 22314. 703/329-6300. **Fax:** 703/329-9130. **Contact:** Rita Grazda, Director of Human Resources. **World Wide Web address:** http://www.avalonbay.com. **Description:** A self-administered and self-managed equity real estate investment trust that specializes in the development, construction, acquisition, and management of apartment communities in the mid-Atlantic and northeastern United States. AvalonBay owns or operates 143 apartment communities in ten states and D.C. **NOTE:** Search and apply for positions online. **Positions advertised include:** Accounting Manager; Sr. Leasing Consultant; Business Information Manager; Director of Rehab Construction; Procurement Analyst. **Corporate headquarters location:** This location. **Listed on:** New York Stock Exchange. **Stock exchange symbol:** AVB.

CB RICHARD ELLIS
7501 Boulders View Drive, Suite 600, Richmond VA 23225. 804/320-5500. **Fax:** 804/320-4839. **Contact:** Human Resources. **E-mail address:** opps@crbe.com. **World Wide Web address:** http://www.cbrichardellis.com. **Description:** A real estate services company offering property sales and leasing, property and facility management, mortgage

banking, and investment management services. **Positions advertised include:** Financial Analyst; Marketing Assistant; Research Assistant; Finance Manager. **Corporate headquarters location:** Los Angeles CA. **Other U.S. locations:** Nationwide. **International locations:** Worldwide. **Number of employees at this location:** 60. **Number of employees worldwide:** 13,500.

LEGUM & NORMAN
4401 Ford Avenue, 12th Floor, Alexandria VA 22302. 703/600-6000. **Toll-free phone:** 800/255-3486. **Fax:** 703/848-0982. **Contact:** Personnel. **E-mail address:** careers@legumnorman.com. **World Wide Web address:** http://www.legumnorman.com. **Description:** A privately owned real estate services company offering property and facility management services. **NOTE:** Submit resume via mail. **Corporate headquarters location:** This location. **Other U.S. locations:** Chicago IL; Ocean City MD.

UNITED DOMINION REALTY TRUST, INC.
400 East Cary Street, Richmond VA 23219. 804/780-2691. **Fax:** 804/343-1912. **Contact:** Human Resources. **World Wide Web address:** http://www.udrt.com. **Description:** One of the largest real estate investment trusts specializing in residential apartment communities in the Southeast. The trust owns 138 properties including over 75,000 apartments in 120 communities, 14 neighborhood shopping centers, and four other commercial properties. Founded in 1972. **NOTE:** Search and apply for positions online. **Positions advertised include:** Construction Manager. **Corporate headquarters location:** This location. **Listed on:** New York Stock Exchange. **Stock exchange symbol:** UDR.

Washington
CB RICHARD ELLIS
1420 Fifth Avenue, Suite 1700, Seattle WA 98101-2314. 206/292-1600. **Contact:** Human Resources. **E-mail address:** opps@cbre.com. **World Wide Web address:** http://www.cbrichardellis.com. **Description:** A fully-integrated real estate and real estate-related service company. **Corporate headquarters location:** Los Angeles CA.

CAPITAL DEVELOPMENT COMPANY
711 Sleater Kinney Road Southeast, Lacey WA 98503. 360/491-6850. **Contact:** Human Resources. **Description:** Engaged in a variety of construction activities including contracting, leasing, and property development and management.

CUSHMAN & WAKEFIELD OF WASHINGTON INC.
1420 Fifth Avenue, Suite 2900, Seattle WA 98101. 206/682-0666. **Contact:** Human Resources. **World Wide Web address:** http://www.cushwake.com/us. **Description:** A real estate services firm offering sales, property management, and appraisal services. **Corporate headquarters location:** New York NY.

DIAMOND PARKING SERVICES, INC.
3161 Elliott Avenue, Suite 200, Seattle WA 98121. 206/284-3100. **Contact:** Personnel. **E-mail address:** hr@diamondparking.com. **World Wide Web address:** http://www.diamondparking.com. **Description:** Owns parking facilities and is involved in real estate. **Corporate headquarters location:** This location. **Number of employees at this location:** 200.

EXPORTS INC.
435 Martin Street, Suite 4000, Blaine WA 98230. 360/332-5239. **Contact:** Human Resources. **Description:** A property management firm involved in the financial management of corporate properties.

OLYMPIC RESOURCE MANAGEMENT
P.O. Box 1780, Poulsbo WA 98370. 360/697-6626. **Physical address:** 19245 10th Avenue NE, Poulsbo WA 98370. **Contact:** Human Resources. **World Wide Web address:** http://www.orm.com. **Description:** Plants and harvests trees sold as timber to the domestic market. This company is also engaged in real estate development. **Parent company:** Pope Resources.

PRUDENTIAL MACPHERSON
18551 Aurora Avenue North, Suite 100, Shoreline WA 98133. 206/546-4124. **Contact:** Personnel Department. **World Wide Web address:** http://www.macphersons.com. **Description:** A real estate company that also operates apartment buildings and provides related services.

Wisconsin
COLDWELL BANKER ACTION REALTY
928 Grand Avenue, Schofield WI 54476. 715/359-0521. **Toll-free phone:** 800/632-2846. **Fax:** 715/359-4826. **Contact:** Human Resources. **E-mail address:** getaction@coldwellbankeraction.com. **World Wide Web address:** http://www.coldwellbankeraction.com. **Description:** A major real estate agency in central Wisconsin. **Parent company:** Coldwell Banker Real Estate Corporation (Parsippany NJ) is one of the three largest residential real estate companies in the United States and Canada in total home sales transactions. The company has 3,500 independently owned and operated offices. **Number of employees at this location:** 75.

WISCONSIN MANAGEMENT COMPANY
2040 South Park Street, Madison WI 53713. 608/258-2080. **Toll-free phone:** 800/480-2080. **Contact:** Human Resources. **World Wide Web address:** http://www.wimci.com. **Description:** A real estate management company that handles apartment complexes, condominiums, and dormitories. **Corporate headquarters location:** This location.

RETAIL

You can expect to find the following types of companies in this section:

Catalog Retailers • Department Stores, Specialty Stores • Retail Bakeries • Supermarkets

---

Employment in retail trade is expected to increase by 1,649,000 jobs or 10.9%, from just over 15 million to 16.7 million. Increases in population, personal income, and leisure time will contribute to employment growth in this industry, as consumers demand more goods.

Alabama

BARNES & NOBLE BOOKSTORES
5850A University Village, Huntsville AL 35806. 256/864-2090. **Contact:** Manager. **World Wide Web address:** http://www.barnesandnoble.com. **Description:** A bookstore chain operating nationwide. This location has a cafe in addition to its comprehensive book departments.

BOOKS-A-MILLION, INC.
402 Industrial Lane, Birmingham AL 35211. 205/942-3737. **Contact:** Human Resources. **E-mail address:** jobs@booksamillioninc.com. **World Wide Web address:** http://www.booksamillioninc.com. **Description:** One of the nation's largest book retailers with a network of more than 200 bookstores in 19 states, primarily in the Southeast. Books-A-Million also operates a book wholesale and distribution subsidiary, American Wholesale Book Company, and an online bookstore at http://www.booksamillion.com. **Positions advertised include:** Director of Internal Audit; Buyer's Assistant. **Corporate headquarters location:** This location. **Subsidiaries include:** American Wholesale Book Company, Inc. **Listed on:** NASDAQ. **Stock exchange symbol:** BAMM. **President/CEO:** Clyde B. Anderson. **Annual sales/revenues:** More than $100 million.

BRUNO'S SUPERMARKETS, INC.
P.O. Box 2486, Birmingham AL 35201. 205/940-9400. **Physical address:** 800 Lakeshore Parkway, Birmingham AL 35211. **Fax:** 205/912-4628. **Contact:** Director of Employee Relations. **E-mail address:** HRRecruiting@brunos.com. **World Wide Web address:** http://www.brunos.com. **Description:** Operates a chain of 169 supermarkets and smaller food and liquor stores in four states. Stores include Food World, Bruno's, Food Fair, Food Max, and Food World Discount Liquors. **Corporate headquarters location:** This location. **Parent company:** AholdUSA. **Listed on:** Privately held. **Annual sales/revenues:** More than $100 million. **Number of employees nationwide:** 13,000.

CVS
901 9th Avenue North, Bessemer AL 35020. 205/426-1664. **Contact:** Human Resources. **World Wide Web address:** http://www.cvs.com. **Description:** CVS operates a chain of more than 5,000 stores in 36 states. Pharmacy operations make up a large portion of the company's business, offering both brand name and generic prescription drugs. CVS stores also offer a range of health and beauty aids, cosmetics, greeting cards, convenience foods, photo finishing services, and other general merchandise. **Corporate headquarters location:** Woonsocket RI. **Number of employees nationwide:** 100,000.

DILLARD'S DEPARTMENT STORES, INC.
3300 Bel Air, Mobile AL 36606. 251/471-1551. **Contact:** Human Resources. **World Wide Web address:** http://www.dillards.com. **Description:** Operates a retail chain offering a full line of fashion brand apparel and home furnishings. Most Dillard's stores are located in suburban shopping centers of the Southwest and Midwest. **Parent company:** Mercantile Stores Company (Cincinnati OH).

PARISIAN, INC.
750 Lakeshore Parkway, Birmingham AL 35211. 205/968-4200. **Contact:** Human Resources. **World Wide Web address:** http://www.parisian.com. **Description:** A chain of fashion specialty stores offering cosmetics, clothing, shoes, and accessories for men, women, and children. Parisian operates 43 department stores throughout the Southeast and Midwest. **Positions advertised include:** Assistant Sales Manager; Sales Manager; Visual Coordinator. **Other U.S. locations:** Nationwide. **Parent company:** Saks Incorporated is a department store holding company that operates approximately 360 stores in 36 states. The company's stores include Saks Fifth Avenue, Parisian, Proffit's, Younker's, Herberger's, Carson Pirie Scott, Boston Store, Bergner's, and Off 5th, the company's outlet store. Saks Incorporated also operates two retail catalogs and several retail Internet sites. **Operations at this facility include:** Administration. **Listed on:** New York Stock Exchange. **Stock exchange symbol:** SKS. **Number of employees at this location:** 850. **Number of employees nationwide:** 7,000.

SAKS INCORPORATED
750 Lakeshore Parkway, Birmingham AL 35211. 205/940-4000. **Contact:** Human Resources. **World Wide Web address:** http://www.saksincorporated.com. **Description:** Parisian operates 43 department stores throughout the Southeast and Midwest. Saks Incorporated is a department store holding company that operates a total of approximately 360 stores in 36 states. The company's stores include Saks Fifth Avenue, Parisian, Proffit's, Younker's, Herberger's, Carson Pirie Scott, Boston Store, Bergner's, and Off 5th, the company's outlet store. Saks Incorporated also operates two retail catalogs and several retail Internet sites. **Positions advertised include:** Corporate Recruiter. **Corporate headquarters location:** This location. **Operations at this facility include:** This location is the corporate headquarters for Saks Incorporated, a specialty department store holding company, and Parisian, a chain of fashion specialty stores offering cosmetics, clothing, shoes, and accessories for men, women, and children. **Listed on:** New York Stock Exchange. **Stock exchange symbol:** SKS.

THOMPSON TRACTOR CO., INC.
P.O. Box 10367, Birmingham AL 35202-0367. 205/849-4267. **Physical address:** 2401 Pinson Valley Parkway, Birmingham AL 35217. **Contact:** Human Resources. **E-mail address:** humanresourcessf@thompsontractor.com. **World Wide Web address:** http://thompsontractor.cat.com. **Description:** Sells, leases, and repairs Caterpillar construction equipment. Founded in 1957. **Positions advertised include:** Heavy Equipment Technicians; Welders; Machinists; Truck Engine Technicians; Lift Truck Technicians; Parts Warehouse Clerks; Power Train Component Specialists; Hydraulics Technicians. **Other U.S. locations:** FL, GA. **Number of employees nationwide:** 1,100.

Alaska

ALASKA COMMERCIAL COMPANY
550 West 64th Avenue, Suite 200, Anchorage AK 99518-1720. 907/273-4600. **Fax:** 907/273-4800. **Contact:** John Stott, Director of Human Resources. **World Wide Web address:** http://www.alaskacommercial.com. **Description:** Operates a retail chain of general merchandise stores. **NOTE:** Employment application available online. **Positions advertised include:** Branch Manager;

Assistant Branch Manager; Department Supervisor; Assistant Department Supervisor; Management Associate; Store Team Leader. **Corporate headquarters location:** This location. **Parent company:** The North West Company. **Annual sales/revenues:** $51 - $100 million. **Number of employees at this location:** 100. **Number of employees nationwide:** 750.

BARNES & NOBLE BOOKSTORES
200 East Northern Lights Boulevard, Anchorage AK 99503. 907/279-7323. **Contact:** Manager. **World Wide Web address:** http://www.bn.com. **Description:** A national bookstore chain operating nationwide. This location also has a cafe and music department.

Arizona

ALBERTSON'S
400 South 99th Avenue, Suite 200, Tolleson AZ 85353. 602/382-5300. **Contact:** Human Resources. **E-mail address:** employment@albertsons.com. **World Wide Web address:** http://www.albertsons.com. **Description:** A full-service supermarket. Founded in 1939. **NOTE:** Search and apply for positions online. **Corporate headquarters location:** Boise ID. **Listed on:** New York Stock Exchange. **Stock exchange symbol:** ABS. **Number of employees nationwide:** 200,000.

BARNES & NOBLE BOOKSTORES
10235 North Metro Parkway East, Phoenix AZ 85051. 602/678-0088. **Contact:** Manager. **World Wide Web address:** http://www.bn.com. **Description:** A discount bookstore chain operating nationwide. This location has a cafe in addition to its comprehensive book departments. **Corporate headquarters location:** New York NY. **Listed on:** New York Stock Exchange. **Stock exchange symbol:** BKS.

BASHAS'
P.O. Box 488, Chandler AZ 85244. 480/895-9350. **Fax:** 480/895-5232. **Physical address:** 22402 South Basha Road, Chandler AZ 85248. **Contact:** Human Resources. **World Wide Web address:** http://www.bashas.com. **Description:** Operates a chain of retail grocery stores. Founded in 1932. **Corporate headquarters location:** This location. **Number of employees nationwide:** 3,400.

COURTESY CHEVROLET
1233 East Camelback Road, Phoenix AZ 85014. 602/279-3232. **Contact:** Human Resources. **World Wide Web address:** http://www.courtesychev.com. **Description:** Provides automobile sales and service. **Corporate headquarters location:** This location. **Listed on:** Privately held. **Number of employees at this location:** 260.

DAVID'S BRIDAL
Ahwatukee Foothills Towne Center, 5043 East Ray Road, Phoenix AZ 85044. 480/785-7300. **Contact:** Human Resources. **E-mail address:** staffing@davidsbridal.net. **World Wide Web address:** http://www.davidsbridal.com. **Description:** One of the nation's largest bridal retailers. The company operates more than 80 David's Bridal stores nationwide. Founded in 1950. **Corporate headquarters location:** Conshohocken PA. **Number of employees nationwide:** 1,500.

DILLARD'S DEPARTMENT STORES, INC.
4700 North Highway 89, Flagstaff AZ 86004. 928/526-5541. **Contact:** Human Resources. **World Wide Web address:** http://www.dillards.com. **Description:** A store location of a major department store chain. The company operates 228 stores in 20 states. Dillard's offers a full line of brand-name fashion apparel and home furnishings. Founded in 1938. **International locations:** Mexico City, Mexico. **Corporate headquarters location:** Little Rock AR. **Listed on:** New York Stock Exchange. **Stock exchange symbol:** DDS.

EARNHARDT FORD
P.O. Box 26878, Tempe AZ 85285-6878. 480/838-6000. **Contact:** Human Resources. **E-mail address:** jobs@earnhardt.com. **World Wide Web address:** http://www.earnhardt.com. **Description:** A retailer of new and used automobiles.

EMPIRE SOUTHWEST COMPANY
1725 South Country Club Drive, Mesa AZ 85210. 480/633-4000. **Contact:** Employment Manager. **E-mail address:** careers@empire-cat.com. **World Wide Web address:** http://www.empire-cat.com. **Description:** A retailer and servicer of Caterpillar equipment. **Corporate headquarters location:** This location. **Other U.S. locations:** Phoenix AZ; Glendale AZ; Kingman AZ; Tucson AZ; Deer Valley AZ; Yuma AZ; Imperial CA. **Subsidiaries include:** Empire Hydraulic Service; Empire Machinery; Empire Transport. **Operations at this facility include:** Administration; Sales; Service.

KMART
12025 North 32nd Street, Phoenix AZ 85028. 602/996-4950. **Contact:** Manager. **E-mail address:** hireme@kmart.com. **World Wide Web address:** http://www.kmartcorp.com. **Description:** The company operates 1,500 Kmart discount stores in 49 states, Puerto Rico, and the Virgin Islands. **Corporate headquarters location:** Troy MI. **Parent company:** Sears Holding Corporation. **Listed on:** NASDAQ. **Stock exchange symbol:** SHLD.

MIDWAY AUTO TEAM
2201 West Bell Road, Phoenix AZ 85023. 602/866-6662. **Fax:** 602/866-6664. **Contact:** Human Resources. **World Wide Web address:** http://www.midwayautoteam.com. **Description:** An automotive dealership. **Corporate headquarters location:** This location. **Number of employees at this location:** 225.

NEW YORK & COMPANY
455 North 3rd Street, Suite 170, Phoenix AZ 85004. 602/252-1250. **Contact:** Manager. **World Wide Web address:** http://www.newyorkandcompany.com. **Description:** A retail location of the national chain of women's moderately priced fashion apparel stores. **Corporate headquarters location:** New York NY.

PEP BOYS
400 South Arizona Avenue, Chandler AZ 85225. 480/899-0822. **Contact:** Store Manager. **World Wide Web address:** http://www.pepboys.com. **Description:** Regional offices for a chain of auto parts supply and service centers. Pep Boys primarily engages in the retail sale of a wide range of automotive parts and accessories, and the installation of automobile components and merchandise through over 400 stores in 24 states. **Corporate headquarters location:** Philadelphia PA. **Listed on:** New York Stock Exchange. **Stock exchange symbol:** PBY.

PETSMART, INC.
19601 North 27th Avenue, Phoenix AZ 85027. 623/580-6100. **Fax:** 623/580-6506. **Contact:** Human Resources. **World Wide Web address:** http://www.petsmart.com. **Description:** Operates more than 800 pet stores in the U.S. and Canada. PETsMART also offers veterinary services, animal adoption centers, grooming services, and obedience classes. **Positions advertised include:** Payroll Specialist; Presentation Support Specialist; Industrial Engineer; Director of Engineering and Facilities; Inventory Coordinator; Financial Analyst; Senior Application Developer; Manager, Database Administration. **Corporate headquarters location:** This location. **Other U.S. locations:** Nationwide. **Listed on:** NASDAQ. **Stock exchange symbol:** PETM.

POWER CHEVROLET PHOENIX
2646 West Camelback Road, Phoenix AZ 85017. 602/242-5555. **Contact:** Human Resources. **World**

Wide Web address: http://www.autonation.com. **Description:** An automotive dealer.

SAFEWAY, INC.
2750 South Priest Drive, Tempe AZ 85282. 480/894-4100. **Recorded jobline:** 480/894-4138. **Contact:** Personnel. **World Wide Web address:** http://www.safeway.com. **Description:** One of the world's largest food retailers. Safeway operates approximately 1,800 stores in the Western, Rocky Mountain, Southwestern, and Mid-Atlantic regions of the United States and in western Canada. Safeway also holds a 35 percent interest in The Vons Companies, Inc., one of the largest supermarket chains in Southern California, and a 49 percent interest in Casa Ley, S.A. de C.V., which operates food/variety, clothing, and wholesale outlet stores in western Mexico. **Positions advertised include:** Telephony Services Manager Service Desk Web Technologist. **Special programs:** Training. **Corporate headquarters location:** Pleasanton CA. **Subsidiaries include:** Dominick's Supermarkets, Inc. is a Chicago-area chain with 112 stores. **Listed on:** New York Stock Exchange. **Stock exchange symbol:** SWY.

SAKS FIFTH AVENUE
2446 East Camelback Road, Phoenix AZ 85016. 602/955-8000. **Contact:** Personnel. **World Wide Web address:** http://www.saksincorporated.com. **Description:** Saks Fifth Avenue is a 62-store chain emphasizing soft-goods products, primarily apparel for men, women, and children. **Corporate headquarters location:** Birmingham AL. **Parent company:** Saks Incorporated is a department store holding company that operates approximately 360 stores in 36 states. The company's stores include Saks Fifth Avenue, Parisian, Proffit's, Younker's, Herberger's, Carson Pirie Scott, Boston Store, Bergner's, and Off 5th, the company's outlet store. Saks Incorporated also operates two retail catalogs and several retail Internet sites. **Operations at this facility include:** This location houses administrative offices. **Listed on:** New York Stock Exchange. **Stock exchange symbol:** SKS.

SANDERSON FORD, INC.
6400 North 51st Avenue, Glendale AZ 85301. 480/922-9395. **Contact:** Human Resources. **World Wide Web address:** http://www.sandersonford.com. **Description:** An automotive dealership.

VF FACTORY OUTLET
2050 South Roslyn Place, Mesa AZ 85208. 480/984-0697. **Contact:** Jose Vega Bon, Store Manager. **World Wide Web address:** http://www.vffo.com. **Description:** A retailer of jeans wear, sportswear, active wear, intimate apparel, and occupational apparel with 50 stores in 27 states. **Positions advertised include:** Management Trainee; Customer Service Representative. **Other area locations:** Tucson AZ.

WALGREEN COMPANY
2222 West Northern Avenue, Suite A101, Phoenix AZ 85021. 602/864-7517. **Fax:** 602/864-0288. **Contact:** Roy Grauer, District Manager. **World Wide Web address:** http://www.walgreens.com. **Description:** Walgreen Company operates one of the largest retail drug store chains in the United States, which sells prescription and nonprescription drugs, cosmetics, toiletries, liquor and beverages, tobacco, and general merchandise. Founded in 1901. **Positions advertised include:** PBM Account Coordinator; Regional Clinical Coordinator; Regional Clinical Manager. **Corporate headquarters location:** Deerfield IL. **Operations at this facility include:** This location is a district office. **Listed on:** New York Stock Exchange. **Stock exchange symbol:** WAG. **Number of employees nationwide:** 179,000.

Arkansas

AFFILIATED FOODS SOUTHWEST
8109 Interstate 30, Little Rock AR 72209. 501/570-0007. **Fax:** 501/562-0792. **Contact:** Human Resources. **E-mail address:** jroystuart@afslr.com **World Wide Web address:** http://www.harvestfoods.com. **Description:** Operates a chain of supermarkets called Harvest Foods. **Corporate headquarters location:** This location. **Listed on:** Privately held. **Number of employees at this location:** 3,200.

BARNES & NOBLE BOOKSTORES
11500 Financial Center Parkway, Little Rock AR 72211 501/954-7646. **Fax**: 501/954-7657. **Contact:** Manager. **World Wide Web address:** http://www.bn.com. **Description:** A bookstore chain operating nationwide. This location has a cafe and music department.

COOK AND LOVE SHOES
11121 Rodney Parham Road, Little Rock AR 72212. 501/221-1833. **Fax:** 501/221-0850. **Contact:** Human Resources. **E-mail address:** info@cookandlove.com. **World Wide Web address:** http://www.cookandloveshoes.com. **Description:** A retail shoe store. **NOTE:** Contact Home Office for all employment inquires. **Positions advertised include:** Store Manager; Sales Associate. **Corporate headquarters location:** Memphis TN 901/525-2181. **Other U.S. locations:** Nashville TN; Jackson MS.

E.C. BARTON & COMPANY
P.O. Box 4040, Jonesboro AR 72403. 870/932-6673. **Fax:** 870/972-1304. **Contact:** Allen Devereux, Director of Personnel. **E-mail address:** allen.devereux@ecbarton.com. **World Wide Web Address:** http://www.ecbarton.com. **Description:** Owners and operators of retail, wholesale, and discount building material stores in eight states. **Corporate headquarters location:** This location. **Operations at this facility include:** Administration; Sales; Service. **Number of employees at this location:** 30. **Number of employees nationwide:** Over 450.

DILLARD'S DEPARTMENT STORES, INC.
900 South Shackleford Street, Little Rock AR 72201. 501/376-5200, ext: 5972. **Contact:** Kim Kingsella, Director of Personnel. **World Wide Web address:** http://www.dillards.com. **Description:** Operates a retail chain. Dillard's offers a full line of fashion brand apparel and home furnishings. Dillard's stores are located primarily in the Southwest and Midwest including Texas, Florida, Louisiana, Oklahoma, Missouri, and Arizona. **NOTE:** Search and apply for positions online. **Corporate headquarters location:** This location. **International locations:** Mexico City, Mexico. **Annual sales/revenues:** More than $100 million. **Number of employees nationwide:** 44,600.

MATTRESS KING
301 South Bowman, Suite 200, Little Rock AR 72211. 501/217-0230. **Fax:** 501/217-0225. **Contact:** Mark Hathaway, Human Resources. **Description:** A bedding retailer, focusing on Sealy Mattress, Inc. products. Founded in 1986. **Corporate headquarters location:** This location. **Other U.S. locations:** Nationwide.

WAL-MART STORES, INC.
702 SW Eighth Street, Bentonville AR 72716. 479/273-4000. **Contact:** Recruiting **E-mail address:** resumix@wal-mart.com. **World Wide Web address:** http://www.walmart.com. **Description:** The world's largest retailer with more than 3,600 facilities in the U.S. and more than 1,570 units in Mexico, Puerto Rico, Canada, Argentina, Brazil, China, Korea, Germany and the UK. Founded in 1962. **Positions advertised include:** Director, Global Procurement; Manager, EEO and Employment Practices; Staff Auditor. **Special programs:** Internships. **Corporate headquarters location:** This location. **Other U.S. locations:** Nationwide. **Listed on:** New York Stock Exchange. **Stock exchange symbol:** WMT. **Annual sales/revenue:** $256 billion. **Number of employees worldwide:** 1.6 million.

California

ALBERTSON'S
1550 East 14th Street, San Leandro CA 94577. 510/483-0881. **Contact:** Human Resources. **E-mail address:** employment@albertsons.com. **World Wide Web**

address: http://www.albertsons.com. **Description:** Operates a nationwide chain of 2,300 food and drug stores in 31 states. **Corporate headquarters location:** Boise ID. **Listed on:** New York Stock Exchange. **Stock exchange symbol:** ABS. **Number of employees nationwide:** 200,000.

ANDRONICO'S MARKET
1109 Washington Avenue, Albany CA 94706. **Fax:** 510/287-5978. **Recorded jobline:** 510/287-5978. **Contact:** Human Resources Department. **E-mail address:** humanresources@andronicos.com. **World Wide Web address:** http://www.andronicos.com. **Description:** Operates a chain of retail grocery stores. Founded in 1929. **NOTE:** Entry-level positions and part-time jobs are offered. **Special programs:** Training. **Corporate headquarters location:** This location. **Other area locations:** Berkeley CA; Danville CA; Emeryville CA; Los Altos CA; Palo Alto CA; San Anselmo CA; San Francisco CA. **Operations at this facility include:** Administration. **Listed on:** Privately held. **Number of employees statewide:** 800.

AVON PRODUCTS INC.
2940 East Foothill Boulevard, Pasadena CA 91121. 626/578-8000. **Toll-free phone:** 800/367-2866. **Contact:** Human Resources. **E-mail address:** jobs@avon.com. **World Wide Web address:** http://www.avoncareers.com. **Description:** Avon Products Inc. is a direct seller of beauty care products, fashion jewelry, gifts, fragrances, and decorative products. Avon, a *Fortune* 500 company, markets its products through a network of 2.8 million independent sales representatives in 135 countries worldwide. **Positions advertised include:** Division Sales Manager. **Corporate headquarters location:** New York NY. **Other U.S. locations:** Newark DE; Atlanta GA; Morton Grove NY; Rye NY; Suffern NY; Springdale OH. **Operations at this facility include:** This location is a distribution center for the West Coast.

BARNES & NOBLE BOOKSTORES
6326 East Pacific Coast Highway, Long Beach CA 90803. 562/431-2253. **Contact:** Manager. **World Wide Web address:** http://www.bn.com. **Description:** A bookstore chain operating nationwide. This location has a cafe and a music department in addition to its book departments. **Corporate headquarters location:** New York NY. **Listed on:** NASDAQ. **Stock exchange symbol:** BKS.

BASKIN-ROBBINS, INC.
1217 North Central Avenue, Glendale CA 91202. 818/240-2131. **Contact:** Manager. **World Wide Web address:** http://www.baskinrobbins.com. **Description:** An ice cream manufacturer that also operates retail locations. **Corporate headquarters location:** Randolph MA. **International locations:** Worldwide. **Parent company:** Dunkin' Brands Inc. **Number of employees nationwide:** 875.

BENO'S FAMILY FASHIONS
1512 Santee Street, Los Angeles CA 90015. 213/748-2222. **Contact:** Personnel. **Description:** Operates a chain of retail stores in California and Nevada selling a wide variety of merchandise, with emphasis on apparel for men, women, and children. More than 55 stores are operated under the name of Beno's. **Corporate headquarters location:** This location. **Number of employees nationwide:** 550.

BROOKS BROTHERS
150 Post Street, San Francisco CA 94108. 415/397-4500. **Contact:** Human Resources Department. **E-mail address:** hr@brooksbrothers.com. **World Wide Web address:** http://www.brooksbrothers.com. **Description:** One location of the specialty clothing store chain. Brooks Brothers operates 80 retail and 72 factory stores in the United States. **NOTE:** Apply in person for selling positions. For management positions send resume to: Attn: BB Employment Specialist, 2395 Riverlane Terrace, Fort Lauderdale FL 33312. **Corporate headquarters location:** New York NY. **International locations:** China; Japan; Taiwan.

BROOKS CAMERA
125 Kearney Street, San Francisco CA 94108. 415/362-4708. **Fax:** 415/362-1436. **Contact:** Michael E. Tinnea, Manager. **E-mail address:** mike@brookscamera.com. **World Wide Web address:** http://www.brookscamera.com. **Description:** A retailer of photography equipment. **Corporate headquarters location:** This location. **Parent company:** Inventory Supply Company, Inc. **Operations at this facility include:** Administration; Sales. **Number of employees at this location:** 10.

CITY CHEVROLET/GEO/VOLKSWAGEN
P.O. Box 85345, San Diego CA 92186. 619/276-6171. **Physical address:** 2111 Morena Boulevard, San Diego CA 92110. **Fax:** 619/276-6194. **Contact:** John Nieman, General Manager. **World Wide Web address:** http://www.city-chevrolet.com. **Description:** Sells new and used automobiles. **Corporate headquarters location:** This location.

DEARDEN'S
700 South Main Street, Los Angeles CA 90014. 213/362-9600. **Contact:** Raquel Bensimon, President. **Description:** A retailer of furniture, appliances, televisions, and audio equipment. **Corporate headquarters location:** This location.

DUNN-EDWARDS CORPORATION
4885 East 52nd Place, Los Angeles CA 90040. 888/337-2468. **Contact:** Human Resources Manager. **World Wide Web address:** http://www.dunnedwards.com. **Description:** The largest employee-owned paint manufacturer in the U.S. Operates 70 stores in Arizona, California, Nevada, New Mexico, and Texas. **Corporate headquarters location:** This location.

eBAY, INC.
2145 Hamilton Avenue, San Jose CA 95125. 408/558-7400. **Contact:** Human Resources. **World Wide Web address:** http://www.ebay.com. **Description:** An online auction site that offers items such as antiques, coins, computers, stamps, and toys. **Positions advertised include:** Senior Software Engineer; Content Manager; Senior QA Engineer; Senior Marketing Data Architect; Web Application Developer; Senior Business Analyst. **Corporate headquarters location:** This location. **Listed on:** NASDAQ. **Stock exchange symbol:** EBAY.

FACTORY 2-U STORES, INC.
15001 South Figueroa Street, Gardena CA 90248. **Fax:** 310/324-9334. **Contact:** Human Resources. **E-mail address:** mailus@factory2-u.com. **World Wide Web address:** http://www.factory2-u.com. **Description:** Operates over 200 Factory 2-U and Family Bargain Center stores, which primarily sell in-season family apparel and housewares at discounted prices. **NOTE:** Entry-level positions are offered. **Positions advertised include:** Import Assistant; Lease Administrator. **Corporate headquarters location:** This location. **Other U.S. locations:** AZ; LA; NV; NM; OK; OR; TX; WA. **Listed on:** NASDAQ. **Stock exchange symbol:** FTUS. **Annual sales/revenues:** More than $100 million. **Number of employees at this location:** 250. **Number of employees nationwide:** 6,000.

FORTY-NINER SHOPS, INC.
6049 East Seventh Street, Long Beach CA 90840. 562/985-7854. **Contact:** Rebecca Behar-Johnson, Applications/Recruitment. **E-mail address:** 49erjobs@csulb.edu. **World Wide Web address:** http://www.csulb.edu/aux/49ershops. **Description:** Operates the bookstore, copy center, and food services on California State University's Long Beach campus. **Positions advertised include:** Accounting Cash Room Assistant; Sales Manager, Catering; Manager, University Dining Plaza; Convenience Stores Manager. **Corporate headquarters location:** This location. **Number of employees at this location:** 450.

FREDERICK'S OF HOLLYWOOD
6255 Sunset Boulevard, Los Angeles CA 90028. 323/466-5151. **Contact:** Human Resources. **E-mail**

address: jobs@fredericks.com. **World Wide Web address:** http://www.fredericks.com. **Description:** A specialty retailer operating a chain of women's intimate-apparel stores throughout the United States. The company also has a national mail-order apparel business selling lingerie, bras, dresses, sportswear, leisurewear, swimwear, hosiery, specialty men's wear, and accessories. **Positions advertised include:** Associate Buyer; Creative Manager; **Corporate headquarters location:** Hollywood CA.

GAP INC.
Two Folsom Street, San Francisco CA 94105. 650/952-4400. **Contact:** Personnel. **World Wide Web address:** http://www.gapinc.com. **Description:** A nationwide retailer of moderately priced casual apparel for men, women, and children. The company operates over 1,800 stores under the names Gap, GapKids, BabyGap, Banana Republic, and Old Navy Clothing Company. **Positions advertised include:** Creative Director; Senior Financial Analyst; Strategy Manager; Merchandise Planning Manager; Marketing Director. **Corporate headquarters location:** This location. **Other U.S. locations:** Nationwide. **International locations:** Canada; France; Germany; Japan; United Kingdom. **Listed on:** New York Stock Exchange. **Stock exchange symbol:** GPS.

GELSON'S
P.O. Box 1802, Encino CA 91426-1802. 818/906-5700. **Physical address:** 16400 Ventura Boulevard, Suite 240, Encino CA 91436. **Fax:** 818/788-4018. **Recorded jobline:** 800/700-0912. **Contact:** Human Resources Department, Attention: Recruitment. **E-mail address:** personnel@gelsons.com. **World Wide Web address:** http://www.gelsons.com. **Description:** General offices for Gelson's Markets, which operates 13 Gelson's and two Mayfair supermarkets in the greater Los Angeles area. **Corporate headquarters location:** Compton CA. **Parent company:** Arden Group, Inc. **Listed on:** NASDAQ. **Stock exchange symbol:** ARDNA. **Number of employees nationwide:** 1,900.

GOTTSCHALKS
7 River Park Place East, Fresno CA 93720. 559/434-4800. **Fax:** 559/434-4666. **Contact:** Renee Jones, Director of Recruitment. **E-mail address:** hr@gottschalks.com. **World Wide Web address:** http://www.gottschalks.com. **Description:** A full-line fashion department store. Founded in 1904. **NOTE:** Entry-level positions and part-time jobs are offered. This location also hires seasonally. **Positions advertised include:** Advertising Copywriter; Programmer Analyst. **Special programs:** Internships; Training. **Corporate headquarters location:** This location. **Other U.S. locations:** AK; ID; NV; OR; WA. **Listed on:** New York Stock Exchange. **Stock exchange symbol:** GOT. **Annual sales/revenues:** $667 million. **Number of employees at this location:** 500. **Number of employees nationwide:** 5,000.

THE GYMBOREE CORPORATION
700 Airport Boulevard, Suite 200, Burlingame CA 94010. 650/579-0600. **Contact:** Human Resources. **World Wide Web address:** http://www.gymboree.com. **Description:** Operates a chain of retail stores that sell children's active wear and accessories. The company also franchises Gymboree Play and Music Programs for children and their parents. **Positions advertised include:** Designer; Technical Designer; Business Systems Manager; International Transportation Manager; Director of Leasing; Merchandise Planner; Inventory Control Analyst; Benefits Manager; Java Programmer; Payroll Assistant; Revenue Accountant; Production Artist. **Corporate headquarters location:** This location. **Parent company:** Gym-Mark, Inc. **Listed on:** NASDAQ. **Stock exchange symbol:** GYMB. **Number of employees at this location:** 100. **Number of employees nationwide:** 3,700.

HARRIS AND FRANK INC.
17629 Ventura Boulevard, Encino CA 91316. 818/783-2739. **Contact:** Personnel Department. **Description:** A specialty fashion store chain of men's and women's clothing including a tuxedo rental department. Harris and Frank operates 19 store locations. **Operations at this facility include:** Regional Headquarters.

HOT TOPIC
18305 East San Jose Avenue, City of Industry CA 91748. 626/839-4681. **Fax:** 626/581-9263. **Contact:** Personnel. **E-mail address:** jobs@hottopic.com. **World Wide Web address:** http://www.hottopic.com. **Description:** Operates a chain of mall-based retail outlets. Hot Topic's product line features clothing and accessories relating to various alternative music-related lifestyles. Founded in 1988. **Positions advertised include:** Internet Customer Service Representative; Database Analyst; Business Analyst; Help Desk Associate; Loss Prevention Auditor. **Corporate headquarters location:** This location. **Other U.S. locations:** Nationwide. **Listed on:** NASDAQ. **Stock exchange symbol:** HOTT. **Annual sales/revenues:** Over $400 million.

KRAGEN AUTO PARTS
4240 International Boulevard, Oakland CA 94601. 510/532-1240. **Contact:** Regional Recruiter. **Description:** A retailer and distributor of automotive aftermarket products. **Company slogan:** Whatever it takes. **Operations at this facility include:** Sales; Service.

LONGS DRUG STORES
141 North Civic Drive, Walnut Creek CA 94596. 925/937-1170. **Fax:** 925/522-7202. **Contact:** Employment Manager. **E-mail address:** employment@longs.com. **World Wide Web address:** http://www.longs.com. **Description:** Longs Drug Stores owns and operates a chain of more than 400 retail drug stores that offer a broad range of pharmaceuticals and personal care products. **Positions advertised include:** Construction Contracts Coordinator; Administrative Assistant, Pharmacy; Project Manager; Store Operations Analyst. **Corporate headquarters location:** This location. **Listed on:** New York Stock Exchange. **Stock exchange symbol:** LDG.

MACY'S WEST
50 O'Farrell Street, San Francisco CA 94102. 415/397-3333. **Contact:** Human Resources. **World Wide Web address:** http://www.macys.com. **Description:** A location of the retail department store chain. **NOTE:** Search and apply for positions online. **Positions advertised include:** Business Manager; Database Administrator; Margin Analyst; Planner; Project Manager; Visual Merchandising Designer. **Corporate headquarters location:** New York NY. **Parent company:** Federated Department Stores.

MACY'S UNION SQUARE
170 O'Farrell Street, San Francisco CA 94102. 415/397-3333. **Contact:** Human Resources. **World Wide Web address:** http://www.macys.com. **Description:** One of three divisions of R.H. Macy Company (New York NY). Macy's Union Square operates 50 stores regionally as part of the full-line department store chain. **Corporate headquarters location:** New York NY. **Operations at this facility include:** Divisional Headquarters. **Parent company:** Federated Department Stores.

MAIL BOXES ETC.
6060 Cornerstone Court West, San Diego CA 92121. 858/455-8800. **Fax:** 858/625-3159. **Contact:** Human Resources. **E-mail address:** jobs@mbe.com. **World Wide Web address:** http://www.mbe.com. **Description:** Operates through two wholly owned subsidiaries. Mail Boxes Etc. provides franchisees with a system of business training, site location, marketing, advertising programs, and management support designed to assist the franchisee in opening and operating MBE Centers. **Positions advertised include:** Technical Trainer Supervisor; Senior Programmer Analyst; Product Development Specialist. **Corporate headquarters location:** This location. **Parent**

company: UPS. **Listed on:** New York Stock Exchange. **Stock exchange symbol:** UPS.

MARSHALLS OF SAN FRANCISCO
901 Market Street, San Francisco CA 94103. 415/974-5369. **Contact:** Human Resources. **World Wide Web address:** http://www.marshallsonline.com. **Description:** An off-price retail organization providing wide assortments of men's, women's, and children's apparel, footwear, accessories, and selected home furnishings at over 500 locations nationwide. **NOTE:** Search and apply for positions online. **Positions advertised include:** Cashier; Merchandise Associate; Processor. **Corporate headquarters location:** Framingham MA. **Parent company:** TJX. **Listed on:** New York Stock Exchange. **Stock exchange symbol:** TJX.

MAY DEPARTMENT STORES COMPANY
6160 Laurel Canyon Boulevard, North Hollywood CA 91606. 818/508-5226. **Contact:** Employment Office. **World Wide Web address:** http://www2.mayco.com. **Description:** Owns and operates a chain of 491 department stores in 46 states. **Corporate headquarters location:** St. Louis MO. **Listed on:** New York Stock Exchange. **Stock exchange symbol:** MAY.

MELISSA DATA
22382 Avenida Empressa, Rancho Santa Margarita CA 92688-2112. 949/589-5200. **Toll-free phone:** 800/800-6245. **Fax:** 949/589-5211. **Contact:** Human Resources. **E-mail address:** hr@melissadata.com. **World Wide Web address:** http://www.melissadata.com. **Description:** A catalog retailer of direct mail software. **Positions advertised include:** Sales Engineer. **Corporate headquarters location:** This location.

NETFLIX
100 Winchester Circle, Los Gatos CA 95032. 408/540-3700. **Contact:** Human Resources. **World Wide Web address:** http://www.netflix.com. **Description**: The world's largest online movie rental service, with more than 4 million subscribers. **Positions advertised include:** Lead QA Engineer; Manager, SOX Compliance; Payroll Assistant; Program Director, Customer Service; Search Engineering; Sr. Accountant; Sr. Database Administrator; Sr. Embedded AV Software Engineer. **Listed on:** NASDAQ. **Stock exchange symbol:** NFLX. **Number of employees nationwide:** 1,200.

NORDSTROM, INC.
285 Winston Drive, San Francisco CA 94132. 415/753-1344. **Toll-free phone:** 888/282-6060. **Contact:** Human Resources Department. **World Wide Web address:** http://www.nordstrom.com. **Description:** A specialty retailer that sells apparel, shoes, and accessories. Nordstrom operates more than 60 stores, with over 20 clearance, boutique, and leased shoe departments in 12 department stores in Hawaii and Guam. Founded in 1901. **Positions advertised include:** Accessories Sales Associate. **Corporate headquarters location:** Seattle WA. **Other area locations:** Statewide. **Listed on:** New York Stock Exchange. **Stock exchange symbol:** JWN.

OAKLEY, INC.
1 Icon, Foothill Ranch CA 92610. 949/951-0991. **Fax:** 949/454-1071. **Contact:** Human Resources. **World Wide Web address:** http//www.oakley.com. **Description:** A maker and retailer of high performance sunglasses and sports goggles. **Positions advertised include:** Apparel Development Manager; Brand Manager; Business Systems Analyst; Equipment Technician; Eyewear Test Engineer. **Corporate headquarters location:** This location. **Listed on:** New York Stock Exchange. **Stock exchange symbol:** OO.

ORCHARD SUPPLY HARDWARE
SEARS HARDWARE STORES
6450 Via Del Oro, San Jose CA 95119. 408/281-3500. **Fax:** 408/365-2690. **Contact:** Human Resources. **E-mail address:** jobsosh@sears.com. **World Wide Web address:** http://www.osh.com. **Description:** Operates more than 250 retail stores nationwide. Products are primarily geared toward home repair and maintenance projects. Founded in 1931. **NOTE:** Address resumes to: Orchard Supply Hardware, Attention: Human Resources, P.O. Box 49027, San Jose CA 95161-9027. **Company slogan:** We are committed to providing our customers with legendary customer service. **Positions advertised include:** Manager, Imports; Training Manager; Direct Loss Prevention Manager. **Special programs:** Internships; Training; Summer Jobs. **Corporate headquarters location:** This location. **Other U.S. locations:** Nationwide. **Parent company:** Sears, Roebuck and Company. **Number of employees at this location:** 300. **Number of employees nationwide:** 13,000.

PACIFIC SUNWEAR
3450 East Miraloma Avenue, Anaheim CA 92806-2101. 714/414-4000. **Fax:** 714/701-4294. **Contact:** Human Resources. **E-mail address:** careers@pacificsunwear.com. **World Wide Web address:** http://www.pacsun.com. **Description:** A surf and skateboard style clothing retailer. **NOTE:** Search and apply for positions or submit resume online. **Positions advertised include:** Buyer; Designer; Director of Merchandise Planning; Director, Loss Prevention; Distribution Center Operations Manager; HR Generalist Coordinator; Instructional Designer; Manager, Corporate Facilities; Manager, Internal Audit. **Special programs:** Internships. **Corporate headquarters location:** This location. **Other U.S. locations:** Nationwide. **Listed on:** NASDAQ. **Stock exchange symbol:** PSUN. **Annual sales/revenues:** $1 billion.

RALEY'S & BEL AIR
500 West Capitol Avenue, West Sacramento CA 95605. 916/373-3333. **Contact:** Ronnie Cobb, Corporate Recruiter. **E-mail address:** jobs@raleys.com. **World Wide Web address:** http://www.raleys.com. **Description:** A large supermarket chain with more than 145 locations in Northern California and Nevada. Raley's owns and operates Bel Air Markets (also at this location) a supermarket chain in San Francisco. **NOTE:** Entry-level positions are offered. Interested candidates may apply online. **Positions advertised include:** Financial Analyst; Loss Prevention Agent. **Special programs:** Internships. **Corporate headquarters location:** This location. **Subsidiaries include:** Food Source; Nob Hill Foods. **Operations at this facility include:** Divisional Headquarters.

RALPHS GROCERY COMPANY
P.O. Box 54143, Los Angeles CA 90054. 310/884-9000. **Physical address:** 1100 West Artesia Boulevard, Compton CA 90200. **Recorded jobline:** 310/884-4642. **Contact:** Personnel. **World Wide Web address:** http://www.ralphs.com. **Description:** Operates a chain of grocery stores throughout California. **Corporate headquarters location:** This location. **Parent company:** The Kroger Company (Cincinnati OH). **Listed on:** New York Stock Exchange. **Stock exchange symbol:** KR.

REDENVELOPE, INC.
201 Spear Street, Third Floor, San Francisco CA 94105. 415/371-9100. **Fax:** 415/371-1134. **Contact:** Human Resources. **E-mail address:** jobs@redenvelope.com. **World Wide Web address:** http://www.redenvelope.com. **Description:** Sells unique gift items through its website and seasonal catalogs. **Positions advertised include:** Software Engineer; Receptionist; Assistant Merchandise Manager; Merchandise Assistant.

SAFEWAY, INC.
5918 Stoneridge Mall Road, Pleasanton CA 94588-3229. 925/467-3000. **Contact:** Jean Hughes, Manager of Corporate Human Resources. **World Wide Web address:** http://www.safeway.com. **Description:** One of the world's largest food retailers. The company operates approximately 1,820 stores in the western, Rocky Mountain, southwestern, and mid-Atlantic

regions of the United States and in western Canada. **Positions advertised include:** Procurement Specialist; Federal Tax Manager; Strategic Pricing Analyst; Store Designer; Real Estate Manager. **Corporate headquarters location:** Phoenix AZ. **Other U.S. locations:** Nationwide. **International locations:** Canada. **Subsidiaries include:** Casa Ley, S.A. de C.V. operates food/variety, clothing, and wholesale outlet stores in western Mexico; The Vons Companies, Inc. is one of the largest supermarket chains in southern California. **Listed on:** New York Stock Exchange. **Stock exchange symbol:** SWY. **President/CEO:** Steven A. Burd. **Annual sales/revenues:** $35.5 billion. **Number of employees nationwide:** 111,000. **Number of employees worldwide:** 208,000.

SAKS FIFTH AVENUE
384 Post Street, San Francisco CA 94108. 415/986-4300. **Contact:** Director of Human Resources Department. **World Wide Web address:** http://www.saksincorporated.com. **Description:** Saks Fifth Avenue is a 62-store chain emphasizing soft-goods products, primarily apparel for men, women, and children. **Corporate headquarters location:** New York NY. **Other area locations:** Palo Alto CA. **Parent company:** Saks Incorporated operates approximately 360 stores in 36 states. The company's stores include Saks Fifth Avenue, Parisian, Proffit's, Younker's, Herberger's, Carson Pirie Scott, Boston Store, Bergner's, and Off 5th, the company's outlet store. Saks Incorporated also operates two retail catalogs and several retail Internet sites. **Listed on:** New York Stock Exchange. **Stock exchange symbol:** SKS.

SAVE MART SUPERMARKETS
P.O. Box 4278, Modesto CA 95352. 209/577-1800. **Physical address:** 1800 Standiford Avenue, Modesto CA 95350. **Contact:** Kit Serpa, Employment Supervisor. **Description:** Operates more than 120 grocery stores in Northern and Central California.

SHARPER IMAGE CORPORATION
650 Davis Street, San Francisco CA 94111. 415/445-6000. **Contact:** Deborah Baker-Reyes, Human Resources. **World Wide Web address:** http://www.sharperimage.com. **Description:** A retailer of a wide variety of gifts in the following categories: automotive, outdoor and garden, travel and luggage, electronics, health and fitness, personal care, and home and safety. **Positions advertised include:** Account Manager; Human Resources Generalist; Senior Programmer/Analyst; Internet Content Specialist; Loss Prevention Specialist; Assistant Electronics Engineer. **Corporate headquarters location:** This location. **Listed on:** NASDAQ. **Stock exchange symbol:** SHRP.

THE SHERWIN-WILLIAMS COMPANY INC.
1450 Sherwin Avenue, Emeryville CA 94608. 510/420-7232. **Contact:** Human Resources Manager. **World Wide Web address:** http://www.sherwin.com. **Description:** Sherwin-Williams Company manufactures, sells, and distributes coatings and related products. Sherwin-Williams labeled architectural and industrial coatings are sold through company-owned specialty paint and wall covering stores. The Sherwin-Williams Company also manufactures paint under the Acme, Dutch Boy, Kem-Tone, Lucas, Martin-Senour, Minwax, Pratt & Lambert, Rogers, and Thompson brand names, as well as private labels, and markets its products to independent dealers, mass merchandisers, and home improvement centers. **Special programs:** Internships. **Corporate headquarters location:** Cleveland OH. **Other U.S. locations:** Nationwide. **Operations at this facility include:** This location is a support office for area stores and a facility for manufacturing emulsion paints. **Listed on:** New York Stock Exchange. **Stock exchange symbol:** SHW.

SMART & FINAL, INC.
600 Citadel Drive, Commerce CA 90040. 323/869-7500. **Fax:** 323/427-3443. **Contact:** Human Resources Department. **E-mail address:** hr@smartandfinal.com. **World Wide Web address:** http://www.smartandfinal.com. Smart and Final operates 230 nonmembership stores in six western states and northern Mexico. Founded in 1871. **NOTE:** Mail resumes to: Smart & Final, Inc., Attention: Human Resources, P.O. Box 512377, Los Angeles CA 90051-0377. **Positions advertised include:** Logistics supervisor; Operations Manager; Senior Payroll Coordinator; Warehouse Supervisor. **Corporate headquarters location:** This location. **Other U.S. locations:** AZ; CA; FL; NV. **International locations:** Mexico. **Listed on:** New York Stock Exchange. **Stock exchange symbol:** SMF. **Annual sales/revenues:** $1.7 billion. **Number of employees at this location:** 600. **Number of employees nationwide:** 5,000.

THE VONS COMPANIES, INC.
5918 Stoneridge Mall Road, Pleasanton CA 94588-3229. 925/467-3000. **Contact:** Human Resources. **World Wide Web address:** http://www.vons.com. **Description:** One of the largest operators of supermarkets and drugstores in Southern California. Vons's Super Combo stores offer video rental, dry cleaning, and photo development services in addition to traditional grocery store and drugstore products. Vons owns five EXPO stores that offer discount drugs and warehouse foods; operates a milk-processing plant; and manages ice cream, delicatessen, meat processing, and baking facilities. **NOTE:** Search and apply for positions online. **Corporate headquarters location:** This location. **Parent company:** Safeway, Inc. **Listed on:** New York Stock Exchange. **Stock exchange symbol:** SWY.

WEST MARINE
P.O. Box 50070, Watsonville CA 95077-0070. 831/728-2700. **Contact:** Human Resources. **E-mail address:** jobs@westmarine.com. **World Wide Web address:** http://www.westmarine.com. **Description:** Operates 400 West Marine stores and BoatU.S. Marine Centers in 38 states, Puerto Rico, and Canada. **Positions advertised include:** Account Management Screener; Accountant; Assistant Category Manager, Lifestyle; AVP Of Internet; Direct Marketing Analyst; Direct Marketing Manager; International Sales Rep; Internet Production Manager; Inventory Control Specialist; Marketing Coordinator; Merchandise Financial Analyst; Merchandise Planner; New Store Analyst; Planning Analyst; Retail Financial Analyst; Sales Auditor; Space Management Coordinator; Sr. Director Planning & Replenishment; Sr. Sales Tax Analyst; Store Planner.

WHEREHOUSE ENTERTAINMENT
2230 Carson Street, Carson CA 90810. 310/516-4221. **Fax:** 310/516-9057. **Contact:** Human Resources. **World Wide Web address:** http://www.wherehousemusic.com. **Description:** A retailer of prerecorded music and videos. **Special programs:** Internships. **Corporate headquarters location:** This location. **Subsidiaries include:** Leopolos; Odyssey; Paradise Music; Record Shop; Rocky Mountain Records. **Parent company:** Trans World Entertainment. **Listed on:** Privately held. **Number of employees at this location:** 230. **Number of employees nationwide:** Over 5,000.

WILLIAMS-SONOMA, INC.
3250 Van Ness Avenue, San Francisco CA 94109. 415/421-7900. **Fax:** 415/616-8462. **Contact:** Human Resources. **World Wide Web address:** http://www.williams-sonomainc.com. **Description:** A retailer of cookware, serving equipment, and other specialty items. Products are sold both through retail stores and mail order catalogs with the following brand names: Williams-Sonoma, Hold Everything, Gardener's Eden, Pottery Barn, and Chambers. **NOTE:** Search and apply for positions online. **Positions advertised include:** QA Analyst; Assistant Buyer; Internet Creative Manager; Catalog Production Manager; Compensation Analyst; Senior Internal Auditor; Senior Financial Analyst; Merchandise Coordinator; Senior Liquidation Analyst; Front Desk Receptionist. **Corporate headquarters location:** This location. **Listed on:** New York Stock Exchange. **Stock**

exchange symbol: WSM. **Number of employees at this location:** 1,400.

Colorado

ALPINE LUMBER COMPANY
5800 North Pecos, Denver CO 80221. 303/458-8733. **Contact:** General Manager. **World Wide Web address:** http://www.alpinelumber.com. **Description:** A retail lumberyard. Founded in 1963. **Corporate headquarters location:** This location. **Other area locations include:** Brighton CO; Denver CO.

AUTOZONE
1108 Bonforte Boulevard, Pueblo CO 81001-1805. 719/542-9000. **Contact:** Human Resources. **World Wide Web address:** http://www.autozone.com. **Description:** A do-it-yourself, retail auto parts chain, specializing in foreign and domestic parts. **Corporate headquarters location:** Memphis TN. **Listed on:** New York Stock Exchange. **Stock exchange symbol:** AZO.

BMC WEST
6400 Arapahoe Avenue, Boulder CO 80303. 303/442-5382. **Contact:** General Manager. **World Wide Web address:** http://www.bmcwest.com. **Description:** A lumber and hardware retailer. **Corporate headquarters location:** Boise ID. **Parent company:** Building Materials Holding Corporation. **Listed on:** NASDAQ. **Stock exchange symbol:** BMHC.

BARNES & NOBLE BOOKSTORES
960 South Colorado Boulevard, Glendale CO 80246. 303/691-2998. **Fax:** 303/691-9193. **Contact:** Manager. **World Wide Web address:** http://www.bn.com. **Description:** Barnes & Noble Bookstores is a bookstore chain operating nationwide. **Corporate headquarters location:** New York NY. **Operations at this facility include:** This location houses the district headquarters as well as a bookstore. **Listed on:** New York Stock Exchange. **Stock exchange symbol:** BKS.

BURT CHEVROLET, INC.
5200 South Broadway, Englewood CO 80110. 303/761-0333. **Contact:** Employment Administrator. **E-mail address:** jobs@burt.com. **World Wide Web address:** http://www.burt.com. **Description:** A new and used automobile dealership. **NOTE:** Send resumes to: Burt Automotive Network, Attn: Employment Administrator, 10301 East Araphahoe Road, Centennial CO 80112.

CHRISTY SPORTS, LLC
875 Parfet Street, Lakewood CO 80215. 303/237-6321. **Fax:** 303/274-4589. **Contact:** Human Resources. **World Wide Web address:** http://www.christysports.com. **Description:** Operates Christy Sports, SportStalker, and Powder Tools sporting goods stores. The company specializes in retail skiing, snowboarding, and sport clothing. In addition, Christy Sports offers patio furniture and several golf retail stores. **NOTE:** Entry-level positions are offered. **Special programs:** Training; Summer Jobs. **Corporate headquarters location:** This location. **Other U.S. locations:** UT. **Number of employees at this location:** 75. **Number of employees nationwide:** 500.

CURRENT, INC.
1005 East Woodman Road, Colorado Springs CO 80920. 719/594-4100. **Contact:** Personnel. **World Wide Web address:** http://www.currentinc.com. **Description:** Prints and markets greeting cards, stationery, and checks. **Corporate headquarters location:** St. Paul MN. **Other U.S. locations:** Nationwide. **Parent company:** Deluxe Corporation.

EMPIRE OLDSMOBILE/HONDA
P.O. Box 200336, Denver CO 80220. 303/399-1950. **Physical address:** 6160 East Colfax Avenue, Denver CO 80220. **Contact:** Judy Grinestaff, Payroll Supervisor. **Description:** An automobile dealership.

THE FOSS COMPANY
1224 Washington Avenue, Golden CO 80401. 303/279-3373. **Contact:** Personnel Manager. **World Wide Web address:** http://www.fossco.com. **Description:** A general store, post office, pharmacy, and liquor store. This location is also headquarters for Ski Country Decanters, H.J. Foss Apparel, and The Golden Ram Restaurant. **Corporate headquarters location:** This location. **Operations at this facility include:** Administration; Sales; Service.

FURNITURE ROW COMPANY
13333 East 37th Avenue, Denver CO 80239. 303/371-8560. **Contact:** Human Resources. **World Wide Web address:** http://www.furniturerow.com. **Description:** A retail furniture dealer with 270 stores in 31 states. **Corporate headquarters location:** This location.

GALLERIA LIGHTING & DESIGN
239-B Detroit Street, Denver CO 80206. 303/592-1223. **Toll-free phone:** 800/332-2066. **Fax:** 303/534-2566. **Contact:** Human Resources. **World Wide Web address:** http://www.dbwrite.com. **Description:** Galleria Lighting & Design sells lighting fixtures in both retail and wholesale markets. **Positions advertised include:** Sales Executive. **Parent company:** QED. **Listed on:** Privately held. **Annual sales/revenues:** $51 - $100 million. **Number of employees at this location:** 30. **Number of employees nationwide:** 200.

IKON OFFICE SOLUTIONS
7173 South Havana Street, Suite A, Englewood CO 80112. 720/875-8300. **Contact:** Lynn Hannblom, Director of Human Resources. **World Wide Web address:** http://www.ikon.com. **Description:** Engaged in the retail sale and service of Canon office equipment and supplies. **Positions advertised include:** Sales Manager; Account Executive. **Corporate headquarters location:** Valley Forge PA. **Other U.S. locations:** Nationwide. **Operations at this facility include:** Administration; Regional Headquarters; Sales; Service. **Listed on:** New York Stock Exchange. **Stock exchange symbol:** IKN.

LEWAN & ASSOCIATES, INC.
1400 South Colorado Boulevard, P.O. Box 22855, Denver CO 80222. 303/759-5440, **Contact:** Human Resources. **World Wide Web address:** http://www.lewan.com. **Description:** A retail office products dealer. **Positions advertised include:** Enterprise Solution Sales Account Executive; New Business Development Representative. **Corporate headquarters location:** This location.

MOUNTAIN STATES MOTORS
1260 South Colorado Boulevard, Denver CO 80246. 303/757-7751. **Contact:** Frank Murray, Office Manager. **World Wide Web address:** http://www.vwdenver.com. **Description:** An automobile dealership specializing in Volkswagen sales and service.

ROCKY MOUNTAIN CHOCOLATE FACTORY, INC.
265 Turner Drive, Durango CO 81303. 970/247-4943. **Fax:** 970/382-7371. **Contact:** Human Resource Supervisor. **E-mail address:** employment@rmcf.com. **World Wide Web address:** http://www.rmcf.com. **Description:** A retail distributor of candy products including chocolate covered fruit, fudge, and caramel apples. The company operates over 200 retail stores worldwide. Founded in 1981. **NOTE:** Part-time jobs and second and third shifts are offered. This location also hires seasonally. **Special programs:** Internships; Summer Jobs. **Corporate headquarters location:** This location. **Other U.S. locations:** Nationwide. **International locations:** Canada; Taiwan; United Arab Emirates. **Listed on:** NASDAQ. **Stock exchange symbol:** RMCF. **Number of employees at this location:** 120. **Number of employees nationwide:** 400.

THE SANBORN MAP COMPANY
1935 Jamboree Drive, Suite 100, Colorado Springs CO 80920. 719/593-0093. **Fax:** 719/528-5093. **Contact:** Human Resources. **E-mail address:** employment@sanborn.com. **World Wide Web**

address: http://www.sanbornmap.com. **Description:** The Sanborn Map Company produces high-quality, detailed maps. Founded in 1866. **Positions advertised include:** GIS Technicians; System Administrator.

7-ELEVEN, INC.
7167 South Alton Way, Englewood CO 80112. 303/740-9333. **Fax:** 303/220-1062. **Recorded jobline:** 800/711-5627. **Contact:** Human Resources. **World Wide Web address:** http://www.7-eleven.com. **Description:** The 7-Eleven convenience store chain is one of the largest store chains in the world. **Corporate headquarters location:** Dallas TX. **Operations at this facility include:** This location serves as the regional headquarters of 7-Eleven convenience stores in Colorado and Utah. **Listed on:** New York Stock Exchange. **Stock exchange symbol:** SE. **Number of employees at this location:** 3,500.

SPORTS AUTHORITY
705 West Hampden Avenue, Englewood CO 80110. 303/789-5266. **Fax:** 303/863-2243. **Contact:** Human Resources. **World Wide Web address:** http://www.sportsauthority.com. **Description:** Operates a chain of retail sporting goods stores. **Positions advertised include:** Department Manager. **Other U.S. locations:** Nationwide. **Listed on:** NASDAQ.

SUN ENTERPRISES INC.
8877 North Washington Street, Thornton CO 80229. 303/287-7566. **Fax:** 303/287-7716. **Contact:** Gerald Bieker, Controller. **E-mail address:** sun@sunent.com. **World Wide Web address:** http://www.sunent.com. **Description:** A retailer of motorcycles, ATVs, watercraft, snowmobiles, power equipment, and related parts and accessories. **Annual sales/revenues:** $11 - $20 million. **Number of employees at this location:** 45.

ULTIMATE ELECTRONICS, INC.
321 West 84th Avenue, Suite A, Thornton CO 80260. 303/412-2500. **Fax:** 303/412-2501. **Contact:** Human Resources. **World Wide Web address:** http://www.ultimateelectronics.com. **Description:** A specialty retailer of home entertainment and consumer electronics. The company operates stores under the SoundTrack, Audio King, and Ultimate Electronics names. Founded in 1968. **NOTE:** Entry-level positions and second and third shifts are offered. **Positions advertised include:** Accounting Manager; Financial Analyst; General Manager; Graphic Designer; Copywriter. **Special programs:** Training. **Corporate headquarters location:** This location. **Other area locations:** Arvada CO; Aurora CO; Boulder CO; Colorado Springs CO; Denver CO; Fort Collins CO; Littleton CO. **Other U.S. locations:** Albuquerque NM; Las Vegas NV; Murray UT; Orem UT; Salt Lake City UT. **Listed on:** NASDAQ. **Stock exchange symbol:** ULTE. **Annual sales/revenues:** More than $100 million. **Number of employees at this location:** 700. **Number of employees nationwide:** 1,600.

WAL-MART STORES, INC.
7455 West Colfax Avenue, Lakewood CO 80214. 303/274-5211. **Contact:** Human Resources. **World Wide Web address:** http://www.walmartstores.com. **Description:** Wal-Mart Stores is a retail merchandise chain operating full-service discount department stores, combination grocery and discount stores, and warehouse stores requiring membership. Founded in 1962. **Corporate headquarters location:** Bentonville AR. **Listed on:** New York Stock Exchange. **Stock exchange symbol:** WMT.

WILD OATS MARKETS
3375 Mitchell Lane, Boulder CO 80301. 303/440-5220. **Contact:** Human Resources. **World Wide Web address:** http://www.wildoats.com. **Description:** Owns and operates more than 100 health food supermarkets in the U.S. and Canada. **Positions advertised include:** Communications Manager; Compensation Analyst; Director of Design; HR Management systems Manager; Plan Development Manager; Pricing Specialist. **Corporate headquarters location:** This location. **Other U.S. locations:** Nationwide. **Listed on:** NASDAQ. **Stock exchange symbol:** OATS.

Connecticut

AMERICAN FROZEN FOODS, INC.
155 Hill Street, Milford CT 06460. 203/882-6200. **Toll-free phone:** 800/233-5554. **Fax:** 203/882-6231. **Contact:** Bill Rappoport, Vice President of Sales. **World Wide Web address:** http://www.americanfoods.com. **Description:** Operates a customized shop-at-home food delivery service, delivering meats, vegetables, juices, desserts, and convenience items directly to the consumer. **Positions advertised include:** Sales Representative; Sales Manager; Independent Sales Agent. **Corporate headquarters location:** This location. **Other U.S. locations:** Nationwide. **Number of employees nationwide:** 1,200.

BARNES & NOBLE BOOKSTORES
1599 Southeast Road, Farmington CT 06032. 860/678-9494. **Contact:** Manager. **World Wide Web address:** http://www.barnesandnoble.com. **Description:** A bookstore chain. This location also has a cafe and music department. **Corporate headquarters location:** New York NY. **Other U.S. locations:** Nationwide.

CDW CORPORATION
2 Enterprise Drive, Shelton CT 06484. 203/929-6684. **Contact:** Human Resources **World Wide Web address:** http://www.cdw.com. **Description:** CDW a provider of technology products and services for business, government and education. Founded in 1984. **NOTE:** Entry-level positions are offered. **Special programs:** Internships. **Corporate headquarters location:** Vernon Hills IL. **Other U.S. locations:** Chicago IL; Mettawa IL; Voorhees NJ; Eatontown NJ; Herndon VA **International locations:** Canada. **Listed on:** NASDAQ. **Stock exchange symbol:** CDWC. **Annual sales/revenues:** More than $5.7 billion. **Number of employees nationwide:** 4,000.

CARVEL CORPORATION
175 Capital Boulevard, Suite 400, Rocky Hill CT 06067-4448. 860/257-4448. **Contact:** Human Resources. **World Wide Web address:** http://www.carvel.com . **Description:** Engaged in the manufacture of ice cream products and franchising operations for the chain of Carvel Ice Cream stores. **Corporate headquarters location:** This location.

ETHAN ALLEN INC.
Ethan Allen Drive, P.O. Box 1966, Danbury CT 06811. 203/743-8000. **Contact:** Christine Bonnel, Human Resources. **World Wide Web address:** http://www.ethanallen.com. **Description:** An international retailer of home furnishings operating approximately 350 retail locations. Founded in 1932. **Positions advertised include:** Retail Production Coordinator; Merchandise Manager, Soft Goods; Advertising Production Manager; Interior Design/Sales Professional; Designer, Store Planner. **Corporate headquarters location:** This location. **Listed on:** New York Stock Exchange. **Stock exchange symbol:** ETH.

KMART STORES
881 Wolcott Street, Waterbury CT 06705. 203/753-2191. **Contact:** Human Resources. **World Wide Web address:** http://www.kmart.com. **Description:** One location in the discount store chain.

MACYS
575 Union Street, Waterbury CT 06702. 203/757-1131. **Contact:** Human Resources. **World Wide Web address:** http://www.mayco,com. **Description:** A fashion department store with 44 locations in the New England/New York area. **Positions advertised include:** General Sales Associate; Commission Sales Associate; Cosmetics Beauty Advisor. **Parent company:** May Department Stores Company.

STEW LEONARD'S FARM FRESH FOODS
100 Westport Avenue, Norwalk CT 06851. 203/847-7214. **Contact:** Recruiting Manager. **World Wide**

Web address: http://www.stew-leonards.com. **Description:** One of the world's largest retail dairy and food stores. Founded in 1969. **Special programs:** Internships. **Internship information:** Culinary and bakery internships are offered. **Corporate headquarters location:** This location. **Other U.S. locations:** Danbury CT; Yonkers NY. **Annual sales/revenues:** $51 - $100 million. **Number of employees at this location:** 700. **Number of employees nationwide:** 1,400.

Delaware

A.H. ANGERSTEIN, INC.
315 New Road, Wilmington DE 19805. 302/996-3500. **Fax:** 302/995-1640. **Contact:** Rob Sanderson, Personnel Director. **E-mail address:** angersteins@angersteins.com. **World Wide Web address:** www.angersteins.com. **Description:** A family-owned and operated store engaged in the retail sale of building materials, glass fixtures and kitchen and bathroom appliances. **NOTE:** Call or send an e-mail message to inquire about current job openings.

AVON PRODUCTS INC.
2100 Ogletown Road, Newark DE 19712. 302/453-7700. **Fax:** 302/453-7952. **Contact:** Gwen Leon, Recruiter. **E-mail address:** gwen.leon@avon.com. **World Wide Web address:** http://www.avon.com. **Description:** The world's largest direct seller of beauty care products, fashion jewelry, gifts, fragrances and decorative products. **NOTE:** See website for current job openings and to apply online. **Positions advertised include:** Merchandise Control Supervisor; Facilities Engineering Supervisor. **Corporate headquarters location:** New York NY. **Operations at this facility include:** Customer Service; Distribution.

HAPPY HARRY'S INC.
326 Ruthar Drive, Newark DE 19711. 302/366-0335. **Contact:** Dennis Gossert, Director of Personnel. **World Wide Web address:** http://www.happy.com. **Description:** The largest drug store in Delaware, with locations in eastern Maryland, southeastern Pennsylvania and southern New Jersey. **NOTE:** See website for current job openings and to apply online. For positions at retail locations, apply in person at the individual store. **Positions advertised include:** Warehouse Picker; Pharmacist. **Corporate headquarters location:** This location. **Other area locations:** Statewide. **Operations at this facility include:** Administration; Distribution.

O.A. NEWTON & SON COMPANY
16356 Sussex Highway, P.O. Box 397, Bridgeville DE 19933. 302/337-8211. **Contact:** Robert Rider, Jr., President. **E-mail address:** rob.riderjr@oanewton.com. **World Wide Web address:** http://www.oanewton.com. **Description:** A company with diversified divisions in agriculture, construction and the design/manufacturing of materials handling equipment.

MACY'S
Christiania Mall, Christiania-Stanton Road, Newark DE 19702. 302/366-5800. **Contact:** Human Resources. **World Wide Web address:** http://www.macys.com. **Description:** One location of the Federated department store chain. **NOTE:** See website or visit store to inquire about current job openings. **Corporate headquarters location:** New York NY. **Parent company:** Federated Department Stores Inc.

THINGS REMEMBERED
Concord Mall, 4737 Concord Pike, Wilmington DE 19803. 302/478-8108. **Contact:** Human Resources. **World Wide Web address:** http://www.thingsremembered.com. **Description:** A company and retail chain specializing in personalized gifts. Founded in 1966. **NOTE:** Call or visit store to inquire about current job openings. **Corporate headquarters location:** Cleveland OH.

District Of Columbia

GIANT FOOD, INC.
1050 Brentwood Road NE, Washington DC 20018. 202/281-3900. **Contact:** Human Resources. **World Wide Web address:** http://www.giantfood.com. **Description:** Operates a retail supermarket chain of approximately 200 stores. **Corporate headquarters location:** Landover MD. **Other U.S. locations:** DE; NJ; VA.

LORD & TAYLOR
5255 Western Avenue NW, Washington DC 20015. 202/362-9600. **Contact:** Human Resources. **World Wide Web address:** http://www.lordandtaylor.com. **Description:** A full-line department store carrying clothing, accessories, and home furnishings, with 54 stores in ten states. Founded in 1826. **NOTE:** Part-time jobs are offered. **Positions advertised include:** General Sales Associate; Commission Sales Associate; Cosmetics Beauty Advisor. **Corporate headquarters location:** New York NY. **Parent company:** The May Department Stores Company. **Listed on:** New York Stock Exchange. **Stock exchange symbol:** MAY.

Florida

B&B CORPORATE HOLDINGS, INC.
P.O. Box 1808, Tampa FL 33601. 813/621-6411. **Physical address:** 927 U.S. Highway 301 South, Tampa FL 33619. **Contact:** Linda Toledo, Director of Human Resources. **World Wide Web address:** http://www.bnbch.com. **Description:** Operates a chain of supermarkets and convenience stores under the USave name. Founded in 1923. **Positions advertised include:** Meat Cutter; Produce Clerk; Management Trainee. **Corporate headquarters location:** This location. **Subsidiaries include:** U-Save Supermarkets. **Operations at this facility include:** Administration.

W.S. BADCOCK CORPORATION
P.O. Box 497, Mulberry FL 33860. 863/425-4921. **Physical address:** 200 Phosphate Boulevard, Mulberry FL 33860. **Contact:** Jim Vernon, Director of Personnel. **World Wide Web address:** http://www.badcock.com. **Description:** Operates a chain of retail furniture stores. **Corporate headquarters location:** This location.

BARNES & NOBLE BOOKSTORES
23654 U.S. 19 North, Clearwater FL 33765. 727/669-1688. **Contact:** Manager. **World Wide Web address:** http://www.bn.com. **Description:** A bookstore chain. This location also has a cafe and a music department. **Other area locations:** Statewide.

BEALL'S DEPARTMENT STORES
P.O. Box 25207, Bradenton FL 34206. **Physical address**: 1806 38th Avenue East, Bradenton FL 34208. 941/747-2355. **Contact:** Human Resources. **World Wide Web address:** http://www.beallsinc.com. **Description:** Operates a department store chain. **Positions advertised include:** Area Sales Manager; Visual Merchandiser; Assistant Store Manager. **Corporate headquarters location:** This location.

BODY SHOP OF AMERICA, INC.
6225 Powers Avenue, Jacksonville FL 32217-2215. 904/737-0811. **Contact:** Judy Anderson, Assistant Controller. **Description:** A retail store offering apparel for juniors.

BURDINES – MACY'S
22 East Flagler Street, 4th Floor, Miami FL 33131. 305/577-1998. **Contact:** Human Resources. **World Wide Web address:** http://www.burdinesflorida.com. **Description:** Operates a retail department store chain. **Positions advertised include:** Cosmetic Beauty Advisor; Cosmetic Counter Manager; Loss Prevention Associate; Merchandise Processor; Sales Associate; Receiving Associate; Sales Support Coordinator; Selling Supervisor; Visual Merchandiser; Associate Manager; Department Manager; Merchant Processing Manager; Merchant Team Manager; Sales Manager; Store Manager; Visual Manager. **Corporate headquarters location:** This location. **Parent company:** Federated Department Stores, Inc.

CED (CONSOLIDATED ELECTRICAL DISTRIBUTORS, INC.)
4910A Adamo Drive, Tampa FL 33605. 813/248-6699. **Contact:** Manager. **World Wide Web address:** http://www.ced.com. **E-mail address:** opps@cbre.com. **Description:** A retail store that specializes in the sale of electrical supplies. **Positions advertised include:** Maintenance Associate: Painter.

CHAMPS SPORTS
303 US 301 Boulevard, Bradenton FL 34205. 941/748-5392. **Fax:** 941/741-7170. **Contact:** Sue Campbell, Vice President of Human Resources. **World Wide Web address:** http://www.champssports.com. **Description:** A specialty sporting goods retailer located in the Desoto Square Mall. Products include hard goods, apparel, footwear, and accessories. **Special programs:** Internships. **Corporate headquarters location:** This location. **Other U.S. locations:** Nationwide. **Parent company:** Foot Locker Inc. **Listed on:** New York Stock Exchange. **Stock exchange symbol:** Z. **Number of employees at this location:** 115.

CHICO'S FAS
11215 Metro Parkway, Fort Myers FL 33912. 239/277-6200. **Fax:** 941/277-7035. **Contact:** Human Resources. **E-mail address:** humanresources@chicos.com. **World Wide Web address:** http://www.chicos.com. **Description:** A manufacturer and retailer of women's apparel and accessories. Founded in 1983. **Corporate headquarters location:** This location. **Other U.S. locations:** Nationwide. **Listed on:** NASDAQ. **Stock exchange symbol:** CHS. **Annual sales/revenues:** More than $100 million.

CLAIRE'S ACCESSORIES
11401 NW 12th Street, Miami FL 33172. 305/436-8816. **Contact:** Manager. **World Wide Web address:** http://www.claires.com. **Description:** A specialty store offering women's accessories with over 2,200 locations in the United States and Canada. **NOTE:** For corporate positions, call human resources at 847/765-1100.

BILL CURRIE FORD
5815 North Dale Mabry Highway, Tampa FL 33614. 813/876-8181. **Fax:** 813/554-5354. **Contact:** Mark Jensen, Human Resources. **E-mail address:** resumes@billcurrie.com. **World Wide Web address:** http://www.billcurrie.com. **Description:** A Ford new and used car dealer. **Positions advertised include:** Customer Service Agent.

DILLARD'S DEPARTMENT STORES, INC.
6901 22nd Avenue North, Saint Peterburg FL 33710. 727/341-6000. **Contact:** Human Resources. **World Wide Web address:** http://www.dillards.com. **Description:** This location is the Florida divisional headquarters. Overall, Dillard's Department Stores operates over 220 stores in 20 states. Dillard's offers a full line of fashion apparel and home furnishings. Founded in 1938. **Corporate headquarters location:** Little Rock AR. **Operations at this facility include:** Sales. **Listed on:** New York Stock Exchange. **Stock exchange symbol:** DDS. **Annual sales/revenues:** More than $100 million.

ECKERD CORPORATION
P.O. Box 4689, Clearwater FL 33758. 727/395-6000. **Physical address:** 8333 Bryan Dairy Road, Largo FL 33777. **Recorded jobline:** 727/395-6443. **Contact:** Human Resources. **World Wide Web address:** http://www.eckerd.com. **Description:** One of the largest drug store chains in the United States, with over 1,715 stores in 13 states. The stores feature general merchandise, prescription and over-the-counter drugs, and photo development services. Nonpharmacy merchandise at Eckerd stores includes health and beauty aids, greeting cards, and other convenience products. The Eckerd Vision Group operates 47 optical superstores and 30 optical centers with one-hour service. Insta-Care Pharmacy Service centers provide prescription drugs and offer patient record and consulting services to health care institutions. **Positions advertised include:** Pharmacist; Pharmacy Technician; Store Management; Photo Lab Management. **Special programs:** Internships. **Corporate headquarters location:** This location. **Parent company:** JC Penney. **Listed on:** New York Stock Exchange. **Stock exchange symbol:** JCP. **Number of employees at this location:** 1,000. **Number of employees nationwide:** 75,000.

FARM STORES
5800 NW 74th Avenue, Miami FL 33166. 305/471-5141. **Contact:** Human Resources. **World Wide Web address:** http://www.farmstores.com. **E-mail address:** info@farmstores.com. **Description:** Operates a regional chain of convenience stores. **Corporate headquarters location:** This location.

GOLDEN BEAR GOLF INC.
11780 U.S. Highway 1, Suite 400, North Palm Beach FL 33408. 561/626-3900. **Contact:** Linda Clark, Personnel Administrator. **World Wide Web address:** http://www.nicklaus.com. **Description:** Franchises golf practice and instruction facilities, operates golf schools, constructs golf courses through Weitz Golf International (also at this location), and sells consumer golf products and apparel. **Corporate headquarters location:** This location. **Operations at this facility include:** Service. **Listed on:** NASDAQ. **Stock exchange symbol:** JACK.

HOME SHOPPING NETWORK, INC.
One HSN Drive, St. Petersburg FL 33729. 727/872-1000. **Contact:** Human Resources. **World Wide Web address:** http://www.homeshoppingnetwork.com. **Description:** A holding company that owns and operates Home Shopping Club, Inc. (HSC), which offers jewelry, hard goods, soft goods, cosmetics, and other items via live television presentations; the Internet Shopping Network, which delivers online shopping; and HSN Direct division, which produces and airs infomercials and distributes infomercial products. **Corporate headquarters location:** This location. **Parent company:** USA Networks Inc. **Listed on:** NASDAQ. **Stock exchange symbol:** USAi. **Number of employees nationwide:** 4,500.

KANE FURNITURE
5700 70th Avenue North, Pinellas Park FL 33781. 727/545-9555. **Fax:** 727/548-0552. **Contact:** Human Resources Department. **World Wide Web address:** http://www.kanesfurniture.com. **E-mail address:** humanresources@kanesfurniture.com. **Description:** A furniture retailer. **Positions advertised include:** Sales Consultant; Store Office Customer Service; Visual Merchandiser; In Store Warehouse Personnel; Delivery Driver; Helpers; Warehouse Assistants; Furniture Repair Technician. **Corporate headquarters location:** This location. **Operations at this facility include:** Administration. **Listed on:** Privately held. **Number of employees at this location:** 250. **Number of employees nationwide:** 750.

KASH 'N KARRY FOOD STORES
3801 Sugar Drive, Tampa FL 33619. 813/620-1139. **Contact:** Human Resources. **World Wide Web address:** http://www.kashnkarry.com. **Description:** An operator of retail food and liquor stores. **Positions advertised include:** Cashier; Meat Cutter; Deli Clerk; Produce Clerk; Bookkeeper; Pharmacist; Truck Driver; Front End Clerk; Stocker; Bakery Clerk; Cake Decorator; Store Manager; Department Manager; Warehouse Selector. **Corporate headquarters location:** This location. **Number of employees nationwide:** 8,400.

LIL CHAMP FOOD STORES INC.
P.O. Box 23180, Jacksonville FL 32241. 904/464-7200. **Physical address:** 8930 Western Way, Suite 4, Jacksonville FL 32256. **Contact:** Manager. **World Wide Web address:** http://www.thepantry.com. **Description:** A chain of retail grocery and convenience stores. Stores operate under the names Depot, ETNA, Express Stop, Food Chief, Handy-Way, Kangaroo, Lil' Champ, Quick Stop, Smokers Express, Sprint, The

Pantry, Wicker Mart, and Zip Mart. **Corporate headquarters location:** This location. **Listed on:** NASDAQ. **Stock exchange symbol:** PTRY.

MARTINE'S CORPORATION
120 East Main Street, Suite A, Pensacola FL 32502. 850/429-8640. **Contact:** Human Resources. **Description:** Operates fast-food establishments, liquor stores, and shopping centers.

MAYORS JEWELERS
14051 NW 14th Street, Sunrise FL 33323. 954/846-8000. **Fax:** 954/846-2787. **Recorded jobline:** 800/223-6964x5408. **Contact:** Human Resources. **E-mail address:** clientservices@mayors.com. **World Wide Web address:** http://www.mayors.com. **Description:** A retailer, merchandiser, and distributor of jewelry, watches, sunglasses, fragrances, and collectibles. **Corporate headquarters location:** This location. **Other U.S. locations:** Nationwide. **Operations at this facility include:** Administration; Distribution. **Number of employees at this location:** 500.

OFFICE DEPOT
2200 Old Germantown Road, Delray Beach FL 33445. 561/278-4800. **Contact:** Human Resources. **World Wide Web address:** http://www.officedepot.com. **Description:** Operates a chain of large-volume office-products warehouse stores that sell brand name office merchandise primarily to small and medium-sized businesses. **Corporate headquarters location:** This location. **Other U.S. locations:** Nationwide. **International locations:** Canada. **Listed on:** New York Stock Exchange. **Stock exchange symbol:** ODP. **Number of employees nationwide:** 33,000.

POTAMKIN SOUTH
21111 South Dixie Highway, Miami FL 33189. 305/238-0000. **Contact:** General Manager. **World Wide Web address:** http://www.potamkinsouth.com. **Description:** An automobile dealership. **Special programs:** Internships. **Other U.S. locations:** Nationwide. **Listed on:** Privately held. **Number of employees at this location:** 115.

PUBLIX SUPER MARKETS, INC.
1936 George Jenkins Boulevard, Lakeland FL 33815. 863/688-1188. **Recorded jobline:** 863/680-5265. **Contact:** Human Resources Department. **World Wide Web address:** http://www.publix.com. **Description:** Operates a chain of retail supermarkets with 691 stores in Alabama, Florida, Georgia, and South Carolina. The company also produces dairy, delicatessen, and bakery items through four plants and conducts distribution operations through more than eight facilities in Florida and Georgia. Founded in 1930. **Company slogan:** Where shopping is a pleasure. **Special programs:** Summer Jobs. **Corporate headquarters location:** This location. **Other U.S. locations:** AL; FL; GA; SC. **Listed on:** Privately held. **CEO:** Howard Jenkins. **Annual sales/revenues:** More than $100 million. **Number of employees at this location:** 5,000. **Number of employees nationwide:** 122,000.

ROBB & STUCKY
13170 South Cleveland Avenue, Fort Myers FL 33907. 239/936-8541. **Fax:** 239/437-6286. **Contact:** Sharon Dill, Director of Human Resources. **E-mail address:** personnel@robbstuckey.net. **World Wide Web address:** http://www.robbstucky.com. **Description:** A chain of furniture stores that also offers interior design services.

SEARS, ROEBUCK & CO.
9501 Arlington Expressway, Suite 785, Jacksonville FL 32225. 904/727-3255. **Contact:** Human Resources. **World Wide Web address:** http://www.sears.com. **Description:** One location of the nationwide department store chain. **Positions advertised include:** District Sales Manager. **Corporate headquarters location:** Chicago IL. **Listed on:** New York Stock Exchange. **Stock exchange symbol:** S.

SOUND ADVICE, INC.
2501 Southwest 32nd Avenue, Hallandale FL 33009. 954/922-4434. **Contact:** Human Resources. **E-mail address:** hr@soundadvice-fl.com. **World Wide Web address:** http://www.wegivesoundadvice.com. **Description:** Operates retail stores that sell and service audio and video equipment for the home and automobile markets. **Corporate headquarters location:** This location.

WINN-DIXIE STORES, INC.
P.O. Box B, Jacksonville FL 32203-0297. 904/783-5000. **Physical address:** 5050 Edgewood Court, Jacksonville FL 32254. **Fax:** 904/783-5235. **Contact:** Human Resources. **E-mail address:** hr@winn-dixie.com. **World Wide Web address:** http://www.winn-dixie.com. **Description:** Winn-Dixie operates supermarkets and stores in the 14 Sunbelt states under the names Winn-Dixie, Marketplace, and Buddies. Winn-Dixie also operates 20 warehousing and distribution centers and a host of manufacturing and processing facilities. A subsidiary of the company operates 12 stores in the Bahamas. **Positions advertised include:** Corporate Finance; Marketing Associate; Corporate Accounting Associate; Human Resources Associate; Information Technology Department; Logistics Associate; Manufacturing Associate; Sales Manager. **Corporate headquarters location:** This location. **Listed on:** New York Stock Exchange. **Stock exchange symbol:** WIN. **President/CEO:** Al Rowland. **Number of employees nationwide:** 120,000.

Georgia

IVAN ALLEN OFFICE FURNITURE
730 Peachtree Street NE, Suite 200, Atlanta GA 30308. 404/760-8700. **Fax:** 404/760-8670. **Contact:** Human Resources Manager. **E-mail address:** hr@ivanallen.com. **World Wide Web address:** http://www.ivanallen.com. **Description:** Engaged in the retail sale of office furniture. **Positions advertised include:** Project Designer; Inside Sales Administrator; Sales – Account Executive; Bid Representative; Small Business Development Representative. **Corporate headquarters location:** Atlanta GA. **Other area locations:** Albany GA; Augusta GA; Athens GA. **Other U.S. locations:** Chattanooga TN; Knoxville TN; Huntsville AL. **Operations at this facility include:** Administration; Sales. **CEO:** H. Inman Allen.

AVON PRODUCTS INC.
425 Horizon Drive, Suwannee GA 30024. 770/271-6100. **Contact:** Human Resources. **World Wide Web address:** http://www.avoncareers.com. **Description:** A direct seller of beauty care products, fashion jewelry, gifts, fragrances, and decorative products. Avon, a *Fortune* 500 company, markets its products through a network of 2.8 million independent sales representatives in 135 countries worldwide. **NOTE:** Salespeople are considered independent contractors or dealers and most work part-time. If you are interested in becoming a sales representative, please call 800/FOR-AVON, or visit the company's Website for more information. Please visit website to search for jobs and apply online. **Positions advertised include:** Customer Service Specialist; Bilingual Customer Service Specialist; Quality Assurance Supervisor. **Special program:** Internships. **Corporate headquarters location:** New York NY. **Other area locations:** Statewide. **Other U.S. locations:** Nationwide. **International locations:** Worldwide. **Listed on:** New York Stock Exchange. **Stock exchange symbol:** AVP. **CEO:** Andrea Jung.

BARNES & NOBLE BOOKSTORES
7660 North Point Parkway, Suite 200, Alpharetta GA 30022. 770/993-8340. **Contact:** Manager. **World Wide Web address:** http://www.bn.com. **Description:** A bookstore chain operating nationwide. This location also has a cafe and music department. **Office hours:** Monday – Thursday, 9:00 a.m. – 10:00 p.m.; Friday – Saturday, 9:00 a.m. – 11:00 p.m.; Sunday 9:00 a.m. – 9:00 p.m. **Other area locations:** Statewide. **Other U.S. locations:** Nationwide.

GENE EVANS FORD, INC.
4355 Jonesboro Road, Union City GA 30291. 770/964-9801. **Toll-free phone:** 800/992-9801. **Fax:** 770/306-6715. **Contact:** Hiring Coordinator. **World Wide Web address:** http://www.geneevansford.com. **Description:** An automobile dealer. **NOTE:** Please visit website for online application form. **Corporate headquarters location:** This location. **Operations at this facility include:** Sales; Service.

HAVERTY FURNITURE COMPANIES, INC.
P.O. Box 420099, Atlanta GA 30342-0099. 404/443-2900. **Physical address:** 780 Johnson Ferry Road, Suite 800, Atlanta GA 30342. **Fax:** 404/443-4170. **Contact:** Vice President of Human Resources. **E-mail address:** hr@havertys.com. **World Wide Web address:** http://www.havertys.com. **Description:** A full-service home furnishings retailer with more than 100 showrooms in 14 states. Founded in 1885. **Positions advertised include:** Sales Associate; Visual Coordinator. **Special programs:** Training. **Corporate headquarters location:** This location. **Other U.S. locations:** Nationwide. **Listed on:** New York Stock Exchange. **Stock exchange symbol:** HVT. **Annual sales/revenues:** More than $100 million. **Number of employees nationwide:** 4,180.

THE HOME DEPOT
2455 Paces Ferry Road, Atlanta GA 30339-4024. 770/433-8211. **Contact:** Human Resources. **World Wide Web address:** http://www.homedepot.com. **Description:** Operates retail warehouse stores that sell a wide assortment of building materials and home improvement products, primarily to the do-it-yourself and home remodeling markets. The company operates 1,232 full-service, warehouse-style stores. Founded in 1978. **NOTE:** Please visit website to search for jobs and apply online. **Positions advertised include:** Senior Systems Specialist; Merchandising Leadership Personnel; Inventory Supervisor; Administrative Assistant; Manager of Finance; Loss Prevention Business Specialist. **Special programs:** Internships. **Corporate headquarters location:** This location. **Other U.S. locations:** Nationwide. **International locations:** Canada; Mexico. **Listed on:** New York Stock Exchange. **Operations at this facility include:** Atlanta Store Support. **Stock exchange symbol:** HD. **CEO:** Bob Nardelli. **Annual sales/revenues:** More than $100 million. **Number of employees nationwide:** 300,000.

THE JONES COMPANY
P.O. Box 2149, Waycross GA 31501. 912/285-4011. **Physical address:** 215 Tindleton Street, Waycross GA 31501. **Fax:** 912/285-5610. **Contact:** Employment. **World Wide Web address:** http://www.jonescoinc.com. **Description:** Owns and operates Flash Foods retail convenience stores. **Corporate headquarters location:** This location.

LEATH FURNITURE
4370 Peachtree Road NE, 4th Floor, Atlanta GA 30319. 404/848-0880. **Contact:** Human Resources. **E-mail address:** hr@leathfurniture.com. **World Wide Web address:** http://www.leathfurniture.com. **Description:** Leath Furniture owns and operates twenty-six retail furniture stores and two distribution centers. **Corporate headquarters location:** This location. **Other U.S. locations:** IL; IN; IA; MI; WI. **Operations at this facility include:** Administrative offices.

NATIONAL VISION
296 Grayson Highway, Lawrenceville GA 30045. 770/822-3600. **Fax:** 770/822-6206. **Recorded jobline:** 888/261-3937. **Contact:** Human Resources. **E-mail address:** jobs@nationalvision.com. **World Wide Web address:** http://www.nationalvision.com. **Description:** National Vision operates five separate retail divisions offering a variety of products and services for eye care and eyewear needs. **Positions advertised include:** Legal Secretary; Human Resources Generalist. **Corporate headquarters location:** This location. **Listed on:** American Stock Exchange. **Stock exchange symbol:** NVI. **Number of employees worldwide:** 2,930.

NEIMAN MARCUS
3393 Peachtree Road NE, Atlanta GA 30326. 404/266-8200. **Toll-free phone:** 800/555-5077. **Contact:** Human Resources Manager. **World Wide Web address:** http://www.neimanmarcus.com. **Description:** A retailer of men's and women's apparel, fashion accessories, precious jewelry, fine china, and moderately priced crystal and silver. Neiman Marcus has 33 stores nationwide. **NOTE:** Entry-level positions are offered. **Corporate headquarters location:** Dallas TX. **Other area locations:** Lawrenceville GA. **Other U.S. locations:** Nationwide. **Subsidiaries include:** Bergdorf Goodman Stores (NY); NM Direct, a direct marketing company. **Operations at this facility include:** Administration; Sales; Service. **Listed on:** New York Stock Exchange. **Stock exchange symbol:** NMG/A. **President/CEO:** Burton Tansky. **Number of employees nationwide:** 15,400.

MACY'S SOUTH
223 Perimeter Center Parkway NE, Atlanta GA 30346. 770/913-4000. 4123. **Contact:** Human Resources. **World Wide Web address:** http://www.federated-fds.com. **Description:** Operates Rich's-Macy's, Lazarus-Macy's, and Goldsmith-Macy's in the Southeastern states. **NOTE:** Please visit http://www.retailology.com to search for jobs and apply online. **Positions advertised include:** Assistant Buyer; Beauty Advisor – Various Brands; Bedding Specialist; Hair Stylist; Loss Prevention Associate; Manager – Seasonal Planning; Regional Merchandise Manager; Sales Associate – Various Departments; Stock/Support Associate. **Corporate headquarters location:** This location. **Other U.S. locations:** Southeastern U.S. **Parent company:** Federated Department Stores, Inc. **Listed on:** New York Stock Exchange. **Stock exchange symbol:** FD. **Number of employees nationwide:** 15,500.

RBM OF ATLANTA, INC.
7640 Roswell Road, Atlanta GA 30350-4839. 770/390-0700. **Fax:** 770/395-7521. **Contact:** Office Manager. **World Wide Web address:** http://www.atlanta.mercedescenter.com. **Description:** A retail dealer and servicer of Mercedes-Benz automobiles.

TARGET STORES
4502 Old Union Road, Tifton GA 31794. 229/387-3000. **Contact:** Human Resources Department. **World Wide Web address:** http://www.target.com. **Description:** A national chain of upscale discount retail stores. **NOTE:** Please visit http://www.targetcorp.com to search for jobs. **Positions advertised include:** Operations Senior Group Leader; Facility Operations Manager; Group Leader; Regional Transportation Supervisor; Facility Operations Group Leader. **Corporate headquarters location:** Minneapolis MN. **Other U.S. locations:** Nationwide. **Operations at this facility include:** The Southeast's distribution center for Target retail stores. **Listed on:** New York Stock Exchange. **Stock exchange symbol:** TGT. **CEO:** Bob Ulrich. **Number of employees nationwide:** 245,000.

TRONCALLI NISSAN
1625 Church Street, Decatur GA 30033. 404/292-3853; 404/292-6828. **Contact:** General Sales Manager. **World Wide Web address:** http://www.troncallinissan.com. **Description:** A franchised dealer of Nissan, Jaguar, and Chrysler-Plymouth automobiles. **NOTE:** Please visit website for online application form.

Hawaii

FOODLAND
3536 Harding Avenue, Honolulu HI 96816. 808/732-0791. **Contact:** Human Resources. **E-mail address:** services@foodland.com. **World Wide Web address:** http://www.foodland.com. **Description:** Operates 24 Foodland supermarkets. **Corporate headquarters location:** This location.

MACY'S
1450 Ala Moana Boulevard, Honolulu HI 96814. 808/941-2345. **Contact:** Human Resources. **World Wide Web address:** http://www.macysjobs.com. **Description:** A department store. **Positions advertised include:** Beauty Advisor, Various Cosmetics Brands; Cosmetics Sales; Commission Sales, Women's Shoes; Counter Manager; Loss Prevention Agent; Sales Associate. **Corporate headquarters location:** Cincinnati OH. **Other area locations:** Statewide. **Parent company:** Federated Department Stores, Inc.

SAFEWAY STORES, INC.
680 Iwilei Road, Suite 590, Honolulu HI 96817. 808/524-4554. **Contact:** Human Resources. **World Wide Web address:** http://www.safeway.com. **Description:** Operates approximately 1,700 stores in the Western, Rocky Mountain, Southwestern, and Mid-Atlantic regions of the United States and in western Canada. **Corporate headquarters location:** Pleasanton CA. **Operations at this facility include:** This location houses the district offices for Safeway supermarkets. **Listed on:** NASDAQ. **Stock exchange symbol:** SWY. **Annual sales/revenues:** $36 billion.

Idaho

ALBERTSON'S, INC.
250 East Parkcenter Boulevard, Boise ID 83706. 208/395-6200. **Toll-free phone:** 877/932-7948 **Fax:** 208/395-4880. **Contact:** Human Resources. **E-mail address:** employment@albertsons.com. **World Wide Web address:** http://www.albertsons.com. **Description:** One of the largest retail food-drug chains in the United States. **Positions advertised include:** Accountant II; Customer Service Manager; Marketing Manager; Systems Engineer and Network Optimization Specialist. **Internship information:** Offers full-time internships that rotate through various departments. **Corporate headquarters location:** This location. **Other U.S. locations:** Nationwide. **Listed on:** New York Stock Exchange. **Stock exchange symbol:** ABS. **Annual sales/revenues:** $37.9 billion. **Number of employees nationwide:** 240,000.

BARNES & NOBLE BOOKSTORES
1315 North Milwaukee Street, Boise ID 83704. 208/375-4454. **Contact:** Manager. **World Wide Web address:** http://www.barnesandnoble.com. **Description:** A bookstore chain operating nationwide. This location has a cafe and music department in addition to its book departments. There is also a B. Dalton Bookseller store located at the Karcher Mall in Nampa. **Listed on:** New York Stock Exchange. **Stock exchange symbol:** BKS.

MACY'S
918 West Idaho Street, Boise ID 83702. 208/388-7004. **Contact:** Julie Strickler, Human Resources. **World Wide Web address:** http://www.macys.com. **Description:** Macy's Northwest is a department store operation in the Pacific Northwest. **NOTE:** Apply for positions online at www.macys.com or in person. **Positions advertised include:** Regional Bridal Manager; Sales Associate. **Corporate headquarters location:** Seattle, WA. **Parent company:** Federated Department Stores. Inc.

JCPENNEY COMPANY, INC.
300 North Milwaukee, Boise ID 83704. 208/376-0555. **Fax:** 208/376-0050. **Contact:** Store Manager. **World Wide Web address:** http://www.jcpenney.com. **Description:** This location is a retail store. JCPenney Company, Inc. is an international retail merchandise sales and service corporation. **Special programs:** Internships. **NOTE:** Some positions listed on the website; visit the store to submit an application for current positions. **Corporate headquarters location:** Plano TX. **Operations at this facility include:** Retail sales; salon; window covering. **Listed on:** New York Stock Exchange. **Stock exchange symbol:** JCP. **CEO:** Myron Ullman III. **Other U.S. locations:** Nationwide.

Illinois

ACE HARDWARE CORPORATION
2200 Kensington Court, Oak Brook IL 60523. 630/990-6600. **Fax:** 630/990-1742. **Contact:** Human Resources. **World Wide Web address:** http://www.acehardware.com. **Description:** A dealer-owned cooperative operating through 5,100 hardware retailers in 62 countries. Ace Hardware Corporation also produces a line of hand and power tools, plumbing products, lawn and garden products, cleaning supplies, and manufactures a line of paint. **NOTE:** Apply online at the company's website. **Positions advertised include:** Associate Web Designer; Corporate Communications Manager; Financial Reporting Analyst; Web Network Systems Engineer. **Corporate headquarters location:** This location.

ALBERTSON'S INC.
3030 Cullerton Drive, Franklin Park IL 60131. **Toll-free phone:** 800/964-1434. **Fax:** 888/541-5793. **Contact:** Human Resources. **E-mail address:** employment@albertsons.com. **World Wide Web address:** http://www.albertsons.com. **Description:** One of the largest retail food-drug chains in the United States, Albertson's is selling its retail operations across the country to grocer Supervalu Inc., drugstore chain CVS Corp. and an investment group. **Internship information:** Offers full-time internships that rotate through various departments. **Corporate headquarters location:** Boise ID. **Other U.S. locations:** Nationwide. **Listed on:** New York Stock Exchange. **Stock exchange symbol:** ABS. **Annual sales/revenues:** $37.9 billion. **Number of employees nationwide:** 240,000.

ALDI INC.
2080 West Main Street, Batavia IL 60510. 630/879-8100. **Contact:** Human Resources. **World Wide Web address:** http://www.aldi.us. **Description:** Operates a chain of discount grocery stores throughout the Midwest. **NOTE:** Apply in person. **Corporate headquarters location:** Essen, Germany.

BARNES & NOBLE BOOKSTORES
1550 West 75th Street, Downers Grove IL 60516. 630/663-0181. **Contact:** Manager. **World Wide Web address:** http://www.barnesandnobleinc.com. **Description:** One location of the nationwide bookstore chain. This location has a cafe in addition to its book department. **NOTE:** Apply online or at the nearest retail location. **Positions advertised include:** Book Seller; Music Seller; Café Attendant; Department Manager; Community Relations Manager. **Corporate headquarters location:** New York NY. **Other U.S. locations:** Nationwide. **Listed on:** NASDAQ. **Stock exchange symbol:** BNBN.

BRIDGESTONE/FIRESTONE RETAIL & COMMERCIAL OPERATIONS
333 East Lake Street Bloomingdale IL 60108. 630/259-9000. **Contact:** Human Resources. **World Wide Web address:** http://www.bfmastercare.com. **Description:** This location is the support center and headquarters for the Bridgestone/Firestone retail stores operations of Bridgestone Corporation. **NOTE:** Entry-level positions and part-time jobs are offered. Apply online at the website. **Corporate headquarters location:** This location. **Other U.S. locations:** Nationwide. **International locations:** Worldwide. **Parent company:** Bridgestone Corp.

CARSON PIRIE SCOTT & COMPANY
One South State Street, Chicago IL 60603. 312/641-7000. **Fax:** 312/641-7088. **Contact:** Hiring Manager. **World Wide Web address:** http://www.carsons.com. **Description:** The department store chain's flagship store in downtown Chicago. Overall, Carson Pirie Scott & Company operates a department store chain with about 30 Midwest locations. **Parent company:** Bon-Ton Stores Inc. operates 279 stores in secondary and metropolitan markets in 23 northeastern, Midwestern, and Great Plains states under the names of Bon-Ton, Bergner's, Boston Store, Carson Pirie Scott, Elder-Beerman, Herberger's, and Younkers. **NOTE:** This

chain has several locations throughout the Chicago area, Illinois, and the Midwest. To apply, see the corporate website for open positions; or visit the nearest store location. **Listed on:** New York Stock Exchange. **Stock exchange symbol:** BONT.

DOMINICK'S FINER FOODS
711 Jorie Boulevard, Oak Brook IL 60523. 630/891-5000. **Toll-free phone:** 877/723-3929. **Fax:** 630/891-5210. **Contact:** Human Resources. **World Wide Web address:** http://www.dominicks.com. **Description:** Operates a chain of retail grocery stores throughout the Chicago area. **NOTE:** Apply online at this company's website. **Corporate headquarters location:** This location. **Parent company:** Safeway Inc. **Operations at this facility include:** Administration.

FORTUNE BRANDS INC.
520 Lake Cook Road, Deerfield IL 60015. 847/484-4400. **Contact:** Human Resources. **World Wide Web address:** http://www.fortunebrands.com. **Description:** A consumer products company offering home and office products, golf equipment, and spirits and wine. **Brand names include:** Jim Beam, Master Lock, Moen, El Tesoro, Acco, Dekuyper, Titlelist; Footjoy. **NOTE:** For positions with a specific Fortune Brand company, see its corporate website for links to the its subsidiaries' websites. **Corporate headquarters location:** This location. **Listed on:** New York Stock Exchange. **Stock exchange symbol:** FO.

HOME NURSERY, INC.
P.O. Box 307, Edwardsville IL 62025. 618/656-1470. **Contact:** Employment Manager. **World Wide Web address:** http://www.homenursery.com. **Description:** A nursery engaged in the wholesale and retail sale of lawn and garden supplies. **Operations at this facility include:** Administration; Accounting.

JC PENNEY COMPANY, INC.
3 Woodfield Mall, Schaumburg IL 60173. 847/240-5000. **Contact:** Human Resources. **World Wide Web address:** http://www.jcpenney.net. **Description:** A national retail service corporation with department stores in most major American cities. JC Penney sells apparel, home furnishings, and leisure lines in catalogs and 1,900 retail stores. **Corporate headquarters location:** Dallas TX. **Other U.S. locations:** Ford City IL; Lombard IL; North Riverside IL. **Operations at this facility include:** Regional Headquarters. **Listed on:** New York Stock Exchange. **Stock exchange symbol:** JCP.

JEWEL OSCO
1955 West North Avenue, Melrose Park IL 60160. 708/531-6000. **Fax:** 708/531-6047. **Contact:** Employment Manager. **World Wide Web address:** http://www.jewelosco.com. **Description:** Operates a chain of retail food stores. **NOTE:** For store management positions, e-mail resumes. For retail positions, apply at the nearest Jewel Osco location. For pharmacy employment, send resume to Recruiting Department, 3030 Cullerton, Franklin Park, IL 60130; fax: 888/541-5793; or e-mail: pharmacyrecruiting@Albertsons.com. When sending a resume, please indicate department of interest. Special programs: Internships; Store Management Training. **Corporate headquarters location:** This location.

K'S MERCHANDISE
3103 North Charles Street, Decatur IL 62526. 217/875-1440. **Fax:** 217/875-6978. **Contact:** Human Resources. **World Wide Web address:** http://www.catalog.ksmerchandise.com. **Description:** A retail catalog showroom chain. **Positions advertised include:** Store Manager Trainee; Jewelry Assistant; Jewelry Manager; Jeweler Promotional Coordinator; Jeweler. **Corporate headquarters location:** This location. **Operations at this facility include:** Administration; Manufacturing; Sales; Service.

NEW YORK & COMPANY
4190-E North Harlem Avenue, Chicago IL 60634. 773/625-9684. **Contact:** Human Resources. **E-mail address:** recruiting@nyandcompany.com. **World Wide Web address:** http://www.nyandcompany.com. **Description:** New York & Company sells moderately priced women's fashions through a chain of retail stores. **NOTE:** See website for corporate job listings. To apply for retail positions, visit the nearest store location. **Operations at this facility include:** This location houses administrative offices. **Parent company:** The Limited, Inc.

SAKS FIFTH AVENUE
700 North Michigan Avenue, Chicago IL 60611. 312/944-6500. **Contact:** Human Resources. **World Wide Web address:** http://www.saksincorporated.com. **Description:** Saks Fifth Avenue is a 62-store chain emphasizing soft-goods products, primarily apparel for men, women, and children. **NOTE:** See website for job listings and apply online. **Parent company:** Saks Incorporated is a department store holding company that operates approximately 360 stores in 36 states. **Operations at this facility include:** This location is a part of the nationwide specialty department store chain. **Listed on:** New York Stock Exchange. **Stock exchange symbol:** SKS.

SEARS, ROEBUCK & CO.
3333 Beverly Road, Hoffman Estates IL 60179. 847/286-2500. **Contact:** Director of Human Resources. **World Wide Web address:** http://www.sears.com. **Description:** Operates a chain of department stores. **Corporate headquarters location:** This location. **Subsidiaries include:** Sears Holdings Corporation's businesses include Kmart, The Great Indoors, Lands' End, and Orchard Supply Hardware. **Listed on:** New York Stock Exchange. **NOTE:** For corporate positions, apply online. For retail positions, visit the nearest retail location. **Stock exchange symbol:** S.

THE SHERWIN-WILLIAMS COMPANY
619 Howard Street, Evanston IL 60202. 847/869-9030. **Contact:** Human Resources. **World Wide Web address:** http://www.sherwin.com. **Description:** Sherwin-Williams Company manufactures, sells, and distributes coatings and related products. Sherwin-Williams labeled architectural and industrial coatings are sold through company-owned specialty paint and wallcovering stores. The Sherwin-Williams Company also manufactures paint under the Acme, Dutch Boy, Kem-Tone, Lucas, Martin-Senour, Minwax, Pratt & Lambert, Rogers, and Thompson brand names, as well as private labels, and markets its products to independent dealers, mass merchandisers, and home improvement centers. **NOTE:** Apply in person at this location. See website for corporate job listings. **Corporate headquarters location:** Cleveland OH. **Operations at this facility include:** This location is a retail and wholesale outlet.

SPIEGEL, INC.
3500 Lacey Road, Downers Grove IL 60515. 630/986-8800. **Fax:** 630/769-2012. **Contact:** Human Resources. **E-mail address:** careers@spgl.com. **World Wide Web address:** http://www.spiegel.com. **Description:** A retailer of goods and services for the home, as well as current fashions for women, men, and children. **Positions advertised include:** Recruiter. **Corporate headquarters location:** This location. **Subsidiaries include:** Eddie Bauer, Inc.

STRATFORD HALL
6253 West 74th Street, Box 2001, Bedford Park IL 60499-2001. 800/628-9028. **Contact:** Human Resources. **World Wide Web address:** http://www.stratfordhall.com. **Description:** Engaged in the catalog sale of personalized holiday cards for businesses. **Corporate headquarters location:** This location.

TRUE VALUE COMPANY
8600 West Bryn Mawr Avenue, Chicago IL 60631-3505. 773/695-5000. **Contact:** Human Resources. **E-mail address:** jobs@truevalue.com. **World Wide Web address:** http://www.truevaluecompany.com. **Description:** A *Fortune* 500 company that operates the

True Value, Home & Garden Showplace, and Taylor Rental national retail chains. **NOTE:** Apply online. **Positions advertised include:** Import Logistics Manager; Import Coordinator; Inventory Analyst; Field Marketing Manager; Retail Project Supervisor; Accounts Payable Manager; Transportation Compliance Analyst. **Corporate headquarters location:** This location.

VALUE CITY FURNITURE
15770 S. La Grange Road, Orland Park IL 60462. 708/226-8121. **Fax:** 708/226-8177. **Contact:** John Jacobe, General Manager. **E-mail address:** John.Jacobe@vcf.com. **World Wide Web address:** http://www.vcf.com. **Description:** A furniture retailer with over 100 stores throughout the Midwestern, Eastern, and Southern United States. **Positions advertised include:** Delivery Driver; General Warehouse Worker; Sales Professional; Service Technician; Visual Merchandiser. **Other U.S. locations:** Nationwide.

WALGREEN COMPANY
200 Wilmot Road, Deerfield IL 60015. 847/914-2500. **Contact:** Personnel Recruiting. **World Wide Web address:** http://www.walgreens.com. **Description:** Walgreen operates one of the largest retail drug store chains in the United States, which sells prescription and nonprescription drugs, cosmetics, toiletries, liquor and beverages, tobacco, and general merchandise. **Corporate headquarters location:** This location.

XPEDX
3555 North Kimball Avenue, Chicago IL 60618. 773/463-0822. **Fax:** 773/463-4862. **Contact:** Human Resources. **World Wide Web address:** http://www.xpedx.com. **Description:** A retailer of paper and office products. **Corporate headquarters location:** This location. **Parent company:** International Paper Company. **Operations at this facility include:** Administration; Sales; Service. **Listed on:** New York Stock Exchange. **Stock exchange symbol:** IP.

Indiana

BARNES & NOBLE BOOKSTORES
3748 East 82nd Street, Indianapolis IN 46240. 317/594-7525. **Contact:** Human Resources. **World Wide Web address:** http://www.bn.com. **Description:** A discount bookstore chain. This location has a cafe and music department in addition to its comprehensive book departments. **Other U.S. locations:** Nationwide.

FINISH LINE INC.
3308 North Mitthoeffer Road, Indianapolis IN 46235. 888/777-3949. **Fax** 317/613-6701. **Contact:** Human Resources. **E-mail address:** hr@finishline.com. **World Wide Web address:** http://www.thefinishline.com. **Description:** Finish Line Inc. operates retail stores that offer a broad selection of current men's, women's, and children's brand name athletic and leisure footwear, active-wear, and accessories. **Positions advertised include:** Store Cash Reconciliation Associate; Controller; Human Resources Specialist; Staff Attorney; Paralegal; Loss Prevention Officer; In-Store Production Coordinator; Product Merchandiser; Senior Tax Accountant. **Corporate headquarters location:** This location.

GRIFFITH MENARD'S
6050 West Ridge Road, Gary IN 46408. 219/838-6134. **Contact:** Human Resources. **World Wide Web address:** http://www.menards.com. **Description:** An electronics, hardware, and home supplies retail outlet. Menard's sells building materials; electricity and lighting equipment; doors, windows, floor supplies and carpeting; home heating equipment; plumbing tools and supplies; and electronics.

KITTLE'S FURNITURE
8600 Allisonville Road, Indianapolis IN 46250. 317/849-5300. **Fax:** 317/579-7394. **Contact:** Human Resources. **E-mail address:** mrenskers@kittles.com. **World Wide Web address:** http://www.kittles.com. **Description:** A fine furniture and appliance retailer consisting of 17 stores located throughout the Midwest. **Positions advertised include:** Information Technology Manager; Sales Manager. **Corporate headquarters location:** This location.

KROGER'S
2864 Charlestown Road, New Albany IN 47150. 812/944-7016. **Contact:** Human Resources. **World Wide Web address:** http://www.kroger.com. **Description:** A supermarket.

MARSH SUPERMARKETS, INC.
9800 Crosspoint Boulevard, Indianapolis IN 46256. 317/845-9137. **Contact:** Human Resources. **E-mail address:** resume@marsh.net. **World Wide Web address:** http://www.marsh.net. **Description:** The company operates Marsh Supermarkets, LoBill Foods, Village Pantry Convenience Stores in Indiana and Ohio, and CSDC, a convenience store distribution company. Founded in 1931. **Positions advertised include:** Chef; Meat Cutter; Floral Department Manager; Pharmacist; Sea Food Manager; Cashier; Espresso Bar Server; Cake Decorator. **Corporate headquarters location:** This location.

SHOE CARNIVAL, INC.
4595 University Drive, Evansville IN 47712. 812/421-2260. **Contact:** Human Resources. **World Wide Web address:** http://www.shoecarnival.com. **Description:** Operates specialty shoe stores.

SUPERVALU INC.
4815 Executive Boulevard, Fort Wayne IN 46808. 260/483-2146. **Contact:** Human Resources. **E-mail address:** careers@supervalu.com. **World Wide Web address:** http://www.supervalu.com. **Description:** One of the nation's largest food retailers and distribution companies, supplying grocery, health and beauty aids, and general merchandise products to over 4,000 customers. In the corporate retail sector, SUPERVALU operates over 300 stores under the following names: Bigg's, Cub Foods, Shop 'n Save, Save-A-Lot, Scott's Foods, Laneco, and Hornbachers. **Corporate headquarters location:** Eden Prairie MN. **Listed on:** New York Stock Exchange. **Stock exchange symbol:** SVU.

TJ MAXX
3301 Maxx Road, Evansville IN 47711. 812/424-0932. **Contact:** Human Resources. **World Wide Web address:** http://www.tjmaxx.com. **Description:** TJ Maxx operates a chain of discount stores. **Corporate headquarters location:** Framingham MA. **Other U.S. locations:** Nationwide. **Parent company:** The TJX Companies, Inc. owns both TJ Maxx and Marshall's. **Operations at this facility include:** This location is a retail distribution and loss control center.

Iowa

BARNES & NOBLE BOOKSTORES
4550 University Avenue, West Des Moines IA 50266-1025. 515/221-9171. **Fax:** 515/226-0930. **Contact:** Store Manager. **E-mail address**: Careers@bn.com. **World Wide Web address:** http://www.barnesandnobleinc.com. **Description:** A bookstore chain operating 900 stores nationwide. This location has a cafe and music department in addition to its book comprehensive departments. **Positions Advertised Include**: Merchandise Analyst; Assistant Buyer; Computer Operator; Editor-Sparknotes; Production Manager-Sparknotes. **Corporate headquarters location:** New York NY. **Other area locations:** Cedar Rapids IA; Coralville IA; Waterloo IA. **Other U.S. locations:** Nationwide. **Listed on:** New York Stock Exchange. **Stock exchange symbol:** BKS. **Number of employees worldwide:** 37,000.

TRUCK COUNTRY
4300 NE 14th Street, Des Moines IA 50313. 515/265-7361. **Toll-free phone:** 888/201-6222. **Fax:** 563/556-3420. **Contact:** Erik Thoms. **E-mail address:** ErikThoms@truckcountry.com. **World Wide Web address:** http://www.truckcountry.com. **Description:** Truck Country is one of the largest Freightliner dealers

in the U.S. **NOTE:** Search posted listings and apply online. **Positions advertised include:** Diesel Technician, Lot Assistant/Detailer, Office Manager, Outside Parts Sales, Parts Counter Salesperson, Shipping & Receiving, Service Manager, Assistant Service Manager, Service Advisor, Inventory Control Clerk, Truck Transfer Driver, Business Analyst, Custodian.

VON MAUR, INC.
6565 Brady Street, Davenport IA 52806. 563/388-2744. **Fax:** 563/388-2242. **Contact:** Denise Holtz, Recruiting Manager. **E-mail address**: dholtz@vonmaur.com. **World Wide Web address:** http://www.vonmaur.com. **Description:** A department store carrying a full line of clothing, shoes, and accessories for men, women, and children. **NOTE**: Search posted openings and apply online. **Positions advertised include:** Buyer; Department Manager; Management Trainee; Retail Manager. **Corporate headquarters location:** This location. **Other U.S. locations:** Nationwide. **Listed on:** Privately held. **Number of employees at this location:** 300. **Number of employees nationwide:** 2,800.

Kansas
BARNES & NOBLE BOOKSTORES
6130 SW 17th Street, Topeka KS 66615. 785/273-9600. **Fax:** 785/273-7125. **Contact:** Manager. **World Wide Web address:** http://www.barnesandnobleinc.com. **Description:** A bookstore chain operating 900 stores nationwide. This location has a cafe and music department in addition to its book departments. **Positions advertised include:** Book Seller; Café Seller; Music Seller; Receiver; Lead Position; Head Cashier; Community Relations Manager; Assistant Store Manager; Store Manager; District Manager. **Corporate headquarters location:** New York NY. **Other area locations:** Leawood KS; Wichita KS. **Other U.S. locations:** Nationwide. **Listed on:** New York Stock Exchange. **Stock exchange symbol:** BKS. **Number of employees worldwide:** 37,000.

DUCKWALL-ALCO STORES, INC.
401 Cottage Avenue, Abilene KS 67410. 785/263-3350. **Fax:** 785/263-1789. **Contact:** Dan Curoe, Vice President of Training & Recruiting. **E-mail address:** dcuroe@duckwall.com. **World Wide Web address:** http://www.duckwall.com. **Description:** A regional retailer operating 170 ALCO discount stores and over 90 Duckwell variety stores in small towns in 21 Midwest states. It distributes a full-line of 35,000 sundry discount items. Founded in 1901. **Positions advertised include:** Management Trainee; Assistant Manager; Store Manager; Store Associate. **Special programs:** Management Training Program; full-time and part-time positions. **Corporate headquarters location:** This location. **Listed on:** NASDAQ. **Stock exchange symbol:** DUCK. **Annual sales/revenues:** $4.5 million. **Number of employees at this location:** 200. **Number of employees nationwide:** 5,200.

MICROTECH COMPUTERS, INC.
4921 Legends Drive, Lawrence KS 66049. 785/841-9513. **Fax:** 785/841-1809. **Contact:** Personnel. **Email address**: hr@microtechcomp.com. **World Wide Web address:** http://www.microtechcomp.com. **Description:** Develops, manufactures, markets, installs, and services personal computers and related equipment. Primary customers are end users, retailers, corporations, and government agencies. Founded in 1986. **NOTE:** Openings posted through local media ads. **Corporate headquarters location:** This location. **Other area locations:** Shawnee Mission KS; Topeka KS. **Subsidiaries include:** A-Plus Open; MicroOpen; Atipa Technologies. **Listed on:** Privately held. **Annual sales/revenues:** $5 million. **Number of employees:** 80.

SHEPLER'S
6501 West Kellogg, Wichita KS 67209. 316/946-3600. **Fax:** 316/946-3652. **Contact:** Kara Hunt, Human Resources. **E-mail address:** khunt@sheplers.com. **World Wide Web address:** http://www.sheplers.com. **Description:** Engaged in retail, catalog, and Internet sales of Western-style apparel operating 19 stores in 9 central and western states. **Positions advertised include:** Internet Graphic Artist; Bi-lingual Customer Service Representative; Department Supervisor. **Special programs:** Internships. **Corporate headquarters location:** This location. **Operations at this facility include:** Corporate Administration and Catalog Warehouse. **Listed on:** Privately held. **Number of employees at this location:** 350. **Number of employees nationwide:** 1,500.

Kentucky
GALL'S INC.
2680 Palumbo Drive, P.O. Box 54308, Lexington KY 40509. 859/266-7227. **Fax:** 859/269-3492. **Recorded jobline:** 859/266-7227, extension 5627. **Contact:** Human Resources. **E-mail address:** resume@galls.com. **World Wide Web address:** http://www.galls.com. **Description:** A retailer of public safety equipment and apparel. **Positions advertised include:** Accounts Receivable Applications Supervisor; Staff Accountant–Reconciliation Specialist; Collections Representative. **Corporate headquarters location:** This location. **Subsidiaries include:** DynaMed. **Parent company:** Aramark Corporation. **Number of employees at this location:** 275.

KROGER DISTRIBUTION WAREHOUSE
111 Copper Creek Drive, Powderly KY 42367. 270/338-6661. **Contact:** Human Resources. **World Wide Web address:** http://www.kroger.com. **Description:** A grocery retail chain that operates 2,500 grocery stores, 800 convenience stores, 400 jewelry stores, 500 supermarket fuel centers and 42 manufacturing facilities in 32 states. **Positions advertised include:** Distribution Order Selector. **Corporate Headquarters location:** Cincinnati Ohio. **Other area locations:** Statewide. **Other U.S. locations:** Nationwide. **Parent company:** The Kroger Co. **Operations at this facility include:** Distribution; Warehousing. **Listed on:** New York Stock Exchange. **Stock exchange symbol:** KR. **Number of employees nationwide:** 290,000.

Louisiana
SCP POOL CORPORATION
109 Northpark Boulevard, 4th Floor, Covington LA 70433. 985/892-5521. **Contact:** Jane Manuel. **E-mail address:** jobs@scppool.com. **World Wide Web address:** http://www.scppool.com. **Description:** Operates over 200 service centers in North America and Europe that distribute swimming pool supplies and related equipment. **Positions advertised include:** Accounts Receivable Manager; Branch Manager; CDL Driver; Counter Sales Person; Customer Service Representative; Office Manager; Operations Manager; Outside Sales; Purchaser; Receptionist; Warehouse Manager. **Special programs:** Educational Reimbursement Program. **Corporate headquarters location:** This location. **Other U.S. locations:** Nationwide. **Listed on:** NASDAQ. **Stock exchange symbol:** POOL. **Annual sales/revenues:** $370 million. **Number of employees nationwide:** Over 2,500.

SOUTHEAST FOODS
1001 North 11th Street, Monroe LA 71207-2230. 318/388-1884. **Fax:** 318/322-0110. **Contact:** Chuck Desmond. **Description:** Owns and operates a franchised food store chain. **Corporate headquarters location:** This location. **Operations at this facility include:** Administration. **CEO:** Jim Creel. **Number of employees at this location:** 30. **Number of employees nationwide:** 750.

Maine
BARNES & NOBLE BOOKSTORES
9 Market Place Drive, Augusta ME 04330. 207/621-0038. **Contact:** Local store Manager. **E-mail address**: Careers@bn.com. **World Wide Web address:** http://www.barnesandnobleinc.com. **Description:** A bookstore chain operating 900 stores nationwide. This location has a cafe and music department. **Positions advertised include**: Merchandise Analyst; Assistant Buyer; Computer Operator; Editor-Sparknotes; Production Manager-Sparknotes. **Corporate headquarters location:** New York NY. **Other U.S.**

locations: Nationwide. **Listed on:** New York Stock Exchange. **Stock exchange symbol:** BKS. **Chairman:** Leonard S. Riggio. **Annual sales/revenues:** $5.2 billion. **Number of employees worldwide:** 37,000.

G.H. BASS & COMPANY
100 Clarks Pond Parkway, South Portland ME 04106. 207/761-7059. **Toll-free phone:** 800/950-2277 **Fax:** 207/791-4909. **Contact:** Human Resources. **E-mail address:** bassresumes@pvh.com. **World Wide Web address:** http://www.pvh.kenexa.com. **Description:** G.H. Bass & Company operates over 200 factory outlet stores. **Positions Advertised Include:** Buyer/Calvin Klein; Technical Designer; Designer III/PVH; Design Textile. **Corporate headquarters location:** New York NY. **Parent company:** Phillips-Van Heusen Corporation. **Listed on:** New York Stock Exchange.

DARLING'S INC.
P.O. Box 277, Brewer ME 04412. 207/941-1240. **Physical address:** 96 Parkway South, Bangor ME 04401. **Contact:** Ron Francis, Corporate office personnel. **World Wide Web address:** http://www.darlings.com. **Description:** This location houses the corporate and accounting offices for the four Darling's automobile dealerships. **Corporate headquarters location:** This location. **Other area locations:** Augusta ME; Lewiston ME, Waterville ME.

HANNAFORD BROS. COMPANY
P.O. Box 1000, Portland ME 04104. 207/885-2592. **Physical address:** 145 Pleasant Hill Road, Scarborough ME 04074. **Toll-free phone**: 800/213-9040. **Contact:** Mindy, Human Resources. **E-mail address:** working@hannaford.com. **World Wide Web address:** http://www.hannaford.com. **Description:** A multiregional food retailer. Supermarkets operate primarily under the names Shop 'n Save, Wilson's, and Sun Foods. **NOTE:** Search posted openings on-line. **Positions advertised include:** Retail System Specialist; Department Manager Trainee; Store Loss Prevention Coordinator; Meat Manager; Warehouse Order Selector; Pharmacy Opportunities. **Corporate headquarters location:** This location. **Other U.S. locations:** MA; NH; NY; VT.

KITTERY TRADING POST
P.O. Box 904, Route 1, Kittery ME 03904-0904. 207/439-2700. **Toll-free phone:** 888/587-6246. **Contact:** Human Resources. **World Wide Web address:** http://www.kitterytradingpost.com. **Description:** A large retail store that sells a wide variety of sporting goods including clothing, footwear, camping gear, shooting and archery equipment, cross country skis, kayaks, and fishing gear. **NOTE:** Search posted openings and apply on-line. Please visit website for online application form.

L.L. BEAN, INC.
One Casco Street, Freeport ME 04033. 207/865-4761. **Toll-free phone:** 800/441-5713. **Fax:** 207/552-3080. **Contact:** Keith Comash, Human Resources. **E-mail address:** recruit@llbean.com. **World Wide Web address:** http://www.llbean.com. **Description:** A mail order sporting goods and clothing retailer. All types of outdoor clothing and gear are available both at the Freeport retail location (open 24 hours) and through regular seasonal catalogs. **Positions advertised include:** Apparel Designers – Men's and Women's. **Number of employees nationwide:** 4,000.

SHAW'S SUPERMARKETS
205 Spencer Drive, Wells ME 04090. 207/646-9616. **Fax**: 207/646-5347. **Contact:** Human Resources. **E-mail address:** resume@shaws.com. **World Wide Web address:** http://www.shaws.com. **Description:** This is the distribution center and regional office location of the Shaw's Supermarkets chain of grocery stores, serving as the hub for the retail locations throughout the state of Maine. Founded 1860. **NOTE:** Please visit website for online application form. **Corporate headquarters location:** East Bridgewater MA. **Other area locations:** Statewide. **Other U.S. locations:** CT; MA; NH; RI; VT. **Parent company:** J. Sainsbury plc. **Operations at this facility include:** Regional Headquarters. **Number of employees nationwide:** 30,000.

WAL-MART STORES, INC.
80 Waterville Common, Waterville ME 04901. 207/877-8774. **Fax**: 207/784-1338. **Contact:** Manager. **E-mail address**: ejobs@walmart.com. **World Wide Web address:** http://www.walmart.com. **Description:** Wal-Mart Stores is one of the largest retail merchandise chains in the country. **NOTE**: Search posted openings nationwide and apply on-line. No paper resumes are accepted and telephone contact is discouraged. Applicants are invited to visit in-store hiring center. **Positions advertised include**: Associate Manager, Customer Intelligence; Business Manager Online Media. **Corporate headquarters location:** Bentonville AR. **Other area locations:** Sanford ME. **Listed on:** New York Stock Exchange. **Stock exchange symbol:** WMT.

Maryland

BARNES & NOBLE BOOKSTORES
620 Marketplace Drive, Bel Air MD 21014. 410/638-7023. **Fax:** 410/6387029. **Contact:** Lori Stark. **World Wide Web address:** http://www.bn.com. **Description:** A bookstore chain. This location also features a cafe and music department. **Corporate headquarters location:** New York NY. **Other U.S. locations:** Nationwide. **Listed on:** New York Stock Exchange. **Stock exchange symbol:** BKS.

DISTRICT PHOTO, INC.
10501 Rhode Island Avenue, Beltsville MD 20705. 301/937-5300. **Contact:** Human Resources. **Description:** Engaged in the retail sale of photographic equipment and supplies. District Photo also provides amateur photofinishing services.

DURON PAINTS & WALL COVERINGS
10406 Tucker Street, Beltsville MD 20705-2297. 301/937-4600. **Toll-free phone:** 800/723-8766. **Fax:** 301/595-0435. **Contact:** Human Resources. **E-mail address:** employment@duron.com. **World Wide Web address:** http://www.duron.com. **Description:** A manufacturer and wholesaler of paint and related products. **Positions advertised include:** Collector Adjuster; Computer Technician; Inside Sales Counter Representative; Machine Operator; Maintenance Technician; Material Handler Associate; Paint Maker Associate; Technician. **Corporate headquarters location:** This location. **Other U.S. locations:** Nationwide. **Operations at this facility include:** Administration; Manufacturing; Regional Headquarters; Research and Development; Sales; Service. **Listed on:** Privately held. **Number of employees at this location:** 375. **Number of employees nationwide:** 1,500.

JOS. A. BANK CLOTHIERS INC.
500 Hanover Pike, Hampstead MD 21074. 410/239-5728. **Fax:** 410/239-5868. **Recorded jobline:** 800/520-4473. **Contact:** Human Resources. **E-mail address:** jobs@jos-a-bank.com. **World Wide Web address:** http://www.josbank.com. **Description:** A retailer of men's clothing. Founded in 1905. **NOTE:** Entry-level and seasonal positions are offered. **Positions advertised include:** Planner; Finance and Accounting Specialist; Marketing Manager; Catalog Developer; Accounts Payable Clerk. **Special programs:** Tuition Reimbursement Program. **Corporate headquarters location:** This location. **Other U.S. locations:** Nationwide. **Listed on:** NASDAQ. **Stock exchange symbol:** JOSB. **Sales/revenues:** $210 million. **Number of employees at this location:** 300. **Number of employees nationwide:** 1,400.

RODMAN'S DISCOUNT FOOD & DRUG
4301 Randolph Road, Silver Spring MD 20906. 301/230-8930. **Contact:** Human Resources. **World Wide Web address:** http://www.rodmans.com. **Description:** A retailer of drugs, appliances, cameras, health and beauty aids, beer, and wine. **Corporate headquarters location:** This location. **Other area**

locations: Rockville MD; Wheaton MD. **Other U.S. locations:** Washington DC.

SAFEWAY, INC.
7595 Greenbelt Road, Greenbelt MD 20770. 301/345-0150. **Contact:** Employment Supervisor. **World Wide Web address:** http://www.safeway.com. **Description:** A regional food store with approximately 1,700 locations in North America. **Positions advertised include:** Shopper Administrator; Staff Pharmacist; Auditor. **Corporate headquarters location:** Pleasanton CA. **Other U.S. locations:** Nationwide. **International locations:** Canada. **Subsidiaries include:** Randall's Food Markets, Incorporated; Carr-Gottstein Foods Company; Dominick's Supermarkets, Incorporated; The Vons Companies, Incorporated. **Operations at this facility include:** Regional Headquarters. **Listed on:** New York Stock Exchange. **Stock exchange symbol:** SWY.

SAKS FIFTH AVENUE
5555 Wisconsin Avenue, Chevy Chase MD 20815. 301/657-9000. **Contact:** Personnel Director. **World Wide Web address:** http://www.saksincorporated.com. **Description:** A 62-store chain emphasizing soft-goods products, primarily apparel for men, women, and children. **Parent company:** Saks Incorporated operates approximately 360 stores in 36 states. Saks Incorporated also operates two retail catalogs and several retail Internet sites. **Special programs:** Scholarship Program; Wellness Program. **Corporate headquarters location:** Birmingham AL. **Description: Operations at this facility include:** This location is a part of the nationwide specialty department store chain. **Listed on:** New York Stock Exchange. **Stock exchange symbol:** SKS.

SATURN OF SALISBURY
30275 Winner Boulevard, Delmar MD 21875. 410/896-3800. **Toll-free phone:** 800/297-0857. **Contact:** Human Resources Manager. **World Wide Web address:** http://www.saturnofsalisbury.com. **Description:** Saturn auto dealer for Salisbury Maryland. **Positions advertised include:** Finance Manager; New Vehicle Sales Associate; Lot Porter; Sales Manager.

SEARS, ROEBUCK & CO.
7103 Democracy Boulevard, Bethesda MD 20817. 301/469-4000. **Contact:** Human Resources. **World Wide Web address:** http://www.sears.com. **Description:** Sears, Roebuck & Co. is a retailer of apparel, home, and automotive products and related services. **Positions advertised include:** Sales Manager; Project Manager; Call Center Team Manager; Pricing & Signing Lead; Custom Window Designer; Technical Manager; Auto Center Manager; Repair Team Manager; Repair Services Requisition. **Corporate headquarters location:** Hoffman Estates IL. **Other U.S. locations:** Nationwide. **Listed on:** New York Stock Exchange. **Stock exchange symbol:** S. **Sales/revenue:** Approximately $41 billion. **Number of employees nationwide:** 289,000.

SHERWIN-WILLIAMS COMPANY
2325 Hollins Ferry Road, Baltimore MD 21230. 410/625-8257. **Contact:** Human Resources. **E-mail address:** Darlene.Bergeron@sherwin.com. **World Wide Web address:** http://www.sherwin.com. **Description:** Manufactures, sells, and distributes coatings and related products. Sherwin-Williams labeled architectural and industrial coatings are sold through company-owned specialty paint and wallcovering stores. The Sherwin-Williams Company also manufactures paint under the Acme, Dutch Boy, Kem-Tone, Lucas, Martin-Senour, Minwax, Pratt & Lambert, Rogers, and Thompson brand names, as well as private labels, and markets its products to independent dealers, mass merchandisers, and home improvement centers. **Special programs:** Internships; Training. **Corporate headquarters location:** Cleveland OH. **Listed on:** New York Stock Exchange. **Stock exchange symbol:** SHW. **CEO/Chairman:** Chris Conner. **Sales/revenue:** Over $5 billion.

THE STATIONERY HOUSE INC.
1000 Florida Avenue, Hagerstown MD 21740. 301/739-4487. **Toll-free phone:** 800/638-3033. **Fax:** 301/739-7981. **Contact:** Human Resources Director. **E-mail address:** hrdirector@stationaryhouse.com. **World Wide Web address:** http://www.stationaryhouse.com. **Description:** A catalog retailer of a wide range of holiday greeting cards for corporations. **Corporate headquarters location:** This location.

Massachusetts

ROBERT ALLEN FABRICS
225 Foxboro Boulevard, Mansfield MA 02035. 508/851-6600. **Fax:** 508/337-7905. **Contact:** Human Resources. **E-mail address:** careers@robertallendesign.com. **World Wide Web address:** http://www.robertallendesign.com. **Description:** Robert Allen Fabrics is a fabric retailer. **Office hours:** Monday - Friday, 8:30 a.m. - 5:00 p.m. **Corporate headquarters location:** This location. **Other U.S. locations:** Nationwide.

APPLESEED'S
30 Tozer Road, Beverly MA 01915. 978/922-2040. **Fax:** 978/922-7001. **Contact:** Human Resources. **E-mail address:** jobs@appleseeds.com. **World Wide Web address:** http://www.appleseeds.com. **Description:** A retailer of women's clothing through its stores and catalog.

BJ'S WHOLESALE CLUB
One Mercer Road, P.O. Box 9601, Natick MA 01760. 508/651-7400. **Fax:** 508/651-8631. **Contact:** Staffing Department. **E-mail address:** jobs@bjs.com. **World Wide Web address:** http://www.bjs.com. **Description:** Membership club retailer of bulk merchandise from grocery items to electronics, automotive accessories and vacations. **Positions advertised include:** Programmer Analyst; Lead Database Administrator; Sr. Information Security Specialist. **Corporate headquarters location:** This location. **Listed on:** New York Stock Exchange. **Stock exchange symbol:** BJ.

BARNES & NOBLE BOOKSTORES
395 Washington Street, Boston MA 02108. 617/426-5184. **Contact:** Manager. **World Wide Web address:** http://www.bn.com. **Description:** A discount bookstore chain. **Corporate headquarters location:** New York NY. **Other U.S. locations:** Nationwide.

BIG Y FOODS INC.
2145 Roosevelt Avenue, P.O. Box 7840, Springfield MA 01102. 413/784-0600. **Fax:** 413/732-7350. **Contact:** Human Resources. **World Wide Web address:** http://www.bigy.com. **Description:** Operates a chain of over 40 supermarkets. **Positions advertised include:** In-Store Systems specialist; Internal Auditor; Network Administrator; Programmer Analyst; Sr. Accountant. **NOTE:** Users may apply for positions online. **Special programs:** Internships. **Other area locations:** Statewide. **Other U.S. locations:** CT. **Corporate headquarters location:** This location. **Operations at this facility include:** Administration. **Listed on:** Privately held. **Number of employees nationwide:** 7,200.

BORDERS BOOKS & MUSIC
10-24 School Street, Boston MA 02108. 617/557-7188. **Fax:** 617/557-4476. **Contact:** Hiring Manager. **World Wide Web address:** http://www.bordersstores.com. **Description:** One location of the discount bookstore chain offering over 200,000 book titles, as well as music and videos. Borders also provides year-round events including live musical performances, author readings, kids programs, book groups, and art exhibitions.

THE BRICK COMPUTER COMPANY
80 Turnpike Road, Ipswich MA 01938. 978/356-1228. **Fax:** 267/948-5354. **Contact:** Human Resources. **World Wide Web address:** http://www.brickcomputers.com. **Description:** Sells laptops through a mail-order catalog.

CAMBRIDGE SOUNDWORKS, INC.
100 Brickstone Square, Andover MA 01810. 978/623-4400. **Fax:** 978/475-5922. **Contact:** Human Resources. **World Wide Web address:** http://www.hifi.com. **Description:** A factory-direct retailer that designs and manufactures stereo and home theater speakers under the Cambridge SoundWorks brand name. **Corporate headquarters location:** This location. **Listed on:** NASDAQ. **Stock exchange symbol:** HIFI.

CASUAL MALE CORPORATION
555 Turnpike Street, Canton MA 02021. 781/828-9300. **Contact:** Human Resources. **World Wide Web address:** http://www.casualmale.com. **Description:** Engaged in the retail sale of footwear and apparel. Casual Male Corporation sells footwear through self-service licensed shoe departments in mass merchandising department stores, through full- and semiservice licensed shoe departments in department and specialty stores, on a wholesale basis, and through its Fayva and Parade of Shoes chains of shoe stores. The company is also involved in the retail sale of apparel through its chain of Casual Male Big & Tall men's stores and also through its chain of Work 'n Gear work clothing stores. **Positions advertised include:** Bank Reconciliation Clerk; Marketing Database Administrator; Production Designer. **Corporate headquarters location:** This location.

CHARRETTE CORPORATION
P.O. Box 4010, Woburn MA 01888-4010. 781/935-6000. **Physical address:** 31 Olympia Avenue, Woburn MA 01801. **Fax:** 781/497-7810. **Contact:** Lawrence Mansfield, Director of Human Resources. **E-mail address:** csullivan@charette.com. **World Wide Web address:** http://www.charrette.com. **Description:** Offers a variety of products and services to design professionals. Products include a wide range of art, design, and office products from mat boards and paints, to furniture and software. Services include digital imaging, offset printing, reprographics, and blueprinting. **NOTE:** Entry-level positions are offered. **Special programs:** Internships. **Corporate headquarters location:** This location. **Other U.S. locations:** Nationwide. **Listed on:** Privately held. **Annual sales/revenues:** $51 - $100 million. **Number of employees at this location:** 350. **Number of employees nationwide:** 750.

COLUMBIA MOTORS
1817 Washington Street, Hanover MA 02339. 781/826-8300. **Contact:** Human Resources. **E-mail address:** sales@columbiamotors.com. **World Wide Web address:** http://www.columbiamotors.com. **Description:** A Pontiac, GMC, Buick, car dealership.

CSN STORES
800 Boylston Street, Suite 1600, Boston MA 02199. 617/532-6100. **Fax:** 617/532-6800. **Contact:** Recruiting. **E-mail address:** jobs@csnstores.com. **World Wide Web address:** http://www.csnstores.com. **Description:** An online retailer. **Positions advertised include:** Customer Care Representative.

CUMBERLAND FARMS, INC.
777 Dedham Street, Canton MA 02021. 781/828-4900. **Fax:** 781/828-9012. **Contact:** Human Resources. **World Wide Web address:** http://www.cumberlandfarms.com. **Description:** Cumberland Farms operates a chain of 1,100 retail convenience stores and gas stations. **Positions advertised include:** Financial Analyst; Sr. Staff Accountant. **Corporate headquarters location:** This location. **Listed on:** Privately held. **Number of employees at this location:** 700. **Number of employees nationwide:** 7,000.

DEMOULAS SUPERMARKETS INC.
875 East Street, Tewksbury MA 01876. 978/851-8000. **Contact:** President of Operations. **Description:** Operates a grocery store chain with locations throughout northern and eastern Massachusetts. **Corporate headquarters location:** This location.

DUNKIN' DONUTS OF AMERICA INC.
130 Royall Street, Canton MA 02021. 781/961-4000. **Contact:** Human Resources. **World Wide Web address:** http://www.dunkindonuts.com. **Description:** Develops and franchises Dunkin' Donuts shops that sell coffee, donuts, and baked goods. **Positions advertised include:** Sr. Financial Analyst; Sr. Coordinator, Leadership and Organizational Development; Director, Global Communications; Sr. IT Analyst. **Corporate headquarters location:** This location. **Subsidiaries include:** Togo; Baskin Robbins. **Parent company:** Allied Domecq Retailing USA.

FILENE'S BASEMENT CORPORATION
25 Corporate Drive, Suite 400, Burlington MA 01803. 617/348-7000. **Fax:** 617/348-7159. **Contact:** David Abelson, Personnel. **World Wide Web address:** http://www.filenesbasement.com. **Description:** Operates specialty stores offering assortments of fashionable, nationally recognized brands and private-label family apparel and accessories. **Corporate headquarters location:** This location. **Other U.S. locations:** CT; DC; IL; ME; MN; NH; NJ; NY; PA; RI; VA.

GEERLINGS & WADE
960 Turnpike Street, Canton MA 02021. 781/821-4152. **Toll-free phone:** 800/782-WINE. **Contact:** Human Resources Department. **E-mail address:** careers@geerwade.com. **World Wide Web address:** http://www.geerwade.com. **Description:** Provides personal wine-buying services to consumers through direct marketing. The company purchases imported and domestic wines and delivers them directly to the customer's home or office. **Corporate headquarters location:** This location.

GROSSMAN'S INC.
90 Hawes Way, Stoughton MA 02072-1163. 781/297-3300. **Contact:** Human Resources, Department D. **Description:** Operates a chain of discount home center outlets with 51 locations in four states. **Positions advertised include:** Manager, Assistant Manager; Department Head.

J.L. HAMMETT COMPANY
P.O. Box 859057, Braintree MA 02185. 781/848-1000. **Toll-free phone:** 800/955-2200. **Physical address:** One Hammett Place, Braintree MA 02184. **Fax:** 781/848-3869. **Contact:** Human Resources. **World Wide Web address:** http://www.hammett.com. **Description:** Distributes educational supplies and equipment through catalog and retail stores. **Corporate headquarters location:** This location. **Operations at this facility include:** Administration; Regional Headquarters; Sales; Service.

THE HARVARD COOPERATIVE SOCIETY
1400 Massachusetts Avenue, Cambridge MA 02138. 617/499-2000. **Contact:** Human Resources. **World Wide Web address:** http://www.thecoop.com. **Description:** A member-owned, collegiate department store selling a broad range of merchandise from clothing, books, and music, to housewares, electronics, and prints. **Corporate headquarters location:** This location.

JANNELL MOTORS
2000 Washington Street, Hanover MA 02339. 781/982-4500. **Fax:** 781/982-4535. **Contact:** Human Resources. **E-mail address:** sales@jannell.com. **World Wide Web address:** http://www.jannell.com. **Description:** A Ford dealership on the South Shore.

JOAN FABRICS CORPORATION
100 Vesper Executive Park, Tyngsboro MA 01879-2710. 978/649-5626. **Contact:** Human Resources. **Description:** Engaged in the manufacturing of woven and knitted fabrics for furniture and automotive manufacturers. The company also operates retail fabric stores nationwide. **Corporate headquarters location:** This location. **Other U.S. locations:** Hickory NC; Troy MI.

KOHL'S
139 Church Street, Pembroke MA 02359. 781/826-3696. **Fax:** 781/982-4535. **Contact:** Human Resources. **World Wide Web address:** http://www.kohls.com. **Description:** A clothing department store. **NOTE:** Visit store location to apply for hourly positions; apply online for executive positions.

MACY'S
450 Washington Street, Boston MA 02111. 617/357-3000. **Recorded jobline:** 800/603-6229. **Contact:** Human Resources. **World Wide Web address:** http://www.macys.com. **Description:** One location of the department store chain. **Positions advertised include:** Beauty Advisor; Bridal Consultant; Cosmetic Business Manager; Counter Manager; Fine Jewelry Service Associate; Furniture Service Associate Selling Specialist; Women's Shoe Service Specialist; Department Sales Manager; Group Sales Manager; Human Resources Coordinator; Merchandise Manager. **Corporate headquarters location:** New York City.

PRINCESS HOUSE, INC.
470 Myles Standish Boulevard, Taunton MA 02780. 508/823-0711. **Contact:** Human Resources. **World Wide Web address:** http://www.princesshouse.com. **Description:** A national direct sales company specializing in crystal and china. **Corporate headquarters location:** This location. **Parent company:** Colgate-Palmolive Company. **Operations at this facility include:** Administration; Service.

REDCATS USA
35 United Drive, West Bridgewater MA 02379. 508/583-8110. **Fax:** 508/588-7994. **Contact:** Human Resources. **E-mail address:** chadwicksjobs@brylane.com. **World Wide Web address:** http://www.brylane.com. **Description:** A multichannel retailer with 10 catalogs and 10 e-commerce websites. **Positions advertised include:** Art Director; Associate Product Manager; collateral Designer; Creative Director; Fashion Designer; Operations Manager; Web Designer. **Corporate headquarters location:** New York NY. **Other area locations:** Taunton MA.

RITZ CAMERA
South Shore Plaza, 250 Granite Street, Braintree MA 02184. 781/843-4619. **Contact:** Hiring Manager. **World Wide Web address:** http://www.ritzcamera.com. **Description:** One location of the camera shop and photo developer chain.

SAKS FIFTH AVENUE
Prudential Center, Boston MA 02199. 617/262-8500. **Contact:** Human Resources. **World Wide Web address:** http://www.saksincorporated.com. **Description:** Saks Fifth Avenue is a 62-store chain emphasizing soft-goods products, primarily apparel for men, women, and children. **Corporate headquarters location:** New York NY. **Parent company:** Saks Incorporated operates approximately 360 stores in 36 states. Saks Incorporated also operates two retail catalogs and several retail Internet sites. **Listed on:** New York Stock Exchange. **Stock exchange symbol:** SKS.

SEARS, ROEBUCK & CO.
Route 6 and 118, Swansea Mall Drive, Swansea MA 02777. 508/324-6500. **Contact:** Human Resources. **World Wide Web address:** http://www.sears.com. **Description:** One location of the department chain store. **Listed on:** NYSE. **Stock exchange symbol:** S.

SHAW'S SUPERMARKETS
P.O. Box 600, East Bridgewater MA 02333-0600. 508/378-7211. **Physical address:** 750 West Center Street, East Bridgewater MA. **Contact:** Human Resources. **World Wide Web address:** http://www.shaws.com. **Description:** Administrative offices of the New England supermarket chain. Shaw's Supermarkets has locations throughout New England. **Corporate headquarters location:** This location. **Other U.S. locations:** CT; ME; MA; NH; RI; VT. **Subsidiaries include:** Star Markets; Wild Harvest. **Parent company:** J Sainsbury plc.

STAPLES, INC.
500 Staples Drive, Framingham MA 01702. 508/253-5000. **Contact:** Human Resources. **World Wide Web address:** http://www.staples.com. **Description:** Staples is a retailer of discount office products. The company operates over 350 office superstores in 18 states and the District of Columbia. **Positions advertised include:** Recruiting Specialist; Loss Prevention Manager; Senior Business Analyst; Business Development Associate; Customer Relations Manager. **Corporate headquarters location:** This location. **Other U.S. locations:** Nationwide. **Listed on:** NASDAQ. **Stock exchange symbol:** SPLS. **Number of employees at this location:** 850. **Number of employees nationwide:** 15,700.

THE STOP & SHOP COMPANIES, INC.
1385 Hancock Street, Quincy MA 02169. 781/380-8000. **Fax:** 617/689-4545. **Contact:** Human Resources. **World Wide Web address:** http://www.stopandshop.com. **Description:** A national supermarket retail chain. **Corporate headquarters location:** This location.

STRIDE-RITE CORPORATION
191 Spring Street, P.O. Box 9191, Lexington MA 02421. 617/824-6000. **Fax:** 617/824-6549. **Contact:** Human Resources. **E-mail address:** staffing@striderite.com. **World Wide Web address:** http://www.striderite.com. **Description:** Manufactures and distributes children's footwear. The company also operates retail stores. **Positions advertised include:** Director of IT Compliance; Marketing Manager, E-Commerce and Web Marketing; Designer; Merchandising Analyst; Sr. Collections Specialist; Key Account Manager. **Corporate headquarters location:** This location. **Listed on:** New York Stock Exchange. **Stock exchange symbol:** SRR.

THE TJX COMPANIES, INC.
770 Cochituate Road, Framingham MA 01701. 508/390-1000. **Fax:** 508/390-2650. **Recorded jobline:** 888/JOB-S597. **Contact:** Staffing Specialist. **E-mail address:** jobs@tjx.com. **World Wide Web address:** http://www.tjx.com. **Description:** The TJX Companies, Inc. is one of the world's largest off-price retailers. It consists of T.J. Maxx, Marshall's, Home Goods, A.J. Wright, Winners Apparel Ltd. in Canada, and T.K. Maxx in Europe. **NOTE:** Entry-level positions, part-time jobs, and second and third shifts are offered. **Positions advertised include:** Buyer; Attorney; AVP Marketing/Advertising; Business Analyst; Communications and Procedures Specialist; Engineering Project Manager; Enterprise Security Analyst; Event Marketing Manager; Lease Auditor. **Special programs:** Internships; Training; Co-ops; Summer Jobs. **Corporate headquarters location:** This location. **Other U.S. locations:** Nationwide. **International locations:** Canada; Europe. **Listed on:** New York Stock Exchange. **Stock exchange symbol:** TJX. **Annual sales/revenues:** More than $100 million. **Number of employees at this location:** 2,000. **Number of employees nationwide:** 60,000.

TALBOTS INC.
One Talbots Drive, Hingham MA 02043. 781/749-7600. **Contact:** Human Resources. **World Wide Web address:** http://www.talbots.com. **Description:** Talbots is a leading specialty retailer and cataloger of women's classic apparel, shoes, and accessories. Talbots operates 1,083 stores in the U.S., Canada, and the UK, and distributes approximately 48 million catalogs annually. The company also operates a chain of Talbots for Kids stores. Founded in 1947. **Positions advertised include:** Project Manager; Store Planner; Business Analyst; LAN Analyst; Purchasing Coordinator; Sourcing Manager; Sr. IT Auditor. **Other U.S. locations:** Nationwide. **Listed on:** New York Stock Exchange. **Stock exchange symbol:** TLB.

VICTORY SUPERMARKETS
75 North Main Street, Leominster MA 01453. 978/840-2200. **Contact:** Human Resources. **World Wide Web address:** http://www.victorysupermarkets.com. **Description:** A grocery store chain with 20 outlets located in Massachusetts and New Hampshire. **Parent company:** Hannaford Supermarkets. **Other area locations:** Clinton MA; Fitchburg MA; Gardner MA; Marlborough MA; Uxbridge MA.

WEARGUARD CORPORATION
141 Longwater Drive, Norwell MA 02061. 781/871-4100. **Contact:** Kathy Gillis, Director of Training. **E-mail address:** employment@wearguard.com. **World Wide Web address:** http://www.wearguard.com. **Description:** WearGuard is a leading direct marketer of work clothing serving over 2 million businesses and individuals and, in association with Sears Shop at Home, markets Workwear and Big and Tall Men's Clothing catalogs under the Sears name. **Parent company:** ARAMARK. **Positions advertised include:** Web Technician. **Operations at this facility include:** This location is a retail store and catalog marketer.

WHITE HEN PANTRY, INC.
41 Montvale Avenue, Stoneham MA 02180. 781/438-1140. **Fax:** 781/438-9354. **Contact:** General Manager. **World Wide Web address:** http://www.whitehenpantry.com. **Description:** White Hen Pantry operates a chain of convenience food stores. **Corporate headquarters location:** Elmhurst IL. **Parent company:** Clark Retail Enterprises, Inc. **Operations at this facility include:** This location houses administrative offices.

Michigan
ACO HARDWARE INC.
23333 Commerce Drive, Farmington Hills MI 48335-2764. 248/471-0100. **Fax:** 248/615-2696. **Contact:** Human Resources Department. **E-mail address:** hmrs@acohardware.com. **World Wide Web address:** http://www.acohardware.com. **Description:** Operates over 60 hardware stores throughout southeast Michigan. **NOTE:** Entry-level positions are offered. **Positions advertised include:** Store Management Trainee. **Corporate headquarters location:** This location. **Other area locations:** Statewide. **Listed on:** Privately held. **Number of employees at this location:** 200. **Number of employees worldwide:** 1,300.

BORDERS GROUP, INC.
100 Phoenix Drive, Ann Arbor MI 48108. 734/477-1100. **Contact:** Human Resources Department. **E-mail address:** jobsr1@bordersstores.com. **World Wide Web address:** http://www.bordersgroup.com. **Description:** Operates Borders Books, one of the nation's largest retail bookselling chains. Borders Group also operates Waldenbooks. Founded in 1933. **Positions advertised include:** Marketing Systems Specialist; Replenishment Manager; Category Manager, Multimedia; Senior Tax Specialist; Accounts Payable Representative; Copy Editor; Content Editor; Allocation Analyst; Storage Administrator. **Corporate headquarters location:** This location. **Listed on:** New York Stock Exchange. **Stock exchange symbol:** BGP. **Annual sales/revenues:** $3.4 billion. **Number of employees worldwide:** Over 32,000.

CHAMPS SPORTS
Southland Mall, 23000 Eureka Road, Space 102, Taylor MI 48180. 734/287-9092. **Contact:** Jim Bennett, Director of Field Recruiting. **E-mail address:** jbennett2@champssports.com. **World Wide Web address:** http://www.champssports.com. **Description:** A specialty/sporting goods retailer. Products include athletic equipment, apparel, footwear, and accessories. **Corporate headquarters location:** Bradenton FL. **Other U.S. locations:** Nationwide. **International locations:** Canada; Puerto Rico. **Parent company:** Foot Locker, Incorporated Group.

KMART CORPORATION
3100 West Big Beaver Road, Troy MI 48084. 248/643-1000. **Contact:** Human Resources. **E-mail address:** hireme@kmart.com. **World Wide Web address:** http://www.kmartcorp.com. **Description:** One of the largest retailers in the United States. Kmart Corporation operates approximately 1,000 discount general merchandise department stores throughout the United States, Puerto Rico, the U.S. Virgin Islands, and Guam. **Special programs:** Internships. **Corporate headquarters location:** This location. **Other U.S. locations:** Nationwide. **Parent company:** Sears Holding Corporation. **Listed on:** Over-The-Counter. **Stock exchange symbol:** KMRTQ. **Annual sales/revenues:** $30 billion. **Number of employees nationwide:** 212,000.

MEIJER INC.
2929 Walker Avenue NW, Grand Rapids MI 49544. 269/453-6711. **Toll-free phone:** 800/219-9150. **Fax:** 616/735-7569. **Contact:** Employment Manager. **E-mail address:** careers@meijer.com. **World Wide Web address:** http://www.meijer.com. **Description:** One of the largest privately owned retail companies in the Midwest. The company operates 99 superstores throughout Michigan, Ohio, Indiana, and Illinois. Founded in 1934. **Positions advertised include:** Internal Auditor; Deployment Coordinator; Performance Measurement Analyst; Pharmacy Team Leader; Staff Pharmacist. **Corporate headquarters location:** This location. **Other area locations:** Statewide. **Other U.S. locations:** IN; IL; KY; NJ; OH. **Number of employees nationwide:** 75,000.

MICHIGAN LUMBER COMPANY
P.O. Box 766, Flint MI 48501. 810/232-4108. **Physical address:** 1919 Clifford Street, Flint MI 48503. **Toll-free phone:** 800/282-5707. **Fax:** 810/232-7169. **Contact:** Personnel Department. **E-mail address:** info@michiganlumber.com. **World Wide Web address:** http://www.michiganlumber.com. **Description:** A retailer of lumber and related materials. **Corporate headquarters location:** This location. **Number of employees at this location:** 100.

SPARTAN STORES INC.
850 76th Street SW, P.O. Box 8700, Grand Rapids MI 49518-8700. 616/878-2000. **Contact:** Human Resources. **E-mail address:** human_resources@spartanstores.com. **World Wide Web address:** http://www.spartanstores.com. **Description:** Owns and operates a chain of grocery stores. **Positions advertised include:** Inventory Control Clerk; Technical Analyst; Category Manager. **Special programs:** Tuition Reimbursement Program. **Corporate headquarters location:** This location. **Other area locations:** Statewide. **Other U.S. locations:** OH. **Listed on:** NASDSAQ. **Stock exchange symbol:** SPTN. **Number of employees nationwide:** 7,400.

Minnesota
AVEDA CORPORATION
4000 Pheasant Ridge Drive, Blaine MN 55449. 763/783-4000. **Fax:** 763/783-6850. **Contact:** Human Resources. **E-mail address:** jobs@aveda.com. **World Wide Web address:** http://www.aveda.com. **Description:** Manufactures perfume, makeup, and other beauty products. Aveda Corporation also operates salons and retail stores. **Positions advertised include:** Administrative Assistant; Accounts Payable Supervisor; Benefits Assistant; CR New Business Coordinator. **Special programs:** Internships. **Internship information:** Candidates should check the company's website for application procedures. **Corporate headquarters location:** This location. **Other U.S. locations:** New York NY. **International locations:** Worldwide. **Parent company:** Estee Lauder Companies, Inc.

BACHMAN'S INC.
6010 Lyndale Avenue South, Minneapolis MN 55419. 612/861-7600. **Fax:** 612/861-7748. **Recorded jobline:** 612/861-9242. **Contact:** Personnel. **E-mail address:** jobs@bachmans.com. **World Wide Web address:** http://www.bachmans.com. **Description:** A retail florist, landscaper, garden center, nursery, and greenhouse with 20 retail locations. **NOTE:** Seasonal positions available. **Positions advertised include:**

Landscape Designer; Customer Service Correspondent. **Special programs:** Internships. **Corporate headquarters location:** This location. **Number of employees at this location:** 1,000.

BEST BUY COMPANY, INC.
7601 Penn Avenue South, Richfield MN 55423. 612/291-1000. **Fax:** 952/947-2422. **Contact:** Human Resources. **World Wide Web address:** http://www.bestbuy.com. **Description:** A national retailer of consumer electronics, appliances, and home office products. **NOTE:** Search and apply for positions online. **Corporate headquarters location:** This location. **Other U.S. locations:** Nationwide. **Listed on:** New York Stock Exchange. **Stock exchange symbol:** BBY. **Annual sales/revenues:** More than $100 million. **Number of employees at this location:** 1,500. **Number of employees nationwide:** 100,000.

DOWNTOWN JAGUAR LOTUS LAND ROVER MINNEAPOLIS
222 Hennepin Avenue, Minneapolis MN 55401. 612/371-1400. **Contact:** Stacy Droun, Controller. **E-mail address:** info@downtownjaguar.com. **World Wide Web address:** http://www.downtownjaguar.com. **Description:** A new and used automobile dealership. **Parent company:** Luther Automobile Dealerships.

FASTENAL COMPANY
2001 Theurer Boulevard, P.O. Box 978, Winona MN 55987. 507/454-5374. **Contact:** Human Resources. **E-mail address:** great2b@fastenal.com. **World Wide Web address:** http://www.fastenal.com. **Description:** Markets and distributes threaded fasteners such as bolts, nuts, screws, studs, and washers, as well as other related construction supplies such as cutting tools, paints, chains, pins, machinery keys, concrete anchors, masonry drills, flashlights, batteries, sealants, metal framing systems, wire rope, and related accessories through company-operated stores. **Positions advertised include:** Customer Service Representative; Sales Support Representative; Store Manager. **Listed on:** NASDAQ. **Stock exchange symbol:** FAST. **Number of employees nationwide:** 870.

GABBERTS FURNITURE AND DESIGN STUDIO
3501 Galleria, Edina MN 55435. 952/927-1500. **Contact:** Linda Hoflander. **E-mail address:** lhofflander@gabberts.com. **World Wide Web address:** http://www.gabberts.com. **Description:** A retail furniture store and design showroom. **Corporate headquarters location:** This location. **Number of employees nationwide:** 200.

GANDER MOUNTAIN COMPANY
180 East Fifth Street, Suite 1300, Saint Paul MN 55101. 651/325-4300. **Toll-free phone:** 888/5-GANDER. **Contact:** Human Resources. **E-mail address:** greatjobs@gandermountain.com. **World Wide Web address:** http://www.gandermountain.com. **Description:** Retailer that serves the needs of outdoor lifestyle enthusiasts, with a particular focus on hunting, fishing, and camping. **Positions advertised include:** Technical Services Support Coordinator; District Loss Prevention Manager; IS Project Manager; VP Logistics; Systems Business Analyst; Product Manager/Buyer **Corporate headquarters location:** This location. **Listed on:** New York Stock Exchange. **Stock exchange symbol:** GMTN.

HOIGAARD'S
3550 South Highway 100, St. Louis Park MN 55416. 952/929-1351. **Contact:** Personnel. **World Wide Web address:** http://www.hoigaards.com. **Description:** A retailer of sporting goods.

HOLIDAY STATIONSTORES
4567 West 80th Street, Bloomington MN 55437. 952/832-8530. **Toll-free phone:** 800/745-7411. **Fax:** 952/832-8551. **Recorded jobline:** 952/832-8585. **Contact:** Recruiting Department. **E-mail address:** jobs@holidaystationstores.com. **World Wide Web address:** http://www.holidaystationstores.com. **Description:** Operates retail convenience stores/gas stations with over 300 locations in 11 states. **Positions advertised include:** Assistant Manager; Sales Associate; Night Manager. **Special programs:** Internships; Training. **Corporate headquarters location:** This location. **Other U.S. locations:** IA; ID; MI; MT; ND; NE; SD; WA; WI; WY. **Parent company:** Holiday Companies. **Listed on:** Privately held. **Annual sales/revenues:** More than $100 million. **Number of employees at this location:** 500. **Number of employees nationwide:** 6,000.

JCPENNEY COMPANY, INC.
Miller Hill Mall, 1600 A Miller Trunk Highway, Duluth MN 55811. 218/727-8111. **Contact:** Human Resources. **World Wide Web address:** http://www.jcpenney.com. **Description:** JCPenney sells apparel, home furnishings, and leisure lines in catalogs and 1,100 stores. **NOTE:** Search and apply for positions online. Positions also advertised in the *Duluth News Tribune*. **Corporate headquarters location:** Plano TX. **Operations at this facility include:** This location is a department store.

KMART CORPORATION
1734 Mall Drive, Duluth MN 55811. 218/727-0816. **Contact:** Personnel. **World Wide Web address:** http://www.kmart.com. **Description:** Kmart Corporation is a mass merchandising company with retail outlets in 49 states, Puerto Rico and the Virgin Islands. Kmart provides employment opportunities in store, pharmacy, corporate and distribution-center operations. This store has a pharmacy and photo center. **NOTE:** Visit the store to complete an application and discuss available positions. **Corporate headquarters location:** Hoffman Estates IL. **Parent company:** Sears Holdings Corp. **Number of employees nationwide:** 144,000.

KNOWLAN'S SUPER MARKETS INC.
111 East County Road F, Vadnais Heights MN 55127. 651/483-9242. **Contact:** Chris Thinnes, Human Resources Director. **World Wide Web address:** http://www.knowlans.com. **Description:** Owns and operates two Knowlan's stores and the Festival Foods chain of retail grocery stores in the northern suburbs of Minneapolis and St. Paul. **Corporate headquarters location:** This location. **Other area locations:** White Bear Lake MN; Andover MN: Brooklyn Park MN; Hugo MN; Lexington/Circle Pines MN.

KOHL'S DEPARTMENT STORE
2115 Miller Trunk Highway, Duluth MN 55811. 218/722-9699. **Contact:** Human Resources. **World Wide Web address:** http://www.kohls.com. **Description:** Kohl's sells apparel, shoes, accessories, home products, and housewares through 500 locations nationwide. **Corporate headquarters location:** Menomonee Falls WI. **Number of employees nationwide:** 50,000.

LUND FOOD HOLDINGS, INC.
7752 Mitchell Road, Eden Prairie MN 55344. 952/927-3663. **Contact:** Human Resources. **E-mail address:** Human.Resources@LFHI.com. **World Wide Web address:** http://www.lundsmarket.com. **Description:** Lund Food Holdings operates about 20 Lunds and Byerly's upscale grocery markets in the Twin Cities area of Minnesota. **Corporate headquarters location:** This location.

PROVELL, INC.
11100 Wayzata Boulevard, Suite 680, Minneapolis MN 55305. 952/258-2000. **Fax:** 952/258-2100. **Contact:** Human Resources. **E-mail address:** receptionist@provell.com. **World Wide Web address:** http://www.provell.com. **Description:** Markets general merchandise through catalogs. Products include computers, home office, home decor, consumer electronics, home improvements, and sporting/fitness goods.

REGIS CORPORATION
7201 Metro Boulevard, Minneapolis MN 55439. 952/947-7777. **Fax:** 952/947-7700. **Contact:** Human

Resources. **World Wide Web address:** http://www.regiscorp.com. **Description:** The world's largest company in the hair salon industry. REGIS Corporation has salon franchise locations all over the world. **Positions advertised include:** JDE Programmer/Analyst; Lease Payables Analyst; Merchandise Buyer. **Corporate headquarters location:** This location. **Other U.S. locations:** Nationwide. **International locations:** Worldwide. **Listed on:** New York Stock Exchange. **Stock exchange symbol:** RGS.

SNYDERS DRUG STORES
14525 Highway Seven, Minnetonka MN 55345. 952/935-5441. **Fax:** 952/936-2512. **Contact:** Human Resources. **World Wide Web address:** http://www.snyderdrug.com. **Description:** Operates a chain of 120 retail drug stores in Minnesota, Wisconsin, and Montana. **Corporate headquarters location:** This location. **Listed on:** Privately held. **Parent company:** Katz Group (Canada). **Annual sales/revenues:** More than $100 million. **Number of employees at this location:** 125. **Number of employees nationwide:** 1,300.

SPEEDWAY SUPERAMERICA LLC
2060 Centre Point Boulevard, Suite 1, Mendota Heights MN 55120. 651/454-7776. **Toll-free phone:** 800/328-2927. **Contact:** John Klompenhower, Human Resources Manager. **World Wide Web address:** http://www.speedway.com. **Description:** Operates a chain of over 1,700 convenience store/gas stations in 9 states in the Midwest. **NOTE:** Entry-level positions are offered. **Special programs:** Internships. **Corporate headquarters location:** Enon OH. **Parent company:** Marathon Ashland Petroleum, LLC. **Operations at this facility include:** Administration; Regional Headquarters. **Number of employees at this location:** 100. **Number of employees nationwide:** 10,000.

SUPERVALU INC.
11840 Valley View Road, Eden Prairie MN 55344. 952/828-4000. **Contact:** Human Resources. **E-mail address:** super.careers@supervalu.com. **World Wide Web address:** http://www.supervalu.com. **Description:** One of the nation's largest grocery companies. with 1,546 retail grocery locations. In addition, it provides food distribution and related logistics services, including warehouse management, transportation, procurement, contract manufacturing, and logistics engineering and management services for the retail grocery channel. **Positions advertised include:** Buyer; Category Manager; Risk Control Manager; Staff Accountant. **Corporate headquarters location:** This location. **Other U.S. locations:** Nationwide. **Listed on:** New York Stock Exchange. **Stock exchange symbol:** SVU. **Annual sales/revenues:** More than $100 million. **Number of employees nationwide:** 56,000.

TARGET
1000 Nicollet Mall, Minneapolis MN 55403. 612/304-6073. **Fax:** 612/370-5502. **Contact:** Human Resources. **World Wide Web address:** http://www.target.com. **Description:** Target is a leading general merchandise retail company. **Corporate headquarters location:** This location. **Other area locations:** Statewide. **Other U.S. locations:** Nationwide. **Subsidiaries include:** Target Financial Corporation; Target Commercial Interiors. **Listed on:** New York Stock Exchange. **Stock exchange symbol:** TGT.

THRIFTY WHITE STORES
6901 East Fishlake Road, Suite 118, Maple Grove MN 55369. 763/513-4300. **Fax:** 763/513-4380. **Contact:** Shannon Kadlec, Human Resources. **E-mail address:** skadlec@thriftywhite.com. **World Wide Web address:** http://www.thriftywhite.com. **Description:** Operates an employee-owned retail drugstore chain with over 50 rural locations in Minnesota, the Dakotas, Iowa, and Montana. **Positions advertised include:** Pharmacist. **Corporate headquarters location:** This location. **Operations at this facility include:** Administration; Sales. **Number of employees at this location:** 60. **Number of employees nationwide:** 1,150.

UNITED HARDWARE DISTRIBUTING COMPANY
5005 Nathan Lane North, Plymouth MN 55442. 763/559-1800. **Contact:** Human Resources. **World Wide Web address:** http://www.unitedhardware.com. **Description:** United Hardware Distributing Company is a dealer-owned hardware distributor that provides products, retail programs, and support services to independent retailers. **Corporate headquarters location:** This location.

WAL-MART STORES, INC.
4740 Mall Drive, Hermantown MN 55811. 218/727-1310. **Contact:** Human Resources. **World Wide Web address:** http://www.walmart.com. **Description:** Wal-Mart Stores is one of the largest retail merchandise chains in the country, operating full-service discount department stores, combination grocery and discount stores, and warehouse stores requiring membership. Founded in 1962. **Corporate headquarters location:** Bentonville AR.

WEDGE COMMUNITY CO-OP
2105 Lyndale Avenue South, Minneapolis MN 55405. 218/722-3336. **Fax:** 612/874-7275. **Contact:** Human Resources. **E-mail address:** wedgehr@wedge.coop. **World Wide Web address:** http://www.wedge.coop. **Description:** The Wedge Co-op is a full-service natural food grocery store. Offers natural and organic in-store bakery, dairy, full-service deli, full-service meat counter, juice bar, produce, bulk foods, health and body care, general merchandise and grocery, as well as classes and catering. **NOTE:** See website for current job openings and to download application, or apply in person. **Positions advertised include:** Deli Manager; Deli Baker; Co-op Partners Wholesale Produce Buyer; Meat and Seafood Manager; Health and Body Care (HBC) Worker; Meat & Seafood Shift Lead; Grocery Stocker.

WINMARK CORPORATION
4200 Dahlberg Drive, Suite 100, Minneapolis MN 55422-4837. 763/520-8500. **Toll-free phone:** 800/567-6600. **Fax:** 763/520-8410. **Contact:** Personnel. **E-mail address:** lgoff@winmarkcorporation.com. **World Wide Web address:** http://www.winmarkcorporation.com. **Description:** A retail franchiser that sells a variety of new and used merchandise. **Positions advertised include:** Account Manager; Software Developer; Field Operations Manager. **Corporate headquarters location:** This location. **Subsidiaries include:** Music Go Round; Once Upon A Child; Play It Again Sports; Plato's Closet.

Mississippi

BARNES & NOBLE BOOKSTORES
15246 Crossroads Parkway, Gulfport MS 39503. 228/832-8906. **Fax:** 228/832-8293. **Contact:** Human Resources. **E-mail address:** d91careers@bn.com. **World Wide Web address:** http://www.barnesandnobleinc.com. **Description:** A bookstore chain operating nationwide. This location has a cafe in addition to its comprehensive book departments. **Positions advertised include:** Assistant Store Manager; Department Manager. **Corporate headquarters location:** New York NY. **Other area locations:** Statewide. **Other U.S. locations:** Nationwide. **Listed on:** New York Stock Exchange. **Stock exchange symbol:** BKS. **Annual sales/revenues:** $4.8 billion. **Number of employees nationwide:** 40,000.

SAKS INCORPORATED
P.O. Box 10327, Jackson MS 39289. 601/968-4400. **Physical address:** 3455 Highway 80 West, Jackson MS 39209. **Contact:** Human Resources. **World Wide Web address:** http://www.saksincorporated.com. **Description:** A department store holding company that operates approximately 360 stores in 36 states. The company's stores include Saks Fifth Avenue, Parisian, Younker's, Herberger's, Carson Pirie Scott, Club Libby Lu, Boston Store, Bergner's, and Off 5th, the company's outlet store. Saks Incorporated also operates two retail

catalogs and several retail Internet sites. **Positions advertised include:** Customer Contact Center Representative; Saks Direct Sales Associate; Construction Controller; Contract Administrator; Senior Programmer Analyst; EGC Marketing Coordinator. **Corporate headquarters location:** Birmingham AL. **Operations at this facility include:** Divisional Headquarters and Operations Center. **Listed on:** New York Stock Exchange. **Stock exchange symbol:** SKS. **Annual sales/revenues:** $6 billion.

Missouri

AUTOZONE
9710 Page Avenue, Overland MO 63132. 314/428-9955. **Contact:** Human Resources. **World Wide Web address:** http://www.autozone.com. **Description:** A do-it-yourself retail auto parts chain specializing in foreign and domestic parts. The company operates over 2,700 stores in 40 states. **Corporate headquarters location:** Memphis TN.

JOHN FABICK TRACTOR COMPANY
One Fabick Drive, Fenton MO 63026. 636/343-5900. **Contact:** Personnel Director. **World Wide Web address:** http://www.johnfabick.com. **Description:** Offers retail sales and service of new and used Caterpillar products including diesel engines, electric generator sets, road construction and earth moving equipment, mining equipment, materials handling equipment, and oil and gas pipe equipment. **Number of employees at this location:** 200.

FAMOUS-BARR COMPANY
601 Olive Street, St. Louis MO 63101. 314/444-3111. **Fax:** 314/444-3175. **Contact:** Bob Becherer, Executive Recruiting Manager. **World Wide Web address:** http://www.mayco.com. **Description:** Operates a retail department store chain with over 20 stores throughout Missouri, Illinois, and Indiana. **Positions advertised include:** Sales Associate. **Corporate headquarters location:** This location. **Parent company:** The May Department Store Company.

FOOD FOR LESS
8985 Jennings Station Road, Jennings MO 63136. 314/867-8100. **Contact:** Human Resources. **Description:** Food For Less operates a chain of supermarkets; conducts bakery and creamery operations; and owns and operates a full-line warehouse and distribution facility.

JCPENNEY COMPANY INC.
METRO DISTRICT OFFICE
90 West County Court, St. Louis MO 63122. 314/965-5969. **Contact:** Personnel Manager. **World Wide Web address:** http://www.jcpenney.com. **Description:** This location houses administrative offices for the major domestic retailer, with 1,100 store operations in all 50 states and Puerto Rico. The dominant portion of the company's business consists of providing merchandise and services to customers through stores and catalog operations. Overall, JCPenney operates and manages almost 600 full-line stores, and more than 1,060 small soft-line stores. **Positions advertised include:** Management Trainee. **Corporate headquarters location:** Plano TX. **Operations at this facility include:** Administration.

KMART
11978 St. Charles Rock Road, Bridgeton MO 63044. 314/739-8800. **Contact:** Personnel Department. **E-mail address:** hireme@kmart.com. **World Wide Web address:** http://www.kmart.com. **Description:** Kmart is one of the nation's largest owners and operators of general merchandising stores. The company operates 1,500 Kmart outlets in 49 states, Puerto Rico, and the Virgin Islands. **NOTE:** Submit resume online. **Corporate headquarters location:** Troy MI. **Operations at this facility include:** This location is a retail store that includes a pharmacy and food court. **Number of employees worldwide:** 144,000.

THE MAY DEPARTMENT STORES COMPANY
611 Olive Street, St. Louis MO 63101. 314/342-6300. **Contact:** Manager of Human Resources. **World Wide Web address:** http://www.maycompany.com. **Description:** A retail organization with 13 department store companies and a discount shoe division. These department store companies operate under various names including Filene's, Lord & Taylor, and Kaufmann's. **Corporate headquarters location:** This location. **Number of employees worldwide:** 127,000.

MEDICINE SHOPPE INTERNATIONAL INC.
1100 North Lindbergh Boulevard, St. Louis MO 63132. 314/993-6000. **Toll-free phone:** 800/325-1397. **Fax:** 314/872-5370. **Contact:** Human Resources. **World Wide Web address:** http://www.medshoppe.com. **Description:** Medicine Shoppe International operates and franchises retail drug stores.

MICHAEL'S STORES
2155 Zumbehl Road, Bogey Hills Plaza, St. Charles MO 63303. 636/947-6379. **Contact:** Human Resources. **World Wide Web address:** http://www.michaels.com. **Description:** A nationwide specialty retailer of art, crafts, and decorative items and supplies. **NOTE:** Search and apply for positions online. **Corporate headquarters location:** Irving TX. **Other U.S. locations:** Nationwide.

NEIMAN MARCUS
100 Plaza Frontenac, St. Louis MO 63131. 314/567-9811. **Contact:** Human Resources Manager. **E-mail address:** slcareers@neimanmarcus.com. **World Wide Web address:** http://www.neimanmarcus.com. **Description:** A retail department store. **Positions advertised include:** Buyer; Merchandiser; Designer. **Special programs:** Internships. **Corporate headquarters location:** Dallas TX. **Parent company:** The Neiman Marcus Group, Inc. operates three specialty retailing businesses: Neiman Marcus, Bergdorf Goodman, and Contempo Casuals. Combined, these three chains offer high-quality men's and women's apparel, fashion accessories, precious jewelry, fine china, and moderately priced crystal and silver. **Operations at this facility include:** Sales; Service. **Listed on:** New York Stock Exchange. **Stock exchange symbol:** NMG.

NETTIE'S FLOWER GARDEN INC.
3801 South Grand Boulevard, St. Louis MO 63118. 314/771-9600. **Contact:** Personnel Office. **Description:** A retail florist specializing in fresh and artificial flowers, supplies, and custom decorating.

O'REILLY OZARK
233 South Patterson Avenue, Springfield MO 65802. 417/862-6708. **Contact:** Director of Human Resources. **E-mail address:** resume@oreillyauto.com. **World Wide Web address:** http://www.oreillyauto.com. **Description:** O'Reilly Ozark operates 1000 automotive supply stores in 17 states offering aftermarket parts, tools, supplies, equipment, and accessories. Founded in 1957. **NOTE:** Apply online or via e-mail. **Other U.S. locations:** Midwest. **Listed on:** NASDAQ. **Stock exchange symbol:** ORLY.

QUALEX
2838 Market Street, St. Louis MO 63103. 314/652-1300. **Contact:** Human Resources Department. **Description:** Wholesalers of photographic supplies and retailers of photo-finishing services. **Number of employees at this location:** 100.

RADIOSHACK
371 South County Center Way, P.O. Box 515371, St. Louis MO 63129. 314/892-1800. **Contact:** Store Manager. **World Wide Web address:** http://www.radioshack.com. **Description:** A store location of the national consumer electronics retailer. Overall, RadioShack operates through more than 7,000 stores worldwide. **Corporate headquarters location:** Fort Worth TX. **Parent company:** InterTAN, Inc. (Fort Worth TX). **Listed on:** New York Stock Exchange. **Stock exchange symbol:** RSH.

SAKS FIFTH AVENUE
1142 Independence Center, Independence MO 64057. 816/795-7432. **Contact:** Christine Shuey, Store Manager. **World Wide Web address:** http://www.saksincorporated.com. **Description:** This location houses the business offices. Overall, Saks Fifth Avenue is a 62-store chain emphasizing soft-goods products, primarily apparel for men, women, and children. **Parent company:** Saks Incorporated.

SCHNUCK MARKETS, INC.
11420 Lackland Road, St. Louis MO 63146-6928. 314/994-9900. **Toll-free phone:** 800/459-HIRE. **Contact:** Employment Manager. **World Wide Web address:** http://www.schnucks.com. **Description:** Operates a chain of 100 supermarkets. **Positions advertised include:** Pharmacists. **Corporate headquarters location:** This location. **Other U.S. locations:** IL; IN; WI; MS; TN. **Number of employees nationwide:** 2,530.

WILLIAM A. STRAUB INC.
8282 Forsyth Boulevard, St. Louis MO 63105. 314/725-2121. **Toll-free phone:** 866/725-2121. **Fax:** 314/725-2123. **Contact:** Paul Poe, General Manager. **Description:** Owners and operators of a chain of retail grocery stores. **President:** Jack Straub, Jr.

J.D. STREETT & COMPANY INC.
144 Weldon Parkway, Maryland Heights MO 63043. 314/432-6600. **Contact:** Personnel. **World Wide Web address:** http://www.jdstreett.com. **Description:** Retailers and wholesale marketers of petroleum products. **Corporate headquarters location:** This location.

SUNTRUP FORD CITY
10700 Page Boulevard, St. Louis MO 63132. 314/429-4455. **Contact:** Personnel Director. **World Wide Web address:** http://www.suntrup.com. **Description:** A dealer of new and used automobiles.

SUPERVALU INC.
7100 Hazelwood Avenue, Hazelwood MO 63042. 314/524-4000. **Contact:** Human Resources. **E-mail address:** super.careers@supervalu.com. **World Wide Web address:** http://www.supervalu.com. **Description:** One of the nation's largest food retailers and distribution companies. In the corporate retail sector, SUPERVALU operates over 1,500 stores in 39 states under the following names: bigg's, Cub Foods, Shop 'n Save, Save-A-Lot, Scott's Foods, Laneco, and Hornbachers. **Corporate headquarters location:** Eden Prairie MN. **Subsidiaries include:** Hazelwood Farms Bakeries manufactures frozen bakery products. **Listed on:** New York Stock Exchange. **Stock exchange symbol:** SVU.

WALGREEN CO.
440 North Highway 67, Florissant MO 63031. 314/837-5500. **Contact:** Personnel Department. **World Wide Web address:** http://www.walgreens.com. **Description:** Walgreen's is one of the largest retail drug store chains in the United States, which sells prescription and nonprescription drugs, cosmetics, toiletries, liquor and beverages, tobacco, and general merchandise. **NOTE:** Search and apply for positions online. **Operations at this facility include:** This location is the district office.

Montana

STEEL ETC. LLP
P.O. Box 1279, Great Falls MT 59403. 406/761-4848. **Physical address:** 302 3rd Street South, Great Falls MT 59405. **Contact:** Human Resources. **E-mail address:** lena@steel-etc.com. **Description:** Steel Inc. operates an automotive parts store, an industrial hardware store, a steel company, and a scrap yard. **Other U.S. locations:** WY.

Nebraska

BED, BATH & BEYOND
2960 Pine Lake Road, Lincoln NE 68516. 402/420-6767. **Fax:** 908/688-0141. **Contact:** Human Resources. **E-mail address:** employment@bedbath.com. or careers@ bedbath.com. **World Wide Web address:** http://www.bedbath.com. **Description:** Nationwide chain of domestic merchandise and furniture stores. Founded in 1971. **Positions advertised include:** Store Manager; Department Manager; Sales Associate; District Human Resources Representative. **Corporate headquarters:** Union NJ. **Other area locations:** Statewide. **Other U.S. locations:** Nationwide. **Listed on:** NASDAQ. **Stock exchange symbol:** BBBY.

THE BUCKLE, INC.
2407 West 24th Street, Kearney NE 68845. 308/236-8491. **Fax:** 308/236-4493. **Contact:** Human Resources. **World Wide Web address:** http://www.buckle.com. **Description:** The Buckle, Inc. is a retailer of casual apparel for young men and women. The company operates over 300 retail stores in 38 states. **Positions advertised include:** Store Manager; Area Manager; District Manager; Full-time and Part-time Sales; Management Development. **Special Programs:** Internships. **Corporate headquarters location:** This location. **Other U.S. locations:** Nationwide. **Listed on:** New York Stock Exchange. **Stock exchange symbol:** BKE.

CABELA'S INC.
One Cabela Drive, Sidney NE 69160. 308/254-5505. **Fax:** 308/254-4500. **Contact:** Employment Specialist. **World Wide Web address:** http://www.cabelas.com. **Description:** The largest mail-order, retail, and Internet outfitter of hunting, fishing, and outdoor gear in the world. Founded in 1961. **Positions advertised include:** Sr. Systems Architect; Financial Analyst; Retail Merchandiser; Graphic Designer; Sr. Programmer/Analyst; Copywriter; Construction Project Manager. **Corporate headquarters location:** This location. **Other U.S. locations:** Kearney NE; Owatonna MN; Prairie du Chien, WI; East Grand Forks MN, Mitchell SD; Dundee MI; Kansas City KS; Hamburg PA; Wheeling WV.

GORDMANS
12100 West Center Road, Omaha NE 68144. 402/691-4000. **Fax:** 402/691-4269. **Fax:** 402/691-4269. **Contact:** Human Resources Manager. **E-mail address:** hr@gordmans.com. **World Wide Web address:** http://www.gordmans.com. **Description:** Operates a chain of off-price department stores. Features brand name furniture, clothing, jewelry, accessories, and shoes. **Positions advertised include:** Store Manager; Assistant Manager; Buyer for Toys; Guest Services Manager. **Corporate headquarters location:** This location. **Other U.S. locations:** CO; IL; IA; KS; MO; ND; OK; SD, WI. **Number of employees at this location:** 200. **Number of employees nationwide:** 2,500.

PAMIDA, INC.
8800 F Street, Omaha NE 68127. 402/339-2400. **Recorded jobline:** 800/284-7270. **Contact:** Human Resources. **E-mail address:** bhackett@pamida.com **World Wide Web address:** http://www.pamida.com. **NOTE:** Please see website for online application form. **Description:** A general merchandise retailer operating nearly 160 stores in 15 Midwestern states. **NOTE:** Entry-level positions are offered. **Positions advertised include:** Pharmacist; Assistant Team Leads; Store Team Leader; Store Team Leader in Training. **Special programs:** Training. **Corporate headquarters location:** This location. **Parent company:** Shopko Stores, Inc. **Listed on:** New York Stock Exchange. **Stock exchange symbol:** SKO. **Annual sales/revenues:** More than $100 million. **Number of employees at this location:** 400. **Number of employees nationwide:** 5,000.

VALMONT INDUSTRIES, INC.
One Valmont Plaza, Omaha NE 68154-5215. 402/963-1000. **Toll-free phone:** 800/825-6668. **Fax:** 402/359-6022. **Contact:** Human Resources. **E-mail address:** hr@valmont.com. **World Wide Web address:** http://www.valmont.com. **Description:** Manufactures irrigation equipment, steel and aluminum poles, tubing,

and fluted poles. **Corporate headquarters location:** This location. **Other area locations:** McCook NE; Valley NE; Waverly NE; West Point NE. **Other U.S. locations:** Nationwide. **Listed on:** NASDAQ. **Stock exchange symbol:** VALM.

Nevada

ALBERTSON'S
4995 South Kietzke Lane, Reno NV 89519. 775/827-5350. **Contact:** Hiring Manager. **World Wide Web address:** http://www.albertsons.com. **Description:** A location of one of the largest food and drug retailers in the United States. The company operates approximately 2,500 stores in 38 states. **Corporate headquarters location:** Boise ID. **Listed on:** New York Stock Exchange. **Stock exchange symbol:** ABS.

BARNES & NOBLE BOOKSELLERS
5555 South Virginia Street, Reno NV 89502. 775/826-8882. **Contact:** Store Manager. **World Wide Web address:** http://www.barnesandnobleinc.com. **Description:** One location of the bookstore chain. This location also has a cafe. **Corporate headquarters location:** New York NY. **Other U.S. locations:** Nationwide.

BLACK & DECKER
3585 South Decatur, Suite A, Las Vegas NV 89103. 702/889-6025. **Contact:** Human Resources. **World Wide Web address:** http://www.bdk.com. **Description:** Black & Decker is a global marketer and manufacturer of products used in and around the home and for commercial applications. Black & Decker is one of the world's largest producers of power tools, power tool accessories, security hardware, and electric lawn and garden tools, as well as one of the largest global suppliers of engineered fastening systems to the markets it serves. **Operations at this facility include:** This location is a retail store. **Listed on:** New York Stock Exchange. **Stock exchange symbol:** BDK.

CHAMPION CHEVROLET
P.O. Box 7277, Reno NV 89510. 775/786-3111. **Physical address:** 800 Kietzke Lane, Reno NV 89502. **Contact:** Office Manager. **E-mail address:** info@championchevroletreno.com. **World Wide Web address:** http://www.championchev.com. **Description:** A dealership that provides new Chevrolet cars and trucks and preowned vehicles.

CIRCUIT CITY STORES, INC.
4811 Kietzke Lane, Reno NV 89509. 775/827-5011. **Contact:** Manager. **World Wide Web address:** http://www.circuitcity.com. **Description:** A store location of one of the largest U.S. retailers of brand name consumer electronics and major appliances, as well as personal computers and music software. **NOTE:** Apply for positions online. **Corporate headquarters location:** Richmond VA.

DESERT BMW OF LAS VEGAS
2333 South Decatur Boulevard, Las Vegas NV 89102. 702/871-1010. **Contact:** Roger Campbell, General Sales Manager. **World Wide Web address:** http://www.autonation.com/dealers/desert/bmw-vegas. **Description:** Rents, leases, repairs, and sells new and used automobiles.

DILLARD'S DEPARTMENT STORES
3200 Las Vegas Boulevard South, Suite 300, Las Vegas NV 89109. 702/734-2111. **Contact:** Store Manager. **World Wide Web address:** http://www.dillards.com. **Description:** A store location of the retail chain. Dillard's offers a full line of brand-name fashion apparel and home furnishings. Dillard's has 300 stores in 29 states. Founded in 1938. **Corporate headquarters location:** Little Rock AR. **Other U.S. locations:** Nationwide.

FAIRWAY CHEVROLET
3100 East Sahara Avenue, Las Vegas NV 89104. 702/641-1400. **Contact:** Human Resources. **World Wide Web address:** http://www.fairwaychevy.com. **Description:** A full service dealership.

THE HOME DEPOT
861 South Rainbow Boulevard, Las Vegas NV 89145. 702/259-3305. **Contact:** Store Manager. **World Wide Web address:** http://www.homedepot.com. **Description:** Operates retail warehouse stores selling a wide assortment of building materials and home improvement products, primarily to the do-it-yourself and home remodeling markets. The company operates more than 1,500 stores (Home Depot, EXPO, and other subsidiary companies). **NOTE:** Apply for positions online. **Corporate headquarters location:** Atlanta GA.

A.C. HOUSTON LUMBER COMPANY
P.O. Box 337410, North Las Vegas NV 89033-7410. 702/681-2901. **Physical address:** 2912 East La Madre Way, North Las Vegas NV 89031. **Contact:** Denise Nichols, Human Resources. **E-mail address:** dnichols@houstonlumber.com. **World Wide Web address:** http://www.achoustonlumber.com. **Description:** This is the main store location of the retailer of lumber and related products. **Positions advertised include:** Truss Designers. **Corporate headquarters location:** This location. **Other U.S. locations:** CA; CO; ID; NM.

JONES WEST FORD
3600 Keitzke Lane, Reno NV 89502. 775/829-3200. **Toll-free phone:** 800/527-3673. **Contact:** Jay Costet, Sales Manager. **World Wide Web address:** http://www.jwford.com. **Description:** An automotive dealership.

LEVITZ FURNITURE CORPORATION
91 South Martin Luther King Boulevard, Las Vegas NV 89106. 702/366-9097. **Contact:** Human Resources. **E-mail address:** careers@levitz.com. **World Wide Web address:** http://www.levitz.com. **Description:** A store location of the national furniture store chain. **Corporate headquarters location:** Woodbury NY. **Other area locations:** Henderson NV.

MERVYN'S CALIFORNIA DEPARTMENT STORES
3871 South Carson Street, Carson City NV 89701-5538. 775/887-8800. **Contact:** Human Relations Coordinator. **World Wide Web address:** http://www.mervyns.com. **Description:** One location of the 187-store chain. **Corporate headquarters location:** Hayward CA. **Other U.S. locations:** Nationwide. **Parent company:** Target Corporation. **Sales/revenue:** $4 billion. **Number of employees nationwide:** 28,000.

NEIMAN MARCUS
3200 Las Vegas Boulevard South, Las Vegas NV 89109. 702/731-3636. **Contact:** Personnel. **World Wide Web address:** http://www.neimanmarcus.com. **Description:** A department store with a cafe. Founded in 1907. **NOTE:** Entry-level positions are offered. **Positions advertised include:** Department Manager. **Special programs:** Training. **Corporate headquarters location:** Dallas TX. **Parent company:** Neiman Marcus Group. **Listed on:** New York Stock Exchange. **Stock exchange symbol:** NMGA. **Number of employees at this location:** 300.

RALEY'S SUPERMARKET & DRUG CENTER
2105 West Williams Avenue, Fallon NV 89406. 775/423-7114. **Contact:** Manager. **World Wide Web address:** http://www.raleys.com. **Description:** A grocery store location of the chain of supermarkets. Raley's operates more than 50 stores in Nevada and Northern California. **NOTE:** Search and apply for corporate positions online. **Corporate headquarters location:** West Sacramento CA. **Other U.S. locations:** Nationwide.

THE SHERWIN-WILLIAMS COMPANY
1606 South Commerce Street, Las Vegas NV 89102. 702/386-5700. **Contact:** Human Resources. **World Wide Web address:** http://www.sherwin.com. **Description:** Sherwin-Williams manufactures, sells, and distributes coatings and related products. Sherwin-

Williams labeled architectural and industrial coatings are sold through company-owned specialty paint and wallcovering stores. **Special programs:** Management Training Program; Internships. **Corporate headquarters location:** Cleveland OH. **Other U.S. locations:** Nationwide. **Operations at this facility include:** This location houses the district offices. **Listed on:** New York Stock Exchange. **Stock exchange symbol:** SHW. **Sales/revenue:** Over $5 billion.

SILVER STATE INTERNATIONAL TRUCKS
2255 Larkin Circle, P.O. Box 1680, Sparks NV 89431. 775/685-6000. **Toll-free phone:** 800/950-2443. **Fax:** 775/685-6015. **Contact:** Manager. **World Wide Web address:** http://www.itctrucks.com. **Description:** An international truck dealership that leases and sells trucks to consumers and industrial customers. **Positions advertised include:** Service Technicians. **Parent company:** Interstate Truck Center.

TOYS 'R US, INC.
5000 Smithridge Drive, Reno NV 89502. 775/827-8697. **Contact:** Store Manager. **World Wide Web address:** http://help.toysrus.com. **Description:** Toys 'R Us operates 1,600 retail toy stores throughout the United States and 500 stores in 27 countries. **Corporate headquarters location:** Paramus NJ. **Other U.S. locations:** Nationwide. **Operations at this facility include:** This location is a retail outlet for the international toy store. **Listed on:** New York Stock Exchange. **Stock exchange symbol:** TOY. **Sales/revenue:** Over $11 billion. **Number of employees worldwide:** 113,000.

WESTPOINT STEVENS, INC.
3993 Howard Hughes Parkway, Suite 250, Las Vegas NV 89109. 702/866-2283. **Contact:** Human Resources. **E-mail address:** wphuman.resources@wpstv.com. **World Wide Web address:** http://www.westpointstevens.com. **Description:** An outlet store for West Point Stevens, a manufacturer of bedding, bath, and kitchen towels. **Special programs:** Internships; Tuition Reimbursement Program. **Other U.S. locations:** Nationwide. **Number of employees nationwide:** 13,000.

New Hampshire

BARNES & NOBLE BOOKSTORES
235 Daniel Webster Highway, Nashua NH 03060. 603/888-0533. **Contact:** Local store Manager. **E-mail address**: Careers@bn.com. **World Wide Web address:** http://www.barnesandnobleinc.com. **Description:** A bookstore chain operating 900 stores nationwide. This location has a cafe and music department in addition to its book comprehensive departments. **NOTE:** Search nationwide openings and use on-line employment application. **Positions Advertised Include**: Merchandise Analyst; Assistant Buyer; Computer Operator; Editor-Sparknotes; Production Manager-Sparknotes. **Corporate headquarters location:** New York NY. **Other U.S. locations:** Nationwide. **Listed on:** New York Stock Exchange. **Stock exchange symbol:** BKS. **Chairman: sales/revenues:** $5.2 billion. **Number of employees worldwide:** 37,000.

BROOKSTONE COMPANY
1 Innovation Way, Merrimack NH 03054 603/880-9500. **Fax:** 603/577-8008. **Contact:** Human Resources. **E-mail address:** hr@brookstone.com. **World Wide Web address:** http://www.brookstone.com. **Description:** Operates a chain over 200 specialty retail stores. **NOTE**: Search posted openings on-line. **Positions advertised include:** Retail Buyer; Creative Director; Art Director; Copywriter; Benefits Administrator; Mail Order Planner; General Ledger Specialist; Project Manager; Merchandise Coordinator. **Corporate headquarters location:** This location. **Listed on:** NASDAQ. **Stock exchange symbol:** BKST.

CCA GLOBAL PARTNERS
670 North Commercial Street, Manchester NH 03101. 800/450-7595. **Fax:** 603/626-3444. **Contact:** Lisa Miles, Human Resources. **World Wide Web address:** http://www.ccaglobal.com. **Description:** Engaged in the flooring, mortgage lending, lighting, formalwear, and biking industries. **Positions advertised include:** Member Relations Specialist; Senior Vice President; Executive Assistant; Training Specialist; Corporate Accountant; National Program Specialist; Sales Associate; Web Manager; Warehouse Worker.

PC CONNECTION
730 Milford Road, Merrimack NH 03054. 603/446-3383. **Toll-free phone:** 888/213-0260. **Contact:** Human Resources. **World Wide Web address:** http://www.pcconnection.com. **Description:** A mail-order retailer of PCs and computer peripheral equipment. **NOTE:** Search posted openings and apply online. **Positions advertised include:** Senior Web Developer; Technical Architect; Account Manager. **Corporate headquarters location:** This location. **Other area locations:** Dover NH; Keene NH. **Other U.S. locations:** Marlborough MA; Fairfield CT; Rockville MD; Boca Raton FL. **Listed on:** NASDAQ. **Stock exchange symbol:** PCCC. **Number of employees nationwide:** 1,300.

SHAW'S SUPERMARKETS
1600 Woodbury Avenue, Portsmouth NH 03801. 603/436-0323. **Contact:** Human Resources. **E-Mail address:** Ptc0344@shaws.com. **World Wide Web address:** http://www.shaws.com. **Description:** A supermarket chain. Founded in 1860. **NOTE:** Search posted openings and apply online at corporate website. **Positions advertised include:** Grocery Clerk, LaCarte Clerk; Grocery Crew Leader Overnight; Part Time Personnel Coordinator; Loss Prevention Store Detectives; Customer Service Representative; Grocery Receiver. **Corporate headquarters location:** East Bridgewater MA. **Other area locations:** Statewide. **Other U.S. locations:** CT; ME; RI; VT

CB SULLIVAN COMPANY
15 West Alice Avenue, Hooksett NH 03106. 603/624-4752. **Toll-free phone:** 800/321-2889. **Fax:** 800/428-6954. **Contact:** Human Resources Department. **World Wide Web address:** http://www.cbsullivan.com . **Description:** Distributes supplies to beauty salons and barbershops. CB Sullivan also operates retail stores throughout New England. **Corporate headquarters location:** This location. **Other area locations:** Hinsdale NH; Lebanon NH; Nashua NH; Newington NH; Salem NH. **Other U.S. locations:** ME; MA; RI; TX; VT.

TIBO LUMBER
112 High Street, Boscawen NH 03303. 603/796-2974. **Fax:** 603/796-2739. **Contact:** Human Resources. **World Wide Web address:** http://www.tibo.com. **Description:** Sells lumber, hardware, and building materials and supplies to contractors. The company also runs Distinctive Kitchens, and Northeastern Truss and Structural Components. **Other area locations:** Statewide. **Number of employees at this location:** 100.

New Jersey

BJ'S WHOLESALE CLUB
1910 Deptford Center Road, Deptford NJ 08096. 856/232-8880. **Contact:** Human Resources. **E-mail address:** 44689.intjobpost.255@openhireresumes.com. **World Wide Web address:** http://www.bjswholesale.com. **Description:** A bulk distributor of merchandise from electronics to groceries. **Positions advertised include:** Assistant Store Manager; Overnight Merchandise Manager; Loss Prevention Manager; Meat Manager. **Corporate headquarters location:** Natick MA. **Parent company:** Waban Inc.

BURLINGTON COAT FACTORY
1830 Route 130, Burlington NJ 08016. 609/387-7800. **Contact:** Human Resources. **E-mail address:** careers@coat.com. **World Wide Web address:** http://www.coat.com. **Description:** An off-price apparel discounter. Product lines consist of brand name apparel including coats, sportswear, children's wear,

men's wear, juvenile furniture, linens, shoes, and accessories. **NOTE:** Search for positions online. **Positions advertised include:** Director of Internet Marketing; Website Copywriter; Merchandise Planner. **Corporate headquarters location:** This location. **Listed on:** New York Stock Exchange. **Stock exchange symbol:** BCF.

CDW
1690 Oak Street, Lakewood NJ 08701. 732/370-3801. **Fax:** 732/886-0567. **Contact:** Human Resources. **World Wide Web address:** http://www.cdw.com. **Description:** A catalog retailer of brand-name Macintosh and IBM-compatible personal computer software, accessories, and peripherals. **Corporate headquarters location:** Vernon Hills IL. **Other U.S. locations:** Gibbsboro NJ; Wilmington OH. **International locations:** Canada; England; France; Germany; Mexico; Sweden; The Netherlands. **Operations at this facility include:** Sales; Service.

EDMUND INDUSTRIAL OPTICS
101 East Gloucester Pike, Barrington NJ 08007. 856/573-6250. **Fax:** 856/573-6295. **Contact:** Cathy Hillias-Slocum, Human Resources Generalist. **E-mail address:** humanresources@edmundoptics.com. **World Wide Web address:** http://www.edmundoptics.com. **Description:** Edmund Scientific Company is a retail supplier of industrial optics, lasers, telescopes, and precision optical instruments through two mail-order catalogs. Founded in 1942. **NOTE:** Entry-level positions are offered. **Positions advertised include:** Programmer/Developer; Catalog Production Associate; Graphic Artist. **Special programs:** Internships. **Corporate headquarters location:** This location. **Other U.S. locations:** Tucson AZ. **International locations:** China; Japan; United Kingdom. **Listed on:** Privately held. **Annual sales/revenues:** $51 - $100 million. **Number of employees at this location:** 190.

EPSTEIN, INC.
P.O. Box 902, Morristown NJ 07963-0902. 973/538-5000. **Contact:** Personnel. **Description:** A department store offering a wide range of fashions and other soft and hard goods. **Corporate headquarters location:** Cedar Knolls NJ. **Other U.S. locations:** Bridgewater NJ; Princeton NJ; Shrewsbury NJ. **Operations at this facility include:** Sales.

FOODARAMA SUPERMARKETS
922 Highway 33, Building 6, Suite 1, Freehold NJ 07728. 732/462-4700. **Contact:** Human Resources. **World Wide Web address:** http://www.foodarama.com. **Description:** Foodarama operates supermarkets in the states of New Jersey, New York, and Pennsylvania. **Corporate headquarters location:** This location.

THE GREAT ATLANTIC & PACIFIC TEA COMPANY
2 Paragon Drive, Montvale NJ 07645. 201/573-9700. **Contact:** Personnel. **World Wide Web address:** http://www.aptea.com. **Description:** The Great Atlantic & Pacific Tea Company maintains approximately 700 retail supermarkets throughout the East Coast, the Mid-Atlantic region, and Canada. **Positions advertised include:** Compensation Analyst; Human Resources Supervisor; Accountant; Voice Analyst; Coordinator. **Corporate headquarters location:** This location. **Operations at this facility include:** This location houses administrative offices. **Listed on:** New York Stock Exchange. **Stock exchange symbol:** GAP. **Number of employees at this location:** 650. **Number of employees nationwide:** 43,000.

HANOVER DIRECT, INC.
1500 Harbor Boulevard, Weehawken NJ 07086. 201/863-7300. **Fax:** 201/272-3280. **Contact:** Personnel. **E-mail address:** njjobapps@hanoverdirect.com. **World Wide Web address:** http://www.hanoverdirect.com. **Description:** A direct marketing company that sells products manufactured by other companies through its 12 core catalogs structured into operating groups. **NOTE:** Entry-level positions are offered. **Positions advertised include:** Analyst. **Corporate headquarters location:** This location. **Other U.S. locations:** San Diego CA; San Francisco CA; Hanover PA; De Soto TX; Roanoke VA; La Crosse WI. **Operations at this facility include:** Administration; Divisional Headquarters; Sales. **Listed on:** American Stock Exchange. **Stock exchange symbol:** HNV. **Annual sales/revenues:** More than $100 million. **Number of employees at this location:** 250. **Number of employees nationwide:** 3,000.

KMART CORPORATION
7401 Tonnelle Avenue, North Bergen NJ 07047. 201/868-1960. **Contact:** Human Resources. **World Wide Web address:** http://www.kmartcorp.com. **Description:** One of the largest nonfood retailers in the United States. The company operates over 2,000 stores nationwide under the Kmart name, with more than 50 Kmart stores located in the New York metropolitan area. All stores offer a broad range of discounted general merchandise, both soft and hard goods. **Corporate headquarters location:** Troy MI. **Operations at this facility include:** Administration; Divisional Headquarters; Service. **Listed on:** New York Stock Exchange. **Stock exchange symbol:** KM. **Number of employees at this location:** 1,700. **Number of employees nationwide:** 330,000.

LINENS 'N THINGS
6 Brighton Road, Clifton NJ 07015. 973/778-1300. **Fax:** 973/815-2990. **Contact:** Personnel. **World Wide Web address:** http://www.lnthings.com. **Description:** A specialty retailer selling linens, home furnishings, and domestics. Linens 'n Things operates over 230 stores nationwide. **Positions advertised include:** Analyst; Tax Analyst; Inventory Analyst; Store Support Coordinator. **Corporate headquarters location:** This location.

PATHMARK STORES INC.
200 Milik Street, Carteret NJ 07008. 732/499-3000. **Fax:** 732/499-4250. **Contact:** Human Resources. **E-mail address:** employment@pathmark.com. **World Wide Web address:** http://www.pathmark.com. **Description:** A diversified retailer engaged primarily in the operation of large supermarket/drug stores. Its Rickel Home Center division is among the largest do-it-yourself home center chains in the nation. The company's retail stores are located in the Mid-Atlantic and New England. **Positions advertised include:** Store Clerk; Store Engineer; Store Maintenance Mechanic; Merchandiser; Cashier; Night Crew Associate; Cart People; Maintenance Clerk; Cake Decorator. **Corporate headquarters location:** This location.

POPULAR CLUB PLAN
22 Lincoln Place, Garfield NJ 07026. 973/471-4300. **Contact:** Human Resources. **World Wide Web address:** http://www.popularclub.com. **Description:** Operates a full-service, mail-order catalog operation offering apparel, housewares, personal care products, jewelry and related items. **Office hours:** Monday – Friday. 8:00 a.m. – 8:30 p.m. **Corporate headquarters location:** This location.

SPENCER GIFTS INC.
6826 Black Horse Pike, Egg Harbor Township NJ 08234. 609/645-3300. **Contact:** Human Resources. **World Wide Web address:** http://www.spencergifts.com. **Description:** A retailer of novelty, joke, and gift items. **Operations at this facility include:** Administration; Sales; Service. **Number of employees nationwide:** 4,000.

STRAUSS DISCOUNT AUTO
9A Brick Plant Road, South River NJ 08882. 732/390-9000. **Contact:** Human Resources Administrator. **World Wide Web address:** http://www.straussauto.com. **Description:** Engaged in the retail trade of automotive aftermarket products. **Positions advertised include:** Store Manager; Assistant Store Manager; Service Department Manager; Auto Technician; Service Writer. **Corporate headquarters location:** This location. **Listed on:**

Privately held. **Number of employees at this location:** 200. **Number of employees nationwide:** 2,200.

SYMS CORPORATION
One Syms Way, Secaucus NJ 07094. 201/902-9600. **Fax:** 201/902-0758. **Contact:** John Tyzbir, Personnel Director. **E-mail address:** hr@syms.com. **World Wide Web address:** http://www.syms.com. **Description:** Syms Corporation operates a chain of 38 off-price apparel stores located throughout the Northeast, Midwest, Southeast, and Southwest. **Corporate headquarters location:** This location.

TOYS 'R US
1 Geoffrey Way, Wayne NJ 07470-2030. 973/617-3500. **Contact:** Director of Employment. **World Wide Web address:** http://www.toysrus.com. **Description:** One of the largest children's specialty retailers in the world. The company operates over 1,450 stores worldwide. Founded in 1948. **NOTE:** Entry-level positions are offered. **Special programs:** Training. **Corporate headquarters location:** This location. **Other U.S. locations:** Nationwide. **Subsidiaries include:** Babies 'R Us; Kids 'R Us. **Listed on:** New York Stock Exchange. **Stock exchange symbol:** TOY. **Annual sales/revenues:** More than $100 million. **Number of employees at this location:** 1,400. **Number of employees worldwide:** 94,000.

UNITED RETAIL GROUP, INC.
365 West Passaic Street, Rochelle Park NJ 07662. 201/845-0880. **Toll-free phone:** 800/963-2744. **Contact:** Human Resources Manager. **World Wide Web address:** http://www.unitedretail.com. **Description:** A leading nationwide specialty retailer of plus-size women's apparel and accessories. The company operates 502 stores in 36 states, principally under the names The Avenue and Sizes Unlimited. Founded in 1987. **Positions advertised include:** Regional Sales Director; District Sales Manager; Store Manager; Assistant Manager; Sales Associate. **Corporate headquarters location:** This location. **Subsidiaries include:** United Retail Incorporated.

UNITEDAUTO GROUP, INC.
2555 Telegraph Road, Bloomfield Hills MI 48302-0954. 248/648-2500. **Fax:** 248/648-2525. **Contact:** Human Resources. **World Wide Web address:** http://www.unitedauto.com. **Description:** Operates car dealerships. **Corporate headquarters location:** This location. **Listed on:** New York Stock Exchange. **Stock exchange symbol:** UAG.

VILLAGE SUPERMARKET, INC.
733 Mountain Avenue, Springfield NJ 07081. 973/467-2200. **Contact:** John Jay Sumas, Personnel Director. **World Wide Web address:** http://www.shoprite.com. **Description:** Operates 23 supermarkets in New Jersey and Pennsylvania. **Corporate headquarters location:** This location. **Other area locations:** Bernardsville NJ; Chester NJ; Florham Park NJ; Livingston NJ; Morristown NJ; The Orchards NJ; Union NJ. **Parent company:** Wakefern Food Corporation.

ZALLIE SUPERMARKETS
1230 Blackwood-Clementon Road, Clementon NJ 08021. 856/627-7585. **Contact:** Vice President of Human Resources. **Description:** This location houses administrative offices for the chain of six Shop-Rite supermarkets. **Corporate headquarters location:** This location.

New Mexico

A TO Z TIRE & BATTERY, INC.
613 Broadway Street, Albuquerque NM 87102-3907. 505/247-0134. **Contact:** Jessica Henry. **E-mail address:** jhenry@atoztire.com. **World Wide Web address:** http://www.atoztire.com. **Description:** A retailer and wholesaler of batteries, tires, and automotive services with 21 locations in five states. Founded in 1926. **NOTE:** Application available for download online. **Corporate headquarters location:** Amarillo TX. **Number of employees nationwide:** 200.

BTWW RETAIL
dba WESTERN WAREHOUSE
11205 Montgomery Boulevard NE, Albuquerque NM 87111-2648. 505/296-8344. **Fax:** 505/296-0278. **Contact:** Human Resources Administrator. **World Wide Web address:** http://www.westernwarehouse.com. **Description:** A retailer of western apparel. This location also hires seasonally. Founded in 1961. **NOTE:** Part-time jobs are offered. Search and apply for positions online. **Corporate headquarters location:** Dallas TX. **Other U.S. locations:** AZ; CA; CO. **Listed on:** Privately held.

ALLSUP'S CONVENIENCE STORES
2112 Thornton Street, Clovis NM 88101. 505/769-2311. **Fax:** 505/769-2564. **Contact:** Human Resources. **World Wide Web address:** www.allsups.com. **Description:** Operates more than 300 convenience stores throughout New Mexico and West Texas. Founded in 1956. Family owned and operated. **NOTE:** See website to download application. Bring the completed application and a resume to the store of choice or to the home office. **Positions advertised include:** Store Associate; Store Manager; Area Supervisor Trainee. **Corporate headquarters location:** This location.

BARNES & NOBLE BOOKSTORES
3701 Ellison Drive NW, Albuquerque NM 87114. 505/792-4234. **Contact:** Manager. **World Wide Web address:** http://www.bn.com. **Description:** A bookstore chain operating nationwide. This location has a cafe in addition to its book department. **Corporate headquarters location:** New York NY.

BLOCKBUSTER VIDEO
4411 San Mateo NE, Suite A, Albuquerque NM 87109. 505/888-4777. **Contact:** Manager. **World Wide Web address:** http://www.blockbuster.com. **Description:** A video retail store operating as part of the nationwide chain. Blockbuster operates approximately 8,500 stores nationwide and in 28 countries. **NOTE:** Search and apply for positions online or at local store. **Corporate headquarters location:** Dallas TX. **Parent company:** Viacom Inc.

CIRCLE K CORPORATION
397 Alameda Boulevard NW, Albuquerque NM 87113. 505/898-6492. **Toll-free phone:** 800/861-8614. **Contact:** Store Manager. **World Wide Web address:** http://www.circlek.com. **Description:** Circle K Corporation operates approximately 2,000 convenience stores in 18 states and 4,000 international locations. **NOTE:** Apply for positions online or visit a local store. **Corporate headquarters location:** Phoenix AZ. **Parent company:** Alimentation Couche-Tard Inc., Quebec, Canada.

FURR'S FAMILY DINING
6100 Central Avenue SE, Albuquerque NM 87108. 505/265-1022. **Fax:** 505/256-1831. **Contact:** Manager. **World Wide Web address:** http://www.furrs.net. **Description:** Part of a restaurant chain that includes Furr's Fresh Buffet. **NOTE:** Apply in person. **Positions advertised include:** Manager; Cook; Line Server; Dining Room Attendant; Dishwasher; Checker; Cashier. **Corporate headquarters location:** Dallas TX. **Other area locations:** Statewide.

HORACE NISSAN & HYUNDAI INC.
4300 East Main Street, Farmington NM 87402. 505/327-0366. **Fax:** 505/327-0879. **Contact:** Owner/Manager. **World Wide Web address:** http://www.horacenissan.com. **Description:** A new and used car dealership.

OFFICE DEPOT, INC.
350 Eubank Boulevard NE, Albuquerque NM 87123. 505/237-1040. **Contact:** Human Resources. **World Wide Web address:** http://www.officedepot.com. **Description:** Office Depot, Inc. is one of the nation's leading office products dealers with more than 1,000 stores in 11 countries. Founded in 1986. **NOTE:** Search and apply for positions online. **Corporate headquarters location:** Delray Beach FL.

OFFICEMAX
3301 Mineaul Boulevard NE, Suite A, Albuquerque NM 87107. 505/889-9696. **Contact:** Store Manager. **World Wide Web address:** http://www.officemax.com. **Description:** A retail store specializing in the sale of office supplies and equipment with more than 1,000 stores. **NOTE:** Search and apply for positions online. **Corporate headquarters location:** Itasca IL.

PEERLESS TYRE COMPANY
3010 Cerrillos Road, Santa Fe NM 87509. 505/473-0900. **Contact:** Dale Brown, Division Manager. **World Wide Web address:** http://www.peerlesstyreco.com. **Description:** Provides tires, shocks, and batteries to both the general public and area dealers. **Other area locations:** Albuquerque NM; Farmington NM.

QUALITY PONTIACBUICK GMC
7901 Lomas Boulevard NE, Albuquerque NM 87110. 505/765-1300. **Contact:** Business Manager. **World Wide Web address:** http://www.qualitydeal.com. **Description:** A new- and used-car dealership selling Pontiac, GMC, and Buick automobiles.

RADIOSHACK
1625 Rio Bravo Boulevard SW, Suite 23, Albuquerque NM 87105. 505/877-0110. **Contact:** Human Resources. **World Wide Web address:** http://www.radioshack.com. **Description:** Part of the 7,000-unit retail store chain specializing in the sale of electronic and computer products. **NOTE:** Search for corporate positions online. Apply for all jobs online. **Corporate headquarters location:** Fort Worth TX. **Listed on:** New York Stock Exchange. **Stock exchange symbol:** RSH.

RICO MOTOR COMPANY
220 South Fifth Street, Gallup NM 87301. 800/523-7426. **Fax:** 505/863-3538. **Contact:** Human Resources. **World Wide Web address:** http://www.ricoautocomplex.com. **Description:** An automobile dealership selling Pontiac, GMC, and Buick brand vehicles.

SEARS, ROEBUCK & CO.
1000 South Main Street, Broadmoor Center, Roswell NM 88201. 505/627-5204. **Contact:** Manager. **World Wide Web address:** http://www.sears.com. **Description:** One of 870 Sears, Roebuck & Co. stores, a retailer of apparel, home, and automotive products and related services. **NOTE:** Search and apply for positions online. **Corporate headquarters location:** Chicago IL. **Listed on:** NASDAQ. **Stock exchange symbol:** SHLD.

SMITH'S FOOD AND DRUG STORES
4700 Tramway Boulevard NE, Albuquerque NM 87111. 505-292-5484. **Contact:** Human Resources. **World Wide Web address:** http://www.smithsfoodanddrug.com **Description:** Operates a chain of 126 supermarkets/pharmacies in seven southwestern states. **NOTE:** Apply for positions online. **Corporate headquarters location:** Salt Lake City UT. **Parent company:** Kroger Company.

7-ELEVEN FOOD STORES
12801 Menaul Boulevard NE, Albuquerque NM 87112. 505/292-6922. **Contact:** District Manager. **World Wide Web address:** http://www.seveneleven.com. **Description:** This location is the district office of the convenience store chain that includes 24,000 stores worldwide. There are more than 20 stores in Albuquerque and one store in Rio Rancho. **Corporate headquarters location:** Dallas TX. **Operations at this facility include:** District Headquarters.

TARGET STORES
2725 North Main Street, Roswell NM 88201. 505/623-0445. **Contact:** Human Resources. **World Wide Web address:** http://www.target.com. **Description:** Target Corporation is a leading general merchandise retail company. **NOTE:** Search and apply for positions online. **Corporate headquarters location:** Minneapolis MN.

WAL-MART STORES, INC.
4500 North Main, Roswell NM 88201. 505/623-2062. **Contact:** Human Resources. **World Wide Web address:** http://www.walmart.com. **Description:** Wal-Mart Stores is the largest retail merchandise chain in the country, operating full-service discount department stores, combination grocery and discount stores, and warehouse stores requiring membership. Founded in 1962. **NOTE:** See website for current job openings and to apply online. **Corporate headquarters location:** Bentonville AR.

WALGREENS DRUG STORE
1401 West Pierce Street, Carlsbad NM 88220. 505/887-0380. **Toll-free phone:** 866/925-4473. **Contact:** Manager. **World Wide Web address:** http://www.walgreens.com. **Description:** Walgreen's operates one of the largest retail drug store chains in the United States, selling prescription and nonprescription drugs, cosmetics, toiletries, liquor and beverages, tobacco, and general merchandise. **NOTE:** For store positions, apply online or at the nearest store. More information available online for positions in areas of pharmacy, retail management, technology, corporate, full- and part-time store, managed care, and distribution center positions.

WILD OATS MARKET
1090 South St. Francis Drive, Santa Fe NM 87505-1654. 505/983-5333. **Fax:** 505/986-6087. **Contact:** Human Resources. **World Wide Web address:** http://www.wildoats.com. **Description:** A natural food stores featuring massage therapists and coffee and juice bars. Founded in 1987. **NOTE:** See website for current job openings and to apply online. Employment inquiries can also be made in person at the store's customer service desk. **Corporate headquarters location:** Boulder CO. **Other area locations:** Albuquerque NM.

New York

ANN TAYLOR STORES CORPORATION
7 Times Square, New York NY 10036. 212/500-2920. **Fax:** 212/536-4410. **Contact:** Human Resources. **E-mail address:** recruitment@anntaylor.com. **World Wide Web address:** http://www.anntaylor.com. **Description:** Ann Taylor is a leading national specialty retailer of women's apparel, shoes, and accessories sold primarily under the Ann Taylor brand name. The company operates 824 stores nationwide. **Corporate headquarters location:** This location. **Other locations:** Nationwide. **Subsidiaries include:** Ann Taylor Stores; Ann Taylor Loft; Ann Taylor Factory Stores. **Listed on:** New York Stock Exchange. **Stock exchange symbol:** ANN. **Annual sales/revenues:** $1.4 billion. **Number of employees:** 10,900.

BARNES & NOBLE CORPORATION
122 Fifth Avenue, 2nd Floor, New York NY 10011. 212/633-3300. **Contact:** Human Resources. **E-mail address:** careersnyc@bn.com. **World Wide Web address:** http://www.barnesandnobleinc.com. **Description:** A bookstore chain operating 900 stores nationwide. **NOTE:** Resumes may be either sent to the above mailing address, e-mail address, fax, or posted on: http://www.barnesandnobleinc.com/jobs/index.html. **Positions advertised include:** Director of Financial Planning and Analysis; Human Resources Manager; Store Operations Administrative Assistant; Marketing Coordinator; Database Administrator; Web Production Engineer; Product Development Engineer. **Corporate headquarters location:** This location. **Other locations:** Nationwide. **Operations at this facility include:** Corporate administration. **Listed on:** New York Stock Exchange. **Stock exchange symbol:** BKS. **Chairman:** Leonard S. Riggio. **Annual sales/revenues:** $5.2 billion. **Number of employees worldwide:** 37,000.

BARNEYS NEW YORK, INC.
575 Fifth Avenue, New York NY 10017. 212/229-7300. **Fax:** 212/450-8489. **Contact:** Human Resources. **E-mail address:** hr@barneys.com. **World Wide Web address:** http://www.barneys.com. **Description:** A national specialty retailer offering upscale men's and

women's apparel collections from both American and international designers operating eight full-price stores and 12 outlets nationwide. Founded in 1923. **NOTE:** For retail positions, contact the appropriate store. **Positions advertised include:** Buyer; Customer Service Representative. **Corporate headquarters location:** This location. **Operations at this facility include:** Administration; Sales; Service. **Listed on:** Over The Counter. **Stock exchange symbol:** BNNY. **Annual sales:** $371 million. **Number of employees:** 1,300.

BLOOMINGDALE'S, INC.
1000 Third Avenue, New York NY 10022. 212/705-2000. **Contact:** Human Resources. **World Wide Web address:** http://www.bloomingdales.com. **Description:** Operates a chain of 25 department stores in 10 states, mostly in New York and California. Founded in 1872. **Positions advertised include:** Graphic Designer; Gross Margin Planner; Line Cook; Marketing Analyst; Designer Apparel Sales Associate; Vendor Selling Specialist; Fine Jewelry Sales Associate; Juniors Sales Associate. **Corporate headquarters location:** This location. **Other U.S. locations:** Washington DC; Boca Raton FL; Miami FL; Palm Beach FL; Chicago IL; Boston MA; Minneapolis MN; Philadelphia PA. **Parent company:** Federated Department Stores Inc. (Cincinnati OH**Chairman/CEO:** Michael Gould. **Annual sales/revenues:** $1.7 billion. **Number of employees:** 9,800.

BROOKS BROTHERS
346 Madison Avenue, New York NY 10017. 212/682-8800. **Contact:** BB Employment Specialist. **E-mail address:** jdesmar@brooksbrothers.com. **World Wide Web address:** http://www.brooksbrothers.com. **Description:** Operates over 160 retail stores and factory outlets in the United States and 75 in Southeast Asia. Founded in 1818. **NOTE:** Resumes may be sent to the human resources office at 100 Phoenix Avenue, Enfield CT 06083. 800/249-6947 ext. 2324. Fax: 860/741-3171. **Positions advertised include:** Draftsperson; Editor; General Manager; Human Resources Manager; Management Trainee; Operations/Production Manager; Purchasing Agent/Manager; Receptionist; Reporter; Secretary; Stock Clerk; Systems Analyst. **Corporate headquarters location:** This location. **Parent company:** Retail Brand Alliance, Inc. (Enfield CT). **Annual sales/revenues:** 635 million.

CACHÉ, INC.
1440 Broadway, 5th Floor, New York NY 10018. 212/575-3248. **Fax:** 212/944-2842. **Contact:** Margarita Croasdaile, Human Resources Manager. **World Wide Web address:** http://www.cache.com. **Description:** Owns and operates 220 upscale women's apparel specialty stores. **Corporate headquarters location:** This location. **Other locations:** Nationwide. **Listed on:** NASDAQ. **Stock exchange symbol:** CACH. **Annual sales/revenues:** $200 million. **Number of employees:** 2,000.

D'AGOSTINO SUPERMARKETS, INC.
1385 Boston Post Road, Larchmont NY 10538-3904. 914/833-4000. **Contact:** Human Resources. **World Wide Web address:** http://www.dagnyc.com. **Description:** A supermarket chain offering a full line of grocery, produce, and meats. The company operates more than 23 stores serving Westchester County, and New York City. Founded in 1932. **NOTE:** Employment inquiries should be directed to: Frank Tucciarone, Director of Associate Development, 257 West 17th Street, New York NY 10011; phone: 917/606-0280; fax: 917/606-0367; email: ftucciarone@dagnyc.com. **Positions advertised include:** Cashier; Department Manager; Management Trainee; Retail Sales Worker. **Special programs:** Internships. **Corporate headquarters location:** This location. **Number of employees at this location:** 50. **Number of employees statewide:** 1,150.

THE DRESS BARN, INC.
30 Dunnigan Drive, Suffern NY 10901. 845/369-4500. **Fax:** 845/369-4829. **Contact:** Human Resources. **E-mail address:** hrrecruit@dressbarn.com. **World Wide Web address:** http://www.dressbarn.com. **Description:** Operates a chain of 750 women's apparel stores nationwide. **Corporate headquarters location:** This location. **Listed on:** NASDAQ. **Stock exchange symbol:** DBRN. **Chairman:** Elliot S. Jaffe. **Annual sales/revenues:** $717 million. **Number of employees:** 8,900.

ECKERD DRUG
7245 Henry Clay Boulevard, Liverpool NY 13088-3571. 315/451-8000. **Contact:** Cathleen Patterelli, Human Resources Director. **E-mail address:** cpatt3@eckerd.com. **World Wide Web address:** http://www.eckerd.com. **Description:** The company operates one of the largest chains of super drug stores in the Northeast under the name Eckerd Drugs. Eckerd Drug Store Division has over 250 drug stores located in New York, Pennsylvania, Vermont, and New Hampshire. **Parent company:** Eckerd Corporation (Largo FL). **Operations at this facility include:** One of the nine nationwide distribution centers.

FINLAY ENTERPRISES, INC.
529 Fifth Avenue, New York NY 10017. 212/808-2800. **Fax:** 212/557-3848. **Contact:** Personnel Manager. **E-mail address:** humanresources@fnly.com. **World Wide Web address:** http://www.finlayenterprises.com. **Description:** Operates through its subsidiary, Finlay Fine Jewelry Corporation, which sells jewelry through over 950 department store locations in the United States. **Corporate headquarters location:** This location. **Subsidiaries/affiliates include:** Thomas H. Lee; Finlay Fine Jewelry Corporation. **Listed on:** NASDAQ. **Stock exchange symbol:** FNLY. **Chairman/President/CEO:** Arthur E. Reiner. **Number of employees:** 6,500.

FOOT LOCKER, INC.
112 West 34th Street, New York NY 10120. 212/720-3700. **Fax:** 866/855-4510. **Contact:** Larry Haley, Regional HR Director. **E-mail address:** lhaley@footlocker.com. **World Wide Web address:** http://www.footlocker.com. **Description:** Formerly the Venator Group, Foot Locker, Inc. is a global retailer with stores and related support facilities in 22 countries. The company retails and distributes a broad range of footwear, apparel, and department store merchandise through more than 2,000 specialty stores and general merchandise stores. Founded in 1894. **NOTE:** Entry-level positions are offered. **Positions advertised include:** Finance Associate; Human Resources Specialist; Information Systems Engineer; Legal Associate; Logistics Specialist; Real Estate Analyst. **Corporate headquarters location:** This location. **International locations:** Worldwide. **Subsidiaries include:** Champ Sports; East Bay; Foot Locker; Kids Foot Locker; Lady Foot Locker. **Listed on:** New York Stock Exchange. **Stock exchange symbol:** FL. **Annual sales/revenues:** $4.5 billion. **Number of employees at this location:** 450. **Number of employees nationwide:** 24,000. **Number of employees worldwide:** 25,000.

FORTUNOFF
1300 Old Country Road, Westbury NY 11590. 516/832-9000. **Fax:** 516/832-1999. **Contact:** Personnel Manager. **E-mail address:** westburyhr@fortunoff.com. **World Wide Web address:** http://www.fortunoff.com. **Description:** Fortunoff offers a wide range of merchandise including home furnishings, fine jewelry, and fine silver. **Positions advertised include:** Buyer; Administrative Assistant; Call Center Representative; Training Manager; Sales Associate; Warehouse Clerk. **Corporate headquarters location:** This location. **Other locations:** Nationwide. **Annual sales/revenues:** $425 million. **Number of employees:** 3,000.

GAMESTOP
687 Broadway, New York NY 10012. 212/473-6571. **Contact:** Store Manager. **World Wide Web address:** http://www.gamestop.com. **Description:** Retails computer software, hardware, video games, accessories, and books. **Corporate headquarters location:** Grapevine TX. **Other U.S. locations:** Nationwide.

International locations: Worldwide. **Listed on:** New York Stock Exchange. **Stock exchange symbol:** GME.

HANNAFORD BROTHERS
900 Central Avenue, Albany NY 12206. 518/438-7296. **Contact:** Retail Employment Specialist. **E-mail address:** retail_opportunities@hannaford.com. **World Wide Web address:** http://www.hannaford.com. **Description:** A chain of grocery stores and distribution centers in the New England states and New York. Hannaford Brothers also operates as a retailer of food, general merchandise, and drug store products. **NOTE:** Apply either at local supermarket or send application materials to: Retail Employment Specialist, Hannaford Bros. Co., Mail Sort #7800, Portland ME 04104. **Corporate headquarters location:** Scarborough ME. **Other locations:** CT; RI; MA; ME; NH; NY; VT. **Parent company:** Delhaize America (Salisbury NC).

KEY FOOD STORES CO-OPERATIVE, INC.
1200 South Avenue, Staten Island NY 10314. 718/370-4200. **Fax:** 718/370-4225. **Contact:** Human Resources. **Description:** A private co-operative of 115 independently owned food stores and supermarkets throughout the New York metropolitan region. Founded in 1937. **Corporate headquarters location:** This location. **Other locations:** Bronx NY; Brooklyn NY; Queens NY; Manhattan NY; Staten Island NY; Yonkers NY. **CEO:** Richard Pallitto. **Annual sales/revenues:** $445 million. **Number of employees:** 150.

LILLIAN VERNON CORPORATION
445 Hamilton Avenue, White Plains NY 10601-1807. 914/925-1200. **Contact:** Human Resources. **E-mail address:** bgarti@lillianvernon.com. **World Wide Web address:** http://www.lillianvernon.com. **Description:** Lillian Vernon markets gift, household, gardening, decorative, Christmas, and children's products through a variety of specialty catalogs. Founded in 1951. **Corporate headquarters location:** This location. **Other U.S. locations:** Virginia Beach VA. **Listed on:** American Stock Exchange. **Stock exchange symbol:** LVC. **Annual sales/revenues:** $247 million. **Number of employees at this location:** 165. **Number of employees nationwide:** 1,400.

LIMITED BRANDS
1114 Avenue of the Americas, 24th Floor, New York NY 10036. 212/884-3000. **Contact:** Recruitment. **World Wide Web address:** http://www.limited.com. **Description:** Operates 3,800 stores and controls six retail brands, which include Victoria's Secret, Express, Bath & Body Works, The Limited, The White Barn Candle Company, and Henri Bendel. **Special programs:** Internships. **Listed on:** New York Stock Exchange. **Stock exchange symbol:** LTD. **Annual sales/revenues:** $940 million. **Number of employees at this location:** 300. **Number of employees nationwide:** 14,000.

LORD & TAYLOR
424 Fifth Avenue, New York NY 10018. 212/391-3344. **Contact:** Human Resources. **World Wide Web address:** http://www.lordandtaylor.com. **Description:** A full-line department store operating 85 stores nationwide offering clothing, accessories, home furnishings, and many other retail items. Founded in 1826. **Positions advertised include:** General Sales Associate; Commission Sales Associate; Cosmetics Beauty Advisor. **Parent company:** The May Department Stores Company (St. Louis MO).

MACY'S EAST
151 West 34th Street, New York NY 10001. 212/695-4400. **Fax:** 212/494-1057. **Contact:** Human Resources. **World Wide Web address:** http://www.macys.com. **Description:** Macy's East, part of the Federated Department Stores family, sells family apparel, home furnishings, and other merchandise from 115 stores in the eastern U.S. with the largest department store in the world at this location. **Positions advertised include:** Art Director; Assistant Buyer; Buyer/Merchandising Buyer; Associate Giftwrap & Extra's Buyer; Divisional Operations Director; Fire Safety Director; Macintosh Technical Support Representative; Assortment Management Planner; Publicity Coordinator; Regional Merchandise Manager; Systems Administrator. **Corporate headquarters location:** This location. **Parent company:** Federated Department Stores, Inc. (Cincinnati OH). **Chairman/CEO:** Harold (Hal) D. Kahn. **Annual sales/revenues:** $5 billion. **Number of employees:** 33,200.

NINE WEST GROUP
Nine West Plaza, 1129 Westchester Avenue, White Plains NY 10604-3529. 914/640-6400. **Fax:** 914/640-3499. **Contact:** Melissa Tavino, Human Resources. **E-mail address:** jobs@ninewest.com. **World Wide Web address:** http://www.ninewest.com. **Description:** A manufacturer and retailer of women's shoes. **Positions advertised include:** Planner; Director of Product Development; Corporate Technical Director; Product Data Maintenance Specialist; Sample Coordinator; Merchandise Processor; Design Assistant; Allocations Manager. **Corporate headquarters location:** This location. **Other U.S. locations:** Nationwide. **Parent company:** Jones Apparel Group. **Listed on:** New York Stock Exchange. **Stock exchange symbol:** JNY.

NEW YORK & COMPANY
450 West 33rd Street, 5th Floor, New York NY 10001. 212/884-2000. **Contact:** Career Opportunities. **Contact:** Marilyn O'Brien, Personnel Director. **E-mail address:** recruiting@nyandcompany.com. **World Wide Web address:** http://www.helmsleyhotels.com. **Description: World Wide Web address:** http://www.nyandcompany.com. **Description:** A specialty retailer of moderately priced women's apparel. The company operates more than 500 retail stores in 45 states. Founded in 1918. **Positions advertised include:** Manager of Training and Development. **Corporate headquarters location:** This location.

THE PENN TRAFFIC COMPANY
P.O. Box 4737, Syracuse NY 13221. 315/453-7284. **Physical address:** 1200 State Fair Boulevard, Syracuse NY 13221. **Fax:** 315/453-8240. **Contact:** Human Resources. **E-mail address:** resumes@penntraffic.com. **World Wide Web address:** http://www.penntraffic.com. **Description:** A food retailer and wholesaler. The company operates over 200 supermarkets in New York, Pennsylvania, Ohio, and West Virginia under the names Big Bear, Quality Markets, P&C Foods, and Bi-Lo Foods. Founded in 1942. **Positions advertised include:** Help Services Analyst. **Special programs:** Internships; Training. **Corporate headquarters location:** This location. **Other area locations:** Jamestown NY. **Other U.S. locations:** Columbus OH; DuBois PA. **Listed on:** NASDAQ. **Stock exchange symbol:** PNFT. **Sales/revenue:** Over $2 billion. **Number of employees at this location:** 2,000. **Number of employees nationwide:** 16,000.

PICK QUICK FOODS INC.
83-10 Rockaway Boulevard, Ozone Park NY 11416. 718/296-9100. **Fax:** 718/296-6203. **Contact:** Human Resources. **Description:** A grocery retailer. **Corporate headquarters location:** This location.

PRICE CHOPPER SUPERMARKETS
GOLUB CORPORATION
501 Duanesburg Road, P.O. Box 1074, Schenectady NY 12306. 518/355-5000. **Recorded jobline:** 888/670-JOBS. **Contact:** Human Resources. **World Wide Web address:** http://www.pricechopper.com. **Description:** Operates a chain of grocery stores, gas stations, and convenience stores located in Connecticut, Massachusetts, New York, Pennsylvania, and Vermont. **Special programs:** Internships; Apprenticeships; Training; Co-ops; Summer Jobs. **Corporate headquarters location:** This location. **Parent company:** Golub Corporation (also at this location). **Number of employees at this location:** 18,000.

QUALITY MARKETS
101 Jackson Avenue, Jamestown NY 14701. 716/664-

6010. **Contact:** Human Resources. **World Wide Web address:** http://www.qualitymarkets.com. **Description:** Regional office of a chain of retail grocery stores. **Parent company:** The Penn Traffic Company (Syracuse NY). **Operations at this facility include:** This location is an office and distribution center. **Listed on:** NASDAQ. **Stock exchange symbol:** PNFT.

RAYMOUR & FLANIGAN FURNITURE INC.
2780 Ridge Road West, Rochester NY 14626. 716/225-9455. **Contact:** Human Resources. **World Wide Web address:** http://www.raymourflanigan.com. **Description:** A retail furniture store offering living room sets, dining room sets, bedroom sets, kitchen furniture, and desks. **Corporate headquarters location:** Liverpool NY. **Other U.S. locations:** MA; CT; PA; NJ. **Number of employees nationwide:** Over 2,300.

SAKS FIFTH AVENUE
611 Fifth Avenue, New York NY 10022. 212/753-4000. **Contact:** Employment Manager. **World Wide Web address:** http://www.saksincorporated.com. **Description:** Saks Fifth Avenue is a 62-store chain emphasizing soft-goods products, primarily apparel for men, women, and children. **Special programs:** Internships. **Corporate headquarters location:** Birmingham AL. **Other U.S. locations:** Nationwide. **Parent company:** Saks Incorporated. **Operations at this facility include:** This location is a part of the nationwide specialty department store chain. **Listed on:** New York Stock Exchange. **Stock exchange symbol:** SKS. **Sales/revenue:** $5.9 billion. **Number of employees nationwide:** Approximately 55,000.

SEARS, ROEBUCK & CO.
1425 Central Avenue, Albany NY 12205. 518/454-3000. **Contact:** Human Resources. **World Wide Web address:** http://www.sears.com. **Description:** A retailer of apparel, home, and automotive products and related services for families throughout North America. **Corporate headquarters location:** Hoffman Estates IL. **Other U.S. locations:** Nationwide. **Operations at this facility include:** One location of the nationwide retail department store chain. **Listed on:** New York Stock Exchange. **Stock exchange symbol:** S. **Sales/revenue:** Over $41 billion. **Number of employees nationwide:** 289,000.

TRANS WORLD ENTERTAINMENT CORPORATION
38 Corporate Circle, Albany NY 12203. 518/452-1242. **Fax:** 518/862-9519. **Contact:** Human Resources. **E-mail address:** jobs@twec.com. **World Wide Web address:** http://www.twec.com. **Description:** A music and video retailer. Trans World owns approximately 1,000 stores throughout the United States and Puerto Rico including Coconuts, Record Town, Camelot Music, Music Express, Planet Music, Strawberries, and Saturday Matinee. **Positions advertised include:** Computer Operator; Customer Care Agent; Entry Level Recruiter; IT Executive; Lease Compliance Manager; Senior Accountant; Web Graphic Designer. **Corporate headquarters location:** This location. **Listed on:** NASDAQ. **Stock exchange symbol:** TWMC. **Annual sales/revenues:** More than $100 million. **Number of employees at this location:** 800.

WESTERN BEEF, INC.
47-05 Metropolitan Avenue, Ridgewood NY 11385. 718/456-3048. **Contact:** Human Resources. **World Wide Web address:** http://www.westernbeef.com. **Description:** A warehouse supermarket chain in the metropolitan New York area that provides a full-line of value-priced perishable and grocery products. In addition to operating 14 supermarkets, the company is also a meat and poultry distributor. **Positions advertised include:** Store Manager; Assistant Store Manager; Deli Manager.

North Carolina

BELK STORES SERVICES INC.
2801 West Tyvola Road, Charlotte NC 28217-4500. 704/357-1000. **Toll-free phone:** 866/235-5443. **Fax:** 704/357-1876. **Contact:** Human Resources. **World Wide Web address:** http://www.belk.com. **Description:** Operates 260 department stores located in 14 southeastern states. **Special programs:** Internships. **Corporate headquarters location:** This location. **Other U.S. locations:** East and Southeast U.S. **Number of employees nationwide:** 17,800.

CATO CORPORATION
8100 Denmark Road, Charlotte NC 28273-5975. 704/554-8510. **Fax:** 704/551-7246. **Contact:** Lynne Morton, Recruiter. **E-mail address:** catjobs@catocorp.com. **World Wide Web address:** http://www.catofashions.com. **Description:** Owns and operates over 500 stores in 22 states. **Positions advertised include:** Human Resources File Clerk; Programmer Analyst; Store Development Coordinator; Store Analyst; Jewelry Buyer; Technical Specialist. **Corporate headquarters location:** This location. **Other U.S. locations:** Southeast, South, East, and Middle U.S. **Number of employees nationwide:** 7,500.

DICK'S SPORTING GOODS
8809 JW Clay Boulevard, Charlotte NC 28262. 704/295-4411. **Contact:** Store Manager. **World Wide Web address:** http://www.dickssportinggoods.com. **Description:** A sporting goods retailer with over 250 stores in 34 states. **Positions advertised include:** Certified Fitness Trainer; Running Specialist; Cashier. **Corporate headquarters location:** Pittsburgh PA. **Other area locations:** Statewide. **Other U.S. locations:** Nationwide.

FAMILY DOLLAR STORES, INC.
10401 Old Monroe Road, P.O. Box 1017, Charlotte NC 28201-1017. 704/847-6961. **Fax:** 704/845-0582. **Contact:** Mary D. Lauzon, Corporate Recruiter. **E-mail address:** mlauzon@familydollar.com. **World Wide Web address:** http://www.familydollar.com. **Description:** Owns and operates a chain of more than 5,000 discount stores. The company provides merchandise for family and home needs. Stores are located in 43 states. Founded in 1959. **NOTE:** Entry-level positions and second and third shifts are offered. **Positions advertised include:** Data Integrity Analyst; Accounts Payable Clerk; Human Resources Customer Services Center Representative; Store Planner; Maintenance Assistant; Division Recruiter; Construction Secretary; Claims Consultant; Buyer; Web Developer. **Corporate headquarters location:** This location. **Listed on:** New York Stock Exchange. **Stock exchange symbol:** FDO. **Number of employees nationwide:** 37,000.

FOOD LION, LLC
P.O. Box 1330, Salisbury NC 28145-1330. 704/633-8250. **Physical address:** 2110 Executive Drive, Salisbury NC 28147. **Fax:** 704/637-2581. **Contact:** Recruiting Manager. **World Wide Web address:** http://www.foodlion.com. **Description:** Owns a chain of discount retail food stores with approximately 1,200 stores operating in 11 southeastern and Mid-Atlantic states. Founded in 1957. **Positions advertised include:** Produce Sales Manager; Corporate Recruiter; FT Grocery Associate; Physical Security Systems Technician; Service Associate. **Corporate headquarters location:** This location. **Parent company:** Delhaize America Inc. **Listed on:** New York Stock Exchange. **Stock exchange symbol:** DEG. **Number of employees nationwide:** 84,000.

HARRIS TEETER, INC.
P.O. Box 10100, Matthews NC 28106-0100. 704/844-3100. **Physical address:** 701 Crestdale Drive, Matthews NC 28105. **Toll-free phone:** 800/432-6111. **Contact:** Director of Personnel. **E-mail address:** jfranklin@harristeeter.com. **World Wide Web address:** http://www.harristeeter.com. **Description:** Operates a regional supermarket chain with over 140 stores in five southeastern states. **Corporate headquarters location:** This location. **Other U.S. locations:** FL; GA; SC; TN; VA. **Parent company:** Ruddick Corporation (Charlotte NC) is a diversified holding company operating through wholly-owned

subsidiaries American & Efird, Inc.; and Ruddick Investment Company. **Listed on:** New York Stock Exchange. **Stock exchange symbol:** RDK. **Number of employees nationwide:** 13,900.

INGLES MARKETS, INC.
P.O. Box 6676, Asheville NC 28816. 828/669-2941. **Physical address:** 2913 US Highway 70 West, Black Mountain NC 28711-9103. **Fax:** 828/669-3678. **Contact:** Human Resources/Recruiting. **E-mail address:** recruit@ingles-markets.com. **World Wide Web address:** http://www.ingles-markets.com. **Description:** Operates over 200 supermarkets in North Carolina, South Carolina, Georgia, Tennessee, Virginia, and Alabama. Ingles Markets also owns and operates a milk processing and packaging plant. **Positions advertised include:** Retail Pharmacist. **Corporate headquarters location:** This location. **Listed on:** NASDAQ. **Stock exchange symbol:** IMKTA. **Number of employees nationwide:** 6,512.

JC PENNEY
246 North New Hope Road, Eastridge Mall, Gastonia NC 28054. 704/864-4775. **Contact:** Human Resources. **World Wide Web address:** http://www.jcpenney.com. **Description:** A nationwide chain of retail department stores. Founded 1902. **Corporate headquarters location:** Plano TX. **Other area locations:** Statewide. **Other U.S. locations:** Nationwide. **Operations at this facility include:** Sales; Customer Service. **Listed on:** New York Stock Exchange. **Stock exchange symbol:** JCP. **Number of employees nationwide:** 147,000.

LOWE'S COMPANIES, INC.
1502 River Road, P.O. Box 1111, North Wilkesboro NC 28656. 336/658-4000. **Fax:** 336/658-4766. **Contact:** Human Resources. **World Wide Web address:** http://www.lowes.com. **Description:** A discount retailer of consumer durables, building supplies, and home products for the do-it-yourself and home improvement markets. The company operates over 900 retail stores in 45 states, primarily in the south central and southeastern regions of the United States. **Positions advertised include:** Corporate Counsel; Customer Care Associate; Designer; Director, Various Departments; Engagement Manager; Forecast Analyst; Human Resources Manager. **Special programs:** Internships. **Corporate headquarters location:** This location. **Listed on:** New York Stock Exchange. **Stock exchange symbol:** LOW. **Annual sales/revenues:** More than $100 million. **Number of employees nationwide:** 153,000.

LOWE'S FOODS
P.O. Box 24908, Winston-Salem NC 27114. 336/659-0180. **Fax:** 336/768-4702. **Contact:** Human Resources. **E-mail address:** jobs@lowesfoods.com. **World Wide Web address:** http://www.lowesfood.com. **Description:** Operates a food store chain. **Parent company:** Alex Lee. **Corporate headquarters:** This location.

OFFICE DEPOT
SALES AND OPERATIONS CENTER
5809 Long Creek Park Drive, Charlotte NC 28269. 704/597-8501. **Fax:** 704/598-2873. **Contact:** Human Resources. **E-mail address:** jobs@officedepot.com. **World Wide Web address:** http://www.officedepot.com. **Description:** Office Depot is a wholesale and retail dealer of office supplies. Both Wilson Office Products (a division of Office Depot) and Office Depot offer over 11,000 different business products. **Positions advertised include:** Business Development Manager; Consultant Service; Account Manager. **Corporate headquarters location:** Delray Beach FL. **Other U.S. locations:** Nationwide. **International locations:** Worldwide. **Operations at this facility include:** This location supplies office products to contract customers. **Listed on:** New York Stock Exchange. **Stock exchange symbol:** ODP.

SONIC AUTOMOTIVE INC.
6415 Idlewild Road, Suite 109, Charlotte NC 28212. 704/566-2400. **Contact:** Human Resources. **E-mail address:** jobopportunities@sonicautomotive.com. **World Wide Web address:** http://www.sonicautomotive.com. **Description:** Operates a nationwide car dealership chain. Sonic Automotive also provides parts and services. **Corporate headquarters location:** This location. **Listed on:** New York Stock Exchange. **Stock exchange symbol:** SAH.

VARIETY WHOLESALERS, INC.
3401 Gresham Lake Road, Raleigh NC 27615. 919876-6000. **Fax:** 252/430-2499. **Contact:** Francis Winslow, Human Resources Manager. **E-mail address:** fwinslow@vwstores.com. **World Wide Web address:** http://www.vwstores.com. **Description:** Operates a chain of retail variety stores. **Corporate headquarters location:** This location. **Other area locations:** Henderson NC.

WELCOME HOME, LLC
309 Raleigh Street, Wilmington NC 28412. 910/791-4312. **Toll-free phone:** 800/348-4088. **Fax:** 910/791-4945. **Contact:** Human Resources. **World Wide Web address:** http://www.welcomehomestores.com. **Description:** A retailer of giftware and home decor including fragrances, candles, framed art, furniture, and seasonal gifts. The company operates over 100 stores in 36 states. **Corporate headquarters location:** This location. **Other U.S. locations:** Nationwide.

North Dakota

DAN'S SUPERMARKET
835 South Washington Street, Suite 4, Bismarck ND 58504. 701/258-2127. **Fax:** 701/258-0064 **Contact**: Dan Bosch. **E-mail address:** dbosch@danssupermarket.com. **World Wide Web address:** http://www.dansupermarket.com. **Description:** A retail food store. **NOTE:** Apply at individual store locations. **Positions advertised include:** Cashier; Meat Wrapper; Deli; Produce Worker. **Other area locations:** Dickinson; Mandan; Rapid City; Gillette. **Corporate headquarters location:** This location.

VANITY SHOPS, INC.
P.O. Box 547, Fargo ND 58107. 701/237-3330. **Fax:** 701/237-4692. **Physical address:** 1001 25th Street, North, Fargo ND 58102. **Contact:** Human Resources. **E-mail address**: vanity@vanityshops.com. **World Wide Web address:** http://www.vanityshops.com. **Description:** A clothing retailer for girls and young women with over 150 stores across the country. **Corporate headquarters:** This location. **Other area locations:** Jamestown,; Grand Forks; Bismarck; Dickinson; Minot. **Other U.S. locations:** Nationwide. **Operations at this facility include:** Development of product lines and visual merchandising plans, advertising, and general support of company stores.

Ohio

ABERCROMBIE & FITCH
P.O. Box 182168, Columbus OH 43218. 614/283-6500. **Physical address:** 6301 Fitch Path, New Albany OH 43054. **Fax:** 614/283-6710. **Contact:** Human Resources Department. **E-mail address:** awesomejobs@abercrombie.com. **World Wide Web address:** http://www.abercrombie.com. **Description:** A retailer of casual clothing for young men and women. Abercrombie & Fitch operates over 200 company-owned locations nationwide. Founded in 1892. **NOTE:** Entry-level positions are offered. **Positions advertised include:** Financial Analyst; Asset Protection Auditor; Purchasing Director; Regional Maintenance Supervisor; Merchandiser; Planner; Allocator; Sourcing Manager; Production Assistant; E-Commerce Developer; CAD Designer; Graphic Designer; Technical Designer. **Corporate headquarters location:** This location. **Other U.S. locations:** Nationwide. **Listed on:** New York Stock Exchange. **Stock exchange symbol:** ANF. **Annual sales/revenues:** More than $100 million.

BARNES & NOBLE BOOKSTORES
3685 West Dublin Granville Road, Columbus OH 43235. 614/798-0077. **Fax:** 614/798-0074. **Contact:** Manager. **World Wide Web address:** http://www.bn.com. **Description:** One location of the

nationwide chain of bookstores. This location also has a cafe and music department. **Corporate headquarters location:** New York NY. **Listed on:** New York Stock Exchange. **Stock exchange symbol:** BKS.

BIG LOTS INC.
300 Phillipi Road, Columbus OH 43228. 614/278-6800. **Fax:** 614/278-6676. **Contact:** General Office Recruiting. **E-mail address:** careers@biglots.com. **World Wide Web address:** http://www.biglots.com. **Description:** One of the nation's largest retailers of close-out merchandise, toys and furniture. The company operates approximately 2,500 stores nationwide. **Positions advertised include:** Store Help Desk Specialist; DC Routing Coordinator; Merchandise Coordinator; Allocation Analyst; Human Resources Development Specialist; Corporate Help Desk Specialist; Data Network Analyst; Payroll Coordinator. **Corporate headquarters location:** This location. **Listed on:** New York Stock Exchange. **Stock exchange symbol:** BLI.

CRAFT HOUSE INC.
5570 Enterprise Boulevard, Toledo OH 43612. 419/536-8351. **Toll-free phone:** 800//537-0295. **Fax:** 419/536-4159. **Contact:** Personnel. **World Wide Web address:** http://www.crafthouse.net. **Description:** A mail-order catalog company and distributor of such hobby products as sun catchers, paint-by-numbers, and model cars.

DILLARD'S DEPARTMENT STORES, INC.
3011 Westgate Mall, Fairview Park OH 44126. 440/333-3000. **Contact:** Human Resources Department. **World Wide Web address:** http://www.dillards.com. **Description:** Operates a regional group of traditional department stores offering branded fashion and private label merchandise. The stores feature fashion apparel, home furnishings, and electronics. Dillard's operates approximately 230 stores located primarily in the Southeast, Southwest, and Midwest regions of the United States. **Other area locations:** Akron OH; Canton OH; Cincinnati OH; Cleveland OH; Toledo OH; Youngstown OH.

ELDER-BEERMAN STORES CORPORATION
3155 El-Bee Road, Dayton OH 45439. 937/296-2700. **Fax:** 937/296-2948. **Contact:** Manager of Recruiting. **E-mail address:** recruiting@elder-beerman.com. **World Wide Web address:** http://www.elder-beerman.com. **Description:** Operates a chain of retail department stores. **Special programs:** Executive Training Program. **Corporate headquarters:** This location.

FEDERATED DEPARTMENT STORES, INC.
7 West Seventh Street, Cincinnati OH 45202. 513/579-7000. **Contact:** Human Resources. **World Wide Web address:** http://www.federated-fds.com. **Description:** Operates over 400 department stores nationwide. The retail segments include Bloomingdale's, The Bon Marche, Burdine's, Lazarus, Rich's, Goldsmith's, and Sterns. **Positions advertised include:** Staff Auditor; Claims Representative. **Special programs:** Internships. **Corporate headquarters location:** This location. **Listed on:** New York Stock Exchange. **Stock exchange symbol:** FD.

GEYERS' MARKET INC.
280 East Main Street, Lexington OH 44904-1194. 419/884-1373. **Contact:** Human Resources. **E-mail address:** ej@geyers.com. **World Wide Web address:** http://www.geyers.com. **Description:** A grocery market. **Positions advertised include:** Retail Manager. **Corporate headquarters location:** This location. **Operations at this facility include:** Sales; Service. **Listed on:** Privately held. **Number of employees at this location:** 325.

JCPENNEY CATALOG FULFILLMENT CENTER
5555 Scarborough Boulevard, Columbus OH 43232. 614/863-8800. **Contact:** Employment and Personnel Relations Manager. **World Wide Web address:** http://www.jcpenney.net. **Description:** A catalog fulfillment center for the major national retail merchandise sales and services corporation. **Corporate headquarters location:** Dallas TX.

THE KROGER COMPANY
1014 Vine Street, Cincinnati OH 45202-1100. 513/762-4000. **Contact:** Human Resources. **World Wide Web address:** http://www.kroger.com. **Description:** Operates more than 2,200 supermarkets and convenience stores. Kroger also has 37 food processing plants that supply over 4,000 private label products to its supermarkets. **Positions advertised include:** Internal Auditor; Administrative Support Personnel. **Corporate headquarters location:** This location. **Listed on:** New York Stock Exchange. **Stock exchange symbol:** KR. **Number of employees worldwide:** 300.

THE LIMITED STORES, INC.
3 Limited Parkway, Columbus OH 43230. 614/415-7000. **Contact:** Recruiting Office. **World Wide Web address:** http://www.limitedbrands.com. **Description:** Operates a nationwide chain of retail stores offering careerwear, sportswear, lingerie, and children's clothing. **Corporate headquarters location:** This location. **Parent company:** Limitedbrands (Also at this location). **Listed on:** New York Stock Exchange. **Stock exchange symbol:** LTD. **Annual sales/revenues:** $638 million.

STERLING JEWELERS INC.
375 Ghent Road, Akron OH 44333. 330/668-5000. **Contact:** Recruitment Manager. **World Wide Web address:** http://www.sterlingcareers.com. **Description:** Operates over 1,000 jewelry stores nationwide. **Positions advertised include:** Senior Programmer/Analyst; Benefits Administrator. **Corporate headquarters location:** This location. **Subsidiaries include:** Belden Jewelers; Goodman Jewelers; J.B. Robinson Jewelers; Kay Jewelers; LeRoy's Jewelers; Osterman Jewelers; Rogers Jewelers; Shaw's Jewelers; Weigfield Jewelers. **Parent company:** Signet Group plc. **Operations at this facility include:** Administration; Service. **Listed on:** NASDAQ. **Stock exchange symbol:** SIGY. **Number of employees at this location:** 1,700. **Number of employees nationwide:** 12,000.

VICTORIA'S SECRET STORES
Four Limited Parkway East, Reynoldsburg OH 43068. 614/577-7000. **Fax:** 614/577-7047. **Contact:** Human Resources. **World Wide Web address:** http://www.limitedbrands.com. **Description:** Victoria's Secret operates a women's lingerie and clothing chain with over 1,000 shops nationwide. **Positions advertised include:** Accounting Processor; Director, Human Resources; Divisional Planning Manager; Insurance Analyst. **Parent company:** Limited Brands. **Operations at this facility include:** This location houses divisional headquarters administrative offices. **Listed on:** New York Stock Exchange. **Stock exchange symbol:** LTD. **Number of employees at this location:** 800.

ZALES JEWELERS
2169 Richland Mall, Mansfield OH 44906. 419/529-0566. **Contact:** Human Resources. **World Wide Web address:** http://www.sales.com. **Description:** One location of the 2,300 retail jewelry store chain. **NOTE:** For sales associate positions, apply at store location. For management positions, mail resume to: Manager of Staffing, Corporate Staffing, MS 5B-12, Zale Corporation, 901 West Walnut Hill Lane, Irving TX 75038-1003. **Corporate headquarters:** Irving TX. **Listed on:** New York Stock Exchange. **Stock exchange symbol:** ZLC.

Oklahoma
LOVE'S COUNTRY STORES
P.O. Box 26210, Oklahoma City OK 73126. 405/749-1744. **Physical address:** 10601 North Pennsylvania Avenue, Oklahoma City OK 73120. **Toll-free phone:** 800/388-0983. **Fax:** 800/655-6830. **Contact:** Carl

Martincich, Human Resources. **E-mail address:** hr@loves.com. **World Wide Web address:** http://www.loves.com. **Description:** Operates more than 140 retail convenience stores, travel stops, and restaurants in the Midwest. **Positions advertised include:** Accounts Payable Specialist; Credit Lead; Worker's Compensation Claims Manager. **Special programs:** Internships. **Corporate headquarters location:** This location. **Other U.S. locations:** CO; KS; NM; TX. **Listed on:** Privately held. **Sales/revenues:** Over $1 billion. **Number of employees nationwide:** 2,000.

Oregon

FRED MEYER, INC.
3800 SE 22nd Avenue, Portland OR 97202. 503/232-8844. **Contact:** Human Resources. **E-mail address:** fredmeyer@webhire.com. **World Wide Web address:** http://www.fredmeyer.com. **Description:** Operates a chain of approximately 400 retail stores offering a wide range of food, products for the home, apparel, fine jewelry, and home improvement items. **Corporate headquarters location:** This location. **Other U.S. locations:** AK; CA; ID; MT; UT; WA. **Parent company:** The Kroger Company.

ROTH I.G.A. FOODLINERS
1130 Wallace Road NW, Salem OR 97304. 503/393-9427. **Contact:** Kathy Moreland, Human Resources. **World Wide Web address:** http://www.iga.com. **Description:** Operates an area retail grocery chain with a number of local outlets. **Corporate headquarters location:** Salem OR. **Other U.S. locations:** Nationwide.

SAFEWAY STORES, INC.
12032 SE Sunnyside Road, P.O. Box 523, Clackamas OR 97015. 503/698-1121. **Recorded jobline:** 503/657-6400. **Contact:** Human Resources. **World Wide Web address:** http://www.safeway.com. **Description:** Safeway Stores, Inc. is one of the world's largest food retailers. The company operates approximately 1,665 stores in the western, Rocky Mountain, southwestern, and mid-Atlantic regions of the United States and in western Canada. **Corporate headquarters location:** Pleasanton CA. **Operations at this facility include:** One location of the retail chain that also produces baked goods and dairy products.

Pennsylvania

AMERICAN EAGLE OUTFITTERS
150 Thorn Hill Drive, Warrendale PA 15086. 724/776-4857. **Fax:** 724/779-5568. **Contact:** Jeff Skogelind, Vice-President of Human Resources. **E-mail address:** cooljobs@ae.com. **World Wide Web address:** http://www.ae.com. **Description:** A specialty retailer selling casual clothing and accessories for men and women. American Eagle Outfitters operates approximately 800 stores throughout the United States. **NOTE:** Employment matters are best handled through the website. **Positions advertised include:** Database Administrator; Business Analyst; Inventory Control Coordinator; Visual Manager. **Corporate headquarters location:** This location. **Listed on:** NASDAQ. **Stock exchange symbol:** AEOS. **Number of employees nationwide:** 6,000.

BARNES & NOBLE BOOKSTORES
5909 Peach Street, Erie PA 16509. 814/864-6300. **Contact:** Human Resources. **World Wide Web address:** http://www.bn.com. **Description:** A discount bookstore chain with locations nationwide. In addition to its book departments, this location also has a cafe and music department. **Positions advertised include:** Retail; Corporate. **Other U.S. locations:** Nationwide.

BLOCKBUSTER VIDEO
1101 North Atherton Street, State College PA 16803-2927. 814/238-6379. **Contact:** Store Manager. **World Wide Web address:** http://www.blockbuster.com. **Description:** A video rental store and part of the nationwide chain. Blockbuster operates approximately 2,000 outlets across the country. **Positions advertised include:** Field Operations; Local Retail Store.

THE BON-TON
2801 East Market Street, York PA 17402. 717/757-7660. **Contact:** Sue Hulme, Manager of Executive Employment. **E-mail address:** cshorts@bonton.com. **World Wide Web address:** http://www.bonton.com. **Description:** A regional department store chain operating 139 department stores and two furniture stores in 16 states. **NOTE:** Entry-level positions are offered, and online application is preferred. **Positions advertised include:** BSR Analyst; Administrative Assistant; Instant Credit Telephone Representative. **Special programs:** Training; Summer Jobs. **Corporate headquarters location:** This location. **Other U.S. locations:** MD; MA; NJ; NY; WV. **Listed on:** NASDAQ. **Stock exchange symbol:** BONT. **Number of employees at this location:** 500. **Number of employees nationwide:** 12,000.

BRIDGESTONE/FIRESTONE, INC.
180 Sheree Boulevard, Suite 2000, Exton PA 19341. 610/594-6181. **Contact:** Bob Pierce, Personnel Manager. **World Wide Web address:** http://www.bridgestone-firestone.com. **Description:** This location is a zone office responsible for supporting and directing more than 250 retail stores throughout the Northeast. **Corporate headquarters location:** Nashville TN. **Other U.S. locations:** Nationwide. **Parent company:** Bridgestone Corporation. **Operations at this facility include:** Administration; Service.

BURLINGTON COAT FACTORY
339 Sixth Avenue, Pittsburgh PA 15222-2515. 412/765-1499. **Contact:** Ron Giannandrea, Store Manager. **World Wide Web address:** http://www.coat.com. **Description:** An apparel discounter for men, women, and children with 345 locations in 42 states. **NOTE:** Employment opportunities are available at the corporate, distribution, and retail levels. Please send your application/resume correspondingly: corporate.employment@coat.com, warehouse.opportunities@coat.com, or employment.opportunities@coat.com. Resumes can also be mailed to human resources at 1830 Route 130, Burlington NJ 08016. **Corporate headquarters location:** Burlington NJ.

BUSY BEAVER BUILDING CENTERS INC.
3130 William Pitt Way, Building A6, Pittsburgh PA 15238. 412/828-2323. **Contact:** Personnel. **World Wide Web address:** http://www.busybeaver.com. **Description:** Busy Beaver is a chain of building supply stores. **Positions advertised include:** General Manager; Store Manager; Administrative Manager; Sales Manager; Full/Part Time Sales; Front End Department; Stock & Warehouse. **Corporate headquarters location:** This location. **Operations at this facility include:** This location houses purchasing offices.

CHARMING SHOPPES, INC.
450 Winks Lane, Bensalem PA 19020. 215/245-9100. **Recorded jobline:** 800/543-2562. **Contact:** Phil Brunone, Director of Human Resources. **E-mail address:** hr@charming.com. **World Wide Web address:** http://www.charmingshoppes.com. **Description:** A retail holding company. **Positions advertised include:** Sr. Production Control Analyst; Tech Desk Analyst; Disbursement Analyst; Sr. Designer; Accounting Manager. **Special programs:** Internships. **Corporate headquarters location:** This location. **Subsidiaries include:** Fashion Bug; Lane Bryant; Catherines Plus Sizes; Crosstown Traders, Inc. **Listed on:** NASDAQ. **Stock exchange symbol:** CHRS. **Number of employees worldwide:** 24,000.

DAVID'S BRIDAL
1001 Washington Street, Conshohocken PA 19428. 610/943-5000. **Fax:** 610/642-7642. **Contact:** Fred Postelle, Vice President of Human Resources. **E-mail address:** careers@davidsbridal.net. **World Wide Web address:** http://www.davidsbridal.com. **Description:** Sells a full line of bridal merchandise including apparel and accessories through 240 stores. **Special programs:**

Internships. **Corporate headquarters location:** This location. **Number of employees at this location:** 215.

DEB SHOPS, INC.
9401 Bluegrass Road, Philadelphia PA 19114. 215/676-6000. **Contact:** Ms. Pat Okun, Office Manager. **E-mail address:** careers@debshops.com. **World Wide Web address:** http://www.debshops.com. **Description:** A chain of specialty apparel stores offering moderately priced, coordinated sportswear, dresses, coats, and accessories for juniors. The company operates 300 stores in 40 states. **NOTE:** See a complete list of current openings at http://www.hotjobs.com. Online application encouraged. **Corporate headquarters location:** This location. **Other U.S. locations:** Nationwide. **Listed on:** NASDAQ. **Stock exchange symbol:** DEBS. **Number of employees at this location:** 200. **Number of employees nationwide:** 2,500.

DURON PAINTS AND WALLCOVERINGS
711 First Avenue, King of Prussia PA 19406. 610/962-9927. **Fax:** 610/962-9859. **Contact:** Human Resources. **E-mail address:** employment@duron.com. **World Wide Web address:** http://www.duron.com. **Description:** A retailer and wholesaler of paints, wallcoverings, window treatments, and related items**Positions advertised include:** Inside Counter Sales Representative; Material Handler; Order Processing Purchasing Clerk; Technician. **Parent company:** Sherwin-Williams. **Operations at this facility include:** Administration; Regional Headquarters; Sales.

THE FINISH LINE, INC.
196 West Moreland Mall, Route 30 East, #114, Greensburg PA 15601-3593. 724/832-8025. **Contact:** Manager. **E-mail address:** hr@finishline.com. **World Wide Web address:** http://www.thefinishline.com. **Description:** Operates a chain of retail stores offering a broad selection of men's, women's, and children's brand-name athletic and leisure footwear, activewear, and accessories. **NOTE:** Apply online for current retail and corporate openings. **Corporate headquarters location:** Indianapolis IN.

GENERAL NUTRITION COMPANIES, INC.
GENERAL NUTRITION CENTERS (GNC)
300 Sixth Avenue, Pittsburgh PA 15222. 412/288-4600. **Fax:** 412/288-2074. **Contact:** Corporate Recruiter. **E-mail address:** corporaterecruiter@gnc-hq.com. **World Wide Web address:** http://www.gnc.com. **Description:** General Nutrition's products are sold through a network of more than 4,800 company and franchised locations in all 50 states and 16 foreign countries. Founded in 1935. **NOTE:** Entry-level positions are offered. **Positions advertised include:** Associate Brand Manager; Promotion Coordinator; Applications Analyst. **Special programs:** Summer Jobs. **Corporate headquarters location:** This location. **Other U.S. locations:** Nationwide. **Number of employees at this location:** 600. **Number of employees nationwide:** 10,000.

LOWE'S HOME CENTERS, INC.
249 Lowe's Boulevard, State College PA 16803. 814/237-2100. **Contact:** Human Resources. **World Wide Web address:** http://www.lowes.com. **Description:** A discount retail store selling consumer durables, building supplies, and home products for the do-it-yourself and home improvement markets. Overall, the company conducts operations through 1,255 retail stores in 49 states. Products sold include tools; lumber; building materials; heating, cooling, and water systems; and specialty goods. **NOTE:** See website for a list of current openings with detailed application information.

NEW YORK & COMPANY
9th and Market Streets, Gallery Market East, Philadelphia PA 19107. 215/627-2550. **Contact:** Manager. **E-mail address:** recruiting@nyandcompany.com. **World Wide Web address:** http://www.nyandcompany.com. **Description:** A store location of the national women's moderately priced specialty apparel store chain. **NOTE:** Resumes should be sent to 450 West 33rd Street, 5th Floor, New York NY 10001. **Corporate headquarters location:** New York NY. **Parent company:** Limited, Inc. owns over 2,300 stores nationwide operating under such names as The Limited, Express, Victoria's Secret, Lane Bryant, and Size Unlimited, and also operates a mail order catalog business. **Operations at this facility include:** Sales; Service. **Listed on:** New York Stock Exchange. **Stock exchange symbol:** LTD.

PENN TRAFFIC COMPANY
RIVERSIDE BI-LO FOODS
P.O. Box 607, DuBois PA 15801. 814/375-3663. **Physical address:** Shaffer Road, Route 255, Dubois PA 15801. **Contact:** Cathy Huey, Human Resources. **Description:** A food retailer, wholesaler, and producer. The company operates more than 110 supermarkets in New York, Pennsylvania, Vermont, and New Hampshire under the names Riverside Markets, Quality Markets, BiLo Foods and P&C Foods. Penn Traffic Company also operates wholesale food distribution businesses. **Corporate headquarters location:** Syracuse NY.

PEP BOYS
3111 West Allegheny Avenue, Philadelphia PA 19132. 215/227-9000. **Contact:** Human Resources. **World Wide Web address:** http://www.pepboys.com. **Description:** Primarily engaged in the retail sale of a wide range of automotive parts and accessories, and the installation of automobile components and merchandise. Pep Boys operates 595 stores in 36 states. **Corporate headquarters location:** This location. **Operations at this facility include:** Administration. **Listed on:** New York Stock Exchange. **Stock exchange symbol:** PBY. **Number of employees at this location:** 700. **Number of employees worldwide:** 22,000.

RENT-WAY, INC.
One Rent-Way Place, Erie PA 16505. 814/455-5378. **Fax:** 814/461-5483. **Contact:** Recruiting Coordinator. **E-mail address:** employment@rentway.com. **World Wide Web address:** http://www.rentway.com. **Description:** Offers rental-purchase programs to customers on a short-term basis. **Positions advertised include:** Assistant Store Manager; Store Manager; Customer Service Associate. **Corporate headquarters location:** This location. **Other U.S. locations:** Nationwide. **Listed on:** New York Stock Exchange. **Stock exchange symbol:** RWY. **Annual sales/revenues:** More than $100 million.

RITE AID CORPORATION
30 Hunter Lane, Camp Hill PA 17011. 717/761-2633. **Fax:** 717/972-3971. **Contact:** Gina Grundusky, Corporate Recruiter. **E-mail address:** recruiter@riteaid.com. **World Wide Web address:** http://www.riteaid.com. **Description:** Operates 3350 retail drug stores in 28 states. Founded in 1939. **Positions advertised include:** Coordinator; Assistant Store Manager; Systems Engineer; Shift Supervisor; Payment Coordinator; Customer Service Representative; Insurance Coordinator; Senior Auditor; Pharmacist. **Special programs:** Internships. **Corporate headquarters location:** This location. **Other U.S. locations:** Nationwide. **Subsidiaries include:** Payless Drug Stores. **Listed on:** New York Stock Exchange. **Stock exchange symbol:** RAD. **Annual sales/revenues:** More than $100 million.

RITE AID PHARMACY
200 Chamber Plaza, Charleroi PA 15022-1605. 724/489-0870. **Contact:** Manager. **World Wide Web address:** http://www.riteaid.com. **Description:** A retail drugstore. **Corporate headquarters location:** Harrisburg PA. **Parent company:** Rite Aid Corporation operates 3350 retail drug stores in 28 states. Subsidiary Payless Drug Stores offers over 45,000 different items. **Listed on:** New York Stock Exchange. **Stock exchange symbol:** RAD.

7-ELEVEN, INC.
2711 Easton Road, Willow Grove PA 19090. 215/672-5711. **Contact:** Human Resources. **World Wide Web address:** http://www.7-eleven.com. **Description:** 7-Eleven is one of the world's largest retailers, with approximately 7,000 7-Eleven convenience units in the United States and Canada. **Corporate headquarters location:** Dallas TX. **Operations at this facility include:** This location houses administrative offices.

STRAWBRIDGE'S
801 Market Street, Philadelphia PA 19107. 215/829-0346. **Contact:** Personnel. **World Wide Web address:** http://www.strawbridges.com. **Description:** Operates a chain of department stores in Pennsylvania, Delaware, and New Jersey. **Special programs:** Internships. **Parent company:** Federated Department Stores. **Number of employees nationwide:** 12,000.

SUPERVALU EASTERN REGION
3900 Industrial Road, P.O. Box 2261, Harrisburg PA 17105. 717/232-6821. **Contact:** Human Resources. **Description:** Supervalu is a full-service grocery wholesaler and retailer, operating 1,500 stores in 40 states and supplying 2,240 customer stores. **Operations at this facility include:** This location is a distribution center. **Number of employees nationwide:** 57,000.

UNI-MARTS, INC.
477 East Beaver Avenue, State College PA 16801-5690. 814/234-6000. **Contact:** Human Resources. **World Wide Web address:** http://www.uni-mart.com. **Description:** An independent regional operator of over 282 convenience stores located in the Mid-Atlantic region. **Positions advertised include:** Store Sales Clerk; Store Manager; Assistant Store Manager; Store Supervisor; Clerical. **Corporate headquarters location:** This location. **Other U.S. locations:** DE; MD; NY.

URBAN OUTFITTERS
1627 Walnut Street, 5th Floor, Philadelphia PA 19103. 215/569-3131. **Fax:** 800/959-8795. **Contact:** Human Resources. **World Wide Web address:** http://www.urbn.com. **Description:** A clothing and housewares retail chain. **Positions advertised include:** Buyer; Divisional Merchandise Manager; Accounts Payable Associate; IT Operations Manager; Sr. Network Engineer. **Corporate headquarters location:** This location. **Listed on:** NASDAQ. **Stock exchange symbol:** URBN.

WAWA INC.
260 West Baltimore Pike, Wawa PA 19063. 610/358-8000. **Contact:** Personnel Director. **World Wide Web address:** http://www.wawa.com. **Description:** Wawa is a convenience store chain with operations throughout Pennsylvania. **Corporate headquarters location:** This location. **Operations at this facility include:** This location houses administrative offices.

WEIS MARKETS, INC.
1000 South Second Street, P.O. Box 471, Sunbury PA 17801. 570/286-4571. **Fax:** 570/286-3286. **Contact:** Jim Kessler, Director of Management and Development. **World Wide Web address:** http://www.weis.com. **Description:** Operates 157 supermarkets in five states. **Positions advertised include:** POS Maintenance Technician; Fleet Maintenance Body Mechanic; Cashier; Store Manager; Clerk; Manager Trainee. **Special programs:** Internships. **Corporate headquarters location:** This location. **Other U.S. locations:** MD; NJ; NY; VA; WV. **Listed on:** New York Stock Exchange. **Stock exchange symbol:** WMK.

Rhode Island

BARNES & NOBLE BOOKSTORES
1350-B Bald Hill Road, Warwick RI 02886. 401/826-8885. **Contact:** Manager. **World Wide Web address:** http://www.bn.com. **Description:** A bookstore chain operating nationwide. This location has a cafe and music store in addition to its book department. **Other area locations:** Middletown RI; Smithfield RI.

BROOKS ECKERD PHARMACY
50 Service Avenue, Warwick RI 02886. 401/825-3900. **Fax:** 401/468-2699. **Contact:** Roy Greene, Director of Human Resources. **E-mail address:** careers@brookseckerd.com. **World Wide Web address:** http://www.brookseckerd.com. **Description:** Fourth largest U.S. drugstore chain. Operates over 330 retail drugstores throughout New England and the east coast. **NOTE:** See website current positions and application instructions. For corporate positions, send resume and salary requirements to the above address. **Positions advertised include:** EDI Coordinator; Manager of Merchandising Support; Patient Care Center Phone Representative; Graphic Artist/Communications Specialist; Technical Support Center Analyst; Pharmacy Technician; Manager; Assistant Manager; Sales Associate. **Corporate headquarters location:** This location. **Other U.S. locations:** CT; MA; ME; NH; VT. **Parent company:** The Jean Coutu Group, Inc. **Listed on:** Toronto Stock Exchange. **Stock exchange symbol:** PJC-SVA.TO. **President and CEO:** Michel Coutu. **Number of employees nationwide:** 8,900.

CVS
One CVS Drive, Woonsocket RI 02895. 401/765-1500. **Contact:** Human Resources. **World Wide Web address:** http://www.cvs.com. **Description:** CVS operates a chain of drugstores throughout the United States. CVS stores also offer a broad range of health and beauty aids, cosmetics, greeting cards, convenience foods, photo finishing services and other general merchandise. Founded in 1963. **NOTE:** See website for current job openings, to apply online and application instructions. Some individual stores cannot accept online applications. **Positions listed include:** Corporate Attorney; Customer Service Representative; Legal Assistant; IS Lead Architect; Senior Accountant; Senior Graphic Designer; Project Manager; Pricing Assistant. **Special programs:** Internships available. **Corporate headquarters location:** This location. **Other U.S. locations:** Nationwide. **Listed on:** New York Stock Exchange. **Stock exchange symbol:** CVS. **Annual sales/revenues:** More than $100 million.

VENDA RAVIOLI INC.
265 Atwells Avenue, Providence RI 02903. 401/421-9105. **Fax:** 401/421-6280. **Contact:** Human Resources. **E-mail address:** info@vendaravioli.com. **World Wide Web address:** http://www.vendaravioli.com. **Description:** A store and café selling gourmet pasta, specialty foods and kitchenware. Affiliated with the gourmet Italian restaurant Costantino's Ristorante & Caffe. **NOTE:** Inquire in person about current job openings in retail sales, food preparation and administration.

South Carolina

BABIES 'R US
605 Haywood Road, Greenville SC 29607. 864/297-9444. **Contact:** Human Resources. **E-mail address:** bruregion3@toysrus.com. **World Wide Web address:** http://www2.toysrus.com. **Description:** A retailer of baby and young children's products at over 165 stores nationwide. Founded in 1996. **NOTE:** Resumes are requested to be sent by e-mail. **Positions advertised include:** Assistant Manager; Cashier; Management; Sales Executive; Services Sales Representative; Stock Clerk. **Other area locations:** Augusta SC; Columbia SC; Greenville SC; North Charleston SC. **Other U.S. locations:** Nationwide. **Parent company:** Toys "R" Us, Inc. (Paramus NJ).

BI-LO, INC.
P.O. Drawer 99, Mauldin SC 29662. 864/234-1600. **Physical address:** 208 Industrial Boulevard, Greenville SC 29607. **Fax:** 864/234-6999. **Contact:** Scott Santos, Senior Vice President of Human Resources. **E-mail address:** bilohr@aholdusa.com. **World Wide Web address:** http://www.bi-lo.com. **Description:** Operates a supermarket chain with stores in South Carolina, North Carolina, Georgia, and Tennessee. **NOTE:** Second shifts offered. Resumes should be submitted online via the company Website. **Positions advertised**

include: Perishable Management Auditor. **Corporate headquarters location:** This location. **Parent company:** Ahold USA. **Annual sales/revenues:** $3.6 billion. **Number of employees:** 26,000.

CALE YARBOROUGH HONDA/MAZDA
2723 West Palmetto Street, Florence SC 29501. 843/669-5556. **Fax:** 843/667-0964. **Contact:** William Howell, Services Manager. **World Wide Web address:** http://www.caleyarboroughhonda.com. **Description:** An automobile dealership that sells new and used Hondas and Mazdas as well as other vehicles. Cale Yarborough Honda/Mazda also offers automobile repair services. **Positions advertised include:** Automotive Mechanic.

HAMRICK'S, INC.
742 Peachoid Road, Gaffney SC 29341. 864/489-6095. **Fax:** 864/489-8734. **Contact:** Michael McCabe, Director of Personnel. **E-mail address:** jobs@hamricks.com. **World Wide Web address:** http://www.hamricks.com. **Description:** Operates a chain of men's clothing stores. These stores are located in the southeastern United States at 20 different locations. **Positions advertised include:** Assistant Store Manager; District Manager; Retail Management Trainee. **Corporate headquarters location:** This location. **Other U.S. locations:** GA; NC; TN.

South Dakota

AUSTAD'S
2801 E 10th Street, Sioux Falls SD 57103. 605/331-4653. **Toll-free phone:** 800/444-1234. **Contact:** Human Resources. **E-mail address:** hr@austadgolf.com. **World Wide Web address:** http://www.austads.com. **Description:** A mail order company specializing in golf equipment. **NOTE:** Send resumes via e-mail with "Careers" as the subject. **Corporate headquarters location:** This location. **Other U.S. locations:** Blaine MN; Maplewood MN; Woodbury MN; Lincoln NE; Omaha NE; Fargo ND.

CORRAL WEST RANCHWEAR
1615 North Harrison, Pierre SD 57501. 605/224-8802. **Toll-free phone:** 800/688-9888. **Contact:** Human Resources. **E-mail address:** hr@corralewest.com. **World Wide Web address:** http://www.corralwest.com. **Description:** A western-wear apparel and work-wear retail chain with over 95 stores throughout the United States. In addition to its retail stores, Corral West also operates an e-commerce business based in Wyoming. **NOTE:** Contact individual stores about current openings, or see website. **Corporate headquarters location:** Cheyenne WY. **Other area locations:** Spearfish SD. **Other U.S. locations:** Nationwide.

SHOPKO STORES INC.
1845 Haines Avenue, Rapid City SD 57701. 605/342-1551. **Contact:** Human Resources. **E-mail address:** careers@shopko.com. **World Wide Web address:** http://www.shopko.com. **Description:** A department store. Founded in 1962. **NOTE:** See website to apply online, or visit the store to apply in person. **Positions advertised include:** Overnight Supervisor; Overnight Freight Team Members; General Merchandise Specialist; Apparel Specialist. **Corporate headquarters location:** Green Bay WI. **Other area locations:** Aberdeen; Mitchell; Sioux Falls, Watertown. **Other U.S. locations:** Nationwide. **Subsidiaries include:** Pamida Stores; ShopKo Express Rx. **Listed on:** New York Stock Exchange. **Stock exchange symbol:** SKO.

Tennessee

CATHERINES STORES CORPORATION
3742 Lamar Avenue, Memphis TN 38118. 901/363-3900. **Contact:** Human Resources. **E-mail address:** great.jobs@catherines.com. **World Wide Web address:** http://www.catherines.com. **Description:** Catherine's Stores Corporation is a specialty retailer of women's plus-size clothing and accessories, operating 400 stores nationwide. **NOTE:** Search for positions through Monster.com. **Corporate headquarters location:** This location. **Other U.S. locations:** Nationwide. **Subsidiaries include:** Added Dimensions; PS Plus Sizes; and The Answer. **Number of employees at this location:** 450. **Number of employees nationwide:** 3,800.

CRACKER BARREL OLD COUNTRY STORE, INC.
P.O. Box 787, Lebanon TN 37088-0787. 615/444-5533. Physical address: 305 Hartmann Drive, Lebanon TN 37087. **Fax:** 615/443-9476. **Contact:** Judy Brodhead, Employment Coordinator. **World Wide Web address:** http://www.crackerbarrelocs.com. **Description:** Operates a restaurant/retail chain with over 430 locations. Founded in 1969. NOTE: Search and apply for positions online. **Positions advertised include:** Accounting Manager; Manager of Financial Planning and Analysis; Construction Project Manager; Sr. Restaurant Analyst; Sr. Tax Research Analyst. **Corporate headquarters location:** This location. **Parent company:** CBRL Group, Inc. **Listed on:** NASDAQ. **Stock exchange symbol:** CBRL. **Annual sales/revenues:** More than $100 million. **Number of employees at this location:** 700.

DOLLAR GENERAL CORPORATION
100 Mission Ridge Drive, Goodlettsville TN 37072. 615/855-4000. **Recorded jobline:** 800/909-5627. **Contact:** Human Resources Department. **World Wide Web address:** http://www.dollargeneral.com. **Description:** Operates 6,700 general merchandise stores in 29 states. Founded in 1939. **NOTE:** Entry-level positions and second and third shifts are offered. Search and apply for positions online. **Positions advertised include:** Financial Analyst; Fleet Operations Supervisor; Programmer; Sr. Staff Accountant. **Corporate headquarters location:** This location. **Listed on:** New York Stock Exchange. **Stock exchange symbol:** DG. **Annual sales/revenues:** More than $100 million. **Number of employees at this location:** 1,000. **Number of employees nationwide:** 57,000.

FRED'S INC.
4300 New Getwell Road, Memphis TN 38118. 901/365-8880. **Fax:** 901/328-0354. **Contact:** Human Resources. **E-mail address:** H2@fredsinc.com. **World Wide Web address:** http://www.fredsinc.com. **Description:** Operates 530 discount general merchandise stores and 245 pharmacies in 14 southeastern states. The company also markets goods and services to 37 franchised stores. Founded in 1947. **Listed on:** NASDAQ. **Stock exchange symbol:** FRED. **Number of employees nationwide:** 9,000.

GOODY'S FAMILY CLOTHING, INC.
P.O. Box 22000, Knoxville TN 37933-2000. 865/966-2000. **Physical address:** 400 Goodies Lane, Knoxville TN 37922. **Fax:** 865/777-4220. **Contact:** Personnel. **World Wide Web address:** http://www.goodysonline.com. **Description:** An apparel retailer for women, men, and children. The company operates more than 335 stores in 18 states. **NOTE:** For corporate positions, fax resume to number above. Search and apply online for store positions. **Corporate headquarters location:** This location. **Other U.S. locations:** AL; AR; FL; GA; IL; IN; KY; LA; MO; MS; NC; OH; OK; SC; TN; TX; VA; WV. **Listed on:** NASDAQ. **Stock exchange symbol:** GDYS. **Chairman/CEO:** Robert M. Goodfriend. **Number of employees nationwide:** 4,335.

TRACTOR SUPPLY COMPANY (TSC)
200 Powell Place, Brentwood TN 37027. 615/366-4600. **Contact:** Human Resources. **World Wide Web address:** http://www.mytscstore.com. **Description:** With 430 stores in 30 states, TSC is one of the largest operators of retail farm stores throughout the United States. The company sells farm maintenance products, animal products, general maintenance products, lawn and garden products, light truck equipment, and work clothing. **Positions advertised include:** Database Administrator; EDI Coordinator; Manager, Merchandise Control Team; Telecommunications Engineer. **Corporate headquarters location:** This

location. **Listed on:** NASDAQ. **Stock exchange symbol:** TSCO. **Number of employees nationwide:** 2,200.

WILLIAMS-SONOMA, INC.
4300 Concorde Road, Memphis TN 38118. 901/795-2625. **Contact:** Human Resources Director. **World Wide Web address:** http://www.williams-sonoma.com. **Description:** Williams-Sonoma is a retailer of cookware, serving equipment, and other specialty items. Products are sold both through retail stores and mail-order catalogs under the brand names Williams-Sonoma, Hold Everything, Gardener's Eden, Pottery Barn, and Chambers. **NOTE:** Search and apply for positions online. **Positions advertised include:** General Operations Manager; Maintenance Manager. **Operations at this facility include:** This location is the company's distribution center.

Texas

ANCIRA ENTERPRISES INC.
6111 Bandera Road, San Antonio TX 78238-1643. 210/681-4900. **Contact:** Human Resources. **World Wide Web address:** http://www.ancira.com. **Description:** Sells new and used automobiles including Chevrolet, Subaru, and Volkswagen. This location also has a service, parts, and body shop. **Corporate headquarters location:** This location.

W.O. BANKSTON LINCOLN MERCURY
4747 LBJ Freeway, Dallas TX 75244. 972/233-1441. **Fax:** 972/386-8292. **Contact:** Human Resources. **World Wide Web address:** http://www.bankstonlincoln.com. **Description:** A car dealer offering both new and used vehicles. **Other area locations:** Frisco TX; Lewisville TX; Dallas TX; Irving TX; Grand Prairie TX.

BLOCKBUSTER ENTERTAINMENT GROUP
1201 Elm Street, Suite 2100, Dallas TX 75270. 214/854-3000. **Fax:** 214/854-3241. **Contact:** Personnel Director. **World Wide Web address:** http://www.blockbuster.com. **Description:** Operates a chain of video rental and music retail stores. There are approximately 7,100 Blockbuster locations worldwide. **NOTE:** Please visit website to search for jobs and apply online. Entry-level positions are offered. **Positions advertised include:** Human Resources Manager; IT Executive; Loss Prevention Representative; Sales Representative. **Corporate headquarters location:** This location. **Other U.S. locations:** Nationwide. **International locations:** Worldwide. **Parent company:** Viacom. **Listed on:** New York Stock Exchange. **Stock exchange symbol:** BBI. **Number of employees worldwide:** 89,000.

THE BOMBAY COMPANY, INC.
550 Bailey Avenue, Suite 700, Fort Worth TX 76107-2111. 817/870-1847. **Fax:** 817/348-7090. **Recorded jobline:** 817/339-3799. **Contact:** Human Resources. **E-mail address:** hr@us.bombayco.com. **World Wide Web address:** http://www.bombayco.com. **Description:** A specialty retailer of ready-to-assemble home furnishings, prints, and accessories. Products are sold through over 400 Bombay Company and Alex & Ivy Stores. **Positions advertised include:** Internet Marketing Business Development Manager; On-Line Store Manager; Human Resources Generalist; Buyer – Lighting and Candles. **Special programs:** Internships. **Corporate headquarters location:** This location. **Other U.S. locations:** Nationwide. **International locations:** Canada. **Listed on:** New York Stock Exchange. **Stock exchange symbol:** BBA. **Number of employees nationwide:** 4,000.

BRIDGESTONE AMERICAS HOLDING, INC. /FIRESTONE, INC.
6050 South Padre Island A, Corpus Christi TX 78412. 361/993-1375. **Contact:** Sandy Scarbro, Human Resources. **World Wide Web address:** http://www.bridgestone-firestone.com. **Description:** An automotive services and manufacturing company. **Corporate headquarters location:** Nashville TN. **Operations at this facility include:** This location is a district office for south Texas.

BROOKSHIRE BROTHERS INC.
P.O. Box 1688, Lufkin TX 75902. 936/634-8155. **Physical address:** 1201 Ellen Trout Drive, Lufkin TX 75904. **Contact:** Human Resources. **World Wide Web address:** http://www.brookshirebrothers.com. **Description:** Operates a retail grocery chain. **NOTE:** Please visit website to submit your resume online. **Corporate headquarters location:** This location.

COMPUSA INC.
14951 North Dallas Parkway, Dallas TX 75254. 972/982-4000. **Fax:** 972/982-4942 **Contact:** Human Resources. **World Wide Web address:** http://www.compusa.com. **Description:** CompUSA Inc. operates over 218 high-volume computer superstores in 54 metropolitan areas throughout the United States. **Positions advertised include:** Media Buyer; Senior CRM Programmer; Front End Manager; Tax Accountant; Staff Accountant; DC Warehouse Manager; Lease Analyst; Sales Manager in Training. **Corporate headquarters location:** This location. **Other U.S. locations:** Nationwide. **Parent company:** Grupo Sanborns. **Listed on:** Privately held.

DAVIS FOOD CITY INC.
P.O. Box 8748, Houston TX 77249-8748. 713/695-2826. **Physical address;** 1111 West Cavalcade Street, Houston TX 77009. **Fax:** 713/695-4057. **Contact:** Human Resources. **E-mail address:** employment@davisfoodcity.com. **World Wide Web address:** http://www.davisfoodcity.com. **Description:** Operates a grocery store chain. **Positions advertised include:** Meat Department Personnel; Produce Department Personnel; Front-End Managers; Store Management. **Corporate headquarters location:** This location.

DUNLAP COMPANY
200 Bailey Avenue, Suite 100, Fort Worth TX 76107. 817/336-4985. **Contact:** Human Resources. **World Wide Web address:** http://www.dunlaps.com. **Description:** Operates a chain of department stores with over 50 locations. The stores operate under the following names: Dunlaps, McClurkans, Kerr's; M.M. Cohn, Heironimus, Stripling & Cox, Porteus, and The White House. Founded in 1892. **NOTE:** Applicants interested in retail sales should apply at the closest store location. **Corporate headquarters location:** This location. **Other U.S. locations:** Nationwide. **Operations at this facility include:** Administration. **Listed on:** Privately held. **President:** Edward Martin.

FERGUSON ENTERPRISES, INC.
19 Burwood Lane, San Antonio TX 78216. 210/344-4950. **Fax:** 210/344-1253. **Contact:** Human Resources. **E-mail address:** resumes@ferguson.com. **World Wide Web address:** http://www.ferguson.com. **Description:** A retail and wholesale distributor of plumbing supplies. **Positions advertised include:** Sales/Management Trainee; Controller Trainee. **Corporate headquarters location:** This location. **Other U.S. locations:** Nationwide.

FIESTA MART INC.
1530 Independence Boulevard, Missouri City TX 77489. 281/261-0200. **Contact:** Human Resources. **World Wide Web address:** http://www.fiestamart.com. **Description:** Operates a chain of grocery stores throughout Texas. **Corporate headquarters location:** This location. **Other area locations:** Dallas/Ft. Worth; Austin; Waco TX.

FIRST CASH, INC.
690 East Lamar Boulevard, Suite 400, Arlington TX 76011. 817/460-3947. **Contact:** Human Resources. **World Wide Web address:** http://www.firstcash.com. **Description:** Acquires, establishes, and operates pawn and short-term loan stores. First Cash also operates more than 25 check-cashing stores. **Corporate headquarters location:** This location. **Other U.S. locations:** CA; OR; VA: DC; IL; MD; MO; OK; SC. **International locations:** Mexico.

FOLEY'S
1110 Main Street, Houston TX 77002. 713/405-7035. **Contact:** Human Resources. **World Wide Web address:** http://www2.shopmay.com. **Description:** One location of the department store chain operating through over 50 stores. **NOTE:** Apply online at the company's website or at the nearest Foley's store location. **Positions advertised include:** General Sales Associate; Commission Sales Associate; Cosmetics Beauty Advisor; Fine Jewelry Associate. **Parent company:** The May Department Stores Company.

FOOD BASKET IGA
1926 North Bryant Boulevard, San Angelo TX 76903. 325/658-5602. **Contact:** Human Resources. **Description:** A grocery store chain with locations throughout Texas. **Corporate headquarters location:** This location.

FOXWORTH-GALBRAITH
P.O. Box 799002, 17111 Waterview Parkway, Dallas TX 75252. 972/437-6100. **Fax:** 972-454-4251. **Contact:** Human Resources. **World Wide Web address:** http://www.foxgal.com. **Description:** A building materials retailer. **Corporate headquarters locations:** This location. **Other area locations:** Statewide. **Other U.S. locations:** AZ; CO; NM. **Listed on:** Privately held.

FRIENDLY CHEVROLET COMPANY, INC.
2754 North Stemmons Freeway, Dallas TX 75207. 214/920-1900. **Contact:** Trisha Casey, Human Resources Manager. **World Wide Web address:** http://www.friendlychevy.com. **Description:** A dealership of both new and used automobiles.

GAMESTOP
2250 William D. Tate Avenue, Grapevine TX 76051. 817/424-2000. **Fax:** 817/424-2800. **Contact:** Human Resources. **World Wide Web address:** http://www.gamestop.com. **Description:** A national retailer of interactive games and accessories. Operates more than 475 stores in the United States and Puerto Rico under the names Babbage's, Software Etc., Gamestop, SuperSoftware, and Planet X. **NOTE:** Address correspondence to the attention of Michelle. **Corporate headquarters location:** This location. **Listed on:** New York Stock Exchange. **Stock exchange symbol:** GME. **CEO:** R. Richard Fontaine.

GILLMAN COMPANIES
10595 West Sam Houston Parkway South, Houston TX 77099. 713/477-8801. **Toll-free phone:** 800/933-7809. Physical address: 2000 Goodyear Drive, Houston TX 77017. **Fax:** 713/776-4849. **Contact:** Human Resources. **World Wide Web address:** http://www.gillmanauto.com. **Description:** An automobile dealership group. Gillman operates dealerships selling Acura, Honda, Hyundai, Lincoln, Mazda, Mercury, Mitsubishi, Nissan, Subaru, and Suzuki automobiles. Founded in 1938. **NOTE:** See corporate website for list of Human Resources contact by dealer.

HEB GROCERY COMPANY
P.O. Box 839999, San Antonio TX 78283. 210/938-8000. **Physical address**: 646 South Main Avenue, San Antonio TX 78204. **Recorded jobline:** 210/938-5222. **Contact:** Human Resources. **E-mail address:** careers@heb.com. **World Wide Web address:** http://www.heb.com. **Description:** Operates a chain of retail grocery stores. Founded in 1905. **NOTE:** Interested jobseekers should contact the jobline before sending a resume. **Office hours:** Monday - Friday, 8:00 a.m. - 5:00 p.m. **Corporate headquarters location:** This location. **Listed on:** Privately held. **President:** Charles Butt.

JC PENNEY COMPANY, INC.
6501 Legacy Drive, Plano TX 75024. Dallas TX 75301. 972/431-1000. **Contact:** Human Resources. **World Wide Web address:** http://www.jcpenney.net. **Description:** JC Penney Company is a national retail merchandise sales and service corporation with department stores nationwide. JC Penney sells apparel, home furnishings, and leisure lines in catalogs and 1,111 stores. **NOTE:** Jobseekers should apply online or at a nearby store location. This store also has positions in its Hair and Nail Salons, Portrait Galleries and Optical Departments. **Positions advertised include:** Intimate Apparel Technical Designer; Bindery Equipment Operator; Department Manager Trainee; Claims Specialist; Fit Model; Administrative Support. **Special programs:** Internships. **Corporate headquarters location:** This location. **Other U.S. locations:** Nationwide. **Operations at this facility include:** This location houses administrative offices. **Listed on:** New York Stock Exchange. **Stock exchange symbol:** JCP. **Number of employees worldwide:** 267,000.

MAC HAIK CHEVROLET INC.
11711 Katy Freeway, Houston TX 77079. 281/497-6600. **Contact:** Human Resources. **World Wide Web address:** http://www.machaikchevy.com. **Description:** An automobile dealership.

MATTRESS GIANT
2344 Greencrest Boulevard, Rockwall TX 75087. 972/772-3969. **Toll-free phone:** 800/442-6823. **Contact:** Human Resources. **World Wide Web address:** http://www.mattressgiant.com. **Description:** With more than 250 stores nationwide, Mattress Giant is a leading retailer of bedding. **NOTE:** Part-time positions offered. Apply online. **Positions advertised include:** Sales Professionals; Store Porter.

MEN'S WEARHOUSE
5803 Glenmont Drive, Houston TX 77081. 713/664-3692. **Contact:** Human Resources Department. **World Wide Web address:** http://www.menswearhouse.com. **Description:** One of the largest off-price retailers of men's tailored business attire in the United States. The stores offer designer brand-name and private-label suits, sports jackets, slacks, dress shirts, and accessories at discount prices. **Positions advertised include:** Operations Manager; Customer Service Assistant; Wardrobe Consultant; Tailor, Store Manager; Professional Truck Driver. **Corporate headquarters location:** This location. **Other U.S. locations:** Nationwide. **International locations:** Canada. **Listed on:** New York Stock Exchange. **Stock exchange symbol:** MW.

MICHAEL'S STORES, INC.
P.O. Box 619566, Dallas TX 75261-9566. 972/409-1300. **Physical address:** 8000 Bent Branch Drive, Irving TX 75063. **Contact:** Human Resources. **World Wide Web address:** http://www.michaels.com. **Description:** A nationwide specialty retailer of art, crafts, and decorative items and supplies. Michael's Stores operates 628 stores in 48 states, Canada, and Puerto Rico. **NOTE:** Jobseekers interested in hourly positions should apply at the nearest store. **Positions advertised include:** Training Designer; Construction Coordinator; Associate Buyer; Administrative Assistant; Set-up Coordinator; Senior Program Analyst. **Corporate headquarters location:** This location. **Listed on:** New York Stock Exchange. **Stock exchange symbol:** MIK.

MINYARD FOOD STORES, INC.
777 Freeport Parkway, Coppell TX 75019. 972/393-8333. **Fax:** 972/304-3828. **Contact:** Human Resources. **E-mail address:** jobs@minyards.com. **World Wide Web address:** http://www.minyards.com. **Description:** A retail grocery chain with more than 70 stores. Stores include Minyard Food Stores, Sack 'n Save, and Carnival Food Stores. **NOTE:** Jobseekers interested in management or corporate positions should submit their resumes to the home office in Coppell. For store positions, jobseekers should visit the nearest location to complete an application. **Corporate headquarters location:** This location. **Listed on:** Privately held.

MOORE SUPPLY COMPANY
P.O. Box 448, Conroe TX 77305. 936/756-4445. **Physical address**: 200 West Loop 336 North, Conroe

TX 77301. **Fax:** 936/441-8468. **Contact:** Human Resources. **World Wide Web address:** http://www.mooresupply.com. **Description:** Engaged in the retail and wholesale of plumbing supplies, lavatory supplies, tubs, and toilets. **NOTE:** This company has retail and warehouse locations throughout Texas. For warehouse positions, contact Ross Ryon at 214/351-6411. For management positions, contact Karen Landry at kvlandry@lcr-m.com or at 800/888-9915x4214. **Operations at this facility include:** Administration.

MUSTANG TRACTOR & EQUIPMENT COMPANY
P.O. Box 1373, Houston TX 77252. 713/460-7232. **Fax:** 713/690-2287. **Recorded jobline:** 713/460-7267. **Contact:** Human Resources. **World Wide Web address:** http://www.mustangcat.com. **Description:** Sells and services Caterpillar heavy equipment and engines. **Special programs:** Development Sales/Management Training. **NOTE:** This company has locations throughout Texas. See its website for locations and job listings. **Corporate headquarters location:** This location.

ANTHONY NAK FINE JEWELRY
800 Brazos Street, Suite 410, Austin TX 78701. 512/454-7029. Fax: 512/454-7031. **Contact:** Human Resources. **E-mail address:** retail@anthonynak.com. **World Wide Web address:** http://www.anthonynak.com. **Description:** A specialty art jewelry store known for its appeal to movie stars and other high-profile people. **NOTE:** Apply during store hours or mail resume.

THE NEIMAN MARCUS GROUP, INC.
1618 Main Street, Dallas TX 75201. 214/573-5688. **Contact:** Human Resources. **World Wide Web address:** http://www.neimanmarcus.com. **Description:** Operates two specialty retailing businesses: Neiman Marcus and Bergdorf Goodman. Combined, these two chains offer men's and women's apparel, fashion accessories, jewelry, fine china, and moderately priced crystal and silver. **NOTE:** Neiman Marcus has all corporate and retail job openings listed on its corporate website. **Corporate headquarters location:** This location. **Subsidiaries include:** NM Direct is a direct marketing company, which advertises primarily through the use of such specialty catalogs as Neiman Marcus and Horchow.

NICHOLS FORD
2401 East Interstate 20 at Campus Drive, Fort Worth TX 76119. 817/429-7750. **Contact:** Human Resources. **World Wide Web address:** http://www.nicholsford.com. **Description:** A new and used car dealership.

OFFICE DEPOT, INC.
2209 Rutland Drive, Suite A100, Austin TX 78758. 512/837-8999. **Fax:** 512/837-1221. **Contact:** Human Resources. **World Wide Web address:** http://www.officedepot.com. **Description:** One of the nation's leading office products dealers. This company has locations throughout Texas and the United States. **Corporate headquarters location:** Delray Beach FL. **Subsidiaries include:** Viking Office Products is a direct mail marketer. **Listed on:** New York Stock Exchange. **Stock exchange symbol:** ODP.

OSHMAN'S SPORTING GOODS INC.
2320 Maxwell Lane, Houston TX 77023. 713/928-3171. **Contact:** Human Resources. **World Wide Web address:** http://www.oshmans.com. **Description:** Offers a broad line of sporting goods and equipment as well as active sports apparel. Most stores operate under the name SuperSports USA. **Corporate headquarters location:** This location.

PARK PLACE MOTORCARS
4023 Oak Lawn Avenue, Dallas TX 75219. 214/526-8701. **Toll-free phone:** 888-354-7176. **Fax:** 214/443-8270. **Contact:** Human Resources. **World Wide Web address:** http://www.parkplacetexas.com. **Description:** A new and pre-owned car dealership for Mercedes-Benz, Porsche, Lexus, and Audi automobiles. Motocars, its parent company, has several dealerships throughout Dallas and Texas. **NOTE:** This company's website lists job openings for its corporate office and its dealerships. Entry-level positions are offered. **Corporate headquarters location:** This location. **Other area locations:** Houston TX; Plano TX.

PIER 1 IMPORTS
P.O. Box 961020, Fort Worth TX 76161-0020. 817/878-8000. **Contact:** Staffing Manager. **World Wide Web address:** http://www.pier1.com. **Description:** Pier 1 Imports is engaged in the specialty retailing of handcrafted decorative home furnishings and accessories imported from approximately 50 countries around the world. The company also owns CargoKids, a children's furniture and accessories store. **NOTE:** The company's website lists all management positions for its corporate office, distribution centers and retail stores. Jobseekers interested in hourly retail positions can also visit the nearest store. **Positions advertised include:** Merchandise Planner; Check Collector; Payroll Tax Specialist; Allocations Analyst; Assistant Manager; Distribution Center Associates; Divisional Visual Manager; Retail Sales Associate. **Corporate headquarters location:** This location. **Other U.S. locations:** Nationwide. **Listed on:** New York Stock Exchange. **Stock exchange symbol:** PIR. **Number of employees worldwide:** 18,000.

RADIOSHACK
300 West Third Street, Suite 200, Fort Worth TX 76102. 817/415-3700. **Fax:** 817/415-3243. **Recorded jobline:** 817/415-2949. **Contact:** Employment Opportunities. **World Wide Web address:** http://www.radioshack.com. **Description:** Sells a wide variety of consumer electronic parts and equipment through more than 7,000 stores nationwide. **Corporate headquarters location:** This location. **Listed on:** New York Stock Exchange. **Stock exchange symbol:** RSH.

RALSTON DRUG AND DISCOUNT LIQUOR
3147 Southmore Boulevard, Houston TX 77004. 713/524-3045. **Contact:** Human Resources. **Description:** Operates discount liquor and drug stores with 18 local outlets.

RANDALLS FOOD MARKETS
3663 Briar Park, Houston TX 77042.**Fax:** 713/435-2499. **Recorded jobline:** 713/268-3404. **Contact:** Recruiter. **E-mail address:** employment@randalls.com. **World Wide Web address:** http://www.randalls.com. **Description:** Operates 138 retail grocery stores in Texas. It is a subsidiary of Safeway Inc., a chain with stores throughout the United States and Canada. **Corporate headquarters location:** This location. **Listed on:** New York Stock Exchange. **Stock exchange symbol:** SWY.

RENT-A-CENTER
5700 Tennyson Parkway, 3rd Floor, Plano TX 75024. 972/801-1100. **Toll-free phone:** 800/275-2696. **Fax:** 972/943-0119. **Contact:** Staffing. **World Wide Web address:** http://www.rentacenter.com. **Description:** Rents furniture, appliances, stereos, and other furnishings and equipment. **Special programs:** Internships. **Corporate headquarters location:** This location. **Other U.S. locations:** Nationwide. **Listed on:** NASDAQ. **Stock exchange symbol:** RCII. **Number of employees nationwide:** 15,400.

RICE EPICUREAN MARKETS INC.
5333 Gulfton Street, Houston TX 77081. 713/662-7700. **Contact:** Human Resources. **E-mail address:** employment@riceepicurean.com. **World Wide Web address:** http://www.riceepicurean.com. **Description:** Operates and manages a chain of five food stores in the Houston area. **NOTE:** All positions require an application which can found on the company's website. **Positions advertised include:** Cashier; Sacker; Meat Cutters; Maid; Bakery Attendants. **Office hours:** Monday - Friday, 8:00 a.m. - 5:00 p.m. **Corporate headquarters location:** This location. **Operations at this facility include:** Administration.

JACK ROACH FORD
6445 Southwest Freeway, Houston TX 77074. 281/588-5000. **Contact:** Human Resources. **World Wide Web address:** http://www.jackroach.com. **Description:** A new and used vehicle dealership.

SAKS FIFTH AVENUE
13550 North Dallas Parkway, Dallas TX 75240. 972/458-7000. **Contact:** Human Resources Manager. **World Wide Web address:** http://www.saksincorporated.com. **Description:** Saks Fifth Avenue is a retail chain emphasizing soft-goods products, primarily apparel for men, women, and children. **NOTE:** Jobseekers interested in management positions should apply online at the company's website. Jobseekers interested in sales positions can apply online at the website or visit the nearest store location. **Corporate headquarters location:** Birmingham AL. **Parent company:** Saks Incorporated operates approximately 380. The company's stores include Saks Fifth Avenue, Parisian, Proffit's, Younker's, Herberger's, Carson Pirie Scott, Boston Store, Bergner's, and Off 5th, the company's outlet store. Saks Incorporated also operates two retail catalogs and several retail Internet sites. **Listed on:** New York Stock Exchange. **Stock exchange symbol:** SKS. **Number of employees nationwide:** 55,000.

SOUTHLAND CORPORATION
P.O. Box 711, Dallas TX 75221. 214/828-7011. **Physical address:** 2711 North Haskell Avenue, Suite B10, Dallas TX 75204-2906. **Fax:** 214/841-6688. **Recorded jobline:** 866/471-1562. **Contact:** Human Resources. **World Wide Web address:** http://www.7eleven.com. **Description:** Owns and operates 7-Eleven convenience stores. **NOTE:** Jobseekers interested in hourly retail positions should call the recorded jobline between 7 a.m. and 11 p.m. CST to speak with a recruiter. Jobseekers interested in corporate and divisional positions should apply online at the company's website. **Corporate headquarters location:** This location. **Listed on:** New York Stock Exchange. **Stock exchange symbol:** SE. **Number of employees nationwide:** 33,000.

SPORTS SUPPLY GROUP, INC.
P.O. Box 7726, 1901 Diplomat Drive, Dallas TX 75234. 972/484-9484. **Fax:** 972/884-7465. **Recorded jobline:** 972/884-7280. **Contact:** Human Resources. **E-mail address:** dallashr@sportsupplygroup.com. **World Wide Web address:** http://www.sportsupplygroup.com. **Description:** A catalog retailer of sporting goods and recreational products. **NOTE:** Fax or e-mail resumes with cover letters including a salary history. **Positions advertised include:** Outbound Sales Associate; Customer Care Associate; Government Sales Associate; Staff Accountant; Inside Sales Associate. **Corporate headquarters location:** This location. **Other U.S. locations:** Alabama. **Number of employees nationwide:** 250.

STAR FURNITURE COMPANY
P.O. Box 219169, Houston TX 77218-9169. 281/492-5445. **Physical address:** 16666 Barker Springs Road, Houston TX 77084. **Fax:** 281/579-5909. **Contact:** Paige Olson, Human Resources Director. **World Wide Web address:** http://www.starfurniture.com. **Description:** Engaged in the retail sale of home furnishings. **NOTE:** Full-time and part-time shifts are offered. **Positions advertised include:** Sales Consultant; Office Associate; Service Assistant; Warehouse Worker; Driver's Helper. **Corporate headquarters location:** This location. **Other area locations:** Austin TX; Bryan TX; San Antonio TX. **Parent company:** Berkshire Hathaway Inc. **Listed on:** Privately held.

STERLING McCALL TOYOTA
9400 Southwest Freeway, Houston TX 77074. 713/270-3900. **Contact:** Human Resources. **World Wide Web address:** http://www.sterlingmccalltoyota.com. **Description:** Sells and services automobiles. **NOTE:** See website for job listings and contact information. **Positions advertised include:** Line Technician; Salesperson.

STRAUS-FRANK COMPANY/CAR QUEST
P.O. Box 600, San Antonio TX 78292-0600. 210/226-0101. **Contact:** Peggy Mamirez, Human Resources Manager. **Description:** A wholesaler of automobile parts. Straus-Frank Company is a partner with GPI who owns the retail chain automotive parts store Car Quest. **NOTE:** Car Quest has locations throughout Texas and the United States. Apply in person at the nearest location. See website for locations and addresses. **Corporate headquarters location:** This location.

STRIPLING & COX
6370 Camp Bowie Boulevard, Fort Worth TX 76116. 817/738-7361. **Contact:** Human Resources. **Description:** A department store offering men's and women's apparel and home furnishings. **Other area locations:** Arlington TX. **Parent company:** The Dunlop Company (Fort Worth TX).

SUPER S FOODS
401 Isom Road, Building 100, San Antonio TX 78216. 210/344-1960. **Fax:** 210/341-6326. **Contact:** Human Resources. **Description:** A corporate division of the retail grocery store chain Super S Foods. Super S Foods has stores throughout Texas. **NOTE:** A completed application must be mailed or faxed to the company. The application can be found on the company's website. **Positions advertised include:** Store Manager; Assistant Store Manager; Market Manager; Produce Manager. **Corporate headquarters location:** This location. **Parent company:** Mass Marketing, Inc.

TOM THUMB FOOD & PHARMACY
3663 Briar Park, Houston TX 77042. **Fax:** 713/435-2499. **Recorded jobline:** 214/355-7444. **Contact:** Recruitment Office. **E-mail address:** employment@tomthumb.com. **World Wide Web address:** http://www.tomthumb.com. **Description:** A chain of supermarkets, including Randall's stores. **Special programs:** Internships. **Corporate headquarters location:** Houston TX. **Parent company:** Safeway. **Operations at this facility include:** Sales; Service. **Listed on:** New York Stock Exchange. **Stock exchange symbol:** SWY.

TUESDAY MORNING CORPORATION
6250 LBJ Freeway, Dallas TX 75240. 972/387-3562. **Contact:** Human Resources. **World Wide Web address:** http://www.tuesdaymorning.com. **Description:** Operates a chain of over 400 discount retail stores under the name Tuesday Morning Inc. The stores sell close-out gift and houseware merchandise at prices ranging from 50 percent to 80 percent below retail prices. **Positions advertised include:** Store Manager; Assistant Store Manager; Senior Store Associate; Store Associate. **NOTE:** The stores are open to the public 10 times a year only for four- to eight-week sales events. **Corporate headquarters location:** This location. **Other U.S. locations:** Nationwide. **Listed on:** NASDAQ. **Stock exchange symbol:** TUES.

UNITED SUPERMARKETS
7830 Orlando Avenue, Lubbock TX 79423. 806/792-0220. **Contact:** Human Resources. **E-mail address:** info@unitedtexas.com. **World Wide Web address:** http://www.unitedtexas.com. **Description:** This chain of supermarkets has more than 40 stores in Texas. **NOTE:** This company provides a list of all its locations on its website. For retail positions, apply at the nearest location. **Special programs:** Manager Training. **Corporate headquarters location:** This location.

VF FACTORY OUTLET
805 Factory Outlet Drive, Hempstead TX 77445-5604. 979/826-8277. **Contact:** Human Resources. **World Wide Web address:** http://www.vffo.com. **Description:** One location of a discount retailer of jeanswear, sportswear, activewear, intimate apparel, and occupational apparel. **NOTE:** Jobseekers interested in management positions should mail their resumes to: Human Resources Manager, Dept. W., VF Outlet, 801 Hill Avenue, Reading PA 19610-3026. Jobseekers interested in other positions should apply online or at the nearest store location. **Positions advertised**

include: Store Management Trainee; Sales Associates; Warehouse Security Associates; Custodial Maintenance. **Corporate headquarters location:** Reading PA. **Other area locations:** Corsicana TX; Le Marque TX; Livingston TX; Mineral Wells TX; San Marcos TX; Sulphur Springs TX. **Other U.S. locations:** Nationwide.

WALGREEN COMPANY
8590 Long Point Road, Houston TX 77055. 713/468-7815. **Contact:** Human Resources. **World Wide Web address:** http://www.walgreens.com. **Description:** Walgreen is a retail drug store chain with more than 3,600 stores nationwide. The company sells prescription and proprietary drugs and also carries cosmetics, toiletries, tobacco, and general merchandise. **NOTE:** Apply online for corporate, support, and retail positions. **Corporate headquarters location:** Deerfield IL. **Listed on:** New York Stock Exchange. **Stock exchange symbol:** WAG.

WHOLE FOODS MARKET INC.
550 Bowie Street, Austin TX 78703. 512/477-4455. **Contact:** Human Resources. **World Wide Web address:** http://www.wholefoodsmarket.com. **Description:** Operates a chain of 180 natural foods supermarkets in 30 states, Washington DC, Canada, and the UK. **Positions advertised include:** Business Systems Analyst; National Replenishment Coordinator; Purchasing Systems Team Lead; Senior Buyer/Product Developer. **Corporate headquarters location:** This location. **Listed on:** NASDAQ. **Stock exchange symbol:** WFMI.

ZALE CORPORATION
901 West Walnut Hill Lane, Mail Station 5B-12, Irving TX 75038. 972/580-4000. **Fax:** 972/580-5266. **Contact:** Manager of Corporate Staffing. **World Wide Web address:** http://www.zalecorp.com. **Description:** A specialty retail firm engaged in selling fine jewelry and related products. **Positions advertised include:** Real Estate Attorney; Records Clerk; Curriculum Designer; Merchandise Planning Director. **Corporate headquarters location:** This location. **Other U.S. locations:** Nationwide. **Listed on:** New York Stock Exchange. **Stock exchange symbol:** ZLC. **Number of employees worldwide:** 20,000.

Utah

BARNES & NOBLE
1104 East 2100 South, Salt Lake City UT 84106. 801/463-2610. **Contact:** Store Manager. **World Wide Web address:** http://www.bn.com. **Description:** A bookstore chain operating nationwide. This location has a cafe and music department in addition to its book department. **Corporate headquarters location:** New York NY. **Listed on:** New York Stock Exchange. **Stock exchange symbol:** BKS.

BURLINGTON COAT FACTORY
340 East University Parkway, Orem UT 84058-7602. 801/224-1700. **Contact:** Human Resources. **E-mail address:** employment.opportunities@coat.com. **World Wide Web address:** http://www.coat.com. **Description:** An apparel discount store. **NOTE:** Please contact the local store to learn about immediate employment opportunities. Corporate headquarters address is ATTN: Field Recruiting Department, 1830 Route 130, Burlington NJ 08016. **Positions advertised include:** Department Sales Manager; Customer Service Manager; Customer Service Supervisor; Receiving Supervisor; Sales Associate; Cashier; Computer Operator; Accounting Room Auditor; Loss Prevention Personnel; Fitting Room Sales Associate; Maintenance Personnel. **Corporate headquarters location:** Burlington NJ. **Other area locations:** Murray UT. **Other U.S. locations:** Nationwide.

KEN GARFF AUTOMOTIVE GROUP
531 South State Street, Salt Lake City UT 84111. 801/521-6111. **Contact:** Human Resources. **World Wide Web address:** http://www.kengarff.com. **Description:** An automotive dealer group with six locations and 14 automotive product lines. **NOTE:** See website for current job openings and to apply online. Entry-level positions are offered. **Special programs:** Apprenticeships; Training. **Corporate headquarters location:** This location.

NORDSTROM, INC.
50 South Main Street, Salt Lake City UT 84144-2012. 801/322-4200. **Contact:** Human Resources Department. **World Wide Web address:** http://www.nordstrom.com. **Description:** A specialty retailer that sells apparel, shoes, and accessories for the family. Nordstrom, Inc. also has a mail-order catalog division. **NOTE:** Visit the store to inquire about current job openings, or apply online. **Corporate headquarters location:** Seattle WA. **Other area locations:** Murray UT; Orem UT. **Other U.S. locations:** Nationwide.

SMITH'S FOOD & DRUG STORES
828 South 900 West, Salt Lake City UT 84104. 801/364-2548. **Contact:** Human Resources. **World Wide Web address:** http://www.smithsfoodanddrug.com. **Description:** Smith's Food & Drug Stores are designed for one-stop shopping and have specialty departments such as one-hour photo processing, hot prepared foods, delicatessen, seafood counter, frozen yogurt counter, bakery, florist, and pharmacy. **NOTE:** Please visit website to search for jobs and apply online, or apply in person. **Positions advertised include:** Retail Personnel; Pharmacy Workers; Manufacturers; Corporate Personnel. **Special programs:** Internships. **Parent company:** The Kroger Company. **Listed on:** New York Stock Exchange. **Stock exchange symbol:** KR.

SPORTS AUTHORITY
5550 South 900 East, Murray UT 84117. 801/263-3633. **Contact:** Human Resources. **World Wide Web address:** http://www.sportsauthority.com. **Description:** A retailer of outdoor goods such as athletic wear, hunting gear, fishing gear, and camping gear. **NOTE:** See website for current job openings, or contact the store. **Positions advertised include:** Store Associate; Store Manager. **Corporate headquarters location:** Denver CO. **Other U.S. locations:** Nationwide.

Vermont

BURLINGTON DRUG COMPANY
91 Catamount Drive, P.O. Box 1001, Milton VT 05468. 802/893-5105, extension 327. **Fax:** 802/893-5110. **Contact:** Maria Burns, Human Resources Director. **E-mail address:** maria@bddow.com. **Description:** Sells tobacco, candy, health and beauty aids, groceries, and beverages. **Positions advertised include:** Computer Programmer.

GREEN MOUNTAIN COFFEE ROASTERS, INC.
33 Coffee Lane, Waterbury VT 05676. 802/244-5621. **Toll-free phone:** 800/545-2326. **Fax:** 802/244-4745. **Contact:** Kari Larkin, Recruiter. **E-mail address:** jobs@gmcr.com. **World Wide Web address:** http://www.greenmountaincoffee.com. **Description:** Produces over 70 varieties of coffee, which are sold to over 7,000 wholesale customers including supermarkets, convenience stores, resorts, and office delivery services under the Newman's Own Organics and Green Mountain Coffee brands as well as through catalogs and the Internet. Founded in 1981. **Positions advertised include:** Maintenance Technician; Production Supervisor; Part-time Retail Associate; Facility Cleaner. **Corporate headquarters location:** This location. **Other locations:** AZ; CA; CT; FL; MA; NH; NY; PA. **Parent company:** Green Mountain Coffee, Inc. **Listed on:** NASDAQ. **Stock exchange symbol:** GMCR. **Annual sales/revenues:** $137 million. **Number of employees at this location:** 200. **Number of employees worldwide:** 717.

THE ORVIS COMPANY INC.
Historic Route 7A, Manchester VT 05254. 802/362-1300. **Fax:** 802/362-0141. **Contact:** Aniko Balzer, Human Resources Manager of Recruitment and Training. **E-mail address:** careers@orvis.com. **World Wide Web address:** http://www.orvis.com.

Description: The company sells hunting and fishing clothing, home furnishings, and country life gifts as well as arranging guided fishing and hunting trips. The company also operates over 40 company stores in the U.S. and Britain and runs fly-fishing and shooting seminars. Founded in 1856. **Positions advertised include:** Buyer/Product Development Specialist; Associate Art Director. **Corporate headquarters location:** This location. **Other area locations:** Sunderland VT. **Other U.S. locations:** Roanoke VA. **Listed on:** Privately held.

Virginia

ADVANCE AUTO PARTS, INC.
5673 Airport Road NW, Roanoke VA 24012. 540/362-4911. **Fax:** 540/561-6930. **Contact:** Director of Human Resources. **World Wide Web address:** http://www.advanceautoparts.com. **Description:** Operates a chain of 2,800 auto part stores in 40 states, Puerto Rico, and the Virgin Islands. **NOTE:** Submit application online. **Corporate headquarters location:** This location. **Listed on:** New York Stock Exchange. **Stock exchange symbol:** AAP. **Number of employees nationwide:** 41,000.

CAMELLIA FOODS
P.O. Box 2320, Norfolk VA 23501. 757/855-3371. **Contact:** Human Resources. **Description:** Operates three chains of grocery stores: Meatland, Food City, and Fresh Pride. **Corporate headquarters location:** This location.

CIRCUIT CITY STORES, INC.
9954 Mayland Drive, Richmond VA 23233-1464. 804/527-4000. **Toll-free phone:** 888/773-2489. **Fax:** 804/527-4086. **Contact:** Staffing & Planning. **E-mail address:** cc-jobs@circuitcity.com. **World Wide Web address:** http://www.circuitcity.com. **Description:** One of the largest U.S. retailers of brand-name consumer electronics and major appliances, as well as personal computers, music, and software. Circuit City has over 600 Circuit City and Circuit City Express stores in operation nationwide. Founded in 1949. **NOTE:** Search and apply for positions online. **Positions advertised include:** Accounting Analyst; Business Development Manager; Direct Marketing Analyst; Human Resources Manager' Inventory Manager; Programmer. **Special programs:** Internships. **Office hours:** Monday - Friday, 8:30 a.m. - 5:00 p.m. **Corporate headquarters location:** This location. **Other U.S. locations:** Nationwide. **Listed on:** New York Stock Exchange. **Stock exchange symbol:** CC. **Annual sales/revenues:** Nearly $10 billion. **Number of employees at this location:** 3,000. **Number of employees nationwide:** 45,000.

DOLLAR TREE STORES, INC.
500 Volvo Parkway, Chesapeake VA 23320. 757/321-5000. **Fax:** 757/321-5555. **Contact:** Human Resources. **World Wide Web address:** http://www.dollartree.com. **Description:** An operator of discount variety stores offering merchandise for $1. The company operates more than 2,500 stores in 48 states. **NOTE:** Search and apply for positions online. **Positions advertised include:** Payroll Manager; Marketing Communications Coordinator; Corporate Recruiter. **Corporate headquarters location:** This location. **Subsidiaries include:** Dollar Tree Distribution, Inc.; Dollar Tree Management, Inc. **Listed on:** NASDAQ. **Stock exchange symbol:** DLTR. **Number of employees nationwide:** 4,500.

HECHT'S
685 North Glebe Road, Arlington VA 22203-2199. 703/558-1200. **Contact:** Human Resources. **World Wide Web address:** http://www.hechts.com. **Description:** A general merchandise and apparel retailer, operating 61 stores. **NOTE:** Apply for positions online. **Parent company:** Federated Department Stores, Inc.

LORD & TAYLOR
7950 Tysons Corner Center, McLean VA 22102. 703/506-1156. **Contact:** Human Resources. **World Wide Web address:** http://www.lordandtaylor.com. **Description:** A full-line department store carrying clothing, accessories, and home furnishings. **NOTE:** Part-time jobs are offered. Request interview online. **Corporate headquarters location:** New York NY. **Parent company:** The May Department Stores Company. **Listed on:** New York Stock Exchange. **Stock exchange symbol:** MAY. **Number of employees at this location:** 300.

NATIONAL AUTOMOBILE DEALERS ASSOCIATION
8400 Westpark Drive, McLean VA 22102. 703/821-7000. **Contact:** Human Resources. **E-mail address:** recruiter@nada.org. **World Wide Web address:** http://www.nada.org. **Description:** A trade organization representing nearly 20,000 new car and truck dealerships. The association publishes a used car guide for dealers that offers insurance information and retirement plans for dealerships. **Corporate headquarters location:** This location. **Operations at this facility include:** Administration; Research and Development; Sales; Service. **Number of employees at this location:** 400.

PEEBLES DEPARTMENT STORES
One Peebles Street, South Hill VA 23970. 434/447-5297. **Contact:** Tim Moyer, Training and Recruitment Director. **World Wide Web address:** http://www.peebles.com. **Description:** Operates a department store chain of 140 stores in 17 states. **NOTE:** Apply for positions online. **Corporate headquarters location:** This location. **Parent company:** State Stores Inc. **Number of employees at this location:** 2,200. **Number of employees nationwide:** 2,340.

S&K FAMOUS BRANDS, INC.
11100 West Broad Street, Glen Allen VA 23060. 804/346-2500. **Fax:** 804/747-3979. **Contact:** Human Resources. **World Wide Web address:** http://www.skmenswear.com. **Description:** Engaged in the retail sale of men's clothing, furnishings, sportswear, and accessories. S&K Famous Brands operates over 240 stores. **NOTE:** Search and apply for positions online. **Positions advertised include:** Visual Communications Manager; Direct Marketing Database Manager. **Corporate headquarters location:** This location. **Listed on:** NASDAQ. **Stock exchange symbol:** SKFB. **Number of employees nationwide:** 1,575.

7-ELEVEN, INC.
7-ELEVEN CONVENIENCE STORES
5300 Shawnee Road, Alexandria VA 22312. 703/642-0711. **Toll-free phone:** 800/547-5711. **Fax:** 703/941-4687. **Recorded jobline:** 800/711-JOBS. **Contact:** Division Recruiter. **World Wide Web address:** http://www.7-eleven.com. **Description:** This location houses administrative offices. 7-Eleven operates 24,000 stores worldwide. Founded in 1927. **NOTE:** Search and apply for positions online. **Positions advertised include:** Field Consultant. **Special programs:** Internships. **Corporate headquarters location:** Dallas TX. **Operations at this facility include:** Divisional Headquarters; Sales; Service. **Listed on:** New York Stock Exchange. **Stock exchange symbol:** SE. **Number of employees nationwide:** 40,000.

Washington

ALBERTSON'S, INC.
14500 15th Avenue NE, Shoreline WA 98155. 206/365-2422. **Contact:** Human Resources. **E-mail address:** employment@albertsons.com. **World Wide Web address:** http://www.albertsons.com. **Description:** A full-service supermarket. **Corporate headquarters location:** Boise ID. **Listed on:** New York Stock Exchange. **Stock exchange symbol:** ABS.

ALL-STAR TOYOTA INC.
13355 Lake City Way NE, Seattle WA 98125. 206/367-0080. **Contact:** Personnel Department. **Description:** A retailer and wholesaler of automobile parts and services.

AMAZON.COM, INC.
605 5th Avenue South, Seattle WA 98104. 206/622-2335. **Contact:** Strategic Growth. **E-mail address:** jobs@amazon.com. **World Wide Web address:** http://www.amazon.com. **Description:** An online store engaged in the sale of books, videos, music, toys, and electronics. Amazon.com also offers online auctions. Founded in 1995. **NOTE:** If sending a resume via e-mail, please be sure the information is in an ASCII-text format. **Positions advertised include:** Technical Program/Product Manager; Senior Buyer; Software Development Engineer. **Corporate headquarters location:** This location. **Other U.S. locations:** New Castle DE; McDonough GA; Coffeyville KS; Cambellsville KY; Lexington KY; Fernley NV. **International locations:** Europe. **Listed on:** NASDAQ. **Stock exchange symbol:** AMZN. **President/CEO:** Jeffrey Bezos.

BJ'S PAINT'N PLACE INC.
6528 Capitol Boulevard South, Suite A, Olympia WA 98501. 360/943-3232. **Contact:** Human Resources. **World Wide Web address:** http://www.bjspaint.com. **Description:** A retail store offering paints, stains, wallpaper, fabric, finishes, brushes, and similar products.

BARNES & NOBLE BOOKSTORES
626 106th Avenue NE, Bellevue WA 98004. 425/451-8463. **Contact:** Human Resources. **World Wide Web address:** http://www.bn.com. **Description:** A bookstore chain operating nationwide. This location has a cafe and music department in addition to its book departments. **Corporate headquarters location:** New York NY. **Listed on:** New York Stock Exchange. **Stock exchange symbol:** BKS.

BARTELL DRUGS
4727 Denver Avenue South, Seattle WA 98134. 206/763-2626. **Contact:** Personnel Department. **E-mail address:** hr@bartelldrugs.com. **World Wide Web address:** http://www.bartelldrugs.com. **Description:** Operates a chain of drug stores in the Seattle area. **Positions advertised include:** Pharmacy Assistant; Pharmacist; Management Trainee. **Corporate headquarters location:** This location. **Number of employees nationwide:** 600.

THE BON MARCHE
602 Northgate Mall, Seattle WA 98101. 206/440-6222. **Contact:** Personnel. **World Wide Web address:** http://www.federated-fds.com. **Description:** Operates a retail department store. **Parent company:** Federated Department Stores. **Number of employees nationwide:** 3,750.

BEN BRIDGE JEWELER
P.O. Box 1908, Seattle WA 98111-1908. 206/448-8800. **Contact:** Human Resources. **World Wide Web address:** http://www.benbridge.com. **Description:** A retailer of fine jewelry and related accessories. **Positions advertised include:** Quality Assurance Specialist; Watchmaker; Clerical and Administrative Associate. **Corporate headquarters location:** This location. **Other U.S. locations:** AL; CA; HI; NV; OR. **Number of employees at this location:** 80. **Number of employees nationwide:** 475.

COSTCO WHOLESALE
845 Lake Drive, Issaquah WA 98027. 425/313-8100. **Fax:** 425/313-8103. **Contact:** Human Resources. **World Wide Web address:** http://www.costco.com. **Description:** A nationwide retailer of food, clothing, and numerous other products at wholesale prices. **Corporate headquarters location:** This location. **Listed on:** NASDAQ. **Stock exchange symbol:** COST. **Annual sales/revenues:** More than $100 million.

EDDIE BAUER, INC.
P.O. Box 97000, Redmond WA 98073-9700. 425/755-6100. **Physical address:** 15010 NE 36th Street, Redmond WA 98052. **Fax:** 425/755-7696. **Contact:** Human Resources. **World Wide Web address:** http://www.eddiebauer.com. **Description:** A multi-unit, private-label retailer and catalog company for apparel and home accessories. **Corporate headquarters location:** This location. **Other U.S. locations:** Nationwide. **Parent company:** Spiegel, Inc. **Listed on:** NASDAQ. **Stock exchange symbol:** SPGLE. **Number of employees at this location:** 1,000. **Number of employees nationwide:** 10,000.

HAGGEN, INC.
TOP FOOD & DRUG
P.O. Box 9704, Bellingham WA 98227. 360/733-8720. **Physical address:** 2211 Rimland Drive, Suite 400, Bellingham WA 98226. **Recorded jobline:** 888/HAG-GENS. **Fax:** 360/752-6424. **Contact:** Human Resources Manager. **E-mail address:** careers@haggen.com. **World Wide Web address:** http://www.haggen.com. **Description:** Operates over 25 grocery stores throughout the Pacific Northwest. **Special programs:** Internships. **Corporate headquarters location:** This location.

NORDSTROM, INC.
1617 Sixth, Suite 500, Seattle WA 98101. 206/628-2111. **Contact:** Personnel. **World Wide Web address:** http://www.nordstrom.com. **Description:** This location is the flagship store of one of the largest independently owned fashion retailers in the United States. The company operates more than 100 full-line stores across the nation. Founded in 1901. **Positions advertised include:** Corporate Expense Keyer; Data Warehouse Analyst; Administrative Assistant; Sales Audit Representative; Senior Accountant; Project Manager; Quality Assurance Analyst. **Corporate headquarters location:** This location. **Listed on:** New York Stock Exchange. **Stock exchange symbol:** JWN. **Annual sales/revenues:** More than $100 million.

NORDSTROM RACK
1601 Second Avenue, Suite 410, Seattle WA 98101. 206/448-8522. **Contact:** Human Resources. **World Wide Web address:** http://www.nordstrom.com. **Description:** Nordstom is one of the largest independently owned fashion retailers in the United States. The company operates more than 60 full-line stores across the nation along with over 20 clearance, boutique, and leased shoe departments in 12 department stores in Hawaii and Guam. Founded in 1901. **Operations at this facility include:** This location is a discounted outlet store. **Listed on:** New York Stock Exchange. **Stock exchange symbol:** JWN. **Annual sales/revenues:** More than $100 million. **Number of employees at this location:** 500.

QUALITY FOOD CENTERS
10116 NE Eighth Street, Bellevue WA 98004. 425/455-3761. **Contact:** Human Resources. **World Wide Web address:** http://www.qfconline.com. **Description:** Operates a chain of retail supermarkets. **Corporate headquarters location:** Cincinnati OH. **Parent company:** The Kroger Company. **Number of employees nationwide:** 2,600.

RECREATIONAL EQUIPMENT INC. (REI)
P.O. Box 1938, Sumner WA 98390. 253/872-2917. **Physical address:** 6750 South 228th Street, Kent WA 98032. **Recorded jobline:** 253/395-4694. **Contact:** Human Resources Department. **World Wide Web address:** http://www.rei.com/jobs. **Description:** A retailer of outdoor clothing and a wide variety of recreational equipment. **NOTE:** Jobseekers may apply and submit resumes online. **Corporate headquarters location:** Kent WA. **Operations at this facility include:** Administration. **Number of employees nationwide:** 3,000.

RITE AID CORPORATION
110 SW 148th Street, Burien WA 98166. 206/835-0166. **Fax:** 206/835-0991. **Contact:** Employee Relations Manager. **World Wide Web address:** http://www.riteaid.com. **Description:** Rite Aid Corporation operates 3800 retail drug stores in 30 states and the District of Columbia. Founded in 1939. **Special programs:** Internships. **Corporate headquarters**

location: Harrisburg PA. **Other U.S. locations:** Nationwide. **Operations at this facility include:** This location houses administrative offices. **Listed on:** New York Stock Exchange. **Stock exchange symbol:** RAD. **Number of employees nationwide:** 40,000.

SOUND FORD INC.
750 Rainier Avenue South, Renton WA 98055. 425/235-1000. **Contact:** Human Resources. **World Wide Web address:** http://www.soundford.com. **Description:** An automotive dealership. **Positions advertised:** Sales; Management.

STARBUCKS COFFEE CORPORATION
P.O. Box 34067, Seattle WA 98124. 206/447-1575. **Physical address:** 2401 Utah Avenue South, Seattle WA 98134. **Fax:** 206/447-0828. **Recorded jobline:** 206/447-4123. **Contact:** Human Resources. **World Wide Web address:** http://www.starbucks.com. **Description:** Sells whole-bean coffees, along with hot coffees and Italian-style espresso beverages through more than 2,500 retail stores worldwide. The company purchases green coffee beans for its coffee varieties from coffee-producing regions throughout the world and custom roasts them. In addition to coffee beans and beverages, the company's stores offer a selection of coffee-making equipment, accessories, pastries, and confections. Also, the company sells whole-bean coffees through specialty sales groups, a national mail-order operation, and supermarkets. **Corporate headquarters location:** This location. **Other U.S. locations:** Nationwide. **International locations:** Worldwide. **Number of employees worldwide:** 37,000.

SUPERVALU INC.
1525 East D Street, Tacoma WA 98421. 253/404-4200. **Fax:** 253/404-4288. **Contact:** Human Resources. **E-mail address:** super.careers@supervalu.com. **World Wide Web address:** http://www.supervalu.com. **Description:** SUPERVALU operates over 1,100 stores under the Bigg's, Cub Foods, Shop'n Save, Save-A-Lot, Scott's Foods, Laneco, and Hornbachers names. **Special programs:** Internships. **Corporate headquarters location:** Eden Prairie MN. **Subsidiaries include:** Hazelwood Farms Bakeries manufactures frozen bakery products. **Operations at this facility include:** This location houses administrative offices. **Listed on:** New York Stock Exchange. **Stock exchange symbol:** SVU. **Number of employees at this location:** 935.

THRIFTWAY STORES INC.
501 S. Grady Way, Renton WA 98055. 425/226-2830. **Fax:** 206/315-4410. **Contact:** Personnel. **World Wide Web address:** http://www.thriftway.com. **Description:** Operates a retail grocery chain with over 100 outlets. **Corporate headquarters location:** This location.

TRI NORTH DEPARTMENT STORES
5700 Sixth Avenue South, Suite 214, Seattle WA 98108-2511. 206/767-7600. **Contact:** Human Resources. **Description:** Owns and operates a chain of retail clothing department stores located primarily throughout the Pacific Northwest. **Corporate headquarters location:** This location.

URM STORES, INC.
P.O. Box 3365, Spokane WA 99220. 509/467-2620. **Physical address:** 7511 North Freya Street, Spokane WA 99217. **Contact:** Personnel Department. **World Wide Web address:** http://www.urmstores.com. **Description:** A grocery and general merchandise business. **Number of employees nationwide:** 2,000.

Wisconsin

AMERICAN GIRL, INC.
8400 Fairway Place, Middleton WI 53562. 608/836-4848. **Fax:** 608/836-1999. **Contact:** Recruiting. **World Wide Web address:** http://www.americangirl.com. **Description:** Operates in four divisions: consumer catalogue and direct mail sales; book publishing, which markets The American Girls Collection and American Girl Library; the magazine division which publishes *American Girl* magazine; and customer programs, which provides programs and special events centered on an American Girl theme. Founded in 1986. **Positions advertised include:** Business Systems Analyst; Sales Representative; Director, Licensing and New Business Development. **Corporate headquarters location:** This location. **Other area locations:** DeForest WI; Eau Claire WI; Wilmot WI. **Other U.S. locations:** Chicago IL. **Parent company:** Mattel, Inc.. **Listed on:** Privately held. **Number of employees at this location:** 750. **Number of employees nationwide:** 1,000.

CAMERA CORNER/CONNECTING POINT, INC.
529 North Monroe Street, P.O. Box 248, Green Bay WI 54305-0248. 920/435-5353. **Fax:** 920/435-3619. **Contact:** Aaron Jamir, Vice President of Technical Services. **E-mail address:** asj@cccp.com. **World Wide Web address:** http://www.cccp.com. **Description:** Sells cameras and computer systems. Camera Corner/Connecting Point also provides service and technical support. **Corporate headquarters location:** This location.

CARSON PIRIE SCOTT & COMPANY
331 West Wisconsin Avenue, Milwaukee WI 53203. 414/347-1152. **Fax:** 414/347-5337. **Contact:** Human Resources Department. **World Wide Web address:** http://www.carsons.com. **Description:** A department store chain, with more than 50 stores located in the Midwest. **Positions advertised include:** Manager, Planning and Allocation; Division Merchandise Manager; Labor Management Staff Planner; Vice President, Divisional Merchandise Manager. **Corporate headquarters location:** This location. **Parent company:** The Bon-Ton Stores, Inc., a subsidiary of Saks Incorporated **Listed on:** New York Stock Exchange. **Stock exchange symbol:** SKS. **Number of employees at this location:** 700. **Number of employees nationwide:** 14,000.

FAMOUS FOOTWEAR
7010 Mineral Point Road, Madison WI 53717-1701. 608/829-3668. **Contact:** Recruitment Manager. **World Wide Web address:** http://www.famousfootwear.com. **Description:** A shoe retailer operating over 920 stores in 50 states plus Guam and Puerto Rico. **Positions advertised include:** Buyer; Controller, Retail Finance; Copywriter; Customer Insight Specialist; Location Planning Manager; Real Estate Associate. **Special programs:** Internships. **Corporate headquarters location:** This location. **Other U.S. locations:** Nationwide. **Parent company:** Brown Shoe Company, Inc. **Number of employees nationwide:** 10,000.

FIGI'S GIFTS INC.
2525 South Roddis Avenue, Marshfield WI 54449. 715/384-1425. **Toll-free phone:** 800/360-6542. **Fax:** 715/384-1177. **Contact:** Gayle Lenz, Human Resources Recruiter. **E-mail address:** gail.lenz@figis.com. **World Wide Web address:** http://www.figis.com. **Description:** A leader in mail-order/catalog food gifts, with a full line of products including cheese, sausage, smokehouse specialties, candy, cookies, nuts, cakes, fruits, plants, and a variety of nonfood gifts. Founded in 1944. **NOTE:** Part-time jobs are offered. This location also hires seasonally. **Special programs:** Internships. **Corporate headquarters location:** This location. **Other area locations:** Neillsville WI; Stevens Point WI. **Parent company:** Fingerhut. **Annual sales/revenues:** More than $100 million. **Number of employees at this location:** 2,250. **Number of employees nationwide:** 2,500.

KOHL'S DEPARTMENT STORE
N56 W17000 Ridgewood Drive, Menomonee Falls WI 53051. 262/703-7000. **Fax:** 262/703-6363. **Contact:** Manager of College Relations. **World Wide Web address:** http://www.kohls.com. **Description:** A value-oriented, family-focused, specialty department store. The company operates nearly 600 stores nationwide. **Positions advertised include:** Senior Compensation Analyst; LAN Technician; Oracle DBA; Senior Systems Analyst; Coordinator Import Compliance;

Manager of Store Finance. **Corporate headquarters location:** This location. **Other U.S. locations:** Nationwide. **Listed on:** New York Stock Exchange. **Stock exchange symbol:** KSS. **Annual sales/revenues:** More than $100 million. **Number of employees at this location:** 1,500. **Number of employees nationwide:** 50,000.

LANDS' END, INC.
One Lands' End Lane, Dodgeville WI 53595. 608/935-9341. **Fax:** 608/935-4260. **Contact:** Human Resources. **World Wide Web address:** http://www.landsend.com. **Description:** A direct merchant of a wide variety of casual clothing for men, women, and children; accessories; shoes; and soft luggage. The company's products are offered through its monthly catalogs, the Internet, and stores. **Positions advertised include:** Middleware Administrator; Quality Assurance Analyst; Planner; HR Generalist; Compensation Analyst; Graphic Designer; Merchandise Manager; Senior Learning Manager. **Corporate headquarters location:** This location. **International locations:** England; Japan. **Parent company:** Sears, Roebuck and Company. **Number of employees worldwide:** 4,700.

MENARD, INC.
4777 Menard Drive, Eau Claire, WI 54703-9604. 715/876-5911. **Fax:** 715/876-2868. **Contact:** Employment Office. **World Wide Web address:** http://www.menards.com. **Description:** Operates a chain of home improvement stores. **Corporate headquarters location:** This location.

MR. G'S INC.
120 North Main Street, Viroqua WI, 54665. 608/637-8271. **Contact:** Human Resources. **Description:** Operates Mr. G's Shoes & Clothing, an apparel store. **Corporate headquarters location:** This location. **Other area locations:** Neenah WI; Racine WI; Shelby WI. **Operations at this facility include:** Administration. **Listed on:** Privately held.

SHOPKO STORES, INC.
P.O. Box 19060, Green Bay WI 54307-9060. 920/497-2211. **Physical address:** 700 Pilgrim Way, Green Bay WI 54304. **Fax:** 920/429-4799. **Contact:** Human Resources. **E-mail address:** careers@shopko.com. **World Wide Web address:** http://www.shopko.com. **Description:** A leading regional retailer operating 141 ShopKo Stores and 218 Pamida stores in 23 states. **Positions advertised include:** Business Analyst; Corporate Traffic Manager; Fleet Equipment Manager; Accountant; Networking Engineering Architect. **Corporate headquarters location:** This location. **Listed on:** New York Stock Exchange. **Stock exchange symbol:** SKO.

STOP-N-GO OF MADISON, INC.
2934 Fish Hatchery Road, Madison WI 53713-3175. 608/271-4433. **Fax:** 608/271-1222. **Contact:** Mark Kiley, Director of Human Resources. **E-mail address:** contact@stop-n-go.com. **World Wide Web address:** http://www.stop-n-go.com. **Description:** Operates a chain of 42 convenience stores in southern Wisconsin and northern Illinois. Founded in 1963. **Positions advertised include:** Customer Service Representative; Sales Manager. **Special programs:** Training; Summer Jobs. **Corporate headquarters location:** This location. **Annual sales/revenues:** $51 - $100 million. **Number of employees nationwide:** 320.

TARGET STORES
4777 South 27th Street, Greenfield WI 53221. 414/282-1000. **Contact:** Personnel. **World Wide Web address:** http://www.target.com. **Description:** A discount department store. **NOTE:** Entry-level positions are offered. **Operations at this facility include:** Sales; Service. **Number of employees at this location:** 215.

Wyoming

KMART CORPORATION
4000 East Second Street, Casper WY 82609. 307/265-0808. **Contact:** Personnel. **World Wide Web address:** http://www.kmart.com. **Description:** Kmart Corporation is a mass merchandising company with retail outlets in 49 states, Puerto Rico and the Virgin Islands. Kmart provides employment opportunities in store, pharmacy, corporate and distribution-center operations. This store has a pharmacy and photo center. **NOTE:** Visit the store to complete an application and discuss available positions. **Corporate headquarters location:** Hoffman Estates IL. **Parent company:** Sears Holdings Corp. **Number of employees nationwide:** 144,000.

MAVERIK COUNTRY STORES, INC.
1014 South Washington Street, P.O. Box 8008, Afton WY 83110. 307/885-3861. **Toll-free phone:** 877/885-3861.**NOTE:** For positions at an individual store, contact the nearest store. The Afton corporate office hires primarily for information systems and accounting positions; direct all inquires for these positions to the relevant department head. **World Wide Web address:** http:// www.maverik.com. **Description:** Operates a chain of convenience stores that include bakeries. Maverik Country Stores operates over 130 locations in the western United States. **Corporate headquarters location:** North Salt Lake UT. **Other U.S. locations:** AZ; CO; ID; MT; NV; UT.

TRANSPORTATION AND TRAVEL

You can expect to find the following types of companies in this section:

Air, Railroad, and Water Transportation Services • Courier Services • Local and Interurban Passenger Transit • Ship Building and Repair • Transportation Equipment • Travel Agencies • Trucking • Warehousing and Storage

---

Transportation occupations are expected to increase by 368,000 jobs, 10% to 4,062,000 jobs. Truck transportation, including couriers and messengers industries will grow by 14%, adding 387,000 new jobs, while more modest growth is projected for rail and water transportation, adding 16,000 new jobs or 9.3%. Demand for truck transportation and warehousing services will expand as many manufacturers concentrate on their core competencies and contract out their product transportation and storage functions. Air transportation occupations will increase by 22,000 jobs, or 16.5%, as passenger and cargo traffic continues to expand in response to increases in population, income, and business activity. The travel arrangement and reservation services industry should add 7,000 jobs, just 3%, increasing to 226,000 jobs, due to use of the Internet and industry consolidation.

Alabama

DEATON INC.
P.O. Box 938, Birmingham AL 35201. 205/798-5555. **Contact:** Jerry Crews, President. **World Wide Web address:** http://www.deatoninc.com. **Description:** Operates a fleet of 350 trucks and 650 flatbed trailers. Founded in 1929. **Parent company:** Old Dominion Freight Lines.

SCHNEIDER NATIONAL CARRIERS
P.O. Box Drawer 500, Evergreen AL 36401. 251/578-2836. **Contact:** Human Resources. **Description:** Provides truckload transportation services through independent contractors and commissioned sales agents. **Corporate headquarters location:** Green Bay WI.

Alaska

ALASKA RAILROAD CORPORATION
P.O. Box 107500, Anchorage AK 99510. 907/265-2437. **Fax:** 907/265-2542. **Contact:** Susan Lindemuth, Human Resources Manager. **E-mail address:** arjobinfo@akrr.com. **World Wide Web address:** http://www.akrr.com. **Description:** A railroad company. **Positions advertised include:** Financial Analyst; Heavy Equipment Operator; Locomotive Electrician; Locomotive Engineer/Conductor Trainee; Locomotive Machinist/Mechanic; Special Agent.

ERA AVIATION, INC.
6160 Carl Brady Drive, Anchorage AK 99502. 907/248-4422. **Fax:** 907/266-8401. **Contact:** Karla Grumman, Personnel Director. **World Wide Web address:** http://www.era-aviation.com. **Description:** An air transportation company. **Positions advertised include:** Aircraft Maintenance Technician; Fleet Service Agent; Ramp Agent/Line Service Technician; Accounts Receivable Clerk. **Corporate headquarters location:** This location. **Other U.S. locations:** Reno NV; Lake Charles LA. **Number of employees at this location:** 750. **Number of employees nationwide:** 900.

NORTHERN AIR CARGO
3900 West International Airport Road, Anchorage AK 99502. 907/249-5137. **Recorded Jobline:** 907/249-5187. **Contact:** Human Resources. **World Wide Web address:** http://www.northernaircargo.com. **Description:** A transportation services company servicing Alaska and the World. Founded in 1956. **Note:** Applications are accepted in-person Monday through Friday from 8:00 a.m. to 6:00 p.m. **Positions advertised include:** Chief Inspector; Logistics Manager; Payroll Clerk; Avionics Technician; Aircraft Mechanic; Manager of Flight Safety; Accounts Payable Clerk.

PACIFIC RIM LOGISTICS, INC.
737 West 5th Avenue, Suite 209, Anchorage AK 99501. 907/277-5191. **Fax:** 907/277-5192. **Contact:** Human Resources. **E-mail address:** info@pacrimlog.com. **World Wide Web address:** http://www.pacrimlog.com. **Description:** Provides complete logistic services including planning, project management, scheduling, estimating, procurement, property tracking, risk evaluation, and community relations. **Positions advertised include:** Contract Administrator; Cost/Project Controls Professional; Administrative Assistant.

Arizona

AMERICAN EXPRESS TRAVEL RELATED SERVICES
20022 North 31st Avenue, Phoenix AZ 85027. 602/537-8500. **Contact:** Human Resources. **World Wide Web address:** http://www.americanexpress.com. **Description:** A diversified travel and financial services company operating in 160 countries around the world. American Express Travel Related Services offers consumers the Personal, Gold, and Platinum cards, as well as revolving credit products such as Optima Cards, which allow customers to extend payments. Other products include the American Express Corporate Card and the Corporate Purchasing Card. Travel Related Services also offers American Express Traveler's Cheques and travel services. Founded in 1850. **Corporate headquarters location:** New York NY. **Other U.S locations:** Fort Lauderdale FL; Jacksonville FL; Greensboro NC. **Parent company:** American Express Company. **Listed on:** New York Stock Exchange. **Stock exchange symbol:** AXP.

JOE CONWAY TRUCKING COMPANY
6509 West Orangewood Avenue, Glendale AZ 85301. 623/937-1684. **Contact:** Gene Cooper, President. **Description:** A trucking company. **Positions advertised include:** Truck Driver. **Corporate headquarters location:** This location. **Number of employees at this location:** 50.

CORPORATE JETS INC.
14600 North Airport Drive, Scottsdale AZ 85260. 480/948-2400. **Fax:** 480/443-7213. **Contact:** Human Resources. **E-mail address:** jobs@cjisdl.com. **World Wide Web address:** http://www.cjisdl.com. **Description:** A full-service, fixed-base corporate jet operator. The company performs a variety of services for corporate jets including refueling and aircraft charter services. **Positions advertised include:** A&P Technician. **Corporate headquarters location:** Pittsburgh PA. **Other U.S. locations:** Dallas TX. **Listed on:** Privately held. **Number of employees at this location:** 80. **Number of employees nationwide:** 700.

OLYMPIAN WORLDWIDE MOVING & STORAGE
2225 South 43rd Avenue, Suite 2, Phoenix AZ 85009. 602/269-2225. **Fax:** 602/233-9810. **Contact:** Diane Davis, Personnel Department. **E-mail address:** ddavis@moveolympian.com. **World Wide Web address:** http://www.moveolympian.com. **Description:** Part of a nationwide company engaged in moving, storing, and distributing products. **Positions advertised include:** CDL Driver; Mover; Helper; Packer; Warehouse Staff. **Special programs:** Internships.

Corporate headquarters location: Hillside IL. **Other U.S. locations:** Nationwide. **Parent company:** The Bekins Company. **Listed on:** Privately held. **Number of employees at this location:** 20. **Number of employees nationwide:** 900.

PENSKE TRUCK LEASING
3519 East 34th Street, Tucson AZ 85713. 520/327-5987. **Contact:** Larry Zitzman, Branch Manager. **World Wide Web address:** http://www.penske.com. **Description:** Offices of the automotive and bulk materials transporting company. **Positions advertised include:** Driver.

SWIFT TRANSPORTATION COMPANY, INC.
P.O. Box 29243, Phoenix AZ 85038-9243. 602/269-9700. **Physical address:** 2200 South 75th Avenue, Phoenix AZ 85043. **Contact:** Human Resources. **World Wide Web address:** http://www.swifttrans.com. **Description:** One of the largest truckload motor carriers in the United States. Swift Transportation Company offers a wide variety of trailers, with more than 5,600 on the road every day. Swift Transportation has more than 2,400 power units to pull the widest variety of vans, flatbeds, and specialty trailers available to the industry. The company also provides full-service equipment leasing, dedicated fleet programs, and third-party logistics services for several major customers. **Positions advertised include:** Revenue Financial Analyst; Research Analyst; Security Officer. **Corporate headquarters location:** This location. **Listed on:** NASDAQ. **Stock exchange symbol:** SWFT. **President/CEO:** Jerry C. Moyes. **Annual sales/revenues:** More than $100 million.

U-HAUL INTERNATIONAL, INC.
2727 North Central Avenue, Phoenix AZ 85004. 602/263-6011. **Contact:** Henry Kelly, Human Resources Director. **World Wide Web address:** http://www.uhaul.com. **Description:** One of the largest consumer truck rental operations in the world, with a fleet of over 158,000 trucks and trailers. The company operates in all 50 states and all Canadian provinces, with 14,000 dealers and over 1,300 U-Haul centers. The company is one of the largest operators of self-storage units in the United States with over 700 storage locations. U-Haul has a computerized, nationwide storage reservation system. U-Haul is one of the world's largest installers of permanent trailer hitches, and is one of the largest retailers of propane fuel. Founded in 1945. **Positions advertised include:** Alarm Analyst; Architectural Imaging Artist; Assistant General Counsel; Budget Analyst; Construction Project Manager; Oracle Programmer/Analyst. **Corporate headquarters location:** This location. **Number of employees nationwide:** 15,500.

U-HAUL TECHNICAL CENTER
11298 South Priest Drive, Tempe AZ 85284. 480/940-0274. **Contact:** Human Resources. **World Wide Web address:** http://www.uhaul.com. **Description:** U-Haul Technical Center provides design, engineering and technical service for U-Haul equipment and products. Maintenance and repair assistance, purchasing supply support and product research and development are some of the functions provided by U-Haul Technical Center. **NOTE:** Search and apply for positions online. **Positions advertised include:** Truck Sales Analyst; Warranty Processing Clerk. **Corporate headquarters location:** Phoenix AZ.

US AIRWAYS
4000 East Sky Harbor Boulevard, Phoenix AZ 85034. **Fax:** 480-693-8813. **Recorded jobline:** 877/292-4562. **Contact:** Human Resources. **World Wide Web address:** http://www.usairways.com. **Description:** US Airways and America West's recent merger creates the fifth largest domestic airline employing nearly 35,000. US Airways, US Airways Shuttle and US Airways Express operate approximately 4,000 flights per day and serve more than 225 communities in the U.S., Canada, Europe, the Caribbean and Latin America. **NOTE:** Search and apply for positions online. **Positions advertised include:** Senior Analyst, Division Finance; Sr. Clerk; Records Specialist; Ground Operations Manager; Ground Operations Supervisor; Airport Quality Assurance Analyst; Manager; Documents Coordinator; Sr. Analyst, Revenue Management; Benefits Specialist; Sr. Analyst, Capacity Planning; Sr. Catering Specialist; Planner; Associate Manager, Media Relations; IMS Database/Systems Administrator; Sr. Analyst, Division Finance; HR Programs Advisor; Online Distribution Director; Web Contents Developer.

VAN TRAN OF TUCSON
3401 East Ajo Way, Tucson AZ 85713-5234. 520/798-1000. **Contact:** Human Resources. **World Wide Web address:** http://www.vantran.org. **Description:** A city-operated transportation service that provides van transportation to handicapped and elderly citizens of Tucson. **NOTE:** Jobseekers must apply in person.

YELLOW TRANSPORTATION INC.
2425 South 43rd Avenue, Phoenix AZ 85009. 602/269-5141. **Contact:** Human Resources. **World Wide Web address:** http://www.myyellow.com. **Description:** A national, long-haul truckload carrier, with over 585 terminal locations in 50 states, Puerto Rico, and Canada. **Corporate headquarters location:** Overland Park KS. **Parent company:** Yellow Corporation. **Listed on:** NASDAQ. **Stock exchange symbol:** YELL. **Number of employees nationwide:** 28,000.

Arkansas

ARKANSAS BEST CORPORATION
P.O. Box 10048, Fort Smith AR 72917-0048. 479/785-6000. **Fax:** 479/785-8912. **Physical address:** 3801 Old Greenwood Road, Fort Smith AR 72903. **Contact:** Human Resources. **World Wide Web address:** http://www.arkbest.com. **Description:** Provides trucking and shipping services nationwide. **Corporate headquarters location:** This location. **Other U.S. locations:** Nationwide. **Subsidiaries include:** ABF Freight System, Inc.; Clipper Group; Data-Tronics Corp.; FleetNet America, LLC; Wingfoot, LLC. **Operations at this facility include:** Administration. **Listed on:** NASDAQ. **Stock exchange symbol:** ABFS. **Number of employees at this location:** 300. **Number of employees nationwide:** 15,000.

FED-EX FREIGHT EAST
2200 Forward Drive, Harrison AR 72601. 870/741-9000. **Fax:** 870/741-0342. **Contact:** Jesse Hancock, Human Resources. **E-mail address:** hr@euronetworldwide.com. **World Wide Web address:** http://www.fedexfreight.fedex.com. **Description:** A trucking company providing scheduled, all-points, regional small shipment carrier service. The truckers ship a wide range of general commodities. The company uses its own drivers, equipment, and documentation process. **Positions advertised include:** Customer Service Representative; Maintenance Administration Systems Support; Programmer Analyst; Staff Accountant; Reliability Analyst; Manager, Quality Assurance; Project Manager. **Corporate headquarters location:** Chantilly VA. **Other U.S. locations:** Nationwide. **Parent company:** Federal Express. **Operations at this facility include:** Administration. **Listed on:** NASDAQ. **Stock exchange symbol:** FDX. **Annual sales/revenues:** More than $18 billion. **Number of employees worldwide:** 142,000.

J.B. HUNT TRANSPORT SERVICES, INC.
615 J.B. Hunt Corporate Drive, P.O. Box 130, Lowell AR 72745. 479/820-0000. **Toll-free phone:** 800/252-4868. **Contact:** Human Resources. **World Wide Web address:** http://www.jbhunt.com. **Description:** Operates one of the largest U.S. truckload carriers of general freight, serving the 48 contiguous states, British Columbia, Ontario, Quebec, and points in Mexico through arrangement with several Mexican carriers. **Positions advertised include:** PeopleSoft Programmer. **Corporate headquarters location:** This location. **Listed on:** NASDAQ. **Stock exchange symbol:** JBHT. **Number of employees nationwide:** 10,450.

USA TRUCK, INC.
P.O. Box 449, Van Buren AR 72957. 479/471-2510. **Fax:** 479/410-8060. **Physical address:** 3200 Industrial Park Drive, Van Buren AR 72956. **Contact:** Roseanne Franceszoni. **World Wide Web address:** http://www.usa-truck.com. **Description:** A trucking company that provides services for retail companies. **Positions advertised include:** Transportation/Traffic Specialist; Driver. **Corporate headquarters location:** This location. **Operations at this facility include:** Administration; Sales. **Listed on:** NASDAQ. **Stock exchange symbol:** USAK.

California
ANCRA INTERNATIONAL LLC
4880 West Rosecrans Avenue, Hawthorne CA 90250. 310/970-8612. **Toll-free phone:** 800/973-5092. **Contact:** Tammy Carson, Human Resources Administrator. **World Wide Web address:** http://www.ancra-llc.com. **Description:** Manufactures cargo restraint equipment for the trucking and aircraft industries including aircraft fittings, winches, cam buckles, o/c buckles, shoring beams, cargo systems, and track. Ancra also maintains off-road and marine divisions. **Corporate headquarters location:** This location. **Other U.S. locations:** Erlanger KY.

CNF, INC.
2855 Campus Drive, San Mateo CA 94403. 650/378-5200. **Contact:** Staffing Services. **E-mail address:** jobs@cnf.com. **World Wide Web address:** http://www.cnf.com. **Description:** A motor freight carrier and air freight forwarder operating in all 50 states. Operations include import/export brokerage, overseas forwarding, and warehousing and distribution services. **NOTE:** Send resumes to: Staffing Services, CNF Inc., P.O. Box 3477, Portland OR 97208. 503/450-2000. Fax: 503/450-2168. **Positions advertised include:** General Clerk. **Corporate headquarters location:** This location. **Other U.S. locations:** Portland OR. **Listed on:** New York Stock Exchange. **Stock exchange symbol:** CNF. **Number of employees nationwide:** 26,000.

CALIFORNIA CARTAGE COMPANY, INC.
3545 Long Beach Boulevard, 5th Floor, P.O. Box 92829, Long Beach CA 90807. 310/537-1432. **Fax:** 562/988-1351. **Contact:** Personnel Director. **World Wide Web address:** http://www.calcartage.com. **Description:** A trucking company that provides freight handling, warehousing, and container freight station operations. **Corporate headquarters location:** This location. **Other area locations:** Carson CA; City of Industry CA; Compton CA; Fontana CA; National City CA; Oakland CA; Vernon CA; Wilmington CA. **Other U.S. locations:** Nationwide.

CATALINA YACHTS INC.
21200 Victory Boulevard, Woodland Hills CA 91367-2522. 818/884-7700. **Fax:** 818/884-3810. **Contact:** Human Resources Department. **World Wide Web address:** http://www.catalinayachts.com. **Description:** Manufactures yachts. **Corporate headquarters location:** This location. **Other U.S. locations:** Largo FL.

CENTRAL TRANSPORT INTERNATIONAL, INC.
550 South Alameda East, Compton CA 90221. **Toll-free phone:** 800/711-6584. **Fax:** 310/632-3880. **Contact:** Human Resources. **E-mail address:** resumes@centraltransportint.com. **Description:** Operates a trucking service. **World Wide Web address:** http://www.centraltransportint.com. **Corporate headquarters location:** Warren MI.

CHIPMAN CORPORATION
dba CHIPMAN MOVING AND STORAGE
1551 Buena Vista Avenue, Alameda CA 94501. 510/748-8700. **Toll-free phone:** 800/825-3866. **Fax:** 510/748-8714. **Contact:** Personnel. **E-mail address:** chipman@chipmancorp.com. **World Wide Web address:** http://www.chipmancorp.com. **Description:** Provides moving and storage services both domestically and internationally. **Corporate headquarters location:** This location. **Other area locations:** Concord CA; Long Beach CA; Sacramento CA; San Jose CA; Valejo CA. **Other U.S. locations:** Portland OR; Seattle WA.

CROWLEY MARITIME CORPORATION
155 Grand Avenue, Oakland CA 94612. 510/251-7500. **Fax:** 510/251-7788. **Recorded jobline:** 904/727-4287. **Contact:** Personnel. **E-mail address:** resumes@crowley.com. **World Wide Web address:** http://www.crowley.com. **Description:** Provides marine transportation and construction services. **Corporate headquarters location:** This location. **Other area locations:** Statewide. **Other U.S. locations:** Nationwide.

DHL WORLDWIDE EXPRESS
50 California Street, San Francisco CA 94111. 415/677-6100. **Contact:** Human Resources. **E-mail address:** hr_jobs@us.dhl.com. **World Wide Web address:** http://www.dhl.com. **Description:** An air express network that, through its subsidiaries, services national and foreign markets in over 190 countries. **Corporate headquarters location:** Plantation FL. **Subsidiaries include:** DHL Airways Inc. **Parent company:** DHL International Ltd.

EAGLE GLOBAL LOGISTICS
19600 Western Avenue, Torrance CA 90501. 310/972-5500. **Contact:** Manager of Human Resources. **World Wide Web address:** http://www.eaglegl.com. **Description:** Provides international air and ocean freight forwarding services. **Positions advertised include:** Managing Director; Operations Manager. **Corporate headquarters location:** Houston TX. **Other area locations:** Sacramento CA; San Diego CA; San Jose CA. **Other U.S. locations:** Nationwide. **International locations:** Worldwide. **Listed on:** NASDAQ. **Stock exchange symbol:** EGL.

FEDERAL EXPRESS CORPORATION (FEDEX)
950 Tower Lane, Suite 770, Foster City CA 94404. 650/578-5100. **Fax:** 650/866-2235. **Recorded jobline:** 888/513-2294. **Contact:** Recruitment Specialist. **World Wide Web address:** http://www.fedex.com. **Description:** One of the world's largest express transportation companies serving 212 countries worldwide. FedEx ships approximately 3.2 million packages daily. FedEx operates more than 45,000 drop-off locations, and has a fleet that consists of more than 640 aircraft and 44,5000 vehicles. Founded in 1973. **Corporate headquarters location:** Memphis TN. **Listed on:** New York Stock Exchange. **Stock exchange symbol:** FDX. **Number of employees at this location:** 100. **Number of employees nationwide:** 148,000.

FEDEX FREIGHT WEST
P.O. Box 649002, San Jose CA 95164. 408/268-9600. **Contact:** Human Resources Department. **World Wide Web address:** http://www.fedexfreight.com. **Description:** A trucking company. **Corporate headquarters location:** This location. **Parent company:** FedEx. **Listed on:** New York Stock Exchange. **Stock exchange symbol:** FDX.

GENERAL STEAMSHIP AGENCIES, INC.
575 Redwood Highway, Suite 200, Mill Valley CA 94941-3007. 415/389-5200. **Fax:** 415/389-9020. **Contact:** Human Resources. **E-mail address:** hr@gensteam.com. **World Wide Web address:** http://www.gensteam.com. **Description:** Operates a shipping agency. **Corporate headquarters location:** This location.

LAIDLAW TRANSIT, INC.
4337 Rowland Avenue, El Monte CA 91731. 626/448-9446. **Contact:** Personnel Director. **E-mail address:** careers@laidlawjobs.com. **World Wide Web address:** http://www.laidlawtransit.com. **Description:** Provides bus service for many districts of Los Angeles County and charter bus service to private customers. The company is also a school bus contractor. **Other area**

locations: Culver City CA; Los Angeles CA. **Parent company:** Laidlaw, Inc. provides solid waste collection, compaction, transportation, treatment, transfer and disposal services; provides hazardous waste services; operates hazardous waste facilities and wastewater treatment plants; and operates passenger and school buses, transit system buses, and tour and charter buses. **Corporate headquarters location:** Kansas City KS. **Listed on:** American Stock Exchange. **Stock exchange symbol:** GLL.

ORIENT OVERSEAS CONTAINER LINE INC. (OOCL)
17777 Center Court Drive, Suite 500, Cerritos CA 90703. 562/499-2600. **Fax:** 562/435-2750. **Contact:** Human Resources. **E-mail address:** hrinfo@oocl.com. **World Wide Web address:** http://www.oocl.com. **Description:** Provides a containerized cargo distribution system to shippers worldwide. **NOTE:** Entry-level positions and part-time jobs are offered. **Company slogan:** We take it personally. **Special programs:** Internships. **Corporate headquarters location:** This location. **Other U.S. locations:** Nationwide. **International locations:** Worldwide. **Parent company:** Orient Overseas Ltd. **Number of employees worldwide:** 4,000.

PORT OF OAKLAND
530 Water Street, Oakland CA 94607. 510/627-1100. **Contact:** Manager of Personnel and Employee Services. **E-mail address:** perstech@portofoakland.com. **World Wide Web address:** http://www.portofoakland.com. **Description:** Operates Oakland International Airport, maritime facilities, and commercial real estate properties. **NOTE:** The above e-mail address may be used to request an application. **Special programs:** Internships. **Corporate headquarters location:** This location. **Operations at this facility include:** Administration; Service. **Number of employees at this location:** 600.

PORT OF STOCKTON
P.O. Box 2089, Stockton CA 95201. 209/946-0246. **Physical address:** 2201 West Washington Street, Stockton CA 95203. **Toll-free phone:** 800/344-3213. **Fax:** 209/941-0537. **Contact:** Human Resources. **E-mail address:** humanresources@stocktonport.com. **World Wide Web address:** http://www.portofstockton.com. **Description:** Provides berthing and warehousing facilities for inbound and outbound marine shipping. The port also provides domestic offices and warehouse space, and has land available for industrial development. **Corporate headquarters location:** This location. **Operations at this facility include:** Administration. **Annual sales/revenues:** $11 - $20 million. **Number of employees at this location:** 80.

SAN JOSE INTERNATIONAL AIRPORT
1732 North First Street, Suite 600, San Jose CA 95112. 408/501-7600. **Recorded jobline:** 408/277-5627. **Contact:** Human Resources. **World Wide Web address:** http://www.sjc.org. **Description:** Operates and manages the city's airport facilities. The airport is a city-funded department, and all airport staff are City of San Jose employees. **NOTE:** Employment applications must be obtained from the City of San Jose's Human Resources Department.

THAI AIRWAYS INTERNATIONAL PUBLIC COMPANY LIMITED
222 North Sepulveda Boulevard, Suite 1950, El Segundo CA 90245. 310/640-0097. **Fax:** 310/322-8728. **Contact:** Janet Mazon, Personnel Coordinator. **World Wide Web address:** http://www.thaiair.com. **Description:** An international passenger and freight air carrier. **NOTE:** Flight crews are only hired through the Bangkok, Thailand location. **Corporate headquarters location:** Bangkok, Thailand. **Other U.S. locations:** Nationwide. **Operations at this facility include:** Regional Headquarters. **Number of employees at this location:** 50. **Number of employees nationwide:** 100.

UPS SUPPLY CHAIN SOLUTIONS
1778 Carr Road, Calexico CA 92231. 760/357-5888. **Fax:** 760/357-5889. **Contact:** Human Resources. **World Wide Web address:** http://www.ups-scs.com. **Description:** A leader in global transportation and logistics. The company's services range from integrated logistics programs to traditional freight forwarding and customs brokerage. UPS SCS develops, implements, and delivers worldwide supply chain solutions for its clients. Founded in 1933. **NOTE:** Entry-level positions are offered. **Special programs:** Internships. **Corporate headquarters location:** Alpharetta GA. **Other U.S. locations:** Nationwide. **International locations:** Worldwide. **Parent company:** UPS. **Listed on:** New York Stock Exchange. **Stock exchange symbol:** UPS.

WALLACE TRANSPORT INC.
9290 East Highway 140, P.O. Box 67, Planada CA 95365. 209/382-0131. **Fax:** 209/382-1235. **Contact:** Dixie Allred, Director of Personnel & Safety. **World Wide Web address:** http://www.wallacetransport.com. **Description:** A common carrier trucking firm. **Corporate headquarters location:** This location. **Other area locations:** Fresno CA; Rancho Cucamonga CA.

Colorado

AMERICOLD LOGISTICS, LLC
4475 East 50th Avenue, Denver CO 80216. 303/320-0333. **Recorded jobline:** 866/KOOL-JOB. **Contact:** Personnel. **E-mail address:** employment@amclog.com. **World Wide Web address:** http://www.americold.net. **Description:** Operates refrigerated warehouse facilities that store frozen and refrigerated food products for various food distributing and processing companies. **Corporate headquarters location:** Atlanta GA. **Other U.S. locations:** Portland OR.

ASPEN DISTRIBUTION INC.
11075 East 40th Avenue, Denver CO 80239. 303/371-2511. **Contact:** Personnel. **World Wide Web address:** http://www.aspendistribution.com. **Description:** A local trucking company and public warehouse.

ASSOCIATED GLOBAL SYSTEMS
16075 East 32nd Avenue, Aurora CO 80011. 720/858-0200. **Contact:** Human Resources. **E-mail address:** careers@agsystems.com. **World Wide Web address:** http://www.agsystems.com. **Description:** An air transportation company offering domestic, international, and same-day services. **Corporate headquarters location:** New Hyde Park NY.

BAX GLOBAL
16075 East 32nd Avenue, Suite B, Aurora CO 80011. 720/859-6240. **Fax:** 720/859-6298. **Toll-free phone:** 800/525-3720. **Contact:** Human Resources. **World Wide Web address:** http://www.baxglobal.com. **Description:** Bax Global offers business-to-business freight delivery through a worldwide network of offices in 124 countries, with 155 offices in the U.S. **Other area locations:** Grand Junction CO. **Other U.S. locations:** Nationwide. **International locations:** Worldwide. **Parent company:** The Brink's Company.

GRAND VALLEY TRANSIT
201 South Avenue, Grand Junction CO 81501. 970/256-7433. **Contact:** Ralph Power, Executive Director. **World Wide Web address:** http://www.grandvalleytransit.com. **Description:** Provides transportation services to people with disabilities.

GREYHOUND BUS LINES
12881 Highway 61, Sterling CO 80751. 970/522-5522. **Contact:** Human Resources. **World Wide Web address:** http://www.greyhound.com. **Description:** Greyhound is a major nationwide bus route service operator, with more than 3,000 stop facilities throughout the United States. Greyhound also offers passenger express bus service, sightseeing services, airport ground transportation, and independent charter bus services. **Corporate headquarters location:** Dallas TX. **Operations at this facility include:** This

location is a local bus terminal.

GROUP VOYAGERS, INC.
dba GLOBUS & COSMOS
5301 South Federal Circle, Littleton CO 80123. 303/703-7000. **Toll-free phone:** 800/851-0728. **Fax:** 303/795-6615. **Contact:** Jackie Boyd, Recruiter. **Description:** Provides travel packages to more than 70 countries on all seven continents. **NOTE:** Entry-level positions and part-time jobs are offered. **Positions advertised include:** Oracle Financial Programmer; C+ Developer; Air Associate. **Special programs:** Training. **Office hours:** Monday - Friday, 7:00 a.m. - 6:00 p.m. **Corporate headquarters location:** This location. **Other U.S. locations:** Pasadena CA. **International locations:** Worldwide. **Number of employees at this location:** 290.

LAIDLAW TRANSIT SERVICES, INC.
6345 North Colorado Boulevard, Commerce City CO 80022. 303/288-1939. **Contact:** Human Resources. **World Wide Web address:** http://www.laidlawtransit.com. **Description:** Provides urban busing services. **Corporate headquarters location:** Overland Park KS. **Parent company:** Provides solid waste collection, compacting, transportation, treatment, transfer, and disposal services; provides hazardous waste services; operates hazardous waste facilities and wastewater treatment plants; and operates passenger and school buses, transit systems buses, and tour and charter buses.

Connecticut

AMERICAN EXPRESS TRAVEL RELATED SERVICES
64 Pratt Street, 3rd Floor, Hartford CT 06103. 860/987-5500. **Contact:** Human Resources. **World Wide Web address:** http://www.americanexpress.com. **Description:** A diversified travel and financial services company operating in 160 countries around the world. **Corporate headquarters location:** Cambridge MA. **Other U.S. locations:** Nationwide. **Listed on:** New York Stock Exchange. **Stock exchange symbol:** AXP.

BRADLEY INTERNATIONAL AIRPORT CONNECTICUT DEPARTMENT OF TRANSPORTATION
Schoephoester Road, Windsor Locks CT 06096. 860/292-2000. **Contact:** Human Resources. **World Wide Web address:** http://www.bradleyairport.com. **Description:** New England's second largest airport. Bradley International Airport serves western New England with international and domestic flights. **NOTE:** Resumes should be addressed to Connecticut Department of Transportation, P.O. Box 317546, Newington CT 06131.

CONNECTICUT LIMO
230 Old Gate Lane, Milford CT 06460. 203/878-6800. **Fax:** 203/783-6992. **Contact:** Human Resources. **E-mail address:** employment@ctlimo.com. **World Wide Web address:** http://www.ctlimo.com. **Description:** A shuttle bus service that provides transportation to and from John F. Kennedy International Airport (New York NY); LaGuardia International Airport (New York NY); Newark International Airport (Newark NJ); and Bradley International Airport (Windsor Locks CT.) **Positions advertised include:** Reservation Agent; Mechanic. **Corporate headquarters location:** This location.

DHL
340 Wilson Avenue, Norwalk CT 06854. 203/655-7900. **Toll-free phone**: 800/225-5345. **Contact:** Human Resources. **World Wide Web address:** http://www.dhl.com. **Description:** An international freight forwarder, serving customers in over 135 countries. **NOTE:** Call 954/888-7000 for Human Resources. **Corporate headquarters location:** Plantation FL. **Other U.S. locations:** Nationwide.

FEDEX
347 State Street, North Haven CT 06473. **Toll-free phone:** 800/463-3339. **Contact:** Human Resources. **World Wide Web address:** http://www.fedex.com. **Description:** One of the world's largest express transportation companies serving 212 countries worldwide. FedEx ships approximately 3 million packages daily through an operating fleet of over 600 aircraft, 39,500 vehicles, 2,000 ship sites, 33,800 drop boxes, and Internet shipping. **Corporate headquarters location:** Memphis TN. **Other U.S. locations:** Nationwide. **Listed on:** New York Stock Exchange. **Stock exchange symbol:** FDX.

GENESEE & WYOMING INC.
66 Field Point Road, Greenwich CT 06830. 203/629-3722. **Fax:** 203/661-4106. **Contact:** Human Resources. **World Wide Web address:** http://www.gwrr.com. **Description:** Operates 18 railroads with 4,700 miles of track in the United States, Canada, Australia, and Mexico. Founded in 1895. **NOTE:** The Human Resources Department is in the Rochester NY location. Please fax resumes to 716/328-8622. **Subsidiaries include:** Allegheny & Eastern Railroad, Inc. (Punxsatawney PA); Buffalo & Pittsburgh Railroad, Inc. (Punxsatawney PA); Illinois & Midland Railroad, Inc. (Springfield IL); Portland & Western Railroad, Inc. (Albany OR); Rail Link, Inc., which provides switching, rail freight, coal loading and unloading, and locomotive leasing in North America; Rochester & Southern Railroad, Inc. (Rochester NY); Willamette & Pacific Railroad, Inc. (Albany OR). **Other U.S. locations:** IL; NY; OR; PA. **International locations:** Australia; Bolivia; Canada; Mexico. **Listed on:** NASDAQ. **Stock exchange symbol:** GNWR. **President/CEO:** Mortimer B. Fuller III.

LAIDLAW TRANSIT SERVICES
80 Logan Street, Bridgeport CT 06607. 203/330-2600. **Contact:** Human Resources. **World Wide Web address:** http://www.laidlaw.com. **Description:** Laidlaw Transit Services operates over 200 transit lines. Laidlaw also provides transportation management services for municipalities, transit authorities, and organizations. **Parent company:** Laidlaw Inc. provides solid waste collection, compaction, transportation, treatment, transfer, and disposal services; provides hazardous waste services; operates hazardous waste facilities and wastewater treatment plants; and operates passenger and school buses, transit system buses, and tour and charter buses. **Operations at this facility include:** This location of Laidlaw Transit owns and operates school buses for the Bridgeport public school system.

OMI CORPORATION
Metro Center, One Station Place, 7th Floor North, Stamford CT 06902. 203/602-6700. **Contact:** Human Resources. **World Wide Web address:** http://www.omicorp.com. **Description:** A large bulk shipping company with interests in 46 ocean-going bulk carriers, tankers, and gas carriers. OMI also provides logistics, crewing, technical, and commercial operations for international clients. The company has interests in OMI Petrolink Corporation and in Chiles Offshore Corporation, which operates 14 drilling rigs. **Corporate headquarters location:** This location. **Subsidiaries include:** OMI Marine Services, LLC. **Listed on:** New York Stock Exchange. **Stock exchange symbol:** OMM.

STOLT-NIELSEN TRANSPORTATION GROUP LTD.
800 Connecticut Avenue, 4th Floor East, Norwalk CT. 203/838-7100. **Fax:** 203/299-0067. **Contact:** Human Resources. **World Wide Web address:** http://www.stoltnielsen.com. **Description:** Operates the world's largest fleet of bulk chemical, oil, acid, and specialty liquid tankers. **Parent company:** Stolt-Nielsen S.A.

Delaware

BURRIS LOGISTICS, INC.
501 Southeast 5th Street, Milford DE 19963. 302/839-4531. **Toll-free phone:** 800/805-8135. **Fax:** 302/839-5175. **Contact:** Human Resources Department. **E-mail address:** wilma.carey@burrislogistics.com. **World**

Wide Web address: http://www.burrislogistics.com. **Description:** Operates refrigerated and frozen food warehousing and distribution systems. The company serves retail, wholesale and manufacturing customers. **NOTE:** Call or send an e-mail message to inquire about current job openings. **Other area locations:** Harrington DE; New Castle DE. **Other U.S. locations:** FL; VA; MD; PA; SC.

DELAWARE RIVER AND BAY AUTHORITY
P.O. Box 71 New Castle DE 19720. 302/571-6438. **Fax:** 302/571-6420. **Contact:** Human Resources. **E-mail address:** hrdept@drba.net. **World Wide Web address:** http://www.drba.net. **Description:** Provides vital transportation links between Delaware and New Jersey, as well as economic development in Delaware and the four southern counties of New Jersey.

District Of Columbia

AAA MID-ATLANTIC
701 15th Street NW, Washington DC 20005. 202/331-3000. **Recorded jobline:** 866/AAA-JOBS. **Contact:** Human Resources. **World Wide Web address:** http://www.aaamidatlantic.com. **Description:** Provides insurance, travel, and a wide variety of services to motorists through a network of more than 50 branch offices. **Positions advertised include:** Insurance Counselor.

AMERICAN BUS ASSOCIATION
700 13th NW, Suite 575, Washington DC 20005-5923. 202/842-1645. **Fax:** 202/842-0850. **Contact:** Human Resources. **World Wide Web address:** http://www.buses.org. **Description:** Represents the intercity busing industry. **Corporate headquarters location:** This location.

SECURITY MOVING & STORAGE
1701 Florida Avenue NW, Washington DC 20009-2697. 202/234-5600. **Fax:** 202/234-3513. **Contact:** Human Resources. **World Wide Web address:** http://www.sscw.com. **Description:** Provides general storage, cold storage, freight forwarding, moving and packing, and international trading services. **Positions advertised include:** Mover; Driver; Warehouseman. **Corporate headquarters location:** This location. **Number of employees at this location:** 160.

Florida

ALAMO RENT-A-CAR
2301 Northwest 33rd Avenue, Miami FL 33142. 305/638-1026. **Toll-free phone:** 800/462-5266. **Contact:** Human Resources. **World Wide Web address:** http://www.alamo.com. **Description:** One of the nation's leading car rental companies. **Corporate headquarters location:** This location. **Operations at this facility include:** Administration. **Listed on:** Privately held.

ALTERMAN TRANSPORTATION GROUP
8344 Morning Glory Road North, Jacksonville FL 32210. 904/378-8233. **Contact:** Human Resources. **World Wide Web address:** http://www.alterman.com. **Description:** An interstate trucking company that specializes in the transport of perishable goods.

BLACKBEARD'S CRUISES
P.O. Box 66-1091, Miami FL 33266. 954/734-7111. **Physical address**: 3700 Hacienda Boulevard, Suite G, Davie FL 33314. **Contact:** Human Resources. **E-mail address:** jobs@blackbeard-cruises.com. **World Wide Web address:** http://www.blackbeard-cruises.com. **Description:** A cruise line that sails to the Bahamas. **Positions advertised include:** Cook; Dive Instructor; Engineer.

BUDGET GROUP, INC.
2900 North University Drive, Coral Springs FL 33065. 954/340-5885. **Contact:** Human Resources. **World Wide Web address:** http://www.bgi.com. **Description:** A holding company. **Corporate headquarters location:** This location. **Subsidiaries include:** Budget Airport Parking; Budget Car Sales, Inc.; Budget Rent A Car Corporation; Cruise America, Inc.; Premier Car Rental; Ryder TRS, Inc.; Van Pool Services, Inc.

CSX TRANSPORTATION
500 Water Street, Jacksonville FL 32202-4423. 904/359-3100. **Contact:** Human Resources. **World Wide Web address:** http://www.csxt.com. **Description:** A railroad company that transports a variety of products for the agricultural, automotive, mining, food, and consumer markets. **Positions advertised include:** Assistant Road-master; Assistant Terminal Trainmaster; Boilermaker; Carman; Clerk; Communications Maintainer; Machinist; Police; Road Electrician; Utility Worker; Yard Worker. **Parent company:** CSX Corporation.

CARNIVAL CORPORATION
CARNIVAL CRUISE LINES
Carnival Place, 3655 NW 87th Avenue, Miami FL 33178-2428. **Toll-free phone:** 888/227-6482. **Contact:** Human Resources. **World Wide Web address:** http://www.carnival.com. **Description:** A travel holding company. **NOTE:** This firm does not accept unsolicited resumes. Please only respond to advertised openings. **Positions advertised include:** International Sales; Information Systems; Hotel Operations; Guest Relations; Executive Sales; Embarkation People; Technical Operations; Ship Board Personnel; Revenue Management Accounting; Reservations; Operations Accounting; Office Sales; Marketing; Management Advisory Services; Loss Prevention; Corporate Environmental Compliance; Consumer Research. **Subsidiaries include:** Carnival Cruise Lines (also at this location) operates nine cruise ships serving the Caribbean and Mexican Riviera; Holland America Line operates seven cruise ships serving primarily the Caribbean and Alaska through the Panama Canal; Windstar Cruises operates three sail-powered vessels that call on locations inaccessible to larger ships; Holland America Westours markets sightseeing tours both separately and as a part of Holland America Line cruise/tour packages.

CELEBRITY CRUISES
1050 Caribbean Way, Miami FL 33132. 305/262-6677. **Contact:** Human Resources. **E-mail address:** celebritycruises@celebrity.com. **World Wide Web address:** http://www.celebrity-cruises.com. **Description:** Operates an ocean cruise line that sails to Alaska, Bermuda, the Caribbean Islands, Europe, Hawaii, and South America. **Corporate headquarters location:** This location.

COSTA CRUISE LINES
200 South Park Road, Hollywood, FL 33021. 954/266-5600. **Contact:** Personnel Manager. **World Wide Web address:** http://www.costacruises.com. **Description:** An ocean cruise line.

CROWLEY AMERICAN TRANSPORT, INC.
P.O. Box 2110, Jacksonville FL 32203-2110. 904/727-2200. **Physical address:** 9487 Regency Square Boulevard, Jacksonville FL 32225. **Recorded jobline:** 904/727-4287. **Contact:** Human Resources. **World Wide Web address:** http://www.crowley.com. **Description:** An ocean freight company. **Positions advertised include:** Specialist Support Services; Security Information Administrator; Freight Service Coordinator; Inter Model Dispatcher.

FLORIDA EAST COAST RAILWAY COMPANY
353 Florida Avenue, Fort Pierce FL 34950. 772/461-8657. **Contact:** Gloria S. Taylor, Director of Human Resources. **Description:** A railway transportation company. **Corporate headquarters location:** This location. **Operations at this facility include:** Administration. **Number of employees at this location:** 200. **Number of employees nationwide:** 1,000.

FLORIDA ROCK INDUSTRIES
P.O. Box 4667, Jacksonville FL 32201. 904/355-1781. **Physical address:** 155 East 21st Street, Jacksonville FL 32206. **Contact:** Bob Banks, Director of Human

Resources. **Description:** Manufactures concrete aggregates. Florida Rock & Tank Lines (also at this location) transports oil and gasoline. Sunbelt Transport (also at this location) is a flatbed transportation company. **Corporate headquarters location:** This location. **Operations at this facility include:** Administration. **Listed on:** New York Stock Exchange. **Stock exchange symbol:** FRK.

LAND SPAN, INC.
P.O. Box 95007, Lakeland FL 33804. 863/688-1102. **Physical address**: 1020 Griffin Road, Lakeland FL 33805. **Contact:** Human Resources. **World Wide Web address:** http://www.landspan.com. **Description:** An interstate trucking company that transports dry and refrigerated freight. **Positions advertised include:** Driver. **Other U.S. locations:** Norcross GA; Chicago IL; Hagerstown MD; Charlotte NC; El Paso TX; Fort Worth TX. **Parent company:** Watkins Associated Industries, Inc. **Number of employees at this location:** 300.

LANDSTAR
P.O. Box 19139, Jacksonville FL 32245-9939. **Physical address**: 13410 Sutton Park Drive South, Jacksonville FL 32224. **Toll-free phone:** 800/235-4466. **Contact:** Susan Ramsey, Human Resources Director. **World Wide Web address:** http://www.landstar.com. **Description:** Landstar Ligon provides truckload transportation services through independent contractors and commissioned sales agents. **Positions advertised include:** Staff Accountant; Permit Representative; Director of Facility Operations; Credit Analyst; Trailer Utilization Coordinator; Log Compliance Representative; Contract Research Representative; Trip Envelope Processor; Per Diem Representative. **Parent company:** Landstar System, Inc. is divided into specialized freight transportation segments. Landstar is one of the only publicly traded trucking companies relying on independent owner-operators rather than salaried company drivers, with the company owning just 10 percent of the trucks in its fleet. Subsidiaries of Landstar System, Inc. include Landstar Expedited, Inc.; Landstar Express America, Inc.; Landstar Gemini, Inc.; Landstar Inway, Inc.; Landstar ITCO, Inc.; Landstar Poole, Inc.; Landstar Ranger, Inc.; Landstar T.L.C., Inc.; Landstar Transportation Service, Inc. **Listed on:** NASDAQ. **Stock exchange symbol:** LSTR.

LUHRS CORPORATION
255 Diesel Road, St. Augustine FL 32084. 904/829-0500. **Toll-free phone:** 800/882-4342. **Fax:** 904/829-0683. **Contact:** Erica Stegerwald, Personnel Manager. **E-mail address:** customerservice@luhrs.com. **World Wide Web address:** http://www.luhrs.com. **Description:** Manufactures fiberglass boats. **Corporate headquarters location:** This location. **Operations at this facility include:** Administration; Manufacturing; Sales; Service. **Number of employees at this location:** 375.

MARITRANS INC.
302 Knights Run Avenue, Suite 1200, Tampa FL 33602. 813/209-0600. **Fax:** 813/221-3179. **Contact:** Human Resources. **E-mail address:** hr@maritrans.com. **World Wide Web address:** http://www.maritrans.com. **Description:** Maritrans provides marine transportation for petroleum and oil storage terminals. The company also offers a full package of oil distribution services including product exchanges, marine transportation, scheduling, terminal storage, and automated truck rack delivery systems. **Positions advertised include:** Major Projects Associate; Project Engineer; Lighting Coordinator; VCE Associate; Tug Rebuilding Associate; Executive Assistant. **Corporate headquarters location:** This location. **Listed on:** New York Stock Exchange. **Stock exchange symbol:** TUG.

McKENZIE TANK LINES, INC.
122 Appleyard Drive, Tallahassee FL 32304. 850/576-1221. **Contact:** Paulette McElroy, Human Resources Director. **World Wide Web address:** http://www.mckenzietank.com. **Description:** An interstate trucking company.

NORWEGIAN CRUISE LINES
7665 NW 19th Street, Miami FL 33126. 305/436-4000. **Contact:** Human Resources. **World Wide Web address:** http://www.ncl.com. **Description:** An ocean cruise line. **Positions advertised include:** Accounting Clerk; Business Analyst; Business Project Manager; Corporate & Crew Supervisor; CRS Administrator; Credit Clerk; Office Administrator; Land Agent; Production Show Supervisor; Revenue Specialist; Yield Management Supervisor.

REGAL MARINE INDUSTRIES, INC.
2300 Jetport Drive, Orlando FL 32809. 407/851-4360. **Fax:** 407/857-1256. **Contact:** Kim Evans, Director of Human Resources. **E-mail address:** regal@regalboats.com. **World Wide Web address:** http://www.regalboats.com. **Description:** Manufactures pleasure boats.

ROYAL CARIBBEAN
1050 Caribbean Way, Miami FL 33132. 305/379-2601. **Contact:** Human Resources. **World Wide Web address:** http://www.rccl.com. **Description:** An ocean cruise line that operates 22 ships sailing to the Caribbean, the Bahamas, Bermuda, Mexico, Alaska, the Mediterranean, Europe, the Greek Isles, Panama Canal, Hawaii, Scandinavia/Russia, and the Far East. **NOTE:** Job seekers are encouraged to submit their resume on-line, so that they may be considered for job opportunities as they become available. **Positions advertised include:** Accounting Clerk; Clerical Administrative Representative; Call Center Representative; Corporate Communication Representative; Culinary Associate; Customer Service Representative; General Manager; Guest Satisfaction Representative; Bar Manager; Hotel Director; Human Resources Manager; Unix System Administrator; Logistics Coordinator; Technical Superintendent; Hotel Purchasing Manager; Safety & Environmental Auditor; Guest Vacation Sales; Marketing Research Manager; Information Analyst; Vacation Sales Specialist; Quality Assurance Manager. **Corporate headquarters location:** This location. **Listed on:** New York Stock Exchange. **Stock exchange symbol:** RCL. **CEO:** Richard D. Fain. **Number of employees nationwide:** 15,000.

RYDER SYSTEM, INC.
3600 NW 82nd Avenue, Miami FL 33166. 305/500-3726. **Contact:** Human Resources. **World Wide Web address:** http://www.ryder.com. **Description:** Leases trucks, hauls automobiles, provides contract carriage and logistics services, and provides school bus transportation. Truck leasing operations are conducted in the United States, Puerto Rico, United Kingdom, Germany, and Poland with over 78,000 vehicles. The company provides maintenance, leasing, and related supplies, and also maintains over 27,000 non-leased trucks. **Positions advertised include:** Administrative Assistant; Benefit Analyst; Branch Rental Manager; Coordinator; Asset Utilization Director; Market Research & Support Sales Director; Account Executive; Management Trainee; International Finance Manager; Market Research & Sales Support; Supply Management Manager; Supply Chain Marketing Consultant; Finance Manager; Service Manager; Service Support Leader; Staff Accountant; Tax Specialist; Customer Logistics Coordinator; Business Financial Analyst. **Corporate headquarters location:** This location. **Other U.S. locations:** Nationwide. **International locations:** Canada; Continental Europe; England; Mexico; Singapore; South America. **Listed on:** NASDAQ. **Stock exchange symbol:** R. **Number of employees worldwide:** 30,000.

SEABOURN
6100 Blue Lagoon Drive, Suite 400, Miami FL 33126. 305/463-3000. **Toll-free phone:** 800/223-0764. **Fax:** 305/463-3035. **Contact:** Human Resources. **World Wide Web address:** http://www.seabourn.com. **Description:** An ocean cruise line that calls at ports

worldwide. **Positions advertised include:** Hotel Officer; Waiter; Waitress; Chef De Partie; Assistant Waiter; Assistant Waitress; Class 2, 3 Deck Officer; Ventilation Officer; Electrical Electronics Engineer; International Sales; Switchboard Operator; Regional Sales Manager; Security Operations Manager; Sales Representative; Corporate Training & Development Specialist; Business Analyst; Cruise Sales Consultant. **Corporate headquarters location:** This location. **Listed on:** New York Stock Exchange. **Stock exchange symbol:** CCL.

TNT LOGISTICS
P.O. Box 40083, Jacksonville, FL 32203. 904/928-1400. **Toll-free phone:** 888/LOG-ISTX. **Fax:** 904/928-1547. **Contact:** Human Resources. **World Wide Web address:** http://www.tntlogistics.com. **Description:** A third party logistics provider. Founded in 1980. **NOTE:** Entry-level positions and second and third shifts are offered. **Positions advertised include:** Business Development Manager; Internal Auditor; Logistics Engineer; Logistics Project Manager; Supervisor; Systems Engineer; Transportation Administrator; Transportation Technician. **Special programs:** Internships; Training. **Office hours:** Monday - Friday, 8:00 a.m. - 5:00 p.m. **Corporate headquarters location:** This location. **International locations:** Argentina; Brazil; Canada; Mexico; United Kingdom. **Listed on:** New York Stock Exchange. **Stock exchange symbol:** TP. **Annual sales/revenues:** More than $100 million. **Number of employees worldwide:** 116,000.

WELLCRAFT MARINE
1651 Whitfield Avenue, Sarasota FL 34243. 941/753-7811. **Fax:** 941/751-7876. **Contact:** Noemi S. Vento, 941/753-7811 ext 553. Human Resources. **E-mail address:** venton@wellcraft.com. **World Wide Web address:** http://www.wellcraft.com. **Description:** Manufactures a variety of boats including cruisers, fishing boats, sport boats, and high-performance speed boats. **Corporate headquarters location:** Minneapolis MN.

WINDJAMMER BAREFOOT CRUISES
P.O. Box 190120, Miami Beach FL 33119. 305/672-6453. **Physical address**: 1759 Bay Road, Miami Beach FL 33139. **Toll-free:** 800-327-2601. **Contact:** John Horn, Personnel Director. **E-mail address:** info@windjammer.com. **World Wide Web address:** http://www.windjammer.com. **Description:** A cruise line that operates six ships sailing to the Caribbean.

Georgia

AIRTRAN AIRWAYS
1800 Phoenix Boulevard, Suite 104, Atlanta GA 30349. 770/994-8258. **Toll-free phone:** 800/965-2107. **Contact:** Human Resources. **World Wide Web address:** http://www.airtran.com. **Description:** A low-fare airline operating more than 600 flights a day to over 40 destinations. **Positions advertised include:** Flight Attendant; Interiors Engineer; Maintenance Planner; Manager Customer Relations; Manager of Financial Planning and Control; Ramp Agent. **Corporate headquarters location:** This location. **Parent company:** AirTran Holdings. **Listed on:** New York Stock Exchange. **Stock exchange symbol:** AAI. **Number of employees nationwide:** 6,700.

AMERICAN AIRLINES, INC.
Hartsfield International Airport, Atlanta GA 30331. **Toll-free phone:** 800/433-7300. **Contact:** Human Resources. **World Wide Web address:** http://www.aa.com. **Description:** Provides scheduled jet service to more than 170 destinations primarily throughout North America, the Caribbean, Latin America, Europe, and the Pacific. **NOTE:** Please visit website to fill out an employment interest form. **Corporate headquarters location:** Fort Worth TX. **Parent company:** AMR Corporation. **Listed on:** New York Stock Exchange. **Stock exchange symbol:** AMR. **President/CEO:** Gerard J. Arpey. **Number of employees nationwide:** 100,000.

ATLANTIC SOUTHEAST AIRLINES (ASA)
100 Hartsfield Centre Parkway, Suite 800, Atlanta GA 30354-1356. 404/766-1400. **Fax:** 404/209-0162. **Contact:** Employment Department. **World Wide Web address:** http://www.flyasa.com. **Description:** One of Atlanta's largest regional airlines and a Delta connection carrier. Founded in 1979. **NOTE:** Jobseekers can request an application by sending a self-addressed, stamped envelope to this location. **Corporate headquarters location:** This location. **Other U.S. locations:** Nationwide. **Parent company:** Delta Air Lines. **Listed on:** New York Stock Exchange. **Stock exchange symbol:** DAL. **President:** W.E. Barnette. **Number of employees nationwide:** 5,500.

CSX TRANSPORTATION
1590 Marietta Boulevard, NW, Atlanta GA 30318. 404/350-5383. **Recorded jobline:** 800/521-1658. **E-mail address:** jobs@csxt.com. **Contact:** Human Resources Department. **World Wide Web address:** http://www.csx.com. **Description:** Provides national and international rail service. **Special programs:** Internships; Co-ops. **Corporate headquarters location:** Jacksonville FL. **Parent Company:** CSX Corporation.

DELTA AIR LINES
P.O. Box 20706, Hartsfield Atlanta International Airport, Atlanta GA 30320-6001. 404/715-2600. **Recorded jobline:** 800/659-2580. **Contact:** Personnel. **E-mail address:** delta.careers@delta.com. **World Wide Web address:** http://www.delta.com. **Description:** One of the largest airlines in the United States. The company provides scheduled air transportation for passengers, freight, and mail on an extensive route that covers most of the country and extends to 58 foreign nations. The route covers 218 domestic cities in 48 states, the District of Columbia, Puerto Rico, the U.S. Virgin Islands, and 131 cities abroad. Major domestic hubs include the Atlanta, Dallas/Fort Worth, Salt Lake City, and Cincinnati ports, with minor hubs located in Los Angeles and Orlando. Founded in 1929. **NOTE:** Please visit website to search for jobs. E-mailed resumes are preferred. Entry-level positions are offered. **Positions advertised include:** Accountant; Income Tax Analyst; Corporate Communications Manager; Employee and Workplace Safety Manager; International Logistics Manager; Program Specialist – Market Planning and Intelligence; Project Leader – Finance; Senior Analyst – Financial Planning and Analysis; Senior Change Consultant; Senior Project Manager – Facilities; Senior Propulsion Engineer; Accounting Supervisor; Boarding Gate/Ticket Counter; Ramp Operator; Air Logistic Worker. **Special programs:** Internships; Co-ops. **Corporate headquarters location:** This location. **Subsidiaries include:** Comair Inc.; Southeast Airlines, Inc. **Listed on:** New York Stock Exchange. **Stock exchange symbol:** DAL. **CEO:** Gerald Grinstein. **Number of employees nationwide:** 81,000.

HERTZ CORPORATION
4751 Best Road, Suite 400, Atlanta GA 30337. 404/530-2990. Fax: 404/530-2962. **Contact:** John Kreitner, Employee Relations. **E-mail address:** jkreitner@hertz.com. **World Wide Web address:** http://www.hertz.com. **Description:** Area offices for the national transportation services organization. Hertz Corporation operates nationally through three divisions: the Rent-A-Car Division, the Car Leasing Division, and the Equipment Rental and Leasing Division. **Positions advertised include:** Heavy Equipment Mechanic; Branch Manager; Management Trainee; Suburban Sales Representative; Financial Analyst. **Corporate headquarters location:** Park Ridge NJ. **Other U.S. locations:** Nationwide. **International locations:** Worldwide. **Parent company:** Ford Motor Company. **President/CEO:** Craig R. Koch. **Number of employees worldwide:** 28,900.

IFF INC.
P.O. Box 45505, Atlanta GA 30320. 404/305-9433. **Physical address:** 452-A Plaza Drive, Cottage Park GA 30349. **Fax:** 404/209-6741. **E-mail address:**

peter.halpaus@iffusa.com. **Contact:** Peter Halpaus. **World Wide Web address:** http://www.iffusa.com. **Description:** A forwarder of international freight. Founded in 1983. **Corporate headquarters location:** This location. **Other U.S. locations:** Charlotte NC; Greenville SC; Richmond VA. **President:** Jeff Smith.

METROPOLITAN ATLANTA RAPID TRANSIT AUTHORITY (MARTA)
2424 Piedmont Road NE, Atlanta GA 30324-3311. 404/848-5000. **Fax:** 404/848-5687. **Recorded jobline:** 404/848-5627. **Contact:** Recruiting. **World Wide Web address:** http://www.itsmarta.com. **Description:** Operates the bus and subway systems for the city of Atlanta. **NOTE:** You may also apply by contacting the Georgia Department of Labor in the metropolitan Atlanta area. **Positions advertised include:** Director – Infrastructure and System Management; Senior IT Program Manager; Planning/Research Project Coordinator; Transit Police Officer; Performance Administrator; Strategic Planner; Manager of Compensation; ITS/GIC Analyst; Technical Engineer. **Special programs:** Internships. **Corporate headquarters location:** This location. **Operations at this facility include:** Administration.

ROADWAY EXPRESS INC.
2701 Moreland Avenue SE, Atlanta GA 30315. 404/361-0861. **Fax:** 404/361-0988. **Contact:** Personnel Manager. **World Wide Web address:** http://www.roadway.com. **Description:** Operates a freight consolidation and distribution terminal for one of the largest common carriers in the United States, with terminals in more than 633 cities nationwide. Founded 1930. **NOTE:** Please visit website to search for jobs. **Corporate headquarters location:** Akron OH. **Other area locations:** Statewide. **Other U.S. locations:** Nationwide. **International locations:** Puerto Rico; Guam; Mexico; Canada. **Parent company:** Yellow Roadway. **Listed on:** NASDAQ. **Stock exchange symbol:** YELL. **Number of employees worldwide:** 24,800.

UNITED PARCEL SERVICE (UPS)
55 Glenlake Parkway NE, Atlanta GA 30328. 404/828-6000. **Fax:** 404/828-6440. **Recorded jobline:** 888/967-5877. **Contact:** Human Resources. **World Wide Web address:** http://www.ups.com. **Description:** United Parcel Service is a package pickup and delivery service organization, providing service to all 50 states and to more than 185 countries and territories worldwide. The company delivers approximately 12 million packages daily. **NOTE:** Please visit website to search for jobs and apply online. **Positions advertised include:** Contact Manager; CSC Industrial Engineer; Print Production Supervisor; Strategic Customer Communications Supervisor; Project Design Specialist; Treasury Specialist; Contract Administrator; Brand Identity Manager; Database Marketing Specialist; Junior Finance Specialist; Plant Engineering Designer; Associate Financial Analyst; Lead Accountant; Warehouse Associate; Paralegal; Regional Account Manager. **Special programs:** Internships. **Corporate headquarters location:** This location. **Other U.S. locations:** Nationwide. **International locations:** Worldwide. **Operations at this facility include:** This location houses the administrative offices. **Listed on:** New York Stock Exchange. **Stock exchange symbol:** UPS. **CEO:** Michael Eskew. **Number of employees nationwide:** 355,000.

WATKINS ASSOCIATED INDUSTRIES
1958 Monroe Drive NE, Atlanta GA 30324. 404/872-3841. **Fax:** 404/872-2812. **Contact:** Human Resources. **Description:** Operates a variety of companies, including trucking company, real estate development, door and window manufacturing, and seafood processing. **Corporate headquarters location:** This location. **Other U.S. locations:** Nationwide. **International locations:** Canada; Mexico; Puerto Rico. **President/CEO:** Mike Watkins. **Number of employees nationwide:** 9,000.

YELLOW TRANSPORTATION
1892 Airport Industrial Park Drive SE, Marietta GA 30060. 770/952-9341. **Contact:** Human Resources Department. **World Wide Web address:** http://www.myyellow.com. **Description:** Yellow Freight Systems, Inc. is a national long-haul truckload carrier, with over 400 terminal locations. **NOTE:** Please visit website to search for jobs. **Corporate headquarters location:** Overland Park KS. **Operations at this facility include:** This location operates one of the company's 17 nationwide hub stations.

Hawaii

ALEXANDER & BALDWIN, INC.
P.O. Box 3440, Honolulu HI 96801-3440. 808/525-6611. **Physical address:** 822 Bishop Street, Honolulu HI 96813-3924. **Contact:** Ruthann S. Yamanaka, Vice President of Human Resources. **World Wide Web address:** http://www.alexanderbaldwin.com. **Description:** A diversified corporation whose businesses include property development and management, ocean transportation, and food products. **Corporate headquarters location:** This location. **Other U.S. locations:** CA. **Subsidiaries include:** Matson Navigation Company; A&B Properties, Maui Office; Kahului Trucking & Storage; Kauai Coffee Company; Kauai Commercial Company. **Listed on:** NASDAQ. **Stock exchange symbol:** ALEX.

HAWAIIAN AIRLINES
P.O. Box 30008, Honolulu HI 96820. 808/835-3700. **Physical address:** 3375 Koapaka Street, G-350, Honolulu HI 96819. **Fax:** 808/835-3649. **Recorded jobline:** 808/835-3730. **Contact:** Human Resources. **World Wide Web address:** http://www.hawaiianair.com. **Description:** A regional airline for passengers, cargo, and mail over a route consisting of six major Hawaiian islands, cities on the West Coast, and some cities in the South Pacific. **NOTE:** Applications and resumes accepted for open positions only. Search and apply online at http://www.hapeople.com. **Positions advertised include:** Call Center Business Liaison; Computer Operator; Coordinator, Cargo Sales & Service; Director, Data Marketing; Director, Internet Marketing; Infrastructure Manager; Technical Writer. **Corporate headquarters location:** This location. **Other U.S. locations:** Los Angeles CA; San Francisco CA; Las Vegas NV; Portland OR; Seattle WA. **Operations at this facility include:** Administration; Research and Development; Sales. **Listed on:** American Stock Exchange. **Stock exchange symbol:** HA. **Number of employees nationwide:** 3,400.

Illinois

ABF FREIGHT SYSTEM, INC.
1970 Weisbrook Drive, Oswego IL 60543. 630/966-0606. **Toll-free phone:** 800/610-5544. **Fax:** 800/599-2810 **Contact:** Branch Manager. **World Wide Web address:** http://www.abfs.com. **Description:** One of the nation's largest motor carriers. **NOTE:** Apply online at website. Special programs: Management Training. **Positions advertised include:** Drivers; Office Clerk; Operations Supervisor; Quotation Analyst; Industrial Engineer. **Corporate headquarters location:** Fort Smith, AK.

ACE DORAN HAULING & RIGGING COMPANY
5529 Dial Drive, Granite City IL 62040. 618/797-0047. **Contact:** Human Resources. **World Wide Web address:** http://www.acedoran.com. **Description:** Provides truck transportation of heavy and specialized commodities such as steel, aluminum, self-propelled vehicles in excess of 15,000 pounds, and construction equipment. **NOTE:** For driver positions, apply online. For all other positions, send resumes to: Ace Doran Hauling & Rigging Company, Human Resources, 1601 Blue Rock Street, Cincinnati OH 45223.

A1 TRAVEL
1506 Wabash Avenue, Springfield IL 62704. 217/546-1090. **Contact:** Hiring Manager. **Description:** A travel agency. A1 Travel also offers classes for individuals

who are considering becoming travel consultants. **Corporate headquarters location:** This location.

ALLIANCE SHIPPERS, INC.
15515 South 70th Court, Orland Park IL 60462. 708/802-7000. **Contact:** Manager. **World Wide Web address:** http://www.alliance.com. **Description:** Transports packages for businesses and consumers throughout the world. **Corporate headquarters location:** This location. **International locations:** Worldwide.

ALLIED VAN LINES
700 Oakmont Lane, Westmont IL 60559. 630/570-3000. **Fax:** 630/570-3606. **Contact:** Human Resources. **World Wide Web address:** http://www.alliedvan.com. **Description:** A moving company whose major markets are household goods moving and specialized transportation services. **NOTE:** To see job listings and to apply, visit the corporate website at http://www.careers.sirva.com. **Positions advertised include:** Customer Service Manager; Transportation Manager; IT Quality Assurance Analyst; Claims Adjustor. **Corporate headquarters location:** This location. **Parent company:** SIRVA. **Number of employees at this location:** 690.

BEKINS VAN LINES
330 South Mannheim Road, Hillside IL 60162. 708/547-2000. **Fax:** 708/547-3228. **Contact:** Human Resources. **World Wide Web address:** http://www.bekins.com. **Description:** A moving and storage company. **Positions advertised include:** Driver. **Corporate headquarters location:** This location. **Parent company:** The Bekins Company. **Operations at this facility include:** Service. **Listed on:** Privately held.

CH2M HILL
8501 West Higgins Road, Suite 300,Chicago IL 60631-2801. 773/693-3809. **Contact:** Human Resources. **World Wide Web address:** http://www.ch2m.com. **Description:** A group of employee-owned companies operating under the names CH2M Hill, Inc., Industrial Design Corporation, Operations Management International, CH2M Hill International, and CH2M Hill Engineering. The professional staff includes specialists in environmental engineering, waste management, water management, transportation, industrial facilities, and a broad spectrum of infrastructure systems. **NOTE:** This company has offices throughout Chicago, Illinois and the United States. See website for job listings and apply online. **Operations at this facility include:** This location provides transportation and environmental engineering services.

CARRY TRANSIT
7830 West 71st Street, Bridgeview IL 60455. 800/777-2288. **Contact:** Neil Desmond, Human Resources. **E-mail address:** ndesmond@carrytransit.com. **World Wide Web address:** http://www.carrytransit.com. **Description:** Operates one of the nation's largest fleets of stainless steel food grade tankers, serving as a liquid and dry bulk distribution partner to various food products manufacturers. **Positions advertised include:** Local Truck Driver; Truck Driver CDL; Trucking Terminal Manager. **Corporate headquarters location:** This location.

CONSOER TOWNSEND ENVIRODYNE ENGINEERS, INC.
303 East Wacker Drive, Suite 600, Chicago IL 60601. 312/938-0300. **Fax:** 312/938-1109. **Contact:** Director of Human Resources. **E-mail address:** jobs@cte-eng.com. **World Wide Web address:** http://www.cte-eng.com. **Description:** Provides engineering consulting for highways, airports, and waste management projects. **NOTE:** Apply online at the company's website or e-mail resumes.

ELGIN, JOLIET & EASTERN RAILWAY COMPANY
1141 Maple Road, Joliet IL 60432. 815/740-6760. **Fax:** 815/740-6757. **Contact:** Human Resources. **World Wide Web address:** http://www.tstarinc.com. **Description:** A common carrier freight line. **NOTE:** Resumes only accepted for open positions. The company's website provides job listings. Apply online or fax or e-mail resumes. **Positions advertised include:** Motor Car Repairman; Trainman/Remote Control/Locomotive Engineer Trainee. **Other U.S. locations:** IN. **Parent company:** Transtar (Monroeville PA). **Operations at this facility include:** Service.

FEDERAL EXPRESS CORPORATION (FEDEX)
500 Commerce Street, Aurora IL 60504. 630/820-1061. **Toll-free phone:** 800/463-3339. **Contact:** Human Resources. **World Wide Web address:** http://www.fedex.com. **Description:** One of the world's largest express transportation companies serving 212 countries worldwide. FedEx ships approximately 3.2 million packages daily. FedEx operates more than 45,000 drop-off locations, and has a fleet that consists of more than 640 aircraft and 44,5000 vehicles. **NOTE:** Apply online at the company's website. **Corporate headquarters location:** Memphis TN. **Other U.S. locations:** Nationwide. **Operations at this facility include:** This location is a World Service Center.

GATX CORPORATION
500 West Monroe Street, 42nd Floor, Chicago IL 60661. 312/621-6200. **Fax:** 312/621-8062. **Contact:** Human Resources. **E-mail address:** jobs@gatx.com. **World Wide Web address:** http://www.gatx.com. **Description:** A holding company engaged in the lease and sale of rail cars and storage tanks for petroleum transport; equipment and capital asset financing and related services; the operation of tank storage terminals, pipelines, and related facilities; the operation of warehouses; and distribution and logistics support. Founded in 1898. **NOTE:** Entry-level positions are offered. **Positions advertised include:** Payroll Specialist; Senior Financial Analyst. **Special programs:** Internships. **Office hours:** Monday - Friday, 8:30 a.m. - 4:45 p.m. **Corporate headquarters location:** This location. **Other U.S. locations:** Nationwide. **International locations:** Worldwide. **Subsidiaries include:** American Steamship Company; GATX Capital Corporation; GATX Logistics; GATX Terminals Corporation; General American Trans. **Operations at this facility include:** Administration. **Listed on:** New York Stock Exchange. **Stock exchange symbol:** GMT.

GE CAPITAL CORPORATION
540 West Northwest Highway, Barrington IL 60010. 847/277-4000. **Contact:** Human Resources. **World Wide Web address:** http://www.gecareers.com. **Description:** GE Capital Corporation is one of the largest vehicle leasing and financing companies in the United States and Canada, providing fleet and related management services to corporate clients. **Parent company:** General Electric Company. **Operations at this facility include:** This location provides automobile leasing and financing. **Listed on:** New York Stock Exchange. **Stock exchange symbol:** GE.

GE CAPITAL RAILCAR SERVICES
161 North Clark Street, Chicago IL 60601. 312/853-5000. **Contact:** Employment Manager. **World Wide Web address:** http://www.gecareers.com. **Description:** A major lessor of railcars in North America. The company's primary areas of business are: leasing and managing railcar equipment, financing, car repair and maintenance, and wheel services. The company's fleet includes covered hoppers, tank cars, boxcars, intermodal cars, pressure differential cars, coal cars, and other specialty cars. The company offers a full variety of lease types and equipment management services. **Special programs:** Internships. **Other U.S. locations:** El Cerrito CA; Englewood CO; Atlanta GA; Oak Brook IL; Albany NY; Bala-Cynwyd PA; Houston TX. **Parent company:** General Electric Company.

ILLINOIS CENTRAL RAILROAD COMPANY
455 North Cityfront Plaza Drive, Chicago IL 60611-5317. 312/755-7500. **Contact:** Human Resources. **World Wide Web address:** http://www.cn.ca.

Description: Operates one of the largest rail networks in the United States. The company's network includes 2,700 miles of main lines; 1,700 miles of passing, yard, and switching track; and 300 miles of secondary main lines. The company serves land shippers in Illinois, Louisiana, Michigan, Alabama, Kentucky, and Tennessee. Illinois Central's equipment consists of locomotives; freight cars; work equipment; and highway trailers and tractors. **NOTE:** Apply online. **Positions advertised include:** Communication Technician. **Corporate headquarters location:** This location. **Parent company:** Canadian National Railway.

LAIDLAW TRANSIT, INC.
SCHOOL BUS DIVISION
1240 East Diehl Road, Suite 100, Naperville IL 60563. 630/955-0003. **Fax:** 630/955-0653. **Contact:** Human Resources. **World Wide Web address:** http://www.laidlawschoolbus.com. **Description:** Provides busing services. **NOTE:** Apply online. **Positions advertised include:** School Bus Driver; Dispatcher; Mechanic; Safety Supervisor; Location Manager. **Parent company:** Laidlaw, Inc. provides solid waste collection, compaction, transportation, treatment, transfer and disposal services; provides hazardous waste services; operates hazardous waste facilities and wastewater treatment plants; and operates passenger and school buses, transit system buses, and tour and charter buses.

LANDSTAR EXPRESS AMERICA, INC.
2136 12th Street, Suite 106, Rockford IL 61104. 815/226-2170. **Contact:** Human Resources. **World Wide Web address:** http://www.landstar.com. **Description:** Performs expedited and emergency air and truck freight services. **Corporate headquarters location:** Jacksonville FL. **Parent company:** Landstar System, Inc. is divided into specialized freight transportation segments: Landstar Carrier Group and Landstar Logistics. **Listed on:** NASDAQ. **Stock exchange symbol:** LSTR.

LANDSTAR CARRIER GROUP
P.O. Box 7013, Rockford IL 61125-7013. 815/972-5000. **Physical address:** 1000 Simpson Road, Rockford IL 61102. **Contact:** Human Resources. **World Wide Web address:** http://www.landstar.com. **Description:** Provides truckload transportation services through independent contractors and commission sales agents. **Corporate headquarters location:** Jacksonville FL.

MERIDIAN RAIL
1545 State Street, Chicago Heights IL 60411. 708/757-8223. **Contact:** Human Resources. **World Wide Web address:** http://www.meridianrail.com. **Description:** Manufactures and markets replacement and original equipment products for the railroad industry. Products include railroad tracks, wheels, brake shoes, and signals. **Other area locations:** Cicero IL (Manufacturing).

MESSENGER MOUSE
7818 Forest Hills Road, Loves Park IL 61111. 815/877-2224. **Contact:** Human Resources. **Description:** Offers package delivery services to companies and individual consumers throughout Illinois and Wisconsin.

SPRINGFIELD AIRPORT AUTHORITY
1200 Capital Airport Drive, Springfield IL 62707-8419. 217/788-1060. **Contact:** Human Resources. **World Wide Web address:** http://www.flyspi.com. **Description:** Operates the Capital Airport. Founded in 1947. **Corporate headquarters location:** This location.

TTX COMPANY
101 North Wacker Drive, Chicago IL 60606. 312/853-3223. **Contact:** Human Resources. **World Wide Web address:** http://www.ttx.com. **Description:** A rail transportation company.

USF HOLLAND
8601 West 53RD Street, McCook IL 60525. 708442-8200. **Toll-free phone:** 800/442-5424. **Fax:** 708/442-6996. . **Contact:** Human Resources. **World Wide Web address:** http://www.usfreightways.com. **Description:** U.S. Freightways offers assembly and distribution, domestic and international freight forwarding, and logistics. **Positions advertised include:** Operations Supervisor.

UNITED AIRLINES, INC. (UAL)
P.O. Box 66100, Chicago IL 60666. 847/700-4000. **Physical address:** 1200 East Algonquin Road, Elk Grove Township IL 60007. **Fax:** 847/700-5287. **Contact:** Human Resources. **World Wide Web address:** http://www.ual.com. **Description:** United Airlines services 159 airports in the United States and 32 foreign countries in Europe, North and South America, and Asia. Domestic hubs are located in Chicago, Denver, San Francisco, and Washington DC. International hubs are located in Japan and England. **Special programs:** Internships. **Corporate headquarters location:** This location. **Operations at this facility include:** Administration; Sales.

VAPOR BUS INTERNATIONAL
1010 Johnson Drive, Buffalo Grove IL 60089. 847/777-6429. **Fax:** 847/520-2225. **Contact:** Dennis E. Huebner, Director Human resources. **Description:** Manufactures transit, shuttle, commuter, and tour coach bus doors. **Corporate headquarters location:** This location.

Indiana
AIR ROAD EXPRESS
3150 Chief Lane, Indianapolis IN 46241. 317/390-6500. **Toll-free phone:** 800/899-3812. **Contact:** Jim Lape, Human Resources Director. **World Wide Web address:** http://www.airroad.com. **Description:** An air transportation company. **Positions advertised include:** Company Driver; Owner Operator.

AMERICAN COMMERCIAL LINES HOLDINGS LLC (ACL)
1701 East Market Street, P.O. Box 610, Jeffersonville IN 47130. 812/288-0100. **Fax:** 812/288-0413. **Contact:** Human Resources. **World Wide Web address:** http://www.acbl.net. **Description:** A large, diversified transportation network operating in North and South America. American Commercial Lines Holdings also operates marine construction facilities and river terminals, and provides communications and repair services. **NOTE:** Entry-level positions, part-time jobs, and second and third shifts are offered. **Special programs:** Internships. **Office hours:** Monday - Friday, 8:00 a.m. - 5:00 p.m. **Corporate headquarters location:** This location. **Other U.S. locations:** New Orleans LA; St. Louis MO. **International locations:** Argentina; Venezuela. **Subsidiaries include:** ACBL; ACT; Jeffboat; Louisiana Dock Company; Watercom. **CEO:** Stephen A, Frasher.

ATLAS WORLD GROUP, INC.
1212 St. George Road, Evansville IN 47711. 812/424-4326. **Fax:** 812/421-7155. **Contact:** Pam Brio. **E-mail address:** pambrio@atlasworldgroup.com. **World Wide Web address:** http://www.atlasvanlines.com. **Description:** A worldwide common carrier, principally engaged in the transportation of used household goods, general commodities, special products, and freight forwarding. **Positions advertised include:** Driver. **Corporate headquarters location:** This location.

CELADON GROUP, INC.
9503 East 33rd Street, Indianapolis IN 46235. 317/972-7000. **Toll-free phone:** 800/235-2366. **Fax:** 317/890-1619. **Contact:** Personnel. **World Wide Web address:** http://www.celadontrucking.com. **Description:** An international truckload carrier specializing in freight shipments between the United States, Canada, and Mexico. **Corporate headquarters location:** This location. **Other U.S. locations:** Laredo TX. **Subsidiaries include:** Cheetah Transportation (Mooresville NC); Gerth Transportation (Ontario,

Canada); Jaguar Transportation (Mexico); and Zipp Express (Indianapolis IN). **President:** Stephen Russell.

DOMETIC CORPORATION
509 South Poplar Street, Lagrange IN 46761. 260/463-2191. **Contact:** Human Resources. **World Wide Web address:** http://www.dometic.com. **Description:** Manufactures a variety of products for recreational vehicles. The company's products include air conditioning systems, antennae, awnings, heating systems, ovens and ranges, refrigerators, roof vents, icemakers, and generators.

GD LEASING COMPANY
2399 East 15th Avenue, Gary IN 46402. 219/881-0215. **Contact:** Human Resources. **World Wide Web address:** http://www.falcon.com. **Description:** A truck driving company servicing the continental United States and Canada.

MORGAN DRIVE AWAY, INC.
THE MORGAN GROUP, INC.
26084 County Road 6, Suite 5, Elkhart IN 46514. 574/266-7702. **Toll-free phone:** 800/289-7565. **Contact:** Personnel. **World Wide Web address:** http://www. morgrp.com. **Description:** Arranges transportation services for the movement and delivery of manufactured houses and recreational vehicles. Morgan Drive Away also arranges the movement of commercial vehicles, office trailers, automobiles, buses, and other vehicles and freight. The company operates a network of approximately 1,900 independent owner-operators and drivers, and 1,100 part-time drive-away employees in 108 offices nationwide. **Parent company:** The Morgan Group, Inc. (also at this location) manages the delivery of manufactured homes, commercialized equipment, and related equipment. The company operates through more than 100 offices nationwide. Subsidiaries of the parent company include: Interstate Indemnity; Morgan Finance, Inc. **Listed on:** American Stock Exchange. **Stock exchange symbol:** MG.

STARCRAFT MONARCH MARINE
201 Starcraft Drive, P.O. Box 517, Topeka IN 46571. 260/593-2500. **Contact:** Human Resources Department. **World Wide Web address:** http://www.starcraftmarine.com. **Description:** Manufactures marine products including power motors and pleasure boating equipment. **Corporate headquarters location:** Goshen IN.

THUNDERBIRD PRODUCTS CORPORATION
P.O. Box 1003, Decatur IN 46733-5003. 260/724-9111. **Physical address:** 2200 West Monroe Street, Decatur IN 46733. **Contact:** Human Resources. **World Wide Web address:** http://www.thunderbirdboats.com. **Description:** Engaged in boat building and repairing services.

TRANSPO
901 East Northside Boulevard, South Bend IN 46617. 574/232-9901. **Fax:** 219/239-2309. **Contact:** Personnel. **World Wide Web address:** http://www. transpo.com. **Description:** Provides transportation planning services and offers research on alleviating and managing traffic. Founded in 1975. **Corporate headquarters location:** Kirkland WA.

Iowa

HEARTLAND EXPRESS, INC.
2777 Heartland Drive, Coralville IA 52241. 319/545-1175. **Fax:** 319/545-1349. **Contact:** Human Resources. **E-mail address:** careers@heartlandexpress.com. **World Wide Web address:** http://www.heartlandexpress.com. **Description:** An irregular-route carrier that is authorized to transport general commodities in interstate commerce throughout the 48 contiguous states. **NOTE:** Driver recruiting: 800/441-4953. **Positions advertised include:** Professional Driver; Owner Operator; Recruiting Verification Clerk; Safety Data Entry Clerk; MIS Desktop Support; Road Breakdown Coordinator. **Corporate headquarters location:** This location. **Other U.S. locations:** Nationwide. **Operations at this facility include:** Administration; Divisional Headquarters; Regional Headquarters; Sales; Service. **Listed on:** NASDAQ. **Stock exchange symbol:** HTLD. **Chairman/ President/CEO/ Secretary:** Russell A. Gerdin. **Annual sales/revenues:** $341 million. **Number of employees nationwide:** 2,000.

Kansas

AIR MIDWEST, INC.
dba US AIRWAYS EXPRESS
2203 Air Cargo Road, Wichita KS 67209. 316/944-2563 **Fax:** 316/945-0947 **Contact:** Human Resources. **World Wide Web address:** http://www.airlineapps.com/transition/76/jobs.asp. **E-mail address:** support@airlineapps.com. **Description:** A regional subsidiary of Mesa Air Group providing scheduled passenger and airfreight service in the lower Midwest region of the U.S. The company operates turboprop aircraft as US Airways Express under agreement at US Airways' hub operations in Pittsburgh, Philadelphia, Kansas City MO, and Tampa, as well as code-sharing with Midwest Express and US Airways. Air Midwest also operates as Mesa Airlines in Albuquerque NM. **NOTE:** Resumes sent by e-mail should be in Microsoft Word or Adobe Acrobat Reader format. **Positions advertised include:** Pilot; Crew Tracker; Dispatcher; Flight Simulator Instructor; Flight Attendant; Maintenance Worker. **Corporate headquarters location:** Phoenix AZ. **Other area locations:** Dodge City KS; Great Bend KS; Manhattan KS; Shawnee Mission; Topeka KS. **Parent company:** Mesa Airlines, Inc. (Farmington NM). **Operations at this facility include:** Administration; Sales; Service. **Listed on:** NASDAQ. **Stock exchange symbol:** MESA. **President:** Greg Stephens. **Annual sales/revenues:** $497 million. **Number of employees at this location:** 100. **Number of employees nationwide:** 3,100.

COLLINS INDUSTRIES, INC.
P.O. Box 2946, Hutchinson KS 67504-2946. 620/663-5551. **Physical address:** 15 Compound Drive, Hutchinson KS 67502. **Fax:** 620/663-1630. **Contact:** Human Resources. **World Wide Web address:** http://www.collinsind.com. **Description:** Designs, manufactures, and sells ambulances, specialty vehicles, and products which include school buses, shuttle buses, commercial bus chassis, road construction equipment, wheelchair lifts, medical support vans, and terminal trucks used to move trailers and containers in warehouses. Founded in 1971. **NOTE:** Application materials can be sent to parent company headquarters or directly to the subsidiary. **Positions advertised include:** Master Painter; Chassis Painter; Customer Service Representative; Engineer; Production Manager; Sales Representative. **Corporate headquarters location:** This location. **Other area locations:** South Hutchinson KS. **Other U.S. locations:** FL; TX. **Subsidiaries include:** Capacity of Texas, Inc. (terminal trucks); Collins Bus Corporation; Lay-Mor (road construction); Mid Bus Corporation (small school buses); Waldon Equipment; Wheeled Coach Industries (ambulances); World Trans, Inc. (commercial buses). **Listed on:** NASDAQ. **Stock exchange symbol:** COLL. **Chairman:** Don L. Collins. **Annual sales/revenues:** $200 million. **Number of employees nationwide:** 1,000.

SEABOARD CORPORATION
9000 West 67th Street, Shawnee Mission KS 66202. 913/676-8800. **Fax:** 913/676-8872. **Contact:** Personnel. **World Wide Web address:** http://www.seaboardcorp.com. **Description:** A diversified international food processing and transportation company specializing in pork products and overseas shipping and milling as well as power generation. Seaboard Corporation operates an ocean-liner service for cargo, with routes running between Florida and Latin America; and operates bulk carriers in the Atlantic Basin. **NOTE:** Apply online only. Paper applications not accepted. **Positions advertised include:** Senior Program Analyst. **Corporate headquarters location:** This location. **Other area locations:** Feed mills in Leoti and Rolla KS. **Other**

U.S. locations: Marine Division in Miami FL. **Operations at this location include:** Corporate Headquarters for Seaboard Corp.; Seaboard Farms, Inc.; and Commodity, Trading & Milling Division. **Listed on:** American Stock Exchange. **Stock exchange symbol:** SEB. **Annual sales/revenues:** $1.8 billion. **Number of employees nationwide:** 5,000. **Number of employees worldwide:** 9,500.

Kentucky

LANDSTAR SYSTEM, INC.
dba RISK MANAGEMENT CLAIM SERVICES, INC.
1850 Lantaff Boulevard, Suite 107, P.O. Box 70, Madisonville KY 42431. 270/821-0400. **Toll-free phone:** 800/435-4010. **Contact:** Human Resources. **World Wide Web address:** http://www.landstar.com. **Description:** Landstar System, Incorporated is a North American multimodal transportation services company, which is divided into specialized freight transportation segments. Risk Management Services, Inc. provides risk and claims management services to Landstar's operating subsidiaries. **Positions advertised include:** Owner Operator. **Corporate headquarters location:** Jacksonville FL. **Other U.S. locations:** Romulus MI; Springfield VA. **Subsidiaries include:** Landstar Expedited, Incorporated; Landstar Express America, Incorporated; Landstar Gemini, Incorporated; Landstar Inway, Incorporated; Landstar ITCO, Incorporated; Landstar Ligon, Incorporated; Landstar Poole, Incorporated; Landstar Ranger, Incorporated; Landstar T.L.C., Incorporated; Landstar Transportation Service, Incorporated. **Listed on:** NASDAQ. **Stock exchange symbol:** LSTR. **Number of employees nationwide:** 2,500.

SAFETRAN SYSTEMS CORPORATION
2400 Nelson Miller Parkway, Louisville KY 40223. 502/244-7400. **Toll-free phone:** 800/626-2710. **Fax:** 502/253-3764. **Contact:** Manager of Human Resources. **E-mail address:** resumes.engineering@invensys.com. **World Wide Web address:** http://www.safetran.com. **Description:** Manufactures railroad accessories and safety devices including electrical control systems, electro-mechanical signal devices, and communication systems. **Positions advertised include:** Financial Controller/Senior Project Accountant. **Other U.S. locations:** Rancho Cucamonga CA; Louisville KY. **Parent company:** Invensys, Inc. **Operations at this facility include:** Administration; Divisional Headquarters; Manufacturing; Research and Development; Sales; Service. **Number of employees at this location:** 250. **Number of employees nationwide:** 700.

Louisiana

DELTA QUEEN STEAMBOAT COMPANY
Robin Street Wharf, 1380 Port of New Orleans Place, New Orleans LA 70130-1890. 504/586-0631. **Toll-free phone:** 800/543-1949. **Fax:** 504/585-0630. **Contact:** Human Resources Manager. **World Wide Web address:** http://www.deltaqueen.com. **Description:** Owns and operates two steamboat cruise lines: the *Delta Queen* and the *Mississippi Queen*. Founded in 1890. **NOTE:** Online applications are available. **Positions advertised include:** Full-time Crew for the *Delta Queen* and the *Mississippi Queen*. **Parent company:** Delaware North Companies, Incorporated.

FOREST LINES
P.O. Box 53425, New Orleans LA 70153-3425. 504/529-1300. **Physical address:** 650 Poydras Street, Suite 1700, New Orleans LA 70153-3425. **Toll-free phone:** 888/354-5274. **Fax:** 504/593-6401. **Contact:** Human Resources. **E-mail address:** fli-seafarers-employmt@intship.com. **World Wide Web address:** http://www.forest-lines.com. **Description:** A company that ships freight across the Atlantic Ocean to deep water and inland river ports. **Corporate headquarters location:** This location. **Other U.S. locations:** New York NY; Washington D.C.; Houston TX; Chicago IL. **International locations:** Singapore **Parent company:** International Shipholdings, Incorporated. **Operations at this facility include:** Administration. **Number of employees at this location:** 225. **Number of employees nationwide:** 800.

NEW ORLEANS COLD STORAGE & WAREHOUSE COMPANY
P.O. Box 26308, New Orleans LA 70186. 504/944-4400. **Physical address:** 3401 Alvar Street, New Orleans LA 70126. **Toll-free phone:** 800/782-2653. **Fax:** 504/944-8539. **Contact:** Human Resources. **E-mail address:** info@nocs.com. **World Wide Web address:** http://www.nocs.com. **Description:** Through its Warehousing Division, the company offers refrigerated storage and distribution, and through its Transport Division, conveys a wide variety of temperature-sensitive products to destinations throughout the U.S. **Corporate headquarters location:** This location. **Other U.S. locations:** Charleston SC; Houston TX. **Operations at this facility include:** Administration; Service.

PHI, INCORPORATED
P.O. Box 90808, Lafayette LA 70509. 337/235-2452. **Physical address:** 2001 SE Evangeline Thruway, Lafayette LA 70508. **Fax:** 337/272.4232. **Contact:** Recruiting. **E-mail address:** resumes@phihelico.com. **World Wide Web address:** http://www.phihelico.com. **Description:** Provides aviation services to the offshore oil, onshore mining, international, air medical and technical services industries. **NOTE:** For Air Medical Group Pilot and Technician positions, contact John Sage at jsage@phihelico.com. For Oil & Gas Pilot, Oil & Gas Technician, and Contract Pilot positions, contact Jim Palmer at jpalmer@phihelico.com. **Corporate headquarters location:** This location. **Other U.S. locations:** Nationwide. **Operations at this facility include:** Overhaul; Maintenance. **Listed on:** NASDAQ. **Stock exchange symbol:** PHELK. **Chairman/CEO:** Al A. Gounsoulin.

SEACOR MARINE LLC
P.O. Box 2291, Morgan City LA 70381. 985/385-3475. **Physical address:** 5005 Railroad Avenue, Morgan City LA 70380. **Fax:** 985/385-1130. **Contact:** Personnel. **E-mail address:** domestic@seacormarine.com. **World Wide Web address:** http://www.seacormarine.com. **Description:** Operates a large fleet of diversified marine support vessels primarily dedicated to supporting offshore oil and gas exploration and development. **NOTE:** Crewmembers on OSV's and Anchor Boats must hold a Merchant Mariner's Document. Entry-level positions are available. **Positions advertised include:** Captain; Mate; Licensed Engineer; Able Seaman; QMED/Oiler; Ordinary Seaman; Wiper; First Captain; Second Captain; Unlicensed Engineer; Deckhand. **Corporate headquarters location:** Houston TX. **International locations:** Worldwide. **Parent company:** SEACOR Holdings Incorporated. **Listed on:** New York Stock Exchange. **Stock exchange symbol:** CKH. **President/CEO/Chairman:** Charles Fabrikant. **Annual sales/revenues:** $406 million. **Number of employees worldwide:** 3,100.

Maine

WASHBURN & DOUGHTY ASSOCIATES, INC.
P.O. Box 296, East Boothbay ME 04544. 207/633-6517. **Physical address:** 7 Enterprise Street, East Boothbay ME 04544. **Fax:** 207/633-7007. **Contact:** Human Resources. **E-mail address:** info@washburndoughty.com. **World Wide Web address:** http://www.washburndoughty.com. **Description:** Washburn & Doughty runs a shipyard where the company manufactures steel and aluminum vessels and barges. **Corporate headquarters location:** This location.

Massachusetts

AAA AUTO CLUB
900 Hingham Street, Rockland MA 02370. 781/871-5880. **Contact:** Human Resources. **E-mail address:** humanresources@aaasne.com. **World Wide Web address:** http://www.aaasne.com. **Description:** Provides insurance, travel, and related services to motorists through a network of over 50 branch offices. **Positions advertised include:** Dispatcher Road

Services Call Center; Call Counselor; Auto Travel Call Counselor; Insurance Customer Service Representative; Travel Agent; Membership Processor; Security Guard; Auto Travel Route Marker; Human Resource Assistant; Non Radio Dispatcher; Executive Assistant.

AMERICAN EXPRESS TRAVEL RELATED SERVICES
One State Street, Ground Level, Boston MA 02109. 617/723-8400. **Contact:** Human Resources. **World Wide Web address:** http://www.americanexpress.com. **Description:** A full-service travel agency. Founded in 1850. **Corporate headquarters location:** Cambridge MA. **Parent company:** American Express is a diversified travel and financial services company operating in 160 countries. **Positions advertised include:** Administrative Assistant; Team Leader Consumer Travel. **NOTE:** Submit resumes and apply online. **Listed on:** Privately held. **Number of employees nationwide:** 3,700.

AMERICAN OVERSEAS MARINE CORPORATION
116 East Howard Street, Quincy MA 02169. 617/786-8300. **Contact:** Human Resources. **E-mail address:** hr@gdamsea.com. **World Wide Web address:** http://www.gdamsea.com. **Description:** Provides supplies and support to ships for the U.S. Navy and maritime academies. **Positions advertised include:** Port Engineer; Program Manager. **Corporate headquarters location:** Falls Church VA. **Other U.S. locations:** CT; IL; MI; NJ; RI; SC. **Parent company:** General Dynamics is a major producer of nuclear submarines and land systems. The company has two main divisions: the Electric Boat Division designs and builds nuclear submarines including the Seawolf class attack submarine and the New Attack submarine; The Land Systems Division designs and builds armored vehicles such as the M1 Series of battle tanks for the U.S. Army, the U.S. Marine Corps, and a number of international customers. General Dynamics also has coal mining operations, provides ship management services for the U.S. government on prepositioning and ready reserve ships, and leases liquefied natural gas tankers. **Listed on:** New York Stock Exchange. **Stock exchange symbol:** GD.

CSL INTERNATIONAL
55 Tozer Road, Beverly MA 01915. 978/922-1300. **Fax:** 978/922-1772. **Contact:** Human Resources. **World Wide Web address:** http://www.csl.ca. **Description:** A bulk freight shipping company that specializes in self-unloading bulk carriers. **Parent company:** Canada Steamship Lines (Montreal, Quebec, Canada). **International locations:** Manitoba; Nova Scotia; Ontario; Singapore.

CAPE AIR/NANTUCKET AIRLINES
660 Barnstable Road, Hyannis MA 02601. 508/771-6944. **Toll-free phone:** 800/352-0714. **Contact:** Personnel. **World Wide Web address:** http://www.flycapeair.com. **Description:** An air transportation company with direct service to Cape Cod and the islands.

CAREY LIMOUSINE OF BOSTON
161 Broadway, Somerville MA 02145. 617/623-8700. **Contact:** Kevin Muldenatto, General Manager. **Description:** A limousine service and executive travel specialist. Carey Limousine offers services for business meetings, airport transfers, dinner/theater events, weddings, and sightseeing activities. **Positions advertised include:** Accountant/Auditor. **Corporate headquarters location:** This location. **Parent company:** Carey International. **Operations at this facility include:** Administration; Sales; Service. **Listed on:** Privately held. **Number of employees at this location:** 50.

GARBER TRAVEL
660 Beacon Street, Boston MA 02215. 617/353-2100. **Contact:** Paul Woods, Human Resources. **E-mail address:** pwoods@garbertravel.com. **World Wide Web address:** http://www.garber.com. **Description:** A travel agency. **Other U.S. locations:** Nationwide.

KELLAWAY TRANSPORTATION
One Kellaway Drive, P.O. Box 750, Randolph MA 02368. 781/961-8200. **Contact:** Human Resources. **E-mail address:** kellaway@kellaway.com. **World Wide Web address:** http://www.kellaway.com. **Description:** An intermodal distribution company. **Corporate headquarters location:** This location. **Parent company:** RoadLink USA.

LILY TRANSPORTATION CORPORATION
145 Rosemary Street, Needham MA 02494. 781/449-8811. **Toll-free phone:** 800/248-LILY. **Contact:** Human Resources. **E-mail address:** hr@lilytransportation.com. **World Wide Web address:** http://www.lily.com. **Description:** A truck rental and leasing company. **Positions advertised include:** CDL Class A Truck Driver; CDL Class B Truck Driver; Truck Mechanic. **Corporate headquarters location:** This location. **Other U.S. locations:** CT; ME; NH; NJ; NY; RI; VT.

MASSACHUSETTS BAY TRANSPORTATION AUTHORITY (MBTA)
10 Park Plaza, Boston MA 02116. 617/222-5000. **Contact:** Human Resources. **World Wide Web address:** http://www.mbta.com. **Description:** Operates the subways, trolleys, buses, and commuter train lines.

MASSACHUSETTS PORT AUTHORITY (MASSPORT)
One Harborside Drive, Suite 200S, East Boston MA 02128-2909. 617/428-2800. **Contact:** Human Resources. **World Wide Web address:** http://www.massport.com. **Description:** Owns and operates Logan International Airport and the public terminals of the Port of Boston. The Massachusetts Port Authority operates an engineering department and environmental unit at this facility.

PROVIDENCE AND WORCESTER RAILROAD COMPANY
75 Hammond Street, Worcester MA 01610. 508/755-4000. **Contact:** Human Resources. **World Wide Web address:** http://www.pwrr.com. **Description:** Providence and Worcester Railroad Company is an interstate freight carrier conducting railroad operations in Massachusetts, Rhode Island, and Connecticut. The railroad operates on approximately 470 miles of track. Freight traffic is interchanged with Consolidated Rail Corporation (ConRail) at Worcester MA and New Haven CT; with Springfield Terminal Railway Company at Gardner MA; and with New England Central Railroad at New London CT. Through its connections, Providence and Worcester Railroad links approximately 78 communities through its lines. Founded in 1847. **Corporate headquarters location:** This location. **Other U.S. locations:** Plainfield CT; Cumberland RI. **Operations at this facility include:** This location is the main freight classification yard and the locomotive and car maintenance facility. **Listed on:** American Stock Exchange. **Stock exchange symbol:** PWX. **Number of employees nationwide:** 140.

ROLLS ROYCE NAVAL MARINE
110 Norfolk Street, Walpole MA 02081. 508/668-9610. **Fax:** 508/668-5638. **Contact:** Human Resources. **Description:** Manufactures marine propulsion systems.

TIGHE WAREHOUSING & DISTRIBUTION, INC.
45 Holton Street, Winchester MA 01890. 781/729-5440. **Fax:** 781/721-5862. **Contact:** Human Resources. **E-mail address:** personnel@tighe-co.com. **World Wide Web address:** http://www.tighe-co.com. **Description:** Provides warehousing, transportation, and related distribution services. **Positions advertised include:** Class A CDL Driver; Warehouse Forklift Operations.

Michigan

AAA MICHIGAN
One Auto Club Drive, Dearborn MI 48126. 313/336-1598. **Toll-free phone:** 800/AAA-MICH. **Fax:** 313/436-7188. **Contact:** Human Resources. **E-mail address:** jobs@aaamich.com. **World Wide Web address:** http://www.autoclubgroup.com/michigan. **Description:** Provides insurance, travel, and a wide variety of services to motorists through a network of over 50 branch offices. **NOTE:** Part-time positions are offered. **Positions advertised include:** Travel Agent; Life Insurance Agent; Actuarial Analyst; Senior Actuarial Analyst; Senior Information Technology Auditor; Senior Support Specialist; Sales Compliance Manager; Business Consultant; Senior Marketing Research Consultant; Business Consultant. **Special programs:** Internships; Tuition Reimbursement Program. **Corporate headquarters location:** This location. **Other area locations:** Statewide. **Number of employees nationwide:** 4,000.

CENTRAL TRANSPORT INTERNATIONAL
12225 Stephens Road, Warren MI 48089. 586/939-7000. **Toll-free phone:** 800/334-4883. **Contact:** Personnel Director. **E-mail address:** resumes@centraltransportint.com. **World Wide Web address:** http://www.centraltransportint.com. **Description:** A trucking company serving the United States, Canada, and Mexico. **Positions advertised include:** Accountant; Telemarketer; Administrative Assistant; Billing Specialist; Accountant; Operations Coordinator; Sales Account Executive; National Sales Representative. **Special programs:** Tuition Assistance Program. **Corporate headquarters location:** This location. **Other U.S. locations:** Nationwide. **International locations:** Canada; Mexico. **Number of employees at this location:** 700. **Number of employees worldwide:** 4,000.

NTB
6601 Sloan Highway, Lansing MI 48917. 517/322-2252. **Fax:** 616/878-5587. **Contact:** Kristin Donbrock. **E-mail address:** hr@ntbtrk.com. **World Wide Web address:** http://www.ntbtrk.com. **Description:** A trucking company. **Positions advertised include:** Dispatcher. **Corporate headquarters location:** Byron Center MI. **Other area locations:** Carlton MI. **Other U.S. locations:** Tipp City OH.

Minnesota

BURLINGTON NORTHERN SANTA FE CORP.
176 East Fifth Street, 1st Floor, St. Paul MN 55101. 651/298-2121. **Contact:** James Dailey, Placement Center. **World Wide Web address:** http://www.bnsf.com. **Description:** Operates a railroad system that transports coal, agricultural commodities, and industrial products. **Special programs:** Internships. **Corporate headquarters location:** Fort Worth TX. **Operations at this facility include:** Administration. **Listed on:** New York Stock Exchange. **Stock exchange symbol:** BNI.

CARLSON COMPANIES, INC.
CARLSON MARKETING GROUP
P.O. Box 59159, Minneapolis MN 55459. 763/212-5000. **Physical address:** 701 Carlson Parkway, Minnetonka MN 55305. **Contact:** Human Resources. **World Wide Web address:** http://www.carlson.com. **Description:** A highly diversified corporation doing business through a variety of subsidiaries. Business areas include hotels, restaurant operations, and retail and wholesale travel. Carlson Marketing Group (also at this location) provides a variety of marketing services for sporting events and airlines; incentive programs for employees of other companies; and strategic consulting services to help client companies create customer/brand loyalty. **Corporate headquarters location:** This location. **Number of employees nationwide:** 50,000.

DART TRANSIT COMPANY
P.O. Box 64110, St. Paul MN 55164-0110. **Physical address:** 800 Lone Oak Road, St. Paul MN 55121. **Toll-free phone:** 800/366-9000. **Fax:** 651/683-1650. **Contact:** Katy Winecke, Human Resources Representative. **E-mail address:** kwinecke@dart.net. **World Wide Web address:** http://www.dartadvantage.com. **Description:** A trucking company with land-based transportation services throughout the United States, Canada, and Mexico. **NOTE:** Entry-level positions, part-time jobs, and second and third shifts are offered. See website for specific instructions on applying for Driver positions. **Positions advertised include:** Driver; Fleet Manager; Operations Floater. **Special programs:** Internships; Summer Jobs. **Corporate headquarters location:** Eagan MN. **Other U.S. locations:** Dallas TX. **Annual sales/revenues:** More than $100 million. **Number of employees at this location:** 225. **Number of employees nationwide:** 1,000.

GE CAPITAL FLEET SERVICES
3 Capital Drive, Eden Prairie MN 55344. 952/828-1000. **Contact:** Human Resources. **World Wide Web address:** http://www.gefleet.com. **Description:** One of the largest vehicle leasing companies in the United States and Canada, providing fleet financing and related management services to corporate clients. **NOTE:** Search and apply for positions online at http://www.gecareers.com. **Parent company:** General Electric Company (Fairfield CT) operates in the following areas: aircraft engines; appliances; broadcasting; industrial; materials; technical products and systems; and capital services.

GENMAR HOLDINGS INC.
2900 IDS Center, 80 South Eighth Street, Minneapolis,. MN 55402. 612/339-7600. **Contact:** Human Resources. **World Wide Web address:** http://www.genmar.com. **Description:** A manufacturer of several brands of recreational boats.

JEFFERSON PARTNERS L.P.
2100 East 26th Street, Minneapolis MN 55404-4101. 612/332-8745. **Recorded jobline:** 800/767-5333x426. **Fax:** 612/359-3437. **Contact:** Linda Gil, Human Resources. **E-mail address:** lindag@jeffersonlines.com. **World Wide Web address:** http://www.jeffersonlines.com. **Description:** An intercity bus line and travel company. **Corporate headquarters location:** This location. **Other U.S. locations:** Fort Smith AR; Des Moines IA; Kansas City MO; Oklahoma City OK; Tulsa OK. **Operations at this facility include:** Administration; Sales; Service. **Listed on:** Privately held. **Number of employees at this location:** 65. **Number of employees nationwide:** 265.

MESABA AIRLINES
1000 Blue Gentian Road, Suite 200, Eagan MN 55121. 651/367-5000. **Contact:** Human Resources. **E-mail address:** employment@mesaba.com. **World Wide Web address:** http://www.mesaba.com. **Description:** A scheduled passenger airline carrier that provides service to 109 U.S. and Canadian cities. Operates as a Northwest Airlink affiliate. **Positions advertised include:** Pilot. **Corporate headquarters location:** This location. **Other U.S. locations:** Detroit MI; Memphis TN. **Parent company:** MAIR Holdings, Inc. **Listed on:** NASDAQ. **Stock exchange symbol:** MAIR. **Number of employees at this location:** 300. **Number of employees nationwide:** 1,400.

METRO TRANSIT
570 Sixth Avenue North, Minneapolis MN 55411. 612/349-7558. **Fax:** 612/349-7566. **Contact:** Human Resources. **E-mail address:** HR.inquiries@metc.state.mn.us. **World Wide Web address:** http://www.metrotransit.org. **Description:** A division of the Metropolitan Council, the regional planning agency serving the Twin Cities seven-county metropolitan area. Metro Transit operates the Hiawatha light-rail line, 118 bus routes, and 9 contract service routes. Metro Transit employs 1,506 drivers (367 are part-time drivers), 468 mechanics, and 549 administrative/clerical staff.

MINNESOTA COACHES
425 East 31st Street, Hastings MN 55033-3691. 651/437-9648. **Fax:** 651/437-1302. **Contact:** Human

Resources. **World Wide Web address:** http://www.minnesotacoaches.com. **Description:** Provides school bus and charter motor coach services throughout the state. **NOTE:** Download application form online and submit by mail or fax.

NORTHWEST AIRLINES
2700 Lone Oak Parkway, Mailstop A1415, Eagan MN 55121-1534. 612/726-3600. **Fax:** 612/726-2524. **Recorded jobline:** 612/726-3600. **Contact:** Personnel. **E-mail address:** nwajobs@nwa.com. **World Wide Web address:** http://www.nwa.com. **Description:** The world's fourth largest airline and one of America's oldest carriers. Northwest Airlines serves more than 750 cities in 120 countries on 6 continents. The U.S. system spans 49 states and the District of Columbia. Hub cities are located in Amsterdam, Detroit, Minneapolis/St. Paul, Memphis, and Tokyo. Maintenance bases are in Duluth, Minneapolis/St. Paul, and Tokyo. Founded in 1926. **Positions advertised include:** Avionics Engineer; Electrical Engineer; Power Plant Engineer; Systems Engineer; Information Technology Auditor; Commodity Manager; Reporting Manager; Sr. Sourcing Analyst Sr. Specialist Inflight Technical Communication. **Special programs:** Co-ops. **Corporate headquarters location:** This location. **Other U.S. locations:** Nationwide. **Operations at this facility include:** Administration; Divisional Headquarters; Sales. **Listed on:** NASDAQ. **Stock exchange symbol:** NWA. **Number of employees worldwide:** 32,460.

PADELFORD PACKET BOAT COMPANY
Harriet Island, St. Paul MN 55107. 651/227-1100. **Toll-free phone:** 800/543-3908. **Fax:** 651/227-0543. **Contact:** Human Resources. **E-mail address:** info@riverrides.com. **World Wide Web address:** http://www.riverrides.com. **Description:** Padelford Packet Boat Company provides Mississippi riverboat cruises in St. Paul and Minneapolis. Operations include sightseeing cruises, dinner cruises, and private charters from April through October. **Positions advertised include:** Boat Crew Member; Boat Crew Chief; Office Crew Member; Photographer. **Operations at this facility include:** Administration; Service.

C.H. ROBINSON WORLDWIDE, INC.
8100 Mitchell Road, Eden Prairie MN 55344. 952/937-8500. **Contact:** Human Resources. **World Wide Web address:** http://www.chrobinson.com. **Description:** A worldwide transportation, logistics, and sourcing company founded in 1905. **NOTE:** Search and apply for positions online at http://www.chrwjobs.com. **Positions advertised include:** Business Analyst; Data Architect; IT Project Manager; Order Entry Clerk; Produce Sales; Senior Retail Business Analyst; Transportation Sales; Transportation Support. **Corporate headquarters location:** This location. **Other U.S. locations:** Nationwide. **International locations:** Worldwide. **Listed on:** NASDAQ. **Stock exchange symbol:** CHRW. **Number of employees worldwide:** 4,800.

SIGNATURE FLIGHT SUPPORT
3800 East 70th Street, Minneapolis MN 55450-1107. 612/726-5700. **Fax:** 612/726-5032. **Contact:** Human Resources Representative. **World Wide Web address:** http://www.signatureflight.com. **Description:** A fixed-base aviation operator at the Minneapolis-St. Paul International Airport. Signature Flight Support provides fuel, hangar, avionics, maintenance, and parts services to the corporate aircraft market. **Corporate headquarters location:** Orando FL. **International locations:** Worldwide. **Parent company:** BBA Group PLC.

THERMO KING CORPORATION
314 West 90th Street, Bloomington MN 55429. 952/887-2200. **Fax:** 952/885-3404. **Contact:** Victoria Allen, Human Resources Manager. **E-mail address:** victoria_allen@irco.com. **World Wide Web address:** http://www.thermoking.com. **Description:** Serves the refrigeration and air conditioning needs of buses and tractor-trailer centers. Thermo King is a world leader in temperature-controlled transport. **NOTE:** Search and apply for positions online at http://www,ingersollrand.com. **Corporate headquarters location:** This location. **Other U.S. locations:** Montgomery AL; Louisville GA; Hastings NE. **Parent company:** Ingersoll-Rand Co. **Operations at this facility include:** Administration; Divisional Headquarters; Manufacturing; Regional Headquarters; Research and Development; Sales; Service. **Number of employees at this location:** 850. **Number of employees nationwide:** 2,000.

TRANSPORT CORPORATION OF AMERICA, INC.
1715 Yankee Doodle Road, Eagan MN 55121. 651/686-2500. **Toll-free phone:** 800/345-0479. **Fax:** 651/994-5785. **Contact:** Human Resources. **E-mail address:** humanresources@transportamerica.com. **World Wide Web address:** http://www.transportamerica.com. **Description:** Freight carried by Transport America includes department-store merchandise, furniture, and consumer, grocery, industrial, and paper products. The company provides pick up and delivery on tight schedules for companies that depend on just-in-time inventories. Founded in 1984. **NOTE:** Apply online or in person. Entry-level positions are offered. **Positions advertised include:** Cargo Claims Supervisor; Fleet Manager; Planner; Director of Safety; ERS Coordinator. **Corporate headquarters location:** This location. **Operations at this facility include:** Administration; Sales; Service. **Number of employees worldwide:** 1,370.

Mississippi

CAGY INDUSTRIES, INC.
P.O. Box 1109, Columbus MS 39703. 662/329-7732. **Fax:** 662/329-7729. **Contact:** Human Resources. **E-mail address:** cagy@cagy.com. **World Wide Web address:** http://www.cagy.com. **Description:** A holding company for various railroads and railroad services corporations. **Subsidiaries include:** Columbus & Greenville Railway Company; Chattooga & Chickamauga Railway Company; Luxapalila Valley Railroad Company; Railway Management, Inc. **Number of employees at this location:** 90.

K.L.L.M. TRANSPORT SERVICES INC.
135 Riverview Drive, Richland MS 39218. 601/939-2545. **Toll-free phone:** 800-925-5556. **Contact:** Human Resources. **World Wide Web address:** http://www.kllm.com. **Description:** K.L.L.M. transports truckload quantities of various commodities, specializing in temperature-controlled shipments. **Positions advertised include:** Driver. **Number of employees at this location:** 2,000.

MCH TRANSPORTATION CO.
3180 Utica Street, Jackson MS 39209-7339. 601/353-9382. **Toll-free phone:** 800/824-5142. **Fax:** 601/355-9055. **Contact:** Helen Boler. **World Wide Web address:** http://www.mchtrans.com. **Description:** A specialized trucking company. Founded in 1986. **Corporate headquarters location:** This location. **Other area locations:** Tupelo MS; Olive Branch MS.

NORTHROP GRUMMAN SHIP SYSTEMS
P.O. Box 149, Pascagoula MS 39568-0149. 228/935-5318. **Physical address:** 1000 Access Road, Pascagoula MS 39567. **Fax:** 228/935-3629. **Contact:** Dorothy Shaw, Director of Staffing, Recruiting and Employment. **E-mail address:** dorothy.shaw@ngc.com. **World Wide Web address:** http://www.ss.northropgrumman.com. **Description:** Provides design, engineering, construction, and life cycle support services for major surface ships to the U.S. Navy, U.S. Coast Guard, international navies, and commercial companies of all types. **Positions advertised include:** Materials Analyst; Project Coordinator; Executive Assistant; Financial Analyst; Information Security Engineer; Director, Warfare Integration Center; Security Manager; Technical Writer; Accountant; Structural Engineer; Electrical Engineer. **Other area locations:** Biloxi MS; Escatawpa MS; Gulfport MS; Moss Point MS; Ocean Springs MS.

Other U.S. locations: Avondale LA. **Parent company:** Northrop Grumman Corporation, a global aerospace and defense company. **Listed on:** New York Stock Exchange. **Stock exchange symbol:** NOC. **Annual sales/revenues:** $25 billion. **Number of employees nationwide:** 18,000. **Number of employees worldwide:** 100,000.

SOUTHEASTERN FREIGHT LINES
130 Riverview Drive, Richland MS 39218. 601/420-0465. **Toll-free phone:** 866/700-7335. **Fax:** 601/939-3556. **Contact:** Human Resources. **E-mail address:** jobs@sefl.com. **World Wide Web address:** http://www.sefl.com. **Description:** A trucking company that provides assembly and distribution services throughout the south. **Positions advertised include:** Dock/Operations Supervisor; Freight Handler; Pick-up and Delivery Driver. **Corporate headquarters:** Lexington SC. **Other area locations:** Jackson MS; Tupelo MS. **Other U.S. locations:** VA; NC; SC; TN; GA; FL; AL; LA; TX.

THE TRAVEL COMPANY
605 North Park Drive, Suite D, Ridgeland MS 39157. 601/991-1922. **Toll-free phone:** 800/844-1133. **Fax:** 601/991-1865. **Contact:** Human Resources. **E-mail address:** travelmail22@yahoo.com. **World Wide Web address:** http://www.thetravelcoinc.com. **Description:** A travel agency. Founded in 1983. **Corporate headquarters location:** This location. **Operations at this facility include:** Sales; Service. **Listed on:** Privately held. **Number of employees at this location:** 15. **Number of employees nationwide:** 35.

Missouri

AAA
12901 North 40 Drive, St. Louis MO 63141-8699. 314/523-7350. **Contact:** Personnel Department. **E-mail address:** personnel@aaamissouri.com. **World Wide Web address:** http://www.ouraaa.com. **Description:** Provides insurance, travel advice, and a wide variety of services to motorists through a network of over 50 branch offices. **Positions advertised include:** Corporate Travel Counselor; Customer Care Representative; Executive Secretary; Marketing Database Analyst; Member Service Counselor; Programmer Analyst; Sales Agent; Sales Assistant; Travel Counselor; Ticket Coordinator; Travel Accounting Clerk. **Corporate headquarters location:** Heathrow FL. **Other U.S. locations:** Nationwide. **Operations at this facility include:** Administration; Regional Headquarters; Service. **Number of employees at this location:** 400. **Number of employees nationwide:** 850.

ACF INDUSTRIES INC.
AMERICAN RAILCAR INDUSTRIES
620 North 2nd Street, St. Charles MO 63301-2075. 636/940-6000. **Contact:** Recruitment Officer. **World Wide Web address:** http://www.americanrailcar.com. **Description:** Manufactures, leases, and sells railroad freight and tank cars; acquires, owns, leases, and sells to industrial corporations special purpose freight and tank cars and provides maintenance for such cars in its lease fleet; and manufactures freight and tank car parts, piggy-back trailer hitches, and tank car valves.

CASSENS TRANSPORT COMPANY, INC.
2000 Mraz Lane, Fenton MO 63026. 636/343-2161. **Fax:** 636/343-4268. **Contact:** Recruiter. **Description:** Engaged in a variety of trucking services, excluding local trucking. **Number of employees at this location:** 600.

CLIPPER CRUISE LINE
11969 Westline Industrial Drive, Suite 10, St. Louis MO 63146-3220. 314/655-6700. **Fax:** 314/655-6670. **Contact:** Personnel. **E-mail address:** employment.global@nwship.com. **World Wide Web address:** http://www.clippercruise.com. **Description:** A cruise line. **Parent company:** INTRAN.

ENTERPRISE RENT-A-CAR
600 Corporate Park Drive, St. Louis MO 63105. 314/512-5000. **Contact:** Human Resources. **World Wide Web address:** http://www.erac.com. **Description:** Enterprise Rent-A-Car is an automobile rental and leasing agency. **Number of employees at this location:** 100.

EXEL TRANSPORTATION
5310 St. Joseph Avenue, St. Joseph MO 64502. 816/387-4200. **Contact:** Human Resources. **World Wide Web address:** http://www.exel.com. **Description:** One of the country's leading providers of single-source transportation services to some of the largest shippers in the world. The company provides a full complement of logistics management services such as dedicated fleet, warehousing, and risk management, as well as the component services involved in these activities. With over 90 offices across North America, Exel is one of the largest transportation services companies in the United States. The company's areas of operation include Intermodal, Trucking Services; Carload, International, Dimensional Traffic; Consolidation & Distribution Services; and its newest division, Air Freight. Services include double stack, trailers, and containers on rail cars; trucks; and ocean-going transportation.

GE TRANSPORTATION SYSTEMS
321 SE County Road AA, Blue Springs MO 64014. 816/229-3345. **Contact:** Human Resources. **World Wide Web address:** http://www.ge.com. **Description:** A supplier of signal and control products to railroads throughout the world. The company sells its products to Class I and short-line freight railroads and to mass rail transit customers. Products are designed to improve the safety and productivity of railroad train operations and include a broad line of railroad signal and train control systems and related components and services, as well as customized asset management services.

HERTZ RENT-A-CAR
THE HERTZ CORPORATION
Lambert International Airport, 10278 Natural Bridge Road, St. Louis MO 63134. 314/426-7555. **Contact:** Personnel. **World Wide Web address:** http://www.hertz.com. **Description:** Area offices for one of the nation's leading transportation services organizations are at this location. Overall, the company operates nationally through several divisions: Rent-A-Car Division (car rental services); Car Leasing Division; and Equipment Rental and Leasing Division. Hertz is also engaged in joint-venture truck leasing operations with Penske Corporation (Hertz Penske Truck Leasing) at 600 locations. **Parent company:** RCA Corporation.

INTRAV INC.
11969 Westline Industrial Drive, St. Louis MO 63146. 314/655-6700. **Toll-free phone:** 800/456-8100. **Fax:** 314/655-6670. **Contact:** Human Resources Director. **E-mail address:** employment.global@nwship.com. **World Wide Web address:** http://www.intrav.com. **Description:** Intrav organizes, markets, and operates escorted, international travel programs. **NOTE:** Search and apply for positions online. **Corporate headquarters location:** This location. **Parent company:** Kuoni (Switzerland).

JIFFY DELIVERY
6185 Olive Boulevard, St. Louis MO 63130. 314/725-5600. **Contact:** Gordie Webb, Manager. **Description:** An express package delivery service. **Positions advertised include:** Truck Driver. **Operations at this facility include:** Service.

MADISON WAREHOUSE CORPORATION
4300 Planned Industrial Drive, St. Louis MO 63120. 314/382-3700. **Fax:** 314/383-1909. **Contact:** Human Resources Department. **E-mail address:** hrstlouis@madisonwarehouse.com. **World Wide Web address:** http://www.madisonwarehouse.com. **Description:** A general warehousing and storage company. **Positions advertised include:** Forklift Operator; Clerk; Operation Manager.

MAYFLOWER TRANSIT, INC.
13390 Lakefront Drive, Saint Louis MO 63101. 314/344-4300. **Contact:** Human Resources. **World Wide Web address:** http://www.mayflower.com. **Description:** A diversified holding company whose subsidiaries provide a variety of transportation-related services including household moving services; services for goods that require special handling; and storage and distribution, freight forwarding, and flatbed hauling of containerized shipments. Mayflower Transit also owns and operates moving and storage agencies; provides school bus service to school districts; provides on-demand transportation services for local communities; operates a school bus dealership; sells tractor trailers; operates a road equipment maintenance facility; and sells moving supplies, equipment, and uniforms to agents and owner operators. Mayflower also provides a variety of insurance services including property and casualty coverage. **Positions advertised include:** Underwriting Administrator; Chief IT Architect; Data Center Operations Analyst. **Corporate headquarters location:** This location. **Parent company:** UniGroup Inc.

ROADWAY EXPRESS INC.
205 Soccer Park Road, Fenton MO 63026. 636/349-5300. **Contact:** Personnel Manager. **World Wide Web address:** http://www.roadway.com. **Description:** Operates a freight consolidation and distribution terminal for one of the largest common carriers in the United States, with terminals in more than 633 cities nationwide. **NOTE:** All candidates follow the same career path: Management Trainee, 10 weeks; Dock Supervisor, one to five years. All hiring is done through the Missouri Department of Employment. Please contact this location for more information. **Corporate headquarters location:** Akron OH. **Other U.S. locations:** Nationwide. **Parent company:** Roadway Services is a transportation holding company with subsidiaries involved in long-haul, airfreight, small package, and custom logistics services. Subsidiaries of Roadway Services include Roadway Global Air with worldwide airfreight service through 230 service centers; Roadway Package System with 271 terminals in the United States and a dozen in Canada; and four regional short-haul freight carriers. The company also offers indirect service to Latin America, Guam, Europe, the Middle East, and the Pacific Rim. **Number of employees worldwide:** 25,000.

SABRELINER CORPORATION
7733 Forsyth Boulevard, Suite 1500, St. Louis MO 63105-1821. 314/863-6880. **Contact:** Human Resources. **World Wide Web address:** http://www.sabreliner.com. **Description:** Sabreliner Corporation manages sophisticated aviation products, services, and training programs; repairs, modifies, and remanufactures aircraft; maintains and overhauls aircraft engines and specialized industrial engines; and sells aircraft parts.

UNION PACIFIC RAILROAD
674 South 20th Street, Lexington, MO 64067. 660/259-6606. **Contact:** Human Resources. **World Wide Web address:** http://www.up.com. **Description:** the largest railroad in North America, covering 23 states. **NOTE:** Search and apply for positions online. **Parent company:** Union Pacific Corporation is a diversified conglomerate including railroad, holding companies, oil and petroleum exploration and development, real estate, waste management, and other operations. Through its subsidiaries, the company owns over 22 million acres of undeveloped property for oil production, interest in the Black Butte mine, industrial waste facilities, three landfills in Oklahoma and Utah, and 17,835 miles of rail, which link the Pacific and Gulf Coasts with the Midwest. Subsidiaries include Skyway Freight Systems and USPCI, Inc. **Number of employees nationwide:** 47,000.

UNITED VAN LINES INC.
One United Drive, Fenton MO 63026. 636/343-3900. **Fax:** 636/349-8794. **Contact:** Human Resources. **E-mail address:** hr@unigroupin.com. **World Wide Web address:** http://www.unitedvanlines.com. **Description:** Offices of the international household goods moving service. **Parent company:** UniGroup Inc., also at this location.

XTRA LEASE
1801 Park 270 Drive, Suite 400, St. Louis MO 63146. 314/579-9300. **Toll-free phone:** 800/325-1453. **Fax:** 314/542-2150. **Contact:** Human Resources. **E-mail address:** humanresources@xtra.com. **World Wide Web address:** http://www.xtralease.com. **Description:** Leases trailers, containers, and chassis to railroads as well as trailers for over-the-road use. Operates 90 locations in North America. **NOTE:** Complete job profile form online. **Corporate headquarters location:** This location. **Parent company:** XTRA Corporation.

YELLOW FREIGHT SYSTEMS, INC.
400 Barton Street, St. Louis MO 63104. 314/772-2905. **Fax:** 314/865-7201. **Contact:** Personnel Department. **World Wide Web address:** http://www.myyellow.com. **Description:** A national long-haul truckload carrier, with over 585 terminal locations in 50 states, Puerto Rico, and many Canadian provinces. **NOTE:** Search for positions online. Submit resume and letter of interest to local facility. **Corporate headquarters location:** Overland Park KS. **Parent company:** Yellow Corporation. **Number of employees worldwide:** 28,000.

Nebraska

UNION PACIFIC CORPORATION
1400 Douglas Street, Omaha NE 68179. 402/544-4000. **Toll-free phone:** 888/870-8777. **Fax:** 402/271-6408 **Contact:** Human Resources. **World Wide Web address:** http://www.up.com. **Description:** Provides transportation, computer technology, and logistics services. Union Pacific Corporation operates in three divisions: Union Pacific Railroad; Overnite Transportation; and Union Pacific Technologies. **Corporate headquarters location:** This location. **Listed on:** New York Stock Exchange. **Stock exchange symbol:** UNP. **Number of employees nationwide:** 47,000.

WERNER ENTERPRISES, INC.
P.O. Box 45308, Omaha NE 68145-0308. 402/895-6640. **Physical address:** 14507 Frontier Road, Omaha NE 68138. **Toll-free phone:** 800/228-2240. **Fax:** 402/894-3927. **Recorded jobline:** 800/937-6374. **Contact:** Human Resources. **E-mail address:** hr@werner.com. **World Wide Web address:** http://www.werner.com. **Description:** Provides transportation services. **Positions advertised include:** Customer Service Manager; Driver Recruiter; Human Resource Generalist; Night Fleet Coordinator; Safety Supervisor; Accounting Clerk; Customer Service Assistant; Health Insurance Coordinator; Security Gate Guard. **Special programs:** Internships. **Corporate headquarters location:** This location. **Listed on:** NASDAQ. **Stock exchange symbol:** WERN. **Number of employees nationwide:** 12,100.

Nevada

ATA AIRLINES, INC.
5757 Wayne Newton Boulevard, P.O. Box 11027, Las Vegas NV 89111. 702/261-3610. **Contact:** Human Resources. **E-mail address:** jobs@iflyata.com. **World Wide Web address:** http://www.ata.com. **Description:** An commercial airline serving major business centers and popular vacation destinations through scheduled service and charter operations. **Corporate headquarters location:** Indianapolis IN. **Listed on:** NASDAQ. **Stock exchange symbol:** ATAH. **Number of employees nationwide:** 7,200.

AMERCO
1325 Airmotive Way, Suite 100, Reno NV 89502-3239. 775/688-6300. **Contact:** Human Resources. **World Wide Web address:** http://www.amerco.com. **Description:** Amerco is the holding company for U-Haul International, Amerco Real Estate Company, Republic Western Insurance Company, and Oxford Life Insurance Company. U-Haul rents trucks, trailers, and

support items to the do-it-yourself mover in the United States and Canada. Amerco Real Estate Company operates and manages nonresidential buildings. Republic Western provides auto insurance to U-Haul rental customers. Oxford provides life and health insurance to employees. **Corporate headquarters location:** This location. **Listed on:** New York Stock Exchange. **Stock exchange symbol:** AOPRA. **Number of employees nationwide:** 18,300.

CSAA (CALIFORNIA STATE AUTOMOBILE ASSOCIATION)
3312 West Charleston, Las Vegas NV 89102. 702/870-9171. **Contact:** Personnel. **E-mail address:** jobreqs@csaa.com. **World Wide Web address:** http://www.csaa.com. **Description:** As the AAA member organization for Northern California, Nevada and Utah, CSAA is a nonprofit membership organization offering a range of automotive and travel services. **Positions advertised include:** Supervisor, Resolution Center; Tow Truck Operator; Call Center Quality Assurance Analyst; Field Stationary Engineer; Sales Representative; Claim Coordinator. **Other U.S. locations:** Nationwide. **Parent company:** AAA (Automobile Association of America). **Number of employees:** 6,000.

GRAY LINE LAS VEGAS SIGHTSEEING TOURS
795 East Tropicana, Las Vegas NV 89119. 702/384-1234. **Toll-free phone:** 800/634-6579. **Fax:** 702/735-4638. **Contact:** Human Resources. **E-mail address:** gltourslv@coachusa.us. **World Wide Web address:** http://www.graylinelasvegas.com. **Description:** Provides guided tours of Las Vegas. **Other U.S. locations:** Nationwide. **International locations:** Worldwide.

LAS VEGAS COLD STORAGE
1201 Searles Avenue, Las Vegas NV 89101. 702/649-8002. **Contact:** Human Resources. **Description:** Operates cold storage warehousing facilities used by other companies.

OZBURN-HESSEY LOGISTICS
450 Lillard Drive, Sparks NV 89434. 775/355-2150. **Contact:** Human Resources. **E-mail address:** hr@ohlogistics.com. **World Wide Web address:** http://www.ohlogistics.com. **Description:** A commercial and household warehousing company. **Corporate headquarters location:** Nashville TN. **Other U.S. locations:** Nationwide.

PRESTIGE TRAVEL AMERICAN EXPRESS
6175 Spring Mountain Road, Las Vegas NV 89146. 702/251-5552. **Toll-free phone:** 800/553-0204. **Contact:** Human Resources. **Description:** A travel agency with 21 locations in the greater Las Vegas area. **Corporate headquarters location:** This location.

RENO-TAHOE INTERNATIONAL AIRPORT
P.O. Box 12490, Reno NV 89510. 775/328-6452. **Physical address:** 2001 East Plum Lane, Reno NV 89502. **Fax:** 775/328-6519. **Contact:** Paul Fillo, Human Resources. **E-mail address:** pfillo@renoairport.com. **World Wide Web address:** http://www.renoairport.com. **Description:** An international aviation transportation center. The airport serves major and commuter airlines, numerous charter airline flights, cargo carriers, general aviation aircraft, and military aircraft. **NOTE:** Faxed applications must be followed up with original documents in the mail. A resume may be submitted in addition to, but not instead of, any portion of the application. **Positions available include:** HVAC Technician; Building Maintenance Electrician; Project Manager; Training Coordinator; Senior Director of Engineering and Facilities. **Parent company:** Airport Authority of Washoe County.

SWIFT TRANSPORTATION COMPANY, INC.
1455 Hulda Way, Sparks NV 89431. 775/359-5161. **Fax:** 775/359-5155. **Toll-free phone:** 800/800-6066. **Contact:** Ted DeRoos, Terminal Manager. **World Wide Web address:** http://www.swifttrans.com. **Description:** One of the largest truckload motor carriers in the United States, Swift Transportation offers a wide variety of trailers to its customers, and as well as providing full-service equipment leasing, fleet programs, and third-party logistics services for its major clientele. The company has more than 2,400 power units and 37 full-service terminals. **NOTE:** Entry-level positions are offered. **Corporate headquarters location:** Phoenix AZ. **Other U.S. locations:** Nationwide. **Listed on:** NASDAQ. **Stock exchange symbol:** SWFT. **Number of employees nationwide:** 6,700.

US AIRWAYS, INC.
P.O. Box 11091, Las Vegas NV 89111. 702/261-5344. **Contact:** Personnel Department. **World Wide Web address:** http://www.usairways.com. **Description:** US Airways offers service to 187 cities in the United States, Canada, Mexico, the Caribbean, France, England, Spain, Italy, The Netherlands, and Germany. The company's primary hubs are in Charlotte, Pittsburgh, Baltimore/Washington, and Philadelphia. **NOTE:** Unsolicited resumes not accepted. **Special programs:** Internships. **Corporate headquarters location:** Arlington VA. **Listed on:** OTC. **Stock exchange symbol:** UAWGQ. **Sales/revenue:** Approximately $7 billion. **Number of employees nationwide:** 28,300.

New Hampshire

C&J TRAILWAYS
185 Grafton Drive, Portsmouth NH 03801. 603/430-1100. **Toll-free phone:** 800/258-7111. **Fax:** 603/433-8960. **Contact:** Human Resources. **E-mail address:** pdionne@cjtrailways.com. **World Wide Web address:** http://www.cjtrailways.com. **Description:** Provides transportation from the seacoast to Boston MA. Offers early morning and late night transportation. Founded in 1968. **Positions advertised include:** Customer Service Provider; Driver; Fleet Mechanic.

FIRST STUDENT INCORPORATED
522 Route 10, Piermont NH 03779. 603/272-4188. **Contact:** Chuck Perkins. **E-mail address:** ChuckPerkins@fs.firstgroupamerica.com. **World Wide Web address:** http://www.firststudentinc.com. **NOTE:** Search posted openings nationwide on-line. **Description:** A school-bus company providing transportation for students to and from school and for chartered trips. First Student serves Nashua, Londonderry, and the Lakes area. **Positions advertised include:** Bus Drivers; Repair Shop Manager; Manager in Training. **Corporate headquarters location:** Cincinnati OH. **Parent Company:** First Group America. **Number of employees at this location:** 10.

GARBER TRAVEL
111 Main Street, Nashua NH 03060. 603/883-1546. **Toll-free phone**: 800/225-4570. Ext.: 1075. **Fax:** 603/883-4616. **Contact:** Paul Woods, Director of Human Resources. **E-mail address:** jobs@garbertravel.com. **World Wide Web address:** http://www.garber.com. **Description:** A travel agency. **NOTE:** Jobseekers should send resume or application form to: 27 Boylston Street, Chestnut Hill MA 02467. **Corporate headquarters location:** Chestnut Hill MA. **Other area locations:** Hanover NH; Manchester NH; Portsmouth NH. **Other U.S. locations:** CA; IL; VT; VA. **International locations:** Canada; United Kingdom.

UNITED AIRLINES
Manchester Airport, Manchester NH 03103. 800/241-6522. **World Wide Web Address**: http://www.united.com. **Description**: United Airlines is the second largest air carrier in the world. **NOTE**: Offers applications online for currently open positions. **Positions advertised include**: Flight Attendant; Transportation, Logistics and Warehouse, Communications, Sales, Public Relations. **Parent Company**: UAL Corporation.

New Jersey

BAX GLOBAL
896 Frelinghuysen Avenue, Newark NJ 07114. 973/954-2000. **Fax:** 973/954-2030. **Contact:** Human

Resources. **World Wide Web address:** http://www.baxglobal.com. **Description:** Bax Global offers business-to-business freight delivery through a worldwide network of offices in 124 countries, with 155 offices in the U.S. **Other area locations:** Secaucus NJ. **Other U.S. locations:** Nationwide. **International locations:** Worldwide.

CR ENGLAND
403 Dultys Lane, Burlington NJ 08016. 609/387-2766. **Contact:** Human Resources. **World Wide Web address:** http://www.crengland.com. **Description:** A trucking company providing freight services. **Positions advertised include:** Driver.

CENDANT CORPORATION
10 Sylvan Way, Parsippany NJ 07054-0642. 973/428-9700. **Fax:** 973/496-5966. **Contact:** Human Resources. **E-mail address:** cendant.jobs@cendant.com. **World Wide Web address:** http://www.cendant.com. **Description:** Provides a wide range of business services including dining services, hotel franchise management, mortgage programs, and timeshare exchanges. Cendant Corporation's Real Estate Division offers employee relocation and mortgage services through Century 21, Coldwell Banker, ERA, Cendant Mortgage, and Cendant Mobility. The Travel Division provides car rentals, vehicle management services, and vacation timeshares through brand names including Avia, Days Inn, Howard Johnson, Ramada, Travelodge, and Super 8. **Positions advertised include:** Commercial Marketing Associate; Mortgage Processor; Staff Accountant; Financial Analyst; International Treasury Manager; Marketing Manager; Executive Assistant; Regional Business Consultant; Staff Accountant; Director; Finance Manager; Administrative Assistant; Marketing Communications Manager. **Corporate headquarters location:** New York NY. **Listed on:** New York Stock Exchange. **Stock exchange symbol:** CD. **Number of employees at this location:** 1,100. **Number of employees worldwide:** 28,000.

DPT
1200 Paco Way, Lakewood NJ 08701. 732/367-9000. **Contact:** Personnel. **E-mail address:** confidence@dptlabs.com. **World Wide Web address:** http://www.dptlabs.com. **Description:** Packages and ships pharmaceutical products manufactured by other companies. **Positions advertised include:** Associate Scientist; Industrial Engineer; Engineering Manager; Facilities Maintenance Supervisor.

HARBOUR INTERMODAL LTD.
1177 McCarter Highway, Newark NJ 07104. 973/481-6474. **Contact:** Human Resources. **Description:** Provides local intermodal transportation services in the greater New York Harbor area. The company also develops and sells equipment for intermodal services including waterborne vessels and mobile and fixed heavy materials handling equipment for transporting and sorting containers, trailers, and general cargo.

THE HERTZ CORPORATION
225 Brae Boulevard, BS – 0034, Park Ridge NJ 07656. 201/307-2000. **Fax:** 201/307-2644. **Contact:** Employee Relations. **World Wide Web address:** http://www.hertz.com. **Description:** A large rental company that leases new and used cars and industrial and construction equipment in 130 countries worldwide. The company also sells used cars in the United States, Australia, New Zealand, and Europe. **Positions advertised include:** Manager of Benefits Accounting; Sr. Accountant; Business Analyst; Web Developer; Director of Website Marketing and Strategy; Manager of Partnership Marketing. **Corporate headquarters location:** This location.

INTTRA INC.
One Upper Pond Road, Morris Corporate Center II, Building E, Parsippany NJ 07054. 973/263-5100. **Fax:** 973/263-5969. **E-mail address:** jobs@inttra.com. **World Wide Web address:** http://www.inttra.com. **Description:** INTTRA creates efficiencies for the ocean transportation industry by standardizing and optimizing traditionally inefficient processes. INTTRA enables shippers, freight forwarders, third party logistics providers, brokers, importers, and industry portals to manage the scheduling, booking, documentation, Bills of Lading, and tracking of cargo and the negotiation of freight services across multiple shipping lines in a single integrated process. **Positions advertised include:** Business Analyst/Product Designer; Product Manager; Quality Assurance/EDI Analyst; Technical Support Manager; Technical Support Technician. **Corporate headquarters location:** This location.

JEVIC TRANSPORTATION INC.
600-700 Creek Road, Delanco NJ 08075. 856/461-7111. **Toll-free phone:** 800/257-0427. **Fax:** 856/764-7224. **Contact:** Human Resources. **World Wide Web address:** http://www.jevic.com. **Description:** Jevic Transportation is a trucking company providing freight services. **Corporate headquarters location:** This location. **Operations at this facility include:** This location houses a dispatching center.

LAIDLAW TRANSIT
LAIDLAW EDUCATIONAL SERVICES
3349 Highway 138, Building 1, Unit D, Wall NJ 07719. 732/556-0255. **Contact:** Human Resources. **World Wide Web address:** http://www.laidlaw.com. **Description:** Laidlaw Educational Services provides school bus transportation services. **NOTE:** Entry-level positions and part-time jobs are offered. **Company slogan:** Laidlaw - we carry the nation's future. **Special programs:** Apprenticeships; Training. **Corporate headquarters location:** Lawrenceville NJ. **Other U.S. locations:** Nationwide. **Operations at this facility include:** This location houses administrative offices. **Listed on:** New York Stock Exchange. **Annual sales/revenues:** $21 - $50 million. **Number of employees nationwide:** 60,000.

MAERSK-SEALAND
Giralda Farms, Madison Avenue, P.O. Box 880, Madison NJ 07940-0880. 973/514-5000. **Contact:** Human Resources Department. **World Wide Web address:** http://www.maersksealand.com. **Description:** Maersk-Sealand ships large containers. **Operations at this facility include:** This location houses the northeast regional headquarters operations. **Parent company:** A.P. Moller Group.

TITAN PRT SYSTEMS, INC.
118 Mill Road, Park Ridge NJ 07676. 201/930-0300. **Contact:** Human Resources. **Description:** Designs, manufactures, and installs monorail transportation systems. **Corporate headquarters location:** This location. **Operations at this facility include:** Administration; Research and Development.

UNITED AIRLINES, INC.
Newark International Airport, Newark NJ 07114. 973/624-6925. **Toll-free phone:** 800/241-6522. **Contact:** Human Resources. **World Wide Web address:** http://www.ual.com. **Description:** An air carrier that provides transportation of people and goods through more than 1,100 daily scheduled flights at 100 airports in the United States, Canada, and Mexico. **NOTE:** Search for positions online. **Corporate headquarters location:** Elk Grove Township IL. **Parent company:** UAL, Inc. **Listed on:** New York Stock Exchange. **Stock exchange symbol:** UAL.

UNITED PARCEL SERVICE (UPS)
One Clover Place, Edison NJ 08837. **Toll-free phone:** 800/622-3593. **Contact:** Human Resources. **World Wide Web address:** http://www.upsjobs.com. **Description:** UPS provides package delivery services nationwide. **Positions advertised include:** Principal; Automotive Mechanic; Regional Account Manager. **Operations at this facility include:** This location is a package-handling center. **Number of employees worldwide:** 370,000.

New Mexico

AIRPORT SHUTTLE
2909 Yale Boulevard SE, Albuquerque NM 87106. 505/765-1234. **Contact:** Human Resources Department. **Description:** An airport shuttle service providing transportation to and from airports across New Mexico. **NOTE:** Apply in person.

ECLIPSE AVIATION
2503 Clark Carr Loop SE, Albuquerque NM 87106. 505/241-8806. **Fax:** 505/241-8800. **Contact**: Human Resources. **E-mail address:** recruit@eclipseaviation.com. **World Wide Web address:** http://www.eclipseaviation.com. **Description:** Designs, certifies, and produces affordable jet aircraft. **NOTE:** See website for current job openings and application instructions.

MESA AIRLINES PILOT DEVELOPMENT
1296 West Navajo Street, Farmington NM 87401. 505/326-5909. **Contact:** Human Resources. **World Wide Web address:** http://www.mesa-air.com. **Description:** Provides regularly scheduled commuter and cargo airline services to 161 cities, 41 states, Canada, Mexico, and the Bahamas. **NOTE:** Search and apply for positions online at http://www.airlineapps.com. **Corporate headquarters location:** Phoenix AZ.

SOUTHWEST AIRLINES COMPANY
3601 Spirit Drive SE, Albuquerque NM 87106. 505/842-4022. **Contact:** Human Resources. **World Wide Web address:** http://www.southwest.com. **Description:** A national airline company with service to 58 cities in the United States. **NOTE:** Job application information available online. **Corporate headquarters location:** Dallas TX. **Number of employees nationwide:** 31,000.

New York

AIR FRANCE
125 West 55th Street, New York NY 10019. 212/830-4000. **Contact:** Air France Recruitment. **E-mail address:** mail.resume@airfrance.fr. **World Wide Web address:** http://www.airfrance.com. **Description:** An international airline serving 20 U.S. cities. Founded in 1933. **NOTE:** Part-time, seasonal, second shift and third shift jobs are offered. Electronic copies of resumes/applications are only accepted in Word format, and if the position applied for is indicated. **Positions advertised include:** Manager of National Account Sales; Account Representative; Accountant; Administrative Assistant; Sales Executive. **Corporate headquarters location:** Paris, France. **Other area locations:** JFK Airport NY; Newark Airport NJ. **Other locations:** Worldwide. **Number of employees at this location:** 830. **Number of employees worldwide:** 49,000.

AIR INDIA
570 Lexington Avenue, 15th Floor, New York NY 10022. 212/407-1300. **Fax:** 212/407-1415. **Contact:** Human Resources Department. **World Wide Web address:** http://www.airindia.com. **Description:** An international airline with routes to major cities throughout the world. **NOTE:** Most positions are only open to Indian citizens belonging to certain caste levels who meet the company's stated requirements. **Corporate headquarters location:** Mumbai, India. **Listed on:** Government owned.

ALSTOM TRANSPORT
353 Lexington Avenue, Suite 1100, New York NY 10016. 212/557-7259. **Fax:** 212/972-4404. **Contact:** Human Resources. **World Wide Web address:** http://www.transport.alstom.com. **Description:** ALSTOM Transport provides rail signal and control systems worldwide. These systems are designed for diverse applications in mainline railways, heavy rail transit, light rail transit, commuter rail, high-speed rail, and automated guideway transit. **Corporate headquarters location:** Hornell NY. **Other area locations:** Hornell NY; Rochester NY. **Other U.S. locations:** CA; CT; District of Columbia; NJ; VA; WA. **Parent company:** Alstom (Paris, France).

AVANT SERVICES CORPORATION
60 East 42nd Street, New York NY 10165. 212/687-5145. **Fax:** 212/370-1452. **Contact:** Personnel Manager. **Description:** A delivery company. **NOTE:** Entry-level positions, part-time jobs, and second and third shifts are offered. **Positions advertised include:** Administrative Assistant; Assistant Manager; Driver. **Special programs:** Summer Jobs.

BAX GLOBAL
19 Ransier Drive, Building-B, West Seneca NY 14224. 716/677-2040. **Fax:** 716/677-2043. **Contact:** Human Resources. **World Wide Web address:** http://www.baxglobal.com. **Description:** A business-to-business shipping service operating on an international level. **Other U.S. locations:** Nationwide. **Other international locations:** Worldwide.

CAMP SYSTEMS INC. (CSI)
Long Island MacArthur Airport, 999 Marconi Avenue, Ronkonkoma NY 11779-7299. 631/588-3200. **Toll-free phone:** 877/411-2267. **Contact:** Human Resources. **E-mail address:** careers@campsys.com. **World Wide Web address:** http://www.campsys.com. **Description:** Camp Systems Inc. (CSI) performs computerized aircraft maintenance and management services. **Positions advertised include:** Aircraft Analyst. **Corporate headquarters location:** This location. **Subsidiaries include:** CAMP Europe SAS; Daniel Systems.

COURTESY BUS COMPANY
107 Lawson Boulevard, Oceanside NY 11572. 516/766-5678. **Fax:** 516/678-0253. **Contact:** Personnel Office. **Description:** Provides bus service to local school districts, as well as a range of charter services through several area locations. **Positions advertised include:** Automotive Mechanic; Driver.

DELAWARE OTSEGO CORPORATION
One Railroad Avenue, Cooperstown NY 13326-1110. 607/547-2555. **Fax:** 607/547-9834. **Contact:** Barbara Rogers, Human Resources. **Description:** Delaware Otsego Corporation is a nonrail holding company. The principal asset is the New York, Susquehanna, and Western Railway Corporation, which provide rail transportation service to customers in New York, New Jersey, and Pennsylvania. The company is also engaged in a real estate project to further develop the traffic base of the railroad. **Corporate headquarters location:** This location.

EL AL ISRAEL AIRLINES LIMITED
15 East 26th Street, 6th Floor, New York NY 10010. 212/768-9200. **Fax:** 212/852-0641. **Contact:** Personnel Department. **World Wide Web address:** http://www.elal.co.il. **Description:** An Israeli government-owned international air carrier operating a route system that includes major United States cities, and destinations in Israel, Europe, and Africa. Founded in 1948. **Corporate headquarters location:** Ben Gurion Airport, Israel. **Annual sales/revenues:** $1.1 billion. **Number of employees:** 3,224.

GLOBAL GROUND
111 Great Neck Road, Great Neck NY 11021. 516/487-8610. **Fax:** 516/498-1534. **Contact:** Human Resources. **Description:** A nationwide aviation service company providing contracting services to airlines and airports including loading/unloading, cleaning planes, fueling planes, and cargo services. **Special programs:** Internships. **Corporate headquarters location:** This location. **Subsidiaries include:** Hudson Aviation Services, Inc. **Number of employees at this location:** 45.

LIBERTY LINES TRANSIT INC.
475 Saw Mill River Road, P.O. Box 624, Yonkers NY 10703. 914/969-6900. **Fax:** 914/376-6440. **Contact:** Human Resources. **E-mail address:** jobs@libertylines.com. **World Wide Web address:** http://www.libertylines.com. **Description:** One of the largest and most diversified bus services in the Yonkers/Westchester area. Services include commuter

and transit bus operations. Founded in 1953. **Positions advertised include:** Bus Driver. **Corporate headquarters location:** This location. **Operations at this facility include:** Administration; Service. **President:** Jerry D'Amore.

LINDBLAD SPECIAL EXPEDITIONS
96 Morton Street, 9th Floor, New York NY 10014. 212/765-7740. **Contact:** Human Resources. **World Wide Web address:** http://www.specialexpeditions.com. **Description:** A cruise line operator with destinations throughout the Pacific and the Caribbean including the Galapagos Islands, Mexico's Baja Peninsula, Alaska, Antarctica, Arctic Norway, and Costa Rica, as well as up the Colorado and Snake Rivers. **Positions advertised include:** Steward; Deckhand; Physician.

THE LONG ISLAND RAILROAD COMPANY
Sutphin Boulevard Jam, Hicksville NY 11801. 516/733-3900. **Contact:** Human Resources. **World Wide Web address:** http://www.lirr.org. **Description:** Operates one of the oldest active railroads in the United States. The company has extensive commuter passenger and freight service railroad operations, primarily between New York City and numerous points on Long Island. The Long island Railroad Company is one of the busiest passenger railroad operators in the United States. **NOTE:** Application materials should be sent to: Human Resources-SR, Mail code 1155-IT-NET, MTA Long Island Rail Road, Jamaica Station, Jamaica NY 11435. **Positions advertised include:** Assistant Conductor; Electrician. **Corporate headquarters location:** This location. **Parent company:** Metropolitan Transportation Authority. (New York NY).

MTA BUS COMPANY
12815 28th Avenue, Flushing NY 11354. 718/445-3100. **Contact:** Kathleen O'Shea, Director of Human Resources. **Description:** A public transportation firm providing express and local service in Queens and Manhattan with more than 270 buses operating on nearly 20 routes. **Positions advertised include:** Bus Operator; Cleaner/Shifter; Foreman. **Special programs:** Internships. **Office hours:** Monday - Friday, 8:30 a.m. - 4:30 p.m. **Corporate headquarters location:** This location. **Operations at this facility include:** Administration. **Number of employees at this location:** 700.

McALLISTER TOWING AND TRANSPORTATION COMPANY, INC.
17 Battery Place, Suite 1200, New York NY 10004. 212/269-3200. **Fax:** 212/509-1147. **Contact:** Nancy Errichiello, Director of Personnel. **World Wide Web address:** http://www.mcallistertowing.com. **Description:** A marine services firm providing ship docking, deep-sea and coastal towing, oil transportation, bulk transportation, special projects such as positioning tunnel and bridge segments and other services for the transportation industry. McAllister also offers full-service, in-house capabilities through a complete packaged transportation service provided to shippers. The company operates one of the largest fleets of tugs and barges on the East Coast and in the Caribbean, with ship docking services in New York NY, Philadelphia PA, Norfolk VA, Charleston SC, Jacksonville FL, Baltimore MD, and Puerto Rico. Founded in 1864. **Corporate headquarters location:** This location. **Other locations:** FL; MD; PR; SC. **President:** Capt. Brian A. McAllister.

METROPOLITAN TRANSPORTATION AUTHORITY (MTA)
347 Madison Avenue, New York NY 10017-3739. 212/878-7000. **Fax:** 212/878-7227. **Contact:** Human Resources Division. **E-mail address:** mtahr@mtahq.org. **World Wide Web address:** http://www.mta.nyc.ny.us. **Description:** A public benefit corporation primarily devoted to obtaining funding for mass transportation in the New York City area, as well as serving as the headquarters for the MTA's constituent agencies. **Positions advertised include:** Police Radio & Communications Specialist; Senior Executive Secretary; Summons Administrator; Business Programs Deputy Director; Financial Analyst; Facilities Manager; Facilities Operation and Support Director; Crime Analyst; Communications Operator. **Annual sales/revenues:** $4 billion. **Number of employees:** 64,169.

SWISSPORT USA
JFK International Airport, Building 151, East Hanger Road, Jamaica NY 11430. 718/656-6135. **Fax:** 718/244-7560. **Contact:** Human Resources Department. **World Wide Web address:** http://www.swissport.com. **Description:** Provides a wide range of ground-handling services for airlines and airports. Services include maintenance, inspections, spare parts inventory, into-plane fueling, cargo handling, cabin cleaning, and ramp services. Swissport USA also operates reservation centers for airlines. **Parent company:** Alpha Airports Group.

TIX INTERNATIONAL GROUP
201 Main Street, Nyack-On-Hudson NY 10960. 845/358-1007. **Fax:** 845/358-1266. **Contact:** Human Resources. **World Wide Web address:** http://www.tixtravel.com. **Description:** A full-service travel agency and ticket broker for concerts, sports, and theater events. **Corporate headquarters location:** This location.

USF RED STAR EXPRESS INC.
34 Wright Avenue, Auburn NY 13021. 315/253-2721. **Fax:** 315/255-4258. **Contact:** Human Resources. **E-mail address:** hr@usfredstar.com. **World Wide Web address:** http://www.old.usfc.com/usfredstar/careers.asp. **Description:** A trucking company that serves as a national shipping agent for other companies. **Corporate headquarters location:** This location. **Number of employees at this location:** 150.

WE TRANSPORT INC.
303 Sunnyside Boulevard, Plainview NY 11803. 516/349-8200. **Contact:** Mary Prioli, Personnel Manager. **Description:** An area school bus and van transportation company. **Special programs:** Internships. **Corporate headquarters location:** This location. **Number of employees at this location:** 70.

North Carolina
HATTERAS YACHTS
110 North Glenburnie Road, New Bern NC 28560-2799. 252/633-3101. **Contact:** Human Resources. **World Wide Web address:** http://www.hatterasyachts.com. **Description:** Hatteras Yachts builds, sells, and repairs fiberglass yachts. **NOTE:** Hatteras Yachts does not accept unsolicited faxed resumes. Please search for jobs and apply online at http://www.brunswick.com. **Positions advertised include:** Customer Service Process Representative; Director of Quality and Process Improvement; Fiberglass Application Engineer; Industrial Designer/Class A Surfacer; Interior Designer; Lean Six Sigma Black Belt. **Corporate headquarters location:** This location. **Parent company:** Brunswick Corporation. **Listed on:** New York Stock Exchange. **Stock exchange symbol:** BC. **Number of employees nationwide:** 21,000.

LANDSTAR EXPRESS AMERICA, INC.
1901 Associates Lane, Suite A1, Charlotte NC 28217. 704/424-9912. **Toll-free phone:** 800/927-7074. **Contact:** Human Resources. **E-mail address:** employment@landstar.com. **World Wide Web address:** http://www.landstar.com. **Description:** Performs expedited and emergency air and truck freight services. **Corporate headquarters location:** Jacksonville FL. **Other U.S. locations:** Rockford IL. **Listed on:** NASDAQ. **Stock exchange symbol:** LSTR.

TRIANGLE TRANSIT AUTHORITY
P.O. Box 13787, Research Triangle Park NC 27709. 919/485-7473. **Fax:** 919/485-7547. **Contact:** Christy Whittington, Human Resources Administrator. **E-mail address:** jobs@ridetta.org. **World Wide Web address:** http://www.ridetta.org. **Description:** Offers access to various methods of transportation including bus services, vanpooling, and carpooling to the Triangle

Park area. The TTA is currently planning to expand their services to include a railway system. **Positions advertised include:** Mechanic; Bus Operator; Dispatcher/Supervisor; Service Attendant.

Ohio

AIRBORNE EXPRESS
ABX AIR, INC.
145 Hunter Drive, Wilmington OH 45177. 937/382-1229. **Fax:** 937/383-3838. **Contact:** Recruitment. **E-mail address:** abx.recruiter@airborne.com. **World Wide Web address:** http://www.abxair.com. **Description:** A delivery service company providing overnight, next-afternoon, and second-day delivery options; same-day courier service; logistics management; and air freight, ocean transport, and customs clearance for international customers. **NOTE:** Resumes accepted for posted positions only. **Positions advertised include:** Aircraft Maintenance Instructor; Human Resources Generalist; HVAC Mechanic; Part-Time Sorter; Weekend Sorter; Teen Sorter; Seasonal Sorter. **Corporate headquarters location:** Seattle WA. **Parent Company:** Airborne Express.

AIRSTREAM INC.
419 West Pike Street, Jackson Center OH 45334. 937/596-6849. **Fax:** 937/596-6539. **Contact:** Cindy Oakley, Human Resources. **World Wide Web address:** http://www.thorindustries.com. **Description:** Develops, manufactures and markets recreational vehicles including travel trailers and motor homes. Founded in 1980. **Parent company:** Thor Industries, Inc.

ENTERPRISE RENT-A-CAR
24690 Sperry Drive, Westlake OH 44145. 440/885-6944. **Fax:** 440/345-7470. **Contact:** Laura Taddeo, Human Resources. **E-mail address:** laura.taddeo@erac.com. **World Wide Web address:** http://www.enterprise.com. **Description:** A car rental agency. **NOTE:** Job seekers may also apply on-line at the above URL. **Positions advertised include:** Branch Manager; Accountant; Driver; Lot Attendant. **Special programs:** Internships. **Special programs:** Management Training Program; Internships. **Corporate headquarters location:** This location.

EXEL LOGISTICS
501 West Schrock Road, Westerville OH 43081-8966. 614/890-1730. **Contact:** Human Resources. **World Wide Web address:** http://www.exel-logistics.com. **Description:** One of the world's leading providers of third-party logistics systems. The company provides transportation, distribution, warehousing, and related supply chain solutions within the automotive, chemical, consumer, healthcare, retail, and technology industries. **Parent company:** NFC International Logistics and Moving Services.

FALCON TRANSPORT COMPANY
650 North Meridian Road, Youngstown OH 44509. 330/793-5604. **E-mail address:** mjester@falcontransport.com. **Contact:** Personnel. **World Wide Web address:** http://www.falcontransport.com. **Description:** A flatbed truck and van company that transports various products including auto parts.

ROADWAY EXPRESS INC.
P.O. Box 471, Akron OH 44309-0471. 330/384-1717. **Physical address:** 1077 Gorge Boulevard, Akron OH 44310. **Contact:** Human Resources. **World Wide Web address:** http://www.roadway.com. **Description:** A leading less-than-truckload motor carrier. **Corporate headquarters location:** This location. **Other area locations:** Cincinnati OH; Copley OH; Dayton OH. **Parent company:** Roadway Corporation. **Listed on:** NASDAQ. **Stock exchange symbol:** ROAD. **Number of employees nationwide:** 24,800.

Oklahoma

DOLLAR THRIFTY AUTOMOTIVE GROUP INC.
5310 East 31st Street, 5th floor, Dollar Thrifty Plaza Complex, Tulsa OK 74135. 918/665-3930. **Contact:** Human Resources. **World Wide Web address:** http://www.dtag.com. **Description:** Through its brands, Dollar Rent-A-Car and Thrifty Car Rental, the company serves both the airport and local car rental markets, with a fleet of over 82,000 cars and more than 1,200 rental locations spanning the globe. **NOTE:** Unsolicited resumes and applications are not accepted. **Positions advertised include:** AS-400/RPG Project Programmer; Section Manager, Internal Audit. **Special programs:** Education Assistance Plan; Health Club Membership. **Corporate headquarters location:** This location. **Subsidiaries include:** Dollar Rent-A-Car; Thrifty Car Rental; Thrifty Car Sales. **Listed on:** New York Stock Exchange. **Stock exchange symbol:** DTG. **Sales/revenue:** $56.8 million. **Number of employees worldwide:** 8,000.

HERTZ RENTAL CORPORATION
10401 North Pennsylvania Avenue, Oklahoma City OK 73120. 405/749-3655. **Contact:** Employee Relations. **World Wide Web address:** http://www.hertz.com. **Description:** A car rental company with approximately 6,500 locations operating in 143 countries. **NOTE:** Do not mail resumes. Call the company directly to set up an appointment. **Positions advertised include:** Account Control Representative; Fleet Accountant; Internal Auditor; Recovery Specialist; Management Trainee; Instant Return Representative; Business Analyst; Computer Operator; Intern; Java Architect; Oracle Application DBA; Programmer Analyst; Telecommunications Analyst. **Corporate headquarters location:** Park Ridge NJ. **Other area locations:** Tulsa OK. **Operations at this facility include:** Administration; Sales; Service. **Subsidiaries include:** Hertz Equipment Rental Corporation; Hertz Claim Management Corporation; Hertz Local Edition. **Parent company:** Ford Motor Company. **Listed on:** New York Stock Exchange. **Stock exchange symbol:** F. **Number of employees at this location:** Over 1,000.

Oregon

AMERICAN AIRLINES, INC.
7000 NE Airport Way, Portland OR 97218. 503/249-4450. **Contact:** Human Resources. **World Wide Web address:** http://www.aa.com. **Description:** Provides scheduled jet service to more than 170 destinations, primarily throughout North America, Latin America, Europe, and the Pacific. American Airlines, Inc.'s Passenger Division is one of the largest passenger airlines in the world. Founded in 1934. **NOTE:** Jobseekers are encouraged to apply via the Website: http://www.aacareers.com. **Parent company:** AMR Corporation's operations fall within three major lines of business: the Air Transportation Group, the SABRE Group, and the AMR Management Services Group. The Air Transportation Group consists primarily of American Airlines, Inc.'s Passenger and Cargo Division and AMR Eagle, Inc., a subsidiary of AMR Corporation.

AMERICAN EXPRESS TRAVEL SERVICES
400 SW 4th Avenue, Portland OR 97204. 206/441-8622. **Toll-free phone:** 800/227-5868. **Contact:** Team Leader. **World Wide Web address:** http://www.americanexpress.com. **Description:** A travel agency. **Positions advertised include:** Corporate Travel Counselor; Leisure Travel Counselor; Outside Sales Representative. **Office hours:** Monday - Friday 8:30am-5:30pm. **International locations:** Worldwide.

AZUMANO CARLSON WAGONLIT TRAVEL
320 SW Stark Street, Suite 600, Portland OR 97204. 503/223-6245. **Toll-free phone:** 800/777-2018. **Fax:** 503/294-6474. **Contact:** Human Resources. **E-mail address:** jobs@azumano.com. **World Wide Web address:** http://www.azumano.com. **Description:** A travel agency. Founded in 1949. **Positions advertised include:** Cruise Agent. **Other U.S. locations:** Denver CO; Vancouver WA.

COLUMBIA HELICOPTERS, INC.
P.O. Box 3500, Portland OR 97208. 503/678-1222. **Fax:** 503/678-5841. **Physical address:** Aurora State Airport, 14452 Arndt Road NE, Aurora OR 97002.

Contact: Personnel Department. **E-mail address:** rosep@colheli.com. **World Wide Web address:** http://www.colheli.com. **Description:** Offers external-load, heavy-lift helicopter services. Founded in 1957. **Positions advertised include:** Aviation Field Mechanic; Ground Service Attendant; Helicopter Log Hooker; Knot Bumper; 2-Person Watch Team; Copilot; Timber Cutter; Aviation Field Electrician/Mechanic.

COUNTRY COACH INC.
135 E 1st Avenue, P.O. Box 400, Junction City OR 97448. 541/998-3720. **Toll-free phone:** 800/547-8015. **Contact:** Human Resources Department. **E-mail address:** dbedore@counrtycoach.com. **World Wide Web address:** http://www.countrycoach.com. **Description:** Manufactures recreational vehicles and coaches. The company's motorcoach lines include Affinity, Allure, Concept, Intrigue, Magna, Prevost H3-45 Conversion, and Prevost XL Conversion.

FREIGHTLINER, LLC
4747 North Channel Avenue, Portland OR 97217-7699. 503/745-8000. **Toll-free phone:** 800/385-4357. **Fax:** 503/745-8921. **Contact:** Human Resources Department. **World Wide Web address:** http://www.freightliner.com. **Description:** Manufactures and markets heavy-duty trucks and chassis. **Positions advertised include:** Customs Manager; Project Planning Engineer; Senior Design Engineer; Senior Manufacturing Release Analyst. **Corporate headquarters location:** This location.

THE GREENBRIER COMPANIES, INC.
One Centerpointe Drive, Suite 200, Lake Oswego OR 97035. 503/684-7000. **Fax:** 503/684-7553. **Contact:** Jeanne Onchi, Human Resources. **World Wide Web address:** http://www.gbrx.com. **Description:** Operates in two primary business segments: manufacturing and refurbishing railcars and marine vessels; and leasing and managing surface transportation equipment and providing related services. **Corporate headquarters location:** This location. **International locations:** Canada; Germany; Mexico; Poland. **Subsidiaries include:** Gunderson Inc.

INTERSTATE DISTRIBUTOR COMPANY
10110 SW Ridder Road, Wilsonville OR 97070. 503/682-1097. **Fax:** 800/795-1034. **Contact:** Human Resources. **E-mail address:** resumes2@intd.com. **World Wide Web address:** http://www.intd.com. **Description:** A transportation/trucking company operating in the Western United States, the Midwest, and the East Coast. **Positions advertised include:** Shop Service Writer; Front Desk Receptionist; Corporate Accountant; Driver Recruiter/Orientation Facilitator; Customer Service Representative; Road Call Coordinator; Shop Foreman; Mechanic. **Corporate headquarters location:** Tacoma WA.

MONACO COACH CORPORATION
91320 Coburg Industrial Way, Coburg OR 97408. 541/686-8011. **Toll-free phone:** 800/634-0855. **Fax:** 541/681-8899. **Contact:** Human Resources. **World Wide Web address:** http://www.monaco-online.com. **Description:** Monaco Coach Corporation is one of the nation's leading manufacturers of high-line motor coaches. The company has five distinct lines: the Windsor, the Dynasty, the Executive, the Crowne Royale Signature Series, and Royale Coach bus conversions. **Corporate headquarters location:** This location.

TRIMET
4012 SE 17th Street, Portland OR 97202. 503/962-7635. **Fax:** 503/962-7440. **Recorded jobline:** 503/962-3000. **Contact:** Human Resources. **E-mail address:** jobs@trimet.org. **World Wide Web address:** http://www.tri-met.org. **Description:** Operates area bus and rail service. **Positions advertised include:** Bus Driver; Manager Fare Equipment Systems.

Pennsylvania

AAA MID-ATLANTIC
1801 Market Street, Ten Penn Center, Ground Floor, Philadelphia PA 19103. 215/399-1180. **Contact:** Human Resources. **World Wide Web address:** http://www.aaamidatlantic.com. **Description:** Provides insurance, travel, and a wide variety of services to motorists through a network of over 50 branch offices. **Positions advertised include:** Business Systems Analyst; Insurance Counselor; Retail Agent; Office Supervisor; Travel Agent. **Corporate headquarters location:** Heathrow FL. **Other U.S. locations:** Nationwide.

AMERICAN EXPRESS TRAVEL RELATED SERVICES
2 PPG Place, Market Square, Pittsburgh PA 15222. 412/577-6911. **Contact:** Human Resources. **Description:** Provides travel services including trip planning, reservations, and ticketing for corporate clients. **Parent company:** American Express Company is a diversified travel and financial services company operating in 160 countries around the world. American Express Travel Related Services offers consumers the Personal, Gold, and Platinum Cards, as well as revolving credit products such as Optima Cards, which allow customers to extend payments. Other products include the American Express Corporate Card, which helps businesses manage their travel and entertainment expenditures; and the Corporate Purchasing Card, which helps businesses manage their expenditures on supplies, equipment, and services.

AMTRAK
30th Street Station, 2nd Floor South, Box 43, Philadelphia PA 19104. 215/349-1108. **Recorded jobline:** 877/268-7251. **Contact:** Patricia Kerins, Human Resources Manager. **E-mail address:** necjobs@amtrak.com. **World Wide Web address:** http://www.amtrak.com. **Description:** Manages and operates an interstate passenger rail service with connections throughout the United States. **NOTE:** This office is responsible for hiring in Philadelphia PA and Wilmington DE. **Positions advertised include:** Project Director Desktop Architecture; Sr. Analyst Procurement Planning; Sr. Estimator. **Special programs:** Internships. **Operations at this facility include:** Administration; Divisional Headquarters; Regional Headquarters; Sales; Service.

B-FAST CORPORATION
660 Newtown-Yardley Road, Newtown PA 18940. 215/860-5600. **Contact:** James Affleck, Director of Human Resources. **Description:** Provides ground support services for general aviation aircraft including demand line services such as fueling, ground handling, and storage of aircraft.

BOMBARDIER TRANSPORTATION
1501 Lebanon Church Road, Pittsburgh PA 15236-1491. 412/655-5700. **Contact:** Human Resources. **World Wide Web address:** http://www.bombardier.com. **Description:** A manufacturer of rapid transit systems including rail systems such as the Bay Area Rapid Transit (BART) in San Francisco CA, and people movers conveyors found in airports and other public facilities. **Positions advertised include:** Manufacturing Control Analyst; Sr. Quality Engineer; Hardware Engineer; Project Manager. **Number of employees nationwide:** 800.

CONSOLIDATED RAIL CORPORATION (CONRAIL)
2001 Market Street, 16th Floor, Philadelphia PA 19103. 215/209-5099. **Recorded jobline:** 215/209-5006. **Contact:** Human Resources. **World Wide Web address:** http://www.conrail.com. **Description:** A railroad company. **NOTE:** Electronic resumes and faxed resumes are not accepted. **Corporate headquarters location:** This location.

CONTINENTAL AIRLINES CARGO FREIGHT FACILITY
Cargo City, West PAC Building C-2, Door 9, Philadelphia PA 19153. 215/492-4301. **Contact:** Human Resources Manager. **World Wide Web address:** http://www.continental.com. **Description:** Provides air transportation services. **NOTE:** Resumes

should be sent to Continental Airlines main cargo facility at Terminal D, Philadelphia PA 19153.

GE TRANSPORTATION SYSTEMS
2901 East Lake Road, Erie PA 16501. 814/875-5145. **Contact:** Human Resources. **World Wide Web address:** http://www.getransportation.com. **Description:** A supplier to the railroad, transit, marine and mining industries. GE provides freight and passenger locomotives, railway signaling and communications systems, information technology solutions, marine engines, motorized drive systems for mining trucks and drills, replacement parts, and value added services. **Positions advertised include:** Quality Engineer; Compressed Air Systems Engineer; Product Manager; Six Sigma Black Belt; Material Analyst; Test Engineer; Lead Systems Engineer.

LIBERTY TRAVEL
1606 Chestnut Street, Philadelphia PA 19103. 215/972-0200. **Contact:** Human Resources. **World Wide Web address:** http://www.libertytravel.com. **Description:** A travel agency with 200 retail locations. **Other U.S. locations:** Nationwide. **Number of employees nationwide:** 1,000.

MARITRANS INC.
EASTERN OPERATIONS GROUP
2 International Plaza, Suite 335, Philadelphia PA 19113. 610/595-8000. **Contact:** Human Resources. **World Wide Web address:** http://www.maritrans.com. **Description:** Operates storage terminals. **Parent company:** Maritrans Inc. provides marine transportation for the petroleum distribution process, delivering about 10.6 billion gallons a year, and owns oil storage terminals. Maritrans offers a full line of distribution services including product exchanges, marine transportation, scheduling, terminal storage, and automated truck rack delivery systems. Marispond Inc. serves the growing international need for oil spill contingency planning and spill management in U.S. waters. This business capitalizes on Maritrans' spill response capabilities and is growing into the related areas of safety training and dry cargo contingency planning. **NOTE:** See website for a complete listing of shoreside and seagoing positions with detailed application information. **Corporate headquarters location:** Tampa FL.

W.C. McQUAIDE, INC.
153 Macridge Avenue, Johnstown PA 15904. 814/269-6000. **Toll-free phone:** 800/456-0292. **Fax:** 814/269-6189. **Contact:** Human Resources. **World Wide Web address:** http://www.mcquaide.com. **Description:** A freight carrier. **Corporate headquarters location:** This location. **Other U.S. locations:** NJ; NY; OH; WV. **Operations at this facility include:** Administration; Sales; Service. **Number of employees at this location:** 200. **Number of employees nationwide:** 415.

PILOT AIR FREIGHT CORPORATION
314 North Middletown Road, P.O. Box 97, Lima PA 19037. 610/891-8100. **Fax:** 610/565-4267. **Contact:** Bill Morgan, Human Resources Director. **E-mail address:** hr@pilotair.com. **World Wide Web address:** http://www.pilotair.com. **Description:** A freight forwarding company. **Corporate headquarters location:** This location. **Other area locations:** Allentown PA; Folcroft PA. **Operations at this facility include:** Administration. **Number of employees at this location:** 85.

SERVICE BY AIR INC.
850 Calcoon Hook Road, Sharon Hill PA 19079. 610/586-5050. **Toll-free phone:** 800/719-0001. **Fax:** 610/586-5511. **Contact:** Human Resources. **World Wide Web address:** http://www.servicebyair.com. **Description:** An air transportation company. **NOTE:** All resumes must indicate location of interest and be sent to: Service By Air Inc., Human Resources, 55 East Ames Court, Plainview NY 11803.

A. STUCKI COMPANY
2600 Neville Road, Pittsburgh PA 15225. 412/771-7300. **Fax:** 412/771-7308. **Contact:** John Faryniak, President. **World Wide Web address:** http://www.stucki.com. **Description:** A manufacturer of load stabilizers and related equipment for the railroad industry.

US AIRWAYS
1000 Commerce Drive, Building One, 4th Floor, Pittsburgh PA 15275. 412/472-2400. **Contact:** Human Resources Recruiting Department. **World Wide Web address:** http://www.usairways.com. **Description:** A leading air carrier at Pittsburgh International, US Airways has 175 flights per day. US Airways has regional, national, and international scheduled air services and express cargo operations. The company's primary hubs are in Philadelphia PA, Pittsburgh PA, Charlotte NC, and Baltimore MD/Washington DC. **NOTE:** Search and apply for positions online.

UNION SWITCH & SIGNAL INC.
1000 Technology Drive, Pittsburgh PA 15219. 412/688-2400. **Toll-free phone:** 800/351-1520. **Contact:** Human Resources. **E-mail address:** jobs@switch.com. **World Wide Web address:** http://www.switch.com. **Description:** Designs, engineers, produces, distributes, and services integrated railway signaling and automation and control systems. The company provides after-sale service of integrated railway signaling, automation and control systems, and related component products that provide a variety of train control and rail operations management capabilities. The company's customers include all Class 1 freight railroads and virtually all major rail-based transit systems in the United States, as well as rail transportation in select foreign countries. **Positions advertised include:** Manager, Hardware/Software Engineering; Project Engineer; Mechanical Engineer. **Parent company:** Ansaldo Signal. **President/CEO:** James Sanders.

WABTEC CORPORATION
1001 Air Brake Avenue, Wilmerding PA 15148. 412/825-1000. **Fax:** 412/825-1019. **Contact:** Patricia Pagnanelli, Human Resources Manager. **World Wide Web address:** http://www.wabco-rail.com. **Description:** A manufacturer of locomotive air brakes. **Listed on:** New York Stock Exchange. **Stock exchange symbol:** WAB.

Rhode Island

AMERICAN CANADIAN CARIBBEAN LINE, INC.
461 Water Street, P.O. Box 368, Warren RI 02885. 401/247-0955. **Toll-free phone:** 800/556-7450. **Fax:** 401/247-2350. **Contact:** Human Resources. **E-mail address:** info@accl-smallships.com. **World Wide Web address:** http://www.accl-smallships.com. **Description:** Operates a fleet of three small cruise ships that sail to destinations in the United States, Canada, the Caribbean and Central America. **NOTE:** See website for open positions and to apply online. **Positions advertised include:** Captain; First Mate; Engineer; Cruise Director; Chef; Assistant Chef; Steward/Stewardess; Deckhand; Destination Specialist. **Corporate headquarters location:** This location. **Listed on:** Privately held. **President:** Nancy E. Blount.

Tennessee

CENTRAL PARKING CORPORATION
2401 21st Avenue South, Nashville TN 37212. 615/297-4255. **Contact:** Human Resources. **World Wide Web address:** http://www.parking.com. **Description:** A leading provider of parking services in the United States. The company operates over 3,700 parking facilities in 38 states, and the District of Columbia. The company provides management services to multilevel parking facilities and surface lots. **NOTE:** Search and apply for positions online. **Positions advertised included:** Chief Internal Auditor. **Corporate headquarters location:** This location. **Other U.S. locations:** Nationwide. **International locations:** Chile; Germany; Ireland; Malaysia; Mexico; Puerto Rico; Spain; the Netherlands; United Kingdom. **Listed on:**

New York Stock Exchange. **Stock exchange symbol:** CPC. **Chairman/CEO:** Monroe J. Carell, Jr.

EXEL TRANSPORTATION SERVICES INC.
965 Ridge Lake Boulevard, Suite 103, Memphis TN 38120. 901/767-4455. **Fax:** 901/767-1929. **Contact:** Human Resources. **World Wide Web address:** http://www.exel.com. **Description:** One of the country's leading providers of single-source transportation services to some of the largest shippers in the world. The company provides a full complement of logistics management services such as dedicated fleet, warehousing, and risk management, as well as the component services involved in these activities. Services offered include double stack, trailers, and containers on rail cars; trucks; and ocean-going transportation. **Corporate headquarters location:** England. **Other U.S. locations:** Nationwide.

MEMPHIS INTERNATIONAL AIRPORT
2491 Winchester Road, Suite 113, Memphis TN 38116-3856. 901/922-8000. **Contact:** Human Resources. **World Wide Web address:** http://www.memphisairport.org. **Description:** An international airport. **Parent Company:** Memphis-Shelby County Airport Authority.

PREMIER TRANSPORTATION SERVICES
581 South 2nd Street, Memphis TN 38126. 901/577-7777. **Fax:** 901/577-7765. **Contact:** Human Resources. **E-mail address:** info@premierofmemphis.com. **World Wide Web address:** http://www.premierofmemphis.com. **Description:** Provides a variety of passenger ground transportation services: Chauffeured Limousine & Sedan, School Service, Convention and Ground Transportation, Contract Transportation Management, Casino Transportation, Taxicab Services.

SEA RAY BOATS, INC.
2600 Sea Ray Boulevard, Knoxville TN 37914. 865/522-4181. **Contact:** Human Resources. **World Wide Web address:** http://www.searay.com. **Description:** One of the nation's leading manufacturers of recreational pleasure boats. Sea Ray offers a line of nearly 60 models in seven product families including sport boats, sport cruisers, sport yachts, and yachts. **NOTE:** Search and apply for positions online. **Positions advertised include:** Manufacturing Engineer; Production Supervisor. **Parent company:** Brunswick Corporation.

SIGNATURE FLIGHT SUPPORT
2488 Winchester Road, Memphis TN 38116. 901/345-4700. **Fax:** 901/345-4733. **Contact:** Personnel. **World Wide Web address:** http://www.signatureflight.com. **Description:** Engaged in flight support operations including fueling, ground handling, passenger services, maintenance, and fuel purchasing. **NOTE:** Contact local HR Representative for employment information. **Corporate headquarters location:** Orlando FL. **Other U.S. locations:** Nationwide. **Parent company:** BBA Aviation. **Number of employees nationwide:** 1,300.

SWIFT TRANSPORTATION
P.O. Box 30788, Memphis TN 30788. 901/332-2500. **Physical address**: 1940 East Brooks Road, Memphis TN 38130. **Contact:** Recruiting. **World Wide Web address:** http://www.swifttrans.com. **Description:** An irregular-route truckload carrier transporting a wide range of commodities in the United States, Canada, and Mexico. The principal types of freight transported are packages, retail goods, nonperishable foodstuffs, paper and paper products, household appliances, furniture, and packaged petroleum products. **Positions advertised include:** Corporate Driver. **Corporate headquarters location:** Phoenix AZ. **Operations at this facility include:** Administration; Customer Service; Marketing; Purchasing; Sales; Service. **Number of employees at this location:** 450. **Number of employees nationwide:** 20,000.

VOLVO PENTA MARINE PRODUCTS
200 Robert Wallace Drive, Lexington TN 38351. 731/968-0151. **Contact:** Human Resources. **World Wide Web address:** http://www.volvo.com/volvopenta. **Description:** Manufactures outboard motors and engines. The company also manufactures replacement parts and accessories, offers boat rentals, and provides related financial services.

Texas

AMR CORPORATION
4333 Amon Carter Boulevard, Euless TX 76039. 817/963-1234. **Fax:** 817/967-9641. **Contact:** Human Resources. **World Wide Web address:** http://www.amrcorp.com. **Description:** Operates American Airlines, one of the largest airline carriers in the world. With its sister companies American Eagle and American Connection, American Airlines transports approximately 88 million passengers annually. It also has a partnership with British Airways. **NOTE:** In addition to its corporate headquarters, American Airlines has positions throughout airports and other offices in Texas. See website for listings and apply online. **Positions advertised include:** Application Development Manager; Financial Auditors; Commodity Managers; Editor – Spirit Magazine; Lead Call Center Engineer; Operations Research Consultant. **Listed on:** New York Stock Exchange. **Stock exchange symbol:** AMR. **Number of employees worldwide:** 90,000.

ABILENE AERO INC.
2850 Airport Boulevard, Abilene TX 79602. 325/677-2601. **Fax:** 325/671-8018. **Contact:** General Manager. **E-mail address:** jcrawford@abileneaero.com. **World Wide Web address:** http://www.abileneaero.com. **Description:** Operates a small airport offering flight instruction, charter and pilot service, aircraft fueling, parts, and maintenance. Founded in 1968. **Corporate headquarters location:** This location.

AMERICAN MAYFLOWER TRANFER
1735 West Crosby Road, Carrolton TX 75006. 972/466-1111. **Toll-free phone:** 800/648-7825. **Fax:** 972/233-3921. **Contact:** Human Resources. **World Wide Web address:** http://www.mayflower.com. **Description:** Offers a full range of moving and storage services to both commercial and individual customers. **Positions advertised include:** Driver. **Parent company:** Unigroup Inc.

BALDWIN DISTRIBUTION SERVICES
P.O. Box 51618, Amarillo TX 79159. 806/383-7650. **Physical address:** 7702 Broadway Drive, Amarillo TX 79108. 806/383-7650. **Toll-free phone:** 800/692-1333. **Contact:** Recruiting. **World Wide Web address:** http://www.baldwin-dist.com. **Description:** Provides long-haul trucking services. Baldwin Distribution Services operates in 48 states, Canada, and Mexico. **NOTE:** Contact Recruiting office at 866/4-BALDWIN. Recruiting office is located at I 40 & Loop 335, Amarillo TX. **Positions advertised include:** Long Haul Driver; Lease Purchase Operator. **Corporate headquarters location:** This location. **President/CEO:** Dudley Baldwin.

BLUE WHALE MOVING COMPANY
8291 Springdale Road, Suite 100, Austin TX 78724. 512/328-6688. **Fax:** 512/454-1463. **Contact:** Human Resources. **E-mail address:** bluewhale@bluewhale.com. **World Wide Web address:** http://www.bluewhale.com. **Description:** Provides both furniture storage and moving services throughout Texas. Founded in 1985.

BOWDEN TRAVEL SERVICE
CLEBURNE TRAVEL
1643 West Henderson Street, Suite A, Cleburne TX 76033-4174. 817/641-3477. **Toll-free phone:** 800/426-9336. **Fax:** 817/641-4477. **Contact:** Human Resources. **World Wide Web address:** http://www.bowdentravel.com. **Description:** A travel agency. **Annual sales/revenues:** Less than $5 million.

BUDGET RENT A CAR CORPORATION
13536 Preston Road, Suite 104, Dallas TX 75240. 972/720-0420. **Contact:** Human Resources. **World**

Wide Web address: http://www.budgetrentacar.com. **Description:** A car and truck rental service. **Positions advertised include:** Agency Operator. **Other area locations:** Statewide. **Other U.S. locations:** Nationwide. **Parent company:** Cendant Corporation. **Listed on:** New York Stock Exchange. **Stock exchange symbol:** CD.

BURLINGTON NORTHERN AND SANTA FE RAILWAY COMPANY
P.O. Box 961057, Fort Worth TX 76161-0057. 817/352-1000. **Physical address:** 2600 Lou Menk Drive, Second Floor, Fort Worth TX 76131. **Toll-free phone:** 800/795-2673. **Contact:** Human Resources. **World Wide Web address:** http://www.bnsf.com. **Description:** A railroad transportation company operating on 24,500 miles of track in 25 western states and 2 Canadian provinces. The company is one of the largest haulers of low-sulfur coal and grain in North America. **NOTE:** No phone calls regarding employment. Faxed resumes are not accepted. Please visit website to search for jobs and apply online. **Positions advertised include:** Auditor; Maintenance of Way Truck Driver; Management Trainee – Various Departments; Manager of Marketing Budgets; Manager of Organization Effectiveness; Manager of Technology Services; Senior Analyst; Senior Operations Research Specialist; Track Measurement Technician. **Special programs:** Internships. **Corporate headquarters location:** This location. **Listed on:** New York Stock Exchange. **Stock exchange symbol:** BNI. **Number of employees worldwide:** 38,000.

CAPITAL METRO
2910 East Fifth Street, Austin TX 78702. 512/389-7400. **Fax:** 512/369-6010. **Recorded jobline:** 512/389-7450. **Contact:** Human Resources. **E-mail address:** application@capmetro.org. **World Wide Web address:** http://www.capmetro.austin.tx.us. **Description:** Operates the public bus system for the metropolitan Austin area. **NOTE:** Contact Human Resources directly at 512/389-7445. Please visit website for a listing of jobs and download application form. Resumes are accepted for additional information, but you must complete an application. **Positions advertised include:** Fleet Mechanic; Marketing Coordinator; Data Analyst; Budget Analyst. **Office hours:** Monday – Friday, 8:00 a.m. – 5:00 p.m. **Corporate headquarters location:** This location.

CENTRAL FREIGHT LINES, INC.
P.O. Box 2638, Waco TX 76702. 254/772-2120. **Toll-free phone:** 800/782-5036. **Physical address:** 5601 West Waco Drive, Waco TX 76710. **Fax:** 254/741-5251. **Contact:** Human Resources. **E-mail address:** recruitingoffice@centralfreight.com. **World Wide Web address:** http://www.centralfreight.com. **Description:** One of the largest regional motor carriers in the United States operating through 77 terminals. Founded in 1925. **Corporate headquarters location:** This location. **Other area locations:** Statewide. **Other U.S. locations:** Nationwide.

CITY MACHINE & WELDING, INC.
P.O. Box 51018, Amarillo TX 79159-1018. 806/358-7293. **Physical address:** 9701 Interchange 552, Amarillo TX 79124. **Fax:** 806/358-7906. **Contact:** Human Resources. **World Wide Web address:** http://www.cmwelding.com. **Description:** Manufactures transport trailers and performs welding services. **President:** L.A. Oeschger.

COACH USA, INC.
950 McCarty Drive, Houston TX 77029. 713/888-0104. **Toll-free phone:** 888/262-2487. **Fax:** 713/888-0257. **Contact:** Human Resources. **World Wide Web address:** http://www.coachusa.com. **Description:** One of the largest bus transportation companies. Among its services are sightseeing tours in major metropolitan cities. **Other U.S. locations include:** CA; CT; GA; MN; MD; NJ; NY; NC. **International locations:** Canada. **Parent company:** Stagecoach International (United Kingdom). **Listed on:** New York Stock Exchange. **Stock exchange symbol:** CUI.

COMDATA CORPORATION
6000 Western Place, Suite 900, Fort Worth TX 76107. 817/731-2895. **Contact:** Human Resources. **E-mail address:** resumes@comdata.com. **World Wide Web address:** http://www.comdata.com. **Description:** Provides transaction processing and information services to the transportation, gaming, and retail industries. Comdata links more than 20,000 telecommunication ports of entry, processing over 100 million transactions per year. **NOTE:** Please visit website to view job listings. Send resumes to the corporate office at Attention Human Resources, Comdata Corporation, 5301 Maryland Way, Brentwood TN 37027. Fax to 615/370-7828. **Parent company:** Ceridian Corporation. **Listed on:** New York Stock Exchange. **Stock exchange symbol:** CEN.

CONTINENTAL AIRLINES
18201 Viscount Road, Houston TX 77032-4330. 281/821-6539. **Fax:** 713/324-5940. **Contact:** Human Resources. **World Wide Web address:** http://www.continental.com. **Description:** One of the largest airlines in the United States, offering flights to 149 domestic and 117 international locations daily. Operating through its major hubs in Newark, Houston, Cleveland, and Guam. Continental offers extensive service to Latin America and Europe. Founded in 1934. **NOTE:** Entry-level positions and second and third shifts are offered. Apply online. **Corporate headquarters location:** This location. **Subsidiaries include:** Continental Express. **Listed on:** New York Stock Exchange. **Stock exchange symbol:** CAL. **Number of employees nationwide:** 42,900.

DALLAS AREA RAPID TRANSIT (DART)
P.O. Box 660163, Dallas TX 75266-7240. 214/749-3259. **Fax:** 214/749-3636. **Recorded jobline:** 214/749-3690. **Contact:** Human Resources. **World Wide Web address:** http://www.dart.org. **Description:** A nonprofit, rapid transit system serving the Dallas metropolitan area. **Positions advertised include:** Contract Specialist; Maintenance Specialist; Fare Inspector; Bus Operator; Rail Operator; Train Operator; Mechanic; DART Police Officer; Bus Mechanic. **Number of employees at this location:** 2,925.

DALLAS-FORT WORTH INTERNATIONAL AIRPORT
P.O. Drawer 619428, DFW Airport TX 75261-9428. 972/574-8888. **Fax:** 972/574-5732. **Physical address:** 3200 East Airfield Drive, DFW Airport TX 75261. **Recorded jobline:** 972/574-8024. **Contact:** Human Resources. **World Wide Web address:** http://www.dfwairport.com. **Description:** An international airport with flights worldwide on 25 commercial airlines and several charter airlines. **NOTE:** Security screening positions for the airport can be found on the National Transportation Security Administration's website (http://www.tsa.gov.) All other positions can be found on the DFW Airport's website. **Positions advertised include:** AVP Airport Real Estate; Budget Analyst; Energy Plant Operations/Maintenance Technician; Organizational Development Manager.

DELTA AIR LINES, INC.
2008 Terminal E Row East, Dallas TX 75201. 972/456-1173. **Contact:** Human Resources. **E-mail address:** delta.careers@delta.com. **World Wide Web address:** http://www.delta.com. **Description:** One of the largest airlines in the United States. The company provides scheduled air transportation for passengers, freight, and mail on an extensive route that covers most of the country and extends to 32 foreign nations. The route covers 205 domestic cities in 46 states, the District of Columbia, Puerto Rico, the U.S. Virgin Islands, and 47 cities abroad. Major domestic hubs of Delta include Atlanta, Dallas-Fort Worth, Salt Lake City, and Cincinnati with minor hubs in Los Angeles and Orlando. Delta has over 550 aircraft in its fleet. Founded in 1929. **NOTE:** All hiring is done through Delta Air Lines, Inc., Recruitment and Employment Office, P.O. Box 20530, Atlanta GA 30320. 404/715-2600. **Corporate headquarters location:** Atlanta GA.

Listed on: New York Stock Exchange. **Stock exchange symbol:** DAL. **Number of employees worldwide:** 60,000.

DYNAMEX INC.
1870 Crown Drive, Dallas TX 75234. 214/561-7500. **Fax:** 214/561-7499. **Contact:** Human Resources. **World Wide Web address:** http://www.dynamex.com. **Description:** Offers customized warehousing and local outsourcing delivery services for companies without private trucks or delivery vehicles. Founded in 1985. **Listed on:** American Stock Exchange. **Stock exchange symbol:** DDN.

FFE TRANSPORTATION SERVICES, INC.
P.O. Box 655888, Dallas TX 75265-5888. 214/630-8090. **Physical address:** 1145 Empire Central Place, Dallas TX 75247-4309. **Contact:** Human Resources. **NOTE:** For additional information, driver applicants can call 800/569-9233; owner/operator applicants can call 800/569-9298; administrative and maintenance applicants can call 800/569-9200. All applicants can also apply online via the website. **World Wide Web address:** http://www.ffeinc.com. **Description:** Provides trucking and transportation services nationwide.

FM INDUSTRIES, INC.
8600 Will Rogers Boulevard, Fort Worth TX 76140. 817/293-4220. **Fax:** 817/551-5801. **Contact:** Human Resources. **World Wide Web address:** http://www.fmionline.net. **Description:** Produces hydraulic cushioning systems for railroad freight cars.

FEDERAL EXPRESS CORPORATION (FEDEX)
1220 Riverbend, Dallas TX 75247. 800/GOF-EDEX. **Contact:** Recruiting. **World Wide Web address:** http://www.fedex.com. **Description:** One of the world's largest express transportation companies serving 215 countries worldwide. FedEx ships approximately 3.2 million packages daily. FedEx operates more than 45,000 drop-off locations, and has a fleet that consists of more than 640 aircraft and 44,5000 vehicles. **Corporate headquarters location:** Memphis TN. **Other U.S. locations:** Nationwide. **International locations:** Worldwide. **Listed on:** New York Stock Exchange. **Stock exchange symbol:** FDS.

GREYHOUND LINES INC.
P.O. Box 660606, Dallas TX 75266-0606. 972/789-7000. **Physical address**: 15110 Dallas Parkway, Dallas TX 75248. **Contact:** Human Resources. **World Wide Web address:** http://www.greyhound.com. **Description:** One of the country's largest private transportation networks. Greyhound conducts regular route, package express, charter, and food service operations. The fleet consists of over 1,650 buses that travel to more than 2,600 destinations.

GULFMARK OFFSHORE
5 Post Oak Circle, Suite 1170, Houston TX 77024. 713/963-9522. **Contact:** Human Resources. **World Wide Web address:** http://www.gulfmark.com. **Description:** Provides offshore marine transportation and erosion control services. **International locations:** Worldwide. **Listed on:** NASDAQ. **Stock exchange symbol:** GMRK.

J.B. HUNT TRANSPORT SERVICES, INC.
5701 West Kiest Boulevard, Dallas TX 75236. 214/330-2015. **Toll-free phone**: 800/643-3622. **Contact:** Human Resources. **World Wide Web address:** http://www.jbhunt.com. **Description:** A major freight transportation company. **Corporate headquarters location:** Lowell AR. **Listed on:** NASDAQ. **Stock exchange symbol:** JBHT.

KITTY HAWK AIR CARGO
1515 West 20th Street, P.O. Box 612787, DFW Airport TX 75261. 972/456-2200. **Contact:** Human Resources. **E-mail address:** jobs@kha.com. **World Wide Web address:** http://www.khcargo.com. **Description:** Provides charter management and cargo services.

LUMINATOR
1200 East Plano Parkway, Plano TX 75074. 972/424-6511. **Fax:** 972/423-0255. **Contact:** Greg Evans, Human Resources. **World Wide Web address:** http://www.luminatorusa.com. **Description:** Manufactures aircraft parts, bus products, and rail products. Luminator aircraft products include batteries, lamps, searchlights, interiors, and crew stations. Bus products include flip-out signs and voice systems. Rail products include various types of lighting, flip dot sign systems, electronic maps, voice systems, and air diffusers. **Positions advertised include:** Credit Manager; Cost Accountant; Program Manager. **Corporate headquarters location:** This location. **Parent company:** Mark IV Industries.

MARTINAIRE INC.
1616 West 23rd Street, Dallas TX 75261. 972/456-8410. **Fax:** 972/349-5750. **Contact:** Tony Holcomb, Maintenance Director. **E-mail address:** tholcomb@martinaire.com. **World Wide Web address:** http://www.martinaire.com. **Description:** An air cargo carrier operating a fleet of 20 aircraft. **Positions advertised include:** Pilot.

NEWPARK SHIPBUILDING & REPAIR INC.
2102 Broadway, Houston TX 77012. 713/847-4600. **Toll-free phone:** 888/399-9283. **Fax:** 713/847-4601. **Contact:** Human Resources. **World Wide Web address:** http://www.fwav.com. **Description:** Manufactures barges, towboats, and riverboats for a wide range of customers. **Corporate headquarters location:** Houston TX. **Other area locations:** Galveston TX; Pasadena TX. **Operations at this facility include:** Administration. **Parent company:** Firstwave Marine. **Operations at this facility include:** Service.

PORT OF HOUSTON AUTHORITY
P.O. Box 2562, Houston TX 77252-2562. 713/670-2400. **Physical address:** 111 East Loop North, Houston TX 77029. **Fax:** 713/670-2400. **Contact:** Human Resources. **E-mail address:** PHA-Resumes@poha.com. **World Wide Web address:** http://www.portofhouston.com. **Description:** Administers and regulates the Port of Houston Authority. Responsibilities include fire and safety protection along the 50-mile Houston Ship Channel. The Port Authority owns 43 general cargo wharves, two liquid-cargo wharves, and many other facilities. **NOTE:** Interested jobseekers must submit completed applications along with their resumes. A list of positions and the application can be found on the website. **Positions advertised include:** Sergeant; Vessel Services Superintendent; Mechanic. **Special programs:** Internships. **Internship information:** The Port of Houston Authority runs programs throughout the year. For more information, see the website or call Deborah Garner at 731/670-216. **Office hours:** Monday – Friday, 8:00 a.m. – 5:00 p.m.

RAILAMERICA, INC
4040 Broadway, Suite 200, San Antonio TX 78209. 210/841-7600. **Contact:** Human Resources. **E-mail address:** employment@railamerica.com. **World Wide Web address:** http://www.railamerica.com. **Description:** A leading operator of short line railroads nationwide. **Positions advertised include:** Electrician. **NOTE:** Send resumes to: RailAmerica, Inc., Employment, 5300 Broken Sound Boulevard Northwest, Boca Raton FL 33487.

SABRE HOLDINGS COMPANY
3150 Sabre Drive, Southlake TX 76092. 682/605-1000. **Fax:** 682/605-8267. **Contact:** Human Resources. **World Wide Web address:** http://www.sabre-holdings.com. **Description:** A giant in the travel reservation industry. This company owns and manages the popular website Travelocity. It also manages the reservations system used by travel agents to book airline seats, hotel rooms, rental cars and cruises. **NOTE:** Apply online. **Positions advertised include:** Senior Business Systems Analyst; Sales Analyst; IT Project Management Senior; Marketing

Communications Manager; Senior Data Warehouse Developer; Insides Sales Representative. **Special programs:** Internships. **Other U.S. locations:** CA; FL; NV; NY; WA; Washington DC. **Listed on:** New York Stock Exchange. **Stock exchange symbol:** TSG.

SKY HELICOPTERS
2559 South Jupiter Road, Dallas TX 75201. 214/349-7000. **Contact:** Human Resources. **World Wide Web address:** http://www.skyhelicopters.com. **Description:** Engaged in helicopter transportation for both public and private use.

SOUTHWEST AIRLINES COMPANY
P.O. Box 36644, Dallas TX 75235-1644. 214/792-4213. **Physical address:** 2702 Love Field Drive, Dallas TX 75235. **Fax:** 214/792-7015. **Recorded jobline:** 214/792-4803 (Dallas TX); 602/389-3738 (Phoenix AZ). **Contact:** SWA People Department. **World Wide Web address:** http://www.southwest.com. **Description:** A major short-haul, low-fare, high-frequency, point-to-point carrier in the United States. Southwest Airlines, a *Fortune* 500 company, flies to 59 cities in 31 states and offers over 2,900 flights daily. **NOTE:** On its website, this airline provides job listings; job requirements, and resume and application procedures. See website before applying for any position. **Positions advertised include:** Clerical; Aircraft Appearance Technician; Mechanic; Flight Attendant; Pilot, Provisioning Agent; Reservation Sales Agent; System Administrator; Accountant; Attorney. **Special programs:** Internships. **Corporate headquarters location:** This location. **Other U.S. locations:** Nationwide. **Listed on:** New York Stock Exchange. **Stock exchange symbol:** LUV. **Number of employees worldwide:** 32,000.

TIDEWATER
2000 West Sam Houston Parkway South, Suite 1280, Houston TX 77042. 713/470-5300. **Fax:** 713/470-0077. **Contact:** Human Resources. **World Wide Web address:** http://www.tdw.com. **Description:** Provides offshore marine services. **NOTE:** See this company's website for job listings. **Corporate headquarters location:** New Orleans, LA.

UNITED PARCEL SERVICE (UPS)
660 Fritz Drive, Coppell TX 75019. 972/471-7171. **Recorded jobline:** 888/877-0924. **Contact:** Human Resources. **World Wide Web address:** http://www.ups.com. **Description:** United Parcel Service is a parcel pickup and delivery service organization that provides service to all 50 states and to more than 185 countries and territories worldwide. The company delivers approximately 12 million packages daily. **NOTE:** The jobline lists mainly part-time positions, including those at other Texas locations. Apply online. **Positions advertised include:** Account Executive; Regional Account Manager.

VIA METROPOLITAN TRANSIT
1021 San Pedro, San Antonio TX 78212. 210/362-2240. **Recorded jobline:** 210/362-2002. **Contact:** Human Resources. **E-mail address:** hr.emp@viainfo.net. **World Wide Web address:** http://www.viainfo.net. **Description:** A bus line for the city of San Antonio. **NOTE:** Apply at Human Resources office. **Positions advertised include:** Strategic Planning Coordinator; Shop Attendant; Bus Operator; Paratransit Operator; Substitute Teacher; Temporary Clerical Pool. **Office hours:** Monday – Friday, 7:30 a.m. – 5:00 p.m. **Corporate headquarters location:** This location.

VIRTUOSO
500 Main Street, Suite 400, Fort Worth TX 76102. 817/870-0300. **Fax:** 817/870-4645. **Contact:** Susan Spain, Strategic Growth & Recruitment. **E-mail address:** humanresources@virtuoso.com. **World Wide Web address:** http://www.virtuoso.com. **Description:** A travel consortium specializing in leisure travel. **NOTE:** Apply online.

Utah

A&K RAILROAD MATERIALS
1505 South Redwood, P.O. Box 30076, Salt Lake City UT 84130. 801/974-5484. **Toll-free phone:** 800/453-8812. **Fax:** 801/972-2041. **Contact:** Human Resources. **E-mail address:** info@akrailroad.com. **World Wide Web address:** http://www.akrailroad.com. **Description:** A wholesaler of materials used to build railroads. **Corporate headquarters location:** This location. **Other U.S. locations:** Nationwide.

AMERICOLD LOGISTICS, LLC
755 East 1700 South, Clearfield UT 84106. 801/773-6886. **Toll-free phone:** 888/484-4877. **Fax:** 801/773-0887. **Contact:** Human Resources. **World Wide Web address:** http://www.amclog.com. **Description:** A freezer/storage company that operates a refrigerated food warehouse facility for frozen food products. **NOTE:** Please visit website to search for jobs and apply online. **Corporate headquarters location:** Atlanta GA. **Other U.S. locations:** Nationwide.

CENTRAL REFIGERATED SERVICE, INC.
575 West 2100 South, West Valley City UT 84120. 801/225-2299. **Toll-free phone:** 800/777-9100. **Fax:** 800/688-1152. **Contact:** Vicki Bird, Human Resources. **E-mail address:** vicki@centralref.com. **World Wide Web address:** http://www.centralref.com. **Description:** A full-service truckload carrier with operations that include inner-city local deliveries, private fleet conversions, team/solo driver regional and long haul dedicated fleets, and team/solo driver regional and long haul truckload delivery. Operations are open 24 hours a day, seven days a week, including holidays. **NOTE:** For driver positions, see website http://www.centraltruckdrivingjobs.com for job openings and application instructions. For non-driver positions, submit resume by mail, fax, or e-mail. **Corporate headquarters location:** This location.

C.R. ENGLAND & SONS, INC.
P.O. Box 27728, Salt Lake City UT 84127-0728. 801/972-2712. **Physical address:** 4701 West 2100 South, Salt Lake City UT 84120. **Toll-free phone:** 800/356-5046. **Contact:** Human Resources. **E-mail address:** For Driver positions – debbier@crengland.com; For Staff positions – carriejo@crengland.com. **World Wide Web address:** http://www.crengland.com. **Description:** A long-haul trucking company. **NOTE:** For Driver positions, please visit website for application form. **Positions advertised include:** Driver. **Corporate headquarters location:** This location. **President:** Eugene England. **CEO:** Daniel England.

MORRIS MURDOCK TRAVEL
240 East Morris Avenue, Salt Lake City UT 84115. 801/487-9731. **Toll-free phone:** 800/888-6699. **Fax:** 801/483-6338. **Contact:** Personnel Manager. **World Wide Web address:** http://www.morrismurdock.com. **Description:** A large travel agency. **Corporate headquarters location:** This location. **Other area locations:** Statewide. **Other U.S. locations:** ID; MT. **CEO:** Mark Slack.

ROADWAY EXPRESS INC.
1234 South 3200 West, Salt Lake City UT 84104. 801/973-7399. **Fax:** 801/975-9916. **Contact:** Human Resources. **World Wide Web address:** http://www.roadway.com. **Description:** Operates a freight consolidation and distribution terminal for one of the largest common carriers in the United States, with terminals nationwide. The company operates in all 50 states. Founded in 1930. **NOTE:** Apply in person during the hours of 8:00 a.m. – 4:00 p.m., Monday – Friday. **Corporate headquarters location:** Akron OH. **Other U.S. locations:** Nationwide. **Subsidiaries include:** Roadway Services is a transportation holding company with subsidiaries involved in long-haul, airfreight, small package, and custom logistics services. Other subsidiaries of the parent company include Roadway Global Air, with worldwide air freight service through 230 service centers; Roadway Package System, with 271 terminals in the United States and a dozen in

Canada; Roadway Express, a motor freight transportation company that offers service in all 50 states, Canada, and Mexico; and four regional short-haul freight carriers. **Parent company:** YRC Worldwide. **Number of employees nationwide:** 24,800.

SKYWEST, INC.
444 South River Road, St. George UT 84790. 435/634-3000. **Fax:** 435/634-3105. **Contact:** Personnel Department. **World Wide Web address:** http://www.skywest.com. **Description:** A holding company that owns SkyWest Airlines and Atlanta-based Atlantic Southeast Airlines (ASA). **NOTE:** Please visit website to search for jobs and to apply online. **Positions advertised include:** Flight Attendant; Customer Service Agent; Ramp Agent; Cross Utilized Agent. **Special programs:** Internships. **Corporate headquarters location:** This location. **Operations at this facility include:** Administration. **Listed on:** NASDAQ. **Stock exchange symbol:** SKYW.

UNITED PARCEL SERVICE (UPS)
2040 Parkway Boulevard, Suite 100, West Valley City UT 84119. 801/973-1409. **Fax:** 801/973-3795. **Contact:** Human Resources Manager. **World Wide Web address:** http://www.ups.com. **Description:** A package pickup and delivery service organization providing service to all 50 states and to more than 185 countries and territories worldwide, delivering approximately 12 million packages daily. **NOTE:** Please visit http://www.upsjobs.com to search for jobs. **Corporate headquarters location:** Atlanta GA. **Other area locations:** Statewide. **Other U.S. locations:** Nationwide. **International locations:** Worldwide.

U.S. XPRESS ENTERPRISES, INC.
1901 West 2100 South, Salt Lake City UT 84119. 800/363-3401. **Contact:** Human Resources. **World Wide Web address:** http://www.usxpress.com. **Description:** A nationwide truckload carrier. **NOTE:** For driver positions, call or see website http://www.xpressdrivers.com. **Corporate headquarters location:** Chattanooga TN. **Operations at this facility include:** Terminal facility. **Listed on:** NASDAQ. **Stock exchange symbol:** XPRSA.

UTAH TRANSIT AUTHORITY
P.O. Box 30810. Salt Lake City UT 84130-0810. 801/262-5626. **Physical address:** 3600 South 700 West, Salt Lake City UT 84119. **Toll-free phone:** 888/743-3882. **Recorded jobline:** 801/287-4617. **Contact:** Human Resources. **E-mail address:** jobs@utabus.com. **World Wide Web address:** http://www.rideuta.com. **Description:** Operates the mass transit bus system. **Positions advertised include:** Mechanics Helper; Part-Time Security Officer. **Corporate headquarters location:** This location. **Other area locations:** Orem UT; Ogden UT.

YELLOW TRANSPORTATION
2410 South 2700 West, West Valley City UT 84119. 801/977-6200. **Fax:** 801/977-6220. **Contact:** Human Resources Manager. **World Wide Web address:** http://www.myyellow.com. **Description:** Operates a fleet of some 8,300 tractors and 33,000 trailers from nearly 340 terminals throughout North America. **NOTE:** Please visit website to search for jobs and apply online. **Corporate headquarters location:** Overland Park KS. **Parent company:** YRC Worldwide.

Vermont

NEW ENGLAND CENTRAL RAILROAD, INC.
2 Federal Street, Suite 201, St. Albans VT 05478. 802/527-3500. **Fax:** 802/527-3482. **Recorded jobline:** 561/226-6800. **Contact:** Human Resources. **E-mail address:** employment@railamerica.com. **World Wide Web address:** http://www.railamerica.com. **Description:** A railroad company operating 366 miles of tracks between East Albugh VT and New London CT serving Vermont, New Hampshire, Massachusetts, and Connecticut. **NOTE:** Unsolicited resumes are not accepted. **Positions advertised include:** Track Inspector; Customer Service Representative; Mechanic; Train Service Employee. **Parent company:** RailAmerica, Inc. (Boca Raton FL).

VERMONT TRANSIT COMPANY INC.
345 Pine Street, Burlington VT 05401. 802/864-6811. **Fax:** 802/862-7812. **Contact:** Human Resources. **World Wide Web address:** http://www.vermonttransit.com. **Description:** A bussing company that serves Vermont, New Hampshire, Maine, New York, and Massachusetts. **NOTE:** Apply online or at the terminal. **Positions advertised include:** Terminal Employee; Maintenance Technician; Service Worker; Motorcoach Operator. **Corporate headquarters location:** This location. **Other locations:** Boston MA; Portland ME; Rutland VT; White River Junction VT.

Virginia

AMERICAN TRUCKING ASSOCIATIONS, INC.
2200 Mill Road, Alexandria VA 22314-4677. 703/838-1700. **Fax:** 703/836-5880. **Contact:** Kay Perkins, Vice President of Personnel. **World Wide Web address:** http://www.trucking.org. **Description:** This national federation of the trucking industry represents all types of trucking companies. **Corporate headquarters location:** This location.

BAE SYSTEMS NORFOLK SHIP REPAIR
750 West Berkley Avenue, Norfolk VA 23523. 757/494-4000. **Fax:** 757/494-4031. **Recorded jobline:** 757/494-2964. **Contact:** Human Resources Manager. **E-mail address:** human_resources.norshipco@baesystems.com. **World Wide Web address:** http://www.norshipco.com. **Description:** Performs non-nuclear ship repair, modernization, conversion, and overhaul. **Positions advertised include:** Outside Machinist. **Parent company:** BAE Systems.

BOATU.S.
880 South Pickett Street, Alexandria VA 22304. 703/823-9550. **Fax:** 703/461-4395. **Recorded jobline:** 703/461-4691. **Contact:** Evelyn Matey, Director of Human Resources. **E-mail address:** humanresources@boatus.com. **World Wide Web address:** http://www.boatus.com. **Description:** One of the largest national associations of recreational boat owners. BoatU.S. provides marine insurance to its members, representation in Congress, water towing services, and discount boating equipment. Founded in 1966. **NOTE:** Search for positions online. **Positions advertised include:** Graphic Designer; Marketing Coordinator; Personal Liability Adjuster; UNIX System Administrator. **Corporate headquarters location:** This location. **Operations at this facility include:** Administration; Sales; Service. **Number of employees at this location:** 500. **Number of employees nationwide:** 1,000.

BRENCO, INC.
2580 Frontage Road, P.O. Box 389, Petersburg VA 23804. 804/732-0202. **Fax:** 804/732-4722. **Contact:** Human Resources. **E-mail address:** resumes@brencoqbs.com. **World Wide Web address:** http://www.brencoqbs.com. **Description:** Manufactures tapered roller bearings and component parts for railroad cars. The company sells tapered roller bearings to most major railroads and railroad car builders worldwide. Automotive forgings are sold principally to automobile manufacturers. **Positions advertised include:** Production Worker; Product Development Engineer; Manufacturing Engineer; Electrician. **Corporate headquarters location:** This location. **Subsidiaries include:** Quality Bearing Service specializes in bearing reconditioning and the sale of replacement bearings; Rail Link, Inc. provides third-party contract switching services to large industrial rail users. **Parent company:** AMSTED Industries Inc.

CI TRAVEL
CRUISE INTERNATIONAL
101 West Main Street, Suite 800, Norfolk VA 23510. 757/627-8000. **Toll-free phone:** 888/734-0775.

Contact: Human Resources. **World Wide Web address:** http://www.citravel.com. **Description:** An ocean cruise line.

CSX CORPORATION
P.O. Box 85629, Richmond VA 23285-5629. 804/782-1400. **Fax:** 904/359-3932. **Physical address:** 901 East Cary Street, Richmond VA 23219. **Contact:** Human Resources. **World Wide Web address:** http://www.csx.com. **Description:** An operator of container ship lines, railcars, and barges. CSX also provides intermodal and logistics services, operates a resort, and conducts real estate activities. The company's rail system consists of 23,000 miles of track in 23 states and Canada. **NOTE:** Search for jobs online. Application procedures vary according to position. **Corporate headquarters location:** Jacksonville FL. **Listed on:** New York Stock Exchange. **Stock exchange symbol:** CSX. **Annual sales/revenues:** $7.8 billion. **Number of employees worldwide:** 40,000.

GENERAL DYNAMICS CORPORATION
2941 Fairview Park Drive, Suite 100, Falls Church VA 22042-4523. 703/876-3000. **Fax:** 703/876-3125. **Contact:** Human Resources. **World Wide Web address:** http://www.generaldynamics.com. **Description:** General Dynamics is involved in business aviation and aircraft services, land and amphibious combat systems, mission-critical information systems and technologies, and shipbuilding and marine systems. The company is a leading supplier of sophisticated defense systems to the United States and its allies. Founded in 1952. **NOTE:** Search and apply for positions online. **Corporate headquarters location:** This location. **Other U.S. locations:** CT; MI; NJ; OH; RI. **Listed on:** New York Stock Exchange. **Stock exchange symbol:** GD. **Annual sales/revenues:** $16.6 billion. **Number of employees at this location:** 60. **Number of employees nationwide:** 31,000. **Number of employees worldwide:** 67,000.

LANDSTAR GOVERNMENT TRANSPORTATION
6225 Brandon Avenue, Suite 320, Springfield VA 22150. 703/912-6808. **Contact:** Human Resources. **World Wide Web address:** http://www.landstar.com. **Description:** The government transportation services office of one of the largest multimodal transportation service companies in North America. **NOTE:** Resumes should be sent to Landstar System, Inc., P.O. Box 19135, Jacksonville FL 32245. **Corporate headquarters location:** Jacksonville FL. **Other U.S. locations:** Madisonville KY; Romulus MI. **Parent company:** Landstar System, Inc. is divided into specialized freight transportation segments. Its business is a mix of regular accounts and spot hauls. Subsidiaries of the parent company include: Landstar Expedited, Inc.; Landstar Express America, Inc.; Landstar Gemini, Inc.; Landstar Inway, Inc.; Landstar ITCO, Inc.; Landstar Ligon, Inc.; Landstar Poole, Inc.; Landstar Ranger, Inc.; Landstar T.L.C., Inc.; and Landstar Transportation Service, Inc. **Listed on:** NASDAQ. **Stock exchange symbol:** LSTR. **Number of employees nationwide:** 2,500.

METRO MACHINE CORPORATION
P.O. Box 1860, Norfolk VA 23501. 757/543-6801. **Contact:** Don Fisher, Personnel Director. **World Wide Web address:** http://www.memach.com. **Description:** Engaged in shipbuilding and repair. **Other U.S. locations:** Philadelphia PA.

NORFOLK SOUTHERN CORPORATION
3 Commercial Place, Norfolk VA 23510-9227. 757/629-2600. **Recorded jobline:** 800/214-3609. **Contact:** Manager of Recruiting. **E-mail address:** careers@nscorp.com. **World Wide Web address:** http://www.nscorp.com. **Description:** A railroad freight transportation and holding company controlling Norfolk Southern Railway, and subsidiaries. The company's rail lines extend 21,800 miles through 22 eastern states, the District of Columbia and the province of Ontario. **NOTE:** Entry-level positions are offered. **Special programs:** Internships. **Corporate headquarters location:** This location. **Other U.S. locations:** Nationwide. **Listed on:** New York Stock Exchange. **Stock exchange symbol:** NSC. **Annual sales/revenues:** More than $100 million. **Number of employees nationwide:** 28,000.

NORTHROP GRUMMAN NEWPORT NEWS
4101 Washington Avenue, Newport News VA 23607. 757/380-2000. **Recorded jobline:** 757/380-2142. **Contact:** Human Resources. **World Wide Web address:** http://www.nn.northropgrumman.com. **Description:** Engaged in the design, construction, repair, overhaul, and refueling of conventional and nuclear-powered merchant and naval surface ships and submarines. **Positions advertised include:** Designer; Medical Records Supervisor; Engineer; Rigger; VCS Product Planner; Operations Coordinator; Construction Manager; Sr. Engineer; Project Engineer; Financial Analyst. **Corporate headquarters location:** This location. **Parent company:** Northrop Grumman. **Operations at this facility include:** Administration; Manufacturing; Research and Development. **Listed on:** New York Stock Exchange. **Stock exchange symbol:** NOC. **Number of employees at this location:** 17,000.

OVERNITE TRANSPORTATION, INC.
1000 Semmes Avenue, P.O. Box 1216, Richmond VA 23218-1216. 804/231-8000. **Fax:** 804/231-8895. **Recorded jobline:** 804/291-5627. **Contact:** Human Resources. **E-mail address:** jobs@overnite.com. **World Wide Web address:** http://www.overnite.com. **Description:** A trucking company that transports goods nationwide. **NOTE:** Search for positions online. Mail for fax resume. **Positions advertised include:** Customer Service Associate. **Corporate headquarters location:** This location. **Other U.S. locations:** Nationwide. **Parent company:** Overnite Corporation. **Listed on:** NASDAQ. **Stock exchange symbol:** OVNT. **Annual sales/revenues:** More than $100 million.

QED SYSTEMS, INC.
4646 North Witchduck Road, Virginia Beach VA 23455. 757/490-5000. **Fax:** 757/490-5027. **Contact:** James Lyons, Human Resources Manager. **E-mail address:** jobs@qedsysinc.com. **World Wide Web address:** http://www.qedsysinc.com. **Description:** A government contracting facility. QED Systems, Inc. handles marine engineering, manufactures technical manuals, and performs shipboard inspections. Founded in 1970. **Positions advertised include:** Accounting Supervisor. **Corporate headquarters location:** This location. **Other area locations:** Chesapeake VA.

SWISSPORT USA
Washington Dulles International Airport, 45025 Aviation Drive, Suite 350, Dulles VA 20166. 703/742-4300. **Fax:** 703/742-4321. **Contact:** Human Resources. **E-mail address:** william.rodriguez@swissport-usa.com. **World Wide Web address:** http://www.swissport.com. **Description:** Provides a wide range of ground-handling services for airlines and airports. Services include maintenance, inspections, spare parts inventory, into-plane fueling, cargo handling, cabin cleaning, and ramp services. Swissport USA also operates reservation centers for airlines. Founded in 1964. **Parent company:** Alpha Airports Group. **Annual sales/revenues:** More than $100 million. **Number of employees at this location:** 50. **Number of employees nationwide:** 6,000.

US AIRWAYS, INC.
2345 Crystal Drive, Arlington VA 22227. 703/872-7000. **Contact:** Senior Vice President of Human Resources. **World Wide Web address:** http://www.usairways.com. **Description:** Provides air transportation of passengers, property, and mail; reservations and ground support services to commuter carriers; aircraft remarketing; aircraft appraisal services; general aviation and spare parts sales; fixed-based operations; fuel services; and other aviation-related activities. **NOTE:** Search and apply for positions online. **Positions advertised include:** Fleet Service Agent; Aircraft Maintenance Technician.

Corporate headquarters location: This location. **Listed on:** New York Stock Exchange. **Stock exchange symbol:** U. **Annual sales/revenues:** More than $100 million.

Washington

AAA SEATTLE
330 Sixth Avenue North, Seattle WA 98109. 206/448-5353. **Contact:** Human Resources. **E-mail address:** hr@aaawa.com. **World Wide Web address:** http://www.aaawa.com. **Description:** Provides insurance, travel, and a wide variety of services to motorists through a network of over 50 branch offices. **Corporate headquarters location:** Heathrow FL.

AIR VAN MOVING GROUP
1111 80th Street Southwest, Everett WA 98203. 425/348-4113. **Toll-free phone:** 800/326-3683. **Contact:** Personnel Director. **World Wide Web address:** http://www.navlagent.com/airvan. **Description:** A freight forwarding company with operations in domestic moving services. **Corporate headquarters location:** This location.

AMERICAN AIRLINES, INC.
Seattle-Tacoma International Airport, Seattle WA 98158-1277. 206/433-3951. **Contact:** Human Resources. **World Wide Web address:** http://www.americanair.com. **Description:** Provides scheduled jet service to more than 170 destinations throughout North America, the Caribbean, Latin America, Europe, and the Pacific. **NOTE:** All resumes should be sent to: American Airlines, Inc., Human Resources, P.O. Box 619616, Mail Drop 5105, DFW Airport TX 75261-9040. **Corporate headquarters location:** Fort Worth TX. **Parent company:** AMR Corporation's operations fall within three major lines of business: the Air Transportation Group, the SABRE Group, and the AMR Management Services Group.

BEKINS NORTHWEST
6501 216th Street SW, Mount Lake Terrace WA 98043. 425/775-8950. **Fax:** 206/527-1429. **Contact:** Personnel Director. **E-mail address:** hr@nekins.net. **World Wide Web address:** http://www.bekinsnorthwest.com. **Description:** Engaged in the transporting and warehousing of household goods, office and industrial equipment, electronics, and business records. Founded in 1903. **Corporate headquarters location:** Seattle WA.

CONSOLIDATED FREIGHTWAYS
805 Broadway, Suite 205, Vancouver WA 98660. 360/993-4100. **Contact:** Personnel. **E-mail address:** cinfo@cfwy.com. **World Wide Web address:** http://www.cfwy.com. **Description:** A motor freight carrier and air freight forwarder operating in all 50 states. Operations include export/import brokerage, overseas forwarding, and warehousing and distribution services. **Corporate headquarters location:** Vancouver WA. **Listed on:** NASDAQ. **Stock exchange symbol:** CFWY.

CONTINENTAL VAN LINES INC.
P.O. Box 3963, Seattle WA 98124-3963. 206/937-2261. **Physical address:** 4501 West Marginal Way SW, Seattle WA 98106. **Contact:** Personnel. **E-mail address:** jobs@continentalvan.com. **World Wide Web address:** http://www.continentalvan.com. **Description:** Engaged in interstate moving and storage. **Positions advertised include:** Class A Drivers; Packers; Loaders/Drivers; Customer Service Staff. **Corporate headquarters location:** Fort Wayne IN.

DHL
4450 E. Marginal Way S. Seattle WA 98134. **Toll-free phone:** 800/225-5345. **Contact:** Recruiting. **World Wide Web address:** http://www.dhl.com. **Description:** A domestic and international air express, air, and ocean freight services company. Operations include both domestic and international door-to-door, next-day delivery, and door-to-airport freight services. Airborne Express operates a fleet of more than 14,000 delivery vehicles. **Positions advertised include:** Claims Examiner; Corporate Accountant; Customer Service Representative; International Accounting Specialist; Payroll Coordinator.

DANZAS AEI
600 Oakesdale Avenue SW, Suite 101, Renton WA 98055. 425/917-2600. **Contact:** Personnel. **World Wide Web address:** http://www.danzas.com. **Description:** A leading provider of logistics solutions. Services include air, road, rail, and sea transportation, as well as distribution and warehousing. **Corporate headquarters location:** Darien CT. **International locations:** Worldwide.

EZ LOADER BOAT TRAILERS INC.
P.O. Box 3263, Spokane WA 99220-3263. 509/489-0181. **Physical address:** 717 North Hamilton Street, Spokane WA 99202. **Contact:** Human Resources. **World Wide Web address:** http://www.ezloader.com. **Description:** Manufactures boat trailers. **Corporate headquarters location:** This location. **Operations at this facility include:** Administration; Manufacturing; Research and Development.

EXPEDITORS INTERNATIONAL OF WASHINGTON, INC.
1015 Third Avenue, 12th Floor, Seattle WA 98104. 206/674-3400. **Contact:** Personnel. **World Wide Web address:** http://www.expd.com. **Description:** Engaged in the business of international air and ocean freight forwarding. The company also acts as a customs broker in its domestic overseas offices. **Positions advertised include:** Staff Accountant; Administrative Assistant; EDI Coordinator; Database Administrator; Senior JAVA Developer; IS Project Manager; UI Designer. **Corporate headquarters location:** This location. **Listed on:** NASDAQ. **Stock exchange symbol:** EXPD.

FOSS MARITIME
660 West Ewing Street, Seattle WA 98119. 206/281-3800. **Contact:** Personnel Department. **E-mail address:** fossjobs@foss.com. **World Wide Web address:** http://www.fossmaritime.com. **Description:** Provides maritime carrier services; deep-sea forum services; domestic, coastwide, and intercoastal transportation; and ship repair and services. **Corporate headquarters location:** This location.

HOLLAND AMERICA LINE WESTOURS
300 Elliott Avenue West, Seattle WA 98119. 206/281-3535. **Fax:** 206/281-7110. **Contact:** Personnel. **World Wide Web address:** http://www.hollandamerica.com. **Description:** Owns hotels, cruise ships, and sail ships, and operates a motor coach transportation division.

HORIZON AIR
P.O. Box 68977, Seattle WA 98168. 206/241-6757. **Toll-free phone:** 800/356-5993. **Contact:** Human Resources. **World Wide Web address:** http://www.horizonair.com. **Description:** A passenger and freight air transportation company.

LAIDLAW TRANSIT INC.
1720 East Fairview Avenue, Spokane WA 99207. 509/482-7270. **Contact:** Human Resources. **World Wide Web address:** http://www.laidlawtransit.com. **Description:** Provides bus service for Seattle and charter bus service to private customers. The company is also a school bus contractor. **Parent company:** Laidlaw, Inc. provides solid waste collection, compaction, transportation, treatment, transfer, and disposal services; provides hazardous waste services; operates hazardous waste facilities and wastewater treatment plants; and operates passenger and school buses, transit system buses, and tour and charter buses. **Corporate headquarters location:** Mt. Lake Terrace WA. **Listed on:** American Stock Exchange. **Stock exchange symbol:** GLL.

LYNDEN INC.
P.O. Box 3757, Seattle WA 98124-3757. 206/241-8778. **Physical address:** 18000 International Boulevard, Suite 800, Seattle WA 98188. **Fax:** 206/243-8415. **Contact:** Personnel Department. **World**

Wide Web address: http://www.lynden.com. **Description:** Provides transportation and construction services for barge, air freight, and trucking companies. **Corporate headquarters location:** This location.

ORIENT OVERSEAS CONTAINER LINE LTD. (OOCL)
18912 North Creek Parkway, Suite 208, Bothell WA 98011. 425/488-5080. **Contact:** Human Resources. **World Wide Web address:** http://www.oocl.com. **Description:** An international containerized transportation company. OOCL owns and operates several container vessels, terminals, and chassis throughout the world. The company also maintains a support group consisting of several depots, warehouses, and trucking companies to support its ocean-based transport operations. **Corporate headquarters location:** Hong Kong. **International locations:** Worldwide.

PRINCESS TOURS
2815 Second Avenue, Suite 400, Seattle WA 98121. 206/336-6000. **Fax:** 206/336-6100. **Contact:** Personnel. **World Wide Web address:** http://www.princess.com. **Description:** Operates rail and motorcoach tours in Alaska and the Canadian Rockies for land-only touring, or in conjunction with cruise ships. The company also owns and operates seasonal and year-round hotels in Alaska. **Corporate headquarters location:** This location. **Other U.S. locations:** AK. **Operations at this facility include:** Administration; Sales. **Number of employees at this location:** 150. **Number of employees nationwide:** 300.

PUGET SOUND FREIGHT LINES INC.
P.O. Box 24526, Seattle WA 98124. 206/623-1600. **Physical address:** 3720 Airport Way South, Seattle WA 98134. **Contact:** Personnel Department. **E-mail address:** hr@psfl.com. **World Wide Web address:** http://www.psfl.com. **Description:** A regional common carrier using both company drivers and owner/operators in truckload operations. **Corporate headquarters location:** This location. **Other U.S. locations:** OR.

SAS CARGO
27 South 161st Street, Seattle WA 98158. 206/433-5151. **Fax:** 201/896-3724. **Contact:** Human Resources. **World Wide Web address:** http://www.sascargo.com. **Description:** A cargo shipping company.

SCANDINAVIAN AIRLINES
1301 Fifth Avenue, Suite 3101, Seattle WA 98101. 206/682-5252. **Fax:** 206/625-9057. **Contact:** Human Resources. **World Wide Web address:** http://www.scandinavian.net. **Description:** Scandinavian Airlines is an air transport company. **Operations at this facility include:** This location is the western regional sales office.

SHURGARD STORAGE CENTERS INC.
1155 Valley Street, Suite 400, Seattle WA 98109. 206/624-8100. **Fax:** 206/624-1645. **Contact:** Human Resources. **World Wide Web address:** http://www.shurgard.com. **Description:** Specializes in the self-storage industry. Shurgard Storage Centers Inc. is a self-administered, real estate investment trust. As one of the largest self-storage center operators in the United States, the company operates over 280 storage centers nationally and abroad. Shurgard owns approximately 60 percent of these centers. **Corporate headquarters location:** This location. **Listed on:** New York Stock Exchange. **Stock exchange symbol:** SHU.

TODD PACIFIC SHIPYARDS CORPORATION
P.O. Box 3806, Seattle WA 98124. 206/623-1635. **Physical address:** 1806 16th Avenue SW, Seattle WA 98134. **Fax:** 206/442-8505. **Contact:** Personnel. **E-mail address:** jobs@toddpacific.com. **World Wide Web address:** http://www.toddpacific.com. **Description:** Engaged in the construction, maintenance, and repair of commercial ships, both domestic and foreign, and of ships for the U.S. Navy and other government agencies. **Positions advertised include:** Project Manager; Senior Financial Analyst; CVN Zone Manager.

US AIRWAYS, INC.
International Boulevard, Seatac WA 98158. 206/433-7853. **Contact:** Manager. **World Wide Web address:** http://www.usairways.com. **Description:** US Airways offers service to 155 cities in the United States, Canada, the Bahamas, Bermuda, Puerto Rico, the Virgin Islands, France, and Germany. The company's primary hubs are located in Charlotte, Pittsburgh, Baltimore/Washington, and Philadelphia. **Corporate headquarters location:** Arlington VA. **Parent company:** United Airlines, Inc.

Wisconsin

AAA WISCONSIN
8401 Excelsior Drive, Madison WI 53717. 608/257-6222. **Fax:** 608/836-7240. **Contact:** Human Resources. **E-mail address:** applyonline@aaawisc.com. **World Wide Web address:** http://www.autoclubgroup.com/wisconsin. **Description:** Provides travel insurance and a wide variety of motorist services to its members through a network of 14 branch offices. **NOTE:** Entry-level positions are offered. Unsolicited resumes are not accepted. **Positions advertised include:** Member Representative. **Special programs:** Training. **Corporate headquarters location:** This location. **Other U.S. locations:** Nationwide. **Parent company:** AAA.

ACE WORLD WIDE
ACE PROFESSIONAL SERVICES
6275 ACE Industrial Drive, Cudahy WI 53110. 414/762-2100. **Fax:** 414/762-0071. **Contact:** Dave Blair, President. **E-mail address:** dave.blair@aceworldwide.com. **World Wide Web address:** http://www.aceworldwide.com. **Description:** ACE Professional Services (APS) is the administrative offices for ACE World Wide, an international moving and storage company.

AIR WISCONSIN AIRLINES CORPORATION
W6390 Challenger Drive, Suite 203, Appleton WI 54914-9120. 920/739-5123. **Fax:** 920/749-7588. **Recorded jobline:** 888/354-4505. **Contact:** Employee Relations. **E-mail address:** hrmail@airwis.com. **World Wide Web address:** http://www.airwis.com. **Description:** As the largest independently held regional airline in the United States, Air Wisconsin Airlines Corporation (AWAC), provides commercial air travel for US Airways Express and United Express. AWAC is also a ground-handler for United Airlines in 20 cities throughout the country. **Positions advertised include:** Director of Information Systems and Services; Flight Following Auditor; Shift Supervisor; Technical Acceptance Specialist. **Corporate headquarters location:** This location. **Number of employees nationwide:** 2,600.

AMERICOLD LOGISTICS, LLC
110th Street and Highway 54, P.O. Box 675, Plover WI 54467. 715/421-3200. **Fax:** 715/424-3921. **Toll-free phone:** 888/484-4877. **Contact:** Ed Ely, Regional HR Director. **E-mail address:** eely@amclog.com. **World Wide Web address:** http://www.americold.net. **Description:** Provider of temperature-controlled food distribution services. **Corporate headquarters location:** Atlanta GA. **Other area locations:** Babcock WI: Tomah WI. **Other U.S. locations:** Nationwide. **Operations at this facility include:** Warehousing. **Number of employees nationwide:** 6,000.

CARVER BOAT CORPORATION
7090 Markham Drive, P.O. Box 1010, Pulaski WI 54162-1010. 920/822-1600. **Fax:** 920/822-8820. **Contact:** Human Resources. **World Wide Web address:** http://www.carveryachts.com. **Description:** A manufacturer of cabin cruisers and yachts. **Positions advertised include:** Bilingual Supervisor; CAD Drafter; Manufacturing Supervisor.

LAIDLAW TRANSIT SERVICES
4605 Pflaum Road, Madison WI 53718. 608/223-0610. **Toll-free phone:** 888/820-1026. **Contact:** Human

Resources Department. **E-mail address:** careers@laidlawjobs.com. **World Wide Web address:** http://www.laidlawtransit.com. **Description:** Provides bus service for Madison and provides charter bus service to private customers. The company is also a school bus contractor. **Parent company:** Laidlaw International, Inc.

MAXAIR INC.
West 6381 Columbia Drive, Outagamie County Airport, Appleton WI 54914-9167. 920/738-3020. **Toll-free phone:** 800/833-1544. **Fax:** 920/738-3026. **Contact:** Human Resources. **World Wide Web address:** http://www.maxair-inc.com. **Description:** Provides air chartering services and airplane rentals, and operates a flight school.

MIDWEST AIR GROUP, INC.
6744 South Howell Avenue, HQ-22, Oak Creek WI 53154. 414/570-4000. **Toll-free phone:** 800/452-2022. **Fax:** 414/570-9666. **Contact:** Personnel. **E-mail address:** meacareers@midwestairlines.com. **World Wide Web address:** http://www.midwestairlines.com. **Description:** The parent company of Midwest Airlines, an airline specializing in passenger air transportation throughout the Midwest. **NOTE:** Unsolicited resumes are not accepted. **Positions advertised include:** Accounting and Reporting Specialist; Facility Maintenance Technician; Power Plant Engineer. **Corporate headquarters location:** This location. **Listed on:** American Stock Exchange. **Stock exchange symbol:** MEH.

PALMER JOHNSON YACHTS
61 Michigan Street, P.O. Box 109, Sturgeon Bay WI 54235. 920/743-4412. **Contact:** Human Resources. **World Wide Web address:** http://www.palmerjohnson.com. **E-mail address:** info@pjflorida.com. **Description:** Builds, refits, brokers, and charters luxury high-performance yachts. Founded in 1918. **Positions advertised include:** Design Engineer; Joiner; Mechanic; Rigger; Upholsterer; Electrician; Painter; Welder; Sales Executive. **Corporate headquarters location:** This location. **Other U.S. locations:** Fort Lauderdale FL.

QUALITY LOGISTICS SYSTEMS
2100 Shawano Avenue, P.O. Box 10291, Green Bay WI 54307. 920/496-3860. **Fax:** 920/496-3868. **Contact:** David Lyneis, Operations Manager. **E-mail address:** info@qualitylogistics.com. **World Wide Web address:** http://www.qualitylogistics.com. **Description:** Manufactures packaging, and provides warehousing, support, distribution, and logistics services. **Corporate headquarters location:** This location. **Other U.S. locations:** Dallas TX; Chicago IL; Meridian MS.

SCHNEIDER NATIONAL, INC.
3101 South Packerland Drive, P.O. Box 2545, Green Bay WI 54306-2545. 920/592-2000. **Toll-free phone:** 800/558-6767. **Fax:** 920/592-3252. **Contact:** Human Resources. **E-mail address:** recruiting@schneider.com. **World Wide Web address:** http://www.schneider.com. **Description:** Offers a wide range of transportation and logistics services. Schneider National's transportation sector offers van, intermodal, flatbed, and bulk tank services. Founded in 1935. **NOTE:** Entry-level positions, part-time jobs, and second and third shifts are offered. **Positions advertised include:** Application Development Technical Architecture; Business Analyst; Data communication Analyst; Desktop Integration Specialist; Infrastructure Architect; Project Manager; Facility Manager; Logistics Manager. **Special programs:** Internships; Training; Co-ops; Summer Jobs. **Corporate headquarters location:** This location. **Other U.S. locations:** Nationwide. **International locations:** Canada; Mexico. **Listed on:** Privately held. **Annual sales/revenues:** More than $100 million. **Number of employees nationwide:** 16,000.

TAX AIRFREIGHT
dba TAX-AIR
5975 South Howell Avenue, P.O. Box 70911, Milwaukee WI 53207. 414/769-6565. **Toll-free phone:** 800/242-6565. **Fax:** 414/769-0529. **Contact:** Recruiting Manager. **E-mail address:** careers@taxair.com. **World Wide Web address:** http://www.taxair.com. **Description:** A non-union, less-than-truckload carrier that transports industrial, commercial, and retail goods throughout the upper Midwest. **Corporate headquarters location:** This location.

MISCELLANEOUS WHOLESALING

You can expect to find the following types of companies in this section:

Exporters and Importers • General Wholesale Distribution Companies

Jobs in wholesale trade are projected to grow by 8.4%, adding 476,000 jobs, compared with the 13% rate of growth projected for all industries combined. Growth will vary, however, depending on the sector of the economy with which individual wholesale trade firms are involved. Consolidation of the industry into larger firms and the spread of new technology (such as electronic commerce) should have their greatest effect on the two largest occupational groups in wholesale trade—office and administrative support, and sales and related occupations. However, as firms provide a growing array of support services, many new jobs will be created and the roles of many workers will change.

Alabama

MOORE-HANDLEY, INC.
P.O. Box 2607, Birmingham AL 35202. 205/663-8011. **Toll-free phone:** 800/633-3848. **Contact:** Bill Rush, Director of Human Resources. **World Wide Web address:** http://www.moorehandley.com. **Description:** A wholesale distributor of plumbing and electrical supplies, power and hand tools, lawn and garden equipment, and other hardware and building materials products. Customers, located mainly in the Southeast, include retail home centers, hardware stores, building materials dealers, combination stores, and some mass merchandisers. In connection with its wholesale distribution activities, Moore-Handley offers a wide range of marketing, advertising, and other support services designed to assist customers in maintaining and improving their market positions. These support services include computer-generated systems for the control of inventory, pricing, and gross margin, as well as advertising and store installation and design services. **Positions advertised include:** Sales Specialist. **Corporate headquarters location:** This location. **Other U.S. locations:** Nationwide. **Listed on:** NASDAQ. **Stock exchange symbol:** MHCO. **Number of employees at this location:** 405.

Arizona

ABATIX CORPORATION
3011 East Broadway, Suite 300, Phoenix AZ 85040. 602/323-1941. **Toll-free phone:** 800/889-5186. **Fax:** 602/323-1942. **Contact:** Human Resources. **E-mail address:** hr@abatix.com. **World Wide Web address:** http://www.abatix.com. **Description:** A distributor of safety supplies, construction tools, clean-up equipment, and general safety products such as protective clothing and eyewear. The company supplies products to the asbestos and lead abatement, hazardous material remediation, and construction markets. Abatix Environmental Corporation has seven distribution centers in Texas, California, Arizona, Nevada, and Washington. **NOTE:** Please send resumes to 8201 Eastpoint Drive, Suite 500, Dallas TX 75227. **Corporate headquarters location:** Dallas TX. **Listed on:** NASDAQ. **Stock exchange symbol:** ABIX.

W.W. GRAINGER
3231 West Virginia Avenue, Phoenix AZ 85009. 602/269-3115. **Contact:** Human Resources. **World Wide Web address:** http://www.grainger.com. **Description:** Distributes a variety of equipment and components to the industrial, commercial, contracting, and institutional markets nationwide. Products include equipment and components for motors, air tools, hydraulic products, refrigeration items, power and hand tools, office equipment, computer supplies, storage equipment, replacement parts, industrial products, safety items, and sanitary supplies. **Corporate headquarters location:** Lake Forest IL. **Other U.S. locations:** Nationwide. **Listed on:** New York Stock Exchange. **Stock exchange symbol:** GWW.

IKON OFFICE SOLUTIONS
P.O. Box 12369, Scottsdale AZ 85267. 602/468-4500. **Contact:** Human Resources. **World Wide Web address:** http://www.ikon.com. **Description:** A wholesaler and distributor of copy machines, fax machines, and related office supplies. **Corporate headquarters location:** Malvern PA. **Listed on:** New York Stock Exchange. **Stock exchange symbol:** IKN.

MOTION INDUSTRIES INC.
2611 South Roosevelt, Suite 102, Tempe AZ 85282. 480/921-9800. **Fax:** 480/921-9198. **Contact:** Human Resources. **E-mail address:** jobs@motion-ind.com. **World Wide Web address:** http://www.motionindustries.com. **Description:** Distributes power transmission equipment. **Corporate headquarters location:** Birmingham AL. **Other area locations:** Tucson AZ; Yuma AZ. **Parent company:** Genuine Parts Company. **Listed on:** New York Stock Exchange. **Stock exchange symbol:** GPC.

California

A-MARK PRECIOUS METALS INC.
429 Santa Monica Boulevard, Suite 230, Santa Monica CA 90401. 310/319-0200. **Fax:** 310/319-0279. **Contact:** Human Resources. **E-mail address:** hr@amark.com. **World Wide Web address:** http://www.amark.com. **Description:** A precious metals wholesaler that buys and sells gold, silver, and platinum coins. Clients include banks, brokerage houses, refiners, jewelers, investment advisors, coin dealers, and government mint officials. **Positions advertised include:** Senior Accountant; Shipping and Receiving Specialist. **Number of employees at this location:** 25.

ABATIX ENVIRONMENTAL CORPORATION
14068 Catalina Street, San Leandro CA 94577. 510/614-2340. **Toll-free phone:** 800/365-5795. **Fax:** 510/614-2350. **Contact:** Human Resources. **E-mail address:** hr@abatix.com. **World Wide Web address:** http://www.abatix.com. **Description:** Supplies safety, construction, fire and water restoration and homeland security products. **Corporate headquarters location:** Dallas TX. **Other area locations:** Santa Fe Springs CA. **Other U.S. locations:** Phoenix AZ; Las Vegas NV; New Orleans LA; Houston TX; Seattle WA. **Listed on:** NASDAQ. **Stock exchange symbol:** ABIX.

CENTRAL GARDEN & PET COMPANY
1340 Treat Boulevard, Suite 600, Walnut Creek CA 94597. 925/948-4000. **Contact:** Personnel Department. **World Wide Web address:** http://www.centralgardenandpet.com. **Description:** One of the nation's largest suppliers and merchandisers of lawn, garden, and pet products and a major distributor of pool supplies. **Corporate headquarters location:** This location. **Other U.S. locations:** Nationwide. **Listed on:** NASDAQ. **Stock exchange symbol:** CENT. **Number of employees nationwide:** 1,450.

THE COAST DISTRIBUTION SYSTEM
350 Woodview Avenue, Morgan Hill CA 95037. 408/782-6686. **Fax:** 408/782-7790. **Contact:** Human Resources. **World Wide Web address:** http://www.coastdistribution.com. **Description:** One of North America's largest distributors of parts and accessories to the recreational vehicle and boating

industries. Products include awnings, electrical and plumbing items, towing equipment and hitches, appliances, marine electronics and safety equipment, and various accessories and consumables. **Corporate headquarters location:** This location. **Other area locations:** Visalia CA. **Other U.S. locations:** Nationwide. **International locations:** Canada.

ITOCHU INTERNATIONAL INC.
180 Montgomery Street, Suite 2360, San Francisco CA 94104. 415/399-3700. **Contact:** General Manager. **E-mail address:** recruiting@itochu.com. **World Wide Web address:** http://www.itochu.com. **Description:** An international, multi-business trading and investment company. Itochu International specializes in developing and sponsoring profitable opportunities in international and domestic commerce, industry, and finance, both as a principal and as an agent. **Corporate headquarters location:** New York NY. **Parent company:** Itochu Corporation.

McJUNKIN CORPORATION
2064 East University Drive, Rancho Dominguez CA 90220-6419. 310/605-5392. **Fax:** 310/537-2464. **Contact:** Human Resources. **World Wide Web address:** http://www.mcjunkin.com. **Description:** A distributor of pipe, valves, fittings, power transmission products, and general industrial products. **Corporate headquarters location:** Charleston West Virginia. **Operations at this facility include:** Sales.

McMASTER-CARR SUPPLY COMPANY
P.O. Box 54960, Los Angeles CA 90054. 562/695-2449. **Physical Address:** 9630 Norwalk Boulevard, Santa Fe Springs CA 90670. **Contact:** Personnel. **E-mail address:** recruiting@mcmaster.com. **World Wide Web address:** http://www.mcmaster.com. **Description:** A distributor of industrial products and supplies including a complete line of products for maintaining a manufacturing facility. The company's broad customer base includes most major manufacturers in North America, as well as many major industrial firms in South and Central America, the Middle and Far East, and Africa. **Corporate headquarters location:** Chicago IL. **Other U.S. locations:** Atlanta GA; Dayton NJ; Cleveland OH. **Listed on:** Privately held.

PETERSON TRACTOR COMPANY
P.O. Box 5258, San Leandro CA 94577. 510/357-6200. **Physical address:** 955 Marina Boulevard, San Leandro CA 94577. **Fax:** 510/357-0634. **Contact:** Rich Hasper, Director of Human Resources. **E-mail address:** hr@petersonholding.com. **World Wide Web address:** http://www.petersontractor.com. **Description:** A wholesaler of Caterpillar heavy construction equipment and diesel engines. Peterson also has retail locations. **NOTE:** Search and apply for positions online. **Positions advertised include:** Project Manager; Sales Representative; Technician Welder; Inventory Clerk. **Corporate headquarters location:** This location. **Operations at this facility include:** Administration; Sales; Service.

QUADREP TECHNOLOGIES
34700 Pacific Coast Highway, Suite 305, Capistrano Beach CA 92624. 949/429-6670. **Fax:** 949/429-6685. **Contact:** Personnel. **World Wide Web address:** http://www.quadrep.com. **Description:** Markets electronic components and system solutions to southern California businesses. **Corporate headquarters location:** This location.

WILBUR-ELLIS COMPANY
CONNELL BROS. COMPANY
345 California Street, 27th Floor, San Francisco CA 94104. 415/772-4000. **Fax:** 415/772-4011. **Contact:** Human Resources. **World Wide Web address:** http://www.wilburellis.com. **Description:** International merchants and distributors involved in importing and exporting goods. Wilbur-Ellis trades agricultural feed and chemical products. **Corporate headquarters location:** This location. **Operations at this facility include:** Administration.

Colorado

CORPORATE EXPRESS
One Environmental Way, Broomfield CO 80021. 303/664-2000. **Fax:** 303/664-3474. **Contact:** Personnel. **World Wide Web address:** http://www.corporateexpress.com. **Description:** A business-to-business supplier of office and computer products and services. The company supplies products through a direct sales staff and direct mail catalogs. **Corporate headquarters location:** This location. **International locations:** Worldwide. **Parent company:** Buhrmann. **Listed on:** New York Stock Exchange. **Stock exchange symbol:** BUH.

JHB INTERNATIONAL INC.
1955 South Quince Street, Denver CO 80231. 303/751-8100. **Contact:** Personnel. **World Wide Web address:** http://www.jhbinternational.snapmonkey.net. **Description:** Wholesales and exports buttons and thimbles.

Connecticut

BARNES GROUP INC.
123 Main Street, Bristol CT 06010. 860/583-7070. **Contact:** James Pappas, Human Resources. **World Wide Web address:** http://www.barnesgroupinc.com. **Description:** Barnes Group distributes repair and replacement products such as fasteners, hardware, automotive parts, gas welding supplies, and industrial aerosols. The company also manufactures and distributes a wide variety of custom metal parts for mechanical purposes and machined and fabricated parts as well as assemblies. **Positions advertised include:** Administrative Services Assistant; Division Controller; Cost Analyst; Senior Internal Control Analyst. **Listed on:** New York Stock Exchange. **Stock exchange symbol:** B.

COE & BROWN COMPANY
P.O. Box 4215, Hamden CT 06514-0215. 203/288-9211. **Physical address:** 295 Treadwell Street, Hamden CT 06514. **Contact:** Human Resources. **Description:** A wholesale distributor of a wide range of industrial supplies.

THE ROBERT E. MORRIS COMPANY
17 Talcott Notch Road, Farmington CT 06032-0487. 860/678-0200. **Contact:** Human Resources. **World Wide Web address:** http://www.robertemorris.com. **Description:** A distributor of machines and machine tooling. Founded in 1941. **Office hours:** Monday - Friday, 8:00 a.m. - 4:45 p.m. **Other U.S. locations:** Nationwide. **Listed on:** Privately held. **Information Systems Manager:** Glenn Eigabroadt.

SWISS ARMY BRANDS, INC.
One Research Drive, P.O. Box 874, Shelton CT 06484-0874. 203/929-6391. **Contact:** Steve Rexford, Director of Human Resources. **World Wide Web address:** http://www.swissarmy.com. **Description:** An importer and marketer of Forschner cutlery and Swiss Army knives. **Corporate headquarters location:** This location. **Listed on:** NASDAQ. **Stock exchange symbol:** SABI.

Florida

BAKER DISTRIBUTING COMPANY
7892 Baymeadows Way, Jacksonville FL 32256. 904/733-9633. **Fax:** 904/733-6722. **Contact:** Doris Spears, Payroll Manager. **E-mail address:** info@bakersdist.com. **World Wide Web address:** http://www.bakerdist.com. **Description:** A wholesaler of industrial heating and cooling equipment.

CAIN AND BULTMAN, INC.
2145 Dennis Street, Jacksonville FL 32204. 904/356-4812. **Contact:** Marc Kimball, Human Resources. **E-mail address:** marckimball@cain-bultman.com. **World Wide Web address:** http://www.cain-bultman.com. **Description:** A wholesale distributor of carpets and vinyl floor coverings.

EDWARD DON & COMPANY
2200 SW 45th Street, Fort Lauderdale FL 33019. 954/983-3000. **Contact:** Human Resources.

Description: Distributes furniture and equipment to restaurants, hotels, and schools. **World Wide Web address:** http://www.don.com. **Positions advertised include:** Operations Supervisor; Transportation Manager; Sales Representative; International Sales Representative; Driver. **Operations at this facility include:** Administration; Divisional Headquarters; Sales. **Listed on:** Privately held. **Number of employees at this location:** 270. **Number of employees nationwide:** 1,200.

HUGHES SUPPLY INC.
P.O. Box 2273, Orlando FL 32802-2273. 407/841-4755. **Physical address:** One Hughes Way, Orlando FL 32805. **Contact:** Human Resources Director. **World Wide Web address:** http://www.hughessupply.com. **Description:** A wholesale distributor of electrical, plumbing, building, and pool supplies. **Positions advertised include:** Outside Sales. **Corporate headquarters location:** This location. **Listed on:** New York Stock Exchange. **Stock exchange symbol:** HUG.

LINDER INDUSTRIAL MACHINERY COMPANY
P.O. Box 4589, Plant City FL 33563. 813/754-2727. **Fax:** 815/754-0772. **Physical address:** 1601 South Frontage Road, Plant City FL 33563-2014. **Contact:** Roxanne Taylor, Human Resources Coordinator. **World Wide Web address:** http://www.linderco.com. **Description:** A distributor of construction and mining equipment. **Number of employees at this location:** 200.

Georgia

AMERICASMART
240 Peachtree Street NW, Suite 2200, Atlanta GA 30303. 404/220-3000. **Toll-free phone:** 800/285-6278. **Fax:** 678/686-5181. **Contact:** Personnel. **E-mail address:** hrdepartment@americasmart.com. **World Wide Web address:** http://www.americasmart.com. **Description:** Houses a campus of wholesale buying facilities for gift, home furnishings, apparel, and area rug buyers. **NOTE:** Entry-level positions are offered. No phone calls regarding employment. **Positions advertised include:** Showroom Manager; Property Manager; Copier Services Technician. **Office hours:** Monday - Friday, 8:30 a.m. - 5:30 p.m. **Corporate headquarters location:** This location. **Parent company:** AMC, Inc. (also at this location) is an international trade show organizer for the wholesale and retail industries. **CEO:** John Portman. **Annual sales/revenues:** $51 - $100 million.

APEX SUPPLY
3300 Breckinridge Boulevard, Suite 100, Duluth GA 30096. 770/449-7000. **Toll-free phone:** 800/395-2739. **Fax:** 770/263-4834. 441-8674. **Contact:** Human Resources. **World Wide Web address:** http://www.apexsupply.com. **Description:** A wholesale distributor of plumbing, heating, air conditioning, industrial piping products, cabinetry, appliances, and tools. The company's three major businesses are plumbing, heating and air conditioning, and building specialty products. The company distributes a variety of products including major brand names such as Kohler, Price-Pfister, Jacuzzi, Delta, and State; Trane, Honeywell, and Reznor; Jamesbury, Sarco, Nibco, Asahi, Weldbend, and US Pipe; Timberlake, Millbrook, and Plato; GE, Magic-Chef, Kitchen Aid, and Sub Zero; and Makita and Ridgid. **NOTE:** Entry-level positions are offered. Please visit website to search for jobs and apply online. **Positions advertised include:** Warehouse Operator; Outside Sales Associate. **Special programs:** Internships; Co-ops. **Corporate headquarters location:** Atlanta GA. **Other area locations:** Statewide. **Other U.S. locations:** SC; TN; FL. **Parent company:** The Home Depot. **Operations at this facility include:** Administration; Sales; Service. **Listed on:** New York Stock Exchange. **Stock exchange symbol:** HD.

FOX APPLIANCE PARTS OF ATLANTA
P.O. Box 16217, Atlanta GA 30321. 404/363-3313. **Physical address:** 5375 North Parkway, Lake City GA 30260. **Contact:** Robert Taylor, Office Manager. **World Wide Web address:** http://www.foxparts.com. **Description:** A wholesale distributor of parts for major appliances and heating and air conditioning products. Founded in 1948. **NOTE:** Please visit website for online application form. **Corporate headquarters location:** This location. **Other area locations:** Statewide. **Operations at this facility include:** Administration; Sales.

FULTON SUPPLY COMPANY
342 Nelson Street SW, Atlanta GA 30313. 404/688-3400. **Fax:** 404/522-0249. **Contact:** Human Resources. **E-mail address:** cwilliams@fultonsupply.com. **World Wide Web address:** http://www.fultonsupply.com. **Description:** A wholesaler of industrial tools. Founded in 1914. **Corporate headquarters location:** This location. **Other U.S. locations:** AL; FL; SC.

REDMAX/KOMATSU ZENOAH AMERICA, INC.
4344 Shackleford Road, Suite 500, Norcross GA 30093. 770/381-5147. **Toll-free phone:** 800/291-8251. **Fax:** 770/381-5150. **Contact:** Human Resources. **World Wide web address:** http://www.redmax.com. **Description:** Imports and wholesales gas-powered, hand-held outdoor equipment including leaf blowers and brush trimmers for commercial use. **Corporate headquarters location:** This location. **Parent company:** Komatsu Japan.

ULINE
2165 Northmont Parkway, Duluth GA 30096. 770/495-0102. **Toll-free phone:** 800/958-5463. **Fax:** 770/495-7504. **Contact:** Human Resources. **E-mail address:** ulinejobs@uline.com. **World Wide Web address:** http://www.uline.com. **Description:** Uline is a nationwide leading distributor of packaging and industrial supplies. **Positions advertised include:** Administrative Assistant; Custodian, Customer Service Representative; Operations Analyst; Warehouse Management; Warehouse Supervisor; General Warehouse; Sales Representative. **Corporate headquarters location:** Waukegan IL. **Other U.S. locations:** Breinigsville PA; Eagan MN; Duluth GA; Coppell TX. **Operations at this facility include:** Manufacturing; Administrative.

YAMAHA MOTOR MANUFACTURING CORPORATION
1000 Georgia Highway 34 East, Newnan GA 30265. 770/254-4000. **Contact:** Human Resource Manager. **World Wide Web address:** http://www.yamaha-motor.com. **Description:** A wholesale distributor of motorized products including motorcycles, ATV's, snowmobiles, golf carts, outboards, and power products. **NOTE:** Please visit website to search for jobs, and for more specific details on applying for positions. **Positions advertised include:** Leasing Specialist; Regional Technical Advisor; District Service Representative; Marine Sales/Technical Support Coordinator; Regional Service Representative; Business Analyst; Buyer; District Manager Inside Sales. **Corporate headquarters location:** Cypress CA. **Other area locations:** Kennesaw GA. **Operations at this facility include:** This location manufactures ATVs, Golf Cars, and Water Vehicles, in addition to housing the Yamaha Golf-Car Company.

Illinois

BOWE BELL & HOWELL COMPANY
760 South Wolf Road, Wheeling IL 60090-6232. 847/675-7600. **Contact:** Human Resources. **E-mail address:** recruiting@bowebellhowell.com. **World Wide Web address:** http://www.bowebellhowell.com. **Description:** Provides document management solutions and services, including cutting, packaging, inserting, plastic card, sorting, integrity, print-on-demand, and software solutions. **NOTE:** See the website for job listings and to apply online. **Operations at this facility include:** Administrative; Production.

THE DOALL COMPANY
254 North Laurel Avenue, Des Plaines IL 60016-4398. 847/824-8191. **Toll-free phone:** 800/923-6255. **Fax:**

847/824-4340. **Contact:** Human Resources. **E-mail address:** info@doall.com. **World Wide Web address:** http://www.doall.com. **Description:** The DoALL Company manufactures and distributes machine tools and other supplies primarily for the metalworking and industrial markets. **NOTE:** Submit resume by e-mail.

EDWARD DON & COMPANY
2500 South Harlem Avenue, North Riverside IL 60546. 708/442-9400. **Toll-free phone:** 800/777-4366. **Fax:** 708/442-0436. **Contact:** Bill Doucette, Human Resources Manager. **World Wide Web address:** http://www.don.com. **Description:** Distributes food service equipment and supplies. **NOTE:** Apply online. **Positions advertised include:** Technical Operations Manager; CAD Operator; Customer Service Representative; Credit Representative; Sales Representative. **Special programs:** Internships. **Corporate headquarters location:** This location. **Listed on:** Privately held.

W.W. GRAINGER
100 Grainger Parkway, Lake Forest IL 60045. 847/535-1000. **Contact:** Human Resources. **World Wide Web address:** http://www.grainger.com. **Description:** Distributes a variety of equipment and components to the industrial, commercial, contracting, and institutional markets nationwide. The company operates 337 branches in all 50 states and Puerto Rico. Products include equipment and components for motors, air tools, hydraulic products, refrigeration items, power and hand tools, office equipment, computer supplies, storage equipment, replacement parts, industrial products, safety items, cold weather clothing, and sanitary supplies. **NOTE:** This company provides job listings for this location and its other locations on its website. Apply online. **Corporate headquarters location:** This location.

GRAINGER PARTS
P.O. Box 3074, Northbrook IL 60062. 847/498-1920. **Fax:** 847/559-6301. **Contact:** Human Resources. **World Wide Web address:** http://www.grainger.com. **Description:** Distributes repair and replacement parts to industrial and commercial markets. **Parent company:** W.W. Grainger, Inc. **Operations at this facility include:** Administration; Divisional Headquarters; Sales; Service.

LAWSON PRODUCTS, INC.
1666 East Touhy Avenue, Des Plaines IL 60018. 847/827-9666. **Toll-free phone:** 800/448-8985. **Fax:** 847/827-0083. **Contact:** Human Resources. **World Wide Web address:** http://www.lawsonproducts.com. **Description:** Distributes a variety of industrial parts and fasteners for machinery, automobiles, and other industrial products. **NOTE:** Apply online.

CHARLES LEVY CIRCULATING COMPANY
815 Ogden, Lisle IL 60532. 630/353-2500. **Contact:** Steve Damiani, Human Resources. **World Wide Web address:** http://www.chaslevy.com. **Description:** A wholesale distributor of magazines, books, videos, cassettes, CDs, and other consumer products. **Corporate headquarters location:** Melrose Park IL. **Other U.S. locations:** Grand Rapids MI; Philadelphia PA. **Operations at this facility include:** Sales; Service. **Listed on:** Privately held.

MCMASTER-CARR SUPPLY
600 County Line Road, Elmhurst IL 60126. 630/833-0300. **Fax:** 630/993-3008. **Contact:** Human Resources. **E-mail address:** rita.lally@mcmaster.com. **World Wide Web address:** http://www.mcmaster.com. **Description:** Publishes a catalog of more than 420,000 industrial supplies used in a multitude of different fields. McMaster keeps 98% of that merchandise on their own warehouse shelves and ready to ship as soon as orders are placed. **Positions advertised include:** Accountant; Customer Service; Data Entry; Marketing Research Assistant; Proofreader; Warehouse Distribution Specialist. **Other U.S. locations:** Atlanta GA, Cleveland OH, Los Angeles CA, Dayton NJ.

NEW HOLLAND CONSTRUCTION
245 East North Avenue, Carol Stream IL 60188. 630/260-4000. **Contact:** Human Resources. **World Wide Web address:** http://www.newholland.com. **Description:** Distributes parts for industrial equipment including tractors and backhoes.

THE RELIABLE CORPORATION
P.O. Box 1502, Ottawa IL 61350-9914. 800/735-4000. **Contact:** Human Resources. **World Wide Web address:** http://www.reliable.com. **Description:** A wholesaler of a wide variety of office supplies sold primarily through a mail-order catalog. **Corporate headquarters location:** This location. **Parent company:** Boise Cascade. **Operations at this facility include:** Administration.

ROSCOR CORPORATION
1061 Feehanville Drive, Mount Prospect IL 60056. 847/299-8080. **Fax:** 847/803-8089. **Contact:** Human Resources. **E-mail address:** opportunities@roscor.com. **World Wide Web address:** http://www.roscor.com. **Description:** Distributes industrial video equipment.

UNITED STATIONERS SUPPLY COMPANY
2200 East Golf Road, Des Plaines IL 60016. 847/699-5000. **Fax:** 847/699-8046. **Contact:** Personnel. **World Wide Web address:** http://www.unitedstationers.com. **Description:** A wholesale distributor of office supplies, furniture, and machines. **Corporate headquarters location:** This location. **Other U.S. locations:** Nationwide. **Operations at this facility include:** Administration; Sales; Service.

WEBER MARKING SYSTEMS, INC.
711 West Algonquin Road, Arlington Heights IL 60005. 847/364-8500. **Fax:** 847/364-8575. **Contact:** Shirley Hurley, Vice President of Human Resources. **E-mail address:** hrdept@webermarketing.com. **World Wide Web address:** http://www.webermarking.com. **Description:** An international distributor of product identification addressing, labeling, industrial, and marking machines and devices. Weber Marking Systems also operates several sales locations. **Corporate headquarters location:** This location.

Indiana

DO IT BEST CORPORATION
P.O. Box 801, Fort Wayne IN 46801. 260/748-5300. **Physical address:** 6502 Nelson Road, Fort Wayne IN 46803. **Fax:** 260/748-5608. **Contact:** Human Resources. **World Wide Web address:** http://doitbest.com. **Description:** A cooperative wholesale supplier of hardware, lumber, and building materials to retailers throughout the world. **Positions advertised include:** Accounting Supervisor; Account Executive; Web Developer; Public Relations Coordinator; Communications Coordinator; Retail Store Designer; Retail Development Specialist. **Special programs:** Internships; Co-ops. **Corporate headquarters location:** This location. **Other U.S. locations:** Nationwide. **President and CEO:** Bob Taylor.

LASALLE BRISTOL
601 Country Road 17, Elkhart IN 46516. 574/295-4400. **Fax:** 574/295-5290. **Contact:** Human Resources. **World Wide Web address:** http://www.lasallebristol.com. **Description:** A wholesaler and manufacturer of furniture, lighting, flooring, and plumbing for the manufactured home and recreational vehicle industries. **Corporate headquarters location:** This location.

LEISURE DISTRIBUTORS INC.
4220 East Morgan Avenue, Evansville IN 47715. 812/473-9684. **Contact:** Human Resources. **Description:** Distributes patio and fireplace equipment including gas grills, fireplaces, and gas logs.

Kansas

IBT INC.
9400 West 55th Street, Merriam KS 66203. 913/677-3151. **Toll-free phone:** 800/332-2114. **Fax:** 913/362-1413. **Contact:** Sean Beaver, Human Resources. **E-**

mail address: sbeaver@ibtinc.com. **World Wide Web address:** http://www.ibt-recruiting.com. **Description:** Manufacturer and distributor of belts, bearings, transmission products and other industrial products with 48 service centers in 11 Midwest states. In addition to industrial supplies, the company distributes rubber hoses, belting products, electrical supplies, and material-handling equipment, as well as providing engineering and media production services. Founded in 1949. **NOTE:** Search postings and apply on-line. **Corporate headquarters location:** This location. **Other area locations:** Statewide. **Operations at this facility include:** Regional Account Manager; Administration; Warehouse; Central Distribution Center. **Number of employees:** 120.

Maine

EMERY-WATERHOUSE COMPANY, INC.
P.O. Box 659, Portland ME 04104. 207/283-0236 **Fax:** 207/775-5206. **Physical address:** 7 Rand Road, Portland ME 04104. **Toll-free phone:** 800/283-0236. **Contact:** Holly Ballwag, Human Resources Department. **E-mail address:** info@emeryonline.com. **World Wide Web address:** http://www.emery-waterhouse.com. **Description:** A hardware wholesaler. Emery-Waterhouse sells hardware and various seasonal items to retail businesses. Founded in 1842. **Corporate headquarters location:** This location.

Maryland

AIRGAS
2900 52nd Avenue, Hyattsville MD 20781. 301/981-3702. **Fax:** 301/864-4875. **Contact:** Jamie Weatherford. **E-mail address:** james.weatherford@airgas.com. **World Wide Web address:** http://www.airgas.com. **Description:** Distributor of industrial, medical, and specialty gases and related equipment, safety supplies and MRO products and services to industrial and commercial customers. **Positions advertised include:** Filler (First Shift). **Corporate headquarters location:** Radnor PA. **Other U.S. locations:** Nationwide. **Listed on:** New York Stock Exchange. **Stock exchange symbol:** ARG. **Chairman and CEO:** Peter McCausland.

R.E. MICHEL COMPANY INC.
6761 Waterview Court, Glen Burnie MD 21060. 410/863-1323. **Contact:** Human Resources. **E-mail address:** hr@remichel.com. **World Wide Web address:** http://www.remichel.com. **Description:** A wholesale distributor of air conditioning, heating, and refrigeration parts and supplies. **Positions advertised include:** Counter Sales Representative; Driver; Information Systems Help Desk Associate; Sales Representative; Warehouse Worker. **Office hours:** Monday – Friday, 8:00 a.m. – 4:00 p.m. – 11:00 a.m. **Other area locations:** Statewide. **Other U.S. locations:** Nationwide.

Massachusetts

AIR COMPRESSOR ENGINEERING COMPANY INC.
P.O. Box 738, Westfield MA 01806. 413/568-2884. **Physical Address:** 17 Meadow Street, Westfield MA 01085-3221. **Contact:** Human Resources. **World Wide Web address:** http://www.aircompressoreng.com. **Description:** Engaged in the wholesale of new and used metalworking machinery.

BRAUN NORTH AMERICA
400 Unicorn Park Drive, Woburn MA 01801. 781/939-8300. **Toll-free phone:** 800/BRA-UN11. **Contact:** Human Resources. **World Wide Web address:** www.braun.com. **Description:** Distributes a variety of consumer products including coffee makers, juicers, and razors, all of which are manufactured by Braun in Germany. **Parent company:** The Procter & Gamble Company.

IKON OFFICE SOLUTIONS
204 Second Avenue, Waltham MA 02154. 781/487-5100. **Contact:** Human Resources. **World Wide Web address:** http://www.ikon.com. **Description:** A wholesaler and distributor of copy machines, fax machines, and related office supplies. **Positions advertised include:** Major Account Representative; Sales Manager. **Other U.S. locations:** Nationwide. **International locations:** Worldwide. **Listed on:** New York Stock Exchange. **Stock exchange symbol:** IKN.

W.B. MASON
59 Centre Street, P.O. Box 111, Brockton MA 02303-0111. 508/586-3434. **Contact:** Human Resources. **World Wide Web address:** http://www.wbmason.com. **Description:** Distributes a wide range of office supplies, primarily to businesses. **Positions advertised include:** Credit and Collections Rep; A/R Analyst; Accounts Payable Manager; Assistant Controller; Fleet/Safety Manager. **Corporate headquarters location:** This location. **Other area locations:** Auburn MA; Boston MA; Hyannis MA; Woburn MA. **Other U.S. locations:** North Haven CT; Secaucus NJ; Cranston RI.

Michigan

DIVERSIFIED DATA PRODUCTS
1995 Highland Drive, Suite D, Ann Arbor MI 48108. 734/677-7878. **Fax:** 734/677-0938. **Contact:** Human Resources. **Description:** Supplies individuals and businesses with consumable parts for computer printers including ribbons and drums. **Corporate headquarters location:** This location.

EVANS-SHERRATT COMPANY
13050 Northend Avenue, Oak Park MI 48237-3405. 248/584-5500. **Fax:** 248/584-5510. **Contact:** Human Resources. **E-mail address:** esoakpark@evans-sherratt.com. **World Wide Web address:** http://www.evans-sherratt.com. **Description:** Engaged in the wholesale trade and servicing of professional office and consumer equipment and supplies. **Corporate headquarters location:** This location. **Other area locations:** Petosky MI; Grand Rapids MI. **Other U.S. locations:** OH; WV; PA. **Number of employees at this location:** 100.

McNAUGHTON-McKAY ELECTRIC COMPANY
1357 East Lincoln Avenue, Madison Heights MI 48071-4134. 248/582-2343. **Fax:** 248/399-6828. **Contact:** Kathy Gollin, Vice President of Human Resources. **E-mail address:** gollink@mc-mc.com. **World Wide Web address:** http://www.mc-mc.com. **Description:** Engaged in the wholesale trade of electrical appliances and equipment. **Corporate headquarters location:** This location. **Other area locations:** Ann Arbor MI; Flint MI. **Other U.S. locations:** OH; NC; SC; GA. **Number of employees nationwide:** 850.

MICHIGAN CAT
24800 Novi Road, Novi MI 48375. 248/348-6520. **Toll-free phone:** 888/MIC-HCAT. **Contact:** Wes Winn, Human Resources Manager. **E-mail address:** wes.winn@michigancat.com. **World Wide Web address:** http://www.michigancat.com. **Description:** Sells and services Caterpillar construction equipment and engines. Founded in 1944. **Positions advertised include:** Service Technician; Heavy Equipment Service Technician. **Special programs:** Internships; Apprenticeships; Training; Co-ops; Summer Jobs. **Corporate headquarters location:** Wixom MI. **Other area locations:** Statewide. **Listed on:** New York Stock Exchange. **Stock exchange symbol:** CAT. **Annual sales/revenues:** $400 million.

H.J. OLDENKAMP COMPANY
4669 East Eight Mile Road, P.O. Box 865, Warren MI 48090. 586/756-0600. **Toll-free phone:** 800/462-6047. **Fax:** 586/756-1045. **Contact:** Personnel. **World Wide Web address:** http://www.oldenkamp.com. **Description:** Engaged in the wholesale trade of materials including Formica, laminates, and cabinets. Founded in 1946. **Corporate headquarters location:** This location. **Other area locations:** Highland Park MI. **Number of employees at this location:** 100.

PRODUCTION TOOL SUPPLY
8655 East Eight Mile Road, Warren MI 48089-4030. 586/755-5258. **Toll-free phone:** 800/270-5779. **Fax:**

586/755-4921. **Contact:** Human Resources. **E-mail address:** warren.mgr@pts-tools.com. **World Wide Web address:** http://www.pts-tools.com. **Description:** A distributor of industrial tools, including precision measuring instruments, fasteners, tool room machinery, hand tools, power tools, and carbide inserts. **Corporate headquarters location:** This location. **Other area locations:** Lansing MI; Novi MI; Grand Rapids MI; Redford MI; Madison Heights MI; Roseville MI; Jackson MI. **Other U.S. locations:** Cleveland OH. **Listed on:** Privately held. **Number of employees at this location:** 260. **Number of employees nationwide:** 600.

REPROGRAPHICS ONE INC.
36060 Industrial Road, Livonia MI 48150. 734/542-8800. **Fax:** 734/542-8480. **Contact:** Human Resource Director. **World Wide Web address:** http://www.reprographicsone.com. **Description:** Supplies reproduction, plotting, art, and drafting products and services to corporate entities. **Corporate headquarters location:** This location.

F.B. WRIGHT COMPANY
9999 Mercier Avenue, P.O. Box 770, Dearborn MI 48121. 313/843-8250. **Fax:** 313/843-8450. **Contact:** Human Resources. **World Wide Web address:** http://www.fbwright.com. **Description:** A distributor of a variety of hoses, gaskets, and fittings. **Corporate headquarters location:** This location. **Other area locations:** Grand Rapids MI; Saginaw MI. **Other U.S. locations:** Toledo OH. **Number of employees at this location:** 100.

Minnesota
BELL INDUSTRIES
580 Yankee Doodle Road, Suite 1200, Eagan MN 55121. 651/450-9020. **Fax:** 651/450-0844. **Contact:** Human Resources. **World Wide Web address:** http://www.bellrpg.com. **Description:** A wholesaler of parts and equipment for recreational vehicles, ATVs, boats, and mobile homes. **Other U.S. locations:** Germantown WI; Grand Rapids MI. **Parent company:** Bell Industries.

CUMMINS NPOWER
1600 Buerkle Road, White Bear Lake MN 55110. 651/636-1000. **Contact:** Human Resources. **E-mail address:** npowerhr@cummins.com **World Wide Web address:** http://www.npower.cummins.com. **Description:** Cummins NPower distributes Cummins and Onan products in the Upper Midwest. **Parent company:** Cummins Inc. **NOTE:** Call to inquire about current job openings. Submit resume by mail or e-mail.

ECOLAB INC.
370 North Wabasha Street, St. Paul MN 55102-2233. 651/293-2233. **Contact:** Human Resources. **World Wide Web address:** http://www.ecolab.com. **Description:** Ecolab provides cleaning, sanitizing, and maintenance products and services for the food service, lodging, health care, laundry, dairy, and food and beverage processing markets in the United States, Canada, Latin America, Asia, and Europe. Products include dispensers, kitchen supplies, cleaners, sanitizers, janitorial products, textile care products, and commercial pest control items. **Listed on:** New York Stock Exchange. **Stock exchange symbol:** ECL.

GUARDIAN BUILDING PRODUCTS DISTIBUTION
5110 Main Street Northeast, Fridley MN 55421. 763/571-5100. **Toll-free phone:** 800/328-7862. **Fax:** 763/571-5186. **Contact:** Human Resources. **World Wide Web address:** http://www.gbpd.com. **Description:** A wholesaler of building supplies including ceiling tiles, coatings, gutters, nails, roofing, screws, siding, and ventilation equipment. **Corporate headquarters location:** Greer SC. **Parent company:** Guardian Industries.

HOBART CORPORATION
1610 Broadway Street NE, Minneapolis MN 55413. 612/379-7544. **Fax:** 612/331-1051. **Contact:** Human Resources. **World Wide Web address:** http://www.hobartcorp.com. **Description:** Sells and services commercial food preparation equipment used in the food service industry and in the retail food/supermarket industry. **Corporate headquarters location:** Troy OH. **Parent company:** Illinois Tool Works Inc. **Operations at this facility include:** Administration; Regional Headquarters; Sales; Service.

IKON BUSINESS SERVICES
2740 West 80th Street, Bloomington MN 55431. 952/888-8000. **Fax:** 952/885-3666. **Contact:** Human Resources. **World Wide Web address:** http://www.ikon.com. **Description:** Resells computers, fax machines, and other office equipment. **Positions advertised include:** Account Executive; Systems Analyst Manager. **Operations at this facility include:** Regional Office; Sales; Service.

NAPCO INTERNATIONAL INC.
11055 Excelsior Boulevard, Hopkins MN 55343. 952/931-2400. **Fax:** 952/931-2402. **Contact:** Linda Monte, Human Resources Administrator. **E-mail address:** lmonte@napcointl.com. **World Wide Web address:** http://www.napcointl.com. **Description:** A manufacturer of defense-related products. **NOTE:** Call to inquire about current job openings. **Corporate headquarters location:** This location. **Parent company:** JATA LLC. **Operations at this facility include:** Sales; Service. **Number of employees at this location:** 85.

NAVARRE CORPORATION
7400 49th Avenue North, New Hope MN 55428. 763/535-8333. **Fax:** 763/533-2156. **E-mail address:** info@navarre.com. **World Wide Web address:** http://www.navarre.com. **Description:** A leading distributor of propriety and non-propriety home entertainment PC software, music and DVD. The company's customers include a wide spectrum of national and regional retailers. This customer base includes mass merchants, specialty stores, wholesalers, and e-retailers. The company operates a business-to-business web site, navarre.com providing product fulfillment to both traditional and e-commerce retailers. **Positions advertised include:** Paralegal; Accounts Payable Specialist; Warehouse. **Corporate headquarters location:** This location. **Other U.S. locations:** Nationwide. **Listed on:** NASDAQ. **Stock exchange symbol:** NAVR.

Missouri
CUMMINS GATEWAY
7210 Hall Street, St. Louis MO 63147. 314/389-5400. **Contact:** John Wagner, President. **World Wide Web address:** http://www.gateway.cummins.com. **Description:** Distributes diesel engines and parts for diesel engines. Cummins Gateway also provides service for diesel engines. **Number of employees at this location:** 100.

LAMMERT FURNITURE COMPANY
501 South Lindbergh Boulevard, St. Louis MO 63131. 314/993-1111. **Contact:** Human Resources. **Description:** A wholesaler and retailer of home and commercial furnishings. The company is also engaged in contract design.

SUMNER GROUP, INC.
2121 Hampton Avenue, St. Louis MO 63139. 314/645-0769. **Fax:** 314/633-8005. **Contact:** Personnel Department. **Description:** A wholesale supplier of office equipment and an authorized Canon dealer, specializing in the sale of copying and duplicating equipment. **Corporate headquarters location:** This location. **Other U.S. locations:** Little Rock AR. **Number of employees at this location:** 300. **Number of employees nationwide:** 450.

Nebraska
DUTTON-LAINSON COMPANY
P.O. Box 729, Hastings NE 68902-0729. 402/462-4141. **Fax:** 402/460-4612. **Contact:** Human Resources. **World Wide Web address:** http://www.dutton-

lainson.com. **Description:** A wholesaler of electrical apparatus and equipment and a metal manufacturer for the marine, hardware, and health care industries. The company also operates the Cornhusker Press, a full-service printer. **Corporate headquarters location:** This location. **Operations at this facility include:** Administration; Divisional Headquarters; Manufacturing; Regional Headquarters; Research and Development; Sales; Service. **Listed on:** Privately held.

Nevada

W.W. GRAINGER
2401 Western Avenue, Las Vegas NV 89102. 702/385-6833. **Contact:** Human Resources. **World Wide Web address:** http://www.grainger.com. **Description:** Distributes a variety of equipment and components to the industrial, commercial, contracting, and institutional markets worldwide. The company has 337 branches in all 50 states and Puerto Rico, and a catalog that lists 78,000 items. Products include equipment and components for motors, air tools, hydraulic products, refrigeration items, power and hand tools, office equipment, computer supplies, storage equipment, replacement parts, industrial products, safety items, cold weather clothing, and sanitary supplies. **Listed on:** New York Stock Exchange. **Stock exchange symbol:** GWW.

IKON OFFICE SOLUTIONS
680 Pilot Road, Las Vegas NV 89119-4441. 702/795-3366. **Contact:** Human Resources. **World Wide Web address:** http://www.ikon.com. **Description:** Distributes, sells, and repairs office equipment including photocopiers, fax machines, and printers. **Other U.S. locations:** Nationwide. **Listed on:** New York Stock Exchange. **Stock exchange symbol:** IKN.

KAR PRODUCTS INC.
12755 Moya Boulevard, Reno NV 89506. 775/786-0811. **Contact:** Human Resources. **E-mail address:** barnesjobs@bd-bgi.com. **World Wide Web address:** http://www.careersatbd.com. **Description:** A distributor of nuts, bolts, and a variety of other fasteners. **Corporate headquarters location:** Des Plaines IL. **Other U.S. locations:** Fairburn GA; Monroe Township NJ; Irving TX. **International locations:** Ontario, Canada. **Parent company:** Barnes Group Inc.

New Jersey

CCA INDUSTRIES INC.
200 Murray Hill Parkway, East Rutherford NJ 07073. 201/330-1400. **Contact:** Human Resources Department. **E-mail address:** humanresources@ccaindustries.com. **World Wide Web address:** http://www.ccaindustries.com. **Description:** Distributes a wide variety of health and beauty products manufactured by other companies using CCA's formulations. The majority of its sales are made to retail drug and food chains and mass merchandisers. **Listed on:** NASDAQ. **Stock exchange symbol:** CCAM.

CREATIVE HOBBIES, INC.
900 Creek Road, Bellmawr NJ 08031-1687. 856/933-2540. **Contact:** Personnel. **World Wide Web address:** http://www.creative-hobbies.com. **Description:** A wholesale distributor of hobby ceramics supplies including clay, kilns, pottery wheels, tools, glazes, and decorating supplies.

ENOVATION GRAPHIC SYSTEMS, INC.
15 Twinbridge Drive, Pennsauken NJ 08110. 856/488-7200. **Contact:** Personnel. **World Wide Web address:** http://www.enovationgraphics.com. **Description:** Distributes graphic arts equipment and systems.

McMASTER-CARR SUPPLY COMPANY
473 Ridge Road, Dayton NJ 08810. 732/329-6666. **Contact:** Recruiting Department. **E-mail address:** recruiting@mcmaster.com. **World Wide Web address:** http://www.mcmaster.com. **Description:** Distributes industrial products and supplies primarily through catalog sales. Products are sold worldwide. **NOTE:** Mail employment correspondence to: Recruiting, McMaster Supply Company, P.O. Box 4355, Chicago IL 60680-4355. **Positions advertised include:** Customer Service Representative. **Corporate headquarters location:** Elmhurst IL. **Operations at this facility include:** Service.

VAN LEEUWEN
777 Alexander Road, Princeton NJ 08540. 609/580-0088. **Contact:** Human Resources. **World Wide Web address:** http://www.vanleeuwen.com. **Description:** Distributes pipes, valves, and fittings, serving both domestic and overseas customers. **NOTE:** If applying for a warehouse position, please contact Martin Curley, Operations Manager; for an office position, contact Jim Gallagher, Regional Manager. **Corporate headquarters location:** This location.

New Mexico

ALBUQUERQUE BOLT & FASTENER
2926 Second Street NW, Albuquerque NM 87107. 505/345-5869. **Contact:** Human Resources. **Description:** A retailer and wholesaler of bolts and fasteners for various industries.

New York

ATELIER ESTHETIQUE INC.
386 Park Avenue South, Suite 1409, New York NY 10016. 212/725-6130. **Contact:** Human Resources. **World Wide Web address:** http://www.aeinstitute.net. **Description:** A wholesaler of cosmetic products and equipment. This location also houses a beauty school.

DYNAMIC INTERNATIONAL LIMITED, INC.
58 Second Avenue, Brooklyn NY 11215. 718/369-4160. **Fax:** 718/369-2210. **Contact:** Human Resources. **Description:** Dynamic Classics sells and distributes a diverse line of exercise equipment, sport bags, luggage, and gift products, which are distributed nationwide. The majority of sales are to catalog showrooms, drug chains, sporting goods chains, distributors, chain stores, discount stores, and the premium trade.

ITOCHU INTERNATIONAL INC.
335 Madison Avenue, New York NY 10017. 212/818-8000. **Fax:** 212/818-8543. **Contact:** Recruiting, Human Resources. **E-mail address:** recruiting@itochu.com. **World Wide Web address:** http://www.itochu.com. **Description:** A diversified international trading company with markets that include textiles, metals, machinery, foodstuffs, general merchandise, electronics, chemicals, and energy. The company has import/export, distribution, finance, investment, transportation, and joint venture operations, all of which contribute to an annual business volume of over $12 billion. Itochu International is also engaged in direct investments and partnerships in many additional industries including high-technology manufacturing, retailing, fiber optics, satellite communications, and real estate development. **Corporate headquarters location:** This location. **Other locations:** AL; CA; CO; GA; IL; MO; WA. **Parent company:** Itochu Corporation.

MARUBENI AMERICA CORPORATION
450 Lexington Avenue, 35th Floor, New York NY 10017-3907. 212/450-0100. **Fax:** 212/450-0700. **Contact:** Human Resources. **E-mail address:** info@marubeni-usa.com. **World Wide Web address:** http://www.marubeni-usa.com. **Description:** An international trading firm that provides importing and exporting services to and from Japan. Operations are conducted through seven groups: Metals & Minerals Group; Machinery Group; Petroleum Group; General Merchandise Group; Chemical & Plastics Group; Textile Group; and Grain, Marine, & Other Products Group. **Corporate headquarters location:** This location. **Other U.S. locations:** Nationwide. **Subsidiaries include:** Don Juan Sportswear Inc.; It Fabrics Inc. **Parent company:** Marubeni Corporation (Japan).

MITSUBISHI INTERNATIONAL CORPORATION
655 Third Avenue, New York NY 10017. 212/605-2000.

Fax: 212/605-2597. **Contact:** Human Resources. **World Wide Web address:** http://www.mitsubishiintl.com. **Description:** Mitsubishi International operates through several trading divisions and related support divisions including Petroleum, Steel, Foods, Chemicals, Machinery, Textile, Non-Ferrous Metals, Ferrous Raw Materials, Lumber and Pulp, and General Merchandise. Regional offices are located throughout the United States. **Corporate headquarters location:** This location. **Other U.S. locations:** Nationwide. **Subsidiaries include:** Mitsubishi Trust & Banking Corporation (also at this location, 212/838-7700) is a bank with diverse activities that include real estate and foreign exchange services. **Parent company:** Mitsubishi Corporation of Japan. **Annual sales/revenues:** $119 million. **Number of employees at this location:** 400. **Number of employees nationwide:** 850.

MITSUI & CO., LTD.
200 Park Avenue, New York NY 10166. 212/878-4000. **Fax:** 212/878-4800. **Contact:** Human Resources. **World Wide Web address:** http://www.mitsui.com. **Description:** An international trading firm engaged in a wide range of import and export activities. **Corporate headquarters location:** Tokyo, Japan. **Other U.S. locations:** Nationwide. **Operations at this facility include:** Administration; Divisional Headquarters; Regional Headquarters; Sales. **Listed on:** NASDAQ. **Stock exchange symbol:** MITSY. **Annual sales/revenues:** $4.2 billion. **Number of employees:** 36,116.

UOP/XEROX
2344 Flatbush Avenue, Brooklyn NY 11234. 718/252-6500. **Fax:** 718/252-8585. **Contact:** Human Resources. **Description:** Sells and services copiers, fax machines, laser printers, and other types of office equipment.

North Carolina
BRADY DISTRIBUTING COMPANY
P.O. Box 19269, Charlotte NC 28219. 704/357-6284. **Physical address:** 2708 Yorkmont Road, Charlotte NC 28208. **Fax:** 704/357-1243. **Contact:** Human Resources Manager. **World Wide Web address:** http://www.bradydist.com. **Description:** Distributes coin-operated vending machines and arcade games. **Corporate headquarters location:** This location. **Other U.S. locations:** Miami FL; Orlando FL; Memphis TN. **Number of employees nationwide:** 120.

CASHWELL APPLIANCE PARTS, INC.
P.O. Box 2549, Fayetteville NC 28302-2549. 910/323-1111. **Physical address:** 3485 Clinton Road, Fayetteville NC 28301. **Toll-free phone:** 800/277-1220. **Fax:** 910/323-5067. **Toll-free fax:** 800/277-2877. **Contact:** Human Resources. **World Wide Web address:** http://www.cashwells.com. **Description:** Distributes bathroom fans, ceiling fans, dryers, electrical equipment parts, and washers. **Positions advertised include:** Warehouse Worker. **Other area locations:** Raleigh NC; Wilmington NC; Asheville NC; Charlotte NC; Greensboro NC. **Operations at this facility include:** Distribution.

L.R. GORRELL CO.
P.O. Box 33395. Raleigh NC 27636. 919/821-1161. **Physical address:** 544 Pylon Drive, Raleigh NC 27606. **Fax:** 919/832-1542. **Contact:** Employment. **E-mail address:** raleigh@lrgorrell.com. **World Wide Web address:** http://www.lrgorrell.com. **Description:** A distributor of parts for heating and cooling equipment. Founded in 1951. **NOTE:** Entry-level positions are offered. **Corporate headquarters location:** This location. **Other area locations:** Asheville NC; Greensboro NC; Charlotte NC; Wilmington NC. **Other U.S. locations:** Greenville SC; North Charleston SC. **Operations at this facility include:** Manufacturing; Administration; Warehousing. **Listed on:** Privately held.

GRAINGER
2533 North Chester Street, Gastonia NC 28052. 704/861-9239. 9235. **Fax:** 704/866-7054. **Contact:** Michael Kenney, Manager. **World Wide Web address:** http://www.grainger.com. **Description:** A national supplier of industrial equipment such as motors, pumps, and safety maintenance equipment. Grainger distributes a variety of equipment and components to the industrial, commercial, contracting, and institutional markets. **Positions advertised include:** Outside Sales Account Manager; Branch Manager; Warehouse Associate; Customer Service Associate. **Corporate headquarters location:** Chicago IL. **Other area locations:** Statewide. **Other U.S. locations:** Nationwide. **International locations:** Worldwide. **Listed on:** New York Stock Exchange. **Stock exchange symbol:** GWW.

HONEYWELL SENSOTEC, INC.
1100 Airport Road, Shelby NC 28150. 704/482-9582. **Contact:** Human Resources. **E-mail address:** hrdepartment2@sensotec.com. **World Wide Web address:** http://www.sensotec.com. **Description:** Supplies components to the automotive, truck, appliance, heating, and aerospace industries. **Corporate headquarters location:** Columbus OH. **International locations:** Worldwide. **Parent company:** Honeywell International.

Ohio
BARNES DISTRIBUTION
1301 East Ninth Street, Suite 700, Cleveland OH 44114. 216/416-7200. **Contact:** Human Resources. **E-mail address:** barnesfsjobs-midwest@bd-bgi.com. **World Wide Web address:** http://www.barnesdistribution.com. **Description:** A direct-to-user distributor of expendable parts and supplies for the industrial, transportation, and heavy-equipment maintenance markets. Founded in 1927. **Positions advertised include:** Senior Materials Planner; Purchasing Analyst. **Corporate headquarters location:** Bristol CT. **Parent company:** Barnes Group, Inc. is a diversified manufacturer of critical parts and supplies for a wide range of industrial applications.

CORPORATE EXPRESS
1170 Highlander Parkway, Richfield OH 44286. 330/523-3000. **Toll-free phone**: 888/238-6329. **Contact:** Human Resources. **World Wide Web address:** http://www.corporateexpress.com. **Description:** Distributes a complete range of office machinery and supplies. **Other area locations:** Cincinnati OH; Cleveland OH; Columbus OH.

THE GARICK CORPORATION
13600 Broadway Avenue, Cleveland OH 44125. 216/581-0100. **Toll-free phone:** 800/242-7425. **Fax:** 216/475-0616. **Contact:** Don English, Vice President of Associate Relations. **E-mail address:** don.english@garick.com. **World Wide Web address:** http://www.garick.com. **Description:** Develops, manufactures, and supplies construction, landscape, and nursery materials. The Garick Corporation's products include Alabama Auburn, Animal Karpet, Dynacushion Play Mats, Equestrian Karpet, Kids Karpet, The Original Bark Bale, and Trail Karpet. **Positions advertised include:** Customer Service Manager. **Special programs:** Internships. **Corporate headquarters location:** This location. **Operations at this facility include:** Administration; Research and Development; Sales; Service. **Parent company:** Fairmount Minerals.

IDG SCALLAN SUPPLY COMPANY
9407 Meridian Way, West Chester OH 45069. 513/942-9100. **Toll-free phone:** 800/722-5526. **Fax:** 513/942-9101. **Contact:** Human Resources. **Description:** A wholesaler of industrial supplies, cutting tools, and hand tools.

LENNOX INDUSTRIES INC.
3750 Brookham Drive, Suite A, Grove City OH 43123. 614/871-7216. **Contact:** Human Resources. **World Wide Web address:** http://www.lennox.com. **Description:** Lennox Industries is a distributor of air conditioners and heating units. **Corporate headquarters location:** Dallas TX. **Operations at this facility include:** This location is a warehouse.

MARCONI
1122 F Street, Lorain OH 44052. 440/288-1122. **Toll-free phone:** 800/800-1280. **Fax:** 440/246-4171. **Contact:** Human Resources Manager. **World Wide Web address:** http://www.marconi.com. **Description:** Marconi Power provides network power systems for telecommunications, Internet, and cable television. **Corporate headquarters location:** London UK. **Other area locations:** Cleveland OH; North Ridgeville OH. **Other U.S. locations:** CA; IL; NY; PA; TX. **International locations:** Worldwide.

PARTS ASSOCIATES INC.
12420 Plaza Drive, Cleveland OH 44130. 216/433-7700. **Toll-free phone:** 800/321-1128. **Fax:** 216/433-9051. **Contact:** Howard Gillespie, Human Resources Department. **World Wide Web address:** http://www.pai-net.com. **Description:** A national distributor serving the automotive, fleet, industrial, maintenance, mining, and off-road equipment markets. Founded in 1948. **Positions advertised include:** Sales Representative.

EJ THOMAS COMPANY
6161 Wiehe Road, Cincinnati OH 45237. 513/841-0880. **Contact:** Human Resources. **Description:** A wholesaler of chemicals and hangers for laundry and dry cleaning companies. **Other area locations:** Columbus, OH.

Oregon

ABC BUILDING PRODUCTS
3610 SE 29th Avenue, Portland OR 97202. 503/239-6543. **Fax:** 239-0131. **Contact:** Human Resources. **World Wide Web address:** http://www.abcsupply.com. **Description:** A leading distributor of building products including insulation, industrial metals, roofing materials, vinyl siding, and millwork. Founded in 1991.

BLACKWELL'S BOOK SERVICES
6024 SW Jean Road, Building G, Lake Oswego OR 97035-8598. 503/684-1140. **Contact:** Human Resources. **World Wide Web address:** http://www.blackwell.com. **Description:** Distributes and sells books to libraries.

BURNS BROTHERS INC.
4800 SW Meadows Road, Suite 475, Lake Oswego OR 97035. 503/697-0666. **Contact:** Human Resources. **Description:** A diversified manufacturer, wholesaler, and retailer of auto parts, accessories, and fuel. Other activities include real estate development and the wholesaling of battery-powered lighting products. **Corporate headquarters location:** This location.

FASTENAL COMPANY
4882 Industry Drive, Central Point OR 97502. 541/770-5411. **Contact:** Human Resources. **World Wide Web address:** http://www.fastenal.com. **Description:** A wholesaler and distributor of industrial fasteners. Founded in 1967. **Corporate headquarters location:** Winona MN. **Listed on:** NASDAQ. **Stock exchange symbol:** FAST.

W.W. GRAINGER
6335 North Basin Avenue, Portland OR 97217. 503/283-0366. **Fax:** 503/285-8624. **Contact:** Human Resources. **World Wide Web address:** http://www.grainger.com. **Description:** Distributes a variety of equipment and components to the industrial, commercial, contracting, and institutional markets nationwide. Products include equipment and components for motors, air tools, hydraulic products, refrigeration items, power and hand tools, office equipment, computer supplies, replacement parts, industrial products, safety items, cold weather clothing, and storage equipment. Founded in 1927. **Corporate headquarters location:** Lake Forest IL. **Other U.S. locations:** Nationwide. **Listed on:** New York Stock Exchange. **Stock exchange symbol:** GWW.

IKON OFFICE SOLUTIONS
12100 SW Garden Place, Portland OR 97223. 503/620-2800. **Fax:** 503/620-3500. **Contact:** Human Resources. **World Wide Web address:** http://www.ikon.com. **Description:** A wholesaler and distributor of copy machines, fax machines, and related office supplies. **Positions advertised include:** Document Specialist; Account Executive; Associate Sales Representative; Major Account Executive; Account Manager; Customer Service Representative; Copy/Mail Operator. **Corporate headquarters location:** Malvern PA. **International locations:** Worldwide. **Listed on:** New York Stock Exchange. **Stock exchange symbol:** IKN.

JEWETT-CAMERON TRADING COMPANY LTD.
32275 NW Hillcrest, P.O. Box 1010, North Plains OR 97133. 503/647-0110. **Fax:** 503/647-2272. **Contact:** Don Boone, CEO. **World Wide Web address:** http://www.msipro.com. **Description:** A supplier to the building supply and home improvement trades located throughout the western United States and the islands of the South Pacific. The company operates in the following business segments: warehouse distribution and direct sales of building materials to home improvement centers; export of finished building materials to overseas customers; and specialty wood products for government and industrial sales, primarily on a contract-bid basis. **Corporate headquarters location:** Tigard OR. **Subsidiaries include:** Jewett-Cameron Lumber Corporation; Jewett-Cameron South Pacific Ltd.; Material Supply International.

Pennsylvania

ALMO CORPORATION
2709 Commerce Way, Philadelphia PA 19154. 215/698-4000. **Fax:** 215/698-4080. **Contact:** Human Resources. **E-mail address:** employment@almo.com. **World Wide Web address:** http://www.almo.com. **Description:** A multiregional distributor of computer products, consumer electronics, major appliances, and specialty wire and cable. **NOTE:** Entry-level positions are offered. **Corporate headquarters location:** This location. **Other U.S. locations:** MA; MD; MO; WI. **Operations at this facility include:** Administration; Divisional Headquarters; Sales. **Number of employees at this location:** 90.

APPLIED INDUSTRIAL TECHNOLOGIES
4350 H Street, Philadelphia PA 19124. 215/744-6330. **Contact:** Personnel. **E-mail address:** career@applied.com. **World Wide Web address:** http://www.applied.com. **Description:** Distributes bearings and power transmission equipment. **NOTE:** Please visit http://www.monster.com for current employment opportunities. **Corporate headquarters location:** Cleveland OH. **Other area locations:** Statewide. **Other U.S. locations:** Nationwide. **Listed on:** New York Stock Exchange. **Stock exchange symbol:** AIT.

FAIRMONT SUPPLY COMPANY
401 Technology Drive, Canonsburg PA 15317. 724/514-3900. **Fax:** 724/514-3889. **Contact:** Human Resources. **E-mail address:** humanresources@fairmontsupply.com. **World Wide Web address:** http://www.fairmontsupply.com. **Description:** An industrial supply, wholesaling company. **Operations at this facility include:** Customer service.

FASTENAL COMPANY
1225 Mid Valley Drive, Jessup PA 18434. 570/307-0992. **Fax:** 570/307-0441. **Contact:** Human Resources. **World Wide Web address:** http://www.fastenal.com. **Description:** A full-line, industrial distributor with products including fasteners, construction accessories, strut and pipe hangers, and power tools. Fastenal Company is one of the largest fastener distributors in the United States. Founded in 1967. **Corporate headquarters location:** Winona MN.

GILES & RANSOME, INC.
2975 Galloway Road, Bensalem PA 19020. 215/639-4300. **Fax:** 215/245-2831. **Contact:** Richard Smith, Manager of Personnel. **E-mail address:** rsmith@ransome.com. **World Wide Web address:** http://www.ransome.cat.com. **Description:** A regional

distributor of Caterpillar heavy construction and industrial equipment including diesel engines and generators, construction vehicles, and material-handling equipment. **Positions advertised include:** Technical Trainer. **Corporate headquarters location:** This location.

HYDRO SERVICE AND SUPPLIES, INC.
1426 Manning Boulevard, Levittown PA 19057. 215/547-0332. **Fax:** 215/547-5734. **Contact:** Human Resources. **E-mail address:** jobs@hydroservice.com. **World Wide Web address:** http://www.hydroservice.com. **Description:** Sells and services water ultrapurification laboratory equipment. **NOTE:** Mail employment correspondence to: Human Resources, P.O. Box 12197, Research Triangle Park NC 27709. **Corporate headquarters location:** Research Triangle Park NC.

IKON OFFICE SOLUTIONS
70 Valley Stream Parkway, Malvern PA 19355. 610/296-8000. **Fax:** 478/471-2417. **Contact:** Kathy Brodhag, Director of Human Resources. **World Wide Web address:** http://www.ikon.com. **Description:** Markets and distributes office equipment and paper products. IKON Office Solutions is one of the largest independent copier distribution networks in North America. **Positions advertised include:** Enterprise Test Manager; Senior IT Manager; Senior Supply Chain Analyst; Online Marketing Manager; Senior Help Desk Technician; Paralegal. **Special programs:** Internships. **Corporate headquarters location:** This location. **Operations at this facility include:** Administration. **Number of employees at this location:** 225.

HENRY F. MICHELL COMPANY
P.O. Box 60160, King of Prussia PA 19406. 610/265-4200. **Fax:** 610/337-7726. **Contact:** Human Resources. **World Wide Web address:** http://www.michells.com. **Description:** Henry F. Michell Company is a horticultural wholesaler. **Positions advertised include:** Assistant to Production Manager.

PEIRCE-PHELPS, INC.
2000 North 59th Street, Philadelphia PA 19131. 215/879-7000. **Contact:** Human Resources. **E-mail address:** jobs@peirce.com. **World Wide Web address:** http://www.peirce.com. **Description:** Distributes a variety of electrical appliances including washers, dryers, and air conditioners.

UNITED REFRIGERATION INC.
11401 Roosevelt Boulevard, Philadelphia PA 19154. 215/698-9100. **Contact:** Human Resources. **World Wide Web address:** http://www.uri.com. **Description:** A worldwide distributor of refrigerators, air conditioners, and heating equipment. Founded in 1947. **Corporate headquarters location:** Philadelphia PA. **Other U.S. locations:** Nationwide. **International locations:** Canada; France; United Kingdom.

WESTINGHOUSE LIGHTING CORPORATION
12401 McNulty Road, Philadelphia PA 19154. 215/671-2000. **Fax:** 215/767-3720. **Contact:** Personnel Director. **World Wide Web address:** http://www.westinghouselighting.com. **Description:** A wholesaler of light bulbs, lighting fixtures, replacement glassware, wall plates, lighting hardware, and other products. **Corporate headquarters location:** This location. **International locations:** Mexico; Germany; United Kingdom; China; Hong Kong; Taiwan. **Operations at this facility include:** Sales. **Number of employees at this location:** 125. **Number of employees nationwide:** 2,500.

South Carolina

W.W. GRAINGER
730 Congaree Road, Greenville SC 29607. 864/288-0110. **Fax:** 864/297-1799. **Contact:** Human Resources. **World Wide Web address:** http://www.grainger.com. **Description:** A national supplier of products to the industrial, commercial, contracting, and institutional markets. Products include equipment and components for motors, air tools, hydraulic products, refrigeration items, power and hand tools, office equipment, computer supplies, replacement parts, industrial products, safety items, cold weather clothing, and storage equipment. Founded in 1927. **Positions advertised include:** Customer Service Associate; Outside Sales Territory Manager; Account Manager; Warehouse Associate; Distribution Associate; Project Manager. **Annual sales/revenues:** $5 billion.

IKON OFFICE SOLUTIONS
7 Technology Circle, Columbia SC 29203. 803/758-5555. **Toll-free phone:** 800/476-6779. **Contact:** Melissa Kitchings, Human Resources. **E-mail address:** mkitchin@ikontech.com. **World Wide Web address:** http://www.ikon.com. **Description:** Distributes, sells, and repairs office equipment including photocopiers, fax machines, and printers. **Positions advertised include:** Account Executive. **Corporate headquarters location:** Malvern PA. **Other U.S. locations:** Nationwide. **International locations:** Worldwide. **Annual sales/revenues:** $5.3 billion. **Number of employees statewide:** 300. **Number of employees worldwide:** 37,000.

ORDERS DISTRIBUTING COMPANY, INC.
P.O. Box 17189, Greenville SC 29606. 864/288-4220. **Physical address:** 1 Whitlee Court, Greenville SC 29607. **Fax:** 864/458-7348. **Contact:** Carole Lister, Human Resources Coordinator. **World Wide Web address:** http://www.ordersdistributing.com. **Description:** A supplier of a broad range of floor coverings including hardwood, vinyl, carpet, and ceramic. Founded in 1955. **Corporate headquarters location:** This location. **Other locations:** Greensboro NC; Johnson City TN; Roanoke VA.

Tennessee

AIRCON CORPORATION
2873 Chelsea Avenue, P.O. Box 80446, Memphis TN 38108-0446. 901/452-0230. **Toll-free phone:** 800/238-9140. **Fax:** 901/452-0264. **Contact:** Human Resources Manager. **Description:** A wholesaler of air pollution and dust control systems and equipment.

DANKA OFFICE IMAGING COMPANY, INC.
1638 Sycamore View Road, Memphis TN 38134. 901/387-5603. **Contact:** Personnel. **World Wide Web address:** http://www.danka.com. **Description:** A wholesaler of photocopiers, printers, and fax machines. Founded in 1977. **NOTE:** Search and apply for positions online. **Corporate headquarters location:** St. Petersburg FL.

INGRAM
One Ingram Boulevard, La Vergne TN 37086. 615/793-5000. **Toll-free phone:** 800/395-4340. **Fax:** 615/213-5192. **Contact:** Human Resources. **World Wide Web address:** http://www.ingrambook.com. **Description:** A distributor of Christian books, music, and gift items. **Corporate headquarters location:** This location. **Other U.S. locations:** Harrison AR; Bakersfield CA; Portland OR; Newport TN; Dallas TX. **Parent company:** Ingram Book Company. **Listed on:** Privately held. **Number of employees at this location:** 250. **Number of employees nationwide:** 610.

LENOIR EMPIRE FURNITURE
1625 Cherokee Road, Johnson City TN 37604. 423/929-7283. **Fax:** 423/929-7040. **Contact:** Human Resources Department. **World Wide Web address:** http://www.hfnet.com/lenoirempirefurniture. **Description:** A discount distributor of home furnishing including bedroom, living room, and dining room furniture.

METAL ROOFING WHOLESALERS
1178 Topside Road, Louisville TN 37777. 865/379-7777. **Toll-free phone:** 877/646-6382. **Fax:** 865/982-4222. **Contact:** Human Resources. **World Wide Web address:** http://www.metalroofingwholesalers.com. **Description:** A wholesaler and distributor of metal roofing products.

ORGILL BROTHERS & COMPANY
3742 Tyndale Drive, Memphis TN 38125. 901/754-8850. **Fax:** 901/752-8989. **Contact:** Human Resources. **World Wide Web address:** http://www.orgill.com. **Description:** A hardware distributor. Founded in 1847. **Parent company:** West Union Corporation. **Listed on:** Privately held.

Texas

ACR GROUP, INC.
3200 Wilcrest Drive, Suite 440, Houston TX 77042-6039. 713/780-8532. **Fax:** 713/780-4067. **Contact:** Human Resources. **E-mail address:** humanresources@acrgroup.com. **World Wide Web address:** http://www.acrgroup.com. **Description:** A wholesale distributor of heating, ventilation, air conditioning, and refrigeration equipment, parts, and supplies. ACR Group's products include motors, fiberglass air handling products, sheet metal products, copper tubing, flexible duct, controls, grilles, registers, and pipe vents. The company has 18 distribution outlets in the United States. Founded in 1990. **Corporate headquarters location:** This location. **Other U.S. locations:** Western and Southern U.S. **Subsidiaries include:** ACH Supply (CA); ACR Supply, Inc. (TX and LA); Contractors Heating & Supply, Inc. (CO, TX, and NM); Florida Cooling Supply, Inc. (FL); Heating and Cooling Supply, Inc. (NV); Total Supply, Inc. (GA, TN). **President/CEO:** Alex Trevino, Jr.

AMC INDUSTRIES
P.O. Box 171290 San Antonio TX, 78217. 210/545-2566. **Physical address:** 3535 Metro Parkway, San Antonio TX 78247. **Fax:** 210/545-2977. **Contact:** Human Resources. **Description:** A wholesale distributor of water well parts. **Corporate headquarters location:** This location. **Other U.S. locations:** Austin TX; Houston TX; Pharr TX; Buda TX.

ABATIX CORPORATION
8201 Eastpoint Drive, Suite 500, Dallas TX 75227. 214/381-0322. **Toll-free phone:** 888/222-8499. **Fax:** 214/381-9513. **Contact:** Human Resources. **E-mail address:** hr@abatix.com. **World Wide Web address:** http://www.abatix.com. **Description:** A supplier of industrial safety supplies, construction tools, general safety products such as protective clothing and eyewear, and clean-up equipment. Abatix Corporation has eight distribution centers serving customers throughout the Southwest, Midwest, and the Pacific Coast. **NOTE:** Please visit website to view job listings. **Corporate headquarters location:** This location. **Other area locations:** Houston TX. **Other U.S. locations:** AZ; CA; NV; WA. **President/CEO:** Terry W. Shaver. **Listed on:** NASDAQ. **Stock exchange symbol:** ABIX.

CELEBRITY, INC.
P.O. Box 6666, Tyler TX 75710. 903/509-0153. **Physical address:** 4520 Old Troup Highway, Tyler TX 75707. **Contact:** Human Resources. **World Wide Web address:** http://www.celebrity-inc.com. **Description:** A supplier of artificial flowers, foliage, flowering bushes, and other decorative accessories to craft stores and other specialty retailers and to wholesale florists throughout North America and Europe. Celebrity imports over 7,000 home accent, decorative accessory, and giftware items including artificial floral arrangements; floor planters and trees; a wide range of decorative brass and textile products; and a broad line of seasonal items such as Christmas trees, wreaths, garlands and other ornamental products. **Corporate headquarters location:** This location.

W.W. GRAINGER
2701 West Kingsley Road, Garland TX 75040. 972/278-8110. **Contact:** Human Resources. **World Wide Web address:** http://www.grainger.com. **Description:** W.W. Grainger is a national supplier of industrial equipment such as motors, pumps, and safety maintenance equipment. The company distributes a variety of equipment and components to the industrial, commercial, contracting, and institutional markets. Products are sold through local branches and include equipment and components for motors, air tools, hydraulic products, refrigeration items, power and hand tools, office equipment, computer supplies, replacement parts, industrial products, safety items, cold weather clothing, and storage equipment. Founded in 1927. **Operations at this facility include:** This location sells industrial supplies. **Other area locations:** Statewide. **Other U.S. locations:** Nationwide.

HALLIBURTON COMPANY
Lincoln Plaza, 500 N. Akard, Suite 3600, Dallas TX 75201. 214/978-2600. **Fax:** 214/978-2611. **Contact:** Human Resources. **World Wide Web address:** http://www.halliburton.com. **Description:** A leading diversified energy services, engineering, construction, maintenance, and energy equipment company. **NOTE:** Job listings and application process information is available at the company's website. **Operations at this facility include:** Administration; Training. **Special programs:** Internships; Apprenticeships; Graduate. **Corporate headquarters location:** This location. **Other U.S. locations:** Nationwide. **Listed on:** New York Stock Exchange. **Stock exchange symbol:** HAL.

THE C.D. HARTNETT COMPANY
P.O. Box 1989, Weatherford TX 76086. 817/594-3813. **Physical address:** 300 North Main Street, Weatherford TX, 76086. **Contact:** Human Resources. **E-mail address:** resume@cd-hartnett.com. **World Wide Web address:** http://www.cd-hartnett.com. **Description:** Distributes groceries to convenience stores and food service companies. Products include produce, dairy items, frozen food, and candy. Founded in 1904.

HI-LINE
2121 Valley View Lane, Dallas TX 75234. 972/247-6200. **Toll-free number:** 800/944-5463. **Fax:** 800/860-8254. **Contact:** Human Resources. **E-mail address:** careers@hi-line.com. **World Wide Web address:** http://www.hi-line.com. **Description:** A distributor of fasteners including nuts, bolts, screws, and rivets; terminals including solder splice connectors, mechanical lugs, and ferrules; cable lugs; battery terminals; insulating materials including shrink tubing, grommets, and specialty tape; wiring accessories; drill bits; and various other industrial products. Founded in 1959. **NOTE:** To be considered for a Territory Sales Manager position, complete an online application at the company's website. **Corporate headquarters location:** This location. **Operations at this facility include:** Administration; Sales. **Number of employees at this location:** 160.

IKON OFFICE SOLUTIONS
7401 East Ben White Boulevard, Building 2, Austin TX 78741-7418. 512/385-5100. **Contact:** Human Resources. **E-mail address:** resumes@ikon.com. **World Wide Web address:** http://www.ikon.com. **Description:** IKON Office Solutions is one of the largest independent copier distribution networks in North America. **Positions advertised include:** Recruiter/Trainer; Strategic Account Sales Analyst; Major Account Executive. **Operations at this facility include:** This location is a sales and service center.

JOHNSON SUPPLY AND EQUIPMENT
10151 Stella Link Road, Houston TX 77025. 713/661-6666. **Toll-free number:** 800/833-5455. **Contact:** Human Resources. **World Wide Web address:** http://www.johnsonsupply.com. **Description:** A supplier of air conditioning systems and equipment. **NOTE:** This company has several locations throughout Texas. Each location manages its applicant screening and hiring. See the company's website for additional locations.

PASSAGE SUPPLY COMPANY
P.O. Box 971395, El Paso TX 79997-1395. 915/778-9377. **Fax:** 915/772-9602. **Contact:** Ron Passage, General Manager. **Description:** A heating and cooling systems distributor. **Corporate headquarters location:** This location.

RENTAL SERVICE CORPORATION (RSC)
16225 Park Ten Place, Suite 200, Houston TX 77084. 281/578-5600. **Contact:** Human Resources. **World Wide Web address:** http://www.rentalservice.com. **Description:** A wholesale and rental that provides a wide variety of construction and industrial equipment for industrial users and homeowners. RSC has two sister companies, Prime Energy and Prime Industrial. **NOTE:** This company's website lists Texas-area job openings. Check website for contact information. **Corporate headquarters location:** This location. **Parent company:** Atlas Copco Group. **Operations at this facility:** Regional Office.

SHEPLER'S
9103 East Almeda Road, Houston TX 77054. 713/799-1150. **Toll-free phone:** 800/729-1150. **Fax:** 713/799-8431. **Contact:** Human Resources Manager. **E-mail address:** human.resources@shelpers.com. **World Wide Web address:** http://www.cmcsheplers.com. **Description:** A supplier of concrete accessories, highway products, and form systems. **NOTE:** Entry-level positions are offered. This company has locations throughout Texas. See website for additional locations. **Special programs:** Internships; Training. **Corporate headquarters location:** This location. **Parent company:** CMC Steel Group. **Operations at this facility include:** Administration; Sales.

Utah

ARNOLD MACHINERY
2975 West 2100 South, P.O. Box 30020, Salt Lake City UT 84130. 801/972-4000. **Fax:** 801/974-4080. **Contact:** Human Resources. **World Wide Web address:** http://www.arnoldmachinery.com. **Description:** A wholesaler of mining, construction, and material handling equipment. **Corporate headquarters location:** This location. **Other U.S. locations:** OR; NV; AZ; ID; MT. **CEO:** Russ Fleming.

MARKER USA
1070 West 2300 South, Suite A, Salt Lake City UT 84119. 801/972-0404. **Fax:** 801/972-3938. **Contact:** Human Resources. **World Wide Web address:** http://www.markerusa.com. **Description:** Distributes ski equipment and apparel. **NOTE:** Entry-level positions and part-time jobs are offered. **Corporate headquarters location:** This location. **Other U.S. locations:** West Lebanon NH.

RED MAN PIPE & SUPPLY COMPANY
485 North 400 West, North Salt Lake City UT 84054-2776. 801/298-4605. **Fax:** 801/295-9191. **Contact:** Human Resources. **E-mail address:** jobs@red-man.com. **World Wide Web address:** http://www.red-man.com. **Description:** A wholesale distributor of pipes, valves, and fittings. **NOTE:** Contact the store to inquire about current job openings. **Other area locations:** Roosevelt UT; Vernal UT. **Other U.S. locations:** Nationwide.

Virginia

FAXPLUS, INC.
1011 Arlington Boulevard, Suite 375, Arlington VA 22209. 703/807-1000. **Fax:** 703/527-4308. **Contact:** Human Resources. **World Wide Web address:** http://www.faxplusinc.com. **Description:** Sells and services digital copiers, fax machines, and other office products primarily to the government. Founded in 1986. **Corporate headquarters location:** This location.

W.W. GRAINGER
1401 Sewells Point Road, Norfolk VA 23502. 757/855-3153. **Fax:** 757/855-9542. **Contact:** Human Resources. **World Wide Web address:** http://www.grainger.com. **Description:** Distributes a variety of equipment and components to the industrial, commercial, contracting, and institutional markets nationwide. The company operates 337 branches in all 50 states and Puerto Rico. Products include equipment and components for motors, air tools, hydraulic products, refrigeration items, power and hand tools, office equipment, computer supplies, storage equipment, replacement parts, industrial products, safety items, cold weather clothing, and sanitary supplies. **NOTE:** Search and apply for positions online. **Corporate headquarters location:** Lake Forest IL. **Listed on:** New York Stock Exchange. **Stock exchange symbol:** GWW.

NOLAND COMPANY
80 29th Street, Newport News VA 23607. 757/928-9000. **Fax:** 757/928-9170. **Contact:** Human Resources. **World Wide Web address:** http://www.noland.com. **Description:** Noland is an independent wholesale distributor of mechanical equipment and supplies to the construction industry and manufacturing, with nearly 100 locations across the eastern and southern United States. **Positions advertised include:** Internal Auditor. **Listed on:** NASDAQ. **Stock exchange symbol:** NOLD. **Number of employees nationwide:** 1,400.

Washington

ABATIX ENVIRONMENTAL CORPORATION
1808 B Street NW, Suite 190, Auburn WA 98001. 253/735-1960. **Fax:** 214/381-9513. **Contact:** Human Resources. **E-mail address:** hr@abatix.com. **World Wide Web address:** http://www.abatix.com. **Description:** A full-line supplier of durable and nondurable supplies to the asbestos and lead abatement, hazardous material remediation, and construction industries. Products include industrial safety supplies, construction tools, general safety products such as protective clothing and eyewear, and clean-up equipment. **Corporate headquarters location:** Dallas TX. **Listed on:** NASDAQ. **Stock exchange symbol:** ABIX.

APPLIED INDUSTRIAL TECHNOLOGIES
2747 R.W. Johnson Boulevard SW, Olympia WA 98512. 360/754-4363. **Contact:** Human Resources. **E-mail address:** career@applied.com. **World Wide Web address:** http://www.applied.com. **Description:** A distributor of bearings, power transmitters, hydraulic power units, and rubber products for use in various industries. **Corporate headquarters location:** Cleveland OH. **Listed on:** New York Stock Exchange. **Stock exchange symbol:** AIT.

FERGUSON
4100 West Marginal Way SW, Seattle WA 98106. 206/682-8700. **Contact:** Administrative Manager. **World Wide Web address:** http://www.ferguson.com. **Description:** A wholesale distributor of industrial pipe, valves, and fittings for commercial, industrial, marine, and nuclear applications. The company is also engaged in the distribution of valve automation products. **Corporate headquarters location:** Newport News VA. **Parent company:** Wolseley Company. **Operations at this facility include:** Administration; Sales.

FISHERIES SUPPLY COMPANY
1900 North Northlake Way, Suite 10, Seattle WA 98103. 206/632-4462. **Contact:** Personnel Department. **World Wide Web address:** http://www.fisheries-supply.com. **Description:** A wholesaler of marine hardware and supplies. **Corporate headquarters location:** This location.

GRAINGER
5706 East Broadway Avenue, Spokane WA 99212. 509/535-9882. **Contact:** Human Resources. **World Wide Web address:** http://www.grainger.com. **Description:** Distributes equipment and components to the industrial, commercial, contracting, and institutional markets nationwide. Products include equipment and components for motors, air tools, hydraulic products, refrigeration items, power and hand tools, office equipment, computer supplies, storage equipment, replacement parts, industrial products, safety items, cold weather clothing, and sanitary supplies. **Positions advertised include:** Outside Sales Account Manager; Market Development Specialist. **Corporate headquarters location:** Chicago IL. **Listed on:** New York Stock Exchange. **Stock exchange symbol:** GWW.

HUGHES SUPPLY INC
10013 Martin Luther King Jr. Way South, Seattle WA

98178. 206/722-4800. **Fax:** 206/722-9477. **Contact:** Personnel. **World Wide Web address:** http://www.hughessupply.com. **Description:** A company engaged in the wholesale of industrial waterworks supplies. **Corporate headquarters location:** Orlando FL.

JENSEN DISTRIBUTION SERVICES
314 West Riverside Avenue, P.O. Box 3708, Spokane WA 99201. 509/624-1321. **Toll-free phone:** 800/234-1321. **Fax:** 509/838-2432. **Contact:** Personnel. **E-mail address:** darrelanc@jensenonline.com. **World Wide Web address:** http://www.jensenonline.com. **Description:** A wholesale distributor of hardware goods. **Corporate headquarters location:** This location.

MODERN MACHINERY
22431 83rd Avenue South, Kent WA 98032. 253/872-3500. **Fax:** 253/872-3519. **Contact:** Human Resources. **World Wide Web address:** http://www.pneco.com. **Description:** Engaged in the sale and service of construction and logging equipment.

NC MACHINERY COMPANY
P.O. Box 3562, Seattle WA 98124. 425/251-9800. **Contact:** Human Resources. **World Wide Web address:** http://www.ncmachinery.com. **Description:** Sells heavy equipment including generators, backhoes, and asphalt cutters as part of Caterpillar's worldwide dealer network. **Number of employees nationwide:** 600.

SEATTLE MARINE FISHING SUPPLY COMPANY
P.O. Box 99098, Seattle WA 98199-0098. 206/285-5010. **Physical address:** 2121 West Commodore Way, Seattle WA 98199. **Fax:** 206/285-7925. **Contact:** Personnel Department. **World Wide Web address:** http://www.seamar.com. **Description:** A wholesaler of marine supplies and hardware.

West Virginia

McJUNKIN CORPORATION
P.O. Box 513, Charleston WV 25322. 304/348-5211. **Physical address:** 835 Hillcrest Drive, Charleston WV 25311. **Fax:** 304/348-4922. **Contact:** Human Resources. **E-mail address:** infomcj@mcjunkin.com. **World Wide Web address:** http://www.mcjunkin.com. **Description:** A privately held distributor of pipes, valves, fittings, instrumentation and controls, oil country tubular goods, drilling supplies, and mining supplies. **NOTE:** Accepts unsolicited resumes. **Corporate headquarters location:** This location. **Number of employees at this location:** 1,600.

WALKER MACHINERY COMPANY
1400 East Dupont Avenue, Belle WV 25015-1217. 304/949-6400. **Toll-free phone:** 800/642-8203. **Fax:** 304/949-7380. **Contact:** Human Resources. **E-mail address:** jtravis@walker-cat.com. **World Wide Web address:** http://www.walker-cat.com. **Description:** Engaged in the sale and service of Caterpillar-brand industrial machinery and equipment. **NOTE:** Email resumes, or send to: Cecil I. Walker Machinery Company, Attn: Human Resources Department, P.O. Box 2427, Charleston WV 25329. **Positions advertised include:** Management Trainee; Mechanic; Warehouseman. **Other area locations:** Statewide. **Other U.S. locations:** Jackson OH. **Listed on:** Privately held. **Number of employees at this location:** 650.

Wisconsin

AERIAL COMPANY, INC.
2300 Aerial Drive, P.O. Box 197, Marinette WI 54143. 715/735-9323. **Toll-free phone:** 800/950-4942. **Fax:** 715/735-9112. **Contact:** Human Resources Department. **World Wide Web address:** http://www.aerialcompany.com. **Description:** A wholesale distributor of professional beauty salon products. **Number of employees nationwide:** 650.

AMERICAN FLOOR COVERING
2914 Latham Drive, Suite B, Madison WI 53713. 608/276-3440. **Fax:** 608/276-3441. **Contact:** Human Resources. **Description:** A wholesale distributor of floor covering materials including ceramic tile and industrial flooring supplies.

APPLIED INDUSTRIAL TECHNOLOGIES
2400 North Sandra Street, Appleton WI 54911-8666. 920/739-5351. **Fax:** 920/739-8453. **Contact:** Personnel. **E-mail address:** sc0301@applied.com. **World Wide Web address:** http://smp.applied.com. **Description:** A distributor of bearings, power transmission components, fluid power components and systems, industrial rubber products, linear components, tools, safety products, general maintenance and a variety of mill supply products. **Corporate headquarters location:** Cleveland OH. **Other area locations:** Statewide. **Other U.S. locations:** Nationwide. **Listed on:** New York Stock Exchange. **Stock exchange symbol:** AIT. **Number of employees worldwide:** 4,300.

AUTOMATIC FIRE PROTECTION
3265 North 126th Street, Suite B, Brookfield WI 53005. 262/781-9665. **Toll-free phone:** 800/686-9665. **Fax:** 262/781-1152. **Contact:** Human Resources. **E-mail address:** klewandowski@autofire.com. **World Wide Web address:** http://www.autofire.com. **Description:** Sells and services equipment for industrial, institutional, and commercial applications.

THE BOELTER COMPANIES
11100 West Silver Spring Road, Milwaukee WI 53225. 414/461-3400. **Toll-free phone:** 800/392-3278. **Fax:** 414/535-4963. **Contact:** Human Resources. **World Wide Web address:** http://www.boelter.com. **Description:** A wholesale distributor of restaurant supplies and equipment. **Positions advertised include:** Retail Sales Representative. **Corporate headquarters location:** This location. **Other area locations:** IL; MI; MN.

GUSTAVE A. LARSON COMPANY
W233 N2869 Roundy Circle West, P.O. Box 910, Pewaukee WI 53072-0910. 262/542-0200, extension 243. **Toll-free phone:** 800/829-9609. **Fax:** 262/542-1400. **Contact:** Susie Klein, Human Resources Director. **E-mail address:** susie.klein@galarson.com. **World Wide Web address:** http://www.galarson.com. **Description:** A wholesale distributor of a broad range of HVACR equipment, parts, and supplies. **Other area locations:** Statewide. **Other U.S. locations:** Nationwide. **Operations at this facility:** Administration; Sales; Service; Distribution.

PATCH PRODUCTS INC.
1400 East Inman Parkway, Beloit WI 53511. 608/362-6896. **Contact:** Human Resources Director. **E-mail address:** carolr@patchproducts.com. **World Wide Web address:** http://www.patchproducts.com. **Description:** A wholesale manufacturer of toys and games. **Positions available include:** Public Relations Coordinator/Copywriter. **Corporate headquarters location:** This location.

WARD ADHESIVES
N27 W23539 Paul Road, Pewaukee WI 53072. 262/523-6300. **Fax:** 262/523-6301. **Contact:** Human Resources. **Description:** A wholesale distributor of industrial adhesives to major local manufacturers. **Corporate headquarters location:** This location.